W9-BKT-274

Personal Financial Planning: Theory and Practice

11TH EDITION

COLLEGE FOR
FINANCIAL PLANNING®
A **KAPLAN** COMPANY

At press time, this edition contains the most complete and accurate information currently available. Due to the nature of advanced designation examinations, however, information may have been added recently to the actual test that does not appear in this edition. Please contact the publisher to verify that you have the most current edition.

This publication is designed to provide accurate and authoritative information in regard to the subject matter covered. It is sold with the understanding that the publisher is not engaged in rendering legal, accounting, or other professional services. If legal advice or other expert assistance is required, the services of a competent professional should be sought.

PERSONAL FINANCIAL PLANNING: THEORY AND PRACTICE, 11TH EDITION
©2020 The College for Financial Planning, Inc. All rights reserved.

The text of this publication, or any part thereof, may not be reproduced in any manner whatsoever without written permission from the publisher.

CLU®, ChFC®, Registered Health Underwriter®, RHU®, REBC® Chartered Life Underwriter®, Chartered Financial Consultant®, Registered Employee Benefits Consultant®, Chartered Advisor for Senior Living™, and CASL™ are registered trademarks of The American College.

CPCU®, ARM®, and AIC® are registered trademarks of the American Institute for CPCU and the Insurance Institute of America.

CFP®, CERTIFIED FINANCIAL PLANNER™, and CFP® are certification marks or registered certification marks of Certified Financial Planner Board of Standards, Inc.

Published by The College for Financial Planning, Inc.

Printed in the United States of America.

ISBN: 978-1-07-880979-5

About the Contributing Authors

Michael Angell, MS, CFP®, EA

- Associate Professor, The College for Financial Planning
- MS, Finance, The College for Financial Planning
- BS, Mathematics, Creighton University
- Federally licensed tax practitioner with a nationally recognized firm
- Former Registered Representative in Securities
- Over 20 years of experience in banking, insurance, investments, retirement planning, estate planning, and charitable philanthropic organizations
- Co-author of The College for Financial Planning/Kaplan's CFP® Exam Prep Review Books 1–7, 2020
- Co-author of The College for Financial Planning/Kaplan's CFP® Exam Required Education Course Materials, 2020

Sara Stolberg Berkowicz, Ph.D., MS, CFP®, CDFA™

- Assistant Professor, The College for Financial Planning
- Ph.D., Personal Financial Planning, Kansas State University
- MS, Financial Planning, The College for Financial Planning
- BA, Political Science, State University of New York at Binghamton
- Mediator, Association for Conflict Resolution and Northwestern University
- Co-author of The College for Financial Planning/Kaplan's CFP® Exam Prep Review Books 1–7, 2020
- Co-author of The College for Financial Planning/Kaplan's CFP® Exam Required Education Course Materials 2020

Jennifer N. Coombs, MSF, CSRIC®, CRPC®

- Associate Professor, The College for Financial Planning

- MS Finance, The College for Financial Planning

- BS, Finance/Political Science, Clarkson University

- Co-author of The College for Financial Planning/Kaplan's CFP® Exam Prep Review Books 1–7, 2020

- Co-author of The College for Financial Planning/Kaplan's CFP® Exam Required Education Course Materials, 2020

Mike Harris, CFP®, MPAS®, CRPC®, AAMS®, AWMA®, CMFC®, CRPC®

- Professor and Chair, Retirement Studies, The College for Financial Planning

- Former Senior Content Specialist, Kaplan Financial Education

- BS in management from the United States Air Force Academy, Colorado Springs, Colorado

- MDiv, Southwestern Baptist Theological Seminary

- MS, Financial Planning, College for Financial Planning

- Served in the United States Air Force for seven years in Oklahoma, California, Idaho, England, and New Mexico

- Former senior relationship manager for a large nonprofit organization

- Over 25 years of experience in the insurance and securities business

- Former general securities representative and life and health insurance agent

- Co-author of Kaplan University/Financial Education's Personal Financial Education Cases and Applications, 10th edition textbook and instructor guide

- Co-author of Kaplan University/Financial Education's CFP® Exam Prep Review Books 1–7, 2017–2018

- Co-author of The College for Financial Planning/Kaplan's CFP® Exam Prep Review Books 1–7, 2019–2020

- Co-author of Kaplan University/Financial Education's CFP® Exam Required Education Course Materials 2017

- Co-author of Kaplan's CFP® Exam Required Education Course Materials 2018–2019

- Co-author of The College for Financial Planning/Kaplan's CFP® Exam Required Education Course Materials 2020

James Maher, MBA, CLU®, ChFC®, CFP©, APMA®

- Professor and Chair, General Principles, Planning Practice, and Insurance, The College for Financial Planning

- Former Senior Content Specialist, Kaplan Financial Education

- Former securities and insurance instructor, Kaplan Financial

- Former insurance representative – General Securities

- BBA from Florida International University

- MBA from Purdue University Global

- Co-author of Kaplan Financial Education's *Personal Financial Planning Cases and Applications, 6th–8th editions* textbook and instructor manual

- Co-author of Kaplan University/Financial Education's *Personal Financial Planning Cases and Applications, 9th Edition* textbook and instructor manual

- Co-author of Kaplan Financial Education's *Personal Financial Planning Theory and Practice, 5th–7th Editions* textbook and instructor manual

- Co-author of Kaplan University/Financial Education's *Personal Financial Planning Theory and Practice, 8th Edition* textbook and instructor manual

- Co-author of the *Kaplan Schweser Review for the CFP® Certification Examination, 12th–13th editions*

- Co-author of the *Kaplan Schweser Review for the CFP® Certification Examination, July–November 2010, March–November 2011*, and *2012–2013 Exams*

- Co-author of Kaplan University/Financial Education's *CFP® Exam Prep Review Books 1–7, 2014–2018*

- Co-author of The College for Financial Planning/Kaplan's *CFP® Exam Prep Review Books 1–7, 2019–2020*

- Co-author of the *Kaplan University/Kaplan Schweser Certification Examination Education Program, 6th–11th Editions* materials

- Co-author of Kaplan University/Financial Education's *CFP® Exam Required Education Course Materials 2014–2017*

- Co-author of Kaplan's *CFP® Exam Required Education Course Materials 2018–2019*

- Co-author of The College for Financial Planning/Kaplan's *CFP® Exam Required Education Course Materials 2020*

Cindy R. Riecke, MSF, CFP®, CRPC®, FPQP®, ChFC®, CLU®

- Professor, College for Financial Planning

- Former Senior Director, Kaplan Financial Education

- BS in Business Administration from Louisiana State University

- MSF from Purdue University Global

- CFP Board Council on Education, 2020

- CFP Board Ethics CE Advisory Group, 2017–2020

- Member of the Financial Planning Association

- Former Director of Marketing Development for an international insurance and financial services company

- Co-author of Kaplan Financial Education's *Personal Financial Planning Cases and Applications, 5th–8th editions* textbook and instructor manual

- Co-author of Kaplan University/Financial Education's *Personal Financial Planning Cases and Applications, 9th Edition* textbook and instructor manual

- Co-author of Kaplan Financial Education's *Personal Financial Planning Theory and Practice, 4th–7th editions* textbook and instructor manual

- Co-author of Kaplan University/Financial Education's *Personal Financial Planning Theory and Practice, 8th Edition* textbook and instructor manual

- Co-author of the *Kaplan Schweser Review for the CFP® Certification Examination, 9th–13th editions*

- Co-author of the *Kaplan Schweser Review for the CFP® Certification Examination, July–November 2010, March–November 2011, and 2012–2013 Exams*

- Co-author of Kaplan University/Financial Education's *CFP® Exam Prep Review Books 1–7, 2014–2018*

- Co-author of The College for Financial Planning/Kaplan's *CFP® Exam Prep Review Books 1–7, 2019–2020*

- Co-author of the *Kaplan University/Kaplan Schweser Certification Examination Education Program, 4th–11th Editions* materials

- Co-author of Kaplan University/Financial Education's *CFP® Exam Required Education Course Materials 2014–2017*

- Co-author of Kaplan's *CFP® Exam Required Education Course Materials 2018–2019*

- Co-author of The College for Financial Planning/Kaplan's *CFP® Exam Required Education Course Materials 2020*

Calvin Barclay Roper, III, Ph.D., MSF

- Assistant Professor, The College for Financial Planning
- American Association of Individual Investors
- Pocatello Estate Planning Council
- Co-author of The College for Financial Planning/Kaplan's CFP® Exam Prep Review Books 1–7, 2020
- Co-author of The College for Financial Planning/Kaplan's CFP® Exam Required Education Course Materials 2020

Christopher Woerhle, JD, LL.M

- Professor and Chair, Tax and Estate Planning, The College for Financial Planning
- Adjunct Professor, Widger School of Law, Villanova University
- LLM, Taxation, Villanova University
- JD, Villanova University
- AB, English, Cornell University
- Former Chair, Pensions and Retirement, The American College
- Member, Pennsylvania Bar
- Council for Advancement and Support of Education (CASE)
- Served in high-level positions managing planned giving and development for universities, the performing arts, and healthcare institutions
- Co-author of The College for Financial Planning/Kaplan's CFP® Exam Prep Review Books 1–7, 2020
- Co-author of The College for Financial Planning/Kaplan's CFP® Exam Required Education Course Materials 2020

Preface

Personal Financial Planning: Theory and Practice was written in response to numerous pleas from instructors and students requesting a fundamental financial planning textbook. Through this text, the contributing authors hope to convey their knowledge of financial planning and reflect their enthusiasm for the subject.

This text is written for graduate and undergraduate students who are interested in acquiring an in-depth understanding of personal financial planning from a professional planning viewpoint. The text is also intended to serve as a reference for practicing professional financial planners.

Content and Themes

The Financial Planner's Pyramid of Knowledge is depicted throughout this text. The base of the pyramid identifies the core knowledge that every financial planner should possess. Chapters 8–17 detail this foundation of knowledge on which a successful financial planning profession can be built. The second layer of the pyramid, presented in chapters 6 and 7, focuses on the basic financial planning tools a financial planner must be familiar with and capable of implementing. The third and fourth layers of the pyramid, presented in chapters 1–5, describe the basic financial planning skills every professional financial planner should possess. Finally, the pyramid's pinnacle explores the financial planning profession and the ethical responsibilities faced by a professional financial planner. Chapters 18 and 19 cover these topics.

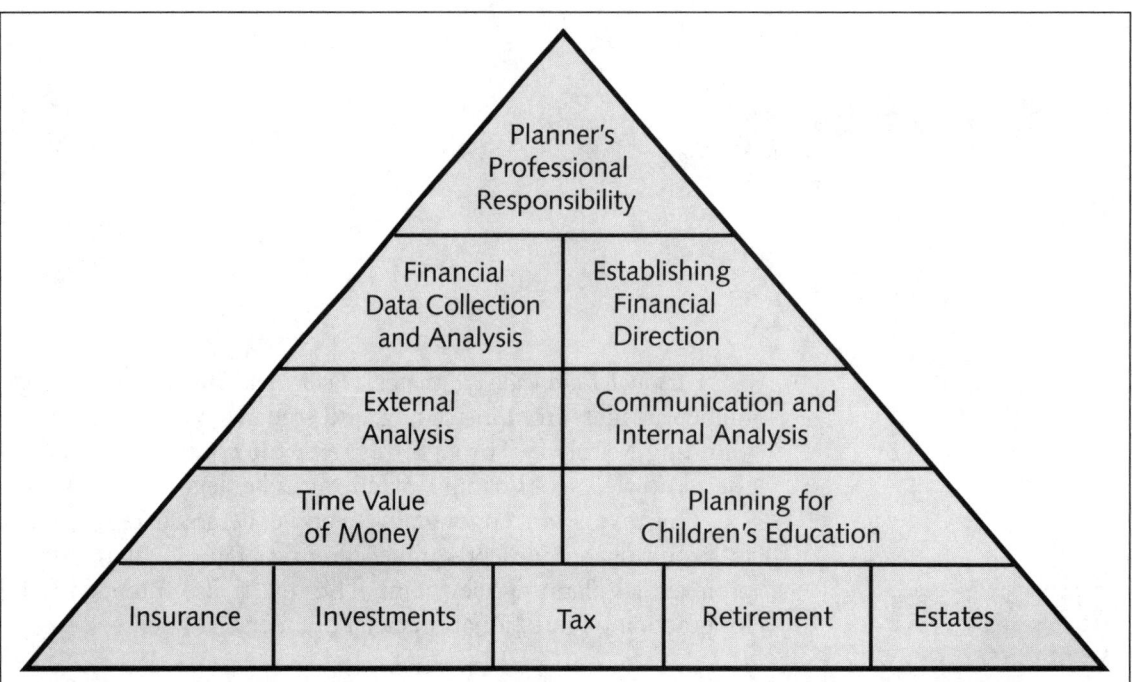

Throughout the text, two themes are identified. The first theme of the text is that personal financial planning is about attaining financial goals and managing financial risks. There are perhaps as many goals as there are clients. Generally, the majority of clients want to achieve one or more of the following goals: to attain financial security for themselves, to accumulate assets to fund their children's education, to save a specific lump sum to cover future expenditures, or to prepare their assets for transfer to heirs. There are many risks threatening the attainment of these goals, including disability, poor health, and untimely death. This text will identify these risks and present ways to manage them.

The second theme emphasized throughout the text is that the professional practice of personal financial planning emphasizes data collection and analysis. For the professional financial planner, this requires knowledge of external environmental influences and skill at data collection, interviewing, and administering questionnaires. Analytical skills are invaluable when applying time-value-of-money concepts and when preparing and analyzing personal financial statements. Excellent communication skills, including displaying empathy and using verbal and nonverbal pacing, are essential when dealing with clients. Finally, helping clients set reasonable goals that are objectively measurable in time and form and using good follow-up and evaluation skills are most valuable to the professional financial planner.

Special Features

A variety of tools and presentation methods are used throughout this text to assist in the learning process. The following are some of the features presented in this text that are designed to enhance the readers' understanding and learning process.

Section Break Features

■ **The financial planner's pyramid of knowledge**—The financial planning pyramid is shown on every section break to focus the student's attention to the section topic. We have shaded the corresponding area on the pyramid to identify the broad knowledge topic discussed in the section. The pyramid's intricacies are discussed more fully in Chapter 1.

■ **Knowledge level: In Brief**—The knowledge level In Brief section allows us to be more specific on the topics covered in the section. The topics are listed by difficulty, with the easier topics at the top, medium topics in the middle, and more difficult topics at the bottom. This was done to help the student be aware of and prepared for the difficulty of the topics. It also allowed us to give a brief keyword overview of the section.

■ **Goal and risk identification**—Common goals and risks are identified on the section break to focus the reader's attention on the ever-present conflict between goal attainment and risk avoidance.

■ **Data collection and analysis requirements**—Data collection and data analysis requirements are identified to help the reader become adept at identifying relevant information.

Chapter Features

■ **Where on the Web**—Each chapter has a Where on the Web section that provides the reader with useful website domains.

■ **Bold keywords**—Keywords appear in boldfaced type throughout the text to assist in the identification of important concepts and terminology. Keyword definitions appear in the margin for quick access to important concepts.

■ **Examples**—Examples are used frequently to illustrate the concepts being discussed.

■ **Exhibits**—The written text is enhanced and simplified by using exhibits where appropriate.

11th Edition Changes

■ All tax numbers, tax tables, and threshold amounts have been updated through 2020.

■ The Insurance section has been updated to reflect 2020 inflation-adjusted dollar amounts that affect several key Social Security concepts, such as the Social Security wage base, the primary insurance amount (PIA), and the maximum family benefit. The discussion of Medicare has been updated to illustrate the impact of the 2020 Medicare premiums, copayments, and deductibles.

■ The Investment section has been reorganized and edited in order to present the material in a more clear and concise manner.

■ The Tax section has been updated for 2020 law changes released.

■ Retirement statistics and limits have been updated for 2020.

■ The Estate Planning section has been updated to reflect the federal transfer tax rates, exemptions, and credits that are in effect in 2020.

Contents

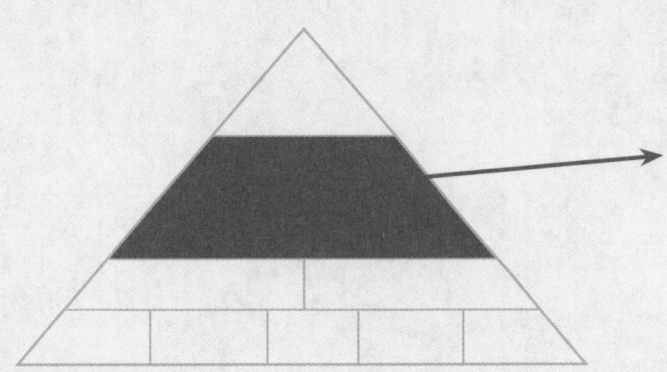

- Personal financial planning

- The Financial Planner's Pyramid of Knowledge

- The external environment

- Communication skills of the financial planner

- Internal analysis

- Life cycle positioning

- Financial statement preparation

- Ratio analysis and comparison to benchmarks

- Trend analysis

- Sensitivity and risk analysis

- Establishing and defining the client-planner relationship

- Gathering information necessary to fulfill the engagement

- Analyzing and evaluating the client's current financial status

- Developing the recommendations

- Communicating the recommendations

- Implementing the recommendations

- Monitoring the recommendations

- Practicing within professional and regulatory standards

1 Basic Financial Planning Skills

CHAPTERS

Risks	Goals
■ Inadequate data collection	■ Establish appropriate mission statement
■ Incorrect data analysis	■ Establish goals
■ Miscommunication to client	■ Establish objectives
■ Poor strategy	■ Select a strategy
■ No client buy-in	

Data Collection	Data Analysis
■ Economic information	■ Economic analysis
■ Legal information	■ Personal financial analysis
■ Personal information	■ Savings analysis
■ Financial information	■ Investment analysis
■ Tax returns	■ Risk tolerance of client
■ Mission	■ Strategic alternatives
■ Goals	
■ Objectives	
■ Strategic alternatives	

Introduction to Personal Financial Planning

LEARNING OBJECTIVES

After learning the material in this chapter, you will be able to do the following:

- Define personal financial planning

- Discuss the benefits of personal financial planning

- Explain how the financial planning process promotes efficient allocation of a client's resources

- Explain how financial success is a relative concept

- Identify why people hire professional financial planners

- Describe the Financial Planner's Pyramid of Knowledge and explain the importance of each component

PERSONAL FINANCIAL PLANNING DEFINED

Personal financial planning
The process of formulating, implementing, and monitoring multifunctional decisions that enable an individual or family to achieve financial goals

Comprehensive **personal financial planning** is the process of formulating, implementing, and monitoring multifunctional decisions that enable an individual or family to achieve financial goals. Personal financial planning involves the management of personal financial risks through cost benefit analysis. It capitalizes on personal and financial strengths and opportunities while managing financial risks and weaknesses. Financial planning professionals and those studying financial planning should understand and appreciate the comprehensive nature of a competently prepared personal financial plan and what it is intended to accomplish for the person who implements it effectively.

BENEFITS OF PERSONAL FINANCIAL PLANNING

Benefits of personal financial planning
- *Goals identified are more likely to be achieved*
- *Helps to clearly identify risk exposures*
- *Is proactive rather than reactive*
- *Creates a framework for feedback, evaluation, and control*
- *Establishes measurable goals and expectations*
- *Develops an improved awareness of financial choices*
- *Provides an opportunity for an increased commitment to financial goals*

A financial plan integrates a financial mission, goals, and objectives into one cohesive plan that allocates financial resources consistently. Individuals and families with no formal financial plan actually have an informal financial plan, which is reflected by their historical pattern of financial decisions and financial behavior. For example, consistent late debt repayments suggest a pattern (plan), and such a pattern eventually leads to financial consequences. Conversely, consistent long-term savings and investment without any formal plan creates a pattern (plan) that also leads to financial consequences. The historical pattern of personal or family financial behavior is as difficult to change as is any other personal habit. Thus, the professional financial planner is not only a strategist and planner but may also be a counselor and a financial "therapist."

There are many **benefits of personal financial planning.** Perhaps the most important benefit is that goals identified and planned for are more likely to be achieved. The planning process helps clearly recognize risks that can undermine goals. Once identified, these risks can be managed with a variety of techniques. The financial planning process is one of learning, growing, and choosing wisely. The process is proactive rather than reactive, thus giving clients more control over their financial status. By using a more logical, systematic, and rational approach to decision making, clients make better strategic choices regarding the use of resources. The process also creates a framework for feedback, evaluation, and control. It establishes measurable goals and expectations that can be compared to actual results.

During the financial planning process, the client develops an improved awareness of financial choices and how internal and external environments affect those choices. The process also provides the client an opportunity to increase commitment to selected goals. When clients and their families understand what they want to achieve, why they want to accomplish it, and how and when it can be attained, they often take ownership of their financial plan and become more committed to it.

A comprehensive personal financial plan helps to establish rationality and reality and eliminate the client's unrealistic ideas and wishful thinking. For example, many people want to retire early and maintain their preretirement lifestyle while currently spending more than 100% of their personal disposable income with no plan to save or invest. A comprehensive personal financial plan will quickly demonstrate the irrationality of such an approach and assist the client in identifying those changes necessary to achieve a more realistic plan.

The financial planning process also brings financial order and discipline. This process instills confidence that goals can be achieved and identifies the behavioral changes necessary to accomplish those goals. It provides a forum for rationalizing the need for change and helps to view change as an opportunity rather than a threat.

Financially successful individuals—not necessarily those who are wealthy but rather those who meet their financial goals—tend to do more financial planning to prepare themselves for the inevitable changes in their internal and external environments. They tend to make more informed financial decisions. They also tend to better anticipate both the short- and long-term consequences of their decisions. Conversely, individuals who are not as financially successful tend to underestimate the value of planning and may attribute their lack of financial success to uncontrollable factors such as a poor economy, foreign competition, government interference, or just bad luck.

There are no absolutes in financial planning any more than there are absolutes about anything in the future. Financial planning will not guarantee desired results; however, it will increase the probability of clients achieving their financial goals. Clients who believe in financial planning generally learn the importance of managing the various risks that could have a negative impact on their plans.

FINANCIAL SUCCESS IS A RELATIVE CONCEPT

Financial success
For most individuals, financial success means accomplishing one's financial goals

Financial success means different things to different people. The fisherman who lives in a poor village in a developing country and has a slightly larger boat than most of the other local fishermen may feel financially successful. The millionaire whose friends are all billionaires may feel less financially successful. In a way, financial success is a comparison with the client's own benchmarks or standards. Thus, from the client's perspective, financial success is both relative and subjective. The professional financial planner needs to keep in mind that, to a particular client, financial success is a relative concept, the description of which may be subjectively determined by the client.

Subjectivity
Relating to the client's perception of reality

Objectivity
Relating to facts without distortion by personal feelings or prejudices

While **subjectivity** tends to dominate the client's thinking about financial success, **objectivity** should dominate the planner's thinking about financial planning. Accomplishing specific goals is objectively determined if objectively defined. Risks that exist in the external environment are objective and real to the professional planner. The client may have a subjective perception of the same risks. For example, the risk of untimely death can be measured actuarially, regardless of the subjective perception of the client. Another example of objectivity is recognizing the risk of permanent disability for a particular job. Consider an example of an NFL running back. The number of running backs who are disabled each year is a predictable percentage, league-wide. Regardless of how the players subjectively feel about their chances of suffering a disabling injury, it is mathematically objective that a certain percentage of running backs will be injured and will be unable to play in any given year. With full knowledge of this objective risk and its catastrophic financial consequences, a professional financial planner would strongly advise his running back client to purchase long-term disability insurance that pays benefits if the player is injured while playing professional football. Most professional planners would agree with that advice even though the policy premiums will be extremely high. The premiums are high because the insurers also understand the objective risks, and they set premiums that will cover losses and earn a profit.

RESOURCE ALLOCATION IN FINANCIAL PLANNING

Financial planning involves making financial choices and allocating scarce resources. People make choices because scarcity exists. At any moment in time, all people want the highest level of overall satisfaction from their choices. Most people are aware from an early

Personal utility curves
Economic curves that describe the satisfaction that an individual receives from a selected item or additional units of that item

Opportunity cost
The highest-valued alternative not chosen; represents what is forgone by choosing another alternative

age that there are alternative financial choices to be made, such as whether to consume today or defer consumption until later. The internal psychological analysis that people perform when they decide among alternatives is a subjective evaluation resulting from the application of their own **personal utility curves** to the alternatives identified and presented to them. Personal utility curves are subjectively based and reflect our knowledge, values, and beliefs and, therefore, may be quite different for each person. Some individuals place a high value on spending time alone, while some value spending time with others in social settings. If a client believes there is no tomorrow, he may as well consume today. If, however, he believes in a long future during which he plans not to work, he may be willing to forego consumption today, deferring those unconsumed resources for the future.

When making choices, we are faced with alternatives. Each alternative poses risks and consequences. Doing nothing is one alternative. The highest-valued alternative not chosen is called the **opportunity cost**. Opportunity cost represents what is forgone by choosing another alternative. For example, if a client chooses to spend $2,500 on a cruise as an alternative to saving for the future, the opportunity cost is the value of the $2,500 in the client's investment portfolio. Five years after taking the cruise, the client has fond memories and beautiful photos of the trip. Alternatively, had he not taken the cruise and invested the money in a well-structured investment portfolio for those five years, he might have significantly increased the value of his portfolio.

When choosing among alternatives, clients need a framework for comparison. When making comparisons, human nature tends to discount anything in the future in favor of immediate gratification. In the cruise example above, the client decided to spend the $2,500 now to take the cruise, even though he objectively knew that the money might increase significantly in five years if invested wisely. For this client, the current subjective satisfaction expected from taking the cruise is worth more today than the increased future value of the investment portfolio.

Once a financial planner presents a client with a framework of objective alternatives that identifies the opportunity cost associated with each choice, the client can make a more informed, more rational choice among alternatives. In this way, the financial planning process promotes efficient allocation of a client's resources and avoids commitment of resources to more costly, less rational choices.

WHY DO PEOPLE HIRE PROFESSIONAL FINANCIAL PLANNERS?

Many people seek the advice of professionals, such as doctors, lawyers, and accountants, on a regular basis. Generally, professionals have a more comprehensive knowledge of their subject field than does the public. In some cases, it is simply a matter of opportunity cost. It may be less expensive—in total satisfaction and cost—to retain an expert than to invest the time to learn to do it ourselves. We may lack the day-to-day cognitive references, financial benchmarks, and comparisons needed to know when a plan is competent or attainable. Even when people have a limited knowledge of financial planning, they may lack the confidence to make important decisions based on that limited knowledge. People hire professional financial planners because they believe that doing so is more effective and efficient than attempting to create and implement a financial plan on their own.

The public has a reasonable expectation that a professional financial planner is knowledgeable and competent in the financial planning field. The planner should have an understanding of objective risks in the environment, such as the risks of untimely death, health issues, disability, property loss, and negligence lawsuits and awards. The public can reasonably expect that a professional financial planner will have knowledge of life expectancies and, thus, an understanding of the average expected number of retirement years. Planners should know that in general it takes 60–80% of preretirement income to maintain a lifestyle during retirement. Planners should know that for low-income workers, Social Security may provide an adequate wage replacement, but for highly paid workers, it may only replace a small percentage of preretirement income. Professional planners should know the risk of inflation and its historical patterns. Planners should also know the historical investment returns for various classes of assets and which asset allocation choices have produced the best overall investment returns for selected risk levels. This text will broaden the professional financial planner's knowledge and skill base in all of these areas.

THE FINANCIAL PLANNER'S PYRAMID OF KNOWLEDGE

The Financial Planner's Pyramid of Knowledge, as depicted in Exhibit 1.1, is presented throughout this text. The Pyramid identifies the skills and basic tools that the financial planner must possess as well as the core topics of which the planner must be knowledgeable. Just as the strength of any structure depends on a solid foundation, the success of any professional financial planner relies on a well-built foundation of knowledge, competency, and skill. The base of the Financial Planner's Pyramid of Knowledge identifies the core knowledge and skill sets that every financial planner should possess. Collectively, these competencies make up the financial planner's toolkit—a foundation on which a successful profession in financial planning can be established. Out of necessity in this text, these skills, tools, and competencies are presented individually; however, they are not performed sequentially or independently. Rather, they are performed simultaneously throughout the many aspects of the financial planning process.

EXHIBIT 1.1 Financial Planner's Pyramid of Knowledge

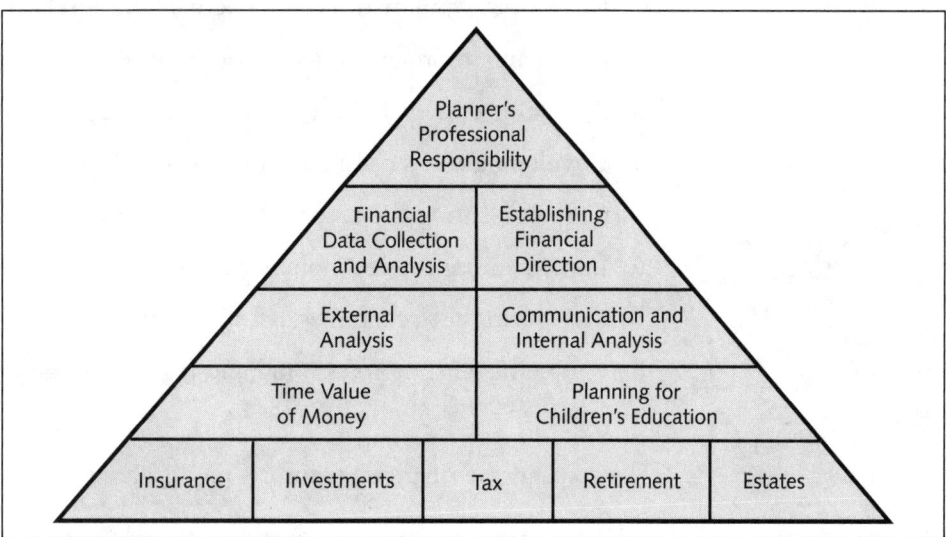

Throughout the text, we also focus on two themes. The first theme of the text is that personal financial planning involves attaining financial goals and managing financial risks. There are perhaps as many goals as there are clients. Generally, the majority of clients are looking to achieve one or more of the following goals: to attain financial security for themselves, to create an accumulation of assets to fund their children's education, to save a specific lump sum to cover future expenditures, or to prepare their assets for transfer to heirs. There are many risks threatening the attainment of these goals, includ-

Emotional intelligence
The ability to recognize and assess emotional expressions in themselves and their clients

Active listening
Paying full attention to what clients are saying and responding by paraphrasing their comments, thus gaining a full understanding of what clients are attempting to communicate

ing disability, ill health, or untimely death. The text will identify these risks and suggest ways for managing them.

The second theme emphasized throughout the text is that the professional practice of personal financial planning emphasizes data collection and analysis. For the professional financial planner, this requires a good education in external environmental influences and good data collection skills for interviewing and administering questionnaires. Analytical skills are invaluable when applying time value of money concepts and when preparing and analyzing personal financial statements. Excellent communication skills, including **emotional intelligence** and **active listening**, are essential when gathering information and communicating with clients. Finally, helping clients set reasonable goals that are objectively measurable in time and form and using good follow-up and evaluation techniques are most valuable to the professional financial planner.

Basic Financial Planning Skills

The first section of the text explains that the practice of personal financial planning requires the financial planner to master good communication, data collection, and analysis skills. These skills are necessary when applying financial planning tools and working with clients. The planner must be aware that individuals generally progress through **financial phases** during their lives. These phases include the asset accumulation phase, the conservation/protection phase, and the distribution/gifting phase. These phases are not mutually exclusive. For example, a client may function in two phases simultaneously. If a professional planner can identify which phase or phases a client is in, the planner will have better insight into the client's financial behavior and a better understanding of the client's approach to goals and risks.

Financial phases
These phases include the asset accumulation phase, the conservation/protection phase, and the distribution/gifting phase

This section also identifies the process of establishing financial direction. The seven steps in the financial planning process are based on the eight job task domains of Certified Financial Planner Board of Standards, Inc.:

1. Establishing and defining the client-planner relationship (Step 1)

2. Gathering information necessary to fulfill the engagement (Step 2)

3. Analyzing and evaluating the client's current financial status (Step 3)

4. Developing the recommendations (Step 4)

5. Communicating the recommendations (Step 5)

6. Implementing the recommendations (Step 6)

7. Monitoring the recommendations (Step 7)

8. Practicing within professional and regulatory standards (Takes place throughout all seven steps)

The steps in the financial planning process are further discussed in Chapter 5.

Financial mission
A broad and enduring statement that identifies the client's long-term purpose for wanting a financial plan

Financial goals
High-level statements of financial desires that may be for the short or the long term

Financial objectives
Statements of financial desire that contain time and measurement attributes, making them more specific than financial goals

A broad and enduring statement that identifies the client's long-term purpose for wanting a financial plan is called a **financial mission,** which begins the process. Once the mission has been identified and embraced, the planner must consider relevant internal and external environmental information. The planner should use objective analysis and rational judgment to guide the client to effective decision making. The client's **financial goals** are high-level statements of financial desires that may be for the short or the long term and the client's **financial objectives** are statements that contain time and measurement attributes, making them more specific than financial goals. These are then identified and prioritized so that feasible alternative strategies can be created. After examining the alternatives, the planner helps the client select the optimal strategy. The recommendations will then be implemented and monitored, but this does not mean the process is finished. The responsible financial planner will then monitor the recommendations that were implemented by providing regular feedback to the client on the plan's performance. All of these activities should be performed in a professional manner and within any applicable regulatory standards.

Basic Financial Planning Tools

Time value of money
The concept that money received today is worth more than the same amount of money received sometime in the future

The second section of the text identifies two basic financial planning tools: **time value of money** and planning for children's education.

Chapter 6 discusses time value of money (TVM) concepts, one of the most useful and important concepts in finance and personal financial planning. The chapter includes in-depth discussions of TVM concepts, such as present value, future value, loan amortization, net present value (NPV) and internal rate of return (IRR), yield to maturity, debt management, and the inflation rate.

Chapter 7 covers developing a plan for funding children's education, which is a primary financial goal of many parents. Education funding is a common area of concern for those seeking financial planning advice, because paying for higher education is one of the largest financial burdens a family will face. In this discussion, the various issues that parents should consider when setting goals for financing their children's education are discussed. The types of financial aid information that can be gathered from a college's financial aid office are also examined, and the importance of the Expected Family Contribution (EFC) formula in student financial aid application is explained. Also discussed are the major student financial assistance programs available and how time value of money concepts are used to help calculate the cost of a child's education.

Core Topics

Chapters 8–11 are dedicated to insurance planning. Chapter 8 discusses the legal foundation of insurance and the transference of risks using insurance contracts. Chapter 9 identifies the risks associated with premature death, catastrophic illness, disability, and the need for long-term care. Also discussed is self-insurance, business uses of life insurance, health savings accounts (HSAs), Health Care Reimbursement Arrangements (HCRAs), equity indexed annuities (EIAs), and Section 1035 exchanges. Other employee benefits are also discussed. Chapter 10 identifies the risks to property and liability exposures. Chapter 11 covers Social Security and other types of social insurance.

Chapters 12–17 provide an introduction to investments, income tax, retirement, and estate planning. Chapter 12 and Supplements A, B, and C offer a discussion on investment planning. Chapter 12 introduces investment goals and the risks that threaten those goals and discusses modern portfolio theory and investment strategies. Supplement 12A discusses investing in lending securities, such as bonds. Supplement 12B covers equity securities, namely common and preferred stock. Supplement 12C discusses mutual funds.

Chapters 13 and 14 cover individual income tax and tax planning and the formation and taxation of business entities. Chapter 13 includes discussions on the objectives of the federal income tax law, the tax rate structures under which income can be taxed, how to perform tax calculations to determine a client's income tax liability, the types of IRS rulings issued as guidance to taxpayers, payroll taxes, the various civil penalties imposed on tax law violators, and the various tax-advantaged investment options available to taxpayers. Chapter 14 identifies the several types of business entities that a businessowner may choose as a legal form of business and characterizes each type of business entity with regard to formation requirements, operation, ownership restrictions, tax treatment, legal liability risk, and management operations. The chapter goes on to discuss the basic factors that a businessowner should consider when selecting a legal form of business and explains how each type of business entity differs with regard to simplicity of formation and operation, ownership restrictions, limited liability, management operations, and tax characteristics.

Chapters 15 and 16 discuss retirement planning. Chapter 15 identifies and explains the major factors that affect retirement planning. Chapter 16 provides an introduction to employer-sponsored and individual retirement plans, including qualified retirement plans, other tax-advantaged retirement plans, and nonqualified plans.

Chapter 17 presents the goals of efficient and effective wealth transfer, during life or at death, and the risks that are associated with such transfers. This chapter introduces estate planning, describes the estate planning process, discusses the objectives of and the benefits derived from planning an estate, lists the types of client information necessary to conduct this planning, and describes the probate process and its advantages and disadvantages. Chapter 17 also explains the gift and estate tax system, identifies the basic strategies for transferring wealth through gifting, explains the purpose of the federal estate tax, defines the marital deduction and how it affects estate planning, and discusses the various estate tax reduction techniques available.

The Financial Planning Profession

Chapter 18 describes the financial planning profession today and describes and differentiates financial institutions from individual financial professionals. The chapter outlines the methods of compensation and closes with ideas about developing and maintaining a practice. Chapter 19 covers the ethical responsibilities of a financial planner, provides a legal framework for malpractice and civil liability, and details the CFP Board Code of Ethics and Standards of Conduct (Code and Standards), which covers the Code of Ethics, duties owed to clients, CFP Board, Firms, and subordinates. In addition, the seven-step financial planning process outlined in the Code and Standards is discussed and analyzed.

WHERE ON THE WEB

Association for Financial Counseling and Planning Education **www.afcpe.org**

Barron's Online **www.barrons.com**

Bloomberg **www.bloomberg.com**

Certified Financial Planner Board of Standards, Inc. **www.cfp.net**

Financial Planning Association **www.fpanet.org**

Forbes Magazine **www.forbes.com**

Fortune Magazine **www.fortune.com**

Kiplinger **www.kiplinger.com**

Money Magazine **www.money.cnn.com**

National Association of Personal Financial Advisors **www.napfa.org**

Society of Financial Service Professionals **national.societyoffsp.org**

Wall Street Journal **www.wsj.com**

Yahoo Finance **www.finance.yahoo.com**

DISCUSSION QUESTIONS

1. What is personal financial planning?

2. What does it mean to consider financial success a relative concept?

3. How does the financial planning process promote efficient allocation of a client's resources?

4. Why do people hire professional financial planners?

5. What does the Financial Planner's Pyramid of Knowledge identify?

6. How can a client benefit from the personal financial planning process?

7. What concepts must the professional financial planner balance in order to create a successful financial plan?

8. Through what activities is the personal financial planner expected to guide the client?

External Environmental Analysis

LEARNING OBJECTIVES

After learning the material in this chapter, you will be able to do the following:

- Differentiate between the external and internal environments in which financial planning occurs

- Discuss how external environmental factors link to the different areas of financial planning

- Give examples of how external environmental factors might affect clients from different economic levels

- Give reasons why external environmental analysis is important

- Explain how economic factors, such as interest rates, taxes, and inflation, affect areas of financial planning

- Define the several phases and important extreme points that make up a business cycle and describe their effect on the economy

- Calculate the inflation rate

- Define the consumer price index, the gross domestic product deflator, and the producer price index

- Explain how changes in monetary and fiscal policy affect the economy

- Discuss the different types of financial institutions and negotiable instruments

- Explain how FDIC coverage works

- Identify federal consumer protection/bankruptcy laws and give a brief description of each

- List federal programs that offer protection for workers on the job site

- Give examples of how other external environmental factors—social, technological, political, and taxation—affect a client's personal financial plan

THE EXTERNAL ENVIRONMENT

The success of a client's financial planning is affected by both internal and external environmental factors. Internal environmental forces, which will be examined fully in subsequent chapters, include a client's current and projected financial situation, risk tolerance, discipline regarding savings and investments, consumption patterns, and financial goals. Exhibit 2.1 shows how the internal environment fits within the external environment.

EXHIBIT 2.1 Internal and External Environments

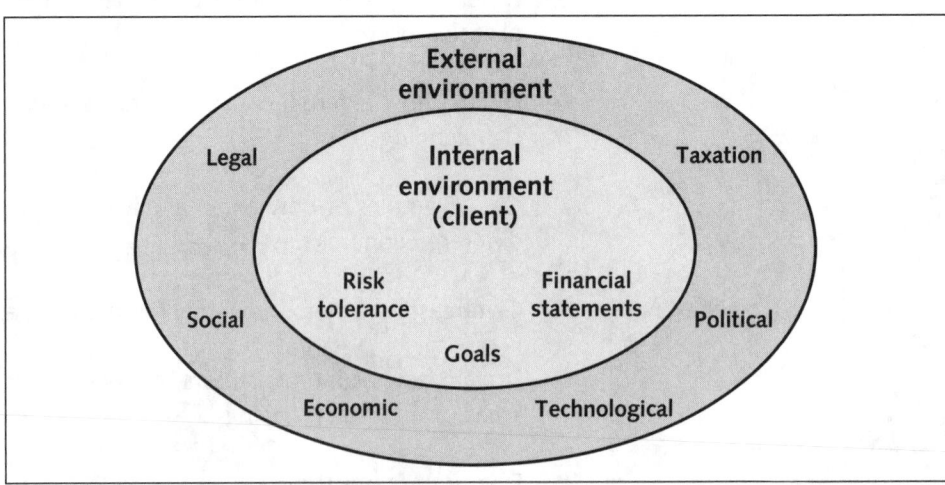

External environment
The whole complex of factors independent of the client that influence the financial planning process, including economic, legal, social, technological, political, and taxation factors

The **external environment** is made up of a variety of factors, or sub-environments, that are broad in scope but have at least some influence on the financial planning process. The external environment includes economic, legal, social, technological, political, and taxation factors. An abbreviated list of factors for each of the external environmental influences is presented in Exhibit 2.2.

EXHIBIT 2.2 Abbreviated List of External Factors*

Economic Factors	Legal Factors
Gross domestic product (GDP)	Antitrust acts
Inflation (Consumer Price Index)	Consumer protection acts
Interest rates	Bankruptcy acts
Trade payments	Securities acts
Consumer income/debt/spending	Forms of business organization
Unemployment	Employer/employee relations
Population age	Workers' compensation
Index of leading economic indicators	Continuation of benefits (COBRA)
	Social Security

Social Factors	Technological Factors
Age of population life expectancy	Current state of technology
Customs and beliefs	Creation of new technology
Attitudes and motivations	Human and business solutions
Status symbols/social institutions	Advances in service and engineering

Political Factors	Taxation Factors
Form of government	Income taxes (federal and state)
Political ideology/stability	Property taxes
Foreign trade policy	Transfer taxes (gift and estate)
Degree of government protectionism	Payroll taxes
	Sales taxes

*There are many other factors than those listed; however, a full discussion of all factors is beyond the scope of this text.

This chapter describes the external environment in which financial planning occurs. The external environment is characterized by opportunities and threats. For the financial planner, the purpose of studying the external environment is to scan for those opportunities and threats that may relate to particular clients and their financial goals. The financial planner may forecast external trends (or use experts to forecast trends) to help clients achieve goals and avoid external risks.

As stated previously, external environmental factors include economic, legal, social, technological, political, and taxation forces. Everyone is influenced by these forces to differing degrees as shown by the selected examples in Exhibit 2.3.

Because some clients are more affected by certain environmental factors than others, it is the financial planner's responsibility to decide the influences relevant to a particular client at a particular time.

EXHIBIT 2.3 External Environmental Impact on Financial Planning (Selected Examples)

Client's economic level	External Environmental Forces					
	Economic	Legal	Social	Political	Taxation	Technological
High income	• Gross domestic product • Interest rates	• Antitrust • Form of business organization	• Status symbols • Life expectancy	• Political ideology/ stability	• Income and transfer taxes • Property taxes	• Investments • Internet
Middle income	• Inflation • Interest rates	• Form of business organization • Employer/ employee relationships • Consumer protection • COBRA • Social Security	• Customs/ beliefs • Life expectancy	• Foreign trade policy	• Property taxes • Income taxes • Payroll taxes	• Investments • Jobs • Electronic tax filing • Internet
Low income	• Unemployment • Inflation	• Workers' compensation • Consumer protection • COBRA • Social Security	• Social institutions • Life expectancy • Customs/ beliefs	• Government protectionism	• Sales taxes • Payroll taxes	• Electronic tax filing • Internet

Analyzing the External Environment

External environmental analysis
The process of identifying and monitoring the environment in which a client lives and the opportunities and threats that are present

External environmental analysis is important for a variety of reasons.

■ External trends and particular events play a significant role in changing the world and the behavior of individuals.

■ Changes in external forces impact beliefs, economics, unemployment, inflation, and a society's well-being.

■ The external environment shapes the way people live, work, spend, save, and reason.

Professional financial planners need to understand these forces and should develop a method for staying abreast of the changes in the external environment.

When performing an external environmental analysis, the financial planner must determine the relevance of one or more external environmental factors for each client. The relevance of such factors may depend on the client's age, goals, net worth, or income. Consider the following examples.

E X A M P L E   Bryan is 70 years old and married, has five adult children and seven grandchildren, and has a net worth of $25 million. One of his goals is to leave as much money as he can to his heirs. Because the tax environment incorporates gift taxes, estate taxes, generation-skipping transfer taxes, and in some cases state inheritance taxes, the tax environment is highly relevant to Bryan's personal financial planning.

E X A M P L E   Jeni, age 36, is married, has three young children, and has debts in excess of her assets. She was injured on the job and may never return to work. Although the tax environment may have some relevance to Jeni, it will be a minor influence relative to Bryan's circumstances. The legal environment, which addresses consumer protection, bankruptcy, workers' compensation, Medicaid, COBRA, Social Security disability benefits, and civil lawsuits, may be of utmost importance to Jeni.

Why Study the External Environment?

Regular observation and monitoring of the external environment is essential to providing high-quality financial planning services to clients. Financial planners may study the external environment formally or informally. Formal study will usually include university-level courses in economics, taxation, political science, sociology, and the legal environment. The external environment may also be studied informally using a variety of sources, such as general economic and business periodicals, books, academic and professional journals, websites, newspapers, government statistical studies, and by obtaining environmental briefings from various information providers. Financial planners should also take continuing professional education courses to stay abreast of the ever-changing external environment.

The Economic and Legal Environments

The external environment—particularly the economic and legal environment—exerts far-reaching yet often subtle influence on accomplishing financial goals and reducing risks. For example, consider an economic environment characterized by low interest rates, modest growth, and low inflation. Such an environment is ideal for businesses to prosper and for investors to achieve excellent investment returns with relatively moderate levels of risk. Alternatively, periods of high interest rates and growing inflation are not as suitable for businesses, investors, or retirees, who, living on fixed incomes, are losing purchasing power. The legal environment, especially consumer protection, is important because it establishes the legal rules by which consumers must abide and creates the legal rights to which consumers are entitled.

IMPORTANCE OF THE ECONOMIC ENVIRONMENT

Of all the external environments, the economic environment has the most direct influence on personal financial planning. The economic environment includes many factors, such as gross domestic product, inflation rates, interest rates, trade payments, consumer income/debt/spending, unemployment, population age, and the index of leading economic indicators. Interest rates, inflation, unemployment, and gross domestic product play a key role in real investment returns and, therefore, in the attainment of financial goals.

Professional financial planners must understand the current economic environment to better forecast the economic future. By identifying the opportunities and threats that lie ahead, planners can help clients adapt to that future. The planner needs an understanding of the current economy's general condition, the current interest rate environment, the current inflation rate, and recent changes in monetary and fiscal policy. The planner must have the ability to anticipate each element's behavior and its potential effect on a client's financial plan. Exhibit 2.4 illustrates several selected economic factors and their relationship to various areas of financial planning.

EXHIBIT 2.4 The Economic Environment and Financial Planning

Selected Economic Factors	Financial Planning Areas Affected	How They Are Affected
Interest rates	Investment returns	Inversely
	Purchasing power and, therefore, the costs of goods and services in the future including education, retirement funding, and health care	Inversely
Taxes	Redistribution of income through government	Directly
	Production of goods	Inversely
	Distribution of wealth	Directly
Inflation	The cost of goods, services, money, and unemployment	Directly
Unemployment	Wage rates and other costs/expansion/contraction/consumption	Inversely
Monetary and fiscal policy	Economic expansion/contraction/expectations	Directly

Remember, these economic factors are not mutually exclusive but interrelated. As Exhibit 2.4 illustrates, one economic factor may influence several areas of financial planning in different ways. Professional financial planners need to interpret the external economic environment accurately so they can adjust their clients' financial plans accordingly.

The General Economy

The economy is a resource-allocation market system that achieves its objectives through a pricing mechanism. Prices are essentially determined in the marketplace at the point where supply and demand reach equilibrium. If supply or demand is affected, prices will change.

In the News

When the Pope lifted the ban on eating meat on Friday for Catholics in 1966, the average price per pound of fish dropped 12.5%. However, with the current awareness of health issues, the price of fish has risen faster than general inflation. Thus, if demand is affected, prices will also be affected. (Frederick W. Bell, "The Pope and the Price of Fish," American Economic Review 58 [December 1968]: 1346–1350)

Demand
The quantity of a particular good that people are willing to buy; heavily dependent on price

Demand curve
The graphic depiction that illustrates the relationship between a particular good's price and the quantity demanded

Demand

The **demand** for a particular good is the quantity people are willing to buy. Demand is heavily dependent on price. The **demand curve** (Exhibit 2.5) illustrates the general relationship between a particular good's price and the quantity demanded.

EXHIBIT 2.5 The Demand Curve

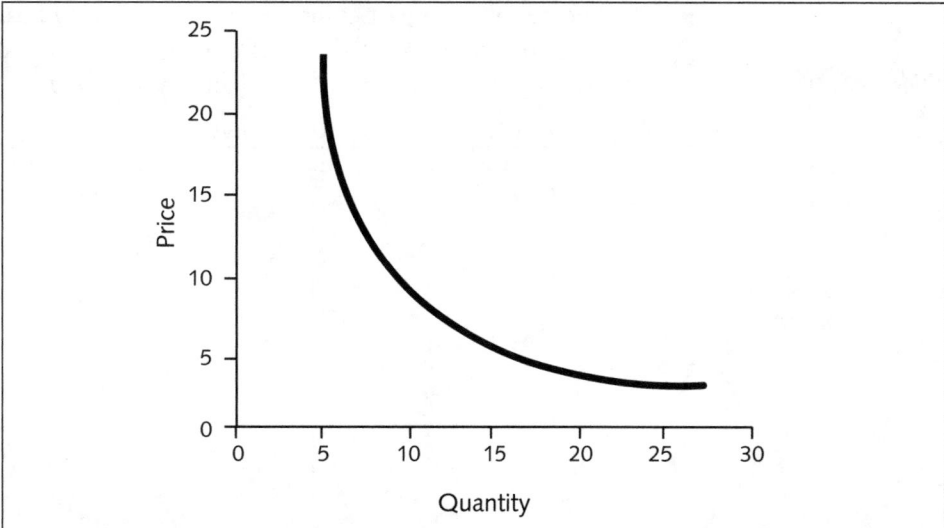

Substitution effect
The phenomenon in which consumers substitute less expensive goods for similar, more expensive goods; this is one of two reasons why the demand curve slopes downward

Changes in quantity demanded
The movements along the demand curve in response to a change in price

Downward sloping demand indicates that if the price increases, the quantity demanded will fall. Conversely, when the price falls, quantity demanded increases. There are two reasons demand declines when the price increases. The first is that consumers will substitute other, less expensive goods when the price for a particular good rises. This phenomenon is called the **substitution effect**. The second reason demand declines is that consumers curb consumption when prices rise. For example, assume Exhibit 2.5 shows the demand curve for Ben's consumption of ice cream. If the price of ice cream is $5 per pint, Ben will consume 15 pints of ice cream. However, if the price of ice cream increases to $8 per pint, Ben will consume only 10 pints of ice cream. Ben could substitute cupcakes for ice cream or simply reduce his overall consumption of desserts. These movements along the demand curve in response to a change in price are called **changes in quantity demanded**.

When the entire curve shifts to the right or the left, we say that there is a **change in demand**. When the curve shifts, quantity demanded at each price level changes. The average income or standard of living is a key determinant of demand. As incomes increase, individuals demand and purchase more goods at each price level. The size of the market and the price and availability of related, substitute goods also influence the demand for a particular good.

Change in demand
This occurs when the entire curve shifts to the right or left as the quantity demanded at each price level changes

EXHIBIT 2.6 Effects of Selected Events on the Demand Curve

Event	Effect on Demand Curve
Increase in the price of the good	Downward movement along the demand curve
Increase in average income	Upward (right) shift of demand curve
Increase in population	Upward shift of demand curve
Increase in the price of related goods	Upward shift of demand curve
Increase in the price of complement goods	Downward (left) shift of demand curve
Increase in taste preference	Upward shift of demand curve
Increases in price and economic expectations	Upward shift of demand curve

The opposite event (e.g., a decrease in average income) will result in an opposite effect on the demand curve (downward shift in the demand curve). Any changes or influences other than the price of a good cause a shift in the demand curve. Price changes simply cause movement along the demand curve.

Supply

Supply
The quantity of a particular good businesses are willing to produce or sell

The **supply** of a particular good is the quantity businesses are willing to produce and sell. The **supply curve** (Exhibit 2.7) depicts the general relationship between the market price of a particular good and the quantity supplied.

EXHIBIT 2.7 The Supply Curve

Supply curve
Depicts the general relationship between the market price of a particular good and the quantity supplied

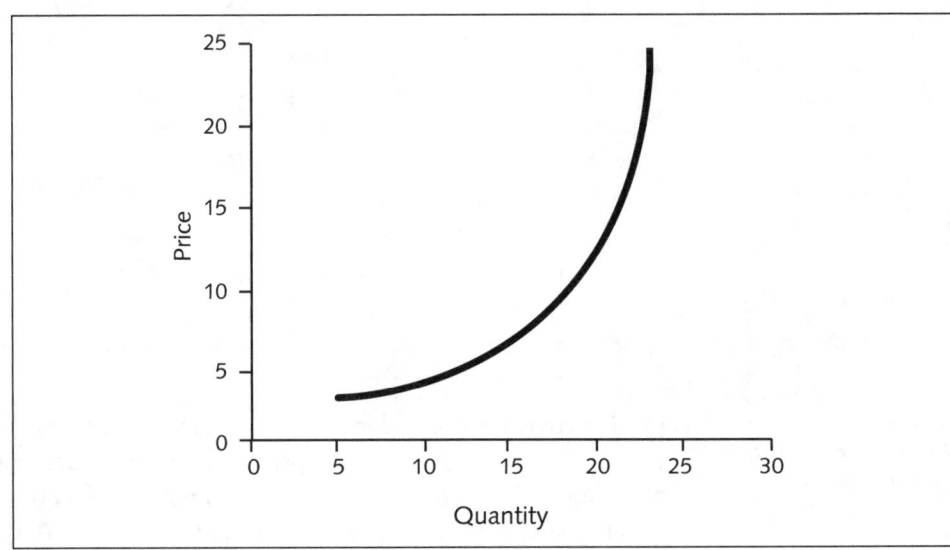

EXHIBIT 2.8 Effects of Selected Events on the Supply Curve

Event	Effect on Supply Curve
Increase in the price of the good	Upward movement along the supply curve
Increase in technology	Upward (right) shift of supply curve
Increase in input prices	Downward (left) shift of supply curve
Increase in the price of related goods	Upward shift of supply curve

Diminishing Marginal Utility

Law of diminishing marginal utility
As the rate of consumption increases, the marginal utility derived from consuming additional units of a good will decline

The **law of diminishing marginal utility** states that as the rate of consumption increases, the marginal utility derived from consuming additional units of a good will decline. **Marginal utility** is the additional utility received from the consumption of an additional unit of a good. For example, if Eddie's favorite food is steak, he might eat steak often. However, if Eddie ate steak for n consecutive days for dinner, the enjoyment, or utility, that he received from the dinner would be higher the first day than on the last.

Marginal utility
The additional utility received from the consumption of an additional unit of a good

Price Elasticity

Price elasticity
The quantity demanded of a good in response to changes in that good's price; a good is elastic when its quantity demanded responds greatly to price changes (luxuries) and inelastic when its quantity demanded responds little to price changes (necessities)

Price elasticity is the quantity demanded of a good in response to changes in that good's price. The percentage of change in quantity demanded divided by the percentage of change in price is a relative measure of price elasticity (PE). The formula for elasticity of demand is as follows:

$$\frac{\text{\% Change in Quantity Demanded}}{\text{\% Change in Price}} = \frac{\left(\dfrac{Q_1 - Q_0}{Q_0}\right)}{\left(\dfrac{P_1 - P_0}{P_0}\right)}$$

Goods differ in their elasticity. A good is elastic when its quantity demanded responds greatly to price changes (PE > 1). Luxuries such as movie tickets and liquor could be considered elastic because they are, generally, highly price sensitive. A good is inelastic when its quantity demanded responds little to price changes (PE < 1). Milk and electricity, considered necessities by some, will remain in demand no matter what the price. **Unit-elastic demand** exists when the percentage of change in quantity demanded is exactly equal to the percentage of change in price, ignoring the direction of the change (PE = 1).

Unit-elastic demand
The percentage of change in quantity demanded is exactly equal to the percentage of change in price, ignoring the direction of the change (PE = 1); a change in price results in no change to total revenue

E X A M P L E   Assume that in a given year U.S. gasoline consumption was 2.563 million gallons per day at an average price of $1.53 per gallon. Several years later, the average price of gasoline rose to $2.27 per gallon, and consumption was 3.288 million barrels per day. We can calculate the price elasticity (PE) of gasoline for this period as follows:

$$\frac{\text{\% Change in Quantity Demanded}}{\text{\% Change in Price}} = \frac{\left(\dfrac{3.288 - 2.563}{2.563}\right)}{\left(\dfrac{2.27 - 1.53}{1.53}\right)} = \frac{28.29\%}{48.37\%} = .585$$

Because PE < 1, we conclude that the demand for this period's gasoline is inelastic.

Price elasticity can also have an effect on a company's total revenues. When the demand for a good is price inelastic, a price decrease reduces total revenues. When the demand is price elastic, a price decrease increases total revenue. In the case of unit-elastic demand, a price decrease results in no change in total revenue.

E X A M P L E   Consider a gas company that derives its revenues from the price of gasoline (an inelastic good). The company typically sells 1 million gallons per day at $5.50 per gallon. This translates into sales of $5.5 million per day. If the price of gasoline increases to $6 per gallon, revenues increase to $6 million per day, giving the company an extra $500,000 of revenue.

With inelastic goods, the demand curve becomes vertical because the price has no effect on the quantity demanded. However, the curve may shift right or left depending on various factors.

E X A M P L E   To explain unit-elastic demand and its effects on company revenues, consider a grocer selling apples for $1 per pound. He typically sells 500 pounds a week for a gross revenue of $500. One week, he decided to raise the price of apples to $2 per pound and only ended up selling 250 pounds and maintaining a gross revenue of $500. Because the change in price had no effect on total revenue, this good is said to be perfectly unit-elastic.

Equilibrium

Equilibrium
The state of the market where quantity demanded equals quantity supplied

In a competitive market, prices are free to adjust to changes in supply and consumer demand. When the price of a good is such that the quantity supplied equals the quantity demanded, the market for that good is said to be in **equilibrium**. The conditions of a competitive market encourage price movement toward equilibrium. For example, if more apples are grown than are demanded, the price for apples will fall, which will encourage consumers to buy. Similarly, if consumers are demanding more bananas than producers are supplying, the price of bananas will rise, discouraging consumers from buying. These adjustments continue until the market prices of apples and bananas achieve equal quantities of supply and demand—equilibrium.

EXHIBIT 2.9 Equilibrium

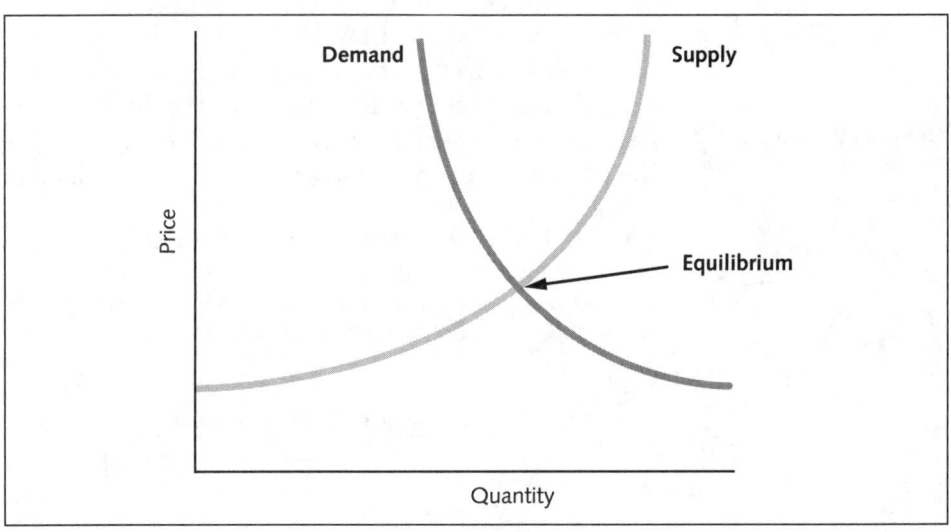

Business Cycles

Business cycles

Swings in total national output, income, and employment marked by widespread expansion or contraction in many sectors of the economy

Business cycles are swings in total national output, income, and employment marked by widespread expansion or contraction in many sectors of the economy. These cycles generally occur because of shifts in aggregate demand. The financial planner should be familiar with the impact of business cycles on the economy, as different investments will not perform the same during various phases of a business cycle. For example, cyclical industries such as the automobile or housing industry generally perform well during an economic expansion and poorly during a contraction.

The business cycle (as depicted in Exhibit 2.10) consists of two general phases, expansion and contraction, and two points, peak and trough. Each phase of the business cycle passes into the next phase and is characterized by different economic conditions.

The expansion phase ends and moves into the contraction phase at the upper turning point, or peak. Similarly, the contraction phase gives way to expansion at the lower turning point, or trough. The emphasis here is not so much on high or low business activity as on the dynamic aspects of the rise and fall of business activity.

EXHIBIT 2.10 A Hypothetical Business Cycle

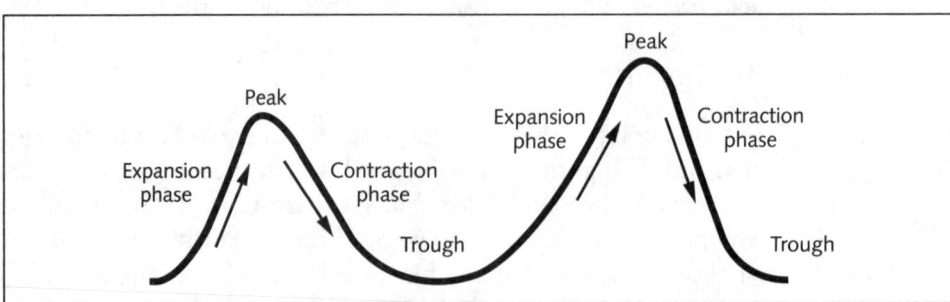

Note: The actual business cycle is not as symmetrical as drawn here. The pattern is more irregular and unpredictable. See Exhibit 2.12 for an illustration of the changes in the actual business cycle.

Business Cycle Components and Their Effect on the Economy

Expansion phase
One of the two general business cycle phases characterized by a rise in business sales, growth of the gross domestic product, and a decline in unemployment

Peak
The point in the business cycle that appears at the end of the expansion phase when most businesses are operating at full capacity and gross domestic product is increasing rapidly

Contraction phase
One of the two general business cycle phases characterized by a fall in business sales, decreased growth of the gross domestic product, and increased unemployment

Trough
The point in the business cycle that appears at the end of the contraction phase when most businesses are operating at their lowest capacity levels and the gross domestic product is at its lowest

Recession
A decline in real gross domestic product for two or more successive quarters

Depression
A persistent recession that brings a severe decline in economic activity

The **expansion phase** leads to the peak. During the expansion phase, business sales rise, gross domestic product (GDP)—which is the value of all goods and services produced in the United States—grows, and unemployment declines.

The **peak** appears at the end of the expansion phase when most businesses are operating at full capacity and GDP is increasing rapidly. The peak is the point at which GDP is at its highest and exceeds the long-run average GDP. Usually employment levels also peak at this point. (See Exhibit 2.11 for a depiction of the relationship between long-run GDP and the business cycle.)

The **contraction phase** leads to the trough. During the contraction phase, business sales fall, GDP growth falls, and unemployment increases.

The **trough** occurs at the end of the contraction phase where businesses are generally operating at their lowest capacity. The trough point is characterized by the lowest GDP growth. Unemployment is rapidly increasing and finally peaks when sales fall rapidly.

Recession is a decline in real GDP for two or more successive quarters characterized by the following:

- Declining consumer purchases
- Expanding business inventories
- Decreasing capital investment
- Decreasing demand for labor
- High unemployment
- Falling commodity prices
- Decreasing business profits
- Falling interest rates due to reduced demand for money

Depression is a persistent recession that brings a severe decline in economic activity.

EXHIBIT 2.11 The Business Cycle and GDP

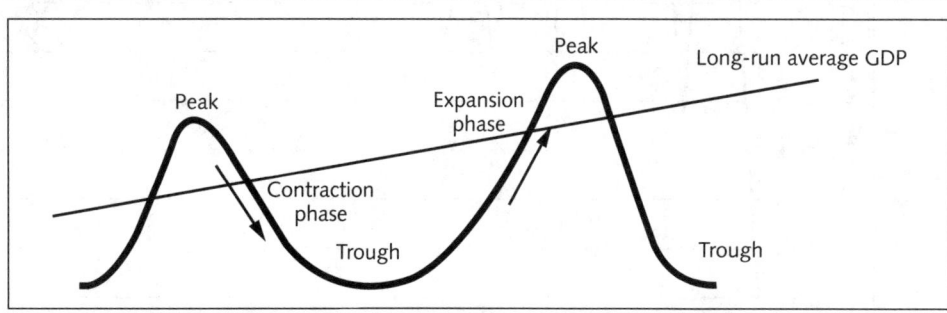

While there are many economic variables that fluctuate during the business cycle, certain economic variables always show greater fluctuation than others. **Capital formation** rises and falls significantly with expansion and contraction, usually leading the trend. **Durable goods**, also a trend leader, are subject to highly erratic patterns of demand. It is the economy's durable, or capital, goods sector that by far shows the greatest cyclical fluctuation. There is good reason to believe that the movement of durable goods represents key causes in the direction of expansion or contraction. **Consumption movements**, which lag behind trends, seem to be the effect of the business cycle phase rather than the cause.

Capital formation
Production of buildings, machinery, tools, and other equipment that will help economic participants produce in the future

Durable goods
Products that are not consumed or quickly disposed of and can be used for several years, such as automobiles, furniture, and computers

Consumption movements
Economic variables that fluctuate during the business cycle; describe changes in consumer purchases

Business Cycle Theories

Two opposing types of theories attempt to explain the fluctuations in the business cycle: external theories and internal theories. External theories find the root of the business cycle in the fluctuations of something outside the economic system, such as wars, revolutions, political events, rates of population growth and migration, discoveries of new resources, scientific and technological discoveries, and innovation. Internal theories look for mechanisms within the economic system that give rise to self-generating business cycles. Thus, every expansion breeds recession and contraction. Every contraction, in turn, breeds revival and expansion in a quasi-regular, repeating, never-ending chain. Each peak and valley, however, is higher than the last and leads to growth in the economy over the long term despite the business cycle.

Actual Business Cycle

The actual business cycle for the United States as depicted below has averaged growth of approximately 3% per year. Growth, as measured by gross domestic product (GDP), will exceed the average in some years, whereas in other years growth will be less than the average. Exhibit 2.12 illustrates the actual change in GDP as a percentage. Note that the graph appears to move horizontally across the page. However, because all years except four have positive growth, the amount of business done has actually increased virtually every year since 1932. At a 3% average growth rate, American business was 11.3 times larger in 2014 than in 1932.

EXHIBIT 2.12 Annual Change in Gross Domestic Product 1932–2019

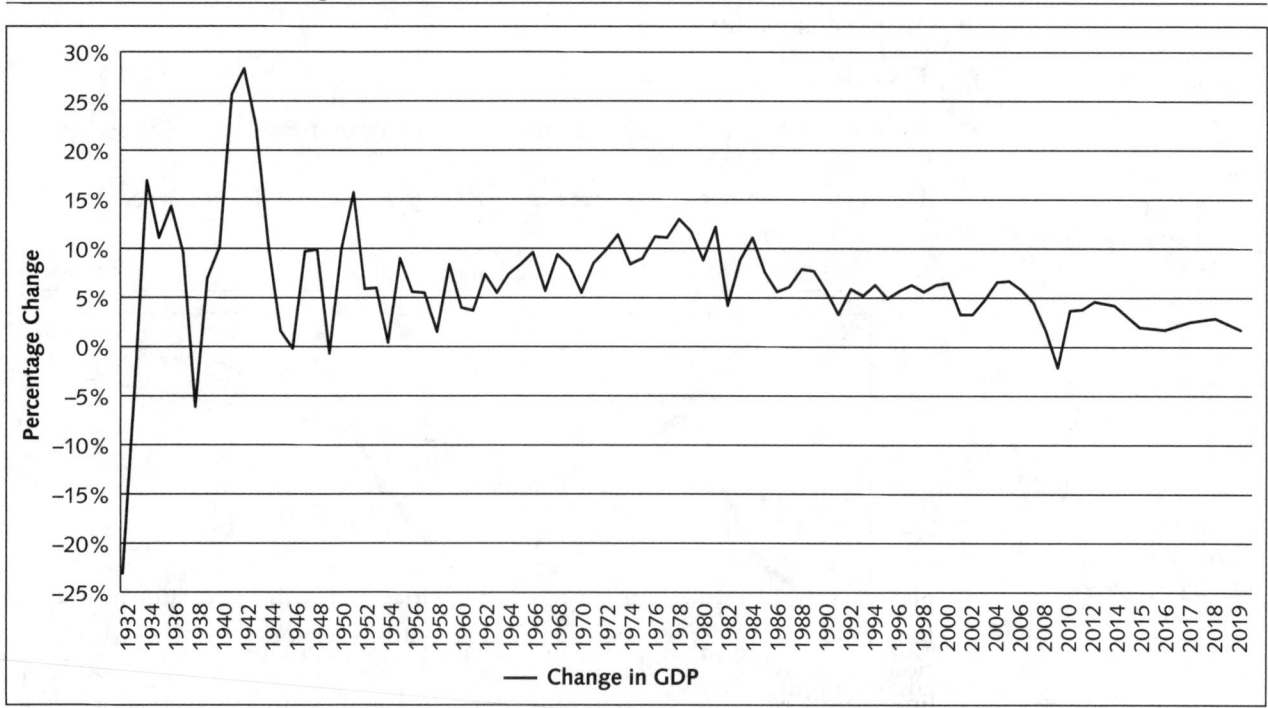

Source: U.S. Department of Commerce Bureau of Economic Analysis, www.bea.gov/national /index.htm (accessed May 20, 2020).

Inflation

Inflation
An increase in the price level of goods and services

Deflation
The opposite of inflation; it occurs when the general level of prices is falling

Disinflation
A decline in the rate of inflation

Moderate inflation
Inflation characterized by slowly rising prices

Galloping inflation
Inflation that occurs when money loses its value very quickly, and real interest rates can be negative 50% or 100% per year

Inflation is another important element affecting the economic environment. Inflation is an increase in the price of goods and services. Inflation increases the cost of buying a home, durable goods, and consumption goods. For retirees on fixed incomes, substantial increases in inflation can dramatically affect their financial plan. Likewise, for wage earners, the rate of inflation may sometimes be greater than the individual's wage increases, resulting in a loss of purchasing power. Professional financial planners need to understand how the rate of inflation is calculated, how it affects the economy, and how it is measured.

The opposite of inflation is **deflation**, which occurs when the general level of prices is falling. **Disinflation** is the term used to denote a decline in the rate of inflation. **Moderate inflation** is characterized by slowly rising prices. **Galloping inflation** occurs when money loses its value very quickly, and real interest rates can be negative 50% or 100% per year. During a period of galloping inflation, people hold only the absolute minimum of cash needed for daily transactions. Financial markets are in turmoil or disappear, and funds are generally allocated by rationing rather than by interest rates. People hoard goods, buy houses, and never lend money at the low nominal interest rate. Remember, though, that during periods of inflation, all prices and wages do not increase at the same rate.

Calculating Inflation

Inflation denotes a rise in the general level of prices. The rate of inflation is the rate of change in the general price level and is calculated as follows:

Inflation rate (year t):

$$\frac{\text{Price level (year } t) - \text{Price level (year } t-1)}{\text{Price level (year } t-1)} \times 100$$

E X A M P L E   Last year Abby paid $30,000 for her college tuition. This year Abby will pay $31,500 for tuition, with the increase solely attributable to inflation. Calculate the inflation rate for Abby's education expense.

Answer: The inflation rate attributable to Abby's increase in tuition is 5%, calculated as follows.

$$\frac{\$31,500 - \$30,000}{\$30,000} \times 100 = 5\%$$

Effects of Inflation

Unexpected inflation causes a redistribution of income and wealth among different classes of people in our economy. Changes are created in the relative prices and outputs of different goods or sometimes in output and employment for the economy as a whole. The major redistributive impact of inflation occurs through its effect on the real value of people's wealth. In general, unanticipated inflation redistributes wealth from creditors to debtors. Said another way, unanticipated or unforeseen inflation helps those who have previously borrowed money and hurts those who have loaned money. An unanticipated decline in inflation has the opposite effect. If, however, inflation is anticipated, prices adjust as expected and there is little redistribution of wealth.

Inflation affects the real economy in two specific areas: total output and economic efficiency. The relationship between prices and output is not necessarily direct. Inflation may be associated with a higher or a lower level of output and employment. Generally, the higher the inflation rate, the greater the changes in relative prices of goods. Distortions occur when price changes accelerate relative to changes in costs and demand.

Real interest rate adjustment
The rate of interest expressed in dollars of constant value (adjusted for inflation) and equal to the nominal interest rate, less the rate of inflation

Price index
A weighted average of the prices of numerous goods and services (e.g., the Consumer Price Index, the gross domestic product deflator, the gross national product deflator, and the Producer Price Index)

Consumer Price Index (CPI)
A price index that measures the cost of a market basket of consumer goods and services purchased for day-to-day living

Gross domestic product (GDP)
The value of all goods and services produced in the country; GDP is the broadest measure of the general state of the economy

If inflation persists for a long period, markets begin to adapt, and an allowance for inflation is built into the market interest rate. This is known as the **real interest rate adjustment**. This phenomenon is consistent with anticipated price increases.

Measures of Inflation

A **price index** is a weighted average of the prices of numerous goods and services. The best known price indexes are the Consumer Price Index (CPI), the gross domestic product (GDP) deflator, the gross national product (GNP) deflator, and the Producer Price Index (PPI).

The **Consumer Price Index (CPI)** measures the cost of a market basket of consumer goods and services, including prices of food, clothing, housing, property taxes, fuels, transportation, medical care, college tuition, and other commodities purchased for day-to-day living. The CPI is constructed by weighting each price according to the economic importance of the commodity in question. Each item is assigned a fixed weight proportional to its relative importance in consumer expenditure budgets.

The **gross domestic product (GDP)** is the market value of final goods and services produced within a country over a specific period, usually a year. The GDP deflator is the ratio of nominal GDP to real GDP and gives an overall measure of prices in the economy. Real GDP only measures increases or decreases in production output. Nominal GDP is affected by changes in prices as well as increases and decreases in production. The GDP deflator is a broader price index than the CPI. In addition to consumer goods, the GDP deflator includes prices for capital goods and other goods and services purchased by businesses and government.

Exhibit 2.13 presents data for both the CPI and GDP deflator. Even though the two indexes are based on different market baskets of goods with different base years, the two measures of the annual rate of inflation are quite similar. The differences between these two measures of inflation have been small, usually only a few tenths of a percentage point per year. The closeness of the two rates is not a surprise because consumer spending makes up about two-thirds of GDP.

EXHIBIT 2.13 Consumer Price Index and GDP Deflator Percentage Change 1986–2019

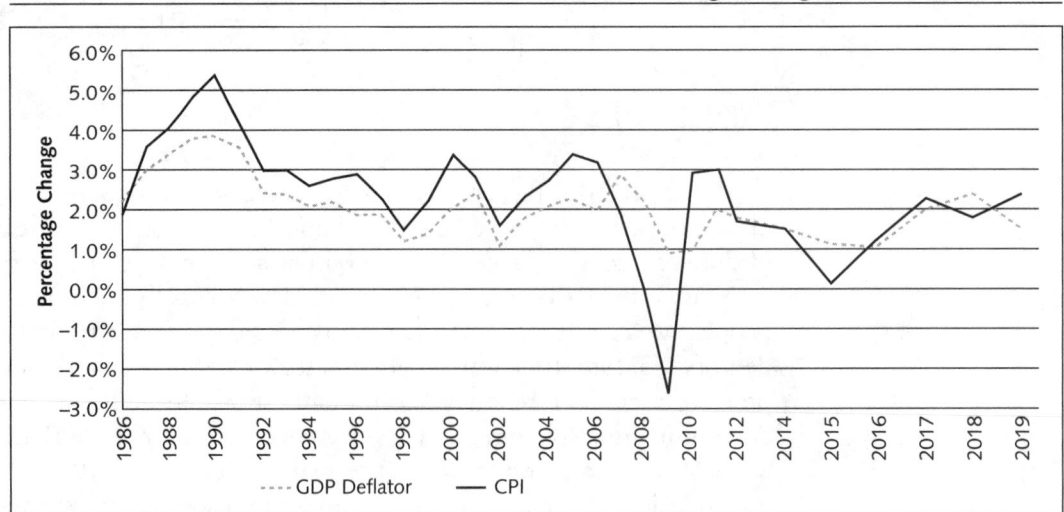

Sources: U.S. Department of Labor and http://data.worldbank.org/indicator/NY.GDP.DEFL.KD.ZG (accessed May 20, 2020).

Price indexes are not problem-free. The cost of living, as estimated by the CPI, is considered overestimated in the situation where consumers substitute relatively inexpensive goods for relatively expensive goods. The CPI does not accurately capture changes in the quality of goods. Although the CPI is modified from time to time, the CPI is not corrected for quality improvements in goods and services.

The GNP deflator is the ratio of nominal gross national product to real gross national product. The difference between gross domestic product and gross national product is subtle. GDP measures goods and services produced within the country, regardless of the citizenship of the owners. For example, automobiles produced at a Honda plant in Ohio would be included in the United States' GDP. GNP, on the other hand, measures goods and services produced by citizens of the country regardless of where they are produced. For example, wages paid to an American working for Honda in Tokyo would be included in GNP but not in GDP.

Producer Price Index (PPI)

A group of indexes that measures the average change in the selling prices received by domestic producers of goods and services over time

The **Producer Price Index (PPI)** is the oldest continuous statistical series published by the Labor Department. It is a group of indexes that measures the average change in the selling prices received by domestic producers of goods and services over time. PPIs measure price change from the perspective of the seller, in contrast with the Consumer Price Index (CPI), which measures price change from the purchaser's perspective. Sellers' and purchasers' prices may differ due to sales and excise taxes, distribution costs, and government subsidies.

For professional planners, the CPI is a good proxy for overall consumer price changes. However, due to the general nature of the market basket of goods described previously, it is likely that many clients' inflation experience will be different from the general CPI. Consider the fact that many people have fixed-rate mortgages rather than rent; thus the cost of the housing payment (principal and interest) associated with the mortgage payment is unaffected by inflation. The property taxes and insurance costs on the home, however, are subject to inflation, as are any maintenance or repair costs. Also consider that some households will need to factor in the effect of inflation on their savings plans for their children's education, whereas other households are relatively unaffected by the costs of higher education. The planner with clients on a fixed income can review a line-item budget to determine which costs are subject to inflation and adjust their overall financial plan accordingly. Having seen some of the more dominant ways individuals are affected by inflation, realize that all individuals are affected in a consequential way by inflation because they pay for groceries, clothing, automobiles, fuel, and medical care.

Monetary and Fiscal Policy

Monetary policy and fiscal policy exert far-reaching influence on the economic environment. Competent financial planners must identify changes in monetary and fiscal policy that will be the most beneficial and most detrimental to their client's financial goals and objectives. Once identified, the planner should forecast the likelihood of the important policy changes and adjust the financial plan accordingly.

Monetary Policy

Federal Reserve (Fed)

The banking and financial system developed under the Federal Reserve Act of 1913; it makes the basic policy decisions that regulate the country's money and banking systems

The **Federal Reserve (Fed)** is charged with three primary responsibilities:

1. To maintain sustainable long-term economic growth

2. To maintain price levels that are supported by that economic growth

3. To maintain full employment

The Fed goes about its mission primarily using the tools of monetary policy. The Fed controls the money supply, which enables it to significantly impact short-term interest rates. The Fed will follow a loose, or easy, monetary policy when it wants to increase the money supply and thus expand the level of income and employment. In times of inflation and when it wants to constrict the money supply, the Fed will follow a tight monetary policy.

Easy monetary policy   When the Fed wants to stimulate the money supply, it lowers the cost of short-term loans to commercial banks. The money supply increases, resulting in the circulation of more money. This leads to more funds available for banks to lend and, ultimately, to a decline in short-term interest rates.

Tight monetary policy   When the Fed wants to tighten the money supply, it raises the cost of short-term borrowing for commercial banks. The money supply is restricted, resulting in less money available for banks to lend. This leads to an increase in short-term interest rates.

The Fed has several methods for controlling the money supply, including adjusting the reserve requirements, adjusting the Federal Reserve discount rates, and using open market operations.

The **reserve requirement** for a member bank of the Federal Reserve is the percentage of deposit liabilities that must be held in reserve. As this requirement is increased, less money is available to be loaned to customers, resulting in a restriction of the money supply. Conversely, as reserve requirements are decreased, more money is made available for loans.

The **Federal Reserve discount rate** is the rate at which member banks can borrow funds from the Federal Reserve to meet reserve requirements. When the Fed raises the discount rate, it increases short-term borrowing costs and discourages member banks from borrowing funds. This causes the money supply to contract. The Fed will lower the discount rate when it wants to increase the money supply. Banks are able to borrow funds at lower rates and lend more money, which increases the money supply.

Note that the Federal Reserve discount rate is the borrowing rate from the Federal Reserve, and differs from the federal funds rate, which is the overnight lending rate between member banks.

Open market operations is the process by which the Federal Reserve purchases and sells government securities in the open market. The Fed buys government securities to cause more money to circulate, resulting in lower interest rates, increased lending, and growth of the money supply. The Fed sells government securities to restrict the money supply. As investors purchase government securities, more money leaves circulation, which increases interest rates and decreases lending.

Fiscal Policy

Taxation, expenditures, and debt management of the federal government is called **fiscal policy**. Economic growth, price stability, and full employment are other goals that may be pursued by changes in fiscal policy.

Changes in taxation affect corporate earnings, disposable earnings, and the overall economy. As tax rates increase, corporations' after-tax income declines, which reduces their ability to pay dividends. This may cause the price for equities to decrease. Tax rate increases also reduce an individual's disposable income and limit the amount of money entering the economy. The demand for tax-free investments is also influenced by changes in taxation levels. As increases in proportional tax rates occur, the attractiveness of tax-free instruments also increases, reducing yields.

Deficit spending occurs when governmental expenditures exceed tax collections. By selling debt securities to the public to finance deficits, Treasury securities compete with other issuers of debt securities. This demand drives the value of debt down because

Reserve requirement
The percentage of deposit liabilities that must be held in reserve by a member bank of the Federal Reserve; as the reserve requirement is increased, less money is available to be loaned, resulting in a restriction of the money supply

Federal Reserve discount rate
The rate at which Federal Reserve member banks can borrow funds to meet reserve requirements; the Fed will lower the discount rate when it wants to increase the money supply

Open market operations
The process by which the Federal Reserve purchases and sells government securities in the open market

Fiscal policy
Taxation, expenditures, and debt management of the federal government

Deficit spending
Occurs when governmental expenditures exceed the government's tax collections

of the increased supply of debt, causing the yields on debt instruments to rise to meet competition.

The Nature of Interest Rates

Discount rate
Interest rate charged by the Federal Reserve on a loan made to a member bank

Nominal interest rate
Stated interest rate without considering the effect of inflation

Real interest rate
Nominal interest rate considering the effect of inflation

The economic environment is greatly influenced by interest rates. Decreases in interest rates are often followed by periods of economic expansion, whereas increases are generally followed by economic contractions. Investment returns and purchasing power are just two of the areas that are affected by the rise and fall of interest rates. Simply stated, the interest rate is the price of money. The **discount rate** is the interest rate charged by the Fed on a loan that it makes to a member bank. The **nominal interest rate** is the stated interest rate without considering the effect of inflation. The return on investments in terms of real goods and services is a real interest rate measure. The return in terms of dollars is an absolute measure. The real interest rate measures the quantity of goods we receive tomorrow for goods forgone today. The **real interest rate** is obtained by correcting nominal or dollar interest rates for the rate of inflation.

Expansion and Recession

As discussed earlier, the economy is in a constant state of flux. Some economic factors tend to expand the economy, and others tend to contract the economy. In the following section, the factors that contribute to the economy's rise and fall are discussed.

Periods of economic expansion are characterized by high employment, high resource demand, and output in excess of the historical gross domestic product average of 3%. As the economy expands, real wages rise, as do real interest rates. Higher interest rates decrease capital expenditures, and higher resource costs increase overall costs and reduce aggregate demand, ultimately ending the expansionary period.

Periods of recession are characterized by high unemployment, low resource demand, falling real wages, and decreasing real interest rates. The economy eventually pulls itself out of recession as prices for money and resources fall.

Recall Exhibit 2.10 (the drawing of the business cycle) with its peaks and troughs. The peaks are simply the top of the expansion, and the troughs, the bottom of the recession. Each is characterized by high and low real interest rates and changes in nonfarm hourly payroll. Real interest rates are at their highest at the peak and at their lowest at the trough. The rate of change in nonfarm hourly labor costs is at its highest at peaks and at its lowest in troughs.

A reasonable question to ask at this point is whether the economy is self-correcting. It appears to be so, although slowly. This slowness is evidenced by a recession's prolonged high unemployment and below-capacity utilization. As a result of the belief that the economy is too slow to self-correct, there is widespread support for monetary and fiscal policy stimulation during periods of recession and, alternatively, for monetary and fiscal restriction during periods of excessive economic expansion. Thus, monetary and fiscal policy tools are used to guide the economy to stability and long-run prosperity. The degree of policy discretion remains controversial. Some economists believe in less discretion and more constant growth models, including the management of money supply, inflation, unemployment, and budget deficits, while others believe in greater discretion and aggressive monetary and fiscal management.

Forecasting the Economy—Index of Leading Economic Indicators

Index of leading economic indicators
A composite index of 10 variables that has had a reasonable track record in predicting recessions; it has accurately predicted every recession since 1950 but has also predicted five that did not happen

Can anyone successfully predict the future economy? Some say that monitoring the gross domestic product is useful in forecasting the economy. Others look to the **index of leading economic indicators**. Monitoring both GDP and the index may be the best approach to forecasting the economy.

GDP is the value of all goods and services produced in the country. It is the broadest measure of the general state of the economy. The historical growth rate is approximately 3%. Growth of GDP less than 2% is considered low and signals a possible recession. Growth in excess of 4% is robust and suggests the possibility of expansion. Monitoring GDP growth is useful in forecasting the peaks and troughs in the economy.

Another indication of future economic activity of which financial planners should be keenly aware is the index of leading economic indicators. This index is a composite index of 10 variables. It has had a reasonable track record in predicting recessions and has accurately predicted every recession since 1950 but has also predicted five that did not happen. When the index declines for three months in a row, it signals a slowdown in economic growth. The index only predicts the direction of economic activity and not the magnitude. The 10 components listed below make up the index.

1. Length of average work week in hours, manufacturing

2. Initial weekly claims for unemployment

3. New orders placed with manufacturers for consumer goods

4. Percentage of companies receiving slower deliveries from supplier

5. Contracts and orders for new plant and equipment

6. Permits for new housing starts

7. Interest rate spread, 10-year Treasury bond less federal funds rate

8. S&P 500 Index

9. Money supply (M2)

10. Index of consumer expectations

Lagging economic indicators
Economic statistics that fall or rise 3–12 months after the general economy

In addition to leading economic indicators, there are **lagging economic indicators**. These economic statistics fall or rise 3 to 12 months after the general economy. The lagging index gives a good picture of where the economy has been. The following are seven components of the lagging index for the United States:

1. Average duration of unemployment

2. Inventories to sales ratio, manufacturing and trade

3. Labor cost per unit of output, manufacturing

4. Average prime rate

5. Commercial and industrial loans

6. Consumer installment credit to personal income ratio

7. Consumer price index for services

Although the word *recession* for some investors may have a less-than-positive connotation in periods of declining economic growth, interest rates generally fall, making the purchases of fixed instruments prior to the decline in interest rates an attractive investment opportunity. Likewise, generally the best time to buy stocks and hold them through economic recovery may be when the economy is at its worst.

How fast should the economy be growing? At first, many people might think, "The faster the better." A quickly growing economy could lead to more business, more wealth, and more jobs. Everyone would win. However, over time, high growth rates have been found to be unsustainable because they can lead to higher inflation. This brings higher interest rates to fight inflation. Thus, unsustainable booms have been followed by harmful busts. One way to measure how fast an economy can grow in the medium term without causing inflation is the "potential GDP." When thinking about an economy, the sustainable rate of growth would most essentially be a combination of productivity growth plus labor force growth. Productivity is the GDP divided by the number of workers each year. For example, if labor productivity grows by 1% a year and the labor force grows by 2% a year, then the "potential GDP" for that economy would be 3%. If the economy was actually growing by 4%, then its growth would be unsustainable over the long term. Excess growth can eventually lead to inflation and higher interest rates to fight that inflation. However, when the actual GDP growth rate is above the potential GDP growth rate, the current unemployment should improve. On the other hand, if this economy was only growing at 1% (2% below potential GDP), inflation and interest rates will be low, but unemployment will be high.

Potential GDP is a useful concept for evaluating the growth rates of different countries. A country with a rapidly rising labor force should grow faster than a country with a slower growing labor force. Also, productivity enhancements help an economy grow. Potential GDP can also inform evaluations of how fast an economy should be growing now compared to former times. For example, China's labor force grew strongly during the 1990–2000s. As the labor force growth slows, either productivity must leap ahead or the economy will not be able to sustain the rapid growth rates of former years. Finally, comparing actual GDP growth to potential GDP growth can diagnosis if an economy is underperforming or is unsustainably high. That should be the starting point for any fiscal or momentary policy decisions. Finally, the best measure of potential GDP is real potential GDP. This is potential GDP with an adjustment to remove inflation.

IMPORTANCE OF THE LEGAL ENVIRONMENT

The legal environment is another component of the external environment that may have far-reaching influence on risk exposure and the accomplishment of financial goals. The rules of property ownership, consumer rights and protections, worker rights and protections, investor rights and protections, and the rules regarding formation of a business are established within this environment. With a high level of competence and knowledge of the legal environment, the personal financial planner can guide clients toward their financial goals while avoiding legal risks and protecting the clients' rights.

Torts

Tort

A private wrong; an infringement on the rights of another

A **tort** (private wrong) is an infringement on the rights of another. The wrongdoer, also known as a tortfeasor, creates a right in the damaged party to bring a civil action. Intentional torts—battery (harmful touching), assault (threat causing apprehension), libel (written falsehood), slander (oral falsehood), false imprisonment (unlawfully holding against will), trespass to land, invasion of privacy, and intentional infliction of emotional

Unintentional tort
Failure to act in a reasonably prudent manner, thereby causing harm to another

distress—are not covered by liability insurance. An **unintentional tort** results from negligence and is defined as the failure to act in a reasonably prudent manner, thereby causing harm to another. Elements of unintentional torts include duty, breach of duty, causation, and actual loss. When determining whether negligence is present, ask, "Did the person exercise the proper degree of care to carry out his duty, and if not, was that the cause of the actual loss suffered by the other party?" If so, the person performing the act may be liable for negligence.

Negligence

Negligence
The failure to act in a way that a reasonably prudent person would have acted under similar circumstances

Negligence is defined as the failure to act in a way that a reasonably prudent person would have acted under similar circumstances. Types of liability created from negligent behavior include the following:

■ *Strict (absolute) liability*—Liability without regard to negligence or fault. It applies to damage resulting from some extraordinarily dangerous activity or other statutorily defined activity (e.g., product liability, hazardous materials, blasting operations). Negligence does not have to be proved; however, defenses may be allowed to refute or lessen liability. Workers are indemnified for employment-connected injuries regardless of who was at fault (e.g., workers' compensation). In these cases, negligence does not have to be proved on the part of the employer, nor are defenses permitted by the employer to refute or lessen liability.

■ *Negligence per se*—The act itself constitutes negligence, thereby relieving the burden to prove negligence (e.g., drunk driving).

Res ipsa loquitur
"The act speaks for itself"; negligence can be assumed from the character of the outcome without evidence of wrongdoing on the part of the tortfeasor

Burden of proof is initially borne by the injured party. Standard of proof in most civil cases is the preponderance of the evidence (greater than 50%). Other concepts to consider include **res ipsa loquitur** ("the act speaks for itself"). *Res ipsa loquitur* is a doctrine of the law of negligence under which negligence can be assumed from the character of the outcome without evidence of wrongdoing on the part of the tortfeasor. For example, if an airplane crashes due to engine failure and, prior to takeoff, a maintenance company checked the engine, the maintenance company may be found negligent based on the concept of *res ipsa loquitor* even though there is not enough physical evidence to determine how or why the engine failed.

Damages

A tort can result in two forms of injury: bodily injury and property damage. Bodily injury may lead to medical expense, loss of income, pain and suffering, and mental anguish. The damages for bodily injury can be:

■ special damages to compensate for measurable losses;

■ general damages to compensate for intangible losses (pain and suffering); or

■ punitive damages—amounts assessed against the negligent party as punishment.

Collateral source rule
Damages assessed against a negligent party should not be reduced simply because the injured party has other sources of recovery available

Property damage is usually measured by the actual monetary loss.

The **collateral source rule** holds that damages assessed against a negligent party should not be reduced simply because the injured party has other sources of recovery available such as insurance or employee benefits (health or disability insurance).

Vicarious Liability

Under the doctrine of **vicarious liability**, parents and guardians may be liable for the acts of minors and mentally incompetent people in their care. Likewise, employers may be vicariously liable for the acts of their employees.

Defenses to Negligence

There are various defenses available to alleged negligent parties that can relieve them of legal liability in spite of negligent behavior.

Assumption of the risk—The injured party fully understood and recognized the dangers that were involved in an activity and voluntarily chose to proceed. This defense is not available in all states.

Negligence on the part of the injured party—This can be either contributory negligence, where there is evidence that the injured party did not look out for his own safety, or comparative negligence, where the amount of damage is adjusted to reflect the injured party's proportion of contribution to the cause of the injury (same with multiple defendants). Contributory negligence theories usually cause the entire action to fail, thus effecting a harsh result. Many states allow recovery for that portion of damage not caused by the injured party (comparative negligence). The "last clear chance" rule may apply. This rule states that a claimant who is endangered by his own negligence may recover if the defendant had a last clear chance to avoid the accident and failed to do so.

Property Ownership

Property ownership rules are generally determined by individual states and will be discussed in Chapter 17: Introduction to Estate Planning.

Consumer Protection

Consumer protection laws are passed at both the state and federal levels. Federal laws preempt state laws where the state law provides less protection than the federal law. However, states do have the right to grant their citizens additional protection in excess of federal laws.

Consumer protection laws accomplish their goals by affecting contractual obligations. Without the right to enforce contracts, there would certainly be less private enterprise. Thus, certain consumer protection laws allow for the rescission of illegal contracts and provide for monetary damages or injunctive relief for the injured party.

Federal consumer protection began with the creation of the **Federal Trade Commission (FTC)** in 1914. Its charge was to keep competition free and fair and to protect consumers. The FTC promotes competition through the enforcement of antitrust laws. It also ensures consumer protection by trade practice regulation prohibiting "unfair or deceptive acts or practices in commerce."

The FTC also prohibits the unfair and deceptive advertising of prices and practices, such as **bait-and-switch promotions**. Credit and packaging also fall under FTC regulation. Federal credit regulations are a response to the magnitude of credit transactions. The laws include the regulation of credit extension and discrimination and the collection and dissemination of credit report information. Laws also regulate consumer warranties and debt collection practices. What follows is a brief description of several FTC laws that have a direct effect on consumers.

Vicarious liability
One person may become legally liable for the torts of another (e.g., parent/child, employer/employee acting in the scope of employment)

Federal Trade Commission (FTC)
The federal organization created in 1914 to keep competition free and fair and to protect U.S. consumers

---

Bait-and-switch promotion
Deceptive sales practice in which a business advertises a low price for an item in order to engage customers and then advise them that the advertised item is no longer available or is of substandard quality, attempting to entice the customers to purchase a more expensive product

EXHIBIT 2.14 The FTC and Federal Consumer Protection Laws

Law	Purpose
Fair Packaging and Labeling Act	Prohibit deceptive labeling and require disclosure
Equal Credit Opportunity Act	Prohibit discrimination in granting credit
Fair Credit Reporting Act	Regulate the consumer credit reporting industry
Fair Credit Billing Act	Regulate consumer credit billing practices
Truth in Lending Act	Require disclosure of terms
Magnuson-Moss Warranty Act	Regulate consumer product warranty
Fair Debt Collection Act	Prevent abusive or deceptive debt collection practices
Federal bankruptcy laws	Adjust consumer debt and allow for a fresh start
Consumer protection at state level	Protect against unfair business practices
Antitrust legislation	Prevent monopolistic price practices
Federal Trade Commission Act	Prohibit unfair and deceptive acts of commerce

The Equal Credit Opportunity Act of 1975 was designed to prohibit discrimination when extending credit to consumers. The law prohibits those to whom it applies from discouraging a consumer from seeking credit on the basis of sex, race, religion, marital status, national origin, or because of the receipt of welfare payments.

The Fair Credit Reporting Act applies to anyone preparing or using a credit report in connection with extending credit, selling insurance, or hiring or terminating an employee. The purpose of the law is to prevent unjust injury to an individual because of inaccurate or arbitrary information in a credit report. It is also designed to prevent undue invasion of privacy in the collection and dissemination of a person's credit record or information. The law gives consumers the right to require the reporting agency to reveal the information given in a credit report and the right to correct incorrect information or explain the consumer's version regarding disputed facts. The act is designed to cover credit-reporting agencies, not individual businesses. A consumer has 60 days to make a written request as to the nature of information received upon which an adverse credit decision was made. If challenged, the credit agency must investigate and respond to the consumer within 30 days of the challenge.

The Fair Credit Billing Act (FCBA) provides a mechanism for consumers to correct credit card billing errors. The consumer must provide a written billing complaint to a creditor within 60 days of receiving the alleged erroneous bill. The creditor must acknowledge the complaint within 30 days and explain the alleged error in writing or correct the error within two billing periods not to exceed 90 days.

The Consumer Credit Protection Act (also known as the Truth in Lending Act) imposes a duty on persons regularly extending credit to private individuals to inform those individuals fully as to the cost of the credit, including financial charges and the annual percentage rate of interest (APR). The purpose of the law is to promote informed decisions about the cost and use of credit.

The Magnuson-Moss Warranty Act covers express consumer warranties. The terms of the warranty must be simple and in readily understandable language, and if the price of the product is greater than $10, the warranty must be labeled as "full" or "limited."

The Fair Debt Collection Practices Act (FDCPA) applies to agencies and individuals whose primary business is the collection of debts for others. The law regulates collectors by prohibiting the collector from physically threatening the debtor or from using obscene language. The collector cannot falsely represent himself as an attorney or threaten the debtor with arrest or garnishment unless the collector can and intends to do so. The collector must disclose that he is a collector and must limit telephone calls to after 8:00 am and before 9:00 pm. The collector cannot telephone repeatedly with the intent to annoy the debtor. The collector cannot place collect calls to the debtor or use any unfair or unconscionable means to collect the debt.

The Fair and Accurate Credit Transaction Act (FACTA) passed in 2003 requires each of the nationwide consumer reporting companies—Equifax, Experian, and TransUnion—to provide a consumer with a free copy of his credit report, at his request, once every 12 months. Finally, the Credit Card Accountability Responsibility and Disclosure Act of 2009 (CARD Act) was enacted to establish fair practices and to enable consumers to better understand their credit transactions.

Bankruptcy
The financial condition when a debtor is determined by the court to be unable to pay creditors

Consumers and businesses receive further protection from creditors through the federal bankruptcy laws. **Bankruptcy** proceedings are held in a separate federal bankruptcy court with the filing of a voluntary (debtor) or involuntary (creditor-forced) petition. When a debtor is determined by the court to be unable to pay creditors, the court will provide or order relief in either liquidation (also known as Chapter 7) or adjusted debts (Chapter 13). Businesses and the self-employed may also enter bankruptcy under reorganization (Chapter 11). Debtor rehabilitation is the main objective of the bankruptcy proceeding allowing the consumer or business entity a fresh start.

With Chapter 7 bankruptcy, individuals are required to relinquish their assets to satisfy the claims of creditors. An individual is permitted, however, to retain certain assets because it is exempt under federal bankruptcy law or under the laws of the debtor's home state. These assets include interest in personal household goods; clothing, books, animals, and so forth. Once Chapter 7 bankruptcy is completed, most debts are discharged completely and the debtor is no longer responsible for their repayment; however, there are certain nondischargeable debts. These nondischargeable debts include back taxes (going back three years); those debts based upon fraud, embezzlement, misappropriation, or defalcation against the debtor acting in a fiduciary capacity; alimony; child support; intentional tort claims; property or money obtained by the debtor under fraudulent or false pretenses; student loans (unless paying the loan will impose an undue hardship on the debtor or the debtor's dependents); unscheduled claims (those not listed while filing for bankruptcy); claims from prior bankruptcy action in which the debtor was denied a discharge; consumer debts of more than $500 for luxury goods or services owed a single creditor within 40 days of relief; cash advances aggregating more than $1,000 as extensions of open-end consumer credit obtained by the debtor within 20 days of the order relief; and judgments or consent decrees awarded against the debtor for liability incurred as a result of the debtor's operation of a motor vehicle while intoxicated.

Chapter 13 bankruptcy tends to be more favorable for creditors because they receive at least some portion of what is owed to them. Chapter 7 bankruptcy does not guarantee that creditors will receive anything. To qualify for Chapter 13, the individual must be a wage earner or have regular income. Also, the debtor's noncontingent, liquidated, unsecured debts must amount to less than $419,275, and secured debts must amount to less than $1,257,850. Payments to creditors are reduced according to an established plan. The debtor is not required to relinquish assets in order to discharge debts.

In 2005, the Bankruptcy Abuse Prevention and Consumer Protection Act (BAPCPA) was passed. The act makes the abuse of the bankruptcy laws more difficult for those debtors who have the capacity to pay. It forces many consumers to file under Chapter 13 (adjustments of debts) rather than Chapter 7 (discharge of debts). The law also increases creditor protection for retirement accounts to those who declare bankruptcy. With BAPCPA 2005, all retirement plans (including non-ERISA plans, or IRAs) are protected in bankruptcy proceedings. Traditional and Roth IRAs are currently protected to a total value of $1,362,800, with adjustments for inflation made every three years (the next adjustment is in 2022). SEP, SIMPLE, and rollover accounts are not subject to this exemption amount.

Certain states have moved to protect citizens from unfair and deceptive acts and practices by enacting legislation that closes gaps in federal law or provides additional protection for consumers under the state law. An example of such state consumer protection is state-ordered lemon laws dealing with defective new automobiles. This legislation creates public or private remedies for undesirable activities (illegal activities under the law). Public remedies include injunction, restitution, fines, and revocation of licenses. Private remedies include loss recovery, punitive damages, injunctions, rescission, and redhibition.

The purpose of **antitrust legislation** is to protect consumers from monopolistic price practices and to protect investors by promoting fair competition. A **monopoly** is a single seller of a well-defined product with no valid substitute. Usually monopolies exist in industries with high barriers to entry, meaning it is cost prohibitive for new producers to enter the market. Because there is no competition, monopolies can control the market price of their products by adjusting output. Multiple sellers of goods can also engage in monopolistic practices when there is a small number of producers with a high incentive to collude. Such groups are called oligopolies. The Organization of Petroleum Exporting Countries (OPEC) is an example of an **oligopoly**. Some of the most important antitrust legislation includes the Sherman Act and the Clayton Act.

The Sherman Act states, "Every contract, combination…or conspiracy in restraint of trade is illegal." It also states, "Every person who shall monopolize or attempt to monopolize shall be guilty of a misdemeanor."

The Clayton Act contains several sections that regulate monopolization, pricing practices, and competition. The following four sections are of particular interest to financial planners.

Section 2 prohibits sellers from discriminating in price between similarly situated buyers of goods (not services) where the effect of such discrimination may be to substantially lessen competition or create a monopoly (Robinson-Patman Act). The objective is to prevent large firms from using predatory pricing practices to drive out small competitors. Section 3 states that persons engaged in commerce may not contract, lease, or sell where the effect of the contract, lease, or sale may be to substantially lessen competition or tend to create a monopoly. This legislation deals with tying contracts, exclusive dealing, and requirements contracts. Section 7 states that corporate mergers are illegal if they tend to create a monopoly in any line of business. Section 8 prohibits persons from being directors of competing corporations. Again, the legislation is intended to prohibit a lessening of competition.

The Federal Trade Commission Act protects consumers through trade practice regulation. The act prohibits unfair methods of competition in or affecting commerce or deceptive acts or practices in commerce. The Federal Trade Commission enforces the Clayton Act provisions on price discrimination, tying and exclusive contracts, mergers and acquisitions, and interlocking directories. The FTC Act is broader in scope than the Sherman Act or the Clayton Act and may be used to curtail activities that prevent fair competition but do not rise to the level regulated by the Sherman or Clayton Acts.

Worker Protection (Employer/Employee Relations)

Worker protection is another facet of the legal environment. There are two fundamental areas of worker protection: job safety and financial security. The reasons for these protections are the same as those for consumer protection, except that they apply specifically to employees.

The Occupational Safety and Health Act (OSHA) ensures safe and healthy working conditions for employees. The Secretary of Labor issues federal standards for safe employment environments to safeguard employees' health.

Antitrust legislation
Laws passed to protect consumers from monopolistic price practices and to protect investors by promoting fair competition

Monopoly
A single seller of a well-defined product with no valid substitutes

Oligopoly
Small number of rival seller firms; incentive to collude; high barrier to entry

Workers' compensation acts are enacted both at the federal and state level and impose a form of strict liability on employers for accidental injuries occurring in the workplace. The legislation essentially removes the right of the injured employee to sue the employer for acts of ordinary negligence and replaces that right with the right to collect benefits—solely funded by employers—from an administrative agency. Workers' compensation protects against financial losses due to accidental injury, death, or disease resulting from employment. Generally, workers' compensation is the exclusive remedy to employment accidents. However, courts are now carving out exceptions to the exclusive remedy rule, recognizing that workers' compensation laws may not adequately compensate workers with the greatest injuries and for situations that exceed normal negligence on the employer's part.

Other federal programs that offer protection for workers are discussed in the following paragraphs.

Unemployment compensation is a federal and state financial security program that provides for temporary payments to workers who, through no fault of their own, become unemployed. Unemployment benefits are funded with a tax on employers based on an extensive rating system.

Social Security is a federal financial security program for providing some replacement income lost due to retirement, disability, and survivorship. Additionally, Social Security provides a death benefit and Medicare benefits, all of which are thoroughly discussed in Chapter 11.

The Employee Retirement Income Security Act (ERISA) was passed to protect the financial security of employees by protecting employee rights in qualified retirement plans. Chapter 16 discusses ERISA and qualified retirement plans.

The Consolidated Omnibus Budget Reconciliation Act of 1986 (COBRA) requires that employees and certain dependents of employees be allowed to continue their group health insurance coverage following a qualifying loss of coverage. Chapter 9 contains a discussion of COBRA.

Financial Institutions

Commercial Banks

Commercial banks are chartered under federal and state regulations. They offer numerous consumer services, such as checking, savings, loans, safe-deposit boxes, investment services, financial counseling, and automatic payment of bills. Approximately 5,000 commercial banks exist nationwide with over 77,000 branch offices. Depositors in a federally chartered commercial bank are protected against loss by the Federal Deposit Insurance Corporation (FDIC). The basic FDIC-insured amount of a depositor is $250,000. Deposits maintained in different categories of legal ownership are separately insured. A more detailed discussion of FDIC follows later in this section.

Savings and Loan Associations

The purpose of savings and loan associations (S&Ls), also known as thrift institutions, is to accept savings and provide home loans. They can also make installment loans for consumer products (e.g., automobiles and appliances). S&Ls may not provide demand deposits (such as checking accounts with a commercial bank); however, they may offer interest-bearing negotiable order of withdrawal (NOW) accounts, which are similar to demand deposit accounts. Accounts maintained at savings and loan associations are eligible for FDIC protection.

S&Ls are either mutual or corporate. The mutual savings and loans, which are more common, have the depositors as the actual owners of the association (shareowners).

Corporate savings and loans operate as corporations and issue common and preferred stock to denote ownership.

Mutual Savings Banks

A mutual savings bank (MSB) is similar to a savings and loan association (S&L). Historically, they accepted deposits in order to make housing loans, but they primarily compete for consumer loans and offer interest-bearing NOW accounts. Technically, the depositors of savings are the owners of the institution. MSBs are state chartered and have either FDIC insurance or a state-approved insurance. They are not, however, permitted in all states. Most are located in the Northeast.

Credit Unions

Credit unions are not-for-profit cooperative ventures. They are developed to pool the deposits of members. These funds are used to invest or lend to members/owners. Members are usually joined by a common bond such as work, union, or fraternal association, and regulations make it possible for people to remain members of a credit union after the common bond has been severed. Credit unions with federal charters have their accounts insured up to $250,000 through the National Credit Union Share Insurance Fund (NCUSIF), administered by the National Credit Union Administration (NCUA), that provides the same safety as deposits insured by the FDIC. Credit unions accept deposits and make loans for consumer products. They also make home loans. Employment-related credit unions typically use payroll deductions for deposits and loan repayments, often offer free term life insurance up to certain limits, and usually offer free credit life insurance.

Money Market Mutual Funds

A mutual fund is an investment company that raises money by selling shares to the public and investing the money in a diversified portfolio of securities. The investments are professionally managed with securities purchased and sold at the discretion of the fund manager. Many mutual fund companies have created money market mutual funds (MMMFs) that serve as money market accounts. The accounts can be used for cash management.

An MMMF is a mutual fund that pools the cash of many investors and specializes in earning a relatively safe and high return by buying securities that have short-term maturities (always less than one year). The average maturity for the portfolio cannot exceed 120 days (portfolios have an average maturity of ≤60 days). This reduces price swings so that the money funds maintain a constant share value. Securities are bought and sold almost daily in money markets that result in payment of the highest daily rates available to small investors. Money deposited in mutual funds is not insured by the federal government; however, MMMFs are considered extremely safe because of the high quality of the securities. Accounts in money market mutual funds provide a convenient and safe place to keep money while awaiting alternative investment opportunities.

Stock Brokerage Firms

A stock brokerage firm is a licensed financial institution that specializes in selling and buying investment securities. These firms usually receive a commission for the advice and assistance they provide. Commissions are based on the buy/sell orders they execute. Stock brokerage firms usually offer money market fund accounts where clients may place money while waiting to invest in stocks and bonds. Money held in a money market mutual fund at a stock brokerage firm is not insured against loss by any government agency; however, most brokerage firms purchase private insurance against such losses.

Financial Services Companies

Financial services companies are national or regional corporations that offer a number of financial services to consumers, including traditional checking, savings, lending, credit card accounts, and MMMFs as well as advice on investments, insurance, real estate, and general financial planning. Financial services companies are also referred to as nonbank banks because they provide limited traditional banking services, either accepting deposits or making commercial loans, but not both.

FDIC Insurance

Any person or entity can have FDIC insurance on a deposit. A depositor does not have to be a U.S. citizen or even a resident of the United States. The FDIC insures deposits in some, but not all, banks and savings associations. Federal deposit insurance protects deposits that are payable in the United States. The FDIC does not insure the following items:

- Deposits that are payable only overseas

- Securities, mutual funds, and similar types of investments

- Creditors (other than depositors) and shareholders of a failed bank or savings association

- Treasury securities (bills, notes, and bonds) purchased by an insured depository institution on a customer's behalf

All types of deposits received by a qualifying financial institution in its usual course of business are insured. For example, savings deposits, checking deposits, deposits in NOW accounts, Christmas club accounts, and time deposits (including certificates of deposit, or CDs) are all FDIC-insured deposits. The FDIC also insures the following:

- Cashiers' checks, money orders, officers' checks, and outstanding drafts

- Certified checks, letters of credit, and travelers' checks for which an insured depository institution is primarily liable, when issued in exchange for money or its equivalent, or for a charge against a deposit account

Deposits in different qualified institutions are insured separately. If an institution has one or more branches, however, the main office and all branch offices are considered to be one institution. Thus, deposits at the main office and at branch offices of the same institution are added when calculating deposit insurance coverage. Financial institutions owned by the same holding company but separately chartered are separately insured. The FDIC presumes that funds are owned as shown on the deposit account records of the insured depository institution. The basic FDIC insured amount of a depositor is $250,000. Accrued interest is included when calculating insurance coverage. Deposits maintained in different categories of legal ownership are separately insured. Accordingly, a depositor can have more than $250,000 insurance coverage in a single institution if the funds are owned and deposited in different ownership categories. The most common categories of ownership are single (or individual) ownership, joint ownership, and testamentary accounts. Separate insurance is also available for funds held for retirement and business purposes. Federal deposit insurance is not determined on a per-account basis. A depositor cannot increase FDIC insurance by dividing funds owned in the same ownership category among different accounts within the same institutions. The type of account (checking, savings, certificate of deposit, outstanding official checks, or other form of deposit) has no bearing on the amount of insurance coverage.

Single Ownership Accounts

A single (or individual) ownership account is an account owned by one person. Single ownership accounts include accounts in the owner's name; accounts established for the benefit of the owner by agents, nominees, guardians, custodians, or conservators; and accounts established by a business that is a sole proprietorship. All single ownership accounts (except retirement accounts) established by, or for the benefit of, the same person are added, and the total is insured up to a maximum of $250,000. If an individual owns and deposits funds in his own name but then gives another person the right to withdraw funds from the account, the account will generally be insured as a joint ownership account.

E X A M P L E   Assume Justin Grant has the accounts listed below. Because the restaurant is Justin's sole proprietorship, its account is considered individually owned by Justin. In this case, $25,000 of Justin's accounts are uninsured by the FDIC.

Depositor	Account Type	Amount Deposited
Justin Grant	Savings account	$125,000
Justin Grant	CD	100,000
Justin Grant	NOW account	25,000
Justin's Restaurant (a sole proprietorship)	Checking	25,000
Total deposited		$275,000
Maximum amount of insurance available		($250,000)
Uninsured amount		$25,000

The Uniform Gifts to Minors Act is a state law that allows an adult to make an irrevocable gift to a minor. Funds given to a minor under the Uniform Gifts to Minors Act are held in the name of a custodian for the minor's benefit. The funds are added to any other single ownership accounts of the minor, and the total is insured up to a maximum of $250,000.

Joint Accounts

A joint account is an account owned by two or more individuals. They are insured separately from single ownership accounts if all of the following conditions are met.

■ All co-owners must be natural persons. This means that legal entities such as corporations or partnerships are not eligible for joint account deposit insurance coverage.

■ Each of the co-owners must have a right of withdrawal on the same basis as the other co-owners. For example, if one co-owner can withdraw funds on his signature alone but the other co-owner can withdraw funds only on the signature of both co-owners, then this requirement has not been satisfied; the co-owners do not have equal withdrawal rights. Likewise, if a co-owner's right to withdraw funds is limited to a specified dollar amount, the funds in the account will be allocated between the co-owners according to their withdrawal rights and insured as single ownership funds. So, for example, if $100,000 is deposited in the names of A and B, but A has the right to withdraw only up to $5,000 from the account, $5,000 is allocated to A and the remainder is allocated to B. The funds, as allocated, are then added to any other single ownership funds of A or B, respectively.

- Each of the co-owners must have personally signed a deposit account signature card. The execution of an account signature card is not required for certificates of deposit; deposit obligations evidenced by a negotiable instrument; or accounts maintained by an agent, nominee, guardian, custodian, or conservator, but the deposit must in fact be jointly owned.

The interests of each individual in all joint accounts he owns at the same FDIC-insured depository institution are added and insured up to $250,000. Each person's interest (or share) in a joint account is deemed equal unless otherwise stated on the deposit account records.

A deposit account held in two or more names that does not qualify for joint account deposit insurance coverage is treated as owned by each named owner as an individual, corporation, partnership, or unincorporated association, as the case may be, according to each co-owner's actual ownership interest. As such, each owner's interest is added to any other single ownership accounts or, in the case of a corporation, partnership, or unincorporated association, to other accounts of such entity, and the total is insured up to $250,000.

Business Accounts

Funds deposited by a corporation, partnership, or unincorporated association are FDIC-insured up to $250,000. Funds deposited by a corporation, partnership, or unincorporated association are insured separately from the personal accounts of the stockholders, partners, or members. To qualify for this coverage, the entity must be engaged in an independent activity. *Independent activity* means that the entity is operated primarily for some purpose other than to increase deposit insurance. Funds owned by a sole proprietorship are treated as the individually owned funds of the sole proprietor. Consequently, funds deposited in the name of the sole proprietorship are added to any other single ownership accounts of the sole proprietor, and the total is insured to $250,000.

Retirement Accounts

Retirement accounts established at FDIC-insured institutions also qualify for FDIC insurance. The total amount insured across all retirement accounts held at a single institution is limited to $250,000. This is provided that the IRA investments are assets eligible for FDIC coverage.

Negotiable Instruments

Negotiable instruments serve two important functions: they serve as an extension of credit and as substitute for money. For an instrument to be negotiable, it must have all of the following requirements on its face:

- In writing
- Signed by maker or drawer
- Contain an unconditional promise or order to pay
- State a fixed amount in money
- Payable on demand or at a definite time
- Payable to order or to bearer, unless it is a check

Commercial paper is a typical form of negotiable instrument, and there are several types.

The first type is known as a draft, and it has three parties in which one person or entity (drawer) orders another (drawee) to pay a third party (payee) a sum of money.

April 1, 2020

On April 1, 2020, pay to the order of Allison $1,000 plus 6% annual interest from April 1, 2021.

To: Acme Publications, Inc.

(signed) **Donna Jones**

A check is a special type of draft that is payable on demand, and the drawee must be a bank. The check writer is the drawer.

A promissory note is another type of commercial paper that is a two-party instrument. With a promissory note, Party A (the maker) promises to pay a specified sum of money to Party B (the payee). The note may be payable on demand or at a definite time. The following example is a promissory note in which Jean Smith is the maker and Kristin Fourroux the payee.

April 1, 2020

I promise to pay to the order of Kristin Fourroux $1,000 plus 6% annual interest on April 1, 2021.

To: Acme Publications, Inc.

(signed) **Jean Smith**

Investor Protection

The *Securities Act of 1933* and the *Securities Exchange Act of 1934* were passed to protect investors and to regulate those providing investment services. Professional financial analysts should be familiar with both of these Acts and the related Acts that followed them.

The Securities Act of 1933 is primarily concerned with new issues of securities or issues in the primary market. The act forbids fraud and deception and requires that all relevant information on new issues be fully disclosed, that new securities be registered with the Securities and Exchange Commission (SEC), and that audited financial statements be filed with the registration statements. When sold, all securities must be accompanied by a prospectus.

Although the Securities Act of 1933 was limited to new issues, the Securities Exchange Act (SEA) of 1934 extended the regulation to securities sold in the secondary markets. The act provided the following.

- Establishment of the Securities and Exchange Commission—The SEC's primary function is to regulate the securities markets.

- Disclosure requirements for secondary market—Annual reports and other financial reports are required to be filed with the SEC before listing on the organized exchanges. These reports include the annual 10K report, which must be audited, and the quarterly 10Q report, which is not required to be audited.

- Registration of organized exchanges—All organized exchanges must register with the SEC and provide copies of their rules and bylaws.

- Credit regulation—Congress gave the Federal Reserve Board the power to set margin requirements for credit purchases of securities. This act also limited securities dealers' indebtedness to 20 times their owners' equity capital.

- Proxy solicitation—Specific rules governing solicitation of proxies were established.

- Exemptions—Securities of federal, state, and local governments, securities that are not traded across state lines, and any other securities specified by the SEC are exempt from registering with the SEC. This includes Treasury bonds and municipal bonds.

- Insider activities—A public report called an insider report must be filed with the SEC in every month that a change in the holding of a firm's securities occurs for an officer, director, or 10% or more of the shareholders. The SEA of 1934 forbids insiders profiting from securities held less than six months and requires these profits be returned to the organization. In addition, short sales are not permitted by individuals considered to be insiders.

- Price manipulation—The SEA of 1934 forbids price manipulation schemes such as wash sales, pools, circulation of manipulative information, and false and misleading statements about securities.

For a complete discussion on Regulatory Requirements, see Appendix C.

Forms of Business Organizations

Each state's legal environment establishes the forms of business organizations that may be created within that state. This chapter introduces the legal forms of business. A more detailed discussion of business organizations is covered in Chapter 14—Business Entities.

There are seven legal forms of organization that a business can use: sole proprietorship, general partnership, limited partnership, limited liability partnership, limited liability company, corporation, and S corporation.

- A sole proprietorship is a business owned by an individual who is personally liable for the obligations of the business.

- A general partnership is an association of two or more persons, who jointly control and carry on a business as co-owners for making a profit. The partners are personally liable for the obligations of the business.

- A limited partnership is an organization in which at least one partner is a general partner and at least one other is a limited partner with limited management participation and limited liability.

- A limited liability partnership (LLP) is usually a professional partnership (CPAs, attorneys) wherein the partners have limited liability to the extent of investment except where personally liable through malpractice. This form protects the individual assets of the partners who do not commit malpractice.

- A limited liability company (LLC) is an entity in which the owners, or members, have limited liability for debts and claims of the business even while participating in management. The governing document is called an operating agreement. Some states prohibit single member LLCs.

- A corporation (C Corporation) is a separate legal entity created by state law and operates under a common name through its elected management. Owners (shareholders) have limited liability.

- An S corporation is a domestic corporation with 100 shareholders or less; comprising individuals (excluding nonresident aliens), estates, certain trusts, and exempt organizations; and having no more than one class of stock.

There are several other forms of business organizations.

- A joint venture is an association formed to perform a single transaction or a series of similar transactions that, for tax purposes, is treated the same as a partnership (although no partnership tax return is filed).

- A syndicate or investment group consists of a number of persons who pool their resources to finance a business venture.

- A business trust involves a number of people who turn over management and legal title of property to one or more trustees who then distribute the profits to the participants (the beneficiaries of the trust).

- A cooperative is an association (may be incorporated) organized to provide an economic service to its members (or shareholders).

IMPORTANCE OF THE SOCIAL ENVIRONMENT

A society's culture affects the way a society lives and what it values. Culture changes slowly, but it does change. How does a changing social environment affect a client's financial plan? Financial planners must accurately assess the social environment and forecast the threats and opportunities that change will bring. Some of the characteristics of a changing social environment include the following:

- Advancing population age

- Increasing life expectancy

- Changing customs, norms, values, folkways, and morals

- Shifts in attitudes and motivations

- Dedication to or alienation from traditional religious beliefs

- Evolving global languages

- Acceptance or rejection of traditional status symbols and social institutions

One likely forecast for the United States is the flow of new cultures from around the globe into the workforce. These modern-day settlers bring new customs and cultures to be assimilated into this country. How they interpret the American dream may determine the country's future social environment.

Statistics show that the U.S. population is aging. At some point, retirees will outnumber active workers. The larger number of retirees will put additional pressure on the finances of the Social Security system. There will be new investment opportunities as our country is faced with the challenges of an aging population with increased life expectancies, geographic mobility, and financial freedom.

IMPORTANCE OF THE TECHNOLOGICAL ENVIRONMENT

Perhaps the most rapidly changing environment is that of technology. Technological advancement has affected our workplace, our homes, and our investment planning. Already, the internet, through large institutions, provides basic financial planning to anyone with access to a computer. Such assistance may include income tax preparation, credit assessment and counseling, mortgage qualification, education planning, preparation of basic personal financial statements, determination of investment selection for Section 401(k) plan contributions, and retirement planning. Why do these institutions provide these services, especially free of charge? The answer is to get more assets under management. Assets under management equals fee revenues. Such technology has displaced some financial planners who were providing the same service for persons in the same market niche. Astute financial planners learn to recognize how the technological environment can best serve them and their clients. Success comes from keeping a constant vigil on the characteristics that make up the technological environment:

- Current state of technology

- Information processing and communication

- Production equipment and processes

- Medical advances

- Creation of new technology

- New patents, trademarks, copyrights

- Human and business solutions

- Biotechnology

- Gene identification and cloning

- Advances in service and engineering

IMPORTANCE OF THE POLITICAL ENVIRONMENT

The political environment is especially important to risk analysis in investments. Political stability means less investment risk. To evaluate the political environment of any country, the financial planner should assess the country's:

- form of government;

- political ideology/stability;

- social unrest;

- relative strength of opposing political groups and views;

- foreign trade policy; and

- degree of government protectionism regarding foreign goods.

This analysis becomes increasingly important as the world moves to a global economy and investors try to diversify investment portfolios using worldwide investments.

IMPORTANCE OF THE TAXATION ENVIRONMENT

Taxation, in its many forms, leaves the taxpayer with less disposable income. In that sense, all taxes, including income taxes, estate transfer taxes, payroll taxes, property taxes, and sales taxes, have a dampening effect on consumer spending and consumption.

Many of the taxes we pay are the result of complex tax laws about which the average taxpayer has little knowledge or understanding. Enter the income tax expert, the transfer tax expert, and even the property tax expert—each offering a specialized knowledge and distinctive expertise.

Some of the taxes we pay are the result of economic choice, some from a lack of understanding of the alternatives. This is especially true in the area of transfer taxes (estate and gift taxes). If people were more keenly aware of the way to avoid transfer taxes, many would. Because of the potential burden of transfer taxes, there is a great opportunity to avoid these transfer taxes through competent tax planning.

The changing nature of taxes and tax legislation has the potential to broadly affect large segments of the financial planning community. Even though transfer taxes affect a small percentage of the U.S. population, those affected are the country's wealthiest. Many of these persons spend substantial amounts to avoid or mitigate the costs of transfer taxes. They spend this money with estate planners, lawyers, CPAs, and insurance professionals because it is cheaper to pay these professionals than to pay the tax. If the transfer tax were eliminated, many of the transaction costs associated with avoiding the transfer tax would also be eliminated. What would happen to the estate-planning bar? What would happen to the insurance professional who sells only multimillion-dollar second-to-die whole life policies? What would happen to the CPA who practices primarily or exclusively in the estate planning area? Perhaps many of the services, products, and devices used to avoid the transfer taxes would disappear.

The tax environment itself is constantly changing. Congress writes new tax laws as frequently as annually. If a professional financial planner is to assist clients in minimizing their legal taxes, thus giving them more disposable income for consumption, savings, and investments, the planner must have a basic education in taxation and must develop ways to remain current in the field.

WHERE ON THE WEB

Board of Governors of the Federal Reserve System **www.federalreserve.gov**

Bureau of Economic Analysis **www.bea.gov**

Bureau of the Fiscal Service **www.fiscal.treasury.gov**

Bureau of Labor Statistics **www.bls.gov**

CPI **www.bls.gov/cpi**

Department of Commerce **www.commerce.gov**

Economy at a Glance **stats.bls.gov/eag/eag.us.htm**

Lawlink (information on bankruptcy)
**www.americanbar.org/groups/departments_offices/
legal_technology_resources/**

National Council on Economic Education **www.councilforeconed.org/**

National Foundation for Credit Counseling **www.nfcc.org**

PPI **www.bls.gov/ppi**

U.S. Census Bureau **www.census.gov**

DISCUSSION QUESTIONS

1. How do the external and internal environments in which financial planning occur differ?

2. What are some examples of how each external environmental factor might affect clients from different economic levels?

3. Why is external environmental analysis so important?

4. How is the external environment analyzed?

5. Why is the economic environment so important to financial planning?

6. What is price elasticity?

7. What is unit-elastic demand?

8. What is marginal utility?

9. What is the law of diminishing marginal utility?

10. How do interest rates, taxes, and inflation affect areas of financial planning?

11. What are the components of the business cycle, and how do they affect the economy?

12. What is the formula for the inflation rate?

13. What are the Consumer Price Index, the gross domestic product deflator, and the Producer Price Index?

14. What is monetary policy?

15. What is fiscal policy?

16. What are the Federal Reserve's three economic goals?

17. What is the index of leading economic indicators?

18. For what is the index of leading economic indicators used?

19. How good is the index of leading economic indicators as a predictor?

20. What are 5 of the 10 components of the index of leading economic indicators?

21. What is negligence?

22. What are considered nondischargeable debts in Chapter 7 bankruptcy?

23. List some examples of federal consumer protection laws.

24. What are some examples of federal programs that offer protection for workers on the job site?

25. Identify two federal securities acts that protect investors.

26. How do the external environmental factors—social, technological, political, and taxation—affect a client's financial plan?

EXERCISES

1. Define the laws of supply and demand.

2. What does it mean if the demand for a product is inelastic?

3. What action might the Federal Reserve take if it wanted to lower interest rates?

4. What is the price adjustment process in a competitive market, and how does it shift?

5. What happens in the marketplace when the supply curve decreases or shifts to the left?

6. Describe what has occurred when the price of a particular product decreases and consumers buy more of that product.

7. Consumer demand for sugar at $.80 per pound results in 1,000 pounds sold. A drop in sugar's price to $.50 per pound results in 1,250 pounds sold. Is the demand for sugar inelastic, elastic, or unit elastic? (Ignore negative signs for PE calculations.)

8. If a substitute good is readily available for a product, is the product demand likely to be elastic or inelastic?

9. Give an example illustrating the law of downward-sloping demand.

10. An increase in the price of product A causes a decrease in the demand for product B. What is the relationship between the two products?

11. Describe reasons for a change in consumer demand.

12. Which of the following might cause an increase in supply?
    A. A decrease in productivity
    B. Fewer sellers in the marketplace
    C. More efficient technology
    D. A decrease in government subsidies

13. Identify several determinants of demand elasticity.

14. If the quantity supplied does not change significantly with a change in price, is the type of supply elastic or inelastic?

15. Define inflation.

16. How would someone living on a fixed income be affected by inflation?

17. When the economy is slowing and unemployment is increasing, what phase of the business cycle is the economy in?

18. Which of the following economic activities represent examples of monetary policy?
    A. The federal funds rate is increased.
    B. The Federal Reserve lowers bank reserve requirements.
    C. The Federal Open Market Committee sells securities.

19. What actions taken by the Fed will lead to increased money supply?

20. Identify the phases and points of a typical business cycle.

21. In a typical business cycle, which phases exhibit periods of increasing employment and increasing output?

PROBLEMS

1. Identify whether each of the following involves a shift in the demand curve or a change in the quantity demanded.
   A. Fish prices fall after Catholics are allowed to eat meat on Fridays.
   B. Auto sales decrease due to increased unemployment.
   C. Gasoline consumption increases as some gasoline taxes are lowered.
   D. After a drought occurs in Louisiana, crawfish sales decrease.

2. If the cost of one year of college education on January 1 of 2018, 2019, and 2020 is $25,000, $16,000, and $27,500, respectively, what was the rate of education inflation for 2018 and 2019? What was the annualized education inflation rate from 2018 to 2020?

3. Erin has the following liquid assets on deposits with her bank, which is an FDIC-insured institution.

Account	Ownership	Balance
CD	Erin	$200,000
Savings	Erin with spouse	$50,000
IRA (money market deposit account)	Erin	$75,000
Checking account	Erin	$90,000

What is the total amount currently insured by the FDIC?

Communication and Internal Environmental Analysis

LEARNING OBJECTIVES

After learning the material in this chapter, you will be able to do the following:

- Explain how a financial planner can successfully communicate respect, trust, and empathy to a client

- List several techniques that reduce the risk of misinterpretation and misunderstanding when communicating with a client

- Identify professional liability risks affecting the financial planner

- List the four phases of thinking through which a client often progresses in the financial planning process

- Describe the auditory learning style, the visual learning style, and the kinetic, or tactile, learning style by discussing how a client with each style prefers to learn

- Identify the five categories that make up a client's internal environment

■ List the factors that make up life cycle positioning

■ Name the life cycle phases through which most financial planning clients eventually progress

■ Explain how a client's tolerance for risk; savings and consumption habits; views about employment, retirement, and leisure time; and attitudes on government (especially taxation) affect the setting of her financial goals

■ Identify special needs that may influence the successful development of a client's financial plan

■ Identify the financial statements and other information needed to develop an accurate assessment of a client's financial position

■ Explain how a client's subjective perception of her financial position affects the objective reality of the financial position provided by a financial planner

COMMUNICATION SKILLS

The importance of a good working relationship between the personal financial planner and the client cannot be overemphasized. This relationship requires excellent interpersonal skills, proficient communication skills, and the ability to educate. As indicated in Exhibit 3.1, these skills are essential to achieving a successful financial plan. Specifically, they are required to efficiently gather accurate information from the client and to educate the client throughout the financial planning process. With a good working relationship, the client is more willing to share information and be less resistant to accepting a planner's advice. A solid relationship is one in which everyone involved is treated with respect, trust, and empathy.

EXHIBIT 3.1 Financial Planner's Pyramid of Knowledge

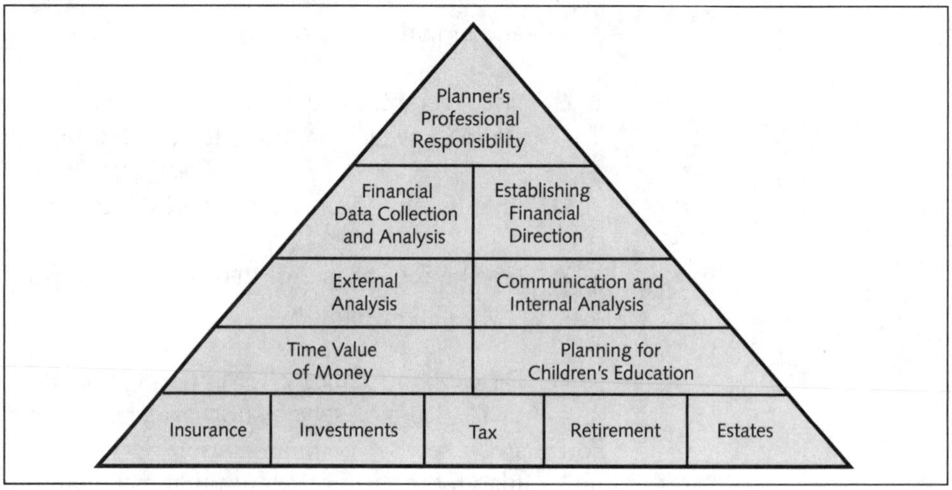

Be Respectful of Your Client

Respect can be conveyed in several ways. One obvious way is the manner in which the client is addressed. When first meeting a client, use a courteous title such as Mr., Ms., or Dr. If later the client indicates a preference to be called by a first name or some other nickname, that desire should be met. Listening to clients, not talking over them, and showing value for their time also portray respect. Always return phone calls when you say you will. Be on time for appointments. Let the client know how long a meeting is expected to last. If you are exceeding the allotted time, ask if the meeting should continue or be rescheduled for another time. These issues may seem elementary, but being mindful of them will assist in developing a professional relationship with your client.

Trust must be developed between the planner and the client. Trust has to be earned, but the process is expedited by showing evidence that others deem you trustworthy. Provide prospective clients with letters of reference from current clients (if permitted), especially those that cite specific examples of how they benefit from your skills. Take care to maintain confidentiality. Clients need to know that any information they share with you will remain strictly confidential. Therefore, if specific examples are provided, make sure the client knows that permission was received before any disclosure.

Respect is shown by being empathetic and viewing the client as an individual. Empathy is the identification with and understanding of another's circumstances, feelings, and motives. Remember that financial success is a relative concept. The client defines success subjectively. The client's definition is based on personal circumstances, feelings, and motives. The financial planner needs to understand the client's perspective and show regard for those views and values.

Communicate With Your Client

A financial planner cannot develop a good relationship with the client without first mastering communication skills. Communications between the financial planner and the client can be difficult because of subjectivity, paradigms, and unspoken words that lead to misinterpretation and misunderstanding.

For example, suppose the client states a desire to take at least one nice vacation each year. The keen financial planner might ask for the vacation destination. Suppose that destination is the Caribbean. The planner may now believe that enough information has been gathered to include this objective into the financial plan. However, enough information has probably not been gathered. The planner might assume the client intends to vacation for one week, because that is the norm in the United States. However, the client may be planning a month-long vacation. In addition, the planner does not know how the client plans to travel. Is she going to fly? If so, does she plan to fly first class or coach? In what type of accommodations does she plan to stay? As you can see, by attributing the financial planner's own standards or by assuming to know the client's standards, the goal of taking one nice vacation a year is easily misinterpreted. This misinterpretation may lead to inappropriate financial planning.

Use Communication Techniques

Fortunately, several communication techniques exist that can greatly reduce the chance of misinterpretation and misunderstanding. Here are a few techniques the financial planner should use when speaking with a client.

Keep the client informed. Tell the client what will happen, what is happening as it happens, and what has happened when it is completed. Although you may be very experienced in the financial planning process, the client is not. Consider the client's perspective. If he does not know what to expect, he will probably be apprehensive. If he is not informed of the significance of particular questions, he may resist answering them or provide only partial information.

Clarify statements and remove ambiguity. Avoid general statements by using clarification techniques such as restating, paraphrasing, and summarizing. Apply the ideas of "is" and "is not." For example, in describing the purpose of property insurance, you may state that property insurance *is* intended to help minimize loss in the event of a disaster. This type of insurance *is not* intended to eliminate loss in the event of a disaster.

Seek information to understand the client's situation and goals. Use open-ended questions to ascertain relevant information. Do not make assumptions. Question everything. Question the answers to the questions. When the client can no longer generate another answer, all the information the client has may be known. However, that does not mean the planner has all of the necessary information. As a result, the planner may need to obtain information from other sources.

Be specific. When communicating with the client, identify the "what, where, when, responsible party, and extent" to describe a task or a result. Avoid the use of slang and colloquialisms. Articulate goals in terms of time, place, and form. A financial plan is useless if it cannot be accurately and precisely communicated to the client.

The Engagement Letter

Engagement letter
A tool of communication between client and financial planner that sets down in writing the information about any agreements or understandings obtained at client/planner meetings, including the plan of action for developing a financial plan, the expected outcome of the engagement, and the method of compensation

An **engagement letter** is a useful tool in communicating with your client. An engagement letter is written near the beginning of the client/planner relationship, usually following the first meeting. The letter should summarize the previous meeting(s) and conversations with the client. This includes the plan of action for developing a financial plan, the expected outcome of the engagement, and the methods and amounts of compensation. Exhibit 3.2 illustrates a sample engagement letter.

EXHIBIT 3.2   Sample Engagement Letter

(Date)

(Name of Client)
(Address of Client)

Dear (Name of Client):

Thank you for meeting with me on *(date)*.   Per our discussions, I understand your goals are as follows:
1. *(list goal)*
2. *(list goal)*
3. *(list goal)*

This letter sets forth our understanding of the terms and objectives of our engagement to provide personal financial planning services to you. The scope and nature of the services to be provided are as follows:

1.   **Review and Evaluation**
       We will review and analyze all information furnished to us including:
       (list items)

2.   **Written Plan**
       Based on our review and analysis, we will prepare a written analysis of your:
       (list items)

       We will also prepare, in writing, specific initial recommendations to address your concerns and issues, including goals, objectives, and risks with respect to:
       (list items)

       Our recommendations will include strategies based on our analysis of your circumstances. Where appropriate, we will include financial illustrations and financial projections to enhance your understanding of the potential outcomes of the alternatives.

       We will meet with you to discuss our analysis and will provide you with a preliminary draft copy of our recommended strategies. You will be given an opportunity to concur with the preliminary recommendations or suggest modifications. Following agreement on your personal financial goals and the strategies to be used to achieve them, we will provide you with a finalized version of the plan.

3.   **Fees**
       Our fee for these services is based on our standard hourly rates and the number of hours required. We expect our fees to be no less than $_____ but not to exceed $_____. We will bill you beginning with our next regular billing cycle. The final payment will be adjusted to reflect actual time expended, not to exceed the maximum total amount quoted for the year, and will be due upon completion of the engagement.

4.   **Implementation**
       We will assist you in implementing the strategies that have been agreed upon. Accordingly, we will be available on an ongoing basis, by telephone or in person, to answer questions, to assist you or your other advisors to take necessary actions, and to make recommendations regarding these matters. We will bill you for these additional services based on time expended at our standard hourly rate.

5.   **Limitation on Scope of Services**

       These services are not intended to include:
       (list items)

We will bill separately for any such additional services provided, based on time expended at our standard hourly rates.

If this letter correctly sets forth your understanding of the terms and objectives of the engagement, please so indicate by signing in the space provided below.

Respectfully yours,

(Name of Planner)
(Name of Firm)

The above letter sets forth my understanding of the terms and objectives of the engagement to provide personal financial planning services.

Signed: _____   Date: _____

PROFESSIONAL LIABILITY

As members of a profession, financial planners are expected to comply with ethical standards and perform their services in accordance with accepted principles and standards. Financial planners who fail to perform such duties may be civilly liable to their clients, for whom they have agreed to provide services, and to third parties, who may have relied upon statements the financial planner has prepared. Civil and criminal liability may also be imposed upon financial planners through statutes such as the federal securities laws.

Common Law Liability to Clients

Common law liability
Liability based on breach of contract, tort of negligence, or fraud

Common law liability to which a financial planner may be subject is based on breach of contract, tort of negligence, or fraud. The failure to perform one's contractual duties is a breach of contract for which one is liable to the party to whom the performance was to be rendered. Thus, if a financial planner has agreed to perform certain services for a client and fails to perform those contractual duties honestly, properly, and completely, the financial planner may be civilly liable. If there has been a breach of contract by a financial planner, courts may award compensatory damages as a remedy to the client.

A financial planner has a duty to exercise the same standard of care that a reasonably prudent and skillful financial planner in the community would exercise under similar circumstances. A violation of generally accepted principles and standards is sufficient evidence of negligence but a financial planner may comply with accepted principles and standards and still be negligent for failure to act with reasonable care. The financial planner, however, is not liable for errors in judgment if made according to accepted practices and with reasonable care or if the client's own negligence or intentional acts contributed significantly to the client's loss.

In an action based on fraud, the client must establish that the financial planner made a false representation of a material fact. The misrepresentation by the financial planner must have been made with the knowledge that it was false (actual fraud) or with reckless disregard for its truth or falsity (constructive fraud). For the fact to be deemed material, the financial planner must have intentionally made the misrepresentation to induce the client to act or discourage the client from acting, and the client must have been injured as a result of his reasonable reliance on the misrepresentation. Damages for common law liability will be equal to the actual or anticipated losses incurred by the client as a result of the breach of contract, negligent act, or fraud and may include the cost of securing the services of another financial planner.

Common Law Liability to Third Parties

Third parties are not clients of the financial planner but are persons who reasonably relied on documents prepared by the financial planner. Traditionally, in common law, a financial planner does not owe contractual duties to third parties unless they are direct parties to or third party beneficiaries of a contract for the planner's services. The financial planner may, however, be subject to tort liability, which is based on negligence in failing to exercise ordinary, reasonable care. If a third party is injured because he reasonably relied on documents prepared by a financial planner who failed to act with reasonable care, the financial planner may be liable and compensatory damages may be awarded.

Statutory Liability

Securities Act of 1933
Federal law that provides rules and regulations related to new issues of investment securities

The financial planner is subject to criminal liability imposed by the Securities Act of 1933, the Securities Exchange Act of 1934, the Investment Advisers Act of 1940 (discussed in Appendix C), and other federal statutes and state criminal codes. The **Securities Act of 1933** provides rules and regulations related to new issues of investment securities such as initial public offerings. Before the issuer can offer the securities to the public, a registration statement that includes financial statements of the firm must be filed with the Securities and Exchange Commission (SEC).

Securities Exchange Act of 1934
Federal law that provides rules and regulations related to the purchase and sale of investment securities in the secondary market

The **Securities Exchange Act of 1934** provides rules and regulations related to the purchase and sale of investment securities in the market after the initial offering. Under this act, persons are liable for false or misleading statements of material facts that are made in applications, reports, documents, and registration statements filed with the SEC. Liability is also imposed on financial planners who have access to material nonpublic information and trade in securities without making a disclosure. It is unlawful to use any manipulative or deceptive device in connection with the sale or purchase of securities such as attempting to defraud, making untrue statements of material facts, and omitting true statements of material facts. The financial planner will be liable to a person who was injured because he purchased or sold securities as a result of such misrepresentation.

Educate Your Client

A significant role of a personal financial planner is that of educator. The client may need to be taught the meaning of common financial planning terminology, such as the time value of money and opportunity costs. The professional financial planner should be an expert in the use of time value of money principles to assist clients in putting financial choices into a logical, systematic, and quantifiable framework. For most clients, the best understood time reference is today. The planner may project that the client will need $1 million at age 62 to quit working (achieve financial independence) and continue to maintain the same preretirement lifestyle. If the client is currently 35 years old, the million dollars and the 27 years until he will need the money may have little relevance. The planner can create relevance and understanding, however, by calculating the need in today's dollars. In this example, $1 million is equal to roughly $100,000 in invested assets or, alternatively, if the client has no investments, $731.25 will need to be saved each month. (This calculation was determined by assuming 324 months of saving $731.25 at an earnings rate of 9% per year to accumulate $1 million at age 62.) The reality of the $100,000 or the $731.25 each month is much more meaningful to the client than the distant $1 million. People understand today's realities and values much better than of those in the future.

Learning styles [auditory, visual, kinetic (or tactile)]
The conditions under which people learn best. Clients whose preferred learning style is auditory learn best by hearing information; clients who prefer a visual learning style learn best by reading and viewing; those who prefer a kinetic, or tactile, style learn best through manipulation and testing information

Clients may need education during the development of goals and objectives or the selection and implementation of the financial strategy. Undoubtedly, clients will need to be educated on many aspects of the financial planning process throughout the relationship. Therefore, the planner should understand how individuals learn. Learning is easier and more effective when people are taught in a manner conducive to their learning style. People who learn best by listening prefer the auditory learning style. Those who prefer to learn by seeing are visual learners. Kinetic, or tactile, learners learn best by doing. Most likely, clients will not know their preferred **learning style**. Exhibit 3.3 may help you gain a better understanding of a client's learning style.

EXHIBIT 3.3 Determining Learning Styles

If Your Client...	Her Learning Style is Most Likely ...	She Should be Educated by...
Talks about situations; expresses emotions verbally; enjoys listening but cannot wait to talk; tends to move lips or subvocalize when reading.	Auditory	Providing verbal instruction and repeating yourself often.
Seems to enjoy watching demonstrations; has intense concentration and ability to visually imagine information; writes things down and takes detailed notes; doodles and looks around studying the environment; often becomes impatient when extensive listening is involved.	Visual	Providing written information, especially charts, graphs, and pictures. This client learns best by studying alone.
Fidgets when reading; is easily distracted when not able to move; expresses emotions physically by jumping and gesturing; does not listen well and tries things out by touching, feeling, and manipulating; needs frequent breaks during meetings.	Kinetic or tactile	Providing exercises or assignments to perform. This client learns best by manipulating and testing information.

Understand the Client's Thinking Phase

The financial planner should be aware that the financial planning process can be both comforting and confusing to a client—comforting because action is being taken to accomplish goals but confusing because this is usually the time when the client realizes the magnitude of the planning choices and decisions required. The planner is responsible for assisting the client throughout this process and providing education and reassurance when necessary. Exhibit 3.4 depicts the common thinking phases that a client often progresses through while establishing a financial plan. The objective is for the client to achieve the high cognitive thinking phase. The financial planner should be knowledgeable about these common phases of thinking and assist the client in progressing through them while establishing financial direction. The planner should help the client transition from the outer edge of the circle to the inner circle in Exhibit 3.4.

EXHIBIT 3.4 Common Thinking Phases

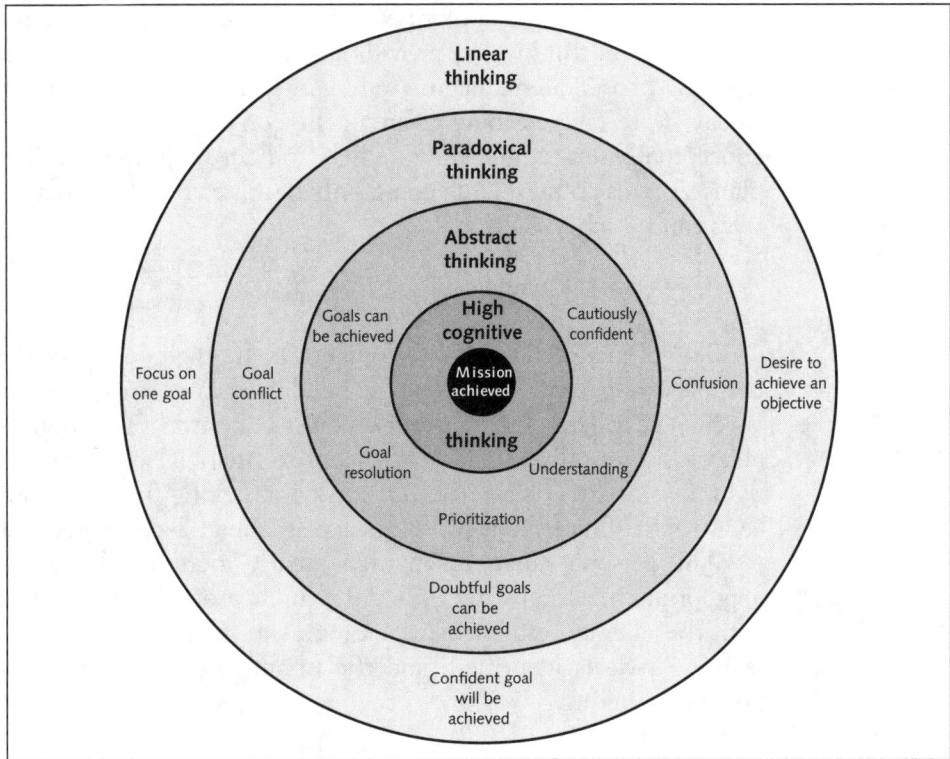

Linear Thinking

Generally, individuals who are just beginning to plan financially are in the outer phase of thinking, referred to as linear thinking. Focusing on accomplishing a particular goal or objective describes the concept of linear thinking. During this phase, an individual's financial plan is compartmentalized and simplistic. The primary interest is in achieving one or two narrow objectives. Confidence that objectives can and will be achieved is high. However, once the individual begins to face the reality that saving for one objective means forgoing funds in another area because funds are limited, confidence in the ability to achieve overall goals is often questioned and the person may give up. During this phase, the client may increase savings or set up a special savings account to save for something only to find that those funds must be used for day-to-day or unexpected expenses. Because of the frequent failure to achieve all goals, clients often give up the idea of developing a financial plan. However, if success is achieved in the linear phase, the client's thinking usually changes from linear to paradoxical.

Paradoxical Thinking

During this phase, the client begins to focus on several simultaneous objectives. As a result, it is during this phase in particular that people become frustrated. They may become overwhelmed with the amount of financial planning required and discover that many of their objectives are in conflict with each other. They often become uncertain of their ability to accomplish any of their financial objectives. Confusion, goal conflict, and ambiguity characterize the paradoxical thinking phase. During this phase an individual often seeks the advice of a financial planner. The financial planner can be of great comfort to clients during this phase by assuring them that goal conflict and confusion are common and can be overcome by good planning.

Abstract Thinking

The skilled financial planner can assist a client in advancing from paradoxical thinking to abstract thinking by providing education and encouragement. During the abstract thinking phase, clients begin to integrate elements of the financial plan into their day-to-day lives. They become aware of the consequences of their financial actions and can conceptually understand how savings and consumption decisions impact their financial plans. At this point, clients commonly become confident that identified goals and objectives can be achieved.

High Cognitive Thinking

The ultimate phase of development is the high cognitive thinking phase. The client becomes enlightened about the financial issues that exist in everyday life. Once this phase is achieved, clients have a great amount of control over their financial future. They are able to successfully integrate their entire financial plan into the other aspects of their lives. During this phase, the mission of achieving financial independence and avoiding catastrophic financial occurrences and financial dependence is most likely achieved.

The personal financial planner greatly increases the probability of developing an appropriate financial strategy and having it properly implemented if a good relationship with the client is established, communication skills are practiced, the client's preferred learning style is identified, and the financial planner understands the client's current phase of thinking.

INTERNAL ANALYSIS

The internal environment defines the way people live, work, spend, save, and think. Internal data about the client are needed to understand the environment in which the client exists and the strengths and weaknesses that are present. Once a good working relationship is developed with the client, and communication lines are open, it is easy to collect most of the internal data needed. The key is to know what information to collect and how to collect it efficiently and accurately. Internal data can be divided into five general categories, which include the following facts about the client:

- Life cycle position

- Attitudes and beliefs

- Special needs

- Financial position

- Perception of his financial situation

Life Cycle Positioning

Life cycle positioning
Using information about a client's age, marital status, dependents, income level, and net worth to help determine goals and risks

Life cycle positioning information is needed because it plays a significant role in affecting a client's goals and behaviors. It also suggests which financial risks currently exist. To identify the client's life cycle position, the planner needs to have the following information about the client:

- Age

- Marital status

- Dependents
- Income level
- Net worth

Age

Age is one of the most important and revealing factors in financial planning. Generally, young people give little thought to retirement goals or wealth-transfer goals. As people age, they become aware that adequate retirement income requires funding. At some time, they begin to seriously plan for this financial goal. In the recent past, it was common for people to become conscious about their "retirement reality" as late as age 50. Today, clients are beginning to become aware of this issue at a much younger age. Perhaps this is the result of the increased amount of readily available information on the cost of retirement and the necessity to plan early.

Marital Status

The second factor that affects goal determination is marital status. The desire to provide for one's dependents creates a host of goals to achieve and risks to avoid. Married couples commonly combine their future economic resources to jointly purchase assets, such as a house, by jointly committing to indebtedness. The purchase of a personal residence through indebtedness, which can be afforded only by combining both incomes, creates an interdependency of one spouse on the other. If one spouse were to suffer unemployment, untimely death, disability, or some other catastrophic event, the commitment to the repayment of the debt may not be met.

Dependents

A third factor affecting the creation of goals is the existence of dependents. Dependents may be children, grandchildren, or elderly parents. Parents commonly have goals of providing education for their children. Education can be an expensive goal that requires substantial expenditures made over a finite period. For example, the average total cost of a college education at a private university in the United States is currently about $46,950 per year, according to *Trends in College Pricing,* a 2017 report from the College Board. If we assume two children and four years in college, the current total cost of such an education would be about $376,000. Whatever the cost, it is probably a substantial amount, on a relative basis, for most 40-year-old clients to take on. Even public university education (in-state) is high—approximately $20,770 for each student per year. Not all parents feel obligated to provide their children with a college education. However, many parents do, and many more wish they were able to do so.

Grandchildren may also be considered dependents. People may have grandchildren as early as in their 30s but more commonly in their 50s or older. The significance of grandchildren is not that they are actual dependents; rather, that grandchildren may signal the initial phase of wealth transfer. Grandparents may find themselves with more assets and income than they feel necessary to sustain their lifestyle. At that point, they may begin to provide financially for their grandchildren.

Other examples of dependencies that affect goals are caring for an aging parent or providing special care to a handicapped child or sibling. Planners should realize that married people with children are not the only ones with dependents. Single, childless people also may have financial dependents by taking on the obligations of aging parents or other loved ones.

Income and Net Worth

Income and net worth are the last two factors concerning life cycle positioning. Substantial income suggests an opportunity to achieve financial goals, as long as the goals are realistic relative to the income. Lower income presents greater challenges in achieving financial security and financial independence. People with a low income and low net worth generally have a more difficult time overcoming financial setbacks. In contrast, a person with substantial net worth is generally less likely to suffer catastrophic consequences from a single financial setback. Substantial net worth also implies a need for increased management of assets and planning. The general rule is that the greater the income or net worth, the greater the interest in tax deferral or avoidance.

Life Cycle Phases and Characteristics

As people progress through their lives, there is a tendency to move subtly but surely among financial objectives because of changes in personal financial circumstances. We have identified and labeled these **life cycle phases** and characteristics as the asset-accumulation phase, the conservation/protection phase, and the distribution/gifting phase. Although not all people move through these phases at the same rate, a sufficient percentage of people do, which enables financial planners to gain valuable insight into their clients' objectives and concerns by identifying which phase or phases their clients are in at a particular time. Exhibit 3.5 illustrates the life cycle phases and the typical characteristics of each phase.

Life cycle phases
Intervals in a client's life cycle that tend to give a planner insight into the client's financial objectives and concerns (asset-accumulation, conservation/protection, and distribution/gifting phases)

EXHIBIT 3.5 Life Cycle Phases and Characteristics

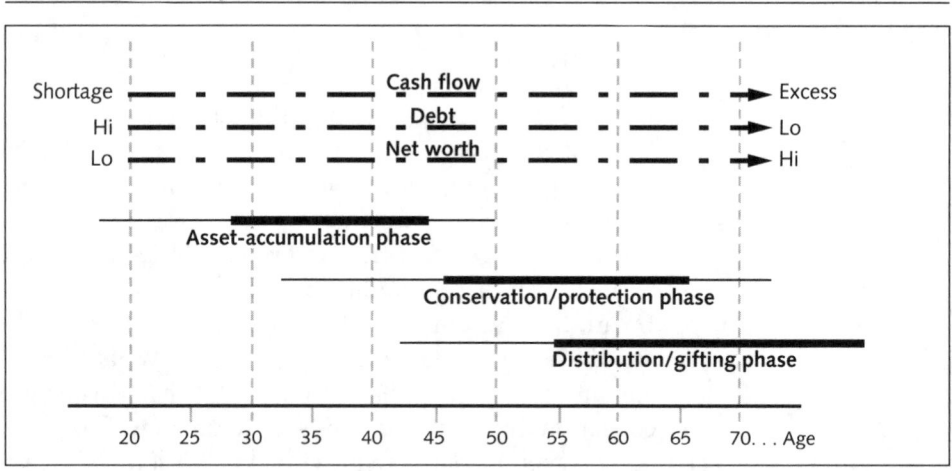

Asset Accumulation

The **asset-accumulation phase** usually begins somewhere between the ages of 20 and 25 and lasts until about age 50. The beginning of this phase is characterized by limited excess funds for investing, a relatively high degree of debt, and a low net worth. At the beginning of this phase, there is generally a low appreciation for the risks that exist. As the person moves through the asset-accumulation phase, cash for investments generally increases, the use of debt as a percentage of total assets decreases, and net worth increases.

Asset-accumulation phase
Life cycle phase through which clients pass; usually begins between the ages of 20 and 25 and lasts until about age 50, characterized by limited excess funds for investing, high degree of debt, and low net worth

Conservation/Protection

**Conservation/
protection phase**
*Life cycle phase through
which clients pass char-
acterized by an increase
in cash flow, assets, and
net worth, with some
decrease in the propor-
tional use of debt*

The **conservation/protection phase** begins when one has acquired some assets, usually in the late 30s or 40s, and may last throughout the work life expectancy. This phase
characterized by an increase in cash flow, assets, and net worth, with some decrease in the
proportional use of debt. People generally become more risk averse as they acquire more
assets. From an investments viewpoint, they are more concerned about losing what they
have acquired than acquiring more. They become aware of and concerned with many
of the risks they ignored at the beginning of the asset-accumulation phase, including an
increased awareness of life's risks (e.g., untimely death, unemployment, and disability).
This is not to say that they have completely left the asset-accumulation phase. At least at
the beginning, they are simultaneously in both phases (trying to accumulate while trying
not to lose what they have).

Making payments for children's education and saving for retirement frequently characterize the conservation/protection phase. It is the time when the client feels a real struggle between current-consumption needs and deferred-
consumption necessities. It is also during this period that the client is most financially
confused because of the conflicting goals and perceived risks. One of the financial planner's greatest opportunities to assist the client exists during this phase.

Distribution/Gifting

**Distribution/
gifting phase**
*Life cycle phase through
which clients pass
characterized by excess
relative cash flows, low
debt, and high relative
net worth*

The **distribution/gifting phase** begins subtly when the person realizes she can afford
to spend money on things she never believed possible. The asset-accumulation and con-
servation/protection phases make this phase possible. At the beginning of this phase, the
person is often simultaneously in both the asset-accumulation and conservation/protec-
tion phases. When parents purchase new cars for adult children, pay for a grandchild's
private school tuition, or take themselves on relatively expensive vacations, they are
likely in the distribution/gifting phase.

The distribution/gifting phase may begin as early as the late 40s and continue until
death. Excess relative cash flows, low debt, and high relative net worth characterize this
phase. At the onset of this phase, the client begins to feel financial pressures declining,
starts to believe life is short and should be enjoyed, and cares less about material things.
Now, clients start asking, "Where did yesterday go?" It is also during this period that life's
risks are put into perspective. Frequently, during this phase, life insurance is reduced
or dropped, deductibles are raised, and the client achieves more financial balance and
confidence.

People are often in two life cycle phases simultaneously, although not necessarily
to the same degree. By determining where the client is in terms of these phases, we can
gain some insight about the person's financial goals, concerns, and behaviors, which will
help serve the client better. Throughout the text, we will refer to whether the client, in
a specific application, is predominantly in the asset-accumulation, conservation/protec-
tion, or distribution gifting phase, or some combination. We do so to put the client's goals
and risks into perspective and gain insight into appropriate financial planning solutions.

Once life cycle positioning is completed, the experienced financial planner can
develop a generic financial plan to meet clients' needs who are in similar life cycle phases.
Exhibit 3.6 illustrates some generalized life cycle positions and the likely goals and risks
associated with each. Remember, however, these are only generalizations. Although
enough information has been obtained to begin developing a client's financial plan, much
more information is required before an accurate financial plan can be developed for a
particular individual.

EXHIBIT 3.6 Selected Life Cycle Positions and Related Goals and Risks

Life Cycle Position	Phase	Common Goals	Risks					
			L	H	D	LTC	P	LB
25- to 35-year-old single (S/25–35); modest income/ net worth	AAP	Savings; investment; wealth accumulation; personal residence; debt management	X	✓	✓	X	✓	✓
25- to 35-year-old married with young, dependent children (MWC/25–35); moderate income/net worth	AAP	Education funding; savings; investment; wealth accumulation; personal residence; debt management	✓	✓	✓	X	✓	✓
40- to 50-year-old with dependent children	AAP, CPP	Retirement planning; education funding; savings; investment; wealth accumulation; debt management	✓	✓	✓	X	✓	✓
62- to 68-year-old; retired with adult children and grandchildren	CPP, DGP	Estate planning	X	✓	X	?	?	✓

Key:
L = Life
H = Health
D = Disability
LTC = Long-term care
P = Property
LB = Liability

✓ = The risk is likely.
X = The risk is not likely.
? = The risk is possible.

AAP = Asset-accumulation phase
CPP = Conservation/protection phase
DGP = Distribution/gifting phase

Client data collection questionnaire
A survey used by financial planners to gather internal data from clients, such as their tolerance for risk and their personal perception of their financial situation, as well as tax-related data, Social Security numbers, information relating to their dependents, and so on

Life cycle positioning is one of the easiest types of internal data to collect. The client is usually comfortable providing this information because it is not too personal and the client probably expects to be asked such questions. This information may be gathered during a face-to-face meeting, a telephone meeting, or by using a **client data collection questionnaire** similar to the one in Appendix 3-A at the end of the chapter.

Attitudes and Beliefs

The second type of internal data identifies the client's attitudes and beliefs. Attitudes and beliefs are important because they play a significant role in affecting the goals and behaviors of individuals. Information that should be gathered includes the client's:

■ risk tolerance levels;

■ savings and consumption habits;

■ views about employment, retirement, and leisure time; and

■ attitude regarding government, especially taxation.

Risk Tolerance Levels

Risk tolerance
The level of risk exposure with which an individual is comfortable

Knowledge of **risk tolerance** levels helps the financial planner determine the types of investments and the style of risk management best suited for the client. The style of risk management refers to the degree to which insurance is sought for mitigation of small to moderate losses. Risk management involves balancing lower premiums and self-reliance for small losses with higher premiums and less loss exposure. Stated risk tolerance levels may be misinterpreted because they are subjective. The statement, "I am not very risk tolerant," may mean different things to different clients. Therefore, additional questioning is needed to ensure understanding. Implementing the communication techniques discussed earlier can assist the planner. In addition to using a client data collection questionnaire, a discussion of the client's past investment decisions can help in assessing the client's risk tolerance level. The concept of risk management will be emphasized throughout the text with special emphasis in the chapters on insurance and investments.

Savings and Consumption Habits

Information regarding a client's savings and consumption habits assists the planner in developing a successful strategic financial plan for the client. If the client does not have a history of consistently saving money, it would be wise to develop a strategy in which money is directed into savings prior to the client receiving a paycheck from the employer. Similarly, if the client has a history of making impulsive large-dollar purchases, it would be wise to discuss ways to institute barriers to this behavior. Historical behavior is the best indicator of future behavior. A good way to collect information about the client's savings and consumption habits is to ask the client detailed questions and to review inflows and outflows for previous years.

Views on Employment, Retirement, Leisure Time

A client's view of employment, retirement, and leisure time is often useful to a financial planner because it provides information about likely behavior. A person who is unhappy with his job or who places a high value on leisure time may be more likely to take spontaneous vacations. The financial planner may want to incorporate these likely-but-unplanned expenditures into the financial strategy. Suppose a client is 55 years old, married with no dependent children, and is unsatisfied with his employment situation. Although this client may intend to work until age 62, the financial planner should be aware that this client might decide to retire earlier than planned, if financially able. The skilled financial planner will develop a strategy that includes contingency plans for various possibilities. Information about a client's views is best gathered through question-and-answer sessions with the client.

Attitude Toward Government

The last type of information about a client's attitudes and beliefs is the attitude toward government fiscal responsibility and taxation. A client who believes that government expenditures are wise and useful to the public would probably be less resistant to taxation than a client who believes that government essentially wastes whatever money it receives. These attitudes toward tax and government translate into financial planning issues in numerous ways. Some clients ignore the role taxes play in financial planning. Other clients are tax conscious and simply view the tax environment as one in which they live and must take into consideration. Still other clients are so focused on tax minimization that they spend extraordinary time and resources on the tax minimization objective, sometimes to the detriment of other goals.

Special Needs

The third type of internal data to be gathered concerns the client's special needs. Special needs may include planning for divorce, remarriage, aging parents, disabled children, terminal illness, nontraditional families, career changes, and unemployment.

Divorce

The financial planner can assist divorcing couples in determining an equitable division of marital assets and planning for the financial changes that accompany the separation of a household. Sources of inflows and outflows may change dramatically, making a review of the client's budget necessary. Other areas for review include:

- legally changing a client's name, changing beneficiaries of retirement plans, and evaluation of retirement funds;

- amending wills and setting up trusts for the benefit of children;

- requiring life insurance from a former spouse for the benefit of the client or children and changing beneficiaries;

- maintaining or acquiring health insurance for the client or children;

- evaluating the need for disability or long-term care insurance; and

- requiring funding from a former spouse for college education of children and assessing education funding requirements.

Remarriage

Many of the areas discussed in divorce planning are relevant in financial planning for remarriage. Besides continuation of insurance for the client and children and review of beneficiary designations, the financial planner should make clients aware of income that will be unavailable after remarriage and discuss integration of families for estate planning and education funding. Frequently, divorce decrees halt alimony payments when the receiver remarries, and Social Security benefits available to the client on the basis of the ex-spouse's earnings generally disappear. Child support, payment of insurance premiums, retirement benefits, and other sources of income from the former spouse may diminish or be eliminated. Finding replacement sources of income or helping the client adjust to a different standard of living is an important role of the financial planner.

When remarriage combines families, the financial planner will have an even larger role. Estate planning and education funding must consider the new couple's relationship with children from each other's previous marriage. A range of questions should be asked, from "Who should inherit the house?" to "How much college tuition would the couple fund?" The financial planner can offer an objective view on the fairness of property gifting and education funding from the perspective of children and stepchildren.

Aging Parents

With the increase in life expectancy, adults may be caring for their aging parents and grandparents for 10 or 20 years. The financial planner can reduce stress for clients faced with prolonged care of an elderly family member by helping them discuss living wills, powers of attorney, and long-term care options with their parents, as well as by helping them prepare financially for medical and living expenses. Two tax advantages that may apply are deductibility of medical expenses paid by the client for a dependent parent and the dependent-care tax credit. Using a loan against life insurance and a reverse mortgage, whereby the homeowner uses the equity in the home to pay expenses, are options that can be discussed with the aging family member. In planning for the care of a client's parents, financial planners must act objectively and with sensitivity.

Disabled Dependents

Many Americans have a child or spouse with a disability. Often, the client with a special-needs dependent is the primary caregiver. The financial planner can assist the client in planning for continuous care for the life of the child or spouse. Wills may need to be modified to provide a custodian for the dependent. Trusts can be created to secure assets for care after the client's death. Second-to-die life insurance, which pays out after both parents have died, may be appropriate for disabled children.

Terminal Illness

Families of a loved one with a terminal illness may come to the financial planner in a state of shock or denial. The financial planner can benefit the terminally ill client and family by retaining a level of detachment and being proactive in addressing financial issues. At the same time, the financial planner must be considerate and empathetic of family members' feelings. Some financial planning topics to address include:

- Estimation of medical or assisted-living expenses for physician, pharmacy, hospital, home health, and hospice care

- Budgeting for medical expenses, loss of income from inability to work or desire not to work, and last wishes

- Coverage provided under health and disability insurance; COBRA options; and government benefits such as Medicare, Medicaid, and Social Security

- Using life insurance benefits through a policy's accelerated benefits clause or through a viatical settlement (the sale of life insurance to a third party)

- Review of investment portfolio goals and time horizons

- Availability of benefits from retirement plans

- Powers of attorney, wills, living wills, and beneficiaries

Nontraditional Families

Unmarried heterosexual couples, domestic partners, and other nontraditional families can benefit greatly from the services of a financial planner. Although same-sex spouses now enjoy the same federal tax benefits as traditional spouses, certain rights and advantages available to married couples are not available to unmarried couples, even if they live together as a family and share common goals. For example, unmarried couples do not qualify for married-filing-jointly income tax status, the unlimited marital deduction for estate taxes, survivorship benefits from Social Security, the ability to direct medical treatment for each other, and legal transfer of assets at death without a will or proper titling of property. It is common for employer-provided retirement benefits and health insurance to be available only to the employee, a spouse, or relative. Besides addressing these disadvantages, the financial planner can help nontraditional families take advantage of their tax status. Because they are not married, both members receive the single standard deduction and may qualify for head of household status, which would reduce their tax liability. Mortgage interest paid on a first and second home is tax deductible. For married couples, this means they can deduct interest on two homes. For unmarried couples, they each can deduct interest on two homes.

Career Change and Unemployment

Career changes and unemployment present similar challenges to the client and his family. The family budget will need revising. Inflows will be reduced, and outflows may increase for job hunting and the purchase of new business clothes, education or training, and resumé preparation. Severance packages and unemployment benefits will help replace lost income for a short period. Health, life, and disability insurance may be eliminated, or premiums may increase. Retirement plans and investment portfolios should be reviewed. The financial planner can assist the client in making these adjustments.

Financial Position

The fourth type of internal data needed is the client's current financial position. This information is so important that it is the focus of Chapter 4. The gathering of information on financial position is the most time consuming step for two reasons. First, the client often does not readily know the answers to the questions. Therefore, some information may need to be collected from third parties, such as stockbrokers, accountants, employers, and lawyers. Second, the financial planner may need to prepare the client's personal financial statements. Financial statements include the statement of financial position (known as a balance sheet when used by a business), the personal statement of cash flows (known as an income statement when used by a business), and the statement of changes in net worth.

Information that needs to be collected to develop these financial statements includes the following:

- Assets

  — Cash, checking accounts, savings accounts

  — Mutual funds, ownership of business, brokerage and retirement accounts

  — Personal residence, jewelry, art collection, automobile

- Liabilities

  — Credit card debt, student loans

  — Auto loan, home mortgage

- Inflows

  — Salaries, bonuses

  — Interest income, employer contributions to retirement plan

- Outflows

  — Rent or mortgage payments, utilities, groceries

  — Insurance premiums, payments on credit cards and other debts, taxes

  — Deposits to savings accounts and retirement plans, donations to charity

In addition to developing financial statements, the financial planner must collect information about the client's insurance policies and coverage, investments, retirement, and other employee benefits. The client's historical tax returns are useful, as is information about any wills, trusts, or other estate planning documents. The planner should be aware of any powers of attorney the client may possess or may have given to others. How to obtain each of these items and how to judge their relevance will be discussed fully in the following chapter.

Client's Perception of Financial Situation

The fifth and final type of internal data is the client's subjective evaluation of her own financial situation. This is how the client thinks she is doing. It allows the financial planner to compare the client's subjective perception to the objective reality of the situation. The greater the gap between the client's subjective perception and economic reality, the greater the education needed. This information may be gathered by using the client data collection questionnaire in Appendix 3-A at the end of this chapter.

A client's internal data changes over time. Therefore, the data should be regularly revisited. If a good client/planner relationship has been developed, the client will notify the financial planner when a major life change occurs. The financial planner, however, should not rely on the client for notification. A competent financial planner will contact the client with sufficient frequency (usually quarterly) to learn how the financial plan is working and to ask if any significant changes have occurred. Contacting clients by phone, email, or in writing should be done in addition to regularly scheduled face-to-face meetings.

WHERE ON THE WEB

Better Business Bureau **www.bbb.org**

CFP® Board Public Website **www.letsmakeaplan.org**

Consumer Federation of America **www.consumerfed.org**

Federal Citizen Information Center **www.gsa.gov**

Federal Trade Commission **www.ftc.gov**

Financial Planning Association **www.onefpa.org**

National Endowment for Financial Education **www.nefe.org**

National Consumers League **www.fraud.org**

DISCUSSION QUESTIONS

1. How does a financial planner successfully communicate respect, trust, and empathy to a client?

2. Which techniques can be used to reduce the risk of misinterpretation and misunderstanding when communicating with a client?

3. What is the purpose of an engagement letter?

4. To what common law liabilities is the financial planner exposed?

5. How do the Securities Act of 1933 and the Securities Exchange Act of 1934 affect financial planners?

6. What four thinking phases does a client progress through during the financial planning process? What can the financial planner do to assist the client in progressing through the common thinking phases? In which phase is it most common for a client to seek the assistance of a financial planner? In which phase is the financial mission most likely to be achieved?

7. Define the auditory learning style, the visual learning style, and the kinetic learning style, and explain how a client with each style prefers to learn.

8. What five categories make up a client's internal environment?

9. Which factors make up a client's life cycle positioning?

10. What are the life cycle phases through which financial planning clients usually pass?

11. Explain how the following affect the setting of financial goals by the client:
    - Risk tolerance
    - Savings and consumption habits
    - Views about employment, retirement, and leisure time
    - Attitudes toward government (especially taxation)

12. What are the special needs that may influence the successful development of a client's financial plan?

13. Which financial statements are needed to develop an accurate assessment of a client's financial position? What other information is important?

14. How does a client's subjective perception of her financial position affect the objective reality of the financial position provided by a financial planner?

EXERCISES

1. Upon your first meeting, how should you address your client?

2. What are some techniques that can be used to clarify statements when speaking with a client?

3. Nancy is a financial planner. Her client, Mr. Martin, is 62 years old and retired. His Social Security and pension plan benefits barely cover his living expenses. His two assets are his personal residence and a brokerage account of $600,000 invested in conservative mutual funds. Nancy advises Mr. Martin to sell all of his mutual fund shares and invest the proceeds in commercial real estate. If Mr. Martin follows Nancy's advice and subsequently loses $300,000, will Nancy be liable for fraud?

4. If you noticed that your client was taking notes and occasionally doodling while you spoke with her, what would you assume her learning style to be? How would you go about educating her regarding financial planning information?

5. If your client is 30 years old, has no children, and has a moderate income and net worth, what are the risks he is most likely seeking to avoid?

6. If your clients are 73 years old, retired, and have adult children and grandchildren and a high net worth, which life cycle phase are they most likely in?

7. What might be the common financial goals of a client who is 24 years old and single with a modest income?

PROBLEMS

1. Write an engagement letter to conduct comprehensive personal financial planning for the Nelsons.

2. Identify their life cycle position and related risks most likely to affect the achievement of the Nelsons' goals.

NELSON FAMILY CASE SCENARIO

The Nelsons recently visited you, their financial planner. After initial discussions and completion of a client data questionnaire similar to the one presented in Appendix 3-A, you have gathered the following information. (The Nelson family will be used throughout the text for various examples and explanations.)

DANA AND DAVID NELSON

As of 12/31/2020

PERSONAL BACKGROUND AND INFORMATION

David Nelson (age 37) is a bank vice president. He has been employed by the bank for 12 years and has an annual salary of $70,000. Dana Nelson (age 37) is a full-time homemaker. David and Dana have been married for eight years. They have two children, John (age 6) and Gabrielle (age 3), and are expecting their third child in two weeks. They have always lived in this community and expect to remain in their current residence indefinitely.

GOALS (not prioritized)

- Save for college education
- Reduce debt
- Save for retirement
- Estate planning
- Invest wisely

APPENDIX 3-A: Client Data Questionnaire

Client Name_____

Date_____

PERSONAL INFORMATION

Your Full Name	Social Security No.
U.S. Citizen? ❑ Yes ❑ No	Date and Place of Birth
Employer	Position
Work Phone	Years with current employer
Married _____ Single _____ Divorced _____	
Spouse's Full Name (if married)	Social Security No.
U.S. Citizen? ❑ Yes ❑ No	Date and Place of Birth
Employer	Position
Work Phone	Years with current employer

Home Address

Home Phone   Home Fax

E-mail address

Previous Marriages

Have you been previously married?   ❑ Yes ❑ No   Has your spouse been previously married?   ❑ Yes ❑ No

Children

Name(s)	Date(s)of Birth	Social Security Number(s)	Tax Dependent
			❑ Yes ❑ No
			❑ Yes ❑ No
			❑ Yes ❑ No
			❑ Yes ❑ No

Grandchildren

Name(s)	Date(s)of Birth	Social Security Number(s)	Tax Dependent
			❑ Yes ❑ No
			❑ Yes ❑ No

Other Income Tax/Financial Dependents

Does anyone other than your children depend on you or your spouse for financial support?   ❑ Yes ❑ No

If so, provide names, ages, and relationships:

Health Issues

Do you or any members of your family have serious health problems?   ❑ Yes ❑ No

Describe:

Professional Advisers (include names, addresses, phone numbers, fax numbers, and e-mail addresses)

Attorney

Accountant (CPA)

Insurance Agent

Banker

Investment Adviser

Page 1   Initial _____ Date _____

APPENDIX 3-A: Client Data Questionnaire (cont.)

FINANCIAL PLANNING GOALS AND OBJECTIVES

Financial Objectives (Please select and indicate degree of importance)	1	2	3	4	5
Retire and maintain preretirement lifestyle					
Retire early - Indicate age _____					
Protection from risks to person/property/liability					
Provide education for children/grandchildren					
Major purchases (car, boat, second home)					
Establish an emergency fund					
Save more					
Invest for safety					
Invest for growth					
Invest for income					
Transfer of wealth					
Minimize income taxes					
Minimize transfer taxes (estates and gifts)					
Other:					

Degree of Importance (1-high/5-low)

Page 2   Initial _____   Date _____

APPENDIX 3-A: Client Data Questionnaire (cont.)

ASSETS

Cash Accounts (indicate current ($) dollar balance for each account)

Type of Account	Your Name	Spouse's Name	Joint w/ Spouse	Other
Cash on hand				
Checking accounts				
Savings accounts				
CDs				
Money market funds				
Treasury securities				
U.S. Savings Bonds				
Total				

Brokerage Accounts (Stocks)

Name of Security	No. of Shares	Market Value

Mutual Funds (Stocks)

Name of Institution (Fund Name)	No. of Shares	Market Value

Mutual Funds (Bonds)

Name of Institution (Fund Name)	No. of Shares	Market Value

Bonds Owned

Name of Institution	Maturity Face Value	Market Value

Page 3   Initial _____   Date _____

APPENDIX 3-A: Client Data Questionnaire (cont.)

Stock Options and/or Stock Purchase Plans

Do you or your spouse participate in a company stock option plan or stock purchase plan?   ☐ Yes   ☐ No

Receivables (owed to you and/or your spouse)

Type	Description	Interest Rate	Amount	Maturity Date
Notes Receivable				
Other Receivables				

Retirement Accounts (indicate vested values)

Type	Description	Fair Market Value You	Fair Market Value Your Spouse
IRA – Regular			
IRA – Roth			
401(k) or 403(b) plan			
Keogh plan			
Pension plan			
Profit-sharing plan			
Employee stock bonus plan			
Employee stock ownership plan			
SEP			
SIMPLE			

Real Estate (Personal Use)

Address	Type*	State Located	Original Cost	Fair Market Value	Current Mortgage Amount

* PR = Personal Residence   VH = Vacation Home

Real Estate (Held for Investment)

Address	Type*	State Located	Original Cost	Fair Market Value	Current Mortgage Amount

* R = Rental   O = Other

Page 4   Initial _____   Date _____

APPENDIX 3-A: Client Data Questionnaire (cont.)

Closely Held Business Interest (attach financial statement if available)

Description	Type of Entity*	Date Acquired	Percentage Owned	Est. Fair Market Value

* P = Proprietorship   PTR = Partnership   S = S corporation   C = C corporation   LLC = Limited Liability Company

Any Other Investments

Description	Date Acquired	Est. Fair Market Value

Personal Use Property

Type	Estimated Fair Market Value
Furniture & household goods	
Jewelry & furs	
Automobiles	
Boats, aircraft	
Recreational vehicles	
Art & antiques	
Other collectibles (stamps, baseball cards)	
Other items of significant value	

Page 5   Initial _____   Date _____

APPENDIX 3-A: Client Data Questionnaire (cont.)

LIABILITIES

	Amount Owed		Monthly Payments	
	You	Spouse	You	Spouse
Bank Loans				
Student Loans				
Insurance Policy Loans				
Personal Loans				
Taxes Payable				
Installment Debt (Automobile)				
Credit Cards				
Other Unpaid Bills				
Alimony/Child Support Obligations				
Charitable Pledges				
Other (_____)				
Other (_____)				
Other (_____)				

Page 6

Initial _____   Date _____

APPENDIX 3-A: Client Data Questionnaire (cont.)

INFLOWS

	You	Spouse	Joint
Employment Income			
Gross Salary			
Bonuses			
Commissions			
Other (Describe_____)			
Investment Income			
Taxable Interest			
Nontaxable Interest			
Dividends			
Net Rental Income			
Business Income			
Annuities			
Social Security Benefits			
Pension/Retirement Plan			
Other (Describe_____)			
Miscellaneous Income (Expected)			
Inheritances			
Alimony			
Child Support			
Other (Describe_____)			

Initial _____   Date _____

APPENDIX 3-A: Client Data Questionnaire (cont.)

INSURANCE

Life Insurance   (Bring in policies)

Type	Policy Owner	Face Amount	Cash Value	Beneficiary	Premium Paid by Employer/ You
Term – You					
Term - Your Spouse					
Permanent – You					
Permanent - Your Spouse					
Other - You (_____)					
Other - Your Spouse (_____)					

General Insurance   (Check the ones you have and bring in the policies and premium statements)

Type
Dental
Health
Short-term disability
Long-term disability
Automobile (Property and Liability)
Homeowners/Renters
Specified Personal Property
Personal Umbrella Liability
Other (_____)
Other (_____)

Page 8   Initial _____   Date _____

APPENDIX 3-A: Client Data Questionnaire (cont.)

RETIREMENT PLANNING AND ESTATE PLANNING

At what age do you and your spouse plan to retire?

_____ You
_____ Spouse

Describe your plans for retirement. Include a description of your retirement lifestyle.

_____
_____
_____
_____
_____
_____
_____

	You		Your Spouse	
	Yes	No	Yes	No
Do you have a recent will?	☐	☐	☐	☐
Are you planning to make any changes to the will?	☐	☐	☐	☐
Do you have an advance medical directive?	☐	☐	☐	☐
Have you given a power of attorney for healthcare and property?	☐	☐	☐	☐

Initial _____ Date _____

Personal Financial Statements
(Preparation and Analysis)

LEARNING OBJECTIVES

After learning the material in this chapter, you will be able to do the following:

- Explain the need for financial statements

- Explain the need for financial statement preparation

- Identify and describe each financial statement, its content, and its objective

- Prepare financial statements

- Identify the tools of financial statement analysis

- Calculate ratios

- Perform financial statement analysis

- Identify the ratios used to determine debt utilization, liquidity, and asset performance

- Discuss the limitations of financial statement analysis

- Define fair market value

- Define liquidity

- List the necessary steps to create a budget

- Discuss the importance of debt management and differentiate between the types of home mortgages

INTRODUCTION

Personal financial statements serve as a fundamental planning tool for the financial planner by providing important financial information and giving the planner an opportunity to analyze the information and use the statements to assist the client in financial decision making. Financial statements are intended to provide information about financial resources available to the client, how these resources were acquired, and what the client has accomplished financially using these resources. Financial statements represent the scoring mechanism for recording and evaluating an individual's financial performance. Information obtained from financial statements can be used to analyze the financial well-being of the client and determine what factors influence the client's earnings and cash flows. Personal financial statements are different from business financial statements primarily in the valuation of assets. Business financial statements use historical values, and personal financial statements use current fair market values.

Financial statements typically used by individuals include the statement of financial position (known as a *balance sheet* when used by a business), the personal statement of cash flows (known as an income statement when used by a business), and the statement of changes in net worth. This chapter will include a discussion of these financial statements, how they are prepared, and where the data are obtained. The chapter provides examples illustrating the different financial statements based on the Nelson family introduced in the previous chapter. Information from the Nelsons is also used to demonstrate a thorough treatment of financial statement analysis including ratio analysis, vertical analysis, and growth analysis.

Decision-Making Uses of Financial Statements and Financial Statement Analysis

Personal financial statements provide planners, clients, and lenders the necessary information to make adequate financial decisions. Clients prepare personal budgets to assist in understanding their spending patterns, gain more control over their financial affairs, and improve the likelihood of reaching their financial goals. As we will see in this chapter, financial statements are used by clients to benchmark goal achievement, by planners to help clients decide financial direction, and by creditors and lenders to make decisions to extend, continue, or call indebtedness. Exhibit 4.1 presents financial actions using the different financial information that can be gathered, the most likely user of the information, and the types of decisions that can be made from gathering and analyzing the financial information.

EXHIBIT 4.1 Financial Information Collection and Analysis

Financial Actions	Likely User	Type of Decision
Preparing personal budgets	Client/planner	Basic planning
Evaluating spending patterns	Client/planner	Efficiency/effectiveness
Determining the financial solvency of the client	Client/planner/ lender	Debt management
Determining whether financial goals are being achieved	Client/planner	Redirect or steady course
Determining whether the client is making adequate progress toward retirement	Client/planner	Capital needs analysis
Evaluating the relative risk and performance of the investment portfolio	Client/planner	Asset allocation
Evaluating the client's use and cost of debt	Client/planner/ lender	Refinance
Determining the adequacy of income replacement insurance	Client/planner	Insurance/estate planning
Determining the adequacy of liquidity for estate planning	Client/planner	Liquidity at death
Evaluating net worth	Client/planner/ lender	Lending
Financial statements required for loans	Lender	Lending

Financial Accounting Standards Board (FASB)

Nongovernmental board that sets the standards for financial statements and generally accepted accounting principles (GAAP)

Rules Regarding Financial Statements

The **Financial Accounting Standards Board** (FASB) is a nongovernmental board that sets the standards for financial statements and generally accepted accounting principles (GAAP). While GAAP generally applies to businesses, the principles are also useful in the development of personal financial statements. The objectives in following such accounting conventions include consistency and comparability in the preparation and presentation of financial statements. Therefore, objective rather than subjective judgments of value should be used in presentation and decision making.

Preparation of Financial Statements

A client is rarely able to provide the financial planner with a complete set of well-documented personal financial statements. The client often does not have the necessary documentation or a clear understanding of his current financial position. With that in mind, the planner can either personally prepare the client's financial statements or have someone else prepare them, usually the client's certified public accountant (CPA). Personally preparing and analyzing a client's financial statements provides the planner with a wealth of information and insight about the client. Because financial statement preparation and analysis are fundamental to financial planning, all competent financial planners should have a basic understanding of the terminology, evaluation and valuation methods, and current and relevant accounting and reporting principles to develop financial statements.

THE STATEMENT OF FINANCIAL POSITION

Statement of financial position
A list of assets, liabilities, and net worth

The **statement of financial position** is a listing of assets, liabilities, and net worth that depicts resources and tells how those resources were obtained or financed. The statement is a financial snapshot of the client at a moment in time (the date of the statement). Historically, the statement of financial position was the primary financial statement given to and relied upon by third parties, especially lenders. This statement was originally designed to meet the needs of creditors who wanted information about assets, collateral, and a person's ability to repay debts (net worth). Now, lenders generally require copies of all personal financial statements, not just the statement of financial position.

Statement of Financial Position Terms and Presentation Order

Assets
Property owned completely or partially by the client

Liquidity
The ability to buy or sell an asset quickly and at a known price

Current assets
Assets expected to be converted to cash within one year

Liability
Money owed by the client

Net worth
The amount of wealth or equity the client has in owned assets

An **asset** is property owned completely or partially by the client. Some examples of assets are cash, investments, personal residences, and automobiles. The classification of the list of assets on the statement of financial position is generally based on liquidity. **Liquidity** is the ability to buy or sell an asset quickly and at a known price. Assets expected to be converted to cash within one year are **current assets**. Therefore, cash and cash equivalents are presented first, followed by assets held as investments, and, finally, assets held for personal use.

A **liability** is money owed by the client. Some examples of liabilities are bank loans, student loans, automobile loans, credit card debt, home mortgages, and taxes owed. On the liability side, liabilities that will or should be paid within one year are presented as current liabilities in their expected order of payoff. Liabilities extending beyond a year are presented as long-term liabilities.

Net worth is the amount of wealth or equity the client has in owned assets. This is the amount of money that would remain after selling all owned assets at their estimated fair market values and paying off all liabilities. The client's net worth is calculated by taking the difference between total assets and total liabilities.

Traditionally, assets are listed on the left side of the statement of financial position and liabilities on the right side. The net worth is shown below liabilities on the right side. Depending on the client and the purpose of the statement of financial position, the categories may be subdivided into more detail. Regardless of the categorization of assets and liabilities, the statement must always balance. The basic statement of financial position formula is assets – liabilities = net worth.

EXHIBIT 4.2 Statement of Financial Position Format

Abbreviated Statement of Financial Position			
Cash and cash equivalents	$ xxx	Current liabilities	$ xxx
Investment assets	xxx	Long-term liabilities	xxx
Personal use assets	xxx	Total liabilities	$ xxx
		Net worth	xxx
Total assets	$ xxx	Total liabilities and net worth	$ xxx

Categories and Classifications of Assets

Cash and Cash Equivalents

Cash and cash equivalents include cash on hand, checking accounts, savings accounts, certificates of deposit, cash value in life insurance policies (if intended for current use as cash and cash equivalents; otherwise, classify permanent insurance policies as investments), money market accounts, income tax refunds due, and accounts receivable that are expected to be collected quickly. These are assets easily converted to cash for regular or emergency expenses and assets that are expected to convert to cash within one year.

Investment Assets

Investment assets include stocks, bonds, mutual funds, real estate, collectibles (e.g., stamps and art) held for investment, cash value in life insurance policies (if not intended for use as cash and cash equivalents), and interests in closely held corporations or businesses. Generally, investment assets are held for growth or income. Assets may also be distinguished in the statement of financial position as tax advantaged or not tax advantaged. This distinction is useful for tax and distribution purposes.

Personal Use Assets

Personal use assets include the personal residence, personal property (e.g., furniture and clothing) jewelry, automobiles, other vehicles, and recreational boats. These assets are generally long lived and are not expected to be liquidated in the short term but are to be used to maintain the client's quality of life.

EXHIBIT 4.3 Commonly Held Assets

Cash and Cash Equivalents	Investments	Personal Use Assets
■ Cash on hand	■ Stocks and bonds	■ Primary residence
■ Checking accounts	■ Certificates of deposit (1 year or more maturity)	■ Vacation home
■ Savings accounts		■ Automobiles
■ Money market accounts	■ Mutual funds	■ Recreational equipment
	■ Real estate	
■ Certificates of deposit (<1 year maturity)	■ Business ownership	■ Household items
	■ Cash value of life insurance (generally)	■ Jewelry
	■ Cash value of pensions	
	■ Retirement accounts	
	■ Collectibles	
	■ Annuities	
	■ Other investment vehicles	

Categories and Classifications of Liabilities

Current Liabilities

Current liability
Debt owed by the client that is expected to be paid off within the year (current ≤ 12 months)

Current liabilities include any short-term credit card debt and unpaid bills. These bills represent money the client currently owes. Unpaid credit card balances, taxes payable, bank loans, and other debts that will or should be paid off within one year are also considered current liabilities.

Long-Term Liabilities

Long-term liability
Debt extending beyond one year (long term > 12 months)

Long-term liabilities are debts that will not be paid off within one year, usually debts of larger assets. Generally, home loans, automobile loans, long-term notes payable, and student loans are considered long-term liabilities. When the debt is long term, the current portion due is listed under current liabilities.

EXHIBIT 4.4 Common Personal Liabilities

Current Liabilities	Long-Term Liabilities
■ Current portion of mortgages due	■ Primary residence mortgage
■ Utility bills due	■ Vacation home mortgage
■ Credit card balances due	■ Other mortgages
■ Insurance premiums due	■ Automobile loans
■ Taxes due	■ Home improvement loans
■ Medical bills due	■ Student loans
■ Repair bills due	■ Other loans

Valuation of Assets and Liabilities

For personal financial statements, assets and liabilities on the statement of financial position are stated at the current fair market value. Presenting assets and liabilities at fair market value is not an easy task. There are problems with the precise determination of fair market value for many of the assets listed. Liabilities are more straightforward in terms of valuation.

Fair market value (FMV)
The price at which an exchange will take place between a willing buyer and a willing seller, both reasonably informed and neither under duress to exchange

Fair market value (FMV) is defined as the price at which an exchange will take place between a willing buyer and a willing seller, both reasonably informed and neither under duress to exchange. Fair market value for certain assets like cash, cash equivalents, some investment account balances, and most liabilities is readily available from institutional statements or by contacting the institution holding the asset. For those assets, a determination can be made. However, for certain other assets, the determination of fair market value is difficult and may require an appraisal by an expert or an estimate by the client. In some cases, the cost of an appraisal is not warranted because the information gained by appraisal is not worth the cost. For example, a small change in the value of a personal residence from year to year may not be relevant to the financial statements, especially where the client has no intent to dispose of the personal residence. The same is true for the valuation of closely held business interests where there is no intent to dispose of the business interests.

The Nelson Family Statement of Financial Position

Exhibit 4.5 is the Nelsons' statement of financial position for December 31, 2019. Exhibit 4.6 is their statement of financial position for December 31, 2020. Notice the changes in net worth, assets, and liabilities. Even though these changes are readily apparent by comparing the numbers, there is no explanation as to what transactions caused those changes. This is one of the weaknesses of the statement of financial position.

For example, in Exhibits 4.5 and 4.6, ABC stock increased from $12,500 to $14,050. Did the Nelsons buy more stock? Did the value of the stock increase? Do the Nelsons still hold the same number of shares? The two statements of financial position do not reveal the answer to these questions. A comparison only reveals an increase in the Nelsons' total assets from $423,072 to $458,947 and an increase in their net worth from $207,626 to $241,573—an increase of $33,947. Is the increase good or bad? Obviously, an increase (for an asset) is better than a decrease, but what was the cause? Once again, the two statements of financial position do not reveal the answer. To answer these questions, other financial statements need to be prepared for the Nelsons: the personal statement of cash flows and the statement of changes in net worth. Once all of the financial statements are prepared, they can be analyzed to gain a better understanding of the underlying financial transactions that occurred during the year. All the financial statements for the Nelsons will be presented and analyzed in this chapter. As you will see, the statement of financial position does not tell the whole financial story.

EXHIBIT 4.5 Nelsons' Statement of Financial Position 12/31/2019

Dana and David Nelson
Statement of Financial Position
12/31/2019

ASSETS			LIABILITIES AND NET WORTH		
Cash/cash equivalents			**Current liabilities**		
JT	Checking account	$1,425	JT	Credit cards	$4,000
JT	Savings account	$950	JT	Mortgage on principal residence	$1,234
			David	Boat loan	$1,493
Total cash/cash equivalents		$2,375	**Total current liabilities**		$6,727
Invested assets			**Long-term liabilities**		
Dana	ABC stock	$12,500	JT	Mortgage on principal residence	$196,654
JT	Education fund	$14,000	David	Boat loan	$12,065
David	Section 401(k) plan	$32,197			
Total invested assets		$58,697	**Total long-term liabilities**		$208,719
Personal use assets			**Total liabilities**		$215,446
JT	Principal residence	$245,000			
JT	Automobile	$18,000			
David	Boat A	$25,000	**Net worth**		$207,626
Dana	Jewelry	$13,000			
JT	Furniture/household	$61,000			
Total personal use assets		$362,000			
Total assets		**$423,072**	**Total liabilities and net worth**		**$423,072**

Notes to financial statements:

◼ Assets are stated at fair market value.

◼ The ABC stock was inherited from Dana's aunt on November 15, 2019. Her aunt originally paid $20,000 for it on October 31, 2010. The fair market value at the aunt's death was $12,000.

◼ Liabilities are stated at principal only.

◼ JT = joint tenancy; client name = separate property

EXHIBIT 4.6 Nelsons' Statement of Financial Position 12/31/2020

Dana and David Nelson
Statement of Financial Position
12/31/2020

ASSETS			LIABILITIES AND NET WORTH		
Cash/cash equivalents			**Current liabilities**		
JT	Checking account	$1,268	JT	Credit cards	$3,655
JT	Savings account	$950	JT	Mortgage on principal residence	$1,370
	Total cash/cash equivalents	$2,218	David	Boat loan	$1,048
			Total current liabilities		$6,073
Invested assets			**Long-term liabilities**		
Dana	ABC stock	$14,050	JT	Mortgage on principal residence	$195,284
JT	Education fund	$15,560	David	Boat loan	$16,017
David	Section 401(k) plan	$38,619	**Total long-term liabilities**		$211,301
David	XYZ stock	$10,000			
	Total invested assets	$78,229			
Personal use assets			**Total liabilities**		$217,374
JT	Principal residence	$250,000			
JT	Automobile	$15,000			
David	Personal watercraft	$10,000			
David	Boat B	$30,000	**Net worth**		$241,573
Dana	Jewelry	$13,500			
JT	Furniture/household	$60,000			
	Total personal use assets	$378,500			
	Total assets	**$458,947**	**Total liabilities and net worth**		**$458,947**

Notes to financial statements:

- Assets are stated at fair market value.
- The ABC stock was inherited from Dana's aunt on November 15, 2019 Her aunt originally paid $20,000 for it on October 31, 2010. The fair market value at the aunt's death was $12,000.
- Liabilities are stated at principal only.
- JT = joint tenancy; client name = separate property

Valuation of Assets and Liabilities—The Nelsons

Reviewing the December 31, 2019, and the December 31, 2020, statements of financial position for the Nelsons, notice that the value of their personal residence has increased by $5,000 ($245,000 – $250,000). If we assume that there were no improvements to the residence, and that we did not have a real estate appraisal, what does the $250,000 value represent? Probably, the planner and client estimated inflation at 2% and rounded the increase in value to $5,000, assuming that real estate generally appreciates at the same rate as inflation. What are the relative merits of such estimation for valuation? If you have no plans to sell an asset but you need a valuation and no ready valuation is available, estimation is a reasonable idea. To rely on a financial statement, you must verify the valuations of important assets and liabilities. In reality, no individual is going to have an annual appraisal for a personal residence, furnishings, automobile, or other personal-use assets. Therefore, the reader of personal financial statements should be skeptical of the valuations given for personal-use assets.

There is always some imprecision in valuing certain assets and liabilities. The extent to which such imprecision is acceptable to the user depends on the particular use of the financial statements. It is frequently appropriate to have the client estimate a value, particularly for a personal residence. Usually clients know what houses have been selling for in their neighborhood and have no intent to dispose of the house. Likewise, it is reasonable to have the client estimate the value of an interest in a closely held business, especially when there is no current intent to dispose of the business interest. Precise valuation may be necessary when the financial statements are used to obtain a loan from a third party and that third party cannot, or will not, accept estimates. For example, if the client is refinancing a home, the mortgage lender may require an appraisal.

Information Sources

The financial planner needs to thoroughly review the client's various assets and liabilities in order to prepare the financial statements. The planner will need to access many different documents to determine valuation, payment schedules, and applicable interest concerns. The detail desired of the financial planning engagement will determine the thoroughness of the planner's assessment of these documents.

EXHIBIT 4.7 Sources and Types of Information for Statement of Financial Position

Source of Information	Types of Information Obtained from Source
Bank statements	Bank balances and possible loan creation or repayments
Investment account statements	Investment account balance and types
Life insurance statements	Cash value of life insurance and any indebtedness
Real estate purchase agreement	Purchase price of real estate
Mortgage notes	Indebtedness of real estate and terms of indebtedness
Auto purchase agreements	Purchase price of automobile
Auto notes	Terms of indebtedness for automobile
Employer benefit statements	Vested and nonvested account balance/options/ contributions by employee and employer to retirement plan
Credit card statements	Purchase price of use assets, balances of credit card indebtedness, payments, interest rates, late charges
Appraisals	Value of the appraised asset
Installment notes	Value of installment notes or liability and terms
Client	All documents and estimates of value regarding assets and liabilities

In the case of the assets and liabilities other than personal-use assets, a wide variety of sources and documents may be used to assist the financial planner in the preparation of the statement of financial position.

Exhibit 4.8 presents each account on the statement of financial position and the best source of information to determine the correct statement of financial position amount. In addition, alternative sources are presented where the cost/benefit of finding precise data does not warrant collection from the best source.

EXHIBIT 4.8 Statement of Financial Position Information by Account Type

Accounts and Account Balances	Best Source of Information for Valuation	Alternative Source
ASSETS		
Cash/cash equivalents		
Checking account	Bank statements	Client/planner estimate
Savings account	Bank statements	
Certificates of deposit	Bank statements	
Invested assets		
Stocks	Brokerage or investment statements	Client/planner estimate
Bonds	Brokerage or investment statements	
Mutual funds	Account statements	
Section 401(k) plan	Account statements	
Section 403(b) plan	Account statements	
IRA/SEP	Account statements	
Investment real estate	Appraisal if warranted	
Personal use assets		
Personal residence	Appraisal if warranted	Client/planner estimate
Personal furniture & fixtures	Appraisal if warranted	
Closely held business interests	Appraisal if warranted	Client/planner estimate
Automobiles	Blue book, bank, credit union	Client/planner estimate
LIABILITIES		
Current liabilities		
Credit card debt	Credit card statements	Client estimate
Bank loans	Lender	Client estimate
Long-term liabilities		
Mortgage loans	Amortization table/lender/annual statements	Client/planner estimate
Auto loans	Coupon/lender	Client/planner estimate
Student loan(s)	Lender/annual statements	Client/planner estimate

Identification of Ownership of Assets and Liabilities

Financial planners find it useful to indicate the type of property ownership and the titling of assets and liabilities on the statement of financial position when preparing financial statements for married persons. Identifying ownership is especially helpful for estate planning and where one individual has separately owned property not subject to the claims of the other spouse's creditors.

Common abbreviations for property ownership and titling on personal statement of financial position are:

Client name = separate property for clients with joint statements
JT = property held jointly with survivorship rights with another (or others)
CP = community property of spouses

Footnotes to the Statement of Financial Position

Generally, footnotes are used to provide additional information or to clarify the item footnoted on the financial statements. Examples of common footnotes to the statement of financial position include:

- assets that are stated at fair market value;

- property title listings;

- existing contingent liabilities (guarantors/cosigned obligations); and

- additional notes regarding property that may be needed at a later date (e.g., basis of gifted property and date of asset acquisition).

THE PERSONAL STATEMENT OF CASH FLOWS

Personal statement of cash flows
Summary of the client's income and expenses during an interval of time, usually one year

The **personal statement of cash flows** presents a summary of the client's cash inflows and outflows during an interval, usually one year. The statement may focus on realized transactions; if so, this is helpful when comparing with budgeted financial goals. The statement may also be prepared pro forma (in advance) and, therefore, can be used for budgeting or projections. The basic equation used in the personal statement of cash flows is:

$$\text{inflows} - \text{outflows} = \text{net cash flow}$$

The bottom line on a personal statement of cash flows shows the amount of **net cash flow** available to the client. As defined in the equation, net cash flow represents the difference between the inflows and the outflows (including committed savings). This calculated cash flow may be a cash flow surplus or a cash flow deficit. Such surplus cash flow may be used for consumption, reduction of debt, additional savings, cash gifts, or the purchase of gifts. If such net positive cash flows are used to reduce debt or are added to savings, statement of financial position ratios will be improved. If the cash flow results in a cash flow deficit, the planner's analysis of the client's financial situation may result in planning opportunities the planner may discover to rectify the situation, creating a surplus.

Statement of Personal Cash Flows Terms and Order of Their Presentation

Inflows

Inflows
All monies received, usually in cash, from employment, investments, and other sources

Inflows include all monies received, usually in cash, from employment, investments, and other sources.

- Employment income includes wages, salaries, bonuses, and commissions.

- Investment income includes interest and dividends from savings and investment accounts, proceeds from the sale of assets, income from annuities, and any other investment-related activities.

- Other inflow sources may include Social Security benefits, child support, alimony, gifts, scholarships, tax refunds, pension income, and any other cash inflow that is received on a regular basis.

Savings

Savings is actually a cash outflow because it reduces income available for expenses. Savings is deferred consumption and will be treated as an increase to assets on the statement of financial position.

Outflows

Outflows are recurring obligations paid, or monthly expenses paid. The three main categories of outflows are fixed, variable, and discretionary.

Fixed outflows/expenses are expenses that remain constant over a period of time and over which the client has little control. Examples of fixed outflows include rent or mortgage payments, insurance premiums, tuition, and loan payments.

Variable outflows/expenses are outflows that fluctuate in amount from time to time over which the client has some control. Examples of variable outflows include food, utilities, and transportation costs.

Discretionary expenses are luxuries or expenses over which the client has complete control. Examples of discretionary expenses are vacations, entertainment expenses, and gifts. Furthermore, some clients do not consider regular donations to religious organizations to be discretionary but consider these outflows to be fixed.

Information Sources

The financial planner will need to thoroughly review the client's various inflow sources and personal outflows to create the personal statement of cash flows. Exhibit 4.9 lists some of the more common sources of financial information that may be used in the collection of data for the preparation of the personal statement of cash flows.

Savings
Deferred consumption

Outflows
Recurring obligations, or monthly expenses paid

Fixed outflows/ expenses
Outflows that remain constant over a period of time and over which the client has little control

Variable outflows/ expenses
Outflows that fluctuate in amount from time to time over which the client has some control

Discretionary expenses
Luxuries or expenses over which the client has complete control

EXHIBIT 4.9 Personal Inflows and Outflows—Sources

Inflows	Information Source
Salary	Form W-2/tax return
Interest (taxable)	Form 1099/tax return
Dividends	Form 1099

Outflows	Information Source
Savings	Bank statements/Section 401(k) plan statements/1099s
Food	Budget/check register/receipts/credit card statement
Clothing	Budget/check register/receipts/credit card statement
Child care	Budget/check register/receipts/credit card statement
Entertainment	Budget/check register/receipts/credit card statement
Utilities	Actual bills/check register/receipts
Auto maintenance	Budget/check register/receipts/credit card statement
Charitable contributions	Checks and receipts
Section 401(k) plan loan repayments	Participant statement
Credit card payments	Credit card statements
Mortgage payments	Mortgage statement
Automobile/boat loan	Loan agreement/check register
Insurance premiums	Invoice/policy/check register
Tuition and education expenses	Invoice/check stubs
Federal income tax (W/H)	Form W-2/tax return
State (and city) income tax	Form W-2/tax return
FICA	Form W-2/tax return
Property tax for real estate	Mortgage statement/check register

Exhibit 4.10 is the Nelsons' personal statement of cash flows showing their inflows, savings, outflows, and net cash flow for 2020.

EXHIBIT 4.10 Personal Statement of Cash Flows

Dana and David Nelson
Personal Statement of Cash Flows
For 2020

INFLOWS		
Salary—David		**$70,000**
Investment income		
Interest income	$900	
Dividend income	$150	$1,050
Total inflows		**$71,050**
Savings		
Reinvestment (interest/dividends)	$1,050	
Section 401(k) plan deferrals	$3,803	
Education fund	$1,000	
Total savings		**$5,853**
Available for outflows		**$65,197**
OUTFLOWS		
Ordinary living expenses		
Food	$6,000	
Clothing	$3,600	
Child care	$600	
Entertainment	$1,814	
Utilities	$3,600	
Auto maintenance	$2,000	
Church	$3,500	
Total ordinary living expenses		**$21,114**
Debt payments		
Credit card payments principal	$345	
Credit card payments interest	$615	
Mortgage payment principal	$1,234	
Mortgage payment interest	$20,720	
Boat loan principal	$1,493	
Boat loan interest	$1,547	
Total debt payments		**$25,954**
Insurance premiums		
Automobile insurance premiums	$900	
Disability insurance premiums	$761	
Homeowners insurance premiums	$950	
Total insurance premiums		**$2,611**
Tuition and education expenses		**$1,000**
Taxes		
FICA and federal income tax (W/H)	$12,855	
State (and city) income tax	$820	
Property tax (principal residence)	$1,000	
Total taxes		**$14,675**
Total outflows		**$65,354**
Net cash flow (deficit)		**($157)**

Compromise in Information Reporting

The personal statement of cash flows is a compromise in information reporting. For an individual, the statement is almost a full cash flow statement. The exceptions, those transactions that are not considered income or expenses but are cash flows, are generally not included in the statement. For example, although conventional corporate accounting would include only the interest portion from any repayment of debt as an expense, personal financial statements commonly include both the principal and the interest in debt repayment as an expense or cash flow for the period (e.g., mortgage payments, credit card payments, and bank loan repayments).

The astute planner will notice that the personal statement of cash flows is neither an accrual statement nor a full cash flow statement. Because the statement is frequently prepared pro forma (in advance) and used as a budget, it is a presentation of recurring inflows and outflows presented in a conventional manner and is, therefore, a compromise. If it were a full statement of cash flows, it would have to consider the acquisition and disposition of all assets for and by cash.

The personal statement of cash flows generally does not consider the sale or purchase of assets during the period, nor does it consider employer matching contributions to qualified retirement accounts. As we will see, another financial statement must be prepared to present the complete financial picture of the client.

The Relationship of the Statement of Financial Position to the Personal Statement of Cash Flows

The statement of financial position represents the financial picture of the individual at a moment in time setting forth assets, liabilities, and net worth. The personal statement of cash flows presents recurring inflows, savings, outflows, and net cash flow over a period of time. The personal statement of cash flows provides a partial picture of what has happened between two statement of financial position dates. As discussed previously, neither statement by itself nor both when taken together present the entire financial picture of the individual. This deficiency creates the need for another financial statement—the statement of changes in net worth—to help further clarify the complete financial picture of the client.

THE STATEMENT OF CHANGES IN NET WORTH

Statement of changes in net worth
Summary of changes from one statement of financial position to the next

Throughout the preparation of the previously mentioned financial statements, we have tried to provide financial information useful to the client and the planner. We now need to be able to explain the changes in net worth between two statements of financial position. The financial statement that allows us to do this is called the **statement of changes in net worth.** To the extent that we have not been able to ascertain all of the exact changes in the net worth, this statement will allow us to do so. Examples of transactions or changes in account balances that would not be included in the personal statement of cash flows are listed below:

- Changes in value for assets due to either appreciation or depreciation

- If an asset other than cash is exchanged for some other assets (real estate for real estate)

- If assets other than cash are received by gift or inheritance (property)

- If assets other than cash are given to charities or noncharitable donees (automobiles, buildings, or investments)

EXAMPLE   Below are some sample transactions and how the transactions affect net worth.

- The client buys $5,000 of furniture on credit. Assets (furniture) increase by $5,000 and liabilities (debt) increase by $5,000; no change in net worth.
- The client's IRA appreciates by $10,000 this year. Assets (IRA) increase by $10,000 and liabilities remain the same, so net worth increases by $10,000.
- The client buys a house for $200,000 with a 5% down payment and financing the balance. Assets decrease by $10,000 (cash) and increase by $200,000 (house), and liabilities increase by $190,000 (mortgage); no change in net worth.

Exhibit 4.11 depicts the statement of changes in net worth for the Nelsons. The Nelsons' net worth statement ties together the overall change in their net worth and reflects each noncash item that was altered during the year. Transactions that were not previously reported on the other statements include:

- an inheritance of $10,000 in XYZ stock from David's grandmother;

- appreciation in value of the jewelry, residence, ABC stock, education fund, and Section 401(k) plan;

- employer contribution to David's Section 401(k) plan ($2,100); and

- a gift of a table to Dana's mother ($1,000 value).

EXHIBIT 4.11 Statement of Changes in Net Worth

Dana and David Nelson
Statement of Changes in Net Worth
For the Year Ending 12/31/2020

Additions to net worth	
Increases in assets:	
Inheritance	
XYZ stock	$10,000
Appreciation of assets:	
Jewelry	$500
Residence	$5,000
Adjustment from exchange:	
Boat B	$30,000
Purchase	
Personal watercraft	$10,000
Appreciation of investments:	
ABC stock	$500
Education fund	$560
Section 401(k) plan	$519
Increase of investment contributions:	
ABC stock	$1,050
Education fund	$1,000
Section 401(k) plan—employee contribution (deferrals)	$3,803
Section 401(k) plan—employer contribution (deferrals)	$2,100
Decrease in liabilities (debt repayments):	
Mortgage on principal residence	$1,234
Boat loan	$1,493
Credit card debt	$345
Total	**$68,104**
Reductions in net worth	
Decrease in assets:	
Checking account	($157)
Depreciation of assets:	
Auto	($3,000)
Gifts	
Table to mother	($1,000)
Adjustment from exchange:	
Boat A	($25,000)
Increase in liabilities	
Addition to boat loan	($5,000)
Total	**($34,157)**
Net change in net worth	**$33,947**

NELSON EXAMPLE RECAP

Recall that the statement of financial position for December 31, 2019 and the statement of financial position for December 31, 2020, do not show the same net worth. Based on this observation, we know that there were circumstances in which the overall financial status of the Nelsons changed during the year.

EXHIBIT 4.12 Spreadsheet Reconciliation of Changes in Net Worth

Asset	12/31/2019 Stmt of Fin Position	Change in Net Worth	12/31/2020 Stmt of Fin Position
Checking account	$1,425	($157)	$1,268
Savings account	$950		$950
ABC stock	$12,500	$1,550	$14,050
Education fund	$14,000	$1,560	$15,560
Section 401(k) plan	$32,197	$6,422	$38,619
XYZ stock	$0	$10,000	$10,000
Principal residence	$245,000	$5,000	$250,000
Automobile	$18,000	($3,000)	$15,000
Personal watercraft	$0	$10,000	$10,000
Boat A	$25,000	($25,000)	$0
Boat B	$0	$30,000	$30,000
Jewelry	$13,000	$500	$13,500
Furniture/household	$61,000	($1,000)	$60,000
Credit cards	($4,000)	$345	($3,655)
Mortgage on residence*	($197,888)	$1,234	($196,654)
Boat loan*	($13,558)	($3,507)	($17,065)
Net worth	**$207,626**	**$33,947**	**$241,573**

* Includes current and long-term liabilities

FINANCIAL ANALYSIS OF PERSONAL FINANCIAL STATEMENTS

Once the statement of financial position, personal statement of cash flows, and statement of changes in net worth have been properly prepared, financial statement analysis can be performed to gain insight into the financial strengths and weaknesses of the client. The financial planner may look upon this activity as a form of diagnosing the financial health of the client. Remember that financial analysis, while somewhat comprehensive, is only one tool of the competent financial planner. Financial analysis by its very nature is limited to the past and, therefore, is not necessarily predictive of the future. Even with its inherent limitations, however, financial statement analysis is a useful and powerful tool to gain insight into the financial well-being of the client.

We begin with a traditional approach to analyzing the financial statements and then broaden our analysis to improve our insights. Our traditional approach utilizes ratio, vertical, and growth analysis.

Financial statement analysis (in general) and ratio analysis (in particular) can assist us in answering the following questions about a client.

■ Can the client financially withstand a sudden negative financial disruption to income (such as unemployment or loss of a significant asset)?

■ Can the client meet short-term obligations?

■ Does the client manage debt well?

- Does the client have an appropriate balance among various classes of expenditures relative to income?

- Is the client's income growing at an appropriate rate?

- Are the client's savings and savings rate appropriate for the given income and income growth?

- Is the client making a satisfactory total return on investments and savings?

- Is the client's net worth growing at an appropriate rate?

- Is the client making satisfactory progress toward funding retirement?

Ratio Analysis

Ratio analysis
The relationship or relative value of two characteristics used to analyze an individual's financial health and to conduct comparison and trend analysis

There are many financial ratios one might use to gain insight into the client's financial well-being. The ratios we have selected are only suggestions. Other financial planners may have ratios they use that we have not presented. Furthermore, some decisions require exhaustive **ratio analysis**, and other decisions are quite simple and may require only the calculation of a few simple ratios. Thus, there is no one set of ratios that needs to be used all of the time, nor is there a particular ratio that is always calculated. The ratios are used to clarify and improve the understanding of the data and are used in comparison with established benchmarks, such as those established in the mortgage lending industry, to make judgments as to their appropriateness for a particular client. We would expect, for example, that at higher income levels, there are greater amounts of savings and larger net worths. Therefore, we must be careful to compare the financial ratios of each individual with relevant benchmarks.

Financial statement analysis is both an art and a science. Although anyone can mathematically calculate ratios, the ability to understand the implications of those ratios and to motivate the client to take actions to affect those ratios where appropriate is truly an art. The art will only come with practice and experience.

Ratio analysis is intended to provide additional perspective on the financial statements. The selection of each numerator and denominator to calculate a particular ratio must be done with care. Not every ratio is relevant for every client. The objective of ratio analysis is twofold: to gain additional insight into the financial situation and behavior of the client and to generate questions for the client to answer to further gain such insight.

The ratios selected for discussion in this chapter are ones the authors have found to be particularly useful. The key to ratio analysis is whether the ratio answers the question asked and then whether there is some standard or benchmark to determine whether the result is appropriate for this particular client. Ratio analysis uses both the statement of financial position and the personal statement of cash flows.

Liquidity Ratios

Liquidity ratios measure the ability of the client to meet short-term financial obligations. They compare current financial obligations such as current liabilities or financial requirements to current assets or cash flows available to meet those financial obligations. These liquidity ratios include the emergency fund ratio and the current ratio.

The Emergency Fund Ratio   The emergency fund ratio assists the planner in determining the ability of the client to withstand a sudden negative financial disruption to cash inflows. Such a financial disruption could occur as a result of a layoff, untimely death, disability, or some other event that causes the cash inflows to cease or be reduced. This ratio is calculated by comparing the amount of liquid assets to the monthly cash outflows/ expenses of the client. The emergency fund ratio should generally be three to six months' of nondiscretionary cash outflows to accommodate unemployment, losses of significant assets, or other unexpected major expenditures.

Reviewing Exhibit 4.6, the statement of financial position dated December 31, 2020, the Nelsons had $2,218 in liquid assets. In reviewing the personal statement of cash flows, they have monthly outflows/expenses totaling $5,446 ($65,354 ÷ 12). A closer review of the monthly expenditures reveals that there are certain outflows that could be reduced if necessary. Assume that the following costs could be eliminated:

Child care[1]	$ 600
Entertainment	1,814
FICA and federal income taxes[2]	12,855
State and city taxes[2]	820
Eliminated cash outflows	$16,089

[1] Dana is a full-time homemaker. In an emergency, child care costs could be eliminated unless the emergency is Dana's death.

[2] If David lost his source of income, the Nelsons would not pay income taxes.

Thus, the real nondiscretionary monthly outflows/expenses are $4,105 ([$65,354 − $16,089] ÷ 12). (Note that in consultation with the Nelsons, the church contribution of $3,500 was not considered discretionary.) The emergency fund ratio (EFR) is calculated by dividing the current assets (numerator) by the monthly nondiscretionary outflows/ expenses (denominator) to provide the result.

$$\text{Emergency fund ratio (EFR)} = \frac{\text{Current assets}}{\text{Monthly nondiscretionary expenses}} = \text{Target of 3 to 6 months}$$

$$\text{Nelsons' EFR } \frac{\$2,218}{\$4,105} = .54 \text{ months}$$

The emergency fund ratio of .54 months is substantially below the target goal of three to six months, suggesting a substantial risk to the overall financial plan. You may observe that the Nelsons could liquidate some of their investments or borrow from David's Section 401(k) plan in the event of an emergency. Although both observations are correct, this course of action would be disruptive to a long-term investment plan. Therefore, we would place building the emergency fund as one of our current objectives with a quantitative target of initially three months, and over a longer period of six months.

Although a client should strive to maintain a three- to six-month EFR using only current assets in the numerator, each client's situation is unique. Some clients may be at little risk of losing income to cover basic living expenses and may desire higher rates of return than can be achieved with checking and savings accounts. In such a case, substitutions for current assets may be made in the EFR calculation. For example, the client may be willing and able to sell marketable securities or obtain a low-interest line of credit.

The Current Ratio The current ratio examines the relationship between current assets and current liabilities. The current ratio indicates the ability to meet short-term obligations. This ratio is calculated by dividing current assets (numerator) by current liabilities (denominator).

$$\text{Current ratio (CR)} = \frac{\text{current assets}}{\text{current liabilities}} = \text{target of 1.0 to 2.0}$$

In reviewing the Nelsons' statement of financial position dated December 31, 2020, we find current assets of $2,218 and current liabilities of $6,073.

$$\text{Nelsons' } CR = \frac{\$2,218}{\$6,073} = .37$$

The current ratio of .37 is low relative to the target of 1.0 to 2.0 and suggests insufficient current assets, too many current liabilities, or some combination of both. Therefore, we would suggest increasing the current ratio to 1.0 over a reasonable period of time. By increasing the emergency fund ratio, the Nelsons may also increase the current ratio.

Debt Ratios and Debt Analysis

Debt ratios indicate how well the person manages debt. Debt is not inherently good or bad. All debt carries some cost, interest costs at least. Quality debt is low in cost and has a term structure that does not exceed the economic life of the asset that created the debt. When a person consistently repays debt as agreed, the repayment creates a history of good credit ratings, the borrower gains confidence in handling debt, and lenders gain confidence in extending credit to the borrower. Excessive debt or expensive debt is a warning sign that default risk is a serious threat. Determining exactly how much debt a person should have is impossible, but various ratios give signals as to the person's ability to handle debt and whether the person may be overextended. The initial debt ratios include total debt to net worth, long-term debt to net worth, debt to total assets, and long-term debt to total assets. These debt ratios are compared from one year to the next in order to identify trends, rather than having a particular target, as with liquidity ratios.

Total Debt to Net Worth

$$\text{Total debt to net worth} = \frac{\text{total debt}}{\text{net worth}}$$

The ratio indicates the portion of a person's assets derived from debt compared to net worth. Generally, we would expect the debt-to-net-worth ratio to decline over a person's lifetime.

Reviewing the two statements of financial position for the Nelsons (December 31, 2019, and December 31, 2020), we find the total debt-to-net-worth ratio to be:

$$12/31/2019 \quad \frac{\$215,446}{\$207,626} = 1.04$$

$$12/31/2020 \quad \frac{\$217,374}{\$241,573} = .90$$

The total debt ratio has improved this year, as a lower proportion of debt indicates less financial risk.

Long-Term Debt to Net Worth   The long-term debt ratio removes short-term debt from the numerator to get a look at the long-term capital structure. The ratio is calculated as follows:

$$\text{Long-term debt to net worth} = \frac{\text{long-term debt}}{\text{net worth}}$$

Net worth should be increasing and long-term debt should be declining over time. Therefore, we expect a decreasing ratio when comparing one year to the next.

Again, after reviewing the two statements of financial position for the Nelsons, we find long-term debt to net worth ratio to be:

$$12/31/2019 \quad \frac{\$208,719}{\$207,626} = 1.01$$

$$12/31/2020 \quad \frac{\$211,301}{\$241,573} = .87$$

Note that the long-term debt-to-net-worth ratios are very close to the total debt to net worth ratios, which suggests that most of the Nelsons' debt is long term. An examination of the Nelsons' long-term debt reveals that the primary debt is the mortgage on the principal residence, which (as opposed to credit card debt) is generally considered high-quality debt.

Total Debt to Total Assets   The ratio of total debt to total assets indicates the proportion of assets furnished by creditors as a percentage of total assets.

$$\text{Total debt to total assets} = \frac{\text{total debt}}{\text{total assets}}$$

Reviewing the Nelsons' two statements of financial position, we find total debt to total assets to be:

$$12/31/2019 \quad \frac{\$215,446}{\$423,072} = .51$$

$$12/31/2020 \quad \frac{\$217,374}{\$458,947} = .47$$

Once again, the ratio has modestly improved over the last year.

Long-Term Debt to Total Assets   The long-term-debt-to-total-assets ratio is a numerator refinement on the previous ratio to focus on long-term debt as a proportion of total assets.

$$\text{Long-term debt to total assets} = \frac{\text{long-term debt}}{\text{total assets}}$$

Once again, we use the two statements of financial position for the Nelsons to determine the long-term debt to total assets:

$$12/31/2019 \quad \frac{\$208,719}{\$423,072} = .49$$

$$12/31/2020 \quad \frac{\$211,301}{\$458,947} = .46$$

The ratio has modestly declined. For the Nelsons, this decline does not add very much insight because of the debt mix. However, for a client with different debt mixes, this ratio could be very revealing.

Debt Analysis

The proper use of debt is to match the economic benefit period of the asset purchased with the repayment period of the debt such that the economic benefit period equals or exceeds the repayment period. We expect that there is a life cycle of indebtedness beginning at the asset accumulation phase, peaking sometime in the conservation/preservation phase, and declining rapidly during or before the gifting phase. Debt is useful for asset accumulation, but it has a cost. Once it is established that the person can manage debt well, lenders are willing to extend more debt up to the point where default risk is increased. At some point, persons who have acquired assets using debt wish to be out of debt to devote the repayment resources to other goals, such as saving for retirement.

Certain types of debt are often thought of as reasonable, such as student loans, mortgages, and auto loans. The underlying assets of education, housing, and transportation create long-lived economic benefits and are expensive. These assets are commonly purchased with some debt financing. Exhibit 4.13 presents the types of debts, the benefits created by those debts, the expected economic benefits period of the asset purchased, and the common repayment period. Many items may be purchased with credit cards; however, credit card debt is considered the worst kind of debt because of its potentially high costs. Many people use credit cards to purchase consumable goods and then find themselves repaying the debt long after the period of consumption. There are some positive ways to use credit cards, such as paying off the balance monthly without increasing overall debt.

EXHIBIT 4.13 Types of Debt: Economic Benefit and Repayment Periods

Type of Debt	Type of Benefit Created	Expected Benefit Period*	Common Repayment Period
Student loans	Education	Lifetime	10 years
Mortgage or principal residence	Shelter	40 years	15–30 years
Auto loans	Transportation	3–10 years	3–5 years
Bank loans	Various	Various	Various
Credit cards	Various[1]	Various	30 days to 1 year[2] or more

*Assumes asset held for entire economic life.

[1] Various, but typically consumption.

[2] If credit cards are paid at the minimum payment, the interest rate may be high (18–21%), and the debt will last a long time.

Consumer Debt Ratio—Non-housing Monthly Debt Service to Monthly Net Income   One of the most commonly used debt management ratios is the consumer debt ratio. This is the ratio of monthly consumer debt payments to monthly net (after-tax) income. Generally, consumer debt refers to debt other than mortgage indebtedness and often includes debt incurred to service automobile and credit card purchases. A generally accepted rule in personal financial planning is that this ratio should not exceed 20%. The ratio is calculated as:

$$\text{Non-housing monthly debt payments} \div \text{Monthly net income} \leq 20\%$$

The Nelson's consumer debt ratio is very good. At 6.97%, they are well below the 20% benchmark. The numerator consists of the credit cards payments and the boat loan payments.

$$\frac{(\$960 \; + \; \$3,040) \div 12}{[\$71,050 - (\$12,855 \; + \; \$820)] \div 12} = \frac{\$333.33}{\$4,781.25} = 6.97\%$$

Monthly Housing Costs to Monthly Gross Income   Mortgage lenders are sophisticated lenders. They have benchmarks for loans secured with real estate used as a personal residence. The first such benchmark is:

$$\frac{\text{Monthly housing costs (PITI)}}{\text{Monthly gross income}} \leq 28\% \text{ monthly gross income}$$

P	=	principal
I	=	interest
T	=	taxes (real estate)
I	=	insurance

Housing costs
Principal and interest to pay the mortgage loan, real estate taxes, and homeowners insurance

Housing costs include the monthly principal and interest to repay the loan, real estate taxes, and homeowners insurance. This sum is divided by monthly gross income (income before taxes and other deductions). Generally, to issue a mortgage loan at prevailing market interest rates, lenders require this ratio to be less than or equal to 28%.

For the Nelsons:

$$\frac{(\$20,720 + \$1,234 + \$1,000 + \$950) \div 12}{\$71,050 \div 12} = \frac{\$1,992}{\$5,921} = 33.6\%$$

This ratio, which for the Nelsons significantly exceeds the benchmark of 28%, suggests that the Nelsons have taken on housing debt in excess of what is reasonable for their income.

Monthly Housing Costs and Other Debt Repayments to Monthly Gross Income   The second ratio that lenders use adjusts the previous numerator to reflect all monthly debt repayments. This ratio should be less than or equal to 36%.

$$\frac{\text{Housing costs} + \text{other monthly debt pyts}}{\text{Monthly gross income}} \leq 36\% \text{ monthly gross income}$$

This ratio of housing costs and all other monthly debt repayments must be less than or equal to 36%. A mortgage applicant must generally meet both the requirements of the 28% benchmark and the 36% benchmark to qualify for a mortgage loan at the best interest rates.

For the Nelsons:

$$\frac{\text{Housing costs + credit cards + boat loan}}{\text{Monthly gross income}} \leq 36\% \text{ monthly gross income}$$

$$\frac{\$1,992 + \left[(\$960 + \$3,040) \div 12\right]}{\$71,050 \div 12} = \frac{\$2,325.33}{\$5,921} = 39.3\%$$

The Nelsons have also exceeded the second benchmark. This should serve as a warning sign that they have too much debt for their current income level. The second housing ratio is not grossly deficient (over the target). If the Nelsons paid off the credit cards and boat with invested assets, the second ratio would be within the established benchmark.

Because these ratios are so widely used by mortgage lenders for both initial mortgage indebtedness and for mortgage refinance, they are useful benchmark ratios to calculate for any client to determine whether the client is at risk of having too much debt. The ratios indicate that monthly housing nondiscretionary costs should not exceed 28% of monthly gross income and that all monthly debt repayments should not exceed 36% of monthly gross income. The second ratio suggests that if the full initial 28% of gross income is used for housing, there is only 8% of gross income left for auto loans, furniture loans, student loans, and monthly credit card repayments. Many clients tend to stretch beyond their means when buying a home and should be cautioned by the planner. These ratios can bring a sense of reality to a client regarding the debt picture and indebtedness decisions. For the Nelsons, when these ratios are reviewed in combination with the consumer debt ratio, it becomes clear that it is not consumer debt that is making their mortgage ratios exceed the benchmark but their housing costs.

Performance Ratios—Savings

Performance ratios are designed to assess the financial flexibility of the client as well as to assess the client's progress toward financial goal achievement. These ratios are the savings ratio and discretionary cash flow plus savings-to-gross-income ratio.

The Savings Ratio   The savings ratio indicates the amount that is actually being saved as a percentage of gross income.

$$\frac{\text{Annual savings (personal and employer-related)}}{\text{Annual gross income}} = \text{annual rate of savings} = \text{target of } 10\%$$

The long-run savings rate for a client is the level of savings that has been achieved on a consistent basis and is reasonably likely to persist. The long-run combined savings rate should be about 10% of gross income if the client begins saving by age 30 expecting to retire at the age of 62. If saving begins later, retirement must be delayed or the savings rate must be increased. For example, beginning to save at age 40 and retiring at 65 would require a 15% savings rate. For these savings rates to be effective, there is also an earnings rate assumption of real market returns on a growth investment portfolio. Unfortunately, many clients do not save enough to create adequate retirement capital. Some clients also do not invest wisely and, therefore, do not achieve growth-oriented portfolio returns.

In reviewing the Nelsons' personal statement of cash flows, Exhibit 4.10, we have determined their savings rate to be:

$$\frac{\$5,853 + \$2,100}{\$71,050} = 11.2\%$$

The Nelsons have a good combined savings rate of 11.2%, which includes the 3% ($71,000 × 3% = $2,100) matching contribution from David's employer.

Net Cash Flows Plus Savings to Annual Gross Income   This ratio indicates the amount that could be saved as opposed to what is saved. The ratio is calculated using net cash flow from the personal statement of cash flows and adding scheduled savings. This sum is then divided by total gross income.

$$\frac{\text{NCF} + \text{savings}}{\text{Annual gross income}} \geq 10\% \text{ target}$$

Reviewing the Nelsons' personal statement of cash flows, we determine that the ratio is:

$$\frac{(\$157) + \$5,853 + \$2,100}{\$71,050} = 11\%$$

Although this ratio is unrevealing for the Nelsons, it may be useful for other clients whose savings rate is lower or where there are significant discretionary cash flows.

Performance Ratios—Investments

Investment performance ratios are designed to assist the reader in understanding the returns on investments. They include income on investments, rate of return on investments, and investment assets to gross income.

Rate of Return on Investments (ROI)   This ratio provides us with a return on investments that we can compare to a previously established benchmark or to an appropriate investment index. The numerator is the change in investment assets from one year to the next (ending investments [EI] – beginning investments [BI]) less any savings or gifts/inheritances received that went into investments. The denominator is the average invested assets. ROI is calculated as:

$$\frac{\text{EI} - \text{BI} - \text{savings} - \text{gifts received}}{\text{Average invested assets}} = \text{target of } 9 - 12\%$$

$$\frac{\text{BI} + \text{EI}}{2} = \text{Average invested assets}$$

Again, using the Nelsons' personal statement of cash flows and statement of financial position, the ROI is calculated to be:

$$\frac{\$78,229 - \$58,697 - \$7,953 - \$10,000}{(\$58,697 + \$78,229) \div 2} = \frac{\$1,579}{\$68,463} = 2.3\%$$

The rate of return on investments for the Nelsons for 2020 was 2.3%. While at first glance that may seem a poor rate of return, it will need to be compared with portfolios with similar asset allocations to determine exactly how the performance compared to a relevant benchmark. Obviously, it is a poor rate of return against the general benchmark of 9–12% needed annually to provide a sufficient capital base for retirement. It may, however, only represent one "down" year among many "up" years that exceeded the target.

Income on Investments   The income on investments is calculated by dividing the income from investment returns by the average invested assets.

$$\frac{\text{Income from investment returns}}{\text{Average invested assets}} = \text{target depends on the client's situation}$$

Using the personal statement of cash flows and the statement of financial position for the Nelsons, we calculate their income on investments to be:

$$\frac{(\$900 + \$150)}{(\$58,697 + \$78,229) \div 2} = \frac{\$1,050}{\$68,463} = 1.5\%$$

The ratio of 1.5% indicates a low level of income from investments. A review of the rate of return on all investments, however, including any unrealized appreciation in investment assets, will provide additional information that may be useful regarding investment performance.

Investment Assets to Annual Gross Income   Calculating investment assets as a percentage of annual gross income provides a peek into the issue of capital needed at retirement. A simple example will help us. Assume that a person about to retire has investment assets devoted to retirement of $1 million, has annual gross income of $100,000, and can invest at a rate of return of 10% with no inflation. The investment asset to income ratio is 10 ($1,000,000 ÷ $100,000), and the client can produce that income in perpetuity. We expect investment assets to be equal to or greater than 10 times preretirement income at normal retirement age. This ratio calculated over time helps us to benchmark the progress toward retirement. The ratio should be about three to four 10 years before retirement and about one 20 years before retirement.

$$\frac{\text{Investment assets}}{\text{Annual gross income}} = \text{Target depends on the client's situation and age}$$

Using the Nelsons' personal statement of cash flows and statement of financial position, the ratio is calculated as:

$$\frac{\$78,229}{\$71,050} = 1.10$$

This investment ratio is excellent for the Nelsons at their age if all the investment assets were held for retirement. Even when the education fund is deducted from the invested assets, the ratio equals .88, which is good progress toward retirement for their age. Exhibit 4.14 gives a summary of the ratio analysis for the Nelsons.

EXHIBIT 4.14 Summary of Ratio Analysis (Targets and Nelsons') Year End 12/31/2020

			Target	Nelsons'
Liquidity ratios				
Emergency fund ratio	$=$	$\dfrac{\text{current assets}}{\text{monthly nondiscretionary expenses}} =$	3–6	.54
Current ratio	$=$	$\dfrac{\text{current assets}}{\text{current liabilities}} =$	1–2	.37
Debt Ratios				
Total debt to net worth	$=$	$\dfrac{\text{total debt}}{\text{net worth}} =$	*	.90
Long-term debt to net worth	$=$	$\dfrac{\text{long-term debt}}{\text{net worth}} =$	*	.87
Total debt to total assets	$=$	$\dfrac{\text{total debt}}{\text{total assets}} =$	*	.47
Long-term debt to total assets	$=$	$\dfrac{\text{long-term debt}}{\text{total assets}} =$	*	.46
Consumer debt ratio	$=$	$\dfrac{\text{non-housing monthly debt payments}}{\text{monthly net income}} =$	≤ 20%	6.97%
Monthly housing costs to monthly gross income	$=$	$\dfrac{\text{monthly housing costs}}{\text{monthly gross income}} =$	≤ 28%	33.6%
Monthly housing costs and other debt repayments to monthly gross income	$=$	$\dfrac{\text{housing costs and debt repayments}}{\text{monthly gross income}} =$	≤ 36%	39.3%
Savings ratios				
Savings ratio	$=$	$\dfrac{\text{personal saving and employer contribution}}{\text{annual gross income}} =$	≤ 10%	11.2%
Net cash flow plus savings to annual gross income	$=$	$\dfrac{\text{net cash flow + savings}}{\text{annual gross income}} =$	> 10%	11%
Performance ratios				
Income on investments	$=$	$\dfrac{\text{dividends and interest}}{\text{average investments}} =$	*	1.5%
Return on investments	$=$	$\dfrac{\text{EI – BI – savings – gifts}}{\text{average investments}} =$	9%–12%	2.3%
Investment assets to annual gross income	$=$	$\dfrac{\text{investment assets}}{\text{annual gross income}} =$	*	1.10

*Target depends on the individual's age or investment objectives.

Vertical Analysis

Vertical Analysis and Common Size Analysis

Vertical analysis of financial statements presents each statement in percentage terms. Usually, the statement of financial position is presented with each item as a percentage of total assets, and the income statement is prepared with each item as a percentage of total income. Percentage items allow us to compare items over time when we have multiple-year financial statements for the same client.

The comparison of one statement on a percentage basis is called common size analysis because the percentages calculated ignore absolute dollars and provide information regarding the stability or instability of each account in percentage terms. Exhibit 4.15 presents the two statements of financial position in a vertical analysis format, and Exhibit 4.16 presents the Nelsons' personal statement of cash flows using vertical analysis.

EXHIBIT 4.15 Statement of Financial Position—Vertical Analysis

Dana and David Nelson
Statement of Financial Position—Vertical Analysis 2020

		12/31/19	12/31/20	Difference
ASSETS				
Cash/cash equivalents				
JT	Checking account	.34%	.28%	−.06%
JT	Savings account	.22%	.21%	−.01%
	Total cash/cash equivalents	.56%	.48%*	−.08%*
Invested assets				
Dana	ABC stock	2.96%	3.06%	.10%
JT	Education fund	3.31%	3.39%	.08%
JT	Section 401(k) plan	7.61%	8.42%	.81%
David	XYZ stock	.00%	2.18%	2.18%
	Total invested assets	**13.88%**	**17.05%**	**3.17%**
*Includes rounding differences				
Personal use assets				
JT	Principal residence	57.91%	54.47%	−3.44%
JT	Automobile	4.25%	3.27%	−.98%
David	Personal watercraft	.00%	2.18%	2.18%
David	Boat A	5.91%	.00%	−5.91%
David	Boat B	.00%	6.54%	6.54%
Dana	Jewelry	3.07%	2.94%	−.13%
JT	Furniture/household	14.42%	13.07%	−1.35%
	Total personal use assets	85.56%	82.47%	−3.09%
	Total assets	**100%**	**100%**	**0%**
LIABILITIES AND NET WORTH				
Current liabilities				
JT	Credit cards	.95%	.79%	−.16%
JT	Mortgage on principal residence	.29%	.30%	.01%
David	Boat loan	.35%	.23%	−.12%
	Total current liabilities	**1.59%**	**1.32%**	**−.27%**
Long-term liabilities				
JT	Mortgage on principal residence	46.48%	42.55%	−3.93%
David	Boat loan	2.85%	3.49%	.64%
Total long-term liabilities		49.33%	46.04%	−3.29%
Total liabilities		**50.92%**	**47.36%**	**−3.56%**
Net worth		49.08%	52.64%	3.56%
Total liabilities and net worth		**100%**	**100%**	**0%**

EXHIBIT 4.16 Personal Statement of Cash Flows

Dana and David Nelson
Personal Statement of Cash Flows—Vertical Analysis
For 2020

INFLOWS

Salary—David 98.52%

Investment income

Interest income	1.27%	
Dividend income	.21%	1.48%
Total Inflows		**100%**

Savings

Reinvestment (interest/dividends)	1.48%	
Section 401(k) plan deferrals	5.35%	
Education fund	1.41%	
Total savings		**8.24%**
Available for outflows		**91.76%**

OUTFLOWS

Ordinary living expenses

Food	8.45%	
Clothing	5.07%	
Child care	.84%	
Entertainment	2.55%	
Utilities	5.07%	
Auto maintenance	2.81%	
Church	4.93%	
Total ordinary living expenses		**29.72%**

Debt payments

Credit card payments principal	.48%	
Credit card payments interest	.87%	
Mortgage payment principal	1.74%	
Mortgage payment interest	29.16%	
Boat loan principal	2.10%	
Boat loan interest	2.18%	
Total debt payments		**36.53%**

Insurance premiums

Automobile insurance premiums	1.27%	
Disability insurance premiums	1.07%	
Homeowners insurance premiums	1.34%	
Total insurance premiums		**3.67%**

Tuition and education expenses		**1.41%**

Taxes

FICA and federal income tax (W/H)	18.09%	
State (and city) income tax	1.15%	
Property tax (principal residence)	1.41%	
Total taxes		**20.65%**
Total outflows		**91.98%**
Net cash flow (deficit)		**(.22%)**

Growth Analysis

The purpose of growth analysis is to calculate the growth rate of certain financial variables over time using time value of money tools. We expect that increases in gross income will exceed increases in the Consumer Price Index (CPI) by more than 1%. Exhibit 4.17 lists the financial variables for which growth rates should be calculated. The second column presents the growth rates that are appropriate for the particular financial variable.

EXHIBIT 4.17 Financial Variables and Growth Rates

Variable	Growth Rate
Inflation	Should equal CPI
Gross income	Should exceed CPI
Savings increase	Should exceed CPI
Savings rate	Should remain constant or increase
NCF + savings	Should grow modestly
Net worth	Should exceed CPI
Investment assets	Should grow exponentially due to combining returns and savings contributions

Limitations of Financial Statement Analysis

Inflation

Because inflation exists, comparing multiple reporting periods will require adjusting certain numbers either to current dollars (inflated dollars) or to some base percentage or index. Inflation reduces the comparability of multiperiod financial statements and ratios even when adjusted for the inflation. It is especially important to adjust growth rates for income and savings to real dollars. It is also useful to adjust nominal investment returns for inflation to determine real economic returns.

Use of Estimates

Whenever estimates of values are used, even if provided by expert appraisers, there is some risk that the estimated value is different from the actual fair market value. Such risks should be evaluated considering the purpose of the financial statement analysis. For example, net worth may be dependent on the estimated value of personal use assets (which are very difficult to value). Because net worth is used as a denominator for several ratios, an error in the denominator will affect the result of any ratio using that denominator.

Benchmarks

For corporations and industries, there are published financial statements and, therefore, clear benchmarks with which to compare ratios for companies in the same industry. Unfortunately, there are few published personal financial statements and, therefore, fewer clearly established benchmarks for individuals. Recall the housing mortgage ratios where benchmarks exist at 28% and 36% of gross income.

Sensitivity Analysis

Some ratios are more important than others. For example, the long-term savings rate and emergency fund ratio are critical, whereas the current ratio is less so. The relative size of the numerator and denominator may cause some ratios to be more sensitive to changes. Sensitivity analysis allows us to manipulate the numerators and denominators by small increments to determine the impact on the ratio.

Risk Analysis

Risk analysis examines the uncertainty of cash flows to the individual. Uncertainty regarding the asset side of the statement of financial position is called business or investment risk. Specifically, earnings may vary because of fluctuations in the value of investments and personal use assets. Financial risk is the risk on the liability side of the statement of financial position. Indebtedness is accompanied by fixed interest and principal repayments. There is always some risk as to whether debt repayments can be made. The debt/net worth ratio and other debt ratios help to measure the financial risk of the individual.

BUDGETING

Description

Planners and clients should remember that good budgeting is a learned phenomenon and, as such, there is a learning curve (the more you do it, the better you get at it). Budgeting requires planning for the expected, the recurring, and the supposedly unexpected (every month it's something). **Budgeting** is a process of projecting, monitoring, adjusting, and controlling future income and expenditures. It may be used to determine the wage replacement ratio for capital needs analysis for retirement where the client is sufficiently close to retirement to be able to estimate the retirement budget.

Budgeting
A process of projecting, monitoring, adjusting, and controlling future income and expenditures

Steps

1. Start with bank statements, checks, and check stubs for a twelve-month period. Create a spreadsheet of all expenditures by month and category. If needed, retrieve copies of credit card expenditure information for a twelve-month period to assist in determining the amounts and categories of expenditures.

2. Once the dollar amounts are determined per category and month, calculate these as a percentage of gross income. Analyze each category, looking for consistent percentage expenditures to develop a predictive model for that particular expenditure.

3. Identify which costs are sensitive to inflation and which are fixed. Examples include:

   ■ ordinary living expenses (e.g., food, clothing, and utilities);

   ■ home mortgage payments (interest);

   ■ credit card payments (interests); and

   ■ other interest-based payments (e.g., boat payments).

4. Forecast next year's income on a monthly basis.

5. Determine how much expenditures will amount to and in which months the expenditure will occur. Insurance bills are often paid annually or semiannually. If they arrive at the wrong time, they can create havoc with cash flows.

6. Project the budget for the next 12 months.

7. Compare actual expenditures for the month to expected expenditures. Adjust the next 11 months accordingly.

8. Continue to analyze, picking out specific expenditure categories that you can control. Utilities are an example of a cost that can be managed. Long-distance telephone bills may be reduced by changing carriers.

Nelson Budgeting Plan

We are now going to look at how a budgeting plan would help the Nelsons achieve their financial goals. First we will look at the personal statement of cash flows to gauge what costs they are incurring against their income.

EXHIBIT 4.18 Personal Statement of Cash Flows

Dana and David Nelson
Personal Statement of Cash Flows
For 2020

INFLOWS

Salary—David $70,000

Investment income

Interest income	$900	
Dividend income	$150	$1,050
Total inflows		$71,050

Savings

Reinvestment (interest/dividends)	$1,050	
Section 401(k) plan deferrals	$3,803	
Education fund	$1,000	
Total savings		$5,853
Available for outflows		$65,197

OUTFLOWS

Ordinary living expenses

Food	$6,000	
Clothing	$3,600	
Child care	$600	
Entertainment	$1,814	
Utilities	$3,600	
Auto maintenance	$2,000	
Church	$3,500	
Total ordinary living expenses		$21,114

Debt payments

Credit card payments principal	$345	
Credit card payments interest	$615	
Mortgage payment principal	$1,234	
Mortgage payment interest	$20,720	
Boat loan principal	$1,493	
Boat loan interest	$1,547	
Total debt payments		$25,954

Insurance premiums

Automobile insurance premiums	$900	
Disability insurance premiums	$761	
Homeowners insurance premiums	$950	
Total insurance premiums		$2,611
Tuition and education expenses		$1,000

Taxes

FICA and federal income tax (W/H)	$12,855	
State (and city) income tax	$820	
Property tax (principal residence)	$1,000	
Total taxes		$14,675
Total outflows		$65,354
Net cash flow (deficit)		($157)

The next step is to focus on the outflows and what percentage of available inflows they represent. It is also beneficial to break down the amounts further into monthly amounts.

EXHIBIT 4.19 Monthly Amounts

Available for Outflows (Monthly)	$5,433.08	Percentage of Available Income
OUTFLOWS (monthly—percentages rounded)		
Ordinary living expenses		
Food	$500	9.2%
Clothing	$300	5.5%
Child care	$50	.9%
Entertainment	$151.16	2.8%
Utilities	$300	5.5%
Auto maintenance	$167.67	3.1%
Church	$291.67	5.4%
Total ordinary living expenses	**$1,760.50**	**32.4%**
Debt payments		
Credit card payments principal	$28.75	.5%
Credit card payments interest	$51.25	.9%
Mortgage payment principal	$102.83	1.9%
Mortgage payment interest	$1,726.66	31.8%
Boat loan principal	$124.42	2.3%
Boat loan interest	$128.92	2.4%
Total debt payments	**$2,162.83**	**39.8%**
Insurance premiums		
Automobile insurance premiums	$75	1.4%
Disability insurance premiums	$63.42	1.2%
Homeowners insurance premiums	$79.16	1.5%
Total insurance premiums	**$217.58**	**4.1%**
Tuition and education expenses	**$83.33**	**1.5%**

We can now see which outflow percentages are higher than others and thus need greater control. This is where the planner and the client begin to discuss the control of costs and establish a budget. With the Nelsons' ordinary living expenses, we see that a large percentage is devoted to food, clothing, and utilities. These are expenses that can be controlled and managed in order to decrease overall expenditures. The planner would also discuss with the Nelsons what other living expenses could possibly be managed.

Debt payments and insurance premiums are also areas where proper management can control costs. There are several techniques that can decrease premium payments for insurance. For example, increasing deductibles and managing appropriate risks and coverage can have dramatic effects on the costs of premiums. Savings with insurance costs and ordinary living expenses can be used in several ways. They can be used toward savings, investments, emergency funds, self-insurance, or education funding, or they may be used to pay down large amounts of debt. A large portion of the Nelsons' outflows goes toward debt payments. They could use the savings to pay off their credit card debt or make additional principal payments on their boat or home. Mortgage payments have certain tax advantages associated with them, so depending on the situation, the planner should recommend paying off other debts first.

Once the Nelsons have agreed on certain cost controls, the planner can establish a projected monthly budget for next year. The budget should then be strictly adhered to and reviewed each month to make sure the goals of the budget are being met. Adjustments and restructuring can be done for those costs that are proving difficult to manage.

Saving and Consumption Habits

Information about a client's saving and consumption habits assists the planner in developing a successful strategic financial plan for the client. If the client does not have a history of saving money consistently, developing a strategy in which money could be directed into savings before the client receives a paycheck from his employer should be encouraged. Similarly, if the client has a history of making large dollar impulse purchases, creating barriers to discourage this tendency would be wise. Historical behavior is the best indicator of future behavior. Therefore, a good way to collect information about the client's saving and consumption habits is by asking the client about previous saving and consumption habits.

DEBT MANAGEMENT

Personal Use—Assets and Liabilities

Debt is appropriate when matched properly with the economic life of the asset and the ability to repay.

For example, the purchase of an automobile that is expected to be used for three years (36 months) has a maximum realistic economic life of five years (60 months). Ideally, it would be financed over 36 months but certainly no longer than 60 months.

A number of risks should be considered when taking on debt, including:

- a shorter than expected economic life;

- increasing cash outflows for repairs as the asset ages; and

- the change of the initial utility curves of the purchaser during the holding period unexpectedly reducing the overall utility of the asset.

Debt repayment cash flows should be matched to the economic life of the asset. Generally, the cash flows considered are not only the principal and interest to retire the debt. Also included are the cash flows associated with the increase in repairs and maintenance due to asset aging (both real and personal property) as well as the prospect of higher executory costs (insurance and taxes).

Either the cost of the replacement asset will have to be borne entirely by future cash flows or the current asset value will help to offset replacement costs. One question is whether the cost of the new asset is increasing in price more quickly than the old asset. Another question is whether the value of the old asset (exchange value to another buyer) is diminishing more quickly than the debt is being extinguished. If so, the purchaser of such an asset may find that he is in a negative equity position. This is the primary reason that lenders insist on down payments and generally establish a repayment schedule to ensure that the borrower will always be in a positive equity position. Such a position will reduce the likelihood that the borrower will abandon the property.

Home Mortgages

Types of home mortgages include:

- 30-year fixed mortgage;

- 15-year fixed mortgage;

- variable mortgage; and

- balloon mortgage.

Fixed-Rate Mortgages

Fixed-rate mortgages offer a level interest rate for the term of the loan and a fixed payment amortization schedule. An amortization schedule outlines the portion of each payment allocated to interest and the portion allocated to principal reduction. The payments are selected such that at the end of the term (i.e., 15 or 30 years), the principal is completely repaid.

EXAMPLE   If John purchases his home using a 15-year fixed-rate mortgage of $120,000 with a 6.5% interest rate, he will pay 6.5% interest on the outstanding balance every month. His monthly payment will be $1,045.33 for the 15-year term of the loan. For the first month, John owes interest of 6.5% ÷ 12 = .5417% on $120,000, which equals $650. The remaining $395.33 will go toward repayment of the loan principal. After this payment, John owes $120,000 – $395.33 = $119,604.67. The $119,604.67 will be the new balance on which the 6.5% interest is calculated. Thus, for each subsequent payment the portion allocated to interest is reduced and the portion allocated to principal repayment is increased.

Variable-Rate Mortgages or Adjustable Rate Mortgages (ARMs)

With a variable-rate mortgage, or adjustable rate mortgage (ARM), the borrower is charged interest based on a benchmark such as the 90-day Treasury bill rate. The interest rate will change monthly on the basis of changes in the benchmark rate. Variable-rate mortgages typically have amortization schedules with fixed payments. The payment is determined by selecting an interest rate and calculating the payment necessary to retire a fixed-rate mortgage with that interest rate. Because the actual interest rate varies, the portion of the mortgage payment allocated to principal repayment will not always be greater than the previous month's allocation as under a fixed mortgage. If the actual interest rate is much higher than the rate used to calculate the mortgage payment, there will still be principal outstanding at the end of the term. In that case, the borrower will be required to repay the remaining balance in a lump sum. On the other hand, if the actual interest rate is much lower than the rate used to calculate the mortgage payment, the loan will be repaid before the end of the term.

EXAMPLE   Samantha has a 2/6 ARM. Her 30-year mortgage interest rate is currently 4%. This means that Samantha's interest rate cannot increase more than 2% per year or 6% over the life of the loan. The maximum interest rate is 10%.

Many variable-rate mortgages limit the amount by which the interest rate can change on a monthly and yearly basis. For example, an ARM may state that the interest rate can only adjust by .5% each month and no more than 2% per year. Another common feature of adjustable rate mortgages is conversion from a fixed rate after a period of time, usually five to seven years. Most ARMs used for personal residences begin as fixed-rate mortgages and then convert to adjustable rate. The borrower pays a fixed rate of interest, usually lower than that for a comparable fixed-rate mortgage, for five to seven years, and then the interest rate adjusts monthly on the basis of the predetermined benchmark.

Balloon Mortgages

Besides the fixed-rate and variable-rate mortgages, a prospective homeowner may acquire a balloon mortgage. Balloon mortgages can have fixed or adjustable interest rates, but the term will be less than the period required to amortize the loan.

EXAMPLE Teresa obtains a seven-year balloon mortgage of $80,000 with a fixed interest rate of 5.75%. The lender determines Teresa's payments on the basis of a 30-year amortization, which results in a fixed monthly payment of $466.86. Teresa will pay $466.86 per month for seven years. At the end of the seventh year, the outstanding balance on Teresa's loan is $71,386.82. Because the term of the loan is seven years, Teresa will be required to pay off the remaining balance in a lump sum. Instead of paying cash, Teresa will probably refinance, replacing her original $80,000 loan with a new one for $71,386.82.

Mortgage Selection

Several issues must be addressed in the selection of mortgages. They include the length of time expected to stay in the house, cash flow capacity, and risk tolerance. A determination should be made of spread between yields after a quantitative analysis comparison of fixed-to-fixed rates and fixed-to-variable rates.

Historically, if the time expected to be in the house is short, an adjustable rate mortgage (ARM) is more likely the mortgage of choice. This is simply because most ARMs have a 2–3% lower interest rate than a 30-year fixed-rate mortgage and have 2/6 caps (2% maximum interest rate increase per year, 6% life of loan). The downside risk is the prospect of the interest rate increasing periodically, causing the payment to increase proportionally. An advantage of an ARM is that, because of the low initial interest rate, the principal and interest (P&I) payments are low relative to a 30-year fixed-rate mortgage. Therefore, potential borrowers may find it easier to qualify for a mortgage using the traditional lender hurdle rates of 28%/36%.

EXAMPLE When comparing a 15-year to a 30-year fixed rate mortgage, the interest rates will usually be about .5% different assuming the same down payment. The cash flows will differ depending on the interest rate and the size of the mortgage.

	Sales Price	Down Payment	Paid Closing Costs	Mortgage Amount	Term Months	Interest Rate	P & I Payment (rounded)
Fixed 30 Year	$180,000	$36,000	$5,760	$144,000	360	5.5%	$ 818
Fixed 15 Year	$180,000	$36,000	$5,760	$144,000	180	5.0%	$1,139
ARM 30 Year	$180,000	$36,000	$5,760	$144,000	360	3.0%	$ 607

Although the ARM has the current lowest payment, the risk is that at some point in the life of the ARM, the interest rate will be 9%, assuming a 2%/6% cap, at which time the monthly P&I payment would be $1,158.66 over a 30-year period. It should be pointed out that in this particular example, loan qualifying would be easier using the ARM because the initial payment is lower (assuming $200 per month taxes and $75 per month insurance).

- 30-year fixed rate: total monthly housing costs = $818 + $200 + $75 = $1,093; monthly gross income needed to qualify for loan = $1,093 ÷ .28 = $3,903.57.

- 15-year fixed rate: total monthly housing costs = $1,139 + $200 + $75 = $1,414; monthly gross income needed to qualify for loan = $1,414 ÷ .28 = $5,050.

- ARM: total monthly housing costs = $607 + $200 + $75 = $882; monthly gross income needed to qualify for loan = $882 ÷ .28 = $3,150.

If a client has a low tolerance for fluctuating payments, a fixed-rate mortgage should be selected. Assuming a higher risk tolerance, the planner will have to consider the length of expected ownership (shorter term will mitigate risk) and the opportunity cost of alternative investments. It is generally not appropriate to select an ARM (using the first-year teaser rate) simply to qualify for a loan and hope that cash flows will be sufficient to pay for any interest increases.

EXAMPLE   The savings resulting from mortgage selection is a result of (1) the 15-year mortgage causing earlier retirement of the principal indebtedness and (2) the slightly lower interest rate. Many 30-year loans are selected simply as a necessity to meet lender qualification requirements. If no prepayment penalties exist, most of the savings can be achieved by paying a 30-year loan according to a 15-year amortization schedule.

	Number of Payments	Monthly Payment	Total Payments	Loan Principal	Interest Paid
Fixed 30 Year	360	$ 818	$294,480	$144,000	$150,480
Fixed 15 Year	180	$1,139	$205,020	$144,000	$ 61,020
Savings					$ 89,460

The total interest paid is determined by multiplying the amount of the payment by the number of payments and then subtracting the principal borrowed.

WHERE ON THE WEB

BankRate **www.bankrate.com**

Credit Union National Association **www.cuna.org**

Equifax **www.equifax.com**

Federal Citizen Information Center **www.gsa.gov**

DISCUSSION QUESTIONS

1. What is the relationship between GAAP/FASB and personal financial statements?

2. Describe some of the uses of personal financial statements.

3. What is the purpose of the statement of financial position?

4. What items are included on the statement of financial position?

5. Discuss the presentation of the statement of financial position (i.e., how items are listed and why).

6. What is the purpose of the personal statement of cash flows?

7. What items are included on the personal statement of cash flows?

8. Discuss the presentation of the personal statement of cash flows (i.e., how items are listed and why).

9. What is the purpose of the statement of changes in net worth?

10. What items are included on the statement of changes in net worth?

11. Discuss the presentation of the statement of changes in net worth (i.e., how items are listed and why).

12. What are the differences between long-term and current assets/liabilities?

13. Why are financial ratios important to financial planning?

14. What is the importance of keeping accurate and up-to-date financial statements?

15. What is fair market value?

16. What is liquidity?

17. Why do we prepare three different financial statements?

18. Discuss the importance of vertical analysis.

19. What are some of the limitations of personal financial statements?

20. What is the purpose of budgeting?

21. List the different types of home mortgages and their characteristics.

EXERCISES

1. What is the balancing equation for the statement of financial position?

2. What do current assets and current liabilities have in common?

3. Your client purchased new living room furniture for $6,500 last month. Which financial statement(s) would this purchase affect and how?

4. How would each of the following items affect net worth?
   A. Repayment of a loan using funds from a savings account
   B. Purchase of an automobile – 25% down payment/75% financed
   C. The S&P 500 increases, and the client has an S&P 500 index mutual fund
   D. Interest rates increase, and the client has a substantial bond portfolio

5. Lauren and Herb have the following assets and liabilities:

Liquid assets	$6,750
Investment assets	$16,250
Personal residence	$125,000
Current liabilities	$3,100
Long-term liabilities	$86,000

   Calculate their total assets, total liabilities, and net worth.

6. Calculate the current ratio based on the facts given in the previous question.

7. After reviewing Kenny and Jane's financial statements, the following information was determined:

Liquid assets	$3,976
Investment assets	$10,738
Annual nondiscretionary expenses	$13,913
Current liabilities	$9,247

   Calculate this couple's emergency fund ratio. Does the ratio fall within the target goal?

8. After reviewing Matt and Jennifer's personal statement of cash flows, the following information was determined:

Mortgage principal	$5,467
Mortgage interest	$21,500
Property tax	$2,000
Homeowners insurance premium	$1,800

   The couple has monthly gross income of $9,500. According to benchmarks set by mortgage lenders, has this couple taken on debt in excess of what is reasonable for their income?

9. In addition to the information given in Exercise 8, Matt and Jennifer had other annual debt payments of $11,600. Calculate the monthly housing costs and other debt repayments to monthly gross income ratio. Do Matt and Jennifer qualify for a mortgage loan?

10. Marisa and Bryant have the following assets and liabilities:

Checking account	$2,000
Personal residence	$125,000
Savings account	$3,000
CDs	$5,000
Automobile	$13,500
Stocks	$10,000
Mortgage	$80,000
Auto loan	$5,000

Determine their net worth.

11. Use the following items to determine total assets, total liabilities, net worth, total cash inflows, and total cash outflows:

Net monthly salary	$2,280
Rent	$750
Savings account balance	$2,000
Auto loan payment	$416
Money market mutual fund	$4,800
Clothing expense	$150
Value of home computer	$1,200
Groceries expense	$220
Entertainment expense	$130
Value of autos	$10,800
Student loan payment	$212
Utilities	$510
Laundry expense	$46
Insurance premium	$368
Balance of student loan	$8,625

Note: Inflow and outflow items are shown monthly.

12. The Coopers have a net worth of $250,000 before any of the following transactions:

   ■ Paid off credit cards of $9,000 using a savings account

   ■ Transferred $5,000 from checking to their Traditional IRAs

   ■ Purchased $2,500 of furniture with credit

What is the Coopers' net worth after these transactions?

13. What are the advantages of performing vertical analysis on financial statements?

14. Explain how inflation limits financial statement analysis.

15. Bart has a history of making large dollar impulse purchases. As Bart's planner, what could you do to help remedy this situation?

PROBLEMS

1. Given the following information, develop a beginning-of-the-year statement of financial position.

Beginning date   January 1, 2020
End date   December 31, 2020
Client name   Frank and Lois Fox

	Beginning Balance	Ending Balance	Income/Expenses Amount (Yearly)
Section 401(k) plan deferrals			$750
Section 401(k) plan—Frank	$0	$1,500	
Section 403(b) plan deferrals			$990
Section 403(b) plan—Lois	$0	$990	
Auto loan	$15,432	$10,436	
Auto loan interest			$381
Auto loan principal			$4,996
Auto maintenance			$600
Automobile—Frank	$20,000	$18,000	
Automobile—Lois	$5,750	$5,175	
Automobile insurance premiums			$2,124
Checking	$10,000	$15,570	
Child support			$2,400
Clothing			$3,600
Credit card	$10,870	$10,417	
Credit card payments interest			$1,707
Credit card payments principal			$453
Entertainment			$4,200
FICA and federal income tax (W/H)			$11,449
Food			$4,800
Furniture/household	$36,000	$34,000	
Go-cart	$0	$1,200	
Homeowners insurance premiums			$534
Jewelry	$6,000	$6,100	
Maid/child care			$4,800
Mortgage on residence	$72,960	$72,164	
Mortgage payment interest			$5,808
Mortgage payment principal			$796
Personal residence	$85,000	$89,250	
Property tax (principal residence)			$850
Reinvestment in savings account/trust			$5,675
Salary—Frank			$25,000
Salary—Lois			$33,000
Savings	$13,500	$14,175	
Savings account/trust fund interest			$5,675
Trust fund	$100,000	$105,000	
Tuition and education expenses			$2,893
Utilities			$2,100

Additional transactions:

Made a joint gift of bedroom furniture with a fair market value of $2,000 to Frank's little sister
Section 401(k) plan employer match = 3% of income
Bought a go-cart for their son for $1,200

2. Use the data in Problem 1 to create a personal statement of cash flows.

3. Use the data in Problem 1 to create a statement of changes in net worth.

4. Use the data in Problem 1 to create an end-of-the-year statement of financial position.

5. Use the results from problems 1–4 to calculate the following ratios for year-end:
   a. Emergency fund
   b. Current ratio
   c. Total debt to net worth
   d. Long-term debt to net worth
   e. Total debt to total assets
   f. Long-term debt to total assets
   g. Monthly housing costs to monthly gross income
   h. Monthly housing costs and other debt repayments to monthly gross income
   i. Savings ratio
   j. Net cash flow plus savings to annual gross income
   k. Income on investments
   l. Return on investments
   m. Investment assets to annual gross income

6. Discuss the financial position of the Foxes as based on the ratios you calculated in the previous problem.

7. Prepare a vertical analysis of the end-of-the-year statement of financial position and the personal statement of cash flows for the Foxes.

8. Lisa recently bought a house for $150,000 using a fixed 30-year home loan with a 5% interest rate. She used 20% of the amount toward the down payment and paid the $5,000 in closing costs out of pocket. How much mortgage interest can Lisa expect to pay during the course of this loan?

Establishing Financial Direction: The Financial Planning Process

▌ LEARNING OBJECTIVES

After learning the material in this chapter, you will be able to do the following:

■ Identify the seven steps of the financial planning process used to establish financial direction

■ Assist clients in identifying an appropriate financial mission

■ Gather client data and identify external and internal environmental information that is relevant for a particular client

■ Assist clients in determining goals, expectations, and objectives

■ Determine a client's financial status and analyze internal strengths and weaknesses, as well as external environmental opportunities and threats

- Develop a financial plan by formulating appropriate financial strategies

- Assist clients in analyzing and selecting the financial strategy that best meets their needs and desires

- Assist clients in implementing and monitoring their financial plans

THE FINANCIAL PLANNING PROCESS

The first step in the financial planning process, establishing and defining the client-planner relationship, has been discussed in Chapter 3. Once this step is completed, the financial planner now begins to establish financial direction by gathering the information necessary to fulfill the engagement and then analyzing and evaluating the client's current financial status. These steps, and the subsequent steps in the financial planning process, are illustrated in Exhibit 5.1.

EXHIBIT 5.1 The Financial Planning Process

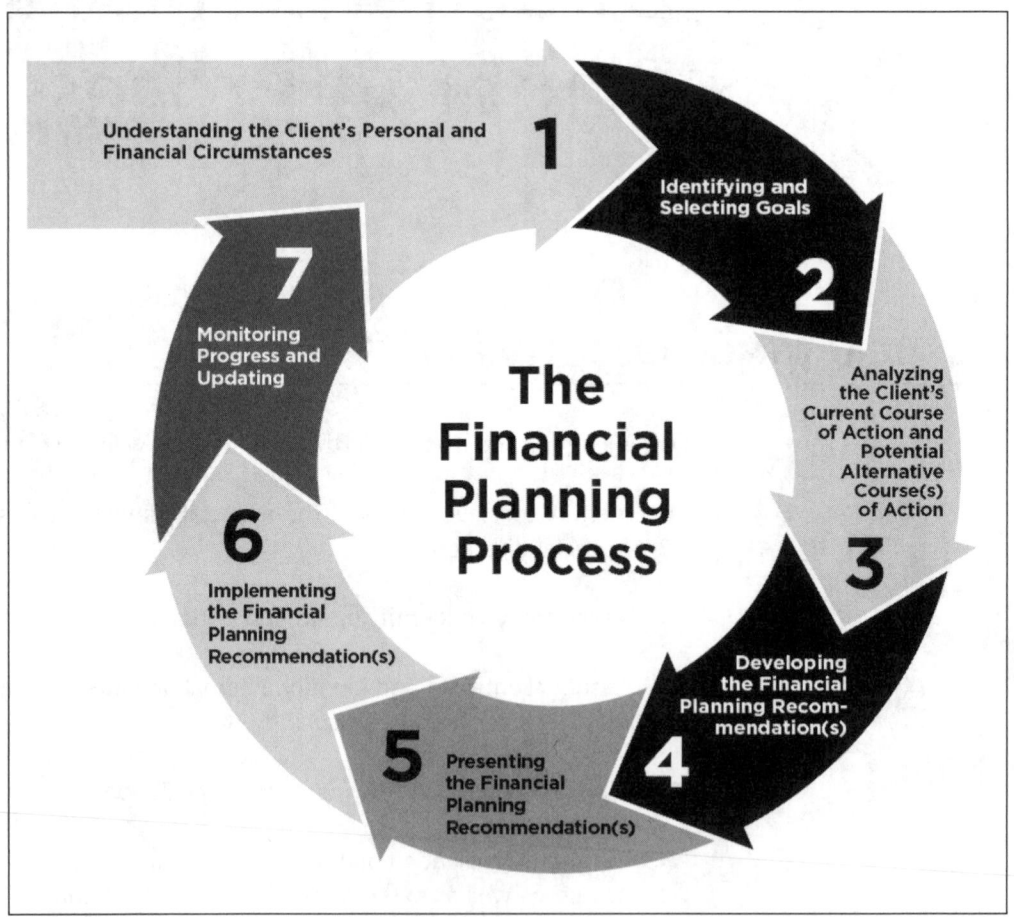

Source: CFP Board - Roadmap to the Code of Ethics and Standards of Conduct

Steps

1. Understanding the client's personal and financial circumstances.

2. Identifying and selecting goals.

3. Analyzing the client's current course of action and potential alternative course(s) of action.

4. Developing the financial planning recommendation(s).

5. Presenting the financial planning recommendation(s).

6. Implementing the financial planning recommendation(s).

7. Monitoring progress and updating.

The seven steps of the financial planning process are completed in sequential order because each step depends on the previous step. The elimination of any step may result in the loss of direction and, possibly, an inappropriate financial strategy. Furthermore, the financial planner must periodically monitor the external and internal environments so that changes in the environment may be responded to appropriately. Monitoring is a continuous and ongoing process that does not end once the plan has been implemented. Modifications to the plan must be made as changes in situations and circumstances require.

To establish financial direction in a manner that is concise and systematic, we recommend the use of the "Client/Planner Worksheet for Establishing Financial Direction" (Exhibit 5.2). The application of this worksheet will be demonstrated throughout this chapter. Notice that the worksheet has a header for the client's name and date, a footer for the planner's name, a section for the financial mission, a section for financial goals and objectives, and a section in which each goal or objective is identified and classified as a need or want, with the want objectives ranked from 1 (nice to have) to 5 (of great importance).

The process of interviewing the client and gathering necessary paperwork could take several weeks. Financial planners may find it helpful to ask the client to provide bank statements, pay stubs, investment account statements, and insurance policies at the data-gathering meeting. A completed client questionnaire may also be requested before the meeting. Having these support documents will speed the analysis phase and allow the planner to ask pointed questions during the data-gathering meeting.

EXHIBIT 5.2 Client/Planner Worksheet—Blank Form

**Client/Planner Worksheet for
Establishing Financial Direction**

Client Name_____   Date_____

FINANCIAL MISSION
1. Educate the client as to what a financial mission is and the importance of it being broad and enduring.
2. Working with your client, develop a financial mission that your client is willing to embrace.

_____
_____

Financial Goals & Objectives
1. Discuss and explain common financial goals with client.
2. Identify goals the client is interested in achieving.
3. Write client objective under appropriate goal classification.
4. Ensure all "need" objectives have been identified and documented.
5. Classify each objective as a want or a need; remember to remain objective.
6. For each "want" objective, the client must assign a weight between 1 and 5 (1 = objective would be nice to have, 5 = objective is of great importance).

Goal:	Need	Want
Objectives:		
	•	•____
	•	•____
	•	•____

Goal	Need	Want
Objectives:		
	•	•____
	•	•____
	•	•____

Goal:	Need	Want
Objectives:		
	•	•____
	•	•____
	•	•____

Goal:	Need	Want
Objectives:		
	•	•____
	•	•____
	•	•____

Planner's Name _____

STEP 1: UNDERSTANDING THE CLIENT'S PERSONAL AND FINANCIAL CIRCUMSTANCES

As discussed in Chapter 3, financial planners must establish relationships of trust and open communication with their clients. During this first step of the financial planning process, the client-planner relationship is defined as expectations that are set for both parties. The financial planner discusses the services to be provided and the methods and sources of compensation. The parties also discuss decision-making and the duration of the relationship.

At this meeting, the planner may help the client develop a financial mission statement. A **financial mission** is a broad and enduring statement that identifies the client's long-term purpose for creating a financial plan. Because the mission statement is broad

Financial mission
Broad and enduring statement that identifies the client's long-term purpose for creating a financial plan

and enduring, it should not change throughout the planning process. The purpose of a financial mission is twofold. First, it ensures a common understanding between the client and the planner as to why the financial plan is being created and implemented. Second, it provides a basis for the creation of feasible alternative goals, objectives, and strategies, and for selecting among strategic alternatives. Throughout this text, it is assumed that the financial mission for most clients is to achieve financial independence and avoid catastrophic financial occurrences that could result in financial dependence.

Appropriate financial planning requires a holistic approach. All aspects of a client's past, present, and projected financial situation need to be evaluated. It is inappropriate to focus only on one or two aspects of a client's situation because all aspects are interrelated and interdependent. This is why developing an appropriate financial mission is so important. The financial planner can use the "Client/Planner Worksheet for Establishing Financial Direction" to begin formalizing the financial planning process when working with the client.

Exhibit 5.3 identifies how the Nelsons, a couple introduced at the end of Chapter 3, might complete the Financial Mission section of the "Client/Planner Worksheet for Establishing Financial Direction." When completing the Financial Mission section, the first step is for the financial planner to communicate with and educate the client so that a realistic, enduring, and broad financial mission is developed. Once the client has adopted the mission, it should be documented on the worksheet. Throughout this chapter, we will assume the Nelsons have embraced the following mission: "To achieve financial independence and avoid catastrophic financial occurrences resulting in financial dependence."

EXHIBIT 5.3 Client/Planner Worksheet—Financial Mission

**Client/Planner Worksheet for
Establishing Financial Direction**

Client Name   Dana and David Nelson   **Date** February 16, 2021

FINANCIAL MISSION
1. Educate the client as to what a financial mission is and the importance of it being broad and enduring.
2. Working with your client, develop a financial mission that your client is willing to embrace.

   To achieve financial independence and avoid catastrophic financial occurrences that may result in financial dependence.

Identifying Relevant Environmental Information

Once the client-planner relationship is established and the mission is adopted, the financial planner gathers data needed to analyze and evaluate the client's financial status. In this step, the financial planner identifies the relevant external and internal environmental information that applies to the client. The planner should apply the skills and information discussed in Chapter 2, External Environmental Analysis, to identify external environmental information that is current and relevant to the client. The planner must also be able to identify the relevant information that has been collected about the client. Lessons learned in Chapter 3, Communication and Internal Environmental Analysis, should also be applied during this step. It is important to keep the mission in mind to determine whether information is relevant. Only relevant information should be listed to keep the amount of information collected manageable. During this step, it is important to gather and list only the facts. Analysis will be conducted and conclusions will be drawn later while developing the SWOT Analysis, during Step 3: Analyzing the client's current course of action and potential alternative course(s) of action.

External and internal environmental information has been gathered and determined to be relevant to the Nelsons; it is listed next.

Relevant external environmental information is as follows.

■ Mortgage rates are 5% for 30 years and 4.5% for 15 years, fixed.

■ Gross domestic product (GDP) is expected to grow at less than 3%.

■ Inflation is expected to be 2.6%.

■ Expected return on investment is 8% for common stocks, 9% for small company stocks, and 1.1% for U.S. Treasury bills.

■ College education costs are $15,000 per year ($75,000 for 5 years).

Relevant internal environmental information is as follows.

■ David has been employed at the bank for 12 years, has a salary of $70,000, and they have a gross income of $71,050.

■ The Nelsons are in the asset-accumulation phase.

■ Relevant financial ratios, identified in Chapter 4, are as follows:

— Current assets to monthly nondiscretionary expenses ratio is 0.54.

— Housing costs to gross income ratio is 33.6%.

— All debt payments to gross income ratio is 39.3%.

— Annual savings to annual gross income ratio is 11.2%.

— Investment asset ratio is 1.10 for the previous year.

■ The entire family is insured under David's employer's health plan (PPO). For covered expenses, a $1,000 in-network deductible and a $2,000 out-of-network deductible apply, after which 80%/20% coinsurance applies in-network and 60%/40% applies out-of-network. There is a stop-loss limit of $20,000 annually in-network and $30,000 annually out-of-network. The entire monthly premium of $1,123.54 is paid by David's employer.

■ David's employer provides group term life insurance equal to two times his current salary.

■ David has a private disability insurance policy covering accidental disability for "own occupation" with a 30-day elimination period. The benefit is $2,700 per month until his normal Social Security retirement age. David pays the annual premium of $761.

■ The Nelsons have a homeowners insurance (HO-3) policy with dwelling extension and replacement cost on contents. The deductible is $250 with an annual premium of $950.

■ David currently contributes 5.43% of his salary into the company's Section 401(k) plan. The company contributes dollar-for-dollar up to 3%. David's maximum contribution is 16%. David's assets within the plan are currently earning 8.5%, based on his investment choices within the plan.

■ David and Dana are in the 15% marginal federal income tax bracket.

STEP 2: IDENTIFYING AND SELECTING GOALS

Goals
High-level statements of financial desire that may be for the short term or the long term

Paradoxical thinking
The second phase of a client's thinking process when setting financial direction in which a client tries to focus on several simultaneous objectives, causing confusion, goal conflict, and ambiguity. The paradoxical thinking phase is where a client often seeks the advice of a financial planner.

The next part of the financial planning process is Step 2: Identifying and selecting goals. Goals are high-level statements of desires that may be for either the short term or the long term. Short-term goals are those that will occur within five years. Long-term goals are those that will occur sometime beyond five years. Identifying goals requires the client to consider all aspects of a financial plan. If all goals are identified and prioritized, the client is less likely to overlook some goals while focusing on others. Performing this process of defining and prioritizing goals, however, often results in the client entering the second common phase of thinking—**paradoxical thinking.** As the client advances to the paradoxical thinking level, he also may begin to become discouraged or frustrated with the process because of a new awareness of the extent of financial planning required to achieve multiple and often conflicting goals. During this phase, the planner should keep explanations simple and discuss goals in present dollar value terms because future value terms may be more difficult for the client to understand.

Goals are critical to the planning engagement because they define what the client wants to achieve and direct the overall process. If this stage of the process is not given the full attention it requires, the rest of the planning process lacks focus and becomes misguided.

Financial goals should be quantified in dollar amounts and have established time frames. Quantifying goals makes it easier to estimate required savings and establish patterns that lead to success. Several goals will include personal and economic assumptions. These assumptions may include, but are not limited to, the following:

- **Personal assumptions**, based on client-related variables, such as retirement age(s), life expectancy(ies), income needs, risk factors, time horizon, and special needs

- **Economic assumptions**, based on economic-based data or performance (current and/or historic), such as inflation rates and investment returns

The specific assumptions that are embedded in the plan require a collaborative exchange between the planner and the client. It is important to remember that the assumptions and goals will shift over time and that calculations are merely estimates. However, any decisions concerning material assumptions within the plan must be disclosed and vetted with the client.

An individual who seeks financial planning services is often motivated by a specific situation or set of circumstances. Early in the planning relationship, these motivating factors can be transformed into well-defined goals that the client aims to achieve. Although achieving these goals becomes central to the plan, the planner must account for issues that the client may not have considered independently. For example, a planner is responsible for conducting a risk analysis of the client's situation and instituting protection against events that can cause unanticipated financial difficulty, hindering long- or short-term goals as a result. If the client were to experience a period of disability, the ensuing financial losses could have consequences on short-term and long-term education planning goals. The planner must anticipate these risks and focus the attention of the client on the interrelated nature of every goal. In addition, personal financial planning should incorporate and responsibly manage financial needs that exist for all clients, such as retirement and estate planning. In the initial phase of the data-gathering process, a discussion must be held regarding these long-term needs, as well as implications of not addressing other issues immediately. After all goals, assumptions, timelines, and risks have been explored, the planner and client can collaborate to rank financial objectives in order of importance. In prioritizing one goal over another, the planner must take care to point out the impact to other goals that arise as a result of the choice.

Generally, financial goals can be divided into the following five categories, each of which will be discussed fully in subsequent chapters.

- *Insurance planning and employee benefits*—The goal is to mitigate the risks of catastrophic losses to persons, property, and liability by maintaining appropriate insurance coverage while paying efficient premiums. Also included in this category are benefits available to employees, including group life, health, and disability insurance.

- *Investment planning*—The goal is to save and invest to accumulate capital for retirement, wealth transfer, and other expenditure objectives, such as the purchase of personal property, education funding, lump-sum payments, and emergencies.

- *Tax planning*—The goal is to arrange income tax affairs to mitigate income tax liability and take advantage of incentives in the income tax law as appropriate.

- *Retirement planning*—The goal is to provide inflation-protected retirement income at an appropriate age for full life expectancy, conservatively estimated.

- *Estate planning*—The goal is to have a proper estate plan consistent with transfer goals.

The financial planner can again use the "Client/Planner Worksheet for Establishing Financial Direction" to assist in establishing financial goals. As the Nelsons' financial planner, you should work with and educate them so that they become familiar with the common financial goals. Next, you should assist them in identifying the goals they are interested in achieving. Once they understand the importance and interdependence of all common financial goals, the goals should be documented in the Financial Goals section of the worksheet. Exhibit 5.4 identifies the goals that are relevant to the Nelsons.

EXHIBIT 5.4 Establishing Financial Direction—Financial Goals

**Client/Planner Worksheet for
Establishing Financial Direction**

Client Name_____**Dana and David Nelson**_____ Date_____**February 16, 2021**_____

FINANCIAL MISSION

1. Educate the client as to what a financial mission is and the importance of it being broad and enduring.

2. Working with your client, develop a financial mission that your client is willing to embrace.

**To achieve financial independence and avoid catastrophic financial
occurrences that may result in financial dependence.**

Financial Goals and Objectives

1. Discuss and explain common financial goals with client.

2. Identify goals the client is interested in achieving.

Goal: Mitigate risk of catastrophic losses by maintaining appropriate insurance coverage while paying efficient premiums.		
Objectives:	Need	Want
	☐	☐____

Goal: Provide inflation-protected retirement income, assuming a life expectancy of 92 years of age.		
Objectives:	Need	Want
	☐	☐____

Goal: Develop an appropriate estate plan consistent with transfer goals.		
Objectives:	Need	Want
	☐	☐____

Goal: Arrange income tax affairs to minimize income tax liability and take advantage of tax law incentives.		
Objectives:	Need	Want
	☐	☐____

Goal: Accumulate capital, through saving and investing, for the purchase of personal property, education, and emergencies.		
Objectives:	Need	Want
	☐	☐____

Developing Financial Objectives

Goals are further defined by the development of financial objectives. Objectives are more specific than goals. Several objectives may be developed for each goal category and should include time and measurement attributes when appropriate.

The client usually engages in paradoxical thinking during this step. The client often becomes confused and frustrated because of the conflict between unlimited wants and limited resources. The planner can greatly assist the client by presenting information in a clear, concise, systematic, and objective manner.

Once objectives have been identified for each goal category, each objective must then be classified as either a want or a need. Generally, the client is more focused on identifying the want objectives. Therefore, the planner is responsible for ensuring that all of the need objectives are identified. To this end, the planner should keep the mission and relevant environmental factors in mind when assisting the client in the development of financial objectives.

Distinguishing between a want and need can be difficult for clients because subjectivity and strong desires become issues. This potential difficulty can be eliminated by asking two questions of each objective:

■ Is this objective necessary to accomplish the financial mission?

■ Does the law require that this objective be implemented?

If the answer to either of these questions is yes, the objective is a need. If the answer to both of these questions is no, the objective is a want.

For example, under the goal of protection against risk, the objectives of property insurance for an old car and auto liability coverage may have been identified. If the planner asks the questions above in reference to auto insurance, we find that in this case auto insurance is a want objective. Implementation of this objective is not necessary to accomplish the mission of achieving financial independence and avoiding catastrophic financial occurrences, nor does law require it because it is an older car and is paid for in full. However, liability insurance may be a need objective because state law requires all licensed automobile owners to carry liability insurance. If the Nelsons are involved in an accident for which they are at fault, lack of liability coverage will likely jeopardize their assets.

Objectives classified as wants are further analyzed by having the client attach weights to them. Assigning weights to objectives allows the planner and the client to objectively evaluate a subjective desire. A weight expresses the importance or desirability of an objective relative to the others by assigning it a number between 1 and 5. A 5 should be assigned to a want objective of great importance—something the client has a strong desire to achieve. A 1 should be assigned to a want objective that the client would like to have but could do without if the objective is not achieved. The weight assignment will be used during strategy selection to assist in determining which want objectives will be implemented. It is probable that not all of the want objectives will be achieved; however, all of the need objectives must be implemented to achieve the financial mission and comply with the law. Therefore, objectives classified as needs do not require weight assignment.

Exhibit 5.5 identifies a partial list of objectives that are important to the Nelsons. Throughout this chapter, we will address only a partial list of objectives in order to keep the amount of material manageable.

EXHIBIT 5.5 Client/Planner Worksheet—Financial Objectives

Client/Planner Worksheet for
Establishing Financial Direction

Client Name ___Dana and David Nelson_____   **Date** ___February 16, 2021_____

FINANCIAL MISSION
1. Educate the client as to what a financial mission is and the importance of it being broad and enduring.
2. Working with your client, develop a financial mission that your client is willing to embrace.

   To achieve financial independence and avoid catastrophic financial occurrences that may result in financial dependence.

Financial Goals & Objectives
1. Discuss and explain common financial goals with client.
2. Identify goals the client is interested in achieving.
3. Write client objective under appropriate goal classification.
4. Ensure all "need" objectives have been identified and documented.
5. Classify each objective as a "want" or a "need." Remember to remain objective.
6. For each "want" objective, the client must assign a weight between 1 and 5. (1 = objective would be nice to have, 5 = objective is of great importance).

Goal: Mitigate risk of catastrophic losses by maintaining appropriate insurance coverage while paying efficient premiums.		
Objectives:	**Need**	**Want**
Within 6 months, modify Life Insurance to include 20-year level term for $500,000.	✔	☐ ____
Within 6 months, modify Disability Insurance to include disability by sickness.	✔	☐ ____
Within 6 months, modify Health Insurance to include major medical with $10,000 deductible due to lifetime limit.	✔	☐ ____

Goal: Provide inflation-protected retirement income, assuming a life expectancy of 92 years of age.		
Objectives:	**Need**	**Want**
Retire at age 67 with an 80% wage replacement, thereby, maintaining lifestyle.	✔	☐ ____
Retire at age 62 with an 80% wage replacement, thereby, maintaining lifestyle.	☐	✔ _5_

Goal: Develop an appropriate estate plan consistent with transfer goals.		
Objectives:	**Need**	**Want**
Develop a will for David, within three months.	✔	☐ ____
Develop a will for Dana, within three months.	✔	☐ ____

Goal: Arrange income tax affairs so that income tax liability is minimized and to take advantage of tax law incentives.		
Objectives:	**Need**	**Want**
Reduce tax payments to the minimum amount allowable by law.	☐	✔ _5_
Within 2 months, increase contributions into Section 401(k) plan to ensure adequate retirement income and to reduce income tax liability.	✔	☐ ____

Goal: Accumulate capital, through saving and investing, for the purchase of personal property, education, and emergencies.		
Objectives:	**Need**	**Want**
Purchase a $200,000 home in Key West within 5 years.	☐	✔ _4_
Save for college tuition so that money is available when John, Gabrielle, and new baby begin college.	☐	✔ _3_
Purchase a new car in two years, twelve years, and at retirement.	☐	✔ _2_
Eliminate credit card debt within six years.	☐	✔ _3_

STEP 3: ANALYZING THE CLIENT'S CURRENT COURSE OF ACTION AND POTENTIAL ALTERNATIVE COURSE(S) OF ACTION

Analyzing and evaluating the client's current course of action and potential alternative course(s) of action, Step 3 of the financial planning process, employs knowledge from all financial disciplines:

- Insurance planning and employee benefits
- Investment planning
- Income tax planning
- Retirement planning
- Estate planning

SWOT analysis
An analysis that helps the financial planner understand how internal and external environmental factors impact the client's financial situation. The acronym SWOT stands for strengths, weaknesses, opportunities, and threats.

This step involves identifying strengths, weaknesses, opportunities, and threats. A **SWOT** (strengths, weaknesses, opportunities, and threats) **analysis** is a useful tool to assist the planner in converting several bits of relevant information into an understandable format. The analysis helps the planner understand how the internal and external environments impact the client's situation—a critical element to developing feasible and responsive strategies. A SWOT analysis is developed by listing the client's internal strengths and weaknesses and the external environment's opportunities and threats. Once the strengths, weaknesses, opportunities, and threats are identified, the planner systematically analyzes the SWOT list to assist in the generation of feasible alternative strategies.

When identifying strengths, the planner should consider the internal and financial data collected from the client. Client strengths, such as appropriate consumption and savings behaviors and positive attitudes and beliefs with regard to financial planning and financial stability, also should be considered. The planner should indicate whether the timing of the plan is appropriate to the client's goals and objectives and whether the client's subjective perception of her financial situation is similar to the planner's objective appraisal of the client's financial situation. The planner should consider areas in which the client has adequate insurance coverage for life, health, disability, long-term care, property, and liability. Finally, the financial ratios that meet or exceed recommended levels should be listed.

When identifying weaknesses, the planner again should consider the internal and financial data collected from the client. Client weaknesses, such as poor savings behaviors, unwise consumption habits, a poor attitude toward financial planning, special needs, and financial instability, should be identified. The planner should indicate whether the timing of the plan is appropriate for the client and whether the client's subjective perception of his financial situation is dissimilar to the objective financial situation. The planner should consider areas in which the client has inadequate insurance coverage for life, health, disability, long-term care, property, and liability. Finally, the financial ratios that do not meet recommended levels should be listed.

When identifying external environmental opportunities, the planner should consider monetary trends, favorable interest rates and inflation levels, technological breakthroughs, governmental controls, favorable changes in income tax rules, social attitudes toward businesses, and the emergence of new industries. The planner should also list favorable trends and forecasts that may positively impact the client's financial plan.

When identifying external environmental threats, the planner should consider unfavorable interest rates and inflation forecasts, technological breakthroughs, governmental controls, adverse changes in income tax rules, public distrust of businesses, and emergence of new industries. The planner also should list unfavorable trends and forecasts that may negatively impact the client's financial plan.

Using the Nelsons as an example, the following SWOT may be developed:

Strengths	■ David's job in a stable industry that provides the family with sufficient income ■ Net worth is reasonable for the Nelsons' ages ■ Investment assets-to-income ratio exceeds the target ratio for the Nelsons' ages
Weaknesses	■ Insufficient annual savings to drive goals ■ Inadequate life and disability insurance ■ Inappropriate investment risk ■ Too much debt ■ Unrealistic goals for current savings and investments ■ Deficient health insurance policy ■ No estate planning ■ Poor housing-cost-to-income ratio
Opportunities	■ Mortgage rates favorable for refinancing ■ High expected return on investments in stocks ■ Low expected inflation rate ■ Low current interest rates ■ Leading economic index signaling expansion
Threats	■ Current cost of college (room and board, tuition) is $15,000 per year per child ■ Slow economy and high unemployment; investments may not provide expected returns

STEP 4: DEVELOPING THE FINANCIAL PLANNING RECOMMENDATION(S)

Several financial, environmental, and internal client aspects must be considered and analyzed before feasible strategies can be formulated for the client and a financial plan developed. This is illustrated in Exhibit 5.6 below. Note that input from other advisors—an estate planning attorney, accountant or CPA, for example—is necessary in most cases.

EXHIBIT 5.6 Strategy Formulation

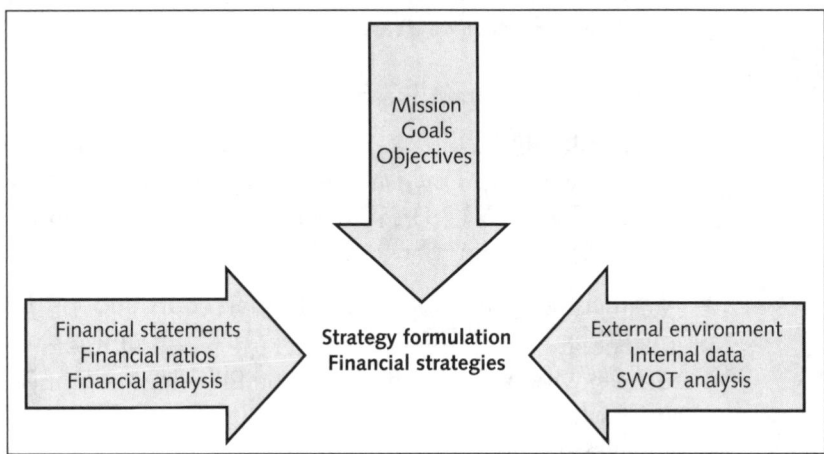

When developing the financial plan, the client's financial situation must be analyzed using financial data collection techniques (Chapter 4). The external environment and its effect on the client also must be considered (Chapter 2). In addition, the client's internal data and life cycle positioning must be understood (Chapter 3). Note that, throughout this process, the client's mission, goals, and objectives must remain central to the development of strategies.

When formulating feasible strategies, the planner should begin by developing an abbreviated income statement to identify the client's current cash flow situation. Then, the planner should identify the costs associated with implementing the need objectives and add the required cash outflows necessary to meet the need requirements to the existing cash flow. This will provide an estimate of the cash flow required to implement a plan that will accomplish the need objectives. Do not be concerned that the addition of these costs may cause the net cash flow to be negative. If a negative net cash flow exists, it may help bring the client into financial reality.

Using the Nelsons as an example and the initial income statement information gathered in Chapter 4, we can estimate the costs for implementing the need objectives.

EXHIBIT 5.7 Abbreviated Statement of Cash Flows

Income	$71,050
Savings	(5,853)
Ordinary living expenses	(21,114)
Other payments	(25,954)
Insurance payments	(2,611)
Tuition and education	(1,000)
Total taxes	(14,675)
Net cash flow (deficit)	$ (157)

The estimated costs for implementing the need objectives for the Nelsons are listed next.

Acquire appropriate amount of insurance

- Life—Add 20-year level term of $500,000, for an estimated cost of $500.

- Disability—Modify coverage to include disability by sickness, at an estimated cost of $1,400.

- Health—Add major medical with $10,000 deductible because of lifetime limit, at an estimated cost of $1,000.

Retire and maintain lifestyle

- David should save 10% of his salary due to his age. Because his company matches 3%, David should save at least 7% in his Section 401(k) plan. David is currently saving 5.43% ($3,803/$70,000). Therefore, he intends to increase his Section 401(k) plan savings by $1,099 (1.57%).

- By increasing his Section 401(k) plan contributions, David will reduce his tax payments by $165 ($1,099 @ 15% = $164.85 rounded to nearest dollar). Therefore, the change in cash flow is an increased outflow of $934 ($1,099 – $165).

Reduce debt

- The Nelsons should increase their payments toward their credit card debt; however, no estimated amounts will be identified at this time. This objective will be addressed when selecting a strategy with the client.

Prepare wills

■ David and Dana should each create a will. The estimated cost of having a will drawn up is $500 each, for a total of $1,000.

The Nelsons currently have a cash flow deficit of $157; however, the implementation of all need objectives would increase the deficit by $4,834 [$2,900 for insurance, $934 for Section 401(k) plan contributions, $1,000 for wills] for a total deficit of $4,991 ($4,834 + $157).

EXHIBIT 5.8 Net Cash Flows After Implementation of Need Objectives

Net cash flow	$ (157)
Life insurance	(500)
Disability insurance	(1,400)
Health insurance	(1,000)
Additional Section 401(k) plan contributions	(1,099)
Reduction of tax resulting from Section 401(k) plan contributions	165
Drafting of wills	(1,000)
Net cash flow after implementation of need objectives	$ (4,991)

Often, as in the case of the Nelsons, the analysis of the abbreviated income statement and the addition of costs associated with need objectives indicate a cash shortage. Therefore, either more cash inflow, less cash outflow, or a combination of the two is required. Common sources of available cash flows to increase inflows or reduce outflows include:

■ cutting discretionary expenses such as entertainment, vacations, utilities, and charitable contributions;

■ refinancing mortgages to reduce payment or decrease the debt term;

■ raising insurance deductibles to reduce premiums;

■ making use of tax-advantaged savings; and

■ obtaining additional income from employment.

After determining the cash flow situation, including the implementation of need objectives, the next step is to develop strategies that (1) create a positive net cash flow; (2) at the same time, resolve weaknesses identified in the SWOT analysis; and (3) accomplish, at a minimum, the need objectives. Therefore, the planner should consider each of the common methods to increase cash inflow or reduce cash outflow, the opportunities identified in the SWOT analysis, and each of the objectives previously identified by the client and the planner.

While developing alternative strategies, the planner must determine how each strategy might affect cash flow and the client's objectives. Remember, all need objectives should be resolved first, and then the want objectives should be considered. These alternative strategies will be presented to the client and, with the assistance of the planner, the client will ultimately choose which strategy to implement.

Revisiting the SWOT analysis and taking advantage of the available external opportunities indicate that the Nelsons should refinance their home. Refinancing their home mortgage at 5% will reduce their annual mortgage payment by $9,206.04, or ($1,829.48 − $1,062.31) × 12. [Assume a 30-year mortgage at 5%: $n = 360$, $i = 0.416667$ (5 ÷ 12),

PV = 197,888 (includes the balance of closing costs not paid at closing), and PMT = 1.062.31.] During analysis of the financial statements and tax returns, it was discovered that the Nelsons' income taxes are currently overwithheld annually by $5,744. This type of discovery is common, and an adjustment to increase receivables will be made on a future balance sheet. The combination of refinancing the home and properly adjusting their income tax withholdings will increase the Nelsons' cash flow by $14,950.04.

If we now compare the total cash flow deficit of $4,991 to the newly found cash inflows of $14,950.04, we find that the Nelsons now have a positive net cash flow of $9,959.04. Some of this positive cash flow should be used to reduce credit card debt. The remainder of the cash flow may be used to achieve some of the want objectives, to create an emergency fund, or increase savings and investments. The expense for the wills is not a recurring expense and will add $1,000 to cash flow in future years.

Recall that the two want objectives most important to the Nelsons (each with a 5 ranking) were to minimize payment of income taxes and to retire at age 62. The next most important objective, with a 4 ranking, was to purchase a home in Key West, Florida.

The objective of minimizing the payment of income taxes was resolved while focusing on the need objectives. For David to retire at age 62, he will need the exceptional investment returns (greater than the 8.5% rate he is currently earning) on his retirement investments. Purchasing a $200,000 home in Key West will require annual savings of $6,684 for five years to create a 20% down payment, then monthly mortgage payments of $1,174.02 ($14,088 annually). (See Supplement at the end of this chapter for detailed calculations.)

The Nelsons have already taken advantage of refinancing and tax savings, so they must now consider cutting discretionary expenses, raising deductibles on insurance, or obtaining additional income. Raising deductibles is usually the next option considered because this strategy has little impact on daily life or the overall financial plan. Clients seem to be more resistant to cutting discretionary expenses or obtaining additional income because those options can have a significant impact on the clients' daily lives.

STEP 5: PRESENTING THE FINANCIAL PLANNING RECOMMENDATION(S)

When presenting a recommendation, the practitioner must make a reasonable effort to assist the client in understanding the client's current situation, the recommendation itself, and its impact on the ability to meet the client's goals, needs, and priorities. In doing so, the practitioner must avoid presenting the practitioner's opinion as fact.

The practitioner must communicate the factors critical to the client's understanding of the recommendations. These factors may include, but are not limited to, the following:

- Personal and economic assumptions

- Interdependence of recommendations

- Material advantages and disadvantages

- Risks

- Time sensitivity

The practitioner should indicate that while the recommendations may meet the client's goals, needs, and priorities, changes in personal and economic conditions could alter the projected progression of the plan. Changes include, but are not limited to, updates to monetary or fiscal policy, family status, career, investment performance, and/or health.

If there are conflicts of interest that have not been previously disclosed, these issues and their impact on the recommendations should be addressed at this time.

Presenting recommendations provides the practitioner an opportunity to further assess whether the potential options meet client expectations, whether the client is willing to act on the recommendations, and whether modifications are necessary.

Ideally, recommendations are written and prepared in a clear, understandable manner. Thorough and thoughtfully crafted recommendations can prepare the adviser to systematically walk the client through the decision-making process.

Abstract thinking

The third phase of a client's thinking process in establishing financial direction, in which a client becomes aware of the consequences of financial actions and understands how day-to-day savings and consumption decisions impact a financial plan

The selection of strategy recommendations is made simpler when analyzed in a quantitative manner. It also helps the client move on to the **abstract-thinking** level. The Strategy Selection Worksheet, shown in Exhibit 5.9, can assist in this analysis. During the evaluation of each alternative, the planner should discuss with the client actions that must be taken; what must occur to implement the strategy; and how the strategy might change the client's current consumption and savings behavior, existing savings rate, time horizon, and asset allocation.

While considering the previously mentioned issues, the client should answer the following questions with the planner's assistance:

- How easy can I implement this strategy?

- How committed am I to implementing this strategy, considering the required action and sacrifices?

The client should respond to each of these questions using a weighting scale of 1 to 5. For the first question, a 5 would indicate the strategy is *very easy* to implement. For the second, a 5 would indicate the client is *very committed* to implementing the strategy. The answer weightings of each question are multiplied to result in a ranking for that strategy. The strategies with the highest rankings are the ones most likely to be successful.

The ranking of the *want* objectives include one additional measure. The weight of the objective identified on the "Client/Planner Worksheet for Establishing Financial Direction" should be considered when obtaining the ranking for that strategy. Again, the strategies with the highest rankings are most likely to be successful and therefore should be seriously considered. Exhibit 5.9 indicates how the Nelsons may have completed the Strategy Selection Worksheet.

EXHIBIT 5.9 Strategy Selection Worksheet

Strategy Selection Worksheet

Client Name <u>Dana and David Nelson</u>   **Date** <u>February 16, 2021</u>

a) List strategy options.
b) For each strategy option, indicate the objective(s) that is resolved.
c) Discuss, with the client, the impact of implementing the objective.
d) For each strategy option, the client should answer the following questions by ranking the answers 1 to 5.
   - ✓ How easy will it be to implement this strategy? (A 5 ranking indicates very easy to implement.)
   - ✓ How committed am I to implementing this strategy? (A 5 ranking indicates very committed.)
e) For "want" objectives, consider the original importance ranking that was identified when completing the **Client/Planner Worksheet**.

Strategy (Discuss how each strategy impacts relevant objectives)	Benefits of Implementing Strategy	Behavior Change Required	Ease of Implementation	Commitment Level	Ranking
Refinance Home	Increases annual cash flow by $9,206	None	5	5	25
Adjust tax withholdings	Increases annual cash flow by $5,744	None	5	5	25
Increase contributions to Section 401(k) plan	Takes advantage of tax-free savings	None, since other strategies will increase current cash flow	5	5	25
Raise Insurance Deductibles	Increases cash flow by $200	Acceptance of additional risk	5	3	15
Cut discretionary expenses	Increases annual cash flow by maximum of $2,414	Do not use paid babysitters, eliminate entertainment expenses, etc.	1	2	2
Dana acquires part-time job	Increases annual cash flow	Put Gabby in daycare	2	1	2
David acquires a second job	Increases annual cash flow	Spend less time with family	2	1	2

After completing the Strategy Selection Worksheet, the Nelsons have decided to refinance their home, adjust their tax withholdings, and increase David's contributions to the Section 401(k) plan. This increase in cash flow will allow them to meet all of their need objectives. They have also decided to use the surplus cash flow to reduce their credit card debt and to begin making deposits into an emergency fund. The Nelsons now realize that purchasing a vacation home in Key West is not reasonable at this time and have decided to revisit this objective in five years. David also realizes that retiring at age 62 may not be possible unless the investment objectives for retirement are achieved; however, he has made a commitment to increase his Section 401(k) plan contributions each time he gets a raise until he reaches the maximum allowable amount.

David and Dana do not want to raise their insurance deductibles because they enjoy the peace of mind of not having a considerable cash outlay in the event of an insurance claim. They do not want to acquire additional employment because spending time with family is very important to both of them.

Communicating the Recommendations

When the planner communicates recommendations to clients, it is important to engage them through meaningful interpersonal (one-on-one) communication. As recommendations are made, a planner becomes both an advisor—actually making the recommendations, and a counselor—offering professional guidance during the client's decision-making process. Active listening and emotional intelligence, both discussed in Chapter 1, are also critical. Planners should use open-ended questions to clarify clients' understanding of the plan recommendations. Refer to "Chapter 3: Communication and Internal Environmental Analysis" for more information regarding open-ended questions and other key communication techniques.

STEP 6: IMPLEMENTING THE FINANCIAL PLANNING RECOMMENDATION(S)

The financial planner is responsible for implementing the client's financial planning recommendation(s) *unless* specifically excluded from the Scope of Engagement. The client is responsible for accepting or rejecting recommendations. In the event that a planner does not have implementation responsibilities, the client and planner collaborate to determine whether implementation responsibilities are retained by the planner and/or delegated to the client or a team of specialists.

The practitioner's responsibilities may include, but are not limited to, the following:

- Identifying activities necessary for implementation

- Determining division of activities between the practitioner and the client

- Referring to other professionals

- Coordinating with other professionals

- Sharing of information as authorized

- Selecting and securing products and/or services

If there are conflicts of interest, sources of compensation, or material relationships with other professionals or advisers that have not been previously disclosed, such conflicts, sources, or relationships must be disclosed at this time.

When referring the client to other professionals or advisers, the financial planning practitioner must indicate the basis on which the practitioner believes the other professional or adviser may be qualified. If the practitioner is engaged by the client to provide only implementation activities, the scope of the engagement must be mutually defined in accordance with Step 1 of the Practice Standards. This scope may include matters such as the extent to which the practitioner will rely on information, analysis, or recommendations provided by others.

The financial planning practitioner must investigate products or services that reasonably address the client's needs. The products or services selected to implement the recommendation(s) must be suitable to the client's financial situation and consistent with the client's goals, needs, and priorities.

At all times, a planner must use professional judgment in selecting the products and services that are in the client's best interest. Professional judgment incorporates both qualitative and quantitative information.

Products and services selected by the practitioner may differ from those of other practitioners or advisers. More than one product or service may exist that can reasonably meet the client's goals, needs, and priorities.

The practitioner must make all disclosures required by applicable regulations.

Above all, the planner's role in coordinating the activities of the client and the other advisers is critical, for in the absence of implementation, the plan has minimal value.

STEP 7: MONITORING PROGRESS AND UPDATING

The purpose of Step 7 of the financial planning process is to clarify the role of the practitioner in the monitoring and updating process. By specifying this responsibility, the client's expectations are more likely to be in alignment with the level of oversight and updating that the practitioner intends to provide.

When engaged in monitoring and updating, the practitioner must make a reasonable effort to define and communicate the specific items that will be subject to oversight. By defining the items to be monitored, the frequency of monitoring, and the communication method(s), the client is provided reassurance and is able to appropriately set expectations.

The monitoring process may reveal the need to reinitiate steps of the financial planning process. Consequently, the current scope of the engagement may need to be modified.

Earlier in the financial planning process, the planner established a client file and a system for periodic review and revision. The scope of engagement defined the planner's role in monitoring. Due to liability concerns, many companies require that the planning engagement be terminated within a certain period, such as six months or one year, and that a new engagement must be created if the relationship continues past that point. If the planner is managing investments or products, the expectation is that the planner will monitor the performance of investments, products, and the general economic environment.

At regularly scheduled reviews with the client, the planner evaluates the progress toward the client's goals and whether shifts to the prior strategies and recommendations need to be made. In addition to economic or investment-related changes, the client's personal objectives, health status, income, or other circumstances may have changed. If this is the case, the financial planner returns to the early steps of the process, reevaluates goals, and gathers additional data to make recommendations that meet the client's new requirements.

When changes in the economy, tax laws, or other issues arise that are likely to affect the client's financial situation, the planner informs the client that the implemented financial planning recommendations are being monitored for potential updates. Step 7 creates a cyclical process, allowing the updates that arise from monitoring to be smoothly integrated into the plan.

WHERE ON THE WEB

Association for Financial Counseling and Planning Education **www.afcpe.org**

Bloomberg **www.bloomberg.com**

Bureau of Economic Analysis (U.S. Department of Commerce) **www.bea.gov**

Bureau of Labor Statistics (U.S. Department of Labor) **www.bls.gov**

CPI Homepage (U.S.) **www.bls.gov/cpi**

Economy at a Glance (U.S.) **stats.bls.gov/eag/eag.us.htm**

Forbes Magazine **www.forbes.com**

National Association of Personal Financial Advisors **www.napfa.org**

Service Corps of Retired Executives **www.score.org**

U.S. Small Business Administration **www.sba.gov**

DISCUSSION QUESTIONS

1. What are the seven steps of the financial planning process?

2. What is the definition of a financial mission?

3. What are the main activities that take place during Step 2 of the financial planning process: Identifying and selecting goals?

4. What are the most common financial goals developed during the planning process?

5. How do financial goals and financial objectives differ?

6. Why must a financial planner keep abreast of the external environment?

7. How does client subjectivity affect the establishment of financial objectives?

8. What is the difference between *need* and *want* objectives?

9. What questions can be asked of financial objectives to determine if the objective is a *need* or a *want*?

10. What does the acronym SWOT stand for?

11. During Step 3 of the financial planning process—Analyzing the client's current course of action and potential alternative course(s) of action—how can a SWOT analysis be useful to a financial planner?

12. What must be considered when formulating planning alternatives?

13. What are common methods to increase cash inflow or reduce cash outflow?

14. What should be considered when selecting strategies to implement?

15. How can the planner improve the probability of successful implementation of strategies?

16. How often should the recommendations within a financial plan be monitored?

EXERCISES

1. Assume Nicholas and Ashley contacted you, a financial planner, to assist them in saving for a car, their children's education, and a boat. Which thinking phase are they probably demonstrating?

2. What would you do if a client came to you insisting that his financial mission was to buy a 1965 Mustang?

3. If you were working with a client to distinguish between a want and a need objective and the client wanted to categorize buying a vacation home as a need, what would you do?

4. What would you say or do to help clients in understanding the difference between a goal and an objective?

PROBLEMS

1. Assume your clients, Alex and Megan, have multiple objectives requiring monthly cash flows of $400, $250, $150, $750, and $325, respectively. Also assume that their current net cash flow per month is $380.
   A.   What technique would you use to bring Alex and Megan into economic reality?
   B.   How would you distinguish between *need* and *want* objectives?
   C.   Where might you look for additional available cash flows to meet their objectives?

2. Assume Ben and Abby have hired you as their financial planner. Upon brief investigation, you collect the following information. The couple has been married for five years and have no children. They take expensive vacations several times a year. Both have good jobs and both save the maximum allowed in their Section 401(k) plans. The mortgage on their house is at a 6% rate. The current mortgage rate is 3.75%. Their credit card balance has been approximately $1,500 for some time, and they make minimum payments each month. The couple has a monthly net cash flow deficit of $98. What would be your recommendations to increase their monthly net cash flow?

CHAPTER 5 SUPPLEMENT

Calculations for Retirement Needs and Key West Home for the Nelsons

Retirement Needs Analysis Using Capital Needs Analysis and the Annuity Method

Step 1 Determine gross dollar needs.

We assume the Nelsons wish to maintain their current lifestyle at retirement. At retirement, the Nelsons will have eliminated Social Security taxes (FICA), Section 401(k) plan contributions, child care expenses, and disability insurance premiums. We also assume that the recommendations were implemented by the Nelsons.

Current salary	$70,000
FICA	− 5,355 (calculated at the 7.65% FICA rate)
Section 401(k) plan contributions	− 4,900
Child care expenses	− 600
Disability insurance premiums	− 2,161
	$56,984 yearly retirement need in today's dollars

Step 2 Determine net dollar needs.

We estimate David's Social Security benefits at age 67 to be $24,756 per year in today's dollars. Because David's ideal would be to retire at age 62, we estimate the Social Security benefit at that age to be $17,220 in today's dollars.

Gross retirement needs	$56,984
Social Security benefits	−17,220
	$39,764 net retirement need per year

Step 3 Calculate inflated preretirement dollar needs.

n	=	25 (62 − 37)
i	=	2.6 (inflation estimate)
PV	=	−$39,764
PMT	=	$0
FV	=	$75,539.50 (first-year need for retirement)

Step 4 Calculate capital need at retirement.

n	=	30 (92 − 62) Expect to live to age 92
i	=	5.75049 {[(1.85 ÷ 1.026) − 1] × 100} (return on investments of 8.5%)
FV	=	$0
PMT	=	−$75,539.50
PV_{AD}	=	$1,129,573.05 (total capital needed at retirement)

Step 5 Calculate yearly deposits to savings.

n	=	25 (62 − 37)
i	=	8.5 (Estimated return on investment)
FV	=	$1,129,573.05
PV	=	−$62,669 [Section 401(k) plan + stocks at end of 2018]
PMT	=	$8,235.28 needs to be saved each year to achieve goal
Required savings		$6,336.40
Current savings		−7,000.00 (includes employer contribution)
		$1,235.28 additional savings required

Key West house purchase

n	=	5
i	=	9 (estimated return on investment)
PV	=	$0
FV	=	$40,000 (20% × $200,000)
PMT	=	$6,683.70 required savings

Key West mortgage payment

n	=	360 (30 × 12)
i	=	0.6667 (8 ÷ 12) (assumes 8% interest on 30-year mortgage in 5 years)
PV	=	−$160,000 ($200,000 − $40,000 down payment)
FV	=	$0
PMT	=	$1,174.02 monthly payment

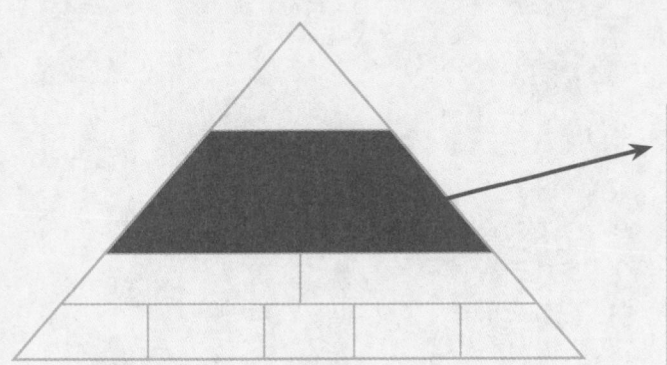

- The power of compound interest
- Basic tools for time value of money
- Future value of an ordinary annuity
- Future value of an annuity due
- Present value of a dollar
- Present value of an ordinary annuity
- Present value of an annuity due
- Financial aid programs for education
- Tax advantages related to education

- Uneven cash flows
- Internal rate of return and net present value
- Yield to maturity
- Solving for terms or yield
- Serial payments

- Discount rate selection
- Rule of 72
- Education funding
- Investments for education

2

Basic Financial Planning Tools

CHAPTERS

6 Time Value of Money

7 Education Funding

▸ **Risks**	▸ **Goals**		▸ **Data Collection**	▸ **Data Analysis**
■ Misunderstanding the impact of inflation ■ Failure to understand compounding	■ Understanding the importance of time value of money to financial planning ■ Adequate resources for education of children		■ Financial aid programs ■ Financial aid information of client ■ Current cost of education ■ Inflation rate ■ Expected earnings rate ■ Tax-advantaged education programs	■ Projected cost of education ■ Education funding choices ■ Education funding analysis ■ Investment selections

Time Value of Money

LEARNING OBJECTIVES

After learning the material in this chapter, you will be able to do the following:

■ Define the time value of money (TVM) concept and explain its importance to financial planning

■ Define the terms present value and future value and illustrate their roles in the calculation of compound interest

■ Calculate the future value and the present value of a dollar

■ List and explain the tools used in TVM analysis

■ Calculate the present and future values of an ordinary annuity and an annuity due

■ Explain the differences between an ordinary annuity and an annuity due

■ Reconcile the difference between an ordinary annuity and an annuity due

■ Prepare an amortization table for debt repayment

■ Explain and apply the Rule of 72

■ Understand how unequal cash flows and serial payments affect the future value of an investment

■ Compare and contrast the concepts of net present value (NPV) and internal rate of return (IRR)

■ Define yield to maturity and explain how it is used to determine a bond's earned interest

■ Explain how solving for term given the other variables is useful in debt management

■ Understand how inflation affects the real rate of return of an investment

■ Define perpetuities and explain how they affect financial planning

UNDERSTANDING TIME VALUE OF MONEY

Time value of money (TVM) is one of the most useful and important concepts in finance and personal financial planning. Essentially, the concept of TVM is money received today is worth more than the same amount of money received sometime in the future. A dollar received today is worth more than a dollar received one year from today because the dollar received today can be invested and will be worth more in one year. Alternatively, a dollar to be received a year from now is worth less than a dollar today. Comparisons of funds received and paid at the same time are necessary to solve many financial planning problems and to make sound financial decisions. Thus, TVM calculations are fundamental to financial planning. The TVM calculation is a tool that allows financial planners to properly plan a client's goals and objectives.

The two values used in TVM analysis are future value and present value. **Future value** is the future dollar amount to which a sum certain today will increase when compounded at a defined interest rate over a period of time. **Present value** is the current dollar value of a future sum when discounted at a defined interest rate over a period of time. Future value is calculated using a process called compounding. Present value is calculated using a process called discounting. Suppose, for example, a dollar was invested in a bank savings account paying 5% annual interest. At the end of the year, the dollar would have grown to $1.05. The initial dollar would be referred to as the present value. The 5% represents the interest rate. The term is for one year. Therefore, the $1.05 equals the future value. The interest earned (in this case, $.05) is compensation for delaying consumption for one year. We will discuss compounding and discounting later in the chapter.

There are numerous important questions in financial planning that can be answered using TVM concepts:

■ If I have a certain dollar amount today, how much will it be worth at some time in the future if it is invested at a certain rate of interest?

■ If I invested a certain dollar amount at regular intervals and at a constant interest rate, how much would I accumulate at some future date?

■ If I wanted to save for the college education of my children, how much would I need to save starting today at regular intervals to pay for that education?

Future value
The future dollar amount to which a sum certain today will increase compounded at a defined interest rate over a period of time

Present value
The current dollar value of a future sum discounted at a defined interest rate over a period of time

- If I wanted to pay off my home mortgage early, what amount would I need to add to each monthly payment?

- What is the present value of my expected Social Security retirement benefits?

- How much investment capital will I need to retire at a particular age in order to maintain my desired retirement lifestyle?

All of these questions and many other financial planning questions can be answered by applying TVM concepts.

FUTURE VALUE AND THE POWER OF COMPOUND INTEREST

Compound interest
Interest earned on interest

Understanding **compound interest** is essential to understanding the future value of money. Compound interest is interest earned on interest. Compounding occurs when interest earned is reinvested in the same investment and interest is then earned on both the principal and the reinvested interest. Mathematically, the growth is exponential (a power function as opposed to a linear function).

If the entire $1.05 in the previous example remained in the investment for a second year earning 5% interest annually, the future value at the end of the second year would be $1.1025:

$$FV = PV (1 + i)$$

$$FV = \$1.05 (1 + 0.05)$$

$$FV = \$1.1025$$

The interest earned in the second year, $.0525, reflect the interest on the original dollar ($.05) and the interest on the $.05 earned in the first year ($.0025).

The mathematical expression for compounding interest at a constant rate is:

$FV = PV (1 + i)^n$, where n represents the number of periods (term) the investment is to be held.

Notice that i must be expressed in the same terms as n (e.g., yearly, semiannually, quarterly, or monthly). If i is expressed as an annual interest or earnings rate, n must also be expressed annually.

To illustrate the compounding of interest, assume $2,000 is invested by a 25-year-old in an individual retirement account (IRA) and left for 5 years earning 12% interest compounded annually. What would be the future value of the investment at the end of 5 years when our investor is age 30?

$$FV = PV (1 + i)^n$$

$$FV = (\$2,000) (1.12)^5$$

$$FV = (\$2,000) (1.7623) \text{ [The exact mathematical factor obtained using a calculator.]}$$

$$FV = \$3,524.68$$

Future value calculations of this type can be performed in a variety of ways using the tools available for TVM calculations. Generally, the illustrated examples in this chapter have been calculated using an HP 10bII+ calculator. (Keystrokes are the same for each calculator.) Where multiple steps were required to solve a problem, we did not round the intermediate steps. If you are attempting to calculate the problems in the chapter and are using table factors or a different calculator, or if you round intermediate steps, you may receive an answer slightly different from that calculated in the chapter. Where we used table factors, you will notice some rounding error. Where we used mathematical exponentials, you will notice differences from calculator or table results. For example, if the problem just listed had been calculated with rounded interest, the answer would be $3,524.60 (rounding error of $.08).

BASIC TOOLS FOR TIME VALUE OF MONEY (TVM) ANALYSIS

Cash flow timeline
TVM analysis tool that graphically depicts cash inflows (cash received) and cash outflows (cash deposited or invested) over a certain period (the term)

In addition to mathematical equations, there are a number of other tools a financial planner can use to understand TVM problems, help the client answer TVM questions, and present quantitative information to clients. Among these tools are **cash flow time-lines**, TVM tables, financial calculators, cash flow computer software, and accumulation schedules. We will illustrate the various tools of TVM by calculating the future value for the previous example ($2,000 invested for 5 years earning 12% interest compounded annually).

Timelines

Timelines are a useful tool to visualize both inflows and outflows. Exhibit 6.1 shows a timeline based on the previous example. Notice the $2,000 invested in time period 0 is listed with a parenthesis, indicating it is an outflow from the investor. Respectively, the future value of $3,524.68 is presented as an inflow to the investor at time period 5.

EXHIBIT 6.1   Cash Flow Timeline

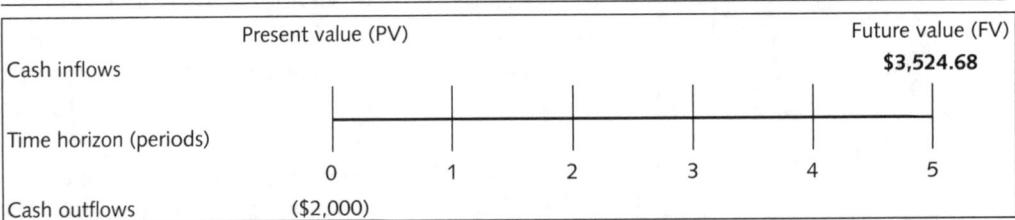

The more complex the TVM problem, the more useful a timeline can be in illustrating the positions of the cash flows.

TVM Tables

TVM tables represent the various values for combinations of i and n. These tables can be found in the Appendix (B-1 through B-6). The Future Value of a Dollar table is necessary to calculate the answer to our problem. The amounts given in the table represent the value of a dollar deposited today (to be received in the future) and compounded at a defined rate (i) for a defined period (n). The interest factor in Table 1 for 12% and 5 years is 1.7623 (rounded). This number is the equivalent of $(1.12)^5$, or $(1.12)(1.12)(1.12)(1.12)(1.12) = 1.7623$. Thus, when using TVM tables, the future value formula is also represented as FV = PV × (Exhibit 6.2 factor at 12% for 5 years). In our example, $2,000 × 1.7623 = $3,524.60.

EXHIBIT 6.2   Future Value Factor of a Dollar (Excerpt from Appendix B-2)

Period	2%	4%	6%	8%	10%	12%
1	1.0200	1.0400	1.0600	1.0800	1.1000	1.1200
2	1.0404	1.0816	1.1236	1.1664	1.2100	1.2544
3	1.0612	1.1249	1.1910	1.2597	1.3310	1.4049
4	1.0824	1.1699	1.2625	1.3605	1.4641	1.5735
5	1.1041	1.2167	1.3382	1.4693	1.6105	**1.7623**

Notice the tables have been rounded off to four decimals for presentation convenience. The rounding in the tables will cause a slight error in calculation. The amount of the error in the example just listed is $.08: $3,524.60 (1.7623 × $2,000) versus $3,524.68 (1.762341683 × $2,000).

Financial Calculators

A wide variety of useful hand-held financial calculators may be used to accurately calculate the solution to TVM problems. Financial calculators are fairly inexpensive and more accurate and flexible than the TVM tables. Calculators are also useful when the financial planner is out of the office and unable to access computer-based TVM software.

The following are among the most widely used financial calculators:

■ Hewlett Packard HP 10bII and 10bII+

■ Hewlett Packard HP 12C

■ Hewlett Packard HP 17BII

■ Texas Instruments TI BA II Plus

■ Sharp EL-733A

Each of these has its own mathematical algorithm for solving TVM problems, and to master each calculator requires some practice. Regardless of which calculator you select, you should review your calculator's user manual and become familiar with the various keys. Familiarity with the following keys is essential:

■ [PV] = stores/calculates the present value

■ [FV] = stores/calculates the future value

■ [PMT] = stores/calculates the amount of each payment

■ [N] = stores/calculates the total number of payments or periods

■ [I/YR] = stores/calculates the interest or discount rate

In calculating the TVM problems throughout this chapter and this text, the HP 10bII+ is used.

Illustrated below are the HP 10bII+ keystrokes used to solve the previous future value problem.

Keystroke	Display
2000 [+/−] [PV]	−2,000.0000
5 [N]	5.0000
12 [I/YR]	12.0000
0 [PMT]	0.0000
[FV]	3,524.6834

Computer Software

Essentially, computer software uses the same or similar mathematical algorithms as the hand-held calculators. In fact, TVM software testers usually use a hand-held calculator to ensure the computer algorithm's accuracy. TVM software and application software using TVM concepts are widely available to aid both individuals and practitioners.

Accumulation Schedules

Knowing the future value of a deposit made today is useful for investment planning for expenditures. It is also useful to know both the amount of interest earned and the balance of an investment account on a yearly or periodic basis. To determine the investment interest accumulation on a periodic basis, prepare a basic accumulation schedule similar to Exhibit 6.3.

EXHIBIT 6.3   Accumulation Schedule

Year (Col 1)	Beginning Balance (Col 2)	Interest (Col 3)	Ending Balance (Col 2) + (Col 3) = (Col 4)
1	$2,000.00	$240.00	$2,240.00
2	$2,240.00	$268.80	$2,508.80
3	$2,508.80	$301.06	$2,809.86
4	$2,809.86	$337.18	$3,147.04
5	$3,147.04	$377.64	$3,524.68
Totals	**$2,000.00**	**$1,524.68**	**$3,524.68**

Column 1 is the year in question, Column 2 is the account balance at the beginning of each year, Column 3 is the interest earned during the year (Column 2 × 12%), and Column 4 is the balance at the year end for each year (Column 2 + Column 3). The Total row shows the original amount deposited, $2,000; interest earned over the 5 years, $1,524.68, and the final balance, $3,524.68. As we will demonstrate, this type of schedule can be expanded or modified to illustrate the extinguishment of debt and is useful for a variety of other illustrative purposes.

Although TVM tables and accumulation schedules are useful for learning, professional financial planners do not generally rely on them. Rather, they rely on hand-held financial calculators or computer software. The remaining calculations in this chapter will be illustrated using the HP 10bII+ financial calculator.

FUTURE VALUE OF AN ORDINARY ANNUITY (FV$_{OA}$)

Annuity
A series of deposits or payments of equal size deposited over a finite number of equal-interval periods

Ordinary annuity
Deposits or payments are made at the end of each period

Annuity due
Deposits or payments are made at the beginning of each period

Future value of an ordinary annuity
The future amount to which a series of deposits of equal size will equal when deposited over a finite number of equal-interval periods, based on a defined interest rate, when the deposits are made at the end of each period

Thus far we have calculated the future value of a single deposit made at the beginning of a period. Now consider, instead of a single deposit, that a series of deposits are made into an account. Instead of our previous example of the $2,000 deposited once in the IRA, our investor deposits $2,000 each year in the IRA for 5 years, earning an annual rate of return of 12%. The series of deposits of equal size is known as an **annuity** when deposited over a finite number of equal-interval periods. It will make a difference whether the deposits are made at the end of each period (known as an **ordinary annuity**) or deposited at the beginning of each period (known as an **annuity due**). The ordinary annuity is quite common in investments and debt repayment and is sometimes referred to as a payment made in arrears. An annuity due calculation is commonly used in education funding and for retirement planning.

To demonstrate the calculation of the **future value of an ordinary annuity**, assume David deposits $2,000 per year at year end for 5 years into an IRA earning 12% annually.

Your financial calculator has a feature (generally a BEG or END or a combination BEG/END key) that will allow you to switch between an ordinary annuity (use END) and an annuity due (use BEG). Calculate the future value of the ordinary annuity using the following keystrokes (using the HP 10bII+):

Keystroke	Display
5[N]	5.0000
12[I/YR]	12.0000
2000 [+/−] [PMT]	−2,000.0000
0[PV]	0.0000
[FV]	12,705.6947

FUTURE VALUE OF AN ANNUITY DUE (FV$_{AD}$)

Future value of an annuity due
The future value to which a series of deposits of equal size will amount when deposited over a definite number of equal-interval periods, based on a defined interest rate, and the deposits are made at the beginning of each period

The calculation for an annuity due is exactly the same as the ordinary annuity, except the first deposit or payment for the annuity due is made at the beginning of the period rather than at the end. This is quite common for education funding calculations where the institution demands tuition payments be made in advance rather than in arrears. Making payments at the beginning of the period creates one additional compounding period when compared to payments made at the end of the period. For this reason, the **future value of an annuity due** will always be greater by one period's interest than the same deposits made for an ordinary annuity of the same term and interest rate. Other common uses of the annuity due concept are for rents and retirement income, which are both commonly paid in advance.

We can solve the problem using the HP 10bII+. Notice that the calculator should be set to BEG mode (using the BEG key or the BEG/END key, depending on the calculator used) mode to indicate an annuity due calculation.

Keystroke	Display
[■][BEG/END]	0.0000 BEG
5[N]	5.0000
12[I/YR]	12.0000
2000 [+/−][PMT]	−2,000.0000
0[PV]	0.0000
[FV]	14,230.3781

The annuity due has an account balance at the end of year 5 of $14,230.38, although the ordinary annuity had an account balance of $12,705.69. The difference of $1,524.69 is equal to the total interest earned in the fifth year ($12,705.69 × .12 = $1,524.68).

PRESENT VALUE OF A DOLLAR (PV)

This calculation is used to determine the current value of a sum of money to be received in a future year based on a specific discount rate. For many financial planning decisions, such as education funding or retirement funding, it is important to determine the present value of a future amount rather than the future value of a present amount. In this section, we explain how to calculate the present value of a future investment amount. To illustrate, suppose an investor wanted to have $20,000 in 5 years and could earn an annual return of 8%. How much must be invested today to meet the goal of $20,000 in 5 years?

Keystroke	Display
20000 [FV]	20,000.0000
8 [I/YR]	8.0000
5[N]	5.0000
0[PMT]	0.0000
[PV]	−13,611.6639

PRESENT VALUE OF AN ORDINARY ANNUITY (PV$_{OA}$)

Present value of an ordinary annuity
The value today of a series of equal payments made at the end of each period for a finite number of periods discounted at a defined interest rate

An investor or a business commonly receives a series of equal payments for a finite period from debt repayment, from a life insurance settlement, from an annuity, or as a pension payment. The question usually asked is, "What is the present value of such a series of payments?" Remember the ordinary annuity assumed that each payment is made at the end of each period (arrears). For example, consider receiving $25,000 per year for the next 5 years with each payment made at year end. Also assume an interest (discount) rate of 8%. What is the present value in dollars of that income stream? The **present value of an ordinary annuity** is calculated as follows:

Keystroke	Display
5[N]	5.0000
8 [I/YR]	8.0000
25000[PMT]	25,000.0000
0[FV]	0.0000
[PV]	−99,817.7509

▌PRESENT VALUE OF AN ANNUITY DUE (PV$_{AD}$)

Present value of an annuity due
The value today of a series of equal payments made at the beginning of each period for a finite number of periods discounted at a defined interest rate

The difference between the **present value of an annuity due** and the present value of an ordinary annuity is the annuity due's payments are made at the beginning of each period rather than at the end, as for an ordinary annuity. This makes the present value of an annuity due always larger than the present value of an ordinary annuity with the same payments over the same time period. The annuity due calculation is quite common in financial planning and is most often used for education funding and for retirement capital needs analysis. Using the previous problem as an education funding problem where the parent is to pay $25,000 each year for 5 years with payments occurring at the beginning of each year and the interest (discount) rate is 8%, we can calculate the present value of the annuity due. (For simplicity, we have assumed an inflation rate of zero.)

Keystroke	Display
[■][BEG/END]	0.0000 BEG
5[N]	5.0000
8 [I/YR]	8.0000
25000[PMT]	25,000.0000
0[FV]	0.0000
[PV]	−107,803.1710

▌OTHER TVM CONCEPTS

Uneven cash flows
Investment returns or deposits that are neither single interval deposits nor equal payments

Net present value (NPV)
The difference between the initial cash outflow (investment) and the present value of discounted cash inflows (i.e., NPV = PV of CF − cost of investment)

Internal rate of return (IRR)
The discount rate that causes cash inflows to equal cash outflows, thus allowing comparison of rates of return on alternative investments

Now that we have a better understanding of the concepts and basic mathematics and mechanics of TVM, it is time to discuss some of the common TVM applications. Included in these applications are **uneven cash flows,** combining sum certains with annuities, **net present value (NPV), internal rate of return (IRR),** yield to maturity (YTM), solving for term, selecting the interest rate, serial payments, perpetuities, education funding, and capital needs analysis for retirement. In the next section of this chapter, we will present the basics of most of these TVM concepts. YTM will be covered more extensively in Chapter 12 Supplement A (Fixed-Income Securities). We will defer coverage of education funding until Chapter 7 (Education Funding) and capital needs analysis until Chapter 15 (Introduction to Retirement Planning).

Uneven Cash Flows

Investment returns or deposits are not always single interval deposits or equal payments. For example, assume an investor deposits $400, $500, $600, and $700 into an investment account at the end of each of four years, respectively. How much would the investment be worth if the interest rate was a constant 8% annually?

Using a financial calculator (HP 10bII+), we can easily calculate the problem by using the uneven cash flow keys. The first step in the calculation determines the present value of the uneven deposits. The second step calculates the future value. The keystrokes for the uneven cash flow problem are below:

Step 1

Keystroke	Display
0 [CFj]	0.0000
400 [+\−] [CFj]	−400.0000
500 [+\−] [CFj]	−500.0000
600 [+\−] [CFj]	−600.0000
700 [+\−] [CFj]	−700.0000
8[I/YR]	8.0000
[■][NPV]	1,789.8600

Step 2

Keystroke	Display	
[PV]	−1,789.8600	(This step inputs the NPV from Step 1 as the PV for Step 2.)
4[N]	4.0000	
8[I/YR]	8.0000	
0[PMT]	0.0000	
[FV]	2,435.0848	

Combining Sums Certain With Annuities

For some investments, such as bonds, the investment returns are received in the form of both an annuity and a sum certain. Assume an investor purchased a 3-year $1,000 corporate bond paying $30 interest twice a year (semiannually) and then paying $1,000 (the maturity value) back to the holder at the end of the 3-year period. If the holder expected an 8% annual return, what amount should be paid for the bond at the beginning of the 3-year period? Assume the interest is paid as an ordinary annuity (arrears). The solution can be easily calculated using the following keystrokes:

Keystroke	Display
6[N]	6.0000
4 [I/YR]	4.0000
30[PMT]	30.0000
1000[FV]	1,000.0000
[PV]	−947.5786

Net Present Value Analysis

Net present value analysis (NPV) is a commonly used TVM technique employed by businesses and investors to evaluate the cash flows associated with capital projects and capital expenditures. The concept is common to capital budgeting. NPV analysis helps determine whether one should select one capital investment over another capital investment. The result of the analysis is in terms of dollars. The method discounts the future cash flows at an appropriate discount rate and allows the present value of inflows to be compared to the present value of outflows. This technique is important to financial planners in helping clients decide which investment projects to consider undertaking.

The model itself is deterministic, that is, it assumes information is known about the future (e.g., cash flows). The NPV model assumes all reinvestments of cash flows received are made at the weighted average cost of the capital of the firm or the required rate of return of the investor.

NPV equals the difference between the initial cash outflow (investment) and the present value of discounted cash inflows. For example, if the present value of a series of cash flows is $200 and the initial outflow is $150, the NPV equals $50. Businesses generally look for investments with a positive NPV.

E X A M P L E   Assume you are a financial planner debating whether to purchase a copy machine. You currently pay $.12 per copy for reproducing materials and expect to make 3,000 copies per month. The copier you are considering costs $5,000 and is expected to last 5 years with a $1,000 salvage value. Your cost for reproducing on the new copier would be $.07 per copy. Assuming a 12% discount rate, what is the net present value of the copier?

To solve this problem, first convert the relevant data to monthly figures. If you purchase a copy machine, each copy would save you $.05 ($.12 − $.07 = $.05). If you made 3,000 copies per month, you would save $150 per month ($.05 × 3,000 = $150). Then calculate the present value of the cash flows discounted at 12% (1% monthly). The keystrokes for this calculation (using the HP 10bII+) are shown below:

Keystroke	Display	
5000 [+/−] [CFj]	−5,000.0000	Initial investment
150 [CFj]	150.0000	Monthly positive cash flow savings
59 [■] [Nj]	59.0000	59 months
1150 [CFj]	1,150.0000	Final monthly cash flow savings of $150 plus the salvage value of $1,000
1 [I/YR]	1.0000	Monthly interest
[■] [NPV]	2,293.7054	

The positive NPV indicates the purchase of the copy machine would be recommended. The purchase will essentially save $2,293.71, in today's dollars, over the life of the machine.

Internal Rate of Return (IRR)

The internal rate of return is the discount rate that equates the discounted cash inflows and outflows of a specific investment or project. IRR calculations allow the financial planner to compare rates of return on alternative investments of unequal size and investment amounts. The NPV model and the IRR model make different assumptions regarding the reinvestment rate of cash flows received during the period of investment. Recall that NPV assumes the reinvestment rate to be the weighted average cost of capital or the required return. The IRR calculation assumes the reinvestment rate equals the IRR. NPV is considered a superior model to IRR when comparing investment projects of unequal lives because assuming reinvestment at the required return is more reasonable than at the IRR.

The formula below describes the basic present value model used for discounting cash flows.

$$PV = \frac{CF_1}{(1 + k)^1} + \frac{CF_2}{(1 + k)^2} + \cdots + \frac{CF_n}{(1 + k)^n}$$

PV = the value of the security or asset today
CF_n = the cash flow for a particular period, n
k = the discount rate or IRR
n = the number of cash flows to be evaluated

The formula states that the PV of a series of cash flows is equal to each cash flow divided by 1 plus the discount rate raised to a power equal to the period in which the cash flow occurs.

The internal rate of return is the exact discount rate (labeled k in the formula) that makes the discounted future cash inflows equal to the initial cash outflow, or investment. One of the underlying assumptions in the equation is that the cash flows received during the investment period will be reinvested at the investment's internal rate of return.

E X A M P L E   Megan owns 1 share of Praha, Inc., stock. She purchased this share of stock 3 years ago for $50. The current market value of the stock is $40 per share. Since buying the stock, the following dividends have been paid:

Dividend year 1 (end)	$4.80 per share
Dividend year 2 (end)	$5.90 per share
Dividend year 3 (end)	$7.25 per share

What is the IRR that Megan has earned on her investment? Because the IRR is the rate of discount that equalizes the cash inflows and outflows, using a financial calculator is the easiest method. The financial calculator keystrokes (HP 10bII+) are shown below.

Keystroke	Display	
50[+\−] [CFj]	−50.0000	
4.8 [CFj]	4.8000	
5.9 [CFj]	5.9000	
47.25[CFj]	47.2500	($40 current market value + $7.25 dividend)
[■][IRR]	5.5695	

Yield to Maturity

Yield to maturity (YTM) is the calculation of the rate of return that will make the discounted cash flows of a bond equal to the current price of that bond. This calculation is the application of the IRR model to bond investments. YTM is generally calculated on the basis of semiannual coupon payments (even with zero-coupon bonds). Financial planners need to understand YTM to begin understanding bonds and other debt investments.

Three adjustments must be made to calculate YTM for a bond that makes semiannual coupon payments.

■ n—The number of periods is determined by multiplying the number of years by 2 so as to reflect two coupon payments per year. For example, the n for a 10-year bond would be 20 to reflect 20 coupon payments.

- PMT—The coupon rate is stated as a percentage of the face value ($1,000) of the bond. Therefore, a 10% coupon bond will pay a total of $100 each year ($50 twice per year). The adjustment is to divide the $100 by 2 to reflect the two payments of $50 during the year.

- YTM—The YTM that will be calculated will be a semiannual YTM rate. Therefore, multiply the calculated YTM by 2 to determine the annual YTM.

E X A M P L E   Julian is considering the purchase of a 5-year $1,000 bond selling for $1,162.22. What is the YTM for this bond if it has a 12% coupon, paid semiannually? The yield to maturity is 8% annually, or 4% per semiannual interest payment.

To calculate the yield to maturity using a financial calculator:

Keystroke	Display	
10[N]	10.0000	Term of the bond expressed for semiannual payments (5 × 2)
1162.22 [+\–][PV]	–1,162.2200	The current cost of the bond
60[PMT]	60.0000	The semiannual interest payment for a 12% annual coupon
1000 [FV]	1,000.0000	Maturity value of the bond
[I/YR]	4.0000	Yield to maturity (multiply by 2 = 8%)

Solving for Term Given the Other Variables

Solving for term n (or on the calculator N) determines the period necessary (in days, months, quarters, or years) to save or pay at a given rate to accomplish a stated goal. This type of analysis is particularly useful in debt management, such as determining the term to:

- pay off student loans;
- pay off a mortgage;
- save for college education; and
- save for a special purchase (e.g., car, home, or vacation).

E X A M P L E   Margaret bought a house using a mortgage loan of $240,000 issued for 15 years at 6.25% per year on May 1. Her first payment was June 1. Now, on January 1 of the following year, she has made 7 payments of $2,057.81 and has 173 payments remaining and a remaining mortgage balance of $234,256.20. Margaret wants to know how many more months she will have to pay if she increases her monthly payment by $500 to $2,557.81. Using a financial calculator (HP 10bII+), we calculate the term using the following keystrokes:

Keystroke	Display	
234256.20[PV]	234,256.2000	Current balance
0 [FV]	0.0000	Future value
2557.81 [+\–][PMT]	–2,557.8100	New payment
6.25 ÷ 12 = 0.5208[I/YR]	0.5208	Monthly interest rate
[N]	124.7745	Number of payments remaining

Margaret is thus able to reduce her remaining payments from 173 to 125 (rounded) by increasing her monthly payment by $500 to $2,557.81. Her last payment (payment 125) will be $1,982.12.

Selecting the Rate of Interest for Accumulating or Discounting

When utilizing TVM analysis, the planner must frequently decide which interest rate or earnings rate to use. The choices include the expected earnings for a particular investment, the client's **opportunity cost**, the risk-free rate, the Consumer Price Index (CPI), the specific inflation rate for particular services (education and medical), or the **real rate of return**, which accommodates both the nominal interest rate and a measure of inflation.

Opportunity cost

When faced with investment alternatives, it is the highest-valued alternative not chosen—it represents what is forgone by choosing another alternative; when discounting a future sum or series of payments back to present value, it is the composite rate of return on the client's assets with similar risk to the assets being examined

Real rate of return

The nominal rate of return adjusted for inflation

Generally, when projecting the future value of an investment, either a lump-sum investment or one made with annuity contributions, the appropriate compounding rate will be the expected rate of return for that particular investment. When discounting a future sum or series of payments back to present value, however, either the client's opportunity cost or the risk-free rate of return will be used. The client's opportunity cost is usually the composite rate of return on the client's assets with similar risk to the assets being examined. The risk-free rate is the Treasury rate for the selected period or term.

When calculating future retirement income needs, it is common to use the general Consumer Price Index (CPI) as the inflation rate, although in the case of college education, the recent and projected rate of inflation for college education should be used.

Financial planners should use an inflation-adjusted interest rate for calculating retirement capital needs or education funding because the costs in the future are generally increasing at one rate (the inflation rate) and the investments are growing at a different rate (the earnings rate). Thus, the way to make the increasing cash outflows equal is to treat them as real dollars of purchasing power and use an inflation-adjusted discount rate that takes into consideration the interest rate and inflation rate. The combination of the nominal earnings rate reduced mathematically by the inflation rate is known as the real rate of return.

The loss of purchasing power is one of the risks investors must overcome to achieve their financial goals. Real economic returns reflect the earnings from an investment above the inflation rate. However, simply subtracting the rate of inflation from the nominal interest rate will not yield the real economic rate of return. Real economic returns must be calculated by using the following formula:

$$\left(\frac{1 + R_n}{1 + I} - 1\right) \times 100$$

R_n = nominal rate of return
I = inflation rate

Assume $1,000 is invested at the beginning of the year and earns 10%, resulting in a balance at the end of the year of $1,100. Also assume that over the same period inflation has been 4%. Thus, $1,040 at the end of the year is equal to the initial investment of $1,000 at the beginning of the year, in terms of real dollars or purchasing power. The real return is equal to the difference between the earnings from interest ($100) and the increase as a result of inflation ($40), which is $60, divided by the initial investment adjusted for inflation ($1,040). This result equals a real rate of return of 5.77%.

■ Conceptually, the return of 5.77% makes sense in that the absolute return was 10% and the inflation rate was 4%, with the difference being 6%:

$$\left(\frac{(1 + 0.10)}{(1 + 0.04)} - 1\right) \times 100 = 5.7692$$

■ The nominal earnings from interest for this investment are $100. The real earnings are $57.69 in today's dollars ($60.00 ÷ 1.04 = $57.69).

Serial Payments

Serial payment

A payment that increases at a constant rate (usually, the rate of inflation) on an annual basis

A **serial payment** is a payment that increases at a constant rate (usually inflation) on an annual basis. There are situations when investors are more comfortable increasing payments or deposits on an annual basis because the investor is expecting increases in income with which to make those increasing payments. Examples include investment deposits, life insurance premiums, education needs, retirement needs, or any lump-sum future expenditure.

Serial payments differ from fixed annuity payments (both ordinary annuities and annuities due) because the payments are increasing at a constant rate. The result is the initial serial payment will be less than a fixed annuity payment but the last payment will be greater than the fixed annuity payment.

E X A M P L E   Alex wants to start his own business in 3 years, and he needs to accumulate $100,000 (in today's dollars) to reach his goal. Alex expects a 4% inflation rate and an 8% rate of return on his investments. What serial payment should Alex make at the end of each year to attain his goal?

The serial payment is calculated by adjusting the interest rate for inflation to determine the real economic rate of return (nominal rate 8%, adjusted for inflation, 4%). This adjustment is accomplished using the following formula:

$$\left(\frac{1 + R_n}{1 + I} - 1\right) \times 100$$

$$\left(\frac{1 + 0.08}{1 + 0.04} - 1\right) \times 100 = 3.8462$$

Therefore, the real rate of return used for the calculation is 3.8462. The serial payment calculation is as follows:

0 [PV]
100000 [FV]
3 [N]
[(1.08 ÷ 1.04) − 1] × 100 = 3.8462 [I/YR]
Solve for [PMT] −32,083.53
−32,083.53 [+/−] × 1.04 = 33,366.87 (payment at the end of year 1)
33,366.87 × 1.04 = 34,701.55 (payment made at end of year 2)
34,701.55 × 1.04 = 36,089.61 (payment made at end of year 3)

The exhibit below proves the increasing payments are correct.

EXHIBIT 6.4 Schedule of Investment

Year	Beginning Balance Needed	Deposit (Payments)	8% Interest Earned	Accumulation Ending Balance
1	$100,000.00	$33,366.87	$0.00	$33,366.87
2	$104,000.00	$34,701.55	$2,669.35	$70,737.77
3	$108,160.00	$36,089.61	$5,659.02	$112,486.40
End of Year 3	**$112,486.40**	**$104,158.03**	**$8,328.37**	**$112,486.40**

Note: Alex could have saved $34,649.58 per year. An annuity of this amount would have provided him with the same future value of $112,486.40. This payment is calculated as follows:

$$FV = \$112,486.40$$
$$n = 3$$
$$i = 8$$
$$PMT = \$34,649.58$$

Notice that the payment of $34,649.58 is greater than the first serial payment but less than the last one.

Perpetuities

A perpetuity is a payment cash flow stream that remains constant. An example of a common perpetuity is preferred stock, which generally pays a set dividend each year. To determine the value of this type of payment stream, simply divide the payment (PMT) by the discount rate (i):

$$PV = \frac{PMT}{i}$$

EXAMPLE   Gleason Corporation always pays a $4 preferred stock dividend, and the client's required rate of return is 10%. The value of the preferred stock equals $40 as illustrated below:

$$PV = \frac{PMT}{i}$$
$$PV = \frac{\$4}{0.10}$$
$$PV = \$40$$

OTHER TVM TOOLS

Timelines, mathematics, TVM tables, accumulation schedules, financial calculators, and computer software are basic tools of TVM analysis. There are other TVM tools, including amortization tables and the Rule of 72. An understanding of each of these tools will assist the financial planner solve other complex TVM problems.

Amortization table
TVM tool used primarily to illustrate the amortization, or extinguishments, of debt. The table presents the number of years of indebtedness, the beginning balance, level payments, interest amount, principal reduction, and ending balance of indebtedness.

Amortization Tables

An **amortization table** is an extension of the accumulation schedules illustrated earlier in the chapter. Amortization tables are primarily used to illustrate the amortization, or extinguishment, of debt. Initially we create a table with the beginning balance of the debt, a level payment, the portion of the payment that is interest, the portion of the payment that is used to reduce the principal indebtedness, and the ending balance of the indebtedness for each year.

EXHIBIT 6.5   Amortization Table (Blank)

Month (Col 1)	Beginning Balance (Col 2)	Payment (Col 3)	6.25% Interest (Col 4) = 6.25% ÷ 12 × (Col 2)	Principal Reduction (Col 5) = (3) – (4)	Ending Mortgage Balance (Col 6) = (2) – (5)
—	—	—	—	—	—
—	—	—	—	—	—

The beginning balance of the indebtedness less the principal amount of reduction will equal the ending balance of the indebtedness. The remainder of the payment was interest as determined in the interest amount column. The common usage for amortization tables is for mortgages, but they can be used to illustrate any indebtedness repayment schedule.

E X A M P L E   Josh secures a $240,000 mortgage with the first payment to be made in January and repaid over 15 years on a monthly basis at 6.25% annual interest.

PV	=	$240,000	Mortgage amount
n	=	180 months	Term in months
i	=	6.25 ÷ 12	Interest per month
PMT	=	–$2,057.8166	Payment of an ordinary annuity
FV_{12}	=	$230,023.66	Balance of mortgage after 12 payments

Notice that Column 2 of Exhibit 6.6 is the beginning balance of indebtedness of $240,000. Josh then makes 12 monthly payments of $2,057.81 (total $24,693.72) during year 1 of which $14,717.44 is interest, and the remainder, $9,976.34, is used to reduce the mortgage balance so that at the end of year 1, Josh owes $230,023.66 on the mortgage (Column 6).

The amortization table can be extended for the full 15 years and illustrates exactly when the balance of the mortgage will reach any certain amount, the amount of interest for a given period, and the amount of principal reduction during a given period. The table may be presented for only one year, as above, or yearly or monthly for the entire indebtedness period. If the mortgage begins some time other than January, the table can be modified so that the mortgage interest expense for each calendar year for estimating the mortgage interest income tax deduction for federal income tax.

EXHIBIT 6.6   Mortgage Amortization Table

Month (Col 1)	Beginning Balance (Col 2)	Payment (Col 3)	6.25% Interest (Col 4) = 6.25% ÷ 12 × (Col 2)	Principal Reduction (Col 5) = (3) – (4)	Ending Mortgage Balance (Col 6) = (2) – (5)
Yr 1 Jan	$240,000.00	$2,057.81	$1,250.00	$807.81	$239,192.19
Yr 1 Feb	$239,192.19	$2,057.81	$1,245.79	$812.02	$238,380.17
Yr 1 Mar	$238,380.17	$2,057.81	$1,241.56	$816.25	$237,563.92
...	...	...	...	...	...
Yr 1 Dec	$230,878.98	$2,057.81	$1,202.49	$855.32	$230,023.66
Total Yr 1		**$24,693.72**	**$14,717.44**	**$9,976.34***	

*rounding error of $0.06

Mortgage amortization calculations may be quickly performed using a financial calculator. Using the previous example, upon calculating the mortgage payment, the financial calculator can provide the amortization details for any period of time during the amortization. To determine the amount of interest and principal paid in the first year and the remaining balance after 12 payments, the calculation is as follows using the HP 10bII+:

240000 [PV]
0 [FV]
180 [N]
6.25 ÷ 12 = .5208 [I/YR]
Solve for [PMT] −2,057.81

Without clearing, enter:

1 [INPUT] 12
[■] [AMORT] (AMORT is the shift function of the [FV] key)

The display will now show 1 – 12. Pressing the [=] key will toggle through the principle paid in months 1–12 (9,976.34), the interest paid in months 1–12 (14,717.44), and the principal balance remaining after 12 months (230,023.66). Any combination of months may be entered and the amortization details for that period will be displayed. For example, entering 13 [INPUT] 24 [■] [AMORT] will display the amortization details for year 2 of the mortgage. Provided the calculator is not cleared, it is not necessary to reenter the mortgage terms to input a different period of months.

Qualified residence interest expense may be deductible for taxpayers who itemize their deductions on their federal income tax return. The mortgage company sends the interest payer a Form 1098 (Mortgage Interest Statement) providing the payer with the amount of interest paid for the prior year. For example, Josh should have received a Form 1098 for the first year of $14,717.44 interest paid.

The Rule of 72

Frequently, professionals want to approximate rates of interest or the time needed to achieve a certain financial goal when the interest rate or the time, but not both, is known. The professional may need only an estimate rather than a mathematically precise answer or does not have access to the appropriate tool to perform precise calculations.

Rule of 72

A method of approximation that estimates the time it takes to double the value of an investment where the earnings (interest) rate is known (by dividing 72 by the interest rate); it can also estimate the earnings (interest) rate necessary to double an investment value if the time is known (by dividing 72 by the period of investment)

The **Rule of 72** is such a method of approximation. Initially used by accountants, it is now used by financial planners to estimate the time it takes to double the value of an investment when the interest rate is known. Alternatively, the Rule of 72 will estimate the interest rate necessary to double an investment value if the time is known. The Rule of 72 states if you know a rate of return, you can determine the time it takes to double the value of the investment by dividing 72 by the interest rate. For example, if the annual interest rate is 6%, then 72 ÷ 6 = 12. Therefore, if a dollar is invested at 6% for 12 years, it should be equal to $2 at the end of the 12-year term. Conversely, if the term is known to be 12 years and you need an amount to double during that term, you can divide 72 by 12 to determine the interest rate necessary (72 ÷ 12 = 6). Therefore, you would need an interest rate of 6% in order to double your investment in 12 years.

EXHIBIT 6.7 Rule of 72 Examples

Interest Rate	Period to Double (*n*)
4%	18.0
6%	12.0
8%	9.0
9%	8.0
10%	7.2

Although the Rule of 72 is extremely helpful as an approximator and a control on the reasonableness of an answer determined by a calculator or computer, it has a small error, especially at extremely low or high rates or terms. Consider, for example, how long it would take to double $1 if the rate of interest were 72% annually. According to the Rule of 72, 72 ÷ 72 = 1, indicating to us that we should double our money in one year, but we know that the value at the end of one year is $1.72, not $2. Many financial planners are using the Rule of 72 without considering the error factor. Exhibit 6.8 is a table of the error percentage rate for the Rule of 72 at various interest rates.

The error rate is calculated in the following using the actual value of $2 as the numerator and the actual calculated amount as the denominator to get the error percentage. The minus signs indicate that the actual value is less than the Rule of 72 estimated by the calculated percentage. The values that are not bracketed are greater than the Rule of 72 estimated by the calculated percentage indicated. For example, at 1%, the actual value of $1 at 1% for 72 periods is $2.047, or 2.4% above $2.

EXHIBIT 6.8 Error Rate Using the Rule of 72

Interest Rate	Error %
1	2.4
2	2.0
3	1.6
4	1.3
5	1.0
6	0.6
7	0.3
8	0.05
9	−0.4
10	−0.6
11	−0.9
12	−1.3
13	−1.4
14	−1.8
15	−2.1
18	−3.1
24	−4.7
40	−7.6
50	−8.5
72*	−14.0

*The error rate for a given interest rate equal to or greater than 72% will always be 14%.

As you can see from Exhibit 6.8, the error rate as a percentage of the future value can range from +2.4% to −14%. Therefore, although the Rule of 72 is a good approximation, especially at interest rates between 6% and 10%, it loses some of its precision when outside the 6–10% interest rate range.

The Rule of 72 can also be used to approximate the effects of inflation in retirement. The doubling time for an asset growing at the rate of inflation will also give the time it will take for prices to double. Prices doubling is the same thing as inflation cutting purchasing power in half. The long-term inflation rate since the establishment of the Federal Reserve is about 3% (72 ÷ 3 = 24 years). Thus, a person retiring at 65 will see prices double in the general economy by about the time he is 89. Age 89 is approximately the life expectancy of an average 65-year-old couple retiring today.

WHERE ON THE WEB

American Savings Education Council **www.asec.org**

Financial Industry Regulatory Authority (FINRA) **www.finra.org**

Investor Desktop, Financial and Insurance Calculators **www.investordesktop.com**

Kiplinger **www.kiplinger.com**

U.S. News **www.usnews.com**

DISCUSSION QUESTIONS

1. What is the time value of money (TVM) concept, and why is it so important in financial planning?

2. What are the important questions in financial planning that can be answered using TVM concepts?

3. What is meant by present value and future value, and how are these two concepts used in the calculation of compound interest?

4. What are the basic tools used in TVM analysis?

5. How are TVM tables computed?

6. What is the difference between the future value of an ordinary annuity (FV_{OA}) and the present value of an ordinary annuity (PV_{OA})?

7. What is the difference between the future value of an annuity due (FV_{AD}) and the present value of an annuity due (PV_{AD})?

8. When would you use an ordinary annuity or an annuity due in financial planning?

9. What are some TVM concepts other than annuities?

10. How do unequal cash flows affect the future value of an investment?

11. How do net present value (NPV) and internal rate of return (IRR) differ in financial planning calculations?

12. What is yield to maturity (YTM), and how is it used to determine a bond's interest rate?

13. How is the concept of solving for term given the other variables useful in debt management?

14. What alternative rate choices exist when selecting the rate of interest for accumulating or discounting?

15. How is the real return of an investment affected by the inflation rate?

16. How do serial payments affect the future value of an investment?

17. How can amortization tables and the Rule of 72 help solve present TVM problems?

EXERCISES

1. Calculate the present value of $10,000 to be received in exactly 10 years, assuming an annual interest rate of 9%.

2. Calculate the future value of $10,000 invested for 10 years, assuming an annual interest rate of 9%.

3. Calculate the present value of an ordinary annuity of $5,000 received annually for 10 years, assuming a discount rate of 9%.

4. Calculate the present value of an annuity of $5,000 received annually that begins today and continues for 10 years, assuming a discount rate of 9%.

5. Calculate the future value of an ordinary annuity of $5,000 received for 10 years, assuming an interest rate of 9%.

6. Calculate the future value of an annual annuity of $5,000 beginning today and continuing for 10 years, assuming an interest rate of 9%.

7. Mike borrows $240,000 at 8% for a mortgage for 15 years. Prepare an annual amortization table assuming the first payment is due January 30 of the current year exactly 30 days after the loan.

8. Joan invested $5,000 in an interest-bearing account earning an 8% annual rate of interest compounded monthly. How much will the account be worth at the end of 5 years, assuming all interest is reinvested at the 8% rate?

9. Callie expects to receive $50,000 in 2 years. Her opportunity cost is 10% compounded monthly. What is the sum worth to Callie today?

10. Lola purchased a zero-coupon bond 9 years ago for $600. If the bond matures today and the face value is $1,000, what is the average annual compound rate of return (calculated semiannually) that Lola realized on her investment?

11. Today Evan put all of his cash into an account earning an annual interest rate of 10%. Assuming he makes no withdrawals or additions to this account, approximately how many years must Evan wait to double his money? Use the Rule of 72 to determine the answer.

12. Anthony has been investing $1,500 at the end of each year for the past 12 years. How much has he accumulated, assuming an interest rate of 8% compounded annually?

13. Dennis has been dollar cost averaging in a mutual fund by investing $1,000 at the beginning of every quarter for the past 5 years. He has been earning an average annual compound rate of return of 11% compounded quarterly. What is the value of the fund today?

14. Casey, injured in an automobile accident, won a judgment that provides him $2,500 at the end of each 6-month period over the next 3 years. If the escrow account that holds Casey's settlement award earns an average annual rate of 10% compounded semiannually, how much was the defendant initially required to pay Casey to compensate him for his injuries?

15. Stacey wants to withdraw $3,000 at the beginning of each year for the next 5 years. She expects to earn 8% compounded annually on her investment. What lump sum should Stacey deposit today?

16. Gary wants to purchase a beach condo in 7 years for $100,000. What periodic payment should he invest at the beginning of each quarter to attain the goal, assuming an annual interest rate of 11%, compounded quarterly?

17. Ann purchased a car for $25,000. She is financing the auto at a 10% annual interest rate, compounded monthly for 4 years. What payment is required at the end of each month to finance Ann's car?

18. Josh purchased a house for $215,000 with a down payment of 20%. What is the amount of his monthly payment assuming the balance is financed at 10% over 30 years?

19. Chase purchased a house for $300,000. He put 20% down and financed the remaining amount over 30 years at 8%. How much interest will he pay over the life of the loan assuming he pays the loan as agreed? (Round to the nearest dollar.)

PROBLEMS

1. Lucy wants to give her son $80,000 on his wedding day in 4 years. How much should she invest today at an annual interest rate of 9.5% compounded annually to have $80,000 in 4 years? Alternatively, how much would she need to invest today if she could have her interest compounded monthly? Explain which interest option would be most beneficial to Lucy.

2. Rachel, who just turned 18, deposits a $15,000 gift into an interest-bearing account earning a 7.5% annual rate of interest. How much will she have in the account when she retires at age 60, assuming all interest is reinvested at the 7.5% rate? If Rachel decided she only needed $300,000 at retirement, could she retire at 59? Explain.

3. Kerri won the lottery today. She has two options. She can receive $30,000 at the end of each year for the next 15 years or take a lump-sum distribution of $200,000. Her opportunity cost is 12% compounded annually. Based on present values, which option should she choose?

4. Darrin wants to donate $8,000 to his church at the beginning of each year for the next 20 years. What lump sum should Darrin deposit today if he expects to earn 11% compounded annually on his investment? Alternatively, how much should he deposit if he wants to have $50,000 left at the end of the 20 years?

5. James deposited $800 at the end of the past 16 years to purchase his granddaughter, Kali, a car. James earned 8% interest compounded annually on his investment. If the car Kali chooses costs $22,999, would she have enough money in the account to purchase the vehicle? What would be the deficit or surplus?

6. Brenda has been investing $150 at the beginning of each month for the past 20 years. How much has she accumulated, assuming she has earned an 11% annual return compounded monthly on her investment? If instead of earning 11%, Brenda was only able to earn 10% (compounded monthly), how much would her payments need to be to have the same accumulated amount?

7. Kenneth took out a loan today to purchase a boat for $160,000. He will repay the loan over 30 years at 9% interest (with payments occurring monthly). What will be his remaining principal balance at the end of the first year?

8. Cody estimates his opportunity cost on investments at 9% compounded annually. Which of the following is the best investment opportunity?
   - To receive $100,000 today
   - To receive $400,000 at the end of 15 years
   - To receive $1,500 at the end of each month for 10 years compounded monthly
   - To receive $75,000 in 5 years and $100,000 5 years later
   - To receive $75,000 in 5 years and $175,000 10 years later

9. Patricia and Scott are ready to retire. They want to receive the equivalent of $30,000 in today's dollars at the beginning of each year for the next 20 years. They assume inflation will average 4% over the long run, and they can earn an 8% compound annual after-tax return on investments. What lump sum do Patricia and Scott need to invest today to attain their goal?

10. Margaret wants to retire in 9 years. She needs an additional $200,000 in today's dollars in 10 years to have sufficient funds to finance this objective. She assumes inflation will average 5% over the long run, and she can earn a 4% compound annual after-tax rate of return on investments. What serial payment should Margaret invest at the end of the first year to attain her objective?

11. Kristi wants to buy a house in 10 years. She estimates she will need $200,000 at that time. She currently has a zero-coupon bond with a market value of $4,600 that she will use as part of the required amount. The zero-coupon bond has a face value of $10,000 and will mature in 10 years. The bond has a semiannual effective interest rate of 4.323%. In addition to the bond, she wants to save a monthly amount to reach her goal. What is Kristi's required monthly payment made at the beginning of each month in order to accumulate the $200,000, including the zero-coupon bond, at an assumed interest rate of 11%?

Education Funding

LEARNING OBJECTIVES

After learning the material in this chapter, you will be able to do the following:

■ Discuss the various issues that parents should consider when setting goals for financing their children's education

■ List the types of financial aid information that can be gathered from a college's financial aid office

■ Explain the importance of the Expected Family Contribution (EFC) formula in student financial aid application

■ Describe the major student financial assistance programs available through the U.S. Department of Education

■ Describe the campus-based financial aid programs available to college students

■ Describe the several financial aid programs available to college students

■ List the benefits of qualified tuition programs (QTPs)

■ Describe the various income tax-saving financial aid vehicles

■ Understand how time value of money concepts are used to help calculate the cost of a child's education

INTRODUCTION

One of the most common financial planning goals of parents is to provide an education for their children. Education funding is a common area of concern for those seeking financial planning advice because paying for higher education is one of the largest financial burdens a family will face. Even clients with high income levels must take into account paying for their children's tuition and school-related expenses. Recently, education costs have dramatically outpaced inflation. Over the past 10 years, tuition at public colleges and universities throughout the country has increased at a rate approximately twice as much as the Consumer Price Index (CPI). Also, recent trends show an increase in the number of years students remain in college and increased requirements for postgraduate education. Along with the expense of a home and taxes, providing for a child's education is one of the largest expenses for families and one of the most important decisions.

EXHIBIT 7.1 Average Published Tuition and Fees in 2019 Dollars by Sector, 1989–1990 to 2019–2020

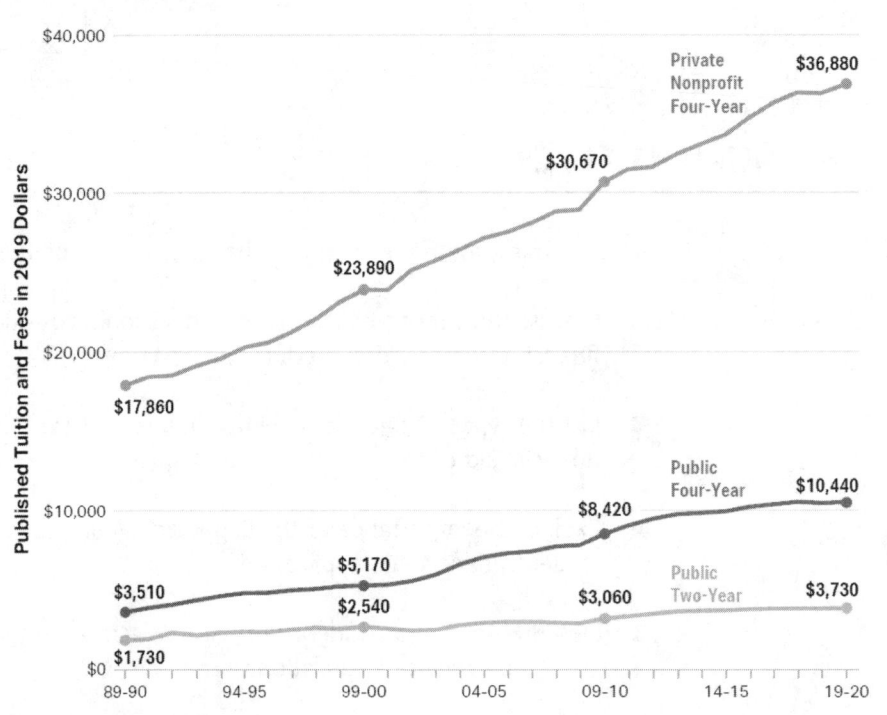

Source: Trends in College Pricing 2019. Copyright 2019 by College Entrance Examination Board. www.collegeboard.org

This chapter discusses how to develop a plan for funding a child's education by addressing the issues that must be raised, the information that must be gathered, and the goals that should be set, taking the family's circumstances into account. Once the goals have been set, the implementation of the plan will depend on the sources of funding available, which may include a savings campaign, financial aid, and various payment options. Once the plan is designed and the strategies have been identified, action must be taken to implement and monitor the plan.

ISSUES AND GOALS

To formulate a plan that best meets the needs of the particular family, goals must be identified and agreed upon and appropriate provisions made to achieve those goals. The key is to set feasible, realistic goals.

When formulating a plan for the education of a child, one of the most significant considerations is how much time there is before the child enters college. There are many options available for parents of very young children who are years away from entering college. Those parents with children nearing college age or currently entering college do not have as many options and savings methods. It cannot be stressed enough that, as with most areas of planning, time is crucial in planning for a child's education. Time allows consistent and persistent contributions toward savings vehicles, allowing them to grow and, hopefully, meet or surpass the cost of tuition. Meanwhile, inflation will continue to drive tuition costs higher over time. It will clearly be less stressful and easier to manage costs, however, with the benefit of 10, 15, or more years of saving versus evaluating options, one's ability to pay, and formulating a plan during the student's junior or senior year in high school. In addition to concerns about college tuition, families should decide whether they want to fund private elementary and secondary school education for their children. A family should also decide whether to provide some or all funding for graduate or professional school education.

One way for parents to ultimately defray the cost of education is paying for only a portion of the child's college expenses and leaving some of the expenses to be paid by the child. Some view this method as a way of building character for the child and educating the child in accepting responsibility, without forcing the child to assume all the financial responsibility for college-related expenses (that may burden the child with overwhelming loans and debt when beginning a career). Again, decisions such as these will depend on the preferences and desires of the parents. However, most parents do not consider that the person their child will marry will also, in all probability, bring college debt to the marriage. Combining two moderate college debts can be a major burden on a young family as they begin married life.

During the goal-setting process, some individuals struggle with the notion of sending their children to public elementary or secondary school, while investing resources to a college education fund. This decision is often based on the quality of the public education available to the child. The parents should also consider that, while private elementary and secondary education will require additional funds, there may be a return on that investment; the child may obtain a more advanced education and perhaps acceptance to prestigious colleges that may provide scholarships or less-stringent financial aid requirements. Of course, these are issues that a financial planner should discuss with the parents so they can make an informed decision based on their own circumstances. Although there are many important issues and financial decisions to be made regarding elementary and secondary education, the majority of this chapter will deal with preparation and planning for a child's college expenses.

Parents should be reminded that families are in a better position to fund college expenses over a long period because their income will likely increase in future years. In addition, with a longer investment time horizon there exists a higher probability of positive returns in funds invested for educational purposes, as well. This will motivate some parents to begin a savings regimen that does not meet all the financial requirements right away but can be increased as the years progress and provide an incentive to increase savings as college years grow nearer.

INFORMATION GATHERING

During the goal-setting process, financial planners must forecast anticipated tuition and related expenses. This forecasting can be accomplished by first determining current tuition and related expenses for the schools in the area and for the schools that the parents believe would be most appropriate for the child. This information can be found by calling the school's administrative office. Additionally, there are numerous college guides in bookstores and local libraries that provide tuition and room and board expenses at colleges and universities throughout the country.

Once these expenses are obtained, the financial planner must adjust these expenses to account for inflation until the child enters college. The planner must assume a tuition inflation rate, probably between 3% and 5% greater than CPI per year for college and related expenses, and then calculate the anticipated expenses for each year the child will attend college. The following example uses a 6% tuition inflation rate.

EXAMPLE

Assumptions:

- Child's current age—10 years
- Anticipated college age—18–22 years
- Current tuition and room and board—$13,000 per year
- Tuition inflation rate—6%

Estimated costs [future value (FV) or actual cost] of tuition and room and board:

- Freshman year—$20,720, (PV = +/–13,000, N = 8, I/YR = 6)
- Sophomore year—$21,963, (PV = +/–13,000, N = 9, I/YR = 6)
- Junior year—$23,281, (PV = +/–13,000, N = 10, I/YR = 6)
- Senior year—$24,678, (PV = +/–13,000, N = 11, I/YR = 6)

Once these expenses have been identified and adjusted for inflation, one can determine the estimated four-year cost of a college education. As will be discussed in this chapter, depending on how much money will be available when the child enters college, a formula can be used to determine how much money must be invested to meet the amount of savings necessary for college (i.e., the Expected Family Contribution). Other expenses that should be considered include books and school supplies, transportation, travel expenses, and entertainment, as shown in Exhibit 7.2—College Expenses Checklist.

Because college is a major investment, families should carefully evaluate potential schools. Some of the information families should obtain includes a copy of the documents describing the school's accreditation and licensing, current school tuition, and on-campus room and board. Also, families should ask about the school's loan default rate. The default rate is the percentage of students who attend the school, obtain federal student loans, and ultimately fail to repay the loan. This information is important because schools with high default rates may not be eligible to obtain federal aid for certain federal financial assistance programs. This may also indicate that students are poorly matched with the school.

EXHIBIT 7.2 College Expenses Checklist

These are the college expenses that most families should keep in mind when planning for payment of a child's education:

- Tuition and tuition-related expenses
- Books, school supplies, and equipment (calculator and computer)
- Lodging
- Meals
- Transportation
- Entertainment (school sporting events) and leisure (health club)
- Travel expenses
- Tutoring (if necessary)
- Extracurricular (fraternity or sorority dues)
- Clothing and attire
- Other considerations particular to the student or family

If a school advertises its job placement rates, it must also publish the most recent employment statistics, graduation statistics, and any other information that would justify its representations. Another relevant item of information is the school's refund policy. If a student enrolls but never attends classes, the student should be refunded the majority of his money. If a student begins attending classes but leaves before completing his coursework, the student may be able to receive a partial refund. Many state university systems allow for prepayment of tuition at current prices for enrollment in the future. Prepaid Tuition Plans are discussed later in this chapter.

A prospective student can obtain the following financial aid availability information from a school:

- Availability of financial assistance, including information on all federal, state, local, private, and institutional financial aid programs
- Procedures and deadlines for submitting financial aid program applications
- The school's process for determining a financial aid applicant's eligibility
- The school's method for determining a student's financial need
- The school's method for determining each type and amount of assistance in a student's financial aid package
- How and when the student will receive financial aid
- The school's method for determining whether the student is making satisfactory academic progress and the consequences if the student is not (whether the student continues to receive federal financial aid depends, in part, on whether the student makes satisfactory academic progress)
- If the student is awarded a job through the Federal Work-Study program, what type of job is involved, the amount of hours the student must work, the duties of the student in that job, the rate of pay, and how and when the student will be paid
- The availability and counseling procedures of the school's financial aid office

The client may also wish to ask the school for a copy of its equity-in-athletics report. Any coeducational school where a student can receive federal financial aid that has an interschool athletic program must prepare an equity-in-athletics report giving financial and statistical information for men's and women's sports. This information is designed to advise students of a school's commitment to providing equitable athletic opportunities for its male and female students.

The client should also be encouraged to consult with high school counselors, local employers, and the state higher education agency. These are invaluable sources of information for those exploring options of higher education.

DETERMINING FINANCIAL NEED

Free Application for Federal Student Aid (FAFSA)

An application form that must be submitted by a college student to become eligible for federal financial aid

As mentioned earlier, most financial aid packages depend heavily on the financial need of the student. Therefore, it is important to evaluate whether a client may have the requisite financial need when estimating costs of tuition and availability of funds for college.

The financial aid process is initiated by filling out financial aid forms available from high schools, the United States Department of Education, or from the college the student will attend. This financial aid application form is called a **Free Application for Federal Student Aid (FAFSA)**. A FAFSA must be submitted by the student applicant to become eligible for federal financial aid. The student can obtain and complete a FAFSA application in one of the following ways:

- Complete and mail a paper FAFSA, which can be obtained from the student's high school, potential college, or college where attending

- Have the student's school submit the completed FAFSA electronically

- Use FAFSA on the web (**www.fafsa.ed.gov**), which is quickly becoming the most common means of application

Colleges usually appoint an agency to conduct an analysis of the financial need of the student and the student's family. The completed information on the FAFSA is sent to colleges requested by the applicant. The college may also have the applicant complete other forms to enable the college to conduct its own needs analysis of the student. Once the student is accepted to a college, the college may inform the student of any available financial aid.

Expected Family Contribution (EFC)

A formula that indicates how much of a student's family's resources ought to be available to assist in paying for the student's college education

When applying for student financial assistance, the information reported by the applicant is used in a formula established by Congress. The formula is called the **Expected Family Contribution (EFC)** for a child's education. The EFC indicates how much of a student's family's resources ought to be available to assist in paying for the student's education. Some of the factors used in this calculation include taxable and nontaxable income, assets, and benefits, such as unemployment and Social Security.

Although low-income families are more likely to qualify for financial aid than higher-income families, higher-income families should not be discouraged from applying for aid because the EFC formula also takes into account various factors including the number of children in private school or college, the size of the family, the number of years until the parents' retirement, and large financial burdens, such as medical bills. The EFC calculation is used to determine eligibility for financial aid programs, except for unsubsidized student loans and PLUS loans, which are provided regardless of financial need. If the EFC is below a certain amount, the student may be eligible for financial aid, such as a Federal Pell Grant, assuming other eligibility requirements are met. Such eligibility requirements include the cost of attendance at the school (tuition, room and board, and related expenses); full-time, half-time, or part-time status; and academic standing.

There is no maximum EFC because the EFC used in a calculation depends on where the student attends school and the cost of attendance at that school. When the student consults with the school's financial aid administrator, the financial aid administrator will calculate the student's financial need by subtracting the student's EFC from the cost of attendance at the school. The remaining figure equals the student's financial need. The formula is as follows:

Tuition/cost of attendance	$ Amount
− Expected Family Contribution (EFC)	−$ Amount
= Financial need	$ Amount

As is evident from the above calculation, a student may have financial need at one school but not another because financial need depends on the cost of attendance, whereas the student's EFC remains constant for the year regardless of which school the student attends. If circumstances warrant it, financial aid administrators can, at their discretion, adjust the cost of attendance or adjust data in calculating a student's EFC. More information on the EFC calculation can be obtained through the Federal Student Aid Information Center at **http://studentaid.ed.gov**.

At this point, most individuals ask how they can reduce their EFC. In other words, how can a family reduce the amount of money it is expected to contribute to a child's education in order to receive more financial assistance? There are various methods that a family can use to reduce EFC. First, however, one must determine the dependency status of the student.

The income and assets of the student's family will be counted only if the student is considered dependent on the parents. If the student applying for financial aid is independent, only the student's income and assets will be considered. The reasoning behind this rule is that a student who has access to parental support should not be able to reap the benefits of student financial aid programs to the exclusion of those needy, independent students who do not have access to parental support. Some of the criteria that will result in a student being considered independent are the following:

- Born before January 1, 1997 (for the 2020–2021 academic year)

- Married

- Enrolled in a master's or doctorate program

- Has legal dependents (other than a spouse or children) who live with the student and receive more than one-half of their support from the student

- Has children who receive more than half their support from the student

- An orphan or ward of the court, or was a ward of the court until age 18

- A veteran of the U.S. Armed Forces, or currently serving on active duty

- Legally emancipated minor

Another common method for reducing a family's EFC is creating a trust for the child and diminishing the family's estate through gifts. This may create problems, however, because the child's own assets will be considered in the child's financial needs analysis. A family may also reduce its EFC by providing all information surrounding the factors that tend to diminish their EFC, such as large medical bills and more than one child in the family attending college. Finally, the school's financial aid adviser may be able to adjust a family's EFC if the circumstances so require. Here, the burden is on the family or student to communicate information to the financial aid adviser that may reduce the EFC.

FINANCIAL AID PROGRAMS

The United States Department of Education has the following major student financial assistance programs:

- Federal Pell Grant
- Stafford Loan
- PLUS Loan
- Consolidation Loan
- Federal Supplemental Educational Opportunity Grant (FSEOG)
- Federal Work-Study

These federal programs are the largest sources of student aid in the United States. According to the U.S. Department of Education, available student aid topped $186.7 billion in 2018–2019.

EXHIBIT 7.3 Undergraduate Student Aid by Source (in Billions), 2018–2019

Pell Grants	$28.2
Other Federal Grant Programs	$11.3
State Grants	$12.2
Institutional Grants	$52.4
Private and Employer Grants	$12.7
Federal Loans	$54.2
Federal Work-Study	$0.9
Education Tax Credits and Deductions	$14.8
Total	**$186.7**

Source: Trends in Student Aid 2018–2019. College Entrance Examination Board. www.collegeboard.org. (Numbers in the table are rounded)

The following subsections identify and describe these federal programs as well as some state and other programs.

Federal Pell Grants

Pell Grant

A grant from the federal government awarded to undergraduate students who have not earned bachelor's or professional degrees; the EFC calculation, which is based on one's financial need, is used to determine a student's eligibility for a Pell Grant and how much is awarded to a student

A Federal **Pell Grant** is not a loan; rather, it is a grant from the federal government that does not require repayment. The EFC calculation, which is based on one's financial need, is used to determine a student's eligibility for a Pell Grant and how much is awarded to a student. Pell Grants are awarded to undergraduate students who have not earned bachelor's or professional degrees. Graduate, professional, and postgraduate students generally are not awarded Pell Grants. Each year's awards depend on program funding for that year. A student can receive only one Pell Grant award per year. A student must be enrolled on at least a half-time basis to qualify.

Stafford Loans

Stafford Loan

The primary type of financial aid provided by the United States Department of Education; Stafford loans are either subsidized or unsubsidized

The **Stafford Loan** is the primary type of financial aid provided by the United States Department of Education. Stafford Loans are either subsidized or unsubsidized. There is no interest charged on the subsidized loan until repayment of the loan begins, which is typically six months after one of the following occurs:

■ Graduation

■ Leaving school

■ Dropping below half-time status

Half-time status is considered half of the minimum hours to be considered full time. For instance, if a school on a semester basis has a 12-hour minimum requirement each semester for a student to be considered full-time, the student is considered half-time if he is enrolled in at least 6 credit hours each semester.

A subsidized loan is based on the financial need of the student as determined by the EFC formula. An unsubsidized Stafford Loan is a loan in which the borrower is charged interest on the principal from the moment of disbursement until the loan is paid off. Those who receive unsubsidized loans have the option of allowing the interest to be capitalized (which means that the interest accumulates and is added to the principal during the life of the loan until principal reduction payments are required) or paying the interest as it accrues. The process of capitalization costs more over the long term because the interest that accumulates is added to the principal balance, and subsequent interest is charged on the entire outstanding balance. However, some students or their families may not be in a financial position to pay the interest while the student is in school, and the capitalization method lets them postpone payment. The interest rates for the 2019–2020 academic year were 4.53% for undergraduate subsidized and unsubsidized loans. Rates of 6.08% apply for graduate or professional unsubsidized loans.

When Stafford Loans are disbursed to a student, an origination fee of 1.059% is charged. Thus, when determining the amount of funds through Stafford Loans required for a school term, the student must remember that the disbursement for a $7,000 Stafford Loan, for example, will only be $6,925.87 ($7,000 × 1.059% = $74.13, and $7,000 − $74.13 = $6,925.87).

Repayment of Stafford Loans begins after a grace period of six months following graduation, leaving school, or dropping below half-time enrollment. The subsidized Stafford Loan is attractive because no interest is charged and no principal payment is required during the six-month grace period. Essentially, the student has received a free loan during school and for six months thereafter under the subsidized loan program. Once the grace period is over, however, the subsidized loan begins to accrue interest, and principal and interest reduction payments must begin. Although interest is charged during the grace period on an unsubsidized Stafford Loan, no repayment of principal or interest is required during the grace period. If the interest is not paid on an unsubsidized loan during the grace period, it accrues and continues to be capitalized.

Students may obtain a deferment of the loan, which is a temporary postponement of payments on the loan. If the student has a subsidized loan, interest will not be charged during the period of deferment. For unsubsidized loans, the interest is capitalized during deferment unless the student chooses to pay the interest as it accrues during deferment. A deferment is allowed only after proving special circumstances to the agency, sender, or holder of the loan. The most common circumstances that may give rise to a deferment of repayment on a Stafford Loan include the following:

- At least half-time enrollment at a postsecondary school

- Economic hardship (for up to three years)

- Former student's inability to attain full-time employment (for up to three years)

Forbearance is a period when repayment of a loan is temporarily postponed for reasons that do not qualify for a deferment. Although forbearance also postpones repayment, subsidized loans accrue interest during the period of forbearance. Direct Stafford Loans can be repaid under several payment plans. Each payment plan has a different term ranging from 10 (the standard term) to 25 years.

Under certain conditions, Stafford Loans may be canceled or recipients may receive repayment assistance. One of the following conditions must be met for the loan to be canceled:

- Death of the student or borrower (i.e., parent of student)

- The borrower becomes totally and permanently disabled

- The student is a full-time teacher for five consecutive years in a designated elementary or secondary school serving students from low-income families

- The loan is discharged in bankruptcy

- The student's school closes before the student completes the program

- The school falsely certifies the loan

Repayment assistance may be available to students who serve in the military or become registered nurses and serve in eligible facilities in areas experiencing a nursing shortage.

PLUS Loans

**Parent Loans for
Undergraduate
Students (PLUS
Loans)**
*Loans that allow parents
with good credit histories to borrow funds
for a child's education
expenses*

Parent Loans for Undergraduate Students (PLUS Loans) allow parents with good credit histories to borrow funds for a child's education expenses. The child must be a dependent student enrolled at least half time in an eligible program at an eligible school. The parents complete a PLUS Loan application and Promissory Note with the school's financial aid office. As long as the parents do not have an adverse credit history, they may be entitled to receive a loan equal to the cost of attendance less any other available financial aid.

For instance, if the cost of attendance is $7,500 and the student has $5,000 in other financial aid, the parents may borrow up to $2,500. The interest rate on a new PLUS Loan is fixed at 7.08% (2019–2020). Interest accrues on the loan from the moment of disbursement until the loan is paid off. A fee of 4% is deducted from the funds disbursed to help defray the cost of the loan to the government. At least two disbursements of funds are made because no installment may exceed half of the loan amount.

Normally, parents must begin repaying PLUS Loans within 60 days after the final loan disbursement for the current academic year. Parents must commence repayment of both principal and interest while the student is in school. The same rules that apply to deferment or forbearance of Stafford Loans apply to PLUS Loans. However, because PLUS Loans are not subsidized, interest will continue to accrue and will thus be capitalized during the period of deferment or forbearance. PLUS Loans generally must be repaid within 10 years, although extended repayment terms of up to 25 years may be available.

Consolidation Loans

Consolidation loan

A loan that provides borrowers with a way to consolidate various types of federal student loans with separate repayment schedules into one loan

A **consolidation loan** provides borrowers with a vehicle to consolidate various types of federal student loans with separate repayment schedules into one loan. The Consolidation Loan Program benefits student and parent borrowers by extending the term of repayment, requiring only one payment per month, and in some cases providing a lower interest rate than on one or more of the loans. The interest rate is based on the weighted average of the interest rates on the loans being consolidated. The school's financial aid adviser can explain the many combinations of consolidation loan options.

Campus-Based Student Financial Aid

There are three campus-based programs that are administered directly by the financial aid office at participating schools:

- The Federal Supplemental Education Opportunity Grant (FSEOG) Program
- The Federal Work-Study Program
- The Federal Perkins Loan Program

Each program extends aid based on financial need of the student and the availability of funds at the school.

The Federal Supplemental Education Opportunity Grant Program

Federal Supplemental Education Opportunity Grant (FSEOG)

Campus-based student financial aid grant awarded to undergraduate students with low EFCs that gives priority to students who receive federal Pell Grants

An **FSEOG** is a grant, an outright gift, which does not require repayment. The FSEOG is awarded to undergraduate students with low EFCs who have not obtained a bachelor's or professional degree and gives priority to students who receive Federal Pell Grants. The difference between a Federal Pell Grant and an FSEOG is that the United States Department of Education guarantees that each eligible school will receive sufficient funds to pay Federal Pell Grants to all eligible students, whereas an FSEOG is paid to eligible students only if funds are available. Once all available FSEOG funds are used at the school, remaining eligible students will not receive an FSEOG. The FSEOG is in the range of $100 to $4,000 per academic year. The amount paid depends on the level of need, the time of application, and the school's funding level.

The Federal Work-Study Program

Federal Work-Study Program

Campus-based student financial aid program that enables undergraduate and graduate students to earn money for education expenses through jobs that pay at least current minimum wages but do not exceed the award received through the program

Federal Work-Study programs enable undergraduate and graduate students with financial need to earn money for education expenses through jobs that pay at least current minimum wages. Some jobs may pay higher hourly rates depending on the work done and skill required. The amount earned through the Federal Work-Study program cannot exceed the award received through the program. Federal Work-Study jobs may be on campus or off campus depending on the employer participating in the program.

The Federal Perkins Loan Program

Federal Perkins Loan

Campus-based, low-interest student loan program that provided financial aid to undergraduate and graduate students that had exceptional financial need

Although the Perkins loan program officially ended on September 30, 2017, it is worthy of mention because students may still have these loans. The final loans were approved for disbursement through June 30, 2018. Prior to the program end, Perkins loans were low interest rate loans funded by the federal government but administered by individual schools. These loans were available both to undergraduate and graduate students. They were need-based and were available to students who were attending on at least a half-time basis and who had an exceptional financial need.

Limits applied to the amount of funds that were borrowed. These loans featured a 5% interest rate, which was not charged during the period that the individual was a student. In addition, borrowers were not charged interest until nine months following graduation, leaving school, or dropping to less than half time, at which time repayment begins. Repayment is typically for 10 years.

For more information about federal education programs and financial aid applications, visit the United States Department of Education's website at **www.ed.gov**.

State Governmental Aid

Most states have programs that are very similar to the federal student financial aid programs previously discussed. The state programs rely heavily on the student's financial need and superior academic performance. States also require that the student be a resident of the state and attend a college or university in that state. Information on a given state's financial aid programs can be obtained from the school or the state's Department of Education.

Other Financial Aid Sources

Aid Directly from the Institution

Each school has its own method of providing aid through loans, scholarships, discounts, and campus jobs. The school's financial aid adviser should adequately explain to the student the school's available options and programs. Some schools will allow a student to pay tuition on a monthly installment plan, which may provide more flexibility to the student and parents. Other schools may offer discounts or scholarships for superior athletic or academic performance either before or after enrollment. The school has an incentive to entice superior athletes and academic students in order to increase their level of top students and to better compete with other schools, which in turn enhances the school's image.

Aid from Armed Forces

The U.S. Armed Forces have numerous programs and scholarships that may pay for tuition, fees, and books for those who enlist or enroll in the military. The student may also receive monthly payments for other expenses. Information regarding the many programs available through the U.S. Armed Forces can be obtained from the college attended or from the Administrative Office of the desired branch of military. Visit any of the following websites for Armed Forces aid:

- **www.goarmy.com/rotc**
- **www.goarmy.com/benefits/education-benefits.html**
- **www.gibill.va.gov**
- **www.marines.mil**
- **www.af.mil**
- **www.uscg.mil**
- **www.navy.mil**

Other Grants, Scholarships, and Fellowships

There are many forms of scholarships that are awarded by groups that are separate and apart from the school and state or federal government. For instance, there are numerous civic organizations, such as the American Legion, the Knights of Columbus, and the Boy Scouts of America, that award scholarships based on need, merit, and the student's or parents' affiliation with that civic organization. Of course, there are various types of scholarships available to students who have high grades and high standardized (entrance) test scores, including National Merit Scholarships. Also, scholarships can be provided through a particular church or religious organization. Although finding out about these scholarships will take some effort, it may prove to be time well spent.

In addition to scholarships, which typically do not include funds for living expenses, many organizations offer grants and fellowships. Grants and fellowships are similar to scholarships in that the funds awarded do not require repayment. Grants, however, are need-based awards, and fellowships are generally awarded to graduate students on the basis of academic merit and include living expenses as well as funds for tuition and fees.

TAX ADVANTAGES FROM EDUCATION EXPENSES AND TAX ISSUES

Although much time has been spent in this chapter discussing the costs of education and the increase in education expenses, there is some tax relief available. There are various vehicles available that allow the family or taxpayer who bears the brunt of education expenses to realize tax savings and benefits.

Qualified Tuition Programs (QTPs)

Also known as 529 plans, QTPs allow individuals to either participate in Prepaid Tuition Plans in which tuition credits are purchased for a designated beneficiary for payment or waiver of higher education expenses or participate in College Savings Plans in which contributions of money are made to an account to eventually pay for qualified higher education expenses of a designated beneficiary

Qualified Tuition Programs

One popular vehicle used to prepare for college tuition and related costs is the **Qualified Tuition Program (QTP)**. QTPs are also commonly referred to as 529 plans after IRC Section 529. The Internal Revenue Code permits the states to enact and tailor their own QTPs within the parameters established by Section 529. All 50 states have 529 plans, and tax laws have made it possible for institutions of higher education to establish their own 529 plans. In addition to state-sponsored plans and plans associated with a specific college or university, the Tuition Plan Consortium, a nonprofit consortium of independent colleges and universities, offers a national Prepaid Tuition Plan for private institutions.

The Benefits of QTPs

The benefits of QTPs are as follows:

- Growth is tax-deferred.

- Distributions from QTPs are excludable from gross income if used to pay for qualified education expenses. There is no limit on the amount of qualified educational expenses that can be withdrawn income tax-free for higher education expenses each year. Since January 1, 2018, up to $10,000 per year can be withdrawn from a 529 plan for K-12 tuition.

- The contributor can remove assets from the taxable estate.

- QTPs generally charge low commissions and have low management fees.

■ Many states provide state tax deductions or tax exemptions for at least a portion of contributions.

■ The contributor or owner has full control of the asset and can change the beneficiary.

Although each state's QTP legislation varies and has different features, all provide for at least one of two types of plans: Prepaid Tuition Plans and College Savings Plans. QTPs allow individuals to participate in either Prepaid Tuition Plans, whereby tuition credits are purchased for a designated beneficiary for payment or waiver of higher education expenses, or College Savings Plans, whereby contributions of money are made to an account to eventually pay for qualified K-12 or higher education expenses of a designated beneficiary.

QTPs are attractive to states because they can provide incentives to residents and nonresidents (depending on the state's individual plan) to invest in higher education and into that state's educational system. These plans are inexpensive for states to run, as many states provide turn-key contracts to financial services firms or investment companies to professionally manage the statewide plan.

Prepaid Tuition Plans

Prepaid Tuition Plans
Plans where prepayment of college tuition is allowed at current prices for enrollment in the future; in other words, a parent can lock in future tuition at current rates

Prepaid Tuition Plans allow prepayment of tuition at current rates for enrollment in the future. In other words, the parent can lock in future tuition at current rates. Participating in a school's prepayment program presupposes that the child will ultimately attend that school. The parents also assume the risk that the child may not meet the school's academic and admission requirements. Starting a tuition prepayment plan years in advance prevents the student from choosing his own college. Other risks include the possibility that the student may be the recipient of a scholarship to that or another college and the QTP would not be used for qualified expenses, negating the tax advantages. Moreover, the college chosen for tuition prepayment, although a well-respected and accredited school, could have a less-than-desirable curriculum in the student's major or area of interest. The client should weigh these risks with the benefits obtained at the particular school through tuition prepayment. Unused prepaid tuition benefits can be transferred to another family member held for possible future use. Refund and transfer options are available, but it is recommended that the family fully investigate the terms and conditions of the specific Prepaid Tuition Plan in order to understand the consequences if the student attends a different college, fails to meet academic qualifications, or does not attend college. Prepaid tuition plans are becoming less common. Whereas 18 states once offered plans, the number has recently diminished to 11.

College Savings Plans

College Savings Plan
Offered only by states, state-sponsored organizations, and eligible educational institutions. The contribution rules are the same as those for prepaid tuition plans. In this type of plan, tuition is not being prepaid, but, rather, a tax-advantaged savings plan is established from which tax-free distributions are made to pay for qualified education expenses.

College savings plans may be offered only by states, state-sponsored organizations, and eligible educational institutions. The contribution rules are the same as those for prepaid tuition plans. In this type of plan, tuition is not being prepaid, but, rather, a tax-advantaged savings plan is established from which tax-free distributions are made to pay for qualified education expenses. The investment options offered in college savings plans often include stock mutual funds, bond mutual funds, and money market mutual funds. Some plans offer age-based portfolios that automatically shift toward more conservative investments as the beneficiary gets closer to college age.

A significant advantage of the college savings plan over the prepaid tuition plan is that it does not restrict where the child beneficiary may attend college. Rather, the private savings plan permits open enrollment and is available for either out-of-state public university costs or private university costs without any loss of account value. Also, while most prepaid tuition plans are established solely for tuition and mandatory fees, the typical college savings plan may be used for qualified education expenses beyond tuition and mandatory fees. Qualified education expenses may include tuition, fees, books, or supplies required for attendance and room and board (for a student attending at least half time). However, unlike the prepaid tuition plan, funds in the college savings plan are not guaranteed by the sponsoring state, and, if the contributor is unhappy with the performance of the college savings plan, the only real alternative is to roll over the account to a different college savings plan.

The following table illustrates the major differences between a prepaid tuition plan and college savings plan.

Prepaid Tuition Plan	College Savings Plan
Inflation-based performance	Market-based performance
Suitable for risk-averse investor	Suitable for risk-tolerant investor
May offer state-guaranteed return on assets	No state-guaranteed return on assets
Usually restricted enrollment options	Open enrollment
May restrict out-of-state tuition costs and, if less than in-state, may not refund difference	Available for out-of-state tuition costs without any refund difference
Covers tuition and mandatory fees only	In addition to tuition and mandatory fees, covers books, required supplies, and room and board (students attending at least half time)

Taxes and the QTP

As discussed, a student's financial aid eligibility depends on the student's financial condition and the financial condition of her family. The existence of a QTP may affect the formula calculation for a student depending on the type of plan involved. For instance, a College Savings Plan is deemed an asset of the owner/contributor of the account.

Contributions to QTPs are deemed to qualify for the annual gift tax exclusion. A five-year averaging election for purposes of the gift tax annual exclusion may be applied to the transfer. If one's contributions exceed $15,000 (2020), the contributor is permitted to spread out one contribution over a five-year period. For example, if Walter (father-contributor) contributes $35,000 to a QTP account for Joey (beneficiary-child) in one year, Walter can elect to spread this contribution over five years—that is, $7,000 per year—and avoid a gift tax [less than the $15,000 (2020) exclusion]. The QTP thus permits the owner/contributor to shift his taxable estate to the beneficiary.

Any distribution or in-kind benefit transferred within 60 days under a QTP to the credit of a new designated beneficiary who is a family member of the old designated beneficiary will not be treated as a distribution and thus is exempt from income taxation and penalty. A change in the designated beneficiary of an interest in a QTP will not be treated as a distribution if the new beneficiary is a family member of the old beneficiary.

Except to the extent provided in the regulations, a tuition program maintained by a private institution is not treated as qualified unless it has received a ruling or determination from the IRS that the program satisfies applicable requirements. This exclusion from gross income for qualified education expenses was extended to distributions from QTPs established and maintained by an entity other than a state.

QTPs are extremely useful tools that provide significant tax savings, allow for substantial investments for a child's education, and, if used correctly, provide a tool for avoidance of gift and estate taxes. When comparing the tax savings alone from a QTP College Savings Plan versus a taxable account, the tax benefits can be substantial. If a family contributes $300 per month to a taxable account earning 10% annually for 16 years, the accumulated value of the account will be approximately $100,000 if the assumed federal and state tax rates total 34%. However, if that same $300 monthly contribution is made for 16 years into a QTP earning 10% annually, the account will be worth approximately $140,000. The difference is a tax savings of approximately $40,000.

Coverdell Education Savings Accounts (ESAs)

Coverdell Education Savings Account (Coverdell ESA)

An investment account established with cash contributions that grow tax-free within the account; money withdrawn from the account remains free from tax or penalty if the funds are used for qualified educational expenses; if not, the earnings are subject to income tax and a 10% penalty

Coverdell Education Savings Accounts (Coverdell ESAs), formerly known as Educational IRAs, were also authorized by the Taxpayer Relief Act of 1997. Coverdell ESAs are designed to offer tax benefits to individuals who wish to save money for a child or grandchild's qualified education expenses. A Coverdell is an investment account established with cash that is not tax-deductible. The contributions are made for the benefit of children under age 18. The contributions are allowed to grow tax-free within the account. Money withdrawn from the account is free from tax or penalty if the funds are used for qualified education expenses. If the funds are used for anything other than qualified education expenses, the earnings are subject to income tax and a 10% penalty.

Coverdell ESAs permit up to $2,000 in annual contributions, whereas QTPs allow larger contributions. However, if the individual family plans to contribute only $2,000 or less annually to the student/beneficiary's college fund, Coverdell ESAs might be more attractive because they offer the same tax benefits as 529 plans and the owner/contributor has the power to direct the specific investments. A person contributing funds to a Coverdell ESA may also contribute funds to a QTP in the same year for the same beneficiary.

A Coverdell can be established for any child under age 18 by a parent, grandparent, other family members or friends, or even the child, as long as the contributor who establishes the account does not have $220,000 ($110,000 for single) or more of modified family annual gross income (the 2020 phaseout is $190,000 to $220,000 for married filing jointly and $95,000 to $110,000 for single filers). If money from the Coverdell is not used for qualified education expenses by the designated beneficiary by the time the beneficiary turns 30, the beneficiary will need to take a distribution and pay both tax and a 10% penalty on the accumulated earnings or the funds may be rolled over into a Coverdell for a family member of the original beneficiary.

No contributions can be made to the account once the beneficiary turns 18. Distributions or withdrawals from Coverdell ESAs comprise of principal and earnings. The principal portion is always excluded from taxation, whereas earnings are excluded if used to pay for qualified education expenses. Although contributors may establish more than one account in a given child's name, the aggregate maximum annual contribution is $2,000. Withdrawals are tax free whether the student is enrolled full time, half time, or less than half time as long as the withdrawals do not exceed the child's qualified education expenses.

The definition of qualified education expenses (beyond undergraduate or graduate level courses) that may be paid tax-free from a Coverdell ESA include qualified elementary and secondary school expenses. These expenses include (1) tuition, fees, academic tutoring, special need services, books, supplies, and other equipment incurred in connection with the enrollment or attendance of the beneficiary at a public, private, or religious school providing elementary or secondary education (kindergarten through grade 12) as determined under state law; (2) room and board, uniforms, transportation, and supplementary items or services (including extended day programs) required or provided by such a school in connection with such enrollment or attendance of the beneficiary; and (3) the purchase of any computer technology or equipment or internet access and related services, if such technology, equipment, or services are to be used by the beneficiary and the beneficiary's family during any of the years the beneficiary is in school. The Tax Cuts and Jobs Act of 2017 broadened the definition of qualified education expenses for 529 plans to include up to $10,000 per year of K-12 tuition. This has made Coverdell ESA less important but they would still be available for clients who wished to withdraw more than $10,000 per year for K-12 expenses costs other than tuition.

Traditional IRA

Generally speaking, if a taxpayer withdraws funds from his traditional IRA before age 59½, the taxpayer is required to pay a 10% early withdrawal penalty on all or part of the amount withdrawn. However, the 10% penalty does not apply if a taxpayer withdraws funds from a traditional IRA to pay for qualified higher education expenses for the taxpayer, the taxpayer's spouse, or the child or grandchild of the taxpayer or taxpayer's spouse. Unlike a Coverdell, the taxpayer will owe federal income tax on the amount withdrawn.

Roth IRA

Roth IRA

An IRA created by the Taxpayer Relief Act of 1997; contributions to a Roth IRA are nondeductible; qualified distributions are excluded from an individual's taxable income; distributions used for qualified educational expenses can also avoid the 10% penalty

The **Roth IRA** does not provide tax deductions for contributions. However, contributions grow tax-free within the Roth IRA. Contributions are limited to $6,000 in 2020, plus an additional $1,000 for taxpayers who are age 50 or older. Contributions can be made as late as the due date of the individual's tax return for the previous tax year. Since 2020, contributions to all IRAs (both traditional and Roth IRAs) can be at any age as long as there is earned income. Even older people age 72 and beyond can contribute to an IRA if they or their spouse have earned income. This has always been true for Roth IRAs. The SECURE Act changed the law to allow contributions to traditional IRAs for people at any age. Contributions to Roth IRAs are phased out for joint filers with adjusted gross income between $196,000–$206,000 for 2020, and for single taxpayers with adjusted gross income between $124,000–$139,000 for 2020. The range for taxpayers who are married but file separately is $0–$10,000.

A distribution from a Roth IRA is not includable in the owner's gross income if it is a qualified distribution, or to the extent that it is a return of the owner's contributions to the Roth IRA. Qualified distributions are distributions that occur after a five-year holding period and for one of the following four reasons:

- Death
- Disability
- Attainment of age 59½
- First-time home purchase (limit of $10,000)

If a distribution is not a qualified distribution and it exceeds contribution (and conversions) to Roth IRAs, the distribution will be subject to income tax and may be subject to the 10% penalty. However, these excess distributions can avoid the 10% penalty if the proceeds are used for qualified higher education costs. Qualified higher education expenses are tuition, fees, and room and board. The taxpayer is always able to withdraw amounts up to his total contribution without income tax or penalty.

In short, Roth IRAs may be an even more attractive vehicle for education savings than Coverdell ESAs because the age of the student is irrelevant (vs. the 30-year-old limit) and because contribution limits are higher. In addition, funds in a Roth IRA not used for education can be used for retirement. On the other hand, distributions from a Roth IRA will raise the EFC in the future. This effect takes place after a two-academic-year delay. Thus,

Roth IRA distributions could be used to pay for the last two years of schooling and other assets, especially assets in the child's name, could be used for the first years.

The American Opportunity Tax Credit

American Opportunity Tax Credit

A tax credit available for qualified tuition, enrollment fees, books, and course materials for the first four years of post-secondary education for the taxpayer, spouse, or dependent

The **American Opportunity Tax Credit** is equal to 100% of the first $2,000 in qualified education expenses and 25% of the next $2,000, for a total of $2,500. Students are eligible during their first four years of college. In addition, books and course materials are eligible for the credit. In order to qualify for the full credit, modified adjusted gross income is limited to $80,000 for single taxpayers and $160,000 for joint filers. The American Opportunity Tax Credit is not available to married taxpayers who file separate returns. Up to 40% of the credit is refundable.

Modified AGI Phaseout for the American Opportunity Tax Credit

	2020
Married filing jointly	$160,000–$180,000
All other taxpayers	$80,000–$90,000

The Lifetime Learning Credit

Lifetime Learning Credit

A tax credit available to pay for tuition and enrollment fees for undergraduate or graduate degree programs

The **Lifetime Learning Credit** is available for tuition and enrollment fees for undergraduate or graduate degree programs or courses that help students acquire or improve job skills. The lifetime learning credit provides a tax credit for qualified college tuition and fees per family of $2,000 per year. The taxpayer must spend $10,000 annually on qualified expenses to qualify for the full credit. This credit is based on a 20% factor of the qualified expenses.

The Lifetime Learning Credit can be claimed for an unlimited number of years. If two or more children in the same household incur qualified expenses in the same year, the parents may claim a Lifetime Learning Credit or an American Opportunity Tax Credit for both children, or a Lifetime Learning Credit for one child and an American Opportunity Tax Credit for the other. However, only one credit is allowed per child per year. Also note that the maximum credit of $2,000 applies to the family, not per student as with the American Opportunity Tax Credit. For 2020, this credit is phased out when modified adjusted gross income (AGI) is between $59,000 and $69,000 for single taxpayers ($118,000–$138,000 for joint returns). No credit can be claimed if modified AGI is above $69,000 for single taxpayers or more than $138,000 for joint filers.

Taxpayers may claim an American Opportunity Tax Credit or Lifetime Learning Credit for a taxable year and exclude from gross income amounts distributed from a Coverdell ESA or QTP on behalf of the same student as long as the distribution is not used for the same expenses for which a credit was claimed.

Series EE United States Savings Bonds (EE Bonds)

If used to pay for qualified higher education expenses at an eligible institution or state tuition plan, EE bonds bestow significant tax savings—that is, no federal income tax is due on the interest

Series EE Bonds

Another vehicle that may be used to save for college is **Series EE United States Savings Bonds (EE bonds)**. EE bonds are useful tools for college tuition. The electronic (paper bonds were discontinued as of January 1, 2012) EE bonds are sold at 100% of face value in any denomination from $25 to $10,000 and are eligible to earn interest for up to 30 years. Since May 2005, the interest rate applied to EE bonds is fixed for the life of the bond (with the rate for new issues adjusted semiannually).

If used to pay for qualified higher education expenses at an eligible institution or state tuition plan, EE bonds bestow significant tax savings—that is, no federal income tax is payable on the interest. This interest exclusion is subject to phaseout based on adjusted gross incomes greater than $82,350 for single taxpayers and $123,550 for married filing jointly taxpayers for 2020. To attain tax-free status, EE bonds must be purchased in the name of one or both parents of the student/child. The parent(s) must be the owners of the bond and at least 24 years old before the first day of the month of the issue date of the bond. Also, the owners must redeem the bonds in the same year that the student/child's qualified higher education expenses are paid. In addition, Series I bonds have the same tax benefits as EE bonds for purposes of qualified higher education costs.

Uniform Gift to Minors Act

Uniform Gift to Minors Act (UGMA)
Allows parents to put cash and securities in a custodial account for a child

The **Uniform Gift to Minors Act (UGMA)** allows parents to put cash and securities in a custodial account for a child. UGMA accounts give the child full ownership of the assets at the age of majority (age 18 or 21, depending on the state). If the child is under age 19, all income over $2,200 for 2020 earned by the assets is taxed at the parent's marginal federal income tax rates. If the child is 19 years or older, the income earned by the assets is taxed at the child's tax rate. In 2020, the kiddie tax rules apply to full-time students under age 24 at the end of the year who do not provide more than 50% of their own support. Notably, this is considered an asset of the child and is considered in determining financial aid. Therefore, the account can significantly reduce a student's eligibility for need-based financial aid.

Uniform Transfers to Minors Act

Uniform Transfers to Minors Act (UTMA)
Allows parents to put cash, securities, and real property in a custodial account for a child

The **Uniform Transfers to Minors Act (UTMA)** is similar to the Uniform Gift to Minors Act. It provides for the transfer of assets to a custodial account for the benefit of a minor. The tax treatment of the income earned on the assets is the same as for UGMA, and an UTMA account is considered an asset of the child for financial aid purposes. There are differences between the two acts. UTMA is more flexible than UGMA. Parents may transfer real property as well as cash and securities to an UTMA account. Because both UTMAs and UGMAs are considered the child's asset when determining financial aid, these accounts should usually be the first money spent to pay for qualified higher education expenses. This will help position the student for higher need-based aid in future years.

Interest on Education Loans

Up to $2,500 of interest paid on student loans for undergraduate and graduate education may be deducted as an adjustment to the taxpayer's AGI. The loaned funds must have been spent on tuition and enrollment fees, books, supplies, equipment, room and board, transportation, or other necessary expenses. For 2020, the amount of the student loan interest deduction is phased out for joint taxpayers with modified adjusted gross incomes (AGI) of between $140,000 and $170,000. There is no deduction if modified AGI is $170,000 or more. For single taxpayers, the loan interest deduction is phased out when modified AGI is between $70,000 and $85,000. No interest deduction can be taken if modified AGI is $85,000 or more.

Employer's Educational Assistance Program

Employer's Educational Assistance Program

Under this program, an employer can pay for an employee's undergraduate tuition, enrollment fees, books, supplies, and equipment while these employer benefits are excluded from the employee's income up to $5,250

Under the **Employer's Educational Assistance Program**, an employer can pay for an employee's tuition (both graduate and undergraduate), enrollment fees, books, supplies, and equipment while these employer benefits are excluded from the employee's income up to $5,250.

Taxpayers are not eligible to claim the deduction and an American Opportunity Tax Credit or Lifetime Learning Credit in the same year for the same student. A taxpayer may not claim a deduction for amounts taken into account in determining the amount excludable resulting from a distribution (i.e., the earnings and the contribution portion of a distribution) from a Coverdell or the amount of interest excludable with respect to education savings bonds.

Equity Lines of Credit

A home equity loan or line of credit is yet another vehicle that can be used to fund college-related expenses. Because home equity loans are secured by a house, the interest rate on a home equity loan may be lower than rates for an unsecured student loan. Many state schools do not consider the value of the home when determining eligibility for financial aid, but numerous private colleges take equity in the home into account. If equity in the home is considered in the financial aid equation, a home equity loan could decrease home equity and possibly improve one's eligibility for financial aid. Furthermore, the interest on home equity loans used for college costs was deductible from the taxpayer's AGI. This ended on December 31, 2017. As a general rule, using home equity loans and lines of credit to pay for higher education expenses should be a last resort, or at least done after researching all other options, rates, and conditions for alternative funding. Borrowing too much against the home could result in foreclosure or other difficult situations.

HIGHLIGHTS OF TAX BENEFITS FOR HIGHER EDUCATION

The following exhibit provides the highlights of the various tax benefits covered in this section.

EXHIBIT 7.4 Highlights of Tax Benefits for Higher Education for 2020

	American Opportunity Tax Credit	Lifetime Learning Credit	Coverdell Education Savings Account	Traditional and Roth IRAs	Student Loan Interest	Section 529 Plans (QTPs)	Education Savings Bond Program
What is your benefit?	Credits can reduce the amount of tax you must pay		Earnings are not taxed	No 10% additional tax on early withdrawal	Above the line (for AGI) deduction of interest	Earnings are not taxed	Interest is not taxed
What is the annual limit?	Up to $2,500 per student	Up to $2,000 per family	$2,000 contribution per beneficiary	Amount of qualifying expenses	$2,500	None	Amount of qualifying expenses
What expenses qualify besides tuition and required enrollment fees?	None		Books Supplies Equipment. Room and board if at least a half-time student. Payments to qualified tuition program including K-12	Books Supplies Equipment. Room and board if at least a half-time student	Books Supplies Equipment. Room and board. Transportation. Other necessary expenses	Books Supplies Equipment. Room and board if at least a half-time student. Up to $10,000 per year for K-12 tuition	Payments to Coverdell ESAs. Payments to qualified tuition programs
What education qualifies?	First 4 years of undergraduate	All undergraduate and graduate					
What are some of the other conditions that apply?	Must be enrolled at least half-time in a degree program.		Can also contribute to qualified tuition programs in the same year. Cannot contribute after 18th birthday of beneficiary. Must withdraw assets by age 30		Must have been at least half-time student in a degree program.	Distribution is excluded from gross income. American Opportunity Tax and Lifetime Learning Credits are permitted in the same year but not for the same expenses.	Applies only to qualified Series EE bonds issued after 1989 or Series I bonds
In what income range do benefits phase out?	MAGI. Single $80,000–$90,000. MFJ $160,000–$180,000	MAGI. Single $59,000–$69,000. MFJ $118,000–$138,000	MAGI. Single $95,000–$110,000. MFJ $190,000–$220,000	No phaseout[1]	MAGI. Single $70,000–$85,000. MFJ $140,000–$170,000	No phaseout	MAGI. Single $82,350–$97,350. MFJ $123,550–$153,550

[1] Phaseouts exist at time of contribution. They are not relevant for withdrawals.

EDUCATION FUNDING/SAVINGS REGIMEN EXAMPLE

Now that all sources of education funding have been discussed and the investment vehicles and tax benefits identified, the most pressing issue is how much the parent or family needs to save now to pay for the child's college education. Calculating the cost of a child's college education through a savings plan is always a helpful exercise.

There are numerous ways to calculate the funding necessary to pay for a child's college education. In the following example, Scott plans to pay for the college education of his daughter, Hannah. As a general rule, Scott should establish a savings schedule for Hannah's college fund. This savings schedule can be created using the time value of money concepts discussed in Chapter 6.

The type of information needed to conduct this analysis includes the age of the child, the age the child will attend college, the parents' after-tax annual earnings rate, the current cost of tuition, related costs and books, and the tuition inflation rate. Scott is willing to fund Hannah's room and board either out of his own pocket when those expenses are incurred or by Hannah working to pay them.

Hannah is one day old, and Scott anticipates that Hannah will be 18 years old when she begins college. Scott expects to earn an after-tax annual rate of return over the 18-year period of 11%. The current cost of tuition, tuition-related expenses, and books and equipment at Hannah's projected category of schools is $25,000 per year. The rate of increase of tuition and tuition-related expenses is assumed to be 6%. The CPI inflation rate for this 18-year period is assumed to be 4%, which is less than the rate of increase of tuition. Therefore, to be conservative, the higher rate of 6% for tuition increases will be used instead of the CPI inflation rate. Other assumptions and necessary data for this exercise are as follows.

- Scott's annual investment, or savings payments, will commence at the end of each year from now until the day Hannah starts college (expected to be in 18 years).

- Scott will stop making savings payments once Hannah starts college so that he can pay for Hannah's monthly room and board expenses.

- Scholarship money and financial aid will not be considered in these calculations.

- Scott will postpone his decision whether to place any burden of education-related expenses on Hannah while she is in school (i.e., work or loans) until a later date.

- Scott desires to fund all college education expenses without having to borrow any funds.

This problem can be viewed in terms of a timeline (below) from year zero until year 21.

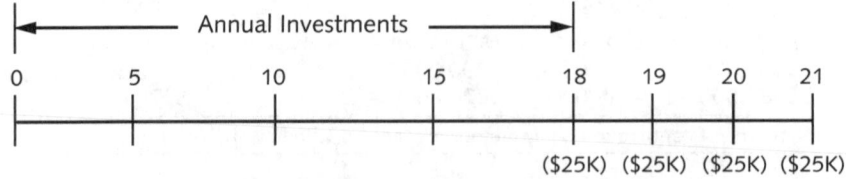

Using what is referred to as the uneven cash flow method, there are two series of cash flows that are important: 1) the cash flows invested annually into the account by Scott over an 18-year span and 2) the four annual payments out of the account starting at the beginning of year 18 and continuing through year 21 for Hannah's college education.

Step 1 Determine the Cost of College Tuition for the Four-Year Period, in Today's Dollars

The first step in this calculation is to determine the present value of the four consecutive annual payments of tuition in years 18 through 21 as of period zero, which is the present day. Using a financial calculator, enter a cash flow of zero for 18 years and a cash flow of $25,000 for the next four years. Then, discount these cash flows to the present day by an adjusted, assumed interest rate of 4.72%. The interest rate of 11% is adjusted for the annual increase in tuition of 6% as follows:

$$\left(\frac{1+ \text{assumed interest rate}}{1+ \text{assumed tuition increase rate}} -1 \right) \times 100 = \text{adjusted assumed annual rate}$$

Formula calculation pertaining to Scott and Hannah's circumstances:

Scott's annual interest rate: $1 + 0.11 = 1.11$

Scott's assumed tuition inflation rate: $1 + 0.06 = 1.06$

$$[(1.11 \div 1.06) -1] \times 100 = 4.72\%$$

Earnings from the interest per year are thus assumed in the calculation to be 4.72%. The net present value (NPV) of the four cash flows of $25,000 (today's dollars) at the beginning of years 18 through 21 equals $40,760.80.

This calculation is illustrated step by step on the following chart, using an HP 10bII+ calculator:

Keystroke	Display
[■][C ALL]	0.0000
0 [CFj]	0.0000
0 [CFj]	0.0000
17[■][Nj]	17.0000
25000[CFj]	25,0000.0000
4[■][Nj]	4.0000
[(1.11 [÷] 1.06) [–] 1] [x] 100 [=] 4.7170 [I/YR]	4.7170
[■][NPV]	40,760.8043

Step 2 Determine the Annual Payments Needed to Fund College Tuition Costs

The next step is to determine the annual payments from year zero through the end of year 17 that are needed to fund the outgoing cash flows for tuition at the beginning of years 18 through 21. Using a financial calculator, the required annual investment or payment is $5,292.50. This calculation is broken down step by step on the following chart, using an HP 10bII+ calculator in END mode:

Keystroke	Display
40,760.80 [PV]	40,760.8043
18 [N]	18.0000
11 [I/YR]	11.0000
0 [FV]	0.0000
[PMT]	5,292.4998

Therefore, Scott must save $5,292.50 per year, at the end of each year, beginning one year from now, the start of year zero, and continuing until the end of year 17 (a total of 18 payments) so that when Hannah attends college at the start of year 18, Scott can pay for her college education.

INVESTMENT STRATEGIES TO ACCOMPLISH EDUCATION GOALS

Financial planners should keep in mind that the investment strategies employed by the family should rely heavily on the amount of time until the child will be enrolled in school. In other words, the time horizon is probably the most important factor (besides risk tolerance) to consider in deciding what securities to invest in, how much to invest, and when to invest. The more time before the child enrolls in school, the more options and time for accumulation of principal and growth for a savings regimen will be available for the parents or family.

Using the education funding example above, if Scott wants to completely pay for his one-day-old daughter Hannah's college tuition, he has a time horizon of 18 years to invest enough money to fund four years of tuition. The funds Scott invests will have numerous years to grow and accumulate, and Scott's risk tolerance for investments will be higher than those parents who start to save for their children's college expenses years after they are born. Scott could invest in more growth- and equity-oriented funds with higher potential rates of return.

Compare Scott's situation to that of Katie, a parent with a 10-year-old daughter named April. Katie will have only eight years to save and invest money to pay for four years of college for April. Katie does not have the luxury of time. Furthermore, Katie cannot tolerate as much risk as Scott because there is less time to recover from a bear market. Therefore, Katie would probably invest substantially more conservatively than Scott.

As discussed earlier in this chapter, QTPs follow this investment principle. QTPs generally require a decrease in risk levels of investments the closer the child gets to the targeted year to begin college. This method is referred to as age-banding. Various QTP managers will generally comply with the sequence illustrated in the exhibit below.

EXHIBIT 7.5 Age-Banding Example

Student's age	Stocks	Bonds	Money market/cash
0–13	70–100%	0–30%	0
14–17	25–40%	35–50%	10–40%
18+	0–10%	20–30%	60–80%

Depending on the specifics of a state's QTP legislation, which varies from one state to another, managers of QTPs must comply with this decrease (or a similar decrease) in the percentage of investment in growth and equity funds because, as the child ages, the risk of losing principal and interest is too great considering that the prospect of attending college hangs in the balance.

Finally, after completing the analysis and a savings plan has been developed and saving has begun, the contributor must monitor and reassess the plan on a consistent, periodic basis (at least annually). This review process is necessary because the parents' financial situation may change or the goals may be changed. If a family experiences a significant increase in income or finances, an increase in the savings amount may be made in order to alleviate the risks of the assumptions made in the analysis, or to broaden the potential colleges and universities the child may consider. If a family experiences a decrease in income or finances, it may be more realistic to lower the expectations or assumptions in the analysis or determine whether the family would qualify for financial aid or assistance, such as a Pell Grant.

Other assumptions may also change over time. For instance, in our earlier example, Scott's daughter, Hannah, may prove to be an extraordinary student or athlete, and the increased likelihood of her receiving a scholarship could be factored into Scott's plan.

In conclusion, the education funding savings plan should be developed and implemented as early as possible to take advantage of time-horizon principles. Once the plan is in place, the plan should be monitored and updated because numerous assumptions and unknowns enter into the analysis. The amount necessary to fund college must be identified, but the family can attempt to minimize the contributions it must make through identifying the issues addressed previously, setting goals, gathering the necessary information regarding financial aid, school loans, scholarships and other assistance, maximizing tax benefits, choosing the best investment vehicles for themselves, and making choices that are best suited to the family's needs, expectations, and desires.

WHERE ON THE WEB

College Board (a not-for-profit education association that created and controls the SAT and PSAT/NMSQT Examinations) **www.collegeboard.org**

College Savings Plans Network (the official website for State 529 plans/QTPs; affiliated with the National Association of State Treasuries; provides links on the internet to individual state plans) **www.collegesavings.org**

Education Commission of the States **www.ecs.org**

Federal Student Aid—Information for Financial Aid Professionals **ifap.ed.gov**

National Association for College Admission Counseling **www.nacacnet.org**

National Association of Student Financial Aid Administrators **www.nasfaa.org**

The SmartStudent™ Guide to Financial Aid (discusses financial aid eligibility and calculations; student loan analysis; scholarship availability) **www.finaid.org**

Information on college savings, calculators, 529 plan rankings, financial aid, scholarships, and other ways to save and pay for college **www.savingforcollege.com**

DISCUSSION QUESTIONS

1. What are the issues and goals of education funding?

2. What education funding information should students and parents collect?

3. How is financial need determined?

4. What is a Federal Pell Grant?

5. What are Stafford Loans?

6. What is the difference between a subsidized student loan and an unsubsidized student loan?

7. What are PLUS Loans?

8. What is a Consolidation Loan?

9. What campus-based student financial aid is available?

10. What are the tax advantages and issues with respect to education expenses?

11. What are the benefits of Qualified Tuition Plans, and how are they taxed?

12. What are Prepaid Tuition Plans, and how do they work?

13. How do contributions to QTPs affect gift taxes?

14. What is a Coverdell Education Savings Account?

15. How can a Roth IRA be used for education funding?

16. What is the maximum credit permitted with the American Opportunity Tax Credit?

17. What are the eligibility requirements to use a lifetime learning credit?

18. What are Series EE bonds?

19. What is the Uniform Gift to Minors Act?

20. What is the Employer's Educational Assistance Program?

EXERCISES

1. Compare and contrast grants, scholarships, and fellowships.

2. Compare and contrast subsidized and unsubsidized Stafford Loans.

3. Shawna, age 18, recently graduated from high school with a 3.6 GPA. Shawna currently lives at home and works part-time as an office assistant. She has been accepted to Texas State University. Her parents cannot afford to assist her with expenses. She wants to obtain a college education but is having trouble affording tuition and other college expenses. What financial aid programs would you recommend to Shawna and why?

4. Karen, age 20, is in her second year at the University of California. She will not be able to hold down a part-time job and complete her bachelor's degree program in four years. She will receive approximately $30,000 from a trust fund left to her by her grandmother on her 22nd birthday. What federal aid programs are available to Karen? Would you recommend that Karen borrow against the trust fund in order to support herself during the next two years? Why or why not?

5. Gordon and Rhonda want to start saving now for their two-year-old daughter's college education. Tuition and fees at a four-year public university are currently $25,000 per year, and tuition has increased approximately 7% each year. How much should Gordon and Rhonda expect to pay for college when their daughter turns 18? (Calculate the expected cost for each age and add them.)

6. Christian and Emily have two children, Bethany, age 5, and Taylor, age 7. Christian's parents would like to pay for Bethany and Taylor's college education. They are considering gifting the money to Bethany and Taylor by setting up savings accounts for them. Would you recommend this approach? Why or why not? If not, whom should the grandparents pass the money to and why?

7. Brandon and Myra are married and have an adjusted gross income of $55,000. They have two children, Beth, age 18, and Brett, age 20. Both Beth and Brett are full-time students attending the local university. Are Brandon and Myra eligible to take advantage of any education tax credits? If so, which ones, and what is the maximum credit they are allowed?

8. Leslie is in her third year of college and has received subsidized Stafford Loans to help her pay for college. She does not have to borrow any more money before she receives her degree. She wants to immediately start paying off her student loans. Given the choices for repaying student loans, what would you recommend to Leslie?

9. Brad was recently awarded financial aid through his university. Although the aid helped, he still needs more financial aid than the school offered. What would you recommend to Brad to help him pay for college?

10. Tyra plans to attend the local university next year. Her parents make too much money to qualify for federal aid programs, but Tyra still needs assistance. What financial aid, if any, is available for Tyra?

11. Julie's parents would like to assist her with the cost of college tuition. Tuition and fees are estimated at $13,000 per school year. Julie's parents apply and qualify for a PLUS Loan. How much can they borrow?

12. John and Sue, both age 30, have a child born today. They plan to save the maximum amount in their respective IRAs until their child goes to college in 18 years. Would you recommend a Roth IRA or a Coverdell ESA? Explain.

13. David intends to open a QTP Savings Plan for his daughter but wants to know whether he can direct the specific investments himself. Can David direct where and how much of the contributions are invested? Can David direct how much of the funds are used to purchase stock or bonds? Explain.

14. In the prior exercise, David was interested in placing a percentage of the QTP funds into stocks and a percentage into bonds. What is this principle called? Also, provide an example as to how it is used.

15. Robby plans to attend college but cannot afford tuition. He decides to apply for federal financial aid. Generally, how will Robby's financial aid eligibility be calculated?

16. Bob established a QTP College Savings Plan for his son Ricky at age 5. When Ricky turned 18, Ricky decided not to attend college and began working as a bartender in the Bahamas. Can Ricky withdraw funds from the QTP account, which has a value of $100,000? What can Bob do (if anything) with the account?

17. Claire established a QTP College Savings Plan for Matt, her son. While Matt was attending college, he asked Claire for money to buy a ski boat. Claire agreed, withdrew $10,000 from the QTP account, and purchased the boat for Matt in his name. Will this $10,000 withdrawal and payment be taxed, and if so, whose tax rate will be used? Would it be important to know what portion of the $10,000 represents contributions and what portion represents earnings from interest? Explain.

18. Let's take Exercise 17 one step further. Would there be any penalty assessed on the $10,000 withdrawal? Would it be important to know what portion of the $10,000 is contributed and what portion is interest?

19. What if, in Exercise 17, Matt had received a full scholarship for his remaining years in college, the semester before Claire gave him $10,000 for the boat?

PROBLEMS

1. Rena and Hunter Alesio have two children, ages 5 and 7. The Alesios want to start saving for their children's education. Each child will spend 6 years at college and will begin at age 18. College currently costs $20,000 per year and is expected to increase at 6% per year. Assuming the Alesios can earn an annual compound return of 12% and inflation is 4%, how much must the Alesios deposit at the end of each year to pay for their children's educational requirements until the younger child is out of school? Assume that education expenses are withdrawn at the beginning of each year and that the last deposit will be made at the beginning of the last year of the younger child.

2. Chelsea was recently divorced and has two children. The divorce decree requires that she pay 1/3 of the college tuition cost for her children. Tuition cost is currently $15,000 per year and has been increasing at 7% per year. Her son and daughter are 12 and 16, respectively, and will attend college for four years beginning at age 18. Assume that her after-tax rate of return will be 9% and that general inflation has been 4%. How much should she save each month, beginning today for the next 5 years, to finance both children's education?

3. Ken and Amy Charvet have two children, ages 4 and 6. The Charvets want to start saving for their children's education. Each child will spend 5 years in college and will begin at age 18. College currently costs $30,000 per year and is expected to increase at 7% per year. Assuming the Charvets can earn an annual compound investment return of 12% and inflation is 4%, how much must the Charvets deposit at the end of each year to pay for their children's educational requirements until the younger child goes to school? Assume that education expenses are withdrawn at the beginning of each year and that the last deposit will be made at the beginning of the first year of the younger child.

4. Barry and Virginia have a 5-year-old son, Daniel. They have plans for Daniel to attend a 4-year private university at age 18. Currently, tuition at the local private university is $15,000 per year and is expected to increase at 7% per year. Assuming Barry and Virginia can earn an annual compound return of 10% and inflation is 4%, how much do Barry and Virginia need to start saving per year, starting today, to be able to pay for Daniel's college education? Assume their last payment is made at the beginning of Daniel's first year in college.

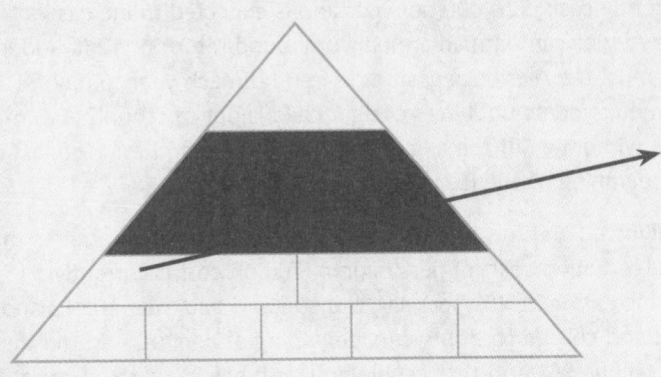

- Risk
- Perils and hazards
- Adverse selection
- Insurable losses
- Law of insurance contracts
- Insurance policy features
- Selecting an insurance company
- Risk management process

- Measuring needs related to premature death
- Characteristics of life, health and disability policies
- Annuities
- Long-term care insurance

- Automobile insurance
- Homeowners insurance
- Liability insurance
- Property insurance
- Business insurance

- Social Security insurance and benefits
- Taxation of Social Security benefits
- Medicare benefits

3 | Insurance Planning

CHAPTERS

Risks	Goals
■ Untimely death	■ Appropriate insurance coverage and reasonable premiums for the risks identified to person, property, and/ or liabilities of the client.
■ Disability	
■ Unemployment	
■ Medical illness	
■ Long-term health care	
■ Damage to property	
■ Tort liability	

Data Collection	Data Analysis
■ Life insurance policies	■ Life insurance policy analysis
■ Disability policies	■ Health insurance policy analysis
■ Employer benefit summaries	■ Disability insurance policy analysis
■ Health plan policies	
■ Long-term care policies	■ Homeowners policy analysis
■ Automobile policies	■ Automobile insurance analysis
■ Homeowners policies, riders, etc.	■ Liability insurance analysis
■ Personal liability umbrella policies	■ Business insurance analysis
■ Business policies	

An Introduction to Insurance and Risk Management

LEARNING OBJECTIVES

After learning the material in this chapter, you will be able to do the following:

■ Define risk and the different types of risk, and understand how risk impacts the personal financial planning process

■ Understand the insurable loss exposures faced by the typical client

■ Understand the responses to pure risk and how they can be incorporated into a risk management plan

■ Define insurance and understand how it is used as a risk management tool

■ Distinguish between a peril and a hazard and understand how each relates to the need for insurance

- Define adverse selection and explain its impact on insurance

- Summarize the requisites for an insurable risk and understand what distinguishes insurance from gambling

- Explain the elements of a valid contract and identify the distinguishing features of an insurance contract

- Understand the reason for, and the effect of, various contractual features in an insurance contract

- Know the different types of authority given to agents to act on behalf of an insurance company

- Understand the methods of loss valuation

- Know the insurance company rating agencies and how they evaluate the financial condition of insurers

- Define risk management and explain the steps in the risk management process

INTRODUCTION

Proper insurance coverage is essential to a client's financial plan. Most people do not have the right types and amounts of insurance coverage. Financial planners must have a basic understanding of risk and insurance in order to properly assist their clients in evaluating their current insurance coverage and to determine their future insurance needs. For most clients, basic insurance needs can be covered with life insurance, health insurance, disability insurance, homeowners or renters insurance, long-term care insurance, automobile insurance, and personal liability insurance. This section of the text is designed as an introduction to the various types of insurance. Chapter 8 discusses risk, the legal foundation of insurance, and the transfer of risk using insurance contracts. Chapter 9 identifies risks to the individual, namely premature death, catastrophic illness, disability, and the need for long-term care. Chapter 10 identifies the risks associated with property and liability exposures. Chapter 11 covers the types and availability of social insurance.

UNDERSTANDING RISK

Risk
The chance of loss, possibility of loss, uncertainty, or a variation of actual from expected results

Risk is the chance of loss, possibility of loss, uncertainty, or a variation of actual from expected results. An insured homeowner knows that one will not likely experience a house fire, but the possibility of fire exists, and the consequences could be financially devastating. Thus, the homeowner transfers the risk of fire to an insurance company by paying an insurer a premium to cover the risk.

RISK CLASSIFICATION

Pure vs. Speculative Risk

Pure risk
A risk in which the results are either a loss or no loss

Speculative risk
A risk with three possible outcomes: profit, loss, or no loss

A **pure risk** is one in which the results are either loss or no loss (e.g, death). While death is a certainty, there is still risk in determining when each person will die. A **speculative risk**, on the other hand, is one where there is potential for profit as well as loss or no loss. Entrepreneurs regularly encounter speculative risk when they begin a new business or sell a new product. Speculative risks are generally undertaken voluntarily and are not insurable.

Consider the risks associated with the purchase of a home. A speculative risk is the potential fluctuation in the value of the house after purchase. The market value of the home could remain the same as the original purchase price, increase, or decline. Also, a variety of pure risks are associated with home ownership, such as the risk of a fire, flood, or theft of property. If a theft occurs, the insured will suffer a loss; however, the condition of the house remains the same. To summarize, a pure risk has two possible outcomes—loss or no loss—while a speculative risk has three: profit, loss, or no loss. Therefore, only pure risks are commercially insurable.

Dynamic vs. Static Risk

Dynamic risk
A risk that results from changes in society or the economy (e.g., inflation)

Static risk
A risk dependent on factors other than a change in society or the economy (e.g., natural disaster)

Risks that can be classified in terms of whether they are affected by society or the economy are called **dynamic risks**. For example, changes in technology can make a company's product obsolete, leading to great financial loss. Dynamic losses are difficult to predict; therefore, insurance companies are not inclined to assume this type of risk.

Static risks, on the other hand, involve losses that would occur regardless of changes in society or the economy (e.g., death of a family's breadwinner). Losses that result from static risks tend to occur with regularity and are generally predictable. For this reason, insurance companies are generally willing to accept these types of risks.

Subjective vs. Objective Risk

Subjective risk
A person's unique perception of risk; varies greatly from individual to individual

Objective risk
The relative variation of an actual loss to an expected loss

Subjective risk is a person's perception of risk and varies greatly among individuals. Consider two people, each having slept only two hours in the last two days, who need to drive home from work late at night. The first person drinks coffee habitually and considers an hour's drive no problem, thus reflecting a low level of subjective risk. The second person does not drink coffee and is tired. One should either not drive home or drive carefully because one has fallen asleep behind the wheel before under similar circumstances. The second person's perception is an example of high subjective risk. A perception of low subjective risk may result in less than prudent conduct, whereas a perception of high subjective risk is more likely to result in prudent conduct.

Objective risk does not depend on a particular person's perception, but rather, the relative variation of an actual loss to an expected loss.

For example, suppose an auto insurer has 1,000 new cars insured each year. On average, 100 cars, or 10% of the car owners, file collision claims each year. If in the first year, 110 car owners file claims, and the next year only 90 filed claims, there is a 10-car variation each year, equaling a 10% objective risk. Objective risk varies *inversely* with the number of exposures involved. As the number of exposures increases, the insurance company can more accurately predict future loss experience based on the law of large numbers (to be discussed later in the chapter).

Particular vs. Fundamental Risk

Particular risk
Personal risk that involves a possible loss for an individual or a small group

Fundamental risk
An impersonal risk that involves a possible loss for a large group

Risks can also be classified in terms of how large a population they affect. **Particular risks** are personal and involve a potential loss to an individual or a small group of individuals rather than a large segment of the population. Theft of a family's personal property is an example of particular risk. **Fundamental risks**, on the other hand, are impersonal and involve a potential loss for a large group. For example, the possibility of rising waters during a hurricane is a fundamental risk.

Financial vs. Nonfinancial Risk

Financial risk
A risk that involves a monetary loss

Nonfinancial risk
A risk that involves a non-monetary loss

Whether a risk involves financial loss is another means of classification. **Financial risks** involve monetary losses. The possibility that a family may be faced with a significant loss of income in the event of an income producer's disability is an example of a financial risk. **Nonfinancial risk** may also be associated with a breadwinner's disability, such as pain and suffering. Generally, insurance is intended for financial losses, although some liability policies will compensate for nonfinancial losses that give rise to legal liability. For example, pain and suffering caused by the insured is covered by a liability policy if it gives rise to liability for monetary damages.

Probability of Loss

Actuary
A person who manages and measures risk

Insurance companies employ highly skilled professionals, known as actuaries, who are experts in the fields of mathematics, statistics, and probability theory. The **actuary**, or team of actuaries, is typically responsible for predicting the losses for various risk pools, calculating required reserves, and producing premium rates that will cover losses while producing a profit for the insurer. The actuary must strike a delicate balance in pricing risks because the insurer's products must compete favorably in a highly competitive market. In addition, both the market and regulatory authorities demand that the insurer remain in a position of financial strength.

For an actuary to estimate how many losses will occur in a given year, one must know the chance of loss for members of a given risk pool. The chance of loss is more commonly referred to as the probability of loss and measures the long-term frequency in which an event occurs.

For example, if 700 out of 100,000 homes suffer a fire each year, the probability of a fire can be calculated as 700 ÷ 100,000, or 0.007. For each individual member of the pool, the probability of loss is a moot point. Whether the probability is 7 in 1,000 or 7 in 100, the insured's concern is that it could be one's home that burns and that such a loss would be financially devastating. Probability analysis provides useful information for the insurer, however, because it allows the insurer to determine the number of insureds who will suffer losses and, therefore, to estimate the aggregate claims. The expected total cost of claims can then be evenly distributed among the members of the pool in the form of policy premiums.

Note that probability represents the long-term chance. This implies that numerous events must occur before the probability can be calculated with reasonable accuracy. To illustrate, consider how one might determine the probability of a tossed coin landing on heads. The probability is .5 (or a 50% chance), but suppose one does not know this chance. To discover the probability of tossing a head, assume the coin is tossed 10 times. With many iterations of the same test, some will obtain 5 out of 10 heads, but others will not. One may erroneously conclude that the probability is .7 (7 out of 10) when 7 heads turn up. In order to calculate the true probability, one must toss the coin several thousand times, recording each of the results. Perhaps there were 5,021 heads, resulting in a better estimate of the true probability (5,021 ÷ 10,000 = 0.5021) than tossing the coin just 10 times.

How does probability relate to objective risk? Objective risk is the chance that predictions about losses will be wrong given certain probabilities. The more reliable the probability figures are, the more accurate the predictions will be, and thus a lower objective risk will be the result.

Law of Large Numbers

Law of large numbers
The chance that predicted results will reflect true results increases as the number of exposures increases

Probability figures must be determined over time. The previous coin toss example illustrates that the more times one repeats an experiment, the more likely the true probability will be revealed. Therefore, the larger the number of exposure units, the more likely the predictions will be accurate. A related conclusion is that the **law of large numbers** helps reduce objective risk, which depends on the variation in, or uncertainty of, possible outcomes.

For example, consider the risk faced by an insurer that has 1,000 insureds in a life insurance pool versus that of an insurer with 100,000 insureds. If the probability of death is 5 in 1,000, or .005, the insurer with the smaller pool estimates that 5 people in the pool will die this year. The larger insurer estimates that 500 people will die. Suppose 5 additional people in each pool die. For the smaller insurer, the extra deaths result in a 100% increase in claims beyond what was originally predicted. For the larger insurer, however, the 5 additional deaths result in an increase of only 1%. Because there are more observations in the larger pool, the variation in possible outcomes declines, which reduces the insurer's objective risk.

RESPONSES TO PURE RISK

Individuals and businesses may respond to pure risk exposures in one or more of the following ways:

- Risk avoidance
- Risk reduction
- Risk retention
- Risk transfer

Risk Avoidance

Risk avoidance
The avoidance of any chance of loss

Risk avoidance is simply the avoidance of any chance of loss. If the probability of loss becomes zero, there is no risk of future losses. How does one eliminate the possibility of dying in an airplane crash? Avoid air travel.

Avoidance works for some, but not all possible, loss exposures. If one risk is avoided, another risk may likely appear in its place. For example, the person who wishes to avoid dying in a plane crash can certainly avoid flying, but then how does one get from one place to another? Perhaps using a car, but many people would also prefer to avoid dying in an automobile accident. So, those persons would have to walk, which in turn involves its own inherent risks.

Certain risks can be avoided; however, some risks are potentially frequent and severe and some people will simply avoid all chance of the risks occurring. For example, some doctors have left private practice because of the fear of medical malpractice suits. They find other ways to earn a living (e.g., teaching or research), thus avoiding the risk of a malpractice suit completely.

Risk Reduction

Risk reduction involves taking measures that reduce the frequency or severity of losses. A person who cannot avoid driving faces the risk of an auto accident but has several risk reduction devices at one's disposal. Taking a defensive driving class and practicing defensive driving techniques are means of reducing the probability of being involved in an accident. In much the same way, wearing a seatbelt reduces the possibility that one will sustain injuries in an automobile accident.

Risk reduction measures are undertaken only when the costs are feasible. To minimize the severity of injuries sustained in a car accident, one might decide to purchase the safest automobile on the market; however, if that automobile costs $50,000, it may be cost prohibitive.

Certain risk reduction techniques that reduce the severity of losses, such as seat belts, may give some drivers a false sense of security. These drivers may more readily exhibit risky behaviors, such as speeding, which increases the probability of loss from an accident and, thus, mitigates the reduction of risk gained by wearing a seatbelt.

Risk Retention

When a person or firm is exposed to risk and decides to bear all or part of the financial burden if a loss occurs, this is known as **risk retention**, and may occur in one of two forms, active or passive.

Active risk retention means that one is fully aware of the chance for loss and consciously plans to retain all or part of the risk. The person who has a $100,000 home may choose to retain the first $500 of any loss through a deductible, whereas the person with a $1,500 automobile may choose to retain the whole risk of automobile damage by not carrying comprehensive and collision coverage because the severity of loss is low.

Passive risk retention is being unaware of a risk but taking no steps to manage it properly. When another risk management method is not chosen, retention is selected by default.

Risk Transfer

Risk transfer involves shifting the probability of loss to another party, such as an insurance company. The purchase of insurance is often an economical method of transferring a pure risk. Three other techniques for handling risk transference include contracts, hedging, and incorporation. **Contractual agreements** may include guarantees at the time of sale, often known as warranties. **Hedging** is a means of trying to match profit on one transaction to the expected loss of another. In stock market transactions, a speculator can hedge unfavorable price fluctuations by buying and/or selling option contracts. **Incorporation** results in limited liability for businessowners. When a business is operated as a sole proprietorship or a partnership, liability is unlimited for the owner(s); however, if a business is incorporated, stockholder liability is limited and the risk of insufficient funds or assets to meet the demands of business expenses rests with the corporation or is shifted to creditors.

Risk reduction
Taking measures that reduce the frequency or severity of losses

Risk retention
Bearing all or part of the financial burden in the event of a loss

Active risk retention
One is fully aware of the chance for loss and consciously plans to retain all or part of the risk

Passive risk retention
Being unaware of a risk, but taking no steps to manage it properly

Risk transfer
Shifting the probability of loss to another party, such as an insurance company

Contractual agreements
Often include guarantees at the time of sale; often known as warranties

Hedging
A means of trying to match profit on one transaction to the expected loss of another

Incorporation
Results in limited liability for businessowners

INSURANCE AS A RISK MANAGEMENT TOOL

Individuals and businesses can obtain protection against certain risks of financial loss through the use of insurance. While there are many ways to suffer a financial loss, insurance is designed to deal specifically with the financial consequences of pure risks. As you will recall, pure risk involves situations in which there is only the possibility of loss or no loss. The possibility of loss when owning property is an example of pure risk. A homeowner is confronted with the possibility that something may damage the home and the potential consequences are loss or no loss.

Insurance is a mechanism through which risk is transferred to an insurer, evidenced by a promise to pay, in exchange for an equitable premium. The insurer agrees to indemnify the losses incurred by the insured, to pay other financial benefits, or to provide services related to the risk. By combining a large number (pool) of similar (homogenous) exposure units (risks), the overall losses of the pool can be predicted due to the law of large numbers. The result is that the potential losses of each member (unit) are shared with the other members of the pool in the form of policy premiums. In the same manner as the overall losses of the group, premiums can be estimated only because of the law of large numbers. Insurance is, therefore, a unique device capable of transferring a large amount of individual risk at a disproportionately reduced cost.

Insurance

A mechanism through which risk is transferred to an insurer, evidenced by a promise to pay, in exchange for an equitable premium

Transfer of Losses

Insurance transfers the risk of loss to the insurer who is a financial intermediary that specializes in assuming risk. The insured pays the insurer a premium and the insurer agrees that if certain events (losses) occur, compensation will be provided to the insured to pay for the consequences of the insured's losses. In exchange, the insurer provides the insured with a legally binding contract, called the insurance policy, that defines covered losses, how those losses will be valued, and what duties are owed by each party to the contract. Almost any risk can be transferred for the right price. Of course, the greater the chance that a loss will occur, the higher the insurance premium and the lower the likelihood that an insurance company will agree to insure the potential loss.

Sharing Losses With Others

Cooperation and sharing are essential to the insurance process. Insureds facing similar risks of loss are pooled together. The insurer mathematically predicts the expected losses for the entire pool, divides the cost of those losses among each insured, and adds a charge for the insurer's operating expenses and profit margin.

Each insured contributes a fair share of money to the pool. Those who pose a greater amount of risk contribute more to the pool. Actuarial science allows insurance companies to estimate losses and, thus, to calculate premiums for each person in the pool.

For example, assume First Mutual Insurance Company has a life insurance pool of 1,000 30-year-old males. Each insured joined the pool because he was concerned about dying during the year and wanted to leave money behind to cover his financial obligations. Human life expectancy is quite predictable, so the actuary can determine with considerable certainty how many of those in this particular pool will die during the year. Suppose the actuary determines that two of the 1,000 men in the pool will die this year. If each man in the pool purchased $100,000 of life insurance coverage, this means that the actuary expects the insurer to pay $200,000 in claims for the year. If the $200,000 in claims (losses) is divided among the 1,000 people in the pool, each person's share is $200. The insurer will add a charge for expenses and profit, perhaps $50 per insured. Thus, the cost of insurance (premium) for each person in the pool for that year will be $250.

Each insured in the pool voluntarily pays $250 for the security of knowing that if he is one of the two insureds to die, his beneficiary will receive $100,000. At the same time, each insured hopes that he does not die and that his $250 will be paid as someone else's death claim.

Notice that in the second year, only 998 insureds are left in the pool if two did in fact die the preceding year. Suppose the actuary determines that, once again, only two people in the pool will die. For the $100,000 death benefit to be paid on each claim, the insurer must again collect a total of $200,000. When this amount is spread over 998 insureds, each is now responsible for $200.40. When the insurer's expenses (again, assume they are $50) are added, the total premium charged is $250.40. This premium is slightly higher than for the previous year. Note that it would be even higher had the actuary determined that three or more people in the pool would likely die the following year.

Because death rates increase as people get older, life insurance premiums rise at an increasing rate. This occurs because the number of people dropping out of the pool increases each year due to death and lapsing policies. Thus, fewer persons remain in the pool to share the expense of future death claims.

Self-Insurance

Self-insurance is essentially the retention of a known risk and, where applicable, the related administrative functions that are typically performed by an insurer. Self-insurance is most often practiced in mid- to large-sized organizations with ample cash reserves. Affluent families will also self-insure by retaining risks that would traditionally be insured. When self-insuring, one normally establishes reserves for future losses in lieu of purchasing insurance.

By self-insuring a portion of their risk, organizations seek to gain more control over their cost of risk while potentially improving loss coverage and limits. Additionally, the organization is in control of claims processing and loss control, and self-insurance may improve cash flow provided the organization experiences losses equal to or less than expected and they manage the program efficiently. However, unless certain provisions are made, the company remains highly vulnerable to unexpected catastrophic losses that could dramatically exceed the loss reserves set aside by the company.

Protected Self-Insurance Program

Under a protected self-insurance program, the business or another entity keeps and administers the manageable, predictable risk within its operations and transfers the catastrophic risk to an insurer. Insurance on the excess is placed with specific and aggregate limits so the entity can know the future cost of protection.

First, the insured organization must determine the maximum amount that it can absorb for the particular line of insurance. Second, the organization creates a loss fund limit in the amount of the losses it expects to incur in a given period. This amount is based on the organization's loss history and future inflation.

When losses exceed the self-insured retention, specific excess insurance, known as *stop-loss coverage*, finances the losses, typically at 100%, up to a specified maximum limit. Thus, the insured organization is protected from losses above the self-insured retention, up to the excess limits of the excess insurance.

Pure Self-Insurance

Large organizations having significant cash reserves on hand may choose to self-insure against both predictable and catastrophic risks. In these cases, a reserve fund is created in the amount of the losses expected to incur in a given period, assuming the probability that a catastrophic loss may occur.

CAUSES OF INSURED LOSSES

Perils

Peril
The proximate, or actual, cause of a loss

Too often the concept of risk, or the chance of loss, is confused with the terms *peril* and *hazard*. A **peril** is the proximate or actual cause of a loss. Some common examples of perils are fire, windstorm, tornado, earthquake, burglary, and collision.

Open perils policy
A policy in which all perils or causes of loss are covered unless they are specifically listed in the exclusions section

Insurance policies may be written in either an open-perils or named-perils format. Historically, open perils policies were called "all-risks" policies because they covered all risks of loss (perils) not specifically excluded. The name *all-risks* proved to be somewhat misleading to the typical consumer, implying that "all" risks were covered. As a result, the industry has moved toward the use of the term *open perils* to describe this type of coverage agreement. An **open perils policy** is one in which all perils or causes of loss are covered unless specifically listed in the exclusions section. A **named perils policy** provides protection against losses caused by the perils specifically listed in the policy. Because there is always a chance of loss being caused by an unknown peril, an open perils policy is preferable to a named perils policy. Consequently, the open perils policy premium is higher because it provides broader coverage.

Named perils policy
A policy that provides protection against losses caused by the perils specifically listed in the policy

Hazards

Hazard
A condition that creates or increases the likelihood of a loss occurring

A **hazard** is a condition that creates or increases the likelihood of a loss occurring.

Physical Hazard

Physical hazard
A tangible condition or circumstance that increases the probability of a peril occurring and/or the severity of damages that result from a peril

A **physical hazard** is a tangible condition or circumstance that increases the probability of a peril occurring and/or the severity of damages that result from a peril. Common examples of physical hazards include poor lighting, icy roads, storing gasoline in a household garage, and defective wiring.

Moral Hazard

Moral hazard
A character flaw or level of dishonesty that causes or increases the chance for loss

Moral hazard is a character flaw or level of dishonesty that causes or increases the chance for loss. In property insurance claims, a good example of a moral hazard is arson. Fraud in auto and health claims also occurs frequently. Unfortunately, these types of losses result in premium increases for all insureds. When insureds submit an inflated or intentionally caused claim, they are stealing from all insureds including themselves.

Morale Hazard

Morale hazard
Indifference to a loss based on the existence of insurance

Morale hazard is the indifference to loss based on the existence of insurance. Certain people think that because they have insurance there is no need to be concerned about protecting their property. As a direct result, the chance of loss is increased. Persons may feel that because they are insured, there is no reason to lock their homes or cars. This should not be confused with a moral hazard, which, for example, would be burning their house down or purposely damaging their own car to collect insurance.

Adverse Selection

Adverse selection

The increased tendency of higher-than-average risks (people who need insurance the most) purchasing or renewing insurance policies

Adverse selection is the increased tendency of higher-than-average risks (i.e., people who need insurance the most) to purchase or renew insurance policies. Calculating insurance premiums depends on the existence of a balance of both favorable and unfavorable risks in the pool. When higher-than-average loss levels occur among a group of insureds, meaning a greater proportion of bad versus good risks, adverse selection may be the problem.

For instance, if someone with no insurance needs surgery, lives in a flood-prone area, or has recently acquired a life-threatening disease, that person is more likely to desire insurance coverage. Adverse selection makes insurance less affordable for all insureds. One could conclude that if all people were to purchase insurance only when they knew that they would incur a financial loss, then insurance would not exist. The premiums insurers collect would be depleted before all the claims could be accounted for, thus causing insurance companies to go out of business.

The problem of adverse selection is primarily managed through effective underwriting, which is the process of selecting and classifying insureds according to their respective risk levels. Each level of risk can be thought of as a pool, and the insureds within a given pool must share similarities in expected losses so they can be charged a premium representative of their risk levels. Although a person with a terminal illness may wish to purchase life insurance (a clear example of adverse selection), the underwriting process should detect the condition and the underwriter should reject the application for insurance.

INSURABLE LOSSES

Insurance vs. Gambling

Many people view insurance and gambling as similar activities. A common statement is, "Insurance is a gamble because the insurance company and the insured are betting if and when an unfortunate event will occur." Although in insurance there are monetary transactions that take place on the basis of chance, insurance and gambling are inherently different.

Insurance allows the insured to transfer a risk to the insurer, whereas gambling creates a risk where none previously existed. In gambling, the risk of loss is created when the transaction itself occurs. For example, when a card player bets $100 on a hand against the dealer, one has immediately created a speculative risk (risk of gain or loss) for oneself. Insurance takes the consequences of a pure risk (loss, no loss) and makes them manageable for the insured.

Requisites for an Insurable Risk

Several conditions must exist before a risk is considered insurable.

- A large number of homogeneous (similar) exposure units.

- Insured losses must be accidental from the insured's standpoint.

- Insured losses must be measurable and determinable.
- Losses must not pose a catastrophic risk for the insurer.

A Large Number of Homogeneous (Similar) Exposure Units

The insurance process depends on the establishment of fair and properly priced premiums for insureds. If accurate estimates of the probability of an occurrence are to be made, a large number of cases must be considered. The law of large numbers states that in order to predict the average frequency and severity of a loss with accuracy, a sufficient number of homogeneous exposure units must be present within each class.

Homogeneous and heterogeneous groups are two distinct entities. If dissimilar exposure units are placed in the same group to be observed, predictions on their loss experience will likely be inaccurate. Imagine a pool of homeowners that consists of people from California, Texas, Montana, and Maine. Because the natural disaster perils each state faces are considerably different, the resulting expected loss predictions would be imprecise. To estimate losses for homeowners in California as one group and to make separate loss estimates for persons living in the other states as another makes more sense. The exposure units must be homogeneous, or similar in nature, to obtain an accurate measure of the underlying probability for the loss experience of an insured group.

Insured Losses Must be Accidental From the Insured's Standpoint

To be insurable, losses need to be unintentional and unexpected from the insured's perspective. If not for this requirement, moral hazards would be created and encouraged; if intentional losses were paid, premiums would skyrocket. As a direct result, fewer people would purchase insurance. This, in turn, would change the ability of companies to predict probabilities based on a large number of homogeneous units.

Insured Losses Must be Measurable and Determinable

To prevent fraud, insurance companies' policies state whether a loss is covered and how much will be paid for that loss. A loss must be both measurable and determinable as to reason, time, location, and price before accurate loss predictions can be made. Difficult risks to predict include flood, earthquake, and nuclear contamination. Losses that are difficult to measure and determine include sentimental value of property (such as the value of a family photograph) and cash losses. Although proving that a house or car existed and what each was worth is straightforward, proving how much cash one had on hand at the time a wallet is stolen is not as easy. Thus, insurers typically provide very limited coverage for losses of cash, while they readily pay for fire damage to houses and for theft of automobiles.

Losses Must Not Pose a Catastrophic Risk for the Insurer

Logically, an insurer cannot provide coverage against a loss that could cause financial insolvency. Dangerous risks for an insurer include those that are not accurately predictable and those that can cause damage to a significant portion of the insurer's pool.

Recall that insurable losses must be predictable and measurable. Otherwise, the insurer cannot accurately estimate the appropriate premium for the coverage. A war is an example of a risk that is not predictable. No statistical trend exists that can be used to determine future losses. For this reason, insurers virtually never provide coverage for war-related losses.

Another source of catastrophic risk for an insurer is any peril, such as a hurricane, that could cause loss to a significant portion of the insureds in the pool. Imagine the loss exposure faced by an insurer that sells property insurance only in Florida. With the hurricane risk faced by a large portion of that state, one massive storm could damage a significant portion of the insured's property. Compare this situation with an insurer that sells coverage in all 50 states and only a small portion of its business is in Florida. In this case, a hurricane in Florida would not be as financially devastating to the insurer.

THE LAW OF INSURANCE CONTRACTS

A contract is valid only if the legal system enforces the terms and conditions. Our legal system has established certain principles upon which insurance contracts are based and interpreted when claims or disputes arise.

Elements of a Valid Contract

The elements of a valid contract include the following:

- Offer and acceptance
- Legal competency of all parties
- Consideration
- Legal purpose

Offer and Acceptance

A valid contract exists only if based on the mutual assent, or the meeting of the minds of the contracting parties. Mutual assent consists of a valid offer made by one party and an acceptance of that offer by the other party. In most cases, an offer is made by the prospective insured to an insurer, via the agent, by filling out and signing an application that is accompanied by an initial premium. Next, the insurance company must decide whether to accept, make a counteroffer, or reject the offer. For a contract to become effective, the insurer or the agent acting on behalf of the company must accept the offer.

Legal Competency of All Parties

The law requires that both the offeror and offeree be legally competent. Most people are considered legally competent, so it is easier to explain which people are deemed legally incompetent. These may include insane persons, intoxicated persons, and minors. Those under age 18 are subject to special state provisions in order to provide a basis for competency.

Entering into a contract with someone who is incompetent is not specifically illegal; however, it may be inadvisable. This is because the contract is generally voidable at the option of the incompetent party once he becomes competent or once someone responsible for the incompetent party discovers the existence of the contract.

Suppose Joe, 16, buys a life insurance policy and pays premiums until he is 18 years old. If upon turning 18, Joe becomes legally competent, he may be able to void the contract on the grounds that he was not competent when he first entered into the contract. By voiding the contract, Joe is stating that he never wanted to be a part of it and is entitled to a refund of all premiums paid. Yet, had Joe died during the two years the policy was in force, the insurer would have been legally required to pay the death claim. Therefore, from the insurer's standpoint, entering into a contract with anyone who is not legally competent is ill-advised.

Consideration

Each party to a contract must provide something of value, known as *consideration*. Payment (or the promise of payment) of the first premium along with the statements made in the insurance application are generally consideration on the part of the insured. The insurer's consideration is the promise to pay losses covered by the policy and uphold the terms of the policy.

Legal Purpose

In a court of law, a contract deemed to have an illegal purpose, or a purpose that is against the public interest in general, is invalid. Any insurance contract that promotes actions contrary to the public interest is unenforceable. For example, an insurer will not pay the beneficiary of a life insurance policy if that beneficiary murdered the insured. To do so would encourage murder, which is illegal and against public policy. Recall that moral hazards are character flaws in persons who may intentionally create losses. They are willing to commit illegal acts to profit from insurance. If insurance policies did not eliminate coverage for illegal activities, they would encourage crime and, thus, be against public policy.

Legal Principles of Insurance Contracts

As a legally enforceable contract, a life insurance contract contains three legal principles.

The Principle of Indemnity

Insurance is a contract of indemnity, which means that a person is entitled to compensation only to the extent that a financial loss has occurred. Insurance exists only to indemnify a person's losses, not to place one in a better financial position than before the loss occurred. If an insured could profit from the perils covered by insurance policies, one would have an incentive to make sure those perils constantly occurred.

In some cases, an insured will exaggerate an insurance claim violating the **principle of indemnity**. If the insured suffers a theft of a leather jacket purchased at a discount store for $100 yet tells the insurance company the jacket was a designer item that cost $1,000, and the insurer pays the claim without question, the insured has actually made a profit from the insurance, which is clearly a violation of the principle of indemnity and also an obvious moral hazard.

People fail to realize that any excessive money an insurance company pays for incurred losses will ultimately result in higher premiums being charged to everyone in the pool. As a result, even when insureds manage to violate the principle of indemnity without being caught, they are only taking money from themselves and others in the pool.

One way insurers enforce the principle of indemnity is by including a subrogation clause in property and liability policies. The **subrogation clause** states that the insured cannot indemnify oneself from both the insurance company and a negligent third party for the same claim. If the insured collects against the policy, he then relinquishes the right to collect damages from the negligent party.

Principle of indemnity
A person is entitled to compensation only to the extent that financial loss has been suffered

Subrogation clause
States that the insured cannot indemnify oneself from both the insurance company and a negligent third party for the same claim

The Principle of Insurable Interest

Principle of insurable interest

To have an insurable interest, an insured must be subject to emotional or financial hardship resulting from damage, loss, or destruction

An insured must be subject to emotional or financial hardship resulting from damage, loss, or destruction of property in order to have an insurable interest. The **principle of insurable interest** as a legal principle is clearly congruent with the principle of indemnity. For example, if Susan is allowed to insure a building she does not own and has no financial interest in, she has every incentive to destroy the building.

In property and liability insurance, an insurable interest must be present both at the time of policy inception and at the time of loss. In the case of life insurance, an insurable interest is necessary only when the policy is issued. These rules exist in part because life insurance is a long-term contract, whereas property and liability contracts are short-term contracts, usually renewed at six-month or one-year intervals. To require a property owner to give up insurance on property one no longer owns does not impose a financial burden. On the other hand, the policyowner who insures a spouse for 20 years and then gets divorced might suffer a severe financial penalty and loss of investment if the policy were automatically terminated due to the loss of insurable interest.

The Principle of Utmost Good Faith

Principle of utmost good faith

Requires that the insured and the insurer both be forthcoming with all relevant facts about the insured risk and the coverage provided for that risk

Also known as the principle of fair dealing, the **principle of utmost good faith** requires that both the insured and the insurer be forthcoming with all relevant facts about the insured risk and the coverage provided for that risk. Recall that to have a binding contract, both a valid offer and a valid acceptance must be present, which together constitute mutual assent. Unless all pertinent facts are revealed by the insured in the application process, the insurer does not have a valid offer on which to base its acceptance. The same is true of any counteroffer the insurer might make to the insured before binding coverage.

Throughout the life of the insurance policy, it is presumed that both parties will tell each other the truth about all matters relevant to the contract. If this standard of honesty is not upheld, then the insured could commit insurance fraud (thus violating the principle of indemnity). Similarly, the insurer could refuse to pay claims for which the insured is legally entitled to receive compensation. The insurer is expected to comply with all terms of the contract and all provisions of the insurance law in the state(s) where it operates. The legal system recognizes three different areas of enforcement that apply to the insured:

1. Warranty

2. Representation

3. Concealment

Warranty

Promise made by the insured to the insurer that is part of the insurance contract to which the insurer must adhere

Warranty   A **warranty** is merely a promise made by the insured to the insurer that is part of the insurance contract and, as such, must be adhered to. The promise can be that something is true when coverage is applied for (also called an affirmative warranty), or it can be a promise that the insured will or will not do something during the life of the policy (promissory warranty). Historically, any violation of a warranty was grounds for the contract being voided; however, most U.S. jurisdictions have determined that statements made on an application for insurance coverage are not affirmative warranties but are representations. The legal effects of representations are covered next.

The effect of a breach of a promissory warranty is much clearer and more severe. For example, a homeowner promises to purchase and maintain a security system for the home as part of the insurance contract. The homeowner decides to save money, so he disconnects the security service. If a burglary occurs three months later, the insurer likely will not have to pay the claim because a breach of a warranty is grounds for voiding a policy.

Representation

Statement made by the proposed insured to the insurer in the application process

Representation   **Representations** are statements made by the proposed insured to the insurer in the application process. Material (relevant) misrepresentations give the insurer the right to void the policy once they are discovered. Why? Once again, mutual assent is a necessary element to any contract. If the proposed insured lied to the insurer during the application (offer) process, the insurer has not received a valid offer and mutual assent was never reached.

The misrepresentation must be material before the insurer may void the policy and ultimately deny payment of a claim. The test of materiality is simple: if the insurer had known the truth, would it have affected the insurer's underwriting decision to such an extent that the policy would not have been issued? For example, if Carmen states on her application for life insurance that she does not smoke when in fact she does, this misstatement definitely would have affected the insurer's underwriting decision. While coverage might have still been sold to Carmen, she would have been placed into a different underwriting class and, thus, charged a higher premium.

Now, suppose Carmen's life insurance application asked if she had ever been seen by a doctor for any medical condition over the past five years (which is a very vague question), and she answered, "No." In reality, she had been seen once a year for an annual check-up and was treated for the flu two years ago. If the insurer discovered the misrepresentation and wanted to void the policy, it would have to prove that knowing she had annual check-ups plus one case of the flu would have changed the underwriting decision. In reality, this type of routine medical treatment probably would not affect the underwriting decision, so the insurer would be barred from voiding the policy.

Concealment

When the insured is silent about a fact that is material to the risk

Concealment   **Concealment** occurs when the insured is silent about a fact that is material to the risk. If an insured does not reveal material information that he knows and that is not specifically asked about, he has concealed that information. Contrast the notion of concealment with that of misrepresentation. A misrepresentation is an untruthful answer to a question, whereas concealment is not revealing a fact that is of importance to the insurer.

In practice, most insurers do not void coverage on the grounds of concealment because it is very difficult to prove. U.S. law requires the insurer to prove that the concealed information was important to the underwriting process and that the insured knew that it was important but intentionally kept it a secret. This is a very difficult standard of proof because the typical consumer has no way of knowing precisely what is or is not relevant to an underwriter's decision.

Legal Form

Although not required to be written, the form and content of an insurance contract are generally governed by state law. Each contract must be filed and approved by a state regulatory agency before the insurance policy may be sold in that state.

Distinguishing Characteristics of Insurance Contracts

Adhesion

Adhesion

A characteristic of insurance that means insurance is a take-it-or-leave-it contract. The proposed insured must accept (or adhere to) the contract as written without any bargaining over the terms and conditions

In most cases, two parties form a contract through the bargaining process. In insurance, however, this is not the case because insurance is a contract of **adhesion**. Adhesion means the insured must accept the contract as written without any bargaining over the terms and conditions. Most insurance companies today use standardized policy forms that may not be modified by the insurer to meet an individual need, and in the vast majority of cases, the proposed insured cannot bargain over the specific terms and conditions contained in the contract.

If the drafter of the contract (in this case, the insurer) leaves the contract ambiguous in any way, such ambiguities will be interpreted in favor of the person who was not allowed to bargain over the terms of the contract (in this case, the insured). This legal doctrine imposes a stringent burden on insurers to use very precise wording in their contractual products. The test of ambiguity is, "How would a reasonable layperson (not an insurance expert) interpret the contract?" If a court determines that a contractual provision is ambiguous to the average person, it will interpret the provision in a manner that is most favorable to the insured.

Aleatory

Aleatory
A characteristic of insurance meaning that monetary values exchanged by each party in an insurance agreement are unequal

Monetary values exchanged by each party to an insurance contract are commonly unequal. This is known as the **aleatory** feature of an insurance contract. While the insured pays a small premium, the insurer might ultimately have to pay a large dollar amount as the result of a claim. There have been a few cases, for example, when the insured died within a few days of the life insurance policy's issuance. Perhaps one $80 premium payment was made, yet the insurer had to pay a $250,000 death claim. On the other hand, an insured might pay premiums for years and never submit a claim, especially with homeowners or automobile insurance.

Unilateral

Unilateral
Only the insurer agrees to a legally enforceable promise

Insurance policies are unilateral contracts because only one party, the insurer, agrees to a legally enforceable promise to provide the coverages shown in the policy and to abide by all terms and conditions of the policy as long as the insured pays the premiums. On the other hand, the insured is not legally obligated to pay premiums. Although the insured must continue to pay premiums to keep the insurance protection in force, the insurer cannot legally force an insured to remain in the contract and to continue paying premiums.

Conditional

Conditional
Insurer is only obligated to compensate the insured if certain conditions are met

Every contract lists provisions or conditions that outline the duties of each party involved. An insurance policy is **conditional** in that the insurer is obligated to compensate the insured only if certain conditions are met. Therefore, every insured should carefully read and understand the conditions listed in a policy before the application is signed.

THE LAW OF AGENCY

Agents and Brokers

The financial planner should understand the relationship between insurers, insureds, agents, and brokers. Often clients will not be aware of potential conflicts of interest inherent in certain agent-insurer or broker-insurer relationships. The financial planner has a responsibility to make clients aware of these relationships and inform them of the various methods of obtaining recommended insurance coverage.

An **agent** is a legal representative of the insurer and has authority to enter into agreements on its behalf. Agents are used by insurance companies as a marketing and sales tool. Types of agencies include general agencies, branch agencies, independent agencies, and surplus-lines agencies. In contrast, **brokers** are legal representatives of the insured and can offer products from many insurers. They are usually licensed to sell insurance products, which facilitates issuance of insurance policies.

A **general agent** is an independent businessperson who represents only one insurer in a designated territory. The general agent is responsible for hiring, training, and paying other agents to work under the supervision of the agency. The general agent is compensated by commissions received from the insurance company for sales produced by the agency, and the insurer may provide some financing for office expenses.

Insurance companies may also market their products via a branch office. The manager in charge of the office is an agent similar to a general agent with respect to duties and compensation, but the manager is an employee of the insurer rather than an independent contractor. The difference between the general agent and the branch manager would not be apparent to the public, and their relationship with insureds is identical.

Independent agents are insurance agents that represent multiple unrelated insurers. Conflicts of interest may arise in the independent agency system because commissions are based on the product line offered and which insurer writes the policy. Agents may have an incentive to sell products that offer higher commissions and may be under pressure to maintain a certain level of product sales offered by the insurance companies they represent in order to maintain a sales contract.

Sometimes the policy requested by a consumer is not available from any insurer that is licensed to do business in the state (an admitted insurer). In this situation, **surplus lines agents** will be employed. These agents have the authority to place business with non-admitted (out-of-state) insurers when the proper type of insurance is not available within the state.

Agency Relationships

Because brokers are representatives of the insured and not of the insurer, insurance companies are not bound by statements made by the broker to the insured. Disagreements will not involve the insurer. Instead, the broker and the insured will be the parties involved if legal controversy arises.

An agent, on the other hand, is designated by an insurance company as a legal representative. Thus, the insurer, known as the principal in the relationship, is generally responsible for statements made by the agent to the insured. The authority of an agent is derived from three sources: express authority, implied authority, and apparent authority.

Express authority is the actual authority an insurance company gives representatives (agents) via the agent's written contract and involves powers that are explicitly given or denied to the agent by the insurer. Usually these are stated in the agency contract between the agent and the insurer. One typical power is the ability to solicit applicants for insurance products. Limits on the amount of insurance the agent can offer may be included in the contract as an additional restriction. The insurance company is responsible for the acts of its agents per express authority.

Implied authority is the authority that the public reasonably perceives the agent to possess, even without express authority. This type of authority gives the agent the power to perform any incidental act required in fulfilling the obligations of the agency agreement. For example, the agent may have an express authority to deliver policies to the insured. Accepting the first premium due under the policy would be an implied power of the agent. Under implied authority, an insurer is liable for the acts of an agent even if the agent knowingly misled the insured.

Agent
Legal representative of the insurer that has authority to enter into agreements on its behalf

Broker
Legal representative of the insured who can offer products from many insurers

General agent
An independent businessperson who represents only one insurer for a designated territory

Independent agent
An agent that represents multiple insurers

Surplus lines agent
An agent who is licensed to place coverage with nonadmitted insurers

Express authority
The actual authority an insurance company gives representatives (agents) via the agent's written contract

Implied authority
The authority that the public reasonably perceives the agent to possess, even without express authority

Apparent authority
*The insured is led to
believe that the agent
has authority, either
express or implied,
where no such authority
actually exists*

Apparent authority is when the insured is led to believe that the agent has authority, either express or implied, where no such authority actually exists. The insurer may be liable for misrepresentations made by the agent even if it is unaware of such acts.

E X A M P L E   An insurer may be liable for unauthorized actions of agents if the company was aware of their actions but did nothing to stop them. Apparent authority is based on this principle of estoppel. For example, an agent who has an insurer's logo on one's stationery and on the office's signage has the apparent authority to represent that insurer to the public. If the insurer withdraws the agent's authority but does not make certain the company's logo is removed from the stationery and the sign, the insurer could still be bound by the future actions of the agent.

IMPORTANT FEATURES OF INSURANCE CONTRACTS

Exclusions

Exclusions are a necessary part of every insurance contract because not every peril or property can be covered in every policy. Moreover, some items are simply uninsurable because they do not meet the requisites of an insurable risk.

The exclusions found in an insurance contract specifically outline items that will not be covered. The doctrine of concurrent causation makes it necessary for even a named perils policy to include numerous exclusions. Concurrent causation exists when a loss can be attributed to more than one peril. The law states that if at least one of the contributing perils is covered, the insurer must pay the entire loss. For example, while a named perils policy may cover fire, the insurer may not wish to cover fires that result from an earthquake. If the insurer does not specifically state that fires caused by earthquake are excluded from coverage, when an earthquake occurs and even a small fire results, the entire loss will have to be paid.

Insurers may exclude coverage for perils (e.g., war and flood), losses (the cost of a private hospital room when a semiprivate room is sufficient), or specific items of property (money over $200 and valuable papers are generally excluded from homeowners insurance coverage).

Riders and Endorsements

**Riders
(endorsements)**
*Written additions to an
insurance contract that
modify the original pro-
visions*

Riders and **endorsements** are two terms used interchangeably by the insurance industry to describe written additions to an insurance contract that modify the original provisions. They make it possible to slightly customize an insurance contract to fit an individual's needs by extending coverage, changing premiums, or making corrections to the policy that take precedence over any conflicting terms in the preprinted policy form.

Valuation of Insured Losses

Insurance policies must not only specify what is covered and excluded, but they must also explain how losses will be paid. Without valuation provisions in the policy, the insured and the insurer would have numerous disputes over how much a particular claim is worth.

For example, property insurance policies typically value losses in one of three ways:

1. Replacement cost

2. Actual cash value

3. Agreed-upon value

Replacement Cost

Replacement cost is the current cost of replacing property with new materials of like kind and quality. If, for example, a house were damaged by fire, the damaged carpet would be replaced with new carpet, even though the old carpet was somewhat worn and soiled. Replacement cost is often found by comparing what was once owned with what is currently on the market. Many homeowners policies have replacement cost provisions covering the dwelling and other structures.

Actual Cash Value (ACV)

Actual cash value is equal to replacement cost minus functional depreciation. For example, if the functional life of a roof is 20 years and it is destroyed after 5 years, the roof is assumed to be 25% depreciated at the time of the loss. The insurer would thus pay 75% of the roof's replacement cost if the policy valued losses on an ACV basis.

From the standpoint of a homeowner, ACV coverage can impose a serious financial burden if a severe loss occurs on older property. Replacement cost coverage is more often suggested, even though it is more expensive. Virtually all automobile policies use ACV, rather than replacement cost, because automobiles depreciate so rapidly. The cost of providing replacement cost coverage on autos would be too high for most consumers.

Actual cash value
Calculated as replacement cost minus functional depreciation

Agreed-Upon Value

Because valuing certain losses is so difficult, amounts paid for a loss are agreed upon by the insurer and the insured at the time a policy is issued. In writing this type of contract, no violation of the principle of indemnity occurs because the insurer will generally agree to a value that is reflective of the property's fair market value. Fine artwork and antiques are often insured under the valued policy principle. Life insurance is a valued policy because it is impossible to determine the precise value of a person's life objectively and/or calculate the replacement cost of a person.

Deductible
A stated amount of money the insured is required to pay on a loss before the insurer will make any payments under the policy

Co-payments
In health insurance policies, amounts an insured must pay in addition to the deductible to receive certain covered services

Deductibles and Co-Payments

A **deductible** is a stated amount of money the insured is required to pay on a loss before the insurer will make any payments under the policy. Deductibles help eliminate small claims, reduce premiums, and decrease morale hazards. Deductibles are used mainly in property, health, and automobile insurance contracts. Disability policies use an elimination period, which is a waiting period, measured in days, which must be satisfied before benefits become payable. This elimination period essentially acts as a time deductible.

Co-payments are nominal amounts an insured must pay to obtain certain covered services and are commonly used in health insurance policies. For example, an insured might have to pay a $10 co-payment for each visit to a doctor's office.

Coinsurance

Coinsurance
The percentage of finan-cial responsibility the insured and the insurer must share under the policy

Coinsurance defines the percentage of financial responsibility that the insured and the insurer must share under the policy. As used in property insurance, coinsurance provisions encourage all insureds to cover their property for at least a stated percentage of the property's value or else suffer a financial penalty. Because the vast majority of property losses are partial, without coinsurance clauses, many insureds would attempt to save money on insurance by purchasing less insurance than the full value of their property. While underinsuring is not an illegal practice, it presents a problem for the underwriter and actuary who base expected loss estimates, and thus premiums, on the full value of the properties in the pool.

The amount paid on a property insurance claim with a coinsurance clause is determined by comparing several values. If the insured purchases coverage that meets or exceeds the coinsurance requirement (usually 80% of replacement value for homeowners insurance), payment on a claim for a loss will be the least of the face value of the policy, replacement cost, or actual expenditures (minus any deductible). However, if the insured purchases coverage that is less than the coinsurance requirement (e.g., 60% of the replacement value), then payment on a claim for a loss will be the greater of the actual cash value or the result of the following formula subject to the face value of the policy:

$$\frac{\text{Amount of coverage purchased}}{\text{Coinsurance requirement}} \times \text{Replacement cost}$$

EXAMPLE   Nicholas owns a home with a replacement value of $300,000 and a depreciated actual cash value equal to 50% of the replacement value. He purchases $200,000 of insurance with a coinsurance requirement of 80%. If Nicholas experiences a $100,000 loss, the insurance company will pay the greater of:

$$\text{Actual cash value} = 50\% \times \$100,000 = \$50,000$$

or

$$\frac{\text{Amt purchased}}{\text{Coinsurance}} \times \text{Replacement cost} = \frac{\$200,000}{80\% \times \$300,000} \times \$100,000 = \$83,333$$

Because the coinsurance formula results in the greater value, Nicholas will receive $83,333 for his $100,000 loss (minus any deductible).

As used in medical insurance indemnity policies, coinsurance refers to the percentage paid by the insurer and the insured for claims after the deductible has been met and before the stop-loss limit is reached. For example, in a plan with 80/20 coinsurance, a $500 deductible, and a $1,000 stop-loss limit, the insured would pay 100% of costs until the $500 deductible was reached. After the first $500 in claims, the insured would pay 20% of costs until claims reached $5,500 ($1,000 stop-loss ÷ 20% coinsurance + $500 deductible) and then 0%. The insurance company would be responsible for 100% of all further covered claims during that policy period.

INDIVIDUAL LOSS EXPOSURES AND INSURANCE COVERAGES

Perils That Can Reduce and/or Eliminate the Ability to Earn Income

The three main types of pure risk that can interrupt one's earned income stream are dying too soon, living too long, and disability.

Dying Too Soon

The risk of a person dying before reaching full life expectancy is known as premature death. In most cases, a person who dies prematurely has a number of potential financial obligations, including a family to support, a mortgage to pay, and children to send through college. To prevent economic upheaval for surviving dependents, proper financial and estate planning using life insurance will provide for dependents in the event of the premature death of an income producer.

Living Too Long

While it may sound ridiculous to say that someone lived "too long," the risk of outliving one's financial resources (called *superannuation*) exists. Medical and technological advances have led to substantial increases in human life expectancy. Currently, the average person retiring at age 65 is expected to live another 20 years. Approximately 50% of all retirees will live beyond the average life expectancy of 20 years. How does one guarantee that savings and other assets will last until death? Various financial planning products make it possible to ensure that one does not outlive one's assets.

Disability

An unexpected accident or illness may result in high medical costs along with the inability to work and earn income. The cost of medical treatment continues to rise at a rate that exceeds general inflation. The cost of providing a lifetime of medical care, while simultaneously being unable to earn an income, can be astronomical. Long-term disability insurance can be used to mitigate this risk.

Perils That Can Destroy or Deplete Existing Assets

Along with earned income, various assets such as cash, real estate, and automobiles are acquired throughout one's lifetime. Even if the individual's ability to earn income is never hindered, financial loss could result if existing assets are destroyed or lost. The two main exposures that exist in this category are damage to property and legal liability for injuries inflicted upon others.

Damage to Property

A host of perils threaten an individual's property, including natural disasters, crimes, and careless accidents. The financial consequences of these perils and their resulting damage can be severe.

Damage to property can result in one of two types of financial losses: direct and indirect. A direct loss is an immediate result of an insured peril. The cost of repairing fire damage to one's house is a direct loss. An indirect loss occurs as a result of a direct property loss. The types of expenses that are incurred as indirect losses are numerous. If a section of a fire-damaged house is being rented out, the lost rent due to the property being uninhabitable is an example of an indirect loss. In addition, the family also has to pay for the cost of hotel accommodations until the house can be repaired, which is another indirect loss resulting from the fire damage. If the hotel does not accept pets, the family will have to pay a kennel or other boarding facility to keep the pets until the home is repaired. All of these expenses add up quickly and can easily exceed the cost of the direct property loss.

Legal Liability for Injuries Inflicted Upon Others

Under the U.S. legal system, one is held legally liable if one causes bodily injury or property damage to another. Personal savings and other assets can be seized to pay for legal liability.

Liability risk is especially dangerous from a financial standpoint because there is no upper limit on the amount of loss one can suffer. Consider the physician who treats 20 to 40 patients each day. If one of those patients is injured as a result of the doctor's malpractice, and a court finds the doctor guilty of malpractice, the injured patient might be awarded millions of dollars in damages. In addition to the damages claimed by the injured party, the insured also suffers another loss: the cost of settling or defending lawsuits. A person found to be free of causing an injury could still have enormous legal bills.

CHARACTERISTICS OF INSURANCE COMPANIES

Types of Ownership

Stock Insurance Company

Stock insurance company
Operate for-profit and owned by stockholders

A **stock insurance company** is operated for profit and is owned by stockholders who purchase shares of the insurance company. The capital received provides funding for operating expenses until premiums and investment earnings are sufficient. Stockholders receive a return on their investment through dividends and capital appreciation of the shares of the company. The board of directors, whose members are elected by the shareholders, declares dividends at its discretion.

Mutual Insurance Company

Mutual insurance company
Owned by policyholders and distributes profit in the form of policy dividends

In contrast to stock insurance companies, **mutual insurance companies** are owned by the policyholders. Most mutual insurance companies operate in the same manner as stock insurance companies and distribute profits in the form of policy dividends to policyholders.

Insurance Underwriting

Underwriters
Classify proposed insureds in a way as to adequately protect the insurance company from adverse selection

To combat the difficulty with loss prediction, especially dealing with adverse selection, insurance companies employ underwriters. **Underwriters** classify proposed insureds in a way as to adequately protect the insurance company from adverse selection. Actuaries develop rates that can be translated into insurance premiums based on particular risk characteristics. The underwriter decides which risk characteristics describe the individual or group applying for coverage. After determining relevant risk exposures, the underwriter will designate the prospect as insurable or uninsurable according to company guidelines. If the potential insured is deemed insurable, the underwriter will determine the appropriate premium to charge based on the actuarial table and level of risk associated with the insured.

Reinsurance

Reinsurance provides sharing of risk across two or more insurance providers. With reinsurance, a company can reduce the exposure to risk of catastrophic loss that could result in insolvency. One method of reinsurance is excess-loss. Under this method, the reinsurer is liable for losses that exceed a specified limit, thereby protecting the original insurer from large claims. The reinsurer will receive premiums from many policies but will likely have only a few claims. Many firms that self-insure for employer-provided health insurance reinsure using the excess-loss method.

E X A M P L E   Company A is willing to expose itself to a maximum of $500,000 of risk (retention limit). Reinsurer B accepts the risk in excess of Company A's $500,000 retention limit. For acceptance of the excess risk, Reinsurer B receives a premium from Company A.

Insurance Regulation

Insurance regulation is intended to create and maintain a market that prevents insurers from placing themselves at risk of insolvency or engaging in abusive market behavior. Historically, the insurance industry has been regulated by state governments. In 1945, with the passage of the McCarran-Ferguson Act, regulation of insurance companies was explicitly given to the states.

Each state has an insurance regulator, often known as the Commissioner, or Administrator, of Insurance, who is either appointed by the governor or elected by registered voters. The Commissioner oversees the execution of state laws related to the insurance industry. Among the Commissioner's duties are licensing insurance agents and companies, approving proposed rate changes, investigating consumer complaints, reviewing insurance forms, and regularly auditing insurance companies to ensure solvency.

National Association of Insurance Commissioners (NAIC)

The National Association of Insurance Commissioners (NAIC) is a voluntary association of the insurance regulators of the 50 states, the District of Columbia, and the four U.S. territories (American Samoa, Guam, Puerto Rico, and the Virgin Islands). The purpose of the NAIC is not to serve as a regulatory body but instead to provide a common forum of interaction for matters that transcend the states. The association exists as a collaborative effort to increase the effectiveness of insurance regulation through the development of common standards, practices, and model legislation.

NAIC Criteria

The NAIC provides assistance to the states' solvency efforts in numerous ways. Among these are uniform statutory financial reporting requirements, solvency screening through financial analysis systems and peer review, and the subsequent reporting of deficiencies to regulatory officials. The NAIC examines all insurers' financial conditions on site and assists with regulatory action when an insurer's financial condition fails to meet established standards.

Risk-Based Capital Model Act   The NAIC established a regulatory capital framework for insurance companies when it introduced the Risk-Based Capital Model Act. States that have adopted the act require insurance companies to file annual reports detailing the following risks:

- Risks associated with assets of the insurer

- Risks associated with adverse experience of the insurer related to liabilities and obligations (underwriting risk)

- Interest rate risk associated with the insurer's business (for life insurance products)

- Other relevant business risks as outlined in the RBC instructions

Risk-based capital model (RBCM)
Adjusts an insurer's capital base according to the amount and types of risk to which it is exposed

The **risk-based capital model (RBCM)** adjusts an insurer's capital base according to the amount and types of risk to which it is exposed. Risk-based capital ratios are measured against minimum established guidelines. If four or more of these ratios fall outside the minimum guidelines, regulatory action may be required.

Regulatory action involves either an attempted rehabilitation or declaration of the insurance company's insolvency. A state insurance department is authorized to take over, or seize, an insurance company if the state can show to the applicable state court that the insurer will be unable to meet its contractual obligations to policyholders.

SELECTING AN INSURANCE COMPANY

Several rating agencies specialize in the financial assessment of insurers. Due to recent financial crises encountered by some insurers, the evaluations of these companies have become more and more important to consumers. The ratings of these agencies reflect their opinions of the insurance companies' financial condition and their ability to meet their obligations to policyowners.

The financial stability of an insurance company is essential for all types of insurance. These ratings may be of greater significance to life insurance policy-owners due to the long-term nature of the life insurance contract. Policyowners need to be concerned with financial stability for obvious investment reasons, and, as a professional, the financial planner should be diligent when recommending insurance products.

Rating Agencies

Four major private rating agencies evaluate the financial condition of insurers and make their ratings available to the public. The examined elements of the insurance companies vary between the rating companies and include recent performance, financial statements, leverage, and management stability. External factors such as competition, diversification, and market presence may also be considered. Each organization provides a description of its analysis and defines its rating scores (see Exhibit 8.1).

A.M. Best, Inc., has been providing ratings for insurance companies since 1899. Specializing in insurance companies, it is the largest and longest-established company devoted to issuing in-depth reports and financial-strength ratings.

Fitch Investors Service, Inc., provides credit opinions for over 800 insurance companies.

Moody's Investors Service is a source for credit ratings, research, and the risk analysis of thousands of companies, including insurers. Generally, Moody's analyzes the financial condition of a company at its request, using internal and external information. The company also rates some companies with only available public information.

Standard & Poor's Corporation provides two types of ratings. Claims-paying ability ratings are issued by request of a company. There is a cost to the requesting company for this service. Qualified solvency ratings are issued using public information only and are free of charge.

When purchasing insurance products, the consumer ideally will use a company that has received a top-tier rating from the majority of the agencies. For safety's sake, any company that has received a low-tier rating from any of the agencies should be avoided.

EXHIBIT 8.1 Insurer Ratings

Rating Service	Ratings (from highest to lowest)
A.M. Best	A++ through S
Standard & Poor's	AAA through D
Moody's	Aaa through C
Fitch Ratings	AAA through D

Additional Considerations

Besides agency financial ratings, consumers should also consider the following when deciding on an insurance provider:

- Asset size and age of the company

- Track record

- Financial operating ratios

- Lapse ratio—percentage of policies that are terminated each year

- Average policy size

- Product lines offered

- Average investment returns

- Form of ownership

THE RISK MANAGEMENT PROCESS

Risk management is a systematic process for identifying, evaluating, and managing pure risk exposures faced by a firm or individual. The six steps in the risk management process include:

1. determining the objectives of the risk management program;

2. identifying the risks to which the company or individual is exposed;

3. evaluating the identified risks as to the probability of outcome and potential loss;

4. determining alternatives for managing risks and selecting the most appropriate alternative for each risk;

5. implementing a risk management plan based on the selected alternatives; and

6. periodically evaluating and reviewing the risk management program.

Determining the Objectives of the Risk Management Program

The first step in the risk management process is determining the goals of the risk management program. Unfortunately, this step in the process is one of the most ignored. Due to vague risk management objectives, many parts of a client's risk management program are not cohesive. Risk management objectives can range from obtaining the most cost-effective protection against risk to continuing income after a loss.

Identifying the Risk Exposures

The next step is to identify all possible pure risk exposures of the client. Though it is difficult to generalize risks that companies face due to differences in structure and conditions, potential exposures mirror those described for individuals. Businesses, of course, are concerned with damage to existing assets and any perils that might interrupt their ability to generate income. As most businesses generate income through the efforts of their personnel, risk managers are also concerned with the recruitment, selection, hiring, training, health, and welfare of personnel.

For a corporate risk manager to identify the risks that the company faces, one must delve into the operations of the firm. Some common methods of research are physical inspection, risk analysis questionnaires, flow process charts, review of financial statements, and reports on past losses.

For the individual consumer, identifying risks is a somewhat simpler process. Analyzing and valuing the properties owned or leased, recognizing activities that could result in injuries to others, and determining how to protect one's ability to generate an income are all reasonably straightforward activities.

Evaluating the Identified Risks

Loss frequency
Expected number of losses that will occur within a given period

Loss severity
Potential size or damage of a loss

The next logical step in the risk management process is to evaluate the potential frequency and severity of losses. **Loss frequency** is the expected number of losses that will occur within a given period. **Loss severity** refers to the potential size or damage of a loss. By identifying loss frequency and severity, a risk manager can prioritize the urgency of dealing with each specific risk.

Recall that probability is useful when applied to large numbers. Relying solely on probability-based predictions for an individual, however, is not recommended. Of greater concern to the individual is the potential severity of the losses that occur. The person who owns a $200,000 home has a maximum possible severity of loss on that asset equal to $200,000. This would be, for the vast majority of consumers, a high severity loss. On the other hand, the person who owns a car worth $1,500 has a fairly low severity loss potential. To the particular person, the $1,500 loss might lead to significant averse consequences, however, and could possibly affect income generation if he could no longer drive to work.

Determining and Selecting the Best Risk Management Alternative

Insurance is neither necessary, nor is it even available, for every risk of loss an individual faces. Choosing the appropriate risk management tool depends largely on the potential severity and frequency of encountered loss exposures. Where more than one tool is deemed appropriate, the costs and benefits of each should be examined to determine which is most economical and beneficial.

As discussed earlier, there are generally four ways to manage a risk: avoidance, reduction, retention, or transference. How does one know the best risk management technique for a particular risk? Exhibit 8.2, based on the frequency and severity of expected losses, can be used as a general guideline for selecting an appropriate risk management tool.

EXHIBIT 8.2 Risk Management Guidelines

	High Frequency	Low Frequency
High Severity	Avoidance	Insurance
Low Severity	Retention/Reduction	Retention

The first type of loss exposure is a combination of high severity and high frequency. This is perhaps the most serious type of exposure and is often handled by avoidance. Assume John applies for the position of chauffeur for Divine Limousine Company. He has previously been arrested for miscellaneous misdemeanors and convicted twice for driving while intoxicated. Clearly, John is an unsafe driver and hiring him as an employee creates potential liability for Divine Limousine. Therefore, Divine Limousine should avoid this exposure by not hiring John.

Exposures that are low in frequency and high in potential severity are best handled by insurance. The high-severity losses can leave a person in a dire financial position, yet their low frequency makes sharing the cost of losses with others economically feasible. Examples of high-severity/low-frequency loss exposures include fire damage to a house and a loss due to an automobile collision.

The remaining types of losses are both low severity in nature. Transferring low-severity losses to an insurer is not economically feasible because the insurer will have substantial expenses associated with processing numerous small claims. The risk of low-severity losses is generally retained. When low-severity losses occur with high frequency, their aggregate impact can have financially devastating effects. Thus, it is suggested that high-frequency, low-severity losses are retained and controlled in an effort to reduce frequency. For an individual, low-severity losses include dings on cars, road-damaged tires, and minor injuries and illnesses.

Implementing a Risk Management Plan Based on the Selected Alternatives

The risk management plan must reflect the chosen response to risk. If risk reduction is the appropriate response to a given risk, the proper risk reduction program must be designed and implemented. If a decision is made to retain a risk, the individual or company must determine whether a reserve fund will be used. If the response to a given risk is to transfer the risk through insurance, an assessment and selection of an insurer are usually followed by planning meetings and the purchase of appropriate insurance products.

Periodically Evaluating and Reviewing the Risk Management Program

The purpose of periodic evaluation and review is twofold. First, the risk management process does not take place independent of external influences. Circumstances change over time along with risk exposures. The risk management technique that was most suitable last year may not be the most prudent solution this year, and adjustments may have to be made to the plan. Second, errors in judgment may occur and periodic reviews allow the risk manager to discover these errors and revise the risk management plan as needed.

WHERE ON THE WEB

A.M. Best, Inc. **www.ambest.com**

Fitch Ratings Insurance Group **www.fitchratings.com**

Independent Insurance Agents and Brokers of America
www.independentagent.com

Insurance Information Institute **www.iii.org**

Investor Desktop **www.investordesktop.com**

Moody's Investors Service **www.moodys.com**

National Association of Insurance Commissioners **www.naic.org**

Property Casualty Insurers Association of America
www.pciaa.net

Standard & Poor's **www.standardandpoors.com**

DISCUSSION QUESTIONS

1. What is risk?

2. What are the different types of risk, and how does each impact the personal financial planning process?

3. What is the difference between subjective and objective risk?

4. Name the common responses to risk. For which of the response(s) is insurance an appropriate risk management tool?

5. How does a peril differ from a hazard, and how does each relate to the need for insurance?

6. What is adverse selection, and how does it affect the insurance contract?

7. What are the requisites for an insurable risk, and what distinguishes insurance from gambling?

8. What are the elements of a valid contract? What distinguishing features do insurance contracts possess?

9. What are the reasons for and the effects of various contractual features in insurance contracts?

10. What is the principle of indemnity?

11. What is the principle of insurable interest?

12. What is a contract of adhesion?

13. Distinguish between an agent and a broker.

14. Differentiate between a general agent, an independent agent, and a surplus lines agent.

15. Describe the various types of agent authority.

16. What are the insurable loss exposures faced by the typical individual consumer?

17. What are the various insurance company rating agencies? Describe each.

18. What are the steps in the risk management process?

19. How do frequency of loss and severity of loss affect risk management?

EXERCISES

1. Briefly explain the difference between pure and speculative risk. Give an example.

2. Name three perils that could cause a loss around a home or apartment. What are the hazards that may increase the probability of these perils?

3. Explain the difference between moral hazard and morale hazard. Give two examples of each.

4. Differentiate between gambling and insurance.

5. How would an insurer reduce or manage the risk of adverse selection in a group dental insurance program?

6. John has an insurance policy for $150,000 on a building located at 175 Pine Street. The policy expires December 31, 2020. John sold the property to Bill on October 31, 2020, for $150,000. That very night, the building burned to the ground. Can John collect on the policy? If so, how much? If not, what legal characteristics would prevent him from collecting? Will John get any money from the insurer?

7. Which of the following people have an insurable interest in Mike's life?
   A. Angel, Mike's 25-year-old daughter
   B. James, Mike's 30-year-old son
   C. Cassie, Mike's ex-wife and Angel's mother
   D. John, Mike's employer
   E. Donna, Mike's daughter-in-law
   F. Scott, Mike's business partner
   G. Rita, Mike's fiancée

8. Leon is the risk manager for ABC, Inc. He has evaluated the following risks in terms of frequency and severity and asks your opinion as to which risk management tool(s) to use:

		Probability/ Frequency	Severity per Occurrence
A.	Fire destroys factory	0.0001	$10,000,000
B.	Loss of property through employee theft	0.1	$1,000
C.	On-the-job employee disability	0.01	$1,500,000
D.	Loss due to misplaced inventory (computer)	0.1	$2,000
E.	Loss due to failure to reduce energy bill (lights off, air conditioner off on weekends)	0.02	$400
F.	Air conditioning unit failure (compressor)	0.01	$2,000

Managing Life, Health, and Disability Risks

LEARNING OBJECTIVES

After learning the material in this chapter, you will be able to do the following:

- Identify the risks associated with premature death

- Measure the needs related to premature death

- Determine disability income and long-term care needs

- List and define the various types of term life insurance

- List and define the various types of whole life insurance

- List and define the various types of universal life insurance

- Distinguish between term, whole life, and universal life insurance, and explain their advantages and disadvantages

- List and define the various types of annuities

- ■ Explain the differences between annuities and life insurance contracts

- ■ Describe the important policy provisions and contractual features of life and annuity contracts

- ■ Understand the taxation of life insurance and annuities

- ■ Be familiar with important policy provisions and major contractual features of individual health coverage

- ■ Discuss health savings accounts (HSAs) and high-deductible health plans (HDHPs)

- ■ Describe the important policy provisions and contractual features of long-term care insurance

- ■ Describe the important policy provisions and major contractual features of individual health and disability coverage

- ■ List and describe the primary types of employer-provided group health and disability coverage

- ■ Be familiar with the history of managed care and understand today's prevalent methods of health care delivery

- ■ Explain how group health coverage may be continued or transferred when employment terminates

- ■ List and describe the primary types of employer-provided health and disability coverage

- ■ Discuss the various business uses of life insurance

- ■ Describe the types of nonqualified benefits often provided to key employees of a company

- ■ Be familiar with other employee benefits, such as Section 125 plans, flexible spending accounts, fringe benefits, voluntary employee benefit associations (VEBAs), and prepaid legal services

▎INTRODUCTION

Life, health, and disability risks include premature death, catastrophic illness, the inability to work, and the need for long-term care. Although these risks are generally low in frequency, they are potentially catastrophic in severity. Thus, the financial planner must assist the client in mitigating the impact of these risks by selecting and implementing appropriate insurance coverage. This chapter examines each of the above catastrophic risks and describes insurance products, particularly life and health insurance, that can mitigate those risks.

Life insurance is a fundamental element in a comprehensive financial plan for most clients, particularly those with dependents. The financial planner should be familiar with each type of life insurance in order to identify and meet client needs.

Health insurance is crucial for each member of the family because an uninsured illness can disrupt income security and reduce personal wealth. Therefore, the financial planner needs to be familiar with major medical insurance, disability insurance, and long-term care insurance.

IDENTIFYING RISKS ASSOCIATED WITH PREMATURE DEATH

Predicting the timing of a person's death may be impossible, but protecting the survivors against the financial distress they can suffer from the loss of an income provider is possible. The purchase of life insurance is one of the most effective methods of protecting against the financial consequences of an untimely death. Financial planners must be able to recognize and quantify two fundamental needs for the capital generated by a life insurance policy: replacing income and preserving assets.

Inadequate Financial Resources

The loss of an income producer may have a significant financial impact on the surviving dependent family members, which can be addressed by using life insurance proceeds.

Providing Income for the Readjustment Period

When a breadwinner dies, the family's income diminishes, and, as a result, the surviving family members likely experience a lower standard of living. Ultimately, the family may adjust the standard of living to fit the new income level, or other family members may be able to work to replace the lost income of the deceased. Moreover, a family usually encounters an unsettling and emotionally stressful readjustment period after the loss of a loved one. The surviving spouse and other dependents will require time to process grief and resume their lives. In some situations, a surviving spouse may have to be re-educated and trained to enter the workforce for the first time. Life insurance made paid directly to the family members or heirs of one's estate can replace lost income and provide for the family's financial support during this period of readjustment.

Providing Financial Support for Dependents

When an income producer has dependents, the dependents' financial well-being is the major concern. The mother who is the sole support for her children concerns herself with how their financial needs will be met if she dies prematurely. A life insurance policy guarantees that when the insured dies, a certain amount of money will be available to support her dependents.

When considering how much money is required for this particular life insurance need, a number of questions must be addressed. First, who actually qualifies as a dependent? For income tax purposes, most people are able to claim only children as dependents. However, other people may be financially dependent on the insured, such as the insured's parents who are elderly and on a fixed income and a spouse who either does not work outside the home or does not earn enough income to survive without the insured's wages. Responsible financial planning considers the needs of all dependents, not just those of minor children.

Secondly, how much financial support should be given to the various dependents? Should dependent children be supported until they are 18 years old, or should they be supported until they complete college? What standard of living does the insured wish to guarantee for survivors? Many questions must be answered before the insured can determine how much life insurance to purchase and maintain.

Earmarking Funds for Specific Goals

In addition to providing survivors with income, insureds may also wish to provide survivors with funds to achieve specific goals, such as paying off a mortgage or providing funds for the education expenses of each child.

Estate Preservation

People work throughout their lives to accumulate wealth. A common fear shared by many people is that their assets will be depleted by the time they die. The following types of postmortem expenses that are imposed upon surviving dependents validate this concern.

Funeral Expenses

Each person has specific preferences about how one's body should be handled after death, such as cremation, burial, being placed in a mausoleum, and even having the body donated to medical science. In fact, some of the choices can be very costly. The final ceremonies or services held for the deceased person, whether they include a simple memorial service or an elaborate funeral, must also be paid. These costs vary according to the decedent's preferences and are normally much higher than expected. When determining the amount of life insurance to carry, disposal and ceremonial expenses should always be taken into consideration.

Probate Expenses

After death, a person's estate normally goes through probate court for final settlement of most financial matters. The probate process provides for the distribution of the deceased's assets that fall within the terms of the decedent's will and for payment of debts. Life insurance proceeds may be used to expedite the prompt settlement of a person's probate estate, including the payment of court costs, taxes, and outstanding debts.

Taxes

During the probate process, federal and state estate taxes, accrued property taxes, and federal and state income taxes for the current year, as well as any back taxes due, will be collected by the appropriate agencies. If cash is not available to pay these taxes, assets may have to be liquidated to satisfy the debts. Life insurance can provide the cash necessary to satisfy the tax liabilities.

Debt Retirement

Most people die with outstanding debts such as credit card balances, unpaid bills, student loans, and automobile loans. A fund may be established to retire some or all of a decedent's debts.

MEASURING NEEDS RELATED TO PREMATURE DEATH

Generally, the following three methods are used to determine the financial needs related to premature death:

1. The human life value approach

2. The financial needs approach

3. The capital retention approach

Human Life Value Approach

Human life value approach
Uses projected future earnings as the basis for measuring life insurance needs

The **human life value (HLV) approach** uses projected future earnings as the basis for measuring life insurance needs. The HLV approach projects the individual's income throughout his remaining work life expectancy. Then, using an appropriate discount rate, the present value of the future earnings is determined. Note that cash flows are adjusted downward by amounts that would have otherwise been used for personal consumption and for the payment of taxes on income. The net amount is known as the FSE (family's share of earnings).

E X A M P L E   Alex, who is married and the father of four, is age 45 and expects to work to age 65. He earns $70,000 per year and expects annual salary increases of 5%. Alex expects inflation to be 4% over his working life. His personal consumption is equal to 10% of after-tax earnings, and his combined federal and state marginal tax bracket is 20%.

Step 1 Calculate the family's share of earnings (FSE).

Annual earnings	=	$70,000
Annual taxes	=	$70,000 × .20 = $14,000
Personal consumption	=	(After-tax income × consumption %)
	=	[($70,000 – $14,000) × .10)]
	=	($56,000 × .10)
	=	$5,600

FSE = Annual earnings – (annual taxes + annual personal consumption)
   = $70,000 – ($14,000 + $5,600)
   = $70,000 – $19,600
   = **$50,400**

Step 2 Calculate work life expectancy (WLE).

WLE = Expected age of retirement – current age
   = 65 – 45
   = 20 years

Step 3 Calculate the future value of the family share of earnings (FSE) over Alex's work life expectancy (WLE).

PMT = –$50,400
i   = 5%
n   = 20
FV = $1,666,524

Step 4 Determine the human life value (HLV).

FV = $1,666,524

i = 4%

n = 20

PV = $760,580 = HLV

Financial needs approach

Evaluates the income replacement needs of one's survivors in the event of untimely death

Financial Needs Approach

The **financial needs approach** evaluates the income replacement and lump-sum needs of survivors in the event of an income producer's untimely death. The effect of inflation over the years is taken into consideration when using this approach.

A family that loses an income producer is likely to have the following common needs:

Lump-sum (cash) needs

Final expenses and debts

Mortgage liquidation or payment fund

Education expenses

Emergency expenses

Income (cash flow) needs

Readjustment period

Dependency period

Spousal life income (pre- and post-retirement)

Income (Cash Flow) Needs

The deceased's survivors are accustomed to a particular lifestyle. Most breadwinners will want to make sure that their dependents will not suffer a decrease in their standard of living.

Final Expenses and Debts

Final expense fund

Fund requiring immediate access by survivors to pay for final expenses and debts of the decedent

A fund for final expenses and debts, commonly known as a **final expense fund**, is needed immediately by the survivors, to pay for a deceased's out-of-pocket medical expenses prior to death, funeral costs, and other unplanned expenditures. Estate administration expenses, federal estate taxes, state death taxes, inheritance taxes, and income taxes must also be funded from a source outside the estate, such as a loan, if no liquid assets are in the estate to cover the costs.

Mortgage Liquidation or Payment Fund

The family may choose to set aside funds to pay off an existing mortgage at the time of the breadwinner's death. If no mortgage prepayment penalty exists, this can be an effective way to reduce the cash flow needs of the surviving family members. A fund may also be established from which monthly mortgage payments are made, as it may be advantageous for the surviving spouse to utilize the annual mortgage interest deduction for income purposes. In some respects, there is an offsetting effect. If a client chooses to pay off the mortgage, life insurance proceeds will be required to cover that. However, if the mortgage is paid off, the ongoing monthly financial need is less, which will require less capital for the future. The reverse is also true. Maintaining the mortgage lowers the amount of life insurance needed earlier. However, it raises the monthly income need and thus can increase the life insurance need for ongoing monthly expenses. In all, a planner needs to help the client find a solution that matches her unique circumstances.

Education Expenses

If an education funding plan is not in place, funds may be set aside for private or secondary school and for college and postcollege education. If the survivors choose not to set aside funds, and education expenses will occur in the future, these expenses should be factored into the life income needed by the family.

Emergency Expenses

The purpose of this fund is to provide survivors with a cash reserve for unforeseen expenses that may arise as the family makes a transition to life without the deceased.

Readjustment Period Income Needs

Readjustment period
The period of time that lasts for one to two years following the death of a breadwinner

The **readjustment period** typically lasts for one to two years following the death of a breadwinner. During this period, the family should receive approximately the same amount of income it received while the deceased was alive. Families will usually have certain nonrecurring expenses as they adjust to a new lifestyle. For a family that will experience a decline in its standard of living, this period income allows the family to achieve the necessary readjustment.

Dependency Period Income Needs

Dependency period
The period of time during which others (the deceased's spouse, children and, in some cases, parents) would have been dependent on the deceased

The **dependency period** is one in which others (the deceased's spouse, children, and, in some cases, parents) would have been dependent on the deceased. In most cases, income needs are largest during this period. The length of the dependency period is determined by the number of dependents, their ages, and the deceased's contribution to the family's total income.

Spousal Lifetime Income Needs

Blackout period
The period of time beginning when Social Security benefits to the surviving spouse are discontinued (usually when the last child reaches age 16) and ending when the spouse begins to receive Social Security retirement benefits at age 60 or later

At some point, the children will no longer be dependent upon the surviving spouse; however, the surviving spouse may still need to replace a part of the wage earner's income, especially if the spouse does not work outside the home. Surviving spouses who reenter the workforce after years at home may often find it difficult to find employment that enables them to maintain the prior standard of living. Therefore, arranging a lifetime income for the surviving spouse may be advisable.

Two income periods should be considered: (1) the **blackout period** and (2) the period during which the surviving spouse receives Social Security benefits. The blackout period refers to the period of time beginning when survivor Social Security benefits to the spouse are discontinued (usually when the last child reaches age 16) and ending when the spouse begins to receive Social Security retirement benefits at age 60 or later. During the blackout period, income must be provided by employment, insurance, investments, or some other source. Once Social Security benefits resume, the amount of supplemental income may be reduced.

If both spouses earned an income prior to death, a smaller percentage of total family income must be replaced upon one of the spouse's deaths. If, however, the sole breadwinner of the family has died, the ability (or desire) of the surviving spouse to secure employment must be considered.

In most cases, the children of the deceased will be entitled to Social Security benefits (see Chapter 11, Social Security benefits). The benefits received by the spouse, as caretaker of the children and on behalf of the children, will decrease the income needs of the family during the dependency period. In addition, if parents were dependents of the deceased, any Social Security benefits received by them as a result of the death of their adult child may also decrease their income needs during the period.

E X A M P L E   Assume Frank is a consultant who earns $72,000 annually. His spouse, Julie, is a homemaker, and they have one child, Betty. Frank is covered by a $200,000 life insurance policy. The couple assumes an average annual inflation rate of 3%.

Frank and Julie have set the following goals and assumptions:

Income needed—readjustment period (one year)	$ 72,000/yr
Income needed—dependency period	$ 48,000/yr
Income needed—"empty nest" period	$ 36,000/yr
Estate expenses and debts	$ 15,000
Education fund needed (in today's dollars)	$180,000
Emergency fund	$ 15,000
Investment assets (cash/cash equivalents)	$100,000
Julie's life expectancy	85 years
Discount rate	6%

Given the information provided, how much life insurance should Frank purchase?

Step 1 Calculate the family's income (cash flow) needs for each period.

	Readjustment (1 year)	Child's Age (4–16)	Child's Age (17–18)	Blackout Period (Age 46–60)	Retirement (25 years)
Annual income needed	$72,000	$48,000	$48,000	$36,000	$36,000
OASDI (Social Security)	26,400	26,400	10,800	0	18,000
Net annual income needed (PMT)	45,600	21,600	37,200	36,000	18,000
Inflation-adjusted interest rate $i = \left(\dfrac{1.06}{1.03} - 1\right) \times 100 =$	2.9126	2.9126	2.9126	2.9126	2.9126
Years needed	1	11	2	15	25
PV of net annual income needed (use begin mode)	$45,600	$206,677	$73,347	$445,092	$325,730
PV of total annual income needed: $1,096,446					

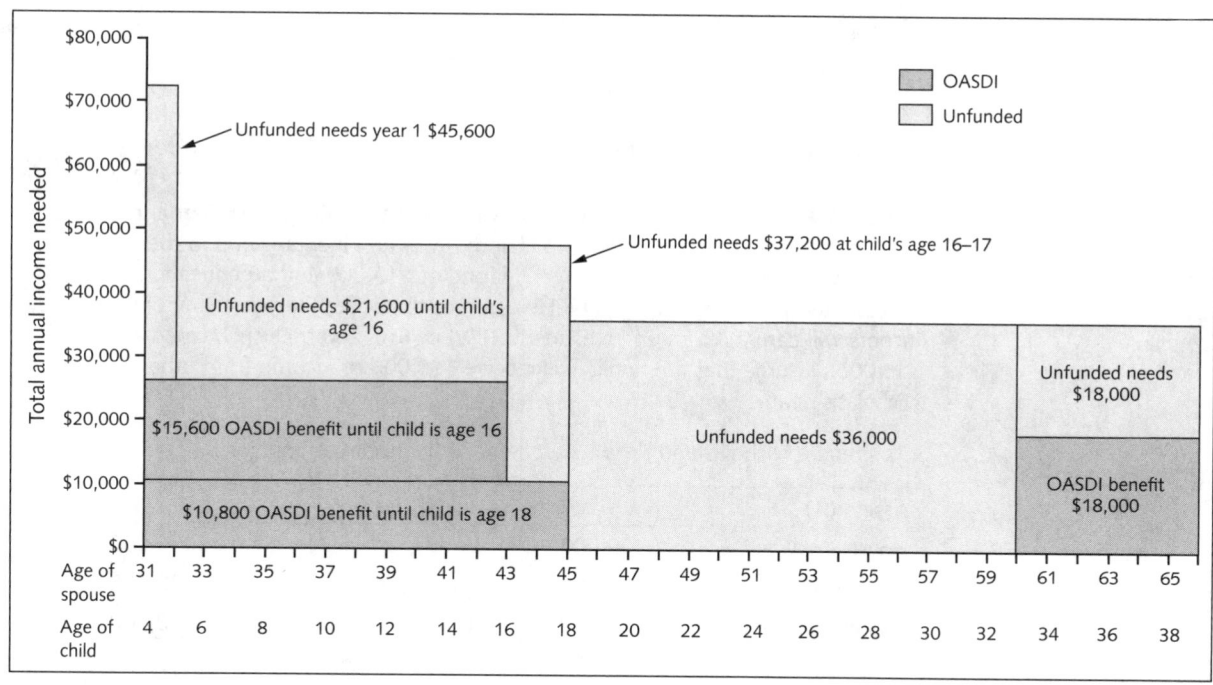

Step 2 Calculate the family's lump-sum funding needs.

Final expenses and debts	$ 15,000
Education fund needed (in today's dollars)	180,000
Emergency fund	15,000
Total lump-sum funding needs	**$ 210,000**

Step 3 Calculate the life insurance death benefit needed.

Total need	$ 1,306,446 ($1,096,446 + $210,000)
Less life insurance already in place	– 200,000
Less liquid assets	– 100,000
Net death benefit needed	**$1,006,446**

Capital Retention Approach

Capital retention approach
Provides a death benefit amount that, along with the family's other assets, is sufficient to provide a level of investment income that covers the projected needs of the family without having to invade the death benefit principal

Unlike the financial needs approach, the **capital retention approach** provides a death benefit amount that, along with the family's other assets, is sufficient to provide a level of investment income that covers the projected needs of the family without having to invade the death benefit principal. Other income-producing assets may be available, which will reduce the required death benefit. In other words, under this approach, survivor income needs are met from the earnings of the other assets. As a result, the income-producing assets remain available for distribution to the children or other heirs.

The capital retention approach involves three steps:

1. *Prepare a statement of financial position*—Prepare a list all of assets and liabilities to arrive at a projected statement of financial position at death. Assets should include any life insurance from other sources, such as existing personal policies, coverage through employers, or death benefits available through retirement plans.

2. *Calculate the capital available for income*—Subtract liabilities, cash needs, and non-income-producing capital from total assets.

3. *Determine the amount of additional capital required*—Compare the family's income objectives with other sources of income available, such as Social Security.

EXAMPLE   Nicholas wants to provide his family with $60,000 of annual income in the event of his death. He wants to provide his children with an inheritance upon the death of his spouse, Kelly. He also wants to establish an emergency fund of $15,000 and an education fund of $60,000 for his children and pay off the mortgage. He assumes that, over the years, any principal used to provide income will earn a return on investment (ROI) of 6%, and that final expenses upon his death will be $15,000. Assume that the family will receive $20,000 of income from other sources each year after Nicholas's death.

1. Prepare Nicholas and Kelly's statement of financial position.

Assets (A)		Liabilities (L)	
House	$300,000	Mortgage	$220,000
Automobiles	30,000	Auto loans	20,000
Personal property	25,000	Credit card debt	10,000
Investments	20,000	Total liabilities	$250,000
Life insurance	200,000	Net worth (A − L)	$325,000
Total	$575,000	Total liabilities and net worth	$575,000

2. Calculate the capital available for income.

Total assets	$575,000
Less:	
Mortgage	$220,000
Other liabilities	30,000
Emergency fund	15,000
Education fund	60,000
Final expenses	15,000
Non-income-producing capital	135,000
(Equity in home, autos, personal property)	
Total deductions	$475,000
Capital available for income (CAI)	$100,000

3. Determine the amount of additional capital required.

Annual income objective for the family	$60,000
Less:	
Capital currently available for income	− 6,000
(CAI × ROI = $100,000 × 0.06)	
Annual income from other sources	− 20,000
Annual income shortfall	$ 34,000
Total additional capital required to cover shortfall	$566,667
(Shortfall/ROI − $34,000 ÷ 0.06)	

Unlike the financial needs approach, the capital retention approach has the advantages of simplicity and preservation of capital and may offer protection from inflation (rising costs). A key disadvantage, however, is the larger amount of life insurance needed so that assets may be preserved for heirs.

INDIVIDUAL LIFE INSURANCE POLICIES

Life insurance is a contractual means by which an individual transfers the risk of loss from death to an insurance company. The policyowner exchanges a stated premium for a promise to pay a stated death benefit. The insurer combines a large number of similar risks into groups or pools. Using the law of large numbers, the insurer's actuaries can predict the number of deaths that will occur during a given period with a fairly high level of accuracy. Policy premiums can then be calculated according to an underwriting class. Although it is impossible to determine which insureds will die, it is possible to know the probability of how many within the pool will die. As a result, life insurance becomes a viable mechanism for transferring a risk that would otherwise result in an economically devastating loss.

Consumers have a wide array of life insurance choices. Policies vary on the basis of the term of coverage, the flexibility of the premium or death benefit, whether the policy has cash value, and whether the underlying interest rate assumptions are fixed or variable. In addition, riders and other options, such as waiver of premium or accidental death benefit, can be added to a policy to suit the client's needs.

Life insurance policies commonly are classified in the following categories:

- Term
- Whole life
- Universal life

Term Life Insurance

Term life insurance
Provides temporary life insurance protection for a given period

Renewable
A feature whereby the policyowner may continue a term policy for an additional period without evidence of insurability at a premium based on the insured's current or attained age

Convertible
A term policy that may be exchanged for a cash value life insurance policy without evidence of insurability

Annual renewable term (ART)
Term insurance issued for one year; renewable for subsequent periods to a stated age without evidence of insurability

Term life insurance is commonly known as pure insurance because it provides nothing more than death benefit protection for a temporary or limited period, and the death benefit is paid only if the insured dies during the period. Term life insurance has no cash value, although some long-term policies build up a small reserve to cover future mortality costs and expenses. This reserve is depleted by the end of the policy term.

Most term life insurance policies are **renewable**, which gives the policyowner the right to continue coverage for an additional period without evidence of insurability at a premium based on the insured's current or attained age. The period of renewal may be the same length as the original term period. The majority of term life insurance policies are also **convertible**, which means that the term policy may be exchanged for a cash value life insurance policy without evidence of insurability. Together, the renewability and convertibility features protect the policyowner against the loss of insurability.

Types of Term Insurance Policies

There are several forms of term insurance available in the market today that vary by premium and death benefit design.

Annual Renewable Term **Annual renewable term (ART)**, also known as yearly renewal term (YRT), is coverage issued for one year, and the policyowner can renew for a subsequent period up to a maximum age without evidence of insurability. Premiums increase each year as the insured ages.

A key advantage of annual renewable term insurance is that no evidence of insurability is required at the time of renewal. One disadvantage, however, is that premiums are re-evaluated at the end of each annual term and will increase as the pool of insured ages and the death rate begins to increase. Because the rate of death rises at an increasing rate with age, the premiums for this type of policy may become prohibitively expensive as the insured gets older. Although initially less expensive than an ordinary whole life insurance policy, ART premiums will far exceed the level premium for the whole life policy as the insured ages. Exhibit 9.1 illustrates a comparison of the premium cost per $1,000 of insurance of an ART policy with an ordinary whole life policy. Notice how the exponential increase of the annual renewable term premium reflects the increased probability of mortality as age increases.

EXHIBIT 9.1 Annual Renewable Term Premium and Premium for Ordinary Whole Life

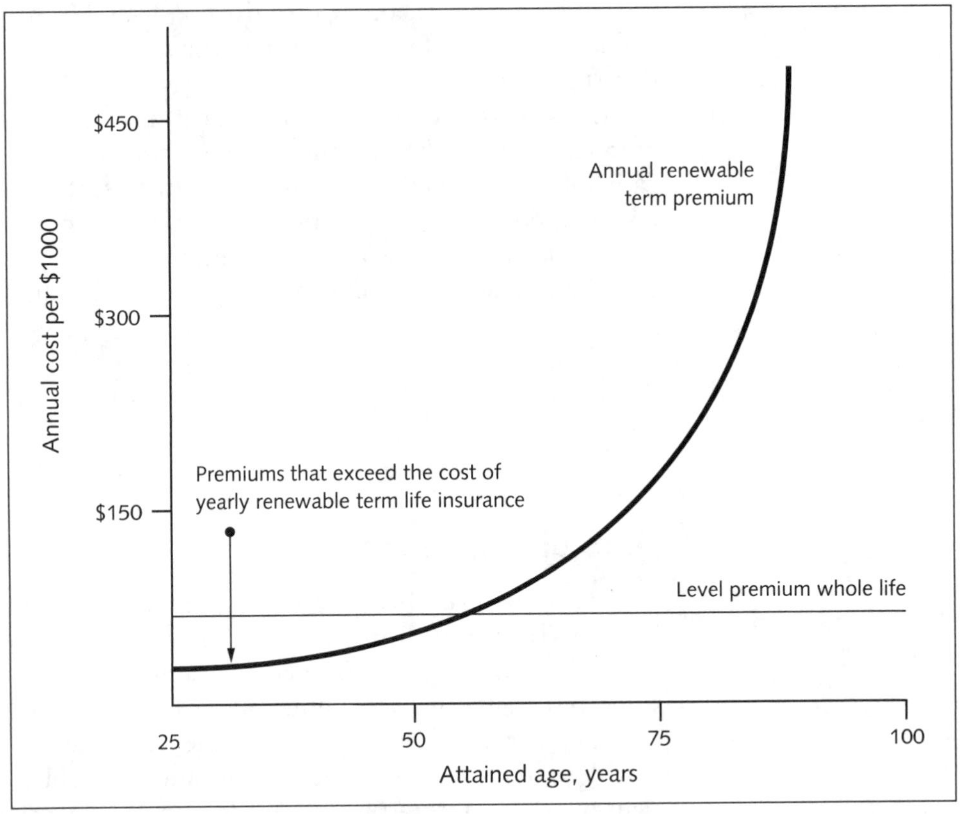

Level Term

Level term insurance features a level death benefit and a level premium for a stated period of time. Level premium periods for this type of policy are typically 5, 10, 15, and 20 years. However, 35-year and 40-year level term policies may be available at younger ages. In most cases, premiums for the early years of the term are higher than those for an annual renewable term policy. This overpayment in early years funds the coverage for later ages when premiums for an ART policy would have been exceedingly expensive and unaffordable. Premiums for the level term period normally reflect the average of ART premiums, with discounting applied for time value of money. Therefore, the cash outlay for a fixed-period, level term policy is less than if the insured had purchased an annually renewable term policy for the same number of years. Note, however, that after the initial level term period, premiums often increase annually, unless the insured is in good health and, in some cases, provides additional evidence of insurability.

Decreasing Term

Decreasing term insurance features a level premium with a decreasing death benefit. In some policies, premiums discontinue a few years before the coverage ends. Decreasing term policies are most commonly used to provide a death benefit to pay off a mortgage in the event a breadwinner dies. Because mortgage balances decrease over time, a decreasing term policy may be the most appropriate type of life insurance to meet this need.

Level term
A policy with a level death benefit and a fixed level premium for a stated period

Decreasing term
Term insurance that features a level premium with a decreasing death benefit

Reentry term

A policy under which the insurer may renew coverage at a lower premium rate if the insured provides satisfactory evidence of insurability

Reentry Term **Reentry term** is a life insurance policy under which the insurance company may renew coverage at a lower premium rate than would otherwise apply, provided that, at the time of renewal, the insured furnishes satisfactory evidence of insurability (e.g., medical exam). The ability to apply for lower rates may or may not be guaranteed in the contract. Rate schedules are provided in the policy, and a guaranteed maximum rate that the policyowner must pay is also provided if the insured no longer qualifies for preferred rates. Reentry term policies reward an insured who remains in good health, and they maintain the insurance coverage of those who no longer qualify as preferred risks. Some level term policies have reentry provisions at the end of each level term period.

Term Life Insurance Policy Riders

Rider

Provides additional coverage for something specifically not covered within the primary policy

A **rider** provides additional coverage for something specifically not covered within the primary policy. The rider is added to the primary policy, and the policyholder pays an extra amount to cover the cost of the rider. A discussion of common term policy riders follows.

Waiver of premium rider

Waives the premium due on a policy while the insured is disabled

Waiver of Premium The **waiver of premium rider** prevents the policy from lapsing because of nonpayment of premiums during the insured's disability. If the insured is disabled, premium payments are not required during the period of disability. In most cases, however, total disability is required. Definitions of disability can range from own occupation (i.e., unable to perform the material and substantial duties of the insured's regular occupation) to any occupation (i.e., unable to engage in any paying work).

Standard elimination (waiting) periods vary from 90 days to six months. In other words, for a 90-day elimination period, 90 days must pass before premiums are waived. Therefore, the policyowner must continue to pay premiums during the waiting period, but, in many cases, the company will return the premiums paid during the waiting period and will continue to waive the premiums until the end of the disability.

Note that premiums waived on behalf of the policyowner are not considered loans and, as such, need not be repaid. During the period in which premiums are waived, all features and benefits of the policy continue just as if the insured were paying the premiums.

Accidental death benefit rider

A policy rider that pays the beneficiary an additional death benefit if the insured dies accidentally, as defined in the rider

Accidental Death Benefit The **accidental death benefit rider** pays the beneficiary an additional death benefit if the insured dies accidentally, as defined in the rider. The definition of *accident* usually requires that death occur within 90 days of a purely unexpected event and not be related to any medical condition of the insured. The accidental death benefit rider is typically provided in the form of double indemnity, whereby the rider pays a benefit equal to the face value of the base policy. The result is double the amount of the initial death benefit.

Accelerated death benefit rider

Allows the policyowner to receive a portion of the policy's death benefit during the insured's lifetime if the insured contracts a terminal illness

Accelerated Death Benefit The **accelerated death benefit rider** allows the policyowner to receive a portion of the policy's death benefit before death, if the insured contracts a terminal illness and/or has a limited life expectancy. This rider is also known as a living benefit rider and is often provided without additional cost.

Return of premium rider

Returns the premium paid for a policy (less any administrative charges, fees, or rider premiums) to the policyowner at the end of the policy term

Return of Premium The **return of premium rider** returns the premium paid for a policy (less any administrative charges, fees, or rider premiums) to the policyowner at the end of the policy term. If the insured dies before the end of the policy term, the beneficiary will receive the death benefit and the amount of premiums paid up to death.

Spouse and child insurance riders
Provide life insurance coverage on the lives of the insured's spouse or children

Spouse and Child Insurance   **Spouse and child insurance riders** provides life insurance coverage on the lives of the insured's spouse and/or children. One child rider usually covers all children of the insured.

Advantages

Maximum Coverage per Premium Dollar   Because term insurance provides pure death protection for a specified, temporary period only, term insurance is less expensive over the short term than a cash value whole life policy that provides coverage for the insured's lifetime. Term insurance premiums must cover only mortality, administrative expenses, and profit margin. Because part of the premium is not allocated for cash value accumulation, a term insurance policy is less expensive than a cash value policy.

Meets Temporary Need for Coverage   Insurance protection under term insurance is temporary. The insurer provides coverage for a specified period only; therefore, term insurance is ideal for a temporary need, such as the payoff of a mortgage in the event of a breadwinner's death.

Protects Insurability   A person with a current need for a large amount of coverage but with limited funds can obtain a lower cost term policy to provide protection. Later, if the policy is convertible, the term policy can be converted to a cash value, permanent policy at the same death benefit level, even if the insured develops a medical condition that renders him uninsurable.

Limitations

Cost Prohibitive at Older Ages   Perhaps the most notable limitation of term insurance is the increase of premiums based on the aging of the insured, making term insurance impractical for many older people desiring coverage.

No Savings Feature   A term life insurance policy does not possess the cash value feature found in an ordinary whole life policy (see next section). Term life insurance's primary function is to provide pure death protection. If one's goal is to accumulate wealth for retirement or education funding through an insurance policy, term life is inappropriate.

No Lifetime Coverage   If the insured has a lifetime need for coverage, a term life insurance policy is not an appropriate option. Term life insurance is designed to provide coverage for a limited period and is priced to provide affordability during the early to mid portion of an insured's lifetime. However, term life insurance becomes increasingly uneconomical as the insured enters her later years and approaches life expectancy. Term life insurance should never be viewed as a form of lifetime protection because it generally may not be renewed after age 65 or 70. A convertibility feature provides an exception to the limited potential for lifetime protection with term life insurance. Some term life insurance policies have the ability to be converted into permanent policies without evidence of insurability. The client would have to remember to convert the term life insurance policy into a permanent policy at some point in the future based on the contract's terms and conditions.

Whole life insurance
Provides coverage during the lifetime of the insured as long as the premiums are paid according to the policy contract

Whole Life Insurance

Whole life insurance provides coverage during the lifetime of the insured, as long as the premiums are paid according to the policy contract. Whole life insurance accumulates a cash value that is available to the policyowner through withdrawals and loans during the insured's lifetime.

A whole life policy offers permanent protection for the insured's "whole life" at a relatively moderate premium, because mortality costs and other expenses are spread over the full policy period (usually to age 100). All whole life policies involve the prepayment of future mortality costs.

Characteristics

Guaranteed Cash Value and Death Benefit   In addition to the permanent coverage whole life insurance provides, the policy is often purchased for the low-risk, tax-deferred cash accumulation feature. Cash value in a traditional whole life policy increases at a steady rate, equaling the policy face amount at age 100.

A traditional whole life insurance policy generates a fairly low rate of return that is unattractive to many consumers, so traditional whole life should not be purchased solely for investment purposes. However, permanent insurance can be used as part of an overall investment and risk management plan. The insurance protection can serve as a risk management component, and the cash value can be appropriate as a low-risk, tax-deferred component of an overall investment program.

Exhibit 9.2 illustrates the cash value feature of a level premium, whole life insurance policy. Notice the original cost per thousand of $13.50 is substantially greater than the $1.95 per thousand mortality cost at the inception of the policy.

EXHIBIT 9.2 The Savings Element of a Level-Premium, Whole Life Insurance Policy

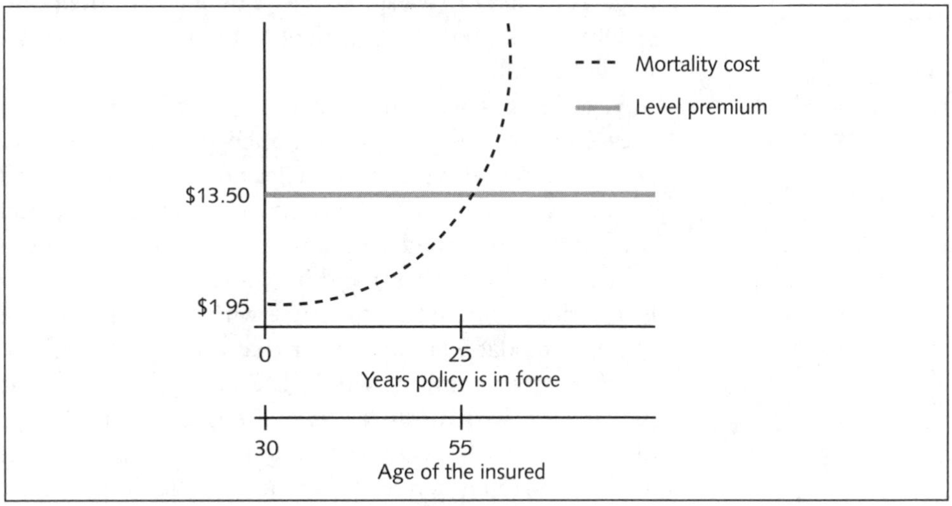

Legal reserve
A fund that is accumulated and maintained by the insurer to meet future obligations, such as administrative expenses and mortality charges

Level Premium   Unlike term life insurance, for which premiums may increase with age, a whole life policy involves a level premium payable for the life of the policy. A whole life policy steadily builds cash values by prepaying premiums in the earlier years with the excess accumulating, thereby subsidizing higher mortality expenses in the later years. The excess premiums in the early years are kept in a **legal reserve**, which is a fund that is accumulated and maintained by the insurer to meet future obligations, such as administrative expenses and mortality charges.

Mortality charge
The amount of money the insurance company charges for providing a death benefit

Mortality Charge   All whole life policies include a **mortality charge**, which is the amount of money the insurance company charges for providing the death benefit. Few people die at younger ages, so the mortality charge is fairly low. As the insureds age, however, the chance of death increases and so does the mortality charge.

Administrative Costs and Insurer Profit   As with all types of insurance, whole life premiums cover not only mortality charges, but administrative expenses and a profit margin as well.

Cash value

Increases over the life of the policy as long as the premiums are paid according to the contract

A whole life policy's savings element, or **cash value**, increases over the life of the policy as long as the premiums are paid according to the contract. The policy may be surrendered for the cash value (surrender charges may apply), or cash may be borrowed under a loan provision.

Types of Whole Life Policies

Ordinary (straight) life policy

A continuous-premium whole life policy in which premiums are paid regularly until either death or age 100

An **ordinary (straight) life policy** is a continuous-premium policy in which premiums are paid regularly until either death or age 100. The insured may choose from various premium modes, including annual, semiannual, quarterly, or monthly. Of the types of whole life policies, the ordinary life policy provides the maximum permanent death protection for the lowest possible premium, but consumers should be aware that the premium must be paid continuously, even past retirement, until death. If the insured survives to age 100, the face amount will be paid to the policyowner as a living benefit.

Limited-payment policy

Permanent life insurance for which premiums are payable for a limited number of years, after which the policy becomes paid up for its stated face amount

Paid-up policy

A policy for which no future premium payments are due; remains in effect for life

Under a **limited-payment policy**, the insurance is permanent, and the insured has lifetime protection. Premiums, however, are payable for only a limited number of years, after which the policy becomes paid up for the stated face amount. A **paid-up policy** is one for which no future premium payments are due, but the policy remains in effect for life. Because the years in which premiums are paid are fewer than those of an ordinary life policy, limited-payment premiums are higher.

The premiums for a limited-payment policy may be fixed for any number of years (e.g., 10 years) or to a stated age. The name of the policy reflects the premium period; for example, if a premium payment is for 10 years, the policy is usually known as a 10-pay whole life policy.

Individuals who anticipate a limited number of high-income years during which they can most afford life insurance premium payments often choose limited-payment policies. Limited-payment policies are not suited for individuals with a restricted amount of financial resources and a need for a large death benefit.

Modified whole life

Premiums are lower for the first few years after policy issue, typically three to five years, and increase to a higher level premium thereafter

Under a **modified whole life** policy, premiums are lower for the first few years (typically three to five years) and increase to a higher level premium thereafter. Modified life is traditional whole life insurance with a unique premium payment arrangement designed to accommodate a policyowner that anticipates higher income in the future.

Single premium whole life

Single lump-sum payment made at policy issue with no future premiums due

A **single premium whole life** policy requires a single lump-sum payment made at policy issue with no future premiums due. Single premium whole life may be suitable for a person with a cash windfall and a death benefit need; however, adverse income tax implications may render this type of policy inappropriate. Even though single premium whole life policies build immediate cash value, they may be classified as modified endowment contracts (MECs) and, as such, may be subject to taxation and penalties on loans or withdrawals. (Refer to the Modified Endowment Contracts section in this chapter for additional information.)

Current assumption whole life

Uses new-money interest rates and current mortality assumptions to determine cash values

A **current assumption whole life** (CAWL) policy uses new-money interest rates and current mortality assumptions to determine cash values. In essence, the insurer shares the investment experience and profits with the policyowner. Interest rates may fluctuate with the experience of the insurer, but the policy also has a stated guaranteed minimum interest rate. Mortality costs vary, as well, with maximum mortality charges stated in the policy.

Variable life
A fixed-premium, whole life policy in which the death benefit and cash values fluctuate on the basis of the performance of subaccounts sometimes referred to as separate accounts

Joint life
Covers two or more lives under one policy at a cost lower than premiums for multiple separate policies

First-to-die policy
Pays the face amount upon the first death of two or more insureds

Last-to-die policy
Makes a death benefit payment upon the last death of multiple insureds

Nonparticipating
A policy that does not pay dividends

Participating
A policy that pays dividends

Variable life, a type of whole life insurance with a fixed premium, has a death benefit and cash values that fluctuate on the basis of the performance of subaccounts, which are professionally managed portfolios of debt and equity securities. The policyowner directs the investment of the policy's cash values among these subaccounts and bears all the investment risk. If the investment experience is weak, the death benefit amount may be reduced but will never fall below the original face amount.

Because variable life insurance policies are securities-based products, they are subject to regulation at both the state and federal levels. Agents and brokers who sell variable life products must be licensed to sell both life insurance and securities.

Joint life insurance covers two or more lives under one policy at a cost lower than multiple, separate policies. A **first-to-die policy** pays the face amount upon the first death of two or more insureds. Spouses may use this type of policy to provide for mortgage payments or education funding. A **last-to-die policy**, also known as a survivorship policy, pays the death benefit upon the last death of multiple insureds and is an effective estate planning tool when the unlimited marital deduction is used and estate taxes are due at the death of the surviving spouse. Premiums usually are based on the underwriting characteristics of the individual with the longest life expectancy.

Dividend Options   A whole life policy that pays dividends is considered a participating policy. Policies that do not pay dividends are considered **nonparticipating**. Dividends declared by the insurer are never guaranteed because they are considered to be a refund of excess policy premiums that remain with the insurer as a result of excess earnings, expense savings, and better-than-anticipated mortality experience. Owners of **participating** whole life policies are entitled to receive policy dividends declared by the insurer. Following are the several dividend options available to policyowners.

Cash   Under the cash option, a policyowner will receive a check on the policy anniversary equal to the full amount of the declared dividend. In most cases, cash dividends are payable only after the policy has been in force for a certain period.

Dividends to Reduce Premium   With the dividends to reduce premium option, dividends are applied toward the payment of the premium, with the policyowner paying the difference, if any, between the total premium and the annual dividend.

Dividends to Accumulate at Interest   When the dividends to accumulate at interest option is chosen, dividends are left on deposit with the insurance company and interest is earned on the dividends. The amount accumulated is added to the death benefit if the insured dies, or to the cash value if the policy is surrendered. The interest earned is taxable as ordinary income in the year earned.

Paid-Up Additions   If the policyowner chooses the paid-up additions option, dividends are used to purchase additional paid-up life insurance coverage, which increases the policy's total death benefit and cash value. The additional amount is what a single premium equal to the dividends would purchase for the same whole life plan. No evidence of insurability is required.

One-Year Term Insurance   Under the one-year term insurance option, dividends are used to purchase one-year term insurance. This is sometimes referred to as the fifth dividend option. In many cases, the face amount of the term insurance policy is the death benefit amount that an annual premium equal to the dividend amount will purchase as annually renewable term. Alternately, the dividends can be used to purchase a one-year term policy equal to the cash value of the original policy. Any remaining dividends are used to purchase increments of paid-up life insurance or accumulate at interest.

Nonforfeiture Options   During the insured's lifetime, the nonforfeiture options apply if the policy is discontinued. Under this provision, the insured does not forfeit the cash value accumulation but chooses how the policy's cash value will be used.

Cash Surrender Value   The cash surrender value option allows the policyowner who ceases premium payments and no longer has a need for the original life insurance protection to surrender the policy and receive the policy's cash surrender value (cash value less any surrender charges). Policyowners who surrender policies may incur an income tax liability on the cash value that exceeds the policy's cost basis.

Reduced Paid-Up Insurance   With the reduced paid-up insurance option, the net cash value of the original life insurance policy is used as a net single premium to purchase a lesser amount of fully paid-up insurance and is suitable for the policyowner who wants to maintain some level of permanent death protection but wants no future premium outlay. The insurance purchased under this option is the same type of policy as the policy being discontinued. The face amount of the new policy depends on the cash value of the original policy, current age of the insured, and policy expenses.

Extended Term Insurance   The extended term insurance option uses the net cash surrender value of the original policy as a net single premium to purchase a term insurance policy with a face amount equal to that of the original policy and is most appropriate for someone who wants to preserve death protection equal to the original policy's net face value for a limited time. The extended term coverage will require no future premium payments, but it will last only as long as the original policy's cash value will support it, on the basis of the insured's attained age.

Whole Life Insurance Policy Riders

Waiver of Premium   A waiver of premium rider ensures that valuable insurance coverage is not lost if the policyholder is unable to pay premiums because of a disability. With this rider, the insurance company waives all premiums should the insured become totally disabled.

Accidental Death Benefit   The accidental death benefit rider pays the beneficiary an additional death benefit if the insured dies accidentally, as defined in the rider. The definition of *accident* usually requires that death occur within 90 days of a purely unexpected event and not be related to any medical condition of the insured. An accidental death benefit is termed *double indemnity* when twice the face amount is paid for an accidental death.

Spouse and Child Insurance   Spouse and child insurance riders allow the policyowner to purchase term insurance on the spouse and children of the insured.

Term insurance rider
Offers additional term life insurance on the insured

Term Insurance Rider   A **term insurance rider** offers additional term life insurance on the insured. Premiums are usually guaranteed for a specified number of years; thereafter, premiums may increase annually. Often, the rider can be converted into permanent insurance on an attained age basis.

Living Benefits Rider   The living benefits rider, also known as an accelerated death benefit rider, gives the policyowner access to a portion of the policy's eligible death benefit if the insured is diagnosed with a terminal illness with a life expectancy of 12 months or less. (Some states have established other life expectancy periods once terminal illness is diagnosed.)

Paid-up insurance rider

Increases the whole life death benefit protection and builds additional cash value

Paid-Up Insurance Rider   The **paid-up insurance rider** is an economical way to increase the death benefit protection and build additional cash value. Premiums for this rider are used to purchase additional, paid-up whole life insurance in addition to the original whole life death benefit.

Advantages

Fixed Premiums   In traditional whole life policies, premiums remain fixed for the duration of the policy.

Tax-Deferred Accumulation   The policyowner pays no current income tax on the cash value accumulation of a whole life policy.

Lifetime Coverage   Whole life policies provide death benefit protection over the insured's lifetime, as long as premiums are paid as stipulated in the policy.

Limitations

Inflexible Premiums   Policyowners cannot modify whole life premiums in the event their financial situation changes. Therefore, much-needed death benefits may lapse if policyowners become ill, unemployed, or find themselves in unfavorable financial circumstances. In some cases, riders can protect the policyowner from several adverse situations.

Gradual Cash Value Growth   Cash values can be insignificant in the early years of a whole life policy but steadily increase over the duration of the policy. Compared with other tax-deferred investments, such as IRAs or Section 401(k) plans, the internal rate of return of a whole life policy may be low.

Surrender Charges   An insurer may penalize a policyowner for canceling a whole life policy, especially during the first few years of the policy, and the penalty is administered through a surrender charge, which is deducted from the cash value. Because the insurer's major expenses associated with the policy issuance are incurred up front (e.g., underwriting cost and agent's commission), the insurer imposes a surrender charge so it can recover some of the costs should the policy be terminated.

Universal Life Insurance

Universal life insurance

Gives policyowners the ability to adjust the premiums, death benefit, and cash values up or down to meet individual needs (within certain limits)

Universal life insurance allows policyholders, within certain limits, to adjust the premium, cash value, or death benefit up or down to meet individual needs. In comparison to whole life policies, which are based on the long-term return of an insurer's general account, universal life premiums are based on a current assumed interest rate that is equal to or (usually) greater than the policy's guaranteed interest rate. Therefore, some of the investment risk is shifted from the insurer to the policyowner.

The basic structure of how a universal life insurance policy operates is a bit complex. Mortality charges based on the insured's age and the policy's net amount at risk, along with the policy's administrative expenses, are deducted from the premium due. The amount left is credited to the policy's cash value, which is then credited with interest, usually at current interest rates, to result in the end-of-period cash surrender value. Exhibit 9.3 illustrates the basic structure of a universal life policy.

EXHIBIT 9.3 Structure of a Universal Life Policy

Death Benefit Options

Option A (Option 1)   Option A pays a level death benefit. The net amount of risk (NAR) for a universal life policy is the difference between the cash value and the death benefit. Therefore, for an Option A policy, the NAR decreases as the cash value increases, as Exhibit 9.4 illustrates.

EXHIBIT 9.4 Death Benefit Options

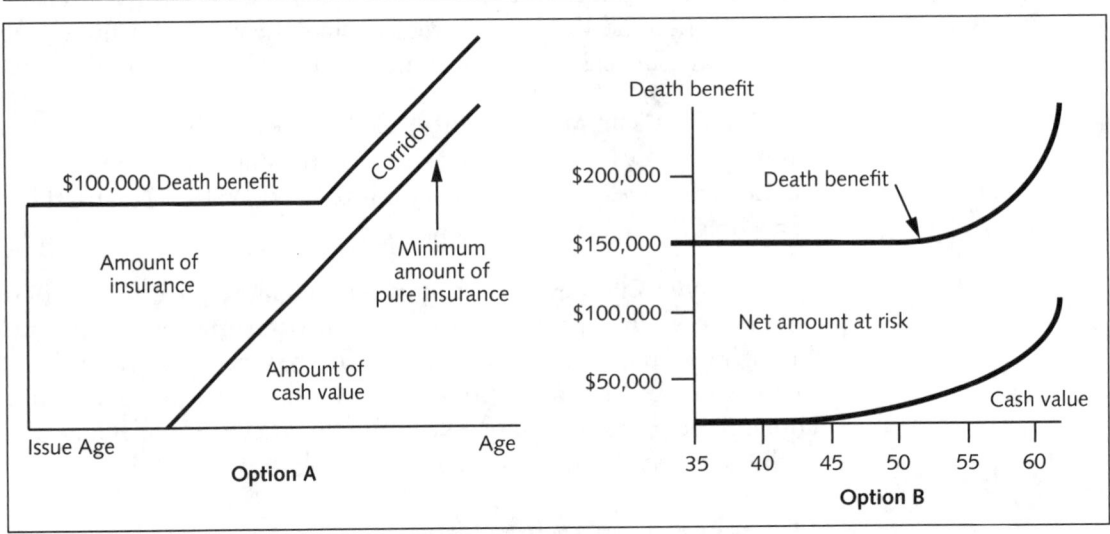

In some cases, an Option A death benefit will begin to increase in the later years, as a result of the tax law that imposes a "DEFRA corridor" of NAR if the cash value becomes too large (as defined by law) relative to the death benefit. This corridor is named after the Deficit Reduction Act of 1984, and it imposes minimum death benefits at certain NAR levels to prevent the policy from becoming more like an investment and less like a life insurance policy.

Option B (Option 2)   Option B provides an increasing death benefit, which is the death benefit plus the cash value. As a result, the NAR under this option remains level throughout the policy.

Premium Payments

Universal life policyowners can choose the amount of premium they pay into their policies, subject to insurer minimums and maximums. However, this premium flexibility can be a disadvantage in cases where insufficient premiums will cause the policy to lapse. For this reason, many insurers require a target, or planned, premium for a given number of years, after which policyowners can determine the premiums paid into the policy. As long as the policy has enough cash value to cover mortality charges and administrative expenses, additional premiums may not be required.

Variable Universal Life

In the 1980s, the life insurance industry unveiled variable universal life (VUL) insurance, a type of universal life insurance policy in which one could buy insurance with the option to invest in managed portfolios called subaccounts, sometimes referred to as separate accounts. Unlike whole life policies, VUL policyholders could actually see a breakdown of the premium payments, expense charges, earnings, and policy values on periodic statements. Because securities are used as variable universal life investment options, agents and brokers who sell variable life products must be licensed to sell both life insurance and securities.

Variable universal life (VUL) insurance

Combines the investment component of variable life and the premium, death benefit, and cash value flexibility features of universal life

Flexible Premiums and Death Benefits   A **variable universal life (VUL) insurance** policy combines the investment component of variable life insurance with the premium, death benefit, and cash value flexibility features of universal life insurance. VUL policies have increasing or decreasing death benefits and flexible premium payments that mirror universal life policies.

Self-Directed Investment Accounts   As with variable life, the policyowner directs the investment of the policy's cash values and bears the investment risk; the cash value is maintained in one or more subaccounts. The cash values reflect the policyowner's pro rata share of assets held in the subaccount and are subject to fluctuations similar to other securities-based products.

Variable Universal Life Policy Structure   The basic structure of a VUL policy is the same as a universal life policy, with mortality charges and administrative expenses being deducted from the policy's cash value and the cash value being credited with interest and/or performance, which is dependent on the asset allocation of the cash value.

Riders and Optional Benefits

Universal life and variable universal life have riders available that are similar to those of other life policies.

Waiver of Premium   The waiver of premium (or waiver of monthly deductions) rider waives mortality and expense charges if the insured becomes totally and permanently disabled before a stated age, usually age 65. The policy continues as if the policyowner were paying an amount equal to these charges. Insurers have recently developed an upgraded form of the traditional waiver of premium rider that pays the target premium of the policy, rather than paying only the mortality and expense charges. This feature allows the policy to continue in a manner similar to how it was likely being funded before an insured's disability. Most waiver of premium riders require that a waiting period be satisfied before the waiver of monthly deductions can begin.

Accidental Death Benefit Rider   The accidental death benefit rider pays the beneficiary an additional death benefit if the insured dies accidentally, as defined in the rider. The definition of accident usually requires that death occur within 90 days of a purely unexpected event and not be related to any medical condition of the insured. An accidental death benefit is termed *double indemnity* when twice the face amount is paid for an accidental death.

Other insured rider
Offers level term insurance coverage on the insured's spouse or children

Living benefits rider
Gives the policyowner access to a portion of the policy's eligible death benefit if the insured is diagnosed with a terminal illness and has a life expectancy of 12 months or less

Other Insured Rider   The **other insured rider** offers level term insurance coverage on the insured's spouse or children. Most often, coverage is convertible to permanent insurance at specified ages.

Living Benefits Rider   The **living benefits rider**, also known as an *accelerated death benefit rider*, gives the policyowner access to a portion of the policy's eligible death benefit if the insured is diagnosed with a terminal illness and has a life expectancy of 12 months or less. (Some states have established other life expectancy periods once terminal illness is diagnosed.)

Advantages

Flexible Premium   The ability to adjust the amount of premium payments is beneficial when financial circumstances change.

Flexible Death Benefit   Universal life offers cost-effective increases in the death benefit without the need to purchase a separate policy; however, proof of insurability may be required. The death benefit can also be decreased if the current death benefit is no longer needed by the policyowner.

Current Assumptions   Because interest rates and mortality are based on current experience, the accumulated value of a universal life policy is often higher than that of a whole life policy. In addition, the overall cost for a universal life policy may be lower than that of a whole life policy.

Limitations

Flexible Premium   Policyowners may decide not to make premium payments at certain times, resulting in a significant decrease in the accumulated value or the lapse of the policy. Owners of universal life policies must be disciplined enough to make the premium payments needed to yield the desired accumulated value and keep the policy in force.

Fewer Guarantees   The accumulated value of a universal life policy can drop to zero if sufficient premiums are not paid. In addition, the target premium for some policies may not keep the policy in force into later years. As a result, the premium required to keep the policy in force may actually be higher than a whole life premium.

On the other hand, a whole life policy is guaranteed to have a specified cash value and death benefit at any given time as long as premiums are paid. Although universal life policies can guarantee a minimum accumulated cash value and death benefit, the premium necessary for the guarantee may not be much less than a whole life policy.

Equity-Indexed Universal Life (EIUL)

Equity-indexed universal life (EIUL)

A universal life policy that offers an upside potential for cash value growth with limited downside risk

The **equity-indexed universal life** policy form first emerged in the late 1990s shortly after equity-indexed annuities gained popularity. EIUL appeals to clients who want upside potential for cash value growth with limited downside risk. Most policies guarantee that returns will not drop below 0%, and in return, the policies will share in the upside by placing a cap, or maximum percentage, that limits the extent to which the policyowner participates in the performance of the index. Most contracts have a fixed account to and from which policy values can be exchanged without incurring a fee; in addition, a policy may have a no-lapse guarantee rarely exceeding five years. The usual and customary riders of universal life policies also are available on most EIUL policies.

Modified Endowment Contracts (MECs)

Modified endowment contract (MEC)

A life insurance policy that exceeds its net level (7-pay) premium during the first seven years or during the seven years following a material change of the policy

According to the Internal Revenue Code, in order for life insurance contracts to receive favorable tax treatment, they must meet the federal tax law definition of life insurance. As a result, a net level premium is established by the Internal Revenue Code for each policy. If the cumulative premium payments exceed the net level premium for the policy during the first seven years of the contract or seven years following a material change to the contract, the policy becomes a **modified endowment contract (MEC)**. The premium is called the 7-pay premium and depends on the amount of the policy's death benefit and the age and life expectancy of the insured.

If the policy is or becomes a MEC, the policyholder may be subject to additional taxes and penalties on any distributions (other than the death benefit) from the policy during the life of the insured. Any distribution (including loans or withdrawals) from a MEC will be taxed on a LIFO (last-in, first-out) basis, which means that policy income or gains are taxed first at the time of distribution. The distribution is then includible in taxable income, up to the amount the account value exceeds the basis in the policy. Once all of the gain is loaned or withdrawn, subsequent distributions are considered a return of basis. In addition, a 10% penalty is assessed to any taxable amount, unless the policyowner has attained age 59½ or older.

EXHIBIT 9.5 Feature Comparison of Common Life Insurance Policies

	Term Life	Whole (Ordinary) Life	Universal Life	Variable Life	Variable Universal Life	Equity Indexed Universal Life
Premium amount	Increasing or level	Fixed; may decrease if dividends are used to reduce premiums	Adjustable at policyowner's discretion, subject to minimum and maximum limits	Fixed; may decrease if earnings used to reduce premiums	Adjustable at policyowner's discretion, subject to minimum and maximum limits; required premiums may increase or decrease based on investment performance of subaccounts	Adjustable at policy-owner's discretion, subject to minimum and maximum limits; the maximum required premium is based on the minimum guaranteed return
Death benefits	Fixed or decreasing	Fixed; will increase if dividends are used to purchase paid-up additions	Option A: Level (increases at DEFRA corridor) Option B: Increases by amount of cash value	Has a guaranteed minimum but can increase if investment experience on cash value is favorable	No long-term guarantee No lapse riders can be purchased for a limited number of years Option A: Level (increases at DEFRA corridor) Option B: Increases by amount of cash value	No long-term guarantee No lapse riders can be purchased for a limited number of years Option A: Level (increases at DEFRA corridor) Option B: Increases by amount of cash value
Policyowner's control over cash value investments	N/A	None	None	Complete	Complete	None
Rate of return on cash value investment	N/A	Fixed; may also pay dividends, which vary	Minimum guaranteed rate, but may be higher depending on current interest rates	No minimum guarantee, but positive investment experience can yield lofty returns	No minimum guarantee, but positive investment experience can yield lofty returns	Minimum guarantee lower than standard universal life
Use	Limited resources, large and/or temporary need, no lifetime coverage	Maximum guarantees, minimum flexibility, lifetime coverage	No investment responsibility, maximum flexibility, lifetime coverage (requires disciplined funding)	Requires investment responsibility, minimal flexibility, lifetime coverage	Requires investment responsibility, moderate flexibility, lifetime coverage (requires discipline funding and reasonable investment performance)	Requires a certain level of risk tolerance to hold through down markets Lifetime coverage (requires disciplined funding and reasonable performance of the underlying index)

Group Life Insurance

Group life insurance covers a large group of insureds under a single master contract. The employer holds the master contract and is responsible for making premium payments to the insurer. The employer can fund premium payments in whole or in part and, in many cases, the employee pays no portion of the premium. If employees pay part of the premiums, the employer generally collects the employee contributions through payroll deductions.

Group insurance is typically less expensive than individual insurance because of the savings the insurer realizes in lower administrative expenses and underwriting costs. Individual underwriting is not required of group insurance participants, so no evidence of insurability is required and no medical examinations are necessary. The employer may set up its requirements for eligibility. Eligibility requirements for a typical plan might include that participating employees be full-time workers and satisfy a minimum probationary period.

Group Term Insurance

Group term life insurance is the most common form of group life insurance selected by employers. Group term life insurance offers the same benefits as an individual term life insurance policy. Group term premiums, like those of individual term policies, increase with age. When an employer provides group term insurance, there is no tax consequence to the employee on the premium paid by the employer if the death benefit under the policy does not exceed $50,000. The imputed cost of coverage in excess of $50,000 must be included in income using the IRS Premium Table and is subject to Social Security and Medicare taxes (IRC Section 79). The actual premiums paid by the employer for group term insurance are tax deductible by the employer as a business expense.

The amount of coverage provided by an employer through a group term plan must be determined by some formula that precludes adverse selection on the part of employees. Most employers provide employees with either a flat amount of coverage, such as $25,000, or coverage equal to a multiple of the employee's annual salary. In some cases, employees are allowed to purchase additional amounts of coverage in prespecified multiple amounts. The insurer may require proof of insurability for optional higher coverage amounts.

A covered employee typically has the right to convert a group term policy, upon termination from the company, to a regular cash value policy at a rate based on his attained age. The insurer usually grants a 31-day grace period after an employee withdraws from the group in which basic death benefits remain in effect. The conversion privilege is, in one respect, advantageous to the insured because no evidence of insurability is required upon conversion. However, adverse selection comes into play with group conversions as those who are uninsurable or are not easily insurable eagerly opt for the conversion privilege, and those who can be favorably underwritten discover much better values in the individual market.

Group Whole Life Insurance

Group whole life insurance allows the insured to obtain death benefit coverage, as well as accumulate a level of savings through the policy's cash value. Group whole life insurance is not a frequently chosen employee benefit because it does not have the tax advantages of group term life insurance. Generally, the employee must report the premiums paid by the employer for a group whole life policy as taxable income.

Group Universal Life Insurance

Some employers offer group universal life plans. Often, these policies serve as optional supplements to the more traditional group term plans. In most cases, employees pay the entire cost of the coverage; the premiums are paid through payroll deductions, resulting in some administrative cost savings for the insurer. The savings are then passed on to employees in the form of lower premiums. Most plans allow the employee to purchase coverage up to a specified maximum face value without providing evidence of insurability.

Group Variable Universal Life (GVUL) Insurance

The newest addition to many employers' optional benefits program is group variable universal life (GVUL) insurance. Major insurers are beginning to introduce GVUL policy forms designed and priced specifically for large groups; they feature very low expenses and surrender charges that range from low down to zero. The result is a readily available alternative for life insurance protection that provides a tax-favored investment, even in the early years of the policy. Because GVUL policies involve mortality and administrative expenses, they should be purchased only by those in need of the protection element.

LIFE INSURANCE POLICY SELECTION

The first step in selecting an insurance policy is to determine the type of product that best suits the needs of the prospective policyowner. Policy cost, duration of the need, amount of coverage, and risk tolerance all must be considered during the process. Term insurance policies are almost always the least expensive in the short term, especially at younger ages. Over the long term, however, they are generally the most expensive and, absent an unexpected accident or the early onset of terminal illness, rarely result in a death benefit being paid. If the need is long term and permanent insurance is required, a higher initial premium must be accounted for in the budgeting process. Universal life policies have more premium flexibility, and premiums are generally lower than traditional whole life policies. Prospective policyowners with higher risk tolerances may be inclined to opt for a variable product.

Once the most appropriate type of life insurance policy is determined, it is necessary to identify the resources for premium payments. When a premium range has been established and budgeted for, policies from various insurers should be compared. Today, this is usually done using one of three methods. First, the National Association of Insurance Commissioners (NAIC) has adopted interest-adjusted cost indices as a method of comparing life insurance policies. There are two types of interest-adjusted cost indices: the interest-adjusted surrender cost index and the interest-adjusted net payment cost index. The interest-adjusted surrender cost is a measure of the true anticipated cost of keeping a policy in force, adjusted for interest, for a specified number of years (usually 10 or 20) and then surrendering it for its cash value. The net payment cost index assumes that the policy remains in force, adjusted for interest, until the insured dies. Today, interest-adjusted cost indices are widely used for policy comparisons.

A second method of policy comparison uses a surrender cost index, which compares cash value levels and costs, assuming that at some point in the future the policy will be surrendered for its cash value. The net payment cost index compares the cost of the death benefit provided. Policyowners can compare future costs, for example, in 10 to 20 years, assuming that premiums are continuously paid and the policy's cash value remains in the policy.

LIFE INSURANCE POLICY ILLUSTRATIONS

Policy illustrations show important policy features and values, on a guaranteed and current basis, and show how a policy is structured and how it can be expected to perform.

Please note that policy illustrations are not forecasts of future performance. They project what policy values could be if the policy performed at illustrated rates, assuming insurer variables, such as investment performance, remain steady. Prospective policyowners should not confuse the policy illustration with the actual policy. Illustrations show some values that are contractually guaranteed, but they also usually show nonguaranteed values as well.

Policy illustrations reflect assumptions pertaining to interest, mortality, loading, and lapse rates. Assumed policy interest rates will probably differ from actual interest/growth rates in the future. As a result, the policy's actual performance will differ from that of the policy illustrated. Care should be taken, however, to project reasonable interest rates and show mortality rates that reflect insurer experience. Policy loads should be sufficient to cover expenses and the insurer's profit margin, so that prospective policyowners are not misled.

LIFE INSURANCE POLICY REPLACEMENT

The decision to replace one policy with another should be made with caution. The methodology for such a decision includes gathering facts, calculations, and benchmark comparisons. One such comparison uses the Belth price of protection model:

$$CPT = \frac{(P + CV_0)(1+i) - (CV_1 + D)}{(DB - CV_1)(0.001)}$$

CPT	=	cost per thousand
P	=	annual premium
CV_0	=	cash value at beginning of year
i	=	net after-tax earning rate
CV_1	=	cash value at year end
D	=	current dividend
DB	=	death benefit

Belth Benchmark Table

Age	Benchmark price of insurance per $1,000
<30	$1.50
30–34	$2.00
35–39	$3.00
40–44	$4.00
45–49	$6.50
50–54	$10.00
55–60	$15.00
60–64	$25.00
65–69	$35.00
70–74	$50.00
75–79	$80.00
80–84	$125.00

(Joseph M. Belth, author)

To use this model, the insured should calculate the cost per thousand (CPT) for one's current insurance and compare the result to the appropriate Belth benchmark per thousand. If the CPT is more than twice the benchmark price, the insured should consider replacement.

E X A M P L E   Joan is 62 years old and has a whole life policy with the following features:

- Annual premium = $800
- Cash value on January 1, 2020 = $400,000
- Cash value on December 31, 2020 = $405,000
- After-tax earning rate = 4.2%
- Current dividend = $600
- Death benefit = $750,000

$$CPT = \frac{(P + CV_0)(1 + i) - (CV_1 + D)}{(DB - CV_1)(0.001)}$$

$$CPT = \frac{(\$800 + \$400,000)(1 + 0.042) - (\$405,000 + \$600)}{(\$750,000 - \$405,000)(0.001)}$$

$$CPT = \$34.88$$

The Belth benchmark for a 62-year-old individual is $25. The CPT for Joan's current insurance is less than $50 (2 × $25), so she should retain her current policy.

LIFE INSURANCE POLICY PROVISIONS

Grace Period

Grace period
Amount of time following the premium due date in which the policyowner may pay the overdue premium

Life insurance policies allow for a **grace period** (typically 31 days) after the premium due date in which the policyowner may pay the overdue premium. During this grace period, the policy remains in force. In some cases, interest may be charged on the overdue premium. If the insured dies within the grace period, the insurer deducts the premium (and, in some cases, pro rata premium) from the death benefit payable to the beneficiary.

Incontestability Clause

Incontestability clause
Prevents the insurer from canceling the policy after it has been in force for two years in the event the life insurer discovers material misrepresentation or concealment

The **incontestability clause** in a life insurance policy prevents the insurer from canceling the policy after it has been in force usually for two years in the event the life insurer discovers material misrepresentation or concealment.

Entire Contract Clause

Entire contract clause
Maintains that the life insurance policy and the policyowner's application compose the complete life insurance contract

The **entire contract clause** maintains that the life insurance policy and the policyowner's application compose the complete life insurance contract. As a result, any statements made on the application are part of the contract and, if these statements are false, can be used as basis to void or alter the contract.

Misstatement of Age or Gender Provision

Misstatement of age or gender provision
If a misstatement is made, the insurer can adjust the face amount to the amount the premium would have purchased had the age or gender been correctly stated

The **misstatement of age or gender provision** provides that, if a misstatement of age or gender is discovered after the policy is issued, the life insurance company can adjust the face amount of the policy to an amount that the premium would have purchased had the insured's age or gender been correctly stated. Usually, the misstatement of age or gender is discovered after the insured dies, when the insurance company receives a death certificate showing the correct information.

E X A M P L E   Suppose Abby is age 45 and she incorrectly states her age as 35 on a life insurance application for a $100,000 policy. Based on the information provided, she is charged a $100 monthly premium for her policy. The insurer, however, would have charged Abby $200 per month had it known she were 45. If she dies and the insurer discovers the misstatement of age, it will recalculate her death benefit on the basis of the premium amount she should have paid. Because she paid only half as much as she should have ($100 instead of $200), the insurer will pay only half the death benefit, or $50,000.

Policy Assignment

Absolute assignment
All life insurance policy ownership rights are transferred to a designated assignee

An assignment is an agreement under which the policyowner (the assignor) transfers some of the ownership rights in a policy to another party (the assignee). Two types of assignments are available, absolute and collateral.

An **absolute assignment** is an assignment of a life insurance policy under which the policyowner transfers all policy ownership rights to a designated assignee.

Collateral assignment
A life insurance policy is transferred to a creditor as security for a loan or debt

A **collateral assignment** is the assignment of a life insurance policy to a creditor as security for a loan or debt. The creditor is entitled to receive the proceeds or cash value of the policy only to the extent of the amount of the unpaid debt. The assignment will terminate when the debt is paid.

Suicide Clause

Suicide clause
Asserts that, if the insured commits suicide within a specified period of time, the policy will be voided and premiums will be refunded to the beneficiary

To mitigate the risk that a person will purchase a life insurance policy in contemplation of suicide, a life insurance policy includes a **suicide clause**. The clause asserts that, if the insured commits suicide within a specified period, the policy will be voided and premiums will be refunded to the beneficiary. Most suicide clauses have a specified time limit of two years.

Reinstatement Clause

Reinstatement clause
Outlines the conditions under which a lapsed policy may be reinstated

A life insurance policy will lapse if the premium payments are not paid by the insured as stated in the policy. The **reinstatement clause** in a policy outlines the conditions under which a lapsed policy may be reinstated. In most cases, evidence of insurability is not needed if the reinstatement takes place within 31 days of grace period expiration. Thereafter, the policy may be reinstated during the reinstatement period (up to five years) with submission of unpaid premiums plus interest and satisfactory evidence of insurability.

Policy Loan Provision

Policy loan provision
Allows the policyowner to borrow (with interest) against the cash surrender value of a permanent insurance policy

A **policy loan provision** allows the policyowner to borrow (with interest) against the cash value of a permanent insurance policy. Any loans and interest payments outstanding at the time of the insured's death will be deducted from the death benefit.

Automatic Premium Loan

Automatic premium loan
Directs the insurance company to pay an overdue premium by making a loan against the policy's cash value if the overdue premium remains unpaid upon the expiration of the grace period

Some whole life policies include a provision for an **automatic premium loan** (APL), which directs the insurance company to pay an overdue premium by making a loan against the policy's cash value if the overdue premium remains unpaid upon the expiration of the grace period. The policyowner must specifically request the provision either on the initial coverage application or in writing at a later date. As with the policy loan provision, any outstanding loans and interest payments at the insured's death will be withheld from the death benefit paid to the beneficiary.

Beneficiary Designations

Revocable beneficiary
Can be changed by the policyowner (who may or may not be the insured) at any time

Irrevocable beneficiary
Cannot be changed without the beneficiary's consent

The proceeds of a life insurance policy are distributed upon death to a beneficiary selected by the policyowner. A life insurance beneficiary can be an individual, a group of individuals, the insured's estate, or an entity, such as a charity or business.

The two types of beneficiary designations are revocable and irrevocable. A **revocable beneficiary** can be changed by the policyowner at any time. An irrevocable beneficiary cannot be changed without the beneficiary's consent. An **irrevocable beneficiary** must give consent before the policyowner can change the beneficiary designation and is often used in divorce settlements to guarantee one parent with a death benefit in the event the other parent dies.

The **primary beneficiary** of a life insurance policy is the party designated by the policyowner to receive the death benefit. A **contingent beneficiary** is an individual, group, or entity designated to receive the policy proceeds if the primary beneficiary dies before the insured. A contingent beneficiary can be secondary (receives a benefit if primary beneficiary predeceases the insured) or tertiary (receives a benefit when both the primary and secondary beneficiaries predecease the insured).

If the primary beneficiary is deceased, and all contingent beneficiaries are deceased or simply not named in the policy, the death benefit proceeds will be paid to the policyowner or to the policyowner's estate if the deceased insured was also the policyowner. In this event, the proceeds will be included in the probate estate and therefore subject to additional costs and delays.

Aviation Exclusion

Although no longer a common exclusion in policies issued today, the aviation exclusion denies coverage for those who die in noncommercial flights, such as private pilots, passengers, and military pilots. The death benefit is not paid; however, premiums are usually returned to the beneficiary.

War Exclusion

The **war exclusion** allows the insurer to deny a death claim if the insured's death is related to war or military service. In lieu of paying the death benefit, premiums are usually returned to the beneficiary with interest.

Survivorship Clause

The **survivorship clause**, also known as the common disaster clause, in a life insurance policy requires that a beneficiary survive the insured by a specified period (usually 30 or 60 days) in order to receive the death benefit proceeds. Otherwise, the policy proceeds will be paid as though the beneficiary had predeceased the insured.

Simultaneous Death Provision

A situation may arise in which the insured and the beneficiary both die within a short time of each other in an accident and it is not readily determinable who died first. Patterned after the Uniform Simultaneous Death Act, which has been adopted by most states, the simultaneous death provision establishes that the proceeds of the life insurance policy will be distributed as though the insured survived the beneficiary. If more than one beneficiary has been named on the policy, the next in the line of succession shall receive the proceeds. If no other beneficiaries are designated, the proceeds will be paid to the policyowner or the policyowner's estate if the deceased insured was also the policyowner.

Primary beneficiary
The party designated by the policyowner to receive death benefits

Contingent beneficiary
An individual, group, or entity designated to receive the policy proceeds if the primary beneficiary predeceases the insured

War exclusion
Allows the insurer to deny a death claim if the insured's death is related to war or military service

Survivorship clause
Requires that a beneficiary survive the insured by a specified period (usually 30 to 60 days) in order to receive the death benefit proceeds

LIFE INSURANCE SETTLEMENT OPTIONS

Settlement options
Allow the policyowner or beneficiary to choose either cash or one of several alternatives to how the death benefit proceeds will be paid

Most life insurance policies provide **settlement options** to a beneficiary as an alternative to receiving a lump sum check at the death of an insured. Moreover, these available alternatives may protect a beneficiary who is unable to manage a large lump sum of cash.

Interest Only

Interest-only option
The insurance company retains the death benefit and pays the primary beneficiary interest on that sum

Under the **interest-only option**, the insurance company retains the death benefit and pays the primary beneficiary interest on that sum. In some cases, the primary beneficiary may be given the right to withdraw some or all of the proceeds in a lump sum. The policyowner or primary beneficiary may name a contingent beneficiary to receive the balance of the proceeds at the primary beneficiary's death.

Fixed Amount

Fixed-amount option
Specifies that a designated amount of income will be provided to the beneficiary on a regular basis until the proceeds and accumulated interest are depleted

The **fixed-amount option** specifies that a designated amount of income will be provided to the beneficiary on a regular basis until the proceeds and accumulated interest are depleted. If the beneficiary dies with a balance of unpaid proceeds and accumulated interest, the balance is paid to a contingent beneficiary or included in the deceased beneficiary's estate.

Fixed Period

Fixed-period option
The beneficiary will receive the maximum periodic payments that the death benefit proceeds will purchase for a specified period

If the **fixed-period option** is chosen, the beneficiary will receive the maximum periodic payments that the death benefit proceeds will purchase for a specified period. If the beneficiary dies within the payment period, the balance is paid to a contingent beneficiary or included in the estate of the deceased beneficiary.

Life Income

Life income option
Allows the beneficiary to receive a specified periodic payment, usually for life

The **life income option** allows the beneficiary to receive a specified periodic payment, usually for life. The amount of the proceeds and the life expectancy of the beneficiary at the time of the insured's death are used to determine the amount of life income payable.

Life Income With Period Certain

Life income with period certain option
Provides an income to the beneficiary for life or a specified period, if longer

The **life income with period certain option** provides an income to the beneficiary for life or a specified period, if longer. The balance of the payments will be made to a contingent beneficiary if the primary beneficiary dies during the certain period. For example, a life income with 20 years certain option will provide a specified amount for at least 20 years (either to the primary beneficiary, if living, or to a contingent beneficiary, if the primary dies) or longer if the primary beneficiary outlives the 20-year period.

Life Income With Refund

Life income with refund option
The life insurance company agrees that if the primary beneficiary dies before the total amount paid under the option equals the proceeds of the policy, the company will pay the difference to a contingent beneficiary

Under the **life income with refund option**, the life insurance company agrees that if the primary beneficiary dies before the total amount paid under the option equals the proceeds of the policy, the life insurance company will pay the difference to a contingent beneficiary either in a lump sum or installments.

Joint and Last Survivor

Joint and last survivor income option

Provides joint beneficiaries a stated amount of income during their lives, and a continuation of the original or reduced amount for the remaining beneficiaries' lives

The **joint and last survivor income option** provides joint beneficiaries a stated amount of income during their lives, and a continuation of the original or reduced amount for the remaining beneficiaries' lives. A period certain may also be stipulated as part of this option.

ANNUITY CONTRACTS

An annuity is a contract designed to provide payments to the holder at specified intervals, usually for a fixed period, for the annuitant's life, or for the lives of two or more joint annuitants. Sold by insurance companies, annuities are commonly used to supplement retirement benefits. Similar to life insurance benefits, annuity payments are based on the pooling of the risk and life expectancy of a group.

Annuities may be classified in a number of ways, but generally they are categorized according to the time when the benefit payments begin (immediate or deferred annuity), by the method of premium payment (flexible or single premium annuity), or by the form of annuity payment (fixed or variable).

Types of Annuities

Immediate vs. Deferred

The insured has the option of having annuity payments made monthly, quarterly, semiannually, or annually. In addition, the insured may also specify whether the annuity payments should be immediate or deferred.

Immediate annuity

One in which the first annuity payment is made one payment interval from the purchase date

Immediate Annuities   An **immediate annuity** is one in which the first annuity payment is made one payment interval from the purchase date. Immediate annuities are purchased with a single lump-sum premium.

Deferred annuity

Provides income at some date in the future

Deferred Annuities   A **deferred annuity** provides income at some date in the future. The most popular form of a deferred annuity is a retirement annuity in which monetary value accumulates for a number of years and is paid in installments when the insured reaches retirement. A deferred annuity is purchased with either a single premium or periodic level premiums.

Flexible Premium vs. Single Premium

Flexible premium annuity

Allows the insured the option to vary premium deposits

Flexible Premium Annuities   A **flexible premium annuity** allows the insured the option to vary premium deposits. The amount of retirement income will relate directly to the accumulated sum in the annuity when it becomes due and payable. Under a flexible premium plan, the insured spreads payments over a designated period by making periodic premium payments.

Single premium annuity

An annuity purchased with a single lump sum

Single Premium Annuities   An annuity purchased with a single lump sum is known as a **single premium annuity**. Proceeds from life insurance policies may be used to purchase single premium annuities at special rates under a life income settlement option. Single premium annuities can be either immediate or deferred.

Fixed, Variable, and Equity Indexed Annuities

Fixed annuity

Insurer agrees to credit a specified interest rate over a stated period

Fixed Annuities   **Fixed annuities** are those in which the insurer agrees to credit a specified interest rate over a stated period. In addition, the insurance company can guarantee a certain annuity payment amount upon annuitization. A fixed annuity provides more security of principal than a variable annuity, but it has limited upside potential.

Variable annuity

Does not guarantee specific payments but has a potential for greater returns

Subaccounts

Portfolios of stocks and/or bonds that are professionally managed according to a specific investment objective

Accumulation units

Units of measurement that, when combined, equal the total account value of a variable annuity

Variable Annuities   Variable annuities do not guarantee specific annuity payments; however, they have potential for greater returns. In a **variable annuity**, the annuity owner chooses to allocate funds among one or more **subaccounts**. Subaccounts, sometimes referred to as separate accounts, are portfolios of stocks and/or bonds that are professionally managed according to specific investment objectives. Gains and losses are credited and debited to the annuity using what are known as **accumulation units**. Accumulation units are the units of measurement that, when combined, equal the total account value of a variable annuity.

The owner of a variable annuity accepts more short-term volatility because the value of the annuity fluctuates with the stock and bond markets, which is simply the trade-off between risk and return.

Equity indexed annuities (EIAs)

Based on the simple concept of returns that are equal to a percentage, or participation rate, of a popular market index (e.g., S&P 500)

Equity Indexed Annuities (EIAs)   **Equity indexed annuities (EIAs)** are based on the simple concept of returns that are equal to a percentage, or participation rate, of a popular market index (e.g., S&P 500). The credited rate is capped at a percentage of the increase in the index, which limits the upside. The insurer buys bonds to mature at a value sufficient to make good on its guarantee of the principal amount, and uses the remainder to invest in options, which, if in the money, can be exercised; thus, profits are available to share with the annuitant according to the participation rate.

An owner of an EIA enjoys features and benefits of both fixed and variable annuities. Although the upside of the index can work in one's favor, a guaranteed return of principal (not a guaranteed return) provides some downside protection for an individual who cannot afford to place any of the retirement funds at risk.

EIAs are a good fit for an individual who cannot afford to risk the principal investment but desires a potentially higher rate of return than one would receive from a fixed annuity, such as a person nearing retirement but wanting to (partially) participate in marketlike returns.

The EIA provides the annuitant with downside protection during the accumulation phase. Similarly, it provides protection against reduced income payments due to market decline. However, the participant will often be subject to surrender charges, sometimes for a substantial period of time. Also, money withdrawn before the completion of the contract may change the manner in which the return on that money was calculated.

Deferred income annuities (DIA)

Guarantee income for life or a certain period of time, however, the future income start dates are chosen at contract issuance

Deferred income annuities (DIA), also known as longevity annuities, guarantee income for life or a certain period of time. One unique characteristic of these types of annuities is that the future income start dates are chosen at contract issuance. Generally, for most deferred annuity contracts, the contract owner would make that decision at some point in the future.

The elected income start date may be any time after the first contract year and generally up to age 85. Premium payments may be single premium or flexible premium. The income start date for annuity benefits will be the same regardless of when the premium payments were made into the contract.

DIA annuity purchase rates (annuitization rates) are established at the time of the initial premium payment or subsequent premium payments. The annuity purchase rates will vary depending on when the premiums are paid. This differs from a typical deferred annuity. With a deferred annuity, if the contract owner decides to annuitize, the annuity purchase rates are determined at the time of annuitization, not when the premium payments are made into the contract.

On July 1, 2014, the U.S. Department of the Treasury and the Internal Revenue Service (IRS) issued final rules regarding **qualified longevity annuity contracts (QLACs)**, an insurance option that ensures retirees have a stream of regular income throughout their advanced years. QLACs are a type of deferred income annuity (DIA). QLACs provide an income stream that begins at an advanced age and continues throughout the individual's life. The final rules made longevity annuities accessible to 401(k) plans and other employer-sponsored individual account plans and IRAs by amending the required minimum distribution (RMD) regulations so that longevity annuity payments will not need to begin prematurely in order to comply with RMD regulations.

The following are key provisions of the final regulations covering QLACs purchased on or after July 2, 2014:

■ *Maximum age at commencement of income.* The QLAC contract must provide that distributions under the contract commence not later than a specified annuity starting date stated in the contract. The specified annuity starting date must be no later than the first day of the month following the employee's attainment of age 85.

■ *Maximum allowed investment.* A 401(k) or similar plan, or IRA, may allow plan participants to use up to 25% of their account balance or $125,000, whichever is less, to buy a QLAC without concern about noncompliance with the age 70½ minimum distribution requirements.

■ *Allowing return of premium (ROP) death benefit.* A longevity annuity in a plan or IRA can now provide that, if buying retirees die before or after the age when the annuity begins making payments (i.e., annuitization), the premiums they paid but have not yet received as annuity payments will be returned to their accounts and can be paid to their beneficiaries.

■ *Protecting persons against unintentional payment of excess longevity annuity premiums.* Individuals who inadvertently exceed the 25% or $125,000 limits on premium payments are allowed to correct the excess without disqualifying the purchase.

■ *Allowing more flexibility in issuing QLACs.* When the contract is issued, the contract (or a rider or endorsement with respect to that contract) must state that the contract is intended to be a QLAC.

Annuitization

Annuitization refers to the irrevocable exchange of a lump-sum amount for a periodic income stream. Annuitization is the same process that occurs with various life insurance settlement options, because the beneficiary is exchanging a lump-sum death benefit for one of several common forms of periodic annuity payments, the timing of which and the guarantees, if any, will vary among the numerous options and income streams.

Straight Life Annuity

Often referred to as a pure life annuity, a **straight life annuity** provides a lifetime income to the annuitant regardless of how long the annuitant lives. After the annuitant dies, no further annuity payments are made by the insurer. For a given purchase price, the highest amount of lifetime income per dollar spent is earned through the pure life annuity.

A straight life annuity provides no guaranteed minimum number of payments the insurer must make, and the dependents of the annuitant receive nothing from the contract once the annuitant has died. Therefore, the pure life annuity is ideal for the person

Qualified longevity annuity contracts (QLACs)

An insurance option that ensures retirees have a stream of regular income throughout their advanced years

Annuitization

An irrevocable exchange of a lump-sum amount for a periodic income stream

Straight life annuity

Provides a lifetime income to the annuitant regardless of how long the annuitant lives

who needs maximum income over his lifetime and has no living dependents to whom to leave the assets.

Life annuity with period certain
Guarantees the greater of a life income to the annuitant or a minimum number of payments to the annuitant's beneficiary

Life Annuity With Period Certain

A **life annuity with period certain** guarantees the greater of a life income to the annuitant or a minimum number of payments to the annuitant's beneficiary. Two common guarantee options are the 10-year period certain and the 20-year period certain. If the annuitant dies before the guarantee period expires, a named beneficiary receives the remaining guaranteed payments. If the annuitant outlives the guarantee period, payments continue until the annuitant's death.

Installment refund annuity
The insurer promises to continue periodic payments after the annuitant has died until the sum of all annuity payments equals the purchase price of the annuity

Installment Refund Annuity

The **installment refund annuity** continues periodic payments after the annuitant has died until the sum of all annuity payments equals the purchase price of the annuity.

Cash Refund Annuity

Cash refund annuity
Provides that, upon the death of an annuitant before payments totaling the purchase price have been made, the excess of the amount paid by the purchaser over the total annuity payments received will be paid in one sum to designated beneficiaries

In cases where an annuitant dies before periodic payments equal or exceed the price paid for the annuity, the insurer pays a lump sum equal to the difference between the price paid and the total payments received by the annuitant to the beneficiary of the annuity.

Joint and Survivor Annuity

Joint and survivor annuity
Based on the lives of two or more annuitants

A **joint and survivor annuity** is based on the lives of two or more annuitants, most often husband and wife. Annuity payments are made until the death of the last annuitant. A joint and 100% survivor annuity pays the full monthly payment to both parties and continues the same payment to the survivor. Some persons, however, choose a joint and survivor annuity that pays the survivor only a portion of the payment that was paid on both lives. For example, a joint and 75% survivor annuity would pay the survivor 75% of the payment received during both annuitants' lifetimes. Joint and last survivor is the most popular form of multilife (2+ annuitants) annuities.

TAXATION OF LIFE INSURANCE AND ANNUITIES

Tax Treatment of Life Insurance

A life insurance contract receives favorable tax treatment in a number of ways. First, death proceeds paid to beneficiaries are generally excluded from taxable income. Second, earnings on the cash value are not taxable until withdrawn. If the insured dies without surrendering the policy or withdrawing the cash value, the cash value accumulated will never be subject to income tax. Third, excluding modified endowment contracts (MECs), loans against a life insurance policy are tax-free. Fourth, under Section 1035 of the Internal Revenue Code, exchanges of one life insurance policy for another or for an annuity or qualified long-term care policy will not result in any recognition of gain. The owner's cost basis for the original life insurance policy will transfer to the new policy or contract.

Taxation of Lifetime Benefits

Dividends

Generally, dividends distributed are not taxable; instead, they are considered a return of a portion of premium payments that reduce the policyowner's basis. If dividends distributed exceed total premiums paid, the excess dividends are taxed to the owner as ordinary income in the year earned.

Withdrawals

Withdrawals from a life insurance policy receive FIFO (first-in, first-out) treatment. In other words, withdrawals of principal are tax-free until the accumulated premiums (less any prior withdrawals or loans) have been paid out (IRC §72(e)).

Modified endowment contracts (MECs) will be subject to LIFO (last-in, first-out) treatment for the life of the policy and a 10% penalty on taxable gains withdrawn before age 59½. (See the Modified Endowment Contracts section in this chapter.)

Cash Surrenders

When the owner of a policy surrenders a life insurance contract, the insurer is no longer obligated to pay the death benefit to the beneficiary. The policyowner will receive the cash surrender value of the policy by one of three methods: lump-sum payment, interest payments, or installment payments. Under the **lump-sum payment method**, the total cash value of the life insurance policy is paid to the policyowner. The gain at surrender equals the cash surrender value minus the investment in the contract (basis), taxed as ordinary income. The investment in the contract equals the premiums paid minus any dividends received minus any outstanding loans or withdrawals.

Upon cash surrender of the policy, the owner may choose to leave the cash value proceeds with the insurer and receive only interest payments on the cash value. Known as the interest only option, the interest is taxable as ordinary income when received or credited to the payee.

Under the **installment payment method**, the policyowner receives the cash value and accrued interest over a period, usually in fixed amounts. This payment method is similar to an annuity, and each payment will include a return of basis and interest. The basis portion is excludable from taxable income and is calculated by using the exclusion ratio, or the ratio of the basis to the total expected payments.

For example, Brigette selected the installment payment option on a policy with a cash value of $150,000. She will receive $1,000 per month for the remainder of her life, which according to life expectancy tables will be 20 more years.

Total expected payments = $1,000 × 12 × 20 = $240,000

Brigette's tax basis = $150,000

Exclusion ratio = $150,000 ÷ $240,000 = 0.625

Thus, 62.5%, or $625, of each payment is excludable from gross income.

If the beneficiary who chose the installment method for receipt of death benefits survives beyond her life expectancy, the annuity payments will retain the original exclusion ratio for income tax purposes. If the beneficiary dies before the projected life expectancy, no basis can be recovered and annuity payments will end.

Lump-sum payment method

The total cash value of the life insurance policy is paid to the policyowner

---

Installment payment method

The policyowner receives the cash value and accrued interest over a period, usually in fixed amounts

Section 1035 Exchanges

Section 1035 exchange

Provides for the replacement of an existing insurance-based contract for a newer insurance-based contract without having to pay taxes on any gain in the original contract

Internal Revenue Code Section 1035 provides for an exchange of an existing insurance-based contract for a newer insurance-based contract without having to pay taxes on any gain in the original contract. A **Section 1035 exchange** can provide new opportunities for flexibility and tax-deferred accumulation without paying taxes on the cash value growth. Note that the tax on the contract's gain is merely deferred, not eliminated.

IRC Section 1035 provides the postponement of taxes resulting from an exchange of:

- two life insurance contracts;

- a life insurance contract for an endowment insurance contract, an annuity contract, or a qualified long-term care insurance policy;

- two annuity contracts;

- an annuity contract for a qualified long-term care insurance policy;

- an endowment insurance contract for an annuity contract or a qualified long-term care insurance policy;

- two endowment insurance contracts, if the new contract provides for regular payments beginning on a date no later than the date payments would have begun under the contract that was exchanged; or

- two qualified long-term care insurance policies.

The basis for the new contract is the same as the basis in the original contract, plus any premiums paid into the new contract, less any dividends received for the new policy. New sales and surrender charges may be imposed on the new contract.

An exchange of an annuity contract for a life insurance policy cannot be accomplished tax-free. This is because the life insurance policy is taxed more favorably (notably, the income-tax-free nature of the policy's death benefit) than the annuity (that does not have a tax-free death benefit).

Transfer for Value

If an existing policy is transferred for valuable consideration, the insurance proceeds are includable in the gross income of the transferee to the extent the proceeds exceed the basis. Thus, the usual income tax exclusion for life insurance proceeds is lost. Instances in which the transfer of a policy does not result in inclusion of proceeds in the income of the transferee are:

- a transfer to the insured;

- a transfer to a business partner of the insured;

- a transfer to a partnership of which the insured is a partner;

- a transfer to a corporation of which the insured is an officer or shareholder; and

- a transfer that results in the transferee's basis being determined by reference to the transferor's basis, such as a gift.

Premiums

Generally, premium payments for individual life insurance policies are not tax-deductible. Life insurance premiums that are considered alimony, however, are tax-deductible to the payor and taxable as income to the recipient for pre-2019 divorce decrees.

Taxation of Benefits Received After Death

The beneficiary of a life insurance policy generally has the same options for payment as the policyowner does when surrendering a contract. However, the taxation of proceeds may be different. A lump-sum death benefit received as a result of the insured's death is excludable from gross income and is tax-exempt for income tax purposes. Under the interest-only payment option, the insurer pays interest earned on the death benefit to the beneficiary. Because these distributions are 100% interest and 0% death benefit, they are fully includable in the gross income of the beneficiary. Installment payments generally will be made in the form of an annuity, and each payment will include a return of basis and interest. The return of basis component is equal to the ratio of the face value of the policy to the total amount of expected payments to be received.

For example, Benjamin selected the installment payment option on a policy with a face value of $300,000. He will receive $1,750 per month for the remainder of his life, which according to life expectancy tables will be 25 more years.

Total expected payments = $1,750 × 12 × 25 = $525,000

Benjamin's tax basis = $300,000

Exclusion ratio = $300,000 ÷ $525,000 = 0.5714

Thus, 57.14%, or approximately $1,000, of each payment is excluded from gross income.

Viatical Agreements

Terminal Illness   When the insured of a life insurance policy owns a policy and becomes terminally ill (defined as having a life expectancy of 24 months or less), the policyowner may sell the policy to a third party without the proceeds being subject to income tax. This type of settlement, known as a **viatical agreement**, occurs when a third-party purchaser will receive the death benefit of the policy upon the death of the insured and will incur an income tax liability for proceeds that exceed the purchase price and any subsequent premiums paid.

Chronic Illness   Another type of viatical agreement with the same tax advantages for the insured is the sale of a life insurance policy whereby the proceeds are used to pay for long-term care for the insured. In this case, the insured must be chronically ill or suffer from substantial cognitive impairment, or be unable to perform at least two of six activities of daily living (ADLs). ADLs are discussed in the Long-Term Care section of this chapter.

Viatical agreement
The owner of a policy covering a terminally ill insured sells a life insurance policy to a third party without the proceeds being subject to income tax

Annuities

Each payment from a fixed annuity is considered a partially tax-free return of basis and partially taxable income, using the exclusion ratio. In general, the numerator for the exclusion ratio is the total investment in the annuity. The denominator is the total expected return from the annuity. Unlike an annuity resulting from a life insurance settlement, an annuity payment from a purchased annuity that occurs beyond the original life expectancy is fully taxable as ordinary income to the annuitant. If the annuitant dies before full recovery of basis, the unrecovered basis may be deducted on the decedent's final IRS 1040 form.

Part of each fixed annuity payment an annuitant receives is considered to be a return of principal, which is not taxed; however, the remaining portion of the payment is taxable because it consists of earnings. The exclusion ratio determines the nontaxable portion of each payment indicated by the following formula:

$$\frac{\text{Investment in the contract}}{\text{Expected return}}$$

The exclusion ratio is no longer used once the principal in the contract has been fully paid out to the annuitant. In other words, when the entire amount of principal has been exhausted, the entire annuity payment will be taxable as ordinary income.

INDIVIDUAL HEALTH INSURANCE

Prudent financial planning includes preparation for the financial impact of a serious injury or illness. Not only may medical bills be incurred, but a loss of income might also occur if the ill or injured person is unable to continue working. The probability of needing medical attention during one's life is very high. However, the severity of the illness and the ultimate cost of treatment are unknown. For example, treating the flu is generally affordable for most people, but obtaining a heart or liver transplant is not.

Purpose

Individual health insurance coverage allows individuals to customize their own insurance package. Health insurers typically allow an insured to choose from a wide array of coverage to meet individual needs. A direct relationship exists between the amount of coverage desired and the price of the premium, which means that as more coverage is chosen, the premium increases.

Cost Concerns

Most people who have health insurance coverage today obtain it through either a group plan or a social insurance program. Individual health coverage is not as popular as group coverage. With individual health coverage, the insured may have to pay the full cost of the coverage, and individual health coverage may not be as comprehensive or generous as that offered through group plans.

Major medical insurance
Health insurance that provides broad coverage of all reasonable and necessary expenses associated with an illness or injury, whether incurred at a doctor's office, a hospital, or the insured's home

Major Medical Insurance

Characteristics

Major medical insurance is designed to provide broad coverage of all reasonable and necessary expenses associated with an illness or injury, whether incurred at a doctor's office, a hospital, or the insured's home. Some major medical policies are stand-alone coverage that pays for a wide range of medical services. Others are written in conjunction with a basic medical plan to provide coverage in excess of that provided by the basic coverage. Many consumers are attracted to major medical insurance because it generally covers a wide range of expenses, including hospitalization charges, physician and surgeon's fees, physical therapy, prescription drugs, wheelchairs, and other medical supplies.

Major medical policies have a few exclusions. Self-inflicted injuries, injuries sustained in war, and elective cosmetic procedures are typically not covered.

Most major medical policies have a deductible ranging from $500 to as high as $10,000. The deductible normally applies per person per year, with a maximum number of aggregate deductibles per family. After the deductible has been met, the insurer typically pays the majority of the remaining usual and customary expenses, subject to a coinsurance amount. **Usual and customary expenses** are health care costs that are consistent with the average rate or charge for identical or similar services in a particular geographical area. **Coinsurance** is the cost sharing of health care expenses between the insured and the insurer, with common amounts ranging from 60%/40% to 80%/20%. In these examples, the insurer would pay either 60% or 80% of covered medical expenses above the deductible, and the insured would be responsible for the remainder. A **stop-loss limit** is the dollar amount of covered benefits to which the coinsurance provision is applied, but it does not include the deductible. Once the stop-loss limit is reached, the insurer pays 100% of all covered expenses for the rest of the year.

For example, Ryan and Sherri have a major medical policy with a $1,000 deductible, 70%/30% coinsurance, and a stop-loss limit of $20,000. Last summer, Ryan suffered from gallstones that resulted in surgery. The medical bills covered by Ryan and Sherri's plan totaled $45,000. No other claims were incurred during the year. Ryan and Sherri's major medical policy would pay as follows:

	Insurer	Ryan and Sherri
Total bills	$45,000	
Less deductible		$1,000
Balance	$44,000	
Coinsurance (of $20,000)	$14,000	$6,000
Ryan and Sherri maximum out-of-pocket		$7,000 ($1,000 deductible + $6,000 coinsurance payment)

Note: Ryan's medical expenses exceeded the policy's $20,000 stop-loss limit. The maximum out-of-pocket for this policy is $7,000 per year. The insurance company is responsible for the remaining $38,000 ($14,000 coinsurance plus $24,000 remaining balance).

2010 Health Care Reform Legislation

The Patient Protection and Affordable Care Act of 2010 and the Health Care and Education Reconciliation Act of 2010 made sweeping changes to the American health care system. For example, most people who are not eligible for Medicare, Medicaid, or other government-provided health care must maintain certain minimum levels of health care coverage. However, the penalty for individuals not having qualified health care coverage was reduced zero for months after December 31, 2018. Refundable tax credits help make health care coverage more affordable for low-income earners.

The legislation provides that plans covering dependents must allow coverage for adult children until age 26, prohibit lifetime coverage limits for essential health benefits, and require plans to provide preventive services without charging deductibles, copayments, or coinsurance. Insurers cannot cancel coverage after an insured gets sick unless there was fraud in the application.

Usual and customary expenses
Health care costs that are consistent with the average rate or charge for identical or similar services in a particular geographic area

Coinsurance
The cost sharing of covered health care expenses between the insured and the insurer

Stop-loss limit
A dollar amount of covered benefits to which the coinsurance provision is applied, but it does not include the deductible; once the stop-loss limit is reached, the insurer pays 100% of all covered expenses

The Affordable Care Act defines essential health benefits to include the following:

- Ambulatory patient services, emergency services, and hospitalization

- Maternity and newborn care and pediatric services, including oral and vision care

- Mental health and substance use disorder services, including behavioral health treatment

- Prescription drugs and laboratory services

- Rehabilitative services and devices

- Preventive and wellness services and chronic disease management

In addition, insurers may no longer impose pre-existing conditions or exclusions or deny coverage based on pre-existing conditions for children under age 19 (not applicable to grandfathered plans). Most plans are prohibited from imposing pre-existing condition exclusions and denials of coverage based on pre-existing conditions for any insured. Insurers cannot impose higher deductibles, copayments, or coinsurance for emergency services provided by an out-of-network provider. Plans are required to provide women with direct access to in-network OBs and GYNs and children with in-network pediatricians (i.e., no preauthorization or referral from primary care physician is necessary). Employer-provided health plans are also prohibited from establishing eligibility rules that discriminate in favor of higher-paid employees.

Medical Expense Insurance

Basic Medical Insurance Coverage

Traditionally, there have been three basic coverages an insured could purchase to provide for a specific type of medical expense: hospital expense insurance, surgical expense insurance, and physician's expense insurance.

Hospital expense insurance provides payment for expenses incurred by the insured while in the hospital. Coverage under hospital expense insurance includes a daily hospital benefit and a miscellaneous expense benefit. The daily hospital benefit pays a specified amount for room and board charges incurred during each day the insured is hospitalized and may be paid on a reimbursement basis, subject to a maximum daily limit, or it may be a flat amount per day. Also, some plans have a maximum number of days covered, such as 90 or 180 days.

A lump-sum benefit may be paid if the patient incurs miscellaneous expenses for items, such as x-rays, medications, surgical supplies, and use of an operating room. The miscellaneous expense benefit may be subject to a maximum dollar amount. This expense would be subject to the 2010 health care reform legislation.

Caution must be exercised in purchasing this type of coverage because many expensive procedures are now performed outside of a hospital. Also, physician's and surgeon's fees are billed separately from hospital services, so hospital expense coverage does not provide for payment of those fees. Purchasing only hospital expense coverage is not sufficient to meet the needs of most individuals.

Surgical expense insurance may be added to a hospital expense insurance policy to provide for the payment of the surgeon's fees, even when surgery is not performed in a hospital. Insurers typically base maximum benefits payable on a generic list of surgical procedures and their estimated costs, but some other benefit determination formula may be used. This expense would also be subject to the limitations imposed by the 2010 health care reform legislation.

Hospital expense insurance
Provides payment for expenses incurred by the insured while in the hospital

Surgical expense insurance
May be added to a hospital expense insurance policy to provide payment of surgeon's fees, even when procedures are not performed in a hospital

Physician's expense insurance pays for fees charged by physicians who provide the insured with nonsurgical care. Treatment can be administered in the doctor's office, the patient's home, or the hospital. Once again, this expense would also be subject to the 2010 health care reform legislation limits.

Physician's expense insurance
Pays for fees charged by physicians that provide nonsurgical care

Limitations

Basic medical coverage, sometimes referred to as indemnity coverage, sets rigid limits on the amount payable for any one event. The maximum benefit provided for any single illness or injury may not be enough to pay the actual expenses incurred. Although having this coverage is better than having no coverage at all, insureds must be aware that benefit levels are restricted.

HEALTH SAVINGS ACCOUNTS (HSAs)

Health savings account (HSA)
Special account that is used to pay for current and future medical expenses in conjunction with a high-deductible health plan (HDHP)

Health savings accounts (HSAs) are special accounts used to pay for current and future medical expenses in conjunction with a high-deductible health plan (HDHP). Although HSAs are commonly offered through an employer, they are not employer-owned accounts; rather, they are individually owned accounts. Therefore, it is the individual who makes decisions regarding participation, contributions, usage, and distributions. The individual also chooses the trustee, or custodian, as well as how funds within the account will be invested.

Eligibility

To be eligible for an HSA, an individual must be covered by an HDHP, cannot be covered by other health insurance or enrolled in Medicare, and cannot be claimed as a dependent on another's tax return. Children are not eligible to establish their own HSAs. However, spouses can establish their own HSAs, provided the spouse meets the normal eligibility requirements. Neither income limits restricting contributions exist, nor are there any earned income requirements that must be met before one can establish an HSA.

High-deductible health plan (HDHP)
A health plan, often used in conjunction with a health savings account (HSA); the HSA is used to pay for expenses up to the deductible amount

High-Deductible Health Plan (HDHP)   Except for preventive care, HDHPs do not cover first-dollar medical expenses and are the responsibility of the individual HSA owner. The individual has the option to use his HSA to pay for these expenses.

As long as certain requirements are met, the HDHP can be an HMO, PPO, or indemnity plan. The HDHP must meet the following requirements to be used in conjunction with an HSA.

The minimum deductibles for 2020 are:

- $1,400 for self-only coverage; and

- $2,800 for family coverage.

In 2020, the maximum annual out-of-pocket, including deductibles and co-payments are:

- $6,900 for self-only coverage; and

- $13,800 for family coverage

Note that the minimum HSA deductibles and maximum annual out-of-pocket amounts are indexed annually for inflation.

Contribution Rules   Contributions to HSAs can be made by the employer, the individual, or both. Employer contributions are not taxable to the employee (excluded from income and wages). Individual contributions are treated as an above-the-line deduction.

Individuals can make a one-time transfer from their IRA to an HSA, subject to the contribution limits applicable for the year of the transfer.

In 2020, the maximum contributions to an HSA from all sources are:

- $3,550 for self-only coverage; and

- $7,100 for family coverage.

These amounts are indexed annually.

For individuals age 55 and older, an additional catch-up contribution of $1,000 is allowed.

Contributions must stop once an individual is eligible for Medicare.

Employees can make contributions to their HSAs through a salary reduction arrangement within a cafeteria plan (Section 125 plan). These elections can change on a monthly basis (unlike salary reduction contributions to an FSA). Contributions to HSAs through a cafeteria plan are pretax and not subject to individual or employment taxes.

The HSA owner's employer can make cafeteria plan contributions on the individual's behalf unless the individual elects to not have such contributions made (negative elections).

Employer contributions are always excluded from an employee's income (pretax) and must be comparable for all employees participating in the HSA. Self-employed, partnership members and S corporation shareholders are normally not considered employees and therefore are ineligible to receive employer contributions; however, they can make deductible HSA contributions on their own behalf.

Distributions   An employer cannot place restrictions on an individual's use of HSA distributions. However, reasonable limitations as to frequency and size of distributions can be placed on the individual by the HSA's custodian or trustee.

The individual has the option to save HSA funds for the future by using alternative resources to pay for current medical expenses. If an individual makes withdrawals from an HSA for purposes other than a qualifying medical expense, the withdrawals will be subject to income tax and a 20% penalty. The 20% penalty does not apply to withdrawals made after the individual reaches age 65, dies, or becomes disabled. Over-the-counter medicines and drugs (other than insulin) do not qualify without a doctor's prescription.

Individual account holders must file Form 8889 on their annual federal tax returns and report the amount of their distributions used for qualified medical expenses.

Tax-free distributions can be taken for qualified medical expenses of a person covered by an HDHP, the spouse of the individual (even if not covered by the HDHP), and any dependent of the individual (even if not covered by the HDHP).

Transfers and Rollovers   Rollovers from HSAs are permitted once per year. A rollover to a new HSA must be completed within 60 days; direct trustee-to-trustee transfers of HSA amounts are not subject to the rollover restriction. Therefore, multiple trustee-to-trustee transfers are allowed in a single year. Direct rollovers from Section 401(k), 403(b), and 457 plans are not permitted.

Treatment of HSAs upon Death   If the spouse is the beneficiary, the spouse inheriting the HSA is treated as the owner. To the extent the spouse is not the beneficiary, the account will no longer be treated as an HSA upon the death of the individual. Instead, the account will become taxable to the decedent in the decedent's final tax return if the estate is the beneficiary, or it will be taxable to the recipient.

The taxable amount will be reduced by any qualified medical expenses incurred by the deceased individual before death and paid by the recipient of the HSA and further reduced by the amount of estate tax paid because of inclusion of the HSA in the deceased individual's estate.

Trustees and Custodians   Banks, credit unions, insurance companies, and previously approved IRA or Archer MSA trustees or custodians are eligible to serve as trustees. The HSA trustee must report all distributions annually to the individual on Form 1099 SA. Trustees are not required to determine whether distributions are used for medical purposes; this is the individual's responsibility. Trustee or custodian fees can be paid from the assets in the HSA account without being subject to taxes or penalties. They can also be paid directly by the beneficiary without being counted toward the HSA contribution limits.

Advantages   The HSA has many advantages. Among these are no "use it or lose it rules" such as those that apply to flexible spending arrangements (FSAs). All amounts in the HSA are fully vested, and unspent balances in accounts remain in the accounts until spent. The HSA encourages the account holder to be a more conscientious consumer of medical care and to shop around for the best value for health care. Furthermore, the owner's funds can be left to grow through investment earnings, in much the same way and with the same investment options as IRAs.

Disadvantages   The primary disadvantage of an HSA lies in the fact that many have enrolled in HSA programs, but many have not actually established an HSA. Among those who have established an HSA, the majority are not funding them adequately. Rather, they have purchased an HDHP, and without funding the HSA, large numbers of Americans lack the resources to fund the first-dollar expenses associated with an HDHP, and many of them are at risk of not receiving the health coverage the HSA was designed to provide.

▌LONG-TERM CARE INSURANCE

Long-term care insurance
Provides coverage for nursing home stays and other types of routine care that are not covered by other health insurance

Skilled nursing care
Daily nursing care and rehabilitation services ordered and monitored by a physician

Intermediate nursing care
Occasional nursing and rehabilitative care ordered and monitored by a physician

An elderly person might be able to live alone but may need assistance each day with dressing and bathing. Medical expense policies (including Medicare) neither cover these types of expenses, nor do they pay for stays in extended care facilities, such as nursing homes. **Long-term care insurance** provides coverage for nursing home stays and other types of assistance with activities of daily living that are not covered by other health insurance. The premium charged for long-term care coverage depends on the insured's age, the insured's health condition, and the level of benefits chosen.

There are seven types of coverage:

1. **Skilled nursing care** is the highest level of medical care and is provided by traditional nursing homes. Daily nursing care is provided, along with rehabilitation services, and the patient's care is ordered and monitored by a physician.

2. **Intermediate nursing care** is similar to skilled nursing care, except that care is provided occasionally rather than on a daily basis. Again, a physician must order and monitor this type of treatment.

Custodial care
Provides assistance with the regular tasks of daily life, such as eating, dressing, bathing, and taking medications

Home health care
Part-time skilled nursing care and rehabilitative therapy provided at the patient's home

Assisted living facilities
Apartment-style housing combined with support services and basic health care

Adult day care
Basic assistance and supervision provided outside the home usually during the primary caregiver's working hours

Hospice care
Care that provides dignity and comfort to terminally ill patients

Defined-period approach
Long-term care coverage provided for a specified period following an elimination period

Pool-of-money concept
Long-term care coverage provided up to a specific dollar amount, regardless of time

Tax-qualified long-term care insurance
Policies that meet standards established with the passage of the Health Insurance Portability and Accountability Act of 1996 (HIPAA)

3. **Custodial care** provides assistance with the regular tasks of daily life, such as eating, dressing, bathing, and taking medications. These services normally can be provided by nonmedical personnel and do not have to be ordered or supervised by a physician.

4. **Home health care** allows the patient to remain at home and receive part-time skilled nursing care, rehabilitative therapy, and other necessary assistance. Depending on the level of treatment needed, services may be provided by skilled professionals or nonmedical personnel.

5. **Assisted living facilities** (ALFs) provide apartment-style housing, support services, and basic health care for individuals who need help with the tasks of daily life. Some assisted living facilities are connected with skilled nursing facilities and allow patients to transfer back and forth as required by their health status.

6. **Adult day care** is provided for persons who need assistance and supervision during times when a spouse or other family caregiver must work. The purpose of adult day care is quite similar to that of infant and child day care—to allow family members living with a person who cannot take care of oneself to maintain their careers.

7. **Hospice care** is care for the terminally ill and can take place at the patient's home, a hospice care center, a hospital, or a nursing facility. Unlike most health care services, hospice care does not seek to cure the patient of an ailment. Rather, the goals of hospice care are providing pain management, emotional and spiritual support, and treatment that provides the patient with dignity and comfort.

The need for long-term care insurance is often overlooked in the financial planning process. When an individual requires long-term care that other health insurance will not cover, assets may be quickly depleted paying for such care. In extreme cases, some people ultimately liquidate all assets so they can qualify for long-term care benefits through the Medicaid (welfare) program. As many long-term care facilities are not Medicaid providers, the insured's choice of care facilities may be severely restricted.

Benefits

Long-term care insurance is a recent innovation prompted by the extension of life provided by today's technology. The two benefit approaches used are the defined-period approach and the pool-of-money approach. The **defined-period approach** is the more popular method and provides coverage for a defined period following an elimination period generally ranging from 30 to 365 days. Benefits may be provided for a specified period or until death. Under the **pool-of-money concept**, the insured is covered up to a specific dollar amount regardless of the period.

Most of the features of other health insurance policies are also found in long-term care insurance policies, including an elimination period and waiver of premium. When determining the appropriateness and desirable characteristics of long-term care insurance, financial planners should consider the benefits available under Medicare, Medicaid, the client's assets, and family health history.

Tax-Qualified Long-Term Care Insurance   A class of long-term care insurance policies called **tax-qualified long-term care insurance** was established with the passage of the Health Insurance Portability and Accountability Act of 1996 (HIPAA). Policies that meet standards set forth in this act state on their cover and in marketing materials that the policy is intended to be a qualified plan. The word *intend* or *intended* is used because the federal government does not have a mechanism for certifying that policies are qualified. However, a policy that clearly does not meet the standards cannot state that it is intended to be a qualified plan.

A tax-qualified (TQ) long-term care insurance policy is any contract that provides only coverage of qualified long-term care services and meets the following additional requirements.

- The contract must not provide for a cash surrender value or other money that can be paid, assigned, borrowed, or pledged.

- Refunds under the contract (other than refunds paid upon the death of the insured or complete surrender or cancellation of the contract) and dividends may be used only to reduce future premiums or to increase future benefits.

- The contract must meet certain consumer protection standards (see Exhibit 9.6).

- The contract must coordinate benefits with Medicare (unless Medicare is a secondary payor) unless the contract is an indemnity or per diem contract.

EXHIBIT 9.6   Consumer Protection Standards

To qualify for favorable tax treatment under HIPAA, a long-term care policy must have certain consumer protection features. These protections include the following:

- All contracts must be guaranteed renewable.
- Pre-existing conditions can be excluded up to a maximum of six months after issue. (If a new contract replaces another contract, the new contract must recognize the previous contract's satisfaction of the insured's six-month pre-existing condition.)
- Contracts cannot require prior hospitalization before paying nursing home benefits or require prior institutionalization before paying home care benefits.
- Contracts cannot exclude any specific illnesses (such as Alzheimer's disease).
- Contracts must provide protection against unintentional lapses because of a physical or cognitive impairment.
- Companies cannot utilize postclaims underwriting.
- Contracts providing home care benefits cannot restrict allowable care to only skilled care and must provide coverage for a meaningful length of time.
- Contracts must offer inflation protection.
- Companies must offer a nonforfeiture option.

Qualified long-term care services
As defined by HIPAA, include necessary diagnostic, preventative, therapeutic, caring, treating, rehabilitative services, and maintenance or personal care services required by a chronically ill or cognitively impaired person and provided by a plan prescribed by a licensed health care practitioner

Chronically ill individual
A person who has an illness or injury resulting in the inability to perform, without substantial assistance, at least two of the six activities of daily living for a period expected to last at least 90 days

Activities of daily living (ADLs)
Eating, bathing, dressing, transferring from bed to chair, toileting, and continence

Qualified long-term care services include necessary diagnostic, preventative, therapeutic, caring, treating, rehabilitative services, as well as maintenance or personal care services that are required by a chronically ill or cognitively impaired person. These services are provided in accordance with a plan of care prescribed by a licensed health care practitioner.

A **chronically ill individual** is any person certified within the previous 12 months by a licensed health practitioner as (1) being unable to perform at least two **activities of daily living (ADLs)** for a period expected to last at least 90 days owing to a loss of functional capacity, (2) requiring substantial supervision to protect the person from threats to health and safety because of severe cognitive impairment, or (3) having a similar level of disability as designated by some future regulation.

Under the ADL trigger, the policy must take into account at least five of the following ADLs in determining whether an individual is chronically ill: eating, toileting, transferring, bathing, dressing, and continence.

Plans that do not meet these requirements are considered non-tax-qualified (NTQ) long-term care insurance, and the plans are identified by one or more of the following characteristics:

1. The physical impairment does not need to be expected to last at least 90 days.

2. The physical impairment requirement can be met with just one ADL impairment.

3. The physical impairment requirement can be met with an impairment with two or more of any ADLs.

4. Fewer than five ADLs can be assessed in determining whether an individual is chronically ill.

5. The physical impairment requirement can be met with an impairment of instrumental activities of daily living (IADLs) only.

6. The physical impairment requirement can be met without reference to the need for substantial assistance.

7. The insured can qualify for benefits:
   - because of a medical necessity;
   - without a severe cognitive impairment; and
   - without a plan of care submitted to the insurance company.

8. The benefits reimburse for actual charges but do not coordinate with Medicare.

9. The plan pays benefits for services received from unskilled providers or family members.*

10. The plan pays benefits for services not related to caring for the insured.

11. The plan pays for capital improvements to a home.

12. The plan includes a cash payment return of premium at lapse that pays in excess of the premiums paid for the policy.

*A tax-qualified (TQ) long-term care insurance plan can also pay benefits for unskilled providers or family members and does not have to coordinate benefits with Medicare if the benefits are paid without regard to actual cost and are referred to as *indemnity plans*. In contrast, plans that are concerned with actual cost are referred to as *reimbursement plans*.

HIPAA allows favorable tax treatment for premiums paid to and benefits received from qualified plans. Premiums paid by the individual are deductible as medical expenses for itemized deduction purposes, depending on the individual's age. Exhibit 9.7 outlines the maximum annual premium allowed to be deducted for 2019 and 2020 income tax purposes. If an employer pays for long-term care insurance, the premiums are tax-deductible to the employer and are not taxable income to the employee. Long-term care benefits cannot be included in a cafeteria plan or a flexible spending account on a tax-advantaged basis. In other words, if the premiums are deducted from the employee's pay, they must be deducted on an after-tax basis. Regardless of who makes the premium payments, benefits received from qualified long-term plans are excluded from income.

EXHIBIT 9.7 Maximum Allowable Federal Income Tax Deduction for Long-Term Care Premiums (2019–2020)

Age of insured	2019 Maximum deduction	2020 Maximum deduction
40 or younger	$420	$430
41–50	$790	$810
51–60	$1,580	$1,630
61–70	$4,220	$4,350
Older than 70	$5,270	$5,430

Long-Term Care Needs

Many people overlook the need to protect against the expenses associated with the special nonmedical care created by prolonged illness or old age. Serious health problems, cognitive impairment, and lack of mobility can have a devastating impact on a family's financial security. Statistics show that over 70% of people over the age of 65 will encounter a long-term care need during their lifetime.

Long-term care insurance can help cover the costs associated with providing assistance with the activities of daily living that individuals cannot perform on their own. Long-term care insurance pays for the costs of caring for a person who requires daily assistance from someone else. Long-term care insurance can help protect against the financial hardship due to a lengthy illness commonly occurring from old age.

Exhibit 9.8 lists some questions to consider when determining long-term care insurance needs.

EXHIBIT 9.8 Long-Term Care—Things to Consider

- What is your family medical history?
- Does this history show a predisposition for long life and a need for residency in a nursing home?
- Does this history show that medical assistance was needed during old age? If so, what general type?
- Do you have assets (e.g., investments) that will provide income during your old age?
- Do you anticipate any other income during your old age?
- What is the current daily/monthly rate for nursing homes in your area?
- What is the projected future daily/monthly rate for nursing homes in your area?
- Other considerations:

_____
_____
_____
_____

DISABILITY INCOME INSURANCE

Overview

Disability income
insurance
A type of insurance
that provides a replace-
ment income while the
insured is unable to
work because of illness
or injury

Disability income insurance provides replacement income while the insured is unable to work because of illness or injury. Premiums for this coverage are a function of the insured's health, occupation, gender, age, and the level of income benefits provided by the policy. Most insureds purchase either a flat dollar amount of coverage, such as $2,000 per month, or coverage that replaces some portion of predisability earnings (such as 60%–80%).

To qualify for disability income, one must become disabled, as defined by the policy, while the policy is in force and remain so until the elimination (waiting) period has ended. Once these qualifications are met, monthly indemnity will be made payable at the end of each month of disability. Premiums for disability insurance are based partially on **morbidity** rates for the benefit term. The morbidity rate is the probability of a person becoming disabled.

Morbidity
Relates to the probability
of becoming disabled

Disability insurance may cover injuries only or injuries and illness. Coverage for injury and illness is preferred but will result in a higher premium. Injury is defined in the policy as either accidental bodily injury or bodily injury by accidental means. **Accidental bodily injury** requires only that the injury incurred be accidental. **Bodily injury by accidental means** requires accidental injury by accidental means.

Accidental bodily
injury
Only the injury incurred
is accidental

Bodily injury by
accidental means
Requires accidental injury
by accidental means

Thus, if Max's co-worker intentionally drops a computer monitor on Max's foot, Max's disability insurance would provide coverage if it provides for accidental bodily injuries. Max would not be covered, however, if his policy defined injury as bodily injury by accidental means, because the co-worker intentionally dropped the monitor. The definition of *illness* usually precludes pre-existing conditions and may require a probationary period.

Disability Income Needs

During an individual's income-earning years, the probability of becoming disabled is greater than the probability of death. As a result, a client should make sure that he is protected against loss of income due to a disability.

Disability Needs Analysis Questionnaire

Exhibit 9.9 is a disability needs analysis questionnaire that addresses an individual's income needs should a disability occur. The questionnaire can help determine how much disability income insurance is required to maintain the current lifestyle of the breadwinner and family. Please note that some costs, such as medical expenses, may actually increase during periods of disability and should be taken into consideration when calculating income needs.

EXHIBIT 9.9 Disability Needs Analysis Questionnaire

Monthly Expenses

Mortgage or Rent	$_____
Food	$_____
Clothing	$_____
Utilities	$_____
Medical/Dental	$_____
Personal Care	$_____
Automobile Expenses	$_____
Tuition	$_____
Insurance Premiums	$_____
Loans/Credit Card Payments	$_____
Other: _____	$_____
Other: _____	$_____
Other: _____	$_____
Other: _____	$_____
Other: _____	$_____
Other: _____	$_____

Total $_____

Monthly Gross Earned Income

Insured	$_____
Spouse	$_____

Total $_____

Income from Other Sources (use after-tax amounts)

Group Disability Insurance	$_____
Mortgage Insurance	$_____
Creditor Insurance	$_____
Disability Pension Benefits	$_____
Investment Income	$_____

Total $_____

After calculating total expenses, subtract any income that will continue during disability, including spousal income and income from other sources.

Total monthly expenses	$_____
Total monthly income	$_____
Maximum amount of monthly disability income	$_____

Characteristics

Definitions of Disability

A key feature of disability income insurance is the definition of *disability*, which specifies what constitutes a disability for the purposes of receiving policy benefits. Unless the insured's condition complies with the disability definition in the policy, the insurer does not pay income benefits. Different types of disability definitions exist, including any occupation, own occupation, and a combination of the two, known as the *split definition*.

Any occupation
Definition of disability in which an insured is considered totally disabled if the duties of any occupation cannot be performed

Any Occupation   A person insured under the **any occupation** definition is considered totally disabled if she cannot perform the duties of any occupation. The courts have interpreted this clause to mean any occupation for which the insured is suited by education, experience, and training. Thus, a disabled brain surgeon can draw benefits from the policy even if she is still able to work at a fast food restaurant. But, if the surgeon is able to teach, lecture, or do research related to her field of expertise, then the insurer would likely not consider her to be disabled.

Own occupation
Definition of disability in which an insured is considered totally disabled if the insured cannot perform the substantial and major duties of the insured's own occupation

Own Occupation   The **own occupation** definition is much more accommodating than the any occupation definition, because it states that the insured must be able to perform the substantial and major duties of his own occupation or he is considered disabled. This means that a surgeon who cannot perform surgery because of a broken hand is considered totally disabled even if he moves to a hospital administration position.

Split Definition   Many disability income insurance policies today include a combination of the any and own occupation definitions. Typically, the own occupation definition of disability applies only during the first one to five years after an illness or injury occurs; after that, the any occupation definition applies.

Features

Elimination period
The amount of time that must pass before benefits are paid

Elimination Period   Short-term disability benefits normally begin to pay within several days of the date of disability. However, long-term policies require the insured to satisfy an **elimination**, or waiting, **period**, ranging in length from of one month to one year, in an effort to reduce small claims and to help reduce the level of moral hazard associated with fraudulent claims. As one might expect, the premium increases as the elimination period gets shorter.

Short-term disability
Provides coverage for up to two years

Long-term disability
Provides coverage for specified term greater than two years, until specified age, or until death

Benefit Period   Disability insurance distinguishes between short-term and long-term coverage. **Short-term disability** typically provides coverage for up to two years. Many employers offer group short-term disability insurance that provides employees with a percentage of their salary while disabled. **Long-term disability** typically provides coverage until normal retirement age, until death, or for a specified term longer than two years. Some employers offer group long-term disability insurance with premiums generally paid for by the employee. Employer-sponsored plans are usually not portable and terminate when the employee leaves the firm, unless the reason for leaving employment is directly related to the disability.

Waiver of Premium   The waiver of premium removes the requirement for the policyowner to make premium payments after the insured has satisfied the elimination period. In most cases, premiums paid during the elimination period are refunded upon commencement of benefits and do not resume until the insured is deemed no longer disabled.

Riders

Partial disability rider
The insured cannot perform all of the substantial and material duties of the job

Partial Disability Rider   Many policies include automatically, or by adding a policy rider, coverage for partial disability, which is defined as a disability that prevents the insured from performing some, but not all, of the substantial and material duties of the job, with exact definitions varying among policies. The **partial disability rider** provides payments that are less than those paid for total disability, but these benefits usually last for only a short time (such as six months). By covering a partial disability in this manner, the insurer gives the insured some incentive to return to work sooner rather than later.

Cost-of-living adjustment (COLA) rider

Increases benefits being received by the policyowner each year; based on an index, such as the CPI

Cost-of-Living Adjustment (COLA) Rider   Disability insurance claims often result in benefit payments that last for a number of years. A cost-of-living adjustment is made to the benefit each year to protect benefits from the effects of inflation for as long as the insured remains disabled. The increases are normally based on either the Consumer Price Index (CPI) with a cap or a fixed-percentage rate that is elected at the time of application by the policyowner, usually ranging from 2%–5% and computed on either a simple or compounded basis. Please note that this benefit does not increase the monthly benefit from the date of policy issue but provides for an increase in benefits that are actually being paid.

Future Increase Option Rider   The future increase option protects future earnings by allowing the policyowner to increase the potential monthly benefit as the insured gets older and earns more, regardless of any health changes. The rider guarantees insurability for a certain period of time (normally to age 55) for an additional premium. Please note that this option affects the monthly benefit; in other words, the potential benefit paid in the event a disability occurs is increased.

Automatic Increase Rider   The automatic increase rider raises the total monthly benefit coverage each year for a specified number of years (a common increase is 5% per year for five years). Premiums will increase as the monthly coverage increases, and the rider is often used to have the monthly benefit coverage keep pace with inflation.

Residual benefits provision

Policyowner receives a percentage of the disability benefit on the basis of the percentage of income loss due to sickness or injury

Residual Benefits   Under the **residual benefits provision,** or rider, the policyowner receives a percentage of the disability benefit on the basis of the percentage of income loss due to sickness or injury. The benefit payable is equal to a proportionate amount of the monthly benefit.

E X A M P L E   Assume Dr. Turner earns $10,000 per month as a practicing physician. She becomes disabled and returns to work as a consultant earning $6,000 per month, resulting in a drop in income of 40%. Dr. Turner had a disability income policy with a residual benefits provision and a monthly benefit of $5,000. Under the residual benefit provision of the policy, she would receive a benefit of $2,000 (40% of the $5,000) per month.

Taxation of Benefits

Individual disability income insurance premiums are generally not tax-deductible by the insured. As a result, benefit payments received during a period of disability are not subject to income taxation.

Integration of Benefits

Financial planners should realize that Social Security may provide disability benefits to a disabled person; however, the Social Security definition of disability is much more restrictive than most definitions used in private disability income insurance. In addition, the Social Security program requires the disabled person to wait five months before receiving benefits and prove that he cannot engage in any gainful employment and that the disability is expected to last at least 12 months or result in death.

A disability income policy may integrate with Social Security disability coverage. A policy that integrates with Social Security reduces benefits payable by the amount of Social Security benefits the disabled person is eligible to receive. This type of coverage is less expensive than a similar policy that does not integrate with Social Security because the insurer expects to pay out lower benefits if the insured is disabled for a long time.

The insured may have a $2,000 monthly disability benefit provided by the policy, but if one is also eligible for a $1,200 monthly Social Security disability benefit, the individual policy might pay only $800 per month. When shopping for an individual disability income policy, the insured should be aware that some policies contain such integration provisions.

Termination of Benefits

Benefit payments cease at either the end of the benefit period or the date when the insured is no longer disabled, whichever occurs first.

EXHIBIT 9.10 Long-Term Disability Insurance Checklist

Feature	Desirable coverage
Amount of benefit	60%–70% of gross pay
Benefit term	Work life expectancy
Covered conditions	Injury and illness
Elimination period	Based on client's liquid assets and emergency fund
Definition of disability	Own occupation or split definition
Integration	To reduce premiums, integration with Social Security or workers' compensation may be desirable

Health and Disability Insurance Policy Provisions

Pre-Existing Conditions

Pre-existing condition
A medical condition that required treatment during a specified period before the insured's effective date

A **pre-existing condition** is a medical condition that required treatment during a specified period (e.g., six months) before the insured's effective date of coverage under a health insurance plan. In some policies, the definition of *pre-existing condition* includes medical conditions known to the insured, even though no medical care was provided for the condition during the specified period. A **pre-existing conditions clause** excludes coverage for pre-existing conditions for a specified period, such as 12 months, after the effective date of coverage and is used to control adverse selection. As noted earlier, the use of pre-existing conditions clauses in health insurance plans has been restricted by the 2010 health care reform legislation.

Preexisting conditions clause
Excludes coverage for pre-existing conditions for a specified period, such as 12 months, after the effective date of coverage

Grace Period

The grace period is the time (usually 31 days) beyond the premium due date during which an insurance premium payment may be made without cancellation of the coverage. During the grace period, the policy remains in force.

Reinstatement

Included in every health insurance policy is a procedure for policy reinstatement if coverage lapses because of nonpayment of premium. The reinstatement clause specifies a time limit within which the insured may reinstate the policy and indicates whether proof of insurability is required. Reinstated policies usually have pre-existing clauses that exclude coverage for illnesses incurred during a given period.

Time Limit on Certain Defenses

The time limit on certain defenses is an optional provision that may be used in noncancelable or guaranteed renewable health insurance contracts. Similar to an incontestability clause in a life insurance policy, it states that the insurer may not contest the validity of the contract, except in cases of fraud, after it has been in force for a certain period (typically two years).

Rights of Renewability

Noncancelable
Insurer guarantees the renewal of the policy for a given period or to a stated age without an increase in premium

Noncancelable

A health or disability insurance policy that is **noncancelable** provides the greatest amount of security for the insured. The insurance company guarantees the renewal of the policy for a given period or to a stated age. In addition, the insurer may not make changes to the policy, including increases in premiums.

Guaranteed Renewable

Guaranteed renewable
The insurer is required to renew the policy for a specified period, regardless of changes in the insured's health (premiums may be increased) by class of insureds

If a health or disability insurance policy is **guaranteed renewable**, the insurance company is required to renew a policy for a specified period (e.g., to age 65), regardless of changes in the health of the insured. Under this agreement, premiums must be paid when due, and renewal of the policy is at the sole discretion of the insured. The insurance company, however, reserves the right to increase premiums as deemed necessary, as long as the premium increase is for an entire class of insureds.

Conditionally renewable
Cannot be canceled by the insurer during the policy term, but insurer may refuse to renew the contract for another term if certain conditions exist

Conditionally Renewable

A policy that is **conditionally renewable** cannot be canceled by the insurance company during the policy term (usually one year), but it may refuse to renew the contract for another term if certain conditions exist as stipulated in the policy.

Optionally renewable
The insurer may not cancel the policy during the term, but the insurer may decline to renew the policy for a subsequent term

Optionally Renewable

Under a policy that is **optionally renewable**, the insurance company may not cancel the policy during the term (usually one year), but it may decline to renew the policy for a subsequent term. Hence, very little security to the insured is provided.

▌GROUP HEALTH INSURANCE

Most medical expense insurance coverage sold today is in the form of a group policy. Pooling together a large number of employees lowers the administrative costs of providing coverage, and adverse selection is usually reduced. As a result, more features and benefits are usually provided through a group health insurance plan.

Eligibility

To be eligible for group health care coverage, one must be a member of a group that has come together for some purpose other than to purchase insurance. Some examples of eligible groups are debtor-creditor groups, labor union groups, multiple-employer trusts, trade and professional associations, and any single employer group. Most eligible groups require participants to:

■ be a full-time employee (or a qualifying member) of the group;

■ satisfy a probationary period; and

■ be actively at work the day coverage begins.

Characteristics

Group underwriting procedures are different from those for individual health coverages. Instead of looking at each insured on an individual basis, the underwriter looks at the overall composition of the group. All employees in the group are automatically eligible for coverage under a group contract.

The employer holds the master contract, and employees are given individual coverage certificates. The employer generally pays most, or all, of the premium, which further prevents adverse selection. The employer is responsible for enrolling new employees and collecting any premiums due from employees. The insurer thus saves a great deal on administrative expenses, and those savings are passed on to the employer or employees in the form of lower premiums.

Basic and Major Medical

Group basic medical insurance provides coverage for hospital, surgical, and physician's expenses that are similar to those discussed previously under Individual Health Coverage. Basic medical plans have low maximum limits on coverage and are often used in conjunction with major medical plans.

Group major medical expense coverage is also very similar to individual major medical coverage. The two main types of group major medical plans are supplemental and comprehensive. **Group supplemental plans**, often attached to basic medical expense coverage, allow the employer to use more than one provider for coverage, offer first-dollar coverage, or use different contribution rates for basic and supplemental coverage.

Comprehensive major medical is a stand-alone coverage that provides a broad range of medical services and high limits of coverage. Deductibles are usually low, and employees pay some percentage of all medical expenses above the deductible, subject to some maximum out-of-pocket dollar limit. As with individual plans, these group major medical plans cover all necessary medical expenses unless they are specifically excluded in the contract. Coverage under these plans has expanded to pay for items, such as extended care facilities, home health care centers, hospice care, ambulatory care, birthing centers, diagnostic x-ray and laboratory services, radiation therapy, supplemental accident benefits, prescription drugs, and vision care.

Group supplemental plans
Often attached to basic medical expense coverage, these policies allow the employer to use more than one provider for coverage, offer first-dollar coverage, or use different contribution rates for basic and supplemental coverage

Comprehensive major medical
Stand-alone coverage that provides a broad range of medical services and high limits of coverage

E X A M P L E   Assume that Alexander's employer offers him comprehensive group major medical coverage. The policy has a $250 per person annual deductible and after that pays 80% of all covered charges. The policy further limits Alexander's out-of-pocket expenses to $1,000 per year (including the deductible). After Alexander has spent $1,000 of his own money, the insurer will pay 100% of covered medical expenses.

If Alexander is involved in a boating accident and incurs $1,250 of medical expenses, he must pay the first $250 of the covered expenses as his deductible. Then, the insurer will pay 80% of the remaining $1,000, or $800, and Alexander will pay 20%, or $200. If two months later, Alexander suffers another injury, he does not have to pay the $250 deductible again because he has a "per person per year" deductible. He only has to pay 20% of his medical expenses. Once he has paid $1,000 out of his pocket for the entire year (including the deductible), his insurer will begin paying 100% of all covered expenses.

Health Care Reimbursement Arrangements (HCRAs)

Health care reimbursement arrangements (HCRAs) are employer-sponsored health-spending accounts that allow employees to accumulate funds for health expenses. Under these plans, an employer sets up an HCRA on behalf of a covered employee and deposits a certain amount of money into the plan each year. Funds that accumulate in the HCRA tax-free are used to reimburse the employee for qualified medical expenses, such as medical bills, prescription drugs, health insurance deductibles, and health insurance premiums. HCRAs differ from health savings accounts (HSAs) because all of the contributions into an HCRA are made by the employer.

Employers that sponsor HCRAs frequently provide high-deductible health plans as well. Once the funds in the HCRA are depleted, the employee's health expenses are covered by the high-deductible health plan, after any co-payment, coinsurance, or deductible requirements are met. If funds remain in the HCRA at the end of the year, they can be rolled over to the following year and used for future health expenses.

Offering an HCRA in conjunction with a high-deductible health plan can be much less expensive for employers. Employees may benefit, too, from having more control over their health care. HCRAs are becoming increasingly popular as employers look for ways to cut health care costs without sacrificing flexible health benefits.

Dental and Vision

Many medical health insurance plans do not provide coverage for dental or vision care. However, most companies today offer supplemental plans for vision and dental coverage to their employees. Preventive care is usually encouraged, so routine checkups are often covered. As a result, they are quite popular with employees, even when the employees must pay 100% of the cost of coverage.

GROUP DISABILITY INCOME INSURANCE

Group disability income insurance is structured in much the same fashion as individual disability income coverage. Under a group disability income plan, however, payments are based on the disability being either long term or short term. Generally, short-term disability payments are made from either the first day of injury resulting from an accident or the eighth day of disability resulting from sickness. Benefits are payable on a weekly basis for a specified benefit period. Long-term disability coverage will pay when short-term benefits expire or when the insured has satisfied the required long-term elimination period. Long-term disability benefits under a group plan are usually paid until the disability ends or until the insured reaches age 65, whichever occurs first; however, the employee should check the term of benefits because they may not be as long as the employee's remaining work life expectancy.

Health Insurance and Managed Care

Various forms of health insurance and discount plans are available on the market. The most prevalent plans today are preferred provider organizations (PPOs), point of service (POS), consumer-driven health plans (CDHPs), and either a health care savings account (individual) or a health care reimbursement account (group) is used in combination with a high-deductible health plan (HDHP). Although traditional major medical and health maintenance organizations are still available, they are rarely seen today.

Health Maintenance Organizations (HMOs)   HMOs share the common goals of comprehensive care, delivery of services, and cost control. An HMO assumes the responsibility and risk of providing a broad range of services to members, including preventive medical services, such as checkups and mammograms, in exchange for a fixed monthly or annual enrollment fee. HMOs usually allow their members very little choice of service providers. The patient must generally use a contract provider, or no benefits will be paid. A copayment usually must be paid by the insured for each office visit.

Primary care doctors are either salaried employees of the HMO, or they are in private practice and receive a monthly fee (capitation payment) for each patient they agree to treat, whether or not the patient receives care. Specialists may also be salaried employees or they may be in private practice and receive fees for only the services they provide.

HMO enrollments have declined sharply, particularly in the private sector. Many believe this is primarily a result of the highly restrictive utilization requirements that were placed on members and an overall public dissatisfaction with the care provided. The traditional HMO plan has virtually disappeared, thereby spawning myriad of managed care models that address many of the shortcomings of the traditional HMO.

Preferred provider organization (PPO)

A contractual arrangement between the insured, the insurer, and the health care provider that allows the insurer to receive discounted rates from service providers

Preferred Provider Organizations (PPOs)   A **preferred provider organization (PPO)** is merely a contractual arrangement between the insured, the insurer, and the health care provider that allows the insurer to receive discounted rates from service providers. PPOs are structured in much the same way as HMOs with two main exceptions: (1) members are allowed to use non-PPO providers, although they pay higher deductibles and coinsurance than required when they use PPO doctors, and (2) primary care doctors (as well as specialists) are paid on a fee-for-service basis rather than as employees under the traditional HMO.

PPOs offer insureds a greater choice of health care providers than most HMOs. Many find the HMO concept objectionable because benefits are not provided if the covered person uses a doctor outside of the HMO's network of providers (in other than an emergency). Although the insured pays more out-of-pocket by going outside the network of preferred providers offered by a PPO, medical benefits are still payable but at a reduced level.

Advantages and Disadvantages   Managed health care companies are highly competitive and often improve services or reduce costs to gain market share. Most managed health care plans are service-oriented and focus on assisting the patient to receive the most appropriate care for the money. To maintain quality of care, managed care plans provide coordination and continuity in the process of delivering care that is deemed medically necessary.

The primary disadvantage of managed care is reduced choice for the patient. Although many managed care plans allow the insured to go outside the network of preferred providers, most plans do not allow physicians to perform certain procedures without prior approval from the plan, which reduces the patient's options for care. Furthermore, some managed care organizations put gag clauses in their contracts with providers that require the provider to remain silent about treatment options for the patient if the managed care plan excludes coverage for those procedures, such as experimental bone marrow transplants. Much criticism focuses on the fact that nonmedical personnel are controlling the medical options offered to patients by their doctors. As a result of this criticism, several states have passed laws restricting or prohibiting the use of gag clauses in managed care plans.

Coverage for Retirees

Historically, many companies continued group health insurance coverage for their retired employees, although Medicare was the primary payor of benefits and the group plan served to fill coverage gaps in the Medicare program. The employer would pay some or all of the premiums on the retiree's coverage. In 1993, however, the Financial Accounting Standards Board (FASB) began requiring employers to recognize (on the balance sheet) the present value of the cost of providing retiree coverage during the employee's active working years. This ruling had a very negative effect on the earnings of employers, so many employers have stopped offering paid benefits to retirees.

Another problem employers face when they offer paid health benefits to retirees is the tendency of U.S. courts to prohibit a reduction in benefits after retirement. If an employer offers a retiree benefits, it may have to continue those benefits as long as the retiree chooses, potentially creating a rather lengthy commitment for the employer that could prove financially burdensome during periods of reduced sales or profits.

Coverage for Elderly Employees

Employees who are 65 and older and who are also eligible for Medicare benefits still must be eligible for the employer's group health coverage. The group plan is the primary payor of benefits, and Medicare is the secondary payor.

Coordination of Benefits

Because of the rising number of dual-income families across America today, insurers have taken measures to prevent insureds from receiving benefits twice for the same ailment. One such measure is known as the **coordination of benefits (COB) clause**. The goal of this measure is to avoid duplicate payments for a single service. COB is used in all group health insurance plans to prevent the insured who is covered by both his own employer's plan and his spouse's plan from receiving more than 100% of the actual cost of health care received.

Coordination of benefits (COB) clause
Prevents an insured from receiving greater than 100% of the cost of health care received when covered by multiple insurance policies

Termination of Benefits

Upon permanent termination of employment with a company, one may still maintain group health insurance benefits for 31 days in order to have adequate time to replace the group insurance with individual insurance. If new employment provides health insurance for the terminated employee, the previous employer's coverage automatically expires, even if the 31-day period has not elapsed.

Consolidated Omnibus Budget Reconciliation Act (COBRA)

Consolidated Omnibus Budget Reconciliation Act (COBRA)
Requires certain employers to provide previously covered persons with the same coverage received before discontinuation of coverage

Employees and dependents previously covered under a group health insurance may have that group coverage extended under a federal law known as the **Consolidated Omnibus Budget Reconciliation Act (COBRA)**. COBRA requires certain employers to provide the previously covered persons (including dependents and spouses) with the same coverage received before unemployment or another event affecting health care coverage. The benefit recipient must pay the full cost of the coverage, however, which may be prohibitively expensive if the recipient is unemployed. The employer is also allowed to charge up to 2% of the premium to cover administrative expenses, but under no circumstances may the employee be charged more than 102% of the total cost of the plan during the period of coverage.

To continue health insurance coverage through COBRA, the group coverage must terminate because of a qualifying event, including:

- voluntary or involuntary termination of the employee (except for gross misconduct);

- death of the covered employee;

- reduction of employee's hours from full time to part time;

- divorce or legal separation of covered employee from spouse;

- employee becomes eligible for Medicare; and

- a dependent child is no longer eligible for coverage under the employee's plan, as would be the case when the child was no longer a student, reached a certain age, or got married.

COBRA applies only to employees who offer a group health plan and have at least 20 employees. Affected employers must offer coverage for a specified period, depending on the type of qualifying event:

- Termination or part-time status, 18 months

- Death of covered employee, 36 months

- Divorce or legal separation, 36 months

- Loss of dependent status, 36 months

- Medicare eligibility, 36 months

- Up to 29 months if employee meets Social Security definition of disabled, or up to 36 months if the beneficiary experiences, during a period of COBRA coverage, a second COBRA qualifying event

Taxation of Group Health Benefits

Currently, employer-provided medical expense coverage is not taxable as income to the employee, and the premiums paid by the employer are tax-deductible as a business expense. Employer-paid premiums for disability income coverage are not taxed as current income to the employee, but if a disability occurs, the benefits paid by the plan are taxable as income to the employee. If the employee pays the entire cost of disability income coverage, the premiums are not tax-deductible for the employee. However, any disability benefits received from an employee-paid policy are not subject to income tax. If the employer and employee share the cost of disability income coverage, disability benefits that are attributable to employer contributions are taxable as income to the employee.

BUSINESS USES OF LIFE INSURANCE AND OTHER EMPLOYEE BENEFITS

Buy-Sell Agreements

Owners of closely held businesses are concerned about what might occur if one of the owners dies. Surviving owners want to make certain that the economic value of the corporate interest is preserved, and this may not be the case if the interest passes to the deceased owner's family members. The surviving owners also would like to avoid interference from the deceased shareholder's family. If surviving owners want to meet these objectives by purchasing the deceased owner's interest, they most often want to be certain that they will have the economic resources to do so. A **buy-sell agreement** funded with life insurance will often meet the concerns of the owners.

Buy-sell agreement

An arrangement in which a deceased owner's share of a business is purchased by using the life insurance proceeds from a policy on the deceased owner's life

Types of Buy-Sell Agreements

The three basic types of buy-sell agreements are a cross-purchase arrangement, an entity purchase agreement, and a wait-and-see agreement. The arrangements differ in terms of policy ownership, ease of administration, disparity of premiums, and whether the remaining shareholders receive a step-up in basis at the deceased shareholder's death.

Cross-Purchase Agreements

Cross-purchase agreement

Each owner of the corporation purchases an insurance policy on the other shareholders; the death proceeds are used to purchase a deceased owner's shares

With a **cross-purchase agreement**, each owner of the corporation purchases an insurance policy on the other shareholders. The purchaser is both owner and beneficiary of the policies. Upon the death of a shareholder, the other shareholders are able to use the life insurance proceeds to purchase the deceased owner's shares.

There are several advantages to the cross-purchase form of the buy-sell agreement. Under the traditional stepped-up basis rules, the family of the deceased owner will have a tax basis equal to the fair market value of the decedent's stock at the date of death, thus avoiding any income tax consequences resulting from the sale. The fair market value of the shares should be defined by the buy-sell agreement.

The life insurance proceeds received by the surviving owners are not subject to income taxation. For newly purchased shares, the corporate shareholders will be entitled to a tax basis equal to the purchase price. The stepped-up basis should reduce future income taxes if the surviving shareholders later sell their interests. The insurance proceeds are not subject to the claims of corporate creditors. The creditor protection exists because the proceeds are paid directly to the individual shareholders.

However, the cross-purchase form of the buy-sell agreement has several disadvantages. The plan is difficult to administer if numerous shareholders are required to purchase a policy on all of the other shareholders. For example, for five owners to cross-purchase life insurance would require 20 policies (five owners purchasing four policies on the other owners). The number of policies can multiply even further if disability coverage is also part of the buy-sell agreement.

Another disadvantage of the cross-purchase agreement is that the age or the insurable status of the partners can create a disparity in premiums. Younger or healthier owners may incur higher premiums to cover older and less healthy owners. A possible solution to this problem is to have the corporation raise salaries to cover the premium (and any tax payable on the additional salary) paid by each owner.

Entity Purchase Agreements

Entity purchase agreement

The corporation owns policies on the lives of the shareholders; at the death of a shareholder, the corporation buys the deceased shareholder's interest in the company with the insurance proceeds

With an **entity purchase agreement**, the corporation owns policies on the lives of the shareholders. When a shareholder dies, the corporation buys the deceased shareholder's interest in the company with the insurance proceeds. A major advantage of the entity purchase agreement is that it is easier to administer for multiple shareholders. An additional advantage to an entity purchase buy-sell is that the corporation bears the premium differences associated with age disparities among shareholders.

The corporation will not recognize income for tax purposes when it receives the insurance proceeds. The corporation must, however, show the effect of the entire transaction (proceeds received and redemption of the deceased's stock) on the earnings and profits of the corporation. The earnings and profits increase with the life insurance proceeds received and decrease as a result of the stock redemption. Therefore, the corporation must pay attention to the overall net effect on earnings and profits and consider how that might affect the dividend policy to shareholders.

A key disadvantage of the entity purchase agreement is that the remaining shareholders do not get the benefit of a stepped-up basis when the corporation purchases the deceased shareholder's interest. In other words, the continuing shareholders retain their original cost basis in the company. Compared with the cross-purchase agreement, the entity purchase agreement creates greater capital gains upon the ultimate disposition of shares if made before death of the surviving owners. After the stock redemption is completed, however, the corporate assets should be relatively unchanged (the insurance proceeds have been used to purchase the deceased's interest), but each owner now enjoys a greater percentage of ownership.

Wait-and-See Agreements

Wait-and-see agreement

A hybrid version of the cross-purchase and entity-purchase buy-sell agreement that allows the businessowners to wait until an owner dies or retires before deciding whether the surviving owners or the business entity will purchase the deceased or retired owner's share

The respective advantages and disadvantages of cross-purchase and entity-purchase buy-sell agreements may make it difficult for businessowners to decide which type of agreement better meets their needs. Even if the owners initially select a plan, their circumstances or the business's circumstances may later change and their initial choice of plan may no longer be suitable.

The **wait-and-see agreement** is a hybrid version of the cross-purchase and entity-purchase buy-sell agreement that allows the businessowners to wait until an owner dies or retires before deciding whether the surviving owners or the business entity will purchase the deceased or retired owner's share. With a wait-and-see agreement, the ultimate purchaser of a deceased or retired owner's interest might be the business itself, the other businessowners, or some combination of the business and the other owners.

To implement a wait-and-see agreement, each businessowner buys and names himself the beneficiary of a life insurance policy on the life of every other owner. This is the same as with a cross-purchase plan; unlike a cross-purchase plan, a wait-and-see plan typically gives the business entity the right of first refusal to purchase all or part of the interest of an owner who dies. If the business doesn't purchase the interest or purchases only part of it, the other owners then have the right to purchase any remaining portion of the interest. If the other owners fail to purchase the entire remaining interest, the business entity must purchase it. This assures there will be a buyer for the deceased owner's entire interest.

As with a cross-purchase plan, the life insurance proceeds are received by the other owners rather than the business entity. If the business entity elects to purchase the interest of a deceased owner, the other owners must either loan the policy proceeds to the business or use the proceeds as a contribution to capital. The surviving owners get an increase in basis if they use the proceeds to purchase the interest directly from the estate of the deceased owner or if they use the proceeds as a contribution to capital so the business entity can make the purchase.

A wait-and-see agreement has some of the same potential disadvantages as a cross-purchase agreement. For example, the number of policies required may become cumbersome if there are numerous owners, and there may be inequities in the premium payments if there are considerable age differences between the owners. The major advantage of a wait-and-see approach is the flexibility it provides in determining who will purchase a deceased or retired owner's interest in the business.

Disability Buy-Sell Arrangements

Owners of closely held corporations should also consider ownership transfer in the event of an owner's disability for the same reasons they would consider a buy-sell agreement that takes effect at death.

Disability buy-sell policies pay benefits when an owner is totally disabled, and usually after at least a one-year elimination period. The policies pay benefits in the form of a lump sum or payments over several years, and in some cases, a combination of the two. In most cases, insurers will provide a benefit up to 80% of the value of the business.

Estate Tax Treatment of Buy-Sell Arrangements

With a cross-purchase agreement, the proceeds from the life insurance are not included in the deceased shareholder's estate. Because the deceased is not the owner of the policy, the insurance proceeds payable at death are not included in the estate.

With an entity purchase buy-sell, however, the estate tax consequences can become more significant when the deceased shareholder has a controlling interest. Under IRC Section 267, a shareholder who owns more than a 50% interest either directly or indirectly is deemed to control a corporation. In this case, the shareholder has an ownership interest in the life insurance policy because of the shareholder's ability to designate a beneficiary, as well as other ownership interests. The fact that the majority shareholder controls interest in the policy results in the proceeds being includable in the deceased's estate. Thus, the after-tax returns on life insurance policies can be substantially reduced if estate taxes are owed as a result of the life insurance proceeds being included in the estate.

Nonqualified Plans

Nonqualified plans are usually used to supplement qualified plans for key employees beyond the qualified plan 415 limit. These plans are not subject to the same ERISA rules as qualified plans and, as a result, they do not benefit from the same tax advantages as qualified plans or other tax-advantaged plans.

Nonqualified deferred compensation (NQDC) plans are a common type of nonqualified plan. Under these plans, part of the employee's compensation is deferred and not paid until some time in the future, such as after the employee retires. If the plan is structured properly, the employee does not pay income taxes on the deferred compensation until the year it is actually received. The employer can deduct the deferred compensation in the same year the employee reports it as income.

Nonqualified plans normally involve no more than a promise to pay from the employer, which is where life insurance often becomes involved. Because there is a substantial risk of loss to the executive, one must accept the promise to pay as the only guarantee of receiving the compensation that could have been paid presently. Corporate-owned life insurance (COLI) provides an excellent means of matching promised benefits with a tax-efficient funding vehicle that provides added security and peace of mind for the executive.

Executive Bonus Plans

Executive bonus plan
A discriminatory fringe benefit that provides life insurance to key employees with tax-deductible dollars

An **executive bonus plan** is a discriminatory fringe benefit that provides life insurance to key employees with tax-deductible dollars. In this arrangement, the employee purchases a personal life insurance plan and names a beneficiary. The business pays the policy premium to the insurer and can deduct the premiums as long as the total payments on behalf of the employee are considered reasonable compensation. The employee pays income taxes on the premium; however, the business can bonus both the premium and tax liability amounts. This is known as a gross-up bonus plan, and total payments must be considered reasonable compensation in this case as well.

The business has several benefits with an executive bonus plan. Premium payments are deductible, the plan is easy to administer, no IRS reporting is required, the plan can be discriminatory, and the plan can be terminated at any time.

There are also advantages to the key employee:

- The business pays most or all of the employee's costs

- The employee's beneficiary receives an income-tax-free death benefit

- The employee owns and controls the policy and the cash values

- The policy is portable; an employee can take it when she leaves the company

Split-Dollar Plans

Split-dollar plan
An agreement between an employer and employee who share the costs and benefits associated with a life insurance policy

Under a **split-dollar plan**, a business provides permanent life insurance on the life of its executives, using corporate funds. Unlike other nonqualified benefit plans, split-dollar plans usually provide that the business will recover the cost of the plan. In split-dollar plans, the agreements are most often between an employer and an employee who share (or split) the costs and the benefits associated with a life insurance policy. The objective of the arrangement is to assist the employee (again, usually an executive) with his life insurance needs by using the financial resources of the employer. When the insured employee dies, the corporation recovers its premium outlay, with the balance of the policy proceeds being paid to the employee's designated beneficiary or beneficiaries. The arrangement is best suited for an executive in the early stage of his employment career because the split-dollar plan requires a reasonable length of time to build up adequate cash value for the employer. There are two basic policy ownership methods by which the split-dollar arrangement may be established: the collateral assignment method and the endorsement method.

Collateral assignment split dollar
An arrangement in which an employer is obligated to make interest-free loans to the employee in the amount of the policy premium; the employee then makes a collateral assignment of the policy to the employer for the amount of premium paid by the employer

Collateral Assignment Method   Under the **collateral assignment split dollar** method, the employee-insured is the policyowner. The employer is obligated to make interest-free loans to the employee in the amount of the premium that the employee has agreed to pay. The employee then makes a collateral assignment of the policy to the employer for the amount of premium paid by the employer.

At the insured employee's death, the employer, as collateral assignee, recovers the loan amount from the death proceeds. The remainder of the death benefit is then paid to the employee's designated beneficiary.

Endorsement Method   Under the **endorsement split dollar** method, the employer owns the policy and is responsible for making all premium payments. When the insured employee dies, the split beneficiary designation provides for the employer to receive a portion of the death benefit equal to its premium outlay, with the remainder of the death proceeds payable to the employee's designated beneficiary. The method gets the name from the employee's rights that are protected by endorsing the policy over to the employer, thus giving the employee the right to name the residual beneficiary. A significant advantage of the endorsement method is that the employer owns the excess cash values in the insurance policy (whereas in the collateral assignment method, this excess is owned by the employee). As a result, the endorsement method is typically used for an employee who is not a shareholder in the corporation.

Endorsement split dollar

An arrangement in which the employer owns the policy and is responsible for making all premium payments; when the insured employee dies, the employer receives a portion of the death benefit equal to its premium outlay, with the remainder of the death proceeds payable to the employee's designated beneficiary

Methods Compared

Attribute	Collateral Assignment	Endorsement
Owner of policy	Employee	Employer
Tax treatment of policy premiums	Nondeductible	Nondeductible
Employer's portion of death proceeds	Employer is refunded loan equal to premiums paid	Equal to amount of cash value
Employee's portion of death proceeds	Remainder to employee's beneficiary	Remainder to employee's beneficiary

Disadvantage of Either Form   A significant disadvantage of either split-dollar ownership form is that the employee must pay income taxes each year on the economic benefit derived from the arrangement. The economic benefit is usually measured by the Table 2001 cost to the employee. In addition, any payment made by an employer under a split-dollar arrangement must be accounted for either as a loan (collateral assignment method) or as compensation (endorsement method) to the employee.

Key Person Life Insurance

Key person life insurance

After the death of a key employee, used to recruit and train a replacement and compensate the company for lost business

Key person life insurance protects a business upon the loss of a key employee. The tax-free proceeds from the policy can be used to recruit and train a replacement and compensate the company for lost business during the transition.

For small businesses, key employees have a more direct effect on the bottom line. If the key employee's departure is planned, as in the case of retirement, a businessowner can prepare for the loss and take steps to minimize the impact. However, if the employee dies, the loss is unpredictable and leaves the business exposed to financial risks. The income-tax-free death benefit from a key person life insurance policy can greatly reduce the financial risks associated with the loss of a key person.

Key person life insurance is often required to obtain funding for the business. Investors want an assurance that they can recover their investment in the business in the event a key employee dies.

Business Overhead Expense Insurance

Business overhead expense insurance

Helps a business meet its liabilities in the event a significant income producer becomes disabled

Some employees are essential to the success of the business. This is often the case when the business relies on the knowledge and expertise of professionals, such as physicians, attorneys, and accountants. **Business overhead expense insurance** helps the business meet its liabilities in the event a significant income producer becomes disabled and can be structured to meet the needs of an individual business. Elimination periods vary, and policies may require total or partial disability. Benefit periods generally extend up to two years. In most cases, benefits are paid whether the disability is expected to be temporary or permanent. Expenses covered by business overhead expense insurance are outlined in the policy and may include rent or mortgage payments, utilities, administrative salaries, the salary of a replacement employee, property taxes, and other fixed expenses. However, the owner's salary is not covered under this policy, but instead, it is covered by an individual disability insurance policy.

Other Employee Benefits

Section 125 Plans

Employers can offer their employees a choice between cash and a variety of nontaxable qualified benefits under IRC Section 125. Also known as **cafeteria plans, Section 125 plans** provide qualified benefits, including health care, dental and vision care, accident and health insurance, group term life insurance, and adoption assistance. These benefits are excludable from the employee's gross income, and the employee is not deemed to be in constructive receipt of the benefits.

Section 125 (cafeteria plan)
A plan in which employers offer their employees a choice between cash and a variety of nontaxable qualified benefits that are excludable from the employee's income

Cafeteria plans must not discriminate in favor of highly compensated employees in terms of contribution amounts and benefits provided. In addition, all employees must be covered under the plan at the beginning of the year following their third anniversary of employment. If a plan is found to be discriminatory, highly compensated employees are taxed on the benefits.

Flexible Spending Accounts (FSAs)

Employers also may offer **flexible spending accounts** to employees under a cafeteria plan that provides coverage under which specified, incurred expenses may be reimbursed. FSAs are typically funded by employee salary reductions and allow employees the benefit of paying for their health-care related expenses with pretax income. FSAs include health and dental accounts for expenses not reimbursed by any other health or dental plan, and dependent care assistance programs. If both types of expenses are reimbursed under the FSA, separate accounts are maintained for each type of expense. Note that if the FSA account balance is not used by 2½ months after the close of the contribution year, the account balance is forfeited.

Flexible spending account (FSA)
An account typically funded by employee salary reductions that allows employees the benefit of paying for their health-care-related expenses with pretax income

Fringe Benefits

Meals and lodging furnished for the employer's convenience. These benefits are excludable from the employee's gross income and, in many cases, can be provided on a discriminatory basis. Meals must be furnished on the employer's premises; lodging, which must be provided on the employer's premises, must be a condition of the employee's employment. In addition, both meals and lodging must be received by the employee solely for the convenience of the employer.

Qualified adoption assistance plans. These expenses include court costs, attorney's fees, and any adoption expenses directly related to the legal adoption of a "qualified child." Costs for a qualified child do not include expenses associated with surrogate parenting or the adoption of a spouse's child. The maximum excludable amount for all years is $14,300 per child (2020). In 2020, the exclusion will begin to phase out for taxpayers with adjusted gross income above $214,520 and will be completely phased out at $254,520.

Education assistance programs. These plans offer income-tax-free reimbursement for education expenses incurred by an employee when acquiring knowledge to perform his job or improve job skills. Covered expenses include tuition, fees, books, and other necessary supplies. Currently, the maximum amount of reimbursement is $5,250 annually.

Dependent care assistance plans. Under these plans, employers can reimburse employees for child care expenses, or they can actually provide day care for employees' dependents. Employees receive benefits income tax-free, and expenses paid by employers are tax-deductible as Section 162 compensation. Qualified dependent care expenses must be for dependent care, not education. These expenses include the cost of a sitter, preschool and kindergarten expenses, after-school care for children under age 13, and summer camp for children under age 13. Benefits must be made available on a nondiscriminatory basis.

Other fringe benefits. FICA and FUTA are not paid on the benefit amounts for the following fringe benefits, which are excludable from gross income:

- Qualified employee discounts that are made on a nondiscriminatory basis

- "No additional cost" services that are offered to employees free or at a bargain price; the employer cannot incur any significant additional cost to provide the benefits, which include vacant hotel rooms, airline tickets, and cable TV services, and the benefits must be nondiscriminatory

- De minimis fringe benefits, such as personal use of an employer's fax machine or copier, or meals before, during, or after an employee's work shift if the employer provides food service

- Qualified moving expense reimbursement was repealed for the years 2018–2025 for all people except active duty members of the armed forces and their families

- Working-condition fringes provided to an employee that would otherwise be deductible by the employee as an employee business expense, had the employee paid for the services; nondiscrimination rules do not apply (examples of working-condition fringes include payment of industry journal subscriptions and the use of a company vehicle)

- Qualified tuition reduction provided by an educational organization for education up to, but not including, the graduate level

Voluntary Employees' Benefit Associations (VEBAs)

Voluntary Employee Benefit Association (VEBA)
A tax-exempt trust authorized by IRC Section 501(c)(9); in a VEBA, an employer makes tax-free deposits to the plan on an employee's behalf

A VEBA is a tax-exempt trust authorized by IRC Section 501(c)(9). In a VEBA, an employer makes tax-free deposits on an employee's behalf to the plan. The employee's account is credited with tax-free investment earnings, and an employee may obtain tax-free reimbursements for medical expenses and insurance premiums payments from the account.

Generally, VEBAs are managed by the membership or trustees/fiduciaries chosen by the employee membership. VEBAs do not pay taxes on net earnings if arranged as a tax-exempt trust or nonprofit organization.

Prepaid Legal Services

Prepaid legal services
Under this arrangement, law firms, in exchange for a monthly payment, provide specific legal services at no or greatly reduced cost

Under this arrangement, law firms, in exchange for a monthly payment, provide specific legal services at no or greatly reduced cost. Employers can deduct the cost of such a plan and, if the plan is a qualified group legal services plan under Section 120 of the Internal Revenue Code, any services provided under the plan are income tax-free when received by the employees.

Services often include the drafting of wills and other legal documents, conferences with attorneys, and domestic legal work. Representation in civil and criminal matters may be available but is usually limited in scope.

WHERE ON THE WEB

A.M. Best Company **www.ambest.com**

American Council of Life Insurers **www.acli.org**

Centers for Medicare and Medicaid Services **www.cms.gov**

Fitch Ratings **www.fitchratings.com**

America's Health Insurance Plans **www.ahip.org**

Insure.com (S & P ratings)
www.insure.com/interactive-tools/sandp/newtool1.jsp

Long-Term Care **longtermcare.acl.gov/**

Medicare **www.medicare.gov**

Moody's Investors Service **www.moodys.com**

National Hospice and Palliative Care Organization **www.nhpco.org**

Standard & Poor's Index Services **us.spindices.com**

TIAA Life Insurance Information **www.tiaa.org**

U.S. Government's Agency for Healthcare Research & Quality
www.ahrq.gov

DISCUSSION QUESTIONS

1. What are some of the potential losses associated with the risk of premature death? How can life insurance reduce (or eliminate) the effect of these losses?

2. What are the three recognized methods for measuring the needs related to premature death?

3. What is used as the basis for risk measurement under the human value life approach to identifying life insurance needs?

4. What specific needs make up the financial needs approach to the amount of life insurance needed?

5. How do term, whole life, and universal life insurance differ? What are the advantages and disadvantages of each policy?

6. Identify the various types of term life insurance.

7. Identify the various types of whole life insurance.

8. Identify and discuss the death benefit options offered in a universal life insurance policy.

9. What differentiates variable life insurance from variable universal life insurance?

10. At what threshold is an employee taxed on group term life insurance provided by an employer?

11. How do annuities differ from life insurance contracts?

12. What are the various types of annuities?

13. What are the tax implications of life insurance and annuities?

14. What are the various contractual provisions and options that pertain to life and annuity contracts?

15. What are the major types of individual health coverage?

16. What are the important policy provisions and major contractual features of individual health coverage?

17. What are the major types of employer-provided group health insurance coverage?

18. What are the important policy provisions and major contractual features of group health coverage?

19. What is the purpose of disability income insurance? What are some of the various definitions of disability?

20. What are the major types of disability coverage?

21. What are the important policy provisions and major contractual features of disability income insurance?

22. What is the tax treatment of health and disability insurance coverage?

23. How do indemnity plans and managed care plans differ?

24. How can group health coverage be continued or transferred when employment terminates?

EXERCISES

1. Comment on each of the following statements concerning the methods of providing life insurance protection.
   - An insurance company can use three approaches to provide life insurance protection: term insurance, which is temporary; whole life insurance, which is permanent protection that builds up a reserve or savings component; and universal life, which is protection that accrues cash value at interest rates usually higher than the guaranteed interest rate.
   - Term insurance is a form of life insurance in which the death proceeds are payable in the event of the insured's death during a specified period, and nothing is paid if the insured survives past the end of the period.
   - The net premium for term insurance is determined by the morbidity rate for the attained age of the individual.
   - Because death rates rise at an increasing rate as ages increase, the net premium for term insurance also rises at an increasing rate.
   - Universal life insurance offers the policyowner more flexibility than traditional whole life insurance.

2. Identify circumstances for which the following types of life insurance would be most appropriate:
   - Term insurance
   - Whole life insurance
   - Variable life insurance
   - Universal life insurance
   - Variable universal life insurance

3. Compare the primary functions of life insurance and annuities.

4. Discuss the following types of annuities:
   - Immediate versus deferred
   - Flexible premium versus single premium
   - Fixed versus variable

5. Identify and describe the features of a major medical plan.

6. Identify and describe the features of a long-term disability insurance policy.

7. Comment on the need for long-term care insurance.

8. Frank, age 45, is married to Julie. Frank makes $120,000 per year. He has two children, ages 9 and 10. He pays income taxes of $26,000 per year and FICA taxes of $5,000 per year. Frank consumes $20,000 per year of the family's expenses. He expects raises of 4% annually and plans to retire at age 65. He expects inflation to be 3%. Using the human life value approach, calculate the required amount of life insurance.

9. Describe the distinguishing features of whole life, universal life, variable life, and variable universal life in terms of premium amount, death benefit, the policyowner's control over investment, and the expected rate of return from the cash value invested.

10. Calculate the amount of money a major medical insurance policy will pay if:
    - the surgeon's charge is $12,500;
    - there is an 80/20 coinsurance clause;
    - the deductible is $500; and
    - the usual and customary charge for this surgery is $10,000.

11. Briefly explain the purpose of an elimination period in a long-term disability policy.

12. Differentiate between an HMO and a PPO.

13. What are the qualifying events that allow for COBRA benefits? What is the maximum benefit period for each qualifying event?

PROBLEMS

Problem 1

Julian, age 27, has two children, ages 4 and 3, from his first marriage. He is now married to Margaret. The children live with their mother, Alice. Julian and Margaret each make $26,000 per year and have recently bought a house for $100,000, with a $95,000 mortgage. They have the following life, health, and disability insurance coverage:

Life Insurance

	Policy A	Policy B	Policy C
Insured	Julian	Julian	Margaret
Face amount	$250,000	$78,000	$20,000
Type	20-year level term	Group term	Group term
Annual premium	$250	$156	$50
Premium payor	Trustee	Employer	Employer
Beneficiary	Trustee*	Alice	Julian
Policyowner	Trust	Julian	Margaret

*Children are beneficiaries of the trust required by divorce decree.

Health Insurance   Julian and Margaret are covered under Julian's employer plan, which is a PPO plan with a $500 in-network deductible per person per year and a $1,500 out-of-network deductible per person per year, an in-network 80/20 coinsurance clause with a family annual out-of-pocket maximum of $2,500, and an out-of-network 60/40 coinsurance clause with a family maximum out-of-pocket of $4,500.

Long-Term Disability Insurance   Julian is covered by an own occupation policy, with premiums paid by his employer. The benefit equals 60% of his gross pay after a 180-day elimination period. The policy covers both sickness and accidents. The benefit period is five years (60 months). Margaret is not covered by disability insurance.

1. Assume that Julian dies. Who would receive the proceeds of the insurance policies?

2. Does Julian have adequate life insurance?

3. Is Julian's health and disability coverage adequate? If not, why not?

4. Should Margaret have disability insurance? Why or why not?

5. Are any of the premiums or benefits received from the life, health, or disability insurance taxable to Julian and Margaret?

Problem 2

Richard graduated from a state university with a Bachelor of Science degree in accounting. He has been employed at Knoth & Cartez, a small local accounting firm (50 employees) for almost seven years. He makes $62,000 per year. Richard has been married to Marianne for six years. She graduated from a private university with a Bachelor of Science degree in elementary education. She is employed as a fourth-grade teacher at Riverside Preparatory School. She makes $35,000 per year. Richard and Marianne have three children: Carlos, age four; and twin girls, Maria and Anna, age two.

The Richards have the following insurance:

Health Insurance   Health insurance is provided for the entire family by Knoth & Cartez. The family is covered by an HMO. Doctor's visits are $10 per visit, prescriptions are $5 for generic brands and $10 for other brands, and there is no co-payment for hospitalization in semiprivate accommodations. Private rooms are provided when medically necessary. For emergency treatment, a $50 copayment is required.

Life Insurance   Richard has a $50,000 group term life insurance policy through Knoth & Cartez. Marianne has a $20,000 group term policy through Riverside Preparatory School. The owners of the policies are Richard and Marianne, respectively, with each other as the respective beneficiary.

Disability Insurance   Richard has disability insurance through the accounting firm. Short-term disability benefits begin for any absence due to accident or illness over six days and will continue for up to six months at 80% of his salary. Long-term disability benefits are available if disability continues over six months. If Richard is unable to perform the duties of his own current position, the benefits provide him with 60% of his gross salary while disabled until recovery, death, retirement, or age 65 (whichever occurs first). All disability premiums are paid by Knoth & Cartez. Marianne currently has no disability insurance.

1. What happens to the family's health insurance if Richard is terminated from his job? What are the alternatives?

2. Does Richard have adequate life insurance?

3. Does either of the group term policies cause taxable income to Richard and Marianne?

4. Should Marianne have disability insurance?

CASE SCENARIO

Use the information provided to answer the following questions regarding the Nelson family.

NELSON FAMILY CASE SCENARIO
DANA AND DAVID NELSON
As of 12/31/2020

Personal Background and Information

David Nelson (age 37) is a bank vice president. He has been employed there for 12 years and has an annual salary of $70,000. Dana Nelson (age 37) is a full-time homemaker. David and Dana have been married for eight years. They have two children, John (age 6) and Gabrielle (age 3), and are expecting their third child in two weeks. They have always lived in this community and expect to remain indefinitely in their current residence.

General Goals (Not Prioritized)

- Save for college education
- Reduce debt
- Save for retirement
- Estate planning
- Invest wisely

Insurance Information

Health Insurance

The entire family is insured under David's employer's health plan (PPO). For covered expenses, a $1,000 in-network deductible and a $2,000 out-of-network deductible apply, after which 80%/20% coinsurance applies in network and 60%/40% applies out of network. There is a stop-loss limit of $20,000 annually in network and $30,000 annually out of network. The entire monthly premium of $1,123.54 is paid by David's employer.

Life Insurance

David's employer provides group term life insurance equal to two times David's current salary. The premium is paid entirely by his employer, and Dana is the primary beneficiary. No contingent beneficiary is named.

Disability Insurance

David's employer also offers a contributory group long-term disability insurance program toward which the employer contributes 60% of the $158.54 monthly premium. David is a participant in the program, which provides a monthly disability income benefit equal to 70% of his current salary, payable to his Social Security normal retirement age, provided that he remains disabled per the policy's "own occupation" definition of disability. David must satisfy a 90-day elimination period before he is eligible to begin receiving benefits.

David's employer doesn't offer dental or vision coverages and the Nelsons have not obtained any private form of individual dental or vision insurance benefits.

Homeowners Insurance

The Nelsons have an HO-3 policy with replacement cost on contents. There is a $250 deductible. The annual premium is $950.

Automobile Insurance

The Nelsons have automobile liability and bodily injury coverage of $100,000/$300,000/$100,000. They have both comprehensive coverage and collision. The deductibles are $250 (comprehensive) and $500 (collision). The annual premium is $900.

Relevant External Environmental Information

- Mortgage rates are 5.0% for 30 years and 4.5% for 15 years, fixed.

- Gross domestic product is expected to grow at less than 3%.

- Inflation is expected to be 2.6%.

- Expected return on investment is 8% for common stocks, 9% for small company stocks, and 1.1% for U.S. Treasury bills.

- College education costs are $15,000 per year.

Investment Information

The bank offers a Section 401(k) plan in which David is an active participant. The bank matches contributions dollar for dollar up to 3% of David's salary. David currently contributes 5.43% of his salary. His employer's plan allows for employee contributions of up to 16% of salary. In the Section 401(k) plan, the Nelsons have the opportunity to invest in a money market fund, a bond fund, a growth and income fund, and a small-cap fund. The Nelsons consider themselves to have a moderate investment risk tolerance. David's assets within the plan are currently earning 8.5%, based on his investment choices within the plan.

Income Tax Information

David and Dana tell you that they are in the 12% federal income tax bracket. They pay $820 annually in state and local income taxes.

Education Information

John is 6 years old and currently attending first grade at a private school. Gabrielle is 3 years old. She will attend private school from pre-kindergarten through high school. The current balance of the college fund is $14,000. They expect to contribute $1,000 at the end of each year to this fund.

Gifts, Estates, Trusts, and Will Information

David has made Dana his primary beneficiary on his Section 401(k) plan, and the children are the contingent beneficiaries. Because most of their assets are owned jointly, David doesn't see the need for a will. Dana also does not have a will.

Dana and David Nelson
Statement of Financial Position
12/31/2019

ASSETS			LIABILITIES AND NET WORTH	
Cash/cash equivalents			**Current liabilities**	
JT	Checking account	$1,425	JT Credit cards	$4,000
JT	Savings account	$950	JT Mortgage on principal residence	$1,234
			David Boat loan	$1,493
Total cash/cash equivalents		$2,375	**Total current liabilities**	$6,727
Invested assets			**Long-term liabilities**	
Dana	ABC stock	$12,500	JT Mortgage on principal residence	$196,654
JT	Education fund	$14,000	David Boat loan	$12,065
David	Section 401(k) plan	$32,197		
Total invested assets		$58,697	**Total long-term liabilities**	$208,719
Personal-use assets			**Total liabilities**	$215,446
JT	Principal residence	$245,000		
JT	Automobile	$18,000		
David	Boat	$25,000	**Net worth**	$207,626
Dana	Jewelry	$13,000		
JT	Furniture/household	$61,000		
Total personal-use assets		$362,000		
Total assets		$423,072	**Total liabilities and net worth**	$423,072

Dana and David Nelson
Statement of Financial Position
12/31/2020

ASSETS			LIABILITIES AND NET WORTH		
Cash/cash equivalents			**Current liabilities**		
JT	Checking account	$1,268	JT	Credit cards	$3,655
JT	Savings account	$950	JT	Mortgage on principal residence	$1,370
	Total cash/cash equivalents	$2,218	David	Boat loan	$1,048
				Total current liabilities	$6,073
Invested assets			**Long-term liabilities**		
Dana	ABC stock	$14,050	JT	Mortgage on principal residence	$195,284
JT	Education fund	$15,560	David	Boat loan	$16,017
David	Section 401(k) plan	$38,619		**Total long-term liabilities**	$211,301
David	XYZ stock	$10,000			
	Total invested assets	$78,229			
Personal use assets				**Total liabilities**	$217,374
JT	Principal residence	$250,000			
JT	Automobile	$15,000			
David	Personal watercraft	$10,000		**Net worth**	$241,573
David	Boat	$30,000			
Dana	Jewelry	$13,500			
JT	Furniture/household	$60,000			
	Total personal-use assets	$378,500			
Total assets		$458,947		**Total liabilities and net worth**	$458,947

Notes to financial statements:

- Assets are stated at fair market value.

- The ABC stock was inherited from Dana's aunt on November 15, 2019. Her aunt originally paid $20,000 for it on October 31, 2010. The fair market value at the aunt's death was $12,000.

- Liabilities are stated at principal only.

- JT = joint tenancy; client name = separate property

Dana and David Nelson
Personal Statement of Cash Flows
For 2020

INFLOWS

Salary—David		$70,000
Investment income		
Interest income	$ 900	
Dividend income	$ 150	$ 1,050
Total inflow		**$71,050**
Savings		
Reinvestment (interest/dividends)	$ 1,050	
Section 401(k) plan deferrals	$ 3,803	
Education fund	$ 1,000	
Total savings		**$ 5,853**
Available for outflows		**$65,197**

OUTFLOWS

Ordinary living expenses		
Food	$ 6,000	
Clothing	$ 3,600	
Child care	$ 600	
Entertainment	$ 1,814	
Utilities	$ 3,600	
Auto maintenance	$ 2,000	
Church	$ 3,500	
Total ordinary living expenses		**$21,114**
Debt payments		
Credit card payments principal	$ 345	
Credit card payments interest	$ 615	
Mortgage payment principal	$ 1,234	
Mortgage payment interest	$20,720	
Boat loan principal	$ 1,493	
Boat loan interest	$ 1,547	
Total debt payments		**$25,954**
Insurance premiums		
Automobile insurance premiums	$ 900	
Disability insurance premiums	$ 761	
Homeowners insurance premiums	$ 950	
Total insurance premiums		**$ 2,611**
Tuition and education expenses		**$ 1,000**
Taxes		
FICA and federal income tax (W/H)	$12,855	
State (and city) income tax	$ 820	
Property tax (principal residence)	$ 1,000	
Total taxes		**$14,675**
Total outflows		**$65,354**
Net cash flow (deficit)		**($157)**

1. The Nelsons wish to evaluate and update their life insurance coverage. David would like to have enough insurance to provide the family with 60% of his current salary. ABC stock and XYZ stock have average annual returns of 9%. The education fund is invested 100% in U.S. Treasuries. David's Section 401(k) plan is invested 50% in a diversified common stock fund and 50% in a small company stock fund. Using the capital retention approach, an interest rate of 8%, and ignoring Social Security benefits, how much additional life insurance do the Nelsons need? Evaluate David's group term life insurance from an income tax perspective as well.

2. Evaluate the Nelsons' disability insurance coverage, and determine what portion of the policy premium is taxable and what portion of the benefit would be income taxable if received.

3. Assume that the Nelsons incurred medical expenses of $30,000 in 2020.

   All covered services were received in network. What was the total cost to the Nelsons for these services?

Personal Property and Liability Insurance

LEARNING OBJECTIVES

After learning the material in this chapter, you will be able to do the following:

■ Identify the need for homeowners, auto, and liability umbrella insurance coverages

■ List and define the basic coverages provided by a homeowners policy

■ Be aware of the various homeowners forms that are available

■ Understand and explain the various contractual options and provisions in homeowners insurance

■ List and define the basic coverages provided by a personal automobile insurance policy

■ Understand and explain the various contractual options and provisions in a personal automobile insurance policy

■ Identify the need for a personal umbrella liability policy and explain its distinguishing characteristics

■ Identify the coverages available to businesses and businessowners

INTRODUCTION

Often a home is the largest investment a family will make. Although the frequency of perils causing financial loss to the home is small, the severity of loss is potentially large. Therefore, it is important that this valuable asset be protected against damage and destruction. The professional financial planner should be knowledgeable about the property risks as well as the liability risks associated with a client's property. Although property insurance protects the assets the client already owns, liability insurance protects the client against financial loss from legal action. Therefore, coverage for both property and liability risks is an essential part of a client's financial plan.

Automobiles are major assets owned by numerous individuals. The personal automobile policy (PAP) mitigates the risk of loss to the automobile and those involved in an automobile accident. For a client, automobile insurance may be among the most expensive aspects of owning a car. Another type of insurance, a personal umbrella liability policy, provides coverage in excess of the liability coverage provided in the homeowners and automobile policies.

Various types of insurance coverage, such as the commercial package policy, the businessowners policy, and professional liability insurance, provide protection for businessowners and self-employed professionals.

This chapter introduces each of these types of insurance to help the planner understand and evaluate the client's property and liability needs and recommend appropriate coverage.

PERSONAL PROPERTY AND LIABILITY INSURANCE

The U.S. legal system holds individuals responsible for the bodily injuries and property damage they cause to others due to their negligence. When one is legally liable for injuries to another, the law requires that payment be made for those injuries along with the possibility of punitive damages being assessed to punish the defendant. Where money is not available to make the necessary restitution, future wages along with other assets may be seized, potentially jeopardizing an individual's future standard of living. Liability insurance provides the insured with financial protection against lawsuits and other claims for damages that result from the insured's actions.

This chapter discusses the three policies most commonly used to protect against personal property and liability risks: homeowners insurance, automobile insurance, and liability umbrella insurance. Homeowners and automobile insurance are package policies that provide both property and liability coverage in one contract. The personal liability umbrella policy provides a layer of personal liability protection above the coverage provided under the homeowners and automobile policies, in the unfortunate event that those policies do not provide adequate compensation to the injured parties.

Each of the following discussions is based on the standard policy forms drafted by the Insurance Services Office (ISO). Because insurance is regulated at the state level, each state may require certain modifications to the standard ISO form. Thus, the ensuing discussions are general in nature. Absolute statements cannot be made about a particular policy without reading the policy thoroughly.

Homeowners (HO) Insurance: Basic Coverage

Homeowners (HO) insurance is a package insurance policy that provides both property and liability coverage for the insured dwelling, other structures, personal property, and loss of use. Each homeowners insurance form consists of two sections: Section I provides property coverage, and Section II provides liability coverage.

Levels of Coverage

A **peril**, as defined in a homeowners insurance policy, is a cause of financial loss. The level of coverage afforded by a homeowners insurance policy is determined by the perils it covers.

Named-perils coverage. **Named-perils coverage** protects from perils that are specifically listed in the policy.

EXHIBIT 10.1 List of Covered Perils

Basic Named Perils

1. Fire	7. Vehicles
2. Lightning	8. Smoke
3. Windstorm	9. Vandalism or malicious mischief
4. Hail	10. Explosion
5. Riot or civil commotion	11. Theft
6. Aircraft	12. Volcanic eruption

Broad Named Perils: Basic Named Perils 1–12, plus 13–18:

13. Falling objects

14. Weight of ice, snow, and sleet

15. Accidental discharge or overflow of water or steam

16. Sudden and accidental tearing apart, cracking, burning, or bulging of a steam, hot water, air conditioning, or automatic fire protective sprinkler system, or from within a household appliance

17. Freezing of a plumbing, heating, air conditioning, or automatic fire sprinkler system, or of a household appliance

18. Sudden and accidental damage from artificially generated electrical current

Open-perils coverage. **Open-perils coverage** is designed to protect against all perils except those specifically excluded from coverage. This increased coverage results in a higher premium for the insured.

Perils Generally Excluded

The following perils are excluded from most homeowners policies.

Movement of the ground. Property damage arising from earth movement is excluded. This includes damage from an earthquake, volcanic eruption, or landslide.

Ordinance or law. A loss due to an ordinance or law that regulates the construction, repair, or demolition of a building or structure is excluded.

Damage from water. Property damage from the following are specifically excluded from coverage under the homeowners policy:

- Floods, surface water, waves, tidal water, and overflow or spray of a body of water

---

Homeowners insurance

A package insurance policy that provides both property and liability coverage for the insured dwelling, other structures, personal property, and loss of use

Named-perils coverage

Protects from perils that are specifically listed in the policy

Open-perils coverage

Coverage designed to protect against all perils except those specifically excluded from coverage

- Water below the surface of the ground that exerts pressure on or seeps through a building, sidewalk, driveway, foundation, swimming pool, or other structure

- Water backing through sewers or drains

Coverage for naturally occurring floods is available through the National Flood Insurance Program (NFIP) offered by the federal government. Residential flood insurance provides coverage for physical loss from a flood. Loss settlement is on an actual cash value basis, but replacement cost is available for a one- to four-family dwelling that is occupied by the owner at least 80% of the year. Coverage is subject to the standard exclusions and a deductible. A flood policy is enforceable immediately during the first 30 days that coverage is available in a community. After the 30th day, there is a 30-day waiting period for coverage to be effective. There are some private insurance companies that may also offer flood insurance in certain locations. Coverage for sewer backup is available in some areas as an endorsement to the HO policy.

War or nuclear hazard. Property damage from war or nuclear hazard, including radiation, or radioactive contamination is excluded. If a radiation leak from a nuclear power plant near an insured's home contaminates the property, there is no coverage for the loss.

Power failure. Losses due to power failure caused by an uninsured peril, such as a freezer thawing out and its contents spoiling because of local power plant malfunctions, are not covered. If, however, a covered peril, such as fire or lightning on the premises causes the power failure, the resulting damage is covered.

Intentional act. If a loss is discovered to be an intentional act on the part of any insured, it is not covered. For example, one cannot intentionally burn the house down and recover insurance benefits.

Neglect. If an insured fails to use all reasonable and necessary means to save and preserve the property during or after the loss, or when the property is endangered by an insured peril, the loss is not covered.

Section I Coverage

Section I, which protects property and belongings, helps the policyowner repair, rebuild, or completely replace a house, furniture, and belongings in the event of a casualty. Section I provides the types of coverage listed below:

- Coverage A: Dwelling

- Coverage B: Other structures

- Coverage C: Personal property

- Coverage D: Loss of use

- Additional coverage: Debris removal, damage to trees, credit card loss

Coverage A: Dwelling

Dwelling
Residential structure covered under a homeowners policy

Coverage A provides coverage for repair or replacement of damage to a **dwelling**, a residential structure covered under a homeowners policy. This section also covers attached structures and building materials on the premises. The homeowner typically buys an amount of coverage equal to the replacement cost of the dwelling and, in some cases, will be required to carry even more if the property is mortgaged. A mortgage lender usually demands an amount of coverage on the dwelling at least equal to the total amount of the mortgage.

Replacement cost
The amount necessary to purchase, repair, or replace the dwelling with materials of the same or similar quality at current prices

Actual cash value (ACV)
The depreciated value of the insured property

Covered losses to the dwelling and other structures are paid on the basis of replacement cost with no deduction for depreciation. **Replacement cost** is the amount necessary to purchase, repair, or replace the dwelling with materials of the same or similar quality at current prices. If the insured does not carry insurance of at least 80% of the replacement cost (coinsurance) at the time of a partial loss, the insured will receive the larger of the following:

■ **Actual cash value (ACV)** for the part of the dwelling that is damaged

■ [Insurance carried ÷ (coinsurance % × replacement value)] × amount of loss

E X A M P L E Amanda owns a home with a replacement value of $280,000 and a depreciated actual value equal to 50% of the replacement value. She purchases $200,000 of insurance with a coinsurance requirement of 80%. If Amanda experiences a $100,000 loss, the insurance company will pay the greater of:

$$\text{Actual cash value} = 50\% \times \$100,000 = \$50,000 \text{ or}$$

$$\frac{\text{Insurance Purchased}}{\text{Coinsurance}} \times \text{Amount of Loss} =$$

$$\frac{\$200,000}{80\% \times \$280,000} \times \$100,000 = \$89,286, \text{less any deductible}$$

Because the coinsurance formula results in the greater value, Amanda will receive $89,286, less any applicable deductible. It is important to remember that the homeowners insurance policy will only cover up to the policy limit. Even if a policyholder has the required 80% multiplied by the replacement cost of the dwelling in coverage, the policy will not pay out more than its limit or face amount.

Certain properties attached to the dwelling or considered an integral part of the dwelling are covered only on an actual cash value basis. These properties include awnings, household appliances, outdoor antennas, outdoor appliances, and nonbuilding structures.

Coverage B: Other Structures

Coverage B provides coverage for small, detached structures on the dwelling property. These **other structures** include detached garages, small greenhouses, storage buildings, and gazebos. The limit of insurance in Coverage B is typically 10% of the Coverage A (dwelling) limit. Like the dwelling coverage, this coverage pays on a replacement cost basis.

Note that detached structures used for business purposes are not covered under Section B of a personal homeowners policy. Additionally, Section B does not apply to any structure rented to someone who is not a tenant of the dwelling, unless the structure is used solely as a private garage.

Other structures
Structures not attached to a dwelling, such as detached garages, small greenhouses, storage buildings, and gazebos

Coverage C: Personal Property

Under Coverage C, personal property refers to the belongings possessed by the policyowner and personal property of any resident family members. This property includes furniture, clothing, electronics, and other personally owned possessions, regardless of where the property is located at the time of loss. The limit of insurance for Coverage C is typically 50% of the Coverage A (dwelling) limit.

Note that the standard HO form provides only actual cash value (ACV) coverage on personal property. An optional endorsement is available to increase coverage up to the replacement cost, and this option is recommended for most homeowners. Because the contents of a home depreciate rapidly, a homeowner could suffer a serious financial loss if replacement cost coverage were not provided.

Consider the price of a man's suit, which is about $300. Assume that after a short time, a homeowner's suits depreciate to a value of $150 each and the homeowner loses five suits in a fire. Under the ACV option, the insurer will only pay the depreciated value of the suits at the time of loss, in this case a total of $750. If the homeowner has an optional replacement cost endorsement, the insurance company will pay the entire replacement cost of the suits.

Certain kinds of personal property have maximum dollar limits on the amount that will be paid for any loss. A typical HO policy contains the following limits of liability:

- $200—cash and currency, bank notes, bullion, coin collections, and medals

- $500—loss of business use property not on premises

- $1,500—securities, manuscripts, stamp collections, valuable papers, and airline tickets

- $1,500—theft of jewelry, watches, gems, precious metals, and real furs

- $1,500—watercraft (including motor and trailer), trailers (not boat affiliated), and equipment

- $1,500—loss of electronic apparatus

- $2,500—theft of firearms

- $2,500—theft of silverware, goldware, pewterware, and similar property

- $2,500—loss of business use property on premises

Property with considerable value, such as jewelry, furs, or stamp collections, may be protected by additional amounts of insurance beyond the limits listed above. These items may be covered under a **scheduled personal property endorsement**. This endorsement provides open-peril coverage under the same terms as if separate contracts were purchased for each type of property. Types of property that may be covered under this type of endorsement may include jewelry, musical instruments, silverware, fine art, cameras, furs, coin collections, and stamp collections. In most cases, the amount for which an item is insured is considered the value of the item if a loss occurs.

Certain items of personal property are excluded from coverage because they are either uninsurable or outside the normal range of property owned by the typical homeowner. Because there is an unusual risk exposure for these types of property, the homeowner must request special coverage outside the homeowners coverage. The following types of personal property are specifically excluded from coverage under a homeowners policy:

- Animals, birds, and fish

- Articles separately described and specifically insured

- Motorized land vehicles used off premises

- Property of roomers or boarders not related to the insured

- Aircraft and parts

- Furnishings on property rented out to others

- Property held as samples, held for sale, or sold but not delivered

- Business data, credit cards, and funds transfer cards

- Business property held away from the residence premises

Scheduled personal property endorsement
Provides open-peril coverage under the same terms as if separate contracts were purchased for each type of property; the amount for which an item is insured is considered the value of the item if a loss occurs

Coverage D: Loss of Use

Loss of use

Coverage that provides reimbursement to an insured homeowner for additional living expenses or loss of fair rental value

Additional living expenses

The difference between the cost of living in temporary arrangements and the normal costs that would have been incurred had there been no loss

Loss of fair rental value

The gross rental value less charges and expenses that do not continue during the period in which the property is uninhabitable

Loss of use coverage may provide reimbursement to an insured homeowner for additional living expenses or loss of fair rental value.

Additional living expenses. Loss of use coverage provides repayment of any extra living expenses incurred as the result of having to live elsewhere while the home is being restored following a Coverage A loss. **Additional living expenses** are defined as the difference between the cost of living in temporary arrangements and the normal costs that would have been incurred had there been no loss. Typically, coverage is limited to a maximum of 20% of the Coverage A (dwelling) limit.

Assume that Betsy cannot live in her house for several weeks because of severe damage that is covered by her homeowners policy. She incurs hotel charges of $4,000, pays $1,500 for meals, and has $150 in laundry costs while living away from home. Had there been no loss, her expenses for her home, meals, and laundry would have been $3,250. Loss of use protection would provide $2,400 in additional living expenses to compensate her for the extra costs associated with being temporarily displaced from her home while it is being repaired ($4,000 + $1,500 + $150 – $3,250 = $2,400).

Loss of fair rental value. Under Coverage D, an insured lessor may recover the loss of fair rental value on property held for rental purposes. Benefits for **loss of fair rental value** are paid on the basis of the gross rental value less charges and expenses that do not continue during the period in which the property is uninhabitable. In this case, coverage is usually limited to a maximum of 20% of the Coverage A (dwelling) limit.

Suppose Janice owns a house in which she rents a section to a university student for $300 per month. The house is deemed uninhabitable for two months after a fire. Each month, she has maintenance expenses for this section of the house totaling $50, which she does not incur during the repair of the house. Janice can recover $500 [($300 – $50) × 2] for the loss of rent during the restoration of the house.

If a civil authority prevents an insured from using the premises because of damage by a covered peril to a neighborhood, loss of use coverage typically will be provided for up to two weeks. This is a unique feature of the HO form, considering that the insured need not directly experience any damage to the property to collect for loss of use. Consider the various forest fire episodes in California. If a civil authority orders a homeowner to vacate the premises because of the spread of fire in the area, loss of use coverage can provide reimbursement of additional living expenses incurred as a result of the evacuation.

Preferred Provisions

Exhibit 10.2 summarizes the preferred provisions of homeowners insurance.

EXHIBIT 10.2 Homeowners Checklist

Part A – Dwelling	■ Replacement cost
	■ Open perils
Part B – Other Structures	■ Replacement cost
	■ Open perils
Part C – Personal Property	■ Replacement cost*
	■ Open perils*
	■ Scheduled items
Part D – Loss of Use	■ Additional living expenses
	■ Loss of fair rental value
Riders	■ Extra coverage for valuable personal property
	■ Aircraft
	■ Watercraft
	■ Furnishings on property rented out to others
	■ Business property
	■ Earthquake insurance
	■ Sewer backup coverage

*An endorsement is required for HO-3 policies.

Section II Coverage

Coverage E: Personal Liability

Coverage E protects the insured homeowner and all resident family members against liability for bodily injury and property damage that may occur on or off the insured's premises due to negligence. The basic limit for liability is $100,000 per occurrence, although this limit may be increased. An **occurrence** is an accident, including exposure to conditions, that results in bodily injury or property damage during the policy period. For example, covered occurrences may include a guest to an insured's home falling on a patch of ice on the walkway, or a dog biting a mail carrier on or off the insured's premises. Coverage E only applies if the insured is found to be legally liable.

As part of the coverage, the insurer pays all defense and settlement costs associated with a claim for damages made by an injured party. Personal liability coverage does not, however, cover the homeowner for liability arising from the operation of a business in the home.

Occurrence
An accident, including exposure to conditions, which results in bodily injury or property damage during the policy period

EXAMPLE Mr. Smith owns a home in Central Florida, which he has insured with a standard homeowners policy. He has an adventurous dog that tends to wander around the neighborhood. If Mr. Smith's dog bites a pedestrian on or off his property, his standard homeowners policy's liability coverage (Coverage E: Personal Liability) will cover him up to the policy limits for any damage or negligence as a result of his dog (dog bite lawsuit) for which he is found legally liable. Coverage F: Medical Payments to Others may also be applied for any medical bills, typically up to $1,000 for coverage of an occurrence on or off the insured property.

EXAMPLE Mr. Smith is on vacation in California. While golfing with friends, he slices his drive into an adjacent fairway and hits another golfer, causing several thousand dollars' worth of medical bills. This is an additional case or occurrence that Mr. Smith's liability coverage within his homeowner's policy (Coverage E: Personal Liability) would protect him against litigation up to the policy limit because he is legally liable for his negligent drive of his golf ball. Coverage F: Medical Payments to Others may also be applied for any medical bills, typically up to $1,000.

EXAMPLE Mr. Smith decided to have a backyard party that included a campfire for his guests to roast marshmallows. The wind picks up and blows the flames from the campfire onto his neighbor's house, causing several thousand dollars in damages. This would be an additional occurrence, and Mr. Smith would be covered for up to the liability limits of his homeowners insurance policy.

Coverage F: Medical Payments to Others

This coverage pays necessary medical expenses of others that result from bodily injury. Bodily injuries must arise out of the insured's activities, premises, or animal(s) on or off the insured's property. Medical expenses must be incurred within three years of the accident; however, this coverage will not pay for medical expenses incurred by the insured or any regular resident of the household, except a residence employee (e.g., a maid or butler).

On the surface, this coverage may seem to duplicate the coverage provided in Coverage E; however, there is an important difference between the two. Coverage F is a no-fault coverage that will automatically pay for bodily injuries, whereas Coverage E pays for both bodily injuries and property damage for which the insured is legally liable. Generally, Coverage F will pay up to $1,000 per person per occurrence. For example, if five people become ill from the food at Marie's dinner party, each person may receive up to $1,000 to cover any necessary medical expenses.

EXAMPLE Suppose Vada hosts a party at her house and invites Katie. While dancing on the coffee table, Katie slips, falls, and is injured. Vada rushes Katie to the hospital. Coverage F will pay up to the policy limit for Katie's medical expenses incurred by the incident, even though her injuries are her own fault, because they occurred on Vada's premises. If, on the following day, Katie files a lawsuit against Vada, asking her for $1 million for pain and suffering damages, Vada's homeowners policy will defend Vada, but if a court determines that Katie's injuries were her own fault, it may deny payment to Katie under the theory that Vada is not legally liable.

Medical Payment Exclusions to Coverage E and Coverage F

Neither Coverage E nor Coverage F will pay for the following injuries or damages:

- That are expected or intended by the insured

- Resulting from the insured's business or professional activities

- Resulting from the rental of premises; however, coverage will be provided when (1) part of an insured location is rented on an occasional basis or solely as a residence to no more than two roomers or boarders and (2) part of an insured location is rented out as an office, school, studio, or private garage

- Arising out of premises the insured owns, rents, or leases to others that have not been declared an insured location

- Arising out of the ownership or use of watercraft, motorized vehicles, and aircraft (however, certain vehicles and watercraft are covered for liability):

  — Trailers that are not connected to a motorized land conveyance

  — A vehicle designed primarily for use off public roads that the insured does not own or that the insured does own but that are on an insured location

- — Motorized golf carts while being used on a golf course

- — Vehicles not subject to motor vehicle registration that include lawnmowers, motorized wheelchairs, and vehicles in dead storage on the insured location

- — Nonmotorized watercraft (e.g., canoes and rowboats)

- — Low-powered boats the insured owns or rents and small (less than 26 feet long) sailboats

- — Model and hobby aircraft that are not designed to carry people or cargo

- — Note that the exclusions of watercraft liability are very detailed; any time the insured plans to purchase, rent, or use a watercraft, the HO policy should be consulted to determine whether coverage exists

- ■ Caused by war or nuclear weapons of any kind

- ■ Caused by the transmission of a communicable disease

- ■ Arising out of sexual molestation, corporal punishment, or physical or mental abuse

- ■ Resulting from the use, sale, manufacture, delivery, transfer, or possession of a controlled substance (other than legally obtained prescription drugs)

- ■ Note that liability for injuries to a residence employee (e.g., a maid or butler) is generally covered; this type of liability coverage is provided to protect the homeowner who needs to hire domestic help but who is not required to purchase workers' compensation coverage for such employees

Exclusions to Coverage E Only

Certain exclusions pertain only to Coverage E of the policy, including the following:

- ■ Damage to property of any insured (should be covered under Section I)

- ■ Damage to premises the insured is renting or has control of, unless caused by fire, smoke, or explosion

- ■ Contractual liability; however, two types of contractual liability are covered: (1) where the insured has entered into a contract that directly relates to the ownership, maintenance, or use of an insured location, and (2) where the liability of others is assumed by the insured in a contract prior to an occurrence

- ■ Liability for loss assessments charged against the insured as a member of an association or organization of property owners (e.g., a condominium association charges individual unit owners for damage to community property)

- ■ Liability for injuries to employees that falls under a workers' compensation or other disability law

- ■ Liability for bodily injury or property damage for which the insured is also covered by a nuclear energy liability policy

Exclusions to Coverage F Only

Coverage F will not provide coverage for the following bodily injuries:

- ■ Sustained by the insured or any family member

- ■ Sustained by a regular resident of an insured location

- Sustained by a residence employee of the insured that occur outside of the scope of employment

- Sustained by anyone eligible to receive benefits for their injuries under a workers' compensation or similar disability law

- Resulting from nuclear reaction radiation, regardless of cause

EXHIBIT 10.3 Summary of Liability Exclusions Applicable to Coverage E and F

Exclusion	Coverage E: Personal Liability	Coverage F: Medical Payments
Intentional injury	✓	✓
Business and professional activities	✓	✓
Rental of property	✓	✓
Professional liability	✓	✓
Uninsured premises	✓	✓
Motor vehicles	✓	✓
Watercraft	✓	✓
Aircraft	✓	✓
War	✓	✓
Communicable disease	✓	✓
Sexual molestation or abuse	✓	✓
Nuclear exclusion	✓	✓
Workers' compensation	✓	✓
Controlled substance	✓	✓
Contractual liability	✓	—
Property owned by or in custody of insured	✓	—
Residence employee away from premises	—	✓
Persons residing on premises	—	✓

HOMEOWNERS (HO) INSURANCE: BASIC FORMS

The basic homeowners (HO) insurance forms available are as follows:

- HO-2: Broad Form (named perils)

- HO-3: Special Form (open perils)

- HO-4: Tenants or Renters

- HO-5: Comprehensive Form (open perils, coverages A, B, C, and D)

- HO-6: Condominium Owners

- HO-8: Modified Form for Special Risks

HO-2: Broad Form

The HO-2 policy provides broad coverage for the dwelling and personal property. In addition, this form broadens certain perils and adds other perils.

HO-3: Special Form

This is the most popular and widely purchased of the basic homeowners policies, accounting for nearly 80% of all homeowners policies sold today. Under an HO-3 policy, real property is covered on an open-perils basis, unless the peril is specifically excluded by the policy. Personal property is covered on a named-perils basis.

An HO-3 policy covers all of the perils listed in an HO-2 policy and any other peril not excluded. The value of the HO-3 is that this form will cover certain unusual losses not specifically named as perils in the HO-2. For example, suppose an insured homeowner with an HO-2 policy, who lives in a rural area, owns a shed that is damaged when a neighbor's livestock gets loose. Because none of the named perils addresses this particular situation, the loss will not be covered. However, had the shed been insured under an HO-3 policy, the damage would have been covered because an HO-3 policy generally has no such exclusions.

HO-4: Tenants or Renters

HO-4 is designed for tenants who do not own their dwelling. In such cases, the tenant has a need only for personal liability coverage, plus coverage for contents and loss of use. The HO-4 policy does not protect the actual building or dwelling (Coverage A or Coverage B), which should be covered by the landlord's policy.

Tenants or Renters provides protection against losses caused by the 18 perils listed in an HO-2 policy. The minimum amount of coverage sold under the HO-4 is $4,000 of personal property coverage (Coverage C). Coverage D (Loss of Use) limit is commonly equal to 30% of the Coverage C limit.

HO-5: Comprehensive Form

The HO-5 is similar to the HO-3 except that Coverage C (personal property) for an HO-5 policy is written on an open-perils basis. The HO-5 was withdrawn from use in 1984 but was reintroduced by the ISO in 2000. In the interim, an HO-15 endorsement was added to an HO-3 policy to provide coverage similar to that of an HO-5 policy.

HO-6: Condominium Owners

The insurance needs of condominium owners differ from those of single-family residence owners because the condo property's common areas (e.g., elevators, hallways, lobbies, and laundry rooms) are covered by insurance policies owned by the condo association. An HO-6 policy provides coverage for the condo owner's personal belongings and any owned structural part of the building. In most cases, the minimum amount of insurance that must be purchased for Coverage C (personal property) under an HO-6 is $6,000. Loss of use coverage is limited to 40% of Coverage C. The HO-6 policy does provide liability protection.

HO-8: Modified Form for Special Risks

The HO-8 policy provides coverage for those who live in an older home whose replacement cost exceeds its market value. The HO-8 policy uses a functional replacement cost provision for loss. Under the functional replacement cost, the insurance company agrees to pay the amount necessary to repair damage, but the coverage cannot be more than the materials and labor that make the dwelling functionally equivalent to its original style. The HO-8 policy covers basic perils only. Liability and medical payments coverage are also part of the policy.

EXHIBIT 10.4 Summary of Covered Perils

	HO-2	HO-3	HO-4	HO-5	HO-6	HO-8
Coverage A: Dwelling	Broad	Open	N/A	Open	Limited	Basic
Coverage B: Other Structures	Broad	Open	N/A	Open	N/A	Basic
Coverage C: Personal Property	Broad	Broad*	Broad	Open	Broad	Basic
Coverage D: Loss of Use	Broad	Open	Broad	Open	Broad	Basic

*Can be endorsed with HO-15 endorsement to provide coverage for personal property on an open-perils basis and can be endorsed to provide loss settlement for personal property on a replacement cost basis

HOMEOWNERS (HO) INSURANCE: ADDITIONAL COVERAGES

Additional coverage is available under homeowners insurance policies. Most of these may be included in an HO-3 policy without additional cost, and not all additional coverage features are available on all policies:

- All-risk coverage for property while it is being moved from one place to another and for an additional 30 days thereafter

- Removal of debris from covered property damaged by an insured peril

- A fire department service charge up to $1,000 for loss by an insured peril; however, a fire department call for rescuing a cat from a tree or people in a home being threatened by a flood is not covered

- The cost of reasonable repairs to protect the property from further damage after a covered loss occurs

- Damage to trees, shrubs, plants, and lawns from all covered perils except for wind (often limited to 5% of the dwelling coverage but not more than $1,000 for any one tree or plant)

- Up to $1,000 per loss for assessments against an insured by a group of property owners arising from loss or damage to property jointly owned by all of the members collectively (e.g., condominium owners)

- Costs resulting from damage to property arising from the collapse of a building caused by an insured peril in addition to several circumstances per the insurance contract

- Damage caused by breakage of glass or safety glazing material that is part of the building, storm doors, or storm windows

- Up to $2,500 for damage to landlord's furnishings in an apartment on the insured's dwelling premises

- Up to $500 for loss due to unauthorized use of credit cards, fund transfer cards, forgery of checks, acceptance of counterfeit money, and any incurred court costs or attorney fees may be available

- Theft coverage for property of students while away at school
- Damage caused by the accidental discharge of water from a waterbed

HOMEOWNERS (HO) INSURANCE: ENDORSEMENTS

Several endorsements are available for homeowners policies at an additional cost, including the following:

Replacement Cost for Personal Property

All of the forms previously discussed provide personal property coverage on the basis of actual cash value (ACV) of the personal property. With this endorsement, covered losses are paid on the basis of what it costs to replace the property without a deduction for depreciation.

Inflation Protection

An inflation protection endorsement provides for an annual pro rata increase in the limits of liability under Coverages A, B, C, and D. The insured specifies the percentage increase, for example 6%, when the endorsement is purchased.

Assume the homeowner chooses an inflation protection endorsement with an annual pro rata increase of 6%. The homeowner's house, originally insured for $200,000, would have coverage of $212,000 at the end of the year.

Because it is uncommon for a home to increase in value at precisely the same rate of inflation, the inflation protection endorsement is not a comprehensive form of protection against inflation and should not be a substitute for regular and careful review of adequate insurance coverage.

Earthquake Endorsement

An earthquake endorsement can be added to Section I of a homeowners policy to provide coverage for earthquakes, landslides, and earth movement. A minimum deductible of $250 applies to any one loss and up to a 10% deductible of the total amount of applicable insurance may apply to the loss.

Water Backup Coverage

This endorsement to Section I of a homeowners policy provides coverage for loss to property as a result of water that backs up through a sewer or drain. An overflow from a sump is also covered, even if the overflow is the result of a mechanical failure of the sump.

Building Law and Ordinance Coverage

Coverage under this endorsement arises from a homeowner's legal responsibility to abide by building laws, ordinances, and codes. If a homeowner is legally required to demolish a partially destroyed house, or if the building codes require more-costly construction methods or materials in the replacement or restoration of a structure, this endorsement provides coverage on the basis of the extra costs.

Personal Injury

Section II of the standard HO policy protects the insured only against liability for bodily injury and property damage. An insured may be liable for personal injury or damage to someone's reputation as well. The HO policies can be endorsed to provide limited personal injury protection to the insured. This endorsement adds coverage for the following unintentional offenses (remember that if the loss is intentionally caused, the policy will not provide coverage):

- False arrest, detention or imprisonment, or malicious prosecution

- Libel, slander, defamation of character, or violation of the right of privacy

- Invasion of right of private occupation, wrongful eviction, or wrongful entry

Open Perils

An endorsement may be purchased to change coverage to open perils from broad perils.

HOMEOWNERS (HO) INSURANCE: CONTRACTUAL CONDITIONS

Section I Conditions

Loss Settlement

This condition specifies how certain property items will be valued (e.g., ACV basis or replacement cost basis). The coinsurance provision of the policy is also contained in this clause.

Duties After a Loss

The insured is required to fulfill a number of obligations before the loss can be settled. Immediately after the loss, the insured must perform the following duties:

- Give notice to the insurance company or agent

- Protect the property against any further damage

- Prepare an inventory of loss to the building and personal property

- File written proof of the loss with the insurance company, within the company's time constraints; the insurer must provide a state-approved form for the proof of loss

Appraisal

This clause gives the insured the right to dispute the amount of settlement offered by the insurer. If the insured and the insurer disagree on the amount of loss, either party may demand an appraisal by a competent appraiser. Both the insurer and the insured hire their own appraisers. If the two appraisers cannot reach an agreement on the loss amount, an umpire mediates their differences. Each party pays for its own appraiser, and both the insured and the insurer equally share the expense of hiring the umpire.

Settlement at Insurer's Option

The insurer retains the right to repair or replace any part of damaged property with similar property, as long as it notifies the insured of this right within 30 days after receiving the insured's sworn proof of loss.

Mortgage Clause

Because many homes are mortgaged property, the insurer includes this clause to protect the mortgagee's (lender's) interest in the insured home. This clause gives the mortgagee important rights. The mortgagee has the right to receive payment for valid claims on the property to the extent of its interest, even if the insurer has denied the insured's claim (which would happen in the case of misrepresentation by the insured or an intentionally caused loss). The mortgagee also has the right to receive notice of policy cancellation or nonrenewal at least 10 days before the coverage on the property ends.

This clause also imposes certain obligations on the mortgagee. The mortgagee is responsible for notifying the insurer if there is a change in ownership or occupancy of the mortgaged property. The mortgagee must also pay any homeowner premiums that are due but that the insured has neglected to pay and file proof of loss statements if the insured fails to do so.

Abandonment of Property

The insurance company does not have to accept property abandoned by an insured. A homeowner who suffers fire damage, for example, might try to force the insurer to take control of the house and be responsible for cleanup, repairs, and even mortgage payments.

Recovered Property

When the insured or the insurer recovers property for which the insurer has already paid a claim (as might be the case following a theft), each must notify the other party of the recovery. The insured then has the option to return the recovered property to the insurer or keep the recovered property. If the insured keeps the property, the loss payment must be adjusted accordingly.

Loss to a Pair or a Set

When there has been a loss to a pair or a set (such as a partial loss of a set of china or the theft of only one earring), the insurer may either repair or replace the damaged or lost items or pay the difference between the value of the property as a set (before the loss) and the value after the loss.

Other Insurance

When a loss covered under one policy is also covered by another policy, the insured cannot collect from each policy in full. To do so would place the insured in a better position after the loss than before the loss, thus violating the principle of indemnity. The Other Insurance clause states that when more than one policy covers a loss, each insurer will pay only a proportion of the loss based on the limits of coverage provided in the policy.

Suppose Erin has two homeowners policies. One provides a limit of $50,000; the other provides a limit of $100,000. Erin's house is worth only $100,000; after a fire destroys it, she will collect a proportion of the loss from each insurer. Because the first insurer provides one-third of all coverage provided ($50,000 ÷ $150,000), it will pay one-third of the loss, or $33,333. The second insurer will pay two-thirds of the loss, or $66,667.

Suit Against the Insurance Company

This clause gives the insured the right to sue the insurer only after complying with all the policy provisions and requires that the suit be brought within one year of the date of the loss.

Loss Payment

After an agreement is reached regarding the amount of loss to provide, the insurer has 60 days to pay the insured.

No Benefit to Bailee

Bailee
A party that holds the property of another

A **bailee** is a party that holds the property of another. If the insured has left property with a bailee, such as a moving company or dry cleaner, the insurer will not pay for loss or damaged property on behalf of the bailee. This clause does not say that claims by the insured will not be paid; it merely states that the coverage will not protect or benefit the bailee. If, for example, a fire on the premises of a dry cleaner destroyed the insured's personal property, the insurer would pay the insured's claim; however, the insurer would then subrogate against, or seek restitution from, the dry cleaner.

Volcanic Eruption Period

All volcanic eruptions occurring within a 72-hour period are considered one occurrence. Because volcanoes tend to erupt gradually over a period of days, this clause protects the insured from having to pay a new deductible for each eruption.

Section II Conditions

Limit of Liability

The insurer will not pay more than the policy's coverage limit for each occurrence, regardless of the number of suits or claims filed against the insured for any one event.

Duties After a Loss

The insured is expected to give notice of any accident or occurrence to the insurer or its agent. The insured must also promptly forward to the insurer all summons and demand letters. The insured must cooperate and assist the insurer in the investigation and settlement of any claims. Finally, the insured must not voluntarily make payments for anything other than first aid at the time a bodily injury is sustained.

Duties of an Injured Person—Coverage F

An injured person or a representative must give the insurer written proof of a claim as soon as practical after a loss and give the insurer permission to obtain medical records of the injured person. The injured person must also submit to a physical exam by the insurer's doctor if instructed to do so by the insurer.

Payment of Claim—Coverage F

This clause states that paying any claim under Coverage F is in no way an admission of liability by the insurer or the insured.

Bankruptcy of Insurance Company

The bankruptcy or insolvency of any insurer does not terminate coverage or relieve the insurer of its obligations under the policy.

Sections I and II Conditions

Concealment or Fraud

Dishonesty either before or after a loss may void the policy. Examples of dishonesty that will void the policy include intentionally concealing or misrepresenting material facts and intentionally causing losses.

Cancellation and Nonrenewal

State laws regarding the insurer's right of cancellation and nonrenewal vary, so it is important to examine the specific policy to understand the law. Generally, however, the insured may cancel the policy at any time by notifying the insurer, whereas the insurer may cancel the policy only for nonpayment of premium, material misrepresentation of fact, or a substantial change in the risk. In most cases, the insurer must provide a 10-day notice of cancellation only when it is canceling a newly issued policy or when it is canceling for nonpayment of premium. Other cancellations and nonrenewals usually require a 30-day notice. Cancellations generally result in a pro rata refund of unused premium.

Assignment

For a homeowners policy, the insured may not assign rights under the policy without the insurer's written consent.

Subrogation

The insurer may require the insured to assign rights of recovery for payments made by the insurer. This allows the insurer to take over the insured's subrogation rights against negligent third parties. The insurer does not, however, subrogate for claims made under Coverage F of the policy.

EXHIBIT 10.5 Summary of Common Homeowners Insurance Policies

	HO-2 (Broad Form)	HO-3 (Special Form)	HO-8 (For Older Homes)	HO-4 (Renter's Contents Broad Form)	HO-6 (For Condominium Owners)
Perils covered	Perils 1–18	All perils except those specifically excluded from buildings; perils 1–18 on personal property	Perils 1–12	Perils 1–18	Perils 1–18
Section 1: Property coverages/limits					
House and any other attachments	Amount based on replacement cost, minimum $15,000	Amount based on replacement cost, minimum $20,000	Amount based on actual cash value of the home, minimum $15,000	Improvements and betterments coverage up to 10% of the amount of personal property coverage	$1,000 on owner's additions and alterations to the unit
Detached buildings	10% of insurance on the home	10% of insurance on the home	10% of insurance on the home	Not covered	Included in Dwelling Coverage
Trees, shrubs, plants, etc.	5% of insurance on the home, $500 maximum per item	5% of insurance on the home, $500 maximum per item	5% of insurance on the home, $250 maximum per item	10% of personal property insurance, $500 maximum per item	10% of personal property insurance, $500 maximum per item
Personal property (contents)	50% of insurance on the home	50% of insurance on the home. Covers same as Broad Form	50% of insurance on the home	Chosen by the tenant to reflect the value of the items, minimum $6,000	Chosen by home owner to reflect the value of the items, minimum $6,000
Loss of use and/or add'l living expense	20% of insurance on the home	20% of insurance on the home	10% of insurance on the home	30% of personal property insurance	40% of personal property insurance
Credit card, forgery, counterfeit money	$500	$500	$500	$500	$500
Section 2: Liability coverage/limits					
Comprehensive personal liability	$100,000	$100,000	$100,000	$100,000	$100,000
Damage to property of others	$250–$500	$250–$500	$250–$500	$250–$500	$250–$500
Medical payments	$1,000	$1,000	$1,000	$1,000	$1,000

*Special limits apply on a per-occurrence basis (e.g., per fire or theft): money, coins, bank notes, precious metals (e.g., gold and silver), $200; securities, deeds, stocks, bonds, tickets, and stamps, $1,500; watercraft and trailers, including furnishings, equipment, and outboard motors trailers other than for watercraft, $1,500; trailers other than for watercraft, $1,500; jewelry, watches, and furs, $1,500; silverware and goldware, $2,500; guns, $2,500.

AUTOMOBILE INSURANCE

Automobile insurance is required in every state, although to varying degrees. Mandatory automobile insurance laws expressly require the purchase of liability insurance before owning or operating a motor vehicle. Some states require the purchase of no-fault coverage that pays for bodily injuries on a first-party basis. Each state implicitly requires automobile insurance by compelling motorists to be financially responsible for a minimum amount of bodily injury and property damage.

In addition to these statutory requirements, many people purchase automobile insurance because their automobiles are financed and the lender requires the borrower to carry coverage for direct physical damage to the auto. Many people purchase increased amounts of automobile insurance because they recognize that the financial burden associated with an automobile accident could be devastating. One at-fault accident could result in thousands of dollars of damage, and the insured would be responsible for those damages. In addition, with most new cars costing into the tens of thousands of dollars, the damage to the insured's vehicle could be very costly to repair.

The owner and operator of an automobile should be concerned about the following losses:

- Damage to or loss of the insured's vehicle

- Injury to the insured or family members

- Legal liability for injuries and damages done to other persons or property

PERSONAL AUTO POLICY (PAP) COVERAGES

Personal automobile policy (PAP)
Provides physical damage insurance, medical payments, liability coverage, and uninsured motorist protection

No-fault insurance
Used in states that require drivers to carry insurance for their own protection; places limits on the insured's ability to sue other drivers for damages

The **personal automobile policy (PAP)** is an insurance package policy that can protect against the three major losses listed above. A PAP may be used to provide physical damage insurance, medical payments, liability coverage, and uninsured motorist protection. These policies may also provide no-fault benefits in states that require this type of protection. **No-fault insurance** is used in states that require drivers to carry insurance for their own protection and also places limits on the insured's ability to sue other drivers for damages. Under this type of insurance, each insurance company pays only for its insured driver's damages, up to policy limits, regardless of who was at fault for the accident. Most insurers use the Insurance Services Office (ISO) Program; however, various state laws may result in different policy provisions and coverage. Therefore, policyowners should carefully read each policy.

Policy Overview

Eligible Vehicles

The PAP may be used to insure four-wheel passenger automobiles, pickup trucks, and vans that are owned by individuals or leased by individuals for at least six months. The vehicle must be owned by an individual or by a married couple who are residents of the same household. Pickups and vans must have a gross vehicle weight of less than 10,000 pounds and not be used primarily for business purposes (other than farming, ranching, or the installation, maintenance, or repair of equipment or furnishings). The policy may be used to insure one vehicle or all the vehicles owned in a household (usually subject to a maximum of four vehicles on one policy). To save premium dollars, all the vehicles in one household should be insured on the same policy rather than insuring each vehicle with a separate policy.

The PAP may be used to insure vehicles that are used for pleasure and recreation (e.g., motorcycles, recreational vehicles, or golf carts). An endorsement is used to provide coverage when it is used for these types of vehicles.

Policy Design

Throughout the personal automobile policy, "you" and "your" refer to the named insured and spouse. "We," "us," and "our" refer to the insurance company. Policy language is usually simplified as much as possible while maintaining the required legal form.

The PAP is arranged into six parts listed as follows:

- Part A: Liability Coverage

- Part B: Medical Payments Coverage

- Part C: Uninsured Motorists Coverage

- Part D: Coverage for Damage to Your Auto

- Part E: Duties After an Accident or Loss

- Part F: General Provisions

Parts A through D are four separate types of coverage that may be included in a PAP. Each part has its own insuring agreement, insured persons covered, and exclusions. Each type of coverage is effective by declaration in the policy and payment of premium for the coverage.

Part A: Liability Coverage

In the PAP's Liability Coverage section, the insurance company agrees to pay damages caused by an accident, up to the policy limit, for which the insured is legally responsible. The insurer retains the right to defend or settle any claim or suit, and settlement and defense costs are paid in addition to the policy limits.

Covered Persons and Autos

Definition of "Insured." An insured is defined in Part A as the following:

- You or any family member, for the ownership, maintenance, or use of any auto or trailer (this includes the use of borrowed autos and even rental cars)

- Any person using your covered auto with permission or belief of right to use

- Any organization that is responsible for the conduct of someone driving your covered auto (e.g., an employer or charitable organization)

- Any organization that is responsible for your conduct or the conduct of a family member while you are driving a nonowned automobile (e.g., an employer that might be responsible for your actions when you are using a coworker's car for business purposes)

Primarily, coverage is provided for the insured or spouse residing in the same household (referred to as "you" in the policy) or any family member for the use of any auto or trailer. "Family member" refers to a person related to the named insured by blood, marriage, adoption, or a foster child residing with the insured. The insured and family members are covered when operating any auto, which includes both the covered auto and rented or borrowed vehicles.

Individuals other than the named insured and family members are covered while using the covered auto. The person using the vehicle, however, must have a reasonable belief that he has the right to do so.

Coverage under a PAP extends to an individual or organization held vicariously liable for damage or injury. Vicarious liability exists when one party is liable for the negligent actions of another, even though the first party was not directly responsible for the injury. The following parties would be covered under a PAP:

E X A M P L E   Those who are vicariously liable for the operation of the insured automobile. Assume Erin is the insured under a PAP policy, which covers her 2014 Mustang. She uses this automobile to run an errand for her employer, Bobby. While running the errand, Erin collides with Don's vehicle and injures him. Don not only brings suit against Erin for damages, he also sues Bobby as Erin's employer. Under the PAP, Bobby is covered in addition to Erin because, as Erin's employer, Bobby is vicariously liable for the injuries she causes.

E X A M P L E   Those held vicariously liable for the operation of a nonowned vehicle by the named insured or family member. Assume Jenni is insured under a PAP policy. Jenni borrows Reggie's 2012 Hummer to call on a client of Eddie, her employer. Jenni rear ends Peggy's vehicle. Peggy is injured and files suit against both Jenni and Eddie as Jenni's employer. Jenni's PAP policy will provide coverage for Eddie's vicarious liability. However, it will not cover Reggie should he be sued as owner of the Hummer. Reggie would, however, be covered under his own PAP.

"Covered Auto" Defined. "Your covered auto" is defined as any of the following:

- Any vehicle shown in the policy declarations

- Any new vehicle in addition to those shown in the declarations, but only for a specified period (policies vary, most often for a 14- or 30-day period) or until the new vehicle is reported to the insurer; the insurer will charge a premium from the date the vehicle was acquired, and the new vehicle will have the broadest coverage provided on any declared vehicle for the specified period

- Any new vehicle that replaces a vehicle shown in the declarations; the new vehicle will have the same coverage as the vehicle it replaced, and the insured must report the new vehicle within 30 days only if coverage for damage to your auto is desired

- Any trailer the insured owns

- Any auto or trailer that the insured does not own but that is used as a temporary substitute while a covered vehicle is unavailable because of loss, breakdown, repair, service, or destruction

Exclusions

PAP liability coverage is quite broad in nature. However, it excludes coverage for the following persons and situations.

- *Vehicle used by auto dealer*—No coverage is provided for any auto dealer or other person in the automobile business who is driving your car. A person in the automobile business should have coverage under his own policy.

- *Bodily injury to an employee*—No coverage is provided for injuries to an employee; such injuries are most often covered by workers' compensation. One exception is that the insured will be covered for liability for injuries to a domestic employee.

- *Insured's owned property*—Liability insurance is designed to pay for damages caused by the insured to third parties. By definition, liability insurance does not pay for damages to the insured's owned property. Therefore, in an auto accident, damages to the insured's car and its contents are not paid by the liability coverage Part A. Damage to the car would be covered by the PAP's Part D–Damage to Your Auto, and damage to contents of the vehicle may be covered by homeowners coverage.

- *Property in the insured's care, custody, and control*—Along the same lines as the previous exclusion, this one prohibits the insured from recovering under his own liability insurance for items that are not true liability losses. When property, such as a rental car is damaged in an automobile accident, the PAP treats it as if it were the insured's owned auto. The insured may not use the liability coverage to pay for damages to the rental car.

- *Intentional acts*—Any person who intentionally causes an auto accident is not covered for liability by the policy.

- *Public livery*—Coverage is not provided for any person or vehicle while transporting people or property for a fee. A share-the-expense car pool is not considered a for-fee activity and is, thus, covered.

- *Commercial vehicles used in business*—This exclusion eliminates coverage for business use of automobiles but then gives back coverage for business use of any private passenger auto, owned pickup or van, or temporary or substitute pickup or van. The intent is to limit business coverage on autos to either private passenger autos or owned pickups and vans.

- *Using auto without permission*—No coverage is provided for any person who uses an automobile without having a reasonable belief that he has permission to do so.

- *Regular use of nonowned or nondeclared auto*—Coverage is not provided when the insured has the regular use of an automobile that is not shown on the declarations page, either because the employer provides a company car or because the insured owns a nondeclared vehicle. If the insured has a company vehicle, the employer should provide coverage or the insured should declare the vehicle as a nonowned vehicle and purchase coverage for the vehicle. Recall that the named insured is covered while using any auto. If this exclusion were not in the policy, the insured could own 10 vehicles and buy coverage on only one but have coverage on all 10. This exclusion makes it clear that the insurer will only cover owned vehicles that have been declared and for which a premium has been paid.

- *Autos with fewer than four wheels*—Motorcycles and recreational vehicles having fewer than four wheels must be specifically insured under a different policy. No coverage is provided for these types of vehicles, whether they are owned or borrowed.

Coverage Limits

Split limits

Lists the per-person bodily injury limit, the per occurrence bodily injury limit for all bodily injuries, and the property damage limit

The limits of coverage for Part A are shown on the declarations page, and in most cases, represent three separate liability coverage limits—two for bodily injury, and one for property damage. These **split limits** are often written as 50/100/25 and are expressed in thousands. All limits are on a per-occurrence basis. The first number represents a per person bodily injury limit. A per person limit of $50,000 indicates that any one injured person may not receive more than $50,000 for bodily injuries. The second number represents a per-occurrence bodily injury limit for all bodily injuries. If this limit were $100,000, the insurer would pay up to $100,000 for all the bodily injuries sustained in one accident, regardless of the number of persons injured. The third number represents the property damage limit and specifies the most the insurer will pay for all property damage caused by one accident.

E X A M P L E   Alan carried 50/100/25 coverage and had a major accident deemed to be his fault. The following claims were filed by injured parties in the other vehicle: Stephen sustained $75,000 in bodily injuries, Scott sustained $22,000 in bodily injuries, and Cheryl sustained $53,000 in bodily injuries. Alan, the driver, incurred $17,000 in automobile repair and rental car costs. Barbara, a nearby homeowner on whose lawn the two cars ultimately landed, sustained $9,000 in lawn and shrubbery damage. All claims are settled in the order mentioned previously.

First, address the bodily injury claims. Stephen is allowed to collect only $50,000 because that is the per-person limit. Note that Stephen will likely sue for the $25,000 deficiency. Scott may collect the full $22,000. Cheryl will collect only $28,000 because, at that point, the $100,000 per occurrence limit has been reached. Claims are paid in the order that they are settled, not on a pro rata basis, so it is important that claimants begin the settlement process as soon as possible.

Next, consider the property damage claims. The policy provides a total of $25,000 of coverage, yet there is a total of $26,000 in property damage claims. Thus, the insurer will pay all of Alan's damages ($17,000), and Barbara will receive only $8,000.

Increased Limits in Another State

As mentioned, all states require some minimum level of financial responsibility or automobile liability insurance. When the insured in one state drives to another state and has an accident, the insured must generally have sufficient limits to meet the requirements of the state in which the accident occurred. In most cases, PAPs providing at least minimum coverage in the home state will provide additional coverage up to the minimum requirements of a visited state.

E X A M P L E   A driver from Arizona who has only the minimum required limits of 25/50/25 who drives to Texas, where the minimum limits are 30/60/30, would be expected to have those coverage limits if an accident occurred in Texas. The PAP automatically provides the increased limits required by state law. Therefore, the Arizona driver's policy would pay up to 30/60/30 if an accident occurred while in Texas.

Please note that this policy provision never reduces the limits of liability the insured has purchased. If a Texas driver with the 30/60/30 coverage limits drives to Arizona, his policy will pay up to those limits for any accident. The policy will not reduce the amount of coverage provided to 25/50/25.

Loss Sharing With Other Coverage

When more than one auto policy covers a loss, the general rule is that insurance on the automobile is primary, while insurance on the driver is excess.

E X A M P L E   If Caitlin borrows Joshua's car and has an accident while driving his car, Joshua's PAP coverage will pay first. When Joshua's limits of coverage have been exhausted, Caitlin's policy will pay on an excess basis. If more than one policy is primary (e.g., if an automobile is declared and covered by two separate policies), the policies share losses on a proportionate basis (similar to homeowners insurance).

Part B: Medical Payments

Medical payments
A no-fault, first-party insurance coverage designed to pay for bodily injuries sustained in an auto accident

Medical payments are optional no-fault, first-party coverage designed to pay for bodily injuries sustained in an auto accident. Expenses must be incurred within three years of the auto accident. Limits of insurance are provided on a per-person, per-occurrence basis. A typical limit of coverage is $5,000 per person per occurrence. This means that if four covered persons are injured in an auto accident, each may collect up to $5,000 for reasonable and necessary medical and funeral expenses.

Who Is Covered?

An insured in this coverage is defined as any of the following:

- You or any family member while occupying a motor vehicle

- You or any family member as a pedestrian when struck by a motor vehicle

- Any other person while occupying your covered auto

Exclusions

Medical payment coverage excludes the following.

- *Public livery*—No coverage is provided while the vehicle is used to carry persons or property for a fee.

- *Auto used as a residence*—Although trailers are included as covered autos, this exclusion prevents someone from having medical payments coverage on a house trailer. This type of nonstandard risk must be specifically insured.

- *Injury while working*—Any benefits that are payable under workers' compensation or other disability benefit laws preclude coverage under this policy.

- *Using auto without permission*—No coverage is provided for any person who uses an automobile without having a reasonable belief that he has permission to do so.

- *Regular use of nonowned or nondeclared auto*—When the insured has the regular use of an automobile that is not shown on the declarations page, either because the employer provides a company car or because the insured owns a nondeclared vehicle, coverage is not provided.

- *Autos with fewer than four wheels*—Motorcycles and recreational vehicles with fewer than four wheels must be specifically insured under a different policy. No coverage is provided for these types of vehicles, regardless of whether they are owned or borrowed.

- *Auto used in insured's business*—The same exclusion that was discussed in Part A applies here. Coverage is provided for private passenger autos used in business and for owned pickups and vans used in business.

- *War and nuclear hazard injuries*—Consistent with other policies, this coverage does not apply to any injuries sustained because of acts of war or because of nuclear contamination or radioactive hazards.

- *Racing*—No coverage is provided when the vehicle is located inside a racing facility or when the vehicle is practicing for, preparing for, or competing in any type of racing or speed contest.

Part C: Uninsured Motorists

Purpose

Because so many drivers do not obey financial responsibility and compulsory automobile insurance laws, the PAP offers insureds the option of purchasing uninsured motorist coverage that covers damages caused by an uninsured or underinsured motorist.

What Is Covered?

Part C will pay for bodily injuries and, in many states, property damages that are sustained by an insured because of an uninsured or underinsured motorist. In other words, this coverage will pay what the uninsured, at-fault motorist's liability insurance should have paid had it been in place.

Who Is Covered?

An insured for this coverage is defined as follows:

- You or any family member

- Any other person occupying your covered auto

- Any person who might also be entitled to damages (e.g., a spouse or child) for the injuries sustained by a person described above

Definitions of an Uninsured/Underinsured Motorist

Uninsured/ underinsured motorist

Motorist without liability coverage or whose insurer cannot or will not pay the claim, hit-and-run driver, or motorist with insufficient liability coverage according to state law

An **uninsured or underinsured motorist** is one who has no liability coverage, has limits of liability coverage less than those required by the insured's home state law, is an unidentified hit-and-run driver, or has liability insurance but whose insurer cannot or will not pay the claim. For the insured to collect from this coverage, the uninsured or underinsured driver must be at fault in the accident.

Exclusions and Limitations

Many of the exclusions contained in Part B are repeated in this coverage:

- Public livery

- Regular use of nonowned auto

- Injury while working

- Regular use of nondeclared auto

- Using auto without permission

- Auto used in insured's business

In addition, the insurer will not pay for any bodily injuries when the insured or legal representatives settle a bodily injury claim without the insurer's consent. Furthermore, this coverage will not pay for punitive damages.

Part D: Coverage for Damage to Your Auto

Coverage D provides direct damage coverage on your covered auto, plus any nonowned auto. A nonowned auto is any private passenger auto, pickup, van, or trailer not owned by or furnished for the use of a family member that is in your (or a family member's) custody. This would include a borrowed car, a rental car, and a temporary substitute auto.

Two Coverages Available

Part D provides the insured with two different direct damage coverages: collision and comprehensive. The insured may purchase one, both, or neither of these coverages. Automobile lenders will generally require the insured to carry both coverages.

Collision is defined under Part D as "the upset of your covered auto or its impact with another vehicle or object." Therefore, this provision covers damages incurred in an accident involving other vehicles or those sustained when an automobile runs off the road and into a tree.

Comprehensive, or **other-than-collision,** coverage protects the insured against the following perils: missiles or falling objects, fire, theft, explosion, earthquake, windstorm, hail, water or flood, malicious mischief or vandalism, riot or civil commotion, contact with a bird or animal, and breakage of glass. These perils are typically viewed as accidental and out of the insured's control. Thus, the premium for this coverage is lower than that for collision coverage.

Collision
Auto insurance coverage that protects the insured against upset and collision damages

Comprehensive (other-than-collision)
Auto insurance coverage that protects the insured's auto against perils out of the insured's control, such as missiles or falling objects, fire, theft, earthquake, hail, flood, and vandalism

---

Dispute Resolution (Appraisal Clause)

If the insured and the insurer do not agree on the amount of a loss, the insured may demand an appraisal process similar to that provided for in a homeowners policy.

Loss Payment

The insurer retains the sole option either to pay for repairs or to declare the vehicle a total loss and pay the actual cash value of the vehicle, less any deductible. The collision coverage deductible is typically twice as high as the other-than-collision (comprehensive) deductible. In most cases, insureds should carry a minimum $250 other-than-collision deductible and $500 collision deductible. Higher (and lower) deductibles are also available; however, higher deductibles generally reduce premiums.

Loss Sharing With Other Policies

When more than one auto policy covers a loss, the general rule is that insurance on the automobile is primary, while insurance on the driver is excess.

E X A M P L E   If Ben borrows Justin's car and has an accident, Justin's collision damage coverage will be primary. Ben's policy will pay on an excess basis but will not pay more than the loss and will still require Ben to pay his own deductible.

If more than one policy is primary (e.g., if an automobile is declared and covered by two separate policies), the policies share losses on a proportionate basis (similar to homeowners insurance).

Exclusions

Many of the exclusions described in other coverages also apply here:

- Public livery

- Custom furnishings on a pickup or van

- Using auto without permission

- Radar detectors

- Racing

- Most electronic equipment, except permanently installed sound reproducing equipment [this generally includes global positioning systems (GPSs), scanning and television monitor receivers, and personal computers]

- War

- Nuclear damages

As with most direct property coverages, the PAP excludes coverage for normal wear and tear and ordinary maintenance losses, such as road damage to tires. Loss caused by destruction or confiscation by governmental authorities, as could occur if the insured vehicle were involved in a crime, is also excluded. Losses to nonowned autos are not covered when the auto is used or maintained by anyone in the automobile business.

Finally, no coverage is provided for a rental vehicle if the insured has purchased a loss damage waiver from the rental car company. Loss damage waivers relieve the insured of liability for damage to the rented vehicle, so the insurer will not provide coverage.

Part E: Duties After an Accident or Loss

After a loss, the insured should notify the insurer, file proof of loss, and cooperate with the insurer in the investigation and settlement of any claim. In addition, the insured must file a police report to have theft coverage for a stolen vehicle or to have uninsured motorist coverage for a hit-and-run incident.

Part F: General Provisions

There are several general provisions and conditions of the auto policy that are similar to those contained in the HO policies. One, however, deserves special attention: the PAP coverage territory.

The PAP provides coverage only in the United States, Puerto Rico and other U.S. territories and possessions, and Canada. When the insured travels to Mexico (where auto accidents are automatically criminal offenses) or to any other country outside the coverage territory, the PAP is not effective. If the insured intends to drive in such a locale, the appropriate local coverages must be arranged.

▌ LEGAL LIABILITY

Intentional interference
Intentional act committed against another that causes injury

Slander
Verbal statement that causes harm to another

Libel
Written statement that causes harm to another

A client may be exposed to three types of risk: torts (civil wrongs), breach of contract, and crimes (public wrongs). Liability insurance will cover certain classes of torts but not breaches of contract or criminal offenses. If a court decides that an individual is liable for a civil wrong that causes injury to another, the individual will be required to make restitution, usually in the form of monetary compensation.

The three general types of torts related to liability are intentional interference, strict and absolute liability, and negligence. **Intentional interference** is an intentional act committed against another that causes injury. Many of the actions that fall under intentional interference are also criminal acts and would not be covered under liability insurance. Slander and libel, however, are usually covered under personal liability insurance policies. **Slander** is defamation or harm caused by a verbal statement, and **libel** is defamation caused by a written statement.

Strict and absolute liability

Liability resulting from law; strict liability allows for defense, and absolute liability does not

Under **strict and absolute liability**, one party is held legally liable regardless of who is responsible for the injury. Workers' compensation laws are examples of absolute liability. Under workers' compensation laws, the employer is liable for any injury to an employee engaged in business activities. Even if the employee causes injury to himself, the employer will be liable unless the employer can prove the injury was due to intoxication or failure to follow orders. If workers' compensation laws provided for absolute liability, the employer would be liable even if the employee were intoxicated. Under strict liability, responsible parties have few options for defense, but under absolute liability, the responsible party has no options for defense.

Negligence

Tort caused by acting without reasonable care

Direct negligence

Involves acts or omissions directly attributable to an individual

Vicarious acts

Negligent acts performed by someone else but for which the individual is held at least partially responsible

If an individual causes harm to another by failing to act with appropriate care, he will be subject to liability due to **negligence**. In determining whether an individual has used appropriate care, the courts use the prudent person standard. The standard is met if a reasonable person confronted with the same circumstances would have performed the same acts. **Direct negligence** refers to acts or omissions directly attributable to an individual. An individual may also be liable for **vicarious acts**, which are negligent acts performed by someone else but for which the individual is held at least partially responsible. For example, in many states bartenders are vicariously liable for the negligent acts of intoxicated patrons. Liability insurance generally covers both types of negligence.

PERSONAL UMBRELLA LIABILITY POLICY

Purpose

Personal umbrella liability policy

Coverage designed to provide a catastrophic layer of liability coverage on top of the individual's homeowners and automobile insurance policies

The **personal umbrella liability policy** is designed to provide a catastrophic layer of liability coverage on top of the individual's homeowners and automobile insurance policies. The standard amount of coverage is $1 million, although higher limits may be purchased. The need for this policy is largely dictated by the insured's personal wealth. The more the insured stands to lose, the more likely it is that an umbrella policy is a suitable purchase.

Characteristics

Most insurers will require the insured to maintain certain underlying limits of coverage through an HO and a PAP; if the insured also has other liability exposures to insure, such as watercraft liability, minimum limits of coverage will be required for those policies as well.

In most cases, the policy provides the insured with a large amount of coverage at an affordable price. The coverage provided is generally quite broad and may even provide coverages in addition to those provided by the underlying policies. For example, the policy might provide personal injury coverage (e.g., for defamation of character or false arrest) even though the underlying HO policy does not cover this type of incident. Where these additional coverages are provided, the insured is usually required to pay a **self-insured retention** (SIR) for each loss. The SIR is similar to a deductible.

Self-insured retention

A payment similar to a deductible that an insured is usually required to pay for each loss under a personal liability umbrella policy (PLUP)

Where both an umbrella and underlying policy cover a loss, the umbrella does not pay any claims until the underlying coverage has been exhausted. From there, the umbrella picks up with no SIR imposed on the insured.

EXAMPLE   If Carol has an HO policy with a Coverage E (Personal Liability) limit of $200,000 and a $1 million umbrella policy and is held liable for bodily injuries totaling $700,000, her HO policy will pay the first $200,000 of the claims, and then the umbrella policy will pay the remaining $500,000.

Exclusions

Umbrella liability forms are nonstandard, so it is difficult to generalize about what exclusions will be included in each policy. Certain exclusions almost universally found in these policies include damage to the insured's property, injuries sustained by the insured or a family member, injuries that were intentionally inflicted or caused by the insured, injuries to another party that should be paid under a workers' compensation law, and business and professional liability incidents.

BUSINESS AND PROFESSIONAL USE OF PROPERTY AND LIABILITY INSURANCE

Some of the policies used by businesses to cover property and liability include the commercial package policy, inland marine policies, the businessowners policy, business liability insurance, workers' compensation, business automobile, business liability umbrella policies, professional insurance, and errors and omissions.

The ISO has developed a commercial insurance program including a package policy (two or more coverages).

The Commercial Package Policy (CPP)

Commercial package policy (CPP)
Property and liability coverage combined into a single policy used by businesses

Used by businesses, a **commercial package policy (CPP)** is property and liability coverage combined into a single policy. The advantages of such a policy include lower premiums and fewer gaps in overall coverage. Workers' compensation coverage and surety coverages are not part of a CPP. A CPP policy format includes (1) a declarations page, (2) a policy conditions page, and (3) two or more coverage parts or forms (property, general liability, crime, boiler and machinery, inland marine, commercial auto, or farm). Each part or form of a CPP will specify covered property, additional coverages, extension of coverages, other provisions, deductibles, coinsurance, valuation provisions, optional coverages, and a cause-of-loss form. Coverages for causes of loss are basic, broad, special, or earthquake form. These forms are similar to the parallel homeowners forms. Business interruption insurance may be added. Also, a builders-risk-coverage form can be added to a CPP for buildings under construction.

Inland Marine Policies

Inland marine policies cover domestic goods in transit, property held by bailees, mobile equipment and property, property of certain dealers, and means of transportation and communication. They may also be used to increase coverage limits on nonmovables, such as furs and jewelry.

The Businessowners Policy (BOP)

The businessowners policy is specifically designed for the needs of small to medium-size businesses, covers buildings and business personal property, and is available in two forms: basic and special. The basic form covers listed perils, as distinguished from the special form, which covers all perils not excluded. The policy has a standard $500 deductible and covers business liability for bodily injury and property damage.

Business Liability Insurance

General liability is the legal liability arising out of business activities not related to autos, motorized vehicles, aircraft, and employee (workers' compensation) injuries. Liability issues, not including the exceptions mentioned, are covered by commercial general liability (CGL) policies. CGL can be written either as a stand-alone policy or as a part of a commercial package policy (CPP). The usual coverage, Coverage A, is for bodily injury, property damage, and legal defense, but has significant exclusions. Coverage B is for personal and advertising injury liability, and Coverage C covers medical payments.

Workers' Compensation

Most businesses are required to carry insurance providing workers' compensation insurance, employer liability insurance, and other state insurance. Part One, workers' compensation insurance, covers benefits provided by the insurer (state). Part Two covers lawsuits by employees injured in the course of employment but not covered by state workers' compensation law. Part Three provides coverage for other listed states (e.g., business trips).

Business Auto

The business auto coverage form is used to insure the private passenger and commercial auto exposures of all businesses other than garages, truckers, and motor carriers. Because of the specialized nature of these businesses and their unique coverage needs, separate forms were designed to cover these risks. This form includes coverage for liability and physical damage. Uninsured Motorists, Medical Payments, and Underinsured Motorists coverage can be added by endorsement.

Business Umbrella Liability

Businesses may use commercial umbrella liability policies for excess coverage on liability beyond the coverage provided by a firm's basic liability policy.

Malpractice Insurance

Malpractice insurance
Used where the deficient conduct of the insured provider of professional services may result in damages

Most people understand **malpractice insurance** as liability insurance for health service providers, especially physicians and surgeons. Malpractice insurance, however, is available for all professional service providers and generally covers intentional as well as unintentional negligent acts committed by the insured. A typical policy will have a maximum per-incident limit and an aggregate limit. The insurer is usually allowed to settle claims out of court without obtaining consent from the insured.

Errors and Omissions

Errors and omissions insurance

Provides protection against loss from negligent acts, errors, and omissions by the insured

Errors and omissions insurance provides protection against loss from negligent acts, errors, and omissions by the insured. Many professionals (e.g., real estate agents, insurance agents, accountants, stockbrokers, attorneys, and engineers) need errors and omissions coverage for negligent acts, omissions, or failure to act within their own profession that may cause legal liability. Policies usually have large deductibles ($1,000 or more).

A special type of errors and omissions coverage, called Directors and Officers Errors and Omissions insurance, is available for business executives. Directors and officers insurance provides protection against liability due to mismanagement. Policies usually have high deductibles and require that the insured be financially responsible for a percentage of any claims.

Product Liability

Businesses that manufacture products are subject to liability with respect to those products. Acts that can expose a company to product liability include the following:

- Manufacturing a harmful product

- Selling a defective product

- Packaging the product inappropriately

- Providing insufficient directions or warnings for use

EXHIBIT 10.6   Summary of Insurance for Businesses and Professionals

	Businesses	Professionals
Property Insurance—Buildings	CPP	CPP
Property Insurance—Personalty	CPP	CPP
General Liability Insurance	As needed	As needed
Inland Marine Coverage	If transporting goods	If transporting goods
Business Interruption Coverage	As needed	As needed
Builders' Risk Insurance	If construction	If construction
Workers' Compensation	If employees	If employees
Commercial Auto Insurance	If autos	If autos
Commercial Umbrella Policy	Excess liability coverage	Excess liability coverage
Malpractice	N/A	Yes
Errors and Omissions	N/A	Yes
Product Liability	If manufacturer	N/A

WHERE ON THE WEB

Federal Emergency Management Agency **www.fema.gov**

Independent Insurance Agents and Brokers of America **www.independentagent.com**

Insurance Information Institute **www.iii.org**

Insurances Guide **www.insurancesguide.org**

Instant Insurance Quotes **www.insure.com/index.html**

DISCUSSION QUESTIONS

1. Describe the need for homeowners, auto, and liability umbrella insurance coverages.

2. List and define the basic coverages provided by a homeowners policy.

3. List the various homeowners forms.

4. Explain the contractual options and provisions in homeowners insurance.

5. List and define the basic coverages provided by the personal automobile policy (PAP).

6. Explain the various contractual options and provisions in a personal automobile policy (PAP).

7. Explain the distinguishing characteristics of a personal umbrella liability policy.

8. What type of coverage does Section 1 of a homeowners policy provide?

9. What type of coverage does Section 2 of a homeowners policy provide?

10. Are intentional acts usually covered by insurance?

EXERCISES

1. What are the three types of property and liability loss exposures facing families and businesses?

2. What is a named-perils policy?

3. Why is it that property insurance policies only pay for the policyowner's insurable interest in a loss?

4. How do property insurance policies determine how losses will be valued?

5. List some examples of the types of property with limited coverage under a typical homeowners policy.

6. List four major exclusions found in homeowners insurance policies pertaining to real property.

7. List the 18 perils that constitute broad coverage.

8. If Joe is injured in an automobile accident, will his own auto policy pay for his medical injuries?

9. Differentiate between the HO-2 and the HO-3 form of homeowners insurance.

10. Jan rents an apartment and has $40,000 of contents coverage. If she is unable to occupy her apartment due to a negligent fire, for how many months could she rent a $700 per month apartment if her damaged apartment rented for $600 per month?

11. Patrice lives in Nebraska, where she carries the state-mandated minimum liability insurance on her car (25/50/25) through her personal automobile policy (PAP). She is driving through Texas and has a wreck. Texas requires minimum liability insurance of 30/60/30. She injures Sherri in an amount equal to $30,000 and Sherri's vehicle in an amount of $35,000. How much will Sherri collect from Patrice's PAP?

12. Pat and Matt are fraternity brothers who frequently drive each other's cars. Their automobiles are insured as follows:

Insured	Insurance Company	Amount
Pat	XYZ Co.	25/50/10
Matt	All Auto	100/300/25

Pat is negligent while driving Matt's car and has an accident, and the bodily injury loss to the other party involved in the accident is $30,000. Which insurer will pay, and how much will be paid?

PROBLEMS

1. Jimmy and Mary Sue, ages 28 and 27, respectively, are married and have a net worth of $100,000. They both work, Jimmy has a 2014 Chevy truck, and Mary Sue has a 2016 Toyota Corolla. They also own a 1966 Indian motorcycle. They rent an apartment and have the following automobile and renter's insurance policies:

Renters Insurance:

■ HO-4 renter's policy without endorsements

■ Content Coverage: $25,000; Liability: $100,000

Automobile Insurance:

■ Both Car and Truck

Type	PAP
Bodily Injury	$25,000/$50,000
Property Damage	$10,000
Medical Payments	$5,000 per person
Physical Damage	Actual Cash Value
Uninsured Motorist	$25,000/$50,000
Comprehensive Deductible	$500
Collision Deductible	$500
Premium (annual)	$2,500

■ What risk exposures are not covered by the HO-4 policy?

■ Comment on the efficiency and effectiveness of the PAP.

■ Is the motorcycle covered under the PAP?

■ Do they have adequate liability coverage? If not, what would you suggest?

2. The Nicholsons recently purchased a new stereo system (FMV $10,000). They asked and received permission to alter their apartment to build speakers into every room. The agreement with the landlord requires them to leave the speakers if they move because they are permanently installed and affixed to the property. The replacement value of the installed speakers is $4,500, and the noninstalled components are valued at $5,500. The cost of the entire system was $10,000. The Nicholsons have an HO-4 policy with $25,000 of content coverage and $100,000 of liability coverage.

   ■ If the Nicholsons were burglarized and had their movable stereo system components stolen, would the burglary be covered under the HO-4 policy, and, if so, for what amount?

   ■ If there was a fire in the Nicholsons' apartment building and their in-wall speaker system was destroyed, would they be covered under the HO-4 policy, and, if so, to what extent?

   ■ If a fire forces the Nicholsons to move out of their apartment for a month and rent elsewhere at a higher cost, would the HO-4 policy provide any coverage?

3. Ken and Mary Claire Powell, both age 40, own their own home, with the land valued at $80,000 and the dwelling with a replacement value of $150,000. They have a total net worth of $550,000. They have the following property/liability insurance coverages:

Homeowners Insurance

The Powells currently have an HO-3 policy with a replacement value endorsement on contents. The policy provides open-perils coverage. The deductible is $250, and the premium is $533.60 per year.

The dwelling coverage is $100,000, contents $50,000, and liability $100,000.

Automobile Insurance

The Powells have full coverage on both cars, including:

   ■ $100,000 bodily injury for one person

   ■ $300,000 bodily injury for all persons

   ■ $50,000 property damage

   ■ $100,000 uninsured motorist

Deductibles

   ■ $500 comprehensive

   ■ $1,000 collision

This insurance includes medical payments, car rentals, and towing.

The cost of the auto insurance is $2,123.50 per year because of the number of speeding tickets Mary Claire has received.

   ■ The Powells suffer a burglary and lose personal property items purchased for $20,000 and having a replacement value of $27,000. How much will the insurance company pay?

   ■ If a fire destroys two-thirds of their house and the loss is $100,000, how much will the insurance company pay?

   ■ Do the Powells have adequate liability coverage?

- What would you recommend regarding their liability coverage?

- While Mary Claire's car was parked in a parking lot next to a school playground, a young student missed a ball being thrown and it dented the hood of Mary Claire's car. The damage was estimated to cost $1,840 to repair. How much will the insurer pay?

CASES

The Bannisters

Derek Bannister, age 26, has been employed for five years at a computer store as a salesperson and trainer. He earns $30,000 per year. His wife, Olga Bannister, age 26, is a German citizen and is employed as a floral designer for a local florist. She earns $28,000 per year. Derek and Olga have been married for two years and have one child, Prissy, age 1.

Insurance Information:

Life Insurance	
Insured	Derek
Owner	Derek
Beneficiary	Olga
Face amount	$50,000
Cash value	0
Type of policy	Term
Settlement option	Lump sum
Premium	Employer-provided

Health Insurance	
Premium	Employer-provided for Derek; Olga and Prissy are dependents under Derek's policy
Coverage	Major medical
	Dental coverage is not provided
Deductible	$250 per person (3-person maximum)
Family out-of-pocket limit	$2,500

Disability Insurance
Neither Derek nor Olga has disability insurance

Automobile Insurance	
Premium	$1,000 total annual premium for both vehicles
Bodily Injury and Property Damage	$10,000/$25,000/$5,000 for each vehicle
Comprehensive	$250 deductible
Collision	$500 deductible

Renter's Insurance	
Type	HO-4
Contents Coverage	$35,000
Premium	$600 annually
Deductible	$250
Liability	$100,000
Medical Payments	$1,000 per person

Homeowners 04 Policy Declaration Page

Policy Number: **H04-123-ZA-996**
Policy Period: **12:01 a.m. Central Time at the residence premises**
From: **January 1, 2020**   To: **December 31, 2020**

Name insured and mailing address:
Derek and Olga Bannister
123 Raleigh Way, Apartment 8
Anytown, State 00001

The residence premises covered by this policy is located at the above address unless otherwise indicated.
Same as above.

Coverage is provided where a premium or limit of liability is shown for the coverage.

Section I Coverages	Limit of Liability	Premium
A. Dwelling	**N/A**	**N/A**
B. Other Structures	**N/A**	**N/A**
C. Personal property	**$35,000**	**$475**
D. Loss of use	**N/A**	**N/A**
Section II Coverages		
A. Personal liability: each occurrence	**$100,000**	**$100**
B. Medical payments to others: each occurrence	**$1,000**	**$ 25**
Total premium for endorsements listed below		
	Policy Total	**$600**

Forms and endorsements made part of this policy:

Number	Edition	Date	Title	Premium
Not applicable.				

DEDUCTIBLE - Section I: **$250**
In case of a loss under Section I, we cover only that part of the loss over the deductible stated.
Section II: Other insured locations: **Not applicable.**

[Mortgagee/Lienholder (Name and address)]
Not applicable.

Countersignature of agent/date	Signature/title - company officer

While on a vacation in Colorado, the Bannisters experienced several unfortunate incidents.

■ A deer collided with their car, causing $800 damage.

■ Derek rented a motorcycle. While riding the motorcycle, his wallet was stolen, but Derek thought he had lost the wallet on the mountain during a fall, so he did not report the loss to the credit card company until he returned home.

■ Derek, not experienced driving in the mountains, collided with another motorcycle on the road causing damage to both motorcycles and injuring Derek. The driver of the other motorcycle, Oscar, suffered a broken arm.

■ Upon returning home, the Bannisters discovered that their apartment building had been destroyed by fire.

1. How much will the insurance company pay to have the front of the car repaired from the collision with the deer?

2. The fire that destroyed the apartment building also destroyed all of their personal property. Although the depreciated or actual cash value of all their property is $8,000, it would cost the Bannisters about $37,000 to replace all of their lost items. How much will the insurance company pay for this loss?

3. Derek's collision with the motorcycle caused $2,000 of damage to Oscar's motorcycle. Will the HO-4 liability policy cover the loss?

4. Oscar, the motorcycle owner, suffered $350 in emergency medical expenses to reset his broken arm caused by the incident. Will the HO-4 cover the loss?

5. In the motorcycle accident, Derek suffered medical expenses of $1,850. Is Derek covered by the HO-4 for this loss?

6. What deficiencies do you think are in the Bannisters' overall insurance program?

CASE SCENARIO

Use the information provided to answer the following questions regarding the Nelson family.

NELSON FAMILY CASE SCENARIO
DANA AND DAVID NELSON
As of 12/31/2020

Personal Background and Information

David Nelson (age 37) is a bank vice president. He has been employed there for 12 years and has an annual salary of $70,000. Dana Nelson (age 37) is a full-time homemaker. David and Dana have been married for eight years. They have two children, John (age 6) and Gabrielle (age 3), and are expecting their third child in two weeks. They have always lived in this community and expect to remain indefinitely in their current residence.

General Goals (Not Prioritized)

- Save for college education
- Reduce debt
- Save for retirement
- Estate planning
- Invest wisely

Insurance Information

Health Insurance

The entire family is insured under David's employer's health plan (PPO). For covered expenses, a $1,000 in-network deductible and a $2,000 out-of-network deductible apply, after which 80%/20% coinsurance applies in network and 60%/40% applies out of network. There is a stop-loss limit of $20,000 annually in network and $30,000 annually out of network. The entire monthly premium of $1,123.54 is paid by David's employer.

Life Insurance

David's employer provides group term life insurance equal to two times David's current salary. The premium is paid entirely by his employer, and Dana is the primary beneficiary. No contingent beneficiary is named.

Disability Insurance

David's employer also offers a contributory group long-term disability insurance program toward which the employer contributes 60% of the $158.54 monthly premium. David is a participant in the program, which provides a monthly disability income benefit equal to 70% of his current salary, payable to his Social Security normal retirement age, provided that he remains disabled per the policy's "own occupation" definition of disability. David must satisfy a 90-day elimination period before he is eligible to begin receiving benefits.

David's employer doesn't offer dental or vision coverages and the Nelsons have not obtained any private form of individual dental or vision insurance benefits.

Homeowners Insurance

The Nelsons have an HO-3 policy with replacement cost on contents. There is a $250 deductible. The annual premium is $950.

Automobile Insurance

The Nelsons have automobile liability and bodily injury coverage of $100,000/$300,000/$100,000. They have both comprehensive coverage and collision. The deductibles are $250 (comprehensive) and $500 (collision). The annual premium is $900.

Relevant External Environmental Information

- Mortgage rates are 5.0% for 30 years and 4.5% for 15 years, fixed.

- Gross domestic product is expected to grow at less than 3%.

- Inflation is expected to be 2.6%.

- Expected return on investment is 8% for common stocks, 9% for small company stocks, and 1.1% for U.S. Treasury bills.

- College education costs are $15,000 per year.

Investment Information

The bank offers a Section 401(k) plan in which David is an active participant. The bank matches contributions dollar for dollar up to 3% of David's salary. David currently contributes 5.43% of his salary. His employer's plan allows for employee contributions of up to 16% of salary. In the Section 401(k) plan, the Nelsons have the opportunity to invest in a money market fund, a bond fund, a growth and income fund, and a small-cap fund. The Nelsons consider themselves to have a moderate investment risk tolerance. David's assets within the plan are currently earning 8.5%, based on his investment choices within the plan.

Income Tax Information

David and Dana tell you that they are in the 12% federal income tax bracket. They pay $820 annually in state and local income taxes.

Education Information

John is 6 years old and currently attending first grade at a private school. Gabrielle is 3 years old. She will attend private school from pre-kindergarten through high school. The current balance of the college fund is $14,000. They expect to contribute $1,000 at the end of each year to this fund.

Gifts, Estates, Trusts, and Will Information

David has made Dana his primary beneficiary on his Section 401(k) plan, and the children are the contingent beneficiaries. Because most of their assets are owned jointly, David doesn't see the need for a will. Dana also does not have a will.

Dana and David Nelson
Statement of Financial Position
12/31/2019

ASSETS			LIABILITIES AND NET WORTH		
Cash/cash equivalents			**Current liabilities**		
JT	Checking account	$1,425	JT	Credit cards	$4,000
JT	Savings account	$950	JT	Mortgage on principal residence	$1,234
			David	Boat loan	$1,493
Total cash/cash equivalents		$2,375	**Total current liabilities**		$6,727
Invested assets			**Long-term liabilities**		
Dana	ABC stock	$12,500	JT	Mortgage on principal residence	$196,654
JT	Education fund	$14,000	David	Boat loan	$12,065
David	Section 401(k) plan	$32,197			
Total invested assets		$58,697	**Total long-term liabilities**		$208,719
Personal-use assets			**Total liabilities**		$215,446
JT	Principal residence	$245,000			
JT	Automobile	$18,000			
David	Boat	$25,000	**Net worth**		$207,626
Dana	Jewelry	$13,000			
JT	Furniture/household	$61,000			
Total personal-use assets		$362,000			
Total assets		$423,072	**Total liabilities and net worth**		$423,072

Dana and David Nelson
Statement of Financial Position
12/31/2020

ASSETS			LIABILITIES AND NET WORTH		
Cash/cash equivalents			**Current liabilities**		
JT	Checking account	$1,268	JT	Credit cards	$3,655
JT	Savings account	$950	JT	Mortgage on principal residence	$1,370
	Total cash/cash equivalents	$2,218	David	Boat loan	$1,048
				Total current liabilities	$6,073
Invested assets			**Long-term liabilities**		
Dana	ABC stock	$14,050	JT	Mortgage on principal residence	$195,284
JT	Education fund	$15,560	David	Boat loan	$16,017
David	Section 401(k) plan	$38,619		Total long-term liabilities	$211,301
David	XYZ stock	$10,000			
	Total invested assets	$78,229			
Personal-use assets			Total liabilities		$217,374
JT	Principal residence	$250,000			
JT	Automobile	$15,000			
David	Personal watercraft	$10,000	Net worth		$241,573
David	Boat B	$30,000			
Dana	Jewelry	$13,500			
JT	Furniture/household	$60,000			
	Total personal-use assets	$378,500			
Total assets		**$458,947**	Total liabilities and net worth		**$458,947**

Notes to financial statements:

■ Assets are stated at fair market value.

■ The ABC stock was inherited from Dana's aunt on November 15, 2019. Her aunt originally paid $20,000 for it on October 31, 2010. The fair market value at the aunt's death was $12,000.

■ Liabilities are stated at principal only.

■ JT = joint tenancy; client name = separate property.

Dana and David Nelson
Personal Statement of Cash Flows
For 2020

INFLOWS

Salary—David		$70,000
Investment income		
Interest income	$ 900	
Dividend income	$ 150	$ 1,050
Total inflow		**$71,050**
Savings		
Reinvestment (interest/dividends)	$ 1,050	
Section 401(k) plan deferrals	$ 3,803	
Education fund	$ 1,000	
Total savings		**$ 5,853**
Available for outflows		**$65,197**

OUTFLOWS

Ordinary living expenses		
Food	$ 6,000	
Clothing	$ 3,600	
Child care	$ 600	
Entertainment	$ 1,814	
Utilities	$ 3,600	
Auto maintenance	$ 2,000	
Church	$ 3,500	
Total ordinary living expenses		**$21,114**
Debt payments		
Credit card payments principal	$ 345	
Credit card payments interest	$ 615	
Mortgage payment principal	$ 1,234	
Mortgage payment interest	$20,720	
Boat loan principal	$ 1,493	
Boat loan interest	$ 1,547	
Total debt payments		**$25,954**
Insurance premiums		
Automobile insurance premiums	$ 900	
Disability insurance premiums	$ 761	
Homeowners insurance premiums	$ 950	
Total insurance premiums		**$ 2,611**
Tuition and education expenses		**$ 1,000**
Taxes		
FICA and federal income tax (W/H)	$12,855	
State (and city) income tax	$ 820	
Property tax (principal residence)	$ 1,000	
Total taxes		**$14,675**
Total outflows		**$65,354**
Net cash flow (deficit)		**($157)**

1. Evaluate the Nelsons' personal property and liability insurance coverage.

2. What business and professional insurance coverage(s) may be relevant to the Nelsons?

3. The Nelson's homeowners insurance provides dwelling coverage for $180,000 with an 80% coinsurance requirement. On March 31, 2020, a stampeding herd of cattle ran through their house, causing $100,000 of damage to the home and $40,000 of damage to furniture and other personal property. How much of the $140,000 of damage will be paid for by their insurance? Assume the replacement value for the home is $240,000.

4. A deer ran into the Nelsons' car while they were on a trip to the supermarket. The damage to the car was $3,000, and Dana, the driver, required $1,200 of medical care in the emergency room (she was not admitted to the hospital). What portion of the accident expenses will be Dana and David's responsibility to pay, if any?

Social Security and Other Social Insurance

LEARNING OBJECTIVES

After learning the material in this chapter, you will be able to do the following:

■ Identify the major categories of benefits administered by the Social Security Administration

■ Understand how the Social Security program works

■ List the eligibility requirements that must be satisfied for a person to qualify as a Social Security beneficiary

■ Calculate a worker's average indexed monthly earnings (AIME) and primary insurance amount (PIA)

■ Discuss how "bend points" affect a worker's Social Security benefit

■ Understand how early and late retirement options affect a worker's Social Security benefit

- List the ways that a worker's Social Security benefit might be reduced

- Explain how modified adjusted gross income affects the taxation of Social Security benefits

- Understand how Medicare is structured and the benefits it offers

OVERVIEW OF THE U.S. SOCIAL SECURITY SYSTEM

Social Security benefits were never intended to provide total financial support upon retirement. Social Security was created to supplement one's pension, savings, investments, and assets. Typically, individuals who retire need 70–80% of their preretirement income to maintain their same preretirement standard of living.

Although Social Security can supplement other sources of retirement income, it generally replaces only a portion of a worker's preretirement income. Workers earning more than the maximum Social Security wage base ($137,700 in 2020) receive a lower percentage of their preretirement income than lower earning workers because the maximum retirement benefit is based on the Social Security wage base.

Retirement benefit
The most familiar Social Security benefit, full retirement benefits are payable at full retirement age, with reduced benefits as early as age 62, to anyone who has obtained at least a minimum amount of Social Security credits

From a financial planning standpoint, professionals should understand Social Security and the various benefits that are available. This chapter provides a basic overview of the Social Security system and its benefits. Six major categories of benefits are administered by the Social Security Administration: (1) retirement benefits, (2) disability benefits, (3) family benefits, (4) survivors benefits, (5) Medicare, and (6) Supplemental Security Income (SSI) benefits. SSI benefits are not funded by Social Security taxes but are funded by the general Treasury.

The **retirement benefit** is the most familiar Social Security benefit. Full retirement benefits are payable at full retirement age, with reduced benefits available as early as age 62, to anyone who has obtained at least a minimum amount of Social Security credits. Based on a change in Social Security law in 1983, the age when full retirement benefits are paid began to rise in 2000 from age 65 and increases to age 67 for people born in 1962 and later. Those workers who delay retirement beyond the full retirement age will receive a special increase in their retirement benefits when they ultimately retire.

Disability benefit
Social Security benefit available to recipients who have a severe physical or mental impairment that is expected to prevent them from performing substantial work for at least one year or result in death, and who have the sufficient amount of Social Security credits

The **disability benefit** is payable at any age to workers who have sufficient credits under the Social Security system. Recipients must have a severe physical or mental impairment that is expected to prevent them from performing any substantial work for at least one year or result in death. According to Social Security guidelines, earnings of $1,260 or more per month (in 2020) are considered substantial for someone who is not blind. The disability insurance program has built-in incentives to smooth the transition back to the workforce, including continuation of benefits and health care coverage.

Family benefit
Social Security benefit available to certain family members of workers eligible for retirement or disability benefits

The **family benefit** is provided to certain family members of workers eligible for retirement or disability benefits. Such family members include spouses age 62 or older, spouses under age 62 but caring for a child under age 16, unmarried children under 18, unmarried children under age 19 and full-time students in secondary schools, and unmarried children of any age who were disabled before age 22. The **survivors benefit** applies to certain members of the worker's family if the worker earned sufficient Social Security credits. Family members entitled to survivors benefits include those listed for family benefits, and may also include the worker's parents if the worker was their primary means of support. A special one-time payment of $255 may be made to the spouse or minor children upon the death of a Social Security covered worker.

Survivors benefit
Social Security benefit available to surviving family members of a deceased, eligible worker

Medicare
A federal health insurance plan for those who have attained full retirement age or have been disabled whether retired or still working

Supplemental Security Income (SSI)
Program administered by the Social Security Administration and funded by the general Treasury that is available to those at full retirement age or disabled who have a low income and few assets

The next benefit, **Medicare**, provides hospital and medical insurance. People who are 65 and older, have received disability benefits for at least two years, or are on kidney dialysis treatment and in end-stage renal failure automatically qualify for Medicare.

Finally, **Supplemental Security Income (SSI)** (funded by general tax reve-nues, not by Social Security taxes) is another benefit of monthly payments to those disabled or at full retirement age who have a low income and few assets. Generally, those who receive SSI will also qualify for Medicaid, food stamps, and other public assistance.

THE HISTORY OF SOCIAL SECURITY BENEFITS

Ever-changing social and economic conditions have dictated the social welfare structure of the United States. During its infancy, the country's economy was predominantly agricultural. As late as 1870, over half of the nation's adult workers were farmers. Then, the country transformed. With the advent of the Industrial Revolution, the country began to specialize. One of the consequences of this industrialization and specialization was more dependence on wages and income to maintain and provide for the family.

Federal, state, and local governmental bodies throughout the country recognized the inherent risks in an industrialized and ever-specializing economy. The perception was that such risks could best be handled through an approach dominated by a philosophy of social insurance. Social insurance is the act of contributing financing over time to social programs to provide protection as a matter of right to everyone without regard to need. Social insurance has its roots in workers' compensation laws dating back to as early as 1908. Various social and other retirement programs were developed and implemented in piecemeal fashion. In addition, the federal government began programs to provide benefits to those who served in the military.

The Depression of the 1930s compelled action by the federal government. State and local governmental entities could not shoulder the immense needs of so many Americans. The federal government extended loans and grants to the states to provide relief and created special programs. By 1935, however, President Franklin D. Roosevelt proposed that Congress enact economic security legislation, resulting in the passage of the Social Security Act signed into law August 14, 1935.

The Social Security Act established two national social insurance programs: old-age benefits and unemployment benefits. The old-age benefits were intended for retired workers employed in industry and commerce, and unemployment benefits were for breadwinners faced with limited employment opportunities. Congress added benefits for dependents of retired and deceased workers in 1939.

By 1950, the Social Security program was expanded to cover a number of jobs that had previously been excluded. The range of the program was further broadened by the inclusion, in 1956, of disability insurance for severely disabled workers aged 50 or older and for adult disabled children of deceased or retired workers. The requirement of attaining age 50 was removed in 1960, and disability benefits were available to widows and widowers by 1967. An annual **cost-of-living adjustment (COLA)** based on the Consumer Price Index was implemented through legislation in 1972, as was the delayed retirement credit that increased benefits for workers retiring after the full retirement age.

COLA
Cost-of-living adjustment provided for Social Security benefits

Medicaid
Provides medical assistance for persons with low incomes and resources

The Medicare program was established through the 1965 amendments to the Social Security Act. The program provided for medical coverage for those age 65 or older, regardless of income. Legislation passed in 1965 also created **Medicaid**, which provides medical assistance for persons with low incomes and resources. Medicare and Medicaid have been subject to numerous legislative changes since 1965. In 1972, the state-administered assistance programs for the aged, blind, and disabled were replaced by the essentially federally administered SSI program.

The 1983 amendments made coverage compulsory for federal civilian employees and for employees of nonprofit organizations; in addition, state and local governments were prohibited from opting out of the system. Gradual increases in the age of eligibility for full retirement benefits from age 65 to age 67 were implemented for those retiring in 2000 or later. Benefits also became subject to income tax for those with higher incomes.

SOCIAL SECURITY TAXES AND CONTRIBUTIONS

Although the Social Security retirement benefits program is thought by many to be one of the most complicated and confusing programs created, the basic concept is quite simple. The basic theory is that employees, employers, and self-employed individuals pay Social Security taxes (FICA) during their working years. These payments are pooled in special trust funds. Contributing workers become covered workers, meaning that they will fall under the Social Security umbrella of benefits after contributing for approximately 10 years, and they will receive retirement benefits based on those contributions.

FICA stands for the **Federal Insurance Contributions Act**, the law allowing paycheck deductions for Social Security and Medicare taxes that are used to pay for Social Security benefits. A portion of these FICA taxes pays part of the Medicare coverage. Separate and apart from Social Security taxes, general tax revenues are used to finance Supplemental Security Income, commonly referred to as SSI. Administered by the Social Security Administration, the SSI program pays benefits to persons who have limited income and assets.

FICA (Federal Insurance Contributions Act)
The law allowing Social Security taxes, including Medicare, to be deducted from paychecks

OASDI
Old Age, Survivors, and Disability Insurance, commonly referred to as Social Security

Both employers and employees pay the taxes for Social Security and Medicare. An employer and employee each pay 6.2% of the employee's gross salary up to a limit of $137,700 (2020) for **Old Age, Survivors, and Disability Insurance (OASDI)**. The salary limit may rise annually on the basis of annual increases in average wages. Self-employed workers pay 12.4% (6.2% × 2) of their taxable income up to the same salary limit. The Medicare portion of the Social Security tax is 1.45% for employers and employees each and 2.9% for self-employed workers. For example, if an employee earns a salary of $150,000 in 2020, the first $137,700 of the employee's salary will be taxed at a rate of 7.65% (6.2% + 1.45%), and the remaining $12,300 will be subject to a tax of only 1.45%. The employer pays the same amount as the employee. A Medicare surtax of 0.9% applies to wages, compensation, and self-employment income in excess of certain thresholds. These thresholds include $250,000 for married couples filing joint returns and $200,000 for single individuals. Exhibit 11.1 shows the complete listing of Medicare surtax filing status thresholds.

EXHIBIT 11.1 Medicare Surtax Filing Status Thresholds

Filing Status	Threshold Amount
Married filing jointly	$250,000
Married filing separate	$125,000
Single	$200,000
Head of household (with qualifying person)	$200,000
Qualifying widow(er) with dependent child	$200,000

Source: Internal Revenue Service (www.irs.gov)

E X A M P L E   Mr. and Mrs. Jones, a married couple filing jointly, have a combined salary of $300,000. The first $250,000 will be taxed at the rate of 1.45%, and the next $50,000 will be taxed at the rate of 2.35% (1.45% + 0.9%).

The 0.9% Medicare surtax is paid only by the employee or self-employed person, and there is no employer share.

An additional Medicare surtax of 3.8% applies to the net investment income of taxpayers whose modified adjusted gross income (MAGI) exceeds certain thresholds. These thresholds are $250,000 for married couples filing jointly and $200,000 for single individuals. The 3.8% surtax applies to net investment income, which generally includes total gross income from interest, dividends, annuities, royalties, and rents, as well as net taxable gain from the disposition of property. The surtax does not apply to distributions from most retirement plans and IRAs or the excludible gain from the sale of a taxpayer's personal residence.

E X A M P L E   Sue has MAGI of $240,000 and a filing status of single. She has net investment income of $50,000. Of that $50,000, $40,000 is subject to the Medicare 3.8% surtax (the lesser of her net investment income or the amount by which her MAGI exceeds $200,000).

THE SOCIAL SECURITY TRUST FUNDS AND THEIR RELATIVE SOLVENCY

The U.S. Social Security system operates on a pay-as-you-go basis. Social Security taxes are collected and divided among several trust funds. The federal Old Age, Survivors, and Disability Insurance (OASDI) Trust Fund pays retirement and survivors benefits and receives 5.3% of the FICA tax. The federal Disability Insurance (DI) Trust Fund pays benefits to workers with disabilities and their families and receives 0.9% of the FICA tax. OASI and DI are the two trust funds used for payment of Social Security benefits.

The two Medicare trust funds are the federal Hospital Insurance (HI) Trust Fund, which pays for services covered under the hospital insurance provisions of Medicare (Part A), and the federal Supplementary Medical Insurance (SMI) Trust Fund, which pays for services covered under the medical insurance provisions of Medicare, known as Part B. The SMI Trust Fund is partially funded by the general fund of the Treasury, with the remainder funding coming from monthly premiums paid by the individuals enrolled in Part B.

EXHIBIT 11.2 Sources of Funding to Social Security Trust Funds

OASI Trust Fund	5.3% (limited to the maximum taxable earnings)
DI Trust Fund	0.9% (limited to the maximum taxable earnings)
HI Trust Fund	1.45% (all earnings taxed) (In 1993, the Omnibus Budget Reconciliation Act of 1993 abolished the ceiling on taxable earnings for Medicare.)
SMI Trust Fund	-0- (no FICA taxes used; funded by general federal tax revenues and monthly premiums paid by enrollees)

Tax revenues are deposited into the trust funds daily. Social Security benefits are paid from these funds. Money that is not needed to pay benefits is invested daily in U.S. government bonds. This method of investing leftover funds into U.S. government bonds is called the "partial reserve" method of funding, which has been used since 1983. The goal is to receive more revenue than that which is paid out so as to accumulate large reserve funds to aid in paying benefits to the increasing number of retired workers. The increase in retired workers represents a society that is living longer as a result of medical improvements, better health information, and less stressful lifestyles. The number of retired workers will continue to rise because of the baby boom generation (born from 1946 to 1964) that has begun to retire in the past few years.

The trust funds are governed by The Board of Trustees of the Social Security and Medicare Trust Funds, whose members are the Secretary of the Treasury, Secretary of Labor, Secretary of Health and Human Services, Commissioner of Social Security, and two public trustees with four-year terms. By law, the trust funds can be used only to pay Social Security benefits and for administrative costs of the program. However, legislation has been adopted to help control future HI program costs and to extend the retirement age to receive retirement benefits. These and other measures may help extend the useful life of the trust funds.

SOCIAL SECURITY BENEFITS—ELIGIBILITY AND CALCULATIONS

Covered Workers and Insured Status

To qualify for retirement benefits, a worker must be "fully insured," which means that a worker has earned a certain number of credits of coverage under the Social Security system. Since 1978, credits of coverage have been determined on the basis of annual earnings. In other words, earning a designated amount of money, regardless of when it was earned during the year, will credit the worker with one credit of coverage for that year. In 2019, the designated amount for one credit of coverage was $1,360, while in 2020, the amount is $1,410. Thus, workers who earned at least $5,440 were credited with four credits of coverage for 2019, and workers who earn at least $5,640 are credited with four credits of coverage for 2020. No worker may earn more than four credits in one year, regardless of earnings. Exhibit 11.3 lists the designated amounts for a credit of coverage, dating back to 1989.

EXHIBIT 11.3 Designated Amounts of Earnings Needed for One Credit of Social Security Coverage

Year	Amount of Earnings Needed to Receive a Credit for One Quarter	Year	Amount of Earnings Needed to Receive a Credit for One Quarter
1991	$540	2006	$970
1992	$570	2007	$1,000
1993	$590	2008	$1,050
1994	$620	2009	$1,090
1995	$630	2010	$1,120
1996	$640	2011	$1,120
1997	$670	2012	$1,130
1998	$700	2013	$1,160
1999	$740	2014	$1,200
2000	$780	2015	$1,220
2001	$830	2016	$1,260
2002	$870	2017	$1,300
2003	$890	2018	$1,320
2004	$900	2019	$1,360
2005	$920	2020	$1,410

Source: Social Security Administration (www.ssa.gov)

For most persons, 40 credits of coverage (10 years of work in employment covered by Social Security) or one credit of coverage earned per year beginning the calendar year after the insured attains age 21 with a minimum of six credits. Fully insured workers are entitled to the benefits under the Social Security system, although some benefits, such as survivors benefits, are available to "currently" (although not necessarily fully) insured individuals. Currently insured workers are those individuals who have at least six credits of coverage out of the previous 13 quarters.

Social Security Beneficiaries

As indicated, Social Security benefits are paid upon retirement, disability, or death, if the eligibility requirements are satisfied. The worker's spouse and children also may be eligible to receive benefits when the worker satisfies eligibility requirements. Generally, monthly Social Security benefits can be paid to the following persons:

- A disabled insured worker under full retirement age

- A retired insured worker at age 62

- The spouse of a retired or disabled worker entitled to benefits who

  — is at least 62 years old; or

  — is caring for a child under age 16 or disabled

- The divorced spouse of a retired or disabled worker entitled to benefits if age 62 and married to the worker for at least 10 years and not remarried by age 60

- The divorced spouse of a fully insured worker who has not yet filed a claim for benefits if both are at least age 62, were married for at least 10 years, and have been finally divorced for at least 2 continuous years

- The dependent, unmarried child of a retired or disabled worker entitled to benefits, or of a deceased insured worker if the child is

  — under age 18,

  — under age 19 and a full-time elementary or secondary school student, or

  — age 18 or over but under a disability that began before age 22

- The surviving spouse (including a surviving divorced spouse) of a deceased insured worker if the widow(er) is age 60

- The disabled surviving spouse (including a surviving divorced spouse in some cases) of a deceased insured worker if the widow(er) is age 50

- The surviving spouse (including a surviving divorced spouse) of a deceased insured worker, regardless of age, if caring for an entitled child of the deceased who is either under age 16 or disabled before age 22

- The dependent parents of a deceased insured worker at age 62

In addition to monthly survivor benefits, a lump-sum death payment of $255 is payable upon the death of an insured worker. Exhibit 11.10 provides a summary of those eligible for OASDI benefits and the percentages of the worker's primary insurance amount (PIA) that each beneficiary will receive. The PIA is the retirement benefit that the worker will receive if he retires at full retirement age.

Social Security Retirement Benefits—A Closer Look

The most commonly known Social Security benefit is the retirement benefit. Until 2000, full retirement age, the age at which full retirement benefits are available to the retiree, was 65 years old. The age at which full benefits are paid began to rise in the year 2000. Exhibit 11.4 shows the phase-in, which raises the full retirement age with full benefits to age 67.

EXHIBIT 11.4 Age Full Retirement Benefits Begin

Full Retirement Age with Full Benefits	Year Born
65 years	Before 1938
65 years, 2 months	1938
65 years, 4 months	1939
65 years, 6 months	1940
65 years, 8 months	1941
65 years, 10 months	1942
66 years	1943–1954
66 years, 2 months	1955
66 years, 4 months	1956
66 years, 6 months	1957
66 years, 8 months	1958
66 years, 10 months	1959
67 years	1960–present

People who delay retirement beyond full retirement age receive an increase in their benefit when they do retire (up to age 70). People who take early retirement, currently as early as age 62, receive an actuarially reduced monthly benefit. (Early and late retirement options are discussed later in this chapter.)

When engaging in financial planning for an individual, it may be appropriate to calculate the individual's expected Social Security retirement benefit or ask the client to request a Social Security statement and consider the benefit in that individual's retirement plan. Some financial planners, however, choose not to consider the estimated retirement benefit in order to be conservative in developing a financial plan. Others justify exclusion of Social Security retirement benefits from financial planning based on fear of drastic changes to the Social Security system through legislative action or through economically driven forces. The exclusion of estimated Social Security benefits would greatly increase the amount of retirement savings needed to prepare for retirement.

The Social Security Statement

Social Security Statement, Form SSA-7005

A written report, mailed by the Social Security Administration to all workers age 25 and over who are not yet receiving Social Security benefits; provides an estimate of the worker's eventual Social Security benefits and instructions on how to qualify for those benefits

The Social Security Administration automatically mails a **Social Security Statement, Form SSA-7005,** to all workers age 25 and over who are not yet receiving Social Security benefits. The Social Security Statement should prove to be a valuable tool in the process of personal financial planning for the worker and her family. The statement provides an estimate of the worker's eventual Social Security benefits and instructions on how to qualify for those benefits.

The Social Security Statement (1) includes the worker's lifetime earnings history, as reported to the Social Security Administration; (2) estimates the amount of Social Security taxes (FICA) and Medicare taxes (FICA-Med) that the worker and employer (if applicable) have paid; (3) and forecasts the ultimate benefits to be paid to the worker and family through retirement, disability, and/or survivorship. It is important to review the lifetime earnings history because mistakes in the earnings history can lower a worker's monthly benefits.

The mail-out campaign is designed to keep the worker informed as to his earnings history and to ensure the accuracy and completeness of the Social Security Administration's records. If any earnings are incorrect or incomplete, the worker can notify the Social Security Administration of the problem well in advance of the time of the worker's retirement age. The statement also serves as a quick and reliable reference to the worker for use in financial planning and forecasting, whether done by the individual worker or by a financial planner. The statement will be mailed to the individual worker roughly three months prior to her birthday and will continue to be mailed at or near that time every year until the worker begins to receive Social Security benefits.

Workers can request a Social Security Statement at any time from the Social Security Administration. A statement can be requested by the worker from the Social Security Administration by filling out and mailing a Request for a Social Security Statement, SSA Form 7004 or by requesting it online at **www.ssa.gov**. Applicants can also obtain the request form by calling Social Security at 1-800-772-1213 and asking for Form SSA-7004. The Social Security Administration will also answer questions and set up appointments with representatives at local Social Security offices through the toll-free number.

The Retirement Benefit Calculation

Average indexed monthly earnings (AIME)

Dollar amount used to calculate Social Security benefits. Actual earnings are adjusted (or indexed for inflation) to calculate the AIME.

Determining a worker's retirement benefit requires specific, detailed information pertaining to age, earnings history, and the worker's retirement date. Social Security benefits are based on earnings averaged over most of a worker's lifetime. Actual earnings are first adjusted or indexed to current dollars to account for changes in average wages since the year the earnings were received. Then, the Social Security Administration calculates the **average indexed monthly earnings (AIME)** (pronounced either "Amy" or "A-I-M-E") during the 35 years in which the applicant had the most earnings and applies a formula to these earnings to arrive at a basic benefit, which is referred to as the **primary insurance amount (PIA)**. The Social Security retirement benefit is based on the worker's PIA. The PIA determines the amount the applicant will receive at his full retirement age. The PIA is indexed to the Consumer Price Index (CPI) annually.

Primary Insurance Amount (PIA)

Amount on which a worker's retirement benefit is based. The PIA determines the amount the applicant will receive at full retirement age. The PIA is indexed to the Consumer Price Index (CPI) annually.

Calculating the Worker's Average Indexed Monthly Earnings (AIME)

To determine a worker's AIME, the worker's annual earnings from the calendar year after the worker attains age 21 to age 62 must be converted into current dollars by multiplying the worker's total annual earnings for each year by an indexing factor. The indexing factor is the result of dividing the national average wage for the year in which the worker attains age 60 by the national average wage for the actual year being indexed. For instance, to calculate the indexing factor for 1982 for a worker born in 1954, the indexing factor for 1982 is determined by dividing the national average wage for 2014 (when the worker attained age 60), which was $46,481.52, by the national average wage for 1982 (the year being indexed), which was $14,531.34, yielding a factor of 3.19871. Exhibit 11.5 provides national average wages from 1966 to 2018.

EXHIBIT 11.5 National Average Wage Indexing Series, 1966–2018

Year	Amount	Year	Amount	Year	Amount
1966	$4,938.36	1984	$16,135.07	2002	$33,252.09
1967	$5,213.44	1985	$16,822.51	2003	$34,064.95
1968	$5,571.16	1986	$17,321.82	2004	$35,648.55
1969	$5,893.76	1987	$18,426.51	2005	$36,952.94
1970	$6,186.24	1988	$19,334.04	2006	$38,651.41
1971	$6,497.08	1989	$20,099.55	2007	$40,405.48
1972	$7,133.80	1990	$21,027.98	2008	$41,334.97
1973	$7,580.16	1991	$21,811.60	2009	$40,711.61
1974	$8,030.76	1992	$22,935.42	2010	$41,673.83
1975	$ 8,630.92	1993	$23,132.67	2011	$42,979.61
1976	$ 9,226.48	1994	$23,753.53	2012	$44,321.67
1977	$ 9,779.44	1995	$24,705.66	2013	$44,888.16
1978	$10,556.03	1996	$25,913.90	2014	$46,481.52
1979	$11,479.46	1997	$27,426.00	2015	$48,098.63
1980	$12,513.46	1998	$28,861.44	2016	$48,642.15
1981	$13,773.10	1999	$30,469.84	2017	$50,321.89
1982	$14,531.34	2000	$32,154.82	2018	$52,145.80
1983	$15,239.24	2001	$32,921.92		

Source: Social Security Administration (www.ssa.gov)

Next, each year's annual earnings must be multiplied by the corresponding indexing factor to arrive at the indexed earnings for the years from age 22 to 60. Note that the indexing factor will always equal 1 for the years in which the worker is 60 or older. After all annual earnings are indexed or converted to current dollar amounts, the highest 35 years of indexed earnings are added together for a total. The sum of the highest 35 years is then divided by 420 (which represents 35 years multiplied by 12 months per year). This yields the average amount of monthly earnings for all indexed years; hence, the name average indexed monthly earnings, or AIME. Once the worker's AIME is determined, the next step in determining the worker's retirement benefit is to calculate the primary insurance amount, or PIA.

Calculating the Worker's Primary Insurance Amount (PIA)

Generally, the PIA is the actual Social Security retirement benefit for the retiree who retires at full retirement age. For those who retire early or late and for family or surviving beneficiaries, the PIA is not the actual amount of the benefit, but the PIA is used to determine their actual benefit.

The PIA is a figure derived from the worker's AIME. The PIA is calculated by applying a benefit formula to AIME. This benefit formula changes from year to year and depends on the worker's first year of eligibility, that is, when the worker turns 62, becomes disabled, or dies.

Bend points

The three separate percentages of portions of the AIME that are summed to arrive at the PIA

The PIA is the sum of three separate percentages of portions of the AIME known as the **bend points**. For 2020, these portions are the first $960 of AIME, the amount of AIME between $960 and $5,785, and the AIME over $5,785. For individuals who first become eligible for retirement benefits or disability insurance benefits in 2020 or who die in 2020 before becoming eligible for benefits, their PIA will be the sum of:

> 90% of the first $960 of their AIME *plus*
> 32% of their AIME over $960 up to $5,785 *plus*
> 15% of their AIME that exceeds $5,785.

The sum of these three calculations is rounded down to the next lower multiple of $.10 (if it is not already a multiple of $.10). For calculations in subsequent years, it is useful to know how to determine a given year's bend points. Exhibit 11.6 shows the established bend points from 1985 through 2020.

EXHIBIT 11.6 Bend Point Table

Dollar Amounts (bend points) in PIA Formula		
Year	First	Second
1985	$280	$1,691
1986	$297	$1,790
1987	$310	$1,866
1988	$319	$1,922
1989	$339	$2,044
1990	$356	$2,145
1991	$370	$2,230
1992	$387	$2,333
1993	$401	$2,420
1994	$422	$2,545
1995	$426	$2,567
1996	$437	$2,635
1997	$455	$2,741
1998	$477	$2,875
1999	$505	$3,043
2000	$531	$3,202
2001	$561	$3,381
2002	$592	$3,567
2003	$606	$3,653
2004	$612	$3,689
2005	$627	$3,779
2006	$656	$3,955
2007	$680	$4,100
2008	$711	$4,288
2009	$744	$4,483
2010	$761	$4,586
2011	$749	$4,517
2012	$767	$4,624
2013	$791	$4,768
2014	$816	$4,917
2015	$826	$4,980
2016	$856	$5,157
2017	$885	$5,336
2018	$895	$5,397
2019	$926	$5,583
2020	$960	$5,785

Source: Social Security Administration (www.ssa.gov)

Figures for the PIA rise each year based on a cost-of-living adjustment (COLA) that is applied to reflect changes in the cost of living. Recent COLAs, which are based on inflation, are shown in Exhibit 11.7.

EXHIBIT 11.7 Cost of Living Adjustment (COLA) Per Year

Year	COLA	Year	COLA
1996	2.9%	2008	5.8%
1997	2.1%	2009	0.0%
1998	1.3%	2010	0.0%
1999	2.5%	2011	3.6%
2000	3.5%	2012	1.7%
2001	2.6%	2013	1.5%
2002	1.4%	2014	1.7%
2003	2.1%	2015	0.0%
2004	2.7%	2016	0.3%
2005	4.1%	2017	2.0%
2006	3.3%	2018	2.8%
2007	2.3%	2019	1.6%

Annual COLA increases are determined by October of each year and go into effect for monthly benefit checks received in January of the following year.

Early and Late Retirement Options

Workers entitled to retirement benefits can currently take early retirement benefits as early as age 62. The worker will receive a reduced benefit because he will receive more monthly benefit payments than if the worker had waited and retired at full retirement age. The reduction to one's monthly benefit for early retirement is permanent. Conversely, a delayed or postponed retirement will permanently increase the monthly retirement benefit for a worker.

For each month of early retirement, a worker will receive a reduction in her monthly retirement benefit of 0.5555%, or 1/180, for each month of early retirement taken up to the first 36 months. For subsequent months of early retirement, the permanent reduction percentage is 0.4167%, or 1/240, per month.

E X A M P L E   Vada, a fully insured worker begins receiving retirement benefits 11 months before her full retirement age. Her monthly retirement benefit will be reduced by 11/180ths (approximately 6.11%). If Vada's monthly retirement benefit at full retirement age (FRA) were $1,000, she would receive $938.80 per month for the remainder of her life, subject to COLA adjustments.

Although the FRA will increase to age 67, workers will still have the option of taking early retirement at age 62. However, the reduction percentage that is applied to the monthly retirement benefit will increase until 2027. Before 2000, those who retired at age 62 received 80% of their retirement benefit, but the increase in full retirement age has increased the number of months from 62 until FRA. For instance, in 2020, covered workers who retire at age 62 were born in 1958. That means their FRA is 66 years and 8 months. Thus, retiring at 62 is 4 years and 8 months early or 56 months early. The first 36 months are penalized 5/9 of a percent per month (0.5555% per month), which is a total of 20%. The remaining 20 months are penalized 5/12 of a percent per month (0.4167% per month) for an additional reduction of 8.33%. Thus, the total reduction would be 28.33% less than their full retirement benefit. By 2022, a covered worker retiring at age 62 (FRA would be 67) will receive only 70% of his monthly retirement benefit. Exhibit 11.8, which was compiled by the Social Security Administration, shows the phasein of the Social Security full retirement age and accompanying reductions for early retirement at age 62.

EXHIBIT 11.8 Social Security Full Retirement and Reductions* by Age

Year of Birth	Full Retirement Age	Age 62 Reduction Months	Monthly Percentage Reduction	Total Percentage Reduction
1937 or earlier	65	36	0.555	20.00
1938	65 and 2 months	38	0.548	20.83
1939	65 and 4 months	40	0.541	21.67
1940	65 and 6 months	42	0.535	22.50
1941	65 and 8 months	44	0.530	23.33
1942	65 and 10 months	46	0.525	24.17
1943-1954	66	48	0.520	25.00
1955	66 and 2 months	50	0.516	25.84
1956	66 and 4 months	52	0.512	26.66
1957	66 and 6 months	54	0.509	27.50
1958	66 and 8 months	56	0.505	28.33
1959	66 and 10 months	58	0.502	29.17
1960 and later	67	60	0.500	30.00

*Percentage monthly and total reductions are approximate because of rounding. The actual reductions are 0.555%, or five-ninths of 1%, per month for the first 36 months and 0.416%, or five-twelfths of 1%, for subsequent months.
Source: Social Security Administration (www.ssa.gov)

No matter what a worker's full retirement age is, she may start receiving benefits as early as age 62. She also can retire at any time between age 62 and full retirement age; however, if she starts at one of these early ages, her benefits are reduced a fraction of a percent for each month before her full retirement age.

E X A M P L E   Assume Betty, a worker born in 1958, decided to retire on her 62nd birthday. Assume that her full retirement benefit would have been $1,429.20 at age 66 and eight months, her full retirement age. If she retires at age 62, what will her monthly retirement benefit be?

The answer is $1,025.00 (decreased to the next lower multiple of 10 cents). As shown in Exhibit 11.8, Betty is retiring 56 months early, and her total percentage reduction is 28.28% ($1,429.20 × 71.72% = $1,025.02).

E X A M P L E   What if Betty retires at age 64 and 10 months? What will be her permanent monthly retirement benefit (subject to COLA increases)?

In this case, Betty is retiring 22 months early. Therefore, her total percentage reduction is 12% (22 months × 0.5555% per month = 12%, rounded off). Her permanent monthly retirement benefit (subject to COLA increases) will be $1,258 (rounded).

For those covered individuals who postpone retirement, that is, take late retirement, the monthly retirement benefit and the benefit paid to the surviving spouse will increase, as shown in Exhibit 11.9.

EXHIBIT 11.9 Percentage Increases For Delayed Retirement

Increase for Year Born	Annual Percentage Each Year of Late Retirement (Up to Age 70)	After Age
1939	7.0%	65 and 4 months
1940	7.0%	65 and 6 months
1941	7.5%	65 and 8 months
1942	7.5%	65 and 10 months
1943 and later	8.0%	66

Source: Social Security Administration (www.ssa.gov)

Those taking delayed retirement receive a permanent increase to their monthly retirement benefit.

Although the calculations explained above can provide estimates of what benefits a retiring worker may receive, a financial planner should have the client obtain his entire earnings history up to the moment of retirement from the Social Security Administration to get the most accurate benefit estimate.

Reduction of Social Security Benefits

Besides early retirement, there are two other ways beneficiaries' benefits can be reduced. The first method is through reduction of benefits on the basis of earnings, referred to as the **retirement earnings limitations test**. The other method is through taxation of Social Security benefits. Both of these measures reduce beneficiaries' net benefits.

A person can continue to work even though he is receiving Social Security retirement benefits. The earnings received by the beneficiary cannot exceed certain limitations without triggering a reduction in Social Security benefits. Beneficiaries can earn up to the limitation and receive all of their benefits, but if those earnings exceed the designated limit for the calendar year, then some or all benefits will be withheld. The law provides an annual earnings limitation of $18,240 for those under the full retirement age for 2020. The Social Security Administration deducts $1 in benefits for each $2 earned by those beneficiaries above annual earnings limitation. In the year that the retiree reaches full retirement age, $1 in benefits will be deducted for each $3 earned above the given year's limit, but only for earnings before the month the retiree reaches full retirement age. For 2020, the limit for earnings in the year the retiree reaches full retirement age is $48,600. The earnings limitation increases every year as median earnings nationwide increase.

If a beneficiary's earnings exceed the limitation, that beneficiary's benefits will be reduced, depending on her age. The beneficiary must file an annual report of her earnings to the Social Security Administration by April 15 of the year following the year worked and must provide the exact earnings for that year and an estimate for the current year. The filing of a federal tax return with the IRS does not satisfy the filing requirement with the Social Security Administration. Also, wages count toward the earnings limitation when they are earned, not when paid, whereas income for the self-employed normally counts when paid, not earned. If other family members receive benefits based on the beneficiary's Social Security record, then the total family benefits may be affected by the beneficiary's earnings that exceed the earnings limitation. In such a case, the Social Security Administration will withhold not only the worker's benefits but also those benefits payable to family members.

Retirement earnings limitations test

One of the ways in which Social Security benefits are reduced on the basis of earnings

E X A M P L E   George is 64 years old and, despite being retired from his occupation as an attorney, earned $20,000 in 2020 while working as a golf instructor at a local golf course. George's monthly retirement benefit from Social Security is normally $2,500, which totals $30,000 for the entire year. Because George exceeded the retirement earnings limitation, how much money will be deducted from George's retirement benefit for 2020?

George's total earnings in 2020	$20,000
Earnings limitation	($18,240)
Remainder excess	$ 1,760
One-half deduction	÷ 2
	$ 880

The Social Security Administration will thus deduct $880 from George's benefits for the year. George will receive $29,120 in retirement benefits ($30,000 annual retirement benefit less $880 reduction). George's total income for 2020 would be $49,120, instead of $50,000.

Another commonly asked question is this: What income counts toward the retirement earnings limitation? Generally, only wages and net self-employment income count; income from savings, investments, and insurance does not. The following is a nonexclusive list of income sources that DO NOT count toward the earnings limitation:

- Pension or retirement pay
- Section 401(k) plan and IRA withdrawals
- Dividends and interest from investments
- Capital gains
- Rental income
- Workers' compensation benefits
- Unemployment benefits
- Court-awarded judgments, less components of award that include lost wages
- Contest winnings

TAXATION OF SOCIAL SECURITY BENEFITS

Modified adjusted gross income
On the 1040 federal tax return, modified adjusted gross income is the sum of adjusted gross income, nontaxable interest, and foreign-earned income

Separate and apart from the earnings limitations, some beneficiaries may be required to pay taxes on their Social Security benefits. For persons with substantial income in addition to Social Security benefits, up to 85% of their annual benefits may be subject to federal income tax. The Social Security Administration is concerned with beneficiaries' **modified adjusted gross income**. On the 1040 Federal tax return, modified adjusted gross income is the sum of adjusted gross income, nontaxable interest, and foreign-earned income.

Generally, up to 50% of Social Security benefits are subject to federal income taxes for beneficiaries who file a federal tax return as an individual and have a modified adjusted gross income between $25,000 and $34,000. For those with a modified adjusted gross income over $34,000, up to 85% of their Social Security benefits will be subject to federal income taxation. For those beneficiaries that file a joint federal tax return and have a modified adjusted gross income with their spouse between $32,000 and $44,000, up to 50% of their Social Security benefits will be subject to federal income taxes. Finally, if beneficiaries filing a joint tax return have a modified adjusted gross income that exceeds

$44,000, up to 85% of their Social Security benefits will be subject to federal income taxation.

To summarize, for persons with substantial income in addition to their Social Security benefits, up to 85% of their annual benefits may be subject to federal income tax. The amount of benefits subject to federal income tax for taxpayers with modified adjusted gross income under $34,000 ($44,000 if married filing jointly) is the smaller of the following:

- One-half of their benefits

- One-half of the amount by which their adjusted gross income, plus tax-exempt interest, plus foreign-earned income, plus one-half of their Social Security, exceeds

    — $25,000 if single,

    — $25,000 if married and not filing a joint return and did not live with a spouse at any time during the year,

    — $32,000 if married and filing a joint return, and

    — $0 if married and not filing a joint return and did live with a spouse at any time during the year.

OTHER SOCIAL SECURITY BENEFITS

Disability Benefits and Disability Insured

Benefits are payable at any age to people who have enough Social Security credits and who have a severe physical or mental impairment that is expected to prevent them from doing substantial work for one year or more, or who have a condition that is expected to result in death. Essentially, workers are insured for disability if they are fully insured and, except for persons who are blind or disabled before age 31, have a total of at least 20 credits of coverage during the 40-quarter period ending with the quarter in which the worker became disabled. Workers who are disabled before age 31 must have total credits of coverage equal to one-half the calendar quarters that have elapsed since the worker reached age 21, ending in the quarter in which the worker became disabled. However, a minimum of six credits is required.

Earnings of $1,260 or more per month for 2020 are considered substantial for some-one who is not blind. The disability program includes incentives to smooth the transition back into the workforce, including continuation of benefits and health care coverage. Disability under the Social Security system is defined as an inability to engage in sub-stantial gainful activity by reason of a physical or mental impairment expected to last at least 12 months or to result in death. The impairment must be of such severity that the applicant is not only unable to do his previous work but cannot, considering age, educa-tion, and work experience, engage in any other kind of substantial gainful work that exists in the national economy.

Family Benefits

If an individual is eligible for retirement or disability benefits, other members of the individual's family might receive benefits as well. Family members who may receive benefits include the following:

- A spouse caring for a child under age 16, or caring for a child who was disabled before age 22

- A child, if the child is unmarried and under age 18, under age 19 but still in secondary school, or age 18 or older but disabled before age 22

For those workers who are entitled to retirement or disability benefits, an ex-spouse could also be eligible for benefits on the worker's record.

The child's benefit stops the month before the child reaches 18, unless the child is unmarried and is either disabled or is a full-time elementary or secondary school student. Approximately five months before the child's 18th birthday, the person receiving the child's benefits will get a form explaining how benefits can continue. A child whose benefits stop at 18 can have them start again if the child becomes disabled before reaching 22 or becomes a full-time elementary or secondary school student before reaching 19. If the child continues to receive benefits after age 18 due to a disability, the child also may qualify for SSI disability benefits. When a student's 19th birthday occurs during a school term, benefits can be continued up to two months to allow completion of the school term.

Survivors Benefits

If a worker earned enough Social Security credits during his or her lifetime, certain members of the worker's family may be eligible for benefits when the worker dies. The family members of a deceased worker who may be entitled to survivors benefits include:

- a widow or widower age 60, age 50 if disabled, or any age if caring for a child under age 16 or a disabled child,

- a child of the deceased worker, if the child is unmarried and under age 18, under age 19 but still in school, or age 18 or older but disabled, and

- parents of the deceased worker, if the deceased worker was their primary means of support, and dependent parent(s) is(are) age 62 or older.

A special one-time payment of $255 may be made to a deceased worker's spouse or minor children upon death. If a spouse was living with the beneficiary at the time of death, the spouse will receive a one-time payment of $255. The payment may be made to a spouse who was not living with the beneficiary at the time of death or an ex-spouse if the spouse or ex-spouse was receiving Social Security benefits based on the deceased's earnings record. If there is no surviving spouse, a child (or children) eligible for benefits on the deceased's work record in the month of death may claim the payment.

EXHIBIT 11.10 Summary of Social Security OASDI Benefits

	Assuming Full Retirement Age of the Worker			
	Retirement	Survivorship		Disability
	Fully Insured (2)	Fully Insured (2)	Currently Insured (3)	(4)
Participant	100%	Deceased	Deceased	100%
Child under 18 (6)	50%	75%	75%	50%
Spouse with child under 16 (7)	50%	75%	75%	50%
Spouse, full retirement age (1)	50%	100%	0%	50%
Spouse, age 62 (1)	32.5%–35%	(8)	0%	35%
Spouse, age 60 (1)	N/A	71.5%	0%	N/A
Dependent parent, age 62	0%	75%/82.5% (5)	0%	0%

(1) Includes divorced spouse if married at least 10 years (unless they have remarried). Survivors benefits are also available to divorced spouse if remarried after age 60.

(2) Fully insured is 40 credits of coverage or 1 credit for each year after age 21 but before age 62.

(3) Currently insured is at least 6 credits of coverage in the last 13 quarters.

(4) Disability insured is based on age as follows:

- Before age 24—must have 6 credits of coverage in the last 12 quarters

- Age 24 through 30—must be covered for half of the available credits after age 21

- Age 31 or older—must be fully insured and have 20 credits of coverage in the last 40 quarters

(5) Parent benefit is 82.5% for one parent and 75% for each parent if two parents.

(6) Child under age 19 and a full-time student in secondary school or of any age and disabled before age 22 also qualifies.

(7) Spouse with child disabled before age 22 also qualifies.

(8) Benefit is prorated for months between age 60 and full retirement age.

THE MAXIMUM FAMILY BENEFIT

When a person dies, her survivors receive a percentage of the worker's Social Security benefits ranging from 75% to 100% each. There is a limit on the amount of monthly Social Security benefits that may be paid to a family called the **maximum family benefit**, which is determined through a formula based on the worker's PIA. Although the limit varies, it is equal to roughly 150–180% of the deceased worker's PIA. If the sum of the family members' benefits exceeds the limit, the family members' benefits are proportionately reduced. For old-age and survivor family benefits, the formula computes the sum of four separate percentages of portions of the worker's PIA.

The following are the bend points for the maximum family benefit formula for 2020, with percentage calculations:

Maximum family benefit
The limit on the amount of monthly Social Security benefits that may be paid to a family

150% of the first $1,226 of the worker's PIA, plus

272% of the worker's PIA over $1,226 through $1,770, plus

134% of the worker's PIA over $1,770 through $2,309, plus

175% of the worker's PIA over $2,309.

MEDICARE BENEFITS

Medicare is a federal health insurance plan for people who are 65 and over, whether retired or still working. People who are disabled or have permanent kidney failure can get Medicare at any age. The Health Care Financing Administration, part of the U.S. Department of Health and Human Services, administers Medicare. Medicare is the nation's largest health insurance program, covering over 61.2 million individuals. There are four parts to Medicare: Hospital Insurance (Part A), Medical Insurance (Part B), Medicare Advantage (Part C), and Prescription Drug Coverage (Part D).

Generally, individuals who are age 65 and over qualify for Medicare. Also, individuals who have received Social Security disability benefits for at least two years automatically qualify for Medicare. All other individuals must file an application for Medicare.

Medicare Part A: Hospital Insurance is paid for by a portion of the Social Security tax. Part A helps pay for necessary medical care and services furnished by Medicare-certified hospitals, inpatient hospital care, skilled nursing care, home health care, hospice care, and other services. The number of days that Medicare covers care in hospitals and skilled nursing facilities is measured by the **benefit period**. A benefit period begins on the first day a patient receives services as a patient in a hospital or skilled nursing facility and ends after the patient has been released for 60 consecutive days. There is no limit to the number of benefit periods a beneficiary may have in a single year.

Benefit period
The number of days that Medicare covers care in hospitals and skilled nursing facilities

The benefit period is identified because deductibles, coinsurance, and premiums relate to the benefit period instead of the calendar year. For instance, for coverage under Medicare Part A in 2020, a deductible of $1,408 applies per benefit period. For the 61st through the 90th day of each benefit period, the insured individual must pay $352 per day in the form of coinsurance. Any days over 90 in a benefit period are considered lifetime reserve days. There are 60 lifetime reserve days available with a coinsurance amount of $704 per day. Lifetime reserve days do not renew with each new benefit period. It is important, therefore, to determine the number of days used in each benefit period.

EXHIBIT 11.11 Medicare Deductible, Coinsurance, and Premium Amounts for 2020

Hospital Insurance (Part A)

- **Deductible**—$1,408 per benefit period

- **Coinsurance**—$352 per day for days 61–90, per benefit period; $704 per day for days 91–150 for each lifetime reserve day (total of 60 lifetime reserve days—nonrenewable)

- **Skilled nursing facility coinsurance**—$176 per day for days 21–100, per benefit period

- **Hospital insurance premium**—$458 per month (paid only by individuals who are not otherwise eligible for premium-free hospital insurance and have fewer than 30 credits of Medicare covered employment)

- **Reduced hospital insurance premium**—$252 for individuals with 30 to 39 quarters of coverage

Medical Insurance (Part B)

- **Deductible**—$198 per year

- **Monthly premium**—$144.60*

*Premium is higher for high-income enrollees
Source: Social Security Administration (www.ssa.gov)

Medicare Part A helps pay for up to 90 days of inpatient hospital care during each benefit period. Covered services for inpatient hospital care include semiprivate room and meals, operating and recovery room costs, intensive care, drugs, laboratory tests, x-rays, general nursing services, and any other necessary medical services and supplies. Convenience items such as television and telephones provided by hospitals in private rooms (unless medically necessary) are generally not covered. Medicare will not pay for custodial services for activities of daily living such as eating, bathing, and getting dressed. However, Medicare will pay for skilled nursing facility care for rehabilitation, such as recovery time after a hospital discharge. Part A may pay for up to 100 days in a participating skilled nursing facility in each benefit period. Medicare pays all approved charges for the first 20 days relating to skilled nursing facility care, and then the patient pays a coinsurance amount for days 21 through 100. Medicare may also pay the full, approved cost of covered home health care services, which includes part-time or intermittent skilled nursing services prescribed by a physician for treatment or rehabilitation of homebound patients. Normally, the only cost to the insured for home health care is a 20% coinsurance charge for durable medical equipment such as wheelchairs and walkers.

Medicare Part B pays for 80% of approved charges for most covered services. Unless an individual declines Part B medical insurance protection, the premium will automatically be deducted from her Social Security check. Medicare Part B usually does not cover charges for routine physical examinations or services unrelated to the treatment of injury or illness. Dental care, dentures, cosmetic surgery, hearing aids, and eye examinations are not covered by Part B. Part B covers a limited number of outpatient prescription drugs that are not typically self-administered and that are provided in a hospital outpatient department or doctor's office.

Prescription drug coverage under Medicare Part D is available to everyone who is covered under Medicare. Enrollees pay a monthly premium. There is also an annual deductible and a co-payment requirement. Various plans are available with differing premiums and benefit levels.

2020 Outpatient Prescription Coverage (Part D)

Medicare Part D pays for prescription drugs using four stages. First, there is the Part D deductible of $435 in 2020. Next comes the initial coverage using copayments and coinsurance. This lasts until the patient and the plan have paid $4,020 in 2020 in this stage of coverage. The third stage is called the "coverage gap" or the "donut hole." Initially, there was no help from Part D for these expenses. Over time, Part D has covered more and more of the expenses in this range, but it does not cover all expenses. In 2020, the "donut hole" is considered closed because Medicare Part D is now involved in paying some portion of all expenses in this category. The maximum a person pays in this category is 25%. Once the person has spent $6,350 out-of-pocket in 2020, the patient is out of the coverage gap and into the "catastrophic coverage" stage. Most of the remaining expenses are paid by Medicare Part D, but there are still some copayments and coinsurance costs borne by the person.

Source: Centers for Medicare & Medicaid Services
(See www.cms.hhs.gov or www.medicare.gov for updates)

Various plans under Medicare are available to insureds. The original Medicare Plan is the means by which most individuals get their Medicare Part A and Part B benefits. This is the traditional payment-per-service arrangement whereby the individual insured may go to any doctor, specialist, or hospital that accepts Medicare, and Medicare pays its share after services are rendered. Medicare carriers and fiscal intermediaries are private insurance organizations that handle claims under the original Medicare Plan. Carriers handle Part B claims, and fiscal intermediaries handle Part A plans. The Social Security Administration does not handle claims for Medicare payments.

Medicare Advantage
A managed care plan that uses a network of doctors, hospitals, and health care providers approved by Medicare

Medical savings account (MSA)
Used to pay the out-of-pocket medical expenses of an insured enrolled in a high-deductible insurance plan

Furthermore, an individual may opt to enroll in a Medicare managed care plan called **Medicare Advantage** (Medicare Part C). These plans are offered by private Medicare-approved companies and are networks of doctors, hospitals, and other health care providers that agree to give care in return for a set monthly payment from Medicare. Individuals are eligible to enroll in Medicare Advantage if they are enrolled in Medicare Parts A and B, pay the Part B premium, do not have end-stage renal disease, and live in the plan's service area.

Another option under Medicare Advantage is a high-deductible insurance plan and a **medical savings account (MSA)**. Funds from the MSA can be used to pay the out-of-pocket medical expenses of an insured enrolled in a high-deductible insurance plan. Medicare will pay the premium and make contributions to the MSA. These contributions are equal to the amount Medicare would pay to a Medicare Advantage plan in the individual's area less the premium for the high-deductible insurance plan.

Many private insurance companies sell Medicare supplemental insurance policies, Medigap and Medicare SELECT. These supplemental policies help bridge the coverage gaps in the original Medicare plan. These supplemental policies also help pay Medicare's coinsurance amounts and deductibles, as well as other out-of-pocket expenses for health care.

When a worker is first enrolled in Part B at age 65, there is a six-month open enrollment period for Medigap plans. During the time of open enrollment, the health status of the applicant cannot be used as a reason to refuse a Medigap policy or charge more than other open enrollment applicants. However, the insurer may require a six-month waiting period for coverage of pre-existing conditions. If, however, the open enrollment period has expired, the applicant may be denied a policy on the basis of health status or may be charged higher rates.

Other Medicare Health Plan Choices

Medicare offers alternative methods of obtaining Medicare benefits through other health plan choices. Choices that vary by area include coordinated care or Medicare managed care plans, such as health maintenance organizations (HMOs), HMOs with a point of service option, provider sponsored organizations (PSOs), and preferred provider organizations (PPOs). These plans involve specific groups of doctors, hospitals, and other providers who furnish care to an insured member of the plan, such as many employer-sponsored plans throughout the country. Medicare managed care plans not only provide the same services covered by Part A and Part B, but most Medicare managed plans also offer a variety of additional benefits such as preventative care, prescription drugs, dental care, eyeglasses, and other items not covered by the original Medicare Plan. The cost of these extra benefits varies among the plans.

Other Medicare health plan choices beyond the original Medicare plan and Medicare managed care plans include Private Fee-for-Service Plans, Medicare medical savings account plans (MSAs), and religious fraternal benefits plans. These plans provide all services covered by both Part A and Part B, as well as a variety of additional benefits. MSAs are funded through a lump-sum payment from traditional Medicare to obtain a high deductible insurance policy. Any remaining balance can be used by the beneficiary for payment of medical expenses not covered by traditional Medicare or for other use. This amount could be subject to taxation if not used for medically related purposes. For information about these various health plan choices, visit the official internet site of Medicare at **www.medicare.gov,** which is very helpful and provides many links to other informative sources.

Applying for Medicare Benefits and Coverage

If a worker applies for retirement or survivor benefits before her 65th birthday, there is no need to file a separate application for Medicare. The worker will receive information in the mail before she turns 65, explaining what needs to be done. Coverage starts automatically at age 65, even without receiving a Medicare card in the mail.

Those who are not receiving Social Security benefits must file an application for Medicare benefits. Spouses can qualify for Medicare Part A at age 65 on the basis of the other spouse's work record if the other spouse is eligible for monthly Social Security benefits or if the other spouse is receiving Social Security disability benefits. Applications should be submitted three months before the applicant's 65th birthday. If the worker does not enroll and delays taking Part B for one year, that worker's monthly premiums for Part B will increase. For every 12 months the worker could have used Part B but does not take it, the monthly premium increases by 10%. If the worker decides to delay opting into Part B because of the worker's current group health plan coverage (if applicable), the worker may be able to avoid the increased monthly premium by applying for Part B either while participating in the group coverage or within eight months after the employment ends or group health coverage ends, whichever occurs first.

Even if an individual continues to work after turning 65, she should sign up for Part A of Medicare. Part A may help defray some costs not otherwise covered by group health plans. Applying for Part B may or may not be advantageous if the worker has health insurance through an employer. The worker would be required to pay the monthly Part B premium, yet Part B benefits may be of limited value because the employer plan will be the primary source of payment of medical bills.

SUPPLEMENTAL SECURITY INCOME BENEFITS

SSI makes monthly payments to individuals with low incomes and few assets. In order to obtain SSI benefits, an individual must be age 65, disabled, or blind. The definition of disability is satisfied when the individual is unable to engage in any substantial gainful activity because of a physical or mental problem expected to last at least one year or result in death. Children as well as adults can qualify for SSI disability payments. As its name implies, Supplemental Security Income supplements the beneficiary's income up to various levels, depending on where the beneficiary lives. If an otherwise eligible SSI applicant lives in another's household and receives support from that person, the federal SSI benefit is reduced by one-third.

The federal government pays a basic rate, which is $783 (2020) per month for one person and $1,175 (2020) per month for married couples. Some states supply additional funds to qualified individuals. To ascertain the SSI benefit rates in a certain state, the financial planner or client can contact a local Social Security office in that state, or visit the Social Security Administration's website. Generally, individuals who receive SSI benefits also qualify for Medicaid, food stamps, and other public assistance.

FILING FOR SOCIAL SECURITY BENEFITS

The Social Security Administration reports that many people fail to file claims with the Social Security Administration or fail to do so in a timely fashion. Individuals should file for Social Security or SSI disability benefits as soon they become too disabled to work or for survivors benefits when a family breadwinner dies. Social Security benefits do not start automatically. Social Security will not begin payment of benefits until the beneficiary files an application. When filing for benefits, applicants must submit documents that show eligibility, such as a birth certificate for each family member applying for benefits, a marriage certificate if a spouse is applying, and the most recent W-2 forms or tax returns.

To file for benefits, obtain information, or to speak to a Social Security representative, individuals must call the Social Security Administration's toll-free number, 1-800-772-1213, or visit the Social Security Administration's website. The toll-free number can be used to schedule an appointment at a local Social Security office. The Social Security Administration treats all calls confidentially. Periodically, a second Social Security representative will monitor incoming and outgoing telephone calls to ensure accurate and courteous service.

SOCIAL SECURITY CHANGES FOR 2019–2020

Each year, the Social Security Commissioner issues a Fact Sheet summarizing the changes in Social Security. Exhibit 11.12 contains the Commissioner's Fact Sheet for 2019 and 2020.

EXHIBIT 11.12 Social Security Changes for 2019–2020

Fact Sheet

SOCIAL SECURITY

2020 SOCIAL SECURITY CHANGES

Cost-of-Living Adjustment (COLA):

Based on the increase in the Consumer Price Index (CPI-W) from the third quarter of 2018 through the third quarter of 2019, Social Security and Supplemental Security Income (SSI) beneficiaries will receive a 1.6 percent COLA for 2020. Other important 2020 Social Security information is as follows:

Tax Rate	2019	2020
Employee	7.65%	7.65%
Self-Employed	15.30%	15.30%

NOTE: The 7.65% tax rate is the combined rate for Social Security and Medicare. The Social Security portion (OASDI) is 6.20% on earnings up to the applicable taxable maximum amount (see below). The Medicare portion (HI) is 1.45% on all earnings. Also, as of January 2013, individuals with earned income of more than $200,000 ($250,000 for married couples filing jointly) pay an additional 0.9 percent in Medicare taxes. The tax rates shown above do not include the 0.9 percent.

	2019	2020
Maximum Taxable Earnings		
Social Security (OASDI only)	$132,900	$137,700
Medicare (HI only)	No Limit	
Quarter of Coverage		
	$1,360	$1,410
Retirement Earnings Test Exempt Amounts		
Under full retirement age	$17,640/yr. ($1,470/mo.)	$18,240/yr. ($1,520/mo.)
NOTE: One dollar in benefits will be withheld for every $2 in earnings above the limit.		

Social Security National Press Office   Baltimore, MD

EXHIBIT 11.12 Social Security Changes for 2019–2020 (continued)

The year an individual reaches full retirement age	$46,920/yr. ($3,910/mo.)	$48,600/yr. ($4,050/mo.)
NOTE: Applies only to earnings for months prior to attaining full retirement age. One dollar in benefits will be withheld for every $3 in earnings above the limit.		
Beginning the month an individual attains full retirement age	None	

	2019	2020
Social Security Disability Thresholds		
Substantial Gainful Activity (SGA)		
Non-Blind	$1,220/mo.	$1,260/mo.
Blind	$2,040/mo.	$2,110/mo.
Trial Work Period (TWP)	$ 880/mo.	$ 910/mo.
Maximum Social Security Benefit: Worker Retiring at Full Retirement Age		
	$2,861/mo.	$3,011/mo.
SSI Federal Payment Standard		
Individual	$ 771/mo.	$ 783/mo.
Couple	$1,157/mo.	$1,175/mo.
SSI Resource Limits		
Individual	$2,000	$2,000
Couple	$3,000	$3,000
SSI Student Exclusion		
Monthly limit	$1,870	$1,900
Annual limit	$7,550	$7,670
Estimated Average Monthly Social Security Benefits Payable in January 2020		
	Before 1.6% COLA	After 1.6% COLA
All Retired Workers	$1,479	$1,503
Aged Couple, Both Receiving Benefits	$2,491	$2,531
Widowed Mother and Two Children	$2,888	$2,934
Aged Widow(er) Alone	$1,400	$1,422
Disabled Worker, Spouse and One or More Children	$2,141	$2,176
All Disabled Workers	$1,238	$1,258

This press release was produced and disseminated at U.S. taxpayer expense.

OTHER ISSUES

Effect of Marriage or Divorce on Benefits

Marriage or divorce may affect one's Social Security benefits, depending on the kind of benefits received. If a worker receives retirement benefits on the basis of his own earnings record, the worker's retirement benefits will continue whether he is married or divorced. If an individual receives benefits on the basis of his spouse's record, the individual's benefits will cease upon divorce, unless the individual is age 62 or older and was married at least 10 years. Widows and widowers, whether divorced or not, will continue to receive survivors benefits upon remarriage if the widow or widower is age 60 or older. Disabled widows and widowers, whether divorced or not, will continue to receive survivors benefits upon remarriage if the disabled widow or widower is age 50 or older.

For all other forms of Social Security benefits, benefits will cease upon remarriage, except in special circumstances. When a person marries, it is presumed that at least one person in the marriage can provide adequate support. Likewise, Social Security benefits may recommence based on the previous spouse's benefits if the marriage ends.

Change of Name

If an individual changes her name because of marriage, divorce, or a court order, that individual must notify the Social Security Administration of the name change so that the Social Security Administration will be able to show the new name in its records and properly credit that individual for earnings. This will ensure that the individual's work history will be accurately recorded and maintained.

Leaving the United States

Beneficiaries who are U.S. citizens may travel or live in most foreign countries without affecting their eligibility for Social Security benefits. However, there are a few countries where Social Security checks cannot be sent. These countries currently include Cuba and North Korea. In general, the Social Security Administration will not send payments to persons in Azerbaijan, Belarus, Kazakhstan, Kyrgyzstan, Moldova, Tajikistan, Turkmenistan, Ukraine, and Uzbekistan. Exceptions may be made for certain eligible recipients in these countries.

Beneficiaries should inform the Social Security Administration of their plans to go outside the United States for a trip that lasts 30 days or more. By providing the name of the country or countries to be visited and the expected departure and return dates, the Social Security Administration will send special reporting instructions to the beneficiaries and arrange for delivery of checks while abroad.

WHERE ON THE WEB

Centers for Medicare and Medicaid Services **www.cms.gov**

Medicare Rights Center **www.medicarerights.org**

National Organization of Social Security Claimants' Representatives **www.nosscr.org**

Social Security Online (official website of the U.S. Social Security Administration) **www.ssa.gov**

Social Security Disability **www.ssa.gov/disability**

Social Security Forms **www.ssa.gov/forms**

U.S. Government website for Medicare **www.medicare.gov**

DISCUSSION QUESTIONS

1. For purposes of Social Security and disability benefits, what is the meaning of substantial work in 2020?

2. When was Social Security legislation passed?

3. When was Social Security legislation passed to include a cost-of-living adjustment (COLA)?

4. How are Social Security benefits financed?

5. Is there a maximum payroll amount to which Social Security taxes apply?

6. To qualify for OASDI disability benefits, what definition of disability must be met?

7. Describe the six major benefits under the Social Security program.

8. Identify and describe the benefits available to those covered under OASDI.

9. How would a person who is entitled to Social Security benefits become ineligible for benefits?

10. What are the coverages that make up the Medicare program?

11. Define and explain the meaning of fully insured, currently insured, and disability insured under the OASDI program.

12. What are the requirements to be fully insured under OASDI?

13. What Social Security benefits are available to the dependents of a deceased worker who was only currently insured?

14. What Social Security benefits would a fully insured worker have that a currently insured worker would not have until achieving fully insured status?

15. What requirements must a person satisfy to collect Social Security (OASDI) disability income benefits?

16. How is Social Security funded?

17. To qualify for Social Security OASDI benefits, how many credits of coverage does one need? How is a credit determined?

18. How is OASDI insured status determined, and why is it important?

19. How are monthly payments under OASDI determined?

20. What is normal retirement age for OASDI benefits for someone born in 1959?

21. Is a recipient of Social Security benefits subject to purchasing-power risk?

22. What are the four benefits payable under the OASDI program?

EXERCISES

1. Michael was 33 and had two dependent children, ages 4 and 6, who are cared for by their mother when he died this year. He had accumulated 20 credits of coverage under Social Security at the time of his death. To what benefits are his survivors entitled under Social Security?

2. In 2020, James earned $5,000 from employment subject to Social Security between January 1 and March 31. He was then unemployed for the remainder of the year. How many credits of coverage did he earn for Social Security for 2020?

3. Charles, age 38, has just died. He was credited with the last 30 consecutive credits of coverage since he left school. He did not work before leaving school. Which of the following persons are eligible to receive Social Security survivor benefits as a result of Charles's death?
   A. Bill, Charles's 16-year-old son
   B. Dawn, Charles' 18-year-old daughter
   C. Margaret, Charles's 38-year-old widow
   D. Betty, Charles's 60-year-old dependent mother

4. Under Social Security (OASDI), what benefits are available to the survivors of a deceased who was currently insured?

5. Which of the following persons are eligible to receive immediate survivor income benefits on the basis of a deceased worker's primary insurance amount (PIA) under OASDI (Social Security)?
   1. A surviving spouse caring for an under-16-year-old child
   2. Unmarried children under age 18 who are dependents
   3. Unmarried disabled children who became disabled before age 22
   4. Any surviving divorced spouse over 50, with no children who was married to decedent for over 10 years and who is disabled

6. How is a worker's insured status determined under Social Security?

7. Philip began his professional corporation single practitioner CPA firm 38 years ago at age 25. He worked profitably as a sole practitioner for the full 38 years and is now age 63 and 2 months. He retired December 31, 2019. On January 1, 2020, he sold his practice for $400,000 to be received in four equal annual installments beginning on January 1, 2020. Is Philip eligible for Social Security retirement benefits during 2020? Why or why not? What would be the ramifications if Philip started his Social Security benefits now?

PROBLEMS

1. Larry was married at the following ages and to the following wives. Larry is fully insured and is 62 and married to Dawn.

	Wife	Current Age	Larry's Age at Marriage	Current Marital Status	Length of Marriage
1	Alice	62	20	Single	10 years, 1 month
2	Betty	63	31	Single	10 years, 1 month
3	Claire	64	42	Single	9 years
4	Dawn	65	53	Married	9 years

Who among the former wives/wives may be eligible to receive Social Security retirement benefits on the basis of Larry's earnings if Larry is 1) retired, or 2) not retired?

2. Rob earned $62,000 in 2020. Calculate his FICA contribution for the year. How much did his employer pay toward FICA?

3. Last year, Michelle, filing single, received $10,400 in Social Security benefits. For the entire year, she had adjusted gross income of $28,000. How much, if any, of her Social Security benefit is taxable?

4. Mike is 68 years old in 2020. He has a full-time job working as a masseur. This year he anticipates earning $32,000 from his job. How much, in dollars, will Mike's Social Security benefits be reduced?

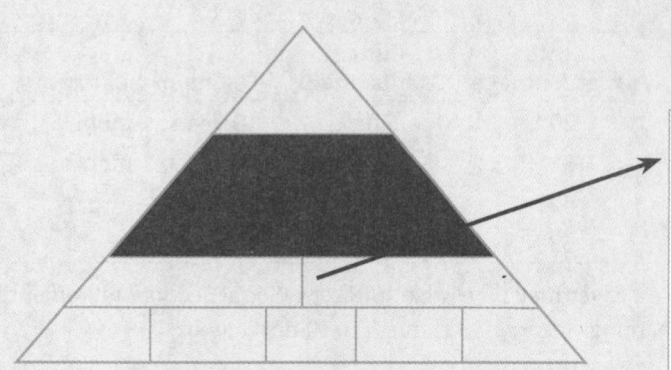

4

Investment, Income Tax, Business, Retirement, and Estate Planning

CHAPTERS

Risks	Goals
■ Unrealized financial planning goals	■ Minimize tax liability
■ Investment losses	■ Match business goals with entity formation
■ Systematic and unsystematic risk	■ Ensure inflation-protected retirement income
■ Excessive tax liability (income, estate, gift)	■ Efficient transfer of assets
■ Excessive general liability exposure	
■ Outliving one's assets	
■ Failure to provide for survivors	
■ Inefficient distribution of estate assets	
■ Failure to meet assisted living and end-of-life care needs	

Data Collection	Data Analysis
■ Business entity characteristics	■ Liquidity needs
■ Financial statements	■ Investment portfolio risks and returns benchmark comparison
■ Family health history	■ Tax efficiency of investments
■ Projected inflation rate	■ Tax-saving strategies
■ Investment history	■ Retirement needs analysis
■ Risk tolerance	■ Adequacy of life insurance and other wealth transfer techniques
■ Tax returns and information forms	
■ Current investment and asset allocation	
■ Life insurance policies and property titles	
■ Retirement plan and deferred compensation information	
■ Estate planning documents and trust information	

Introduction to Investment Concepts

LEARNING OBJECTIVES

After learning the material in this chapter, you will be able to do the following:

■ Describe the steps involved in the investment planning process

■ List the most common investment goals and how to achieve them

■ Explain the difference between direct investing and indirect investing

■ Differentiate between systematic risk and unsystematic risk

■ Define lending investments and ownership investments

■ Identify attributes of an investment in tangible assets (collectibles) or natural resources (oil and gas wells)

■ Describe the two common measures of risk: beta and standard deviation

■ Understand how to calculate several measures of investment return

411

- Define the efficient frontier, and explain its role in modern portfolio theory

- Describe the capital asset pricing model (CAPM), the capital market line (CML), and the security market line (SML)

- Describe the efficient market hypothesis

- Describe the basic principles of behavioral finance

INTRODUCTION TO INVESTING

As this text's opening chapters point out, the professional financial planner's purpose is to assist clients in achieving their financial goals and objectives, while simultaneously helping them manage personal and financial risks. Investment planning and portfolio evaluation are key elements in achieving many financial planning goals, such as saving for retirement, saving for children's education, and the accumulation and preservation of wealth. This chapter will provide the financial planner with the background and reference information necessary to develop a solid foundation of investment planning—an essential ingredient in the financial planning process.

Investing is based on the concept that forgoing immediate consumption provides for greater future consumption. Investing provides an opportunity for discretionary funds to grow and accumulate over time. Therefore, the first step in developing a sound financial plan is to save rather than spend. This current sacrifice implies an expectation that funds saved today will provide for greater expenditures in the future.

Without the ability to invest and grow through savings, interest income, dividend payments, rental income, and capital appreciation, investors would have difficulty achieving their financial goals. However, financial growth is only one element to consider in achieving financial goals. Taxes, inflation, and other risks stand in the way.

THE INVESTMENT PLANNING PROCESS

This process begins with a client establishing a clear set of goals and developing and implementing an investment strategy that is in agreement with the goals. The formal steps in the investment planning process include determining whether the client has the means to invest, establishing the time horizon for investment based on the client's financial objectives, and ascertaining the appropriate level of risk and return for the investment portfolio based on the investor's risk tolerance and required rate of return. Investment planning requires a thorough review of the client's current financial situation. The investment professional needs to assist the client in making the proper financial choices to help the client meet the goals. In order to provide effective investment counseling, the advisor should examine and review the client's financial goals, risk tolerance, tax situation, liquidity needs, and financial statements.

■ ESTABLISHING FINANCIAL GOALS

Financial or investment goals are the objectives that a client wishes to accomplish through the investing process. Ultimately the investment choices that a client will make is dictated by their investment goals.

The time horizon for goals can be short, intermediate, or long. Short-term goals are commonly fulfilled within two years, and include saving for small purchases or for a down payment on an automobile. Intermediate goals are often accomplished within 2 to 10 years, and include funding a child's college education or saving for a down payment on a home. Long-term goals generally take over 10 years to achieve, and include saving for retirement.

Investment Policy Statement

Investment policy statement
A written document that sets forth a client's objectives, as well as limitations on the investment manager

An **investment policy statement** (IPS) is a written document that sets forth a client's objectives, as well as limitations on the investment manager. This document also gives guidance to the investment manager and provides a means for evaluating investment performance. Specifically, the objectives portion of the statement should include the desired portfolio return as well as the client's risk tolerance. To determine the client's risk tolerance, many advisors use a questionnaire. In addition, advisors use the following constraints as part of an IPS:

■ Investment time horizon

■ Liquidity needs of the investor during the investment period

■ Tax status of the investor's portfolio

■ Laws and regulations that may affect the investor's portfolio

■ Any unique circumstances and/or investor preferences (e.g., a pending inheritance)

Typical Financial Planning Goals

Purchasing a home is likely one of the largest financial commitments clients will make during their lifetimes. Most people begin the process by saving for a few years to accumulate a down payment. If the price of an average home is $150,000, many people attempt to make a down payment of approximately $30,000, or 20%. Generally, the average time to save for a down payment is between two and five years. This short period offers minimal opportunity for growth and deters the client from incurring a significant amount of investment risk. Therefore, the appropriate types of securities or investments for this situation are relatively conservative.

One typical goal for parents is funding their children's college education. The cost of tuition and fees ranges from a few thousand dollars to nearly $60,000 per school year. In some cases, parents will pay the entire cost of education from their current income. However, with tuition costs increasing at a rate of approximately 5–7% per year, parents are finding it increasingly difficult to pay for a child's college education. As a result, many parents are beginning to plan and save for college as soon as their child is born, giving themselves an investment time horizon of approximately 18 years. Other parents with young children may not have the resources to begin planning for college until the child is beginning high school. In their case, the time horizon for saving and investing is closer to four or five years. Clearly, the 18-year time horizon presents a longer compounding period of growth and a greater amount of risk tolerance than does the shorter time horizon.

Even individuals and couples without children or those whose children choose not to attend college still need to plan for retirement. Today's Social Security system may not provide enough income for most individuals to maintain their current standard of living during retirement. Consequently, the burden of funding retirement falls mainly upon the individual. As people become more knowledgeable about financial planning, they are beginning to save earlier for retirement. Someone who is 25 years old has approximately 40 years to save for retirement, assuming retirement begins around age 65. Others will not begin to save until much later but will still have a long-term investment time horizon because the average person may spend 10 to 20 years or longer in retirement. Therefore, the total investment period may still last for 40 or more years.

In each of these cases, accomplishing the specific financial planning goal requires that the individual save and invest funds for a certain period. However, because the time horizon of each goal is different, the ability to tolerate fluctuation in the value of the invested assets varies. For example, investors can tolerate more fluctuation when planning for retirement than when saving for a down payment on a home.

Budgeting

The purpose of budgeting is to manage the amount of income and expenses on a monthly basis. For most people, income is reasonably fixed in the short term, while expenses may vary widely throughout the year. For example, some items are paid monthly, such as utilities, mortgage payments, and phone bills, but other items are paid semiannually, such as automobile insurance. In addition, certain expenses are necessities, or nondiscretionary, such as mortgage payments, groceries, and utilities—while other expenses are discretionary, such as dining out or purchasing new clothes. By identifying necessary and discretionary monthly expenses, one can then begin to find ways to reduce expenses and increase savings. For those who live on a relatively fixed income or salary, the only way to increase savings is to reduce expenditures.

Methods of Increasing Savings

Reducing expenditures, especially discretionary expenditures, is an excellent way to increase cash flow for investment. One way to accomplish this is a savings method called "pay yourself first." Paying yourself first means that the first bill paid every pay period is a deposit to his savings. This method of savings is particularly effective for people without savings discipline because it can be accomplished automatically. For instance, a mutual fund account can be set up to automatically draft a certain amount of investment dollars from a checking account every month or each pay period. Paying yourself first ensures saving on a regular basis and promotes living within a budget.

Another method to increase savings over time is to allocate a portion of future raises and other increases in household income to savings. As increases in salary occur, increases in savings should occur simultaneously. If a person was able to live on $4,000 last month and received a 5% raise, the person should be able to live on less than $4,200 next month and can allocate up to $200 of the raise to savings.

Elective savings programs, such as Section 401(k) plans (cash or deferred arrangements), are another method of increasing personal savings and net worth. These plans facilitate automatic savings in the form of a payroll deduction on a pretax basis. Employee salary deferrals are usually accompanied by employer-matching contributions, which are like free money, and individuals should take full advantage of these contributions. A Section 401(k) plan can facilitate both the "pay yourself first" and the allocating raises methods of increasing savings.

E X A M P L E   One of the most important steps in achieving financial goals is to begin sooner rather than later. Time is a great asset in achieving financial planning objectives. For example, a 25-year-old saving $2,000 per year for 10 years will accumulate more by age 65 than a 35-year-old saving $2,000 for 30 years. Although the younger investor invested only one-third of the amount of the older investor, the younger investor has more assets at age 65. How can this be? The simple answer is time. Exhibit 12.1 demonstrates this concept using three different earnings rates.

EXHIBIT 12.1 Time/Savings Example (Accumulation at Age 65)

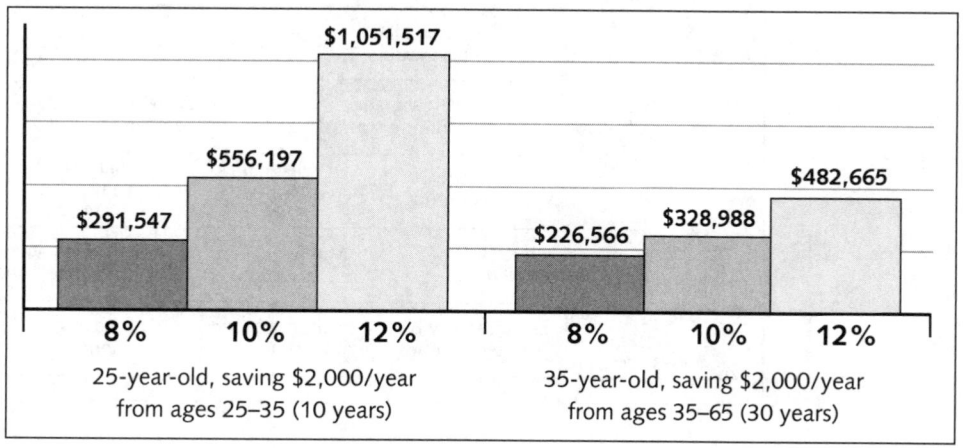

Direct vs. Indirect Investing

Direct investing
A process of investing where investors purchase actual securities

Indirect investing
A process of investing where investors invest in companies that invest directly in securities

Investing in bonds or stocks can be accomplished by purchasing the actual securities or by investing in companies that purchase the actual securities. **Direct investing** occurs when investors purchase actual securities. For example, an investor who purchased an IBM corporate bond or Microsoft's common stock would be investing directly. Direct investing can be accomplished by investing through a brokerage account.

Indirect investing is a process of investing in securities (e.g., mutual funds) that invest directly. Mutual funds are companies that invest in stocks, bonds, and other various securities. Over the last 20 years, indirect investing has gained in popularity. In fact, there are currently more investment companies (mutual funds) than there are listed securities.

▌INVESTMENT RISKS

Individuals, corporations, and institutions all invest to accumulate wealth. The investor's returns, however, are indeterminable at the inception of the investment because of uncertainty. This uncertainty is a risk that is perceived and managed differently by individual investors. Risk can be thought of as the uncertainty of future outcomes or defined as the probability of an adverse result. In either case, investors expect higher returns when they accept higher levels of uncertainty or risk. The two most important investment strategies that assist investors in managing investment risk are portfolio diversification and asset allocation. They both facilitate the achievement of a fundamental investment goal: obtaining the highest possible return while assuming the lowest amount of risk.

EXHIBIT 12.2 The Risk Pyramid

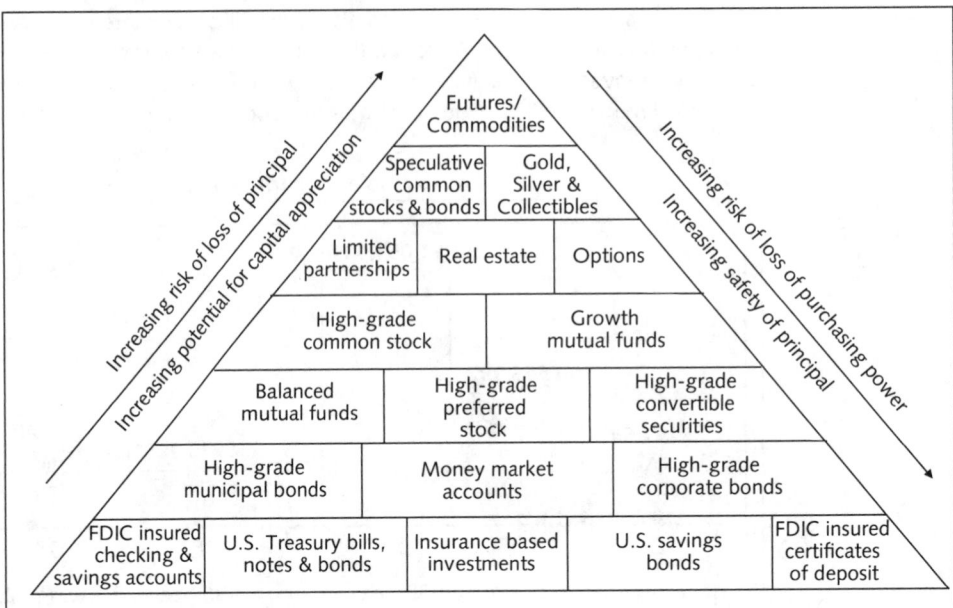

Investors must accept a certain level of risk. Some investors think they can avoid all risks; however, certain risks influence all securities, such as the risk of inflation and fluctuations in interest rates. Even the most conservative investors, invested in the least risky fixed-income securities, are subject to purchasing power risk (inflation) and interest rate risk (changes in interest rates). Other types of risk may only affect a single security, industry, or country. On the basis of these differences, there are two broad categories of risk: systematic risks and unsystematic risks. Exhibit 12.3 summarizes the types of risks under each category.

EXHIBIT 12.3 Systematic and Unsystematic Risks

Systematic Risks	Unsystematic Risks
Purchasing power risk	Business risk
Reinvestment rate risk	Financial risk
Interest rate risk	Default risk
Market risk	Country risk
Exchange rate risk	Liquidity risk
	Marketability risk
	Tax risk

Systematic Risks

Systematic risks
Investment risks impacted by broad macroeconomic factors that influence all securities

Systematic risks are investment risks impacted by broad macroeconomic factors that influence all securities. These risks include purchasing power risk, reinvestment rate risk, interest rate risk, market risk, and exchange rate risk. Diversification cannot eliminate all systematic risk because at least one of these factors affects every security. To recall the components of systematic risk, use the mnemonic *PRIME*, which uses the first letter of each risk source.

Purchasing Power Risk

Purchasing power risk
A systematic risk in which inflation erodes the real value of the investor's assets

The risk that inflation will erode the real value of the investor's assets is referred to as **purchasing power risk**. As the price of goods increases, the purchasing power of assets decreases. The objective of investment planning is to generate returns in excess of inflation to ensure that the real value of assets does not erode. Unanticipated inflation is the main cause of purchasing power risk. Bonds held to maturity are likely to suffer from purchasing power risk because maturity values and coupon payments remain constant regardless of price changes.

Reinvestment Rate Risk

Reinvestment rate risk
A systematic risk in which earnings (cash flows) distributed from current investments cannot be reinvested at a rate of return equal to the expected yield of the current investments

Reinvestment rate risk is the risk that earnings (cash flows) distributed from current investments cannot be reinvested at a rate of return equal to the expected yield of the current investments. For example, if a bond purchased today yields 4% and market rates subsequently decline, interest payments from the bond cannot be reinvested at 4%; thus, the overall realized return will decline. Zero-coupon bonds (bonds that do not make regular periodic interest payments), are not subject to reinvestment rate risk during the term of the bond because payments are not made to the investor until maturity.

Interest Rate Risk

Interest rate risk
A systematic risk in which changes in interest rates affect the value of securities

The risk that changes in interest rates will affect the value of securities is known as **interest rate risk**. An inverse relationship exists between the value of fixed investments and changes in interest rates: as interest rates increase, the value of bonds decreases. Rising interest rates generally have a negative effect on stocks as well. Reasons for this negative pressure include the increased discount rate used for valuation of cash flows, increased borrowing costs for corporations (thus, an expectancy of lower earnings), and increased yields on alternative investments, such as bonds.

Market Risk

Market risk
A systematic risk describing the tendency of stocks to move in concert with the market

The tendency for securities to move in concert with the market is **market risk**. When the market is rising, stocks have a tendency to increase in value. Conversely, most stocks tend to fall with declines in the overall market. Often, a move in the market is prefaced by some change in the economic environment.

In addition, certain events, such as wars and economic collapse, could have a large impact on a client's portfolio. Forecasting and planning for these types of events may be difficult, but communicating their possibility over a long-term investment horizon is important for financial planners. If a sudden disruption in the market occurs, the financial planner should recommend that the client remain focused on the long term and avoid implementing financial decisions based solely on emotion.

Exchange Rate Risk (Foreign Currency Risk)

Exchange rate risk
A systematic risk due to the potential change in the relationship between the value of the dollar (or investor's currency) and the value of the foreign currency during the period of investment; also known as foreign currency risk

Exchange rate risk is the risk that a change in the relationship between the value of the dollar (or investor's currency) and the value of the foreign currency will occur during the period of investment. This risk affects investments in foreign stocks and bonds as well as domestic corporations that export products or import factors of production.

E X A M P L E   John invests $1 million in the Orval Corporation based in Mexico. If the conversion rate for pesos to dollars is 10:1, John must invest 10 million pesos in Orval Corporation. Orval Corporation does extremely well, and John is able to sell his interest for 15 million pesos. If John attempts to convert the pesos into dollars when the exchange rate has changed to 12:1, he will receive $1,250,000 (15,000,000 ÷ 12).

This gain comprises a 50% (5,000,000 pesos) gain on the investment and a loss of 16.67% [(10 pesos per dollar ÷ 12 pesos per dollar) – 1], or $250,000, from the change in the currency rate. The net result is a 25% gain on the original investment; however, it is only half of the gain generated from the appreciation of Orval Corporation.

Unsystematic Risks

> **Unsystematic risks**
> *Types of investment risks unique to a single company, industry, or country that can be eliminated by portfolio diversification*

Unsystematic risks are unique to a single security, company, industry, or country and include default risk, business risk, financial risk, and country risk. Unlike systematic risk, these risks can be eliminated through diversification. Several studies have found that unsystematic risk declines significantly with a portfolio consisting of as few as 10 randomly chosen stocks. As more stocks are added to a portfolio, the losses of one company in the portfolio will have less impact on the total performance of the portfolio.

EXHIBIT 12.4 Total Portfolio Risk

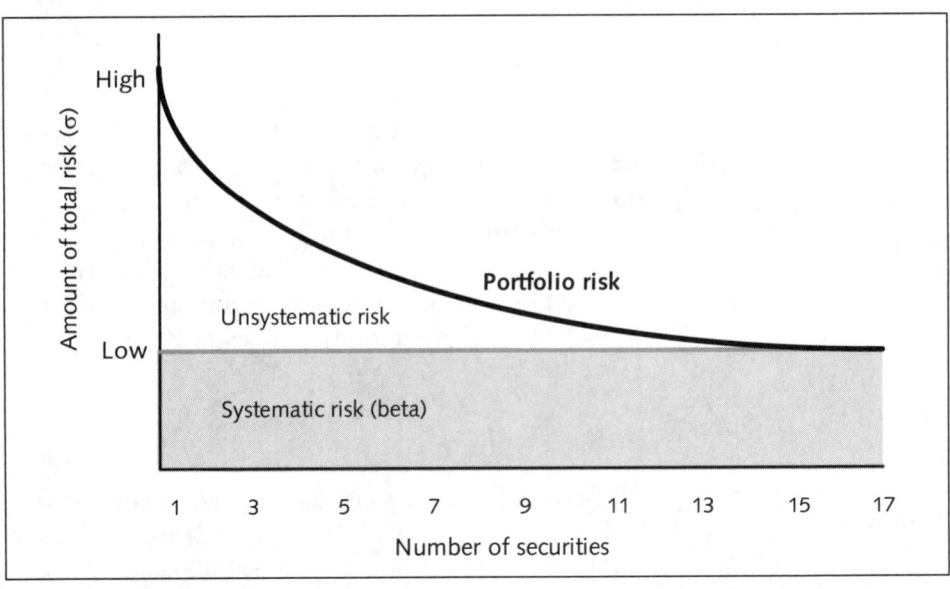

Exhibit 12.4 illustrates the concept of diversification. As more securities are added to the portfolio, the overall risk of the portfolio declines. There are several other points of interest. First, unsystematic risk can be reduced and effectively eliminated. This is not the case for systematic risk. Systematic risk cannot be eliminated because it represents the risk to all securities. Systematic risk is generally measured by beta, whereas total risk (systematic risk + unsystematic risk) is measured by standard deviation. For portfolios that have significantly reduced unsystematic risk, beta is a good measure of total risk. Conversely, when unsystematic risk is not reduced, beta does a poor job of estimating total risk.

> **Business risk**
> *An unsystematic risk based on predictability of operating income for a specific business; dependent upon management and industry characteristics*

Business Risk

Business risk, or the level of risk associated with the specific business, includes the speculative nature of the business, the management of the business, and the philosophy of the business. Different types of businesses will have different levels of risk. For instance, searching for oil is generally riskier than operating a grocery store; however, each has unique risks. Business risk is also related to the uncertainty of operating income. Utility companies have relatively stable and predictable income streams and, therefore, have lower business risk. Because cyclical companies, such as auto manufacturers, have unsteady or fluctuating operating income levels, they have higher business risk.

Financial Risk

Financial risk
An unsystematic risk based on the inclusion of debt in the capital structure of a firm, which affects the return on equity (ROE) for a company

Financial risk is based on the inclusion of debt in the capital structure of a firm. The decision to finance some of the firm's assets with debt creates additional risk which is absorbed by shareholders. Specifically, the use of debt magnifies the return on equity (ROE) and makes gains and losses more volatile.

E X A M P L E   For example, a firm that is financed with 75% debt (25% equity) will have an ROE four times larger than a similar firm with the same net income and financed 100% with equity. This financial leverage occurs because the return is based on a smaller amount of equity. In this example, the equity of the leveraged company is one-fourth that of the nonleveraged firm, so that returns and losses for the leveraged firm will be four times larger on a percentage basis. Financial risk is associated with the liability side of the firm's balance sheet.

	Company A	Company B
Net income	$50,000	$50,000
Debt	$0	$300,000
Equity	$400,000	$100,000
ROE	12.5%	50%

Default Risk

Default risk
An unsystematic risk associated with the inability of a business to service its debt

The risk that a business will be unable to service its debt is **default risk**. Bonds issued by both corporations and municipalities are subject to default risk. Rating agencies, such as Moody's and Standard & Poor's, rate bonds issued by corporations and municipalities from the highest grade to default. Obligations of the U.S. government are considered free from default risk. In addition, equity investments are not subject to default risk.

Country Risk

Country risk
An unsystematic risk associated with the potential adverse effect of changes in a country's laws or political situation

International investments are subject to **country risk**, which is the unique risk associated with a particular country and the potential adverse effect of changes in a country's laws or its political situation. These risks include political and economic risks. The United States is generally thought to have the lowest country risk because its political and economic systems are the most stable. An investor is able to minimize country risk by investing in several countries in various parts of the world.

Liquidity and Marketability Risk

Liquidity
The ability to sell an investment quickly and at a competitive price, with no loss of principal and minimal price concession

Liquidity is the ability to sell an investment quickly and at a competitive price, with no loss of principal and minimal price concession. If the security markets do not have sufficient liquidity to absorb a trade, the trader may find that a price concession is necessary to execute the trade. **Marketability** refers to the ability of an investor to find a ready market where the investor may sell an investment to a willing buyer. Real estate is marketable but may not be liquid. Treasury bills are both liquid and marketable. Liquidity and marketability may be realized as points along a continuum, with cash and cash equivalents being the most liquid and most marketable.

Tax Risk

Marketability
The ability of an investor to find a ready market where the investor may sell an investment to a willing buyer

Tax risk is the risk that taxation of investment gains or losses will adversely affect a investor's investment return. An investor must take into consideration how a country's tax laws may potentially affect the after-tax return of an investment.

Tax risk
The uncertainty associated with the tax laws that may impact the ownership and/or disposition of investment assets

Risk and Return

An investment's risk and expected return have a direct relationship. As the level of risk increases, the expected return increases. Meanwhile, as the level of risk declines, the expected return declines. Thus, to achieve higher returns, an investor must accept the trade-off of greater risk and typically more volatile returns.

Risk Tolerance

Risk tolerance
An estimate of the level of risk an investor is willing to accept within a portfolio

Risk tolerance is an estimate of the level of risk that an investor is willing to accept in a portfolio. Certain investors are unwilling to accept any risk, whereas others invest in only the riskiest securities. A planner estimates a client's tolerance for risk using two common methods. The first method is to develop a clear understanding of the client's investment preferences and investment history. This information provides a basis for determining how comfortable a client is with investments in equities, fixed-income securities, and other risky securities. The second method is to use a questionnaire designed to elicit the client's feelings about risky assets and their overall comfort level given certain changes in the portfolio. When combined, these two methods can guide the planner toward accurately assessing a client's risk tolerance.

▌INVESTMENT CHOICES

The level of risk and the specific risks investors must face greatly influence their choice of investments. Investors today have a wide variety of investment options, ranging from interest-bearing checking accounts to sophisticated derivatives. Although investments can be extremely complicated and risky, as in the case of derivatives, investments generally fall within one of two categories: lending investments or ownership investments.

Lending Investments

Savings accounts and bonds are examples of lending investments. When cash is deposited into a savings account, the owner has loaned money to the bank and will receive interest payments. The bank will then lend money to others in the form of mortgages or other debt instruments. Interest may be based on a fixed rate, or it may vary based on a variable-rate benchmark, such as the 90-day Treasury bill rate.

Bonds are more structured investments than savings accounts. Bonds have specific maturity dates, stated face values, and defined interest (coupon) payments. Although a savings account is, in effect, an indefinite loan, bonds have a specific maturity date. This date is the time at which the borrower (bond issuer) must repay the loan to the lender (bondholder).

Bonds generally have a par value (face value) of $1,000. Bond issuers compensate the bondholder by making specified interest payments. These interest payments, generally paid semiannually, are based on an interest rate called the coupon rate. A bond with a stated coupon rate of 4% will pay interest of $20 ($1,000 × 4% ÷ 2) twice per year for a total of $40 per year. These coupon payments continue for the life of the bond. Therefore, a 30-year bond will generally make 60 coupon payments. At the time the bond matures, the investor will receive the par value of the bond.

Bonds provide investors with a certain level of security because they generally make regular, specified payments to the bondholders. Many investors, especially retired individuals, rely on these coupon payments as a source of income.

Ownership Investments in Business (Common and Preferred Stock)

Ownership investments take the form of common or preferred stock. Common stockholders accept the risks inherent in owning a company. Although bondholders have a right to be repaid funds that were loaned, common stockholders have invested in the potential future profitability of the business. If the company is successful, the value of the common stock will increase. If the company is unsuccessful, then the value of the common stock will decline. Investors in common stock are rewarded for accepting risk in two ways. The first is through appreciation in the value of the stock. The second is from earnings that are paid to the shareholders in the form of dividends. A dividend is a payment made by the corporation to the shareholders as their share of the profits of the corporation.

Common stockholders assume more risk than bondholders because, in the event of bankruptcy, bondholders are paid before stockholders. Investors require higher returns for common stock to compensate for the increased risks associated with owning equity securities. In addition, equities tend to have more price volatility than bonds.

Preferred stock has the characteristics of both bonds and common stock. Similar to bonds, preferred stock generally pays a fixed payment, called a preferred stock dividend, which is determined as a percentage of the par value of the preferred stock. Preferred stock is valued similarly to bonds and is subject to many of the same risks as bonds. Some preferred stocks have mandatory redemption dates that occur 30 years or more after issuance; however, most bonds typically mature within 30 years. Some preferred stocks have no redemption features, similar to common stocks, and continue for the life of the company unless retired.

Ownership Investments in Real Estate

Real estate is another type of ownership asset that is valuable to investors. Stocks, bonds, money market securities, and derivatives are all intangible financial assets, whereas real estate is a tangible asset. Investments in real estate are characterized by the following attributes:

- Each parcel of land or real estate is unique in its location and composition

- Real estate is immovable

- Land is virtually indestructible

- Limited supply

Real estate investment trust (REIT)

A form of indirect ownership of real estate that invests in real estate, short-term construction loans, and mortgages

An investor can choose from a variety of real estate investments, including residential real estate, commercial real estate, partnerships and limited partnerships, developed land, undeveloped land, and **real estate investment trusts** (REITs). REITs invest in real estate, short-term construction loans, and mortgages. Like closed-end companies, some REITs are publicly traded on the exchanges and can sell at premiums or discounts to net asset value. As a result, the REIT investor achieves diversification and marketability that is generally lacking with a real estate limited partnership. The advantages of investing in real estate include the generation of cash flow, depreciation deductions, and low correlation to other asset classes.

Derivatives

Derivatives

Securities whose value is based on the value of some other security

Derivatives are securities whose value is based on the value of some other security. For example, an ABC option contract will derive its value from the value of ABC stock. Changes in the value of ABC stock will cause the associated option contract to also change in value.

Options

Options

Derivatives that give the holder, or buyer, the right to sell or purchase the underlying asset

Call option

A derivative that gives the holder the right to purchase the underlying asset, generally a stock, at a specified price within a specified period

Put option

A derivative that gives the holder the right to sell the underlying asset, generally a stock, at a specified price within a specified period

Exercise price

The price at which an underlying stock may be sold (put) or purchased (call) by the holder of an option

Premium

The cost of an option contract

Options are derivatives that give the holder, or buyer, the right to sell or purchase the underlying asset. **Call options** give the holder the right to purchase the underlying asset, generally a stock, at a specified price within a specified period.

Put options give the holder the right to sell the underlying asset, generally a stock, at a specified price within a specified period. Options can be either bought or sold (also referred to as "written"). Therefore, there are four unique positions that an investor can take with an option: to buy a call option, to sell (write) a call option, to buy a put option, or to sell (write) a put option. However, investors will often combine multiple option positions or combine an option position with a stock position to create different risk-return characteristics.

The **exercise price** of an option contract is the price at which the underlying stock may be sold (put) or purchased (call) by the holder of the option. The **premium** for any option is simply the cost of the option contract. The premium is generally impacted by the following factors: the price of the underlying security, the exercise price of the underlying security, the time until the option expires, the volatility of the underlying security, and the risk-free rate of return. Each option contract represents 100 shares of the underlying stock.

What are the reasons that an investor might enter into an option contract? As with most derivatives, options can be used for specific purposes or simply as a leveraged investment. Investors who believe that the underlying security is going to appreciate may purchase call options. Investors will generally sell call options when they believe that the underlying security is going to remain flat or decline in value. Often, when an investor is holding a long position in a stock that has appreciated rapidly within a short period of time, the investor will sell (write) a call option to generate the premium for additional income.

Put options are often purchased to establish a floor or to protect against a decline in the value of a long position in a stock. For example, an investor might own ABC stock and be concerned that it is overvalued. In this case, the investor might purchase a put option at a level slightly below the current market price. In the event that the stock decreased in value, the investor could sell the stock at the exercise price. In other words, a put option provides downside protection by establishing the minimum price at which the investor will be able to sell the ABC stock.

Put options can be sold by an investor to generate an option premium for a stock that the investor believes will increase in price and that he may own or wish to own. If the investor is correct and the stock does increase, the investor will receive the option premium as income. In the event that the stock goes down and someone puts the stock to the investor (forces the investor to purchase the stock), the investor probably will still believe that the stock was a good stock to own. A summary of the maximum economic gain and loss, with respect to basic option positions, is shown in Exhibit 12.5.

EXHIBIT 12.5 Options: Maximum Gain or Loss

Option Position	Maximum Gain	Maximum Loss
Buy Call	Unlimited	Amount of premium paid
Buy Put	Exercise price less amount of premium paid	Amount of premium paid
Write Call	Amount of premium received	Unlimited (if naked)
Write Put	Amount of premium received	Exercise price less amount of premium received

LEAPS

Long-term Equity Anticipation Securities (LEAPS) are long-term options that allow investors to establish positions that can be maintained for up to three years. LEAPS provide investors with a longer term view of the market as a whole or on an individual stock. LEAPS can be purchased on a limited number of individual stocks and indexes. Equity LEAPS can provide long-term stock market investors an opportunity to benefit from the growth of large capitalization companies without having to directly purchase the stock.

Long-term Equity Anticipation Securities (LEAPS)
Long-term options that generally have expiration dates of up to three years

Warrants

Similar to a call option, a **warrant** is essentially a long-term call option giving the owner the right to purchase the stock of the issuing corporation. Warrants give the owner the right to purchase a specified number of common stock shares for a specified period of time at a specified price. A warrant has the following characteristics which differentiate it from a call option:

Warrants
A long-term, customized call option to purchase the stock of a given corporation within a specified period of time

- A warrant is issued by a corporation, whereas a call is written by an individual

- A warrant is customized to fit the needs of the issuing corporation and owner, whereas a call includes standardized terms

- A warrant typically has a maturity date of at least several years, whereas a call generally has an expiry date of no more than nine months

If corporations issue warrants, they usually do so in conjunction with a new bond issue or preferred stock issue. These warrants give the bond or stock purchaser a sweetener or equity kicker, making the particular issue more attractive to buyers. As a result, issuing the bond or preferred stock with a warrant will typically permit the issuer to lower the coupon or dividend rate on the offering.

Futures

Futures contract
An agreement between two parties to make or take delivery of a specified amount of a commodity or financial asset at a future time, place, and unit price

Unlike options, which give the holder a right to purchase or sell a specific security, a **futures contract** is an agreement to transact something in the future. Generally, purchasing (selling) a futures contract obligates the buyer (seller) to take delivery (make delivery) of a specific commodity at a specific time in the future. Because a futures contract is an agreement to make or take delivery in the future, the investor will be required to put up a good faith deposit, known as an initial margin, until the agreement is fulfilled.

Over time, the futures contract, which is required to be marked to the market on a daily basis, will generate gains and losses. Each of these daily gains and losses will either add to or reduce the initial margin. If the initial amount put up is reduced to a level below the maintenance margin, the investor will be required to restore the initial margin. Both the initial margin percentage and the maintenance margin amount are set at the inception of the contract.

Speculators and hedgers use futures contracts for different reasons. Speculators use futures contracts as a leveraged investment. Government studies have suggested that approximately 90% of individual investors who speculate in futures lose money. The majority of these investors invest in futures contracts only once. Unlike speculators, hedgers use futures contracts to reduce or offset certain risks.

For example, farmers who sell commodities, such as cotton, are concerned about decreasing commodity prices. To offset this risk, farmers can sell futures contracts to ensure that the cotton produced sells at a specific price. This type of hedge, referred to as a short hedge, protects against decreasing prices.

Other investors who hedge using futures contracts include manufacturers who use commodities as raw material. For example, if a furniture manufacturer is concerned about rising lumber prices, the manufacturer might purchase lumber futures contracts to lock in the price at which he will buy lumber in the future. This type of hedge, referred to as a long hedge, protects against rising prices. The following table summarizes the two types of hedge positions.

Hedger	Cash Position	Hedge Needed	Action
Grower	Long	Short	Sell futures contracts
Manufacturer	Short	Long	Buy futures contracts

In general, derivatives provide investors with a variety of speculative and hedging strategies that would not be available using traditional investment alternatives and allow for a more complete market.

Tangible Assets

These investments take the form of either collectibles or, sometimes, precious metals (e.g., gold or silver). Collectibles (e.g., baseball cards) may provide the dual benefits of maintaining a collection and possible capital appreciation. However, the collectibles market is inefficient and is characterized by an inherent lack of liquidity. Alternatively, precious metals derive their value from factors that are external to the financial markets (e.g., with the purchase of gold, an investor's fear of inflation). As a result, the price of precious metals often moves inversely (i.e., has a negative correlation) with the prices of stocks. Therefore, investing in gold bullion or silver may be used as a hedge against a declining, or bearish, stock market.

Natural Resources

An investment in natural resources includes an investment in oil and gas properties or timber lands. There are three ways to invest in natural resources:

- Direct investing in the properties or lands via (typically) a limited partnership

- Investing in the stock of companies who develop the natural resources

- Investing in mutual funds that specialize in natural resources

A major advantage of investing in natural resources is the pass-through of certain tax benefits, such as deductions for depletion and/or intangible drilling costs. Natural resources also have historically exhibited some negative correlation with that of financial assets (stocks and bonds). However, a major disadvantage of such an investment is the higher degree of risk, particularly if the activity involves exploratory drilling for oil wells.

MEASURES OF RISK

We defined risk earlier in the chapter as the probability of an adverse result. In the field of investments and financial planning, risk is generally measured in terms of volatility.

Beta

Beta

A commonly used measure of systematic risk that is derived from regression analysis

Beta is a commonly used measure of risk derived from regression analysis. Beta measures systematic risk and provides an indication of the volatility of a portfolio compared to the market. The market is defined as having a beta of 1.0. Portfolios with a beta greater than 1.0 are more volatile than the market, whereas portfolios with a beta less than 1.0 are less volatile than the market. A portfolio with a beta of 1.5 is considered to be 50% more volatile than the market. Similarly, a portfolio with a beta of 0.7 is considered to be 30% less volatile than the market.

Because beta only measures systematic risk, it is a good measure of risk for fully diversified portfolios. Diversified portfolios have minimal unsystematic risk, which means that beta is capturing the majority of the risk of the portfolio. However, when the diversification of the portfolio is low and the portfolio has a substantial amount of unsystematic risk, beta does not capture all of the volatility within the portfolio. Beta is more appropriate for portfolios and mutual funds that are well-diversified and, therefore, highly correlated to the market.

Standard Deviation

Standard deviation

Measures both total volatility and total risk (systematic and unsystematic risk) of the portfolio

Unlike beta, **standard deviation** measures a portfolio's total risk (volatility). Standard deviation is a statistical measure of how far actual returns deviate from the mean (average) return.

Normal Probability Distribution

A normal probability distribution is characterized by a single peak in the center, which is the location of the arithmetic mean of the series of observations. The series of observations, normally referred to as a bell curve, implies a 50% chance that an observation selected at random will fall to the right of the mean and a 50% chance that it will fall to the left of the mean. A bell curve is illustrated in Exhibit 12.6.

EXHIBIT 12.6 Normal Probability Distribution

Normal curve is symmetrical

Mean, median, and mode are equal

EXHIBIT 12.7 Area Under the Curve

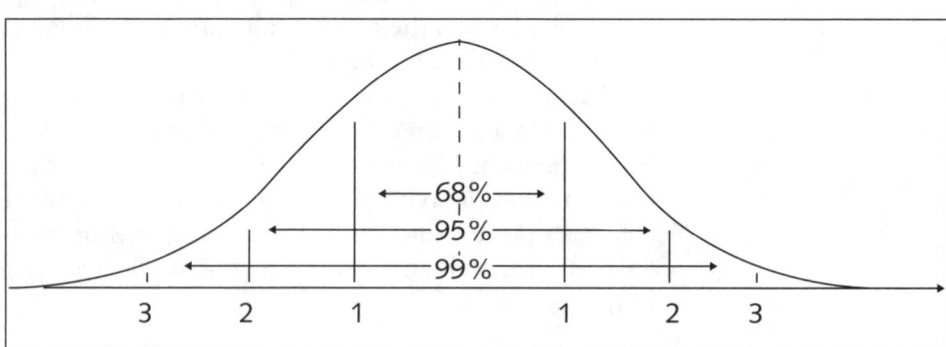

When interpreting standard deviation, a return (observation) will occur 68% of the time within one standard deviation of the mean, 95% of the time within two standard deviations of the mean, and 99% of the time within three standard deviations of the mean as shown in Exhibit 12.7. Returns falling outside of three standard deviations are considered outliers.

Semivariance

Semivariance

Measures the variability of returns that fall below the average or expected return

Semivariance is another statistical measure of risk. In contrast to standard deviation, semivariance only considers the downside risk of an investment. Specifically, semivariance measures the variability of returns that fall below the average or expected return.

Critics of standard deviation state that investors do not complain, nor are they concerned, about volatility above the average return. Rather, investors are only concerned about volatility below the average return. Therefore, a portfolio manager with a large standard deviation may be punished for having superior positive returns. Semivariance attempts to correct for this perceived flaw by only considering returns and volatility below the expected or average return.

▌ MEASURES OF RETURN

Financial advisors and planners use a variety of measures of return, including, but not limited to, holding period return, arithmetic mean, geometric mean, internal rate of return, and real rate of return. Each of these calculations of return has certain advantages and disadvantages.

Simple Rate of Return

A **simple rate of return** for an investment is calculated by dividing its total return (income earned plus capital appreciation divided by the original investment) by the number of years that the investor has held the asset. This computation results in an annualized noncompounded rate of return.

E X A M P L E   Eugene owned an investment that generated a total return of 25% over the past five years. His simple rate of return is 5% (25% ÷ 5).

Compound Rate of Return

The **compound rate of return** computation for an investment assumes that all interim proceeds, such as interest and repayment of principal, are reinvested (thereby generating additional return) over the holding period. This return is easily calculated with a financial calculator using the time-value-of-money keys or the uneven-cash-flow and net-present-value keys.

E X A M P L E   Allison deposits $1,000 in a one-year CD that pays an annual interest rate of 3% compounded monthly. She will have a total of $1,030.42 ($1,000 +/–PV; 1 × 12 N; 3 ÷ 12 I/YR; solve for FV) in her account at the end of the year. Therefore, Allison's compound rate of return is 3.04% ($1,000 +/–PV; $1,030.42 FV; 1 N; solve for I/YR).

Annual Percentage Rate and Effective Annual Rate

The nominal **annual percentage rate (APR)** is the yearly cost of funds expressed as a percentage. However, the nominal APR does not take compounding into consideration. If a lender advertises a 1.25% monthly rate, the APR is 15% (1.25% × 12).

The **effective annual rate (EAR)** is the annual percentage rate taking into consideration the impact of compounding. This calculation provides the annual rate of interest of an investment or debt when compounding occurs more than once per year.

$$EAR = [1 + (i \div n)]^n - 1$$

i = annual interest rate
n = number of periods

If an investor has a certificate of deposit paying monthly interest based on annual rate of 1.75%, the effective annual rate will be more than 1.75% due to the effect of compounding. This is a result of a greater principal onto which the interest is calculated each month. The resulting effective annual rate is 1.77%.

E X A M P L E   Janine carries a balance on her credit card. The nominal APR is 14.99% compounded daily. The effective annual rate is actually 16.17%, calculated as follows:

$$EAR = [1 + (.1499 \div 365)]^{365} - 1 = .1617, \text{ or } \mathbf{16.17\%}$$

Holding Period Return

Holding period return
Measures the total return an investor receives over a specific time period

The **holding period return** (HPR) measures the total return an investor receives from an investment over a specific time period.

$$HPR = \frac{\text{ending value of investment} - \text{beginning value of investment} +/- \text{cash flows}}{\text{beginning value of investment}}$$

E X A M P L E   Glen purchased a stock for $50 per share. Later, he sells the stock for $75 per share. During his period of ownership, the stock paid dividends of $10. The holding period return equals 70% as follows:

$$HPR = \frac{\$75 - \$50 + \$10}{\$50} = 70\%$$

Is 70% an acceptable return? At first, you might think that a 70% return is great. However, we have no idea how long the investment was held. Therefore, there is no way to compare an HPR to other alternative investments, such as the risk-free rate of return. Because the HPR ignores the time value of money, it is not commonly used as a return measure.

Arithmetic Mean

Arithmetic mean
A measure of investment return that is the result of averaging periodic returns

The **arithmetic mean** is a measure of investment return that is the result of averaging periodic returns.

E X A M P L E   Assume a client had the following returns for four consecutive years:

Year	Return
1	12%
2	3%
3	10%
4	15%

The arithmetic mean equals 10%, calculated as follows:

$$AM = \frac{12\% + 3\% + 10\% + 15\%}{4} = 10\%$$

Geometric Mean

Geometric mean
A method of calculating the internal rate of return based on periodic rates of return

The **geometric mean** is a method of calculating the internal rate of return based on periodic rates of return.

E X A M P L E   Assume a client had the following returns for four consecutive years (same example as above):

Year	Return
1	12%
2	3%
3	10%
4	15%

The geometric mean equals 9.91%, calculated as follows:

PV = –1

FV = (1 + .12)(1 + .03)(1 + .10)(1 + .15) = 1.4593

n = 4

Solve for i = 9.91%

Using the same series of returns (12%, 3%, 10%, and 15%) has resulted in a different outcome for the arithmetic mean and the geometric mean. This difference is a result of the geometric mean taking into consideration the compounding of the investment returns over time.

In this case, the geometric mean is less than the arithmetic mean. Will this always be the case? No, but the geometric mean will always be less than or equal to the arithmetic mean. They will be equal only when the periodic returns are identical. The difference between the two measures will increase as the volatility in returns increases.

E X A M P L E   John invests $100 at the beginning of the year. At the end of the year, his investment is worth $200. At the end of the following year, his investment is worth $100. The returns for the two years are as follows:

Year	Beginning of the Year	End of the Year	Rate of Return
1	$100	$200	100%
2	$200	$100	–50%

The arithmetic mean equals 25%, calculated as follows:

$$AM = \frac{100\% - 50\%}{2} = 25\%$$

The geometric mean equals 0.00%, calculated as follows:

PV = –$100
FV = $100
n = 2
i = 0%

Obviously, a big difference exists between a 25% return and a 0% return. Therefore, the arithmetic mean is not as practical for evaluating investment returns as the geometric mean.

Internal Rate of Return

Internal rate of return
A measure of return that equates discounted future cash flows to the present value of an asset

Internal rate of return (IRR) is one of the most common measures of return. This measure equates discounted future cash flows to the present value of an asset. Consider the basic present value model:

$$PV = \frac{CF_1}{(1+r)^1} + \frac{CF_2}{(1+r)^2} + \cdots + \frac{CF_n}{(1+r)^n}$$

PV = Present value of future cash flows

CF_n = Cash flows for period n

n = Number of cash flows in the analysis

r = Internal rate of return

An important assumption of this model is that any cash flows that occur before the end of the investment will be reinvested at the IRR. If these cash flows are not reinvested at the IRR, the actual return received will be different than expected.

E X A M P L E   A bond selling at par ($1,000) with an annual coupon rate of 10% (coupon payments of $100) will have an IRR of 10%. If the annual coupon payments of $100 are reinvested at a rate of return of 10%, the actual return received by the investor will be 10%. However, if the coupon payments are invested at a rate of return less (or greater) than 10%, the actual return the investor receives will be less (or greater) than 10%. This is an example of reinvestment rate risk.

Real Rate of Return

Nominal return
The stated return from an investment

Real rate of return
The nominal rate of return adjusted for inflation

As discussed earlier in the chapter, inflation erodes returns and the purchasing power of assets. Therefore, financial planners should understand both nominal returns and real returns. The **nominal return** is the stated return from the investment. The **real rate of return**, sometimes referred to as the inflation-adjusted rate of return, is the nominal return adjusted for inflation.

$$\text{Real return} = \left[\frac{(1+R_n)}{(1+I)} - 1 \right] \times 100$$

R_n = nominal rate of return

I = rate of inflation

E X A M P L E　Renee owns a corporate bond with a coupon rate of 6.00%. If the annual inflation rate is 3.5%, her real rate of return on the bond is 2.42%, calculated as follows:

$$\left[\frac{(1+0.06)}{(1+0.035)}-1\right]\times100=(1.0242-1)\times100=2.4155 \ \ (\text{rounded to } 2.42)$$

MODERN PORTFOLIO THEORY

> **Modern portfolio theory (MPT)**
> A theory created by Harry Markowitz that describes portfolio diversification gained by combining securities with varying characteristics

The familiar adage, "Don't put all your eggs in one basket" reminds us that it is safer to spread your risk around than to concentrate in one area. This simple truth is especially applicable to investing. Investors diversify risk by investing in more than one security and more than one asset class. Through diversification, investors are able to reduce the risk of their investment portfolios. Diversification involves the acquisition of assets that have different risk characteristics in order to mitigate portfolio risk.

The reason diversification works is that unsystematic risks can be minimized by adding additional securities to the portfolio. Similarly, adding additional asset classes to a portfolio can minimize or reduce the unique risks associated with a specific asset class.

Modern portfolio theory (MPT) is based on this diversification process. Harry Markowitz, considered the father of MPT, developed this theory using the following assumptions:

- Investors consider each investment opportunity as being represented by a probability distribution of expected returns over a specified holding period

- Investors estimate the risk of the portfolio on the basis of the variability of returns

- Investors base decisions solely on expected return and risk; therefore, their indifference curves are a function of expected return and the expected variance of returns only

- Investors base their indifference to alternative investments on the maximization of wealth over a specified period, and this indifference diminishes as they get beyond this period

- For a given level of risk, investors prefer higher returns to lower returns

Efficient Frontier

> **Efficient frontier**
> Consists of investment portfolios with the highest expected return for a given level of risk

Markowitz found that by combining different asset classes and varying the weightings of each asset class, he could create portfolios that had higher returns with less volatility (risk). Markowitz used standard deviation (σ) as a measure of risk. The portfolios that had the highest expected return [E(r)] for the given level of risk referred to as efficient portfolios. By combining these efficient portfolios, he created the **efficient frontier**.

EXHIBIT 12.8 The Efficient Frontier

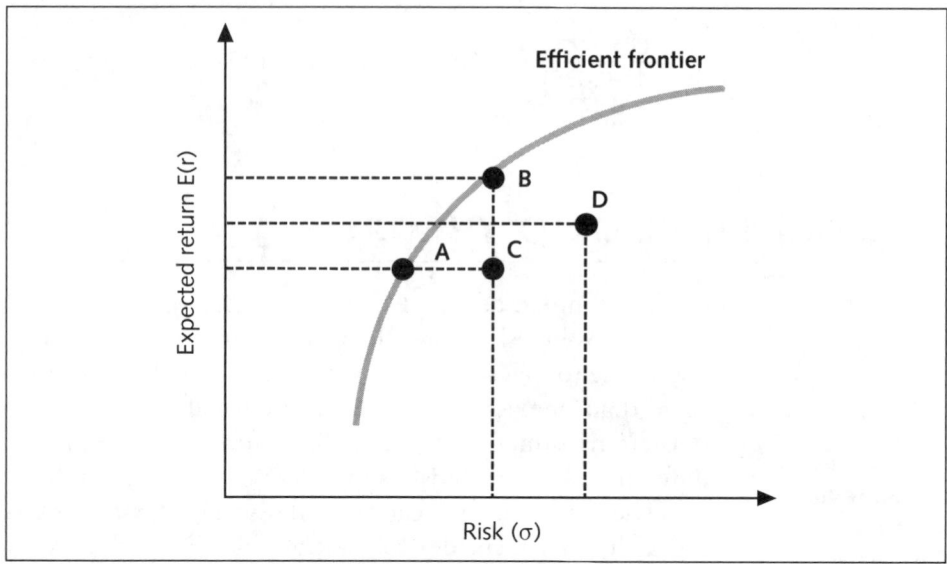

The efficient frontier consists of portfolios with the highest expected return for a given level of risk. Notice in Exhibit 12.8 above that only portfolios A and B are efficient portfolios. Portfolio A is more efficient than Portfolio C because it has the same expected return with less risk. Portfolio B is more efficient than Portfolio C because it has a much higher expected return for the same level of risk. Portfolio B is also more efficient than Portfolio D because B has a higher expected return and less risk. Markowitz came up with the following three rules for choosing efficient portfolios:

- For any two portfolios with the same expected return, choose the one with the lower risk

- For any two portfolios with the same risk, choose the one with the higher expected return

- Choose any portfolio that has a higher expected return and lower risk

Portfolios C and D are inefficient because they have not maximized the return for a given level of risk. Portfolios do not exist above the efficient frontier because the efficient frontier consists of the most efficient portfolios (portfolios of assets with the highest expected return for a given level of risk).

Each risk-averse investor (a fundamental assumption of modern portfolio theory) will choose to establish a portfolio lying somewhere on this efficient frontier by implementing her own set of indifference curves. **Indifference curves,** which graphically represent the risk-reward trade-off that the investor is willing to make, will cross the efficient frontier in two locations, lie tangent to the efficient frontier, or not intersect the efficient frontier at all. The portfolio that lies at the point of tangency is the optimal portfolio for the investor. The efficient frontier, investor's indifference curves, and an optimal portfolio are illustrated in Exhibit 12.9.

Indifference curves

A graphical representation of the risk-reward trade-off that an investor is willing to make

EXHIBIT 12.9 Indifference Curves

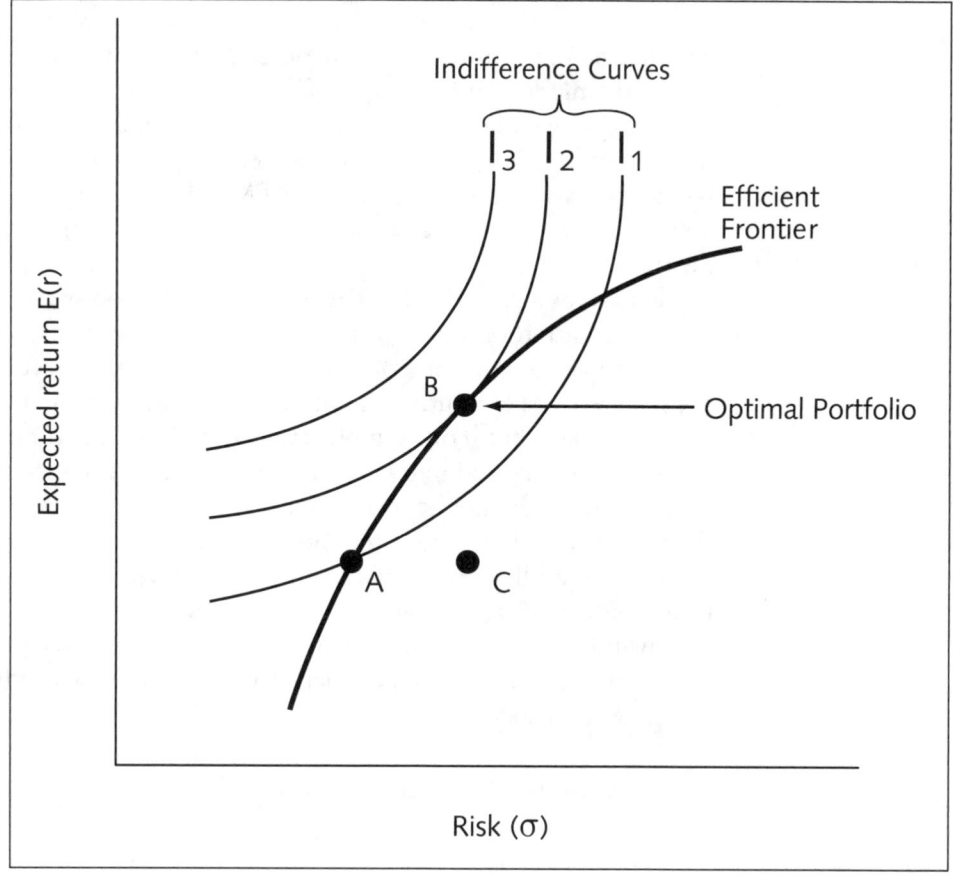

Markowitz developed a model to estimate the efficient frontier by using security standard deviations, correlation coefficients, and expected returns in calculating the standard deviation of a multiasset portfolio and the expected return of a portfolio.

These calculations are the foundation for most of the asset allocation software packages used by financial planners. The purpose of these software packages is to build an investment portfolio capable of accomplishing the goals of the client, while matching the level of risk in the portfolio to the investor's risk tolerance. Most financial planners who provide investment counseling use some type of mean-variance optimization software to determine an optimum portfolio or asset allocation based on a client's goals, risk tolerance, time horizon, tax situation, and economic forecasts.

The goal in using these software packages is to build an efficient portfolio for the client. Remember that an efficient portfolio is one that has the highest level of return (in practice, the return should be an after-tax return) for the given level of risk.

Capital Asset Pricing Model

Capital asset pricing model (CAPM)

An asset pricing model that developed from Markowitz's efficient frontier and from the introduction of a risk-free asset

The **capital asset pricing model** (CAPM) is an asset pricing model that was developed from Markowitz's efficient frontier and from the introduction of a risk-free asset.

$$r_i = r_f + (r_m - r_f)\beta_i$$

r_i = expected return for a stock
r_m = market rate of return
r_f = risk-free rate of return
β_i = beta, measures systematic risk of a particular stock

This model is actually made up of two separate components. One component is known as the *stock risk premium* and is the part of the model reflected by the following formula: $(r_m - r_f)\beta_i$, where r_m is the market return, r_f is the risk-free return, and β_i is the beta coefficient of the stock. The other component is the *market risk premium* and is the part of the model reflected by the following formula: $r_m - r_f$, where r_m is the market return and r_f is the risk-free return. The stock risk premium may compel the individual to invest in a particular stock, whereas the market risk premium provides incentive to invest in the securities market in general. The CAPM accounts for the impact of systematic risk only and does not take into consideration unsystematic risk, which is assumed to have been diversified away.

Finally, as a part of MPT, the major contribution of the CAPM to investment theory was the creation of a quantitative investment risk measure and a statistical association with the investment's rate of return. Specifically, the CAPM allows analysts to compute the required rate of return for an investment and compare it to the expected rate of return for that investment. For example, if the CAPM required rate of return is higher than the investment's expected rate of return, all other investment considerations being equal, the investment should not be made. Conversely, if the CAPM required rate of return is lower than the investment's expected rate of return, a decision to invest is warranted.

As you recall from the discussion of Markowitz, any portfolio that lies on the efficient frontier is considered an efficient portfolio, and thus, it has the highest level of return for the given level of risk. However, by introducing a risk-free asset (r_f), a new set of portfolios can be created that is more efficient than the Markowitz efficient frontier. Exhibit 12.10 illustrates this concept.

EXHIBIT 12.10   Capital Market Line

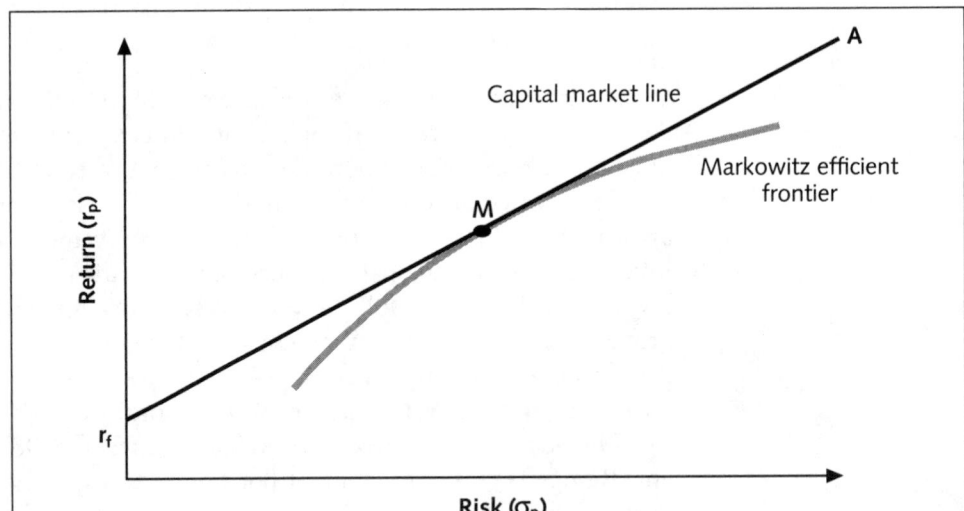

The capital market line (CML) is the new efficient frontier. However, instead of providing a maximum return, as did the efficient frontier of Markowitz, the CML provides an expected return based on the level of risk. The equation for the CML is written as follows:

$$r_p = r_f + \sigma_p \left[\frac{r_m - r_f}{\sigma_m} \right]$$

r_p = expected return of the portfolio
r_f = risk-free rate of return
r_m = market rate of return
σ_m = standard deviation of the market
σ_p = standard deviation of the portfolio

The CML provides an expected return for a portfolio based on the expected return of the market, the risk-free rate of return, and the standard deviation of the portfolio in relation to the standard deviation of the market. The CML is generally used to evaluate diversified portfolios. The security market line (SML), which is derived from the CML and is the same as the CAPM, allows us to evaluate individual securities for use in a diversified portfolio.

The SML is written as follows:

$$r_i = r_f + (r_m - r_f)\beta_i$$

r_i = expected return for asset i
r_f = risk-free rate of return
r_m = market rate of return
β_i = beta of asset i

The security market line determines the expected return for an asset (r_i) on the basis of its beta and the expectations about the market and the risk-free rate.

E X A M P L E If the beta of ABC Company is 1.2 and the market return is expected to be 13% with a risk-free return of 3%, then the expected return of ABC is 15%, as follows:

$r_i = r_f + (r_m - r_f)\beta_i$

$r_i = 0.03 + 1.2 (0.13 - 0.03) = 0.15$, or 15%

Therefore, on the basis of the level of systematic risk of ABC Company, the stock should earn a return of 15%. The SML helps identify how the characteristics of a portfolio will be impacted when a security is added to the portfolio.

Asset Allocation

Asset allocation
The distribution of investments in a portfolio by asset class

The primary purpose of a mean-variance optimization model is to determine an efficient allocation for an investor's portfolio based on the goals of the client and tolerance for risk. An **asset allocation** is the specific distribution of investment asset classes within a portfolio. By including a target asset allocation in an Investment Policy Statement (IPS), the financial planner presents an investor with a guide as to how much of the portfolio should be invested in each asset class. Exhibit 12.11 illustrates three possible asset allocations: one for a conservative investor, one for a moderate investor, and one for an aggressive investor.

EXHIBIT 12.11 Sample Asset Allocations

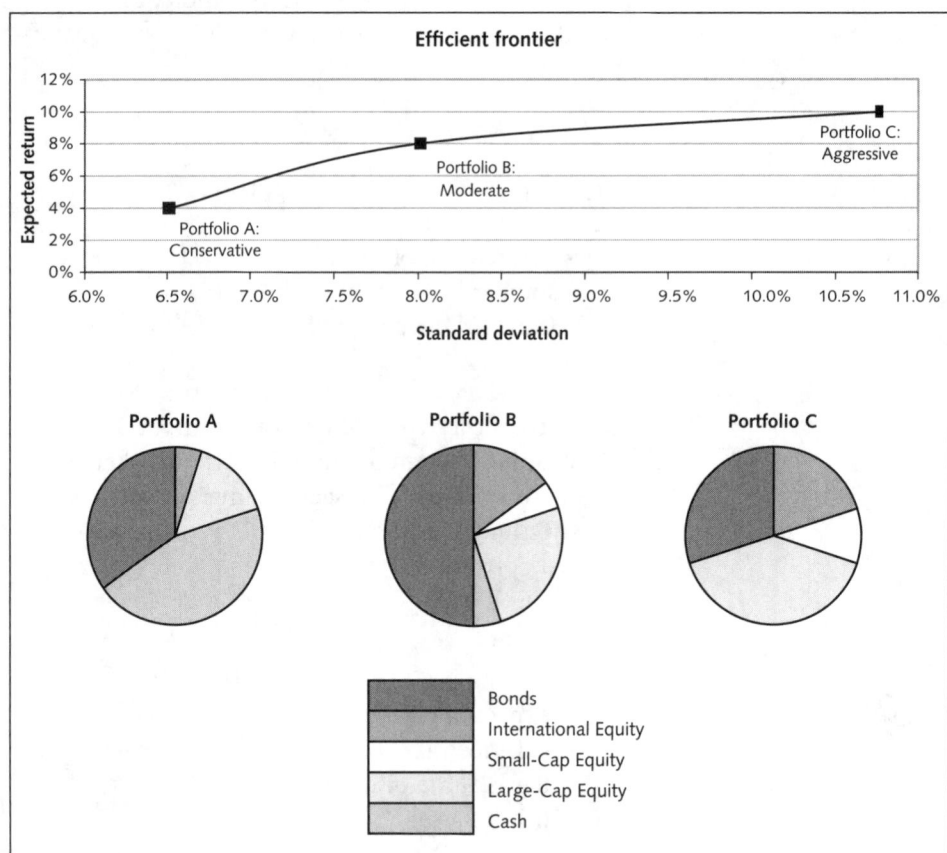

Strategic Asset Allocation

The purpose of strategic asset allocation is to determine an appropriate allocation based on the long-term financial goals of the client. Accordingly, the risk tolerance of the client is assessed in conjunction with the current phase of the client's life cycle. When implementing a strategic asset allocation, once the allocation is determined, it remains constant until (typically) some life-changing event occurs. Because the investment performance of the selected asset classes is different, rebalancing must take place to bring the portfolio in line with the strategic mix. However, changing market conditions play a small role in determining the appropriate asset mix.

Tactical Asset Allocation

In contrast to the strategic approach, tactical asset allocation (TAA) continuously adjusts the asset allocation and class mix in an attempt to take advantage of changing market conditions and overall investor sentiment. When implementing a TAA, portfolio adjustments are driven solely by perceived changes in the market values of the asset classes, and little consideration is given to the long-term financial goals of the client. In essence, TAA is a market timing portfolio management approach that is intended to take advantage of perceived market inefficiencies (and opportunities for investor profit).

Selection of a Type of Asset Allocation

The type of asset allocation to use likely depends on the investor's or manager's portfolio management style. Certainly, an investor or manager who believes in active portfolio management (and that the market is inherently inefficient) will tend towards tactical asset allocation. Alternatively, an investor or manager who adopts more of a long-term buy-and-hold strategy (passive management style) will find strategic asset allocation to be preferable. Above all, a thoughtful analysis of these asset allocation techniques, that accounts for both one's time horizon and investment preferences, serves as a key factor impacting long-term portfolio performance and, therefore, is of the highest importance to financial planners, managers, and investors.

Asset Allocation Using Mutual Funds

Research (by Brinson, Hood, Beebower, 1986, and Vanguard, 2003) has shown that asset allocation is the most important factor in determining long-term variation (risk) in portfolio returns. According to their studies, asset allocation may account for more than 90% of such variation. Obviously, asset allocation is an important facet of the investment planning process. How, then, can mutual funds be used in implementing such an asset allocation strategy?

Early in the investment planning process, the financial planner, together with the client, identifies the client's goals, objectives, and risk tolerance. Once these have been determined, the planner will often help the client select an appropriate asset allocation. In other words, the planner assists the client in determining what portion of the client's assets should be invested in cash, fixed-income investments, equity investments, real estate, international investments, and so on. The asset allocation decision usually involves a narrowing process, in which the allocation to fixed-income investments is separated into municipal (tax-free) versus taxable and an appropriate average duration is chosen. Similarly, the equity portion of the portfolio will be subdivided into core, value, and growth investment styles and then separated into large, mid, and small capitalization equities. International investments are generally separated into large capitalization or emerging markets and could be divided into different regions or countries around the world.

EXAMPLE James and Stacey, ages 40 and 37, respectively, would like to develop an investment plan for their retirement. Assume that after evaluating the timing of their goal and through discussions with them, their financial planner classifies them as moderately aggressive investors. Also, assume that an appropriate asset allocation for them is a portfolio that is 80% equity (60% domestic equities and 20% foreign equities) and 20% fixed-income investments, with no allocation to cash or money markets. The allocation might be further divided as shown in the following table.

Equities		Fixed Income	
Large-cap value	10%	Taxable fixed income	8%
Large-cap core	20%	Municipal fixed income	8%
Large-cap growth	10%	Foreign fixed income	4%
Mid-cap growth	10%		
Small-cap growth	10%		
Large-cap foreign	20%		
Total equity allocation	80%	Total fixed-income allocation	20%

The above asset allocation provides James and Stacey with an investment portfolio that is heavily weighted toward equity investments. This equity allocation is divided between domestic and foreign and between large, mid, and small capitalization securities. The fixed-income allocation is also divided between domestic and foreign, as well as taxable and municipal (nontaxable).

Once the asset allocation decision has been made, mutual funds can be used as the vehicle to implement the investment plan. Planners and investors should select mutual funds that are consistent with the concepts and underlying assumptions of the asset allocation process. Specifically, an asset allocation for a client's portfolio should be derived through a **mean-variance optimization model** to determine the highest level of return (based on combinations of asset classes and different weightings of asset classes) for a specified level of risk. This level of risk is generally the client's risk level or risk tolerance.

Mean-variance optimization model
Used to determine the highest level of return (based on combinations of asset classes and different weightings of asset classes) for a specified level of risk tolerance

A mean-variance optimization model generally uses all of the following inputs for each asset class represented in the model:

- Historical return or expected return for each asset class

- Standard deviation of each asset class (historical or expected)

- Correlation coefficients (historical or expected) for each asset class compared to all other asset classes

Most of the time, these inputs for the asset classes are derived from indexes that represent the asset class. For example, the large-cap equity asset class is usually represented by the S&P 500 Index. Small-cap equities are often represented by the Russell 2000® Index, and fixed-income securities may be represented by one of the J.P. Morgan Indices.

Because the assumptions used in the model are derived from indexes, selected funds should have characteristics consistent with the index they are representing. This means that if there is an allocation to the large-cap growth-asset class, then the fund selected to represent this asset class should have risk and return characteristics consistent with that index. However, this does not mean that index funds are the only choice for implementing an asset allocation strategy because all highly correlated funds deserve investment consideration.

As with all facets of financial planning, the investment planning process is not complete at implementation. The portfolio selections and allocations must be monitored on a continual basis to ensure that the quality of the investments has not changed and that the allocations and risk tolerance of the client have not significantly changed. This monitoring process generally includes quarterly, semiannual, or annual performance measurement reports and subsequent client meetings.

An investment performance report should include sufficient information to determine whether the investment portfolio has performed as intended and what, if any, changes should be made to the investment portfolio. The report should indicate the return for the overall portfolio, as well as the return for each asset class. These returns should be reported for the recent quarter and the past year, three-year, and five-year periods (if available). Each of these returns should be compared to an appropriate benchmark to determine the performance of the fund or investment.

In addition to return information, performance reports should provide the investor with information about the risk characteristics of the overall portfolio. This includes measures for standard deviation and, possibly, beta.

DIVERSIFICATION

As previously discussed, the goal of diversification is to reduce unsystematic risk within a portfolio. Diversification is achieved by structuring an individual's investment portfolio with an appropriate combination of aggressive, moderate, and conservative investments.

Covariance

Covariance
A measure of the extent to which two variables move in a predictable manner to one another, either positively or negatively

Covariance, which is a nonstandardized version of the correlation coefficient, measures the extent to which two variables move in a predictable manner to one another, either positively or negatively. If two assets move together simultaneously, either up or down, they have perfect positive covariance. Conversely, if the assets move exactly opposite one another, they exhibit perfect negative covariance. Finally, if the assets move in completely independent directions, their covariance is zero. The range for covariance is negative infinity to positive infinity. A drawback of covariance is that there are no boundaries within which to measure the relationship between two stocks. The concept of covariance is the key to minimizing the standard deviation of an overall portfolio and, therefore, managing risk.

Correlation Coefficient

Correlation coefficient (R)
A statistical measure of the direction and strength of the relationship between two sets of data

The **correlation coefficient**, generally denoted by the symbol **R**, is a statistical measure generated from a regression analysis that provides insight into the relationship between two securities, two portfolios, or two indexes. The correlation coefficient indicates the direction of the relationship between the two indexes or securities and the strength between the two items. The correlation coefficient ranges between +1.0 and –1.0. At +1.0, there is perfect positive correlation between the two items. In other words, the two items will move together over time. At –1.0, there is perfect negative correlation between the two items. The two items will move in opposite directions over time. At a correlation of zero, there is no relationship between the two items and they will move independent of each other. Exhibit 12.12 depicts these relationships.

The correlation coefficient is key to the concept of asset allocation. When the correlation coefficient between two asset classes is less than 1.0, combining the asset classes will reduce the overall risk of the investment portfolio. The lower the correlation, the lower the standard deviation of the combined portfolio and, therefore, the lower the risk.

EXHIBIT 12.12 Correlation Coefficient

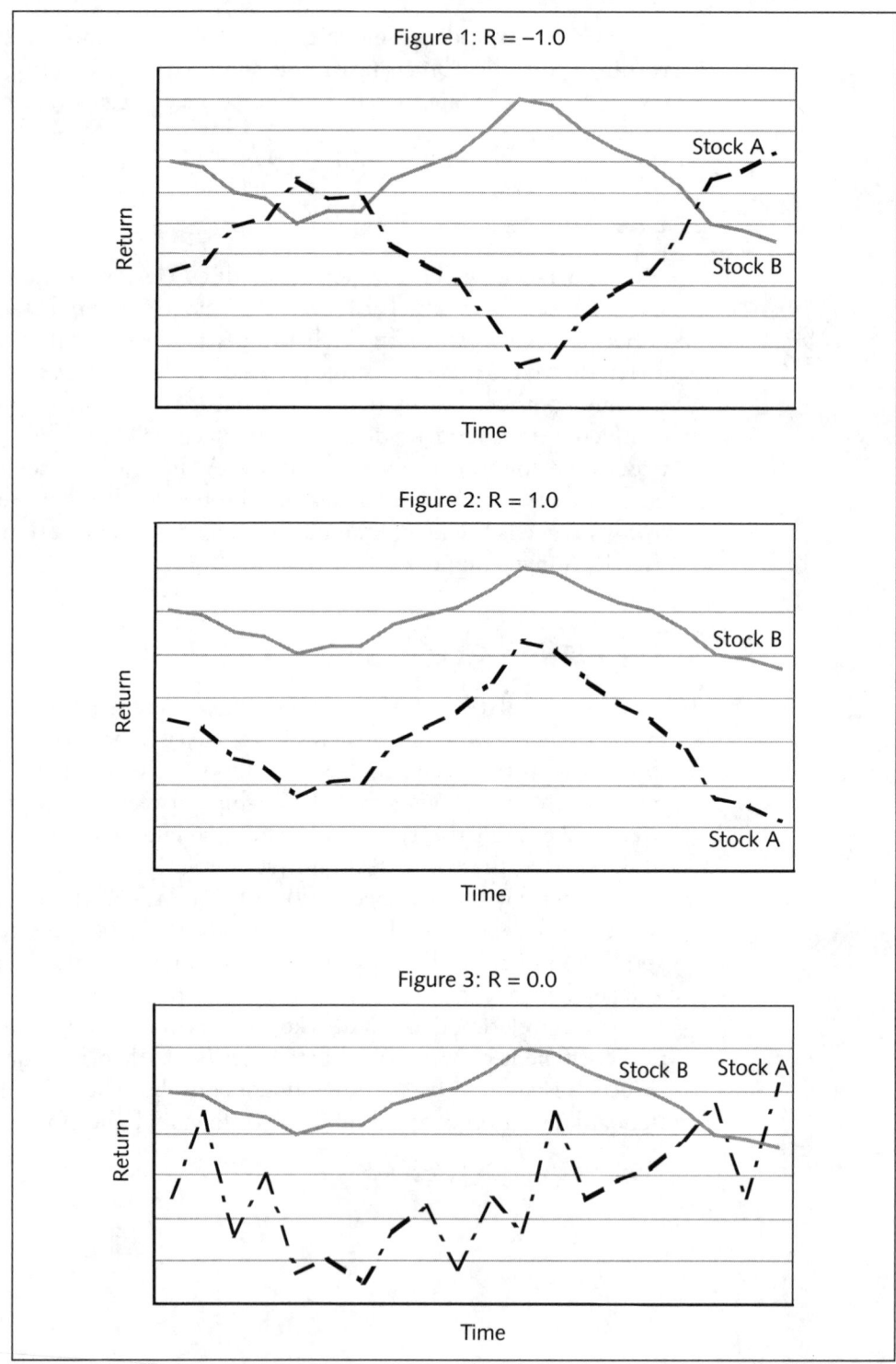

Coefficient of Determination

Coefficient of determination (R^2)

A modern portfolio theory statistic that indicates the percentage change in a portfolio or mutual fund that can be explained by changes in the market

The **coefficient of determination (R^2)** is calculated by squaring the correlation coefficient. The coefficient of determination describes the percentage of variability of returns of an asset that can be explained by changes in the returns of another asset. For example, assume that the correlation coefficient between portfolio X and the S&P 500 index is .95. The coefficient of determination would be $(.95)^2 = .9025$. This means that approximately 90% of the variability of portfolio X is explained by changes in the index. The remaining 10% of the movement of portfolio X is caused by other variables. If we consider the S&P 500 index as a measure of the market, the 10% would be considered unsystematic risk.

INVESTMENT STRATEGIES AND THEORIES

Efficient Market Hypothesis

Efficient market hypothesis

A theory that suggests that securities are priced fairly and efficiently by the market, and investors are unable to consistently outperform the market on a risk-adjusted basis

Random walk

An unpredictable pattern that describes the movement of security prices over time

The **efficient market hypothesis** (EMH) is a theory that suggests that the market prices securities fairly and efficiently and investors are unable to consistently outperform the market on a risk-adjusted basis. In fact, the EMH states that securities prices reflect all historical information. Therefore, analyzing historical information using technical or fundamental analysis will not provide an advantage in investing. The only information that will affect the price of a security will be new, unknown information. As new information affecting a security is released, the price of the security will increase if the information is positive and decrease if the information is negative. Because new information is by its very nature unknown, it is random, or unpredictable. Thus, security prices should follow a **random walk**, or an unpredictable pattern.

The efficient market hypothesis is often evaluated under three forms: the weak, semistrong, and strong. The level of information thought to be efficiently incorporated into a security's price differs between the three EMH forms.

The weak form asserts that a security's price reflects information related to its trading data including price information, volume information, and short-interest information. Under this form, analyzing trends in the price of a security is irrelevant because the price of a security should already fully reflect this information.

The semistrong form states that a security's price not only reflects its trading data but also all publicly available information related to the security. This public information includes analysis of the company's products, management, fixed and variable cost structure, earnings, and cash flow and analysis of the industry in which the company is included.

The strong form goes even farther than the other forms. This form asserts that all public and private information is included in the price of a security. Therefore, even corporate inside information will not allow investors to outperform the market on a consistent basis.

The types of market information considered relevant in attaining above-market rates of return for each form of the EMH are summarized in Exhibit 12.13.

EXHIBIT 12.13 Efficient Market Hypothesis: Three Forms

Form of EMH	Relevant Information
Weak	Insider information and credible fundamental analysis
Semistrong	Insider information
Strong	Nothing

Is the efficient market hypothesis correct? Are markets so efficient that investors are unable to consistently outperform on a risk-adjusted basis? These questions have been plaguing the investment community for decades without a definitive answer. For our purposes, it is fair to say many of the aspects of the EMH are correct. Stock prices will generally move because of new information. Investors may find it difficult to outperform the market on a consistent basis, as evidenced by the thousands of mutual funds that do not outperform the market each year (especially after adjusting for transaction costs and expenses).

Anomalies

Occurrences in the stock market that are not supported by the concept of the efficient market hypothesis

However, there are counterarguments to the validity of the EMH. **Anomalies** are occurrences in the stock market that are not supported by the concept of an efficient market. For example, if a method of trading results in superior returns, the trading method implies that the market is not perfectly efficient. Numerous anomalies have been studied at great length throughout the years. Some of these anomalies end up supporting the EMH based on the extended research, whereas others remain unexplained by the EMH principles. The most common anomalies are listed below:

■ The *price-to-earnings (P/E) ratio effect* suggests that higher returns may be attainable with portfolios comprised of securities with low P/E ratios. This effect is also a fundamental premise of value investing, which is the practice of mega-investors such as Warren Buffett.

■ The *small or neglected firm effect* relates to the number of security analysts who follow smaller companies. When fewer analysts follow a stock, the security may not be as efficiently priced and may result in undervalued stocks.

■ The *January effect* suggests that stocks have a tendency to decline during the month of December and move up significantly in early January. This anomaly likely is the result of tax selling and buying, which are most prevalent during the months when the anomaly is observed.

■ The *Value Line® enigma* relates to stocks that are rated 1 on Value Line's scale of 1–5 ratings (with 1 being the highest rating and a recommended buy). Historically, these stocks have had a tendency to outperform lower rated stocks by Value Line, a noted source of investment research.

Finally, it is fair to say that the markets are efficient, without defining the level of efficiency, and that it is difficult for professional portfolio managers to outperform the market. In addition, certain markets are more efficient than others. For example, the U.S. large-cap equity market is more efficient than the international emerging equity market. This is due to the fact that the U.S. large-cap market has fewer barriers to entry, and the financial statements of large publicly traded U.S. companies are readily available and reviewed by analysts. The degree to which one subscribes to a given level of market efficiency directly influences his decision to implement an active or passive investment strategy.

Active vs. Passive Investing

Active and passive investment strategies are commonly used approaches to investing. Active management is an attempt to outperform the returns that are available to investors who use a passive approach. To secure higher returns, active managers attempt to find undervalued or mispriced securities. Active management often requires more research and support than passive strategies. Therefore, the expenses associated with active management are generally higher than for passively managed approaches.

A passive approach to investment management does not rely on the discovery of undervalued securities. Instead, this approach assumes that investors will be unable to consistently outperform the market over the long term. As a result, managers will not employ active strategies and will maintain a well-diversified portfolio, often based on an asset allocation strategy. Over time, the portfolio may have to be rebalanced because of different rates of return for different asset classes within the portfolio. One commonly employed method of passive investing is the use of index funds.

Indexing

Investors often ask, "How did my portfolio perform compared to the market?" The market is generally represented by an index, or benchmark, such as Standard & Poor's 500 Index. These indexes provide investors with a baseline for performance comparison within different segments of the market.

Indexing is the concept of investing in the same securities and in the same proportions represented by an index. For instance, an investor might purchase the same securities that make up the S&P 500 Index. However, purchasing 500 stocks and purchasing them in the correct proportions requires a substantial investment. Therefore, investors will often invest in index mutual funds. These funds provide an inexpensive method for investors to receive the performance of an index without the hassle of having to mimic the structure of the index.

Indexing has proven to be an effective investment strategy. Historical return results indicate that the majority of active managers do not produce returns in excess of returns earned by indexes or index mutual funds.

Market Timing

Market timing is a strategy whereby investors attempt to be fully invested in periods of upward movements in the market and to be out of the market when prices are declining. This type of strategy can be applied to equities, fixed-income securities, or portfolios. Knowing when to buy and when to sell is the inherent difficulty with this strategy. Although there are a vast number of methods to time the market, many of which can be found on the internet, the majority of academic studies indicate that outperforming the market by attempting to time its rise and fall is neither reliable nor repeatable.

Buy and Hold

The buy-and-hold strategy is the conceptual opposite of market timing. This strategy, in its purest form, means that no purchases for or sales from an investor's existing portfolio will be transacted over a long period (i.e., investment time horizon). Buy and hold is a passive management strategy and is supported by the efficient market hypothesis.

The buy-and-hold strategy features three advantages:

- The investor can minimize the transaction costs in the acquisition and trading of securities.

- The investor's income tax obligations (particularly income tax liabilities or tax due) may be managed more effectively.

- The strategy ensures that the investor will not be out of the market during an upturn in prices or its most profitable trading days.

Behavioral Finance

Behavioral finance is a branch of personal finance that proposes psychology-based theories to explain investor behavior and stock market anomalies. Behavioral finance argues that investors are not nearly as rational as believed by traditional finance theorists. Critics of behavioral finance contend that the theory is merely a collection of market anomalies that are not correlated to irrational investor behavior and that these anomalies eventually will be priced out of the market. To advance the understanding of personal decisions in financial matters, prominent behavioral finance researchers have proposed the following theories:

- People's decisions are often affected by how the problem or opportunity is framed.

- Investors usually fear losses much more than they value gains. Accordingly, they will most often choose the smaller of two potential gains if it avoids a sure loss. This behavior is also known as prospect theory.

- People tend to look for information that supports their previously established decision, even if that decision was imprudent. This helps explain why investors tend to hold onto losing stock far too long before selling. This behavior is also known as confirmation bias.

- An investor's personal experiences and gender can play a significant role in investment planning.

Behavioral finance
A branch of personal finance that proposes psychology-based theories to explain investor behavior and stock market anomalies

WHERE ON THE WEB

CME Group (Futures & Options Trading) **www.cmegroup.com**

Commodity Futures Trading Commission **www.cftc.gov**

MSN Money **www.moneycentral.msn.com/investor**

Investor Guide **www.investorguide.com**

Investor's Clearinghouse **www.investoreducation.org**

National Futures Association **www.nfa.futures.org**

North American Securities Administrators Association **www.nasaa.org**

Securities and Exchange Commission—Investor Education and Assistance **www.sec.gov/investor/teachers.shtml**

DISCUSSION QUESTIONS

1. How does investment planning fit into the overall framework of financial planning?

2. What investment goals are common to most investors, and how are these goals achieved?

3. What are two methods of increasing the savings rate for an investor?

4. How are systematic risk and unsystematic risk different?

5. Compare lending investments and ownership investments.

6. What are the benefits of owning real estate in an investment portfolio?

7. What are two types of derivatives?

8. What are the differences in the obligations and rights with regard to option and futures contracts?

9. What is the difference between direct and indirect investing?

10. Describe the basic theoretical assumption of behavioral finance.

11. How are the two common measures of risk—beta and standard deviation—different?

12. What are the differences between strategic and tactical asset allocation?

13. How are the nominal rate of return and real rate of return different?

14. What is the efficient frontier and what is its role in modern portfolio theory?

15. What type of information is conveyed by the correlation coefficient?

16. What is the efficient market hypothesis (EMH)?

17. What makes market timing such a difficult investment strategy?

18. What are anomalies and how do they provide a counterargument to the validity of the EMH?

19. What is indexing and how is it used in investment planning?

20. What is the difference between active and passive portfolio management?

EXERCISES

1. List five systematic risks and explain each.

2. List five unsystematic risks and explain each.

3. Compare and contrast common and preferred stock.

4. ABC stock has recently had a market correction. If Bill likes the long-term prospects of the stock, what option position(s) might he choose and why?

5. Harry bought XYZ Company stock 15 years ago. The stock has greatly appreciated, and he is concerned about a correction. List two alternatives that he could implement to minimize losses in the event of a correction.

6. The efficient market hypothesis is often evaluated under three forms. Identify each form and explain how each incorporates information into a security's price.

7. Discuss the two major components of the capital asset pricing model (CAPM).

PROBLEMS

1. Michael invests $10,000 in Bonsai, Inc., which is based in Japan. The conversion rate at the time of the investment is 100 yen to $1. Michael sells his interest six months later for 1,750,000 yen. However, the exchange rate now is 125 yen to $1. What is Michael's return on the investment (before yen to dollars), return due to exchange rate risk, and net result on the original investment?

2. Kyle purchases 100 shares of Superstock for $6,500. One year later, he sells the lot when the stock is trading for $79 per share. Superstock does not pay dividends. What is Kyle's holding period return?

3. Based on the following chart, calculate the arithmetic mean and geometric mean for the 5-year period.

Year	Return
1	10%
2	–5%
3	18%
4	6%
5	1%

4. Eric recently purchased furniture for his family room on his credit card. If the nominal APR is 5.95% (compounded monthly), what is the effective annual rate?

5. Janet has a portfolio that has a correlation with the market of 0.8 and a standard deviation of 20%. Determine how much unsystematic risk is within Janet's portfolio.

6. JEM stock has a beta coefficient of 1.35, and the market has a rate of return of 8.50%. The risk-free rate of return is 1.75%. Calculate the expected rate of return for this stock.

7. Sandra expects to earn a long-term after-tax rate of return of 10%. If inflation is expected to continue at 3%, what is Sandra's real rate of return?

8. If portfolio A has a coefficient of determination of 0.81 when compared to the S&P 500 Index, what portion of the portfolio's risk is considered unsystematic risk?

9. Lucas invested $15,000 into a 5-year CD that pays an annual interest rate of 3.5% compounded quarterly. What will be his annual compound rate of return after the 5 years?

Supplement A: Fixed-Income Securities

LEARNING OBJECTIVES

This supplement provides information on fixed-income securities. The following topics are covered:

- Bond concepts

- Valuation

- Measures of return

- Types, risks, and volatility of fixed-income securities

- Term structure of interest rates

- Duration and immunization

BASIC CONCEPTS OF LENDING SECURITIES

Fixed-income securities
Securities with specified payment dates and amounts, primarily bonds

Lending securities
Securities wherein the investor lends funds to the issuer in exchange for a promise of a stream of periodic interest payments and a repayment of the loaned principal at maturity

Coupon payments
Interest payments paid to the bondholder on a semiannual basis and based on a percentage of the par value of the bond

Maturity
The period through which the issuer has control over the bond proceeds and the period it must continue to pay coupon payments

As described in this chapter, **fixed-income securities**, including bonds, are known as **lending securities**. A bond investor lends funds to the issuer in exchange for a promised stream of periodic interest payments and a repayment of the loaned principal at maturity. These interest payments are called coupon payments and are often paid on a semiannual basis, or twice per year. **Coupon payments** are based on a percentage of the par value, or face value, of the bond, which is typically $1,000. For example, a bond that contains a 5% coupon will pay $50 per year (generally, $25 twice per year) for the life of the bond.

Bonds provide investors with an alternative to other types of securities and can be used for the purpose of diversifying portfolios or providing income to individuals who need a stream of cash flows. Although bonds generally have lower returns than equity investments, they are less risky than equities and provide higher returns than bank certificates of deposit and savings accounts.

A variety of entities issue bonds, including domestic and foreign governments and domestic and foreign companies; however, the U.S. federal government, agencies, municipalities, and domestic corporations issue the majority of the fixed-income securities. Bonds may be issued in public markets or private offerings and each offer different characteristics.

One of the key features of a bond is the length of its term, or **maturity**. The maturity of the bond indicates the period through which the issuer has control over the bond proceeds and must continue to pay coupon payments. The maturity of a bond also affects the yield that is received by the investor. Usually, the yield that is received by the investor will be higher for longer maturity bonds. However, as we will see later, this potential for higher yields depends on the shape of the yield curve. The maturity also affects the volatility of the bond and can affect other types of risk associated with the bond.

VALUATION OF FIXED-INCOME SECURITIES

As with most financial securities, the value of a bond is equal to the present value of the expected future cash flows. Conceptually, the cash flows of a bond are straightforward: fixed-coupon payments on a periodic basis and a return of principal at maturity. To determine the present value of a bond, these expected cash flows are discounted at an appropriate discount rate, which depends on the market yields being offered on comparable fixed-income securities. The value of a bond is determined in the same manner as the value of an annuity, by using time value of money concepts.

Basic Calculation Example

EXAMPLE   Assume a three-year junk bond (face value of $1,000) is issued by XYZ Company that pays an 8% coupon semiannually ($40 twice each year). What is the value of the bond if comparable bonds are yielding 10%?

$$V = \frac{CF_1}{(1+y)^1} + \frac{CF_2}{(1+y)^2} + \frac{CF_3}{(1+y)^3} + \frac{CF_4}{(1+y)^4} + \frac{CF_5}{(1+y)^5} + \frac{CF_6}{(1+y)^6}$$

$$V = \frac{40}{(1.05)^1} + \frac{40}{(1.05)^2} + \frac{40}{(1.05)^3} + \frac{40}{(1.05)^4} + \frac{40}{(1.05)^5} + \frac{1,040}{(1.05)^6}$$

$$V = 38.10 + 36.28 + 34.55 + 32.91 + 31.34 + 776.06$$

$$V = \$949.24 \text{ (The bond should sell for } \$949.24)$$

Each cash flow is discounted by first raising the sum of 1 plus the periodic discount rate to the power in which the cash flow occurs and then dividing the cash flow by this amount. For example, the present value of the first cash flow is equal to $40 divided by 1.05 [1 + (10% ÷ 2)] resulting in a discounted value of $38.10. We used 5%, because it is half of the 10% yield, to reflect the semiannual coupon payments.

The value of a bond can also be calculated using a financial calculator. Using the previous example, a bond's value would be calculated using the following inputs:

Present Value of a Bond		
n	= 6 (3 years × 2)	Semiannual periods
i	= 5 (10 ÷ 2)	Discount rate or YTM
PMT	= $40 ($80 ÷ 2)	Semiannual coupon
FV	= $1,000	Maturity value
PV	= ($949.24)	Present value

MEASURES OF RETURN

One of the important issues relating to bonds is the determination of various measures of return. Investors in fixed-income securities will be rewarded with interest or coupon payments, capital appreciation (or loss), and the reinvestment of coupon payments. Each of the following types of returns takes into consideration some or all of these factors.

Current Yield

Current yield
A bond's annual coupon payment divided by the current market price

The **current yield** (CY) of a bond is an indication of the income or cash flow an investor will receive on the basis of the coupon payment (in dollars) and the current market price. The formula for calculating the current yield is:

$$\text{Current yield} = \frac{\text{Annual coupon payment}}{\text{Current market price}}$$

E X A M P L E For example, a 10-year bond that has a 4.5% coupon rate and is currently selling for $850 will have a current yield of 5.29%, calculated as follows:

$$CY = \frac{\$1,000 \times 4.5\%}{\$850}$$

$$CY = \frac{\$45}{\$850}$$

$$CY = 5.29\%$$

This type of measure is useful for determining the income or cash flow that can be earned on the purchase of a bond. For example, a person living on a fixed income might choose to invest in fixed-income securities if the yield is sufficiently high enough to cover living and other expenses. Notice that the calculation does not consider appreciation of the bond or reinvestment of the coupon payments.

Yield to Maturity

Yield to maturity (YTM)

The compounded rate of return on a bond purchased at the current market price and held to maturity

In the previous section, we illustrated the method for determining the price of a bond, which is based on its cash flows and the discount rate. The discount rate used in the calculation is generally the **yield to maturity (YTM)** and is determined by solving for the earnings rate that equates the current market price of the bond to the discounted cash flows from the bond. In calculating the yield to maturity, you would solve for the y that equates the present value of the bond to the discounted cash flows from the bond.

$$PV = \frac{CF_1}{(1+y)^1} + \frac{CF_2}{(1+y)^2} + \frac{CF_3}{(1+y)^3} + \frac{CF_4}{(1+y)^4} + \frac{CF_5}{(1+y)^5} + \ldots + \frac{CF_n}{(1+y)^n}$$

PV = present value
CF_n = cash flow for period n
y = yield to maturity
n = number of periods

E X A M P L E   Calculating yield to maturity using this formula is a long and arduous process. Instead, a financial calculator is recommended to calculate the yield to maturity, using the present value of the bond, term of the bond, coupon payments, and par value. For example, a 30-year bond that pays a coupon payment of 5% semiannually and is selling for $1,149.45 has a yield to maturity of 4.12%, calculated as follows:

Present Value of a Bond			
PV	=	($1,149.45)	Current market price
n	=	60 (30 years × 2)	Semiannual periods
PMT	=	$25 ($50 ÷ 2)	Semiannual coupon
FV	=	$1,000	Maturity value
i	=	2.06 × 2 = 4.12%	Yield to maturity

The calculation of the yield to maturity is based on certain important assumptions. First, the calculation assumes that the investor will hold the bond until it matures and the calculation accounts for the timing of the cash flows. Second, this calculation also assumes that any cash flows that occur during the life of the bond will be reinvested at the calculated yield to maturity rate of return. This is an important limitation of the model. If the reinvestment rate differs from the yield to maturity, then the actual yield received on the bond will be different from the expected yield calculated at inception. Specifically, if the reinvestment rate is less than the yield to maturity, then the actual yield earned on the bond will be less than the calculated yield to maturity. If the reinvestment rate is greater than the yield to maturity, then the actual yield earned on the bond will be greater than the calculated yield to maturity.

As stated, the calculation assumes that the bond is held until it matures. If the investor sells the bond before maturity and the bond is sold at either a premium or discount, the actual yield will differ from the calculated yield to maturity, because of the capital gain or loss. A premium occurs when the bond sells for a price greater than par, while a discount occurs when the price of a bond is less than par. Note the following relationships among the price of a bond, the coupon rate, the current yield, and the yield to maturity.

Bond Selling At			Relationship		
Par	Coupon rate	=	Current yield	=	Yield to maturity
Discount	Coupon rate	<	Current yield	<	Yield to maturity
Premium	Coupon rate	>	Current yield	>	Yield to maturity

Yield to Call (YTC)

Yield to call (YTC)

The expected return on a bond from the purchase date to the first date that the bond may be called

Yield to call (YTC) is the rate of return that equates the present value of the bond (purchase price) to the expected cash flows, adjusted for the call feature. Calculating yield to call is performed using the same method as that used to calculate yield to maturity, with two adjustments. A bond containing a call feature generally allows the issuer the right to call the bond before maturity, but usually at a premium above par value. Therefore, in the calculation of yield to call, the number of periods needs to be adjusted to reflect the shorter term of the bond resulting from the call feature and the future value must be adjusted to reflect the premium paid by the issuer.

For example, assume a 30-year bond ($1,000) that pays a coupon rate of 5% semiannually is selling for $1,149.45, has a yield to maturity of 4.12%, and has a call provision. If the call provision provides that the bond may be called in five years at 103 (meaning 103% of the par value), then the yield to call equals 2.38%, calculated as follows:

Present Value of a Bond		
PV	= ($1,149.45)	Current market price
n	= 10 (5 years × 2)	Semiannual periods
PMT	= $25 ($50 ÷ 2)	Semiannual coupon payments
FV	= $1,030 (103% × $1,000)	Par value plus call premium
i	= 1.19 × 2 = 2.38%	Yield to call

Note that the yield to call is different from the yield to maturity. Investors who are considering the purchase of a callable bond should calculate both the YTM and the YTC in case the issuer decides to call the bond. The lesser of the YTM or YTC is the more conservative estimate of the actual yield.

Comparing Corporate Returns and Municipals Returns

The taxable bond market and the tax-exempt bond market make up the U.S. bond market. The taxable bond market consists of U.S. Treasury bonds, U.S. government agency bonds, and corporate bonds. The tax-exempt bond market consists of bonds issued by municipalities, which includes states, counties, cities, and parishes. The exemption from federal income tax is the reason municipal bonds are referred to as tax exempt. Interest from bonds issued by municipalities is exempt from federal income tax and, in some cases, exempt from state income tax. Interest from U.S. Treasury securities is subject to federal income tax, but not subject to state income tax. Corporate bond interest and interest derived from U.S. agency bonds are subject to federal and state income tax. Because various types of bonds have different tax treatment, planners must compare yields for different bonds on a consistent basis. This comparison can be performed on an after-tax basis or a pretax basis.

Taxable equivalent yield

A method for investors to compare the yield on municipal bonds with the yield on taxable (e.g., corporate) bonds

An investor can convert a municipal bond yield to a taxable equivalent yield (TEY) using the following formula:

$$TEY = \frac{\text{tax-exempt yield}}{1 - \text{marginal tax rate}}$$

EXAMPLE For example, Tom, who is in the 35% tax bracket, is considering the purchase of a Big State municipal bond that is offering a 3% yield, while comparable, credit-worthy corporate bonds are offering a yield of 4.5%. To determine which bond is preferred, on the basis of yield, Tom could determine the taxable equivalent yield for the municipal bond, as illustrated:

$$\text{TEY} = \frac{0.03}{1-0.35} = 0.04615 = 4.62\%$$

Because the taxable equivalent yield equals 4.62%, the municipal bond yield of 3% is preferable to the corporate bond yield of 4.5%. The comparison can also be made on an after-tax basis by multiplying the taxable yield of the corporate bond by the difference between 1 and the marginal tax rate, as follows:

$$\text{After-tax yield} = 0.045 \times (1 - 0.35) = 0.02925 = 2.93\%$$

Because the 3% tax-free municipal yield is greater than the 2.93% after-tax corporate bond yield, the municipal bond appears to be the better choice, on the basis of yield.

Generally, a tax-exempt entity should never purchase a municipal bond over a taxable bond because pretax yields on taxable instruments are generally higher than yields for tax-exempt securities of similar risk. Similarly, municipal bonds should not be used in tax-deferred accounts, such as IRAs and Section 401(k) plans.

TYPES OF FIXED-INCOME SECURITIES

The Money Market

Money market
Consists of debt securities that have the following characteristics: short-term maturity, low credit risk, and high liquidity

The **money market** consists of debt securities that have the following characteristics: short-term maturity, low credit risk, and high liquidity. These securities include U.S. Treasury bills, commercial paper, certificates of deposit, banker's acceptances, repurchase agreements, and eurodollars.

Treasury Bills (T-bills)

The U.S. Treasury issues 4-week, 8-week, 13-week, 26-week, and 52-week bills in $100 denominations. The Treasury auctions these bills on a weekly basis. In addition to being purchased directly from the Treasury, these securities may be purchased and sold in the secondary market.

Treasury bills are issued at a discount or percentage of face value. If an investor paid $997.27 for a $1,000 bill, the bill will mature at its face value of $1,000, providing the investor with income of $2.73. Because T-bills have a maturity date of no more than one year, they are not subject to the original issue discount taxation rules that apply to other bonds. Interest income from the bill, which is not taxable until the bill matures, is taxed at ordinary federal income tax rates but is not subject to state income tax.

Commercial Paper

Commercial paper consists of a private sector company's issue of short-term, unsecured promissory notes. This type of debt is issued in denominations of $100,000 or more and serves as a substitute for short-term bank financing. Maturities for commercial paper are 270 days or less and are often backed by lines of credit from banks. In comparison to Treasury bills, these instruments have a slightly higher default risk and are slightly less liquid. Therefore, commercial paper has slightly higher yields than T-bills of similar term structures.

Certificates of Deposit

Negotiable certificates of deposit (also known as jumbo CDs) are deposits of $100,000 or more placed with commercial banks at a specific stated rate of interest. These short-term securities can be bought and sold in the open market. These instruments usually yield slightly higher returns than T-bills because they have more default risk and less marketability.

Banker's Acceptances

Banker's acceptances are securities that act as a line of credit issued from a bank. Companies that are too small to issue commercial paper will use banker's acceptances to fund short-term debt needs. When using a banker's acceptance, the bank usually acts as an intermediary between the American company and the foreign company. For example, an American importer may request acceptance financing from its bank when the foreign company will not provide credit. As a result, the importer's bank agrees to pay the foreign supplier on behalf of the importer. The importer is then contractually obligated to repay the bank within three to six months. In turn, the importer's bank may sell the obligation at a discount to obtain immediate cash. These securities usually have slightly higher interest rates than commercial paper, reflecting greater default risk and less liquidity.

Repurchase Agreements

Securities dealers use repurchase agreements (known as "repos") to finance large inventories of marketable securities from one to a few days. The issuer or seller both sells and agrees to repurchase the underlying security at a specified price and date. The repurchase price is higher than the selling price, creating the required return to compensate the holder for participating in the repurchase agreement. The opposite of the repo is the reverse repurchase agreement (or reverse repo). In a reverse repo, the dealer buys government securities from another dealer and then sells them back later at a higher price.

Eurodollars

Eurodollars are U.S. dollar-denominated deposits at banks outside the United States. The average deposit is in the millions and has a maturity of less than six months. Therefore, the market for this investment is generally only the largest financial institutions and the only way for individuals to invest is indirectly through a money market mutual fund. A variation on the eurodollar time deposit is the eurodollar CD (or euro CD). This type of CD shares the same characteristics as its domestic counterpart except that the obligation is the liability of a non-U.S. bank. Accordingly, euro CDs are less liquid and, therefore, offer a slightly higher yield than domestic CDs. Generally, only the largest financial institutions invest in the eurodollar market. Similar to eurodollars, individual investors may participate in the eurodollar market indirectly through the use of money market mutual funds.

Government Debt Securities

U.S. Treasury Notes and Bonds

U.S. Treasury notes and bonds have virtually the same characteristics with the exception of maturity. Specifically, U.S. Treasury notes are issued with a maturity date of no more than 10 years, whereas U.S. Treasury bonds have a maturity of 30 years. The minimum purchase amount for both types of securities is $100. Treasury notes and bonds pay interest on a semiannual basis. As with Treasury bills, pricing for notes and bonds is done through the auction process. Treasury notes and bonds are considered default risk-free and are exempt from income taxation at both the state and local levels. For federal income tax purposes, all interest from either obligation is taxable at ordinary income tax rates in the year earned.

Treasury Inflation-Protected Securities (TIPS)

Treasury inflation-protected securities (TIPS)

Marketable securities whose principal is adjusted by changes in the Consumer Price Index (CPI)

In 1997, the Treasury began issuing notes and bonds that are indexed with the Consumer Price Index (CPI) referred to as **Treasury inflation-protected securities (TIPS)**. These securities have the same basic characteristics as non-inflation-adjusted Treasury notes and bonds, except for the inflation-adjustment feature.

The interest rate paid on these securities is determined through the auction process, just as the other Treasury obligations; however, the principal value of the bond is adjusted for changes in the CPI. Thus, the semiannual interest payments received by the investor are determined by multiplying the inflation-adjusted principal value by one-half of the stated coupon payment.

One of the primary risks to which fixed-income securities are subject is changes in interest rates, both from devaluation in principal and from loss of purchasing power. The indexed Treasuries provide protection from both of these risks, making them an attractive security for investors concerned about rising inflation and devaluation due to loss of purchasing power.

Treasury STRIPS

Treasury STRIPS

Acronym for Separate Trading of Registered Interest and Principal of Securities, a program that permits investors to hold and trade the individual interest and principal components of eligible Treasury notes and bonds as separate securities

The **Treasury STRIPS** (Separate Trading of Registered Interest and Principal of Securities) program permits investors to hold and trade the individual interest and principal components of eligible Treasury notes and bonds as separate securities. The Treasury does not issue or sell STRIPS directly to investors. STRIPS can be purchased and held only through financial institutions and government securities brokers/dealers who are the parties that separate the original security into its components.

When a Treasury fixed-principal or inflation-indexed note or bond is stripped, each interest payment becomes a separate zero-coupon security, as does the principal payment. Each component has its own identifying number and can be held or traded separately. For example, a Treasury note with 10 years remaining to maturity consists of a single principal payment at maturity and 20 interest payments, one every six months for 10 years. When this note is converted to STRIPS form, each of the 20 interest (coupon) payments and the principal payment become a separate (zero-coupon) security. STRIPS are also called zero-coupon securities because the only time investors receive a payment during the life of STRIPS is when they mature.

U.S. Savings Bonds

Savings bonds, a part of the federal government debt structure, include Series E, EE, H, HH, and I bonds. Historically purchased for patriotic reasons, these bonds may be purchased and used for funding education costs and gifting.

Series EE Savings Bonds

The Treasury issued the new Series EE savings bond beginning July 1, 1980, in order to replace the older Series E bond. The interest rate earned on Series EE savings bonds is a fixed rate determined by the U.S. Treasury Department, with a new rate announced each May and November. The electronic (paper bonds were discontinued as of January 1, 2012) EE savings bond is sold at 100% of face value. Series EE bonds reach original maturity 20 years after the date of issue and continue to earn interest until they reach final maturity 30 years after the date of issue. Bonds may be redeemed at any time, subject to the following restrictions and penalties: (1) bonds must be held for at least 12 months, and (2) if a bond that is less than five years old is redeemed, the penalty is the forfeiture of the last three months of interest.

One of the attractions of Series EE bonds is the special tax treatment of the income attributable to these securities. Interest earned from bonds that are issued at a discount, such as zero-coupon bonds and STRIPS, must be reported as taxable income on an annual basis even though cash may not be received during the year. Because of the special tax treatment afforded Series EE bonds, however, the interest accrued on these securities is generally not taxed on an annual basis, but rather upon redemption. However, taxpayers are permitted to make an election to include for tax purposes the income from these securities on an annual basis. This elected tax treatment can be beneficial under certain circumstances, such as for a child with income under the standard deduction. In such a case, basis can be established without incurring tax.

Another tax benefit of Series EE bonds is that the interest earned on these securities can be completely excluded from taxable income if the proceeds from the bonds are used for qualified higher education costs of the taxpayer, spouse, or dependents. These costs include books, tuition, and fees for these family members.

Series HH Savings Bonds

Unlike Series EE bonds that are sold for cash, Series HH savings bonds could be only acquired through an exchange of Series E or EE bonds or with redemption proceeds of another H bond (and savings notes issued prior to 1970). Series HH bonds were issued at 100% of the face amount until September 1, 2004, when they were discontinued. Series HH bonds pay interest semiannually at a fixed rate set on the date of issuance and adjusted on the 10th anniversary. The interest payments are required to be included in income for federal income tax purposes.

Series HH bonds have an original maturity period of 10 years and have been granted one 10-year extension of maturity with interest, bringing their final maturity to 20 years. Series HH bonds were issued only in registered physical form and are not transferable. In other words, Series HH bonds are not marketable securities.

Series I Savings Bonds

The Treasury offers Series I savings bonds in an attempt to provide individuals a way to accrue income and protect the purchasing power of their investment. Series I bonds are issued at 100% of the face value. The bonds have an interest-paying life of 30 years after issue and cease to increase in value on that date. Like EE and HH bonds, Series I bonds are not transferable or marketable.

The Series I bond earnings rate is a combination of two separate rates: a fixed rate of return and a semiannual inflation rate. Each May and November, the Treasury announces a fixed rate of return that applies to all Series I bonds issued during the six-month period beginning with the effective date of the announcement, May 1 or November 1. The fixed rate for any given Series I bond remains the same for the life of the bond.

In addition, every May and November, the Treasury announces a semiannual inflation rate based on changes in the Consumer Price Index for all urban consumers (CPI-U). The semiannual inflation rate announced in May is a measure of inflation from the previous October through March; the rate announced in November is a measure of inflation from the previous April through September. The CPI-U is published monthly by the Department of Labor's Bureau of Labor Statistics. The semiannual inflation rate is then combined with the fixed rate of the Series I bond to determine the bond's earnings rate for the next six months. In the rare event that the CPI-U is negative during a period of deflation and the decline in the CPI-U is greater than the fixed rate, the redemption value of Series I bonds remains the same until the earnings rate becomes greater than zero.

Series I bonds receive special income tax treatment. The interest from Series I bonds is not subject to state and local income tax. Interest is accrued for Series I bonds and is not taxable until redeemed. In addition, the interest can be completely excluded from taxable income if the proceeds are used for qualified higher education expenses of the taxpayer, spouse, or dependents.

Series I bonds can be redeemed at any time 12 months after the issue date. The owner will receive the original investment plus the earnings; however, Series I bonds are meant to be long-term investments. So, if a Series I bond is redeemed within the first five years, there is a three-month earnings penalty. Exhibit 12A.1 illustrates the differences among the three types of savings bonds.

EXHIBIT 12A.1 Summary of U.S. Savings Bonds

	Series EE	Series HH	Series I
Range of denominations	$25 to $10,000	No longer issued	$25 to $10,000
Purchased	With cash (electronically)	By exchanging E or EE bonds	With cash (electronically)
Maturity date	20 years (30-year interest earning period)	20 years	30 years
Interest rate	Fixed rate	1.5% fixed rate	Combination of fixed and variable rates
Interest payments	Accrues	Paid semiannually	Accrues
Taxation of interest	Deferred	Taxed annually	Deferred
Interest can be completely excluded for qualified higher education costs	Yes (if not above phaseout)	Not eligible	Yes (if not above phaseout)

Municipal Bonds

Municipal bonds
Debt instruments issued by municipalities (states, counties, parishes, cities, or towns)

Municipalities include states, counties, parishes, cities, and towns. These government agencies issue debt instruments, referred to as **municipal bonds**. The unique characteristic of municipal bonds is their income tax treatment. The interest from municipal bonds is not subject to federal income tax and, in some cases, is not subject to state income tax. Although the yields on municipals are generally lower than those of Treasuries, their special tax treatment makes them the choice for higher income investors because of their

General obligation bonds

A municipal bond backed by the full faith, credit, and taxing power of the municipality

Revenue bonds

A municipal bond backed by a specific source of revenue

higher after-tax yields. Two common types of municipal bonds are general obligation bonds and revenue bonds.

General obligation bonds are backed by the full faith and credit of the government issuing the debt and are repaid through taxes collected by the governmental body. Because these bonds are backed by the taxing authority of the municipality, they are only subject to minimal default risk.

Revenue bonds are issued by government bodies to raise funds to finance specific revenue-producing projects. Examples of revenue bonds include airport revenue bonds, college and university revenue bonds, hospital revenue bonds, sewer revenue bonds, toll road revenue bonds, and water revenue bonds. These bonds are not backed by the full faith and credit of the issuing body. Instead, the interest and principal are repaid from revenue generated from the project that was financed with the bond proceeds. Because the revenue generated from the project may differ from what is expected, these bonds are riskier than general obligation bonds and, thus, require higher yields for similar maturities.

There are other differences between municipal bonds besides sources of repayment. For example, municipal bonds may be either term bonds or serial bonds. The principal for term bonds is repaid in full upon maturity, whereas serial bonds require that the municipality retire a certain amount of the bond issue each year.

Corporate Bonds

Corporations raise funds by issuing both equity and debt obligations. Debt obligations provide corporations with a method of raising needed capital funds without diluting the ownership of the entity; however, excessive amounts of debt can strain the financial health of the company by using precious resources for debt service. In general, debt increases the leverage of a company, and specifically, it impacts the return on equity. Excessive use of debt can cause increased fluctuations in the share price of the common stock.

The corporate bond market is typically classified by the type of issuer. The five broad categories of corporate bonds are banks and finance companies, industrials, public utilities, transportations, and international. Each of these categories can be further subdivided. For example, transportation can be divided into airlines, railroads, and trucking. Along with bond ratings, these subcategory classifications can assist investors in analyzing and comparing various debt issues.

Bond indenture agreement

The legal document that sets forth the repayment schedules, restrictions, and promises between the issuer of a corporate bond and the borrower

The **bond indenture agreement** is the legal document that sets forth the repayment schedules, restrictions, and promises between the issuer and the borrower. Information that may be found in the indenture agreement includes call provisions, sinking fund provisions, collateral provisions, and conversion options.

Call Provisions

Call provision

Right to redeem the bond issue before maturity

A **call provision** provides the issuer of the debt instrument the right to redeem the bond issue prior to maturity. Generally, a call provision will require the issuer to pay a premium if the bond issue is redeemed before maturity. When interest rates decline, call provisions allow the issuer to redeem the outstanding debt and reissue it at a lower interest rate. By refinancing the debt, companies can save significant amounts of interest payments that would have been paid to the creditors.

Sinking Fund Provisions

> **Sinking funds**
> Funds usually held by trustee to ensure repayment of borrowed principal

Sinking funds may be established and funded by the bond issuer each year and may accumulate to pay off debt upon maturity. These funds are usually held by a trustee to ensure the repayment of the borrowed principal. Such a fund is included to reduce the default risk associated with some bond issues.

Collateral Provisions

> **Mortgage bond**
> Bond secured by real property

Bonds may be unsecured or secured. A secured bond has a claim on specific assets of the issuing company in the event of liquidation. A **mortgage bond** is secured by real property, such as real estate holdings. Generally, a mortgage bond will have a lien on the specified property, but it could have a lien on all assets of the firm. A mortgage bond may be open ended, limited open ended, or closed ended, which indicates the degree to which additional debt may be issued against the same property.

> **Collateral trust bonds**
> Bonds secured by securities issued by other companies

Collateral trust bonds are usually secured by stocks and bonds of other companies held in trust. For companies with insufficient real property, providing a lien on securities held by the company is a method of providing security to creditors. The investments that are pledged act as collateral for the loan.

Companies are willing to provide security for bond issues to reduce and minimize interest payments and expense. The market interest rate required for secured bonds will be less than that of unsecured bonds.

> **Debentures**
> Unsecured corporate bonds whose holders have no claim to specific assets of the issuing corporation

Unsecured bonds are called **debentures**. Investors who hold debentures do not have a claim to specific assets of the corporation. However, if liquidation occurs, debenture holders, who are general creditors of the issuing corporation, will be paid only after secured creditors have been repaid. Subordinated debentures have an even lower claim on assets than general creditors, such as debenture holders.

Zero-Coupon Bonds

> **Zero-coupon bond**
> A bond that does not pay periodic coupon or interest payments

A **zero-coupon bond** is a bond that does not pay periodic coupon or interest payments; therefore, this bond will always sell at a deep discount from (less than) par. As a result, the only cash flow that occurs and needs to be considered in the valuation of a zero-coupon bond is the maturity value or principal value. Although coupon payments are not actually paid, the number of periods that are used when valuing a zero is the same as if the coupon payments were being paid. In other words, the number of periods will equal the number of years until maturity of the bond multiplied by 2. Therefore, the valuation methodology of a zero-coupon bond will be consistent with, and comparable to, the valuation methodology of a coupon-paying bond.

Corporations may favor zero-coupon bonds because they have an extended period to use the borrowed money without the obligation of making periodic interest payments. Thus, these bonds can be an effective cash management tool. Investors favor zero-coupon bonds because the heavily discounted bond price means they can purchase more bonds with the same amount of investment dollars and can time the maturity of the bonds to coincide with future financial needs and expenses.

Convertible Bonds

Convertible bonds

Hybrid securities that permit the holder to acquire shares of common stock from the issuing company by exchanging the currently held debt security for a specific number of common stock shares

Corporate bonds may contain provisions permitting the conversion of the fixed-income security into equity securities. **Convertible bonds** are hybrid securities that permit the holder to acquire shares of common stock from the issuing company by exchanging the currently held debt security according to a specific formula. Similar to an option contract, the holder's ability to convert the current security into common stock is a right, not an obligation. The conversion decision hinges on the value of the stock upon conversion. If the value of the stock after conversion would be less than the value of the bond, then the investor should hold on to the fixed-income security.

Convertible securities allow the issuer to reduce the cost of interest for a bond issue by paying a lower yield. The lower yield is a result of the buyer purchasing not only a steady stream of cash flows, but also an option to convert the bond to common stock.

Convertible securities provide investors with several advantages over nonconvertible securities. They provide the holder with a steady stream of income and the ability to participate in the growth of the underlying company. Convertible bonds have a relatively low correlation to other bonds and only a moderate correlation to stocks, providing investors the opportunity to diversify a portfolio. Convertible securities are senior securities in terms of liquidation and are highly marketable.

Asset-Backed Securities

Asset-backed securities

Bundled securities issued against some type of asset-linked debts, such as mortgages

Asset-backed securities, such as mortgage-backed securities and collateralized mortgage obligations, contain more uncertainty with regard to their cash flows. First, coupon payments and repayment of principal are based on payments made by the mortgagors, who often have the right to prepay principal. Prepayments cause the schedule of cash flows to change, which adjusts the value of the bond. The second issue related to asset-backed securities is the potential for defaults. Clearly, in a large pool of mortgages, some of the mortgages may result in default. In such a case, the cash flows are affected, causing the value of the bond to change. Each of these issues can be incorporated into the projection of the expected cash flows and, therefore, incorporated into the valuation of the asset-backed securities.

Mortgage-Backed Securities

Mortgage-backed securities (MBSs)

Ownership claims on a pool of mortgages

Mortgage-backed securities (MBSs) are ownership claims against a pool of mortgages. The originating mortgage lender will sell loans to investors in the secondary market. These investors pool mortgages together and sell interests in the pool to other investors. This process of transforming nonpublicly traded securities into marketable assets is known as **securitization**.

Securitization

The process of transforming nonnegotiable securities into negotiable securities

Mortgage-backed securities are often referred to as pass-through securities because the monthly mortgage payments are passed along to the holders of the MBSs, less a small servicing fee. These monthly mortgage payments consist of scheduled interest and principal payments, as well as unscheduled principal prepayments. These unscheduled principal prepayments result from borrowers making additional principal payments on their loans or paying off loans, such as in the case of refinancing.

Because MBSs are backed by mortgages (all of which are secured by real property, with many backed by the government), they have little credit risk. However, MBSs are subject to other risks. Similar to other fixed-income obligations, these securities are subject to fluctuations in interest rates. As interest rates increase, the value of the MBS decreases; as interest rates decrease, the value of the MBS increases.

Because MBSs pass through payments on a monthly basis, the investor must reinvest these cash flows in some other investment. This reinvestment rate risk impacts MBSs in the same manner as other fixed-income securities that have cash flows occurring during the life of the security.

Prepayment risk
The risk that homeowners will pay off their loans before the scheduled loan maturity date

Unlike other fixed-income obligations, MBSs are subject to **prepayment risk**, which is the risk that homeowners will pay off their loans before the scheduled loan maturity date. Because the value of these securities is based on the schedule of cash flows, any mortgage prepayments will impact the return an investor receives. In addition to creating uncertainty as to the timing of the cash flows, these prepayments present a situation in which the investor must reinvest the additional principal payments, possibly at a lower interest rate. Ultimately, this propagates the reinvestment rate risk.

The majority of the mortgage-backed securities have been issued by three agencies: the Federal National Mortgage Association (FNMA or Fannie Mae), the Government National Mortgage Association (GNMA or Ginnie Mae), and the Federal Home Loan Mortgage Corporation (FHLMC or Freddie Mac).

Collateralized Mortgage Obligations (CMOs)

Collateralized mortgage obligations (CMOs)
Mortgage-backed securities that are divided into tranches

Due to the popularity of the mortgage-backed securities, private investment firms have created their own pass-through securities, known as **collateralized mortgage obligations (CMOs)**. Collateralized mortgage obligations are similar to MBSs in that they are backed by mortgages. However, they differ from MBSs in that the cash flow associated with the pool of mortgages is divided into repayment periods called tranches. In the traditional MBS, the cash flow an investor will receive each month includes a pro rata share of principal and interest.

The principal repayment method for collateralized mortgage obligations is different from the method for MBSs. As described, tranches, or repayment periods, are established to dictate when an investor will receive principal repayments. Each of the tranches will receive regular interest payments, with the investors of the first tranche receiving all principal payments until they are completely repaid their principal. Once the obligations of the first tranche are satisfied, all principal payments are made to the second tranche and so on, until all of the tranches are repaid. The holders of the CMOs of the first tranche have less interest rate risk than the holders of the CMOs of the last tranche because the maturity is longer for these securities.

Promissory Notes

A promissory note is a private transaction between a lender and a borrower commonly used to finance business operations or expansion. The structure of a promissory note is similar to that of a bond (i.e., it generally involves a fixed amount and time of payment), and many of the same investment considerations that apply to a bond are also relevant to a promissory note. The present value of a promissory note is found using time value of money principles and discounting back future cash flows from the note at a specified discount rate over the stipulated time period of the note.

Rating Agencies

Rating agencies are responsible for assisting investors in evaluating the default risk of fixed-income securities. Bond rating agencies analyze the financial information of thousands of companies attempting to determine a credit rating for the various debt issues in the market. The two largest and most popular rating agencies are Standard & Poor's and Moody's. Their credit rating systems are listed in Exhibit 12A.2.

EXHIBIT 12A.2 Standard Credit Rating Systems

Bonds	Standard & Poor's	Moody's
Investment grade		
■ High grade	AAA–AA	Aaa–Aa
■ Medium grade	A–BBB-	A–Baa
Noninvestment grade		
■ Speculative	BB+–B	Ba–B
■ Default	CCC–D	Caa–C
Overall range	AAA–D	Aaa–C

Investment grade bonds have a high probability of timely payment of both interest and repayment of principal, and noninvestment grade bonds are those in which a significant risk exists surrounding interest or principal payments.

The rating agencies generally provide the same rating for a specific debt issue. In some cases, there may be a slight difference between the ratings of a specific issue by the different agencies; this difference is referred to as a split rating.

RISKS OF FIXED-INCOME SECURITIES

Fixed-income securities can provide substantial returns to investors; however, there are a variety of risks to which investors of fixed-income securities are subject, including the following:

Systematic Risks	Unsystematic Risks
Interest rate risk	Default risk
Reinvestment rate risk	Call risk
Purchasing power risk	

Interest Rate Risk

Interest rate risk is the risk that fluctuations in interest rates will adversely impact the value of a security. This risk is generally the greatest risk for a bond investor. There is an inverse relationship between changes in interest rates and bond prices. As interest rates fall, bond prices increase. Conversely, as interest rates rise, the value of bonds declines.

Planners should understand that a decline in the value of a bond, which is attributable to an increase in interest rates, is of little relevance to an investor holding the bond to maturity. In such a case, the decline in value of the bond is simply a reflection of the change in market interest rates. The investor will still receive the scheduled coupon payments and the par value upon maturity. For an investor who sells before maturity, an increase in interest rates means that the investor will incur a capital loss. Interest rate risk impacts bonds, bond portfolios, and bond mutual funds.

Default Risk

As discussed previously, investing in a fixed-income obligation is a process of lending money. The bond issuer is effectively borrowing money from the investor in return for a promise to make periodic interest (coupon) payments and repay the principal at the maturity of the bond. However, because bonds are often issued with maturities exceeding 10, 20, and 30 years, there is a risk that the financial well-being of the bond issuer will change over this long period. In some cases, the financial health of a company will be in such turmoil that the company cannot uphold its promise to repay the borrowed proceeds. The risk that this might occur is referred to as default, or credit, risk. Rating agencies, such as Standard & Poor's and Moody's, provide investors with analysis of the financial stability of companies and their ability to service their debt.

Another issue of default risk is the impact that a change in a company's financial well-being will have on the value of a bond issue. When a company's financial health diminishes, it increases the probability of default. Because of this increased likelihood of default, as small as it may be, the market value of the bond will decline relative to other bonds with similar characteristics. Therefore, it is not simply a matter of default, but also how changes in the general financial health of the bond issuer impact the price of a fixed-income security.

Reinvestment Rate Risk

Simply put, reinvestment rate risk is the risk that cash flows received during the holding period of an investment will not be able to be invested at a rate that is at least as great as the expected internal rate of return of the original investment.

Purchasing Power Risk

Purchasing power risk, also referred to as inflation risk, is the risk that inflation will erode the purchasing power of the investor's assets. Bondholders can especially be impacted by purchasing power risk. For example, if an investor owns a bond with a coupon rate of 3% when inflation is 4%, the investor is losing purchasing power at a rate of 1% per year. As discussed, there are certain inflation-adjusted bonds, such as those issued by the U.S. Treasury, that can help minimize the adverse impact of inflation.

Call Risk

For bonds that have a call feature, there is a risk that the bond will be called from the investor prior to maturity. Bond issuers will generally call a bond when interest rates decline, which means that the investor will have to reinvest the proceeds in an environment of lower interest rates.

VOLATILITY OF FIXED-INCOME SECURITIES

Volatility is defined as the magnitude and frequency of changes in the price of a security, such as bonds, within a given time period. The two key factors that influence volatility are the coupon rate and maturity.

Coupon Rate

The volatility in a bond's price is inversely related to the bond's coupon payment when interest rates change. A bond with a higher coupon rate is more stable with regard to interest rate changes than is a bond with a lower coupon rate. A zero-coupon bond's value will generally be more volatile than a bond with a 5% coupon.

Maturity

A bond with a longer term is subject to more volatility in an environment of changing interest rates than is a bond with a shorter term. A 30-year Treasury bond will be more volatile than a five-year Treasury note when interest rates change. This is illustrated in Exhibit 12A.3.

E X A M P L E   Bond A is a five-year high-yield bond with a 10% coupon rate. Bond B is a 30-year high-yield bond, also with a 10% coupon rate. Because Bond B has a longer maturity, it will experience more volatility when interest rates change.

EXHIBIT 12A.3 Impact of Maturity on Bond Volatility

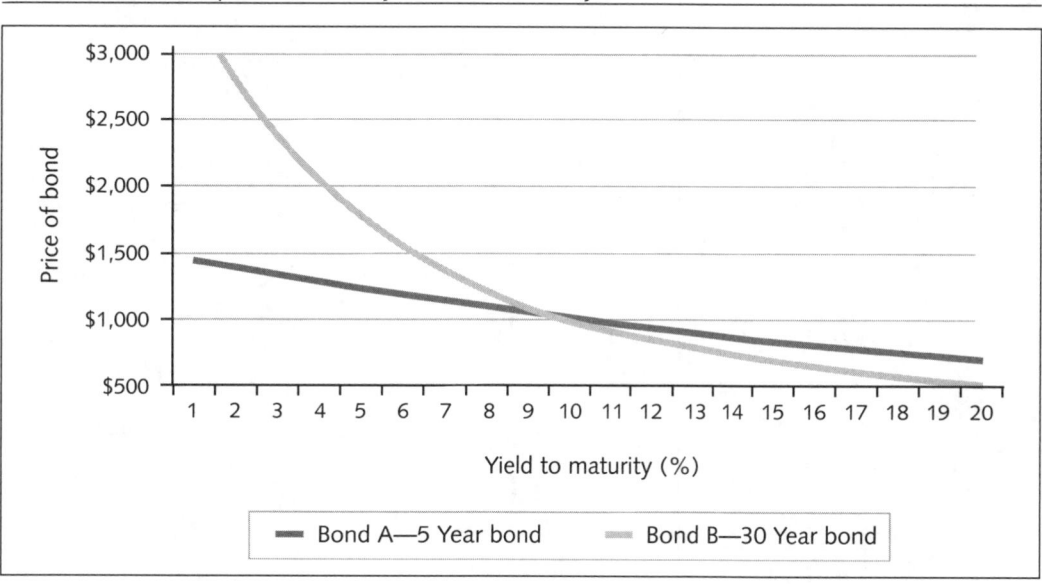

Notice that Bond B's slope is steeper than Bond A's. At a YTM of 10%, the price of both bonds is equal at $1,000. When interest rates decrease, the price of Bond B increases more than Bond A. When interest rates increase, the price of Bond B decreases more than Bond A.

TERM STRUCTURE OF INTEREST RATES

Yield Curves

Yield curves

Graphical representations that reflect current market interest rates for various bond maturities

Traditionally, interest rates for bonds have been reflected in graphical representations called **yield curves**. These yield curves reflect current market interest rates for various bond maturities. The most popular of these yield curves is the Treasury yield curve, which depicts current yields for Treasury securities. The yield curve is generally upward sloping, indicating that yields on longer-term bonds are higher than yields on shorter-term bonds.

However, there have been times when the structure of interest rates has caused the yield curve to be shaped differently. The yield curve is generally described as upward sloping (normal), flat, or downward sloping (inverted) as shown in Exhibit 12A.4.

EXHIBIT 12A.4 Yield Curves

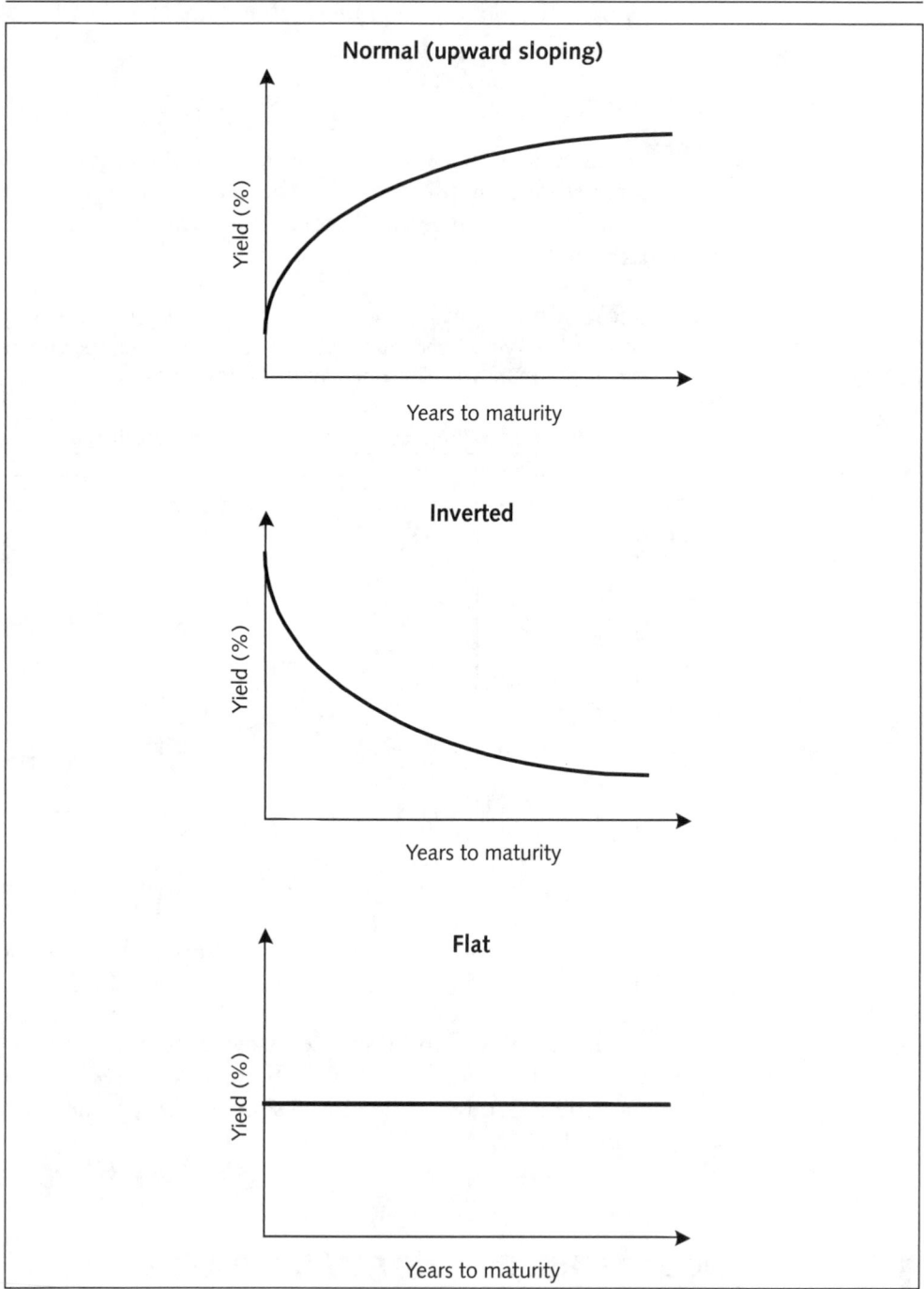

The most important point regarding yield curves is that their shape varies according to changes in the economic cycle; therefore, they may be used to make predictions about the future state of the economy.

- A normal or positive yield curve occurs during periods of economic expansion and generally predicts that market interest rates will rise in the future.

- An inverted yield curve occurs when the Federal Reserve has tightened credit in an inflationary economy. This type of curve predicts interest rates will fall and, sometimes, can signal an upcoming economic recession.

- A flat yield curve occurs when the economy is peaking and, therefore, no change in future interest rates (particularly down) is expected.

The Treasury yield curve is often used as a benchmark for other fixed-income securities. The Treasury yield curve is an effective benchmark for pricing bonds and determining yields of bonds in other sectors because it is not impacted by credit risk or liquidity risk. Treasuries are backed by the full faith and credit of the U.S. government and, as a result, are not subject to credit risk. The Treasury market is extremely liquid because it is the largest and most actively traded bond market.

The traditional method for valuing or pricing non-Treasury bonds has been to use the yield on the Treasury yield curve for the appropriate maturity, plus a premium for additional risk.

An alternative way to conceptualize the valuation of bonds is to consider them as a series of individual cash flow, each one an independent zero-coupon bond. For example, a 10-year, 3% coupon Treasury note could be viewed as 20 separate and distinct zero-coupon bonds. These individual cash flows can then be valued on the basis of market yields for zero-coupon Treasuries with similar maturities.

Yield Curve Theories

Several theories attempt to explain the reason for the shape of the yield curve. These include the expectations theory, the liquidity theory, the preferred habitat theory, and the market segmentation theory.

The Expectations Theory

Expectations theory
Yield curve theory asserting long-term interest rates are based on expectations about future short-term interest rates

The **expectations theory** asserts that long-term rates are based on expected future short-term rates. In other words, forward rates should indicate the market's perception of which direction rates will be moving. For example, an upward-sloping yield curve would indicate that future short-term rates would be increasing; a flat yield curve indicates that future short-term rates will remain constant; and a downward, or inverted, yield curve represents the expectation that short-term rates will be declining. One shortcoming of this theory is that it does not reflect the inherent increased risk or uncertainty in longer-term bonds.

The Liquidity Preference Theory

Liquidity preference theory
Yield curve theory asserting long-term bonds have greater yields to compensate investors for increased interest rate risk

According to the **liquidity preference theory**, investors prefer certainty and expect to be compensated for uncertainty. This theory incorporates a liquidity premium into the expectations theory model. Under this theory, investors require a premium for the increased exposure to interest rate risk inherent in long-term bonds. Yield curves generally will be upward sloping, reflecting a higher premium for longer term bonds.

The Preferred Habitat Theory

Preferred habitat theory
Yield curve theory asserting financial institutions prefer to match asset maturities to liability maturities

The **preferred habitat theory** is similar to the market segmentation theory (described in the next paragraph), and it states that institutions (generally financial institutions) prefer to match the maturity of their assets to that of their liabilities. In other words, institutions generally try to match the maturity or duration of their assets and liabilities. Under this theory, institutions have an incentive to shift their maturities or duration if the premium for the switch is significant enough. Therefore, it is possible to have any shape yield curve under this theory.

Market Segmentation Theory

Market segmentation theory
Yield curve theory asserting yields are determined by the laws of supply and demand for specific bond maturities

According to the **market segmentation theory**, interest rates for varying maturities are determined by supply and demand. Institutions may have liabilities that are short term, intermediate term, or long term and will generally want to match the maturity of their assets with the maturity of their liabilities. As a result, there are certain types of institutions that lend and borrow using different categories of maturities. This results in a separate market for short-term borrowings, intermediate-term borrowings, and long-term borrowings. Each maturity market has its own balance between supply and demand, creating the possibility of a yield curve of almost any shape.

▌DURATION AND IMMUNIZATION

Duration
Provides a time-weighted measure of a security's cash flows in terms of payback

The concept of **duration**, developed by Frederick Macaulay in 1938, provides a time-weighted measure of a security's cash flows in terms of payback. Duration is defined as the average time it takes a bondholder to receive the interest and principal from a bond in present value dollars. This number can be used by bond investors to measure a bond's price volatility compared with those issues of equal coupon rates and different maturity dates.

Duration can be used for the following:

■ Measuring of a bond's volatility

■ Estimating the change in the price of a bond on the basis of changes in interest rates

■ Immunizing a bond or bond portfolio against interest rate risk

Calculating Duration

EXAMPLE   Consider a three-year corporate bond selling for $973.27, paying interest annually, with a face value of $1,000, a coupon rate of 5%, and a YTM of 6%.

Year	Cash Flow	PV of CF	PV × Year
1	$50.00	$47.17	$47.17
2	$50.00	$44.50	$89.00
3	$1,050.00	$881.60	$2,644.80
Total		$973.27	$2,780.97

Duration is then determined by dividing $2,780.97 by the current market price of the bond ($973.27). Calculating duration for a bond requires the following steps.
1. List the years
2. List the cash flows
3. Determine the present value of the cash flows using the year and the YTM for the bond, 6%
4. Multiply the year number by the present value (e.g., 2 × 44.50 = 89.00)
5. Sum the last column and divide by the current market price

The duration of this bond is determined by dividing the sum in the last column by the current market price of the bond, yielding **2.8573 years** ($2,780.97 ÷ $973.27).

Duration as a Measure of a Bond's Volatility

Duration provides investors with a method to easily compare a bond's volatility to the volatility of other bonds. Simply, bonds with higher durations are more volatile when interest rates change than bonds with lower durations. Therefore, the volatility of bonds increases as the duration increases. The main factors that impact a bond's duration are coupon rate, maturity, and yield to maturity.

Coupon Rate

The coupon rate of a bond and its duration have an inverse relationship. The duration of a bond cannot exceed the maturity of a bond. Generally, the duration of a bond is less than its term to maturity. A bond's duration will equal its maturity only if the bond is a zero-coupon bond.

When the coupon rate is increased, the investor is receiving cash flows more quickly, decreasing the time the investor must wait to be paid back the initial investment. A quicker payback means a shorter duration.

Term to Maturity

The term to maturity of a bond and its duration have a direct relationship. Bonds with greater maturities have longer durations. However, the increase in duration is at a diminishing rate. Exhibit 12A.5 illustrates this point. This graph shows the duration for a bond with a 10% coupon and a 10% YTM, calculated for maturities ranging between 1 year and 30 years.

EXHIBIT 12A.5 Duration at Various Maturities for a 10% Coupon Bond with 10% YTM

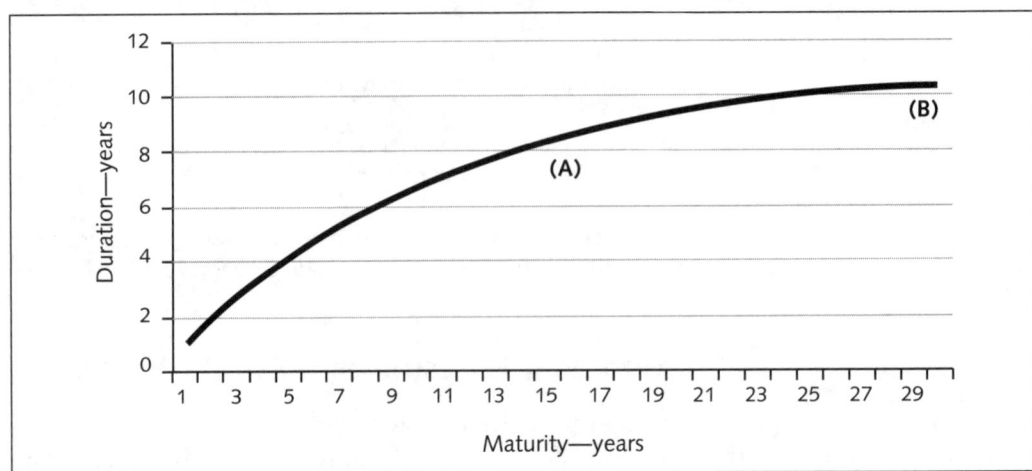

As shown, duration is directly impacted by maturity, however, at a decreasing rate. In this graph, the duration for a maturity of 15 years is approximately 8.4 years (A), and the duration for a maturity of 30 years is only 10.4 years (B). Although the actual maturity doubled, the duration of the bond increased by only two years.

Yield to Maturity

As with the coupon rate of a bond, the market interest rate, or current yield to maturity, is inversely related to duration. As the level of interest rates increases, the durations of bonds decrease, and, if interest rates decrease, durations will increase. A reduction in market interest rates results in a lower reinvestment rate for coupon payments, which extends the payback period for the bond.

Bond Price Changes

Another important application of duration is its use in determining the price change in a bond or bond portfolio on the basis of changes in interest rates. As interest rates change, bond prices are impacted. Exposure to interest rate risk is a significant variable to fixed-income investors. What is the percentage of change in the bond or bond portfolio, given a specific change in interest rates? The answer to this question can be determined by understanding the relationship between a bond's price and its duration. As we discussed, coupon, maturity, and YTM all impact duration. These same factors also determine the price of a bond. Therefore, duration can assist us in determining the estimated change in the price of a bond on the basis of changes in interest rates. The following formula provides an estimate, based on the duration and the change in market interest rates, of the percentage change in the price of a bond:

$$\frac{\Delta P}{P} = -D \left[\frac{\Delta y}{1+y} \right]$$

$\Delta P/P$ = percentage change in the price of a bond
D = duration of the bond
y = yield to maturity for the bond
Δy = change in YTM as a decimal

As the formula describes, the estimated change in the price of a bond equals the duration of a bond divided by one plus the YTM and multiplied by the change in interest rates.

E X A M P L E How much will the price of a bond with a price of $974.22 and a duration of 2.8 years increase if its YTM changed from 8% to 7.5%? (Assume a 7% coupon rate)

$$\frac{\Delta P}{P} = -2.8 \left[\frac{-.005}{1+0.08} \right]$$

$$\frac{\Delta P}{P} = 0.01296$$

The price of the bond should increase by 0.01296, or 1.3%, resulting in a new price of $986.88 (1.013 × $974.22).

Using Duration to Immunize Bond Portfolios

As noted in the previous section, interest rate risk is one of the major concerns of fixed-income investors, and managers of fixed-income portfolios. When interest rates increase, the price of bonds will decline. However, an offsetting position must be considered. As interest rates increase, the reinvested coupon payments can be invested at higher rates, offsetting the decline in the value of the bond. This offsetting of price and reinvested coupon payments is illustrated in the following table.

Interest Rates Move	Value of Bond (Inverse to Interest Rates)	Value of Reinvested Coupon Payments (Direct to Interest Rates)
↑	↓	↑
↓	↑	↓

As demonstrated previously, when interest rates increase, the value of bonds declines, but the value of reinvested coupon payments increases. Similarly, as interest rates decline, bond prices increase and the value of reinvested coupon payments decreases. This offsetting is the basis for immunizing a bond or bond portfolio against interest rate risk.

Immunization is the concept of minimizing the impact of changes in interest rates on the value of investments. The goal of immunization is to protect the bond portfolio against interest rate fluctuations and reinvestment rate risk. The purpose of immunization is to provide a stable compound rate of return that equals the calculated YTM at the purchase of the bond, despite interest rate fluctuations. The portfolio is considered immunized if the realized rate of return is at least as great as the computed YTM calculated at inception. Another way to think of immunization is that a bond portfolio is immunized when the actual future value is at least as great as had been expected at inception.

A bond portfolio is initially immunized at the point of duration. Therefore, if an investor were to match the duration of a bond portfolio to the time horizon of his goal, his portfolio would be initially immunized. This can be easily accomplished with a zero-coupon bond. An investor who had a cash need in 10 years could simply purchase a 10-year, zero-coupon bond and hold it to maturity. This will eliminate all reinvestment rate risk and interest rate risk. However, purchasing a zero-coupon bond with the desired maturity may not always be feasible. Although not as ideal as a zero-coupon bond, an ordinary coupon bond can effectively immunize a portfolio.

Matching the duration to the investor's cash need immunizes the portfolio against initial changes in interest rates. As time passes, however, the bond portfolio will need to be rebalanced so that the duration and remaining time continue to match. Rebalancing should be done once or twice per year. If rebalancing is performed more frequently than twice per year, transaction costs will minimize any benefits derived through the strategy.

Immunization

Minimizing the impact of changes in interest rates on the value of investments

Traditional Methods of Immunizing Bond Portfolios

Traditional strategies for immunizing bond portfolios from interest rate risk include the ladder strategy, the barbell strategy, and the bullet strategy.

The Ladder Strategy

Ladder strategy
Portfolio immunization strategy that uses a portfolio of bonds with staggered maturities

The **ladder strategy** is accomplished by establishing a portfolio of bonds with staggered maturities. For example, ten $20,000 bonds could be purchased with maturities ranging from one to ten years for a total portfolio value of $200,000. The shorter maturity bonds would be less subject to price fluctuation than the longer term bonds, and they would combine to provide the desired duration. This approach provides two advantages. First, because there is a combination of long- and short-term bonds in the portfolio, the laddered portfolio will provide higher yields than a portfolio consisting entirely of short-term bonds. Second, because one bond matures each year, cash is regularly available to the investor.

The Barbell Strategy

Barbell strategy
Portfolio immunization strategy that uses a portfolio of short- and long-term bonds

When using the **barbell strategy**, one-half of the portfolio is invested in short-term bonds, and the other half is invested in long-term bonds. The long-term end of the barbell allows the investor to lock in attractive long-term interest rates, whereas the short-term end ensures that the investor will have the opportunity to invest in other assets if the bond market declines in value. For example, a $200,000 fixed-income portfolio might be invested as $100,000 in five-year bonds and $100,000 in 15-year bonds.

The Bullet Strategy

Bullet strategy
Portfolio immunization strategy that uses a portfolio of bonds with similar maturities

When investors purchase a series of bonds with similar maturities, focused around a single point in time, they are utilizing a **bullet strategy**. Like the previous two strategies, the portfolio is created to achieve the desired duration. For example, assume that an investor wants all of the bonds to mature in 10 years. Therefore, using the bullet strategy, the investor buys two bonds immediately, two bonds two years from now, and two more bonds four years from now. As a result, the bonds purchased immediately have a maturity date of 10 years, the bonds purchased two years later have maturity dates of eight years, and the bonds purchased four years later have maturity dates of six years.

WHERE ON THE WEB

Bloomberg **www.bloomberg.com**

Bureau of the Fiscal Service **www.publicdebt.treas.gov**

CNN Money **money.cnn.com**

Ginnie Mae (GNMA) **www.ginniemae.gov**

Marketwatch from Dow Jones **www.marketwatch.com**

Moody's Investors Service **www.moodys.com**

MSN Money **www.msn.com/en-us/money**

Securities Industry and Financial Markets Association (formerly the Bond Market) **www.sifma.org**

Standard & Poor's **www.standardandpoors.com**

Treasury Direct (U.S. Savings Bonds) **www.savingsbonds.gov**

Supplement B:
Equity Securities

LEARNING OBJECTIVES

This supplement provides information on equity securities. The following topics are covered:

- Characteristics of equities

- Types of common stock

- Preferred stock

- Foreign securities

- Risks associated with equities

- Measures of return

- Equity markets

- Market indexes and averages

- Market positions

- Margin accounts

- Trading securities

- Methods of security analysis

- Valuation models

BASIC CONCEPTS OF OWNERSHIP INVESTMENTS

What Ownership Means

Dividends

Distributions of cash or additional shares of stock paid to the shareholders of a corporation

Declaration date

Date on which a corporation's board of directors declares a dividend payment creating an obligation on the company to make a dividend payment to shareholders

Record date

The date at which an owner of the common stock of a corporation is entitled to receive the dividend payment

Ex-dividend date

The date on which the market reflects the dividend payment

Payable date

The date that the dividend will actually be paid

Dividend reinvestment plans (DRIPs)

Dividends are automatically reinvested into the company's stock without the use of a broker

Ownership securities are securities that represent some form of ownership interest in a corporation. Corporations are artificial, legal entities whose creation and operation are controlled by state statutes. To become a corporation, a business must incorporate within a state. As part of the incorporation process, and as one method of raising additional capital, a corporation may issue shares of common stock. Holders of these shares have certain rights and benefits, including the right to receive dividends, the right to vote on corporate issues, the right to limited liability, and, finally, the right to ultimate distribution of assets in the event of liquidation.

Numerous risks are inherent in owning common stock. The primary reason that investors are willing to accept these risks is that equities have earned significantly higher returns than other types of investments over long periods. Common stock returns consist of two primary sources, dividends and capital appreciation.

Dividends

Companies have positive net income when their earnings are greater than their expenses. A company's excess earnings may be reinvested into the business in the form of new or existing projects or paid to the shareholders of the corporation in the form of **dividends**.

Four dates are important when discussing payment of a dividend: the **declaration date**, the **record date**, the **ex-dividend date**, and the **payable date**. The board of directors declares a dividend payment, which creates an obligation for the company to make a dividend payment to shareholders. The record date represents the date on which an investor needs to be an owner of the common stock to be entitled to receive the dividend payment. The ex-dividend date is two business days before the date of record. Because most trades settle three days after the trade date, a customer must purchase the stock three business days before the date of record to qualify for the dividend.

Finally, the payable date is simply the date on which the dividend will actually be paid to the shareholders of record. Therefore, someone who sells shares after the record date, but before the payable date, will receive the dividend payment.

Many companies allow investors to automatically reinvest dividends rather than receive them in cash. These **dividend reinvestment plans (DRIPs)** allow investors to accumulate wealth over time by reinvesting cash dividends back into their equity holdings. DRIPs have traditionally been programs established by corporations to allow their shareholders to purchase additional shares without a broker and to automatically reinvest dividend payments. These programs can provide cost-efficient investing for the average investor.

Capital Appreciation

Capital appreciation
The form of return the investor receives when a company chooses to retain the earnings and invest in additional projects; appreciation of the stock

A company may choose to retain the earnings it has generated and invest in additional projects. In this case, the owner or investor receives the return in the form of appreciation of the stock, which is referred to as **capital appreciation**. Capital appreciation is simply an increase in the market price of the common stock.

Voting

Statutory voting
One vote per share of common stock

Cumulative voting
A shareholder casts votes equal to the number of vacant positions on the board of directors multiplied by the number of shares owned, allocated in any way the shareholder wishes

Proxy voting
Authorizing an agent to cast the votes for the shareholder

In addition to the returns from dividend income and capital appreciation, owners of common stock have voting rights. These voting rights include the right to vote for the board of directors and the right to vote on corporate issues such as certain mergers and acquisitions.

Voting can take the form of statutory voting or cumulative voting. **Statutory voting** authorizes one vote per share of common stock for each item on the ballot, such as seats on the board of directors. **Cumulative voting** may be advantageous for small/minority shareholders by giving them a greater opportunity to offset the votes of large shareholders. With cumulative voting, a shareholder casts votes equal to the number of vacant positions on the board of directors multiplied by the number of shares owned, allocated in any way the shareholder wishes. In addition, voting can be done in person or by proxy. **Proxy voting** involves sending a written authorization to an agent to cast the votes for the shareholder.

Maintaining Ownership Percentage

Preemptive right
Allows shareholders to maintain ownership percentage by requiring new issues of stock to be offered first to current shareholders

Some companies permit owners to maintain their ownership percentage in the event of any new offering of company stock. For example, an investor who owns 10% of a company might be given the opportunity to purchase 10% of any new stock offering. This right, known as a **preemptive right**, allows the investor to maintain the current ownership percentage. A rights offering allows stockholders to purchase common stock below the current market price during the subscription period. Stockholders may exercise their rights, sell them, or let them expire.

Liability

Because corporations are separate legal entities, they are generally responsible for all debts and claims arising from all sources. As a result, shareholders are protected from personal liability.

TYPES OF EQUITY SECURITIES

Common Stock

Common stock
Ownership interest in a company

Common stock represents an ownership interest in a firm. If the company succeeds, the investor will receive returns from the investment. However, if the company does not perform well, then the value of the stock will decline. Because there are thousands of companies, a classification system has been developed to categorize equity securities. One classification system is based on the type of stock. This classification system includes defensive stocks, cyclical stocks, blue-chip stocks, growth stocks, income stocks, interest-sensitive stocks, value stocks, and technology stocks.

Defensive Stocks

Defensive stocks
Stock of companies that are relatively unaffected by general fluctuations in the economy

Stocks that are relatively unaffected by general fluctuations in the economy are considered **defensive stocks**. These companies tend to have steady (although slow) growth, become popular during economic recessions, and lose popularity during economic booms. Many of these companies provide products that are necessary for everyday life. Thus, the demand for these products will not be adversely affected by changing economic cycles. Defensive stocks are usually found in the following industries:

- Utilities
- Soft drinks
- Groceries
- Candy
- Drugs/pharmaceuticals
- Tobacco

Another way to think of defensive stocks is that they have low systematic risk because they are not greatly affected by changes in the economy and the market. Therefore, these securities will typically have low betas relative to the overall market.

Cyclical Stocks

Cyclical stocks
Stock of companies that tend to prosper in expanding economies and perform poorly during down business cycles

Cyclical stocks tend to prosper during economic expansion and perform poorly during a downturn in the business cycle. When the economy is growing, demand strengthens, and these companies are able to make large profits. When the economy is in a downturn, these companies are hurt by declines in demand and are less profitable. In recessions, they employ cost-cutting measures to improve the bottom line (earnings) and, as a result, these companies end up in a healthy financial position for the next economic upturn. The companies regarded as cyclicals usually have large investments in plant and equipment and, therefore, high fixed costs. These stocks come from industries that include the following:

- Automobiles
- Cement
- Paper
- Airlines
- Railroads

- Machinery
- Steel

Because these stocks typically perform well when the economy is booming and perform poorly when the economy is in recession, cyclical stocks are highly correlated with the overall stock market. In addition, these stocks will typically have higher betas relative to the overall market.

Blue-Chip Stocks

Blue-chip stocks
Stock issued by older, well-established companies that maintain the ability to pay dividends both in years the company has income and in years the company has losses

Stocks issued by highly regarded investment quality companies are called **blue-chip stocks**. These older, well-established companies tend to maintain their ability to pay dividends both in years the company has income and in years the company has losses. These companies are often leaders in their respective industries. They tend to offer investors quality investments with steady dividend streams and relatively consistent growth.

Growth Stocks

Growth stocks
Stock issued by companies whose sales, earnings, and market share are growing at higher rates than the average or the general economy

Growth stocks are stocks issued by companies that have sales, earnings, and market share growing at higher rates than the average or the general economy. Many blue-chip stocks can also be classified as growth stocks. Because these companies are growing and expanding, they typically do not pay large dividends. Most of the earnings generated from these companies are reinvested in the company to support future growth. These companies are expected to grow and appreciate more rapidly than other companies.

Price appreciation is appealing to investors because it remains untaxed until the appreciation is recognized (i.e., there is no taxable gain until the stock is sold and the gain is recognized for tax purposes). This growth acts as an income tax deferral and allows for higher compounding returns. Because investors trying to accumulate wealth do not usually need current income, these stocks match their financial needs better than other investments due to smaller dividends and tax deferred appreciation.

Emerging growth stocks are a subset of growth stocks, comprised of smaller and younger companies. These companies have survived the early years and are beginning to grow and expand. Emerging growth stocks have great potential for investment but are also subject to tremendous risk.

Income Stocks

Income stock
Stock issued by companies in the maturity phase of the industry life cycle and that pay out the majority of their earnings in the form of dividends

As discussed earlier, dividends are one of the two ways investors benefit from investing in common stock. Some stocks are attractive because they make large divided payments relative to other firms. Often these companies are in the maturity phase of the industry life cycle and pay out the majority of their earnings in the form of dividends. Utilities are a good example of an **income stock**.

Interest-Sensitive Stocks

Interest-sensitive stock
Stock issued by companies whose performance is largely affected by changes in interest rates

Because the performance of some companies is largely affected by changes in interest rates, their stock is considered **interest-sensitive stock**. For example, the housing industry is more productive and has more demand when interest rates are low because it is cheaper for consumers to purchase homes. When interest rates rise, the cost of purchasing of a home goes up, causing the demand for a new home to decline. These trends also affect lumber, plumbing, furnishing, and household equipment companies. Rising interest rates cause the cost of debt to increase; therefore, companies that have large amounts of debt may have increasing interest expense. These companies, like consumers, have the opportunity to refinance their debt during periods of low interest rates.

Some of the companies heavily affected by interest rates are:

- insurance companies,
- savings and loans, and
- commercial banks.

Value Stocks

Value stocks

Stock trading at prices that are low given the stock's historical earnings and current asset value

Stocks trading at prices that are low given their historical earnings and current asset value are referred to as **value stocks**. These securities tend to have low price-to-earnings ratios and tend to be out of favor in the market. Value investment managers attempt to find these high-quality companies that are temporarily undervalued by the market in hopes that the market will recognize their true value and their price will increase.

Technology Stocks

Technology stocks

Stocks of companies involved in high-technology fields categorized by above-average earnings potential and high risk

Technology stocks are part of the broader technology sector that encompasses the research, development, and distribution of technology based products. These stocks include companies that are involved in electronics, data storage, computer software, robotics, and life science companies. Companies in this sector sell and service tech-based equipment, networking systems, and online services to businesses, governmental agencies, and home users. Tech stocks offer the investor large potential gains coupled with high risk because of business uncertainty and fierce competition. Therefore, the typical tech stock investor must have a high risk tolerance, and be prepared to assume a high level of risk.

Preferred Stock

Preferred stock

A type of stock that has characteristics of both fixed-income investments and of common stock in that dividend payments must be paid each year before paying a dividend to the common shareholders

Cumulative preferred stock

Preferred stock that requires receipt of previously unpaid preferred dividends before common shareholders receive dividend payments

Participating preferred stock

Preferred stock that receives dividend based on the performance of the firm in addition to the specified preferred dividend

Preferred stock has characteristics of both fixed-income investments and of common stock. Shareholders of preferred stock generally receive dividends each year equal to a stated percentage of the par value of the stock if declared by the company. For example, a $100 par, 5.5% issue of preferred stock pays a dividend of $5.50 each year for each share owned. The corporation must satisfy these dividend payments before paying a dividend to the common shareholders. If the corporation is required to pay any unpaid preferred dividends from prior years before paying a dividend to the common stockholders, the stock is referred to as **cumulative preferred stock**.

Preferred stock also may be participating, which means that preferred shareholders share in the profits of the corporation. With **participating preferred stock**, the preferred shareholders generally receive dividend payments. Then, holders of common stock receive dividends equal to the amount paid to the preferred shareholders. Additional funds for dividends are then allocated between the participating preferred and common shareholders, according to stock agreements.

Preferred stock has a preferential right over common shareholders to the assets of the corporation. This right must be satisfied before the common shareholders receive any assets upon liquidation. However, secured and unsecured creditors will be compensated before preferred shareholders receive any assets of the corporation.

Convertible preferred stock
Preferred stock that includes the right to convert preferred stock into a specific number of common shares at the option of the stockholder

Foreign securities
Securities issued by non-U.S. firms

American depositary receipts (ADRs)
Certificates issued by U.S. banks representing ownership in shares of stock of a foreign company that are held on deposit in a bank in the firm's home country

Convertible preferred stock has a conversion right that allows holders to redeem or trade in the preferred stock for a specified number of common stock shares. Convertible preferred stock provides the safety of a fixed-income security with the growth potential associated with common stock.

Foreign Securities

Foreign securities may provide significant benefits to U.S. investors. First, securities issued outside the United States have substantial return potential. Many of the countries outside the United States are less developed and, therefore, provide opportunities for significant growth. Second, foreign markets are generally not as efficient as the U.S. market and, consequently, provide opportunities to find undervalued securities. Third, foreign securities provide diversification benefits. The returns and movements in the equity markets of most foreign countries are not highly correlated with that of the U.S. market. Therefore, adding foreign asset classes to a portfolio may increase the efficiency of the portfolio.

Foreign securities are generally classified as being from developed countries or emerging markets. Developed countries include Canada, Japan, England, and France. Emerging markets include those countries with significant growth potential that are currently underdeveloped. Examples of emerging markets are Argentina, Brazil, and Chile.

American Depositary Receipts (ADRs)

American depositary receipts (ADRs) are one of the easiest methods of acquiring individual foreign securities. They are certificates issued by U.S. banks representing ownership in shares of stock of a foreign company that are held on deposit in a bank in the firm's home country. ADRs are denominated in U.S. dollars and pay dividends in U.S. dollars. Although they are denominated in U.S. currency, they do not protect holders from exchange rate risk. Changes in currency rates between the firm's currency and the U.S. dollar will be reflected by a change in the value of the ADR.

ADRs are considered cross-listed because the foreign shares are listed on the U.S. stock exchange as well as the foreign exchange. One of the benefits of ADRs is that the foreign company must satisfy the requirements of U.S. exchanges, including compliance with U.S. Generally Accepted Accounting Principles (GAAP) and certain disclosure and reporting requirements.

Purchasing Foreign Shares on Foreign Stock Exchanges

Direct purchases of foreign securities on foreign exchanges are more difficult than indirect purchases. However, with the advance of technology, the process has simplified. Establishing a brokerage account in a foreign country or using a foreign branch of a U.S. broker can accomplish the purchase of foreign shares on foreign exchanges. The foreign transactions require completion in the local currency. Monitoring direct foreign investments is certainly more difficult than monitoring a mutual fund.

RISKS OF EQUITY SECURITIES

As with all securities and investments, certain inherent risks (both systematic and unsystematic) associated with equity investments must be considered. Some of the investment risks that we will discuss include market risk, interest rate risk, business risk, financial risk, exchange rate risk, and country risk.

Market Risk

Market risk represents the tendency for changes in the market to influence the prices of equities. When the market is on the rise, most stocks increase in value. Conversely, stocks tend to fall with declines in the market. Often, a move in the market is prefaced by some change in the broad economic environment.

Interest Rate Risk

Interest rate risk is one of the major risks affecting fixed-income securities and bond portfolios. Equity securities also are affected by changes in interest rates. When interest rates rise, there is negative pressure on the value of common stocks and when interest rates fall, stocks tend to increase in value. The three primary reasons for this relationship are increased borrowing costs, attractiveness of alternative investments, and the valuation of securities.

Increased Borrowing Costs   Most companies use debt to finance capital expansion and acquire assets. The cost of debt is interest payments. When interest rates rise, the cost of future borrowing will increase. This increased borrowing cost can cause earnings to decline. When earnings decrease, the value of the company is reduced. Therefore, changes in interest rates have a direct impact on the cost of borrowing and, thus, on the earnings of a firm.

Attractiveness of Alternative Investments   When interest rates rise, so do the corresponding yields on fixed-income securities. As yields increase, bonds become more attractive. Investors become unwilling to assume the additional risk inherent in equities when the spread between the expected return on bonds and stocks is small. Therefore, as investors decrease investments in equities so that they can take advantage of the fixed-income yields, there is downward pressure on the equity market, causing it to decline.

The Value of Equities   The value of a security today is the sum of the discounted future cash flows expected from the investment. As interest rates rise, the discount rate used to value a security must also increase. Because an increase in the discount rate results in a lower valuation, stocks generally decline when interest rates rise.

Business Risk

Business risk is a risk associated with a specific business, which includes the speculative nature of the business, the management of the business, and the philosophy of the business. Different types of businesses will have different levels of risk. For instance, we generally consider technology securities to be more risky than defensive stocks.

Business risk can also be thought of as the uncertainty of operating income. Utility companies have relatively stable and steady operating income streams and, therefore, have lower business risk. Because they have unsteady or fluctuating operating income levels, cyclical companies (such as auto manufacturers) have higher business risk.

Financial Risk

The method by which firms acquire their assets is directly related to financial risk or financial leverage. With regard to their capital structure, companies may use debt through the issuance of bonds, or they may issue equity securities. When companies choose debt to finance the purchase of additional assets, the level of financial risk increases. This increased leverage is the same as for individuals when they use margin to purchase securities.

E X A M P L E Consider two firms that each earn $50,000 of net income. Both firms are in the same business, and each has $400,000 of assets. Company A has not issued debt and has financed all of its assets with equity. Company B has issued $300,000 of debt and $100,000 of equity.

	Company A	Company B
Net income	$50,000	$50,000
Debt	$0	$300,000
Equity	$400,000	$100,000
ROE (return on equity)	12.5%	50%

Notice that while each company's earnings and assets are the same, the return on equity is quite different. This disparity results from the different capital structure of each firm. Because Company B has chosen to use debt as a method of financing, it has increased the leverage of the firm. However, Company B's returns are likely to be more volatile over time than Company A's returns.

Exchange Rate Risk

The uncertainty of returns in foreign investments due to changes in the value of a foreign currency relative to the valuation of the investor's domestic currency is referred to as exchange rate risk. A foreign investment is subject not only to the inherent risk of the investment, but also to the risk that the foreign currency will weaken relative to the domestic currency, decreasing the gains (or increasing the losses) from the investment.

Country Risk

International investments are subject to country risk, which is the unique risk associated with a particular country. These risks include both political and economic risks. The United States is generally thought to have the lowest country risk because its political and economic systems are considered the most stable.

MEASURES OF RETURN

The primary purpose of investing is to earn a positive return. Investors seek investments that are consistent with their risk and return preferences in an attempt to achieve financial goals. Therefore, investors should understand and be able to calculate the returns from equity securities. There are several methods of calculating returns from equity securities, each with distinct advantages and disadvantages.

Time-Weighted and Dollar-Weighted Returns

Time-weighted returns
A method of determining an internal rate of return by evaluating the performance of portfolio managers without the influence of additional investor deposits or withdrawals to or from the portfolio

Dollar-weighted returns
A method of determining the internal rate of return that an individual investor earned on the basis of the investor's particular cash flow into and out of the portfolio

Although time-weighted returns and dollar-weighted returns are both methods of determining an internal rate of return, they have very different purposes. **Time-weighted returns** are used to evaluate the performance of portfolio managers separate from the influence of additional investor deposits or withdrawals. **Dollar-weighted returns** are used to determine the rate of return an individual investor earned on the basis of the investor's particular cash flows into and out of a portfolio. The example comparing Portfolios A and B illustrates the difference between dollar-weighted returns and time-weighted returns.

Assume we are comparing two portfolios, A and B. Over a four-year period, they each earn exactly the same return per period. However, each portfolio has a different set of investor deposits and withdrawals.

Portfolio A

Period	Investor Cash Flows	Beginning of Period Value	End of Period Value	Periodic Rate of Return
0	($1,000)	$1,000	$1,200	20.00%
1	$400	$800	$700	–12.50%
2	($300)	$1,000	$1,400	40.00%
3	$200	$1,200	$1,000	–16.67%
4	$1,000	—	—	—
DWR =	8.2311%		TWR =	5.2034%

Portfolio B

Period	Investor Cash Flows	Beginning of Period Value	End of Period Value	Periodic Rate of Return
0	($1,000)	$1,000	$1,200	20.00%
1	($400)	$1,600	$1,400	–12.50%
2	$400	$1,000	$1,400	40.00%
3	($400)	$1,800	$1,500	–16.67%
4	$1,500	—	—	—
DWR =	2.0245%		TWR =	5.2034%

Note: Negative cash flows are deposits and positive cash flows are withdrawals.

Using the uneven cash flow keys of a financial calculator, we have calculated the dollar-weighted return (DWR) for Portfolio A to be 8.23% and the DWR for Portfolio B to be 2.02%. Is it reasonable to use a methodology that results in drastically different returns when each portfolio produced the same periodic rates of return? The answer depends on our goal. To evaluate the overall return for the portfolio, we want to use DWR. This provides investors with their actual return. For portfolio managers, DWR is generally not used. This is because managers do not control the timing of additional investments into the portfolio or withdrawals from the portfolio. A more accurate measure of the portfolio manager's ability is the time-weighted return (TWR).

The TWR for Portfolios A and B is calculated as follows (r = return for given period; n = number of periods):

$$\text{TWR} = [(1 + r_1)(1 + r_2)(1 + r_3)...(1 + r_n)^{1/n} - 1] \times 100$$

$$(1 + .20)(1 - .1250)(1 + .40)(1 - .1667)^{1/4} - 1 = .0520338 \times 100 = 5.2034\%$$

Total Return

Total return

The sum of the capital appreciation/depreciation on an investment plus any income or earnings generated by the investment

Total return may be thought of as the sum of:

- the capital appreciation/depreciation on the underlying principal of the investment; and

- any income or earnings generated from that investment.

For example, a typical annual dividend paid (income or earnings) on a stock is 2%. If, in addition, the market value of the stock increases 6% from the beginning of the year to year end, the investor would have a total return on the stock of 8% (2% income + 6% capital appreciation). Whether an investor values the income or capital growth component of total return more highly (or both are valued equally) depends on both tax status and cash flow needs.

Dividend Yield

Dividend yield

The measure of a security's annual dividend payment as a percentage of the current market price

The measure used to compare the dividend payments from one company to another is called the **dividend yield** and is calculated as follows:

$$DY = \frac{\text{annual dividend per share}}{\text{current market price}}$$

If XYZ Company is paying an annual dividend of $4 per share and the current market price of the stock is $50, then the dividend yield of XYZ equals 8% ($4 ÷ $50). The dividend yield measure is useful for selecting stocks for inclusion in a portfolio of an investor who needs income derived from the portfolio.

▌ EQUITY MARKETS AND BENCHMARKS

Primary Market

Primary market

The market where new issues of securities are first offered to the public

Initial public offering (IPO)

First offering of equity securities to the general public

The **primary market** is the place where securities are initially offered to the public. These security offerings are in the form of **initial public offerings**, commonly referred to as IPOs. IPOs allow businesses and entrepreneurs access to the capital markets. Business owners may issue additional shares to the public to raise capital for the expansion and growth of their business. Although an IPO will dilute the ownership of the existing shareholders, it can provide the capital and resources necessary to dramatically expand the business.

Underwriting

Underwriting

The process by which investment bankers purchase an issue of securities from a firm and resell it to the public

To issue shares to the public, companies enlist the assistance of investment bankers to underwrite the stock issue. In the process of **underwriting** an IPO, the investment banker may assume some of the risk associated with selling the securities to the public. For example, an investment banker might agree to purchase an issue for $12 per share and then resell the issue to the public for $13 per share. This $1 profit is referred to as an underwriter's spread. In addition, underwriters often help the issuing firm determine its financial needs and the best investment vehicle to achieve the desired capital target.

Firm commitment
Equity underwriting in which the underwriter purchases the entire issue at a specific price from the firm and resells it on the open market

Standby underwriting
Equity underwriting in which the underwriter purchases any securities remaining after an initial offering

Best efforts agreement
Equity underwriting in which the firm agrees to repurchase any securities remaining after the initial offering is made by the underwriter

Private placement
A corporation selling a new issue of securities to a small group of institutions or sophisticated individual investors

Underwriting can take one of four forms: firm commitment, standby underwriting, best efforts, and private placement.

Firm Commitment   With a **firm commitment**, the underwriter purchases the entire issue of securities at a specific price, then attempts to sell it at a higher price. This arrangement shifts all risk to the underwriter. If the issue cannot be resold at a price above the purchase price, the underwriter will lose money on the transaction. Often, a syndicate of underwriters will be set up to spread the potential risk.

Standby Underwriting   When the underwriter purchases the remaining securities at a predetermined price after an initial offering (usually to existing shareholders/owners), the form of underwriting is called **standby underwriting**. This type of underwriting may reduce the issuer's risk, but it will increase the underwriter's risk.

Best Efforts   Under a **best efforts agreement**, the underwriter sells as much of the issue as possible, and the remainder is returned to the issuing company. No risk is shifted to the underwriter. This arrangement occurs when the issuing company is confident that the issue will be sold or the underwriter is concerned about the financial stability of the company.

Private Placement   The main attraction of a **private placement** is the lack of registration requirements associated with an IPO, resulting in less expense and less time. Generally, the issue can be placed quickly and at a low cost. Bonds have been the most common privately placed issues. A private placement cannot be sold to more than 35 unaccredited investors. An unaccredited investor is one who does not fit into one of the following categories:

- Net worth of more than $1 million

- Gross income in excess of $200,000 for each of the past two years, with the anticipation of the same level of income ($300,000 if the investor is a married couple)

In addition to reduced costs, private placements avoid the registration requirements of the SEC and the public's access to information that occurs when conforming to SEC requirements. Although private placements are limited to 35 unaccredited investors, there is no limit to the number of accredited investors.

Secondary Market

Secondary market
The market where investors can buy and sell securities with other investors

The **secondary market** is where investors buy and sell securities that have been issued previously in the primary markets. The secondary market provides liquidity to the capital markets and allows for the efficient trade of public securities.

- The first market is the exchange (auction) market where listed securities trade and includes the New York Stock Exchange (NYSE) and the over-the-counter (OTC) market.

- The second market provides a method of trading unlisted securities (OTC and Nasdaq).

Third market
Over-the-counter trading of equity shares that are listed on an exchange

- The **third market** consists of stocks traded both on the organized exchanges and on the OTC market. This market is especially important when the exchange is not trading a security or when trading occurs outside the normal operating hours of the exchange.

Fourth market
Composed of institutional traders who trade without the help of brokers

■ The **fourth market** is commonly used by institutions (e.g., pension funds) that trade in very large volumes among themselves without the help of brokers (INSTINET).

EXHIBIT 12B.1 Secondary Market

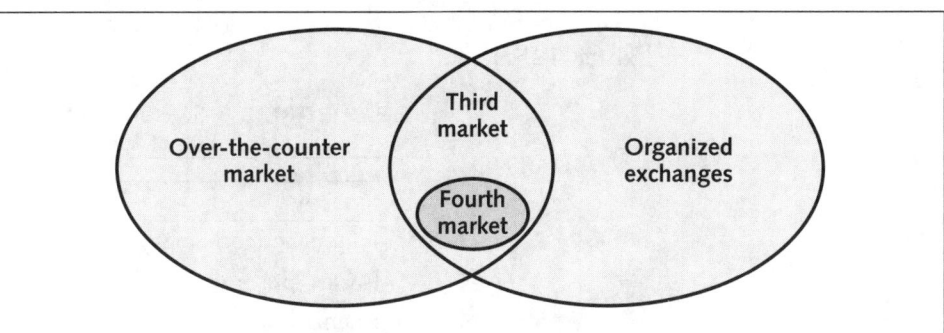

Market Indexes and Averages

The purpose of a market index or average is to provide information to investors and advisers concerning the overall movement and performance of the securities markets. Most securities are positively correlated with their respective index; the securities tend to increase when their index is increasing and decrease when their index is decreasing.

Dow Jones Industrial Average

Dow Jones Industrial Average (DJIA)
A financial index that is a price-weighted average of 30 leading industrial stocks used to measure the status of the equity market

The **Dow Jones Industrial Average** (DJIA), probably the best-known financial index in the United States, is a price-weighted average of 30 leading industrial stocks used to measure the status of the equity market. The 30 stocks currently included in the DJIA are identified in Exhibit 12B.2.

EXHIBIT 12B.2 DJIA Stocks (As of July 15, 2020)

3M	ExxonMobil	Nike
American Express	Goldman Sachs	Pfizer
Apple	Home Depot	Procter & Gamble
Boeing	IBM	Raytheon Technologies
Caterpillar	Intel	Travelers Companies Inc.
Chevron	Johnson & Johnson	United Healthcare
Cisco Systems	JPMorgan Chase	Verizon
Coca-Cola	McDonald's	Visa
Disney	Merck	Walmart
Dow Chemical	Microsoft	Walgreens

The DJIA consists of stocks that are considered blue-chip stocks. Although these companies are often leaders in their industry, the composition of the average does change over time. However, the DJIA does have fundamental shortcomings as it fails to reflect payment of cash dividends, ignores stock dividends of less than 10%, fails to account for the number of shares outstanding, and consists of a biased sample of stocks. Even with these shortcomings, the DJIA is highly correlated with other broader market indexes, such as the S&P 500. The correlation coefficient between the DJIA and the S&P 500 is greater than 95%. A high correlation indicates that the DJIA is an adequate representation of the market in spite of its fundamental weaknesses.

Standard & Poor's 500 Index

Standard & Poor's Index (S&P 500)

A financial index of 500 U.S. equities chosen for market size, liquidity, and industry group representation

The **Standard & Poor's Index** (S&P 500) traditionally has been the measure of the U.S. large capitalization market used by academics and financial service professionals. The index consists of 500 U.S. equities chosen for market size, liquidity, and industry group representation. These 500 stocks are represented by the industries described in Exhibit 12B.3.

EXHIBIT 12B.3 S&P 500 Sector Breakdown
(As of April 30, 2020)

Industry	As % of 500
Information technology	25.7%
Health care	15.4%
Financials	10.6%
Communication services	10.8%
Consumer discretionary	10.5%
Industrials	7.9%
Consumer staples	7.4%
Utilities	3.3%
Real estate	2.9%
Energy	3.0%
Materials	2.5%

Market capitalization

The product of the number of outstanding common stock shares and current stock price

The S&P 500 is a market capitalization-weighted index. This means that a company's **market capitalization** (outstanding shares multiplied by the current stock price) is represented in the index. Market capitalization indexes typically provide a better measure of the market than averages such as the DJIA. (However, the DJIA is highly correlated with the S&P 500.)

Russell Indexes

Russell 2000® Index

A well-known index used to benchmark small capitalization companies

All of the U.S. Russell indexes are market capitalization weighted and are subsets of the Russell 3000® Index, which represents 99% of the U.S. equity market. The **Russell 2000® Index** is an index that is used to benchmark small capitalization companies. The Russell 1000® Index represents the thousand largest companies in the Russell 3000® Index. Russell also maintains numerous value and growth indexes that allow for comparisons with various portfolio manager styles.

Wilshire 5000 Index

Wilshire 5000 Index

A financial index consisting of over 5,000 U.S.-based companies; often used as a measure of the overall market within the United States

The **Wilshire 5000 Index** is another well-known index that is used as a measure of the U.S. broad market. This index consists of over 5,000 U.S.-based companies and is often used as a measure of the overall market within the United States.

MSCI EAFE Index

MSCI EAFE Index

An index measuring the international securities markets

The **MSCI EAFE** (Morgan Stanley Capital International Europe, Australasia, and Far East) **Index** is a measure of the international securities markets. This index provides an indication of how a portfolio consisting of companies outside the United States might perform over time and is probably the best known measure of international markets.

Benchmarks

The indexes just discussed can be used to compare portfolio results and evaluate an investment manager's performance. Although many investors use comparisons with other managers as a measure of performance, benchmarks should also be examined for comparative purposes. A good benchmark includes the following characteristics:

- Unambiguous—the composition and weighting of the components of the benchmark must be clearly delineated

- Investable—the option to invest in the benchmark is available

- Measurable—the benchmark's return should be calculated on a relatively frequent basis

- Appropriate—the benchmark must be consistent with the manager's investment philosophy and style

- Reflective of current investment opinions—the manager has current investment knowledge of the securities that make up the benchmark

- Specified in advance—the benchmark should be constructed before the beginning of the evaluation period

These six properties improve the usefulness of a benchmark as an investment management tool and allow for a better measure of a portfolio manager's performance.

PURCHASING EQUITY SECURITIES

Long Positions

Long position
The purchase of a stock in hopes that it will appreciate over time

The most prevalent type of position investors take is a long position. A **long position** is the purchase of a stock in hopes that it will appreciate over time. If a stock is purchased for $45 and is sold for $100, then the stock has increased in price, resulting in a gain of $55.

Short Positions

Short position
A type of position investors take by selling borrowed shares in hopes that the stock price will decline over time

Investors also may benefit when they find securities that are believed to be overvalued. A short sale allows the investor to profit from the decline in the value of the security. A short sale is selling shares that are not owned by the investor. This transaction is accomplished by borrowing shares of a stock from a broker. Once the shares are sold in the market, the investor is credited with the proceeds. However, the investor must, at some point, replace the borrowed shares. This is known as covering the **short position** and is accomplished by purchasing the shares in the market and replacing the shares that were borrowed.

The short seller will profit if the shares can be purchased at a price less than the price at which the shares were sold. If the stock appreciates after the shares are sold short, the investor will lose money.

Two technical issues must be discussed regarding short selling. The first concerns dividend payments that occur before closing the short position. A short sale involves borrowing stock and selling it in the market. At the time of a short sale, two investors believe that they own the stock and are entitled to receive any dividend payment that is declared and paid. However, the company declaring the dividend will only recognize one owner (the third party who purchased the shares in the market) and will only make one dividend payment. Therefore, the short seller has the responsibility to make up the other dividend payment to the party from whom the stock was originally borrowed.

The second issue is that a short seller is required to have a margin account and post margin as if the investor were acquiring stock. If the stock increases, then the short seller may be required to restore the margin.

E X A M P L E   Allison sells short 100 shares of ALC stock currently trading at $35 per share. The initial margin requirement is 50%. If the price of ALC stock declines to $25 and Allison covers her short position by repurchasing the stock, what is her gain in both dollars and as a percentage?

Allison's investment		$1,750 (100 shares × 0.5 × $35)
Short sale proceeds		$3,500
Cost to repurchase	–	$2,500
Dollar gain	=	**$1,000**
Percentage gain	=	**57.14%** ($1,000 ÷ $1,750)

Margin Accounts

Cash accounts

A type of brokerage account that requires all securities purchased by the investor to be paid for in full without any indebtedness

Margin accounts

A type of brokerage account that allows the investor to borrow funds from the broker to purchase additional securities without adding cash to the account

An investor opens a brokerage account as either a cash account or a margin account. **Cash accounts** require that all securities purchased by the investor be paid for in full without any indebtedness. If a cash account is fully invested in securities, then the only way to purchase additional securities is to add cash to the account or sell some of the current securities to generate cash. In contrast, **margin accounts** allow the investor to borrow funds from the broker to purchase additional securities without adding cash to the account. Margin accounts give investors flexibility and the ability to use leverage.

Margin accounts require that the account owner pay for a certain percentage of the cost of an investment. The margin percentage that must be established for the purchase of a security is referred to as the initial margin. The Federal Reserve Board sets the minimum initial margin percentage, which is currently 50%. Therefore, the initial purchase of a security requires the investor to put up at least 50% of the initial purchase.

In addition to the amount that initially must be put up by the investor, the investor must maintain an equity position in the account that equals or exceeds the maintenance margin. The maintenance margin is typically 35%, which means that the equity in the account must equal or exceed 35%. However, some securities may require a higher maintenance requirement. If the equity in the account drops below the maintenance margin, then the account holder receives a margin call from the broker. A margin call is a request for funds in order to restore the account equity to the maintenance margin.

Determining the Price for a Margin Call

Account equity is defined as the market value of the securities in the account less any outstanding debt. The equity percentage equals the account equity divided by the market value of the securities. The price at which a margin call is received occurs when the equity percentage drops below the maintenance margin.

EXAMPLE   Lauren purchases 100 shares of Solvent Company for $104 per share. Lauren uses a margin account with a 50% initial margin for the purchase and is concerned about receiving a margin call. If the maintenance margin equals 35%, then Lauren will receive a margin call if the stock falls below $80 per share, as illustrated:

$$\text{Margin call} = \frac{\text{debit balance}}{1 - \text{maintenance margin}}$$

$$\text{Margin call} = \frac{\$52}{1 - 0.35} = \$80$$

(Note: The debit balance is 50% of the cost per share of $104.)

Determining How Much to Deposit to Restore Account Equity

If the stock or account drops below the price at which there is a margin call, then the account owner must deposit sufficient funds to restore the account equity to the maintenance margin. This amount can be determined by asking two questions. How much equity does the broker require? How much equity does the investor currently have?

Using the above example, assume that the stock drops in value to $70. In this case, Lauren would be required to deposit $6.50 per share ($24.50 – $18.00).

Required Equity		Current Equity Position	
Current value of stock	$70.00	Current value of stock	$70.00
Equity %	35%	Loan amount	(52.00)
Required equity	$24.50	Current equity	$18.00

The investor must maintain an equity position of 35%, which is the given maintenance margin. Because the price of the stock is currently $70, Lauren must have $24.50 ($70 × 35%) of equity in her account. To determine Lauren's current equity position, subtract the outstanding debt from the value of the stock. Because her current equity position equals $18, and she must have $24.50 of equity, Lauren must fund the account with the difference of $6.50 per share for a total of $650 (100 shares × $6.50).

Trading Securities

Investors should be aware of the different types of orders that can be used to acquire shares of common stock. The four standard types of orders include market orders, limit orders, stop loss orders, and stop limit orders. All orders are considered day orders unless otherwise specified. If an order is not filled within the trading day, it will expire. Orders can be good for a specific time, or they can be good-til-canceled. Time limits are often used with limit and stop orders because they are not as likely as market orders to be filled during the day.

Market Order

Market order
Type of securities order that requires the trade be made at the best current market price

Most orders are **market orders**. In fact, 75–80% of all orders have traditionally been market orders and these orders have the highest priority. A market order is an order to buy or sell a security at the best current market price. These orders must be filled before the other types of orders are considered. Although these are the fastest orders, they do not have limits or a specific price and, therefore, are subject to the fluctuations and time lines of the market.

Limit Order

Limit order
Type of securities order that requires the trade be made at a specified price or better

The objective of a **limit order** is to acquire or sell a security at a specific price—that is, one that is better than the market at the time the order is placed. The price acts as a ceiling for purchases and a floor for sales, and the order will be held until filled or canceled. Limit orders are maintained in chronological order. Higher priced purchase limit orders take priority over lower priced purchase limit orders. Even if the price for the stock is below (or above) the limit order, there is no guarantee that it will be filled.

E X A M P L E   David, a seasoned investor, has reviewed all the relevant financial information and has determined that the Ashbey Corporation is worth $45 per share. While the stock is trading between $48 and $50, he places a limit order at $45. This will ensure that if the order is filled to purchase shares of Ashbey Corporation, David's price will be no higher than $45. If Ashbey continues to trade above $45, David's order will not be filled.

Stop Loss Order

Stop loss order
A type of securities order that becomes a market order when the security's price reaches a specific level

Stop loss orders are used to protect investors against large losses. If the market price reaches a certain point, the stop order will turn into a market order. For instance, an investor who is long in a security might place a stop order 10 points below the current market price to protect the appreciation of the stock against serious declines in market price. Likewise, these orders can be used to limit losses in connection with short sales.

E X A M P L E   Steve purchased Roland, Inc. for $29 per share. The stock is now trading at $73 per share. He has an unrecognized gain of $44. If Steve is concerned about the price of the stock declining, he can place a stop order at $70. If the stock price drops to $70, a market order is placed immediately. However, the order may be filled at $69 or $68. The stop order protects his profit position.

Stop Limit Order

Stop limit order
A type of securities order that becomes a limit order when the security's price reaches a specific level

Stop limit orders are similar to stop loss orders except they turn into limit orders when triggered. The stop order price and the limit order price are both specified. Stop limit orders are the least used type of order.

E X A M P L E   If Dina owns 5,000 shares of Prez's Pretzels, which is selling for $35 per share, and she is concerned about the price dropping, she may want to place a stop limit order. If she places the order "sell 5,000 shares at $32 stop, $30 limit," and the price drops to $32, the broker will attempt to sell the stock for $32 but will not sell below the $30 limit order.

Good-Til-Canceled Order

Good-til-canceled order
An order to buy or sell a security at a specific or limit price that lasts until the order is completed or canceled

A **good-til-canceled (GTC) order** is an order to buy or sell a security at a specific or limit price that lasts until the order is completed or canceled. A GTC order will not be executed until the limit price has been reached, regardless of the time frame. Investors often use GTC orders to set a limit price that is far away from the current market price. Some brokerage firms may limit the time a GTC order can remain in effect and may charge more for executing this type of order.

METHODS OF ANALYSIS

The two primary forms of analysis used by security analysts to determine whether a particular security should be purchased or, if already owned, should be sold are technical analysis and fundamental analysis.

Technical Analysis

Technical analysis
The search for identifiable and recurring stock price patterns

Technical analysis is an attempt to determine the demand side of the supply/demand equation for a particular stock or set of stocks. This method is based on the belief that studying the history of security trades will help predict future movements. Technical analysts (or chartists, due to their reliance on charts) believe that the history of the stock price will tell the whole story of the security and that there is no need to be concerned with earnings, financial leverage, product mix, and management philosophy. Recall that technical analysis is in direct contradiction to the efficient market hypothesis that, at all levels, states that the current price already reflects all historical price data. Technical analysts believe that basic economic assumptions support the theory of technical analysis.

- The interaction between supply and demand is the foundation for the value of all goods and services.

- Both rational and irrational factors control supply and demand. The market weighs each of these factors.

- The market and individual securities tend to move in similar trends that endure for substantial lengths of time.

- Variations in the relationship between supply and demand can change prevailing trends.

- Shifts or variations in supply and demand can be detected in the movement of the market.

Technical analysts use a variety of techniques to predict the trend of the market, such as moving averages, relative strength analysis, contrary opinion rules, and breadth of the market indicators. One of the most significant stock price and volume techniques is called the Dow theory.

The Dow theory, developed initially by Charles H. Dow and later expanded by William Hamilton, is the basis for many of the theories of technical analysis. The Dow theory suggests three types of price movements. Primary moves are the first type of movement and represent large trends that last anywhere from one to four years. These moves are considered to be bull or bear markets for up or down moves, respectively. The second type of movement is called an intermediate move that is a temporary change in movement called a technical correction. The time frame for these corrections is generally less than two months. The final type of movement is referred to as a ripple that occurs during both primary and secondary movements and represents a small change in comparison to the first two movements. The belief is that all three of these movements are occurring at the same time.

The Dow theory uses the Dow Jones Industrial Average (DJIA) and the Dow Jones Transportation Average (DJTA) as indicators of the market. This theory is based on the concept that measures of stock prices, such as averages and indexes, should move coincidentally. Thus, if the DJIA is moving upward, the DJTA should also be increasing. Support from both market indicators would suggest a strong bull market. Likewise, if both averages are declining, there is considerable support for a strong bear market. When the averages are moving in opposite directions, the future direction of stock prices is unclear.

Fundamental Analysis

Fundamental analysis
The analysis of a stock's value using basic, publicly available data, such as the stock's earnings, sales, risk, and industry analysis

Fundamental analysis is the process of determining the intrinsic value of a security. This intrinsic value is generally thought of as the present value of future cash flows (often the dividend stream of an equity security). Through fundamental analysis, investors attempt to determine what the company is worth. Once the value is determined, it is compared to the market value of the security. If the market value of the security is less than the intrinsic value, then the investor will purchase the security. If the market value of the security is greater than the intrinsic value, the investor should sell shares currently held or delay the purchase of shares.

The process of determining the value of a security encompasses many aspects. The fundamental analyst incorporates broad macroeconomic trends, industry analysis, and company analysis into an estimate of a security's value. The analysis of broad economic trends includes analyzing growth of the economy, analyzing monetary and fiscal policy, interest rates, unemployment, consumer spending, and inflation. Analysts look at industry data to determine market competitiveness, strengths and weaknesses, and other factors that impact the value of a security within the context of its industry. At the company level, fundamental analysts use financial statement analysis, valuation models, and ratio analysis to assist in determining the company's worth. Once forecasts about future cash flows are developed, a fundamental analyst uses valuation models to determine the value of the company.

Fundamental analysts may be further differentiated according to where they begin (and finish) their analysis. A top-down fundamental analyst begins with researching the overall economy and current state of the secondary market. Specifically, such an analyst then selects an industry (or industry sector) that he believes will perform best over an upcoming time frame. Finally, the analyst then screens a database of securities within that industry to find acceptable companies (and acceptable stocks) in which to recommend investment.

The other type of fundamental analyst, the bottom-up fundamental analyst, begins with an examination of the company's fundamentals and then considers the financial prospects for the industry in which the company operates. Indeed, because of emphasis first and foremost on the security itself, the bottom-up analyst is sometimes known as a stock-picker. Finally, this type of analyst then considers the prospects for the overall economy.

VALUATION MODELS

One of the components of selecting a stock in which to invest is determining its intrinsic value using one of the following valuation models.

Valuing Preferred Stock

Because preferred stock generally pays a fixed dividend and often has no maturity, it is considered a perpetuity. In other words, the dividend continues indefinitely. Therefore, we can use the no-growth (perpetuity) dividend discount model to value a preferred stock.

$$V = \frac{D}{r}$$

The value of a preferred stock equals the dividend (D) divided by the required rate of return of the investor (r). For example, if a preferred stock is paying a dividend of $6 and the investor's required rate of return equals 12%, the intrinsic value of the preferred stock should equal $50, as follows:

$$V = \frac{\$6}{0.12} = \$50$$

If the current market price of the security were greater than $50, the investor should not purchase the preferred stock as an investment. However, if the stock was trading at a price of $50 or less, the purchase of the security would be a wise decision.

Constant Growth Dividend Discount Model

Common stock dividends typically do not remain steady over time. Generally, the dividend grows over time. Assuming a constant rate of growth for the dividend, we can expand the above model to accommodate the growth component of the dividend stream. The following formula is used to value a common stock with a constant growing dividend:

$$V = \frac{D_1}{r - g}$$

The value of a common stock equals the dividend one period from today (D_1) divided by the difference between the investor's required rate of return (r) and the expected growth rate of the dividend (g).

E X A M P L E   JEM stock is paying a current annual dividend of $6, which is growing at a constant rate of 4% per year. If the investor's required rate of return equals 12%, then the intrinsic value of the common stock equals $78:

$$V = \frac{\$6 \times (1.04)}{0.12 - 0.04} = \$78$$

D_1 must be determined by multiplying the current dividend (D_0) by one plus the growth rate ($1 + g$). The model is based on a constant growing dividend and on the required return of the investor. Notice that the model will be meaningless if the growth rate (g) equals or exceeds the required rate of return of the investor (r). This model is most appropriate for mature companies.

Multistage Growth Dividend Discount Model

The multistage (variable) growth dividend discount model assumes that the growth rate of the stock's dividend is not constant but rather changes (either up or down). This model is most appropriately used for a company in the growth phase. To determine the intrinsic value of a stock using this model, follow a three-step process.

1. Compute the value of each future dividend until the growth rate stabilizes.

2. Use the constant growth dividend discount model to compute the remaining intrinsic value of the stock at the beginning of the year when the dividend growth rate stabilizes.

3. Use the uneven cash flow method to solve for the net present (intrinsic) value of the stock.

EXAMPLE   Consider CPM stock with a current dividend of $1 per share and a current market price of $25.56 per share. The current dividend is expected to grow for three years at a rate of 3% annually and then 2% annually thereafter. Assume an investor's required rate of return is 6%.

1. Compute the value of each future dividend until the growth rate stabilizes (Years 1–3).
    D_1 = $1.00 × 1.03 = **$1.03**
    D_2 = $1.03 × 1.03 = **$1.06**
    D_3 = $1.06 × 1.03 = **$1.09**

2. Use the constant growth dividend discount model to compute the remaining intrinsic value of the stock at the beginning of the year when the dividend growth rate stabilizes (Year 4).
    D_4 = $1.09 × 1.02 = $1.11
    V = $1.11 ÷ (0.06 – 0.02) = **$27.75**

3. Use the uneven cash flow method to solve for the net present (intrinsic) value of the stock.
    CF_0 = $0
    CF_1 = $1.03
    CF_2 = $1.06
    CF_3 = $1.09 + $27.75 = $28.84
    I/YR = 6%
    Solve for NPV = $26.13

In this example, the intrinsic value of the stock is **$26.13**.

Price-to-Earnings (P/E) Ratio

P/E ratio

A measure of how much the market is willing to pay for each dollar of earnings of a company

The **P/E ratio** is a measure of how much the market is willing to pay for each dollar of earnings of a company. The ratio is determined by dividing the current market price of the security by the earnings per share (EPS) for the company:

$$P/E = \frac{\text{current market price}}{\text{earnings per share}}$$

EXAMPLE   If XYZ stock is trading at $50 per share and has earnings per share of $4, its P/E ratio equals 12.5.

The P/E ratio may be used to compare companies within an industry. Better quality companies generally have higher P/E ratios than lower quality companies. Investors are willing to pay more for each dollar of earnings from a high-quality company.

Valuing the Company vs. Valuing the Stock

Up to this point, we have limited our valuation methodology to those stocks that pay dividends. With preferred stock, we use the valuation of a perpetuity to determine its price. Similarly, we valued common stock with a constant growing dividend. What about those companies that do not regularly pay dividends? Our focus simply needs to shift from the valuation of the stock to the valuation of the company. Instead of looking at the cash flows from the security, we need to address the cash flows that are generated by the company.

By using the models developed for finding the present value of a stream of cash flows, we can obtain the value of the company. The inputs in the model are the relevant cash flows and the discount rate.

Free cash flow to equity

Term that describes the available cash after meeting all of the firm's operating and financial needs; used to calculate the value a company

The term **free cash flow to equity** describes the available cash after meeting all of the firm's operating and financial needs and is generally calculated as follows:

	Revenue
−	Operating expenses
=	**Earnings before interest, taxes, and depreciation (EBITDA)**
−	Depreciation
−	Amortization
=	**Earnings before interest and taxes (EBIT)**
−	Interest
−	Taxes
=	Net income
+	Depreciation
+	Amortization
=	**Cash flow from operations**
−	Preferred dividends
−	Capital expenditures
−	Working capital needs
−	Principal repayments (loan)
+	Proceeds from new debt issues
=	**Free cash flow to equity**

Once the cash flow is forecasted, then it can be used to value the company. The discount rate that is used can be derived from reviewing comparable companies in the market or by using models such as the capital asset pricing model.

Once the value of the company is established, then the value of the stock can be derived from the company's valuation. However, valuing the share price of the stock is not as simple as dividing the value of the company by the outstanding shares of common stock. The value of the company reflects an inherent control premium. This premium reflects the ability to change the board of directors, change the dividend policy, and influence the business opportunities that are undertaken. The concept of the control premium can be seen in the market any time a company acquires another company. The acquiring company is willing to pay more than the current market price of the stock because it is acquiring control. Therefore, the value of a share of stock as listed on an exchange has been discounted from the proportionate value of the company because the stock represents a minority interest.

WHERE ON THE WEB

American Association of Individual Investors **www.aaii.com**

American Stock Exchange **www.amex.com**

Barron's Online **www.barrons.com**

Bloomberg.com **www.bloomberg.com**

MSN Money **www.msn.com/en-us/money**

CNN Money **www.money.cnn.com**

S&P Dow Jones Indices **us.spindices.com**

Kiplinger **www.kiplinger.com**

Nasdaq **www.nasdaq.com**

NYSE Euronext (NYSE Group, Inc. and Euronext, N.V. combined) **www.nyse.com**

TD Ameritrade **www.tdameritrade.com**

U.S. Securities and Exchange Commission **www.sec.gov**

Yahoo Finance **finance.yahoo.com**

Supplement C: Mutual Funds

LEARNING OBJECTIVES

This supplement provides additional information on mutual funds. The following topics are covered:

■ Types of investment companies

— Unit investment trusts
— Exchange-traded funds
— Closed-end investment companies
— Open-end investment companies (mutual funds)
— Hedge funds

■ Mutual fund fees

■ Mutual fund classification

■ Advantages of mutual funds

■ Types and objectives of mutual funds

■ Mutual fund selection

■ Performance measures

■ Mutual fund selection issues

TYPES OF INVESTMENT COMPANIES

Investment companies

Financial services companies that sell shares of stock to the public and use the proceeds to invest in a portfolio of securities

Investment companies are financial services companies that sell shares of stock to the public and use the proceeds to invest in a portfolio of securities. Although each investor or shareholder may have a relatively small investment in total, the funds of all shareholders pooled together allow the investment company to create a widely diversified portfolio with certain economies of scale. The four types of investment companies are unit investment trusts, exchange-traded funds, closed-end funds, and open-end investment companies (mutual funds).

Investment companies are generally nontaxable entities. These companies do not pay federal or state income tax. Instead, investment companies act as flow-through entities or conduits whereby interest income, dividends, and capital gains all flow through from the investment company to the shareholders and are reported on the investor's individual tax return. The income that flows through retains its character as to ordinary income or capital gain and is allocated to each shareholder based on the number of shares owned. The tax treatment of investment companies is similar in concept to the tax treatment of partnerships and S corporations.

In addition to meeting specific requirements of the Internal Revenue Code, investment companies are also regulated by the Securities and Exchange Commission (SEC) under the Investment Company Act of 1940. Investment companies are also regulated under the Securities Act of 1933, the Securities Exchange Act of 1934, and the Investment Advisors Act of 1940. For more information on these acts, see Appendix C at the end of the text.

Unit Investment Trusts

Unit investment trust (UIT)

A registered investment company that is passively managed and may invest in stocks, bonds, or other securities

A **unit investment trust** (UIT) is a registered investment company that is passively managed and may invest in stocks, bonds, or other securities. Investors generally purchase units, which are sold at net asset value plus a commission, with the idea that they will hold the units until they mature. As income is earned and securities mature, investors receive both income (interest and/or dividends) and principal from the trust.

In the case of a UIT that invests in stocks, the trust will have a defined maturity date, at which time the investor will have the option of rolling over the proceeds, receiving a pro rata distribution of the UIT's underlying securities, or receiving cash from the investment.

UITs are known as unmanaged, or passively managed, funds because professional managers initially select securities to be included in the portfolio, and those securities are generally held until they mature. For example, a UIT investing in municipal bond securities may have a portfolio of municipal bonds with staggered maturities. These bonds will generally be held until they mature. As coupon payments are received from the bond issuer, they are passed along to the unit holders. When a bond matures, the face value will be passed through to the unit holders. Although the holdings of UITs are monitored, the securities within the fund generally remain the same throughout the life of the fund.

The traditional UIT invested in fixed-income securities. Today, however, there are a variety of UITs available to meet the objectives and risk tolerances of investors. UITs invest in a wide array of securities, including municipal bonds, corporate bonds, U.S. government bonds, international bonds, and mortgage-backed securities.

Exchange-Traded Funds (ETFs)

Exchange-traded fund (ETF)

A type of investment company whose investment objective is to achieve the same return as a particular market index

Exchange-traded funds (ETFs) are portfolios or baskets of stocks that are traded on an exchange. ETFs are index-based equity instruments that represent ownership in either a fund or a unit investment trust and give investors the opportunity to buy and sell shares of an entire stock portfolio as a single security. Common examples include QQQ (Nasdaq-100 Index) and SPDRs (Standard & Poor's Depositary Receipts, tracking the S&P 500 index or sectors of the index). Unlike mutual funds, ETFs can be purchased and sold throughout the day. In addition, they can be bought on margin and sold short. ETFs typically have lower annual expenses than mutual funds.

Exchange-traded funds are usually passively managed (however, some are now actively managed) and attempt to track a specific index or sector within the index. Although ETFs are traded on exchanges, investors may be able to buy or redeem shares from the fund family, generally in 50,000-share blocks. The price of ETF shares is based on the value of the underlying securities; however, it may not be equal to NAV because of supply and demand for the shares. Although the price of ETF shares may trade at a discount or premium, the difference should be minimal.

In most cases, the annual expense ratio for ETF shares is lower than for the majority of index mutual funds. However, ETF shares that are purchased using a broker require a commission to be paid. Depending on the commission and the size of the investment, one alternative may be better than the other. ETFs have low turnover and, therefore, lower taxable distributions than most mutual funds. When there is a substantial amount of mutual fund share redemptions, the manager is forced to liquidate some of the underlying securities to generate enough cash for redemptions. This does not occur in ETFs because shares are either sold or redeemed in-kind.

Most mutual funds have cash that is not invested, which is a result of new contributions into the fund or cash that is maintained for redemptions. ETFs do not have this cash management problem and may have better performance than mutual funds.

International Exchange-Traded Funds (ETFs)

International ETFs are passively managed foreign index funds designed after Standard & Poor's Depositary Receipts (SPDRs), which track the S&P 500 index. They are similar to open-end investment companies (mutual funds) in that they are open ended and the shares trade at or near net asset value (NAV). However, as with closed-end funds, international ETFs trade in the secondary market.

International ETFs, along with the other methods of foreign investing, provide investors with numerous advantages over investing solely in domestic equities. When foreign investment is combined with domestic investment, advantages include higher potential returns, lower levels of risk, and greater portfolio efficiency.

Closed-end fund

A type of investment company whose shares trade in the same manner that publicly traded stocks trade in the secondary market

Closed-End Investment Companies

A **closed-end fund** is a type of investment company whose shares trade in the same manner that publicly traded stocks trade in the secondary market. Shares of closed-end funds are listed on a stock exchange or trade in the over-the-counter market. Because shares trade in the same manner as other stocks, their prices are subject to the fluctuations in the supply and demand for the shares in the market. Although the value of securities held within the fund is relatively easy to determine, the share price for the fund will rarely be directly equal to the value of the underlying securities. The shares will generally sell at a premium or discount relative to the net asset value of the fund.

After the initial public offering, a closed-end fund will generally not issue additional shares. Unlike an open-end fund, a closed-end fund's capitalization is considered fixed, because it generally does not add assets to the fund after initial capitalization.

Because the pool of assets to be invested for a closed-end fund is fixed and shares are not redeemed, the manager of a closed-end fund has a great deal of flexibility in managing the assets within the fund. For example, the closed-end fund manager does not have to plan for cash redemptions as with a mutual fund (open-end investment company). This characteristic of closed-end funds allows the manager to invest in less liquid securities that may have higher expected returns than more liquid securities.

Closed-end funds invest in a wide array of securities, including municipal bonds, corporate bonds, U.S. government bonds, international bonds, mortgage-backed securities, convertible securities, domestic equities, and foreign equities. A particularly interesting closed-end fund is known as an equity dual-purpose fund. This type of fund invests primarily in securities of U.S. companies but has two classes of shares. The first class of shares consists of income shares that receive all dividend income, but no capital appreciation. The second class of shares consists of capital shares that receive all capital appreciation, but no dividend income. An investor interested in income only, such as a retiree, might purchase the first class of shares.

One likely reason that closed-end funds have not been as popular as open-end funds is that the fees generated by the fund managers and operators of closed-end funds are not as high as those of open-ended funds. Good performance in an open-end fund attracts significant increases in fund assets, resulting in a larger base of assets upon which to charge the management fee. A closed-end fund that has great performance may have shares selling at a premium, but additional funds are generally not forthcoming. Therefore, increasing the management fees through an open-end mutual fund is easier than a closed-end fund.

Another reason that closed-end funds may not be as popular as open-end funds is the requirement of a broker to buy or sell shares for a closed-end fund. With an open-end fund, an investor must simply call the fund to request the shares be redeemed. The process of purchasing mutual fund shares directly from a fund family is easier than setting up a brokerage account and purchasing closed-end fund shares. In addition, open-end funds are easier for investors to comprehend because their share price is based solely on the price of the underlying securities.

Open-End Investment Companies (Mutual Funds)

Mutual funds
Open-end investment companies that sell shares of stock to the public and use the proceeds to invest in a portfolio of securities on behalf of their shareholders

Mutual funds are investment vehicles that provide individual investors and institutional investors easy access to capital markets. They are a type of investment company that sells shares of stock to the public and uses the proceeds to invest in a portfolio of securities on behalf of its shareholders. The many benefits to investing in mutual funds will be discussed in this section.

Over the past few decades, mutual funds have become the predominant method for small investors to gain access to equity and fixed-income investments. The growing popularity of mutual funds is evidenced by the increasing number of mutual funds available to investors as well as the amount of assets invested in mutual funds. In the United States,

Open-end investment company

An investment company whose capitalization constantly changes as new shares are sold and outstanding shares are redeemed

Net asset value (NAV)

The price at which shares of an open-end investment company are sold. The NAV of a fund is determined by subtracting total liabilities from total assets of the fund and dividing the difference by the outstanding shares.

there are more than 8,000 mutual funds, which means that there are more mutual funds than there are listed equity securities. Assets invested in mutual funds have increased to almost $18 trillion at the end of 2018.

Open-end investment companies are referred to as open-end because they are not limited in the number of shares that can be sold. The total capitalization of these funds is constantly changing. Some investors are purchasing shares while others are redeeming their shares. All shares are sold by the mutual fund family and redeemed by the mutual fund family. Investors must be provided with specific information when purchasing mutual funds. The prospectus contains information regarding the fund's investment policies, objectives, sales charge, performance, and management expenses.

The price at which shares are sold is referred to as **net asset value** (NAV). Subtracting total liabilities from total assets (cash + current value of securities) of the fund and dividing the difference by the outstanding shares determines the net asset value of the fund. Each day, as the prices of the underlying securities change in value, so will the NAV for the fund. All shares will be purchased for and redeemed at NAV. However, commissions and other sales charges may be charged against the purchase or redemption of shares.

Mutual fund shares are either purchased directly from the fund family or purchased through a broker. Purchases made directly with the fund family are processed by mail, telephone, internet, or by visiting office locations. Shares purchased through a broker or other financial services person will ordinarily be charged a commission or a sales charge. These fees compensate the broker as an investment adviser.

EXHIBIT 12C.1 The Structure of a Mutual Fund

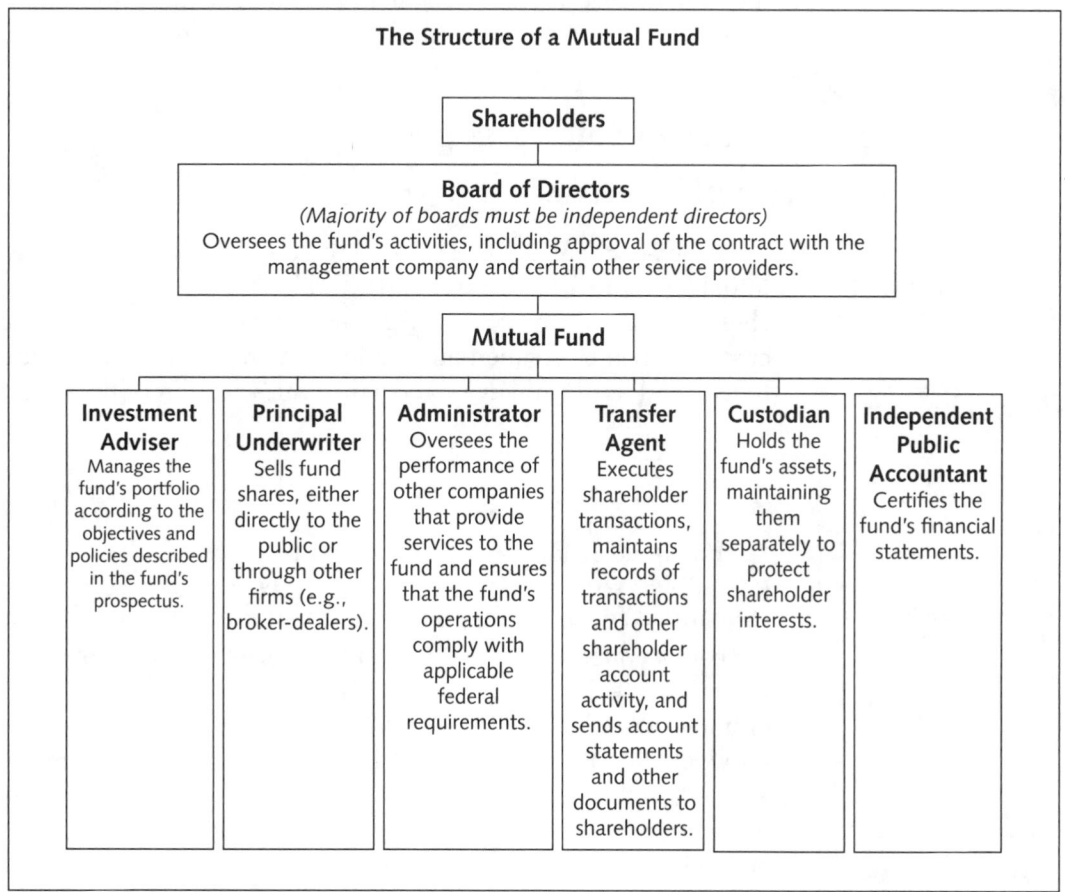

Source: *A Guide to Understanding Mutual Funds,* Investment Company Institute, Washington, DC, 2007

Hedge Funds

Hedge funds

An unregistered, privately offered, managed pool of capital for wealthy, financially sophisticated investors

A **hedge fund** is an unregistered, privately offered, managed pool of capital for wealthy, financially sophisticated investors. The fund typically implements a wide array of trading strategies, including, but not limited to, heavy borrowing and selling short, in an attempt to achieve a superior return for investors. A hedge fund strives to capture market inefficiencies and uses active management techniques. Unlike mutual fund managers, whose compensation solely depends on the amount of assets under management, hedge fund managers are paid on the basis of fund performance sometimes taking up to 20% of the profits, plus a base fee of up to 2% of the assets under management.

An investor of considerable means who is most interested in managing the risk of possible loss from an investment is the most likely type of investor in a hedge fund. In addition, an investor who is very concerned about the skill and expertise of the portfolio manager should strongly consider contributing to a hedge fund. Conversely, such a fund is usually beyond the financial means of the smaller investor who is looking for capital growth or current income, the two primary investment objectives of mutual fund shareholders.

MUTUAL FUND FEES

Just like other service providers, investment professionals charge fees for the management of an investor's assets. Fees are charged by the mutual fund company and by financial service professionals who sell mutual funds to their clients. These fees are generally categorized into loads or sales charges and operating expenses.

Loads or Sales Charges

Front-End Load

Front-end load

A sales charge based on the initial investment into a mutual fund

Front-end load is simply a term to describe a sales charge based on the value of the initial investment into the mutual fund. This load is incurred when an investor purchases shares of a mutual fund from a commission-based financial adviser. The sales charge is used to compensate the investment professional (usually someone unrelated to the fund itself) for advice related to the selection of the mutual fund.

Back-End Load

Back-end load

A sales charge incurred upon the sale or redemption of mutual fund shares rather than at the time of purchase

Back-end load is a term also used to describe a contingent deferred sales charge (CDSC) or redemption fee. However, the sales charge is incurred upon the sale or redemption of mutual fund shares rather than at the time of purchase. Today, many of the back-end loads found in mutual funds are in the form of a declining redemption fee, such that the percentage sales charge declines each year that the fund is held. For example, a fund might charge a 5% declining redemption fee. In such a case, an investor would pay 5% of the amount invested into the fund for redemption within the first year, 4% within the second year, and so on. After five years, no redemption fee would be charged. A back-end load is typically assessed on the lesser of the redemption value or the initial investment value.

Other Mutual Fund Fees

12b-1 Fees

12b-1 fee

A fee that pays for the services of brokers who sell mutual funds and who maintain the client relationship

Under the Investment Company Act of 1940, Section 12b-1, fees are permitted to pay for marketing and distribution expenses directly from a fund's asset base. The so-called **12b-1 fee** charged by the mutual fund company is used to pay for the services of brokers who sell the mutual funds and who maintain the client relationships. This fee is often paid in the form of trailing commissions, where commissions are paid to the broker over a period of years. The maximum 12b-1 fee that can be charged is 75 basis points per year. However, a separate 25 basis points can be charged as a "service fee," which effectively raises the total annual fee to 100 basis points or 1% of assets.

Management Fee

Management fee

A fee charged by an investment adviser for the management of a mutual fund's assets

The **management fee**, which is typically a predetermined annual percentage of the portfolio's asset value, is the fee charged by the investment adviser for the management of the fund assets. This fee is generally the single largest expense of a mutual fund and is included in the expense ratio.

Expense Ratio

Expense ratio

An indication of the annual fund expenses, stated as a percentage of total assets

The **expense ratio** is disclosed by all mutual funds in the fund prospectus and is an indication of the annual fund expenses, stated as a percentage of total assets. Included in this figure are the management fee, the 12b-1 fee, and other operating expenses related to running and operating the fund. The expense ratio does not include any applicable sales charges and is calculated by dividing a fund's expenses by its net average assets.

An investor should realize that reducing the expense ratio by 1% is essentially the same as increasing the rate of return by 1%. Therefore, managing the expenses paid for the management of mutual fund assets is an important element of the investment planning process.

MUTUAL FUND CLASSIFICATION

Mutual funds may be classified as either no-load funds or load funds. No-load funds are sold directly by the fund to the investor and do not charge front- or back-end loads.

Load funds

Mutual funds that charge either a front-end load or back-end load

Load vs. No-Load Funds

Mutual funds that charge either a front-end load or a back-end load are considered **load funds**. As stated previously, sales charges are used to compensate the brokers or sales force for their sales efforts. Note that funds without a typical front-end or back-end load that have a 12b-1 fee exceeding 25 basis points (.25% or .0025) are also considered load funds. Only if the 12b-1 fee is 25 basis points or less can the fund be called a no-load fund. Generally, **no-load funds** are purchased directly through the mutual fund family without the assistance of a broker.

No-load funds

Mutual funds purchased directly through the mutual fund family without the assistance of a broker

Classes of Load Fund Shares

Many fund families that offer load funds have different classes of shares that contain various sets of loads and expenses. Although there are no legal requirements as to the classification of shares of a load fund, most of the industry follows a similar classification system. Shares are generally categorized into three classes, known as class A shares, class B shares, and class C shares:

- Class A shares—these shares usually charge a front-end load with a lower 12b-1 fee.

- Class B shares—these shares usually charge a deferred redemption fee plus a higher 12b-1 fee. In addition, many of the class B shares will have a conversion feature that automatically converts the class B shares to class A shares after a period of years. The advantage of the conversion feature is that the investor will save expenses because the 12b-1 fee is lower for class A shares than for class B shares. However, the trend over the past several years has been for mutual funds to eliminate this share class.

- Class C shares—these shares often have a level deferred sales charge (often 1%), plus a higher 12b-1 fee. However, these shares do not convert to class A shares.

Many fund families have additional classes of shares that have a variety of features and fees. As a result, investors should carefully review the prospectus of each fund to determine the actual fees charged to shareholders.

Expense Ratios for Different Types of Funds

High-quality funds may have high or low expense ratios. However, as a general rule, the higher the expenses of the mutual fund, the more the fund manager will have to overcome to achieve strong return performance.

What expense ratio is appropriate for a mutual fund? The answer to this question depends on the objectives of the mutual fund. For example, actively managed funds (those that frequently buy and sell securities) require more research and support than passively managed index funds. Therefore, most actively managed funds will have higher expense ratios than passively managed funds. Similarly, it is more costly to manage international equities than domestic equities (usually 1–1.5%) because there are many more companies internationally than within the United States. In addition, the availability of accounting and financial information outside the United States is not as robust, making research more difficult and more costly. Therefore, international equity funds tend to have higher expense ratios relative to domestic equity funds.

ADVANTAGES OF MUTUAL FUNDS

Mutual funds provide many benefits to investors including access to a diversified portfolio with professional management and other benefits that are not found in other securities including low initial investment amounts, tax efficiency, liquidity, transaction cost efficiency, and shareholder services.

Overall, the dramatic growth of mutual funds has provided a great opportunity to the small investor. This growth has allowed an increasing number of individuals access to professional money managers, in both Section 401(k) plans and taxable investment accounts. When considering mutual fund investments, however, investors must be careful to understand the risks inherent in investing in the underlying securities when selecting a particular mutual fund.

Low Initial Investment

Most mutual funds have very low minimum investment requirements, allowing smaller investors access to many choices of mutual funds. In fact, most mutual funds have minimums of $1,000 or less. These low minimum investment requirements allow individuals, who would otherwise be precluded from such investments, access to the equity and fixed-income markets.

Diversification

Mutual funds provide an easy way to diversify a portfolio at a low cost. Some mutual funds have as many as 2,000 different securities in a single portfolio. This broad diversification, coupled with a low minimum investment requirement, achieves investor portfolio diversification at a very low outlay.

Ease of Access

Investors can purchase mutual funds easily. Mutual funds can be purchased directly from the mutual fund family or through a broker, bank, or other financial institution. To invest in a mutual fund directly through the fund family, an investor must call the fund family for an account application and prospectus, complete the application, and return the application to the fund family with a check for the amount of the initial investment. Investing in a mutual fund through a broker is as easy as calling the broker and requesting the purchase of the mutual fund. Usually, a brokerage account must be established before the purchase of the mutual fund can be made.

Professional Management

The same benefits that institutional investors find with professional portfolio managers can be found in mutual funds. The manager is constantly evaluating the holdings of the funds and alternative investment choices. Managers either have research departments or access to research that assists them in attempting to achieve above-average returns. Individual investors may find it difficult to match the performance of professional managers over time and through different markets. Therefore, mutual funds provide access to professional management without subjecting investors to the same restrictions on minimum account size.

Liquidity

Investors of mutual funds are always able to redeem their shares because mutual funds are required to redeem shares when requested by investors. These shares will be redeemed at the next available net asset value minus any applicable sales charge.

Transaction Cost Efficiency

Because mutual funds generally have hundreds of millions (and sometimes billions) of dollars under management, they enjoy economies of scale with regard to transaction costs. Many of their investment trades can be executed for pennies per share or less. These transaction costs are significantly less on a per share and dollar basis than most individuals could achieve on their own.

Variety of Mutual Funds

Green fund
A fund that invests in environmentally friendly companies

With more than 8,000 mutual funds available today, an investor has a plethora of choices in which to invest. There are mutual funds that can meet almost any investor's objectives, whether a growth fund, a sector fund, or a **green fund**.

Shareholder Services

Mutual funds provide investors with a variety of services that they would not have with an individual portfolio of securities. Basic services such as reporting may include monthly or quarterly statements that provide investors with a variety of information about their investments. This information generally includes the number of shares owned, net asset value of those shares, and total value of the mutual fund investment. In addition, statements will often provide information on investors' rate of return and tax basis in the fund.

Dollar cost averaging
The process of purchasing securities over time by investing a predetermined amount at regular intervals

Other services that are extremely helpful in accomplishing certain financial goals include automatic investing into the fund, often called **dollar cost averaging**. Investors can set up a mutual fund account such that an automatic electronic transfer of a certain dollar amount from the investor's checking or savings account is invested into the fund on a certain day each month regardless of market conditions or market prices. This allows an investor to automatically invest on a periodic basis, similar to payroll reduction with a Section 401(k) plan. The effect of this technique is to increase the number of shares gradually over a long period of time.

Like automatic investing, automatic withdrawals or sales services may also be provided. Individuals who need a certain sum of money every month can set up a directive to the mutual fund to automatically sell a certain number of shares to provide for this income need. The proceeds from the sale are then transferred into the investor's checking or savings account.

Other services that are common to mutual funds include automatic reinvestment of dividends and capital gain distributions, check-writing privileges, maintaining the shareholder adjusted tax basis, and telephone and wire redemptions. All of these services provide convenience and flexibility to investors that would not be provided by a single individual portfolio.

TYPES AND OBJECTIVES OF MUTUAL FUNDS

Although the classification system for mutual funds is not completely standardized or precise, there are certainly specific types and objectives of mutual funds that can be discussed. Mutual funds can be categorized into equity funds, bond funds, hybrid funds, or money market funds. As Exhibit 12C.2 shows, at the end of 2018, there were 4,753 equity funds, 2,174 bond funds, 783 hybrid funds, and 368 money market funds.

EXHIBIT 12C.2 Number of Mutual Funds (Year-End 2018)

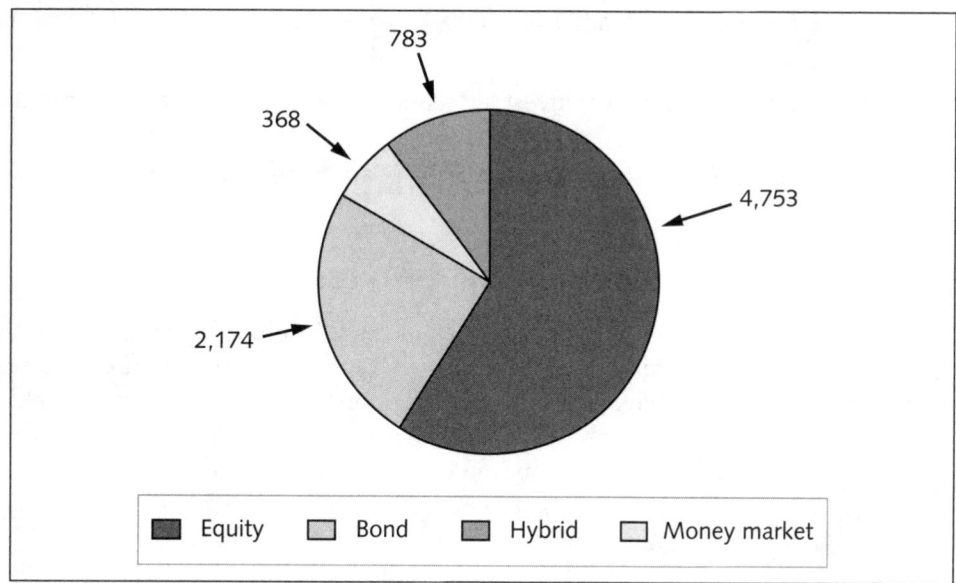

Source: *2019 Investment Company Fact Book*, Investment Company Institute, Washington, DC

EXHIBIT 12C.3 Types of Mutual Funds

Stock Funds

■ *Growth*: Invested in stocks of companies that are growing rapidly, these funds are focused on stocks that generate capital gains rather than income and are oftentimes further categorized as large cap; mid cap, or aggressive; or small cap, or growth (*cap* stands for capitalization and references the market size of the company's outstanding stock issues).

■ *Income*: An income fund emphasizes current income over growth. The fund's objectives are accomplished by investing in the stocks of companies with long histories of dividend payments, such as utility companies or blue-chip stocks.

■ *Growth and income*: These funds invest in securities offering potentially increasing value. They are primarily interested in so-called *value stocks*, or stocks that are underpriced relative to a stock that exhibits similar risk and return characteristics.

■ *Index*: These funds invest in securities designed to mirror a selected market index, such as the Standard & Poor's 500 Index. They track the selected index's performance and buy and sell securities in a manner that mirrors its composition.

■ *Sector*: A fund that restricts its investments to a particular sector of the market, such as energy or health care. Such fund tends to be more volatile than a more diversified fund and/or portfolio.

Bond Funds

■ *Corporate bond funds*: These funds seek a high level of income by investing two-thirds or more of their portfolios in corporate bonds and have no explicit restrictions on average maturity.

■ *U.S. government bond funds*: These funds purchase securities issued by the U.S. Treasury or an agency of the U.S. government. Investors in these funds seek current income and maximum safety.

EXHIBIT 12C.3 Types of Mutual Funds (continued)

Hybrid Funds

- *Asset allocation funds:* These funds focus on providing a diversified portfolio by investing across various asset classes, including equities, bonds, and money markets.
- *Balanced funds:* These funds invest in fixed percentages of equity, bond, and money market securities.

Foreign Funds

- *International mutual funds:* Invest in securities of companies that are located outside the United States.
- *Global mutual funds:* Invest in securities that are traded worldwide, including U.S. issues.

Money Market Mutual Funds

Money market mutual funds

A mutual fund that invests in money market instruments, such as Treasury bills and negotiable CDs

Money market mutual funds provide investors the opportunity to earn money market returns with the added benefits of ease of access and liquidity. Investors who have a portion of their portfolio invested in cash, or those who create cash by selling other long-term securities, can use money market mutual funds as an appropriate, competitive money market investment or as a temporary holding place for cash. In addition, an investor can choose to invest in either taxable or tax-exempt money market mutual funds, depending on the investor's tax situation.

With such short maturities, these funds have minimal interest rate risk, and because of the quality and diversity of the investments, these funds have little or no credit risk. However, they are subject to reinvestment rate risk and purchasing power risk.

Money market mutual funds have net asset values set at $1 per share. However, the NAV may fall below $1 if the investments perform poorly. Interest for these funds is earned and credited on a daily basis. Most of these funds allow investors check-writing privileges as long as a minimum balance is maintained. This check-writing feature allows competitive short-term returns with the flexibility of a checking account.

Unlike some fixed-income and equity mutual funds, money market mutual funds do not charge front-end loads or redemption fees. However, a fee is charged for the management of the assets within the fund.

Fixed-Income Mutual Funds

Fixed-income (or bond) mutual funds

A mutual fund that invests in fixed-income securities ranging in maturity of several months to 30 years or longer. Bond funds invest in numerous bond issues to diversify the investment portfolio from default risk.

Fixed-income, or **bond, mutual funds** invest primarily in fixed-income securities ranging in maturity from several months to 30 years or longer. Like money market mutual funds, bond funds invest in numerous bond issues to diversify the investment portfolio from default risk. Fixed-income funds provide investors with current income, making them ideal for retired investors who need continuing income generated by their investments for retirement expenditures. In addition, bond funds are appropriate for investors wishing to allocate a certain portion of their portfolio to fixed-income securities.

The risks investors accept when using bond funds are the same risks that any investor faces with fixed-income securities. Because mutual fund portfolios are well diversified, there is minimum default risk associated with bond mutual funds. As with other fixed-income securities, purchasing power risk is a relevant factor to consider when investing in bond mutual funds. However, the most significant risk associated with bond mutual funds is interest rate risk. Just as the value of an individual bond will decline when interest rates increase, so will the value of a bond mutual fund. Conversely, as interest rates decrease, the value of bond mutual funds will increase.

Bond mutual funds may have a variety of fees, costs, and expenses, including management fees, sales charges (both front-end and deferred), and 12b-1 fees. Regarding management fees, some of the objectives require higher management fees than others. For example, a fund that matches the Barclays Capital U.S. Aggregate Bond Index will require less cost and time than a fund that is actively managed, because no research is required to determine which securities to select. Most bond funds have an expense ratio of 1% or below, with higher expenses for actively managed and international bond funds.

Equity Mutual Funds

Equity mutual funds
A mutual fund that invests primarily in equity or ownership type securities, such as preferred stock and common stock

Equity mutual funds invest primarily in equity (ownership interest) securities, such as common stocks, and have a variety of objectives (as shown in Exhibit 12C.3). These funds have become tremendously popular over the last few decades and, in fact, make up the highest percentage of total assets invested in mutual funds (see Exhibit 12C.4).

EXHIBIT 12C.4 How Mutual Fund Assets are Invested (Year-End 2018)

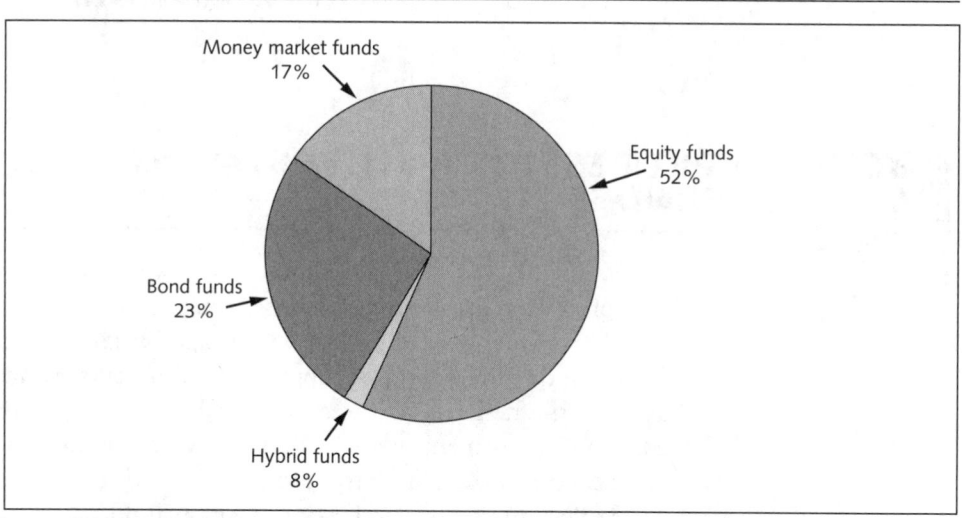

Source: *2019 Investment Company Fact Book*, Investment Company Institute, Washington, DC

As we previously discussed, equities have had higher returns than have fixed-income securities, and equity mutual funds provide investors easy access to common stock securities in an efficient method. The public's increased awareness of higher potential returns is a major contributing factor to the popularity of equity mutual funds.

Just as bond mutual funds have a variety of risks, so do equity mutual funds. One of the most important risks that an equity mutual fund investor must consider is market risk. Recall that market risk is the risk that movements in the market will have a detrimental effect on the value of an investment. There is a strong tendency for equities and equity mutual funds to fluctuate in the same direction and at a similar rate as the entire market. If the market has a sudden decline, most equity funds will also decline in value.

For those investors who invest similar amounts on a monthly basis into an equity mutual fund, temporary declines in the market and equity funds provide the opportunity to invest at lower prices. Equity funds are, however, usually more volatile than bond funds but historically have earned higher returns over a long-term time horizon.

Hybrid (or Balanced) Funds

Hybrid (or balanced) mutual funds

A mutual fund that invests in a combination of cash, fixed-income securities, and equity securities

Hybrid, or **balanced, mutual funds** are mutual funds that cannot be categorized into any of the three types of fund classifications discussed previously (money market, bond, or equity). These funds generally have an objective of investing in a balanced fashion, such that a portion of the portfolio is invested in cash, fixed-income securities, and equity securities.

Investors can build appropriate asset allocation portfolios by investing in a combination of selected money market funds, bond funds, and equity funds. Alternatively, investors can simply select a hybrid fund, such as an asset allocation fund, that meets their asset allocation objective and use it as their only or primary investment vehicle.

Foreign Funds

Foreign funds

Securities that provide investors with the easiest method of investing in foreign markets in the context of a diversified portfolio

Today, numerous mutual funds have the objective of investing internationally. These **foreign funds** provide investors with an easy method of investing in foreign markets within a diversified portfolio. Foreign funds have a variety of objectives, ranging from regions of the world to size of the market.

HOW DO PROFESSIONAL INVESTMENT ADVISERS SELECT MUTUAL FUNDS?

With the thousands of mutual funds available to investors, how does an investor or a professional investment adviser select a mutual fund for inclusion in a portfolio? In other words, what distinguishes an appropriate mutual fund from an inappropriate mutual fund? In general, an appropriate fund is one that meets the client's objectives and has the best risk-adjusted historical performance compared with similar funds. In addition, investment advisers should review information regarding the fund's performance, costs, taxation, portfolio turnover, and services offered.

Professionals use databases of mutual fund information, such as Morningstar, to help narrow the thousands of mutual funds down to a few that meet the objectives of the investor. These databases contain a substantial amount of information about each mutual fund and allow advisers to establish specific criteria and search through voluminous information quickly to select appropriate funds for clients. Much of this information comes from the mutual fund prospectus; the remainder comes from the database company's analysis of the funds.

PERFORMANCE MEASURES

As described in Chapter 12, the concepts of modern portfolio theory have been widely accepted among financial practitioners. These MPT statistics provide insight into the fund's risk-return characteristics.

The three most common performance measures used with mutual funds include Jensen's alpha, Sharpe ratio, and Treynor ratio. In addition, we will examine the information ratio which is a relatively new risk-adjusted measure for portfolio evaluation.

These performance measures provide a method of quantifying the risk-adjusted performance of investments, including mutual funds.

Jensen's Alpha

Jensen's alpha
An absolute measure of performance indicating how the actual performance of an investment compares with the expected performance

Jensen's alpha is an absolute measure of performance indicating how the actual performance of the investment compares with the expected performance. Specifically, alpha is measured as the portfolio's actual or realized return in excess of (or deficient to) the return predicted by the capital asset pricing model. A positive alpha means that the portfolio manager has added value on an absolute basis compared with the required return based on the level of investment risk undertaken. A negative alpha means that the manager has underperformed.

$$\alpha_p = \overline{r_p} - \left[\overline{r_f} + \left(\overline{r_m} - \overline{r_f} \right) \beta_p \right]$$

α_p = alpha

r_p = actual return of the portfolio

r_f = risk-free rate of return

β_p = beta of the portfolio

r_m = market rate of return

E X A M P L E   A higher alpha indicates that the actual return of the investment is better than what was expected, based on the level of risk of the investment. For instance, if the actual return of a portfolio is 12% and the expected return was 7%, then the alpha equals 5%. In other words, the portfolio performed five percentage points better than expected on a risk-adjusted basis. Similarly, a negative alpha implies that the return of the investment was less than expected based on the level of risk. An alpha of zero means that the investment performed as expected.

Sharpe Ratio

Sharpe ratio
A measure of risk-adjusted portfolio performance that uses standard deviation as the risk measure

The **Sharpe ratio** is also a measure of risk-adjusted performance. However, like the Treynor ratio, it is a relative measure of performance, meaning that the ratio by itself has little or no meaning. The ratio is meaningful only when compared to alternative investments. Unlike Treynor and Jensen, which use beta as the risk measure, Sharpe uses standard deviation. Because Sharpe uses standard deviation, this ratio incorporates total risk (both systematic and unsystematic risk) into the calculation.

$$S_p = \frac{\overline{r_p} - \overline{r_f}}{\sigma_p}$$

S_p = Sharpe ratio

r_p = actual return of the portfolio

r_f = risk-free rate of return

σ_p = standard deviation of the portfolio

E X A M P L E   If ABC growth mutual fund returned 12%, while the risk-free rate was 3% and the standard deviation was 20%, then the Sharpe ratio would equal 0.45. Again, the ratio of 0.45 has no meaning in and of itself; however, when compared with alternative investments, it becomes meaningful. Consider, for instance, the Sharpe ratios for the following mutual funds.

Fund name	Sharpe ratio
High Growth Mutual Fund	1.20
S&P 500 Index Mutual Fund	0.95
ABC Growth Mutual Fund	0.45
XYZ Growth Mutual Fund	0.30

Clearly, on a risk-adjusted basis, XYZ Growth Mutual Fund (0.30 Sharpe ratio) and ABC Growth Mutual Fund (0.45 Sharpe ratio) are mediocre performing funds. Two better alternatives appear to be the High Growth Mutual Fund (1.20 Sharpe ratio) and the S&P 500 Index Mutual Fund (.95 Sharpe ratio).

Treynor Ratio

Treynor ratio
A measure of risk-adjusted portfolio performance that uses beta as the risk measure

The **Treynor ratio** is a similar relative performance measure to the Sharpe ratio except for its measure of risk. Treynor uses beta as its measure of risk. Therefore, the same issues with regard to the use of beta in the calculation of alpha also apply to the calculation of the Treynor ratio.

$$T_p = \frac{\overline{r_p} - \overline{r_f}}{\beta_p}$$

T_p = Treynor ratio
r_p = actual return of the portfolio
r_f = risk-free rate of return
β_p = beta of the portfolio

The Treynor ratio also evaluates the incremental return above the risk-free rate of return. Alternative investments should be ranked in order from the highest to the lowest ratio. The investment with the highest Treynor ratio is the one that has the highest risk-adjusted return.

If all of the performance measures provide a quantification of the risk-adjusted return of investments, should the rankings, from highest to lowest, for each of the three measures be the same? The answer to this question is that "it depends." Specifically, it depends on the value of R^2 (coefficient of determination). If R^2 is high (at least 0.75), then the three performance measures will provide similar rankings. However, if R^2 is not high, then the three performance measures may not provide similar rankings. This inconsistency occurs because of the use of beta instead of standard deviation as the measure of risk in two of the performance measures.

Information ratio
A ratio of expected return to risk as measured by standard deviation that seeks to quantify the amount of incremental risk undertaken by a portfolio manager to achieve an excess return

Information Ratio

The **information ratio** is the ratio of expected return to risk as measured by standard deviation that seeks to quantify the amount of incremental risk undertaken by a portfolio manager to achieve an excess return.

$$IR = \frac{R_P - R_B}{\sigma_A}$$

IR = information ratio

R_P = average rate of return for a given time period

R_B = average rate of return on the benchmark portfolio; CAPM's required rate of return may be used

σ_A = standard deviation of portfolio returns

This ratio reduces to the Sharpe ratio when the benchmark portfolio is a constant-return, risk-free asset and is extremely difficult to interpret when the alpha for the subject portfolio is negative. Therefore, the information ratio should be used only when the alpha is positive (i.e., the portfolio manager has added value) and the beta is meaningful. Because the information ratio measures return and risk only relative to a benchmark, using the right benchmark is crucial to getting an accurate measure.

Coefficient of Variation

Coefficient of variation
A relative measure of total risk per unit of expected return

The **coefficient of variation (CV)** is a relative measure of total risk per unit of expected return and is used to compare investments with varying rates of return and standard deviations. The CV is computed by dividing the standard deviation of an asset by its average or mean return. When using this ratio to compare two alternatives, the one with the lower CV is usually the preferable choice.

E X A M P L E   ABC stock has a mean return of 10.75% and a standard deviation of 7.18%. XYZ stock has a mean return of 20% and a standard deviation of 12%. Therefore, if an investor is solely basing an investment decision on the amount of total risk, the choice would most likely be ABC stock because this stock has a lower standard deviation. However, in determining the CV for each stock, ABC stock has a CV of 0.6679, whereas XYZ stock has a CV of only 0.60. This means that ABC stock has more total risk per unit of expected return; thus, the investor may instead choose to invest in XYZ stock.

ISSUES TO LOOK FOR WHEN MANAGING PORTFOLIOS OF MUTUAL FUNDS

Once an investment strategy, including one that involves mutual funds, has been implemented, the portfolio must be monitored. Certain aspects of mutual funds should be monitored to be certain that the fund is performing as anticipated. The issues to consider include changing asset size, style drift, manager changes, built-in gains, and portfolio turnover.

Changing Asset Size

When mutual funds have good performance for several consecutive years, new money flows to these funds, making their asset base much larger. This asset accumulation can result in a change in the basic dynamics of the fund (this is especially true for funds that invest in small-cap and mid-cap asset classes). Therefore, when a small-cap mutual fund dramatically increases its asset base, the fund may no longer be able to invest the additional assets as efficiently or effectively as it had in the past. If this occurs, returns could suffer and assets may begin to leave the fund. To prevent this problem, some funds will close temporarily to new investors, thus limiting the asset base of the fund to protect the dynamics of the fund.

Style Drift

As part of the asset allocation process, the large-cap equity allocation is often segregated into value, growth, and core styles. The purpose of this segregation is to have one growth fund, one value fund, and one core fund, for example. What happens, though, if the value fund begins adopting more of a growth style? Suddenly, the diversified portfolio becomes more heavily weighted toward growth, which results in style drift. Even though the portfolio has potential for strong performance with the new allocation, it is likely that when the growth style goes out of favor, the portfolio may decline significantly. Therefore, the fund's style should remain consistent with the stated objective.

Manager Changes

The reason mutual fund managers are well compensated is that they make the buy-and-sell decisions, which cause the fund to have good or poor performance. Because the manager is responsible for the performance of the fund, it is important to watch for changes in the management structure. In most cases, one person manages the fund; in other cases, a team manages the fund. A change in investment management means that there is increased risk that the fund will not be managed as before and, therefore, historical returns may be less significant in predicting future returns.

Built-In Gains

Mutual funds normally have appreciated securities within their portfolio. This appreciation is considered a built-in gain inside the mutual fund. Selling these appreciated securities by the mutual fund causes income to be recognized for income tax purposes by the fund, which is passed through to the investor. Investors who purchase shares of mutual funds having these built-in gains may subject themselves to potential taxable income without any associated economic gain. The built-in gain on mutual funds can range widely and depends on past performance of the fund. Investors should be cautious when purchasing mutual funds with large amounts of unrecognized appreciation.

Portfolio Turnover

The costs of buying and selling securities within a mutual fund are reflected in the portfolio turnover ratio. In many instances, aggressive growth funds may contain an annual turnover rate of 100% or more. A 100% turnover rate means the fund replaces the entire portfolio annually. If the fund achieves superior returns, the strategy of buying and selling is working; if not, the strategy is possibly subjecting investors to undue costs.

The portfolio turnover rate reflects a fund's holding period. If a fund has a turnover rate of 100% or more, the fund generally is holding its securities for less than one year. Therefore, all capital gain distributions are likely to be short-term and subject to the maximum tax rate.

WHERE ON THE WEB

American Association of Individual Investors **www.aaii.com**

American Stock Exchange **www.amex.com**

Bloomberg **www.bloomberg.com**

Closed-End Fund Association **www.cefa.com**

MSN Money **www.msn.com/en-us/money**

CNN Money **www.money.cnn.com**

Investment Company Institute **www.ici.org**

Kiplinger **www.kiplinger.com**

Morningstar **www.morningstar.com**

Mutual Fund Investor's Center **www.mfea.com**

Trustnet (Unit Investment Trust Info) **www.trustnet.com**

13

Individual Income Tax and Tax Planning

▌ LEARNING OBJECTIVES

After learning the material in this chapter, you will be able to do the following:

■ List the objectives of the federal income tax law and give examples of each

■ Name three different tax rate structures under which income can be taxed and discuss how those rate structures differ

■ Perform the calculation to determine a client's income tax liability

■ Describe the types of IRS rulings issued as guidance to taxpayers and IRS agents

■ List the various civil penalties imposed on taxpayers who violate the tax law

■ Understand the IRS audit selection and screening process

■ Identify the various payroll taxes imposed on individuals through the Federal Insurance Contributions Act (FICA) and the Federal Unemployment Tax Act (FUTA)

■ Discuss the difference between tax avoidance and tax evasion

■ Discuss the various tax-advantaged investment options available to taxpayers

INCOME TAX PLANNING

One of the most important areas of financial planning is income tax planning. Income taxes have an impact on almost every business and investment decision as well as many personal decisions. The objective of tax planning is to pay the lowest tax legally permissible consistent with overall financial planning objectives. The financial planner must not only consider the tax ramifications of a proposed action or transaction but must also develop an appropriate tax planning strategy consistent with the client's goals and objectives.

Effective tax planning has been complicated over the years by constant changes to the tax law. The federal income tax system in the United States is among the most complex tax systems in the world. Changes have been made frequently to the Internal Revenue Code (IRC) in an attempt to raise revenues for the federal government or accomplish other social goals.

History

Under the U.S. Constitution, any direct tax imposed by Congress was required to be apportioned among the individual states based on that state's relative population. In 1913, the Sixteenth Amendment to the U.S. Constitution was ratified, which allowed Congress to levy taxes on all income without apportionment among the states.

The Sixteenth Amendment states, "The Congress shall have the power to lay and collect taxes on incomes, from whatever source derived, without apportionment among the several states, and without regard to any census or enumeration."

After 1913, Congress exercised its taxing authority with the passage of several revenue acts, adding to the complexity of the income tax system. In an attempt to resolve confusion, Congress combined the separate sources of the tax law in 1939. This legislation, named the Internal Revenue Code of 1939, systematically arranged all previous legislation and provided the basis for a standardized income tax law.

The 1939 Code was revised in 1954 and again in 1986. The governing federal income tax law today is the Internal Revenue Code of 1986, as amended. In 2017, sweeping legislation was passed in the form of the Tax Cuts and Jobs Act.

Objectives of the Federal Income Tax Law

There are several objectives of the federal income tax law. These objectives can be classified as revenue raising, economic, and/or social in nature.

The revenue-raising objective is the most important. The primary goal of taxation is to provide the resources necessary to fund governmental expenditures. Individual income taxes provide 53% of the annual revenues of the federal government.

EXHIBIT 13.1 Internal Revenue Collections by Principal Sources (2019)

Total Internal Revenue Collections	Business Income Taxes	Individual Income Taxes	Employment Taxes	Estate and Gift Taxes	Excise Taxes
3,564,583,961	277,057,735	1,981,650,716	1,207,553,842	17,565,044	80,756,624

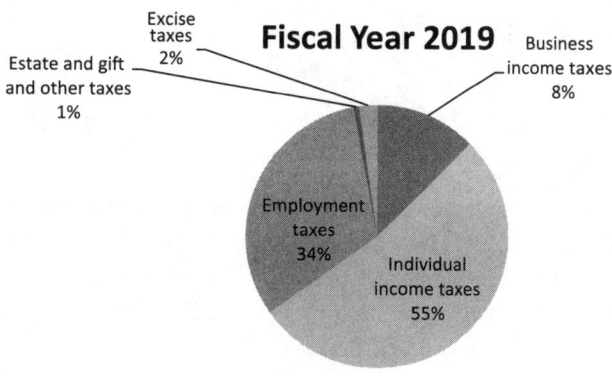

Internal Revenue Collections by Type of Tax (2020)
Internal Revenue Service, Data Book, 2019, Publication 55-B,
Washington, DC, June 2020

The federal income tax system also addresses certain economic goals. Taxation is a major tool used by the government to achieve the goals of economic growth and full employment. During periods of recession, taxes can be lowered, thereby increasing the disposable income in the hands of taxpayers. This can allow individuals to spend more money, which can increase demand, resulting in economic growth.

Social objectives are also accomplished through effective income tax legislation. The Internal Revenue Code (the Code) contains many economic incentives designed to encourage certain social behavior. For example, contributions to charitable organizations are socially desirable. Therefore, to encourage contributions, the Code permits limited deductions for contributions of money or property to qualified charitable organizations. In addition, the Code provides various tax benefits for homeowners and those saving for retirement.

INDIVIDUAL INCOME TAX RATES

Tax rates are applied to an individual's taxable income to determine the amount of tax due. Currently, income can be taxed under three different rate structures: ordinary tax rates, capital gain tax rates, and alternative minimum tax (AMT) rates.

Ordinary Rates

Once taxable income has been calculated, the income must be separately classified as ordinary or capital, because different tax rates may apply to capital gains.

Ordinary income includes any income that arises from services or from property that is not classified as a capital asset. Salaries, interest, dividends, rents, and income

Ordinary income
Any income that arises from services or from property that is not classified as a capital asset

earned from a sole proprietorship, partnership, S corporation, or LLC/LLP are all considered ordinary income.

If the taxpayer's income is classified as ordinary income, the tax on this income is calculated on the basis of one of four rate tables. The appropriate tax rate table is chosen on the basis of the individual's filing status, which is one of the following:

- Married individuals filing joint returns (includes qualifying widow/widower)

- Married individuals filing separate returns

- **Head of household**

- Single

The income tax rate tables are graduated, meaning that the rates increase as taxable income increases. The ordinary income tax rates are the same for each filing status; however, the taxable income thresholds for which these rates apply vary between the tables. Ordinary income tax rates are 10%, 12%, 22%, 24%, 32%, 35%, and 37%. These tax tables are contained in Appendix 13.1.

Capital Gain Rates

Taxpayers may be eligible to use lower tax rates when they incur a gain upon the disposition of certain types of assets, known as capital assets. Several factors must be present for a gain to be afforded preferential treatment. In general, the asset must be:

- a capital asset;

- sold or exchanged; or

- held long term.

Capital Asset

The Internal Revenue Code defines a **capital asset** by listing the types of assets that are not considered capital. All other assets disposed of are presumably capital assets. The following types of assets are not considered capital assets:

- Accounts or notes receivable arising in the ordinary course of a trade or business

- Copyrights or creative works held by the creator

- Inventory or property held for sale to customers in the ordinary course of the taxpayer's trade or business

- Depreciable real or personal property used in a trade or business

- A U.S. government publication held by a taxpayer who received it other than by purchase

Assets that are not capital assets can be remembered most easily by using the mnemonic ACID, which is the first letter of the first four types of assets listed.

Therefore, property held for personal use is a capital asset, as is property used for the production of income. Examples of capital assets include securities held for investment, a personal residence, and a personal automobile.

Head of household
The filing status that identifies a taxpayer as an unmarried individual who maintains a household for another and satisfies certain conditions set forth in the Internal Revenue Code

Capital asset
Broadly speaking, all assets are capital except those specifically excluded by the Internal Revenue Code; excluded assets include property held for resale in the normal course of business (inventory), trade accounts and notes receivable, and depreciable property and real estate used in a trade or business

Sale
Transfer of property for an amount of money or money equivalent that is fixed or determinable

Exchange
Transfer of property for property other than money

Sale or Exchange

Gains or losses from the disposition of property will not qualify as a capital gain or loss unless the property is disposed of by a sale or exchange. A **sale** is a transfer of property for an amount of money or money equivalent that is fixed or determinable. An **exchange** is a transfer of property for property other than money.

It is generally not difficult to determine whether a sale or exchange has occurred. However, the Internal Revenue Code has provided for several situations in which capital gain treatment is afforded even though a sale or exchange has not occurred. For example, capital loss treatment is allowed for a security that becomes worthless during the year, even though no sale or exchange has occurred.

Long-Term Holding Period

Once it has been determined that the asset is a capital asset that has been sold or exchanged, the taxpayer may qualify for lower capital gain tax rates if the property is held long term. In general, a capital asset is held long term if the taxpayer owned the asset for more than one year (i.e., a year and one day). The date the asset is disposed of is part of the holding period. For example, if property is acquired on March 3, 2019, the property will need to be sold on or after March 4, 2020, to be considered long-term.

Tax Treatment of Long-Term Capital Gains   If the taxpayer recognizes a **long-term capital gain**, which is a gain from a sale of a capital asset that has been held for more than one year, the gain may be taxed at a lower rate than the individual's ordinary income tax rate. Following are the long-term capital gains (LTCG) tax rates.

Long-Term Capital Gains Rate	Single Taxpayer	Married Filing Jointly	Head of Household	Married Filing Separately
0%	Up to $40,000	Up to $80,000	Up to $53,600	Up to $40,000
15%	$40,001–$441,450	$80,001–$496,600	$53,601–$469,050	$40,001–$248,300
20%	Over $441,450	Over $496,600	Over $469,050	Over $248,300

If the asset is a collectible, such as a work of art, or if the asset is small business stock (as defined in Section 1202), the recognized gain is taxed at a maximum capital gain rate of 28%. In addition, capital gains on sales of depreciable real estate are taxed at a maximum rate of 25%, to the extent of any unrecaptured straight-line depreciation on the property. The following table summarizes the different capital gain rates.

EXHIBIT 13.2 Capital Gain Rates

Type of Capital Asset	Minimum Holding Period	2020 Maximum Rate
Collectibles (antiques, etc.) or Section 1202 stock	Greater than 1 year	28%
Depreciable real estate	Greater than 1 year	25%
Other capital assets	Greater than 1 year	Depends on taxpayer's AGI

Short-term capital gain
A gain from a sale or exchange of a capital asset that has been held for one year or less

Qualified dividends
Dividends received from domestic corporations and foreign corporations incorporated in a U.S. possession, such as Puerto Rico

Capital loss
A loss from the sale or exchange of a capital asset

Net investment tax
A Medicare tax on investment income for taxpayers whose modified gross income (MAGI) exceeds certain thresholds

Long-term capital gain
A gain from a sale or exchange of a capital asset that has been held for more than one year

Tax Treatment of Short-Term Capital Gains   A **short-term capital gain** is a gain from a sale or exchange of a capital asset that has been held one year or less. It receives no special treatment and is taxed as ordinary income.

Tax Treatment of Qualified Dividends   **Qualified dividends** are dividends received from domestic corporations and foreign corporations incorporated in a U.S. possession, such as Puerto Rico. Taxpayers may elect to use the long-term capital gain tax rates for qualified dividends.

Tax Treatment of Capital Losses   A **capital loss** is a loss from the sale or exchange of a capital asset. An individual taxpayer may deduct capital losses only to the extent of capital gains plus the lesser of $3,000 ($1,500 for the taxpayer filing as married filing separately) or the net capital loss. The net capital loss is the excess of capital losses for the year over capital gains for the year.

E X A M P L E   For example, if an individual not filing as married filing separately has a short-term capital loss of $200 and a long-term capital loss of $3,700, the taxpayer is permitted to deduct $3,000 from ordinary income. The remaining loss of $900 ($200 + $3,700 − $3,000) can be carried forward to later years indefinitely until it is absorbed. The short-term loss is utilized first, so the carryover is $900 of long-term capital loss.

Net Investment Income Tax

A 3.8% tax is levied on net investment income of tax payers with MAGI exceeding applicable thresholds listed below.

Filing Status	Threshold Amount
Married filing jointly	$250,000
Married filing separately	$125,000
Single	$200,000
Head of household (with qualifying person)	$200,000
Qualifying widow(er) with dependent child	$250,000

The tax is 3.8% of the lesser of net investment income or the excess of modified adjusted gross income over the threshold amount. This tax is in addition to any other taxes on the investment income (ordinary or capital gain).

For an estate or trust, the tax is 3.8% of the lesser of (1) undistributed net investment income or (2) the excess of AGI over the dollar amount at which the highest income tax bracket applicable to an estate or trust begins. The tax does not apply to nonresident aliens and certain charitable trusts.

Net investment income is gross investment income reduced by certain investment-related expenses, such as investment interest expense, investment brokerage fees, royalty-related expenses, and state and local taxes allocable to items included in net investment income.

Net investment income includes (but is not limited to) interest, dividends, capital gains, rental and royalty income, nonqualified annuities, income from businesses involved in the trading of financial instruments or commodities, and businesses that are passive activities to the taxpayer. In addition to these types of income, net investment income includes gains such as those from the sale of stocks, bonds, and mutual funds, capital gain distributions from mutual funds, gain from the sale of investment real estate, and gains from the sale of partnership or S corporation interests.

The gain that is excludable from a taxpayer's gross income under Section 121 on the sale of a personal residence is not subject to the tax, but all or a portion of any excess is taxable if the taxpayer's MAGI exceeds the threshold for their filing status. Another exception is a distribution from most retirement plans and IRAs. While the distribution is not subject to the tax, its inclusion in the taxpayer's MAGI may force the taxpayer over the threshold and make net investment income taxable. Tax-exempt bond interest is also exempt from the tax.

E X A M P L E   Jane has MAGI of $220,000 and has a filing status of single. She has net investment income of $25,000. Of that, $20,000 will be subject to the net investment income tax of 3.8% (the lesser of the amount her MAGI exceeds the threshold or the net investment income).

E X A M P L E   Paul and Cindy sold their home this year and had a gain of $650,000 on the sale. Their MAGI is $175,000 in the year of the sale (before including the capital gain on the home sale), and they had net investment income of $10,000. Because the couple's MAGI is now $325,000, the net investment income tax of 3.8% will apply to $75,000 ($325,000 − $250,000) of their total net investment income.

Alternative Minimum Tax Rates

Alternative minimum tax (AMT)
System designed to ensure that individuals with large deductions and other tax benefits pay at least a minimum amount of tax

The **alternative minimum tax (AMT)** is a separate tax system that parallels the regular tax system. The AMT system was designed to ensure that individuals with large deductions and other tax benefits pay at least a minimum amount of tax.

The AMT calculation begins with the individual's taxable income, which is adjusted to arrive at alternative minimum taxable income (AMTI). AMT tax rates are then applied to AMTI, resulting in the tentative minimum tax. If the tentative minimum tax exceeds the individual's regular tax liability, the excess amount is the alternative minimum tax. The AMT calculation is summarized in the table below.

EXHIBIT 13.3 Alternative Minimum Tax Calculation

	Taxable income
+	Positive AMT adjustments
−	Negative AMT adjustments
=	Taxable income after AMT adjustments
+	Tax preferences (always positive)
=	**Alternative minimum taxable income (AMTI)**
−	AMT exemption
=	Minimum tax base
×	AMT rate
=	**Tentative AMT**
−	Regular income tax on taxable income
=	**AMT**

A taxpayer may incur an AMT liability if he has one or more of the following items of deduction or income, which are added back to the taxpayer's taxable income to determine AMTI:

- State and local income taxes

- Real property taxes

- Interest income on certain private activity bonds purchased before January 1, 2009 and after December 31, 2010

- Exercise of incentive stock options

- Gain on sale of certain small business stock (as defined in Section 1202)

Adjustments made to taxable income in the basic individual AMT formula (see previous page) may be either positive or negative; most adjustments relate to timing differences because of the regular income tax and AMT rules. A positive adjustment is made when the deduction allowed for regular income tax purposes exceeds the deduction allowed for AMT purposes. A negative adjustment is made when the deduction allowed for AMT purposes exceeds that for regular income tax purposes.

EXHIBIT 13.4 Adjustments to Taxable Income (2020)

Adjustment	Regular Tax	Individual AMT	Positive/Negative
Standard deduction amount	Allowed	Disallowed	Positive
Itemized deduction— income and property taxes	Allowed	Disallowed	Positive

A taxpayer may have to pay the AMT if the taxpayer's taxable income for regular income tax purposes, combined with any AMT tax adjustments and preference items, exceeds (2020):

- $72,900 if the filing status is that of a single taxpayer;

- $56,700 for a filing status of married filing separately (MFS); or

- $113,400 for a married taxpayer filing jointly (MFJ).

These exemption amounts begin to be phased out in 2020 on a one-for-four basis when the MFJ taxpayers' AGI exceeds $1,036,800, and for all other taxpayers (except estates and trusts) when AGI exceeds $518,400.

The tentative minimum tax is applied at 26% of AMTI up to $197,900 ($98,950 for MFS). AMTI exceeding $197,900 ($98,950 for MFS) is taxed at 28%.

DETERMINING INCOME TAX LIABILITY

Of all the sources providing revenues to the federal government, individual income tax is the largest. Calculating an individual's income tax liability can be very complicated. The tax liability itself is a product of the taxpayer's taxable income, which is summarized in the following formula:

EXHIBIT 13.5 Taxable Income

Total income (from whatever source derived)	$xx,xxx
Less: exclusions from gross income	(x,xxx)
Gross income	$xx,xxx
Less: deductions for adjusted gross income	(x,xxx)
Adjusted gross income (AGI)	$xx,xxx
Less: the larger of:	
standard deduction or itemized deductions	(x,xxx)
Taxable income	$xx,xxx

Total Income and Gross Income

Gross income
The Internal Revenue Code Section 61(a) defines gross income as "all income from whatever source derived"

Exclusion
Income exempt from tax and not included in a taxpayer's gross income

The tax computation begins with the determination of the taxpayer's total income. The Internal Revenue Code Section 61(a) defines **gross income** as "all income from whatever source derived." In general, all income is taxable unless Congress has specifically exempted the income from taxation. In tax terminology, this exemption is called an **exclusion** and is income exempt from tax and not included in a taxpayer's gross income.

In determining gross income, the taxpayer may exclude many different types of income received. Some of the more common types of income that may be excluded are as follows:

- Most retirement plan salary deferrals

- Accident insurance proceeds

- Bequests received

- Child support payments received

- Certain employee fringe benefits

- Gain on the sale of a personal residence (limited)

- Gifts received

- Group term life insurance premiums paid by an employer (limited)

- Interest received from municipal bonds

- Life insurance proceeds received (unless the policy is subject to transfer for value rules)

- Meals and lodging (furnished for the convenience of the employer on the employer's premises)

- Scholarship grants (for tuition and books of a degree candidate)

- Workers' compensation

The amount of income remaining after removing the exclusions is termed the taxpayer's gross income. Gross income is generally the starting point for the federal individual income tax return (Form 1040).

E X A M P L E During 2020, Joe received salary of $60,000, dividends of $2,000, tax-exempt interest of $500, and a gift of $20,000 from his parents. Joe has total income for 2020 of $82,500, because total income is based on income from all sources. However, Joe's gross income reported on his tax return is $62,000, the sum of the $60,000 salary and the $2,000 taxable dividend income. The remaining $500 of tax-exempt interest income and $20,000 gift is excluded from gross income.

Adjusted Gross Income (AGI)

Above-the-line deduction (deduction for AGI)
An above-the-line deduction that reduces gross income directly

Adjusted gross income
A determination peculiar to individual taxpayers that represents gross income less business expenses, expenses attributable to the production of rent or royalty income, the allowed capital loss deduction, and certain personal expenses (deductions for AGI)

The gross income can be reduced further by allowed deductions. Deductions that reduce gross income directly are referred to as **above-the-line deductions (deductions for AGI)**. The line referred to in this phrase is **adjusted gross income (AGI)**. A determination peculiar to individual taxpayers that represents gross income less business expenses, expenses attributable to the production of rent or royalty income, the allowed capital loss deduction, and certain personal expenses (deductions for AGI).

AGI is a very important concept for individual income taxation. It represents the basis for calculating percentage limitations on certain itemized deductions such as the charitable and medical itemized deductions. AGI also serves as a benchmark for passive rental real estate losses.

In determining adjusted gross income, the taxpayer may reduce gross income by the following:

- Ordinary and necessary expenses incurred in a trade or business

- Net capital losses (limited)

- Deductible employer share of self-employment tax paid

- Alimony paid to an ex-spouse (This applies only if the divorce was finalized before 1/1/19. For divorce decrees finalized or amended on or after 1/1/19 alimony paid is not deductible.)

- Certain payments to a Keogh, SIMPLE, or SEP retirement plan

- Contributions to a traditional IRA (limited)

- Forfeited interest penalty for premature withdrawal of time deposits

- Self-employed health insurance premiums and qualified long-term care premiums

- Interest paid on qualifying education loans (limited)

Deductions for AGI are more favorable than itemized deductions because they are generally subject to fewer limits than itemized deductions, and they do not require the taxpayer to itemize to receive a benefit from the deduction. They also reduce AGI, which reduces calculated hurdles for itemized deductions, and can reduce phased-out items.

Itemized Deductions and the Standard Deduction

Several deductions are allowed to reduce adjusted gross income. This type of deduction is often referred to as a **below-the-line deduction (deduction from AGI).**

The **basic standard deduction** is the amount allowed all taxpayers who do not itemize their deductions. It represents the government's estimate of tax-deductible expenses a taxpayer might have. The allowed standard deduction is based on the tax year and the taxpayer's filing status. The allowed basic standard deductions for 2020 are summarized in the table below.

Below-the-line deduction (deduction from AGI)
Deduction that is allowed to reduce adjusted gross income

Basic standard deduction
The amount allowed all taxpayers who do not itemize their deductions

EXHIBIT 13.6 Allowed Basic Standard Deduction

Filing Status	Basic Standard Deduction 2020
Single	$12,400
Married, filing jointly/SS*	$24,800
Head of household	$18,650
Married, filing separately	$12,400

*SS—Surviving spouse

Taxpayers who have deductible expenses in excess of the standard deduction may choose to itemize and deduct these itemized expenses instead of taking the standard deduction. These expenses, referred to as **itemized deductions**, are generally personal expenses. In addition, some of the itemized deductions have separate AGI limitations that may reduce their deductibility.

Itemized deductions
Deductions in excess of the standard deduction that are used in lieu of the standard deduction

E X A M P L E   For example, medical expenses are only deductible to the extent they exceed 7.5% of the taxpayer's AGI. If an itemizing taxpayer's AGI is $100,000 and he incurs unreimbursed medical expenses during the year of $10,500, only $3,000, or $10,500 − ($100,000 × 7.5%), of the medical expenses is deductible.

The following is a brief list of some of the more common itemized deductions. Note that some of the deductions listed below are subject to AGI or income limitations.

- Medical expenses*

- State and local income taxes, real estate taxes, and personal property taxes (Note that the deduction for taxes is capped at $10,000, aggregately.)

- Mortgage interest

- Investment interest*

- Charitable contributions*

- Casualty losses from a federally declared disaster*

   * AGI or income limited

E X A M P L E   Mary is a single taxpayer, age 45. In 2020, she paid mortgage interest of $3,500, real estate taxes of $1,500, and state income taxes of $2,000 and incurred medical expenses of $600. Assuming Mary's AGI is $50,000, her itemized deductions would total $7,000 ($3,500 + $1,500 + $2,000). The medical expenses are not deductible as itemized deductions because they do not exceed 7.5% of Mary's AGI. Because Mary is a single taxpayer, her standard deduction would be $12,400 for 2020, and therefore it would be beneficial for Mary to use the standard deduction in 2020.

Not everyone is entitled to the standard deduction. No standard deduction is allowed for the following individuals:

- A married person filing a separate return if his spouse itemizes deductions
- A nonresident alien
- An individual filing a tax return for a period of less than 12 months

The basic standard deduction is reduced under the Tax Code for an individual who may be claimed as a dependent of another taxpayer for a taxable year beginning in the calendar year in which the individual's taxable year begins. The basic standard deduction is limited to the greater of $1,100 (2020) or the sum of $350 and the individual's earned income, limited to $12,400 (2020).

In addition to the basic standard deduction, a taxpayer will be entitled to an additional standard deduction if the taxpayer is blind or turns 65 by the end of the tax year.

EXHIBIT 13.7 Additional Standard Deduction

Filing Status	2020 Additional Standard Deduction
Single	$1,650
Married, filing jointly/SS	$1,300
Head of household	$1,650
Married, filing separately	$1,300

Determining Who Is a Dependent

Dependent
An individual who meets the definition of a qualifying child or a qualifying relative and who can be listed by a taxpayer on an income tax return

Qualifying child
A taxpayer may claim an individual as a dependent if the individual satisfies all of the following requirements: relationship, abode, age, support, citizenship, and joint return

Qualifying relative
A taxpayer may claim an individual as a dependent if the individual satisfies all of the following requirements: relationship, support, gross income, citizenship, and joint return

To use either the qualifying widow(er)/surviving spouse status after the year of a spouse's death or the head of household filing status, the taxpayer must have a qualifying child or qualifying relative as a dependent. The qualifying person on the taxpayer's return also applies to whether or not a taxpayer may use the child tax credit or the child and dependent care credit. In all cases, the dependent's Social Security number or taxpayer identification number must be on the return.

Per tax code, a dependent can be claimed if an individual is either a **qualifying child** or **qualifying relative** of the taxpayer. In order to claim an individual as a dependent, the individual must either be a qualifying child or a qualifying relative of the taxpayer. Certain tests must be met before an individual will satisfy either definition.

Requirement	Qualifying Child	Qualifying Relative
Relationship test	Must be taxpayer's: child, stepchild, foster child, brother, stepbrother, sister, stepsister, or a descendent of any of the previously listed	Not a qualifying child as identified in column 2; either bears a specified relationship to the taxpayer, including parent, in-law, niece, nephew, aunt, or uncle; or is unrelated to the taxpayer, but the individual resided in the taxpayer's principal home during the tax year
Income test	N/A	Gross income must be less than the standard deduction amount for a single person; nontaxable income, such as Social Security benefits, when used as support by the individual, counts toward the threshold
Residence test	Must have lived with the taxpayer more than half of the taxable year	A parent does not have to reside in the same household with the taxpayer
Age test	The individual must pass an age test (meet one of the following): under age 19 at the close of the tax year; is a full-time student and under age 24 at the close of the tax year; or, is totally and permanently disabled at any time during the tax year	N/A
Support test	Dependent must not have provided more than 50% of own support (scholarships do not count)	Taxpayer must have provided more than 50% of support
Dependents test	Individual cannot claim any other individual as a dependent	Individual cannot claim any other individual as a dependent
Filing	The individual may not file a joint return for the tax year (unless the only reason a return was filed was to obtain a refund of tax withheld)	The individual may not file a joint return for the tax year (unless the only reason a return was filed was to obtain a refund of tax withheld)
Citizenship	The individual generally must also be a U.S. citizen, U.S. national, or resident of the United States, Canada, or Mexico	The individual generally must also be a U.S. citizen, U.S. national, or resident of the United States, Canada, or Mexico

NOTE: **Relatives who do not have to live with you.** A person related to you in any of the following ways does not have to live with you all year as a member of your household to meet the "Member of Household or Relationship Test" (IRS Pub 501).

• Your child, stepchild, foster child, or a descendant of any of them (e.g., your grandchild). (A legally adopted child is considered your child.)

• Your brother, sister, half brother, half sister, stepbrother, or stepsister.

• Your father, mother, grandparent, or other direct ancestor, but not foster parent.

• Your stepfather or stepmother.

• A son or daughter of your brother or sister.

• A son or daughter of your half brother or half sister.

• A brother or sister of your father or mother.

• Your son-in-law, daughter-in-law, father-in-law, mother-in-law, brother-in-law, or sister-in-law.

Any of these relationships that were established by marriage are not ended by death or divorce.

As long as all the tests are met, an individual can be identified as a dependent for a person who dies during the year, without a reduction.

Taxable Income and Tax Rates

Taxable income is calculated by reducing the adjusted gross income by the standard or itemized deduction. Taxable income is the tax base upon which the tax rates are applied to determine the taxpayer's tax liability before credits.

The tax rate schedule is based on the current tax year and the individual's filing status. The 2020 tax rates for all filing statuses are listed in Appendix 13.1.

Tax Credits

Once the individual's tax liability is determined, it may be reduced further by any allowable tax credits. Tax credits result in a direct, dollar-for-dollar reduction in tax liability. A credit may be refundable or nonrefundable. Most credits are nonrefundable, meaning that the credit can reduce an individual's tax liability to zero but not below zero. Common tax credits include the foreign tax credit, the child and dependent care credit, the child tax credit, the American Opportunity Tax Credit, and the Lifetime Learning Credit.

▌IRS GUIDANCE

Letter Ruling
A written statement issued by the National Office of the IRS that gives guidance on the way the IRS will treat a prospective or contemplated transaction for tax purposes

Determination Letter
A written statement issued by an IRS district director that applies the principles and precedents announced by the National Office to a given set of facts

Due to the complexity of the federal tax law, the IRS often issues guidance as to how it will treat certain transactions for tax purposes. This guidance is often given using Letter Rulings, Determination Letters, Revenue Rulings, Revenue Procedures, and Technical Advice Memoranda.

A **Letter Ruling** is essentially a statement by the IRS of the way it will treat a prospective or contemplated transaction for tax purposes. In response to a written request from a taxpayer, the National Office prepares the Letter Ruling. A ruling is generally honored only with respect to the specific taxpayer to whom the ruling was issued. Other taxpayers cannot assume that the IRS will apply the Letter Ruling to them, even if they engage in the same transaction set out in the Letter Ruling. It does, however, give other taxpayers an idea of the IRS's application of the law.

A **Determination Letter** is a written statement issued by a District Director of the IRS. The letter applies the principles and precedents announced by the National Office to a given set of facts. Determination letters are issued only if the issue can be resolved on the basis of clearly established rules. They are typically used when establishing a qualified retirement plan, such as a pension or profit-sharing plan.

Revenue Rulings
Official interpretation on how the law should be applied to a specific set of facts

Private Letter Rulings
Statements issued for a fee upon a taxpayer's request that describe how the IRS will treat proposed transactions for tax purposes

Revenue Procedures
Statements reflecting the internal management practices of the IRS that affects the rights and duties of taxpayers

Internal Revenue Bulletin (IRB)
Announces official rulings and procedures of the IRS and publishes Treasury Decisions, Executive Orders, Tax Conventions, legislation, court decisions, and other items of general interest

Technical Advice Memoranda
Advice or guidance in memorandum form furnished by the National Office of the IRS to IRS agents who request such advice or guidance during an audit

The National Office of the IRS issues **Revenue Rulings**. They provide an official interpretation on how the law should be applied to a specific set of facts. They are typically issued because of many requests for **Private Letter Rulings** with respect to an area of the tax law. Private Letter Rulings are statements issued for a fee upon a taxpayer's request that describe how the IRS will treat proposed transactions for tax purposes. Taxpayers may rely on Revenue Rulings in determining the tax consequences of their transactions; however, taxpayers must determine whether their facts closely resemble the facts presented in the ruling.

Revenue Procedures are statements reflecting the internal management practices of the IRS that affect the rights and duties of taxpayers.

The **Internal Revenue Bulletin (IRB)** announces official rulings and procedures of the IRS and publishes Treasury Decisions, Executive Orders, Tax Conventions, legislation, court decisions, and other items of general interest. Rulings and procedures reported in the IRB do not have the force and effect of Treasury tax regulations, but they may be used as precedents. In contrast, any documents not published in the IRB cannot be relied on, used, or cited as precedents in the disposition of other cases.

Technical Advice Memoranda give advice or guidance in memorandum form and are furnished by the National Office of the IRS. An IRS agent typically requests the memorandum during an audit. The purpose of technical advice is to help IRS personnel close cases and maintain consistent holdings throughout the IRS.

PENALTIES AND INTEREST

Various civil penalties are imposed on taxpayers and tax return preparers who violate the tax law. Included in the civil penalties are failure-to-file penalties, failure-to-pay-tax penalties, accuracy-related penalties, and fraud penalties.

Failure-to-File-Tax-Return Penalty

Failure-to-file penalty
A civil penalty imposed on taxpayers and tax return preparers who fail to file tax returns according to the requirements of tax law

The **failure-to-file penalty** was enacted to ensure the timely filing of tax returns. Generally, a return is considered filed on the date it is delivered to the IRS.

The penalty is 5% of the amount of tax required to be shown on the return for each month or fraction of a month that the failure continues, up to a maximum penalty of 25% of the unpaid tax. If the return is filed more than 60 days after the due date or the extended due date, the minimum penalty is the lesser of $435 or 100% of the unpaid tax. If a taxpayer can show that there was reasonable cause for the failure to file the return, the IRS will not assess the penalty. The penalty period runs from the due date of the tax return, including extensions, to the date the IRS actually receives the return.

The failure-to-file penalty is reduced by any failure-to-pay penalty.

Failure-to-Pay-Tax Penalty

Failure-to-pay-tax penalty
A civil penalty imposed on taxpayers who, without reasonable cause, fail to pay the tax shown on their return

The **failure-to-pay-tax penalty** is imposed on taxpayers who, without reasonable cause, fail to pay the tax shown on a return. The penalty is one-half of 1% of the tax shown for each month or fraction of a month that it is not paid, up to a maximum penalty of 25%.

E X A M P L E   Jim files his tax return 40 days after the due date. He remits a check for $7,000 that represents the balance of the tax due. Jim's failure-to-file and failure-to-pay penalties total $700, calculated as follows:

Failure-to-pay ($7,000 × .5% × 2 months)		$70
Failure-to-file ($7,000 × 5% × 2 months)		$700
Less: failure-to-pay penalty	(70)	$630
Total penalty		$700

Interest is generally payable whenever any tax or civil penalty is not paid when due, even if the taxpayer has been granted an extension of time to pay the tax. Interest on unpaid tax liabilities runs from the last day prescribed by the Tax Code for payment to the date paid.

Accuracy-Related Penalties

Accuracy-related penalty
A penalty of 20% of the portion of the tax underpayment attributable to negligence, substantial understatement of tax, or substantial valuation misstatement without intent to defraud

The **accuracy-related penalty** is a penalty of 20% of the portion of the tax underpayment attributable to negligence, substantial understatement of tax, or substantial valuation misstatement without intent to defraud.

Negligence includes any failure to make a reasonable attempt to comply with the tax laws, exercise reasonable care in return preparation, and keep proper books and records or properly substantiate items. If the IRS has evidence that the taxpayer was negligent, the taxpayer must establish that he was not negligent by a preponderance of the evidence.

A substantial understatement of income tax occurs when an individual fails to report on his income tax return the appropriate amount of tax that should be imposed, and this understatement exceeds the larger of (1) 10% of the correct tax or (2) $5,000.

Substantial valuation misstatement occurs when a taxpayer undervalues or overvalues property or services, resulting in the understatement of income tax liability. The valuation misstatement is considered substantial if the value claimed on the return is 200% or more of the correct value. However, the penalty does not apply unless the understatement of tax liability exceeds $5,000.

E X A M P L E   Scott, who is in the 32% marginal tax rate, contributes artwork to a charitable organization and claims a deduction of $40,000. Assuming the actual fair market value of the art is $18,000, Scott would be subject to the 20% accuracy-related penalty because the overstatement of the asset's value was more than 200% of the correct value and the understatement of tax liability is more than $5,000.

The accuracy-related penalty does not apply with respect to any portion of an underpayment if the taxpayer has a reasonable cause for the position taken on the return. The determination of whether a taxpayer acted with reasonable cause and in good faith is made on a case-by-case basis, taking into account all pertinent facts and circumstances.

Fraud Penalties

The fraud penalty is 75% of the portion of the tax underpayment attributable to the fraud. The IRS must prove that there was an underpayment and that the underpayment was attributable to fraud.

Fraud penalty
A penalty levied against a taxpayer by the IRS after it has proven an underpayment of tax by the taxpayer and proven that the underpayment was attributable to a willful attempt to evade tax

For the **fraud penalty** to apply, there must be a willful attempt to evade tax. The taxpayer must have intended to mislead the IRS or conceal information to prevent the collection of taxes. Civil fraud has not been clearly defined, but courts have inferred fraudulent intent from factors, such as understatement of income, failure to file tax returns, and failure to cooperate with tax authorities.

The fraud penalty does not apply with respect to any portion of an underpayment if the taxpayer has a reasonable cause for the position taken on the return. In addition, the imposition of the fraud penalty precludes the imposition of the accuracy-related penalty on the same underpayment.

▌AUDIT PROCESS

A goal of the IRS is to promote the highest degree of compliance with the Internal Revenue Code. Tax compliance is a voluntary process. Without some sort of audit process, the IRS would have no means by which to ensure compliance with the law. In an **audit**, the IRS examines a tax return "to determine if income, expenses, and credits are being reported accurately" (Publication 556). Before conducting an audit, the IRS must use a screening process to determine which taxpayers will be subject to audit, who will perform the audit, and what type of audit will be conducted.

Audit
When the IRS examines a tax return "to determine if income, expenses, and credits are being reported accurately" (Publication 556)

The percentage of returns audited each year varies depending on the IRS's available staff. Returns on which all or most of the income is subject to withholding and where taxpayers did not itemize their deductions are the returns least likely to be audited.

Discriminant Index Function (DIF) system

A mathematical technique used to classify tax returns as to their examination potential

Selection and Screening Process

The IRS employs various methods and procedures for identifying and selecting individual returns for examination.

One selection method employed by the IRS is the **Discriminant Index Function (DIF) system**. The DIF system is a mathematical technique used to classify tax returns as to their examination potential. Under this system, returns are divided into different audit classes. Weights are then assigned to certain return characteristics according to a formula that varies with each audit class. These weights are added to arrive at the total DIF score for the return. Returns with the highest DIF scores are made available to the examination division of the IRS for manual screening.

Although DIF scores indicate examination potential, tax examiners must manually screen returns to identify issues in need of examination and to eliminate returns that do not warrant an audit. Depending on the complexity of the issues involved and the degree of auditing skills required to perform the examination, either revenue agents or tax auditors manually screen individual returns.

If an audit examination is to be conducted, a classification check sheet is prepared and attached to the return. The check sheet lists significant items to be considered and identifies whether a correspondence audit, an office audit, or a field audit will be performed. Which type of audit to conduct is determined on the basis of the complexity of the return and which type of audit is most conducive to effective and efficient tax administration.

Correspondence audit

An audit conducted almost entirely by written correspondence and telephone contact with the taxpayer and typically involves simple issues

Office audit

The audit is conducted at the IRS office near the taxpayer's home and usually involve issues too complicated to be resolved by mail, such as travel and entertainment expenses, income from rents, and large itemized deductions

Types of Audits

A **correspondence audit** is conducted almost entirely by written correspondence and telephone contact with the taxpayer. These audits typically involve simple issues, such as itemized deductions, IRA contribution limits, and self-employment tax.

Office audits usually involve issues too complicated to be resolved by mail, such as travel and entertainment expenses, income from rents, and large itemized deductions. In most cases, the audit is conducted at the IRS office near the taxpayer's home. The taxpayer is informed that his tax return is being audited and is usually requested to furnish certain information.

Field audits are conducted for complex individual returns with business or other financial activities. IRS revenue agents handle field audits, as opposed to office audits, which are conducted by less-experienced tax auditors. These audits are typically conducted at the taxpayer's business or wherever the taxpayer's books are maintained. Before the field audit begins, the examiner makes a precontact analysis of the return to determine which items should be examined.

Field audit

An audit conducted for complex individual returns with business or other financial activities. IRS revenue agents handle field audits, as opposed to office audits, which are conducted by less-experienced tax auditors and are typically conducted at the taxpayer's business or wherever the taxpayer's books are maintained.

Outcomes of Audits

Once the audit is complete, there are four possible outcomes to determinations made by the examiner:

- No change to the return—the examiner proposes no change in the taxpayer's tax liability.

- Taxpayer agrees with examiner's findings—if the taxpayer agrees with the examiner's proposed changes, the taxpayer signs an agreement form and pays any additional taxes and interest owed. The taxpayer may even receive a refund because of the audit.

- Taxpayer does not agree with examiner's findings—if the taxpayer does not agree with the examiner's proposed changes, the taxpayer has the right to appeal. The IRS will send the taxpayer a *30-day letter* notifying the taxpayer of his right to appeal the proposed changes within 30 days. If the taxpayer does not respond within 30 days, the IRS will send a *90-day letter*, which is a notice of deficiency.

  — The notice of deficiency officially informs the taxpayer that the IRS has determined that a tax deficiency exists and details the basis for and the amount of the deficiency. Once an individual has received a 90-day letter, he may pay the deficiency, file a Tax Court petition, or take no action.

- Taxpayer partially agrees with examiner's findings—the taxpayer agrees with some, but not all, of the examiner's proposed changes.

If a taxpayer has exhausted all of his administrative remedies, he may litigate a case in court. The following chart details the court system as it applies to tax litigation.

EXHIBIT 13.8 Income Tax Appeal Procedure

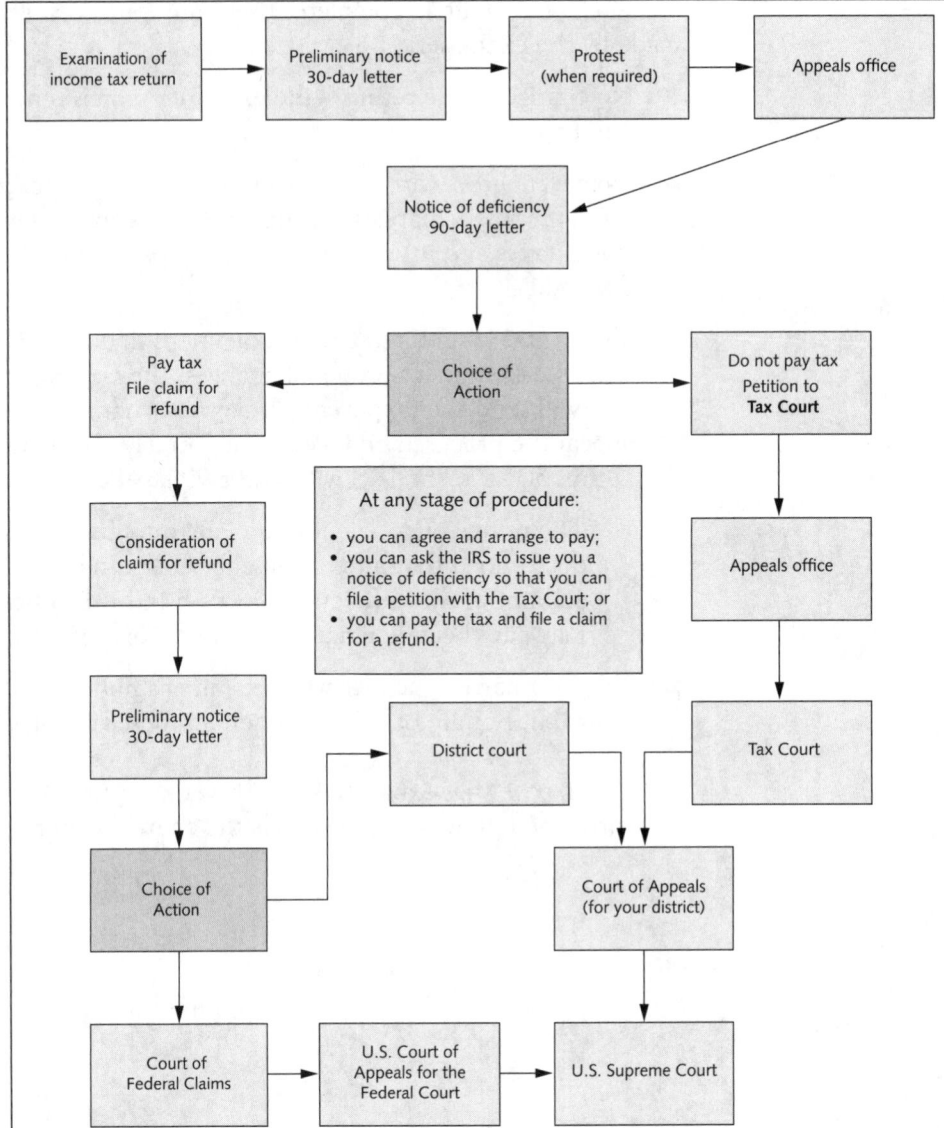

The litigation begins in a court of original jurisdiction, or trial court. The U.S. Tax Court, U.S. District Court, and U.S. Court of Federal Claims are all trial courts that may hear tax cases.

- The U.S. Tax Court tries only tax cases. The taxpayer does not pay the alleged deficiency but files suit against the IRS Commissioner to stop the collection of tax. The court consists of 19 judges, and a jury trial is not available. The Small Case Division may try the case if the deficiency is equal to or less than $50,000.

- The U.S. District Court tries tax cases as well as many other types of civil and criminal cases. The taxpayer pays the alleged deficiency and files suit against the U.S. government for a refund. There are approximately 90 district courts, and a jury trial is available. If the taxpayer has filed for bankruptcy, the Federal Bankruptcy Division may try the case.

- The U.S. Court of Federal Claims tries tax cases as well as other cases against the federal government. The taxpayer pays the alleged deficiency and files suit against the U.S. government for a refund. The court consists of 16 judges, and a jury trial is not available.

The table below summarizes the courts of original jurisdiction.

EXHIBIT 13.9 Courts of Original Jurisdiction

	U.S. Tax Court	U.S. District Court	U.S. Claims Court
Number of courts	1	Approx. 90	1
Number of judges	19	1 (per court)	16
Jurisdiction	National	District	National
Subject matter	Tax only	Criminal and civil	Claims against govt.
Pay deficiency?	No	Yes	Yes
Jury available?	No	Yes	No
Where to appeal	U.S. Court of Appeals	U.S. Court of Appeals	U.S. Court of Appeals—Fed. Circuit

The appropriate appellate court depends on which trial court hears the case. If the case is tried in the Tax Court or District Court, the appeals are taken to the U.S. Court of Appeals. Appeals from the Claims Court are taken to the U.S. Court of Appeals for the Federal Circuit.

PAYROLL TAXES

The federal government, through the Federal Insurance Contributions Act (FICA), imposes employment taxes on employers, employees, and self-employed individuals. These taxes provide for a federal system of old age, survivors, disability, and hospital insurance.

The Federal Unemployment Tax Act (FUTA) provides for payments of unemployment compensation to workers who have lost their jobs.

FICA Taxes for Employers and Employees

The Federal Insurance Contributions Act (FICA) created several different programs designed to prevent people from becoming poverty stricken. The two most important and well-recognized programs created by FICA are Old Age, Survivors, and Disability Insurance (OASDI), better known as Social Security, and the Hospital Insurance (HI) program, better known as Medicare Part A. These taxes have different tax rates, and only the OASDI tax has a wage base limit.

Contributions to these programs are made by salary reductions for employees and by direct payments to the government by employers and self-employed individuals. FICA taxes are imposed on employees at a combined rate of 7.65% in 2020. This rate represents the total of the 6.2% rate for the OASDI portion and the 1.45% rate for the HI portion. The OASDI rate is applied to the employee's total wages for the year, up to the taxable wage base ($137,700 in 2020) for the Social Security portion of the tax. The employer is required to make a matching contribution for each employee. There is no wage ceiling on the Medicare (hospital insurance) portion of the tax.

EXAMPLE   If Tom earns a salary of $150,000 in 2020 for ABC Company, he will have $10,712 withheld from his paycheck for FICA taxes, computed as follows:

Social Security portion (6.2% × $137,700)	$8,537
Medicare portion (1.45% × $150,000)	$2,175
Total FICA taxes	$10,712

In 2020, Tom would have had 6.2% deducted as the Social Security portion from his check ($8,537). ABC Company will be required to pay the amount withheld from Tom's paycheck, plus the company's own contribution. ABC's contribution would be 6.2% up to the taxable wage base for the Social Security portion ($137,700 in 2020) and 1.45% for the Medicare portion. ABC Company will also receive a deduction for its share of the FICA taxes paid.

Additional Medicare Tax

Additional Medicare tax

A Medicare tax of 0.9% paid by taxpayers above certain income thresholds that is in addition to the 2.9% Medicare tax

The **Additional Medicare Tax** has a tax rate of 0.9%. An individual is liable for the Additional Medicare Tax if the individual taxpayer's wages, other compensation, or self-employment income (combined with a spouse if filing as married filing jointly) exceeds the thresholds listed below for the taxpayer's filing status.

Filing Status	Threshold Amount
Married filing jointly	$250,000
Married filing separately	$125,000
Single	$200,000
Head of household (with qualifying person)	$200,000
Qualifying widow(er) with dependent child	$200,000

Unlike the 2.9% Medicare tax, which is divided between an employer and an employee share, only the employee pays the full 0.9% tax. This tax is in addition to the 1.45% employee share regular Medicare tax. The tax is applied to the amount of income that is in excess of the threshold for the taxpayer's filing status.

Employers are required to begin collecting the Additional Medicare Tax from employees in the first payroll period the employee's compensation from the employer exceeds $200,000. Only the amount in excess of $200,000 is subject to the payroll tax deduction. The employer does not match the employee contribution of the Additional Medicare Tax.

If an employee who files as MFJ does not have income exceeding $250,000 when the spouses combine their income and file their income tax return, or when the spousal incomes are combined and the amount of Additional Medicare Tax that should have been paid is less than what was deducted, any excess payments can be refunded to the taxpayer when the income tax return is filed.

Additionally, if a taxpayer expects to have income above the threshold for the taxpayer's filing status when combined with a spouse's income, and/or any self-employment income, the taxpayers may ask for additional federal income tax withheld by the employers, even though neither taxpayer's compensation will reach the $200,000 threshold. A self-employed taxpayer may make additional estimated tax payments to cover this contingency as well.

It must be emphasized that this is in addition to the 2.9% that is assessed on all compensation and net self-employment income.

Self-Employment Tax

Self-employment tax
Tax paid by self-employed individuals that is based on net earnings, not on the individual's wages. Because the self-employed must bear the burden of both the employer and employee portion of FICA, the self-employment tax rate is 15.3% (up to the taxable wage base)— double the employee's rate of 7.65% in 2020. Net SE income exceeding the TWB is taxed at the 2.9% Medicare tax rate, which has no income ceiling, and is added to the SE tax calculated for the SE income up to the TWB.

Self-employed individuals must bear the burden of both the employer and employee portion of FICA taxes. Therefore, the **self-employment tax** rate is 15.3% (in 2020), double the employee's rate of 7.65% [subject to the taxable wage base (TWB) limit]. If the net earnings exceed the taxable wage base, the Medicare tax of 2.9% is levied on the amounts that exceed the TWB. This tax is calculated on Schedule SE, which is attached to the individual's Form 1040.

Self-employment tax is calculated in the same fashion as FICA tax; however, the tax is based on net earnings from self-employment, not on the individual's wages. The net earnings from self-employment is the gross income from the trade or business, less any allowable deductions. Before applying the income tax rates, net earnings may be reduced by 7.65%, which represents the deductible employer share of the FICA tax.

EXAMPLE   If Andrea owns her own business and during 2020 her income after allowed deductions is $200,000, she will incur $22,431.10 in self-employment tax, calculated as follows:

Net earnings from self-employment	$200,000
Less: 7.65% of net earnings	(15,300)
Amount subject to self-employment tax	$184,700
Social Security portion (12.4% × $137,700)	$17,074.80
Medicare portion (2.9% × $184,700)	$5,356.30
Total self-employment taxes	$22,431.10

Andrea will report the self-employment tax on her income tax return and receive a deduction of $11,216 the employer deductible share of the self-employment tax in 2020. This amount will be deducted in arriving at adjusted gross income (above-the-line deduction).

EXHIBIT 13.10 Form 1040—Adjustments to Income

1	Wages, salaries, tips, etc. Attach Form(s) W-2		**1**
2a	Tax-exempt interest	**2a**	**b** Taxable interest. Attach Sch. B if required	**2b**
3a	Qualified dividends	**3a**	**b** Ordinary dividends. Attach Sch. B if required	**3b**
4a	IRA distributions	**4a**	**b** Taxable amount	**4b**
c	Pensions and annuities . . .	**4c**	**d** Taxable amount	**4d**
5a	Social security benefits . . .	**5a**	**b** Taxable amount	**5b**
6	Capital gain or (loss). Attach Schedule D if required. If not required, check here ▶ ☐		**6**
7a	Other income from Schedule 1, line 9		**7a**
b	Add lines 1, 2b, 3b, 4b, 4d, 5b, 6, and 7a. This is your **total income** ▶		**7b**
8a	Adjustments to income from Schedule 1, line 22		**8a**
b	Subtract line 8a from line 7b. This is your **adjusted gross income** ▶		**8b**
9	**Standard deduction or itemized deductions** (from Schedule A) . .	**9**	
10	Qualified business income deduction. Attach Form 8995 or Form 8995-A	**10**	
11a	Add lines 9 and 10		**11a**
b	**Taxable income.** Subtract line 11a from line 8b. If zero or less, enter -0-		**11b**

Standard Deduction for—
- Single or Married filing separately, $12,200
- Married filing jointly or Qualifying widow(er), $24,400
- Head of household, $18,350
- If you checked any box under *Standard Deduction*, see instructions.

For Disclosure, Privacy Act, and Paperwork Reduction Act Notice, see separate instructions.   Cat. No. 11320B   Form **1040** (2019)

SCHEDULE 1
(Form 1040 or 1040-SR)

Department of the Treasury
Internal Revenue Service

Additional Income and Adjustments to Income

▶ **Attach to Form 1040 or 1040-SR.**
▶ **Go to** *www.irs.gov/Form1040* **for instructions and the latest information.**

OMB No. 1545-0074

20**19**

Attachment
Sequence No. **01**

Name(s) shown on Form 1040 or 1040-SR

Your social security number

At any time during 2019, did you receive, sell, send, exchange, or otherwise acquire any financial interest in any virtual currency? . . . . ☐ Yes ☐ No

Part I	Additional Income		
1	Taxable refunds, credits, or offsets of state and local income taxes	**1**	
2a	Alimony received	**2a**	
b	Date of original divorce or separation agreement (see instructions) ▶		
3	Business income or (loss). Attach Schedule C	**3**	
4	Other gains or (losses). Attach Form 4797	**4**	
5	Rental real estate, royalties, partnerships, S corporations, trusts, etc. Attach Schedule E .	**5**	
6	Farm income or (loss). Attach Schedule F	**6**	
7	Unemployment compensation	**7**	
8	Other income. List type and amount ▶		
		8	
9	Combine lines 1 through 8. Enter here and on Form 1040 or 1040-SR, line 7a	**9**	

Part II	Adjustments to Income		
10	Educator expenses	**10**	
11	Certain business expenses of reservists, performing artists, and fee-basis government officials. Attach Form 2106	**11**	
12	Health savings account deduction. Attach Form 8889	**12**	
13	Moving expenses for members of the Armed Forces. Attach Form 3903	**13**	
14	Deductible part of self-employment tax. Attach Schedule SE	**14**	
15	Self-employed SEP, SIMPLE, and qualified plans	**15**	
16	Self-employed health insurance deduction	**16**	
17	Penalty on early withdrawal of savings	**17**	
18a	Alimony paid	**18a**	
b	Recipient's SSN . . . . ▶		
c	Date of original divorce or separation agreement (see instructions) ▶		
19	IRA deduction	**19**	
20	Student loan interest deduction	**20**	
21	Tuition and fees. Attach Form 8917	**21**	
22	Add lines 10 through 21. These are your **adjustments to income.** Enter here and on Form 1040 or 1040-SR, line 8a	**22**	

For Paperwork Reduction Act Notice, see your tax return instructions.   Cat. No. 71479F   Schedule 1 (Form 1040 or 1040-SR) 2019

Federal Unemployment Tax Act

The Federal Unemployment Tax Act (FUTA) provides for payments of unemployment compensation to workers who have lost their jobs. Most employers pay both a federal and state unemployment tax. The employee is not responsible for paying unemployment tax.

Federal unemployment taxes are imposed on employers who pay wages of $1,500 or more during any calendar quarter during the year or who employ at least one individual for at least a part of a day in any 20 or more different weeks during the current or previous year. There are different limits for an employer of farm workers. For many years the FUTA rate has been 6.2%, and it was applied to the first $7,000 the employer pays each employee as wages during the year. Therefore, the maximum FUTA payment required for a covered employee was $434 ($7,000 × 6.2%). In most cases, where an employer has paid state unemployment taxes, a credit of up to a maximum of 5.4% could be taken to reduce the amount of FUTA due. The effective tax rate then became 0.6%.

TAX AVOIDANCE VS. TAX EVASION

Tax avoidance
The legal minimization of taxes, which is accomplished by applying knowledge of the IRC and the Treasury regulations to an individual's income tax situation

The goal of most income tax planning is to reduce and minimize the amount of tax a person must pay to the government. **Tax avoidance** is the legal minimization of taxes. This avoidance is accomplished by applying knowledge of the Internal Revenue Code (also referred to as the Tax Code) and the Treasury regulations to an individual's income tax situation. Every individual has the right to reduce his tax burden within the scope of the law.

The taxpayers' legal right to minimize or reduce personal income taxes has been upheld by the courts. In the case of *Commissioner v. Newman*, Judge Learned Hand wrote:

> Over and over again courts have said that there is nothing sinister in so arranging one's affairs so as to keep taxes as low as possible. Everybody does so, rich or poor, and all do right, for nobody owes any public duty to pay more than the law demands; taxes are enforced extractions, not voluntary contributions. To demand more in the name of morals is mere cant.

Tax planning and tax avoidance involve only legal actions. Tax planning is the process of arranging one's actions in light of their tax consequences. In many cases, tax planning can be accomplished simply by changing the form of a transaction. For example, if an individual is invested in tax-exempt bonds, the individual is not required to pay tax on the interest income earned by the bonds, and therefore his tax liability is less than if he invested in taxable bonds.

Tax evasion
Any of the various fraudulent methods by which a taxpayer may pay less than his proper tax liability

Whereas tax avoidance is the term applied to the legal interpretation of the tax laws to minimize *tax liabilities*, **tax evasion** is the term generally applied to any of the various fraudulent methods by which a taxpayer may pay less than his proper tax liability.

For example, if an individual works part time at home babysitting the neighbors' children or mowing lawns for others, the income received must be reported as income on the individual's income tax return. Because the babysitting income may not be reported to the government by the individual's neighbors, the individual may decide illegally to exclude the income from the tax return.

This example of tax evasion may lead to additional tax liability, as well as interest and penalties, if the tax return is audited. The amount of interest and penalties depends on the amount of understatement. Criminal tax evasion can even lead to fines and an occasional jail sentence.

TAX-ADVANTAGED INVESTMENTS

One goal shared by most financial planners and their clients is the minimization of all current and future taxes. Because taxes are often an individual's highest expenditure each year, effective reduction of taxes is of extreme importance.

Although Congress has significantly reduced the opportunities available to minimize income taxes, there are still a few opportunities available for investors interested in or already involved in tax-advantaged investments. Included in these opportunities are investments in tax-exempt securities, investment in tax shelters and vacation homes, use of tax-advantaged employee benefits, use of acceleration/deferral techniques, and awareness of other tax-reduction opportunities.

Investment in Tax-Exempt Securities

As a rule, interest income is taxable regardless of its source. However, interest income from certain state and local bonds and interest on educational savings bonds is excluded from income for federal income tax purposes.

Interest on obligations of a state, territory, U.S. possession (such as Puerto Rico), or any of their political subdivisions is nontaxable. If an individual has money to invest, one may wish to invest in state bonds if income tax reduction is an important goal. It should be noted, however, that state governments typically offer lower interest rates on these bonds than the rate offered on taxable investments. Therefore, to determine whether an investment in a tax-exempt security is a wise choice, one can calculate an interest rate that a tax-exempt investment must earn to break even with the higher rate offered by a taxable investment. The formula to determine the break-even interest rate is:

Taxable interest rate × (1 − marginal tax rate) = tax-free rate

E X A M P L E   Joe has a 35% marginal income tax rate, and he would like to invest in State of Kentucky bonds. If similar taxable investments yield 10%, Joe must earn a rate of return on the State of Kentucky bonds of at least 6.5%, or 10% x (1 − 35%), to make this a worthwhile investment.

In addition to state bonds, interest on U.S. savings bonds such as Series EE bonds may be either tax deferred or tax exempt. The interest earned on the bond can be tax deferred until the year the bond matures or is redeemed by the individual. The taxpayer can also elect to recognize the interest income as it is earned instead of deferring the recognition until redemption or maturity. The interest income from a Series EE bond is completely tax-free if the bond was issued after 1989 and if the accrued interest and principal amount of the bond are used to pay for qualified education expenses of the taxpayer, spouse, or dependents, subject to AGI limitations.

Tax Shelters and Passive Activities

Under prior law, an individual could reduce or eliminate her tax liability by investing in tax shelters that produced losses that could be used to offset other income. These shelters often created paper losses in excess of the amount of capital the investor provided, causing the tax shelter business to grow into a thriving industry.

Typically, tax shelters took the form of limited partnerships, thus allowing losses to flow through to the individual partners. In the first few years of the partnerships' operation, losses were generally high due to low revenues and high expenses, such as interest, taxes, and accelerated depreciation.

The Tax Reform Act of 1986 significantly curtailed the benefits available to investors in tax shelters by the introduction of the passive activity loss limits. Passive activities include all rental operations and all other businesses in which the taxpayer does not materially participate. An individual meets the material participation test only if he is involved in the operation of the activity on a regular, continuous, and substantial basis.

Although there are many exceptions, a taxpayer will be considered a material participant if she spends more than 500 hours in the activity during the year or if she spends more than 100 hours in the activity and no other individual spends more time on the activity. If the investor is not a material participant, the activity is considered passive. Investors have two rules that govern deductibility of a loss from a passive activity. Under the **at-risk rule**, a taxpayer can deduct losses only to the extent of the amount the taxpayer has at risk in the investment (amount invested). Losses in amounts in excess of the amount at risk in the investment are suspended until the taxpayer increases the amount invested in the passive activity, either by additional investment or by a profit from the activity. Under the **passive loss rule**, passive losses may only offset income from the same or another passive activity. If the passive activity is a publicly traded partnership (master limited partnership), losses from that activity may only be offset by income from the same publicly traded partnership. Investors may not use passive activity losses to offset ordinary taxable income, such as salary, interest, and dividends. If a loss is disallowed (suspended) under the passive loss rule, it can subsequently be utilized when the taxpayer disposes of the activity.

Even though deductions for passive losses are generally disallowed, there are situations in which a taxpayer would benefit by investing in a tax shelter. For example, if the taxpayer has an investment in a passive activity that is generating income, any passive losses could be used to offset the passive income. In addition, a taxpayer may deduct a limited amount of loss against active income when the taxpayer invests in rental real estate.

A taxpayer who actively participates in a rental real estate activity may deduct up to $25,000 ($12,500 for taxpayers married but filing separately) of losses annually. A taxpayer is considered an active participant if he participates in management decisions such as approving new tenants and owns at least a 10% interest in the activity. The allowance is reduced by 50% of the excess of the individual's AGI over $100,000 ($50,000 for MFS) and is therefore completely phased out when the taxpayer's AGI reaches $150,000 ($75,000 for MFS).

At-risk rule

A taxpayer can deduct losses only to the extent of the amount the taxpayer has at risk in the investment (amount invested). Losses in amounts in excess of the amount at risk in the investment are suspended until the taxpayer increases the amount invested in the passive activity, either by additional investment or by a profit from the activity.

Passive loss rule

Passive losses may only offset income from another passive activity. If the passive activity is a publicly traded partnership (master limited partnership), losses from that activity may only be offset by income from the same publicly traded partnership.

Acceleration of Deductions

In addition to pursuing tax-advantaged investments, the taxpayer may take advantage of opportunities to accelerate income tax deductions or defer income tax gains. This also referred to as *deduction clustering*. However, this must be looked at in concert with the alternative minimum tax (AMT) implications. Some of these deductions are added back to regular taxable income to arrive at alternative minimum taxable income (AMTI), exposing the taxpayer to a possible AMT liability. This liability is the difference between the tax due on regular taxable income and the tax due on AMTI.

The Internal Revenue Code allows individual taxpayers to claim deductions for various personal, investment, and business expenses. The deduction can generally be claimed in the year in which the expenses are paid; therefore, individuals have some flexibility with respect to the timing of deductions. A taxpayer wishing to reduce or eliminate a potential tax liability can accelerate deductions by prepaying the expense. For example, state income taxes can be paid during the current tax year rather than waiting until the following year when the tax is due. Taxpayers can also make additional contributions to charity before the close of the tax year, resulting in an income tax deduction in the current year.

Deferral of Tax Gains

When a taxpayer disposes of property, any resulting gain is usually reported, or recognized, on the individual's income tax return in the year of disposition. However, there are several situations where a taxpayer can dispose of property and defer recognition of the gain until a later date.

Section 1031 of the Tax Code allows a taxpayer to exchange certain types of domestic (U.S.) real estate property without recognizing a gain. These like-kind exchanges are afforded beneficial tax treatment. If property other than like-kind property, commonly called **boot**, is received in the exchange, gain may be recognized.

Boot

Property (other than like-kind property) that qualifies as a tax gain when received in a property exchange

If a taxpayer is not required to recognize gain from a real estate like-kind exchange, the basis of the property received by the taxpayer must be reduced by the unrecognized (deferred) gain, resulting in recognition of the deferred gain when the acquired property is subsequently sold.

E X A M P L E   Jack received vacant land worth $60,000 in exchange for vacant land with a tax basis to Jack of $35,000. Assuming the vacant land qualifies as like-kind property, Jack's realized gain of $25,000 ($60,000 – $35,000) will not be reported on his income tax return. Jack's basis in the land received will be $35,000 ($60,000 – $25,000 deferred gain).

Taxpayers do not always dispose of their property intentionally. Occasionally, property is lost due to theft or to a casualty, such as a fire or storm. When this occurs, the taxpayer may receive some sort of compensation, such as insurance proceeds. The proceeds received may even exceed the taxpayer's basis in the property, resulting in a gain. Absent special provisions, the gain would be fully taxable in the year of the conversion, resulting in a potential financial hardship for the taxpayer.

Section 1033 of the Internal Revenue Code allows a taxpayer (even a related one) who undergoes an involuntary conversion to postpone recognition of the gain. If the amount reinvested in the replacement property equals or exceeds the amount realized, the realized gain is not recognized. If the amount reinvested in the replacement property is less than the amount realized, the gain is recognized to the extent the proceeds are not reinvested.

Normally, the taxpayer has a two-year time period from the end of the taxable year in which any gain is realized from an involuntary conversion (e.g., fire) to replace the property. However, if a condemnation of real property by a governmental authority is the reason for the conversion, this time period is extended to three years from the end of the taxable year in which any gain is realized. The general requirement to apply

Section 1033 is that the replacement property must be similar in service or use to the involuntarily converted property.

SUMMARY OF VALUATION RULES FOR SECTIONS 1031 AND 1033

	Section 1031 Real Estate Exchanges	Section 1033 Involuntary Conversions
Realized gain =	FMV of all property received – adjusted basis of all property given up	amount realized – adjusted basis of old property

Recognized gain occurs if boot received =	Recognized gain* occurs if boot received
	
	 ■ LESSER of:
	    ■ Boot received
	    ■ Realized gain
	
	 *Recognized gain also occurs if appreciated boot is given up	

Recognized gain =		amount realized but not reinvested in new property (limited to realized gain)
Deferred gain =	realized gain – recognized gain	realized gain – recognized gain
Basis in like-kind property received =	FMV of property received in exchange – deferred gain	
Basis in new property =		FMV of property at acquisition – deferred gain

Exemption Opportunities

The Tax Code has traditionally provided tax breaks for homeowners, including the allowance of deductions for mortgage interest and property taxes. The tax law also provides for the exclusion of some or all of the gain on the sale of a residence. The provision applies to residence sales as frequently as every two years, to gains in amounts up to $250,000 for single taxpayers and $500,000 for married taxpayers.

The exclusion is applicable to the sale of a residence owned by the taxpayer and used as a principal residence for two of the five years preceding the sale. If the taxpayer fails the use or ownership test, a partial exclusion may be available if the home is sold due to a change in employment, health, or other unforeseen circumstances. The allowed exclusion is based on a ratio of the number of qualifying months to 24 months.

Under the Mortgage Forgiveness Debt Relief Act of 2007, the gain exclusion has been expanded for surviving spouses. Because the $500,000 exclusion required filing of a joint income tax return, surviving spouses could only take advantage of the full $500,000 gain exclusion in the year of a spouse's death. Effective for sales and exchanges occurring after December 31, 2007, surviving single spouses qualify for the up-to-$500,000 exclusion amount (all other rules apply) for sales occurring up to two years from the date of death of the other spouse. It is important to understand that the two years expires with the second anniversary of the actual date of death and not just occurring in the second tax year after death. For example, if a spouse dies February 15, 2020, and the surviving spouse sells the residence February 1, 2022, the rule applies. If the residence is sold March 1, 2022, the surviving spouse is treated as single and only qualifies for up to $250,000 of gain exclusion.

E X A M P L E   Mary, a single taxpayer, owned and used her home as a principal residence for 18 months. She then sold her home because of a new job in another city, realizing a gain on the sale of $300,000. Mary would be entitled to an exclusion of $187,500 ($250,000 × 18/24), resulting in a reportable capital gain of $112,500 ($300,000 – $187,500).

If a married couple filing jointly does not meet the conditions for claiming the full $500,000 exclusion, the excludible gain will be the sum of the exclusion that each spouse would be entitled to if both were single. For this purpose, each spouse is treated as owning the home for the period that either spouse owned the home.

E X A M P L E   When Al and Susan were married, Susan moved into the home Al had owned and had been using as his principal residence for over 20 years. They used the home as their principal residence for six months, then sold the home (gain of $600,000) because of a new job. The couple can exclude $312,500 of the gain because Al will receive the full $250,000 exclusion and Susan will be entitled to a partial exclusion of $62,500 ($250,000 × 6/24).

Another exemption opportunity exists for taxpayers owning vacation homes. If the home is rented to others for 14 days or less during the year, any rental income from the home is excludible from the taxpayer's gross income, no matter how much rent is charged.

CONCLUSION

The federal tax system in the United States is among the most complex tax systems in the world. A financial planner must realize the importance of gaining a comprehensive understanding of the tax law because income taxes are often the largest single expenditure of a client in a given year.

Although changes to the law have made income tax avoidance much more difficult over the last few years, many tax planning opportunities still exist. It is the financial planner's duty to a client to be aware of these opportunities to prevent the client from paying more tax than he is obligated to pay.

WHERE ON THE WEB

American Bar Association **www.abanet.org**

American Institute of Certified Public Accountants (CPA/PFS) **www.aicpa.org**

Certified Financial Planner Board of Standards, Inc. **www.cfp.net**

Financial Planning Association **www.fpanet.org**

Internal Revenue Service **www.irs.gov**

National Association of Personal Financial Advisors **www.napfa.org**

National Association of State Boards of Accountancy **www.nasba.org**

National Association of Tax Professionals **www.natptax.com**

RIA (Research Institute of America) Thomson Tax and Accounting **www.riathomson.com**

Society of Financial Service Professionals **www.financialpro.org**

DISCUSSION QUESTIONS

1. What are the objectives of federal income tax law?

2. What is the alternative minimum tax?

3. What is a capital asset?

4. What is the formula for determining a client's income tax liability?

5. What are some of the types of government rulings issued as guidance to taxpayers and IRS agents?

6. When taxpayers violate the tax laws, what civil penalties might they expect to incur?

7. What payroll taxes did the Federal Insurance Contributions Act and the Federal Unemployment Tax Act create?

8. What tax-advantaged investment options are available to taxpayers?

EXERCISES

1. Joe, a self-employed individual, earns $150,000 in self-employment income. How much self-employment tax will Joe owe for for 2020?

2. Kay sold the following investments during the current year:

Property	Date Sold*	Date Acquired*	Sales Price	Adjusted Basis
ABC stock	2/3/CY	1/2/PY	$3,300	$1,300
Bond	2/5/CY	2/5/PY	$1,200	$1,400
Land	4/5/CY	5/4/PY	$4,300	$3,400

   * CY = current year; PY = prior year

   What is the amount of net long-term gain and net short-term gain on the sale of the investments?

3. Cindy sold 300 shares of XYZ stock for $5,200. She had paid $3,000 for the stock. Commissions of $300 on the sale and $180 on the purchase were paid.

   What is Cindy's amount realized and her gain realized, respectively, on this sale?

4. Don, age 61, incurred $28,000 of medical expenses in the current year. His insurance company reimbursed him $6,000. Assuming his AGI is $100,000, what is the amount of medical expense deduction Don can claim for the year?

5. The Durrs are a married couple with two school-age children they fully support. Use the following information about their 2020 finances to answer the following question.

Gross income	$91,350
Deductions for AGI	$6,000
Itemized deductions	$14,800

   Assuming the Durrs file a joint income tax return, what is their taxable income for 2020?

6. Susan, a single taxpayer, sold her home because she has a new job in another city. On the sale date, she had owned the home and used it as a personal residence for 18 months. What is the maximum gain that Susan can exclude on the sale of the residence?

7. During the current year, Scott had long-term capital losses of $2,000 and short-term capital losses of $1,500. If this is the first year he has experienced capital gains or losses, what amount of these losses may Scott deduct this year? Assume Scott files as single for federal income tax.

8. Pablo, a single individual, purchased a new personal residence for $375,000. Pablo sold the property 12 months later for $550,000 so he could take a new job that involved a promotion. How much gain must Pablo recognize?

9. David exchanged an apartment complex that he had owned for 8 years for farmland. The farmland was worth $1,050,000, and David's basis in the apartment complex was $475,000. David received $100,000 cash in the transaction. How much is David's gain realized and gain recognized because of this exchange?

10. Doug and Susan, ages 45 and 40, are married and file a joint return for 2020. The following pertains to their return for the year:

Adjusted gross income	$61,600
Itemized deductions	$26,000

   What is their taxable income and tax liability for 2020?

11. Joe is a single taxpayer who has taxable income of $175,000, including the capital gain. During the current year, he sold the following assets:

Investment	Gain
ABC Company stock	$4,500
XYZ Company stock	$1,000
Baseball card collection	$2,000
Corporate bonds	$6,000
Antiques	$8,000

   All of the assets were held longer than one year. How will Joe be taxed on the capital gains?

12. Susan filed her tax return 70 days after the due date. She remitted a check for $8,000 that represented the balance of the tax due. Calculate her total failure-to-file and failure-to-pay penalties.

13. Jim is in the 32% marginal income tax rate, and he would like to invest in State of Louisiana bonds. If similar taxable investments yield 9%, how much must Jim earn to make this a worthwhile investment?

14. Allison is age 12 and has the following income:

Investment income	$1,800
Income from a summer job	$2,200

Assuming her parents list Allison as a dependent on their income tax return, what is her taxable income for 2020?

15. Billy sold the following investments during the year:

Description	Holding Period	Gain/(Loss)
ABC Stock	Short-term	$30,000
XYZ Stock	Long-term	$45,000
Bonds	Short-term	($20,000)
Real estate	Long-term	($60,000)

As a taxpayer who files with his spouse as married, filing jointly, what is the net short-term or long-term gain or loss, and how much must Billy include or deduct in the current year?

PROBLEMS

1. David and Sue are married and file a joint return. They have two children, Billy and Suzy, ages 8 and 6, respectively.

   David is a self-employed real estate appraiser, and the results for his business for the current year are as follows (he paid self-employment tax of $4,705):

Gross receipts	$50,000
Expenses:	
Advertising	$900
Insurance	$1,000
Interest	$500
Dues	$700
Depreciation	$1,200
Office rent	$12,000

   Sue, who is employed by a marketing company, earned a salary of $40,000 for the current year. She participates in the company Section 401(k) plan and made contributions to the plan of $6,000 for the current year (the company does not provide any matching contributions).

   David and Sue also received the following income during the year:

   Interest:

Second National Bank, Dallas	$1,100
State of Louisiana Municipal Bonds	$500

Qualified dividends:

ABC Company cash dividend	$350
XYZ Company cash dividend	$400

They sold their principal residence after owning and living in the home for five years. The following information relates to the sale of the residence:

- Sales price $700,000
- Original cost $150,000

David and Sue incurred the following expenses during the current year:

- Real estate taxes $10,000
- Mortgage interest $4,500
- Sales taxes $800

Assuming David paid $5,000 in alimony to his ex-wife, calculate the couple's taxable income for 2020.

2. Scott and Laura are married and file a joint income tax return. They have taxable income for the current year of $65,000. In arriving at taxable income, they took the following deductions:

Mortgage interest	$8,000
Real estate taxes	$10,000
State income taxes	$8,000
Charitable contributions	$300

In addition, Scott and Laura received the following tax-exempt interest:

Municipal bonds	$600
Private activity bonds issued in 2005	$3,000

Laura also exercised incentive stock options (ISOs) during the year. The option entitled her to purchase 500 shares at $50 per share. The stock was worth $110 per share at the time of exercise.

Calculate the couple's AMTI before considering the AMT exemption amount.

3. Steve and Elaine exchange real estate investments. Steve gives up property with an adjusted basis of $250,000 (FMV $400,000). In return for this property, Steve receives property with a FMV of $300,000 (adjusted basis $200,000) and cash of $100,000.

What are Steve and Elaine's realized, recognized, and deferred gains because of the exchange?

4. Anne, a CPA employed by a CPA firm, is an unmarried taxpayer. She earned a salary of $100,000 for the current year (2020) and did not participate in the firm's Section 401(k) plan.

Anne also received the following income and incurred the following expenses during the year:

Income:		
	Interest	$2,000
	Ordinary dividends	$900
Expenses:		
	Medical (unreimbursed)	$1,500
	Real estate taxes	$7,000
	Mortgage interest	$5,000
	Interest on auto loan	$2,500

Ignoring any credits, how much lower would Anne's tax liability have been had she made a deductible employee contribution ($12,000) to the Section 401(k) plan?

CASE SCENARIO

Use the information provided to answer the following questions regarding the Nelson family.

NELSON FAMILY CASE SCENARIO
DANA AND DAVID NELSON
As of January 1, 2020

Personal Background and Information

David Nelson (age 37) is a bank vice president. He has been employed there for 12 years and has an annual salary of $70,000. Dana Nelson (age 37) is a full-time home-maker. David and Dana have been married for eight years. They have two children, John (age 6) and Gabrielle (age 3), and are expecting their third child in two weeks. They have always lived in this community and expect to remain indefinitely in their current residence.

General Goals (Not Prioritized)

- Save for college education
- Reduce debt
- Save for retirement
- Estate planning
- Invest wisely

Insurance Information

Health Insurance

The entire family is insured under David's employer's health plan (PPO). For covered expenses, a $1,000 in-network deductible and a $2,000 out-of-network deductible apply, after which 80%/20% coinsurance applies in-network and 60%/40% applies out-of-network. There is a stop-loss limit of $20,000 annually in-network and $30,000 out-of-network annually. The entire monthly premium of $1,123.54 is paid by David's employer.

Life Insurance

David's employer provides group term life insurance equal to two times his current salary. The premium is paid entirely by his employer, and Dana is the primary beneficiary. No contingent beneficiary is named.

Disability Insurance

David's employer also offers a contributory group long-term disability insurance program toward which the employer contributes 60% of the $158.54 monthly premium. David is a participant in the program, which provides a monthly disability income benefit equal to 70% of his current salary, payable to his Social Security normal retirement age, provided that he remains disabled per the policy's "own occupation" definition of disability. David must satisfy a 90-day elimination period before he is eligible to begin receiving benefits.

David's employer doesn't offer dental or vision coverage, and the Nelsons have not obtained any private form of individual dental or vision insurance benefits.

Homeowners Insurance

The Nelsons have an HO-3 policy with replacement cost on contents. There is a $250 deductible. The annual premium is $950.

Automobile Insurance

The Nelsons have automobile liability and bodily injury coverage of $100,000/$300,000/$100,000. They have both comprehensive coverage and collision. The deductibles are $250 (comprehensive) and $500 (collision). The annual premium is $900.

Relevant External Environmental Information

- Mortgage rates are 5.0% for 30 years and 4.5% for 15 years, fixed.

- Gross domestic product is expected to grow at less than 3%.

- Inflation is expected to be 2.6%.

- Expected return on investment is 8% for common stocks, 9% for small company stocks, and 1.1% for U.S. Treasury bills.

- College education costs are $15,000 per year.

Investment Information

The bank offers a Section 401(k) plan in which David is an active participant. The bank matches contributions dollar for dollar up to 3% of David's salary. David currently contributes 5.43% of his salary. His employer's plan allows for employee contributions of up to 16% of salary. In the Section 401(k) plan, the Nelsons have the opportunity to invest in a money market fund, a bond fund, a growth and income fund, and a small-cap stock fund. The Nelsons consider themselves to have a moderate investment risk tolerance. David's assets within the retirement plan are currently earning 8.5%, based on his investment choices within the plan.

Income Tax Information

David and Dana tell you that they are in the 12% federal income tax bracket. They pay $820 annually in state and local income taxes.

Education Information

John is 6 years old and currently attending first grade at a private school. Gabrielle is 3 years old. She will attend private school from pre-kindergarten through high school. The current balance of the college fund is $14,000. They expect to contribute $1,000 at the end of each year to this fund.

Gifts, Estates, Trusts, and Will Information

David has made Dana his primary beneficiary on his Section 401(k) plan, and the children are the contingent beneficiaries. Because most of their assets are owned jointly, David doesn't see the need for a will. Dana also does not have a will.

Dana and David Nelson
Statement of Financial Position
12/31/2019

ASSETS			LIABILITIES AND NET WORTH		
Cash/cash equivalents			**Current liabilities**		
JT	Checking account	$1,425	JT	Credit cards	$4,000
JT	Savings account	$950	JT	Mortgage on principal residence	$1,234
			David	Boat loan	$1,493
Total cash/cash equivalents		$2,375	**Total current liabilities**		$6,727
Invested assets			**Long-term liabilities**		
Dana	ABC stock	$12,500	JT	Mortgage on principal residence	$196,654
JT	Education fund	$14,000	David	Boat loan	$12,065
David	Section 401(k) plan	$32,197			
Total invested assets		$58,697	**Total long-term liabilities**		$208,719
Personal-use assets			**Total liabilities**		$215,446
JT	Principal residence	$245,000			
JT	Automobile	$18,000			
David	Boat	$25,000	**Net worth**		$207,626
Dana	Jewelry	$13,000			
JT	Furniture/household	$61,000			
Total personal-use assets		$362,000			
Total assets		$423,072	**Total liabilities and net worth**		$423,072

Dana and David Nelson
Statement of Financial Position
12/31/2020

ASSETS			LIABILITIES AND NET WORTH		
Cash/cash equivalents			**Current liabilities**		
JT	Checking account	$1,268	JT	Credit cards	$3,655
JT	Savings account	$950	JT	Mortgage on principal Residence	$1,370
Total cash/cash equivalents		$2,218	David	Boat loan	$1,048
			Total current liabilities		$6,073
Invested assets			**Long-term liabilities**		
Dana	ABC stock	$14,050	JT	Mortgage on principal Residence	$195,284
JT	Education fund	$15,560	David	Boat loan	$16,017
David	Section 401(k) plan	$38,619	**Total long-term liabilities**		$211,301
David	XYZ stock	$10,000			
Total invested assets		$78,229			
Personal-use assets			**Total liabilities**		$217,374
JT	Principal residence	$250,000			
JT	Automobile	$15,000			
David	Personal watercraft	$10,000	**Net worth**		$241,573
David	Boat B	$30,000			
Dana	Jewelry	$13,500			
JT	Furniture/household	$60,000			
Total personal-use assets		$378,500			
Total assets		$458,947	**Total liabilities and net worth**		$458,947

Notes to financial statements:
- Assets are stated at fair market value.
- The ABC stock was inherited from Dana's aunt on November 15, 2019. Her aunt originally paid $20,000 for it on October 31, 2010. The fair market value at the aunt's death was $12,000.
- Liabilities are stated at principal only.
- JT = joint tenancy; client name = separate property.

Dana and David Nelson
Personal Statement of Cash Flows
For 2020

INFLOWS		
Salary—David		$70,000
Investment income		
Interest income	$900	
Qualified dividends	$150	$1,050
Total inflow		**$71,050**
Savings		
Reinvestment (interest/dividends)	$1,050	
Section 401(k) plan deferrals	$3,803	
Education fund	$1,000	
Total savings		**$5,853**
Available for outflows		**$65,197**
OUTFLOWS		
Ordinary living expenses		
Food	$6,000	
Clothing	$3,600	
Child care	$ 600	
Entertainment	$1,814	
Utilities	$3,600	
Auto maintenance	$2,000	
Church	$3,500	
Total ordinary living expenses		**$21,114**
Debt payments		
Credit card payments principal	$345	
Credit card payments interest	$615	
Mortgage payment principal	$1,234	
Mortgage payment interest	$20,720	
Boat loan principal	$1,493	
Boat loan interest	$1,547	
Total debt payments		**$25,954**
Insurance premiums		
Automobile insurance premiums	$900	
Disability insurance premiums	$761	
Homeowners insurance premiums	$950	
Total insurance premiums		**$2,611**
Tuition and education expenses		**$1,000**
Taxes		
FICA and federal income tax (W/H)	$12,855	
State (and city) income tax	$820	
Property tax (principal residence)	$1,000	
Total taxes		**$14,675**
Total outflows		**$65,354**
Net cash flow (deficit)		**($157)**

1. Calculate the Nelsons' taxable income and tax liability for 2020 (ignoring any credits).
2. Are the Nelsons subject to the alternative minimum tax? If so, what is their AMT for 2020?
3. The Nelsons exchanged their boat (Boat A) plus $5,000 for Boat B on December 31, 2020. David had paid $22,000 for Boat A a few years ago. What are the realized gain and recognized gain from this transaction?
4. If David increased his contributions to maximize his employer's match to his Section 401(k) plan, what would be the reduction in the Nelsons' tax liability in 2020?

APPENDIX 13.1 2020 Tax Rates and Brackets

2020 TAX RATES AND BRACKETS

Single—Schedule X

If taxable income is:

Over	But not over	The tax is	Of the amount over
$ 0	$ 9,875	$ 0 + 10%	$ 0
$ 9,875	$ 40,125	$ 987.50 + 12%	$ 9,875
$ 40,125	$ 85,525	$ 4,617.50 + 22%	$ 40,125
$ 85,525	$163,300	$ 14,605.50 + 24%	$ 85,525
$163,300	$207,350	$ 33,721.50 + 32%	$163,300
$207,350	$518,400	$ 47,367.50 + 35%	$207,350
$518,400	-----------	$156,253.00 + 37%	$518,400

Married Filing Jointly or Qualifying Widow(er)—Schedule Y-1

If taxable income is:

Over	But not over	The tax is	Of the amount over
$ 0	$ 19,750	$ 0 + 10%	$ 0
$ 19,750	$ 80,250	$ 1,975.00 + 12%	$ 19,750
$ 80,250	$171,050	$ 9,235.00 + 22%	$ 80,250
$171,050	$326,600	$ 29,211.00 + 24%	$171,050
$326,600	$414,700	$ 66,543.00 + 32%	$326,600
$414,700	$622,050	$ 94,735.00 + 35%	$414,700
$622,050	-----------	$167,307.50 + 37%	$622,050

Married Filing Separately—Schedule Y-2

If taxable income is:

Over	But not over	The tax is	Of the amount over
$ 0	$ 9,875	$ 0 + 10%	$ 0
$ 9,875	$ 40,125	$ 987.50 + 12%	$ 9,875
$ 40,125	$ 85,525	$ 4,617.50 + 22%	$ 40,125
$ 85,525	$163,300	$14,605.50 + 24%	$ 85,525
$163,300	$207,350	$33,721.50 + 32%	$163,300
$207,350	$311,025	$47,367.50 + 35%	$207,350
$311,025	-----------	$83,653.75 + 37%	$311,025

Head of Household—Schedule Z

If taxable income is:

Over	But not over	The tax is	Of the amount over
$ 0	$ 14,100	$ 0 + 10%	$ 0
$ 14,100	$ 53,700	$ 1,410.00 + 12%	$ 14,100
$ 53,700	$ 85,500	$ 6,162.00 + 22%	$ 53,700
$ 85,500	$163,300	$ 13,158.00 + 24%	$ 85,500
$163,300	$207,350	$ 31,830.00 + 32%	$163,300
$207,350	$518,400	$ 45,926.00 + 35%	$207,350
$518,400	-----------	$154,793.50 + 37%	$518,400

APPENDIX 13.2 Form W-2

22222	a Employee's social security number		
	OMB No. 1545-0008		
b Employer identification number (EIN)		1 Wages, tips, other compensation	2 Federal income tax withheld
c Employer's name, address, and ZIP code		3 Social security wages	4 Social security tax withheld
		5 Medicare wages and tips	6 Medicare tax withheld
		7 Social security tips	8 Allocated tips
d Control number		9	10 Dependent care benefits
e Employee's first name and initial Last name Suff.		11 Nonqualified plans	12a
		13 Statutory employee Retirement plan Third-party sick pay	12b
		14 Other	12c
			12d
f Employee's address and ZIP code			

15 State Employer's state ID number	16 State wages, tips, etc.	17 State income tax	18 Local wages, tips, etc.	19 Local income tax	20 Locality name

Form **W-2** Wage and Tax Statement   **2020**   Department of the Treasury—Internal Revenue Service

Copy 1—For State, City, or Local Tax Department

Business Entities

LEARNING OBJECTIVES

After learning the material in this chapter, you will be able to do the following:

■ Identify the different types of business entities that a businessowner may choose as a legal form of business

■ Characterize each type of business entity listed below with regard to formation requirements, operation, ownership restrictions, tax treatment, legal liability risk, and management operations:

    — Sole proprietorship

    — Partnership

    — Limited liability partnership

    — Corporation

    — S corporation

    — Limited liability company

■ List the basic factors that a businessowner should consider when selecting a legal form of business

- Explain how each type of business entity is different with regard to simplicity of formation and operation, ownership restrictions, limited liability, management operations, and tax characteristics

- Discuss family limited partnerships and how FLPs are used in estate planning

- Discuss taxation and legal liabilities of partnerships, corporations, and S corporations

- Discuss the components of the financial statements used by business entities

BUSINESS ENTITIES

One of the major decisions confronting a businessowner from a tax and legal perspective concerns selecting the form in which the business will operate. The businessowner can choose from several different business forms, each with its own advantages and disadvantages.

Businessowners may choose to run their business as a sole proprietorship, a partnership, a limited liability partnership (LLP), a corporation, or a limited liability company (LLC). Each of these business forms has different formation requirements, tax rules, legal liability risk, and type of management.

Once a business entity has been created, the next step is operating the business. The type of entity chosen will help determine which individuals will be responsible for making the day-to-day business decisions.

Another consideration in the selection of a legal form of business entity is the legal liability of the owners. A major concern of businessowners is the preservation and growth of personal assets, especially in today's litigious society. Therefore, it is critical to select a form of business entity that not only provides the desired asset protection but also allows the appropriate level of freedom to run the company.

Income tax considerations play an important role in the selection of a business entity. Although many of the entities are taxed in a similar fashion, each entity is subject to a set of rules that provides the businessowner with tax consequences that are either advantageous or detrimental. The following sections detail the different tax consequences of the formation and operation of sole proprietorships, partnerships, limited liability partnerships (LLPs), corporations, and limited liability companies (LLCs). Beginning in 2018, there is a deduction for pass-through income of 20% allowed to a noncorporate taxpayer, including a trust or estate, who has qualified business income (QBI) from a partnership, S corporation, or sole proprietorship. The calculation is complex and will not be covered in this book. The student should only be aware that it exists.

The creator of a new business can choose from several legal business forms. The owner must carefully analyze the available options to determine which type of business entity is most appropriate. As a personal financial planner, it is important to understand the different types of business forms available. The most common forms and their basic characteristics are discussed in this chapter.

SOLE PROPRIETORSHIP

Sole proprietorship
A business owned and controlled by one person who is personally liable for all debts and claims against the business

Proprietor
The owner of a sole proprietorship

A **sole proprietorship** is a business owned and controlled by one person who is personally liable for all debts and claims against the business. Separate financial records are regularly maintained. However, for tax purposes, the sole proprietorship is not treated as a separate taxable entity. Rather, the income and deductions of the business are reported directly on the individual owner's federal income tax return (Schedule C of Form 1040).

Advantages of a sole proprietorship include its ease of formation and its simplicity of operation and taxation. **Proprietors** own all business property and need not consult partners or other managers before making business decisions. In addition, this form of business entity may provide some state and federal tax advantages over other entities. For example, if the proprietorship incurs a loss for the year, the loss will be reported on the individual's income tax return, where it may provide immediate tax relief because the loss may be deductible against other taxable income.

Management Operation and Decision Making of a Proprietorship

The proprietor is responsible for the day-to-day operation of the business and is responsible for making all of the business decisions. This allows for great flexibility in the operation of the business. For example, the owner may choose to add a new line of business or discontinue an existing line of business without the approval of others.

Legal Liability of a Proprietorship

The major disadvantage of the sole proprietorship is that the proprietor has unlimited personal liability for the indebtedness of the sole proprietorship. Business liabilities may be satisfied from the owner's personal assets, and any personal liabilities may be satisfied from the business assets. The owner may purchase business liability insurance. This insurance does not exempt the owner from creditor's claims, but it does provide protection against lawsuits.

Taxation of a Proprietorship

Although separate financial records are maintained for tax purposes, the sole proprietorship is not treated as a separate taxable entity.

Tax Ramifications of Formation of a Proprietorship

The formation of a sole proprietorship is very straightforward. No formal transfer of assets to the business is required to enable a proprietorship to engage in business activities. Also, the owner generally is not required to file documents with local authorities (except perhaps for a business license), unless the owner is planning to operate the business under an assumed name. When a sole proprietorship is established, there are no federal income tax ramifications.

Tax Ramifications of Business Operation of a Proprietorship

When the proprietorship generates income and incurs losses, it is not required to file a separate federal income tax return. Instead, the income or loss from the business is reported directly on Schedule C of the proprietor's individual income tax return, Form 1040. When reported, the income or loss is combined with the proprietor's other income to determine the taxpayer's adjusted gross income (AGI). The income from the business is taxed at ordinary income tax rates applicable to individual taxpayers and is generally subject to self-employment taxes.

Schedule C of Form 1040 is used to report the name of the proprietor, as well as the name, address, and accounting method of the proprietorship. This form also contains separate sections to report income earned by the business, such as gross receipts, and expenses incurred by the business, such as advertising, supplies, and wages paid. A sole proprietorship generally may deduct ordinary and necessary business expenses as incurred. A self-employed businessowner is allowed an above-the-line (for AGI) deduction for appropriate contributions to retirement plans, and, in amounts not to exceed net earnings from self-employment, 100% of health insurance premiums and qualified long-term care premiums paid.

The net profit or loss from Schedule C is reflected on the individual income tax return Form 1040. If Schedule C reflects a net profit for the year, this profit is subject to self-employment tax. Self-employment tax is calculated in the same fashion as FICA tax; however, the tax is based on net earnings from the sole proprietorship instead of wages. Before applying the tax rates, net earnings are reduced by 7.65%, which is the deductible share of the self-employment tax rate.

EXHIBIT 14.1 Schedule 1 of Form 1040

Part I	**Additional Income**		
1	Taxable refunds, credits, or offsets of state and local income taxes	1	
2a	Alimony received	2a	
b	Date of original divorce or separation agreement (see instructions) ▶		
3	Business income or (loss). Attach Schedule C	3	
4	Other gains or (losses). Attach Form 4797	4	
5	Rental real estate, royalties, partnerships, S corporations, trusts, etc. Attach Schedule E	5	
6	Farm income or (loss). Attach Schedule F	6	

To terminate a sole proprietorship, the taxpayer need only cease operations, pay off all vendors, and report final income or loss on Schedule C of Form 1040 in the tax year the business is terminated.

E X A M P L E If Stan owns his own proprietorship business, and during 2020 his business income after allowed deductions is $300,000, he would incur $22,728.45 in self-employment tax, calculated as follows:

Net earnings from sole proprietorship	$300,000
Less 7.65% of net earnings	($22,950)
Amount subject to self-employment tax	$277,050
Social Security portion (12.4% × $137,700)	$17,074.80
Medicare portion (2.9% × $277,050)	8,034.45
Total self-employment taxes	$25,109.25

The self-employment tax is calculated on Schedule SE, which is attached to the proprietor's Form 1040. The proprietor is allowed a deduction for deductible share (employer share) of the self-employment tax paid, or $12,554.63, in the example. This amount will be deducted in arriving at adjusted gross income (above-the-line deduction). In addition, Stan would be subject to the 0.9% Additional Medicare tax in excess of his applicable threshold. The tax is not a deductible expense. The amount would depend on Stan's filing status.

▌PARTNERSHIP

Partnership

An association of two or more entities or individuals that operate as co-owners of a business for the purpose of making a profit

Partner

An individual, corporation, trust, estate, or other partnership that has an ownership interest in a partnership

A **partnership** is an association of two or more entities or individuals that operate as co-owners of a business for the purpose of making a profit. Generally, forming a partnership is a simple process because formality is ordinarily unnecessary. The partnership form of business is very flexible because there are no limitations on the number of **partners**, and partners can be individuals, corporations, trusts, estates, and even other partnerships. There are two types of partnerships—general and limited. These differ primarily in the nature of the rights and obligations of the partners. General partnerships are owned entirely by general partners. Each partner can act on behalf of the partnership. A limited partnership is a partnership formed under the limited partnership laws of a state. This partnership must have at least one general partner and at least one limited partner.

Management Operation and Decision Making of a Partnership

Ordinarily, when a partnership is formed, a partnership agreement is drafted outlining the identity of the partners, the division of profits and losses, and the duties of each partner in the management of the partnership business.

General partnership

A type of business entity owned entirely by general partners, each of whom can act on behalf of the partnership

General Partnership

In a **general partnership**, the general partners participate in the management of the partnership and are directly responsible for the day-to-day operation of the business. With management and ownership consolidated among the same individuals, partners are relatively free to change operating policy. Thus, the partnership can change its operational direction at any time.

Limited partnership

In a limited partnership, limited partners are not allowed to participate in the management of operations but generally are allowed to vote on major changes affecting the structure of the partnership

Limited Partnership

In a **limited partnership**, limited partners are not allowed to participate in the management of the partnership affairs. If the limited partners do participate in management, they will become general partners and lose their limited liability status. It should be noted that even though limited partners are not allowed to participate in management, they generally are entitled to vote on major changes affecting the structure of the partnership, such as a change in the type of investments purchased.

Legal Liability of a Partnership

General Partnership

General partnerships are owned entirely by general partners. While the partnership form of business has many advantages, it also has several disadvantages. The most significant disadvantage is the unlimited personal liability of the partners.

A general partner has unlimited liability for the acts of the partnership, the other partners, and obligations made by any partner or the partnership in the performance of partnership duties. If the partnership assets are insufficient to satisfy the liabilities of the partnership, the partnership's creditors can collect against the personal assets of the general partners. The creditors have the right to make any one partner, or several partners, satisfy the entire amount of the partnership's obligations. As a result, one partner may have to make good on the partnership's obligations and then may not be able to recover these amounts from the other partners.

Limited Partnership

A limited partner is liable for partnership indebtedness only to the extent of the capital the partner has contributed or agreed to contribute. In this respect, the limited partner is treated as an investor, liable only for the amount of his investment. Although the status of a limited partner generally provides the individual with limited liability, the limited liability status may disappear, and the partner would be liable as a general partner under any of the following circumstances.

- The surname of the limited partner is included in the partnership name. This does not apply if there is a general partner with the same surname.

- The limited partner acts as a general partner by participating in the management of the business operations.

- The limited partner learns that the firm is defectively formed and fails to withdraw from the partnership.

Taxation of a Partnership

For federal income tax purposes, each general partner's share of partnership trade or business income is considered self-employment income, subject to self-employment taxes. A limited partner, however, is not allowed to participate in the management and control of the business and, therefore, is not subject to self-employment taxes on partnership earnings. A limited partner's income and losses are generally considered passive and subject to the passive activity rules, and a general partner's income and losses are ordinary.

Flow-through or conduit entity
A type of business entity in which the results of business operations are reported directly on the owner's income tax return

A partnership is similar to a sole proprietorship in that both entities are **flow-through or conduit entities** for federal income tax purposes. In other words, the results of business operations for both entities are reported directly on the owner's income tax return. For federal income tax purposes, partners must take into account their distributive share of partnership taxable income and any additional items the partnership is required to report separately, such as interest and dividend income. Consequently, the partnership is not, as an entity, subject to federal income tax. The partnership items of income and expense are completely taxable to the partners at their own personal income tax rates but are reported initially on the partnership tax return (Form 1065) and then reported to each partner (Form K-1).

Tax Ramifications of Formation of a Partnership

Partners may form a partnership by contributing cash, property, or services to the partnership in exchange for an ownership interest. When a partner contributes cash or property to the partnership, no gain or loss is recognized and the partner's basis in the partnership is equal to the value of the cash contributed or the adjusted basis of the property contributed. If a partner contributes personal or professional services to the partnership, the partner must recognize ordinary compensation income for the value of the services. The amount of income recognized becomes the partner's basis in the partnership interest.

EXAMPLE   Assume Tom contributes the following to the ABC partnership in exchange for a 50% general partnership interest in the partnership:

Contribution	Fair market value
Cash	$10,000
Land (Tom's basis is $40,000)	$50,000
Services	$ 5,000

Tom would recognize ordinary income of $5,000, the value of the services he contributed to the partnership. His basis in the partnership interest would be $55,000 ($10,000 + 40,000 + 5,000).

Tax Ramifications of Business Operation of a Partnership

Once the partnership has been created, it is treated for federal income tax purposes as an aggregate of the separate partners, rather than as a separate taxable entity. The partnership itself is not required to pay any income tax, but must file an information return, Form 1065, detailing the items of income and expense that will be reported on the partner's individual income tax return.

Partners must take into account their distributive share of partnership taxable income and any separately stated items in computing their individual taxable incomes. Generally, a partner's interest in the partnership's capital and profits determines the partner's share of income, gain, loss, deduction, or credit. The partners may change the traditional allocation of tax items through the partnership agreement. This special allocation of an item or items must have a substantial economic effect to be valid. In many cases, special allocations allow the benefits of deductions to pass to those partners who have a greater use for such deductions.

Each partner's distributive share of items is reported on Form 1065 Schedule K-1, which is furnished by the partnership to both the Internal Revenue Service (IRS) and to each partner. Schedule K-1 details the partner's share of partnership ordinary income, which is the net profit or loss resulting from the partnership's trade or business. If the partner is a general partner, this allocation of ordinary income will be subject not only to ordinary income tax but also to self-employment tax, similar to a proprietorship.

Form 1065 Schedule K-1 also reflects various items that must be reported separately from ordinary income. These separately stated items—dividend income, interest income, and capital gains—are reported also on the partner's individual income tax return.

The partner's adjusted taxable basis in the partnership interest must be adjusted each year to reflect the allocated items of income and expense. Adjusted taxable basis is increased by a partner's distributive share of both taxable and nontaxable partnership income and is decreased by the partner's share of partnership losses, nondeductible expenses, and distributions.

Continuing with the example of ABC, if the partnership reported earnings of $40,000 for the first year, Tom, a 50% partner, would report $20,000 of ordinary income on his federal income tax return even if no cash was actually distributed. His basis in the partnership after the first year would be adjusted to $75,000 ($55,000 original basis + $20,000 of allocated income). Because Tom is a general partner, the $20,000 distributable share of partnership earnings would also be subject to self-employment tax.

Tax Ramifications of Withdrawals or Distributions from a Partnership

Partners may withdraw cash or property from the partnership to meet their needs or as advance payments of their share of partnership income. Regardless of the reason for the withdrawal, the recipient partner generally recognizes no gain on the distribution. Instead, the withdrawal is treated as a return of capital that reduces the partner's adjusted taxable basis in the partnership. For example, if Tom, the ABC partner, withdrew the $20,000 earned, his adjusted taxable basis would return to $55,000. Once the partner's basis has been reduced to zero, any additional withdrawals taken from the partnership result in a capital gain to the partner.

The dissolution or termination of a general or limited partnership, family limited partnership (FLP), and a limited liability partnership (LLP) is more complex. The events that can trigger a termination of a partnership are varied, and the requirements to dissolve a partnership are not encompassed by this textbook.

FAMILY LIMITED PARTNERSHIP

Family limited partnership (FLP)
A limited partnership of family members that is used to generate valuation discounts for estate and gift tax purposes on the transfer of the limited interest in the partnership

A **family limited partnership (FLP)** is an estate planning technique utilizing a limited partnership of family members. The arrangement is generally structured so that a senior family member transfers appreciating, capital-intensive property, such as real estate, to a limited partnership in return for a minimal general partnership interest (typically 1%) and a significant limited partnership interest (typically 99%). Over the senior family member's lifetime, the limited partnership interests are transferred to junior family members by gift or sale.

One of the primary objectives of the family limited partnership arrangement is to generate valuation discounts for estate and gift tax purposes on the transfer of the limited interest in the partnership. The estate and gift tax value of a limited partnership interest in a properly structured family limited partnership typically is determined by applying minority interest and lack of marketability discounts.

- *Minority interest discount*—A reduction in value of an asset transferred is often allowed if the asset transferred represents a minority interest in a business. A minority interest is any interest that, in terms of voting, is not a controlling interest. Because minority owners cannot control the business or compel its sale or liquidation, outside buyers would not be willing to pay the same amount for a minority interest as they would for a majority or controlling interest.

- *Lack of marketability discount*—A reduction in value of an asset transferred is often allowed if the asset transferred has an inherent lack of marketability. Limited partnership interests in a family limited partnership are more difficult to sell than interests in other assets such as publicly traded stock. Therefore, a discount is often allowed for the lack of marketability.

The family limited partnership has many advantages. One of the major advantages is that the senior family member can retain control of the business because the senior family member is the only family member with a general partnership interest. (Limited partners are not allowed to participate in the management of the business.) Additional advantages of this technique include creditor protection and the ability to place restrictions on transfers of limited partnership interests by junior family members. Also, it can allow income shifting from higher to lower tax bracket family members.

Management Operation and Decision Making of a Family Limited Partnership

The management of a family limited partnership is the same as that of a limited partnership. The general partner manages the partnership and is directly responsible for the day-to-day operation of the business. Thus, the partnership can change its operational direction at any time.

Legal Liability of a Family Limited Partnership

The general partner (senior family member) has unlimited liability for the acts of the partnership, the other partners, and obligations made by any partner or the partnership in the performance of partnership duties. The limited partners (junior family members) are treated as investors, liable only for the amount of each of their investments, and their respective shares of profits and losses are subject to the passive activity rules.

Taxation of a Family Limited Partnership

The partnership agreement governs how partnership income is divided among the partners. Generally, both general and limited partners share income and cash flow on the basis of their percentage interest in the partnership. The taxable income of the FLP is reported annually and allocated to each partner on the basis of that partner's percentage interest. The allocation is noted on Form K-1 issued to each partner. Usually, the general partner annually distributes at least enough cash to pay the income tax liability attributable to each partner. Distributions from the partnership are not taxable to the extent the partner has basis in the partnership interest. Distributions to the extent of basis are return of capital. The partnership itself (unlike a corporation) is not subject to tax because it passes through all items of income and deduction to the partners.

LIMITED LIABILITY PARTNERSHIP

A **limited liability partnership (LLP)** is similar to a general partnership, except an LLP provides additional liability protection to the partners. Only certain professionals (such as attorneys and accountants) are eligible for LLPs.

Management Operation and Decision Making of a Limited Liability Partnership

Limited liability partnership (LLP)
A form of business entity similar to a general partnership, except that an LLP provides additional liability protection to the partners

The management of an LLP is the same as that of a general partnership. The partners participate in the management of the partnership and are directly responsible for the day-to-day operation of the business. With management and ownership consolidated among the same individuals, partners are relatively free to change operating policy. Thus, the partnership can change its operational direction at any time.

Legal Liability of a Limited Liability Partnership

In an LLP, partners are personally liable for their own acts of wrongdoing, but their personal assets (those outside the partnership entity) are protected from claims arising from the wrongful acts of other partners. This liability protection in many states extends only to tort law, not contract law.

Taxation of Limited Liability Partnerships

For federal income tax purposes, an LLP is treated in the same fashion as a partnership. The LLP is considered a conduit, or flow-through entity, which is not subject to federal income tax. Partners must take into account their distributive share of partnership taxable income and any additional items the partnership is required to report separately.

CORPORATION

C corporation
A business entity created by state law that is separate and distinct from its shareholders

Shareholders
The owners of a corporation who elect the corporation's board of directors

A corporation (regular **C corporation**) is an entity created by state law that is separate and distinct from its **shareholders** (owners). A corporation can be closely held if owned by a few shareholders, or publicly held if owned by many shareholders.

The shareholders enjoy limited liability—they can lose only the amount they have invested in the corporation. They do not represent the corporation but vote for a board of directors, which determines corporate policy and appoints officers. The officers manage the corporation.

Management Operation and Decision Making of a Corporation

Directors
Individuals who, acting as a group known as the board of directors, manage the business affairs of a corporation

Board of directors
The governing body of a corporation whose members are elected by shareholders

Corporations have management advantages over other business forms. With a corporation, there is a separation of management from ownership so that the mere ownership of corporate stock does not give the owner the right to participate in management. The management is centralized, with the directors and officers handling management of corporate affairs.

Directors are the individuals who, acting as a group known as the **board of directors**, manage the business affairs of a corporation. Elected by the shareholders, the board of directors is the governing body of a corporation. Directors may be shareholders or individuals with no financial interest in the corporation. The directors are responsible for selecting the officers and for the supervision and general control of the corporation.

Officers

Individuals appointed by a corporation's board of directors to carry out the board's policies and make day-to-day operating decisions

Officers of a corporation are individuals appointed by the board of directors. Like directors, officers may be shareholders or individuals with no financial interest in the corporation. The officers are responsible for carrying out the board's policies and for making day-to-day operating decisions.

The decisions made by the officers and directors are based in part on the corporation's bylaws. Bylaws are the regulations of a corporation that, subject to statutory law and the articles of incorporation, provide the basic rules for the conduct of the corporation's business affairs.

Legal Liability of a Corporation

The shareholders' liability for the acts, omissions, debts, and other obligations of the corporation generally is limited to the shareholders' capital contributions. There are several situations, however, in which the shareholders will be held personally liable for the debts of the corporation.

- A lender to a closely held corporation requires that the primary shareholders guarantee the loan to the corporation. If this is the case, the shareholders are liable to the extent of their guarantees, in addition to their capital contributions.

- A court may ignore the legal fiction of the corporation as an entity (pierce the corporate veil) when the corporation has been used to perpetuate fraud, circumvent law, accomplish an illegal purpose, or otherwise evade law.

- The courts may disregard the corporate form of business entity if the corporation is not maintained as a separate entity from its shareholders. This arises occasionally in the case of closely held corporations.

Taxation of a Corporation

A corporation is an entity created under state law that is separate and distinct from its owners. It may be formed only through compliance with state incorporation statutes. For federal income tax purposes, the corporation is treated as a separate taxable entity, not as a flow-through or conduit entity.

Tax Ramifications of Formation of a Corporation

When a corporation is formed, cash or property is generally transferred to the corporation in exchange for shares of stock. When cash is transferred to the corporation, the transferor will recognize no gain or loss for federal income tax purposes. The transferor will have a basis in the shares received equal to the cash transferred.

In the case of property transfers, no gain or loss will be recognized if the transfer meets the requirements of Section 351. Section 351 provides that gain or loss is not recognized if property is transferred to a corporation in exchange for stock in the corporation, and, if immediately after the transfer, the transferors are in control of the corporation.

Tax Ramifications of Business Operation of a Corporation

A corporation is treated as a separate entity for federal income tax purposes. Computing a corporation's income tax liability can be complicated. The tax liability itself is a product of the corporation's taxable income, which is summarized in the formula shown in Exhibit 14.2.

EXHIBIT 14.2 Corporate Taxable Income Formula

Total income (from whatever source derived)	$xx,xxx
Less exclusions from gross income	(x,xxx)
Gross income	$xx,xxx
Less deductions	(x,xxx)
Taxable income	$xx,xxx

Total income and gross income—The tax computation begins with the determination of the corporation's total income, from whatever source derived. In general, all income is taxable unless Congress has specifically exempted the income from taxation. In tax terminology, income exempt from tax and not included in a taxpayer's gross income is referred to as an exclusion. The amount of income remaining after removing the exclusions is the corporation's gross income, which is generally the starting point for the corporate income tax return (Form 1120).

Deductions—Several deductions are allowed to reduce gross income in arriving at corporate taxable income. Fewer restrictions are placed on corporate deductions than are placed on individual deductions because all activities of a corporation are considered business activities. For example, casualty losses incurred in a federally declared disaster area are fully deductible by a corporation but are subject to a $100 floor and a 10% of AGI limitation for individuals.

Some deductions are allowed only for corporations. For example, corporations are allowed a deduction for dividends received from other corporations. The amount of the **dividends-received deduction (DRD)** is based on the percentage owned by the corporation receiving the dividend. If the dividend-receiving corporation owns less than 20% of the dividend-paying corporation, the dividends-received deduction will be 50% of the dividend actually received. Exhibit 14.3 summarizes the dividend-received deduction for different ownership levels.

Dividends-received deduction (DRD)
A deduction for dividends received by one corporation from another corporation. The amount of the DRD is based on the percentage owned by the corporation receiving the dividend.

EXHIBIT 14.3 Dividend-Received Deduction Based on Corporate Ownership Level

Ownership %	DRD
Less than 20%	50%
At least 20% and less than 80%	65%
At least 80% (affiliated corporations)	100%

EXAMPLE If ABC Company owns 15% of XYZ Company, and XYZ pays a $10,000 dividend during the year to ABC Company, ABC will include the $10,000 of dividend income in its gross income. However, ABC will be entitled to a dividends-received deduction of $5,000 ($10,000 × 50%).

Taxable income and tax—The corporate taxable income is calculated by subtracting allowed deductions from the corporation's gross income. The tax on this income is generally taxed at the 21% rate for all corporations effective in 2020. However, the investment income of a personal holding company will generally still be taxed at the 35% rate.

If a corporation incurs a net operating loss (NOL) for the year, the loss may be carried forward indefinitely. When the NOL is used in a future year, it may only offset 80% of the income for that year.

Personal service corporation—A **personal service corporation (PSC)** is defined as a C corporation in which substantially all of the activities involve the performance of services in the fields of health, law, engineering, architecture, accounting, actuarial science, or consulting, and substantially all of the stock is owned by employees. The taxable income of a personal service corporation is taxed at the regular corporate income tax rate of 21%. Prior to the TCJA, PSCs were potentially subject to corporate tax rates as high as 35%. However, corporate tax rates were permanently reduced to 21%. Thus, PSCs may in some cases be an attractive business entity option for tax sensitive, self-employed professionals.

Personal service corporation (PSC)

A C corporation in which substantially all of the activities involve the performance of services in the fields of health, law, engineering, architecture, accounting, actuarial science, or consulting

Tax Ramifications of Withdrawals or Distributions From a Corporation

One of the major tax disadvantages of the corporate legal form of business entity is the **double taxation of dividends** paid by the corporation to its shareholders. Double taxation refers to the taxation of income at the corporate level and the subsequent taxation of dividend distributions at the individual shareholder's level. However, this impact is lessened because qualified dividends are taxed at the relatively low long-term capital gains rates. There is no deduction from the taxable income of a corporation for dividends distributed to shareholders.

Double taxation of dividends

The taxation of income at the corporate level and the subsequent taxation of dividend distributions at the individual shareholder's level

E X A M P L E   If a corporation has taxable income of $1,000 that is taxed at the 21% rate, there will only be $790 remaining to distribute to shareholders. If the shareholders are in the 35% tax bracket, the $790 dividend received will result in an additional tax of $119 (15% capital gains rate for qualified dividends), leaving the shareholder with only $671 in cash.

S CORPORATION

An **S corporation** is a special type of corporation for federal income tax purposes. The corporation is formed like a regular corporation (with limited liability as a separate entity) under state law; however, it is treated similarly to a partnership for income tax purposes. Therefore, all items of corporation income and deduction are passed through to the shareholders and reported on their personal income tax returns. The entity itself files an informational tax return (Form 1120S).

These corporations are called S corporations because they must satisfy the requirements of Subchapter S of the Internal Revenue Code to receive this special tax treatment. The essential elements of an S corporation include that the corporation must be a domestic corporation and may not have more than 100 shareholders. In addition, nonresident aliens, C corporations, partnerships, and certain trusts are not allowed to hold stock in an S corporation.

S corporation

A special type of corporation formed under state law like a regular corporation; however, for income tax purposes, is treated similar to a partnership

Management Operation and Decision Making of an S Corporation

S corporations are identical to regular corporations in terms of their management characteristics. However, closely held S corporations are often managed in a similar fashion to partnerships.

Legal Liability of an S Corporation

As with regular corporations, one of the major advantages of the S corporation is the limited liability enjoyed by shareholders.

The shareholders' liability for the acts, omissions, debts, and other obligations of the corporation generally is limited to the shareholders' capital contributions. There are several situations, however, in which the S corporation's shareholders are personally liable for the debts of the corporation.

■ A lender to a closely held corporation requires that the primary shareholders guarantee the loan to the corporation. If this is the case, the shareholders are liable to the extent of their guarantees, in addition to their capital contributions.

■ A court may ignore the legal fiction of the corporation as an entity (pierce the corporate veil) when the corporation has been used to perpetuate fraud, circumvent law, accomplish an illegal purpose, or otherwise evade law.

■ The courts may disregard the corporate form of entity if the corporation is not maintained as a separate entity from its shareholders. This arises occasionally in the case of closely held corporations.

Taxation of an S Corporation

Even though an S corporation is similar to a regular, or C corporation, in that it is an entity created under state law that is separate and distinct from its owners, the federal income tax treatment of an S corporation is similar to the treatment of a partnership.

In order for a corporation to be taxed according to the rules of Subchapter S, an election must be filed on Form 2553 within 2 months and 15 days after the corporation's taxable year begins. A corporation must meet all of the following requirements at all times for the S election to be initially and continually valid.

■ *Maximum of 100 shareholders*—An S corporation cannot have more than 100 eligible shareholders. Members of a family who own stock are treated as a single taxpayer (attribution rules).

■ *Eligible shareholders*—Ownership of S corporation stock is restricted to individuals who are U.S. citizens or residents, estates, certain trusts, and charitable organizations. Nonresident aliens, C corporations, and partnerships are prohibited from holding stock in an S corporation.

■ *Domestic corporation*—The corporation must be an eligible corporation created under the laws of the United States or of any state.

- *Eligible corporation*—Insurance companies, domestic international sales corporation (DISCs), and certain financial institutions are not eligible for S corporation status.

- *One class of stock*—The corporation is allowed only one class of outstanding stock. The shares generally must provide identical rights to all shareholders. However, an S corporation may have two classes of stock if the only difference is that one class has voting rights and the other class does not.

Tax Ramifications of Formation of an S Corporation

An S corporation is formed in the same manner as a C corporation, with the rules of Section 351 applying to transfers of property to the corporation. Therefore, under qualifying circumstances, property can be transferred to the corporation without gain or loss recognition by the transferors receiving stock.

Conceptually, the computation of a shareholder's basis in S corporation stock is similar to that for partners in a partnership. Both calculations are designed to ensure that there is neither a double taxation of income nor double deduction of expenses.

Tax Ramifications of Business Operation of an S Corporation

Once the S corporation election has been made, the corporation is treated for federal income tax purposes in a similar fashion to that of a partnership. The S corporation itself is generally not required to pay any income tax but must file an information return, Form 1120S, detailing the items of income and expense that will be reported on the shareholder's individual income tax return.

Shareholders must take into account their distributive share of corporate taxable income and any separately stated items in computing their taxable incomes. A shareholder's weighted-average ownership in the stock of the company determines the share of income, gain, loss, deduction, or credit. Special allocations are not allowed with S corporations. All items of income must be allocated on the basis of pro rata ownership.

Each shareholder's distributive share of items is reported on Schedule K-1, which is furnished by the S corporation to both the IRS and the shareholder. The K-1 for an S corporation is similar to that of a partnership, except the K-1 for an S corporation does not include a reconciliation of capital accounts or a line for guaranteed payments.

The S corporation K-1 details the shareholder's share of partnership ordinary income, which is the net profit or loss resulting from the corporation's trade or business. Ordinary income allocated to a shareholder from an S corporation is not subject to self-employment tax. The Schedule K-1 also reflects various items that must be reported separately from ordinary income. These separately stated items, which include dividend income, interest income, and capital gains, are afforded special treatment on the shareholder's individual income tax return.

LIMITED LIABILITY COMPANY

Limited liability company (LLC)
A relatively new and versatile form of business entity created under state law by filing articles of organization

Members
The owners of an LLC who can be individuals, partnerships, trusts, corporations, or other LLCs

A **limited liability company** (LLC) is a relatively new type of business entity and is one of the most versatile. An LLC is created under state law by filing articles of organization. Its owners, referred to as **members**, can be individuals, partnerships, trusts, corporations, or other LLCs. A limited liability company is a business entity that is generally able to provide the limited personal liability of corporations and the flow-through or conduit taxation of partnerships or S corporations.

One reason for the versatility of LLCs is that they can be taxed as a sole proprietorship, partnership, C corporation, or S corporation. Generally, however, LLCs are treated as general partnerships for federal income tax purposes. If the LLC is taxed as a partnership or sole proprietorship, all items of LLC income and expense are reported on the individual member's income tax return. Unlike a general partnership or sole proprietorship, however, members are not personally liable for the obligations of the LLC. This protection from personal liability for members, coupled with the favorable flow-through federal income tax treatment, has made the LLC a popular choice as a business entity.

Management Operation and Decision Making of a Limited Liability Company

Articles of organization
Document filed in compliance with state law to create a limited liability company (LLC)

Managers
Individuals who are responsible for the maintenance, administration, and management of the affairs of a limited liability company

When an LLC is formed through the filing of **articles of organization**, the LLC is registered with the state. When drafting the articles of organization, the members of the LLC must determine whether the LLC will be managed directly by all of its members, or if the administration of the LLC will be delegated to one or more managers.

Managers are individuals who are responsible for the maintenance, administration, and management of the affairs of the LLC. In most states, the managers serve a particular term and report to and serve at the discretion of the members. Specific duties of the managers may be detailed in the articles of organization or the operating agreement of the LLC. In some states, the members of an LLC may also serve as the managers.

Legal Liability of a Limited Liability Company

A member of an LLC has no personal liability for the debts or obligations of the LLC. This limited liability applies to members who participate in management and those who do not. The ability to participate in management and still have limited liability is one of the most attractive features of LLCs. A member who participates in management is similar to a general partner in a partnership, except the member of the LLC has limited liability.

Taxation of a Limited Liability Company

An LLC with two or more owners is generally treated as a partnership for federal income tax purposes, unless it elects to be treated as a corporation. The election to be treated as a corporation is made by checking a box on IRS Form 8832, the Entity Classification Election form. If the LLC has only one member, it may be treated as a sole proprietorship, unless the LLC elects to be taxed as an S corporation in those states that permit one-member LLCs. In some states, the LLCs that elect to be treated as a corporation for federal income tax purposes are also permitted to elect small business treatment, causing the LLC to be taxed as an S corporation. The election of S corporation treatment for an LLC is accomplished in the same manner as a regular C corporation, by the filing of Form 2553.

A major advantage of an LLC is the limited liability of its members. The protection of owners from personal liability for obligations of the entity, coupled with the flow-through federal income tax treatment, has spurred the enactment of LLC legislation in most states.

Tax Ramifications of Formation of a Limited Liability Company

Generally, limited liability companies are classified as partnerships for federal income tax purposes. As such, the income tax consequences applicable to the formation of an LLC are identical to those applicable to a partnership. When a member contributes cash or property to the LLC, no gain or loss is recognized, and the member's basis in the LLC interest is equal to the value of the cash contributed or the basis of the property contributed. If a member instead contributes services to the LLC, the member must recognize ordinary income for the value of the services contributed.

Tax Ramifications of Business Operation of a Limited Liability Company

An LLC with two or more members can be taxed as a partnership or a corporation. If the LLC is classified as a partnership for income tax purposes, the LLC must file an information return, Form 1065, detailing the items of income and expense that will be reported on the member's individual income tax return. The members receive a Schedule K-1 detailing their allocable amounts of income, loss, deduction, and credit. If the LLC is classified as a corporation, the LLC must file Form 1120 and is responsible for any tax on business income.

If the LLC is composed of only one member, all results from the business will be reported directly on Schedule C of the member's individual income tax return, unless the LLC makes a timely election to be treated as an S corporation. Therefore, the income from the business is taxed at the member's individual income tax rate.

SELECTING THE PROPER BUSINESS LEGAL FORM

The selection of an appropriate business legal form has probably never been as challenging as it is today. Each business entity has its own characteristics that make it more suitable or attractive in a particular situation. The basic factors that should be considered in selecting a business entity include simplicity of formation and operation, ownership restrictions, limited liability, management operations, and tax characteristics. Exhibit 14.4 summarizes some of the more critical legal liability and tax considerations for various business entities.

EXHIBIT 14.4 Summary of Legal Liability and Tax Considerations for Various Business Entities

	Sole Proprietor	Partnership*	LLP	LLC**	S Corp	Corporation
What type of liability do the owners have?	Unlimited	General partnership—unlimited; Limited partnership—limited	Limited	Limited	Limited	Limited
What federal tax form is required to be filed for the organization?	Form 1040, Schedule C	Form 1065	Form 1065	Form 1040, Schedule C, Form 1065, Form 1120, or Form 1120S	Form 1120S	Form 1120
Under what concept is the organization taxed?	Individual level	Flow-through/conduit	Flow-through/conduit	LLCs can be taxed as sole proprietorships, partnerships, C corporations, or S corporations	Flow-through/conduit	Entity level
On what tax form is the owner's compensation reported?	Form 1040, Schedule C	Schedule K-1	Schedule K-1	Form 1040, Schedule C, or Schedule K-1; or Form W-2 and Schedule K-1; or Form W-2	Form W-2 and Schedule K-1	Form W-2 (dividends are reported on Form 1099-DIV)
What is the nature of the owner's income from the organization?	Self-employment income	Self-employment income for general partners; ordinary income for limited partners	Self-employment income	Self-employment income; or W-2 income and ordinary income; W-2 income	W-2 income and ordinary income	W-2 income and dividend income

Flow-through/conduit: all items of income flow from the entity to the individual partner's/owner's/member's return while retaining the character of the income at the entity level.

* Limited partners will generally not have self-employment income.

**The LLC will have the same tax characteristics and attributes as the type of entity it has elected for taxation.

Simplicity of Formation and Operation

If the main factor in the determination of a business legal form is simplicity of formation, either the sole proprietorship or the general partnership is the business form of choice. No special documents need to be prepared for a sole proprietorship or general partnership to begin activities. However, it is customary for a general partnership to draft a written partnership agreement, and the partnership must file a separate income (informational) tax return each year.

The formation of a limited partnership requires the filing of a certificate of limited partnership with the Secretary of State in the state where the partnership is being organized. Otherwise, the operation of the limited partnership is similar to the general partnership in that income and losses are allocated to the partners, and the limited partnership is required to file a separate informational tax return each year.

A corporation is often the most expensive form of entity to organize and operate. If the corporate form is selected, the businessowners must prepare a certificate of incorporation, articles of incorporation, and bylaws, and must pay filing fees. Corporations must file annual reports with the state and must file annual federal income tax returns and state franchise tax returns. An S corporation also must make an initial election to be treated as an S corporation for tax purposes.

A limited liability company is formed by filing articles of organization with the state in which the entity is to be registered. This process is similar to filing articles of incorporation for a corporation. Limited liability companies are generally classified as partnerships for federal income tax purposes. As such, the income tax consequences applicable to an LLC are almost identical to those applicable to a partnership.

Ownership Restrictions

Some business forms place restrictions on the number and types of owners. The ownership structure of the business must be considered before selecting a type of business entity.

C corporations are extremely flexible in the number and types of owners allowed. A regular C corporation can have an unlimited number of shareholders, and the shareholders are not limited to individuals. However, ownership of an S corporation is limited to 100 eligible shareholders. Eligible shareholders are individuals who are U.S. citizens or residents, estates, certain trusts, and charitable organizations. Nonresident aliens, C corporations, and partnerships are prohibited from holding stock in an S corporation.

No limit is placed on the number of members of an LLC. In addition, almost any type of entity may be a member. This flexibility in the number and types of owners makes an LLC more attractive than an S corporation in many situations.

A sole proprietorship can have only one owner. Therefore, this type of business form is unacceptable for joint owners of a business. No limit is placed on the number of partners in a general or limited partnership; however, a limited partnership must have at least one general partner and at least one limited partner.

Limited Liability

A major concern of most businessowners is the risk of personal liability. As a result, the limited liability company, although relatively new, has become a very popular business form. Members of an LLC have no personal liability for the debts or obligations of the LLC. The ability to participate in management without assuming personal liability for debt is one of the most attractive features of an LLC. Limited liability status also applies to C corporations and S corporations.

A general partner has unlimited liability for the acts of the partnership, the other partners, and obligations made by any partner or the partnership in the performance of partnership duties. If the partnership assets are insufficient to satisfy the liabilities of the partnership, the partnership's creditors can collect against the personal assets of the general partners. Therefore, if legal liability is a major concern for the business, a general partnership is a poor choice of business form.

Management Operations

Another consideration in the selection of a business legal form is the structure and flexibility provided to management.

The management of sole proprietorships and partnerships is straightforward. With a sole proprietorship, the proprietor is responsible for the day-to-day operation of the business and for making all of the business decisions. This allows for great flexibility in the operation of the business. With partnerships, the general partners participate directly in the management of the partnership and are directly responsible for the day-to-day operation of the business. Limited partners are not allowed to participate in management.

Corporations have management advantages and disadvantages over other business forms. One advantage is that there is a separation of management from ownership so that the mere ownership of corporate stock does not give the owner the right to participate in the management. The management is centralized, with the directors and officers handling management of corporate affairs. A disadvantage, however, is that the decision process may become time consuming and expensive because of the formalities involved.

In the case of an LLC, the members of the LLC must determine initially whether the LLC will be managed directly by all of its members, similar to a partnership, or if the administration of the LLC will be delegated to one or more managers, similar to a corporation.

Tax Characteristics

Startup Losses

A business that expects losses in the first few years of operation will typically opt for a different type of business legal form than that of a business expecting immediate profits. If the business expects losses, a flow-through entity, such as a partnership, S corporation, or limited liability corporation is generally the entity of choice. Losses will flow through to the owners of the entity and can generally be used immediately to offset other income at the individual level.

In contrast, losses incurred by a C corporation can only benefit the corporation. Therefore, several years may pass before the loss can be utilized against corporate profits.

Double Taxation of Dividends

As discussed previously in this chapter, one of the major tax disadvantages of the corporate form is the double taxation of dividends paid by the corporation to its shareholders. Double taxation refers to the taxation of income at the corporate level and the subsequent taxation of dividend distributions at the individual shareholder's level. There is no deduction from the taxable income of a corporation for dividends distributed to shareholders. This double taxation may be an incentive to discourage the use of the regular C corporation form.

BUSINESS ENTITY FINANCIAL STATEMENTS

We discussed several types of financial statements used by individuals in Chapter 4. Business entities also use financial statements to report their financial condition.

Balance Sheet

Balance sheet
A financial statement that reports a business's assets, liabilities, and net worth on a given date

In a business context, the functional equivalent of the personal statement of financial position is the balance sheet. Like the personal statement of financial position, the business **balance sheet** is a snapshot of the company's financial standing at an instant in time. The balance sheet reports the company's assets, liabilities, and net worth, which is often referred to as stockholder's equity or retained capital in the business context. As with an individual, a company's net worth equals its assets minus its liabilities.

A balance sheet shows several types of assets and liabilities that are unique to businesses and that do not appear on an individual's statement of financial position. Examples of these business assets include the following:

- Accounts receivable

- Inventory

- Land and buildings

- Machinery and equipment

- Certain intangible assets, such as copyrights, patents, and business goodwill

Examples of business liabilities include:

- Accounts payable

- Accrued expenses

- Certain contingent liabilities, such as lawsuits, warranties, and company guarantees of loan repayment

Income Statement

Income statement
A financial statement that reports a business's income and expenses over a given period

The functional equivalent of the personal statement of cash flows in a business context is the **income statement**. Also known as the profit and loss statement (or simply, P&L statement), the income statement shows all the income and expenses of the business over a given period. That is, it shows how profitable (or not profitable) the business actually is. As noted earlier, whether these profits are reported at the business entity level or are reported by the businessowner(s) individually depends on whether the business is organized as a regular, or C, form of corporation or as a sole proprietorship, partnership, or some other form of pass-through entity.

Pro forma income statement
A financial statement that projects a business's income and expenses for the future rather than reporting the past

A **pro forma income statement** is similar to the business income statement except that it projects for the future rather than reporting the past. Pro forma income statements are an important tool for planning future business operations. If the projections accurately predict a decline in business profitability, the businessowner can make operational changes, such as increasing prices or decreasing costs, before these events actually occur. The pro forma statement is created first by estimating gross profit and total expenses for the coming year or years and then accounting for any taxes that will be due on the net profit.

Statement of cash flows
A financial statement that reflects the cash inflows and outflows of a business and reconciles the net changes in cash between two balance sheets

Cash flows from operations
Cash inflows or outflows that are generated by a company's actual business activities as opposed to incidental activities such as investing or borrowing

Cash flows from investing
Cash inflows or outflows resulting from a business's buying and selling of investments

Cash flows from financing
Cash inflows from a business's issuance of additional debt (bonds) or equity (stocks) and cash outflows for the repayment of debt (principal)

Statement of Cash Flows

One statement that is typically used only in businesses is the **statement of cash flows**. The statement of cash flows assists in the reconciliation of the business income statement to changes between two balance sheets. For a given period, the statement of cash flows reflects the inflows and outflows of the business and the net changes in cash between two balance sheets. It also identifies the changes in some of the accounts from one balance sheet to the next. Typically, there are three components of the statement of cash flows.

■ **Cash flows from operations** are the cash inflows or outflows that were generated by the company's actual business activities, as opposed to incidental activities such as investing or borrowing. These cash flows are important to investors and lenders because they indicate whether the business is successful in generating cash from its core business activities.

■ Cash flows from investing include the cash outflows used to acquire investments and the cash inflows from the sale of investments. Investments may include not only intangible assets such as stocks and bonds but also physical assets such as the company's plants and equipment.

■ **Cash flows from financing** include cash inflows from the issuance of additional debt (bonds), or equity (stocks), and cash outflows for the repayment of debt (principal). Increases in cash flows are created, for example, when the business increases long-term indebtedness (i.e., obtains a loan) and receives cash at the inception of the transaction.

Note that the statement of cash flows used by businesses is not the same statement as the personal statement of cash flows, which we discussed in Chapter 4 in the context of individuals. The personal statement of cash flows is more analogous to the income statement in the business context.

WHERE ON THE WEB

Bureau of National Affairs (Search for BNA Portfolios) **www.bna.com**

Cornell Law School **www.law.cornell.edu**

Internal Revenue Service **www.irs.gov**

LSU Libraries Federal Agencies Directory **www.lib.lsu.edu/gov/index.html**

National Association of Tax Professionals **www.natptax.com**

RIA (Research Institute of America) Thomson Tax and Accounting **www.ria.thomson.com**

Small Business Center **www.quicken.com/small_business**

Small Business Taxes and Management **www.smbiz.com**

Tax and Accounting Sites Directory **www.taxsites.com**

U.S. Small Business Administration **www.sba.gov**

DISCUSSION QUESTIONS

1. What are the different types of business entities that a businessowner may choose as a legal form of business?

2. How is a limited liability partnership (LLP) taxed?

3. What are the differences between general and limited partners?

4. How does each type of business entity differ regarding the personal liability of owners?

5. What are the tax ramifications of withdrawals or distributions from a C corporation?

6. What type of business entity should owners choose if they expect the business to produce losses in the first few years?

7. What is the tax treatment of a limited liability corporation?

8. What type of business entity should an owner choose if simplicity of formation and operation is a major priority?

9. What are the components of a financial statement for a business entity?

EXERCISES

1. A bookkeeper performed services for ABC Partnership and, in lieu of her normal fee, accepted a 20% unrestricted capital interest in the partnership with a fair market value of $7,500. How much income from this arrangement should the bookkeeper report on her income tax return?

2. An S corporation has the following information for its taxable year:

Net income before the items below	$60,000
Salary to employee	(18,000)
Rental income	22,000
Rental expenses	(29,000)
Net income	$35,000

John is a 40% owner of the S corporation, and he performs services for the business. What is John's self-employment income from the corporation, subject to self-employment tax?

3. During the year, Susan purchased 5 shares of an S corporation's 100 shares of common stock outstanding. She held the shares for 146 days during the taxable year. If the S corporation reported taxable income of $200,000, how much must Susan include on her personal income tax return?

4. Alpha Company (a C corporation) owns 25% of Zeta Company. During the year, Zeta Company paid a $30,000 dividend to Alpha Company. For tax purposes, how will Alpha Company treat the dividend received?

5. Mark received a 70% capital interest in a general partnership by contributing the following:

Item transferred	Mark's basis	FMV
Land	$60,000	$100,000
Debt (on land)	N/A	(50,000)
Inventory	$10,000	$8,000
Services	N/A	$2,500

What is Mark's basis in the partnership after the contribution?

6. Brooke Industries, Inc. (a C corporation) had the following income and loss items during the year:

Gross receipts	$200,000
Cost of goods sold	(50,000)
Dividend income from ABC Corp. (Brooke owns 15% of ABC)	$ 20,000
Operating expenses	(40,000)
Net operating loss carryforward	(12,000)

What is Brooke Industries' taxable income for the year?

7. In its first year of business, Sanifone Corp (a C corporation) had gross income of $160,000 and deductions of $40,000. The company also paid a qualified dividend of $20,000 to its only shareholder, Joe, who files as single for income tax reporting and has compensation of $457,000 before considering his Sanifone dividend. What are the tax implications to Sanifone and Joe?

8. Tommy is a general partner in RichTech, a general partnership. Tommy received a K-1 from the partnership, which contained the following items:

Partnership taxable income	$200,000
Dividend income	$2,500
Long-term capital gain (on investments)	$6,000

How much self-employment tax will Tommy have to pay in 2020?

9. What is the management structure of a C corporation?

10. What are the requirements for an S Corporation?

11. What are the components of a balance sheet?

PROBLEMS

1. Hugh is a single taxpayer with no children. He is a self-employed real estate appraiser, and the results for his business for the current year are as follows:

Gross receipts	$150,000
Expenses:	
Advertising	$ 2,000
Insurance	$ 1,000
Dues	$ 1,500
Office rent	$12,000
Meals and entertainment	$ 800

Hugh also received the following income during the year:

Interest	$1,100
Dividends	$1,400

Hugh incurred the following expenses during the year:

Real estate taxes	$9,000
Mortgage interest	$5,000

Assuming Hugh was divorced in 2018 and paid $10,000 in alimony to his ex-wife in 2020, calculate his taxable income and self-employment tax for tax year 2020.

2. Pete is a single taxpayer with no dependents. During the year, he invested $40,000 in an S corporation. He received the following information on the K-1 from the S corporation:

Net income before salary	$60,000
Salary to Pete (S corporation)	$18,000
Interest income	$ 2,000
Qualified dividend income	$ 1,000
Long-term capital gain	$ 4,500
Charitable contributions	$ 2,000

Pete also received a distribution of $5,500 from the S corporation, and earned a salary of $50,000 at his full-time job. Calculate Pete's taxable income in 2020.

3. Doug, a single taxpayer, will be starting a new business in 2020. He is not sure whether to operate the business as a C corporation or S corporation. Given the following estimates of income and expenses, determine the total tax that would be due under either scenario.

Gross profit	$150,000
Operating expenses (excluding salary)	(60,000)
Salary paid to Doug	$50,000
Cash distribution to Doug	$10,000

APPENDIX 14.1 Schedule C of Form 1040

| SCHEDULE C
(Form 1040 or 1040-SR)

Department of the Treasury
Internal Revenue Service (99) | **Profit or Loss From Business**
(Sole Proprietorship)
▶ Go to *www.irs.gov/ScheduleC* for instructions and the latest information.
▶ **Attach to Form 1040, 1040-SR, 1040-NR, or 1041; partnerships generally must file Form 1065.** | OMB No. 1545-0074
2019
Attachment
Sequence No. **09** |

Name of proprietor		Social security number (SSN)

A Principal business or profession, including product or service (see instructions)
B Enter code from instructions ▶

C Business name. If no separate business name, leave blank.
D Employer ID number (EIN) (see instr.)

E Business address (including suite or room no.) ▶ _____
City, town or post office, state, and ZIP code

F Accounting method: **(1)** ☐ Cash **(2)** ☐ Accrual **(3)** ☐ Other (specify) ▶ _____

G Did you "materially participate" in the operation of this business during 2019? If "No," see instructions for limit on losses . ☐ Yes ☐ No

H If you started or acquired this business during 2019, check here . . . . ▶ ☐

I Did you make any payments in 2019 that would require you to file Form(s) 1099? (see instructions) . . . . . . ☐ Yes ☐ No

J If "Yes," did you or will you file required Forms 1099? . . . . ☐ Yes ☐ No

Part I   Income

1	Gross receipts or sales. See instructions for line 1 and check the box if this income was reported to you on Form W-2 and the "Statutory employee" box on that form was checked . . . . ▶ ☐	**1**	
2	Returns and allowances	**2**	
3	Subtract line 2 from line 1	**3**	
4	Cost of goods sold (from line 42)	**4**	
5	**Gross profit.** Subtract line 4 from line 3	**5**	
6	Other income, including federal and state gasoline or fuel tax credit or refund (see instructions)	**6**	
7	**Gross income.** Add lines 5 and 6 . . . . ▶	**7**	

Part II   Expenses. Enter expenses for business use of your home **only** on line 30.

8	Advertising	**8**		**18**	Office expense (see instructions)	**18**	
9	Car and truck expenses (see instructions).	**9**		**19**	Pension and profit-sharing plans .	**19**	
10	Commissions and fees .	**10**		**20**	Rent or lease (see instructions):		
11	Contract labor (see instructions)	**11**		**a**	Vehicles, machinery, and equipment	**20a**	
12	Depletion	**12**		**b**	Other business property . . .	**20b**	
13	Depreciation and section 179 expense deduction (not included in Part III) (see instructions).	**13**		**21**	Repairs and maintenance . . .	**21**	
				22	Supplies (not included in Part III) .	**22**	
				23	Taxes and licenses	**23**	
				24	Travel and meals:		
14	Employee benefit programs (other than on line 19) . .	**14**		**a**	Travel	**24a**	
15	Insurance (other than health)	**15**		**b**	Deductible meals (see instructions)	**24b**	
16	Interest (see instructions):			**25**	Utilities	**25**	
a	Mortgage (paid to banks, etc.)	**16a**		**26**	Wages (less employment credits) .	**26**	
b	Other	**16b**		**27a**	Other expenses (from line 48) . .	**27a**	
17	Legal and professional services	**17**		**b**	Reserved for future use . . .	**27b**	

28	**Total expenses** before expenses for business use of home. Add lines 8 through 27a . . . . . . ▶	**28**	
29	Tentative profit or (loss). Subtract line 28 from line 7	**29**	
30	Expenses for business use of your home. Do not report these expenses elsewhere. Attach Form 8829 unless using the simplified method (see instructions). **Simplified method filers only:** enter the total square footage of: (a) your home: _____ and (b) the part of your home used for business: _____ . Use the Simplified Method Worksheet in the instructions to figure the amount to enter on line 30	**30**	
31	**Net profit or (loss).** Subtract line 30 from line 29. • If a profit, enter on both **Schedule 1 (Form 1040 or 1040-SR), line 3** (or **Form 1040-NR, line 13**) and on **Schedule SE, line 2.** (If you checked the box on line 1, see instructions). Estates and trusts, enter on **Form 1041, line 3.** • If a loss, you **must** go to line 32.	**31**	
32	If you have a loss, check the box that describes your investment in this activity (see instructions). • If you checked 32a, enter the loss on both **Schedule 1 (Form 1040 or 1040-SR), line 3** (or **Form 1040-NR, line 13**) and on **Schedule SE, line 2.** (If you checked the box on line 1, see the line 31 instructions). Estates and trusts, enter on **Form 1041, line 3.** • If you checked 32b, you **must** attach **Form 6198.** Your loss may be limited.	**32a** ☐ All investment is at risk. **32b** ☐ Some investment is not at risk.

For Paperwork Reduction Act Notice, see the separate instructions.   Cat. No. 11334P   Schedule C (Form 1040 or 1040-SR) 2019

APPENDIX 14.1 Schedule C of Form 1040 (continued)

Schedule C (Form 1040 or 1040-SR) 2019   Page **2**

Part III	**Cost of Goods Sold** (see instructions)

33 Method(s) used to
value closing inventory: **a** ☐ Cost   **b** ☐ Lower of cost or market   **c** ☐ Other (attach explanation)

34 Was there any change in determining quantities, costs, or valuations between opening and closing inventory?
If "Yes," attach explanation . . . . ☐ Yes   ☐ No

35	Inventory at beginning of year. If different from last year's closing inventory, attach explanation . . .	**35**	
36	Purchases less cost of items withdrawn for personal use	**36**	
37	Cost of labor. Do not include any amounts paid to yourself	**37**	
38	Materials and supplies	**38**	
39	Other costs	**39**	
40	Add lines 35 through 39	**40**	
41	Inventory at end of year	**41**	
42	**Cost of goods sold.** Subtract line 41 from line 40. Enter the result here and on line 4	**42**	

Part IV	**Information on Your Vehicle.** Complete this part **only** if you are claiming car or truck expenses on line 9 and are not required to file Form 4562 for this business. See the instructions for line 13 to find out if you must file Form 4562.

43 When did you place your vehicle in service for business purposes? (month, day, year) ▶ ____ / ____ / ____

44 Of the total number of miles you drove your vehicle during 2019, enter the number of miles you used your vehicle for:

a Business _____ **b** Commuting (see instructions) _____ **c** Other _____

45 Was your vehicle available for personal use during off-duty hours? . . . . ☐ Yes   ☐ No

46 Do you (or your spouse) have another vehicle available for personal use? . . . . ☐ Yes   ☐ No

47a Do you have evidence to support your deduction? . . . . ☐ Yes   ☐ No

b If "Yes," is the evidence written? . . . . ☐ Yes   ☐ No

Part V	**Other Expenses.** List below business expenses not included on lines 8–26 or line 30.

--	
--	
--	
--	
--	
--	
--	
--	
48 Total other expenses. Enter here and on line 27a	**48**

Schedule C (Form 1040 or 1040-SR) 2019

APPENDIX 14.2 Schedule SE

SCHEDULE SE
(Form 1040 or 1040-SR)

Self-Employment Tax

OMB No. 1545-0074

20**19**

Department of the Treasury
Internal Revenue Service (99)

► Go to *www.irs.gov/ScheduleSE* for instructions and the latest information.
► **Attach to Form 1040, 1040-SR, or 1040-NR.**

Attachment
Sequence No. **17**

Name of person with self-employment income (as shown on Form 1040, 1040-SR, or 1040-NR)

Social security number of person
with **self-employment** income ►

Before you begin: To determine if you must file Schedule SE, see the instructions.

May I Use Short Schedule SE or Must I Use Long Schedule SE?

Note: Use this flowchart **only if** you must file Schedule SE. If unsure, see *Who Must File Schedule SE* in the instructions.

Did you receive wages or tips in 2019?

No → Are you a minister, member of a religious order, or Christian Science practitioner who received IRS approval **not** to be taxed on earnings from these sources, **but** you owe self-employment tax on other earnings? — Yes →

No ↓

Are you using one of the optional methods to figure your net earnings (see instructions)? — Yes →

No ↓

Did you receive church employee income (see instructions) reported on Form W-2 of $108.28 or more? — Yes →

No ↓

You may use Short Schedule SE below

Yes → Was the total of your wages and tips subject to social security or railroad retirement (tier 1) tax **plus** your net earnings from self-employment more than $132,900? — Yes →

No ↓

Did you receive tips subject to social security or Medicare tax that you **didn't** report to your employer? — Yes →

No ↓

No ← Did you report any wages on Form 8919, Uncollected Social Security and Medicare Tax on Wages? — Yes →

You must use Long Schedule SE on page 2

Section A—Short Schedule SE. Caution: Read above to see if you can use Short Schedule SE.

1a Net farm profit or (loss) from Schedule F, line 34, and farm partnerships, Schedule K-1 (Form 1065), box 14, code A	**1a**	
b If you received social security retirement or disability benefits, enter the amount of Conservation Reserve Program payments included on Schedule F, line 4b, or listed on Schedule K-1 (Form 1065), box 20, code AH	**1b**	( )
2 Net profit or (loss) from Schedule C, line 31; and Schedule K-1 (Form 1065), box 14, code A (other than farming). Ministers and members of religious orders, see instructions for types of income to report on this line. See instructions for other income to report	**2**	
3 Combine lines 1a, 1b, and 2	**3**	
4 Multiply line 3 by 92.35% (0.9235). If less than $400, you don't owe self-employment tax; **don't** file this schedule unless you have an amount on line 1b . . . . ►	**4**	
Note: If line 4 is less than $400 due to Conservation Reserve Program payments on line 1b, see instructions.		
5 **Self-employment tax.** If the amount on line 4 is: • $132,900 or less, multiply line 4 by 15.3% (0.153). Enter the result here and on **Schedule 2 (Form 1040 or 1040-SR), line 4,** or **Form 1040-NR, line 55.** • More than $132,900, multiply line 4 by 2.9% (0.029). Then, add $16,479.60 to the result. Enter the total here and on **Schedule 2 (Form 1040 or 1040-SR), line 4,** or **Form 1040-NR, line 55** .	**5**	
6 **Deduction for one-half of self-employment tax.** Multiply line 5 by 50% (0.50). Enter the result here and on **Schedule 1 (Form 1040 or 1040-SR), line 14,** or **Form 1040-NR, line 27**	**6**	

For Paperwork Reduction Act Notice, see your tax return instructions.   Cat. No. 11358Z   Schedule SE (Form 1040 or 1040-SR) 2019

APPENDIX 14.2 Schedule SE (continued)

Schedule SE (Form 1040 or 1040-SR) 2019	Attachment Sequence No. **17** Page **2**
Name of person with self-employment income (as shown on Form 1040, 1040-SR, or 1040-NR)	Social security number of person with **self-employment** income ▶

Section B—Long Schedule SE

Part I   **Self-Employment Tax**

Note: If your only income subject to self-employment tax is **church employee income,** see instructions. Also see instructions for the definition of church employee income.

A   If you are a minister, member of a religious order, or Christian Science practitioner **and** you filed Form 4361, but you had $400 or more of **other** net earnings from self-employment, check here and continue with Part I . . . . ▶ ☐

1a   Net farm profit or (loss) from Schedule F, line 34, and farm partnerships, Schedule K-1 (Form 1065), box 14, code A. **Note:** Skip lines 1a and 1b if you use the farm optional method (see instructions)   . | **1a** |

b   If you received social security retirement or disability benefits, enter the amount of Conservation Reserve Program payments included on Schedule F, line 4b, or listed on Schedule K-1 (Form 1065), box 20, code AH | **1b** (   )

2   Net profit or (loss) from Schedule C, line 31; and Schedule K-1 (Form 1065), box 14, code A (other than farming). Ministers and members of religious orders, see instructions for types of income to report on this line. See instructions for other income to report. **Note:** Skip this line if you use the nonfarm optional method (see instructions) . . . . | **2** |

3   Combine lines 1a, 1b, and 2 . . . . | **3** |

4a   If line 3 is more than zero, multiply line 3 by 92.35% (0.9235). Otherwise, enter amount from line 3   . | **4a** |
   Note: If line 4a is less than $400 due to Conservation Reserve Program payments on line 1b, see instructions.

b   If you elect one or both of the optional methods, enter the total of lines 15 and 17 here . . . . . | **4b** |

c   Combine lines 4a and 4b. If less than $400, **stop;** you don't owe self-employment tax. **Exception:** If less than $400 and you had **church employee income,** enter -0- and continue . . . . ▶ | **4c** |

5a   Enter your **church employee income** from Form W-2. See instructions for definition of church employee income . . . . | **5a** |
b   Multiply line 5a by 92.35% (0.9235). If less than $100, enter -0- . . . . | **5b** |

6   Add lines 4c and 5b . . . . | **6** |

7   Maximum amount of combined wages and self-employment earnings subject to social security tax or the 6.2% portion of the 7.65% railroad retirement (tier 1) tax for 2019 . . . . | **7** | 132,900 |

8a   Total social security wages and tips (total of boxes 3 and 7 on Form(s) W-2) and railroad retirement (tier 1) compensation. If $132,900 or more, skip lines 8b through 10, and go to line 11 . . . . | **8a** |
b   Unreported tips subject to social security tax (from Form 4137, line 10) . . | **8b** |
c   Wages subject to social security tax (from Form 8919, line 10) . . . . . | **8c** |
d   Add lines 8a, 8b, and 8c . . . . | **8d** |

9   Subtract line 8d from line 7. If zero or less, enter -0- here and on line 10 and go to line 11 . . . ▶ | **9** |

10   Multiply the **smaller** of line 6 or line 9 by 12.4% (0.124) . . . . | **10** |

11   Multiply line 6 by 2.9% (0.029) . . . . | **11** |

12   **Self-employment tax.** Add lines 10 and 11. Enter here and on **Schedule 2 (Form 1040 or 1040-SR), line 4,** or Form 1040-NR, line 55 . . . . | **12** |

13   **Deduction for one-half of self-employment tax.**
   Multiply line 12 by 50% (0.50). Enter the result here and on **Schedule 1 (Form 1040 or 1040-SR), line 14,** or Form 1040-NR, line 27 . . . . | **13** |

Part II   **Optional Methods To Figure Net Earnings** (see instructions)

Farm Optional Method. You may use this method only if **(a)** your gross farm income¹ wasn't more than $8,160, **or (b)** your net farm profits² were less than $5,891.

14   Maximum income for optional methods . . . . | **14** | 5,440 |

15   Enter the **smaller** of: two-thirds (⅔) of gross farm income¹ (not less than zero) **or** $5,440. Also include this amount on line 4b above . . . . | **15** |

Nonfarm Optional Method. You may use this method only if **(a)** your net nonfarm profits³ were less than $5,891 and also less than 72.189% of your gross nonfarm income,⁴ **and (b)** you had net earnings from self-employment of at least $400 in 2 of the prior 3 years. **Caution:** You may use this method no more than five times.

16   Subtract line 15 from line 14 . . . . | **16** |

17   Enter the **smaller** of: two-thirds (⅔) of gross nonfarm income⁴ (not less than zero) **or** the amount on line 16. Also include this amount on line 4b above . . . . | **17** |

¹ From Sch. F, line 9, and Sch. K-1 (Form 1065), box 14, code B.
² From Sch. F, line 34, and Sch. K-1 (Form 1065), box 14, code A—minus the amount you would have entered on line 1b had you not used the optional method.
³ From Sch. C, line 31; and Sch. K-1 (Form 1065), box 14, code A.
⁴ From Sch. C, line 7; and Sch. K-1 (Form 1065), box 14, code C.

Schedule SE (Form 1040 or 1040-SR) 2019

APPENDIX 14.3 Form 1065—Schedule K-1

651119

| | | | Final K-1 | Amended K-1 | OMB No. 1545-0123 |

Schedule K-1
(Form 1065)
Department of the Treasury
Internal Revenue Service

20**19**

For calendar year 2019, or tax year

beginning / / 2019   ending / /

Partner's Share of Income, Deductions, Credits, etc.   ▶ See back of form and separate instructions.

Part III	**Partner's Share of Current Year Income, Deductions, Credits, and Other Items**	
1	Ordinary business income (loss)	15	Credits

Part I **Information About the Partnership**

A Partnership's employer identification number

B Partnership's name, address, city, state, and ZIP code

C IRS Center where partnership filed return ▶

D ☐ Check if this is a publicly traded partnership (PTP)

Part II **Information About the Partner**

E Partner's SSN or TIN (Do not use TIN of a disregarded entity. See inst.)

F Name, address, city, state, and ZIP code for partner entered in E. See instructions.

G ☐ General partner or LLC member-manager   ☐ Limited partner or other LLC member

H1 ☐ Domestic partner   ☐ Foreign partner

H2 ☐ If the partner is a disregarded entity (DE), enter the partner's:
   TIN _____   Name _____

I1 What type of entity is this partner? _____

I2 If this partner is a retirement plan (IRA/SEP/Keogh/etc.), check here ☐

J Partner's share of profit, loss, and capital (see instructions):

	Beginning	Ending
Profit	%	%
Loss	%	%
Capital	%	%

Check if decrease is due to sale or exchange of partnership interest . . ☐

K Partner's share of liabilities:

	Beginning	Ending
Nonrecourse . . $	$	
Qualified nonrecourse financing . . . $	$	
Recourse . . . $	$	

☐ Check this box if Item K includes liability amounts from lower tier partnerships.

L **Partner's Capital Account Analysis**

Beginning capital account . . . $ _____
Capital contributed during the year . . $ _____
Current year net income (loss) . . . $ _____
Other increase (decrease) (attach explanation) $ _____
Withdrawals & distributions . . . $ (_____)
Ending capital account . . . . $ _____

M Did the partner contribute property with a built-in gain or loss?
   ☐ Yes   ☐ No   If "Yes," attach statement. See instructions.

N **Partner's Share of Net Unrecognized Section 704(c) Gain or (Loss)**
   Beginning . . . . $ _____
   Ending . . . . $ _____

2	Net rental real estate income (loss)		
3	Other net rental income (loss)	16	Foreign transactions
4a	Guaranteed payments for services		
4b	Guaranteed payments for capital		
4c	Total guaranteed payments		
5	Interest income		
6a	Ordinary dividends		
6b	Qualified dividends		
6c	Dividend equivalents	17	Alternative minimum tax (AMT) items
7	Royalties		
8	Net short-term capital gain (loss)		
9a	Net long-term capital gain (loss)	18	Tax-exempt income and nondeductible expenses
9b	Collectibles (28%) gain (loss)		
9c	Unrecaptured section 1250 gain		
10	Net section 1231 gain (loss)		
		19	Distributions
11	Other income (loss)		
		20	Other information
12	Section 179 deduction		
13	Other deductions		
14	Self-employment earnings (loss)		

21 ☐ More than one activity for at-risk purposes*
22 ☐ More than one activity for passive activity purposes*
*See attached statement for additional information.

For IRS Use Only

For Paperwork Reduction Act Notice, see Instructions for Form 1065.   www.irs.gov/Form1065   Cat. No. 11394R   **Schedule K-1 (Form 1065) 2019**

APPENDIX 14.3 Form 1065—Schedule K-1 (continued)

Schedule K-1 (Form 1065) 2019   Page **2**

This list identifies the codes used on Schedule K-1 for all partners and provides summarized reporting information for partners who file Form 1040 or 1040-SR. For detailed reporting and filing information, see the separate Partner's Instructions for Schedule K-1 and the instructions for your income tax return.

1. **Ordinary business income (loss).** Determine whether the income (loss) is passive or nonpassive and enter on your return as follows.

	Report on
Passive loss	See the Partner's Instructions
Passive income	Schedule E, line 28, column (h)
Nonpassive loss	See the Partner's Instructions
Nonpassive income	Schedule E, line 28, column (k)

2. **Net rental real estate income (loss)** — See the Partner's Instructions
3. **Other net rental income (loss)**

Net income	Schedule E, line 28, column (h)
Net loss	See the Partner's Instructions

4a. **Guaranteed payment Services** — See the Partner's Instructions
4b. **Guaranteed payment Capital** — See the Partner's Instructions
4c. **Guaranteed payment Total** — See the Partner's Instructions
5. **Interest income** — Form 1040 or 1040-SR, line 2b
6a. **Ordinary dividends** — Form 1040 or 1040-SR, line 3b
6b. **Qualified dividends** — Form 1040 or 1040-SR, line 3a
6c. **Dividend equivalents** — See the Partner's Instructions
7. **Royalties** — Schedule E, line 4
8. **Net short-term capital gain (loss)** — Schedule D, line 5
9a. **Net long-term capital gain (loss)** — Schedule D, line 12
9b. **Collectibles (28%) gain (loss)** — 28% Rate Gain Worksheet, line 4 (Schedule D instructions)
9c. **Unrecaptured section 1250 gain** — See the Partner's Instructions
10. **Net section 1231 gain (loss)** — See the Partner's Instructions
11. **Other income (loss)**

Code		Report on
A	Other portfolio income (loss)	See the Partner's Instructions
B	Involuntary conversions	See the Partner's Instructions
C	Sec. 1256 contracts & straddles	Form 6781, line 1
D	Mining exploration costs recapture	See Pub. 535
E	Cancellation of debt	
F	Section 743(b) positive adjustments	
G	Section 965(a) inclusion	
H	Income under subpart F (other than inclusions under sections 951A and 965)	See the Partner's Instructions
I	Other income (loss)	

12. **Section 179 deduction** — See the Partner's Instructions
13. **Other deductions**

A	Cash contributions (60%)	
B	Cash contributions (30%)	
C	Noncash contributions (50%)	
D	Noncash contributions (30%)	
E	Capital gain property to a 50% organization (30%)	See the Partner's Instructions
F	Capital gain property (20%)	
G	Contributions (100%)	
H	Investment interest expense	Form 4952, line 1
I	Deductions—royalty income	Schedule E, line 19
J	Section 59(e)(2) expenditures	See the Partner's Instructions
K	Excess business interest expense	See the Partner's Instructions
L	Deductions—portfolio (other)	Schedule A, line 16
M	Amounts paid for medical insurance	Schedule A, line 1, or Schedule 1 (Form 1040 or 1040-SR), line 16
N	Educational assistance benefits	See the Partner's Instructions
O	Dependent care benefits	Form 2441, line 12
P	Preproductive period expenses	See the Partner's Instructions
Q	Commercial revitalization deduction from rental real estate activities	See Form 8582 instructions
R	Pensions and IRAs	See the Partner's Instructions
S	Reforestation expense deduction	See the Partner's Instructions
T	through U	Reserved for future use
V	Section 743(b) negative adjustments	
W	Other deductions	See the Partner's Instructions
X	Section 965(c) deduction	

14. **Self-employment earnings (loss)**

Note: If you have a section 179 deduction or any partner-level deductions, see the Partner's Instructions before completing Schedule SE.

A	Net earnings (loss) from self-employment	Schedule SE, Section A or B
B	Gross farming or fishing income	See the Partner's Instructions
C	Gross non-farm income	See the Partner's Instructions

15. **Credits**

A	Low-income housing credit (section 42(j)(5)) from pre-2008 buildings	
B	Low-income housing credit (other) from pre-2008 buildings	
C	Low-income housing credit (section 42(j)(5)) from post-2007 buildings	See the Partner's Instructions
D	Low-income housing credit (other) from post-2007 buildings	
E	Qualified rehabilitation expenditures (rental real estate)	
F	Other rental real estate credits	
G	Other rental credits	

Code		Report on
H	Undistributed capital gains credit	Schedule 3 (Form 1040 or 1040-SR), line 13, box a
I	Biofuel producer credit	See the Partner's Instructions
J	Work opportunity credit	
K	Disabled access credit	
L	Empowerment zone employment credit	
M	Credit for increasing research activities	See the Partner's Instructions
N	Credit for employer social security and Medicare taxes	
O	Backup withholding	
P	Other credits	

16. **Foreign transactions**

A	Name of country or U.S. possession	
B	Gross income from all sources	Form 1116, Part I
C	Gross income sourced at partner level	

Foreign gross income sourced at partnership level

D	Reserved for future use	
E	Foreign branch category	
F	Passive category	Form 1116, Part I
G	General category	
H	Other	

Deductions allocated and apportioned at partner level

I	Interest expense	Form 1116, Part I
J	Other	Form 1116, Part I

Deductions allocated and apportioned at partnership level to foreign source income

K	Reserved for future use	
L	Foreign branch category	
M	Passive category	Form 1116, Part I
N	General category	
O	Other	

Other information

P	Total foreign taxes paid	Form 1116, Part II
Q	Total foreign taxes accrued	Form 1116, Part II
R	Reduction in taxes available for credit	Form 1116, line 12
S	Foreign trading gross receipts	Form 8873
T	Extraterritorial income exclusion	Form 8873
U	through V	Reserved for future use
W	Section 965 information	See the Partner's Instructions
X	Other foreign transactions	

17. **Alternative minimum tax (AMT) items**

A	Post-1986 depreciation adjustment	
B	Adjusted gain or loss	See the Partner's Instructions and the Instructions for Form 6251
C	Depletion (other than oil & gas)	
D	Oil, gas, & geothermal—gross income	
E	Oil, gas, & geothermal—deductions	
F	Other AMT items	

18. **Tax-exempt income and nondeductible expenses**

A	Tax-exempt interest income	Form 1040 or 1040-SR, line 2a
B	Other tax-exempt income	See the Partner's Instructions
C	Nondeductible expenses	See the Partner's Instructions

19. **Distributions**

A	Cash and marketable securities	
B	Distribution subject to section 737	See the Partner's Instructions
C	Other property	

20. **Other information**

A	Investment income	Form 4952, line 4a
B	Investment expenses	Form 4952, line 5
C	Fuel tax credit information	Form 4136
D	Qualified rehabilitation expenditures (other than rental real estate)	
E	Basis of energy property	See the Partner's Instructions
F	through G	
H	Recapture of investment credit	See Form 4255
I	Recapture of other credits	See the Partner's Instructions
J	Look-back interest—completed long-term contracts	See Form 8697
K	Look-back interest—income forecast method	See Form 8866
L	Dispositions of property with section 179 deductions	
M	Recapture of section 179 deduction	
N	Interest expense for corporate partners	
O	through Y	
Z	Section 199A information	
AA	Section 704(c) information	
AB	Section 751 gain (loss)	See the Partner's Instructions
AC	Section 1(h)(5) gain (loss)	
AD	Deemed section 1250 unrecaptured gain	
AE	Excess taxable income	
AF	Excess business interest income	
AG	Gross receipts for section 59A(e)	
AH	Other information	

APPENDIX 14.4 Corporation Form 1120-S

Form **1120-S**	**U.S. Income Tax Return for an S Corporation**	OMB No. 1545-0123
Department of the Treasury Internal Revenue Service	▶ Do not file this form unless the corporation has filed or is attaching Form 2553 to elect to be an S corporation. ▶ Go to *www.irs.gov/Form1120S* for instructions and the latest information.	**20**19

For calendar year 2019 or tax year beginning	, 2019, ending	, 20

A S election effective date	**TYPE OR PRINT**	Name	**D** Employer identification number
B Business activity code number (see instructions)		Number, street, and room or suite no. If a P.O. box, see instructions.	**E** Date incorporated
C Check if Sch. M-3 attached ☐		City or town, state or province, country, and ZIP or foreign postal code	**F** Total assets (see instructions) $

G Is the corporation electing to be an S corporation beginning with this tax year? ☐ Yes ☐ No   If "Yes," attach Form 2553 if not already filed

H Check if: **(1)** ☐ Final return **(2)** ☐ Name change **(3)** ☐ Address change **(4)** ☐ Amended return **(5)** ☐ S election termination or revocation

I Enter the number of shareholders who were shareholders during any part of the tax year . . . . ▶ ----------------------------

J Check if corporation: **(1)** ☐ Aggregated activities for section 465 at-risk purposes **(2)** ☐ Grouped activities for section 469 passive activity purposes

Caution: Include **only** trade or business income and expenses on lines 1a through 21. See the instructions for more information.

Income	**1a**	Gross receipts or sales	**1a**		
	b	Returns and allowances	**1b**		
	c	Balance. Subtract line 1b from line 1a		**1c**	
	2	Cost of goods sold (attach Form 1125-A)		**2**	
	3	Gross profit. Subtract line 2 from line 1c		**3**	
	4	Net gain (loss) from Form 4797, line 17 (attach Form 4797)		**4**	
	5	Other income (loss) (see instructions—attach statement)		**5**	
	6	**Total income (loss).** Add lines 3 through 5 . . . . ▶		**6**	

Deductions (see instructions for limitations)	**7**	Compensation of officers (see instructions—attach Form 1125-E)	**7**	
	8	Salaries and wages (less employment credits)	**8**	
	9	Repairs and maintenance	**9**	
	10	Bad debts	**10**	
	11	Rents	**11**	
	12	Taxes and licenses	**12**	
	13	Interest (see instructions)	**13**	
	14	Depreciation not claimed on Form 1125-A or elsewhere on return (attach Form 4562)	**14**	
	15	Depletion **(Do not deduct oil and gas depletion.)**	**15**	
	16	Advertising	**16**	
	17	Pension, profit-sharing, etc., plans	**17**	
	18	Employee benefit programs	**18**	
	19	Other deductions (attach statement)	**19**	
	20	**Total deductions.** Add lines 7 through 19 . . . . ▶	**20**	
	21	**Ordinary business income (loss).** Subtract line 20 from line 6	**21**	

Tax and Payments	**22a**	Excess net passive income or LIFO recapture tax (see instructions) . . .	**22a**		
	b	Tax from Schedule D (Form 1120-S)	**22b**		
	c	Add lines 22a and 22b (see instructions for additional taxes)		**22c**	
	23a	2019 estimated tax payments and 2018 overpayment credited to 2019	**23a**		
	b	Tax deposited with Form 7004	**23b**		
	c	Credit for federal tax paid on fuels (attach Form 4136)	**23c**		
	d	Reserved for future use	**23d**		
	e	Add lines 23a through 23d		**23e**	
	24	Estimated tax penalty (see instructions). Check if Form 2220 is attached . . . . . ▶ ☐		**24**	
	25	**Amount owed.** If line 23e is smaller than the total of lines 22c and 24, enter amount owed . . .		**25**	
	26	**Overpayment.** If line 23e is larger than the total of lines 22c and 24, enter amount overpaid . . .		**26**	
	27	Enter amount from line 26: **Credited to 2020 estimated tax** ▶ **Refunded** ▶		**27**	

Sign Here	Under penalties of perjury, I declare that I have examined this return, including accompanying schedules and statements, and to the best of my knowledge and belief, it is true, correct, and complete. Declaration of preparer (other than taxpayer) is based on all information of which preparer has any knowledge.			May the IRS discuss this return with the preparer shown below? See instructions. ☐ Yes ☐ No
	▶ Signature of officer	Date	▶ Title	

Paid Preparer Use Only	Print/Type preparer's name	Preparer's signature	Date	Check ☐ if self-employed	PTIN
	Firm's name ▶			Firm's EIN ▶	
	Firm's address ▶			Phone no.	

For Paperwork Reduction Act Notice, see separate instructions.   Cat. No. 11510H   Form **1120-S** (2019)

APPENDIX 14.4 Corporation Form 1120-S (continued)

Form 1120-S (2019)   Page **2**

Schedule B	Other Information (see instructions)		Yes	No

1 Check accounting method: **a** ☐ Cash   **b** ☐ Accrual

      c ☐ Other (specify) ▶ _____

2 See the instructions and enter the:

a Business activity ▶ _____   **b** Product or service ▶ _____

3 At any time during the tax year, was any shareholder of the corporation a disregarded entity, a trust, an estate, or a nominee or similar person? If "Yes," attach Schedule B-1, Information on Certain Shareholders of an S Corporation . .

4 At the end of the tax year, did the corporation:

a Own directly 20% or more, or own, directly or indirectly, 50% or more of the total stock issued and outstanding of any foreign or domestic corporation? For rules of constructive ownership, see instructions. If "Yes," complete (i) through (v) below . . . .

(i) Name of Corporation	(ii) Employer Identification Number (if any)	(iii) Country of Incorporation	(iv) Percentage of Stock Owned	(v) If Percentage in (iv) Is 100%, Enter the Date (if any) a Qualified Subchapter S Subsidiary Election Was Made

b Own directly an interest of 20% or more, or own, directly or indirectly, an interest of 50% or more in the profit, loss, or capital in any foreign or domestic partnership (including an entity treated as a partnership) or in the beneficial interest of a trust? For rules of constructive ownership, see instructions. If "Yes," complete (i) through (v) below . . . .

(i) Name of Entity	(ii) Employer Identification Number (if any)	(iii) Type of Entity	(iv) Country of Organization	(v) Maximum Percentage Owned in Profit, Loss, or Capital

5a At the end of the tax year, did the corporation have any outstanding shares of restricted stock? . . . .

If "Yes," complete lines (i) and (ii) below.

(i) Total shares of restricted stock . . . . ▶ _____

(ii) Total shares of non-restricted stock . . . . ▶ _____

b At the end of the tax year, did the corporation have any outstanding stock options, warrants, or similar instruments? .

If "Yes," complete lines (i) and (ii) below.

(i) Total shares of stock outstanding at the end of the tax year . ▶ _____

(ii) Total shares of stock outstanding if all instruments were executed ▶ _____

6 Has this corporation filed, or is it required to file, **Form 8918,** Material Advisor Disclosure Statement, to provide information on any reportable transaction? . . . .

7 Check this box if the corporation issued publicly offered debt instruments with original issue discount . . . . ▶ ☐

If checked, the corporation may have to file **Form 8281,** Information Return for Publicly Offered Original Issue Discount Instruments.

8 If the corporation **(a)** was a C corporation before it elected to be an S corporation **or** the corporation acquired an asset with a basis determined by reference to the basis of the asset (or the basis of any other property) in the hands of a C corporation **and (b)** has net unrealized built-in gain in excess of the net recognized built-in gain from prior years, enter the net unrealized built-in gain reduced by net recognized built-in gain from prior years. See instructions . . . . . ▶ $ _____

9 Did the corporation have an election under section 163(j) for any real property trade or business or any farming business in effect during the tax year? See instructions . . . .

10 Does the corporation satisfy one or more of the following? See instructions . . . .

a The corporation owns a pass-through entity with current, or prior year carryover, excess business interest expense.

b The corporation's aggregate average annual gross receipts (determined under section 448(c)) for the 3 tax years preceding the current tax year are more than $26 million and the corporation has business interest expense.

c The corporation is a tax shelter and the corporation has business interest expense.

If "Yes," complete and attach Form 8990.

11 Does the corporation satisfy **both** of the following conditions? . . . .

a The corporation's total receipts (see instructions) for the tax year were less than $250,000.

b The corporation's total assets at the end of the tax year were less than $250,000.

If "Yes," the corporation is not required to complete Schedules L and M-1.

Form **1120-S** (2019)

APPENDIX 14.4 Corporation Form 1120-S (continued)

Form 1120-S (2019)   Page **3**

Schedule B	Other Information (see instructions) (continued)	Yes	No
12	During the tax year, did the corporation have any non-shareholder debt that was canceled, was forgiven, or had the terms modified so as to reduce the principal amount of the debt?		
	If "Yes," enter the amount of principal reduction . . . . ▶ $ _____		
13	During the tax year, was a qualified subchapter S subsidiary election terminated or revoked? If "Yes," see instructions .		
14a	Did the corporation make any payments in 2019 that would require it to file Form(s) 1099?		
b	If "Yes," did the corporation file or will it file required Form(s) 1099?		
15	Is the corporation attaching Form 8996 to certify as a Qualified Opportunity Fund?		
	If "Yes," enter the amount from Form 8996, line 14 . . . . ▶ $		

Schedule K		Shareholders' Pro Rata Share Items		Total amount
Income (Loss)	1	Ordinary business income (loss) (page 1, line 21)	**1**	
	2	Net rental real estate income (loss) (attach Form 8825)	**2**	
	3a	Other gross rental income (loss)	**3a**	
	b	Expenses from other rental activities (attach statement)	**3b**	
	c	Other net rental income (loss). Subtract line 3b from line 3a	**3c**	
	4	Interest income	**4**	
	5	Dividends: **a** Ordinary dividends	**5a**	
		b Qualified dividends	**5b**	
	6	Royalties	**6**	
	7	Net short-term capital gain (loss) (attach Schedule D (Form 1120-S)) . . .	**7**	
	8a	Net long-term capital gain (loss) (attach Schedule D (Form 1120-S)) . . .	**8a**	
	b	Collectibles (28%) gain (loss)	**8b**	
	c	Unrecaptured section 1250 gain (attach statement)	**8c**	
	9	Net section 1231 gain (loss) (attach Form 4797)	**9**	
	10	Other income (loss) (see instructions) . . . Type ▶	**10**	
Deductions	11	Section 179 deduction (attach Form 4562)	**11**	
	12a	Charitable contributions	**12a**	
	b	Investment interest expense	**12b**	
	c	Section 59(e)(2) expenditures **(1)** Type ▶ _____ **(2)** Amount ▶	**12c(2)**	
	d	Other deductions (see instructions) . . . . Type ▶	**12d**	
Credits	13a	Low-income housing credit (section 42(j)(5))	**13a**	
	b	Low-income housing credit (other)	**13b**	
	c	Qualified rehabilitation expenditures (rental real estate) (attach Form 3468, if applicable) . .	**13c**	
	d	Other rental real estate credits (see instructions) Type ▶ _____	**13d**	
	e	Other rental credits (see instructions) . . . Type ▶ _____	**13e**	
	f	Biofuel producer credit (attach Form 6478)	**13f**	
	g	Other credits (see instructions) . . . . . Type ▶	**13g**	
Foreign Transactions	14a	Name of country or U.S. possession ▶ _____		
	b	Gross income from all sources	**14b**	
	c	Gross income sourced at shareholder level	**14c**	
		Foreign gross income sourced at corporate level		
	d	Reserved for future use	**14d**	
	e	Foreign branch category	**14e**	
	f	Passive category	**14f**	
	g	General category	**14g**	
	h	Other (attach statement)	**14h**	
		Deductions allocated and apportioned at shareholder level		
	i	Interest expense	**14i**	
	j	Other	**14j**	
		Deductions allocated and apportioned at corporate level to foreign source income		
	k	Reserved for future use	**14k**	
	l	Foreign branch category	**14l**	
	m	Passive category	**14m**	
	n	General category	**14n**	
	o	Other (attach statement)	**14o**	
		Other information		
	p	Total foreign taxes (check one): ☐ Paid ☐ Accrued . . . . ▶	**14p**	
	q	Reduction in taxes available for credit (attach statement)	**14q**	
	r	Other foreign tax information (attach statement)		

Form **1120-S** (2019)

APPENDIX 14.4 Corporation Form 1120-S (continued)

Form 1120-S (2019)   Page **4**

Schedule K		Shareholders' Pro Rata Share Items *(continued)*	Total amount	
Alternative Minimum Tax (AMT) Items	15a	Post-1986 depreciation adjustment	15a	
	b	Adjusted gain or loss	15b	
	c	Depletion (other than oil and gas)	15c	
	d	Oil, gas, and geothermal properties—gross income	15d	
	e	Oil, gas, and geothermal properties—deductions	15e	
	f	Other AMT items (attach statement)	15f	
Items Affecting Shareholder Basis	16a	Tax-exempt interest income	16a	
	b	Other tax-exempt income	16b	
	c	Nondeductible expenses	16c	
	d	Distributions (attach statement if required) (see instructions)	16d	
	e	Repayment of loans from shareholders	16e	
Other Information	17a	Investment income	17a	
	b	Investment expenses	17b	
	c	Dividend distributions paid from accumulated earnings and profits	17c	
	d	Other items and amounts (attach statement)		
Reconciliation	18	**Income (loss) reconciliation.** Combine the amounts on lines 1 through 10 in the far right column. From the result, subtract the sum of the amounts on lines 11 through 12d and 14p	18	

Schedule L	Balance Sheets per Books	Beginning of tax year		End of tax year	
	Assets	(a)	(b)	(c)	(d)
1	Cash				
2a	Trade notes and accounts receivable				
b	Less allowance for bad debts	( )		( )	
3	Inventories				
4	U.S. government obligations				
5	Tax-exempt securities (see instructions)				
6	Other current assets (attach statement)				
7	Loans to shareholders				
8	Mortgage and real estate loans				
9	Other investments (attach statement)				
10a	Buildings and other depreciable assets				
b	Less accumulated depreciation	( )		( )	
11a	Depletable assets				
b	Less accumulated depletion	( )		( )	
12	Land (net of any amortization)				
13a	Intangible assets (amortizable only)				
b	Less accumulated amortization	( )		( )	
14	Other assets (attach statement)				
15	Total assets				
	Liabilities and Shareholders' Equity				
16	Accounts payable				
17	Mortgages, notes, bonds payable in less than 1 year				
18	Other current liabilities (attach statement)				
19	Loans from shareholders				
20	Mortgages, notes, bonds payable in 1 year or more				
21	Other liabilities (attach statement)				
22	Capital stock				
23	Additional paid-in capital				
24	Retained earnings				
25	Adjustments to shareholders' equity (attach statement)				
26	Less cost of treasury stock		( )		( )
27	Total liabilities and shareholders' equity				

Form **1120-S** (2019)

APPENDIX 14.4 Corporation Form 1120-S (continued)

Form 1120-S (2019) Page **5**

Schedule M-1 Reconciliation of Income (Loss) per Books With Income (Loss) per Return

Note: The corporation may be required to file Schedule M-3. See instructions.

1	Net income (loss) per books		5	Income recorded on books this year not included on Schedule K, lines 1 through 10 (itemize):	
2	Income included on Schedule K, lines 1, 2, 3c, 4, 5a, 6, 7, 8a, 9, and 10, not recorded on books this year (itemize) _____		a	Tax-exempt interest $ _____	
3	Expenses recorded on books this year not included on Schedule K, lines 1 through 12 and 14p (itemize):		6	Deductions included on Schedule K, lines 1 through 12 and 14p, not charged against book income this year (itemize):	
a	Depreciation $ _____		a	Depreciation $ _____	
b	Travel and entertainment $ _____		7	Add lines 5 and 6	
			8	Income (loss) (Schedule K, line 18). Subtract line 7 from line 4	
4	Add lines 1 through 3				

Schedule M-2 Analysis of Accumulated Adjustments Account, Shareholders' Undistributed Taxable Income Previously Taxed, Accumulated Earnings and Profits, and Other Adjustments Account (see instructions)

		(a) Accumulated adjustments account	**(b)** Shareholders' undistributed taxable income previously taxed	**(c)** Accumulated earnings and profits	**(d)** Other adjustments account
1	Balance at beginning of tax year				
2	Ordinary income from page 1, line 21 . . .				
3	Other additions				
4	Loss from page 1, line 21	( )			
5	Other reductions	( )			( )
6	Combine lines 1 through 5				
7	Distributions				
8	Balance at end of tax year. Subtract line 7 from line 6				

Form **1120-S** (2019)

APPENDIX 14.5 Form 8832

Form **8832**
(Rev. December 2013)

Department of the Treasury
Internal Revenue Service

Entity Classification Election

OMB No. 1545-1516

▶ Information about Form 8832 and its instructions is at *www.irs.gov/form8832*.

Type or Print	Name of eligible entity making election	Employer identification number
	Number, street, and room or suite no. If a P.O. box, see instructions.	
	City or town, state, and ZIP code. If a foreign address, enter city, province or state, postal code and country. Follow the country's practice for entering the postal code.	

▶ Check if: ☐ Address change   ☐ Late classification relief sought under Revenue Procedure 2009-41
☐ Relief for a late change of entity classification election sought under Revenue Procedure 2010-32

Part I   **Election Information**

1   **Type of election** (see instructions):

a ☐ Initial classification by a newly-formed entity. Skip lines 2a and 2b and go to line 3.
b ☐ Change in current classification. Go to line 2a.

2a   Has the eligible entity previously filed an entity election that had an effective date within the last 60 months?

☐ **Yes.** Go to line 2b.
☐ **No.** Skip line 2b and go to line 3.

2b   Was the eligible entity's prior election an initial classification election by a newly formed entity that was effective on the date of formation?

☐ **Yes.** Go to line 3.
☐ **No.** Stop here. You generally are not currently eligible to make the election (see instructions).

3   Does the eligible entity have more than one owner?

☐ **Yes.** You can elect to be classified as a partnership or an association taxable as a corporation. Skip line 4 and go to line 5.
☐ **No.** You can elect to be classified as an association taxable as a corporation or to be disregarded as a separate entity. Go to line 4.

4   If the eligible entity has only one owner, provide the following information:

a   Name of owner ▶ ....
b   Identifying number of owner ▶ ....

5   If the eligible entity is owned by one or more affiliated corporations that file a consolidated return, provide the name and employer identification number of the parent corporation:

a   Name of parent corporation ▶ ....
b   Employer identification number ▶ ....

For Paperwork Reduction Act Notice, see instructions.   Cat. No. 22598R   Form **8832** (Rev. 12-2013)

APPENDIX 14.5 Form 8832 (continued)

Form 8832 (Rev. 12-2013)   Page **2**

| **Part I** | **Election Information** (Continued) |

6   Type of entity (see instructions):

a   ☐ A domestic eligible entity electing to be classified as an association taxable as a corporation.
b   ☐ A domestic eligible entity electing to be classified as a partnership.
c   ☐ A domestic eligible entity with a single owner electing to be disregarded as a separate entity.
d   ☐ A foreign eligible entity electing to be classified as an association taxable as a corporation.
e   ☐ A foreign eligible entity electing to be classified as a partnership.
f   ☐ A foreign eligible entity with a single owner electing to be disregarded as a separate entity.

7   If the eligible entity is created or organized in a foreign jurisdiction, provide the foreign country of
organization ▶ ....

8   Election is to be effective beginning (month, day, year) (see instructions) . . . . ▶ _____

9 Name and title of contact person whom the IRS may call for more information	**10** Contact person's telephone number

Consent Statement and Signature(s) (see instructions)

Under penalties of perjury, I (we) declare that I (we) consent to the election of the above-named entity to be classified as indicated above, and that I (we) have examined this election and consent statement, and to the best of my (our) knowledge and belief, this election and consent statement are true, correct, and complete. If I am an officer, manager, or member signing for the entity, I further declare under penalties of perjury that I am authorized to make the election on its behalf.

Signature(s)	**Date**	**Title**

Form **8832** (Rev. 12-2013)

APPENDIX 14.5 Form 8832 (continued)

Form 8832 (Rev. 12-2013)   Page **3**

Part II	**Late Election Relief**

11   Provide the explanation as to why the entity classification election was not filed on time (see instructions).

Under penalties of perjury, I (we) declare that I (we) have examined this election, including accompanying documents, and, to the best of my (our) knowledge and belief, the election contains all the relevant facts relating to the election, and such facts are true, correct, and complete. I (we) further declare that I (we) have personal knowledge of the facts and circumstances related to the election. I (we) further declare that the elements required for relief in Section 4.01 of Revenue Procedure 2009-41 have been satisfied.

Signature(s)	Date	Title

Form **8832** (Rev. 12-2013)

APPENDIX 14.5 Form 8832 (continued)

General Instructions

Section references are to the Internal Revenue Code unless otherwise noted.

Future Developments

For the latest information about developments related to Form 8832 and its instructions, such as legislation enacted after they were published, go to *www.irs.gov/form8832*.

What's New

For entities formed on or after July 1, 2013, the Croatian Dionicko Drustvo will always be treated as a corporation. See Notice 2013-44, 2013-29, I.R.B. 62 for more information.

Purpose of Form

An eligible entity uses Form 8832 to elect how it will be classified for federal tax purposes, as a corporation, a partnership, or an entity disregarded as separate from its owner. An eligible entity is classified for federal tax purposes under the default rules described below unless it files Form 8832 or Form 2553, Election by a Small Business Corporation. See *Who Must File* below.

The IRS will use the information entered on this form to establish the entity's filing and reporting requirements for federal tax purposes.

Note. An entity must file Form 2553 if making an election under section 1362(a) to be an S corporation

A new eligible entity should not file Form 8832 if it will be using its default classification (see Default Rules below).

Eligible entity. An eligible entity is a business entity that is not included in items 1, or 3 through 9, under the definition of **corporation** provided under *Definitions*. Eligible entities include limited liability companies (LLCs) and partnerships.

Generally, corporations are not eligible entities. However, the following types of corporations are treated as eligible entities:

1. An eligible entity that previously elected to be an association taxable as a corporation by filing Form 8832. An entity that elects to be classified as a corporation by filing Form 8832 can make another election to change its classification (see the *60-month limitation rule* discussed below in the instructions for lines 2a and 2b).

2. A foreign eligible entity that became an association taxable as a corporation under the foreign default rule described below.

Default Rules

Existing entity default rule. Certain domestic and foreign entities that were in existence before January 1, 1997, and have an established federal tax classification generally do not need to make an election to continue that classification. If an existing entity decides to change its classification, it may do so subject to the 60-month limitation rule. See the instructions for lines 2a and 2b. See Regulations sections 301.7701-3(b)(3) and 301.7701-3(h)(2) for more details.

Domestic default rule. Unless an election is made on Form 8832, a domestic eligible entity is:

1. A partnership if it has two or more members.

2. Disregarded as an entity separate from its owner if it has a single owner.

A change in the number of members of an eligible entity classified as an **association** (defined below) does not affect the entity's classification. However, an eligible entity classified as a partnership will become a disregarded entity when the entity's membership is reduced to one member and a disregarded entity will be classified as a partnership when the entity has more than one member.

Foreign default rule. Unless an election is made on Form 8832, a foreign eligible entity is:

1. A partnership if it has two or more members and at least one member does not have limited liability.

2. An association taxable as a corporation if all members have limited liability.

3. Disregarded as an entity separate from its owner if it has a single owner that does not have limited liability.

However, if a qualified foreign entity (as defined in section 3.02 of Rev. Proc. 2010-32) files a valid election to be classified as a partnership based on the reasonable assumption that it had two or more owners as of the effective date of the election, and the qualified entity is later determined to have a single owner, the IRS will deem the election to be an election to be classified as a disregarded entity provided:

1. The qualified entity's owner and purported owners file amended returns that are consistent with the treatment of the entity as a disregarded entity;

2. The amended returns are filed before the close of the period of limitations on assessments under section 6501(a) for the relevant tax year; and

3. The corrected Form 8832, with the box checked entitled: Relief for a late change of entity classification election sought under Revenue Procedure 2010-32, is filed and attached to the amended tax return.

Also, if the qualified foreign entity (as defined in section 3.02 of Rev. Proc. 2010-32) files a valid election to be classified as a disregarded entity based on the reasonable assumption that it had a single owner as of the effective date of the election, and the qualified entity is later determined to have two or more owners, the IRS will deem the election to be an election to be classified as a partnership provided:

1. The qualified entity files information returns and the actual owners file original or amended returns consistent with the treatment of the entity as a partnership;

2. The amended returns are filed before the close of the period of limitations on assessments under section 6501(a) for the relevant tax year; and

3. The corrected Form 8832, with the box checked entitled: Relief for a late change of

entity classification election sought under Revenue Procedure 2010-32, is filed and attached to the amended tax returns. See Rev. Proc. 2010-32, 2010-36 I.R.B. 320 for details.

Definitions

Association. For purposes of this form, an association is an eligible entity taxable as a corporation by election or, for foreign eligible entities, under the default rules (see Regulations section 301.7701-3).

Business entity. A business entity is any entity recognized for federal tax purposes that is not properly classified as a trust under Regulations section 301.7701-4 or otherwise subject to special treatment under the Code regarding the entity's classification. See Regulations section 301.7701-2(a).

Corporation. For federal tax purposes, a corporation is any of the following:

1. A business entity organized under a federal or state statute, or under a statute of a federally recognized Indian tribe, if the statute describes or refers to the entity as incorporated or as a corporation, body corporate, or body politic.

2. An association (as determined under Regulations section 301.7701-3).

3. A business entity organized under a state statute, if the statute describes or refers to the entity as a joint-stock company or joint-stock association.

4. An insurance company.

5. A state-chartered business entity conducting banking activities, if any of its deposits are insured under the Federal Deposit Insurance Act, as amended, 12 U.S. C. 1811 et seq., or a similar federal statute.

6. A business entity wholly owned by a state or any political subdivision thereof, or a business entity wholly owned by a foreign government or any other entity described in Regulations section 1.892-2T.

7. A business entity that is taxable as a corporation under a provision of the Code other than section 7701(a)(3).

8. A foreign business entity listed on page 7. See Regulations section 301.7701-2(b)(8) for any exceptions and inclusions to items on this list and for any revisions made to this list since these instructions were printed.

9. An entity created or organized under the laws of more than one jurisdiction (business entities with multiple charters) if the entity is treated as a corporation with respect to any one of the jurisdictions. See Regulations section 301.7701-2(b)(9) for examples.

Disregarded entity. A disregarded entity is an eligible entity that is treated as an entity not separate from its single owner for income tax purposes. A "disregarded entity" is treated as separate from its owner for:

• Employment tax purposes, effective for wages paid on or after January 1, 2009; and

• Excise taxes reported on Forms 720, 730, 2290, 11-C, or 8849, effective for excise taxes reported and paid after December 31, 2007.

APPENDIX 14.5 Form 8832 (continued)

Form 8832 (Rev. 12-2013)   Page **5**

See the employment tax and excise tax return instructions for more information.

Limited liability. A member of a foreign eligible entity has limited liability if the member has no personal liability for any debts of or claims against the entity by reason of being a member. This determination is based solely on the statute or law under which the entity is organized (and, if relevant, the entity's organizational documents). A member has personal liability if the creditors of the entity may seek satisfaction of all or any part of the debts or claims against the entity from the member as such. A member has personal liability even if the member makes an agreement under which another person (whether or not a member of the entity) assumes that liability or agrees to indemnify that member for that liability.

Partnership. A partnership is a business entity that has at least two members and is not a corporation as defined above under *Corporation.*

Who Must File

File this form for an eligible entity that is one of the following:

• A domestic entity electing to be classified as an association taxable as a corporation.

• A domestic entity electing to change its current classification (even if it is currently classified under the default rule).

• A foreign entity that has more than one owner, all owners having limited liability, electing to be classified as a partnership.

• A foreign entity that has at least one owner that does not have limited liability, electing to be classified as an association taxable as a corporation.

• A foreign entity with a single owner having limited liability, electing to be an entity disregarded as an entity separate from its owner.

• A foreign entity electing to change its current classification (even if it is currently classified under the default rule).

Do not file this form for an eligible entity that is:

• Tax-exempt under section 501(a);

• A real estate investment trust (REIT), as defined in section 856; or

• Electing to be classified as an S corporation. An eligible entity that timely files Form 2553 to elect classification as an S corporation and meets all other requirements to qualify as an S corporation is deemed to have made an election under Regulations section 301.7701-3(c)(v) to be classified as an association taxable as a corporation.

All three of these entities are deemed to have made an election to be classified as an association.

Effect of Election

The federal tax treatment of elective changes in classification as described in Regulations section 301.7701-3(g)(1) is summarized as follows:

• If an eligible entity classified as a partnership elects to be classified as an association, it is deemed that the partnership contributes all of its assets and liabilities to the association in exchange for stock in the association, and immediately thereafter, the partnership liquidates by distributing the stock of the association to its partners.

• If an eligible entity classified as an association elects to be classified as a partnership, it is deemed that the association distributes all of its assets and liabilities to its shareholders in liquidation of the association, and immediately thereafter, the shareholders contribute all of the distributed assets and liabilities to a newly formed partnership.

• If an eligible entity classified as an association elects to be disregarded as an entity separate from its owner, it is deemed that the association distributes all of its assets and liabilities to its single owner in liquidation of the association.

• If an eligible entity that is disregarded as an entity separate from its owner elects to be classified as an association, the owner of the eligible entity is deemed to have contributed all of the assets and liabilities of the entity to the association in exchange for the stock of the association.

Note. For information on the federal tax consequences of elective changes in classification, see Regulations section 301.7701-3(g).

When To File

Generally, an election specifying an eligible entity's classification cannot take effect more than 75 days prior to the date the election is filed, nor can it take effect later than 12 months after the date the election is filed. An eligible entity may be eligible for late election relief in certain circumstances. For more information, see *Late Election Relief,* later.

Where To File

File Form 8832 with the Internal Revenue Service Center for your state listed later.

In addition, attach a copy of Form 8832 to the entity's federal tax or information return for the tax year of the election. If the entity is not required to file a return for that year, a copy of its Form 8832 must be attached to the federal tax returns of all direct or indirect owners of the entity for the tax year of the owner that includes the date on which the election took effect. An indirect owner of the electing entity does not have to attach a copy of the Form 8832 to its tax return if an entity in which it has an interest is already filing a copy of the Form 8832 with its return. Failure to attach a copy of Form 8832 will not invalidate an otherwise valid election, but penalties may be assessed against persons who are required to, but do not, attach Form 8832.

Each member of the entity is required to file the member's return consistent with the entity election. Penalties apply to returns filed inconsistent with the entity's election.

If the entity's principal business, office, or agency is located in:	Use the following Internal Revenue Service Center address:
Connecticut, Delaware, District of Columbia, Florida, Illinois, Indiana, Kentucky, Maine, Maryland, Massachusetts, Michigan, New Hampshire, New Jersey, New York, North Carolina, Ohio, Pennsylvania, Rhode Island, South Carolina, Vermont, Virginia, West Virginia, Wisconsin	Cincinnati, OH 45999

If the entity's principal business, office, or agency is located in:	Use the following Internal Revenue Service Center address:
Alabama, Alaska, Arizona, Arkansas, California, Colorado, Georgia, Hawaii, Idaho, Iowa, Kansas, Louisiana, Minnesota, Mississippi, Missouri, Montana, Nebraska, Nevada, New Mexico, North Dakota, Oklahoma, Oregon, South Dakota, Tennessee, Texas, Utah, Washington, Wyoming	Ogden, UT 84201
A foreign country or U.S. possession	Ogden, UT 84201-0023

Note. Also attach a copy to the entity's federal income tax return for the tax year of the election.

Acceptance or Nonacceptance of Election

The service center will notify the eligible entity at the address listed on Form 8832 if its election is accepted or not accepted. The entity should generally receive a determination on its election within 60 days after it has filed Form 8832.

Care should be exercised to ensure that the IRS receives the election. If the entity is not notified of acceptance or nonacceptance of its election within 60 days of the date of filing, take follow-up action by calling 1-800-829-0115, or by sending a letter to the service center to inquire about its status. Send any such letter by certified or registered mail via the U.S. Postal Service, or equivalent type of delivery by a designated private delivery service (see Notice 2004-83, 2004-52 I.R.B. 1030 (or its successor)).

If the IRS questions whether Form 8832 was filed, an acceptable proof of filing is:

• A certified or registered mail receipt (timely postmarked) from the U.S. Postal Service, or its equivalent from a designated private delivery service;

• Form 8832 with an accepted stamp;

• Form 8832 with a stamped IRS received date; or

• An IRS letter stating that Form 8832 has been accepted.

APPENDIX 14.5 Form 8832 (continued)

Specific Instructions

Name. Enter the name of the eligible entity electing to be classified.

Employer identification number (EIN). Show the EIN of the eligible entity electing to be classified.

 Do not put "Applied For" on this line.

Note. Any entity that has an EIN will retain that EIN even if its federal tax classification changes under Regulations section 301.7701-3.

If a disregarded entity's classification changes so that it becomes recognized as a partnership or association for federal tax purposes, and that entity had an EIN, then the entity must continue to use that EIN. If the entity did not already have its own EIN, then the entity must apply for an EIN and not use the identifying number of the single owner.

A foreign entity that makes an election under Regulations section 301.7701-3(c) and (d) must also use its own taxpayer identifying number. See sections 6721 through 6724 for penalties that may apply for failure to supply taxpayer identifying numbers.

If the entity electing to be classified using Form 8832 does not have an EIN, it must apply for one on Form SS-4, Application for Employer Identification Number. The entity must have received an EIN by the time Form 8832 is filed in order for the form to be processed. An election will not be accepted if the eligible entity does not provide an EIN.

 Do not apply for a new EIN for an existing entity that is changing its classification if the entity already has an EIN.

Address. Enter the address of the entity electing a classification. All correspondence regarding the acceptance or nonacceptance of the election will be sent to this address. Include the suite, room, or other unit number after the street address. If the Post Office does not deliver mail to the street address and the entity has a P.O. box, show the box number instead of the street address. If the electing entity receives its mail in care of a third party (such as an accountant or an attorney), enter on the street address line "C/O" followed by the third party's name and street address or P.O. box.

Address change. If the eligible entity has changed its address since filing Form SS-4 or the entity's most recently-filed return (including a change to an "in care of" address), check the box for an address change.

Late-classification relief sought under Revenue Procedure 2009-41. Check the box if the entity is seeking relief under Rev. Proc. 2009-41, 2009-39 I.R.B. 439, for a late classification election. For more information, see *Late Election Relief,* later.

Relief for a late change of entity classification election sought under Revenue Procedure 2010-32. Check the box if the entity is seeking relief under Rev. Proc.

2010-32, 2010-36 I.R.B. 320. For more information, see *Foreign default rule,* earlier.

Part I. Election Information

Complete Part I whether or not the entity is seeking relief under Rev. Proc. 2009-41 or Rev. Proc. 2010-32.

Line 1. Check box 1a if the entity is choosing a classification for the first time (i.e., the entity does not want to be classified under the applicable default classification). Do not file this form if the entity wants to be classified under the default rules.

Check box 1b if the entity is changing its current classification.

Lines 2a and 2b. 60-month limitation rule. Once an eligible entity makes an election to *change* its classification, the entity generally cannot change its classification by election again during the 60 months after the effective date of the election. However, the IRS may (by private letter ruling) permit the entity to change its classification by election within the 60-month period if more than 50% of the ownership interests in the entity, as of the effective date of the election, are owned by persons that did not own any interests in the entity on the effective date or the filing date of the entity's prior election.

Note. The 60-month limitation does not apply if the previous election was made by a newly formed eligible entity and was effective on the date of formation.

Line 4. If an eligible entity has only one owner, provide the name of its owner on line 4a and the owner's identifying number (social security number, or individual taxpayer identification number, or EIN) on line 4b. If the electing eligible entity is owned by an entity that is a disregarded entity or by an entity that is a member of a series of tiered disregarded entities, identify the first entity (the entity closest to the electing eligible entity) that is not a disregarded entity. For example, if the electing eligible entity is owned by disregarded entity A, which is owned by another disregarded entity B, and disregarded entity B is owned by partnership C, provide the name and EIN of partnership C as the owner of the electing eligible entity. If the owner is a foreign person or entity and does not have a U.S. identifying number, enter "none" on line 4b.

Line 5. If the eligible entity is owned by one or more members of an affiliated group of corporations that file a consolidated return, provide the name and EIN of the parent corporation.

Line 6. Check the appropriate box if you are changing a current classification (no matter how achieved), or are electing out of a default classification. Do not file this form if you fall within a default classification that is the desired classification for the new entity.

Line 7. If the entity making the election is created or organized in a foreign jurisdiction, enter the name of the foreign country in which it is organized. This information must be provided even if the entity is also organized under domestic law.

Line 8. Generally, the election will take effect on the date you enter on line 8 of this form,

or on the date filed if no date is entered on line 8. An election specifying an entity's classification for federal tax purposes can take effect no more than 75 days prior to the date the election is filed, nor can it take effect later than 12 months after the date on which the election is filed. If line 8 shows a date more than 75 days prior to the date on which the election is filed, the election will default to 75 days before the date it is filed. If line 8 shows an effective date more than 12 months from the filing date, the election will take effect 12 months after the date the election is filed.

Consent statement and signature(s). Form 8832 must be signed by:

1. Each member of the electing entity who is an owner at the time the election is filed; or

2. Any officer, manager, or member of the electing entity who is authorized (under local law or the organizational documents) to make the election. The elector represents to having such authorization under penalties of perjury.

If an election is to be effective for any period prior to the time it is filed, each person who was an owner between the date the election is to be effective and the date the election is filed, and who is not an owner at the time the election is filed, must sign.

If you need a continuation sheet or use a separate consent statement, attach it to Form 8832. The separate consent statement must contain the same information as shown on Form 8832.

Note. Do not sign the copy that is attached to your tax return.

Part II. Late Election Relief

Complete Part II only if the entity is requesting late election relief under Rev. Proc. 2009-41.

An eligible entity may be eligible for late election relief under Rev. Proc. 2009-41, 2009-39 I.R.B. 439, if **each** of the following requirements is met.

1. The entity failed to obtain its requested classification as of the date of its formation (or upon the entity's classification becoming relevant) or failed to obtain its requested change in classification solely because Form 8832 was not filed timely.

2. Either:

a. The entity has not filed a federal tax or information return for the first year in which the election was intended because the due date has not passed for that year's federal tax or information return; or

b. The entity has timely filed all required federal tax returns and information returns (or if not timely, within 6 months after its due date, excluding extensions) consistent with its requested classification for all of the years the entity intended the requested election to be effective and no inconsistent tax or information returns have been filed by or with respect to the entity during any of the tax years. If the eligible entity is not required to file a federal tax return or information return, each affected person who is required to file a federal tax return or information return must have timely filed all such returns (or if not timely, within 6 months after its due date, excluding extensions) consistent with the

APPENDIX 14.5 Form 8832 (continued)

Form 8832 (Rev. 12-2013)   Page **7**

entity's requested classification for all of the years the entity intended the requested election to be effective and no inconsistent tax or information returns have been filed during any of the tax years.

3. The entity has reasonable cause for its failure to timely make the entity classification election.

4. Three years and 75 days from the requested effective date of the eligible entity's classification election have not passed.

Affected person. An affected person is either:

• with respect to the effective date of the eligible entity's classification election, a person who would have been required to attach a copy of the Form 8832 for the eligible entity to its federal tax or information return for the tax year of the person which includes that date; or

• with respect to any subsequent date after the entity's requested effective date of the classification election, a person who would have been required to attach a copy of the Form 8832 for the eligible entity to its federal tax or information return for the person's tax year that includes that subsequent date had the election first become effective on that subsequent date.

For details on the requirement to attach a copy of Form 8832, see Rev. Proc. 2009-41 and the instructions under *Where To File.*

To obtain relief, file Form 8832 with the applicable IRS service center listed in *Where To File,* earlier, within 3 years and 75 days from the requested effective date of the eligible entity's classification election.

If Rev. Proc. 2009-41 does not apply, an entity may seek relief for a late entity election by requesting a private letter ruling and paying a user fee in accordance with Rev. Proc. 2013-1, 2013-1 I.R.B. 1 (or its successor).

Line 11. Explain the reason for the failure to file a timely entity classification election.

Signatures. Part II of Form 8832 must be signed by an authorized representative of the eligible entity and each affected person. See *Affected Persons,* earlier. The individual or individuals who sign the declaration must have personal knowledge of the facts and circumstances related to the election.

Foreign Entities Classified as Corporations for Federal Tax Purposes:

American Samoa—Corporation
Argentina—Sociedad Anonima
Australia—Public Limited Company
Austria—Aktiengesellschaft
Barbados—Limited Company
Belgium—Societe Anonyme
Belize—Public Limited Company
Bolivia—Sociedad Anonima
Brazil—Sociedade Anonima
Bulgaria—Aktsionerno Druzhestvo
Canada—Corporation and Company
Chile—Sociedad Anonima
People's Republic of China—Gufen Youxian Gongsi

Republic of China (Taiwan)
    —Ku-fen Yu-hsien Kung-szu
Colombia—Sociedad Anonima
Costa Rica—Sociedad Anonima
Croatia—Dionicko Drustvo
Cyprus—Public Limited Company
Czech Republic—Akciova Spolecnost
Denmark—Aktieselskab
Ecuador—Sociedad Anonima or Compania Anonima
Egypt—Sharikat Al-Mossahamah
El Salvador—Sociedad Anonima
Estonia—Aktsiaselts
European Economic Area/European Union
    —Societas Europaea
Finland—Julkinen Osakeyhtio/Publikt Aktiebolag
France—Societe Anonyme
Germany—Aktiengesellschaft
Greece—Anonymos Etairia
Guam—Corporation
Guatemala—Sociedad Anonima
Guyana—Public Limited Company
Honduras—Sociedad Anonima
Hong Kong—Public Limited Company
Hungary—Reszvenytarsasag
Iceland—Hlutafelag
India—Public Limited Company
Indonesia—Perseroan Terbuka
Ireland—Public Limited Company
Israel—Public Limited Company
Italy—Societa per Azioni
Jamaica—Public Limited Company
Japan—Kabushiki Kaisha
Kazakstan—Ashyk Aktsionerlik Kogham
Republic of Korea—Chusik Hoesa
Latvia—Akciju Sabiedriba
Liberia—Corporation
Liechtenstein—Aktiengesellschaft
Lithuania—Akcine Bendroves
Luxembourg—Societe Anonyme
Malaysia—Berhad
Malta—Public Limited Company
Mexico—Sociedad Anonima
Morocco—Societe Anonyme
Netherlands—Naamloze Vennootschap
New Zealand—Limited Company
Nicaragua—Compania Anonima
Nigeria—Public Limited Company
Northern Mariana Islands—Corporation
Norway—Allment Aksjeselskap
Pakistan—Public Limited Company
Panama—Sociedad Anonima
Paraguay—Sociedad Anonima
Peru—Sociedad Anonima
Philippines—Stock Corporation
Poland—Spolka Akcyjna
Portugal—Sociedade Anonima

Puerto Rico—Corporation
Romania—Societe pe Actiuni
Russia—Otkrytoye Aktsionernoy Obshchestvo
Saudi Arabia—Sharikat Al-Mossahamah
Singapore—Public Limited Company
Slovak Republic—Akciova Spolocnost
Slovenia—Delniska Druzba
South Africa—Public Limited Company
Spain—Sociedad Anonima
Surinam—Naamloze Vennootschap
Sweden—Publika Aktiebolag
Switzerland— Aktiengesellschaft
Thailand—Borisat Chamkad (Mahachon)
Trinidad and Tobago—Limited Company
Tunisia—Societe Anonyme
Turkey—Anonim Sirket
Ukraine—Aktsionerne Tovaristvo Vidkritogo Tipu
United Kingdom—Public Limited Company
United States Virgin Islands—Corporation
Uruguay—Sociedad Anonima
Venezuela—Sociedad Anonima or Compania Anonima

 See Regulations section 301.7701-2(b)(8) for any exceptions and inclusions to items on this list and for any revisions made to this list since these instructions were printed.

Paperwork Reduction Act Notice

We ask for the information on this form to carry out the Internal Revenue laws of the United States. You are required to give us the information. We need it to ensure that you are complying with these laws and to allow us to figure and collect the right amount of tax.

You are not required to provide the information requested on a form that is subject to the Paperwork Reduction Act unless the form displays a valid OMB control number. Books or records relating to a form or its instructions must be retained as long as their contents may become material in the administration of any Internal Revenue law. Generally, tax returns and return information are confidential, as required by section 6103.

The time needed to complete and file this form will vary depending on individual circumstances. The estimated average time is:

Recordkeeping .   .   .   . 2 hr., 46 min.

**Learning about the
law or the form** .   .   .   . 3 hr., 48 min.

**Preparing and sending
the form to the IRS** .   .   .   .   . 36 min.

If you have comments concerning the accuracy of these time estimates or suggestions for making this form simpler, we would be happy to hear from you. You can write to the Internal Revenue Service, Tax Forms and Publications, SE:W:CAR:MP:TFP, 1111 Constitution Ave. NW, IR-6526, Washington, DC 20224. Do not send the form to this address. Instead, see *Where To File* above.

15

Introduction to Retirement Planning

LEARNING OBJECTIVES

After learning the material in this chapter, you will be able to do the following:

■ Define financial security

■ Identify and understand the major factors that affect retirement planning

■ Understand the work life expectancy/retirement life expectancy dilemma

■ Explain the impact that timeliness of savings has on savings accumulation

■ Discuss the balance that must be achieved between increasing and decreasing retirement income needs

■ Define the wage replacement ratio and explain how it is used to estimate retirement income needs

■ Differentiate between the top-down approach and the budgeting approach to calculating the wage replacement ratio

■ Discuss the qualitative factors that affect retirement planning

■ Differentiate among the three capital needs analysis calculations: the pure annuity model; the capital preservation (CP) model; and the purchasing power preservation (PPP) model

■ Determine capital needs for various clients

■ Make projections to prepare a capital needs analysis presentation

INTRODUCTION

One of the main financial planning goals for many people is long-term financial security and independence. This goal is realized when individuals are financially secure enough to live at their desired comfort level without the need for employment income. Financial security at retirement requires individuals to plan carefully. Unfortunately, the majority of American workers have no idea how much money they will need to fund their retirement. When coupled with changes in Social Security, tax laws, the economy, and the value structure of our society, retirement planning becomes a necessary but difficult and time-consuming process. Because of the complex nature of retirement planning, financial planners often are enlisted to provide direction and guidance. This chapter discusses the fundamental concepts that financial planners must know to effectively plan for a client's retirement. Chapter 16 discusses the characteristics of actual retirement plans.

BASIC FACTORS AFFECTING RETIREMENT PLANNING

Several basic factors affect retirement planning. The following areas must be considered: the remaining work life expectancy (WLE), the retirement life expectancy (RLE), basic savings concepts, the annual income needed (needs), the wage replacement ratio (WRR), the sources of retirement income, inflation, investment returns, and other qualitative factors.

REMAINING WORK LIFE EXPECTANCY (RWLE)

Work life expectancy (WLE)
The number of years a person spends in the workforce, generally 30–40 years

Remaining work life expectancy (RWLE)
The work period remaining at a certain point in time prior to retirement

Work life expectancy (WLE) is the period of time a person is in the work force, generally 30–40 years. There has been a substantial decline in the overall WLE because of increased education, which causes later entry into the workforce and earlier than normal retirement.

Remaining work life expectancy (RWLE) is the work period that remains at a certain point in time before retirement. For example, a 50-year-old client who expects to retire at age 62 has a RWLE of 12 years. Determining the remaining work life expectancy is important for the financial planner because this figure tells the planner the remaining number of years the client has to save for retirement. In the past, normal retirement age was most often age 65 because this age was the retirement age historically set forth by the Social Security Administration. Today, however, the average retirement age is several years less than age 65, with age 62 being a common retirement age, especially when one spouse earns less than the other spouse.

Exhibit 15.1 presents a skewed distribution of all retirees' retirement ages. Notice that the area identified as A represents 93% of the area of the curve, illustrating that approximately 93% of all individuals retire between ages 62 and 65 (inclusive).

EXHIBIT 15.1 Average Retirement Age (United States)

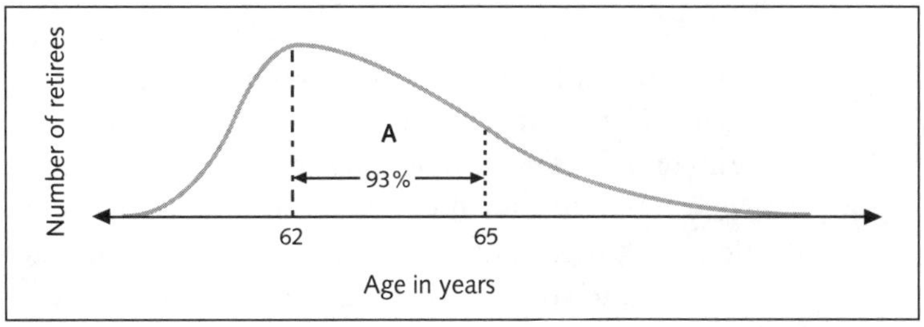

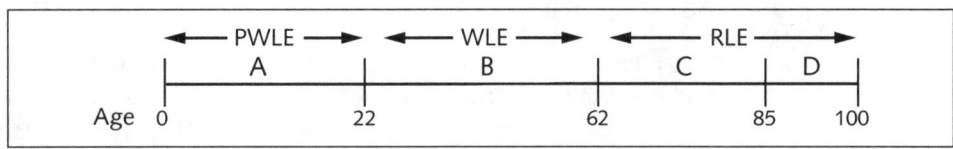

RETIREMENT LIFE EXPECTANCY (RLE)

Retirement life expectancy (RLE)

The time period beginning at retirement and extending until death; the period of retirement that must be funded

Retirement life expectancy (RLE) is the time period beginning at retirement and extending until death. Although the average RLE for a group of 65-year-olds is approximately 20 years, many clients may live beyond this statistical average. In 1900, the average life expectancy for a newborn was 47 years. The average life expectancy in the United States has risen to 78.93 years for those born in 2020. This increase in life expectancy, and the corresponding increase in RLE, is a direct result of a decline in the death rate, especially the birth mortality rate. The overall death rate has declined because of medical and technological advances in disease diagnoses, cures, and prevention. With each new medical advancement, life expectancy will, no doubt, increase. However, even these numbers do not tell the real life expectancy story. First, *life expectancy* is defined as the time until half the defined population has expired. Thus, by definition, everyone who is reasonably healthy has at least a 50% probability of living longer than their "life expectancy." Second, for retirees and those approaching retirement, the important numbers are not life expectancy at birth, but remaining life expectancy in retirement. Third, the life expectancy of more educated and more wealthy individuals is longer than those who are struggling to get by.

The WLE-RLE Relationship

A financial planner needs to understand the relationship between WLE and RLE. If either period changes, the other period is affected. Exhibit 15.2 presents the work life expectancy/retirement life expectancy dilemma.

EXHIBIT 15.2 The WLE/RLE Dilemma

Area A represents the prework life expectancy (PWLE) and lasts until the person enters the workforce on a full-time basis. Generally, the PWLE ends between ages 18 and 26, with the average age being 22. Area B, the WLE, represents the period of working years before retirement. This period begins at the end of the PWLE and ends at the beginning of C, the RLE, usually around age 62. The RLE (Area C) generally lasts to age 85, but may continue beyond age 100. With a longer RLE period to finance and a shortened WLE in which to save and accumulate assets, careful planning is needed to meet the funding requirements for a financially secure retirement.

SAVINGS CONCEPTS

The savings amount, the savings rate, the timing of savings, and investment decisions are important concepts in retirement planning. If our society were adequately saving for retirement beginning at an early age, people would be saving about 10% of their gross annual income and investing in a broad portfolio of growth investments over their entire work life. They would be ever mindful of investment returns and inflation to ensure sufficient savings. Unfortunately, workers save at a much lower rate than is necessary, are not investment savvy, and are, generally, insensitive to the impact of inflation.

Savings Amount

In general, persons who begin the financial security planning process at an early age (25–30) should save 10–15% of their gross annual pay. If individuals do not begin at an early age, then they must save a greater amount of their gross pay to compensate for the missed years of contributions and compounding. Exhibit 15.3 shows how much individuals must save if they choose to wait until later years to begin saving for retirement.

EXHIBIT 15.3 Required Savings Rate for Retirement

Age Beginning Regular and Recurring Savings*	Savings (As Percentage of Gross Pay) Rate Required to Create Appropriate Capital*
25–35	10–13%
35–45	15–18%
45–55	20–25%
55–65	30–35%

*Assumes appropriate asset allocation for reasonable-risk investor through accumulation year; also assumes normal salary increases and an 80% wage replacement ratio at Social Security normal retirement age.

Exhibit 15.3 illustrates a major problem with delaying retirement savings. Namely, many individuals find it difficult to begin saving such large amounts even if they are accustomed to saving. Saving requires foregoing current consumption, and most individuals find it difficult to decrease consumption by 20–30%, especially when they have been accustomed to maintaining a certain standard of living for long periods.

Savings Rate

The savings rate is an important concern in financial planning. Overall savings rates had declined over the past decade until the United States fell into a period of recession a few years ago. Facing uncertain economic times, Americans began to cut expenses and increased savings. The U.S. personal savings rate, as reported by the Federal Reserve Bank of St. Louis, was 6.8% in 2016, 7.9% in 2019, and was rising into double digits in early 2020.

Timing of Savings

The earlier a person begins to save, the greater the number of future compounding periods available before retirement. A greater number of compounding periods leads to a lower required savings rate and a larger accumulation of capital at retirement. When saving is delayed, the power of compounding is lost, and individuals must compensate by saving a greater percentage of their disposable income.

E X A M P L E   Ann saves $3,000 a year from age 25 to 34 inclusively and invests in an account earning 8% annually. Ann stops investing at age 34 but does not withdraw the accumulation until age 65. Ann's accumulation at age 65 is $472,300 even though she only deposited $30,000. In contrast, Bob saves $3,000 a year from age 35 to 65 inclusively and invests in an account similar to Ann's, earning 8% annually. Even though Bob saved $93,000 more than Ann, he will have accumulated $102,300 less than Ann at age 65. The deposits and balances for Ann and Bob at age 65 are presented in Exhibit 15.4.

EXHIBIT 15.4 Time/Savings Example (Accumulation at Age 65)

	Ann	Bob
Total Invested (OA)	$30,000	$93,000
Balance at 65	$472,300	$370,000
Earnings Rate	8%	8%

Even though Bob invested more than three times as much as Ann, Ann has 28% more than Bob at age 65. This result demonstrates the power of compound earnings over the longer period of 41 years versus 31 years. Exhibit 15.5 shows this phenomenon graphically.

EXHIBIT 15.5 Accumulation Example

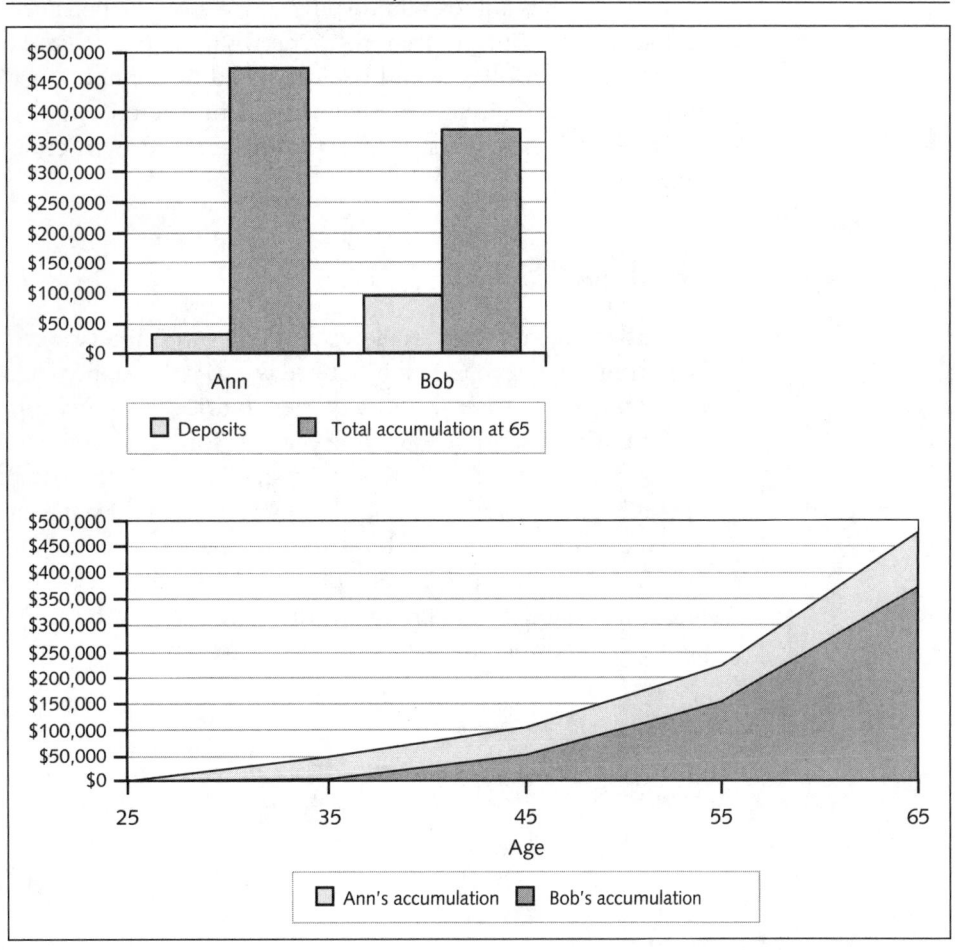

This example highlights the importance of starting early and not withdrawing money early. However, while Ann's results are clearly superior to Bob's, why would she want to stop saving for her future? If she would have simply continued to invest the same amount each year, her balance at 65 would have been $839,400 instead of $472,300. Also, if inflation averaged 3% per year, her balance at retirement of $472,300 would only be worth around $98,400 in her age 25 dollars (present value). If she would have continued to save at the same pace, her $839,400 would have been worth approximately $175,000 in age 25 dollars (present value). No matter how much better Ann did than Bob, retiring today with a nest egg of $98,400 is worse than retiring with $175,000. Actually, a retirement nest egg of $175,000 today is clearly inadequate to maintain even a middle-class lifestyle during a retirement period that could last 30 years.

INVESTMENT DECISIONS

A fundamental understanding of investment decisions and their consequences is essential to retirement planning. In this chapter, we will briefly identify some of the relationships between investments and retirement planning. More in-depth investment information is provided in Chapter 12 of this book.

All assets do not have the same historical investment returns. When planning for retirement, it is important to have an historical perspective of investment returns for various investment alternatives. One would expect that when investors are young, their investment portfolios would be dominated by common stocks because they generally can afford the risk. As investors near retirement, their asset allocation generally shifts to lower risk alternatives while still maintaining some growth component to mitigate the risk of inflation.

Inflation

Inflation
An increase in the price level of goods and services

Inflation causes a loss of purchasing power. If a retiree has a fixed retirement income beginning at age 65 and inflation is 2% (the approximate average rate for the past 20 years), the retiree would experience a loss in purchasing power of 18% in 10 years, 33% in 20 years, and 45% in 30 years. If inflation were to increase to an average annual rate of 3%, which is the 100-year average in the U.S., the retiree would experience a loss in purchasing power of 26% in 10 years, 46% in 20 years, and 60% in 30 years. Although Social Security retirement benefits are inflation adjusted, many private pension plans are not. Accordingly, the financial planner must account for inflation when projecting retirement needs and advise clients to save accordingly. Exhibit 15.6 illustrates the decline in purchasing power that a 2% inflation rate can cause over a 50-year span.

EXHIBIT 15.6 Impact of Inflation

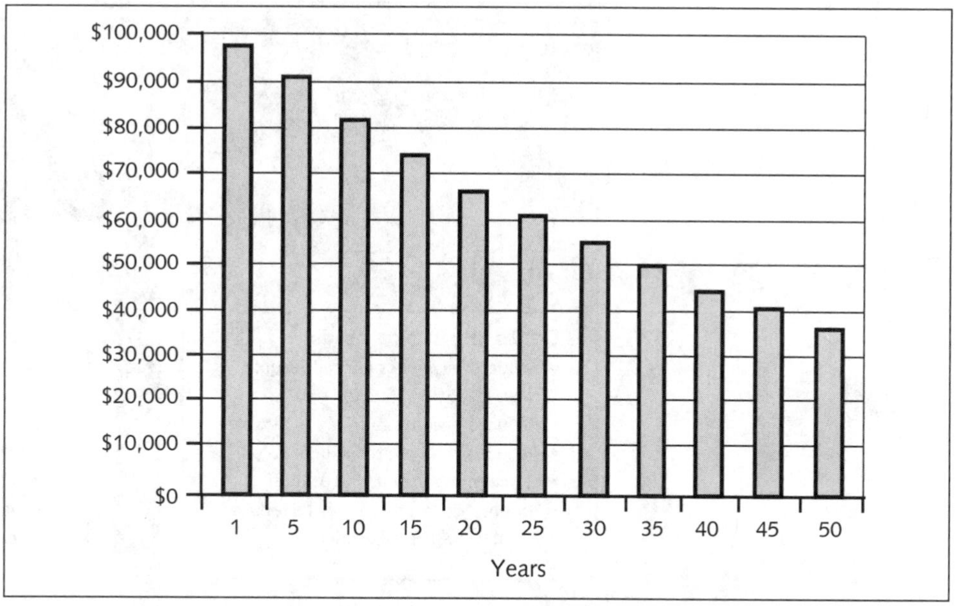

DEFINING RETIREMENT GOALS (NEEDS)

How much income does a person need to be financially independent? Most individuals entering retirement intend to maintain at least the same lifestyle they had before retirement. Clients generally do not radically reduce their expenses downward unless it is necessary. When a retirement budget is prepared, it should include amounts similar to the preretirement budget, with a few adjustments. Some costs in retirement will decrease, while others will increase. The reduced costs in retirement may include: (1) the elimination of costs associated with employment (e.g., certain clothing costs, parking, some meal costs); (2) the elimination of mortgage costs if the mortgage debt is scheduled to be repaid by retirement; (3) the elimination of costs associated with raising children (e.g., tuition and clothes); (4) the elimination of payroll costs (FICA); and (5) the elimination of savings, because the plan will require the use of accumulated savings. For some individuals, retirement can bring increased spending on travel and other lifestyle changes. Often, retirees are at risk for increases in health care costs. Exhibit 15.7 presents lists of potential decreasing and increasing costs when entering retirement.

EXHIBIT 15.7 Balancing Increasing and Decreasing Retirement Income Needs

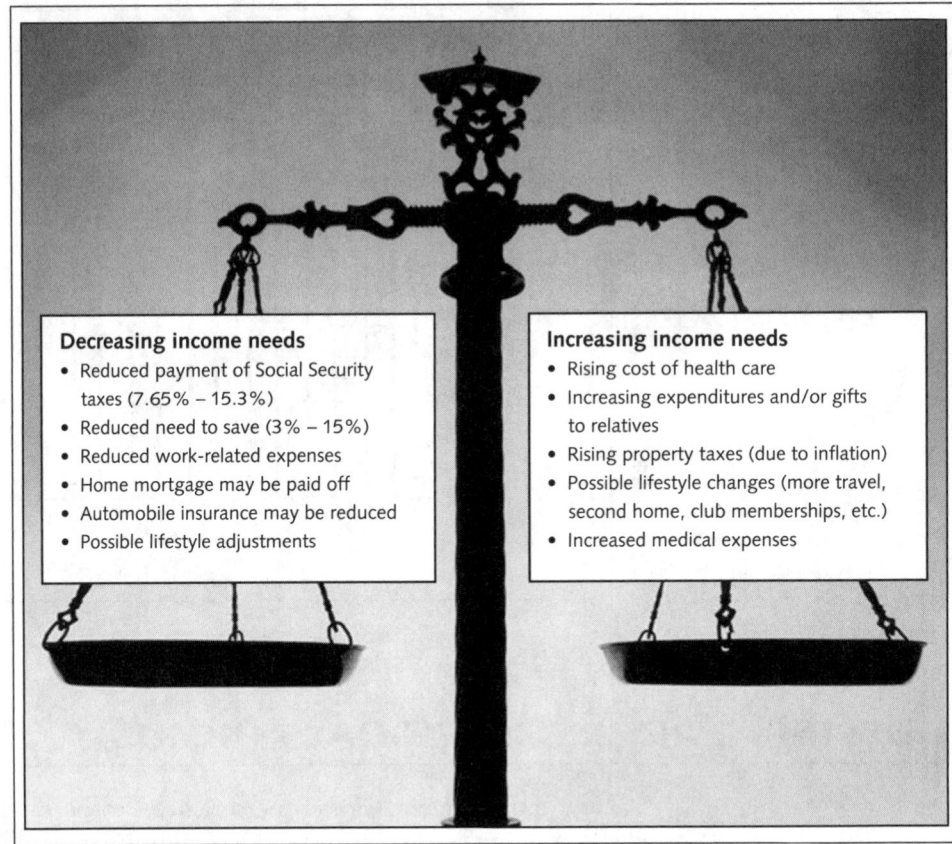

Decreasing income needs
- Reduced payment of Social Security taxes (7.65% – 15.3%)
- Reduced need to save (3% – 15%)
- Reduced work-related expenses
- Home mortgage may be paid off
- Automobile insurance may be reduced
- Possible lifestyle adjustments

Increasing income needs
- Rising cost of health care
- Increasing expenditures and/or gifts to relatives
- Rising property taxes (due to inflation)
- Possible lifestyle changes (more travel, second home, club memberships, etc.)
- Increased medical expenses

Planning for Retirement—Pretax or After Tax

Retirement needs may either be planned for on a pretax basis or an after-tax basis. Many financial planners calculate needs in pretax dollars believing that pretax is what their clients best understand. The pretax assumption is that clients are more likely to know their gross income than to know their net after-tax cash flow. Therefore, planners sometimes create retirement plans on a pretax basis, and the clients simply pay whatever income taxes for which they are liable out of their gross retirement income, similar to what clients do during preretirement years. Many CPAs think in terms of after-tax dollars and plan for retirement on an after-tax basis. After-tax planning assumes that income taxes are paid before other retirement needs. Planning can be effective either way as long as the client understands the difference between pretax and after-tax planning.

▌WAGE REPLACEMENT RATIO (WRR)

Wage replacement ratio (WRR)

An estimate of the percentage of income needed at retirement compared to earnings prior to retirement

The **wage replacement ratio (WRR)** is an estimate of the percentage of annual income needed during retirement compared to income earned prior to retirement. The wage replacement ratio or percentage is calculated by dividing the amount of money needed on an annual basis in retirement by the preretirement income. For example, if a client in the last year of work (prior to retirement) earns $100,000, and that client needs $80,000 in the first retirement year to maintain the same preretirement lifestyle, the wage replacement ratio (WRR) is 80% (80,000 ÷ 100,000).

Calculating the Wage Replacement Ratio

There are two methods to calculate the wage replacement ratio: the top-down approach and the budgeting approach (or bottom-up approach).

Top-Down Approach

The top-down approach is commonly used with younger clients where expenditure patterns are likely to change dramatically over time. As clients approach retirement age, a more precise wage replacement ratio should be calculated using a budgeting approach. This approach estimates the wage replacement ratio using common sense and percentages.

E X A M P L E   To illustrate, assume a 40-year-old client earns $50,000 a year, pays 7.65% of his gross pay in Social Security payroll taxes, and saves 10% of his gross income annually. If we assume that any work-related savings resulting from retirement are expected to be completely offset by additional spending adjustments during retirement, and that the client wants to maintain his exact preretirement lifestyle, we would expect that the client would need a wage replacement ratio of 82.35% (100% − 7.65% − 10%).

$50,000 =	100.00%	of salary
(5,000) =	(10.00%)	current savings
(3,825) =	(7.65%)	payroll taxes
$41,175 =	82.35%	wage replacement ratio

Notice that the client is currently living on 82.35% of his gross pay. The remaining 17.65% is allocated to FICA taxes and savings. Therefore, the 82.35% is a reasonable estimate, or proxy, of the amount necessary, as a percentage of current income, to maintain the preretirement lifestyle.

Budgeting Approach

The second method used to calculate the wage replacement ratio is called the budgeting approach. This approach used with older clients because, as a person nears retirement, it is possible to examine the actual expenditure patterns of the individual. In cooperation with the client, the planner can determine which costs in the current (preretirement) budget will change (plus or minus) in the retirement budget and thus determine, with greater precision than the top-down approach, an estimate of actual retirement needs.

E X A M P L E   Clients A and B each earn $100,000 in preretirement income. Client A has arranged her financial affairs so she will have no mortgage payment or car payment during retirement. Client B, on the other hand, expects to continue to have both a mortgage payment and a car payment throughout the majority of his retirement years. Exhibit 15.8 illustrates that Client A will need a 59.1% WRR, and Client B will need a 79.6% WRR. The difference is due to Client B's $15,000 mortgage payment and $5,500 car payment.

EXHIBIT 15.8 Budgeting Approach to Wage Replacement Ratio

	Clients A & B Budget	Client A Retirement Budget	Client B Retirement Budget
Annual income (current) budget	$100,000	$100,000	$100,000
Expenses:	Current	Retirement	Retirement
Income and payroll taxes	$27,650	$20,000	$20,000
Food	4,800	4,800	4,800
Utilities/phone	2,400	2,400	2,400
Mortgage	15,000	0	15,000
Health insurance	1,000	1,000	1,000
Auto insurance	1,000	1,000	1,000
Entertainment	5,000	5,000	5,000
Clothing	2,000	1,500	1,500
Auto maintenance/operation	1,000	750	750
Auto payment	5,500	0	5,500
Charity	4,800	4,800	4,800
Savings	12,000	0	0
Miscellaneous	17,850	17,850	17,850
Total expenses	$100,000	$59,100	$79,600
Wage replacement percentage needed		**59.1%**	**79.6%**

Does a person really need the same wage replacement percentage throughout the entire retirement period? There are clear indications that consumption slows dramatically as people age. The 70–80% wage replacement ratio is probably most appropriate from the beginning of retirement, regardless of age, until one's late 70s. A person's consumption beyond age 80 declines primarily as a result of limited mobility. Although this may be correct for society at large, certain individuals will incur dramatic medical costs during the latter part of their retirement period. Therefore, although most who study retirement expenditures would suggest a consumption function similar to the one provided in Exhibit 15.9, such a model may not apply to a particular individual.

EXHIBIT 15.9 Real Consumption by Age

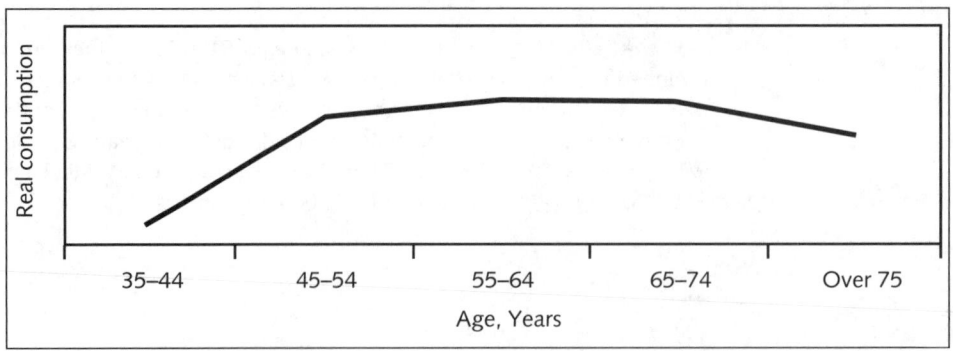

Exhibit 15.10 presents the adjustments from preretirement to retirement in terms of estimated percentages. Notice that many of the adjustments in Exhibit 15.10 will be client-specific.

EXHIBIT 15.10 Adjustments from Preretirement to Retirement

Adjustments to Expenditures Needed From Preretirement Income to Retirement Income	
Adjustments that decrease income needs:	
■ No longer pay Social Security taxes	Savings of 7.65–15.3%
■ No longer need to save for retirement	Savings of 3–15%
■ May no longer pay home mortgage	May decrease income needs
■ No longer pay work-related expenses	*
■ Auto insurance may be reduced	*
■ Possible lifestyle adjustments	*
Adjustments that may increase income needs:	
■ Increasing cost of health care	*
■ Lifestyle changes	*
■ Increase in travel	*
■ Second home	*
■ Clubs and activities	*
■ Expenditures on family/gifts/grandchildren	*
■ Increased property taxes	*
■ Need to continue saving for vehicle replacements/ maintenance and major home repairs/maintenance	*

* Amounts must be estimated for each individual.

Many financial planners conclude that most clients need at least 70–80% of their pre-retirement current income to retire and maintain their preretirement lifestyle. Although many clients would fall into this range, there are also those particularly frugal clients who may need as little as 40% of preretirement income and others who need substantially more than the 80% wage replacement ratio.

THE SOURCES OF RETIREMENT INCOME

Historically, retirees generally relied on three sources of income for retirement: Social Security, private pension plans, and personal savings. Today, the reality for many retirees is a fourth leg: working during retirement, either on a full- or part-time basis. Why the fourth leg? For some retirees who haven't saved enough for retirement, work is an economic necessity to help make ends meet. For other retirees, work is an optional activity that gives them something productive to do with their time. Surveys of baby boomers often show an expectation or willingness to work long past the traditional retirement ages of 62, 65, or even 70. Whatever their reasons, many retirees will include work during retirement as a part of their retirement plan. All four of these sources complement each other to provide adequate retirement income. Exhibit 15.11 shows the average amount of income for the average retiree from each of these four sources.

EXHIBIT 15.11 Retirement Income Sources

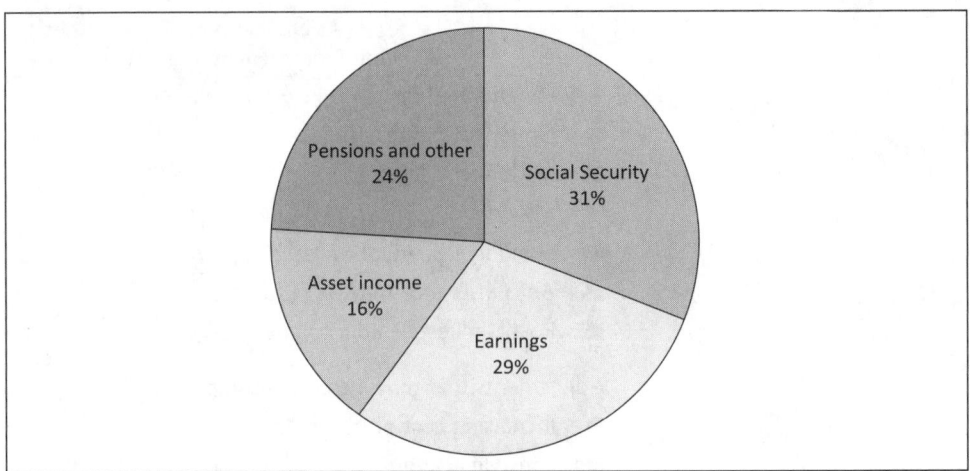

Source: Social Security Administration, *Fast Facts and Figures about Social Security*, 2015 (the latest update as of May, 2020)

Social Security

Social Security provides the foundation of retirement earnings. Social Security covers almost all occupational groups (except 25% of state and local government employees) with retirement benefits adjusting for inflation. It is considered the safety net of a secure income, but for most income levels it will not be a sufficient source of income replacement during retirement. As illustrated in Exhibit 15.12, Social Security may be an adequate wage replacement for lower- wage earners to maintain their lifestyle, but it is clearly inadequate to provide sufficient replacement income for middle- to upper-wage earners. (Social Security and Social Security benefits are covered in detail in Chapter 11.)

EXHIBIT 15.12 Social Security Retirement Benefits as a Percentage of Earnings

Base Year's Average Earnings	Annual Retirement Benefit	Percentage of Earnings Replaced
$20,000	$10,572	52.86%
$40,000	$14,748	36.87%
$80,000	$23,112	28.89%
$100,000	$27,288	27.29%
$200,000	$35,256	17.63%

Source: Social Security Administration Quick Benefit Calculator (www.ssa.gov)
Assumptions: Client was born in 1954 and retires in 2020.

Private Pension and Company-Sponsored Retirement Plans

Private pension plans are the second source of retirement income. Private pension plans provided by employers are covered in Chapter 16. As you will see, private pension plans have dramatically changed over the last few years from employer-sponsored and funded plans to employee self-reliance plans, putting more and more emphasis on personal savings as the primary source of retirement income for middle- to upper-wage workers.

Personal Savings

Personal savings is the third source of retirement income and the one most influenced by the individual. The more personal savings put aside for retirement, the larger the accumulation at retirement and the larger the retirement income for the individual.

Whenever a retiree has income from invested assets, it can mean a substantially higher overall retirement income. The median income of those retirees with asset income is more than twice as large as the income of retirees with no asset income. As Exhibit 15.13 illustrates, retirees without asset income are concentrated in the lowest income categories.

EXHIBIT 15.13 Income Categories of Retirees

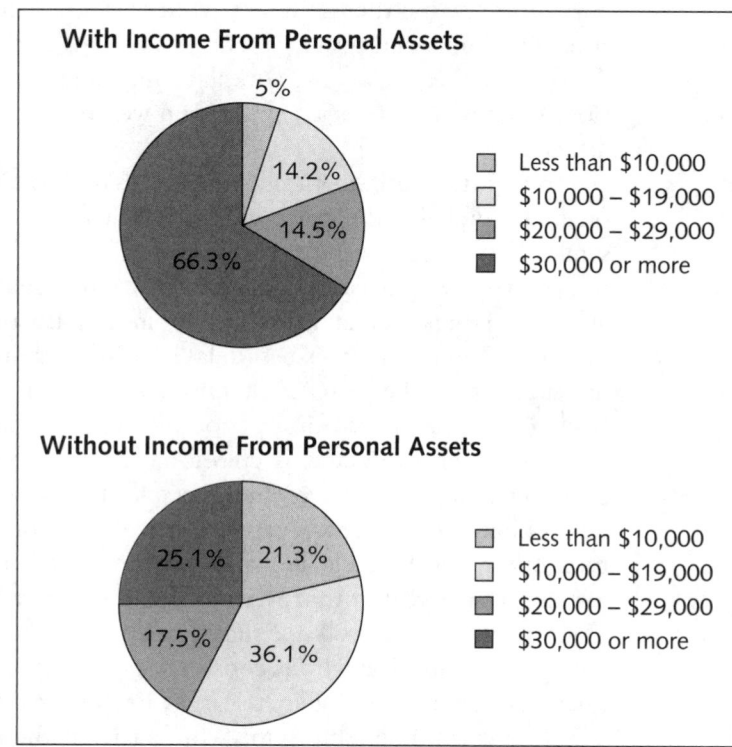

Source: Social Security Administration, *Income of the Aged Chartbook*

WORK

According to the U.S. Bureau of Labor Statistics, over 40% of Americans age 55 and older were employed in 2017. Though many preretirees expect to work during their traditional retirement years, the unfortunate reality is that unpredictable events such as layoffs, downsizing, illness, and family obligations often curtail their plans.

QUALITATIVE FACTORS IN RETIREMENT— ADVISING CLIENTS

Qualitative factors associated with retirement are no less important than the financial or quantitative factors. Qualitative factors include involuntary versus voluntary retirement, emotional and psychological factors such as loss of self- esteem and boredom, and the decision to relocate.

The best overall advice financial planners can give their clients is to know themselves and their support systems, have a well-planned qualitative plan for retirement, and have a system in place to maintain their egos and self-esteem. Many individuals in our culture define themselves by what they do. The mere act of going to work may be a ritual or a habit that provides that person with a sense of self-worth and a purpose in life. A trusted colleague at the workplace may be a source of support and personal gratification. Voluntary retirement, even when well planned, means change—and change is often difficult.

Involuntary retirement, if perceived as undesirable, can have as devastating an impact on an individual as the death of a loved one or a bitter divorce. The client may follow the same psychological pattern of grief: shock, anger, denial, and acceptance. Financial planning professionals need to be aware of the emotional affect retirement can have on clients and realize that when an individual is emotionally troubled, major decisions—financial or otherwise—are sometimes best delayed. Rather than abruptly making important financial decisions, it may be better to do minimal financial maneuvering during a grieving period. Such grieving may last for a period of a year or longer. Trying to optimize the financial situation when the client is emotionally unable to determine her goals or priorities is probably counterproductive and may add stress to the situation.

A client's decision to change physical locations after retirement (for example, move to another state) should be carefully considered over a long period of planning. Some retirees do not realize that when they move, they will have a completely new environment to adjust to, as well as a substantial loss of their former support system of friends and family. An individual who is considering moving should conduct a trial transition over a number of years, spending increasingly longer periods at the desired location. This gradual adjustment will help determine whether what the retiree believes will actually enhance retirement will, in fact, be true. Persons considering retiring abroad will encounter even more of a challenge, thereby necessitating more detailed planning.

SUMMARY OF FACTORS AFFECTING RETIREMENT PLANNING

Financial planners may encounter clients who subjectively "feel" they are financially secure because they have a good job and/or a good net worth. If a good job is lost through premature death, disability, layoff, termination, unexpected illness, or other events, or if the net worth decreases dramatically, the client's financial security is suddenly lost. In most instances, the client's actual determination of financial security is subjective rather than objective. Therefore, the financial planner must be the intermediary between the client's subjective feelings and the overall objective of financial security.

Other factors that complicate the retirement planning process include at least two societal issues. Society has become more mobile with the traditional family unit deteriorating. Having lost the close connection to family, older individuals may not be able to depend on family members to provide retirement assistance. Thus, there is a greater need for financial independence for each individual. In addition, because society seems to place more value on youth than on age and wisdom in the workplace, retirees have less chance of being hired for part-time employment, which could supplement retirement income.

Many people begin planning for retirement too late in life and save too little to effectively meet retirement capital accumulation needs. Some people do not even consider retirement funding until they are in their 40s. Even when people do save, many of them make poor investment choices and, therefore, have poor investment returns.

In addition, inflation erodes purchasing power. For recipients of fixed incomes, inflation is like a progressive tax causing declining purchasing power. Exhibit 15.14 lists the factors that challenge effective retirement planning and the negative impact associated with each factor.

EXHIBIT 15.14 Factors that Negatively Affect Retirement Planning and their Impact on the Planning Process

Factor	Impact
Reduced WLE	Insufficient savings period
Increased RLE	Increased capital needs
Reduced family reliance	Fewer alternatives in retirement
Reduced ability to work	Fewer alternatives in retirement
Planned too late	Fewer compounding periods
Low savings rate	Unable to meet capital requirements
Inflation	Reduced purchasing power
Poor earnings rate and asset allocation	Unable to meet capital requirements

Long-term financial security does not happen automatically. It requires careful planning, a clear understanding of quantified goals, and identification and management of the risks involved. Retirement planning requires the collection, analysis, and projection of data and must be conducted meticulously and conservatively.

RISKS TO FINANCIAL INDEPENDENCE

There are many risks to achieving financial independence. Selected risks are identified in Exhibit 15.15. People should begin saving at an early age, save a sufficient amount, invest wisely, and not underestimate retirement needs or the impact of inflation. The risks identified in Part B of Exhibit 15.15 are more thoroughly discussed in the chapters on risk management and insurance.

EXHIBIT 15.15 Summary of Factors Affecting Retirement Planning

Factor	Risk	Mitigator
Part A: Risks Discussed in this Chapter		
Work Life Expectancy (WLE)	Shortened because of untimely death, disability, health, unemployment	Life insurance, disability insurance, health insurance, education, training, experience, diet, exercise
Retirement Life Expectancy (RLE)	Lengthened	Adequate capital accumulation, possible immediate annuity
Savings rate, amount, and timing	Too low and too late	Save more; start early; asset allocation
Inflation	Greater than expected	Realistically project inflation rate and income needs
Retirement income needs	Underestimated	Use wage replacement estimators
Investment returns	Inadequate to amass needed retirement capital	Knowledge of investments; broad portfolio of diversified investments and proper asset allocation
Sources of retirement income	Overestimation of Social Security benefits, private pension plans, work or personal income (or adverse changes in taxation of such income)	Conservatively estimate and plan for such income; monitor income projections and tax policy
Part B: Risks Discussed in Risk Management and Insurance Chapters		
Qualitative factors including changes in lifestyle, employment, and major assets	Unexpected cost increases due to changes in personal situation; losses due to perils	Plan conservatively to provide for the unexpected; property and liability insurance

CAPITAL NEEDS ANALYSIS

Capital needs analysis

The process of calculating the amount of investment capital needed at retirement to maintain the desired lifestyle and mitigate the impact of inflation during the retirement years

Capital needs analysis is the process of calculating the amount of investment capital needed at retirement to maintain the desired lifestyle and mitigate the impact of inflation during the retirement years. There are three commonly used models for analyzing capital needs: the pure annuity model, the capital preservation model, and the purchasing power preservation model.

Basic Planning—Pure Annuity Model

The following steps are used to determine the capital necessary at the beginning of retirement to fund the retirement period:

Step 1 Calculate WRR. Determine the wage replacement ratio (WRR) today using one of the two methods identified earlier (top-down or budgeting).

Step 2 Determine gross dollar needs. Determine the wage replacement amount in today's dollars from Step 1.

Step 3 Determine net dollar needs. Reduce the result from Step 2 by any expected Social Security benefits in today's dollars or other benefits that are indexed to inflation.

Step 4 Calculate preretirement dollar needs adjusted for inflation. Inflate the result from Step 3 to the retirement age at the CPI rate to determine the first annual retirement payment.

Step 5 Calculate capital needed at retirement age. Calculate the present value at retirement of an annuity due (BEGin mode) for an annual payment equal to the result from Step 4 over the full retirement life expectancy (estimate life expectancy conservatively at 90–95) and use the inflation-adjusted earnings rate.

Step 6 Determine the amount to save during the work life expectancy. Discount the capital needed at retirement using the savings rate and investment earnings rate, being mindful as to whether the client is expected to save annually or more frequently, and whether the client is expected to save under an annuity due or an ordinary annuity scheme.

E X A M P L E   Mary Jones, age 41, currently earns $80,000. Her wage replacement ratio is determined to be 80%. She expects that inflation will average 3% for her entire life expectancy. She expects to earn 10% on her investments and retire at age 62, living possibly to age 90. She has sent for and received her Social Security benefit statement, which indicated that her Social Security retirement benefit in today's dollars adjusted for early retirement is $12,000 per year.

1. Calculate Mary's capital needed at retirement at age 62.

2. Calculate the amount she must save monthly, at month end, assuming she has no current savings to accumulate the capital needed for retirement at age 62.

3. Calculate the amount she must save monthly, at month end, assuming that she has $50,000 in current retirement savings.

    Calculate her capital needed at retirement at age 62.

Step 1	80% WRR		
Step 2	($80,000 × 0.80)	= $64,000	Total needs in today's dollars
Step 3		−12,000	Less Social Security in today's dollars
		$52,000	Annual amount needed in today's dollars
Step 4	n	= 21 (62 − 41)	
	i	= 3 (inflation rate)	
	PV	= $52,000 (Step 3)	
	PMT	= 0	
	FV	= $96,735.32 (Step 4) First-year needs for retirement	
Step 5	n	= 28 (90 − 62)	
	i	= 6.7961 {[(1 + earnings rate) ÷ (1 + inflation rate)] − 1} × 100 [(1.10 ÷ 1.03) − 1] × 100	
	FV	= 0	
	PMT$_{AD}$	= $96,735.32 (from Step 4)	
	PV$_{AD@62}$	= $1,278,954.46 (Step 5 – amount needed at age 62)	

Calculate the amount she must save monthly, at month end, assuming she has no current savings to accumulate the capital needed for retirement at age 62.

FV$_{@62}$	= $1,278,954.46 (from Step 5)
n	= 252 (21 years × 12 months)
i	= 0.8333 (10 ÷ 12) I/YR is 10%
PV	= 0
PMT$_{OA}$	= $1,502.09 (monthly savings necessary)

Calculate the amount she must save monthly, at month end, assuming she has $50,000 in current retirement savings.

$FV_{@62}$	= $1,278,954.46
n	= 252
i	= 0.8333
PV	= –$50,000
PMT_{OA}	= $1,026.70 (monthly savings necessary)

Accurate Assumptions Are Essential

Assumptions are made for the wage replacement ratio, the work life expectancy, the retirement life expectancy, inflation, investment earnings, Social Security, and any other benefits. If these assumptions are inaccurate, the projection using those assumptions will be flawed. The wage replacement ratio should be carefully calculated, especially for a client near retirement. Estimating life expectancy usually begins with the IRS tables and is conservatively estimated at 90–95, owing to the risk of outliving retirement money. Where family history indicates a particularly long life expectancy, that age could be increased. The estimate of the work life expectancy is critical, as one less year of work means one less year of retirement savings and account growth. It also means one more year of retirement withdrawals. Conversely, working one additional year or so may make an otherwise unworkable retirement plan work quite nicely because of the additional year of savings, the additional year of earnings accumulation, and one less year of consumption.

The assumptions regarding inflation and earnings rates are obviously essential ingredients in capital needs analysis. Historical data are available for inflation; however, inflation is difficult to predict. Perhaps the best estimate is the inflation rate from the most recent three to five years. Investment earnings rates are dependent on the client's asset allocation and the markets but can be estimated for a well-diversified portfolio over a long period. Conservatively estimating inflation (increase it a bit) and earnings (decrease a bit) is wise in retirement planning. Such estimation provides a little conservatism in case one or more of the assumptions are not realized. Social Security benefits and pension benefits that are inflation protected should be carefully determined and documented. The retirement plan and capital needs analysis can be adjusted on an annual basis as information becomes more certain.

As one might expect, small changes in earnings, life expectancy, and needs may have a dramatic impact on the retirement plan. The uncertainty of these assumptions can be accommodated in some of the latest retirement planning software packages that incorporate Monte Carlo analysis (MCA). MCA uses a random-number generator for data input into a software package that will provide an output with specific probabilities of outcomes. MCA provides insight into the most likely outcome, but with other possible outcomes. This analysis provides the financial planner with a best-case scenario and a worst-case scenario with which to make decisions.

Advanced Planning—Capital Preservation (CP) Model

Pure annuity model
The basic capital needs analysis approach that is generally prepared on a pretax basis

The basic capital needs analysis is a **pure annuity model**, generally prepared on a pretax basis. The annuity concept means that if all of the assumptions occur exactly as expected, the person will die exactly at the assumed life expectancy with a retirement account balance of zero. There is a substantial risk that many clients could outlive their assets using this annuity approach. Therefore, they will actually need more money at retirement. Two models used to mitigate the risk of outliving money are the capital pres-

Capital preservation (CP) model

This model maintains the original balance needed at retirement under the pure annuity model for the entire retirement life expectancy.

ervation model and the purchasing power preservation model. The **capital preservation model** maintains the original balance needed at retirement under the pure annuity model for the entire retirement life expectancy. The purchasing power preservation model maintains the purchasing power of the original pure annuity capital balance at retirement for the entire retirement life expectancy. In spite of any conservatism that we may have built into the annuity model with our assumptions, it is always possible that one or more of our assumptions will be unrealized. To mitigate the risk of the assumptions being overly optimistic, we can make use of a capital preservation model or a purchasing power preservation model rather than a simple annuity model to determine capital needs. These two additional models help to overcome the risks of the pure annuity model (primarily, the risk of running out of money, or superannuation).

Recall that the capital amount needed under the pure annuity model for Mary Jones at age 62 calculated was $1,278,954.46. If we discount that amount at the expected earnings rate of 10%, we can then determine the additional amount of capital necessary to leave an estate of $1,278,954.46 at the projected life expectancy.

$$n = 28$$

$$i = 10$$

$$FV_{@90} = \$1,278,954.46 \text{ (amount at life expectancy)}$$

$$PV_{@62} = \$88,686.99$$

$$1,367,641.45 = 88,686.99 + 1,278,954.46 \text{ (amount needed for capital preservation model)}$$

Thus, the capital preservation model will require $88,686.99 more at retirement than the pure annuity model, but it will reduce the risk of superannuation. Such an increase in capital will also require that savings be increased in Exhibit 15.16 that presents parts B and C of the Mary Jones example.

EXHIBIT 15.16 Comparison of the Capital Preservation Model with the Annuity Model (Mary Jones)

	CP Model		Annuity Model	
	No savings	Savings	No savings	Savings
	B	C	B	C
$FV_{@62}$	$1,367,641.45	$1,367,641.45	$1,278,954.46	$1,278,954.46
n	252	252	252	252
i	0.8333	0.8333	0.8333	0.8333
PV	0	−$50,000	0	−$50,000
PMT_{OA}	$1,606.25	$1,130.86	$1,502.09	$1,026.70

Even though the capital preservation model would increase the savings need of Mary Jones by about $100 per month, it would diminish many of the risks in the traditional capital needs annuity approach.

Advanced Planning—Purchasing Power Preservation (PPP) Model

Purchasing power preservation (PPP) model

A capital needs analysis method that assumes the client will have a capital balance of equal purchasing power at life expectancy as he did at retirement

An even more conservative approach to capital needs analysis is the **purchasing power preservation model**.

The calculation steps under the purchasing power preservation model are essentially the same as the steps in the capital preservation model, with the exception that an inflation-adjusted interest rate is used.

$n = 28$

$i = 6.7961$

$FV = 1,278,954.46$

$PMT = \$96,735.32$ (amount needed the first year of retirement)

$PV_{AD@62} = \$1,481,866.64$ (capital needed for purchasing power preservation model)

The additional accumulation at retirement using a purchasing power model is $202,912.18 greater than the pure annuity approach.

The amounts in B and C in the exhibit would change.

EXHIBIT 15.17 Comparison of the Purchasing Power Preservation Model with the Annuity Model (Mary Jones)

	PPP model		Annuity model	
	No savings	Savings	No savings	Savings
	B	C	B	C
$FV_{@62}$	$1,481,866.64	$1,481,866.64	$1,278,954.46	$1,278,954.46
n	252	252	252	252
i	0.8333	0.8333	0.8333	0.8333
PV	0	−$50,000	0	−$50,000
PMT_{OA}	$1,740.41	$1,265.02	$1,502.09	$1,026.70

EXHIBIT 15.18 Capital Needs Analysis Summary for Mary Jones

	Annuity model	CP model	PPP model
Capital needed at retirement (A)	$1,278,954.46	$1,367,641.45	$1,481,866.64
Monthly savings with no initial balance (B)	$1,502.09	$1,606.25	$1,740.41
Monthly savings with $50,000 initial balance (C)	$1,026.70	$1,130.86	$1,265.02

There are other methods of alleviating risk in projections, including sensitivity analysis, that are beyond the scope of this text, most of which would be covered in a full semester course on retirement planning.

WHERE ON THE WEB

AARP (formerly American Association of Retired Persons) **www.aarp.org**

American Society on Aging **www.asaging.org**

International Foundation for Retirement Education **www.infre.org**

MSN.money: Retirement and Wills
www.moneycentral.msn.com/retire/home.asp

National Council on Aging **www.ncoa.org**

Senior Law Homepage **www.seniorlaw.com**

Social Security Online **www.ssa.gov**

The Retire Early Homepage **www.retireearlyhomepage.com**

U.S. Administration on Aging **www.aoa.gov**

U.S. Census Bureau **www.census.gov**

DISCUSSION QUESTIONS

1. What is the U.S. savings rate?

2. List the steps necessary to calculate capital needs analysis.

3. What is the difference between capital needs analysis prepared on an annuity basis and capital needs analysis prepared using a capital preservation model? A purchasing power preservation model?

4. What are the four sources of retirement income?

5. What are the two methods for determining the wage replacement ratio?

6. Which method for determining the wage replacement ratio is appropriate for a client who is 50 years old? Why?

7. How is financial security defined?

8. List the financial factors that affect retirement planning.

9. Should retirement planning (capital needs analysis) be prepared on a pretax basis or an after-tax basis? Why?

10. What percentage of retirement income is provided by Social Security for the average retiree?

11. Does Social Security favor lower-wage or higher-wage individuals in terms of retirement benefits and wage replacement? How and why?

12. What is one of the main goals for many individuals regarding personal financial planning?

13. When is financial security realized?

14. What is the WLE?

15. What is the RWLE?

16. How has life expectancy changed over the past century?

17. How and why does the timing of savings affect the ultimate amount of accumulation?

18. How does inflation affect retirement planning?

19. What adjustments are normally made to the preretirement budget to arrive at the retirement budget?

20. What is the wage replacement ratio?

21. Does the wage replacement ratio remain constant over the retirement life expectancy?

22. What wage replacement ratio does Social Security provide for a worker with $20,000 income?

23. What is capital needs analysis?

24. What advanced models are used to perform capital needs analysis?

EXERCISES

1. Donna, age 45, is self-employed and earns $70,000 annually. She is fairly settled in her lifestyle. She currently saves 15% of her gross income. Her mortgage payment (principal and interest) is fixed at $1,166.67 per month. She has scheduled her mortgage payments to cease at retirement. On the basis of the information given, what do you expect Donna's wage replacement ratio to be?

2. Kim, age 30, begins saving $2,500 per year at year-end, continues for 8 years, and then stops saving. Joy, age 40, begins saving $2,500 per year at year-end and saves continuously until age 65. Assume that both Kim and Joy earn a 12% return compounded annually. Calculate the total amount of savings and the accumulated balance for Kim and Joy, respectively, at age 65. Explain the difference.

Use the following information for Exercises 3–10:

Mike, age 48, has $60,000 saved for retirement. He is currently saving 10% of his annual income of $50,000 on a monthly basis. His employer matches his savings contributions with $1,500 annually, paid on a monthly basis. Mike projects that inflation will be 3.5%, and he can earn 9.5% before and during retirement. Mike needs a wage replacement ratio of 75% of his preretirement income. He plans to retire at age 62 with Social Security benefits of $10,000 in today's dollars. His life expectancy is age 90.

3. How much will Mike's salary be at age 62, assuming his income increases yearly equal to the inflation rate?

4. How much are the Social Security benefits expected to be at age 62?

5. What will be Mike's retirement income need in the first year of retirement, taking into consideration his anticipated Social Security income?

6. How much capital will Mike need at age 62 to fund his retirement?

7. How much will Mike have at age 62, assuming he continues his current savings and investment program?

8. How much additional monthly savings would be required for Mike to retire at age 62?

9. After reflection, Mike wants to know at what age he can retire, assuming he continues to follow his current savings plan. Make a schedule for years 62, 64, and 66 so Mike can make some informed decisions.

10. You remind Mike that if he waits until age 66 to retire, he will receive $14,344 in Social Security benefits in today's dollars rather than the reduced benefit of $10,000 he would receive at age 62. Would this additional cash flow suggest that he could retire at age 66, or perhaps earlier?

11. Marion, age 65, is a pensioner who receives a fixed pension of $17,500 for life from her employer's pension plan. Marion also receives $12,000 currently from Social Security. Marion is concerned about how inflation will affect her rent, food, and other expenses. She estimates that inflation will be 3% per year for the next 10 years. What loss of purchasing power will she have in today's dollars in 10 years?

12. George, a financial planner, has determined that Dennis, his client, needs $2 million at age 66 to retire by using an annuity model based on a retirement income of $150,337.75 per year for 24 years to age 90. If the earnings rate was 10% and the inflation rate was 3%, what additional amount would be needed at age 66 to provide a capital preservation model solution?

13. Referring to Exercise 12, what additional amount would Dennis need at age 66 to fund a purchasing power presentation model?

PROBLEMS

Bill, age 45, wants to retire at age 60. He currently earns $60,000 per year. His goal is to replace 80% of his preretirement income. He wants the retirement income to be adjusted for inflation. Bill has an investment portfolio valued at $150,000, which is currently earning 10% average annual returns. Bill expects inflation to average 3% and, based on his family health, predicts he will live to age 90. Bill is currently saving 7% of his gross income at each year-end and expects to continue this level of savings. Bill wants to ignore any Social Security benefits for purposes of retirement planning.

1. What will Bill's annual income needs be at age 60?

2. Will the need be for an ordinary annuity or an annuity due?

3. How much total capital will Bill need at age 60?

4. How much capital will Bill have at age 60?

5. Will Bill have enough income at retirement?

6. What is the earliest age that Bill could retire utilizing the current savings and investment plan?

7. How much would Bill need to increase his savings on an annual basis to meet his goal of retiring at age 60?

8. Even assuming that Bill increases his savings to an appropriate amount, what are the risks that may affect the success of the plan?

9. How could the capital needs analysis be modified to reduce the risks identified above?

Basic Retirement Plans

LEARNING OBJECTIVES

After learning the material in this chapter, you will be able to do the following:

- Describe a qualified retirement plan

- Identify and articulate the characteristics of qualified retirement plans

- Describe some disadvantages of qualified retirement plans

- Define vesting and list two accepted vesting schedules

- Identify the reasons for the creation of qualified retirement plans

- Calculate and determine the benefits of tax deferral in a qualified retirement plan

- Identify the various types of qualified retirement plans

- Distinguish between pension and profit-sharing plans

- Distinguish between defined benefit plans and defined contribution plans

- Distinguish between noncontributory and contributory plans

- Describe the operations and benefits of a Section 401(k) plan

- Distinguish between Keogh and corporate plans

- Identify other tax-advantaged retirement plans

- Describe IRAs, SEPs, SIMPLEs, and Section 403(b) plans

- Describe distributions from qualified retirement plans and other tax-advantaged retirement plans

- Describe and identify nonqualified plans

- Clarify why nonqualified plans are useful to employers

RETIREMENT PLANS

In the previous retirement chapter, we discussed the four general sources of funding used to provide retirement income: Social Security, private retirement plans, personal savings, and earned income from employment. We determined that the retirement benefits from Social Security alone provided a poor wage replacement ratio during retirement except for those beneficiaries who are the lowest wage earners. This chapter provides an introduction to private retirement plans, including qualified retirement plans, other tax-advantaged retirement plans, and nonqualified plans. Exhibit 16.1 illustrates the various types of retirement plans.

EXHIBIT 16.1 Retirement Plans

Qualified Plans		Tax-Advantaged Plans	Nonqualified Plans
Pension Plans	**Profit-Sharing Plans**		
Traditional defined benefit pension	Profit-sharing plans	SEPs	Nonqualified deferred compensation plans
Cash balance pension plans	Stock bonus plans	IRAs (including Roth)	Nonqualified stock option plans
Money purchase pension plans	ESOPs	Section 403(b) plans (including Roth)	Incentive stock option plans
Target benefit pension plans	Section 401(k) plans	SIMPLE (IRA)	Phantom stock plans
DB(k) plans	Thrift plans	SIMPLE 401(k)	Restricted stock
	SIMPLE 401(k)	Roth 401(k)	Employee stock purchase plans (ESPP)
	Age-based, profit-sharing plans		Junior class shares
			Stock appreciation rights (SARs)
			Section 457 plans

QUALIFIED RETIREMENT PLANS

Qualified retirement plans are sponsored by either a self-employed individual or another employer. The word qualified means the plan meets Internal Revenue Service requirements. To encourage retirement savings, Congress has created or approved various types of qualified plans that provide tax advantages for the employer who sponsors the plan and the employees who participate in the plan.

Exhibit 16.2 summarizes the advantages and disadvantages of qualified plans.

EXHIBIT 16.2 Advantages and Disadvantages of Qualified Retirement Plans

Advantages/Rules	Disadvantages	Limits
■ Employer contributions are deductible	■ Costs	**Covered Compensation**
■ Employer contributions are not subject to payroll taxes	■ Limits	$285,000 (2020)
	■ Min. participation reqs.	**Defined Benefit**
■ Employee contributions are pretax (except Roth and thrift)		$230,000 (2020)
	■ Min. vesting reqs.	**Defined Contribution**
■ Earnings are tax deferred	■ Top-heavy rules	Lesser of 100% comp. or $57,000 (2020)
■ 10-year forward averaging or pre-1974 capital gains treatment	■ Minimum contribution rules	**Salary Deferral***
■ ERISA protection	■ Reporting reqs.	$19,500 (2020)
■ Net unrealized appreciation	■ Disclosure reqs.	Sections 401(k), 403(b), 457, and SARSEP
	■ Nondiscrimination reqs.	
	■ Highly compensated limits	*Before catch-up contribution
	■ Minimum coverage reqs.	
	■ Testing reqs.	**Testing**
	■ Key employee limits	50/40 Coverage Test—DB Plans
	■ Employee contributions and salary deferrals are subject to payroll taxes	Ratio % Test
		Average Benefit % Test
		Section 401(k) ACP
		Section 401(k) ADP

Characteristics of Qualified Retirement Plans

Employer Contributions Are NOT Subject to Federal Income Tax

Unlike most business transactions that result in an income tax deduction for one party and taxable income for another party, contributions made to qualified retirement plans result in a mismatch of income and deductions. Employer contributions to a qualified plan are deductible by the employer for income tax purposes for the year in which they were made, but they are not included in current employee taxable income until distributed to the employee. This favorable tax treatment is a major advantage for both employers and employees. Employers receive a current deduction for the contribution, whereas employees receive deferral of income. Because of this favorable tax treatment, however, qualified retirement plans must satisfy numerous nondiscrimination requirements to ensure a certain percentage of the nonhighly compensated employees are benefiting from the plan.

Employer Contributions Are NOT Subject to Payroll Tax

Another major advantage of contributions to qualified retirement plans is that employer contributions are not subject to payroll tax. This means compensation in the form of qualified retirement plan contributions will avoid the expense for the Federal Insurance Contributions Act (FICA). Such avoidance benefits both the employer and the employee because both parties are required to pay this tax. If the same amount of money contributed to a qualified retirement plan is paid as employee compensation, then both the employer and the employee would be required to pay FICA taxes.

Employee Pretax Contributions Are NOT Subject to Federal Income Tax

Similar to employer contributions, employee contributions to qualified retirement plans generally are not includable in the employee's current taxable income. Therefore, employees can save a portion of their income on a pretax basis. Income contributed to a qualified retirement plan will avoid federal and, in most cases, state income taxes at the time of deferral to a qualified retirement plan. An example of a qualified retirement plan that allows these pretax employee contributions is the Section 401(k) plan. There are certain other qualified retirement plans that provide for employee after-tax contributions, such as thrift plans, Roth 401(k) plans, and certain defined benefit plans.

Employee Contributions ARE Subject to Payroll Tax

Unlike the payroll tax treatment of employer contributions, employee contributions to qualified retirement plans generally are subject to payroll tax. Therefore, contributions made by employees will be subject to FICA taxes for both the employer and the employee. This is why an employee's Form W-2 may have different income amounts for federal income tax and Social Security purposes.

EXHIBIT 16.3 Form W-2

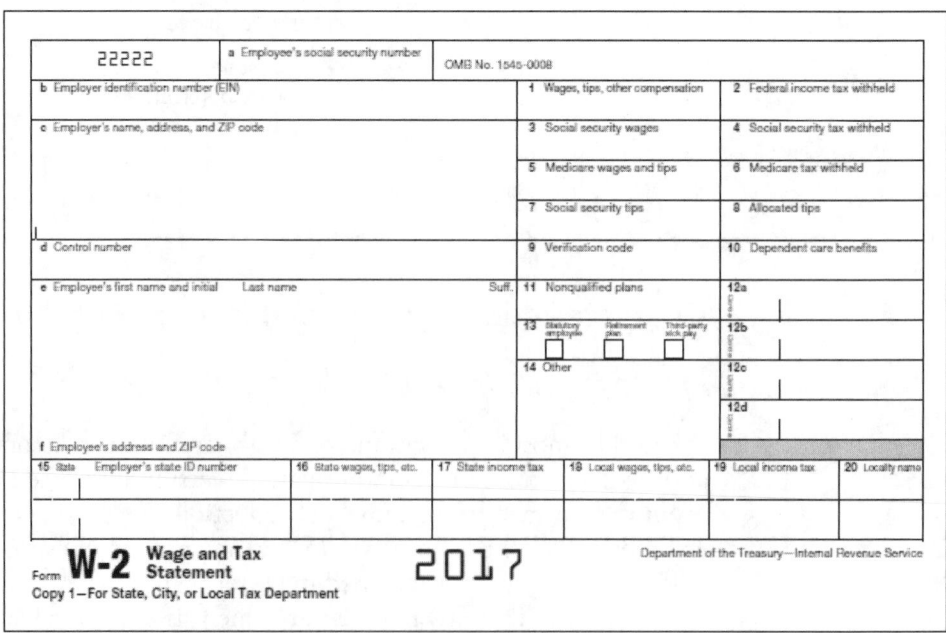

Tax-Deferred Growth

Assets that are contributed to a qualified retirement plan are held in trust for the benefit of the participants or their beneficiaries. Qualified retirement plan trusts are tax-exempt entities; therefore, the earnings accruing from contributions from both employers and employees grow income tax deferred until distributed. The tax-deferred growth of both contributions and earnings is a significant benefit provided by qualified retirement plans.

Special Income Tax Averaging

There is a provision for special 10-year-forward income tax averaging on lump-sum distributions made from qualified retirement plans. This provision may reduce the federal income tax liability for taxpayers taking a full and complete distribution from a qualified retirement plan. Only those taxpayers who were born before January 2, 1936, however, are eligible for this special provision.

In addition to receiving special income tax averaging, taxpayers born before January 2, 1936, may also be eligible to receive capital gains treatment on a portion of their lump-sum distribution. The portion of a distribution that may receive capital gains treatment is that which is attributable to participation in the qualified plan before 1974. Because of this qualifying date, fewer clients will qualify for this special tax treatment each year.

Net Unrealized Appreciation

In general, distributions from qualified retirement plans are made in cash and are taxable as ordinary income. There is an exception, however, for lump-sum distributions of employer securities (generally stock) that have appreciated while being held in a qualified retirement plan. When such securities are distributed (typically in the form of a lump-sum distribution) from a qualified retirement plan, the appreciation above the cost basis, called net unrealized appreciation (NUA), is not subject to income tax upon distribution. In addition, the net unrealized appreciation will be taxed as a capital gain (not as ordinary income), when the securities are subsequently sold. With the large disparity between ordinary income tax rates and capital gains tax rates, this exception provides significant benefits to taxpayers who receive qualifying distributions of employer securities. However, this special treatment is not available for distributions from individual retirement accounts (IRAs). Therefore, a rollover of otherwise qualifying securities from a qualified retirement plan to an IRA will eliminate this potential benefit. It is important to note, however, that the cost basis in these shares (the value of the shares at the time of contribution to the plan) is taxed as ordinary income at the time of the lump-sum distribution.

ERISA Protection

Assets held in a qualified retirement plan are protected from creditors by the Employee Retirement Income Security Act (ERISA). ERISA prohibits the alienation of benefits, which means that the benefits of the qualified retirement plan may be used only by the participant or by the participant's family members. Therefore, even those unfortunate individuals who are forced into bankruptcy have protection for their qualified retirement plan assets. In 2005, the Bankruptcy Abuse Prevention and Consumer Protection Act (BAPCPA) created protection for up to $1 million (indexed) for contributory IRAs and unlimited protection for eligible IRA rollovers.

Small Business Tax Credit

America has a huge problem. About 40% of American workers are employed by firms that do not offer a retirement plan for their workers. To help alleviate this problem, the law offers an income tax credit to small employers to encourage them to start offering a retirement plan. The previous law was updated in 2020 by the SECURE Act. Now the employer's tax credit for retirement plan start-up costs is the lesser of 50% of the qualified plan start-up costs or the greater of $500 or $250 times the number of nonhighly compensated employees eligible to participate in the plan.

Retirement Plans as Part of a Compensation Package

From the perspective of the employees in the labor market, many qualified retirement plans essentially have become part of their overall compensation package. The employee recognizes the need for retirement savings and typically accepts an overall compensation package as salary, retirement plan, and other employee fringe benefits, rather than just salary.

This does not suggest that the employee chooses the qualified retirement plan. The employer chooses the type of qualified retirement plan, and it usually becomes part of an overall compensation package offered to current and future employees. The employees then evaluate the complete compensation package, given their personal goals and opportunity costs, to make appropriate employment decisions. Today, employees are aware of the benefits of using a qualified retirement plan's taxable income deferral as an alternative to receiving additional current compensation, which would be currently subject to income tax.

In the late 1990s, many employees chose to work for companies that provided minimal salaries but offered employee stock options. Employees recognized these high-tech companies as having tremendous growth potential. Employees were willing to sacrifice current income in hopes that their employer's stock would appreciate significantly enough to compensate them for their current sacrifice of higher salaries elsewhere.

Microsoft is a good example of this phenomenon. Base salaries were small, but the right to participate in the ownership of the company was tremendously enticing to potential employees. As it turns out, many of these employees became quite wealthy because of their stock options and other fringe benefits.

Disadvantages of Qualified Retirement Plans

Qualified retirement plans were created by Congress to provide incentives for employers to sponsor and promote retirement savings. Congress has known for some time that Social Security would not provide an adequate wage replacement for many workers. However, whenever Congress creates a plan that proffers income tax relief or tax advantage, there are usually costs, limitations, or disadvantages to the successful implementation of such a plan. Some of these disadvantages are discussed next.

Costs to Qualify the Plan

To establish a qualified retirement plan, employers must have a legal plan document drafted by a pension attorney or one preapproved by the IRS (a prototype plan). The plan document sets forth the rules for administration of the plan, provides for how benefits are earned and allocated to employees, and names the classes of employees that will benefit under the plan. Generally, there are attorney costs to having a plan document drafted. A determination letter is often obtained from the Internal Revenue Service (IRS) to ensure that the plan meets the requirements of Internal Revenue Code (IRC) Section 401(a).

The determination letter assures the plan sponsor that the plan meets the requirements to be a qualified retirement plan. EGTRRA 2001 allows some small employers to receive determination letters without paying a fee.

Many financial institutions have prototype plans available to their clients. Prototype plans are qualified retirement plan documents that have already been approved by the IRS as meeting the requirements of IRC Section 401(a). These prototype plans usually allow only a few options for the client to select regarding the plan's operation. These options are selected by the client on an adoption agreement. The remainder of the document is a standard form. Prototype plans are inexpensive to establish and are preapproved by the IRS.

Costs to Fund the Plan

To meet qualification requirements, qualified retirement plans must be funded on a regular basis. Pension plans must be funded at least annually, whereas contributions to profit-sharing plans must be only substantial and recurring and are not mandatory each year. Employer-deductible plan contributions may be as much as 25% of covered payroll for defined contribution plans and even higher for defined benefit plans. During years of poor earnings, funding a qualified plan can be a substantial drain on a company's cash flow.

Costs of Administering the Plan

Qualified retirement plans require ongoing administration and maintenance. Information compliance tax returns (such as IRS Form 5500) must be filed with the IRS annually. Allocation of contributions to employees' accounts, or determination of accrued benefits, also must be completed at least annually for most plans. Other administrative duties include annual testing to comply with IRS regulations and amending the plan document for tax law changes. In addition to performing administrative duties, the plan sponsor must retain and supervise an investment adviser to ensure that plan assets are managed for the sole benefit of participants and their beneficiaries. Defined benefit plans require the services of an actuary each year. The plan sponsor may outsource each of these tasks to a third-party administrator or other provider.

Annual Compensation Limit

The Internal Revenue Code limits the amount of compensation that can be considered for purposes of funding qualified retirement plans. This compensation limit, although indexed, was an attempt to limit the contribution to highly compensated employees and increase the contributions to nonhighly compensated employees. Exhibit 16.4 illustrates the annual compensation limits for the years from 1993 to 2020.

EXHIBIT 16.4 Annual Compensation Limit (1993–2020)

Year	Compensation Limit	Year	Compensation Limit
1993	$235,850	2007	$225,000
1994	$150,000	2008	$230,000
1995	$150,000	2009	$245,000
1996	$150,000	2010	$245,000
1997	$160,000	2011	$245,000
1998	$160,000	2012	$250,000
1999	$160,000	2013	$255,000
2000	$170,000	2014	$260,000
2001	$170,000	2015	$265,000
2002	$200,000	2016	$265,000
2003	$200,000	2017	$270,000
2004	$205,000	2018	$275,000
2005	$210,000	2019	$280,000
2006	$220,000	2020	$285,000

For 2020, up to $285,000 of compensation can be considered for purposes of funding a qualified plan on behalf of a participant. Any income earned above this limit is disregarded. The compensation limit is indexed annually to the CPI in $5,000 increments. When an employer wants to provide benefits on earnings above the annual limit, it is generally done in the form of deferred compensation, which does not have the same tax benefits as qualified plans.

Eligibility Requirements

Minimal standards need to be met by an employee in order to be eligible to participate in a qualified retirement plan provided by an employer. Generally, all employees who are at least age 21 and have one year of service (defined as 1,000 hours within a 12-month period) are considered eligible for the plan. As the number of eligible employees for the plan increases, so does the number that must benefit under the plan for the plan to remain qualified. Obviously, an increase in the number of employees under the plan increases the cost of the plan. Union employees, who are covered by a separate collective bargaining agreement, are not required to be covered by their employer's qualified retirement plan. The reason for the exception of union employees is that these individuals generally have retirement benefits provided by the union, and employers generally are required to contribute to these union plans.

Coverage Requirements for Employees

A qualified retirement plan must benefit a broad range of employees, not just the highly compensated. Although there are exceptions, in general, employers are required to cover 70% of the eligible nonhighly compensated employees. For defined benefit plans only, the employer also must cover 50 employees or 40% of those eligible, whichever is less. Coverage under the plan means that the employee is somehow benefiting, either from employer contributions or from the ability to defer employee taxable income in the plan [such as a Section 401(k) plan]. Highly compensated employees are defined as those employees who owned more than 5% of the company stock or had income above a certain limit in the previous year ($130,000 in 2020). An election also is available that allows only the top 20% of wage earners to be considered highly compensated. Nonhighly compensated employees are those employees who are not classified as highly compensated.

As long as the qualified retirement plan meets the coverage requirement, it is permitted to exclude certain groups of eligible employees from participating in the plan. For example, salaried employees or commissioned employees might be excluded from the plan as a class. These types of class exclusions may reduce the employer's contribution to the plan and reduce the overall cost of the plan. The plan must meet the basic coverage rules, however, and the class exclusions should be considered in the overall context of employee compensation and as a business decision.

Vesting Requirements

Vesting
An employee's nonforfeitable right to receive a present or future pension benefit

Vesting is the process by which employees accrue benefits in the form of ownership provided by an employer's contribution. In the context of qualified retirement plans, an employee is vested when he has ownership rights to the contributions (or benefits) provided by the employer. In general, employees vest over a specific period.

The two standard vesting schedules preapproved by the IRS are referred to as cliff and graduated vesting. The cliff vesting schedule requires an employee to complete a certain number of years of service such as three or five; the number depends on whether a defined benefit or defined contribution plan is being considered. In a defined benefit plan, for instance, after five years of service (one year of service defined as 1,000 hours within a 12-month period), the employee is fully or 100% vested, meaning that the employee has ownership rights to all previous employer contributions and any contributions made on his behalf in the future. Graduated vesting allows employees to become partially vested over a period of years. In the case of three-to-seven-year graduated vesting for defined benefit plans, employees accrue ownership rights as shown in Exhibit 16.5.

EXHIBIT 16.5 Defined Benefit Vesting Schedules

Vesting Schedule (5-Year Cliff)			Vesting Schedule (3–7 Year Graduated)	
Years of Service	Portion Vested		Years of Service	Portion Vested
1	0%		1	0%
2	0%		2	0%
3	0%		3	20%
4	0%		4	40%
5	100%		5	60%
			6	80%
			7	100%

Graduated vesting allows those employees who worked for four years, for example, to leave the company with some benefit; whereas, under the five-year-cliff vesting schedule, such employees would receive nothing from the contributions made by the employer and nothing from the earnings on employer contributions. Contributions and the earnings on contributions made by the employee [such as with a Section 401(k) plan], however, are always 100% vested and remain the property of the employee.

The vesting schedule an employer selects could be more liberal than the prescribed vesting schedules under the Internal Revenue Code. For instance, instead of choosing a five-year-cliff vesting schedule, an employer may elect to have employees' accounts vest over four years at 25% each year. However, the employer may not select a vesting schedule that is more restrictive than the five-year-cliff or three-to-seven-year graduated methods for defined benefit plans.

Defined contribution plans, employer-matching contributions, and top-heavy defined benefit plans are required to vest at least as quickly as a three-year-cliff or two-to-six-year graduated vesting schedule (see Exhibit 16.6).

EXHIBIT 16.6 Vesting for Defined Contribution Plans, Matching Contributions, and Top-Heavy Defined Benefit Plans

Vesting Schedule (3-Year Cliff)		Vesting Schedule (2–6 Year Graduated)	
Years of Service	Portion Vested	Years of Service	Portion Vested
1	0%	1	0%
2	0%	2	20%
3	100%	3	40%
4	100%	4	60%
5	100%	5	80%
6	100%	6	100%

Top-Heavy Plans

Under IRC Section 416(g), defined benefit retirement plans are considered top heavy if more than 60% of the benefits are attributable to a group of owners and officers called key employees. If a plan is top heavy, there are two consequences. First, the standard vesting schedules are required to be shortened (cliff vesting to three years and graduated using a two-to-six-year schedule) such that benefits vest more quickly for the nonkey employee group. Second, there are certain minimum contributions that must be provided to the nonkey employees on the basis of the benefits accrued or contributions made for the key employees. The top-heavy rules ensure that a defined benefit retirement plan actually benefits the rank-and-file employees of the company, not just owners and officers. The Pension Protection Act of 2006 requires that all employer contributions to a defined contribution plan vest at least as quickly as one of the two accelerated vesting schedules. Again, an employer may use a schedule that vests more quickly than the accelerated schedules.

Disclosure Requirements

The employer is required to provide a summary of the details of the qualified retirement plan to employees, participants, and beneficiaries under pay status. The employer also is required to provide to the plan participants notices of any plan amendments or changes. These documents help to inform the employee of his rights under ERISA and of the rights of the qualified retirement plan.

Annual Testing of Qualified Retirement Plans

As described previously, many recurring requirements must be met to maintain a qualified retirement plan. Therefore, annual testing is necessary to ensure that the plan continues to meet each of these requirements.

BENEFITS OF TAX DEFERRAL

For an employee who participates in a qualified retirement plan, tax deferral is perhaps the biggest benefit. Neither the contributions to the plan nor the earnings on these contributions are currently subject to income tax. The expectation is that in retirement, when distributions begin, the plan participant will be in a lower income tax bracket than during the working years.

E X A M P L E   A client's employer will either pay the client $1,000 that is subject to payroll and income tax (see A), or contribute $1,000 to a qualified retirement plan (see B) on his behalf. The client would save the net received from A and earn 12% per year for 40 years. The contribution made to the qualified retirement plan (B) is made by the employer.

	A		B	
	Not Tax-Advantaged		Qualified Plan	
Deposit	$1,000.00		$1,000.00	
Less	76.50	Payroll tax	0.00	Payroll tax
Less	240.00	24% assumed income tax rate	0.00	Tax rate
Net deposited	$ 683.50		$1,000.00	
PV	$ 683.50		$1,000.00	
i	9.12%	(12% × 0.76) (24% income tax rate)	12%	
n	40 years		40 years	
FV	$22,243.31		$93,050.97	
Net of tax	$22,243.31		$70,718.74	(24% tax bracket)

The above example (A) assumes that the 12% earnings is subject to income tax each year, thus the use of the 9.12 earnings rate $(1 - \text{tax rate})(ER) = [(1 - 0.24) \times 12] = 9.12\%$. However, even if we assumed a portfolio of non-dividend-paying stocks that were only subject to capital gains rates of 15% at the end of 40 years, the advantage would still be to the qualified retirement plan.

	A	B
	Not Tax-Advantaged	Qualified Plan
Deposit	$683.50	$1,000.00
PV	$683.50	$1,000.00
n	40	40
i	12%	12%
FV	$63,600.34	$93,050.97
Tax rate	15% on capital gains ($63,600.34 – $683.50)	24% on ordinary income
Net after tax	$63,600.34 ($63,600.34 – $9,437.53 capital gains tax)	$70,718.74 [FV × (1 – 0.24)]

The difference between A and B in both examples is partially due to the payroll tax, which was not applicable to the qualified retirement plan, and partially due to the current income tax on the non-tax-advantaged fund (A).

TYPES OF QUALIFIED RETIREMENT PLANS

Qualified retirement plans may be classified as:

- pension or profit-sharing plans;
- defined benefit plans, defined contribution plans, target/age-weighted (hybrid) plans;
- contributory or noncontributory plans; and
- corporate or Keogh plans.

Exhibit 16.7 identifies 11 common types of qualified retirement plans.

EXHIBIT 16.7 Qualified Retirement Plans

Type	Pension Plans		Profit-Sharing Plans
Defined benefit plans	(1)	Traditional defined benefit pension plan	None
	(2)	Cash balance pension plan	
Defined contribution plans	(1)	Target benefit pension plan	(1) Profit-sharing plan
	(2)	Money purchase pension plan	(2) Section 401(k) plan
			(3) Thrift plan
			(4) Stock bonus plan
			(5) Employee stock ownership plan
			(6) Age-based profit-sharing plan
			(7) New comparability plan

Pension Plans

Pension plan
A qualified plan structured to provide a regularly paid, fixed sum at retirement

The legal requirement or "promise" of a **pension plan** is to either regularly pay a fixed sum of money at retirement (defined benefit pension plans) or to make a stated contribution to the pension plan (defined contribution pension plans). Because of this promise, pension plans have certain requirements and characteristics. Pension plans require mandatory funding. In general, this means that pension plans must be funded on an annual basis, regardless of whether the company has sufficient cash flow. The reason for annual funding is to ensure that sufficient assets will be available to fulfill the promise of a pension during retirement.

Pension plans are permitted to allow in-service withdrawals only to participants still employed with the company who are age 62 or over. An in-service withdrawal is an employee distribution while the employee is still in the active service of the employer. However, loans are not considered in-service withdrawals.

Pension plans are limited to investing no more than 10% of the qualified retirement plan assets in employer securities. To be consistent with the underlying promise of the pension plan, the investments of the qualified retirement plan should be reasonably diversified to limit the amount of risk undertaken by the portfolio.

There is a limit on contributions to defined contribution pension plans. An employer can contribute up to, and in some cases exceed, 25% of aggregate covered compensation. Contributions to defined benefit pension plans may exceed 25% of covered compensation if a higher amount is actuarially determined to assure the promised benefits. The term *covered compensation* describes the portion of payroll that may be considered for qualified retirement plan purposes. These high contribution limits provide ample opportunity for the employer to fulfill the promise of pension benefits.

There are four types of pension plans, as indicated in Exhibit 16.7. Each type of plan differs from the others in complexity and costs. The traditional defined benefit pension plan is the most complex and costly, requiring the annual services of an actuary. The money purchase pension plan is the least complex and least costly. A prototype plan for a money purchase pension plan is available from almost any financial institution. A target benefit pension plan is a special type of money purchase plan. Each pension plan has particular applications that make it a better choice than the others depending on the employer-sponsor's goals; the number of participants; and the census of participants, including length of service, age, and compensation levels. Cash balance pension plans are a special type of defined benefit pension plan and are beyond the scope of this text.

Small businesses tend to avoid pension plans because of the strict mandatory funding requirement. Small businesses prefer profit-sharing plans or other tax-advantaged retirement plans that permit more discretion over the funding of contributions.

Profit-Sharing Plans

Profit-sharing plan
A qualified defined contribution plan featuring a flexible (discretionary) employer-contribution provision. Profit-sharing plans are structured to offer employees participation in company profits that they may use for retirement purposes

A **profit-sharing plan** is a qualified defined contribution plan featuring a flexible (discretionary) employer contribution provision. The funding discretion is allowed regardless of cash flows or profits. An employer is permitted to fund a profit-sharing plan (including stock bonus plans) in any amount up to 25% of aggregate covered employee compensation.

The legal promise of a profit-sharing plan is to defer taxes rather than provide retirement benefits. There is no particular time requirement for the deferral of taxes. The deferral period could be until retirement, or the plan may be designed to allow in-service withdrawals as early as after two years of participation. The plan document (the plan legal description) will dictate what is, or is not, permitted.

Stock bonus plan
A defined contribution profit-sharing plan in which all employer contributions are in the form of employer stock. Distributions to participants can be made in the form of employer stock.

Unlike the restriction of pension plans, profit-sharing plans do not have restrictions on the amount of employer securities that can be purchased within the plan. Profit-sharing plans are permitted to invest 100% of the qualified retirement plan assets in employer securities. **Stock bonus plans** and employee stock ownership plans (ESOPs) are examples of profit-sharing type plans that often invest entirely in employer securities.

There are seven different profit-sharing plans, as shown in Exhibit 16.7. Each one has a particular application depending on costs; complexity; sponsor goals; and the census of employees, including age, length of service, and compensation levels.

Section 401(k) profit-sharing plan
A defined contribution profit-sharing plan that gives participants the option of reducing their taxable salary and contributing the salary reduction on a tax-deferred basis to an individual account for retirement purposes

The most common type of profit-sharing plan is the **Section 401(k) profit-sharing plan**. This plan is the most popular self-reliant qualified retirement plan and gets its name after Section 401(k) of the Internal Revenue Code. The Section 401(k) plan permits an employee to save, on a pretax basis, $19,500 (indexed to inflation in $500 increments) in 2020, or a certain percentage of income per year. In some cases, that savings is matched, or partially matched, by the employer. Employer-matching contributions typically range from $0.50 to $1.00 per dollar contributed by the participant, often with an overall limit as to the maximum matching contribution by the employer. For example, the employer may match dollar for dollar on the first 6% of compensation deferred by the participant.

The advantage of this kind of plan to the employer is that the funding is heavily employee dependent and self-reliant. Advantages to the employee are the size of the pretax savings, any employer match, and the prospects for a substantial accumulation over the work life expectancy.

E X A M P L E   Assume Joe, age 25, participates in a Section 401(k) plan, and his annual salary is $50,000. Joe contributes 6% annually to his Section 401(k) plan, and the contribution is matched $0.50 per dollar by his employer. Joe intends to contribute the same amount each month for the next 40 years. Assume that Joe can earn 10% annually, compounded monthly, on his and his employer's contributions and balances. How much will Joe accumulate at age 65 assuming no increase in salary or in the amount of the monthly contribution?

$$PV = 0$$
$$n = 480 \ (40 \times 12) \text{ months}$$
$$i = 0.8333 \ (10 \div 12)$$
$$PMT_{OA} = \$375.00 \ [(50{,}000 \times 6\%) + (50{,}000 \times 3\%)] \div 12$$
$$FV_{@65} = \$2{,}371{,}529.84$$

The accumulation is substantial. Joe and his employer deposited only $180,000 ($375 × 12 × 40), and at age 65, Joe has accumulated $2,371,530. The assumed rate of return is excellent in the example, but Joe started saving early and reaped the benefits of a long period of compounding. In actual practice, we would hope and expect that as Joe's salary increased, he would maintain at least a 6% savings rate, as opposed to the $375 per month, thus increasing his contributions with each raise. Joe's contribution, as well as the employer match, would increase with each increase in salary, thus increasing the deposits and the accumulation at age 65.

The Section 401(k) plan has become one of the most popular and widely used qualified retirement plans. The plan is self-reliant and easily understood by employees and is popular with employers because it is relatively inexpensive, as employees provide most of the funding.

Section 401(k) plans [and Section 403(b) plans] may allow a participant to elect to have all or a portion of the participant's elective deferrals under the plan treated as Roth contributions. As with contributions to Roth IRAs, these participant-elective deferrals would be subject to current taxation (not tax deferred) but would be exempt from taxation when distributed if certain requirements were met. These after-tax contributions can accumulate in the Roth account on a tax-deferred basis. This addition to Section 401(k) plans may be one of the most beneficial enhancements of qualified plans that has been seen in many years.

Legislation created plans known as solo Section 401(k) plans or individual Section 401(k) plans. These plans cover only one participant (a businessowner) or only a businessowner and spouse.

Employee elective deferrals do not count against the plan limit for employer contributions. Also, plans allowing elective deferrals may allow for additional catch-up contributions for employees age 50 and older. In 2020, the maximum catch-up contribution is $6,500.

Exhibit 16.8 summarizes the major differences between pension plans and profit-sharing plans.

EXHIBIT 16.8 Major Differences Between Pension and Profit-Sharing Plans

Plan Features	Pension Plans	Profit-Sharing Plans
In-service withdrawals	Permitted for employees age 62 or older	Permitted after 2 years
Mandatory funding	Yes	No
Percentage of employer stock permitted in the plan	10%	100%
Employer contribution limit	25% of aggregate covered compensation (defined contribution plans)	25% of aggregate covered compensation

Defined Benefit and Defined Contribution Plans

Qualified retirement plans are characterized as either defined benefit or defined contribution plans. In a defined benefit plan, the contributions are actuarially determined to produce a certain future retirement benefit under a formula. The annual funding for a defined benefit plan depends on six factors: (1) the life expectancies of the participants, (2) the mortality experience in the employee group, (3) the earnings rate and expected earnings rate on plan assets, (4) the expected wage increases of employees, (5) the expected inflation rate associated with plan costs, and (6) the expected turnover rate of employees. An actuary makes an annual analysis of the six variables to determine the annual funding. Obviously, defined benefit plans are both costly and complex. There are two defined benefit plans, the traditional **defined benefit pension plan** and the cash-balance pension plan, as well as a hybrid plan called a DB(k), which combines a defined benefit plan with a Section 401(k) provision. Generally, large corporations use these where the costs of administration, including actuarial costs, can be spread over a large number of employee participants. Small businesses will occasionally make use of defined benefit plans, though typically in very limited situations. For instance, a highly paid older professional (such as a doctor or lawyer) with a few young, lower-income staff employees might be an excellent candidate for a defined benefit plan.

Defined benefit plan assets are invested and managed by the employer, as trustee, or by an outside trustee. Actuaries for defined benefit plans determine the annual funding necessary to assure payment of the future promised benefit to be paid at normal retirement age (frequently age 65). Contributions to defined benefit plans generally are provided by the employer only. Because the employer is responsible for meeting the benefit obligations, it bears the investment risk for the funding. If the performance of the fund assets is better than expected, contributions can be reduced. If investment returns are less than expected, however, the employer is required to make higher contributions than anticipated.

The benefits payable under a defined benefit plan commonly are paid as a lifetime annuity, although some plans provide a cash-out option at retirement. The older a person is when entering into the plan, the greater the funding requirements; therefore, defined benefit plans are said to favor older-age entrants and long-term employees.

There is some risk that the employer will be unable to sustain the payment of retirement benefits from a defined benefit plan, so sponsors of these plans generally are required to participate in the Pension Benefit Guarantee Corporation (PBGC) termination insurance program. The PBGC is a federal corporation created under ERISA that guarantees benefits to participants of defined benefit plans. Plan sponsors make premium payments to the PBGC based on the number of plan participants and the level of plan funding. The PBGC does not guarantee the full amount of benefits but only a set amount as limited by

Defined benefit pension plan

A retirement plan that specifies the benefits that each employee receives at retirement. Defined benefit plans actuarially determine the benefit to be paid at normal retirement age.

law ($69,750 in 2020). The PBGC does not guarantee benefits of defined contribution plans.

Defined contribution plans specify the annual employer current contribution (as opposed to an ultimate future benefit). The investment risk in a defined contribution plan is borne by the participant; therefore, the final benefit is not guaranteed and will be dependent on the participant's account balance.

There are two defined contribution pension plans and seven defined contribution profit-sharing plans. Usually, defined contribution plan funding is borne solely by the employer [except for the Section 401(k) plan and thrift plan], but the assets are maintained in each participant's individual account. The investment risk is borne by the participants, and the investment of the plan assets is often self-directed, meaning the plan participant chooses which investment option(s) to invest the participant's plan contributions (deferrals and employer contributions) from a menu of investment options offered by the plan. Defined contribution plans favor younger participants who have a longer compounding and accumulation period. Unlike defined benefit plans, defined contribution profit-sharing plans have no annual mandatory funding requirement. Thus, accumulations in these accounts are dependent on the contributions made and the earnings performance.

Exhibit 16.9 summarizes the characteristics and differences between defined benefit and defined contribution plans.

Defined contribution plan

A retirement plan that specifies the annual employer current contribution. The amount of benefit received by an employee depends on the account balance at retirement.

EXHIBIT 16.9 Characteristics of Selected Retirement Plan

	Defined Benefit	Defined Contribution
Plan typically benefits older, long-term employees	Yes	No
Requires PBGC insurance	Yes	No
Benefits insured by PBGC	Yes	No
Actuarial costs	Yes	No
Can encourage early retirement	Yes	Possibly
Can provide benefits based on prior service	Yes	No
Maximum annual benefit $230,000 (2020)	Yes	No
Higher plan costs and complexity	Yes	No
Individual accounts	No	Yes
Contribution is percentage of compensation	No	Yes
Investment risk	Employer	Employee
Annual additions limited to lesser of 100% of comp. or $57,000 (2020)	No	Yes
Forfeitures reduce plan costs	Yes	Possibly
Assets in plan	Commingled funds	Separate accounts

Target/Age-Weighted Plans

Target benefit pension plans and age-weighted profit-sharing plans allow for higher contributions for older plan participants.

A traditional **target benefit pension plan** is a hybrid between a defined contribution pension plan and a traditional defined benefit plan. The traditional target benefit pension plan is an age-weighted money purchase pension plan.

The **age-based profit-sharing plan** is a profit-sharing plan with an age-weighted factor in the allocation formula. Because the plan allocations are age weighted, older plan participants are favored.

Target benefit pension plan

An age-weighted money purchase pension plan; a hybrid between a defined contribution plan and a defined benefit plan

Age-based profit-sharing plan

A profit-sharing plan with an age-weighted factor in the allocation formula

New comparability plan

A defined contribution plan that maximizes the age-weighted discrepancy permitted under the cross-testing provisions of proposed nondiscrimination regulations

The **new comparability plan** represents an attempt to push age weighting to its maximum limit under the cross-testing provisions of nondiscrimination regulations.

Contributory vs. Noncontributory Plans

Qualified retirement plans may be distinguished as either contributory (employee makes some contribution) or noncontributory (employer pays all). Most pension and profit-sharing plans are noncontributory. The common exceptions are the Section 401(k) plan and the thrift plan (an after-tax savings plan).

Corporate vs. Keogh (Self-Employed) Plans

Qualified retirement plans are either corporate sponsored (regular C corporations and S corporations) or Keogh (self-employed, partnerships, LLCs filing as partnerships) plans. Corporations can adopt any of the qualified retirement plans, pension plans, or profit-sharing plans discussed previously, as well as other tax-advantaged plans that are not qualified. Self-employed persons can adopt the majority of qualified retirement plans (except stock bonus and ESOP plans) as well as other tax-advantaged plans.

Keogh plan

A qualified plan for unincorporated businesses

The intent of Congressional legislation regarding self-employed individuals was to put **Keogh plans** in parity with corporate plans. There are two important differences, however, between corporate plans and Keogh plans. The first is the calculation of the maximum contribution allowed by the self-employed person; the second is the availability of loans from the Keogh plan to these self-employed individuals. Any type of qualified plan may be adopted as a Keogh plan (except stock bonus and ESOP plans).

Self-Employed Maximum Contribution Calculation

Forfeitures

Employer contributions that are not fully vested and thus revert to the employer in the event that an employee terminates service

Traditional employees receive a Form W-2 that reflects their earnings for the current year. Maximum annual contributions, referred to as annual additions, to defined contribution plans cannot exceed the lesser of 100% of an employee's compensation or $57,000 in 2020. Annual additions include employer contributions, employee contributions, and **forfeitures** reallocated to plan participants. For example, an employee with compensation of $100,000 in 2020 would be limited to $57,000 in annual additions for a single year.

Unfortunately for self-employed individuals, their maximum contribution calculation is more complicated. These individuals are limited in their contributions to the lesser of 25% of earned income from self-employment or $57,000 for 2020. Earned income from self-employment is different from compensation and is defined as self-employment income reduced by one-half of self-employment tax paid (net self-employment income) and reduced by the retirement plan contribution. Reducing the income that can be used as the base for the retirement plan contribution by the retirement plan contribution creates what is known as a circular equation. To resolve this circular equation, the retirement plan contribution percentage is divided by the sum of one plus the retirement plan contribution percentage. This factor is then multiplied by the difference between self-employment income and one-half self-employment tax paid.

EXAMPLE   Bob has self-employment income of $105,000 and self-employment tax of $14,836 in 2020. His contribution for the tax year is limited to a maximum of $19,516 (see the following calculation).

Keogh Plan Contribution Calculation		
1.	Self-employment income	$105,000	
2.	Less ½ self-employment tax	7,418	½ × $14,836
3.	Equals net self-employment income	97,582	
4.	Less Keogh plan contribution	(19,516)	$97,582 × (0.25 ÷ 1.25)
5.	Equals earned income	78,066	
6.	Times Keogh contribution percentage	× 25%	
7.	Equals Keogh plan contribution	$19,516	

Notice that the contribution of $19,516 is calculated by multiplying $97,582 by 20%, which equals earned income (line 5 above) multiplied by 25%. Therefore, it is not necessary to extend the analysis through steps 5 to 7. Determining the contribution is usually calculated by dividing the plan percentage by the sum of one plus the plan percentage and multiplying the result by the difference between self-employment earnings and the deductible share of self-employment tax. The following table displays the percentage often used for Keogh calculations, depending on the plan contribution percentage limit.

Plan Percentage	Keogh Limit	Plan Percentage	Keogh Limit
1%	0.9901%	14%	12.2807%
2%	1.9608%	15%	13.0435%
3%	2.9126%	16%	13.7931%
4%	3.8462%	17%	14.5299%
5%	4.7619%	18%	15.2542%
6%	5.6604%	19%	15.9664%
7%	6.5421%	20%	16.6667%
8%	7.4074%	21%	17.3554%
9%	8.2569%	22%	18.0328%
10%	9.0909%	23%	18.6992%
11%	9.9099%	24%	19.3548%
12%	10.7143%	25%	20.0000%
13%	11.5044%		

OTHER TAX-ADVANTAGED PLANS

Other than qualified retirement plans, there are individually-sponsored and employer-sponsored retirement plans that are tax advantaged but are not technically qualified plans. Generally, these plans appeal to individuals or small employers because they are less costly to maintain. Tax-advantaged plans typically have lower contribution limits but function much like qualified plans, offering tax deferred earnings; some plans allow tax deductible contributions. Exhibit 16.10 lists these plans.

EXHIBIT 16.10 Other Tax-Advantaged Plans

- Individual retirement account or annuity (IRA)
  — Deductible
  — Nondeductible
- Roth IRA
- Simplified employee pension (SEP) plan
- Savings incentive match plan for employees (SIMPLE)
- Section 403(b) plans (tax-sheltered annuities)

Individual Retirement Accounts (IRAs) or IRA Annuities

In general, the IRA is a tax-deferred investment and savings account that serves as a personal retirement fund for persons with earned income.

An individual worker with earned income at any age in 2020 and afterwards can contribute to an IRA. Annual IRA contributions are limited to the lesser of $6,000 or earned income for 2020. If a married person has a nonworking spouse, the annual contribution limit is increased to $12,000 for 2020. IRA contribution limits are periodically adjusted for inflation in $500 increments.

Deductibility Rules

The deductibility of an IRA contribution is affected by the taxpayer's status as an active participant in an employer-sponsored retirement plan and by the taxpayer's modified adjusted gross income (MAGI). For taxpayers who are not active participants in a qualified plan, SEP, SARSEP, SIMPLE, or Section 403(b) plan, contributions to a traditional IRA are fully deductible, regardless of the taxpayer's MAGI. For taxpayers who are active participants in a qualified plan, SEP, SARSEP, SIMPLE, or Section 403(b) plan, the deduction for traditional IRA contributions is limited (or eliminated) when a taxpayer's adjusted income reaches certain levels. These phaseout levels are listed in Exhibit 16.11.

EXHIBIT 16.11 IRA Current Phaseout Limits

Tax Year	Phaseout Range, by Taxpayer Filing Status	
	Single	Married Filing Jointly
2020	$65,000–$75,000	$104,000–$124,000

An individual will not be considered an active participant in an employer-sponsored retirement plan solely because her spouse is an active participant. However, when only one spouse is an active participant, the nonparticipant spouse will have his deduction phased out at AGI levels between $196,000 and $206,000 in 2020.

Catch-up contributions are available for individuals over 50 years old. Any individual who attains 50 by the end of the taxable year can make additional contributions of $1,000.

Thus, a taxpayer age 50 or older in 2020 could contribute a total of $7,000 to an IRA. This contribution consists of the annual limit plus the catch-up contribution.

Roth IRA

Roth IRA
An individual retirement account in which contributions are made on an after-tax basis and qualifying distributions are made tax free

The **Roth IRA** is a special type of IRA. Contributions to a Roth IRA are made on an after-tax basis. Earnings are not subject to current taxation, and distributions of earnings are generally tax-exempt if certain qualifying conditions are met. Taxpayers can contribute to Roth IRAs with no age restriction and are not forced to receive minimum distributions at age 72 as they are with traditional IRAs. Only taxpayers with incomes less than those listed below qualify to make a contribution to a Roth IRA in 2020.

Taxpayer status	2020 Phaseout MAGI
Single	$124,000–$139,000
Married filing jointly	$196,000–$206,000
Married filing separately	$0–$10,000

Simplified Employee Pensions (SEPs)

Simplified employee pension (SEP)

A tax-deferred, noncontributory retirement plan that uses an individual retirement account (IRA) as the receptacle for contributions

A **simplified employee pension (SEP)** plan is a tax-deferred noncontributory retirement plan that is employer sponsored and similar to a qualified profit-sharing plan with regard to funding requirements and contribution limits. In contrast to qualified profit-sharing plans, SEPs are much easier to implement, are less costly to administer, and are not subject to the same extensive filing requirements. SEPs are funded through employer contributions to an IRA in the name of the employee. All contributions are immediately 100% vested. The funding is discretionary on the part of the employer up to 25% of covered employee compensation to a maximum of $285,000 in 2020, not to exceed $57,000 in 2020. The advantage of a SEP versus an IRA is the significantly higher potential amount of funding.

The plan is uncomplicated and inexpensive, compared with qualified retirement plans. Generally, the individual participant has the responsibility and risk for investment returns. SEPs may not be appropriate for small businesses with permanent part-time employees because part-time employees must be covered under the plan. A major advantage of a SEP is that it can be established and funded as late as the due date of the employer's federal income tax return, including extensions. Qualified plans, on the other hand, must be established by the end of the tax year for which contributions are being made.

SIMPLE IRAs

A savings incentive match plan for employees (SIMPLE) is a tax-deferred, employer-sponsored retirement plan that more closely resembles an IRA. Like the SEP, it has minimal filing requirements. The SIMPLE IRA allows employees to make elective contributions to an IRA up to the lesser of 100% of compensation or $13,500 in 2020.

Catch-up provisions are available for individuals age 50 and above. Any individual who attains age 50 by the end of the tax year may be eligible to make an additional contribution of $3,000 (2020).

The employer is required to provide one of the following two types of benefits to the participants in the plan: (1) provide a dollar-for-dollar match up to 3% of the participant's compensation, or (2) make a contribution of 2% of compensation for each eligible employee without regard to the employee's contribution. All contributions are immediately 100% vested. The benefits are portable; however, withdrawals made within two years of participation are subject to a 25% premature-distribution penalty tax.

The advantage of the SIMPLE IRA over the traditional IRA is the larger amount of contribution allowed. The advantage of the SIMPLE IRA over the SEP is that the SIMPLE IRA is funded mostly through employee contributions, and there is no percentage limit for contributions to a SIMPLE IRA.

To sponsor a SIMPLE IRA, the employer must have fewer than 100 employees. SIMPLE IRAs are essentially governed by the same rules as IRAs. Individual accounts are created, and employees choose the investments from those offered by the plan.

One big disadvantage of a SIMPLE IRA is that no other types of qualified retirement plans are permitted to be simultaneously maintained by the employer. Therefore, if the employer wanted to sponsor a pension or profit-sharing plan, the SIMPLE IRA would have to be terminated. However, the employer, if eligible, can maintain a Section 457 plan for the benefit of its employees.

SIMPLE 401(k)

A Section 401(k) plan may also be structured as a SIMPLE for eligible employers. Employers with 100 or fewer employees earning $5,000 (or more) during the preceding year may adopt a SIMPLE 401(k). The employer may not maintain any other qualified or employer-sponsored plan. However, the employer, if eligible, can maintain a Section 457 plan for the benefit of its employees. The SIMPLE 401(k) is exempt from the special nondiscrimination testing that applies to the traditional Section 401(k).

Participants in a SIMPLE 401(k) may make elective deferrals (similar to the traditional Section 401(k) plan). Deferral limits are less than traditional Section 401(k) plans, $13,500 for 2020, with an additional $3,000 catch-up allowance for participants age 50 and above. The employer-sponsor of the plan must either match those elective deferral amounts, up to 3% of employee compensation, or, alternatively, make a flat (nonelective) contribution of 2% of compensation for all eligible employees. SIMPLE 401(k)s are not subject to the 25% penalty on withdrawals within the first two years of participation. Rather, the penalty for an early withdrawal is the same as for all other plans, 10%. Unlike traditional Section 401(k) employer contributions (where vesting schedules are permissible), the employee is always 100% vested in the contributions made to a SIMPLE 401(k) by the employer.

Historically, the major advantage for employer implementation of the SIMPLE 401(k) option (rather than the SIMPLE IRA) was, as a qualified plan, creditor protection of the assets within the plan. The Bankruptcy Act of 2005 minimized this advantage in part. Specifically, subsequent to October 2005, the first $1 million of assets included in initially established IRAs of any type (including the SIMPLE IRA) are protected from creditor claims. This amount is unlimited for a rollover IRA. Thus, it is anticipated that the use of the SIMPLE 401(k) may recede even further from its admittedly narrow market under law.

Section 403(b) Plans

Section 403(b) plan
A retirement plan similar to a 401(k) plan that is available to certain tax-exempt organizations and to public schools

Congress established Section 403(b) plans to encourage workers in certain tax-exempt organizations to establish retirement savings programs. The name, like that of Section 401(k) plans, refers to the relevant section of the Internal Revenue Code. A **Section 403(b) plan** is a tax-deferred savings and retirement plan that, while not a qualified plan, provides many of the same benefits and is governed by many of the same rules that govern qualified retirement plans. The plan is essentially the Section 401(k) of the not-for-profit industry. Participants contractually reduce their salaries, and elective deferrals are subject to the same limits as the Section 401(k). Contributions are made on a before-tax basis, and the only allowable funding vehicles are mutual funds and tax-sheltered annuities. The contributions and earnings grow tax deferred until distribution, and the benefit received is equal to the account balance at the accumulation date (usually retirement). Similar to the Section 401(k) and other defined contribution plans, the responsibility and risk of investment returns is on the individual participant.

Nonrefundable Credit for Elective Deferrals

A special nonrefundable tax credit is available to low-income and moderate-income savers for elective deferrals or contributions made to a Section 401(k) plan, Section 403(b) plan, eligible deferred-compensation arrangement of a state or local government (a Section 457 plan), SIMPLE, SEP, or IRA.

The maximum annual contribution eligible for the credit is $2,000. The credit rates are based on AGI (adjusted for inflation).

The credit is in addition to any deduction or exclusion that would otherwise apply with respect to the contribution. The credit offsets alternative minimum tax liability as well as regular tax liability. The credit is available to individuals who are age 18 or older, but not individuals who are full-time students or claimed as a dependent on another taxpayer's return.

When figuring this credit, the taxpayer generally must subtract the amount of distributions received from retirement plans from the contributions made. This rule applies for distributions starting two years before the year the credit is claimed and ending with the filing deadline for that tax return. In the case of a distribution from a Roth IRA, this rule applies to any such distributions, whether taxable or not.

DISTRIBUTIONS FROM QUALIFIED AND OTHER TAX-ADVANTAGED PLANS

Distributions from qualified retirement plans and other tax-advantaged plans generally are subject to the following income tax treatment: If the contributions were made pretax, then both contributions and earnings are treated as ordinary income equal to the distribution and thus receive ordinary income tax treatment. If the contributions were made after tax, the contributions are treated as a return of capital, and the earnings are treated as ordinary income.

In general, distributions from qualified retirement plans and other tax-advantaged retirement plans made before age 59½ (except for death or disability, for instance) are penalized by a premature penalty tax of 10%. Annual distributions from qualified retirement plans and other tax-advantaged retirement plans typically must begin no later than the year when the participant attains age 72, although the first distribution may be delayed until April 1 of the following year.

EXHIBIT 16.12 Taxation of Distributions

Contributions	Distribution	Earnings on Contributions
Pretax	Taxable as ordinary income	Ordinary income
After-tax	Nontaxable return of capital	Ordinary income

The two common exceptions to the general income tax treatment of distributions from tax-advantaged retirement accounts are Roth IRA distributions and lump-sum distributions consisting of employer securities. A Roth IRA has nondeductible contributions but generally provides for tax-exempt distributions and is not subject to the rules on minimum distributions at age 72.

As previously discussed, distributions from qualified plans that consist of employer securities may be eligible to receive deferred recognition treatment of the net unrealized appreciation in the securities, with the gains taxable at capital gains rates instead of ordinary income tax rates.

NONQUALIFIED PLANS

Nonqualified plan

A retirement plan that can discriminate in favor of executives but is not eligible for all of the special tax benefits available for qualified or other tax-advantaged retirement plans

A **nonqualified plan** is any retirement plan, savings plan, or deferred-compensation plan or agreement that does not meet the qualified retirement plan tax requirements of the Internal Revenue Code. All qualified retirement plans and other tax-advantaged plans are in some way a form of deferred compensation but with some form of current income tax deduction and/or deferral of taxation on earnings. Most nonqualified retirement plans offer deferral of taxation on earnings but do not allow an immediate tax deduction to the employer. The employer receives a deduction for contributions only when the participant recognizes the distribution as income for income tax purposes. If the nonqualified plan agreement delays receipt of taxable income by the participant, then the employer/sponsor's income tax deduction also is delayed.

Employers use nonqualified plans to provide additional financial benefits that are not, or cannot be, provided in qualified retirement plans. Nonqualified plans can reward employees (usually key executives) on a more selective basis than qualified retirement plans that require broad participation, coverage, and nondiscrimination. An example of one benefit that can be provided by a nonqualified plan is a deferred-compensation plan to provide retirement benefits to a key employee in excess of the limits that may be provided under a qualified retirement plan. Recall that the limit for covered compensation that can be considered for purposes of qualified retirement plans is $285,000 for 2020. Employees who earn exactly $285,000 for 2020 have a much higher wage replacement ratio than those who make $1 million under the same qualified retirement plan. Even though the person is earning $1 million, her qualified retirement plan acts as if she is making only $285,000 for 2020. The deferred-compensation, nonqualified plan is used to mitigate this wage replacement ratio inequity.

Nonqualified plans generally have some risk as to whether the employee/participant will receive the benefits. (A substantial risk of forfeiture or a lack of funding is essential for the plan to defer taxation to the employee/participant.) If there is no substantial risk of forfeiture and the benefit is funded, there is constructive receipt of the funds, and the benefits are currently taxable rather than being deferred. In addition, nonqualified plans are not protected from creditors under ERISA's nonalienation of benefits rules.

A number of nonqualified plans may be used to attract, compensate, and retain key personnel on a discriminatory or selective basis and include deferred- compensation plans, split-dollar life insurance plans, and employee stock option plans.

Deferred Compensation Plans

Deferred compensation plan

A nonqualified plan that is a contractual agreement between the employer and selected employees; takes the form of either salary reduction or salary continuation. Compensation is deferred until retirement, disability, death, or termination of employment, but usually only at normal retirement age.

Nonqualified deferred compensation agreements are contractual arrangements between the employer and selected employees. **Deferred compensation plans** take the form of salary reduction or, more commonly, salary continuation. Either way, compensation is deferred generally until retirement, disability, death, or termination of employment, but usually only at normal retirement age.

The employer does not receive any tax deduction unless and until the employee recognizes taxable income. The presumption is that the executive employee may be in a lower income tax bracket during retirement than during the maximum earnings years of employment. Another reason for using nonqualified plans is to delay the receipt of taxable cash flow to the executive until it is actually needed.

Employee Stock Option Plan

In employee stock option plans, the employer grants to the employee a right (option) to purchase a fixed number of shares of the employer's stock for a set price (exercise price) during a specified period. The purpose of granting such stock options to employees is to align more closely executive compensation to stock performance. These options may be nonqualified stock options (NQSOs) or incentive stock options (ISOs). The NQSO is taxable to the recipient at the time of exercise to the extent of the difference between the fair market value of the stock and the exercise price as ordinary Form W-2 income. The exercise of ISOs does not currently create taxable income for regular income tax purposes, as with NQSOs. There is income, however, for alternative minimum tax purposes created upon the exercise of the ISO. The alternative minimum tax (AMT) may apply when employees exercise ISOs. In addition, the shares acquired through the ISO exercise cannot be sold before one year from the date of exercise or two years from the date of grant. If this holding period is satisfied, the gain upon the sale of the ISO shares will be a long-term capital gain; otherwise, the income will be ordinary. Therefore, ISOs provide some important advantages to the employees but also have certain restrictions on the number that can be granted and when the shares can be sold.

Section 457 Plans

A Section 457 plan is a deferred compensation plan of governmental units, governmental agencies, and non-church-controlled, tax-exempt organizations. In 2020, the amount deferred annually by an employee under a Section 457 plan cannot exceed the lesser of $19,500 or 100% of the employee's compensation currently includable in gross income. In addition, individuals who have attained age 50 may make catch-up contributions. The additional catch-up amount is $6,500 for 2020.

The contribution limit is doubled in the three years before an individual's retirement. During this three-year period (before retirement), the catch-up rule does not apply.

Plan distributions cannot be made before any of the following:

■ The calendar year in which the participant attains age 70½ (Note that the SECURE Act did not change this age to 72)

■ Separation from service

■ An unforeseeable emergency as defined in regulations

Distributions must begin no later than April 1 of the calendar year after the year in which the plan participant attains age 72.

THE FINANCIAL PLANNER'S ROLE IN RETIREMENT PLANNING

The financial planner's role in retirement planning is to assist clients in the accomplishment of their retirement goals. Retirement plans have many tax advantages, business benefits, and other advantages. Financial planners must be able to identify the objectives of the client and assist the client in choosing a retirement plan that meets those objectives.

WHERE ON THE WEB

American Benefits Council **www.appwp.org**

American Society of Pension Professionals and Actuaries **www.asppa.org**

Benefits Link **www.benefitslink.com**

The ESOP Association **www.esopassociation.org**

Employee Benefit Research Institute **www.ebri.org**

Employee Benefits Security Administration **www.dol.gov/ebsa**

Internal Revenue Service **www.irs.gov**

International Foundation of Employee Benefit Plans **www.ifebp.org**

National Institute of Pension Administrators **www.nipa.org**

National Tax Sheltered Accounts Association (403(b) and 457 plans) **www.ntsaa.org**

Pension Benefit Guaranty Corporation (PBGC) **www.pbgc.gov**

Profit Sharing/401(k) Council of America **www.psca.org**

DISCUSSION QUESTIONS

1. What is a qualified retirement plan?

2. What are the advantages of a qualified retirement plan, and what are its disadvantages?

3. What is vesting?

4. What are the standard vesting schedules for defined benefit plans and defined contribution plans?

5. Why were qualified retirement plans created?

6. What are the benefits of tax deferral in a qualified retirement plan and how can they be calculated?

7. What are the different types of qualified retirement plans?

8. How do pension plans and profit-sharing plans differ?

9. How do defined benefit plans and defined contribution plans differ?

10. How do noncontributory plans and contributory plans differ?

11. What is a Section 401(k) plan, and how does it operate?

12. How do Keogh (self-employed) plans and corporate plans differ?

13. What are some examples of tax-advantaged retirement plans?

14. What are IRAs, SEPs, SIMPLEs, and Section 403(b) plans?

15. How are distributions from qualified retirement plans and other tax-advantaged retirement plans the same, and how do they differ?

16. What is a nonqualified plan, and what are some examples of this type of plan?

17. Why are nonqualified plans useful to employers?

18. Which qualified retirement plans permit in-service withdrawals?

19. Which qualified retirement plans require immediate vesting of employer contributions?

EXERCISES

1. Shawna, a 73-year-old single taxpayer, retired two years ago and is receiving a pension of $700 per month from her previous employer's qualified pension plan. She recently started a new job with a discount retail outlet that has no pension plan. She will receive $12,000 in compensation from her current job, as well as the $8,400 from her pension. How much can she contribute to a deductible IRA in 2020?

2. What deductible contribution amount may the following individuals make to an IRA in 2020? Assume none of the persons listed or their spouses participate in an employer-sponsored pension plan, and none are age 50 or over.

Person	Marital Status	AGI
Larry	Single	$ 32,000
Mark	Married	$ 87,000
Lee Anne	Single	$ 56,000
Dennis	Married	$120,000

3. Tom and Denise, both age 45, are married and filed a joint income tax return for the tax year. Tom earned a salary of $70,000 in 2020. Tom and Denise earned interest of $5,000 in 2020 on their joint savings account. Denise is not employed, and the couple had no other income. What amount could Tom and Denise contribute to IRAs to take advantage of their maximum allowable IRA deduction on their 2020 tax return?

4. Evan and Jody, both age 52, are married and filed a joint income tax return for the year 2020. Their 2020 adjusted gross income was $100,000. The couple had no other income, and neither spouse was covered by an employer-sponsored plan. What amount could Evan and Jody contribute to IRAs to take advantage of their maximum allowable IRA deduction on their 2020 tax return?

5. Darlene and Rick are married and file a joint income tax return. They are both covered by a qualified retirement plan. Their 2020 adjusted gross income was $85,000. The couple had no other income. Assuming the couple is under age 50, what amount could Darlene and Rick contribute to a Roth IRA this year?

6. In January of the current year, Phil (age 47) took a $500,000 premature distribution from a rollover IRA, leaving a balance in his IRA of $1 million. On October 31 of the current year, Phil died with the IRA account balance of $1.2 million. Which penalty or penalties will apply to Phil as a result of these facts?

7. What is the maximum deductible contribution to a defined contribution qualified pension plan on behalf of Ann, a self-employed individual whose income from self-employment is $25,000 and whose Social Security taxes are $3,532 in 2020?

8. Refer back to the previous exercise concerning Ann, the self-employed person. What is the maximum Ann could contribute to a profit-sharing plan?

9. Robbins, Inc., a regular C corporation, is considering the adoption of a qualified retirement plan. The company has had fluctuating cash flows in the recent past, and such fluctuations are expected to continue. The average age of nonowner employees is 24, and the average number of years of service is 3 with the high being 4 and the low, 1. Approximately 25% of the 12-person labor force turns over each year. The two owners receive about two-thirds of the total covered compensation. Which is the most appropriate vesting schedule for Robbins, Inc.?

10. What is the minimum number of employees that must be covered in a defined benefit plan to conform to ERISA requirements for a company having 100 eligible employees?

PROBLEMS

1. XYZ Company has two employees: John, who earns $300,000 annually, and his assistant Kim, age 26, who has worked for John for 4 years. Kim earns $20,000. XYZ has a contributory pension plan using graduated vesting. Kim's account balance reflects the following:

Contributions		Earnings From Contributions		Kim's Total Balance
Employee	Employer	Employee	Employer	
$1,500	$2,000	$800	$1,200	$5,500

Reviewing the account and assuming that Kim terminated employment when the account balance was as above after 4 years of employment, how much could she take with her, plan permitting?

2. The following table contains qualified plan information for Yarbrough, Inc., as of 12/31/2020. Yarbrough, Inc., maintains a noncontributory qualified profit-sharing plan with 3-year cliff vesting.

Employee	Compensation	Ownership Interest	Years of Service*	Plan Account Balance*
A	$270,000	5%	2	$20,000
B	$180,000	8%	10	$300,000
C	$130,000	6%	8	$180,000
D	$60,000	1%	3	$27,000
E	$40,000	0%	2	$7,500

* As of 12/31/20

Please answer all of the following questions:
A. What is the total covered compensation for 2020?
B. What is the maximum profit-sharing contribution Yarbrough can make for 2020?
C. Which of the employees is highly compensated?
D. Is the plan top-heavy?
E. If employees D and E quit in January 2021, what are their respective vested balances in the plan?

Introduction to
Estate Planning

▮ LEARNING OBJECTIVES

After learning the material in this chapter, you will be able to do the following:

- Define estate planning and describe the estate planning process

- Discuss the objectives of and the benefits derived from planning an estate

- Explain the risks of failing to plan for estate transfer

- Identify the steps in the estate planning process

- List the types of client information necessary to begin and complete the estate planning process

- Identify the most common estate transfer objectives

- Discuss the types of property ownership interests and how each interest is transferred at death

- Identify and describe the basic essential estate planning documents

- Describe the probate process and list its advantages and disadvantages

- Understand why a unified gift and estate tax system exists

- Define the annual exclusion and explain its tax ramifications

- Explain the concept of gift splitting

- Identify the basic strategies for transferring wealth through the process of making gifts

- Define and explain the purpose of the federal estate tax

- Describe the gross estate, what assets are included in the gross estate, and the expenses and deductions that reduce the gross estate

- Describe how charitable planning impacts estate planning

- Define the marital deduction and explain how it affects estate planning

- Define the generation-skipping transfer tax and explain how it affects estate planning

- List the various estate planning techniques available to reduce the estate tax

BASICS OF ESTATE PLANNING

This chapter presents the goals of efficient and effective wealth transfer, during life or at death, and the risks associated with such transfers. When a personal financial planner begins the estate planning process for a client, certain personal and financial data are collected from the client and analyses of that data are performed. Client interest in the estate planning process generally begins at or near the beginning of the distribution/gifting phase of the client's personal lifecycle. However, all clients need to have at least basic documents (e.g., will, durable power of attorney, and advanced medical directives) and provisions in the will for the care of minor children.

Estate Planning Defined

Estate planning may be broadly defined as the process of accumulation, management, conservation, and transfer of wealth considering legal, tax, and personal objectives. It is financial planning for our inevitable death. The goal of estate planning is the effective and efficient transfer of assets. An effective transfer occurs when the client's assets are transferred to the person or institution intended by the client. An efficient transfer occurs when wealth transfer costs are minimized consistent with the greatest assurance of effectiveness.

The Objectives of Estate Planning

Common objectives of estate planning include transferring (distributing) property to particular persons or entities consistent with client wishes; minimizing all taxes (income, gift, estate, state inheritance, and generation-skipping taxes); minimizing the transaction costs associated with the transfer (costs of documents, lawyers, and the legal probate process); and providing liquidity to the estate to pay for costs which commonly arise, such as taxes, funeral expenses, and final medical costs.

EXHIBIT 17.1 Estate Planning Objectives

- ◼ Fulfill client's property transfer wishes
- ◼ Minimize taxes
- ◼ Minimize costs
- ◼ Provide needed liquidity

Everyone needs a basic estate plan to provide for health care and property decisions and for transferring property according to the individual's wishes. An important estate planning objective is to ensure that the decedent's property is received by the person, persons, or entities that the client desires.

Heir
One who inherits; beneficiary

Risks associated with failing to plan for estate transfer include the transfer of property contrary to the client's wishes, insufficient financial provision for the client's family, and liquidity problems at the time of death. Any of these risks could be catastrophic to the decedent's **heirs** and family. For example, a decedent's assets could be tied up in probate court for an indefinite period if that person has no will or has competing and conflicting heirs. Another consideration in estate planning is the high transfer tax rates. In 2020, for example, the maximum gift tax, estate tax, and generation-skipping transfer tax rate is 40%. These tax rates have been higher than 55% in the past, and it is possible that higher rates will be imposed again in the future.

EXHIBIT 17.2 Risks in Failing to Plan an Estate

- ◼ Client's property transfer wishes go unfulfilled.
- ◼ Taxes are excessive.
- ◼ Transfer costs are excessive.
- ◼ Client's family is not properly provided for.
- ◼ There is insufficient liquidity to cover client's debts.

The Estate Planning Team

The estate planning team consists of the attorney, accountant, life insurance consultant, trust officer, and financial planner. The role of the professional financial planner is to help integrate the work of the estate planning team in developing the overall estate plan.

The estate planning process is complex and can be somewhat confusing. A CPA is usually involved as a member of the estate planning team because the process requires the identification of assets, calculation of the related adjusted tax basis, and other tax issues. An insurance specialist, such as a CLU or ChFC, is usually involved to help ensure liquidity at death and protection for the client from the risks of untimely death. A licensed attorney is almost always a part of the team because the process requires drafting numerous legal documents. The financial planner may serve as the team captain and assist in data collection, analysis, and investment decisions. Although each member of the planning team may individually be an estate expert, each specialty brings with it a particular and unique perspective, the combination of which is more likely to produce a better result for the client. The financial planner, unless a licensed attorney, should be careful not to engage in any act that could be found to be the unauthorized practice of law.

The Estate Planning Process

There are eight basic steps to the estate planning process.

1. Gather client information, including the client's current financial statements.

2. Establish the client's transfer objectives, including family and charitable objectives.

3. Define any problem areas, such as the disposition of assets, liquidity issues, excessive taxes or costs, and other situational needs, such as disability of an identified heir.

4. Determine the estate liquidity needs now and at five-year intervals for the life expectancy of the transferor, including estate transfer costs.

5. Establish priorities for all client objectives.

6. Develop a comprehensive plan of transfer consistent with all information and objectives.

7. Implement the estate plan.

8. Review the estate plan periodically, and update the plan when necessary (especially for changes in family situations).

Steps 1 and 2 are briefly discussed below. An estate planning course would cover steps 3 through 8.

Collecting Client Information and Defining Transfer Objectives

The collection of information is essential to gain a complete financial and family picture of the client and to assist the client in identifying financial risks. Information about prospective heirs and legatees needs to be collected to properly arrange for any transfer that the client wants to make.

To begin the estate planning process, the planner should collect the following:

- Current financial statements

- Family information (i.e., parents, children, any other dependents, their ages, and health status)

- A detailed list of assets and liabilities, including the fair market value, adjusted tax basis, and expected growth rate for all assets, how title is held, and the date acquired

- Copies of medical and disability insurance policies

- Copies of all life insurance policies in force identifying the ownership of each policy, the named insured, and the designated beneficiaries

- Copies of annuity contracts

- Copies of wills and trusts

- Identification of powers of attorney and general powers of appointment

- Copies of all previously filed income tax and gift tax returns (as available)

- Identification of assets previously gifted

- Other pertinent information

Once client and family information is collected, the process of determining the transfer objectives can be completed. Usually, the most important objective of the client is to transfer assets as the client wishes. Secondarily, the client generally wishes to avoid the shrinkage of the estate resulting from costs associated with the transfer. Exhibit 17.3 provides a list of common transfer objectives.

EXHIBIT 17.3 Common Transfer Objectives

- Minimize estate and transfer taxes to maximize the assets received by heirs.
- Avoid probate.
- Use lifetime transfers (gifts).
- Meet liquidity needs at death.
- Plan for children.
- Plan for the incapacity of the transferor.
- Provide for the needs of the surviving spouse.
- Fulfill charitable intentions of the transferor.

BASIC DOCUMENTS INCLUDED IN AN ESTATE PLAN

The basic documents used in estate planning include wills, living wills or medical directives, durable powers of attorney for health care or property, and side letters.

Wills

A **will** is a legal document that provides the testator, or will maker, the opportunity to control the distribution of property and avoid the state's intestacy law distribution scheme. In general, a will is valid when the will maker is at least 18 years old or an emancipated minor and is "of sound mind," that is, possessing **testamentary capacity**. The "sound mind" rules are not as rigorous as the rules that are required to form contracts. In other words, a person who may not have the legal capacity to form a contract may have sufficient legal capacity to make a will.

Intestacy

To die **intestate** is to die without a valid will. In such a case, the state directs how the decedent's property will be distributed by creating a hypothetical will according to the state's **intestacy laws**. One size does not fit all, and the intestacy laws are not likely to distribute property the way every person would wish had he written his own will. There are possible adverse consequences of intestacy. In certain states, a spouse's share of the decedent's estate will be equal to a child's. For example, the surviving spouse's share with one child might be one-half, but with nine children it will be one-tenth. Certain states provide that a spouse's share is only a life estate with the true owner being the children. When there are no children, the surviving spouse may be forced to share with the deceased spouse's parents or brothers and sisters. Although each child's needs may be quite different, children may be treated equally and, therefore, not necessarily equitably. A person who has a will can appoint an executor in the will and, in many states, can specify that the executor serve without posting a bond. Intestacy may require the probate

Will

A legal document used in estate planning that provides the testator, or will maker, the opportunity to control the distribution of property and avoid the state's intestacy law distribution scheme

Testamentary capacity

Having the mental capability to make a will to transfer assets; being of sound mind

Intestate

To die without a valid will

Intestacy laws

State laws that direct how a decedent's property will be distributed when the decedent dies without a will

Administrator
In the event a decedent dies intestate (without a valid will) or where an executor cannot be appointed by the probate court, the court appoints an administrator with powers called letters of administration, which enable the administrator to perform duties set down in the laws of intestacy

court to appoint an **administrator**, who will usually have to furnish a surety bond, thereby raising the costs of administration. The court, not the decedent, will select any administrator of the estate.

Types of Wills

There are three types of wills: holographic, nuncupative (oral), and statutory.

■ **Holographic wills** are handwritten. The material provisions of the will are in the testator's handwriting. The will is dated and signed by the testator and does not need to be witnessed. Holographic wills are valid in most states.

■ **Nuncupative (oral) wills** are dying declarations made before sufficient witnesses. In some states, nuncupative wills may be able to pass personal property only, not real property. The use of nuncupative wills is fairly restricted and is not permitted in all states.

■ **Statutory (formal) wills** are generally drawn by an attorney, complying with the statutes for wills of the domiciliary state. They are usually signed in the presence of two witnesses. A person who is a beneficiary under the will usually cannot be a valid witness.

Holographic will
Handwritten will dated and signed by the testator

Nuncupative (oral) will
Dying declarations made before sufficient witnesses

Statutory (formal) will
Generally drawn by an attorney and signed in the presence of witnesses, complying with the statutes for wills of the domiciliary state

A document that amends or revises a prior will is known as a **codicil**.

Common Clauses

Codicil
A document that amends or revises a prior will

Although all wills are different, there are certain clauses that appear in almost all wills. Common clauses that are generally found in even the simplest will include the following:

■ An introductory clause to identify the testator

■ The establishment of the testator's domicile and residence

■ A declaration that this is the last will and testament of the testator

■ A revocation of all prior wills and codicils by the testator

■ The identification and selection by the testator of the executor and successor executor

■ A directive for the payment of debts clause

■ A directive for the payment of taxes clause

■ A disposition of tangible personal property clause

■ A disposition of real estate clause (i.e., the residence and other real estate)

■ Clauses regarding specific bequests of intangibles and cash

Residuary clause
A general provision in a will that provides for the transfer of the balance of any assets not specifically mentioned in the will to someone or to some institution named by the testator

■ A **residuary clause**—the transfer of the balance of any other assets to someone or to some institution (note that the failure to have a residuary clause means that the state intestacy laws will determine the distribution of any assets that are not specifically addressed in the will; also, taxes will be paid from the residuary unless specifically directed otherwise)

■ An appointment and powers clause, naming fiduciaries, guardians, trustees, and so forth

- A testator's signature clause

- An attestation clause, or witness clause

- A self-proving clause, which allows the probate court to find that the will was executed properly without the witnesses having to testify in court

Other Clauses

More sophisticated wills often have additional clauses that dictate specific wishes regarding the handling of the estate. Additional clauses may include the following.

- A **simultaneous death clause**—In the event that both spouses die simultaneously, this clause provides a presumption of which spouse dies first.

- A **survivorship clause**—This clause provides that the beneficiary must survive the decedent for a specified period in order to receive the inheritance or bequest. This clause prevents property from being included in two different estates in rapid succession. For transfers to qualify for the estate tax marital deduction, the survival period included in a survivorship clause for a spouse can be no longer than six months.

- A **disclaimer clause**—A disclaimer clause simply reminds the heir that disclaiming inheritances may be an effective tool in estate planning. A disclaimer allows property to pass from one party to another without gift tax consequences.

- A no-contest clause—This clause discourages heirs from contesting the will by substantially decreasing or eliminating their bequest if they file a formal contest to the will.

- A spendthrift clause—This clause bars transfer of a beneficiary interest to a third party and stipulates that the interest is not subject to claims of the beneficiary's creditors. This clause is usually ineffective in a will.

Power of Attorney

People frequently need another trusted person to make decisions for them regarding property or to make health care decisions for them under certain circumstances. A power of attorney is the legal document that allows the trusted person to act in one's place. It gives the right to one person, the **attorney-in-fact** (the power holder), to act in the place of the other person, the **principal** (power giver). A power of attorney may be very broad or very specific. For example, a power of attorney might limit the attorney-in-fact's authority to paying the principal's bills or be broad enough to allow the attorney-in-fact to handle all of the principal's financial affairs. All powers are revocable by the giver and cease at the death of giver. A durability feature should be included if the giver intends that the power survive the incapacity or disability of the giver. The principal (the power giver) must be at least 18 years old and legally competent.

Durable Power of Attorney for Health Care or Property

A specific form of power of attorney is a **durable power of attorney issued either for health care or for property**. These powers are frequently issued to separate persons or, in the case of property, a financial institution. The power of attorney for health care or property eliminates the necessity to petition a local court to appoint a guardian ad litem

---

Simultaneous death clause
In the event that both spouses die simultaneously, this clause provides a presumption that one spouse (predetermined) predeceased the other spouse

Survivorship clause
Provides that the beneficiary must survive the decedent for a specified period in order to receive the inheritance or bequest

Disclaimer clause
A common clause in a decedent's will that allows property to pass from one party to another without gift tax consequences

Attorney-in-fact
The person designated by the principal in a power of attorney to act in place of the principal on the principal's behalf

Principal
In a power of attorney document, the person (power giver) who designates another person or persons to act as his attorney-in-fact

Durable power of attorney issued either for health care or for property
A written document enabling the principal to designate another person or persons to act as the principal's attorney-in-fact

Durable feature
The power survives incapacity and disability of the principal

or conservator to make health care or property decisions for a person who is incapacitated. It provides for continuity in the management of affairs in the event of disability and/or incapacity. The power may be springing or immediately effective (nonspringing). Generally, if the power is springing, the document must indicate that the power springs upon disability or incapacity and is not affected by subsequent disability or incapacity. The power is revocable by the principal. Durable powers of attorney are generally less expensive to set up and administer than a living trust or conservatorship. Durable powers of attorney can be abused, so the principal should give serious consideration to choosing the person to hold such power. The **durable feature** means the power survives incapacity and disability of the principal.

Note: A person possessing a durable power of attorney, in most cases, is not permitted to make gifts to himself or other family members (usually in conjunction with estate planning). If the power to gift to charitable or noncharitable donees is a desirable feature of the power of attorney, it should be separately and explicitly stated.

Living Wills and Advance Medical Directives

A living will (also known as an advance medical directive) is not a will at all but rather the maker's last wishes regarding sustaining life. It establishes the medical situations and circumstances in which the maker of the document no longer wants life-sustaining treatment. Such a document, though authorized in all states, must generally meet the formal requirements specified by state statute. A living will, or advance medical directive, only covers a narrow range of situations and usually applies only to terminally ill patients. Generally, a durable power of attorney issued for health care is insufficient to make decisions regarding the termination of life-sustaining procedures.

Side Instruction Letter or Personal Instruction Letter

Side instruction letter
Also known as a personal instruction letter, separate from a will; details the testator's wishes regarding the disposition of tangible possessions (household goods), the disposition of the decedent's body, and funeral arrangements

A **side instruction letter**, or personal instruction letter, details the testator's wishes regarding the disposition of tangible possessions (household goods), the disposition of the decedent's body, and funeral arrangements. Because the side instruction letter exists separately from the will itself, it avoids cluttering the will with small details that may cause conflict among heirs. The letter is given to the executor. The letter may contain information regarding the location of important personal documents, safe deposit boxes, outstanding loans, and other personal and financial information that is invaluable to the executor. Although in most cases, the letter has no legal standing, the executor will generally perform the wishes of the decedent.

THE PROBATE PROCESS DEFINED

The **probate process** proves the validity of any will, supervises the orderly distribution of assets to the heirs, and protects creditors by ensuring that valid debts of the estate are paid. In addition, when a person dies, there must be some legal way for the surviving heirs to obtain legal title to the property inherited. Probate is the legal process that performs the function of changing title to properties that do not change title any other way (e.g., by operation of law or by contract).

Probate process

Proves the validity of any will, supervises the orderly distribution of assets to the heirs, and protects creditors by ensuring that valid debts of the estate are paid. Probate is also the legal process that performs the function of changing property title from a decedent's name to an heir's name.

Exhibit 17.4 identifies the primary duties of an executor or administrator in the probate process. When an executor is named in a valid will, the probate court usually accepts that person and provides the executor with powers called letters testamentary. In the event of intestacy, or where an executor named in a will cannot be appointed by the probate court, the court will appoint an administrator (generally, a family member of the decedent). The court provides any appointed administrator with powers called letters of administration. The main differences between an executor and an administrator are that the decedent chooses the executor, the probate court names the administrator, and the administrator (but not always the executor) must post a bond.

EXHIBIT 17.4 Duties of Executor and/or Administrator

When the Decedent Dies Testate (with a Will)	When the Decedent Dies Intestate (without a Will)
■ The executor: — Locates and proves the will. — Locates witnesses to the will. — Receives letters testamentary from court.	■ The administrator: — May petition court for his own appointment. — Receives letters of administration. — Posts the required bond.

Duties of the Executor or Administrator

■ Locates and assembles property
■ Safeguards, manages, and invests property
■ Advertises in legal newspapers that person has died and creditors and other interested parties are on notice
■ Locates and communicates with potential beneficiaries
■ Pays the expenses of the decedent's estate
■ Pays the debts of the decedent
■ Files federal and state tax returns, such as Forms 1040, 1041, and 706, and makes tax payments
■ Distributes assets to beneficiaries according to the will or the laws of intestacy

Property Passing Through Probate

Property passing through probate includes property disposed of by a will. Also included in probate is property that does not pass by operation of law or by contract, or that is not covered by the will, such as intestate property resulting from the failure to provide a residuary clause. Exhibit 17.5 illustrates various assets that pass through and around probate.

EXHIBIT 17.5 Assets Passing Through and Around the Probate Process

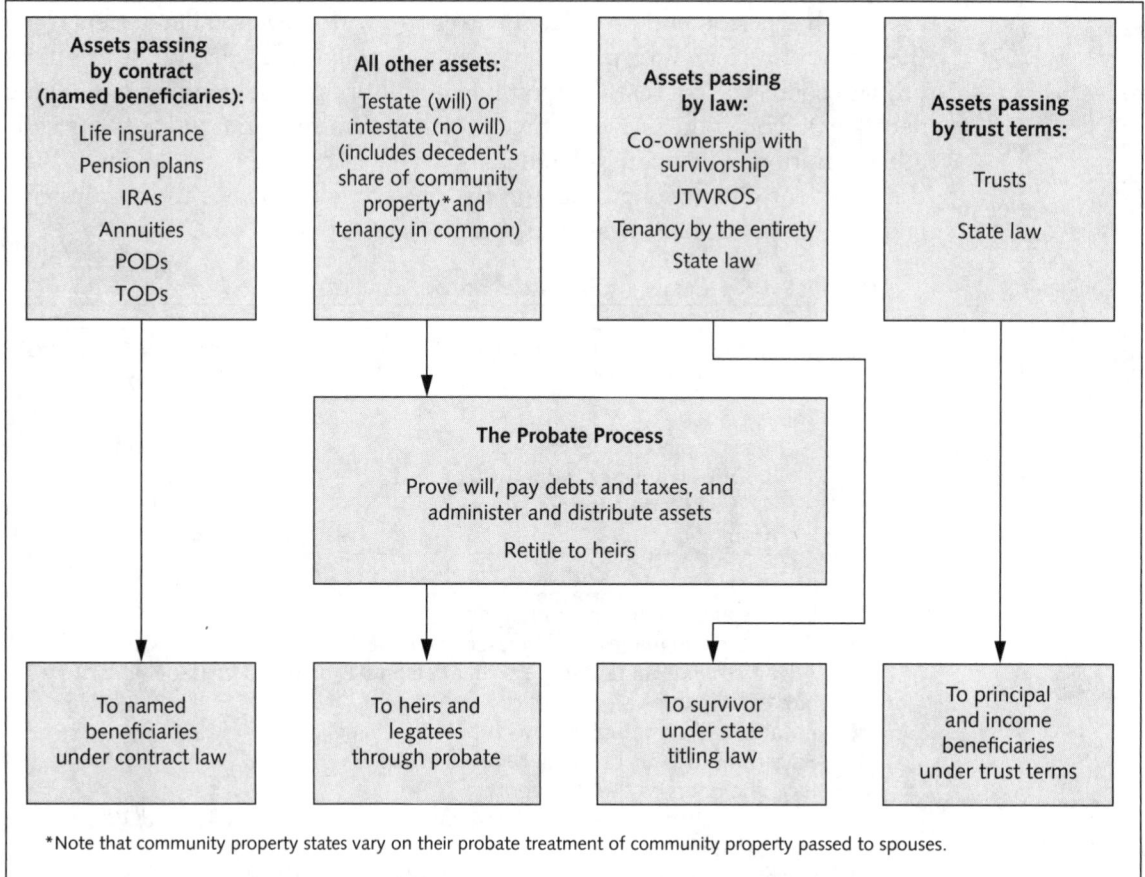

*Note that community property states vary on their probate treatment of community property passed to spouses.

Property Passing Outside of the Probate Process

Property that passes outside of the probate process includes property passing by contract and property passing by operation of law. Property passing by contract includes life insurance proceeds with a named beneficiary, pension plans and IRAs with named beneficiaries, annuities with named joint annuitants, and pay-on-death/transfer-on-death accounts. Property passing by operation of law includes property held as joint tenants with rights of survivorship (JTWROS or tenants by the entirety). Trust property passes outside of probate according to trust terms under state trust laws.

Advantages of the Probate Process

Probate has many advantages. It protects creditors by ensuring that the debts of the estate are paid before distribution to heirs. It implements the disposition objectives of the testator of the valid will. It provides clean title to heirs or legatees. It increases the chances that all parties in interest have notice of the proceedings and, therefore, a right to be heard. Finally, it provides for an orderly administration of the decedent's assets. The probate process requires the executor or administrator to advertise the upcoming probate for a certain period in legal newspapers to give interested parties notice to enter into the process.

Disadvantages of the Probate Process

Probate also has disadvantages. Probate can be both costly and complex. The legal notice requirement, attorney fees, and court costs create some of the costs. Delays are frequently caused by identification of property, valuation, identification of creditors and heirs, court delays, conflicts, and filing of taxes, to name a few. Real property located in a state outside the testator's domicile will require a separate ancillary probate in that state. One of the biggest disadvantages is loss of privacy because probate is open to public scrutiny.

OWNERSHIP AND TRANSFER OF PROPERTY

Property may be described as real property (land and buildings), tangible personal property (moveable property that may be touched and is not affixed to the land), or intangible personal property (stocks, bonds, patents, and copyrights). Some property is specifically titled to a named person or persons. Examples include real estate, automobiles (assuming the state has a motor vehicle title law), stocks, bonds, bank accounts, and retirement accounts. Other property may not have a specific title (e.g., household goods). The law of the state in which a person is domiciled determines the ways in which personal property can be transferred from one person to another, either during life or at death. For real estate, these matters are determined by the law of the state in which the property is located (the "situs"). Not all states have every alternative type or form of property interest. The forms have developed over time for the convenience of the citizens of the states that have adopted these forms.

The financial planning professional needs a working knowledge of the various forms of property interest and how each is transferred. Clients will need to be advised as to the initial ownership form depending on the client's objectives and the process the client will have to go through to transfer the property during life or at death.

Probate and Property Interests (Title and Ownership)

Property interests take several different legal forms and include fee simple, tenancy in common, joint tenancy, tenancy by the entirety, community property, pay-on-death accounts, and transfer-on-death accounts. In addition, there are property ownerships that are less than complete, including life estates, and interests for term.

Fee Simple

Fee simple
The complete individual ownership of property with all rights associated with outright ownership, such as the right to use, sell, gift, alienate, or convey

Fee simple is the complete individual ownership of property with all rights associated with outright ownership, such as the right to use, sell, gift, alienate, or convey. This type of property ownership interest is also known as fee simple absolute.

Tenancy in Common

Tenancy in common
Two or more persons hold an undivided interest in a whole property

Tenancy in common is where two or more persons hold an undivided interest in the whole property. The percentage owned by each party may differ. The property interest is treated as if it were owned outright, and the owner's interest can be used, sold, donated, willed, or passed with or without a will. When one of the owners dies, the other owner does not receive the decedent's interest by right of survivorship. The property passes through the probate process for retitling purposes and will pass under the owner's will or according to the state intestacy laws if the owner does not have a valid will. There is a right of partition, called the right to sever, in the event the owning parties cannot agree.

Joint Tenancy with Right of Survivorship (JTWROS)—Nonspouses or Spouses

Joint tenant | **Joint tenancy** is where two or more persons, called equal owners, hold the same
fractional interest in a property. The persons may be nonspouses or spouses. The right of survivorship (JTWROS) is normally implied. Joint tenants have the right to sever their interest in property without the consent of the other joint tenant, thereby destroying the survivorship right for that portion of the property. For example, if there are two joint tenants and one tenant severs his interest, the joint tenancy is destroyed. If there are three or more joint tenants and one tenant severs his interest, only that portion of the property is now held as tenants in common with the other two tenants. The joint tenancy between the remaining tenants is unaffected and will survive until altered by death or further severed by any of the other joint tenants. Property held JTWROS at the time of death of a tenant passes to the surviving tenant(s) outside of the probate process according to state law regarding survivorship rights.

Joint tenancy
Two or more persons, called equal owners, hold the same fractional interest in a property

Tenancy by the Entirety: JTWROS Between Spouses Only

Tenancy by the entirety is a JTWROS that can only occur between a married couple. Generally, neither tenant is able to sever his interest without the consent of the other tenant spouse. At the death of the first tenant, the property is passed to the surviving spouse according to the state law regarding tenancy by the entirety. Because the state law provides for retitling upon presentation of a legal death certificate, there is no need for this property to go through the probate process.

Tenancy by the entirety
Joint tenancy with right of survivorship (JTWROS) that can only occur between a married couple

Community Property

Community property is a regime recognized in some states where married individuals own an equal undivided interest in all wealth accumulated during the marriage. Spouses may also own separate property that was acquired before marriage, or that was inherited or received by gift during marriage. It is possible to create separate property out of a community property by donating a spouse's interest to the other spouse. Community property does not have a survivorship feature, and thus the decedent's half will generally require the probate process for retitling. If a spouse passes away, one-half of the community property is included in the gross estate of the decedent spouse for estate tax purposes. There is also a step-up to fair market value for both halves of the community property at the death of the first spouse. This is in contrast to property titled as JTWROS or tenancy by the entirety, where only the decedent's one-half interest receives a step-up to fair market value. Community property may be dissolved by death, divorce, or agreement between the spouses.

Community property
A regime where married individuals own an equal undivided interest in all wealth accumulated during marriage

Pay-on-Death (POD) and Transfer-on-Death (TOD) Accounts

Pay-on-death bank accounts are fairly new devices. Most states have adopted these devices for bank accounts (PODs) and/or investment accounts (TODs). Essentially, they provide that if the owner of the account has a named beneficiary for the account, that account will legally transfer to the named beneficiary without going through the probate process. Such transfers reduce transfer transaction costs and may improve liquidity for the named heirs, thereby providing estate liquidity. A similar transfer mechanism has existed for a long time with regard to IRAs and other retirement accounts, annuities, and life insurance where a named person is the beneficiary of the accounts or policy. These beneficiary transfer mechanisms are easy and efficient and avoid the probate process.

Less Than Complete Ownership Interests

Property law also provides for the creation of, or transfer of, less than the full and complete ownership of property. Two of the most common types of less than full ownership are the life estate and the interest for term.

Life Estate

Life estate
An interest in property that ceases upon the death of the owner of the life interest or estate

A **life estate** is an interest in property that ceases upon the death of the owner of the life interest or estate. A life estate provides a right to income, a right to use, or both. It may be thought of as a right for a life term. Generally at the date of death of the party having the life estate, the property is transferred to the person who has the remainder interest. An example of a life estate is where one person leaves the use of his beach house to someone for life and then to a charitable or noncharitable beneficiary when that person dies.

Interest for Term

An interest for term is another example of less than full ownership, but instead of a life interest, the interest is for a definite term. An interest for term could involve an income, a use interest, or both. At the end of the interest for term, the property is either transferred to the remainderman or reverts back to the original owner, such as with a lease.

Methods of Transfer

In general, property ownership can be transferred during life or at death using one of the following three methods: outright, legal, or beneficial. In an outright transfer, the transferee receives both the legal title and beneficial (equitable) interest, or economic, ownership. In a legal transfer, the transferee, such as a trust officer, receives only the legal title but not the beneficial (equitable) interest or economic ownership. In a beneficial transfer, the transferee receives beneficial (equitable) interest or economic ownership, as with a trust beneficiary, but not the legal title.

Transfers During Life (Inter Vivos)

Property ownership transfers during life include transfer by sale, by gift, and by partial gift or sale. Transfer by sale is a transfer for the full value and full consideration (i.e., straight sale or installment sale). Transfer by completed gift is a transfer for less than full fair market value. The concept of a completed gift is where the donor no longer has any control over the property that constituted the gift. When the value received by the transferor in a sale is less than the fair market value of the property, the transfer is called a bargain sale. This type of transaction may be treated as a completed sale for state property law but will be treated by the IRS as a transfer without full and adequate consideration and so will be part gift and part sale of the property.

Transfers at Death (Testamentary)

Transfers at death include transfers by will, by laws of intestacy, by other laws such as jointly held property with a survivorship feature (i.e., JTWROS or tenancy by the entirety), by contract, and by trust. Transfers at death by contract with a named beneficiary include insurance policies, IRAs, retirement plan assets such as Section 401(k) plans, marriage contracts, and annuities. Transfers at death by trust instrument may also include revocable trusts and irrevocable trusts. All revocable trusts become irrevocable at death.

Transfers at death require retitling of the property from the decedent to the new owner. There are various retitling mechanisms, including state laws, which automatically retitle jointly held property where a survivorship feature exists. There are also legal contracts, which call for immediate retitling, such as life insurance and annuities, retirement accounts, and PODs/TODs with named beneficiaries. Where property is not automatically retitled under one of these other mechanisms, it will go through the probate process and either pass under the decedent's will (testate) or following the state laws of intestacy for retitling to the heirs.

Consequences of Property Transfers

The consequences of transfers of property depend on the method of transfer. If the transfer is for less than full consideration, the transfer is by gift. Gift taxes may be due for inter vivos (during life) transfers and are usually paid by the donor-transferor. If the transfer is by sale, there is a loss of the sold asset and the possibility of capital gain taxes; however, the consideration received replaces the asset sold. If the transfer is at death, there are the issues of costs, federal and state estate taxes, delays, and publicity.

▌INTRODUCTION TO TRUSTS

Trust

A legal arrangement, usually provided for under state law, in which property is transferred by a grantor to a trustee for the management and conservation of the property for the benefit of the named beneficiaries

A **trust** is a legal arrangement (usually provided for under state law) in which property is transferred by a grantor to a trustee for the management and conservation of the property for the benefit of the named beneficiaries. The trustee could be either an individual or a financial institution (i.e., a bank). There are usually three parties to a trust: the grantor, the trustee, and the beneficiary. The grantor, or creator, transfers property to a trustee, who takes legal title to those assets for the benefit of all trust beneficiaries. The trustee must adhere to the trust provisions regarding investments, distributions of income and corpus, and eventual termination of the trust. The trust earns income on the trust assets and may distribute that income to those entitled to it, called income beneficiaries. Usually, the grantor has created two types of beneficiaries: the income beneficiary and the remainder beneficiary. The remainder beneficiary receives the trust corpus upon termination of the trust. The income beneficiary and remainder beneficiary may be the same person, which we refer to as a single beneficiary trust. Exhibit 17.6 illustrates the basic structure of a trust.

EXHIBIT 17.6 Structure of a Trust

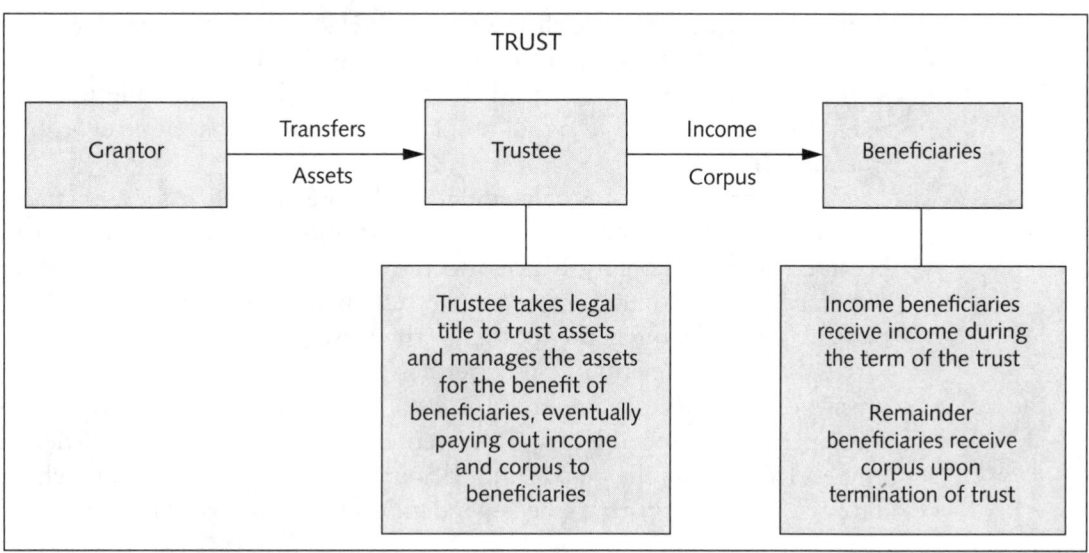

Trusts are created for a variety of purposes, including the avoidance of probate, transfer tax reduction, and the management of the trust assets. Exhibit 17.7 lists some types of trusts and their uses.

EXHIBIT 17.7 Types and Uses of Trusts

Type of Trust	Use of Trust
Living trust (revocable)	Used to manage assets. Protects in emergencies, such as medical. Avoids publicity and costs of probate. Property is included in the gross estate of the grantor (a type of grantor trust).
Irrevocable trusts (inter vivos)	Used to make gifts. Grantor has loss of control. Assets not included in gross estate of grantor unless grantor has reserved an interest (e.g., right to income) in the trust.
Testamentary trusts	Created by the will. Property is included in the gross estate and does not avoid probate. Generally used to manage assets of heirs.
Trust for minors	Manages assets for minors. May shift income tax burden to lower-bracket taxpayer.
Irrevocable life insurance trust (ILIT)	An irrevocable trust, usually created during life, used to hold an insurance policy and thus remove the proceeds from the insured's gross estate. The ILIT usually provides income to the spouse and the remainder interest to children or grandchildren.

Whether a trust is selected depends somewhat on the transfer goals of the grantor, the size of the estate, the nature of the relationship with and the financial competence of the spouse, any income needs of the spouse, the nature of the relationship with and financial security and competence of any adult children, any minor children, and any charitable intentions of the grantor. Where there is a split interest in assets (an income interest to one party and the remainder interest to a different party), a trust is used to reduce the risk that the income party will use all of the assets, leaving nothing for the remaindermen.

Common split interest trusts include the irrevocable life insurance trust, the credit equivalency trust, and QTIP trust, all of which may call for income to the decedent's spouse and the remainder to children or grandchildren. Trusts are also created to provide income to a noncharitable beneficiary (grantor/grantor spouse) with the remainder to a charity.

Trusts are either revocable or irrevocable and are either created during life (inter vivos) or at death (testamentary). If the trust is revocable, the property will be included in the gross estate of the grantor. A revocable trust will avoid the costs and process of probate but will not reduce federal estate taxes because the trust assets will be included in the grantor's gross estate. If the trust is irrevocable, the property will generally not be included in the gross estate of the grantor unless the grantor has reserved an interest, such as the right to receive income, in the trust assets. Irrevocable lifetime trusts are used to reduce estate taxes and to avoid probate. One example is the irrevocable life insurance trust (ILIT).

The inter vivos trust is created during the life of the grantor and may be revocable or irrevocable by the grantor. The property in an inter vivos trust avoids the probate process because the trust property is titled to the trust and not to the decedent. Alternatively, the property used to fund trusts created testamentary (by the will) first goes through the probate process before being retitled to the trust.

Although testamentary trusts neither reduce the estate tax nor avoid the costs and process of probate, they are useful in estate planning to protect the interests of minors, incompetents, or spendthrifts. Testamentary trusts are also useful when there is a split interest (income to one person and the remainder to someone else) such that the grantor did not want either party to be dependent on the other party for interest.

EXHIBIT 17.8 Trusts Summary Box

Established During Life	Probate	Gross Estate	Income Tax	Gift Tax
Revocable	Avoid	Included	To grantor	None at creation
Irrevocable	Avoid	Generally excluded	To trust or beneficiary	May be subject to
Established by Will				
Testamentary	Does not avoid	Included	To trust or beneficiary	Not applicable

Living Trusts

A living trust is one in which the grantor creates an inter vivos trust that is funded with part or all of the grantor's property. The advantage of a living trust is that the property does not pass through probate at death, but rather passes according to the trust provisions and with a minimum of publicity, expense, and delays.

A revocable living trust is revocable during the grantor's life and becomes irrevocable at the grantor's death. The fair market value of the assets in a revocable trust is included in the gross estate of the grantor. The grantor incurs no gift tax at the time of creation of a revocable trust because there is no completed gift.

For an irrevocable trust created during life, the grantor places property into a trust that he cannot rescind or amend. Transfers of property to an irrevocable trust constitute completed gifts, and any gift tax applies at the time the trust is created and funded. Assuming the grantor of the trust has no retained ownership interest in the irrevocable trust assets at death, such assets are generally not included in the grantor's gross estate, thereby providing both income tax and estate tax benefits to the grantor.

Grantor Trusts

A grantor trust is a trust in which the grantor transfers property into a trust but retains some right of enjoyment of the property, usually an income right. The Internal Revenue Code provides that if a grantor has control over the trust, a completed gift has not been made and the trust is not a separate taxable entity. Consequently, all the income, deductions, and credits of the trust pass through to the grantor for income tax purposes.

Later in this chapter, we identify some other trusts that are useful in certain situations and are used to reduce transfer taxes. These application trusts are listed in Exhibit 17.9.

EXHIBIT 17.9 Application Trusts and Their Uses

Application trusts	Trust uses
Credit equivalency trust (B trust—B stands for "bypassing the spouse's estate")	A B trust is usually created by the will (testamentary) and provides an amount equal to any credit equivalency (allowed by the federal estate tax laws) to be placed in trust with the spouse, the usual income beneficiary, and the children or grandchildren, or remaindermen. The principal of the trust is not included in the gross estate of the surviving spouse.
Power of appointment (POA or A) trust	A power of appointment trust is usually created by will (testamentary) providing all income annually to the spouse and with the spouse having a power to invade the principal. The assets in this trust qualify for the unlimited marital deduction at the death of the first spouse. The assets will be included in the gross estate of the surviving spouse to the extent they are not consumed during the surviving spouse's life.
Qualified terminable interest property (QTIP) trust	A testamentary trust whereby the executor elects QTIP status. The assets selected for this trust qualify for the unlimited marital deduction. The surviving spouse must receive all the trust income, paid at least annually. The remaindermen are chosen by the decedent. The assets remaining at the death of the surviving spouse are included in the gross estate of the surviving spouse.
Charitable remainder trusts (CRTs)	Charitable remainder trusts are irrevocable and may be created during life or testamentary. They are created to provide income to noncharitable beneficiaries (sometimes the grantor and/or spouse) with the remainder interest going to a charity at the end of the trust term.

REDUCING THE GROSS ESTATE

Generally speaking, if the amount of the gross estate is small, the amount of the estate tax liability will also be small. Appropriate use of qualified transfers (qualifying transfers directly to medical or educational institutions), gifts less than the annual exclusion amount, and the lifetime use of the exemption equivalency will all reduce the size of the gross estate at death. Obviously, personal consumption and lifetime transfers to charities will also reduce the gross estate. Removing the value of the proceeds of life insurance from the gross estate can dramatically reduce the size of the gross estate. There is generally little value in a decedent having an ownership interest in a life insurance policy where the decedent is the insured. The insured generally does not benefit from the proceeds during life and is usually attempting to benefit heirs at the time of the decedent's death. Why not let heirs (beneficiaries) or an ILIT own the insurance policy on the life of the insured? These are the two preferred financial and estate planning methods of owning life insurance. However, like everything else in financial planning, there are no absolutes, and careful consideration should be given as to who should own any insurance policy for a particular insured.

It is relatively easy to have a zero estate tax liability: either leave the entire taxable estate to a charity or leave the estate to the decedent's spouse in a way that qualifies for the marital deduction. However, the decedent may not have any charitable intentions or may not have a spouse to whom the decedent wants to leave the balance of the estate.

If a decedent first spouse leaves everything in a qualifying way to the surviving spouse, that will cause the deferral of estate tax until the death of the second spouse, which may (and many times does) occur shortly after the first death. In addition, because qualified transfers to a surviving spouse are added to the surviving spouse's personally owned assets to determine the gross estate of the surviving spouse, such transfers could increase the combined federal estate tax rate and amount of tax for the surviving spouse.

There are a wide variety of techniques for reducing the estate tax, all of which would be thoroughly covered in an estate planning course but are beyond the scope of this text. However, consider that only qualified transfers to a spouse qualify for the marital deduction. Is it possible to have a spouse benefit from assets without those assets qualifying for the unlimited marital deduction? The answer is yes, and as a result, the first decedent can transfer an amount equal to the estate tax exemption to nonspouse beneficiaries, simultaneously providing the spouse with a life income interest from that same transfer. Because this type of transfer is a so-called split interest (an income interest to the spouse and a remainder interest to someone else), the arrangement calls for a trust.

The Use of Life Insurance in Estate Planning

The federal estate tax return (Form 706) must be filed and the tax must generally be paid within nine months of the decedent's death. Thus, estate liquidity planning is essential and may require the purchase of life insurance because the life insurance proceeds are quickly available from the insurer upon presentation of a proper death certificate.

There is usually a need for liquid assets when someone dies. The hospital wants to be paid, the funeral home and cemetery must be paid, and creditors want to be paid. Even the costs associated with getting a death certificate from the coroner must be paid. Often the need for liquidity at death is satisfied with life insurance proceeds because life insurance is one of the quickest sources of liquidity. The beneficiary needs only to send a certified copy of the death certificate to the insurer, and the proceeds are generally paid immediately. Although insurance is an effective tool to provide liquidity at death, the proceeds of such insurance will be included in the decedent's gross estate if the insured (decedent) has any incidents of ownership in the life insurance policy at death, if the proceeds are payable to the decedent's estate, or if the decedent gifted the policy within three years of death. Therefore, it is wise for either the beneficiary of the insurance policy or an irrevocable life insurance trust to own the life insurance on the insured. Either of these arrangements will avoid including the life insurance proceeds in the insured's (decedent's) gross estate. The beneficiary-owner can then loan to the estate the cash needed for liquidity, keeping the policy proceeds from inclusion in the decedent-insured's gross estate.

COMMON ESTATE PLANNING MISTAKES

Invalid, Out-of-Date, or Poorly Drafted Wills

Having an invalid, out-of-date, or poorly drafted will can be detrimental to estate planning. No one wants to spend time developing an estate plan only to have it fall apart due to an inadequate will. An invalid will subjects the estate to intestacy laws that may distribute property contrary to the decedent's wishes. A will may be deemed invalid because it does not meet statutory requirements or because the decedent has moved to another state or domicile and has not reflected the new state's laws in the will. An outdated will often fails to minimize estate taxes because it does not contemplate changes in the tax law. Poorly drafted wills generally lack residuary clauses or other common drafting specificities, which can leave estate issues unresolved.

Simple Wills ("Sweetheart" or "I Love You" Wills)

A simple will leaves everything to the decedent's spouse. Leaving everything to a spouse can cause an overqualification of the estate because it fails to take advantage of the credit equivalency for the first spouse who dies. The second spouse to die may pay estate taxes that could have been avoided with a credit equivalency trust or bequest. There is also the risk of mismanagement of assets. Assets may be put in the hands of a spouse who does not have the education, experience, training, or desire to manage them efficiently and effectively.

Improperly Arranged or Inadequate Life Insurance

Improperly arranged or inadequate life insurance can defeat successful estate planning. If an insurance policy is arranged improperly, the proceeds will be included in the decedent's gross estate. Inclusion will occur when the policy is owned by the decedent, the proceeds are made payable to the estate, or the decedent has any incidents of ownership. Inclusion will also occur if the decedent gifted the policy to someone else within the last three years of the decedent's life.

An insurance policy is also improperly arranged when the beneficiary is ill equipped (emotionally, in legal capacity, or because of young age) to receive and manage those assets. A trust may provide the necessary management of the insurance needs.

Another way an insurance policy can be improperly arranged is when the decedent fails to name a contingent beneficiary. If the original beneficiary predeceases the decedent and there is no contingent beneficiary, the proceeds may be placed back in the estate, where the proceeds may be subject to creditor claims, state inheritance laws, federal estate taxes, or all three.

Another improper arrangement of life insurance that should be avoided is when the policy is owned by the spouse on the insured's life, and the spouse then names a child the beneficiary. At the death of the insured, the spouse has made a gift to the child.

An insurance policy is generally inadequate when it does not cover the needs of the insured, including survivor needs and estate liquidity needs. Survivor needs are generally calculated as the present value of the lost income (net of taxes and the decedent's consumption) over the remaining work life expectancy. An industry rule is to use 10 times salary to offset inflation. However, this may not provide sufficient estate liquidity where the majority of the other assets in the estate are both large in value and illiquid (real estate or a closely held business).

Possible Adverse Consequences of Jointly Held Property

Although having jointly held property with rights of survivorship offers some benefits, it can also pose several problems. One problem is that the decedent may not be able to direct the property to the person or entity he wishes because the survivor obtains complete ownership of the property. Another problem is that creating jointly held property might result in a completed gift. The consequence of this may be a federal and state gift tax liability as well as an estate tax liability.

Estate Liquidity Problems

Insufficient cash assets and inadequate planning are two estate liquidity problems that should be avoided. When there are insufficient cash assets and estate planning has been inadequate, the estate may be forced to liquidate assets when they are not fully valued or have not reached their potential value. The result is that assets may have to be sold at less than full value.

Wrong Executor/Trustee/Manager

Having the wrong executor/trustee/manager can cause several problems in the estate plan. When the named executor/trustee is incapable of administering the estate efficiently and effectively, it can make costs increase as a result of poor estate management. It can also cause potential conflicts of interest when there are proximity problems or family conflicts.

▌THE UNIFIED GIFT AND ESTATE TRANSFER TAX SYSTEM

The federal estate tax is a method of raising revenue for the federal government. It is also a method of social reallocation of wealth. The estate tax system prevents large masses of wealth from being transferred from one generation to subsequent generations. When a taxpayer with a large estate dies, a large portion of the estate will be paid to the federal government in the form of estate tax and thus will be reallocated to other members of society.

The unified estate and gift transfer tax system exists to prevent individuals (donors) from freely transferring property to others (donees) in an attempt to minimize income and estate tax. Congress, ever mindful of the resolve and ingenuity with which some taxpayers try to avoid federal taxes, established an excise tax for gifts during life. The excise tax is applied to the transfer of property gratuitously during life. In 1976, Congress unified the gift and estate tax schedules to prevent taxpayers from manipulating transfers during life and death.

Unified gift and estate transfer tax system
Unified tax transfer system created by Congress to ensure that at the time of transfer of property, either during life (gifts) or at death (bequests), the transferor will pay the same tax rate or amount for the transfer

The general theory behind the **unified gift and estate transfer tax system** is that at the time of transfer of property, either during life (gifts) or at death (bequests), the transferor will pay the same tax rate or amount for the transfer. Later in the chapter, we will point out major differences between transfers made during life and those made at death. Observe in Exhibit 17.10 that the maximum gift and estate tax rate in 2020 is 40%. As with many other types of taxes, there are ways to arrange one's financial affairs to reduce or eliminate the transfer tax, thus preserving a greater portion of the estate for heirs.

EXHIBIT 17.10 Unified Tax Rate Schedule for Gifts and Estates for 2020

More than $0 but not over $10,000	**18%** of such amount
More than $10,000 but not more than $20,000	$1,800 plus **20%** of any amount over $10,000
More than $20,000 but not more than $40,000	$3,800 plus **22%** of any amount over $20,000
More than $40,000 but not more than $60,000	$8,200 plus **24%** of any amount over $40,000
More than $60,000 but not more than $80,000	$13,000 plus **26%** of any amount over $60,000
More than $80,000 but not more than $100,000	$18,200 plus **28%** of any amount over $80,000
More than $100,000 but not more than $150,000	$23,800 plus **30%** of any amount over $100,000
More than $150,000 but not more than $250,000	$38,800 plus **32%** of any amount over $150,000
More than $250,000 but not more than $500,000	$70,800 plus **34%** of any amount over $250,000
More than $500,000 but not more than $750,000	$155,800 plus **37%** of any amount over $500,000
More than $750,000 but not more than $1,000,000	$248,300 plus 39% of any amount over $750,000
More than $1,000,000	$345,800 plus 40% of any amount over $1,000,000

The estate and gift tax rates and credit exemption amount for 2020 are as shown in Exhibit 17.11.

EXHIBIT 17.11 Estate and Gift Tax Rates and Credit Exemption Amount for 2020

Calendar Year	Estate, Gift, and GST Tax Exemption	Highest Estate and Gift Tax Rates
2020	$11,580,000	40%

Most property inherited from a decedent receives a stepped-up basis equal to its fair market value on the date of death or on the alternate valuation date (AVD) if the decedent's estate elected to use the AVD on the federal estate tax return. Property inherited from a decedent is always considered to be long-term property for purposes of the capital gains tax.

THE FEDERAL GIFT TAX SYSTEM

Purpose and Definition

Gift
In estate planning, a direct transfer of property or cash made during life

Recall that one of the estate planning objectives mentioned earlier in this chapter was the effective and efficient transfer of property. What could be more effective or efficient than a direct **gift** from the client during life to a loved one? First, because the client is still living, the transferor can ensure the completion of the gift. Second, the direct gift generally has little transaction cost except perhaps the cost to change the title to the asset (such as when retitling a car in the name of the donee). Third, the client (transferor) is able to see the beneficial effect of his transfer and the joy the gift brings to the donee while also enjoying the pleasure of making the gift. Unfortunately, whenever a gift is made, the client loses control of the asset given and loses income from the asset, which may be needed currently or at some point in the future. The creation of a joint bank account is not a gift until the joint tenant removes the money for his own benefit. Also, the client has financially empowered the donee (transferee), which may turn out to be ill advised. The transferee may not use the property wisely, as the transferor intended, or may no longer behave in a way in which the transferor desired. Even with these noted disadvantages, lifetime gifts remain a cornerstone of estate planning for the reasons stated here and for the reasons discussed next.

If the overall objective of the client is estate reduction, it may be wise to transfer the property with the greatest potential for future appreciation rather than cash or property that has already appreciated. A gift of property will be valued for gift tax purposes at the fair market value as of the date of the gift or transfer. Therefore, any future appreciation on the transferred property will be to the transferee (donee) and, thus, out of the transferor's gross estate. Property that commonly has substantial future appreciation includes (1) business interests, (2) real estate, (3) art or other collections, (4) investment securities (stocks and bonds), and (5) other intangible rights (patents, copyrights, and royalties). Thus, the selection of property for gifting requires careful financial and estate planning consideration.

Annual Exclusion

Annual exclusion

A result of a de minimis rule by Congress to eliminate the need for taxpayers to keep an account of, or report, small gifts. All individuals are allowed to gift, tax-free, up to $15,000 (for 2020) per donee per year.

All individuals are allowed to gift, tax free, up to $15,000 (for 2020) per donee per year. This **annual exclusion** is a result of a de minimis rule by Congress to help reduce reporting requirements of taxpayers for small gifts. However, to qualify for the annual exclusion, the gift must be of a present interest, which means that the donee can currently benefit from the gift. If the gift is of a future interest, such as a gift of a remainder interest in a trust, the gift does not qualify for the annual exclusion. The annual exclusion amount is indexed to the CPI.

Split gift

A joint gift made by spouses that has the effect of doubling the annual exclusion of gifts to the donee. A split gift requires the consent of the spouse and spouse's signature on Form 709.

If a person (transferor) is married and joins with his spouse to use both annual exclusions for a particular donee, the exclusion is effectively increased to $30,000 per donee per year. When one donor makes the gift but the donor's spouse consents and agrees to use their annual exclusion for that donee, then the joint gift is called a **split gift**. A gift tax return (Form 709) is required for all split gifts, and both spouses are required to sign the gift tax return. In addition, if an election to split gifts is made, it applies to all gifts made from both spouses during the year while the spouses were married. Only gifts made while the donors are married qualify for split gift treatment.

Not all joint gifts are subject to gift splitting. Gifts of community property, for example, do not require gift splitting because each spouse is deemed to own one-half of any community property. Therefore, any gift of community property is a joint gift not subject to gift splitting. Gift splitting was enacted to equalize community and noncommunity property states. Because gifts of community property are not considered gift splits, a return is not required unless the gifts constitute taxable gifts (i.e., exceed $30,000 to an individual recipient).

E X A M P L E   Gift Splitting

Kelly made the following gifts in the current year:

Gift	Donee	Value
Cash	Nephew	$15,000
6-month CD	Niece	8,000
Antique rifle	Friend	20,000
Bonds in trust—Life estate to	Father	60,000
Remainder to:	Niece	18,000
	Total	$121,000

Kelly's total taxable gifts for the current year equal $68,000 as described below:

Donee	FMV	Less Annual Exclusion	Total Taxable Gifts
Nephew	$15,000	$15,000	0
Niece	8,000	8,000	0
Friend	20,000	15,000	5,000
Father	60,000	15,000	45,000
Niece	18,000	Not available	18,000
Total gifts	$121,000	$53,000	$68,000

All of Kelly's gifts qualified for the annual exclusion except the gift to her niece consisting of the remainder interest in a trust. Because her niece is unable to currently use the gift, it is not a gift of a present interest and, therefore, does not qualify for the annual exclusion. All of the other gifts qualify because they are of a present interest.

E X A M P L E   Gift Splitting Comparison

John and Mary made the following gifts during the current year:

	From John	From Mary	Total
To son, Paul	$40,000	$16,000	$56,000
To daughter, Virginia	40,000	6,000	46,000
To granddaughter, Terry	20,000	4,000	24,000
	$100,000	$26,000	$126,000

A comparison of gift splitting and not using gift splitting is provided for John and Mary's taxable gifts below.

If Gift Splitting Is Elected (the Parties Must Split All Gifts Made During Year)

	From John	From Mary	Total
To Paul	$28,000	$28,000	$56,000
To Virginia	23,000	23,000	46,000
To Terry	12,000	12,000	24,000
Total gross gifts	$63,000	$63,000	$126,000
Less annual exclusions			
For Paul	$15,000	$15,000	$30,000
For Virginia	15,000	15,000	30,000
For Terry	12,000	12,000	24,000
Total exclusions	$42,000	$42,000	$84,000
Current taxable gifts	$21,000	$21,000	$42,000

If Gift Splitting Is Not Elected

	From John	From Mary	Total
To Paul	$40,000	$16,000	$56,000
To Virginia	40,000	6,000	46,000
To Terry	20,000	4,000	24,000
Total gross gifts	$100,000	$26,000	$126,000
Less annual exclusions			
For Paul	$15,000	$15,000	$30,000
For Virginia	15,000	6,000	21,000
For Terry	15,000	4,000	19,000
Total exclusions	$45,000	$25,000	$70,000
Current taxable gifts	$55,000	$1,000	$56,000

An election to the split gifts in the above example results in a decrease in the total taxable gifts from $56,000 to $42,000. The $14,000 difference is a result of the couple not making full use of their annual exclusions when they don't use gift splitting ($56,000 – $42,000 = $14,000).

Applicable Credit Amount; Lifetime Exemption

In addition to the annual exclusion, a lifetime gift and estate tax credit is used to offset the gift and estate tax on inter vivos and testamentary transfers. This credit allows taxpayers to transfer during life assets totaling $11,580,000 (for 2020) without incurring any transfer tax. This amount is known as the applicable exclusion amount or the lifetime exemption amount.

EXHIBIT 17.12 Applicable Exclusion (Lifetime Exemption) Amount and Applicable Credit Amount

	2020
Applicable exclusion (lifetime exemption) amount	$11,580,000
Applicable credit amount	$4,577,800

The $11,580,000 exemption amount is a cumulative lifetime total and applies to all taxable gifts made during life. Any portion of the exemption amount that remains unused at death is applied toward the estate tax.

Portability Between Spouses

The $11,580,000 lifetime exemption amount is portable between spouses. Portability means that a surviving spouse may use any portion of a predeceased spouse's exemption amount that remained unused when the predeceased spouse died. For example, if the predeceased spouse used none of her exemption during life or at death, the surviving spouse could potentially have a $23,160,000 exemption. The surviving spouse may apply the predeceased spouse's unused exemption amount both to lifetime transfers and to transfers at death.

The restrictions on portability are as follows.

■ The predeceased spouse must have died after December 31, 2010.

■ The predeceased spouse's estate must have filed a timely estate tax return and made an election to permit the surviving spouse to use the deceased spouse's unused exemption amount.

■ If a surviving spouse has more than one predeceased spouse, only the unused exemption amount of the last predeceased spouse is available.

E X A M P L E   James and Margaret are married. James made no taxable gifts during his life. When he died in 2020, his taxable estate was $3 million. Because James used only $3 million of his $11,580,000 exemption amount when he died, Margaret can add his $8,580,000 unused exemption to her own $11,580,000 exemption amount for a total of $20,160,000. Margaret can apply the $20,160,000 exemption amount to lifetime taxable gifts and when she dies, her estate can apply any remaining amount against her estate tax.

Qualified Transfers

Qualified transfer
A payment made directly to an educational institution for tuition and fees or to a medical provider for medical expenses for the benefit of someone else

Certain transfers, called qualified transfers, are not subject to gift tax. A **qualified transfer** is a payment made directly to an educational institution for tuition and fees or directly to a medical provider for medical expenses for the benefit of someone else. These qualified transfers allow taxpayers to effectively transfer wealth to others without being subject to gift tax. However, to qualify for this treatment, the payments must be paid directly to the specific institution.

E X A M P L E   Jennifer, who is single, gave an outright gift of $60,000 to her friend, Tiffany, who needed the money to pay her medical expenses. Because the gift was made to Tiffany instead of being paid directly to the medical institution, it cannot be considered a qualified transfer. However, the gift is of a present interest and, therefore, qualifies for the $15,000 annual exclusion. Therefore, Jennifer has made a taxable gift of $45,000 and must file a gift tax return to report the gift. If Jennifer had paid the medical expenses directly to the medical institution for Tiffany, the entire $60,000 received for Tiffany would have escaped gift taxes. In addition, Jennifer would have been able to give Tiffany another $15,000 that would qualify for the annual exclusion.

Because qualified transfers are not subject to gift tax and there is no limitation on the amount of the qualified transfer, it allows family members to provide assistance to other family members without worrying about transfer taxes. In addition, families can make use of the rules to minimize gift tax within the family by allowing, for example, grandparents to pay for college education for their grandchildren instead of making taxable gifts to the parents, who would, in turn, pay for the college expenses. Although qualified transfers are often used in family situations, the gift tax exclusion for qualified transfers is not limited to family members; it is available even if the donor is unrelated to the person who benefits from the transfer.

Gifts to Spouses

Marital deduction

unlimited deduction for transfers of property to a spouse during life (gifts) or at death (bequests)

The law provides an unlimited marital deduction for gifts and bequests to a spouse, including a same-sex spouse. To be eligible for the gift tax **marital deduction**, however, the donee spouse must be a citizen of the United States. When the donee spouse is a non-citizen, there is a special annual exclusion that shelters allows gifts of up to $157,000 per year to the non-citizen spouse (in 2020).

The estate tax marital deduction for non-citizen spouses is discussed later in this chapter.

Payments for Support

Payments for legal support

transfers to children that are essentially legal support obligations; exempt from gift tax rules

Payments for legal support are transfers to children that are essentially legal support obligations. Payments of support are exempt from the gift tax rules.

Reporting and Paying Taxes

Taxable gifts are reported on the federal gift tax return, Form 709. The gift tax return is due April 15 but may be extended until October 15, as with individual income tax returns. However, the gift tax is not extended as a result of the extension of time to file and is therefore due on April 15, similar to individual income tax. The donor is liable for any gift tax due. The gift tax return is also used to report transfers that are subject to generation-skipping transfer tax, which is discussed later in the chapter.

EXHIBIT 17.13 Basic Strategies for Transferring Wealth Through Gifting

Generally, if the objective of the transferor is to reduce the size of his gross estate, he can use the following lifetime gifting techniques to achieve a lower gross estate at death:

- Make optimal use of qualified educational transfers (pay tuition for children and grandchildren from private school through professional education).

- Pay medical costs for children, grandchildren, and heirs directly to provider institutions.

- Make optimal use of the $15,000 annual gift exclusion ($30,000 if the gift is made jointly with the spouse). Example: John is married to Joan and has 3 adult children who all have stable marriages, and there are 7 grandchildren. John and Joan can gift $390,000 per year without incurring any gift tax: $30,000 × 13 transferees (3 children, 3 spouses, 7 grandchildren)

- A spouse may make unlimited lifetime gifts to a spouse who is a U.S. citizen.

- If the above four strategies are completely exhausted, the transferor can begin using his applicable exclusion amount ($11,580,000) while still paying no gift tax until the summation of lifetime taxable gifts exceeds the lifetime credit equivalency amount.

- Any gift tax paid on gifts prior to three years of death is also excluded from the gross estate of the transferor. This is discussed later in this chapter.

EXHIBIT 17.14 Form 709

Form **709**

Department of the Treasury
Internal Revenue Service

United States Gift (and Generation-Skipping Transfer) Tax Return

▶ Go to *www.irs.gov/Form709* for instructions and the latest information.

(For gifts made during calendar year 2019)

▶ See instructions.

OMB No. 1545-0020

20**19**

Part 1—General Information

1 Donor's first name and middle initial		**2** Donor's last name	**3** Donor's social security number
4 Address (number, street, and apartment number)			**5** Legal residence (domicile)
6 City or town, state or province, country, and ZIP or foreign postal code			**7** Citizenship (see instructions)

		Yes	No
8	If the donor died during the year, check here ▶ ☐ and enter date of death _____ , _____ .		
9	If you extended the time to file this Form 709, check here ▶ ☐		
10	Enter the total number of donees listed on Schedule A. Count each person only once ▶		
11a	Have you (the donor) previously filed a Form 709 (or 709-A) for any other year? If "No," skip line 11b		
b	Has your address changed since you last filed Form 709 (or 709-A)?		
12	**Gifts by husband or wife to third parties.** Do you consent to have the gifts (including generation-skipping transfers) made by you and by your spouse to third parties during the calendar year considered as made one-half by each of you? (See instructions.) (If the answer is "Yes," the following information must be furnished and your spouse must sign the consent shown below. **If the answer is "No," skip lines 13–18.**)		
13	Name of consenting spouse	**14** SSN	
15	Were you married to one another during the entire calendar year? See instructions		
16	If line 15 is "No," check whether ☐ married ☐ divorced or ☐ widowed/deceased, and give date. See instructions ▶		
17	Will a gift tax return for this year be filed by your spouse? If "Yes," mail both returns in the same envelope		
18	**Consent of Spouse.** I consent to have the gifts (and generation-skipping transfers) made by me and by my spouse to third parties during the calendar year considered as made one-half by each of us. We are both aware of the joint and several liability for tax created by the execution of this consent.		

Consenting spouse's signature ▶   Date ▶

19	Have you applied a DSUE amount received from a predeceased spouse to a gift or gifts reported on this or a previous Form 709? If "Yes," complete Schedule C	

Part 2—Tax Computation

1	Enter the amount from Schedule A, Part 4, line 11	**1**	
2	Enter the amount from Schedule B, line 3	**2**	
3	Total taxable gifts. Add lines 1 and 2	**3**	
4	Tax computed on amount on line 3 (see *Table for Computing Gift Tax* in instructions)	**4**	
5	Tax computed on amount on line 2 (see *Table for Computing Gift Tax* in instructions)	**5**	
6	Balance. Subtract line 5 from line 4	**6**	
7	Applicable credit amount. If donor has DSUE amount from predeceased spouse(s) or Restored Exclusion Amount, enter amount from Schedule C, line 5; otherwise, see instructions	**7**	
8	Enter the applicable credit against tax allowable for all prior periods (from Sch. B, line 1, col. C)	**8**	
9	Balance. Subtract line 8 from line 7. Do not enter less than zero	**9**	
10	Enter 20% (0.20) of the amount allowed as a specific exemption for gifts made after September 8, 1976, and before January 1, 1977. See instructions	**10**	
11	Balance. Subtract line 10 from line 9. Do not enter less than zero	**11**	
12	Applicable credit. Enter the smaller of line 6 or line 11	**12**	
13	Credit for foreign gift taxes (see instructions)	**13**	
14	Total credits. Add lines 12 and 13	**14**	
15	Balance. Subtract line 14 from line 6. Do not enter less than zero	**15**	
16	Generation-skipping transfer taxes (from Schedule D, Part 3, col. G, total)	**16**	
17	Total tax. Add lines 15 and 16	**17**	
18	Gift and generation-skipping transfer taxes prepaid with extension of time to file	**18**	
19	If line 18 is less than line 17, enter **balance due.** See instructions	**19**	
20	If line 18 is greater than line 17, enter **amount to be refunded**	**20**	

Attach check or money order here.

Sign Here

Under penalties of perjury, I declare that I have examined this return, including any accompanying schedules and statements, and to the best of my knowledge and belief, it is true, correct, and complete. Declaration of preparer (other than donor) is based on all information of which preparer has any knowledge.

▶ _____
Signature of donor   Date

May the IRS discuss this return with the preparer shown below? See instructions. ☐ Yes ☐ No

Paid Preparer Use Only

Print/Type preparer's name	Preparer's signature	Date	Check ☐ if self-employed	PTIN
Firm's name ▶			Firm's EIN ▶	
Firm's address ▶			Phone no.	

For Disclosure, Privacy Act, and Paperwork Reduction Act Notice, see the instructions for this form.   Cat. No. 16783M   Form **709** (2019)

EXHIBIT 17.14 Form 709 (continued)

Form 709 (2019)   Page **2**

| SCHEDULE A | Computation of Taxable Gifts (Including transfers in trust) (see instructions) |

A   Does the value of any item listed on Schedule A reflect any valuation discount? If "Yes," attach explanation . . . . . . Yes ☐   No ☐

B   ☐ ◄ Check here if you elect under section 529(c)(2)(B) to treat any transfers made this year to a qualified tuition program as made ratably over a 5-year period beginning this year. See instructions. Attach explanation.

Part 1—Gifts Subject Only to Gift Tax. Gifts less political organization, medical, and educational exclusions. See instructions.

A Item number	B • Donee's name and address • Relationship to donor (if any) • Description of gift • If the gift was of securities, give CUSIP no. • If closely held entity, give EIN	C	D Donor's adjusted basis of gift	E Date of gift	F Value at date of gift	G For split gifts, enter ½ of column F	H Net transfer (subtract col. G from col. F)
1							

Gifts made by spouse—complete **only** if you are splitting gifts with your spouse and he/she also made gifts.

Total of Part 1. Add amounts from Part 1, column H . . . . ►

Part 2—Direct Skips. Gifts that are direct skips and are subject to both gift tax and generation-skipping transfer tax. You must list the gifts in chronological order.

A Item number	B • Donee's name and address • Relationship to donor (if any) • Description of gift • If the gift was of securities, give CUSIP no. • If closely held entity, give EIN	C 2632(b) election out	D Donor's adjusted basis of gift	E Date of gift	F Value at date of gift	G For split gifts, enter ½ of column F	H Net transfer (subtract col. G from col. F)
1							

Gifts made by spouse—complete **only** if you are splitting gifts with your spouse and he/she also made gifts.

Total of Part 2. Add amounts from Part 2, column H . . . . ►

Part 3—Indirect Skips and Other Transfers in Trust. Gifts to trusts that are indirect skips as defined under section 2632(c) or to trusts that are currently subject to gift tax and may later be subject to generation-skipping transfer tax. You must list these gifts in chronological order.

A Item number	B • Donee's name and address • Relationship to donor (if any) • Description of gift • If the gift was of securities, give CUSIP no. • If closely held entity, give EIN	C 2632(c) election	D Donor's adjusted basis of gift	E Date of gift	F Value at date of gift	G For split gifts, enter ½ of column F	H Net transfer (subtract col. G from col. F)
1							

Gifts made by spouse—complete **only** if you are splitting gifts with your spouse and he/she also made gifts.

Total of Part 3. Add amounts from Part 3, column H . . . . ►

(If more space is needed, attach additional statements.)   Form **709** (2019)

EXHIBIT 17.14 Form 709 (continued)

Part 4—Taxable Gift Reconciliation

1	Total value of gifts of donor. Add totals from column H of Parts 1, 2, and 3	**1**	
2	Total annual exclusions for gifts listed on line 1 (see instructions)	**2**	
3	Total included amount of gifts. Subtract line 2 from line 1	**3**	

Deductions (see instructions)

4	Gifts of interests to spouse for which a marital deduction will be claimed, based on item numbers _____ of Schedule A	**4**		
5	Exclusions attributable to gifts on line 4	**5**		
6	Marital deduction. Subtract line 5 from line 4	**6**		
7	Charitable deduction, based on item numbers _____ less exclusions	**7**		
8	Total deductions. Add lines 6 and 7		**8**	
9	Subtract line 8 from line 3		**9**	
10	Generation-skipping transfer taxes payable with this Form 709 (from Schedule D, Part 3, col. G, total)		**10**	
11	**Taxable gifts.** Add lines 9 and 10. Enter here and on page 1, Part 2—Tax Computation, line 1		**11**	

Terminable Interest (QTIP) Marital Deduction. (See instructions for Schedule A, Part 4, line 4.)

If a trust (or other property) meets the requirements of qualified terminable interest property under section 2523(f), and:

a. The trust (or other property) is listed on Schedule A; and

b. The value of the trust (or other property) is entered in whole or in part as a deduction on Schedule A, Part 4, line 4, then the donor shall be deemed to have made an election to have such trust (or other property) treated as qualified terminable interest property under section 2523(f).

If less than the entire value of the trust (or other property) that the donor has included in Parts 1 and 3 of Schedule A is entered as a deduction on line 4, the donor shall be considered to have made an election only as to a fraction of the trust (or other property). The numerator of this fraction is equal to the amount of the trust (or other property) deducted on Schedule A, Part 4, line 6. The denominator is equal to the total value of the trust (or other property) listed in Parts 1 and 3 of Schedule A.

If you make the QTIP election, the terminable interest property involved will be included in your spouse's gross estate upon his or her death (section 2044). See instructions for line 4 of Schedule A. If your spouse disposes (by gift or otherwise) of all or part of the qualifying life income interest, he or she will be considered to have made a transfer of the entire property that is subject to the gift tax. See *Transfer of Certain Life Estates Received From Spouse* in the instructions.

12   Election Out of QTIP Treatment of Annuities

☐ ◀ Check here if you elect under section 2523(f)(6) **not** to treat as qualified terminable interest property any joint and survivor annuities that are reported on Schedule A and would otherwise be treated as qualified terminable interest property under section 2523(f). See instructions. Enter the item numbers from Schedule A for the annuities for which you are making this election ▶

SCHEDULE B   Gifts From Prior Periods

If you answered "Yes" on line 11a of page 1, Part 1, see the instructions for completing Schedule B. If you answered "No," skip to the Tax Computation on page 1 (or Schedule C or D, if applicable). Complete Schedule A before beginning Schedule B. See instructions for recalculation of the column C amounts. Attach calculations.

A Calendar year or calendar quarter (see instructions)	B Internal Revenue office where prior return was filed	C Amount of applicable credit (unified credit) against gift tax for periods after December 31, 1976	D Amount of specific exemption for prior periods ending before January 1, 1977	E Amount of taxable gifts

1	Totals for prior periods	**1**	
2	Amount, if any, by which total specific exemption, line 1, column D, is more than $30,000	**2**	
3	Total amount of taxable gifts for prior periods. Add amount on line 1, column E, and amount, if any, on line 2. Enter here and on page 1, Part 2—Tax Computation, line 2	**3**	

(If more space is needed, attach additional statements.)   Form **709** (2019)

EXHIBIT 17.14 Form 709 (continued)

Form 709 (2019)   Page **4**

SCHEDULE C   Deceased Spousal Unused Exclusion (DSUE) Amount and Restored Exclusion

Provide the following information to determine the DSUE amount and applicable credit received from prior spouses. Complete Schedule A before beginning Schedule C.

A Name of deceased spouse (dates of death after December 31, 2010, only)	B Date of death	C Portability election made?		D If "Yes," DSUE amount received from spouse	E DSUE amount applied by donor to lifetime gifts (list current and prior gifts)	F Date of gift(s) (enter as mm/dd/yy for Part 1 and as yyyy for Part 2)
		Yes	No			
Part 1—DSUE RECEIVED FROM LAST DECEASED SPOUSE						
Part 2—DSUE RECEIVED FROM PREDECEASED SPOUSE(S)						

TOTAL (for all DSUE amounts applied from column E for Part 1 and Part 2) . . . . ▶

1	Donor's basic exclusion amount (see instructions)	**1**
2	Total from column E, Parts 1 and 2	**2**
3	Restored Exclusion Amount (see instructions)	**3**
4	Add lines 1, 2, and 3	**4**
5	Applicable credit on amount in line 4 (see *Table for Computing Gift Tax* in the instructions). Enter here and on line 7, Part 2—Tax Computation	**5**

SCHEDULE D   Computation of Generation-Skipping Transfer Tax

Note: Inter vivos direct skips that are completely excluded by the GST exemption must still be fully reported (including value and exemptions claimed) on Schedule D.

Part 1—Generation-Skipping Transfers. List items from Schedule A first, then items to be reported on Schedule D, including any transfers subject to an Estate Tax Inclusion Period (ETIP).

A Item number (from Schedule A, Part 2, col. A, then ETIP transfers, if any)	B Description (only for ETIP transfers)	C Value (from Schedule A, Part 2, col. H, or close of ETIP described in col. B)	D Nontaxable portion of transfer	E Net transfer (subtract col. D from col. C)
1				
Gifts made by spouse (for gift splitting only)				

(If more space is needed, attach additional statements.)   Form **709** (2019)

EXHIBIT 17.14 Form 709 (continued)

Part 2—GST Exemption Reconciliation (Section 2631) and Section 2652(a)(3) Election

Check here ▶ ☐ if you are making a section 2652(a)(3) (special QTIP) election. See instructions.

Enter the item numbers from Schedule A of the gifts for which you are making this election ▶ ----------------------------------

1	Maximum allowable exemption (see instructions)	**1**
2	Total exemption used for periods before filing this return	**2**
3	Exemption available for this return. Subtract line 2 from line 1	**3**
4	Exemption claimed on this return from Part 3, column C, total below	**4**
5	Automatic allocation of exemption to transfers reported on Schedule A, Part 3. To opt out of the automatic allocation rules, you must attach an "**Election Out**" statement. See instructions	**5**
6	Exemption allocated to transfers not shown on line 4 or line 5 above. **You must attach a "Notice of Allocation."** See instructions	**6**
7	Add lines 4, 5, and 6	**7**
8	Exemption available for future transfers. Subtract line 7 from line 3	**8**

Part 3—Tax Computation

A Item number (from Schedule D, Part 1)	B Net transfer (from Schedule D, Part 1, col. E)	C GST exemption allocated	D Divide col. C by col. B	E Inclusion ratio (Subtract col. D from 1.000)	F Applicable rate (multiply col. E by 40% (0.40))	G Generation-skipping transfer tax (multiply col. B by col. F)
1						
Gifts made by spouse (for gift splitting only)						
Total exemption claimed. Enter here and on Part 2, line 4, above. May not exceed Part 2, line 3, above . . .		**Total generation-skipping transfer tax.** Enter here; on page 3, Schedule A, Part 4, line 10; and on page 1, Part 2—Tax Computation, line 16				

(If more space is needed, attach additional statements.)   Form **709** (2019)

THE FEDERAL ESTATE TAX SYSTEM

Purpose and Definition

Federal estate tax
An excise tax on the right to transfer assets by a decedent

The **federal estate tax** is an excise tax on the right to transfer assets by a decedent. To properly determine the estate tax liability, the executor must first determine what assets are included in the gross estate. Generally, the gross estate includes all property that the decedent owned at death at the fair market value of the decedent's interest.

The gross estate (Exhibit 17.15, line 1) less the enumerated deductible expenses (lines 2–6) equals the adjusted gross estate (line 8). From the adjusted gross estate (line 7) are three deductions: (1) the value of property left to a qualified charity and (2) the value of qualified property left to the decedent's spouse and (3) state death taxes paid. The net result of the adjusted gross estate (line 7) less any state death taxes paid (line 10), any marital deduction (line 9) and any charitable deduction (line 8) equals the taxable estate (line 11).

Following the determination of the taxable estate, any taxable gifts (transfers that did not qualify for the annual exclusion) made after 1976 are added to determine the tentative tax base (line 11 + line 12 = line 13). The tentative tax (line 14) is calculated using the Unified Estate and Gift Tax Schedule. From the tentative tax are subtracted any credits, such as previous gift tax paid (line 15) and the applicable credit amount (line 16), to determine the federal estate tax liability (line 17).

EXHIBIT 17.15 The Estate Tax Formula

(1)	Gross estate (GE)		$ _____	Gross estate
	Less deductions:			
(2)	Last medical	$ _____		
(3)	Administrative costs	$ _____		
(4)	Funeral	$ _____		
(5)	Debts	$ _____		
(6)	Losses during estate administration	$ _____	$ _____	Deductions
(7)	Equals: adjusted gross estate (AGE)		$ _____	Adjusted gross estate
(8)	Less: charitable deduction	$ _____		
(9)	Less: marital deduction	$ _____		
(10)	Less: state death tax paid	$ _____	$ _____	
(11)	Equals: taxable estate (TE)		$ _____	Taxable estate
(12)	Add: previous taxable gifts (post-1976)		$ _____	Post-1976 gifts
(13)	Equals: tentative tax base (TTB)		$ _____	Tentative tax base
(14)	Tentative tax (TT)		$ _____	Tentative tax
	Less: credits			
(15)	Previous gift tax deemed paid	$ _____		
(16)	Applicable credit amount	$ _____		
(17)	Equals: federal estate tax liability (FETL)		$ _____	Federal estate tax liability

Reporting and Paying Taxes

Federal estate tax is reported on the federal estate tax return (Form 706). The federal estate tax return is due nine months from the date of death but may be extended six months. However, an extension of time for filing does not extend the time for paying the estate tax. Therefore, unless permitted by one of the statutory exceptions, estate tax is payable nine months after the date of death.

The Gross Estate

The financial planner must have a clear understanding of the size of the client's **gross estate** in order to develop a meaningful estate plan. The size and types of assets included in the gross estate will directly determine which planning techniques should be implemented. Exhibit 17.16 illustrates most of the asset types that may be included in the gross estate as covered in Section 2033 (the relevant code section) of the Internal Revenue Code.

Gross estate

All assets included in a decedent's estate, including but not limited to cash, stocks, bonds, annuities, retirement accounts, notes receivable, personal residences, automobiles, art collections, life insurance proceeds, and income tax refunds due

EXHIBIT 17.16 Assets Included in the Gross Estate

Cash
Stocks and bonds
Annuities
Retirement accounts
Notes receivable
Personal residence
Other real estate
Household goods
Automobiles
Business interests
Proceeds of life insurance
Collections (art, wine, jewelry)
Vested future rights
Outstanding loans due decedent from others
Income tax refunds due
Patents/copyrights
Damages owed decedent
Dividends declared and payable
Income in respect of decedent
Decedent's share of property held with others
Other tangible personal property

*List may not be all inclusive.

Note that the gross estate includes the decedent's interest in any jointly held property and the proceeds of life insurance on the decedents life where (1) the decedent had any incidents of ownership in the policy at the time of death, (2) the decedent had assigned (gifted) the insurance to someone else within three years of the decedent's death, or (3) the proceeds are payable to the decedent's estate. The valuation of property included in the gross estate is either the fair market value at the date of death or, if properly elected, the value for the alternate valuation date (six months from the date of death or date of sale if it occurs between the date of death and the alternate valuation date). The alternate valuation date is provided to give relief to a decedent who happened to die on a date when the gross estate was valued very highly as a result of the temporary market conditions. Certain requirements must be met in order to elect the alternate valuation date.

Deductions From the Gross Estate

Adjusted gross estate
Gross estate less deductions provided for by law in recognition that the entire value of the gross estate will not be transferred to the heirs due to costs, debts, and certain other deductions

Once the assets are identified and the value of the gross estate is determined, the next step is to determine the allowed deductions to arrive at the **adjusted gross estate** (see Exhibit 17.15). The deductions are provided in recognition that the entire value of the gross estate will not be transferred to the heirs because of costs, debts, and certain other deductions.

The adjusted gross estate is determined by deducting the following:

- Funeral expenses
- Last medical costs
- Administration expenses
- Debts
- Losses during estate administration

Funeral Costs

Reasonable expenditures related to the funeral, such as interment costs, burial plot, grave marker, and transportation of the body to the place of burial, are deductible for estate tax purposes.

Last Medical Costs

Medical costs related to the decedent's last illness are deductible from the gross estate as long as they are not deducted on the decedent's final federal income tax return.

Administrative Expenses

Any expenses related to the administration of the estate are deductible from either the estate tax return (Form 706) or the estate's income tax return (Form 1041). These expenses generally include attorney and accountant fees for preparing the estate tax return, the final Form 1040, and the estate income tax return and expenses related to the retitling of assets through the probate process. These costs may also include appraisal and valuation fees necessary to determine values of assets included in the gross estate for estate tax purposes.

Debts

All debts of the decedent are deductible from the gross estate. These debts include any amounts the decedent was obligated to pay while alive, plus interest accrued to the date of death. Debts generally include such items as outstanding mortgages, income tax due, credit card balances, and other miscellaneous outstanding debts.

Losses During Estate Administration

Any losses to the estate during the period of administration, including casualty and theft losses, are deductible expenses to the extent they exceed insurance reimbursements.

State Death Taxes

There is also a deduction for death taxes actually paid to any state. The deduction for the state death taxes paid is not deducted to arrive at the adjusted gross estate; instead, the state death taxes are deducted from the adjusted gross estate at the same time both the charitable and marital deductions are made to arrive at the taxable estate. (See Exhibit 17.15, line 10).

THE CHARITABLE DEDUCTION

Definition

Charitable deduction
A charitable contribution made as a gift to a qualified organization

Internal Revenue Code 170(c) defines a charitable contribution as a gift made to a qualified organization. To qualify for a **charitable deduction**, a contribution must be made to one of the following organizations:

- A state or possession of the United States or any subdivision thereof

- A corporation, trust, or community chest, fund, or foundation that is situated in the United States and is organized exclusively for religious, charitable, scientific, literary, or educational purposes or for the prevention of cruelty to children or animals

- A veteran's organization

- A fraternal organization operating under the lodge system

- A cemetery company

The IRS publishes a list (Publication 78) of organizations that have applied for and received tax-exempt status under section 501 of the Internal Revenue Code.

Types of Charitable Bequests

Direct Charitable Bequests

A direct charitable bequest of any property to a qualifying organization is fully deductible from the gross estate in arriving at the taxable estate.

Charitable remainder trust (CRT)
A split-interest trust; if created during life, the income goes to one or more parties, usually the grantor, or grantor and spouse for life, and upon the income beneficiary's death, the principal (remainder) is transferred to a charity; if the CRT is created testamentary, the usual income beneficiary is the spouse for life

Charitable Trusts

A **charitable remainder trust (CRT)** is an estate planning vehicle used to reduce the impact of income and estate taxes. A CRT is created by transferring property to a charitable trust. Although the property transferred to the trust may be cash, it generally consists of appreciated property. Because it is a nontaxable entity, the CRT can dispose of property without incurring taxable income upon the disposition. The trust is established so that an income interest, which may be in the form of an annuity or a unitrust payment, is paid to either the donor or a family member of the donor. At the termination of the income interest, which generally occurs at the death of the income beneficiary, the remaining assets in the CRT are transferred to the charity named in the trust document. Because there are two beneficiaries—the income beneficiary or annuitant and the named charity of a CRT—the CRT is considered a split-interest trust.

Charitable remainder trusts can be established during life or at the death of the donor. CRTs that are established during life provide several benefits. First, the donor will receive an income tax deduction equal to the value of the property transferred to the trust less the value of the income stream that is expected to be received by the income beneficiary. Second, although all or part of the trust assets will be included in the donor's gross estate if the donor reserved the right to income from the CRT during his life, the donor's estate is entitled to a charitable deduction for the value of the remainder interest that passes to charity. Third, the CRT provides an income stream to the donor or the donor's family member. Finally, if the property transferred to the trust was highly appreciated, the trust is able to dispose of the property without current income taxation. CRTs that are established at death are primarily used to reduce the estate tax and to provide an income stream to one of the donor's heirs.

Charitable lead trust (CLT)
A split-interest trust where a charity is the income beneficiary, and there is a noncharitable remainderman

In some cases, the income beneficiary is the charity with the remaining property being passed to one of the donor's heirs. This type of arrangement is called a **charitable lead trust (CLT)**. A CLT is generally used to transfer property to heirs in the future while paying gift tax at the current valuation of the property. Any appreciation in the value of the property will escape transfer tax.

THE MARITAL DEDUCTION

Definition

A marital deduction occurs when the decedent's estate claims as a deduction from the adjusted gross estate an unlimited qualifying bequest or transfer of property to a surviving spouse. This treatment parallels the unlimited marital deduction for gifts and for gift tax purposes. If the surviving spouse is not a U.S. citizen, a bequest to the spouse does not qualify for the marital deduction unless a qualified domestic trust (QDOT) is used, as discussed later in this chapter.

Qualifications for the Marital Deduction

Terminable interest
An interest that ends upon an event or contingency

To qualify for the marital deduction, the property must be included in the decedent's gross estate and passed to the decedent's spouse. This includes a spouse in a same-sex marriage. The interest in the property must not be a terminable interest. A **terminable interest** is an interest that ends upon an event or contingency. In other words, if the spouse initially gets the interest in the property and then later this interest terminates upon some event (usually death) and the interest passes to someone else, it is a terminable interest. Terminable interests do not qualify for the unlimited marital deduction unless they meet one of the exceptions to the terminable interest rule.

The following are some exceptions to the terminable interest rule.

■ When the only condition of a bequest is that the survivor spouse lives for a period not exceeding six months, the marital deduction is allowed if the surviving spouse actually lives for the period specified.

■ When there is a right to the income from the property for life coupled with a general power of appointment.

- When there is a bequest to a spouse of income from a charitable remainder annuity trust or a charitable remainder unitrust and the spouse is the only noncharitable beneficiary.

- Certain marital trusts are exceptions to the terminable interest rule (i.e., qualified terminable interest property, or QTIP).

Direct Bequests to a Spouse

Direct bequest (to a spouse)

The first spouse who dies leaves everything outright to the surviving spouse

In a **direct bequest**, the first spouse who dies leaves everything outright to the surviving spouse. The estate of the decedent spouse gets a 100% marital deduction equal to the adjusted gross estate. Any property that is not consumed by the surviving spouse during life will be included in the gross estate of the surviving spouse. The advantages of direct bequests are that they are simple and inexpensive. The surviving spouse gets unfettered control over all of the assets of the decedent. One disadvantage of this approach is that a direct bequest may overqualify the estate because the first spouse to die does not take advantage of the decedent's available applicable credit amount or its equivalency. Overqualification means that the decedent failed to make use of his applicable exclusion opportunity to pass his exemption equivalency amount ($11,580,000 for 2020) to someone other than the spouse and still pay no estate tax. If an estate is overqualified, the total estate tax on the death of the second spouse may be greater than it would have been had they arranged their affairs differently. Another disadvantage is that the first spouse is unable to retain control over the ultimate disposition of the assets.

Qualified Terminable Interest Property (QTIP) Trust

Qualified terminable interest property (QTIP) trust

Allows a terminable interest to be passed to a surviving spouse and the property to still qualify for the unlimited marital deduction; the election is made by the executor on IRS Form 706

If a direct bequest to a spouse is determined to be inappropriate and the decedent wishes no transfer tax at the first death, the alternatives are a QTIP or a power of appointment trust. A **qualified terminable interest property trust**, sometimes called a C trust or a Q trust, allows a terminable interest to be passed to a surviving spouse and the property to still qualify for the unlimited marital deduction. The election is made by the executor on IRS Form 706. There are certain rules associated with QTIPs that must be followed to qualify the transfer for the unlimited marital deduction.

Any income from the trust must be payable to the surviving spouse at least annually and for life. The trust income cannot be payable to anyone other than the surviving spouse. The trust assets will be included in the gross estate of the surviving spouse at death to the extent they are not consumed during the surviving spouse's lifetime. The first spouse to die determines the ultimate disposition of the property from the trust (names the remainder beneficiaries) in the trust provisions. This is an especially useful device when the surviving spouse is not the parent of the children of the decedent spouse.

Power of Appointment Trust

Power of appointment trust

Allows a terminable interest to be passed to a surviving spouse and the property to still qualify for the marital deduction; unlike a QTIP trust, no election is required

A **power of appointment trust**, sometimes called an A trust, allows a terminable interest to be passed to a surviving spouse and the property to still qualify for the marital deduction. Unlike a QTIP trust, no election is required. The rules require that income from the trust be payable to the surviving spouse at least annually for life. Any assets in the trust when the surviving spouse dies will be included in the gross estate of the surviving spouse. The surviving spouse is given a general power of appointment (the power to appoint the assets to anyone, including himself) over the property during life or at death.

The first spouse to die does not control the ultimate disposition of the property because the surviving spouse has a general power of appointment over the trust assets.

OPTIMIZING THE MARITAL DEDUCTION

If the objective of the married decedent is to have a zero-tax-liability estate, he can simply leave all assets in a qualifying way to the surviving spouse. The problem with such a strategy is that it fails to utilize the decedent's right to leave the applicable exclusion amount ($11,580,000 for 2020) to someone other than the spouse. Therefore, all assets, less the applicable exclusion amount, can be left to the spouse in a qualifying way and still have a zero estate tax liability for the estate of the first spouse to die. Although the $11,580,000 is left to another heir, the decedent may provide that income from the property is to be paid exclusively to the surviving spouse while the spouse is alive. The common method of leaving the applicable exclusion amount where the spouse has a need for the income from such assets is called a bypass trust. In the event a spouse has no need for the income or assets from the credit equivalency amount, the spouse can disclaim, as discussed next. Keep in mind, however, that bequests to surviving spouses who are not U.S. citizens must meet special requirements to qualify for the marital deduction, as described later in this section.

The Bypass Trust (Credit Equivalency)

Bypass trust (B trust)
Avoids inclusion in, or bypasses, the surviving spouse's gross estate; the assets transfer to a future generation free of estate taxes; the purpose of a bypass trust is to take advantage of the applicable credit amount

A **bypass trust** avoids inclusion in, or bypasses, the surviving spouse's gross estate. The assets transfer to a future generation free of estate taxes. The purpose of a bypass trust (B trust) is to take advantage of the applicable credit amount. The property does not qualify for the unlimited marital deduction when the first spouse dies, but it escapes taxation because it is covered by the estate tax applicable exclusion amount. A common scenario is for the first spouse to leave everything to the surviving spouse except for the credit equivalent amount, which goes into a bypass trust. The surviving spouse may be the income beneficiary of the bypass trust and may also be able to invade the trust for health, education, maintenance, or support (HEMS). When the surviving spouse dies, the bypass trust assets are not included in that spouse's gross estate but rather pass to children or other heirs.

A bypass trust can be used instead of an outright bequest to heirs who are not sophisticated or mature enough to handle property. In addition, the bypass trust is used where the surviving spouse needs the income from the trust but wants to avoid inclusion of the assets in the surviving spouse's gross estate. In this case, the choice of the trust over the simple bequest may give the transferor some peace of mind. Often, highly appreciating assets are placed into the bypass trust. This freezes the value for estate tax purposes for the spouses at the death of the first spouse. A bypass trust may also be called a credit equivalency trust, a credit shelter trust, a family trust, or a B trust.

The Mechanics of the Bypass Trust (Credit Equivalency)

Recall that the property that qualified for the marital deduction reduced the taxable estate of the decedent and that the amount of such transfer is unlimited. Also recall that each individual has a lifetime exemption (Exhibit 17.12) and that this exemption would be lost to the first spouse were he to transfer to the surviving spouse all of his property in a way that qualifies for the marital deduction. A credit equivalency (bypass) trust can be used to avoid these problems. Usually testamentary, a credit equivalency trust is provided for in the will with a provision to fund the trust with an amount equal to the current (at the time of death) applicable exclusion amount with the spouse having a lifetime interest in the income and the remaindermen being someone else, usually children. Such a transfer does not qualify for the marital deduction, and those assets will not be included in the gross estate of the surviving spouse when he dies. The assets are included in the taxable estate of the grantor but will not result in any federal estate tax liability as demonstrated in the following example.

E X A M P L E   Sherri and Gary are married with two children. They each have property worth $15 million. Each spouse has a will bequeathing all property to the surviving spouse.

Calculation of the total estate tax paid, assuming Gary dies first on January 3, 2020 (assume the applicable credit amount and estate tax rates remain the same when Sherri dies but that she is not eligible for the portability provision):

	Gary	Sherri	
Assets	$15,000,000	$15,000,000	
Inheritance		$15,000,000	
Gross estate	$15,000,000	$30,000,000	
Marital deduction	(15,000,000)	-0-	
Taxable estate	-0-	$30,000,000	
Tentative tax	-0-	11,945,800	
Applicable credit	-0-	(4,577,800)	(2020)
Estate tax	$-0-	$7,368,000	
Total estate tax paid by family	$7,368,000		

Calculation of the total estate tax paid assuming Gary dies on January 3, 2020, using a maximized credit equivalency trust with the children as beneficiaries (assume the applicable credit amount and estate tax rates remain the same when Sherri dies):

	Gary	Sherri	
Assets	$15,000,000	$15,000,000	
Inheritance	-0-	$3,420,000	
Gross estate	$15,000,000	$18,420,000	
Marital deduction	(3,420,000)	-0-	
Taxable estate	$11,580,000	$18,420,000	
Tentative tax	$4,577,800	$7,313,800	
Applicable credit	(4,577,800)	(4,577,800)	(2020)
Estate tax	$ -0-	$2,736,000	
Total estate tax paid by family	$2,736,000		

Conclusion: By using the credit equivalency trust, the family saved $4,632,000 ($7,368,000 without shelter – $2,736,000 with shelter = $4,632,000 savings) in estate tax. This savings is a result of the couple taking full advantage of the applicable credit amount by placing the applicable exclusion amount of funds at the first death in a credit equivalency trust for the children. Sherri can receive income from the trust for the remainder of her life and have the right to withdraw limited amounts of principal. The credit equivalency trust assets will pass untaxed to the children at Sherri's death.

Effect of Portability

As discussed earlier, current tax law allows for the portability of the $11,580,000 (in 2020) applicable exclusion amount between spouses. The portability feature reduces the need for bypass planning because with portability, the predeceased spouse's applicable exclusion amount is not necessarily wasted if the predeceased spouse does not utilize it in his estate. If certain requirements are met, the unused applicable exclusion amount may be available to the surviving spouse. For example, a married couple with total assets of $23,160,000 in assets might elect to use no applicable exclusion amount in the estate of the first spouse to die and instead use the entire $23,160,000 exclusion when the second spouse dies.

There are some restrictions on the use of the portability feature, however. For example, under the portability provision, only the unused exemption amount of the last predeceased spouse is available to a surviving spouse. If a surviving spouse remarries and the second spouse also predeceases the surviving spouse, the unused exemption amount of the first predeceased spouse is no longer available. A second example is that a timely estate tax return must be filed for the first spouse to die, and the executor for the first spouse to die must elect on the Form 706 Estate Tax Return to allow the surviving spouse to use portability. Many people neglect to file the estate tax return if no estate tax will be due and thus forfeit the benefits of portability.

Use of Disclaimers

Disclaimer
The refusal of the receipt of an estate; the use of disclaimers allows an individual to disclaim or renounce receiving any part of an estate

A **disclaimer** allows a spouse or anyone else to disclaim or renounce receiving any part of a bequest. A specific direction to disclaim is not necessary in the will or trust device. If the spouse disclaims property, his interest in and control over the property is extinguished. Because disclaimers must be made within nine months of the decedent's death, the surviving spouse may find it difficult to give up property at a time when he may not be feeling emotionally or financially secure. When a person disclaims, he is not making a gift but rather is simply bypassed.

Alien Surviving Spouses

Qualified domestic trust (QDOT)
For a noncitizen spouse who was a U.S. resident at the time of the decedent's death, the marital deduction is allowed if the property is placed in a QDOT that passes to the noncitizen surviving spouse

Section 2056(d) disallows the unlimited marital deduction if the surviving spouse is not a U.S. citizen. If a noncitizen spouse becomes a U.S. citizen before the federal estate tax return is filed (Form 706 within nine months), Section 2056(d) does not apply. For a noncitizen spouse who was a U.S. resident at the time of the decedent's death, the marital deduction is allowed if the property is placed in a **qualified domestic trust (QDOT)** that passes to a noncitizen surviving spouse. The trust document for a QDOT requires at least one trustee to be a U.S. citizen or a U.S. corporation. The trustee must have a right to withhold estate tax on distribution of assets or income and must meet requirements of the U.S. Treasury. The executor must make an irrevocable election to establish a QDOT.

GENERATION-SKIPPING TRANSFER TAX (GSTT)

Generation-skipping transfer tax (GSTT)
A tax in addition to the unified gift and estate tax designed to tax large transfers that skip a generation (i.e., from grandparent to grandchild)

The **generation-skipping transfer tax (GSTT)** is in addition to the unified gift and estate tax and is designed to tax large transfers that skip a generation (i.e., from grandparent to grandchild). The purpose of the tax is to collect potentially lost tax dollars from the skipped generation. Were it not for the generation-skipping tax, one could leave all of one's assets to a grandchild and avoid the unified gift and estate tax on the middle generation. The current unified tax scheme would tax from the first to the second generation and from the second to the third generation. For a transfer made from the first generation directly to the third generation, some unified gift and estate tax is avoided. The generation-skipping transfer tax attempts to make up for that loss of tax.

The GSTT rate is the highest marginal rate for the unified gift and estate tax rates (40% in 2020). There are several exceptions to this tax. First, the annual exclusion also applies to a generation-skipping transfer ($15,000 in 2020). Second, there is a lifetime exemption per donor ($11,580,000 in 2020). Unlike the gift tax and estate tax exemption, the GSTT lifetime exemption is not portable between spouses. There is also an exception for transfers to a person of a skipped generation where a parent has predeceased the transferee prior to the transfer. For example, if a parent died, the grandparent may donate or devise to the grandchild without the grandchild being considered a skip person. In effect, the grandchild steps into the shoes of the deceased parent. An unrelated person 37½ years younger than the donor-transferor is considered a skip person. A spouse of a person in a nonskip generation is not a skip person because they are assigned to their spouse's generation. For example, a brother's wife who is 40 years younger than the donor is not a skip person. Finally, qualified transfers, such as medical costs and tuition paid directly to the provider, are also excluded from GSTT. Gift splitting is available for the annual exclusion exceptions as long as both spouses elect to split gifts.

THE ROLE OF THE FINANCIAL PLANNER IN ESTATE PLANNING

Estate planning is very personal and requires the financial planner to seek out the particulars that characterize each client's individual situation and goals. Financial planners must be able to ascertain the objectives of the client while forecasting the long-range ramifications of the plan.

Reducing the estate tax is a matter of taking full advantage of various planning opportunities (summarized in Exhibit 17.17). Initially, getting the life insurance out of the gross estate is generally a wise idea. The next step for most clients is to make full use of the qualified transfers to educational and medical institutions. Then, the client should be encouraged to make optimal use of the annual exclusion ($15,000 or $30,000 if split) on a yearly basis. At some time, either during life or at death, the client should make effective use of the applicable exclusion amount ($11,580,000 at death for 2020) by transferring these assets so as to avoid inclusion in the surviving spouse's gross estate. Then the spouse who has accomplished all of the above can leave the balance of the gross estate to his spouse in a qualifying way and, thus, have an estate tax liability of zero. Charitable contributions during life will reduce his gross estate, and the income on those transferred assets will not be taxed to the transferor. Charitable transfers at death are deductible from the adjusted gross estate and thus are not taxable.

EXHIBIT 17.17 Estate Tax Reduction Techniques

There are several techniques to reduce estate tax:

- Do not overqualify the estate. Use the applicable exclusion amount.
- Do not underqualify the estate. Use an appropriate amount for the marital deduction, generally to reduce estate tax to zero.
- Generally, remove life insurance from the estate of the client.
- Change the ownership of life insurance or use irrevocable life insurance trust (must remove all incidents of ownership).
- Use lifetime gifts. Make use of annual exclusions with gift splitting.
- Use basic trusts.
- Use charitable contributions, transfers, and trusts

Estate planning calls for a broad range of sophisticated talents. An attorney and CPA may need to be called into the estate team at this point, if not before, to cover the legal and tax aspects.

CONCLUDING COMMENTS ON THE UNIFICATION SCHEME OF GIFTS AND ESTATES

Although it may appear that the unification scheme (the unified tax table) for gifts and estates provides equality or parity for transfers during life or at death, there are at least four important distinctions.

First, the annual exclusion of $15,000 per donee per year that is provided for gifts is essentially lost if the transfer does not occur until death. Thus, the annual exclusion is a perishable right, the total value of which declines with each passing year. A married couple with four children and two grandchildren can transfer $180,000 ($30,000 to each descendent) per year total during life to the six donees without any gift tax consequences. If this money is not transferred by gift or consumed by the decedent, it will be included in the gross estate at the decedent's death and may be subject to estate tax.

The second, and perhaps the most important, advantage of making lifetime gifts is that any future appreciation of any asset transferred is not included in the gross estate of the transferor at death. For example, suppose William gave his son, James, some XYZ.com stock, with a fair market value of $15,000. William (donor) pays no gift tax on the transfer because it is equal to the annual exclusion amount of $15,000 in 2020. Now assume that James holds the stock for 10 years; at the end of the 10-year period, the stock is worth $300,000, and William dies. No part of the value of the stock is included in William's gross estate. If William had retained the stock, he would have had to include the entire $300,000 in his gross estate. Thus, for assets that appreciate, transfers during life are more advantageous than transfers at death in reducing the gross estate.

Third, if any gift tax is paid on gifts made, that gift tax is also not included in the gross estate of the donor unless such gift tax is paid on gifts made within three years of death.

DISCUSSION QUESTIONS

1. What is estate planning, and what are its objectives?

2. What risks are associated with failing to plan for an estate transfer?

3. Which professionals make up the estate planning team?

4. What steps make up the estate planning process?

5. What client information needs to be gathered to begin a successful estate transfer?

6. What are some common estate transfer objectives?

7. What are the basic documents used in estate planning?

8. What is the probate process, and what are its advantages and disadvantages?

9. Why is having a will important?

10. What are the three types of wills, and how do they differ?

11. What are some provisions typically found in wills?

12. What is a power of attorney?

13. What is a durable power of attorney for health care?

14. What are the definitions of the terms community property, separate property, and tenancy by the entirety?

15. What are the types of property ownership interests, and how are they transferred at death?

16. What are the duties of the executor/administrator of a will?

17. What is a living trust?

18. What is a grantor trust?

19. How can the gross estate be reduced?

20. What are the common estate planning mistakes?

21. What is the applicable credit amount, and how does it affect an individual's federal estate tax liability?

22. How can the annual gift tax exclusion be used as an estate planning tool?

23. What is gift splitting?

24. What are qualified transfers?

25. When is the gift tax return due?

26. What are the advantages and disadvantages of the unlimited marital deduction?

27. What are the steps in calculating the estate tax?

28. What are at least three estate planning techniques available to reduce gift and estate taxes?

29. When is the estate tax return due?

30. What are the applicable credit amounts against federal gift and estate taxes for 2020?

31. On which IRS form do you deduct funeral expenses?

32. What is a trust, and what are the benefits of creating one?

33. What are different types of trusts that can be created?

34. What is the generation-skipping transfer tax?

EXERCISES

1. Which of the following people need estate planning?
   1. Steve, who has a wife, 1 small child, and a net worth of $350,000.
   2. Earl, married with 9 children, 6 grandchildren, and a net worth of $4,000,000.
   3. Ellen, divorced, whose only son is severely mentally challenged.
   4. Mary, who is single, has a net worth of $150,000, and has 2 cats she considers her children.

2. Place the following estate planning steps in their proper order.
   1. Establish priorities for estate objectives.
   2. Prepare a written plan.
   3. Define problem areas including liquidity, taxes, etc.
   4. Gather client information and establish objectives.

3. Which arrangements are plausible when dealing with unanticipated incapacity.

4. Describe why each of the following would be considered potential problems of an estate plan.
   1. Ancillary probate
   2. A will that includes funeral instructions
   3. A will that attempts to disinherit a spouse and/or minor children

5. Describe each of the following common provisions in a well-drafted will.
   1. Establishment of the domicile of testator
   2. An appointment and powers clause
   3. A survivorship clause
   4. A residuary clause

6. Which of the following statements is(are) NOT correct?
   1. A durable power of attorney for health care is always a direct substitute for a living will.
   2. A living will only covers a narrow range of situations.
   3. A living will must generally meet the requirements specified by state statute.
   4. Many well-intentioned living wills have failed because of vagueness and/or ambiguities.

7. Marleen has a general power of appointment over the assets in a trust established by her mother. Which of the following statements regarding the power is(are) CORRECT?
   1. Marleen can appoint the trust assets to pay for the needs of her mother.
   2. Marleen can appoint money to Marleen's creditors.
   3. Marleen must only appoint money using an ascertainable standard (health, education, maintenance, and support).
   4. If Marleen were to die, Marleen's gross estate would include the trust assets, although they were not previously appointed to Marleen.

8. Describe each of the following property ownership arrangements.
   1. Tenancy in common
   2. Joint tenancy with right of survivorship
   3. Tenancy by the entirety
   4. Community property

9. Which of the following statements regarding joint tenancy is(are) CORRECT?
   1. Under a joint tenancy, each tenant has an undivided interest in the property.
   2. Joint tenancies may only be established between spouses.
   3. Community property is the same as joint tenancy and has been adopted in many states.
   4. Assuming a spousal joint tenancy, the full value of the property will be included in the gross estate of the first spouse to die without regard to the contribution of each spouse.

10. Generally speaking, which of the following property is included in the probate estate?
    1. Property owned outright in one's own name at the time of death.
    2. An interest in property held as a tenant in common with others.
    3. Life insurance, and other death proceeds, payable to one's estate at death.
    4. The decedent's half of any community property.

11. Describe at least 3 advantages and 3 disadvantages of the probate process.

12. Identify alternatives to probate regarding disposition of property.

13. John and Mary are married and are both 36 years old with one child, Patrick, age 6. What documents does the couple need for estate planning?

14. Given Mark's assets below, which will go through the probate process if Mark dies?

Life insurance	Face	$100,000	Beneficiary is Mary
IRA	Balance	$200,000	Beneficiary is Mary
Personal residence	Value	$280,000	Titled JTWROS with Mary
Automobile	Value	$4,000	Owned by Mark

15. Ann is married to Roy. They have no children. Given that Ann has the following assets, what could she do to reduce her gross estate?

Life insurance	Face	$2,000,000	Owner is Ann
Cash	Amount	$4,000,000	Owner is Ann

16. During 2020, Bob gave $100,000 to his son and $100,000 to his daughter. Bob's wife, Lori, also gave $5,000 to their son. No other gifts were made during the year. Bob and Lori elected to split the gifts on their gift tax returns. What is the amount of taxable gifts made by Bob and Lori?

17. Which of the following situations would not constitute a taxable transfer under the gift tax statutes?
    1. Frank creates an irrevocable trust under the terms of which his son is to receive income for life and his grandson the remainder at his son's death.
    2. Frank, with personal funds, purchases real property and has the title conveyed to himself and his brother as joint tenants with right of survivorship.
    3. Frank creates a trust giving income for life to his wife providing that, at her death, the corpus is to be distributed to their daughter. Frank reserves the right to revoke the trust at any time.

18. Stephen created a joint bank account for himself and his friend, Anna. When is there a gift to Anna?

19. During 2020, Mark and Lydia made joint gifts of the following items to their son:
    1. A bond with an adjusted basis of $13,000 and a fair market value of $40,000
    2. Stock with an adjusted basis of $22,000 and a fair market value of $33,000
    3. An auto with an adjusted basis of $13,000 and a fair market value of $15,000
    4. An interest-free loan of $6,000 for a computer (for the son's personal use) on January 1 that was paid by their son on December 31 (assume the applicable federal rate was 2% per annum)

    What is the gross amount of gifts includable in Mark and Lydia's gift tax returns for this year?

20. Tamara, who is single, gave an outright gift of $50,000 to a friend, Heather, who needed the money to pay her medical expenses. In filing the gift tax return, how much is Tamara entitled to exclude?

21. Which of the following represent(s) taxable gifts?
    1. The transfer of wealth by a parent to a dependent child that represents legal support.
    2. Payment of a child's tuition to Loyola Law School by a parent.
    3. Payment of $20,000 from a grandparent to a grandchild for educational purposes.
    4. Payment of $15,000 of medical bills for a friend paid directly to the medical institution.

22. Victor wants to begin a program of lifetime giving to his 3 grandchildren and 5 great-grandchildren. He wants to control the amount of annual gifts to avoid the imposition of federal gift tax, and he does not desire to use any of his or his wife Veronica's applicable credit amount. Veronica is willing to split each gift over a period of 10 years. What is the total amount of gifts, including gift splitting, that Victor can give over the 10-year period? (Assume the annual exclusion for all years is the same as for 2020.)

23. Rodney and his wife, Lois, have 4 children, each over the age of majority, 2 grandchildren over age 21, and 6 minor grandchildren. Rodney and Lois want to make gifts to their children and grandchildren sufficient to make maximum use of the tax provisions providing for annual exclusions from federal gift tax. Considering that desire only, what is the total amount of gifting that Rodney and Lois can make during 2020?

24. Kurt died on July 31. His assets and their fair market value at the time of his death were:

Cash	$150,000
Personal residence	$7,500,000
Life insurance on Kurt's life	$3,500,000
Series EE bonds	$200,000

    Kurt had a balance on his residence mortgage of $150,000. What is the total of Kurt's gross estate?

25. Evelyn died on August 1 this year. What is her gross estate?
    - Two years ago, Evelyn gave cash of $30,000 to her friend. No gift tax was paid on the gift.
    - Evelyn held property jointly with her brother. Each paid $2 million of the total purchase price of $4 million. Fair market value of the property at date of death was $7 million.
    - In 2012, Evelyn purchased a life insurance policy on her own life and gave it as a gift to her sister. Evelyn retained the right to change the beneficiary. Upon Evelyn's death, her sister received $5 million under the policy.
    - In 2004, Evelyn gave her son a summer home (fair market value in 2004, $1 million). Evelyn continued to use it until her death pursuant to an understanding with her son. The fair market value at the date of death was $2 million.

26. Jane died on May 2, 2020, leaving an adjusted gross estate of $18 million at the date of death. Under the terms of the will, $3,750,000 was bequeathed outright to her husband. The remainder of the estate was left to her mother. No taxable gifts were made during her lifetime. In computing the taxable estate, how much should the executor claim as a marital deduction?

27. Joshua died in 2020 with a taxable estate of $18 million. He had made no previous taxable gifts during his lifetime. How much is his federal estate tax?

28. Identify at least 3 alternative methods of limiting, reducing, or avoiding federal estate taxes.

29. Which of the following transfers qualify for the unlimited marital deduction?
    1. Outright bequest to resident alien spouse
    2. Property passing to citizen spouse in QTIP
    3. Income beneficiary of CRT is a nonresident alien spouse (trust is not a QDOT)
    4. Outright bequest to resident spouse who, prior to the decedent's death, was not a citizen but who, after the decedent's death and before the estate return was filed, became a U.S. citizen

30. Who among the following would be skip persons for purposes of the GSTT? Matt, the transferor, is 82 years old.
    ■ Tim, the grandson of Matt, whose mother, Bonnie, is living but whose father, Ben, son of Matt, is deceased.
    ■ Mindy is the great-grandchild of Matt. Both Mindy's parents and grandparents are living.
    ■ Sharon is the 21-year-old wife of Matt's second son, Alan, age 65.

31. Rosalie, who is single, is diagnosed with a serious disease and expects to be completely incapacitated in three years. Rosalie has two daughters and two grandchildren. She has $500,000 in net worth including her principal residence. Which of the following estate planning tools would you recommend for Rosalie?
    1. Set up a durable power of attorney.
    2. Immediately gift annual exclusion amounts to children and grandchildren.
    3. Set up a revocable living trust.
    4. Set up an irrevocable living trust.
    5. Set up a QTIP trust.

32. On April 30 Dennis transfers property to a trust which he retains the right to revoke. The trust is to pay Kim 5% of the trust assets valued annually for her life, with the remainder to be paid to a qualified charity. On August 31, Dennis dies and the trust becomes irrevocable. Identify the type of trust.

PROBLEMS

1. Kristi and Patrick are married, and both are 35 years old with 2 children, Christopher (age 4) and Andrew (age 2). The couple has simple wills that leave everything to each other. They have asked you to help them update their wills. What would you recommend?

2. Tomas is a wealthy golfer who would prefer that his assets not be subject to public scrutiny when he dies. What tools can he use to accomplish his goal?

3. George owns the following property:
    1. Boat (fee simple)
    2. Condominium on the beach (tenancy in common with his brother and sister)
    3. House and two cars with his wife, Ann (tenancy by the entirety)
    4. Checking account with his son, Bill (POD)
    5. Karate business (JTWROS with his partner, Eric)

    Which items will go through probate? Which property could he sell without the consent of a co-owner?

4. Neal is a widower with a taxable estate of $15 million. He had made no taxable lifetime gifts. What is his federal estate tax due before the applicable credit if he dies in 2020? What is the amount of the applicable credit?

5. Denise and Barry are married and own total assets with a fair market value of $16 million, all of which are in Barry's name alone. Barry leaves his entire estate to Denise, and Denise leaves her entire estate to their children. Assume Barry dies in January 2020 and Denise dies in November 2020. What is the total amount of federal estate tax that will be paid on the two estates? (Assume the fair market value of the estate is unchanged when Denise dies and Denise is not entitled to take advantage of the portability provision.)

6. In 2020, Georgia gave a $10,000 cash gift to her friend, Mary. How much is the taxable gift?

7. For each of the past 10 years, Jessica has given $16,000 to each of her 6 grandchildren and $26,000 each to her son and daughter. What is the total amount of taxable gifts? (Assume the annual exclusion for all 10 years is the same as 2020.)

8. Ken and Libby have the following assets:
    - $800,000 house in Ken's name
    - $1,100,000 investment account in Libby's name
    - $16,000,000 in rental property jointly owned as JTWROS
    - $300,000 beach condo that Libby co-owns with her sister as tenants in common

    They have 2 adult children and have made no previous taxable gifts. How much can they transfer to the children free of all transfer tax in a lifetime transfer in 2020?

9. Charles is an 85-year-old widower with 2 sons and a daughter, 3 grandchildren, and a 27-year-old girlfriend. He has an estate currently worth $650,000, including a house worth $300,000. His estate also includes a life insurance policy on his life with a face value of $120,000, and the primary beneficiaries are his children. Charles was recently diagnosed with Alzheimer's disease. The doctors predict a rapid progression and recommend that Charles go into a nursing home soon. He currently has a will that leaves all of his assets equally to his children. He has not taken advantage of any other estate planning techniques. Which of the following would you recommend to Charles while he still has all his mental faculties, and why?
    1. Create a living will, a general power of attorney, and a power of attorney for health care.
    2. Transfer ownership of his residence to his children so that it will not be counted as a resource when he goes into the nursing home.
    3. Create an irrevocable trust containing all of his assets and naming his children as beneficiaries.
    4. Create a revocable trust containing all of his assets and naming his children as beneficiaries.
    5. Create a QTIP trust naming his girlfriend as the income beneficiary and his children as the remaindermen beneficiaries.

CASE SCENARIO

Use the information provided to answer the following questions regarding the Nelson family.

NELSON FAMILY CASE SCENARIO
DANA AND DAVID NELSON
As of 1/1/2020

Personal Background and Information

David Nelson (age 37) is a bank vice president. He has been employed there for 12 years and has an annual salary of $70,000. Dana Nelson (age 37) is a full-time homemaker. David and Dana have been married for eight years. They have two children, John (age 6) and Gabrielle (age 3), and are expecting their third child in two weeks. They have always lived in this community and expect to remain indefinitely in their current residence.

General Goals (Not Prioritized)

■ Save for college education

■ Reduce debt

■ Save for retirement

■ Estate planning

■ Invest wisely

Insurance Information

Health Insurance

The entire family is insured under David's employer's health plan (PPO). For covered expenses, a $1,000 in-network deductible and a $2,000 out-of-network deductible apply, after which 80%/20% coinsurance applies in network and 60%/40% applies out of network. There is a stop-loss limit of $20,000 annually in network and $30,000 annually out of network. The entire monthly premium of $1,123.54 is paid by David's employer.

Life Insurance

David's employer provides group term life insurance equal to two times David's current salary. The premium is paid entirely by his employer, and Dana is the primary beneficiary. No contingent beneficiary is named.

Disability Insurance

David's employer also offers a contributory group long-term disability insurance program toward which the employer contributes 60% of the $158.54 monthly premium. David is a participant in the program, which provides a monthly disability income benefit equal to 70% of his current salary, payable to his Social Security normal retirement age, provided that he remains disabled per the policy's "own occupation" definition of disability. David must satisfy a 90-day elimination period before he is eligible to begin receiving benefits.

David's employer doesn't offer dental or vision coverages and the Nelsons have not obtained any private form of individual dental or vision insurance benefits.

Homeowners Insurance

The Nelsons have an HO-3 policy with replacement cost on contents. There is a $250 deductible. The annual premium is $950.

Automobile Insurance

The Nelsons have automobile liability and bodily injury coverage of $100,000/$300,000/$100,000. They have both comprehensive coverage and collision. The deductibles are $250 (comprehensive) and $500 (collision). The annual premium is $900.

Relevant External Environmental Information

- Mortgage rates are 5.0% for 30 years and 4.5% for 15 years, fixed.

- Gross domestic product is expected to grow at less than 3%.

- Inflation is expected to be 2.6%.

- Expected return on investment is 8% for common stocks, 9% for small company stocks, and 1.1% for U.S. Treasury bills.

- College education costs are $15,000 per year.

Investment Information

The bank offers a Section 401(k) plan in which David is an active participant. The bank matches contributions dollar for dollar up to 3% of David's salary. David currently contributes 5.43% of his salary. His employer's plan allows for employee contributions of up to 16% of salary. In the Section 401(k) plan, the Nelsons have the opportunity to invest in a money market fund, a bond fund, a growth and income fund, and a small-cap fund. The Nelsons consider themselves to have a moderate investment risk tolerance. David's assets within the plan are currently earning 8.5%, based on his investment choices within the plan.

Income Tax Information

David and Dana tell you that they are in the 12% federal income tax bracket. They pay $820 annually in state and local income taxes.

Education Information

John is 6 years old and currently attending first grade at a private school. Gabrielle is 3 years old. She will attend private school from pre-kindergarten through high school. The current balance of the college fund is $14,000. They expect to contribute $1,000 at the end of each year to this fund.

Gifts, Estates, Trusts, and Will Information

David has made Dana his primary beneficiary on his Section 401(k) plan, and the children are the contingent beneficiaries. Because most of their assets are owned jointly, David doesn't see the need for a will. Dana also does not have a will.

Dana and David Nelson

Statement of Financial Position

12/31/2019

ASSETS			LIABILITIES AND NET WORTH		
Cash/cash equivalents			**Current liabilities**		
JT	Checking account	$1,425	JT	Credit cards	$4,000
JT	Savings account	$950	JT	Mortgage on principal residence	$1,234
			David	Boat loan	$1,493
Total cash/cash equivalents		$2,375	**Total current liabilities**		$6,727
Invested assets			**Long-term liabilities**		
Dana	ABC stock	$12,500	JT	Mortgage on principal residence	$196,654
JT	Education fund	$14,000	David	Boat loan	$12,065
David	Section 401(k) plan	$32,197			
Total invested assets		$58,697	**Total long-term liabilities**		$208,719
Personal-use assets			**Total liabilities**		$215,446
JT	Principal residence	$245,000			
JT	Automobile	$18,000			
David	Boat	$25,000	**Net worth**		$207,626
Dana	Jewelry	$13,000			
JT	Furniture/household	$61,000			
Total personal-use assets		$362,000			
Total assets		$423,072	**Total liabilities and net worth**		$423,072

Dana and David Nelson
Statement of Financial Position
12/31/2020

ASSETS			LIABILITIES AND NET WORTH		
Cash/cash equivalents			**Current liabilities**		
JT	Checking account	$1,268	JT	Credit cards	$3,655
JT	Savings account	$950	JT	Mortgage on principal residence	$1,370
	Total cash/cash equivalents	$2,218	David	Boat loan	$1,048
				Total current liabilities	$6,073
Invested assets			**Long-term liabilities**		
Dana	ABC stock	$14,050	JT	Mortgage on principal residence	$195,284
JT	Education fund	$15,560	David	Boat loan	$16,017
David	Section 401(k) plan	$38,619		Total long-term liabilities	$211,301
David	XYZ stock	$10,000			
	Total invested assets	$78,229			
Personal-use assets			Total liabilities		$217,374
JT	Principal residence	$250,000			
JT	Automobile	$15,000			
David	Personal watercraft	$10,000	Net worth		$241,573
David	Boat B	$30,000			
Dana	Jewelry	$13,500			
JT	Furniture/household	$60,000			
	Total personal-use assets	$378,500			
Total assets		**$458,947**	**Total liabilities and net worth**		**$458,947**

Notes to financial statements:

- Assets are stated at fair market value.
- The ABC stock was inherited from Dana's aunt on November 15, 2019. Her aunt originally paid $20,000 for it on October 31, 2010. The fair market value at the aunt's death was $12,000.
- Liabilities are stated at principal only.
- JT = joint tenancy; client name = separate property.

Dana and David Nelson
Personal Statement of Cash Flows
For 2020

INFLOWS

Salary—David $70,000

Investment income

Interest income	$ 900	
Dividend income	$ 150	$ 1,050
Total inflow		**$71,050**

Savings

Reinvestment (interest/dividends)	$ 1,050	
Section 401(k) plan deferrals	$ 3,803	
Education fund	$ 1,000	
Total savings		**$ 5,853**
Available for outflows		**$65,197**

OUTFLOWS

Ordinary living expenses

Food	$ 6,000	
Clothing	$ 3,600	
Child care	$ 600	
Entertainment	$ 1,814	
Utilities	$ 3,600	
Auto maintenance	$ 2,000	
Church	$ 3,500	
Total ordinary living expenses		**$21,114**

Debt payments

Credit card payments principal	$ 345	
Credit card payments interest	$ 615	
Mortgage payment principal	$ 1,234	
Mortgage payment interest	$20,720	
Boat loan principal	$ 1,493	
Boat loan interest	$ 1,547	
Total debt payments		**$25,954**

Insurance premiums

Automobile insurance premiums	$ 900	
Disability insurance premiums	$ 761	
Homeowners insurance premiums	$ 950	
Total insurance premiums		**$ 2,611**
Tuition and education expenses		**$ 1,000**

Taxes

FICA and federal income tax (W/H)	$12,855	
State (and city) income tax	$ 820	
Property tax (principal residence)	$ 1,000	
Total taxes		**$14,675**
Total outflows		**$65,354**
Net cash flow (deficit)		**($157)**

1. Given David's current attitudes about the necessity for a will for himself and Dana, what problems has David created should he or Dana die today?

2. What provisions should David have in his will?

3. What provisions should Dana have in her will?

4. Assume that David and Dana have implemented recommendations for debt repayment to increase their discretionary cash available and increase life insurance coverage on David to a total of $450,000. The disability coverage has been changed to add coverage for illness as well as accident. As their financial planner, what other insurance coverages should you recommend to the Nelsons?

APPENDIX 17.1 JFK, Jr.'s Last Will and Testament

The Last Will and Testament of John F. Kennedy, Jr.

John F. Kennedy, Jr., planned to leave the bulk of his holdings to his wife, Carolyn Bessette-Kennedy, or their children. But John and Carolyn died together in a plane crash in July of 1999 without leaving any issue (children). Therefore, his property will go to the children of his sister, Caroline Kennedy Schlossberg. The bulk of his estate is left to the beneficiaries of a trust he established in 1983. Kennedy also left the scrimshaw set, or carved whale ivory set, once owned by his father to nephew John B.K. Schlossberg. Kennedy's cousin, Timothy P. Shriver was named executor of the will. Kennedy's estate is reportedly worth $100 million.

I, JOHN F. KENNEDY, JR., of New York, New York, make this my last will, hereby revoking all earlier wills and codicils. I do not by this will exercise any power of appointment.

FIRST: I give all my tangible property (as distinguished from money, securities and the like), wherever located, other than my scrimshaw set previously owned by my father, to my wife, Carolyn Bessette-Kennedy, if she is living on the thirtieth day after my death, or if not, by right of representation to my then living issue, or if none, by right of representation to the then living issue of my sister, Caroline Kennedy Schlossberg, or if none, to my said sister, Caroline, if she is then living. If I am survived by issue, I leave this scrimshaw set to said wife, Carolyn, if she is then living, or if not, by right of representation, to my then living issue. If I am not survived by issue, I give said scrimshaw set to my nephew John B.K. Schlossberg, if he is then living, or if not, by right of representation to the then-living issue of my said sister, Caroline, or if none, to my said sister Caroline, if she is then living. I hope that whoever receives my tangible personal property will dispose of certain items of it in accordance with my wishes, however made unknown, but I impose no trust, condition or enforceable obligation of any kind in this regard.

SECOND: I give and devise all my interest in my cooperative apartment located at 20-26 Moore Street, Apartment 9E, in said New York, including all my shares therein and any proprietary leases with respect thereto, to my said wife, Carolyn, if she is living on the thirtieth day after my death.

THIRD: If no issue of mine survive me, I give and devise all my interests in real estate, wherever located, that I own as tenants in common with my said sister, Caroline, or as tenants in common with any of her issue, by right of representation to Caroline's issue who are living on the thirtieth day after my death, or if none, to my said sister Caroline, if she is then living. References in this Article THIRD to "real estate" include shares in cooperative apartments and proprietary leases with respect thereto.

FOURTH: I give and devise the residue of all the property, of whatever kind and wherever located, that I own at my death to the then trustees of the John F. Kennedy Jr. 1983 Trust established October 13, 1983 by me, as Donor, of which John T. Fallon, of Weston, Massachusetts, and I are currently the trustees (the "1983 Trust"), to be added to the principal of the 1983 Trust and administered in accordance with the provisions thereof, as amended by a First Amendment dated April 9, 1987 and by a Second Amendment and Complete Restatement dated earlier this day, and as from time to hereafter further amended whether before or after my death. I have provided in the 1983 Trust for my children and more remote issue and for the method of paying all federal and state taxes in the nature of estate, inheritance, succession and like taxes occasioned by my death.

FIFTH: I appoint my wife, Carolyn Bessette-Kennedy, as guardian of each child of our marriage during minority. No guardian appointed in this will or a codicil need furnish any surety on any official bond.

APPENDIX 17.1 JFK, Jr.'s Last Will and Testament (continued)

SIXTH: I name my cousin Anthony Stanislaus Radziwill as my executor; and if for any reason, he fails to qualify or ceases to serve in that capacity, I name my cousin Timothy P. Shriver as my executor in his place. References in this will or a codicil to my "executor" mean the one or more executors (or administrators with this will annexed) for the time being in office. No executor or a codicil need furnish any surety on any official bond. In any proceeding for the allowance of an account of my executor, I request the Court to dispense with the appointment of a guardian ad litem to represent any person or interest. I direct that in any proceeding relating to my estate, service of process upon any person under a disability shall not made when another person not under a disability is a party to the proceeding and has the same interest as the person under the disability.

SEVENTH: In addition to other powers, my executor shall have power from time to time at discretion and without license of court: To retain, and to invest and reinvest in, any kind or amount of property; to vote and exercise other rights of security holders; to make such elections for federal and state estate, gift, income and generation-skipping transfer tax purposes as my executor may deem advisable; to compromise or admit to arbitration any matters in dispute; to borrow money, and to sell, mortgage, pledge, exchange, lease and contract with respect to any real or personal property, all without notice to any beneficiary and in such manner, for such consideration and on such terms as to credit or otherwise as my executor may deem advisable, whether or not the effect thereof extends beyond the period settling my estate; and in distributing my estate, to allot property, whether real or personal, at then current values, in lieu of cash.

APPENDIX 17.2 Marilyn Monroe's Last Will and Testament

The Will of Marilyn Monroe

The legendary icon, who tragically committed suicide in 1962, left most of her fortune to her friends and family.

I, MARILYN MONROE, do make, publish and declare this to be my Last Will and Testament.

FIRST: I hereby revoke all former Wills and Codicils by me made.

SECOND: I direct my Executor, hereinafter named, to pay all of my just debts, funeral expenses and testamentary charges as soon after my death as can conveniently be done.

THIRD: I direct that all succession, estate or inheritance taxes which may be levied against my estate and/or against any legacies and/or devises hereinafter set forth shall be paid out of my residuary estate.

FOURTH: (a) I give and bequeath to BERNICE MIRACLE, should she survive me, the sum of $10,000.00.
(b) I give and bequeath to MAY REIS, should she survive me, the sum of $10,000.00.
(c) I give and bequeath to NORMAN and HEDDA ROSTEN, or to the survivor of them, or if they should both predecease me, then to their daughter, PATRICIA ROSTEN, the sum of $5,000.00, it being my wish that such sum be used for the education of PATRICIA ROSTEN.
(d) I give and bequeath all of my personal effects and clothing to LEE STRASBERG, or if he should predecease me, then to my Executor hereinafter named, it being my desire that he distribute these, in his sole discretion, among my friends, colleagues and those to whom I am devoted.

FIFTH: I give and bequeath to my Trustee, hereinafter named, the sum of $100,000.00, in Trust, for the following uses and purposes:

(a) To hold, manage, invest and reinvest the said property and to receive and collect the income therefrom.
(b) To pay the net income therefrom, together with such amounts of principal as shall be necessary to provide $5,000.00 per annum, in equal quarterly installments, for the maintenance and support of my mother, GLADYS BAKER, during her lifetime.
(c) To pay the net income therefrom, together with such amounts of principal as shall be necessary to provide $2,500.00 per annum, in equal quarterly installments, for the maintenance and support of MRS. MICHAEL CHEKHOV during her lifetime.
(d) Upon the death of the survivor between my mother, GLADYS BAKER, and MRS. MICHAEL CHEKHOV to pay over the principal remaining in the Trust, together with any accumulated income, to DR. MARIANNE KRIS to be used by her for the furtherance of the work of such psychiatric institutions or groups as she shall elect.

SIXTH: All the rest, residue and remainder of my estate, both real and personal, of whatsoever nature and wheresoever situate, of which I shall die seized or possessed or to which I shall be in any way entitled, or over which I shall possess any power of appointment by Will at the time of my death, including any lapsed legacies, I give, devise and bequeath as follows:
(a) to MAY REIS the sum of $40,000.00 or 25% of the total remainder of my estate, whichever shall be the lesser,
(b) To DR. MARIANNE KRIS 25% of the balance thereof, to be used by her as set forth in ARTICLE FIFTH (d) of this my Last Will and Testament.
(c) To LEE STRASBERG the entire remaining balance.

SEVENTH: I nominate, constitute and appoint AARON R. FROSCH Executor of this my Last Will and Testament. In the event that he should die or fail to qualify, or resign or for any other reason be unable to act, I nominate, constitute and appoint L. ARNOLD WEISSBERGER in his place and stead.

EIGHTH: I nominate, constitute and appoint AARON R. FROSCH Trustee under this my Last Will and Testament. In the event he should die or fail to qualify, or resign or for any other reason be unable to act, I nominate, constitute and appoint L. Arnold Weissberger in his place and stead.

Marilyn Monroe (L.S.)

SIGNED, SEALED, PUBLISHED and DECLARED by MARILYN MONROE, the Testatrix above named, as and for her Last Will and Testament, in our presence and we, at her request and in her presence and in the presence of each other, have hereunto subscribed our names as witnesses this 14th day of January, One Thousand Nine Hundred Sixty-One

APPENDIX 17.3 Power of Attorney

United States of America
State of Louisiana
Parish of Jefferson

Be it known, that on this _____ day of _____, in the year _____:

1. Before me, the undersigned authority, a Notary Public duly commissioned and qualified in and for the State and Parish set forth above, therein residing, and in the presence of the undersigned competent witnesses, personally came and appeared: _____ a person of the full age of majority and domiciled in St. Rose, Louisiana (the "Principal"), who declared that the Principal appoints his children, _____ (the "Agent," whether one or more, with either authorized to act alone), as the Principal's true and lawful agent and attorney-in-fact, general and special, granting unto the Agent full power and authority for the Principal and in the Principal's name and behalf, and to the Principal's use, to conduct, manage and transact all of the Principal's affairs, business, concerns and matters of whatever nature or kind, without any reservation whatsoever, except as hereinafter specifically set forth and subject to the following effective date. The Power of Attorney shall not become effective unless and until a personal physician of the Principal certifies in writing that the Principal is mentally or physically incapable of administering her affairs. In furtherance of this general grant of authority to the Agent, but not in limitation thereof, the Principal specifically authorizes the Agent to perform all of the following acts and exercise all of the following powers for the Principal and in the Principal's name.

2. To open all letters or correspondence addressed to the Principal and answer them.

3. To open accounts with any bank, brokerage or other entity; to deposit funds (whether represented by cash, checks or otherwise) in any account maintained by or for the Principal with any bank or other entity; to endorse all checks, bills of exchange and other instruments; to withdraw funds from any account maintained by the Principal with any bank or other person; to sign checks, bills or exchange and other instruments; to deposit any obligation with any bank or other entity for collection.

4. To represent the Principal in the Principal's capacity as a creditor or obligee of any person; to collect any funds or things owed the Principal by any person; and to attend any meeting of creditors in which the Principal may be interested and to vote in the Principal's name on all matters that may be submitted to the meeting.

5. To represent the Principal in the Principal's capacity as a stockholder of any corporation, partner in any partnership, beneficiary of any trust or member of any association or entity or as a security holder thereof. This authority shall include (but is not limited to) the authority to execute consent agreements and to attend any meetings of stockholders, partners, members, or beneficiaries or security holders of any corporation, partnership, association, trust or entity and to agree or vote (or execute proxies in favor of others to agree or vote) in the name of the Principal on all questions, including merger, sale, consolidation, any type of reorganization or matters.

6. To borrow any amounts of money for the Principal and in the Principal's name upon such terms and conditions as the Agent may in the Agent's sole discretion deem appropriate.

7. To sell, exchange, donate, transfer, or convey any property, whether immovable (real), movable (personal), tangible or intangible or corporeal or incorporeal, including stocks, bonds, notes, bills or any other security, belonging to the Principal or any interest therein and to receive the price or other consideration thereof.

8. To make gifts or other gratuitous transfers of any property belonging to the Principal either outright or in trust (including the forgiveness of debt), to any of the Principal's descendants or to the agent.

9. To purchase, acquire by exchange or otherwise acquire any property for and in the name of the Principal and to make payment therefore out of the Principal's funds or assets.

10. To create servitudes, building restrictions, other real rights, easements and covenants of any kind that burden, benefit or otherwise affect any property of the Principal.

11. To accept donations.

12. To lease, rent, let or hire (as lessor) any property belonging to the Principal.

13. To lease, rent, hire or let (as lessee) any property.

APPENDIX 17.3 Power of Attorney (continued)

14. To encumber, mortgage, pledge, pawn or otherwise grant any security interest in any property of the Principal, whether to secure obligations of the Principal or any other person or entity.

15. To grant or convey oil, gas, and other mineral leases, net profits interests, production payments, royalty interests, mineral servitudes and other interests in oil, gas and any other minerals on or under any property of the Principal; to sign division orders and transfer orders; to grant rights-of-way and easements; and otherwise to execute documents incident to the exploration for oil, gas or other minerals on or underlying property of the Principal.

16. To enter into transactions pursuant to which the Principal is lessee, grantee or vendee under or of any oil, gas or mineral lease, net profits interest, production payment, royalty deed, mineral servitude or any other interest in oil, gas or other minerals.

17. To undertake any obligations for the Principal, to act for the Principal in agreeing to guarantee any obligations of others or agreeing to defend and indemnify any person or entity against any claims, obligations or liabilities.

18. To act for the Principal and be the Principal's substitute in all cases in which the Principal may be appointed the agent or attorney of others.

19. To refer matters to arbitration and to initiate, prosecute, defend and otherwise represent the Principal in any judicial or arbitration proceeding (whether as plaintiff or defendant) and to settle and compromise any claim, dispute or proceeding; to apply for and obtain any attachments, sequestrations, injunctions, and appeals, give the requisite security, and sign the necessary bonds.

20. To represent the Principal in connection with any succession or estate in which the Principal may be or become interested (whether as heir, legatee, creditor, executor, administrator or otherwise), including the execution of any acceptance or renunciation thereof on the Principal's behalf; to apply for the administration thereof, and to demand, obtain and execute all orders and decrees as the Agent may deem proper; to settle, compromise, and liquidate the Principal's interest therein; and to receive and receipt for all property to which Principal may be entitled in respect of successions or estates.

21. To acknowledge any debt of the Principal.

22. To settle and compromise any dispute or matter involving the Principal.

23. To file any United States, State or other tax returns (including but not limited to income tax returns); to apply for extensions of time to file tax returns; and to represent the Principal in connection with any matter or dispute relating to United States, State or other taxes.

24. The Principal further authorizes and empowers the Agent to take any other action concerning the affairs, business or assets of the Principal as fully, completely and effectively and for all intents and purposes with the same validity as though the action had been expressly provided for herein and as though the Principal had taken the action in person.

25. The transactions entered into by the Agent for the Principal shall be on such terms and conditions as to payment and otherwise as the Agent may in the Agent's sole discretion determine.

26. The Agent is authorized to make, sign and execute in the name of the Principal all agreements, contracts, and instruments that may be necessary or convenient in the Agent's sole discretion to carry out transactions entered into by the Agent for the Principal or to enable the Agent fully to exercise the powers granted herein and to include therein any terms, conditions and provisions that the Agent shall deem appropriate and to bind the Principal thereby as fully as though each instrument had been signed by the Principal in person.

27. The agency created by this Power of Attorney shall be "durable" as provided by Louisiana Civil Code article 3027(B) and shall not be deemed revoked by the Principal's disability or incapacity.

28. The Principal agrees to ratify and confirm all actions that the Agent shall take pursuant to this Power of Attorney.

29. References herein to one gender shall be deemed to include the other whenever appropriate.

30. The term "property" means all kinds of property, whether movable, immovable, real, personal, mixed, corporeal, incorporeal, tangible or intangible. The term "entity" includes natural persons, corporations, partnerships, trusts, associations and any other form of legal entity and governmental and political organizations.

APPENDIX 17.3 Power of Attorney (continued)

31. THUS DONE AND PASSED in multiple originals on the date first above written in the presence of the undersigned competent witnesses, who sign their names with the Principal and me, Notary, after reading of the whole.

WITNESSES:

_____

_____

Print Name: _____

Principal _____

Print Name: _____

_____
Notary Public

APPENDIX 17.4 Medical Power of Attorney

Medical Power of Attorney

1. BE IT KNOWN, that on this _____ day of _____, in the year 20xx:

2. BEFORE ME, the undersigned authority, a Notary Public duly commissioned and qualified in and for the State and Parish set forth above, therein residing, and in the presence of the undersigned competent witnesses, personally came and appeared: (The "Principal"), who after being duly sworn, declared that the Principal appoints his children, _____ (the "Agent", whether one or more, with either authorized to act alone), as the Principal's true and lawful agent and attorney-in-fact, granting unto the Agent full power and authority regarding the matters set forth below.

3. <u>Durability</u>. This agency is "durable" and shall not be deemed revoked by the Principal's disability or incapacity.

HEALTH CARE

4. The Principal grants unto the Agent full power and authority regarding the following health care matters that the Principal could exercise on the Principal's own behalf, if capable of doing so. The Principal specifically authorizes the Agent to:

    4.1 <u>Medical Records.</u>   Have access to any medical information in any form regarding the Principal's physical condition, and to execute such consents as may be necessary to obtain such medical information.

    4.2 <u>Professionals.</u>   Retain, compensate and discharge any health care professionals the Agent deems necessary to examine, evaluate or treat the Principal, whether for emergency, elective, recuperative, convalescent or other care.

    4.3 <u>Institutionalization.</u>   Admit the Principal to any health care facility recommended by a qualified health care professional, whether for physical or mental care or treatment, and remove the Principal from such institution at any time, even if contrary to medical advice.

    4.4 <u>Treatment.</u>   Consent on the Principal's behalf to tests, treatment, medication, surgery, organ transplant or other procedures, and to revoke that consent, even if contrary to medical advice.

    4.5 <u>Chemical Dependency.</u>   Consent on the Principal's behalf to a course of treatment for chemical dependency, whether suspected or diagnosed, and to revoke such consent.

    4.6 <u>Pain Relief.</u>   Consent on the Principal's behalf to pain relief procedures, even if they are unconventional or experimental, even if they risk addiction, injury or foreshortening the Principal's life.

    4.7 <u>Releases.</u>   Release from liability any health care professional or institution that acts on the Principal's behalf in reliance on the Agent.

PERSONAL CARE

5. The Principal grants unto the Agent full power and authority regarding the following personal care matters that the Principal could act on the Principal's own behalf, if capable of doing so. The Principal specifically authorizes the Agent to:

    5.1 <u>Home Care.</u>   Provide for the Principal's continued maintenance and support. As nearly as possible, the Principal expressly authorizes the Agent to maintain the Principal's accustomed standard of living. The Agent shall provide the Principal with a suitable place to live by maintaining the Principal in the Principal's family residence or apartment (home), paying principal, interest, taxes, insurance and repairs as necessary. The Agent may retain or discharge domestic servants, attendants, companions, nurses, sitters or other persons who provide care to the Principal and the Principal's home. The Agent may authorize purchases of food, clothing, medical care and customary luxuries on the Principal's behalf.

    5.2 <u>Institutional Care.</u>   Arrange and contract for institutional health care (hospital, retirement facility, nursing home, hospice or other) on the Principal's behalf if recommended by the Principal's physician. If reasonably advised that the Principal's return home is unlikely because of the Principal's condition, the Agent may sell, exchange, lease, sublease or dispose of the Principal's home and such of its contents as are no longer useful to the Principal and are not specifically bequeathed in the Principal's will, all on such terms as to price, payment and security as the Agent deems reasonable.

    5.3 <u>Religious Needs.</u>   Continue the Principal's affiliation with the Principal's church, keeping the Principal accessible to the Principal's clergy, members and other representatives, continuing and renewing any pledge made by the

APPENDIX 17.4 Medical Power of Attorney (continued)

Principal whether for capital, operations or other purposes, and generally to assist the Principal in maintaining the Principal's church relationships to the extent the Principal's health permits.

5.4   Companions and Recreation.   Hire, discharge, direct and compensate such companions as may be necessary for the Principal's health, recreation, travel, and general well-being.

5.5   Funeral Arrangements.   Arrange and contract for the Principal's funeral including appropriate arrangements and instruction for the Principal's funeral service or memorial service, including purchase of a burial plot or other appropriate disposition of the Principal's body. The Agent shall comply with any known written instructions as the Principal may have or leave.

5.6   Curator or Guardian.   Nominate on the Principal's behalf any person the Agent deems qualified, including the Agent, as the Principal's curator, undercurator, curator ad hoc, guardian, or conservator or any other fiduciary office the Principal has a right to nominate or designate, to waive any bond on the Principal's behalf and to grant to that fiduciary or representative any powers that the Principal might extend on the Principal's own behalf.

REFUSAL OF MEDICAL TREATMENT

6.   The Principal declares that the Principal does not wish the Principal's dying to be prolonged artificially through extraordinary or heroic means if the Principal's condition is terminal. Even over the objection of members of the Principal's family, the Principal authorizes the Agent to:
6.1   Withdraw or Withhold Life Support.   Sign on behalf of the Principal any documents, waivers or releases necessary to withdraw, withhold or cease any procedure calculated only to prolong the Principal's life, including the use of a respirator, cardiopulmonary resuscitation, surgery, dialysis, blood transfusion, antibiotics, antiarrhythmic and pressor drugs or transplants if two licensed physicians, one of whom is the Principal's attending physician, have personally examined the Principal and the Principal's attending physician has noted in the Principal's medical records that the Principal's condition is terminal and irreversible.

6.2   Nourishment.   Refuse or discontinue intravenous or parenteral feeding, hydration, misting and endotracheal or nasogastric tubes, if advised that no undue pain will be caused to the Principal.

DECLARATION

7.   Contemplating that the Principal's medical care may be rendered in Louisiana, or that state law might apply, the Principal has executed a Declaration Concerning Life-Sustaining Procedures ("Declaration") pursuant to State Revised Statues 40:1299.58.1 and following as amended, a copy of which is attached. The Principal declares that by executing that Declaration the Principal does not intend to limit or reduce the powers over the Principal's person elsewhere granted to the Agent in this agency, but rather to convey to the Agent any additional powers as are necessary to make or carry out the terms of that Declaration.

8.   THUS DONE AND PASSED in multiple originals on the date first above written in the presence of the undersigned competent witnesses, who signed their names with the Principal and me Notary, after reading of the whole.

WITNESSES:

_____

_____

Print Name:_____   Principal

_____

Print Name:_____

_____

Notary Public

APPENDIX 17.5 Living Will

Living Will Declaration

This Declaration is made on the _____ day of _____, 20xx, pursuant to the Louisiana Natural Death Act, La. R.S. 40:1299.58.1 *et seq.*

I,_____, being of sound mind, willfully and voluntarily make known my desire that my dying shall not be artificially prolonged under the circumstances set forth below and do hereby declare:

If at any time I should have an incurable injury, disease or illness certified to be a terminal and irreversible condition or a continual profound comatose state with no reasonable chance of recovery by two physicians who have personally examined me, one of whom shall be my attending physician, and the physicians have determined that my death will occur whether or not life-sustaining procedures are utilized and where the application of life-sustaining procedures would only serve to prolong artificially the dying process, I direct that such procedures (including but not limited to artificial means of respiration, hydration and/or nutrition) be withheld or withdrawn and that I be permitted to die naturally with only the administration of medication or the performance of any medical procedure deemed necessary to provide me with comfort care.

In the absence of my ability to give direction regarding the use of such life-sustaining procedures, it is my intention that this Declaration shall be honored by my family and physician(s) as the final expression of my legal right to refuse medical or surgical treatment and accept the consequences from such refusal.

I understand the full import of this Declaration, and I am emotionally and mentally competent to make this Declaration. Terms used in this Declaration shall have the meanings prescribed in the Louisiana Natural Death Act, La. R.S. 40:1299.58 *et seq.*, as amended now or hereafter.

_____
Declarant

Metairie, Jefferson Parish, Louisiana

The declarant has been personally known to me, and I believe the declarant to be of sound mind. Both witnesses are competent adults who are not entitled to any portion of the estate of the declarant upon declarant's decease. The declarant signed this Declaration in our presence on the date set forth above.

_____
Witnesses

_____
Witnesses

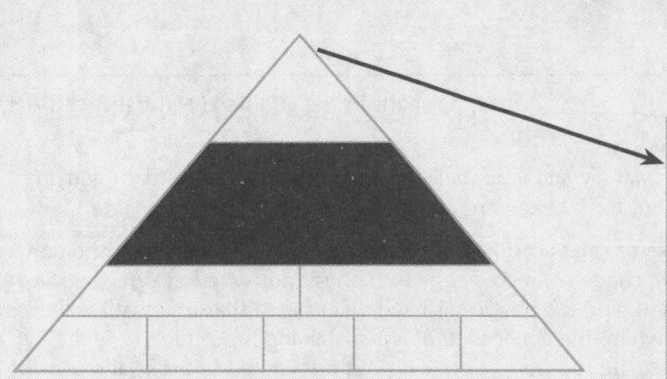

- Financial planning institutions
- Financial planning professionals
- The Code of Ethics and Standards of Conduct
- State laws
- Civil liability

- Developing a financial planning practice
- Maintaining competence
- Developing clients

- Practicing competently, ethically, and legally
- Procedures regarding discipline
- Civil liability

5 | The Financial Planning Profession

CHAPTERS

▷ Risks	▷ Goals	▷ Data Collection	▷ Data Analysis
■ Incompetence of planner	■ The competent, legal, and ethical practice of financial planning	■ Financial planning institutions	■ Maintaining professional competence
■ Improper practice		■ Financial planning professionals	■ Continuing education
■ Unethical practice		■ The Code of Ethics	■ Practicing lawfully and ethically
■ Illegal practice		■ Standards of Conduct	■ Building a practice
■ Professional discipline		■ Malpractice laws	
■ Civil liability		■ Disciplinary rules	
		■ Civil liability	

The Practice of Financial Planning

LEARNING OBJECTIVES

After learning the material in this chapter, you will be able to do the following:

- Describe various types of financial planning institutions

- Identify the types of services that are provided by the various types of financial planning institutions

- List the common credentials associated with the financial planning industry

- Discuss common compensation methods for professional financial planners

- Identify essential aspects of building a financial planning practice and maintaining clients

- Discuss the importance of continuing education for financial planners

INTRODUCTION

The professional financial planner understands that the overall purpose of personal financial planning is to assist clients in achieving their goals and objectives. While most of those goals are financial, many are more qualitative than quantitative. The planner realizes that personal financial planning is about the adaptation of the individual client's strengths and weaknesses in an environment characterized by opportunities and risks.

The planner must possess a wide variety of skills and knowledge with which to assess the client's current financial situation, help the client establish realistic financial goals, and develop a plan or strategy for accomplishing those goals.

To be successful, the financial planning professional should have a working knowledge of the concepts within the financial planner's pyramid of knowledge.

EXHIBIT 18.1 Financial Planner's Pyramid of Knowledge

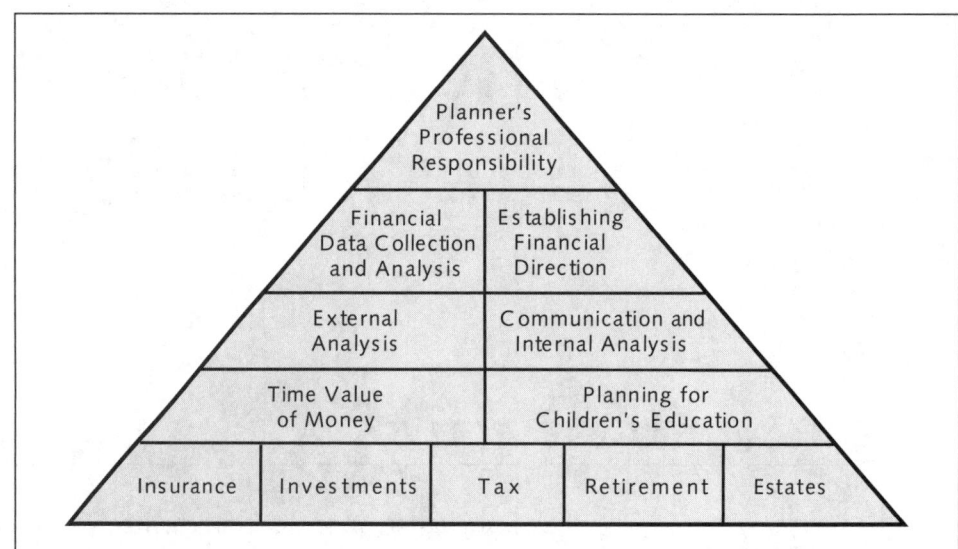

THE FINANCIAL PLANNING PROFESSION

The financial planning profession is comprised of a diverse group of individuals and institutions. Certain practitioners maintain individual private practices. Other financial planners work for accounting firms, law firms, insurance companies, personal financial planning firms, brokerage houses, mutual funds, banks, and other financial institutions that provide financial planning-related services.

Financial Planning Institutions

Accounting Firms

Accounting firms provide accounting, tax, and auditing-related services. Traditionally, these services were limited to preparing tax returns, preparing financial statements, business consulting, and business and individual tax planning. Today, accounting firms are providing even more services related to financial planning. These services include assistance in investment planning, retirement planning, and estate planning.

The American Institute of Certified Public Accountants (AICPA) has been actively assisting Certified Public Accountants (CPAs) in the development of financial planning practices in recent years. They provide training for members at national conferences and have instituted the Personal Financial Specialist (PFS) designation which is devoted solely to financial planning. The AICPA has also established relationships with other financial services firms that allow CPAs to deliver more financial planning services to their new and existing clients.

Law Firms

Attorneys have always been an integral part of developing and implementing financial and estate plans. Because attorneys draft legal documents, they are in a good position to provide additional services to their clients. Law firms have commonly drafted wills, powers of attorney, trusts, qualified plan documents, and partnership agreements. Their traditional services include tax planning, estate planning, and retirement and benefit planning.

Insurance Companies

Insurance companies primarily sell life, health, and/or property and casualty insurance products. Many insurance companies are expanding their services to include other areas of financial planning, particularly estate planning and retirement planning. Some have their own proprietary mutual funds.

Personal Financial Planning (PFP) Firms

These firms are generally small and specialize in a particular market niche. Some PFP firms manage assets and others provide comprehensive financial planning or sell products.

Brokerage Houses

Many brokerage houses provide global financial management and advisory services, including financial planning, securities underwriting, and trading and brokering. Some brokerage firms provide research, banking and insurance services, and investment banking. Brokerage houses are currently changing the nature of their businesses from transaction oriented to more service and planning related. These new services include retirement and estate planning.

Mutual Funds

Numerous mutual fund companies now provide financial planning assistance to better serve their clients and differentiate from their competition. To achieve this, mutual fund companies have established personal counselors for their large customers, while providing generic planning on the internet for all customers.

Banks

Banks offer a wide range of financial planning services. Core product offerings include checking and savings accounts, mortgages, loans, and other credit products. In addition, banks now offer comprehensive brokerage services such as stocks, bonds, mutual funds, investments, and retirement planning. They may also offer estate planning services through their trust departments.

EXHIBIT 18.2 Summary of Financial Planning Institutions

Common Practice Areas	Accounting Firms	Law Firms	Insurance Companies	PFP Firms	Brokerage Houses	Mutual Funds	Banks
Insurance			✓	✓	✓		✓
Investments	✓		✓	✓	✓	✓	✓
Tax	✓	✓		✓			
Retirement	✓	✓	✓	✓	✓	✓	✓
Estate Planning	✓	✓	✓	✓	✓		✓

In an effort to attract clients and increase assets under management, firms and individual practices are expanding services to include all elements of financial planning. This newfound diversification provides clients with one-stop shopping. Firms have accomplished changes and expansion by maintaining their traditional expertise, such as tax planning for accounting firms and investment advice for brokerage houses, and hiring specialists in the other areas. Thus, the institutions continue to dominate service and training in one specific area but have the capacity, through company experts, to cover all aspects of financial planning. In addition, the institutions themselves continue to expand as the competition increases, in order to spread the costs of experts and additional services over the greatest number of clients and the amount of assets under management.

The consolidation of the various practice areas will provide an opportunity for lower-to-middle-income clients to have access to better financial planning services. Those services may become less personal, however, with planning services offered over the internet and within financial apps. Meanwhile, the wealthiest clients will likely continue to seek the services of a team of professionals, generally from more than one institution. Individuals with large investments generally seek independent, objective advice, which may be difficult to obtain from a single institution.

Financial Planning Professionals

The public perceives, and has a reasonable expectation, that those who practice financial planning are competent and ethical. Many financial professionals are licensed at the state and federal levels in specific areas such as insurance and/or securities. They are not specifically regulated, however, for their financial planning activities, with the exception of the CERTIFIED FINANCIAL PLANNER™, who is certified by Certified Financial Planner Board of Standards, Inc. (CFP Board). Individuals who have only an elementary understanding of one or two functional areas are not prepared to assist clients faced with complex choices in a changing environment. Although there are many competent, highly trained and highly credentialed individuals practicing financial planning, there are many more holding themselves out as financial planners who are not trained, competent, or credentialed. Unfortunately, the practice of financial planning lacks uniform educational standards, professional competence standards, and commitment to one profession with a self-regulating set of ethical standards.

Many financial planning professionals attempt to distinguish themselves by earning financial planning designations. The following three sections briefly describe some of the more common credentials for individuals who work in the financial planning area.

Financial Planning Designations

Certified Financial Planner™ (CFP®) CFP® certification, perhaps the most recognized and respected financial planning certification, is awarded by CFP Board. CFP® certificants are individuals who have met CFP Board's education, examination, experience, and ethics requirements. These individuals are committed to high standards of ethical conduct and must complete biennial continuing education requirements. Additional information about CFP Board and its Code of Ethics and Standards of Conduct is provided in the following chapter.

Chartered Financial Consultant® (ChFC®) The ChFC® credential is a financial planning designation awarded by The American College of Financial Services to individuals who complete the required education program, meet the experience requirements, and agree to adhere to a code of ethics.

Personal Financial Specialist™ (PFS™) The PFS™ designation is granted exclusively to CPAs who wish to specialize in personal financial planning. The PFS™ credential is a financial planning designation awarded by the AICPA to candidates who have met the CPA education requirements, have the minimum hours of financial planning experience, and successfully complete an exam.

EXHIBIT 18.3 Summary of Financial Planning Designations

	Education/Experience	Exam	Ethics	Continuing Education	Designating Organization
CFP®	Bachelor's degree and three years of financial planning-related experience (or two years of apprenticeship experience meeting additional requirements)	6 hours (two 3-hour sessions in one day)	Yes	30 hours every two years; includes 2 hours for ethics	CFP Board
ChFC®	Nine-course financial planning curriculum from The American College of Financial Services and three years of business experience	Two-hour exam for each of the nine courses	Adherence to The American College's Code of Ethics	30 hours every two years (mandatory for certain designees who matriculated after 06/30/1989; voluntary for others)	The American College of Financial Services
PFS™	Candidates must be CPAs and practice in the area of financial planning for a minimum number of hours per year	Comprehensive seven and one-quarter hour exam covering six financial planning topic areas	Adherence to the AICPA's Code of Professional Conduct	60 hours of CPE every three years; earned through classes, research, and work experience	AICPA, only to members who meet the requirements

Other Designations Held by Financial Services Professionals

Chartered Life Underwriter® (CLU®) The CLU® designation is awarded by The American College of Financial Services to insurance and financial services professionals who have met the College's three-year business experience requirement, passed eight college-level education courses (five required, three electives), and agreed to abide by the Code of Ethics.

Chartered Financial Analyst® (CFA®)   This designation is awarded by CFA Institute to experienced financial analysts who pass three examinations covering economics, financial accounting, portfolio management, securities analysis, and ethics, and complete four years of relevant work experience.

Certified Public Accountant (CPA)   The CPA designation is awarded by the American Institute of Certified Public Accountants (AICPA) to accountants who pass the AICPA's Uniform CPA Examination and satisfy the work experience and statutory and licensing requirements of the state(s) in which they practice.

Other Licenses Held by Financial Services Professionals

Attorney (JD)   As mentioned in the previous section, some attorneys provide financial planning services. Generally, those who provide these services specialize in estate or tax planning. The attorney is typically part of a financial planning team and may provide specific legal advice to a client, prepare legal documents, and consult on estate and tax planning issues.

Insurance Agent   Insurance agents are licensed by a state or states to sell or give advice on insurance products, including life, health, disability, property, and casualty insurance. Financial planning services will vary based on the type of agent. Independent insurance agents sell products for more than one insurance company, whereas exclusive insurance agents represent only one company.

Securities Analyst   These professionals are usually employed by investment brokers, banks, mutual fund managers, or other investment institutions to conduct investment research and analyze the value of securities, financial condition of a company, group of companies, or industry sector. Based on their analysis, securities analysts will make specific investment recommendations.

Registered Investment Adviser (RIA)   Registered investment advisers are individuals (or firms) providing securities advice for compensation. They must be registered with the Securities and Exchange Commission (SEC) or appropriate state securities agencies. Financial planning services provided by RIAs include recommendations of stocks, bonds, mutual funds, and other investments.

The Dodd-Frank Wall Street Reform and Consumer Protection Act, which changed the original Investment Advisers Act of 1940 thresholds for registration with the SEC, was signed into law on July 21, 2010. As of July 2011, advisers with assets under management of $100 million or more will continue to register as investment advisers with the SEC (unless an exemption applies). Advisers with assets under management of less than $100 million may be required to register with the SEC or with the state in which they maintain clients.

Real Estate Broker   Real estate brokers are licensed by the state or states in which they practice. These individuals arrange for the purchase or sale of property in return for a commission. Financial planning services provided by real estate brokers are limited and may include helping customers finance a real estate purchase through their contacts with banks, savings and loans, and mortgage bankers.

Compensation Methods

The methods of compensation for professional financial planners are as diverse as the planners themselves and include fee-only planners, fee-based planners, commission-based planners, and those receiving fees for assets under management. In recent years, there has been a move toward fee-only and fee-based planners due to the public's perception of a conflict of interest for commission-based planners.

Fee-Only Planners

Fee-only planners typically charge an hourly rate for advice or a fixed fee for a defined engagement. These planners do not receive commissions, and, therefore, their compensation is not contingent on the purchase or sale of a product. Many attorneys, CPAs, and CFP® certificants are compensated as fee-only financial planners.

Fee-Based Planners

Fee-based planners are compensated by both fees and commissions that are contingent on the purchase or sale of financial products.

Commission-Based Planners

Commission-based planners are compensated solely by commissions that are contingent on the purchase or sale of financial products. These products are used in the implementation of a financial plan.

Fees for Assets Under Management

Some planners are fee-only for advice and, if they take investment assets under management, will charge a monthly, quarterly, or annual fee of some percentage of the overall portfolio value. Fees charged for the management of assets are predominantly based on a percentage of assets. The percentage charged will generally be lower as the size of the client's portfolio increases.

Compliance Issues

There are few regulations by state and federal agencies regarding financial planners as a group. However, most financial planners render some sort of advice in areas that are regulated by the federal and/or state government. Planners selling stocks and bonds, insurance products, or real estate or providing legal or tax advice are required to have licenses for the specific services they provide. In addition, most planners providing investment advice must register with their state as well as the SEC in accordance with the Investment Advisers Act of 1940. In the absence of government regulation of financial planners, those planners who are CFP® certificants have voluntarily chosen to be regulated by a professional regulatory organization, CFP Board.

Financial planners who work in the securities industry may need to register with the Financial Industry Regulatory Authority (FINRA). FINRA is a self-regulatory agency overseen by the SEC that enforces standards of practice upon its members for the protection of investors. Member firms of FINRA are entitled to participate in investment banking and securities sales sponsored by FINRA members. Employees of member firms who engage in securities transactions must register with FINRA as registered representatives, which includes passing a qualification examination that tests the employees' understanding of securities products and laws.

SECURITIES INDUSTRY ESSENTIALS (SIE) EXAM

The SIE exam is FINRA's new general industry knowledge exam testing basic information such as products, risks, the structure and function of the securities industry and its regulatory agencies, and knowledge of regulated and prohibited practices. Although ideal for university students and career changers, anyone can sit for the exam without prior association with a firm. The range of topics covered on the SIE exam includes:

- Knowledge of Capital Markets

- Understanding Products and their Risks

- Understanding Trading, Customer Accounts, and Prohibited Activities

- Overview of the Regulatory Framework

In an effort to make it easier to start a financial services career or to simply prove mastery of basic industry knowledge, FINRA does not require sponsorship with a firm to sit for the SIE exam. However, to become registered with FINRA and seek a representative level role with an employer, candidates must also pass a revised, specialized knowledge qualification exam (or "top-off"), applicable to their job function with the firm.

With a low exam fee and no firm sponsorship requirement, the SIE exam is ideal for university students looking to get a head start on a financial services career and, most importantly, stand out to potential employers by proving mastery of basic industry knowledge and the ability to pass a high-stakes examination.

The SIE exam consists of 75 multiple-choice questions, plus 10 additional experimental questions. The breakdown is as follows:

Sections	% of Exam	# of Exam Questions
Knowledge of Capital Markets	16%	12
Understanding Products and their Risks	44%	33
Understanding Trading, Customer Accounts and Prohibited Activities	31%	23
Overview of Regulatory Framework	9%	7
TOTAL	100%	75

After passing the SIE exam, a candidate has up to four years to pass the representative-level "top-off" exam for registration with FINRA and association with a firm.

The SIE exam will act as a prerequisite exam—to become registered with FINRA and seek a representative level role with an employer, candidates must also pass a revised, specialized knowledge qualification exam (or "top-off") applicable to their job function with the firm.

EXHIBIT 18.4 Required FINRA Exams

Securities Transaction	Qualification Exam Required
Mutual funds (open-end)	Series 6
Variable annuities[1]	
Variable life insurance[1]	
Unit investment trusts	
Municipal fund securities (e.g., Section 529 plans, Coverdells)	
Corporate securities	Series 7
Mutual funds	
Money market funds	
REITs	
Asset-backed securities	
Mortgage-backed securities	
Options	
Government securities	
Venture capital	
Direct participation programs	Series 22
Municipal securities	Series 52
Equity traders	Series 55
Corporate securities	Series 62
Closed-end funds	
Money market funds	
REITs	
Venture capital	
Unsolicited securities orders from firm's clients (excludes municipal securities and limited partnerships)	Series 11
Government securities	Series 72
Government agency securities	
Mortgage-backed securities	
Investment advice	Series 65/66

[1]Individuals must also be state insurance licensed.

Many financial planners are investment advisers under the SEC definition and are required to register as such. According to SEC regulations, an investment adviser is a person who:

■ provides advice or issues reports or analyses regarding securities;

■ is in the business of providing such services; and

■ provides such services for compensation.

Exceptions include the following:

- Banks and bank holding companies

- Lawyers, accountants, engineers, or teachers, if their advisory services are solely incidental to their professions

- Brokers or dealers, if their advisory services are solely incidental to their business as brokers or dealers

- Publishers of newspapers, newsmagazines, or business or financial publications of general and regular circulation

- Persons whose advice is related only to securities that are direct obligations of or guaranteed by the United States

The SEC prohibits misstatements or misleading omissions in connection with purchases or sales of securities or investment advice. An investment adviser owes his clients undivided loyalty and may not engage in activity that creates any conflict of interest.

DEVELOPING A PROFESSIONAL PRACTICE

Building a Practice

Like any other service-oriented professional practice, a personal financial planning practice will grow and develop slowly. The professional developing a practice generally begins by writing a business or strategic plan that identifies the specific market niche of clients to be targeted and establishes goals and objectives for the practice. The planner assesses the competition for that market niche, the external environment, and internal strengths and weaknesses. The planner should implement an appropriate business strategy selected from a number of alternatives. Finally, the planner must monitor and adjust the practice on a continuing basis.

Choosing a market niche is perhaps the most important strategic decision a professional can make to develop a long-lasting, viable practice. An individual planner cannot be all things to all clients. Therefore, a professional planner must direct attention to the areas of specialization that he can penetrate and that will allow him to prosper. An appropriate approach to developing a practice is to scan the environment for a market niche that is not being well served or for a newly developing market need that is underserved or will soon be underserved.

Once a market niche is selected, the planner must effectively promote the professional services that are relevant to that particular niche. Finding the best form of promotion depends on the market demographics, the external environment, and the professional's strengths and weaknesses.

Some clients may feel insecure, skeptical, and vulnerable when engaging professional services. Therefore, clients must not only have confidence in the planner's technical abilities but must also feel that they can trust the planner. After all, they are entering into a relationship in which they must divulge personal financial information to the planner. With that in mind, a successful marketing plan might begin with promoting to an already existing client base. Such client-centered marketing is a good start because planners and their clients have already developed a relationship. In addition, planners are already familiar with their clients' concerns and needs. If planners are developing new practices, an alternative option may be to partner with other professionals who do not provide the services the planner expects to provide.

The pursuit of new clients is more of a challenge, as the ability to win the client's trust and confidence is a substantial obstacle in the sale of professional services. Clients of less than competent practitioners do not leave those practitioners just because a more competent professional becomes available. Many clients lack the ability to assess a practitioner's competence and, even if they can, they may fear and resist changing practitioners. Thus, many clients stay with poor practitioners simply because the relationship is familiar. An understanding of this phenomenon should lead the developing professional to understand that he must be creative and patient when developing a practice. Marketing to new clients may take the form of referrals, networking, educational and professional seminars, teaching financial planning courses, and direct advertising. The development of a successful practice will require a variety of promotional tools used in combination, consistent with an overall marketing and development plan.

Maintaining Clients

As mentioned, a high level of interpersonal trust is the key to long-term planner-client relationships. Regular contact, honesty, sincerity, and effective communication help develop the personal relationships that are essential to maintaining clients. Regular written communications, telephone conversations, lunch meetings, and other social activities help develop these personal relationships.

Although regular contact is important, perhaps the most essential key to a good planner-client relationship is the ability of the planner to truly listen. Clients should feel that the planner listens to their concerns, cares about their futures, and respects them. According to researchers at the University of Minnesota, on average, people spend nearly half of their communication time listening. Good listening is an active process that requires knowledge of a few basic skills and a great deal of practice. Many professionals are in such a habit of selling that they do not stop to listen. Suggestions regarding successful listening include taking notes during client meetings, restating what the client has just said and obtaining client acknowledgement, and requesting clarification when an issue is unclear. Active listening improves interpersonal skills, human relations, and personal selling opportunities. Nurturing client relationships takes time but will greatly benefit the planner in the long run and may result in additional business referrals.

Education and Continuing Education

The professional financial planner must obtain an initial education followed by a lifetime of continuing professional monitoring and education. The economy and financial environment are complex and constantly changing, as are some of the functional areas of financial planning. The risks to life, health, working ability, property, and liability change. The tax laws are complex and change so frequently that the average client may not be able to keep up or understand them. While investment information is readily available today, discerning relevant and useful facts requires more than an elementary understanding. Competent financial planning professionals make staying up to date with these changes a major priority throughout their professional careers.

Technology

A substantial part of the financial planning profession involves data collection and analysis. Fortunately, with the computer software available today, planners can harness vast amounts of financial and economic data. Financial planners who are setting up practices or upgrading their software and network systems should consider the following:

- Planning software for creating financial statements

- Software for evaluating recommendations and alternatives

- Monte Carlo simulation software to evaluate effects of various economic conditions on financial goals

- Data management tools for collecting, storing, and protecting client data

- Data mining/sorting tools to identify clients affected by legal, tax, or economic changes

---

WHERE ON THE WEB

American Bar Association **www.americanbar.org**

American Institute of Certified Public Accountants (CPA/PFS) **www.aicpa.org**

Certified Financial Planner Board of Standards, Inc. **www.cfp.net**

CFA Institute (CFA designation) **www.cfainstitute.org**

Financial Industry Regulatory Authority (FINRA) (NASD and NYSE consolidation) **www.finra.org**

Financial Planning Association **www.onefpa.org**

Financial Planning Magazine **www.financial-planning.com**

National Association of Insurance Commissioners **www.naic.org**

National Association of Personal Financial Advisors **www.napfa.org**

National Association of State Boards of Accountancy **www.nasba.org**

North American Securities Administrators Association **www.nasaa.org**

Securities and Exchange Commission **www.sec.gov**

Small Business Administration **www.sba.gov**

Society of Financial Service Professionals **national.societyoffsp.org**

U.S. Chamber of Commerce **www.uschamber.com**

DISCUSSION QUESTIONS

1. What are the primary differences in services provided by accounting firms and law firms?

2. Generally, which types of financial planning firms specialize in investment planning?

3. Generally, which types of financial planning firms specialize in estate planning?

4. How is the internet changing the financial planning industry?

5. What is the most recognized and respected financial planning certification?

6. What are the differences between CFP® certification and the CFA® charter?

7. Describe the fee-only compensation method.

8. What is one of the most important strategic decisions that must be made when developing a financial planning practice?

9. What can a planner do to improve the planner-client relationship?

Ethical Responsibilities

LEARNING OBJECTIVES

After learning the material in this chapter, you will be able to do the following:

- Compare and contrast ethics, law, and code of ethics

- Define Certified Financial Planner Board of Standards, Inc. (CFP Board)

- Describe CFP Board's Code of Ethics and Standards of Conduct

- Describe the structure of CFP Board's Code of Ethics and Standards of Conduct and provide the role of each part

- List the six principles of the Code of Ethics

- Explain how the commingling of funds is regulated under the Standards of Conduct

- Discuss the requirements of the Standards of Conduct

- Explain the provisions of the Practice Standards

■ Discuss the Fitness Standards for Candidates and Professionals Eligible for Reinstatement

■ Compare the three distinct standards or burdens of proof to illustrate the different treatment of a CFP® certificant at various stages of disciplinary proceedings

■ Differentiate among the four forms of discipline that can be applied by the Disciplinary and Ethics Commission

INTRODUCTION

CFP Board's Code of Ethics and Standards of Conduct
The set of principles of conduct that regulates behavior of CFP® certificants

Certified Financial Planner Board of Standards, Inc.
An independent professional regulatory organization that regulates financial planners

This chapter identifies, describes, and explains ethical principles for those involved in the financial planning industry through an analysis of the **CFP Board's Code of Ethics and Standards of Conduct** established by **Certified Financial Planner Board of Standards, Inc.** (CFP Board). The CFP Board occasionally updates its Code of Ethics and Standards of Conduct. While the changes have always been incremental, the key changes were adopted March 29, 2018, and made effective as of October 1, 2019. The basis for this material is to broaden the fiduciary standard to all financial advice and financial planning. Previously, the fiduciary standard only applied when doing financial planning or material elements of financial planning.

This chapter provides an overview of several important provisions of the Code of Ethics and Standards of Conduct. The full text provided in Appendix F for review. The most current version of the Code and Standards can also be downloaded at *https://www.cfp.net/for-cfp-professionals/professional-standards-enforcement/code-and-standards*.

ETHICS, LAW, AND CODES OF ETHICS

Ethics
The discipline of dealing with the moral principles or values that guide an individual

Law
Rules of conduct established by a government or other authority that command and encourage behavior considered right and prohibit behavior considered wrong

Analyzing the Code of Ethics and Standards of Conduct as it pertains to CFP® certificants proves to be an excellent guide for all of those involved in the financial planning field. First, however, it is important to distinguish among ethics, law, and codes of ethics.

Ethics is the discipline of dealing with the moral principles or values that guide an individual. When a decision must be made about a certain act, ethics aid an individual in determining what is right and wrong. In other words, ethical behavior is doing or not doing what one feels is right from within. Morals relate to one's conscience, character, and social relations. Morals form one's behavior and dictate whether one engages in conduct that is considered to be right or wrong. Thus, each individual's set of morals and values forms the ethics or ethical behavior of that individual.

Law is defined as rules of conduct established by a government or other authority that command and encourage behavior considered right and prohibit behavior considered wrong. Law and ethics differ in that laws apply to everyone, under certain authority, and compliance with laws is mandatory for those individuals. If the law is broken, that person is subject to punishment by government authorities. A violation of or deviation from one's ethics, on the other hand, does not necessarily subject that person to punishment.

Code of ethics
A set of principles of conduct that governs a group of individuals and usually requires conformity to professional standards of conduct

A **code of ethics** is a set of principles of conduct that governs a group of individuals and usually requires conformity to professional standards of conduct. Although the Code of Ethics and Standards of Conduct provides rules for ethical behavior, they are more closely aligned with law. For example, the same rule applies to attorneys concerning state bar ethics codes. The Code of Ethics and Standards of Conduct is considered the set of rules for CFP® certificants because compliance is mandatory, and failure to abide by these rules may result in disciplinary action, such as revocation or suspension of the CFP® certification.

Many professions have codes of ethics or laws of conduct created to promote ethical behavior. No finite set of ethical rules, however, can anticipate all situations or future developments in an industry. To truly satisfy the goal of an ethics code, applicable professionals must do more than merely fulfill the code's minimum requirements. To reach the ideals of a code, there must be a conscientious, good faith commitment by the professionals to the spirit of the standards of the code under all circumstances.

Ethical behavior, which conforms to moral principles, is the aim of CFP Board's Code of Ethics and Standards of Conduct. If financial planners abide by the highest standards of ethical behavior, the financial services industry will maintain or gain public trust. A need exists for a common, accepted set of ethical principles to ensure fair representation and full disclosure in financial planning services. The Standards of Conduct seek to regulate behavior of CFP® certificants with the intent to provide fairness to clients, maintain and increase public trust, and foster accountability. Public trust in the profession is crucial because opportunities for unethical behavior arise frequently in the financial planning profession. If the public loses trust in the advice of CFP® certificants, they will consult other professionals or not seek financial planning services. So compliance with the code of ethics is vital to the profession.

CFP BOARD AND THE CODE OF ETHICS AND STANDARDS OF CONDUCT

CFP Board's Disciplinary and Ethics Commission
A subsidiary board of CFP Board that interprets and applies the Code

CFP Board's Board of Directors
The governing board for the certified financial planning profession

CFP Board is an independent professional regulatory organization that owns the federally registered CFP® and Certified Financial Planner™ marks (the marks) in the United States. CFP Board regulates financial planners through trademark law by licensing individuals who meet CFP Board's certification requirements to use these federally registered marks. **CFP Board's Disciplinary and Ethics Commission** investigates, reviews, and takes appropriate action in connection with alleged violations of the Standards of Conduct.

CFP Board's Board of Directors requires compliance with the Code of Ethics and Standards of Conduct by all those who have been recognized and certified to use the CFP® marks, as well as those who seek certification. Violations may result in a letter of admonition, private censure, suspension, or revocation of the right to use the CFP® marks. Forms of discipline and an explanation of the disciplinary process are established in the Disciplinary Rules and Procedures (the Procedures). The Procedures also explain the disciplinary process. The final authority in all disciplinary matters rests solely with CFP Board and the Disciplinary and Ethics Commission.

CFP Board has several governing documents, rules, and procedures, including the following:

■ Code of Ethics, which states the six Principles constituting the basis for the ethical rules stated in all the other sections

■ Standards of Conduct

- Financial Planning Practice Standards

- Disciplinary Rules and Procedures

- Appeal Rules and Procedures

- Fitness Standards for Candidates and Professionals Eligible for Reinstatement

CFP® certificant
An individual who is currently certified by CFP Board

Professional eligible for reinstatement (PER)
An individual who is not currently certified by CFP Board but who was certified in the past and has an entitlement to potentially use the CFP® marks

Generally, the Code of Ethics and Standards of Conduct applies to CFP® professionals currently certified (CFP® certificants) and professionals eligible for reinstatement (PERs). A **CFP® certificant** is an individual who is currently certified by CFP Board. A **professional eligible for reinstatement** (PER) is an individual who is not currently certified but who was certified by CFP Board in the past and has an entitlement to potentially use the CFP® marks. This includes individuals who have relinquished their certification and who are eligible for reinstatement without being required to pass the current CFP® Certification Examination. For the sake of simplicity, the discussion in this chapter will reference the ethical obligations required by the Code of Ethics and Standards of Conduct in terms of their application to certificants.

NOTE ON CIVIL LIABILITY

The Code of Ethics and Standards of Conduct does not define the conduct expected of CFP® certificants for purposes of civil liability. Nonetheless, there are various areas in which a violation of the Code of Ethics and Standards of Conduct could likely result in civil liability for malpractice or professional negligence if the client sustains damages resulting from the CFP® certificant's action or inaction. For example, a certificant who violates Standard A.3 (Competence), which requires that services be provided competently may be susceptible to a lawsuit for professional negligence or malpractice if a client sustains damages resulting from the incompetence. Likewise, a certificant who violates Standard A.1 (Fiduciary Duty), which requires certificants to select financial products that are consistent with the client's needs could also be liable for the client's damages in a malpractice suit.

CODE OF ETHICS AND PROFESSIONAL RESPONSIBILITY

Principles
Aspirational statements expressing the ethical and professional ideals CFP® certificants are expected to display in their professional activities

The Code of Ethics provides six **Principles**, which express the ethical and professional ideals certificants are expected to display in their professional activities. They are aspirational in character and provide certificants with a source of guidance. The Principles contained in the Code of Ethics form the basis of the Standards of Conduct, Financial Planning Practice Standards, and Disciplinary Rules and Procedures.

Principle 1: Act with honesty, integrity, competence, and diligence. The duty of integrity means honesty in all aspects of the planner's relationship with the client. There can be no deceit or fraud in any statement or omission with a client. Honesty and candor must be more important than the planner's personal benefit. Allowance can be made for innocent error and legitimate differences of opinion, but integrity cannot coexist with deceit or subordination of one's principles. Competence involves both knowledge and skill. If the planner does not have the required knowledge or skill, she can acquire the skill, recommend someone else to provide these aspects of the plan, or limit the planning engagement to only areas in which the planer is competent. Diligence involves a thoroughness in preparation and execution.

Principle 2: Act in the client's best interest. The foundation of the CFP Board Code of Ethics and Standards of Conduct is that a CFP® certificant is held to a fiduciary standard in all financial advice. Formerly, the fiduciary standard was only applied when providing financial planning or material elements of financial planning. CFP Board defines a *fiduciary* as one who acts in the utmost good faith, in a manner he reasonably believes to be in the best interests of the client.

Principle 3: Exercise due care.

Principle 4: Avoid or disclose and manage conflicts of interest.

Principle 5: Maintain the confidentiality and protect the privacy of client information.

Principle 6: Act in a manner that reflects positively on the financial planning profession and the CFP® certification.

STANDARDS OF CONDUCT

Standards of Conduct
Rules established by CFP Board that establish the high standards expected of CFP® certificants, the violation of which may subject a certificant to discipline

The **Standards of Conduct** establish the high standards expected of certificants. They are binding on all certificants who have the right to use the CFP® marks, regardless of their title, type of employment or method of compensation, and regardless of whether they use actually use the CFP® marks. Violations may subject a certificant to discipline.

Certificants engage in a wide range of activities, and some certificants may not perform all of the typical services provided by financial planning professionals. As a result, some of the Standards may not apply to a certificant's specific activity. In addition, when the Standards require a specific action, a certificant is considered to be in compliance with the Standards if the certificant's employer performed the action.

The Standards of Conduct are divided into duties owed to clients, the application of practice standards for the financial planning process, duties to firms and subordinates, and the prohibition on circumvention. Summaries of some of the important Standards of Conduct are discussed in the sections that follow.

Duties Owed to Clients

Fiduciary Duty

A CFP® professional always owes a fiduciary duty to the client when providing financial advice. This means always acting in the best interests of the client by fulfilling three duties: the duty of loyalty, the duty of care, and the duty to follow clients' instructions.

The duty of loyalty has two aspects:

■ Placing the interests of the client above the interests of the CFP® certificant and the firm for which he or she professional works

■ Avoiding conflicts of interest or fully disclosing material conflicts or interest and obtaining the client's informed consent

The duty of care means acting with skill, care, prudence, and thoroughness in light of the client's goals, risk tolerance, and circumstances.

The duty to follow client instructions means implementing the client's objectives, restrictions, and policies in accordance with the terms of the engagement.

The duty of integrity means honesty in all aspects of the planner's relationship with the client. There can be no deceit or fraud in any statement or omission with a client.

If the services include financial planning, the certificant or the certificant's employer must enter into a written agreement governing the financial planning services with the client. The agreement must specify the services to be provided, the duration of the agreement, and procedures for terminating the agreement.

Competence

Besides the fiduciary duty and integrity in all aspects of the relationship, a CFP® certificant is required to be competent. This means certificants must offer advice only in areas in which they are competent to do so and maintain competence in any areas in which they are engaged to provide professional services. Keep in mind that financial planning is broad, and a CFP Board designee may be knowledgeable in many areas but deficient in others. This is particularly true today because financial services are quite complicated. Because of the vast diversity and scope of financial services, few people can be experts in all areas.

By virtue of having earned CFP® certification, a certificant is deemed to be qualified to practice and knowledgeable in the field of financial planning. However, it is neither sufficient simply to assimilate and absorb the common body of knowledge required to obtain CFP® certification, nor is it sufficient simply to acquire the necessary experience. Rather, a certificant must make a continuing commitment to learn and improve. As will be discussed later, CFP Board thus requires certificants to satisfy minimum continuing education requirements.

Generally, the requirement of competence involves certificant-client relationships—the Standards specifically refer to clients in defining the requirements relating to competence. The driving force behind this is that financial planning clients must be protected from incompetence. In certificant-client relationships, a certificant's incompetence can result in damage or loss to the client, not simply a disappointment or disciplinary action for the individual certificant. In addition, incompetence may reflect poorly upon the financial planning profession in general.

Certificants must exercise reasonable and prudent professional judgment when providing professional services to a client. They may only make or implement recommendations that are in the best interests of the client. This depends on the facts and circumstances of the client's situation. In addition, certificants must provide reasonable professional supervision to any subordinate or third party to whom they assign responsibility for any client services. This is yet another safeguard that ultimately benefits the client and strengthens the public's trust in the profession. All of these duties follow from the fiduciary relationship that exists between certificants and their clients.

Certificants must be in compliance with any applicable regulatory requirements governing the professional services they provide to clients. They must also advise their current clients of any suspension or revocation of their CFP® certification.

If the planner is not competent in an aspect of the relationship, the planner must obtain the competence; the engagement must be limited or terminated as necessary; or a competent professional must be found. A CFP® certificant must inform the client of any professional services that were requested by the client that will not be undertaken by the planner.

Diligence

Diligence involves giving a matter to the degree of effort expected in the client-planner relationship, including responding to the client in a timely and sufficiently thorough manner.

Disclose and Manage Conflicts of Interest

This duty involves the provision of financial advice, in particular the disclosure and management of all material conflicts of interest. This gives the client the ability to give informed consent or to reject the unacceptable aspects of the relationship.

A **conflict of interest** exists when a certificant's financial, business, property, or personal interests, relationships, or circumstances impair the certificant's ability to offer objective advice, recommendations, or services. Professional financial planners should recognize the inherent conflicts of interests that may arise in certificant-client relationships. The main reason for providing financial services as a financial planning practitioner is to give the client personalized financial advice that will maximize the client's financial well-being. On the other hand, the certificant is engaged in the financial services industry to earn a living and be compensated for the service. This compensation comes from the client—the same client who has engaged the certificant to improve the client's financial status. Theoretically speaking, this may be a conflict of interest in and of itself. For example, many certificants sell stocks, bonds, mutual funds, life insurance, or annuities and earn commissions from the sale of these products to their clients. This potentially creates an incentive for certificants to recommend products that may provide higher commissions or to refrain from recommending another course of action that may be in the client's best interest but would not provide any commissions. Even if the certificant is not in fact swayed in this scenario, there is an appearance that the interests of the certificant and the client are in conflict. When the appearance of such a conflict exists, it would be impractical for the certificant to disqualify himself from the relationship with the client, because then there would be no circumstance in which a certificant could earn a commission for selling a product to a client. Instead of disqualification or disengagement, the Standards require that a certificant disclose all potential conflicts of interests to the client in writing. The assumption is that, if the certificant discloses the information to the client, the client will feel as if the certificant has nothing to hide, and at the same time, the certificant is reminding himself to remain objective.

CFP Board holds that a CFP® certificant sincerely believing he is acting in the client's best interest is not sufficient to meet the duty to disclose and manage conflicts of interest. When investigating, the CFP Board will look for evidence that a reasonable client would have understood the disclosure and management aspects of the relationship in order for the client to give informed consent. The closer a planner conforms to commonly accepted business practices, the more likely the CFP Board will conclude that proper disclosure was made. Any unclear provisions in the disclosure will be interpreted in the client's favor.

Sound and Objective Professional Judgment

Under this duty, a planner's judgment may not be clouded by the interests of the planner. A CFP® certificant may not solicit or receive any gifts, noncash compensation, or other inducements that can reasonably be perceived to compromise the planner's objectivity or professional judgment.

Professionalism

The duty of professionalism involves showing clients, prospects, and other professionals respect, dignity, and courtesy.

Conflict of interest

Exists when a certificant's financial, business, property, and/or personal interests, relationships, or circumstances impair the certificant's ability to offer objective advice, recommendations, or services

Comply With the Law

The duty of compliance with all laws and regulations is also owed to the client. Besides the planner complying with all laws, rules, and regulations, a CFP® certificant may not intentionally assist in someone else's failure to obey all laws, rules, and regulations.

Confidentiality and Privacy

In general, a CFP® certificant may not disclose nonpublic information for any client, former client, or prospective client without consent. This is true even if the person is not harmed by the disclosure. However, client information may be shared within the purview of normal business relations when necessary. Additionally, a client's information can be shared with an authorized representative working for the client. Client information may also be shared in regard to a legal or enforcement action by a duly authorized representative of the law enforcement community or other applicable regulatory body or to defend against a legal matter brought against the planner on behalf of the client. Finally, all CFP® certificants must take reasonable steps to protect client data in both physical and electronic form.

Provide Information to the Client

A CFP® professional must provide the required information to the client at or before the start of the client engagement. The required information is dependent upon the nature of the engagement. There are two categories—when providing financial advice that does not rise to the level of financial planning according to the Practice Standards and when financial planning is occurring.

When only providing financial advice, the following information is required to be given to the client:

1. A description of the services and products involved

2. How the client pays for the services and products, including any additional charges that might be incurred

3. How the CFP® certificant and the firm are compensated

4. Any websites of governing authorities, self-regulating organizations, or professional organizations that contain the CFP® professional's public disciplinary history or any personal bankruptcy or business bankruptcy in which the planner was materially involved

5. Any other material information about the planner or firm regarding the client's decision to engage or continue to engage in the planning relationship

When providing financial planning, all the information required for financial advice is required, plus the following:

1. The terms of the engagement, including the scope of the engagement, time period, and any limits to the engagement

2. The client's responsibilities—unless excluded in the terms of the agreement, the CFP® certificant is responsible for implementing, updating. and monitoring the recommendations

3. A written disclosure of conflicts of interest and how they will be managed

4. The policies for protecting, handling, and sharing nonpublic information

5. The planner's duties when communicating with the client

Finally, for duties to provide information to the client, a CFP® professional has an obligation to give the client any material updates to the information given to the client previously. Specifically, any material updates to the CFP® professional's disciplinary history or bankruptcy information must be provided to the client within 90 days. The planner is also required to give the client the web pages that pertain to these changes.

Communicating With a Client

There is also a duty to provide accurate information and responses to questions in a timely manner in accordance with the terms of the engagement. All responses must be in a format a client would be reasonably expected to understand.

Certificants may not communicate to clients any false or misleading information related to their professional qualifications or services and may not mislead clients about the potential benefits of their services. Certificants may not fail to disclose or omit facts when disclosure is necessary to avoid misleading clients.

Certificants must disclose the following information to clients and prospective clients:

- An accurate and understandable description of the compensation arrangements being offered

- A general summary of likely conflicts of interest between the client and the certificant, the certificant's employer, or any affiliates or third parties

- Contact information for the certificant and the certificant's employer

If the certificant's services include financial planning, these disclosures must be in writing. The certificant must also make a timely disclosure to the client if any of this information materially changes.

Representing Compensation Method

There are three categories of compensation: fee-only, fee-based, and sales-related compensation. To be fee-only, neither the planner nor any part of the planner's business can receive any sales-related compensation in connection to the services provided to clients.

Fee-based compensation means the planner or the planner's firm receives both fees and sales-related compensation. The CFP Board calls this compensation *fee and commission.*

Sales-related compensation includes any compensation relating to the buying or selling of a client's financial assets other than for providing financial advice. It also includes compensation for referral of a client to an outside professional. It includes all types of commissions, 12b-1 fees, spreads, and revenue sharing arrangements. There are certain exceptions to sales-related compensation listed by the CFP Board.

A CFP® professional's duty to the client when the CFP® certificant's firm misrepresents compensation methods depends on if the CFP® professional controls the firm or not. If the CFP® professional controls the firm, then he may not allow the firm to misrepresent its compensation methods. If the CFP® certificant does not control the firm, then he must correct the firm's misrepresentations when dealing with the client.

Recommending, Engaging, and Working With Additional Persons

A duty a CFP® professional owes to clients involves the manner in which she deals with additional people in the relationship, such as attorneys and accountants. First, the CFP® professional must have a reasonable basis for recommending the additional person to a client. Second, either when the recommendation occurs or before the engagement with the client, the CFP® professional must disclose any economic benefits the planner or the firm will receive for the recommendation.

When dealing with the additional person on behalf of the client, the CFP® certificant must inform the additional person about the scope of the services and the division of responsibilities. The CFP® certificant has a responsibility to inform the client in a timely manner if the additional person is not performing adequately within the scope of the engagement.

Selecting, Using, and Recommending Technology

This duty involves the CFP® certificant only using or recommending technology in which he has an adequate understanding of the assumptions used and which he reasonably believes will produce reliable, objective, and appropriate results.

Refrain From Borrowing or Lending and Commingling Assets

A final duty owed to a client is to refrain from borrowing, lending, or commingling financial assets with the client. The only exceptions from the prohibition on CFP® certificants borrowing from or lending to a client are when the client is a family member or when the client is a money-lending institution. Finally, the CFP® professional and the firm are always prohibited from commingling financial assets with a client. Commingling is the act of mixing property (usually funds) belonging to one party with property belong to someone else; commingling occurs when a planner deposits client funds into his personal bank account. Commingling a client's property with other clients' property is prohibited unless doing so is authorized by law or the certificant has written authorization from each client and sufficient recordkeeping to accurately track the assets. Note that this rule restricts the situations when a certificant may commingle funds, even when the certificant has no negative intent. Even when a certificant has no negative intent, commingling client funds with personal funds may give rise to an appearance of impropriety.

Duties Owed to Firms and Subordinates

A certificant who is an employee or agent must perform professional services with dedication to the lawful objectives of the employer or principal and in accordance with the Code of Ethics. Certificants must also advise their current employers of any renovation or suspension of their CFP® certification.

A CFP® certificant is to provide reasonable care in the supervision of all associates acting for the CFP® certificant. The primary duty of supervision is to follow all rules, regulations, laws, and the CFP® Code of Ethics and Standards of Conduct. If a planner suspects another member of the firm with illegal or unethical behavior, she must promptly disclose it to management. The second duty is to comply with the lawful objectives of the employer. The planner will be subject to discipline by CFP Board for violations of the Code of Ethics and Standards of Conduct that do not conflict with the policies and procedures of the CFP®'s firm.

Duties Owed to CFP Board

One of the most basic of these obligations is that a certificant must meet all CFP® requirements, including continuing education requirements, to retain the right to use the CFP® marks. CFP Board requires 30 hours of continuing education biannually; of these 30 hours, at least 2 hours must cover ethics.

A certificant must notify CFP Board of any changes in contact information, including email addresses, telephone numbers, and physical addresses, within 45 days of the changes. A certificant must also notify CFP Board in writing of any conviction of a crime, other than minor traffic violations, or of any professional suspension or bar within 30 calendar days.

Finally, a certificant must not engage in any conduct that adversely reflects on (1) his integrity or fitness as a certificant, (2) upon the CFP® marks, or (3) upon the profession. The scope of this rule is broader than the other rules pertaining to professionalism, because it applies to any conduct that has an adverse effect on the certificant or the profession. There is some overlap between this requirement and the principle of integrity.

Actions Reflecting Upon the Profession

In the case of *Ibanez v. Florida Department of Business and Professional Regulation, Board of Accountancy*, 512 U.S. 136, 114 S. Ct. 2084, 129 L. Ed. 2d 118 (1994), Ibanez, an attorney, licensed CPA, and CFP® certificant, was reprimanded by the Florida Board of Accountancy for engaging in "false, deceptive, and misleading" advertising. Ibanez referred to her credentials as an attorney, a CPA, and CFP® certificant in her advertising and other communications with the public, placing CPA and CFP® certificant next to her name in her yellow pages listing and in her business cards and law office stationery.

The Florida Board of Accountancy argued that the term *certified* in the phrase *Certified Financial Planner* was misleading to the public because it implied state approval and recognition, when in fact the CFP Board certification is not given by the state. The U.S. Supreme Court rejected this argument and ruled that Ibanez had a constitutional right to promote herself as an attorney/CPA who was also a CFP® certificant. The Court then approvingly stated:

> Noteworthy in this connection, "Certified Financial Planner" and "CFP®" are well-established, protected federal trademarks that have been described as the most recognized designation(s) in the planning field. [Several thousand] persons have qualified for the designation nationwide. Over 50 accredited universities and colleges have established courses of study in financial planning approved by the CFP Board of Standards, Inc., and standards for licensure include satisfaction of certain core educational requirements, a passing score on a certification examination similar in concept to the Bar or CPA examinations, completion of a planning-related work experience requirement, agreement to abide by the CFP Board's *Code of Ethics and Professional Responsibility*, and an annual continuing education requirement.

The Court concluded that Ibanez could use all three credentials in her advertising because doing so was not misleading or false and because she had a constitutional right to commercial speech. The case also casts the CFP® marks in a favorable light, recognizing the credibility that accompanies them. Thus, Ibanez's actions did not mislead the public and did not adversely affect the profession.

THE PRACTICE STANDARDS

Practice Standards

The set of standards that (1) establish the level of professional practice that is expected of certificants engaged in personal financial planning, (2) advance professionalism in the practice of financial planning, and (3) enhance the value of the personal financial planning process

CFP Board established the Board of Practice Standards to draft the **Practice Standards** to ensure that the financial planning practice by certificants is based on agreed-upon norms of practice. The Practice Standards are also in place to advance professionalism in the practice of financial planning and to enhance the value of the personal financial planning process. A Practice Standard establishes the level of professional practice that is expected of certificants engaged in personal financial planning. The facts and circumstances of each particular situation determine the services to be provided.

Practice Standard 1

Understanding the Client's Personal and Financial Circumstances. The formal start of any engagement involves gathering the client's data and documenting it in writing. This includes the obligation of the CFP® certificant to act in the best interests of the client and to inform the client of the firm's policies and procedures. The planner must communicate to the client the need for both quantitative and qualitative data to fulfill the scope of the engagement and to collaborate with the client in obtaining the information. This data is analyzed to determine the client's personal and financial condition. If a planner cannot obtain sufficient data to fulfill the scope of the engagement, the scope of the engagement must be limited to what the data supports or the engagement must be terminated.

The scope of the engagement must be mutually defined by the financial planning practitioner and the client prior to providing any financial planning service. The process of *mutually defining* is accomplished by identifying the services to be provided, disclosing the practitioner's material conflicts of interest and compensation arrangements, determining the client's and practitioner's responsibilities, and establishing the duration of the engagement.

Practice Standard 2

Identifying and Selecting Goals. After discussing the planner's assessment of the client's personal and financial circumstances, the next issue is the client's goals. A client's personal financial goals, needs, and priorities that are relevant to the scope of the engagement and the service(s) being provided must be mutually defined by the financial planning practitioner and the client prior to making and/or implementing any recommendation. One portion of the goal-setting process is understanding that accomplishing one goal may impact other goals. When setting goals, a planner may use reasonable assumptions and estimates of items such as investment returns, inflation rates, tax rates, and other material items. Finally, the planner must inform the client of any goals the client finally selects which are not realistic in the planner's estimation.

Practice Standard 3

Analyzing the Client's Current Course of Action and Potential Alternative Course(s) of Action. A financial planning practitioner must analyze the client's present course of action and evaluate the major advantages and disadvantages of staying the course in the attempt to maximize the potential to meet the goals of the client. The CFP® certificant should also analyze the potential of alternative courses of action along with their major advantages and disadvantages in concert with the client's other goals, facts, and circumstances. This Practice Standard is intended to increase the probability of the practitioner helping the client to achieve the goals and objectives of the financial plan.

Practice Standard 4

Developing the Financial Planning Recommendation(s). The financial planning practitioner shall consider sufficient and relevant alternatives to the client's current course of action in an effort to reasonably meet the client's goals, needs, and priorities. This evaluation, which is done prior to any recommendations, may involve multiple reasonable assumptions, research, or consultation with other competent professionals. This process may result in one alternative, no alternatives, multiple alternatives, or various combinations in relation to the client's current course of action.

The financial planning practitioner must develop recommendations based on the selected alternatives and the current course of action in order to reasonably achieve the client's goals, needs, and priorities. A recommendation may be an independent action, continuation of the current course of action, inaction, or a combination of actions that may need to be implemented collectively. collectively. Each recommendation must consider the following:

1. The assumptions and estimates used to develop the recommendation

2. The basis for the recommendation including how it attempts to maximize the chance of meeting the goal and affecting the client's personal and financial situation

3. The timing and priority of the recommendation and whether the recommendation stands alone or must be implemented in coordination with another recommendation

Practice Standard 5

Presenting the Financial Planning Recommendation(s). A financial planning practitioner must communicate the recommendations to the client and the information that was required to be considered in developing the recommendations in a manner and to an extent reasonably necessary to assist the client in making an informed decision. The practitioner is charged with the responsibility of assisting the client in understanding (1) the client's current situation, (2) the recommendation itself, and (3) the impact of the recommendation on the ability to achieve the client's goals, needs, and priorities. If the client possesses an understanding of the items, the client then can make an informed decision. Presenting recommendations also provides the practitioner the opportunity to further assess whether the recommendations meet the client's expectations, the client's willingness to act on the recommendations, and whether modifications are needed.

Practice Standard 6

Implementing the Financial Planning Recommendation(s). The client and the financial planning practitioner must mutually agree on the implementation responsibilities consistent with the scope of the engagement. The client is responsible for accepting or rejecting recommendations and for retaining or delegating implementation responsibilities. The responsibilities of the financial planning practitioner may include (1) communicating with the client the recommendations being implemented, (2) identifying activities necessary for implementation, (3) determining division of activities between the client and practitioner, (4) handling referrals to and/or coordination with other professionals, (5) sharing of information as authorized, (6) selecting and securing products or services after considering the advantages and disadvantages of the action, product, or services relative to the reasonably available alternatives, and (7) discussing with the client the basis for selecting the products or services recommended and any conflicts of interest. Finally, the CFP® professional must discuss with the client any client selection that deviates from the recommendations.

The financial planning practitioner has the duty to use her judgment in investigating products or services that reasonably address the client's needs and are in the best interests of the client. The planner must discuss with the client any client selection that differs from the actions, products, and services that the planner recommended. Professional judgment incorporates information that is both qualitative and quantitative and, of course, may differ from those of other practitioners or advisers. Over time, implementing recommendations using proper products and services for the client increases the credibility of the profession in the eyes of the public.

Practice Standard 7

Monitoring Progress and Updating—Defining Monitoring Responsibilities. The financial planning practitioner and client must mutually define monitoring responsibilities. This Practice Standard clarifies the role, if any, of the practitioner so that the client's expectations are more likely to be in alignment with the level of monitoring services that the practitioner intends to provide. When monitoring services are engaged, the financial planning practitioner must make a reasonable effort to define and communicate to the client those monitoring activities that the practitioner is able and willing to provide, including an explanation of what is to be monitored, how the actions, products, and services will be monitored, the frequency of monitoring, and the communication method.

A portion of monitoring includes analyzing and updating the client's progress toward goals and reviewing the results with the client. Both quantitative and qualitative data is analyzed during the review process, including any material changes reported by the client.

FITNESS STANDARDS FOR CANDIDATES AND PROFESSIONALS ELIGIBLE FOR REINSTATEMENT

The Disciplinary and Ethics Commission (DEC), a group within CFP Board, has determined specific character and fitness standards for candidates for certification to ensure an individual's conduct does not reflect adversely upon the profession as a whole or upon the CFP® certification marks. These standards are referred to as the Fitness Standards for Candidates and Professionals Eligible for Reinstatement (PERs). CFP Board determined that such standards would benefit individuals interested in attaining CFP® certification. The following conduct (referred to as *Conduct Deemed Unacceptable*) is unacceptable and will *always* bar an individual from becoming certified:

■ Felony conviction for theft, embezzlement, or other financially based crimes

■ Felony conviction for tax fraud or other tax-related crimes

■ Revocation of a financial (registered securities representative, broker-dealer, insurance, accountant, investment advisor, financial planner) professional license, unless the revocation is administrative in nature (i.e., the result of the individual determining not to renew the license by not paying the required fees)

- Felony conviction for any degree of murder or rape

- Felony conviction for any other violent crime within the last five years

The following conduct (referred to as *Conduct Deemed a Presumptive Bar*) is *presumed* to be unacceptable and will bar an individual from becoming certified unless the individual petitions the Disciplinary and Ethics Commission (the "Commission") for consideration, and the Commission grants the petition:

- Two or more personal or business bankruptcies

- Revocation or suspension of a nonfinancial professional (e.g., real estate agent, attorney) license, unless the revocation is administrative in nature (i.e., the result of the individual determining not to renew the license by not paying the required fees)

- Suspension of a financial professional (e.g., registered securities representative, broker-dealer, insurance agent, accountant, investment adviser, financial planner) license, unless the suspension is administrative in nature (i.e., the result of the individual determining not to renew the license by not paying the required fees)

- Felony conviction for nonviolent crimes (including perjury) within the last five years

- Felony conviction for violent crimes other than murder or rape that occurred more than five years ago

Under the procedures outlined in CFP Board's *Disciplinary Rules and Procedures*, the Commission will review other matters that may reflect adversely upon the profession or the CFP® certification marks once the candidate for CFP® certification has successfully completed the education, examination, and experience requirements for certification. These matters include, but are not limited to:

- consumer complaints;

- arbitrations and other civil proceedings;

- felony convictions for nonviolent crimes that occurred over five years ago;

- misdemeanor convictions; and

- employer investigations and terminations.

Candidates for CFP® certification and PERs are required by CFP Board to disclose certain matters on the ethics section of the initial certification application.

Individuals who have conduct that is listed in the *Conduct Deemed a Presumptive Bar* list (discussed previously) or may reflect adversely upon the profession or the CFP® certification marks may petition the Commission for consideration and a determination whether their conduct will bar certification. The basic process for these reviews will be as follows.

- When CFP Board learns that an individual's conduct falls within the *Conduct Deemed Unacceptable* list (previously discussed), CFP Board notifies the individual that he/she is permanently barred from becoming certified.

- The individual submits a written petition for consideration to the CFP Board's Professional Standards Department.

- The individual signs a form agreeing to CFP Board's jurisdiction to review the matter.

- CFP Board reviews the request to confirm that the conduct either falls within the *Conduct Deemed a Presumptive Bar* list or is conduct that may reflect adversely upon the profession or the CFP® certification marks.

- Once confirmed, CFP Board requests all relevant documentation from the individual, and a fee is paid by the individual submitting the petition for consideration.

Once the Disciplinary and Ethics Commission has reviewed the petition, it will make one of the following decisions.

- Grant the petition after determining that the conduct does not reflect adversely on the individual's fitness as a candidate for CFP® certification or upon the profession or the CFP® certification marks, and certification will be issued to the individual.

- Deny the petition but allow the individual to reapply for CFP® certification after a period not to exceed five years. The individual will be required to meet the education, examination, experience, and ethics requirements of CFP® certification at the time of reapplication.

- Deny the petition after determining that the conduct reflects adversely on the individual's fitness as a candidate for CFP® certification or upon the profession or the CFP® certification marks, and certification will be permanently barred.

Disciplinary Rules and Procedures
The rules and regulations for disciplinary proceedings against CFP Board certificants

The Commission's decision regarding a petition for reconsideration may be appealed to the Appeals Committee of the Board of Directors.

DISCIPLINARY RULES AND PROCEDURES

The Standards of Conduct also provide the rules and regulations for disciplinary proceedings against CFP Board designees. The enforcement of the Standards is accomplished through CFP Board's **Disciplinary Rules and Procedures** (the Procedures).

Notes on Burdens of Proof

Burden of proof
The requirement of proving facts to a certain degree of probability. With regard to disciplinary rules and procedures, there are three distinct burdens of proof: (1) preponderance of the evidence, (2) clear and convincing evidence, and (3) evidence beyond a reasonable doubt.

Professional financial planners should understand the various standards of proof that are involved with litigation in general and in disciplinary procedures. A standard of proof, or **burden of proof**, is the requirement of proving facts to a certain degree of probability. There are three distinct burdens of proof: (1) preponderance of the evidence, (2) clear and convincing evidence, and (3) evidence beyond a reasonable doubt. A comparison of the burdens of proof illustrates that different burdens apply at various stages of disciplinary proceedings. Note that burden of proof in disciplinary proceedings is upon CFP Board. The certificant is presumed to be free from ethical violations until proven otherwise.

The Preponderance of the Evidence Standard

Preponderance of the evidence means that the evidence as a whole shows what it was intended to prove with a probability of 51% or more. To say it another way, the evidence tends to prove that the existence of a fact is more likely than not. For example, proof of misconduct by a certificant must be "*established by a preponderance of the evidence.*" In other words, it must be shown that a certificant more than likely violated the Code. In professional negligence or malpractice cases, the standard of proof is generally by a preponderance of the evidence.

The Clear and Convincing Evidence Standard

"*Clear and convincing evidence*" requires more proof or more certainty in the eyes of the fact finder than a preponderance of the evidence. **Clear and convincing evidence** is the measure or degree of proof that will produce in the mind of the fact finder a firm belief or conviction as to allegations sought to be established and has been loosely described as a 75% certainty that a fact has been proven. Under the Procedures, a certificant who has been suspended for over a year must petition the Disciplinary and Ethics Commission for reinstatement and prove by clear and convincing evidence that he has been rehabilitated, has met continuing education requirements, and is fit to use the marks. In other words, the certificant must clearly and convincingly prove that he is worthy of reinstatement, with more certainty than by a preponderance of the evidence but less than that beyond a reasonable doubt.

In litigation involving fraud, usually the party alleging fraud must prove fraud by clear and convincing evidence.

The Beyond a Reasonable Doubt Standard

Beyond a reasonable doubt in evidence means that the fact finder is fully satisfied, entirely convinced, and satisfied to a moral certainty that a fact has been established. The fact finder can have no doubt as to the existence of a fact unless that doubt is unreasonable or irrational. Some define the term as a 99% certainty that the evidence shows as a whole the fact sought to be proven. In criminal proceedings, the burden of proof is beyond a reasonable doubt.

Grounds for and Forms of Discipline

The grounds for discipline under the Procedures are as follows:

- Any act that violates the Standards of Conduct

- Any act that fails to comply with the Practice Standards

- Any act that violates any criminal laws, whether the certificant is convicted or acquitted

- Any act that is the proper basis for professional suspension

- Any act that violates the Disciplinary Rules and Procedures or an order of discipline

- Failure to respond to a request of CFP Board without good cause, or obstruction of CFP Board or staff in the performance of one's duties

- Any false or misleading statement made to CFP Board

Preponderance of the evidence

A measure or degree of proof. With regard to disciplinary rules and procedures, preponderance of the evidence means the evidence as a whole shows what it was intended to prove with a probability of 51% or more.

Clear and convincing evidence

A measure or degree of proof; with regard to disciplinary rules and procedures, clear and convincing evidence means the evidence as a whole shows what it was intended to prove with a probability of 75% or more

Beyond a reasonable doubt

A measure or degree of proof; with regard to disciplinary rules and procedures, beyond a reasonable doubt means the evidence as a whole shows what it was intended to prove with a probability of 99% or more

Private censure
An unpublished written reproach that is mailed to the censured CFP® certificant by the Disciplinary and Ethics Commission

Public letter of admonition
Written reproach of the CFP® certificant's behavior that will normally be published in a press release or other form of publicity selected by the Disciplinary and Ethics Commission

Suspension
May be ordered by the Disciplinary and Ethics Commission for a specified period of time, not to exceed five years, for individuals it deems can be rehabilitated

Revocation
The Disciplinary and Ethics Commission may order permanent revocation of a certificant's right to use the marks and to publish the revocation in a press release or other form of publicity

If grounds for discipline are established, the Disciplinary and Ethics Commission has discretion to use any of the following forms of discipline:

- **Private censure**—an unpublished written reproach that is mailed to the censured certificant by the Disciplinary and Ethics Commission

- **Public letter of admonition**—a publishable written reproach of the certificant's behavior that will normally be published in a press release or other form of publicity selected by the Disciplinary and Ethics Commission

- **Suspension**—may be ordered by the Disciplinary and Ethics Commission for a specified period, not to exceed five years, for individuals it deems can be rehabilitated; the suspension will normally be published in a press release or other form of publicity, unless extreme mitigating circumstances exist; certificants who are suspended may qualify for reinstatement

- **Revocation**—the Disciplinary and Ethics Commission may order permanent revocation of a certificant's right to use the marks and publish the revocation in a press release or other form of publicity; all revocations are permanent

In all cases, the Disciplinary and Ethics Commission can require certificants to complete additional continuing education or other remedial work.

Disciplinary proceedings under the Procedures are commenced upon a written request by any person. After commencement, the matter is referred to the Disciplinary and Ethics Commission. If the Disciplinary and Ethics Commission in its discretion determines to proceed with the investigation, CFP Board provides written notice to the certificant of the investigation and the allegations made, and the certificant has 30 calendar days from the date of service of notice of the investigation to file a written response to the allegations. If a timely response is received, CFP Board staff counsel shall compile all documents and materials and commerce probable cause determination procedures as soon thereafter as is reasonably practicable.

CFP Board staff counsel determines if there is probable cause for disciplinary action and then does one of the following: (1) dismisses the allegations as not warranting further investigation, (2) dismisses the allegations with a letter of caution—recommending remedial action and/or entering appropriate orders, or (3) issues a formal complaint, stating the grounds for discipline and the alleged wrongful conduct of the certificant. Within 20 days, the certificant must respond to all allegations and set forth any defenses or mitigating circumstances. If the certificant fails to file an answer within 20 days of service, the certificant will be in default and the allegations of the complaints will be deemed admitted. CFP Board staff counsel must serve the certificant with an Order of Revocation, stating clearly and with reasonable particularity the grounds for revocation of the certificant's right to use the CFP® marks.

All hearings on complaints seeking disciplinary action against a certificant are required to be conducted by a **hearing panel**. The hearing panel must establish the rules of procedures and evidence to be observed at the hearing. Proof of misconduct is established by a preponderance of the evidence. All testimony at hearings before the hearing panel must be transcribed.

Hearing panel
Panel that establishes the rules of procedures and evidence to be observed at a complaint hearing seeking disciplinary action against a certificant

Report, Findings of Fact, and Recommendation

After the hearing, the hearing panel records its findings of fact and recommendations and submits them to the Disciplinary and Ethics Commission for consideration. The report must recommend that the complaint be dismissed as not proven or refer the matter to the Disciplinary and Ethics Commission with the recommendation of discipline, stating which form of discipline the hearing panel deems appropriate. The hearing panel may also recommend that the Disciplinary and Ethics Commission enter other appropriate orders.

The Disciplinary and Ethics Commission has the power to review any determination made during disciplinary proceedings and to enter any order concerning that determination, including an order directing that further proceedings be conducted. Within 45 days of the hearing, the Disciplinary and Ethics Commission must mail the certificant a final order containing the Commission's findings of fact and, if appropriate, any sanction imposed. Any appeal must be submitted to the Appeals Committee within 30 days after notice of the order is sent to the certificant. Otherwise, the order becomes final.

Conviction of a Crime or Professional Suspension

Conviction of a crime or an order of professional suspension is conclusive evidence and proof of the commission of the act for purposes of disciplinary proceedings. The certificant has a duty to report a conviction or professional suspension to CFP Board within 30 days after the date on which the certificant is notified of the conviction or suspension. After receiving notice that a certificant has been convicted of a crime, other than minor traffic offenses, or has been the subject of professional discipline, CFP Board staff counsel will determine whether an investigation is warranted. If a certificant is convicted of a serious crime or is the subject of a professional suspension, CFP Board shall obtain the record of the conviction or suspension and, if appropriate, file a complaint against the certificant.

Settlement Procedure

Offer of Settlement
A certificant may tender an Offer of Settlement in lieu of a disciplinary hearing

A certificant may tender an **Offer of Settlement** in lieu of a disciplinary hearing. The Offer of Settlement may be made where the public interest and CFP Board permit. A certificant is allowed only one Offer of Settlement during the course of a disciplinary proceeding. If the Offer of Settlement is rejected by the hearing panel, the Offer is deemed void, and the matter will be set for hearing. The certificant will not be prejudiced in any way by the prior Offer, and this Offer will not be given consideration in determination of the issues involved in the pending or any other proceeding. The hearing panel may also make a Counter Settlement Offer to the certificant, subject to the same rules as to an Offer of Settlement.

Required Action After Revocation or Suspension

When an order of revocation or suspension becomes final, the certificant "*shall promptly terminate*" any use of the CFP® marks. Revocation is permanent, and no opportunity for reinstatement is available.

A certificant who has been suspended for less than one year shall be reinstated automatically after expiration of the suspension, provided that the certificant files a request for reinstatement within 30 days after the expiration of the period of suspension. A certificant who has been suspended over one year must petition the Disciplinary and Ethics Commission for reinstatement within six months of the end of the suspension, or reinstatement is relinquished or waived. If the certificant petitions the Disciplinary and Ethics Commission within six months of possible reinstatement, the certificant has the burden of proving by "*clear and convincing evidence*" that the certificant has been rehabilitated, has complied with all applicable disciplinary procedures, and is fit to use the marks.

If the certificant petitions for reinstatement, CFP Board staff counsel will initiate an investigation. The certificant must cooperate with the investigation, and CFP Board staff counsel shall submit a report of the investigation detailing the certificant's past disciplinary record and any recommendation regarding reinstatement. If the certificant is denied reinstatement, the certificant must wait two years to petition again for reinstatement. The second petition for reinstatement must be received by CFP Board within six months of the expiration of the two-year period. If the second petition is not submitted in a timely fashion or is denied, the certificant's right to use the marks is administratively relinquished. If no petition for reinstatement is sought within six months of the expiration of the two-year period for reinstatement, the failure of the individual to file the petition for reinstatement within this six-month time period will result in the individual's right to use the marks being administratively relinquished.

All proceedings and records conducted in accordance with the Procedures are confidential and will not be made public, unless otherwise provided for in the Procedures. The Procedures allow disclosure of disciplinary proceedings if the proceeding is based on criminal conviction or professional suspension, the certificant has waived confidentiality, or disclosure is required by legal process. In proceedings involving a consumer, CFP Board staff may contact the consumer or the certificant's employer to request relevant documents.

THE IMPORTANCE OF ETHICS

While understanding the fundamentals of financial planning is vital to those who aspire to work and interact in the business and financial environments, equally important is recognizing and being able to handle ethical issues that accompany interaction in the finance services industry and that accompany the provision of financial services. The negative effects of unethical practices and actions of a few not only damage the individual engaging in unethical behavior and the victim of such behavior but also damage the image and productivity of the entire industry. Ethics codes and practice standards can significantly help in reducing the incidence of unethical and damaging conduct, as well as providing much needed counsel, tutelage, guidance, and direction to the individual professional.

Certified Financial Planner Board of Standards Inc. owns the marks CFP®, CERTIFIED FINANCIAL PLANNER™, and CFP (with flame logo) in the United States, which it awards to individuals who successfully complete initial and ongoing certification requirements.

Kaplan does not award CFP® certification. The right to use the marks CFP® and CERTIFIED FINANCIAL PLANNER™ is granted by CFP Board to those persons who have met its rigorous educational standards, passed the CFP® Certification Examination, satisfied a work experience requirement, and agreed to abide by CFP Board's Code of Ethics and Professional Responsibility. Only persons registered with CFP Board are permitted to sit for the CFP® Certification Examination. CFP® certification is issued only by CFP Board.

DISCUSSION QUESTIONS

1. Compare and contrast ethics, law, and an ethics code.

2. What is Certified Financial Planner Board of Standards, Inc.?

3. What is the role of CFP Board's Code of Ethics and Standards of Conduct?

4. What is the role of the Standards of Conduct in relation to CFP Board's Code of Ethics and Standards of Conduct?

5. What are a CFP® certificant's responsibilities with respect to client property?

6. What is the role of the Disciplinary Rules and Procedures in relation to the Code of Ethics and Standards of Conduct?

7. What restrictions apply to loans between CFP® certificants and their clients?

8. What are the six principles provided by the Code of Ethics?

9. Explain the term *commingling* and the restrictions on commingling that apply to CFP® certificants.

10. How do the three distinct standards or burdens of proof affect the treatment of a CFP® certificant at various stages of disciplinary proceedings?

11. What four forms of discipline can be applied by the Disciplinary and Ethics Commission?

12. What are the Fitness Standards for Candidates and Professionals Eligible for Reinstatement (PERs)? List the conduct that will always bar an individual from becoming certified.

13. Describe the process of an individual petitioning CFP Board for reconsideration under the Fitness Standards for Candidates and Professionals Eligible for Reinstatement (PERs). What decisions might the Disciplinary and Ethics Commission make regarding a petition for reconsideration?

6 Appendices

APPENDICES

Comprehensive Financial Planning Case

Today is January 1, 2021. Mark and Ava Lane have come to you, a financial planner, for help in developing a plan to accomplish their financial goals. From your initial meeting together, you have gathered the following information.

PERSONAL BACKGROUND AND INFORMATION

Mark Lane (age 30)

Mark is an assistant in the marketing department for Gas & Electric, Inc. His annual salary is $52,000.

Ava Lane (age 30)

Ava is a legal research assistant with the law firm of Sabrio, Johnson & Williams, LLC. Her annual salary is $40,000.

The Children

Mark and Ava have no children from this marriage. Mark has two children, Shawn (age 4) and Ronald (age 3), from a former marriage. Shawn and Ronald live with their mother, Kimberly.

The Lanes

Mark and Ava have been married for two years.

Mark must pay $500 per month in child support until both Shawn and Ronald are age 18. The divorce decree also requires Mark to create an irrevocable life insurance trust for the benefit of the children and contribute $350 per month for payment of life insurance premiums to the trustee, Kimberly's father. There are no withdrawal powers on the part of the beneficiaries. The trust is to be used for the education and/or maintenance of the children in the event of Mark's death. The trustee has the power to invade any trust principal for the beneficiaries at the earlier of Mark's death or when Ronald becomes age 18.

ECONOMIC INFORMATION

- Inflation is expected to be 4% annually.
- Their salaries should increase by 5% for the next 5 to 10 years.
- There is no state income tax.
- The economy is growing slowly; stocks are expected to grow at 9.5%.

Bank Lending Rates

- The 15-year mortgage rate is 3.6%.
- The 30-year mortgage rate is 4.2%.
- The rate for a secured personal loan is 10%.

INSURANCE INFORMATION

Life Insurance

	Policy A	Policy B	Policy C
Insured	Mark	Mark	Ava
Face amount	$300,000	$78,000[1]	$20,000
Type	Whole life	Group term	Group term
Cash value	$2,000	$0	$0
Annual premium	$2,100	$178	$50
Who pays premium	Trustee	Employer	Employer
Beneficiary	Trustee[2]	Kimberly	Mark
Policy owner	Trust	Mark	Ava
Settlement options clause selected	None	None	None

[1] This was increased from $50,000 to $78,000 January 1, 2019.
[2] Shawn and Ronald are beneficiaries of the trust.

Health Insurance

■ Mark and Ava are covered under Mark's employer plan, which is an indemnity plan with a $200 deductible per person per year and an 80/20 major medical coinsurance clause with a family annual stop-loss limit of $10,000.

Long-Term Disability Insurance

■ Mark is covered by an own occupation policy with premiums paid by his employer. The benefits equal 60% of his gross pay after an elimination period of 180 days. The policy covers both sickness and accidents and is guaranteed renewable.

■ Ava is not covered by disability insurance.

Renters' Insurance

■ The Lanes have an HO-4 renters' policy without endorsements.

■ Content coverage is $25,000; liability coverage is $100,000.

Automobile Insurance

■ Both the car and truck are covered.

■ The Lanes do not have any additional insurance on Mark's motorcycle.

Type	Personal auto policy
Bodily injury	$25,000/$50,000
Property damage	$10,000
Medical payments	$5,000 per person
Physical damage	Actual cash value
Uninsured motorist	$25,000/$50,000
Comprehensive deductible	$250
Collision deductible	$500
Premium (annual)	$3,300

INVESTMENT INFORMATION

The Lanes think they need six months' cash flow net of all taxes, savings, vacation, and discretionary cash flow in an emergency fund. They are willing to include in the emergency fund the savings account and Mark's 401(k) plan balance because it has borrowing provisions.

The Amazing.com stock was a gift to Mark from his uncle Bill. At the date of the gift (July 1, 2018), the fair market value of the stock was $3,500. Bill's tax basis was $2,500, and Bill paid gift tax of $1,400 on the gift. Bill had already used up both his lifetime applicable exclusion amount and that year's annual exclusion to Mark.

The K&B stock was a gift to Ava of 100 shares from her uncle Mike. At the date of the gift (December 25, 2018), the fair market value was $8,000 and Mike had paid $10,000 for the stock in 2005 (his tax basis).

The Growth Mutual Fund (currently valued at $13,900) was acquired by Mark over the years 2015 through 2020 with deposits of $1,000, $1,000, $2,000, $2,000, $2,500, and $3,000. The earnings were all reinvested, and Mark received 1099 forms for the income and capital gains during the years of earnings ($0 in 2015, $200 in 2016, $400 in 2017, $400 in 2018, $650 in 2019, and $750 in 2020).

INCOME TAX INFORMATION

The Lanes' federal income tax filing status is married filing jointly. Both the children (Shawn and Ronald) are claimed as dependents on the Lanes' tax return as part of Mark's divorce agreement. The Lanes live in a state that does not have state income tax.

Section 79 Cost from Uniform Premium Table:
Age 30 and under, $.06 per month/per $1,000

RETIREMENT INFORMATION

Mark currently contributes 3% of his salary to his Section 401(k) plan. The employer matches each $1 contributed with $.50 up to a total employer contribution of 3% of salary.

GIFTS, ESTATES, TRUSTS, AND WILL INFORMATION

- Mark has a will leaving all of his probate estate to his children.
- Ava does not have a will.
- The Lanes live in a common law state that has adopted the Uniform Probate Code.

PERSONAL STATEMENT OF CASH FLOWS

Mark and Ava Lane
Personal Statement of Cash Flows (Expected to be Similar in 2021)
January 1, 2020–December 31, 2020

CASH INFLOWS		
Salaries*		
Mark	$52,000	
Ava	40,000	
Investment income**	1,090	
Total inflows		$93,090
CASH OUTFLOWS–SAVINGS AND INVESTMENTS		
Savings—house down payment	$ 2,400	
Reinvestment of investment income	1,090	
Section 401(k) plan contribution	1,560	
Total savings		$ 5,050
FIXED OUTFLOWS		
Child support	$ 7,800	
Life insurance payment (to trustee)	4,200	
Rent	19,200	
Renters' insurance	960	
Utilities	2,880	
Telephone	1,200	
Auto down payment 12/31/20***	7,400	
Auto insurance	6,600	
Gas, oil, maintenance	4,800	
Student loans	6,000	
Credit card debt	3,600	
Loan for furniture	2,400	
Total fixed outflows		$30,261
VARIABLE OUTFLOWS		
Taxes—FICA and withholding both spouses	$12,225	
Food	6,000	
Clothing	2,400	
Entertainment/vacation	3,000	
Total variable outflows		$13,935
Total outflows		$47,266
Net cash flows (deficit)		$ (176)
TOTAL OUTFLOWS		$47,090

*Mark's W-2 will reflect the Section 79 costs of $28,000 in excess group term life insurance, but this is not a cash inflow.

**$340 from dividends and $750 from other investment sources.

***P&I next year will total $3,600.

STATEMENT OF FINANCIAL POSITION

Mark and Ava Lane
Statement of Financial Position
As of January 1, 2021

ASSETS[1]		LIABILITIES[2] & NET WORTH	
Cash and equivalents		**Current liabilities**	
Cash	$ 500	Credit card balance VISA	$ 9,000
Savings account	1,000	Student loan—Mark[3]	3,240
Total cash and equivalents	**$ 1,500**	Auto loan—Ava	2,508
Invested assets		Furniture loan	1,115
Amazing.com stock (100 shares)[4]	$ 5,000	**Total current liabilities**	**$15,863**
K&B stock (100 shares)	7,200		
Growth Mutual Fund	13,900	**Long-term liabilities**	
Section 401(k) plan	1,500	Student loan—Mark	$41,821
Total invested assets	**$27,600**	Auto loan—Ava	12,288
Use assets		Furniture loan	418
Auto—Ava	$18,494	**Total long-term liabilities**	**$54,527**
Truck—Mark	4,000		
Motorcycle—Mark	1,000	**Total liabilities**	**$70,390**
Personal property & furniture	17,750	**Net worth**	**(46)**
Total use assets	**$41,244**		
Total assets	**$70,344**	**Total liabilities & net worth**	**$70,344**

Notes to financial statements:

1. Assets are stated at fair market value.

2. Liabilities are stated at principal only as of January 1, 2019, before January payments.

3. Mark's parents took out the student loans, but he is repaying his parents at a rate of $300 per month. The P & I are from his parents' records.

4. Amazing.com's current dividend is $3.40.

INFORMATION REGARDING ASSETS AND LIABILITIES

Home Furnishings

The furniture was purchased with 20% down and 18% interest over 36 months. The monthly payment is $108.46.

Automobile

The automobile was purchased December 31, 2020, for $37,000 with 20% down and 80% financed over 48 months with payments of $695.16 per month.

Student Loan

The student loans were made in Mark's parents' names and consist of a combination of home equity and PLUS loans. The interest rates vary and Mark pays his parents directly each month.

Stereo System

The Lanes have a sophisticated stereo system (FMV $10,000). They asked and received permission to alter the apartment to build speakers into every room. The agreement with the landlord requires the Lanes to leave the speakers if they move because the speakers are permanently installed and affixed to the property. The replacement value of the installed speakers is $4,500, and the noninstalled components are valued at $5,500. The cost of the system was $10,000, and it was purchased in late 2016.

▌REQUIREMENTS

1. Complete an engagement letter to the Lanes to advise them on financial planning.

2. Complete a client/planner worksheet.

3. Calculate the Lanes' financial ratios.

   a. Comment on any of the above ratios that you think are important.

   b. Describe the Lanes' current financial condition.

4. Identify the Lanes' financial strengths and weaknesses.

5. After reading the case, what additional information would you request from the Lanes to complete your data-gathering phase?

6. Identify the Lanes' likely appropriate mission, goals, and objectives.

7. Make recommendations based on the Lanes' goals and risks in all areas of their financial situation.

Time Value of Money Tables

APPENDIX B-1 Present Value of a Dollar

Present Value of $1

$$\left[\frac{1}{(1+i)^n}\right]$$

Period	1%	2%	3%	4%	5%	6%	7%	8%	9%	10%	11%	12%	13%
1	0.9901	0.9804	0.9709	0.9615	0.9524	0.9434	0.9346	0.9259	0.9174	0.9091	0.9009	0.8929	0.8850
2	0.9803	0.9612	0.9426	0.9246	0.9070	0.8900	0.8734	0.8573	0.8417	0.8264	0.8116	0.7972	0.7831
3	0.9706	0.9423	0.9151	0.8890	0.8638	0.8396	0.8163	0.7938	0.7722	0.7513	0.7312	0.7118	0.6931
4	0.9610	0.9238	0.8885	0.8548	0.8227	0.7921	0.7629	0.7350	0.7084	0.6830	0.6587	0.6355	0.6133
5	0.9515	0.9057	0.8626	0.8219	0.7835	0.7473	0.7130	0.6806	0.6499	0.6209	0.5935	0.5674	0.5428
6	0.9420	0.8880	0.8375	0.7903	0.7462	0.7050	0.6663	0.6302	0.5963	0.5645	0.5346	0.5066	0.4803
7	0.9327	0.8706	0.8131	0.7599	0.7107	0.6651	0.6227	0.5835	0.5470	0.5132	0.4817	0.4523	0.4251
8	0.9235	0.8535	0.7894	0.7307	0.6768	0.6274	0.5820	0.5403	0.5019	0.4665	0.4339	0.4039	0.3762
9	0.9143	0.8368	0.7664	0.7026	0.6446	0.5919	0.5439	0.5002	0.4604	0.4241	0.3909	0.3606	0.3329
10	0.9053	0.8203	0.7441	0.6756	0.6139	0.5584	0.5083	0.4632	0.4224	0.3855	0.3522	0.3220	0.2946
11	0.8963	0.8043	0.7224	0.6496	0.5847	0.5268	0.4751	0.4289	0.3875	0.3505	0.3173	0.2875	0.2607
12	0.8874	0.7885	0.7014	0.6246	0.5568	0.4970	0.4440	0.3971	0.3555	0.3186	0.2858	0.2567	0.2307
13	0.8787	0.7730	0.6810	0.6006	0.5303	0.4688	0.4150	0.3677	0.3262	0.2897	0.2575	0.2292	0.2042
14	0.8700	0.7579	0.6611	0.5775	0.5051	0.4423	0.3878	0.3405	0.2992	0.2633	0.2320	0.2046	0.1807
15	0.8613	0.7430	0.6419	0.5553	0.4810	0.4173	0.3624	0.3152	0.2745	0.2394	0.2090	0.1827	0.1599
16	0.8528	0.7284	0.6232	0.5339	0.4581	0.3936	0.3387	0.2919	0.2519	0.2176	0.1883	0.1631	0.1415
17	0.8444	0.7142	0.6050	0.5134	0.4363	0.3714	0.3166	0.2703	0.2311	0.1978	0.1696	0.1456	0.1252
18	0.8360	0.7002	0.5874	0.4936	0.4155	0.3503	0.2959	0.2502	0.2120	0.1799	0.1528	0.1300	0.1108
19	0.8277	0.6864	0.5703	0.4746	0.3957	0.3305	0.2765	0.2317	0.1945	0.1635	0.1377	0.1161	0.0981
20	0.8195	0.6730	0.5537	0.4564	0.3769	0.3118	0.2584	0.2145	0.1784	0.1486	0.1240	0.1037	0.0868
25	0.7798	0.6095	0.4776	0.3751	0.2953	0.2330	0.1842	0.1460	0.1160	0.0923	0.0736	0.0588	0.0471
30	0.7419	0.5521	0.4120	0.3083	0.2314	0.1741	0.1314	0.0994	0.0754	0.0573	0.0437	0.0334	0.0256
35	0.7059	0.5000	0.3554	0.2534	0.1813	0.1301	0.0937	0.0676	0.0490	0.0356	0.0259	0.0189	0.0139
40	0.6717	0.4529	0.3066	0.2083	0.1420	0.0972	0.0668	0.0460	0.0318	0.0221	0.0154	0.0107	0.0075
45	0.6391	0.4102	0.2644	0.1712	0.1113	0.0727	0.0476	0.0313	0.0207	0.0137	0.0091	0.0061	0.0041
50	0.6080	0.3715	0.2281	0.1407	0.0872	0.0543	0.0339	0.0213	0.0134	0.0085	0.0054	0.0035	0.0022

APPENDIX B-1 Present Value of a Dollar (continued)

Present Value of $1

$$\left[\frac{1}{(1+i)^n}\right]$$

Period	14%	15%	16%	17%	18%	19%	20%	25%	30%	35%	40%	45%	50%
1	0.8772	0.8696	0.8621	0.8547	0.8475	0.8403	0.8333	0.8000	0.7692	0.7407	0.7143	0.6897	0.6667
2	0.7695	0.7561	0.7432	0.7305	0.7182	0.7062	0.6944	0.6400	0.5917	0.5487	0.5102	0.4756	0.4444
3	0.6750	0.6575	0.6407	0.6244	0.6086	0.5934	0.5787	0.5120	0.4552	0.4064	0.3644	0.3280	0.2963
4	0.5921	0.5718	0.5523	0.5337	0.5158	0.4987	0.4823	0.4096	0.3501	0.3011	0.2603	0.2262	0.1975
5	0.5194	0.4972	0.4761	0.4561	0.4371	0.4190	0.4019	0.3277	0.2693	0.2230	0.1859	0.1560	0.1317
6	0.4556	0.4323	0.4104	0.3898	0.3704	0.3521	0.3349	0.2621	0.2072	0.1652	0.1328	0.1076	0.0878
7	0.3996	0.3759	0.3538	0.3332	0.3139	0.2959	0.2791	0.2097	0.1594	0.1224	0.0949	0.0742	0.0585
8	0.3506	0.3269	0.3050	0.2848	0.2660	0.2487	0.2326	0.1678	0.1226	0.0906	0.0678	0.0512	0.0390
9	0.3075	0.2843	0.2630	0.2434	0.2255	0.2090	0.1938	0.1342	0.0943	0.0671	0.0484	0.0353	0.0260
10	0.2697	0.2472	0.2267	0.2080	0.1911	0.1756	0.1615	0.1074	0.0725	0.0497	0.0346	0.0243	0.0173
11	0.2366	0.2149	0.1954	0.1778	0.1619	0.1476	0.1346	0.0859	0.0558	0.0368	0.0247	0.0168	0.0116
12	0.2076	0.1869	0.1685	0.1520	0.1372	0.1240	0.1122	0.0687	0.0429	0.0273	0.0176	0.0116	0.0077
13	0.1821	0.1625	0.1452	0.1299	0.1163	0.1042	0.0935	0.0550	0.0330	0.0202	0.0126	0.0080	0.0051
14	0.1597	0.1413	0.1252	0.1110	0.0985	0.0876	0.0779	0.0440	0.0254	0.0150	0.0090	0.0055	0.0034
15	0.1401	0.1229	0.1079	0.0949	0.0835	0.0736	0.0649	0.0352	0.0195	0.0111	0.0064	0.0038	0.0023
16	0.1229	0.1069	0.0930	0.0811	0.0708	0.0618	0.0541	0.0281	0.0150	0.0082	0.0046	0.0026	0.0015
17	0.1078	0.0929	0.0802	0.0693	0.0600	0.0520	0.0451	0.0225	0.0116	0.0061	0.0033	0.0018	0.0010
18	0.0946	0.0808	0.0691	0.0592	0.0508	0.0437	0.0376	0.0180	0.0089	0.0045	0.0023	0.0012	0.0007
19	0.0829	0.0703	0.0596	0.0506	0.0431	0.0367	0.0313	0.0144	0.0068	0.0033	0.0017	0.0009	0.0005
20	0.0728	0.0611	0.0514	0.0433	0.0365	0.0308	0.0261	0.0115	0.0053	0.0025	0.0012	0.0006	0.0003
25	0.0378	0.0304	0.0245	0.0197	0.0160	0.0129	0.0105	0.0038	0.0014	0.0006	0.0002	0.0001	0.0000
30	0.0196	0.0151	0.0116	0.0090	0.0070	0.0054	0.0042	0.0012	0.0004	0.0001	0.0000	0.0000	0.0000
35	0.0102	0.0075	0.0055	0.0041	0.0030	0.0023	0.0017	0.0004	0.0001	0.0000	0.0000	0.0000	0.0000
40	0.0053	0.0037	0.0026	0.0019	0.0013	0.0010	0.0007	0.0001	0.0000	0.0000	0.0000	0.0000	0.0000
45	0.0027	0.0019	0.0013	0.0009	0.0006	0.0004	0.0003	0.0000	0.0000	0.0000	0.0000	0.0000	0.0000
50	0.0014	0.0009	0.0006	0.0004	0.0003	0.0002	0.0001	0.0000	0.0000	0.0000	0.0000	0.0000	0.0000

APPENDIX B-2 Future Value of a Dollar

Future Value of $1

$(1+i)^n$

Period	1%	2%	3%	4%	5%	6%	7%	8%	9%	10%	11%	12%	13%
1	1.0100	1.0200	1.0300	1.0400	1.0500	1.0600	1.0700	1.0800	1.0900	1.1000	1.1100	1.1200	1.1300
2	1.0201	1.0404	1.0609	1.0816	1.1025	1.1236	1.1449	1.1664	1.1881	1.2100	1.2321	1.2544	1.2769
3	1.0303	1.0612	1.0927	1.1249	1.1576	1.1910	1.2250	1.2597	1.2950	1.3310	1.3676	1.4049	1.4429
4	1.0406	1.0824	1.1255	1.1699	1.2155	1.2625	1.3108	1.3605	1.4116	1.4641	1.5181	1.5735	1.6305
5	1.0510	1.1041	1.1593	1.2167	1.2763	1.3382	1.4026	1.4693	1.5386	1.6105	1.6851	1.7623	1.8424
6	1.0615	1.1262	1.1941	1.2653	1.3401	1.4185	1.5007	1.5869	1.6771	1.7716	1.8704	1.9738	2.0820
7	1.0721	1.1487	1.2299	1.3159	1.4071	1.5036	1.6058	1.7138	1.8280	1.9487	2.0762	2.2107	2.3526
8	1.0829	1.1717	1.2668	1.3686	1.4775	1.5938	1.7182	1.8509	1.9926	2.1436	2.3045	2.4760	2.6584
9	1.0937	1.1951	1.3048	1.4233	1.5513	1.6895	1.8385	1.9990	2.1719	2.3579	2.5580	2.7731	3.0040
10	1.1046	1.2190	1.3439	1.4802	1.6289	1.7908	1.9672	2.1589	2.3674	2.5937	2.8394	3.1058	3.3946
11	1.1157	1.2434	1.3842	1.5395	1.7103	1.8983	2.1049	2.3316	2.5804	2.8531	3.1518	3.4785	3.8359
12	1.1268	1.2682	1.4258	1.6010	1.7959	2.0122	2.2522	2.5182	2.8127	3.1384	3.4985	3.8960	4.3345
13	1.1381	1.2936	1.4685	1.6651	1.8856	2.1329	2.4098	2.7196	3.0658	3.4523	3.8833	4.3635	4.8980
14	1.1495	1.3195	1.5126	1.7317	1.9799	2.2609	2.5785	2.9372	3.3417	3.7975	4.3104	4.8871	5.5348
15	1.1610	1.3459	1.5580	1.8009	2.0789	2.3966	2.7590	3.1722	3.6425	4.1772	4.7846	5.4736	6.2543
16	1.1726	1.3728	1.6047	1.8730	2.1829	2.5404	2.9522	3.4259	3.9703	4.5950	5.3109	6.1304	7.0673
17	1.1843	1.4002	1.6528	1.9479	2.2920	2.6928	3.1588	3.7000	4.3276	5.0545	5.8951	6.8660	7.9861
18	1.1961	1.4282	1.7024	2.0258	2.4066	2.8543	3.3799	3.9960	4.7171	5.5599	6.5436	7.6900	9.0243
19	1.2081	1.4568	1.7535	2.1068	2.5270	3.0256	3.6165	4.3157	5.1417	6.1159	7.2633	8.6128	10.1974
20	1.2202	1.4859	1.8061	2.1911	2.6533	3.2071	3.8697	4.6610	5.6044	6.7275	8.0623	9.6463	11.5231
25	1.2824	1.6406	2.0938	2.6658	3.3864	4.2919	5.4274	6.8485	8.6231	10.8347	13.5855	17.0001	21.2305
30	1.3478	1.8114	2.4273	3.2434	4.3219	5.7435	7.6123	10.0627	13.2677	17.4494	22.8923	29.9599	39.1159
35	1.4166	1.9999	2.8139	3.9461	5.5160	7.6861	10.6766	14.7853	20.4140	28.1024	38.5749	52.7996	72.0685
40	1.4889	2.2080	3.2620	4.8010	7.0400	10.2857	14.9745	21.7245	31.4094	45.2593	65.0009	93.0510	132.7816
45	1.5648	2.4379	3.7816	5.8412	8.9850	13.7646	21.0025	31.9204	48.3273	72.8905	109.5302	163.9876	244.6414
50	1.6446	2.6916	4.3839	7.1067	11.4674	18.4202	29.4570	46.9016	74.3575	117.3909	184.5648	289.0022	450.7359

APPENDIX B-2 Future Value of a Dollar (continued)

Future Value of $1

$$(1+i)^n$$

Period	14%	15%	16%	17%	18%	19%	20%	25%	30%	35%	40%	45%	50%
1	1.1400	1.1500	1.1600	1.1700	1.1800	1.1900	1.2000	1.2500	1.3000	1.3500	1.4000	1.4500	1.5000
2	1.2996	1.3225	1.3456	1.3689	1.3924	1.4161	1.4400	1.5625	1.6900	1.8225	1.9600	2.1025	2.2500
3	1.4815	1.5209	1.5609	1.6016	1.6430	1.6852	1.7280	1.9531	2.1970	2.4604	2.7440	3.0486	3.3750
4	1.6890	1.7490	1.8106	1.8739	1.9388	2.0053	2.0736	2.4414	2.8561	3.3215	3.8416	4.4205	5.0625
5	1.9254	2.0114	2.1003	2.1924	2.2878	2.3864	2.4883	3.0518	3.7129	4.4840	5.3782	6.4097	7.5938
6	2.1950	2.3131	2.4364	2.5652	2.6996	2.8398	2.9860	3.8147	4.8268	6.0534	7.5295	9.2941	11.3906
7	2.5023	2.6600	2.8262	3.0012	3.1855	3.3793	3.5832	4.7684	6.2749	8.1722	10.5414	13.4765	17.0859
8	2.8526	3.0590	3.2784	3.5115	3.7589	4.0214	4.2998	5.9605	8.1573	11.0324	14.7579	19.5409	25.6289
9	3.2519	3.5179	3.8030	4.1084	4.4355	4.7854	5.1598	7.4506	10.6045	14.8937	20.6610	28.3343	38.4434
10	3.7072	4.0456	4.4114	4.8068	5.2338	5.6947	61917	9.3132	13.7858	20.1066	28.9255	41.0847	57.6650
11	4.2262	4.6524	5.1173	5.6240	6.1759	6.7767	74301	11.6415	17.9216	27.1439	40.4957	59.5728	86.4976
12	4.8179	5.3503	5.9360	6.5801	7.2876	8.0642	8.9161	14.5519	23.2981	36.6442	56.6939	86.3806	129.7463
13	5.4924	6.1528	6.8858	7.6987	8.5994	9.5964	10.6993	18.1899	30.2875	49.4697	79.3715	125.2518	194.6195
14	6.2613	7.0757	7.9875	9.0075	10.1472	11.4198	12.8392	22.7374	39.3738	66.7841	111.1201	181.6151	291.9293
15	7.1379	8.1371	9.2655	10.5387	11.9737	13.5895	15.4070	28.4217	51.1859	90.1585	155.5681	263.3419	437.8939
16	8.1372	9.3576	10.7480	12.3303	14.1290	16.1715	18.4884	35.5271	66.5417	121.7139	217.7953	381.8458	656.8408
17	9.2765	10.7613	12.4677	14.4265	16.6722	19.2441	22.1861	44.4089	86.5042	164.3138	304.9135	553.6764	985.2613
18	10.5752	12.3755	14.4625	16.8790	19.6733	22.9005	26.6233	55.5112	112.4554	221.8236	426.8789	802.8308	1477.892
19	12.0557	14.2318	16.7765	19.7484	23.2144	27.2516	31.9480	69.3889	146.1920	299.4619	597.6304	1164.105	2216.838
20	13.7435	16.3665	19.4608	23.1056	27.3930	32.4294	38.3376	86.7362	190.0496	404.2736	836.6826	1687.952	3325.257
25	26.4619	32.9190	40.8742	50.6578	62.6686	77.3881	95.3962	264.6978	705.6410	1812.776	4499.880	10819.32	25251.17
30	50.9502	66.2118	85.8499	111.0647	143.3706	184.6753	237.3763	807.7936	2619.996	8128.550	24201.43	69348.98	191751.1
35	98.1002	133.1755	180.3141	243.5035	327.9973	440.7006	590.6682	2465.190	9727.860	36448.69	130161.1	444509	1456110
40	188.8835	267.8635	378.7212	533.8687	750.3783	1051.668	1469.772	7523.164	36118.86	163437.1	700037.7	2849181	11057332
45	363.6791	538.7693	795.4438	1170.479	1716.684	2509.651	3657.262	22958.87	134106.8	732857.6	3764971	18262495	83966617
50	700.2330	1083.657	1670.704	2566.215	3927.357	5988.914	9100.438	70064.92	497929.2	3286158	20248916	117057734	637621500

APPENDIX B-3 Present Value of an Ordinary Annuity

Present Value of Ordinary Annuity

$$\left[\frac{1 - \frac{1}{(1+i)^n}}{i} \right]$$

Period	1%	2%	3%	4%	5%	6%	7%	8%	9%	10%	11%	12%	13%
1	0.9901	0.9804	0.9709	0.9615	0.9524	0.9434	0.9346	0.9259	0.9174	0.9091	0.9009	0.8929	0.8850
2	1.9704	1.9416	1.9135	1.8861	1.8594	1.8334	1.8080	1.7833	1.7591	1.7355	1.7125	1.6901	1.6681
3	2.9410	2.8839	2.8286	2.7751	2.7232	2.6730	2.6243	2.5771	2.5313	2.4869	2.4437	2.4018	2.3612
4	3.9020	3.8077	3.7171	3.6299	3.5460	3.4651	3.3872	3.3121	3.2397	3.1699	3.1024	3.0373	2.9745
5	4.8534	4.7135	4.5797	4.4518	4.3295	4.2124	4.1002	3.9927	3.8897	3.7908	3.6959	3.6048	3.5172
6	5.7955	5.6014	5.4172	5.2421	5.0757	4.9173	4.7665	4.6229	4.4859	4.3553	4.2305	4.1114	3.9975
7	6.7282	6.4720	6.2303	6.0021	5.7864	5.5824	5.3893	5.2064	5.0330	4.8684	4.7122	4.5638	4.4226
8	7.6517	7.3255	7.0197	6.7327	6.4632	6.2098	5.9713	5.7466	5.5348	5.3349	5.1461	4.9676	4.7988
9	8.5660	8.1622	7.7861	7.4353	7.1078	6.8017	6.5152	6.2469	5.9952	5.7590	5.5370	5.3282	5.1317
10	9.4713	8.9826	8.5302	8.1109	7.7217	7.3601	7.0236	6.7101	6.4177	6.1446	5.8892	5.6502	5.4262
11	10.3676	9.7868	9.2526	8.7605	8.3064	7.8869	7.4987	7.1390	6.8052	6.4951	6.2065	5.9377	5.6869
12	11.2551	10.5753	9.9540	9.3851	8.8633	8.3838	7.9427	7.5361	7.1607	6.8137	6.4924	6.1944	5.9176
13	12.1337	11.3484	10.6350	9.9856	9.3936	8.8527	8.3577	7.9038	7.4869	7.1034	6.7499	6.4235	6.1218
14	13.0037	12.1062	11.2961	10.5631	9.8986	9.2950	8.7455	8.2442	7.7862	7.3667	6.9819	6.6282	6.3025
15	13.8651	12.8493	11.9379	11.1184	10.3797	9.7122	9.1079	8.5595	8.0607	7.6061	7.1909	6.8109	6.4624
16	14.7179	13.5777	12.5611	11.6523	10.8378	10.1059	9.4466	8.8514	8.3126	7.8237	7.3792	6.9740	6.6039
17	15.5623	14.2919	13.1661	12.1657	11.2741	10.4773	9.7632	9.1216	8.5436	8.0216	7.5488	7.1196	6.7291
18	16.3983	14.9920	13.7535	12.6593	11.6896	10.8276	10.0591	9.3719	8.7556	8.2014	7.7016	7.2497	6.8399
19	17.2260	15.6785	14.3238	13.1339	12.0853	11.1581	10.3356	9.6036	8.9501	8.3649	7.8393	7.3658	6.9380
20	18.0456	16.3514	14.8775	13.5903	12.4622	11.4699	10.5940	9.8181	9.1285	8.5136	7.9633	7.4694	7.0248
25	22.0232	19.5235	17.4131	15.6221	14.0939	12.7834	11.6536	10.6748	9.8226	9.0770	8.4217	7.8431	7.3300
30	25.8077	22.3965	19.6004	17.2920	15.3725	13.7648	12.4090	11.2578	10.2737	9.4269	8.6938	8.0552	7.4957
35	29.4086	24.9986	21.4872	18.6646	16.3742	14.4982	12.9477	11.6546	10.5668	9.6442	8.8552	8.1755	7.5856
40	32.8347	27.3555	23.1148	19.7928	17.1591	15.0463	13.3317	11.9246	10.7574	9.7791	8.9511	8.2438	7.6344
45	36.0945	29.4902	24.5187	20.7200	17.7741	15.4558	13.6055	12.1084	10.8812	9.8628	9.0079	8.2825	7.6609
50	39.1961	31.4236	25.7298	21.4822	18.2559	15.7619	13.8007	12.2335	10.9617	9.9148	9.0417	8.3045	7.6752

APPENDIX B-3 Present Value of an Ordinary Annuity (continued)

Present Value of Ordinary Annuity

$$\left[\frac{1 - \frac{1}{(1+i)^n}}{i} \right]$$

Period	14%	15%	16%	17%	18%	19%	20%	25%	30%	35%	40%	45%	50%
1	0.8772	0.8696	0.8621	0.8547	0.8475	0.8403	0.8333	0.8000	0.7692	0.7407	0.7143	0.6897	0.6667
2	1.6467	1.6257	1.6052	1.5852	1.5656	1.5465	1.5278	1.4400	1.3609	1.2894	1.2245	1.1653	1.1111
3	2.3216	2.2832	2.2459	2.2096	2.1743	2.1399	2.1065	1.9520	1.8161	1.6959	1.5889	1.4933	1.4074
4	2.9137	2.8550	2.7982	2.7432	2.6901	2.6386	2.5887	2.3616	2.1662	1.9969	1.8492	1.7195	1.6049
5	3.4331	3.3522	3.2743	3.1993	3.1272	3.0576	2.9906	2.6893	2.4356	2.2200	2.0352	1.8755	1.7366
6	3.8887	3.7845	3.6847	3.5892	3.4976	3.4098	3.3255	2.9514	2.6427	2.3852	2.1680	1.9831	1.8244
7	4.2883	4.1604	4.0386	3.9224	3.8115	3.7057	3.6046	3.1611	2.8021	2.5075	2.2628	2.0573	1.8829
8	4.6389	4.4873	4.3436	4.2072	4.0776	3.9544	3.8372	3.3289	2.9247	2.5982	2.3306	2.1085	1.9220
9	4.9464	4.7716	4.6065	4.4506	4.3030	4.1633	4.0310	3.4631	3.0190	2.6653	2.3790	2.1438	1.9480
10	5.2161	5.0188	4.8332	4.6586	4.4941	4.3389	4.1925	3.5705	3.0915	2.7150	2.4136	2.1681	1.9653
11	5.4527	5.2337	5.0286	4.8364	4.6560	4.4865	4.3271	3.6564	3.1473	2.7519	2.4383	2.1849	1.9769
12	5.6603	5.4206	5.1971	4.9884	4.7932	4.6105	4.4392	3.7251	3.1903	2.7792	2.4559	2.1965	1.9846
13	5.8424	5.5831	5.3423	5.1183	4.9095	4.7147	4.5327	3.7801	3.2233	2.7994	2.4685	2.2045	1.9897
14	6.0021	5.7245	5.4675	5.2293	5.0081	4.8023	4.6106	3.8241	3.2487	2.8144	2.4775	2.2100	1.9931
15	6.1422	5.8474	5.5755	5.3242	5.0916	4.8759	4.6755	3.8593	3.2682	2.8255	2.4839	2.2138	1.9954
16	6.2651	5.9542	5.6685	5.4053	5.1624	4.9377	4.7296	3.8874	3.2832	2.8337	2.4885	2.2164	1.9970
17	6.3729	6.0472	5.7487	5.4746	5.2223	4.9897	4.7746	3.9099	3.2948	2.8398	2.4918	2.2182	1.9980
18	6.4674	6.1280	5.8178	5.5339	5.2732	5.0333	4.8122	3.9279	3.3037	2.8443	2.4941	2.2195	1.9986
19	6.5504	6.1982	5.8775	5.5845	5.3162	5.0700	4.8435	3.9424	3.3105	2.8476	2.4958	2.2203	1.9991
20	6.6231	6.2593	5.9288	5.6278	5.3527	5.1009	4.8696	3.9539	3.3158	2.8501	2.4970	2.2209	1.9994
25	6.8729	6.4641	6.0971	5.7662	5.4669	5.1951	4.9476	3.9849	3.3286	2.8556	2.4994	2.2220	1.9999
30	7.0027	6.5660	6.1772	5.8294	5.5168	5.2347	4.9789	3.9950	3.3321	2.8568	2.4999	2.2222	2.0000
35	7.0700	6.6166	6.2153	5.8582	5.5386	5.2512	4.9915	3.9984	3.3330	2.8571	2.5000	2.2222	2.0000
40	7.1050	6.6418	6.2335	5.8713	5.5482	5.2582	4.9966	3.9995	3.3332	2.8571	2.5000	2.2222	2.0000
45	7.1232	6.6543	6.2421	5.8773	5.5523	5.2611	4.9986	3.9998	3.3333	2.8571	2.5000	2.2222	2.0000
50	7.1327	6.6605	6.2463	5.8801	5.5541	5.2623	4.9995	3.9999	3.3333	2.8571	2.5000	2.2222	2.0000

APPENDIX B-4 Future Value of an Ordinary Annuity

Future Value of Ordinary Annuity

$$\left[\frac{(1+i)^n - 1}{i}\right]$$

Period	1%	2%	3%	4%	5%	6%	7%	8%	9%	10%	11%	12%	13%
1	1.0000	1.0000	1.0000	1.0000	1.0000	1.0000	1.0000	1.0000	1.0000	1.0000	1.0000	1.0000	1.0000
2	2.0100	2.0200	2.0300	2.0400	2.0500	2.0600	2.0700	2.0800	2.0900	2.1000	2.1100	2.1200	2.1300
3	3.0301	3.0604	3.0909	3.1216	3.1525	3.1836	3.2149	3.2464	3.2781	3.3100	3.3421	3.3744	3.4069
4	4.0604	4.1216	4.1836	4.2465	4.3101	4.3746	4.4399	4.5061	4.5731	4.6410	4.7097	4.7793	4.8498
5	5.1010	5.2040	5.3091	5.4163	5.5256	5.6371	5.7507	5.8666	5.9847	6.1051	6.2278	6.3528	6.4803
6	6.1520	6.3081	6.4684	6.6330	6.8019	6.9753	7.1533	7.3359	7.5233	7.7156	7.9129	8.1152	8.3227
7	7.2135	7.4343	7.6625	7.8983	8.1420	8.3938	8.6540	8.9228	9.2004	9.4872	9.7833	10.0890	10.4047
8	8.2857	8.5830	8.8923	9.2142	9.5491	9.8975	10.2598	10.6366	11.0285	11.4359	11.8594	12.2997	12.7573
9	9.3685	9.7546	10.1591	10.5828	11.0266	11.4913	11.9780	12.4876	13.0210	13.5795	14.1640	14.7757	15.4157
10	10.4622	10.9497	11.4639	12.0061	12.5779	13.1808	13.8164	14.4866	15.1929	15.9374	16.7220	17.5487	18.4197
11	11.5668	12.1687	12.8078	13.4864	14.2068	14.9716	15.7836	16.6455	17.5603	18.5312	19.5614	20.6546	21.8143
12	12.6825	13.4121	14.1920	15.0258	15.9171	16.8699	17.8885	18.9771	20.1407	21.3843	22.7132	24.1331	25.6502
13	13.8093	14.6803	15.6178	16.6268	17.7130	18.8821	20.1406	21.4953	22.9534	24.5227	26.2116	28.0291	29.9847
14	14.9474	15.9739	17.0863	18.2919	19.5986	21.0151	22.5505	24.2149	26.0192	27.9750	30.0949	32.3926	34.8827
15	16.0969	17.2934	18.5989	20.0236	21.5786	23.2760	25.1290	27.1521	29.3609	31.7725	34.4054	37.2797	40.4175
16	17.2579	18.6393	20.1569	21.8245	23.6575	25.6725	27.8881	30.3243	33.0034	35.9497	39.1899	42.7533	46.6717
17	18.4304	20.0121	21.7616	23.6975	25.8404	28.2129	30.8402	33.7502	36.9737	40.5447	44.5008	48.8837	53.7391
18	19.6147	21.4123	23.4144	25.6454	28.1324	30.9057	33.9990	37.4502	41.3013	45.5992	50.3959	55.7497	61.7251
19	20.8109	22.8406	25.1169	27.6712	30.5390	33.7600	37.3790	41.4463	46.0185	51.1591	56.9395	63.4397	70.7494
20	22.0190	24.2974	26.8704	29.7781	33.0660	36.7856	40.9955	45.7620	51.1601	57.2750	64.2028	72.0524	80.9468
25	28.2432	32.0303	36.4593	41.6459	47.7271	54.8645	63.2490	73.1059	84.7009	98.3471	114.4133	133.3339	155.6196
30	34.7849	40.5681	47.5754	56.0849	66.4388	79.0582	94.4608	113.2832	136.3075	164.4940	199.0209	241.3327	293.1992
35	41.6603	49.9945	60.4621	73.6522	90.3203	111.4348	138.2369	172.3168	215.7108	271.0244	341.5896	431.6635	546.6808
40	48.8864	60.4020	75.4013	95.0255	120.7998	154.7620	199.6351	259.0565	337.8824	442.5926	581.8261	767.0914	1013.704
45	56.4811	71.8927	92.7199	121.0294	159.7002	212.7435	285.7493	386.5056	525.8587	718.9048	986.6386	1358.230	1874.165
50	64.4632	84.5794	112.7969	152.6671	209.3480	290.3359	406.5289	573.7702	815.0836	1163.909	1668.771	2400.018	3459.507

APPENDIX B-4 Future Value of an Ordinary Annuity (continued)

Future Value of Ordinary Annuity

$$\left[\frac{(1+i)^n - 1}{i}\right]$$

Period	14%	15%	16%	17%	18%	19%	20%	25%	30%	35%	40%	45%	50%
1	1.0000	1.0000	1.0000	1.0000	1.0000	1.0000	1.0000	1.0000	1.0000	1.0000	1.0000	1.0000	1.0000
2	2.1400	2.1500	2.1600	2.1700	2.1800	2.1900	2.2000	2.2500	2.3000	2.3500	2.4000	2.4500	2.5000
3	3.4396	3.4725	3.5056	3.5389	3.5724	3.6061	3.6400	3.8125	3.9900	4.1725	4.3600	4.5525	4.7500
4	4.9211	4.9934	5.0665	5.1405	5.2154	5.2913	5.3680	5.7656	6.1870	6.6329	7.1040	7.6011	8.1250
5	6.6101	6.7424	6.8771	7.0144	7.1542	7.2966	7.4416	8.2070	9.0431	9.9544	10.9456	12.0216	13.1875
6	8.5355	8.7537	8.9775	9.2068	9.4420	9.6830	9.9299	11.2588	12.7560	14.4384	16.3238	18.4314	20.7813
7	10.7305	11.0668	11.4139	11.7720	12.1415	12.5227	12.9159	15.0735	17.5828	20.4919	23.8534	27.7255	32.1719
8	13.2328	13.7268	14.2401	14.7733	15.3270	15.9020	16.4991	19.8419	23.8577	28.6640	34.3947	41.2019	49.2578
9	16.0853	16.7858	17.5185	18.2847	19.0859	19.9234	20.7989	25.8023	32.0150	39.6964	49.1526	60.7428	74.8867
10	19.3373	20.3037	21.3215	22.3931	23.5213	24.7089	25.9587	33.2529	42.6195	54.5902	69.8137	89.0771	113.3301
11	23.0445	24.3493	25.7329	27.1999	28.7551	30.4035	32.1504	42.5661	56.4053	74.6967	98.7391	130.1618	170.9951
12	27.2707	29.0017	30.8502	32.8239	34.9311	37.1802	39.5805	54.2077	74.3270	101.8406	139.2348	189.7346	257.4927
13	32.0887	34.3519	36.7862	39.4040	42.2187	45.2445	48.4966	68.7596	97.6250	138.4848	195.9287	276.1151	387.2390
14	37.5811	40.5047	43.6720	47.1027	50.8180	54.8409	59.1959	86.9495	127.9125	187.9544	275.3002	401.3670	581.8585
15	43.8424	47.5804	51.6595	56.1101	60.9653	66.2607	72.0351	109.6868	167.2863	254.7385	386.4202	582.9821	873.7878
16	50.9804	55.7175	60.9250	66.6488	72.9390	79.8502	87.4421	138.1085	218.4722	344.8970	541.9883	846.3240	1311.682
17	59.1176	65.0751	71.6730	78.9792	87.0680	96.0218	105.9306	173.6357	285.0139	466.6109	759.7837	1228.170	1968.523
18	68.3941	75.8364	84.1407	93.4056	103.7403	115.2659	128.1167	218.0446	371.5180	630.9247	1064.697	1781.846	2953.784
19	78.9692	88.2118	98.6032	110.2846	123.4135	138.1664	154.7400	273.5558	483.9734	852.7483	1491.576	2584.677	4431.676
20	91.0249	102.4436	115.3797	130.0329	146.6280	165.4180	186.6880	342.9447	630.1655	1152.210	2089.206	3748.782	6648.513
25	181.8708	212.7930	249.2140	292.1049	342.6035	402.0425	471.9811	1054.791	2348.803	5176.504	11247.20	24040.72	50500.34
30	356.7868	434.7451	530.3117	647.4391	790.9480	966.7122	1181.882	3227.174	8729.985	23221.57	60501.08	154106.6	383500.1
35	693.5727	881.1702	1120.713	1426.491	1816.652	2314.214	2948.341	9856.761	32422.87	104136.3	325400.3	987794.5	2912217
40	1342.025	1779.090	2360.757	3134.522	4163.213	5529.829	7343.858	30088.66	120392.9	466960.4	1750092	6331512	22114663
45	2590.565	3585.128	4965.274	6879.291	9531.577	13203.42	18281.31	91831.50	447019.4	2093876	9412424	40583319	167933233
50	4994.521	7217.716	10435.65	15089.50	21813.09	31515.34	45497.19	280255.7	1659761	9389020	50622288	260128295	1275242998

APPENDIX B-5 Present Value of an Annuity Due

Present Value of an Annuity Due

$$\left[\frac{1 - \dfrac{1}{(1+i)^{n-1}}}{i} + 1 \right]$$

Period	1%	2%	3%	4%	5%	6%	7%	8%	9%	10%	11%	12%	13%
1	1.0000	1.0000	1.0000	1.0000	1.0000	1.0000	1.0000	1.0000	1.0000	1.0000	1.0000	1.0000	1.0000
2	1.9901	1.9804	1.9709	1.9615	1.9524	1.9434	1.9346	1.9259	1.9174	1.9091	1.9009	1.8929	1.8850
3	2.9704	2.9416	2.9135	2.8861	2.8594	2.8334	2.8080	2.7833	2.7591	2.7355	2.7125	2.6901	2.6681
4	3.9410	3.8839	3.8286	3.7751	3.7232	3.6730	3.6243	3.5771	3.5313	3.4869	3.4437	3.4018	3.3612
5	4.9020	4.8077	4.7171	4.6299	4.5460	4.4651	4.3872	4.3121	4.2397	4.1699	4.1024	4.0373	3.9745
6	5.8534	5.7135	5.5797	5.4518	5.3295	5.2124	5.1002	4.9927	4.8897	4.7908	4.6959	4.6048	4.5172
7	6.7955	6.6014	6.4172	6.2421	6.0757	5.9173	5.7665	5.6229	5.4859	5.3553	5.2305	5.1114	4.9975
8	7.7282	7.4720	7.2303	7.0021	6.7864	6.5824	6.3893	6.2064	6.0330	5.8684	5.7122	5.5638	5.4226
9	8.6517	8.3255	8.0197	7.7327	7.4632	7.2098	6.9713	6.7466	6.5348	6.3349	6.1461	5.9676	5.7988
10	9.5660	9.1622	8.7861	8.4353	8.1078	7.8017	7.5152	7.2469	6.9952	6.7590	6.5370	6.3282	6.1317
11	10.4713	9.9826	9.5302	9.1109	8.7217	8.3601	8.0236	7.7101	7.4177	7.1446	6.8892	6.6502	6.4262
12	11.3676	10.7868	10.2526	9.7605	9.3064	8.8869	8.4987	8.1390	7.8052	7.4951	7.2065	6.9377	6.6869
13	12.2551	11.5753	10.9540	10.3851	9.8633	9.3838	8.9427	8.5361	8.1607	7.8137	7.4924	7.1944	6.9176
14	13.1337	12.3484	11.6350	10.9856	10.3936	9.8527	9.3577	8.9038	8.4869	8.1034	7.7499	7.4235	7.1218
15	14.0037	13.1062	12.2961	11.5631	10.8986	10.2950	9.7455	9.2442	8.7862	8.3667	7.9819	7.6282	7.3025
16	14.8651	13.8493	12.9379	12.1184	11.3797	10.7122	10.1079	9.5595	9.0607	8.6061	8.1909	7.8109	7.4624
17	15.7179	14.5777	13.5611	12.6523	11.8378	11.1059	10.4466	9.8514	9.3126	8.8237	8.3792	7.9740	7.6039
18	16.5623	15.2919	14.1661	13.1657	12.2741	11.4773	10.7632	10.1216	9.5436	9.0216	8.5488	8.1196	7.7291
19	17.3983	15.9920	14.7535	13.6593	12.6896	11.8276	11.0591	10.3719	9.7556	9.2014	8.7016	8.2497	7.8399
20	18.2260	16.6785	15.3238	14.1339	13.0853	12.1581	11.3356	10.6036	9.9501	9.3649	8.8393	8.3658	7.9380
25	22.2434	19.9139	17.9355	16.2470	14.7986	13.5504	12.4693	11.5288	10.7066	9.9847	9.3481	8.7843	8.2829
30	26.0658	22.8444	20.1885	17.9837	16.1411	14.5907	13.2777	12.1584	11.1983	10.3696	9.6501	9.0218	8.4701
35	29.7027	25.4986	22.1318	19.4112	17.1929	15.3681	13.8540	12.5869	11.5178	10.6086	9.8293	9.1566	8.5717
40	33.1630	27.9026	23.8082	20.5845	18.0170	15.9491	14.2649	12.8786	11.7255	10.7570	9.9357	9.2330	8.6268
45	36.4555	30.0800	25.2543	21.5488	18.6628	16.3832	14.5579	13.0771	11.8605	10.8491	9.9988	9.2764	8.6568
50	39.5881	32.0521	26.5017	22.3415	19.1687	16.7076	14.7668	13.2122	11.9482	10.9063	10.0362	9.3010	8.6730

APPENDIX B-5 Present Value of an Annuity Due (continued)

Present Value of Annuity Due

$$\left[\frac{1-\dfrac{1}{(1+i)^{n-1}}}{i}+1\right]$$

Period	14%	15%	16%	17%	18%	19%	20%	25%	30%	35%	40%	45%	50%
1	1.0000	1.0000	1.0000	1.0000	1.0000	1.0000	1.0000	1.0000	1.0000	1.0000	1.0000	1.0000	1.0000
2	1.8772	1.8696	1.8621	1.8547	1.8475	1.8403	1.8333	1.8000	1.7692	1.7407	1.7143	1.6897	1.6667
3	2.6467	2.6257	2.6052	2.5852	2.5656	2.5465	2.5278	2.4400	2.3609	2.2894	2.2245	2.1653	2.1111
4	3.3216	3.2832	3.2459	3.2096	3.1743	3.1399	3.1065	2.9520	2.8161	2.6959	2.5889	2.4933	2.4074
5	3.9137	3.8550	3.7982	3.7432	3.6901	3.6386	3.5887	3.3616	3.1662	2.9969	2.8492	2.7195	2.6049
6	4.4331	4.3522	4.2743	4.1993	4.1272	4.0576	3.9906	3.6893	3.4356	3.2200	3.0352	2.8755	2.7366
7	4.8887	4.7845	4.6847	4.5892	4.4976	4.4098	4.3255	3.9514	3.6427	3.3852	3.1680	2.9831	2.8244
8	5.2883	5.1604	5.0386	4.9224	4.8115	4.7057	4.6046	4.1611	3.8021	3.5075	3.2628	3.0573	2.8829
9	5.6389	5.4873	5.3436	5.2072	5.0776	4.9544	4.8372	4.3289	3.9247	3.5982	3.3306	3.1085	2.9220
10	5.9464	5.7716	5.6065	5.4506	5.3030	5.1633	5.0310	4.4631	4.0190	3.6653	3.3790	3.1438	2.9480
11	6.2161	6.0188	5.8332	5.6586	5.4941	5.3389	5.1925	4.5705	4.0915	3.7150	3.4136	3.1681	2.9653
12	6.4527	6.2337	6.0286	5.8364	5.6560	5.4865	5.3271	4.6564	4.1473	3.7519	3.4383	3.1849	2.9769
13	6.6603	6.4206	6.1971	5.9884	5.7932	5.6105	5.4392	4.7251	4.1903	3.7792	3.4559	3.1965	2.9846
14	6.8424	6.5831	6.3423	6.1183	5.9095	5.7147	5.5327	4.7801	4.2233	3.7994	3.4685	3.2045	2.9897
15	7.0021	6.7245	6.4675	6.2293	6.0081	5.8023	5.6106	4.8241	4.2487	3.8144	3.4775	3.2100	2.9931
16	7.1422	6.8474	6.5755	6.3242	6.0916	5.8759	5.6755	4.8593	4.2682	3.8255	3.4839	3.2138	2.9954
17	7.2651	6.9542	6.6685	6.4053	6.1624	5.9377	5.7296	4.8874	4.2832	3.8337	3.4885	3.2164	2.9970
18	7.3729	7.0472	6.7487	6.4746	6.2223	5.9897	5.7746	4.9099	4.2948	3.8398	3.4918	3.2182	2.9980
19	7.4674	7.1280	6.8178	6.5339	6.2732	6.0333	5.8122	4.9279	4.3037	3.8443	3.4941	3.2195	2.9986
20	7.5504	7.1982	6.8775	6.5845	6.3162	6.0700	5.8435	4.9424	4.3105	3.8476	3.4958	3.2203	2.9991
25	7.8351	7.4338	7.0726	6.7465	6.4509	6.1822	5.9371	4.9811	4.3272	3.8550	3.4992	3.2219	2.9999
30	7.9830	7.5509	7.1656	6.8204	6.5098	6.2292	5.9747	4.9938	4.3317	3.8567	3.4999	3.2222	3.0000
35	8.0599	7.6091	7.2098	6.8541	6.5356	6.2489	5.9898	4.9980	4.3329	3.8570	3.5000	3.2222	3.0000
40	8.0997	7.6380	7.2309	6.8695	6.5468	6.2572	5.9959	4.9993	4.3332	3.8571	3.5000	3.2222	3.0000
45	8.1205	7.6524	7.2409	6.8765	6.5517	6.2607	5.9984	4.9998	4.3333	3.8571	3.5000	3.2222	3.0000
50	8.1312	7.6596	7.2457	6.8797	6.5539	6.2621	5.9993	4.9999	4.3333	3.8571	3.5000	3.2222	3.0000

APPENDIX B-6 Future Value of an Annuity Due

Future Value of Annuity Due

$$\left[\frac{(1+i)^n - 1}{i}\right] \times [1+i]$$

Period	1%	2%	3%	4%	5%	6%	7%	8%	9%	10%	11%	12%	13%
1	1.0100	1.0200	1.0300	1.0400	1.0500	1.0600	1.0700	1.0800	1.0900	1.1000	1.1100	1.1200	1.1300
2	2.0301	2.0604	2.0909	2.1216	2.1525	2.1836	2.2149	2.2464	2.2781	2.3100	2.3421	2.3744	2.4069
3	3.0604	3.1216	3.1836	3.2465	3.3101	3.3746	3.4399	3.5061	3.5731	3.6410	3.7097	3.7793	3.8498
4	4.1010	4.2040	4.3091	4.4163	4.5256	4.6371	4.7507	4.8666	4.9847	5.1051	5.2278	5.3528	5.4803
5	5.1520	5.3081	5.4684	5.6330	5.8019	5.9753	6.1533	6.3359	6.5233	6.7156	6.9129	7.1152	7.3227
6	6.2135	6.4343	6.6625	6.8983	7.1420	7.3938	7.6540	7.9228	8.2004	8.4872	8.7833	9.0890	9.4047
7	7.2857	7.5830	7.8923	8.2142	8.5491	8.8975	9.2598	9.6366	10.0285	10.4359	10.8594	11.2997	11.7573
8	8.3685	8.7546	9.1591	9.5828	10.0266	10.4913	10.9780	11.4876	12.0210	12.5795	13.1640	13.7757	14.4157
9	9.4622	9.9497	10.4639	11.0061	11.5779	12.1808	12.8164	13.4866	14.1929	14.9374	15.7220	16.5487	17.4197
10	10.5668	11.1687	11.8078	12.4864	13.2068	13.9716	14.7836	15.6455	16.5603	17.5312	18.5614	19.6546	20.8143
11	11.6825	12.4121	13.1920	14.0258	14.9171	15.8699	16.8885	17.9771	19.1407	20.3843	21.7132	23.1331	24.6502
12	12.8093	13.6803	14.6178	15.6268	16.7130	17.8821	19.1406	20.4953	21.9534	23.5227	25.2116	27.0291	28.9847
13	13.9474	14.9739	16.0863	17.2919	18.5986	20.0151	21.5505	23.2149	25.0192	26.9750	29.0949	31.3926	33.8827
14	15.0969	16.2934	17.5989	19.0236	20.5786	22.2760	24.1290	26.1521	28.3609	30.7725	33.4054	36.2797	39.4175
15	16.2579	17.6393	19.1569	20.8245	22.6575	24.6725	26.8881	29.3243	32.0034	34.9497	38.1899	41.7533	45.6717
16	17.4304	19.0121	20.7616	22.6975	24.8404	27.2129	29.8402	32.7502	35.9737	39.5447	43.5008	47.8837	52.7391
17	18.6147	20.4123	22.4144	24.6454	27.1324	29.9057	32.9990	36.4502	40.3013	44.5992	49.3959	54.7497	60.7251
18	19.8109	21.8406	24.1169	26.6712	29.5390	32.7600	36.3790	40.4463	45.0185	50.1591	55.9395	62.4397	69.7494
19	21.0190	23.2974	25.8704	28.7781	32.0660	35.7856	39.9955	44.7620	50.1601	56.2750	63.2028	71.0524	79.9468
20	22.2392	24.7833	27.6765	30.9692	34.7193	38.9927	43.8652	49.4229	55.7645	63.0025	71.2651	80.6987	91.4699
25	28.5256	32.6709	37.5530	43.3117	50.1135	58.1564	67.6765	78.9544	92.3240	108.1818	126.9988	149.3339	175.8501
30	35.1327	41.3794	49.0027	58.3283	69.7608	83.8017	101.0730	122.3459	148.5752	180.9434	220.9132	270.2926	331.3151
35	42.0769	50.9944	62.2759	76.5983	94.8363	118.1209	147.9135	186.1021	235.1247	298.1268	379.1644	483.4631	617.7493
40	49.3752	61.6100	77.6633	98.8265	126.8398	164.0477	213.6096	279.7810	368.2919	486.8518	645.8269	859.1424	1145.486
45	57.0459	73.3306	95.5015	125.8706	167.6852	225.5081	305.7518	417.4261	573.1860	790.7953	1095.169	1521.218	2117.806
50	65.1078	86.2710	116.1808	158.7738	219.8154	307.7561	434.9860	619.6718	888.4411	1280.299	1852.336	2688.020	3909.243

APPENDIX B-6 Future Value of an Annuity Due (continued)

Future Value of Annuity Due

$$\left[\frac{(1+i)^n - 1}{i}\right] \times [1+i]$$

Period	14%	15%	16%	17%	18%	19%	20%	25%	30%	35%	40%	45%	50%
1	1.1400	1.1500	1.1600	1.1700	1.1800	1.1900	1.2000	1.2500	1.3000	1.3500	1.4000	1.4500	1.5000
2	2.4396	2.4725	2.5056	2.5389	2.5724	2.6061	2.6400	2.8125	2.9900	3.1725	3.3600	3.5525	3.7500
3	3.9211	3.9934	4.0665	4.1405	4.2154	4.2913	4.3680	4.7656	5.1870	5.6329	6.1040	6.6011	7.1250
4	5.6101	5.7424	5.8771	6.0144	6.1542	6.2966	6.4416	7.2070	8.0431	8.9544	9.9456	11.0216	12.1875
5	7.5355	7.7537	7.9775	8.2068	8.4420	8.6830	8.9299	10.2588	11.7560	13.4384	15.3238	17.4314	19.7813
6	9.7305	10.0668	10.4139	10.7720	11.1415	11.5227	11.9159	14.0735	16.5828	19.4919	22.8534	26.7255	31.1719
7	12.2328	12.7268	13.2401	13.7733	14.3270	14.9020	15.4991	18.8419	22.8577	27.6640	33.3947	40.2019	48.2578
8	15.0853	15.7858	16.5185	17.2847	18.0859	18.9234	19.7989	24.8023	31.0150	38.6964	48.1526	59.7428	73.8867
9	18.3373	19.3037	20.3215	21.3931	22.5213	23.7089	24.9587	32.2529	41.6195	53.5902	68.8137	88.0771	112.3301
10	22.0445	23.3493	24.7329	26.1999	27.7551	29.4035	31.1504	41.5661	55.4053	73.6967	97.7391	129.1618	169.9951
11	26.2707	28.0017	29.8502	31.8239	33.9311	36.1802	38.5805	53.2077	73.3270	100.8406	138.2348	188.7346	256.4927
12	31.0887	33.3519	35.7862	38.4040	41.2187	44.2445	47.4966	67.7596	96.6250	137.4848	194.9287	275.1151	386.2390
13	36.5811	39.5047	42.6720	46.1027	49.8180	53.8409	58.1959	85.9495	126.9125	186.9544	274.3002	400.3670	580.8585
14	42.8424	46.5804	50.6595	55.1101	59.9653	65.2607	71.0351	108.6868	166.2863	253.7385	385.4202	581.9821	872.7878
15	49.9804	54.7175	59.9250	65.6488	71.9390	78.8502	86.4421	137.1085	217.4722	343.8970	540.9883	845.3240	1310.6817
16	58.1176	64.0751	70.6730	77.9792	86.0680	95.0218	104.9306	172.6357	284.0139	465.6109	758.7837	1227.1699	1967.5225
17	67.3941	74.8364	83.1407	92.4056	102.7403	114.2659	127.1167	217.0446	370.5180	629.9247	1063.697	1780.8463	2952.7838
18	77.9692	87.2118	97.6032	109.2846	122.4135	137.1664	153.7400	272.5558	482.9734	851.7483	1490.576	2583.6771	4430.6756
19	90.0249	101.4436	114.3797	129.0329	145.6280	164.4180	185.6880	341.9447	629.1655	1151.210	2088.206	3747.7818	6647.5135
20	103.7684	117.8101	133.8405	152.1385	173.0210	196.8474	224.0256	428.6809	819.2151	1555.484	2924.889	5435.7336	9972.7702
25	207.3327	244.7120	289.0883	341.7627	404.2721	478.4306	566.3773	1318.489	3053.444	6988.280	15746.08	34859.038	75750.5049
30	406.7370	499.9569	615.1616	757.5038	933.3186	1150.387	1418.258	4033.968	11348.98	31349.12	84701.51	223454.60	575250.178
35	790.6729	1013.346	1300.027	1668.994	2143.649	2753.914	3538.009	12320.95	42149.73	140583.9	455560.4	1432302.0	4368325.82
40	1529.909	2045.954	2738.478	3667.391	4912.591	6580.496	8812.629	37610.82	156510.7	630396.5	2450128	9180692.2	33171994.0
45	2953.244	4122.898	5759.718	8048.770	11247.26	15712.07	21937.57	114789.4	581125.2	2826733	13177394	58845813	251899849
50	5693.75	8300.37	12105.35	17654.72	25739.45	37503.25	54596.63	350319.6	2157689	12675177	70871203	377186028	1912864498

Regulatory Requirements

REGULATORY REQUIREMENTS—FEDERAL SECURITIES REGULATION

Introduction

The issuance and sale of corporate securities are extensively regulated by the Securities and Exchange Commission (SEC), a federal agency that administers the Securities Act of 1933, the Securities Exchange Act of 1934, and other federal statutes. A major objective of securities regulation is to protect the investing public by requiring full and correct disclosure of relevant information. Both the federal and state governments require a substantial amount of regulation; however, most is from the federal government because the majority of trading is done across state borders.

The Securities Act of 1933

This securities act is primarily concerned with new issues of securities or issues in the primary market. The term *investment security* is broadly defined as:

> Any note, stock, treasury stock, bond, debenture, evidence of indebtedness, certificate of interest or participation in any profit sharing agreement . . . investment contract . . . or, in general, any interest or instrument commonly known as a "security" or any certificate of interest or participation in . . . receipt for . . . or right to subscribe to or purchase, any of the foregoing.

Securities Act of 1933, Section 2, Subsection (a)(1)

Any transaction in which a person invests money or property in a common enterprise or venture, or an investor who reasonably expects to make a profit primarily or substantially as a result of the managerial efforts of others is regulated by this act.

The 1933 Act requires full disclosure of material information that is relevant to investment decisions and prohibits fraud and misstatements when securities are offered to the public through the mail and/or interstate commerce. Registration statements, including financial statements, must be filed with the Securities and Exchange Commission (SEC) before investment securities can be offered for sale by an issuer. A registration statement, which is filed with the SEC, contains a thorough description of the securities, financial structure, condition, and management personnel of the issuing corporation. It also contains a description of material pending litigation against the issuing corporation. The 1933 Act also requires that a prospectus, based on the information in the registration statement, be given to any prospective investor or purchaser.

Securities that are exempt from registration requirements include:

- intrastate offerings where all offerees and issuers are residents of the state in which issuer performs substantially all of its operations;

- securities issued by a governmental body or nonprofit organization;

- securities issued by a bank, savings institution, common carrier, or farmers' cooperative and subject to other regulatory legislation;

- commercial paper with a maturity date of less than nine months (270 days);

- stock dividends, stock splits, and securities issued in connection with corporate reorganizations; and

- insurance, endowment, and annuity contracts.

Regulation A requires less demanding disclosures and registration for small issues of less than $1.5 million. Regulation D lists those transactions that are exempt from registration requirement:

- Private, noninvestment company sales of less than $500,000 worth of securities in a 12-month period to investors who will not resell the securities within two years

- Private, noninvestment company sales of less than $5 million worth of securities in a 12-month period to:

  — accredited investors—natural persons with annual income of more than $200,000 (or $300,000 jointly with a spouse) or whose net worth exceeds $1 million;

  — investors who are furnished with purchaser representatives who are knowledgeable and experienced regarding finance and business; or

  — up to 35 unaccredited investors that have financial and business knowledge and experience, who are furnished with the same information as would be contained in a full registration statement prospectus.

- Sales of any amount of securities to accredited investors or those furnished with independent purchaser representatives (private placement)

The Securities Exchange Act of 1934 (SEA)

Although the Securities Act of 1933 was limited to new issues, the 1934 Securities Act extended the regulation to securities sold in the secondary markets. The act provides the following.

- Establishment of the SEC—the SEC's primary function is to regulate the securities markets.

- Disclosure requirements for the secondary market—annual reports and other financial reports are required to be filed with the SEC prior to listing on the organized exchanges. These reports include the annual 10K Report, which must be audited, and the quarterly 10Q Report, which is not required to be audited.

- Registration of organized exchanges—all organized exchanges must register with the SEC and provide copies of their rules and bylaws.

- Credit regulation—Congress gave the Federal Reserve Board the power to set margin requirements for credit purchases of securities. Securities dealers' indebtedness was also limited to 20 times their owners' equity capital by this act.

- Proxy solicitation—specific rules governing solicitation of proxies were established.

- Exemptions—securities of federal, state, and local governments, securities that are not traded across state lines, and any other securities specified by the SEC are exempt from registering with the SEC.

- Insider activities—a public report, called an insider report, must be filed with the SEC in every month that a change in the holding of a firm's securities occurs for an officer, director, or 10% or more shareholder. The 1934 SEA forbids insiders profiting from securities held less than six months and requires these profits be returned to the organization. In addition, short sales are not permitted by individuals considered to be insiders.

- Price manipulation—the SEA of 1934 forbids price manipulation schemes, such as wash sales, pools, circulation of manipulative information, and false and misleading statements about securities.

Liability Under the Securities Exchange Act of 1934

The Securities Exchange Act of 1934 relates to the purchase and sale of investment securities in the market (i.e., being public). Section 18 states that a financial planner is liable for false and/or misleading statements of material facts that are made in applications, reports, documents, and registration statements, which are prepared by the financial planner and filed with the SEC. Liability is imposed upon those (including financial planners) who, because of their inside positions, have access to material information (which is not available to the public and which may affect the value of securities) and trade in the securities without making a disclosure.

A financial planner may be liable to a person who purchased or sold securities when it can be established that:

- the statement or omission was material;

- the financial planner intended to deceive or defraud others; and

- as a result of his reasonable reliance upon the misrepresentation, the purchaser or seller incurred a loss.

Criminal liability for willful conduct is imposed by the Securities Act of 1933, the Securities Exchange Act of 1934, the Internal Revenue Act, and other federal statutes, as well as state criminal codes.

The Investment Advisers Act of 1940

An investment adviser is defined as any person who, for compensation and as part of a regular business, engages in the business of advising others on the value of securities or on the advisability of investing in or selling them. The advice can be delivered in person, through publications or writings, or through research reports concerning securities.

To be an investment adviser under both state and federal securities law, a person must meet the following three tests:

- Provides advice, or issues reports or analyses, regarding securities

- Is in the business of providing such services

- Provides such services for compensation (compensation is "the receipt of any economic benefit" including commissions on the sale of products)

Certain organizations and individuals are excluded from the definition of investment adviser:

- Banks and bank holding companies (except as amended by the Gramm-Leach-Bliley Act of 1999)

- Lawyers, accountants, engineers, or teachers, if their performance of advisory services is solely incidental to their professions

- Brokers or dealers, if their performance of advisory services is solely incidental to the conduct of their business as brokers or dealers, and they do not receive any special compensation for their advisory services

- Publishers of bona fide newspapers, news magazines, or business or financial publications of general and regular circulation

- Federally covered investment advisers registered with the SEC

- Any other person the Administrator specifies

- Incidental practice exception is not available to individuals who hold themselves out to the public as providing financial planning, pension consulting, or other financial advisory services

The act generally requires investment advisers entering into an advisory contract with a client to deliver a written disclosure statement on their background and business practices. Form ADV Part II must be given to a client under Rule 204-3, known as the brochure rule. The 1940 Advisers Act and the SEC's rules require that advisers maintain and preserve specified books and records and make them available for inspection.

In accordance with the Investment Adviser Brochure Rule, an investment adviser must furnish each advisory client and prospective client with a written disclosure statement, which may be a copy of Part II of Form ADV, or written documents containing at least the information required by Part II of Form ADV, or such other information as the administrator may require.

Antifraud provisions—Section 206 of the Investment Advisers Act, Section 17 of the Securities Act of 1933, Section 10(b) of the Securities Exchange Act of 1934, and Rule 10b-5 prohibit misstatements or misleading omissions of material facts, fraudulent acts, and practices in connection with the purchase or sale of securities or the conduct of an investment advisory business. An investment adviser owes his clients undivided loyalty and may not engage in activity that conflicts with a client's interest.

Registration of Investment Advisers

Small Advisers—Those with less than $25 million of assets under management (AUM) are regulated by one or more states unless the state in which the adviser has its principal office and place of business has not enacted a statute regulating advisers.

Mid-Sized Advisers—Those with between $25 million and $100 million of AUM are regulated by one or more state if (i) the adviser is registered with the state where it has its principal office and place of business, and (ii) the adviser is "subject to examination" by that state authority.

Large Advisers—Those with more than $100 million of AUM must register with the SEC (unless an exemption is available), and state adviser laws are preempted for these advisers.

Investment Adviser Registration Depository

The Investment Adviser Registration Depository (IARD) is an electronic filing system for Investment Advisers sponsored by the Securities and Exchange Commission (SEC or Commission) and North American Securities Administrators Association (NASAA), with FINRA serving as the developer and operator of the system. The IARD system collects and maintains the registration and disclosure information for Investment Advisers and their associated persons. The IARD system supports electronic filing of the revised Forms ADV and ADV-W, centralized fee and form processing, regulatory review, the annual registration renewal process, and public disclosure of Investment Adviser information.

FINRA does not have regulatory authority over Investment Advisers; however, it was chosen to develop, operate, and maintain the system because of its regulatory business and technical expertise and the success of its web-based licensing and regulation system, Web CRDSM, deployed in 1999. Web CRD is a state-of-the-art web application for the registration of broker-dealers and their representatives. IARD provides regulators with the ability to monitor and process Investment Adviser information via a single, centralized system.

The SEC mandated its Investment Adviser registrants use the system to make all filings with the Commission (effective January 1, 2001). The IARD system satisfies the requirements of the National Securities Markets Improvement Act (NSMIA, 1996), which authorized electronic system registration of Investment Advisers.

IARD provides a mechanism that allows federally regulated Investment Advisers to satisfy the SEC mandate for electronic filing and related public disclosure. The system also offers states similar benefits by facilitating "Notice Filing" requirements for federal filers and registration requirements of state-regulated Investment Advisers. The IARD Program also provides for the registration of Investment Adviser Representatives (RAs) using the Individual Form Filing Functionality in Web CRD.

The IARD Program is composed of four critical components: IA Firm Registration, IA Firm Public Disclosure, IA Representative Registration, and IA Representative Public Disclosure. The Firm Registration component was released into production on January 1, 2001. This allows Investment Adviser firms to file a Form ADV and/or Form ADV-W electronically with the SEC and states. The IA Representative Registration component was implemented in Web CRD March 18, 2002. Release 4.0 in Web CRD enables firms to register their IA representatives online via the Web CRD system. In conjunction with the Release, the Uniform Forms U-4 and U-5 were revised to include the RA registration position code for IA representatives. Both the IA Firm Registration component and the IA Representative Registration component provides the ability to view the information contained on the filings, collect and disburse fees associated with these filings, request reports, and allow joint firms that are both broker-dealers and Investment Advisers, to share filing information between Web CRD and IARD.

Source: Financial Industry Regulatory Authority, Inc., *What is IARD?*, 2009, http://www.iard.com/WhatIsIARD.asp

Due Diligence

Due diligence is the process investment advisors use to make suitable investment recommendations to their clients. The advisor should gather all information necessary to establish proper suitability. This information includes, but is not limited to, the client's age, net worth, risk tolerance, and financial knowledge. Based on the client's objectives, the advisor should conduct due diligence on the various investment choices with the goal to provide investment recommendations that are in the client's best interest.

Investment Company Act of 1940

The Investment Company Act of 1940 requires registration with the SEC and restricts activities of investment companies (including mutual funds). The Investment Company Act of 1940 governs the management of investment companies. This act requires that investment companies register with the SEC, provide prospectuses to investors prior to the sale of shares, disclose the investment goals of the company, have outside members on the board of directors, use uniform accounting practices, and gain approval by shareholders for changes in management.

REFORM OF PREVIOUS ACTS

The Glass-Steagall Act (1933) prohibited commercial banks from acting as investment bankers, established the Federal Deposit Insurance Corporation (FDIC), and prohibited commercial banks from paying interest on demand deposits. This was one of the first of many securities regulation laws that impacted the investment markets. However, the Gramm-Leach-Bliley Act, passed by Congress in November 1999, eliminated many of the restrictions against affiliations among banks, securities firms, and insurance companies.

The act repealed the affiliation sections of the Glass-Steagall Act that prohibited a bank holding company and a securities firm that underwrites and deals in ineligible securities from owning and controlling each other.

It also amended the Bank Holding Company Act (1956) to permit cross-ownership and control among bank holding companies, securities firms, and insurance companies, provided that such cross-ownership and control is effected through a financial holding company that engages in activities that conform to the act.

A bank must register as an investment adviser if it provides investment advice to a registered investment company, provided that, if the bank provides such advice through a "separately identified department or division," that department or division must be deemed to be the investment adviser.

FINRA

The Financial Industry Regulatory Authority (FINRA), is the largest non-governmental regulator for all securities firms doing business in the United States. All told, FINRA oversees nearly 4,850 brokerage firms, about 173,000 branch offices and more than 647,000 registered securities representatives.

Created in July 2007 through the consolidation of National Association of Securities Dealers (NASD) and the member regulation, enforcement and arbitration functions of the New York Stock Exchange, FINRA is dedicated to investor protection and market integrity through effective and efficient regulation and complementary compliance and technology-based services.

FINRA touches virtually every aspect of the securities business—from registering and educating industry participants to examining securities firms; writing rules; enforcing those rules and the federal securities laws; informing and educating the investing public; providing trade reporting and other industry utilities; and administering the largest dispute resolution forum for investors and registered firms. It also performs market regulation under contract for The NASDAQ Stock Market, the American Stock Exchange, the International Securities Exchange and the Chicago Climate Exchange.

Source: Financial Industry Regulatory Authority, Inc., *About the Financial Industry Regulatory Authority*, 2009, http://www.finra.org/AboutFINRA/

CFP® Certification Examination Principal Topics

CERTIFIED FINANCIAL PLANNER BOARD OF STANDARDS, INC.

2015 Principal Knowledge Topics (72 Topics)

The following Principal Knowledge Topics are based on the results of CFP Board's 2015 Job Analysis Study.

The Principal Knowledge Topics serve as the blueprint for the March 2016 and later administrations of the CFP® Certification Examination. Each exam question will be linked to one of the following Principal Knowledge Topics, in the approximate percentages indicated following the general category headings.

The Principal Knowledge Topics serve as a curricular framework and also represent subject topics that CFP Board accepts for continuing education credit, effective January 2016.

Eight Principal Knowledge Topic Categories

A. Professional Conduct and Regulation (7%)

B. General Financial Planning Principles (17%)

C. Education Planning (6%)

D. Risk Management and Insurance Planning (12%)

E. Investment Planning (17%)

F. Tax Planning (12%)

G. Retirement Savings and Income Planning (17%)

H. Estate Planning (12%)

A. Professional Conduct and Regulation

A.1.   CFP Board's Code of Ethics and Professional Responsibility and Rules of Conduct

A.2.   CFP Board's Financial Planning Practice Standards

A.3.   CFP Board's Disciplinary Rules and Procedures

A.4.   Function, purpose, and regulation of financial institutions

A.5.   Financial services regulations and requirements

A.6.   Consumer protection laws

A.7.   Fiduciary

Professional Conduct & Regulation

B. General Principles of Financial Planning

B.8.	Financial planning process
B.9.	Financial statements
B.10.	Cash flow management
B.11.	Financing strategies
B.12.	Economic concepts
B.13.	Time value of money concepts and calculations
B.14.	Client and planner attitudes, values, biases and behavioral finance
B.15.	Principles of communication and counseling
B.16.	Debt management

General Financial Planning Principles

C. Education Planning

C.17.	Education needs analysis
C.18.	Education savings vehicles
C.19.	Financial aid
C.20.	Gift/income tax strategies
C.21.	Education financing

Education Planning

D. Risk Management and Insurance Planning

D.22.	Principles of risk and insurance
D.23.	Analysis and evaluation of risk exposures
D.24.	Health insurance and health care cost management (individual)
D.25.	Disability income insurance (individual)
D.26.	Long-term care insurance (individual)
D.27.	Annuities
D.28.	Life insurance (individual)
D.29.	Business uses of insurance
D.30.	Insurance needs analysis
D.31.	Insurance policy and company selection
D.32.	Property and casualty insurance

Risk Management & Insurance Planning

E. Investment Planning

E.33.	Characteristics, uses and taxation of investment vehicles
E.34.	Types of investment risk
E.35.	Quantitative investment concepts
E.36.	Measures of investment returns
E.37.	Asset allocation and portfolio diversification
E.38.	Bond and stock valuation concepts
E.39.	Portfolio development and analysis
E.40.	Investment strategies
E.41.	Alternative investments

Investment Planning

F. Tax Planning

F.42.	Fundamental tax law
F.43.	Income tax fundamentals and calculations
F.44.	Characteristics and income taxation of business entities
F.45.	Income taxation of trusts and estates
F.46.	Alternative minimum tax (AMT)
F.47.	Tax reduction/management techniques
F.48.	Tax consequences of property transactions
F.49.	Passive activity and at-risk rules
F.50.	Tax implications of special circumstances
F.51.	Charitable/philanthropic contributions and deductions

Tax Planning

G. Retirement Savings and Income Planning

G.52.	Retirement needs analysis
G.53.	Social Security and Medicare
G.54.	Medicaid
G.55.	Types of retirement plans
G.56.	Qualified plan rules and options
G.57.	Other tax-advantaged retirement plans
G.58.	Regulatory considerations
G.59.	Key factors affecting plan selection for businesses

Retirement Savings & Income Planning

G.60.   Distribution rules and taxation

G.61.   Retirement income and distribution strategies

G.62.   Business succession planning

H. Estate Planning

H.63.   Characteristics and consequences of property titling

H.64.   Strategies to transfer property

H.65.   Estate planning documents

H.66.   Gift and estate tax compliance and tax calculation

H.67.   Sources for estate liquidity

H.68.   Types, features, and taxation of trusts

H.69.   Marital deduction

H.70.   Intra-family and other business transfer techniques

H.71.   Postmortem estate planning techniques

H.72.   Estate planning for non-traditional relationships

Contextual Variables

In addition to the Principal Knowledge Topics, other important variables are to be considered when dealing with specific financial planning situations. These are referred to as "Contextual Variables" and are used as part of content development for the CFP® Certification Examination or other case-based scenarios.

More specifically, financial planning situations require the application of financial planning knowledge for different types of clients. Important client details to consider as part of financial planning situations are:

- **Family Status** (traditional family, single parent, same-sex couples, blended families, widowhood)
- **Net Worth** (ultra-high net worth, high net worth, mass affluent, emerging affluent, mass market)
- **Income Level** (high, medium, low)
- **Life or Professional Stage** (student, starting a career, career transition, pre-retirement, retirement)
- **Other Circumstances** (health issues, divorce, change of employment status, aging parents, special needs children)

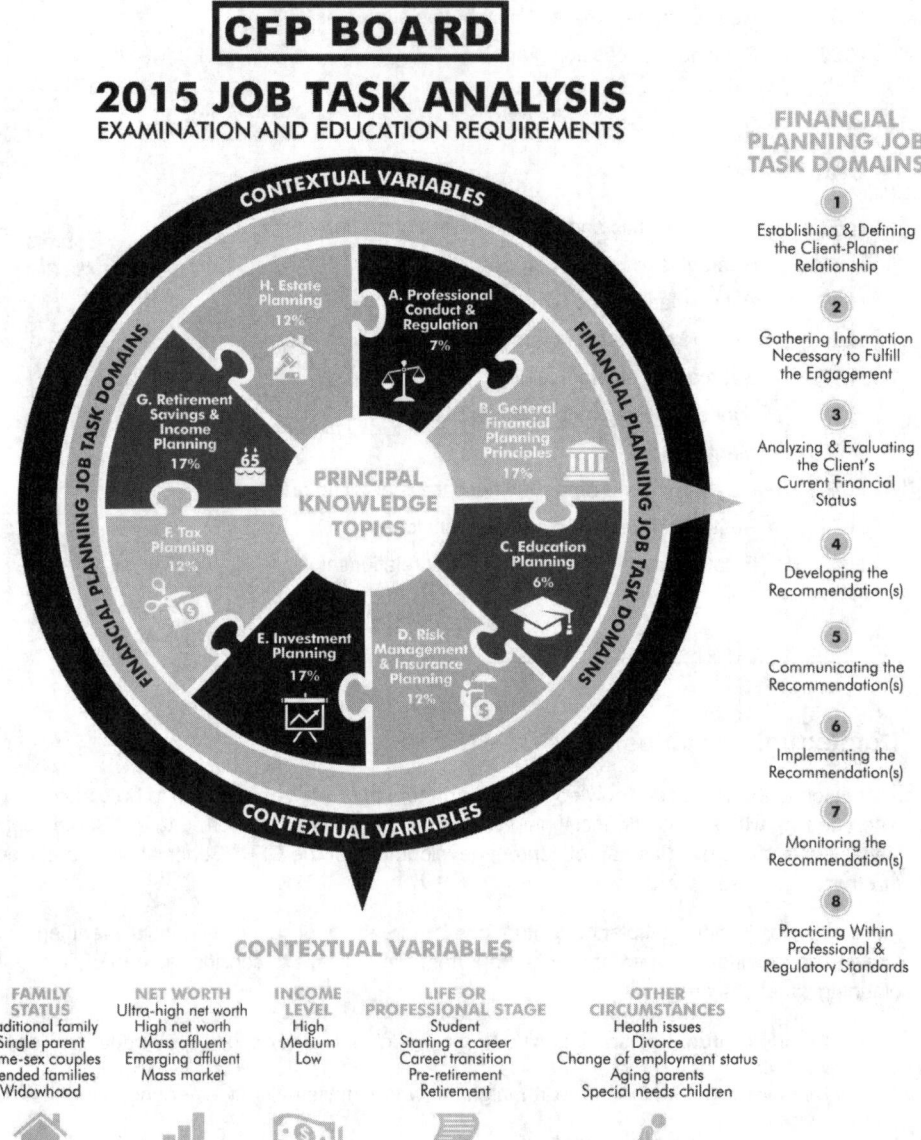

Copyright © 2015 Certified Financial Planner Board of Standards, Inc. All Rights Reserved

CFP® Certification Examination Job Task Domains

CERTIFIED FINANCIAL PLANNER BOARD OF STANDARDS, INC.

2015 Financial Planning Job Task Domains

The following Financial Planning Job Task Domains are based on the results of CFP Board's 2015 Job Analysis Study. The Job Tasks are used to provide guidance for developing content for the CFP® Certification Examination and other case-based scenarios.

Eight Major Domains

1. **Establishing and Defining the Client-Planner Relationship**
2. **Gathering Information Necessary to Fulfill the Engagement**
3. **Analyzing and Evaluating the Client's Current Financial Status**
4. **Developing the Recommendation(s)**
5. **Communicating the Recommendation(s)**
6. **Implementing the Recommendation(s)**
7. **Monitoring the Recommendation(s)**
8. **Practicing within Professional and Regulatory Standards**

1. Establishing and Defining the Client-Planner Relationship

A) Identify the client (e.g., individual, family, business, organization)
B) Discuss the financial planning process
C) Explain scope of services offered
D) Assess and communicate ability to meet the client's needs and expectations
E) Identify and disclose conflicts of interest in client relationships
F) Discuss responsibilities of parties involved
G) Define and document the scope of the engagement
H) Provide client disclosures
   1) Regulatory disclosure
   2) Compensation arrangements and associated potential conflicts of interest

2. Gathering Information Necessary to Fulfill the Engagement

A) Explore with the client their personal and financial needs, priorities and goals
B) Assess the client's level of knowledge, experience and risk tolerance
C) Evaluate the client's risk exposures (e.g., longevity, economic, liability, healthcare)
D) Gather relevant data including:
   1) Summary of assets (e.g., cost basis information, beneficiary designations and titling)
   2) Summary of liabilities (e.g., balances, terms, interest rates)
   3) Summary of income and expenses
   4) Estate planning documents
   5) Education plan and resources
   6) Retirement plan information
   7) Employee benefits

8) Government benefits (e.g., Social Security, Medicare)
9) Special circumstances (e.g., legal documents and agreements, family situations)
10) Tax documents
11) Investment statements
12) Insurance policies and documents (e.g., life, health, disability, liability)
13) Closely held business documents (e.g., shareholder agreements)
14) Inheritances, windfalls, and other large lump sums

3. Analyzing and Evaluating the Client's Current Financial Status

A) Evaluate and document the strengths and vulnerabilities of the client's current financial situation including:
   1) Statement of financial position/balance sheet
   2) Cash flow statement
   3) Capital needs analysis (e.g., insurance, retirement, major purchases)
   4) Asset protection (e.g., titling, trusts, etc.)
   5) Asset allocation
   6) Client liquidity (e.g., emergency fund)
   7) Government benefits (e.g., Social Security, Medicare)
   8) Employee benefits
   9) Investment strategies
   10) Current, deferred and future tax liabilities
   11) Estate tax liabilities
   12) Tax considerations
   13) Income types
   14) Retirement plans and strategies (e.g., qualified plans, IRAs)
   15) Accumulation planning
   16) Distribution planning
   17) Estate documents
   18) Ownership of assets
   19) Beneficiary designations
   20) Gifting strategies
   21) Executive compensation (e.g., deferred compensation, stock options, RSUs)
   22) Succession planning and exit strategy
   23) Risk management (e.g., retained risk and insurance coverage)
   24) Educational financial aid
   25) General sources of financing
   26) Special circumstances (e.g., divorce, disabilities, family dynamics, etc.)
   27) Inheritances, windfalls, and other large lump sums
   28) Charitable planning
   29) Aging and eldercare
   30) Mental capability and capacity issues
B) Identify and use appropriate tools and techniques to conduct analyses including:
   1) Financial calculator
   2) Computer spreadsheet
   3) Financial planning software

4. Developing the Recommendation(s)

A) Evaluate alternatives to meet the client's goals and objectives
   1) Sensitivity analysis (e.g., factors outside of client control)
B) Consult with other professionals as appropriate
C) Develop recommendations considering:
   1) Client attitudes, values and beliefs
   2) Behavioral finance issues (e.g., anchoring, overconfidence, recency)
   3) Their interdependence
D) Document recommendations

5. Communicating the Recommendation(s)

A) Present financial plan and provide guidance
   1) Goals
   2) Assumptions
   3) Observations and findings
   4) Alternatives
   5) Recommendations
B) Obtain feedback from the client and revise the recommendations as appropriate
C) Provide documentation of plan recommendations and any additional disclosures
D) Verify client acceptance of recommendations

6. Implementing the Recommendation(s)

A) Create a prioritized implementation plan with timeline
B) Directly or indirectly implement the recommendations
C) Coordinate and share information, as authorized, with others
D) Define monitoring responsibilities with the client (e.g., explain what will be monitored, frequency of monitoring, communication method(s))

7. Monitoring the Recommendation(s)

A) Discuss and evaluate changes in the client's personal circumstances (e.g., aging issues, change in employment)
B) Review the performance and progress of the plan
C) Review and evaluate changes in the legal, tax and economic environments
D) Make recommendations to accommodate changed circumstances
E) Review scope of work and redefine engagement as appropriate
F) Provide ongoing client support (e.g., guidance, education)

8. Practicing within Professional and Regulatory Standards

A) Adhere to CFP Board's *Standards of Professional Conduct*
B) Manage practice risk (e.g., documentation, monitor client noncompliance with recommendations)
C) Maintain awareness of and comply with regulatory and legal guidelines

CONTEXTUAL VARIABLES

In addition to the Principal Knowledge Topics, other important variables are to be considered when dealing with specific financial planning situations. These are referred to as "Contextual Variables" and are used as part of content development for the CFP® Certification Examination or other case-based scenarios.

More specifically, financial planning situations require the application of financial planning knowledge for different types of clients. Important client details to consider as part of financial planning situations are:

- **Family Status** (traditional family, single parent, same-sex couples, blended families, widowhood)
- **Net Worth** (ultra-high net worth, high net worth, mass affluent, emerging affluent, mass market)
- **Income Level** (high, medium, low)
- **Life or Professional Stage** (student, starting a career, career transition, pre-retirement, retirement)
- **Other Circumstances** (health issues, divorce, change of employment status, aging parents, special needs children)

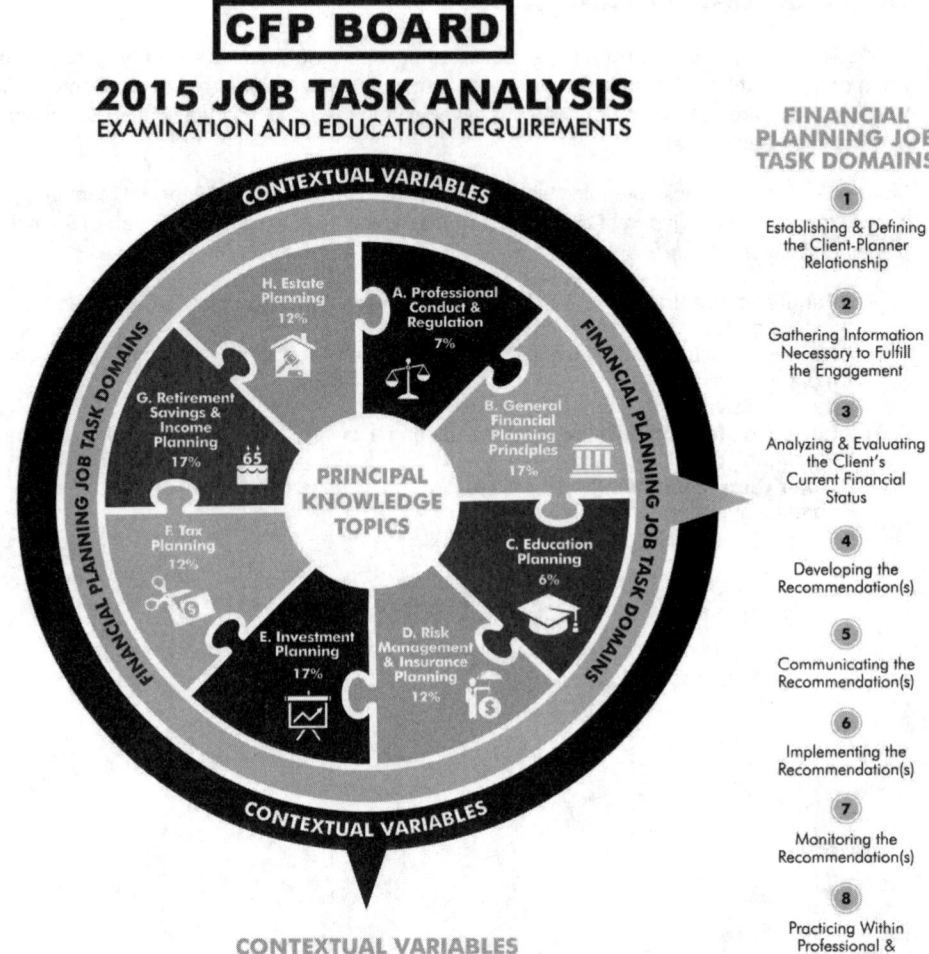

Copyright © 2015 Certified Financial Planner Board of Standards, Inc. All Rights Reserved

APPENDIX F

Code of Ethics and Standards of Conduct
(effective October 1, 2019;
revised March 29, 2018)

CFP BOARD

CODE OF ETHICS AND STANDARDS OF CONDUCT

MARCH 2018

EFFECTIVE DATE: OCTOBER 1, 2019

PREAMBLE

CFP Board's *Code of Ethics and Standards of Conduct* reflects the commitment that all CFP® professionals make to high standards of competency and ethics. CFP Board's *Code and Standards* benefits and protects the public, provides standards for delivering financial planning, and advances financial planning as a distinct and valuable profession. Compliance with the *Code and Standards* is a requirement of CFP® certification that is critical to the integrity of the CFP® marks. Violations of the *Code and Standards* may subject a CFP® professional to discipline.

CODE OF ETHICS

A CFP® professional must:

1. Act with honesty, integrity, competence, and diligence.

2. Act in the client's best interests.

3. Exercise due care.

4. Avoid or disclose and manage conflicts of interest.

5. Maintain the confidentiality and protect the privacy of client information.

6. Act in a manner that reflects positively on the financial planning profession and CFP® certification.

STANDARDS OF CONDUCT

A. DUTIES OWED TO CLIENTS

1. FIDUCIARY DUTY

At all times when providing Financial Advice to a Client, a CFP® professional must act as a fiduciary, and therefore, act in the best interests of the Client. The following duties must be fulfilled:

a. **Duty of Loyalty.** A CFP® professional must:

   i. Place the interests of the Client above the interests of the CFP® professional and the CFP® Professional's Firm;

   ii. Avoid Conflicts of Interest, or fully disclose Material Conflicts of Interest to the Client, obtain the Client's informed consent, and properly manage the conflict; and

   iii. Act without regard to the financial or other interests of the CFP® professional, the CFP® Professional's Firm, or any individual or entity other than the Client, which means that a CFP® professional acting under a Conflict of Interest continues to have a duty to act in the best interests of the Client and place the Client's interests above the CFP® professional's.

b. **Duty of Care.** A CFP® professional must act with the care, skill, prudence, and diligence that a prudent professional would exercise in light of the Client's goals, risk tolerance, objectives, and financial and personal circumstances.

c. **Duty to Follow Client Instructions.** A CFP® professional must comply with all objectives, policies, restrictions, and other terms of the Engagement and all reasonable and lawful directions of the Client.

2. INTEGRITY

a. A CFP® professional must perform Professional Services with integrity. Integrity demands honesty and candor, which may not be subordinated to personal gain or advantage. Allowance may be made for innocent error and legitimate differences of opinion, but integrity cannot co-exist with deceit or subordination of principle.

b. A CFP® professional may not, directly or indirectly, in the conduct of Professional Services:

   i. Employ any device, scheme, or artifice to defraud;

   ii. Make any untrue statement of a material fact or omit to state a material fact necessary in order to make the statements made, in the light of the circumstances under which they were made, not misleading; or

   iii. Engage in any act, practice, or course of business which operates or would operate as a fraud or deceit upon any person.

3. COMPETENCE

A CFP® professional must provide Professional Services with competence, which means with relevant knowledge and skill to apply that knowledge. When the CFP® professional is not sufficiently competent in a particular area to provide the Professional Services required under the Engagement, the CFP® professional must gain competence, obtain the assistance of a competent professional, limit or terminate the Engagement, and/or refer the Client to a competent professional. The CFP® professional shall describe to the Client any requested Professional Services that the CFP® professional will not be providing.

4. DILIGENCE

A CFP® professional must provide Professional Services, including responding to reasonable Client inquiries, in a timely and thorough manner.

5. DISCLOSE AND MANAGE CONFLICTS OF INTEREST

a. **Disclose Conflicts.** When providing Financial Advice, a CFP® professional must make full disclosure of all Material Conflicts of Interest with the CFP® professional's Client that could affect the professional relationship. This obligation requires the CFP® professional to provide the Client with sufficiently specific facts so that the Client is able to understand the CFP® professional's Conflicts of Interest and the business practices that give rise to the conflicts, and give informed consent to such conflicts or reject them. A sincere belief by a CFP® professional with a Material Conflict of Interest that he or she is acting in the best interests of the Client is insufficient to excuse failure to make full disclosure.

   i. In determining whether to infer that a Client has consented to a Material Conflict of Interest, CFP Board will evaluate whether a reasonable Client receiving the disclosure would have understood the conflict and how it could affect the advice the Client will receive from the CFP® professional. The greater the potential harm the conflict presents to the Client, and the more significantly a business practice that gives rise to the conflict departs from commonly accepted practices among CFP® professionals, the less likely it is that CFP Board will infer informed consent absent clear evidence of informed consent. Ambiguity in the disclosure provided to the Client will be interpreted in favor of the Client.

   ii. Evidence of oral disclosure of a conflict will be given such weight as CFP Board in its judgment deems appropriate. Written consent to a conflict is not required.

b. **Manage Conflicts.** A CFP® professional must adopt and follow business practices reasonably designed to prevent Material Conflicts of Interest from compromising the CFP® professional's ability to act in the Client's best interests.

6. SOUND AND OBJECTIVE PROFESSIONAL JUDGMENT

A CFP® professional must exercise professional judgment on behalf of the Client that is not subordinated to the interest of the CFP® professional or others. A CFP® professional may not solicit or accept any gift, gratuity, entertainment, non-cash compensation, or other consideration that reasonably could be expected to compromise the CFP® professional's objectivity.

7. PROFESSIONALISM

A CFP® professional must treat Clients, prospective Clients, fellow professionals, and others with dignity, courtesy, and respect.

8. COMPLY WITH THE LAW

a. A CFP® professional must comply with the laws, rules, and regulations governing Professional Services.

b. A CFP® professional may not intentionally or recklessly participate or assist in another person's violation of these *Standards* or the laws, rules, or regulations governing Professional Services.

9. CONFIDENTIALITY AND PRIVACY

a. A CFP® professional must keep confidential and may not disclose any non-public personal information about any prospective, current, or former Client ("client"), except that the CFP® professional may disclose information:

    i. For ordinary business purposes:

        a) With the client's consent, so long as the client has not withdrawn the consent;

        b) To a CFP® professional's employer, partners, employees, or other persons with whom the CFP® professional is providing services to or for the client, when necessary to perform those services;

        c) As necessary to provide information to the CFP® professional's attorneys, accountants, and auditors; and

        d) To a person acting in a representative capacity on behalf of the client;

    ii. For legal and enforcement purposes:

        a) To law enforcement authorities concerning suspected unlawful activities, to the extent permitted by the law;

        b) As required to comply with federal, state, or local law;

        c) As required to comply with a properly authorized civil, criminal, or regulatory investigation or examination, or subpoena or summons, by a governmental authority;

        d) As necessary to defend against allegations of wrongdoing made by a governmental authority;

        e) As necessary to present a civil claim against, or defend against a civil claim raised by, a client;

        f) As required to comply with a request from CFP Board concerning an investigation or adjudication; and

        g) As necessary to provide information to professional organizations that are assessing the CFP® professional's compliance with professional standards.

b. A CFP® professional may not use any non-public personal information about a client for his or her direct or indirect personal benefit, whether or not it causes detriment to the client, unless the client consents.

c. A CFP® professional, either directly or through the CFP® Professional's Firm, must take reasonable steps to protect the security of non-public personal information about any client, including the security of information stored physically or electronically, from unauthorized access that could result in harm or inconvenience to the client.

d. A CFP® professional, either directly or through the CFP® Professional's Firm, must adopt and implement policies regarding the protection, handling, and sharing of a client's non-public personal information and must provide clients with written notice of those policies.

e. A CFP® professional shall be deemed to comply with this Section if the CFP® Professional's Firm is subject to, and the CFP® professional complies with, Regulation S-P under the federal securities laws or substantially equivalent federal or state laws or rules.

10. PROVIDE INFORMATION TO A CLIENT

a. **When Providing Financial Advice.** When providing or agreeing to provide Financial Advice that does not require Financial Planning in accordance with the Practice Standards, a CFP® professional must provide the following information to the Client, prior to or at the time of the Engagement, and document that the information has been provided to the Client:

    i. A description of the services and products to be provided;

    ii. How the Client pays for the products and services, and a description of the additional types of costs that the Client may incur, including product management fees, surrender charges, and sales loads;

    iii. How the CFP® professional, the CFP® Professional's Firm, and any Related Party are compensated for providing the products and services;

    iv. The location(s), if any, of the webpages of all relevant public websites of any governmental authority, self-regulatory organization, or professional organization that sets forth the CFP® professional's public disciplinary history or any personal bankruptcy or business bankruptcy where the CFP® professional was a Control Person; and

    v. Any other information about the CFP® professional or the CFP® Professional's Firm that is Material to a Client's decision to engage or continue to engage the CFP® professional or the CFP® Professional's Firm.

b. **When Providing Financial Planning.** When providing or required to provide Financial Planning in accordance with the Practice Standards, a CFP® professional must provide the following information to the Client, prior to or at the time of the Engagement, in one or more written documents:

    i. The information required to be provided in Section A.10.a.; and

    ii. The terms of the Engagement between the Client and the CFP® professional or the CFP® Professional's Firm, including the Scope of Engagement and any limitations, the period(s) during which the services will be provided, and the Client's responsibilities. A CFP® professional is responsible for implementing, monitoring, and updating the Financial Planning recommendation(s) unless specifically excluded from the Scope of Engagement.

c. **Other Information.** A CFP® professional also must provide the information required under Sections A.5.a, A.9.d., and A.11.

d. **Updating Information.** A CFP® professional has an ongoing obligation to provide to the Client any information that is a Material change or update to the information required to be provided to the Client. Material changes and updates to public disciplinary history or bankruptcy information must be disclosed to the Client within ninety days, together with the location(s) of the relevant webpages.

11. DUTIES WHEN COMMUNICATING WITH A CLIENT

A CFP® professional must provide a Client with accurate information, in accordance with the Engagement, and in response to reasonable Client requests, in a manner and format that a Client reasonably may be expected to understand.

12. DUTIES WHEN REPRESENTING COMPENSATION METHOD

A CFP® professional may not make false or misleading representations regarding the CFP® professional's or the CFP® Professional's Firm's method(s) of compensation.

a. **Specific Representations**

    i. **Fee-Only.** A CFP® professional may represent his or her or the CFP® Professional's Firm's compensation method as "fee-only" only if:

        a) The CFP® professional and the CFP® Professional's Firm receive no Sales-Related Compensation; and

        b) Related Parties receive no Sales-Related Compensation in connection with any Professional Services the CFP® professional or the CFP® Professional's Firm provides to Clients.

ii. **Fee-Based.** CFP Board uses the term "fee and commission" to describe the compensation method of those who receive both fees and Sales-Related Compensation. A CFP® professional who represents that his or her or the CFP® Professional's Firm's compensation method is "fee-based" or any other term that is not fee-only:

a) May not use the term in a manner that suggests the CFP® professional or the CFP® Professional's Firm is fee-only; and

b) Must clearly state that either the CFP® professional or the CFP® Professional's Firm earns fees and commissions, or that the CFP® professional or the CFP® Professional's Firm are not fee-only.

b. **Sales-Related Compensation.** Sales-Related Compensation is more than a de minimis economic benefit, including any bonus or portion of compensation, for purchasing, holding for purposes other than providing Financial Advice, or selling a Client's Financial Assets, or for the referral of a Client to any person or entity other than the CFP® Professional's Firm. Sales-Related Compensation includes, for example, commissions, trailing commissions, 12b-1 fees, spreads, transaction fees, revenue sharing, referral or solicitor fees, or similar consideration. Sales-Related Compensation does not include:

i. Soft dollars (any research or other benefits received in connection with Client brokerage that qualifies for the "safe harbor" of Section 28(e) of the Securities Exchange Act of 1934);

ii. Reasonable and customary fees for custodial or similar administrative services if the fee or amount of the fee is not determined based on the amount or value of Client transactions;

iii. Non-monetary benefits provided by another service provider, including a custodian, that benefit the CFP® professional's Clients by improving the CFP® professional's delivery of Professional Services, and that are not determined based on the amount or value of Client transactions;

iv. Reasonable and customary fees for Professional Services, other than for solicitations and referrals, the CFP® professional or CFP® Professional's Firm provides to a Client that are collected and distributed by another service provider, including under a Turnkey Asset Management Platform; or

v. A fee the Related Party solicitor receives for soliciting clients for the CFP® professional or the CFP® Professional's Firm.

c. **Related Party.** A person or business entity (including a trust) whose receipt of Sales-Related Compensation a reasonable CFP® professional would view as benefiting the CFP® professional or the CFP® Professional's Firm, including, for example, as a result of the CFP® professional's ownership stake in the business entity. There is a rebuttable presumption that a Related Party includes:

i. Family Members. A member of the CFP® professional's Family and any business entity that the Family or members of the Family Control; and

ii. Business Entities. A business entity that the CFP® professional or the CFP® Professional's Firm Controls, or that is Controlled by or is under common Control with, the CFP® Professional's Firm.

d. **In Connection with any Professional Services.** Sales-Related Compensation received by a Related Party is "in connection with any Professional Services" if it results, directly or indirectly, from Client transactions referred or facilitated by the CFP® professional or the CFP® Professional's Firm.

e. **Safe Harbor for Related Parties.** Sales-Related Compensation received by a Related Party is not "in connection with any Professional Services" if the CFP® professional or the CFP® Professional's Firm adopts and implements policies and procedures reasonably designed to prevent the CFP® professional or the CFP® Professional's Firm from recommending that any Client purchase Financial Assets from or through, or refer any Clients to, the Related Party.

f. **Misrepresentations by a CFP® Professional's Firm.** A CFP® professional who Controls the CFP® Professional's Firm may not allow the CFP® Professional's Firm to make false or misleading representations of compensation method. A CFP® professional who does not Control the CFP® Professional's Firm must correct a CFP® Professional's Firm's misrepresentations of compensation method by accurately representing the CFP® professional's compensation method to the CFP® professional's Clients.

13. **DUTIES WHEN RECOMMENDING, ENGAGING, AND WORKING WITH ADDITIONAL PERSONS**

   a. When engaging or recommending the selection or retention of additional persons to provide financial or Professional Services for a Client, a CFP® professional must:

   i. Have a reasonable basis for the recommendation or Engagement based on the person's reputation, experience, and qualifications;

   ii. Disclose to the Client, at the time of the recommendation or prior to the Engagement, any arrangement by which someone who is not the Client will compensate or provide some other material economic benefit to the CFP® professional, the CFP® Professional's Firm, or a Related Party for the recommendation or Engagement; and

   iii. When engaging a person to provide services for a Client, exercise reasonable care to protect the Client's interests.

   b. When working with another financial or Professional Services provider on behalf of a Client, a CFP® professional must:

   i. Communicate with the other provider about the scope of their respective services and the allocation of responsibility between them; and

   ii. Inform the Client in a timely manner if the CFP® professional has a reasonable belief that the other provider's services were not performed in accordance with the scope of services to be provided and the allocation of responsibilities.

14. **DUTIES WHEN SELECTING, USING, AND RECOMMENDING TECHNOLOGY**

   a. A CFP® professional must exercise reasonable care and judgment when selecting, using, or recommending any software, digital advice tool, or other technology while providing Professional Services to a Client.

   b. A CFP® professional must have a reasonable level of understanding of the assumptions and outcomes of the technology employed.

   c. A CFP® professional must have a reasonable basis for believing that the technology produces reliable, objective, and appropriate outcomes.

15. **REFRAIN FROM BORROWING OR LENDING MONEY AND COMMINGLING FINANCIAL ASSETS**

   a. A CFP® professional may not, directly or indirectly, borrow money from or lend money to a Client unless:

   i. The Client is a member of the CFP® professional's Family; or

   ii. The lender is a business organization or legal entity in the business of lending money.

   b. A CFP® professional may not commingle a Client's Financial Assets with the Financial Assets of the CFP® professional or the CFP® Professional's Firm.

B. **FINANCIAL PLANNING AND APPLICATION OF THE PRACTICE STANDARDS FOR THE FINANCIAL PLANNING PROCESS**

   1. **Financial Planning Definition.** Financial Planning is a collaborative process that helps maximize a Client's potential for meeting life goals through Financial Advice that integrates relevant elements of the Client's personal and financial circumstances.

   2. **Examples of Relevant Elements of the Client's Personal and Financial Circumstances.** Relevant elements of personal and financial circumstances vary from Client to Client, and may include the Client's need for or desire to: develop goals, manage assets and liabilities, manage cash flow, identify and manage risks, identify and manage the financial effect of health considerations, provide for educational needs, achieve financial security, preserve or increase wealth, identify tax considerations, prepare for retirement, pursue philanthropic interests, and address estate and legacy matters.

3. **Application of Practice Standards.** The Practice Standards set forth the Financial Planning process. A CFP® professional must comply with the Practice Standards when:

   a. The CFP® professional agrees to provide or provides (i) Financial Planning; or (ii) Financial Advice that requires integration of relevant elements of the Client's personal and/or financial circumstances in order to act in the Client's best interests ("Financial Advice that Requires Financial Planning"); or

   b. The Client has a reasonable basis to believe the CFP® professional will provide or has provided Financial Planning.

4. **Integration Factors.** Among the factors that CFP Board will weigh in determining whether a CFP® professional has agreed to provide or provided Financial Advice that Requires Financial Planning are:

   a. The number of relevant elements of the Client's personal and financial circumstances that the Financial Advice may affect;

   b. The portion and amount of the Client's Financial Assets that the Financial Advice may affect;

   c. The length of time the Client's personal and financial circumstances may be affected by the Financial Advice;

   d. The effect on the Client's overall exposure to risk if the Client implements the Financial Advice; and

   e. The barriers to modifying the actions taken to implement the Financial Advice.

5. **CFP Board Evaluation.** In a disciplinary proceeding in which a CFP® professional denies CFP Board's allegation that the CFP® professional was required to comply with the Practice Standards, the CFP® professional must demonstrate that compliance with the Practice Standards was not required.

6. **No Client Agreement to Engage for Financial Planning.** If a CFP® professional otherwise must comply with the Practice Standards, but the Client does not agree to engage the CFP® professional to provide Financial Planning, the CFP® professional must either:

   a. Not enter into the Engagement;

   b. Limit the Scope of Engagement to services that do not require application of the Practice Standards, and describe to the Client the services the Client requests that the CFP® professional will not be performing;

   c. Provide the requested services after informing the Client how Financial Planning would benefit the Client and how the decision not to engage the CFP® professional to provide Financial Planning may limit the CFP® professional's Financial Advice, in which case the CFP® professional is not required to comply with the Practice Standards; or

   d. Terminate the Engagement.

C. PRACTICE STANDARDS FOR THE FINANCIAL PLANNING PROCESS

In complying with the Practice Standards, a CFP® professional must act prudently in documenting information, as the facts and circumstances require, taking into account the significance of the information, the need to preserve the information in writing, the obligation to act in the Client's best interests, and the CFP® Professional's Firm's policies and procedures.

1. **Understanding the Client's Personal and Financial Circumstances**

   a. **Obtaining Qualitative and Quantitative Information.** A CFP® professional must describe to the Client the qualitative and quantitative information concerning the Client's personal and financial circumstances needed to fulfill the Scope of Engagement and collaborate with the Client to obtain the information.

      i. Examples of qualitative or subjective information include the Client's health, life expectancy, family circumstances, values, attitudes, expectations, earnings potential, risk tolerance, goals, needs, priorities, and current course of action.

    ii. Examples of quantitative or objective information include the Client's age, dependents, other professional advisors, income, expenses, cash flow, savings, assets, liabilities, available resources, liquidity, taxes, employee benefits, government benefits, insurance coverage, estate plans, education and retirement accounts and benefits, and capacity for risk.

  b. **Analyzing Information.** A CFP® professional must analyze the qualitative and quantitative information to assess the Client's personal and financial circumstances.

  c. **Addressing Incomplete Information.** If unable to obtain information necessary to fulfill the Scope of Engagement, the CFP® professional must either limit the Scope of Engagement to those services the CFP® professional is able to provide or terminate the Engagement.

2. **Identifying and Selecting Goals**

  a. **Identifying Potential Goals.** A CFP® professional must discuss with the Client the CFP® professional's assessment of the Client's financial and personal circumstances, and help the Client identify goals, noting the impact that selecting a particular goal may have on other goals. In helping the Client identify goals, the CFP® professional must discuss with the Client, and apply, reasonable assumptions and estimates. These may include life expectancy, inflation rates, tax rates, investment returns, and other Material assumptions and estimates.

  b. **Selecting and Prioritizing Goals.** A CFP® professional must help the Client select and prioritize goals. The CFP® professional must discuss with the Client any goals the Client has selected that the CFP® professional believes are not realistic.

3. **Analyzing the Client's Current Course of Action and Potential Alternative Course(s) of Action**

  a. **Analyzing Current Course of Action.** A CFP® professional must analyze the Client's current course of action, including the material advantages and disadvantages of the current course and whether the current course maximizes the potential for meeting the Client's goals.

  b. **Analyzing Potential Alternative Courses of Action.** Where appropriate, a CFP® professional must consider and analyze one or more potential alternative courses of action, including their material advantages and disadvantages, whether they help maximize the potential for meeting the Client's goals, and how they integrate the relevant elements of the Client's personal and financial circumstances.

4. **Developing the Financial Planning Recommendation(s)**

From the potential courses of action, a CFP® professional must select one or more recommendations designed to maximize the potential for meeting the Client's goals. The recommendation may be to continue the Client's current course of action. For each recommendation selected, the CFP® professional must consider the following information:

  a. The assumptions and estimates used to develop the recommendation;

  b. The basis for making the recommendation, including how the recommendation is designed to maximize the potential to meet the Client's goals, the anticipated material effects of the recommendation on the Client's financial and personal circumstances, and how the recommendation integrates relevant elements of the Client's personal and financial circumstances;

  c. The timing and priority of the recommendation; and

  d. Whether the recommendation is independent or must be implemented with another recommendation.

5. **Presenting the Financial Planning Recommendation(s)**

A CFP® professional must present to the Client the selected recommendations and the information that was required to be considered when developing the recommendation(s).

6. **Implementing the Financial Planning Recommendation(s)**

   a. **Addressing Implementation Responsibilities.** A CFP® professional must establish with the Client whether the CFP® professional has implementation responsibilities. When the CFP® professional has implementation responsibilities, the CFP® professional must communicate to the Client the recommendation(s) being implemented and the responsibilities of the CFP® professional, the Client, and any third-party with respect to implementation.

   b. **Identifying, Analyzing, and Selecting Actions, Products and Services.** A CFP® professional who has implementation responsibilities must identify and analyze actions, products, and services designed to implement the recommendations. The CFP® professional must consider the basis for each selection, which must include:

      i. How the action, product, or service is designed to implement the CFP® professional's recommendation; and

      ii. The advantages and disadvantages of the action, product, or service relative to reasonably available alternatives.

   c. **Recommending Actions, Products, and Services for Implementation.** A CFP® professional who has implementation responsibilities must recommend one or more actions, products and services to the Client. The CFP® professional must discuss with the Client the basis for selecting an action, product, or service, the timing and priority of implementing the action, product, or service, and describe any Conflicts of Interest concerning the action, product, or service.

   d. **Selecting and Implementing Actions, Products, or Services.** A CFP® professional who has implementation responsibilities must help the Client select and implement the actions, products, or services. The CFP® professional must discuss with the Client any Client selection that deviates from the actions, products, and services the CFP® professional recommended.

7. **Monitoring Progress and Updating**

   a. **Monitoring and Updating Responsibilities.** A CFP® professional must establish with the Client whether the CFP® professional has monitoring and updating responsibilities. When the CFP® professional has responsibilities for monitoring and updating, the CFP® professional must communicate to the Client:

      i. Which actions, products, and services are and are not subject to the CFP® professional's monitoring responsibility;

      ii. How and when the CFP® professional will monitor the actions, products, and services;

      iii. The Client's responsibility to inform the CFP® professional of any Material changes to the Client's qualitative and quantitative information;

      iv. The CFP® professional's responsibility to update the Financial Planning recommendations; and

      v. How and when the CFP® professional will update the Financial Planning recommendations.

   b. **Monitoring the Client's Progress.** A CFP® professional who has monitoring responsibility must analyze, at appropriate intervals, the progress toward achieving the Client's goals. The CFP® professional must review with the Client the results of the CFP® professional's analysis.

   c. **Obtaining Current Qualitative and Quantitative Information.** A CFP® professional who has monitoring responsibility must collaborate with the Client in an attempt to obtain current qualitative and quantitative information concerning the Client's personal and financial circumstances.

   d. **Updating Goals, Recommendations, or Implementation Decisions.** Where a CFP® professional has updating responsibility, and circumstances warrant changes to the Client's goals, recommendations, or selections of actions, products or services, the CFP® professional must update as appropriate in accordance with these *Practice Standards.*

D. DUTIES OWED TO FIRMS AND SUBORDINATES

1. **Use Reasonable Care When Supervising**

   A CFP® professional must exercise reasonable care when supervising persons acting under the CFP® professional's direction, including employees and other persons over whom the CFP® professional has responsibility, with a view toward preventing violations of applicable laws, rules, regulations, and these *Standards*.

2. **Comply with Lawful Objectives of CFP® Professional's Firm**

   A CFP® professional:

   a. Will be subject to discipline by CFP Board for violating policies and procedures of the CFP® Professional's Firm that do not conflict with these *Standards*.

   b. Will not be subject to discipline by CFP Board for violating policies and procedures of the CFP® Professional's Firm that conflict with these *Standards*.

3. **Provide Notice of Public Discipline**

   A CFP® professional must promptly advise the CFP® Professional's Firm, in writing, of any public discipline imposed by CFP Board.

E. DUTIES OWED TO CFP BOARD

1. **Definitions**. The following definitions apply:

   a. **Felony.** A felony offense, or for jurisdictions that do not differentiate between a felony and a misdemeanor, an offense punishable by a sentence of at least one-year imprisonment or a fine of at least $1,000.

   b. **Relevant Misdemeanor.** A criminal offense, that is not a Felony, for conduct involving fraud, theft, misrepresentation, other dishonest conduct, crimes of moral turpitude, violence, or a second (or more) alcohol and/or drug-related offense.

   c. **Regulatory Investigation.** An investigation initiated by a federal, state, local, or foreign governmental agency, self-regulatory organization, or other regulatory authority. A Regulatory Investigation does not include preliminary or routine regulatory inquiries or requests for information, deficiency letters, "blue sheet" requests or other trading questionnaires, or examinations.

   d. **Regulatory Action.** An action or proceeding initiated by a federal, state, local, or foreign governmental agency, self-regulatory organization, or other regulatory authority.

   e. **Civil Action.** A lawsuit, arbitration, or mediation.

   f. **Finding.** A finding includes an adverse final action and a consent decree in which the finding is neither admitted nor denied, but does not include a deficiency letter, examination report, memorandum of understanding, or similar informal resolution of a matter.

   g. **Minor Rule Violation.** A violation of a self-regulatory organization rule designated as a minor rule violation under a plan approved by the U.S. Securities and Exchange Commission. A rule violation may be designated as "minor" under a plan if the sanction imposed consists of a fine of $2,500 or less, and if the sanctioned person does not contest the fine.

2. **Refrain from Adverse Conduct.** A CFP® professional may not engage in conduct that reflects adversely on his or her integrity or fitness as a CFP® professional, upon the CFP® marks, or upon the profession. Such conduct includes, but is not limited to, conduct that results in:

   a. A Felony or Relevant Misdemeanor conviction, or admission into a program that defers or withholds the entry of a judgment of conviction for a Felony or Relevant Misdemeanor;

b. A Finding in a Regulatory Action or a Civil Action that the CFP® professional engaged in fraud, theft, misrepresentation, or other dishonest conduct;

c. A personal bankruptcy or business bankruptcy filing or adjudication where the CFP® professional was a Control Person of the business, unless the CFP® professional can rebut the presumption that the bankruptcy demonstrates an inability to manage responsibly the CFP® professional's or the business's financial affairs;

d. A federal tax lien on property owned by the CFP® professional, unless the CFP® professional can rebut the presumption that the federal tax lien demonstrates an inability to manage responsibly the CFP® professional's financial affairs; or

e. A non-federal tax lien, judgment lien, or civil judgment that has not been satisfied within a reasonable amount of time unless the CFP® professional can rebut the presumption that the non-federal tax lien, judgment lien, or civil judgment demonstrates an inability to manage responsibly the CFP® professional's financial affairs.

3. **Reporting.** A CFP® professional must provide written notice to CFP Board within 30 calendar days after the CFP® professional, or an entity over which the CFP® professional was a Control Person, has:

a. Been charged with, convicted of, or admitted into a program that defers or withholds the entry of a judgment or conviction for, a Felony or Relevant Misdemeanor;

b. Been named as a subject of, or whose conduct is mentioned adversely in, a Regulatory Investigation or Regulatory Action alleging failure to comply with the laws, rules, or regulations governing Professional Services;

c. Had conduct mentioned adversely in a Finding in a Regulatory Action involving failure to comply with the laws, rules, or regulations governing Professional Services (except a Regulatory Action involving a Minor Rule Violation in a Regulatory Action brought by a self-regulatory organization);

d. Had conduct mentioned adversely in a Civil Action alleging failure to comply with the laws, rules, or regulations governing Professional Services;

e. Become aware of an adverse arbitration award or civil judgment, or a settlement agreement, in a Civil Action alleging failure to comply with the laws, rules, or regulations governing Professional Services, where the conduct of the CFP® professional, or an entity over which the CFP® professional was a Control Person, was mentioned adversely, other than a settlement for an amount less than $15,000;

f. Had conduct mentioned adversely in a Civil Action alleging fraud, theft, misrepresentation, or other dishonest conduct;

g. Been the subject of a Finding of fraud, theft, misrepresentation, or other dishonest conduct in a Regulatory Action or Civil Action;

h. Become aware of an adverse arbitration award or civil judgment, or a settlement agreement in a Civil Action alleging fraud, theft, misrepresentation, or other dishonest conduct, where the conduct of the CFP® professional, or an entity over which the CFP® professional was a Control Person, was mentioned adversely;

i. Had a professional license, certification, or membership suspended, revoked, or materially restricted because of a violation of rules or standards of conduct;

j. Been terminated for cause from employment or permitted to resign in lieu of termination when the cause of the termination or resignation involved allegations of dishonesty, unethical conduct, or compliance failures;

   k. Been named as the subject of, or been identified as the broker/adviser of record in, any written, customer-initiated complaint that alleged the CFP® professional was involved in:

      i. Forgery, theft, misappropriation, or conversion of Financial Assets;

      ii. Sales practice violations and contained a claim for compensation of $5,000 or more; or

      iii. Sales practice violations and settled for an amount of $15,000 or more.

   l. Filed for or been the subject of a personal bankruptcy or business bankruptcy where the CFP® professional was a Control Person;

   m. Received notice of a federal tax lien on property owned by the CFP® professional; or

   n. Failed to satisfy a non-federal tax lien, judgment lien, or civil judgment within one year of its date of entry, unless payment arrangements have been agreed upon by all parties.

4. **Provide Narrative Statement.** The written notice must include a narrative statement that accurately and completely describes the Material facts and the outcome or status of the reportable matter.

5. **Cooperation.** A CFP® professional may not make false or misleading representations to CFP Board or obstruct CFP Board in the performance of its duties. A CFP® professional must cooperate fully with CFP Board's requests, investigations, disciplinary proceedings, and disciplinary decisions. Cooperation includes providing to CFP Board all requested information and documents that are in the CFP® professional's possession, custody, or control. A CFP® professional must use best efforts to obtain requested documents, not already provided to CFP Board, from those entities or persons whom the CFP® professional Controls, including the CFP® professional's attorney. If the requested information and documents are not provided, the CFP® professional must explain the efforts undertaken to obtain them, and why those efforts were unsuccessful.

6. **Compliance with *Terms and Conditions of Certification and License*.** A CFP® professional must comply with the *Terms and Conditions of Certification and License*.

F. PROHIBITION ON CIRCUMVENTION

A CFP® professional may not do indirectly, or through or by another person, any act or thing that the *Code and Standards* prohibit the CFP® professional from doing directly.

GLOSSARY

CFP® Professional's Firm(s). Any entity on behalf of which a CFP® professional provides Professional Services to a Client, and that has the authority to exercise control over the CFP® professional's activities, including the CFP® professional's employer, broker-dealer, registered investment adviser, insurance company, and insurance agency.

Client. Any person, including a natural person, business organization, or legal entity, to whom the CFP® professional provides or agrees to provide Professional Services pursuant to an Engagement.

Conflict of Interest. (a) When a CFP® professional's interests (including the interests of the CFP® Professional's Firm) are adverse to the CFP® professional's duties to a Client, or (b) When a CFP® professional has duties to one Client that are adverse to another Client.

Control. The power, directly or indirectly, to direct the management or policies of the entity at the relevant time, through ownership, by contract, or otherwise.

Control Person. A person who has Control.

Engagement. An oral or written agreement, arrangement, or understanding.

Family. Grandparent, parent, stepparent, father-in-law/mother-in-law, uncle/aunt, spouse, former spouse, spousal equivalent, domestic partner, brother/sister, stepsibling, brother-in-law/sister-in-law, cousin, son/daughter, stepchild, son-in-law/daughter-in law, nephew/niece, grandchild, and any other person the CFP® professional, directly or indirectly, supports financially to a material extent.

Financial Advice.

A. A communication that, based on its content, context, and presentation, would reasonably be viewed as a recommendation that the Client take or refrain from taking a particular course of action with respect to:

1. The development or implementation of a financial plan;

2. The value of or the advisability of investing in, purchasing, holding, or selling Financial Assets;

3. Investment policies or strategies, portfolio composition, the management of Financial Assets, or other financial matters;

4. The selection and retention of other persons to provide financial or Professional Services to the Client; or

B. The exercise of discretionary authority over the Financial Assets of a Client.

The determination of whether Financial Advice has been provided is an objective rather than subjective inquiry. The more individually tailored the communication is to the Client, the more likely the communication will be viewed as Financial Advice. The provision of services or the furnishing or making available of marketing materials, general financial education materials, or general financial communications that a reasonable CFP® professional would not view as Financial Advice, does not constitute Financial Advice.

Financial Assets. Securities, insurance products, real estate, bank instruments, commodities contracts, derivative contracts, collectibles, or other financial products.

Financial Planning. A collaborative process that helps maximize a Client's potential for meeting life goals through Financial Advice that integrates relevant elements of the Client's personal and financial circumstances.

Material. Information is material when a reasonable Client or prospective Client would consider the information important in making a decision.

Professional Services. Financial Advice and related activities and services that are offered or provided, including, but not limited to, Financial Planning, legal, accounting, or business planning services.

Related Party. A person or business entity (including a trust) whose receipt of Sales-Related Compensation a reasonable CFP® professional would view as benefiting the CFP® professional or the CFP® Professional's Firm, including, for example, as a result of the CFP® professional's ownership stake in the business entity. There is a rebuttable presumption that a Related Party includes:

a. **Family Members.** A member of the CFP® professional's Family and any business entity that the Family or members of the Family Control; and

b. **Business Entities.** A business entity that the CFP® professional or the CFP® Professional's Firm Controls, or that is Controlled by or is under common Control with, the CFP® Professional's Firm.

Scope of Engagement. The Professional Services to be provided pursuant to an Engagement.

CFP BOARD

CERTIFIED FINANCIAL PLANNER BOARD OF STANDARDS, INC.

1425 K St NW #800 Washington DC 20005
p 800-487-1497 | f 202-379-2299
mail@CFPBoard.org | CFP.net

©2018 Certified Financial Planner Board of Standards, Inc. All rights reserved.

Glossary

12b-1 fee *A fee that pays for the services of brokers who sell mutual funds and who maintain the client relationship*

Above-the-line deduction (deduction for AGI) *An above-the-line deduction that reduces gross income directly*

Absolute assignment *All life insurance policy ownership rights are transferred to a designated assignee*

Abstract thinking *The third phase of a client's thinking process in establishing financial direction, in which a client becomes aware of the consequences of financial actions and understands how day-to-day savings and consumption decisions impact a financial plan*

Accelerated death benefit rider *Allows the policyowner to receive a portion of the policy's death benefit during the insured's lifetime if the insured contracts a terminal illness*

Accidental bodily injury *Only the injury incurred is accidental*

Accidental death benefit rider *A policy rider that pays the beneficiary an additional death benefit if the insured dies accidentally, as defined in the rider*

Accumulation units *Units of measurement that, when combined, equal the total account value of a variable annuity*

Accuracy-related penalty *A penalty of 20% of the portion of the tax underpayment attributable to negligence, substantial understatement of tax, or substantial valuation misstatement without intent to defraud*

Active listening *Paying full attention to what clients are saying and responding by paraphrasing their comments, thus gaining a full understanding of what clients are attempting to communicate*

Active risk retention *One is fully aware of the chance for loss and consciously plans to retain all or part of the risk*

Activities of daily living (ADLs) *Eating, bathing, dressing, transferring from bed to chair, toileting, and continence*

Actual cash value (ACV) *The depreciated value of the insured property*

Actual cash value *Calculated as replacement cost minus functional depreciation*

Actuary *An expert in the fields of mathematics, statistics, and probability theory; responsible for predicting losses for various risk pools, calculating required reserves, and producing premium rates*

Additional living expenses *The difference between the cost of living in temporary arrangements and the normal costs that would have been incurred had there been no loss*

Additional Medicare tax *A Medicare tax of 0.9% paid by taxpayers above certain income thresholds that is in addition to the 2.9% Medicare tax*

Adhesion *A characteristic of insurance that means insurance is a take-it-or-leave-it contract. The proposed insured must accept (or adhere to) the contract as written without any bargaining over the terms and conditions*

Adjusted gross estate *Gross estate less deductions provided for by law in recognition that the entire value of the gross estate will not be transferred to the heirs due to costs, debts, and certain other deductions*

Adjusted gross income *A determination peculiar to individual taxpayers that represents gross income less business expenses, expenses attributable to the production of rent or royalty income, the allowed capital loss deduction, and certain personal expenses (deductions for AGI)*

Administrator *In the event a decedent dies intestate (without a valid will) or where an executor cannot be appointed by the probate court, the court appoints an administrator with powers called letters of administration, which enable the administrator to perform duties set down in the laws of intestacy*

Adult day care *Basic assistance and supervision provided outside the home usually during the primary caregiver's working hours*

Adverse selection *The increased tendency of higher-than-average risks (people who need insurance the most) purchasing or renewing insurance policies*

Age-based profit-sharing plan *A profit-sharing plan with an age-weighted factor in the allocation formula*

Agent *Legal representative of the insurer that has authority to enter into agreements on its behalf*

Aleatory *A characteristic of insurance meaning that monetary values exchanged by each party in an insurance agreement are unequal*

Alternative minimum tax (AMT) *System designed to ensure that individuals with large deductions and other tax benefits pay at least a minimum amount of tax*

American depositary receipts (ADRs) *Certificates issued by U.S. banks representing ownership in shares of stock of a foreign company that are held on deposit in a bank in the firm's home country*

American Opportunity Tax Credit *A tax credit available for qualified tuition, enrollment fees, books, and course materials for the first four years of post-secondary education for the taxpayer, spouse, or dependent*

Amortization table *TVM tool used primarily to illustrate the amortization, or extinguishments, of debt. The table presents the number of years of indebtedness, the beginning balance, level payments, interest amount, principal reduction, and ending balance of indebtedness.*

Annual exclusion *A result of a de minimis rule by Congress to eliminate the need for taxpayers to keep an account of, or report, small gifts. All individuals are allowed to gift, tax-free, up to $14,000 (for 2016) per donee per year.*

Annual Renewable Term (ART) *Term insurance issued for one year; renewable for subsequent periods to a stated age without evidence of insurability*

Annuitization *An irrevocable exchange of a lump-sum amount for a periodic income stream*

Annuity due *Deposits or payments are made at the beginning of each period*

Annuity *A series of deposits or payments of equal size deposited over a finite number of equal-interval periods*

Anomalies *Occurrences in the stock market that are not supported by the concept of the efficient market hypothesis*

Antitrust legislation *Laws passed to protect consumers from monopolistic price practices and to protect investors by promoting fair competition*

Any occupation *Definition of disability in which an insured is considered totally disabled if the duties of any occupation cannot be performed*

Apparent authority *The insured is led to believe that the agent has authority, either express or implied, where no such authority actually exists*

Arithmetic mean *A measure of investment return that is the result of averaging periodic returns*

Articles of organization *Document filed in compliance with state law to create a limited liability company (LLC)*

Asset allocation *The distribution of investments in a portfolio by asset class*

Asset-accumulation phase *Life cycle phase through which clients pass; usually begins between the ages of 20 and 25 and lasts until about age 50, characterized by limited excess funds for investing, high degree of debt, and low net worth*

Asset-backed securities *Bundled-together securities issued against some type of asset-linked debts, such as mortgages*

Assets *Property owned completely or partially by the client*

Assisted living facilities *Apartment-style housing combined with support services and basic health care*

At-risk rule *A taxpayer can deduct losses only to the extent of the amount the taxpayer has at risk in the investment (amount invested). Losses in amounts in excess of the amount at risk in the investment are suspended until the taxpayer increases the amount invested in the passive activity, either by additional investment or by a profit from the activity.*

Attorney-in-fact *The person designated by the principal in a power of attorney to act in place of the principal on the principal's behalf*

Audit *When the IRS examines a tax return "to determine if income, expenses, and credits are being reported accurately" (Publication 556)*

Automatic premium loan *Directs the insurance company to pay an overdue premium by making a loan against the policy's cash value if the overdue premium remains unpaid upon the expiration of the grace period*

Average indexed monthly earnings (AIME) *Dollar amount used to calculate Social Security benefits. Actual earnings are adjusted (or indexed) to calculate AIME.*

Back-end load *A sales charge incurred upon the sale or redemption of mutual fund shares rather than at the time of purchase*

Bailee *A party that holds the property of another*

Bait-and-switch promotion *Deceptive sales practice in which a business advertises a low price for an item in order to engage customers and then advise them that the advertised item is no longer available or is of substandard quality, attempting to entice the customers to purchase a more expensive product*

Balance sheet *A financial statement that reports a business's assets, liabilities, and net worth on a given date*

Bankruptcy   *The financial condition when a debtor is determined by the court to be unable to pay creditors*

Barbell strategy   *Portfolio immunization strategy that uses a portfolio of short- and long-term bonds*

Basic standard deduction   *The amount allowed all taxpayers who do not itemize their deductions*

Behavioral finance   *A branch of personal finance that proposes psychology-based theories to explain investor behavior and stock market anomalies*

Below-the-line deduction (deduction from AGI)   *Deduction that is allowed to reduce adjusted gross income*

Bend points   *The three separate percentages of portions of the AIME that are summed to arrive at the PIA*

Benefit period   *The number of days that Medicare covers care in hospitals and skilled nursing facilities*

Benefits of personal financial planning
- *Creates a framework for feedback, evaluation, and control*
- *Develops an improved awareness of financial choices*
- *Establishes measurable goals and expectations*
- *Goals identified are more likely to be achieved*
- *Helps to clearly identify risk exposures*
- *Is proactive rather than reactive*
- *Provides an opportunity for an increased commitment to financial goals*

Best efforts agreement   *Equity underwriting in which the firm agrees to repurchase any securities remaining after the initial offering is made by the underwriter*

Beta   *A commonly used measure of systematic risk that is derived from regression analysis*

Beyond a reasonable doubt   *A measure or degree of proof; with regard to disciplinary rules and procedures, beyond a reasonable doubt means the evidence as a whole shows what it was intended to prove with a probability of 99% or more*

Blackout period   *The period of time beginning when Social Security benefits to the surviving spouse are discontinued (usually when the last child reaches age 16) and ending when the spouse begins to receive Social Security retirement benefits at age 60 or later*

Blue-chip stocks   *Stock issued by older, well-established companies that maintain the ability to pay dividends both in years the company has income and in years the company has losses*

Board of directors   *The governing body of a corporation whose members are elected by shareholders*

Bodily injury by accidental means   *Requires accidental injury by accidental means*

Bond indenture agreement   *The legal document that sets forth the repayment schedules, restrictions, and promises between the issuer of a corporate bond and the borrower*

Boot   *Property (other than like-kind property) that qualifies as a tax gain when received in a property exchange*

Broker   *Legal representative of the insured who can offer products from many insurers*

Budgeting   *A process of projecting, monitoring, adjusting, and controlling future income and expenditures*

Bullet strategy   *Portfolio immunization strategy that uses a portfolio of bonds with similar maturities*

Burden of proof   *The requirement of proving facts to a certain degree of probability. With regard to disciplinary rules and procedures, there are three distinct burdens of proof: (1) preponderance of the evidence, (2) clear and convincing evidence, and (3) evidence beyond a reasonable doubt.*

Business cycles   *Swings in total national output, income, and employment marked by widespread expansion or contraction in many sectors of the economy*

Business overhead expense insurance   *Helps a business meet its liabilities in the event a significant income producer becomes disabled*

Business risk   *An unsystematic risk based on predictability of operating income for a specific business; dependent upon management and industry characteristics*

Buy-sell agreement   *An arrangement in which a deceased owner's share of a business is purchased by using the life insurance proceeds from a policy on the deceased owner's life*

Bypass trust (B trust)   *Avoids inclusion in, or bypasses, the surviving spouse's gross estate; the assets transfer to a future generation free of estate taxes; the purpose of a bypass trust is to take advantage of the applicable credit amount*

C corporation   *A business entity created by state law that is separate and distinct from its shareholders*

Call option   *A derivative that gives the holder the right to purchase the underlying asset, generally a stock, at a specified price within a specified period*

Call provision   *Right to redeem the bond issue before maturity*

Capital appreciation   *The form of return the investor receives when a company chooses to retain the earnings and invest in additional projects; appreciation of the stock*

Capital asset pricing model (CAPM)   *An asset pricing model that developed from Markowitz's efficient frontier and from the introduction of a risk-free asset*

Capital asset   *Broadly speaking, all assets are capital except those specifically excluded by the Internal Revenue Code; excluded assets include property held for resale in the normal course of business (inventory), trade accounts and notes receivable, and depreciable property and real estate used in a trade or business*

Capital formation *Production of buildings, machinery, tools, and other equipment that will help economic participants produce in the future*

Capital loss *A loss from the sale or exchange of a capital asset*

Capital needs analysis *The process of calculating the amount of investment capital needed at retirement to maintain the desired lifestyle and mitigate the impact of inflation during the retirement years*

Capital preservation (CP) model *A capital needs analysis method that assumes that at life expectancy, the client has exactly the same account balance as the client did at retirement*

Capital retention approach *Provides a death benefit amount that, along with the family's other assets, is sufficient to provide a level of investment income that covers the projected needs of the family without having to invade the death benefit principal*

Cash accounts *A type of brokerage account that requires all securities purchased by the investor to be paid for in full without any indebtedness*

Cash flow timeline *TVM analysis tool that graphically depicts cash inflows (cash received) and cash outflows (cash deposited or invested) over a certain period (the term)*

Cash flows from financing *Cash inflows from a business's issuance of additional debt (bonds) or equity (stocks) and cash outflows for the repayment of debt (principal)*

Cash flows from investing *Cash inflows or outflows resulting from a business's buying and selling of investments*

Cash flows from operations *Cash inflows or outflows that are generated by a company's actual business activities as opposed to incidental activities such as investing or borrowing*

Cash refund annuity *When an annuitant dies before periodic payments equal or exceed the price paid for the annuity, the insurer pays a lump sum equal to the difference between the price paid and the total payments received by the annuitant*

Cash value *Increases over the life of the policy as long as the premiums are paid according to the contract*

Certified Financial Planner Board of Standards, Inc. *An independent professional regulatory organization that regulates financial planners*

CFP Board's Board of Directors *The governing board for the certified financial planning profession*

CFP Board's Disciplinary and Ethics Commission *A subsidiary board of CFP Board that interprets and applies the Code*

CFP Board's Standards of Professional Conduct *The set of principles of conduct that regulates behavior of CFP® certificants*

CFP® certificant *An individual who is currently certified by CFP Board*

Change in demand *This occurs when the entire curve shifts to the right or left as the quantity demanded at each price level changes*

Changes in quantity demanded *The movements along the demand curve in response to a change in price*

Charitable deduction *A charitable contribution made as a gift to a qualified organization*

Charitable lead trust (CLT) *A split-interest trust where a charity is the income beneficiary, and there is a noncharitable remainderman*

Charitable remainder trust (CRT) *A split-interest trust; if created during life, the income goes to one or more parties, usually the grantor, or grantor and spouse for life, and upon the income beneficiary's death, the principal (remainder) is transferred to a charity; if the CRT is created testamentary, the usual income beneficiary is the spouse for life*

Chronically ill individual *A person who has an illness or injury resulting in the inability to perform, without substantial assistance, at least two of the six activities of daily living for a period expected to last at least 90 days*

Clear and convincing evidence *A measure or degree of proof; with regard to disciplinary rules and procedures, clear and convincing evidence means the evidence as a whole shows what it was intended to prove with a probability of 75% or more*

Client data collection questionnaire *A survey used by financial planners to gather internal data from clients, such as their tolerance for risk and their personal perception of their financial situation, as well as tax-related data, Social Security numbers, information relating to their dependents, and so on*

Closed-end fund *A type of investment company whose shares trade in the same manner that publicly traded stocks trade in the secondary market*

Code of ethics *A set of principles of conduct that governs a group of individuals and usually requires conformity to professional standards of conduct*

Codicil *A document that amends or revises a prior will*

Coefficient of determination (R2) *A modern portfolio theory statistic that indicates the percentage change in a portfolio or mutual fund that can be explained by changes in the market*

Coefficient of variation *A relative measure of total risk per unit of expected return*

Coinsurance *The cost sharing of covered health care expenses between the insured and the insurer*

Coinsurance *The percentage of financial responsibility the insured and the insurer must share under the policy*

COLA *Cost-of-living adjustment provided for Social Security benefits*

Collateral assignment split dollar   *An arrangement in which an employer is obligated to make interest-free loans to the employee in the amount of the policy premium; the employee then makes a collateral assignment of the policy to the employer for the amount of premium paid by the employer*

Collateral assignment   *A life insurance policy is transferred to a creditor as security for a loan or debt*

Collateral source rule   *Damages assessed against a negligent party should not be reduced simply because the injured party has other sources of recovery available*

Collateral trust bonds   *Bonds secured by securities issued by other companies*

Collateralized mortgage obligations (CMOs)   *Mortgage-backed securities that are divided into tranches*

College Savings Plan   *A type of QTP similar to Coverdell Education Savings Accounts (Coverdell ESAs) where the owner of the account (the parent or grandparent of the student) contributes cash to the account so that the contributions can grow tax-deferred and, hopefully, realize a higher return on the investment than could be achieved outside of the plan*

Collision   *Auto insurance coverage that protects the insured against upset and collision damages*

Commercial package policy (CPP)   *Property and liability coverage combined into a single policy used by businesses*

Commingling   *The act of mixing property (usually funds) belonging to one party with property belong to another party*

Common law liability   *Liability based on breach of contract, tort, or fraud*

Common stock   *Ownership interest in a company*

Community property   *A regime where married individuals own an equal undivided interest in all wealth accumulated during marriage*

Complements   *Products that are usually consumed jointly; an increase in the price of one will likely decrease the demand for the other*

Compound interest   *Interest earned on interest*

Comprehensive (other-than-collision)   *Auto insurance coverage that protects the insured's auto against perils out of the insured's control, such as missiles or falling objects, fire, theft, earthquake, hail, flood, and vandalism*

Comprehensive major medical   *Stand-alone coverage that provides a broad range of medical services and high limits of coverage*

Concealment   *When the insured is silent about a fact that is material to the risk*

Conditional   *Insurer is only obligated to compensate the insured if certain conditions are met*

Conditionally renewable   *Cannot be canceled by the insurer during the policy term, but insurer may refuse to renew the contract for another term if certain conditions exist*

Conflict of interest   *Exists when a certificant's financial, business, property, and/or personal interests, relationships, or circumstances impair the certificant's ability to offer objective advice, recommendations, or services*

Conservation/protection phase   *Life cycle phase through which clients pass characterized by an increase in cash flow, assets, and net worth, with some decrease in the proportional use of debt*

Consolidated Omnibus Budget Reconciliation Act (COBRA)   *Requires certain employers to provide previously covered persons with the same coverage received before discontinuation of coverage*

Consolidation loan   *A loan that provides borrowers with a way to consolidate various types of federal student loans with separate repayment schedules into one loan*

Consumer Price Index (CPI)   *A price index that measures the cost of a market basket of consumer goods and services purchased for day-to-day living*

Consumption movements   *Economic variables that fluctuate during the business cycle; describe changes in consumer purchases*

Contingent beneficiary   *An individual, group, or entity designated to receive the policy proceeds if the primary beneficiary predeceases the insured*

Contraction phase   *One of the two general business cycle phases characterized by a fall in business sales, decreased growth of the gross domestic product, and increased unemployment*

Contractual agreements   *Often include guarantees at the time of sale; often known as warranties*

Convertible bonds   *Hybrid securities that permit the holder to acquire shares of common stock from the issuing company by exchanging the currently held debt security for a specific number of common stock shares*

Convertible preferred stock   *Preferred stock that includes the right to convert preferred stock into a specific number of common shares at the option of the stockholder*

Convertible   *A term policy that may be exchanged for a cash value life insurance policy without evidence of insurability*

Coordination of benefits (COB) clause   *Prevents an insured from receiving greater than 100% of the cost of health care received when covered by multiple insurance policies*

Co-payments   *In health insurance policies, amounts an insured must pay in addition to the deductible to receive certain covered services*

Correlation coefficient (R)   *A statistical measure of the direction and strength of the relationship between two sets of data*

Correspondence audit *An audit conducted almost entirely by written correspondence and telephone contact with the taxpayer and typically involves simple issues*

Cost-of-living adjustment (COLA) rider *Increases benefits being received by the policyowner each year; based on an index, such as the CPI*

Country risk *An unsystematic risk associated with the potential adverse effect of changes in a country's laws or political situation*

Coupon payments *Interest payments paid to the bondholder on a semiannual basis and based on a percentage of the par value of the bond*

Covariance *A measure of the extent to which two variables move in a predictable manner to one another, either positively or negatively*

Coverdell Education Savings Account (Coverdell ESA) *An investment account established with cash contributions that grow tax-free within the account; money withdrawn from the account remains free from tax or penalty if the funds are used for higher education expenses; if not, the earnings are subject to income tax and a 10% penalty*

Cross-purchase agreement *Each owner of the corporation purchases an insurance policy on the other shareholders; the death proceeds are used to purchase a deceased owner's shares*

Cumulative preferred stock *Preferred stock that requires receipt of previously unpaid preferred dividends before common shareholders receive dividend payments*

Cumulative voting *A shareholder casts votes equal to the number of vacant positions on the board of directors multiplied by the number of shares owned, allocated in any way the shareholder wishes*

Current assets *Assets expected to be converted to cash within one year*

Current assumption whole life *Uses new-money interest rates and current mortality assumptions to determine cash values*

Current liability *Debt owed by the client that is expected to be paid off within the year (current ≤ 12 months)*

Current yield *A bond's annual coupon payment divided by the current market price*

Custodial care *Provides assistance with the regular tasks of daily life, such as eating, dressing, bathing, and taking medications*

Cyclical stocks *Stock of companies that tend to prosper in expanding economies and do poorly during down business cycles*

Debentures *Unsecured corporate bonds whose holders have no claim to specific assets of the issuing corporation*

Declaration date *Date on which a corporation's board of directors declares a dividend payment creating an obligation on the company to make a dividend payment to shareholders*

Decreasing term *Term insurance that features a level premium with a decreasing death benefit*

Deductible *A stated amount of money the insured is required to pay on a loss before the insurer will make any payments under the policy*

Default risk *An unsystematic risk associated with the inability of a business to service its debt*

Defensive stocks *Stock of companies that are relatively unaffected by general fluctuations in the economy*

Deferred annuity *Provides income at some date in the future*

Deferred compensation plan *A nonqualified plan that is a contractual agreement between the employer and selected employees; takes the form of either salary reduction or salary continuation. Compensation is deferred until retirement, disability, death, or termination of employment, but usually only at normal retirement age.*

Deferred income annuities (DIA) *Guarantee income for life or a certain period of time, however, the future income start dates are chosen at contract issuance*

Deficit spending *Occurs when governmental expenditures exceed the government's tax collections*

Defined benefit pension plan *A retirement plan that specifies the benefits that each employee receives at retirement. Defined benefit plans actuarially determine the benefit to be paid at normal retirement age.*

Defined contribution plan *A retirement plan that specifies the annual employer current contribution. The amount of benefit received by an employee depends on the account balance at retirement.*

Defined-period approach *Long-term care coverage provided for a specified period following an elimination period*

Deflation *The opposite of inflation; it occurs when the general level of prices is falling*

Demand curve *The graphic depiction that illustrates the relationship between a particular good's price and the quantity demanded*

Demand *The quantity of a particular good that people are willing to buy; heavily dependent on price*

Dependency period *The period of time during which others (the deceased's spouse, children and, in some cases, parents) would have been dependent on the deceased*

Dependent *An individual who meets the definition of a qualifying child or a qualifying relative and who can be claimed by a taxpayer for an exemption on an income tax return*

Depression *A persistent recession that brings a severe decline in economic activity*

Derivatives *Securities whose value is based on the value of some other security*

Determination Letter   A written statement issued by an IRS district director that applies the principles and precedents announced by the National Office to a given set of facts

Direct bequest (to a spouse)   The first spouse who dies leaves everything outright to the surviving spouse

Direct investing   A process of investing where investors purchase actual securities

Direct negligence   Involves acts or omissions directly attributable to an individual

Directors   Individuals who, acting as a group known as the board of directors, manage the business affairs of a corporation

Disability benefit   Social Security benefit available to recipients who have a severe physical or mental impairment that is expected to prevent them from performing substantial work for at least one year or result in death, and who have the sufficient amount of Social Security credits

Disability income insurance   A type of insurance that provides a replacement income while the insured is unable to work because of illness or injury

Disciplinary Rules and Procedures   The rules and regulations for disciplinary proceedings against CFP Board certificants

Disclaimer clause   A common clause in a decedent's will that allows property to pass from one party to another without gift tax consequences

Disclaimer   The refusal of the receipt of an estate; the use of disclaimers allows an individual to disclaim or renounce receiving any part of an estate

Discount rate   Interest rate charged by the Federal Reserve on a loan made to a member bank

Discretionary expenses   Luxuries or expenses over which the client has complete control

Discriminant Index Function (DIF) system   A mathematical technique used to classify tax returns as to their examination potential

Disinflation   A decline in the rate of inflation

Distribution/gifting phase   Life cycle phase through which clients pass characterized by excess relative cash flows, low debt, and high relative net worth

Dividend reinvestment plans (DRIPs)   Dividends are automatically reinvested into the company's stock without the use of a broker

Dividend yield   The measure of a security's annual dividend payment as a percentage of the current market price

Dividends   Distributions of cash or additional shares of stock paid to the shareholders of a corporation

Dividends-received deduction (DRD)   A deduction for dividends received by one corporation from another corporation. The amount of the DRD is based on the percentage owned by the corporation receiving the dividend.

Dollar cost averaging   The process of purchasing securities over time by investing a predetermined amount at regular intervals

Dollar-weighted returns   A method of determining the internal rate of return that an individual investor earned on the basis of the investor's particular cash flow into and out of the portfolio

Double taxation of dividends   The taxation of income at the corporate level and the subsequent taxation of dividend distributions at the individual shareholder's level

Dow Jones Industrial Average (DJIA)   A financial index that is a price-weighted average of 30 leading industrial stocks used to measure the status of the equity market

Durable feature   The power survives incapacity and disability of the principal

Durable goods   Products that are not consumed or quickly disposed of and can be used for several years, such as automobiles, furniture, and computers

Durable power of attorney issued either for health care or for property   A written document enabling the principal to designate another person or persons to act as the principal's attorney-in-fact

Duration   Provides a time-weighted measure of a security's cash flows in terms of payback

Dwelling   Residential structure covered under a homeowners policy

Dynamic risk   A risk that results from changes in society or the economy (e.g., inflation)

Efficient frontier   Consists of investment portfolios with the highest expected return for a given level of risk

Efficient market hypothesis   A theory that suggests that securities are priced fairly and efficiently by the market, and investors are unable to consistently outperform the market on a risk-adjusted basis

Elimination period   The amount of time that must pass before benefits are paid

Emotional intelligence   The ability to recognize and assess emotional expressions in themselves and their clients

Employer's Educational Assistance Program   Under this program, an employer can pay for an employee's undergraduate tuition, enrollment fees, books, supplies, and equipment while these employer benefits are excluded from the employee's income up to $5,250

Endorsement split dollar   An arrangement in which the employer owns the policy and is responsible for making all premium payments; when the insured employee dies, the employer receives a portion of the death benefit equal to its premium outlay, with the remainder of the death proceeds payable to the employee's designated beneficiary

Engagement letter   A tool of communication between client and financial planner that sets down in writing the information about any agreements or understandings obtained at client/planner meetings, including the plan of action for developing a financial plan, the expected outcome of the engagement, and the method of compensation

Entire contract clause   Maintains that the life insurance policy and the policyowner's application compose the complete life insurance contract

Entity purchase agreement   The corporation owns policies on the lives of the shareholders; at the death of a shareholder, the corporation buys the deceased shareholder's interest in the company with the insurance proceeds

Equilibrium   The state of the market where quantity demanded equals quantity supplied

Equity indexed annuities (EIAs)   Based on the simple concept of returns that are equal to a percentage, or participation rate, of a popular market index (e.g., S&P 500)

Equity mutual funds   A mutual fund that invests primarily in equity or ownership type securities, such as preferred stock and common stock

Equity-indexed universal life (EIUL)   A universal life policy that offers an upside potential for cash value growth with limited downside risk

Errors and omissions insurance   Provides protection against loss from negligent acts, errors, and omissions by the insured

Ethics   The discipline of dealing with the moral principles or values that guide an individual

Exchange rate risk   A systematic risk due to the potential change in the relationship between the value of the dollar (or investor's currency) and the value of the foreign currency during the period of investment; also known as foreign currency risk

Exchange   Transfer of property for property other than money

Exchange-traded fund (ETF)   A type of investment company whose investment objective is to achieve the same return as a particular market index

Exclusion   Income exempt from tax and not included in a taxpayer's gross income

Ex-dividend date   The date on which the market reflects the dividend payment

Executive bonus plan   A discriminatory fringe benefit that provides life insurance to key employees with tax-deductible dollars

Exercise price   The price at which an underlying stock may be sold (put) or purchased (call) by the holder of an option

Expansion phase   One of the two general business cycle phases characterized by a rise in business sales, growth of the gross domestic product, and a decline in unemployment

Expected Family Contribution (EFC)   A formula that indicates how much of a student's family's resources ought to be available to assist in paying for the student's college education

Expense ratio   An indication of the annual fund expenses, stated as a percentage of total assets

Express authority   The actual authority an insurance company gives representatives (agents) via the agent's written contract

External environment   The whole complex of factors independent of the client that influence the financial planning process, including economic, legal, social, technological, political, and taxation factors

External environmental analysis   The process of identifying and monitoring the environment in which a client lives and the opportunities and threats that are present

Failure-to-file penalty   A civil penalty imposed on taxpayers and tax return preparers who fail to file tax returns according to the requirements of tax law

Failure-to-pay-tax penalty   A civil penalty imposed on taxpayers who, without reasonable cause, fail to pay the tax shown on their return

Fair market value (FMV)   The price at which an exchange will take place between a willing buyer and a willing seller, both informed and neither under duress to exchange

Family benefit   Social Security benefit available to certain family members of workers eligible for retirement or disability benefits

Family limited partnership (FLP)   A limited partnership of family members that is used to generate valuation discounts for estate and gift tax purposes on the transfer of the limited interest in the partnership

Federal estate tax   An excise tax on the right to transfer assets by a decedent

Federal Perkins Loan   Campus-based, low-interest student loan provided to undergraduate and graduate students that have exceptional financial need—that is, very low EFCs

Federal Reserve (Fed)   The banking and financial system developed under the Federal Reserve Act of 1913; it makes the basic policy decisions that regulate the country's money and banking systems

Federal Reserve discount rate   The rate at which Federal Reserve member banks can borrow funds to meet reserve requirements; the Fed will lower the discount rate when it wants to increase the money supply

Federal Supplemental Education Opportunity Grant (FSEOG) *Campus-based student financial aid grant awarded to undergraduate students with low EFCs that gives priority to students who receive federal Pell Grants*

Federal Trade Commission (FTC) *The federal organization created in 1914 to keep competition free and fair and to protect U.S. consumers*

Federal Work-Study Program *Campus-based student financial aid program that enables undergraduate and graduate students to earn money for education expenses through jobs that pay at least current minimum wages but do not exceed the award received through the program*

Fee simple *The complete individual ownership of property with all rights associated with outright ownership, such as the right to use, sell, gift, alienate, or convey*

FICA (Federal Insurance Contributions Act) *The law allowing Social Security taxes, including Medicare, to be deducted from paychecks*

Fiduciary *Someone who acts in utmost good faith, in a manner he believes is in the best interest of the client*

Field audit *An audit conducted for complex individual returns with business or other financial activities. IRS revenue agents handle field audits, as opposed to office audits, which are conducted by less-experienced tax auditors and are typically conducted at the taxpayer's business or wherever the taxpayer's books are maintained.*

Final expense fund *Fund requiring immediate access by survivors to pay for final expenses and debts of the decedent*

Financial Accounting Standards Board (FASB) *Nongovernmental board that sets the standards for financial statements and generally accepted accounting principles (GAAP)*

Financial goals *High-level statements of financial desires that may be for the short or the long term*

Financial mission *A broad and enduring statement that identifies the client's long-term purpose for wanting a financial plan*

Financial mission *Broad and enduring statement that identifies the client's long-term purpose for creating a financial plan*

Financial needs approach *Evaluates the income replacement needs of one's survivors in the event of untimely death*

Financial objectives *Statements of financial desire that contain time and measurement attributes, making them more specific than financial goals*

Financial phases *These phases include the asset accumulation phase, the conservation/protection phase, and the distribution/gifting phase*

Financial risk *A risk that involves a monetary loss*

Financial risk *An unsystematic risk based on the inclusion of debt in the capital structure of a firm, which affects the return on equity (ROE) for a company*

Financial success *For most individuals, financial success means accomplishing one's financial goals*

Firm commitment *Equity underwriting in which the underwriter purchases the entire issue at a specific price from the firm and resells it on the open market*

First-to-die policy *Pays the face amount upon the first death of two or more insureds*

Fiscal policy *Taxation, expenditures, and debt management of the federal government*

Fixed annuity *Insurer agrees to credit a specified interest rate over a stated period*

Fixed outflows/expenses *Outflows that remain constant over a period of time and over which the client has little control*

Fixed-amount option *Specifies that a designated amount of income will be provided to the beneficiary on a regular basis until the proceeds and accumulated interest are depleted*

Fixed-income (or bond) mutual funds *A mutual fund that invests in fixed-income securities ranging in maturity of several months to 30 years or longer. Bond funds invest in numerous bond issues to diversify the investment portfolio from default risk.*

Fixed-income securities *Securities with specified payment dates and amounts, primarily bonds*

Fixed-period option *The beneficiary will receive the maximum periodic payments that the death benefit proceeds will purchase for a specified period*

Flexible premium annuity *Allows the insured the option to vary premium deposits*

Flexible spending account (FSA) *An account typically funded by employee salary reductions that allows employees the benefit of paying for their health-care-related expenses with pretax income*

Flow-through or conduit entity *A type of business entity in which the results of business operations are reported directly on the owner's income tax return*

Foreign closed-end funds *Closed-end funds that invest in foreign firms*

Foreign funds *Securities that provide investors with the easiest method of investing in foreign markets in the context of a diversified portfolio*

Foreign securities *Securities issued by non-U.S. firms*

Forfeitures *Employer contributions that are not fully vested and thus revert to the employer in the event that an employee terminates service*

Fourth market   Composed of institutional traders who trade without the help of brokers

Fraud penalty   A penalty levied against a taxpayer by the IRS after it has proven an underpayment of tax by the taxpayer and proven that the underpayment was attributable to a willful attempt to evade tax

Free Application for Federal Student Aid (FAFSA)   An application form that must be submitted by a college student to become eligible for federal financial aid

Free cash flow to equity   Term that describes the available cash after meeting all of the firm's operating and financial needs; used to calculate the value a company

Front-end load   A sales charge based on the initial investment into a mutual fund

Fundamental analysis   The analysis of a stock's value using basic, publicly available data, such as the stock's earnings, sales, risk, and industry analysis

Fundamental risk   An impersonal risk that involves a possible loss for a large group

Future value of an annuity due   The future value to which a series of deposits of equal size will amount when deposited over a definite number of equal-interval periods, based on a defined interest rate, and the deposits are made at the beginning of each period

Future value of an ordinary annuity   The future amount to which a series of deposits of equal size will equal when deposited over a finite number of equal-interval periods, based on a defined interest rate, when the deposits are made at the end of each period

Future value   The future dollar amount to which a sum certain today will increase compounded at a defined interest rate over a period of time

Futures contract   An agreement between two parties to make or take delivery of a specified amount of a commodity or financial asset at a future time, place, and unit price

Galloping inflation   Inflation that occurs when money loses its value very quickly, and real interest rates can be negative 50% or 100% per year

General agent   An independent businessperson who represents only one insurer for a designated territory

General obligation bonds   A municipal bond backed by the full faith, credit, and taxing power of the municipality

General partnership   A type of business entity owned entirely by general partners, each of whom can act on behalf of the partnership

Generation-skipping transfer tax (GSTT)   A tax in addition to the unified gift and estate tax designed to tax large transfers that skip a generation (i.e., from grandparent to grandchild)

Geometric mean   A method of calculating the internal rate of return based on periodic rates of return

Gift   In estate planning, a direct transfer of property or cash made during life

Goals   High-level statements of financial desire that may be for the short term or the long term

Good-till-canceled order   An order to buy or sell a security at a specific or limit price that lasts until the order is completed or canceled

Grace period   Amount of time following the premium due date in which the policyowner may pay the overdue premium

Green fund   A fund that invests in environmentally friendly companies

Gross domestic product (GDP)   The value of all goods and services produced in the country; GDP is the broadest measure of the general state of the economy

Gross estate   All assets included in a decedent's estate, including but not limited to cash, stocks, bonds, annuities, retirement accounts, notes receivable, personal residences, automobiles, art collections, life insurance proceeds, and income tax refunds due

Gross income   The Internal Revenue Code Section 61(a)defines gross income as "all income from whatever source derived"

Group supplemental plans   Often attached to basic medical expense coverage, these policies allow the employer to use more than one provider for coverage, offer first-dollar coverage, or use different contribution rates for basic and supplemental coverage

Growth stocks   Stock issued by companies whose sales, earnings, and market share are growing at higher rates than the average or the general economy

Guaranteed renewable   The insurer is required to renew the policy for a specified period, regardless of changes in the insured's health (premiums may be increased) by class of insureds

Hazard   A condition that creates or increases the likelihood of a loss occurring

Head of household   The filing status that identifies a taxpayer as an unmarried individual who maintains a household for another and satisfies certain conditions set forth in the Internal Revenue Code

Health savings account (HSA)   Special account that is used to pay for current and future medical expenses in conjunction with a high-deductible health plan (HDHP)

Hearing panel   Panel that establishes the rules of procedures and evidence to be observed at a complaint hearing seeking disciplinary action against a certificant

Hedge funds   An unregistered, privately offered, managed pool of capital for wealthy, financially sophisticated investors

Hedging   A means of trying to match profit on one transaction to the expected loss of another

Heir   One who inherits; beneficiary

High-deductible health plan (HDHP)   A health plan, often used in conjunction with a health savings account (HSA); the HSA is used to pay for expenses up to the deductible amount

Holding period return   Measures the total return an investor receives over a specific time period

Holographic will   Handwritten will dated and signed by the testator

Home health care   Part-time skilled nursing care and rehabilitative therapy provided at the patient's home

Homeowners insurance   A package insurance policy that provides both property and liability coverage for the insured dwelling, other structures, personal property, and loss of use

Hospice care   Care that provides dignity and comfort to terminally ill patients

Hospital expense insurance   Provides payment for expenses incurred by the insured while in the hospital

Housing costs   Principal and interest to pay the mortgage loan, real estate taxes, and homeowners insurance

Human life value approach   Uses projected future earnings as the basis for measuring life insurance needs

Hybrid (or balanced) mutual funds   A mutual fund that invests in a combination of cash, fixed-income securities, and equity securities

Immediate annuity   One in which the first annuity payment is made one payment interval from the purchase date

Immunization   Minimizing the impact of changes in interest rates on the value of investments

Implied authority   The authority that the public reasonably perceives the agent to possess, even without express authority

Income statement   A financial statement that reports a business's income and expenses over a given period

Income stock   Stock issued by companies in the maturity phase of the industry life cycle and that pay out the majority of their earnings in the form of dividends

Incontestability clause   Prevents the insurer from canceling the policy after it has been in force for two years in the event the life insurer discovers material misrepresentation or concealment

Incorporation   Results in limited liability for businessowners

Independent agent   An agent that represents multiple insurers

Index of leading economic indicators   A composite index of 10 variables that has had a reasonable track record in predicting recessions; it has accurately predicted every recession since 1950 but has also predicted five that did not happen

Indifference curves   A graphical representation of the risk-reward trade-off that an investor is willing to make

Indirect investing   A process of investing where investors invest in companies that invest directly in securities

Inflation   An increase in the price level of goods and services

Inflows   All monies received from employment, investments, and other sources

Information ratio   A ratio of expected return to risk as measured by standard deviation that seeks to quantify the amount of incremental risk undertaken by a portfolio manager to achieve an excess return

Initial public offering (IPO)   First offering of equity securities to the general public

Installment payment method   The policyowner receives the cash value and accrued interest over a period, usually in fixed amounts

Installment refund annuity   The insurer promises to continue periodic payments after the annuitant has died until the sum of all annuity payments equals the purchase price of the annuity

Insurance   A mechanism through which risk is transferred to an insurer, evidenced by a promise to pay, in exchange for an equitable premium

Intentional interference   Intentional act committed against another that causes injury

Interest rate risk   A systematic risk where changes in interest rates will affect the value of securities

Interest-only option   The insurance company retains the death benefit and pays the primary beneficiary interest on that sum

Interest-sensitive stock   Stock issued by companies whose performance is largely affected by changes in interest rates

Intermediate nursing care   Occasional nursing and rehabilitative care ordered and monitored by a physician

Internal rate of return (IRR)   The discount rate that causes cash inflows to equal cash outflows, thus allowing comparison of rates of return on alternative investments

Internal rate of return   A measure of return that equates discounted future cash flows to the present value of an asset

Internal Revenue Bulletin (IRB)   Announces official rulings and procedures of the IRS and publishes Treasury Decisions, Executive Orders, Tax Conventions, legislation, court decisions, and other items of general interest

Intestacy laws   *State laws that direct how a decedent's property will be distributed when the decedent dies without a will*

Intestate   *To die without a valid will*

Investment companies   *Financial services companies that sell shares of stock to the public and use the proceeds to invest in a portfolio of securities*

Investment policy statement   *A written document that sets forth a client's objectives, as well as limitations on the investment manager*

Irrevocable beneficiary   *Cannot be changed without the beneficiary's consent*

Itemized deductions   *Deductions in excess of the standard deduction that are used in lieu of the standard deduction*

Jensen's alpha   *An absolute measure of performance indicating how the actual performance of an investment compares with the expected performance*

Joint and last survivor income option   *Provides joint beneficiaries a stated amount of income during their lives, and a continuation of the original or reduced amount for the remaining beneficiaries' lives*

Joint and survivor annuity   *Based on the lives of two or more annuitants*

Joint life   *Covers two or more lives under one policy at a cost lower than premiums for multiple separate policies*

Joint tenancy   *Two or more persons, called equal owners, hold the same fractional interest in a property*

Keogh plan   *A qualified plan for unincorporated businesses*

Key person life insurance   *After the death of a key employee, used to recruit and train a replacement and compensate the company for lost business*

Ladder strategy   *Portfolio immunization strategy that uses a portfolio of bonds with staggered maturities*

Lagging economic indicators   *Economic statistics that fall or rise 3–12 months after the general economy*

Last-to-die policy   *Makes a death benefit payment upon the last death of multiple insureds*

Law of diminishing marginal utility   *As the rate of consumption increases, the marginal utility derived from consuming additional units of a good will decline*

Law of large numbers   *The chance that predicted results will reflect true results increases as the number of exposures increases*

Law   *Rules of conduct established by a government or other authority that command and encourage behavior considered right and prohibit behavior considered wrong*

Learning styles [auditory, visual, kinetic (or tactile)]   *The conditions under which people learn best. Clients whose preferred learning style is auditory learn best by hearing information; clients who prefer a visual learning style learn best by reading and viewing; those who prefer a kinetic, or tactile, style learn best through manipulation and testing information*

Legal reserve   *A fund that is accumulated and maintained by the insurer to meet future obligations, such as administrative expenses and mortality charges*

Lending securities   *Securities wherein the investor lends funds to the issuer in exchange for a promise of a stream of periodic interest payments and a repayment of the loaned principal at maturity*

Letter Ruling   *A written statement issued by the National Office of the IRS that gives guidance on the way the IRS will treat a prospective or contemplated transaction for tax purposes*

Level term   *A policy with a level death benefit and a fixed level premium for a stated period*

Liability   *Money owed by the client*

Libel   *Written statement that causes harm to another*

Life annuity with period certain   *Guarantees the greater of a life income to the annuitant or a minimum number of payments to the annuitant's beneficiary*

Life cycle phases   *Intervals in a client's life cycle that tend to give a planner insight into the client's financial objectives and concerns (asset-accumulation, conservation/protection, and distribution/gifting phases)*

Life cycle positioning   *Using information about a client's age, marital status, dependents, income level, and net worth to help determine goals and risks*

Life estate   *An interest in property that ceases upon the death of the owner of the life interest or estate*

Life income option   *Allows the beneficiary to receive a specified periodic payment, usually for life*

Life income with period certain option   *Provides an income to the beneficiary for life or a specified period, if longer*

Life income with refund option   *The life insurance company agrees that if the primary beneficiary dies before the total amount paid under the option equals the proceeds of the policy, the company will pay the difference to a contingent beneficiary*

Lifetime Learning Credit   *A tax credit available to pay for tuition and enrollment fees for undergraduate or graduate degree programs*

Limit order   *Type of securities order that requires the trade be made at a specified price or better*

Limited liability company (LLC)   *A relatively new and versatile form of business entity created under state law by filing articles of organization*

Limited liability partnership (LLP)   *A form of business entity similar to a general partnership, except that an LLP provides additional liability protection to the partners*

Limited partnership   *In a limited partnership, limited partners are not allowed to participate in the management of operations but generally are allowed to vote on major changes affecting the structure of the partnership*

Limited-payment policy   *Permanent life insurance for which premiums are payable for a limited number of years, after which the policy becomes paid up for its stated face amount*

Linear thinking   *The initial phase of a client's thinking process when setting financial direction in which a client focuses on accomplishing one particular goal or narrow objective using a very compartmentalized, simplistic, self-designed financial plan*

Liquidity preference theory   *Yield curve theory asserting long-term bonds have greater yields to compensate investors for increased interest rate risk*

Liquidity   *The ability to sell an investment quickly and at a competitive price, with no loss of principal and little price concession*

Living benefits rider   *Gives the policyowner access to a portion of the policy's eligible death benefit if the insured is diagnosed with a terminal illness and has a life expectancy of 12 months or less*

Load funds   *Mutual funds that charge either a front-end load or back-end load*

Long position   *The purchase of a stock in hopes that it will appreciate over time*

Long-term capital gain   *A gain from a sale or exchange of a capital asset that has been held for more than one year*

Long-term care insurance   *Provides coverage for nursing home stays and other types of routine care that are not covered by other health insurance*

Long-term disability   *Provides coverage for specified term greater than two years, until specified age, or until death*

Long-term Equity Anticipation Securities (LEAPS)   *Long-term options that generally have expiration dates of up to three years*

Long-term liability   *Debt extending beyond one year (long term > 12 months)*

Loss frequency   *Expected number of losses that will occur within a given period*

Loss of fair rental value   *The gross rental value less charges and expenses that do not continue during the period in which the property is uninhabitable*

Loss of use   *Coverage that provides reimbursement to an insured homeowner for additional living expenses or loss of fair rental value*

Loss severity   *Potential size or damage of a loss*

Lump-sum payment method   *The total cash value of the life insurance policy is paid to the policyowner*

Major medical insurance   *Health insurance that provides broad coverage of all reasonable and necessary expenses associated with an illness or injury, whether incurred at a doctor's office, a hospital, or the insured's home*

Malpractice insurance   *Used where the deficient conduct of the insured provider of professional services may result in damages*

Management fee   *A fee charged by an investment adviser for the management of a mutual fund's assets*

Managers   *Individuals who are responsible for the maintenance, administration, and management of the affairs of a limited liability company*

Margin accounts   *A type of brokerage account that allows the investor to borrow funds from the broker to purchase additional securities without adding cash to the account*

Marginal utility   *The additional utility received from the consumption of an additional unit of a good*

Marital deduction   *Unlimited deduction for transfers of property to a spouse during life (gifts) or at death (bequests)*

Market capitalization   *The product of the number of outstanding common stock shares and current stock price*

Market order   *Type of securities order that requires the trade be made at the best current market price*

Market risk   *A systematic risk describing the tendency of stocks to move with the market*

Market segmentation theory   *Yield curve theory asserting yields are determined by the laws of supply and demand for specific bond maturities*

Marketability   *The ability of an investor to find a ready market where the investor may sell an investment to a willing buyer*

Maturity   *The period through which the issuer has control over the bond proceeds and the period it must continue to pay coupon payments*

Maximum family benefit   *The limit on the amount of monthly Social Security benefits that may be paid to a family*

Mean-variance optimization model   *Used to determine the highest level of return (based on combinations of asset classes and different weightings of asset classes) for a specified level of risk tolerance*

Medicaid   *Provides medical assistance for persons with low incomes and resources*

Medical payments   *A no-fault, first-party insurance coverage designed to pay for bodily injuries sustained in an auto accident*

Medical savings account (MSA)   *Used to pay the out-of-pocket medical expenses of an insured enrolled in a high-deductible insurance plan*

Medicare Advantage   *A managed care plan that uses a network of doctors, hospitals, and health care providers approved by Medicare*

Medicare investment tax   *A Medicare tax on investment income for taxpayers whose modified gross income (MAGI) exceeds certain thresholds*

Medicare   *A federal health insurance plan for those who have attained full retirement age or have been disabled whether retired or still working*

Members   *The owners of a limited liability company (LLC) who can be individuals, partnerships, trusts, corporations, or other LLCs*

Misstatement of age or gender provision   *If a misstatement is made, the insurer can adjust the face amount to the amount the premium would have purchased had the age or gender been correctly stated*

Moderate inflation   *Inflation characterized by slowly rising prices*

Modern portfolio theory (MPT)   *A theory created by Harry Markowitz that describes portfolio diversification gained by combining securities with varying characteristics*

Modified adjusted gross income   *On the 1040 federal tax return, modified adjusted gross income is the sum of adjusted gross income, nontaxable interest, and foreign-earned income*

Modified endowment contract (MEC)   *A life insurance policy that exceeds its net level (7-pay) premium during the first seven years or during the seven years following a material change of the policy*

Modified whole life   *Premiums are lower for the first few years after policy issue, typically three to five years, and increase to a higher level premium thereafter*

Money market mutual funds   *A mutual fund that invests in money market instruments, such as Treasury bills and negotiable CDs*

Money market   *Consists of debt securities that have the following characteristics: short-term maturity, low credit risk, and high liquidity*

Monopoly   *A single seller of a well-defined product with no valid substitutes*

Moral hazard   *A character flaw or level of dishonesty that causes or increases the chance for loss*

Morale hazard   *Indifference to a loss based on the existence of insurance*

Morbidity   *Relates to the probability of becoming disabled*

Mortality charge   *The amount of money the insurance company charges for providing a death benefit*

Mortgage bond   *Bond secured by real property*

Mortgage-backed securities (MBSs)   *Ownership claims on a pool of mortgages*

MSCI EAFE Index   *An index measuring the international securities markets*

Municipal bonds   *Debt instruments issued by municipalities (states, counties, parishes, cities, or towns)*

Mutual funds   *Open-end investment companies that sell shares of stock to the public and use the proceeds to invest in a portfolio of securities on behalf of their shareholders*

Mutual insurance company   *Owned by policyholders and distributes profit in the form of policy dividends*

Named perils policy   *A policy that provides protection against losses caused by the perils specifically listed in the policy*

Named-perils coverage   *Protects from perils that are specifically listed in the policy*

Negligence   *The failure to act in a way that a reasonably prudent person would have acted under similar circumstances*

Negligence   *Tort caused by acting without reasonable care*

Net asset value (NAV)   *The price at which shares of an open-end investment company are sold. The NAV of a fund is determined by subtracting total liabilities from total assets of the fund and dividing the difference by the outstanding shares.*

Net cash flow   *Money available after all expenses are accounted for*

Net present value (NPV)   *The difference between the initial cash outflow (investment) and the present value of discounted cash inflows (i.e., NPV = PV of CF − cost of investment)*

Net worth   *The amount of wealth or equity the client has in owned assets*

New comparability plan   *A defined contribution plan that maximizes the age-weighted discrepancy permitted under the cross-testing provisions of proposed nondiscrimination regulations*

No-fault insurance   *Used in states that require drivers to carry insurance for their own protection; places limits on the insured's ability to sue other drivers for damages*

No-load funds   *Mutual funds purchased directly through the mutual fund family without the assistance of a broker*

Nominal interest rate   *Stated interest rate without considering the effect of inflation*

Nominal return   *The stated return from an investment*

Noncancelable   *Insurer guarantees the renewal of the policy for a given period or to a stated age without an increase in premium*

Nonfinancial risk   *A risk that involves a non-monetary loss*

Nonparticipating   *A policy that does not pay dividends*

Nonqualified plan   *A retirement plan that can discriminate in favor of executives but is not eligible for all of the special tax benefits available for qualified or other tax-advantaged retirement plans*

Nuncupative (oral) will   *Dying declarations made before sufficient witnesses*

OASDI   *Old Age, Survivors, and Disability Insurance, commonly referred to as Social Security*

Objective risk   *The relative variation of an actual loss to an expected loss*

Objectivity   *Relating to facts without distortion by personal feelings or prejudices*

Occurrence   *An accident, including exposure to conditions, which results in bodily injury or property damage during the policy period*

Offer of Settlement   *A certificant may tender an Offer of Settlement in lieu of a disciplinary hearing*

Office audit   *The audit is conducted at the IRS office near the taxpayer's home and usually involve issues too complicated to be resolved by mail, such as travel and entertainment expenses, income from rents, and large itemized deductions*

Officers   *Individuals appointed by a corporation's board of directors to carry out the board's policies and make day-to-day operating decisions*

Oligopoly   *Small number of rival seller firms; incentive to collude; high barrier to entry*

Online trading   *A method of buying and selling securities over the internet without the use of a broker*

Open market operations   *The process by which the Federal Reserve purchases and sells government securities in the open market*

Open perils policy   *A policy in which all perils or causes of loss are covered unless they are specifically listed in the exclusions section*

Open-end investment company   *An investment company whose capitalization constantly changes as new shares are sold and outstanding shares are redeemed*

Open-perils coverage   *Coverage designed to protect against all perils except those specifically excluded from coverage*

Opportunity cost   *The highest-valued alternative not chosen; represents what is forgone by choosing another alternative*

Opportunity cost   *When faced with investment alternatives, it is the highest-valued alternative not chosen—it represents what is forgone by choosing another alternative; when discounting a future sum or series of payments back to present value, it is the composite rate of return on the client's assets with similar risk to the assets being examined*

Optionally renewable   *The insurer may not cancel the policy during the term, but the insurer may decline to renew the policy for a subsequent term*

Options   *Derivatives that give the holder, or buyer, the right to sell or purchase the underlying asset*

Ordinary (straight) life policy   *A continuous-premium whole life policy in which premiums are paid regularly until either death or age 100*

Ordinary annuity   *Deposits or payments are made at the end of each period*

Ordinary income   *Any income that arises from services or from property that is not classified as a capital asset*

Other insured rider   *Offers level term insurance coverage on the insured's spouse or children*

Other structures   *Structures not attached to a dwelling, such as detached garages, small greenhouses, storage buildings, and gazebos*

Outflows   *Recurring obligations, or monthly expenses paid*

Own occupation   *Definition of disability in which an insured is considered totally disabled if the insured cannot perform the substantial and major duties of the insured's own occupation*

P/E ratio   *A measure of how much the market is willing to pay for each dollar of earnings of a company*

Paid-up insurance rider   *Increases the whole life death benefit protection and builds additional cash value*

Paid-up policy   *A policy for which no future premium payments are due; remains in effect for life*

Paradoxical thinking   *The second phase of a client's thinking process when setting financial direction in which a client tries to focus on several simultaneous objectives, causing confusion, goal conflict, and ambiguity. The paradoxical thinking phase is where a client often seeks the advice of a financial planner.*

Parent Loans for Undergraduate Students (Plus Loans)   *Loans that allow parents with good credit histories to borrow funds for a child's education expenses*

Partial disability rider   *The insured cannot perform all of the substantial and material duties of the job*

Participating preferred stock   *Preferred stock that receives dividend based on the performance of the firm in addition to the specified preferred dividend*

Participating   *A policy that pays dividends*

Particular risk   *Personal risk that involves a possible loss for an individual or a small group*

Partner   *An individual, corporation, trust, estate, or other partnership that has an ownership interest in a partnership*

Partnership   *An association of two or more entities or individuals that operate as co-owners of a business for the purpose of making a profit*

Passive loss rule   *Passive losses may only offset income from another passive activity. If the passive activity is a publicly traded partnership (master limited partnership), losses from that activity may only be offset by income from the same publicly traded partnership.*

Passive risk retention   *Being unaware of a risk, but taking no steps to manage it properly*

Payable date   *The date that the dividend will actually be paid*

Payments for legal support   *transfers to children that are essentially legal support obligations; exempt from gift tax rules*

Peak   *The point in the business cycle that appears at the end of the expansion phase when most businesses are operating at full capacity and gross domestic product is increasing rapidly*

Pell Grant   *A grant from the federal government awarded to undergraduate students who have not earned bachelor's or professional degrees; the EFC calculation, which is based on one's financial need, is used to determine a student's eligibility for a Pell Grant and how much is awarded to a student*

Pension plan   *A qualified plan structured to provide a regularly paid, fixed sum at retirement*

Peril   *The proximate, or actual, cause of a loss*

Personal automobile policy (PAP)   *Provides physical damage insurance, medical payments, liability coverage, and uninsured motorist protection*

Personal financial planning   *The process of formulating, implementing, and monitoring multifunctional decisions that enable an individual or family to achieve financial goals*

Personal liability umbrella policy   *Coverage designed to provide a catastrophic layer of liability coverage on top of the individual's homeowners and automobile insurance policies*

Personal service corporation (PSC)   *A C corporation in which substantially all of the activities involve the performance of services in the fields of health, law, engineering, architecture, accounting, actuarial science, or consulting*

Personal statement of cash flows   *Summary of the client's income and expenses during an interval of time, usually one year*

Personal utility curves   *Economic curves that describe the satisfaction that an individual receives from a selected item or additional units of that item*

Physical hazard   *A tangible condition or circumstance that increases the probability of a peril occurring and/or the severity of damages that result from a peril*

Physician's expense insurance   *Pays for fees charged by physicians that provide nonsurgical care*

Policy loan provision   *Allows the policyowner to borrow (with interest) against the cash surrender value of a permanent insurance policy*

Pool-of-money concept   *Long-term care coverage provided up to a specific dollar amount, regardless of time*

Power of appointment trust   *Allows a terminable interest to be passed to a surviving spouse and the property to still qualify for the marital deduction; unlike a QTIP trust, no election is required*

Practice Standards   *The set of standards that (1) establish the level of professional practice that is expected of certificants engaged in personal financial planning, (2) advance professionalism in the practice of financial planning, and (3) enhance the value of the personal financial planning process*

Preemptive right   *Allows shareholders to maintain ownership percentage by requiring new issues of stock to be offered first to current shareholders*

Preexisting condition   *A medical condition that required treatment during a specified period before the insured's effective date*

Preexisting conditions clause   *Excludes coverage for preexisting conditions for a specified period, such as 12 months, after the effective date of coverage*

Preferred habitat theory   *Yield curve theory asserting financial institutions prefer to match asset maturities to liability maturities*

Preferred provider organization (PPO)   *A contractual arrangement between the insured, the insurer, and the health care provider that allows the insurer to receive discounted rates from service providers*

Preferred stock   *A type of stock that has characteristics of both fixed-income investments and of common stock in that dividend payments must be paid each year before paying a dividend to the common shareholders*

Premium   *The cost of an option contract*

Prepaid legal services   *Under this arrangement, law firms, in exchange for a monthly payment, provide specific legal services at no or greatly reduced cost*

Prepaid Tuition Plans   *Plans where prepayment of college tuition is allowed at current prices for enrollment in the future; in other words, a parent can lock in future tuition at current rates*

Prepayment risk   *The risk that homeowners will pay off their loans before the scheduled loan maturity date*

Preponderance of the evidence   *A measure or degree of proof. With regard to disciplinary rules and procedures, preponderance of the evidence means the evidence as a whole shows what it was intended to prove with a probability of 51% or more.*

Present value of an annuity due   *The value today of a series of equal payments made at the beginning of each period for a finite number of periods discounted at a defined interest rate*

Present value of an ordinary annuity *The value today of a series of equal payments made at the end of each period for a finite number of periods discounted at a defined interest rate*

Present value *The current dollar value of a future sum discounted at a defined interest rate over a period of time*

Price elasticity *The quantity demanded of a good in response to changes in that good's price; a good is elastic when its quantity demanded responds greatly to price changes (luxuries) and inelastic when its quantity demanded responds little to price changes (necessities)*

Price index *A weighted average of the prices of numerous goods and services (e.g., the Consumer Price Index, the gross domestic product deflator, the gross national product deflator, and the Producer Price Index)*

Primary beneficiary *The party designated by the policyowner to receive death benefits*

Primary Insurance Amount (PIA) *Amount on which a worker's retirement benefit is based. The PIA determines the amount the applicant will receive at full retirement age, based on the year in which the retiree turns 62. The PIA is indexed to the Consumer Price Index (CPI) annually.*

Primary market *The market where new issues of securities are first offered to the public*

Principal *In a power of attorney document, the person (power giver) who designates another person or persons to act as his attorney-in-fact*

Principle of indemnity *A person is entitled to compensation only to the extent that financial loss has been suffered*

Principle of insurable interest *To have an insurable interest, an insured must be subject to emotional or financial hardship resulting from damage, loss, or destruction*

Principle of utmost good faith *Requires that the insured and the insurer both be forthcoming with all relevant facts about the insured risk and the coverage provided for that risk*

Principles *Aspirational statements expressing the ethical and professional ideals CFP® certificants are expected to display in their professional activities*

Private censure *An unpublished written reproach that is mailed to the censured CFP® certificant by the Disciplinary and Ethics Commission*

Private Letter Rulings *Statements issued for a fee upon a taxpayer's request that describe how the IRS will treat proposed transactions for tax purposes*

Private placement *A corporation selling a new issue of securities to a small group of institutions or sophisticated individual investors*

Pro forma income statement *A financial statement that projects a business's income and expenses for the future rather than reporting the past*

Probate process *Proves the validity of any will, supervises the orderly distribution of assets to the heirs, and protects creditors by ensuring that valid debts of the estate are paid. Probate is also the legal process that performs the function of changing property title from a decedent's name to an heir's name.*

Producer Price Index (PPI) *A group of indexes that measures the average change in the selling prices received by domestic producers of goods and services over time*

Professional eligible for reinstatement (PER) *An individual who is not currently certified by CFP Board but who was certified in the past and has an entitlement to potentially use the CFP® marks*

Profit-sharing plan *A qualified defined contribution plan featuring a flexible (discretionary) employer-contribution provision. Profit-sharing plans are structured to offer employees participation in company profits that they may use for retirement purposes*

Proprietor *The owner of a sole proprietorship*

Proxy voting *Authorizing an agent to cast the votes for the shareholder*

Public letter of admonition *Written reproach of the CFP® certificant's behavior that will normally be published in a press release or other form of publicity selected by the Disciplinary and Ethics Commission*

Purchasing power preservation (PPP) model *A capital needs analysis method that assumes the client will have a capital balance of equal purchasing power at life expectancy as he did at retirement*

Purchasing power risk *A systematic risk where inflation will erode the real value of the investor's assets*

Pure annuity model *The basic capital needs analysis approach that is generally prepared on a pretax basis*

Pure expectations theory *Yield curve theory asserting long-term interest rates are based on expectations about future short-term interest rates*

Pure risk *A risk in which the results are either a loss or no loss*

Put option *A derivative that gives the holder the right to sell the underlying asset, generally a stock, at a specified price within a specified period*

Qualified dividends *Dividends received from domestic corporations and foreign corporations incorporated in a U.S. possession, such as Puerto Rico*

Qualified domestic trust (QDOT) *For a noncitizen spouse who was a U.S. resident at the time of the decedent's death, the marital deduction is allowed if the property is placed in a QDOT that passes to the noncitizen surviving spouse*

Qualified longevity annuity contracts (QLACs)   *An insurance option that ensures retirees have a stream of regular income throughout their advanced years*

Qualified long-term care services   *As defined by HIPAA, include necessary diagnostic, preventative, therapeutic, caring, treating, rehabilitative services, and maintenance or personal care services required by a chronically ill or cognitively impaired person and provided by a plan prescribed by a licensed health care practitioner*

Qualified terminable interest property (QTIP) trust   *Allows a terminable interest to be passed to a surviving spouse and the property to still qualify for the unlimited marital deduction; the election is made by the executor on IRS Form 706*

Qualified transfer   *A payment made directly to an educational institution for tuition and fees or to a medical provider for medical expenses for the benefit of someone else*

Qualified Tuition Programs (QTPs)   *Also known as 529 plans, QTPs allow individuals to either participate in Prepaid Tuition Plans in which tuition credits are purchased for a designated beneficiary for payment or waiver of higher education expenses or participate in College Savings Plans in which contributions of money are made to an account to eventually pay for higher education expenses of a designated beneficiary*

Qualifying child   *A taxpayer may claim an individual as a dependent if the individual satisfies all of the following requirements: relationship, abode, age, support, citizenship, and joint return*

Qualifying relative   *A taxpayer may claim an individual as a dependent if the individual satisfies all of the following requirements: relationship, support, gross income, citizenship, and joint return*

Random walk   *An unpredictable pattern that describes the movement of security prices over time*

Ratio analysis   *The relationship or relative value of two characteristics used to analyze an individual's financial health and to conduct comparison and trend analysis*

Readjustment period   *The period of time that lasts for one to two years following the death of a breadwinner*

Real estate investment trust (REIT)   *A form of indirect ownership of real estate that invests in real estate, short-term construction loans, and mortgages*

Real interest rate adjustment   *The rate of interest expressed in dollars of constant value (adjusted for inflation) and equal to the nominal interest rate, less the rate of inflation*

Real interest rate   *Nominal interest rate considering the effect of inflation*

Real rate of return   *The nominal rate of return adjusted for inflation*

Recession   *A decline in real gross domestic product for two or more successive quarters*

Record date   *The date at which an owner of the common stock of a corporation is entitled to receive the dividend payment*

Reentry term   *A policy whereby the insurer may renew coverage at a lower premium rate if the insured provides satisfactory evidence of insurability*

Reinstatement clause   *Outlines the conditions under which a lapsed policy may be reinstated*

Reinvestment rate risk   *A systematic risk where earnings (cash flows) distributed from current investments cannot be reinvested at a rate of return equal to the expected yield of the current investments*

Remaining work life expectancy (RWLE)   *The work period remaining at a certain point in time prior to retirement*

Renewable   *A feature whereby the policyowner may continue a term policy for an additional period without evidence of insurability at a premium based on the insured's current or attained age*

Replacement cost   *The amount necessary to purchase, repair, or replace the dwelling with materials of the same or similar quality at current prices*

Representation   *Statement made by the proposed insured to the insurer in the application process*

Res ipsa loquitur   *"The act speaks for itself"; negligence can be assumed from the character of the outcome without evidence of wrongdoing on the part of the tortfeasor*

Reserve requirement   *The percentage of deposit liabilities that must be held in reserve by a member bank of the Federal Reserve; as the reserve requirement is increased, less money is available to be loaned, resulting in a restriction of the money supply*

Residual benefits provision   *Policyowner receives a percentage of the disability benefit on the basis of the percentage of income loss due to sickness or injury*

Residuary clause   *A general provision in a will that provides for the transfer of the balance of any assets not specifically mentioned in the will to someone or to some institution named by the testator*

Retirement benefit   *The most familiar Social Security benefit, full retirement benefits are payable at full retirement age, with reduced benefits as early as age 62, to anyone who has obtained at least a minimum amount of Social Security credits*

Retirement earnings limitations test   *One of the ways in which Social Security benefits are reduced on the basis of earnings*

Return of premium rider   *Returns the premium paid for a policy (less any administrative charges, fees, or rider premiums) to the policyowner at the end of the policy term*

Revenue bonds   *A municipal bond backed by a specific source of revenue*

Revenue Procedures   *Statements reflecting the internal management practices of the IRS that affects the rights and duties of taxpayers*

Revenue Rulings   *Official interpretation on how the law should be applied to a specific set of facts*

Revocable beneficiary   *Can be changed by the policyowner (who may or may not be the insured) at any time*

Revocation   *The Disciplinary and Ethics Commission may order permanent revocation of a certificant's right to use the marks and to publish the revocation in a press release or other form of publicity*

Rider   *Provides additional coverage for something specifically not covered within the primary policy*

Riders (endorsements)   *Written additions to an insurance contract that modify the original provisions*

Risk avoidance   *The avoidance of any chance of loss*

Risk reduction   *Taking measures that reduce the frequency or severity of losses*

Risk retention   *Bearing all or part of the financial burden in the event of a loss*

Risk tolerance   *An estimate of the level of risk an investor is willing to accept in his portfolio*

Risk tolerance   *The level of risk exposure with which an individual is comfortable*

Risk transfer   *Shifting the probability of loss to another party, such as an insurance company*

Risk   *The chance of loss, possibility of loss, uncertainty, or a variation of actual from expected results*

Risk-based capital model (RBCM)   *Adjusts an insurer's capital base according to the amount and types of risk to which it is exposed*

Roth IRA   *An individual retirement account in which contributions are made on an after-tax basis and qualifying distributions are made tax free*

Roth IRA   *An IRA created by the Taxpayer Relief Act of 1997; contributions to a Roth IRA are nondeductible; qualified distributions are excluded from an individual's taxable income; distributions used for qualified education expenses can also avoid the 10% penalty*

Rule of 72   *A method of approximation that estimates the time it takes to double the value of an investment where the earnings (interest) rate is known (by dividing 72 by the interest rate); it can also estimate the earnings (interest) rate necessary to double an investment value if the time is known (by dividing 72 by the period of investment)*

Rules of Conduct   *Rules established by CFP Board that establish the high standards expected of CFP® certificants, the violation of which may subject a certificant to discipline*

Russell 2000® Index   *A well-known index used to benchmark small capitalization companies*

S corporation   *A special type of corporation formed under state law like a regular corporation; however, for income tax purposes, is treated similar to a partnership*

Sale   *Transfer of property for an amount of money or money equivalent that is fixed or determinable*

Savings   *Deferred consumption*

Scheduled personal property endorsement   *Provides open-peril coverage under the same terms as if separate contracts were purchased for each type of property; the amount for which an item is insured is considered the value of the item if a loss occurs*

Secondary market   *The market where investors can buy and sell securities with other investors*

Section 1035 exchange   *Provides for the replacement of an existing insurance-based contract for a newer insurance-based contract without having to pay taxes on any gain in the original contract*

Section 125 (cafeteria plan)   *A plan in which employers offer their employees a choice between cash and a variety of nontaxable qualified benefits that are excludable from the employee's income*

Section 401(k) profit-sharing plan   *A defined contribution profit-sharing plan that gives participants the option of reducing their taxable salary and contributing the salary reduction on a tax-deferred basis to an individual account for retirement purposes*

Section 403(b) plan   *A retirement plan similar to a 401(k) plan that is available to certain tax-exempt organizations and to public schools*

Securities Act of 1933   *Federal law that provides rules and regulations related to new issues of investment securities*

Securities Exchange Act of 1934   *Federal law that provides rules and regulations related to the purchase and sale of investment securities in the secondary market*

Securitization   *The process of transforming nonnegotiable securities into negotiable securities*

Self-employment tax   *Tax paid by self-employed individuals that is based on net earnings, not on the individual's wages. Because the self-employed must bear the burden of both the employer and employee portion of FICA, the self-employment tax rate is 15.3% (up to the taxable wage base)—double the employee's rate of 7.65% in 2016. Net SE income exceeding the TWB is taxed at the 2.9% Medicare tax rate, which has no income ceiling, and is added to the SE tax calculated for the SE income up to the TWB.*

Self-insured retention   *A payment similar to a deductible that an insured is usually required to pay for each loss under a personal umbrella policy*

Semivariance   *Measures the variability of returns that fall below the average or expected return*

Serial payment   A payment that increases at a constant rate (usually, the rate of inflation) on an annual basis

Series EE United States Savings Bonds (EE Bonds)   If used to pay for qualified higher education expenses at an eligible institution or state tuition plan, EE bonds bestow significant tax savings—that is, no federal income tax is due on the interest

Settlement options   Allow the policyowner or beneficiary to choose either cash or one of several alternatives to how the death benefit proceeds will be paid

Shareholders   The owners of a corporation who elect the corporation's board of directors

Sharpe ratio   A measure of risk-adjusted portfolio performance that uses standard deviation as the risk measure

Short position   A type of position investors take by selling borrowed shares in hopes that the stock price will decline over time

Short-term capital gain   A gain from a sale or exchange of a capital asset that has been held for one year or less

Short-term disability   Provides coverage for up to two years

Side instruction letter   Also known as a personal instruction letter, separate from a will; details the testator's wishes regarding the disposition of tangible possessions (household goods), the disposition of the decedent's body, and funeral arrangements

Simplified employee pension (SEP)   A tax-deferred, noncontributory retirement plan that uses an individual retirement account (IRA) as the receptacle for contributions

Simultaneous death clause   In the event that both spouses die simultaneously, this clause provides a presumption that one spouse (predetermined) predeceased the other spouse

Single premium annuity   An annuity purchased with a single lump sum

Single premium whole life   Single lump-sum payment made at policy issue with no future premiums due

Sinking funds   Funds usually held by trustee to ensure repayment of borrowed principal

Skilled nursing care   Daily nursing care and rehabilitation services ordered and monitored by a physician

Slander   Verbal statement that causes harm to another

Social Security Statement, Form SSA-7005   A written report, mailed by the Social Security Administration to all workers age 25 and over who are not yet receiving Social Security benefits; provides an estimate of the worker's eventual Social Security benefits and instructions on how to qualify for those benefits

Sole proprietorship   A business owned and controlled by one person who is personally liable for all debts and claims against the business

Speculative risk   A risk where a potential for profit as well as loss or no loss exists

Split gift   A joint gift made by spouses that has the effect of doubling the annual exclusion of gifts to the donee. A split gift requires the consent of the spouse and spouse's signature on Form 709.

Split limits   Lists the per-person bodily injury limit, the per occurrence bodily injury limit for all bodily injuries, and the property damage limit

Split-dollar plan   An agreement between an employer and employee who share the costs and benefits associated with a life insurance policy

Spouse and child insurance riders   Provide life insurance coverage on the lives of the insured's spouse or children

Stafford Loan   The primary type of financial aid provided by the United States Department of Education; Stafford loans are either subsidized or unsubsidized

Standard & Poor's Index (S&P 500)   A financial index of 500 U.S. equities chosen for market size, liquidity, and industry group representation

Standard deviation   Measures both total volatility and total risk (systematic and unsystematic risk) of the portfolio

Standby underwriting   Equity underwriting in which the underwriter purchases any securities remaining after an initial offering

Statement of cash flows   A financial statement that reflects the cash inflows and outflows of a business and reconciles the net changes in cash between two balance sheets

Statement of changes in net worth   Summary of changes from one statement of financial position to the next

Statement of financial position   A list of assets, liabilities, and net worth

Static risk   A risk dependent on factors other than a change in society or the economy (e.g., natural disaster)

Statutory (formal) will   Generally drawn by an attorney and signed in the presence of witnesses, complying with the statutes for wills of the domiciliary state

Statutory voting   One vote per share of common stock

Stock bonus plan   A defined contribution profit-sharing plan in which all employer contributions are in the form of employer stock. Distributions to participants can be made in the form of employer stock.

Stock insurance company   Operate for-profit and owned by stockholders

Stop limit order   A type of securities order that becomes a limit order when the security's price reaches a specific level

Stop loss order   *A type of securities order that becomes a market order when the security's price reaches a specific level*

Stop-loss limit   *A dollar amount of covered benefits to which the coinsurance provision is applied, but it does not include the deductible; once the stop-loss limit is reached, the insurer pays 100% of all covered expenses*

Straight life annuity   *Provides a lifetime income to the annuitant regardless of how long the annuitant lives*

Strict and absolute liability   *Liability resulting from law; strict liability allows for defense, and absolute liability does not*

Subaccounts   *Portfolios of stocks and/or bonds that are professionally managed according to a specific investment objective*

Subjective risk   *A particular person's perception of risk; varies greatly from individual to individual*

Subjectivity   *Relating to the client's perception of reality*

Subrogation clause   *States that the insured cannot indemnify oneself from both the insurance company and a negligent third party for the same claim*

Substitutes   *Products that serve similar purposes; an increase in the price of one will cause an increase in the demand for the other*

Substitution effect   *The phenomenon in which consumers substitute less expensive goods for similar, more expensive goods; this is one of two reasons why the demand curve slopes downward*

Suicide clause   *Asserts that, if the insured commits suicide within a specified period of time, the policy will be voided and premiums will be refunded to the beneficiary*

Supplemental Security Income (SSI)   *Program administered by the Social Security Administration and funded by the general Treasury that is available to those at full retirement age or disabled who have a low income and few assets*

Supply curve   *The graphic depiction that shows the relationship between the market price of a particular good and the quantity supplied*

Supply   *The quantity of a particular good businesses are willing to produce or sell*

Surgical expense insurance   *May be added to a hospital expense insurance policy to provide payment of surgeon's fees, even when procedures are not performed in a hospital*

Surplus lines agent   *An agent that has the authority to engage in business with out-of-state insurers in order to meet consumer needs*

Survivors benefit   *Social Security benefit available to surviving family members of a deceased, eligible worker*

Survivorship clause   *Provides that the beneficiary must survive the decedent for a specified period in order to receive the inheritance or bequest*

Survivorship clause   *Requires that a beneficiary survive the insured by a specified period (usually 30 to 60 days) in order to receive the death benefit proceeds*

Suspension   *May be ordered by the Disciplinary and Ethics Commission for a specified period of time, not to exceed five years, for individuals it deems can be rehabilitated*

SWOT analysis   *An analysis that helps the financial planner understand how internal and external environmental factors impact the client's financial situation. The acronym SWOT stands for strengths, weaknesses, opportunities, and threats.*

Systematic risks   *Investment risks impacted by broad macroeconomic factors that influence all securities*

Target benefit pension plan   *An age-weighted money purchase pension plan; a hybrid between a defined contribution plan and a defined benefit plan*

Tax avoidance   *The legal minimization of taxes, which is accomplished by applying knowledge of the IRC and the Treasury regulations to an individual's income tax situation*

Tax evasion   *Any of the various fraudulent methods by which a taxpayer may pay less than his proper tax liability*

Tax risk   *The uncertainty associated with the tax laws that may impact the ownership and/or disposition of investment assets*

Taxable equivalent yield   *A method for investors to compare the yield on municipal bonds with the yield on taxable (e.g., corporate) bonds*

Tax-qualified long-term care insurance   *Policies that meet standards established with the passage of the Health Insurance Portability and Accountability Act of 1996 (HIPAA)*

Technical Advice Memoranda   *Advice or guidance in memorandum form furnished by the National Office of the IRS to IRS agents who request such advice or guidance during an audit*

Technical analysis   *The search for identifiable and recurring stock price patterns*

Technology stocks   *Stocks of companies involved in high-technology fields categorized by above-average earnings potential and high risk*

Tenancy by the entirety   *Joint tenancy with right of survivorship (JTWROS) that can only occur between a married couple*

Tenancy in common   *Two or more persons hold an undivided interest in a whole property*

Term insurance rider   *Offers additional term life insurance on the insured*

Term life insurance   *Provides temporary life insurance protection for a given period*

Terminable interest   *An interest that ends upon an event or contingency*

Testamentary capacity   *Having the mental capability to make a will to transfer assets; being of sound mind*

Retirement life expectancy (RLE)   *The time period beginning at retirement and extending until death; the period of retirement that must be funded*

Third market   *Over-the-counter trading of equity shares that are listed on an exchange*

Time value of money   *The concept that money received today is worth more than the same amount of money received sometime in the future*

Time-weighted returns   *A method of determining an internal rate of return by evaluating the performance of portfolio managers without the influence of additional investor deposits or withdrawals to or from the portfolio*

Tort   *A private wrong; an infringement on the rights of another*

Total return   *The sum of the capital appreciation/depreciation on an investment plus any income or earnings generated by the investment*

Treasury inflation-protected securities (TIPS)   *Marketable securities whose principal is adjusted by changes in the Consumer Price Index (CPI)*

Treasury STRIPS   *Acronym for Separate Trading of Registered Interest and Principal of Securities, a program that permits investors to hold and trade the individual interest and principal components of eligible Treasury notes and bonds as separate securities*

Treynor ratio   *A measure of risk-adjusted portfolio performance that uses beta as the risk measure*

Trough   *The point in the business cycle that appears at the end of the contraction phase when most businesses are operating at their lowest capacity levels and the gross domestic product is at its lowest*

Trust   *A legal arrangement, usually provided for under state law, in which property is transferred by a grantor to a trustee for the management and conservation of the property for the benefit of the named beneficiaries*

Underwriters   *Classify proposed insureds in a way as to adequately protect the insurance company from adverse selection*

Underwriting   *The process by which investment bankers purchase an issue of securities from a firm and resell it to the public*

Uneven cash flows   *Investment returns or deposits that are neither single interval deposits nor equal payments*

Unified gift and estate transfer tax system   *Unified tax transfer system created by Congress to ensure that at the time of transfer of property, either during life (gifts) or at death (bequests), the transferor will pay the same tax rate or amount for the transfer*

Uniform Gift to Minors Act (UGMA)   *Allows parents to put cash and securities in a custodial account for a child*

Uniform Transfers to Minors Act (UTMA)   *Allows parents to put cash, securities, and real property in a custodial account for a child*

Unilateral   *Only the insurer agrees to a legally enforceable promise*

Uninsured/underinsured motorist   *Motorist without liability coverage or whose insurer cannot or will not pay the claim, hit-and-run driver, or motorist with insufficient liability coverage according to state law*

Unintentional tort   *Failure to act in a reasonably prudent manner, thereby causing harm to another*

Unit investment trust (UIT)   *A registered investment company that is passively managed and may invest in stocks, bonds, or other securities*

Unit-elastic demand   *The percentage of change in quantity demanded is exactly equal to the percentage of change in price, ignoring the direction of the change (PE = 1); a change in price results in no change to total revenue*

Universal life insurance   *Gives policyowners the ability to adjust the premiums, death benefit, and cash values up or down to meet individual needs (within certain limits)*

Unsystematic risks   *Types of investment risks unique to a single company, industry, or country that can be eliminated by portfolio diversification*

Usual and customary expenses   *Health care costs that are consistent with the average rate or charge for identical or similar services in a particular geographic area*

Value stocks   *Stock trading at prices that are low given the stock's historical earnings and current asset value*

Variable annuity   *Does not guarantee specific payments but has a potential for greater returns*

Variable life   *A fixed-premium, whole life policy in which the death benefit and cash values fluctuate on the basis of the performance of subaccounts sometimes referred to as separate accounts*

Variable outflows/expenses   *Expenses that fluctuate from time to time over which the client has some control*

Variable universal life (VUL) insurance   *Combines the investment component of variable life and the premium, death benefit, and cash value flexibility features of universal life*

Vesting   *An employee's nonforfeitable right to receive a present or future pension benefit*

Viatical agreement   The owner of a policy covering a terminally ill insured sells a life insurance policy to a third party without the proceeds being subject to income tax

Vicarious acts   Negligent acts performed by someone else but for which the individual is held at least partially responsible

Vicarious liability   One person may become legally liable for the torts of another (e.g., parent/child, employer/employee acting in the scope of employment)

Voluntary Employee Benefit Association (VEBA)   A tax-exempt trust authorized by IRC Section 501(c)(9); in a VEBA, an employer makes tax-free deposits to the plan on an employee's behalf

Wage replacement ratio (WRR)   An estimate of the percentage of income needed at retirement compared to earnings prior to retirement

Wait-and-see agreement   A hybrid version of the cross-purchase and entity purchase buy-sell agreement that allows the businessowners to wait until an owner dies or retires before deciding whether the surviving owners or the business entity will purchase the deceased or retired owner's share

Waiver of premium rider   Waives the premium due on a policy during the period the insured is disabled

War exclusion   Allows the insurer to deny a death claim if the insured's death is related to war or military service

Warrants   A long-term, customized call option to purchase the stock of a given corporation within a specified period of time

Warranty   Promise made by the insured to the insurer that is part of the insurance contract to which the insurer must adhere

Whole life insurance   Provides coverage during the lifetime of the insured as long as the premiums are paid according to the policy contract

Will   A legal document used in estate planning that provides the testator, or will maker, the opportunity to control the distribution of property and avoid the state's intestacy law distribution scheme

Wilshire 5000 Index   A financial index consisting of over 5,000 U.S.-based companies; often used as a measure of the overall market within the United States

Work life expectancy (WLE)   The number of years a person spends in the workforce, generally 30–40 years

Yield curves   Graphical representations that reflect current market interest rates for various bond maturities

Yield to call (YTC)   The expected return on a bond from the purchase date to the first date that the bond may be called

Yield to maturity (YTM)   The compounded rate of return on a bond purchased at the current market price and held to maturity

Zero-coupon bond   A bond that does not pay periodic coupon or interest payments

Index

Required Disclaimers:

CFA Institute does not endorse, promote, or warrant the accuracy or quality of the products or services offered by Kaplan. CFA Institute, CFA®, and Chartered Financial Analyst® are trademarks owned by CFA Institute.

Certified Financial Planner Board of Standards Inc. owns the certification marks CFP®, CERTIFIED FINANCIAL PLANNER™, and federally registered CFP (with flame design) in the U.S., which it awards to individuals who successfully complete initial and ongoing certification requirements. The College for Financial Planning®, a Kaplan company, does not certify individuals to use the CFP®, CERTIFIED FINANCIAL PLANNER™, and CFP (with flame design) certification marks. CFP® certification is granted only by Certified Financial Planner Board of Standards Inc. to those persons who, in addition to completing an educational requirement such as this CFP® Board-Registered Program, have met its ethics, experience, and examination requirements.

The College for Financial Planning®, a Kaplan company, is a review course provider for the CFP® Certification Examination administered by Certified Financial Planner Board of Standards Inc. CFP Board does not endorse any review course or receive financial remuneration from review course providers.

GARP® does not endorse, promote, review, or warrant the accuracy of the products or services offered by Kaplan of FRM® related information, nor does it endorse any pass rates claimed by the provider. Further, GARP® is not responsible for any fees or costs paid by the user to Kaplan, nor is GARP® responsible for any fees or costs of any person or entity providing any services to Kaplan. FRM®, GARP®, and Global Association of Risk Professionals™ are trademarks owned by the Global Association of Risk Professionals, Inc.

CAIAA does not endorse, promote, review or warrant the accuracy of the products or services offered by Kaplan, nor does it endorse any pass rates claimed by the provider. CAIAA is not responsible for any fees or costs paid by the user to Kaplan nor is CAIAA responsible for any fees or costs of any person or entity providing any services to Kaplan. CAIA®, CAIA Association®, Chartered Alternative Investment Analyst℠, and Chartered Alternative Investment Analyst Association® are service marks and trademarks owned by CHARTERED ALTERNATIVE INVESTMENT ANALYST ASSOCIATION, INC., a Massachusetts non-profit corporation with its principal place of business at Amherst, Massachusetts, and are used by permission.

Notes

W9-BSX-294

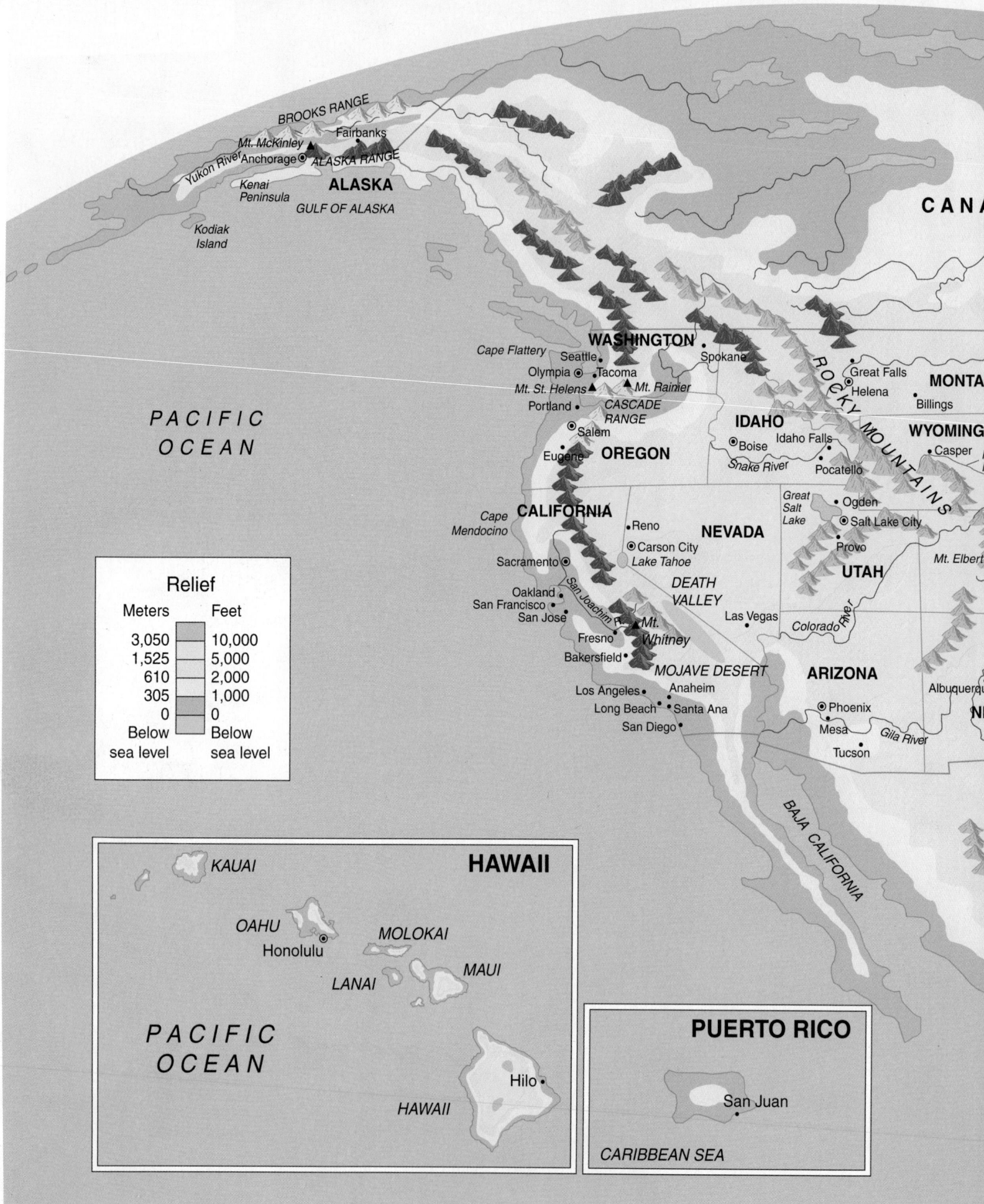

BROOKS RANGE
Fairbanks
Mt. McKinley ▲
Yukon River Anchorage ◉ ALASKA RANGE
ALASKA
Kenai Peninsula
GULF OF ALASKA
Kodiak Island

CANA

PACIFIC OCEAN

Cape Flattery
WASHINGTON
Seattle
Olympia ◉ Tacoma
Mt. St. Helens ▲ ▲ Mt. Rainier
Portland
CASCADE RANGE
Salem ◉
Eugene
OREGON

Spokane

Great Falls
Helena
MONTAN
Billings

IDAHO
Boise ◉ Idaho Falls
Snake River
Pocatello
WYOMING
Casper
Ne R.

Cape Mendocino
CALIFORNIA
Reno
Carson City ◉
Lake Tahoe
NEVADA

Great Salt Lake
Ogden
Salt Lake City ◉
Provo
UTAH
Mt. Elbert ▲

Sacramento ◉

Oakland
San Francisco
San Jose
San Joachim R.
Fresno
Bakersfield
▲ Mt. Whitney
DEATH VALLEY
Las Vegas

Colorado River

MOJAVE DESERT
Los Angeles
Long Beach
Anaheim
Santa Ana
San Diego
ARIZONA
Phoenix ◉
Mesa
Tucson
Albuquerque
NE
Gila River

ROCKY MOUNTAINS

BAJA CALIFORNIA

Relief

Meters		Feet
3,050		10,000
1,525		5,000
610		2,000
305		1,000
0		0
Below sea level		Below sea level

HAWAII

KAUAI

OAHU
Honolulu ◉
MOLOKAI
LANAI
MAUI

PACIFIC OCEAN

Hilo

HAWAII

PUERTO RICO

San Juan

CARIBBEAN SEA

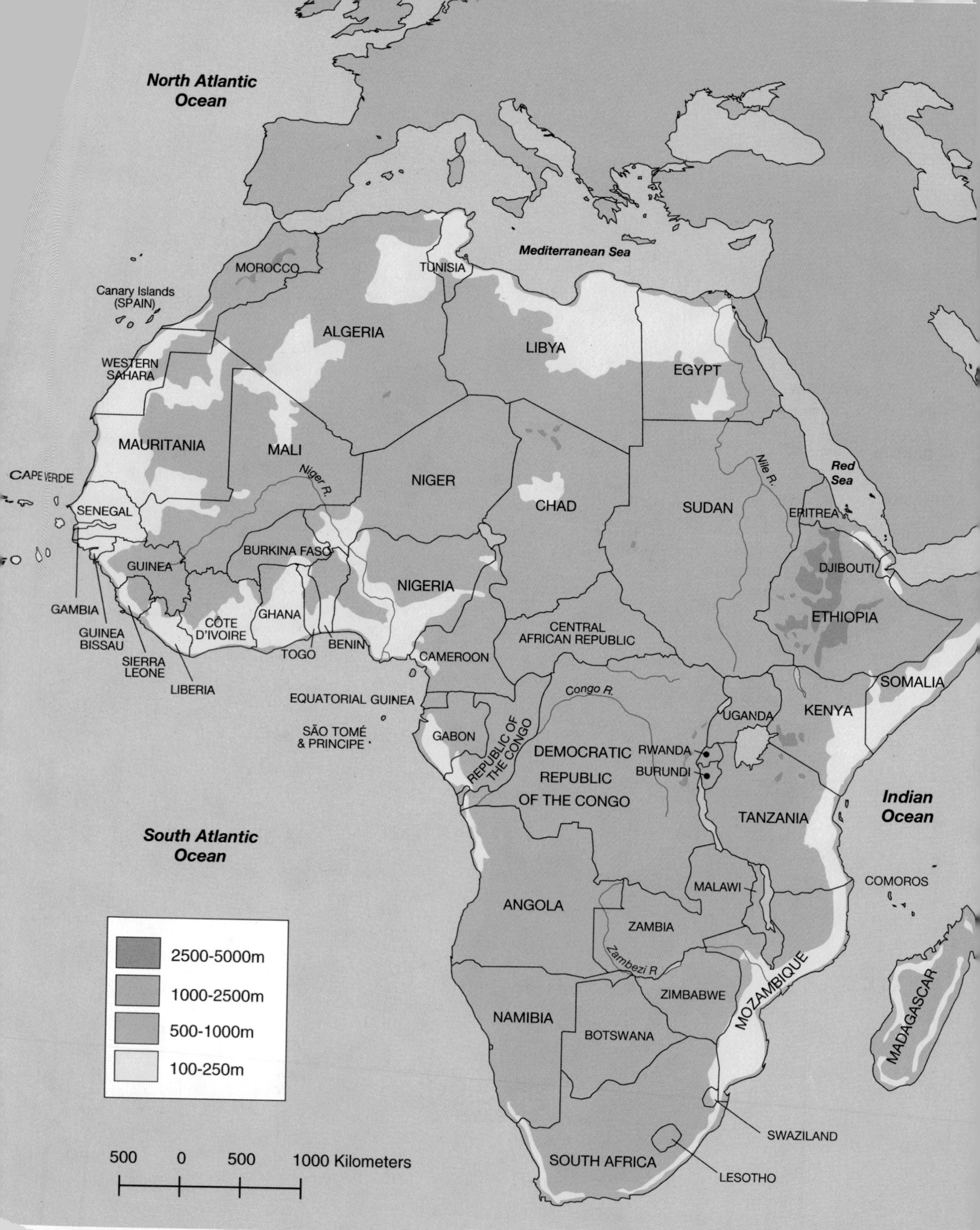

Sixth Edition

The African-American Odyssey

VOLUME 2

Darlene Clark Hine
Northwestern University

William C. Hine
South Carolina State University

Stanley Harrold
South Carolina State University

PEARSON

Boston   Columbus   Indianapolis   New York   San Francisco   Upper Saddle River
Amsterdam   Cape Town   Dubai   London   Madrid   Milan   Munich   Paris   Montréal   Toronto
Delhi   Mexico City   São Paulo   Sydney   Hong Kong   Seoul   Singapore   Taipei   Tokyo

Editor-in-Chief: Dickson Musslewhite
Publisher: Charlyce Jones Owen
Editorial Assistant: Maureen Diana
Program Manager: Beverly Fong
Managing Editor: Ann Marie McCarthy
Project Manager: Emsal Hasan
Director of Marketing: Brandy Dawson
Executive Marketing Manager: Wendy Albert
Operations Specialist: Mary Ann Gloriande
Director of Media: Brian Hyland
Digital Media Editor: Thomas Scalzo
Senior Art Director: Maria Lange
Interior Design: S4Carlisle Publishing Services
Cover Design: Redkite Productions
Cartographer: International Mapping
Full-Service Production and Composition: S4Carlisle Publishing Services
Full Service Project Manager: Mary Tindle
Manager, Rights and Permissions: Barbara Ryan
Printer/Binder: Courier/Kandallville
Cover Printer: Lehigh Phoenix

Dedicated To

Alma J. Clark McIntosh
(1951–2012)

Roy Harrold
(1950–2011)

Peter J. Hine
(1953–2012)

Credits and acknowledgments for materials borrowed from other sources and reproduced, with permission, in this textbook appear on pages **C-1** to **C-2**.

© 2014, 2011, 2008 by Pearson Education, Inc., Upper Saddle River, New Jersey, 07458.
Pearson Education. All rights reserved. Printed in the United States of America. This publication is protected by Copyright and permission should be obtained from the publisher prior to any prohibited reproduction, storage in a retrieval system, or transmission in any form or by any means, electronic, mechanical, photocopying, recording, or likewise. To obtain permission(s) to use material from this work, please submit a written request to Pearson Education, Inc., Permissions Department, One Lake Street, Upper Saddle River, New Jersey 07458 or you may fax your request to 201-236-3290.

Many of the designations by manufacturers and seller to distinguish their products are claimed as trademarks. Where those designations appear in this book, and the publisher was aware of a trademark claim, the designations have been printed in initial caps or all caps.

Library of Congress Cataloging-in-Publication Data
Hine, Darlene Clark, author.
 The African-American odyssey / Darlene Clark Hine, William C. Hine, and
Stanley Harrold. — Sixth edition.
        volumes cm
 Includes index.
  ISBN 978-0-205-94704-1
 1. African Americans. 2. African Americans—History. I. Hine, William C. II. Harrold, Stanley. III. Title.
 E185.H533 2013
 973.00496073—dc23

                        2013016281

V011

Student Edition:	Volume 1	Volume 1 a la carte
ISBN 10: 0-205-94045-5	ISBN 10: 0-205-94704-2	ISBN 10: 0-205-94974-6
ISBN 13: 978-0-205-94045-5	ISBN 13: 978-0-205-94704-1	ISBN 13: 978-0-205-94974-8
Instructor Review Copy	Volume 2	Volume 2 a la carte
ISBN 10: 0-205-94904-5	ISBN 10: 0-205-94749-2	ISBN 10: 0-205-94973-8
ISBN 13: 978-0-205-94904-5	ISBN 13: 978-0-205-94749-2	ISBN 13: 978-0-205-94973-1

Brief Contents

Contents

Part V   The Great Depression and World War II 472

CHAPTER 18

Black Protest, the Great Depression, and the New Deal, 1929–1940 474

CHAPTER 19

Meanings of Freedom: Culture and Society in the 1930s, 1940s, and 1950s, 1930–1950 505

CHAPTER 20

The World War II Era and the Seeds of a Revolution, 1936–1948 535

Maps, Figures, and Tables

Maps

Figures

Tables

Preface

"One ever feels his two-ness,—an American, a Negro; two souls, two thoughts, two unreconciled strivings; two warring ideals in one dark body." So wrote W. E. B. Du Bois in 1897. African-American history, Du Bois maintained, was the history of this double-consciousness. Black people have always been part of the American nation that they helped to build. But they have also been a nation unto themselves, with their own experiences, culture, and aspirations. African-American history cannot be understood except in the broader context of American history. Likewise, American history cannot be understood without African-American history.

Since Du Bois's time, our understanding of both African-American and American history has been complicated and enriched by a growing appreciation of the role of class and gender in shaping human societies. We are also increasingly aware of the complexity of racial experiences in American history. Even in times of great racial polarity, some white people have empathized with black people and some black people have identified with white interests.

It is in light of these insights that *The African-American Odyssey* tells the story of African Americans. That story begins in Africa, where the people who were to become African Americans began their long, turbulent, and difficult journey, a journey marked by sustained suffering as well as perseverance, bravery, and achievement. It includes the rich culture—at once splendidly distinctive and tightly intertwined with a broader American culture—that African Americans have nurtured throughout their history. And it includes the many-faceted quest for freedom in which African Americans have sought to counter white oppression and racism with the egalitarian spirit of the Declaration of Independence that American society professes to embody.

Nurtured by black historian Carter G. Woodson during the early decades of the twentieth century, African-American history has blossomed as a field of study since the 1950s. Books and articles have appeared on almost every facet of black life. Yet this survey is the first comprehensive college textbook of the African-American experience. It draws on recent research to present black history in a clear and direct manner, within a broad social, cultural, and political framework. It also provides thorough coverage of African-American women as active builders of black culture.

The African-American Odyssey balances accounts of the actions of African-American leaders with investigations of the lives of the ordinary men and women in black communities. This community focus helps make this a history of a people rather than an account of a few extraordinary individuals. Yet the book does not neglect important political and religious leaders, entrepreneurs, and entertainers. It also gives extensive coverage to African-American art, literature, and music.

African-American history started in Africa, and this narrative begins with an account of life on that continent to the sixteenth century and the beginning of the forced migration of millions of Africans to the Americas. Succeeding chapters present the struggle of black people to maintain their humanity during the slave trade and as slaves in North America during the long colonial period.

The coming of the American Revolution during the 1770s initiated a pattern of black struggle for racial justice in which periods of optimism alternated with times of repression. Several chapters analyze the building of black community institutions, the antislavery movement, the efforts of black people to make the Civil War a war for emancipation, their struggle for equal rights as citizens during Reconstruction, and the strong opposition these efforts faced. There is also substantial coverage of African-American military service, from the War for Independence through American wars of the nineteenth and twentieth centuries.

During the late nineteenth century and much of the twentieth century, racial segregation and racially motivated violence that relegated African Americans to second-class citizenship provoked despair, but also inspired resistance and commitment to change. Chapters on the late nineteenth and early twentieth centuries cover the Great Migration from the cotton fields of the South to the North and West, black nationalism, and the Harlem Renaissance. Chapters on the 1930s and 1940s—the beginning of a period of revolutionary change for African Americans— tell of the economic devastation and political turmoil caused by the Great Depression, the growing influence of black culture in America, the emergence of black internationalism, and the racial tensions caused by black participation in World War II.

The final chapters tell the story of African Americans in the closing decades of the twentieth century and the dawn of the twenty-first century. They portray the freedom struggles and legislative successes of the civil rights movement at its peak during the 1950s and 1960s and the electoral political victories of the black power movement during the more conservative 1970s and 1980s. Finally, there are discussions of black life in the twenty-first century and the election and reelection of Barack Obama, the first African-American president of the United States.

In all, *The African-American Odyssey* tells a compelling story of survival, struggle, and triumph over adversity. It will leave students with an appreciation of the central place of black people and black culture in this country and a better understanding of both African-American and American history.

WHAT'S NEW IN THE SIXTH EDITION

Every chapter in the sixth edition of *The African-American Odyssey* has been revised and improved with updated scholarship. A new feature at the end of each part, **Connecting the Past**, examines important milestones of the African-American experience over time. These six featured essays examine the evolution of the black church, the development of black autobiography, black migration, desegregation of the military, and black culture. There are new in-depth MyHistoryLab activities that explore events and issues using interactive maps on a key event within the chapters.

Chapter Revision Highlights

Chapter 12 The discussion of the devastating impact that the Civil War had the South has been expanded, and there is more information on widespread disease among African Americans following the War. The Bibliography has been updated.

Chapter 13 There is a new section on the Ellenton riot in South Carolina in 1876. The Bibliography has been updated. There is a new featured essay, **Connecting the Past**, on voting rights and politics, which follows the chapter.

Chapter 14 The discussion of memories of the Civil War among black and white people has been revised. There is more information on the desire among black people to acquire land. The Bibliography has been updated.

Chapter 15 There is additional information on the origins of the term "buffalo soldiers" and on black women in the west including black "cowgirls." The Bibliography has been updated.

Chapter 16 There is a revised discussion of Booker T. Washington's dinner with President Theodore Roosevelt in 1901. Information has been added on the Great Migration, and there is a new table on migration, as well as anew quote from Ida B. Wells anticipating the Chicago race riot in 1919. The Bibliography has been updated.

Chapter 17 There is a new featured essay, **Connecting the Past**, on migration and its impact, which follows the chapter.

Chapter 18 A new discussion of medical experimentation on people besides those involved in the Tuskegee Syphilis Experiment has been added with information about the syphilis experiments in Guatemala and in the Indiana prison population. The Bibliography has been substantially updated with new books on Black Internationalism.

Chapter 19 The Bibliography has been updated with new studies and information about Don Cornelius, creator of "Soul Train."

Chapter 20 There is new information on black radar specialists at Camp Evans during World War II. There is also a new photo of President Eisenhower and Dr. Walter S. McAfee of Camp Evans. A new featured essay, **Connecting the Past,** on the significance of the desegregation of the military, which follows the chapter.

Chapter 21 The discussion on Rosa Parks has been expanded as has that of black women's activism against rape and sexual violence before the 1955–1956 bus boycott. The Bibliography has been updated by adding more books about the civilrights movements in northern urban cities.

Chapter 22 The Introduction to the chapter has been rewritten. There have been revisions to the discussion of the black power movement "From Bullets to Ballots." A new chart of black elected officials has been added. The Bibliography has been updated.

Chapter 23 The discussion of the impact of the Recession of 2008–2011 on black women and black communities has been revised and expanded.

Chapter 24 There is a new discussion of the four stages in the evolution of black politics. Information on the reelection of Barack Obama to a second term is new as is a map of voters and a demographic chart of the 2012 electorate. There is also a new chart depicting select accomplishments of President Obama's first term. The Bibliography has been updated. There is an added a new featured essay, **Connecting the Past**, on the significance of black culture, which follows the chapter.

ABOUT *THE AFRICAN-AMERICAN ODYSSEY*

The many special features and pedagogical tools integrated within *The African-American Odyssey* are designed to make the text accessible to students. They include a variety of tools to reinforce the narrative and help students grasp key issues.

Part-opening timelines thematically organize events in African-American history and provide a reference to the many noteworthy individuals discussed in the chapters.

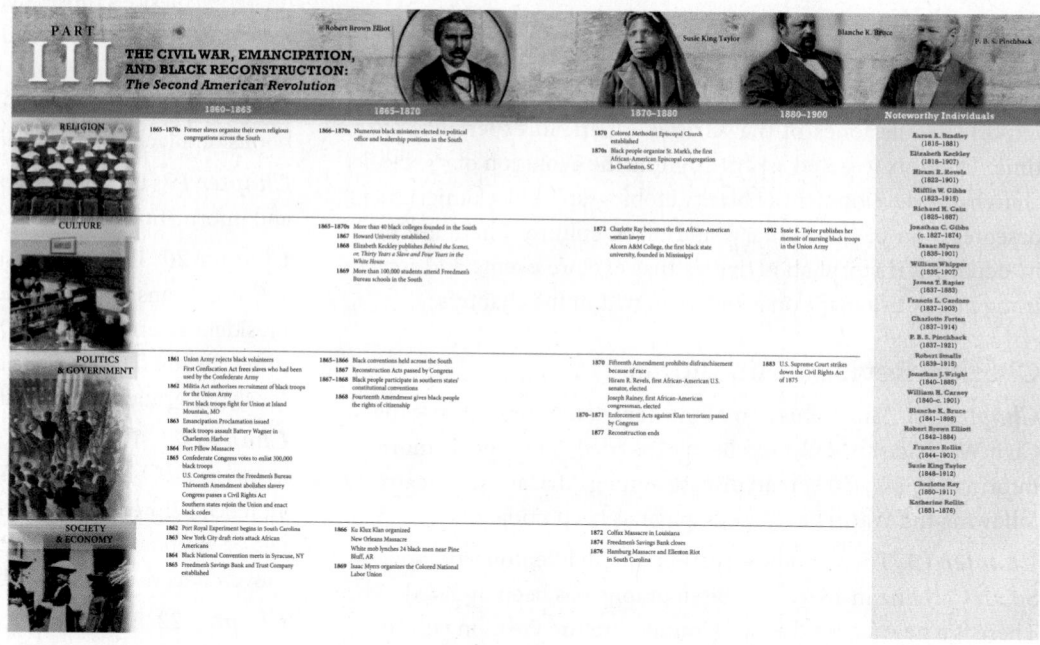

Chronologies are included throughout the chapters to provide students with a snapshot of the temporal relationship among significant events.

Voices boxes provide students with first-person perspectives on key events in African-American history. Brief introductions and study questions help students analyze these primary source documents and relate them to the text.

1861–1863
THE STEPS TO EMANCIPATION

April 1861
Fort Sumter is attacked; Civil War begins

August 1861
General Fremont orders emancipation of slaves in Missouri; Lincoln countermands him

April 1862
Congress provides funds for compensated emancipation; border states spurn the proposal

Summer 1862
Lincoln concludes that Union military victory requires emancipation

January 1, 1863
Emancipation Proclamation takes effect

May 1861
General Butler refuses to return escaped "contrabands" to slavery

August 1861
First Confiscation Act frees captured slaves used by Confederate Army

May 1862
Lincoln revokes General Hunter's order abolishing slavery in South Carolina, Georgia, and Florida

September 22, 1862
Lincoln issues Preliminary Emancipation Proclamation after Battle of Antietam

---

VOICES   A Black Nurse on the Horrors of War and the Sacrifice of Black Soldiers

Susie King Taylor was born a slave in Georgia and learned to read and write in Savannah. She escaped to Union forces in 1862 and served as a nurse and laundress with the First South Carolina Volunteers. In these passages, written years later, she recalls her service with the black men who went into combat and pays tribute to them.

It seems strange how our aversion to seeing suffering is overcome in war,—how we are able to see the most sickening sights, such as men with their limbs blown off and mangled by the deadly shells, without a shudder; and instead of turning away, how we hurry to assist in alleviating their pain, bind up their wounds, and press the cool water to their parched lips, with feelings only of sympathy and pity. . . .

I look around now and see the comforts that our younger generation enjoy, and think of the blood that was shed to make these comforts possible for them, and

see how little some of them appreciate the old soldiers. My heart burns within me at this want of appreciation. There are only a few of them left now, so let us all, as the ranks close, take a deeper interest in them. Let the younger generation take an interest also, and remember that it was through the efforts of these veterans that we older ones enjoy our liberty today.

1. How does Taylor describe what men in combat endure?

2. Who is the object of Taylor's criticism, and why does she offer it?

SOURCE: Susie King Taylor, *Reminiscences of My Life in Camp* (Boston: Taylor, 1902), 31–32, 51–52.

Read on MyHistoryLab Document: An African-American Army Laundress Describes Her Service, 1902

Profile boxes provide biographical sketches that highlight the contributions and personalities of both prominent individuals and ordinary people, illuminating common experiences among African Americans at various times and places.

PROFILE Elizabeth Keckley

BORN A SLAVE IN 1818, ELIZABETH KECKLEY became a dressmaker for First Lady Mary Todd Lincoln and later wrote one of the first personal accounts of life inside the Lincoln White House. Elizabeth Keckley had experienced the exploitation and degradation common to thousands of slave women. She was born in Dinwiddie Court House, Virginia, and spent her childhood as a slave of the Burwell family. She saw slaves beaten and sold away from their families. She even watched as a young boy was sold away from his mother so his owner could buy pigs.

During adolescence, she was loaned to a North Carolina slave owner, where she was beaten and eventually raped. She described what happened: "I was regarded as fair-looking for one of my race, and for four years a white man—I spare the world his name—had base designs upon me. I do not care to dwell upon this subject for it is one that is fraught with pain. Suffice it to say that he persecuted me for four years, and I—I became a mother. The child of which he was the father was the only child I ever brought into the world."

Later, one of the Burwell daughters took Keckley and her son George to St. Louis. She already knew how to sew, and she became a proficient seamstress. She also married a slave, James Keckley, but they soon separated. Keckley was able to purchase herself and her son for $1,200. She also learned to read and write. In 1860 she moved to Washington, DC, and attracted a prosperous clientele that included such prominent politicians' wives as Varma Davis, the wife of Mississippi Senator Jefferson Davis, soon to be president of the Confederacy.

After the Lincolns arrived in Washington, Keckley began making dresses for the First Lady and became Mrs. Lincoln's confidante and traveling companion. She helped convert Mrs. Lincoln, whose family owned slaves in Kentucky, to strong antislavery views. Both women lost sons. Keckley's son George was killed early in the Civil War in Missouri fighting for the Union. Eleven-year-old Willie Lincoln died of a fever in 1862 in the White House. With Mrs. Lincoln's assistance, Keckley founded the Contraband Relief Association to help former slaves in Washington.

In 1868 she published *Behind the Scenes: Or, Thirty Years a Slave and Four Years in the White House.* Although it was a favorable account of life in the Lincoln White House, the book upset the Lincoln family. Keckley denied she had violated Mrs. Lincoln's privacy. "If I have betrayed confidence in anything I have published it has been to place Mrs. Lincoln in better light before the world. My own character as well as the character of Mrs. Lincoln, is at stake, since I have been intimately associated with the lady in the most eventful periods of her life."

Elizabeth Keckley spent the rest of her own life living off the pension from her son's service as a Union soldier. She died in Washington in 1907 at the Home for Destitute Women and Children, which she had helped found years earlier.

Read on MyHistoryLab Document: Elizabeth Keckley, *Behind the Scenes: Or, Thirty Years a Slave, and Four Years in the White House*, 1868

Marginal glossary terms throughout the chapter guide the student to key terms for review.

Like the decision to free the slaves, the decision to employ black troops proceeded neither smoothly nor logically. The commitment to the Civil War as a white man's war was entrenched, and many white northerners opposed the initial attempts to enlist black troops. As with emancipation, Lincoln moved slowly from outright opposition to cautious acceptance to enthusiastic support for enlisting black men in the Union Army.

View on MyHistoryLab Closer Look: Black Union Soldiers

Although black men had fought well in the War for Independence and the War of 1812, they were legally prohibited from joining the regular U.S. Army. The Militia Act of 1792 also barred them from the state militias. In 1861 a few black men were able to join Union units and go off to war. H. Ford Douglas, who had a fair complexion, enlisted in the all-white 95th Illinois Infantry, a volunteer regiment.

The First South Carolina Volunteers

Some Union officers recruited black men long before emancipation was proclaimed and before most white northerners were prepared to accept, much less welcome, black troops. In May 1862 General David Hunter began recruiting former slaves along the South Carolina coast and the sea islands, an area Union forces had captured in late 1861. But some black men did not want to enlist, and Hunter used white troops to force black men to "volunteer" for military service. He managed to organize a 500-man regiment—the **First South Carolina Volunteers**.

First South Carolina Volunteers This black military unit consisted of former slaves recruited in the South Carolina and Georgia low country in 1862 and 1863 for service with Union military forces in the Civil War.

The former slaves were outfitted in bright red pants, with blue coats and broad-brimmed hats. Through the summer of 1862, Hunter trained and drilled the regiment while awaiting official authorization and funds to pay them. When Congress balked, Hunter disbanded all but one company of the regiment that August. The troops were dispersed, unpaid and disappointed. The surviving company was sent to St. Simon's Island off the Georgia coast to protect former slaves.

Second Confiscation Act The 1862 Act freeing all slaves of rebel owners.

Militia Act of 1862 The 1862 Act authorizing Lincoln to enlist black soldiers.

Although Congress failed to support Hunter, it did pass the **Second Confiscation Act** and the **Militia Act of 1862**, which authorized President Lincoln to enlist black men. In Louisiana that fall, two regiments of free black men, the Native Guards, were accepted for federal service, and General Benjamin Butler organized them into the Corps d'Afrique. General Rufus Saxton gained the approval of Secretary of War Edwin Stanton to revive Hunter's dispersed regiment and to recall the company that had been sent to St. Simon's Island.

Connecting the Past essays examine important milestones of the African-American experience over time: evolution of the black church, the emergence of black autobiography, black migration, desegregation of the military, and black culture.

CONNECTING THE PAST

Migration

African-American men, women, and children who participated in the Great Migration to the north, with suitcases and luggage placed in front, Chicago, 1918.

CHICAGO HAD SLIGHTLY MORE THAN 40,000 black residents in 1910. By 2010, more than one million African Americans lived in Chicago and its suburbs. This huge growth in the city's black population was part of the Great Migration, the largest internal movement of people in American history. Yet this massive shift in population was only one of many instances over the long course of history that Africans and their descendants have willingly or unwillingly changed locations.

Early humans roamed from Africa into Asia and Europe as hunters and gatherers about 100,000 years ago. Between the sixteenth and nineteenth centuries, 12 million Africans were forced to endure the horrors of the Middle Passage and the Atlantic slave trade. In the decades before the Civil War, thousands of southern slaves escaped to freedom in the northern states and Canada by way of the underground railroad. In the late 1870s, economic and political oppression led as many as 40,000 former slaves known as Exodusters to leave the South and move west to Kansas and Oklahoma. About the same time a small number of freedmen left the United States and went to Liberia in West Africa.

But it was the twentieth century's Great Migration that prompted recent and profound political and economic changes in American society. Most of these migrants boarded segregated passenger trains in southern towns to travel on the overground railroad to northern and western communities. Unlike the nineteenth century abolitionist movement and the civil rights movement of the 1950s and 1960s, no dynamic organizations or inspirational leaders were involved in this remarkable resettlement. Instead, individuals, husbands, wives, and friends made what was often a heart-wrenching decision to leave the southern communities where they had been born and raised for a strange and distant destination like Chicago, Pittsburgh, or New York City. They did so because, like the slaves who had fled to freedom a century earlier, the migrants wanted a better life. They hoped to liberate themselves from economic dependence, and to escape the segregation and violence that exemplified life in the Jim Crow South.

While life in the North and the West may have been an improvement, black migrants did not suddenly find themselves residing in the Promised Land. White workers resented black competition for unskilled jobs in manufacturing. Labor unions prohibited black membership. White employers' use of black workers as strikebreakers or scabs further alienated white workingmen. Black women were confined to domestic work and denied employment as retail clerks, bank tellers, waitresses, or secretaries. But the "white" and "colored" signs that saturated the South rarely were seen in the North. Buses, streetcars, and passenger trains had open seating. Black people did not have to step aside when white people passed on city sidewalks.

Many myths accompanied the migrants. Black people who already lived in northern cities looked down on the "countrified" ways of the new arrivals and ridiculed the way they talked, dressed, and carried themselves. They disparaged the newcomers' supposed lack of education, low incomes, and inability to maintain stable families. But these perceptions proved to be inaccurate. Migrants had a sense of purpose and commitment. They were better educated than the people they left behind. They had higher incomes and were less likely to be on welfare than African Americans who already resided in the North. They were more likely to be married and remain married. Their children lived in two-parent households.

By the middle of the twentieth century, several million African Americans lived in densely populated urban communities throughout the nation. Here are residents of Harlem on Seventh Avenue on a cold February day in 1956.

The development of black political power was one of the unexpected consequences of the Great Migration. Black men and women voted freely in the North and West. Living together in black neighborhoods afforded them the opportunity to elect black city councilmen, aldermen, and congressmen. By the 1950s, black men from Chicago, Detroit, Philadelphia, and Harlem served in the U.S. House of Representatives. In the 1960s and 1970s, black mayors were elected in Cleveland, Newark, Detroit, and Los Angeles. Democratic presidential candidates Harry Truman in 1948 and John F. Kennedy in 1960 relied on black voters in northern cities to provide them with margins of victory.

The Civil Rights Act of 1964 and the Voting Rights Act of 1965 eradicated Jim Crow in the South. The Great Migration began to reverse itself. Black people who had migrated to northern communities in the 1940s and 1950s began to retire in the 1980s and 1990s to towns and communities they had left as young people. Now, with a shifting racial dynamic in the United States that included the election of an African-American president, there is a new migration. Black people from Africa and the Caribbean increasingly come to America. Between 2000 and 2010, 216,900 Africans moved to the United States. Not all of them will remain, but more will come, attracted to a place where their predecessors were sold and toiled as slaves. Those predecessors and their descendants helped create a vibrant nation that now draws immigrants from nearly every corner of the globe.

1. What specific factors account for the Great Migration?
2. Under what circumstances would you move hundreds of miles from your friends and family?

SUPPLEMENTARY INSTRUCTIONAL MATERIALS

The supplementary package that accompanies *The African-American Odyssey* provides instructors and students with an array of resources that combine sound scholarship, engaging content, and a variety of pedagogical tools and media to enrich the classroom experience and students' understanding of African-American history.

Instructor's Manual

The Instructor's Manual provides instructor resources—lecture and discussion topics, MyHistoryLab resources, and audio/visual resources for each chapter—organized around the learning objectives from the text. The Instructor's Manual is available to adopters for download at Pearson's Instructor Resource Center, www.pearsonhighered.com/irc.

Test Item File

Test materials include multiple-choice, essay, and short-answer questions correlated to the learning objectives from the text. The test item file is available to adopters for download at Pearson's Instructor Resource Center, www.pearsonhighered.com/irc.

My Test

This online test management program allows instructors to select from testing material in the Test Item File to design their own exams. They are available to adopters for download at Pearson's Instructor Resource Center, www.pearsonhighered.com/irc.

PowerPoint Presentations

PowerPoint presentations correlated to the chapters of *The African-American Odyssey* include a full lecture script, a wealth of images and maps, and links to the full array of MyHistoryLab media. They are available to adopters for download at Pearson's Instructor Resource Center, www.pearsonhighered.com/irc.

MyHistoryLab™

MyHistoryLab is a state-of-the-art interactive and instructive solution, designed to be used as a supplement to a traditional lecture course in African-American history, or to completely administer an online course. MyHistoryLab provides access to a wealth of resources, all geared to meet the individual teaching and learning needs of instructors and students. Highlights of MyHistoryLab include:

- The tools you need to engage every student before, during, and after class. An assignment calendar and gradebook allow you to assign specific activities with due dates and to measure your students' progress throughout the semester.
- The **Pearson e-Text** lets students access their textbook anytime, anywhere, and anyway they want, including *listening online*. The e-Text for *The African-American Odyssey* features integrated videos, Explorer activities, documents, images, maps, and interactive self-quizzes.
- A **Personalized Study Plan** for each student, based on Bloom's Taxonomy, arranges activities from those that require less complex thinking—like remembering and understanding—to more complex critical thinking—like applying and analyzing. This layered approach promotes better critical thinking skills, helping students succeed in the course and beyond.

New Features of MyHistoryLab

Two exciting new features of MyHistoryLab are Explorer and MyHistoryLibrary.

- **Explorer** activities connect with topics from the text, engaging students with data visualizations, comparisons of change over time, and data localized to their own communities.
- **MyHistoryLibrary** features 200 documents that enable students to explore the discipline more deeply. Multiple-choice questions for each reading help students review what they've learned—and allow instructors to monitor their performance. The documents are available as e-Texts and audio files.

Acknowledgments

In preparing *The African-American Odyssey*, we have benefited from the work of many scholars and the help of colleagues, librarians, friends, and family.

Special thanks are due to the following scholars for their substantial contributions to the development of this textbook: Hilary Mac Austin, *Chicago, Illinois*; Brian W. Dippie, *University of Victoria*; Thomas Doughton, *Holy Cross College*; W. Marvin Dulaney, *College of Charleston*; Sherry DuPree, *Rosewood Heritage Foundation*; Peter Banner-Haley, *Colgate University*; Robert L. Harris, Jr., *Cornell University*; Wanda Hendricks, *University of South Carolina*; Rickey Hill, *Mississippi Valley State University*; William B. Hixson, *Michigan State University*; Barbara Williams Jenkins, formerly of *South Carolina State University*; Earnestine Jenkins, *University of Memphis*; Hannibal Johnson, *Tulsa, Oklahoma*; Wilma King, *University of Missouri, Columbia*; Karen Kossie-Chernyshev, *Texas Southern University*; Frank C. Martin, *South Carolina State University*; Jacqueline McLeod, *Metropolitan State University of Denver*; Freddie Parker, *North Carolina Central University*; Christopher R. Reed, *Roosevelt University*; Linda Reed, *University of Houston*; Mark Stegmaier, *Cameron University*; Robert Stewart, *Trinity School, New York*; Matthew Whitaker, *Arizona State University*; Barbara Woods, *South Carolina State University*; Andrew Workman, *Mills College*; Deborah Wright, *Avery Research Center, College of Charleston*.

We are grateful to the reviewers through six editions who devoted valuable time to reading and commenting on *The African-American Odyssey*. Their insightful suggestions greatly improved the quality of the text: Leslie Alexander, *The Ohio State University*; Carol Anderson, *University of Missouri, Columbia*; Abel A. Bartley, *University of Akron*; Jennifer L. Baszile, *Yale University*; James M. Beeby, *West Virginia Wesleyan College*; Richard A. Buckelew, *Bethune-Cookman College*; Claude A. Clegg, *Indiana University*; Gregory Conerly, *Cleveland State University*; Delia Cook, *University of Missouri at Kansas City*; Caroline Cox, *University of the Pacific*; Mary Ellen Curtin, *Southwest Texas State University*; Henry Vance Davis, *Ramapo College of NJ*; Roy F. Finkenbine, *Wayne State University*; Dr. Jessie Gaston, *California State University, Sacramento*; Abiodun Goke-Pariola, *Georgia Southern University*; Robert Gregg, *Richard Stockton College of NJ*; Keith Griffler, *University of Cincinnati*; John H. Haley, *University of North Carolina at Wilmington*; Robert V. Hanes, *Western Kentucky University*; Julia Robinson Harmon, *Western Michigan University*; Ebeneazer Hunter, *De Anza College*; Eric R. Jackson, *Northern Kentucky University*; Wali Rashash Kharif, *Tennessee Technological University*;

John W. King, *Temple University*; Joseph Kinner, *Gallaudet University*; Lester C. Lamon, *Indiana University, South Bend*; Eric Love, *University of Colorado-Boulder*; John F. Marszalek, *Mississippi State University*; Kenneth Mason, *Santa Monica College*; Andrew T. Miller, *Union College*; Diane Batts Morrow, *University of Georgia*; Ruddy Pearson, *American College*; Walter Rucker, *University of Nebraska, Lincoln*; Josh Sides, *California State University, Northridge*; Manisha Sinha, *University of Massachusetts, Amherst*; John David Smith, *North Carolina State University at Raleigh*; Marshall Stevenson, *Ohio State University*; Betty Joe Wallace, *Austin Peay State University*; Matthew C. Whitaker, *Arizona State University*; Harry Williams, *Carleton College*; Vernon J. Williams, Jr., *Purdue University*; Leslie Wilson, *Montclair State University*; Andrew Workman, *Mills College*; Marilyn L. Yancy, *Virginia Union University*.

We wish to thank the following reviewers for their insightful comments in preparation for this sixth edition: Leslie Alexander, *The Ohio State University*; Lila Ammons, *Howard University*; Beverly Bunch-Lyons, *Virginia Technical College*; Latangela Crossfield, *Clark Atlanta University*; Linda Denkins, *Houston Community College*; Lillie Edwards, *Drew University*; Jim Harper, *North Carolina Central University*; Dr. Maurice Hobson, *University of Mississippi*; Alyce Miller, *John Tyler Community College*; Zacharia Nchinda, *University of Wisconsin, Milwaukee*; Melinda Pash, *Fayetteville Technical Community College*; Charmayne Patterson, *Clark Atlanta University*; Matthew Schaffer, *Florence Darlington Technical College*; Denise Scifres, *City Colleges of Chicago, Center for Distance Learning*; Linda Tomlinson, *Fayetteville State University*; Angela Winand, *University of Illinois, Springfield*; Erica Woods-Warrior, *Hampton University*.

Many librarians provided valuable help tracking down important material. They include Avery Daniels, Ruth Hodges, Doris Johnson, the late Barbara Keitt, Cathi Cooper Mack, Mary L. Smalls, Ashley Till, and Adrienne Webber, all of Miller F. Whittaker Library, South Carolina State University; James Brooks and Jo Cottingham of the interlibrary loan department, Cooper Library, University of South Carolina; and Allan Stokes of the South Caroliniana Library at the University of South Carolina. Dr. Marshanda Smith and Kathleen Thompson provided important documents and other source material.

Seleta Simpson Byrd of South Carolina State University and Marshanda Smith of Northwestern University provided valuable administrative assistance.

Each of us also enjoyed the support of family members, particularly Barbara A. Clark, Robbie D. Clark, Emily Harrold, Judy Harrold, Carol A. Hine, and Thomas D. Hine.

Finally, we gratefully acknowledge the essential help of the superb editorial and production team at Prentice Hall: Charlyce Jones Owen, Publisher, whose vision got this project started and whose unwavering support saw it through to completion; Maureen Diana, Editorial Assistant; Rochelle Diogenes, Editor-in-Chief of Development; Maria Lange, Creative Design Director; Ann Marie McCarthy, Senior Managing Editor; and Emsal Hasan, Project Manager, who saw it efficiently through production; Marianne Gloriande, Manufacturing Buyer; Wendy Albert, Senior Marketing Manager; Beverly Fong, Program Manager; and Monica Ohlinger Group, who pulled together the book's supplementary material.

We owe a special and heartfelt debt of gratitude to our development editor, the late Gerald Lombardi. Gerald worked closely and conscientiously with us for five editions. This is a better book because of his efforts.

D.C.H.
W.C.H.
S.H.

About the Authors

Darlene Clark Hine

Darlene Clark Hine is Board of Trustees Professor of African-American Studies and Professor of History at Northwestern University. She is a fellow of the American Academy of Arts and Sciences, as well as past president of the Organization of American Historians and of the Southern Historical Association. Hine received her BA at Roosevelt University in Chicago, and her MA and Ph.D. from Kent State University, Kent, Ohio. Hine has taught at South Carolina State University and at Purdue University. She was a fellow at the Center for Advanced Study in the Behavioral Sciences at Stanford University and at the Radcliffe Institute for Advanced Studies at Harvard University. She is the author and/or co-editor of 20 books, most recently *The Black Chicago Renaissance* (Urbana: University of Illinois Press, 2012), *Black Europe and the African Diaspora* (Urbana: University of Illinois Press, 2010), co-edited with Trica Danielle Keaton and Stephen Small; *Beyond Bondage: Free Women of Color in the Americas* (Urbana: University of Illinois Press, 2005), co-edited with Barry Gaspar; and *The Harvard Guide to African-American History* (Cambridge: Harvard University Press, 2000), co-edited with Evelyn Brooks Higginbotham and Leon Litwack. She co-edited a two-volume set with Earnestine Jenkins, *A Question of Manhood: A Reader in U.S. Black Men's History and Masculinity* (Bloomington: Indiana University Press, 1999, 2001); and with Jacqueline McLeod, *Crossing Boundaries: Comparative History of Black People in Diaspora* (Bloomington: Indiana University Press, 2000). With Kathleen Thompson she wrote *A Shining Thread of Hope: The History of Black Women in America* (New York: Broadway Books, 1998), and edited with Barry Gaspar *More Than Chattel: Black Women and Slavery in the Americas* (Bloomington: Indiana University Press, 1996). She won the Dartmouth Medal of the American Library Association for the reference volumes co-edited with Elsa Barkley Brown and Rosalyn Terborg-Penn, *Black Women in America: An Historical Encyclopedia* (New York: Carlson Publishing, 1993). She is the author of *Black Women in White: Racial Conflict and Cooperation in the Nursing Profession, 1890–1950* (Bloomington: Indiana University Press, 1989). She continues to work on the forthcoming book project *The Black Professional Class: Physicians, Nurses, Lawyers, and the Origins of the Civil Rights Movement, 1890–1955*.

William C. Hine

William C. Hine received his undergraduate education at Bowling Green State University, his master's degree at the University of Wyoming, and his Ph.D. at Kent State University. He is a Professor of History at South Carolina State University. He has had articles published in several journals, including *Agricultural History, Labor History,* and the *Journal of Southern History.* He is currently writing a history of South Carolina State University.

Stanley Harrold

Stanley Harrold, Professor of History at South Carolina State University, received his bachelor's degree from Allegheny College and his master's and Ph.D. degrees from Kent State University. He is co-editor of *Southern Dissent*, a book series published by the University Press of Florida. In 1991–1992 and 1996–1997 he had National Endowment for the Humanities Fellowships. In 2005 and 2013 he received NEH Faculty Research Awards. His books include *Gamaliel Bailey and Antislavery Union* (Kent, Ohio: Kent State University Press, 1986), *The Abolitionists and the South* (Lexington: University Press of Kentucky, 1995), *Antislavery Violence: Sectional, Racial, and Cultural Conflict in Antebellum America* (co-edited with John R. McKivigan, Knoxville: University of Tennessee Press, 1999), *American Abolitionists* (Harlow, U.K.: Longman, 2001), *Subversives: Antislavery Community in Washington, D.C., 1828–1865* (Baton Rouge: Louisiana State University Press, 2003), *The Rise of Aggressive Abolitionism: Addresses to the Slaves* (Lexington: University Press of Kentucky, 2004), *Civil War and Reconstruction: A Documentary Reader* (Oxford, U.K.: Blackwell, 2007), and *Border War: Fighting Over Slavery before the Civil War* (Chapel Hill: University of North Carolina Press, 2010). He has published articles in *Civil War History, Journal of Southern History, Radical History Review,* and *Journal of the Early Republic.*

12

The Meaning of Freedom: The Promise of Reconstruction

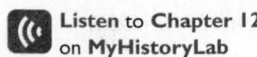
Listen to Chapter 12 on MyHistoryLab

LEARNING OBJECTIVES

12-1 What did freedom mean to nearly four million people who had been slaves?

12-2 How did the government help former slaves acquire land of their own?

12-3 What was the Freedmen's Bureau, its goals, and how effective was it?

12-4 What role did the black church play in African-American life in the post-war decades?

12-5 Why was education so important to African Americans, and what were the ways in which they were able to obtain it?

12-6 Describe the violence directed at southern black people in the aftermath of the war.

12-7 What were the main elements of the separate Reconstruction programs offered by President Johnson and the Radical Republicans in Congress, as well as the South's reaction to these plans?

Many Thousand Gone

No more auction block for me,
No more, no more,
No more auction block for me,
Many thousand gone.
No more driver's lash for me,
No more, no more,
No more driver's lash for me,
Many thousand gone.
No more peck of salt for me,
No more, no more,
No more peck of salt for me,
Many thousand gone.
No more iron chain for me,
No more, no more.
No more iron chain for me,
Many thousand gone.

An African-American emancipation song

What did freedom mean to a people who had endured and survived 250 years of enslavement in America? What did the future hold for nearly four million African Americans in 1865? Freedom meant many things to many people. But to most former slaves, it meant that families would stay together. Freedom meant that women would no longer be sexually exploited. Freedom meant learning to read and write. Freedom meant organizing churches. Freedom meant moving around without having to obtain permission. Freedom meant that labor would produce income for the laborer and not the master. Freedom meant working without the whip. Freedom meant land to own, cultivate, and live on. Freedom meant a trial before a jury if

Students assembled in front of James Plantation School in North Carolina shortly after the Civil War ended in 1865. Compared to many such schools, this one was exceptionally well constructed. Notice the students' clothes and lack of shoes.

FREEDMEN'S SCHOOL.

charged with a crime. Freedom meant voting. Freedom meant citizenship and having the same rights as white people.

Years after slavery ended, a former Texas slave, Margrett Nillin, was asked if she preferred slavery or freedom. She answered unequivocally, "Well, it's dis way, in slavery I owns nothin' and never owns nothin'. In freedom I's own de home and raise de family. All dat causes me worryment and in slavery I has no worryment, but I takes freedom."

The End of Slavery

12-1   **What did freedom mean to nearly four million people who had been slaves?**

With the collapse of slavery, many black people were quick to inform white people that whatever loyalty, devotion, and cooperation they might have shown as slaves had never reflected their inner feelings and attitudes. Near Opelousas, Louisiana, a Union officer asked a young black man why he did not love his master, and the youth responded sharply, "When my master begins to lub me, den it'll be time enough for me to lub him. What I wants is to get away. I want to take me off from dis plantation, where I can be free."

In North Carolina, planter Robert P. Howell was disappointed that a loyal slave named Lovet fled at the first opportunity. "He was about my age and I had always treated him more as a companion than a slave. When I left I put everything in his charge, told him that he was free, but to remain on the place and take care of things. He promised me faithfully that he would, but he was the first one to leave . . . and I did not see him for several years."

Emancipation was traumatic for many former masters. A Virginia freedman remembered that "Miss Polly died right after the surrender, she was so hurt that all the negroes was going to be free." Another former slave, Robert Falls, recalled that his master assembled the slaves to inform them they were free. "I hates to do it, but I must. You all ain't my niggers no more. You is free. Just as free as I am. Here I have raised you all to work for me, and now you are going to leave me. I am an old man, and I can't get along without you. I don't know what I am going to do." In less than a year, he was dead. Falls attributed his master's death to the end of slavery: "It killed him."

Differing Reactions of Former Slaves

Other slaves bluntly displayed their reaction to years of bondage. Aunt Delia, a cook with a North Carolina family, revealed that she secretly had been gaining retribution for the indignity of servitude. "How many times I spit in the biscuits and peed in the coffee just to get back at them mean white folks." In Goodman, Mississippi, a slave named Caddy learned she was free and rushed from the field to find her owner. "Caddy threw down that hoe, she marched herself up to the big house, then, she looked around and found the mistress. She went over to the mistress, she flipped up her dress and told the white woman to do something. She said it mean and ugly. This is what she said: 'Kiss my ass!'"

In contrast, some slaves, especially elderly ones, were apprehensive about freedom. On a South Carolina plantation, an older black woman refused to accept emancipation. "I ain' no free nigger! I is got a marster and mistiss! Dee right dar in de great house. Ef you don' b'lieve me, you go dar an' see."

Reuniting Black Families

As slavery ended, the most urgent need for many freed people was finding family members who had been sold away from them. Slavery had not destroyed the black family. Husbands, wives, and children went to great lengths to reassemble their families after the Civil War.

Watch on **MyHistoryLab Video:** The Meaning of Freedom

Listen on **MyHistoryLab Audio:** Remembering Slavery #2

Read on **MyHistoryLab Document:** Reconstruction: The Struggle to Define the Meaning of Freedom

12-1
12-2
12-3
12-4
12-5
12-6
12-7

For years and even decades after the end of slavery, advertisements in black newspapers appealed for information about missing kinfolk. For example, the *Colored Tennessean* published the following notice on August 5, 1865:

> Saml. Dove wishes to know of the whereabouts of his mother, Areno, his sisters Maria, Neziah and Peggy, and his brother Edmond, who were owned by Geo. Dove of Rockingham County, Shenandoah Valley, Va. Sold in Richmond, after which Saml. and Edmond were taken to Nashville, Tenn., by Joe Mick; Areno was left at the Eagle Tavern, Richmond. Respectfully yours, Saml. Dove, Utica, New York.

In North Carolina a northern journalist met a middle-aged black man "plodding along, staff in hand, and apparently very footsore and tired." The nearly exhausted freedman explained that he had walked almost 600 miles looking for his wife and children, who had been sold four years earlier.

There were emotional reunions as family members found each other after years of separation. Ben and Betty Dodson had been apart for 20 years when Ben found her in a refugee camp after the war. "Glory! glory! hallelujah," he shouted as he hugged his wife. "Dis is my Betty, shuah. I foun' you at las'. I's hunted and hunted till I track you up here. I's boun' to hunt till I fin' you if you's alive."

Other searches had more heart-wrenching results. Husbands and wives sometimes learned that their spouses had remarried during the separation. Believing his wife had died, the husband of Laura Spicer remarried—only to learn after the war that Laura was still alive. Sadly, he wrote to her but refused to meet: "I would come and see you but I know I could not bear it. I want to see you and I don't want to see you. I love you just as well as I did the last day I saw you, and it will not do for you and I to meet."

Tormented, he wrote again pledging his love: "Laura I do not think that I have change any at all since I saw you last—I thinks of you and my children every day of my life. Laura I do love you the same. My love to you never have failed. Laura, truly, I have got another wife, and I am very sorry that I am. You feels and seems to me as much like my dear loving wife, as you ever did Laura."

One freedman testified to the close ties that bound many slave families when he replied bitterly to the claim that he had had a kind master who had fed him and never used the whip: "Kind! yes, he gib men corn enough, and he gib me pork enough, and he neber gib me one lick wid de whip, but whar's my wife?—whar's my chill'en? Take away de pork, I say; take away de corn, I can work and raise dese for myself, but gib me back de wife of my bosom, and gib me back my poor chill'en as was sold away."

Land

12-2 **How did the government help former slaves acquire land of their own?**

As people embraced freedom and left their masters, they wanted land. Nineteenth-century Americans of virtually every background associated economic security with owning land. Families wanted to work land and prosper as self-sufficient yeomen. Former slaves believed their future as a free people was tied to the possession of land. But just as it had been impossible to abolish slavery without federal intervention, it would not be possible to procure land without the assistance of the U.S. government. At first, federal authorities seemed determined to make land available to freedmen.

Special Field Order #15

Shortly after his army arrived in Savannah—after having devastated Georgia— Union General William T. Sherman announced that freedmen would receive land.

FREEDMAN'S VILLAGE, ARLINGTON, VIRGINIA.—[See Page 294.]

Former slaves assembled in a village near Washington, DC. Black people welcomed emancipation, but without land, education, or employment, they faced an uncertain future.

12-1

12-2

12-3

12-4

12-5

12-6

12-7

On January 16, 1865, he issued **Special Field Order #15**. This military directive set aside a 30-mile-wide tract of land along the Atlantic coast from Charleston, South Carolina, 245 miles south to Jacksonville, Florida. White owners had abandoned the land, and Sherman reserved it for black families. The head of each family would receive "possessory title" to 40 acres of land. Sherman also gave the freedmen the use of army mules—hence the slogan, "Forty acres and a mule." (Mules, horses, and other draft animals were essential for plowing fields and harvesting many crops before agriculture became mechanized.)

Within six months, 40,000 freed people were working 400,000 acres in the South Carolina and Georgia low country and on the sea islands. Former slaves generally avoided the slave crops of cotton and rice and instead planted sweet potatoes and corn. They also worked together as families and kinfolk. They avoided the gang labor associated with slavery. Most husbands and fathers preferred that their wives and daughters not work in the fields as slave women had been forced to do. Black women who worked in the homes of white families were increasingly willing to resist what they considered the unreasonable demands of white women.

Special Field Order #15 General William Tecumseh Sherman issued this military directive in January 1865. It set aside lands along the coast from Charleston, South Carolina, to Jacksonville, Florida, for former slaves. President Andrew Johnson revoked the order six months later.

The Port Royal Experiment

Meanwhile, hundreds of former slaves had been cultivating land for three years. In late 1861 Union military forces carved out an enclave around Beaufort and Port Royal, South Carolina, that remained under federal authority for the rest of the war. White planters fled to the interior, leaving their slaves behind. Under the supervision of U.S. Treasury officials and northern reformers and missionaries who hurried south in 1862, ex-slaves began to work the land in what came to be known as the "**Port Royal Experiment**." When Treasury agents auctioned off portions of the land for nonpayment of taxes, freedmen purchased some of it. But northern businessmen bought most of the real estate and then hired black people to raise cotton.

White owners sometimes returned to their former lands only to find that black families had taken charge. Black farmers told one former owner, "We own this land now, put it out of your head that it will ever be yours again." And on one South Carolina sea island, white men were turned back by armed black men.

Port Royal Experiment An effort by northern white missionaries, educators, and businessmen in the Sea Islands near Beaufort, South Carolina, to transform former slaves into educated, reliable, and industrious wage earners. Most of the freedmen did not acquire the land they worked.

The Freedmen's Bureau

12-3 | What was the Freedmen's Bureau, its goals, and how effective was it?

Freedmen's Bureau Congress established the Bureau of Refugees, Freedmen, and Abandoned Lands in February 1865 to assist black and white Southerners left destitute by the Civil War.

12-1
12-2
12-3
12-4
12-5
12-6
12-7

As the war ended in early 1865, Congress created the Bureau of Refugees, Freedmen, and Abandoned Lands—commonly called the **Freedmen's Bureau**. Created as a temporary agency to assist freedmen to make the transition to freedom, the bureau was placed under the control of the U.S. Army, and General Oliver O. Howard was put in command. Howard, a devout Christian who had lost an arm in the war, was eager to aid the freedmen.

The bureau was given enormous responsibilities. It was designed to help freedmen obtain land, gain an education, negotiate labor contracts with white planters, settle legal and criminal disputes involving black and white people, and provide food, medical care, and transportation for black and white people left destitute by the war. However, Congress never provided sufficient funds or personnel to carry out these tasks.

The Freedmen's Bureau never had more than 900 agents spread across the South from Virginia to Texas. Mississippi, for example, had 12 agents in 1866. One agent often served a county with a population of 10,000 to 20,000 freedmen. Few of the agents were black because few military officers were black. John Mercer Langston of Virginia was an inspector of schools assigned to the bureau's main office in Washington, DC; Major Martin R. Delany worked with freedmen on the South Carolina sea islands. Large portions of the South had been devastated by the war. Richmond, Atlanta, Columbia, South Carolina, and Charleston were in ruins. Railroads had been torn up. Factories were destroyed. Sherman's army laid waste to farms, plantations, and towns in Georgia and the Carolinas. Southern planters lost nearly four million human beings they had owned as property and had controlled as labor.

The need for assistance was desperate as thousands of black and white southerners endured disease and extreme privation as the Civil War ended. A terrible smallpox epidemic swept through the South and killed as many as one million newly freed people. The Bureau was overwhelmed as it tried to provide medical care to freedmen and thousands of white people who were suffering and dying from malnutrition, cholera, yellow fever, and pneumonia, as well as smallpox. The bureau established camps for the homeless, fed the hungry, and cared for orphans and the sick as best it could. By 1866 it had distributed more than 13 million rations, consisting of flour, corn meal, and sugar.

In July 1865 the bureau took a first step toward distributing land when General Howard issued Circular 13 ordering agents to "set aside" 40-acre plots for freedmen. But the allocation had hardly begun when the order was revoked, and authorities announced that land already distributed under Sherman's Special Field Order #15 was to be returned to its white owners.

The reason for this reversal was that Andrew Johnson, who had become president after Lincoln's assassination in April 1865, began to pardon hundreds and then thousands of former Confederates and restore their lands to them. General Howard had to tell black people that they had to relinquish the land they thought they had acquired. Speaking to some 2,000 freedmen on South Carolina's Edisto Island in October 1865, Howard pleaded with them to "lay aside their bitter feelings, and to become reconciled to their old masters." A black man shouted a response, "Why, General Howard, why do you take away our lands? You take them from us who are true, always true to the Government! You give them to our all-time enemies. This is not right!"

A committee rejected Howard's appeal for reconciliation and forgiveness and an unhappy black man insisted the government provide land:

> You ask us to forgive the landowners of our island. You only lost your right arm in war and might forgive them. The man who tied me to a tree and gave me 39 lashes and who stripped and flogged my mother and my sister and who will not let me stay in his empty hut except I will do his planting and be satisfied with his price and who combines with others to keep away land from me well knowing I would not have anything to do with him if I had land of my own—that man I cannot well forgive.

📖 Read on MyHistoryLab Document: The Freedmen's Bureau Bill (1865)

THE FREEDMEN'S BUREAU.—Drawn by A. R. Waud.—[See Page 461.]

Freedmen's Bureau agents often found themselves in the middle of angry disputes over land and labor that erupted between black and white southerners. Too often the bureau officers sided with the white landowners in these disagreements with former slaves.

Harper's Weekly, July 25, 1868.

12-1
12-2
12-3
12-4
12-5
12-6
12-7

These appeals moved Howard. He returned to Washington and attempted to persuade Congress to provide land. Congress refused, and President Johnson was determined that white people would get their lands back. It seemed so sensible to most white people. Property that had belonged to white families for generations simply could not be given to freedmen. Freedmen saw it differently. They deserved land that they and their families had worked without compensation for generations. Freedmen believed it was the only way to make freedom meaningful and to gain independence from white people. As it turned out, most freedmen were forced off land they thought should belong to them.

Southern Homestead Act

In early 1866 Congress attempted to provide land for freedmen with the passage of the **Southern Homestead Act**. More than three million acres of public land were set aside for black people and white southerners who had remained loyal to the Union. Much of this land, however, consisted of swampy wetlands or unfertile pinewoods unsuitable for farming. More than 4,000 black families—three-quarters of them in Florida—did claim some of this land, but many lacked the financial resources to cultivate it. Eventually timber companies acquired much of it, and the Southern Homestead Act largely failed.

Southern Homestead Act Congress passed this measure in 1866 that set aside over three million acres of land for former slaves and loyal white Southerners to farm following the Civil War. Most of the land was not fertile or suitable for agriculture, and the act largely failed.

Sharecropping

To make matters worse, by 1866 bureau officials tried to force freedmen to sign labor contracts with white landowners—returning black people to white authority. Black men

VOICES   A Freedmen's Bureau Commissioner Tells Freed People What Freedom Means

In June 1865 Charles Soule, the commissioner of contracts for the Freedmen's Bureau, told freedmen in Orangeburg, South Carolina, what to expect and how to behave in the coming year:

You are now free, but you must know that the only difference you can feel yet, between slavery and freedom, is that neither you nor your children can be bought or sold. You may have a harder time this year than you have ever had before; it will be the price you pay for your freedom. You will have to work hard, and get very little to eat, and very few clothes to wear. If you get through this year alive and well, you should be thankful. . . . You cannot be paid in money, for there is no good money in the District, nothing but Confederate paper. Then, what can you be paid with? Why, with food, with clothes, with the free use of your little houses and plots. You do not own a cent's worth except yourselves.

You do not understand why some of the white people who used to own you do not have to work in the field. It is because they are rich. If every man were poor, and worked in his own field, there would be no big farms, and very little cotton or corn raised to sell; there would be no money, and nothing to buy. Some people must be rich, to pay the others, and they have the right to do no work except to look out after their property.

Remember that all of your working time belongs to the man who hires you: therefore you must not leave work without his leave not even to nurse a child, or to go and visit a wife or husband. When you wish to go off the place, get a pass as you used to, and then you will run no danger of being taken up by our soldiers.

In short, do just about as the good men among you have always done. Remember that even if you are badly off, no one can buy and sell you: remember that if you help yourselves, GOD will help you, and trust hopefully that next year and the year after will bring some new blessing to you.

1. **According to Soule, what is the difference between slavery and freedom?**
2. **Does freedom mean that freed people will have economic opportunities equal to those of white people?**
3. **How should freed people have responded to Soule's advice?**

SOURCE: Ira Berlin et al., "The Terrain of Freedom: The Struggle over the Meaning of Free Labor in the U.S. South," *History Workshop* 22 (Autumn 1986): 108–30.

who refused to sign contracts could be arrested. Theoretically, these contracts were legal agreements between two equals: landowner and laborer. But they were seldom freely concluded. Bureau agents usually sided with the landowner and pressured freedmen to accept unequal terms.

Occasionally, the landowner would pay wages to the laborer. But because most landowners lacked cash to pay wages, they typically agreed to provide the laborer with part of the crop. The laborer, often grudgingly, agreed to work under the supervision of the landowner. The contracts required labor for a full year, and the laborer could neither quit nor strike. Landowners demanded that the laborers work the fields in gangs. Freedmen, however, resisted this system. They sometimes insisted on making decisions involving planting, fertilizing, and harvesting as they sought to exercise independence (see Map 12–1).

Thus, it took time for a new form of agricultural labor to develop. But by the 1870s, the system of **sharecropping** dominated most of the South. There were no wages. Freedmen worked land as families—not in gangs—and not under direct white supervision. The landowner provided seed, tools, fertilizer, and work animals (mules, horses, oxen), and the black family received one-third of the crop. There were many variations on these arrangements, and black families were often cheated out of their fair share of the crop. Without land of their own, they remained under white authority well into the twentieth century.

sharecropping The system following the Civil War in which former slaves worked land owned by white people and "paid" for the use of the land and for tools, seeds, fertilizer, and mules by sharing the crop—usually cotton—with the owner.

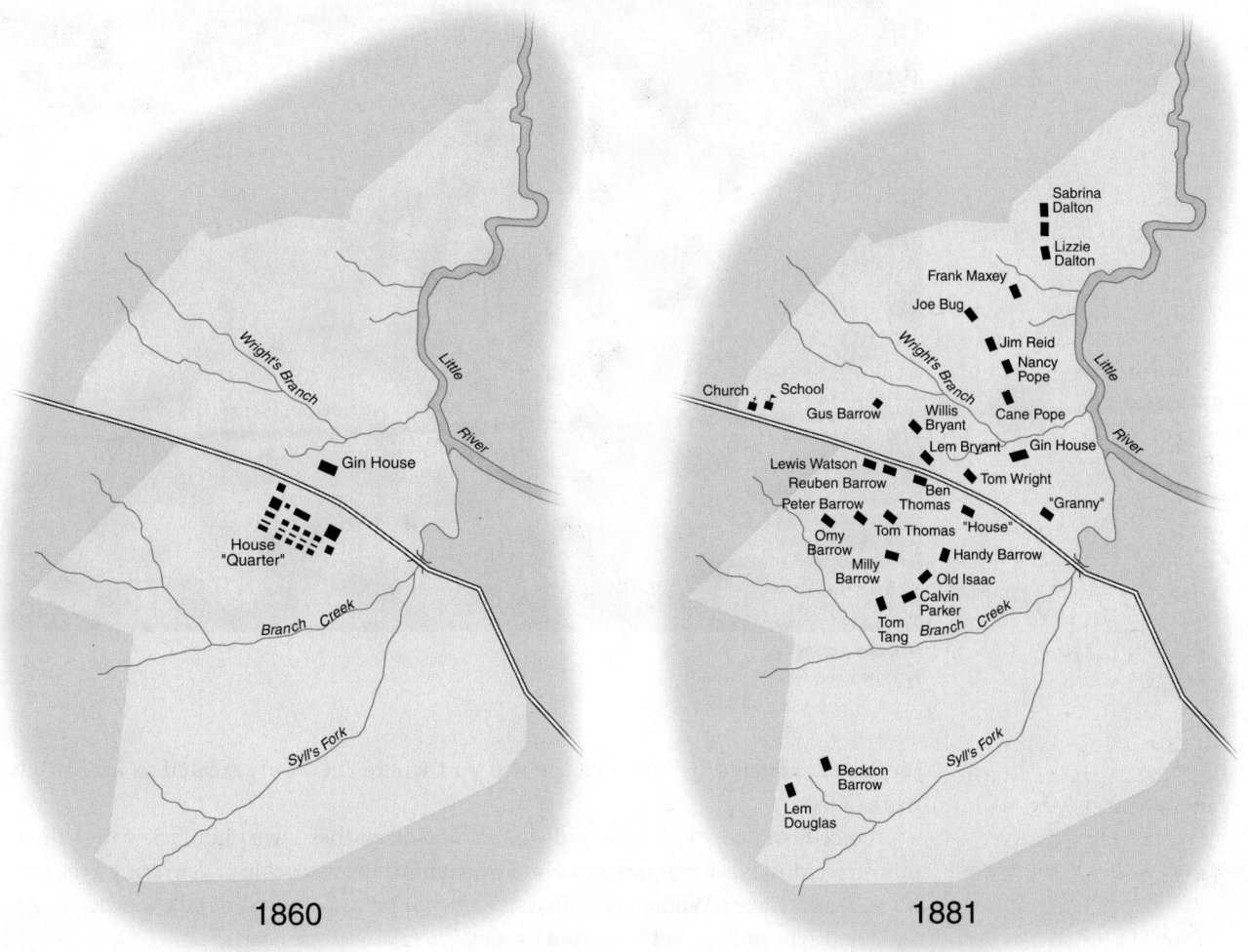

**MAP 12–1 THE EFFECT OF SHARECROPPING ON THE SOUTHERN PLANTATION:
THE BARROW PLANTATION, OGLETHORPE COUNTY, GEORGIA**
With the end of slavery and the advent of sharecropping, black people would no longer
agree to work in fields as gangs. They preferred to have each family cultivate separate
plots of land, thereby distancing themselves as much as possible from slavery and white
supervision.

**Although many freed people worked the same land that they had as
slaves, how does this map suggest the changes experienced by black
people in family life, religion, education, and their relationships with
white people?**

The Black Church

12-4   **What role did the black church play in African-American life
in the post-war decades?**

In the years after slavery, the church became the most important institution among
African Americans other than the family. It filled deep spiritual needs, offered enriching
music, provided charity and compassion to those in need, developed community and
political leaders, and was free of white supervision. Before slavery's demise, free black
people and slaves often attended white churches where they participated in religious

12-1

12-2

12-3

12-4

12-5

12-6

12-7

Freedwomen washing laundry.

services conducted by white clergymen and where they were treated as second-class Christians.

Once liberated, black men and women organized their own churches with their own ministers. Most black people considered white ministers incapable of delivering a meaningful message. Nancy Williams recalled, "Ole white preachers used to talk wid dey tongues widdout sayin' nothin', but Jesus told us slaves to talk wid our hearts."

Northern white missionaries were sometimes appalled by the unlettered and ungrammatical black preachers who nevertheless communicated effectively and emotionally with their parishioners. A visiting white clergyman was impressed and humbled on hearing a black preacher who lacked education but more than made up for it with his devout faith. "He talked about Christ and his salvation as one who understood what he said. . . . Here was an unlearned man, one who could not read, telling of the love of Christ, of Christian faith and duty in a way which I have not learned."

Other black and white religious leaders anguished over what they considered moral laxity and displaced values among the freed people. They preached about honesty, thrift, temperance, and elimination of sexual promiscuity. They demanded an end to "rum-suckers, bar-room loafers, whiskey dealers and card players among the men, and to those women who dressed finely on ill gotten gain."

Church members struggled, scrimped, and saved to buy land and build churches. Most former slaves founded Baptist and Methodist churches. These denominations tended to be more autonomous and less subject to outside control. Their doctrine was usually simple and direct without complex theology. Of the Methodist churches, the African Methodist Episcopal (AME) Church made giant strides in the South after the Civil War.

In Charleston the AME Church was resurrected 40 years after it had been forced to disband during the turmoil over the Denmark Vesey plot in 1822 (see Chapter 8). But by the 1870s, three AME congregations were thriving in Charleston. In Wilmington, North Carolina, the 1,600 members of the Front Street Methodist Church decided to join the AME Church soon after the Civil War ended. They replaced the longtime white minister with a black man.

Hundreds of black churches were founded across the South following the Civil War, and they grew spectacularly in the decades that followed. This illustration shows a congregation crowded into Richmond's First African Baptist Church in 1874.

White Methodists initially encouraged cooperation with black Methodists and helped establish the Colored (now Christian) Methodist Episcopal (CME) Church. However, the white Methodists lost some of their fervor after they failed to persuade the black Methodists to keep political issues out of the CME Church and to dwell instead solely on spiritual concerns.

The Presbyterian, Congregational, and Episcopal churches appealed to the more prosperous members of the black community. Their services tended to be more formal and solemn. Black people who had been free before the Civil War were usually affiliated with these congregations and remained so after the conflict. Well-to-do free black people in Charleston organized St. Mark's Protestant Episcopal Church when they separated from the white Episcopal Church, but they retained their white minister Joseph Seabrook as rector. Poorer black people of darker complexion found churches like St. Mark's unappealing. Ed Barber visited, but only one time:

> *"When I was trampin' 'round Charleston, dere was a church dere called St. Mark, dat all de society folks of my color went to. No black nigger welcome dere, they told me. Thinkin' as how I was bright 'nough to git in, I up and goes dere one Sunday, Ah, how they did carry on, bow and scrape and ape de white folks. . . . I was uncomfortable all de time though, 'cause they were too "hifalootin" in de ways, in de singin', and all sorts of carryin' ons."*

The Roman Catholic Church made modest in-roads among black southerners. There were all-black parishes in St. Augustine, Savannah, Charleston, and Louisville after the Civil War. For generations before the conflict, many well-to-do free people of color in New Orleans had been Catholics, and their descendants remained faithful to the church. On Georgia's Skidaway Island, Benedictine monks established a school for black youngsters in 1878 that survived for nearly a decade.

Religious differences notwithstanding, the black churches, their parishioners, and their clergymen would play a vital role in Reconstruction politics. More than one hundred black ministers were elected to political office after the Civil War.

12-1
12-2
12-3
12-4
12-5
12-6
12-7

Education

12-5   **Why was education so important to African Americans, and what were the ways in which they were able to obtain it?**

Freedom and education were inseparable. To remain illiterate after emancipation was to remain enslaved. One ex-slave master bluntly told his former slave, Charles Whiteside, "Charles, you is a free man they say, but Ah tells you now, you is still a slave and if you lives to be a hundred, you'll STILL be a slave, cause you got no education, and education is what makes a man free!" Almost every freed black person—young or old—desperately wanted to learn. Elderly people were especially eager to read the Bible. During the war and before slavery ended, black people began to establish schools. In 1861 Mary Peake, a free black woman, opened a school in Hampton, Virginia. On South Carolina's sea islands, a black cabinetmaker began teaching openly after having covertly operated a school for years. In 1862 northern missionaries arrived on the sea islands to begin teaching. Laura Towne and Ellen Murray, two white women, and Charlotte Forten, a black woman, opened Penn School on St. Helena's Island as part of the Port Royal Experiment. They enrolled 138 children and 58 adults. By 1863 there were 1,700 students and 45 teachers at 30 schools in the South Carolina low country.

With the end of the Civil War, northern religious organizations, in cooperation with the Freedmen's Bureau, organized hundreds of schools. Classes were held in stables, homes, former slave cabins, taverns, churches, and even—in Savannah and New Orleans—the old slave markets. Former slaves spent hours in the fields and then trudged to a makeshift school to learn the alphabet and arithmetic. In 1865 black ministers created the Savannah Educational Association, raised $1,000, employed 15 black teachers, and enrolled 600 students.

In 1866 the Freedmen's Bureau set aside $500,000 for education. The Bureau furnished the buildings, while former slaves hired, housed, and fed the teachers. By 1869 the Freedmen's Bureau was involved with 3,000 schools and 150,000 students. Even more impressive, by 1870 black people had contributed $1 million to educate their people.

Black Teachers

Although freedmen appreciated the dedication of the white teachers affiliated with the missionary societies, they usually preferred black teachers. The Rev. Richard H. Cain, an AME minister who came south from Brooklyn, New York, said that black people needed to learn to control their own futures: "We must take into our own hands the education of our race. . . . Honest, dignified whites may teach ever so well, but it has not the effect to exalt the black man's opinion of his own race, because they have always been in the habit of seeing white men in honored positions, and respected."

Black men and women responded to the call to teach. Virginia C. Green, a northern black woman, felt compelled to go to Mississippi: "Though I have never known servitude they are . . . my people. Born as far north as the lakes I have felt no freer because so many were less fortunate. . . . I look forward with impatience to the time when my people shall be strong, blest with education, purified and made prosperous by virtue and industry." Hezekiah Hunter, a black teacher from New York, commented in 1865 on the need for black teachers: "I believe we best can instruct our own people, knowing our own peculiarities—needs—necessities. Further—I believe we that are competent owe it to our people to teach them our speciality." And in Malden, West Virginia, when black residents found that a recently arrived 18-year-old black man could read and write, they hired him to teach.

Watch on **MyHistoryLab Video:** The Schools that the Civil War and Reconstruction Created

Read on **MyHistoryLab Document:** Charlotte Forten Describes Life on the Sea Islands, 1864

Charlotte Forten came from a prominent Philadelphia family of color. She joined hundreds of black and white teachers who migrated South during and after the Civil War to instruct the freed people. Some teachers remained for a few months. Others stayed for a lifetime. Charlotte Forten—shown here in an 1866 photograph—taught on the South Carolina sea islands from 1862 to 1864.

In some areas of the South, the sole person available to teach was a poorly educated former slave equipped primarily with a willingness to teach fellow freedmen. One such teacher explained, "I never had the chance of goen to school for I was a slave until freedom. . . . I am the only teacher because we can not doe better now." Many northern teachers, black and white, provided more than the basics of elementary education. Black life and history were occasionally read about and discussed. Abolitionist Lydia Maria Child wrote *The Freedmen's Book,* which offered brief biographies of Benjamin Banneker, Frederick Douglass, and Toussaint Louverture. More often northern teachers, dismayed at the backwardness of the freedmen, struggled to modify behavior and to impart cultural values by teaching piety, thrift, cleanliness, temperance, and timeliness.

Many former slaves came to resent some of these teachers as condescending, self-righteous, and paternalistic. Sometimes the teachers, especially those who were white, became frustrated with recalcitrant students who did not readily absorb middle-class values. Others, however, derived enormous satisfaction from teaching freedmen. A Virginia teacher commented, "I think I shall stay here as long as I live and teach this people. I have no love or taste for any other work, and I am happy only here with them."

Black Colleges

Northern churches and religious societies established dozens of colleges, universities, academies, and institutes across the South in the late 1860s and the 1870s. Most of these institutions provided elementary and secondary education. Few black students were prepared for actual college or university work. The **American Missionary Association**—an abolitionist and Congregationalist organization—worked with the Freedmen's Bureau to establish Fisk in Tennessee, Hampton in Virginia, Tougaloo in Alabama, and Avery in South Carolina. The primary purpose of these schools was to educate black students to become teachers.

In Missouri, the black enlisted men and white officers of the 62nd and 65th Colored Volunteers raised $6,000 to establish Lincoln Institute in 1866, which would become Lincoln University. The American Baptist Home Mission Society founded Virginia Union, Shaw in North Carolina, Benedict in South Carolina, and Morehouse in Georgia. Northern Methodists helped establish Claflin in South Carolina, Rust in Mississippi, and Bennett in North Carolina. The Episcopalians were responsible for St. Augustine's in North Carolina and St. Paul's in Virginia. These and similar institutions formed the foundation for the historically black colleges and universities.

American Missionary Association This religious organization sent teachers and clergymen throughout the South following the Civil War to tend to the spiritual and educational needs of former slaves. It was instrumental in establishing dozens of schools, including Fisk, Hampton, and Avery.

Response of White Southerners

White southerners considered black people's efforts to learn absurd. For generations, white Americans had considered people of African descent abjectly inferior. When efforts were made to educate former slaves, white southerners reacted with suspicion, contempt, and hostility. One white woman told a teacher, "I do assure you, you might as well try to teach your horse or mule to read, as to teach these niggers. They can't learn."

Most white people were well aware that black people could learn. Otherwise, the slave codes that prohibited educating slaves would have been unnecessary. After slavery's end, some white people went out of their way to prevent black people from learning. Countless schools were burned, mostly in rural

View on **MyHistoryLab Closer Look:** Higher Education for African Americans

Black and white land-grant colleges stressed training in agriculture and industry. In this late nineteenth-century photograph, Hampton Institute students learn milk production. The men are in military uniforms, which was typical for males at these colleges. Military training was a required part of the curriculum.

areas. In Canton, Mississippi, black people collected money to open a school—only to have white residents inform them that the school would be burned and the prospective teacher lynched if it opened. The female teacher at a freedmen's school in Donaldsonville, Louisiana, was shot and killed.

Other white southerners grudgingly tolerated black people's desire to acquire an education. One planter conceded in 1870, "Every little negro in the county is now going to school and the public pays for it. This is one hell of [a] fix but we can't help it, and the best policy is to conform as far as possible to circumstances."

Most white people refused to attend school with black people. No integrated schools were established in the immediate aftermath of emancipation. Most black people were more interested in gaining an education than in whether white students attended school with them. When black youngsters tried to attend a white school in Raleigh, North Carolina, the white students stopped going to it. For a brief time in Charleston, black and white children attended the same school, but they were taught in separate classrooms.

Violence

12-6	Describe the violence directed at southern black people in the aftermath of the war.

In the days, weeks, and months after the end of the Civil War, an orgy of brutality and violence swept across the South. White southerners—embittered by their defeat and unable to adjust to the end of slave labor and the loss of millions of dollars worth of slave property—lashed out at black people. There were beatings, murders, rapes, and riots, often with little or no provocation.

Black people who demanded respect, wore better clothing, refused to step aside for white people, or asked to be addressed as "mister" or "missus" were attacked. In South Carolina, a white clergyman shot and killed a black man who protested when another black man was removed from a church service. In Texas, one black man was killed for not removing his hat in the presence of a white man and another for refusing to relinquish a bottle of whiskey. A black woman was beaten for "using insolent language," and a black worker in Alabama was killed for speaking sharply to a white overseer. In Virginia, a black veteran was beaten after announcing he had been proud to serve in the Union Army.

In South Carolina, a white man asked a passing black man whom he belonged to. The black man replied that he no longer belonged to anybody, "I am free now." With that, the white man roared, "Sas me? You black devil!" He then slashed the freedman with a knife. The sheriff of DeWitt County, Texas, shot a black man who was whistling "Yankee Doodle." A Freedmen's Bureau agent in North Carolina explained the intense white hostility: "The fact is, it's the first notion with a great many of these people, if a Negro says anything or does anything that they don't like, to take a gun and put a bullet into him, or a charge of shot." In Texas another Freedmen's Bureau officer claimed that white people simply killed black people "for the love of killing."

There was also large-scale violence. In 1865 University of North Carolina students twice attacked peaceful meetings of black people. Near Pine Bluff, Arkansas, in 1866, a white mob burned a black settlement and lynched 24 men, women, and children. An estimated 2,000 black people were murdered around Shreveport, Louisiana. In Texas, white people killed 1,000 black people between 1865 and 1868.

In May 1866 white residents of Memphis went on a rampage after black veterans forced police to release a black prisoner. The city was already beset with economic difficulties and racial tensions caused in part by an influx of rural refugees. White people, led by Irish policemen, destroyed hundreds of homes, cabins, shacks, churches, and schools in the black section of Memphis. Altogether, 46 black people and two white men died.

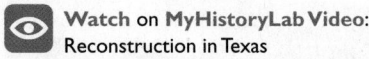

Watch on MyHistoryLab Video:
Reconstruction in Texas

PROFILE   Charlotte E. Ray

CHARLOTTE E. RAY became the first African-American woman to earn a law degree and the first woman admitted to practice law in Washington, DC. She was born on January 13, 1850, in New York City, one of seven children. Her parents were the Rev. Charles B. Ray and his second wife, Charlotte Augusta Burroughs Ray. They were firm believers in the rights of African Americans and in their potential for success.

Charlotte attended Myrtilla Miner's Institution for the Education of Colored Youth in Washington, DC, where Myrtilla Miner, a white educator from New York, was determined to demonstrate that black women were as capable of high moral and mental development as white women.

Charlotte completed high school at Miner's in 1869 and taught at the Normal and Preparatory Department of the recently established Howard University. She also enrolled in law classes at Howard and wrote a thesis analyzing corporations.

She graduated from the law school in 1872 and a month later was admitted to the bar in Washington. She opened an office and planned to practice real estate law. As a real estate lawyer, she could avoid court appearances and the discrimination that women attorneys encountered. She often used her initials, C. E. Ray, so that her clients would not suffer because their legal counsel could be identified as a woman.

Because of the Panic of 1873 and the ensuing economic depression, as well as the difficulties of being a black woman in a white male profession, Ray gave up the practice of law. She supported women's rights and, in 1876, attended the annual meeting of the National American Woman Suffrage Association in New York City. By 1879, she had returned to New York and taught school in Brooklyn. Some time before 1886, she had married, but little is known of her husband. Charlotte Ray died of acute bronchitis on January 11, 1911.

On July 30, 1866, in New Orleans, white people—angered that black men were demanding political rights—assaulted black people on the street and in a convention hall. City policemen, who were mostly Confederate veterans, shot down the black delegates as they fled in panic waving white flags in a futile attempt to surrender. In the assault, 34 black people and three of their white allies died. Federal troops eventually stopped the bloodshed. General Philip H. Sheridan called the riot "an absolute massacre."

Little was done to stem the violence. Most Union troops had been withdrawn from the South and demobilized after the war. The Freedmen's Bureau was usually unwilling and unable to protect the black population. Black people left to defend themselves were usually in no position to retaliate. Instead, they sometimes attempted to bring the perpetrators to justice. In Orangeburg, South Carolina, armed black men brought three white men who had been wreaking violence in the community to the local jail. In Holly Springs, Mississippi, a posse of armed black men apprehended a white man who had murdered a freedwoman.

For black people, the system of justice was thoroughly unjust. Although black people could now testify against white people in court, southern juries remained all white and refused to convict white people charged with harming black people. In Texas during 1865 and 1866, 500 white men were indicted for murdering black people. None were convicted.

The Crusade for Political and Civil Rights

In October 1864 in Syracuse, New York, 145 black leaders gathered in a national convention. Some of the century's most prominent black men and women attended, including Henry Highland Garnet, Frances E. W. Harper, William Wells Brown, Francis L. Cardozo, Richard H. Cain, Jonathan J. Wright, and Jonathan C. Gibbs. They embraced the basic tenets of the American political tradition and proclaimed that they expected to participate fully in it.

Anticipating a future free of slavery, Frederick Douglass optimistically declared "that we hereby assert our full confidence in the fundamental principles of this government . . . the great heart of this nation will ultimately concede us our just claims, accord us our rights, and grant us our full measure of citizenship under the broad shield of the Constitution."

Even before the **Syracuse Convention**, northern Republicans met in Union-controlled territory around Beaufort, South Carolina, and nominated the state's delegates to the 1864

Syracuse Convention A meeting of black leaders in Syracuse, New York, to discuss the future of African Americans following the abolition of slavery. They insisted that black people had earned and deserved the same political and legal rights as white Americans.

Republican national convention. Among those selected were Robert Smalls and Prince Rivers, former slaves who had exemplary records with the Union Army. The probability of black participation in postwar politics seemed promising.

But northern and southern white leaders who already held power would largely determine whether black Americans would gain political power or acquire the same rights as white people. As the Civil War ended, President Lincoln was more concerned with restoring the seceded states to the Union than in opening political doors for black people. Yet Lincoln suggested that at least some black men deserved the right to vote. On April 11, 1865, he wrote, "I would myself prefer that [the vote] were now conferred on the very intelligent, and on those who serve our cause as soldiers." Three days later he was assassinated.

Presidential Reconstruction under Andrew Johnson

12-7 What were the main elements of the separate Reconstruction programs offered by President Johnson and the Radical Republicans in Congress, as well as the South's reaction to these plans?

Vice President Andrew Johnson became president following Lincoln's assassination and initially seemed inclined to impose stern policies on the white South while befriending the freedmen. He announced that "treason must be made odious, and traitors must be punished and impoverished." In 1864 he had told black people, "I will be your Moses, and lead you through the Red Sea of War and Bondage to a fairer future of Liberty and Peace." Nothing proved to be further from the truth. Andrew Johnson was no friend of black Americans.

Born poor in eastern Tennessee and never part of the southern aristocracy, Johnson opposed secession and was the only senator from the seceded states to remain loyal to the Union. He had nonetheless acquired five slaves and the conviction that black people were so inferior that white men must forever govern them. In 1867 Johnson argued that black people could not exercise political power and that they had "less capacity for government than any other race of people. No independent government of any form has ever been successful in their hands. On the contrary, wherever they have been left to their own devices they have shown a constant tendency to relapse into barbarism."

Johnson quickly lost his enthusiasm for punishing traitors. Indeed, he began to placate white southerners. In May 1865 Johnson granted blanket amnesty and pardons to former Confederates willing to swear allegiance to the United States. The main exceptions were high former Confederate officials and those who owned property valued in excess of $20,000, a large sum at the time. Yet even these leaders could appeal for individual pardons. And appeal they did. By 1866 Johnson had pardoned more than 7,000 high-ranking former Confederates and wealthier southerners. Moreover, he had restored land to those white people who had lost it to freedmen.

Johnson's actions encouraged those who had supported secession, owned slaves, and opposed the Union. He permitted longtime southern leaders to regain political influence and authority only months after the end of America's bloodiest conflict. As black people and Radical Republicans watched in disbelief, Johnson appointed provisional governors in the former Confederate states. Leaders in those states then called constitutional conventions, held elections, and prepared to regain their place in the Union. Johnson merely insisted that each former Confederate state formally accept the **Thirteenth Amendment** (ratified in December 1865, it outlawed slavery) and repudiate Confederate war debts.

The southern constitutional conventions excluded black people from the political system and denied them equal rights. As one Mississippi delegate explained, "'Tis nature's law that the superior race must rule and rule they will."

Watch on MyHistoryLab Video:
Presidential Reconstruction

Thirteenth Amendment This amendment to the U.S. Constitution outlawed slavery and involuntary servitude.

12-1
12-2
12-3
12-4
12-5
12-6
12-7

VOICES   A Northern Black Woman on Teaching Freedmen

Blanche Virginia Harris was born in 1842 in Monroe, Michigan, and graduated from Oberlin College in 1860. She became the principal of a black school in Norfolk, Virginia, attended by 230 students. She organized night classes for adults and a sewing society to provide clothing for impoverished students. Later, she taught in Mississippi, North Carolina, and Tennessee. In the following letter she describes her experiences in Mississippi:

23 January 1866

Natchez, Miss.

I have been in this city now nearly five months. . . . The colored teachers three in number, sent out by the [American Missionary] Association to this city, have been brought down here it is true. And then left to the mercy of the colored people or themselves. The distinction between the two classes of teachers (white and colored) is so marked that it is the topic of conversation among the better class of colored people.

My school is very large, some of them pay and some do not. And from the proceeds I pay the board of my sister and myself, and also for the rent of two rooms; rent as well as board is very high so I have to work quite hard to meet my expenses. I also furnish lights, wood and coal. I do not write this as fault-finding, far from it. I shall be thankful if I can in any way help. I sometimes get discouraged. . . .

I have become very much attached to my school; the interest they manifest in their studies pleases me. I will now tell you how I employ my time. From 8 A.M. until 2 P.M. I teach the children. At 3 P.M. I have a class of adults and at night I have night school.

One afternoon we have prayer meeting, another sewing school. And another singing school. I hope my next letter may be more interesting to you.

Very Respectfully,
Blanche Harris

1. **Why was the race of the teacher of such concern?**
2. **What did Harris find difficult about teaching, and what did she find rewarding?**

SOURCE: Ellen NicKenzie Lawson, ed., *The Three Sarahs: Documents of Antebellum Black College Women* (New York: Edward Mellon Press, 1984).

Black Codes

After the election of state and local officials, white legislators gathered in state capitals across the South to determine the status and future of the freedmen. With little debate, the legislatures drafted the so-called **black codes**. Southern politicians gave no thought to providing black people with the political and legal rights associated with citizenship.

The black codes sought to ensure the availability of a subservient agricultural labor supply controlled by white people. They imposed severe restrictions on freedmen, who had to sign annual labor contracts with white landowners. In addition, South Carolina required black people who wanted to establish a business to purchase licenses costing from $10 to $100. The codes permitted black children ages 2 to 21 to be apprenticed to white people and spelled out their duties and obligations in detail. Corporal punishment was legal. Employers were designated "masters" and employees "servants." The black codes also restricted black people from loitering or vagrancy, using alcohol or firearms, hunting, fishing, and grazing livestock. However, the codes did guarantee rights that slaves had not possessed. Freedmen could marry legally, engage in contracts, purchase property, sue or be sued, and testify in court. But black people could not vote or serve on juries. The black codes conceded—barely—freedom to black people.

black codes Laws that were passed in each of the former Confederate states following the Civil War that applied only to black people. While conceding such rights as the right to marry, to contract a debt, or to own property, the codes severely restricted the rights and opportunities of former slaves in terms of labor and mobility.

Black Conventions

Alarmed by these threats to their freedom, black people met in conventions across the South in 1865 and 1866 to protest, appeal for justice, and chart their future. Men who had been free before the war dominated the conventions. Many were ministers, teachers, and artisans. Few had been slaves. Women and children also attended—as spectators, not delegates—but

12-1

12-2

12-3

12-4

12-5

12-6

12-7

women were often influential as they offered comments, suggestions, and criticism. These meetings were hardly militant or radical affairs. Delegates respectfully insisted that white people live up to the principles and rights embodied in the Declaration of Independence and the Constitution.

At the AME church in Raleigh, North Carolina, delegates asked for equal rights and the right to vote. At Georgia's convention, they protested against white violence and appealed for leaders who would enforce the law without regard to color: "We ask not for a Black Man's Governor, nor a White Man's Governor, but for a People's Governor, who shall impartially protect the rights of all, and faithfully sustain the Union."

Delegates at the Norfolk meeting reminded white Virginians that black people were patriotic: "We are Americans. We know no other country. We love the land of our birth." But they protested that Virginia's black code caused "invidious political or legal distinctions, on account of color merely." They requested the right to vote and added that they might boycott the businesses of "those who deny to us our equal rights."

Two conventions were held in Charleston, South Carolina—one before and one after the black code was enacted. At the first, delegates stressed the "respect and affection" they felt toward white Charlestonians. They even proposed that only literate men be granted the right to vote if it were applied to both races. The second convention denounced the black code and insisted on its repeal. Delegates again asked for the rights to vote and testify in court: "These two things we deem necessary to our welfare and elevation." They also appealed for public schools and for "homesteads for ourselves and our children." White authorities ignored the black conventions and their petitions. Instead, they were confident they had relegated the freedmen to a subordinate role.

By late 1865 President Johnson's Reconstruction policies had aroused black people. One black Union veteran summed up the situation: "If you call this Freedom, what do you call Slavery?" Republicans in Congress also opposed Johnson's policies toward the freedmen and the former Confederate states.

The Radical Republicans

Radical Republicans Members of the Republican Party during Reconstruction who vigorously supported the rights of African Americans to vote, hold political office, and have the same legal and economic opportunities as white people.

Radical Republicans, as the more militant Republicans were called, were especially disturbed that Johnson seemed to have abandoned the ex-slaves to their former masters. They considered white southerners disloyal and unrepentant, despite their military defeat. Moreover, Radical Republicans—unlike moderate Republicans and Democrats—were determined to transform the racial fabric of American society by including black people in the political and economic system.

Among the most influential Radical Republicans were Senators Charles Sumner, Benjamin Wade, and Henry Wilson, as well as Congressmen Thaddeus Stevens, George W. Julian, and James M. Ashley. Few white Americans were as dedicated to the rights of black people as these men. They had fought to abolish slavery and were reluctant to compromise. They were honest, tough, and articulate but also abrasive, difficult, self-righteous, and vain. Black people appreciated them, whereas many white people hated them. One black veteran wrote to Charles Sumner in 1869, stating, "Your name shall live in our hearts forever." A white Philadelphia businessman said that Thaddeus Stevens "seems to oppose any measure that will not benefit the nigger."

Radical Proposals

To provide freedmen with land, Stevens introduced a bill in Congress in late 1865 to confiscate 400 million acres from the wealthiest 10 percent of southerners and distribute it free to freedmen. The remaining land would be auctioned off in plots no larger than 500 acres. Few legislators supported the proposal. Even those who wanted fundamental change considered confiscation a violation of property rights.

Instead, Radical Republicans supported voting rights for black men. They were convinced that black men—to protect themselves and to secure the South for the Republican Party—had to have the right to vote.

PROFILE   Aaron A. Bradley

AT A TIME WHEN MANY WHITE PEOPLE considered it a disgrace that even the most reserved, refined, and well-educated black man might serve in political office, Aaron Bradley's presence in politics was outrageous. White southerners regarded him as a dangerous revolutionary. White Republicans, who normally would have been his allies, considered him belligerent and uncooperative. But most freedmen admired and supported him. Like him or not, he was a major figure in Georgia politics during Reconstruction.

Bradley was born a slave in about 1815 in South Carolina. His father was probably white. He belonged to Francis W. Pickens, who was South Carolina's governor when the state seceded (see Chapter 10). For a time, Bradley worked as a shoemaker in nearby Augusta, Georgia. At about age 20, he escaped and went to Boston, where he studied law and met black and white abolitionists.

In 1865 Bradley moved to Savannah, where he took up the cause of the freedmen and opened a school. He worked closely with the city's black longshoremen and low country and sea island rice field workers.

Bradley demanded that black families keep the land they had occupied under Sherman's Special Field Order #15. He believed that they had to have land to prosper. He criticized the Freedmen's Bureau for attempting to force black people off the land and argued that President Johnson should be impeached for supporting Confederate landowners rather than black and white people who were loyal to the Union.

Bradley also insisted that black people deserved the rights to vote, testify in court, and have jury trials. After he urged black farmers to defend their land by force, federal authorities charged him with advocating insurrection. He was sentenced to a year's confinement but was soon paroled. Almost immediately, another fiery speech got him in trouble again, and he had to leave Georgia.

He returned to Boston and renewed his pleas for land for the freedmen. He wrote the head of the Freedmen's Bureau, "My great object is, to give you Back-bone, and as the Chief Justice of 4 millions of Colored people, and Refugees; You can not, and must not, be a Military Tool, in the hands of Andrew Johnson."

In 1867 Bradley returned to Savannah and attacked the system of sharecropping. He complained that freedmen were compelled to work involuntarily and asked that black men be permitted to arm themselves. He also argued that justice would be fairer if the courts included black men. Although the Freedmen's Bureau considered Bradley a troublemaker, he never backed down.

In 1867, black voters elected Bradley to the state constitutional convention, but he was soon expelled. Then he was elected to the state senate—only to be expelled again along with all the black members of the Georgia legislature.

Meanwhile, Bradley carried on a running battle with Savannah's mayor, a former Confederate colonel affiliated with the Ku Klux Klan. He threatened the "KKK and all Bad Men, . . . if you strike a blow the man or men will be followed, and the house in which he or they shall take shelter, will be burned to the ground."

In 1868 Bradley organized black workers to arm themselves to retain the lands that they believed belonged to them. For a month, black men controlled parts of Chatham County outside Savannah. Eventually, federal authorities jailed one hundred of them. Bradley again fled north.

He returned to Georgia in 1870 and reclaimed his senate seat after Congress forced the legislature to seat its black members. He supported measures to remove Savannah's mayor, reduce taxes on workers, and institute an eight-hour workday.

Democrats regained control of Georgia politics in 1872, and Bradley and the Republicans were swept from power. He ran for Congress in South Carolina in 1874 but lost. He supported black migration to Liberia and Florida, but he moved to St. Louis and died there in 1881.

Aaron Bradley was certainly not a typical Reconstruction leader. He maintained few close ties to black or white politicians. He was constantly embroiled in disputes, he did not cooperate with middle-class black leaders, and had no ties with local churches and their clergymen—a rarity among black politicians.

He dressed in expensive and flashy clothes, and he could be pompous, abrasive, and intemperate. White people universally detested him. Yet Bradley remained popular among freedmen.

12-1

12-2

12-3

12-4

12-5

12-6

12-7

Moderate Republicans, however, found the prospect of black voting almost as objectionable as the confiscation of land. They preferred to build the Republican Party in the South by cooperating with President Johnson and attracting loyal white southerners.

The thought of black suffrage appalled northern and southern Democrats. Most white northerners—Republicans and Democrats—favored denying black men the right to vote in

12-1

12-2

12-3

12-4

12-5

12-6

12-7

Read on MyHistoryLab Document: The Colored People of South Carolina Protest the "Black Codes," 1865

Bearing a remarkable resemblance to a slave auction, this scene in Monticello, Florida, shows a black man auctioned off to the highest bidder shortly after the Civil War. Under the terms of most southern black codes, black people arrested and fined for vagrancy or loitering could be "sold" if they could not pay the fine. Such spectacles infuriated many northerners and led to demands for more rigid Reconstruction policies.

their states. After the war, proposals to guarantee the right to vote to black men were defeated in New York, Ohio, Kansas, and the Nebraska Territory. In the District of Columbia, a vote to permit black suffrage lost 6,951 to 35. However, five of the six New England states as well as Iowa, Minnesota, and Wisconsin allowed black men to vote.

As much as they objected to black suffrage, most white northerners objected even more strongly to defiant white southerners. Journalist Charles A. Dana described the attitude of many northerners: "As for negro suffrage, the mass of Union men in the Northwest do not care a great deal. What scares them is the idea that the rebels are all to be let back . . . and made a power in government again, just as though there had been no rebellion."

In December 1865 Congress created the Joint Committee on Reconstruction to determine whether to readmit the southern states to the Union. The committee confirmed reports of widespread mistreatment of black people and white arrogance.

The Freedmen's Bureau Bill and the Civil Rights Bill

In early 1866 Senator Lyman Trumbull, a moderate Republican from Illinois, introduced two major bills. The first was to provide more financial support for the Freedmen's Bureau and extend its authority to defend the rights of black people.

The second proposal became the first **Civil Rights Act** in American history. It made any person born in the United States a citizen (except Indians) and entitled them to rights protected by the U.S. government. Black people would possess the same legal rights as white people. The bill was clearly intended to invalidate the black codes.

Read on MyHistoryLab Document: The Civil Rights Act of 1866

Civil Rights Act This act nullified the black codes and made African Americans citizens with the basic rights of life, liberty, and due process. It was passed over President Andrew Johnson's veto. Its main features were subsequently embedded in the Fourteenth Amendment to the Constitution.

Johnson's Vetoes

Both measures passed in Congress with nearly unanimous Republican support. President Johnson, however, vetoed them. He claimed that the bill to continue the Freedmen's Bureau would greatly expand the federal bureaucracy and permit too "vast a number of agents" to exercise arbitrary power over the white population. He insisted that the Civil Rights Bill benefited black people at the expense of white people: "In fact, the distinction of race and color is by the bill made to operate in favor of the colored and against the white race."

The Johnson vetoes stunned Republicans. Although he had not meant to, Johnson drove moderate Republicans into the radical camp and strengthened the Republican Party. The president did not believe Republicans would oppose him to support the freedmen. He was wrong. Congress overrode both vetoes. The Republicans broke with Johnson in 1866, defied him in 1867, and impeached him in 1868 (failing to remove him from office by only one vote in the Senate).

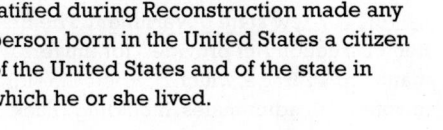 **Read on MyHistoryLab Document:** President Johnson Vetoes the Civil Rights Act of 1866

The Fourteenth Amendment

To secure the legal rights of freedmen, Republicans passed the **Fourteenth Amendment**. This amendment fundamentally changed the Constitution by compelling states to accept their residents as citizens and to guarantee that their rights as citizens would be safeguarded.

Its first section guaranteed citizenship to every person born in the United States. This included virtually every black person. In addition, it made each person a citizen of the state in which he or she resided, defined the specific rights of citizens, and protected those rights against the authority of state governments. Citizens had the right to due process (usually a trial) before they could lose their life, liberty, or property:

Fourteenth Amendment This amendment ratified during Reconstruction made any person born in the United States a citizen of the United States and of the state in which he or she lived.

> All persons born or naturalized in the United States, and subject to the jurisdiction thereof, are citizens of the United States and of the State wherein they reside. No State shall make or enforce any law which shall abridge the privileges or immunities of citizens of the United States; nor shall any State deprive any person of life, liberty, or property, without due process of law; nor deny to any person within its jurisdiction the equal protection of the laws.

Eleven years after Chief Justice Roger Taney declared in the *Dred Scott* decision that black people were "a subordinate and inferior class of beings" who had "no rights that white people were bound to respect," the Fourteenth Amendment vested African Americans with the same rights of citizenship other Americans possessed.

The amendment also threatened to deprive states of representation in Congress if they denied black men the vote. The end of slavery had also made obsolete the Three-Fifths Clause in the Constitution, which had counted slaves as only three-fifths (or 60 percent) of

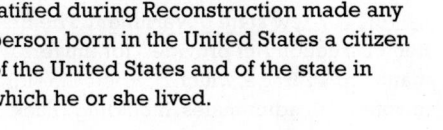 **Read on MyHistoryLab Document:** The Thirteenth, Fourteenth, and Fifteenth Amendments to the Constitution, 1865

12-1
12-2
12-3
12-4
12-5
12-6
12-7

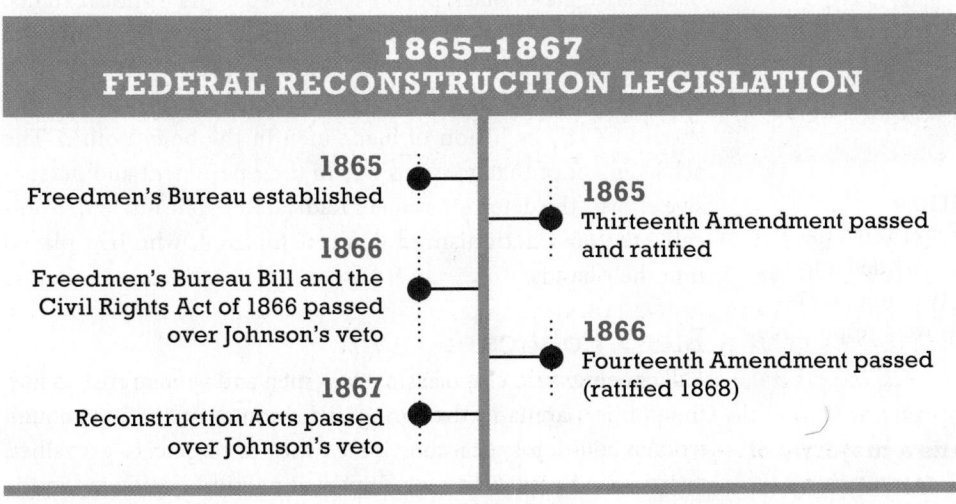

1865–1867 FEDERAL RECONSTRUCTION LEGISLATION

1865
Freedmen's Bureau established

1865
Thirteenth Amendment passed and ratified

1866
Freedmen's Bureau Bill and the Civil Rights Act of 1866 passed over Johnson's veto

1866
Fourteenth Amendment passed (ratified 1868)

1867
Reconstruction Acts passed over Johnson's veto

a white person in calculating a state's population and in determining the number of representatives each state was entitled to in the House of Representatives. Republicans feared that southern states would count black people in their populations without permitting them to vote, thereby gaining more representatives than those states had before the Civil War. The amendment mandated that if any state—northern or southern—did not allow adult male citizens to vote, then the number of representatives it was entitled to in Congress would be reduced in proportion to the number of men denied the right to vote.

Democrats almost unanimously opposed the Fourteenth Amendment. Andrew Johnson denounced it, although he could not prevent its adoption. Except for Tennessee, southern states refused to ratify it. Women's suffragists felt betrayed because the amendment limited suffrage to males. Despite this opposition, the amendment was ratified in 1868.

Radical Reconstruction

By 1867 Radical Republicans in Congress had wrested control over **Reconstruction** from Johnson, and they then imposed policies that brought black men into the political system as voters and officeholders. It was a dramatic development, second in importance only to emancipation and the end of slavery.

Republicans swept the 1866 congressional elections despite the belligerent opposition of Johnson and the Democrats. With two-thirds majorities in the House and Senate, Republicans easily overrode presidential vetoes. Two years after the Civil War, Republicans dismantled the state governments established in the South under Johnson's authority and instituted a new Reconstruction policy.

Republicans passed the first of three **Reconstruction Acts** over Johnson's veto in March 1867. It divided the South into five military districts, each under the command of a general (see Map 12–2). Troops would protect lives and property while new civilian governments were formed. Elected delegates in each state would draft a new constitution and submit it to the voters.

Universal Manhood Suffrage

The Reconstruction Act stipulated that all adult males in the states of the former Confederacy were eligible to vote, except for those who had actively supported the Confederacy or were convicted felons. Once each state had formed a new government and approved the Fourteenth Amendment, it would be readmitted to the Union with representation in Congress.

The advent of Radical Reconstruction was the culmination of the struggle of black people to gain legal and political rights. Since the 1864 black national convention in Syracuse and the meetings and conventions in the South in 1865 and 1866, black leaders had argued that one of the consequences of the Civil War should be the inclusion of black men in the body politic. The achievement of that goal was due to their persistent and persuasive efforts, the determination of Radical Republicans, and, ironically, the obstructionism of Andrew Johnson, who had played into their hands.

Black Politics

Full of energy and enthusiasm, black men and women rushed into the political arena in the spring and summer of 1867. Although women could not vote, they joined men at the meetings, rallies, parades, and picnics that accompanied political organizing in the

---

Reconstruction The 12 years (1865–1877) following the Civil War, during which the former Confederate states were restored to the Union and former slaves became citizens and gained the right to vote and hold political office. It was also a time of violence and terrorism as many southern white people resisted the change in the status of African Americans.

Reconstruction Acts Led by Radical Republicans, Congress divided the South into five military districts. Each former Confederate state (except Tennessee) was to frame a new state constitution and establish a new state government. The first Reconstruction Act provided for universal manhood suffrage, which granted the right to vote to all adult males, including black men.

Explore on MyHistoryLab Map: Congressional Reconstruction

MAP 12–2 CONGRESSIONAL RECONSTRUCTION
Under the terms of the First Reconstruction Act of 1867, the former Confederate states (except Tennessee) were divided into five military districts and placed under the authority of military officers. Commanders in each of the five districts were responsible for supervising the reestablishment of civilian governments in each state.

In which states were African Americans a majority of delegates to that state's constitutional convention?

With the adoption of Radical Republican policies, most black men eagerly took part in political activities. Political meetings, conventions, speeches, barbecues, and other gatherings also attracted women and children.

South. For many freed men and women, politics became as important as religious activities. Black people flocked to the Republican Party and the new Union Leagues.

The **Union Leagues** had been established in the North during the Civil War, but they expanded across the South as quasi-political organizations in the late 1860s. The Leagues were social, fraternal, and patriotic groups in which black people often but not always outnumbered white people. League meetings featured ceremonies, rituals, initiation rites, and oaths. They gave people an opportunity to sharpen leadership skills and gain a political education by discussing issues from taxes to schools.

Union League A social and fraternal organization that stirred political interest and support among black and white Republicans in the South during Reconstruction.

Sit-Ins and Strikes

Political progress did not induce apathy, satisfaction, or contentment among black people. Instead, gaining citizenship, legal rights, and the vote generated more expectations and demands for advancement. For example, black people insisted on equal access to public transportation. In Charleston, South Carolina, black people were permitted to ride only on the outside running boards of the horse- and mule-drawn streetcars. After a Republican rally there in April 1867, black men staged a "sit-in" on one of the vehicles before they were arrested. They wanted to sit on the seats inside. Within a month, after military authorities intervened, the streetcar company gave in. Similar protests occurred in Richmond and New Orleans.

Black workers also struck across the South in 1867. Black longshoremen in New Orleans, Mobile, Savannah, Charleston, and Richmond walked off the job. Black laborers were usually paid less than white men for the same work, which led to labor unrest during the 1860s and 1870s. Sometimes the strikers won, sometimes they lost. In 1869 a black Baltimore longshoreman, Isaac Myers, organized the National Colored Labor Union.

12-1

12-2

12-3

12-4

12-5

12-6

12-7

The Reaction of White Southerners

White southerners grimly opposed Radical Reconstruction. They were outraged that black people could claim the same legal and political rights they themselves possessed. Such a possibility seemed preposterous to people convinced of the absolute inferiority of black people. Benjamin F. Perry, whom Johnson had appointed provisional governor of South Carolina in 1865, captures the depth of this racist conviction: "The African," Perry declared, "has been in all ages, a savage or a slave. God created him inferior to the white man in form, color and intellect, and no legislation or culture can make him his equal. . . . His hair, his form and features will not compete with the caucasian race, and it is in vain to think of elevating him to the dignity of the white man. God created differences between the two races, and nothing can make him equal."

Some white people, taking solace in their belief in the innate inferiority of black people, concluded they could turn black suffrage to their advantage. White people, they assumed, should easily be able to control and manipulate black voters just as they had controlled black people during slavery. White southerners who believed this, however, would be disappointed, and their disappointment would turn to fury.

CONCLUSION

Why were black southerners able to gain citizenship and access to the political system by 1868? Most white Americans did not suddenly abandon 250 years of deeply ingrained beliefs that people of African descent were their inferiors. The advances that African Americans achieved fit into a series of complex political developments after the Civil War. Black people themselves had fought and died to preserve the Union, and they had earned the grudging respect of many white people and the open admiration of others. Black leaders in meetings and petitions insisted that their rights be recognized.

White northerners—led by the Radical Republicans—were convinced that President Johnson was wrong to support policies that permitted white southerners to retain pre–Civil War leaders while the black codes virtually made freedmen slaves again. Republicans were determined that white southerners realize that their defeat had doomed the prewar status quo. Republicans established a Reconstruction program to disfranchise key southern leaders while providing legal rights to freedmen. The right to vote, they reasoned, would enable black people to deal more effectively with white southerners and strengthen the Republican Party in the South.

The result was to make the mid to late 1860s one of the few high points in African-American history. During this period, not only was slavery abolished, but black southerners were able to organize schools and churches, and black people throughout the South acquired legal and political rights that would have been incomprehensible before the war. Yet black people did not stand on the brink of utopia. Most freedmen still lacked land and had no realistic hope of obtaining much, if any, of it. In addition, white violence and cruelty continued almost unabated across much of the South. Still, for millions of African Americans, the future looked more promising than ever before in American history.

CHAPTER TIMELINE

AFRICAN-AMERICAN EVENTS

NATIONAL EVENTS

1862–1864

March 1862
The Port Royal Experiment in South Carolina begins

October 1864
Black national convention in Syracuse, New York

February 1862
Julia Ward Howe publishes the first version of "Battle Hymn of the Republic" in the *Atlantic Monthly*

July 1862
Morrill Land-Grant College Act signed into law

November 1864
President Lincoln reelected

1865–1866

January 1865
General Sherman's Special Field Order #15

March 1865
Freedmen's Bureau established

September–November 1865
Black codes enacted

February 1866
Southern Homestead Act

March 1866
President Johnson vetoes bill to extend the Freedman's Bureau and the Civil Rights Bill

April 1866
Congress overrides Johnson's veto of the Civil Rights Bill

May 1866
Memphis riot

July 1866
Congress enacts new Freedmen's Bureau bill over Johnson's veto; New Orleans riot

April 1865
Lincoln is assassinated; Andrew Johnson succeeds to presidency

May 1865
Johnson begins presidential Reconstruction

June–August 1865
Southern state governments reorganized

December 1865
Thirteenth Amendment to the Constitution ratified

November 1866
Republicans gain greater than two-thirds majorities in House and Senate

1867–1969

Spring–Summer 1867
Union Leagues and the Republican Party organized in southern states

1869
The National Colored Labor Union established under the leadership of Isaac Myers

March 1867
Congress passes the first Reconstruction Act over President Johnson's veto
The United States purchases Alaska from Russia

February 1868
House impeaches President Johnson

May 1868
Senate acquits Johnson by one vote

July 1868
Fourteenth Amendment to the Constitution ratified

November 1868
Ulysses S. Grant elected president

May 1869
Transcontinental railroad completed

On MyHistoryLab

✓ Study and Review on MyHistoryLab

REVIEW QUESTIONS

1. What did freedom mean to ex-slaves? How did their priorities differ from those of African Americans who had been free before the Civil War?

2. What did the former slaves and the former slaveholders want after emancipation? Were these desires realistic? How did former slaves and former slaveholders disagree after the end of slavery?

3. Why did African Americans form separate churches, schools, and social organizations after the Civil War? What role did the black church play in the black community?

4. How effective was the Freedmen's Bureau? How successful was it in assisting ex-slaves to live in freedom?

5. Why did southern states enact black codes?

6. Why did Radical Republicans object to President Andrew Johnson's Reconstruction policies? Why did Congress impose its own Reconstruction policies?

7. Why were laws passed to enable black men to vote?

8. Why did black men gain the right to vote but not possession of land?

9. Did congressional Reconstruction secure full equality for African Americans as American citizens?

RECOMMENDED READING

Ira Berlin and Leslie Rowland, eds. *Families and Freedom: A Documentary History of African-American Kinship in the Civil War Era.* New York: Cambridge University Press, 1997. A collection of documents that conveys the aspirations and frustrations of freedmen.

David W. Blight. *Race and Reunion: The Civil War in American Memory.* Cambridge, MA: Harvard University Press, 2001. This outstanding study shows how white Americans "remembered" the Civil War and reconciled their sectional differences by essentially forgetting the role and contributions of African Americans.

James Conn. *Sick From Freedom: African American Illness and Suffering During the Civil War and Reconstruction.* New York: Oxford University Press, 2012. This pathbreaking account traces the devastating impact that smallpox had on African Americans as they gained their freedom.

W. E. B. Du Bois. *Black Reconstruction in America: An Essay Toward a History of the Part Which Black Folk Played in the Attempt to Reconstruct Democracy in America, 1860–1880.* New York: Russell & Russell, 1935. A classic account of Reconstruction challenging the traditional interpretation that it was a tragic era marked by corrupt and inept black rule of the South.

Eric Foner. *Reconstruction: America's Unfinished Revolution, 1863–1877.* New York: Harper & Row, 1988. The best and most comprehensive account of Reconstruction.

Herbert G. Gutman. *The Black Family in Slavery and Freedom, 1750–1925.* New York: Oxford University Press, 1976. An illustration of how African-American family values and kinship ties forged in slavery endured after emancipation.

Steven Hahn. *A Nation Under Our Feet: Black Political Struggles in the Rural South from Slavery to the Great Migration.* Cambridge, MA: Harvard University Press, 2003. In a sophisticated analysis, Hahn explores how African Americans conceived of themselves as political people and organized from slavery through Reconstruction and disfranchisement to the 1920s.

Tera W. Hunter. *To 'Joy My Freedom: Southern Black Women's Lives and Labors after the Civil War.* Cambridge, MA: Harvard University Press, 1997. An examination of the interior lives of black women, their work, social welfare, and leisure.

Gerald D. Jaynes. *Branches Without Roots: Genesis of the Black Working Class in the American South, 1862–1882.* New York: Pantheon, 1986. Examines the changes in work patterns and the labor of African Americans after slavery.

Leon F. Litwack. *Been in the Storm So Long: The Aftermath of Slavery.* New York: Alfred A. Knopf, 1979. A rich and detailed account of the transition to freedom largely based on recollections of former slaves.

ADDITIONAL BIBLIOGRAPHY

EDUCATION

James D. Anderson. *The Education of Blacks in the South, 1860–1935.* Chapel Hill: University of North Carolina Press, 1988.

Ronald E. Butchart. *Northern Schools, Southern Blacks, and Reconstruction: Freedmen's Education, 1862–1875.* Westport, CT: Greenwood Press, 1981.

Edmund L. Drago. *Initiative, Paternalism, and Race Relations: Charleston's Avery Normal Institute.* Athens: University of Georgia Press, 1990.

Robert C. Morris. *Reading, 'Riting, and Reconstruction: The Education of the Freedmen in the South, 1861–1890.* Chicago: University of Chicago Press, 1981.

Joe M. Richardson. *Christian Reconstruction: The American Missionary Association and Southern Blacks, 1861–1890.* Athens: University of Georgia Press, 1986.

Brenda Stevenson, ed. *The Journals of Charlotte Forten Grimke.* New York: Oxford University Press, 1988.

Heather Andrea Williams. *Self Taught: African-American Education in Slavery and Freedom.* Chapel Hill: University of North Carolina Press, 2005.

LAND AND LABOR

Paul A. Cimbala and Randall M. Miller, eds. *The Freedmen's Bureau and Reconstruction.* New York: Fordham University Press, 1999.

Barbara J. Fields. *Slavery and Freedom on the Middle Ground: Maryland During the Nineteenth Century.* New Haven, CT: Yale University Press, 1985.

Jacqueline Jones. *Labor of Love, Labor of Sorrow: Black Women, Work and Family, from Slavery to the Present.* New York: Basic Books, 1985.

Edward Magdol. *A Right to the Land: Essays on the Freedmen's Community.* Westport, CT: Greenwood Press, 1977.

Claude F. Oubre. *Forty Acres and a Mule: The Freedmen's Bureau and Black Landownership.* Baton Rouge: Louisiana State University Press, 1978.

Dylan C. Penningroth. *The Claims of Kinfolk: African American Property and Community in the Nineteenth-Century South.* Chapel Hill: University of North Carolina Press, 2003.

Roger L. Ransom and Richard Sutch. *One Kind of Freedom: The Economic Consequences of Emancipation.* New York: Cambridge University Press, 1977.

Elizabeth Regosin. *Freedom's Promise: Slave Families and Citizenship in the Age of Emancipation.* Charlottesville: University of Virginia Press, 2002.

Willie Lee Rose. *Rehearsal for Reconstruction: The Port Royal Experiment.* Indianapolis: Bobbs-Merrill, 1964.

Julie Saville. *The Work of Reconstruction: From Slave to Wage Labor in South Carolina, 1860–1870.* New York: Cambridge University Press, 1994.

James D. Schmidt. *Free to Work: Labor, Law, Emancipation, and Reconstruction, 1815–1880.* Athens: University of Georgia Press, 1998.

Leslie A. Schwalm. *A Hard Fight for We: Women's Transition From Slavery to Freedom in South Carolina.* Urbana: University of Illinois Press, 1997.

BLACK COMMUNITIES

John W. Blassingame. *Black New Orleans, 1860–1880.* Chicago: University of Chicago Press, 1973.

Orville Vernon Burton, Jerald Podair, and Jennifer L. Weber, eds. *The Struggle for Equality: Essays on the Sectional Conflict, the Civil War, and the Long Reconstruction.* Charlottesville: University of Virginia Press, 2011.

Cyprian Davis. *The History of Black Catholics in the United States.* New York: Crossroad, 1990.

Robert F. Engs. *Freedom's First Generation: Black Hampton, Virginia, 1861–1890.* Philadelphia: University of Pennsylvania Press, 1979.

William E. Montgomery. *Under Their Own Vine and Fig Tree: The African American Church in the South 1865–1900.* Baton Rouge: Louisiana State University Press, 1993.

Bernard E. Powers Jr. *Black Charlestonians: A Social History, 1822–1885.* Fayetteville: University of Arkansas Press, 1994.

Clarence E. Walker. *A Rock in a Weary Land: The African Methodist Episcopal Church During the Civil War and Reconstruction.* Baton Rouge: Louisiana State University Press, 1982.

James M. Washington. *Frustrated Fellowship: The Black Baptist Quest for Social Power.* Macon, GA: Mercer University Press, 1986.

RETRACING THE ODYSSEY

The Avery Research Center for African-American History and Culture, Charleston, South Carolina. In 1865 the American Missionary Association opened a private school for black youngsters that served the Charleston community until 1954. The renovated structure currently contains an archive, a restored classroom, and exhibits devoted to African-American life in the Carolina low country.

Shaw University and St. Augustine's College, Raleigh, North Carolina. These are two of the many black colleges established during Reconstruction. The Baptists founded Shaw in 1865, and its impressive Estey Hall has survived almost 130 years. The Episcopal Church and the Freedmen's Bureau collaborated to found St. Augustine's in 1867.

Fisk University, Nashville, Tennessee. The American Missionary Association established Fisk in 1866. Magnificent Jubilee Hall is the nation's oldest building dedicated to the higher education of black students. It was completed in 1876. There is an impressive collection of European and American art on the campus at the Carl Van Vechten Art Gallery.

St. Stephen African Methodist Episcopal Church, Wilmington, North Carolina. Following the Civil War, black members of the Front Street Methodist Church withdrew and founded their own church on Red Cross Street. In 1880 they began construction of the current building. For a time parishioners met in the basement while work continued on the imposing and ornate sanctuary above them.

Gullah/Geechee Cultural Heritage Corridor. In 2006 Congress established this 12,000-square-mile corridor that extends along the South Atlantic coast from Wilmington, North Carolina, through South Carolina and Georgia, to Jacksonville, Florida. It was created to recognize the cultural contributions, language, and way of life that has prevailed among people of African descent on the sea islands and the low country since the seventeenth century.

The Meaning of Freedom: The Failure of Reconstruction

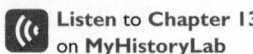

Listen to **Chapter 13**
on **MyHistoryLab**

LEARNING OBJECTIVES

13-1 What political offices were black men elected to—and not elected to—during Reconstruction?

13-2 What issues were of most concern to black political leaders, and what were the results of their attempts to initiate change in the South?

13-3 Why were so many white southerners opposed to black and white Republicans exercising political power?

13-4 Why was the Ku Klux Klan founded, and how effective was it?

13-5 What were the origins and effects of the Fifteenth Amendment and the Enforcement Acts?

13-6 How and why did black and white Republicans lose control of every southern state by 1877?

13-7 What were the methods used and results of attempts to "redeem" the southern states?

> Let us with a fixed, firm, hearty, earnest, and unswerving determination move steadily on and on, fanning the flame of true liberty until the last vestige of oppression shall be destroyed, and when that eventful period shall arrive, when, in the selection of rulers, both State and Federal, we shall know no North, no East, no South, no West, no white nor colored, no Democrat nor Republican, but shall choose men because of their moral and intrinsic value, their honesty and integrity, their love of unmixed liberty, and their ability to perform well the duties to be committed to their charge.
>
> *From a speech delivered in 1872, by Jonathan J. Wright, Associate Justice of the South Carolina Supreme Court*

In 1868, for the first time in American history, thousands of black men would elect hundreds of black and white leaders to state and local offices across the South. Would this newly acquired political influence enable freedmen to complete the transition from slavery to freedom? Would political power propel black people into the mainstream of American society? Equally important, would white southerners and northerners accept black people as fellow citizens?

Events from 1867 to 1877 generated hope that black and white Americans might learn to live together on a compatible and equitable basis. But these developments also raised the possibility that black people's new access to political power would fail to resolve the racial animosity and intolerance that persisted in American life after the Civil War.

These are the first African Americans to serve in the U.S. Congress. Standing, left to right: Robert C. DeLarge, representative, South Carolina; Jefferson Long, representative, Georgia; Seated, left to right: U.S. Senator Hiram R. Revels, Mississippi; Benjamin S. Turner, representative, Alabama; Josiah T. Walls, representative, Florida; Joseph H. Rainey, representative, South Carolina; Robert B. Elliott, representative, South Carolina.

Constitutional Conventions

13-1 What political offices were black men elected to—and not elected to—during Reconstruction?

Black men as a group first entered politics as delegates to constitutional conventions in the southern states in 1867 and 1868. Each of the former Confederate states, except Tennessee, which had already been restored to the Union, elected delegates to these conventions. Most southern white men were Democrats. They boycotted these elections to protest Congress's assumption of authority over Reconstruction and the extension of voting privileges to black men. Thus, the delegates to the conventions that met to frame new state constitutions to replace those drawn up in 1865 under President Johnson's authority were mostly Republicans joined by a few conservative southern Democrats. The Republicans represented three constituencies. One consisted of white northern migrants who moved to the South after the war. They were disparagingly called **carpetbaggers** because they were said to have arrived in the South with all their possessions in a single carpetbag. A second group consisted of native white southerners, mostly small farmers in devastated upland regions of the South who hoped for economic relief from Republican governments. Other southern white people denigrated them as **scalawags**, or scoundrels. African Americans made up the third and largest Republican constituency.

Of the 1,000 men elected as delegates to the 10 state conventions, 265 were black. Black delegates were a majority only in the South Carolina and Louisiana conventions. In most states, including Alabama, Georgia, Mississippi, Virginia, North Carolina, Arkansas, and Texas, black men made up 10 to 20 percent of the delegates. At least 107 of the 265 black delegates had been born slaves. About 40 had served in the Union Army. Several were well-educated teachers and ministers. Others were tailors, blacksmiths, barbers, and farmers. Most went on to hold other political offices.

These delegates produced impressive constitutions. Unlike previous state constitutions in the South, the new constitutions ensured that all adult males could vote, and except in Mississippi and Virginia, they did not disfranchise many former Confederates. They conferred broad guarantees of civil rights. In several states they provided the first statewide systems of public education. These constitutions were progressive, not radical. Black and white Republicans hoped to attract support from white southerners for the new state governments these documents created by encouraging state support for private businesses, especially railroad construction.

Elections

Elections were held in 1868 to ratify the new constitutions and elect officials. The white Democratic response varied. In some states, Democrats boycotted the elections. In others, they participated but voted against ratification, and in still other states they supported ratification and attempted to elect as many Democrats as possible. Congress required only a majority of those voting—not a majority of all registered voters—to ratify the constitutions. In each state, a majority of those voting eventually voted to ratify, and in each state, black men were elected to office.

Black Political Leaders

Over the next decade, 1,465 black men held political office in the South. Although black leaders individually and collectively enjoyed significant political leverage, white Republicans dominated politics during Reconstruction. In general, the number of black officials in a state reflected the

carpetbagger The derogatory term used during Reconstruction to describe northerners who came South following the Civil War to take advantage of political and economic opportunities. They were labeled "carpetbaggers" because they ostensibly carried all of their possessions in a solitary carpetbag.

scalawag The derogatory term used during Reconstruction to identify a native white southerner who supported black and white Republicans. They were considered traitors to their people and the Democratic Party.

🔍 **View on MyHistoryLab Closer Look:** The First Vote

Southern black men cast ballots for the first time in 1867 in the election of delegates to state constitutional conventions. The ballots were provided by the candidates or political parties, not by state or municipal officials. Most nineteenth-century elections were not by secret ballot.

13-1 13-2 13-3 13-4 13-5 13-6 13-7

TABLE 13–1 AFRICAN-AMERICAN POPULATION AND OFFICEHOLDING DURING RECONSTRUCTION IN THE STATES SUBJECT TO CONGRESSIONAL RECONSTRUCTION

	African-American Population in 1870	African-Americans as Percentage of Total Population	Number of African-American Officeholders During Reconstruction
South Carolina	415,814	58.9	314
Mississippi	444,201	53.6	226
Louisiana	364,210	50.1	210
North Carolina	391,650	36.5	180
Alabama	475,510	47.6	167
Georgia	545,142	46.0	108
Virginia	512,841	41.8	85
Florida	91,689	48.7	58
Arkansas	122,169	25.2	46
Texas	253,475	30.9	46
Tennessee	322,331	25.6	20

SOURCE: Eric Foner, Freedom's Lawmakers: A Directory of Black Officeholders During Reconstruction *(New York: Oxford University Press, 1993), xiv; The Statistics of the Population of the United States, Ninth Census (1873), xvii.*

13-1

13-2

13-3

13-4

13-5

13-6

13-7

size of that state's African-American population. Black people were a substantial majority of the population in just Mississippi and South Carolina, and most of the black officeholders came from those two states and Louisiana, where black people were a slight majority. In most states, such as Arkansas, North Carolina, Tennessee, and Texas, where black people made up between 25 and 40 percent of the population, far fewer black men were elected to office (see Table 13-1).

Initially, black men chose not to run for the most important political offices because they feared their election would further alienate angry white southerners. But as white Republicans swept into office in 1868, black leaders reversed their strategy, and by 1870 black men had been elected to many key positions. No black man was elected governor, but Lieutenant Governor P. B. S. Pinchback served one month (December 1872 to January 1873) as governor in Louisiana after the white governor was removed from office. Blanche K. Bruce and Hiram Revels represented Mississippi in the U.S. Senate. Beginning with Joseph Rainey in 1870 in South Carolina, 14 black men served in the U.S. House of Representatives during Reconstruction. Six black men served as lieutenant governors. In Mississippi and South Carolina, a majority of the representatives in state houses were black men, and each of these states had two black speakers of the house in the 1870s. Jonathan J. Wright, quoted at the beginning of this chapter, served seven years as a supreme court justice in South Carolina. Four black men served as state superintendents of education, and Francis L. Cardozo served as South Carolina's secretary of state and then treasurer. During Reconstruction, 112 black state senators and 683 black representatives were elected. There were also 41 black sheriffs, five black mayors, and 31 black coroners. Tallahassee, Florida, and Little Rock, Arkansas, had black police chiefs.

Many of these men—by background, experience, and education—were well qualified. However, others were not. Of the 1,465 black officeholders, at least 378 had been free before the Civil War, 933 were literate, and 195 were illiterate (we lack information about the remaining 337). In addition, 64 had attended college or professional school. In fact, 14 of the leaders had been students at Oberlin College in Ohio, which began admitting both black and female students before the Civil War.

Black farmers and artisans—tailors, carpenters, and barbers—were well represented among those who held political office. There were also

Hiram R. Revels represented Mississippi in the U.S. Senate from February 1870 until March 1871, completing an unexpired term. He went on to serve as Mississippi's secretary of state. He was born free in Fayetteville, North Carolina, in 1822. He attended Knox College in Illinois before the Civil War. In 1874 he abandoned the Republican Party and became a Democrat. By the 1890s he had acquired a sizable plantation near Natchez.

237 ministers and 172 teachers. At least 129 had served in the Union Army, and 46 had worked for the Freedmen's Bureau.

Several black politicians were wealthy, and a few were former slave owners. Antoine Dubuclet, who became Louisiana's treasurer, had owned more than one hundred slaves and land valued at more than $100,000 before the Civil War. Former slave Ferdinand Havis became a member of the Arkansas House of Representatives. He owned a saloon, a whiskey business, and 2,000 acres near Pine Bluff, where he became known as "the Colored Millionaire."

Although black men did not take over any state politically, a few did dominate districts with sizable black populations. Before he was elected to the U.S. Senate, Blanche K. Bruce all but controlled Bolivar County, Mississippi, where he served as sheriff, tax collector, and superintendent of education. Former slave and Civil War hero Robert Smalls was the political "kingpin" in Beaufort, South Carolina. He served in the South Carolina house and senate and in the U.S. House of Representatives. He was also a member of the South Carolina constitutional conventions in 1868 and 1895.

Read on **MyHistoryLab**
Document: An African-American Senator Decries Democratic Political Violence, 1876

The Issues

13-2 | What issues were of most concern to black political leaders, and what were the results of their attempts to initiate change in the South?

Many but not all black and white Republican leaders favored increasing the authority of state governments to promote the welfare of all the state's citizens. Before the Civil War, most southern states did not provide schools, medical care, assistance for the mentally impaired, or prisons. Such concerns—if attended to at all—were left to local communities or families.

Education and Social Welfare

Black leaders were eager to increase literacy and promote education among black people. Republicans created statewide systems of public education throughout the South. It was a difficult and expensive task, and the results were only a limited success. Schools had to be built, teachers employed, and textbooks provided. To pay for it, taxes were increased in states still reeling from the war.

In many rural areas, schools were not built. In other places, teachers were not paid. Some people—black and white—opposed compulsory education laws, preferring to let parents determine whether their children should attend school or work to help the family. Some black leaders favored a poll tax on voting to fund the schools. Thus, although Reconstruction leaders established a strong commitment to public education, the results they achieved were uneven.

Furthermore, white parents refused to send their children to integrated schools. Although no laws required segregation, public schools during and after Reconstruction were invariably segregated. However, black parents were usually more concerned that their children attend school, and were less concerned that the schools were integrated. In any case, the schools in New Orleans were mixed.

Reconstruction leaders also supported higher education. In 1872 Mississippi legislators took advantage of the 1862 federal Morrill Land-Grant Act, which provided states with funds for agricultural and mechanical colleges, to found the first historically black state university: Alcorn A&M College. Although the university was named after white Republican Governor James L. Alcorn, former U.S. Senator Hiram Revels was its first president. The South Carolina legislature created a similar college and attached it to the Methodist-sponsored Claflin University.

Black leaders in the state legislature compelled the University of South Carolina, which had been all white, to admit black students and hire black faculty. As a result, many of the white students and faculty left. Several black politicians enrolled in the law and medical programs at the university. Richard Greener, a black Harvard graduate, served on the university's faculty and was its librarian.

13-1
13-2
13-3
13-4
13-5
13-6
13-7

Despite the costs, Reconstruction leaders also created the first state-supported institutions for the insane, the blind, and the deaf in much of the South. Some southern states during Reconstruction began to offer medical care and public health programs. Some states established orphanages and built prisons. Black leaders also supported revisions to state criminal codes, the elimination of corporal punishment for many crimes, and a reduction in the number of capital crimes.

Civil Rights

Black politicians were often the victims of racial discrimination when they tried to use public transportation and accommodations such as hotels and restaurants. Rather than provide separate arrangements for black customers, white-owned businesses simply excluded black patrons. This was true in the North as well as the South. The Civil War hero Robert Smalls, for example, was ejected from a Philadelphia streetcar in 1864. After protests, the company agreed to accept black riders. In Arkansas, Mifflin Gibbs (see Profile: The Gibbs Brothers) and W. Hines Furbish successfully sued a local saloon after they had been denied service. In South Carolina, Jonathan J. Wright won $1,200 in a lawsuit against a railroad after he had purchased a first-class ticket but had been forced to ride in the second-class coach.

Black leaders' determination to open public facilities to all people revealed deep divisions between themselves and white Republicans. In several southern states they introduced bills to prevent proprietors from excluding black people from restaurants, barrooms, hotels, concert halls, and auditoriums, as well as railroad coaches, streetcars, and steamboats. Many white Republicans and virtually every Democrat attacked such proposals as efforts to promote social equality and gain access for black people to places where they were not welcome. White politicians blocked these laws in most states. Only South Carolina—with a black majority in the house and many black senators—enacted such a law, but it was not effectively enforced. In Mississippi, the Republican Governor James L. Alcorn vetoed a bill to outlaw racial discrimination by railroads. In Alabama and North Carolina, civil rights bills were defeated, and Georgia and Arkansas enacted measures that encouraged segregation.

Economic Issues

Black politicians sought to promote economic development in general and for black people in particular. For example, white landowners sometimes fired black agricultural laborers near the end of the growing season and then did not pay them. Some of these landowners were dishonest, but others were in debt and could not pay their workers. To prevent such abuses, black politicians secured laws that required laborers to be paid before the crop was sold or when it was sold. Some black leaders who had been slaves also wanted to regulate wages, but these proposals failed because most Republicans did not believe states had the authority to regulate wages and prices.

Legislators also enacted measures that protected the land and property of small farmers against seizure for nonpayment of debts. Black and white farmers who lost land, tools, animals, and other property because they could not pay their debts were unlikely to recover financially. "Stay laws" prohibited, or "stayed," authorities from taking property. Besides protecting poor farmers, Republicans hoped these laws would weaken support among white yeomen for the Democratic Party and draw them into the Republican Party.

Land

Black leaders were unable to provide land to landless black and white farmers. Many black and white political leaders believed the state had no right to distribute land. Again, South Carolina was the exception. Its legislature created a state land commission in 1869.

The commission could purchase and distribute land to freedmen. It also gave the freedmen loans on generous terms to pay for the land. Unfortunately, the commission was corrupt and inefficiently managed and had little fertile land to distribute. Yet despite its many difficulties, the commission enabled more than 14,000 black families and a few white families to acquire land in South Carolina. Their descendants still possess some of this land today.

PROFILE   The Gibbs Brothers

Mifflin Gibbs was probably the only African American in the nineteenth century elected to political office in two nations. He served as a city councilman in Victoria, British Columbia, in Canada in the late 1860s, and he was elected a judge in Little Rock, Arkansas, in 1873.

AMONG THE MANY BLACK LEADERS WHO EMERGED DURING Reconstruction were the Gibbs brothers, who had political careers in Arkansas and Florida. Mifflin W. Gibbs and Jonathan C. Gibbs grew up in a well-to-do, free black family in Philadelphia, where their father was a Methodist minister. But their paths diverged, and they spent little time together as adults.

Mifflin was born in 1823 and became a building contractor. By the 1840s, he was an active abolitionist. With the discovery of gold in California in 1849, he went west and eventually established California's first black newspaper, the *Mirror of the Times*. He led a protest in 1851 against a California constitution provision that denied black men the right to vote. In 1858 he left California for Canada, again because gold had been discovered. He spent more than 10 years in Canada as a businessman involved in real estate and a coal company. In 1866 he was elected to the Victoria City Council in British Columbia. He returned to the United States in

1869, and graduated from the law program at Oberlin College in 1870.

Mifflin moved to Arkansas in 1871 and was elected municipal judge in Little Rock in 1873. Although defeated for reelection, he remained involved in the Republican Party and was a delegate to every Republican national convention from 1876 to 1904. In 1897, Republican President William McKinley appointed him U.S. consul to Madagascar, a French island colony off the east coast of Africa, where he served until 1901. He died in 1915, and a black high school in Little Rock was named in his honor.

Jonathan, born in 1827 or 1828, also joined the abolitionist movement. Rejected by 18 colleges because of his color, he finally graduated from Dartmouth in 1852. He then went to Princeton Theological Seminary and became a Presbyterian minister in Troy, New York.

Jonathan attended the 1864 National Black Convention in Syracuse, New York; taught at a freedmen's school in North Carolina; and then spent two years in Charleston, South Carolina. There he joined those black leaders who favored limiting the right to vote to literate men if that restriction were applied both to black and white people.

In 1867, Jonathan moved to Florida, where he became a key Republican leader and the state's highest-ranking black official. He was elected to the 1868 Florida constitutional convention, and the Republican governor appointed him secretary of state. Although defeated for a seat in Congress in 1868, he remained one of Florida's most visible black leaders and was repeatedly threatened by the Ku Klux Klan. In 1873, another Republican governor appointed him state superintendent of education. Jonathan Gibbs died in 1874, but his son Thomas served in the Florida House of Representatives, where he was instrumental in establishing Florida A&M University.

13-1
13-2
13-3
13-4
13-5
13-6
13-7

Although some black leaders were reluctant to use the states' power to distribute land, others had no qualms about raising property taxes so high that large landowners would be forced to sell some of their property to pay their taxes. Abraham Galloway of North Carolina explained, "I want to see the man who owns one or two thousand acres of land, taxed a dollar on the acre, and if they can't pay the taxes, sell their property to the highest bidder . . . and then we negroes shall become the land holders."

Business and Industry

Black and white leaders had an easier time enacting legislation to support business and industry. Like most Americans after the Civil War, Republicans believed that expanding the railroad network would stimulate employment, improve transportation, and generate prosperity. State governments approved the sale of state-supported bonds to finance railroad construction. In Georgia, Alabama, Texas, and Arkansas, the railroad network did expand; however, the bonded debt of these states soared, and taxes increased to pay for it. Moreover, railroad financing was often corrupt. Most of the illegal money wound up in the pockets of white businessmen and politicians. Black politicians rarely had access to large financial transactions.

So attractive were business profits that some black political leaders formed corporations. They invested modest sums and believed—like so many capitalists—that the rewards outweighed the risks. In Charleston, 28 black leaders (and two white politicians) formed a horse-drawn streetcar line they called the Enterprise Railroad to carry freight between the city wharves and the railroad terminal. Black leaders in South Carolina also created a company to extract the phosphate used for fertilizer from riverbeds and riverbanks in the low country. Neither business lasted long. Black men found it far more difficult than white entrepreneurs to finance their corporations.

Black Politicians: An Evaluation

Southern black political leaders on the state level did create the foundation for public education; for state assistance for the blind, deaf, and insane; and for reforming the criminal justice system. They tried (but mostly failed) to outlaw racial discrimination in public facilities and encouraged state support for economic expansion.

But black leaders could not significantly improve the lives of their constituents. Because white Republicans almost always outnumbered them, they could not enact an agenda of their own. Moreover, black leaders often disagreed among themselves about issues and programs. Class and prewar status frequently divided them. Those leaders who had not been slaves and had not been raised in rural isolation were less likely to be concerned with land and agricultural labor. More prosperous black leaders showed more interest in civil rights and encouraging business. Even when they agreed about the need for public education, black leaders often disagreed about how to finance it and whether it should be compulsory.

Republican Factionalism

13-3 Why were so many white southerners opposed to black and white Republicans exercising political power?

Disagreements among black leaders paled compared to the conflicts that divided the Republican Party during Reconstruction. Black and white Republicans often disagreed on political issues and strategy, but the lack of party cohesion and discipline was even more harmful. The Republican Party in the South constantly split into factions as groups fought with each other. Most disagreements were over who should run for and hold political office.

Hundreds of would-be Republican leaders—black and white—sought public offices. If they lost the Republican nomination, they often formed a competing slate of candidates. Then Republicans ran against each other and against the Democrats in the general election. It was not a recipe for political success.

These bitter and angry contests were based less on race and issues than on the desperate desire to gain an office that would pay even a modest salary. Most black and white Republicans were not well off. Public office assured them a modicum of economic security.

Ironically, these factional disputes led to a high turnover in political leadership and the loss of that very economic security. It was difficult for black leaders (and white leaders too) to be renominated and reelected to more than one or two terms. Few officeholders served three or four consecutive terms in the same office during Reconstruction. This made for inexperienced leadership and added to Republican woes.

Opposition

Even if black and Republican leaders had been less prone to fighting among themselves and more effective in adopting a political platform, they might still have failed to sustain themselves for long. Most white southerners led by conservative Democrats remained absolutely

PROFILE   The Rollin Sisters

Frances Rollin Whipper was an author, teacher, political activist, wife, and mother. With her sisters, she was deeply involved in Reconstruction politics in South Carolina.

FEW WOMEN, BLACK OR WHITE, were as influential in Reconstruction politics as the Rollin sisters of South Carolina. Although they could not vote or hold political office, the five sisters, and especially Frances and Katherine, were closely associated with the black and white Republican leadership in South Carolina. With their education, knowledge, and charm, these black women affected political decisions and policies.

The sisters were born and raised in the elite antebellum free black community in Charleston. Their father, William Rollin, a prosperous lumber dealer, was descended from French Catholic Haitians and insisted that his daughters obtain a first-rate education. Frances, who was born in 1844, was sent to Philadelphia to take the "ladies course" at the Quaker's Institute for Colored Youth. At least two of the other sisters attended school in Boston. After the war, Frances joined other members of Charleston's prominent people of color and taught at schools sponsored by the American Missionary Association. She also wrote the biography of the black abolitionist leader Martin Delany. This was the first major nonfiction work a black woman published in America, but she felt compelled to conceal her identity under a male name, Frank A. Rollin.

In 1867 and 1868, as black men were entering the political arena, the Rollin sisters also gravitated to politics. Against her father's wishes, Frances married one of South Carolina's most controversial figures, William Whipper, a black attorney from Philadelphia who settled in Beaufort, South Carolina, after the war. (Whipper was the nephew of the antebellum black Pennsylvania businessman, also named William Whipper, profiled in Chapter 7.) He was elected to the state constitutional convention and then to the South Carolina House of Representatives. Whipper was a tough, able, shrewd, and not altogether honest politician. He enjoyed an expensive lifestyle. Most white people detested him.

While the legislature was in session, the Whippers and the Rollin sisters lived in Columbia, the state capital. There, the sisters were extraordinarily popular. They were well educated, intelligent, refined, and sophisticated. One observer described them as "ravishingly beautiful." Katherine Rollin was frequently seen with white State Senator George W. McIntyre.

The Rollin sisters were enthusiastic proponents of women's rights and women's suffrage who enlisted the wives of prominent black and white Republicans in their cause. Charlotte and Katherine organized a women's rights convention in Columbia in 1870 and formed the South Carolina branch of the American Women's Suffrage Association.

Charlotte Rollin pleaded for the right to vote:

> We ask suffrage not as a favor, not as a privilege, but as a right based on the grounds that we are human beings and as such entitled to human rights. While we concede that woman's ennobling influence should be confined chiefly to the home and society, we claim that public opinion has had a tendency to limit a woman's sphere to too small a circle and until woman has the right of representation this will last, and other rights will be held by insecure tenure.

Their black and white male allies tried to amend South Carolina's constitution to enable women to vote, but the legislature rejected it after a bitter debate.

After the Democrats regained political power in 1877, the Rollin sisters left for the North. Charlotte and Louise settled with their mother in Brooklyn, New York. William and Frances Whipper and their five children moved to Washington, DC, in 1882, where he practiced law and she was a clerk in the General Land Office. Three of their children survived to adulthood. Their sole son, Leigh Whipper, was a prominent stage and screen actor in the 1940s and 1950s. Sometime in the 1890s, Frances joined her husband in Beaufort. She died there in 1901.

opposed to letting black men vote or hold office. As a white Floridian put it, "The damned Republican Party has put niggers to rule us and we will not suffer it." Of course, just because black people voted did not mean they ruled during Reconstruction; however, many white people failed to grasp that. Instead, for most white southerners, the only acceptable political system was one that excluded black men and the Republican Party.

13-1
13-2
13-3
13-4
13-5
13-6
13-7

As far as most white people were concerned, the end of slavery and the enfranchisement of black men did not make black people their equals. They did not accept the Fourteenth Amendment, and they attacked Republican governments and their leaders unrelentingly. White southerners blamed the Republicans for an epidemic of waste and corruption in state government. But most of all, they considered it preposterous and outrageous that former slaves could vote and hold office.

James S. Pike spoke for many white people when he ridiculed black leaders in the South Carolina House of Representatives in 1873:

> The body is almost literally a Black Parliament. . . . The Speaker is black, the Clerk is black, the door-keepers are black, the little pages are black, the chairman of the Ways and Means is black, and the chaplain is coal-black. At some of the desks sit colored men whose types it would be hard to find outside of Congo; whose costume, visages, attitudes, and expression only befit the forecastle of a buccaneer. It must be remembered, also, that these men, with not more than a half a dozen exceptions, have been themselves slaves, and that their ancestors were slaves for generations.

Pike's observations circulated widely in both the North and the South.

White southerners were determined to rid themselves of Republicans and the disgrace of having to live with black men who possessed political rights. White southerners would "redeem" their states by restoring white Democrats to power. This meant not just defeating black and white Republicans in elections but removing them from politics entirely. White southerners believed any means—fair or foul—were justified in exorcising this evil.

The Ku Klux Klan

13-4   **Why was the Ku Klux Klan founded, and how effective was it?**

If the presence of black men in politics was illegitimate—in the eyes of white southerners—then it was acceptable to use violence to remove them. This thinking gave rise to militant terrorist organizations, such as the **Ku Klux Klan**, the Knights of the White Camellia, the White Brotherhood, and the Whitecaps. They were terrorists who resorted to threats, intimidation, beatings, rapes, and murder to restore conservative white Democratic rule and to force black people back into subordination.

The Ku Klux Klan, founded in Pulaski, Tennessee, in 1866, was originally a social club for Confederate veterans who adopted secret oaths and rituals—similar to the Union Leagues but with far more deadly consequences. One of the key figures in the Klan's rapid growth was former Confederate General Nathan Bedford Forrest, who became its leader or grand wizard. The Klan drew its members from all classes of white society, not merely from among the poor. Businessmen, lawyers, physicians, and politicians, as well as farmers and planters, were active in the Klan. The Klan and other armed groups functioned mainly where black people were a large minority and where their votes could affect elections. Klansmen virtually took over areas of western Alabama, northern Georgia, and Florida's panhandle. The Klan controlled the up-country of South Carolina and the area around Mecklenburg County, North Carolina. However, in the Carolina and Georgia low country where there were huge black majorities, the Klan rarely, if ever, appeared.

Although the Klan and similar societies were neither well organized nor unified, they did reduce support for the Republican Party and helped eliminate its leaders. Often wearing hoods and masks to hide their faces, white terrorists embarked on a campaign of violence rarely matched and never exceeded in American history.

Mobs of marauding terrorists beat and killed hundreds of black people—and many white people. Black churches and schools were burned. Republican leaders were threatened or killed. In South Carolina in 1868, the black chairman of the Republican Party, Benjamin F. Randolph,

Ku Klux Klan A secret society founded by former Confederates in Pulaski, Tennessee, in 1866. It transformed itself into a terrorist organization during Reconstruction to drive black and white Republicans from political power in southern states.

 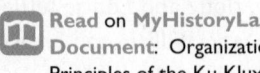
Read on MyHistoryLab
Document: Organization and Principles of the Ku Klux Klan, 1868

((•)) 📖 **Read** on **MyHistoryLab Document:** An Ex-Slave Describes a Ku Klux Klan Ride, Late 1860s

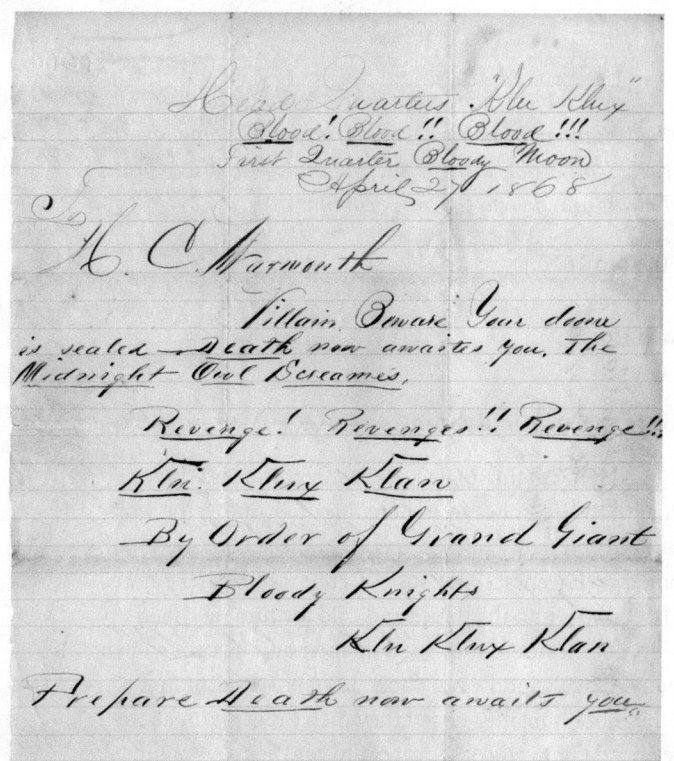

The flowing white robes and cone-shaped headgear associated with the Ku Klux Klan today are mostly a twentieth-century phenomenon. The Klansmen of the Reconstruction era, like these two men in Alabama in 1868, were well armed, disguised, and prepared to intimidate black and white Republicans. The note is a Klan death threat directed at Louisiana's first Republican governor, Henry C. Warmoth.

13-1

13-2

13-3

13-4

13-5

13-6

13-7

was murdered as he stepped off a train. Black legislator Lee Nance and white legislator Solomon G. W. Dill were later slain. In 1870 black lawmaker Richard Burke was killed in Sumter County, Alabama, because he was considered too influential among "people of his color."

As his wife looked on, Jack Dupree—a local Republican leader—had his throat cut and was eviscerated in Monroe County, Mississippi. In 1870 North Carolina Senator John W. Stephens, a white Republican, was murdered. After Alabama freedman George Moore voted for the Republicans in 1869, Klansmen beat him, raped a girl who was visiting his wife, and attacked a neighbor. An Irish-American teacher and four black men were lynched in Cross Plains, Alabama, in 1870. The outlaw John Wesley Hardin openly acknowledged he had killed black Texas state policemen.

White men attacked a Republican campaign rally in Eutaw, Alabama, in 1870, killing four black men and wounding 54 other people. After three black leaders were arrested in 1871 in Meridian, Mississippi, for delivering what many white people considered inflammatory speeches, shooting broke out in the courtroom. The Republican judge and two of the defendants were killed, and in a wave of violence, 30 black people were murdered, including every black leader in the small community. In the same year, a mob of 500 men broke into the jail in Union County, South Carolina, and lynched eight black prisoners accused of killing a Confederate veteran.

Nowhere was the Klan more active and violent than in York County, South Carolina. Almost the entire adult white male population joined in threatening, attacking, and

VOICES   An Appeal for Help against the Klan

H. K. Roberts, a black lieutenant in the South Carolina militia, described Klan terror in York County in late 1870 to Governor Robert K. Scott. Roberts desperately appealed for aid to protect Republicans and defend the black community.

Dec. the 6th 1870.

Antioch P.O.
York County S.C.

To Your Excelency R. K. Scott

Sir I will tell you that on last friday night the 2nd day of this [month] 8 miles from here thier was one of the worst outrages Commited that is on record in the state from 50 to 75 armed men went to the house of Thomas Blacks a colored man fired shots into the house and cald for him he clibed up in the loft of the house they fired up their and he came down jumped out at a window ran about 30 steps was shot down then they shot him after he fell they then draged him about 10 steps and cut his throat from ear to ear their was about 30 bullet holes in his body some 50 to one hundred shots in the house. . . . [They] abused his wife and enquired for one or two more colored men some of the colored people are leaving and a great many lying out in the woods and they reports comes to me evry day that they Ku Kluxs intend to kill us all

out and I heard yesterday that they had 30 stands of arms. . . . I wish you would give me 20 or 25 men or let me enroll that many and I will stop it or catch some of them or send some U S Soldiers on for I tell you their must be something don and that quick to for I do believe that they intend to beat and kill out the Radical party in the upper Counties of the state where the vote is close if we was to have the ellection now the Radicals would turn [out] to vote their ticket I leave the matter with you I hope you will wright back to me by return mail and let me heare what you think you can do for us up here I cant tell whether I can hold my own or not I know some men that stay with us at night for safety but if they come as strong as they were the other night they may kill me and all of my men I remain yours truly as ever.

H.K. Roberts, Lieut.
Commanding Post of State Guards Kings Mountain

1. **Why did Roberts write this letter?**
2. **Would Roberts have had any reason to exaggerate the violence in York County?**
3. **According to Roberts, what motivated white men to attack?**

SOURCE: H. K. Roberts to Governor Robert K. Scott, South Carolina Department of Archives and History.

murdering the black population. Hundreds were beaten and at least 11 were killed. Terrified families fled into the woods. Black leaders sent appeals for help to Governor Robert K. Scott (see Voices: An Appeal for Help against the Klan).

But Scott did not send aid. He had already sent the South Carolina militia into areas of Klan activity, and even more violence had resulted. The militia was made up mostly of black men, and white terrorists retaliated by killing militia officers. Scott could not send white men to York County because most of them sympathized with the Klan. Thus, Republican governors like Scott responded ineffectually. Republican-controlled legislatures passed anti-Klan measures that made it illegal to appear in public in disguises and masks, and they strengthened laws against assault, murder, and conspiracy. Nonetheless, enforcement was weak.

A few Republican leaders did deal harshly and effectively with terrorism. Governors in Tennessee, Texas, and Arkansas declared martial law and sent in hundreds of well-armed white and black men to quell the violence. Hundreds of Klansmen were arrested, many fled, and three were executed in Arkansas. But when Governor William W. Holden of North Carolina sent the state militia after the Klan, he provoked an angry reaction. Subsequent Klan violence in 10 counties helped Democrats carry the 1870 legislative elections, and the legislature then removed Holden from office.

Outnumbered and outgunned, black people in most areas did not retaliate against the Klan, and the Klan was rarely active where black people were in a majority and prepared to defend themselves. In the cause of white supremacy, the Klan usually attacked those who could not defend themselves.

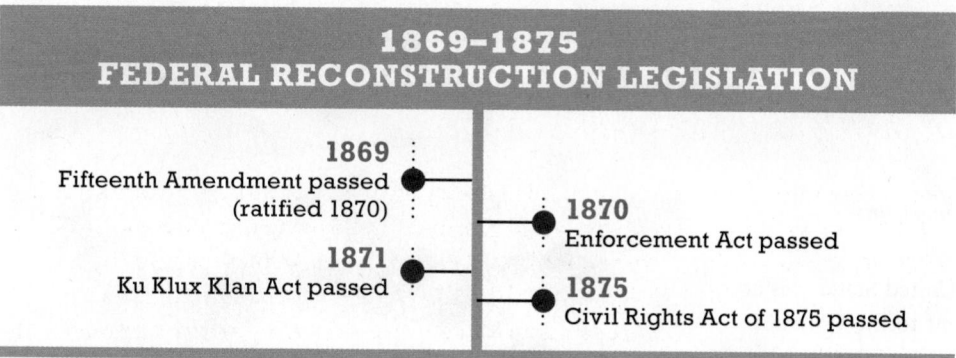

1869–1875
FEDERAL RECONSTRUCTION LEGISLATION

1869
Fifteenth Amendment passed
(ratified 1870)

1870
Enforcement Act passed

1871
Ku Klux Klan Act passed

1875
Civil Rights Act of 1875 passed

The West

During the 1830s the U.S. government forced the Five Civilized Tribes—the Cherokee, Chickasaw, Choctaw, Creek, and Seminole—from their southern homelands to Indian Territory in what is now Oklahoma. By 1860 Native Americans there held 7,367 African Americans in slavery. Many of the Indians fought for the Confederacy during the Civil War. Following the war, the former slaves encountered nearly as much violence and hostility from Native Americans as they did from southern white people. Indians were reluctant to share their land with freedmen, and they vigorously opposed policies that favored black voting rights.

Gradually and despite considerable Indian prejudice, some African Americans managed to acquire tribal land. Also, the Creeks and the Seminoles permitted former slaves to take part in tribal government. Black men served in both houses of the Creek legislature—the House of Warriors and the House of Kings. An African American, Jesse Franklin, served as a justice on the Creek tribal court in 1876. In contrast, the Chickasaw and Choctaw were absolutely opposed to making concessions to freed people. Therefore, the U.S. government ordered federal troops onto Chickasaw and Choctaw lands to protect the former slaves.

Elsewhere on the western frontier, black people struggled for legal and political rights and periodically participated in territorial governments. In 1867, 200 black men voted—although white men protested—in the Montana territorial election. In the Colorado Territory, William Jefferson Hardin, a barber, campaigned with other black men for the right to vote, and in 1865 they persuaded 137 African Americans (91 percent of Colorado's black population) to petition the territorial governor to abolish a white-only voting provision. In 1867 black men in Colorado finally gained the right to vote. Hardin later moved to Cheyenne and was elected to the Wyoming territorial legislature in 1879.

The Fifteenth Amendment

13-5 **What were the origins and effects of the Fifteenth Amendment and the Enforcement Acts?**

The federal government under Republican domination tried to protect black voting rights and defend Republican state governments in the South. In 1869 Congress passed the **Fifteenth Amendment**, which was ratified in 1870. It stipulated that a person could not be deprived of the right to vote because of race: "The right of citizens of the United States to vote shall not be denied or abridged by the United States or by any State on account of race, color, or previous condition of servitude." Black people, abolitionists, and reformers hailed the amendment as the culmination of the crusade to end slavery and give black people the same rights as white people.

Northern black men were the amendment's immediate beneficiaries because, before its adoption, black men could vote in only eight northern states. Yet to the disappointment

Fifteenth Amendment This constitutional amendment stipulated that the right to vote could not be denied on account of race, color, or because a person had been a slave.

✳ EXPLORE ON MYHISTORYLAB

Reconstruction

How did Reconstruction Affect African Americans in the South?

In 1865 at the end of the Civil War, the United States was at a crossroads. The Thirteenth Amendment to the Constitution had abolished slavery, but questions remained on what rights—if any—should be granted to the newly liberated African Americans. White political leaders were divided on how to restore the war-torn southern states to the Union. Many white Southerners expected to continue their ways of life with freed African Americans regarded as their inferiors. Although the subsequent Fourteenth and Fifteenth Amendments were intended to include African Americans in the legal and political fabric of the nation, most white people in the North and South were unwilling to accept black people as their equals. The early promises of Reconstruction for African Americans went unfulfilled.

✳ Explore the Topic on MyHistoryLab

1. **Analysis** *How did voting patterns for Republicans evolve during the Reconstruction period?* Chart voting patterns to understand reasons behind voting trends.

2. **Comparison** *How did literacy rates differ between African Americans and Euro-Americans in the South?* Theorize how this might affect black disenfranchisement.

3. **Response** *What was the land-holding situation for African Americans at the end of the nineteenth century?* Map land tenure to see discrepancies with whites.

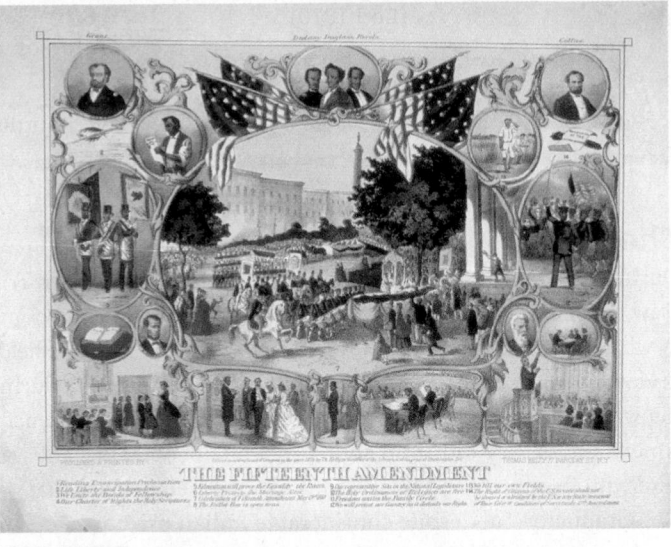

This optimistic 1870 illustration exemplifies the hopes and aspirations generated during Reconstruction as black people gained access to the political system, suggesting that African Americans would soon assume their rightful and equitable role in American society.

RECONSTRUCTION AMENDMENTS TO THE CONSTITUTION

Amendment	Summary	Date
Thirteenth	Abolishes slavery	December 6, 1865
Fourteenth	Ensures equal rights and protections to every person born or naturalized in the United States	July 9, 1868
Fifteenth	Prohibits the denial of the right of vote based on race	February 3, 1870

---

of many, the amendment said nothing about women voting and did not outlaw poll taxes, literacy tests, and property qualifications that could disfranchise citizens.

The Enforcement Acts

Enforcement Acts Also known as the Force Acts, these measures were passed by Congress in the early 1870s to undermine the Ku Klux Klan and other terrorist organizations by authorizing the president to use military force and to suspend the writ of *habeas corpus.*

habeas corpus A court order that a person arrested or detained by law enforcement officers must be brought to court and charged with a crime, not just held indefinitely.

In direct response to the terrorism in the South, Congress passed the **Enforcement Acts** in 1870 and 1871; the federal government thereby expanded its authority over the states. The 1870 act outlawed disguises and masks and protected the civil rights of citizens. The 1871 act—known as the Ku Klux Klan Act—made it a federal offense to interfere with a person's right to vote, hold office, serve on a jury, or enjoy equal protection of the law. Those accused of violating the act would be tried in federal court. For extreme violence, the act authorized the president to send in federal troops and suspend the writ of **habeas corpus**. (*Habeas corpus* is the right to be brought before a judge and not be arrested and jailed without cause.)

Black congressmen, who had long advocated federal action against the Klan, endorsed the Enforcement Acts. Representative Joseph Rainey of South Carolina wanted to suspend the Constitution to protect citizens: "I desire that so broad and liberal a construction be placed on its provisions, as will insure protection to the humblest citizen. Tell me nothing of a constitution which fails to shelter beneath its rightful power the people of a country."

Armed with this new legislation, the Justice Department and Attorney General Amos T. Ackerman moved vigorously against the Klan. Hundreds of Klansmen were arrested—700 in Mississippi alone. Faced with a full-scale rebellion in late 1871 in South Carolina's up-country, President Ulysses S. Grant declared martial law in nine counties, suspended the writ of *habeas corpus*, and sent in the army. Mass arrests and trials followed, but federal authorities permitted many Klansmen to confess and thereby escape prosecution. The government lacked the human and financial resources to bring hundreds of men to court for lengthy trials. Some white men were tried, mostly before black juries, and were imprisoned or fined. Comparatively few Klansmen, however, were punished severely, especially considering the enormity of their crimes.

The North and Reconstruction

13-6 How and why did black and white Republicans lose control of every southern state by 1877?

Although the federal government did reduce Klan violence for a time, white southerners remained convinced that white supremacy must be restored and Republican governments overturned. Klan violence did not overthrow any state governments, but it undermined freedmen's confidence in the ability of these governments to protect them. Meanwhile, Radical Republicans in Congress grew frustrated that the South and especially black people continued to demand so much of their time and attention year after year. There was less and less sentiment in the North to continue support for the freedmen and involvement in southern affairs.

Many northern Republicans lost interest in civil rights issues and principles and became more concerned with winning elections and the economy. By the mid-1870s, there was more discussion in Congress of patronage, veterans' pensions, railroads, taxes, tariffs, the economy, and monetary policy than about rights for black people or the future of the South.

By the 1870s, the American political system was also awash in corruption, which further detracted from concerns over the South. Although President Grant was a man of integrity, many men in his administration were not. They were implicated in scandals involving the construction of the transcontinental railroad, federal taxes on whiskey, and fraud within the Bureau of Indian Affairs. Nor was the dishonesty limited to Republicans. William Marcy "Boss" Tweed and the Democratic machine that dominated New York City were notoriously corrupt.

Many Republicans began to question the necessity for more moral, military, and political support for African Americans. They were convinced that African Americans had demanded too much for too long from the national government. Former slaves had become citizens and had the right to vote and hold political office. Therefore, they did not need additional help or legislation from the federal government. Equality for black people would come from their labor as free men, which would produce wealth and acceptance by white people. Federal legislation, many northern white people believed, could not create equality.

The *Chicago Tribune*, a Republican newspaper, had wearied of black agitation by 1874: "Is it not time for the colored race to stop playing baby? The whites of America have done nobly in outgrowing old prejudices against them. They cannot hurry this process by law. Let them obtain social equality as every other man, woman, and child in the world obtain it,—by showing themselves in their lives the social equals of those with whom they wish to consort. If they do this, year by year the prejudices will die away."

Other northern white people, swayed by white southerners' views of black people, began to doubt the wisdom of universal manhood suffrage. Many white people who had nominally supported black suffrage began to believe the exaggerated complaints about corruption among black leaders and the unrelenting claims that freedmen were incapable of self-government. Some white northerners began to conclude that Reconstruction had been a mistake.

Economic conditions contributed to changing attitudes. A financial crisis—the Panic of 1873—sent the economy into a long slump. Businesses and financial institutions failed, unemployment soared, and prices fell. In 1874 the Democrats recaptured a majority in the House of Representatives for the first time since 1860 and also took control of several northern states.

The Freedmen's Bank

Freedmen's Savings Bank A private financial institution chartered by Congress in 1865. Many black people and organizations deposited funds in the bank, which went bankrupt in 1874.

One of the casualties of the financial crisis was the **Freedmen's Savings Bank**, which failed in 1874. Founded in 1865 when hope flourished, the Freedmen's Savings and Trust Company had been chartered by Congress but was not connected to the Freedmen's Bureau. However, the bank's advertising featured pictures of Abraham Lincoln, and many black people assumed it was a federal agency. Freedmen and black veterans, churches, fraternal organizations, and benevolent societies opened thousands of accounts in the bank. Most of the deposits totaled under $50, and some amounted to only a few cents.

Although the bank had many black employees, its board of directors consisted of white men. They invested the bank's funds in risky ventures, including Washington, DC, real estate. With the Panic of 1873, the bank lost large sums in unsecured railroad loans. To restore confidence, its directors persuaded Frederick Douglass to serve as president and invest $10,000 of his own money to help shore up the bank. Douglass lost his money, and African Americans across the South lost more than $1 million when the bank closed in June 1874. Eventually about half the depositors received three-fifths of the value of their accounts, but many African Americans believed the U.S. government owed them a debt. Well into the twentieth century, they wrote to Congress and the president in unsuccessful efforts to retrieve their hard-earned money.

The Civil Rights Act of 1875

Civil Rights Act of 1875 This federal legislation outlawed racial discrimination in public accommodations such as hotels and restaurants, and in transportation, including railroad coaches and steamboats. The Supreme Court invalidated it in 1883.

Before Reconstruction expired, Congress made one final—some said futile—gesture to protect black people from racial discrimination when it passed the **Civil Rights Act of 1875**. Championed by Senator Charles Sumner of Massachusetts, it was originally intended to open public accommodations—including schools, churches, cemeteries, hotels, and transportation—to all people regardless of race. It passed in the Republican-controlled Senate in 1874, but House Democrats held up passage. It was not enacted until 1875 and then largely as a memorial to Sumner, who had died in 1874. In its final form, the bans on discrimination in churches, cemeteries, and schools were deleted.

The act stipulated "That all persons . . . shall be entitled to the full and equal enjoyment of the accommodations, advantages, facilities, and privileges of inns, public conveyances on land or water, theaters, and other places of public amusement." After its passage, no attempt was made to enforce these provisions, and in 1883 the Supreme Court declared it unconstitutional. Justice Joseph Bradley wrote that the Fourteenth Amendment protected black people from discrimination by states but not by private businesses. Black newspapers likened the decision to the *Dred Scott* case a quarter century earlier.

The End of Reconstruction

Watch on MyHistoryLab Video: The Promise and Failure of Reconstruction

13-7 What were the methods used and results of attempts to "redeem" the southern states?

redemption The term used for the process, often violent, by which white conservative Democrats regained political control of a southern state from black and white Republicans during Reconstruction.

Reconstruction ended as it began—in violence and controversy. Democrats demanded "**redemption**"—a word with biblical and spiritual overtones. They wanted southern states restored to conservative, white political control. By 1875 they had regained authority in all

VOICES Black Leaders Support the Passage of a Civil Rights Act

Black Congressmen Robert Brown Elliott of South Carolina and James T. Rapier of Alabama spoke passionately in favor of the Sumner civil rights bill in 1874. Both men had been free before the war. Both were also lawyers, and although each accumulated considerable wealth, they died in poverty in the 1880s.

[James T. Rapier]

I must confess it is somewhat embarrassing for a colored man to urge the passage of this bill, because if he exhibit an earnestness in the matter and expresses a desire for its immediate passage, straightaway he is charged with a desire for social equality, as explained by the demagogue and understood by the ignorant white man. But then it is just as embarrassing for him not to do so, for, if he remains silent while the struggle is being carried on around, and for him, he is liable to be charged with a want of interest in a matter that concerns him more than anyone else, which is enough to make his friends desert his cause. So in steering away from Scylla I may run upon Charybdis. But the anomalous, and I may add the supremely ridiculous, position of the Negro at this time, in this country, compel me to say something. Here his condition is without comparison, parallel alone to itself. Just that the law recognizes my right upon this floor as a law-maker, but that there is no law to secure to me any accommodations whatever while traveling here to discharge my duties as a Representative of a large and wealthy constituency. Here I am the peer of the proudest, but on a steamboat or car I am not

equal to the most degraded. Is not this most anomalous and ridiculous?

[Robert Brown Elliott]

The results of the war, as seen in Reconstruction, have settled forever the political status of my race. The passage of this bill will determine the civil status, not only of the Negro but of any other class of citizens who may feel themselves discriminated against. It will form the capstone of that temple of liberty begun on this continent under discouraging circumstances, carried on in spite of the sneers of monarchists and the cavils of pretended friends of freedom, until at last it stands in all its beautiful symmetry and proportions, a building the grandest which the world has ever seen, realizing the most sanguine expectations and the highest hopes of those who in the name of equal, impartial and universal liberty, laid the foundation stone.

1. **If black men had the right to vote and serve in Congress, why was a civil rights law needed?**
2. **Who would benefit most from the passage of this bill?**
3. **What distinction does the congressmen draw between social discrimination and political rights?**

SOURCE: *Congressional Record,* 43rd Congress, 1st sess., 1874, vol. II, pt. 1, 565–67; Peggy Lamson, *The Glorious Failure* (New York: Norton, 1973), 181.

the former Confederate states except Mississippi, Florida, Louisiana, and South Carolina (see Map 13–1). Democrats had redeemed Tennessee in 1870 and Georgia in 1871. Democrats had learned two lessons. First, few black men would vote for the Democratic Party—no matter how much white leaders wanted to believe former slaves were easy to manipulate. Second, intimidation and violence would win elections in areas where the number of black and white voters was nearly equal. The federal government had stymied Klan violence in 1871, but by the mid-1870s the government had become reluctant to send troops to the South to protect black citizens.

Violent Redemption

In Alabama in 1874, black and white Republican leaders were murdered, and white mobs destroyed crops and homes. On election day in Eufaula, white men killed seven and injured nearly 70 unarmed black voters. Black voters were also driven from the polls in Mobile. Democrats won the election and "redeemed" Alabama.

White violence marred every election in Louisiana from 1868 to 1876. After Republicans and Democrats each claimed victory in the 1872 elections, black people seized the small town of Colfax along the Red River to protect themselves against a Democratic takeover. They held out for three weeks. Then on Easter Sunday in 1873, a well-armed white

13-1

13-2

13-3

13-4

13-5

13-6

13-7

On January 6, 1874, Robert Brown Elliott delivered a ringing speech in the U.S. House of Representatives in support of the Sumner civil rights bill. Elliott was responding in part to words uttered the day before by Virginia Congressman John T. Harris, who claimed that "there is not a gentleman on this floor who can honestly say he really believes that the colored man is created his equal."

P.S. Duval and Son, Come and join us brothers; Civil War; Philadelphia, PA; ca. 1863. Chicago Historical Society ICHi-22051.

Colfax Massacre At least 105 African Americans were murdered on Easter Sunday in 1873 in Colfax, Louisiana, in the single worst episode of racial violence during Reconstruction.

shotgun policy In Mississippi in 1875, white men resorted to violence and intimidation against black and white Republicans to regain political control of the state for conservative Democrats.

Hamburg Massacre White Democrats attacked black Republicans in July 1876 in the village of Hamburg, South Carolina. Five black men were murdered as the Democrats began a violent effort to redeem the state.

mob attacked the black defenders. At least 105 were killed in the **Colfax Massacre**, the worst single day of bloodshed during Reconstruction. In 1874 the White League almost redeemed Louisiana in a wave of violence. Black people were murdered, courts were attacked, and white people refused to pay taxes to the Republican state government. Six white and two black Republicans were murdered at Coushatta. In September, President Grant finally sent federal troops to New Orleans after 3,500 White Leaguers nearly wiped out the black militia and the Metropolitan Police. But the stage had been set for the 1876 campaign.

At least 105 African Americans were murdered on Easter Sunday in 1873 in Colfax, Louisiana, in the single worst episode of racial violence during Reconstruction.

The Shotgun Policy

In 1875 white Mississippians, no longer afraid the national government would intervene in force, declared open warfare on the black majority. The masks and hoods of the Klan were discarded. One newspaper proclaimed that Democrats would carry the election, "peaceably if we can, forcibly if we must." Another paper carried a bold banner: "Mississippi is a white man's country, and by the eternal God we'll rule it."

White Mississippi unleashed a campaign of violence known as the "**shotgun policy**" that was extreme even for Reconstruction. Many Republicans fled, and others were murdered. In late 1874 an estimated 300 black people were hunted down outside Vicksburg after black men armed with inferior weapons had lost a "battle" with white men. In 1875, 30 teachers, church leaders, and Republican officials were killed in Clinton. The white sheriff of Yazoo County, who had married a black woman and supported the education of black children, fled the state.

Governor Adelbert Ames appealed for federal help, but President Grant refused: "The whole public are tired out with these annual autumnal outbreaks in the South . . . [and] are ready now to condemn any interference on the part of the Government." The terrorism intensified, and many black voters went into hiding on election day, afraid for their lives and those of their families. Democrats redeemed Mississippi and prided themselves that they—a superior race representing the most civilized of all people—were back in control.

In Florida in 1876, white Republicans noted that support for black people in the South was fading. They nominated an all-white Republican slate and even refused to renominate black Congressman Josiah Walls.

The Hamburg Massacre and the Ellenton Riot

South Carolina Democrats were divided between moderate and extreme factions, but they united to nominate former Confederate General Wade Hampton for governor after the **Hamburg Massacre**. The prelude to this event occurred on July 4, 1876—the nation's centennial—when two white men in a buggy confronted the black militia that was drilling on a town street in Hamburg, a small, mostly black town. Hot words were exchanged, and days later, Democrats demanded the militia be disarmed. White rifle club members from around the state arrived in Hamburg and attacked the armory, where 40 black members of the militia defended themselves. The rifle companies brought up a cannon and reinforcements from Georgia. After the militia ran low on ammunition, white men captured the armory. One white man was killed, 29 black men were taken prisoner, and the other 11 fled. Five of the black men identified as leaders were shot down in cold blood. The rifle companies wrecked the town. Seven white men were indicted for murder. All were acquitted.

Two months after the Hamburg killings a false allegation that African Americans had assaulted an elderly white woman gave armed bands of white men the excuse to attack black people in the rural community of Ellenton about 30 miles south of Hamburg. Between 30 and 100 African Americans were slain in the **Ellenton Massacre**, including state legislator Simon Coker. Two white men died. Had it not been for the timely arrival of U.S. troops, more lives would have been lost. No one was charged much less convicted in the Ellenton affair.

The Hamburg Massacre and Ellenton Riot represented the determined effort of South Carolina Democrats to imitate Mississippi's "shotgun policy." It also had forced a reluctant President Grant to send federal troops to South Carolina. In the 1876 election campaign, hundreds of white men in red flannel shirts turned out on mules and horses to support Wade Hampton against incumbent Republican Governor Daniel Chamberlain and his black and white allies. When Chamberlain and fellow Republicans tried to speak in Edgefield, 600 Red Shirts, many of them armed, ridiculed, threatened, and shouted them down.

Democrats beat and killed black people to prevent them from voting. Democratic leaders instructed their followers to treat black voters with contempt: "In speeches to negroes you must remember that argument has no effect on them. They can only be influenced by their fears, superstition, and cupidity. . . . Treat them so as to show them you are a superior race and that their natural position is that of subordination to the white man."

As the election approached, black people in the up-country of South Carolina knew it would be dangerous if they tried to vote. But in the low country, black people went on the offensive and attacked Democrats. In Charleston, a white man was killed in a racial melee. At a campaign rally at Cainhoy, a few miles outside Charleston, armed black men killed five white men.

A few black men supported Hampton and the Red Shirts. Hampton had a paternalistic view of black people, and, although he considered them inferior, he promised to respect their rights. Hampton and the Democrats were more trustworthy than unreliable Republicans; Delany campaigned for Hampton and was later rewarded with an appointment to a minor political post. A few conservative black men during Reconstruction also supported the Democrats and curried their favor and patronage. However, most black people despised them. When one black man gave his support to the Democrats, his wife threw him and his clothes out, declaring she would prefer to "beg her bread" than live with a "Democratic nigger."

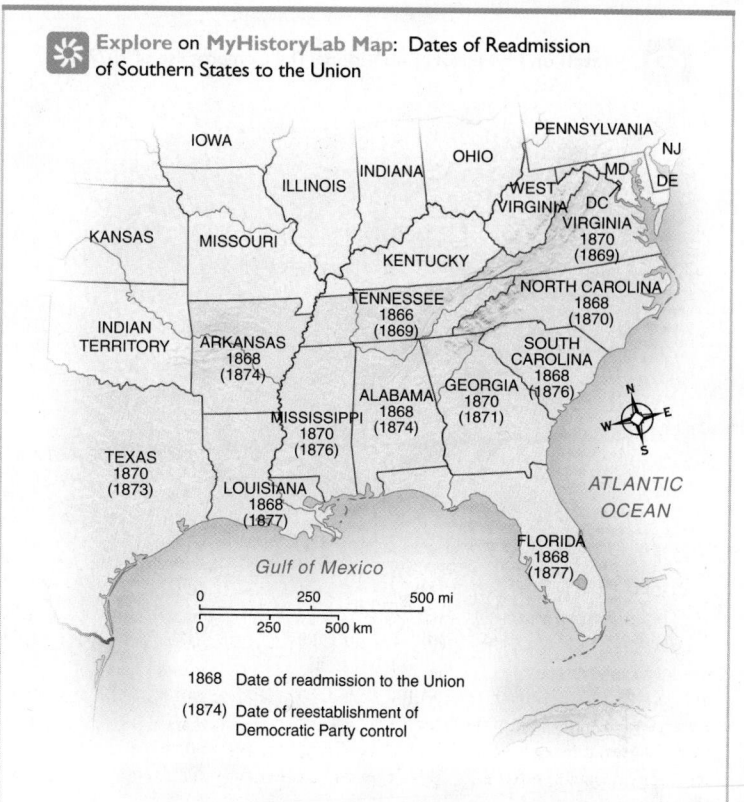

Explore on MyHistoryLab Map: Dates of Readmission of Southern States to the Union

1868 Date of readmission to the Union
(1874) Date of reestablishment of Democratic Party control

MAP 13–1 DATES OF READMISSION OF SOUTHERN STATES TO THE UNION AND REESTABLISHMENT OF DEMOCRATIC PARTY CONTROL
Once conservative white Democrats regained political control of a state government from black and white Republicans, they considered that state "redeemed." The first states the Democrats "redeemed" were Georgia, Virginia, and North Carolina. Louisiana, Florida, and South Carolina were the last. (Tennessee was not included in the Reconstruction process under the terms of the 1867 Reconstruction Act.)

In which states did black and white Republicans hold political control for the shortest and longest periods of time?

Ellenton Massacre Between 30 and 100 African Americans were killed by marauding white men in September 1876 in Aiken County, South Carolina, after an alleged assault by a black man on an elderly white woman.

The "Compromise" of 1877
Threats, violence, and bloodshed accompanied the elections of 1876 in the South, but the national results were confusing and contradictory. Samuel Tilden, the Democratic presidential candidate, won the popular vote by more than 250,000 and had a large lead—185 to 167—over Republican Rutherford B. Hayes in the electoral vote. The 20 remaining electoral votes were in dispute. Both Democrats and Republicans claimed to have won in Florida,

13-1
13-2
13-3
13-4
13-5
13-6
13-7

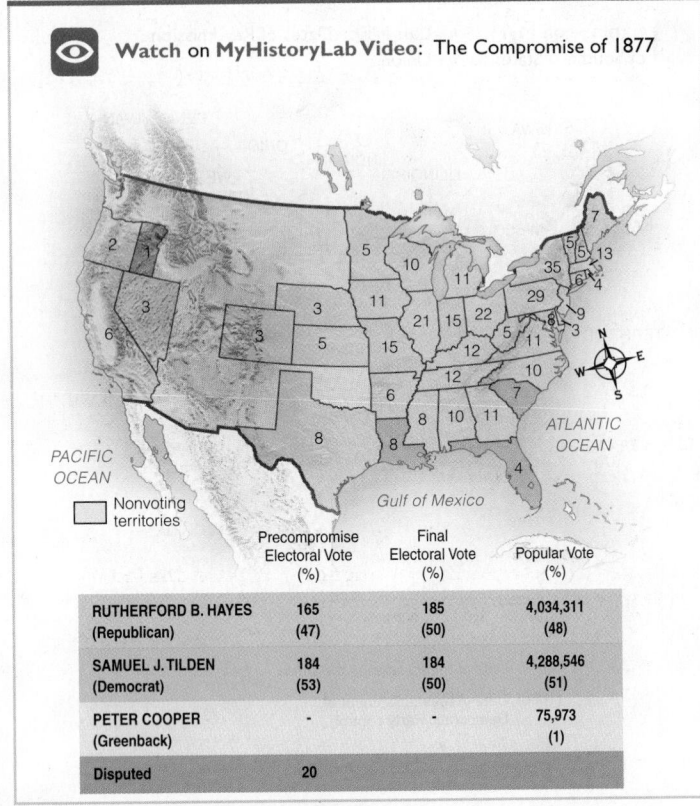

Watch on MyHistoryLab Video: The Compromise of 1877

	Precompromise Electoral Vote (%)	Final Electoral Vote (%)	Popular Vote (%)
RUTHERFORD B. HAYES (Republican)	165 (47)	185 (50)	4,034,311 (48)
SAMUEL J. TILDEN (Democrat)	184 (53)	184 (50)	4,288,546 (51)
PETER COOPER (Greenback)	-	-	75,973 (1)
Disputed	20		

MAP 13–2 THE ELECTION OF 1876

Although Democrat Samuel Tilden appeared to have won the election of 1876, Rutherford B. Hayes and the Republicans were able to claim victory after a prolonged political and constitutional controversy involving the disputed Electoral College votes from Louisiana, Florida, and South Carolina (and one from Oregon). In an informal settlement in 1877, Democrats agreed to accept electoral votes for Hayes from those states, and Republicans agreed to permit those states to be "redeemed" by the Democrats. The result was to leave the entire South under the political control of conservative white Democrats. For the first time since 1867, black and white Republicans no longer effectively controlled any former Confederate state.

What factors explain the loss of political power by southern Republicans?

Compromise of 1877 This informal arrangement between national Democrats and Republicans settled the disputed presidential election of 1876 by permitting Republican Rutherford B. Hayes to become president while allowing Democrats to complete redemption by taking political control of Louisiana, Florida, and South Carolina.

Louisiana, and South Carolina, the last three southern states that had not been redeemed. (There was also one contested vote from Oregon.) Unless Hayes managed to capture all 20 electoral votes of the three contested states (and Oregon), Tilden would be the next president (see Map 13–2).

The constitutional crisis over the outcome of the 1876 election was not resolved until shortly before Inauguration Day in March 1877. An informal understanding known as the **Compromise of 1877** ended the dispute. Democrats accepted a Hayes victory, but Hayes let southern Democrats know he would not support Republican governments in Florida, Louisiana, and South Carolina. In 1877 Hayes withdrew the last federal troops from the South, and the Republican administration in those states collapsed. Democrats immediately took control.

Redemption was now complete. White Democrats controlled each of the former Confederate states. Henry Adams, a black leader from Louisiana, explained what had happened: "The whole South— every state in the South had got into the hands of the very men that held us as slaves."

CONCLUSION

The glorious hopes that emancipation and the Union victory in the Civil War had aroused among African Americans in 1865 appeared forlorn by 1877. To be sure, black people were no longer slave laborers or property. They lived in tightly knit families that white people no longer controlled. They had established hundreds of schools, churches, and benevolent societies. The Constitution now endowed them with freedom, citizenship, and the right to vote. Some black people had even acquired land.

But no one can characterize Reconstruction as a success. The epidemic of terror and violence made it one of the bloodiest eras in American history. Thousands of black people had been beaten, raped, and murdered since 1865 simply because they had acted as free people. Too many white people were determined that black people could not and would not have the same rights that white people enjoyed. White southerners would not tolerate either the presence of black men in politics or white Republicans who accepted black political involvement. Most white northerners and even Radical Republicans grew weary of intervening in southern affairs and became convinced again that black men and women were their inferiors and were not prepared to participate in government. Reconstruction, they concluded, had been a mistake.

Furthermore, black and white Republicans hurt themselves by indulging in fraud and corruption and by engaging in angry and divisive factionalism. But even if Republicans had been honest and united, white southern Democrats would never have accepted black people as worthy to participate in the political system.

Southern Democrats would accept black people in politics only if Democrats could control black voters. But black voters understood this, rejected control by former slave owners, and were loyal to the Republican Party—as flawed as it was.

As grim a turn as life may have taken for black people by 1877, it would get even worse in the decades that followed.

CHAPTER TIMELINE

AFRICAN-AMERICAN EVENTS

NATIONAL EVENTS

1865–1866

1865
The Freedmen's Savings Bank and Trust Company is established

1865
Freedmen's Bureau established

1866
President Johnson vetoes Freedmen's Bureau and civil rights bills; Congress overrides both vetoes
Ku Klux Klan founded in Pulaski, Tennessee

1867–1868

1867–1868
Ten southern states hold constitutional conventions

1867
Howard University established in Washington, DC

1868
Black political leaders elected to state and local offices across the South

1867
Congress takes over Reconstruction and provides for universal manhood suffrage

1868
Fourteenth Amendment to the Constitution ratified
Ulysses S. Grant elected president

1869–1870

1870
Hiram R. Revels elected to the U.S. Senate and Joseph H. Rainey to the U.S. House of Representatives
Congress passes the Enforcement Act

1869
Knights of Labor founded in Philadelphia

1870
Fifteenth Amendment to the Constitution ratified
John D. Rockefeller incorporates Standard Oil Co. in Cleveland

1871–1872

1871
Congress passes the Ku Klux Klan Act

1871
William Marcy "Boss" Tweed indicted for fraud in New York City
Chicago Fire

1872
President Grant reelected
Yellowstone National Park established

1873

1873
The Colfax Massacre occurs in Louisiana

1873
Financial panic and economic depression begin

1875–1876

1875
Blanche K. Bruce elected to the U.S. Senate
Congress passes the Civil Rights Act of 1875
Democrats redeem Mississippi with the "shotgun policy"

1876
Hamburg Massacre and Ellenton riot occur in South Carolina

1875
Whiskey Ring exposes corruption in federal liquor tax collections

1876
Disputed presidential election between Samuel J. Tilden and Rutherford B. Hayes
Gen. George A. Custer and U.S. troops defeated by Sioux and Cheyenne in Battle of Little Big Horn

1877

Last federal troops withdrawn from the South

"Compromise of 1877" ends Reconstruction

On MyHistoryLab

 Study and Review on MyHistoryLab

REVIEW QUESTIONS

1. What issues most concerned black political leaders during Reconstruction?

2. What did black political leaders accomplish and fail to accomplish during Reconstruction? What contributed to their successes and failures?

3. Were black political leaders unqualified to hold office so soon after the end of slavery?

4. To what extent did African Americans dominate southern politics during Reconstruction? Should this era be referred to as "Black Reconstruction"?

5. Why did the Republican Party fail to maintain control of southern state governments during Reconstruction?

6. What was "redemption"? What happened when redemption occurred? What factors contributed to redemption?

7. How and why did Reconstruction end?

8. How effective was Reconstruction in assisting black people to move from slavery to freedom? How effective was it in restoring the southern states to the Union?

RECOMMENDED READING

Eric Foner. *Freedom's Lawmakers: A Directory of Black Officeholders During Reconstruction.* New York: Oxford University Press, 1993. Biographical sketches of every known southern black leader during the era.

John Hope Franklin. *Reconstruction after the Civil War.* Chicago: University of Chicago Press, 1961. An excellent summary and interpretation of the postwar years.

William Gillette. *Retreat from Reconstruction, 1869–1879.* Baton Rouge: Louisiana State University Press, 1979. An analysis of how and why the North lost interest in the South.

Thomas Holt. *Black over White: Negro Political Leadership in South Carolina.* Urbana: University of Illinois Press, 1979.

A masterful and sophisticated study of black leaders in the state with the most African-American politicians.

Michael L. Perman. *Emancipation and Reconstruction, 1862–1879.* Arlington Heights, IL: Harlan Davidson, 1987. Another excellent survey of the period.

Howard N. Rabinowitz, ed. *Southern Black Leaders of the Reconstruction Era.* Urbana: University of Illinois Press, 1982. A series of biographical essays on black politicians.

Frank A. Rollin. *Life and Public Services of Martin R. Delany.* Boston: Lee and Shepard, 1883. This is the first biography of a black leader by an African American. The author was Frances A. Rollin, but she used a male pseudonym.

ADDITIONAL BIBLIOGRAPHY

RECONSTRUCTION IN SPECIFIC STATES AND TERRITORIES

M. Thomas Bailey. *Reconstruction in Indian Territory: A Story of Avarice, Discrimination, and Opportunism.* Port Washington, NY: Kennikat Press, 1972.

Jane Dailey. *Before Jim Crow: The Politics of Race in Post Emancipation Virginia.* Chapel Hill: University of North Carolina Press, 2000.

Edmund L. Drago. *Black Politicians and Reconstruction in Georgia.* Athens: University of Georgia Press, 1982.

———. *Hurrah for Hampton! Black Red Shirts in South Carolina During Reconstruction.* Fayetteville: University of Arkansas Press, 1998.

Luther P. Jackson. *Negro Officeholders in Virginia, 1865–1895.* Norfolk, VA: Guide Quality Press, 1945.

Peter Kolchin. *First Freedom: The Responses of Alabama's Blacks to Emancipation and Reconstruction.* Westport, CT: Greenwood, 1972.

Merline Pitre. *Through Many Dangers, Toils, and Snares: The Black Leadership of Texas, 1868–1900.* Austin, TX: Eakin Press, 1985.

Joe M. Richardson. *The Negro in the Reconstruction of Florida, 1865–1877.* Tallahassee: Florida State University Press, 1965.

Buford Stacher. *Blacks in Mississippi Politics, 1865–1900.* Washington, DC: University Press of America, 1978.

Ted Tunnell. *Crucible of Reconstruction: War, Radicalism and Race in Louisiana, 1862–1877.* Baton Rouge: Louisiana State University Press, 1984.

Charles Vincent. *Black Legislators in Louisiana During Reconstruction.* Baton Rouge: Louisiana State University Press, 1976.

Joel Williamson. *After Slavery: The Negro in South Carolina: 1861–1877.* Chapel Hill: University of North Carolina Press, 1965.

NATIONAL POLITICS: ANDREW JOHNSON AND THE RADICAL REPUBLICANS

Michael Les Benedict. *A Compromise of Principle: Congressional Republicans and Reconstruction.* New York: Norton, 1974.

Dan T. Carter. *When the War Was Over: The Failure of Self-Reconstruction in the South, 1865–1867.* Baton Rouge: Louisiana State University Press, 1983.

Hugh Davis. *We Will Be Satisfied with Nothing Less: The African American Struggle for Equal Rights in the North During Reconstruction*. Ithaca, NY: Cornell University Press, 2011.

Michael W. Fitzgerald. *The Union League Movement in the Deep South*. Baton Rouge: Louisiana State University Press, 1989.

———. *Splendid Failure: Postwar Reconstruction in the American South*. Chicago: Ivan R. Dee, 2007.

Eric L. McKitrick. *Andrew Johnson and Reconstruction, 1865–1867*. Chicago: University of Chicago Press, 1960.

James M. McPherson. *The Struggle for Equality: Abolitionists and the Negro in the Civil War and Reconstruction*. Princeton, NJ: Princeton University Press, 1964.

Hans L. Trefousse. *The Radical Republicans: Lincoln's Vanguard for Racial Justice*. Baton Rouge: Louisiana State University Press, 1969.

EDUCATION, LAND, LABOR, AND THE FREEDMEN'S BANK

Elizabeth Bethel. *Promiseland: A Century of Life in a Negro Community*. Philadelphia: Temple University Press, 1981.

Carol R. Bleser. *The Promised Land: The History of the South Carolina Land Commission, 1869–1890*. Columbia: University of South Carolina Press, 1969.

Sharon Ann Holt. *Making Freedom Pay: North Carolina Freed People Working for Themselves, 1865–1900*. Athens: University of Georgia Press, 2000.

Ward McAfee. *Religion, Race and Reconstruction: The Public Schools in the 1870s*. Albany: State University of New York Press, 1998.

Lynda J. Morgan. *Emancipation in Virginia's Tobacco Belt*. Athens: University of Georgia Press, 1992.

Donald G. Nieman. *To Set the Law in Motion: The Freedmen's Bureau and Legal Rights for Blacks, 1865–1869*. Millwood, NY: KTO, 1979.

Carl R. Osthaus. *Freedmen, Philanthropy and Fraud: A History of the Freedman's Savings Bank*. Urbana: University of Illinois Press, 1976.

Heather Cox Richardson. *The Death of Reconstruction: Race, Labor, and Politics in the Post–Civil War North, 1865–1901*. Cambridge, MA: Harvard University Press, 2001.

VIOLENCE AND THE KU KLUX KLAN

Charles Lane. *The Day Freedom Died: The Colfax Massacre, the Supreme Court and the Betrayal of Reconstruction*. New York: Henry Holt and Co., 2008.

George C. Rable. *But There Was No Peace: The Role of Violence in the Politics of Reconstruction*. Athens: University of Georgia Press, 1984.

Allen W. Trelease. *White Terror: The Ku Klux Klan Conspiracy and Southern Reconstruction*. New York: Harper & Row, 1973.

Christopher Waldrep and Donald G. Nieman, eds. *Local Matters: Race, Crime, and Justice in the Nineteenth Century South*. Athens: University of Georgia Press, 2011.

Lou Falkner Williams. *The Great South Carolina Ku Klux Klan Trials, 1871–1872*. Athens: University of Georgia Press, 1996.

AUTOBIOGRAPHY AND BIOGRAPHY

Mifflin Wistar Gibbs. *Shadow & Light: An Autobiography*. Lincoln: University of Nebraska Press, 1995.

David Joens. *From Slave to State Legislator: John W. E. Thomas: Illinois' First African American Lawmaker*. Carbondale: Southern Illinois University Press, 2012.

Peter D. Klingman. *Josiah Walls*. Gainesville: University Press of Florida, 1976.

Peggy Lamson. *The Glorious Failure: Black Congressman Robert Brown Elliott and Reconstruction in South Carolina*. New York: Norton, 1973.

Edward A. Miller. *Gullah Statesman: Robert Smalls: From Slavery to Congress, 1839–1915*. Columbia: University of South Carolina Press, 1995.

Loren Schweninger. *James T. Rapier and Reconstruction*. Chicago: University of Chicago Press, 1978.

Okon E. Uya. *From Slavery to Public Service: Robert Smalls, 1839–1915*. New York: Oxford University Press, 1971.

RETRACING THE ODYSSEY

Howard University, Washington, DC. The Freedmen's Bureau founded this national university in 1867. Also located on the campus is the Moorland-Spingarn Research Center, one of the country's richest archives in African-American history.

Wilberforce University and the National Afro-American Museum and Cultural Center, Wilberforce, Ohio. Wilberforce University opened in 1856 and was named after English abolitionist William Wilberforce. The African Methodist Episcopal Church took over the school in 1863. It contains exhibits, an art gallery, and a theater, and has a picnic area.

Union Bank Building, Tallahassee, Florida. For a time during Reconstruction, a branch of the Freedmen's Savings and Trust

Company was located here. The building, constructed in 1840, originally served as a planters' bank. It is currently part of the Museum of Florida History and includes its African-American History teacher in-service program.

The Robert Smalls Home, Beaufort, South Carolina. The Civil War hero and black political leader bought this house in 1863. He had lived on the premises as a slave, and it remained in his hands until his death in 1915. (The former Smalls house is a privately owned dwelling today.)

CONNECTING THE PAST

Voting and Politics

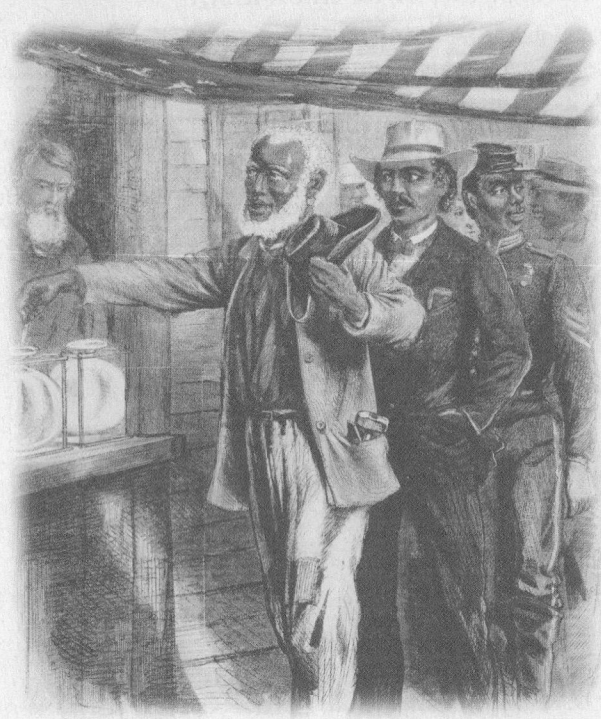

THE FIFTEENTH AMENDMENT TO THE CONSTITUTION, ratified in 1870, explicitly states that the right "to vote shall not be denied or abridged by the United States or any State on account of race, color, or previous condition of servitude." Why then was it necessary for Congress to pass the Voting Rights Act of 1965?

Race and the right to vote have been volatile issues since the creation of the American republic. The Founding Fathers betrayed a deep mistrust of permitting white men to vote who lacked education and had no stake in society through the possession of property or wealth. Slaves could not vote. Women were disfranchised. But in the late 1700s, a few free black men in the Northeastern states of Pennsylvania, New York, Connecticut, Rhode Island, Massachusetts, New Hampshire, and Vermont did vote. In the early nineteenth century, however, as the political system became more democratic for white men, black men in Pennsylvania and Connecticut—and most black men in New York—lost the right to vote.

Following the Civil War, white Southerners and northern Democrats were outraged when Republicans in Congress granted black men the right to vote through Reconstruction legislation and the Fifteenth Amendment. As southern Democrats "redeemed" the former Confederate states, they systematically disfranchised black voters and evaded the Fifteenth Amendment.

To do this, they devised a variety of schemes. Among them were the poll tax, the literacy test, and a requirement that illiterate men could vote only if they could "understand" the Constitution. Several southern states also adopted the grandfather clause, which stipulated that only men who were eligible to vote before 1867 or had fathers or grandfathers who were eligible to vote at that time would be eligible to vote in the late nineteenth century. Violence and intimidation were also used to "persuade" black men and their white allies that they did not want to vote. The U.S. Supreme Court acquiesced in disfranchisement by narrowly defining voting rights for African Americans in a series of cases in the late nineteenth and early twentieth centuries that nullified the Fifteenth Amendment. In tortured logic in one of these cases, Chief Justice Morrison Waite declared that, "The Fifteenth Amendment does not confer the right of suffrage upon anyone." Instead, he claimed, "It prevents the States, or United States, however, from giving preference . . . to one citizen of the United States over another, on account of race, color or previous condition of servitude."

By the early twentieth century, Democrats and Republicans began to hold primary elections to nominate party candidates to run in the general election. Southern Democrats took advantage of this innovation to limit membership in the Democratic Party to white men—and later white women. Only members of the Democratic Party were eligible to vote in the Democratic primary. Because the Republican Party had all but ceased to exist in the

South after Reconstruction and rarely ran candidates for statewide offices, victory in the Democratic primary meant victory in the fall election. Black voters who could still vote in the general election found it a meaningless gesture because the "real" election had been the Democratic primary.

As black men and women migrated North and West in the early and mid-twentieth century, they were able to vote in their new communities. Their increasing political strength enabled them to elect black men and women to local and state offices. They also elected black men from northern cities, including Oscar DePriest, Robert Nix, Adam Clayton Powell, and Charles Diggs, to serve in the U.S. House of Representatives. With the New Deal in the 1930s, black voters began to support Democratic candidates as they abandoned their longstanding loyalty to the Republican Party. In turn, the Democratic Party increasingly relied on those black voters to support their presidential candidates such as Franklin D. Roosevelt, Harry S Truman, and John F. Kennedy. In the meantime, the Supreme Court declared the grandfather clause unconstitutional in 1915 and outlawed the South's white Democratic primary elections in 1944.

During the Civil Rights movement and with unrelenting pressure from President Lyndon B. Johnson, northern Democrats and Republicans in Congress passed—over the bitter opposition of southern Democrats—the Civil Rights Act of 1964 and the Voting Rights Act of 1965. The Voting Rights Act authorized the U.S. Department of Justice to dispatch federal registrars to states and communities that had a history of suppressing voting rights. As a result, the number of black voters and then black officeholders expanded exponentially across the South.

Yet voting rights still is not a dead issue. In the second decade of the twenty-first century, the Republican Party launched a campaign in 30 states to require voter photo identification at the polls. If implemented, the requirement for government-issued identification will adversely affect poorer voters who lack such documentation—especially African Americans, Hispanics, and Native Americans.

1. **Who should be denied the right to vote? Why?**

2. **To prevent fraud, should voters be required to present photo identification to cast a ballot?**

PART IV

SEARCHING FOR SAFE SPACES

W. C. Handy

	1860–1900	1900–1910

RELIGION

1880s–1890s Holiness Movement and Pentecostal churches spread among African Americans

1854 James A. Healey ordained first African-American Roman Catholic priest in Paris

1890 Baptist churches count 1,300,000 southern black members, making them the largest African-American denomination

CULTURE

1887 Black players banned from major league baseball

1890s–1920s Emergence of jazz and the blues among southern blacks

1899 Scott Joplin writes the "Maple Leaf Rag"

1900 James W. Johnson writes "Lift Every Voice and Sing"

1901 Booker T. Washington publishes *Up from Slavery*

1903 W. E. B. Du Bois publishes *The Souls of Black Folk*

1905 The *Defender* begins publication in Chicago

1908 Jack Johnson wins heavyweight championship in boxing

POLITICS & GOVERNMENT

1869–1889 Four black regiments stationed on the Western frontier

1881 First Jim Crow law segregates trains in Tennessee

1882 South Carolina begins to disfranchise black voters

1892 Populist Party attracts many black voters

1896 *Plessy v. Ferguson* upholds "separate but equal" doctrine of racial segregation

1898 First black officers command black troops in the Spanish-American War

1899–1901 George H. White serves as the South's last black congressman to be elected until 1972

SOCIETY & ECONOMY

1867 Independent Order of St. Luke founded

1868 Hampton Institute founded

1870 Howard University Law School founded

1881 Tuskegee Institute founded

1886 Washington County, Texas, race riot

1887 National Colored Farmers' Alliance formed

1892 155 African Americans lynched in the United States

1895 Booker T. Washington addresses the Cotton States Exposition in Atlanta

1896 National Association of Colored Women founded

1903 St. Luke Penny Savings Bank established in Richmond

1904 Boule (Sigma Pi Phi) formed

1905 Niagara Movement begins

1906 Brownsville Affair

Atlanta riot

1908 Springfield riot

National Association of Colored Graduate Nurses founded

1909 NAACP established

Zora Neale Hurston

Countee Cullen

Anna Julia Cooper

| 1910–1920 | 1920–1940 | Noteworthy Individuals |

1920 Baseball's Negro League organized
1922 Claude McKay publishes *Harlem Shadows*
1924 Jessica R. Faucet publishes *There Is Confusion*
1925 Countee Cullen publishes *Color*
Alain Locke publishes *The New Negro*
1926 Carter Woodson organizes Negro History Week
Langston Hughes publishes *The Weary Blues*
1927 James W. Johnson publishes *God's Trombones*
1928 Duke Ellington debuts at the Cotton Club
Claude McKay publishes *Home to Harlem*
1929 Fats Waller's "Ain't Misbehavin" opens on Broadway
1930 James W. Johnson publishes *Black Manhattan*
1933 James W. Johnson publishes his autobiography
Along the Way
1937 Zora Neale Hurston publishes *Their Eyes Were Watching God*

1914 President Woodrow Wilson defends racial segregation
1917–1918 Over 1,000 black men serve as officers in World War I

1920 Nineteenth Amendment grants female suffrage with support from black women
1927 *Nixon v. Herndon* strikes down the white primary laws

1910 Urban League founded
Negro Fellowship League founded
1914 Universal Negro Improvement Association founded
1915 Reemergence of the Ku Klux Klan
1917 East St. Louis riot
Houston riot
1919 Chicago riot
Elaine, Arkansas, riot
Pan-African Congress meets in Paris
Marcus Garvey founds the Black Star Line

1925 National Bar Association founded
A. Philip Randolph founds the Brotherhood of Sleeping Car Porters

1877–1895
White Supremacy Triumphant: African Americans in the Late Nineteenth Century

Listen to Chapter 14
on MyHistoryLab

LEARNING OBJECTIVES

14-1	How important were African Americans in the political system in the late 1800s after Reconstruction ended?
14-2	What methods were employed to disfranchise black voters?
14-3	How, where, and why did segregation of the races begin?
14-4	What were the rules of "racial etiquette"?
14-5	Why were African Americans the victims of such extensive brutality and violence in the South?
14-6	Why did relatively small numbers of African Americans begin to leave the South?
14-7	What economic situation did large numbers of African Americans find themselves caught up in across the South in the late nineteenth century?
14-8	How just was the legal system for black people in the South?

> The supremacy of the white race of the South must be maintained forever, and the domination of the negro race resisted at all points and at all hazards—because the white race is the superior race. This is the declaration of no new truth. It has abided forever in the marrow of our bones, and shall run forever with the blood that feeds Anglo-Saxon hearts.
>
> *Henry Grady, editor of the* Atlanta Constitution, *1887*

> I remember a crowd of white men who rode up on horseback with rifles on their shoulders. I was with my father when they rode up, and I remember starting to cry. They cursed my father, drew their guns and made him salute, made him take off his hat and bow down to them several times. Then they rode away. I was not yet five years old, but I have never forgotten them.
>
> *Benjamin E. Mays on his childhood in Epworth, South Carolina, in 1898*

Black people struggled against a rising tide of white supremacy in the late nineteenth century. White southerners—and most white northerners—had long been convinced that as a race they were superior to black people intellectually and culturally. They were certain that black people—because of their inferiority—could play only a subservient role in society. During slavery, white southerners had taken that subservience for granted. With slavery's end, black people had allied themselves with radical Republicans during Reconstruction and challenged white supremacy as they became citizens and participated in the political system. The federal government established and enforced—although unevenly—the rights of all citizens to enjoy equal protection of the law and due process of law. But the commitment of the Republicans and the federal government wavered, waned, and then collapsed by the mid-1870s.

The Moses Speese family acquired a homestead near Westerville in Custer County, Nebraska. This 1888 photograph shows the extended family assembled in front of their sod house. They have installed a windmill to provide power to pump water from a well. They also possess two teams of horses.

With vivid recollections of the Civil War receding by the late 1800s, antagonism lessened between white southerners and white northerners. Many northern white people had previously expressed considerable sympathy for former slaves and bitter hostility toward southern rebels. But white Americans increasingly came to remember the Civil War less as a conflict directly involving the destiny of four million African Americans and more as a war that was marked by the terrible sacrifices and losses endured by white people. The same white Americans were increasingly preoccupied with the frontier West and with the Industrial Revolution that was transforming American society.

Congress, the president, and especially the Supreme Court abandoned the commitment to protect African Americans' civil and legal rights. Political and judicial leaders embraced a laissez-faire approach to social and economic issues. The government would keep its hands off the expanding railroad, steel, and petroleum industries. Neither would government intervene to safeguard the rights of black citizens. The Supreme Court interpreted the Fourteenth Amendment to protect corporations from government regulation, but it failed to protect the basic rights of black people.

As a result, the conservative white Democrats who had regained power in the South were no more than mildly fearful that the U.S. government or Republicans would intrude as white authority expanded over the lives of southern African Americans in the late nineteenth century. Between 1875 and 1900, black people in the South were gradually excluded from politics, segregated in public life, and denied equal—even basic—rights. They were forced to behave in a demeaning and deferential manner to white people. Most of them were limited to menial agricultural and domestic jobs that left them poor and dependent on white landowners and merchants. They were often raped, lynched, and beaten. Southern justice was systematically unjust.

Unwilling and unable to tolerate such conditions, some African Americans left the South for Africa or the American West. However, most black people remained in the South, where many acquired a semblance of education, some managed to purchase land, and a few even prospered.

Politics

14-1 **How important were African Americans in the political system in the late 1800s after Reconstruction ended?**

In the late nineteenth century, black people remained important in southern politics. Black men served in Congress, state legislatures, and local governments. They received federal patronage appointments to post offices and custom houses. But as southern Democrats steadily disfranchised black voters in the 1880s and 1890s, the number of black politicians declined until the political system was virtually all white by 1900 (see Figure 14–1).

When Reconstruction ended in 1877 and the last Republican state governments collapsed, black men who held major state offices were forced out. In South Carolina, Lieutenant Governor Richard H. Gleaves resigned under protest in 1877: "I desire to place on record, in the most public and unqualified manner, my sense of the great wrong which

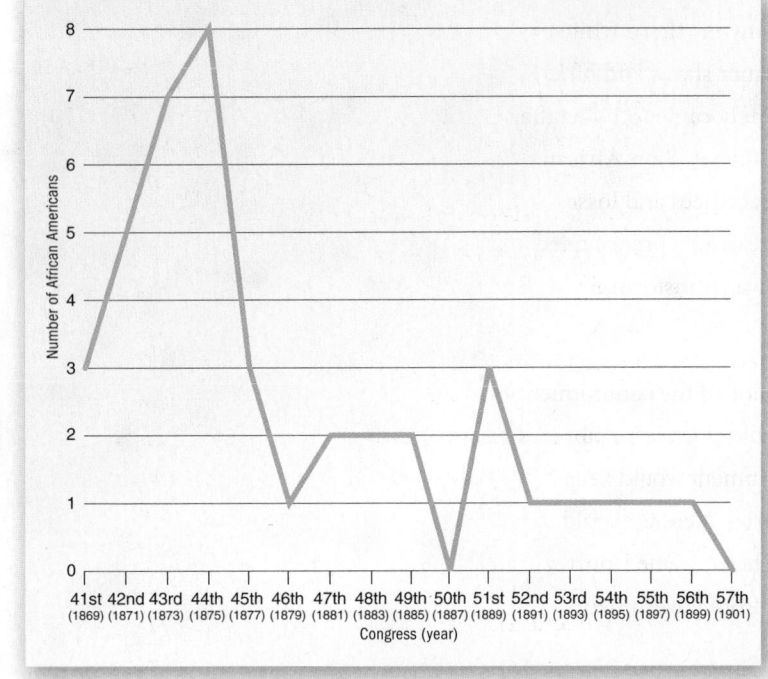

FIGURE 14–1 AFRICAN-AMERICAN REPRESENTATION IN CONGRESS, 1867–1900
Black men served in the U.S. Congress from Joseph Rainey's election in 1870 until George H. White's term concluded in 1901. All were Republicans.

thus forces me practically to abandon rights conferred on me, as I fully believe by a majority of my fellow citizens of this State."

For a time, some conservative white Democrats accepted limited black participation in politics as long as no black leader had power over white people and black participation did not challenge white domination. South Carolina's Governor Wade Hampton even assured black people that he respected their rights and would appoint qualified black men to minor offices. Hampton condescendingly told black people in 1878, "We propose to protect you and give you all your rights; but while we do this you cannot expect that we should discriminate in your favor, and say because you are a colored man, you have the right to rule the State. We say to you that we intend to take the best men we can find to represent the State, and you must qualify yourselves to do so before you can expect to be chosen."

Paternalistic Democrats like Hampton did appoint black men to lower-level positions. Hampton, for example, appointed Richard Gleaves and Martin Delany as trial justices. In turn, some black men supported the Democrats. A few black Democrats were elected to state legislatures in the 1880s. Some had been Democrats throughout Reconstruction. Others had abandoned the Republicans.

Most black voters, however, remained loyal Republicans even though the party had become a hollow shell of what it had been during Reconstruction. Its few white supporters usually shunned black Republicans. The party rarely fielded candidates for statewide elections, limiting itself to local races in regions where Republicans remained strong.

Black Congressmen

Democrats created oddly shaped congressional districts to confine much of the black population of a state to one district, such as Mississippi's third, South Carolina's seventh, Virginia's fourth, and North Carolina's second. A black Republican usually represented these districts, while the rest of the state elected white Democrats to Congress. This diluted black voting strength and reduced the number of white people represented by a black congressman. Thus Henry Cheatham and George H. White of North Carolina, John Mercer Langston of Virginia, and Thomas E. Miller of South Carolina were elected to the House of Representatives long after Reconstruction ended (see Table 14–1).

But these black men wielded only limited power in Washington. They could not persuade their white colleagues to enact significant legislation to benefit their black constituents. They did, however, get Republican presidents to appoint black people to federal positions in their districts—including post offices and custom houses—and they denounced the plight of African Americans. George H. White, for example, rebuked white leaders for their readiness to label black people as inferior while denying them the means to prove otherwise: "It is rather hard to be accused of shiftlessness and idleness when the accuser . . . closes the avenues for labor and industrial pursuits to us. It is hardly fair to accuse us of ignorance when it was made a crime under the former order of things to learn enough about letters to even read the Word of God."

Democrats and Farmer Discontent

Black involvement in southern politics survived Reconstruction, but it did not survive the nineteenth century. Divisions within the Democratic Party and the rise of a new political

TABLE 14–1 BLACK MEMBERS OF THE U.S. CONGRESS, 1860–1901

Dates	Name	State	Occupation	Prewar Status
1. 1870–1879	Joseph H. Rainey	South Carolina	Barber	Slave, then free
2. 1870–1873	Jefferson Long	Georgia	Tailor, storekeeper	Slave
3. 1870–1873	Hiram Revels*	Mississippi	Barber, minister, teacher, college president	Free
4. 1871–1877	Josiah T. Walls	Florida	Editor, planter, teacher, lawyer	Slave
5. 1871–1873	Benjamin Turner	Alabama	Businessman, farmer, merchant	Slave
6. 1871–1873	Robert C. DeLarge	South Carolina	Tailor	Free
7. 1871–1875	Robert B. Elliott	South Carolina	Lawyer	Free
8. 1873–1879	Richard H. Cain	South Carolina	African Methodist Episcopal minister	Free
9. 1873–1875	Alonzo J. Ransier	South Carolina	Shipping clerk, editor	Free
10. 1873–1875	James T. Rapier	Alabama	Planter, editor, lawyer, teacher	Free
11. 1873–1877, 1882–1883	John R. Lynch	Mississippi	Planter, lawyer, photographer	Slave
12. 1875–1881	Blanche K. Bruce*	Mississippi	Planter, teacher, editor	Slave
13. 1875–1877	Jeremiah Haralson	Alabama	Minister	Slave
14. 1875–1877	John A. Hyman	North Carolina	Storekeeper, farmer	Slave
15. 1875–1877	Charles E. Nash	Louisiana	Mason, cigar maker	Free
16. 1875–1887	Robert Smalls	South Carolina	Ship pilot, editor	Slave
17. 1883–1887	James E. O'Hara	North Carolina	Lawyer	Free
18. 1889–1893	Henry P. Cheatham	North Carolina	Lawyer, teacher	Slave
19. 1889–1891	Thomas E. Miller	South Carolina	Lawyer, college president	Free
20. 1889–1891	John M. Langston	Virginia	Lawyer	Free
21. 1893–1897	George W. Murray	South Carolina	Teacher, farmer	Slave
22. 1897–1901	George H. White	North Carolina	Lawyer	Slave

*Revels and Bruce served in the Senate. The 20 remaining black legislators served in the House.

party—the Populists—accompanied successful efforts to remove black people entirely from southern politics.

Militant Democrats opposed the more paternalistic conservatives who took charge after Reconstruction. For the militants, these redeemers seemed too willing to tolerate limited black participation in politics while showing little interest in the needs of white yeoman farmers. Dissatisfied independents, "readjusters," and other disaffected white people resented the domination of the Democratic Party by former planters, wealthy businessmen, and lawyers who often favored limited government and reduced state support for schools, asylums, orphanages, and prisons while encouraging industry and railroads. Nor did the redeemer and paternalistic Democrats always agree among themselves. Some favored agricultural education, boards of health, and even separate colleges for black students. This disunity permitted insurgent Democrats and even Republicans to exploit economic and racial issues to undermine Democratic solidarity.

Many farmers felt betrayed as the Industrial Revolution transformed society. They fed and clothed America, but large corporations, banks, and railroads dominated economic life. Wealth was concentrated in the hands of big industrialists and financiers. Farmers were no longer self-sufficient, admired for hard work and self-reliance. They now depended on banks for loans, were exploited when they bought and sold goods, and were at the mercy of railroads when they shipped their commodities. As businessmen got richer, farmers got poorer.

A sharp decline in the price of cotton between 1865 and 1890 hurt small independent (yeomen) farmers in the South. Many lost their land and were forced into tenant farming and sharecropping. By 1890 most farmers in the Deep South, black and white, worked land they did not own.

In response to their woes, farmers organized. In the 1870s they formed the Patrons of Husbandry, or Grange. Initially a fraternal organization, the Grange promoted economic cooperatives and political involvement. Grangers especially favored government regulation of the rates railroads charged to transport crops. By the 1880s, many hard-pressed farmers turned to Farmers' Alliances, which soon spread from the South into the Midwest and Great Plains. These organizations favored railroad regulation, currency inflation (to increase crop prices and reduce debt), and support for agricultural education. By 1888 many of them joined in the National Farmers' Alliance.

The Colored Farmers' Alliance

Colored Farmers' Alliance A large organization of black southern farmers in the 1880s and 1890s that had as many as one million members who agitated for improved conditions and income for black landowners, renters, and sharecroppers.

The alliances, however, were conservative on racial issues and did not challenge the racial status quo. Excluded from the Southern Alliance, black farmers formed their own **Colored Farmers' Alliance**, which expanded across the South and became one of the largest black organizations in American history. When the white alliances met in St. Louis in 1889, so did the black alliance—in a separate convention. The alliances maintained strict racial distinctions but promised to cooperate to resolve their economic woes.

However, black and white alliance members did not always see their economic difficulties from the same perspective. Some white farmers owned the land that the black farmers lived on and worked. Black men saw their alliance as a way of getting a political education. In 1891, 16 black men organized a branch of the Colored Farmers' Alliance in St. Landry Parish in Louisiana. Their purpose was to help their race and their families and acquire enough information to vote effectively: "This organization is for the purpose of trying to elevate our race, to make us better citizens, better husbands, better fathers and sons, to educate ourselves so that we may be able to vote more intelligently on questions that are of vital importance to our people."

But white people were not certain they wanted black men to vote at all—intelligently or otherwise—and they opposed electing black men to office. Paradoxically, they also encouraged black men to vote as long as the black voters supported candidates the alliances backed. By the late 1880s, alliance-backed candidates in the South were elected to state legislatures, to Congress, and to four governorships.

The Populist Party

Populist Party Also known as the Peoples' Party, the Populists supported inflation; the free and unlimited coinage of silver and gold; government ownership of railroads, telephone, and telegraph companies; and an eight-hour workday. They won state and congressional elections but lost the presidential contests in 1892 and 1896.

By 1892 many alliance members threw their political support to a new political party—the People's Party—generally known as the **Populist Party**. Convinced that neither the Democrats nor the Republicans cared about American farmers and industrial workers, the Populists hoped to wrestle control of the economy from bankers, industrialists, and their allies in the traditional parties and let the "people" shape the country's destiny. The Populists wanted the federal government to take over railroad, telegraph, and telephone companies and to operate a loan and marketing program, known as the subtreasury system, to benefit farmers. They urged southern white men to abandon the Democrats and southern black men to reject the Republicans and unite politically to support the Populists.

The foremost proponent of black and white political unity was Thomas Watson of Georgia. He and other Populist leaders believed economic and political cooperation could transcend racial differences. During the 1892 presidential campaign, Watson explained that black and white farmers faced the same economic exploitation, but that they failed to cooperate with each other because of race:

> The white tenant lives adjoining the colored tenant. Their homes are almost equally destitute of comforts. Their living is confined to bare necessities. They are equally burdened with heavy taxes. They pay the same high rent for gullied and impoverished land. . . .
>
> Now the Peoples' Party says to these two men, You are kept apart that you may be separately fleeced of your earnings. You are made to hate each other because upon that hatred is rested the keystone of the arch of financial despotism which enslaves you both. You are deceived and blinded that you may not see how this race antagonism perpetuates a monetary system which beggars both.

14-1
14-2
14-3
14-4
14-5
14-6
14-7
14-8

Watson, however, was not calling for improved race relations. He opposed economic exploitation that was disguised by race; however, when Democrats accused him of promoting racial reconciliation, he bluntly supported segregation to a black audience:

> They say I am an advocate of social equality between the whites and the blacks. THAT IS AN ABSOLUTE FALSEHOOD, and the man who utter[s] it knows it, I have done no such thing, and you colored men know it as well as the men who formulated the slander. It is best for your race and my race that we dwell apart in our private affairs. It is best for you to go to your churches, and I will go to mine; it is best that you send your children to the colored school, and I'll send my children to mine; you invite your colored friends to your home, and I'll invite my friends to mine.

Watson eventually became a racial demagogue who thoroughly supported white supremacy. But in 1892 he desperately wanted black and white voters to support Populist candidates. The Populists lost the national election that year and again in 1896, although they did win several congressional and governor's races. Southern Democrats, outraged at the Populist appeal for black votes, resorted again to fraud and terror to prevail. When a biracial coalition of black and white Populists took control of Grimes County in east Texas in 1900, Democrats massacred first the black and then the white leaders.

Nor is it a coincidence that in the election of 1892, when the Democrats carried every southern state, there was an explosion of violence. Democrats were determined to destroy the Populist challenge. That year a record 235 people were lynched in the United States.

The Populist challenge heightened southern Democrats' fears that black voters could decide elections if the white vote split. But many black people were suspicious of the Populists and remained loyal to the Republicans. The Republican Party in the South, however, was much weaker than it had been during Reconstruction because many of its supporters could no longer vote. Years before the alliances and the Populists emerged, southern Democrats had begun to eliminate the black vote.

Disfranchisement

14-2 **What methods were employed to disfranchise black voters?**

As early as the late 1870s, southern Democrats worked to undermine black political power. Violence and intimidation, so effective during Reconstruction, continued in the 1880s and 1890s. Frightened, discouraged, or apathetic, many black men stopped voting. White landlords could sometimes intimidate or bribe black sharecroppers and renters not to vote or to vote for the landlord's candidates.

There was also simple injustice. In 1890 black Congressman Thomas E. Miller ran for reelection and won—or so he thought. But he was charged with using illegal ballots and declared the loser. He appealed to the South Carolina Supreme Court, which ruled that although his ballots were printed on the required white paper, it was "of a distinctly yellow tinge." He did not return to Congress.

Evading the Fifteenth Amendment

More militant and determined southern Democrats were unwavering in their efforts to find some "legal" means to prevent black men from voting. However, the Fifteenth Amendment stated that the right to vote could not be denied on "account of race, color, or previous condition of servitude."

White leaders worried that if they imposed what were then legally acceptable barriers to voting—literacy tests, poll taxes, and property qualifications—they would also disfranchise many white voters. But resourceful Democrats found ways around this problem. In 1882, for example, South Carolina passed the Eight Box Law, a primitive literacy test that required

14-1
14-2
14-3
14-4
14-5
14-6
14-7
14-8

14-1
14-2
14-3
14-4
14-5
14-6
14-7
14-8

Listen on **MyHistoryLab** Audio: A Republican Textbook for Colored Voters Excerpt

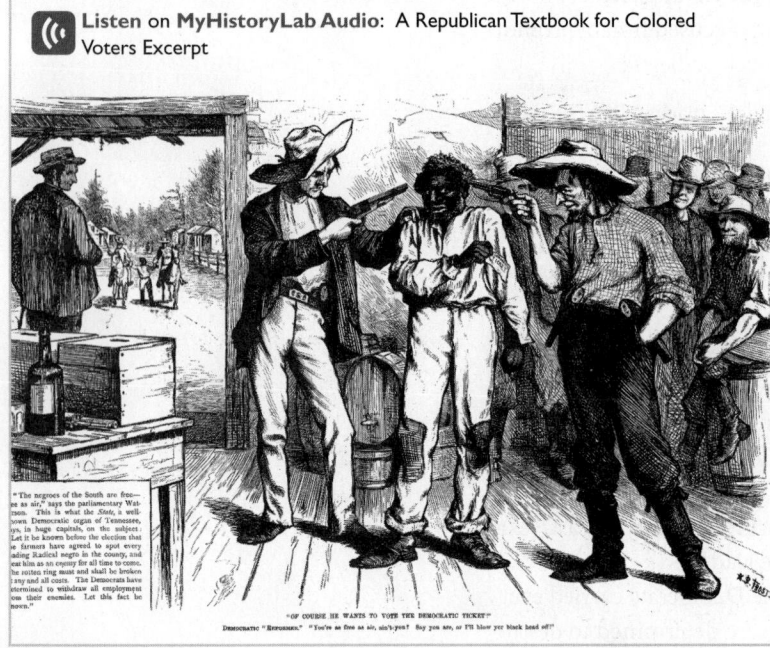

A rural black man "freely" exercises his right to vote. Notice the bottle of whiskey next to the ballot box.

voters to deposit separate ballots for separate election races in the proper ballot box. Illiterate voters could not identify the boxes unless white officials assisted them.

Mississippi

Mississippi made the most successful effort to eliminate black voters without openly violating the Fifteenth Amendment. Black men had continued to vote in Mississippi despite intimidation. In 1889 black leaders from 40 Mississippi counties protested the "violent and criminal suppression of the black vote." In response, white men called a constitutional convention to do away with the black vote.

With a single black delegate and 134 white delegates, the convention adopted complex voting requirements that—without mentioning race—disfranchised black voters. Voting required proof of residency and payment of all taxes, including a $2 poll tax. A person convicted of arson, bigamy, or petty theft—crimes the delegates associated with black people—could not vote. People convicted of so-called white crimes—murder, rape, and grand larceny—could vote.

The new Mississippi constitution also required voters to be literate, but illiterate men could still qualify to vote by demonstrating that they understood the constitution if it was read to them. It was taken for granted that white voting registrars would accept almost all white applicants and fail black applicants seeking to register under this provision.

South Carolina

Black voting had been declining in South Carolina since the end of Reconstruction. In 1876, 91,870 black men voted. In 1888, only 13,740 did. Unhappy that even so few voters might decide an election, U.S. Senator Benjamin R. Tillman won approval for a constitutional convention in 1895. The convention followed Mississippi's lead and created an "understanding clause," but not without a protest from black leaders.

Six black men and 154 white men were elected to the South Carolina convention. Two of the black men—Robert Smalls and William Whipper (see Chapter 13)—had been delegates to the 1868 constitutional convention. The six black men protested black disfranchisement. Thomas E. Miller explained that the basic rights of citizens were at stake: "The Negroes do not want to dominate. They do not and would not have social equality, but they do want to cast a ballot for the men who make their laws and administer the laws. I stand here pleading for justice to a people whose rights are about to be taken away with one fell swoop."

It was for naught. Black voters were disfranchised in South Carolina. White delegates did not even pretend that elections should be fair. William Henderson of Berkeley County admitted,

> We don't propose to have fair elections. We will get left at that every time. . . . I tell you, gentlemen, if we have fair elections in Berkeley we can't carry it. There's no use to talk about it. The black man is learning to read faster than the white man. And if he comes up and can read you have got to let him vote. Now are you going to throw it out. . . . We are perfectly disgusted with hearing so much about fair elections. Talk all around, but make it fair and you'll see what'll happen.

The Grandfather Clause

In 1898 Louisiana added a new twist to **disfranchisement**. Its **grandfather clause** stipulated that only men who had been eligible to vote before 1867—or whose father or grandfather had been eligible before that year—would be qualified to vote. Because virtually no black men had been eligible to vote before 1867—most had just emerged from slavery—the law

disfranchisement White southern Democrats devised a variety of techniques in the late nineteenth and early twentieth centuries to prevent black people from voting. Those techniques included literacy tests, poll taxes, and the grandfather clause as well as intimidation and violence.

grandfather clause A method southern states used to disfranchise black men. It stipulated that only men whose grandfathers were eligible to vote were themselves eligible to vote. The U.S. Supreme Court invalidated the grandfather clause in 1915.

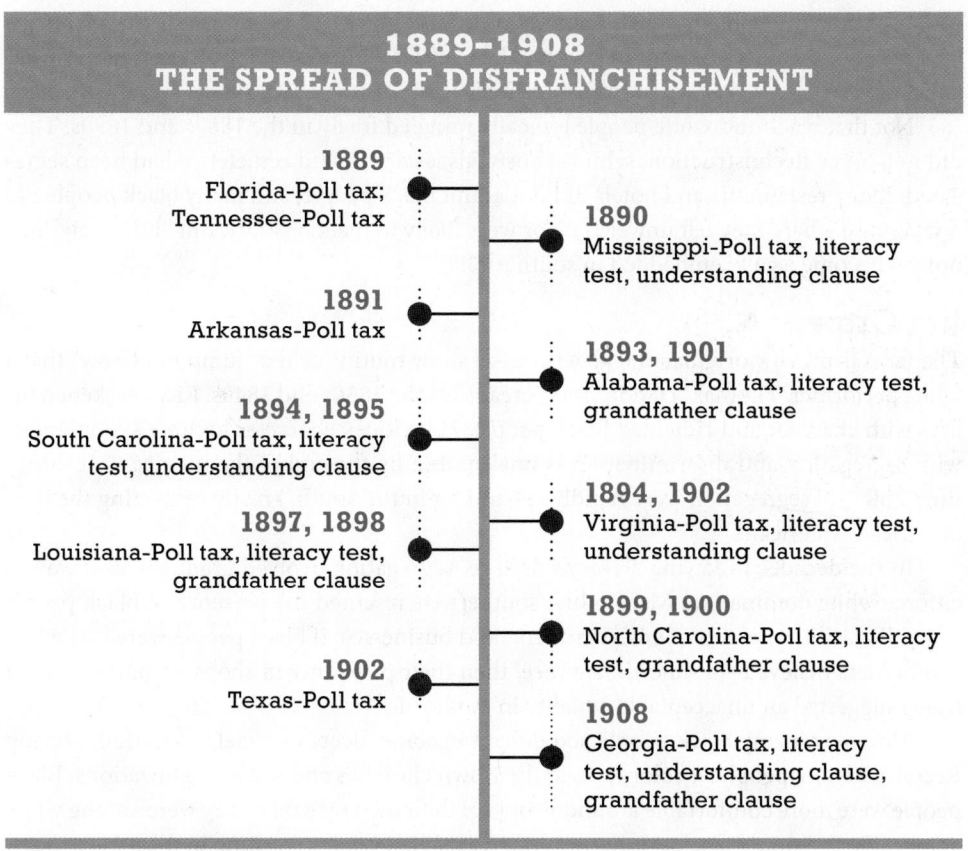

1889–1908
THE SPREAD OF DISFRANCHISEMENT

1889
Florida-Poll tax;
Tennessee-Poll tax

1890
Mississippi-Poll tax, literacy
test, understanding clause

1891
Arkansas-Poll tax

1893, 1901
Alabama-Poll tax, literacy test,
grandfather clause

1894, 1895
South Carolina-Poll tax, literacy
test, understanding clause

1894, 1902
Virginia-Poll tax, literacy test,
understanding clause

1897, 1898
Louisiana-Poll tax, literacy test,
grandfather clause

1899, 1900
North Carolina-Poll tax, literacy
test, grandfather clause

1902
Texas-Poll tax

1908
Georgia-Poll tax, literacy
test, understanding clause,
grandfather clause

Goldfield et al., *The American Journey* (Upper Saddle River, NJ: Prentice Hall, 2004), 550.

immediately disfranchised almost all black voters. In Louisiana in 1896, 130,000 black men voted. In 1904, 1,342 voted.

Except for Kentucky and West Virginia, each southern state had enacted elaborate restrictions on voting by the 1890s. As a result, few black men continued to vote, and none were elected to office.

The "Force Bill"

Republicans in Congress in the meantime had made a final, futile attempt to protect black voting rights. In 1890 Massachusetts Congressman Henry Cabot Lodge introduced a bill to require federal supervision of elections in congressional districts where fraud and intimidation were alleged. White southerners were enraged and labeled it the "Force bill" because they believed—incorrectly—that it would force black rule over white people.

This **Federal Elections Bill** easily passed the House, but it failed in the Senate after a 33-day Democratic filibuster. That ended the last significant congressional attempt to protect black voting rights in the South until the passage of the Voting Rights Act in 1965.

Federal Elections Bill A measure, also known as the Force bill, to protect the voting rights of black men in the South by providing federal supervision of elections. It passed in the House of Representatives but failed in the Senate.

Segregation

14-3   How, where, and why did segregation of the races begin?

When black attorney T. McCants Stewart visited Columbia, South Carolina, in 1885, he told readers of the *New York Age* that he had been pleasantly received and had encountered little discrimination: "I can ride in first class cars on the railroads and in the streets. I can go into saloons and get refreshments even as in New York. I can stop in and drink a glass of

segregation The separation of people based on their race in the use of such public facilities as hotels, restaurants, restrooms, drinking fountains, parks, and auditoriums. In many instances segregation meant the exclusion of black people.

Jim Crow "Jump Jim Crow" was a nineteenth-century dance ridiculing black people that was transformed by the twentieth century into a term meaning racial discrimination and segregation.

14-1
14-2
14-3
14-4
14-5
14-6
14-7
14-8

soda and be more politely waited upon than in some parts of New England." Stewart's visit occurred before most segregation laws had been enacted. In fact, the word **segregation** was almost never used before the twentieth century.

Not that black and white people typically mingled freely in the 1880s and 1890s. They did not. Since Reconstruction, schools, hospitals, asylums, and cemeteries had been segregated. Many restaurants and hotels did not admit black people, and many black people did not venture where they felt unwelcome or were likely to meet hostility. But "Jim Crow" had not yet become legally embedded in southern life.

Jim Crow

The term **Jim Crow** originated with a minstrel show routine called "Jump Jim Crow" that a white performer, Thomas "Daddy" Rice, created in the 1830s and 1840s. Rice blackened his face with charcoal and ridiculed black people. How Rice's character became synonymous with segregation and discrimination is unclear, but by the end of the nineteenth century Jim Crow and segregation were rapidly expanding in the South, greatly restricting the lives of African Americans.

In the decades following slavery's demise, segregation evolved gradually as a way to enforce white domination. Many white southerners resented the presence of black people in public facilities, places of entertainment, and businesses. If black people were—as white southerners believed—a subordinate race, then their proximity in shops, in parks, and on trains suggested an unacceptable equality in public life.

Moreover, many black people acquiesced in some facets of racial separation. During Reconstruction, people of color formed their own churches and social organizations. Black people were more comfortable around people of their own race than they were among white people. Furthermore, black southerners often accepted separate seating in theaters, concert halls, and other facilities that had been previously closed to them. Segregation, they felt, was better than exclusion.

Segregation on the Railroads

Many white people particularly objected to the presence of black people in the first-class coaches of trains. Before segregation laws, white passengers and railroad conductors sometimes forced black people who had purchased first-class tickets into second-class coaches. In 1889 black Baptists from Savannah bought first-class tickets to travel to a convention in Indianapolis. News was telegraphed ahead, and a white mob threatened and beat them at a railroad stop in Georgia. A white man shoved a pistol into the breast of a black woman who had screamed in fear. He demanded, "You G-d d-n heffer, if you don't hush your mouth and get out of here, I will blow your G-d d-n brains out."

In another instance, a young black woman, Mary Church (later Mary Church Terrell), was traveling alone in a first-class coach when the conductor attempted to move her to the second-class car. She stayed but only after warning the conductor that she would send a telegram to her father telling him "you are forcing me to ride all night in a Jim Crow car. He will sue the railroad for compelling his daughter who has a first-class ticket to ride in a second-class car."

The first segregation laws involved passenger trains. Despite the opposition of black politicians, the Tennessee legislature mandated segregation on railroad coaches in 1881. Florida passed a similar law in 1887. The railroads opposed these laws but not because they wanted to protect the rights of black people. Rather, they were concerned about the expense of maintaining separate cars or sections within cars for black and white people. Whether they could pay for a first-class ticket or not, most black passengers were confined to grimy second-class cars crowded with smoking and

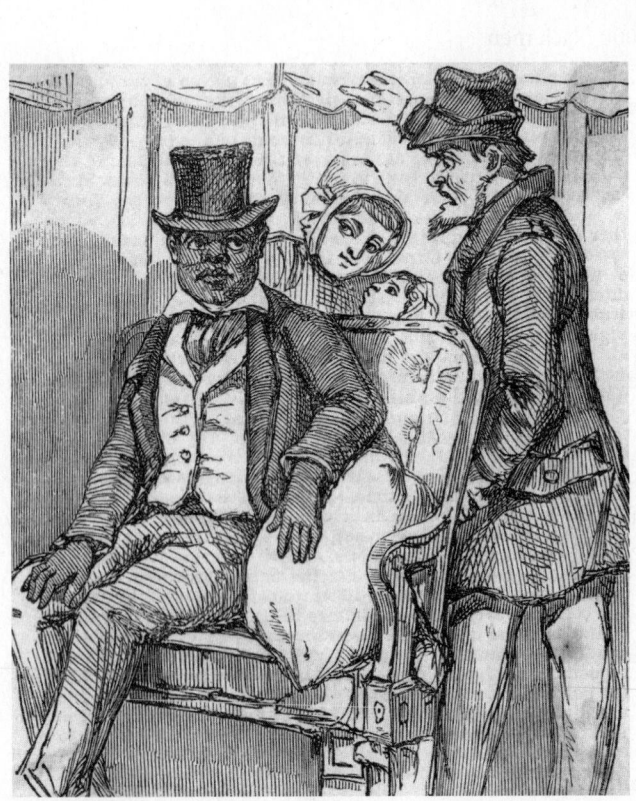

To enforce segregation on a railroad coach, a rather shabbily attired conductor evicts a well-dressed black man from a first-class coach so that he will not pose a danger to a white woman and her child.

tobacco-chewing black and white men. Hitched just behind the smoke-belching locomotive, these cars were filthy with soot and cinders.

Plessy v. Ferguson

In 1891 the Louisiana legislature required segregated trains within the state, despite opposition from a black organization, the American Citizens' Equal Rights Association of Louisiana, the state's 18 black legislators, and the railroads.

In a test case, black people challenged the law and hoped to demonstrate its absurdity by enlisting the support of a black man who was almost indistinguishable from a white person. In 1892 Homer A. Plessy bought a first-class ticket and attempted to ride on the coach designated for white people. Plessy, who was only one-eighth black, was arrested for violating the new law.

In the case—**Plessy v. Ferguson**—Plessy's lawyers argued that segregation deprived their client of equal protection of the law guaranteed by the Fourteenth Amendment. But in 1896 the Supreme Court, in an 8-to-1 decision, upheld Louisiana's segregation statute. Speaking for the majority, Justice Henry Brown ruled that the law, merely because it required separation of the races, did not deny Plessy his rights, nor did it imply he was inferior. The lone dissenter from this "separate but equal" doctrine, Justice John Marshall Harlan—whose father had owned slaves—likened the majority opinion to the *Dred Scott* decision 39 years earlier. Thus, with the complicity of the Supreme Court, the Fourteenth Amendment no longer afforded black Americans equal treatment under the law. After the *Plessy* decision, southern states and cities created an American apartheid—an elaborate system of racial separation.

Streetcar Segregation

Before the automobile, the electric streetcar was the primary form of public transportation in American cities and towns. Beginning with Georgia in 1891, states and cities across the South segregated these vehicles. In some communities, the streetcar companies had to operate separate cars for black and white passengers. In others, they designated separate sections within cars. The companies often resisted segregation, citing the expense of duplicating equipment and hiring more employees.

But black people were bitterly opposed to Jim Crow streetcars. During Reconstruction, they had fended off streetcar discrimination with boycotts and sit-ins. Thirty years later, they tried the same techniques. There were boycotts in at least 25 southern cities between 1891 and 1910. Black people refused to ride segregated cars in Atlanta, Augusta, Jacksonville, Montgomery, Mobile, Little Rock, and Columbia. The boycotts seriously hurt the streetcar companies, and segregation was briefly abandoned in Atlanta and Augusta.

Black people also attempted to form alternative transportation companies in Portsmouth and Norfolk, Virginia, and in Chattanooga and Nashville, Tennessee. In 1905 the black community in Nashville organized a black-owned bus company and committed $25,000 to it. They purchased five buses, but the company failed after a few months.

Segregation Proliferates

Jim Crow proceeded inexorably. "White" and "colored" signs appeared in railroad stations, theaters, auditoriums, and restrooms, and over drinking fountains. Southern white people went to any length to keep black and white people apart. Courtrooms maintained separate Bibles for black and white witnesses "to swear to tell the truth." By 1915 Oklahoma mandated white and colored public telephone booths. New Orleans attempted to segregate customers of black and white prostitutes, but with mixed results.

Although *Plessy v. Ferguson* required "separate but equal" facilities for black and white people, when facilities were made available to black people, they were inferior to those afforded white people. Often, people of color were offered no facilities at all. They were simply excluded. Few hotels, restaurants, libraries, bowling alleys, public parks, amusement parks, swimming pools, golf courses, or tennis courts would admit black people. The only exceptions were black people who accompanied or assisted white people. For example, a black woman caring for a white child could visit a "white-only" public park with the child, but she dare not visit it with her own child.

 Watch on MyHistoryLab Video: Plessy v. Ferguson

Plessy v. Ferguson In 1896, in an 8-to-1 decision, the U.S. Supreme Court ruled that segregation did not violate the equal protection clause of the Fourteenth Amendment. The "separate but equal" doctrine remained the supreme law of the land until the 1954 *Brown v. Board of Education* decision overturned *Plessy*.

Read on MyHistoryLab Document: *Plessy v. Ferguson* Legalizes Segregation, 1896

14-1
14-2
14-3
14-4
14-5
14-6
14-7
14-8

VOICES   Majority and Dissenting Opinions on *Plessy v. Ferguson*

14-1

14-2

14-3

14-4

14-5

14-6

14-7

14-8

The Supreme Court's 8-to-1 decision in Plessy v. Ferguson *sanctioned legal segregation and opened the way for segregation laws throughout the South. The majority opinion ruled that segregation was constitutional so long as both races were provided equal facilities. In practice, of course, the facilities for African Americans were invariably inferior to those for white people.*

From Justice Henry Brown of Michigan's majority opinion:

> The object of the [Fourteenth] amendment was undoubtedly to enforce the absolute equality of the two races before the law, but in the nature of things it could not have been intended to abolish distinctions based upon color, or to enforce social, as distinguished from political, equality, or a commingling of the two races upon terms unsatisfactory to either.
>
> We consider the underlying fallacy of the plaintiff's argument to consist in the assumption that the enforced separation of the two races stamps the colored race with a badge of inferiority. If this be so, it is not by the reason of anything found in the act, but solely because the colored race chooses to put that construction upon it. . . . If the two races are to meet on terms of social equality, it must be the result of natural affinities, a mutual appreciation of each other's merits and a voluntary consent of individuals. . . . Legislation is powerless to eradicate racial instincts or to abolish distinctions based upon physical differences. . . . If one race be inferior to the other socially, the Constitution of the United States cannot put them upon the same plane.

From Justice John Marshall Harlan of Kentucky, the lone dissent:

> In my opinion, the judgment this day rendered will, in time, prove to be quite as pernicious as the decision made by this tribunal in the Dred Scott Case. . . . But it

seems that we have yet, in some of the states, a dominant race, a superior class of citizens, which assumes to regulate the enjoyment of civil rights, common to all citizens, upon the basis of race. The present decision, it may well be apprehended, will not only stimulate aggressions, more or less brutal and irritating, upon the admitted rights of colored citizens, but it will encourage the belief that it is possible, by means of state enactments, to defeat the beneficent purposes which the people of the United States had in view when they adopted the recent amendments of the Constitution, by one which the blacks of this country were made citizens of the United States and of the states in which they respectively reside and whose privileges and immunities, as citizens, the states are forbidden to abridge. . . . What can more certainly arouse race hate, what more certainly create and perpetuate a feeling of distrust between these races, than state enactments which in fact proceed on the ground that the colored citizens are so inferior and degraded that they cannot be allowed to sit in public coaches occupied by white citizens? . . . But in view of the Constitution, in the eyes of the law, there is in this country no superior, dominant, ruling class of citizens. There is no caste here. Our Constitution is color-blind, and neither knows nor tolerates classes among citizens. In respect of civil rights, all citizens are equal before the law.

1. **What does Justice Brown mean when he distinguishes between political and social equality? How does his position compare to that of Congressmen Rapier and Elliott when they argued for civil rights in 1874? (see p. 329)**

2. **How does Justice Harlan counter the majority opinion?**

SOURCE: 163 U.S. 537 United States Reports: *Cases Adjudged in the Supreme Court* (New York: Banks and Brothers, 1896).

Racial Etiquette

14-4   **What were the rules of "racial etiquette"?**

During slavery, white people had insisted that black people act in a subservient manner. Such behavior made white dominance clear. After emancipation, white southerners sought to maintain that dominance through a pattern of racial etiquette that determined how black and white people dealt with each other in their day-to-day affairs.

Black and white people did not shake hands. Black people did not look white people in the eyes. They were supposed to stare at the ground when addressing white men and women. Black men removed their hats in the presence of white people. White men did not remove their hats in a black home or in the presence of a black woman. Black people went to the back door, not the front door, of a white house. A black man or boy was never to look at a white woman. A black man in Mississippi observed, "You couldn't smile at a white woman. If you did you'd be hung from a limb." Touching a white woman, even inadvertently, was a serious offense for a black man.

White customers were always served first, even if a black customer had been the first to arrive. Black women could not try on clothing in white businesses. White people did not use titles of respect—Mr., Mrs., Miss—when addressing black adults. They used first names, "boy" or "girl," or sometimes even "nigger." Older black people were sometimes called "auntie" or "uncle." But black people were expected to use Mr., Mrs., or Miss when addressing white people, including adolescents. "Boss" or "cap'n" might do for a white man.

Violence

14-5 **Why were African Americans the victims of such extensive brutality and violence in the South?**

The late nineteenth-century South was a violent place. Political and mob violence, so prevalent during Reconstruction, continued unabated into the 1880s and 1890s as Democrats often used force to drive the dwindling number of black and white Republicans out of politics.

Washington County, Texas

In 1886 in Washington County in Texas, Democrats were determined to keep the control they had won in 1884 through fraud. Masked Democrats tried to seize ballot boxes in a Republican precinct. But armed black men resisted and killed one of the white men. Eight black men were arrested. A mob of white men in disguise broke into the jail and lynched three of the black men. Three white Republicans fled but convinced federal authorities to investigate. The U.S. attorney twice tried to secure convictions for election fraud. The first trial ended in a hung jury, the second in acquittal. The white Democratic sheriff did not investigate the lynching. But the black man charged with the killing of a white man was sentenced to 25 years in prison.

The Phoenix Riot

In the tiny South Carolina community of Phoenix in 1898, a white Republican candidate for Congress urged black men to fill out an affidavit if they were not permitted to vote. This produced a confrontation with Democrats. Words were exchanged, shots were fired, and the Republican candidate was wounded. White men then went on a rampage through rural Greenwood County. Black men were killed—how many is unknown. Others, including Benjamin Mays's father, as related in one of the quotes that opens this chapter—had to humiliate themselves by bowing down and saluting white men.

The Wilmington Riot

While white men roamed Greenwood County for black victims, an even bloodier riot erupted in Wilmington, North Carolina. Black and white men shared power as Republicans and Populists in Wilmington's government, and white Democrats resented it. With the encouragement of the *Wilmington News and Observer,* the Democrats were determined to

The Pullman Company manufactured and operated passenger, sleeping, and dining cars for the nation's railroads. The company employed black men to serve and wait on passengers, who were usually white people. Black porters and attendants were expected to be properly deferential as they dealt with passengers.

© Collection of The New-York Historical Society, Negative # : 51391.

14-1
14-2
14-3
14-4
14-5
14-6
14-7
14-8

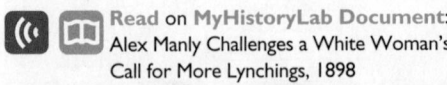

Read on **MyHistoryLab Document:** Alex Manly Challenges a White Woman's Call for More Lynchings, 1898

drive the legitimately elected political leaders from power. Alfred Moore Waddell, a former Confederate and U.S. congressman, vowed in a speech to "choke the Cape Fear [River] with carcasses."

In the midst of this tense situation, Alex Manly, the young editor of a local black newspaper, the *Daily Record,* wrote an editorial condemning white men for the sexual exploitation of black women. Manly also suggested that black men had sexual liaisons with rural white women, which infuriated the white community: "Poor white men are careless in the matter of protecting their women, especially on the farms. . . . Tell your men that it is no worse for a black man to be intimate with a white woman than for a white man to be intimate with a colored woman. . . . Don't think ever that your women will remain pure while you are debauching ours."

A white mob destroyed the newspaper office. Black and white officials resigned in a vain attempt to prevent further violence, but at least a dozen black men—and perhaps more—were murdered. Some 1,500 black residents of Wilmington fled. White people then bought up black homes and property at bargain rates. Waddell was installed as Wilmington's new mayor. Black Congressman George H. White, who represented Wilmington and North Carolina's second district, served the remainder of his term and then moved north. He remarked, "I can no longer live in North Carolina and be a man." White was the last black man to serve in Congress from the South until the election of Andrew Young in Atlanta in 1972.

The New Orleans Riot

Robert Charles was a 34-year-old literate laborer who had migrated to New Orleans from rural Mississippi. Infuriated by lynching, he was tantalized by the prospect of emigration to Liberia promoted by African Methodist Episcopal (AME) Bishop Henry M. Turner. On July 23, 1900, white New Orleans police officers harassed Charles and a friend. One of the officers attempted to beat Charles with a nightstick. Failing to subdue the large black man, the officer then drew a gun. Charles pulled out his own gun, and each man wounded the other. Charles fled but was tracked down to a rooming house where he had secluded himself with a rifle, with which he proceeded to shoot his tormentors. Eventually, a white mob that numbered as many as 20,000 gathered. In the meantime, Charles—an expert marksmen—methodically shot 27 white people, killing seven, including four policemen. Finally, burned out of the dwelling, Charles was shot, and enraged white people stomped his corpse beyond recognition. Four days of rioting ensued. At least a dozen black people were killed and many more injured.

Lynching

Between 1889 and 1932, 3,745 people were lynched in the United States (see Figure 14–2). Two or three people were lynched, on average, every week for 30 years. Most lynchings happened in the South, and black men were usually the victims. Sometimes white people were lynched. In 1891 in New Orleans, 11 Italians were lynched for alleged involvement with the Mafia and for the murder of the city's police chief. For black southerners, violence was an ever-present possibility. Rarely did a sheriff or police officer protect a potential victim; even if one did, that protection was often not enough.

Lynchers were never apprehended, tried, or convicted. Prominent community members frequently encouraged and even participated in lynch mobs. White politicians, journalists, and clergymen rarely denounced lynching in

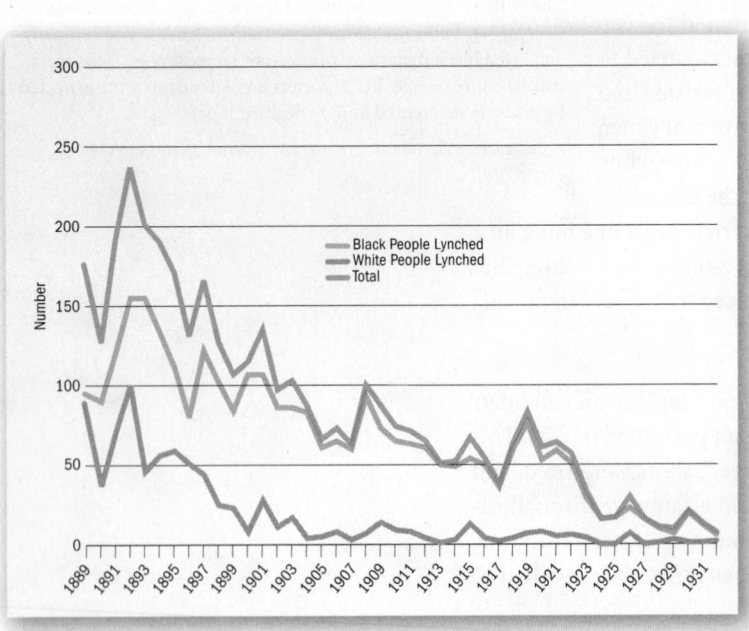

FIGURE 14–2 LYNCHING IN THE UNITED STATES: 1889–1932
Depending on the source, statistics on lynching vary. It was difficult to assemble information on lynching, particularly in the nineteenth century. Not every lynching was recorded.

SOURCE: *The Negro Year Book, 1931–32, 293.*

public. The *Atlanta Constitution* dismissed lynching as relatively inconsequential: "There are places and occasions when the natural fury of men cannot be restrained by all the laws in Christendom."

Lynchings were barbaric, savage, and hideous. Such mob brutality was another manifestation of white supremacy. Black people were murdered, beaten, burned, and mutilated for trivial reasons—or for no reason. Most white southerners justified lynching as a response to the raping of white women by black men. But many lynchings involved no alleged rape. Even in cases when a rape occurred, the person or persons lynched rarely were involved in the crime.

After a white family was murdered in Statesboro, Georgia, in 1904, Paul Reed and Will Cato were convicted of murder and then seized by a mob that invaded the courtroom. They were burned alive in front of a large crowd. Then the violence spread. Albert Roger and his son were lynched "for being Negroes." A black man named McBride attempted to protect his wife who had had a baby three days earlier. He "was beaten, killed, and shot to death."

Mobs often attacked black people who had achieved economic success. In Memphis, Thomas Moss with two friends opened the People's Grocery Company in a black neighborhood. The store flourished, but it competed with a white-owned grocery. "They were succeeding too well," one of Moss's friends observed. After the white grocer had the three black men indicted for conspiracy, black people organized a protest, and violence followed. The three black men were jailed. A white mob attacked the jail, lynched them, and looted their store. Ida B. Wells, a newspaper editor and a friend of Moss, was heartbroken: "A finer, cleaner man than he never walked the streets of Memphis." She considered his lynching an "excuse to get rid of Negroes who were acquiring wealth and property and thus keep the race terrorized and keep the nigger down." Wells began a lifelong crusade against lynching. (See *Profile: Ida Wells Barnett*.)

Although less often than men, black women were also lynched. In 1914 in Wagoner County, Oklahoma, 17-year-old Marie Scott was lynched because her brother had killed a white man who had raped her. In Valdosta, Georgia, in 1918, after Mary Turner's husband was lynched, she publicly vowed to bring those responsible to justice. Although she was eight months pregnant, a mob seized her, tied her ankles together, and hanged her upside down from a tree. Someone slit her abdomen, and her nearly full-term child fell to the ground. The mob stomped the infant to death. They then set her clothes on fire and shot her.

Rape

Although white people often justified lynching as a response to the presumed threat black men posed to the virtue of white women, white men routinely harassed and abused black women. There are no statistics on such abuse, but it surely was more common than lynching. Like lynching, rape demonstrated the power of white men over black men and women.

Black men tried to keep their wives and daughters away from white men. For example, they often refused to permit black women to work as servants in homes where white men were present. One black man commented in 1912, "I believe nearly all white men take, and expect to take, undue liberties with their colored female servants, not only the fathers, but in many cases the sons also." A black man could not easily protect a black woman. He might be killed trying to do so, as an Alabama clergyman pointed out: "White men on the highways and in their stores and on the trains will insult our women and we are powerless to resent it as it would only be an invitation for our lives to be taken."

Many white people believed black women "invited" white males to take advantage of them. Black women were considered inferior, immoral, and lascivious. Therefore, white people reasoned it was impossible to defend the virtue of black women because they had none. Governor Coleman Blease of South Carolina pardoned black and white men found guilty of raping black women. "I am of the opinion," he said in 1913, "as I have always been, and have very serious doubts as to whether the crime of rape can be committed upon a negro."

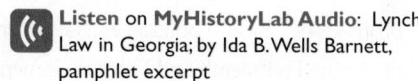

Listen on **MyHistoryLab** Audio: Lynch Law in Georgia; by Ida B. Wells Barnett, pamphlet excerpt

⚜ EXPLORE ON MYHISTORYLAB
Racial Violence in the United States, 1880–1930

What was the relationship between racial inequality and violence in the South by the early 1900s?

Although slavery was abolished by the Thirteenth Amendment, the promises of legal and political equality offered to African Americans under the Fourteenth and Fifteenth Amendments did not last long following the end of Reconstruction. White southerners were determined that African Americans remain a subordinate people in the South. This system of discrimination included the disfranchisement of African Americans. Widespread violence was also employed to maintain white control. African Americans who threatened the status quo were lynched. Victims were often falsely accused of some crime and subsequently murdered without a trial. Lynching was a tool to maintain the social, political, and economic dominance of white southerners over African-American people and their communities.

Lynchings were common and public events in the South. Jesse Washington, a 17-year-old, was accused and found guilty of the murder and rape of a white woman in Waco, Texas, in 1916. Before the sentence could be carried out, he was lynched in front of a crowd of several thousand people.

TOTAL LYNCHINGS IN SELECTED STATES, 1900–1931

State	Total
Alabama	132
Arkansas	127
Florida	170
Georgia	302
Louisiana	172
Mississippi	285
Texas	201

SOURCE: *Lynchings by States and Counties in the United States 1900 to 1931, Research Department, Tuskegee Institute, http://memory.loc.gov/.*

⚜ Explore the Topic on MyHistoryLab

1. **Analysis** *In what regions of the South were lynchings most common?* Consider the reasons behind such patterns.
2. **Consequence** *How did white literacy rates correspond to the frequency of lynchings in particular areas?* Explore the relationship between these two elements.
3. **Response** *How did local economic patterns affect the prevalence of lynchings?* Consider connections between land ownership and violence against African Americans.

Migration

14-6 **Why did relatively small numbers of African Americans begin to leave the South?**

In 1900 AME Minister Henry McNeal Turner despaired for black people in America: "Every man that has the sense of an animal must see that there is no future in this country for the Negro. [W]e are taken out and burned, shot, hanged, unjointed and murdered in every way. Our civil rights are taken from us by force, our political rights are a farce."

It is therefore surprising that more African Americans did not flee poverty, powerlessness, and brutality in the South. As late as 1910, 90 percent of black Americans still lived in the southern states. And of those who left the South, most did not head north along the old underground railroad route. The Great Migration to the northern industrial states did not begin until about 1915. Emigrants of the 1870s or 1880s were more likely to strike out for Africa; move west to Kansas, Oklahoma, and Arkansas; or move from farms to southern towns or cities.

PROFILE Ida Wells Barnett

IDA WELLS BARNETT began life as a slave in 1862 and grew up during Reconstruction. As a young woman, she saw the worst indignities and cruelties that the Jim Crow South could inflict, but she fought back as a journalist, agitator, and reformer.

Wells was one of eight children born to Jim and Lizzie Wells in Holly Springs, Mississippi. After the Civil War, she and her mother learned to read and write at a school for freed people. Her parents and one of her brothers died in the yellow fever epidemic of 1878. Sixteen-year-old Ida became mother and father to her five surviving siblings. She attended Shaw University in Holly Springs (now Rust College) and taught school in Mississippi and Tennessee.

In 1884, a railroad conductor removed Wells from a first-class car. She sued the railroad and won a $500 settlement. "Dusky Damsel Gets Damages," a Memphis newspaper reported. But a higher court reversed the decision.

Wells then took up journalism and wrote a weekly column for the *Living Way*. In 1889, she bought a one-third interest in the *Memphis Free Speech and Headlight*. She wrote about racial issues and criticized black educators for the quality of black schools. In 1892 her friend Thomas Moss was lynched with two other men for the crime of running a successful grocery store. Wells expressed her rage and horror in a fiery editorial, thus beginning a lifelong crusade against lynching.

Wells blamed the white people of Memphis for her friend's murder and pointed out that more black men were lynched for challenging the myth of white superiority than for allegedly raping a white woman. She angered white people even more by writing that white women could be attracted to black men.

She blamed white clergymen and their parishioners for tolerating lynching: "Our American Christians are too busy saving the souls of white Christians from burning in hell-fire to save the lives of black ones from present burning in fires kindled by white Christians."

Wells moved to Chicago and helped draft a pamphlet that criticized the exclusion of black people from the local groups that organized the 1893 World's Fair. In 1895 she married Ferdinand Barnett, the owner of the *Chicago Conservator*.

After a white journalist from Missouri wrote that black women were immoral, "having no sense of virtue and altogether without character," black women including Wells Barnett founded the National Association of Colored Women in 1896.

In 1909, Wells Barnett was one of two black women who supported the founding of the National Association for the Advancement of Colored People (NAACP), although she later broke with the group because of its mostly white board of directors and what she considered its cautious stands. She also helped organize the Negro Fellowship League in 1910.

Wells Barnett became an ardent supporter of black voting rights. She believed that if enough black men and women could vote, their political power would end lynching. In 1913 she helped found the Alpha Suffrage Club, the first black women's suffrage organization in Illinois, and was a delegate to the National American Woman's Suffrage Association meeting in Washington, DC.

Ever an agitator, she found Booker T. Washington's philosophy too timid. She was influenced by the Universal Negro Improvement Association in the 1920s and praised Marcus Garvey as a black leader who "made an impression on this country as no Negro before him had ever done."

She continued to write, campaign, speak out, and organize. She protested the execution of black soldiers after the 1917 Houston riot. She exposed the injustice 12 poor black farmers experienced after the Elaine riot and massacre in 1919 (see p. 428). She supported A. Phillip Randolph and the formation of the Brotherhood of Sleeping Car Porters (see p. 454). In 1928 she ran as a Republican for the state senate. Only death from kidney failure in 1931 ended her efforts to secure justice for black Americans.

  Read on MyHistoryLab Document: Ida B. Wells Challenges White Justifications for Lynchings, 1895

14-1
14-2
14-3
14-4
14-5
14-6
14-7
14-8

Explore on **MyHistoryLab** Activity: Going Back to Africa

The Liberian Exodus

When in 1875 white Democrats redeemed Mississippi with the "shotgun policy," a group of black people from Winona, Mississippi, wrote to Governor Adelbert Ames "to inquire about the possibility of moving to Africa. [W]e the colored people of Montgomery County are in a bad fix for we have no rights in the county and we want to know of you if there is any way for us to get out of the county and go to some place where we can get homes . . . so will you please let us know if we can go to Africa?"

They did not go to Africa, but some black Georgians and South Carolinians did. In 1877 black leaders in South Carolina, including Congressman Richard H. Cain, probate judge Harrison N. Bouey, and Martin Delany, urged black people to migrate to Liberia. Black communities and churches caught "Liberia Fever" while black people in upper South Carolina still felt the trauma of the terror that had ended Reconstruction.

A white journalist described the situation in Chester County: "At some places in this county the desire to shake off the dust of their feet against this Democratic State is so great, that they are talking of selling out their crops and their personal effects, save what they would need in their new home." They were given promising although sometimes inaccurate information about Liberia. One potato in Liberia, they were told, could feed an entire family.

Several black men organized the Liberian Exodus Joint Stock Steamship Company. They raised $6,000 and hired a ship, the *Azor*. The ship left Charleston in April 1878 with 206 migrants aboard, leaving 175 behind because there was not enough room for them. With inadequate food and freshwater and no competent medical care, 23 migrants died at sea. The ship arrived in Liberia on June 3.

In Liberia, several of the migrants prospered. Sam Hill established a 700-acre coffee plantation, and C. L. Parsons became the chief justice of the Liberian Supreme Court. But others did less well, and some returned to the United States. The Liberian Exodus Company experienced financial difficulties and could not pay for further voyages.

In a paradoxical twist in 1890, South Carolina Democrat Matthew C. Butler introduced an emigration bill in the U.S. Senate to appropriate $5 million per year to transport African Americans who volunteered to migrate to Africa. Butler was a former Confederate general who had helped redeem South Carolina. Most African Americans—including Frederick Douglass and Robert Smalls—opposed the legislation, but some, including Henry McNeal Turner, supported it. Butler's bill never passed. (See the *Profile* on Turner in Chapter 15.)

The Exodusters

In May 1879 black delegates from 14 states met in a convention in Nashville presided over by Congressman John R. Lynch of Mississippi. The delegates declared that "the colored people should emigrate to those States and Territories where they can enjoy all the rights which are guaranteed by the laws and Constitution of the United States." They also asked Congress—in vain—for $500,000 for this venture.

Nevertheless, black people headed west. Between 1865 and 1880, 40,000 black people known as **"Exodusters"** moved to Kansas. Benjamin "Pap" Singleton, a charismatic ex-slave from Tennessee, persuaded several hundred to migrate. Six black men were instrumental in founding the Kansas town of Nicodemus in 1877. Named after an African prince who bought his freedom, Nicodemus thrived in the 1880s with a hotel, two newspapers, a general store, a drugstore, a school, and three churches. Several of the businesses were white owned. Edwin P. McCabe, a black native of Troy, New York, settled for a time in Nicodemus, and in 1882 Kansas voters elected him state auditor.

By 1890, however, Nicodemus went into a decline from which it never recovered. Three railroads were built across Kansas, but each avoided Nicodemus, spelling economic ruin for the community. Edwin McCabe moved to Oklahoma and helped found the black town of Langston. Eventually more black people settled in Oklahoma than in Kansas.

Exodusters Black migrants who left the South during and after Reconstruction and settled in Kansas, often in all-black towns.

With their meager belongings, these African Americans await the arrival of a steamboat in about 1878 to transport them to Kansas or perhaps another western location.

By 1900 African Americans possessed 1.5 million acres in Oklahoma worth $11 million. In 1889 Congress enacted legislation eliminating Indian Territory in Oklahoma, dispossessing the Five Civilized Tribes of their land and dismantling tribal government. More than two dozen black towns, including Boley and Liberty, were founded in Oklahoma. There were nearly 50 black towns in the West by the early twentieth century, including Allensworth, California; Blackdom, New Mexico; and Dearfield, Colorado. Other black migrants settled in rural and isolated portions of Nebraska, the Dakotas, and Colorado (see Map 14–1).

Many people who moved west after the Civil War took advantage of the 1862 Homestead Act, which provided 160 acres of federal land free to those who would settle on it and farm it for at least five years. (Alternatively, a settler could buy the land for $1.25 per acre and possess it after six months' residency.) Life on the frontier was often bleak, dreary, and lonely. People lived in sod houses and relied on cow (or buffalo) chips for heat and cooking fuel as they struggled to endure.

Railroads encouraged migration by offering reduced fares. Some western farmers and agents were eager to sell land, but some of it was of little value. Some white residents of Mississippi and South Carolina, which had large black majorities, were glad to see the black people go. However, the loss of cheap black labor alarmed others.

Some black leaders urged black people to stay put. In 1879 Frederick Douglass insisted that more opportunities existed for black people in the South than elsewhere: "Not only is the South the best locality for the Negro on the ground of his political powers and possibilities, but it is best for him as a field of labor. He is there, as he is nowhere else, an absolute necessity." Robert Smalls urged black people to come to his home county of Beaufort, South Carolina, "where I hardly think it probable that any prisoner will ever be taken from jail by a mob and lynched."

Migration within the South

Many black people left the poverty and isolation of farms and moved to villages and towns in the South. Others went to growing black neighborhoods in larger southern

14-1

14-2

14-3

14-4

14-5

14-6

14-7

14-8

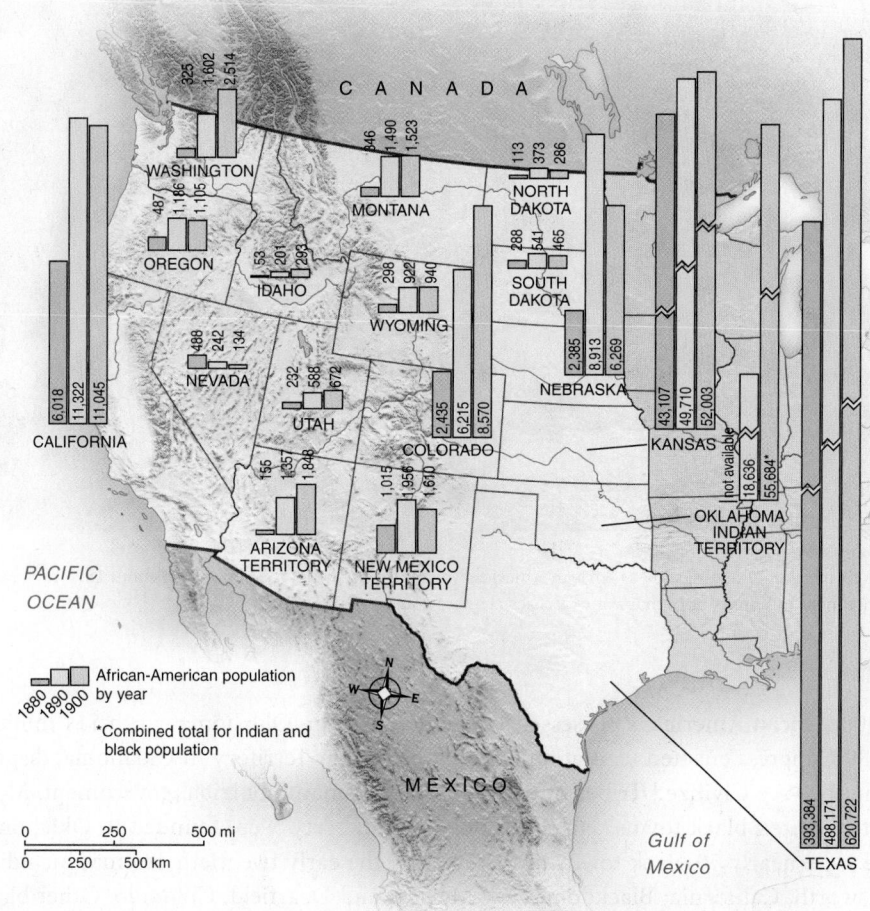

MAP 14–1 AFRICAN-AMERICAN POPULATION OF WESTERN TERRITORIES AND STATES, 1880–1900
Although most African Americans remained in the South following the Civil War, thousands of black people moved west and settled on farms and ranches. Others migrated to small towns that were populated mostly by former slaves.

What motivated several thousand African Americans to move to the Great Plains, Rocky Mountains, and West Coast in the late nineteenth century?

cities like Atlanta, Richmond, and Nashville. Urban areas offered more economic opportunities than rural areas. Although black people were usually confined to menial labor—from painting and shining shoes to domestic service—city work paid cash on a fairly regular basis, whereas rural residents received no money until their crops were sold. Towns and cities also had more entertainment and religious and educational activities. Black youngsters in towns spent more time in school than rural children, who had to work the farms.

Black women had a better chance than black men of finding regular work in a town, although it was usually as a domestic or cleaning woman. This economic situation damaged the black family. Before the increase in migration, a husband and wife headed 90 percent of black families. But with migration, many black men remained in rural areas where they could get farm work, while women went to urban communities. Often these women became single heads of households.

Black Farm Families

14-7 **What economic situation did large numbers of African Americans find themselves caught up in across the South in the late nineteenth century?**

Most black people remained poverty-stricken sharecroppers and renters on impoverished, white-owned land. They were poorly educated. They lacked political power. They were invariably in debt. Many rural black families remained close to involuntary servitude in the decades after Reconstruction.

Many black and white southerners were hardly better off than medieval serfs. They lived in drafty, leaky cabins without electricity or running water. Outdoor toilets created health problems. Medical care was often unavailable. Diets were dreary and unbalanced—mostly pork and cornbread—and deficient in vitamins and protein.

Cultivating Cotton

By the late 1800s, farmers in the Midwest and on the Great Plains had access to expensive labor-saving machinery such as reapers, threshers, and combines that enabled them to cultivate hundreds if not thousands of acres of grain. In the South cotton was unaffected by mechanization until the 1930s and 1940s. From the end of slavery into the twentieth century, black farm families annually grew millions of pounds of cotton by spending hundreds of millions of hours in the fields.

Each spring an older youth or adult walked behind a mule and broke the ground with a plow. At the end of a row, the farmer might shout "haw!" to the mule, and the animal then made a left turn to plow another row. Men, women, and children then planted cotton seeds and supplied fertilizer—guano—to the soil. When the green cotton plants emerged, the weaker plants were removed. From May until July, the field was hoed or chopped repeatedly to remove weeds that competed with the cotton for nutrients.

For generations after the Civil War, African-American men, women, and children planted, tended, and picked cotton.

14-1
14-2
14-3
14-4
14-5
14-6
14-7
14-8

"Lay-by" time came in July and August as the cotton plants matured and the "fruit" or the cotton bolls grew. There was less work during lay-by time, and children sometimes went to school in July and August. The cotton was then picked by hand beginning in the oppressive heat and humidity of August and continuing into September and October. Family members carried large baskets or enormous sacks through the fields as they removed the cotton from the spiny bolls. Because the bolls did not open simultaneously, the fields had to be picked more than once. The larger the family, the larger the labor force, and the more cotton they could harvest.

Benjamin Mays described his experience in the fields as a 12-year-old in early twentieth-century South Carolina: "When it came to picking cotton, my brother Hezekiah and I were the best in the family, and among the best cotton pickers in the county. We often competed with each other to see which could pick the most cotton. . . . 'H. H.' as we called him and I competed all day, from sunup to sundown, . . . when father weighed the cotton that evening, H. H. had picked 424 pounds and I had picked 425."

Picked cotton was stored before it was transported by wagon to the local ginnery. A few cotton gins were still operated with animal or water power; however, by the late nineteenth century steam engines ran the equipment at most ginneries. The modern facility was typically a two-story frame building that featured a large hose-like device that suctioned the cotton from the wagon. A separator then removed debris before a conveyor belt sent the clean cotton to gins that removed the cotton seeds. Then a large hydraulic press compressed the cotton into bales that weighed approximately 500 pounds each. Wagons took the bales to a nearby railroad depot where they were shipped to a textile mill.

Sharecroppers

Most of these black farm families (and many white families) were sharecroppers. Sharecropping had emerged during Reconstruction as landowners allowed the use of their land for a share of the crop. The landlord also usually provided housing, horses or mules, tools, seed, and fertilizer, as well as food and clothing. In return, the landowner received from one-half to three-quarters of the crop.

Read on **MyHistoryLab** Document:
A Sharecrop Contract (1882)

Sharecropping lent itself to exploitation. By law, verbal agreements were considered contracts. In any case, many sharecroppers were illiterate and could not have read written contracts. The landowner informed the sharecropper of the value of the product raised—typically cotton—and the value of the goods provided to the sharecropping family. Black farmers who disputed white landowners put themselves in peril. Although many sharecroppers knew the proprietor's calculations were wrong, they could do nothing about it. Also, cotton brokers and gin owners routinely paid black farmers less than white farmers per pound for cotton. A forlorn ditty in the late nineteenth century captured this inequity:

> A naught's a naught, and a figger's a figger—
> All fer de white man—none fer de nigger!

Read on **MyHistoryLab** Document:
When We Worked on Shares, We Couldn't Make Nothing

Black men were forced to accept the white man's word. One Mississippi sharecropper explained, "I have been living in this Delta thirty years, and I know that I have been robbed every year; but there is no use jumping out of the frying pan into the fire. If we ask any questions we are cussed, and if we raise up we are shot, and that ends it."

Renters

Black farmers preferred renting to sharecropping. As tenants, they paid a flat charge to rent a given number of acres. Payment would be made in either cash—perhaps $5 per acre—or, more typically, in a specified amount of the crop—two bales of cotton per 20 acres. Tenants

VOICES   Cash and Debt for the Black Cotton Farmer

Benjamin E. Mays was born in 1895 in Epworth, South Carolina. He was the youngest and eighth child of parents who had been slaves and whose lives revolved around agriculture. Mays went on to South Carolina State College, to Bates College in Maine, and to the University of Chicago. He became the president of Morehouse College in Atlanta, where he served as a mentor to Martin Luther King, Jr. Mays delivered the eulogy at King's funeral in 1968.

As I recall, Father usually rented forty acres of land for a two-mule farm, or sixty acres if we had three mules. The rent was two bales of cotton weighing 500 pounds each, for every twenty acres rented. So the owner of the land got his two, four, or six bales of cotton out of the first cotton picked and ginned.

To make sixteen bales of cotton on a two-mule farm was considered excellent farming. After four bales were used to pay rent, we would have twelve bales left. The price of cotton fluctuated. If we received ten cents a pound, we would have somewhere between five and six hundred dollars, depending on whether the bales of cotton weighed an average of 450, 475, or 500 pounds. When all of us children were at home we, with our father and mother, were ten. We lived in a four-room house, with no indoor plumbing—no toilet facilities, no running water.

We were never able to clear enough from the crop to carry us from one September to the next. We could usually go on our own from September through February; but every March a lien had to be placed on the crop so that we could get money to buy food and other necessities from March through August, when we would get some relief by selling cotton. Strange as it may seem, neither we nor our neighbors ever raised enough hogs to have meat year round, enough corn and wheat to insure having our daily bread, or cows in sufficient numbers to have enough milk. The curse was cotton. It was difficult to make farmers see that more corn, grain, hogs, and cows meant less cash but more profit in the end. Cotton sold instantly, and that was cash money. Negro farmers wanted to feel the cash—at least for that brief moment as it passed through their hands into the white man's hands!

1. **What might have led to greater independence for people like the Mays family?**
2. **Why were southern black and white families so large?**

SOURCE: *Born to Rebel: An Autobiography* (New York: Charles Scribner, 1971), pp. 5–6. Reprinted by permission of the University of Georgia Press, 2001.

14-1
14-2
14-3
14-4
14-5
14-6
14-7
14-8

usually owned their own animals and tools. As Bessie Jones explained, "You see, a share-cropper don't ever have nothing. Before you know it, the man done took it all. But the renter always have something, and then he go to work when he want to go to work. He ain't got to go to work on the man's time. If he didn't make it, he didn't get it."

Crop Liens

Many sharecroppers and renters were also indebted to a merchant for food, clothing, and farm supplies. The merchant advanced the merchandise but took out a **lien** on the crop. If the sharecropper or renter failed to repay the merchant, the merchant was entitled to all or part of the crop once the landowner had received his payment. Merchants tended to charge high prices and interest rates. They usually insisted that farmers plant cotton before they would agree to a lien. Cotton could be sold quickly for cash.

lien Black and white farmers purchased goods on credit from local merchants. The merchant demanded collateral in the form of a lien on the crop, typically cotton. If the farmer failed to repay the loan, the merchant had a legal right to seize the crop.

Peonage

Many farmers fell deeply into debt. They were cheated. Bad weather destroyed crops. Crop prices declined. Farmers could not leave the land until their debts were paid. If they tried to depart, the sheriff pursued them. This was **peonage**, and it amounted to enslavement, holding thousands of black people across the South in perpetual bondage. Peonage violated

peonage The system that forbade southern farmers, usually sharecroppers and renters, who accumulated debts to leave the land until the debt was repaid—often an impossible task.

federal law, but the law was rarely enforced. White juries acquitted landowners and merchants who were prosecuted for keeping black people in peonage.

Black Landowners

Considering the incredible obstacles against them, black farm families acquired land at an astonishing rate after the Civil War. Many white people refused to sell land to black buyers, preferring to keep them dependent. Black people also found it difficult to save enough money to purchase land even when they could find a willing seller. Still, they managed to accumulate land.

A white Georgia farmer sourly commented that African Americans were desperate to get their own land: "They will almost starve and go naked before they will work for a white man, if they can get a patch of ground to live on and get from under his control."

Some black families had kept land that had been distributed in the Carolina and Georgia low country under the Port Royal Experiment and Sherman's Special Field Order #15 (see Chapter 12). In 1880 black people on South Carolina's sea islands held 10,000 acres of land worth $300,000.

By 1900 more than 100,000 black families owned their own land in the eight states of the Deep South. Black landownership increased more than 500 percent between 1870 and 1900. Most black people possessed small farms of about 20 acres. These small plots were often subsequently subdivided among sons and grandsons, making it harder for their families to prosper. But some black farmers owned impressive estates. Prince Johnson had 360 acres of excellent Mississippi delta land. Freedman Leon Winter was the richest black man in Tennessee, with real estate worth $70,000 in 1889. In Florida, J. D. McDuffy raised melons, cabbages, and tomatoes on an 800-acre farm near Ocala. Texas freedman Daniel Webster Wallace had a 10,000-acre cattle ranch. Few black people inherited large estates. Most of these landowners had been born into slavery. After emancipation, they managed to accumulate land—usually just a few acres at a time.

White Resentment of Black Success

Many white southerners could not tolerate black economic success and lashed out at those who had achieved it. For example, when one rural black man built an attractive new house, white people told him not to paint it—lest it look better than theirs. He accepted the advice and left the dwelling bare.

In the early twentieth century, Henry Watson, a well-to-do black farmer in Georgia, drove a new car to town. Enraged white people forced Watson and his daughter out at gunpoint and burned the vehicle. Watson was told, "From now on, you niggers walk into town, or use that ole mule if you want to stay in this city."

In 1916 Anthony Crawford, the owner of 427 acres of prime cotton land in Abbeville, South Carolina, secretary of the Chapel AME Church, a married man with 16 children, was arrested and then released after he quarreled with a local white merchant over the price of cotton seed. But a mob, infuriated that Crawford spoke so bluntly to a white man, went after him. "When a nigger gets impudent we stretch him out and paddle him a bit," exclaimed one white man. But Crawford resisted and crushed the skull of a white attacker. The mob then stabbed and beat Crawford before the sheriff rescued him and put him in jail. But a second mob broke into the jail and beat him to death. His body was left hanging at the fairgrounds. After his first beating, Crawford had told a friend, "I thought I was a good citizen." The coroner's jury ruled that his death had occurred at the hands of persons unknown.

While pursuing a master's degree at the University of Chicago, Benjamin E. Mays briefly taught English at South Carolina State College in Orangeburg. This is a photo taken from the 1926 college yearbook. He met his second wife, Sadie Grey, while teaching in Orangeburg. She was teaching sociology and also working on a graduate degree at the University of Chicago. Mays's first wife, Ellen Harvin, had died from complications due to child birth in 1923.

14-1
14-2
14-3
14-4
14-5
14-6
14-7
14-8

African Americans and Southern Courts

14-8 How just was the legal system for black people in the South?

The southern criminal justice systems yielded nothing but injustice to black people. Southern lawmakers worried incessantly about what they considered the black crime problem and enacted laws to control the black population. Vagrancy laws made it easy to arrest idle black men or one who was passing through a community. Contract evasion laws ensnared black people who attempted to escape peonage and perpetual servitude.

Segregated Justice

The legal system also became increasingly white after Reconstruction. Black police officers were eliminated, and white policemen acquired a deserved reputation for brutality. Juries were all white by 1900. (No women served on southern juries.) In Alabama, a black man called for a local grand jury insisted on serving until he was beaten and forced to step down. Judges were white men. Most attorneys were white. The few black lawyers faced daunting hurdles. Some black defendants believed—correctly—that they would be convicted and sentenced to a longer term if they retained a black attorney rather than a white one. Court personnel treated black plaintiffs, defendants, and witnesses with contempt, calling them "niggers," "boy," and "gal." Black people were rarely "Mr." or "Mrs." in court proceedings.

A black defendant could not get justice. Black people were more often charged with crimes than white people. They were almost always convicted, regardless of the strength of the evidence or the credibility of witnesses. In one of the few instances when a black man was found not guilty of killing a white man, his attorney advised him to leave town because white people were unlikely to accept the verdict. He fled but returned 20 years later and was castrated by two white men.

Race took precedence in the legal system. Black victims of crime found the law turned against them. In 1897 in Hinds County, Mississippi, a white man beat a black woman with an axe handle. She took him to court, only to have the justice of the peace rule that he knew of "no law to punish a white man for beating a negro woman."

Juries rarely found white people guilty of crimes against black people. In a Georgia case in 1911, the evidence against several white people for holding black families in peonage was so overwhelming that the judge virtually ordered the jury to return a guilty verdict. Nonetheless, after five minutes of deliberation, the jury found the defendants not guilty. Many black and white people were astonished in 1898 in Shreveport, Louisiana, when a jury found a white man guilty of murdering a black man. He was sentenced to five years in prison.

Black people could receive leniency from the judicial system, but it was not justice. They were much less likely to be charged with a crime against another black person, such as raping a black woman, than against a white person. Black people often were not charged with crimes such as adultery and bigamy because white people considered such offenses typical black behavior.

Black defendants who had some personal or economic connection to a prominent white person were less likely to be treated or punished the same way as black people who had no such relationship. In Vicksburg, Mississippi, a black woman watched as the black man who had murdered her husband was acquitted because a white man intervened. Those black people known as "a white man's nigger" had an advantage in court.

Black people received longer sentences and larger fines than white people. In Georgia, black convicts served much longer sentences than white convicts for the same offense—five times as long for larceny, for example. An 80-year-old black preacher went to prison "for what a white man was fined five dollars." In New Orleans, a black man was sentenced to

PROFILE Johnson C. Whittaker

SHORTLY AFTER 6 A.M. ON APRIL 6, 1880, West Point's lone black cadet, Johnson C. Whittaker, was found lying unconscious on the floor of his room in the barracks. He was splattered with blood. His hands were tied together, and his feet were tied to the bed. In the months that followed, Whittaker's case attracted nationwide attention.

Whittaker was born a slave in 1858 near Camden, South Carolina, the son of a house slave and a free man. In 1876 white Republican Congressman Solomon L. Hoge nominated Whittaker to West Point.

During his first year at the military academy, Whittaker roomed with the only other black cadet, Henry O. Flipper. But Flipper graduated in 1877—the first black man to graduate from the academy—and Whittaker spent the next four years completely ostracized as the only remaining black cadet. White cadets refused to associate or room with him. Quiet and studious, he had a creditable academic record, but when he failed an exam in 1878, he had to repeat a year.

When he was found bloody and bound, Whittaker claimed he had been assaulted by three masked men after receiving a warning note the day before. A court of inquiry, however, declared that he had mutilated himself. Whittaker then insisted on a court-martial to prove his innocence. In February 1881, that court-martial convened in New York City.

Whittaker was charged with conduct unbecoming an officer and with lying. After four months of testimony, the court found him guilty. It determined that Whittaker was "shamming"—making it up to avoid failing an exam. Major Asa Bird Gardiner told the court, "Negroes are noted for their ability to sham and feign." Gardiner maintained that Whittaker was unfit: "By his own story the accused has shown himself a coward without one redeeming quality . . . his mental attitude [was] inferior to the average Anglo-Saxon."

The court ordered Whittaker dishonorably discharged, fined $1, and sentenced to a year's hard labor. But in March 1882, President Chester Arthur overturned the verdict. On the same day, Secretary of War Robert Lincoln (Abraham's son) ordered Whittaker discharged from West Point.

Whittaker spent most of the rest of his life working with young black people at South Carolina State College and at Douglass High School in Oklahoma City. He died in South Carolina in 1931. Whittaker had two sons. Both were commissioned officers and served in all-black units in World War I.

Whittaker summed up the meaning of his experience at West Point in a speech after the court-martial found him guilty:

> West Point has tried to take from me honor and good name, but West Point has failed. I have honor and manhood still left me. I have an education which none can take from me. That education has come to me at fearful cost. The government may not wish me to use it in her service, but I shall use it for the good of my fellow men and for the good of those around me. . . . Poverty and sneers can never crush manhood. With God as my guide, duty will be my watchword, I can, I must, I will win a place in life!

In July 1995, President Bill Clinton posthumously awarded Johnson C. Whittaker his commission in the U.S. Army.

---

90 days in jail for petty theft. A black newspaper said it was "three days for stealing and eighty-seven days for being colored."

The Convict Lease System

convict lease system Southern states and communities leased prisoners to privately operated mines, railroads, and timber companies. These businesses forced the prisoners, who were usually black men, to work in brutal, unhealthy, and dangerous conditions. Many convicts died of abuse and disease.

Conditions in southern prisons were wretched. Black prisoners—many incarcerated for vagrancy, theft, disorderly conduct, and other misdemeanors—spent months and years in oppressive conditions and were unrelentingly abused by white authorities. Nonetheless, conditions got worse.

In the late nineteenth century, southern politicians devised the **convict lease system**. Businesses and planters leased convicts from the state to build railroads, clear swamps, cut timber, tend cotton, and work mines. The company or planter had to feed, clothe, and

Black and white men serve on a jury together during Reconstruction but they segregate themselves.

14-1
14-2
14-3
14-4
14-5
14-6
14-7
14-8

house the prisoners. Of course, the convicts were not paid. The state and local community were not only freed of the burden of maintaining prisons and jails but also received revenue. For example, the state of South Carolina was paid $3 per month per prisoner. Some states and counties found this so remunerative that law enforcement officials were encouraged to arrest and convict even more black men so that they could contribute to this lucrative enterprise.

Leased convicts endured appalling conditions. They were shackled and beaten, over-worked, and underfed. They slept on vermin-infested straw mattresses and received little or no medical care. They sustained terrible injuries on the job and at the hands of guards. Diseases proliferated in the camps. Hundreds died. They had, in effect, been sentenced to death for petty crimes.

Businessmen and planters found such cheap labor almost irresistible. Black prisoners found it "nine kinds of hell." It was worse than slavery because these black lives had no value to either the government or the businesses involved in this sordid system. As one employer explained in 1883, "But these convicts; we don't own em. One dies, get another." Convict leasing became such a scandal that several states outlawed it by the early twentieth century.

CONCLUSION

With the end of the Civil War and slavery in 1865, more than four million African Americans had looked with hope and anticipation to the future. Four decades later, there were more than nine million African Americans, and more than eight million of them lived in the South. The crushing burden of white supremacy limited their hopes and aspirations. The U.S. government abandoned black people to white southerners and their state and local governments. The federal government that had affirmed their rights as citizens during Reconstruction ignored the legal, political, and economic situation that entrapped most black southerners.

Although the Thirteenth Amendment abolished slavery, thousands of black people were trapped in peonage or labored as sharecroppers and renters, indebted to white landowners and merchants. Yet more than 100,000 black families managed to acquire their own farms by 1900. Many black farmers had also organized and participated in the Colored Farmers' Alliance and the Populist Party, although it brought few tangible benefits.

The Fourteenth Amendment had guaranteed the rights of citizenship that included due process of law. No state could deprive a person of life, liberty, or property without a court proceeding. The amendment also ensured each citizen equal protection of the law. But the Supreme Court had ruled that racial segregation in public places did not infringe on the right to equal protection of the law. And as for the right to life, by the early 1900s, mobs had lynched hundreds of black people.

The Fifteenth Amendment stipulated that race could not be used to deprive a man of the right to vote. But southern states circumvented the amendment with poll taxes, literacy tests, and the grandfather clause. Thus, by 1900, after black men had held political offices across the South for 30 years, no black person served in an elected political position in any southern state.

White people regarded black Americans as an inferior race not entitled to those rights that the Constitution supposedly guaranteed. What could black people do about the discrimination, violence, and powerlessness they had to endure? What strategies, ideas, and leadership could overcome the burdens they were forced to bear? What chances did they have of overcoming white supremacy? How could black people organize to gain fundamental rights that were guaranteed to them?

CHAPTER TIMELINE

AFRICAN-AMERICAN EVENTS

NATIONAL EVENTS

1875–1880

1880
Cadet Johnson C. Whittaker assaulted at West Point

1877
Reconstruction ends

1880
James Garfield elected president

1880–1890

1881
Tennessee segregates passenger trains
Tuskegee Institute founded

1886
Riot in Washington County, Texas

1887
National Colored Farmers' Alliance formed
Florida segregates passenger trains

1889–1908
Southern states disfranchise black voters

1880s
Southern Farmers' Alliance forms

1881
President Garfield assassinated
Clara Barton establishes the Red Cross

1884
Grover Cleveland elected president

1886
Haymarket affair in Chicago

1887
Congress creates the Interstate Commerce Commission
Dawes Act permits individual Indian families to own reservation land

1888
Benjamin Harrison elected president

1889
Wall Street Journal established

1890–1895

1891
Georgia segregates streetcars

1892
235 people lynched in the United States, 155 of them African American

1890
Eleven Italians lynched in New Orleans
James A. Naismith invents basketball

1892
Populist Party challenges the Democrats and Republicans in national elections
Homestead strike at the Carnegie steel plant near Pittsburgh
Grover Cleveland elected to a second term as president

1893
Panic of 1893 begins economic depression

1895–1900

1896
In *Plessy v. Ferguson,* Supreme Court upholds legal segregation

1898
Phoenix riot in South Carolina
Wilmington riot in North Carolina

1899–1901
George H. White of North Carolina—the South's last black congressman until 1972

1900
New Orleans riot

1896
William McKinley elected president
Populist Party's last national campaign

1898
Eugene V. Debs helps found Socialist Party
United States annexes Hawaii
Spanish-American War

1900
William McKinley reelected president

On MyHistoryLab

✓ Study and Review on MyHistoryLab

REVIEW QUESTIONS

1. How were black people prevented from voting despite the Fifteenth Amendment?

2. How did white Americans justify segregation?

3. Why did the South experience an epidemic of violence and lynching in the late nineteenth century?

4. Why didn't more black people leave the South in this period?

RECOMMENDED READING

Edward L. Ayers. *The Promise of the New South: Life After Reconstruction.* New York: Oxford University Press, 1992. An excellent overview of life in the late nineteenth-century South.

Douglas A. Blackmon. *Slavery by Another Name: The Re-Enslavement of Black Americans from the Civil War to World War II.* New York: Random House, 2009. Thousands of black people were taken into custody and forced into labor in the decades following the Civil War.

Leon Litwack. *Trouble in Mind: Black Southerners in the Age of Jim Crow.* New York: Alfred A. Knopf, 1998. In moving words, black people describe life in a white supremacist society.

Rayford Logan. *The Negro in American Life and Thought: The Nadir, 1877–1901.* New York: Dial Press, 1954. Explorations of the contours and oppressiveness of racism.

Benjamin E. Mays. *Born to Rebel: An Autobiography.* New York: Charles Scribner, 1971. Graphic recollection of growing up black in the rural South at the turn of the century.

C. Vann Woodward. *The Strange Career of Jim Crow.* New York: Oxford University Press, 1955. The evolution of legal segregation in the South.

ADDITIONAL BIBLIOGRAPHY

REGIONAL, STATE, AND LOCAL STUDIES

Charles S. Aiken. *The Cotton Plantation South Since the Civil War.* Baltimore: Johns Hopkins University Press, 1998.

Eric Anderson. *Race and Politics in North Carolina, 1872–1901: The Black Second.* Baton Rouge: Louisiana State University Press, 1981.

David Cecelski and Timothy B. Tyson, eds. *Democracy Betrayed: The Wilmington Race Riot and Its Legacy.* Chapel Hill: University of North Carolina Press, 1998.

Helen G. Edmonds. *The Negro and Fusion Politics in North Carolina, 1894–1901.* Chapel Hill: University of North Carolina Press, 1951.

William Ivy Hair. *Carnival of Fury: Robert Charles and the New Orleans Riot of 1900.* Baton Rouge: Louisiana State University Press, 1976.

Neil R. McMillen. *Dark Journey: Black Mississippians in the Age of Jim Crow.* Urbana: University of Illinois Press, 1989.

David M. Oshinsky. *"Worse Than Slavery": Parchman Farm and the Ordeal of Jim Crow Justice.* New York: Free Press, 1999.

H. Leon Prather. *We Have Taken a City: Wilmington Racial Massacre and Coup of 1898.* Rutherford, NJ: Fairleigh Dickinson University Press, 1984.

George B. Tindall. *South Carolina Negroes, 1877–1900.* Columbia: University of South Carolina Press, 1952.

Vernon Wharton. *The Negro in Mississippi, 1865–1890.* Chapel Hill: University of North Carolina Press, 1947.

BIOGRAPHIES AND AUTOBIOGRAPHIES

Mia Bay. *To Tell the Truth Freely: The Life of Ida B. Wells.* New York: Hill and Wang, 2009.

Albert S. Broussard. *African-American Odyssey: The Stewarts, 1853–1963.* Lawrence: University Press of Kansas, 1998.

Alfreda Duster, ed. *Crusade for Justice: The Autobiography of Ida B. Wells.* Chicago: University of Chicago Press, 1972.

Henry O. Flipper. *The Colored Cadet at West Point.* New York: Arno Press, 1969.

Paula Giddings. *Ida: A Sword Among Lions: Ida B. Wells and the Campaign Against Lynching.* New York: Amistad, Harper Collins, 2008.

John F. Marszalek, Jr. *Court Martial: The Army vs. Johnson Whittaker.* New York: Scribner, 1972.

_____. *A Black Congressman in the Age of Jim Crow: South Carolina's George Washington Murray.* Gainesville: University Press of Florida, 2006.

Linda McMurry. *To Keep the Waters Troubled: The Life of Ida B. Wells.* New York: Oxford University Press, 1998.

Patricia A. Schechter. *Ida B. Wells-Barnett and American Reform, 1882–1930.* Chapel Hill: University of North Carolina Press, 2001.

POLITICS AND SEGREGATION

Grace Hale. *Making Whiteness: The Culture of Segregation in the South, 1890–1940.* New York: Pantheon Books, 1998.

Williamjames Hull Hoffer. *Plessy v. Ferguson: Race and Inequality in Jim Crow America.* Lawrence: University of Kansas Press, 2012.

J. Morgan Kousser. *The Shaping of Southern Politics: Suffrage Restriction and the Establishment of the One-Party South, 1880–1910.* New Haven, CT: Yale University Press, 1974.

Michael Perman. *Struggle for Mastery: Disfranchisement in the South, 1888–1908.* Chapel Hill: University of North Carolina Press, 2001.

Thomas Adams Upchurch. *Legislating Racism: The Billion Dollar Congress and the Birth of Jim Crow.* Lexington: University Press of Kentucky, 2004.

LYNCHING

James Allen, Hinton Als, John Lewis, and Leon F. Litwack. *Without Sanctuary: Lynching Photography in America.* Santa Fe, NM: Twin Palms Books, 2000.

W. Fitzhugh Brundage. *Lynching in the New South: Georgia and Virginia, 1880–1930.* Urbana: University of Illinois Press, 1993.

_____, ed. *Under Sentence of Death: Lynching in the South.* Chapel Hill: University of North Carolina Press, 1997.

Sandra Gunning. *Race, Rape, and Lynching: The Red Record of American Literature, 1890–1912.* New York: Oxford University Press, 1996.

National Association for the Advancement of Colored People. *Thirty Years of Lynching in the United States, 1889–1918.* New York: NAACP, 1919.

Diane Sommerville. *Rape & Race in the Nineteenth Century South.* Chapel Hill: University of North Carolina Press, 2004.

Stewart E. Tolnay and E. M. Beck. *A Festival of Violence: An Analysis of Southern Lynchings, 1882–1930.* Urbana: University of Illinois Press, 1995.

THE WEST

Robert G. Athearn. *In Search of Canaan: Black Migration to Kansas, 1879–80.* Lawrence: Regents Press of Kansas, 1978.

Jacob U. Gordon. *Narratives of African Americans in Kansas, 1870–1992.* Lewiston, NY: Edward Mellon Press, 1993.

Nell Irvin Painter. *Exodusters: Black Migration to Kansas After Reconstruction.* New York: Alfred A. Knopf, 1977.

Quintard Taylor. *In Search of the Racial Frontier: African Americans in the American West, 1528–1990.* New York: Norton, 1998.

MIGRATION, MOBILITY, AND LAND OWNERSHIP

William Cohen. *At Freedom's Edge: Black Mobility and the Southern White Quest for Racial Control, 1861–1915.* Baton Rouge: Louisiana State University Press, 1991.

Pete Daniel. *The Shadow of Slavery: Peonage in the South, 1901–1969.* Urbana: University of Illinois Press, 1972.

Edward Royce. *The Origins of Southern Sharecropping.* Philadelphia: Temple University Press, 1993.

Loren Schweninger. *Black Property Owners in the South, 1790–1915.* Urbana: University of Illinois Press, 1990.

RETRACING THE ODYSSEY

Nicodemus National Historic Site, Nicodemus, Kansas. W. R. Hill was a black real estate agent who founded Nicodemus in 1877. By 1887 over 250 people lived in the town. The absence of a railroad led to a prolonged decline of what had been a small thriving community. Most of the town's original structures have not survived.

Langston, Oklahoma, and Langston University. Langston was one of the many all-black towns established after the Civil War. In 1897 the town set aside 40 acres to create a black land-grant university. The town and university are named for John Mercer Langston, a prominent nineteenth-century black leader and congressman from Virginia.

Historic District, Boley, Oklahoma. Boley was an all-black town incorporated in 1905. Many of the town's residents left when the economy collapsed during the Great Depression. Some of the historic black businesses and buildings still stand.

Black American West Museum and Heritage Center, Denver, Colorado. Founded by Paul Stewart, this museum is dedicated to the black pioneers of the frontier West, including cowboys, soldiers, barbers, and homesteaders. It has artifacts, photographs, recordings, and other memorabilia of nineteenth- and early twentieth-century African Americans. It is located in the former home of Dr. Justina Ford, a pioneer and black woman physician who delivered seven thousand babies of virtually every ethnic background.

African Americans Challenge White Supremacy

 Listen to **Chapter 15**
on MyHistoryLab

LEARNING OBJECTIVES

15-1 What scientific and scholarly ideas were developed to support racism during the late nineteenth century?

15-2 What, according to Booker T. Washington, was the chief purpose of education for black people? To what extent did Washington's critics disagree with his position on black education?

15-3 What role did religion play in the lives of African Americans and in their adjustment to discrimination?

15-4 Why did black men in the U.S. Army engage in combat against Native Americans, the Spanish, and Filipinos?

15-5 What were the major developments among African Americans in businesses and labor unions in the struggle for equality?

15-6 What opportunities existed for African Americans in the legal and medical professions?

15-7 What did African Americans contribute to music in the late nineteenth and early twentieth centuries?

15-8 What contributions did African Americans make to athletics in the late nineteenth and early twentieth centuries?

> The Anglo-Saxon said to the negro, in most haughty tones: "in this great 'battle for bread,' you must supply the brute force while I will supply the brain." . . . He will contribute the public funds to educate the negro and then exert every possible influence to keep the negro from earning a livelihood by means of that education.
>
> They pay our teachers poorer salaries than they do their own; they give us fewer and inferior school buildings and they make us crawl in the dust before the very eyes of our children in order to secure the slightest concessions. . . .
>
> In school, they are taught to bow down and worship at the shrine of men who died for the sake of liberty, and day by day they grow to disrespect us, their parents[,] who have made no blow for freedom. But it will not always be thus!
>
> *Black novelist Sutton E. Griggs in* Imperium in Imperio, *1899*

Industrialization and the rise of large, powerful corporations transformed the American economy in the late nineteenth century. As millions of European immigrants crowded into the cities of the North and Midwest to find jobs in the new factories, agricultural production increased and prices declined, impoverishing many rural southerners. Most black people—nearly eight million—remained in the South, where they struggled to confront white supremacy. Living in a society that sought to disregard their rights and exclude them from its institutions and culture, black Americans increasingly relied on their own resources to forge a path into the future.

Some African Americans turned to education to elevate themselves and their people, but they disagreed about the best approach. Some African-American men sought to advance themselves and prove their worth to American society through military service. By the late nineteenth century, however, black Americans mostly relied on each other and their own communities to sustain themselves. As they had during Reconstruction, they continued to support churches, schools, and colleges. They established businesses and sometimes formed labor unions and went on strike. They founded their own hospitals.

Several hundred African-American cowboys participated in the development of the western cattle empire in the decades after the Civil War. This photo depicts a group of those cowboys near Bonham, Texas, in 1909.

They expressed themselves in music by creating ragtime, jazz, and blues. At times they were allowed to participate with white people in organized sports such as professional boxing, baseball, and college football. More often, they formed their own athletic teams and leagues. African Americans refused to allow white supremacy to prevent them from creating a meaningful place for themselves in American society.

Social Darwinism

15-1 What scientific and scholarly ideas were developed to support racism during the late nineteenth century?

Pseudoscientific evidence and academic scholarship bolstered the conviction of many Americans that white people, especially those of English and Germanic descent—Anglo-Saxons—were culturally and racially superior to nonwhites and even other Europeans. Sociologists Herbert Spencer and William Graham Sumner drew on Charles Darwin's theory of evolution and concluded that life in modern industrial societies mirrored life in the animal kingdom. This theory, called **social Darwinism**, held that through natural selection, the strong would thrive, prosper, and reproduce, while the weak would falter, fail, and die. Life was a struggle. Only the fittest survived.

social Darwinism Derived from Charles Darwin's theory of evolution, Herbert Spencer and William Graham Sumner asserted that life in modern society was competitive and only those individuals who were mentally, emotionally, and physically strong would prevail.

Social Darwinism applied to both individuals and "races." It justified great disparities in wealth, suggesting that such men as John D. Rockefeller and Andrew Carnegie were rich because they were "fit," whereas many European immigrants and most African Americans were poor and unlikely to succeed because they were "unfit." The same logic explained why the United States, Britain, and Germany were stronger and more prosperous than countries such as Spain and Italy and why African, Asian, and Latin American societies seemed backward and primitive. In absorbing this ideology of class and race, many Americans and Europeans came to believe they had a responsibility—a duty—to introduce the political, economic, and religious benefits and values of Western cultures to the "less advanced" and usually darker peoples of the globe. The English poet Rudyard Kipling called this supposed responsibility "the white man's burden."

Social Darwinism led most Protestant white Americans to believe that other Americans could be ranked from superior to inferior based on their race, nationality, and ethnicity. Black people invariably occupied the bottom of this hierarchy, and the eastern and southern European immigrants who were flooding the country ranked slightly above them. Black people were capable, so the reasoning went, of only a subordinate role in a complex and advanced society as it rushed into the twentieth century. And if their position was biologically ordained, why should society devote substantial resources to educating them?

Education and Schools

15-2 What, according to Booker T. Washington, was the chief purpose of education for black people? To what extent did Washington's critics disagree with his position on black education?

A black youngster who wanted an education in the late nineteenth century faced formidable obstacles. Most black people were poor farmers who had few opportunities for an education and even fewer prospects for a career in business or in a profession. It is a testimony to black perseverance that so many black people did manage to acquire an education and free themselves from illiteracy (see Figure 15–1).

15-1
15-2
15-3
15-4
15-5
15-6
15-7
15-8

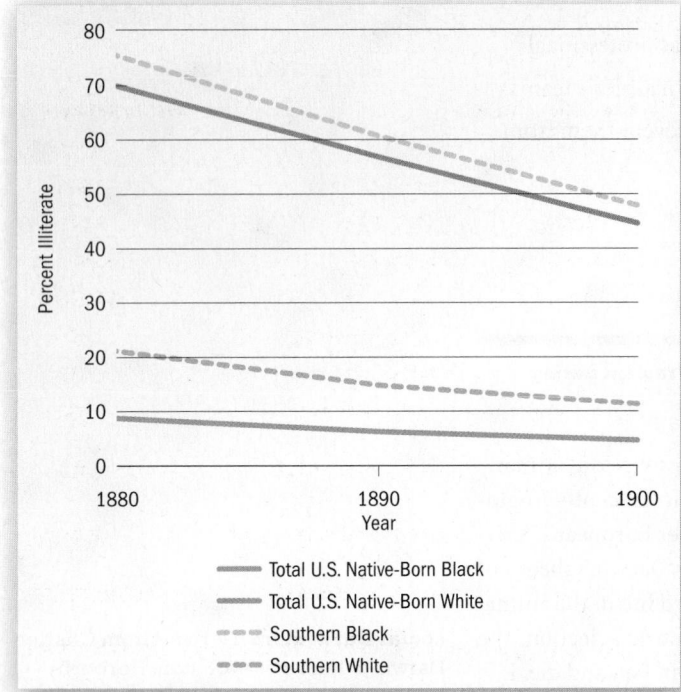

FIGURE 15–1 BLACK AND WHITE ILLITERACY IN THE UNITED STATES AND THE SOUTHERN STATES, 1880–1900
Although more than half of adult black southerners were still illiterate in 1900, black people had made substantial progress in education during the last two decades of the nineteenth century. This progress is especially remarkable considering the difficulties black youngsters and adults faced in acquiring even an elementary education.

Gaining even a rudimentary education was not easy. Rural schools for black children rarely operated for more than 30 weeks a year. Because of the demands of fieldwork, most black youngsters could not attend school on a regular basis. Brothers and sisters sometimes alternated work and school with each other on a daily basis. Benjamin Mays was 19 years old before he went to school for more than four months a year—and even then he had to defy his father's demand that he leave school in February to work on the farm.

Schools were often dilapidated shacks. They lacked plumbing, electricity, books, and teaching materials. Some schools were in churches and homes. Teachers were poorly paid and often poorly prepared. Septima Clark remembered her first teaching experience on Johns Island on the South Carolina coast in the early twentieth century:

> Here I was, a high-school graduate, eighteen years old, principal in a two-teacher school with 132 pupils ranging from beginners to eighth graders, with no teaching experience, a schoolhouse constructed of boards running up and down, with no slats on the cracks, and a fireplace at one end of the room that cooked the pupils immediately in front of it but allowed those in the rear to shiver and freeze on their uncomfortable, hard, back-breaking benches.

Segregated Schools

Although southern states could not afford to support even one first-rate public school system, each of them operated separate schools for black and white children (see Table 15–1). The South had almost no public black high schools. In 1915, not one public black high school existed in 23 southern cities with populations of more than 20,000, including Tampa, New Orleans, Charleston, and Charlotte. But these 23 cities had 36 high schools for white youngsters. In 1897—over the vehement protests of the black community—white officials in Augusta, Georgia, transformed Ware High School, the black secondary school, into a black primary school. The U.S. Supreme Court in 1899 in *Cumming v. Richmond County [Georgia] Board of Education* unanimously refused to accept black parents' contention that this violated the "separate but equal" doctrine announced in the *Plessy v. Ferguson* case three years earlier. Augusta was left with two white high schools—one for males and one for females—and none for black people.

Young black people who sought a secondary education often had to travel to a black college or university that offered a high school program. For example, in 1911, at the age of 16, Benjamin Mays traveled one hundred miles to South Carolina State College and enrolled in the seventh grade. He graduated from high school there in 1916 at the age of 22 and then graduated from Maine's Bates College four years later.

In many communities, black people, with the assistance of churches and northern philanthropists, operated private academies and high schools, such as the Fort Valley

Young African-American children being taught washing and ironing at a primary school in Hampton, Virginia, in the 1890s.

High and Industrial School in Georgia and Mather Academy in Camden, South Carolina, to fill the void the lack of public schools created. Typically students were charged a modest tuition and came from more prosperous families. In 1890, 3,106 black youngsters between the ages of 15 and 19 attended black public or private high schools in the South. By 1910, 26,553 did.

The Hampton Model

Some black and many white people regarded education for black youngsters as pointless. Benjamin Mays's father put little value in education: "My greatest opposition to going away to school was my father. When I knew that I had learned everything that I could in the one-room Brickhouse School and realized how little that was, my father felt . . . that it was all I needed. . . . He was convinced that education went to one's head and made him a fool and dishonest." In 1911 South Carolina's Governor Coleman Blease was even more blunt: "Instead of making an educated negro, you are ruining a good plow hand and making a half-trained fool."

Others were convinced the most appropriate education for a black child was industrial or domestic training. Black youngsters, these people maintained, should learn skills they could teach others and use to become productive members of the community.

Hampton Normal and Agricultural Institute was founded in 1868 in Virginia and was dominated for decades by Samuel Chapman Armstrong, a white missionary with paternalistic inclinations. Hampton trained legions of African Americans and Native Americans to teach skills and embrace hard work, diligence, and Christian morality. Armstrong stressed learning trades, such as shoemaking, carpentry, tailoring, and sewing. Hampton placed little emphasis on critical or independent thinking. Instead, students were taught to conform to middle-class values. Armstrong cautioned against black involvement in politics and acquiesced to Jim Crow racial practices. The chapel walls at Hampton featured pictures of Robert E. Lee and Andrew Johnson.

Booker T. Washington and the Tuskegee Model

Hampton's foremost graduate was Booker T. Washington, who became the nation's leading apostle of industrial training and one of the most remarkable men—black or white—in American history. Washington was born a slave in western Virginia in 1856. His father was an unknown white man. His mother, Jane, raised him in an unimpressive but tidy cabin built of split logs on a small farm. As a child, he worked at a salt works, in coal mines, and as a houseboy for a prominent white family. He learned to read and write at a local school.

Intensely ambitious, Washington set off for Hampton Institute in 1872. While there, he was much affected by Armstrong, his curriculum, and his method of instruction. Washington worked his way through school and taught for two years at Hampton after graduating. In 1881 he accepted an invitation to found a black college in Alabama—Tuskegee Institute. The result was an institution that he forged almost single-handedly and that reflected his experience at Hampton and the influence of Armstrong.

From his arrival at Tuskegee until his death in 1915, Washington worked tirelessly to persuade black and white people that the surest way for black people to advance was by learning skills and demonstrating a willingness to do manual labor. In a famous speech at the Cotton States Exposition in Atlanta in 1895 (see Chapter 16), Washington told his segregated audience, "No race can prosper till it learns that there is as much dignity in tilling a field as in writing a poem. It is at the bottom of life we must begin, and not at the top." He believed that if black people acquired skills and became prosperous small farmers, artisans, and shopkeepers, they would earn the respect and acceptance of white

TABLE 15-1 SOUTH CAROLINA'S BLACK AND WHITE PUBLIC SCHOOLS, 1908–1909

Black Schools		White Schools
2,354	Public Schools	2,712
894	Men Teachers	933
1,802	Women Teachers	3,247
181,095	Total Pupils	153,807
123,481	Average Attendance	107,368
77	Pupils per School	55
63	Pupils per Teacher	35
14.7	Average Number of Weeks of School	25.2
$118.17	Average Yearly Salary for Men Teachers	$479.79
$91.45	Average Yearly Salary for Women Teachers	$249.13
$308,153.16	Total Expenditures	$1,590,732.51

SOURCE: *Department of Education Annual Report, South Carolina, 1908–09, 935, 961.*

School for most southern black students and teachers was a part-time activity. Because of the demands of agriculture, few rural students, black or white, attended school more than six months a year. Few teachers were graduates of four-year college programs. In urban communities and the Upper South, the school year lasted longer and education was better financed. But all public southern schools were segregated.

Read on MyHistoryLab Document: Booker T. Washington, The Atlanta Exposition Address (1895)

15-1

15-2

15-3

15-4

15-5

15-6

15-7

15-8

Read on **MyHistoryLab Document:** Booker T. Washington Advocates Industrial Education for Blacks, 1895

Booker T. Washington was by 1900 the most influential black leader in America. White business and political leaders were reassured by his message that black people themselves were responsible for their economic progress and that people of color should avoid a direct challenge to white supremacy. Although W. E. B. Du Bois appreciated Washington's commitment to the advancement of black people, he believed more emphasis should be placed on developing an educated elite who would take the lead in solving the race problem. Washington was a southerner who looked for practical solutions to the problems of everyday life; Du Bois was a northerner who stressed the need for intellectual advancement.

Read on **MyHistoryLab Document:** W. E. B. Du Bois Describes the Role of the "Talented Tenth" in Black Life, 1903

Americans and eradicate the race problem—all without unseemly protest and agitation.

White political leaders and philanthropists, who were more inclined to support the promotion of trades and skills among black people than an academic and liberal education, praised Washington's message. Steel magnate Andrew Carnegie, impressed by Washington, financed the construction of 29 buildings on the campuses of black schools and colleges. White railroad executive William H. Baldwin provided millions of dollars for black industrial education, and the John F. Slater Fund poured money into vocational education. Julius Rosenwald, the longtime head of Sears and Roebuck, consulted with Washington and contributed liberally to black education across the South. Disciples of Washington and graduates of Tuskegee fanned out across the South as industrial and agricultural training for black youngsters proliferated.

The Morrill Act, which Congress passed in 1862, entitled each state to the proceeds from the sale of federal land (most of it in the West) for establishing land-grant colleges to provide agricultural and mechanical training. However, southern states did not admit black students to their A&M (Agricultural and Mechanical) schools. In 1890, however, a second Morrill Act permitted states to establish and fund separate black land-grant colleges. The 1890 act accelerated the development of practical education through the appropriation of federal money to such institutions as Alcorn A&M in Mississippi, Florida A&M, Southern University in Louisiana, Langston in Oklahoma, and Tuskegee Institute. By 1915 there were 16 black land-grant colleges.

Most of the institutions were not actually colleges. Few of their students graduated with bachelor's degrees, and many of them were enrolled in primary and secondary programs. Most students at the black land-grant schools had to take courses in trades, agriculture, and domestic sciences. Most of the schools required students to do manual labor for which they were paid small sums. Students built and maintained the campuses and raised the food served in the school cafeteria. Many students were in the "normal" curriculum, which prepared them to teach at a time when most states did not require a college degree for a teaching certificate. Students in "normal" schools or programs earned a licentiate of instruction that certified them to teach.

Critics of the Tuskegee Model

Not everyone shared Washington's stress on industrial and agricultural training to the near exclusion of the liberal arts, including literature, history, philosophy, and languages. Washington's program, critics charged, seemed designed to train black people for a subordinate role. Black people, they worried, would continue to labor much as they had in slavery and not far removed from it.

W. E. B. Du Bois, a Fisk- and Harvard-trained scholar, and African Methodist Episcopal (AME) Bishop Henry M. Turner believed education went beyond mere training and the acquisition of skills. It involved intellectual growth. It would confront racial problems, and it would create wise men. According to Du Bois, "The function of the Negro college, then, is clear, it must maintain standards of popular education, it must seek the social regeneration of the Negro, and it must help in the solution of problems of race contact and cooperation. And finally, beyond all this, it must develop men."

Many of the private black colleges resisted the emphasis on agricultural and mechanical training. American Missionary Association schools such as Fisk, Talladega, and Tougaloo; AME schools such as Allen, Paul Quinn, and Morris Brown; and Methodist institutions such as Claflin, Bennett, and Rust still promoted the liberal arts and taught Latin, Greek,

VOICES Thomas E. Miller and the Mission of the Black Land-Grant College

In 1896 the South Carolina General Assembly established the Colored Normal, Industrial, Agricultural and Mechanical College of South Carolina. It derived funds from the Morrill Acts of 1862 and 1890 and from the state itself. Its first president was former black congressman and lawyer Thomas E. Miller. In an address to the Bamberg County Colored Fair in 1897, Miller embraced the Hampton and Tuskegee models as he described the mission of his institution:

> The work of our college is along the industrial line. We are making educated and worthy school teachers, educated and reliable mechanics, educated, reliable and frugal farmers. We teach your sons and daughters how to care for and milk the cows, how to make gilt-edged butter, how to make cheese, what kind of fertilizer each crop needs, the natural strength and productive qualities of the various soils, and last to make a compost heap and how to take care of it. We teach them

how to make a wagon, plow and hoe, how to shoe a horse and nurse him when sick. We teach your children how to keep books and typewrite, we teach your girls how to make a dress or undergarment, how to cook, wash and iron. We teach your boys how to make and run an engine, how to make and control electricity, we teach them mechanical and artistic drawing, house and sign painting.

1. **Given the racism of the 1890s, why was or wasn't agricultural and mechanical training the most suitable education for most black youngsters?**
2. **If a young black person did learn the skills Miller mentioned, was he or she educated for an inferior place in society?**

SOURCE: I. A. Newby, *Black Carolinians, A History of Blacks in South Carolina from 1895 to 1968* (Columbia: University of South Carolina Press, 1973), 263.

---

mathematics, and natural sciences. Henry L. Morehouse of the American Baptist Home Missionary Society explained that the purpose of education was to develop strong minds. He believed gifted intellectuals—a "talented tenth" as he characterized them in 1896—could lead people forward. Du Bois likewise stressed the need for the best-educated 10 percent of the black population to promote progress and advance the race.

Washington did not deny the importance of a liberal arts education, but he believed industry was the foundation to progress:

> On such a foundation as this will grow habits of thrift, a love of work, economy, ownership of property, bank accounts. Out of it in the future will grow practical education, professional education, and positions of public responsibility. Out of it will grow moral and religious strength. Out of it will grow wealth from which alone can come leisure and the opportunity for the enjoyment of literature and the fine arts.

Ultimately, however, Washington was wrong to believe education for black people that focused on economic progress would earn the respect of most white Americans. As Du Bois explained, most white people preferred ignorant and unsuccessful black people to educated and prosperous ones:

> If my own city of Atlanta had offered it to-day the choice between 500 Negro college graduates—forceful, busy, ambitious men of property and self-respect—and 500 black cringing vagrants and criminals, the popular vote in favor of the criminals would be simply overwhelming. Why? Because they want Negro crime? No, not that they fear Negro crime less, but that they fear Negro ambition and success more. They can deal with crime by chain gang and lynch law, or at least they think they can, but the South can conceive neither machinery nor place for the educated, self-reliant, self-assertive black man.

As Chapter 16 discusses, the disagreement among black leaders over education would expand by the early twentieth century into a larger controversy. What began as a conversation over the value of practical education became a passionate debate among Washington, Du Bois, and others over the most effective strategy—accommodation or confrontation—for overcoming Jim Crow and white supremacy.

Church and Religion

15-3 **What role did religion play in the lives of African Americans and in their adjustment to discrimination?**

In a world in which white people so thoroughly dominated the lives and limited the possibilities of black people, the church had long been the most important institution—after the family—that African Americans controlled for themselves. After the Civil War, black people organized their own churches and religious denominations, which thrived as sources of spiritual comfort and centers of social activity. Black clergymen were often the most influential members of the black community.

In 1890 the South had more black Baptists than all other denominations combined. Baptist congregations were more independent and under less supervision by church hierarchy than other denominations. Bishops, for example, in the African Methodist Episcopal Zion Church and the AME Church exercised considerable authority over congregations, as did Methodist and Presbyterian leaders. Many black people (and many southern white people) preferred the autonomy of the Baptist churches (Figure 15–2).

But whatever the denomination, the church was integral to the lives of most black people. It fulfilled spiritual needs through sermons and music. It enabled black people, free from white interference, to plan, organize, and lead. It was a sanctuary for black women, who immersed themselves in church activities. Although church members usually had little money to spare, they helped the sick, the bereaved, and those in need. Congregations also helped thousands of youngsters attend school and college.

The church service itself was the most important aspect of religious life for most black congregations. Parishioners were expected to participate and not merely listen quietly to the minister's sermon. Black people had long considered white church services too sedate. One black school principal believed black people gave added meaning to Christianity; whereas "the white man gives it system, logic and abstraction, the Negro is necessary to impart feeling, sanctioned emotions, heart throes and ecstasy." In most black churches, members punctuated the minister's call with many an "Amen." They testified, shouted, laughed, cried, and sometimes fainted. Choirs provided joyful music and solemn songs.

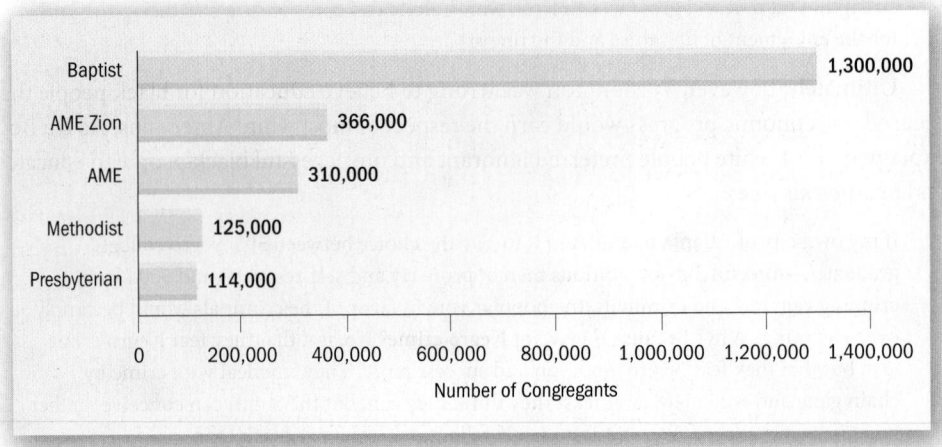

FIGURE 15–2 CHURCH AFFILIATION AMONG SOUTHERN BLACK PEOPLE, 1890
The vast majority of black southerners belonged to Baptist, Methodist, and Presbyterian congregations in the late nineteenth century, although there were about 15,000 black Episcopalians and nationwide perhaps 200,000 black Roman Catholics.

SOURCE: *Edward L. Ayers, The Promise of the New South, 160–61.*

Most congregations did not want scholarly sermons or theologically sound addresses. When Frederick Jones, a well-dressed new black minister in North Carolina, offered a deliberate message brimming with rationality, he was met with silence and rebuked by a senior member of the congregation: "Dese fellers comes out heah wid dere starched shirts, and dey' beaver hats, and dere kid gloves, but dey don't know nuffin b[o]ut 'ligion." The next time Jones preached, he had changed his clothes and delivered a passionate sermon.

Many black ministers had little or no education. Benjamin E. Mays's father told him the clergy did not need an education: "God called men to preach; and when He called them, He would tell them what to say!" Unqualified clergymen who relied on ungrammatical and rhetorical appeals disturbed some black leaders. In 1890 Booker T. Washington claimed that "three-fourths of the Baptist ministers and two-thirds of the Methodists are unfit, either mentally or morally, or both, to preach the Gospel to any one or to attempt to lead any one." W. E. B. Du Bois wanted black churches free of "the noisy and unclean leaders of the thoughtless mob" and the clergy replaced by thoughtful "apostles of service and sacrifice." But a black Alabama farmer observed that solemn and erudite preachers would not survive: "You let a man preach de true Gospel and he won't git many nickels in his pocket; but if he hollers and jumps he gits all the nickels he can hold and chickens besides."

A few black women led congregations. Nannie Helen Burroughs established Women's Day in Baptist churches. Women delivered sermons and guided the parishioners. But she complained that Women's Day quickly became more an occasion to raise money than to raise women.

Nannie Helen Burroughs and other black women came together at the Banner State Woman's National Baptist Convention in the early twentieth century. In addition to her involvement with the Baptist women's movement, Burroughs was devoted to industrial education as well as voting rights for black men and women. She was also active with the National Association of Colored Women, serving as the chair of its anti-lynching committee.

The Church as Solace and Escape

For many black people, the emotional involvement in church services was an escape from their dreary and oppressive daily lives. Growing up in rural South Carolina, Benjamin E. Mays admitted that his Baptist preacher, James F. Marshall, who barely had a fifth-grade education, "emphasized the joys of heaven and the damnation of hell" and that the "trials and tribulations of the world would all be over when one got to heaven." But such messages helped to assuage the impact of white supremacy: "Beaten down at every turn by the white man, as they were, Negroes could perhaps not have survived without this kind of religion."

Clergymen like Marshall refused to challenge white supremacy. Even veiled comments might invite retaliation or lynching. When a visiting minister began to criticize white people to Marshall's congregation, Marshall immediately stopped him. Despite the reluctance of many black clergymen to advocate improvement in race relations, many white people still viewed black religious gatherings as a threat. Black churches were burned and black ministers assaulted and killed with tragic regularity in the late nineteenth-century South.

Black clergymen, like their white counterparts, often stressed middle-class values to their congregations while suggesting that many black people found themselves in shameful situations because of their sinful ways. They urged them to improve their behavior. The black clergyman at Mount Ever Rest Colored Church in rural Mississippi warned his congregation to stop "cussin; lyin; stealin; crap shootin; whisky drinkin; and backbiting one another to de white folks." Black people who had acquired sinful reputations sometimes received funeral sermons that consigned them to eternal damnation. As Benjamin Mays recalled, "The church was usually full at funerals, especially if the deceased had been well known; and when a man of bad reputation died the church was jammed."

Some black clergy publicly opposed white supremacy and insisted that black people stand up for their rights. Bishop Henry M. Turner persistently spoke out on racial matters. In 1883, after the Supreme Court declared the 1875 Civil Rights Act unconstitutional, Turner called the Constitution "a dirty rag, a cheat, a libel and ought to be spit upon by every Negro in the land."

The Holiness Movement and the Pentecostal Church

Not all black people belonged to mainline denominations. For example, the Holiness movement and the emergence of Pentecostal churches affected Methodist and Baptist congregations. Partly in reaction to the elite domination and stiff authority of white Methodism, the Holiness movement gained a foothold among white people and spilled over among black southerners. Holiness churches ordained women such as Neely Terry to lead them. Holiness clergy preached that sanctification allowed a Christian to receive a "second blessing" and feel the "perfect love of Christ." Believers thus achieved an emotional reaffirmation and a new state of grace.

The Church of God in Christ (COGIC) became the leading black Holiness church. After successful revivals in Mississippi and Memphis, two black former Baptists—Charles Harrison Mason and C. P. Jones—founded COGIC in 1907. However, Mason was expelled after reporting that "a flame touched [his] tongue," and his "language changed." He had spoken in tongues. Mason then organized the Pentecostal General Assembly of the Church of God in Christ, and he assigned black men as bishops in Mississippi, Arkansas, Texas, Missouri, and California. In 1911 Mason appointed Lizzie Woods Roberson to lead the Woman's Department, a post she held until 1945. She transformed it into a financial powerhouse for COGIC.

In the meantime, Charles Fox Parham, a white minister, had founded the Pentecostal church in the early twentieth century in Texas. William J. Seymour, who was born a slave in Louisiana, played a key role in the development of the church. After hearing black people speak in tongues in Houston, he went to Los Angeles, where he and others also began to speak in tongues. There he founded what became the Pentecostal church, which grew rapidly.

Charles Harrison Mason joined the Pentecostal movement, and under his leadership the Reorganized COGIC became the leading Pentecostal denomination. It soon spread across the South among black and white people. Although there were tensions between black and white believers, the Pentecostal church was the only significant movement that crossed the racial divide in early twentieth-century America.

Roman Catholics and Episcopalians

Most African Americans belonged to one of the Baptist or Methodist churches. Booker T. Washington reportedly observed that "if a black man is anything but a Baptist or Methodist, someone has been tampering with his religion." Nevertheless, black people also belonged to other churches and denominations—or to no organized religious group.

About 200,000 African Americans were Roman Catholics in 1890. However, they were rarely fully accepted by the church or white Catholics. In the South, they were segregated in separate churches with separate parish schools.

The most prominent black Catholics came from the Healy family. Eliza Clark was a slave who had nine children by Michael Healy, an Irish-Catholic plantation owner in Georgia. Unlike many white men, Healy genuinely

Although he rarely mentioned it, James A. Healy's mother was black and a slave. He graduated from Holy Cross College, was ordained a Roman Catholic priest in Paris in 1854, and became the Bishop of Portland, Maine, in 1875.

© College of The Holy Cross Archives & Special Collections.

PROFILE Henry McNeal Turner

HENRY MCNEAL TURNER began as a supporter of racial harmony and a patriot. As he aged, however, he became disenchanted with the way white Americans contradicted their professed dedication to the principles of fairness and justice by their treatment of black Americans.

Turner was born to free black parents in Newberry, South Carolina, in 1834. After his father's death, he worked in cotton fields and learned to be a blacksmith and carriage maker. He also learned to read and write. Drawn to religion, he was licensed to preach by the Methodist Episcopal Church, a white denomination. In 1859 he moved to Baltimore and was ordained in the AME Church. He then became pastor of Union Bethel Church, the largest black congregation in Washington, DC. During the Civil War, he was a chaplain with the First Regiment of U.S. Colored Troops.

After the war, he briefly worked for the Freedmen's Bureau in Georgia. In an Emancipation Day address in Savannah in 1866 he praised the American flag and predicted that white people would soon accept black people.

Turner became active in Republican politics and was elected to the 1867–1868 Georgia constitutional convention, where he was the only black delegate to favor a literacy requirement for voting. He also supported a measure to help white planters who had not paid their taxes to keep their land. He conceded that "no man in Georgia has been more conservative than I. Anything to please white folks has been my motto."

In 1868 Turner was elected to the Georgia House of Representatives. When white legislators voted to remove the 32 black representatives, he objected: "I shall neither fawn nor cringe before any party, nor stoop to beg for my rights. . . . I am here to demand my rights, and to hurl thunderbolts at the men who dare to cross the threshold of my manhood." The black lawmakers were reinstated.

In 1880 he was elected one of the 12 bishops in the AME Church and became president of Morris Brown College in Atlanta, where he served until 1900. He also became an advocate of emigration to Africa and the Liberian Exodus of 1877. Turner supported women's suffrage and ordained a woman as a deacon in the AME Church in 1888, but the AME Council of Bishops withdrew the appointment.

Turner had little tolerance for those who considered Christianity a white man's religion. He asserted that "God is a Negro" and attacked those who "believe God is a white-skinned, blue-eyed, projecting-nosed, compressed-lipped, and finely-robed white gentleman."

He helped establish and edited a monthly AME newspaper, the *Voice of Missions.* In its pages he took a black nationalist stance and criticized white supremacy and lynching. Growing older and angrier, he told black readers to attack white predators: "Let every Negro in this country who has a spark of manhood in him supply his house with one, two, or three guns . . . and when your domicile is invaded . . . turn loose your missiles of death and blow the fiendish wretches into a thousand giblets."

He denounced black soldiers who fought to suppress the Philippine Insurrection: "I boil over with disgust when I remember that colored men from this country . . . are there fighting to subjugate a people of their own color. . . . I can scarcely keep from saying that I hope the Filipinos will wipe such soldiers from the face of the earth. . . . To go down there and shoot innocent men and take the country away from them, is too much for me to think about."

Embittered and tired, Turner lost faith in the intentions of white people and no longer praised the flag: "I used to love what I thought was the grand old flag, and sing with ecstasy about the Stars and Stripes, but to the Negro in this country the American flag is a dirty and contemptible rag. . . . Without multiplying words, I wish to say that hell is an improvement on the United States where the Negro is concerned."

Turner died of a heart attack in 1915. He was married four times, outliving three wives and all but two of his children.

15-1
15-2
15-3
15-4
15-5
15-6
15-7
15-8

15-1

15-2

15-3

15-4

15-5

15-6

15-7

15-8

cared for Eliza and their children, although by law he could not marry her. The children were educated in northern schools. James A. Healy graduated from the Jesuit-run Holy Cross College in Massachusetts and was ordained a priest in Paris in 1854. He later became a bishop in Portland, Maine.

Patrick Healy also attended Holy Cross and became the first black Jesuit priest in the United States. He served eight years as president of Georgetown University in Washington. Eliza Healy took vows as a nun and was the headmistress of a Catholic school in Vermont. Most white people were unaware of the racial ancestry of the Healys, and members of the family did not openly acknowledge being African American even when other black Catholics asked for their support. Bishop James Healy, for example, refused on three occasions to speak to the Congress of Colored Catholics, an association of black Catholics that met at least four times in northern cities between 1889 and 1893. Its members were mainly concerned with the discrimination they faced in the church and with the educational opportunities that were available—or more often not available—to black Catholic children in church schools.

Augustus Tolton was another African-American priest, and there was no question about his color. Because no American seminary would accept him, he was educated and ordained in 1886 in Rome. For a time, he presided over a parish in Quincy, Illinois, made up mainly of Irish and German Catholics. Unlike Bishop Healy, Tolton did speak to the Congress of Colored Catholics in Philadelphia in 1892.

Mother Mathilda Beasley came from a prominent free black family in Savannah. Her efforts to establish a community of Franciscan nuns in rural Georgia ultimately failed. In New Orleans, where there were many black Catholics of French and Spanish descent, the Sisters of the Blessed Sacrament established a black high school in 1915 that became Xavier University in 1925.

Fairly or not, most African Americans identified black Episcopalians with wealth and privilege. Many black Episcopalians traced their heritage to free black families before the Civil War. By 1903 approximately 15,000 members of black Episcopal parishes worshipped in Richmond, Raleigh, Charleston, and other cities in the North and South.

Red versus Black: The Buffalo Soldiers

15-4 Why did black men in the U.S. Army engage in combat against Native Americans, the Spanish, and Filipinos?

After the Civil War, the U.S. Army was reduced to fewer than 30,000 troops. Congressional Democrats tried to eliminate black soldiers from this small force, but Radical Republicans, led by Massachusetts Senator Henry Wilson, kept the military open to black men. The Army Reorganization Act of 1869 maintained 21 white regiments and four all-black regiments: the 9th and 10th Cavalry Regiments and the 24th and 25th Infantry Regiments. These four regiments spent most of the next three decades on the western frontier. Nearly 12,500 black men served during the late nineteenth century in these segregated units commanded—as black troops had been during the Civil War—by white officers. Unlike in the Civil War, however, many of these white officers were southerners who frequently held black men in low regard.

Military service in the West was wretched for white troops and worse for black soldiers. Too often officers considered black troops lazy, undisciplined, and cowardly. Black regiments were assigned mainly to the New Mexico and Arizona territories and to west Texas because the army thought black people tolerated heat better than white people did. The ancestors of the slaves were "from the tropics," claimed Quartermaster General Montgomery C. Meigs, and "not from the Northern or Southern extremities of Africa but from the Torrid Zone almost entirely." Most black soldiers were thus compelled to endure the hot, dry, and

15-1
15-2
15-3
15-4
15-5
15-6
15-7
15-8

MAP 15–1 MILITARY POSTS WHERE BLACK TROOPS SERVED, 1866–1917
Black troops in the 9th and 10th Cavalries and the 24th and 25th Infantries were
assigned almost exclusively to western military posts from the end of the Civil War until
the early twentieth century.

**Why were African-American troops assigned largely to isolated posts
on the western frontier?**

dusty Southwest desert. Others were sent to Kansas, Colorado, and the Dakotas, where they
confronted howling blizzards, subzero temperatures, and frostbite (see Map 15–1).

Discrimination in the Army

Black troops faced more hardships than adverse weather. The army provided them inferior
food and inadequate housing. Whereas white soldiers received dried apples and peaches,
canned tomatoes, onions, and potatoes, black troops were given foul beef, bad bread, and
canned peas unfit for human consumption. In 1867 white troops at Fort Leavenworth in
Kansas lived in barracks while black troops slept in tents on wet ground. Black regiments
were allotted used weapons and equipment. The army sent its worst horses—often old and
lame—to the black cavalry.

Long stretches of boredom, tedious duty, and loneliness marked army life for black and
white men in the West. Months might pass without combat. Desertion and alcoholism were
endemic, although black soldiers were less likely to desert or turn to drink than were white
troops. In 1877, for example, 18 men deserted from the all-black 10th Regiment, and 184
white soldiers deserted from the all-white 4th Regiment. Black troops realized that although

Listen on MyHistoryLab Audio: What the
Government Is Doing for Our Colored Boys

army life could be harsh and dangerous, it compared favorably to the civilian world, which held few opportunities for them. Army food was poor, but the private's pay of $13 per month was regular. Moreover, black troops developed immense pride as professional soldiers.

How African-American troops came to be identified as buffalo soldiers is uncertain. Comanche and Cheyenne Indians began to refer to black troops as "**buffalo soldiers**" in the 1870s, perhaps because the Plains Indians associated the hair of black men with the shaggy coat of the buffalo, a sacred animal. The wife of a white officer on the western frontier referred to buffalo soldiers in her personal correspondence. Famed artist and sculptor Frederic Remington described black troops as buffalo soldiers in an article in *Century Magazine* in 1889. The 10th Cavalry later displayed a buffalo in their unit emblem.

buffalo soldiers Four regiments of black soldiers that served with the U.S. Army on the western frontier from the 1870s to the 1890s. The Plains Indians called them the buffalo soldiers.

The Buffalo Soldiers in Combat

It was ironic that white military authorities would employ black men to subdue red people. Most black soldiers, however, had no qualms about fighting Indians, protecting white settlers and railroad construction gangs, or apprehending bandits and cattle rustlers. From the late 1860s to the early 1890s, the four black regiments repeatedly engaged hostile Indians. In September 1867, 700 Cheyenne attacked 50 Army scouts along a dry riverbed in eastern Colorado. The scouts held out for over a week until the 10th Cavalry rescued them. For more than 12 months in 1879 and 1880, the 9th and 10th Cavalries fought the Apaches under Chief Victorio in New Mexico and Texas in a campaign of raid and counterraid. The Apaches slipped across the Mexican border and then returned to southwest Texas. In clashes at Rattlesnake Springs and near Fresno Spring, the 10th killed more than 30 Apaches before Victorio fled again to Mexico, where the Mexican Army killed him. But the 9th and 10th Cavalries deserve most of the credit for his defeat, with their dogged pursuit for months over hundreds of miles of rugged terrain.

In 1879, however, 10th Cavalry troops protected Kiowa women and children from Texas Rangers. Black troops also protected Chickasaw and Cherokee farmers from Kiowa and Comanche bands.

In 1890 the 9th Cavalry was sent to the Pine Ridge Reservation in South Dakota, where Sioux Indians were holding a religious ceremony known as the Ghost Dance. Confined to reservations, some Indians—out of desperation and yearning for the past—believed their participation in the Ghost Dance would bring their ancestors and the almost extinct buffalo back to the Great Plains. White people would vanish, and Indian life would return to what it had been decades earlier. White authorities considered the Ghost Dance an act of defiance.

On December 29, the 7th Cavalry attempted to disarm the Sioux at Wounded Knee on the Pine Ridge Reservation. Shooting erupted, and 146 Indian men, women, and children—along with 26 soldiers—were killed. The 9th Cavalry, 108 miles away, rode the next day through a blizzard and arrived tired and freezing to come to the aid of the 7th Cavalry. The 9th spent the remainder of the winter guarding the Sioux. A black private, W. H. Prather, observed, "The Ninth, the Ninth were the first to come, will be the last to leave, we poor devils, and the Sioux are left to freeze."

Read on MyHistoryLab Document: Paul Laurence Dunbar, "The Colored Soldiers," 1896

Several black men who were in the 10th Cavalry enjoy some time to themselves near St. Mary's, Montana, in 1894. Within four years they would be in combat against Spanish troops in Cuba during the Spanish-American War.

Civilian Hostility to Black Soldiers

Despite the gallant performance of the buffalo soldiers, civilians frequently treated them with hostility. In Texas in 1875, Mexicans ambushed five black soldiers, killed two of them, and mutilated their bodies. The next day the infuriated white commander of the 9th Cavalry, Colonel Edward Hatch, rode out with 60 soldiers and apprehended the Mexicans. A local grand jury indicted nine of them for murder, but one was acquitted, and the other eight were released without a trial. Hatch, another white officer, and three buffalo soldiers were then indicted for breaking into and burglarizing the shack where the Mexicans had sought refuge. The charges were dropped, but the five men had to hire their own lawyers.

In 1877, 54 black troops from the 9th Cavalry intervened successfully in a political and ethnic dispute between white and Mexican residents of El Paso, Texas. The 9th was also dispatched to police the so-called Johnson County War in Wyoming between big and small ranchers in 1890. One of the state's U.S. senators, who favored the big ranchers, arranged the deployment of black troops; their presence angered the small ranchers, as it was intended to do. Racial violence and bloodshed soon erupted between residents of the town of Suggs, who had run two black soldiers out of town, and several of the soldiers who had disobeyed orders. The troops were withdrawn after the town was shot up and one soldier killed.

A west Texas newspaper, the *Bellville Countryman,* summarized the attitudes of many white westerners when it complained that "the idea of a gallant and high-minded people being ordered and pushed around by an inferior, ignorant race is shocking to the senses."

Brownsville

One of the worst examples of hostility to black troops, the so-called **Brownsville affair**, also occurred in Texas. In 1906 the 1st Battalion of the 25th Infantry was transferred from Nebraska to Fort Brown in Brownsville, Texas, along the Rio Grande. The black soldiers immediately encountered discrimination from both white people and Mexicans in this border community. More than four out of five of Brownsville's residents were Hispanic. Black people were not permitted in public parks, and white businesses refused to serve them. Civilians provoked and attacked black soldiers.

Shortly after midnight on August 14, about 150 shots were fired in Brownsville. One man died, and a Hispanic policeman and the editor of a Spanish-language newspaper were injured. Black troops were blamed for the violence when clips and cartridges from the army's Springfield rifles were found in the street. Two military investigations concluded that black soldiers did the shooting. The army could not identify the specific soldiers responsible because no one would confess or name the alleged perpetrators.

With no hearing or trial, President Theodore Roosevelt dismissed three companies of black men—167 soldiers—from the army. They were barred from rejoining the military and from government employment and were denied veterans' pensions or benefits. The black community, which had supported Roosevelt, reacted angrily. Booker T. Washington, a Roosevelt supporter, wrote, "There is no law, human or divine, which justifies the punishment of an innocent man." Washington added, "I have the strongest faith in the President's honesty of intention, high mindedness of purpose, sincere unselfishness and courage, but I regret for all these reasons all the more that this thing has occurred."

Republican Senator James B. Foraker of Ohio led a Senate investigation that upheld Roosevelt's dismissals. But Foraker, an opponent of Roosevelt, questioned the guilt of the black men. The clips and cartridges that served as evidence were apparently planted. After Roosevelt left office in 1909, the War Department reinstated 14 of the soldiers. In 1972 the Justice Department determined that an injustice had occurred. The black soldiers were posthumously awarded honorable discharges. Congress awarded the only survivor of the Brownsville affair—Dorsie Willis—$25,000 and the right to treatment at veterans' facilities.

Brownsville affair In 1906, a shooting in Brownsville, Texas, was blamed on black soldiers from the 25th Infantry Regiment. President Theodore Roosevelt summarily dismissed 167 black men from the U.S. Army. Later investigations exonerated the men.

African Americans in the Navy

Naval service was even more unappealing than life in the army. In the late nineteenth century, as the navy made the transition from timber and sail to steam and steel, approximately one sailor in 10 was a black man. Although warships were technically integrated, in that black and white sailors served on them together, white sailors were often hostile to

15-1
15-2
15-3
15-4
15-5
15-6
15-7
15-8

15-1

15-2

15-3

15-4

15-5

15-6

15-7

15-8

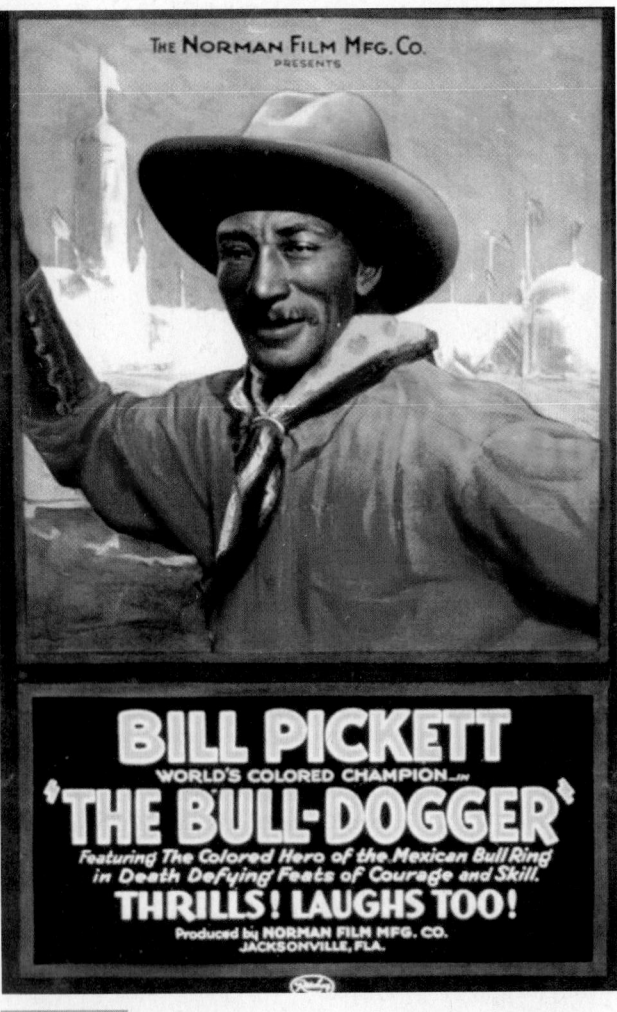

Bill Pickett was an authentic cowboy who became one of the first black movie stars. "The Bull-Dogger" was a 1922 black-and-white silent film aimed at attracting black audiences. (No copies of the film are known to have survived.) Pickett's skill as a bull-dogger was legendary. He would ride alongside a steer, jump off his horse, and grab the animal by the horns. He then wrestled it to the ground by sharply biting the animal's upper lip or nose. Pickett was the hit of the 1904 Cheyenne Frontier Days rodeo in Wyoming.

black sailors. They would not eat or bunk with them or take orders from them. Increasingly, and to enforce a de facto shipboard segregation, black sailors were restricted to stoking boilers and to cooking and serving food to white sailors.

James Conyers was the first black man to enroll as a midshipman at the U.S. Naval Academy in 1872. He faced intense ostracism, and resigned in 1873. Seventy-six years later, in 1949, Wesley A. Brown became the first African American to graduate from the Naval Academy.

The Black Cowboys

Black men before, during, and after the Civil War were familiar with horses and mules. As slaves, they tended animals. Black cavalrymen gained experience with horses. By the 1870s and 1880s, black men joined Mexicans, Native Americans, and white men on the long cattle drives from Texas to Kansas, Nebraska, and Missouri. There were probably no more than a few hundred black cowboys in the late nineteenth and early twentieth centuries.

Tending cattle was monotonous, difficult, and dirty work. Yet it required skill as a rider to manage hundreds of ornery and stinking animals. Cowboys had to tolerate weather that ranged from incredibly hot to bitter cold. They had to eat unappetizing food. There was no bed to sleep in each night, and their closest companion was often the horse they rode.

Black cowhands sometimes endured discrimination and abuse. They had to tame the toughest horses, work the longest hours, and face hostility in saloons, hotels, brothels, and shops in towns like Dodge City, Abilene, or Cheyenne. Still, black cowboys earned the respect of white ranchers and cattle barons. Bose Ikard had been born a slave in Mississippi and went to work for Texas cattleman Charles Goodnight after the Civil War. Goodnight praised Ikard: "He was my detective, banker, and everything else in Colorado, New Mexico, and the other wild country I was in. . . . We went through some terrible trials during those four years on the trail. . . . [Ikard] was the most skilled and trustworthy man I had."

The Black Cowgirls

Several African-American women were "cowgirls." Johanna "Aunt Chona" was of black and Seminole Indian descent, and she rode side saddle and broke untamed horses in Texas. She called it "gentling" them. Henrietta Williams Foster—"Aunt Rittie"—was born a slave in Mississippi and sold to Texas slave owners. As an ex-slave she became an expert rider who could take control of a herd of cattle. Although lacking formal education, she served as a midwife and also treated injured animals. Small in stature, she could be tough, ornery, and would out-cuss most men.

Mary Fields—otherwise known as "Stagecoach Mary"—operated a stagecoach in Montana for eight years. An imposing woman at six feet tall and 200 pounds, she carried a 38 Smith and Wesson and took part in at least one shooting with an angry cowboy. She lived in Cascade, Montana into the twentieth century.

The Spanish-American War

With the West subdued by 1890, many Americans concluded that the United States should expand overseas. European nations had already carved out colonies in Africa and Asia. Many, but by no means all, Americans favored the extension of U.S. authority to Latin America and the Pacific. In 1893 the navy and American businessmen toppled the monarchy in Hawaii, and the United States annexed those islands in 1898.

The same year, the United States went to war to liberate Cuba from Spain. As in the Civil War, black men enlisted, fought, and died. Twenty-two black sailors were among the 266 men who died when the battleship USS *Maine* blew up in Havana harbor; this event helped trigger the war. Many black Americans were convinced, as they had been during previous wars, that their support for the war against Spain would reduce or even eliminate white hostility. E. E. Cooper, editor of the *Washington Colored American,* declared that the war would "cement the races into a more compact brotherhood through perfect unity of purpose and patriotic affinity." The war, he asserted, would help white Americans "unloose themselves from the bondage of race prejudice."

Many black and white Americans, however, questioned the American cause. Some black people saw the war as an effort to extend American racial practices, including Jim Crow, beyond U.S. borders. The Rev. George W. Prioleau, chaplain of the 9th Cavalry, wondered why black Americans supported what he considered a hypocritical war:

> Talk about fighting and freeing poor Cuba and of Spain's brutality. . . . Is America any better than Spain? Has she not subjects in her very midst who are murdered daily without a trial of judge or jury? Has she not subjects in her own borders whose children are half-fed and half-clothed, because their father's skin is black. . . . Yet the Negro is loyal to his country's flag.

Whether or not they harbored doubts, black men by the thousands served in the Spanish-American War and in the Philippine Insurrection that followed it. Shortly before war was declared, the army transferred its four black regiments from the West to Florida to prepare for combat in Cuba. President William McKinley also appealed for volunteers. The War Department designated four of the black volunteer units "immune regiments" because it believed that black men would tolerate the heat and humidity of Cuba better than white troops and that black people were immune or at least less susceptible to yellow fever, which was endemic to Cuba. (Mosquitoes carry yellow fever, but in 1898 most people believed the tropical Caribbean climate caused the disease.)

State militia (national guard) units were also called into federal service, and several states, including Alabama, Ohio, Massachusetts, Illinois, Kansas, Virginia, Indiana, and North Carolina, sent all-black militias, as well as white units. But Georgia's governor refused to permit that state's black militia to serve, and New York would not permit black men to enlist in its militia. The states typically followed the federal example and confined black men to all-black units commanded by white officers, but there were exceptions.

Black Officers

The buffalo soldiers of the 9th and 10th Cavalries and the 24th and 25th Infantries remained under white officers. But the men of several volunteer units insisted they be led by black officers: "No officers, no fight." So for the first time in American history, black men commanded all-black units: the 8th Illinois, the 23rd Kansas, and the 3rd North Carolina. Mindful that many people doubted black men's ability to lead, the colonel of the 8th Illinois cautioned his men, "If we fail, the whole race will have to shoulder the burden." The War Department also permitted black men to serve as lieutenants with other black volunteer units; however, all higher-ranking officers were white men. Charles Young, a black graduate of West Point, was given command of Ohio's 9th Battalion. He served with distinction and was promoted to colonel.

As black and white troops assembled in Georgia and Florida, black men soon realized a U.S. uniform did not lessen white prejudice. White civilians in Georgia killed four black men of the 3rd North Carolina. All-white juries acquitted those who were charged with the murders. After the white proprietor of a drug store in Lakeland, Florida, refused to serve a black soldier at the soda fountain, a mob of black troops gathered. The proprietor was pistol whipped, and a stray bullet killed another white man before the troops were disarmed. In Tampa, where the troops were embarking for Cuba, an all-night riot broke out after drunken white soldiers from Ohio used a black child for target practice. Twenty-seven black soldiers and three white soldiers were seriously wounded. When black troops of the 3rd Alabama regiment adopted an injured crow as the unit mascot, they named it Jim.

Most of the black units never saw combat. White military authorities considered black men unreliable and inadequately trained. Black volunteer units stayed behind in Florida when white units embarked for Cuba. However, the buffalo soldiers did go to Cuba, where they performed well despite the doubts and criticism of some white men. The Spanish troops were impressed enough to give the black men the nickname "smoked yankees."

"A Splendid Little War"

In the summer of 1898, U.S. troops arrived in Cuba. Black men of the 10th Cavalry fought alongside Cuban rebels, many of whom were black. Four black American privates earned the Congressional Medal of Honor. Black and white troops were best remembered for their role in the assault on San Juan and Kettle Hills overlooking Santiago in eastern Cuba. Santiago was the main Spanish naval base in Cuba, and its capture would break Spain's hold over the island.

In this assault, black soldiers from the 24th Infantry and the 9th and 10th Cavalries fought alongside white troops including Theodore Roosevelt's volunteer unit, the Rough Riders. In the fiercest fighting of the war, black and white men were thrown together under withering Spanish fire. Although the outcome was in doubt, they took the high ground overlooking Santiago harbor. White soldiers praised the black troops. One commented, "I am not a negro lover. My father fought with Mosby's Rangers [in the Confederate Army] and I was born in the South, but the negroes saved that fight." In his campaign for vice president in 1900, Theodore Roosevelt stated that black men saved his life during the battle. Later, however, he accused black men of cowardice.

After the War

As hostilities concluded, men of the 24th Infantry agreed to work in yellow fever hospitals after white regiments refused the duty. Some 471 black soldiers contracted yellow fever. Other black troops arrived in Cuba after the war to serve garrison duty. The 8th Illinois and the 23rd Kansas built roads, bridges, schools, and hospitals. The black men were especially pleased at the absence of Jim Crow in Cuba. Some black soldiers considered organizing emigration to Cuba, but nothing came of it. Still other black troops from the 6th Massachusetts joined in the invasion of Puerto Rico as the United States took that island from Spain.

The Philippine Insurrection

With the resounding victory in the war, many Americans decided their nation had an obligation to uplift those less fortunate peoples who had been part of the Spanish empire. Thus, President William McKinley insisted the United States acquire Guam, Puerto Rico, and the Philippines from Spain in the Treaty of Paris that ended the war in December 1898. The Filipinos, like the Cubans, had opposed Spanish rule and expected the American government to support their independence. When they learned that the United States intended to annex the Philippines, the Filipinos, under Emilio Aguinaldo, switched from fighting the Spanish to fighting the occupying U.S. forces.

Would Black Men Fight Brown Men?

Many black and white Americans denounced the effort to take the Philippines. They were unconvinced the Filipinos would benefit from American benevolence. Some wondered how African-American soldiers were helping to lessen racial oppression in the United States by oppressing the Filipinos. AME Bishop Henry Turner termed U.S. intervention in the Philippines an "unholy war of conquest," and Booker T. Washington believed the Filipinos "should be given an opportunity to govern themselves." In a grim attempt to taunt those who proclaimed the superiority of white civilization, a group of black men formed the "Black Man's Burden Association."

Listen on **MyHistoryLab Audio**: The Negro as Soldier

VOICES   Black Men in Battle in Cuba

On October 1, 1898, a letter appeared in the Illinois Record, *a black newspaper, from one of the men in the 10th Cavalry. The author was probably John E. Lewis, and he wrote the letter from Montauk Point on Long Island in New York, where black and white troops were sent after the war. Lewis described the enthusiastic reaction of the Rough Riders to the 9th and 10th Cavalries, but he complained that the black soldiers' contributions were too often ignored.*

The Rough Riders were mustered out on the 12th and 13th [of September], and when Colonel Roosevelt bade the regiment good-bye he paid a glowing tribute to the 9th and 10th Cavalry, especially in saving them from ambush.

Mr. Editor, if your readers could have heard the Rough Riders yell when the 10th Cav. was mentioned as the 'Smoked Yankees' and that they were of a good breed, they would have been doubly proud of the members of their race who rendered such signal service on the battle field. . . .

When a troop of the 10th made their famous charge of 3,000 yards under the command of Capt. [William J.] Beck, the non-commissioned officers, all colored, distinguished themselves in a manner that will redound to the glory of the race. Among those who distinguished themselves are Carter Smith, acting 1st Sergeant, Sgts. Geo. Taylor, James F. Cole, James H. Williams, Smith Johnson and Corpl. Joseph G. Mitchell who was wounded at San Juan.

All are soldiers whose names should go down in history. They never faltered in the thickest of the battle; they encouraged on in a rain of shot and shell and showed by their actions that they were the leaders. They did not hesitate to take the lead, and when that charge was made it was "save your cartridges, don't waste a shot."

The half will never be told of their deeds upon the battlefield. All deserve praise from the private up, but the praise has been given those who should have been in the lead instead of laying in the rear under cover. And yet they say that the black is not fit to lead.

If our war reports would only give credit where credit is due there would be no need writing these poorly composed lines that your readers might know of the deeds and hardships their dear ones have passed through.

You will read that colored troops, or companies did so and so, but the white papers never mention a name and the world only knows one who has done an act of bravery as a Negro soldier, nameless and friendless. It was never mentioned how, at that famous charge of the 10th Cav. And the rescue of the Rough Riders at San Juan Hill, the yell was started by a single trooper of C Troop, 10th Cav. and was carried down the line.

Brave 1st Sgt. Adam Huston at the head of his troop commanded "forward" which seemed into almost certain death. In him the troop found an able leader; Lieut. [E. D.] Anderson who was in command and fell to the rear and when the command "Forward March," was given, the brave Major [Theodore J.] Wint only smiled, for he admired bravery and did not change the command although he knew that the troops was in a desperate position. The troops were carried safely through. . . .

Will it ever be known how Sgt. Thomas Griffith of Troop C cut the wire fence along the line so that the 10th Cav. and Rough Riders could go through?

Never once did these brave men give thought to danger. . . .

The Spaniard would have sent our army home in disgrace had it not been for the daring and almost reckless charge of the Negro regiments. God was with them in that charge and no man who has ever seen the place will say that it was possible to make the charge without being slaughtered. . . .

[Unsigned]

1. **Why is the author of this letter bitter?**
2. **Why did black men fight in the Spanish-American War?**
3. **Does any of this account seem exaggerated or unreliable? Why or why not?**

SOURCE: Willard B. Gatewood Jr., *Smoked Yankees and the Struggle for Empire: Letters from Negro Soldiers, 1898–1902* (Urbana: University of Illinois Press, 1971), 76–78.

15-1
15-2
15-3
15-4
15-5
15-6
15-7
15-8

Nonetheless, black soldiers served throughout the campaign in the Pacific islands. The black troops included the regular 25th and 24th Infantries, the 9th Cavalry, and the 48th and 49th Volunteer Regiments. The Filipino rebels attempted to convince black troops to abandon the cause. Posters reminded "The Colored American Soldier" of injustice and lynching in the United States. White troops did not help by calling Filipinos "niggers." Although many black soldiers had reservations about the fighting, they remained loyal. When the conflict ended with an American victory in 1902, only five black men had deserted. David Fagen of the 24th Infantry joined Filipino forces and became an officer, fighting American troops for two years before he was killed. Two black men from the 9th Cavalry were executed for desertion. Fifteen white deserters had their death sentences commuted.

15-1
15-2
15-3
15-4
15-5
15-6
15-7
15-8

Although black men had served with distinction as professional soldiers for 40 years after the Civil War—on the frontier, in Cuba, and in the Philippines—the army little valued their achievements and sacrifice, as the Brownsville affair showed. White military and political leaders relied on passions and prejudices over evidence of achievement. These circumstances dashed the hopes of those black civilians and soldiers who believed the performance of black troops would demonstrate that black citizens had earned the same rights as other Americans.

Black Business People and Entrepreneurs

15-5 **What were the major developments among African Americans in businesses and labor unions in the struggle for equality?**

As the nineteenth century ended, the American people had become enthralled by their country's scientific, industrial, and agricultural progress. Their enthusiasm for these achievements was exemplified by the fairs and expositions held around the country between 1876 and 1916. Municipal leaders in Philadelphia, New Orleans, Atlanta, Nashville, Buffalo, and St. Louis, among others, were eager to capitalize on the curiosity of thousands of people who would visit these fairs and leave millions of dollars behind to enrich local businesses.

African Americans and the World's Columbian Exposition

There is no better example of this mania for fairs than the World's Columbian Exposition held in Chicago in 1893 to commemorate the four-hundredth anniversary of Christopher Columbus's first voyage to America. The Chicago fair was spectacular. Located on 600 acres on the city's south side, it featured 200 buildings and exhibits from 46 nations. At the center was the White City, a group of white buildings that were illuminated at night by electric lights. The fair's featured attraction was a huge 264-foot-high steel wheel designed by George Ferris that could carry 2,160 riders in its 36 passenger cars. The fair drew 27 million visitors between May and October 1893.

In promoting the technological progress of the American people, visitors enjoyed comparing their society to the other nations that had exhibits. The Dahomey village and its 69 Fon people was perhaps the most sensational and controversial among the fair's black and white visitors. One journalist captured the reaction of many white people to these Africans from a French colony when he wrote, "Sixty-nine of them are here in all their barbaric ugliness." Some African Americans were plainly embarrassed by what they considered a display of primitive culture. However, African Americans who visited the exposition found little overt discrimination or segregation as they took in the exhibits and attractions and dined in the restaurants.

Three black colleges created exhibits that were intended to depict the advances African Americans had achieved since the end of slavery. Wilberforce College won a Columbian Medal and Diploma for its display of academic work by its students that included examples of math, logic, and rhetoric as well as needlecraft and woodwork. The Atlanta University exhibit had photos of the campus with students engaged in nursing, home economics, and crafts. Hampton Institute's display featured dressmaking, tailoring, and woodwork. The Atlanta University representative at the fair proudly proclaimed that his institution's 300 feet of exhibition floor space showed "better than any others, what is being done for the race and what the race is doing for itself."

Colored American Day at the fair was held on August 25, 1893. Some African Americans, including Ida B. Wells, resented having a separate day for black people, and she criticized Frederick Douglass for agreeing to speak at that day's festivities. But the 75-year-old Douglass delivered a blunt address about race in America. He denounced Americans' commitment to white supremacy and their unjust treatment of people of color: "Men talk of the Negro problem. There is no Negro problem. The problem is whether the American people have honesty enough, loyalty enough, honor enough, patriotism enough to live up to their own Constitution."

Obstacles and Opportunities for Employment among African Americans

During planning for the Chicago fair, African Americans, including Ida B. Wells, complained that black people had been excluded on the committees that organized the exposition. But white people rarely elevated African Americans to positions of authority. Well-educated black men and women stood no chance of gaining employment with any major business or industrial corporation in the 1890s. White males not only monopolized management and supervisory positions, but also took nearly every job that did not involve manual labor. In 1899 black novelist Sutton E. Griggs described the frustrations that an educated black man encountered:

> He possessed a first class college education, but that was all. He knew no trade nor was he equipped to enter any of the professions. . . . He would have made an excellent drummer, [salesman] clerk, cashier, government official (county, city, state, or national), telegraph operator, conductor, or anything of such a nature. But the color of his skin shut the doors so tight that he could not even peep in. . . . It is true that such positions as street laborer, hod carrier, cart driver, factory hand, railroad hand were open to him; but such menial tasks were uncongenial to a man of his education and polish.

Although white supremacy and Jim Crow restricted opportunities for educated black people, those same limitations enabled enterprising black men and women to open and operate businesses that served black clientele. By the early twentieth century, black Americans had established banks, newspapers, insurance companies, retail businesses, barbershops, beauty salons, and funeral parlors. Virtually every black community had its own small businesses, markets, street vendors, and other entrepreneurs.

Some black men and women established substantial businesses. In Atlanta, Union Army veteran Alexander Hamilton was a successful building contractor. He supervised construction of the Good Samaritan Building, oversaw the erection of buildings on the Morris Brown College campus, and built many impressive houses on Peachtree Street. Hamilton employed both black and white workmen.

Alonzo Herndon was a former slave who also thrived in Atlanta. His fashionable barbershop on Peachtree Street served well-to-do white men. The shop had crystal chandeliers and polished brass spittoons. Herndon opened two other shops, eventually employing 75 men. He also founded the Atlanta Life Insurance Company, the largest black stock company in the world.

In Montgomery, Alabama, H. A. Loveless, a former slave, became a butcher and then diversified by opening an undertaking establishment and a hack and dray company. By 1900, he also ran a coal and wood yard and sold real estate.

In Richmond, Maggie Lena Walker—the secretary-treasurer of the Independent Order of St. Luke, a mutual benefit society, and a founder of the St. Luke's Penny Savings Bank—became the wealthiest black woman in America. Also in Richmond, former slave John Dabney owned a catering business that served wealthy white Virginians. He catered two state dinners for President Grover Cleveland. He purchased houses and invested in real estate.

Madam C. J. Walker may have been the most successful black entrepreneur of them all. Born Sarah Breedlove in 1867 on a Louisiana cotton plantation, she married at age 14 and was a widowed single parent by age 20. She spent the next two decades struggling to make ends meet. In 1905 with $1.50, she developed a formula to nourish and enrich the hair of black women.

The business rapidly became a thriving enterprise that employed hundreds of black women. She established the company's headquarters in Indianapolis. In the meantime, she married Charles Joseph Walker and took his name and the title Madam. As she accumulated

15-1
15-2
15-3
15-4
15-5
15-6
15-7
15-8

In less than two decades in the early twentieth century, Sarah Breedlove rose from abject poverty to become extraordinarily wealthy as Madam C. J. Walker.

View on **MyHistoryLab Map:** Organizing American Labor in the Late Nineteenth Century

wealth, she shared it generously with Bethune Cookman College and Tuskegee Institute. She was a major contributor to the NAACP's anti-lynching campaign. When she died at age 51 in 1919, she was reportedly a millionaire.

Despite such successes, most black people who went into business had difficulty surviving. Too often they depended on black customers who were themselves poor. White-owned banks were unlikely to provide credit to black business people. And even the wealthiest black entrepreneurs did not come close to possessing the wealth the richest white Americans accumulated.

African Americans and Labor

Thousands of black southerners worked in factories, mills, and mines. Although most textile mills refused to hire black people except as janitors, many black laborers toiled in tobacco and cigar-making facilities, flour mills, coal mines, sawmills, and turpentine camps, and on railroads. Black women worked for white families as servants. Black workers usually were paid less than white men employed in the same capacity. Conversely, white working people frequently complained they were not hired because employers retained black workers who worked for less pay. In 1904 in Georgia, white railroad firemen struck in an attempt to compel management to dismiss black firemen. Antagonism between black and white laborers was chronic.

Unions

When white workers formed labor unions, they usually excluded black workers. The Knights of Labor, however, founded in 1869, was open to all workers (except whiskey salesmen, lawyers, and bankers), and by the mid-1880s counted 50,000 women and 70,000 black workers among its nearly 750,000 members. But by the 1890s, after unsuccessful strikes and a deadly riot in Chicago, the Knights had lost influence to a new organization, the American Federation of Labor (AFL). Founded in 1886, the AFL was ostensibly open to all skilled workers, but most of its local craft unions barred women and black tradesmen. In contrast, the United Mine Workers (UMW), formed in 1890, encouraged black coal miners to join the union rather than serve as strikebreakers. By 1900 approximately 20,000 of the 91,000 members of the UMW were black men. The Industrial Workers of the World, a revolutionary labor organization founded in 1905, brought black and white laborers together in, among other places, the Brotherhood of Timber Workers in the Piney Woods of east Texas.

In 1869 a Baltimore ship caulker, Isaac Myers, organized the National Colored Labor Union, which lasted for seven years. It discouraged strikes and encouraged its members to work hard and be thrifty. However, it lost whatever effectiveness it had when Republican leaders took it over during Reconstruction.

Strikes

During the late nineteenth and early twentieth centuries, most strikes failed because business owners could rely on strikebreakers and the police or national guard to bring the strikes to an often violent end. For a time, black shipyard workers in southern ports achieved success. Black stevedores who loaded and unloaded ships endured oppressive conditions and long hours for low pay. They periodically went on strike in Charleston, Savannah, and New Orleans. The Longshoremen's Protective Union in Charleston won several strikes in the 1870s. In Nashville in 1871 black dockyard workers went on strike, demanding 20 cents an hour. Steamboat owners broke the strike by hiring state convicts for 15 cents an hour.

Black and white laborers who toiled in the Louisiana sugarcane fields earned an average of $13 a week in the 1880s. They were paid in scrip—not cash—that was redeemable only in stores the planters owned, where prices were exorbitant. Workers lived in 12-by-15-foot cabins that they rented from the planters. In some ways, it was worse than slave labor.

15-1
15-2
15-3
15-4
15-5
15-6
15-7
15-8

PROFILE   Maggie Lena Walker

Maggie L. Walker

BY THE EARLY TWENTIETH CENTURY, MAGGIE LENA WALKER was a successful business-woman, community leader, and one of the wealthiest black women in America. She was also an ardent advocate for her race and her gender. She was born Maggie Mitchell in Richmond on July 15, 1867, to Elizabeth Draper, a laundress. Her mother married William Mitchell in 1870. Young Maggie was greatly influenced by the determination, fortitude, and hard work of her mother. Throughout her childhood, she helped her mother wash, iron, and carry laundry.

Maggie Mitchell graduated from a normal school in 1883 and taught primary school. She was a lifelong member of the First African Baptist Church. In 1886 she married Armstead Walker. Her views on marriage were progressive: "Since marriage is an equal partnership, I believe that the woman and the man are equal in power and should by consultation and agreement, mutually decide as to the conduct of the home and the government of the children."

The Independent Order of St. Luke was one of many black mutual aid societies that flourished in the nineteenth century. Black people contributed small sums, and the Order paid benefits either to members who became sick or to their survivors. But the Order was also a fraternal and social organization that stressed racial pride as well as compassion, generosity, and charity.

Maggie Lena Walker became active in the Order at age 14 in 1881. She was elected Grand Matron and became the Right Worthy Grand Secretary in 1899. When she assumed her duties, the Order had $31.61 and 1,080 members. She was a dynamic leader and an inspirational speaker. She traveled extensively and spoke to members. She stressed racial concerns and attacked discrimination and lynching. She appealed to audiences to patronize black enterprises. By the early twentieth century, under Walker's guidance, the Order operated in 22 states. Its membership had increased, and its financial standing had improved. In 1924 its funds totaled $3,480,540.

The Order ran a newspaper, the *St. Luke Herald,* and a bank with Walker as president. She was the first black woman to serve as the chief executive of a bank in the United States. The bank subsequently merged with two other banks and became the Consolidated Bank and Trust Company, with Walker as president. She was especially pleased that the bank enabled black customers to purchase homes. By 1920, 645 black families had acquired their houses with the bank's assistance.

Walker was concerned with the plight of black women and made certain that the Order employed black women in significant positions. In 1909 she paid homage to women of color:

> And the great all absorbing interest, this thing which has driven sleep from my eyes and fatigue from my body, is the love I bear women, our Negro women, hemmed, circumscribed, with every imaginable obstacle in our way, blocked and held down by the fears and prejudices of the whites, ridiculed and sneered at by the intelligent blacks.

Walker became wealthy and lived in a 22-room house. She was involved in community affairs and organizations. She supported Virginia Union University and the Industrial School for Colored Girls. She worked with the Piedmont Tuberculosis Sanitarium for Negroes, served on Richmond's Council for Colored Women and with the Virginia Federation of Colored Women's Clubs, and was among the prominent women who helped organize the Council of Women of the Darker Races. She joined the National Association of Colored Women in 1912 and was active in the NAACP. She was also a committed Republican and ran unsuccessfully for state superintendent of public instruction. She died on December 15, 1934.

Although the state militia had broken previous strikes, 9,000 black and 1,000 white workers responded in 1887 to a call by the Knights of Labor for a new strike. They quit the sugar fields in four parishes (as Louisiana counties are called) to demand more pay. The strike was peaceful, but the governor sent in the militia. The troops fired into a crowd at Pattersonville and killed four people. Local officials killed several strikers who had been taken prisoner. In Thibodaux, "prominent citizens" organized and armed themselves and had martial law declared. More than 35 unarmed black people, including women and children, were killed in their homes and churches. Two black strike leaders were lynched. The strike was broken.

Black washerwomen went on strike in Atlanta in 1881. The women, who washed laundry by hand for white families, refused to do any more until they were guaranteed $1 per 12 pounds of laundry. The strike was well organized through black churches, and it spread to cooks and domestics. A strike committee used persuasion and intimidation to ensure support. Some 3,000 black people joined the strike, and white families went two weeks without clean clothes. However, Atlanta's white community broke the strike. Police arrested strike leaders for disorderly conduct. Black women were fined from $5 to $20. The city council threatened to require each washerwoman to purchase a $25 business license. Although the strike ended without achieving its goal, it demonstrated that poor black women could organize effectively.

Black Professionals

15-6 | **What opportunities existed for African Americans in the legal and medical professions?**

Like business and labor, the medical and legal professions were strictly segregated. Most black physicians, nurses, and lawyers attended all-black professional schools in the late nineteenth century. Black people in need of medical care were either excluded from white hospitals or confined to all-black wards. Since black physicians were denied staff privileges at white hospitals, black people often formed their own hospitals. Most were small with 50 or fewer beds.

Medicine

In 1891 Dr. Daniel Hale Williams established Provident Hospital and Training Institute in Chicago, the first black hospital operated solely by African Americans. In 1894 the Freedmen's Hospital was organized in Washington, DC, and later affiliated with Howard University. Frederick Douglass Memorial Hospital and Training School was founded in Philadelphia in 1895. Dr. Alonzo McClennan and other black physicians established the Hospital and Training School for Nurses in Charleston, South Carolina, in 1897.

In 1900 Williams explained why black medical institutions were necessary:

> In view of this cruel ostracism, affecting so vitally the race, our duty seems plain. Institute Hospitals and Training Schools. Let us no longer sit idly and inanely deploring existing conditions. Let us not waste time trying to effect changes or modifications in the institutions unfriendly to us, but rather let us seek to promote the doctrine of helping and stimulating our race.

By 1890, 909 black (most of whom were male) physicians were practicing in the United States. They served a black population of 7.5 million people. Barred from membership in the American Medical Association, black doctors organized the National Medical Association in Atlanta in 1895. Most black doctors had been educated at seven black medical schools that included Leonard Medical School at Shaw University in Raleigh, Flint-Goodridge Medical College in New Orleans, Meharry Medical School in Nashville, and the Howard University School of Medicine in Washington, DC.

In 1910, in a report issued by the Carnegie Foundation for the Advancement of Teaching, Abraham Flexner recommended improving medical education in the United States by eliminating weaker medical schools. He suggested raising admission standards and expanding laboratory and clinical training in the stronger schools. As a result of these recommendations, 60 of 155 white medical schools closed; among black medical schools, only Howard and Meharry survived. By 1920 there were 3,885 black physicians. Many had completed medical school before the Flexner report was compiled.

The number of black women physicians was declining. In 1890, 90 black women were practicing medicine. By 1920 only 65 were. There were fewer medical schools, and most black and white men considered medicine an inappropriate profession for women. But black women also had to contend with the opposition of white women. Isabella Vandervall was a graduate of New York Medical College and Hospital who was accepted for an internship at the Hospital for Women and Children in Syracuse. When she appeared in person, however, the hospital's female administrator rejected Vandervall, declaring, "We can't have you here! You are colored!"

Nursing was different. By 1920 there were 36 black nurse training schools and 2,150 white nursing schools. White nurses resented the competition from black nurses for positions as private duty nurses. In addition, the black physicians who ran nurse training schools exploited their students by hiring them out, as part of their training, for private duty work but requiring them to relinquish their pay to the schools. Moreover, many people—black and white—regarded black nurses more as domestics than as trained professionals. To confront such obstacles, 52 black nurses met in New York City in 1908 and formed the National Association of Colored Graduate Nurses (NACGN). By 1920 the NACGN had 500 members.

Black physicians and nurses struggled to provide medical care to people who were often desperately ill and sought treatment only as a last resort. Disease and sickness flourished among people who were ill nourished, poorly clad, and inadequately housed. Tuberculosis, pneumonia, pellagra, hookworm, and syphilis afflicted many poor black people—as they also did poor white people. Bessie Hawes, a 1918 graduate of Tuskegee Institute's Nurse Training program, described the situation she faced in rural Alabama:

> A colored family of ten were in bed and dying for the want of attention. No one would come near. I was glad of the opportunity. As I entered the little country cabin, I found the mother in bed. Three children were buried the week before. The father and the remainder of the family were running a temperature of 102–104. Some had influenza, others had pneumonia. No relatives or friends would come near. I saw at a glance I had work to do. I rolled up my sleeves and killed chickens and began to cook. . . . I milked the cow, gave medicine, and did everything I could to help conditions. I worked day and night trying to save them for seven days. I had no place to sleep. In the meantime the oldest daughter had a miscarriage and I delivered her without the aid of any physicians. . . . I only wished that I could have reached them earlier and been able to have done something for the poor mother.

The Law

Unlike black physicians and nurses, who were excluded from white hospitals, black lawyers were permitted to practice in what was essentially a white male court system. But white judges and attorneys did not welcome them. Black defendants and plaintiffs often retained white lawyers in the hope that white legal counsel might improve their chances of receiving justice. As a result, many black attorneys had a hard time making a living from the practice of law.

The American Bar Association (ABA) would not admit black attorneys to membership. William H. Lewis, a graduate of Amherst College and the Harvard Law School who was appointed an assistant U.S. attorney general by President William Howard Taft in 1911, was expelled by the ABA in 1912 when its leaders discovered he was black. They defended his expulsion by claiming the association was mainly a social organization. In 1925 black lawyers—led by Howard Law School graduate George H. Woodson—organized the National Bar Association.

Lutie A. Lytle graduated from the Central Tennessee College of Law and passed the bar examination. She became a member of the faculty at the same institution, and thus was the first African-American woman to become a professor of law in an American law school.

PROFILE A Man and His Horse: Dr. William Key and Beautiful Jim Key

MORE THAN FIVE MILLION PEOPLE visited the 1904 St. Louis World's Fair. Perhaps the most popular attraction was a horse, Beautiful Jim Key, and his African-American owner, Dr. William Key.

On the fair's opening day, President Theodore Roosevelt's feisty 20-year-old daughter Alice, accompanied by Congressman Nicholas Longworth, went to see the horse that had captured the hearts and minds of hundreds of thousands of Americans over the previous seven years. Using his mouth, Beautiful Jim Key plucked the correct letters from a metal frame that contained the alphabet and arranged them to spell "Alice Roosevelt." Then, prompted by a member of the audience, the horse added "Longworth" to Roosevelt's name. It was prophetic. Two years later the Republican congressman married the president's daughter, and she became Alice Roosevelt Longworth.

William Key was born a slave in Winchester, Tennessee, in 1833, the son of a slave woman who had Cherokee ancestry and a white man. From childhood, Key demonstrated an ability to work with and care for animals. He became a self-taught veterinarian whom local black and white people called "Dr. Key."

He also learned the art of diplomacy. During the Civil War he simultaneously helped slaves escape while protecting his owner's two sons who went off to fight for the Confederacy. For these latter efforts, he was arrested by Union officials and threatened with hanging.

Following the war and emancipation, Key acquired enough wealth as a veterinarian to purchase land near Shelbyville, Tennessee. A shrewd businessman and gambler, he sold patent medicine—Keystone Liniment—and regularly won at poker. Dr. Key also purchased an Arabian horse that had been relegated to circus acts in Mississippi. He bred the neglected and weary mare, and she produced a sickly, scrawny colt in 1889 that he named Beautiful Jim Key. Through years of kind training, Key transformed this unimpressive horse into a splendid, talented animal.

The veterinarian had an uncanny capacity to communicate with Beautiful Jim Key, sometimes through indecipherable Cherokee and African words. The horse could add, subtract, multiply, and divide numbers that totaled less than 30. In one show he was asked to multiply four times five, then add five, and subtract three. He promptly plucked the card with 22 from the rack, causing one journalist to wonder, "What will he learn next, square roots?" The brainy horse learned the alphabet and how to read basic names and words. Asked by audience members, he spelled such words as "physics," "constitution," and "Pennsylvania." He could make change by selecting the correct coins out of a specially built National Cash Register.

In 1897 a white entrepreneur and showman from Cincinnati, Albert Rogers, persuaded Dr. Key to collaborate with him, and Rogers managed and promoted the black veterinarian and his horse for the next decade. Key and Rogers stressed the kind and gentle treatment of animals before virtually every audience. (Key never used a whip.) Beautiful Jim Key was eventually inducted into honorary membership in the American Humane Association, its only nonhuman member.

But Beautiful Jim Key's intelligence and knowledge attracted the crowds. In 1897 President William McKinley visited the Nashville World's Fair and sat amazed in the Negro Building as Beautiful Jim Key selected the names of cabinet members from a rack as they were read to him.

With the emergence of Jim Crow, Dr. Key and his horse performed before segregated audiences across the South. When William Key would hold special shows "open to all," the audience was invariably all black.

There were those who doubted the intelligence of Beautiful Jim Key. Some thought the doctor had devised secret means of communicating answers to the horse. In 1901 a group of Harvard professors scrutinized Beautiful Jim Key. After witnessing two performances, the scholars declared that no trickery was involved. Dr. Key had simply educated an intelligent animal.

The man and his horse finally retired to the Key estate near Shelbyville. William Key died at age 76 in 1909. His magnificent horse died at age 23 in 1912.

Few black women were lawyers. Charlotte Ray was the first (see Chapter 12). In 1900 there were 10 black women practicing law compared to over 700 black men and 112,000 white men. Lutie A. Lytle, who graduated from Central Tennessee Law School in 1897, returned to her alma mater and became the first black woman law professor in the United States.

Music

| **15-7** | **What did African Americans contribute to music in the late nineteenth and early twentieth centuries?** |

In the half century after the Civil War, music created and performed by black people evolved into the uniquely American art forms of ragtime, jazz, and blues. The roots of these extraordinary musical innovations are uncertain. Some late nineteenth-century music can be traced to African forms and rhythms. Other sources are slave work songs and spirituals.

Traveling groups of black men, some of them ex-slaves, put on minstrel shows that featured "coon songs" after the Civil War. Many black Americans resented these popular shows as caricatures and exaggerations of black behavior. At least 600 "coon songs" that attracted a predominantly white audience were published by 1900 including "All Coons Look Alike to Me," "Mammy's Little Pickaninny," and "My Coal Black Lady."

Most black people had other forms of musical entertainment. "The Civil Rights Juba," published in 1874, was a precursor to ragtime. In 1871 the Fisk University Jubilee Singers began the first of many fund-raising concert tours that entertained black and white audiences in the United States and Europe for years thereafter with slave songs and spirituals. Other black colleges and universities sent choirs and singers on similar trips.

Ragtime

Ragtime, which emerged in the 1890s, was composed music, written down for performance on the piano. Ragtime pieces were not accompanied by lyrics and not meant to be sung. The creative genius of ragtime, Scott Joplin, was born in Texarkana, Texas, in 1868. He learned to play on a piano his mother bought from her earnings as a maid, and he may have had training in classical music. Joplin learned to transfer complex banjo syncopations to the piano as he fused European harmonies and African rhythms. He played at the World's Columbian Exposition in Chicago in 1893 and soon wrote ragtime sheet music that sold well. In 1899 he composed his best-known tune, the "Maple Leaf Rag," named after a social club (brothel) in Sedalia, Missouri. It sold an astonishing one million copies.

Jazz

Jazz gradually replaced ragtime in popularity in the early twentieth century. Unlike ragtime, jazz was mostly improvised, not composed, and it was not confined to the piano. Jazz incorporated African and European musical elements drawn from such diverse sources as plantation bands, minstrel shows, riverboat ensembles, and Irish and Scottish folk tunes. The first jazz bands emerged around New Orleans where they played at parades, funerals, clubs, and outdoor concerts. Instead of the banjos, pipes, fifes, and violins of earlier black musical groups, these bands relied more on brass, reeds, and drums.

Ferdinand J. La Menthe, regarded as the first prominent jazz musician, was born in 1890 and grew up in a French-speaking family in New Orleans. Young La Menthe played several musical instruments before settling on the piano. He was also a superb composer and arranger. Later he changed his name to Morton and came to be known as Jelly Roll Morton. He played in the "red light" district of New Orleans known as Storyville, where

15-1
15-2
15-3
15-4
15-5
15-6
15-7
15-8

Listen on **MyHistoryLab Audio:** Scott Joplin's Maple Leaf Rag

Scott Joplin (1868–1917) was one of America's most prolific composers, and his name is indelibly linked with ragtime. Although ragtime's popularity faded by the 1920s, Joplin's reputation and compositions were resurrected in 1974 when the Hollywood film *The Sting* relied on Joplin's 1902 rag "The Entertainer" for its soundtrack. In 1976 Scott Joplin was posthumously awarded the Pulitzer Prize for music.

he was also a pool shark and gambler. He moved to Los Angeles in 1917 and to Chicago in 1922, where he led and recorded with "Morton's Red Hot Peppers." He died in 1941.

The Blues

In rural, isolated areas of the South, poor black people composed and sang songs about their lives and experiences. W. C. Handy, the father of the blues, later recalled, "Southern Negroes sang about everything. Trains, steamboats, steam whistles, sledge hammers, fast women, mean bosses, stubborn mules." They accompanied themselves on anything from a guitar to a harmonica to a washboard. They played in juke joints (rural nightclubs), at picnics, in lumber camps, and in urban nightclubs.

Handy, who was born in Florence, Alabama, in 1873, took up music despite the opposition of his devoutly Christian parents. He learned to play the guitar, although his mother and father regarded it as the "devil's plaything." He later led his own nine-man band. In the Mississippi delta in 1903, Handy encountered "primitive," or "boogie," music unlike anything he had heard before. Handy was not initially impressed by the mostly unskilled and itinerant musicians whose lives swirled around cheap whiskey, gambling, prostitution, and violence: "Then I saw the beauty of primitive music. They had the stuff people wanted. It touched the spot. Their music wanted polishing, but it contained the essence. People would pay money for it." Handy composed many tunes, including "Memphis Blues" and "St. Louis Blues."

Handy was not the only musician to "discover" the blues. Gertrude Pridget sang in southern minstrel shows. In 1902 she heard a young black woman in Missouri sing about a lover who had left her. Pridget included the song in her shows. In 1904 she married William "Pa" Rainey and became "Ma" Rainey. She created other "blues" songs based on ballads, hymns, and the experiences of black people. As "Mother of the Blues," Rainey recorded extensively in the 1920s and 1930s.

By 1920 two forms of American music were developing—jazz and the blues. Both drew on African and American musical elements and European styles. But most of all, jazz and the blues represented the experiences of African Americans and the creativity of the musicians who developed and performed the music.

Sports

15-8 **What contributions did African Americans make to athletics in the late nineteenth and early twentieth centuries?**

While talented black musicians were making dramatic innovations, black athletes found that white athletes and sports entrepreneurs increasingly opposed the presence of black men in the boxing ring and on the playing field.

Boxing and Jack Johnson

Black boxers regularly fought white boxers through the end of the nineteenth century, but this offended many white people—especially southerners. In 1892 George Dixon, a black boxer, won the world featherweight title, and some white men cheered his victory, distressing a Chicago journalist: "It was not pleasant to see white men applaud a negro for knocking another white man out. It was not pleasant to see them crowding around 'Mr.' Dixon to congratulate him on his victory, to seek an introduction with 'the distinguished colored gentleman' while he puffed his cigar and lay back like a prince receiving his subjects." Despite such opinions, there was never any official prohibition of interracial bouts.

The success of another black boxer, heavyweight Jack Johnson, angered many white Americans. Johnson was born in Galveston, Texas, in 1878. Between 1902 and 1907 he won 57 bouts against black and white fighters. In 1908 he beat the white heavyweight champion, Tommy Burns, in Australia. Many white fans were unwilling to accept Johnson as the champion and looked desperately for "a great white hope" who could defeat him. Jim Jeffries, a former champion, came out of retirement to take on Johnson. In a brutal fight in Reno, Nevada, in 1910, Johnson knocked out Jeffries in the fifteenth round.

Johnson's personal life, as well as his prowess in the ring, provoked white animosity. Having divorced his black wife, he married a white woman in 1911. Several months later, overwhelmed by social ostracism, she committed suicide. After Johnson married a second white woman, he was convicted of violating the Mann Act, which made it illegal to transport a woman across state lines for immoral purposes. The "immorality" was Johnson's marriage to white women. Sentenced to a year in prison and fined $1,000, Johnson fled to Canada and then to France to avoid punishment. He lost his title to Jesse Willard in 1915 in Havana in the twenty-sixth round in a fight many people believe that Johnson threw. He returned to the United States in 1920 and served 10 months in Leavenworth Prison.

Jack Johnson spars with Marty Cutler in the early twentieth century. Johnson was a superb fighter whose ability to defeat white boxers rankled many white men. But Johnson's involvement with white women infuriated them even more and led to his imprisonment.

Baseball

Baseball became popular after the Civil War. As professional baseball developed in the 1870s and 1880s, both black and white men competed to earn money playing the game. It was not easy. They were the nation's first professional athletes, but professional baseball was unstable. Teams were formed and dissolved with depressing regularity. Players moved from team to team. Some 30 black men played professional baseball in the quarter century after the Civil War.

White players led by A. C. "Cap" Anson of the Chicago White Stockings tried to get club owners to stop signing black men to contracts. Anson, who was from Iowa, resented having to play against black men. In 1887 International League officials rescinded a rule that had permitted them to sign black players. One black player, Weldy Wilberforce Walker, protested the exclusion in a letter to *Sporting Life:* "There should be some broader cause—such as lack of ability, behavior, and intelligence—for barring a player, rather than his color. It is for these reasons and because I think ability and intelligence should be recognized first and last—at all times and by everyone—I ask the question again, 'Why was the law permitting colored men to sign repealed, etc.?'" There was no intelligent answer to Walker's question. But Jim Crow was now on the baseball diamond. Moses Fleetwood Walker—Weldy's brother—was the last black man to play major league baseball with white men until Jackie Robinson joined the Brooklyn Dodgers in 1947.

In reaction to their exclusion, black men formed their own teams. By 1900 there were five black professional teams including the Norfolk Red Stockings, the Chicago Unions, and the Cuban X Giants of New York. The Negro Leagues would be an integral (but not integrated) part of sports for the next half century.

Basketball and Other Sports

James Naismith invented basketball in 1891 in Springfield, Massachusetts. Black youngsters were playing organized basketball by 1906 in the YMCA in New York City and later in YMCAs in Philadelphia and Washington, DC. By 1910–1911 Howard University and Hampton Institute had basketball teams. In horse racing, black jockeys regularly won major races. Willie Simms won the Kentucky Derby in 1894, 1895, 1896, and 1898. Bicycling and bicycle racing were enormously popular by the 1890s, and in 1899 a black rider, Marshall W. "Major" Taylor, won the world championship.

College Athletics

Generally, white colleges and universities in the North that admitted black students would not let them participate in intercollegiate sports. (Southern colleges and universities did not admit black students.) There were, however, exceptions. In 1889, W. T. S. Jackson and William Henry Lewis played football for Amherst College. Lewis was the captain of the team in 1890. As a law school student, Lewis played for Harvard and was named to the Walter Camp All-American team in 1892. (Lewis was later forced out of the American Bar Association because of his color. See the section "The Law" in this chapter.) White institutions with black players often encountered rampant racism. In 1907 the University of Alabama baseball team canceled a game with the University of Vermont because the Vermont squad had two black infielders. Moreover, opposing teams and their fans frequently abused black players.

White colleges and universities occasionally played black institutions. The Yale Law School baseball team, for example, played Howard in 1898. But black college teams were far more likely to play each other. The first football game between two black colleges took place on December 27, 1892, when Biddle University (today Johnson C. Smith University) defeated Livingston College in Salisbury, North Carolina.

Eventually black athletic conferences were formed. The Central Intercollegiate Athletic Association was organized in 1912 with Hampton, Howard, Virginia Union, and Shaw College in Raleigh among its early members. The Southeastern Conference was established in 1913 and consisted of Morehouse, Fisk, Florida A&M, and Tuskegee, among others. It would become the Southern Intercollegiate Athletic Conference (SIAC). In Texas in 1920, five black colleges founded the Southwestern Athletic Conference: Prairie View A&M, Bishop College, Paul Quinn College, Wiley College, and Sam Houston College.

CONCLUSION

White supremacy was debilitating, discouraging, and dangerous, but black Americans could sometimes turn Jim Crow to their advantage. To combat white racism and improve the economic status of black people, educators like Samuel Chapman Armstrong and Booker T. Washington recommended agricultural and mechanical training for black Americans. But critics such as W. E. B. Du Bois stressed the need to cultivate the minds as well as the hands of black people to develop leaders.

Black men served with distinction in all-black military units in the Indian wars, the Spanish-American War, and the Philippine Insurrection. But no matter how loyal or committed black soldiers were, the white majority never fully trusted or displayed confidence in them. African Americans could only react with outrage when President Theodore Roosevelt dismissed 167 black soldiers in 1906 in the Brownsville affair.

As they tried to shape their own destinies in the late nineteenth century, black Americans organized a variety of institutions. Mostly barred from white schools, churches, hospitals, labor unions, and places of entertainment, they developed businesses and facilities to serve their communities in an environment mostly free from white interference. Black people relied on their own experiences and imaginations to create new music. They occasionally participated in sports with white athletes but more often played separately from them as segregation and white hostility spread.

Although black people recognized their churches, hospitals, schools, and businesses were often inadequately financed and usually less imposing than those of white people, they also knew that at a black school or church, in a black store, or in the care of a black physician or nurse, they would not be abused, mistreated, or ridiculed because of their color.

CHAPTER TIMELINE

AFRICAN-AMERICAN EVENTS

NATIONAL EVENTS

1860–1870

1867
Independent Order of St. Luke founded in Baltimore

1868
Hampton Institute founded

1869–1898
Four regiments of black soldiers serve on the western frontier

1862
Morrill Land-Grant Act is passed to support agricultural and mechanical education

1867
United States purchases Alaska from Russia

1869
Cincinnati "Red Stockings" organized as the first professional baseball team

Rutgers and Princeton play the first college football game

1870–1880

1870
Howard University Law School established

1873
Panic of 1873 is followed by major depression

1880–1890

1881
Tuskegee Institute founded

1887
Black players barred from major league baseball

1881
Clara Barton establishes the Red Cross

1890–1900

1891
Dr. Daniel Hale Williams founds Provident Hospital in Chicago

1892
First black college football game: Biddle vs. Livingstone

1895
Booker T. Washington addresses the Cotton States Exposition in Atlanta

1899
Scott Joplin composes the "Maple Leaf Rag"

1890
Second Morrill Act passed

1891
John D. Rockefeller funds the establishment of the University of Chicago

1892
Grover Cleveland elected to a second term as president

1893
World's Columbian Exposition in Chicago

1895
Sears, Roebuck and Company form a retail mail order business

1896
William McKinley elected president

1898
Spanish-American War

1899
Cumming v. Richmond County [Georgia] Board of Education eliminates Augusta's black high school

CHAPTER TIMELINE

AFRICAN-AMERICAN EVENTS

NATIONAL EVENTS

1900–1910

1903
St. Luke Penny Savings Bank established in Richmond with Maggie Lena Walker as president

1906
Brownsville affair

1908
National Association of Colored Graduate Nurses is founded in New York City; Jack Johnson wins the heavyweight championship in boxing

1900
William McKinley reelected president

1901
President McKinley assassinated; Vice President Theodore Roosevelt becomes president

1903
Henry Ford organizes the Ford Motor Co.

Wilbur and Orville Wright launch the first powered aircraft at Kitty Hawk, North Carolina

1904
Theodore Roosevelt reelected president

1908
William Howard Taft elected president

On MyHistoryLab

 Study and Review on MyHistoryLab

REVIEW QUESTIONS

1. How and why did the agricultural and mechanical training that Hampton Institute and Tuskegee Institute offered gain so much support among both black and white people? Why did black colleges and universities emphasize learning trades and acquiring skills?

2. How compatible was the educational philosophy of the late nineteenth century with the era's racial ideology?

3. Of what value was an education for a black person in the 1890s or early 1900s? To what use could a black person put an education?

4. What purpose did the black church serve? What were the strengths and weaknesses of the black church? What roles did black clergymen play in late nineteenth-century America?

5. How could a black soldier justify participating in wars against Native Americans, the Spanish, and the Filipinos? Why did black soldiers serve? How well did they serve?

6. Did black people derive any benefits from the expansion of segregation and Jim Crow?

7. Why did ragtime, jazz, and the blues emerge and become popular?

8. How did segregation affect amateur and professional athletics in the United States?

RECOMMENDED READING

James D. Anderson. *The Education of Blacks in the South, 1860–1931.* Chapel Hill: University of North Carolina Press, 1988. Anderson is highly critical of the education and philosophy promoted and provided by Hampton Institute and Tuskegee Institute.

Edward L. Ayers. *The Promise of the New South: Life After Reconstruction.* New York: Oxford University Press, 1992. This wide-ranging study encompasses almost every aspect of life in the late nineteenth-century South, including religion, education, sports, and music.

Sutton E. Griggs. *Imperium in Imperio.* New York: Arno Press reprint, 1899. This novel describes the formation of a separate black nation in Texas at the end of the nineteenth century.

Leon Litwack. *Trouble in Mind: Black Southerners in the Age of Jim Crow.* New York: Alfred A. Knopf, 1998. The author lets the words of black people of the time, including lawyers, physicians, and musicians, explain what life was like in an age of intense white supremacy.

Leon Litwack and August Meier, eds. *Black Leaders in the Nineteenth Century.* Urbana: University of Illinois Press, 1988. This volume contains 18 brief but valuable biographical essays.

Benjamin E. Mays. *Born to Rebel.* New York: Scribner, 1971. Mays's autobiography includes penetrating insights into religion and education among rural black southerners.

Howard N. Rabinowitz. *Race Relations in the Urban South, 1865–1890.* New York: Oxford University Press, 1978. The author examines black life in Atlanta, Montgomery, Nashville, Raleigh, and Richmond.

Christopher Robert Reed. *"All the World Is Here!" The Black Presence at White City.* Bloomington: Indiana University Press, 2000. Although African Americans were not involved in the planning or management of the World's Columbian Exposition, they did take part in the fair's exhibits and activities.

Mim Eichler Rivas. *Beautiful Jim Key: The Lost History of a Horse and a Man Who Changed the World.* New York: William Morrow, 2005. A fascinating and warm account of how a former slave and an exceptional horse became hugely successful entertainers.

Quintard Taylor. *In Search of the Racial Frontier: African Americans in the American West, 1528–1990.* New York: W. W. Norton, 1998. A fine survey and analysis of African Americans in the West from the sixteenth century to 1990.

ADDITIONAL BIBLIOGRAPHY

EDUCATION

Eric Anderson and Alfred A. Moss, Jr. *Dangerous Donations: Northern Philanthropy and Southern Black Education, 1902–1930.* Columbia: University of Missouri Press, 1999.

James D. Anderson and V. P. Franklin, eds. *New Perspectives on Black Educational History.* Boston: G. K. Hall, 1978.

Peter M. Ascoli. *Julius Rosenwald: The Man Who Built Sears, Roebuck and Advanced the Cause of Black Education in the American South.* Bloomington: Indiana University Press, 2006.

Henry A. Bullock. *A History of Negro Education in the South from 1619 to the Present.* Cambridge, MA: Harvard University Press, 1967.

Mary S. Hoffschwelle. *The Rosenwald Schools in the American South.* Gainesville: University Press of Florida, 2006.

RELIGION

Stephen W. Angell. *Bishop Henry McNeal Turner and African American Religion in the South.* Knoxville: University of Tennessee Press, 1992.

Cyprian Davis. *The History of Black Catholics in the United States.* New York: Crossroad, 1990.

Harold T. Lewis. *Yet with a Steady Beat: The African American Struggle for Recognition in the Episcopal Church.* Valley Forge, PA: Trinity Press International, 1996.

Iain MacRobert. *The Black Roots and White Racism of Early Pentecostalism in the USA.* Basingstoke, England: Macmillan, 1988.

James M. O'Toole. *Passing for White: Race, Religion, and the Healy Family, 1820–1920.* Amherst: University of Massachusetts Press, 2002.

Edwin S. Redkey, ed. *The Writings and Speeches of Henry McNeal Turner.* New York: Arno Press, 1971.

Clarence E. Walker. *A Rock in a Weary Land: The African Methodist Episcopal Church During the Civil War and Reconstruction.* Baton Rouge: Louisiana State University Press, 1982.

THE MILITARY AND THE WEST

John M. Carroll, ed. *The Black Military Experience in the American West.* New York: Liveright, 1973.

Willard B. Gatewood, ed. *Smoked Yankees and the Struggle for Empire: Letters from Negro Soldiers, 1898–1902.* Urbana: University of Illinois Press, 1971.

William Loren Katz. *The Black West.* New York: Touchstone Books, 1996.

William H. Leckie. *The Buffalo Soldiers: A Narrative of the Negro Cavalry in the West.* Norman: University of Oklahoma Press, 1967.

Sara R. Massey, ed. *Black Cowboys of Texas.* College Station: Texas A&M University Press, 2000.

Frank N. Schubert. *Voices of the Buffalo Soldier: Records, Reports, and Recollections of Military Life and Service in the West.* Albuquerque: University of New Mexico Press, 2003.

Paul W. Stewart and Wallace Yvonne Ponce. *Black Cowboys.* Broomfield, CO: Phillips, 1986.

John D. Weaver. *The Brownsville Raid.* New York: W. W. Norton, 1971.

LABOR

Tera W. Hunter. *To 'Joy My Freedom: Southern Black Women's Lives and Labors After the Civil War.* Cambridge, MA: Harvard University Press, 1997.

Gerald D. Jaynes. *Branches Without Roots: Genesis of the Black Working Class in the American South, 1862–1882.* New York: Oxford University Press, 1986.

THE PROFESSIONS

V. N. Gamble. *The Black Community Hospital: Contemporary Dilemmas in Historical Perspective.* New York: Garland, 1989.

Darlene Clark Hine. *Speak Truth to Power: Black Professional Class in United States History.* Brooklyn, NY: Carlson, 1996.

Gertrude Woodruff Marlowe. *A Right Worthy Grand Mission: Maggie Lena Walker and the Quest for Black Economic Empowerment.* Washington, DC: Howard University Press, 2003.

J. Clay Smith, Jr. *Emancipation: The Making of the Black Lawyer, 1844–1944.* Philadelphia: University of Pennsylvania Press, 1993.

———, ed. *Rebels in Law: Voices in History of Black Women Lawyers.* Ann Arbor: University of Michigan Press, 1998.

Susan L. Smith. *Sick and Tired of Being Sick and Tired: Black Women's Health Activism in America, 1890–1950.* Philadelphia: University of Pennsylvania Press, 1995.

Thomas J. Ward, Jr. *Black Physicians in the Jim Crow South.* Fayetteville: University of Arkansas Press, 2003.

MUSIC

W. C. Handy. *Father of the Blues: An Autobiography.* New York: Macmillan, 1941.

John Edward Hasse, ed. *Ragtime, Its History, Composers, and Music.* London: Macmillan, 1985.

William Howland Kenney. *Jazz on the River.* Chicago: University of Chicago Press, 2005.

Alan Lomax. *Mr. Jelly Roll: The Fortunes of Jelly Roll Morton, New Orleans Creole and "Inventor of Jazz."* New York: Grove Press, 1950.

Gunther Schuller. *Early Jazz: Its Roots and Musical Development.* New York: Oxford University Press, 1968.

SPORTS

Ocania Chalk. *Black College Sport.* New York: Dodd, Mead, 1976.

Neil Lanctot. *Negro League Baseball: The Rise and Ruin of a Black Institution.* Philadelphia: University of Pennsylvania Press, 2004.

Robert W. Peterson. *Only the Ball Was White: Negro Baseball: A History of Legendary Black Players and All-Black Professional Teams Before Black Men Played in the Major Leagues.* New York: Prentice Hall, 1970.

Andrew Ritchie. *Major Taylor: The Extraordinary Career of a Championship Bicycle Racer.* San Francisco: Bicycle Books, 1988.

Randy Roberts. *Papa Jack: Jack Johnson and the Era of White Hopes.* New York: Free Press, 1983.

RETRACING THE ODYSSEY

Hampton University, Hampton, Virginia. Founded by Samuel Chapman Armstrong with the assistance of the American Missionary Association, Hampton Normal and Agricultural Institute opened in 1868 to train former slaves (and later Native Americans) in agricultural and mechanical skills. Virginia Hall (1874), Memorial Church (1886), the Hampton Museum, and the giant Emancipation Oak are all located on this picturesque campus overlooking Chesapeake Bay and Hampton Roads.

Tuskegee Institute National Historic Site, Tuskegee, Alabama. What is now Tuskegee University opened in 1881 and remained under the leadership of Booker T. Washington until his death in 1915. His home—The Oaks—was built by students and is now a museum. His grave and memorial are also on the campus, as is the George Washington Carver Museum.

Alonzo F. Herndon Home, Atlanta, Georgia. Herndon was the founder of the Atlanta Life Insurance Company and one of the wealthiest black men in America by the early 1900s. His 15-room mansion with immense white pillars was finished in 1910 and is open to the public. It is furnished with antiques, Roman and Venetian glass, as well as ornate artwork.

Maggie L. Walker National Historic Site, Richmond, Virginia. Built in 1883, this 22-room Victorian mansion was home to the Walker family from 1904 to 1934 and is now open for tours. There is a visitor center that contains exhibits on the life of Maggie Lena Walker and the Jackson Ward community.

Madame C. J. Walker Center, Indianapolis, Indiana. In 1910 C. J. Walker (Sarah Breedlove) moved her thriving hair care and beauty products business from Denver to Indianapolis. The four-story triangular building was completed in 1919 shortly after Walker's death. It housed manufacturing facilities and was home to a beauty college that trained Walker's agents to care for the hair of African-American women and to sell Walker's products. It is currently a community center and theater.

Dunbar Hospital, Detroit, Michigan. This red brick structure was built in 1892 and served as a hospital for Detroit's black community from 1918 to 1928. It is currently operated by the Detroit Medical Society, and it has exhibits, medical devices, photographs, and papers documenting the medical care available to black Detroit.

16

Conciliation, Agitation, and Migration: African Americans in the Early Twentieth Century

((• Listen to Chapter 16
on MyHistoryLab

The wisest among my race understand that the agitation of questions of social equality is the extremest folly, and that progress in the enjoyment of all privileges that will come to us must be the result of severe and constant struggle rather than of artificial forcing. No race that has anything to contribute to the markets of the world is long in any degree ostracized. It is important and right all privileges of the law be ours, but it is vastly more important that we be prepared for the exercises of these privileges.

Booker T. Washington, Atlanta Cotton States and International Exposition, September 18, 1895

Mr. Washington distinctly asks that black people give up, at least for the present three things,—First, political power, Second, insistence on civil rights, Third, higher education of Negro youth,—and concentrate all their energies on industrial education, the accumulation of wealth, and the conciliation of the South.

W. E. B. Du Bois, The Souls of Black Folk, 1903

LEARNING OBJECTIVES

What advice for advancement did Booker T. Washington offer to African Americans?   **16-1**

What were the views of W. E. B. Du Bois on promoting progress among African Americans in early twentieth-century America?   **16-2**

What were the origins and goals of the NAACP?   **16-3**

What role did black women play in advocating reform and in fostering progress among African Americans?   **16-4**

What were the defining characteristics of the black elite?   **16-5**

How did African Americans contribute to the U.S. war effort in World War I?   **16-6**

What were the causes of racial violence in the early twentieth century and why was that violence so intense?   **16-7**

Why did African Americans begin to leave the rural South in the early twentieth century, and what kinds of lives were they able to make for themselves in urban communities?   **16-8**

As the twentieth century dawned, black and white Americans had profoundly different views on the future of black people in America. Most white people believed black Americans were an inferior race capable of little more than manual labor and entitled to only the most basic legal rights. Black Americans rejected those assertions and worked for a more equitable place in society. Black scholar W. E. B. Du Bois announced in 1903 that race would be the century's critical issue: "The problem of the twentieth century is the problem of the

---

Although Tuskegee Institute stressed agricultural and vocational subjects, students did enroll in math, science, and English courses. Here students in a U.S. history class are involved in a discussion of Virginia's founding in the early seventeenth century. Notice that the male and female students are segregated and that the classroom features portraits of three U.S. presidents and several American flags.

color line—the relation of the darker to the lighter races of men in Asia and Africa, in America and the islands of the sea."

Black people refused to accept the inferiority to which they had been consigned. They devised strategies and organized institutions to enable them to prosper in a hostile society. However, African Americans and their leaders disagreed about how to secure the constitutional rights and the material comforts that so many white Americans took for granted. Some, following Du Bois, a founder of the Niagara Movement and the National Association for the Advancement of Colored People (NAACP), favored a frontal assault on discrimination, disfranchisement, and Jim Crow. Others, following Booker T. Washington of the Tuskegee Institute, cautioned against the vigorous pursuit of civil rights and political power and insisted that agricultural and industrial training would generate prosperity and self-sufficiency among people of color.

The emergence of the club movement among black women and other self-help organizations enabled more prosperous black people to aid those suffering from poverty and prejudice. The black elite, often reviled for ostentatious social displays, came to be designated the **Talented Tenth**, and many of them took seriously their responsibilities to aid their brethren.

When the United States entered World War I in 1917, black men responded patriotically, as they had in previous conflicts. They joined a Jim Crow military that was fighting to make the world safe for democracy. But black people in America were not safe, and democracy did not prevail. Racial violence erupted before, during, and after the war.

In the meantime, one of the most important episodes in American history—a vast and prolonged migration of hundreds of thousands of rural black southerners to northern cities—began in earnest after 1910. Drawn mainly by economic opportunities, black people moved to New York, Philadelphia, Cleveland, Chicago, and other urban centers where they became the core of the black working class.

By the 1910s, many Americans were anxious about the rapid economic and social changes that confronted the United States, including industrialization, the rise of powerful corporations, the explosive growth of cities, and the influx of millions of immigrants. Their apprehensions spawned a disparate collection of reform efforts known as the progressive movement. In general, progressives believed America needed a new social awareness to deal with the new social and economic problems. But most of the middle- and upper-class white people who formed the core of the movement showed little interest in white racism and its impact. Indeed, many were racists themselves. They were primarily concerned with the concentration of wealth in monopolies such as Standard Oil, with the pervasive political corruption in state and local governments, and with the plight of working-class immigrants in American cities. They cared deeply about the debilitating effects of alcohol, tainted food, and prostitution, but little about the grim impact of white supremacy. When Upton Sinclair wrote his muckraking novel *The Jungle* in 1906 to expose the exploitation of European immigrants in Chicago meatpacking houses, he depicted black people as brute laborers and strikebreakers.

Talented Tenth Term popularized by W. E. B. Du Bois for the educated black elite of the late nineteenth and early twentieth centuries. The upper 10 percent was supposed to assume responsibility for the leadership and advancement of the remaining 90 percent of African Americans.

16-1
16-2
16-3
16-4
16-5
16-6
16-7
16-8

The reforms of the progressive movement nonetheless offered a glimmer of hope that racial advancement was possible. If efforts were made to improve America, was it not possible also to improve the policies and conditions affecting black Americans? But how much militancy or forbearance was necessary to achieve racial progress? Did it even make sense for black people to demand a meaningful role in a nation that despised them? Perhaps it was wiser to rely on each other rather than plead for white recognition and respect.

Booker T. Washington's Approach

16-1

What advice for advancement did Booker T. Washington offer to African Americans?

Booker T. Washington's commitment to agricultural and industrial education was the basis for his approach to "the problem of the color line." By 1900, Washington was convinced that black men and women who had mastered skills acquired at institutions like Tuskegee and Hampton would be recognized, if not welcomed, as productive contributors to the southern economy. He believed economic acceptance would lead to political and social acceptance.

The Tuskegee leader eloquently outlined his philosophy in the speech he delivered at the opening ceremonies of the Cotton States Exposition in Atlanta in 1895 (see Chapter 15). Black people, he told his segregated audience, would find genuine opportunities in the South. "When it comes to business, pure and simple, it is in the South that the Negro is given a man's chance in the commercial world." Washington added that black people should not expect too much but should welcome menial labor as a first step in the struggle for progress. Ever optimistic, he looked hopefully at what was possible while deprecating those who complained: "Nor should we permit our grievances to overshadow our opportunities." He told white listeners that the lives of black and white southerners were historically linked and that black people were far more loyal and steadfast than newly arrived immigrants: "In our humble way, we shall stand by you with a devotion that no foreigner can approach, ready to lay down our lives, if need be, in defence of yours, interlacing our industrial, commercial, civil, and religious life with yours in a way that shall make the interests of both races one."

Washington reassured white people that cooperation between the races in the interest of prosperity did not endanger segregation: "In all things that are purely social we can be as separate as the fingers, yet one as the hand in all things essential to mutual progress." Finally, Washington implied that black people need not protest because they were denied rights white men possessed. Instead, he urged his black listeners to struggle steadily rather than make defiant demands: "The wisest among my race understand that the agitation of questions of social equality is the extremest folly, and that progress in the enjoyment of all the privileges that will come to us must be the result of severe and constant struggle rather than of artificial forcing." Washington was convinced that as African Americans became productive and made economic progress, white people would concede them their rights.

The speech was warmly received by both white and black listeners and by those who read it when it was widely reprinted. T. Thomas Fortune, the black editor of the *New York Age*, told Washington that he had replaced Frederick Douglass (who died in 1895) as a leader: "It looks as if you are our Douglass, the best equipped of the lot of us to be the single figure ahead of the procession."

But not everyone was complimentary. The black editor of the *Washington Bee*, W. Calvin Chase, complained, "He said something that was death to the Afro-American and elevating to white people." Bishop Henry M. Turner added that Washington "will have to live a long time to undo the harm he has done our race."

16-1

16-2

16-3

16-4

16-5

16-6

16-7

16-8

White people regarded Washington's speech as moderate, sensible, and praiseworthy. Almost overnight he was designated the spokesman for African Americans. Washington took full advantage of the recognition.

Washington's Influence

Booker T. Washington was a complex man. Many people found him unassertive, dignified, and patient. Yet he was ambitious, aggressive, and opportunistic as well as shrewd, calculating, and devious. He had an uncanny ability to elicit a positive response from other people. He became extraordinarily powerful, "the wizard of Tuskegee," in the words of his assistant, Emmett J. Scott.

After the Atlanta speech, Washington's influence soared. He received extensive and mostly positive coverage in black newspapers. Some of that popularity stemmed from admiration for his leadership and agreement with his ideas. But Washington also flattered editors, paid for advertisements for Tuskegee, and subsidized struggling African-American journalists.

He was especially effective in dealing with prominent white businessmen and philanthropists. Washington's management of Tuskegee so impressed William H. Baldwin, vice president of the Southern Railroad, that Baldwin agreed to serve as the chairman of Tuskegee's board. Washington developed support among the nation's industrial elite including steel magnate Andrew Carnegie and Julius Rosenwald, the head of Sears, Roebuck and Company. They trusted Washington's judgment and consulted him before contributing to black colleges and universities. Washington assured them of the wisdom of training black men and women in agricultural and mechanical skills. These students, he reminded donors, would be self-sufficient and productive members of southern society.

For example, Rosenwald traveled to Tuskegee, consulted with Washington, and agreed to contribute several million dollars to construct public schools for black youngsters across the southern states. Between 1913 and 1932, over 5,300 schools ranging in size from one to six classrooms were built. Rosenwald insisted that local communities provide a substantial portion of the funds. Of the $28 million spent on constructing these Rosenwald schools, black communities contributed 19 percent, Rosenwald donated 16.5 percent, white people provided 4.5 percent, and state and local governments provided 60 percent. Some white communities, however, refused to have these schools built even after black people and Rosenwald agreed to share the financial responsibility for the schools. Black children in those communities received little, if any, education.

The Tuskegee Machine

Washington advised black people to avoid politics, but he ignored his own advice. Although he never ran for office or was appointed to a political position, Washington was a political figure to be reckoned with. His connections to white businesspeople and politicians gave him enormous influence. With his influence, connections, and organizational skills, Washington operated what came to be known as the "**Tuskegee Machine**." In 1896 he supported winning Republican presidential candidate William McKinley over the Democratic and Populist William Jennings Bryan. Washington got along superbly with McKinley's successor, Theodore Roosevelt. Although Roosevelt subscribed to social Darwinism (see Chapter 15) and regarded black Americans as inferiors, he respected Washington.

In 1901 Roosevelt invited Washington to dinner at the White House, where Roosevelt's family and a Colorado businessman joined them. Black people applauded, but the white South recoiled in disgust from such a flagrant breach of racial etiquette. Under no circumstances did white people and black people dine together at the same table. South Carolina Senator Benjamin R. Tillman declared, "The action of President Roosevelt in entertaining that nigger will necessitate our killing a thousand niggers in the South before they will learn their place

16-1

16-2

16-3

16-4

Tuskegee Machine As the president of Tuskegee Institute, Booker T. Washington developed an extensive network of contacts that gave him extraordinary influence with white political leaders and philanthropists as well as with black business people, journalists, and college presidents.

16-5

16-6

16-7

16-8

Booker T. Washington had access to and influence among the most powerful political and business leaders in the United States. Here he shares the podium with President Theodore Roosevelt. Washington persuaded Republican leaders like Roosevelt to appoint black men to an assortment of federal offices and convinced businessmen to contribute sizable sums to black colleges and universities. Nevertheless, some African Americans criticized the Tuskegee leader for not speaking out more candidly in opposition to white supremacy and Jim Crow.

again." Roosevelt was unmoved, and he continued to correspond and meet with Washington. Still, Roosevelt never invited Washington for another meal at the Executive Mansion.

Washington and Roosevelt consulted each other on political appointments. In the most notable case, Washington urged Roosevelt to appoint William D. Crum, a black medical doctor, as the collector of customs for the port of Charleston. White southerners, led by Senator Benjamin R. Tillman, delayed confirmation by the Senate for nearly three years. With Washington's assent, Roosevelt appointed black attorney William Lewis as U.S. attorney in Boston. President William Howard Taft later appointed Lewis assistant attorney general. (For more on Lewis, see Chapter 15.)

Most of Washington's political activities were not public. He secretly helped finance an unsuccessful court case against the Louisiana grandfather clause. (The statute disfranchised those voters—black men—whose grandfathers had not possessed the right to vote. See Chapter 14.) Washington funded two cases challenging Alabama's grandfather clause to the Supreme Court, which rejected both on a technicality. He tried to persuade railroad executives to improve the conditions on segregated coaches and in station waiting rooms. He worked covertly with white attorneys to free a black farm laborer imprisoned under Alabama's peonage law. In many of these secret activities, Washington used code names in correspondence to hide his involvement. In the Louisiana case he was identified only as X.Y.Z.

Washington was a conservative leader who did not directly or publicly challenge white supremacy. He was willing to accept literacy and property qualifications for voting if they were equitably enforced regardless of race. He also opposed women's suffrage. He attacked lynching only occasionally. But he did write an annual letter to white newspapers filled with data on lynchings that had been compiled at Tuskegee. Washington let the grim statistics speak for themselves rather than denounce the injustice himself.

Washington founded the National Negro Business League in 1900 and served as its president until he died in 1915. The league brought together merchants, retailers, bankers, funeral directors, and other owners and operators of small enterprises. It promoted black businesses in the black community and brought businessmen together to exchange information. Moreover, the league's annual meetings allowed Washington to develop support for the Tuskegee Machine from black community leaders from across the nation. Similarly, he worked closely with leaders in black fraternal orders such as the Odd Fellows and Pythians.

Opposition to Washington

Years before Washington became prominent, there were black leaders who favored a direct challenge to racial oppression. In 1889 delegates from 23 states met to form the Afro-American League in Chicago. Its main purpose was to press for civil and political rights guaranteed by the Constitution: "The objects of the League are to encourage State and local leagues in their efforts to break down color bars, and in obtaining for the Afro-American an equal chance with others in the avocations of life . . . in securing the full privileges of citizenship." But the league did not flourish, and the Niagara Movement eventually displaced it.

Opposition to Washington's conciliatory stance on racial matters intensified. William Monroe Trotter, the Harvard-educated editor of the *Boston Guardian*, attacked Washington as "the Great Traitor," "the Benedict Arnold of the Negro Race," and "Pope Washington." At a 1903 meeting of the National Negro Business League in Boston, Trotter stood on a chair and interrupted a speech by Washington, defiantly asking, "Are the rope and the torch all the race is to get under your leadership?" Washington ignored him, and the police arrested the editor for disorderly conduct. He spent 30 days in jail for what newspapers labeled "the Boston Riot."

16-1

16-2

16-3

16-4

16-5

16-6

16-7

16-8

W. E. B. Du Bois

16-2   **What were the views of W. E. B. Du Bois on promoting progress among African Americans in early twentieth-century America?**

William Edward Burghardt Du Bois, who was 12 years younger than Booker T. Washington, would eventually eclipse the influence and authority of the Wizard of Tuskegee. Du Bois became the most significant black leader in America during the first half of the twentieth century. Whereas slavery, poverty, and the industrial work ethic fostered at Hampton Institute had shaped Washington's life, Du Bois was born and raised in the largely white town of Great Barrington, Massachusetts. It was a small community where he encountered little overt racism and developed a passion for knowledge.

Du Bois possessed, as he put it, "a flood of Negro blood, a strain of French, a bit of Dutch, but, thank God! no Anglo-Saxon." He graduated from Great Barrington High School at a time when few white and still fewer black youngsters attended more than primary school. He went to Fisk University in Nashville and graduated at age 20. He was the first black man to earn a Ph.D. (in history) at Harvard in 1895, and he pursued additional graduate study in Germany.

Du Bois was perhaps the greatest scholar-activist in American history. He was an intellectual, at ease with words and ideas. He wrote 16 nonfiction books, five novels, and two autobiographies. He was a fearless activist determined to confront disfranchisement, Jim Crow, and lynching. Whereas Washington solicited the goodwill of powerful white leaders and was comfortable with a gradual approach to eradicating white supremacy, Du Bois was impatient with white people who accepted or ignored white domination and had little tolerance for black people who were unwilling to demand their civil and political rights.

Read on **MyHistoryLab** Document: W.E.B. Du Bois, from "Of Mr. Booker T. Washington and Others," 1903

VOICES   W. E. B. Du Bois on Being Black in America

W. E. B. Du Bois's The Souls of Black Folk *(1903) contained perhaps the most eloquent statement ever written on being black in white America. The difficulties of their circumstances, Du Bois believed, create a double consciousness among Americans of African descent.*

After the Egyptian and Indian, the Greek and Roman, the Teuton and Mongolian, the Negro is a sort of seventh son, born with a veil, and gifted with second-sight in this American world,—a world which yields him no true self-consciousness, but only lets him see himself through the revelation of the other world. It is a peculiar sensation, this double-consciousness, this sense of always looking at one's self through the eyes of others, of measuring one's soul by the tape of a world that looks on in an amused contempt and pity. One ever feels his two-ness,—an American, a Negro; two souls, two thoughts, two unreconciled strivings; two warring ideals in one dark body, whose dogged strength alone keeps it from being torn asunder.

The history of the American Negro is the history of this strife,—this longing to attain self-conscious manhood, to merge his double self into a better and truer self. In this merging he wishes neither of the older selves to be lost. He would not Africanize America, for America has too much to teach the world and Africa. He would not bleach his Negro soul in a flood of white Americanism, for he knows that Negro blood has a message for the world. He simply wishes to make it possible for a man to be both a Negro and an American, without being cursed and spit upon by his fellows, without having the doors of Opportunity closed roughly in his face.

1. **Why does Du Bois maintain that a black person cannot be simply an American?**

2. **Would Du Bois agree, based on his concept of double consciousness, that African Americans have a separate identity and culture from other Americans?**

SOURCE: W. E. B. Du Bois, *The Souls of Black Folk* (New York: Library of America, 1903), 8–9.

Du Bois was well aware that he and Washington came from dissimilar backgrounds:

> I was born free. Washington was born a slave. He felt the lash of an overseer across his back. I was born in Massachusetts, he on a slave plantation in the South. My great-grandfather fought with the Colonial Army in New England in the American Revolution. I had a happy childhood and acceptance in the community. Washington's childhood was hard. I had many more advantages: Fisk University, Harvard, graduate years in Europe. Washington had little formal schooling.

The Souls of Black Folk

Du Bois was not always critical of Washington. Following Washington's speech at the Cotton States Exposition in 1895, Du Bois, then a young Harvard Ph.D. teaching at Ohio's Wilberforce University, wrote to praise him: "Let me heartily congratulate you upon your phenomenal success at Atlanta—it was a word fitly spoken." But in 1903, Du Bois, by then an Atlanta University professor, published *The Souls of Black Folk*. One of the major literary works of the twentieth century, it contained the first formal attack on Washington and his leadership.

In a provocative essay, "Of Booker T. Washington and Others," Du Bois conceded it was painful to challenge Washington, a man so highly praised and admired: "One hesitates, therefore, to criticise a life which, beginning with so little, has done so much. And yet the time is come when one may speak in all sincerity and utter courtesy of the mistakes and shortcomings of Mr. Washington's career, as well as the triumphs." Du Bois proceeded to attack Washington for failing to stand up for political and civil rights and higher education for black Americans. Du Bois found even more infuriating Washington's willingness to compromise with the white South and Washington's apparent agreement with white southerners that black people were not their equals: "Mr. Washington represents in Negro thought the old attitude of adjustment and submission . . . and Mr. Washington's programme practically accepts the alleged inferiority of the Negro races."

In concluding, Du Bois stressed that he agreed with Washington on some issues, but he so disagreed on other significant issues that it was vital to oppose Washington's positions:

> So far as Mr. Washington preaches Thrift, Patience, and Industrial Training for the masses, we must hold up his hands and strive with him. . . . But so far as Mr. Washington apologizes for injustice, North or South, does not rightly value the privilege and duty of voting, belittles the emasculating effects of caste distinctions, and opposes higher training and ambition of our brighter minds,—so far as he, the South, or the Nation, does this,—we must unceasingly and firmly oppose them.

Washington worried that the opposition of Trotter, Du Bois, and others would jeopardize the flow of funds from white philanthropists to black colleges and universities. To reconcile with his opponents, he organized a meeting with them, funded by white philanthropists, at Carnegie Hall in New York City in 1904. But Du Bois and other opponents of Washington came to the gathering determined to adopt a radical agenda. When Washington loyalists monopolized the proceedings, Du Bois quit in disgust.

The Talented Tenth

Du Bois, joined by a small cadre of black intellectuals, set out to organize an aggressive effort to secure the rights of black citizens. He was convinced that the advancement of black

Read on **MyHistoryLab** Document: W. E. B. Du Bois Challenges Booker T. Washington, 1903

This early twentieth-century photograph depicts a dapper young W. E. B. Du Bois (1868–1963). He was a key figure in opposing Booker T. Washington's Tuskegee Machine. Du Bois helped found the NAACP and edited its publication, the *Crisis*, for two decades.

 Watch on **MyHistoryLab** Video: The Conflict between Booker T. Washington and W. E. B. Du Bois

Read on **MyHistoryLab** Document: The Niagara Movement, Declaration of Principles, 1905

The founders of the Niagara Movement posed in front of a photograph of the falls when they met at Niagara Falls, Ontario, Canada, in 1905. W. E. B. Du Bois is second from the right in the middle row.
Photographs and Prints Division, Schomburg Center for Research in Black Culture. The New York Public Library, Astor, Lenox, and Tilden Foundations.

people was the responsibility of the black elite, those he called the Talented Tenth, meaning the upper 10 percent of black Americans. Education, he believed, was the key:

> Work alone will not do it unless inspired by the right ideals and guided by intelligence. Education must not simply teach work—it must teach Life. The Talented Tenth of the Negro race must be made leaders of thought and missionaries of culture among people. No others can do this work, and Negro colleges must train men for it. The Negro race, like all other races, is going to be saved by its exceptional men.

The Niagara Movement

In 1905 Du Bois carried the anti-Washington crusade a step further and invited a select group to meet at Niagara Falls in Canada. The 29 delegates to this meeting insisted that black people no longer quietly accept the loss of the right to vote: "We believe that [Negro] American citizens should protest emphatically and continually against the curtailment of their political rights." They also demanded an end to segregation: "All American citizens have the right to equal treatment in places of public entertainment." They appealed for better schools, health care, and housing; protested the discrimination black soldiers endured; and criticized the racial prejudice of most churches as "wrong, unchristian and disgraceful to the twentieth century civilization." Perhaps most important, the Niagara gathering insisted that white people did not know what was best for black people: "We repudiate the monstrous doctrine that the oppressor should be the sole authority as to the rights of the oppressed."

The Niagara Movement that emerged from this meeting attracted 400 members and remained active for years. Du Bois composed annual addresses to the nation designed to arouse black and white support. But the Niagara Movement was no match for the powerful, well-financed Tuskegee Machine. Washington used every means at his disposal to undermine the movement. Black newspaper editors like the *Washington Bee*'s W. Calvin Chase, who had earlier attacked Washington's Atlanta address, were paid to attack Du Bois and praise Washington. Washington dispatched spies to Niagara meetings to report on the organization's activities.

Washington sent a telegram requesting that black lawyer Clifford Plummer infiltrate the first Niagara meeting: "See Plummer at once. Give him fifty dollars. Tell him to go to Buffalo tonight or tomorrow morning ostensibly to attend Elks convention but to report fully what goes on at meeting. . . . Get into meeting, if possible but be sure [to get] name of all who attend and what they do." Washington let it be known that black federal employees might be dismissed if they joined the Niagara Movement.

Niagara members also quarreled among themselves. Du Bois was an inexperienced leader, and difficulties developed between him and Trotter. In 1908 the Niagara Movement virtually collapsed. Most black and white Americans would not support an organization that seemed so uncompromising in its demands.

The NAACP

16-3 **What were the origins and goals of the NAACP?**

As the Niagara Movement expired, the National Association for the Advancement of Colored People (NAACP) came to life. There was no direct link between the demise of the Niagara Movement and the rise of the NAACP. However, the relatively few people—black and white—who felt comfortable with the Niagara Movement's assertive stance on race were inclined to support the NAACP. In its early years the NAACP was a militant organization dedicated to racial justice. White leaders dominated it, and white contributors largely financed it.

A few white progressives were concerned about the rampant racial prejudice manifested so graphically in lynchings, Jim Crow, black disfranchisement, and a vicious riot in 1908 in Springfield, Illinois—Abraham Lincoln's hometown. After a gathering of leaders in January 1909 in New York City, on February 12—Lincoln's birthday—Oswald Garrison Villard called on "all believers in democracy to join a national conference to discuss present evils, the voicing of protests, and the renewal of the struggle for civil and political liberty."

Villard was the president and editor of the *New York Evening Post* and the grandson of abolitionist William Lloyd Garrison. Prominent progressives endorsed the call, including social workers Lillian Wald and Jane Addams, literary scholar Joel E. Spingarn, and respected attorneys Clarence Darrow and Moorfield Storey. Du Bois, Ida Wells Barnett, and Mary Church Terrell were the black leaders most involved in forming the NAACP.

Using the System

The NAACP was determined that black citizens should fully enjoy the civil and political rights the Constitution guaranteed to all citizens. It relied on the judicial and legislative systems in what would be a persistent and decades-long effort to secure those rights. The NAACP won its first major legal victory in 1915 when the Supreme Court overturned Oklahoma's grandfather clause in *Guinn v. United States*. But poll taxes and literacy tests continued to disfranchise black citizens.

In 1917, in a case brought by the Louisville NAACP, the Supreme Court struck down a local law that enforced residential segregation by prohibiting black people and white people from selling real estate to people of the other race. The NAACP also tried in 1918 to secure a federal law prohibiting lynching. With the assistance of Congressman Leonidas Dyer, a white St. Louis Republican, the anti-lynching measure—the Dyer bill— passed in the House of Representatives in 1922 over vigorous Democratic opposition. But the Senate blocked it, and it never became law.

Du Bois and the *Crisis*

Du Bois was easily the most prominent black figure associated with the NAACP during its first quarter century. He became director of publicity and research and edited the NAACP publication called the *Crisis*, while largely leaving leadership and administrative tasks to others.

With the *Crisis*, Du Bois the scholar became Du Bois the propagandist. He denounced white racism and atrocities and demanded that black people stand up for their rights: "Agitate, then, brother; protest, reveal the truth and refuse to be silenced. . . . A moment's let up, a moment's acquiescence, means a chance for the wolves of prejudice to get at our necks." He would not provoke violence, but he would not tolerate mistreatment either: "I am resolved to be quiet and law abiding, but to refuse to cringe in body or in soul, to resent deliberate insult, and to assert my just rights in the face of wanton aggression." These were not the even-tempered, cautious words of Booker T. Washington to which so many Americans had grown accustomed. The *Crisis* became required reading in many black homes. By 1913 it had 30,000 subscribers, whereas the NAACP had only 3,000 members.

Washington versus the NAACP

Villard tried to reassure Washington that the NAACP posed no threat and to gain his support for the new association: "It is not to be a Washington movement, or a Du Bois movement. The idea is that there shall grow out

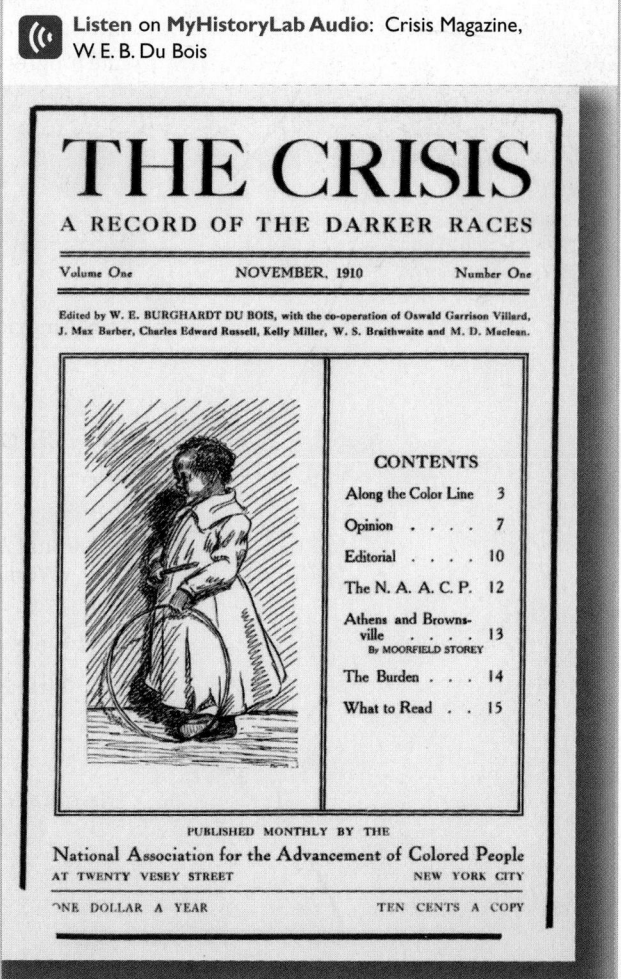

Listen on **MyHistoryLab Audio**: Crisis Magazine, W. E. B. Du Bois

The first issue of the *Crisis* monthly magazine was published in November 1910.

of it, first, an annual conference . . . for the discussion by men of both races of the conditions of the colored people, politically, socially, industrially and educationally."

Many black leaders and members of the NAACP, however, despised Washington and his ideology, and Washington returned the sentiment and worked to subvert the new organization. Washington considered Du Bois little more than the puppet of white people, who dominated the leadership of the NAACP, and the Tuskegee leader declined to debate Du Bois. One of Washington's aides commented that "it would be entirely out of place for Dr. Washington to enter into any discussion with a man occupying the place that Dr. Du Bois does, for the reason that Dr. Washington is at the head of a large institution. . . . Dr. Du Bois, on the other hand, is a mere hired man, as it were, in an institution completely controlled by white people."

Charles Anderson, a Tuskegee loyalist in New York City, wrote to Washington in 1909 that the NAACP was meeting secretly, and he would attempt to disrupt its efforts: "I will find out as much about them as possible and let you know the facts. I am doing all I can to discredit this affair." Washington relied again on allies who were editors of black newspapers to criticize the NAACP.

He also wrote Clark Howell, the white editor of the *Atlanta Constitution*, to attack Du Bois: "I think that it is too bad that an institution like Atlanta University has permitted Dr. Du Bois to go on from year to year stirring up racial strife in the South." Washington told an alumnus of Tuskegee that the main aim of the NAACP was to destroy Washington and Tuskegee: "As a matter of straight fact, this organization is for the purpose of tearing down our work wherever possible and I think none of our friends should give it comfort."

Washington became so obsessed with the NAACP that he was not above manipulating white supremacists to damage those connected with it. When he learned that black and white progressives associated with the NAACP were going to gather at the Café Boulevard in

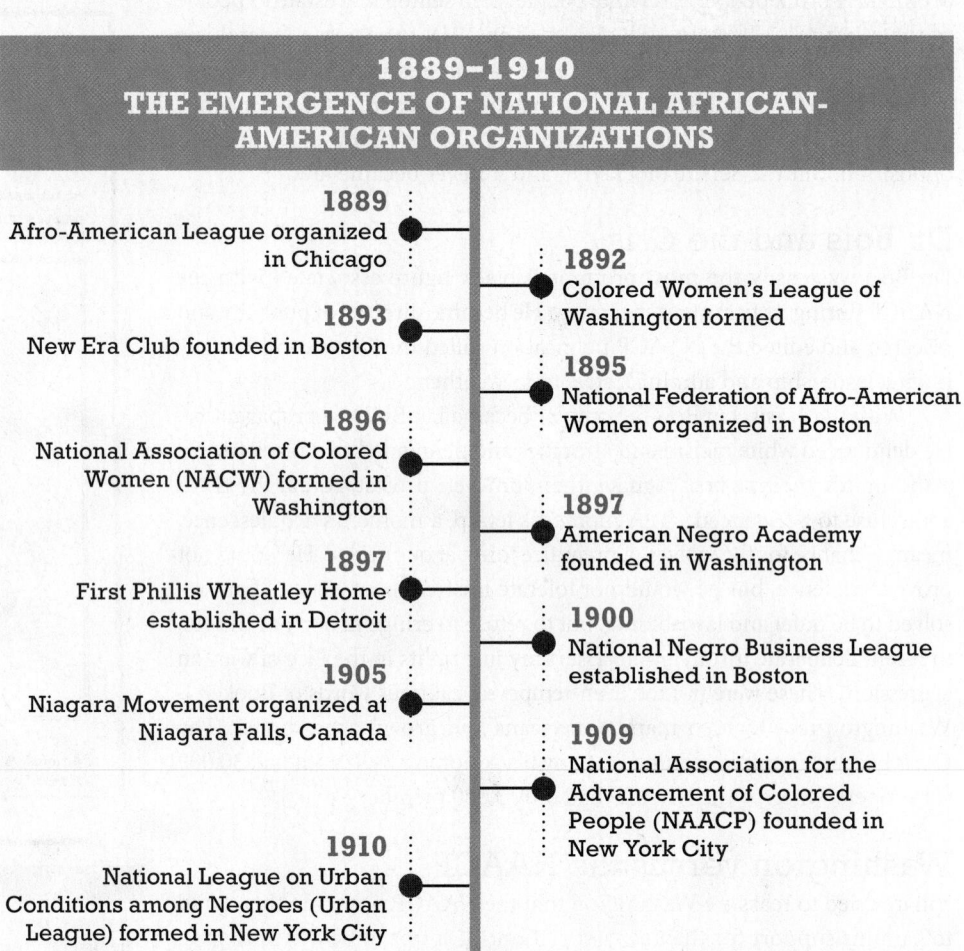

1889–1910
THE EMERGENCE OF NATIONAL AFRICAN-AMERICAN ORGANIZATIONS

1889
Afro-American League organized in Chicago

1892
Colored Women's League of Washington formed

1893
New Era Club founded in Boston

1895
National Federation of Afro-American Women organized in Boston

1896
National Association of Colored Women (NACW) formed in Washington

1897
American Negro Academy founded in Washington

1897
First Phillis Wheatley Home established in Detroit

1900
National Negro Business League established in Boston

1905
Niagara Movement organized at Niagara Falls, Canada

1909
National Association for the Advancement of Colored People (NAACP) founded in New York City

1910
National League on Urban Conditions among Negroes (Urban League) formed in New York City

16-1
16-2
16-3
16-4
16-5
16-6
16-7
16-8

PROFILE Mary Church Terrell

MARY CHURCH TERRELL lived from the year of the Emancipation Proclamation (1863) to the year that the Supreme Court declared segregated schools unconstitutional (1954). During those nine decades, she exemplified the African-American leaders whom Du Bois called the Talented Tenth. The daughter of slaves, she acquired a superb education and became prominent in Washington's black elite. She was ever conscious of her social status, education, and fair complexion. She was dedicated to eliminating Jim Crow and also to the cause of African-American women.

Mary Church was born in Memphis and raised during Reconstruction. She went to Oberlin College where she studied classics, became proficient in languages, and earned an M.A. In 1891 she married Robert H. Terrell, who had earned a law degree at Howard. He was an auditor in the U.S. Treasury Department and became a District of Columbia municipal judge.

Mary Church Terrell immersed herself in literary, social, and political activities. She spearheaded the creation of the Colored Women's League and in 1896 became the first president of the National Association of Colored Women (NACW). She believed that well-to-do black women had a responsibility to assist struggling and poorer women of color.

Terrell was an inspirational speaker. She spoke in 1904 at the International Congress of Women in Berlin—in German, French, and English. Mamie Garvin Fields recalled a speech Terrell delivered in Charleston in 1916:

> Oh, my, when I saw her walk onto that podium in her pink evening dress and long white gloves, with her beautifully done hair, she was the Modern Woman. . . . Regal, intelligent, powerful, reaching out from time to time with

that long glove, she looked and sounded like the Modern Woman that she talked about.

Terrell was active in the NAACP, which was not easy given her close relationship with Booker T. Washington and his wife, Margaret Murray Washington. She could not afford to alienate Washington because he could prevent her husband's reappointment as judge. Terrell managed to convince Washington that she supported him; in fact, she was devoted to the NAACP and its program. She served on its board and spoke forcefully on civil rights. She risked the wrath of President Theodore Roosevelt after she criticized his dismissal of three companies of black soldiers following the Brownsville incident (see Chapter 15). She presented President William Howard Taft with NAACP petitions against lynching. She wrote articles attacking chain gangs, peonage, disfranchisement, and lynching. She worked with progressive organizations, such as the Women's International League for Peace and Freedom, and supported women's suffrage and the Nineteenth Amendment.

The Terrells were active in Washington's black elite—the Four Hundred. They attended balls, concerts, and parties, traveled extensively, and belonged to Washington's most exclusive black congregation, the Lincoln Temple Congregational Church. She was also active in Delta Sigma Theta sorority.

Mary Church Terrell consistently opposed racial discrimination. She protested to Oberlin College when her daughters encountered more prejudice as students than she had. A lifelong Republican, she opposed Democratic President Franklin Roosevelt's inaction on civil rights in the 1930s. At age 87 she demonstrated against an all-white restaurant in Washington, DC.

Mary Church Terrell summed up her legacy in her 1940 autobiography, *A Colored Woman in a White World*: "This is the story of a colored woman living in a white world. It cannot possibly be like a story written by a white woman. A white woman has only one handicap to overcome—that of sex. I have two—both sex and race. I belong to the only group in this country which has two such huge obstacles to surmount. Colored men have only one—that of race."

((• **Listen on MyHistoryLab Audio:** The Progress of Colored Women; Mary Church Terrell, excerpt

16-1
16-2
16-3
16-4
16-5
16-6
16-7
16-8

New York City in 1911, he allowed Charles Anderson to alert the hostile white press, which described the multiracial dinner in the most inflammatory terms: "Fashionable White Women Sit at Board with Negroes, Japs and Chinamen to Promote 'Cause' of Miscegenation" proclaimed one headline. The *New York Press* added, "White women, evidently of the cultured and wealthier classes, fashionably attired in low-cut gowns, leaned over the tables to chat confidentially with negro men of the true African type."

Ultimately, Washington's efforts to ruin the NAACP and reduce its supporters' influence failed. By the time of his death in 1915, the NAACP had 6,000 members and 50 local branches. Its aggressive campaign for civil and political rights replaced Washington's strategy of progress through conciliation and accommodation.

The Urban League

In 1910, black and white progressives founded the National League on Urban Conditions among Negroes in New York City. Soon known simply as the Urban League, its goal was to alleviate conditions black people encountered as they moved into large cities in ever-increasing numbers during the early twentieth century. The Urban League worked to improve housing, medical care, and recreational facilities among black residents who lived in segregated neighborhoods in New York, Philadelphia, Atlanta, Nashville, Norfolk, and other cities. The league also assisted youngsters who ran afoul of the law, and it helped establish the Big Brother and Big Sister movements.

Black Women and the Club Movement

16-4 What role did black women play in advocating reform and in fostering progress among African Americans?

Years before the Urban League and the NAACP were founded, black women began creating clubs and organizations. The local groups that began forming in the 1870s and 1880s, such as the Bethel Literary and Historical Association in Washington, DC, were mainly concerned with cultural, religious, and social matters. But many of the mostly middle-class women active in these clubs eventually became less interested in tea and gossip and more involved with community problems. In 1893 black women in Boston founded the New Era Club. Their monthly magazine, *Woman's Era*, featured articles on fashion, health, and family life.

In 1895 a New Era Club member, Josephine St. Pierre Ruffin, enraged by white journalist James W. Jack's vilification of black women as "prostitutes, thieves, and liars," issued a call to "Let Us Confer Together" that drew 104 black women to a meeting in Boston. The result was the formation of the National Federation of Afro-American Women, which soon included 36 clubs in 12 states. In the meantime, the Colored Women's League of Washington, DC, which had been founded in 1892, appealed in *Woman's Era* for black women to organize a national association at the 1895 meeting of the National Council of Women. At that gathering, representatives from black women's clubs organized the National Colored Woman's League.

The NACW: "Lifting as We Climb"

The two groups—The National Federation of Afro-American Women and the National Colored Woman's League—merged in 1896 to form the National Association of Colored Women (NACW), with Mary Church Terrell elected the first president. The NACW adopted the self-help motto "Lifting as We Climb," and in the reforming spirit of the progressive age they stressed moral, mental, and material advancement. By 1914 the NACW had 50,000 members in 1,000 clubs nationwide.

Middle- and upper-class black club women were sometimes more concerned with the morality and behavior of black men and women than with civil rights and white supremacy. They opposed premarital sex and warned against the evils of alcohol.

There were occasionally unpleasant disagreements and conflicts among the club women. Margaret Murray Washington—Booker T. Washington's wife—served as NACW president from 1912 to 1916, and the organization's *National Notes* was published at Tuskegee until 1922. Not everyone was fond of this arrangement. Ida Wells Barnett claimed that the Tuskegee Machine censored the publication. Meanwhile, Mary Church Terrell found Barnett abrasive and contentious and managed to exclude her from the initial NACW meeting in 1896. There were also regional rivalries, ideological disputes, and sensitivity over the light complexion of leaders like Terrell.

More important than these internal struggles were the efforts of black women to confront the problems black people encountered in urban areas as rural southerners migrated to the cities by the thousands in the second and third decades of the twentieth century. The NACW clubs worked to eradicate poverty, end racial discrimination, and promote education. Members cared for older people, especially former slaves. They aided orphans; provided nurseries, health care, and information on child rearing for working mothers; and established homes for delinquent and abandoned girls.

Phillis Wheatley Clubs

Black women also formed Phillis Wheatley clubs and homes across the nation, named in honor of the eighteenth-century African-American poet (see Chapter 4). The residences offered living accommodations for single, black working women in many cities where YWCAs refused to admit them. Some Phillis Wheatley clubs also provided nurseries and classes in domestic skills. In Cleveland, a nurse named Jane Edna Hunter organized a residence for single, black working women who could not find comfortable and affordable housing. In 1911, she formed the Working Girls' Home Association for cleaning women, laundresses, and private duty nurses. With association members contributing five cents a week, Hunter opened a 23-room residence in 1913 that expanded to a 72-room building in 1917.

Anna Julia Cooper and Black Feminism

"Only the BLACK WOMAN can say 'when and where I enter, in the quiet, undisputed dignity of my womanhood, without violence and without suing or patronage, then and there the whole Negro race enters with me." So wrote Anna Julia Cooper in the late nineteenth century. Not only was Cooper convinced that black women would play a decisive role in shaping the destiny of their people, she labored against the stereotype that black women lacked refinement, grace, and morality.

Cooper was born a slave in Raleigh, North Carolina, in 1858 and graduated from St. Augustine's School. She then earned a bachelor's degree from Oberlin College in 1884. Speaking and writing with increasing confidence and authority, she published *A Voice From the South, by a Black Woman of the South* in 1892. In these essays she stressed the pivotal role that black women would play in the future and chastised white women for their lack of support. In 1900 she addressed the Pan African Conference in London.

Cooper was principal of Washington's famed M Street Colored High School (later Paul Laurence Dunbar High School) from 1901 to 1906. She was forced out in 1906 amid allegations that supporters of the Tuskegee Machine resented her emphasis on academic preparation over vocational training. She went on to teach for four years at Missouri's Lincoln University before returning to M Street High as a teacher. Fluent in French, she earned a Ph.D. at the Sorbonne in Paris.

She was active with the NACW, the NAACP, and the YWCA. Married in 1877, her husband died only two years later. Cooper found time following his death to take in and raise five children. She died in 1964 at age 105.

Women's Suffrage

Historically, many black women had supported women's suffrage. Before the Civil War, many abolitionists, including Mary Ann Shadd Cary, Sojourner Truth, and Frederick Douglass,

Read on **MyHistoryLab**
Document: Anna Julia Cooper Describes the Status of Women in America, 1892

16-1

16-2

16-3

16-4

16-5

16-6

16-7

16-8

PROFILE Jane Edna Hunter and the Phillis Wheatley Association

IN THE EARLY TWENTIETH CENTURY, no one was more committed to improving the lives of young black women than Jane Edna Hunter. Trained as a nurse, she migrated to Cleveland, where she founded the Phillis Wheatley Association.

Born Jane Harris in 1882 in Pendleton, South Carolina, she had a fair complexion because her father was the son of a slave woman and a white overseer. For a time she believed that her light color made her superior to darker friends and family members, especially her mother.

Her beloved father died when she was 10. She had little schooling as a child, but she was able to enroll at Ferguson Williams College in Abbeville, South Carolina, at age 14. Later her mother prodded her to marry Edward Hunter, a man 40 years her senior. The marriage lasted all of 15 months. Jane Edna Hunter never remarried.

She came to reject her color consciousness and embraced her heritage as a black woman: "—I was to be overwhelmed by the realization that I was, above and beyond all, my Mother's child—a Negro; that I was proud of the blood of my ancestors; that my life henceforth was to be a solemn dedication to the people of my Mother's race!"

She received training as a nurse in Charleston at the Canon Street Hospital and Training School for Nurses and then at the Dixie Hospital and Training School at Hampton Institute. In 1905 she moved to Cleveland, Ohio. She immediately encountered difficulties as a young black woman in a big city. In search of a place to stay, she unintentionally knocked on the door of a brothel.

No white hospital would hire her as a nurse, and she worked as a cleaning woman while living in an unsavory boarding house: "In the average rooming house of that period . . . the Negro girl had to pay a dollar and a quarter a week for a small, low-roofed, poorly furnished room. She was charged extra for the use of the laundry and gas. If she wished to invite a caller, she was frequently required to clean the whole house in payment for the privilege. The use of the bath tub, when there was one, was discouraged."

The YWCA in Cleveland did not extend its benevolence to black women, and they were not permitted to live at YWCA residential facilities. Jane Edna Hunter took it upon herself to persuade the white women who ran the YWCA to support the establishment of a separate housing facility for black women. But some black people—"a small group of club women, who blessed with prosperity, had risen from the servant class and now regarded themselves as the arbiters and guardians of colored society"—opposed her efforts.

Nevertheless, the Phillis Wheatley Home opened in 1911. It was named in honor of the former slave who had become a prominent poet in colonial America. The first facility had 23 rooms. Hunter worked with white leaders to expand the size and services of what became the Phillis Wheatley Association. In doing so, black leaders attacked her for being too conciliatory and subservient to white people simply to gain access to their funds.

Ambitious and determined, she earned a law degree and passed the bar in 1926. She presided over the construction of an 11-story residence for black women that was completed in 1927. It featured a beauty school, dining facilities, a nursery school, and the Booker T. Washington Playground. The Phillis Wheatley Association also operated a summer camp for children and served as an employment agency for black women. Critics complained because many of the jobs were as domestics for well-to-do white families and accused Hunter of providing dead-end positions that kept black people in a subordinate status.

Hunter also shrewdly invested in Cleveland real estate and was active for decades in the NACW, even though it included many of the same women who had opposed her efforts. She served as a trustee of Ohio's Central State University. In 1937 she was awarded the NAACP's Spingarn Medal. She retired in 1946. When she died in 1971 she left most of her estate of nearly $500,000 to the Phillis Wheatley Foundation.

had also backed women's suffrage. Cary and Truth tried unsuccessfully to vote after the war. Black women, such as Caroline Remond Putnam of Massachusetts, Lottie Rollin of South Carolina, and Frances Ellen Watkins Harper of Pennsylvania, attended conventions of the mostly white American Woman's Suffrage Association in the 1870s.

Black women were also involved in the long struggle for women's suffrage on the state level. Ida Wells Barnett was a leader in the Illinois suffrage effort. By 1900 Wyoming, Utah, Colorado, and Idaho permitted women to vote, and by 1918 women in 17 northern and western states had gained the vote. But as more women won voting rights, women's suffrage became more controversial. The proposed Nineteenth Amendment to the Constitution drove a wedge between black and white advocates of women's political rights. Many opponents of women's suffrage, especially white southerners, warned that granting women the right to vote would increase the number of black voters. Some white women advocated strict literacy and educational requirements for voting to limit the number of black voters, both women and men.

Only two southern states—Kentucky and Tennessee—ratified the Nineteenth Amendment before its adoption in 1920. Black suffragists understood that the right to vote meant political power, and political power could be exercised to acquire civil rights, improve education, and gain respect. White southerners also grasped the importance of voting rights. Thus, despite the Nineteenth Amendment, most black people in the South—both men and women—remained unable to vote.

The Black Elite

16-5 | **What were the defining characteristics of the black elite?**

Many of the black leaders described by Du Bois as the Talented Tenth formed protest organizations, joined reform efforts, and organized self-help groups. The leaders were middle- and upper-class black people who were better educated than most Americans—black or white.

The American Negro Academy

In 1897, Episcopal priest Alexander Crummell met with 16 other black men in Washington, DC, to form the American Negro Academy. This scholarly organization was made up of "men of African descent" who assembled periodically to discuss and publish works on history, literature, religion, and science. Among those who attended the initial gathering were Du Bois, Paul Laurence Dunbar, Kelly Miller, and Francis Grimke.

Crummell was an elderly but dynamic and distinguished leader who did not hesitate to express his convictions on race, religion, and Africa. He had been born in 1818 in New York and lived in Liberia in the 1850s and 1860s as an Episcopal missionary. Crummell died in 1898, but the Academy survived as a vibrant intellectual and elitist society.

Carter G. Woodson, Alain Locke, Arthur Schomburg, and James Weldon Johnson joined its ranks before the Academy disbanded in 1928. It afforded black intellectuals an opportunity to ponder what it meant to be black in America and develop their racial consciousness, thus nurturing ideas and concepts that would mature during the Harlem Renaissance.

Most members of the Academy supported women's rights and women's suffrage. Consequently, it was ironic that black women were not invited to become members of the Academy, although several black women, including Anna Julia Cooper, Ida Wells Barnett, and Mary Church Terrell, were easily the intellectual equals of the male participants.

The Upper Class

By the early twentieth century, there were several hundred wealthy African Americans. These black aristocrats were as sophisticated, refined, and status conscious as any group in American society. They distanced themselves from less affluent black and white people and

16-1 16-2 16-3 16-4 16-5 16-6 16-7 16-8

lived in expensive houses. Many of them had fair complexions. They were medical doctors, lawyers, and businessmen. Although they possessed vastly more wealth than most Americans, their wealth paled compared to the huge fortunes of the richest American families, such as the Rockefellers, Carnegies, and Vanderbilts.

The black elite formed exclusive organizations that jealously limited membership to the small black upper class. In the 1860s the Ugly Fishing Club was made up of New York City's wealthiest black men. It soon came to be known simply as the Ugly Club, and its membership spread to Newport, Rhode Island; Baltimore; and Philadelphia. In 1904 two wealthy Philadelphia physicians, a dentist, and a pharmacist formed Sigma Pi Phi, better known as Boulé, to provide "inspiration, relaxation, intellectual stimulation, and brotherhood: for male college graduates." Boulé expanded to seven chapters in cities that included Chicago and Memphis, but its membership totaled a mere 177.

Organizations like the Diamondback Club and the Cosmos Club in Washington, the Loendi Club in Pittsburgh, and the Bachelor-Benedict Club in New York sponsored luxurious banquets, dances, and debutante balls. Several of these groups owned ornate clubhouses. These elite societies and cliques competed to demonstrate social exclusivity and preeminence.

Fraternities and Sororities

Among the black elite were also the African Americans who established the Greek-letter black fraternities and sororities. In 1906 seven students at Cornell University formed Alpha Phi Alpha, the first college fraternity for black men. Within a few years, it had chapters at the University of Michigan, Yale, Columbia, and Ohio State. The first black sorority, Alpha Kappa Alpha, was founded in 1908 at Howard University.

Other Greek-letter organizations were launched at Howard: Omega Psi Phi fraternity in 1911, Delta Sigma Theta sorority in 1913, Phi Beta Sigma fraternity in 1914, and Zeta Phi Beta sorority in 1920. In 1911 Kappa Alpha Psi fraternity was founded at Indiana University, and Sigma Gamma Rho sorority was formed in Indianapolis in 1922.

Besides providing college students with an opportunity to enjoy each other's company, the black fraternities and sororities stressed scholarship, social graces, and community involvement. Alpha Phi Alpha created the "Go to High School, Go to College" campaign in 1919. Kappa Alpha Psi adopted the "Guide Right" program to assist black youngsters in 1922. In 1923 Alpha Kappa Alpha opened a mobile health clinic in Mississippi. From 1935 to 1941, during the Great Depression, Alpha Kappa Alpha sponsored free health clinics in Mississippi under the guidance of Dr. Dorothy Ferebee of the Howard University Medical School. It was the first time many black people in that state had received professional medical attention.

African-American Inventors

Among the black elite were inventors and innovators who contributed to the technical and industrial transformation of America during the late nineteenth and early twentieth centuries. Like Thomas Edison, Henry Ford, and Harvey Firestone, these African Americans were mostly self-taught and not college educated. But there was an exception. Shelby J. Davidson had graduated from Howard University and was a lawyer.

As a longtime employee of the auditing department of the Post Office Division of the U.S. Treasury, Davidson became an expert on the new and complex adding machines used to maintain post office accounts. In 1908 he received a patent for an electric device that fed paper into the machines. He worked diligently for years to create a mechanism that would enable large Burroughs adding machines to calculate the ascending rates that post offices charged for money orders. But the attempt to secure a joint patent with Edwin Dowling for their invention failed when it was challenged. Davidson had not maintained the paperwork and drawings to sustain their claim.

As prejudice and discrimination against black federal employees intensified, Davidson resigned his auditing position in 1912. He believed that a less qualified white man was promoted while he was not. He complained to Assistant U.S. Attorney William H. Lewis, who was black, "Had I been white instead of colored I do not doubt at all that I would have been chief of one of the divisions instead of now being on trial, hounded, persecuted and expected to make another record in order to maintain my present rating and this under the most painful and adverse conditions."

Granville Woods was born in Australia in 1856 and grew up in Columbus, Ohio. He developed mechanical skills and became a locomotive engineer. His extensive knowledge of electricity enabled him to win 45 patents. His Synchronous Multiplex Railway Telegraph improved communication among trains and with stations, thereby increasing railroad safety. His invention of an electric railway brake also enhanced safe operations. Thomas Edison challenged Woods's claim to have invented the Multiplex Telegraph, but Woods prevailed. It was one of the rare patent cases that Edison lost.

Lewis Latimer's parents were slaves who had escaped from Virginia to Boston in 1842. Lewis was born in 1848, and as a youngster he sold copies of William Lloyd Garrison's abolitionist newspaper, the *Liberator*. During the Civil War at age 15, Latimer joined the Union Navy. After the war he became a skilled draftsman for a patent law firm. In 1874 Latimer received a patent for a flushing mechanism that improved toilets on railway coaches.

He went on to draft diagrams for Alexander Graham Bell's patent application for the telephone. While working for the U.S. Electric Lighting Company, Latimer invented an improved process for manufacturing carbon filaments for light bulbs that he patented in 1882. He went to work for the Edison Electric Light Company in 1883, and in 1890 he published *Incandescent Lighting: A Practical Description of the Edison System*. He served as the chief draftsman for the General Electric/Westinghouse Board of Patent Control after it was formed in 1896.

Lewis H. Latimer's *Incandescent Lighting: A Practical Description of the Edison System*, published in 1896, was one of the first books on electric lighting.

The men who worked for Thomas Edison before 1885 joined together in 1918 as Edison Pioneers to reminisce about their early experiences and experiments. Latimer was the only African American among them.

Madam C. J. Walker was more an entrepreneur than an inventor (see Chapter 15). However, she did develop a secret chemical formula to nourish and promote the growth of hair among black women. She also created an improved hot comb and the Anti-Kink Walker System to straighten black hair.

Presidential Politics

Since Reconstruction, black voters had supported the Republican Party and its presidential candidates. "The Party of Lincoln" welcomed that support and rewarded black men with federal jobs. Republican presidents Theodore Roosevelt (1901–1909) and William Howard Taft (1909–1913) continued that policy.

FRUSTRATED BY THE REPUBLICANS

However, other presidential actions offset whatever goodwill these appointments generated. Roosevelt discharged three companies of black soldiers after the Brownsville incident in 1906, and Taft tolerated restrictions on black voters in the South and encouraged the development of a "lily white" Republican Party, removing black people from federal jobs in the region.

In 1912 the Republican Party split in a bitter feud between President Taft and Theodore Roosevelt, and Roosevelt's supporters formed the Progressive Party, which nominated him to run against Taft and the Democratic candidate, Woodrow Wilson. But as the delegates at the Progressive convention in Chicago sang the "Battle Hymn of the Republic," southern black men who had come to the gathering stood outside the hall, denied admission by white Progressives.

16-1
16-2
16-3
16-4
16-5
16-6
16-7
16-8

PROFILE George Washington Carver and Ernest Everett Just

GEORGE WASHINGTON CARVER AND ERNEST EVERETT JUST rose from humble beginnings to become eminent biologists. Carver was born in 1864 or 1865 to slave parents in Diamond Grove, Missouri. Eager to learn, he spent much of his youth engaged in menial labor around Missouri, Iowa, and Kansas as he acquired an uneven education. He attended Simpson College and then enrolled at Iowa State University in 1891 at age 25 as its sole black student. He compiled a superb academic record and took charge of the campus greenhouse. He became fascinated with botany and focused on mycology (the study of fungi) and cross-fertilization.

Just was born in Charleston in 1883 and grew up on nearby James Island, where his mother toiled in phosphate mines after the death of his father. He attended local schools and earned a teacher training certificate in 1899 from what is now South Carolina State University. Just went on to Kimball Union Academy in New Hampshire and graduated with honors from Dartmouth College in 1907 with a major in biology and minors in Greek and history.

Just was hired by Howard University and spent the rest of his teaching career there. In 1911 he helped establish Omega Psi Phi, which became a major black fraternity. Although hired to teach English and rhetoric, he soon changed to zoology and biology, the subjects in which he had an abiding interest. He spent several summers at the Marine Biology Laboratory at Woods Hole, Massachusetts, and earned a Ph.D. in zoology from the University of Chicago in 1916.

While Just felt more at home doing research in a laboratory, Carver felt more comfortable experimenting with crops in a field. At the invitation of Booker T. Washington, Carver left a promising career at Iowa State in 1896 to take charge of the agriculture program at Tuskegee Institute. Having studied with two men at Iowa State—James Wilson and Henry C. Wallace—who later became U.S. secretaries of agriculture, Carver established political ties that benefitted Tuskegee. He became the director of the nation's only black agricultural experiment station.

Carver was a superb teacher in and out of the classroom, but he was a less-than-efficient administrator who clashed with Booker T. Washington. Carver sought to make impoverished black farmers more productive and less dependent on cotton. He sponsored outreach programs and farmers' institutes. He discovered hundreds of uses for the protein-rich peanut. And he experimented extensively with sweet potatoes.

Carver became a folk hero by the 1930s with his gregarious personality and self-effacing demeanor. He never married and lived in a student dormitory at Tuskegee. He wore a tattered coat with a fresh flower in the lapel. Though he never earned more than $1,200 a year, he gave more than $60,000 to Tuskegee before he died in 1943.

Just, confronted with the lack of opportunities available to a dedicated black scientist at white universities, pursued his research in the fertilization of marine animals at Woods Hole. But even there he was shunned and patronized. Nevertheless, by 1928 he had published 35 articles, mostly on fertilization. Awarded a grant from the Julius Rosenwald Foundation, he spent much of the 1930s engaged in research in Italy, Germany, and France. In 1939 he published *Biology of the Cell Surface*.

Just married Ethel Highwarden, a Howard faculty member, in 1912. They had three children but later divorced. In 1939 he married Maid Hedwig Schnetzler, a German scientist. Just died of cancer in 1941.

Both George Washington Carver and Ernest Everett Just were awarded the NAACP's Spingarn Medal—Just in 1915 and Carver in 1923.

WOODROW WILSON

It was not a complete shock that militant black leaders like William Monroe Trotter and W. E. B. Du Bois urged black voters to break with the Republican Party and support Woodrow Wilson. Wilson was the reform governor of New Jersey and had been president of Princeton University. Wilson's academic background and his promise to pursue a progressive policy toward black Americans impressed Trotter and Du Bois. Du Bois wrote,

> Wilson is a cultivated scholar and he has brains. We have, therefore, a conviction that Mr. Wilson will treat black men and their interests with foresighted fairness. He will not advance the cause of an oligarchy in the South, he will not seek further means of "jim crow" insult, he will not dismiss black men wholesale from office, and he will remember that the Negro has a right to be heard and considered.

But President Wilson was no friend of black people. Born in Virginia and raised in South Carolina, Wilson had absorbed white southern racial views. Federal agencies and buildings were fully segregated early during Wilson's tenure. In 1914 Trotter and a black delegation met with Wilson to protest segregation in the Treasury Department and the Post Office. Wilson defended separation of the races as a means to avoid friction. Trotter strongly disagreed. Wilson became visibly irritated with Trotter and abruptly ended the meeting.

Black Men and the Military in World War I

16-6 How did African Americans contribute to the U.S. war effort in World War I?

In 1915–1916 Wilson faced more than problems with dissatisfied black people. Relations with Mexico had steadily deteriorated after a revolution and civil war there. War in Europe threatened to draw the United States into conflict with Germany.

The Punitive Expedition to Mexico

In 1914 war almost broke out between the United States and Mexico when U.S. Marines landed at Vera Cruz after an attack on American sailors. Then in March 1916, Francisco "Pancho" Villa, one of the participants in Mexico's civil war, led a force of Mexican rebels across the border into New Mexico in an effort to provoke war with the United States. Fifteen Americans were killed, including seven U.S. soldiers. In response, Wilson dispatched a "punitive expedition" that eventually numbered 15,000 troops under General John J. Pershing. Pershing had acquired the nickname "Black Jack" after commanding black troops in Cuba during the Spanish-American War.

U.S. forces, including the black 10th Cavalry, spent 10 months in Mexico in 1916–1917 in a futile effort to capture Villa. White officers commanded the 10th Cavalry, as had been the case with black troops since the Civil War. But Lieutenant Colonel Charles Young, an 1889 black graduate of West Point, helped lead the regiment.

Young led the black troops against a contingent of Villa's rebels who had ambushed an element of the 13th Cavalry, a white unit, at Santa Cruz de Villegas. Major Frank Tompkins of the 13th was so relieved to be rescued that he reportedly exclaimed to Young, "By God, Young, I could kiss every black face out there." Young supposedly replied, "If you want to, you may start with me." As the probability increased that the United States would enter World War I against Germany, U.S. troops were withdrawn from Mexico in 1917.

Lieutenant Colonel Charles D. Young, an 1889 graduate of the U.S. Military Academy at West Point who served in Cuba, the Philippines, Haiti, and Mexico, was not permitted to command troops during World War I. He returned to military service at the end of the war and was sent to Liberia to help train that country's army. He died while on furlough in Nigeria in 1922.

16-1

16-2

16-3

16-4

16-5

16-6

16-7

16-8

16-1

16-2

16-3

16-4

16-5

16-6

16-7

16-8

World War I

When World War I erupted in Europe in August 1914, most Americans had no intention or desire to participate. Wilson issued a proclamation of neutrality. Running for reelection in 1916 on the slogan "He Kept Us Out of War," Wilson narrowly defeated Republican Charles Evans Hughes. But German submarine attacks on civilian vessels and the loss of American lives infuriated Wilson and many Americans as a gross violation of U.S. neutrality rights. On April 6, 1917, Congress declared war on Germany. Most African Americans supported the war effort. As in previous conflicts, black people sought to demonstrate their loyalty and devotion to the country through military service. "If this is our country," declared Du Bois, "then this is our war. We must fight it with every ounce of blood and treasure."

Some white leaders were less enthusiastic about the participation of black men. One southern governor wondered about the wisdom of having the military train and arm thousands of black men at southern camps and posts. General Pershing insisted on white leadership: "Under capable white officers and with sufficient training, Negro soldiers have always acquitted themselves creditably."

Black Troops and Officers

There were about 10,000 black regulars in the U.S. Army in 1917: the 9th and 10th Cavalry Regiments and the 24th and 25th Infantry Regiments. There were more than 5,000 black men in the navy, but virtually all of them were waiters, kitchen attendants, and stokers for the ships' boilers. The Marine Corps did not admit black men. During World War I, the new Selective Service system drafted more than 370,000 black men—13 percent of all draftees—although none of the local draft boards had black members. Several all-black state National Guard units were also incorporated into federal service.

Although the military remained rigidly segregated, black newspapers and the NAACP campaigned to commission black officers to lead black troops. The War Department created an officer training school at Fort Des Moines, Iowa. Nearly 1,250 black men enrolled—1,000 were civilians, and 250 were enlisted men from the regular regiments—and over 1,000 received commissions. Black officers, however, were confined to the lower ranks. None of the new black officers were promoted above captain, and the overall command of black units remained in white hands.

Lieutenant Colonel Charles Young was eligible to lead black and white troops in World War I. He had already served in Cuba, the Philippines, Haiti, and Mexico. White soldiers complained, however, that they did not want to take orders from a black man, and, over Young's protests, military authorities forced him to retire by claiming he had high blood pressure. Young rode a horse from his home in Xenia, Ohio, to Washington, DC, to prove he was in good health. But he remained on the retired list until he was given command of a training unit in Illinois five days before the war ended.

Discrimination and Its Effects

Most white military leaders, politicians, and journalists embraced racial stereotypes and expected little from black soldiers. As in earlier wars, black troops were discriminated against, abused, and neglected. Some had to drill with picks and shovels rather than rifles. At Camp Hill, Virginia, black troops lived through a cold winter in tents with no floors, no blankets, and no bathing facilities. White men failed to salute black officers, and black officers were denied admission to officers' clubs. Morale among black troops was low, and their performance sometimes reflected it.

Military authorities did not expect to use black troops in combat. The army preferred to employ black troops in labor battalions, as stevedores, in road construction, and as cooks and bakers. Of more than 380,000 black men who served in World War I, only 42,000 went into combat. Black troops represented 3 percent of U.S. combat strength. The army did not prepare black soldiers adequately for combat, but military leaders complained when black soldiers who did face combat performed poorly.

The 368th Infantry Regiment of the 92nd Division came in for especially harsh criticism. Fighting alongside the French in September 1918, the regiment's second and third battalions fell back in disorder. Some men ran. The white regimental commander blamed black officers, and 30 of them were relieved of command. Five officers were court-martialed for cowardice; four were sentenced to death and one to life in prison. All were later freed. But black Lieutenant Howard H. Long argued that the perceptions of white officers caused the poor performance: "Many of the [white] field officers seemed far more concerned with reminding their Negro subordinates that they were Negroes than they were in having an effective unit that would perform well in combat."

Even the white commander of the 92nd Division, General Charles C. Ballou, identified white officers as the main problem: "It was my misfortune to be handicapped by many white officers who were rabidly hostile to the idea of a colored officer, and who continually conveyed misinformation to the staff of the superior units, and generally created much trouble and discontent. Such men will never give the Negro the square deal that is his just due."

Read on MyHistoryLab Document: French Officers Receive Secret Information Concerning Black American Troops, 1918

African-American troops on the march near Verdun in France in 1918.

White officials stressed the weaknesses of the 368th Infantry Regiment and mostly ignored the commendable records of the 369th, 370th, 371st, and 372nd Regiments. The 369th compiled an exemplary combat record. Sent to the front for 91 consecutive days, these "Men of Bronze"—as they came to be known—consisted mainly of soldiers from the 15th Regiment of the New York National Guard. They fought alongside the French and were given French weapons, uniforms, helmets, and food (but not the wine that French soldiers received). They had an outstanding military band led by Jim Europe, one of the finest musical leaders of the early twentieth century. The 369th lived up to their motto, "Let's Go," as they took part in heavy fighting. They never lost a trench or gave up a prisoner. By June 1918 French commanders were asking for all the black troops the Americans could send.

Most French civilians and troops, unfazed by racist warnings from white American officials about the presumed danger black men posed to white women, praised the conduct of black soldiers and accepted them as equals. Following the triumph of the Allies in World War I, French authorities awarded the Croix de Guerre, France's highest military medal, to the men of the 369th, the 371st, and the 372nd Regiments.

Black troops returned to America on segregated ships. The 15th New York National Guard Unit from the 369th Regiment and its famed band were not permitted to join the farewell parade in New York City. Even praise from white Americans was riddled with racist stereotypes. The *Milwaukee Sentinel* was typical: "Those two colored regiments fought well, and it calls for special recognition. Is there no way of getting a cargo of watermelons over there?"

Read on MyHistoryLab Document: The Reverend F. J. Grimke Speaks to African-American Veterans, 1919

Du Bois's Disappointment

The treatment of black soldiers embittered black leaders who had supported American entry in the war. During the war in 1918, Du Bois appealed to black people in the *Crisis* to "close ranks" and support the war:

> We of the colored race have no ordinary interest in the outcome. That which the German power represents today spells death to the aspirations of Negroes and all darker races for equality, freedom and democracy. Let us not hesitate. Let us, while this war lasts, forget our special grievances and close ranks with our own white fellow citizens and the allied nations that are fighting for democracy.

Du Bois's unequivocal support may have been connected to his effort to secure an officer's commission in military intelligence through the intervention of Joel E. Spingarn, chairman of the NAACP board of directors. Du Bois did not get his commission; instead, what he got was criticism for his "close ranks" editorial. William Monroe Trotter said that Du Bois had "finally weakened, compromised, deserted the fight, [and] betrayed the cause of his race." To Trotter, Du Bois was "a rank quitter in the cause for equal rights."

In 1930 Du Bois confessed that he should not have supported intervention in the war:

> I was swept off my feet during the world war by the emotional response of America to what seemed to be a great call to duty. The thing that I did not understand is how easy and inevitable it is for an appeal to blood and force to smash to utter negation any ideal for which it is used. Instead of a war to end war, or a war to save democracy, we found ourselves during and after the war descending to the meanest and most sordid of selfish actions.

By the end of World War I, Du Bois—who had visited black troops in France—could see that black loyalty and sacrifice had not eroded white racism. He wrote defiantly in the *Crisis* that black people were determined to make America yield to its democratic ideals:

> But by the God of heaven, we are cowards and jackasses if now that the war is over, we do not marshal every ounce of our brain and brawn to fight a sterner, longer, more unbending battle against the forces of hell in our own land.
> We return.
> We return from fighting.
> We return fighting.
> Make way for Democracy! We saved it in France, and by the Great Jehovah, we will save it in the United States of America, or know the reason why.

View on MyHistoryLab Closer Look:
African American Soldiers Return Home

Race Riots

16-7 **What were the causes of racial violence in the early twentieth century and why was that violence so intense?**

Despite the reformist impulse of the progressive era and the democratic ideals trumpeted as the United States went to war against Germany, most white Americans clung to social Darwinism and white supremacy. White people reacted with contempt and violence to demands by black people for fairer treatment and equal opportunities in American society. The campaigns of the NAACP, the efforts of the black club women, and the services and sacrifices of black men in the war not only failed to alter white racial perceptions but were sometimes accompanied by a backlash against African Americans. Ten black men still in uniform were lynched in 1919.

Many white Americans concurred with Mississippi Senator James K. Vardaman when he declared in 1914 that white people would not accept black claims for a meaningful political and legal role in America:

> God Almighty never intended that the negro should share with the white man in the government of this country. . . . Do not forget that. It matters not what I may say or others

may think; it matters not what constitutions may contain or statutes provide, wherever the negro is in sufficient numbers to imperil the white man's civilization or question the white man's supremacy the white man is going to find some way around the difficulty. And that is just as true in the North as it is in the South. You need not deceive yourselves about that. The feeling against the negro in Illinois when he gets in the white man's way is quite as strong, more bitter, less regardful of the negro's feelings and conditions than it is in Mississippi.

The racial violence that permeated southern life expanded into northern communities as many white Americans responded with hostility to the arrival of black migrants from the South. Black people defended themselves, and casualties among both races escalated (see Map 16–1).

Atlanta, 1906

In 1906—11 years after Booker T. Washington delivered his Cotton States Exposition address there—white mobs attacked black residents in Atlanta. Several factors aggravated white racial apprehensions in the city. In 1902 four black and four white people had been killed in a riot there. Many rural black people, attracted by economic opportunities, had moved to Atlanta. But white residents considered the newcomers more lawless and immoral than the longtime black residents. The Atlanta newspapers—the *Constitution*, the

MAP 16–1 MAJOR RACE RIOTS, 1900–1923
In the years between 1900 and 1923, race conflicts and riots occurred in dozens of American communities as black people migrated in increasing numbers to urban areas. The violence reached a peak in the immediate aftermath of World War I during the Red Summer of 1919. White Americans—in the North and South—were determined to keep black people confined to a subordinate role as menial laborers and restricted to well-defined all-black neighborhoods. African Americans who had made significant economic and military contributions to the war effort and who had congregated in large numbers in American cities insisted on participating on a more equitable basis in American society.

Were the causes of each of these riots similar, or were the reasons for the upsurge in racial violence unique to each situation?

16-1

16-2

16-3

16-4

16-5

16-6

16-7

16-8

Journal, and the *Georgian*—ran inflammatory accounts about black crime and black men who brutalized white women. However, many of these stories were false or exaggerated. Two white Democrats—Hoke Smith and Clark Howell—were engaged in a divisive campaign for a U.S. Senate seat in 1906, and both candidates stirred up racial animosity. There were also determined and ultimately successful efforts under way to disfranchise black voters in Georgia.

On a warm Saturday night, September 22, 1906, a white man jumped on a box on Decatur Street, one of Atlanta's main thoroughfares, and waved an Atlanta newspaper emblazoned with the headline THIRD ASSAULT. He hollered, "Are white men going to stand for this?" The crowd roared, "No! Save our women!" "Kill the niggers." A five-day orgy of violence followed.

The mayor, police, and fire departments vainly tried to stop the mob. Thousands of white people roamed the streets in search of black victims. Black people were tortured, beaten, and killed. White men pulled black passengers off streetcars. They destroyed black businesses. As white men armed themselves, the police disarmed black men. Black men and women who surrendered to marauding white mobs in hopes of mercy were not spared. Black men who fought back only infuriated the crazed white crowd. Twenty-five black people and one white person died, and hundreds were injured in the riot.

Du Bois hurried home to Atlanta from Alabama to defend his family. He waited on his porch with a shotgun for a mob that never came: "I would without hesitation have sprayed their guts over the grass." In New York, black editor T. Thomas Fortune called for a violent black response: "It makes my blood boil. I would like to be there with a good force of armed men to make Rome howl. I cannot believe that the policy of non-resistance in a situation like that of Atlanta can result in anything but contempt and massacre of the race."

Booker T. Washington looked for a silver lining in the awful affair by noting that "while there is disorder in one community there is peace and harmony in thousands of others." He said that black resistance would merely result in more black fatalities. Washington went to Atlanta and appealed for racial reconciliation.

A Committee of Safety of 10 black and 10 white leaders was formed. Charles T. Hopkins, an influential white Atlantan, warned in strong paternalist terms: "If we let this dependent race be butchered before our eyes, we cannot face God in the judgment day." But little real racial cooperation resulted. Black minister Henry Hugh Proctor worked with white leaders and often seemed to agree with them that Atlanta's main problem was black crime, not white racism.

No members of the white mob were brought to justice. Black Georgia voters were disfranchised. Atlanta's streetcars were segregated. The city had no public high school for black youngsters. The Carnegie Library did not admit black people, and the Atlanta police force had no black officers.

Springfield, 1908

Two years later in August 1908, white citizens of Springfield, Illinois, attacked black residents in an episode that led to the creation of the NAACP in 1909. George Richardson, a black man, was falsely accused of raping a white woman. Although the sheriff got Richardson out of town, a mob tore into Springfield's small black population. Six black people were shot and killed, two were lynched, dozens were injured, and black homes and businesses were wrecked. About 2,000 black people were driven out of Springfield.

Major racial conflicts occurred between 1917 and 1921 in East St. Louis, Illinois; Houston; Chicago; Elaine, Arkansas; and Tulsa. Smaller violent confrontations occurred in Washington, DC; Charleston; Knoxville, Tennessee; Omaha; and Waco and Longview, Texas. Although different incidents sparked each riot, the underlying causes were similar. White residents feared that black migrants would compete for jobs and housing.

East St. Louis, 1917

East St. Louis, Illinois, was a gritty industrial town of nearly 60,000 across the Mississippi River from St. Louis, Missouri. About 10 percent of the inhabitants were black. The town's schools, public facilities, and neighborhoods were segregated. Racial tensions increased in February 1917 after 470 black workers were hired to replace white members of the American Federation of Labor who had gone on strike against the Aluminum Ore Company. On July 1, white people drove through a black neighborhood firing guns. Shortly after, two white plainclothes police officers drove into the same neighborhood and were shot and killed by residents who may have believed the drive-by shooters had returned.

Angry white mobs sought revenge. Black people were mutilated and killed and their bodies thrown into the river. Black homes, many of them little more than cabins and shacks, were burned. Hundreds of black people were left homeless. The police joined the rioters. Thirty-five black people and eight white people died in the violence.

The NAACP sent Du Bois and Martha Gruening to East St. Louis. They compiled a report, "Massacre at East St. Louis," that documented instance after instance of brutality: "Negroes were 'flushed' from the burning houses, and ran for their lives, screaming and begging for mercy. A Negro crawled into a shed and fired on the white men. Guardsmen started after him, but when they saw he was armed, one of them turned to the mob and said: 'He's armed boys. You can have him. A white man's life is worth the lives of a thousand Negroes.'"

To protest the riot, the NAACP organized a silent demonstration in New York City, and thousands of well-dressed black people marched to muffled drums down Fifth Avenue.

Houston, 1917

A month after the East St. Louis riot, black soldiers in Houston attacked police officers and civilians. The Third Battalion of the 24th Infantry recently had been transferred from Wyoming and California to Camp Logan near Houston, where the black troops came face-to-face with Jim Crow. Streetcars and public facilities were segregated. White and Hispanic people regularly called the black troops "niggers."

On August 23 a black soldier tried to prevent a police officer, Lee Sparks, from beating a black woman. Sparks clubbed the soldier and hauled him off to jail. Corporal Charles W. Baltimore attempted to determine what had happened, and he was also beaten and

On July 28, 1917, the NAACP organized a silent march in New York City to protest the East St. Louis, Illinois, race riot, in which 35 black people died, as well as to denounce the ongoing epidemic of lynchings. The marchers were accompanied by the beat of muffled drums.

incarcerated. Although both soldiers were later released, a rumor circulated that Baltimore had been slain. Led by Sergeant Vida Henry, black men sought revenge.

About one hundred armed black soldiers mounted a two-hour assault on the police station. Fifteen white residents—including five policemen—and one Mexican American, four black soldiers, and two black civilians were killed. The army arrested 118 black soldiers and charged 63 of them with mutiny. Three separate court-martials were held. The NAACP retained the son of Texas legend Sam Houston to help defend them. Eight black men, however, agreed to testify against the defendants. Thirteen black troops were hanged (including Corporal Baltimore) after the first court-martial. Later seven more were executed, seven others were acquitted, and the rest were sentenced to prison terms.

While the Houston violence prompted some political and military leaders to call for the abolition of the black regiments, Du Bois eulogized the first 13 black soldiers to be executed: "Thirteen young men, strong men, soldiers who have fought for a country which never was wholly theirs; men born to suffer ridicule, injustice and, at last, death itself." In the meantime, Lee Sparks remained on the Houston police force and killed two black people later that year.

Chicago, 1919

((•)) Read on **MyHistoryLab** Document: The *Chicago Defender* Describes a Race Riot, 1919

Between 1916 and 1919, the black population of Chicago doubled as migrants from the South moved north in search of jobs, political rights, and humane treatment. Many encountered a violent reception. A housing shortage strained the boundaries between crowded, segregated black neighborhoods and white residential areas. After World War I ended in November 1918, racial tensions increased as black men were hired to replace striking white workers in Chicago.

With summer temperatures rising and racial tensions escalating, Ida B. Wells anticipated a major conflict in the pages of the *Chicago Tribune* in early July. "With one Negro dead as a result of the race riot last week, another one very badly injured in the county hospital; with a half-dozen attacks upon Negro children, and one on the Thirty-fifth street car Tuesday, in which four white men beat one colored man, it looks very much like Chicago is trying to rival the south in its race hatred against the Negro."

The Chicago riot began on Sunday, July 27, 1919—one day after black troops were welcomed home with a parade down the city's Michigan Avenue. Eugene Williams, a young black man, was swimming in Lake Michigan and inadvertently crossed the invisible boundary that separated the black and white beaches and bathing areas. He was stoned by white people and drowned. Instead of arresting the alleged perpetrators, the police arrested a black man who complained about police inaction.

Williams's death set off a week of violence that left 23 black people and 15 white people dead. More than 500 were injured, and nearly 1,000 were left homeless after fire raged through a Lithuanian neighborhood. Police often joined white mobs as they attacked black pedestrians and streetcar passengers. Black men formed a barrier along State Street to stop white gangs from the stockyard district. Three regiments of the Illinois National Guard were sent into the streets, but the violence did not end until August 1, when heavy rains kept people indoors.

During the riot, the *Chicago Defender*, the city's black newspaper, reported many violent incidents: "In the early [Tuesday] morning a thirteen-year-old lad standing on his porch at 51st and Wabash Avenue was shot to death by a white man who, in an attempt to get away, encountered a mob and his existence became history. A mounted policeman, unknown, fatally wounded a small boy in the block of Dearborn Street and was shot to death by some unknown rioter."

Elaine, 1919

In 1919, black sharecroppers in and around Elaine, Arkansas, attempted to organize a union and withhold their cotton from the market until they received a higher price.

Deputy sheriffs tried to break up a union meeting in a black church, and one of the deputies was killed. In retaliation, white people killed dozens of black people. No white people were prosecuted, but 12 black men were convicted of the deputy's murder. They were sentenced to death, and 67 other black men received prison terms of up to 20 years. Many were tortured and beaten in jail. Ida Wells Barnett and the Equal Rights League generated enormous publicity about the case. The NAACP appealed the convictions, and in 1923 the Supreme Court overturned them.

Tulsa, 1921

Violence erupted in Tulsa on May 31, 1921, after still another black man was accused of rape. Dick Rowland allegedly assaulted a white woman elevator operator, and rumors circulated that white men intended to lynch him. To protect Rowland, who was later found innocent, black men assembled at the jail as white men also gathered there. Angry words were exchanged, and shooting erupted. Several black and white men died in the chaos that ensued.

Read on MyHistoryLab Document: An NAACP Official Investigates the Tulsa Race Riot of 1921

This is the Greenwood neighborhood of Tulsa, Oklahoma, in flames during the riot in June 1921.

Black men retreated to their neighborhood, known as Greenwood, to protect their families and homes. The governor dispatched the National Guard, and the sheriff sent Rowland to an unknown location. By the morning of June 1, 500 white men confronted about 1,000 black men across a set of railroad tracks. White men in automobiles were cruising around the black residential area. Approximately 50 armed black people defended themselves in a black church near the edge of Greenwood as white men advanced on them. The attackers set fire to the church. As black people fled the burning building, they were shot. More fires were set. About 2,000 black residents managed to escape to a convention hall. Forty square blocks and more than 1,000 of Greenwood's homes, churches, schools, and businesses went up in flames. White men even used aircraft for reconnaissance and to drop incendiary devices on Greenwood. As many as 300 black people and 20 white people may have perished in what was one of the worst episodes of civilian violence in American history until September 11, 2001.

In 2001, a biracial commission recommended that the Oklahoma legislature offer restitution. The legislators declined to set aside funds for survivors, but they did appropriate $750,000 to formulate plans for a museum and memorial. They also created a Greenwood Redevelopment Authority and a scholarship program.

Rosewood, 1923

In January 1923, the small town of Rosewood, Florida, was destroyed, and its black residents were driven out or killed. Rosewood was a mostly black community—it had a few white inhabitants—in the pinewoods of west-central Florida not far from the Gulf of Mexico. On New Year's Day, Fannie Taylor, a married white woman from a nearby town, claimed a black man had raped and beaten her. White people assumed Jessie Hunter was responsible. Other white people believed Mrs. Taylor wanted to divert attention away from herself because she had a white lover who was not her husband.

White men sought Hunter and vengeance. Unable to find him, they beat Aaron Carrier, who may have helped Taylor's white lover escape. The mob killed Samuel Carter after mutilating him. Tensions escalated.

On January 4 an angry mob invaded Rosewood, but the black people there were prepared to defend themselves. Led by Sylvester Carrier and his mother Sarah, many townspeople had congregated in the Carrier home. The mob fired on the residence, killing Sarah

16-1
16-2
16-3
16-4
16-5
16-6
16-7
16-8

Carrier. Two white men who attempted to enter the home were killed. Shooting continued until the mob ran out of ammunition on January 5.

The next day a mob of 250, including Ku Klux Klan members from Gainesville, invaded, burned, and destroyed Rosewood. The community's black residents fled to the woods and swamps with little more than the clothes on their backs, never to return. Rosewood was no more.

The precise number of black people who died will never be known. It may have exceeded one hundred. In 1994 the Florida legislature appropriated $2.1 million to survivors of Rosewood and to families who lost property in the assault. Ten survivors were still alive and collected $150,000 each. But many black people could not verify that they had been in Rosewood in 1923 or that they were kin to people who had owned property there. As a result, much of the money was not disbursed.

The Great Migration

16-8 **Why did African Americans begin to leave the rural South in the early twentieth century, and what kinds of lives were they able to make for themselves in urban communities?**

The Great Migration of African Americans from the rural South to the urban North began as a trickle after the Civil War and became a flood by the second decade of the twentieth century (see Table 16–1). Between 1910 and 1940, 1.75 million black people left the South. As a result, the black population outside the South doubled by 1940. Most of the initial wave of migrants were younger people born in the 1880s and 1890s who had no recollection of slavery but anticipated a better future for themselves and their families in the North.

Why Migrate?

People moved for many reasons. Often they were both pushed from their rural homes and pulled toward urban areas. The push resulted from disasters in southern agriculture in the 1910s. The boll weevil destroyed cotton crops across the South, and floods devastated Mississippi and Alabama in 1915. The pull resulted from labor shortages created by World War I in northern industry and manufacturing. The war interrupted European immigration to the United States, eliminating a main source of cheap labor. At the same time, European governments and the United States placed huge orders for war material with northern factories. Thousands of jobs became available in steel mills, railroads, meatpacking plants, and the automobile industry. Northern businessmen sent labor agents to recruit southern workers.

Many southern white people reacted ambivalently to the loss of black residents. They welcomed the departure of people for whom they had contempt, but they also worried about the loss of tenants and sharecroppers. Southern states and municipalities required labor agents to obtain licenses to recruit workers. Angry white landowners and businessmen forced some of these agents to leave southern towns.

Black newspapers, such as the *Pittsburgh Courier* and especially the *Chicago Defender*, encouraged black southerners to move north. Black railroad porters and dining car employees distributed thousands of copies of the *Defender* throughout the South. One unnamed black man wrote in the *Defender* that sensible men would leave the poverty, injustice, and violence of the South for the cold weather of the North: "To die from the bite of frost is far more glorious than that of the mob. I beg of you, my brothers, to leave that benighted land. You are free men."

A black resident of South Carolina's sea islands explained in 1917 that he left to earn more money: "I could work and dig all year on the Island and best I could do would be to make $100 and take a chance of making nothin'. Well, I figured I could make 'roun' thirty or thirty-five dollars every week and at that rate save possibly $100 every two months." Like

Watch on MyHistoryLab Video: The Great Migration

TABLE 16–1 BLACK POPULATION GROWTH IN SELECTED NORTHERN CITIES, 1910–1920

	1910		1920		
	Number	**Percentage***	**Number**	**Percentage***	**Percentage Increase**
New York	91,709	1.9%	152,467	2.7%	66.3%
Chicago	44,103	2.0	109,458	4.1	148.2
Philadelphia	84,459	5.5	134,229	7.4	58.9
Detroit	5,741	1.2	40,838	4.1	611.3
St. Louis	43,960	6.4	69,854	9.0	58.9
Cleveland	8,448	1.5	34,451	4.3	307.8
Pittsburgh	25,623	4.8	37,725	6.4	47.2
Cincinnati	19,739	5.4	30,079	7.5	53.2
Indianapolis	21,816	9.3	34,678	11.0	59.0
Newark	9,475	2.7	16,977	4.1	79.2
Kansas City	23,566	9.5	30,719	9.5	30.4
Columbus	12,739	7.0	22,181	9.4	74.1
Gary	383	2.3	5,299	9.6	1,283.6
Youngstown	1,936	2.4	6,662	5.0	244.1
Buffalo	1,773	.4	4,511	.9	154.4
Toledo	1,877	1.1	5,691	2.3	203.2
Akron	657	1.0	5,580	2.7	749.3

*"Percentage" refers to percentage of city's population; "Percentage Increase" refers to growth of the black population.
SOURCE: *U.S. Department of Commerce.*

many migrants, he moved more than once. He first went to Savannah and then to Philadelphia before finally settling in New York.

Black people who departed the South (see Table 16–2) escaped the most blatant forms of Jim Crow and the injustice in the judicial system. Black women fled the sexual exploitation of white and black men. Black people in the North could vote. The North also offered better public schools. In the early twentieth century the South had almost no public high schools for black youngsters, and the longer school year in the urban North was not tied to the demands of planting and harvesting crops.

Some black people migrated to escape the dull, bleak, impoverished life and culture of the rural South. One young woman left South Carolina's St. Helena Island in 1919: "[I] got tired of the Island. Too lonesome. Go to bed at six o'clock. Everything dead. No dances, no moving picture show, no nothing. 'Coz every once in a while they would have a dance, but here you could go to 'em every Saturday night. That's why people move more than anything else."

The decision to migrate could take years of pondering and planning. To depart was to leave family, friends, and familiar surroundings behind for the uncertainty, confusion, and rapid pace of urban communities. Migrants often first moved to southern towns or cities and then headed for a larger city. Writer Langston Hughes was born in Joplin, Missouri, in 1902 and moved to Lincoln, Illinois: "I had no sooner graduated from grammar school in Lincoln than we moved from Illinois to Cleveland. My stepfather sent for us. He was working in a steel mill during the war, and making lots of money. But it was hard work, and he never looked the same afterwards."

Some people made the decision to move impulsively. After she was fired from her nursing position at Hampton Institute in Virginia in 1905, Jane Edna Hunter decided to go to Florida but changed her mind:

> En route, I stopped at Richmond, Virginia, to visit with Mr. and Mrs. William Coleman, friends of Uncle Parris.

TABLE 16–2 AFRICAN-AMERICAN MIGRATION FROM THE SOUTH

1910s	550,000
1920s	903,000
1930s	480,000
1940s	1,600,000
1950s	1,400,000
1960s	1,000,000
Total	**5,933,000**

SOURCE: *Adapted from Isabel Wilkerson,* The Warmth of Other Suns: The Epic Story of America's Great Migration. *New York: Random House, Vintage Books, 2010, pp. 161, 217, 218.*

They were at church when I arrived; so I sat on the doorstep to await their return. After these good friends had greeted me, Mrs. Coleman said, 'Our bags are packed to go to Cleveland, Jane. We are going to take you with us.' I was swept off my feet by the cheerful determination of the Colemans. My trunk, not yet removed from the station, was rechecked to Cleveland.

Most migrants maintained a fondness for their southern homes and kinfolk. They returned for holidays, weddings, and funerals. Kelly Miller, who had grown up in South Carolina, spent years as a scholar and teacher at Howard University, but he still had "an attachment for the old state that time and distance cannot destroy. After all, we love to be known as a South Carolinian." Thousands of black migrants routinely sent money home. Over the years, millions of dollars earned in the North flowed into southern communities.

Destinations

Although many black southerners went to Florida, most migrants from the Carolinas and Virginia settled in Washington, DC, Philadelphia, and New York (see Map 16–2). Black people who left Georgia, Alabama, and Mississippi tended to move to Pittsburgh, Cleveland, and Detroit. Migrants from Louisiana, Mississippi, and Arkansas often rode the Illinois Central Railroad to Chicago. Once they experienced a metropolis, many black

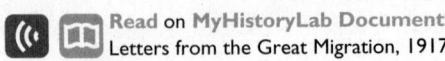
Read on **MyHistoryLab Document:**
Letters from the Great Migration, 1917

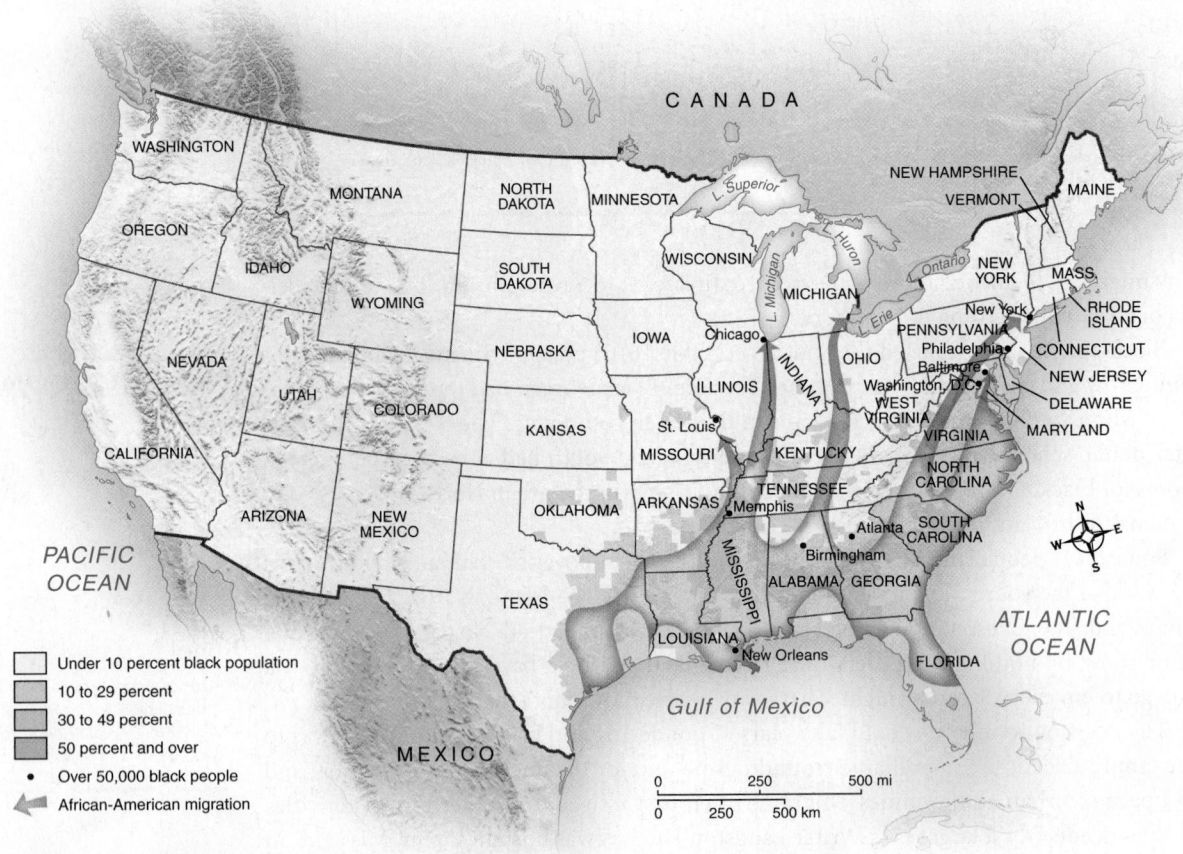

MAP 16–2 THE GREAT MIGRATION AND THE DISTRIBUTION OF THE AFRICAN-AMERICAN POPULATION IN 1920
Although several hundred thousand black southerners migrated north during the second and third decades of the twentieth century in the largest internal migration in American history, most African Americans remained in the southern states.

Why did most African Americans stay in the South if so many opportunities beckoned in the North?

people then resettled in smaller communities. Migrants to Philadelphia, for example, moved on to Harrisburg or Altoona, Pennsylvania, or to Wilmington, Delaware.

Few black southerners moved west to California, Oregon, or Washington. California had only 22,000 black residents in 1910. Substantial black migration west did not occur until the 1930s and 1940s. But in 1920 Mallie Robinson made the long trek west. Deserted by her husband, she set out with her five children (including one-year-old Jackie, who would become a baseball legend) and eight other relatives. They boarded a train in Cairo, Georgia; traveled to Los Angeles; and settled in nearby Pasadena. Mallie's half brother, who had already moved west, assured her she would be closer to heaven in California.

However, most black migrants found their destination was near neither heaven nor the Promised Land. Black people congregated in all-black neighborhoods—Harlem in New York City, Chicago's South Side, Paradise Valley in Detroit, Cleveland's East Side, and the Hill District of Pittsburgh—that later would be called ghettoes. White owners resisted selling or renting property to black people outside of these neighborhoods. And many southern black migrants themselves, wary of white hostility, preferred to live among black people, often friends and family who had preceded them north.

Migration from the Caribbean

Many descendants of Africans who had been slaves in the sugarcane fields of the West Indies joined the migration of black southerners to the North. Between 1900 and 1924, 102,000 West Indians came to the United States. Most came from British colonies including Jamaica, Barbados, Montserrat, and Trinidad and Tobago. But black immigrants also arrived from French-held Guadeloupe and Martinique, the Dutch colonies of Aruba and Curacao, and the Danish Virgin Islands (which the United States acquired in 1917). Some of these migrants were middle-class professionals and skilled workers, but many had been employed as laborers building the Panama Canal from 1904 to 1914.

Although white Americans tended to lump all people of color together, regardless of their complexion or origin, the West Indians often did not mix comfortably with African Americans. Some spoke Dutch and French. Those who came from British islands were usually Anglicans (Episcopalians) and not Baptists or Methodists. Almost all of the newcomers sent money home to families in the West Indies. Moreover, many of the Caribbean arrivals were temporary residents; as many as one-third of them would return to the West Indies. In 1924 Congress restricted immigration to the United States, and migration from the Caribbean dropped drastically.

Northern Communities

Even before the Civil War, most northern cities had small free black populations. By the late nineteenth century, southern migrants began to gravitate to these urban areas and make their presence felt. Black residents established churches, social organizations, businesses, and medical facilities. They gained representation in community and political affairs.

There was less overt segregation in the North. Most northern states and California prohibited racial discrimination in public transportation, hotels, restaurants, theaters, and barbershops. Most of these states also forbade segregated schools. However, enacting such laws and enforcing them were two different matters. Many white businesses and communities ignored the statutes and embraced Jim Crow, especially along the Ohio River in southern Ohio, Indiana, and Illinois.

CHICAGO

As early as 1872, Chicago had a black policeman, and in 1876 John W. E. Thomas became the first black man elected to the Illinois Senate. Black physician Daniel Hale Williams established African-American–staffed Provident Hospital on Chicago's South Side in 1891. By 1900 black Chicagoans were the twelfth largest ethnic group in the city, behind such European immigrant groups as the Irish, Poles, and Germans.

VOICES   A Migrant to the North Writes Home

People who migrated to northern communities often wrote home to describe their new surroundings and experiences and to confess they missed their old homes. One unidentified black man who had moved to Philadelphia made his feelings known to a medical doctor.

Oct. 7, 1919

Philadelphia, Pa.,

Dear Sir:

I take this method of thanking you for yours early responding and the glorious effect of the treatment. Oh. I do feel so fine. Dr. the treatment reach me almost ready to move I am now housekeeping again I like it so much better than rooming. Well Dr. with the aid of God I am making very good I make $75 per month. I am carrying enough insurance to pay me $20 per week if I am not able to be on duty. I don't have to work hard. dont have to mister every little white boy comes along I havent heard a white man call a colored nigger you no now—since I been in the state of Pa. I can ride in the electric street and steam cars any where I get a seat. I dont care to mix with white what

I mean I am not crazy about being with white folks, but if I have to pay the same fare I have learn to want the same accomidation. and if you are the first in a place here shoping you dont have to wait until the white folks get thro tradeing yet amid all this I shall ever love the good old South and I am praying that God may give every well wisher a chance to be a man regardless of his color, and if my going to the front [World War I] would bring about such conditions I am ready any day—well Dr. I dont want to worry you but read between the lines; and maybe you can see a little sense in my weak statement the kids are in school every day I have only two and I guess that all. Dr. when you find time I would be delighted to have word from the good old home state. Wife join me in sending love you and yours.

> 1. **What is the writer's main reason for having migrated?**
>
> 2. **What was more important to this man, better living standards or the sense of liberation he enjoyed in Philadelphia?**

SOURCE: Emmett J. Scott, ed., "Letters of Negro Migrants of 1916–1918," *Journal of Negro History* 4 (July 1, 1919), in Fishel and Quarles, *The Negro American: A Documentary History*, 398–99.

Chicago's black population surged from 1900 to 1930 as migrants poured into the city. Black institutions flourished. In 1912 an NAACP branch was established. By 1920 black Chicago had 80 Baptist and 36 Methodist churches. The Olivet Baptist Church grew from 3,500 members in 1916 to 9,000 by 1922. Because the downtown YMCA barred black men, black people raised $50,000 and Julius Rosenwald of Sears, Roebuck and Company contributed $25,000 to build the Wabash YMCA for the black community in 1913. However, many black Chicagoans considered this a surrender to segregation and insisted that they should be admitted to the white YMCA.

The *Chicago Defender* was the city's leading black newspaper. Its founder, Robert S. Abbott, the son of slaves, began publishing the *Defender* in 1905, and by 1920 it had a nationwide circulation of 230,000. Chicago's first black bank, Jesse Binga's State Bank, was established in 1908, and in 1919 Frank L. Gillespie organized the Liberty Insurance Company.

In 1915 black Chicago's political influence expanded when Oscar DePriest was elected second-ward alderman. Two other black men were elected to the city council by 1918. DePriest was then elected to the U.S. House of Representatives as a Republican in 1928, becoming the first black congressman since North Carolina's George White left the House in 1901.

As the number of black Chicagoans swelled, racial tensions exploded in the 1919 race riot. Competition for jobs was a critical issue. White employers, such as the meatpacking companies, regularly replaced white strikers with black workers. Black men took such jobs because most labor unions would not admit them. But a few weeks before the riot in 1919, the Amalgamated Meatcutters Union tried to sponsor a unity parade of black and white stockyard workers. The police prohibited it because, some observers believed, the meatpacking companies feared that black and white working men might unite.

Housing was an even more divisive issue than employment. Chicago's black population was almost entirely confined to an eight-square-mile area on the South Side east of State Street. Prosperous black people who could afford more expensive housing outside the area could not purchase it because of their race. As the black population grew, housing became more congested, and crime and vice increased.

Langston Hughes described the similar situation his family experienced in Cleveland:

Rents were very high for colored people in Cleveland, and the Negro district was extremely crowded, because of the great migration. It was difficult to find a place to live. We always lived, during my high school years, either in an attic or a basement, and paid quite a lot for such inconvenient quarters. White people on the east side of the city were moving out of their frame houses and renting them to Negroes at double and triple the rents they could receive from others. An eight room house with one bath would be cut up into apartments and five or six families crowded into it, each two-room kitchenette apartment renting for what the whole house had rented for before.

HARLEM

Harlem was a white community in upper Manhattan that had declined by the latter 1800s. It then enjoyed a building boom that occurred in anticipation of the construction of the subway that would link upper Manhattan to downtown New York City by the early twentieth century. But real estate speculators overbuilt and were left with empty houses and apartments. Facing foreclosure, many white property owners sold or rented to black people in Harlem. In 1904 Philip A. Payton formed the Afro American Realty Company, which sold homes and rented apartments to black clients before it failed in 1908.

Harlem's white residents opposed the influx of black people. Some of them formed the Harlem Property Owners' Improvement Corporation in 1910 to block black settlement. Its founder, John G. Taylor, warned in 1913, "We are approaching a crisis, it is a question of whether the white man will rule Harlem or the Negro." However, many white property owners—eager for a profit—preferred to sell to black people rather than maintain white unity.

As thousands of black people moved to Harlem, many left the "Tenderloin" and "San Juan Hill" areas of Manhattan's West Side, where New York's black residents had lived in the nineteenth century. The construction of Pennsylvania Station forced many to vacate the "Tenderloin." Black churches took the lead in the "On to Harlem" movement as they occupied churches white denominations had formerly used. Some black churches were among the largest property owners in Harlem.

St. Philip's Protestant Episcopal Church, the wealthiest black church in the United States—and noted for its solemn services and elite parishioners—moved in 1910 from West 25th Street in the "Tenderloin" to Harlem. In 1911 St. Philip's purchased 10 apartment houses on West 135th Street between Lennox and Seventh Avenues for $640,000. The Rev. Adam Clayton Powell Sr. and the Abyssinian Baptist Church, St. Mark's Episcopal Church, and the African Methodist Episcopal Zion Church ("Mother Zion") also moved to Harlem and acquired extensive real estate holdings there. The black churches helped make Harlem a black community.

As Harlem's black population increased, large houses and apartments were often subdivided among working families that could not rent or buy in other areas of New York. They paid higher prices for real estate than white people did. The average Harlem family paid $9.50 a room per month. White working families paid $6.50 for similar accommodations elsewhere in New York.

By 1920, 75,000 black people lived in Harlem (see Map 16–3). Harlem became the "Negro Capital of the World." Black businesses and institutions, including the Odd Fellows, Masons, Elks, Pythians, the NAACP, the Urban League, and the YMCA and YWCA, moved to Harlem. Black newspapers—the *New York News* and *Amsterdam News*—opened in Harlem to compete with the older *New York Age*. One resident exclaimed, "If my race can make Harlem, good lord, what can't it do?"

16-1 16-2 16-3 16-4 16-5 16-6 16-7 16-8

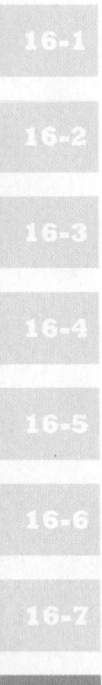

MAP 16–3 THE EXPANSION OF BLACK HARLEM, 1911–1930

Before the American Revolution, Harlem was a small Dutch village located at the northern end of Manhattan island. In the early twentieth century, African Americans transformed it into a thriving black metropolis. Migrants who arrived either after a short trip of just a few miles from the "Tenderloin" or "San Juan Hill" sections of midtown Manhattan or after much longer journeys from the Carolinas or Georgia took over block after block of Harlem homes and apartments.

SOURCE: *From* The Harlem Renaissance *by Steven Watson, copyright © 1955 by Steven Watson. Used by permission of Pantheon Books, a division of Random House, Inc.*

Why did African Americans settle in Harlem and not elsewhere in New York City?

FAMILIES

Migration placed black families under enormous strains. Relatives frequently moved north separately. Fathers or mothers would leave a spouse and children behind as they sought employment and housing. Children might be left with grandparents. Extended family members—cousins, in-laws, brothers, and sisters—crowded into limited living space.

Men generally found more opportunities for work in northern industries than women did. Unskilled labor during and after World War I was in huge demand. In 1915 Henry Ford astounded industrial America when he began to pay employees of the Ford Motor Company in Detroit the unprecedented sum of $5 per day, and that included black men and occasionally black women. Rarely, however, was a black man promoted beyond menial labor. Except for some opportunities in manufacturing during the war, black women were confined to domestic and janitorial work. Mary Ellen Washington recalled the experience in her family: "In the 1920s my mother and five aunts migrated to Cleveland, Ohio, from Indianapolis and, in spite of their many talents, they found every door except the kitchen door closed to them."

Black women employed as domestics lived with white families, worked long hours, and saw more of their white employer's children than they did their own. One maid explained her dreary and unhappy situation:

> I am now past forty years of age and am the mother of three children. My husband died nearly fifteen years ago. . . . For more than thirty years—or since I was ten years old—I have been a servant in one capacity or another in white families.
>
> I frequently work from fourteen to sixteen hours a day. I am compelled . . . to sleep in the house. I am allowed to go home to my own children, the oldest of whom is a girl of 18 years, only once in two weeks, every other Sunday afternoon—even then I'm not permitted to stay all night. . . . I don't know what it is to go to church; I don't know what it is to go to a lecture or entertainment of any kind; I live a treadmill life. . . . You might as well say that I'm on duty all the time—from sunrise to sunrise, every day in the week. I am the slave, body and soul, of this family.

Some vulnerable younger women were lured into prostitution in the intimidating urban environment. Black women's organizations worked to prevent newly arrived migrants from being sexually exploited. They did not always succeed. Some women made a calculated decision to turn sex to their economic advantage. Sara Brooks caustically commented, "Some women woulda had a man to come and live in the house and had an outside boyfriend too, in order to get the house paid for and the bills. They meet a man and if he promises 'em four or five dollars to go to bed, they's grab it. That's called sellin' your own body, and I wasn't raised like that."

Despite the stresses and pressures, most black families survived intact. Most northern black families, although hardly well to do, were two-parent households. Women headed comparatively few families. Fathers were present in 7 of 10 black families in New York City in 1925. But the Great Migration transformed southern peasants into an urban proletariat.

CONCLUSION

In 1900 Booker T. Washington was the nation's most influential black leader. He soothed white people and reassured black Americans as he counseled conciliation, patience, and agricultural and mechanical training as the most effective means to bridge the racial divide. His 1895 speech at the Cotton States Exposition in Atlanta elicited praise from both white and black listeners.

The Wizard of Tuskegee, as Washington was known, had little appreciation for criticism and did not hesitate to attack his opponents, including William Monroe Trotter and W. E. B. Du Bois. He worked to subvert the Niagara Movement and the NAACP. But support for Washington and his conservative strategy diminished as the NAACP openly confronted racial discrimination. Washington died in 1915. By 1920 the NAACP took the lead in the struggle for civil rights as it fought in the courts and legislatures.

The Talented Tenth of black Americans, distinguished by their educational and economic resources, promoted "self-help" through a variety of organizations—from women's groups to fraternities and sororities—to enhance their own status and help less affluent black people.

As black men served in World War I and as thousands of black southerners migrated north, many white Americans became alarmed that African Americans were not as content with their subordinate and isolated status as Booker T. Washington had suggested they were. Some white Americans responded with violence in race riots as they attempted to prevent black Americans from assuming a more equitable role in American society. By 1920, despite white opposition, black Americans had demonstrated they would not accept economic subservience and the denial of their rights.

CHAPTER TIMELINE

AFRICAN-AMERICAN EVENTS

NATIONAL EVENTS

1895–1900

1895
Frederick Douglass dies; Booker T. Washington delivers Cotton States Exposition address

1896
Plessy v. Ferguson

1898
Riot erupts in Wilmington, North Carolina

1900
New Orleans riot

1896
William McKinley is elected president

1898
Spanish-American War

1899
Philippine insurrection begins

1900
President McKinley reelected

1900–1905

1903
W. E. B. Du Bois publishes *The Souls of Black Folk*

1901
McKinley is assassinated; Theodore Roosevelt becomes president

1904
Theodore Roosevelt elected president

1905–1910

1905
Niagara Movement founded at Niagara Falls, Canada; the *Defender* founded in Chicago

1906
Brownsville affair; Atlanta riot

1908
Springfield riot

1909
NAACP is founded

1905
Thomas Dixon publishes *The Clansman;* the film *Birth of a Nation* is based on the novel

1908
William Howard Taft elected president

1910–1915

1910
Urban League founded in New York City

1912
Du Bois endorses Woodrow Wilson for president

1912
Woodrow Wilson elected president

1914
World War I breaks out in Europe

1915–1920

1915
Guinn v. United States overturns the Oklahoma grandfather clause; Booker T. Washington dies

1917
East St. Louis riot; Houston riot

1919
Chicago riot; Elaine, Arkansas riot

1920
Harlem becomes "The Negro Capital of the World"

1921
Tulsa riot occurs

1923
Rosewood destroyed

1916
President Wilson reelected

1917
United States enters World War I

1918
World War I ends

1919
Treaty of Versailles

1920
Nineteenth Amendment (women's suffrage) ratified; Warren Harding elected president

On MyHistoryLab

 ✓ Study and Review on MyHistoryLab

REVIEW QUESTIONS

1. How did the strategies promoted by Booker T. Washington differ from those of W. E. B. Du Bois and the NAACP? Which were more effective?

2. Assess Washington's contributions to the advancement of black people.

3. How did middle-class and prosperous black people try to contribute to progress for their race? Were their efforts effective?

4. Why did most African Americans support U.S. participation in World War I? Was that support justified?

5. What factors contributed to race riots and violence in the World War I era?

6. Why did many black people leave the South in the 1920s? Why didn't this migration begin earlier or later?

7. Why did migrants decide to leave or to stay?

RECOMMENDED READING

W. E. B. Du Bois. *The Souls of Black Folk.* New York: Library of America, 1903. An essential collection of superb essays.

John Hope Franklin and August Meier. *Black Leaders of the Twentieth Century.* Urbana: University of Illinois Press, 1982. Fifteen "minibiographies," including those of Washington, Du Bois, T. Thomas Fortune, and Ida Wells Barnett.

Willard Gatewood. *Aristocrats of Color: The Black Elite, 1880–1920.* Bloomington: Indiana University Press, 1990. An examination of the lives and activities of well-to-do black people.

Lawrence Otis Graham. *One Kind of People: Inside America's Black Upper Class.* New York: HarperCollins, 1999. An informative history and analysis of black America's wealthiest families and organizations.

Louis R. Harlan. *Booker T. Washington: The Making of a Black Leader, 1856–1901.* New York: Oxford University Press, 1972; and *Booker T. Washington: The Wizard of Tuskegee, 1901–1915.* New York: Oxford University Press, 1983. The definitive two-volume biography.

David Levering Lewis. *W. E. B. Du Bois: Biography of a Race, 1868–1919.* New York: Henry Holt and Co., 1993; and *W. E. B. Du Bois: The Fight for Equality and the American Century, 1919–1963.* New York: Henry Holt and Co., 2001. A magisterial and exhaustive account of Du Bois's life and times.

Robert J. Norrell. *Up From History: The Life of Booker T. Washington.* Cambridge, MA: Harvard University Press, 2009. A positive assessment of the Wizard of Tuskegee.

Deborah Gray White. *Too Heavy a Load: Black Women in Defense of Themselves.* New York: Norton, 1999. An exploration of black women's history in the twentieth century.

Isabel Wilkerson. *The Warmth of Other Suns: The Epic Story of America's Great Migration.* New York: Random House, 2010. This is an outstanding discussion and analysis of the people who migrated based on extensive research and marvelous oral histories.

ADDITIONAL BIBLIOGRAPHY

LEADERSHIP CONFLICTS AND THE EMERGENCE OF AFRICAN-AMERICAN ORGANIZATIONS

Tamara L. Brown, Gregory Parks, and Clarenda M. Phillips, eds. *African American Fraternities and Sororities: The Legacy and the Vision.* Lexington: University Press of Kentucky, 2005.

Deborah Davis. *Guest of Honor: Booker T. Washington, Theodore Roosevelt, and the White House Dinner That Shocked a Nation.* New York: Atria Books, 2012.

Kevin K. Gaines. *Uplifting the Race: Black Leadership, Politics, and Culture in the Twentieth Century.* Chapel Hill: University of North Carolina Press, 1996.

Charles F. Kellogg. *NAACP: A History of the National Association for the Advancement of Colored People.* Baltimore: Johns Hopkins University Press, 1967.

August Meier. *Negro Thought in America, 1880–1915.* Ann Arbor: University of Michigan Press, 1967.

Michele Mitchell. *Righteous Propagation: African Americans and the Politics of Racial Destiny After Reconstruction.* Chapel Hill: University of North Carolina Press, 2004.

Jacqueline Moore. *Booker T. Washington and W. E. B. Du Bois and the Struggle for Racial Uplift.* Wilmington, DE: Scholarly Resources, 2003.

Alfred A. Moss, Jr. *American Negro Academy: Voice of the Talented Tenth.* Baton Rouge: Louisiana State University Press, 1981.

B. Joyce Ross. *J. E. Spingarn and the Rise of the N.A.A.C.P.* New York: Atheneum, 1972.

Lawrence C. Ross, Jr. *The Divine Nine: The History of African-American Fraternities and Sororities.* New York: Kensington Books, 2000.

Elliott Rudwick. *W. E. B. Du Bois.* New York: Atheneum, 1968.

Nancy Weiss. *The National Urban League, 1910–1940.* New York: Oxford University Press, 1974.

Shamoon Zamir. *Dark Voices: W. E. B. Du Bois and American Thought, 1888–1903.* Chicago: University of Chicago Press, 1995.

AFRICAN-AMERICAN WOMEN IN THE EARLY TWENTIETH CENTURY

Elizabeth Clark-Lewis. *Living In, Living Out: African American Domestics in Washington, D.C., 1910–1940.* Washington, DC: Smithsonian Institution Press, 1994.

Bettye Collier-Thomas. *Jesus, Jobs, and Justice; African American Women and Religion.* New York: Alfred A. Knopf, 2010.

Anna Julia Cooper. *A Voice from the South.* New York: Oxford University Press, 1988.

Cynthia Neverdon-Morton. *Afro-American Women of the South and the Advancement of the Race, 1895–1925.* Knoxville: University of Tennessee Press, 1998.

Jacqueline A. Rouse. *Lugina Burns Hope: A Black Southern Reformer.* Athens: University of Georgia Press, 1989.

Stephanie J. Shaw. *What a Woman Ought to Be and to Do: Black Professional Women Workers During the Jim Crow Era.* Chicago: University of Chicago Press, 1996.

Rosalyn Terborg-Penn. *African American Women in the Struggle for the Vote, 1850–1920.* Bloomington: Indiana University Press, 1998.

AFRICAN AMERICANS IN THE MILITARY IN THE WORLD WAR I ERA

Arthur E. Barbeau and Florette Henri. *Black American Troops in World War I.* Philadelphia: Temple University Press, 1974.

Edward M. Coffman. *The War to End All Wars: The American Military Experience in World War I.* Madison: University of Wisconsin Press, 1986.

Arthur W. Little. *From Harlem to the Rhine: The Story of New York's Colored Volunteers.* New York: Covici, Friede, 1936.

Bernard C. Nalty. *Strength for the Fight: A History of Black Americans in the Military.* New York: Free Press, 1986.

CITIES AND RACIAL CONFLICT

Michael D'Orso. *Like Judgment Day: The Ruin and Redemption of a Town Called Rosewood.* New York: Boulevard Press, 1996.

St. Clair Drake and Horace R. Clayton. *Black Metropolis: A Study of Negro Life in a Northern City.* 2 vols. Chicago: Harcourt, Brace and Co., 1945.

Sherry Sherrod Dupree. *The Rosewood Massacre at a Glance.* Gainesville, FL: Rosewood Forum, 1998.

Scott Ellsworth. *Death in a Promised Land: The Tulsa Race Riot of 1921.* Baton Rouge: Louisiana State University Press, 1982.

David Fort Godshalk. *Veiled Visions: The 1906 Atlanta Race Riot and the Reshaping of American Race Relations.* Chapel Hill: University of North Carolina Press, 2005.

Robert V. Haynes. *A Night of Violence: The Houston Riot of 1917.* Baton Rouge: Louisiana State University Press, 1976.

Hannibal Johnson. *Black Wall Street, from Riot to Renaissance in Tulsa's Historic Greenwood District.* Austin, TX: Eakin Press, 1998.

David M. Katzman. *Before the Ghetto: Black Detroit in the Nineteenth Century.* Urbana: University of Illinois Press, 1973.

Kenneth L. Kusmer. *A Ghetto Takes Shape: Black Cleveland, 1870–1930.* Urbana: University of Illinois Press, 1976.

Gregory Mixon. *The Atlanta Riot: Race, Class, and Violence in a New South City.* Gainesville: University Press of Florida, 2005.

Kevin J. Mumford. *Interzones: Black/White Sex Districts in Chicago and New York in the Early Twentieth Century.* New York: Columbia University Press, 1997.

Gilbert Osofsky. *Harlem: The Making of a Ghetto, 1890–1930.* New York: Harper & Row, 1966.

Christopher Reed. *The Chicago NAACP and the Rise of Black Professional Leadership, 1910–1966.* Bloomington: Indiana University Press, 1997.

Elliott M. Rudwick. *Race Riot at East St. Louis, July 2, 1917.* Cleveland, OH World Publishing, 1966.

Roberta Senechal. *The Sociogenesis of a Race Riot: Springfield, Illinois, in 1908.* Urbana: University of Illinois Press, 1990.

Allan H. Spear. *Black Chicago: The Making of a Negro Ghetto, 1890–1920.* Chicago: University of Chicago Press, 1967.

Joe William Trotter, Jr. *Black Milwaukee: The Making of an Industrial Proletariat, 1915–1945.* Urbana: University of Illinois Press, 1985.

William Tuttle. *Chicago in the Red Summer of 1919.* New York: Atheneum, 1970.

Lee E. Williams. *Anatomy of Four Race Riots: Racial Conflict in Knoxville, Elaine (Arkansas), Tulsa, and Chicago, 1919–1921.* Hattiesburg: University and College Press of Mississippi, 1972.

THE GREAT MIGRATION

Peter Gottlieb. *Making Their Own Way: Southern Blacks' Migration to Pittsburgh, 1916–1930.* Urbana: University of Illinois Press, 1987.

James Gregory. *The Southern Diaspora: How the Great Migrations of Black and White Southerners Transformed America.* Chapel Hill: University of North Carolina Press, 2005.

James R. Grossman. *Land of Hope: Chicago, Black Southerners, and the Great Migration.* Chicago: University of Chicago Press, 1989.

Florette Henri. *Black Migration, 1900–1920.* Garden City, NY: Anchor Press, 1975.

Carole Marks. *Farewell—We're Good and Gone: The Great Black Migration.* Bloomington: Indiana University Press, 1989.

Milton C. Sernett. *Bound for the Promised Land: African American Religion and the Great Migration.* Durham, NC: Duke University Press, 1997.

Joe William Trotter, Jr., ed. *The Great Migration in Historical Perspective.* Bloomington: Indiana University Press, 1991.

AUTOBIOGRAPHY AND BIOGRAPHY

W. E. B. Du Bois. *Dusk of Dawn.* New York: Harcourt, Brace & Co., 1940.

———. *The Autobiography: A Soliloquy on Viewing My Life from the Last Decade of Its First Century.* New York: International Publishers, 1968.

Rayvon Fouché. *Black Inventors in the Age of Segregation: Granville T. Woods, Lewis H. Latimer & Shelby J. Davidson.* Baltimore: Johns Hopkins University Press, 2003.

Stephen R. Fox. *The Guardian of Boston: William Monroe Trotter.* New York: Atheneum, 1970.

Jane Edna Hunter. *A Nickel and a Prayer.* Cleveland, OH: Elli Kani Publishing, 1940.

Adrienne Lash Jones. *Jane Edna Hunter: A Case Study of Black Leadership, 1910–1950.* Brooklyn, NY: Carlson Publishing, 1990.

Kenneth R. Manning. *Black Apollo of Science: The Life of Ernest Everett Just.* New York: Oxford University Press, 1983.

Linda O. McMurry. *George Washington Carver: Scientist and Symbol.* New York: Oxford University Press, 1981.

Arnold Rampersad. *The Art and Imagination of W. E. B. Du Bois.* Cambridge, MA: Harvard University Press, 1976.

Mary Church Terrell. *A Colored Woman in a White World.* New York: Arno Press reprint, 1940.

Emma Lou Thornbrough. *T. Thomas Fortune.* Chicago: University of Chicago Press, 1970.

Booker T. Washington. *Up from Slavery.* New York: Doubleday, 1901.

RETRACING THE ODYSSEY

The Booker T. Washington National Monument, Hardy, Virginia. Booker T. Washington lived his first nine years on this farm. A museum and restored schoolhouse depict rural life in nineteenth-century America, especially for slaves.

The George Washington Carver National Monument, Diamond, Missouri. George Washington Carver was born a slave here in 1864 or 1865 in a cabin that no longer exists. The 210-acre park has a visitor center that has exhibits on Carver's life as well as a short film about his boyhood. There are also nature trails and the Carver Science Discovery Center.

The 369th Historical Society, New York, New York. The 369th Regiment distinguished itself during World War I in combat alongside French units. Previously it had been the 15th Infantry Regiment of the New York National Guard. The 369th Armory contains a museum that features weapons, equipment, and photos of black troops from World War I to Operation Desert Storm of 1991.

The Greenwood Cultural Center, Tulsa, Oklahoma. The Greenwood Cultural Center has a permanent exhibit of 45 photos taken during the 1921 riot that devastated the Greenwood community. There is also a replica of one of the houses that was destroyed. The center maintains exhibits on other aspects of local black history as well, and it is home to a Jazz Hall of Fame.

African Americans and the 1920s

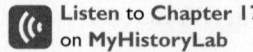
Listen to Chapter 17
on MyHistoryLab

LEARNING OBJECTIVES

17-1 Why was there an increase in intolerance in the 1920s?

17-2 How did the Ku Klux Klan become so influential in the 1920s?

17-3 How did major black organizations confront racial discrimination and promote progress in the 1920s?

17-4 Why did some black men and women who worked as Pullman Porters form a labor union, and what role did A. Philip Randolph play in those efforts to organize these workers?

17-5 Who were some of the men and women involved in the cultural phenomenon known as the Harlem Renaissance, and what were some of their literary, artistic, dramatic, and musical contributions to that movement?

17-6 What was the role of Harlem and its inhabitants in what popularly came to be known as the Jazz Age?

17-7 What opportunities and obstacles confronted black athletes in the 1920s?

> *I, Too*
> I, too, sing America.
> I am the darker brother.
> They send me to eat in the kitchen
> When company comes.
> But I laugh,
> And eat well,
> And grow strong.
> To-morrow
> I'll sit at the table
> When company comes
> Nobody'll dare
> Say to me,
> "Eat in the kitchen"
> Then.
> Besides, they'll see how beautiful I am
> And be ashamed,—
> I, too, am America.
>
> —*Langston Hughes, 1926*

Many Americans had difficulty adjusting to life after World War I. The Allied victory brought little long-term satisfaction or security, and the Senate's rejection in 1919 of the Treaty of Versailles—and therefore membership in the League of Nations—left many Americans disillusioned. The Bolshevik Revolution in Russia in 1917 and labor agitation at home increased anxiety and heightened fears of radicals. Racial and ethnic intolerance escalated as thousands of rural black southerners continued to stream into northern cities, and more than 800,000 immigrants, mostly from Europe, arrived in America in 1920 and 1921.

The fight to stop lynchings was one of the NAACP's most important campaigns in the early twentieth century. In the 1920s the NAACP fought unsuccessfully to secure anti-lynching legislation in Congress. To keep the issue in the public arena, the NAACP persisted with demonstrations and protests like this one at the Crime Conference in Washington, DC.

Americans shunned Europe and its problems and closed their eyes to the imperfections of American society. Enthusiasm for progressive reforms faded as many Americans concluded that government efforts to mitigate poverty, control vice, improve working conditions, and regulate big business had been excessive. Middle-class Americans became preoccupied with making money and acquiring material possessions—usually on credit and for the first time. They were drawn to newly available technological devices— automobiles, radios, and home appliances—that would revolutionize daily living in the twentieth century. Middle-class black consumers also bought these products, but most African Americans in the 1920s were too poor to afford them.

Many native white Americans, convinced that black people and immigrants—especially Jewish and Catholic immigrants—threatened their Anglo-Saxon ethnic purity, ever more fervently embraced social Darwinism. Many sought reassurance in organizations that stressed religious, racial, and national pride. Millions of white Americans joined the revived Ku Klux Klan in the 1920s as it promoted white supremacy, American patriotism, and Protestant values.

Led by the NAACP, African Americans denounced injustice and pressed for inclusion in society, the enforcement of civil rights, and economic opportunities. Black workers— notably the members of the **Brotherhood of Sleeping Car Porters**—organized and demanded recognition and improved working conditions, hours, and wages. But the 1920s also saw hundreds of thousands of African Americans enthusiastically support Marcus Garvey and the **Universal Negro Improvement Association (UNIA)**. Garvey celebrated black nationalism and urged his followers to forsake white America, take pride in themselves, and look to Africa. In addition, the 1920s saw black culture blossom and flourish as the artists, writers, musicians, and entertainers of the Harlem Renaissance celebrated black life and society.

In 1919 and 1920, Americans were bewildered and angered by labor unrest and afraid the communists (or "Reds") in the new Soviet Union would try to incite a revolution in America. There were 3,600 strikes in 1919 as workers who during the war had deferred demands for pay raises and improved working conditions walked off their jobs. More than 300,000 steelworkers in Pittsburgh and Gary, Indiana, struck, including 7,000 unskilled black steelworkers in Pittsburgh. In a demonstration of solidarity with striking shipyard workers, most of Seattle's working people shut the city down in a general strike. Americans were even more alarmed when police officers in Boston went on strike. Many worried that labor agitation was a prelude to revolution.

Political leaders exacerbated these feelings by warning that communists and foreign agents were plotting to overthrow the government. Woodrow Wilson's attorney general, A. Mitchell Palmer, grimly warned Americans of the Red menace and the threat that aliens posed. He ordered 249 aliens deported and some 6,000 arrested and imprisoned, in gross violation of their rights, but it was an action that many Americans approved. Palmer went too far, however, when he predicted the Red revolution would begin in the United States on May 1, 1920. There was no revolution, and confidence in Palmer waned. There

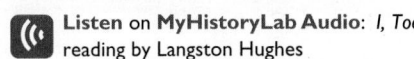
Listen on MyHistoryLab Audio: *I, Too,* reading by Langston Hughes

Brotherhood of Sleeping Car Porters (BSCP) Black men and women who worked on Pullman passenger coaches on the nation's railroads organized this labor union in 1925 with A. Philip Randolph as its leader.

Universal Negro Improvement Association (UNIA) Established in 1914 in Jamaica by Marcus Garvey, it fostered racial pride, African heritage, Christian faith, and economic uplift.

17-1

17-2

17-3

17-4

17-5

17-6

17-7

17-1
17-2
17-3
17-4
17-5
17-6
17-7

Red Scare The widespread fear among many Americans in the years immediately after World War I, from about 1918 to about 1924, that Russia's 1917 Bolshevik Revolution might result in communists attempting to take over the U.S. government.

were, however, several terrorist bombings, including one on Wall Street in September 1920 that killed 33 people. Moreover, evidence indicates that some business leaders supported the Palmer raids to discourage workers from forming and joining labor unions and participating in strikes.

Prompted in part by the **Red Scare**, xenophobia (fear of foreigners) swept the nation in the 1920s. Two Sicilian immigrants who were anarchists, Nicola Sacco and Bartolomeo Vanzetti, were charged in 1920 with a murder that had occurred during a payroll robbery near Boston. They were found guilty and, after a prolonged controversy, were executed in 1927. But their supporters believed the guilty verdict was due more to their foreign origins and radical beliefs than to conclusive proof they had committed the murder.

Varieties of Racism

17-1 Why was there an increase in intolerance in the 1920s?

The entrenched racism of American society found expression in more than one form in the 1920s. There was the sophisticated racism associated with supposedly scholarly studies that reflected the ideology of social Darwinism. There was also the raw bigotry that manifested itself in popular culture and the ideology of the increasingly popular Ku Klux Klan.

Scientific Racism

Many white Americans believed the United States was under siege as European immigrants and black migrants flooded American cities. Pseudoscholars warned about the peril these "inferior" peoples posed. In 1916 Madison Grant published *The Passing of the Great Race*. Grant warned that America was committing "race suicide" because northern Europeans and their descendants—the "Great Race"—were being diluted by inferior people from eastern and southern Europe. Lothrop Stoddard's *The Rising Tide of Color* in 1920 argued that people of color would never be equal to white Americans. Stoddard stated his case unequivocally in 1927:

> Even a general knowledge of historical and scientific facts suffices to show the need for a racial basis to our national life,—as it has been, and as we intend that it shall be. We know that our America is a White America. "America," in the traditional sense of the word, was founded by White men, who evolved institutions, ideals, and cultural manifestations which were spontaneous expressions of their racial temperament and tendencies. And the overwhelming weight of both historical and scientific evidence shows that only so long as the American people remains White will its institutions, ideals, and culture continue to fit the temperament of its inhabitants,—and hence continue to endure.

These racist claims were cloaked in the trappings of legitimate scholarship, and they strengthened the cause of white supremacy in the 1920s and helped to "protect" America from the "threat" of immigration. In 1921 and in 1924, Congress severely restricted immigration from southern and eastern Europe, Latin America, and the Caribbean and prohibited it entirely from Asia.

The Birth of a Nation

In 1915 D. W. Griffith released *The Birth of a Nation*, a cinematic masterpiece and historical travesty based on Thomas Dixon's 1905 novel *The Clansman*. Both the book and the film purported to depict Reconstruction in South Carolina. This was a three-hour black-and-white film without sound. In this epic, immoral and ignorant Negroes joined by shady mulattoes and greedy white Republicans ruthlessly seize control of state government until the heroic and honorable Ku Klux Klan saves the state and rescues its white womanhood. The film was enormously popular. President Wilson had it screened in the White House. It grossed $18 million ($378 million in 2010 dollars) and helped assure a future for Metro Goldwyn Mayer, the studio that produced it. It also distorted perceptions about Reconstruction and black Americans.

The NAACP was enraged by *The Birth of a Nation* and fought to halt its presentation. W. E. B. Du Bois complained in the *Crisis* that in the film "the Negro [was] represented either as an ignorant fool, a vicious rapist, a venal or unscrupulous politician or a faithful but doddering idiot." The film unleashed racist violence. After seeing it in Lafayette, Indiana, an infuriated white man killed a young black man. In Houston, white theatergoers shouted, "Lynch him!" during a scene in which a white actor in blackface pursued the film's star, Lillian Gish. In front of a St. Louis theater, white real estate agents passed out circulars calling for residential segregation.

Thanks largely to NAACP opposition, the film was banned in Pasadena, California; Wilmington, Delaware; and Boston. With an election looming in Chicago, Republican Mayor "Big Bill" Thompson appointed American Methodist Episcopal Bishop Archibald Carey to the board of censors, which temporarily banned the film there. When the sound version of *The Birth of a Nation* was released in 1930, the NAACP renewed its opposition. Ironically, the NAACP campaign may have provided publicity that attracted more viewers to the film. However, the campaign also helped increase NAACP membership.

The glorification of the Ku Klux Klan in D. W. Griffith's *The Birth of a Nation,* reflected in this publicity poster, outraged African Americans. The NAACP protested when the silent film was first distributed in 1915 and again when a sound version was released in 1930. The demonstrations attracted publicity to both the film and the NAACP.

The Ku Klux Klan

17-2   **How did the Ku Klux Klan become so influential in the 1920s?**

The Ku Klux Klan, which had disappeared after Reconstruction, was resurrected a few months after *The Birth of a Nation* was released. On Thanksgiving night in 1915, William J. Simmons and 34 other men gathered at Stone Mountain near Atlanta; in the flickering shadows of a fiery cross, they brought the Klan back to life.

The Ku Klux Klan in the 1920s stood for white supremacy—and more. Klansmen styled themselves as "100 percent Americans" who opposed perceived threats from immigrants as well as black Americans. The Klan claimed to represent white, Anglo-Saxon, Protestant America. With European immigrants flocking to America, William Simmons announced that the United States was no melting pot; rather, "It is a garbage can! . . . When the hordes of aliens walk to the ballot box and their votes outnumber yours, then that alien horde has got you by the throat."

The Klan found enormous support among apprehensive white middle-class Americans in the North and West. Many of them believed the liberal, immoral, and loose lifestyles they associated with urban life, immigrants, and African Americans threatened their religious beliefs and conservative values. The Klan attacked the theory of evolution, fought for the prohibition of alcoholic beverages, and claimed to uphold the "sanctity" of white womanhood. The Ku Klux Klan opposed Jews, Roman Catholics, and black people. Klansmen often used violence. They burned synagogues and Catholic churches. They beat, branded, and lynched opponents.

Read on MyHistoryLab
Document: Hiram Evans Links the Klan to Americanism, 1926

By 1925 the Klan had an estimated five million members, and 40,000 of them marched in Washington, DC, that year. The Klan attracted small businessmen, shopkeepers, clerks, Protestant clergymen, farmers, and professional people. It was open only to native-born white men, but it also had a Women's Order, a Junior Order for boys, and a Tri K Klub for girls. The Klan was active in Oregon, Colorado, Illinois, and Maine, and it became a potent political force in Indiana, Oklahoma, and Texas, where candidates for office who refused to support or join the Klan stood little chance of election.

The Klan was also a moneymaking machine. Its leaders collected millions of dollars in initiation fees, membership dues, and sales of Klan paraphernalia. But the Klan declined rapidly in the late 1920s when its leaders fought among themselves. Its claim to uphold the purity of white womanhood was damaged when one of its leaders, D. C. Stephenson, was charged in Indiana with raping a young woman who subsequently committed suicide. Stephenson was sentenced to life in prison, and the Klan never fully recovered.

Protest, Pride, and Pan-Africanism: Black Organizations in the 1920s

17-3 | **How did major black organizations confront racial discrimination and promote progress in the 1920s?**

African Americans responded to racism and to cultural and economic developments in the 1920s in several ways. The NAACP continued its efforts to secure constitutional rights and guarantees by advocacy in the political and judicial systems. Many working-class black people who had migrated to northern cities were attracted to the racial pride that Marcus Garvey and the UNIA promoted. There were also attempts to foster racial cooperation among peoples of African descent and to exert diplomatic influence through the work of Pan-African Congresses that were held during the first three decades of the twentieth century.

The NAACP

During its second decade, the NAACP expanded its influence and increased its membership. In 1916 James Weldon Johnson (who wrote "Lift Every Voice and Sing") joined the NAACP as field secretary. He played a pivotal role in the organization's development and in its growth from 9,000 members in 1916 to 90,000 in 1920. Johnson traveled tirelessly, recruiting members and establishing branches.

Johnson impressed both black and white people. He got along well with Du Bois—not always an easy task, considering Du Bois's sometimes haughty and acerbic demeanor. Johnson was an excellent diplomat who could negotiate and compromise, but he could also be blunt when necessary. He methodically reported the gruesome details of lynchings, and when some NAACP directors complained in 1921 that these graphic descriptions offended people, Johnson stood his ground: "What we need to do is to root out the thing which makes possible these horrible details. I am of the opinion that this can be done only through the fullest publicity."

In 1918 Johnson hired Walter White to assist him. White was from Atlanta and, like Johnson, a graduate of Atlanta University. White's fair complexion permitted him to move easily among white people to investigate racial discrimination and violence. Although his domineering personality offended some NAACP officials and supporters, White devoted his life to the organization and to racial justice.

Johnson and the NAACP fought hard in Congress to secure passage of the Dyer anti-lynching bill in 1921 and 1922 (see Chapter 16). The legislation ultimately failed, but the NAACP publicized the persistence of barbaric mob behavior in a nation supposedly devoted to fairness and the rule of law. It was the first campaign by a civil rights organization to lobby Congress, and—like the attempt to block *The Birth of a Nation*—it won goodwill for the NAACP.

Johnson blamed the Dyer bill's failure on Republican senators. He charged that the Republican Party took black support for granted because southern Democrats remained committed to white supremacy, and therefore black people had little choice but to vote Republican: "The Republican Party will hold the Negro and do as little for him as possible, and the Democratic Party will have none of him at all." He warned, however, that black voters in the North would abandon the Republicans:

> The Negro can serve notice that he is no longer a part of the agreement by voting in the coming elections in each State against Republicans who have betrayed him, who are in league with the Ku Klux Klan, who are found to be hypocrites and liars on the question of the Negro's essential rights, and by letting them know he has done it. I am in favor of doing the job at once.

Johnson pointed out that black voters in Harlem had elected a black Democrat to the state legislature.

The NAACP continued to rely on the judicial system to protect black Americans and enforce their civil rights. By the 1920s the Democratic Party in virtually every southern state barred black people from membership, which excluded them from voting in Democratic primaries. The result was what was known as "white primaries." Because the Republican Party had almost disappeared in most of the South, victory in the Democratic primary led invariably to victory in the general election. In 1924 the NAACP, in cooperation with its El Paso branch, filed suit over the exclusion of black voters from the Democratic primary in Texas. In 1927 the Supreme Court ruled in *Nixon v. Herndon* that the Democratic primary was unconstitutional—the first victory in what would become a 20-year legal struggle to permit black men and women to vote in primary elections across the South.

In Detroit in 1925, black physician Ossian Sweet and his family moved into an all-white neighborhood. For several nights a mob threatened the Sweet family and other people who defended them. One evening, shots fired from the Sweet home killed a white man. As a result, 12 occupants of the house were charged with murder. The NAACP retained Clarence Darrow and Arthur Garfield Hayes, two of the nation's finest criminal attorneys, to defend the Sweets. The Sweets pleaded self-defense and after two trials were acquitted.

"Up You Mighty Race": Marcus Garvey and the UNIA

With several million enthusiastic followers, Marcus Garvey's UNIA became the largest mass movement of black people in American history. The UNIA enabled black people—often dismissed by the white majority for having no genuine history or culture—to celebrate one another and their heritage and to anticipate a glorious future. Garvey was an energetic, charismatic, and flamboyant leader who wove racial pride, Christian faith, and economic cooperation into a black nationalist organization that by the early 1920s had spread throughout the United States.

Garvey was born in 1887 in the British colony of Jamaica, the eleventh child in a rural family. He quit school at age 14 and became a printer in Kingston, the island's capital. He was promoted to foreman before he was fired during a strike in 1907. He traveled to Costa Rica, Panama, Ecuador, and Nicaragua and became disturbed over the conditions black workers endured in fields, factories, and mines. He returned to Jamaica and set out to educate himself. He spent two years in London, where he sharpened his oratorical and debating skills discussing the plight of black people with Africans and people from the Caribbean.

He returned to Jamaica and founded the UNIA in 1914. With the slogan "One God! One Aim! One Destiny!" he stressed the need for black people to organize for their own advancement. Garvey had read Booker T. Washington's *Up From Slavery* and was much impressed with Washington's emphasis on self-help and progress through education and the acquisition of skills. Garvey also—like Washington—could criticize black people for their lack of progress: "The bulk of our people are in darkness and are really unfit for good society." They had "done nothing to establish the right to equality."

17-1
17-2
17-3
17-4
17-5
17-6
17-7

17-1
17-2
17-3
17-4
17-5
17-6
17-7

VOICES   The Negro National Anthem: "Lift EveryVoice and Sing"

In 1900, to celebrate Abraham Lincoln's birthday, James Weldon Johnson wrote "Lift Every Voice and Sing." His younger brother John Rosamond Johnson composed music to accompany the words. It was published in 1921 and soon thereafter—with the encouragement of the NAACP—the song was embraced as the Negro national anthem.

Lift every voice and sing, 'til earth and heaven ring,
Ring with the harmonies of liberty
Let our rejoicing rise, high as the list'ning skies,
Let it resound loud as the rolling sea.
Sing a song full of the faith that the dark past has taught us,
Sing a song full of the hope that the present has brought us;
Facing the rising sun of our new day begun
Let us march on till victory is won.

Stony the road we trod, bitter the chast'ning rod
Felt in the days when hope unborn had died
Yet with a steady beat, have not our weary feet
Come to the place for which our fathers sighed?
We have come over a way that with tears has been watered,
We have come, treading our path thro' the blood of the slaughtered

Out from the gloomy past, 'til now we stand at last
Where the white gleam of our bright star is cast.

God of our weary years, God of our silent tears
Thou who has brought us thus far on the way
Thou who hast by Thy might, led us into the light
Keep us forever in the path, we pray.
Lest our feet stray from the places, our God, where we met Thee
Lest our hearts, drunk with the wine of the world, we forget Thee
Shadowed beneath Thy hand, may we forever stand
True to our God, true to our native land.

1. To what native land does Johnson refer in the last line: "True to our God, true to our native land"?
2. Do the lyrics apply to all Americans or only to African Americans? Would the song be appropriate as the American national anthem? Why or why not?

SOURCE: James Weldon Johnson wrote "Lift Every Voice and Sing." His younger brother John Rosamond Johnson composed music to accompany the words.

 **Read** on **MyHistoryLab Document:** Marcus Garvey Calls for Black Separatism, 1921

Garvey came to the United States in 1916 just as thousands of African Americans were migrating to cities. A dynamic speaker whose message resonated among the disaffected urban working class, Garvey built the UNIA into a major movement. He urged his listeners to take pride in themselves as they restored their race to its previous greatness: "We must canonize our own saints, create our own martyrs, and elevate to positions of fame and honor black men and women who have made their distinct contributions to our racial history." He reminded people that Africa had a remarkable past: "Africa was peopled with a race of cultured black men, who were masters in art, science and literature; men who were cultured and refined; men, who, it was said, were like the gods. . . . Black men, you were once great; you shall be great again." He insisted that his followers change their thinking: "We have outgrown slavery, but our minds are still enslaved to the thinking of the Master Race. Now take these kinks out of your mind, instead of out of your hair."

With the formation of the New York division of the UNIA in Harlem in 1917, Garvey exhorted, "Up you mighty race!" as he commanded black people to take control of their destiny. Still, he blamed them for their predicament: "That the Negro race became a race of slaves was not the fault of God Almighty . . . it was the fault of the race." Their salvation would result from their own exertion and not from concessions by white people.

Garvey's message and the UNIA spread to black communities large and small. He regularly couched his rhetoric in religious terms, and he came to be known as the Black Moses, a messiah. Garvey dwelled on Christ's betrayal as he identified himself with Jesus:

"If Garvey dies, Garvey lives." "Christ died to make men free, I shall die to give courage and inspiration to my race."

Garvey's followers enjoyed the pageantry, ceremonies, and titles that were a part of the UNIA. The African Legionnaires and the Black Cross Nurses, resplendent in their uniforms,

PROFILE James Weldon Johnson

JAMES WELDON JOHNSON was a man of immense talents: lawyer, diplomat, journalist, teacher, and gifted writer. Most important, he was an effective and dynamic civil rights leader.

Johnson was born in 1871 in Jacksonville, Florida, to parents who had not been slaves. His father was a waiter in a fashionable hotel, and his mother was a schoolteacher. He received his secondary and collegiate education at Atlanta University, where he also earned a master's degree. He read law in the office of a white Jacksonville attorney and was admitted to the Florida bar. In 1902 he moved to New York City.

With his brother John Rosamond and black entertainer Robert Cole, he became part of a successful songwriting team. They contributed two musical numbers to Theodore Roosevelt's 1904 presidential campaign: "You're All Right Teddy" and "The Old Flag Never Touched the Ground." Johnson's connection to the Republican Party and his support for Booker T. Washington helped secure diplomatic appointments for him. Johnson spent seven years as a U.S. consul in Venezuela and Nicaragua. In 1910 he married Grace Neal, the sister of a prominent New York real estate broker.

With the 1912 election of Woodrow Wilson, a Democrat, Johnson's diplomatic career ended. He became an editorial writer for the *New York Age*. He also published anonymously *The Autobiography of an Ex-Colored Man*. In 1916 Joel Spingarn, the president of the NAACP, asked Johnson to take a leadership role with that organization, and Johnson—who had not openly supported the NAACP before Booker T. Washington's death in 1915—became its field secretary.

Johnson spent the next 14 years with the NAACP. In 1920 he became chief executive, responsible for the association's day-to-day operations. He had organized the silent march on Fifth Avenue on July 28, 1917, to protest the East St. Louis riot (see Chapter 16). He publicized lynchings. He recruited members and established new branches. In 1920 in the *Nation*, he documented the mistreatment of Haitians by U.S. troops who had occupied that Caribbean nation. He supported black workers and A. Philip Randolph and the Brotherhood of Sleeping Car Porters. He arranged legal counsel for Ossian Sweet in Detroit in 1925 after Sweet and several of his supporters were charged with murder.

Johnson also managed to write prolifically and imaginatively. In 1920, he wrote "The Creation: A Negro Sermon." He wrote "God's Trombones: Seven Negro Sermons in Verse" in 1927 and many other works of prose and poetry. In 1930 he finished *Black Manhattan*, which traced the cultural contributions of black people to New York City in music, poetry, and theater from the seventeenth to the twentieth century.

Like so many civil rights leaders, Johnson could be inconsistent about racial issues. Though dedicated to the proposition that black and white people should enjoy equal access to public facilities, he supported an all-black YMCA in Harlem and the separate training of black military officers during World War I. He opposed moving the NAACP headquarters from Fifth Avenue to Harlem. He supported building an all-black veteran's hospital at Tuskegee, Alabama, as long as it would be staffed by black physicians and nurses. He appreciated Marcus Garvey's emphasis on black pride, but he considered the back-to-Africa movement to be an attempt to escape from America's racial problems rather than a solution to them.

In 1930 Johnson became a professor of creative writing at Fisk University in Nashville. He left the NAACP as a far more visible and strong organization than he had found it in 1916. At Fisk, he worked with some of the twentieth century's leading black scholars, including Horace Mann Bond, Alrutheus A. Taylor, and E. Franklin Frazier. Historian John Hope Franklin was one of his students. Johnson published his autobiography, *Along the Way,* in 1933. Johnson died in an automobile accident in 1938.

Listen on **MyHistoryLab Audio:** The Creation: A Negro Sermon

17-1
17-2
17-3
17-4
17-5
17-6
17-7

Jamaican-born Marcus Garvey arrived in the United States in 1916 and quickly rose to prominence as the head of the UNIA. Garvey appears here in a 1924 parade in Harlem attired in a uniform similar to those worn by British colonial governors in Jamaica, Trinidad, and elsewhere.

assembled in New York's Liberty Hall and paraded through Harlem. They prayed from *The Universal Negro Catechism* and reflected on their connection to Africa: "O Blessed Lord Jesus, redeem Africa from the hands of those who exploit and ravish her."

Garvey and the UNIA also established businesses that employed nearly 1,000 black people. The weekly newspaper, *Negro World,* promoted Garvey's ideology. In New York City, the Negro Factories Corporation operated three grocery stores, two restaurants, a printing plant, a steam laundry, and a factory that turned out clothes for UNIA members. The association also owned property in other cities. Garvey proudly declared to white Americans that the UNIA "employs thousands of black girls and black boys. Girls who could only be washer women in your homes, we made clerks, stenographers. . . . You will see from the start we tried to dignify our race."

Although Garvey and the UNIA are most frequently associated with urban communities in the North, the UNIA also spread rapidly through the rural South in the 1920s. Black farmers and sharecroppers established UNIA chapters from Virginia to Louisiana, and the Garvey movement and the *Negro World* could be found in such remote communities as Kinston, North Carolina; Ty Ty, Georgia; and Cotton Plant, Arkansas.

Garvey may be best remembered for his proposal to return black people to Africa on the Black Star Line, a steamship company he founded in 1919. Garvey sold stock in the company for $5 a share, and he hoped to establish a fleet with black officers and crews. In 1920 the company purchased the *Yarmouth,* a dilapidated vessel that became the first ship in the fleet. Garvey bought two more ships, the *Kanawha* and the *Booker T. Washington,* but he lacked the money to maintain them or transport anyone to Africa.

Moreover, Garvey knew it was unrealistic to expect several million black residents of the Western Hemisphere to join the back-to-Africa enterprise, but he did believe that the UNIA could liberate Africa from European colonial rule: "Wake up Ethiopia! Wake up Africa! Let us work towards the one glorious end of a free, redeemed and mighty nation." The UNIA adopted a red, green, and black flag for the proposed African republic that represented the blood, land, and race of the African people.

The UNIA attempted to establish a settlement on the Cavalla River in southern Liberia. Garvey also petitioned the League of Nations to permit the UNIA to take over the former German colony of Tanganyika (today's Tanzania) in East Africa. But the major colonial powers in Africa—Britain and France—and the United States thwarted Garvey's plans, and the UNIA never gained a foothold on the continent.

The U.S. government and several black American leaders also worked diligently to undermine Garvey and the UNIA. J. Edgar Hoover and the Bureau of Investigation (the predecessor of the FBI) considered Garvey a threat to the racial status quo. Hoover employed black agents to infiltrate the UNIA and compile information that could be used to deport Garvey, who had never become an American citizen.

Garvey had few friends or admirers among African-American leaders because he and they differed fundamentally on strategy and goals. Garvey deplored efforts to gain legal and political rights within the American system. By appealing to the black masses, he rejected Du Bois's notion that the Talented Tenth would lead the race to liberation. He mocked the NAACP as the "National Association for the Advancement of Certain People." Not long after he arrived in the United States, Garvey visited the NAACP office in New York and disliked what he saw: "There was no representation of the race there that any one could recognize. . . . [Y]ou had to be as near white as possible, otherwise there was no place for

VOICES Marcus Garvey Appeals for a New African Nation

Marcus Garvey and the UNIA offered hope to African Americans in the 1920s. In the following words, Garvey passionately calls for African Americans and West Indians to support the creation of a new African nation:

For five years the Universal Negro Improvement Association has been advocating the cause of Africa for the Africans—that is, that the Negro peoples of the world should concentrate upon the object of building up for themselves a great nation in Africa. . . .

It is only a question of a few more years when Africa will be completely colonized by Negroes, as Europe is by the white race. What we want is an independent African nationality, and if America is to help the Negro peoples of the world establish such a nationality, then we welcome the assistance.

It is hoped that when the time comes for American and West Indian Negroes to settle in Africa, they will realize their responsibilities and duty. It will not be to go to Africa for the purpose of exercising an over-lordship over the natives, . . .

It will be useless, as stated before, for bombastic Negroes to leave America and the West Indies to go to Africa, thinking that they will have privileged positions to inflict upon the race that bastard aristocracy that they have tried to maintain in this Western world at the expense of the masses. Africa shall develop an aristocracy of its own, but it shall be based upon service and loyalty to race. Let all Negroes work toward that end. . . .

The time has really come for the Asiatics to govern themselves in Asia, as the Europeans are in Europe and the Western world, so also is it wise for the Africans to govern themselves at home, and thereby bring peace and satisfaction to the entire human family.

So Negroes, I say, through the Universal Negro Improvement Association, that there is much to live for. I have a vision of the future, and I see before me a picture of a redeemed Africa, with her dotted cities, with her beautiful civilization, with her millions of happy children going to and fro. Why should I lose hope, why should I give up and take a back place in this age of progress? . . .

Africa shall reflect a splendid demonstration of the worth of the Negro, of the determination of the Negro, to set himself free and to establish a government of his own.

1. **Why does Garvey call for a black homeland in Africa? How realistic was this call in the 1920s for nationhood in Africa?**

2. **Who does Garvey believe should lead (or should not lead) the new African nation? What are the qualifications for such leadership?**

3. **What does Garvey think the globe will look like in the future? How will peoples of various colors coexist?**

SOURCE: David Levering Lewis, ed., *The Portable Harlem Renaissance Reader* (New York: Viking Penguin, 1994), 17, 19, 20, 21, 25.

17-1
17-2
17-3
17-4
17-5
17-6
17-7

you as stenographer, clerk or attendant in the office of the National Association for the Advancement of 'Colored' People."

Garvey called Du Bois a "lazy, dependent mulatto." In return, Du Bois described Garvey as "a little, fat black man, ugly but with intelligent eyes and big head," who was "the most dangerous enemy of the Negro race in America and the world . . . either a lunatic or a traitor." A. Philip Randolph, the black labor leader, called Garvey "the supreme Negro Jamaican Jackass," an "unquestioned fool and ignoramus."

Unlike African-American leaders, Garvey believed black and white people had separate destinies, and he regarded interracial cooperation as absurd. Thus, Garvey considered a meeting he had with Ku Klux Klan leaders in Atlanta in 1922 consistent with his racial views: "They are better friends to my race, for telling us what they are, and what they mean, thereby giving us a chance to stir for ourselves . . . every whiteman is a Klansman . . . and there is no use lying about it."

In 1922 Garvey and three other UNIA leaders were indicted on 12 counts of mail fraud in connection with the sale of stock in the Black Star Line. Eight African-American leaders wrote to the U.S. attorney general to insist on his prosecution. Although Garvey was guilty of no more than mismanagement and incompetence, he was found guilty and sent to prison in 1925. President Calvin Coolidge commuted his sentence in 1927, and he was then deported.

With the loss of its inspirational leader, the UNIA declined steadily in the late 1920s and the 1930s. UNIA businesses closed, and its property—including the *Yarmouth*—was sold. Garvey was never permitted to return to the United States, and he died in London in 1940. However, his legacy persisted. The Rev. Earl Little, a Baptist minister and the father of Malcolm X, belonged to the UNIA and admired Garvey. Malcolm X recalled his father's association with Garvey: "I remember hearing that he had black followers not only in the United States but all around the world, and I remember how the meetings always closed with my father saying, several times, and the people chanting after him, 'Up, you mighty race, you can accomplish what you will!'"

The African Blood Brotherhood

In 1919 black men who had migrated to New York City from the Caribbean formed the African Blood Brotherhood as a radical alternative to Marcus Garvey and the UNIA. Cyril Briggs, who had been born in St. Kitts-Nevis in 1888, was the founder. The brotherhood rejected Garvey's reliance on capitalism and his devotion to Christianity. The brotherhood supported Marxism and had ties to the Communist Party.

Edited by Briggs, the African Blood Brotherhood briefly published the *Crusader* in the early 1920s. Unlike the UNIA, the Brotherhood's rejection of private enterprise and mainstream religion prevented it from becoming a mass movement. It never had more than 3,000 supporters.

Pan-Africanism

While Garvey, Du Bois, and Briggs differed on the most appropriate strategy for advancing African Americans, they shared an abiding interest in Africa. Garvey, Du Bois, Briggs, and other black leaders believed people of African descent from around the world should come together to share their heritage, discuss their ties to the continent, and explore ways to moderate—if not eliminate—colonial rule in Africa, a concept termed **Pan-Africanism**.

By 1914 Britain, France, Germany, Portugal, Belgium, Spain, and Italy had established colonies across almost all of Africa. Only Liberia and Ethiopia (then called Abyssinia) remained independent. The Europeans assumed the "white man's burden" in their imperialist "scramble" for Africa. Christian missionaries sought to convert Africans, and European companies exploited Africa's human and natural resources. As they gained control over the continent, the European powers confirmed their conviction that they represented a superior race and culture.

The first Pan-African Congress convened in London in 1900 and was organized principally by Henry Sylvester Williams, a lawyer from Trinidad who had lived in Canada and then London. Du Bois chaired the Committee on the Address to the Nations of the World. He called for the creation of "a great central Negro state of the world." But Du Bois did not insist on the immediate withdrawal of the European powers from Africa. Instead, he offered a modest recommendation that would provide "as soon as practicable the rights of responsible self-government to the black colonies of Africa and the West Indies."

The second Pan-African Congress met in Paris for three days in February 1919 near Versailles, where the peace conference ending World War I was assembled. There were 58 delegates from 16 nations. Du Bois was among the 16 African Americans in attendance. (None of them had been to Africa.) Marcus Garvey did not attend. The delegates took seriously the Fourteen Points that President Wilson had proposed to create a new postwar world. They were especially interested in Wilson's fifth point, which called for the interests of colonial peoples to be given "equal weight" in the adjustment of colonial claims after the war. The congress recommended that the League of Nations assume authority over the former German colonies in Africa. The League later established mandates over those colonies but delegated authority to administer those mandates to Britain, France, and Belgium. Two more Pan-African Congresses met in Brussels and London in the 1920s but also failed to influence the policies of the colonial powers.

Pan-Africanism A movement of people of African descent from sub-Saharan Africa in the early twentieth century that emphasized their identity, shared experiences, and the need to liberate Africa from its European colonizers.

Labor

17-4 Why did some black men and women who worked as Pullman Porters form a labor union, and what role did A. Philip Randolph play in those efforts to organize these workers?

The arrival of thousands of black migrants in American cities during and after World War I changed the composition of the industrial workforce and intensified pressure on labor unions to admit black members. By 1916, 12,000 of the nearly 50,000 workers in the Chicago stockyards were black people. In Detroit, black laborers made up nearly 14 percent of the workforce in the automobile industry. The Ford Motor Company employed 50 black people in 1916 and 2,500 by 1920.

Yet even with the Industrial Revolution and the Great Migration, more than two-thirds of black workers in 1920 were employed in agriculture and domestic service (see Figure 17–1). Less than 20 percent were engaged in manufacturing. Many black men and women remained confined to the rural South. Those who were part of industrial America disproportionately worked in the dreary, dirty, and sometimes dangerous unskilled jobs that paid the least. Still, work in the factories, mills, and mines paid more than agriculture (Figure 17–2). But even those with skills were usually not admitted to the local craft unions that made up the American Federation of Labor (AFL). More than 50 trade unions within the AFL had no black members. Unions that did admit black workers included those representing cigar makers, coal miners, garment workers, and longshoremen.

By the World War I years, the NAACP and the Urban League regularly appealed to employers and unions to accept black laborers. The Urban League attempted to convince

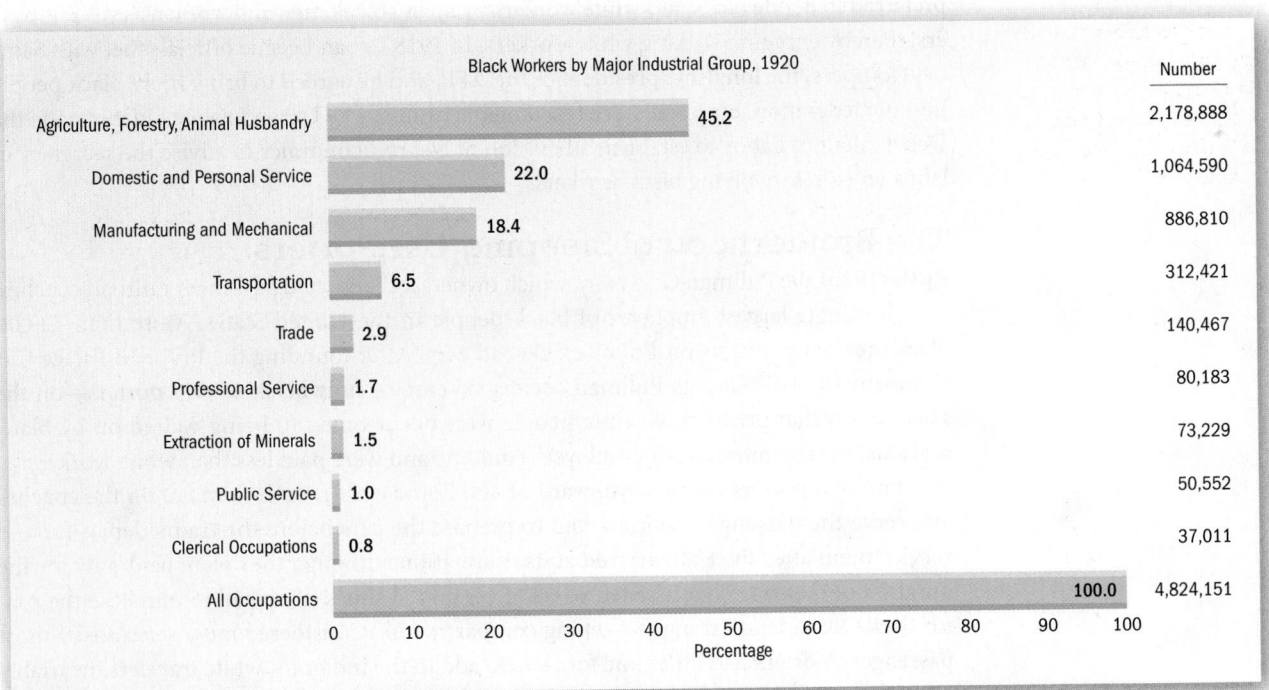

Black Workers by Major Industrial Group, 1920

	Percentage	Number
Agriculture, Forestry, Animal Husbandry	45.2	2,178,888
Domestic and Personal Service	22.0	1,064,590
Manufacturing and Mechanical	18.4	886,810
Transportation	6.5	312,421
Trade	2.9	140,467
Professional Service	1.7	80,183
Extraction of Minerals	1.5	73,229
Public Service	1.0	50,552
Clerical Occupations	0.8	37,011
All Occupations	100.0	4,824,151

FIGURE 17–1 BLACK WORKERS BY MAJOR INDUSTRIAL GROUP, 1920

By 1920 thousands of African Americans had moved to northern cities and were employed in a variety of mostly unskilled and low-paying industrial jobs that nonetheless paid more than farm labor. Still, agriculture remained the largest single source of employment among black people, and agriculture and domestic service together employed more than two-thirds of African-American men and women. About 5 percent were employed in "white-collar" jobs.

SOURCE: Sterling D. Spero and Abram L. Harris, *The Black Worker: The Negro and the Labor Movement* (1928), 81.

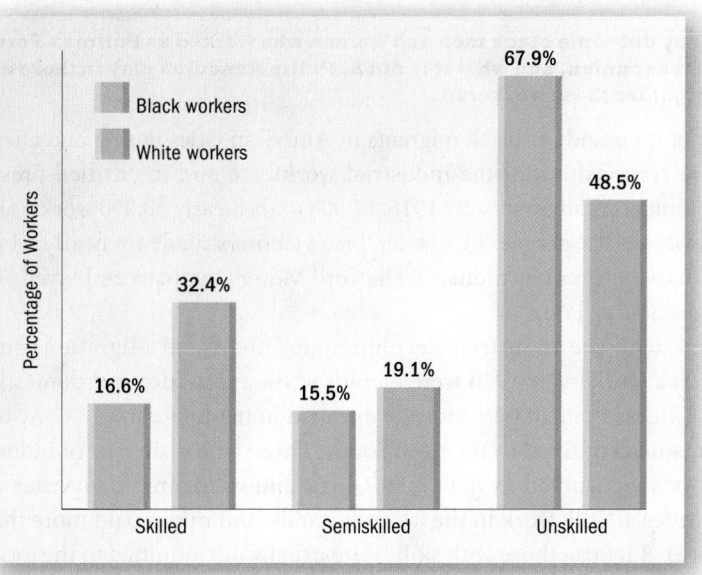

FIGURE 17–2 BLACK AND WHITE WORKERS BY SKILL LEVEL, 1920
Only one-third of black workers, compared to slightly more than one-half of
white workers, found employment in skilled or semiskilled jobs in 1920.
SOURCE: Sterling D. Spero and Abram L. Harris, *The Black Worker: The Negro and the Labor Movement* (1928), 85.

business owners that black employees would be efficient and reliable. But many employers
preferred to divide black and white workers by hiring black men and women as strikebreakers, thereby enraging striking white workers. In 1918 Urban League officials met with Samuel Gompers, the longtime president of the AFL, and he agreed to bring more black people
into the federation, but there were few tangible results. The Urban League did persuade the
Department of Labor to establish a Division of Negro Economics to advise the secretary of
labor on issues involving black workers.

The Brotherhood of Sleeping Car Porters

By the 1920s the Pullman Company, which owned and operated passenger railroad coaches,
was the single largest employer of black people in the United States. More than 12,000
black men were porters on Pullman railroad cars. After founding the Pullman Palace Car
Company in 1867, George Pullman decided to employ only black men as porters—on the
assumption that prosperous white people were accustomed to being waited on by black
servants. Furthermore, black employees could be and were paid less than white workers.

Pullman porters toiled for upward of 400 hours each month to maintain the coaches
and serve the passengers. Porters had to prepare the cars before the train's departure and
service them after the train arrived at its destination, although they were paid only for the
duration of the trip. They assisted passengers, shined shoes (they had to purchase the pol-
ish themselves), and arranged sleeping compartments. Considered mere servants by most
passengers, porters had little time for rest. To add to the indignity, white travelers invariably
referred to these black men as "George," no matter what their actual name was. Porters were
paid an average of $67.50 per month—about $810 per year. But with tips that might average
$600 annually, a porter could earn $1,400 in a year, a decent wage at the time. They had to
buy their own uniforms during their first 10 years of employment.

Although strenuous and time consuming, Pullman employment was the most satisfactory
work many black men could hope to achieve. Barred from business and industry, black men
with college degrees often worked as sleeping car porters. As poorly paid as they were compared
with many white workers, they still earned more than most black schoolteachers. Most of these
Pullman employees regarded themselves as solid, respectable members of the middle class.

It seemed unlikely that men as subservient and unobtrusive as the Pullman porters would form a labor union to challenge one of America's most powerful corporations. But they did. The key figure in this effort was A. Philip Randolph. In 1925 Pullman porters in Harlem invited Randolph to become their "general organizer" as they formed the Brotherhood of Sleeping Car Porters (BSCP). Randolph accepted.

A. Philip Randolph

Randolph was a socialist with superb oratorical skills who had earned a reputation as a radical on the streets of Harlem. He was born in 1889 in Crescent City, Florida. He attended high school at Cookman Institute (later Bethune-Cookman College) and migrated in 1911 to New York City, where he attended City College and joined the Socialist Party. In 1913 he married Lucille Campbell Greene. She was a prosperous beauty shop owner who contributed financially to many of her husband's causes. With Chandler Owen, he founded the *Messenger,* a monthly socialist journal that drew the attention of federal agents because they regarded it as the only radical Negro magazine in the country. Randolph opposed American involvement in World War I. In 1919 Department of Justice officials arrested Randolph and Owen for violating the Espionage Act and held them briefly. They labeled Randolph the most dangerous Negro in America.

Randolph was an improbable radical. He was handsome, dignified, impeccably dressed, and aloof. Save for his color, he could have been mistaken for the sort of Wall Street broker or powerful corporate attorney he detested. But blessed with a rich baritone voice, he "damned the classes and exalted the masses" and maintained an unwavering commitment to economic and racial change. He was one of the nation's foremost protest leaders for more than five decades.

Randolph faced the daunting task of recruiting support for the brotherhood, winning recognition from the Pullman Company, and gaining the union's acceptance by the American Federation of Labor (AFL). There was considerable opposition, much of it from within the black community. Many porters were too frightened to join the brotherhood. Black clergymen counseled against union activities. Black newspapers, including the *Chicago Defender,* opposed the BSCP.

But Randolph persevered with the assistance of Milton Webster, who became vice president of the brotherhood after Randolph assumed the presidency. With the slogan "Service not servitude," the two men recruited members, organized the brotherhood, and attempted to negotiate with the Pullman Company. Pullman executives ignored Randolph's overtures. They instead fired porters who joined the union, infiltrated union meetings with company agents, and organized the Employees' Representation Plan—an alternative company union that they claimed actually represented the black employees.

Although the NAACP and the Urban League supported the BSCP, progress was slow. In 1928 Randolph threatened to call a strike against the Pullman Company, but he called it off after AFL president William Green promised modest assistance to the as-yet-unrecognized union. Green's offer simply saved face for Randolph. It is unlikely that a strike would have succeeded or that most porters would have followed Randolph's leadership and left the trains. The Great Depression of the 1930s brought layoffs and mass resignations from the brotherhood. The AFL barely responded to repeated charges of discrimination by Randolph, the NAACP, and the Urban League. The BSCP nearly collapsed. Not until the passage of legislation during President Franklin D. Roosevelt's New Deal in the mid-1930s did the BSCP make substantial gains.

In this painting by Betsy G. Reyneau, A. Philip Randolph hardly resembles the militant agitator, activist, and labor leader that he was. He became the head of the BSCP, and he eventually rose to power in the AFL. He planned the first March on Washington in 1941 and was responsible for organizing the 1963 March on Washington.

Betsy G. Reyneau, A. Philip Randolph. National Archives.

The Harlem Renaissance

17-5 **Who were some of the men and women involved in the cultural phenomenon known as the Harlem Renaissance, and what were some of their literary, artistic, dramatic, and musical contributions to that movement?**

For most of American history, most Americans have shown little interest in serious literature or intellectual developments. The 1920s were no exception. People were far more fascinated by sports, automobiles, the radio, and popular music than they were by poetry, plays, museums, or novels. Still, the 1920s witnessed a proliferation of creative works by a remarkable group of gifted writers and artists. Among white writers, T. S. Eliot, Ezra Pound, Edith Wharton, Ernest Hemingway, Sinclair Lewis, Eugene O'Neill, Willa Cather, and F. Scott Fitzgerald produced literary works that explored a range of themes but were mostly critical of American life and society. Eliot, Pound, Wharton, Fitzgerald, and Hemingway found American culture so unappealing that they exiled themselves to Europe.

Black intellectuals congregated in Manhattan and gave rise to the creative movement known as the **Harlem Renaissance**. Alain Locke promoted *The New Negro*. Poets, novelists, and painters probed racial themes and grappled with what it meant to be black in America. This renaissance had no precise beginning. As early as 1920, Du Bois wrote in the *Crisis* that the nation was on the verge of a "renaissance of American Negro literature." In 1925 the *New York Herald Tribune* declared that America was "on the edge, if not already in the midst of, what might not improperly be called a Negro renaissance." No matter when it began, the Harlem Renaissance produced stunning artistic works, especially in creative writing, that continued into the 1930s.

Before Harlem

There had certainly been serious cultural developments among African Americans before the 1920s. From 1897 to 1928, the American Negro Academy was a forum for the Talented Tenth as men such as Alain Locke, Kelly Miller, and Du Bois reflected on race and color.

At the turn of the century, novelist Charles W. Chesnutt depicted a young black woman's attempt to pass for white in *The House Behind the Cedars,* and he wrote about racist violence in the post-Reconstruction South in *The Marrow of Tradition.* Ohio poet Paul Laurence Dunbar wrote evocatively of black life, frequently relying on black dialect, before he died at age 34 in 1906. Henry Ossawa Tanner had an illustrious career as a painter. Shortly after he produced "The Banjo Lesson" in 1893, Tanner left for Paris and spent most of the rest of his life in Europe. He died there in 1937.

Carter G. Woodson, the son of Virginia slaves, earned a Ph.D. at Harvard in history and founded in 1915 the Association for the Study of Negro Life and History. He stressed the need for the scholarly examination of Negro history and established the *Journal of Negro History* and the *Negro History Bulletin.* He also founded Associated Publishers to publish books on black history. Woodson wrote several major works, including *The Negro in Our History.* In 1926 he established Negro History Week during February. Not surprisingly, Woodson became known as the "father of Negro history."

During the bloody Red Summer of 1919 when racial violence erupted in Chicago and elsewhere, Claude McKay, a Jamaican who settled—like Marcus Garvey—in New York City, wrote a powerful poem, "If We Must Die," in response to the attacks by white people in Chicago on black residents:

If we must die, let it not be like hogs

Hunted and penned in an inglorious spot,

While round us bark the mad and hungry dogs,

Making their mock at our accurséd lot.

If we must die, O let us nobly die,

Watch on **MyHistoryLab Video:** The Harlem Renaissance

Harlem Renaissance As New York City became a destination for black migrants before, during, and after World War I, most of them settled in Harlem—a large neighborhood in the northern portion of Manhattan Island—which by the 1920s became a center of African-American cultural activities including literature, art, and music.

17-1
17-2
17-3
17-4
17-5
17-6
17-7

Listen on **MyHistoryLab Audio:** *If We Must Die*; poem and reading by Claude McKay

So that our precious blood may not be shed

In vain; then even the monsters we defy

Shall be constrained to honor us though dead!

O kinsmen! We must meet the common foe!

Though far outnumbered let us show us brave,

And for their thousand blows deal one deathblow!

What though before us lies the open grave?

Like men we'll face the murderous, cowardly pack,

Pressed to the wall, dying, but fighting back!

McKay left the United States for the Soviet Union in 1922 and spent the next 12 years in Europe. In 1928, while in France, he wrote *Home to Harlem,* a novel that depicted life among pimps, prostitutes, loan sharks, and petty criminals. McKay was not on cordial terms with the African-American intellectuals who formed the core of the Harlem Renaissance, and he did not consider himself part of the Talented Tenth: "I was an older man and not regarded as a member of the renaissance, but more as a forerunner."

Writers and Artists

Few white Americans and still fewer black Americans had access to a college education in the early twentieth century. Only about 2,000 African Americans were pursuing college degrees by 1920. Yet the writers and artists associated with the Harlem Renaissance were the products of some of the nation's finest schools, and, with the exception of Zora Neale Hurston, they did not come from isolated, rural southern communities. Hurston was born in Notasulga, Alabama, and raised near Orlando in the all-black town of Eatonville, Florida. She attended Morgan State University and Howard University, and graduated from Barnard College. Alain Locke was a native of Philadelphia and Phi Beta Kappa graduate of Harvard. He was the first African American to win a Rhodes scholarship to Oxford University, and he also earned a Ph.D. in philosophy from Harvard. Aaron Douglas was born in Kansas and was an art major at the University of Nebraska.

Carter G. Woodson was born in 1875, the son of slaves. As a young man he toiled in West Virginia coal mines. He worked his way through Berea College and then earned a doctorate in history from Harvard in 1912. In 1915 he founded the Association for the Study of Negro Life and History. Woodson would go on to edit the association's *Journal of Negro History* (now the *Journal of African American History*). In 1926 Woodson founded Negro History Week, which would become Negro History Month. He died in 1950.

Langston Hughes was born in Joplin, Missouri; graduated from high school in Cleveland; and attended Columbia University before he graduated from Pennsylvania's Lincoln University. Jessie Fauset came from a prominent Philadelphia family of color. She was a graduate of Cornell University and a member of Phi Beta Kappa. She earned an M.A. from the University of Pennsylvania in romance languages. Jean Toomer was born in Washington, DC, and was raised largely by his grandparents in a fashionable white neighborhood. Toomer went to the University of Wisconsin and then the Massachusetts College of Agriculture. Wallace Thurman was born in Salt Lake City and attended both the University of Utah and the University of Southern California. Countee Cullen was a native of Lexington, Kentucky, and a Phi Beta Kappa graduate of New York University. Nella Larsen was the only major writer connected to the Harlem Renaissance who did not have a college degree. A native of Chicago, she graduated from the nurse training program at New York City's Lincoln Hospital.

The Harlem Renaissance gradually emerged in the early 1920s and then expanded as more creative figures were drawn to Harlem. In 1923 Jean Toomer published *Cane,* a collection of stories and poetry about southern black life. It sold a mere 500 copies, but it had a major impact on Jessie Fauset and Walter White. Fauset was the literary editor of the *Crisis,* and in 1924 she finished *There Is Confusion,* the first novel published during

17-1

17-2

17-3

17-4

17-5

17-6

17-7

1919–1937
THE HARLEM RENAISSANCE

1919
Claude McKay publishes
"If We Must Die"

1920
Eugene O'Neill's *The Emperor
Jones* opens, featuring Charles
Gilpin; Langston Hughes pub-
lishes *The Negro Speaks of Rivers*

1922
Shuffle Along, by Noble Sissle and
Eubie Blake, opens on Broadway
with Florence Mills and Josephine
Baker; Claude McKay publishes
Harlem Shadows

1923
Jean Toomer publishes *Cane;* the
Cotton Club opens; *Opportunity:
A Journal of Negro Life,* edited by
Charles S. Johnson and supported
by the Urban League, begins
publication

1924
Jessie R. Fauset publishes *There Is
Confusion;* Walter White publishes
The Fire in the Flint; Paul Robeson
stars in Eugene O'Neill's *All God's
Chillun Got Wings*

1925
Countee Cullen publishes *Color;*
James Weldon Johnson publishes
*The Book of American Negro Spiri-
tuals; The New Negro,* edited by
Alain Locke, is published

1926
Langston Hughes publishes *The
Weary Blues;* George Schuyler's
"The Negro-Art Hokum" appears
in the *Nation;* The Savoy Ballroom
opens; Wallace Thurman pub-
lishes one issue of *Fire;*
Florence Mills dies

1927
Langston Hughes publishes *Fine
Clothes to the Jew;* James Weldon
Johnson publishes *God's Trombones:
Seven Negro Sermons in Verse*

1928
Claude McKay publishes *Home
to Harlem;* Duke Ellington's band
appears at the Cotton Club; Nella
Larsen publishes *Quicksand*

1929
Jessie R. Fauset publishes *Plum
Bun;* Wallace Thurman publishes
The Blacker the Berry . . . ; Claude
McKay publishes *Banjo;* Countee
Cullen publishes *The Black Christ;*
Nella Larsen publishes *Passing;*
Fats Waller's *Ain't Misbehavin'*
opens on Broadway

1930
James Weldon Johnson publishes
Black Manhattan

1931
Jessie R. Fauset publishes
The Chinaberry Tree

1933
Jessie R. Fauset publishes her last
novel, *Comedy American Style;*
James Weldon Johnson publishes
his autobiography, *Along the Way*

1934
Wallace Thurman dies

1935
Zora Neale Hurston publishes
Mules and Men

1937
Zora Neale Hurston publishes
Their Eyes Were Watching God

17-1

17-2

17-3

17-4

17-5

17-6

17-7

Artist Aaron Douglas (1899–1979) was born in Topeka, Kansas, and was the sole black student at the University of Nebraska when he graduated in 1922. He moved to Harlem in 1925 and shortly after that visited Paris, where he met celebrated black artist Henry Ossawa Tanner. Douglas returned to Harlem and then taught art at Fisk University in Nashville from 1937 to 1966. His paintings reflected his deep interest in the African-American experience. Notice the Ku Klux Klan as well as black soldiers in this work.

Aaron Douglas, Aspects of Negro Life, *Oil on canvas, 60"×139", Schomburg Center for Research in Black Culture, Art & Artifacts Division, The New York Public Library, Astor, Lenox and Tilden Foundation.*

the renaissance. Her novels explored the manners and color consciousness among well-to-do Negroes. Walter White, who was James Weldon Johnson's assistant at the NAACP, published in 1924 *The Fire in the Flint,* a novel about a black physician who confronted white brutality in Georgia.

In the meantime, the *Crisis,* as well as *Opportunity,* a new publication of the Urban League, published the poetry and short stories of black authors, including Langston Hughes, Countee Cullen, and Zora Neale Hurston. White publishers were also attracted to black literary efforts. In 1925 *Survey Graphic* published a special edition on black life and culture called "Harlem: Mecca of the New Negro." Howard University professor Alain Locke then edited *The New Negro,* which drew much of its material from *Survey Graphic* as well as *Opportunity* and included silhouette drawings with Egyptian motifs by Aaron Douglas. In his opening essay, Locke explained Harlem's literary significance: "Harlem has the same role to play for the new Negro as Dublin has had for the New Ireland or Prague for the New Czechoslovakia."

Disagreements erupted during the Harlem Renaissance over the definition and purpose of black literature. Some, such as Alain Locke, Du Bois, Jessie Fauset, and Benjamin Brawley, wanted black writers to promote positive images of black people in their works. They hoped inspirational literature could help resolve racial conflict in America, and they believed black writers should be included in the larger (and mostly white) American literary tradition. Claude McKay, Langston Hughes, and Zora Neale Hurston disagreed. Their work portrayed the streets and shadows of Harlem and the lives of poor black people. In *The Ways of White Folks,* Hughes ridiculed the notion that writers could promote racial reconciliation. One of his characters derisively declares, "Art would break down color lines, art would save the race and prevent lynchings! Bunk!"

Du Bois commented caustically after he read McKay's bawdy *Home to Harlem,* "I feel distinctly like taking a bath." Du Bois was less than impressed with Jake, the novel's protagonist, who is intimately involved with the reality of life in Harlem that included opium, alcohol, and sex. Alain Locke dismissed McKay as a mere propagandist, and McKay in turn called Locke "a dyed-in-the-wool pussy-footing professor." Black critic George Schuyler's

Read on **MyHistoryLab**
Document: Alain Locke, from *The New Negro,* 1925

"The Negro-Art Hokum" in the *Nation* ridiculed black writers who contended that black people even had their own expressive culture that was separate from that of white people: "As for the literature, painting, and sculpture of Afroamericans—such as there is—it is identical in kind with the literature, painting, and sculpture of white Americans."

Langston Hughes, meanwhile, defended the authenticity of black art and literature but insisted the approval or disapproval of white people and black people was of little consequence:

> We younger Negro artists who create now intend to express our individual dark-skinned selves without fear or shame. If white people are pleased, we are glad. If they are not, it doesn't matter. We know we are beautiful. And ugly too. The tom-tom cries and the tom-tom laughs. If colored people are pleased we are glad. If they are not, their displeasure doesn't matter either. We build our temples for tomorrow, strong as we know how, and we stand on top of the mountain, free within ourselves.

Hughes pursued racial themes in *Fine Clothes to the Jew* (1927), which contained "Red Silk Stockings," a poem that depicted young black women who were tempted by liaisons with white men, a subject that offended some readers:

Red Silk Stockings

Put on yo' red silk stockings,

Black gal.

Go out an' let de white boys

Look at yo' legs.

Ain't nothin' to do for you, nohow.

Round this town.—

You's too pretty.

Put on yo' red silk stockings, gal,

An' tomorrow's chile'll

Be a high yaller.

Go out an' let de white boys

Look at yo' legs.

Even more upsetting to those who wanted to safeguard the reputation of black people was Wallace Thurman, who arrived in New York in 1925. Thurman worked briefly at the *Messenger*, the socialist publication that A. Philip Randolph's BSCP had absorbed. He was a voracious reader with a brilliant mind and an eccentric personality who attracted many admirers. He wrote, "I cannot bear to associate with the ordinary run of people. I have to surround myself with individuals who for the most part are more than a trifle insane."

In 1926 Thurman published *Fire*, a journal that lasted only one issue but managed to incite enormous controversy and leave Thurman deeply in debt. *Fire* included Thurman's short story "Cordelia the Crude," about a prostitute, and a one-act play by Zora Neale Hurston, *Color Struck*. Hurston replicated the speech of rural black southerners while depicting the jealousy a darker woman feels when a light-skinned rival tries to take her man. Black critic Benjamin Brawley complained that with *Fire* "vulgarity had been mistaken for art."

Thurman, who was a dark black man, antagonized still more people when *The Blacker the Berry . . .* was published in 1929. In it he described the tribulations and sorrows of Emma Lou, a young woman who did not mind being black, "but she did mind being too black." The book made it plain that many black people had absorbed a color prejudice that they did not hesitate to inflict on darker members of their own race.

Unlike Thurman, Nella Larsen wrote about black people who were indistinguishable from white people. Her novel *Quicksand* depicted the life of Helga Crane, who, like Larsen herself, had a Danish mother and a black father. In *Passing*, Larsen dealt with a young black woman who passed for white and, indeed, married a white racist.

White People and the Harlem Renaissance

Like many of the writers associated with the Harlem Renaissance, Zora Neale Hurston's pen sliced like a scalpel. She called the white people who took an interest in Harlem "Negrotarians" and her black literary colleagues the "Niggerati." But no matter how they were described, black and white people developed pleasant but often uneasy relationships during the renaissance.

No white man was more attracted to the cultural developments in Harlem than photographer and writer Carl Van Vechten. In 1926 he caused a furor with his novel *Nigger Heaven*. The title, which referred to the balcony where black patrons had to sit in segregated theaters and auditoriums, offended many people. The novel dealt with the coarser aspects of life in Harlem, which irritated Du Bois, Fauset, and Countee Cullen. But Van Vechten wanted a more honest depiction of the black experience, and James Weldon Johnson, Walter White, and Langston Hughes approved of the novel.

Most black writers and artists welcomed the encouragement and financial backing they received from white authors, critics, and publishers. White writers, including Eugene O'Neill, Sherwood Anderson, Sinclair Lewis, and Van Wyck Brooks, were fascinated by black people and interested in the works of black authors. Major publishers, such as Alfred A. Knopf, published the works of Harlem writers. Black and white literary figures gathered for cocktails, small talk, and music at Carl Van Vechten's apartment on West 55th Street.

White attention and support were sometimes accompanied by condescension and disdain. Too many "Negrotarians" considered Harlem and its inhabitants exotic, curious, and uncivilized. They found life in Harlem—its clubs, music, and entertainers, as well as its poetry, prose, and painting—more energetic, lively, and sensual than white life and culture. Black culture was also—many white people believed—unsophisticated and primitive, which is what made it so appealing. Black writers like Langston Hughes, Claude McKay, and Countee Cullen wanted to depict black life realistically—from its gangsters to its gamblers. But they resented the notion that black culture was inherently crude and unrefined.

White patrons like Amy Spingarn, whose husband Joel was president of the NAACP board of directors, and Charlotte Osgood "Godmother" Mason supported black writers and artists. Spingarn helped finance Langston Hughes's education at Lincoln University. "Godmother" Mason was a wealthy widow who financially supported black artists. She worked closely with Alain Locke, who helped identify Langston Hughes, Zora Neale Hurston, and Aaron Douglas, among others, who became her "godchildren." Mason wanted no publicity for herself, but her patronage had its costs. Mason gave Hurston $200 a month and an automobile. She gave Hughes $150 a month plus expensive clothing and writing supplies. In return, Mason demanded that the black writers keep her informed about their activities, and she did not hesitate to tell them when they were not productive enough. She also tried to influence what they wrote. She preferred that black writers confine themselves to exotic themes. As helpful as Mason's financial assistance and personal encouragement were, she created a system of dependency, and Hughes and Hurston finally severed the arrangement. Hughes later fondly recalled, "I can only say that those months when I lived by and through her were the most fascinating and fantastic I have ever known."

Harlem's cultural icons sometimes congregated away from the curiosity and paternalism of white admirers. The plush twin townhouses of A'Lelia Walker at 108–110 West 136th Street also attracted Harlem's literary figures as well as entertainers. Walker was the daughter of black cosmetics

Claude McKay was a major figure of the Harlem Renaissance, a writer whose work provides frank portrayals of black life. His first and most famous work, *Home to Harlem*, was published in 1928 and depicted the gritty, intense nightlife of Harlem.

17-1

17-2

17-3

17-4

17-5

17-6

17-7

millionaire Madam C. J. Walker. Although she read little herself, A'Lelia Walker enjoyed hosting musicians, writers, and artists at "The Dark Tower," named for Countee Cullen's column, "The Dark Tower," that appeared regularly in *Opportunity*. But Harlem artists also gathered in the much less luxurious surroundings of "Niggerati Manor," a rooming house on 267 West 136th Street where Thurman, Hurston, and Hughes resided in the late 1920s.

The profusion of literary works associated with the Harlem Renaissance did not so much end as fade away. Black writers remained active into the 1930s. Hurston wrote her two most important works in the 1930s—*Mules and Men* in 1935 and *Their Eyes Were Watching God* in 1937. Although McKay and Hughes continued to have their work published, the Great Depression that began in 1929 devastated book and magazine sales. Subscriptions to the *Crisis* and *Opportunity* declined, and both journals published fewer works by creative writers. Many black intellectuals left Harlem. James Weldon Johnson and Aaron Douglas went to Fisk University in Nashville.

Du Bois quarreled with the NAACP and returned to Atlanta University. Alain Locke remained on the faculty at Howard University. Jessie Fauset married an insurance executive and took up housekeeping after her last novel was published in 1931. Nella Larsen was charged unjustly with plagiarism. She quit writing and resumed her career as a nurse. Wallace Thurman died an alcoholic in 1934. Countee Cullen taught French at DeWitt Clinton High School in New York City, where James Baldwin was one of his students in the late 1930s.

Harlem and the Jazz Age

17-6 What was the role of Harlem and its inhabitants in what popularly came to be known as the Jazz Age?

As powerful and important as these black literary voices were, they were less popular than the entertainers, musicians, singers, and dancers who were also part of the Harlem Renaissance. Without Harlem, the 1920s would not have been the Jazz Age. From wailing trumpets, beating drums, dancing feet, and plaintive and mournful songs, Harlem's clubs, cabarets, theaters, and ballrooms echoed with the vibrant and soulful sounds of African Americans. By comparison, white music seemed sedate and bland.

Black and white people flocked to Harlem to enjoy themselves—and to break the law. In 1919–1920, the Eighteenth Amendment and the Volstead Act prohibited the manufacture, distribution, and sale of alcoholic beverages. But liquor flowed freely in Harlem's fancy establishments and smoky dives. Musicians and entertainers, like Harlem's working-class residents, had migrated there. The blues and their sorrowful tales of troubled and broken relationships arrived from the Mississippi delta and rural South. Jazz had its origins in New Orleans, but it drew on ragtime and spirituals as it moved up the Mississippi River to Kansas City and Chicago on its way to Harlem.

The Cotton Club was Harlem's most exclusive and fashionable nightspot. Opened in 1923 by white gangster Owney Madden to peddle illegal beer, it catered to well-to-do white people who regarded a trip to Harlem as a foreign excursion. The club's entertainers and waiters were black, but the customers were white. Black patrons were not admitted. The club featured well-choreographed and fast-paced two-hour revues that included a chorus line of attractive young women—all brown skinned, all under age 21, and all over five feet six inches tall. No dark women appeared. Assorted ensembles provided the music. Cab Calloway might sing "She's Tall, She's Tan and She's Terrific" or "Cotton Colored Gal of Mine."

In 1928 Edward K. "Duke" Ellington and his orchestra began a 12-year association with the Cotton Club. Although Ellington had not yet begun to compose his own music in earnest, his band already had an elegant, sophisticated, and recognizable African-American sound. Another club, Connie's Inn, also served a mostly white clientele. Thomas "Fats"

Waller played a rambunctious piano at Connie's. Waller's father was the deacon at the Abyssinian Baptist Church in Harlem, and his mother was the organist. The songs and music their son wrote, including "Honeysuckle Rose" and "Ain't Misbehavin," were hardly sacred, but they were popular. Connie's also put on stunning musical revues, perhaps the best known of which was *Hot Chocolates*. Dancers who performed at Connie's included the legendary Bill "Bojangles" Robinson and Earl "Snakehips" Tucker. A young trumpeter from New Orleans, Louis Armstrong, played briefly at Connie's. Armstrong amazed listeners with his virtuoso trumpet and gravelly voice.

Harlem's black residents were more likely to step into one of Harlem's less pretentious and inexpensive establishments, such as the Sugar Cane. In these places, the beer and liquor were cheap, the food was plentiful, the music was good, and there were no elaborate production numbers. Even less impressive clubs and bars remained open after the legal closing hour of 3 A.M. "Arrangements" were made with the police, who looked the other way as the music and alcohol continued through the night. Musicians from "legal" clubs drifted into the after-hours joints and played until dawn.

Another popular—and sometimes necessary—form of entertainment among Harlemites was the rent party. Housing costs in Harlem were extravagant, and white people and real estate agents refused to rent or sell to black people in most other areas of New York City. To make the steep monthly rent payments, apartment dwellers would push the furniture aside and begin cooking chicken, chitterlings, rice, okra, and sweet potatoes. They would distribute a few flyers and hire a musician or two. The party was usually on a Saturday or a Thursday night. (Most domestic servants had Thursdays off.) Partygoers paid 10 cents to 50 cents for admission. Food and liquor were sold. With a decent crowd, the month's rent was paid.

Song, Dance, and Stage

Black women became popular as singers and dancers in Harlem and then often appeared in Broadway shows and revues. Florence Mills entranced audiences with her diminutive singing voice in several Broadway productions including *Plantation Review, Dixie to Broadway,* and *Blackbirds* before she died of appendicitis in 1927. Adelaide Hall also appeared in *Blackbirds* and later opened her own nightclubs in London and Paris. Ethel Waters worked her way up from smoky gin joints in Harlem basements, where she sang risqué and comic songs, to Broadway shows, and then to films. Years later she toured with Billy Graham's religious revivals.

White men wrote many of the popular Broadway productions that starred black entertainers. In 1921, however, Eubie Blake and Noble Sissle put on *Shuffle Along,* which became a major hit. Its most memorable tune was "I'm Just Wild About Harry." Sissle and Blake's *Chocolate Dandies* in 1924 was created especially for a thin, lanky, dark, and funny young lady named Josephine Baker. But in 1925 Baker moved to Paris, where she starred in the *Revue Nègre,* which created a sensation in the French capital. She remained in France for the rest of her life.

White playwright Eugene O'Neill wrote serious drama involving black people. Charles Gilpin and then Paul Robeson appeared in O'Neill's *Emperor Jones.* Robeson—who had an illustrious career—was a graduate of Rutgers University, where he was an all-American football player. He earned a law degree at Columbia University but abandoned the law for the stage. He appeared in numerous productions, including O'Neill's *All God's Chillun Got Wings,* Shakespeare's *Othello,* Gershwin's *Porgy and Bess,* and Kern and Hammerstein's *Showboat.* He often sang spirituals in his rich voice and later recorded many of them.

Noble Sissle and Eubie Blake were the first two black entertainers who dressed elegantly in tuxedos and not as minstrel players. They collaborated on writing the lyrics and composing the music for *Shuffle Along,* which opened on Broadway in 1921 and played for 504 performances. The show's hit tune was "I'm Just Wild About Harry." In 1948 Harry Truman resurrected it as his campaign song. Truman went on to defeat Republican Thomas Dewey and win the presidency.

PROFILE Bessie Smith

BESSIE SMITH KNEW THE BLUES. She sang the blues. She lived the blues. She was the "Empress of the Blues." During the 1920s no singer in America was more popular than she was.

Bessie was born in poverty in 1894 in Chattanooga, Tennessee. She was one of seven children of a Baptist preacher, William Smith, and his wife, Laura. Bessie's parents and two brothers died while she was a child, and an older sister, Viola, raised the surviving children.

With her brother Andrew accompanying her on the guitar, Bessie began to sing on Chattanooga street corners to earn money for the family, an apprenticeship that shaped her career. In 1912 she toured with a musical group that featured Gertrude "Ma" Rainey. In 1913 she worked in Atlanta for $10 a week plus tips. Her fame spread, and soon she was touring the South. By the 1920s she was singing in Philadelphia and Atlantic City.

Initially her voice was considered too rough for the infant recording industry. But in 1923 Frank Walker signed her to a contract with Columbia Records. She recorded what were known in the 1920s as "race" records, produced for black audiences by white recording companies. Her first recordings included "Downhearted Blues" and "Gulf Coast Blues." Her second session brought "Tain't Nobody's Business If I Do." She sold 780,000 records within months.

In 1925 she recorded "St. Louis Blues" and "Careless Love" with Louis Armstrong—their only recordings together. She toured major cities, including Pittsburgh, Cleveland, and Chicago, in a private railroad coach, and huge crowds lined up at clubs and theaters to hear her. Though it could sound coarse, her striking and appealing voice conveyed her emotions and experiences.

She also knew of what she sang. When she sang "Money Blues," "Pickpocket Blues," or "Empty Bed Blues," she revealed the pathos, but also the humor, that so many black people had experienced. Smith's blues tore at the raw feelings that sociologists and academics missed when they discussed poverty, unemployment, alcoholism, or sexual relationships. Her blues were firmly grounded in African-American oral and musical traditions.

Bessie Smith was not a delicate woman. She was married twice. Her first husband, Earl Love, died shortly after they married. Her second marriage, to Jack Gee, was marked by jealousy, drinking, and physical conflict. They separated in 1930. She had a profusion of lovers—male and female. Her warmest and most enduring relationship was with Richard Morgan, a Chicago bootlegger.

People did not trifle with Bessie Smith. A large lady, over 200 pounds, she ate, drank, and fought to excess. She could be mean, contentious, and violent. She physically attacked others and was herself attacked. But she also had a sweet and loyal side and could be generous and compassionate. However, she seemed fond of some of the sleaziest, most dangerous nightclubs in America. She could not resist Detroit's Koppin Theater, a den of debauchery. She admitted wanting to go where "the funk was flying."

She continued to record even after record sales declined during the Depression. Her last recording session included "Nobody Knows When You're Down and Out." Bessie Smith died at age 43 in 1937 in an automobile accident near Clarksdale, Mississippi. Perhaps Louis Armstrong summed up her musical legacy best: "She used to thrill me at all times, the way she could phrase a note with a certain something in her voice no other blues singer could get. She had music in her soul and felt everything she did."

Sports

17-7 | **What opportunities and obstacles confronted black athletes in the 1920s?**

Sports flourished in the 1920s. Americans worshiped their athletic heroes. Babe Ruth and Jack Dempsey were as well known as President Coolidge. Professional athletics, especially baseball and boxing, expanded dramatically. Professional football and basketball emerged later. Black men had been banned from major league baseball in 1887 (see Chapter 15). Nevertheless, in 1901 Baltimore Orioles manager John J. McGraw signed a black man, Charlie Grant, to play second base. McGraw claimed that Grant was "Chief Tokohoma," a full-blooded Cherokee Indian. Chicago White Sox owner Charles Comiskey knew otherwise, and Grant did not play in the major leagues.

Playing among themselves, black baseball players barely made a living as they moved from team to team in an ever-fluctuating and disorganized system that saw teams come and go with monotonous regularity. No leagues functioned effectively for the black teams and players. Owners of the black teams were sometimes involved in organized crime. William A. Greenlee, for example, the proprietor of the Pittsburgh Crawfords, made most of his money from the numbers racket.

Black players crisscrossed the country on trains and in automobiles as they played each other in small towns and large cities for meager money shared from gate receipts. It was an insecure and nomadic life. The black clubs kept few individual or team statistics, and their financial records were frequently in disarray.

Negro National League A professional baseball league for black players and teams organized in 1912.

Rube Foster

Andrew "Rube" Foster was the father of black baseball in twentieth-century America. He was a crafty pitcher from Texas who combined athletic skills with mental dexterity. In 1911 he founded the Chicago American Giants, and he pitched with them regularly until 1915; after that, he mainly managed the team. A fine athlete, Foster was an even more talented organizer and administrator.

In 1919 in the *Chicago Defender,* he argued for a Negro baseball league. In 1920 he was the catalyst in the formation of the eight-team **Negro National League** and became its president and secretary. It was the first stable black league, with franchises in Kansas City, St. Louis, Indianapolis, Detroit, Dayton, and two teams in Chicago. The eighth team was the Cuban Stars.

Foster and the new league took advantage of the migration of black people to northern cities. The black ball clubs usually played late in the afternoon or in the early evening so fans could attend after a day's work. (This was before night baseball.) Sunday doubleheaders in Chicago or Kansas City might draw 8,000 to 10,000 people. Players were paid regularly, and athletes on Foster's Giants earned at least $175 a month. The biggest obstacle that black teams faced was the lack of their own fields or stadiums. They were forced to rent, often at exorbitant rates, from major league clubs, which frequently kept the profits from concessions.

Black baseball thrived—more or less—in the 1920s, thanks mostly to Foster's dedication. He was a tireless worker and strict disciplinarian, but the pressure may have been too much. He suffered a mental breakdown in 1926 and died in 1930. The loss of Foster—combined with the Depression—disrupted the league system.

Andrew "Rube" Foster was the father of black baseball. An outstanding pitcher, he reportedly taught major-league-great Christy Mathewson how to throw the screwball. He became the owner and manager of the Chicago American Giants, and he was the founder of the Negro National League. His teams won the pennant in 1920, 1921, and 1922. He was elected to the Baseball Hall of Fame in Cooperstown in 1981.

College Sports

Football, baseball, basketball, and track and field were popular at the collegiate level. Amateur sports were less rigidly segregated than professional baseball. Black men played for white northern universities, although few teams had more than one black player. For example, Paul Robeson was on the Rutgers football team in

1916 that played against Frederick Douglass "Fritz" Pollard and Brown University. Pollard was the first black man to play in the Rose Bowl, where Brown lost to Washington State in 1916.

Pollard played professional football in the 1920s. He played for four early National Football League (NFL) teams, including Milwaukee and Providence. In 1921 he became the first African-American head coach in the league when he took charge of the Akron team. Later he coached an independent all-black team, the Chicago Black Hawks. Pollard, who died in 1986, was inducted into the NFL Hall of Fame in 2005.

Black college players on white teams encountered discrimination when the teams traveled. Spectators taunted and threatened them. The Big Ten had an unwritten agreement that basketball coaches would not accept black players. All-white college teams sometimes refused to play schools with black players. In 1920, for example, Virginia's Washington and Lee University canceled a football game against Washington and Jefferson College of Pennsylvania because Charles West, a black man, played in the Washington and Jefferson backfield.

Sports in black colleges and universities thrived in the 1920s. Baseball and football were the most popular spectator events. Traditional rivalries attracted large crowds. Several schools played baseball religiously each Easter Monday. In 1926 Livingstone College defeated Biddle University (now Johnson C. Smith University) before a crowd of 6,000 in Charlotte, North Carolina. With the migration of black people to the North, black colleges began to play football in northern cities. Howard and Lincoln played to a scoreless tie before 18,000 people in Philadelphia on Thanksgiving in 1925. Hampton and Lincoln played at New York's Polo Grounds on the edge of Harlem in 1929 in a game Lincoln won 13–7 before 10,000 spectators.

CONCLUSION

For African Americans, the 1920s must have seemed little more than a depressing continuation of earlier decades. Little appeared to have changed. Racial violence and lynching persisted. *The Birth of a Nation* mocked black people and inflamed racial animosity. "Experts" offered "proof" that people of color were inferior and threatened America's ethnic purity. The Ku Klux Klan became a formidable organization again. Millions of white men joined the Klan, and millions more supported it.

Nevertheless, positive developments in the 1920s gave hope for a more promising future. The NAACP became an organization to be reckoned with as it fought for anti-lynching legislation in Congress and for civil and political rights in the courts. Its membership exceeded 100,000 during the 1920s. Although many black and white Americans ridiculed Marcus Garvey for his flamboyant style and excessive rhetoric, he offered racial pride and self-respect as he enrolled hundreds of thousands of black people in the UNIA.

Black workers made little progress as they sought concessions from big business and representation within the ranks of organized labor. A. Philip Randolph founded the BSCP and began a struggle with both the Pullman Company and the AFL that would begin to pay off in the 1930s.

The Harlem Renaissance was a cultural awakening in literature and the arts that was unprecedented in African-American history. A torrent of words poured forth from novelists, essayists, and poets. Although they disagreed—sometimes vehemently—on the purposes of black art, the writers and artists who were a part of the renaissance had an enduring impact. The renaissance allowed thoughtful and creative men and women to grapple with what it meant to be black in a society in which the white majority had defined the black minority as inferior, incapable, and backward. Hereafter, African Americans were less likely to let other people characterize them in demeaning ways.

Black musicians, dancers, singers, entertainers, and athletes made names for themselves and contributed to popular culture in a mostly urban environment. As the 1930s began, it remained to be seen whether the modest but real progress of the 1920s would be sustained.

17-1
17-2
17-3
17-4
17-5
17-6
17-7

CHAPTER TIMELINE

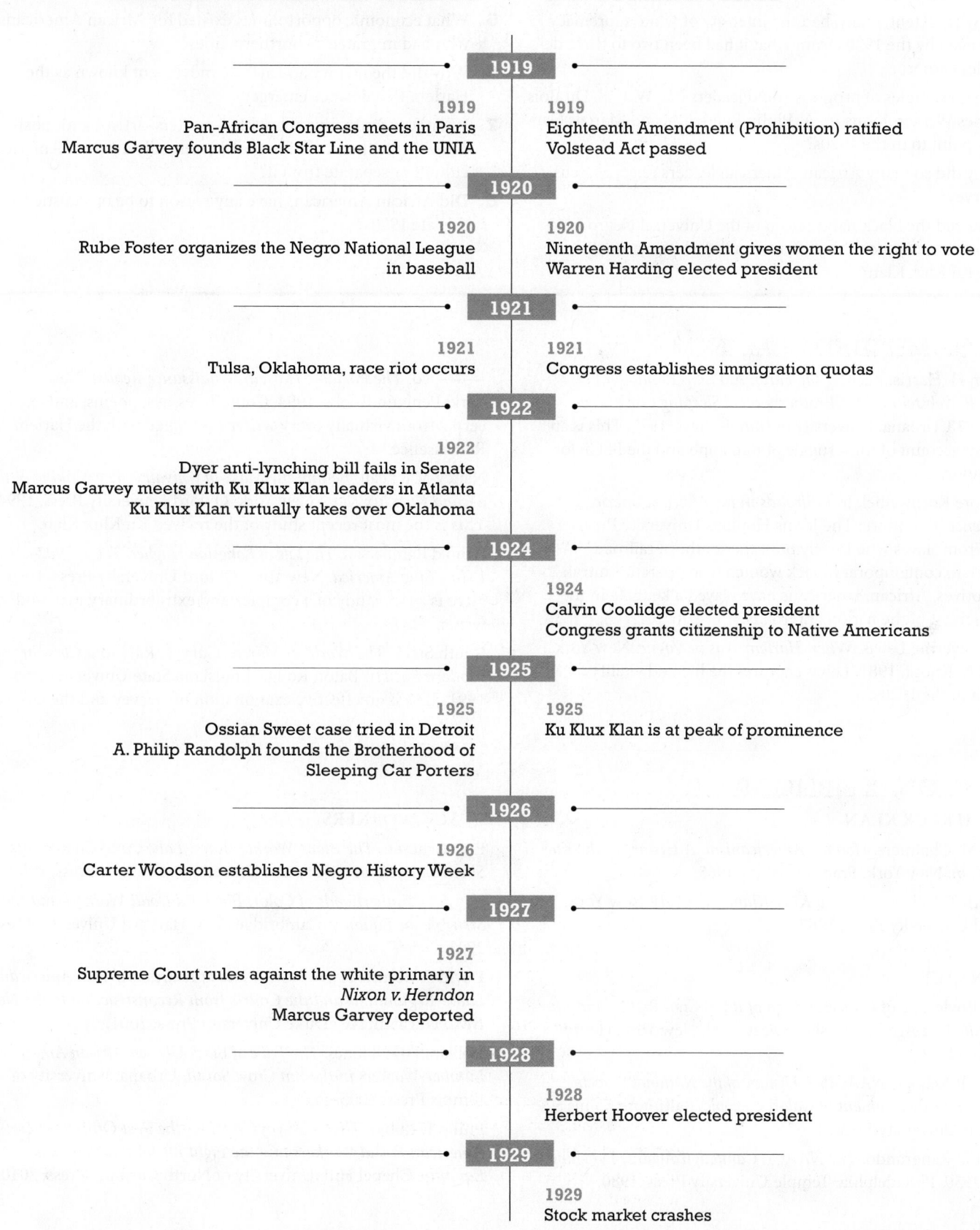

AFRICAN-AMERICAN EVENTS

NATIONAL EVENTS

1919

1919
Pan-African Congress meets in Paris
Marcus Garvey founds Black Star Line and the UNIA

1919
Eighteenth Amendment (Prohibition) ratified
Volstead Act passed

1920

1920
Rube Foster organizes the Negro National League
in baseball

1920
Nineteenth Amendment gives women the right to vote
Warren Harding elected president

1921

1921
Tulsa, Oklahoma, race riot occurs

1921
Congress establishes immigration quotas

1922

1922
Dyer anti-lynching bill fails in Senate
Marcus Garvey meets with Ku Klux Klan leaders in Atlanta
Ku Klux Klan virtually takes over Oklahoma

1924

1924
Calvin Coolidge elected president
Congress grants citizenship to Native Americans

1925

1925
Ossian Sweet case tried in Detroit
A. Philip Randolph founds the Brotherhood of
Sleeping Car Porters

1925
Ku Klux Klan is at peak of prominence

1926

1926
Carter Woodson establishes Negro History Week

1927

1927
Supreme Court rules against the white primary in
Nixon v. Herndon
Marcus Garvey deported

1928

1928
Herbert Hoover elected president

1929

1929
Stock market crashes

On MyHistoryLab

 ✓ Study and Review on MyHistoryLab

REVIEW QUESTIONS

1. To what extent, if any, had the intensity of white supremacy changed by the 1920s from what it had been two to three decades earlier?

2. What examples of progress could leaders like W. E. B. Du Bois, James Weldon Johnson, A. Philip Randolph, and Marcus Garvey point to in the 1920s?

3. Why did so many African-American leaders reject Marcus Garvey?

4. How did the black nationalism of the Universal Negro Improvement Association differ from the white nationalism of the Ku Klux Klan?

5. What economic opportunities existed for African Americans who had migrated to northern cities?

6. Why did the literary and artistic movement known as the Harlem Renaissance emerge?

7. What was distinctive about black writers, artists, and musicians? Were their creative works essentially a part of American culture or separate from it?

8. Did African Americans have any reason to be optimistic by the late 1920s?

RECOMMENDED READING

William H. Harris. *Keeping the Faith: A. Philip Randolph, Milton P. Webster and the Brotherhood of Sleeping Car Porters, 1925–1937.* Urbana: University of Illinois Press, 1977. This is an excellent account of the struggle of Randolph and the BSCP for recognition.

Theodore Kornweibel, Jr. *Railroads in the African American Experience.* Baltimore: The Johns Hopkins University Press, 2010. From slaves who largely built the southern railroad network to contemporary black women who operate Amtrak locomotives, African Americans have played a key role in the development of the nation's railroads.

David Levering Lewis. *When Harlem Was in Vogue.* New York: Alfred A. Knopf, 1981. Lewis captures the life and vitality of Harlem in the 1920s.

————, ed. *The Portable Harlem Renaissance Reader.* New York: Penguin Books, 1994. Contains essays, poems, and excerpts from virtually every writer associated with the Harlem Renaissance.

Nancy MacLean. *Behind the Mask of Chivalry: The Making of the Second Ku Klux Klan.* New York: Oxford University Press, 1994. This is the most recent study of the revived Ku Klux Klan.

Arnold Rampersad. *The Life of Langston Hughes, Vol. 1, 1902–1941: I, Too, Sing America.* New York: Oxford University Press, 1986. Here is a rich study of a complex and extraordinary man and writer.

Judith Stein. *The World of Marcus Garvey: Race and Class in Modern Society.* Baton Rouge: Louisiana State University Press, 1991. This is an effective examination of Garvey and the UNIA.

ADDITIONAL BIBLIOGRAPHY

THE KU KLUX KLAN

David M. Chalmers. *Hooded Americanism: A History of the Ku Klux Klan.* New York: Franklin Watts, 1965.

Kenneth T. Jackson. *The Ku Klux Klan in the City.* New York: Oxford University Press, 1967.

THE NAACP

Kevin Boyle. *Arc of Justice: A Saga of Race, Civil Rights, and Murder in the Jazz Age* [the Ossian Sweet case]. New York: Henry Holt, 2004.

Charles F. Kellogg. *NAACP: A History of the National Association for the Advancement of Colored People.* Baltimore: Johns Hopkins University Press, 1967.

Robert L. Zangrando. *The NAACP Campaign Against Lynching, 1909–1950.* Philadelphia: Temple University Press, 1980.

BLACK WORKERS

Eric Arnesen. *The Black Worker: Race, Labor, and Civil Rights Since Emancipation.* Urbana: University of Illinois Press, 2007.

————. *Brotherhoods of Color: Black Railroad Workers and the Struggle for Equality.* Cambridge, MA: Harvard University Press, 2001.

David E. Bernstein. *Only One Place of Redress: African Americans, Labor Regulations and the Courts from Reconstruction to the New Deal,* Durham, NC: Duke University Press, 2001.

William Powell Jones. *The Tribe of Black Ulysses: African American Lumber Workers in the Jim Crow South.* Urbana: University of Illinois Press, 2005.

Philip F. Rubio. *There's Always Work at the Post Office: African American Postal Workers and the Fight for Jobs, Justice, and Equality.* Chapel Hill: University of North Carolina Press, 2010.

A. PHILIP RANDOLPH AND THE BROTHERHOOD OF SLEEPING CAR PORTERS

Jervis B. Anderson. *A. Philip Randolph: A Biographical Portrait.* New York: Harcourt, Brace, Jovanovich, 1973.

Beth Tompkins Bates. *Pullman Porters and the Rise of Protest Politics in Black America, 1925–1945.* Chapel Hill: University of North Carolina Press, 2001.

Melinda Chateauvert. *Marching Together: Women of the Brotherhood of Sleeping Car Porters.* Urbana: University of Illinois Press, 1998.

Paula F. Pfeffer. *A. Philip Randolph: Pioneer of the Civil Rights Movement.* Baton Rouge: Louisiana State University Press, 1990.

Jack Santino. *Miles of Smiles, Years of Struggle: Stories of Black Pullman Porters.* Urbana: University of Illinois Press, 1989.

Larry Tye. *Rising From the Rails: Pullman Porters and the Making of the Black Middle Class.* New York: Henry Holt, 2004.

MARCUS GARVEY AND THE UNIVERSAL NEGRO IMPROVEMENT ASSOCIATION

Randall K. Burkett. *Garveyism as a Religious Movement: The Institutionalization of a Black Civil Religion.* Metuchen, NJ: Scarecrow Press, 1978.

E. David Cronon. *Black Moses: The Story of Marcus Garvey and the Universal Negro Improvement Association.* Madison: University of Wisconsin Press, 1955.

Marcus Garvey. *Philosophy and Opinions of Marcus Garvey.* New York: Atheneum, 1969.

Theodore Kornweibel, Jr. *Seeing Red: Federal Campaigns Against Black Militancy, 1919–1925.* Bloomington: Indiana University Press, 1998.

THE HARLEM RENAISSANCE

Arna W. Bontemps, ed. *The Harlem Renaissance Remembered.* New York: Dodd, Mead, 1972.

Nathan Huggins. *Harlem Renaissance.* New York: Oxford University Press, 1971.

Bruce Kellner, ed. *The Harlem Renaissance: A Historical Dictionary of the Era.* Westport, CT: Greenwood Press, 1984.

Joyce Moore Turner. *Caribbean Crusaders and the Harlem Renaissance.* Urbana: University of Illinois Press, 2004.

Steven Watson. *The Harlem Renaissance: Hub of African American Culture, 1920–1930.* New York: Pantheon, 1995.

BIOGRAPHIES AND AUTOBIOGRAPHIES

Pamela Bordelon, ed. *Go Gator and Muddy the Water: Writings by Zora Neale Hurston from the Federal Writers' Project.* New York: Norton, 1999.

Wayne F. Cooper. *Claude McKay, Rebel Sojourner in the Harlem Renaissance: A Biography.* Baton Rouge: Louisiana State University Press, 1987.

Robert C. Cottrell. *The Best Pitcher in Baseball: The Life of Rube Foster, Negro League Giant.* New York: New York University Press, 2001.

Thadious M. Davis. *Nella Larsen, Novelist of the Harlem Renaissance: A Woman's Life Unveiled.* Baton Rouge: Louisiana State University Press, 1994.

Robert Hemenway. *Zora Neale Hurston: A Literary Biography.* Urbana: University of Illinois Press, 1977.

Gloria T. Hull. *Color, Sex, and Poetry: Three Women Writers of the Harlem Renaissance.* Bloomington: Indiana University Press, 1987.

George Hutchinson. *In Search of Nella Larsen: A Biography of the Color Line.* Cambridge, MA: Harvard University Press, 2006.

James Weldon Johnson. *Along the Way.* New York: Viking Press, 1933.

Cynthia E. Kerman. *The Lives of Jean Toomer: A Hunger for Wholeness.* Baton Rouge: Louisiana State University Press, 1987.

Eugene Levy. *James Weldon Johnson: Black Leader, Black Voice.* Chicago: University of Chicago Press, 1973.

Michelle R. Scott. *Black Empress in Black Chattanooga: Bessie Smith and the Emerging Urban South.* Urbana: University of Illinois Press, 2008.

RETRACING THE ODYSSEY

The Studio Museum of Harlem, New York City. Founded in 1967, this museum displays a rich and diverse array of art and artifacts by black artists from Africa, the Caribbean, and America and thus maintains the legacy of the Harlem Renaissance.

Abyssinian Baptist Church, New York City. The best-known church in Harlem and home to a huge congregation, it was led for most of the first three-quarters of the twentieth century by the Rev. Adam Clayton Powell, Sr. and then his son, the Rev. Adam Clayton Powell, Jr. The present structure was completed in 1923 and contains a small museum at 132 Odell Clark Place (formerly 132 W. 138th Street).

Paul Laurence Dunbar Home, Dayton, Ohio. Dunbar was born in 1872 in Dayton. He purchased this two-story brick house in 1903 and lived in it until his death in 1906. His mother resided in it until 1936. It is open to the public and features exhibits, artifacts, photos, and papers from Dunbar's life and era.

The Negro Leagues Baseball Museum, Kansas City, Missouri. Devoted to the history of African Americans and baseball from the 1860s to the 1950s, the museum opened in 1991 and contains films, exhibits, and interactive computer stations. Its Field of Legends features 12 life-sized bronze sculptures that honor the men who contributed the most to black baseball.

CONNECTING THE PAST

Migration

African-American men, women, and children who participated in the Great Migration to the north, with suitcases and luggage placed in front, Chicago, 1918.

CHICAGO HAD SLIGHTLY MORE THAN 40,000 black residents in 1910. By 2010, more than one million African Americans lived in Chicago and its suburbs. This huge growth in the city's black population was part of the Great Migration, the largest internal movement of people in American history. Yet this massive shift in population was only one of many instances over the long course of history that Africans and their descendants have willingly or unwillingly changed locations.

Early humans roamed from Africa into Asia and Europe as hunters and gatherers about 100,000 years ago. Between the sixteenth and nineteenth centuries, 12 million Africans were forced to endure the horrors of the Middle Passage and the Atlantic slave trade. In the decades before the Civil War, thousands of southern slaves escaped to freedom in the northern states and Canada by way of the underground railroad. In the late 1870s, economic and political oppression led as many as 40,000 former slaves known as Exodusters to leave the South and move west to Kansas and Oklahoma. About the same time a small number of freedmen left the United States and went to Liberia in West Africa.

But it was the twentieth century's Great Migration that prompted recent and profound political and economic changes in American society. Most of these migrants boarded segregated passenger trains in southern towns to travel on the overground railroad to northern and western communities. Unlike the nineteenth century abolitionist movement and the civil rights movement of the 1950s and 1960s, no dynamic organizations or inspirational leaders were involved in this remarkable resettlement. Instead, individuals, husbands, wives, and friends made what was often a heart-wrenching decision to leave the southern communities where they had been born and raised for a strange and distant destination like Chicago, Pittsburgh, or New York City. They did so because, like the slaves who had fled to freedom a century earlier, the migrants wanted a better life. They hoped to liberate themselves from economic dependence, and to escape the segregation and violence that exemplified life in the Jim Crow South.

While life in the North and the West may have been an improvement, black migrants did not suddenly find themselves residing in the Promised Land. White workers resented black competition for unskilled jobs in manufacturing. Labor unions prohibited black membership. White employers' use of black workers as strikebreakers or scabs further alienated white workingmen. Black women were confined to domestic work and denied employment as retail clerks, bank tellers, waitresses, or secretaries. But the "white" and "colored" signs that saturated the South rarely were seen in the North. Buses, streetcars, and passenger trains had open seating. Black people did not have to step aside when white people passed on city sidewalks.

Many myths accompanied the migrants. Black people who already lived in northern cities looked down on the "countrified" ways of the new arrivals and ridiculed the way they talked, dressed, and carried themselves. They disparaged the newcomers' supposed lack of education, low incomes, and inability to maintain stable families. But these perceptions proved to be inaccurate. Migrants had a sense of purpose and commitment. They were better educated than the people they left behind. They had higher incomes and were less likely to be on welfare than African Americans who already resided in the North. They were more likely to be married and remain married. Their children lived in two-parent households.

The development of black political power was one of the unexpected consequences of the Great Migration. Black men and women voted freely in the North and West. Living together in

By the middle of the twentieth century, several million African Americans lived in densely populated urban communities throughout the nation. Here are residents of Harlem on Seventh Avenue on a cold February day in 1956.

black neighborhoods afforded them the opportunity to elect black city councilmen, aldermen, and congressmen. By the 1950s, black men from Chicago, Detroit, Philadelphia, and Harlem served in the U.S. House of Representatives. In the 1960s and 1970s, black mayors were elected in Cleveland, Newark, Detroit, and Los Angeles. Democratic presidential candidates Harry Truman in 1948 and John F. Kennedy in 1960 relied on black voters in northern cities to provide them with margins of victory.

The Civil Rights Act of 1964 and the Voting Rights Act of 1965 eradicated Jim Crow in the South. The Great Migration began to reverse itself. Black people who had migrated to northern communities in the 1940s and 1950s began to retire in the 1980s and 1990s to towns and communities they had left as young people. Now, with a shifting racial dynamic in the United States that included the election of an African-American president, there is a new migration. Black people from Africa and the Caribbean increasingly come to America. Between 2000 and 2010, 216,900 Africans moved to the United States. Not all of them will remain, but more will come, attracted to a place where their predecessors were sold and toiled as slaves. Those predecessors and their descendants helped create a vibrant nation that now draws immigrants from nearly every corner of the globe.

1. **What specific factors account for the Great Migration?**

2. **Under what circumstances would you move hundreds of miles from your friends and family?**

PART

V

THE GREAT DEPRESSION AND WORLD WAR II

Dizzy Gillespie

	1900–1930	**1930–1935**
RELIGION 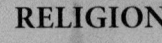	**1919** Father Divine begins what comes to be known as the Peace Mission Movement **1929** Nation of Islam emerges	**1933** Father Divine establishes his Peace Mission in Harlem **1934** Elijah Muhammad becomes leader of the Detroit Temple of Islam
CULTURE 		**1930s–1940s** Heyday of Chicago's Black Renaissance **1930** Duke Ellington's "Mood Indigo" Langston Hughes publishes *Not Without Laughter* **1931** Katherine Dunham forms the Negro Dance Group **1933** Paul Robeson stars in *The Emperor Jones* **1935** Marvel Cooke and Ella Baker publish "The Bronx Slave Market" in the *Crisis*
POLITICS & GOVERNMENT 	**1925** U.S. War College concludes that African Americans are not fit for combat	**1930** NAACP helps block John J. Parker's appointment to the Supreme Court **1932** "Scottsboro Boys" arrested **1933** Franklin D. Roosevelt's "black cabinet" formed
SOCIETY & ECONOMY 	**1899** North Carolina Mutual Life Insurance Company becomes the largest black-owned business in the United States **1908** Binga Bank opens in Chicago	**1930** Fannie Peck founds Detroit Housewives League **1932** Tuskegee Experiment begins **1935** Mary M. Bethune founds the National Council of Negro Women National Negro Congress founded NAACP sues to integrate University of Maryland School of Law

Mahalia Jackson   James Baldwin   Ralph Bunche

| 1935–1940 | 1940–1950 | Noteworthy Individuals |

1936 Jesse Owens wins four gold medals at the Berlin Olympics

1937 Joe Louis wins heavyweight championship

1939 Billie Holiday premiers "Strange Fruit"

Marian Anderson sings at the Lincoln Memorial

"Bojangles" Robinson organizes Black Actors Guild

1940s Black musicians introduce bebop

1940–1948 Oscar Micheaux's films

1940 Richard Wright publishes *Native Son*

1941 Mary Dawson founds the National Negro *Opera* Company

1942 Margaret Walker publishes *For My People*

1945 Nat King Cole becomes the first black star to have his own radio variety show

1947 Jackie Robinson becomes the first black major league baseball player

1948 Alice Coachman becomes the first African-American woman to win an Olympic gold medal

1952 Ralph Ellison publishes *Invisible Man*

1936 African-American voters switch to the Democratic Party

1937 William Hastie named first black federal judge

1938 Oscar DePriest elected, first African-American congressman from the North

1941 U.S. Army forms Tuskegee Air Squadron

1942 Marine Corps accepts first African Americans

1943 Navy officer schools accept African Americans

1944 Adam Clayton Powell elected to Congress

Port of Chicago "mutiny"

U.S. Supreme Court declares "white primaries" unconstitutional

1945 U.S. Army desegregates its Nurse Corps

1946 President Truman creates the Committee on Civil Rights

1948 Executive Order 9981 desegregates the U.S. military

1950 State Department revokes Paul Robeson's passport

1951 House Un-American Activities Committee indicts W. E. B. Du Bois

1954 *Brown v. Board of Education* declares "separate but equal" unconstitutional

---

1936 First National Negro Congress held

1937 Mary M. Bethune organizes conference on the Negro and Negro Youth

1940s Many African Americans move from agriculture to jobs in industry

1941 A. Philip Randolph organizes the March on Washington Movement

1942 CORE founded

1943 Detroit race riots

1944 *An American Dilemma* published

Southern Regional Council established

1946 Journey of Reconciliation begins

1950 Ralph Bunche becomes the first African-American recipient of the Nobel Peace Prize

18

1929–1940

Black Protest, the Great Depression, and the New Deal

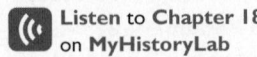 **Listen to Chapter 18 on MyHistoryLab**

LEARNING OBJECTIVES

18-1	What caused the Great Depression of the 1930s and what were the economic effects on blacks in the cities and rural areas?
18-2	What were the varieties of protests continued by blacks during the Great Depression to address economic concerns and challenge racial discrimination?
18-3	How did the New Deal affect African Americans?
18-4	What was the "black cabinet," its purpose, and its goals?
18-5	What role did organized labor play in radicalizing black Americans in the 1930s?
18-6	What was the *Scottsboro* case and what were its consequences?
18-7	What was the Tuskegee study and its impact?

The depression brought everyone down a peg or two.
And the Negro had but a few pegs to fall.

Langston Hughes

The only thing that we not only can, but must do, is voluntarily and insistently to organize our economic and social power, no matter how much segregation it involves. Learn to associate with ourselves and to train ourselves in methods of democratic control within our own group. Run and support our own institutions.

W. E. B. Du Bois

For African Americans, the Great Depression was an era of suffering made worse by the horrors and burdens of American racism as well as a time of profound political change, demographic shifts, and social activism that would lay the foundation for the progress of ensuing decades. At the beginning of

Photographer Margaret Bourke White may not have intended to contrast the American dream of prosperity—for white families—and the harsh realities of life for black Americans in this Depression photograph, but it has become representative of existing racial disparity. The collapse of the economy spurred the search for radical critiques and solutions to deal with the desperate conditions millions of African Americans endured. Separate economic development and the creation of parallel institutions and organizations was one option. But was it practicable?

the economic collapse in late 1929, most African Americans were either trapped in the failing southern agricultural system or eking out a bare existence at the margins of the booming urban economy. The economy's fall pushed many black Americans to the edge of starvation, throwing them off the land and out of the small niches they had carved out in other occupations. Coming out of the southern-dominated Democratic Party, President Franklin Roosevelt's New Deal programs for fighting the Depression might have simply reinforced existing racism, as in fact it did to some extent. But from another perspective, the emerging political power of African-American voters in the North, the development of civil rights organizations, and the growth of an antiracist agenda among radicals and labor unions created the preconditions for a profound change in American politics. Amid economic despair, peonage, lynchings, and labor conflicts, black men, women, and their children saw glimmers of hope in protests against racial segregation and radical critiques of capitalist exploitation. Their protests helped shape the policies and programs of the New Deal. The 1930s were thus the dark dawn of a new era that witnessed, among other significant changes, the rise to prominence of a remarkable cadre of black social scientists.

The Cataclysm, 1929–1933

18-1 **What caused the Great Depression of the 1930s and what were the economic effects on blacks in the cities and rural areas?**

The Great Depression was a cataclysm. National income fell from $81 billion in 1929 to $40 billion in 1932. Americans lost faith in banks, and the resulting panic deepened the despair. Overnight millions of Americans lost their life savings in bank closings and home foreclosures. Americans responded by buying fewer consumer goods; in turn, businesses cut back production, investment, and payrolls. The result was a downward spiral of economic activity made worse by increasing numbers of unemployed. According to the American Federation of Labor (AFL), the number of unemployed people increased from 3,216,000 in January 1930 to 13,689,000 in March 1933 (see Figure 18–1). The standard of living of nearly everyone, from farmers to small businessmen and entrepreneurs to wage laborers, dropped to a fraction of what it had been before 1929.

Most people blamed the stock market crash and Republican President Herbert Hoover for the hard times, but the true explanation is more complicated. Although its causes are hotly debated, the Great Depression was probably the result of several factors, including rampant speculation, corporate capitalism's drive for markets and profits unchecked by federal regulation, the failure of those in the government or private sector to understand how the economy worked, a weak international trading system, overproduction of—and low prices for—many agricultural goods and raw materials, and—most important—the great inequality of wealth and income that limited the purchasing power of millions of Americans.

Watch on MyHistoryLab Video:
The Great Depression

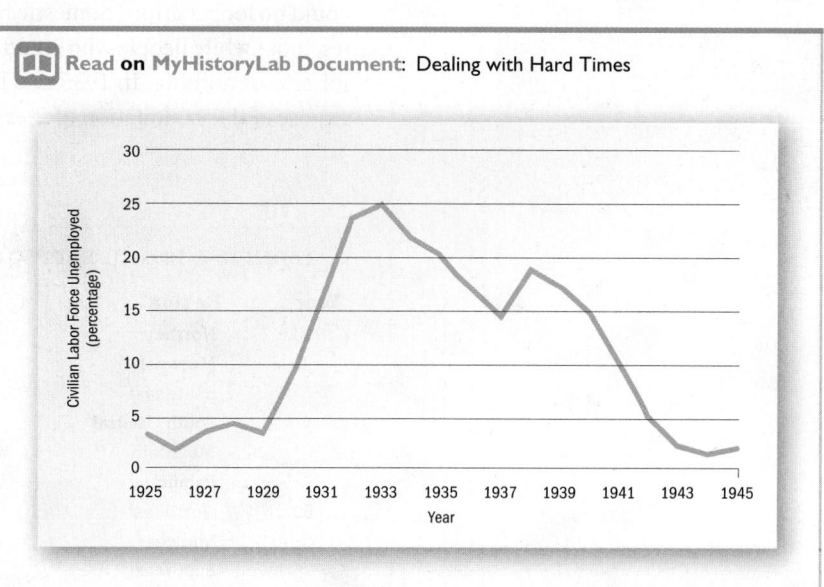

Read on MyHistoryLab Document: Dealing with Hard Times

FIGURE 18–1 UNEMPLOYMENT, 1925–1945
With the collapse of the American economy, unemployment soared in the 1930s. New Deal programs alleviated some of the suffering, but full recovery did not come until the defense industries swung into action with the U.S. entry into World War II.

18-1
18-2
18-3
18-4
18-5
18-6
18-7

Explore on MyHistoryLab Activity: The Great Depression

Harder Times for Black America

The economic collapse hit African Americans particularly hard. Most black people remained in the rural South mired in an exploitive agricultural system. Indeed, the Depression worsened the key problems besetting cash-crop production in the 1920s. Consumer demand for cotton and sugar fell with the depressed economy; however, as farmers grew more of these crops to make ends meet, the supply of these staples increased. The result was a catastrophe, with prices for cotton—still the mainstay of the southern economy—plunging from 18 cents a pound in 1929 to six cents in 1933. Black sharecroppers and tenant farmers, nearly powerless in the rural South, were reduced to starvation or thrown off the land.

The hard times also struck those 1.5 million African Americans who had escaped the South for northern urban communities (see Table 18–1). Even during the prosperous 1920s, black Americans had suffered layoffs, and their living standards had steadily fallen. After 1929 the same forces that impoverished rural Americans swept those in urban areas further toward the economic margins as waves of refugees from the farms crowded into the cities and competed for scarce jobs (see Table 18–2). By 1934, when the federal government noted that 17 percent of white citizens could not support themselves, the figure for black Americans had increased to 38 percent overall. In Chicago, 40 percent of African-American men were unemployed; in Pittsburgh, 48 percent; in Harlem, 50 percent; in Philadelphia, 56 percent; and in Detroit, 60 percent. The figures were even more dire for black workers in southern cities. In Atlanta, Georgia, 65 percent of black workers needed public assistance, and in Norfolk, Virginia, a stunning 80 percent had to apply for welfare.

African Americans lost jobs in those parts of the economy where they had gained a tenuous foothold. Before 1929, jobs in low-status or poorly paid occupations, such as garbage collection, foundries, or domestic service, had been regarded as "Negro work" and hence were generally immune from white competition. As desperation set in, however, white southerners not only competed for these jobs but also used the old tactics of terror and intimidation to compel employers to fire black people. Unions, north and south, continued to exclude African Americans from membership and pressured manufacturers to hire white people.

Black women workers, overwhelmingly concentrated in domestic service and laundry work, were affected even more than black men. There were fewer jobs because many families could no longer afford domestic help. With many impoverished women coming into the cities, those white people who could hire help found they could employ these desperate women for almost nothing. In 1935 two black women, Marvel Cooke and Ella Baker, published an exposé of the exploitation of these women laborers in the *Crisis*. They titled the article "The

TABLE 18–1 DEMOGRAPHIC SHIFTS: THE SECOND GREAT MIGRATION, 1930–1950

Year	Region	Black Population	Total Population	% Black
1930	Northeast	1,146,985	34,427,091	3.33
	Midwest	1,262,234	38,594,100	3.27
	Southeast	7,079,626	25,680,803	27.57
	South Central	2,281,951	12,176,830	18.74
	Mountain	30,225	3,701,789	0.82
	Pacific	90,122	8,622,047	1.05
1950	Northeast	2,018,182	39,477,986	5.11
	Midwest	2,227,876	44,460,762	5.01
	Southeast	7,793,379	32,659,516	23.86
	South Central	2,432,028	14,517,572	16.73
	Mountain	66,429	5,074,998	1.31
	Pacific	507,043	15,114,964	3.35

SOURCE: U.S. Bureau of the Census Release, *1991*, and Statistical Abstract, *1990. Also see Schomburg Center, The New York Public Library*, African American Desk Reference (*New York: John Wiley & Sons, 1999*), 100–101.

Bronx Slave Market" because the buying and selling of labor in New York City reminded them of the old slave marts in the antebellum South. Cooke and Baker described how the street corner market worked: "The Simpson avenue block exudes the stench of the slave market at its worst. Not only is human labor bartered and sold for a slave wage, but human love also is a marketable commodity." The black women gathered on particular street corners and waited as well-to-do white women selected them for a day's labor. They received "wages as low as 15 to 25 cents an hour, some working only two or three hours a day." Some black people were hired but never paid.

African Americans were no strangers to adversity, and many used the survival strategies developed through centuries of hardship to eke out an existence during the first years of the Great Depression. Survival demanded that black women pool their resources and adhere to a collective spirit that found fertile ground in segregated northern neighborhoods. In Chicago, for example, women and their families lived in crowded tenements in which they shared bathrooms and other facilities including hot plates, stoves, and sinks. They bartered and exchanged goods and services because money was so scarce. One woman might dress the hair of a neighbor in return for permission to borrow her dress or use her pots and pans. Another woman might trade bread and sugar or another household staple for milk, beans, or soap. Grandmothers watched over children as their mothers went to look with rising futility for a domestic job. They helped each other as best they could.

Rural black women, like their urban sisters, had to rely on their individual and collective ingenuity to survive. As one observer of black women household heads in rural Georgia noted, "In their effort to maintain existence, these people are catching and selling fish, reselling vegetables, sewing in exchange for old clothes, letting out sleeping space, and doing odd jobs. They understand how to help each other. Stoves are used in common, wash boilers go their rounds, and garden crops are exchanged and shared." Nonetheless, the depth and duration of this downturn strained these mutual aid strategies to the breaking point. By 1933 the clock seemed to have been turned back to 1865, when many African Americans could claim to own little more than their bodies.

Black Businesses in the Depression: Collapse and Survival

Black businessmen and professionals also suffered. African Americans who had built successful businesses and professional practices in medicine and law, for example, faced the same Depression-borne problems as other businesses, but they suffered even more because the communities on which they depended were poorer. Two types of black-owned businesses, banks and insurance companies, illustrate how black enterprises stood or fell during the economic crisis.

The Binga Bank, Chicago's first black-owned-and-operated financial institution, had been founded in 1908 by its president, Jesse Binga (1865–1950), a Detroit-born real estate broker who had worked as a barber and a Pullman porter. Binga had managed the bank so effectively that by 1930 its deposits had grown to more than $1.5 million. Binga once boasted he could lay claim to more footage on State Street, Chicago's principal thoroughfare, than any other man in the city. The Binga Bank was, during its early years, an important symbol of successful black capitalism and as such represented the hopes and aspirations of black Chicagoans. But the bank's assets were too heavily invested in mortgages to black churches

TABLE 18–2 MEDIAN INCOME OF BLACK FAMILIES COMPARED TO THE MEDIAN INCOME OF WHITE FAMILIES FOR SELECTED CITIES, 1935–1936

City and Type of Family	Black	White	Black Income as a Percentage of White Income
Husband–Wife Families			
New York	$980	$1,930	51%
Chicago	$726	$1,687	43%
Columbus	$831	$1,622	51%
Atlanta	$632	$1,876	34%
Columbia	$576	$1,876	31%
Mobile	$481	$1,419	34%
Other Families			
Atlanta	$332	$940	35%
Columbia	$254	$1,403	18%
Mobile	$301	$784	38%

SOURCE: *Median Income of Black Families . . . White Families for Selected Cites, 1935–1936 from An American Dilemma: The Negro Problem and Modern Democracy by Gunnar Myrdal. Copyright © 1944, 1962 by Harper and Row Publishers, Inc. Reprinted by permission of HarperCollins Publishers.*

18-1
18-2
18-3
18-4
18-5
18-6
18-7

18-1

18-2

18-3

18-4

18-5

18-6

18-7

and fraternal societies, many of which could not meet their payments after their members lost their jobs. Binga refused to seize the properties of these community institutions, but his restraint, coupled with financial improprieties, led to the bank's failure. On July 31, 1930, Illinois state bank auditors padlocked the institution and filed a federal misuse-of-funds charge against the once proud financier. Sentenced to prison in 1933, Binga was pardoned by the Governor of Illinois Dwight H. Green on April 12, 1941. He never regained his fortune.

Some black businesses survived the economic cataclysm although often in a much weakened state. Among the businesses still standing when prosperity finally returned in the 1940s were the leading black insurance companies, such as Atlanta Life, Supreme Life, Golden State, and North Carolina Mutual Life. Atlanta Life Insurance Company, for example—founded in 1905 by a former Georgia slave, Alonzo Franklin Herndon—not only survived the Depression but recorded substantial profit. Between 1931 and 1936, its assets increased by more than $1 million. This was in part because insurance companies such as Atlanta Life provided an essential service for African Americans, particularly in an era before government-provided social security, and could thus depend on a continued flow of premiums. And unlike the Binga Bank, Atlanta Life's officers drastically reduced their investments in mortgages in the black community.

The North Carolina Mutual Life Insurance Company, founded in Durham, weathered the Great Depression under the astute leadership of Charles Clinton Spaulding (1874–1952), a former manager of a black cooperative grocery store. In 1899 Spaulding joined with two other African Americans to transform the insurance company into the nation's largest black business. His partners were his uncle, Dr. Aaron McDuffie Moore, Durham's only black physician, and John Merrick, a former slave and leading real estate agent and barber (he owned six barbershops, three for whites and three for blacks). Following on the heels of the great migration to the North, Spaulding expanded the company's territory into Virginia, Maryland, and the District of Columbia. The company adhered to the thrift, hard work, and self-help philosophy so ardently expressed by Booker T. Washington. It is still one of the three largest black-owned insurance companies in the United States.

Many of the 250 black hospitals, clinics, and nursing training schools that black physicians, such as Dr. Daniel Hale Williams, had launched since the 1890s could not survive the ravages of the Depression. Confronting a diminishing clientele and worsening health among black people, some black physicians began encouraging their patients to demand admission to the segregated, government-operated hospitals and clinics. At the outset of the Depression, Dr. Matilda A. Evans (1872–1935) of Columbia, South Carolina, an 1897 graduate of the Woman's Medical College in Philadelphia, mobilized a diverse constituency of black parents, professionals, and religious and business leaders to persuade the state board of health to provide free inoculations and immunization shots to black schoolchildren. Other healthcare professionals volunteered to conduct free medical and dental examinations. When Evans's Columbia Clinic opened in July 1930, over 700 patients showed up. This short-lived clinic reflected Evans's belief that health care was a state responsibility just as important as the provision of free public education. The black South Carolina newspaper, the *Palmetto Leader*, declared in October 1930 that "evidence keeps on piling on top of evidence to the effect that the Columbia Clinic is just proving to be, and will yet stand as the most important effort sponsored for our group in Columbia within the last half century." The deteriorating economic conditions of both the state of South Carolina and its people made it impossible to sustain this effort. But the Columbia Clinic movement taught black people a powerful lesson about how to mobilize to achieve change and thus raised, as Evans anticipated it would, black consciousness about the need to apply pressure on the state for more access to public resources.

A remarkable black woman physician, Dr. Matilda A. Evans (1872–1935) of Columbia, South Carolina, believed in the importance of establishing institutions and organizations that would enable black people to survive and from which they could fight to end racial segregation and discrimination. In the opening decades of the twentieth century, Dr. Evans established two hospitals and founded a nursing training school. She organized the Good Health Association of South Carolina, edited the Negro Health Journal, and served a term as president of the Palmetto Medical Association.

The Failure of Relief

Before Franklin Roosevelt's New Deal, private charities or, as a last resort, state and local governments were responsible for providing relief from economic hardships. Even in good times these institutions provided too little for all those in need. Moreover, African Americans had a much harder time getting aid than white people and were given less when they did get it. The Depression made it impossible for the nation's charitable organizations to meet the needs of more than a small portion of the hungry, homeless, and unemployed millions. In turn, state and local governments could not or would not provide unemployment insurance or increased welfare benefits to ease the suffering of those most vulnerable to the economic disaster. Even when these governments wanted to help, the economic collapse so lowered tax receipts that it became nearly impossible for relief agencies to act.

Despite the need to alleviate the economic disaster, President Hoover hesitated to respond. Steeped in the free-market orthodoxy of his time, he believed government should do little to interfere with the workings of the economy. Nevertheless, Hoover did more to counteract a depression than any previous president had done. He tried to convince businesses that if they retained employees and did not cut wages, they would contribute to the health of the general economy and promote their own best interests. The president also approved loans to banks, railroads, and insurance companies by the Reconstruction Finance Corporation, a federal agency created to rescue large corporations. He hoped these businesses would reinvigorate production, create new jobs, and restore consumer spending. His faith was misplaced. Businesses took the government loans and still laid off workers, much the same way many banks behaved in 2009 after receiving government funds to prevent them from failing.

Hoover's reluctance to use the federal government to intervene in the economy extended to the provision of relief. He suggested that local governments and charities should address the needs of the unemployed, the homeless, and the starving masses. Hoover was not a callous person, but he was trapped in a rigid ideology. He watched with dismay the wandering groups of men, women, and children who began settling into what they called, with grim humor, "Hoovervilles"—sordid clusters of shacks made of tin, cardboard, and burlap next to railroad tracks and dumps. Still, he refused to allow the federal government to provide direct relief.

Hoover's inactivity was bad enough, but his politics were as racist as those of the Democratic Party. Wanting to create a white Republican Party in the South, he cultivated white southerners by attempting to appoint to the U.S. Supreme Court Judge John Parker of North Carolina, who believed in "separate but equal," and by displacing black Republican leaders. Hoover's policy was not new. For decades the national Republican Party had treated black voters with contempt and often declined to reward them with patronage appointments. This policy looked even worse during the early 1930s against the backdrop of black suffering. As NAACP director Walter White put it, Hoover

> sat stolidly in the White House, refusing bluntly to receive Negro citizens who wished to lay before him the facts of their steadily worsening plight or to consider any remedial legislation or governmental action. His attitude toward Negroes caused me to coin a phrase, which gained considerable currency, particularly in the Negro world, in which I described Hoover as "the man in the lily-White House."

Black Protest during the Great Depression

18-2   **What were the varieties of protests continued by blacks during the Great Depression to address economic concerns and challenge racial discrimination?**

During the 1930s African-American men and women initiated their own agenda and determined to use every resource at their disposal to destroy the obstacles to racial justice and barriers to equal opportunity. The NAACP sponsored a legal campaign, led by Charles Houston and Thurgood Marshall, against educational discrimination and political disfranchisement; mobilized black communities; and sustained hope in the struggle. Black people benefited from the New Deal but less than white people did. The disparity between black and white lives was a spur to action. The juxtaposition of black subordination and misery alongside the new forms of federal aid so willingly distributed to white citizens convinced black Americans to intensify their own struggle for their rights as Americans. Many embraced radical critiques of American capitalism, but few ever considered communism a viable alternative to American democracy. Black people would emerge from the Depression more determined than ever to make democracy work for them.

The NAACP and Civil Rights Struggles

During the 1930s the NAACP became a more effective advocate for African-American civil rights. The biracial organization took the lead in pressing the government to protect African-American rights and eliminate the blatant racism in government programs. Part of the reason for this new dynamism was the astute leadership of Walter White, a man whose physical characteristics—he had blond hair and blue eyes—could have easily permitted him to pass for white and turn away from the problems of black people. Instead, he became an insistent voice of protest, personally investigating 42 lynchings and eight race riots, and he was an ardent lobbyist for civil rights legislation and racial justice. Throughout the 1930s African Americans of all hues moved into leadership positions in the NAACP and joined its many branches.

The NAACP's new dynamism became apparent in 1930 when Walter White took a prominent role in the successful campaign to defeat Hoover's nomination of John J. Parker to the Supreme Court. Parker had openly embraced white supremacy, stating, for example, that the "participation of the Negro in politics is a source of evil and danger to both races." The NAACP formed a coalition with the AFL to persuade the Senate to reject Parker's nomination by a vote of 41 to 39. It was the first time since 1854 that the Senate had refused to confirm a nominee to the Court. Although the NAACP could take only part of the credit for Parker's defeat, White trumpeted the victory and let it be known that African Americans would not be silent while "the Hoover administration proposed to conciliate southern white sentiment by sacrificing the Negro and his rights."

Du Bois Ignites a Controversy

The NAACP had critics, even within its own ranks. Many younger black people criticized its focus on civil liberties and deplored it for ignoring the economic misery of most African Americans. In 1934 W. E. B. Du Bois, editor of the NAACP's journal, the *Crisis*, joined the chorus. Criticizing what he considered the group's overemphasis on integration, Du Bois advocated a program of self-determination he hoped would permit black people to develop "an economic nation within a nation." Du Bois acknowledged that this internal economy could meet only part of the needs of the African-American community. But he insisted it could be developed and expanded in many ways: "This smaller part could be so important and wield so much power that its influence upon the total economy of Negroes and the total industrial organization of the United States would be decisive for the great ends towards which the Negro moves."

Black intellectuals attacked Du Bois for advocating "voluntary segregation." Sociologist E. Franklin Frazier, for example, called the idea of black businesses succeeding within a segregated economy a black upper-class fantasy and social myth. Nevertheless, Du Bois held fast to his position that, as long as discrimination persisted, the NAACP should combine its opposition to legal segregation with vigorous support to improve segregated institutions. He was eventually forced from the editorship of the *Crisis*, but his resignation did not end the controversy. By the late 1930s the NAACP had developed a greater emphasis on economic policy and stronger ties to the growing labor movement.

Challenging Racial Discrimination in the Courts

A dramatic expansion of its legal campaign against racial discrimination enhanced the NAACP's effectiveness. Central to this project was the hiring of Charles Hamilton Houston,

Thurgood Marshall (1908–1993), Charles Hamilton Houston (1895–1950), and Donald Gaines Murray. In 1935, attorneys Marshall and Houston handled Donald Murray's suit against the University of Maryland Law School. In 1938 Murray became the first African American to graduate from a southern state school. Thus began the relentless black attack against segregated education in America.

a Harvard-trained African-American lawyer and scholar, to lead it. As vice dean of Howard University Law School, Houston had transformed it into a powerful institution for training black attorneys in civil rights law. At the NAACP, he laid out a plan for a legal program to challenge inequality in education and the exclusion of black people from voting in the South. Houston used lawsuits to force state and local governments to live up to the Constitution and to inspire community organization. "This is no star performance," he said of his strategy. "My ideal of administration is to make the movement self-perpetuating. . . . Our idea should be to press upon the opposition and public that what we have is a real program, sweeping up . . . [from] popular demand."

Houston did not focus directly on eliminating segregation but rather sought to force southern states to equalize their facilities. Studies by the NAACP had revealed great disparities in per capita expenditures for white and black students and huge differences in salaries for white and black teachers. In Georgia, for example, the average annual per pupil expenditure for white students was $36.29, compared with $4.59 for black students. White teachers' salaries averaged $97.88 per month, whereas black teachers received only $49.41. Houston was no supporter of segregation. He hoped to use litigation to secure judgments that would so increase the cost of separate institutions that states would be forced to abandon them.

To execute his agenda, Houston convinced Walter White in 1936 to hire his former student at Howard, Thurgood Marshall. Marshall was born in Baltimore in 1908. His father was a dining-car waiter and club steward. His mother had been a teacher before her marriage. During the 1930s Marshall and Houston focused on bringing greater parity between the pay of black and white teachers, a project they hoped would increase NAACP membership among teachers, their students, and parents. The two men, working with a network of African-American attorneys, also attempted to end discrimination against black students in professional and graduate schools. Inequalities were obvious here because many southern states offered no graduate facilities of any kind to black students. Like other campaigns, this focus on graduate education was intended to establish precedents that might be used to gain equality in other areas and as an organizing tool to strengthen local NAACP branches. The first significant accomplishment in this campaign was the Supreme Court's 1938 decision in *Gaines v. Canada*. The Court ordered the state of Missouri to provide black citizens an opportunity to study law in a state-supported institution. Failure to do so, the Court held, would violate the equal protection of the law clause of the Fourteenth Amendment to the Constitution. Although Lloyd Gaines, the prospective student for whom the case was brought, disappeared before this challenge was resolved, Missouri hastily established a law school for African Americans at the historically black Lincoln University in Jefferson City, the state capital. In the 1940s several southern states, including North Carolina, Texas, Oklahoma, and South Carolina, also established law schools for their black citizens.

The *Gaines* decision encouraged Marshall and the NAACP to persist in challenging the constitutionality of the "separate but equal" doctrine. The case of *Sipuel v. Board of Regents of the University of Oklahoma* (1947) was another such effort. In this case Ada Lois Sipuel sought admission to the law school of the University of Oklahoma at Norman. In accordance with state statutes, she was refused admission but granted an out-of-state tuition award. Marshall argued that this arrangement failed to meet the needs of the state's black citizens. The Supreme Court declared that Oklahoma was obliged under the equal protection clause of the Fourteenth Amendment to provide a legal education for Sipuel. The case established the principle that the states had to provide a separate law school for African-American students in their home states.

Heman Sweatt, a black mail carrier, tested this principle in a suit against the University of Texas Law School. In *Sweatt v. Painter* (1950), the Supreme Court again sided with the NAACP lawyers. In response to Sweatt's initial challenge, Texas had created a separate law school that had inadequate library facilities, faculty, and support staff. It was separate but hardly equal. Marshall and black lawyers in Texas argued that the legal education offered Sweatt at the black law school was so inferior it violated the equal protection clause of the Fourteenth Amendment. Marshall declared, "Whether the University of Texas Law School is compared with the original or new law school for Negroes, we cannot find substantial equality in the educational opportunities offered white and Negro law students by the state. In terms of number of the faculty, variety of courses and opportunity for specialization, size of the student body, scope of the library, availability of law review and similar activities, the University of Texas Law School is superior." These early legal victories laid the legal foundation for the 1954 *Brown v. Topeka Board of Education* decision.

The fight against political disfranchisement also helped mobilize local and state communities and NAACP branches. Nowhere was this more apparent than in Texas. In 1923 the Texas legislature enacted the **Terrell law**, which declared, "In no event shall a Negro be eligible to participate in a Democratic primary election . . . in . . . Texas." In the one-party South, the Democratic primaries were more important than the general elections, which usually merely rubber-stamped the choice made in the primary. Thus, to be denied the right to vote in Democratic Party primaries was to be disfranchised. The NAACP developed a case to test the constitutionality of the Terrell law and began a 20-year battle through the courts. The Texas branches of the NAACP raised money and coordinated local involvement in the campaign to overthrow the Democratic white primary that disfranchised black Texans.

The Texas white primary fight was the most sustained and intense effort that any NAACP chapter undertook during the interwar period. It began in the 1920s and won its first victory when the Supreme Court ruled in 1927 in *Nixon v. Herndon* that the Texas Democratic primary was unconstitutional (see Chapter 17). At the national headquarters, Houston and Marshall orchestrated the assault, and subsequent decisions chipped away at the legal basis for the white primary. Finally, in 1944 the Supreme Court issued a ruling in *Smith v. Allwright* that ended the white primary altogether. It was the NAACP's greatest legal victory to that time. Many more would soon follow.

Terrell law The Terrell law was a Texas law banning African-American participation in the Democratic primary.

Black Women and Community Organizing

Black women made exceptional contributions to the NAACP during the 1930s through their fund-raising and membership drives. Three agitators for racial justice were Daisy Adams Lampkin (c. 1884–1965), Juanita Mitchell (1913–1992), and Ella Baker (1903–1986). These women worked closely with White and the NAACP throughout the Depression and World War II. Lampkin, a native of Washington, DC, in 1915, became the president of the Negro Women's Franchise League, a group dedicated to fighting for the vote. During World War I, she sold some $2 million worth of government Liberty Bonds in black communities in Pennsylvania to help finance the war. In 1930 Walter White enlisted her as regional field secretary of the NAACP, a post she held until she was made national field secretary in 1935. She continued raising funds for the NAACP and played leading roles within organized black womanhood.

The NAACP in the 1930s and 1940s depended on the formidable fund-raising talents of black women like Daisy Lampkin (shown here in a black Baptist church), Ella Baker, and Juanita Mitchell. These women played a major role in building NAACP membership.

Juanita E. Jackson was born in Hot Springs, Arkansas, and raised in Baltimore. She earned a degree in education from the University of Pennsylvania in 1931 and then returned to Baltimore, where she helped found the City-Wide Young People's Forum. This organization encouraged young people to combat such scourges as unemployment, segregation, and lynching. The success of the group prompted Walter White to offer her the leadership of the NAACP's new youth program, which she directed from 1935 to 1938. In 1938 Jackson married fellow civil rights activist Clarence Mitchell, had four sons, and directed the NAACP's voter registration campaigns. In 1950 she received a law degree from the University of Maryland. As the first black woman admitted to practice law in Maryland, she embarked on a series of cases that helped destroy racial segregation on the state's public beaches and in its public schools.

Ella Baker, who became one of the most important women in the civil rights movement of the 1950s and 1960s, began her life's work during the Depression. Born in Norfolk, Virginia, Baker moved to New York City in 1927 and worked as a waitress and as an organizer in radical politics. She was also on the staff of two local newspapers, the *American West Indian News* and the *Negro National News*. Within two years after her arrival, she had cofounded with George Schuyler the Young Negroes' Cooperative League in Harlem. The group practiced collective decision making and attempted to involve all segments of the community in the cooperatives. As she worked with the young men and women, Baker developed a strong belief in grassroots mobilization. She also worked with women's and labor groups, such as the Harlem Housewives Cooperative, the Women's Day Workers and Industrial League, and the YWCA. In 1935 she served as publicity director of the Sponsoring Committee of the National Negro Congress. In 1936 she worked as a teacher with the Works Progress Administration (WPA)—a New Deal organization created to provide jobs for the unemployed—and eventually became one of its assistant supervisors. Walter White was impressed with her relentless organizing and management skills. In 1941, after much persuasion, Baker accepted White's offer to become an assistant field secretary of the NAACP. She traveled across the country and throughout the South, making friendships that would serve her well in the coming decades. From 1943 to 1946, Baker worked as director of NAACP branches and built up the organization's membership. After resigning from the NAACP, she joined the staff of the New York Urban League.

Other black women organized outside the NAACP. Black women in Detroit provide a potent illustration of this kind of activity. On June 10, 1930, 50 black women responded to a call issued by Fannie B. Peck, wife of Rev. William H. Peck, pastor of the 2,000-member Bethel African Methodist Episcopal Church and the president of the Booker T. Washington Trade Association. Out of this initial meeting emerged the Detroit Housewives' League, an organization that combined economic nationalism and black women's self-determination

18-1
18-2
18-3
18-4
18-5
18-6
18-7

to help black families and businesses survive the Depression. Peck had been inspired by M. A. L. Holsey, secretary of the National Negro Business League. Holsey described the directed spending campaigns that enabled housewives in Harlem to consolidate their economic power to persuade businesses to hire black women and children. Fannie Peck became convinced that such an organization would also succeed in Detroit. An admirer recalled that Peck effectively "focused the attention of women on the most essential, yet most unfamiliar factor in the building of homes, communities, and nations, namely, 'The Spending Power of Women.'"

The Detroit organization grew rapidly. By 1934, 10,000 black women belonged to it. According to Peck, the black woman had finally realized "that she has been traveling through a blind alley, making sacrifices to educate her children with no thought as to their obtaining employment after leaving school." The only requirement for membership was a pledge to support black businesses, buy black products, and patronize black professionals, thereby keeping money in the community. The league quickly spread to other cities. Housewives' leagues in Chicago, Baltimore, Washington, Durham (North Carolina), Harlem, and Cleveland used boycotts of merchants who refused to sell black products and employ black children as clerks or stock persons to secure an estimated 75,000 new jobs for black people.

African Americans and the New Deal

18-3   **How did the New Deal affect African Americans?**

In 1932, the third year of the Great Depression, voters elected New York governor Franklin Delano Roosevelt to the presidency with a total of nearly 23 million votes. Roosevelt's lopsided victory over Hoover, who received fewer than 16 million votes, demonstrated the country's loss of faith in the Republican Party and its economic philosophy and heralded the emergence of a new electoral coalition. The new president appealed to the Democratic Party's base of support in the white South, but to this group he added a coalition of western farmers, industrial workers, white ethnic groups in northern cities, and reform-minded intellectuals. For the time being, however, black Americans still clung to the Republican banner. In Chicago, for example, less than 25 percent of black voters voted for Roosevelt. But this was the last election in which the party of Lincoln could take them for granted. To counter the Depression, in his first term Roosevelt inaugurated a multitude of programs—collectively known as the New Deal—that would shift the allegiance of African Americans. Initially his programs continued past patterns of discrimination against African Americans, but by 1935 the New Deal was providing more equal benefits and prompting profound social changes. The result was a new political order that ultimately undermined the edifice of American racism.

Roosevelt and the First New Deal, 1933–1935

During his first one hundred days in office, Roosevelt pressed through Congress a profusion of bold new economic initiatives that came to be known as the first New Deal. To combat the Depression, Roosevelt, unlike Hoover, followed no predetermined plan. Instead, he favored experimentation—tempered by political expediency—over ideology as the guide to federal action. With little resistance Congress passed the president's sprawling and complex laws aimed at overhauling the nation's financial, agricultural, and industrial systems. Most hoped, vainly as it turned out, that these changes would eventually bring a return to prosperity. Meanwhile, Roosevelt moved to counter the immediate suffering of the unemployed with a massive emergency federal relief effort. Many of the first New Deal's programs benefited both white and black people, but the strength of white southerners in the Democratic Party and the nearly complete lack of African-American political power in the South caused much of this early program to be unfairly administered.

Watch on MyHistoryLab Video: The New Deal

The **Agricultural Adjustment Act (AAA),** designed to protect farmers by giving them subsidies to limit production and thereby stabilize prices, illustrates the key benefits and problems African Americans experienced during the first New Deal. The theory underlying the AAA was that lessening production would increase agricultural prices. Essentially, farmers would be paid to grow less. The program provided for sharecroppers and tenant farmers to get part of the subsidies and allowed new rural relief agencies to dispense supplementary income to off-season wageworkers.

This program helped many African Americans, mainly because it pumped billions of dollars into an economic sector on which over 4.5 million black people relied for their livelihood. Also, the AAA was designed to remedy the problems of those farmers—disproportionately African American—who were overreliant on such cash crops as cotton. By 1929 three out of four black farmers, compared with two out of five white farmers, received at least 40 percent of their gross income from cotton. The flow of money from the AAA did, for a time, slow the exodus of black people from farming. Fewer left the farms in the first two years of the program than in the two years before it began. Indeed, from a broader perspective, the New Deal appeared to have slowed the rate at which black people left the land. During the 1930s only 4.5 percent of African Americans abandoned farming, compared with the 8.6 percent who did so during the 1920s.

But if the AAA brought real benefits to black farmers, it was often contrary to protections written into the law, administered unfairly and corruptly. Local control of the AAA resided in the hands of the Extension Service and County Agricultural Conservation Committees, which were supposed to represent all farmers. The county agents, however, were often the planters themselves, and the committees mirrored southern politics as a whole by excluding black people. African Americans were further disadvantaged by the system of unilateral bookkeeping and oppressive credit relations between landlords and tenants. During the first two years of the AAA, black farmers complained bitterly that white landlords simply grabbed and pocketed the millions of dollars of benefit checks they were supposed to forward to tenants. To compound the injury, some planters then evicted the sharecroppers and tenants from the land.

The experience of African Americans with the **National Industrial Recovery Act (NIRA)** mimicked the problems with the AAA. The NIRA was intended to revive manufacturing by allowing industries to cooperate in establishing codes of conduct to govern prices, wage levels, and employment practices, all of which were to be overseen by a National Recovery Administration (NRA). The NRA oversaw the drafting of the codes but faced tremendous resistance from employers and unions in eliminating racial disparities in wage rates and working conditions. Even when African-American advocates did win wage increases for occupations in which black people predominated, the result was often a shift to white labor. These policies prompted some African-American newspapers and protest organizations to claim that "NRA" really stood for the "Negro Removal Agency" or "Negroes Robbed Again." To the relief of many African-American advocates and workers, the Supreme Court declared the NIRA unconstitutional in 1935.

The New Deal's national welfare programs included the Federal Emergency Relief Administration (FERA), the Civilian Conservation Corps (CCC), the Public Works Administration, and the Civil Works Administration (CWA). Although inadequate and unfairly administered on local levels, these programs were often the only thing standing between black people and starvation. FERA provided funds for local and state relief operations to restart and expand their programs. The program pulled millions of people back from the brink of starvation. Because African Americans suffered greater economic devastation, they received benefits at a higher rate than white people. In most cities north and south, 25 to 40 percent of African Americans were on relief rolls that FERA funded wholly or in part. However, many in the Roosevelt administration deemed direct welfare to be morally debilitating, so the government emphasized hiring the unemployed for public works projects. The CWA was a temporary agency created to help people through the winter of 1933–1934.

Agricultural Adjustment Act (AAA) A federal program that provided subsidies to farmers to grow less to help stabilize prices.

Read on **MyHistoryLab Document:** E. E. Lewis, "Black Cotton Farmers and the AAA," 1935

National Industrial Recovery Act (NIRA) Federal law intended to promote the revival of manufacturing by allowing for cooperation among industries.

18-1

18-2

18-3

18-4

18-5

18-6

18-7

VOICES A Black Sharecropper Details Abuse in the Administration of Agricultural Relief

This is one of many letters black sharecroppers sent to the NAACP for assistance to halt the mass evictions and abuse of New Deal relief efforts.

ALABAMA

June 21, 1934

Dear Sir:—

I am writing you these few lines ask you if it is any possible chance of you fining out just why F.E.R.A. office here in . . . refuse to gave me work when I have six in family to care for and also my wife's mother who is over 65 years old and been under the Doctor care for the past seven years of course my wife has a little job but its not with the relief work which some weeks she makes five dollars and some weeks less with four children to take care off which range in age 8–6–4–3 years old and we have $5 per month rent and also $1.74 per week Insurance which that don't enclude Food and Clothing and Fuel to burn. Now Mr. White in the past two and half months I am being going to the relief office trying to get on the relief work and it seem like it is empossible and also just before the first of April I went up to the relief office and explain my case to Mr . . . , the man that gave out the work cards and he gave me a food order for the amount of $2—two dollars and also I got some work to do. But as soon as I got paid for the 24 hours work he came to me to collect $2 for the food order that he gave me and I refuse to gave him $2 and I havent been able to get any more work to do and I have been going up to the office each day sence. But they tell me at the office that they cant gave me work because my wife is working. Of course if that maybe the case I can gave you the name and the address of at least a hundred families where there is two and three in one family who are working on the relief project and I know of at least twenty single men with no one but theirself to take care of and are working twenty-four hours every week and they got to gave their foreman one dollar each every week if they want to stay on the job.

Now Mr. White the white man who my wife work for and my wife told him that they refuse to gave me work because she was working for me and he went up to relief office to see about it But they told him that they didnt cut me out of work because my wife were working but they cut me off because I were unable to do the work. and of course I know that to be very much untrue. The trouble is I refuse to be a fool like so many of my race here and else where around here to pay for a food order that is supose to be giving to the needy free of charge but lots are paying for them and also paying for their job. Of course Mr. White I am colored and when you go up to the relief office The Colored people is treated just as if they were dogs and not human beings. I have been up in the office and I have seen with my own eyes my color kicked and beaten down a whole flight of stairs. I have seen everything done except been murder. Understand Mr. White the little job that my wife has isn't on the relief is a private and everybody that is head of any thing here in the relief office is kin to one another. Now Mr. White the lady that is head of the relief is Mrs. . . . which I saw here once since I was cut off from work and I explained my case to her and she told that she would send a investigator around to my home the next morning whose name is Miss. el;and she told me that when I gave Mr. . . . the $2 for the food order she would O.K. my work card. Mr. White if possible will you please fine out for me just what is the reason they refuse to gave me work when I have six in family and rent to pay. Insurance, Doctor bill, milk bill, buy food and clothing and with only my wife at work it is impossible Mr. White.

1. **Why did the writer seek help from Walter White and the NAACP?**

2. **What were some of the reasons, both implied and noted, that prevented even more black people from protesting economic inequality?**

SOURCE: Herbert Aptheker, ed., *A Documentary History of the Negro People in the United States, 1933–1945*, Vol. 4, New York: Citadel Press, 1974; 1992, pp. 58–60. Reprinted by permission of Bettina Aptheker, Literary Executer, Herbert Aptheker Estate.

The CCC built segregated camps to employ young men and remove them from the poverty and hopelessness of urban areas.

Dayton Jones of the FERA in California devised an ingenious plan that negated the CCC's regulations prohibiting segregation. In a June 26, 1935, letter, Jones shared his proposal for effective internal segregation within the camps with W. Frank Persons, the CCC's director of selections:

It is a known fact that colored boys make efficient kitchen and dining-room aides, and in addition the vast majority of colored youths enjoy this type of work. By being assigned to work as cooks' helpers, kitchen police and in the preparation of raw vegetables for the men such as peeling and slicing potatoes, a good proportion of the colored members in most camps could be absorbed in this manner. Segregation of the colored boys in the mess halls is prevalent in a number of camps by virtue of actual necessity to prevent racial difficulties. Under my plan this segregation would automatically be accomplished because of the fact that kitchen help must necessarily eat at a time other than when the rest of the enrollees take their meals. By assigning these colored boys to this particular type of work the segregation could be accomplished with no one realizing that segregation was being effected.

Despite protests from the NAACP, at least the California camps did institute segregation. Effective August 9, 1935, all CCC districts in California transferred their African-American enrollees into "five colored companies." Yet despite the segregation, former enrollees conceded that their experience in the CCC helped them secure better jobs and a middle-class life after World War II. By the time the CCC was abolished in 1945, more than 200,000 African-American youth had taken part in it.

These relief programs helped many African Americans through the worst parts of the Depression. However, the programs also tended to be less helpful to black people than they were to white people. For example, in its early days the CCC was a tightly segregated institution, with only about 5 percent of its slots going to black youths during its first year. Likewise, although FERA tended to be administered fairly in northern cities, in the South it reached few of those in need.

Black Officials in the New Deal

The first New Deal was not completely bleak for African Americans. In addition to the benefits—however grudgingly disbursed—that New Deal relief programs provided, African Americans also gained new influence and allies within the Roosevelt administration. Their experience reflected the growing availability of highly trained African Americans for government service and the emerging consciousness among white liberals about the problems—and potential electoral power—of black people.

Black people found a staunch ally in First Lady Eleanor Roosevelt. She was revered for her relentless commitment to racial justice. She arranged meetings at the White House for black leaders. She cajoled her husband to consider legislation for black rights. She defied Jim Crow laws by refusing to sit in a "white only" section while attending a meeting in the South. Moreover, she wrote newspaper columns calling for "fair play and equal opportunity for Negro citizens." Roosevelt further endeared herself to black Americans when she resigned her membership in the Daughters of the American Revolution after that organization refused to allow a young black opera singer, Marian Anderson, to perform at its Constitution Hall in Washington in 1939. (Administration officials subsequently arranged for Anderson to perform in front of the Lincoln Memorial on Easter Sunday before a crowd of 75,000. The first song she sang was "My Country, 'Tis of Thee.")

Other liberals joined Eleanor Roosevelt to press for racial justice and seek the appointment of African Americans throughout the government. Early in 1933 President Roosevelt acceded to their request that he appoint someone in his administration to assume responsibility for ensuring that African Americans received fair treatment. He asked Secretary of the Interior Harold Ickes, a former president of the Chicago chapter of the NAACP and a white man whom most black Americans trusted as a friend, to make this happen. Ickes invited Clark Foreman, a young white Georgian who had rejected his region's racism, to handle the assignment. Foreman recognized the irony of a white man representing black people in the government and immediately began to recruit highly trained African Americans. Similar efforts to bring African Americans into government positions were made by Eleanor Roosevelt, Ickes, and other administration officials, such as Secretary of Commerce Daniel Roper and Harry Hopkins, President Roosevelt's relief administrator and confidant. The result was that doors to the government began opening in an unprecedented way.

Read on **MyHistoryLab**
Document: Luther C. Wandall Describes His Experience in the Civilian Conservation Corp (CCC), 1935

Watch on **MyHistoryLab** Video: Responding to the Great Depression: Whose New Deal?

18-1
18-2
18-3
18-4
18-5
18-6
18-7

The Rise of Black Social Scientists

18-4 What was the "black cabinet," its purpose, and its goals?

The Roosevelt administration employed professional black architects, lawyers, engineers, economists, statisticians, interviewers, office managers, and social workers. The Department of Commerce hired Eugene K. Jones, on leave from the National Urban League. The National Youth Administration brought in Mary McLeod Bethune, and the Department of Interior employed William H. Hastie and Robert Weaver. Ira De A. Reid joined the Social Security Administration, and Lawrence W. Oxley worked for the Department of Labor. Ambrose Caliver served in the WPA and the Office of Education.

A core of highly placed African-American social scientists thus became linked in a network called the Federal Council on Negro Affairs, more loosely known as Roosevelt's **"black cabinet."** Mary McLeod Bethune was a leader of this body, which consisted primarily of "New Deal race specialists." It numbered 27 men and three women working mostly in temporary emergency agencies, and it included such stalwarts as housing administrator Robert Weaver. This group met every Friday in Bethune's Washington home. A smaller and younger group met occasionally in Robert Weaver's apartment. This cadre of advisers pressured the president and the heads of federal agencies to adopt and support color-blind policies and lobbied to advance the economic, educational, and social status of black Americans.

black cabinet Informal group of highly placed African-American advisers to President Franklin D. Roosevelt.

Mary McLeod Bethune, and Eleanor Roosevelt, wife of the President of the United States, speaking before an N.Y.A. meeting. Bethune was a key figure in Franklin Roosevelt's Black Cabinet, which included Robert Weaver, Eugene Kinckle Jones, and William H. Hastie.

Social Scientists and the New Deal

Many black intellectuals, scholars, and writers believed the social sciences could be used to adjudicate race relations, and during the New Deal they found greater receptiveness to their work than ever before. Nearly 200 African Americans received Ph.D.s during the 1930s, more than four times the combined total from the previous three decades. Several of these young scholars reached the top ranks of the social sciences, studying the economic, political, and sociological problems of black people with a depth of experience and theoretical sophistication earlier generations of scholars had lacked. In sociology E. Franklin Frazier and Charles S. Johnson took the lead. Frazier's pioneering studies of black families, although now dated, placed him at the forefront of debates on social policy. Throughout the 1930s, as the editor of *Opportunity*, the journal of the Urban League, Johnson published insightful critiques of American racial practices and policies, as well as the work of emerging black novelists, poets, and playwrights. Meanwhile, Ralph Bunche became well known within political science, and Abram Harris and Robert Weaver gained renown in economics.

Historians such as Carter G. Woodson, Lorenzo Greene, Benjamin Quarles, and John Hope Franklin argued that black people had been active agents in the past and not simply the passive objects of white people's actions. Through the Association for the Study of Negro

PROFILE Robert C. Weaver

ROBERT C. WEAVER (1907–1997) was born in Washington, DC. His parents and his teachers at the elite Dunbar High School (which boasted a host of distinguished black alumni, including Charles Houston and William Hastie) instilled in him pride in being a black American. After Dunbar, Weaver went to Harvard, where he earned his undergraduate degree in 1925 and a Ph.D. in economics in 1933, despite the hostility of professors who doubted that black people could do serious intellectual work. Such racist thinking only hardened Weaver's resolve to succeed.

Armed with impressive credentials but bleak job prospects, Weaver returned to Washington, where—together with his Harvard classmate John P. Davis—he founded the Negro Industrial League (NIL) and the Joint Committee on Economic Recovery (JCER) to advocate for black workers. They attracted sponsorships from 24 black and white organizations, including the National Baptist Convention, the African Methodist Episcopal Church, the NAACP, the United Mine Workers, the Elks, the Catholic Interracial Council, and the YWCA. Weaver could soon claim that the NIL and the JCER represented over one million black people.

This broad coalition demanded that the Roosevelt administration appoint black advisers or "experts" to key New Deal agencies. In 1935, Weaver succeeded a white southerner as the adviser on Negro affairs in the Department of the Interior and together with Mary McLeod Bethune became coleader of Roosevelt's "black cabinet."

Weaver remained in government service until 1944. As director of the Office of Race Relations at the United States Housing Authority, he established guidelines that ensured that black workers would be employed on all government-funded housing projects.

Under President John F. Kennedy, Weaver rejoined the government in 1961 and persuaded Kennedy to issue an executive order banning racial discrimination in federal housing programs. In 1966, under Kennedy's successor, Lyndon B. Johnson, Weaver became secretary of housing and urban development, the nation's first African-American cabinet secretary. He spearheaded the passage of the Housing Act of 1968, which expanded opportunities for black home ownership. Weaver died in New York City in 1997.

Life and History and Negro History Week, Woodson and his coworkers Lorenzo Greene, Alrutheus Taylor, and Monroe Work deployed their scholarship to dismiss claims of black inferiority. Their scholarly emphasis on racial pride, achievement, and autonomy raised black morale.

The increasing importance of black scholars became apparent late in the 1930s when the Carnegie Corporation, a philanthropic foundation, sponsored a major study of black life. Although Swedish social scientist Gunnar Myrdal led the study, nearly half of the large staff of scholars were African Americans, and several, particularly Bunche, had a major impact on the work. Published in 1944 as *An American Dilemma*, this massive study profoundly affected public understanding of how racism undermined the progress of African Americans, and it helped set the agenda for the civil rights movement.

18-1

18-2

18-3

18-4

18-5

18-6

18-7

African Americans and the Second New Deal

By late 1935, after two years marked by a slow recovery, much of the first New Deal lay in shambles. The Supreme Court had invalidated major parts of it, and a conservative backlash was emerging against the Roosevelt administration. In response, Roosevelt pressed for a second burst of legislation marked by the passage of the Social Security Act (SSA), the National Labor Relations Act (NLRA), the creation of the WPA, and other measures considerably more radical than those he had established in 1933. The NLRA, for example, helped unions get established and grow. The SSA provided the rudiments of a social welfare system as well as unemployment and retirement insurance. This new set of laws, known as the second New Deal, survived legal challenges and fundamentally changed the United States, particularly by strengthening the role of the federal government.

Roosevelt's leftward political shift helped him win the 1936 presidential election in a landslide. This election cemented a new electoral coalition that yoked the southern wing of the Democratic Party with more liberal farmers and working-class voters who were labor union members in the North and West. The Democratic Party began to win the votes of the large African-American populations in the great cities of the North. The Great Migration had relocated tens of thousands of prospective black voters to northern urban centers, the traditional strongholds of Democratic Party machines, such as in Chicago. Institutionalized housing segregation, combined with the often conscious choice to live in their own neighborhoods, concentrated the black electorate and increased its political power. This power had already appeared in the 1928 election of Republican Oscar De Priest to the U.S. House of Representatives, the first African-American congressman from the North. In 1934, reflecting a shift in partisan allegiance, Chicago's black voters replaced De Priest with Democrat Arthur W. Mitchell. Mitchell, a registered Republican when the Great Depression began, switched to the Democratic Party and thus became the first black Democrat to win a seat in Congress.

Mitchell's election was only the beginning of the change in black people's political identification. The black press fanned the shifting winds, and many more black urban dwellers developed an intense interest in politics. They began to connect political power with the prospect of improving their economic conditions. By the end of the 1930s, black urban voters garnered noteworthy influence in key states such as Illinois, Ohio, Pennsylvania, and New York. This political consciousness led to the election of black state legislators in California, Illinois, Indiana, Kansas, Kentucky, New Jersey, New York, Ohio, Pennsylvania, and West Virginia.

In another indication of change, some Democrats began supporting anti-lynching legislation. Congressman Mitchell gave a strong speech printed in the *Congressional Record* in 1935 supporting President Roosevelt as an anti-lynching advocate. "No President," he declared, "has been more outspoken against the horrible crime of lynching than has Mr. Roosevelt. In speaking of lynching some time ago he characterized it as 'collective murder' and spoke of it as a crime which blackens the record of America." Mitchell told black audiences, "Let me say again, the attitude of the administration at the White House is absolutely fair and without prejudice, insofar as the Negro citizenry is concerned."

So the 1936 election results revealed that Roosevelt had captured the allegiance of most African Americans. Robert Vann, editor of the *Pittsburgh Courier,* urged black people, after casting their ballots, to go home and "turn Lincoln's picture to the wall." There are many complex reasons for this revolution in black political allegiance. The shift to the Democratic Party did not occur without anxiety. Some black people feared that by joining the party they would open the door for even more white southern Democrats to assume national power and thwart black advancement. But by 1936 most African-American voters were willing to take the risk.

The increased participation of African Americans in the Democratic Party sent chills down the spines of the white southern elite. The tension between black Democrats and white conservative Democrats erupted at the party's 1936 convention in Philadelphia. The seating

PROFILE Mary McLeod Bethune

MARY MCLEOD BETHUNE played a powerful role in Roosevelt's black cabinet, but this was only one of the many forums in which she exercised consummate leadership and diplomatic skill. Bethune's life and work link the social reform efforts of post-Reconstruction black women to the civil rights protest activities of the generation emerging after World War II. All the strands of black women's struggle for education, political rights, racial pride, and sexual autonomy are united in her writings, speeches, and organizational work.

Bethune, born on July 10, 1875, near Mayesville, South Carolina, graduated from Scotia Seminary in 1894 and entered Dwight Moody's Institute for Home and Foreign Missions in Chicago. After teaching in mission schools, she settled in Daytona, Florida, where she founded the Daytona Educational and Industrial Institute for Training Negro Girls. Reflecting on her work years later, Bethune recalled, "The school expanded fast. In less than two years I had two hundred fifty pupils. . . . I concentrated more and more on girls, as I felt that they especially were hampered by lack of educational opportunities." Eventually, however, she agreed to merge with Cookman Institute, an educational facility for black boys under the auspices of the Methodist Church. In 1923 the now coeducational institution was renamed Bethune-Cookman College.

During the 1920s Bethune became the leader of the National Association of Colored Women (NACW), a federation of women's clubs. As its president she attempted to turn the organization away from its focus on self-help and moral uplift and toward broader goals. Although she made progress, by 1935 she had become frustrated by the NACW's caution and founded the National Council of Negro Women (NCNW), an "organization of organizations." The women present at the creation of the NCNW were the who's who of black women's activism. They included educators Charlotte Hawkins Brown and Mary Church Terrell, executive director of the National Association of Colored Graduate Nurses Mabel K. Staupers, NAACP national field director Daisy Lampkin, and former president of the Empire State Federation of Women's Clubs Addie W. Hunton, who also led the International Council of Women of the Darker Race. Eventually, the NCNW had 20 national affiliates and 90 local councils in cities, towns, and rural communities across the country. Club engagement strengthened women's resolve to struggle for black rights and provided safe space for them to develop the skills and networks that proved critical in the post–World War II civil rights movement.

With the New Deal, Bethune became a Democratic Party activist and a government official. She had a close relationship with First Lady Eleanor Roosevelt that gave her access to the president that few others enjoyed. She and Eleanor Roosevelt had persuaded the president that the National Youth Administration (NYA) needed a Negro division to ensure that benefits would be distributed fairly, and Bethune was named the NYA's director of Negro affairs. She was the first African-American woman to hold a high position in the government. During the 1936 campaign, Bethune helped convince African Americans that their best interests lay with the Democratic rather than the Republican Party.

One of Bethune's many noteworthy accomplishments was the 1937 conference the Department of Labor held on the "Problems of the Negro and Negro Youth," at which Eleanor Roosevelt delivered a key speech. During the session titled "Security of Life and Equal Protection under the Law," the conference called for a federal anti-lynching law, equal access to the ballot in federal elections, and elimination of segregation and discrimination on interstate trains and buses. This was a virtual blueprint of the agenda of the civil rights movement. No other general meeting on civil rights during the Roosevelt administration generated so much interest, support, and publicity. With this conference, Bethune assumed the middle ground of black politics.

18-1

18-2

18-3

18-4

18-5

18-6

18-7

18-1

18-2

18-3

18-4

18-5

18-6

18-7

of 32 black delegates infuriated southern politicians. The selection of a black Baptist minister to open one session with a prayer outraged South Carolina Senator Ellison D. "Cotton Ed" Smith, who, accompanied by Mayor Burnet Maybank of Charleston and other delegates, marched off the floor, proclaiming that they refused to support "any political organization that looks upon the Negro and caters to him as a political and social equal." Smith declared he was "sick of the whole damn thing." Undaunted, the black minister simply observed that "Brother Smith needs more prayer." The next day when Congressman Mitchell of Illinois took to the floor, Smith repeated his walkout. The South Carolina delegation subsequently adopted a protest resolution denouncing the appearance of black men on the convention's program. Southern white protests, however, had no effect on the political decisions of black men and women. Heeding the advice of the NAACP, they voted their personal interests.

Despite the rise of black Democrats, southern congressmen succeeded in excluding many African Americans from key government programs. For example, they insisted on denying the benefits of the NLRA and the SSA to agricultural laborers and domestic servants. These white southerners could not, however, stop the tilt toward fairer administration of programs or the revival of the push for equal rights, which had lain all but dormant since the end of Reconstruction.

The WPA illustrates the changes that the second New Deal and the increasing shift of African Americans to the Democratic Party wrought. The WPA, with Harry Hopkins as its head, was created to employ the unemployed. Under Hopkins's direction and sustained with $1.39 billion in federal funds, the WPA put thousands of men and women to work building new roads, hospitals, city halls, courthouses, and schools. Under the aegis of the WPA, American citizens built bridges, ports, and water systems. Larger-scale infrastructure projects included the Lincoln Tunnel under the Hudson River connecting New York and New Jersey, the Triborough Bridge system linking Manhattan to Long Island, and the Bonneville and Boulder dams. (Boulder Dam was later renamed the Hoover Dam by a Republican-controlled Congress in 1946.)

The WPA was administered far more fairly than were the first New Deal programs. The national government explicitly rejected racial discrimination and made sure local officials complied. Although far from perfect, by 1939 it had provided assistance to one million black families on a far more equitable basis than ever before.

The same pattern prevailed in the WPA's four arts programs—the Federal Art Project, the Federal Music Project, the Federal Theater Project, and the Federal Writers' Project—which employed thousands of musicians, intellectuals, writers, and artists. A fifth program that was created in 1937, the Historical Records Survey, sent teams of writers, including Zora Neale Hurston, to collect folklore and study ethnic groups. One team collected the life histories of 2,000 former slaves.

Between 1935 and 1943, the WPA helped artists display their talents and made their work widely available. Among the black artists hired to adorn government buildings, post offices, and public parks were Aaron Douglas, Charles Alston, Richmond Barthe, Sargent Johnson, Archibald Motley Jr., and Augusta Savage. Savage was a sculptor who worked in clay, marble, and bronze. She established arts schools in New York City in the 1930s—the Savage School of Arts and Crafts, Savage Studios, and the Uptown Art Laboratory. She became the first director of the Harlem Community Art Center in 1937. Her students included Jacob Lawrence, William Artis, Norman Lewis, and Elton Fax.

One of the most effective New Deal agencies, the WPA offered African Americans numerous opportunities for vocational training. Young men learned from experienced craftsmen. As this 1942 photo illustrates, the intricate lathe operations instruction prepared the trainee with skills that could be used in the defense industries.

The Federal Theater Project established 16 black theater units. Among their most notable productions was a version of *Macbeth* set in Haiti with an all-black cast. White actor John Houseman and black actress Rose McClendon directed the Harlem Federal Theater Project. This project—more than the others—proved controversial due to the fear of communist influence and the leftist political views of some African-American writers and performers.

Organized Labor and Black America

18-5 **What role did organized labor play in radicalizing black Americans during the 1930s?**

The relationship of African Americans to labor unions changed profoundly during the 1930s. Before this time, most local unions affiliated with the national AFL barred black people or restricted them to segregated locals. The railroad unions, which called themselves "brotherhoods," excluded black workers entirely. The New Deal, especially after 1935, did much to transform the labor movement. The NLRA and the militancy of workers provided the opportunity to organize the nation's great mass production industries. Still, leaders of the AFL were unwilling to incorporate into their unions the masses of unskilled workers, many of whom were African American or recent European immigrants. Frustrated by this situation, in 1935 the head of the United Mine Workers, John L. Lewis (1880–1969), and his followers formed the **Committee for Industrial Organization (CIO)** to take on the task.

Unlike the AFL, the CIO was committed to interracial and multiethnic organizing and so enabled more African Americans to participate in the labor movement. Its leaders knew it was in organized labor's best interest to admit black men and women to membership. As one black union organizer said, "We colored folks can't organize without you and you white folks can't organize without us." But it took a massive change in outlook to achieve this unity. By 1940 the CIO had enlisted approximately 210,000 black members. Unions that valued and sustained interracial cooperation included the International Mine, Mill, and Smelter Workers; the Food, Tobacco, and Agricultural Workers Union; and the United Farm Equipment and Metal Workers.

A. Philip Randolph's Brotherhood of Sleeping Car Porters (BSCP) remained with the AFL, but it also benefited from New Deal legislation. In 1934 Congress had amended the Railway Labor Act in a way that helped the BSCP overcome the opposition of the Pullman Company. The law required that corporations bargain in good faith with unions if the unions could demonstrate through elections monitored by the National Mediation Board that they genuinely represented the corporations' employees. The Pullman Company resisted, but in 1937, long after an election certified the BSCP as the workers' representative, the company finally recognized the brotherhood. Then—and only then—did the AFL grant the BSCP full membership as an international union. After more than 12 years, A. Philip Randolph and thousands of black men won their struggles against a giant corporation and a powerful labor organization. These were no small victories.

Although most black people in unions were men, some unions also represented and helped improve the lives of black working women. For example, since the early nineteenth century there had been a rigid hierarchy among workers in the tobacco industry, one of the few areas of the economy outside agriculture or domestic service that employed many black women. Jobs were assigned on the basis of race and gender, with black women receiving the most difficult and tedious job, that of "stemmer." In 1939 stemmer Louise "Mama" Harris instigated a series of walkouts at the I. N. Vaughn Company in Richmond. The strikes, which CIO affiliates—including the white women of the International Ladies Garment Workers Union—supported, led to the formation of the Tobacco Workers Organizing Committee, another CIO affiliate. In 1943 black women union leaders and activists, including Theodosia Simpson and Miranda Smith, were involved in a strike

WPA poster for the all-black production of Macbeth.

Committee for Industrial Organization (CIO) Labor organization that was committed to interracial and multiethnic organizing.

Read the **Document**: National Labor Relations Act, 1935

18-1
18-2
18-3
18-4
18-5
18-6
18-7

VOICES | A. Philip Randolph Inspires a Young Black Activist

In 1928 young E. D. Nixon heard A. Philip Randolph speak, and it changed Nixon's life. He became president of the Montgomery branch of the Brotherhood of Sleeping Car Porters that year and remained in the post until 1964. During that period he played a leading role in mobilizing and organizing the Montgomery bus boycott ignited by Rosa Parks's arrest for refusing to relinquish her seat to a white male passenger. He recalls Randolph's speech in the following passage.

When I heard Randolph speak [in 1928], it was like a light. Most eloquent man I ever heard. He done more to bring me in the fight for civil rights than anybody. Before that time, I figure that a Negro would be kicked around and accept whatever the white man did. I never knew the Negro had a right to enjoy freedom like everyone else. When Randolph stood there and talked that day, it make a different man out of me. From that day on, I was determined that I was gonna fight for freedom until I was able to get some of it for myself.

1. **What does Nixon's reaction to Randolph's speech say about the importance of leadership in the labor movement?**

2. **How did Randolph's speech influence Nixon's later involvement in the struggle for black civil rights?**

SOURCE: Quoted in Studs Turkel, *Hard Times: An Oral History of the Great Depression* (1970; reprint, New York: New Press, pbk ed., 2000), 119.

against the R. J. Reynolds tobacco company to force it to the negotiating table. Smith later became southern regional director of the Food, Tobacco, Agricultural, and Allied Workers of America. It was the highest position a black woman held in the labor movement up to that time.

The Communist Party and African Americans

18-6 **What was the *Scottsboro* case and what were its consequences?**

Throughout the 1930s the Communist Party intensified its support of African Americans' efforts to address unemployment and job discrimination and to seek social justice. The communists' militant antiracism and determination to be interracial attracted some African Americans. The party expelled members who exhibited racial prejudice and gave black men key leadership positions. James Ford, an African American, ran as the party's vice-presidential candidate in the election of 1932. Although few black men and women actually joined the Communist Party, some became increasingly sympathetic to left-wing ideas and prescriptions as the Depression wore on.

Many black workers were drawn to the Communist Party because it criticized the refusal of organized white labor to include them. The communists maintained that "the low standard of living of Negro workers is made use of by the capitalists to reduce the wages of the white workers." They chided "the mis-leaders of labor, the heads of the reformist and reactionary trade union organizations" for refusing to organize black workers. They insisted "this anti-Negro attitude of the reactionary labor leaders helps to split the ranks of labor, allows the employers to carry out their policy of 'divide and rule,' frustrates the efforts of the working class to emancipate itself from the yoke of capitalism, and dims the class-consciousness of the white workers as well as of the Negro workers." Indeed, much of the push for racial equality within the CIO emanated from those connected with the party.

Read on MyHistoryLab Document: Lester B. Granger Calls on Black Workers to Combat Discrimination in Organized Labor, 1934

The International Labor Defense and the "Scottsboro Boys"

The *Scottsboro* case brought the Communist Party to the attention of many African Americans. It began when nine black youths who had caught a ride on a freight train in Alabama were tried, convicted, and sentenced to death for allegedly raping two white women. Their ordeal started on the night of March 25, 1931, when a group of young white hobos accosted them. A fight broke out. The black youths threw the white youths off the train. The losers filed a complaint with the Scottsboro, Alabama, sheriff charging that black hoodlums had assaulted them. The sheriff ordered his deputies to round up every black person on the train. The sweep netted the nine young black men: Ozie Powell, Clarence Norris, Charlie Weems, Olen Montgomery, Willie Robertson, Haywood Patterson, Eugene Williams, Andy Wright, and Roy Wright. The police also discovered two young white women: 19-year-old Victoria Price and 17-year-old Ruby Bates.

Afraid of being arrested and perhaps ashamed of being hobos, Price and Bates falsely claimed that the nine black youths had sexually assaulted them. On the basis of that accusation, the "**Scottsboro Boys**" (ranging in age from 13 to 20) were given a hasty trial. They never had a chance. Their white court-appointed attorney came to court drunk each day. Three days after the trial started and 15 days after their arrest, the jurors found them all guilty. Eight received the death sentence, and the youngest was sentenced to life imprisonment, even though medical examinations of Price and Bates proved that neither had been raped.

While other organizations dawdled or refused to intervene, the Communist Party's International Labor Defense (ILD) rushed to help the "boys" by appealing the conviction and death sentence to the Supreme Court. The case produced two important decisions that reaffirmed black people's right to the basic protections that all other American citizens enjoyed. In *Powell v. Alabama* (1932), the Court ruled that the *Scottsboro* defendants had not been given adequate legal counsel and that the trial had taken place in a hostile and volatile atmosphere. Asserting that the youths' right to due process as set forth in the Fourteenth Amendment had been violated, the Court ordered a new trial. Alabama did as instructed, but the new trial resulted in another guilty verdict and sentences of death or life imprisonment. The ILD promptly appealed, and in *Norris v. Alabama* (1935) the Court decided that all Americans have the right to a trial by a jury of their peers. The systematic exclusion of African Americans from the *Scottsboro* juries, the Court held, denied the defendants

Scottsboro Boys Nine young African-American men unjustly accused of raping two white women in Alabama in 1931. The Supreme Court overturned their convictions in 1937.

The "Scottsboro Boys," a case of southern justice gone awry, attracted international attention and fueled competition between the NAACP and the Communist Party. In this 1937 photograph the NAACP's Juanita E. Jackson Mitchell visits with the Scottsboro Boys, nine unemployed black young men accused of raping two white women mill workers on a Southern Railroad freight car on March 25, 1931. All were sentenced to death, with one exception. Eugene Williams's life was spared because he was only 13. Victoria Price and Ruby Bates recanted their stories, but it made no difference. The U.S. Supreme Court overturned the death convictions and sentences in two landmark cases, one of which established the right of the accused to competent legal counsel.

equal protection under the law, which the Fourteenth Amendment guaranteed. Chief Justice Charles Evans Hughes pointed out that no black citizens had served on juries in the Alabama counties for decades, even though many were qualified to serve. The Court noted that the exclusion was blatant racial discrimination and called for yet another trial.

Despite these stunning defeats and increasing evidence that the "boys" had been falsely convicted, Alabama still pursued the case. Even when Ruby Bates publicly admitted the rape charge had been a hoax, white Alabamians ignored her. Finally, in 1937 Alabama dropped its charges against five of the nine men, and in the 1940s the state released those still in jail. Altogether, nine innocent black men had collectively served some three-quarters of a century in prison. Clarence Willie Norris, however, escaped and fled to Michigan, returning decades later to receive a ceremonious pardon from Governor George Wallace. When a reporter asked Norris how he felt, he declared, "I'm just glad to be free." The experience had taught him "to stand up for your rights, even if it kills you. That's all life consists of."

Debating Communist Leadership

Throughout the *Scottsboro* case, the NAACP tried unsuccessfully to wrest control from the Communist Party. Indeed, as the case evolved, tensions and competition between the Communist Party and the NAACP for leadership of black America flared into open hostility. At first, the NAACP had hesitated to defend accused rapists, but it moved more decisively after the Communist Party had taken the lead.

The contest between the NAACP and the communists reveals the differences between the two groups. The party organized protest marches and demonstrations and used its press to denounce more cautious middle-class organizations. In Harlem, for example, the communists staged a 1931 protest march that attracted over 3,000 black men and women and ended with an address by Ada Wright, the mother of two of the defendants, who praised the ILD for its help. The NAACP countered with a carefully orchestrated campaign that questioned the sincerity and effectiveness of the communists and sought to repair its own reputation as a respectable and effective advocate for African Americans.

Black public opinion divided in its evaluation of the party. Some black men and women applauded the communists. Journalist Eugene Gordon wrote,

> Negro workers think of the countless times Communists have been beaten insensible for defending . . . Negro workers. . . . They see the ILD . . . supported by the Communist Party, rushing to the defense of the nine Negro youths at Scottsboro before other Negro organizations in the country condescended to glance superciliously in their direction. . . . Seeing and hearing all these things, the Negro worker in the United States would be a fool not to recognize the leadership that he has been waiting for since his freedom.

Historian Carter G. Woodson praised the Communist Party in the *New York Age*:

> I have talked with any number of Negroes who call themselves Communists, and I have never heard one express a desire to destroy anyone or anything but oppression. . . . Negroes who are charged with being Communists advocate the stoppage of peonage, equality in employment of labor. . . . If this makes a man "Red," the world's greatest reformers belong to this class, and we shall have to condemn our greatest statesmen, some of whom have attained the presidency of the United States.

But other African Americans ridiculed the party. George Schuyler, a columnist for the *Pittsburgh Courier*, used his razor-sharp wit to castigate the party and persuade black people that its claim to champion African Americans was a lie. Schuyler objected to the communists' "campaign of vilification . . . against the NAACP":

> No Ku Kluxer ever denounced the latter organization more vigorously and unfairly. The Communists know they are lying when they assert time and time again that the NAACP wants to see the boys convicted and is betraying the race. They have quite the same sort of grooved mentality as Ku Kluxers, Garveyites and other race fanatics, black and white. The course they tentatively pursue is held the only true one and whoever takes exception is denounced as an enemy of humanity, even though they may have to change that course in a few months.

PROFILE   Angelo Herndon

IN THE SOUTH, THE COMMUNIST PARTY gravitated toward those areas where black and white laborers were grossly exploited. The party's efforts in Georgia, Alabama, and Mississippi produced black organizers such as Hosea Hudson, Nate Shaw, and Angelo Herndon, who became targets of white supremacists.

In 1932, young organizer Angelo Herndon was arrested, tried, and convicted in Atlanta for inciting insurrection. One of 13 children, Herndon was born May 6, 1913, in Ohio. Seeking better opportunities, Herndon, at age 13, escaped the poverty of his home region to work in the coal mines in Alabama. At 18 he was already a seasoned miner but disillusioned and angry at the exploitation of coal miners. He attended a Communist Party meeting and was impressed by its commitment to equality, both racial and social. He joined the party and poured enormous energy into organizing and recruiting members from among the mine workers and the unemployed. In 1934, Herndon explained why he joined the party:

> All my life I'd been sweated and stepped on and Jim-Crowed. I lay on my belly in the mines for a few dollars a week, and saw my pay stolen and slashed, and my buddies killed. I lived in the worst section of town, and rode behind the "Colored" signs of streetcars, as though there was something disgusting about me? I heard myself called "nigger" and

"darky" and I had to say "Yes, sir" to every white man. . . . I had always detested it, but I had never known that anything could be done about it. And here, all of a sudden, I had found organizations . . . that weren't scared to come out for equality for the Negro people, and for the rights of workers. The Jim-Crow system, the wage-slave system, weren't everlasting after all! It was like all of a sudden turning a corner on a dirty, old street and finding yourself facing a broad, shining highway. . . . I felt then, and I know now, that the Communist program is the only program that the Southern workers—whites and Negroes both—can possibly accept in the long run. It's the only program that does justice to the southern worker's ideas that everybody ought to have an equal chance, and that every man has rights that must be respected.

The party sent Herndon to Atlanta, where he organized an interracial relief group and staged peaceful demonstrations against hunger. This proved his undoing. One week later, while picking up his mail at the post office, he was arrested on the charge that he had violated an old ordinance forbidding black and white people from mingling together. Herndon's trial and conviction made him the best-known African-American communist in the nation. The case underscored the fear that the specter of social equality across racial lines inspired in white southerners. The Communist Party assigned a young black attorney, Benjamin Davis, Jr., to represent Herndon. Davis challenged the constitutionality of the ordinance and of Atlanta's jury system, which excluded African Americans from service. His defense was unsuccessful, and the judge sentenced Herndon to 20 years on a chain gang. The severity of the sentence and the judge's racist sentiments sparked a nationwide movement to free Herndon as black organizations, labor unions, and religious groups joined with the Communist Party to fight for his immediate release. After four years of appeals, in 1937 the Supreme Court, in a 5-to-4 decision, declared Georgia's slave insurrection law unconstitutional and ordered the state to release him.

Although most African Americans applauded the antiracist work that the Communist Party supported and performed, there was no chance they would defect from the traditional American political system, as W. E. B. Du Bois wrote in 1931:

> American Negroes do not propose to be the shock troops of the Communist Revolution, driven out in the front to death, cruelty and humiliation in order to win victories for white workers. . . . Negroes know perfectly well that whenever they try to lead revolution in America, the nation will unite as one fist to crush them and them alone.

18-1
18-2
18-3
18-4
18-5
18-6
18-7

VOICES Hoboing in Alabama

Ralph Ellison, the noted author of the great novel Invisible Man *(1952), here recalls his harrowing experience as a young black "hobo" after the arrest of the "Scottsboro Boys."*

During June of 1933, I found myself traveling by freight train in an effort to reach Tuskegee Institute in time to take advantage of a scholarship granted me. Having little money and no time left in which to earn the fare for a ticket, I grabbed an armful of freight car, a form of illegal travel quite common during the Great Depression. In fact, so many young men, young women, prostitutes, gamblers, and even some quite respectable but impoverished elderly and middle-aged couples were hoboing that it was quite difficult for the railroad to control such passengers. I justify this out of sheer desperation, college being my one hope of improving my condition.

But I was young and adventurous and regarded hoboing as the next best thing to floating down the Mississippi on a raft. My head was full of readings of the Rover Boys and Huckleberry Finn. I converted hoboing into a lark until I found myself in the freight yards of Decatur, Alabama, where two white railroad detectives laying about them with the barrels of long nickel-plated .45 revolvers forced some forty or fifty of us, black and white alike, off the train and ordered us to line up along the tracks. For me, this was a most frightening moment. Not only was I guilty of stealing passage on a freight train, but I realized that I had been caught in the act in the town where, at that very moment, the *Scottsboro* case was being tried. The case and the incident leading to it were widely reported in the black press, and what I had read of the atmosphere of the trial led me to believe that the young men in the case had absolutely no

possibility of receiving a just decision. As I saw it, the trial was a macabre circus, a kangaroo proceeding that would be soon followed by an enactment of the gory rite of lynching, that ultimate form of racial victimage.

I had no idea of what the detectives intended to do with me, but given the atmosphere of the town, I feared that it would be most unpleasant and brutal. I, too might well be a sacrificial scapegoat, simply because I was the same race as the accused young men then being prepared for death. Therefore, when a group of white boys broke and ran, I plunged into their midst, and running far closer to the ground than I had ever managed to do as a high school football running back, I kept running and moving until I came to a shed with a railroad loading dock, under which I scooted; and there I remained until dawn, when I grabbed the first thing that was smoking and headed south.

A few days later I reached Tuskegee, but that scrape with the law—the fear, the horror and sense of helplessness before legal injustice—was most vivid in my mind, and it has so remained.

1. **How does Ellison's experience as a hobo illuminate race relations in the South?**
2. **How did the *"Scottsboro Boys"* case increase Ellison's sense of vulnerability? Why were so many people engaged in "hoboing"? How did the black experience of "hoboing" differ from that of white Americans?**

SOURCE: Ralph Ellison, "Perspective of Literature," in *Going to the Territory* (New York: Vintage Books, 1995), 324–25.

The National Negro Congress

National Negro Congress (NNC)
Organization founded in 1936 to unite African-American protest groups.

The infighting between the Communist Party and other groups doomed a major attempt to unite all the disparate African-American protest groups into the **National Negro Congress (NNC)**. John P. Davis, a Washington-based economist, organized the NNC, modeling it on his experience as the executive secretary of the Joint Committee on National Recovery, a coalition of black groups that pressed for fairness in the early New Deal. The NNC was to be a federation of organizations on a national scale supported by regional councils. Over 800 delegates representing 585 organizations attended its first meeting, held in Chicago in 1936. However, prominent black activists, leaders, and intellectuals were conspicuously absent, notably those associated with the NAACP. A. Philip Randolph was elected president, and Davis became the executive secretary. The group resolved not to be dominated by any one political faction and to build on the strength of all parts of the black community. Although handicapped by lack of funds, the NNC initially worked effectively at the local or community level. With branches in approximately 70 cities, the organization gained for its members increased employment opportunities, better housing, and adequate relief work. The NNC also prodded labor unions, in particular the CIO, to fight for better conditions and higher wages for black workers.

At the NNC's second meeting in Philadelphia in 1937, a skeptical Davis maintained that the Democratic Party would never allow black people to benefit fairly from the New Deal. Eventually the increasing importance of communists in the NNC alienated most other groups and reduced the organization's ability to speak for most black people. By 1940 it was greatly weakened. Randolph was voted out of office, and the once promising NNC became little more than a front group for the Communist Party.

Misuses of Medical Science: The Tuskegee Study

18-7   **What was the Tuskegee study and its impact?**

The 1930s marked the rising prominence of black scholars and intellectuals; paradoxically, the decade also witnessed the worst manifestation of racism in American science. This shocking episode of racial mistreatment occurred in Macon County, Alabama, through medical experimentation on impoverished and vulnerable populations. There, in 1932, U.S. Public Health Service (USPHS) officials initiated several major studies of syphilis, a sexually transmitted disease that can cause paralysis, insanity, heart failure, and eventually death. For the subjects of its program—titled the Tuskegee Study of Untreated Syphilis in the Male Negro—the USPHS recruited 622 black men, all of them poor sharecroppers and the majority illiterate. Of these men, 431 had advanced cases of syphilis. The rest were free of the disease and served as controls for comparison.

Another experiment decades prior to the one is Tuskegee involved people in Guatemala. As historian Susan Reverby explained, "This experiment is the global, rather than the American South, differed from the Study in Alabama in two major ways: government doctors did infect people with syphilis and then did treat them with penicillin." In 1944 the Public Health Service deliberately injected gonorrhea in "volunteers" who were inmates at the Terre Haute Federal Penitentiary in Indiana but abandoned the study when it proved "difficult to get the men to exhibit infection."

The **Tuskegee Study** was called a treatment program, but it turned out to be an experiment, designed to chart the progression and development of a potentially fatal disease. To gain the men's trust, the government doctors centered their work at Tuskegee Institute and hired a black nurse, Eunice Rivers, who convinced the men they had "bad blood" and needed special treatment. Although penicillin, which can cure the disease, became available in the 1940s, the sharecroppers never received it. Instead, they were given ineffective placebos, which they were told would cure them.

Initially the Tuskegee Study was to last only 6 to 12 months, but it was repeatedly extended. The men

Tuskegee Study A medical study by the U.S. Public Health Service of the effects of syphilis on 622 black men. The study ran from 1932 to the 1970s, and the men were given only placebos and no treatment for the disease.

From 1932 to 1972, the U.S. Public Health Service conducted an experiment on approximately 400 black Alabama sharecroppers to trace the evolution of untreated syphilis. The men were never informed that they had the disease, nor were they given penicillin when it became available. On May 16, 1997, President Bill Clinton on behalf of the U.S. government finally apologized for this cruel and clearly racist experiment on human subjects.

18-1

18-2

18-3

18-4

18-5

18-6

18-7

received regular physical examinations, which included a painful lumbar puncture. This insertion of a needle into the spinal cord to obtain fluid for diagnosis often caused the men severe headaches, and in a few isolated cases it resulted in paralysis and even death. For almost 40 years, Tuskegee Study doctors observed the men, keeping careful records of their health and performing autopsies on those who died, but they never treated them for syphilis. So little understood was the Tuskegee Study that men not only remained in the program but believed they were fortunate to have the physical examinations, the hot lunches provided on examination days, and the burial allowance the government guaranteed their families. The medical community knew of the Tuskegee experiment, but the general public learned of it only in 1972 when a reporter broke the story. Black attorney Fred D. Gray of Alabama sued the U.S. government on behalf of the participants and their families, but before the case went to trial, the government made a $9 million settlement to the Tuskegee survivors and the descendants of those who had died.

CONCLUSION

Notable political changes occurred during the early 1930s: the NAACP came of age, black women found their voice, white left-wing leaders joined with black men and women in interracial alliances, organized labor bridged the race chasm, and black voters switched from the Republican to the Democratic Party. The New Deal had stimulated some economic recovery and, more important, laid the basis for a strong national state and a political coalition that, beginning with World War II, would challenge the nation's racial system.

CHAPTER TIMELINE

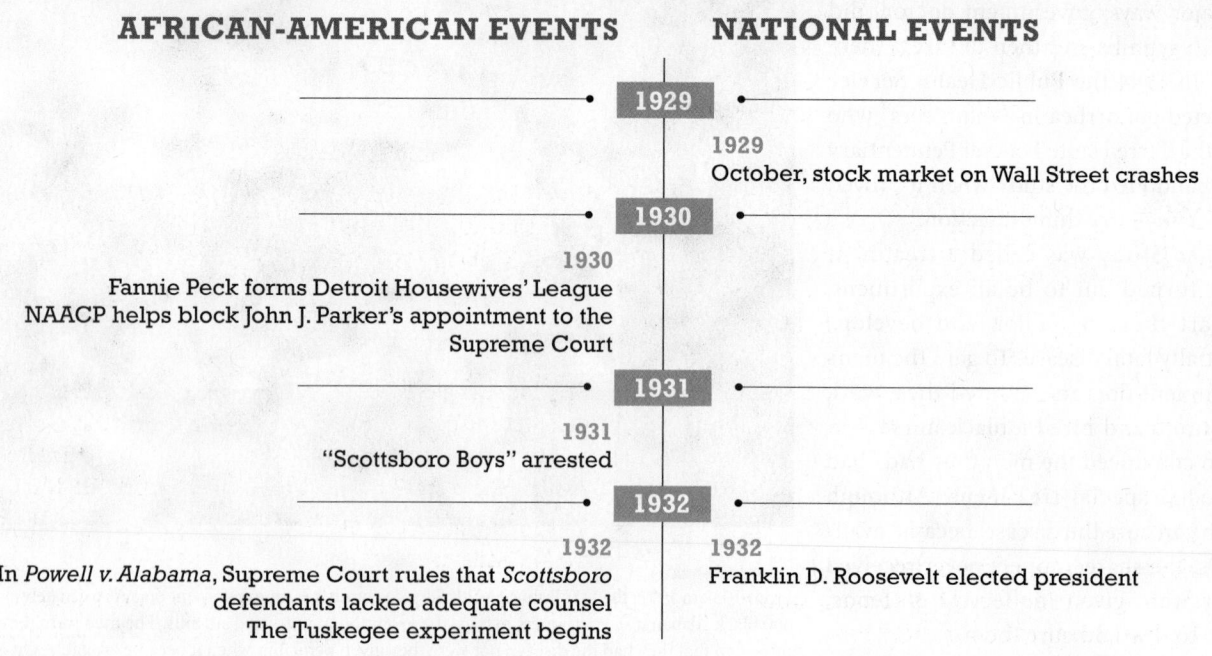

AFRICAN-AMERICAN EVENTS   **NATIONAL EVENTS**

1929

1929
October, stock market on Wall Street crashes

1930

1930
Fannie Peck forms Detroit Housewives' League
NAACP helps block John J. Parker's appointment to the Supreme Court

1931

1931
"Scottsboro Boys" arrested

1932

1932
In *Powell v. Alabama*, Supreme Court rules that *Scottsboro* defendants lacked adequate counsel
The Tuskegee experiment begins

1932
Franklin D. Roosevelt elected president

CHAPTER TIMELINE

AFRICAN-AMERICAN EVENTS	NATIONAL EVENTS
1933	
1933 The "black cabinet" of social scientists formed	**1933** Roosevelt launches the first New Deal
1934	
1934 Elijah Muhammad becomes leader of the Nation of Islam W. E. B. Du Bois resigns from the NAACP	
1935	
1935 Mary McLeod Bethune forms the National Council of Negro Women *Norris v. Alabama* establishes right to trial by a jury of one's peers Free Angelo Herndon Campaign begins National Negro Congress formed	**1935** The CIO is formed Roosevelt's second New Deal—Social Security Act, National Labor Relations Act, and Works Progress Administration
1936	
1936 African Americans shift allegiance to the Democratic Party Mary McLeod Bethune named director of the Division of Negro Affairs	**1936** Roosevelt reelected in a landslide
1937	
1937 William Hastie named first black federal judge Bethune organizes conference on Problems of the Negro and Negro Youth	

On MyHistoryLab

 ✔ Study and Review on MyHistoryLab

REVIEW QUESTIONS

1. Why did African Americans abandon their long association with the Republican Party in favor of the Democratic Party?

2. How did black radicalism influence Roosevelt's New Deal policies and programs?

3. How did black people respond to and survive the Great Depression? How did the experiences of black women during the Depression reflect their race, class, and gender status?

4. How did the New Deal adversely affect black sharecroppers, tenants, and farmers? What were the political, social, and economic repercussions of the large-scale migration of African Americans out of the South during the 1930s?

5. What role did racism play in the Tuskegee experiment and the "Scottsboro Boys" case?

6. Why were W. E. B. Du Bois's editorials in the *Crisis* about segregation so divisive and explosive? How did black activists and scholars respond to the idea of voluntary self-segregation?

RECOMMENDED READING

Martha Biondi. *To Stand and Fight: The Struggle for Civil Rights in Post War New York City*. Cambridge, Harvard University Press, 2003. A persuasive, well-researched history of African-American struggles for civil and economic rights in New York City prior to the advent of the modern civil rights movement.

John Egerton. *Speak Now Against the Day: The Generation Before the Civil Rights Movement in the South*. New York: Alfred A. Knopf, 1994. An excellent survey of the period before the modern civil rights era, with chapters on the Depression in the South and black and white southerners' reactions to it.

James H. Jones. *Bad Blood: The Tuskegee Syphilis Experiment*. New York: Free Press, 1981. A comprehensive study of the Tuskegee experiment.

Robin D. G. Kelley. *Hammer and Hoe: Alabama Communists During the Great Depression*. Chapel Hill: University of North Carolina Press, 1990. A splendid study of the radicalizing activism of steelworkers and farmers during the 1930s. Kelley shows why the communists appealed to black workers.

Koritha Mitchell. *Living with Lynching: African American Lynching Plays, Performance, and Citizenship, 1890–1930*. Urbana: University of Illinois Press, 2012. An uniquely original and brilliant analysis of lynching plays that facilitated the survival of African-American communities during a period of rampant mob violence.

Mark Naison. *Communists in Harlem During the Depression*. Urbana: University of Illinois Press, 1983. A well-researched and clear-sighted study of the Communist Party in Harlem and the National Negro Congress.

Susan M. Reverby. *Examining Tuskegee: The Infamous Syphilis Study and Its Legacy*. Chapel Hill: University of North Carolina Press, 2009. A comprehensive study and brilliant analysis of the African American men involved as patients, their families, and the healthcare professionals who participated in the famous government-financed study of untreated syphilis.

Susan M. Reverby. "'Normal Exposure' and Inoculation Syphilis: A PHS 'Tuskegee' Doctor in Guatemala, 1946–1948." *Journal of Policy History* 23, no. 1 (January 2011): 6–28. The PHS conducted research not only on black men, but also on other male ethnic groups.

Harvard Sitkoff. *A New Deal for Blacks: The Emergence of Civil Rights as a National Issue, Vol. I: Depression Decade*. New York: Oxford University Press, 1978. An important work that presents the New Deal as laying the groundwork for the civil rights movement.

Raymond Wolters. *Negroes and the Great Depression: The Problem of Economic Recovery*. Westport, CT: Greenwood, 1974. A solid survey that covers the Depression's impact on African Americans, the workings of the "black cabinet," and the effects of the New Deal agencies on black Americans.

ADDITIONAL BIBLIOGRAPHY

POLITICS

Adam Fairclough. *Better Day Coming: Blacks and Equality, 1890–2000*. New York: Viking, 2001.

Glenda Elizabeth Gilmore. *Defying Dixie: The Radical Roots of Civil Rights, 1919–1950*. New York: W. W. Norton, 2008.

Kenneth W. Goings. *"The NAACP Comes of Age": The Defeat of Judge John J. Parker*. Bloomington: Indiana University Press, 1990.

Charles V. Hamilton. *Adam Clayton Powell, Jr., the Political Biography of an American Dilemma*. New York: Atheneum, 1991.

Darlene Clark Hine. *Black Victory: The Rise and Fall of the White Primary in Texas*. New edition with essays by Darlene Clark Hine, Steven F. Lawson, and Merline Pitre. Columbia: University of Missouri Press, 2003.

Christopher R. Reed. *The Chicago NAACP and the Rise of Black Professional Leadership, 1910–1966*. Bloomington: Indiana University Press, 1997.

Christopher R. Reed. *The Depression Comes to the South Side: Protest and Politics in the Black Metropolis, 1930–1933*. Bloomington, Indiana University Press, 2011.

Patricia Sullivan. *Days of Hope: Race and Democracy in the New Deal Era*. Chapel Hill: University of North Carolina Press, 1996.

Patricia Sullivan. *Lift Every Voice: The NAACP and the Making of the Civil Rights Movement*. New York: New Press, 2009.

Mark V. Tushnet. *The NAACP's Legal Strategy Against Segregated Education, 1925–1950*. Chapel Hill: University of North Carolina Press, 1987.

Nancy J. Weiss. *Farewell to the Party of Lincoln: Black Politics in the Age of FDR*. Princeton, NJ: Princeton University Press, 1983.

LABOR

Lizabeth Cohen. *Making a New Deal: Industrial Workers in Chicago, 1919–1939*. New York: Cambridge University Press, 1990.

Olen Cole, Jr. *The African-American Experience in the Civilian Conservation Corps*. Gainesville: University Press of Florida, 1999.

Dennis C. Dickerson. *Out of the Crucible: Black Steelworkers in Western Pennsylvania, 1875–1980*. Albany: State University of New York Press, 1986.

August Meier and Elliott Rudwick. *Black Detroit and the Rise of the UAW*. New York: Oxford University Press, 1979.

EDUCATION

Badia Sahar Ahad. *Freud Upside Down: African American Literature and Psychoanalytic Culture*. Urbana: University of Illinois Press, 2010.

Derrick P. Alridge. *The Educational Thought of W.E.B. Du Bois: An Intellectual History*. New York: Teachers College Press, 2008.

James D. Anderson. *The Education of Blacks in the South, 1860–1935*. Chapel Hill: University of North Carolina Press, 1988.

Pero Gaglo Dagbovie. *The Early Black History Movement, Carter G. Woodson and Lorenzo Johnston Greene*. Urbana: University of Illinois Press, 2007.

Richard Kluger. *Simple Justice: The History of* Brown v. Board of Education *and Black America's Struggle for Equality.* New York: Random House, 1976. New rev. ed., 2004.

Kenneth W. Mack. *Representing the Race: The Creation of the Civil Rights Lawyer.* Cambridge, Harvard University Press, 2012.

Thomas J. Ward, Jr. *Black Physicians in the Jim Crow South.* Fayetteville: University of Arkansas Press, 2003.

Zachery R. Williams. *In Search of the Talented Tenth: Howard University Public Intellectuals and the Dilemmas of Race, 1926–1970.* Columbia: University of Missouri Press, 2009.

Francille Rusan Wilson. *The Segregated Scholars: Black Social Scientists and the Creation of Black Labor Studies, 1890–1950.* Charlottesville: University of Virginia Press, 2006.

BLACK RADICALISM

Ramla M. Bandele. *Black Star: African American Activism in the International Political Economy.* Urbana: University of Illinois Press, 2008.

Dan Carter. *Scottsboro: A Tragedy of the American South.* Baton Rouge: Louisiana State University Press, 1969.

Vanessa Northington Gamble. *Making a Place for Ourselves: The Black Hospital Movement, 1920–1945.* New York: Oxford University Press, 1995.

Michael K. Honey. *Southern Labor and Black Civil Rights: Organizing Memphis Workers.* Urbana: University of Illinois Press, 1993.

Jacqueline Jones. *Labor of Love, Labor of Sorrow: Black Women, Work, and the Family From Slavery to the Present.* New York: Basic Books, 1985.

Nicholas Natanson. *The Black Image in the New Deal: The Politics of FSA Photography.* Knoxville: University of Tennessee Press, 1992.

Christopher R. Reed. *The Chicago NAACP and the Rise of Black Professional Leadership, 1910–1966.* Bloomington: Indiana University Press, 1997.

Meredith L. Roman. *Opposing Jim Crow: African Americans and the Soviet Indictment of U.S. Racism, 1928–1937.* Lincoln: University of Nebraska Press, 2012.

Daryl Michael Scott. *Contempt and Pity: Social Policy and the Image of the Damaged Black Psyche, 1880–1996.* Chapel Hill: University of North Carolina Press, 1997.

Mark Solomon. *The Cry Was Unity: Communists and African Americans, 1917–1936.* Jackson: University Press of Mississippi, 1998.

Richard W. Thomas. *Life for Us Is What We Make It: Building Black Community in Detroit, 1915–1945.* Bloomington: Indiana University Press, 1992.

ECONOMICS

Charles T. Banner-Haley. *To Do Good and to Do Well: Middle Class Blacks and the Depression, Philadelphia, 1929–1941.* New York: Garland, 1993.

Alexa Benson Henderson. *Atlanta Life Insurance Company: Guardian of Black Economic Dignity.* Tuscaloosa: University of Alabama Press, 1990.

Robert E. Weems, Jr. *Black Business in the Black Metropolis: The Chicago Metropolitan Assurance Company, 1924–1985.* Bloomington: Indiana University Press, 1996.

BIOGRAPHY AND AUTOBIOGRAPHY

Felix L. Armfield. *Eugene Kinckle Jones: The National Urban League and Black Social Work, 1910–1940.* Urbana: University of Illinois Press, 2012.

Andrew Buni. *Robert L. Vann of the Pittsburgh Courier.* Pittsburgh, PA: University of Pittsburgh Press, 1974.

Cornelius L. Bynum. *A. Philip Randolph and the Struggle for Civil Rights.* Urbana: University of Illinois Press, 2010.

Henry Louis Gates, Jr., and Evelyn Brooks Higginbotham, eds. *African American Lives.* New York: Oxford University Press, 2004.

Joyce A. Hanson. *Mary McLeod Bethune and Black Women's Political Activism.* Columbia: University of Missouri Press, 2003.

Randal Maurice Jelks. *Benjamin Elijah Mays, Schoolmaster of the Movement: A Biography.* Chapel Hill: The University of North Carolina Press, 2012.

Spencie Love. *One Blood: The Death and Resurrection of Charles R. Drew.* Chapel Hill: University of North Carolina Press, 1996.

Jacqueline A. McLeod. *Daughter of the Empire State: The Life of Judge Jane Bolin.* Urbana: University of Illinois Press, 2012.

Genna Rae McNeil. *Groundwork: Charles Hamilton Houston and the Struggle for Civil Rights.* Philadelphia: University of Pennsylvania Press, 1983.

Jeffrey B. Perry, ed. *The Hubert Harrison Reader.* Middletown, CT: Wesleyan University Press, 2001.

Barbara Ransby. *Ella Baker and the Black Freedom Movement.* Chapel Hill: University of North Carolina Press, 2003.

John Herbert Roper, Sr. *The Magnificent Mays: A Biography of Benjamin Elijah Mays.* Columbia: University of South Carolina Press, 2012.

Mark V. Tushnet. *Making Civil Rights Law: Thurgood Marshall and the Supreme Court, 1935–1961.* New York: Knopf, 1994.

Gilbert Ware. *William Hastie: Grace Under Pressure.* New York: Oxford University Press, 1984.

Oscar R. Williams. *George S. Schuyler: Portrait of a Black Conservative.* Knoxville: University of Tennessee Press, 2007.

Roy Wilkins with Tom Mathews. *Standing Fast: The Autobiography of Roy Wilkins.* New York: Da Capo Press, 1994.

BLACK INTERNATIONALISM

Carol Anderson. *Eyes Off the Prize: The United Nations and the African American Struggle for Human Rights, 1944–1955.* Cambridge: Cambridge University Press, 2003.

Kate A. Baldwin. *Beyond the Color Line and the Iron Curtain: Reading Encounters Between Black and Red, 1922–1963.* Durham, NC: Duke University Press, 2002.

Douglas A. Blackmon. *Slavery by Another Name: The Reenslavement of Black Americans from the Civil War to World War II.* New York: Doubleday, 2008.

Tina Campt. *Other Germans: Black Germans and the Politics of Race, Gender, and Memory in the Third Reich*. Ann Arbor: University of Michigan Press, 2003.

Joy Gleason Carew. *Blacks, Reds, and Russians: Sojourners in Search of the Soviet Promise*. New Brunswick, NJ: Rutgers University Press, 2008.

Carole Boyce Davies. *Left of Karl Marx: The Political Life of Black Communist Claudia Jones*. Durham, NC: Duke University Press, 2008.

Mary L. Dudziak. *Cold War Civil Rights: Race and the Image of American Democracy*. Princeton, NJ: Princeton University Press, 2006.

Brent Hayes Edwards. *The Practice of Diaspora: Literature, Translation, and the Rise of Black Internationalism*. Cambridge, MA: Harvard University Press, 2003.

Lashawn Harris. "Running with the Reds: African American Women and the Communist Party During the Great Depression," *Journal of African American History* 94, no. 1 (Winter 2009): 21–43.

Cheryl Higashida. *Black Internationalist Feminism: Women Writers of the Black Left, 1945–1995*. Urbana: University of Illinois Press, 2011.

Clarence Lusane. *Hitler's Black Victims: The Historical Experiences of Afro-Germans, European Black, Africans, and African Americans in the Nazi Era*. New York: Routledge, 2002.

Minkah Makalani. *In the Cause of Freedom: Radical Black Internationalism from Harlem to London, 1917–1939*. Chapel Hill: University of North Carolina Press, 2012.

Erik S. McDuffie. *Sojourning for Freedom: Black Women, American Communism, and the Making of Left Feminism*. Durham, NC: Duke University Press, 2011.

Susan Pennybacker. *From Scottsboro to Munich: Race and Political Culture in 1930*. Princeton, NJ: Princeton University Press, 2009.

Brenda Gayle Plummer. *Rising Wind: Black Americans and U.S. Foreign Affairs, 1935–1960*. Chapel Hill, NC: University of North Carolina Press, 1996.

Cedric J. Robinson. *Black Marxism: The Making of the Black Radical Tradition*. 1983; Reprint, Chapel Hill, NC: University of North Carolina Press, 2000.

Jonathan Rosenberg. *How Far the Promised Land: World Affairs and the African American Civil Rights Movement from the First World War to Vietnam*. Princeton, NJ: Princeton University Press, 2006.

Randi Storch. *Red Chicago: American Communism at its Grassroots, 1928–1935*. Urbana: University of Illinois Press, 2007.

Tyler Stovall. "The Color Line Behind the Lines: Racial Violence in France During the Great War." *American Historical Review* 103, no. 3 (June 1998): 737–69.

Penny Von Eschen. *Race Against Empire: Black Americans and Anticolonalism, 1937–1957*. Ithaca: Cornell University Press, 1997.

Victoria W. Wolcott. *Remaking Respectability: African American Women in Interwar Detroit*. Chapel Hill: University of North Carolina Press, 2001.

Jeff Woods. *Black Struggles, Red Scare: Segregation and Anti-Communism in the South, 1948–1968*. Baton Rouge: Louisiana State University Press, 2004.

RETRACING THE ODYSSEY

Apollo Theater, New York City. When other venues were closed to African Americans, many talented men and women destined to become top performers in twentieth-century America launched their careers at the Apollo Theater. Since the 1930s, performers such as Duke Ellington, Count Basie, Charlie Parker, Bessie Smith, Billie Holiday, and Ella Fitzgerald have graced the Apollo stage. Renowned comedians such as Bill Cosby, Richard Pryor, and Redd Foxx honed their talents here, as well as numerous others.

The Mary McLeod Bethune Council House, Washington, DC. Mary McLeod Bethune, born in 1875 in Mayesville, South Carolina, was one of the most politically engaged black women in the first half of the twentieth century. She was the president of Bethune-Cookman College in Daytona Beach, Florida, when President Franklin Delano Roosevelt appointed her director of Negro affairs of the National Youth Council. An ardent black clubwoman, Bethune is celebrated as the founder, in 1935, and first president of the National Council of Negro Women (NCNW). It remains a significant umbrella group for organizations of black women. The Bethune Museum and Archive Center was her home and headquarters of the NCNW from 1943 to 1966. It contains exhibits and sponsors programs that emphasize the contributions of African-American women to American society. The archive contains important manuscript collections and other research materials pertaining to the NCNW and to black women's history.

Charles H. Wright Museum of African-American History, Detroit, Michigan. This is the largest African-American history museum in America. It sponsors a variety of educational programs throughout the year.

19

Meanings of Freedom: Culture and Society in the 1930s, 1940s, and 1950s

((•)) Listen to Chapter 19 on MyHistoryLab

He would not Africanize America, for America has too much to teach the world and Africa. He would not bleach his Negro soul in a flood of white Americanism, for he knows that Negro blood has a message for the world. He simply wished to make it possible for a man to be both a Negro and an American, without being cursed and spit upon by his fellows, without having the doors of opportunity closed roughly in his face. This, then, is the end of his striving: to be a co-worker in the kingdom of culture, to escape both death and isolation, to husband and use his best powers and his latent genius.

W. E. B. Du Bois, The Souls of Black Folk: Essay and Sketches

W. E. B. Du Bois commented often on the gifts black people had given to America. Even before he wrote the passage that opens this chapter, Du Bois had proclaimed, "We are the first fruits of this new nation. . . . We are the people whose subtle sense of song has given America its only American music, its only American fairy tales, its only touch of pathos and humor amid its money-getting plutocracy." African-American "destiny is not a servile imitation of Anglo-Saxon culture, but a stalwart originality which shall unswervingly follow Negro ideals."

A key theme in black life from the 1930s to the early 1950s was the many strategies African Americans devised to protest second-class citizenship, resist negative racial stereotypes, and end white entrepreneurs' appropriation of black culture. At heart, black cultural workers and creative artists sought to shape the representation of black people

LEARNING OBJECTIVES

How did black institutions support classical music in St. Louis in the 1930s and 1940s?	19-1
How did African Americans merge a distinct aesthetic with a demand for social justice?	19-2
How did swing, big band, and bebop music develop and why were they important for blacks?	19-3
What was the role and presentation of blacks in comic strips, movies, and radio?	19-4
What were the characteristics, developments, artists, and authors of the Chicago Renaissance?	19-5
How did black graphic artists of the 1930s fuse politics and art in their work?	19-6
What were the themes and impact of the work of Richard Wright and Ralph Ellison?	19-7
How did sports figures contribute to black culture?	19-8
What were the alternative religious movements and how did they help African Americans?	19-9

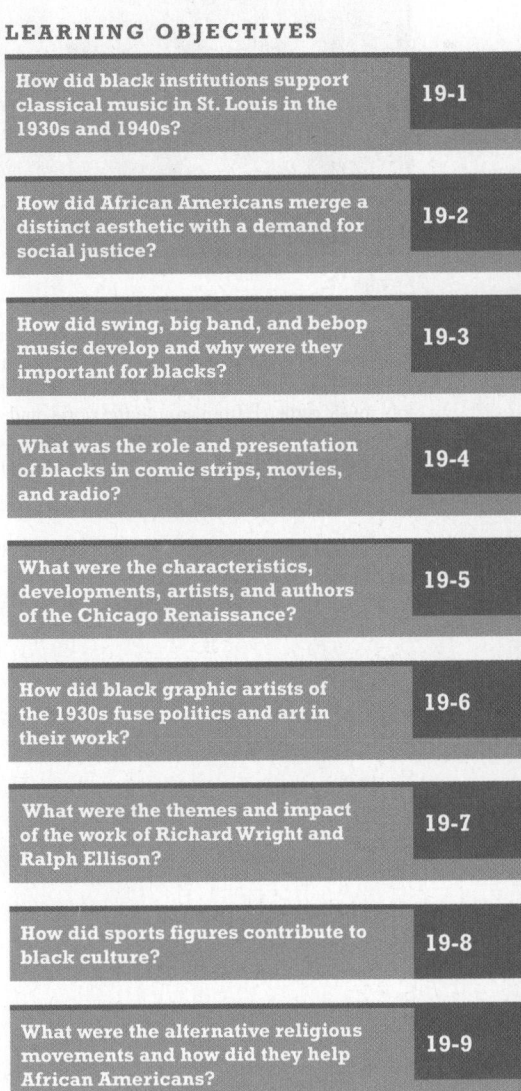

Pitching great Leroy Satchel Paige warms up at New York's Yankee Stadium in 1942.

Singer and actor Paul Robeson (1898–1976) as "Othello" in 1943. A man of astonishing magnetism and creative power, Paul Robeson became, in 1943, the first black actor to play "Othello" in the United States. He was fluent in many languages, produced over 300 recordings of spiritual and folk music gathered from around the world, and appeared in 11 motion pictures. An unflinching proponent of freedom from racism and want, Robeson received the NAACP's Spingarn Medal in 1945.

in American society and to sustain a viable black culture for a rapidly urbanizing people. A central issue in this chapter is the extent to which black culture from the 1930s to the 1950s became a source of strength—cultural power—that helped African Americans define and assert themselves within American society.

Cultural power allowed African Americans to craft positive images of black people that challenged negative distortions and helped to build community. The new black cultural power had to fight the well-worn stereotypes of the dumb and lazy black man, the selfless mammy, and the promiscuous dark Venus. As we have seen throughout this book, black people were disfranchised and socially and economically marginalized. But in the arts, black people drove a small wedge into the wall of racial segregation and discrimination. In literature and the visual and performing arts, talented African Americans, such as singer and actor Paul Robeson, who starred in Shakespeare's *Othello* on Broadway in 1930, novelist Richard Wright, and expatriate singer and dancer Josephine Baker, compelled the attention of white Americans. The 1930s, 1940s, and 1950s—when most black people were suffering from the lingering effects of the Depression and the entrenched Jim Crow regime—were a fertile period in the history of black expressive culture.

Black Culture in a Midwestern City

19-1 How did black institutions support classical music in St. Louis in the 1930s and 1940s?

Beginning in the 1930s, a second wave of black migrants made St. Louis the fifth largest city in the United States. Yet, because of segregation and discrimination, the city's black community developed institutions to address its own educational and cultural needs. Attention has usually focused on St. Louis's contributions to popular culture, but classical music also commanded considerable interest in the city. Black residents struggled to secure training in this genre of music and for opportunities to perform it. Langston Hughes's words recall the possibilities and excitement that life in a midwestern city held for black people:

> St. Louis! The town where Scott Joplin and Tom
> Turpin used to play ragtime. The town that
> W. C. Handy made famous in his great song,
> "The St. Louis Blues." The town where Josephine
> Baker started out as a $15.00 a week waitress, and end[ed] up in Paris as one of the most
> glamorous stars of the international theater. St. Louis, the town that gave a laugh-hungry
> world the joy of E. Simms Campbell and his rib-tickling cartoons of Esquire and King
> Features fame. The town where the riverboats used to run from New Orleans with Louis
> Armstrong's horn blasting the night away.

St. Louis is in the heart of a region often considered remote from the nation's cultural centers. Yet it has produced outstanding black jazz musicians. But not all black musicians wanted to play ragtime and jazz, and many of them resented being relegated to these forms.

A closer look at black support for classical music in St. Louis during the 1930s and 1940s reveals the diversity of black life—even though white St. Louisianians marginalized or ignored the contributions of black artists.

Schools, churches, labor, and media within the St. Louis black community had to create opportunities for black children to study, appreciate, and perform classical music. The two largest black newspapers, the *St. Louis Argus* and the *St. Louis American*, publicized recitals and concerts. Two all-black institutions supported classical music education: Lincoln University in Jefferson City (founded in 1866 as a school created by and for black Civil War veterans and their families) and Sumner High School (founded in 1875 as the first secondary school for black people west of the Mississippi).

By the 1940s Lincoln University had become the institution for training St. Louis musicians, and its music instructors were active in the black cultural affairs. Sumner High School had orchestras, bands, choirs, and glee clubs. Many of its music teachers possessed advanced degrees from prestigious music departments. The most influential teacher was Kenneth Billups, an arranger, composer, and founding director of the Legend Singers, a black professional chorus.

The Legend Singers appeared with the St. Louis Symphony and the Municipal Opera Company (MUNY) in productions of *Show Boat*, where they dressed in demeaning slave costumes. Billups's response to criticism of these appearances indirectly addressed the dilemma of black artists in a racially restrictive environment:

> I've seen situations where I felt inwardly . . . I might have had to do some things; for example, let's take this Showboat thing at MUNY Opera. There is the need of a black chorus to go there, and I had the privilege of doing that with my Legend Singers, simply because one of the first requirements was to have a black chorus.

Black churches, including Antioch Baptist, Central Baptist, and Berea Presbyterian, sponsored religious programs highlighting the works of both black and white composers. Local 197 of the American Federation of Musicians and the St. Louis Music Association, which was the local branch of the National Association of Negro Musicians, promoted black performing organizations and training. These groups sponsored musical organizations and paid for scholarships and summer choirs for boys and girls.

The Black Culture Industry and American Racism

19-2 **How did African Americans merge a distinct aesthetic with a demand for social justice?**

Black American artists had to confront discrimination and exploitation in the culture industry. They could rarely afford to produce and disseminate their work. This power often resided in the hands of record companies, publishers, and the owners of radio stations and film studios. Yet black artists in the 1930s and 1940s shaped an emerging consciousness that would erupt in the 1950s and propel a modern movement for civil rights and social justice. Paul Robeson not only won acclaim as a great performing artist, but he became a leading black internationalist and outspoken critic of colonialism and racism. Robeson became friends with African freedom fighters such as Kwame Nkrumah in Ghana, Jomo Kenyatta in Kenya, and Dr. Nnamdi Azikiwe of Nigeria. In 1945, the NAACP awarded him its prestigious Spingarn Medal. The U.S. State Department, however, revoked Robeson's passport in 1950 because of his support for radical social and economic reform and his practice of black internationalism.

The political content of black art provoked heated debates among black artists. Many black Americans insisted that music, the visual and performing arts, literature, and oratory serve both a political function and an aesthetic purpose. They expected black artists not only

19-1
19-2
19-3
19-4
19-5
19-6
19-7
19-8
19-9

to create beauty but also to use their art to promote freedom across the black diaspora and to forge cultural and political linkages. African-American artists and intellectuals joined with people of African descent throughout the Diaspora to support Ethiopian resistance to Italian aggression in 1935. Still, the disparate reasons for white involvement in the marketing and use of black culture created tension among black artists. Although many white Americans had long appreciated black culture, some had also appropriated it for their own profit.

During the late 1930s and 1940s, corporate America recognized the money that could be made from producing and marketing black culture. But black artists had to be made "acceptable" if they were to be successfully marketed to affluent white consumers. These artists had to compromise, mask, and subordinate their true feelings and expressiveness to earn income from their work. Artists who exhibited the right combination of showmanship, charm, and talent could reap some of the financial rewards their creativity generated. The paradox of the black performer—using your art to entertain your oppressor—was most apparent in music.

The Music Culture from Swing to Bebop

19-3   How did swing, big band, and bebop music develop and why were they important for blacks?

Ironically, the very creativity that white Americans valued and often appropriated depended on the artists' ability to preserve some intellectual and emotional autonomy. Black artists had to juxtapose the requirements of earning a living with the need to remain true to their art. Black musicians continuously had to refine, expand, and perfect their art not only for themselves and each other but also for a white-dominated marketplace. In many respects black music is synonymous with black culture; the experience of segregation or self-imposed separation often made possible the creation of new cultural expressions. Music encapsulates and reflects the core values and underlying tensions and anxieties in black communities. In black music we witness cultural producers developing strategies of resistance to white domination.

The Great Depression wrought havoc on the vibrant black culture industry of the 1920s. Record sales in 1932 were only a sixth of those in 1927. Black musicians like Louis Armstrong had enjoyed a golden age of creativity during the 1920s. The record companies had their separate black music labels and sold thousands of records to southern migrants moving to the big cities. New bands sprouted up from Kansas City to Chicago; Memphis to Detroit; and Washington, DC, to New York. Los Angeles, San Francisco, and Seattle had their own black music enthusiasts and performers. The territorial (traveling) bands took the music to the outposts of black America, and the big bands under Fletcher Henderson, Duke Ellington, Count Basie, and Cab Calloway played in white urban dance halls and ballrooms that admitted black people only as staff or entertainers.

New York was where black musicians felt they had to go to prove themselves. After entertaining affluent white people or providing backup music for the Apollo Theater in Harlem, black musicians discarded their masks of docility and deference and made a different sound in their own space and on their own time in late-night jam sessions. In Harlem's small clubs, such as Monroe's Uptown House and Minton's Playhouse a few blocks from the Apollo, a new kind of jazz was born.

The big band swing style that became popular in the 1930s transformed white American culture. Swing emerged as white bands reduced the music of the more innovative black bandleaders to a broadly appealing formula based on a swinging 4/4 beat, well-blended saxophone sections, and pleasant vocals. The big swing bands of the 1930s played written, arranged music. Swing's popularity helped boost the careers of black and white bandleaders, but it also led to a creative slump that disheartened many younger black musicians. Tired of swing's predictability, they began improvising in the jazz clubs, sharpening their reflexes, ears, and minds.

PROFILE Charlie Parker

CHARLIE PARKER WAS ONE OF THE most innovative and influential of all American musicians. With his inspired saxophone playing, his technical mastery of his instrument, and his melodic, rhythmic, and harmonic innovations, he was an architect of modern jazz, or "bebop." His playing challenged his contemporaries, influenced generations of jazz musicians, and helped transform jazz from entertainment into one of America's most respected art forms. But Parker was also troubled by drug addiction, mental instability, and tumultuous relationships.

Charles Parker Jr. was born on August 29, 1920, in Kansas City, Kansas. In 1927 his family moved across the state line to Kansas City, Missouri. He had little formal musical instruction. But Kansas City had a dynamic jazz scene. Pianist and composer Mary Lou Williams remembered the freewheeling atmosphere: "Now, at this time, which was still Prohibition . . . [m]ost of the night spots were run by politicians and hoodlums, and the town was wide open for drinking, gambling, and pretty much every form of vice. Naturally, work was plentiful for musicians though some of the employers were tough people." Young Parker became a fixture in the local clubs, where he also acquired a heroin habit that plagued him for the rest of his life.

In 1939, Parker left Kansas City for New York, then the jazz capital of the country. There Parker began to sit in, or "jam," at Harlem nightclubs. In 1942 he was back in Kansas City playing in Jay McShann's popular "territory band," which traveled from Lincoln, Nebraska, to New Orleans. During this time he acquired the nickname "Bird."

Parker left the McShann band in 1942 to join pianist Earl Hines's band in New York. In March and April 1943, all the following musicians were in the band with Parker: "Little" Benny Harris, Bennie Green, Wardell Gray, and vocalists Billy Eckstine and Sarah Vaughan. This collection of talent reflected a musical environment that fostered innovation. New ideas spread from musician to musician and in late-night jam sessions. It was from the close collaboration between Parker and Dizzy Gillespie in this period that bebop emerged.

Charlie Parker joined the first bebop big band, formed by Billy Eckstine in 1944. Eckstine's friend and valet, Bob Redcross, remembers a night that year when the band was at its best: "Everybody was on. [Art] Blakey was on; John [Gillespie] was on; Bird was on; Bidd [Johnson] was on; everybody. Man, they upset this place. They had people screaming and hollering."

In 1944 a recording of Parker's composition, "Red Cross," the first to be copyrighted in his name, was released on the Savoy label.

Parker and Gillespie first recorded together commercially in 1945. Gillespie formed his first bebop big band and took it on a tour of the South as part of the "Hepsations-1945" package tour. Also in 1945, Parker led an expanded group at the Spotlite club that included trumpeter Miles Davis, tenor saxophonist Dexter Gordon, bassist Leonard Gaskin, and drummer Stan Levey. During a disastrous trip to California, Parker had a nervous breakdown and spent months at Camarillo State Hospital.

In 1947, when Parker returned to New York, he formed his "classic" quintet, with trumpeter Miles Davis, drummer Max Roach, pianist Duke Jordan, and Tommy Potter on bass. The recordings this quintet produced, four sides on the Savoy label, are the foundation on which much of Parker's reputation rests.

In 1949, in a fitting tribute to Parker's genius by his contemporaries, a New York nightclub, Birdland, was named for him. Charlie Parker died in New York on March 12, 1955.

In the 1940s at least seven musicians—Charlie Parker, Dizzy Gillespie, Thelonious Monk, Bud Powell, Kenny Clarke, Max Roach, and Ray Brown—were among the men most responsible for revolutionizing jazz, ushering in a new sound and dimension that became known, scornfully at first, as *bebop*. Bebop featured complex rhythms and harmonies and highlighted improvisation. Gillespie (1917–1993) said that Kansas City–born Charlie "Yardbird" and then just "Bird" Parker (1920–1955) was "the architect of the style. Yard and I were so close, so wrapped up in one another, that he would think 'three,' and I would say 'four,' and I would say 'seven,' and he'd say 'eight.' . . . It wasn't difficult for us, really together, sometimes it sounded like one horn playing, and sometimes it was one horn, but sometimes it was both of us sounding like one horn."

White America resisted bebop. The nation was about to enter World War II and was too preoccupied to switch from the big band swing ballroom dancing music to bebop. Moreover, because jazzmen played in small, intimate clubs too small for big bands, they had more freedom from the expectations of white society. Bebop music was of such enduring quality, however, that it shaped American popular culture and style for two generations. Before long, bebop became the principal musical language of jazz musicians around the world.

Bebop was a way of life and had its own attendant styles whose nuances depended on class status and, perhaps, age. Gillespie helped create one side of bebop style in dress, language, and demeanor. He began to wear dark glasses on stage to reduce the glare after he had cataract surgery. He grew a goatee because shaving irritated his bottom lip. He wore pegged pants, jackets with wide lapels, and a beret when men were still wearing hats with brims. Other bebop musicians emulated and modified this attire. For example, they wore cashmere jackets without lapels. Beboppers also created their own slang, hip Black English that mingled colorful and obscene language. They also engaged in a freewheeling lifestyle that often included love across the color line. But there was a downside to bebop. Some musicians became drug addicts, engaged in parasitical relationships with women, and spent their money recklessly.

Black working-class young men adopted their own style of talking and hip dressing, reflected in their zoot suits and conked hair. Zoot suits featured high-waisted, baggy, pegged pants and long draped coats. A 16-year-old Malcolm Little (who later took the name Malcolm X) plunged into hipster culture when he moved to Boston. His first zoot suit was sky blue with a matching hat, gold watch chain, and monogrammed belt. To savor this new identity, he recalled, "I took three of those twenty-five cent sepia-toned, while-you-wait pictures of myself, posed the way 'hipsters' wearing their zoots would 'cool it'—hat dangled, knees drawn close together, feet wide apart, both index fingers jabbed toward the floor." He then mastered the lindy hop dance style and took to the floor of the Roseland Ballroom, where he shed his life as an unskilled wageworker and became freer and more empowered. He recalled the ballroom's patrons' escape from their dreary lives: "They'd jam pack that ballroom, the black girls in way out silk and satin dresses and shoes, their hair done in all kinds of styles, the men sharp in their zoot suits and crazy conks, and everybody grinning and greased and gassed."

Bebop was the dominant black music of the war decade, but after 1945 returning veterans preferred a slower-paced music, simple love songs, and melodies. This contributed to bebop's waning and led to more transformations. All artistic innovation extracts a high price. Bebop was no exception. Many of the most talented musicians—like Billie Holiday, discussed later in this chapter—paid that price in lives decimated by drugs, poverty, sickness, and broken relationships. Few black musicians received the respect, recognition, and financial rewards from white America that their creativity warranted. Ultimately, white Americans wanted the art but not the artists.

Popular Culture for the Masses: Comic Strips, Radio, and Movies

19-4 What was the role and presentation of blacks in comic strips, movies, and radio?

The masses of African Americans participated in more accessible black popular culture outlets. Everyone needed relief from the bleakness and despair of the Depression years. Comic strips, radio programs, and movies were affordable forms of artistic creativity that allowed momentary escape. Newspapers were widely shared, and families gathered around the radio for nightly programs of comedy and music. For black city dwellers, the movies offered escape from poverty and want.

The Comics

African Americans quickly noted the difference between the fun that black people made of each other and the mockery white people made of them. These differences were reflected in tone, intent, and sympathetic versus derisive laughter. During the Depression, comic strips in newspapers and comic books featuring superheroes diverted millions of Americans. Comic strips in black newspapers entertained but also affirmed the values and ideals of black people. They portrayed humorous situations and tales of intrigue and action.

The *Philadelphia Independent*, a black paper, ran a serial in the 1930s called "The Jones Family." This strip, drawn by an editorial cartoonist named Branford, was an example of the dual function of entertaining and affirming. The strip centered on the young Jones boy's search for the "good life" of money, success, love, and a happy marriage. But at every turn he confronts a harsh reality. Unable to get a job because of the Depression, he becomes an outlaw and narrowly escapes jail. Constantly "on the run" from oppression, his only consolations are his family and his beautiful, ever-faithful girlfriend.

"The Jones Family" illuminates the gray areas that most African Americans, regardless of their class, faced when attempting to live rational, coherent lives in the northern cities. Although they cherished middle-class values, they often had to live with poverty, crime, and racial oppression. The black comic strips sought to provide entertaining, nonjudgmental prescriptions and blueprints for middle-class life, but to more cynical and alienated black people they seemed to be promoting unattainable values and lifestyles.

Radio and Jazz Musicians and Technological Change

Although there were individual exceptions, African-American jazz musicians embraced the commercial and technological developments that revolutionized the music industry in the 1920s. The phonograph allowed for wide distribution of the music they created, just as the recording studios served as incubators for their creative innovations. By the end of the 1920s, black musicians had embraced electrical recording, and in the 1930s they learned to appreciate microphone amplification—a product of radio technology—which allowed for the dominating rhythmic pulse of electric guitars and bases that would radically change black popular music. By the 1930s jazz musicians were making records that replicated live performances more closely than ever before. Radio and improved record making helped spread black music and ensured its survival.

During the 1930s black musicians, including Duke Ellington, Fats Waller, and Art Tatum, starred in regular radio programs. Many black musicians acquired their first lucrative jobs in radio as full-time staff musicians. Some earned higher salaries than writers, announcers, and white performers. Black musicians succeeded in the radio medium because they were heard and not visible. It was the mastery of their instruments that won audience approval. Perhaps most important, black radio staff musicians could communicate to larger audiences than those who played in clubs and on the traveling circuits. Thus, they enhanced the appeal of their music for a much wider audience.

Radio and Black Disc Jockeys

Chicago was a pioneering center both for recording and performing music. As black music became a commodity, influential black disc jockeys like Al Benson (Arthur B. Leaner was his real name) appeared on the radio and attracted a large following in "Bronzeville." Benson, a migrant from Mississippi, was as skilled a businessman as he was a cultural impresario. He attracted followers drawn by his "black everyman's style." By 1948, he was hosting shows on three radio stations. Readers of the *Defender* voted him the "Mayor of Bronzeville." A determined entrepreneur, Benson arranged "first play rights" with record producers and distributors, catapulting Chicago into a major launch site for new releases. Diverse artists, including bluesman Muddy Waters and gospel singer Mahalia Jackson, benefited from the airplay. Historian Adam Green concludes that because of the power and machinations of black disc jockeys, "black popular music would never again face the disastrous conditions of destitution and near-erasure it faced during the depression."

In the post-Depression and pre-modern Civil Rights era, black disc jockeys played the blues, gospel, and jazz and attracted listeners with their sharp banter and fast, smooth-talking style. The number of black disc jockeys rose from 16 in 1946 to over 500 by 1955. They used their radio shows not only to entertain and to sell records but also to promote the careers of black musicians. As awareness of the buying power of black consumers sank in, both white- and black-owned businesses eagerly sponsored black-appeal radio programs. Black radio stations thus became platforms for independent black music and were essential to the building of black community businesses. Black radio communicated the news, shared announcements, and molded urban black consciousness. Following Benson's lead, a young apprentice, Don Cornelius, would, decades later, launch a legendary music and dance show, "Soul Train," on WCIU-TV (August 17, 1970) in Chicago. Cornelius explained how his start in radio inspired him: "It was with the advent of black radio that I thought black people would watch music television programs oriented toward themselves." "Soul Train" success-fully combined images of blackness with technical proficiency and production control by black people in the white-dominated entertainment industry.

Radio and Race

During the Depression, black actors in radio and film were frequently marginalized, exploited, or excluded. Commercial radio delivered an audience of white consumers to white advertisers, and it denied black people jobs as announcers, journalists, or technicians. White entertainers schooled in blackface minstrelsy portrayed black radio characters. The major labor unions in the entertainment side of the radio industry restricted membership to white people. Still—with its offerings of vaudeville, big bands, drama, and comedy—radio provided relief from the miseries of the Depression to all Americans, black as well as white.

The most popular comedy radio program in the early 1930s—a precursor to the soap operas and sitcoms that were to become staples of radio and television programming—was *The Amos 'n' Andy Show*. The inauguration of this program was a significant moment in radio history. Two white performers, Charles Correll and Freeman Gosden, not only wrote and performed scripts laced with oxymorons and malapropisms but also played the title roles. Skillful showmen, Correll and Gosden ingratiated themselves in Chicago's black community, appearing at parades and posing with black children. The *Chicago Defender* endorsed them, and they received standing ovations at the Regal Theater in Chicago's black South Side. Part of the amusement they generated derived from their mispronounced words, garbled grammar, and their show's minstrel ambience. Each episode highlighted an im-probable situation involving the black cab driver (Amos) and his gullible overweight friend (Andy). Other characters included the scheming con artist Kingfish, his overbearing wife Sapphire, and his domineering mother-in-law, Mama. On radio, Gosden and Correll fur-nished voices for the members of Amos and Andy's fraternal lodge and for an array of other characters. The characters and their humor reinforced unflattering racial and gender ste-reotypes, but the show was not mean-spirited. Some of the characters conducted themselves with dignity, modeling such positive values as marital fidelity, strong families, hard work, and economic independence. An *Amos 'n' Andy* movie, *Check and Double Check*—released in 1930 when hard times made black entertainers grateful for any employment they could get—featured music by Duke Ellington's orchestra. The movie introduced Ellington to a wider audience of affluent white people and enhanced his reputation.

Black audiences recognized the minstrel stereotyping in *Amos 'n' Andy*, yet many of them still enjoyed the show. A vocal component of the ever more sophisticated and urbanized black population, however, complained that this show and other radio programs reinforced negative images—of black women as bossy Sapphires or Mammies and black men as childish clowns—in the nation's consciousness. Educator and activist Nannie Helen Burroughs considered the show demeaning. Robert L. Vann, editor of the *Pittsburgh Courier*, argued that it exploited African Americans for white commercial gain. Vann sponsored a petition to the Federal Communications Commission to ban the show, but his efforts were futile. By the 1940s, *The Amos 'n' Andy Show* was less popular. In the early 1950s, it had a brief life as a television series, this time with black actors. Alvin Childress, an experienced stage actor and director, became Amos, and Spencer Williams, Jr., who had written, directed, and starred in several independent all-black movies, played Andy. Tim Moore assumed the role of the Kingfish of the Mystic Knights of the Sea Lodge. Johnny Lee portrayed the shyster lawyer, Algonquin J. Calhoun.

The show never demonstrated how the characters' race affected their lives or the psychological or economic costs of racism. It taught white America to laugh at striving black men and women. The best-known and most successful African-American actor on network radio in the late 1930s was Eddie Anderson, who played Jack Benny's sidekick Rochester in NBC's *The Jack Benny Show*. Like the characters in *Amos 'n' Andy*, Rochester reinforced negative racial stereotypes. Anderson's rationalization of his role suggests his discomfort with it:

> I don't see why certain characters are called stereotypes. The Negro characters being presented are not labeling the Negro race any more than "Luigi" is labeling the Italian people as a whole. The same goes for "Beulah," who is not playing the part of thousands of Negroes, but only the part of one person, "Beulah." They're not saying here is the portrait of the Negro, but here is "Beulah."

Radio and *Destination Freedom*

Between 1948 and 1950, black writers and actors in Chicago produced a unique local radio program about African-American politics, culture, and history for northern urban audiences (a form of "narrowcasting"). According to historian Barbara Diane Savage, this program, called *Destination Freedom,* "provide[d] a glimpse of the politically creative ways African Americans could use the medium of radio when they had freer rein over it. . . . This kind of broadcast was possible because of black migration and the formation of an urban market of working-class and middle-class African Americans." She concluded that *Destination Freedom,* conceived and written by black journalist and radio scriptwriter Richard Durham (a migrant born in Mississippi), was "by far the single most effective use of radio to teach black history and to make political arguments on behalf of the black quest for freedom." Durham stated his vision of this program with its positive depiction of black lives:

> Somewhere in this ocean of Negro life, with its cross-current and under-currents, lies the very soul of America. . . . It lies there because the real-life story of a single Negro in Alabama walking into a voting booth across a Ku Klux Klan line has more drama and world implications than all the stereotypes Hollywood or radio can turn out in a thousand years."

While Durham enjoyed enormous latitude in developing biographical profiles of black men and women, his power was not absolute. For example, he was not allowed to air a profile of Paul Robeson. In 1950, station WMAQ, despite the success of the program, discontinued it, fearful of the threat of rising anti-communist conservatism. Durham moved on to serve in the 1960s as editor of Elijah Muhammad's publication, *Muhammad Speaks,* and helped Muhammad Ali write his 1977 biography, *The Greatest.*

Race, Representation, and the Movies

In the 1930s and 1940s—after the introduction of sound in motion pictures—black and white producers began to make what were known as **race films** for African-American audiences. Except for these race films, white film executives,

race films Movies made for African-American audiences in the 1930s and 1940s.

Richard Durham (1917–1984) migrated to Chicago with his family in the 1920s. From 1948 to 1950 his unique radio series *Destination Freedom* educated the citizens of Bronzeville about the long black struggle for civil rights.

19-1
19-2
19-3
19-4
19-5
19-6
19-7
19-8
19-9

since the beginning of the film industry, had cast black men and women in roles designed to comfort, reassure, and entertain white audiences. Continuing this trend, African Americans in Hollywood movies of the 1930s were usually cast in servile roles and often portrayed as buffoons. For example, the first black actor to receive major billing in American films, Stepin Fetchit (1902–1985, born Lincoln Theodore Monroe Perry), purportedly earned $2 million in 10 years playing a servile, dim-witted, slow-moving character.

Black performers appeared as servants in many other box-office successes during the Depression era. Among them were Gertrude Howard and Libby Taylor, who played servants to Mae West's characters in *I'm No Angel* (1933) and *Belle of the Nineties* (1934). In *Imitation of Life* (1934), Louise Beavers played a black servant whose light-skinned daughter, played by Fredi Washington, tried to pass for white. The black tap dancer and stage performer Bill "Bojangles" Robinson was featured in four popular films—*The Little Colonel* (1935), *The Littlest Rebel* (1935), *Just Around the Corner* (1938), and *Rebecca of Sunnybrook Farm* (1938)—as a servant to white child star Shirley Temple.

The film that most firmly cemented the role of black Americans as servants in the American consciousness was *Gone with the Wind* (1939). Hattie McDaniel and Butterfly McQueen were the black "stars" in this epic adaptation of Margaret Mitchell's romantic salute to the Old South. McDaniel had played servant or "Mammy" roles throughout the 1930s. The image of Mammy, the headscarf-wearing, obese, dutiful black woman who preferred nurturing white families to caring for her own children, appealed to white America. But in *Gone with the Wind*, McDaniel gave the performance of a lifetime and in 1940 became the first African American to win an Oscar. Many in the black community criticized her for playing "female Tom" roles. McDaniel retorted she would rather play a maid and earn $700 a week than be one and earn $7 a week. In time, however, McDaniel and other black actors—dismayed by their relegation to demeaning roles—formed the **Fair Play Committee** to lobby the white-dominated movie industry for more substantial roles, to get rid of dialect speech, and to ban the term *nigger* from the screen. But in the *Beulah* radio show, which premiered in 1947, McDaniel again played a wise but subservient maid who provides the family that employs her with advice, guidance, and direction.

Eventually, during and after World War II, Hollywood developed more sophisticated race-directed movies. Of particular significance was the positive, even romanticized, portrayal of black Americans in a movie the War Department financed to gain support among African Americans for the U.S. role in World War II. *The Negro Soldier*, directed by Frank Capra in 1944, played to vast audiences of enthusiastic black people. But even before *The Negro Soldier*, some motion pictures had depicted African Americans positively. Paul Robeson made two movies, *The Emperor Jones* (1933) and *Show Boat* (1936), in which he attempted to change how black men and women were represented on screen. He proclaimed in 1934, "In my music, my plays, my films I want to carry always this central idea: to be African. Multitudes of men have died for less worthy ideals; it is even more eminently worth living for." Robeson's films, however, were not box-office successes, and he left the United States for Europe. There his commitment to communism and leftist politics made him a target of the anticommunist hysteria that gripped the United States as the Cold War took hold in the late 1940s (see Chapter 20).

To succeed commercially, African-American filmmakers had to disguise their dissent or appeal to an exclusively black audience. One of the most enterprising black filmmakers, Oscar Micheaux (1884–1951), made films aimed primarily at the black public. White Hollywood directors and producers often ignored or insulted black people. Unlike the dominant Hollywood stereotypes, the black men and women in Micheaux's films were often educated, cultured, and prosperous. Micheaux endowed black Americans with cinematic voice and subjectivity. His films featured middle-class or identity issues such as "passing for white."

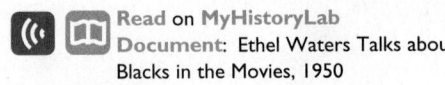

Read on **MyHistoryLab**
Document: Ethel Waters Talks about Blacks in the Movies, 1950

Fair Play Committee Organization formed to promote black actors in the movie industry and improve the image of blacks in film.

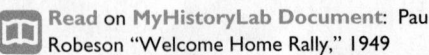

Read on **MyHistoryLab Document:** Paul Robeson "Welcome Home Rally," 1949

19-1
19-2
19-3
19-4
19-5
19-6
19-7
19-8
19-9

Micheaux produced more than 30 feature films between 1919 and 1948. In 1932, he released *The Exile*, the first sound motion picture to be made by, with, and for black Americans. The following year he produced *Veiled Aristocrats*, about passing for white among Chicago's black professional class. The characters in the film are considered "aristocrats" because they are descended from the white gentry of the Old South and Europe. They are "veiled" because of their color. The plot turns on the revelation that the wealthy "white" heroine is actually "colored," which enables her to marry the talented mulatto hero.

Micheaux tried to transform Hollywood without changing it, much as members of the black bourgeoisie struggled to be included in American society. His films capture the dilemma of black double consciousness. As W. E. B. Du Bois put it, black people always experienced that "peculiar sensation," that "sense of always looking at one's self through the eyes of others, of measuring one's soul by the tape of a world that looks on in amused contempt and pity." Black culture existed within and was shaped by American culture, while simultaneously transforming it. To the degree that black Americans had been assimilated, white American culture was also their culture.

The white immigrants who created Hollywood were determined to help marginal and excluded groups like Jews and Italians assimilate into the American mainstream. Hollywood sought to create the illusion that these groups belonged to the power elite. However, these Hollywood entrepreneurs did not do the same for African Americans. Their films during the Depression represented black people as unassimilable. A small cadre of black filmmakers and actors created independent films and showed them in theaters exclusively for black patrons. Following the lead of pioneers like Micheaux, they created an alternative cinema in which they introduced nuanced and fully human characters.

Oscar Micheaux (1884–1951) was born on a farm in Metropolis, Illinois. He became the greatest black filmmaker of his time. He wrote articles for the *Chicago Defender* and a thinly veiled autobiography, *The Conquest: The Story of a Negro Pioneer*, and made dozens of sophisticated films that captured the complexity of African-American life and culture.

The Black Chicago Renaissance

19-5   **What were the characteristics, developments, artists, and authors of the Chicago Renaissance?**

Black culture flourished during the 1930s and 1940s, decades otherwise noted for economic depression and global warfare. African-American musicians thrived in cities as far from Harlem as Kansas City (Missouri), Dallas, Denver, and Oklahoma City. They created a southwestern style of jazz with a blues inflection. Jazz pianist Mary Lou Williams (1910–1981) worked in Kansas City during the 1930s. She recalled, "I found Kansas City to be a heavenly city—music everywhere in the Negro section of town, and fifty or more cabarets rocking on Twelfth and Eighteenth Streets." The southwestern musical style rivaled the West Coast jazz scene (which often included black and Latino musicians) that radiated from Los Angeles to Portland, Seattle, San Francisco, and Oakland. It even reached as far as Honolulu and found patrons in such Asian cities as Yokohama in Japan, Shanghai and Hong Kong on the coast of China, and Manila in the Philippines.

In many respects, however, Black Chicago became the center of black culture innovation and expressivity during the 1930s and 1940s. In contrast to some of the artists of the "Harlem Renaissance," the leading writers in Chicago harbored no illusions that art would solve the problems caused by white supremacy and black subordination. The Chicago writers of the 1930s and 1940s emphasized the idea that black art had to combine aesthetics and function. It had to be art that served the cause of black freedom.

Arna Bontemps (1902–1973) was to the Black **Chicago Renaissance** what Alain Locke had been to the Harlem Renaissance. "The Depression," Bontemps asserted,

Chicago Renaissance Flourishing of the arts that made Chicago the center of black culture in the 1940s.

put an end to the dream world of renaissance Harlem and scattered the band of poets and painters, sculptors, scholars and singers who had in six exciting years made a generation of Americans aware of unnoticed and hitherto unregarded creative talents among Negroes.... What they did not dream was that a second awakening, less gaudy but closer to realities, was already in prospect.... One way or the other, Harlem got its renaissance in the middle twenties, centering around the *Opportunity* contests and the Fifth Avenue Awards Dinners.... Ten years later Chicago reenacted it on WPA [Works Progress Administration] without finger bowls but with increased power.

Born in Louisiana, Bontemps migrated in 1935 from California to Chicago, where he met Richard Wright and joined the South Side Writers Group, which Wright founded in 1936. The group included poet Margaret Walker and playwright Theodore Ward. It offered criticism and moral support to black writers. Bontemps's association with the group influenced his own writing. After 1935 his novels and short stories reflected a restlessness and revolutionary spirit. In 1936 he published *Black Thunder* about the nineteenth-century slave conspiracy led by Gabriel, and in 1939 he published *Drums at Dusk* about the Haitian Revolution and Toussaint Louverture. Richard Wright's writings also celebrated resistance, but with more nuance. He published *Uncle Tom's Children* in 1938 and his masterpiece, *Native Son*, in 1940.

Among the artists who launched their careers on WPA funds were Margaret Walker and Willard Motley. Walker attracted attention when her collected poems, *For My People,* appeared in the Yale Series of Younger Poets. Willard Motley worked with a radio group while writing his novel *Knock on Any Door* (1947), which depicted the transformation of an Italian-American altar boy into a criminal headed for the electric chair. The novel invited comparisons with Wright's *Native Son*.

Before the 1930s, black intellectuals misjudged Chicago's potential to become a center of black culture. In the late 1920s, black social scientists Charles S. Johnson and E. Franklin Frazier expressed disdain for Black Chicago's artistic and intellectual prospects. Frazier proclaimed that "Chicago has no intelligentsia," and in 1923 Johnson asked rhetorically,

Who can write of lilies and sunsets in the pungent shadows of the stockyards? ... It is no dark secret why literary societies fail, [why] there are no Art exhibits or libraries about, why periodicals presuming upon an I.Q. above the age of 12 are not read, why so little literature comes out of the city. No, the kingdom of the second ward [the black neighborhood] has no self-sustaining intelligentsia, and a miserably poor acquaintance with that of the world surrounding it.

Johnson did, however, admit one saving grace in Chicago's cultural wasteland: "It leads these colored United States in its musical aspirations with, perhaps, the best musical school in the race, as these go."

Johnson and Frazier were too harsh. Just as Chicago's industrial economy attracted working-class black people, it also nurtured artists who drew inspiration from and reflected this stratum of moving and striving, strolling and styling black people who wanted to transgress class and geographical lines. These working-class people aspired to enjoy the middle-class life of accomplishment and consumption. A critical pulse point on Chicago's South Side came to be known as Bronzeville. It measured and reflected the lives of ordinary working-class people. As Harlem had its 125th Street, Chicago had 35th and State Street and 47th and South Park (now Martin Luther King, Jr. Drive).

Chicago was heir to the Harlem Renaissance. In 1930 Langston Hughes published *Not Without Laughter*, the first major novel about the black experience in Chicago. Hughes moved to the city himself in 1941 and wrote for the *Chicago Defender*. The city epitomized urban industrial America. As the northern terminus of the Illinois Central Railroad, it had long attracted displaced agricultural workers from the southern cotton fields. By 1930 it had a black population of 233,903. The migrants arrived eager to absorb Chicago's hard-driving blues and jazz culture.

VOICES | Margaret Walker on Black Culture

In 1942 Margaret Walker (1915–1998) published For My People, *the most important collection of poetry written by a participant in the Black Chicago Renaissance before Gwendolyn Brooks's* A Street in Bronzeville *(1945). In a 1992 collection of her essays, Walker reflected on the meaning and significance of black culture:*

Black culture has two main streams: a sociological stream . . . and an artistic stream. . . . In this artistic stream black culture has five branches. These are language, religion, art, music, and literature. . . .

Black music is perhaps the most acceptable of our black culture. The modern world is willing to accept the unique character of African rhythms and the language of the drum. White America, in general, reluctantly admits that black American music is the American music and most indigenous to our culture. In every category or classification of music, moreover, Black America has achieved monumentally. With a broad base of folk music—spirituals and gospel music, seculars (blues, work songs, prison hollers)—individuals have risen in notable achievement in classical, popular, and various forms of jazz. From Black Patti to Marian Anderson and Leontyne Price, the great black American singer has gained worldwide eminence. Roland Hayes, William Warfield, Todd Duncan, the late Ellabelle Davis, Dorothy Maynor, and Mattiwilda Dobbs are notable black artists known the world over. Our blues singers like Bessie Smith, Ma Rainey, and B. B. King; folk singers like Leadbelly, and the greats like Louis Armstrong, Jimmie Lunceford, and Count Basie; great composers like Scott Joplin, Eubie Blake, Charlie Parker, and the incomparable Duke Ellington are significant contributors to the modern world and all represent the undeniable genius of the black American musician.

Individual achievement, while part of our general cultural picture, is not all. It is in language and religion that Black Americans as a group have made a significant contribution to the national fiber of American life and to the modern world. As spiritual creatures we have shown through unmerited suffering that we have a sense of humanity that can enrich the moral fiber and contribute to a new world ethos. Our black culture is aware of human needs and human values. Handicapped as we have been by a racist system of dehumanizing slavery and segregation, our American history of nearly five hundred years reveals that our cultural and spiritual gifts brought from our African past are still intact. It is not only that we are singers and dancers, poets and prophets, great athletes and perceptive politicians—but we are also a body of charismatic and numinous people yet capable of cultic fire as seen in our black churches and still creative enough in intellect to signal the leap forward into a new and humanistic age. We are the authors of the new paradigm. . . .

How then has black culture been disseminated and kept alive? Black culture has survived in the black institutions of Black America. In the black family, the Black Church, the black school, the black press, the black nation, and the black world. This is where our black culture has survived and thrived. This is where it must continue to grow. The ground of common humanity is not yet a reality in the modern world but when it comes as it must in the twenty-first century, Black Africa, and black humanity must be as always the foundation on which it stands and from which it logically proceeds. One world of international brotherhood does not negate the nationalism of black people. It only enforces and re-enforces our common humanity.

1. According to Walker, what external factors influenced and sustained black culture? What are some of the central themes in black culture?

2. What political and symbolic use have African Americans made of black culture?

SOURCE: *On Being Female, Black, and Free/Essays by Margaret Walker, 1932–1992*, edited by Maryemma Graham. Jackson, University of Mississippi Press, 1997. Reprinted by permission of Maryemma Graham.

During the 1920s a discernible class structure among African Americans emerged in Chicago, fueled in part by the new migrants. These men and women expanded the consumer base and gave rise to a cadre of educated professionals and entrepreneurs who developed an appreciation for the arts. The *Black Metropolis*, as social scientists St. Clair Drake and Horace R. Cayton designated Chicago's South Side, became a black city within a city. Black businesses, such as banks and insurance companies, formed the financial foundation. Entrepreneur Walter L. Lee started Your Cab Company and put on the streets each day a half dozen chauffeur-uniformed drivers of vehicles. In the late 1940s, John Johnson would launch a publishing empire with such magazines as *Negro Digest, Jet*, and *Ebony*. These businesses depended less on white patronage than on black support. It was in their best interest to support the arts and provide venues for performances.

Archibald Motley (1891–1981) captures in *Barbecue* (1934) the exuberance and vitality of nightlife in Chicago's Bronzeville. Motley was a major artistic talent during Chicago's Black Renaissance of the 1930s and 1940s.
Oil on canvas, 361/4" × 401/8".

Music was the primary inspiration for the creativity of black cultural movements in America. Avant-garde developments in black music preceded black cultural activity in the visual arts, poetry, drama, dance, literature, film, and sports. Cultural creativity was a potent force for raising consciousness and stirring resentment against oppressive living conditions and economic exploitation in different locations in America.

Within the South Side of Chicago, black musical giants, such as trumpeter Louis Armstrong (1898–1971) and his wife, Lillian Hardin Armstrong (1898–1971), a well-known and respected classically trained pianist, nurtured a distinct jazz culture. "Lil" Armstrong was born in Memphis, Tennessee, and received formal music training at Fisk University, the Chicago College of Music (earning a teaching certificate in 1924), and the New York College of Music (graduated in 1929). She led her own band and arranged, composed, and sang. She played with great performers and befriended Louis Armstrong when he arrived in Chicago. They were married in 1924. Lil Armstrong eventually encouraged her husband to leave King Oliver's Creole Jazz Band and join Fletcher Henderson in New York. The Armstrongs were divorced in 1938. She continued her recording career with Decca records under the name Lil Hardin.

In his autobiography, *Music Is My Mistress*, Duke Ellington remarked,

> Chicago always sounded like the most glamorous place in the world to me when I heard the guys in Frank Holliday's poolroom talking about their travels. . . . They told very romantic tales about nightlife on the South Side. By the time I got there in 1930, it glittered even more . . . the Loop, the cabarets . . . city life, suburban life, luxurious neighborhoods—and the apparently broken-down neighborhoods where there were more good times than any place in the city.

At this point, Ellington was recording some of his best jazz, such as *Mood Indigo* (1930) and *Ko-Ko* (1940). Ellington's stay in Chicago left a powerful impression on vocalist Joe Williams, who recalled,

> I used to arrange my classes so that I could get home in time to hear a program they [Ellington's band] had in Chicago called "Red Hot and Low Down." . . . The program's theme was Ellington's "East St. Louis Toodle-oo." Later on, they changed the theme to "Sepia Panorama." Then they changed it again, to "Take the 'A' Train." But I used to come home early from high school so that I could hear Duke Ellington on the radio.

The seeds that blossomed into full-bodied jazz culture were planted across America at the turn of the century. The most famous musicians, however, all went to or passed through Chicago. As the Chicago Jazz Age came into its own, "Pretty Baby" became the city's theme song. It was written by Tony Jackson, whom Jelly Roll Morton (the self-proclaimed "inventor of jazz") called "maybe the best entertainer the world has ever seen." The South Side, specifically along State Street between 31st and 35th, was the beating heart of the city's Jazz Age. Although Chicago did not replace New York as the major location for the aspiring jazz musician, it was the place you went to prove you had what it took to make a name for yourself.

Gospel in Chicago: Thomas Dorsey

The term *gospel* designates the traditional religious music of the black church. It was nurtured and flourished in Chicago's Holiness, Sanctified, Pentecostal, Baptist, and Methodist churches, in storefronts and in large edifices. Gospel music became the backbone of urban

PROFILE Langston Hughes

LANGSTON HUGHES IDENTIFIED WITH POOR and working-class black people. He used his poetry, prose, and plays to make the dignity and beauty of black people visible and known.

Hughes once referred to himself as "a literary sharecropper." Admirers called him a range of names—for starters, "Poet Laureate of the Negro People." During his career he produced 15 volumes of poetry, two collections of short stories, one novel, two volumes of autobiography—*The Big Sea* (1940), and *I Wonder as I Wander* (1956)—and 15 plays, along with librettos, scripts, essays, songs, translations, anthologies, children's stories, biographies and histories for the young, and two decades of weekly newspaper columns. He recorded the humor, wisdom, dialects, moods, and music of black people. One of the best examples of his social poetry was "The Negro Speaks of Rivers":

> *I've known rivers:*
> *I've known rivers ancient as the world and older*
> *than the flow of human blood in human veins.*
> *My soul has grown deep like the rivers.*
> *I bathed in the Euphrates when dawns were*
> *young.*
> *I built my hut near the Congo and it lulled me to sleep.*
> *I looked upon the Nile and raised the pyramids*
> *above it.*
> *I heard the singing of the Mississippi when Abe*
> *Lincoln went down to New Orleans, and I've seen its*
> *muddy bosom turn all golden in the sunset.*
> *I've known rivers:*
> *Ancient, dusky rivers.*
> *My soul has grown deep like the rivers.*

Hughes was born in Joplin, Missouri, in 1902 and was raised by his maternal grandmother, Mary Langston.

His father, James Hughes, emigrated to Mexico, and his mother, Carrie Langston, remarried. Hughes became fascinated by black urban folk culture, which the Great Migration had transplanted from the rural South. He joined his mother in Cleveland in 1916, attended an integrated high school, and began to publish. Hughes felt ambivalent about his parents, who left him adrift, emotionally and financially. He dropped out of Columbia University in 1922, lived in Harlem, and traveled to Europe and Africa.

With the publication of *The Weary Blues* in 1926, his career took off. The language of the blues enchanted Hughes—its warmth, stoicism, incongruous humor, ironic laughter mixed with tears, and the "pain that was swallowed in a smile." In 1943 he introduced in his *Chicago Defender* column the character Jesse B. Semple, a racially conscious barfly philosopher—unlettered but wise. The college-educated, somewhat uptight narrator of the series interrogates Semple about black life, from love of women and watermelon to the fortunes of rich gospel singers and the whereabouts of leaders who hide from the black people they lead. At one point Semple observed,

> *Not only am I half dead right now from pneumonia,*
> *but everything else has happened to me! I've been cut,*
> *shot, stabbed, run over, hit by a car, and tromped by a*
> *horse. I have also been robbed, fooled, deceived, two-*
> *timed, double-crossed, dealt seconds, and mightily near*
> *blackmailed—but I'm still here! . . . I have been fired,*
> *laid off, and last week given an indefinite vacation, also*
> *Jim Crowed, segregated, barred out, insulted, eliminated,*
> *called black, yellow, and red, locked in, locked out, locked*
> *up, and also left holding the bag.*

In 1932 Hughes visited Moscow, where he felt comfortable and appreciated. He was impressed by the absence of Jim Crow segregation and discrimination and ignored Stalin's oppression and murders. But Hughes never joined the Communist Party. He was an artist who championed black folk culture as authentic American culture.

SOURCE: Poem from *Collected Poems* by Langston Hughes. ©1994 by the Estate of Langston Hughes. Used by permission of Alfred A. Knopf, a division of Random House, Inc.

((⚫ **Listen** on **MyHistoryLab Audio:** *I've Known Rivers*; poem and reading by Langston Hughes

19-1
19-2
19-3
19-4
19-5
19-6
19-7
19-8
19-9

and contemporary black religion and is deeply entrenched in worship. The use of instruments—tambourines, drums, pianos, horns, guitars, and Hammond organs—distinguishes gospel from earlier spiritual and black folk music. During the 1930s and 1940s, it developed its own idioms and performance techniques. There were always tensions between genres of black music, and gospel provoked its share of critics. Members of the older generation deemed it too secular and insufficiently spiritual.

The doctrines of black "folk churches" encouraged free expression, group participation, spontaneous testimonies, prayers, witnessing, and music. Singers and choirs rarely performed the same songs in the same way more than once. The performer paid attention to the quality of the sound and to the careful manipulation of timbre, range, and shading. The style of the delivery used the whole body in synchronized movement. The mechanics of the delivery were designed to intensify the performance, giving it added textual variation and melodic improvisation. Performers expanded a melody by a variety of technical devices, including repetition, shouts, slides, slurs, moans, and grunts. The supporting piano and organ frequently engaged in call-and-response interplay.

Gospel singer Pearl Williams-Jones makes clear the distinction between black church music and music of the other churches: "The traditional liturgical forms of plain chant, chorales, and anthems do not fulfill the needs of traditional black folk religious worship and rituals."

In Chicago, Thomas Dorsey (1899–1993)—one of the leading composers of the blues since the mid-1920s—was most responsible for developing black urban gospel. Dorsey synthesized elements of the blues with religious hymns to create a gospel blues. His gospel pieces, performed with a ragtime-derived, boogie-woogie piano accompaniment, radiated an urban religious spirit. In 1930 Dorsey gained attention when Willie Mae Ford Smith (1904–1994) performed his "If You See My Savior, Tell Him That You Saw Me" at the National Baptist Convention in Chicago. Two years later, in 1932, Dorsey's place in musical history was assured when Theodore Frye, with Dorsey at the piano, performed in the Ebenezer Baptist Church in Chicago his now classic gospel song "Take My Hand, Precious Lord." The song had a profound impact on gospel performers and their audiences. Dorsey's abundant works provided a foundation for shout worship formed in the 1930s and succeeding decades in the urban Protestant churches that transplanted black southerners.

((•)) Listen on **MyHistoryLab** Audio: **"I Sing Because I'm Happy"**; sung by Mahalia Jackson

One of the greatest gospel singers, Chicago-based Mahalia Jackson (1911–1972), promoted Dorsey's songs all over the country on the church circuit and at religious conventions between 1939 and 1944. Jackson once said of the music, "Gospel songs are the songs of hope. When you sing them you are delivered of your burden." During the Depression and World War II, gospel became big business.

Chicago in Dance and Song: Katherine Dunham and Billie Holiday

The influence of the WPA in Chicago was especially reflected in dance. Dance has always been an integral part of African-American life, and the dances of black people have always been important in the American theater. The first performances by black dancers given within and taken seriously by the concert dance world occurred in the 1930s. The first "Negro Dance Recital in America" was performed in 1931 by the New Negro Art Theater Dance Company, cofounded by Edna Buy and Hemsley Winfield. In that same year, Katherine Dunham (1909–2006) founded the Negro Dance Group in Chicago, which survived thanks to WPA support. As Dunham later recalled, "Black dancers were not allowed to take classes in studios in the '30s. I started a school because there was no place for blacks to study dance. I was the first to open the way for black dancers and I was the first to form a black dance company."

Dunham was unique. Trained in anthropology, she studied African-based ritual dance in the Caribbean. In 1938 her troupe stunned an audience with the sexual vitality of its performance of one of her works. When the company, renamed the Katherine Dunham Dance Company, performed in February 1940, audiences and critics were awed. The *New York Times* declared,

> With the arrival of Katherine Dunham on the scene the development of a substantial Negro dance Art begins to look decidedly bright. Her performance with her group at the Windsor Theater may very well become a historic occasion, for certainly never before in all efforts of recent years to establish the Negro dance as a serious medium has there been so convincing and authoritative approach. . . . The potential greatness of the Negro dance lies in its discovery of its own roots and the crucial nursing of them into growth and flower. . . . It is because she has showed herself to have both the objective quality of the student and the natural instinct of the artist that she has done such a truly important job.

What kept audiences returning to Dunham dance performances, however, was the dancer's bold sensuality. A reviewer of *Tropical Revue*, for example, wrote that it was "likely to send thermometers soaring to the bursting point. . . . Tempestuous and torrid, raffish and revealing." The *New York Sun* marveled, "Shoulders, midsections and posteriors went round and round. Particularly when the cynosure was Miss Dunham, the vista was full of pulchritude."

Dunham explained her motivation:

> I felt a new dance form was needed for black people to be able to appear in any theater in the world and be accepted and exciting. One of the prerequisites of art is uniqueness. Rather than taking years to build a classical ballet company for blacks, I decided to create a dance with an authentic base for black people. Through my anthropological work, I studied primitive and folk dances and created the Dunham dance from them.

One of America's premier dance artists, the internationally acclaimed Katherine Dunham (1909–2006) performed in the Boboli Gardens in Florence, Italy, in 1950. A talented choreographer, anthropologist, and writer, Dunham founded one of the first black dance companies. She was an outspoken critic of Jim Crow segregation.

Dunham's success in New York led to film offers. The producers of the all-black musical extravaganza *Cabin in the Sky* hired the dance troupe and gave the featured role of Georgia Brown to Dunham. The role gave Dunham, as the *Times* dance critic wrote, the chance "to sizzle." But it also undermined her seriousness, allowing white audiences to view her as the stereotypical sultry black sexpot.

Nevertheless, the profits from the film funded the dancers' stage performances and Dunham's research. In 1943 Dunham moved to New York and opened the Katherine Dunham School of Arts and Research, which trained artists in dance, theater, literature, and world cultures.

Dunham protested racial segregation, even though it hurt her popularity. In the early 1940s she denounced discrimination. In 1944 in Louisville, Kentucky, Dunham announced after a performance, "We are glad we have made you happy. We hope you have enjoyed us. This is the last time I shall play Louisville because the management refuses to let people like us sit by people like you. Maybe after the war we shall have democracy and I can return." Dunham is important because she was a gifted and talented pioneer in dance whose choreography inspired future generations. She also underscored the responsibility that a black artist had to the black community to fight racism.

Billie Holiday (1915–1959), another great performer whose career took shape during the Depression, also used her art to challenge the oppression of black people. Holiday, popularly known as "Lady Day," began singing at age 15 and was discovered three years later by John Hammond, a Chicago jazz producer and promoter. In 1933 Hammond arranged for Holiday's first recording session, and in 1934 she made her debut at the Apollo Theater in Harlem. An incomparable singer known for subtle and artful improvisation, she left a wealth of recordings.

PROFILE   Billie Holiday and "Strange Fruit"

19-1
19-2
19-3
19-4
19-5
19-6
19-7
19-8
19-9

Billie Holiday (1915–1959) was one of the greatest jazz singers of all time. Between 1935 and 1938, she released some 80 titles on the Brunswick label for marketing to the black jukebox audience.

"STRANGE FRUIT," WHICH BILLIE HOLIDAY first performed in 1939, became her signature piece. It was written by a white schoolteacher who went by the name of Lewis Allan (his real name was Abel Meeropol). While the lyrics capture the brutality of lynching, Holiday's incomparable vocal style and delivery gave the song its political, emotional, and cultural power and made it the anti-lynching anthem:

> Southern trees bear a strange fruit,
> Blood on the leaves and blood at the root,
> Black body swinging in the Southern breeze,
> Strange fruit hanging from the poplar trees.
> Pastoral scene of the gallant South,
> The bulging eyes and the twisted mouth,
> Scent of magnolia sweet and fresh,
> And the sudden smell of burning flesh!
> Here is a fruit for the crows to pluck
> For the rain to gather, for the wind to suck,
> For the sun to rot, for a tree to drop.
> Here is a strange and bitter crop.

"Every time she sang that song," recalled Barney Josephson, a New York nightclub owner, "it was unforgettable. . . . I made her do it as her last number. . . . When she sang 'Strange Fruit' she never moved. Her hands were down. She didn't even touch the mike. With the little light on her face. The tears never interfered with her voice, but the tears would come and just knock everybody in that house out."

Billie Holiday was born Eleanora Fagan in Philadelphia, Pennsylvania, on April 7, 1915, to teenagers Sadie Fagan and Clarence Holiday. She grew up in Baltimore and became arguably the greatest jazz singer ever recorded, a unique improviser and soloist. She set the standards to which future vocalists such as Sarah Vaughan, Carmen McRae, and Lena Horne would aspire. Much attention has focused on the tragic and destructive dimensions of her private life, but it is her musical talent that compels interest and admiration. Holiday used her talent to do more than entertain. She challenged and often disturbed her listeners. While frequently inaccurate, Holiday's autobiography, *Lady Sings the Blues* (1956), and the equally distorted 1972 movie starring Diana Ross emphasize her struggle against sexism and racism within the music world and society. Holiday appeared in two movies. In 1935 she performed in Duke Ellington's *Symphony in Black*, singing "Big City Blues." In 1946 she sang three songs in *New Orleans*, opposite her musical mentor Louis Armstrong. Saxophonist Lester Young, who began recording with Holiday in 1937, gave her the nickname "Lady Day." By the late 1940s, Holiday's addiction to drugs was hurting her career. In 1947 she entered a clinic but could not stay clean. Following her discharge, the police arrested her for possession, and she served nine and one-half months at the Federal Reformatory for Women at Alderson, West Virginia. New York officials revoked her cabaret card and prohibited her from performing in nightclubs in the city. Still, she gave concerts in other cities and on international tours. A year before her death, Holiday recorded her most popular album, *Lady in Satin* (1958). She died in New York City on July 17, 1959. Thousands of friends and fans attended the funeral, a formal requiem high mass held at St. Paul the Apostle Church. She was buried in St. Raymond's Catholic Cemetery in the Bronx.

SOURCE: Lyrics by Lewis Allan © 1939 (renewed). Music Sales Corp. (ASCAP). International copyright secured. All rights reserved. Reprinted by permission.

Black Visual Art

19-6   **How did black graphic artists of the 1930s fuse politics and art in their work?**

Chicago artists, such as Charles White, Elizabeth Catlett, and Eldzier Cortor, and Harlem's Jacob Lawrence celebrated working-class black people while implicitly criticizing the racial hierarchy of power and privilege. Their art belonged to the social realist school that flourished in the 1930s. Social realist art was intensely ideological. It strove to fuse propaganda—both left and right wing—to art to make it socially and politically relevant.

As the Depression worsened, black artists became even more determined to portray the crisis in capitalism. This involved depicting social and racial inequality. Charles White wrote that "paint is the only weapon I have with which to fight what I resent. If I could write I would write about it. If I could talk I would talk about it. Since I paint, I must paint about it."

Defense Worker, a painting by Dox Thrash, reflects these concerns. Completed in 1942, just after the United States had entered World War II, it shows a black worker looming over the horizon. The heroic proletarian imagery alludes to the dream of a racially integrated labor force, equal opportunity, and social reform in the wake of the New Deal and the demand for labor triggered by the war.

The Harmon Foundation sponsored five juried exhibitions (1926–1931, 1933) of the work of black artists. The William E. Harmon Awards for Distinguished Achievement among Negroes celebrated black artists in the hope they would serve as role models for others. William E. Harmon, a real-estate investor from Iowa, established the New York–based foundation in 1925. In the 1930s the WPA established art workshops and art centers in black urban communities such as Chicago (Southside Community Art Center), Cleveland (Karamu House Artist Association), Detroit (Heritage House), and Harlem (Harlem Art Workshop and the Harlem Community Art Center) to teach art to neighborhood young people and provide work for artists. Sculptor Augusta Savage, as the first director of the Harlem Community Art Center, presided over more than 1,500 students enrolled in day and evening classes in drawing, painting, sculpture, printmaking, and design. Among the teachers was Selma Burke (1900–1995), who sculpted the relief of Franklin D. Roosevelt that appears on the dime coin.

The **Federal Arts Project**, another New Deal agency, sponsored the creation of murals that illustrated American ideals in public buildings, such as post offices and schools. Murals by black artists celebrated the heritage, contributions to society, and struggles of African Americans. Aaron Douglas, a leading painter of such public art, spoke about his work and that of his colleagues in a 1936 essay, "The Negro in American Culture":

Federal Arts Project New Deal agency formed to promote the creation of public art.

> One of our chief concerns has been to establish and maintain recognition of our essential humanity, in other words, complete social and political equality. This has been a difficult fight as we have been the constant object of attack by all manner of propaganda from nursery rhymes to false scientific racial theories. . . . In this struggle the rest of the proletariat almost invariably has been arrayed against us. . . . But the Negro artist, unlike the white artist, has never known the big house. He is essentially a product of the masses and can never take a position above or beyond their level.

Douglas and other black artists pressed the WPA to appoint more African Americans to its local boards and to hire them for more projects. The Harlem Artists Guild and the Arts and Crafts Guild in Chicago provided forums where black artists could foster the visual arts and support the social and political issues that affected black people.

19-1
19-2
19-3
19-4
19-5
19-6
19-7
19-8
19-9

Black Literature

19-7	What were the themes and impact of the work of Richard Wright and Ralph Ellison?

Black literature, like black art, has been assessed in terms of what it reveals about the social, cultural, and political landscape at a given historical moment. The most distinguishing feature of black literature may be the way that black writers have attempted to create spaces of freedom in their work, to liberate place, a trait that also marks black religious culture and folk cultural practices, such as storytelling. Black literature, like all black cultural production, is valued both for aesthetic reasons on its own and for the way it represents the struggles of black people to attain freedom. Black writers in the 1930s and 1940s felt obliged to address questions of identity and to define and describe urban life to the dispossessed and impoverished black migrants who moved to the cities. They tried to delineate the dimensions of a shared American heritage by portraying the contributions that African Americans had made to American society. Finally, and perhaps most ambitiously, black writers explored the issue of the rights African Americans were entitled to as Americans and the demands they could and should make on the state and society.

Richard Wright's *Native Son*

In 1940 Richard Wright (1908–1960) published *Native Son*, the first of many important novels by Depression-generation black authors. Reviewers hailed it as "the new American tragedy." Its tale of the downfall of the young Bigger Thomas could be read as a warning about how economic hardship, segregation, and discrimination could lead young black men to lash out in violence and rage. Setting out for an interview for a job as a chauffeur, Bigger meets with his South Side Chicago neighborhood friends who want him to help them rob a grocery store. Bigger's fear of whites prevents him from going along. Instead, he picks a fight to camouflage his fear and avoid committing the crime. Bigger gets the chauffeur's job, which requires him to drive for the wealthy Dalton family. On his first assignment, he is supposed to drive young Mary Dalton to a university lecture. But she talks him into picking up her boyfriend, Jan—a communist—and taking them to a restaurant in the black neighborhood. Jan and Mary are oblivious to the patronizing way they treat Bigger. After dinner Bigger drives them around the city while they drink and make love in the back seat.

When Jan leaves, Bigger takes an intoxicated Mary home. Because Mary is too drunk to walk, Bigger carries her to her room and is putting her to bed when blind Mrs. Dalton comes to check on her daughter. Bigger panics and covers Mary's head with a pillow to keep her quiet. When Mrs. Dalton leaves, Bigger discovers he has smothered Mary. He burns her body in the basement furnace. Not fully grasping what he has done, Bigger writes a ransom note signed with a phony name to make it seem that Mary has been kidnapped. When Mary's remains are discovered, Bigger flees. Fearing she might betray him, Bigger then murders his girlfriend, Bessie. Bigger is captured, tried, and condemned. The remainder of the novel explores the hysteria and bigotry that envelop the case, the harsh criminal justice system, the insensitivity of the Communist Party—which seeks to exploit Bigger's plight—and the poverty and social ills that plagued Chicago's African-American communities during the Depression.

At the center of the drama is Wright's exploration of how Bigger comes to terms with his murder of Mary and Bessie. In conversations with Max, his communist lawyer, he realizes his irrational fear of white people had caused him to kill the two women and that he was a product of his experiences in the ghetto. At the end of the novel he says, "What I killed for I am."

Wright's novel thrust the impact of urbanization and racism on black men and women into the collective consciousness of the American people. One white critic declared, "Speaking from the black wrath of retribution, Wright insisted that history can be punishment. He told us the one thing even the most liberal whites preferred not to hear: that Negroes were far from patient or forgiving, that they were scarred by fear, that they hated every moment of their suppression even when seeming most acquiescent, and that often enough they hated us

19-1
19-2
19-3
19-4
19-5
19-6
19-7
19-8
19-9

the decent and cultivated white men who from complicity or neglect shared in the responsibility of their plight."

In his closing arguments, the lawyer, Max, describes the psychological conditions that led Bigger to kill and warns of the destructive potential of suppressed black rage:

> The hate and fear which we have inspired in him, woven by our civilization into the very structure of his consciousness and into his blood and bones, into the hourly functioning of his personality, have become the justification of his existence. . . . Kill him and swell the tide of pent up lava that will some day break loose, not in a single, blundering crime, but in a wild cataract of emotion that will brook no control.

Native Son was an immediate success. It became a Book-of-the-Month Club selection and has sold millions of copies.

James Baldwin Challenges Wright

Wright's influence on American literature has been immense. He was the first African-American writer to enjoy an international reputation, and he showed that success and militancy were not mutually exclusive. A younger generation of black writers, however, especially James Baldwin (1924–1987), took issue with Wright. African Americans, they argued, need not be portrayed as hapless victims of racism. In his famous 1949 essay, "Everybody's Protest Novel," Baldwin argued that Bigger's tragedy was not that he was black, poor, and scared but that he had accepted "a theology that denies him life, that he admits the possibility of his being sub-human and feels constrained, therefore, to battle for his humanity according to those brutal criteria bequeathed him at his birth. . . . The failure of the protest novel lies in its rejection of life, the human being, the denial of his beauty, dread, power, in its insistence that it is his categorization alone which is real and which cannot be transcended." In turn, Wright accused Baldwin of trying to destroy his reputation and of betraying all African-American writers who wrote protest literature: "All literature is protest. You can't name a single novel that isn't protest."

Baldwin answered Wright in a second essay in 1951 titled "Many Thousand Gone." "Wright's work," Baldwin declared, "is most clearly committed to the social struggle . . . that artist is strangled who is forced to deal with human beings solely in social terms; and who has, moreover, as Wright had, the necessity thrust on him of being the representative of some thirteen million people. It is a false responsibility (since writers are not congressmen) and impossible, by its nature, of fulfillment."

The controversy ended the friendship between Wright and Baldwin, and Baldwin, whose work would soon include many powerful novels and essays, inherited the mantle of "best-known black American male writer" (see Chapter 22).

Ralph Ellison and *Invisible Man*

The most intricate novel about the black experience in America written during this era was Ralph Ellison's (1914–1994) *Invisible Man*, which won the National Book Award for fiction in 1952. Partially autobiographical, it traces the life of a young black man from his early years in a southern school (a thinly disguised Tuskegee Institute) through his migration to New York City. The novel explores class tensions within American society and the black community. It offers a balanced, incisive perspective on the interaction between white and black Americans.

Invisible Man was Ellison's only completed novel. He argued that the black tradition teaches one "to deflect racial provocation and to master and control pain. . . . It is a tradition which abhors as obscene any trading on one's own anguish for gain or sympathy. . . . It takes fortitude to be a man and no less to be an artist. Perhaps it takes even more if the black man would be an artist." He concluded, "It would seem to me, therefore, that the question

Richard Wright (1908–1960) was the first black writer to commandeer serious attention in mainstream American literature. In *Native Son* (1940) and *Black Boy* (1945), Wright provided incisive critiques of American racism. He received support from the Federal Writers Project and in his early works he poignantly portrayed the pathos of black southern migrants to the urban industrial North.

 Read on **MyHistoryLab** Document: Richard Wright, "Are We Solving America's Race Problem?" 1945

19-1
19-2
19-3
19-4
19-5
19-6
19-7
19-8
19-9

of how the 'sociology of his existence' presses upon the Negro writer's work depends upon how much of his life the individual writer is able to transform into art."

Echoing Du Bois's classic characterization of the "twoness" of the African-American character, Ellison observed, "[Black people] are an American people who are geared to what is and who yet are driven by a sense of what it is possible for human life to be in this society."

African Americans in Sports

19-8   **How did sports figures contribute to black culture?**

It is in the arena of professional sports that black Americans have demonstrated what human life can achieve when unconstrained by racism. The experiences of black men and women in American sports are a microcosm of their lives in American society. The privileges whites enjoyed in sports in this era paralleled the disadvantages and exclusions that were a constant part of black life. In the 1930s two black athletes, Jesse Owens and Joe Louis, captured the world's attention and inspired African Americans with pride, hope, and pleasure.

Jesse Owens and Joe Louis

Jesse Owens (1913–1980) was born on an Alabama sharecropping farm but grew up in Cleveland. A talented runner, he studied at Ohio State University and prepared for the 1936 Olympics, which were to be held in Berlin, the capital of Nazi Germany. Many African-American leaders objected to participating in the games because they believed this would help legitimate the Nazi myth of the superiority of the so-called Aryan race. Owens debunked that myth, becoming the first Olympian to win four gold medals. Although Hitler left the stadium to avoid congratulating Owens, African Americans relished Owens's victory over racism.

Joe Louis Barrow (1914–1981) was also a son of Alabama sharecroppers. His family migrated to Detroit when he was 12. Although his mother wanted him to be a violinist, Joe Louis—he dropped the name Barrow—had other interests. As a youth, he won a string of local boxing victories. In 1935 he faced former heavyweight champion Primo Carnera. A record crowd of 62,000 attended the fight in New York, which also had political overtones. Louis was fighting an Italian-American when Benito Mussolini, the fascist dictator of Italy, was about to invade Ethiopia. This was the oldest black independent nation in Africa, and many black Americans admired its ruler, Emperor Haile Selassie. Sports writers and police were amazed to observe everyone cheering when Louis beat Carnera in the sixth round.

Louis won the world heavyweight title against James J. Braddock in 1937 and beat the German Max Schmeling in a symbolic victory over Nazism in 1938. Louis retained the world heavyweight title until 1949.

Breaking the Color Barrier in Baseball

Although African Americans were integrated in track and boxing, professional baseball remained segregated until after World War II. Despite the hardships of the Depression, however, virtually every major black community tried to field its own baseball team. The Negro National League, which had folded in 1932, was revived in 1934, and the Negro American League was formed in 1937. Many of the players in the Negro leagues, including the legendary Josh Gibson, Satchel Paige, Leon Day, and Cool Papa Bell, would have equaled or excelled their white counterparts in the major leagues. Except for Paige, they never had that chance.

In 1947, however, major league baseball, which had had no black players since the departure of Fleetwood Walker in 1887, became integrated again when Jackie Robinson (1919–1972) signed to play with the Brooklyn Dodgers. In 1945 Branch Rickey, the Dodgers' general manager, decided to sign a black ball player to improve

Jackie Robinson (1919–1972) broke baseball's color barrier when he joined the Brooklyn Dodgers in 1947. He silently endured considerable hostility and threats from angry white citizens.

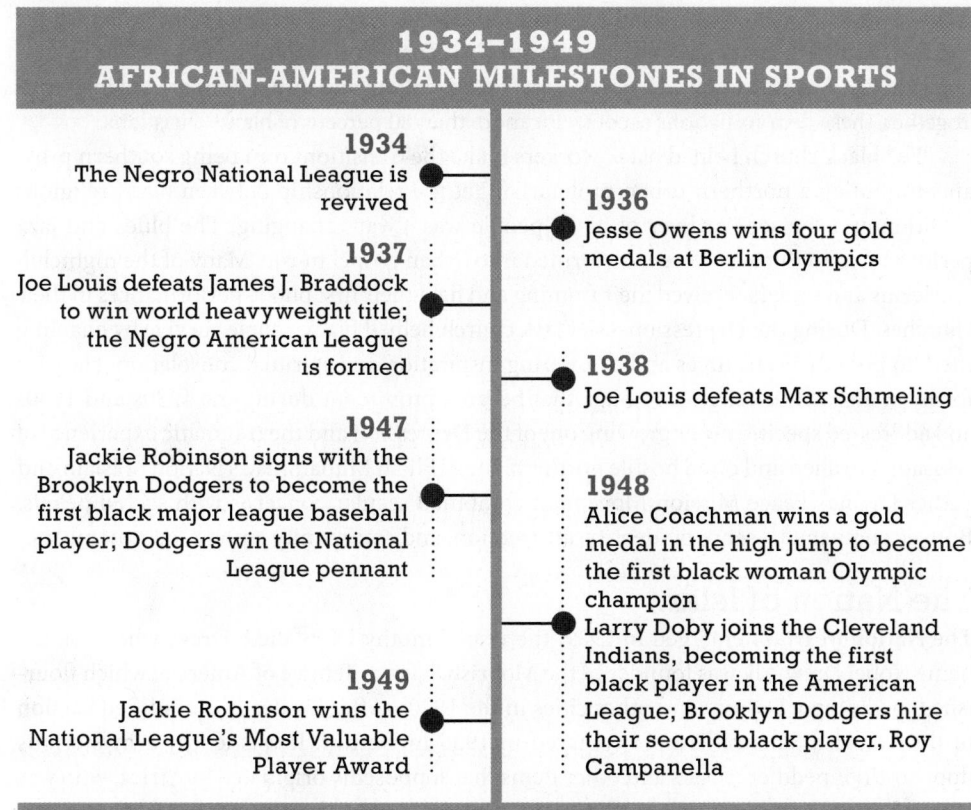

1934–1949
AFRICAN-AMERICAN MILESTONES IN SPORTS

1934
The Negro National League is revived

1936
Jesse Owens wins four gold medals at Berlin Olympics

1937
Joe Louis defeats James J. Braddock to win world heavyweight title; the Negro American League is formed

1938
Joe Louis defeats Max Schmeling

1947
Jackie Robinson signs with the Brooklyn Dodgers to become the first black major league baseball player; Dodgers win the National League pennant

1948
Alice Coachman wins a gold medal in the high jump to become the first black woman Olympic champion
Larry Doby joins the Cleveland Indians, becoming the first black player in the American League; Brooklyn Dodgers hire their second black player, Roy Campanella

1949
Jackie Robinson wins the National League's Most Valuable Player Award

19-1
19-2
19-3
19-4
19-5
19-6
19-7
19-8
19-9

the team's chances of winning the National League pennant and the World Series. After scouting the Negro leagues, he signed 26-year-old Jackie Robinson.

Robinson was the ideal choice, a superb athlete and a man of fortitude and determination. Born in Georgia and raised in southern California, he had been an All-American running back in football at UCLA and then had played baseball for the legendary Kansas City Monarchs of the Negro leagues. Robinson was also committed to black people and racial progress. He played the 1946 season for the Dodgers' minor league team in Montreal, where the Canadians welcomed him and his wife Rachel. But spring training in segregated Florida was difficult. Robinson broke the color barrier when he opened at first base for the Dodgers in April 1947. Taunted, ridiculed, and threatened by some spectators and players, he responded by playing spectacular baseball. He won the Rookie of the Year honors in 1947, and the Dodgers won the National League pennant. Robinson retired in 1957 but remained outspoken on racial issues until his death from diabetes in 1972.

In July 1947 Larry Doby became the first black player in the American League when he joined the Cleveland Indians. As other major league teams also signed black players, the once popular Negro leagues withered.

Watch on MyHistorylab Video: Jackie Robinson and the Integration of Baseball

Black Religious Culture

19-9 **What were the alternative religious movements and how did they help African Americans?**

Just as black religion was the "invisible institution" that helped African Americans survive slavery, the black church was the visible institution that helped hundreds of thousands of migrants adjust to urban life while affirming a set of core values consisting of freedom, justice, equality, and an African heritage. There was, of course, no single "black church." The term is shorthand for a pluralistic collection of institutions, including most prominently seven independent, historic, and black-controlled denominations: the African Methodist Episcopal Church; the

African Methodist Episcopal Zion Church; the Christian Methodist Episcopal Church; the National Baptist Convention, Incorporated; the National Baptist Convention of America, Unincorporated; the Progressive National Baptist Convention; and the Church of God in Christ. Together, these denominations account for more than 80 percent of black Christians.

The black church helped black workers make the transition from being southern peasants to joining a northern urban proletariat. Yet the relationship between black religious tradition and the secular lives of black people was always changing. The blues and jazz performed in nightclubs were transformed into urban gospel music. Many of the nightclub musicians and singers received their training and held their first public performances in their churches. During the Depression, the black church helped black people survive by enabling them to pool their resources and by offering inspiration and spiritual consolation. Here we focus on alternative religious groups that became prominent during the 1930s and 1940s and addressed specific needs growing out of the Depression and the traumatic experience of relocating to alien and often hostile northern cities. Elijah Muhammad's Nation of Islam and Father Divine's Peace Mission Movement combined secular concerns with sacred beliefs. Both strengthened a sense of identity, affirmation, and community among their members.

The Nation of Islam

Nation of Islam Religious movement that combines Islam with black nationalism.

The **Nation of Islam** emerged in 1929, the year Timothy Drew died. Drew, who took the name Nobel Drew Ali, was founder of the Moorish Science Temple of America, which flourished in Chicago, Detroit, and other cities in the 1920s. After his death, a modified version of the Moorish Science Temple emerged in 1930 in Detroit. It was led by a mysterious door-to-door peddler of silks and other items that supposedly originated in Africa, who was known variously as Wallace D. Fard, Master Farad Muhammad, or Wali Farad. He wrote two manuals of instruction, *The Secret Ritual of the Nation of Islam* and *Teaching for the Lost-Found Nation of Islam in a Mathematical Way*. His teachings that black people were the true Muslims attracted many poor residents in Depression-era Detroit. In addition to the beliefs of Nobel Drew Ali, Fard's Nation of Islam also taught a mixture of Koranic principles, the Christian Bible, his own beliefs, and those of nationalist Marcus Garvey.

In 1934, after establishing a Temple of Islam, Fard disappeared, and one of his disciples, Elijah Poole (1897–1975), renamed Elijah Muhammad by Fard, became leader of the Detroit temple and then of a second temple in Chicago. The Nation attracted the attention of federal authorities during World War II when its members refused to serve in the military. Muhammad was arrested in May 1942 on charges of inciting his followers to resist the draft and was imprisoned until 1946. After his release he settled in Chicago and began to expand his movement.

The Nation of Islam taught that black people were the Earth's original human inhabitants who had lived, according to Elijah Muhammad, in the Nile Valley. Approximately 6,000 years ago, a magician named Yakub produced white people. They proved so troublesome that they were banished to Europe, where they began to spread evil. Their worst crime was their enslavement of black people. Elijah Muhammad taught that white supremacy was ending and black people would rediscover their authentic history and culture. To prepare for the coming millennium, he instructed members to adhere to a code of behavior that included abstaining from many traditionally southern black foods, especially pork. Members subscribed to a family-centered culture in which women's role was to produce and rear the next generation. The Nation also demanded part of the South for a black national state.

Father Divine and the Peace Mission Movement

Peace Mission Movement Religious movement led by Father Major Jealous Divine.

Father Major Jealous Divine (c. 1877–1965) was born George Baker in Savannah. Like Elijah Muhammad, little is known about his early life. He captured attention in 1919 when he settled with 20 followers in Sayville, New York, and began what became known in the 1930s as the **Peace Mission Movement**. Divine secured domestic jobs for many of his followers on the surrounding estates and preached a gospel of hard work, honesty, sobriety, equality, and sexual abstinence. He provided free (or nearly free) meals and shelter for anyone who asked. In 1930 he changed his name to Father Divine. His Peace Movement espoused a racially neutral and economically empowering dogma that appealed to poor and needy black and white urbanites by offering them spiritual guidance and mental and physical healing. The movement embodied ideas from the New Thought, Holiness, Perfectionist, and Adventist religions. Hundreds of people traveled to see Father Divine on weekends, feast at his communal banquet table, and listen to his promises of heaven on Earth. The feasts were symbolic of the early Christian Eucharist and became the defining practices of Divine's religion.

In 1931 the police arrested Divine and 80 followers on charges of being a "public nuisance." Three days after a judge sentenced Divine to a year in jail and a $500 fine, the judge died of a heart attack. Divine was quoted as saying, "I hated to do it." The conviction was reversed, and Divine's reputation as a master of cosmic forces soared. Some of his followers believed he was God. Aside from the belief in the divinity of Father Divine, members of the Peace Movement were drawn to the mission's emphasis on ending racial prejudice and economic inequalities.

In 1933 Divine moved his headquarters to Harlem, where his Peace Mission Movement prospered. He eventually purchased key real-estate and housing projects called "heavens." These acquisitions and other businesses in the Midwest enhanced Divine's ability to provide shelter, jobs, and incomes for his followers. He launched the journal *New Day* in 1937 to disseminate his teachings. Divine also protested social injustice and encouraged his followers to become politically engaged. Between 1936 and 1940, he lobbied for a federal anti-lynching law. At the time of Divine's death in 1965, the holdings of the Peace Mission were estimated to be worth $10 million. Father Divine's movement echoed the Protestant ethic: work hard, keep both your mind and body healthy, eat right, dress properly, keep good company, and avoid evil and vice.

CONCLUSION

The Depression caused intense hardship. It was also a period in which black Americans had an unprecedented impact on American culture. Through the medium of radio, black Americans powerfully helped to change American popular entertainment and gave rise to a new urban consciousness and a sense of belonging. Black people excelled in sports, arts, drama, and music. The Works Projects Administration (WPA) funded artists whose cultural productions were accessible, inclusive, and populist.

The Chicago Black Renaissance reflected the positive impact that the WPA had on the lives of hundreds of artists. A new generation of black jazz musicians transformed black music into an art form that won worldwide admiration and emulation. Black musicians weaned Americans from swing to bebop. Gospel music satisfied the needs of the black urban migrants to express their spiritual and communal feelings. Disc jockeys of black-appeal radio programs helped make black music commercially profitable.

These positive changes occurred against a backdrop of discrimination and segregation. Still, some African Americans found satisfying jobs in film and radio while many others were excluded or relegated to stereotypical roles. Negative typecasting motivated innovative black filmmakers to develop alternative films and artistic institutions that allowed the development of a more balanced representation of black life and culture. However, such creative ventures seldom produced the profits that white entrepreneurs reaped from marketing black cultural productions to white consumers. The mass appeal and unparalleled success of entertainers such as Louis Armstrong and Duke Ellington should not obscure the fate of those artists who refused to entertain white America and instead sought to oppose racism and social and economic injustice.

Black counterculture artists had a lasting impact on America and facilitated the spread of black internationalism and anti-colonialism. Black artists reflected a growing pride and a determination to resist complete assimilation into white culture. The comic strips, the Semple stories of Langston Hughes, the black press, the radio broadcast of *Destination Freedom,* and the black church preserved black people's dignity. Black culture prepared black people for the next level of struggle against the American Jim Crow regime and against ideologies of white supremacy across the black diaspora.

CHAPTER TIMELINE

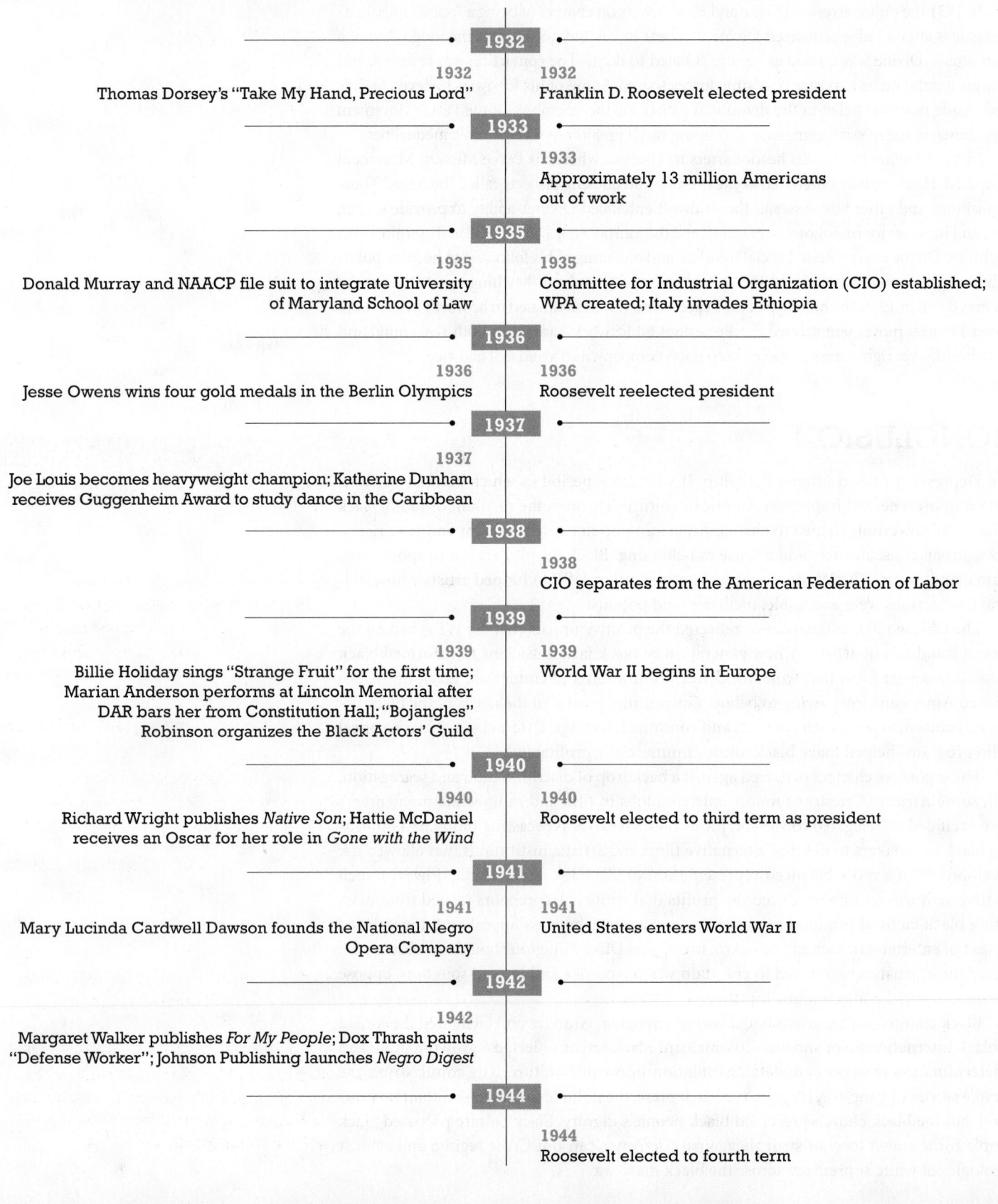

AFRICAN-AMERICAN EVENTS

NATIONAL EVENTS

1932

1932
Thomas Dorsey's "Take My Hand, Precious Lord"

1932
Franklin D. Roosevelt elected president

1933

1933
Approximately 13 million Americans
out of work

1935

1935
Donald Murray and NAACP file suit to integrate University
of Maryland School of Law

1935
Committee for Industrial Organization (CIO) established;
WPA created; Italy invades Ethiopia

1936

1936
Jesse Owens wins four gold medals in the Berlin Olympics

1936
Roosevelt reelected president

1937

1937
Joe Louis becomes heavyweight champion; Katherine Dunham
receives Guggenheim Award to study dance in the Caribbean

1938

1938
CIO separates from the American Federation of Labor

1939

1939
Billie Holiday sings "Strange Fruit" for the first time;
Marian Anderson performs at Lincoln Memorial after
DAR bars her from Constitution Hall; "Bojangles"
Robinson organizes the Black Actors' Guild

1939
World War II begins in Europe

1940

1940
Richard Wright publishes *Native Son*; Hattie McDaniel
receives an Oscar for her role in *Gone with the Wind*

1940
Roosevelt elected to third term as president

1941

1941
Mary Lucinda Cardwell Dawson founds the National Negro
Opera Company

1941
United States enters World War II

1942

1942
Margaret Walker publishes *For My People*; Dox Thrash paints
"Defense Worker"; Johnson Publishing launches *Negro Digest*

1944

1944
Roosevelt elected to fourth term

CHAPTER TIMELINE

AFRICAN-AMERICAN EVENTS

NATIONAL EVENTS

1945

1945
Nat King Cole becomes first black star with his own network (NBC) radio variety show; Johnson Publishing launches *Ebony Magazine*

1945
Roosevelt dies, Truman becomes president; United States drops atomic bombs on Hiroshima and Nagasaki; World War II ends

1947

1947
Jackie Robinson becomes the first black major league baseball player

1948

1948
Alice Coachman becomes the first black woman Olympic champion; Richard Durham broadcasts *Destination Freedom*

1948
Truman elected president

On MyHistoryLab

✓ Study and Review on MyHistoryLab

REVIEW QUESTIONS

1. How did the Great Depression affect black culture? How did the WPA democratize black culture? How did black religious culture change during this era?

2. How did black artists, musicians, filmmakers, and writers negotiate the dilemma of dual consciousness as articulated by Du Bois? Which parts of black art did white corporate executives find easiest to appropriate and shape for white consumption?

3. How did swing-era big band music lead to bebop? What problems did the bebop musicians encounter? How did black music transform American culture? How did African-American musicians make creative use of radio technology?

4. How did radio broadcasts and Hollywood films portray black Americans during the 1930s and 1940s? How did these images affect white Americans' attitudes and behavior toward black Americans? How did these representations contribute to the emergence of an alternative black radio and/or independent black cinema?

5. How did the Chicago Renaissance compare with the Harlem Renaissance?

6. Why did black athletes become prominent during the 1930s and 1940s? What was their impact on American culture? How did the experiences of black sports figures reflect the status of race relations in the United States?

RECOMMENDED READING

William Barlow. *Voice Over: The Making of Black Radio.* Philadelphia: Temple University Press, 1999. A lucid, informative cultural history of black radio and the personalities who made it a powerful instrument for disseminating black music, culture, language, and politics, and for constructing an African-American public sphere.

Pearl Bowser and Charles Musser. *Oscar Micheaux and His Circle: African American Filmmaking and Race Cinema of the*

Silent Era. Bloomington: Indiana University Press, 2005. Informative new perspectives on a great filmmaker and the era in which he worked.

Scott DeVeaux. *BeBop: A Social and Musical History.* Berkeley: University of California Press, 1997. A perceptive study of the creative artistry and lives of the pivotal black professional musicians. Beginning in the jazz age and flourishing during the 1930s and 1940s, they made bebop commercially successful.

Melvin Patrick Ely. *The Adventures of Amos 'n' Andy: A Social History of an American Phenomenon.* New York: Free Press, 1991. A subtle and penetrating examination of the complexities of racial stereotyping in one of the most influential and controversial radio and television programs in the history of media race relations.

Erik S. Gellman. *Death Blow to Jim Crow: The National Negro Congress and the Rise of Militant Civil Rights.* Durham: University of North Carolina Press, 2012. Breaks new ground and deepens our understanding of the militant, radical, anti-racism interracial reformers who founded one of the earliest civil rights movement's organizations.

Darlene Clark Hine and John McCluskey, eds. *The Black Chicago Renaissance.* Urbana: University of Illinois Press, 2012.

A collection of original essays that focus on the lives and work of black creative, literary, visual, and performance artists in Black Chicago Renaissance during the 1930s to the 1950s. Essays focus on Charles White, Richard Wright, Horace Cayton, and Gwendolyn Brooks. It includes a lengthy history of Black Chicago visual artists with representative illustrations of their painting and sculptures.

Barbara Dianne Savage. *Broadcasting Freedom: Radio, War, and the Politics of Race, 1938–1948.* Chapel Hill: University of North Carolina Press, 1999. An illuminating and ingenious social history of African-American men and women who struggled to create a public venue to discuss racial consciousness and the desire for freedom during the 1940s.

ADDITIONAL BIBLIOGRAPHY

ART

Michael D. Harris and Moyo Okediji. *Colored Pictures: Race and Visual Representation.* Chapel Hill: University of North Carolina Press, 2003.

Peter T. Nesbett and Michelle DuBois. *Over the Line: The Art and Life of Jacob Lawrence.* Seattle: University of Washington Press, 2002.

Sharon F. Patton. *African-American Art.* New York: Oxford University Press, 1998.

Richard J. Powell. *Black Art and Culture in the 20th Century.* New York: Thames and Hudson, 1997.

Tyler Stovall. *Paris Noir: African Americans in the City of Light.* Boston: Houghton Mifflin, 1996.

Maren Strange. *Bronzeville: Black Chicago in Picture, 1941–1943.* New York: New Press, 2003.

William E. Taylor and Harriet G. Warkel. *A Shared Heritage: Art by Four African Americans.* Bloomington: Indiana University Press, 1996.

BLACK CHICAGO RENAISSANCE

Wallace Best. *Passionately Human, No Less Divine: Religion and Culture in Black Chicago, 1915–1932.* Princeton, NJ: Princeton University Press, 2005.

Robert Bone. "Richard Wright and the Chicago Renaissance." *Callaloo* 9, no. 3 (1986): 446–68.

Richard Courage and Robert A. Bone. *The Muse in Bronzeville: African American Creative Expression in Chicago, 1932–1950.* New Brunswick, New Jersey: Rutgers University Press, 2011.

Adam Green. *Selling the Race: Culture, Community, and Black Chicago, 1940–1955.* Chicago: University of Chicago Press, 2007.

Anne Meis Knupfer. *The Chicago Black Renaissance and Women's Activism.* Urbana: University of Illinois Press, 2006.

Clovis E. Semmes. *The Regal Theatre and Black Culture.* New York: Palgrave, 2006.

Craig Werner. "Leon Forrest, the AACM and the Legacy of the Chicago Renaissance." *The Black Scholar* 23, no. 3/4 (1993): 10–23.

CULTURE

Christine Acham. *Revolution Televised: Prime Time and the Struggle for Black Power.* Minneapolis: University of Minnesota Press, 2004.

Gerald Early, ed. *"Ain't But a Place": An Anthology of African American Writings About St. Louis.* St. Louis: Missouri Historical Society Press, 1998.

Geneviève Fabre and Robert O'Meally, eds. *History and Memory in African-American Culture.* New York: Oxford University Press, 1994.

Kenneth W. Goings. *Mammy and Uncle Mose: Black Collectibles and American Stereotyping.* Bloomington: Indiana University Press, 1994.

Jacqueline Goldsby. *A Spectacular Secret: Lynching in American Life and Literature.* Chicago: University of Chicago Press, 2006.

Darlene Clark Hine, Trica Danielle Keaton, and Stephen Small, eds. *Black Europe and the African Diaspora.* Urbana: University of Illinois Press, 2009.

Robin D. G. Kelley. *Race Rebels: Culture, Politics, and the Black Working Class.* New York: Free Press, 1994.

Tommy L. Lott. *The Invention of Race: Black Culture and the Politics of Representation.* Malden, MA: Blackwell, 1999.

Mel Watkins. *On the Real Side: Laughing, Lying, and Signifying.* New York: Simon & Schuster, 1994.

Robert E. Weems, Jr. *Desegregating the Dollar: African American Consumerism in the Twentieth Century.* New York: New York University Press, 1998.

Victoria Wolcott. *Remaking Respectability: African American Women in Interwar Detroit.* Chapel Hill: University of North Carolina Press, 2001.

DANCE

Katherine Dunham. *A Touch of Innocence.* London: Cassell, 1959.

Bennetta Jules-Rosette. *Josephine Baker in Art and Life: The Icon and the Image.* Urbana: University of Illinois Press, 2007.

Anthea Kraut. "Between Primitivism and Diaspora: The Dance Performances of Josephine Baker, Zora Neale Hurston, and Katherine Dunham." *Theatre Journal* 55, no. 3 (October, 2003): 433–50.

Susan Manning. *Modern Dance, Negro Dance: Race in Motion.* Minneapolis: University of Minnesota Press, 2004.

FILMS

Donald Bogle. *Brown Sugar: Eighty Years of America's Black Female Superstars.* New York: Crown, 1980.

Thomas Cripps. *Making Movies Black: The Hollywood Message Movie From World War II to the Civil Rights Era.* New York: Oxford University Press, 1993.

Jane M. Gaines. *Fire and Desire: Mixed-Race Movies in the Silent Era.* Chicago: University of Chicago Press, 2001.

Jacqueline Najuma Stewart. *Migrating to the Movies: Cinema and Black Urban Modernity.* Berkeley: University of California Press, 2005.

LITERATURE

Henry Louis Gates and Nellie Y. McKay, eds. *Norton Anthology of African American Literature.* New York: Norton, 1997.

Robert G. O'Meally. *The Craft of Ralph Ellison.* Cambridge, MA: Harvard University Press, 1980.

Arnold Rampersad. *The Life of Langston Hughes.* New York: Oxford University Press, 1986.

Margaret Walker. *Richard Wright, Daemonic Genius: A Portrait of the Man, a Critical Look at His Work.* New York: Morrow, 1988.

Richard Wright. *12 Million Black Voices*, Photos by Edward Rosskam. (1941). Reprint. New York: Basic Books, 2002.

MUSIC AND RADIO

William Barlow. *Looking Up at Down: The Emergence of Blues Culture.* Philadelphia: Temple University Press, 1989.

Thomas Brothers, ed. *Louis Armstrong: In His Own Words.* New York: Oxford University Press, 1999.

John Chilton. *The Song of the Hawk: The Life and Recordings of Coleman Hawkins.* Ann Arbor: University of Michigan Press, 1990.

Linda Dahl. *Morning Glory: A Biography of Mary Lou Williams.* New York: Pantheon Books, 2000.

Miles Davis and Quincy Troupe. *Miles: The Autobiography.* New York: Simon & Schuster, 1989.

Duke Ellington. *Music Is My Mistress.* New York: Da Capo Press, 1973.

John Birks Gillespie and Wilmot Alfred Fraser. *To Be or Not . . . to Bop: Memoirs—Dizzy Gillespie with Al Fraser.* New York: Doubleday, 1979. New ed., University of Minnesota Press, 2009.

Farah Jasmine Griffin. *If You Can't Be Free, Be a Mystery: In Search of Billie Holiday.* New York: Oxford University Press, 2001.

Michael Harris. *The Rise of Gospel Blues: The Music of Thomas Andrew Dorsey in the Urban Church.* New York: Oxford University Press, 1992.

Allan Keiler. *Marian Anderson: A Singer's Journey.* New York: Scribner, 2000.

Robin D. G. Kelley. *Thelonious Monk: The Life and Times of an American Original.* New York: Free Press, 2009.

Jules Schwerin. *Got to Tell It: Mahalia Jackson, Queen of Gospel.* New York: Oxford University Press, 1992.

Alyn Shipton. *Groovin' High: The Life of Dizzy Gillespie.* New York: Oxford University Press, 1999.

Eileen Southern. *The Music of Black Americans: A History.* 2nd ed. New York: Norton, 1983.

Quintard Taylor. *In Search of the Racial Frontier: African Americans in the American West, 1528–1900.* New York: Norton, 1998.

Terry Teachout. *Pops: A Life of Louis Armstrong.* New York: Houghton Mifflin Harcourt, 2009.

J. C. Thomas. *Chasin' the Trane: The Music and Mystique of John Coltrane.* Garden City, NY: Doubleday, 1975.

Dempsey J. Travis. *Autobiography of Black Jazz.* Chicago: Urban Research Press, 1983.

SPORTS

Arthur Ashe, with the assistance of Kip Branch, Ocania Chalk, and Francis Harris. *A Hard Road to Glory: A History of the African-American Athlete.* New York: Warner Books, 1988.

Richard Bak. *Joe Louis: The Great Black Hope.* New York: Da Capo Press, 1998.

Robert Peterson. *Only the Ball Was White: A History of Legendary Black Players and All-Black Professional Teams.* New York: McGraw-Hill, 1984.

Arnold Rampersad. *Jackie Robinson: A Biography.* New York: Alfred A. Knopf, 1997.

Jackie Robinson. *I Never Had It Made.* New York: G. P. Putnam's Sons, 1972.

Jeffrey T. Sammons. *Beyond the Ring: The Role of Boxing in American Society.* Urbana: University of Illinois Press, 1988.

Scott Simon. *Jackie Robinson and the Integration of Baseball.* New York: John Wiley & Sons. 2002.

RELIGION

Claude Andrew Clegg III. *An Original Man: The Life and Times of Elijah Muhammad.* New York: St. Martin's Griffin, 1997.

C. Eric Lincoln and Lawrence H. Mamiya. *The Black Church in the African American Experience.* Durham, NC: Duke University Press, 1990.

Elijah Muhammad. *The True History of Elijah Muhammad: Messenger of Allah (Autobiographically Authoritative).* Atlanta: Secretarius MEMPS Publications, 1997.

Jill Watts. *God, Harlem U.S.A.: The Father Divine Story.* Berkeley: University of California Press, 1992.

Robert Weisbrot. *Father Divine and the Struggle for Racial Equality.* Urbana: University of Illinois Press, 1983.

RETRACING THE ODYSSEY

Harold Washington Library Center, Chicago, Illinois. Named in honor of Harold Washington, Chicago's first African-American mayor, the 10-story library, art, and computer reference center features the Harold Washington Archives and Collections (on the ninth floor), the collection of the Chicago Blues Archive, and the work of several African-American artists. Jacob Lawrence contributed a mural-sized mosaic titled "Events in the Life of Harold Washington" on the north wall of the library.

DuSable Museum of African-American History, Chicago, Illinois. Artist Margaret Goss Burroughs opened the Ebony Museum in 1961 in her home in Chicago. She moved it in 1973 to its present location at Washington Park and renamed it the DuSable Museum of African-American History. The DuSable Museum honors the accomplishments of Jean Baptiste Pointe DuSable, a Haitian-born immigrant who arrived in Chicago in 1779 and was the first non-Indian to settle in the area. The museum houses an extensive collection of artifacts, art, books, and civil rights documents and sponsors a diverse array of cultural and educational programs and exhibits.

Carter G. Woodson Regional Library, Chicago, Illinois. This branch of the Chicago Public Library, named in honor of the "Father of Black History," Carter G. Woodson, contains a wealth of photographs, books, documents, and manuscript collections concerning the artists and authors, women's clubs, and social institutions that detail the Black Chicago Renaissance. The Vivian Harsah Collection of Afro-American History and Literature contains over 70,000 volumes by Langston Hughes, Richard Wright, Gwendolyn Brooks, and Arna Bontemps, among others.

20

The World War II Era and the Seeds of a Revolution

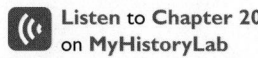

Listen to Chapter 20
on MyHistoryLab

The treatment that the Negro soldier has received has been resented not only by the Negro soldier but by the Negro civilian population as well. In fact, any straight-thinking person with a sense of justice and right, without any respect to color or race, must realize the dangers inherent in the evil practices that have been permitted to exist in the Army. It is not a pleasant thought for Negroes to ponder that their tax money is being spent to help maintain an army that has little regard for the real principles of democracy.

David H. Bradford, the Louisville Courier Journal, *September 2, 1941*

LEARNING OBJECTIVES

How did African Americans use the World War II crisis to protest racial discrimination?	20-1
What role did African-American physicians and nurses play in the struggle to desegregate the military during World War II?	20-2
How did the Tuskegee Airmen contribute to victory in World War II?	20-3
How did the war exacerbate tensions and competition over housing and jobs between black and white Americans?	20-4
What were the positive and negative effects of the Cold War on blacks, both in politics and social life?	20-5

Between 1939 and 1954, the U.S. role in the world was transformed. The victory in World War II of the Allies—the Soviet Union, Great Britain, the United States, and dozens of other countries—over the Axis powers of Germany, Italy, and Japan marked America's emergence as the dominant global power. This international role placed new constraints on the nation's domestic policies, particularly when, after the Axis surrender in 1945, suspicions between the United States and the Soviet Union developed into the Cold War. This period also witnessed the rise of black internationalism. Many African Americans forged close bonds with Africans who fought against European colonialism in Africa. The Cold War lasted until 1989 and led to a vast expansion in the size and power of the federal government, particularly its military. It also greatly influenced domestic politics.

International events replaced the Great Depression as the defining force in the lives of African Americans. In preparing for and fighting World War II, America finally emerged from the Depression and laid the basis for an era of unprecedented prosperity. Industrial and military mobilization resulted in the movement of millions of people, many of them African Americans, from agricultural areas into the cities. This population shift substantially increased black voting

Racial segregation as practiced by the U.S. military reminded African Americans of their second-class status in America. The World War II crisis made impossible continued acquiescence to blatant inequalities. The black "Double V" campaign sought victory against racism on the home and fascism on the foreign fronts.

535

strength in the North and West, which—combined with a moral recoil from the savage racial policies of the Nazis—drove the issue of black equality to the forefront of national politics. Moreover, hundreds of thousands of black men and women learned new skills and ideas while serving in the armed forces, and many resolved to claim their rights. Events abroad and in the United States during the 1940s heightened black consciousness and led to a more aggressive militancy among local leaders and black citizens in southern states.

The Cold War also had a tremendous impact on African Americans and their struggle for freedom. The two sides of this global conflict avoided direct confrontation with each other. Instead, they sought to enlist Africans, Asians, and Latin Americans as proxies. American leaders, trying to convince these peoples of America's virtues as a democracy, were pressed to address the segregation and racial discrimination that remained firmly imbedded in American life. The U.S. Department of State sponsored worldwide tours of outstanding black jazz musicians to represent the positive dimensions of American culture. Still, the advocacy groups and black press that had come of age during the 1930s and 1940s focused attention on fighting racism and demanded the full rights and responsibilities of citizenship for all people. The result was a powerful movement for civil rights that many liberal white Americans and, increasingly, key institutions in the national government supported. Rising opposition to European colonialism in Africa and the development of numerous African independence wars also inspired black American militancy and human rights activism.

These favorable developments, however, provoked strong resistance. Egged on by their politicians, white southerners defended segregation with all the power at their command. The emerging conflict with the Soviet Union prompted many white conservatives to charge that all those seeking to fight racial injustice were agents of the communist enemy. These contrary currents—on one hand, the push for a new democracy, and, on the other, the Cold War mentality—would indelibly stamp the emerging civil rights movement.

On the Eve of War, 1936–1941

20-1 **How did African Americans use the World War II crisis to protest racial discrimination?**

Watch on MyHistoryLab Video:
Origins of World War II

As the world economy wallowed in the Great Depression, the international order collapsed in Europe and Asia. Germany under Adolf Hitler (1889–1945) and Italy under Benito Mussolini (1883–1945) created an alliance, known as the Axis, to control Europe. These fascist dictators advocated a political program based on extreme nationalism that suppressed internal opposition and used violence to gain their will abroad. Germany was the dominant partner in the Axis. Its National Socialist, or Nazi, Party in part blamed communists and foreign powers for the nation's economic depression and loss of power. However, even more than by anticommunism, Hitler was driven by virulent racism and his belief in Anglo-Saxon, or white Aryan, supremacy. Unlike racists in the United States, he blamed Jews for Germany's social and economic problems. The Nazis also despised black people and considered them inferior or subhuman beings. They discriminated against Germans with African ancestors and banned jazz as "nigger" music. Beginning in the mid-1930s, the Germans and Italians embarked on a series of aggressive confrontations and military campaigns that placed much of Central Europe under their power. In August 1939 Germany signed a nonaggression pact with the Soviet Union, a prelude to its September 1 attack on Poland, which the Soviets joined a few weeks later. Poland's allies, Britain and France, reacted by declaring war on Germany, thus beginning World War II.

As Germany and Italy pursued their aggression in Europe, the empire of Japan sought to dominate East Asia. The Japanese considered themselves the foremost power in the Far East and wanted to drive out or supplant both the European states—mainly Britain, France, and the Netherlands—and the United States, which had extensive economic interests and colonial possessions there. (The United States controlled the Philippines, Hawaii, Guam, and other Pacific islands.) Japan's aggressive expansionist policies also led to conflict in the 1930s with the Soviet Union in Manchuria and to a long and bloody war with the Nationalist regime in China. The United States supported China and encouraged the Europeans to resist Japanese demands for economic and territorial concessions in their Asian colonies. Japan's alliance with Nazi Germany and fascist Italy further aggravated United States–Japanese relations, which deteriorated rapidly after the outbreak of World War II in Europe. These tensions led to war on December 7, 1941, when the Japanese bombed American warships at Pearl Harbor, Hawaii, and launched a massive offensive against British, Dutch, and American territory throughout the Pacific.

President Franklin D. Roosevelt watched the events in Europe and Asia during the 1930s with growing concern, but his ability to react was limited. Despite its large economy and large navy, America was not a preeminent military power at the time. Roosevelt had trouble convincing Congress to enlarge the army because a significant segment of the American population, the isolationists, believed the United States had been hoodwinked into fighting World War I and should avoid becoming entangled in another foreign war. During the late 1930s, the president had managed to overcome some of this opposition and had won the authority to increase the size of the nation's armed forces. By early 1940 the United States had instituted its first peacetime draft to provide men for the army and navy.

African Americans and the Emerging International Crisis

Many African Americans responded to the emerging world crisis with growing activism. When Italy invaded Ethiopia—which, along with Liberia and Haiti, was one of the world's three black-ruled nations—in 1935, black communities throughout the United States organized to send it aid. In New York, black nurses under the leadership of Salaria Kee raised money to purchase medical supplies, and black physician John West volunteered to treat wounded Ethiopians at a hospital supported by black American donations. Mass meetings to support the Ethiopians were held in New York City under the auspices of the Provisional Committee for the Defense of Ethiopia and the Ethiopian World Federation. Similar rallies occurred in other large cities while reporters from black newspapers, such as J. A. Rogers of the *Pittsburgh Courier*, brought the horror of this war home to their readers. Although American law forbade citizens to engage in active combat in Ethiopia, over 17,000 African Americans indicated a desire to help Emperor Haile Selassie (r. 1930–1974) resist the Italians. Despite fierce resistance, the Italians won the war in 1936, in part by using poison gas. The conflict alerted many African Americans to the dangers of fascism and fueled even greater interest in and identification with Africa. The flames of black internationalism became even hotter after World War II.

Civil war in Spain stimulated renewed activism among leftist African Americans. In 1936 a fascist-conservative movement led by General Francisco Franco (1892–1975), supported by Germany and Italy, started a civil war to overthrow the left-leaning Spanish Republic. About a hundred African Americans traveled to Spain in 1936–1937 to serve with the Abraham Lincoln Brigade, an integrated fighting force of 3,000 socialist and communist American volunteers. Among the African Americans were two women: Salaria Kee, who nursed the wounded on the battlefield, and Thyra Edwards, who worked for the Medical Bureau and North American Committee to Aid Spanish Democracy. Support of the Abraham

((· Listen on **MyHistoryLab** Audio: Pearl Harbor

20-1

20-2

20-3

20-4

20-5

Lincoln Brigade reflected a commitment by a few African Americans to the communists' vision of internationalism. Mobilization for war, however, would soon bring most black people and their organizations into the fight against fascism abroad and for equality and justice in the United States (the **"Double V" campaign**).

"Double V" campaign Slogan during World War II that stood for victory over fascism abroad and over racism at home for blacks.

A. Philip Randolph and the March on Washington Movement

In 1939 and 1940, the American government, along with the governments of France and Britain, spent so much on arms that the U.S. economy was finally lifted out of the Depression. But the United States mobilized its economy for war and rebuilt its military in keeping with past practices of discrimination and exclusion. As unemployed white workers streamed into aircraft factories, shipyards, and other centers of war production, jobless African Americans were left waiting at the gate. Most aircraft manufacturers, for example, would hire black people only in janitorial positions no matter what their skills were. Many all-white American Federation of Labor (AFL) unions enforced closed-shop agreements that prevented their employers from hiring black workers who were not members of the labor organization. Indeed, many working-class whites were also excluded because of closed-shop agreements. Government-funded training programs regularly rejected black applicants, often reasoning that training them would be pointless given their poor prospects of finding skilled work. The United States Employment Service (USES) filled "whites-only" requests for defense workers. The military itself made it clear that although it would accept black men in their proportion to the population, about 11 percent at the time, it would put them in segregated units and assign them to service duties. The navy limited black servicemen to menial positions. The Marine Corps and the Army Air Corps refused to accept them altogether.

When a young African-American man wrote the *Pittsburgh Courier* and suggested a "Double V" campaign—victory over fascism abroad and victory over racism at home—the newspaper adopted his words as the battle cry for the entire race. Fighting this struggle in a nation at war would be difficult, but the effort led to the further development of black organizations and transformed the national and international worldviews of many African-American soldiers and civilians. Black internationalism was never a more prominent component of black people's consciousness than during the spirited "Double V" campaign in which African-American protest groups and newspapers criticized discrimination at home and fascism abroad. Two months before the 1940 presidential election, the NAACP, the Urban League, and other groups pressed President Roosevelt to act against discrimination in defense programs. The president listened to their protests, but aside from a few token gestures—appointing Howard University Law School dean William Hastie as a "civilian aide on Negro affairs" in the Department of War and promoting Benjamin O. Davis, the senior black officer in the army, to brigadier general—he responded with little of substance. As a result, during late 1940 the NAACP and other groups staged mass protest rallies around the nation. With the election safely won, the president—anxious not to offend white southern politicians he needed to back his war program—refused even to meet with black leaders.

In January 1941 A. Philip Randolph, who was president of the Brotherhood of Sleeping Car Porters and who had been working with other groups to get Roosevelt's attention, called on black people to unify their protests and direct them at the national government. He suggested that 10,000 African Americans march on Washington under the slogan "We loyal Negro-American citizens demand the right to work and fight for our country." In the following

Read on MyHistoryLab Document: A. Philip Randolph Calls on Blacks to Support the Fight for Equality at Home and Abroad, 1941

Horace Pippin's (1888–1946) *Mr. Prejudice* (1943) hammers a wedge of racism through a giant V (the sign of victory). It is a powerful expression of black Americans' ongoing struggle against racial discrimination, segregation, and violence even within a nation at war against fascism and Nazism and the spread of communism.
Horace Pippin (1888–1946), "Mr. Prejudice," 1943. Oil on canvas, 18" × 14".
Philadelphia Museum of Art, Gift of Dr. and Mrs. Matthew T. Moore.

20-1
20-2
20-3
20-4
20-5

months, Randolph helped create the **March on Washington Movement (MOWM)**, which soon became the largest African-American organization since Marcus Garvey's Universal Negro Improvement Association of the 1920s. The MOWM's demands included a presidential order forbidding companies with government contracts from engaging in racial discrimination, eliminating race-based exclusion from defense training courses, and requiring the USES to supply workers on a nonracial basis. Randolph also wanted an order to abolish segregation in the armed forces and the president's support for a law withdrawing the benefits of the National Labor Relations Act from unions that refused to grant membership to black Americans. Unlike the leaders of most other African-American protest groups of the time, Randolph prohibited white involvement and encouraged the black working class to participate.

Many African Americans who had never taken part in the activities of middle-class-dominated groups like the NAACP responded to Randolph's appeal. Soon he alarmed the president by raising the number expected to march to 50,000. Roosevelt, fearing the protest would undermine America's democratic rhetoric and provide grist for the German propaganda mills, dispatched First Lady Eleanor Roosevelt and New York City Mayor Fiorello La Guardia to dissuade Randolph from marching. Their pleas for patience fell on deaf ears, compelling Roosevelt and his top military officials to meet with Randolph and other black leaders. The president offered a set of superficial changes, but the African Americans stood firm in their demands and raised the stakes by increasing their estimate of the number of black marchers coming to Washington to 100,000. By the end of June 1941, the president capitulated and had his aides draft **Executive Order 8802**, prompting Randolph to call off the march. It was a grand moment. "To this day," NAACP leader Roy Wilkins wrote in his autobiography, "I don't know if he would have been able to turn out enough marchers to make his point stick . . . but, what a bluff it was. A tall, courtly black man with Shakespearean diction and the stare of an eagle had looked the patrician Roosevelt in the eye—and made him back down."

Executive Order 8802

On the surface at least, the president's order marked a significant change in the government's stance. It stated in part,

> I do hereby affirm the policy of the United States that there shall be no discrimination in the employment of workers in the defense industry or government because of race, creed, color, or national origin.

The order instructed all agencies that trained workers to administer such programs without discrimination. To ensure full cooperation with these guidelines, Roosevelt created the **Fair Employment Practices Committee (FEPC)** with the power to investigate complaints of discrimination. The order said nothing about desegregation of the military, but private assurances were made that the barriers to entry in key services would be lowered. Over a dozen African-American scientists would participate in the development of radar and in research projects on other secret defense technologies at Camp Evans in New Jersey. Camp Evans was a U.S. Army Signal Corps base and was one of the principal U.S. sites associated with the development of radar.

Executive Order 8802, although it was the first major presidential action countering discrimination since Reconstruction, was no new Emancipation Proclamation. Black excitement with the order soon soured as many industries, particularly in the South, made only token hirings of African Americans. What the black community learned in this instance, and what it would witness repeatedly in the decades to come, was that merely articulating antidiscrimination principles and establishing commissions and committees did not eradicate inequalities. Moreover, the order did not mention union discrimination. Nonetheless, the threat of the march, the issuance of the executive order, and the creation of the FEPC marked the formal acknowledgment by the federal government that it bore some responsibility for protecting black and minority rights in employment. Black activists and their allies would have to continue their fight if the order was to have meaning. Randolph sought to

March on Washington Movement (MOWM) Movement created by A. Philip Randolph to pressure the federal government to end discrimination in the defense industry and government.

Executive Order 8802 Order issued by President Franklin D. Roosevelt in 1941 banning discrimination in employment in defense industries and the federal government.

Fair Employment Practices Committee (FEPC) A committee created by Franklin Roosevelt to investigate complaints of discrimination.

 **Read** on MyHistoryLab
Document: Earl B. Dickerson Talks About the Fair Employment Practices Committee, 1941–1943

20-1

20-2

20-3

20-4

20-5

lead them but would find it difficult to do so because of the opposition of key government agencies—notably the military—as well as the power of southern congressmen and a belief among white people that winning the war took precedence over racial issues.

Race and the U.S. Armed Forces

20-2 What role did African-American physicians and nurses play in the struggle to desegregate the military during World War II?

The demands of A. Philip Randolph and other black leaders and healthcare professionals to end segregation in the armed forces initially met stiffer resistance than their pleas for change in the civilian sector. Black men were expected to serve their country; however, at the beginning of the war, most were assigned to segregated service battalions, relegated to noncombat positions, kept out of the more prestigious branches of the service, and confronted by tremendous obstacles to becoming officers. This was particularly galling because military segregation was a symbol of the rampant discrimination black men and women encountered in their daily lives.

During the prewar mobilization period (1940–1941), black physicians and leaders of their black professional organization, the National Medical Association, remembering the segregation they had experienced during World War I, queried the War Department about their status. In a new war, would black physicians be integrated into the medical corps or required to practice in separate facilities set aside for sick and wounded black soldiers? In a 1940 speech, Dr. G. Hamilton Francis underscored the black doctors' concerns: "Our nation is again preparing to defend itself against aggression from without. Today, we are ready and willing to contribute all of our skill and energy and to wholeheartedly enlist our services as members of the medical profession, but we must be permitted to take our right places, as evidenced by our training, experience, and ability."

Institutional Racism in the American Military

Much of the armed forces' racial policy derived from negative attitudes and discriminatory practices common in American society. Reflecting this ingrained racism, a 1925 study by the American War College concluded that African Americans were physically unqualified for combat duty, were by nature subservient and mentally inferior, believed themselves to be inferior to white people, were susceptible to the influence of crowd psychology, could not control themselves in the face of danger, and lacked the initiative and resourcefulness of white people.

Based on this and later studies, the War Department laid out two key policies in 1941 for the use of black soldiers. Although they would be taken into the military at the same rate as white inductees, African Americans would be segregated and would serve primarily in noncombat units. Responding with disdain for those who criticized these policies, Undersecretary of War Robert Patterson wrote,

> The Army is not a sociological laboratory; to be effective it must be organized and trained according to principles which will insure success. Experiments to meet the wishes and demands of the champions of every race and creed for the solution of their problems are a danger to efficiency, discipline and morale and would result in ultimate defeat. Out of these fundamental thoughts have been evolved broad principles relating to the employment of all persons in the military service.

In creating these policies, the military ignored evidence of the fighting ability that African Americans had shown in previous wars, confirmed by

Fort Monmouth physicist Dr. Walter S. McAfee (1914–1995) is shown with President Dwight D. Eisenhower after a White House ceremony in 1956. He was awarded one of the first Secretary of the Army's Research Fellowships, which provided for his postdoctoral study at Harvard University and at laboratories in Europe and Australia.

PROFILE   Steven Robinson and the Montford Point Marines

These are among the very first African-American men to serve in the U.S. Marine Corps. Beginning in 1942 they trained at a separate facility at Montford Point near Camp Lejeune, North Carolina.

WHEN 17-YEAR-OLD STEVEN ROBINSON joined the military in May 1942, he was among the first African Americans to become a marine. From its founding in 1798 until World War II, the Marine Corps accepted only white men. Although President Roosevelt's Executive Order 8802 ended that racial exclusion, it did not outlaw segregation in the military.

With grim reluctance, the Marine Corps began to accept black men. The commandant of the corps, Major General Thomas Holcomb, disdained the prospect of black marines: "If it were a question of having a Marine Corps of 5,000 whites or 250,000 Negroes, I would rather have the whites." The corps would not allow black men to train with white recruits at Parris Island in South Carolina. Instead, it established a separate training facility for black men at Montford Point in North Carolina.

Robinson immediately encountered hostility as he traveled south for basic training. For the first time, he experienced segregated railroad coaches and stations. He inadvertently entered a white waiting room in Rocky Mount, North Carolina, and was curtly instructed to leave: "So I went out the door and as I went out the door, something [said], look, look back and I looked back, I looked over at the station, at the entrance to the station, and I saw a sign. It had to be three feet in width and maybe five feet in length and it says 'For White Only.'"

During basic training Robinson impressed white drill instructors and officers, and he was promoted to platoon sergeant before departing for the war in the Pacific. On the troop train to the West Coast, black marines were refused service when they tried to buy soda in Arizona. They saw German and Italian prisoners of war enjoying the company of American women in restaurants, bars, and clubs that excluded African Americans.

Doubting their fitness, the Marine Corps did not want black men in combat, and most of the Montford Point marines were assigned support roles in ammunition and depot companies. Nevertheless, the black marines participated in several major amphibious operations in the Pacific, including Iwo Jima.

Robinson and a contingent of black marines went ashore on Iwo Jima on February 19, 1945, and took part in some of the fiercest fighting of World War II. One of Robinson's close friends, Jimmy Wilkins, was mortally wounded: "Jimmy was on my right shoulder about two feet [away] when he got hit. And he was killed . . . everybody liked him in the platoon. I mean, he was just a likable seventeen-year-old young teenager. And I might add, a good Marine." Wilkins was also one of the marines who had not been able to buy a soda in Arizona.

Robinson and other marines were aware that they were fighting to defeat two enemies: "We were fighting the war against the bigotry at home and fighting the war against the bigotry overseas. And we were fighting the war to liberate people who had more liberty than we had."

Photographers and filmmakers generally avoided documenting the activities of the black marines, but Robinson and other black marines witnessed the famous flag raising on Iwo Jima's Mount Suribachi. Robinson would spend 106 days on Iwo Jima. More than 6,000 marines and 21,000 Japanese troops died on the small volcanic island before the Americans gained control.

Nearly 20,000 black men trained at Montford Point during and immediately after World War II. In 1949, as a result of President Harry Truman's Executive Order 9981, the Marine Corps began to integrate, and the separate training facility at Montford Point closed. Black marines would be trained and would fight alongside white marines in Korea, Vietnam, Afghanistan, and Iraq.

Taking advantage of the G.I. Bill of Rights after World War II, Steven Robinson graduated from the University of Pittsburgh and earned a law degree. He practiced law for more than 50 years in Warren, Ohio, where he was active in state and local politics. Robinson died in 2006.

20-1

20-2

20-3

20-4

20-5

the heroism of Doris "Dorie" Miller during the attack on Pearl Harbor. Miller was the son of Texas sharecroppers and had enlisted in the navy in 1938. Like all black sailors in the navy at the time, he had been assigned to mess attendant duty. In other words, he was a cook and a waiter. When the Japanese air force attacked the naval base on December 7, 1941, the 22-year-old Miller was below decks on the battleship U.S.S. *West Virginia*. When his captain was wounded, Miller braved bullets to help move him to a more protected area of the deck.

"above and beyond the call of duty"

DORIE MILLER
*Received the Navy Cross
at Pearl Harbor, May 27, 1942*

This World War II War Department recruitment poster recognizes the heroism of Dorie Miller (1919–1943) at Pearl Harbor. His bravery, however, did not alter the navy's policy of restricting black sailors to the kitchens and boiler rooms of navy vessels.

Read on **MyHistoryLab** Document: Thurgood Marshall, The Legal Attack to Secure Civil Rights, 1942

He then took charge of a machine gun, shooting down at least two and perhaps six enemy aircraft before running out of ammunition. Miller had never before fired the gun. On May 27, 1942, the navy cited him for "distinguished devotion to duty, extraordinary courage and disregard for his own personal safety" and awarded him a Navy Cross, the highest medal that the navy could bestow. It then sent Miller back to mess duty without a promotion.

The Costs of Military Discrimination

Although the War and Navy departments held to the fiction of "separate but equal" in their segregation programs, their policies gave black Americans inferior resources or excluded them entirely. Sick and injured black soldiers were treated in segregated wards in military hospitals. Black physicians could treat only black military personnel. At army camps black soldiers were usually placed in the least desirable spots and denied the use of officers' clubs, base stores, and base recreational facilities. Four-fifths of all training camps were located in the South, where black soldiers were harassed and discriminated against off base as well as on. Even on leave, black soldiers were not offered space in the many hotels the government leased and had to make do with the limited accommodations that had been available to black people before the war. For southern African Americans, even going home in uniform could be dangerous. For example, when Rieves Bell of Starkville, Mississippi, was visiting his family in 1943, three young white men cornered him on a street and attempted to strip off his uniform. Bell fought back and injured one of them with a knife. The army could not save him from the wrath of local civilian authorities who sentenced Bell to three and a half years in the notorious Parchman state penitentiary for the crime of self-defense.

Perhaps most galling was seeing enemy prisoners of war accorded better treatment than African-American soldiers. Dempsey Travis of Chicago recalled his experiences at Camp Shenango, Pennsylvania: "I saw German prisoners free to move around the camp, unlike black soldiers who were restricted. The Germans walked right into the doggone places like any white American. We were wearin' the same uniform, but we were excluded." In 1944 black servicemen stationed at Fort Lawton in Washington State objected to living and working conditions that were inferior to those granted to Italian prisoners of war (POWs). Not only did the Italians receive lighter work assignments than the black Americans, but some Italian POWs were allowed to go to local bars that refused to admit African Americans. The resentment erupted into a riot on August 14, 1944, when black soldiers stoned the barracks housing the Italians. One prisoner was killed, and 24 others were injured. A court-martial convicted 23 black servicemen.

Because of the military's policies, most of the nearly one million African Americans who served during World War II did so in auxiliary units, notably in the transportation and engineering corps. Soldiers in the transportation corps, almost half of whom were black, loaded supplies and drove them in trucks to the front lines. Operating in the Red Ball Express or the later White Ball Express—the names for the trucking operations used to supply the American forces as they drove toward Germany in 1944 and 1945—African Americans braved enemy fire and delivered the fuel, ammunition, and other goods that made the fight possible. Black engineers built camps and ports, constructed and repaved roads, and performed many other tasks to support frontline troops.

Black soldiers performed well in these tasks but were often subject to unfair military discipline. In Europe, many more black soldiers than white soldiers were executed even though African Americans made up only 10 percent of the total number of soldiers stationed there. One of the most glaring examples of unfair treatment was the navy's handling of a "mutiny" at its Port Chicago base north of San Francisco. On July 17, 1944, in the worst home-front disaster of the war, an explosion at the base killed 320 sailors, of whom 202 were black ammunition loaders. In the following month, 328 of the surviving ammunition loaders were sent to fill another ship. When 258 of them refused to do so, they were arrested. Eventually the navy charged 50 men with mutiny, convicted them, and sentenced them to terms of imprisonment ranging from 8 to 15 years at Terminal Island in California. The NAACP's Thurgood Marshall filed a brief arguing that the men had been railroaded into prison because of their race, but to no avail.

Soldiers and Civilians Protest Military Discrimination

In military segregation, black American leaders identified a formidable but vulnerable target. Employing a variety of strategies, they mobilized the black civilian workforce, black women's groups, black college students, and an interracial coalition to resist this blatant inequality. They provoked a public dialogue with government and military officials at a pivotal moment when America's leaders most wanted to present a united democratic front to the world.

Examples of black protest abound. In 1942 the NAACP's journal the *Crisis* and the National Urban League's *Opportunity* published many editorials denouncing military segregation. Walter White traveled across the country and throughout the world visiting camps and making contacts with black soldiers and their white officers. He inundated the War Department and the president with letters citing examples of improper, hostile, and humiliating treatment of black servicemen by military personnel and in the white communities where bases were located. Frustration with continued military intransigence, however, forced William Hastie to resign as an adviser on Negro affairs on January 5, 1943.

Black Women in the Struggle to Desegregate the Military

The role of black women in the struggle to desegregate the military has often been overlooked, but their militancy contributed to the effort. A 1942 editorial in the *Crisis* suggested why:

> The colored woman has been a more potent factor in shaping Negro society than the white woman has been in shaping white society because the sexual caste system has been much more fluid and ill-defined than among whites. Colored women have worked with their men and helped build and maintain every institution we have. Without their economic aid and counsel we would have made little if any progress.

The most prominent example of black women's struggle is found in the history of the National Association of Colored Graduate Nurses. Mabel K. Staupers, its executive director, led an aggressive fight to eliminate quotas in the U.S. Army Nurse Corps. Although many black nurses volunteered during World War II, the navy refused to admit them, and the army allowed few to serve. To draw attention to the unfairness of quotas, Staupers met with First Lady Eleanor Roosevelt in November 1944 and described black

William H. Hastie earned his L.L.B. in 1930 and his S.J.D. in 1935 at Harvard Law School. He taught at Howard University Law School, where he, along with Charles Hamilton Houston, trained the first generation of civil rights lawyers, the most illustrious of whom were Thurgood Marshall and Oliver Hill. In 1943, the NAACP presented Hastie with the Spingarn Medal. Appointed by President Harry Truman in 1949, Hastie became the first black American to serve as a federal judge. He sat on the Third Circuit Court of Appeals until 1971.

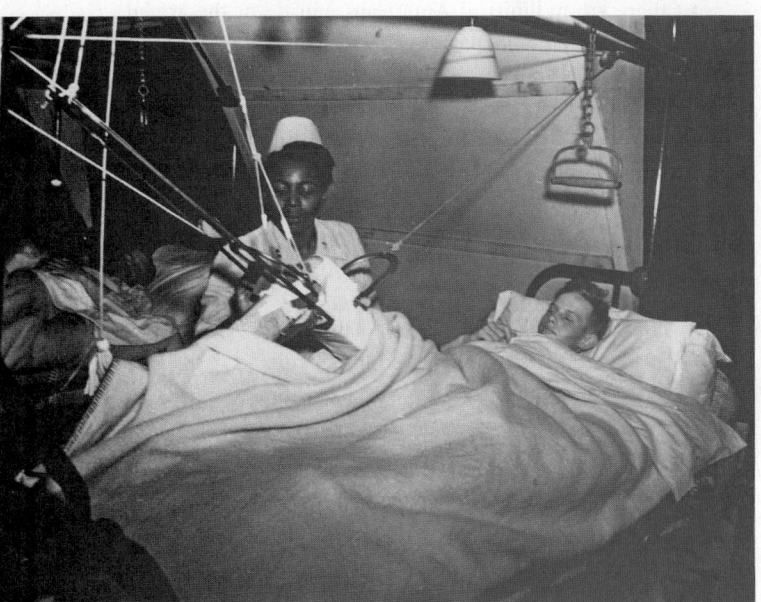

African-American women nurses served at station hospitals at home and abroad. They resented the quotas and discrimination and fought to end segregation in the U.S. military. Still, black nurses such as Lt. Florie E. Grant provided expert care for POWs, as shown in this October 7, 1942, image of her in a hospital ward in England.

VOICES   William H. Hastie Resigns in Protest

In January 1943 William H. Hastie, who had been on leave from his post as dean of the Howard University Law School, resigned as civilian aide to Secretary of War Henry L. Stimson to protest the failure to outlaw discrimination in the military. Hastie had taken the position in 1940, but throughout his tenure he had experienced frustration and hostility in attempting to secure equal treatment for black men and women in uniform. In his letter of resignation, which he published in the Chicago Defender, *he explains that the Army Air Forces' reactionary policies and discriminatory practices were the catalyst to his resignation:*

The Army Air Forces are growing in importance and independence. In the post war period they may become the greatest single component of the armed services. Biased policies and harmful practices established in this branch of the army can all too easily infect other branches as well. The situation had become critical. Yet, the whole course of my dealings with the Army Air Forces convinced me that further expression of my views in the form of recommendations within the department would be futile. I, therefore, took the only course which can, I believe, bring results. Public opinion is still the strongest force in American life.

To the Negro soldier and those who influence his thinking, I say with all the force and sincerity at my command that the man in uniform must grit his teeth, square his shoulders and do his best as a soldier, confident that there are millions of Americans outside of the armed services, and more persons than he knows in high places within the military establishment, who will never cease fighting to remove every racial barrier and every humiliating practice which now confront him. But only by being, at all times a first class soldier can the man in uniform help in this battle which shall be fought and won.

When I took office, the Secretary of War directed that all questions of policy and important proposals relating to Negroes should be referred to my office for comment or approval before final action. In December, 1940, the Air Forces referred to me a plan for a segregated training center for Negro pursuit pilots at Tuskegee. I expressed my entire disagreement with the plan, giving my reasons in detail. My views were disregarded.

Since then, the Air Command has never on its own initiative submitted any plan or project to me for comment or recommendation. What information I obtained, I had to seek out. Where I made proposals or recommendations, I volunteered them.

This situation reached its climax in late December, 1942, when I learned through army press releases sent out from St. Louis and from the War Department in Washington that the Air Command was about to establish a segregated officer candidate school at Jefferson Barracks, Mo., to train Negro officers for ground duty with the Army Air Forces. Here was a proposal for a radical departure from present army practice, since the officer candidate-training program is the one large field where the army is eliminating racial segregation.

Moreover, I had actually written to the Air Command several weeks earlier in an attempt to find out what was brewing at Jefferson Barracks. The Air Command replied as late as December 17, 1942, giving not even the slightest hint of any plan for a segregated officer candidate school. It is inconceivable to me that consideration of such a project had not then advanced far enough for my office to have been consulted, even if I had not made specific inquiry. The conclusion is inescapable that the Air Command does not propose to inform, much less counsel with, this office about its plans for Negroes.

1. **Why did African Americans fight so relentlessly to end segregation in the U.S. military? What did the military represent or symbolize to the nation?**

2. **Under what circumstances did African Americans appear to accept segregation and the establishment of separate programs such as the Tuskegee Airmen? Why, then, did African Americans object to the military's efforts to provide equal but separate facilities and educational programs?**

SOURCE: William H. Hastie, "Why I Resigned," *Chicago Defender*, February 6, 1943. Reprinted courtesy of the *Chicago Defender*.

nurses' troubled relationship with the armed forces. She told Mrs. Roosevelt that 82 black nurses were serving 150 patients at the all-black hospital at Fort Huachuca, Arizona, at a time when the army was complaining of a nursing shortage and debating the need to draft nurses. Staupers cited the practice of using black women to care for German POWs and asked if this was to be the special role of the black nurse in the war: "When our women hear of the great need for nurses in the Army and when they enter the service it is with the high hopes that they will be used to nurse sick and wounded soldiers who are fighting our country's enemies and not primarily to take care of these enemies."

Soldiers and sailors also resisted segregation and discrimination while in the service. They mounted well-organized efforts to desegregate officers' clubs. At Freeman Field, Indiana, for example, one hundred black officers refused to back down when their commanders threatened to arrest them for seeking to use the officers' club. In other bases, African-American soldiers responded with violence to violence, intimidation, and threats. Their actions, although quickly suppressed, prompted the army brass to reevaluate their belief in the military efficiency of discrimination.

The Beginning of Military Desegregation

In response to the militancy of black officers, civil rights leaders, and the press, the War Department made changes and began to reeducate soldiers, albeit in a limited fashion. The Advisory Committee on Negro Troop Policies was charged with coordinating the use of black troops and developing policy on social questions and personnel training. In 1943 the War Department also produced its own propaganda film—*The Negro Soldier*, directed by Frank Capra—to alleviate racial tensions. This patronizing film emphasized the contributions black soldiers had made in the nation's wars since the American Revolution and was designed to appeal to both black and white audiences.

The War Department also attempted to use propaganda to counter black protest groups and the claims of discrimination reported in the black press. The key to this effort was boxer

20-1

20-2

20-3

20-4

20-5

VOICES   Separate but Equal Training for Black Army Nurses?

In August 1944 Mabel Staupers received this reply from Under secretary of War Robert Patterson in response to her query about a segregated training center the army had established at Fort Huachuca, Arizona, for black nurses:

AUGUST 7, 1944

Mrs. Mabel K. Staupers R.N.,
Executive Secretary,
National Association of Colored Graduate Nurses, Inc.,
1790 Broadway,
New York 19, N.Y.

Dear Mrs. Staupers:

Thank you for your letter of July 19 with reference to the establishment of the first basic training center for Army Negro nurses at Fort Huachuca.

In establishing the first basic training center for Army Negro nurses at Fort Huachuca, the War Department desired that these nurses receive the best possible training and the most valuable experience for the type of service they would be required to render as Army nurses. It is the policy of the War Department to assign Negro nurses to those hospitals where there is a substantial number of Negro troops

in relation to the personnel of the entire installation. The trainee at Fort Huachuca will therefore have the advantage of serving in a facility and under conditions parallel to those under which she will serve as an Army nurse.

You may be assured that the facilities for training afforded Negro nurses at Fort Huachuca will in no way be inferior to those of other similar establishments, and in their subsequent assignments these nurses will have full opportunity to render valuable service to the Army.

Sincerely yours,
(Signed) ROBERT P. PATTERSON
ROBERT P. PATTERSON,
Under Secretary of War

1. How does Patterson's letter reflect the military's position that "separate but equal" did not constitute discrimination against African Americans?

2. Why did Mabel Staupers and the National Association of Colored Graduate Nurses object to separate training facilities for black women?

SOURCE: War Department Files, File #2912, National Archives, Washington, DC.

PROFILE   Mabel K. Staupers

MABEL K. STAUPERS WAS BORN IN BARBADOS, in the British West Indies, on February 27, 1890, to Thomas Clarence and Pauline (Lobo) Doyle. Mother and daughter emigrated to New York in 1903. Mabel's father joined them later. In 1917 Mabel became a U.S. citizen. In short order, she married James Max Keaton, from whom she was later divorced, and received her R.N. diploma from Freedmen's Hospital School of Nursing in Washington, DC. She worked as a private-duty nurse in Washington and New York City, where she helped to organize and served as the superintendent from 1920 to 1922 of the Booker T. Washington Sanatorium, an inpatient clinic for African Americans with tuberculosis. This was one of the few facilities in New York that permitted black physicians to treat their patients when they were hospitalized. Most other hospitals denied black medical professionals attending or staff privileges and positions. Staupers further honed her organizing and leadership skills when she became executive secretary of the Harlem Committee of the New York Tuberculosis and Health Association from 1922 to 1934. In 1935 Staupers joined with Mary McLeod Bethune to found the National Council of Negro Women. In 1934 Staupers became the first executive director of the National Association of Colored Graduate Nurses (NACGN) and served until 1949, when she was named the organization's president. Under her stewardship the NACGN officially dissolved in 1951, after black nurses gained membership in the American Nursing Association.

Staupers's organizational and leadership talent was put to its greatest test during World War II. With verve and perfect timing, she mobilized wide-ranging support to end quotas that the military had established to limit the numbers of black nurses in the armed forces nurse corps. While the army initially indicated that it would accept 56 black nurses to work in the hospital units at Camp Livingston in Louisiana and Fort Bragg in North Carolina, the navy refused to accept any black women nurses. The matter came to a head when, in January 1945, President Franklin D. Roosevelt announced his support of legislation to draft nurses. Staupers was appalled that the government would entertain such a notion when hundreds of black women nurses were eager to serve. She led the struggle to end quotas and discrimination against black women nurses in the armed forces. Staupers published her account of this struggle in *No Time for Prejudice: A Story of the Integration of Negroes in Nursing in the United States* (New York: Macmillan, 1961). In recognition of her courageous struggle against racial discrimination, the NAACP awarded Staupers the Spingarn Medal in 1951. An array of honors followed. In 1967, New York Mayor John V. Lindsay gave her a citation that read, "To an immigrant who came to the United States and by Individual Effort through Education and Personal Achievement has become an Outstanding American Leader and Distinguished Citizen of America." She died of pneumonia at her home in Washington, DC, in 1989.

Joe Louis, whom the army believed was "almost a god" to most black Americans. "The possibilities for using him," a secret internal report stated, "are almost unlimited, such as touring the army camps as special instructor on physical training; exhibition bouts, for use in radio or in movies; in a movie appearance a flashback could be shown of Louis knocking out Max Schmeling, the champion of the Germans." The same report also mentioned other prominent black men and women who had "great value in any propaganda programs. Other athletes like Ray Robinson, also track athletes, etc.; name bands like Cab Calloway, [Jimmy] Lunceford; stage, screen and concert stars like Ethel Waters, Bill Robinson, Eddie Anderson, Paul Robeson, etc." This propaganda did little to counter the prejudice and discrimination that most black Americans experienced in their daily lives.

Racism remained strong throughout the war, but the persistent push of protest groups and the military's need for soldiers gradually loosened its grip. After the attack on Pearl

Harbor, the services had to relax their restrictions on African Americans. The navy, previously the most resistant service, began to accept black men as sailors and noncommissioned officers. By 1943 it allowed African Americans into officer training schools. The Marine Corps, exclusively white throughout its history, began taking African Americans in 1942. Black officers were trained in integrated settings in all services except the Army Air Corps. The War Department even compelled recalcitrant commanding officers to recommend black servicemen for admission to the officer training schools, and soon over 2,000 a year graduated.

Many African Americans also saw combat, although under white officers. Several African-American artillery, tank destroyer, anti-aircraft, and combat engineer battalions fought with distinction in Europe and Asia. Military prejudice seemed to be borne out by the poor showing of the all-black 92nd Combat Division in the Italian campaign in 1944–1945, but investigation revealed that its failure was the result of poor training and leadership by its white commander, General Edward M. Almond, who had no confidence in his men. After the Battle of the Bulge, a massive German counterattack in Belgium in December 1944, 2,500 black volunteers fought in integrated units. The army did not repeat the experiment during the rest of the war, but its success laid the groundwork for the eventual end of segregated units. Although subject to many of the same kinds of discrimination as African-American men, African-American women also found expanded opportunities in the military. Approximately 4,000 black women served in the Women's Army Auxiliary Corps.

Mabel Staupers's efforts finally bore fruit in 1945. When the War Department claimed there was a shortage of nurses, Staupers mobilized nursing groups of all races to protest the discrimination against black nurses in the Army and Navy Nurse Corps. There was an immediate groundswell of public support to remove quotas. Buried beneath an avalanche of telegrams from an inflamed public, the War Department declared an end to quotas and exclusion. On January 10, 1945, the army opened its Nurse Corps to all applicants without regard to race. The navy followed suit on January 15. Within weeks, Phyllis Daley became the first black woman inducted into the Navy Nurse Corps. The Army Nurse Corps eventually accepted over 300 black nurses.

The Tuskegee Airmen

20-3 **How did the Tuskegee Airmen contribute to victory in World War II?**

The most visible group of black soldiers served in the Army Air Force. In January 1941 the War Department announced the formation of an all-black pursuit squadron of fighter planes and the creation of a training program at Tuskegee Army Air Field, Alabama, for black pilots.

Unlike all other units in the army, the 99th Squadron and the 332nd Group, made up of the 100th, 301st, and 302nd Squadrons, had black officers. The 99th went to North Africa in April 1943 and flew its first combat mission against the Italian island of Pantelleria in the Mediterranean on June 2. Later the squadron participated in the air battle over Sicily and supported the invasion of Italy. The squadron regularly engaged German pilots in aerial combat. General Benjamin O. Davis, Jr., commanded the 332nd Group when it was deployed to Italy in January 1944. In July, the 99th was added to the 332nd, and the group participated in campaigns in Italy, France, Germany, and the Balkans.

The **Tuskegee Airmen** gained an impressive record. They flew over 15,500 sorties, completed 1,578 missions, and escorted 200 heavy bombers deep into Germany's

Tuskegee Airmen All-black combat air unit during World War II.

VOICES   A Tuskegee Airman Remembers

Virgil Patterson was a Tuskegee Airman. In an oral history told to historian Ben Vinson III, Patterson recalled both the excitement of being an airman and the racism the Tuskegee Airmen endured:

Between December of 1944 and March of 1945 we saw more action. After having muscled into France, the Allies were preparing to make their final thrust at Hitler. I remember when we flew escort for over 1,000 bombers on their way to Germany. It was an awesome sight, seeing bombers in every direction for a 150-mile stretch. Looking down into the sea we saw still more activity, throngs and throngs of ships. During these months our planes bombarded German factories and troop positions that were preparing to repel the Allied invasion. Thankfully, the Germans didn't have use of the French fleet, which had been scuttled. But the Germans did have friends amongst the French, which made the Allied job more difficult.

Part of our responsibilities included strafing radar installations along the coast of France. On one sortie, I was part of a mission of four planes led by a man named Ballard. My wingman was Jefferson. His wingman was a pilot named Daniels. As we came in towards the ground from an altitude of almost 15,000 feet, I suddenly looked back to find Jefferson and noticed that Daniels, who was flying in front of me, was going up in smoke. I pulled up and started following Ballard, who didn't look back. That's when I noticed that Jefferson was being shot down as well. Ballard and I went in as close to the coast as we

dared and fired furiously at our targets. One, two, three . . . fire! One, two, three . . . fire! That was the interval. I shot short bursts while flying above the ocean at nearly 500 miles an hour.

We lost a number of pilots that day. When I returned to base I learned that Faulkner, our squadron leader, who had been flying at 30,000 feet, turned over and went down. They radioed him, knowing that something must have gone wrong. He was probably unconscious because he didn't respond. A poor oxygen connection apparently caused him to pass out during flight. As for Daniels, I learned many years later that he had survived his ordeal and had become a POW. Ironically, once behind enemy lines, the Germans treated him with proper respect. He was an officer, not a *black* officer. It seemed interesting to me to see how black soldiers had to be in the clutches of the enemy before being bestowed some of the honor that they deserved.

1. **What emotions did combat evoke in Patterson?**
2. **What do his comments about the German treatment of black POWs imply about racism in the U.S. military?**
3. **Do you think Patterson and the other Tuskegee Airmen wanted to be treated as officers or as black officers?**

SOURCE: *Flight: The Story of Virgil Richardson, A Tuskegee Airman in Mexico* (New York: Palgrave, 2004), 66–67.

Rhineland. They accumulated 150 Distinguished Flying Crosses, a Legion of Merit, a Silver Star, 14 Bronze Stars, and 744 Air Medals. Coleman Young (1919–1997), mayor of Detroit from 1973 to 1993, was a proud Tuskegee Airman and retained fond memories of his military service.

Technology: The Tuskegee Planes

To fly and participate in combat, the Tuskegee Airmen and the black ground troops who looked after their planes had to overcome more than the racism that cast doubt on black soldiers' ability to fight. They also had to master the technology of complex machines. The 332nd Fighter Group flew more different kinds of fighter planes than any other group of pilots during World War II. They were initially equipped with P-40 Warhawks, then with P-39 Airacobras, later with P-47 Thunderbolts, and finally with the P-51 Mustang, the airplane with which they became most identified. Keeping these different kinds of planes in top form placed extreme pressure on the black mechanics who serviced them. The mechanics had to master the schematics of completely different engines and repair them. Despite the challenges this presented, the Tuskegee mechanics acquired the respect of the airmen and were recognized for their exceptional mechanical abilities during the war. They frequently worked round-the-clock, sleeping and eating in shifts in the airplane hangars.

Standardization was impossible because each type of plane was designed differently from the others. For example, while the P-39's engine was behind the pilot, the P-40's engine was in front of him. Virgil Richardson, one of the Tuskegee mechanics, talked about servicing the P-39: "First of all, you entered the cockpit through a door, as if you were getting into a car. The plane's motor was located behind the pilot, and there was a propeller shaft that came from the motor, under the pilot's seat, to the three-blade metal propeller. P-39s were equipped with a 37-millimeter cannon in the propeller hub. There were also two .50-caliber machine guns in each wing, and two more in the nose. That was substantial armament! The plane had wide, tricycle landing gear . . . [it] was a joy to fly, since there was no torque."

The Transformation of Black Soldiers

A new generation of African Americans became soldiers during World War II, and the experience gave many of them an enhanced sense of themselves and a commitment to the fight for black equality. They returned home with a broader perception of the world and a transformed consciousness. Unlike the black soldiers in World War I, a greater percentage of those drafted at the outset of World War II had attended high school, and more of them were either high school or college graduates. Some black soldiers brought so-called radical ideas with them as they were drafted and sent to segregated installations. The urban and northern black servicemen and women and many of the southern rural recruits had a strong sense of their own self-worth and dignity. In their study of Chicago, sociologists St. Clair Drake and Horace Cayton noted:

> At least half of the Negro soldiers—and Bronzeville's men fall into this class—were city people who had lived through a Depression in America's Black Ghettoes, and who had been exposed to unions, the Communist movement, and to the moods of racial radicalism that occasionally swept American cities. Even the rural southern Negroes were different this time—for the thirty years between the First and Second World War has seen a great expansion of school facilities in the South and distribution of newspapers and radios.

The armed forces first exposed many African Americans to a world outside the segregated South and nurtured a budding international consciousness. Haywood Stephney of Clarksdale, Mississippi, recalled that when he first encountered segregation in the military he simply thought it was supposed to be that way: "Because you grow up in this situation you don't see but one side of the coin. Having not tasted the freedom or the liberty of being and doing like other folks then you didn't know what it was like over across the street. So we accepted it." Like many others, his experiences during the war quickly removed him from "total darkness" and raised fundamental questions about the nation's racial system.

Douglas Conner, another Mississippi veteran, captured the collective understanding of the social and political meaning of the war shared by the men in his unit, the 31st Quartermaster Battalion stationed in Okinawa: "The air people in Tuskegee, Dorie Miller, and the others gave

Tuskegee Airmen Marcellus G. Smith, Louisville, Kentucky, and Roscoe C. Brown, New York, NY, service their airplane in Ramitelli, Italy, March 1945.

The distinguished World War II record of the "Tuskegee Airmen," pilots who trained and fought in all-black fighter squadrons, confounded the expectations of white officers who doubted that black men had the ability or nerve to pilot fighter aircraft.

the blacks a sense that they could succeed and compete in a world that had been saying that 'you're nothing.'" Conner insisted that "because of the world war, I think many people, especially blacks, got the idea that we're going back, but we're not going back to business as usual. Somehow we're going to change this nation so that there's more equality than there is now." The personal transformation that Conner and others experienced, combined with a number of international, national, and regional forces, laid the foundation for a modern freedom movement.

Black People on the Home Front

20-4   **How did the war exacerbate tensions and competition over housing and jobs between black and white Americans?**

Just as they did in the military, African Americans at home fought a dual war against the Axis powers and racism in the United States. Black workers and volunteers helped staff the factories and farms that produced goods for the fight while also purchasing war bonds and participating in other defense activities. The changes the war brought on also created new points of conflict while exacerbating preexisting problems and occasionally igniting full-scale riots. Throughout the war, protest groups and the black press fought employment discrimination and political exclusion.

Black Workers: From Farm to Factory

The war accelerated the migration of African Americans from rural areas to the cities. Even though the farm economy recovered during the war, high-paying defense jobs and other urban occupations tempted many black farmers to abandon the land. By the 1940s the bitter experiences of the previous decades had made it clear there was little future in the cotton fields. Boll weevils, competition from other cotton-growing parts of the world, and mechanization reduced the need for black labor. Indeed, by the end of the war in 1945, only 28 percent of black men worked on farms, down from 41 percent in 1940. More than 300,000 black men left agricultural labor between 1940 and 1944 alone.

The wartime need for workers, backed by pressure from the government, helped break down some barriers to employing African Americans in industry. During the war the number of black workers in nonfarm employment rose from 2,900,000 to 3,800,000, and thousands moved into previously whites-only jobs. African Americans found employment in the aircraft industry, and tens of thousands were employed in the nation's shipyards.

With so many of their men away at war, black women increasingly found work outside the laundry and domestic service that had previously been their lot. Nationally 600,000 black women—400,000 of them former domestic servants—shifted into industrial jobs. As one aircraft worker wryly put it, "Hitler was the one that got us out of the white folks' kitchen." Even those women who stayed in domestic work often saw their wages improve as the supply of competent workers dwindled.

The abundance of industrial jobs helped spur and direct the second phase of the Great Migration, in which some 1.5 million migrants—nearly 15 percent of the population— left the South, swelling the black communities in northern and western cities that had significant war industries. By 1950 the percentage of the nation's black population living in the South had fallen from 77 percent to 68 percent. The most dramatic rise in black population was in southern California. Because of its burgeoning aircraft industry and the success of civil rights groups and the federal government in limiting discrimination, Los Angeles saw its relatively small African-American community increase by more than 340,000 during the war.

Many unions became more open to African-American workers as black men and women took jobs in industries. Between 1940 and 1945, black union membership rose from 200,000 to 1.25 million. Those unions connected to the Committee for Industrial Organization (CIO), particularly the United Automobile Workers, were the most open to black membership, whereas AFL affiliates were the most likely to treat African Americans as second-class members or to exclude them altogether. Some white unionized workers continued to oppose hiring black workers, even going on strike to prevent it, but the union leadership, the government, and employers often deflected their resistance. The growth in black membership did not end racism in unions, even in the CIO, but it did provide African Americans with a stronger foundation on which to protest discrimination in employment.

The FEPC during the War

After President Roosevelt issued the executive order banning job discrimination in defense industries with government contracts, thousands of impoverished black southerners rushed to cities in the Pacific Northwest, especially to Seattle. Wartime Seattle had offered jobs in its shipyards, in logging-truck manufacturing, and at the Boeing aircraft production plants. By 1945, Boeing employed over 1,200 black workers, approximately 3 percent of its labor force. African Americans also accounted for 7 percent of Seattle's shipyard workers. By 1948 black families in Seattle boasted a median income of $3,314, a mere 10 percent lower than the median for the nation's white families. However, the economic good fortune of black workers on the West Coast was not typical of the rest of the country.

In the Midwest and on the East Coast, many African Americans criticized industry's failure to end economic discrimination. In May 1943 President Roosevelt responded to the ineffectiveness of the FEPC. Executive Order 9346 established a new Committee on Fair Employment Practice, increased its budget, and placed its operation directly under the Executive Office of the President. Roosevelt appointed Malcolm Ross, a combative white liberal, to head the committee. Ross initiated nationwide hearings of cases concerning discrimination in the shipbuilding and railroad industries. These proceedings embarrassed some companies and increased compliance with the FEPC's orders. Resistance, however, was more common. In Mobile, Alabama, for example, the white employees of the Alabama Dry Dock and Shipbuilding Company opposed the FEPC's efforts to pressure the company to promote 12 of the 7,000 African Americans it employed in menial positions to racially mixed welding crews. The white workers went on a rampage, assaulting 50 African Americans. The FEPC thereupon withdrew its plan and acquiesced in the traditional Jim Crow arrangements for all work assignments. White workers retained their more lucrative positions. As a result of this kind of intransigence, the committee failed to redress most of the grievances of black workers. An effort to continue the committee after the war was defeated.

Anatomy of a Race Riot: Detroit, 1943

One of the bloodiest race riots in the nation's history took place in 1943 in Detroit, Michigan, where black and white workers were competing fiercely for jobs and housing. Relations between the two communities had been smoldering for months, with fighting in the plants and on the streets, against housing segregation and economic discrimination. The brutality of white police officials was an especially potent factor. Tensions were so palpable that weeks before the riot, the NAACP's Walter White had warned that the city could explode.

The immediate trigger for the riot was a squabble on June 20 between white and black bathers at the segregated city beaches on Belle Isle in the Detroit River. Within hours, 200 white sailors from a nearby base joined the white mob that attacked black men and

Before World War II, few white women and still fewer black women worked in heavy industries, but with so many men in the armed forces, women were recruited for jobs in shipyards and airplane factories, like this aircraft worker. Between 1940 and 1944, the percentage of black women in the industrial workforce increased from 6.8 percent to 18 percent.

women. A rumor that white citizens had killed a black woman and thrown her baby over a bridge spread across the city. Soon the riot was in full swing and spread quickly along Woodward Avenue, the city's major thoroughfare, into Paradise Valley, where some 35,000 southern black migrants had joined, by the spring of 1943, the city's already crowded black population. By Monday morning white men in search of more victims had overrun downtown Detroit. The mayor refused to acknowledge that the situation had gotten out of hand, but by Tuesday evening he could no longer deny the crisis.

Six thousand federal troops had to be dispatched to Detroit to restore order. When the violence ended, 34 people had been killed (25 black and nine white people) and more than 700 injured. Of the 25 black people who died, the Detroit police killed 17. However, the police did not kill any of the white men who assaulted African Americans or committed arson. Property damage was extensive, and one million man-hours were lost in war production.

In the aftermath, the city created the Mayor's Interracial Committee, the first permanent municipal body designed to promote civic harmony and fairness. Despite the efforts of labor and black leaders, many white people in Detroit, including Wayne County prosecutor William E. Dowling, blamed the black press and the NAACP for instigating the riot. Dowling and others accused the city's black citizens of pushing too hard for economic and political equality and insisted that they operated under communist influence. One report concluded that black leaders provoked the riot because they had compared "victory over the axis . . . [with] a corresponding overthrow in the country of those forces which . . . prevent true racial equality." In contrast, black leaders, radical trade unionists, and members of other ethnic organizations, especially Jewish groups, blamed "the KKK, the Christian Front, the Black Dragon Society, the National Workers League, the Knights of the White Camelia, the Southern Voters League, and similar organizations based on a policy of terror and . . . white supremacy."

The G.I. Bill of Rights and Black Veterans

In 1944, President Roosevelt signed the Servicemen's Readjustment Act (known as the "G.I. Bill of Rights"), legislation that would profoundly affect American life and society. It rewarded the sacrifices and accomplishments of black and white veterans in the war with college tuition allowances, stipends for books, and guaranteed loans of up to $2,000 (a substantial sum at the time) at low interest rates, with which to purchase homes or launch small businesses. Congress would eventually pay approximately $14.5 billion for the G.I. Bill's provisions.

By 1947, veterans accounted for half of all college students. The G.I. Bill made possible the upward mobility of a generation of American men who entered professions and trades and purchased homes that would become the basis of future wealth. Between 1950 and 1960, Americans built more than 13 million new homes—11 million of them were in the suburbs, where one-quarter of the entire population relocated after the war. The G.I. Bill fueled the boom in higher education, transportation, and the construction industries that undergirded the postwar prosperity America enjoyed.

While many black veterans benefited from the G.I. Bill of Rights, they never received their fair share of funds and assistance. Mississippi Congressman John E. Rankin sabotaged the transformative potential of the G.I. Bill by insisting that state and local veterans' administrators control the distribution of the benefits. The resulting racial disparities were predictable in southern states. In Mississippi, by the summer of 1947, local officials had approved over 3,000 Veterans Administration home loans, but only two went to African-American veterans. In northern urban areas, real estate agencies and banks practiced "redlining" and denied black men mortgages in desirable areas. The denial of loans and the violence that often erupted when black families attempted to move into suburban areas curtailed upward and outward mobility. Roosevelt may have thought he was signing a color-blind law, but its execution proved otherwise.

Old and New Protest Groups on the Home Front

The NAACP grew tremendously during the war; by the war's end, it stood poised for even greater achievements. Under the editorial direction of Roy Wilkins, the circulation of the NAACP's journal, the *Crisis,* grew from 7,000 to 45,000. During the war, the *Crisis* was one of the most important sources for information about black men and women. The NAACP's membership increased from 50,000 in 1940 to 450,000 at the end of the war. Much of this growth occurred in the South, which by 1945 had more than 150,000 members. Supreme Court victories and especially close monitoring of the "Double V" campaign helped explain these huge increases.

Success, however, bred conflict and ambivalence. Leaders split over the value of integration versus self-segregation and questioned the benefit of relying so heavily on legal cases rather than paying more attention to the concerns and needs of working-class black men and women. Wilkins acknowledged the organization's uncertainty and indecisiveness:

> The war was a great watershed for the NAACP. We had become far more powerful, and now the challenge was to keep our momentum. Everyone knew the NAACP stood against discrimination and segregation, but what was our postwar program to be? Beyond discrimination and segregation, where would we stand on veterans, housing, labor-management relations, strikes, the Fair Employment Practices Commission, organizations at state levels, education? What would we do to advance the fight for the vote in the South? . . . We had a big membership . . . but we didn't know how to use them.

In 1944 southern white liberals joined with African Americans to establish the **Southern Regional Council (SRC)**. This interracial coalition, an important example of the local initiative of private citizens, was devoted to expanding democracy in a region better known for the political and economic oppression and exploitation of its black citizens. The SRC conducted research and focused attention on the political, social, and educational inequalities endemic to black life in the South. Although the events of the 1950s and 1960s would soon overtake its patient, gradualist program, the SRC challenged the facade of southern white supremacy.

In 1942 a far more strident group called the **Congress of Racial Equality (CORE)** was formed. It pursued different tactics from those of the NAACP, Urban League, and other existing civil rights groups. CORE began in Chicago when an interracial group of Christian pacifists gathered to find ways to make America live up to the ideals of equality and justice on which it based its war program. James Farmer and Bayard Rustin were key in getting the group off the ground. Unlike the NAACP, CORE was a decentralized, intensely democratic organization. CORE dedicated itself to the principles of nonviolent direct action as expounded by Indian leader Mohandas Gandhi. During the war this pacifist organization expanded to other cities and challenged segregation in the North with sit-ins and other protest tactics that the civil rights movement would later adopt in the South.

African Americans fought discrimination in many ways. Women were central to these efforts. Throughout the 1940s, in countless communities across the South and the Midwest, black women organized women's political councils and other groups to press for integration of public facilities—hospitals, swimming pools, theaters, and restaurants—and for the right to pursue collegiate and professional studies. Others were galvanized by the war and took advantage of the limited social and political spaces afforded them to create lasting works in the arts, literature, and popular culture. Women whose names would become virtually synonymous with the modern civil rights movement in the 1950s and 1960s helped lay its foundation in the World War II era. For example, Ella Baker was accumulating contacts and sharpening her organizing skills as she served as the NAACP field secretary. Rosa Parks began resisting segregation laws on Montgomery, Alabama, buses during the 1940s.

Black college students also began protesting segregation in public accommodations. The spark that ignited the Howard University campus civil rights movement came in January 1943. Three sophomore women—Ruth Powell from Massachusetts and Marianne Musgrave

Southern Regional Council (SRC) Organization that conducted research and focused attention on social, political, and educational inequality in the South.

Congress of Racial Equality (CORE) Protest group committed to nonviolent direct action.

20-1

20-2

20-3

20-4

20-5

PROFILE Bayard Rustin

Bayard Rustin spent his life actively engaged in civil rights causes. He struggled against discrimination during the 1940s, was special assistant to Martin Luther King, Jr., in the 1950s, acted as a behind-the-scenes architect of the March on Washington in 1963, and was executive director of the A. Philip Randolph Institute. Robert Maas captures his quiet dignity in this 1982 photograph.

BAYARD RUSTIN, THE PREEMINENT STRATEGIST of non-violent resistance, was born on March 17, 1910, in West Chester, Pennsylvania. Rustin worked behind the scenes to give shape and coherence to the modern civil rights movement. During his youth, he belonged to the Young Communist League; however, in the 1940s he, along with Pauli Murray and James Farmer, became staff members of the pacifist organization Fellowship of Reconciliation (FOR) and experimented with Gandhian techniques of nonviolent resistance to racial injustice. In 1942, Rustin and Farmer were active in founding the Congress of Racial Equality (CORE). A year later, Rustin refused to be drafted, rejecting even the traditional Quaker compromise of alternative service in an army hospital.

Convicted of violating the Selective Service Act, he served three years in a federal penitentiary in Kentucky.

While in prison, Rustin honed the philosophy that would guide his life. Rustin wrote,

There are three ways in which one can deal with an injustice. (a) One can accept it without protest. (b) One can seek to avoid it. (c) One can resist the injustice nonviolently. To accept it is to perpetuate it. To avoid it is impossible. To resist by intelligent means, and with an attitude of mutual responsibility and respect, is much the better course.

On release from prison, Rustin became race relations secretary for FOR and participated in countless protest organizations. He organized a Free India Committee to press for the end of British rule in India and directed A. Philip Randolph's Committee Against Discrimination in the Armed Forces. He orchestrated CORE's 1947 Journey of Reconciliation (a precursor to the Freedom Rides of 1961), in which 16 black and white men traveled by bus through the Upper South to test new federal laws prohibiting segregated services in interstate transportation. Outside Chapel Hill, North Carolina, the group was assaulted and arrested. Rustin and three of his colleagues were sentenced to 30 days on a road gang, of which he served 22 days. In the late 1950s Rustin was an adviser to Martin Luther King, Jr., and one of the key figures in the civil rights movement of the 1950s and 1960s.

Rustin, who was gay, fought oppression all his life. After the ebb tide of the civil rights movement, he shifted to combating homophobia. He declared shortly before his death on August 24, 1987, that "the barometer of where one is on human rights questions is no longer the black community, it's the gay community. Because it is the community which is most easily mistreated."

and Juanita Morrow from Ohio—sat at a lunch counter near the campus and were refused service. They demanded to see the manager and vowed to wait until he came. Instead, two policemen arrived who instructed the waitress to serve them. When the check arrived, the trio learned they had been charged 25 cents each instead of the customary 10 cents. They placed 35 cents on the counter, turned to leave, and were arrested. Ruth Powell later reported that "the policeman who arrested us told us we were being taken in for investigation because he had no proof that we weren't 'subversive agents.'" In fact, no charges were lodged against the women. The purpose of their arrest had been to intimidate them, but the incident instead fanned the smoldering embers of resentment in the Howard University student body.

The Transition to Peace

After the German surrender in May 1945 and the Japanese surrender in August 1945, the United States began the transition to peace. Many of the gains of black men and women were wiped away as the armed forces demobilized and the factories began reinstituting the discriminatory hiring systems that were in place before the conflict. Access to fair, decent, and affordable housing remained a sore issue, as did the inequalities in educational opportunities and the continuing scourge of police brutality. Thus, as the country tried to regain its prewar footing, it was clear that segregation and discrimination would face a huge challenge in the coming years and that the African-American community was ready, willing, and able to fight in ways undreamed of in earlier eras.

The Cold War and International Politics

20-5 **What were the positive and negative effects of the Cold War on blacks, both in politics and social life?**

As the defeat of the Axis powers neared in early 1945, the United Nations began planning for the peace. Within a short time, however, the opposing interests of the Soviet Union and the United States led to a long period of intense hostility that became known as the Cold War. This conflict soon led to a division of Europe into two spheres, with the Soviets dominating part of Germany and the nations to its east and a coalition of democratic capitalist regimes allied with the United States in the west. Thereafter, the overriding goal of the United States and its allies was the "containment" of communism. To this end, the **North Atlantic Treaty Organization (NATO)** was formed in 1949 to provide a military counterforce to Soviet power in Europe while American dollars helped rebuild Western Europe's war-shattered economy. The United States forged a similarly close relationship with Japan. Much of the rest of the world, however, became contested terrain during the Cold War.

North Atlantic Treaty Organization (NATO) Military alliance formed to counter the threat posed by the Soviet Union and its allies.

As the nations of Asia and Africa gained independence from colonial domination over the ensuing decades, the United States struggled to keep them out of the Soviet orbit. It did so through foreign aid, direct military force, and, occasionally, through clandestine operations run by the Central Intelligence Agency. These interventions were matched by a rising diplomatic and propaganda effort to convince the emerging nations that the United States was a model to be emulated and an ally to be trusted.

The Cold War had an enormous influence on American society precisely when the powerful movement for African-American rights was beginning to emerge. The long conflict resulted in the rise of a large permanent military establishment in the United States. The reorganized American military enlisted millions of men and women by the early 1950s and claimed most of the national budget. The federal government also grew in power during the war and provided a check on the control that white southerners had exercised over race relations in their region for so long. American policymakers also became concerned about the nation's ability to win the allegiance of Africans and other nonwhite people in the emerging nations. Soviet propaganda could discredit American sincerity by pointing to the deplorable state of race relations within the United States. Hence, during the Cold War, external pressures reinforced domestic efforts to change American racial policy.

America's Cold War propaganda targeted all citizens, black and white. This anticommunism poster was one of many designed to remind Americans of threats to their freedom and to fan the flames of patriotism.

African Americans in World Affairs: W. E. B. Du Bois and Ralph Bunche

The Cold War gave new importance to the voices of African Americans in world affairs. Two men, W. E. B. Du Bois and Ralph Johnson

Bunche (1904–1971), represented alternative strategies for responding to this opportunity. Du Bois was highly critical of American policy. For half a century, he had linked the fate of African Americans with that of Africans, and by 1945 was widely hailed as the "Father of Pan-Africanism." In that year he directed the Fifth Pan-African Congress, which met in Manchester, England. Africans who had been radicalized by World War II dominated the conference and encouraged it to denounce Western imperialism. Du Bois considered the United States a protector of the colonial system and opposed its stance in the Cold War. On returning from the Manchester congress, he declared,

> We American Negroes should know . . . until Africa is free, the descendants of Africa the world over cannot escape their chains. . . . The NAACP should therefore put in the forefront of its program the freedom of Africa in work and wage, education and health, and the complete abolition of the colonial system.

In contrast to Du Bois, scholar-diplomat Ralph Bunche opted to work within the American system. Bunche held a Harvard doctorate in government and international relations and had spent much of the 1930s studying the problems of African Americans. During World War II, the American government found his expertise on Africa of tremendous value, and Bunche became one of the key policymakers for the region. His analysis of events and changes in Africa and the Far East after World War II led to his appointment as adviser to the U.S. delegation at the San Francisco conference that drafted the United Nations (UN) Charter. In 1948 he served as acting mediator of the UN Special Committee on Palestine, and in 1949 he negotiated an armistice between Egypt and Israel. He received the Spingarn Medal of the NAACP in 1949, and in 1950 he became the first African American to receive the Nobel Peace Prize. Although Bunche worked in concert with national policymakers, he was committed to winning independence for African nations and freedom for his own people. As he wrote:

> Today, for all thinking people, the Negro is the shining symbol of the true significance of democracy. He has demonstrated what can be achieved with democratic liberties even when grudgingly and incompletely bestowed. But the most vital significance of the Negro . . . to American society . . . is the fact that democracy which is not extended to all of the nation's citizens is a democracy that is mortally wounded.

Anticommunism at Home

The rising tensions with the Soviet Union affected all aspects of domestic life in the United States. Conservatives used fears of communist subversion to attack anyone who advocated change in America. This included people who were or had been members of the Communist Party, union members, liberals, and those who had fought for African-American rights. The Truman administration (1945–1953) responded to fears of subversion by instituting government loyalty programs. Government employees were dismissed for the merest suspicion of disloyalty. Militant American anticommunism reached a feverish peak in the immediate postwar years and ignited an explosion of red-baiting hysteria that led to the rise of Wisconsin Republican Senator Joseph McCarthy (1909–1957) and the **House Un-American Activities Committee (HUAC).** The relentless pursuit of "communist sympathizers" by McCarthy and HUAC ruined many lives. HUAC hounded people in the media and the entertainment industry. Even so prominent a figure as Du Bois was ripe for attack. On February 8, 1951, HUAC indicted him for allegedly serving as an "agent of a foreign principal" in his work with the Peace Information Center. In November a federal judge dismissed the charges. The government had been unable to prove Du Bois was an agent of communism. Despite his past contributions, fear and personal malice prevented most African-American leaders from defending him.

House Un-American Activities Committee (HUAC) Congressional committee formed to investigate the activities of communists and "communist sympathizers" in America.

Paul Robeson

Paul Robeson (1898–1976) was one of the most tragic victims of these anticommunist witch hunts. This fine scholar and star collegiate athlete, Columbia Law School graduate, consummate performer, and star of stage and screen had always advocated the rights of African Americans and workers. During the 1930s he worked closely with the Communist Party (although he was never a member), becoming one of the most famous defenders of the Soviet Union. Many leftists of the time became disaffected with the Soviet Union after its 1939 pact with Hitler and its brutal repressiveness became clear. Robeson, however, doggedly stuck to his belief in Soviet communism.

In the late 1940s, Robeson's pro-Soviet views and inflammatory statements aroused the ire of the U.S. government and its red hunters. A statement he made at the communist-dominated World Congress of the Defenders of Peace in Paris in 1949 provoked outrage. "It is unthinkable," Robeson said, "that American Negroes would go to war on behalf of those [the United States] who have oppressed us for generations against a country [the Soviet Union] which in one generation has raised our people to full human dignity of mankind." Later in 1949 crowds twice disrupted a Robeson concert in Peekskill, New York, the first time preventing the concert from being held, the second time terrorizing performers and audience members after the concert by throwing rocks at them.

Throughout the 1940s Robeson consistently linked the struggles of black America with the struggles of black Africa, brown India, yellow Asia, black Brazilians and Haitians, and workers throughout Latin America. Robeson also refused to sign an affidavit concerning past membership in the Communist Party. In response, the U.S. State Department revoked his passport in 1950 "because the Department considers that Paul Robeson's travel abroad at this time would be contrary to the best interest of the United States." The travel ban remained in effect until the Supreme Court declared it unconstitutional in 1958.

Robeson had combined his art and his politics to attack racial discrimination, segregation, and the ideology of white supremacy and black inferiority in America. During the Cold War the state would tolerate no such dissent even by a world-acclaimed black artist.

Henry Wallace and the 1948 Presidential Election

Robeson's struggles illustrate how conservative attacks choked off left-wing involvement in the struggle for black equality. The attacks destroyed Robeson's brilliant singing career. The increasing importance of black votes to Democrats, however, meant that key elements of the African-American liberation struggle remained at the center of national politics. Nowhere was this more apparent than in the 1948 presidential election.

President Harry S. Truman was not expected to win this election because he faced a strong challenge from Thomas Dewey, the popular and well-financed Republican governor of New York. A challenge from his former secretary of commerce, Henry Wallace, who had been Roosevelt's vice president from 1941 to 1945, compounded Truman's problems. Wallace ran on the ticket of the communist-backed Progressive Party, which sought to take the votes of liberals, leftists, and civil rights advocates disappointed by Truman's moderation. Wallace also supported a peaceful accommodation with the Soviet Union. To undercut Wallace's challenge, Truman began to press Congress to pass liberal programs.

Black votes in key northern states were central to Truman's strategy for victory. African Americans in these tightly contested areas could make the difference between victory and defeat, so Truman, to retain their allegiance, sought to demonstrate his administration's support of civil rights. In January 1948 he embraced the findings of his biracial Committee on Civil Rights and called for their enactment into law. The committee's report, "To Secure These Rights," was a blueprint for changing the racial caste system in the United States. It recommended passage of federal anti-lynching legislation, ending

20-1

20-2

20-3

20-4

20-5

discrimination at the ballot box, abolishing the poll tax, desegregating the military, and many other measures.

The reaction of white southern politicians was swift and threatening, causing Truman to pause. But as the election neared, fear of black disaffection at the polls became so great that the Democratic convention passed a strong pro-civil rights plank. Many white southerners, led by South Carolina's Governor Strom Thurmond, bolted from the convention and formed their own States' Rights, or "Dixiecrat," Party. In the election, the Dixiecrats carried South Carolina, Alabama, Mississippi, and Louisiana. Wallace carried no state. Dewey carried 13 northern and midwestern states, but Truman won a plurality in the popular vote and a majority in the Electoral College. The failure of the bulwark of white supremacy to prevent the Democratic Party from advocating African-American rights, and Truman's victory, despite the defection of hard-line racists, represented a turning point in American politics.

Desegregating the Armed Forces

The importance of the black vote, the fight for the allegiance of the emerging nations, and the emerging civil rights movement hastened the desegregation of the military. In February 1948 a communist coup in Czechoslovakia raised the possibility of war between the United States and the Soviet Union and heightened concerns among military leaders about African Americans' willingness to serve yet again in a Jim Crow army. When Congress reinstated the draft in March 1948, A. Philip Randolph, who—in a replay of the March on Washington scenario—had formed the League for Non-Violent Civil Disobedience Against Military Segregation in 1947, warned the nation that black men and women were fed up with segregation and Jim Crow and would not take a Jim Crow draft lying down. Black New York Congressman Adam Clayton Powell, Jr., also supported this stance. There were not enough jails in America to hold the black men who would refuse to bear arms in a Jim Crow army, he declared. On June 24, 1948, the Soviet Union heightened tensions even further when it imposed a blockade on West Berlin.

On July 26, Truman, anticipating war between the superpowers and hoping to shore up his support among black voters for the approaching November elections, issued **Executive Order 9981**, which mandated "equality of treatment and opportunity for all persons in the armed services without regard to race, color, religion, or national origin." After Truman signed the order, Randolph and Grant Reynolds, a former minister and co-chair of the League for Nonviolent Civil Disobedience Against Military Segregation, disbanded the organization and called off marches planned for Chicago and New York.

Not until 1950 and the outbreak of the Korean War, however, was Truman's order fully implemented. The Korean War reflected the American Cold War policy of containment, which was intended to stop what American leaders believed to be a worldwide conspiracy orchestrated by Moscow to spread communism. In 1950 the North Koreans, allied with the Soviets, attacked the American-supported government in South Korea and launched a "hot war" in the midst of the Cold War. After the North Koreans invaded South Korea, the United States under UN auspices intervened. Heavy casualties early in the war depleted many white combat units. Thus, early in 1951, the army acted on Truman's executive order and authorized the formal integration of its units in Korea. By 1954 the army

Watch on **MyHistoryLab Video:** The Desegregation of the Military and Blacks in Combat

Executive Order 9981 Order issued by President Harry Truman in 1948 desegregating the armed forces.

Read on **MyHistoryLab Document:** President Truman Integrates the Armed Forces, 1948

Read on **MyHistoryLab Document:** Segregation in the Military During World War II, 1940–1941

African-American civilians demonstrated firm resolve to end racial segregation at home while Americans fought to make the world safe for democracy. The NAACP Detroit branch's 1944 "Parade for Victory" featured pallbearers with caskets as they marched behind a sign that proclaimed "HERE LIES JIM CROW." It conveyed the sentiment, if not the reality. But Jim Crow's days were numbered.

had disbanded its last all-black units, and the armed forces became one of the first sectors of American society to abandon segregation.

CONCLUSION

The years between 1940 and 1954 were a dynamic period of black activism and witnessed a rising international consciousness among African Americans. The quest for racial justice in the military and on the home front became an integral part of the ongoing struggle for economic, political, and social progress. President Roosevelt's Executive Order 8802 was a significant victory for A. Philip Randolph's March on Washington Movement and for black workers, who were able to appeal racial discrimination in defense industries to the FEPC. The rise of fascism in Europe alarmed black and white Americans who correctly perceived ideologies based on racial tyranny and state dominance to be hostile to individual freedom and democracy. World War II profoundly transformed black servicemen and servicewomen.

The Cold War created a climate in America that was both hospitable and hostile to the African-American freedom movement. Radicals such as Paul Robeson and W. E. B. Du Bois found no place in this movement or in American society. Instead, more moderate organizations, such as the NAACP's Legal Defense and Educational Fund, pursued their goals within the ideological and legal constraints of the American political system and met with some success. The coming civil rights movement would, however, soon lead to a more varied, vibrant, and successful challenge to racism.

20-1
20-2
20-3
20-4
20-5

CHAPTER TIMELINE

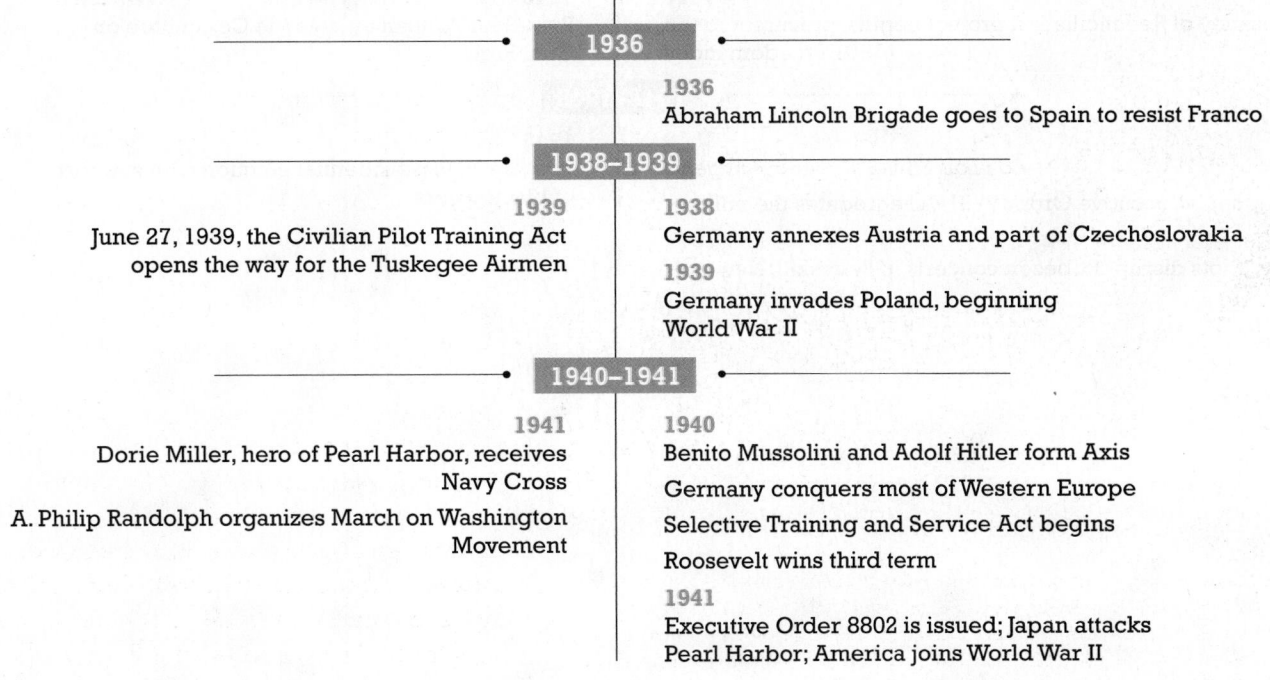

AFRICAN-AMERICAN EVENTS

NATIONAL AND WORLD EVENTS

1936

1936
Abraham Lincoln Brigade goes to Spain to resist Franco

1938–1939

1939
June 27, 1939, the Civilian Pilot Training Act opens the way for the Tuskegee Airmen

1938
Germany annexes Austria and part of Czechoslovakia

1939
Germany invades Poland, beginning World War II

1940–1941

1941
Dorie Miller, hero of Pearl Harbor, receives Navy Cross

A. Philip Randolph organizes March on Washington Movement

1940
Benito Mussolini and Adolf Hitler form Axis

Germany conquers most of Western Europe

Selective Training and Service Act begins

Roosevelt wins third term

1941
Executive Order 8802 is issued; Japan attacks Pearl Harbor; America joins World War II

CHAPTER TIMELINE

AFRICAN-AMERICAN EVENTS

NATIONAL AND WORLD EVENTS

1942–1943

1942

Congress of Racial Equality (CORE) founded in Chicago

Charity Adams (Early) becomes first black commissioned officer in the Women's Army Auxiliary Corps

First black cadets graduate from flying school at Tuskegee, Alabama

1943

William H. Hastie resigns in protest from War Department

Race riots in Mobile, Detroit, and Harlem

The black 99th Pursuit Squadron flies its first combat mission

1942

100,000 Japanese Americans interred in camps

1943

Roosevelt signs G.I. Bill

1944–1955

1944

Adam Clayton Powell, Jr., is elected to U.S. House of Representatives from Harlem

Supreme Court overthrows the white primary in *Smith v. Allwright*

1945

Mabel Staupers secures end to discrimination against black nurses in the military

Du Bois, Bethune, White, and Bunche attend UN founding in San Francisco

Paul Robeson receives NAACP Spingarn Medal

1944

D-Day, Allied invasion of German-occupied France, begins

Roosevelt wins fourth term

Servicemen's Readjustment Act provides funds for housing and education after the war

Battle of the Bulge, last major German counteroffensive

1945

United Nations founded

President Roosevelt dies; Truman becomes president

Germany surrenders

United States bombs Hiroshima and Nagasaki; Japan surrenders

1946–1947

1947

Journey of Reconciliation project begins, precursor to the 1961 Freedom Rides

1946

President Truman creates the Committee on Civil Rights

1948–1949

1948

Ada Lois Sipuel v. Board of Regents

Truman's Executive Order 9981 desegregates the military

1949

Riots disrupt Robeson concerts in Peekskill, New York

1948

Truman wins presidential election with support of black voters

On MyHistoryLab

 ✓ Study and Review on MyHistoryLab

REVIEW QUESTIONS

1. How did World War II change the status of African Americans? What were some of the consequences of so many black servicemen fighting in Europe against fascism and Nazism? How did the Tuskegee Airmen contribute to the Allied victory in Europe?

2. How did black women participate in the campaign to desegregate the U.S. military and in the Abraham Lincoln Brigade? How did Mabel Staupers win acceptance of black women into the military nurses corps?

3. What did the "Double V" campaign accomplish? How did African-American civilians support black servicemen? What institutional resources were African

Americans able to marshal in their campaign against racism at home?

4. How did World War II affect black workers in America? What was the significance of A. Philip Randolph's March on Washington Movement, and how did President Roosevelt respond to it?

5. Why did the Cold War originate, and what was its significance for black activism? How did the World War II era promote the internationalization of African-American consciousness? How did the State Department attempt to downplay black dissent in America, and why?

6. Why did President Truman decide to desegregate the U.S. military?

RECOMMENDED READING

John D'Emilio. *Lost Prophet: The Life and Times of Bayard Rustin.* New York: Simon & Schuster, 2003. A first-rate, well-written, thoughtful biography of a key although often under-appreciated leader in the long struggle for social justice for all Americans.

Mary L. Dudziak. *Cold War Civil Rights: Race and the Image of American Democracy.* Princeton, NJ: Princeton University Press, 2000. An excellent study of Cold War diplomacy and the centrality of race issues, as well as a splendid analysis of the Truman administration's commitment to civil rights.

Darlene Clark Hine. "Black Professional and Race Consciousness: Origins of the Civil Rights Movement, 1890–1950." *Journal of American History* 89, no. 4 (2003): 1279–94. A detailed discussion of the struggle of black physicians and nurses to end the racial segregation of medicine in the armed forces during World War II.

Paula F. Pfeffer. *A. Philip Randolph, Pioneer of the Civil Rights Movement.* Baton Rouge: Louisiana State University Press, 1990. A richly insightful biography of a pioneering labor leader and activist whose March on Washington Movement in 1941 was essential to the formation of the first Fair Employment Practices Committee and the integration of the armed services.

William R. Scott. *The Sons of Sheba's Race: African-Americans and the Italo-Ethiopian War, 1935–1941.* Bloomington: Indiana University Press, 1993. A detailed and illuminating account of African-American responses to the Italian invasion of Ethiopia and the growth of black internationalism.

Laura Wexler. *Fire in a Canebrake: The Last Mass Lynching in America.* New York: Scribner's, 2003. A riveting and sobering account of the lynching by a white mob of four victims on July 25, 1946, in Walton County, Georgia, at Moore's Ford Bridge. The book is a poignant study of the pernicious power of racism in the wake of the global holocaust of World War II.

ADDITIONAL BIBLIOGRAPHY

AFRICAN AMERICANS AND THE MILITARY

Robert Allen. *Port Chicago Mutiny: The Story of the Largest Mass Mutiny in U.S. Naval History.* New York: Warner Books/Amistad Books, 1989.

Martin Binkin and Mark J. Eitelberg with Alvin J. Schexnider and Marvin M. Smith. *Blacks and the Military: Studies in Defense Policy.* Washington, DC: Bookings Institution, 1982.

Richard Dalfiume. *Desegregation of the U.S. Armed Forces: Fighting on Two Fronts, 1939–1953.* Columbia: University of Missouri Press, 1969.

Thomas E. Daniels. "Contributions of Black Americans to Electronic Research, Development, Production Distribution, and Training at Fort Monmouth, 1940-1982." http://www.campusevans.org

Department of Defense. *A History of Army Communications and Electronics at Fort Monmouth, New Jersey, 1917–2007.* Wall Township, NJ: Fort Monmouth Historical Office, 2008.

Charles W. Dryden. *A-Train: Memoirs of a Tuskegee Airman.* Tuscaloosa: University of Alabama Press, 1997.

Charity Adams Earley. *One Woman's Army: A Black Officer Remembers the WAC.* College Station: Texas A&M University Press, 1989.

Darlene Clark Hine. *Black Women in White: Racial Conflict and Cooperation in the Nursing Profession, 1890–1950.* Bloomington: Indiana University Press, 1989.

Ulysses Lee. *The Employment of Negro Troops.* Washington, DC: Center of Military History, 1990.

Melton A. McLaurin. *The Marines of Montford Point: America's First Black Marines.* Chapel Hill: University of North Carolina Press, 2007.

Neil McMillen, ed. *Remaking Dixie: The Impact of World War II on the American South.* Jackson: University Press of Mississippi, 1997.

Mary Penick Motley. *The Invisible Soldier: The Experience of the Black Soldier, World War Two.* Detroit: Wayne State University Press, 1975.

Alan M. Osur. *Blacks in the Army Air Forces During World War II: The Problem of Race Relations.* Washington, DC: Office of Air Force History, 1977.

Lou Potter. *Liberators: Fighting on Two Fronts in World War II.* New York: Harcourt Brace Jovanovich, 1992.

Stanley Sandler. *Segregated Skies: All-Black Combat Squadrons of WWII.* Washington, DC: Smithsonian Institution Press, 1992.

Howard Sitkoff. "Racial Militancy and Interracial Violence in the Second World War." *Journal of American History* 58, no. 3 (1971): 663–83.

Paul Stillwell, ed. *The Golden Thirteen: Recollections of the First Black Naval Officers.* Annapolis, MD: Naval Institute Press, 1993.

Ben Vinson III. *Flight: The Story of Virgil Richardson, a Tuskegee Airman in Mexico.* New York: Palgrave/Macmillan, 2004.

BLACK URBAN STUDIES

Albert Broussard. *Black San Francisco: The Struggle for Racial Equality in the West, 1900–1954.* Lawrence: University Press of Kansas, 1993.

Dominic Capeci. *The Harlem Riot of 1943.* Philadephia: Temple University Press, 1977.

_____. *Race Relations in Wartime Detroit: The Sojourner Truth Housing Controversy of 1942.* Philadelphia: Temple University Press, 1984.

Dominic Capeci and Martha Wilkerson. *Layered Violence: The Detroit Rioters of 1943.* Jackson: University Press of Mississippi, 1991.

Lawrence B. DeGraaf. "Significant Steps on an Arduous Path: The Impact of World War II on Discrimination Against African Americans in the West." *Journal of the West* 35, no. 1 (1996): 24–33.

St. Clair Drake and Horace R. Cayton. *Black Metropolis: A Study of Negro Life in a Northern City.* New York: Harcourt Brace, 1945.

Richard W. Thomas. *Life for Us Is What We Make It: Building Black Community in Detroit, 1915–1945.* Bloomington: Indiana University Press, 1992.

BLACK AMERICANS, DOMESTIC RADICALISM, AND INTERNATIONAL AFFAIRS

Beth Tompkins Bates. *Pullman Porters and the Rise of Protest Politics in Black America, 1925–1945.* Chapel Hill: University of North Carolina Press, 2001.

William C. Berman. *The Politics of Civil Rights in the Truman Administration.* Columbus: Ohio State University Press, 1970.

John Morton Blum. *V Was for Victory: Politics and American Culture During World War II.* New York: Harcourt Brace Jovanovich, 1996.

Gabrielle Simon Edgecomb, *From Swastika to Jim Crow : Refugee Scholars at Black Colleges.* Malabar, FL: Krieger Publishing Company, 1993.

Herbert Garfinkel. *When Negroes March: The March on Washington Movement in the Organizational Politics for FEPC.* New York: Atheneum, 1973.

Erik S. Gellman. *Death Blow to Jim Crow: The National Negro Congress and the Rise of Militant Civil Rights.* Chapel Hill: University of North Carolina Press, 2012.

Erik S. Gellman and Jarod Roll. *The Gospel of the Working Class: Labor's Southern Prophets in New Deal America.* Urbana: University of Illinois Press, 2011.

Joseph Harris. *African American Reactions to War in Ethiopia, 1936–1941.* Baton Rouge: Louisiana State University Press, 1994.

Gerald Horne. *Black and Red: W. E. B. Du Bois and the Afro-American Response to the Cold War.* Albany: State University of New York Press, 1986.

Andrew Edmund Kersten. *Race and War: The FEPC in the Midwest, 1941–46.* Urbana: University of Illinois Press, 2000.

George Lipsitz. *Rainbow at Midnight: Labor and Culture in the 1940s.* Urbana: University of Illinois Press, 1994.

Gail Williams O'Brien. *The Color of the Law: Race, Violence and Justice in the Post–World War II South.* Chapel Hill: University of North Carolina Press, 1999.

Brenda Gayle Plummer. *Rising Wind: Black Americans and U.S. Foreign Affairs, 1935–1960.* Chapel Hill: University of North Carolina Press, 1996.

Linda Reed. *Simple Decency and Common Sense: The Southern Conference Movement, 1938–1963.* Bloomington: Indiana University Press, 1991.

Joe William Trotter and Jared E. Day, eds. *Race and Renaissance: African Americans in Pittsburgh Since World War.* Pittsburgh, PA: University of Pittsburgh Press, 2010.

Patricia Scott Washburn. *A Question of Sedition: The Federal Government's Investigation of the Black Press During World War II.* New York: Oxford University Press, 1986.

AUTOBIOGRAPHY AND BIOGRAPHY

Andrew Buni. *Robert Vann of the Pittsburgh Courier.* Pittsburgh, PA: University of Pittsburgh Press, 1974.

Martin Bauml Duberman. *Paul Robeson: A Biography.* New York: Ballantine Press, 1989.

Kenneth R. Janken. *Rayford W. Logan and the Dilemma of the African American Intellectual.* Amherst: University of Massachusetts Press, 1993.

Spencie Love. *One Blood: The Death and Resurrection of Charles Drew.* Chapel Hill: University of North Carolina Press, 1996.

Manning Marable. *W. E. B. Du Bois: Black Radical Democrat.* Boston: Twayne, 1986.

Constance Baker Motley. *Equal Justice Under Law: An Autobiography.* New York: Farrar, Straus and Giroux, 1998.

Pauli Murray. *Song in a Weary Throat: An American Pilgrimage.* New York: Harper & Row, 1987.

Bayard Rustin. *Troubles I've Seen.* New York: HarperCollins, 1996.

Brian Urquhart. *Ralph Bunche: An American Life.* New York: Norton, 1993.

Gilbert Ware. *William Hastie: Grace Under Pressure.* New York: Oxford University Press, 1984.

Roy Wilkins with Tom Mathews. *Standing Fast: The Autobiography of Roy Wilkins.* New York: Da Capo Press, 1994.

RETRACING THE ODYSSEY

National Museum of the Tuskegee Airmen at Historic Fort Wayne (Detroit, Michigan). This museum documents the achievements of the combat aviators who served as a segregated unit of the U.S. armed forces in World War II. They received their training at the Army Air Corps base in Tuskegee, Alabama. During World War II these black aviators shot down enemy aircraft, bombed barges and enemy power stations, and successfully escorted American bombers on their missions across Europe.

Port Chicago Naval Magazine National Memorial, Concord Naval Weapons Station, California. The memorial contains artifacts and exhibits. Much of the base is now a wildlife preserve.

CONNECTING THE PAST

The Significance of the Desegregation of the U.S. Military

Howard P. Perry, the first African American to enlist in the Marine Corps.

THROUGH THEIR MILITARY SERVICE AFRICAN AMERICANS have played important roles in the construction and preservation of American democracy. Since their participation in the colonial militia and the Continental Army during the American Revolution, through the recent wars against Iraq and in Afghanistan in the twenty-first century, black Americans have viewed military service as a way to prove their loyalty and bravery, and to show their right to freedom and citizenship.

At the birth of the new nation in 1775–1776, black people composed one-fifth of the population. They fought mostly in integrated colonial militias and army regiments during the American Revolution, but it would take over two centuries and many more wars before military integration became permanent national policy. In the Civil War, the Spanish-American War, World War I, and World War II, black and white servicemen fought in racially segregated units in the Army and Navy. (The Marines did not allow black men to serve until 1942.) The desegregation of the military during the 1950s was thus, in many respects, a monumental and historic achievement. Throughout World War II black communities had waged a "Double V" campaign against Fascism and Nazism abroad and racial segregation and discrimination at home. President Harry Truman's Executive Order 9981 ordering the desegregation of the U.S. military in 1948 helped to set the stage for the emergence of the modern civil rights movement. Desegregation in the military preceded the end of legal segregation and Jim Crow in civilian life by more than a decade. Today, the U.S. military is one of the most racially neutral institutions in America.

The War for Independence (1775–1783) was, as scholars now attest, "the first mass slave rebellion in American history." Enslaved black men fought on both sides of the war. Some fought for the British, but even larger numbers joined the Patriot cause, believing that they would be freed as compensation for their service to the new nation. In 1775, Lord Dunmore, Virginia's last royal governor, promised to free any slave or indentured servant in exchange for their military service to the Crown. In response, George Washington, the Patriot commander, initially vacillated but soon allowed the enlistment of free black men in his army. In both the Battle of Bunker Hill and the Battle of Long Island in 1776, African-American soldiers from the northern states "served in twice the proportion of their numbers in the population." By 1781, at the decisive Battle of Yorktown, which ensured American independence, black troops were estimated to make up one-quarter of the Patriot Army. Despite their military service and contributions, however, the American Revolution would remain the unfinished revolution for African Americans.

Slavery endured and flourished until the 1860s when the election of President Abraham Lincoln, followed by the secession of South Carolina and 10 other southern states, ignited the Civil War. Free African Americans who supported the abolition of slavery pressured an initially reluctant Lincoln to make the destruction of slavery a military objective. When Lincoln issued the Emancipation Proclamation in 1863 and also allowed states to raise black militias, the Civil War became an opportunity for African Americans to fight for their own liberation.

During the Civil War, more than 185,000 African Americans fought in the Union Army and Navy. They provided the crucial margin of manpower that facilitated the North's victory. Approximately 29,000 African American men made up one-fourth of the entire naval enrollment. The recruitment and enlistment of African Americans into the Union Army was controversial, however. Frederick Douglass, the leading advocate of arming black men, reminded Lincoln that African Americans had fought well enough to help win American independence and insisted that they were eager and more than qualified to fight for their people's freedom and to preserve that independence. On August 25, 1862, the War Department granted General Rufus Saxton, military governor of South Carolina's Sea Islands, the power to raise five regiments of black troops on the islands, albeit under the command of white officers.

The northern victory in the Civil War preserved the Union and ended slavery. But again, black military service failed to end military segregation and discrimination in the military academies at West Point and Annapolis. The closing decades of the nineteenth century simultaneously witnessed the rise of legal segregation and political disfranchisement and helped to fan the Great Migration from the South to northern cities. Still, black people's desire to serve in the military never wavered. Black public protest against military segregation and discrimination continued during World War I and reached a peak in World War II when a nation with a segregated military fought Germany and Japan, nations that embraced a master race ideology.

Black Americans seized the national crisis of World War II to make their demands for civil and human rights heard. In 1949, Wesley A. Brown became the first black midshipman to graduate from the U.S. Naval Academy (founded in 1845). Representative Adam Clayton Powell, Jr., of New York had interceded on his behalf. One of Brown's classmates was future President Jimmy Carter. The desegregation of the military, one of the most significant institutions in American public life, opened opportunities for black men and women. A generation later Colin Luther Powell, born in Harlem, New York to Jamaican-American parents, reached the highest position in the military when he became the twelfth Chairman of the Joint Chief of Staff (1985–1989), after which he was named the Secretary of State in 2001 by President George W. Bush. Today, African Americans constitute almost 20 percent of service men and women in the U.S. armed forces.

Colin Powell (center), Chairman of the Joint Chiefs of Staff, with Former Vice President Richard Cheney and General Norman Schwarzkopf.

PART VI
THE BLACK REVOLUTION

James Farmer

	1950–1965	1965–1975

RELIGION

1954 Malcolm X becomes minister of Harlem's Temple 7

1963 Malcolm X founds the Muslim Mosque

CULTURE

1959 Miles Davis records *Kind of Blue*

1960 Louis Armstrong's jazz band tours Africa

1963 James Baldwin publishes *The Fire Next Time*

1965 Alex Haley publishes *The Autobiography of Malcolm X*

LeRoi Jones founds the Black Arts Repertory Theater

1966 San Francisco State University sets up nation's first black studies program

1968 Eldridge Cleaver publishes *Soul on Ice*

1969 Harvard University's African-American Studies program established

Robert Chrisman and Nathan Hare start *The Black Scholar*

1970 Imamu Amiri Baraka organizes the Congress of African Peoples

1974 National Council for Black Studies formed

POLITICS & GOVERNMENT

1954 *Brown v. Board of Education* ends "separate but equal"

1955 Brown II decision calls for schools to desegregate with "all deliberate speed"

1957 Federal troops enforce school desegregation in Little Rock, Arkansas

1963 Federal government forces Governor George Wallace to desegregate University of Alabama

1964 Equal Employment Opportunity Commission established

1965 President Lyndon Johnson first uses the term "affirmative action"

Voting Rights Act of 1965 enacted by Congress

1966 Edward Brooke of Massachusetts elected the first black U.S. senator since Reconstruction

Black Panther Party founded

1967 Thurgood Marshall becomes first black Supreme Court justice

1968 Kerner Report released

SOCIETY & ECONOMY

1955 Rosa Parks arrested for refusing to give up her seat on a bus in Montgomery, Alabama

1958 Southern Christian Leadership Conference organized

1960 Black students launch the sit-in movement

SNCC founded

1961 Freedom Riders attacked in Alabama

1962 James Meredith admitted to the University of Mississippi

1963 Medgar Evers assassinated

Martin Luther King, Jr., delivers "I Have a Dream" speech

Baptist church bombed in Birmingham, Alabama

1964 Mississippi Freedom Summer Project

Civil rights workers murdered in Mississippi

Martin Luther King, Jr., awarded Nobel Peace Prize

1965 Watts riot

Selma march

1967 Riots in Detroit, Newark, and other cities

1968 Poor People's Campaign

Martin Luther King, Jr., assassinated

1969 Chicago police kill Black Panther leaders Fred Hampton and Mark Clarke

1970 Jackson State killings

1971 Jesse Jackson founds PUSH

1973 National Black Feminist Organization founded

Barbara Jordan

Eldridge Cleaver

Condoleezza Rice

1975–1990

1990–2001

Noteworthy Individuals

1978 Lewis Farrakhan becomes leader of the Nation of Islam

1989 Barbara Harris is first African-American woman elected bishop of the Episcopal Church

1990 Black Baptists constitute the fourth largest U.S. religious group with 8.7 million members

1991 George A. Stallings consecrated a Roman Catholic bishop

1993 Pope John Paul II apologizes for the Catholic Church's support of slavery

2000 Vashti M. McKenzie is first woman elected bishop of African Methodist Episcopal church

2001 Bishop Wilton D. Gregory elected president of the United States Conference of Catholic Bishops

---

1979 Sugar Hill Gang records "Rapper's Delight"

1980 Toni C. Bambara's *Salt Eaters* wins American Book Award

Molefi Kete Asante publishes *Afrocentricity*

1982 Alice Walker's *The Color Purple* wins Pulitzer Prize

1984 Prince films *Purple Rain*

1986 *The Oprah Winfrey Show* becomes nationally syndicated

1987 Rita Dove wins Pulitzer Prize for poetry

1988 Temple University becomes first college to offer a Ph.D. in African-American studies

1989 N.W.A. records *Straight Outta Compton*

1990 August Wilson's *The Piano Lesson* wins the Pulitzer Prize

1993 Rita Dove becomes Poet Laureate

Toni Morrison becomes the first African American to win the Noble Prize for Literature

2007 Forest Whitaker wins the Best Actor Academy Award

1977 Randall Robinson founds TransAfrica

Patricia Harris becomes the first black woman to serve in the cabinet

1983–1984 Jesse Jackson runs for president

1989 L. Douglas Wilder of Virginia becomes first African-American governor since Reconstruction

1991 Clarence Thomas nominated to the Supreme Court

2001 Colin Powell becomes first African-American secretary of state

2005 Condoleezza Rice becomes secretary of state under George W. Bush

2008 Barack Hussein Obama is elected president of the United States

---

1991 Los Angeles riot after police officers who beat Rodney King are acquitted

1995 Million Man March

1997 Million Woman March

2000 Census records large gains in income and education by African Americans

2005 Hurricane Katrina ravages the city of New Orleans

Ella Baker (1903–1986)
Fannie Lou Hamer (1917–1977)
Rosa Parks (1918–2005)
James Farmer (1920–1999)
Alex Haley (1921–1992)
Medgar Evers (1925–1963)
Malcolm X (1925–1965)
Ralph Abernathy (1926–1990)
Miles Davis (1926–1991)
Coretta Scott King (1927–2006)
Carl Stokes (1927–1996)
Maya Angelou (1928–)
Martin Luther King, Jr. (1929–1968)
Toni Morrison (1931–)
James Brown (1933–2006)
James Meredith (1933–)
Vernon Jordan (1935–)
Eldridge Cleaver (1935–1998)
Bobby Seale (1936–)
Barbara Jordan (1936–1996)
Colin Powell (1937–)
Maxine Waters (1938–)
Marian W. Edelman (1939–)
John Lewis (1940–)
Jesse Jackson (1941–)
Stokely Carmichael (1941–1998)
Muhammad Ali (1942–)
Molefi Kete Asante (1942–)
Aretha Franklin (1942–)
Randall Robinson (1942–)
Huey Newton (1942–1989)
Terri McMillan (1943–)
Angela Davis (1944–)
Alice Walker (1944–)
August Wilson (1945–2005)
Clarence Thomas (1948–)
Jamaica Kincaid (1949–)
Henry Louis Gates (1950–)
Cornell West (1953–)
Condoleezza Rice (1954–)
Oprah Winfrey (1954–)
Anita Hill (1956–)
Spike Lee (1957–)
Barack Obama (1962–)

21

The Long Freedom Movement

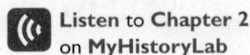 Listen to Chapter 21
on MyHistoryLab

LEARNING OBJECTIVES

21-1 What were the background and conditions of the 1950s that led to the emergence of the national civil rights movement?

21-2 What events led to *Brown v. Board of Education* (1954), and why was it the most important Supreme Court decision of the twentieth century?

21-3 How did white southerners' strategy of massive resistance affect the modern civil rights movement?

21-4 What were the origins and outcome of, and who were the participants in, the Montgomery Bus Boycott?

21-5 What were the goals of the Civil Rights Act of 1957?

21-6 How did the early activism by students differ in tactics and methods from earlier activism?

21-7 Who were the leaders and what were the tactics and effects of their various civil rights activities?

21-8 How did the federal government intermittently support and thwart the long freedom movement?

"What King delivered to blacks there, far more important than whether they got to ride on the bus, was the absence of fear, the ability to be men. . . . Dr. King had this tremendous facility for giving people the feeling they could be bigger and stronger and more courageous and more loving than they thought they could be."

Quoted from the Bayard Rustin Interview, in Howell Raines, My Soul Is Rested (New York: Bantam Books, 1978), 49.

"Up to the mid-1950s, my people were afraid. They figured if they spoke out, they'd be pushed around on their job, or they would lose their job, so they kept silent. In my case, my paycheck came from Chicago, and they couldn't get me fired so easy. So when I saw the opportunity, I knew I could reach out and grab for it."

E. D. Nixon, Pullman Car Porter and NAACP activist. Quoted from Nixon, in Donnie Williams with Wayne Greenhaw, The Thunder of Angels: The Montgomery Bus Boycott and the People Who Broke the Back of Jim Crow (Chicago: Lawrence Hill Books, 2006), 53.

Between 1954 and 1965, the civil rights movement achieved a revolution, transforming the legal and social status of African Americans. Bold movements—beginning with the "Double V" Campaign during World War II, and the NAACP's long legal struggle to overthrow the "separate but equal" doctrine—triumphed in the ***Brown v. Board of Education of Topeka*** decision in 1954. Black men and women protested against segregation and discrimination through the Montgomery Bus Boycott of 1955–1956, and against white-only lunch counters and public transportation. Black protest culminated in massive grassroots campaigns throughout the South in 1963, 1964, and 1965—and changed the face of race relations in the United States. Despite fierce resistance, legally sanctioned segregation, racial discrimination, and disfranchisement fell before a mighty coalition of civil rights groups and their allies. Demonstrations and the pressures of the Cold War compelled high government officials to abandon their early caution. Although racism remained powerful in American life after 1965, and African Americans continued to suffer from severe economic disadvantages, the enlargement of freedom of

At the height of his moral authority, Martin Luther King, Jr. (1929–1968), delivers the memorable "I Have a Dream" speech at the 1963 March on Washington.

opportunity and recognition of African Americans' full citizenship rights transformed America and radiated across the globe.

The heart of the story of the modern civil rights movement is the courage and tenacity people showed in their own communities in their determination to attack segregation and exclusion from the political process. Behind the charismatic leaders and the spectacles of the NAACP's Supreme Court victories and the marches and demonstrations captured so dramatically on television were the ordinary citizens who initiated protests, formulated strategies and tactics, and garnered other essential resources that made collective action work. The people's actions were made effective through their families, churches, voluntary associations, political organizations, women's clubs, labor unions, and colleges. The sacrifices and experience gained in the previous one hundred years of struggle had, by the mid-1950s, accumulated sufficiently to permit an all-out attack on white supremacy. The civil rights movement would be long and bloody, and it would not lead to the Promised Land, but it would change America.

Brown v. Board of Education of Topeka Decision by the Supreme Court in 1954 that overturned the "separate but equal" doctrine.

The 1950s: Prosperity and Prejudice

21-1 | **What were the background and conditions of the 1950s that led to the emergence of the national civil rights movement?**

For most white Americans, the 1950s were an era of unparalleled prosperity, consumer consumption, and a patriarchal business culture. Affluent white Americans fled to the suburbs; by 1960, 52 percent of Americans owned their own homes. The decade is remembered nostalgically as a time of large, stable nuclear families; wives and mothers who stayed at home; and communities untroubled by drugs, crime, and juvenile delinquency. It was a time of backyard barbecues and hula hoops, when nightly television shows like *Ozzie and Harriet* and *I Love Lucy* projected a vision of domestic tranquility.

For most black Americans, however, the 1950s were less blissful. American society remained rigidly segregated in housing and education. Despite the gains African Americans made during the World War II era, Jim Crow still reigned. Although the *Smith v. Allwright* Supreme Court decision in 1944, which declared the "white primary" unconstitutional, helped reenfranchise black voters in Florida, Tennessee, and Texas, Jim Crow restrictions and the threat of white violence kept millions of African Americans from voting in the Deep South. Likewise, although the 1948 *Shelley v. Kramer* Supreme Court decision—which outlawed the restricted residential covenants that had allowed homeowners to refuse to sell, rent, or lease their property to African Americans—was a significant victory, violence and extralegal practices still made housing integration a distant dream.

More important, most African Americans did not benefit from the economic boom of the 1950s that allowed so many white Americans to purchase homes in the suburbs. Moving into urban centers, where the number of factories and jobs were just beginning to decline, African Americans suffered a higher unemployment rate than any other segment of the population. White workers, fearing for their jobs, felt threatened by competition from unemployed black workers. As urban neighborhoods deteriorated, conditions ripened for a massive explosion.

21-1
21-2
21-3
21-4
21-5
21-6
21-7
21-8

The Road to *Brown*

21-2 What events led to *Brown v. Board of Education* (1954), and why was it the most important Supreme Court decision of the twentieth century?

In 1954, with the Supreme Court's decision in *Brown v. Board of Education of Topeka, Kansas*, progress in the desegregation of American society moved into the civilian realm. The *Brown* decision undermined state-sanctioned segregation. The NAACP's legal program of the 1920s and 1930s was largely responsible for this victory. In 1940 the NAACP set up the Legal Defense and Educational Fund (NAACP-LDEF) to attack the legal foundations of race inequality in American education. Thereafter, the NAACP-LDEF fought segregation and discrimination in education, housing, employment, and politics. In the first years of its existence, attorneys for the fund won stunning victories, including a 1944 Supreme Court decision, *Smith v. Allwright*, declaring white primaries unconstitutional, and *Shelley v. Kramer* (1948), outlawing restrictive residential covenants. The life and career of one of the NAACP-LDEF lawyers, Constance Baker Motley, symbolizes the struggle that black professionals, both men and women, waged to overcome racial and gender exclusion as well as the union of disparate forces that planted and nurtured the seeds of the coming revolution. Motley is our guide on the road to *Brown*.

Constance Baker Motley and Black Lawyers in the South

Constance Baker Motley was born in 1921 to immigrant parents, Rachel Huggins and Willoughby Alva Baker, from Nevis, in the British West Indies. She grew up in a tightly knit West Indian community in New Haven, Connecticut. The members of New Haven's black community, including Baker's parents, worked as domestics or in service jobs for Yale University. Baker attended integrated schools and experienced episodic racism, including being refused admission to a local beach and a skating rink. In high school, Baker developed a strong racial consciousness: "My interest in civil rights [was] a very early interest which developed when I was in high school. The fact that I was a Black, a woman, and a member of a large, relatively poor family was also the base of this great ambition [to enter the legal profession]."

The most important event in her early life was the lecture that George Crawford, a 1903 Yale Law School graduate who worked in New Haven as an NAACP lawyer, gave at the local Dixwell Community Center. The talk concerned the Supreme Court decision in *State of Missouri ex rel. Gaines v. Canada*. Crawford explained that the University of Missouri's law school had denied Gaines admission but had offered to pay his tuition expenses to an out-of-state school. The NAACP Legal Committee under Charles H. Houston's leadership won a victory when the Supreme Court ruled that the state had violated the Fourteenth Amendment's mandate that state laws provide equal protection regardless of race. After *Gaines*, states had to furnish within their borders facilities for legal education for black people equal to those offered for white citizens.

Baker desperately wanted to go to law school, but her family could not even afford to send her to college. For a year and a half after graduation from high school in 1939, Baker earned $50 a month varnishing chairs for a building restoration project under the auspices of the National Youth Administration. In 1940, however, Baker came to the attention of Clarence Blakeslee, a local white philanthropist who offered to finance her education after hearing her speak at a meeting of black and white community residents. She attended Fisk University until 1942 and then transferred to New York University, where she graduated in 1943. She then became the second black woman ever to attend Columbia University Law School. In 1946 she married former New York University law student Joel Motley and went to work for the NAACP's LDEF.

Constance Baker Motley first met Thurgood Marshall in October 1945 when he hired her as a law clerk during her second year in law school. Marshall assigned her to work on the

Constance Baker Motley endured many hardships and even assaults as she tried school desegregation cases in the South. Here she leaves the federal court in Birmingham after an unsuccessful attempt to force the University of Alabama to accept a black student.

21-1

21-2

21-3

21-4

21-5

21-6

21-7

21-8

hundreds of army court-martial cases filed after World War II. Motley recalled, "From the first day I knew that this was where I wanted to be. I never bothered interviewing anywhere else. But for this fortuitous event, I do not think that I would have gotten very far as a lawyer. Women were simply not hired in those days."

In the late 1940s, the NAACP-LDEF's attack on inequality in graduate education provided the basis for a full-scale assault on segregation. No longer would the organization be satisfied only to push for fulfillment of the promise of "separate but equal" facilities. In 1948 the University of Oklahoma Law School denied Ada Lois Sipuel admission because she was black. The Supreme Court, signaling it was willing to take a more activist stance, ordered Oklahoma, in *Sipuel v. Board of Regents of the University of Oklahoma*, to "provide [a legal education] for [Sipuel] in conformity with the equal protection clause of the Fourteenth Amendment and provide it as soon as it does for applicants of any other group."

Another case, *Sweatt v. Painter*, which the Supreme Court decided in 1950, began when the University of Texas at Austin attempted to circumvent court orders to admit Heman

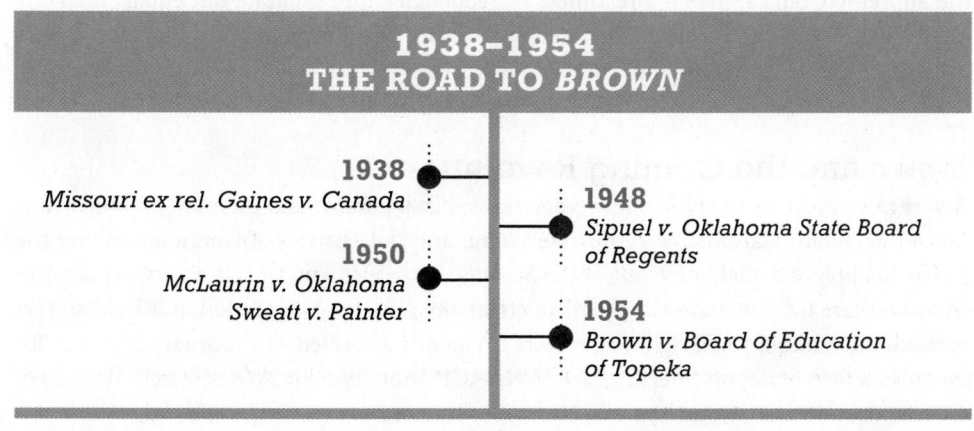

1938–1954
THE ROAD TO *BROWN*

1938
Missouri ex rel. Gaines v. Canada

1948
Sipuel v. Oklahoma State Board of Regents

1950
McLaurin v. Oklahoma
Sweatt v. Painter

1954
Brown v. Board of Education of Topeka

 Read on **MyHistoryLab Document:** *McLaurin v. Oklahoma State Regents* Paves the Way for *Brown,* 1950

This student at the University of Oklahoma was not allowed to sit in a classroom with white students. It took two Supreme Court decisions to end such segregation at the University of Oklahoma.
Corbis-Bettmann.

Sweatt to its law school by creating a separate facility consisting of three basement rooms, a small library, and a few instructors who would lecture to him alone. The court ruled that the university had deprived Sweatt of intangibles such as "the essential ingredient of a legal education . . . the opportunity for students to discuss the law with their peers and others with whom they would be associated professionally in later life."

On the same day the justices ruled in *Sweatt,* they also declared illegal the University of Oklahoma's segregation of George W. McLaurin from white students attending the Graduate School of Education. The University of Oklahoma had admitted McLaurin but made him sit in the hallway at the classroom door, study in a private part of the balcony of the library, and eat in a sequestered part of the lunchroom. When he finally gained a seat in the classroom, it was marked "reserved for colored." In these precedent-setting cases, the Supreme Court signaled a readiness to reconsider the "separate but equal" doctrine of *Plessy* (1896) and to redefine the meaning of the "equal protection of the laws" clause of the Fourteenth Amendment. These cases were important stepping-stones on the road to *Brown.*

Brown and the Coming Revolution

A year after the *Sweatt* and *McLaurin* decisions, black parents and their lawyers filed suits in Kansas, South Carolina, Virginia, Delaware, and the District of Columbia asking the courts to apply the qualitative test of the *Sweatt* case to elementary and secondary schools and to declare the "separate but equal" doctrine invalid in public education. Black lawyers in the South handling civil rights cases were frequently assaulted. On February 27, 1942, for example, a former deputy sheriff attacked NAACP attorney Leon A. Ransom in the hall of the Davidson County Courthouse in Nashville, Tennessee. The *Crisis* reported,

The attack came when Ransom walked out into the hall from the courtroom where he was sitting with Z. Alexander Looby, local NAACP attorney, on a case involving the exclusion of Negroes from a jury. . . . When the scuffle began, Negroes who would have aided Ransom were held back by a former constable (white) named Hill, who drew his gun and shouted: "We are going to teach these northern Negroes not to come down here raising fancy court questions."

At Ransom's death in 1954, Thurgood Marshall eulogized,

Negro Americans, whether they know it or not, owe a great debt of gratitude to Andy Ransom and men like him who battled in the courts down a span of years to bring us to the place we now occupy in the enjoyment of our constitutional rights as citizens, in helping to build up the NAACP legal program step by step, in the skill which he gave to individual cases and to the planning of strategy, Dr. Ransom left a legacy to the whole population.

It was no less difficult for a black woman lawyer to venture into the South in search of justice. Black attorney Derrick Bell, who also worked for the LDEF, said of Motley's work,

Nothing in the Southern lawyers' background could have prepared them for Connie. To them Negro women were either mammies, maids, or mistresses. None of them had ever dealt with a Negro woman on a peer basis, much less on a level of intellectual equality, which in this case quickly became superiority.

Motley was keenly aware of her precarious situation. "Often a southern judge would refer to men attorneys as Mister, but would make a point of calling me 'Connie,' since traditionally Black women in the South were only called by their first name." Housing was another problem. Motley recalled that when in a southern town for a long trial, "I knew that it was going to be impossible to stay in a decent hotel." These lawyers had to depend on the good graces and courage of local people. Motley explained, "Usually in these situations a Black family would agree to put you up. But there was so much publicity involved with civil rights cases that no Black family dared have us—they were too afraid." While in Mississippi arguing a teachers' equalization of salaries case, Motley declared, "A Black doctor invited us to dinner, but that was about it. . . . I wonder how many lawyers have had the experience of preparing for trial in a flophouse. That was the only room I could get."

In the late 1940s, the black parents of children attending Scott's Branch School in Clarendon County, South Carolina, approached Roderick W. Elliott, the chairman of the school board, with a modest request. There were 6,531 black students and only 2,375 white students enrolled in the county's schools. Although the county had 30 buses to convey the white students to their schools, no buses were available to black schoolchildren. Some black students had to walk 18 miles round-trip each day. Once they arrived, they entered buildings heated by wood stoves and lit by kerosene lamps. For a drink of water or to go to the toilet they had to go outdoors.

With the encouragement of African Methodist Episcopal pastor and schoolteacher Rev. Joseph Armstrong DeLaine, the parents mustered the courage to petition the school board for buses. Elliott's reply was short: "We ain't got no money to buy a bus for your nigger children." In 1949 DeLaine went to the NAACP officials in Columbia, and Thurgood Marshall was there. On December 20, 1950, Harry Briggs, a navy veteran, and 24 other Clarendon County residents sued the school district. The case, *Briggs v. Elliott*, was the first legal challenge to elementary school segregation to originate in the South. Meanwhile, however, four other cases in different parts of the country were advancing through the federal courts. These would be combined into one case that would decide the fate of the *Plessy* doctrine of "separate but equal."

The years of preparation and hardship paid off. Motley worked with a dream team of black lawyers and academics, an inner circle of advisers that included Louis Redding from Wilmington, Delaware; James Nabrit from Washington, DC; Robert Ming from Chicago; psychologist Kenneth Clark from New York; and historian John Hope Franklin to prepare the case *Brown v. Board of Education of Topeka* and to argue it before the Supreme Court.

Read on MyHistoryLab Document: *Brown v. Board of Education of Topeka, Kansas, 1954*

In 1950, when the all-white Sumner School in Topeka, Kansas, refused to admit Linda Brown (1943–), her father, Oliver Brown, filed a lawsuit and testified in court that his daughter had to travel an hour and 20 minutes to attend a black school. The Sumner School was only seven blocks away but practiced racial exclusion. Linda became the "named plaintiff" in the landmark U.S. Supreme Court case *Brown v. Board of Education* (1954), which declared unconstitutional laws mandating public school segregation.

Motley, Robert Carter, Jack Greenberg, and Marshall also sought assistance from Spottswood Robinson and Oliver Hill of Richmond, Virginia, and read papers prepared by historians C. Vann Woodward and Alfred Kelly about the original equalitarian intentions of the post–Civil War amendments and other legislation. In his argument, Marshall appealed to the Court to meet the *Plessy* doctrine head on and declare it erroneous:

> It [*Plessy*] stands mirrored today as a legal aberration, the faulty conception of an era dominated by provincialism, by intense emotionalism in race relations . . . and by the preaching of a doctrine of racial superiority that contradicted the basic concept upon which our society was founded. Twentieth century America, fighting racism at home and abroad, has rejected the race views of *Plessy v. Ferguson* because we have come to the realization that such views obviously tend to preserve not the strength but the weakness of our heritage.

By the time Marshall made this argument, black intellectuals, scholars, and activists and their progressive white allies had closed ranks to support integration. To suggest other alternatives as the goal for African Americans was to swim against the current.

During late 1953 and early 1954, Chief Justice Earl Warren persuaded the Court to support Marshall's position. On May 17, 1954, the Court ruled unanimously in favor of the NAACP lawyers and their clients that a classification based solely on race violated the Fourteenth Amendment. In a stirring passage Warren declared,

> We come then to the question presented: Does segregation of children in public schools solely on the basis of race, even though the physical facilities and other 'tangible' factors may be equal, deprive the children of the minority group of equal educational opportunities? We believe that it does. . . . To separate them from others of similar age and qualifications solely because of their race generates a feeling of inferiority as to the status in the community that may affect their hearts and minds in a way unlikely ever to be undone. . . . We conclude that in the field of public education the doctrine of "separate but equal" has no place. Separate educational facilities are inherently unequal.

The *Brown* decision would eventually lead to the dismantling of the entire structure of Jim Crow laws that regulated important aspects of black life in America: movement, work, marriage, education, housing, and even death and burial. The *Brown* decision, more than any other case, signaled the emerging primacy of equality as a guide to constitutional decisions. This and subsequent decisions helped advance the rights of other minorities and women. As Motley reflected, "In the *Brown* case and in the decisions that followed, we blazed a trail for others by showing the competence of Black lawyers."

Brown II

21-3 **How did white southerners' strategy of massive resistance affect the modern civil rights movement?**

A year after the *Brown* decision, in May 1955, the Supreme Court issued a second ruling, commonly known as *Brown II*, which addressed the practical process of desegregation. The Court underscored that the states in the suits should begin prompt compliance with the 1954 ruling and that this should be done with "all deliberate speed." Many black Americans interpreted this to mean "immediately." White southerners hoped it meant a long time or never. Ominously, President Eisenhower seemed displeased with the Court's rulings and refused to put the moral authority of his office behind their enforcement.

Nevertheless, in 1955 and early 1956, desegregation proceeded without hindrance in Maryland, Kentucky, Delaware, Oklahoma, and Missouri. Alabama Governor Jim Folsom declared that his state would obey the courts. Other moderate white southern politicians counseled calm and worked to head off a full-scale conflict with the federal government.

Massive White Resistance

White moderates, however, soon found themselves a shrinking minority, as extremists, determined to maintain white supremacy at any cost, prepared to resist the Court's decisions. The extremists' rhetoric bordered on hysteria but found a receptive audience among many. For example, Jerry Falwell, a young minister from Virginia, explained that black people were the descendants of Noah's son Ham and were destined to be servants because of a curse God had put on him. Falwell also claimed that Moscow had inspired the Supreme Court's decisions. In 1955 leading businessmen, white-collar professionals, and clergy began organizing, in virtually every southern city, White Citizens' Councils dedicated to preserving "the southern way of life" and the South's "sacred heritage of freedom." The councils used their economic and political power to intimidate African Americans who challenged segregation. They fired black people, evicted them, and refused them credit.

Many white politicians took up the banner of massive resistance. Mississippi Senator James O. Eastland called the *Brown* decision a "monstrous crime." The Virginia legislature closed all public schools in Prince Edward County to thwart integration. On March 12, 1956, 96 southern congressmen led by North Carolina's Senator Sam Ervin, Jr., and South Carolina's Senator Strom Thurmond issued "The Southern Manifesto," vowing to fight to preserve segregation and the southern way of life. The manifesto called the *Brown* decisions an "unwarranted exercise of power by the court, contrary to the Constitution." The only southern senators who refused to sign the manifesto were Albert Gore, Sr., of Tennessee and Lyndon B. Johnson of Texas.

The NAACP came under siege after the *Brown* decision as southern states tried to destroy it. By 1957 nine southern states had filed suit to eradicate the organization. Some states, alleging the NAACP was linked to a worldwide communist conspiracy, made membership illegal. Membership plummeted from 128,716 to 79,677, and the association lost 246 branches in the South.

Under these pressures, desegregation ground to a halt. By 1958, 13 school systems had been desegregated. By 1960, two years later, the total had risen to only 17. Massive resistance successfully challenged the possibility of achieving change through court action alone.

◉ **Watch** on **MyHistoryLab Video:** How Did the Civil Rights Movement Change American Schools?

The Lynching of Emmett Till

White southerners' violent reaction to the growing assertiveness of black people found expression in the summer of 1955 in the lynching of 14-year-old Emmett Till of Chicago, an event that helped galvanize the emerging civil rights movement. Till was visiting relatives in the small town of Money, Mississippi. On a dare from his friends, he entered Bryant's grocery store, bought candy, and said "Bye, baby" to Carolyn Bryant, the wife of the owner, as he left. Till was unaware how far white people would go to avenge this small breach of white supremacy's racial etiquette. In the middle of the night a few days after the incident, Bryant's husband and brother-in-law arrived at the small house where Till was staying and kidnapped him at gunpoint. His body was subsequently found in the Tallahatchie River tied to a heavy cotton gin fan. Till had a bullet in his head and had been tortured before his murder. Despite overwhelming evidence and the brave testimony of Mose Wright, Till's uncle, and other local black people, an all-white jury acquitted the two men who lynched Till. In early 1956 the murderers sold their confession

In August 1955, 14-year-old Emmett Till was visiting relatives in Money, Mississippi, when he transgressed the line of racial etiquette by speaking to a white woman in a country store. He paid the ultimate price. The lynching of Emmett Till and the subsequent acquittal of his murderers reflected the low regard in which black life was held in the Jim Crow South and the extent to which whites were determined to maintain the racial status quo.

to *Look* magazine and gloated over their escape from justice. In 2004, new evidence indicated that 10 people may have been involved in the Till lynching.

The Till lynching shaped the consciousness of a generation of young African-American activists. Partly this was due to Till's mother, Mamie Bradley. Unwilling to let America turn away from this crime, she had her son's mangled body displayed in an open casket in Chicago. Thousands of mourners paid their respects, and many committed themselves to fighting the system that made this crime possible. Bradley also traveled around the nation speaking to groups on whom her grief had a profound impact. Myrlie Evers, who would later have a role in the movement, remembered how she felt: "I bled for Emmett Till's mother. I know when she came to Mississippi and appeared at the mass meetings how everyone poured out their hearts to her, went into their pockets when people had only two or three pennies, and gave."

New Forms of Protest: The Montgomery Bus Boycott

21-4 | What were the origins and outcome of, and who were the participants in, the Montgomery Bus Boycott?

Strong local communities formed the core of the civil rights movement in the South, and the deeds of brave individuals often sparked them to action. The first and one of the most important expressions of this process occurred in Alabama's capital city. Blessed with well-organized educational, religious, and other institutions, Montgomery's African-American community of 45,000 was poised to make history.

The Roots of Revolution

The movement in Montgomery did not emerge out of the blue, although it must have seemed that way to many white southerners. It was the result of years of organization and planning by protest groups. In addition to its numerous churches, two black colleges, and other social organizations, Montgomery had a core of protest groups. One, the Women's Political Council (WPC), had been founded in 1946 by Mary Frances Fair Burks, chair of Alabama State College Department of English, after the all-white League of Women Voters had refused to allow black women to participate in its activities. The WPC had only 40 members, all middle-class, courageous, and competent leaders who were willing to stand up to powerful white people. The WPC was joined by a chapter of the NAACP led by E. D. Nixon, a Pullman train car porter and head of the Alabama chapter of the Brotherhood of Sleeping Car Porters. In 1943 Nixon had founded the Montgomery Voters League, which was dedicated to helping African Americans navigate Alabama's tortuous voter registration process. In the decade after 1945, these groups searched for a way to mobilize the black community to challenge white power.

The 1954 *Brown* decision seemed to provide a means to destroy segregation and discrimination in the city. Four days after it was announced, Jo Ann Robinson, a professor at Alabama State College, wrote to Montgomery's mayor on behalf of the WPC reiterating the complaints of the black community about conditions on the city's buses: "Please consider this plea, for even now plans are being made to ride less, or not at all, on our buses." The mayor ignored the warning, and the buses remained as segregated as before. All seemed quiet, but Montgomery's black lawyers and NAACP chapter began laying the groundwork for a test case challenging segregation of the city's bus lines.

On March 2, 1955, a 15-year-old Booker T. Washington High School student, Claudette Colvin, was arrested for refusing to give up her seat on a bus to a white woman. The WPC was ready to use this incident to initiate the threatened bus boycott. E. D. Nixon called 24-year-old Fred D. Gray, who agreed to represent Colvin in her challenge to Jim Crow segregation laws. Gray was one of only two black lawyers in Montgomery. The March 18, 1955, hearings resulted in a guilty verdict, and Claudette was placed on probation in the custody

VOICES   Letter of the Montgomery Women's Political Council to Mayor W. A. Gayle

In this letter threatening a boycott of Montgomery's buses, the Women's Political Council politely asks not for the desegregation of the buses but only for new regulations that would prevent black riders from being forced to move to accommodate white riders.

May 21, 1954

Honorable Mayor W. A. Gayle
City Hall
Montgomery, Alabama

Dear Sir:

The Women's Political Council is very grateful to you and the City Commissioners for the hearing you allowed our representative during the month of March, 1954, when the "city-bus-fare-increase case" was being reviewed. There were several things the Council asked for:

1. A city law that would make it possible for Negroes to sit from back toward front, and whites from front toward back until all the seats were taken.
2. That Negroes would not be asked or forced to pay fare at front and go to the rear of the bus to enter.
3. That buses stop at every corner in residential sections occupied by Negroes as they do in communities where whites reside.

We are happy to report that buses have begun stopping at more corners now in some sections where Negroes live than previously. However, the same practices in seating and boarding the bus continue.

Mayor Gayle, three-fourths of the riders of these public conveyances are Negroes. If Negroes did not patronize them, they could not possibly operate.

More and more of our people are already arranging with neighbors and friends to ride to keep from being insulted and humiliated by bus drivers.

There has been talk from twenty-five or more local organizations of planning a city-wide boycott of buses. We, sir, do not feel that forceful measures are necessary in bargaining for a convenience which is right for all bus passengers. We, the Council, believe that when this matter has been put before you and the Commissioners, that agreeable terms can be met in a quiet and in a sensible manner to the satisfaction of all concerned.

Many of our Southern cities in neighboring states have practiced the policies we seek without incident whatsoever. Atlanta, Macon and Savannah in Georgia have done this for years. Even Mobile, in our own state, does this and all the passengers are satisfied.

Please consider this plea, and if possible, act favorably upon it, for even now plans are being made to ride less, or not at all, on our buses. We do not want this.

Respectfully yours,
The Women's Political Council
Jo Ann Robinson, President

1. **What did the Women's Political Council initially hope to accomplish?**
2. **What does this letter suggest about the importance of black women's political organizations in the early years of the civil rights movement?**

SOURCE: Stewart Burns, *Daybreak of Freedom: The Montgomery Bus Boycott* (Chapel Hill: University of North Carolina Press, 1997), 58.

  Read on **MyHistoryLab Document:** Jo Ann Gibson Robinson Looks Back at the Montgomery Bus Boycott of 1955

21-1
21-2
21-3
21-4
21-5
21-6
21-7
21-8

---

of her parents. Jo Ann Robinson recalled, "Claudette's agonized sobs penetrated the atmosphere of the courthouse. Many people brushed away their own tears." The Colvins were not members of the black social elite in Montgomery, and for various reasons community leaders decided against protesting Claudette's conviction for allegedly "assaulting" the police officers who had dragged her from the bus. They decided to wait for another opportunity to launch a protest movement. Fred Gray, however, decided to appeal Colvin's case.

Rosa Parks

On Thursday, December 1, 1955, Rosa Parks, a 43-year-old department store seamstress and civil rights activist, boarded a city bus and moved to the back where African Americans were required to sit. All seats were taken, so she sat in one toward the middle of the bus. When a white man boarded the bus, the driver ordered Parks to vacate her seat for him. There was nothing unusual in this, but on this fateful day, Parks refused to move. She had not planned

Watch on **MyHistoryLab Video:** African-American Women and the Struggle for Civil Rights

Claudette Colvin was a teenager when she refused to obey the transportation segregation laws in Montgomery.

Montgomery Bus Boycott Refusal from 1955 to 1957 of African Americans in Montgomery, Alabama, to ride the city's buses until the bus lines were desegregated.

 Listen on **MyHistoryLab Audio:** Mass Meeting; speech by Martin Luther King, Jr.

to resist on that day, but, as she later said, she had "decided that I would have to know once and for all what rights I had as a human being and a citizen. . . . I was so involved with the attempt to bring about freedom from this kind of thing . . . I felt just resigned to give what I could to protest against the way I was being treated, and felt that all of our meetings, trying to negotiate, bring about petitions before the authorities . . . really hadn't done any good at all." At the time Parks was portrayed as simply tired, but she had been training for just this kind of challenge for years. When her moment came, she seized it; with this act of resistance, she launched the **Montgomery Bus Boycott** and inspired the modern civil rights struggle for freedom and equality.

The plans of the WPC and NAACP came into play after Parks's arrest for violating Montgomery's transportation laws. She was ordered to appear in court on the following Monday. Meanwhile, E. D. Nixon bailed her out of the city jail and began mobilizing the leadership of the black community behind her. Working in tandem with Nixon, Robinson wrote and circulated a flyer calling for a one-day boycott of the buses followed by a mass meeting of the community to discuss the matter. Robinson took the flyer to the Alabama State College campus, stayed up all night, and, with the help of a colleague, mimeographed 30,000 copies of it. The WPC had planned distribution routes months earlier, and the next day, Robinson and nearly 200 volunteers distributed bundles of flyers to beauty parlors and schools, to factories and grocery stores, and to taverns and barbershops throughout the black neighborhoods.

Montgomery Improvement Association

On December 5, 1955, the black community did not ride the buses, and the movement had begun. Nixon and other community leaders, including Jo Ann Gibson Robinson, who would become its chief strategist, formed a new organization, the Montgomery Improvement Association (MIA), to coordinate the boycott. They selected a 26-year-old minister, Martin Luther King, Jr., as its president. That evening there was an overflowing mass meeting of the black community at the Holt Street Baptist Church to decide whether to continue the boycott. King, with barely an hour to prepare, defined the goals of the boycott and the civil rights movement that followed. In his dramatic voice, he connected the core values of America and of the Judeo-Christian tradition to the goals of African Americans nationwide as well as in Montgomery. Fred Gray and his fiancée were in the church and recalled the impact of King's speech:

> The high point of the meeting was the speech by Dr. Martin Luther King. This was the first time he had spoken to so many people. It was the first speech of his career as a civil rights leader, later to become an internationally known figure. Each of us listened to his words and waited for his next phrase. My fiancée Bernice was in the audience. She later described how King's inspiring speech ignited the crowd and was the motivating factor that was needed to make the protest successful. It was his message and his encouragement and his speech that gave those thousands of African Americans the courage, the enthusiasm and the desire to stay off the buses.

Martin Luther King, Jr.

King's speech electrified the meeting, which unanimously decided to boycott the buses until the MIA's demands were met. The speech also marked the beginning of King's role as a leader of the civil rights movement. King had been raised in a prominent ministerial family with a long history of standing up for African-American rights. His grandfather had led a protest to force Atlanta to build its first high school for African Americans. King's father spoke out

PROFILE Rosa Louise McCauley Parks

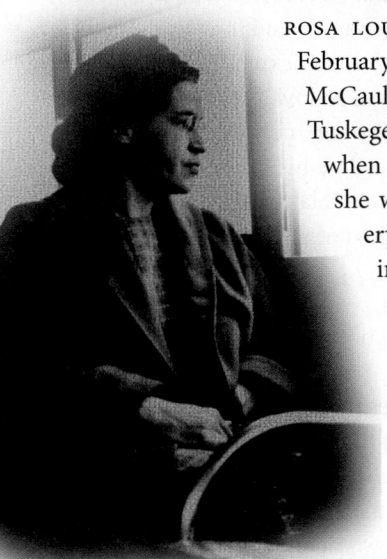

Rosa Parks, in this 1999 photograph by Paul Richards, is venerated as the mother of the civil rights movement and has remained an important symbol of hope and courage.

ROSA LOUISE MCCAULEY PARKS was born on February 4, 1913, to James and Leona (Edwards) McCauley, a carpenter and a schoolteacher, of Tuskegee, Alabama. Her father migrated north when his daughter was two years old. When she was 11, Rosa attended the Montgomery Industrial School for Girls while living with a widowed aunt. In 1932 Rosa married Raymond Parks, who worked in the Atlas Barber Shop in Montgomery. She worked as a department store seamstress. They were both active in the efforts to secure the release of the Scottsboro Boys. Rosa Parks enjoyed a full and busy life, serving as the secretary of the Montgomery branch of the NAACP (1943–1956) and as a member of the African Methodist Episcopal Church. In the late 1940s Rosa Parks worked to mobilize the black Montgomery community to protest white sexualized violence against black women. The assault on Gertrude Perkins, in the 1940s, and on many others black women by white men who were never punished made Parks even more determined in her activism. She participated in voter registration campaigns, and in 1954 she attended the Highlander Folk School, a training center for social change in Monteagle, Tennessee.

On December 1, 1955, when Rosa Parks refused to give up her seat on a Montgomery bus, little could she have anticipated that she would become a living symbol of the African-American quest for freedom, justice, and equality of opportunity. With great dignity and little fanfare, Parks chose to be arrested rather than to comply with the white bus driver's order to move to the back-of-the-bus section reserved for black people. Parks's behavior was a thoughtful reflection of her larger pattern of personal and public resistance. As word of Parks's arrest reverberated through Montgomery's black community, Jo Ann Robinson and members of the Women's Political Council (WPC) swung into action. On December 2, 1955, Robinson wrote and circulated, with assistance from students and club women, 30,000 copies of a flyer that declared, "Another Negro woman has been arrested and thrown in jail because she refused to get up out of her seat on the bus for a white person to sit down. It is the second time since the Claudette Colvin case that a Negro woman has been arrested for the same thing. This has to be stopped. Negroes have rights too, for if Negroes did not ride the buses, they could not operate." Robinson and the WPC asked the community to stay off the buses for a day to show their opposition to bus segregation and their solidarity with Rosa Parks.

The success of the one-day boycott aroused the community and motivated thousands to attend the first mass meeting at the Holt Street Baptist Church and to found, under the leadership of Rev. Martin Luther King, Jr., the Montgomery Improvement Association. A year later, on December 20, 1956, the Supreme Court ruled Alabama's state and local segregation laws unconstitutional. In retaliation, the department store fired Parks. The response was, perhaps, irrelevant.

In 1957 Parks, her husband, and her mother moved to Detroit, where her brother resided. For a quarter of a century, Rosa Parks worked as a special assistant to Congressman John Conyers. In 1979 the NAACP awarded Parks its Spingarn Medal. Detroit named a street, Rosa Parks Boulevard, in her honor. In keeping with a lifetime commitment to social justice and the pursuit of freedom, at the celebration of her seventy-seventh birthday in 1990 at the Kennedy Center in Washington, DC, Parks implored the 3,000 revelers to "pray and work for the freedom of Nelson Mandela and all of our sisters and brothers in South Africa."

Rosa Parks lived a quiet life in Detroit until her death on October 24, 2005, at the age of 92. Her casket lay in state in the rotunda of the U.S. Capitol for two days, an honor usually reserved for presidents, as the nation paid its last respects to this extraordinary woman.

21-1
21-2
21-3
21-4
21-5
21-6
21-7
21-8

for African-American rights as pastor of the Ebenezer Baptist Church. At age 15, King had entered Morehouse College but did not embrace the ministry as his profession until he came under the influence of its president, Dr. Benjamin E. Mays. By age 25, King had been awarded a Ph.D. in theology from Boston University. He moved to Alabama with his wife, Coretta Scott King, to become pastor of the Dexter Avenue Baptist Church in Montgomery.

In addition to his verbal artistry, King had the ability to inspire moral courage and teach people how to maintain themselves under excruciating pressure. King merged the nonviolence advocated by the Indian nationalist leader Mohandas Gandhi with black Christian faith and church culture to create a unique ideology well suited for the civil rights struggle. King declared that the boycott would continue with or without its leaders because the conflict was not "between the white and the Negro" but "between justice and injustice." He told the Montgomery boycotters, "If we are arrested every day, if we are exploited every day, if we are trampled over every day, don't ever let anyone pull you so low as to hate them. . . . We must realize so many people are taught to hate us that they are not totally responsible for their hate." King's faith was tested. As the boycott proceeded, his home was bombed. Segregationists also bombed Nixon's home and those of two other black clergymen and MIA leaders, Ralph Abernathy and Fred Shuttlesworth, and assaulted other boycott participants.

Walking for Freedom

Although men occupied the top leadership positions in the boycott, women were the key to its effectiveness. The boycott lasted more than a year—381 days—and over its course nearly all the black women previously dependent on the buses to get to work refused to ride them. Some walked 12 miles a day. Others had the support of their white women employers, who provided transportation. And many helped organize a car pool of 200 vehicles that proved critical to sustaining the boycott. The community held mass meetings nightly in local churches. Robinson edited the MIA newsletter. Other women supported the boycott in dozens of ways. Some organized bake sales and made door-to-door solicitations to raise the $2,000 per week needed to keep the car pools going. The boycott took 65 percent of the bus company's business, forcing it to cut schedules, lay off drivers, and raise fares. White merchants also suffered. Impressive as it was, the boycott by itself could not end segregation on the buses. Black Montgomery needed a two-pronged strategy of mass local pressure and legal recourse through the courts. The legal backing of the federal government was necessary to end Jim Crow. Thus, NAACP lawyers and MIA's lawyer Fred Gray filed a suit in the names of Claudette Colvin, Mary Louise Smith, and three other women.

Friends in the North

The Montgomery movement was not without allies outside the South. Money poured into the MIA's coffers from concerned Americans. Many northern activists who had long been hoping black southerners would begin just this kind of resistance also swung into action to help. Indeed, black and white activists in many northern cities including New York and Chicago had launched challenges to overthrow housing segregation and promote open access to public beaches and amusement parks. Activist and civil rights groups joined with labor unionists to support issues of economic justice, fair employment, and an end to police corruption and brutality. Two people who were particularly important in the "Long Civil Rights" movement were Bayard Rustin and liberal Jewish lawyer Stanley Levison. Two and a half months into the boycott, Montgomery officials indicted King and one hundred other leaders on charges of conspiracy to disrupt the bus system, and Bayard Rustin arrived in Montgomery. He encouraged the leaders to follow Gandhian practice and submit freely to arrest. In a diary entry, Rustin wrote,

> Many of them did not wait for the police to come but walked to the police station and surrendered. Nixon was the first. He walked into the station and said, "You are looking for me? Here I am." This procedure had a startling effect on both the Negro and the white communities. White community leaders, politicians, and police were dumbfounded. Negroes were thrilled to see their leaders surrender without being hunted down. Soon hundreds of Negroes gathered outside the police station and applauded the leaders as they entered, one by one.

Rustin continued working behind the scenes as one of King's most trusted advisers on nonviolent principles and tactics. Stanley Levison and Ella Baker created a group called In Friendship, which raised money for the boycott. (For more on Ella Baker, see Chapter 18.)

21-1 21-2 21-3 21-4 21-5 21-6 21-7 21-8

Levison was a wealthy attorney committed to social justice. He had worked with the Communist Party, and Rustin had a long history of association with radical groups. Their influence soon attracted the attention of the FBI, which had long been obsessed with black leaders and organizations. King was not a communist, but FBI director J. Edgar Hoover hated him and other black leaders. Hoover called King "the most dangerous man in America," and he pressed his subordinates to prove King was a communist and that the civil rights movement was a Moscow-inspired conspiracy. The FBI began tapping King's telephone and hotel room phones and even threatened to expose his extramarital affairs if he did not commit suicide. By the early 1960s, the FBI had stopped warning King when it uncovered threats to his life.

Victory

As the bus boycott reached the one-year mark, it was obvious that the all-white city government would not budge, no matter how long the boycott lasted. Any white politician who hoped to remain in office had to defend segregation. King and the others who suffered through the ordeal grew discouraged, and in November 1956 their hopes seemed to fade when it became clear the state courts would declare the car pools illegal.

Salvation for the movement came from the cases local women (Claudette Colvin, Aurelia Browder, Susie McDonald, and Mary Louise Smith), Fred Gray, and the NAACP had taken to the federal courts. In keeping with the *Brown* precedent, on November 13, 1956, the Supreme Court in *Browder v. Gayle* ordered an end to Montgomery's bus segregation and overturned the convictions of Colvin and the other women. This decision, unlike the *Brown* decision, also expressly overturned the 1896 *Plessy v. Ferguson* decision because, like *Plessy*, it applied to transportation. Ironically, the ruling was handed down on the same day an Alabama court issued an injunction to end the MIA carpool. The bus company agreed not only to end segregation but also to hire African-American drivers and to treat all passengers with equal respect.

The city's black community rejoiced. On December 21, 1956, black citizens of Montgomery boarded the buses and sat wherever they pleased.

No Easy Road to Freedom: 1957–1960

21-5 **What were the goals of the Civil Rights Act of 1957?**

The victory at Montgomery set an example for future protests. It was the result of a highly organized black community led by committed and capable black leaders. These local efforts were bolstered by the advice and involvement of activists from outside the South, the attention of a sympathetic national press, and, crucially, intervention from the federal courts. But local victories could only go so far, particularly as white resistance intensified. In the three years following the boycott, black southerners and their allies across the nation prepared for a broader movement. At the same time, federal officials outside the judiciary found they could not ignore the white South's incipient rebellion without grave consequences for both the nation and their own power.

Martin Luther King, Jr., and the SCLC

By the end of the campaign in Montgomery, Martin Luther King, Jr., had emerged as a moral leader of national stature. On the advice of Levison, Rustin, and Ella Baker, he helped create a new organization, the **Southern Christian Leadership Conference (SCLC),** to provide an institutional base for continuing the struggle. The SCLC was a federation of civil rights groups, community organizations, and churches that sought to coordinate the burgeoning local movements. King assumed leadership of the SCLC, crisscrossing the nation to build

Southern Christian Leadership Conference (SCLC) Organization spearheaded by Martin Luther King, Jr., to provide an institutional base for the civil rights movement.

support and raise money. The organization also began training black activists, particularly on college campuses, in the tactics of nonviolent protest. Because the ballot was deemed the critical weapon needed to complete school desegregation and secure equal employment opportunity, adequate housing, and equal access to public accommodations, the SCLC focused on securing voting rights for black people. In the three years after the Montgomery Bus Boycott, the SCLC also aided black communities in challenging bus segregation in Tallahassee, Florida, and Atlanta.

The SCLC shared many of the NAACP's goals, but tensions arose between the two organizations. The NAACP's leadership doubted the effectiveness of the protest tactics the SCLC favored. They resented having to divert resources from work on important court cases to defend people arrested in protests and were troubled by the left-wing connections of King's advisers. The fortunes of the NAACP in the South, however, plummeted in the late 1950s as southern states persecuted its members. This left the field to the SCLC. The SCLC and the NAACP worked together, but the tensions over tactics were never far below the surface.

Civil Rights Act of 1957

Despite President Eisenhower's tepid response to *Brown*, Congress proved willing to take a modest step toward ending racial discrimination. Buttressing the Supreme Court's desegregation initiatives, it enacted the Civil Rights Act of 1957, the first such legislation since the end of Reconstruction. To pass the bill, liberals in the Senate were able to end a filibuster by southerners, but the law, for all its symbolic import, was weak. It created a commission to monitor violations of black civil rights and to propose remedies for infringements on black voting. It upgraded the Civil Rights Section into a division within the Justice Department and gave it the power to sue states and municipalities that discriminated on the basis of race. Although an important step on the long road toward black enfranchisement, this act disappointed black activists because it was too weak to counter white reaction and because they felt the Eisenhower administration would not enforce it.

Little Rock, Arkansas

Eisenhower may have had little inclination to support the fight for black rights, but the defiance of Arkansas Governor Orville Faubus forced him to. At the beginning of the school year in 1957, Faubus posted 270 Arkansas national guardsmen outside Little Rock Central High School to prevent nine black youths from entering. Faubus was determined to flout *Brown* and maintain school segregation. When a federal court order forced the governor to allow the children into the school, he simply withdrew the state guard and left the children to face a hate-filled mob.

To defend the sovereignty of the federal courts and the Constitution, Eisenhower had to act. He sent in 1,100 paratroopers from the 101st Airborne Division to Little Rock and put the Arkansas National Guard under federal authority. It was the first time since Reconstruction that troops had been sent to the South to protect the rights of African-American citizens. The troops remained in Little Rock Central High School for the rest of the school year. Governor Faubus closed the Little Rock public schools in 1958–1959. Eight of the nine black students withstood the abuse and curses of segregationists both inside and outside the facility and eventually desegregated the high school. Young African Americans throughout the South would show similar courage.

Read on MyHistoryLab Document: President Eisenhower Uses the National Guard to Desegregate Central High School, 1957

Elizabeth Eckerd, one of nine black students who sought to enroll at Little Rock Central High School in September 1957, endures the taunts of an angry white crowd as she tries to make her way to the school.

Black Youth Stand Up by Sitting Down

21-6 **How did the early activism by students differ in tactics and methods from earlier activism?**

Beginning in 1960, motivated black college students adapted a strategy that the Congress of Racial Equality (CORE) had used in the 1940s—the "sit-in"—and emerged as the vanguard of the civil rights movement. Their distinctive and independent contributions to the black protest movement accelerated the pace of social change. Before long the movement would inspire more northern black and white students. Some high school students in southern cities, including the "Ribault Ten" who integrated Jean Ribault High School in Jacksonville, Florida, in 1966, had to stand up for freedom. As one of the students, Jean Downing, recalled: "Our high school experience was not a pleasant one . . . but someone had to integrate the high schools."

Sit-Ins: Greensboro, Nashville, Atlanta

On February 1, 1960, Joseph McNeil, Franklin McCain, David Richmond, and Ezell Blair, Jr., all freshmen at North Carolina Agricultural and Technical College, decided to desegregate local restaurants by sitting at the lunch counter of Greensboro, North Carolina's Woolworth five-and-dime store. Although black people were welcome to spend their money in the store, they could not eat at the lunch counter, making it a painful symbol of white supremacy. At 4:30 in the afternoon the students sat at the counter. They received no service that day but sat quietly doing their schoolwork until the store closed. The action of these four young men electrified their fellow students, and the next day many others joined them. Soon, black women students from Bennett College and a few white students from the University of North Carolina Women's College joined the protest, and by the fifth day hundreds of young, studious, neatly dressed African Americans crowded the downtown store demanding their rights.

Like the black people of Montgomery, the students in Greensboro acted with forethought and with the support of their community. They had long debated how they could best participate in the desegregation movement. All four of the black students had been members of NAACP college or youth groups and were aware of the currents of change flowing through the South. Although they began the sit-in on their own, it quickly gained the support of the black community. Many people in the North and West—both black and white—also joined the campaign by picketing local stores of the national chains that approved of segregation in the South. After facing the collective power of the black community and their allies for months, white businessmen and politicians gave in to the black community's demands.

The students at Greensboro were not alone in their desire to strike out at discrimination. Indeed, at Fisk University in Nashville, Tennessee, Diane Nash, John

View on MyHistoryLab Closer Look: Second Day of Woolworth's Lunch Counter Sit-in

Four students—from the left, Joseph McNeil, Franklin McCain, Billy Smith, and Clarence Henderson—sit patiently at Woolworth's lunch counter on February 2, 1960, the second day of the sit-in in Greensboro, North Carolina. Although not the first sit-in protest against segregated facilities, the Greensboro action triggered a wave of sit-ins by black high school and college students across the South.

21-1
21-2
21-3
21-4
21-5
21-6
21-7
21-8

Read on **MyHistoryLab** Document: Julian Bond, Sit-ins and the Origins of SNCC (1960)

Lewis, Marion Barry, James Bevel, Curtis Murphy, Gloria Johnson, Bernard Lafayette, and Rodney Powell had begun organizing nonviolent workshops before the Greensboro sit-in. With youthful exuberance and idealism, they determined to follow the Rev. James Lawson's leadership and teaching on nonviolence and Christian brotherhood. Even better organized than their comrades in North Carolina, they had been training intensively for a sit-in campaign. Twelve days after the first sit-ins began, the Nashville group swung into action. Hundreds were arrested, and those who sat suffered insults, beatings, arrest, and torture while in jail. Nonetheless, by May 1960 they had compelled major restaurants to desegregate.

Atlanta, Martin Luther King, Jr.'s home base and the site of a large African-American community, spawned an even more dramatic movement. It began after Spelman College freshman Ruby Doris Smith persuaded her friends and classmates to launch sit-ins in the city. On March 15, 1960, two students at Atlanta University, Julian Bond and Lonnie King, executing a carefully orchestrated plan, deployed 200 sit-in students to 10 different eating places. They targeted government-owned property and public places, including bus and train stations and the state capitol, which should have been willing to serve all customers. At the Federal Building, Bond and his classmates attempted to eat in the municipal cafeteria and were arrested. After hours of incarceration they were released. In earlier years, a jail stint had been a mark of shame, but these students returned to the campus as heroes. The Atlanta sit-in students broadened their campaign demands to include desegregation of all public facilities, black voting rights, and equal access to educational and employment opportunities. On September 27, 1961, the Atlanta business and political elite gave in.

Just as in Greensboro, the students in Nashville, Atlanta, and other southern cities won the support of local people who had not been previously involved in organized resistance. By April 1960 more than 2,000 students from black high schools and colleges had been arrested in 78 southern towns and cities. Local people demonstrated their allegiance to them in numerous ways, but their most effective tactic was the economic boycott. When business began to suffer, white leaders proved willing to negotiate the racial status quo. By the summer, more than 30 southern cities had set up community organizations to respond to the complaints of black citizens.

The Student Nonviolent Coordinating Committee

Recognizing the significance of the region-wide student action and fearing it would soon melt away, SCLC's Ella Baker organized a conference for 150 students at her alma mater, Shaw University, in Raleigh, North Carolina. Baker, who managed operations in SCLC's Atlanta headquarters, chafed under the rigid male leadership of the organization. In contrast, she advocated decentralized leadership and celebrated participatory democracy. Her skepticism about SCLC struck a chord with the students.

Read on **MyHistoryLab** Document: Student Nonviolent Coordinating Committee (SNCC) Statement of Purpose, 1960

Student Nonviolent Coordinating Committee (SNCC) Civil rights organization founded by black college students in 1960 at the initiative of Ella Baker.

On April 15–17, 1960, delegates representing over 50 colleges and high schools from 37 communities in 13 states began discussing how to keep the movement going. Baker addressed the group in a speech entitled "More Than a Hamburger" and became the midwife of a new organization named the **Student Nonviolent Coordinating Committee (SNCC)**. The newest addition to the roster of civil rights associations adhered to the ideology of nonviolence, but it also acknowledged the possible need for increased militancy and confrontation. More accommodating black leaders, even some of those in SCLC, objected to the students' use of direct confrontational tactics that disrupted race relations and community peace.

Freedom Rides

Freedom Rides Effort in 1961 to desegregate interstate bus and rail travel.

The sit-in movement paved the way for the **"Freedom Rides"** of 1961. CORE's James Farmer and Bayard Rustin resolved that it was time for a reprise of their 1947 mission to ride interstate buses and trains in the Upper South. That early effort—a planned bus trip from Washington, DC, to Kentucky—reached only as far as Chapel Hill, North Carolina. There the group of interracial riders met violent resistance, were arrested, and were sentenced to 30 days on a road gang. This new journey tested the Justice Department's willingness to protect the rights of African Americans to use bus terminal facilities on a nonsegregated basis.

The Freedom Rides showed the world how far some white southerners would go to preserve segregation. The first ride ran into trouble on May 4, 1961, when John Lewis, one of the seven black riders, tried to enter the white waiting room of the Greyhound bus terminal in Rock Hill, South Carolina, and was beaten by local white people in full view of the police. The interracial group continued through Alabama toward Jackson, Mississippi, but white violence made escape from Alabama difficult. At Anniston, Alabama, a mob firebombed the bus and beat the escaping riders. Local African Americans led by the Rev. Fred Shuttlesworth took many of the shocked and injured riders to Birmingham.

With the police offering no protection, CORE abandoned the Freedom Rides, and most of the original riders left Alabama. But SNCC activists and students in Nashville refused to let the idea die. At least 20 civil rights workers went to Birmingham, where they vowed on May 20 to ride on to Montgomery. John Lewis remained with the group that arrived in Montgomery. Awaiting them was another angry mob of more than 1,000 white people and not a policeman in sight. This time Lewis was knocked unconscious, and all the riders had to be hospitalized. Even a presidential aide assigned to monitor the crisis was injured.

News services flashed around the world graphic images of the violence, and the federal government resolved to end the bloodletting. Attorney General Robert Kennedy sent 400 federal marshals to restore law and order. Martin Luther King, Jr., and Ralph Abernathy joined the conflict on May 21, as 1,200 men, women, and children met at Abernathy's church. The federal marshals averted further bloodshed by surrounding the building. Only then did Governor John Patterson order the National Guard and state troopers to protect the protesters. When the group arrived in Jackson, Mississippi, white authorities arrested them. By summer's end, more than 300 Freedom Riders had served time in Mississippi's notorious prisons.

((• 📖 **Read** on **MyHistoryLab** Document: Letters from Mississippi Freedom Summer, 1964

On May 14, in Anniston, Alabama, a white mob firebombed this Freedom Riders' bus and attacked passengers as they escaped the flames.

21-1
21-2
21-3
21-4
21-5
21-6
21-7
21-8

PROFILE   Robert Parris Moses

Robert "Bob" Moses instructs volunteers for the Freedom Summer campaign of 1964.

BOB MOSES, ONE OF THE MOST DEDICATED and revered young civil rights activists, was a soft-spoken man possessed of a powerful intellect, iron courage, and a rare purity of moral conviction. Born in Harlem in 1935, Moses was an excellent student. He attended Hamilton College in New York State, and from his readings there in philosophy, including works on Buddhism and existential-ism, he developed a so-phisticated understanding of nonviolent protest, a topic he explored during his graduate stud-ies in philosophy at Harvard.

When Moses learned of the sit-ins in 1960, he went south to participate. It was a fateful trip during which he met Amzie Moore, one of the World War II veterans who had returned home to make Missis-sippi safe for democracy. Moore was the vice president of the state conference of the NAACP branches. The two men developed a deep-seated appreciation for each other's strengths, and Moore convinced Moses to work in Mississippi. By August 1961 Moses was an organizer for the Student Nonviolent Coordinating Committee (SNCC) in the small town of McComb, Mississippi. There his group registered black voters. In early 1962 he be-came the program director of the Council of Federated Organizations and remained in the center of the struggle in Mississippi for the next three years.

The violence of white people and the courage of local black people profoundly affected Moses. In McComb he was arrested, jailed, beaten, and threatened with death. One of the local black people who helped his group was murdered in cold blood by a state senator who was sub-sequently acquitted of the crime by an all-white jury. Moses respected anyone who had the courage to take a stand after suffering a lifetime of such abuse. He sought to give local people the tools to continue to control their lives long after movement organizers had left.

Although Moses refused to become a formal leader of the SNCC forces in Mississippi, the young civil rights worker set an example of nonviolent resistance and encouraged SNCC to avoid developing a hierarchical leadership. In late 1963 Moses became the driving force behind the Freedom Summer project and played a cen-tral role in persuading SNCC to accept white volunteers from the North. He also stood for principle rather than expediency when, at the 1964 Democratic Conven-tion, he rejected the meager deal offered to the Missis-sippi Freedom Democratic Party (discussed later in the chapter).

In 1965 Moses began to drift away from the civil rights movement and toward opposition to the war in Vietnam. Exhausted from his ordeal in the South and seeking to avoid the draft, he emigrated first to Canada and then to the African nation of Tanzania. Moses re-turned after President Jimmy Carter offered amnesty to draft resisters in 1977 and began teaching math and science to inner-city black children. After receiving a MacArthur Foundation "genius grant," he developed the Algebra Project, which uses many of the empowerment strategies pioneered during the civil rights era to help children and their families gain the education they need in a computer-oriented economy.

A Sight to Be Seen: The Movement at High Tide

21-7 | **Who were the leaders and what were the tactics and effects of their various civil rights activities?**

Between 1960 and 1963, the civil rights movement developed the techniques and organiza-tion that would finally bring America face-to-face with the conflict between its democratic ideals and the racism of its politics. Day after day the movement squared off against the die-hard resistance of the white South and created a situation that demanded that the president and Congress take action.

The Election of 1960

One of the persistent fears of white southerners was that black Americans, if armed with the ballot, would possess the balance of political power. The presidential election of 1960 proved this to be true. Initially, many African Americans favored the Republican nominee Richard Nixon, who had advocated strong civil rights legislation. Baseball star Jackie Robinson and many other well-known African Americans were Nixon supporters. It seemed as if the New Deal coalition had weakened and that black citizens would reverse their move into the Democratic Party. The Democratic nominee, Massachusetts Senator John F. Kennedy, in contrast, had done little to distinguish himself to black Americans in the struggles of the 1950s. As the campaign progressed, however, Kennedy made sympathetic statements in support of black protests. Meanwhile, Nixon attempted to strengthen his position with white southern voters and remained silent about civil rights issues, even though the Republican Party had a strong pro–civil rights record.

Shortly before the election, Martin Luther King, Jr., was sentenced to four months in prison for leading a nonviolent protest march in Atlanta. Kennedy telephoned Coretta Scott King to offer his support, while his brother Robert F. Kennedy used his influence to obtain King's release. These acts impressed African Americans and won their support. African-American voters in key northern cities provided the crucial margin that elected John F. Kennedy. In Illinois, for example, with black voters casting 250,000 ballots for Kennedy, the Democrats carried the state by only 9,000 votes.

The Kennedy Administration and the Civil Rights Movement

Early in his administration Kennedy grew concerned about the violence occasioned by the civil rights movement. As the Freedom Rides continued across the Deep South, the activists provoked confrontations and forced the federal government to intervene on their behalf. Kennedy's primary interest at this point was to prevent disorder from getting out of hand and to avoid compromising America's position with the developing nations. But he had little room to maneuver given the power of white southerners in his party and in Congress.

Despite these limitations, Kennedy did aid the cause of civil rights. He issued Executive Order 11063, which required government agencies to discontinue discriminatory policies and practices in federally supported housing, and he named Vice President Lyndon B. Johnson to chair the newly established Committee on Equal Employment Opportunity. Kennedy also nominated Thurgood Marshall to the Second Circuit Court of Appeals on September 23, 1961 (although opposition in the Senate blocked Marshall's confirmation until September 11, 1963). He named journalist Carl Rowan deputy assistant secretary of state. More than 40 African Americans took positions in the new administration, including Robert Weaver, director of the Housing and Home Finance Agency; Mercer Cook, ambassador to Norway; and George L. P. Weaver, assistant secretary of labor. Moreover, Kennedy's brother Robert put muscle into the Civil Rights Division of the Justice Department by hiring an impressive team of lawyers headed by Washington attorney Burke Marshall.

Like Eisenhower, when President Kennedy felt that intractable southern governors were challenging his authority, he acted decisively. On June 25, 1962, one year after James Meredith had filed a complaint of racial discrimination against the University of Mississippi, the U.S. Court of Appeals ruled that the university had to admit him. Governor Ross Barnett vowed to resist, but Kennedy sent 300 federal marshals to uphold the order. Thousands of students rioted at the campus. Two people died, 200 were arrested, and nearly half the marshals were injured. Kennedy did not back down. He federalized the Mississippi National Guard to ensure Meredith's admission. Although isolated and harassed throughout his time at the University of Mississippi, Meredith eventually graduated. Likewise, in June 1963, the Kennedy administration compelled Governor George Wallace to allow the desegregation of the University of Alabama.

21-1
21-2
21-3
21-4
21-5
21-6
21-7
21-8

PROFILE Fannie Lou Hamer

FANNIE LOU HAMER (1917–1977) emerged from the ranks of "local people" in Mississippi to become one of the most powerful leaders and orators of the civil rights movement. Hamer, the youngest of 20 children, grew up in extreme poverty and had only a few years of education. She worked and lived as a timekeeper on a plantation in Ruleville, Mississippi. When SNCC workers came to the community for a voting rights campaign, Hamer was one of the first to participate.

On August 1, 1962, Hamer attempted to register to vote in Indianola, Mississippi. In response, she was fired from her plantation job and evicted

Fannie Lou Hamer, in words and deeds, refused to compromise with racial injustice. This June 1966 photograph by Flip Schule captures Hamer, a tireless organizer, speaking at an evening rally held at Tougaloo College in Mississippi on the last day of the March Against Fear.

from her land. Still, she refused to capitulate and accepted full-time employment as a field secretary for the SNCC, where she worked on the Voter Education Project.

Despite her lack of education, Hamer was a spellbinding orator. Her televised testimony before the 1964 Democratic convention won national support for the MFDP's challenge to the party regulars from Mississippi. The next year Hamer, who had run for the House of Representatives, challenged the seating of the Mississippi congressional delegation. Although unsuccessful, her action paved the way for the Voting Rights Act of 1965.

Although basic civil and voting rights had been won by 1965, most black people in the Mississippi Delta still lived in deep poverty. In 1968 Hamer sought to address this problem by setting up the nonprofit Freedom Farms Corporation as an agricultural cooperative. The mixed results of this last campaign, however, cannot diminish the profound changes that Fannie Lou Hamer was so instrumental in bringing about. She died in 1977.

 Read on **MyHistoryLab Document:** Fannie Lou Hamer, Voting Rights in Mississippi (1962–1964)

Voter Registration Projects

On June 16, 1961, Robert Kennedy urged student leaders to redirect their energies to voter registration projects and to lessen their concentration on direct-action activities. He and Justice Department aides persuaded the students that the free exercise of the ballot would result in profound and significant social change. James Foreman, SNCC's executive director, followed Kennedy's lead. By October 1962 SNCC had joined forces with the NAACP, SCLC, and CORE in the Voter Education Project funded by major philanthropic foundations and administered by the Southern Regional Council. SNCC was responsible for Alabama and Mississippi. Drawing on the expertise of Robert Moses and working with a cadre of local leaders like Amzie Moore, head of the NAACP in Mississippi's Cleveland County, and Fannie Lou Hamer of Ruleville, SNCC opened voter registration schools. When the "graduates" attempted to register to vote, it unleashed a wave of white violence and murder across Mississippi.

The Albany Movement

In Albany, Georgia, the civil rights movement met sophisticated resistance and experienced its most profound defeat up to that time. The movement in Albany began in the summer of 1961 when SNCC members moved into the city to register voters. Local groups decided to form a coalition called the Albany Movement and elected William G. Anderson as its president. The movement's goal expanded from securing the vote to the total desegregation of the town.

In Laurie Pritchett, Albany's police chief, the movement faced an uncommonly sophisticated opponent. Pritchett studied the past tactics of SNCC and King and resolved not to confront the federal government directly and to avoid the violence that brought negative media attention. When students from a black college decided to desegregate the bus terminal, Pritchett arrested them after they entered the white waiting room and attempted to eat in the bus terminal dining room. Shrewdly, he charged the students with violating a city ordinance for failing to obey a law enforcement officer. The Albany Movement decided to invite King and SCLC to aid them and to overwhelm the police department by filling the jails with protesters. King answered the call. On December 16, 1961, he and more than 250 demonstrators were arrested, joining the 507 people already in jail. The plan was to stay in jail to, as Charles Sherrod explained, "break the system down from within. Our ability to suffer was somehow going to overcome their ability to hurt us." King vowed to remain in jail until the city desegregated. Sheriff Pritchett, however, made arrangements to house almost 2,000 people in surrounding jail facilities and trained his deputies in the use of nonviolent techniques. Thus, Pritchett avoided confrontation, violence, and federal intervention.

On December 18, 1961, two days after King's arrest, the city and the Albany Movement announced a truce. King returned to Atlanta, and the city refused to implement the terms of the agreement. When King and Ralph Abernathy returned to Albany in July 1962 for sentencing on their December arrests, they chose 45 days in jail rather than admit guilt by paying a fine. The mass marches resumed, but again Pritchett thwarted King by releasing him from jail to avoid negative publicity. The city's attorney then secured a federal injunction to prevent King and the other leaders from demonstrating. Given his dependence on the federal government, King felt he could not violate the injunction, and he abandoned the protest. For King, the Albany Movement was a failure, his most glaring defeat, and one that called into question the future of the movement.

The Birmingham Confrontation

By early 1963 the movement appeared to be stalled. Black communities in much of the South were strong and well organized, but their efforts had achieved only modest changes. It was impossible to overcome the power of southern state and local governments without the intervention of the federal government, but national politicians, including President Kennedy, remained reluctant to act unless faced with open defiance by white people or with televised violence against peaceful protesters. King and other black leaders knew that if city governments throughout the South followed the model of Sheriff Pritchett in Albany, the civil rights movement might lose momentum. To rejuvenate the movement, SCLC decided to launch a massive new campaign during 1963, the year of the one-hundredth anniversary of the Emancipation Proclamation.

Birmingham, Alabama, a large, tightly segregated industrial city, was chosen as the site for the action. The city was ripe for such a protest, in part because its black community suffered from police brutality and economic, educational, and social discrimination. The Ku Klux Klan terrorized people with impunity. The black community had, however, developed a strong phalanx of protest organizations called the Alabama Christian Movement for Human Rights (ACMHR) led by the Rev. Fred Shuttlesworth. The ACMHR and SCLC planned a campaign of boycotts, pickets, and demonstrations code-named "Project C for Confrontation." Their program would be far more extensive than any before, with demands to integrate public facilities, for guarantees of employment opportunities for black workers in downtown businesses, to desegregate the schools, to improve services in black neighborhoods, and to provide low-income housing. Organizers hoped to provoke the city's public safety commissioner Eugene T. "Bull" Connor, who, unlike Sheriff Pritchett, had a reputation for viciousness. Civil rights leaders believed Connor's conduct would horrify the nation and compel Kennedy to act.

Project C began on April 3 with student sit-ins. Days later, marches began, and Connor, following the lead of Pritchett, arrested all who participated but avoided overt violence. When the state courts prohibited further protests, King and Abernathy, among others, violated the ruling. They were arrested and jailed on Good Friday, April 12, 1963.

Watch on **MyHistoryLab Video**: Photographing the Civil Rights Movement: Birmngham, 1963

While in jail, King received a letter from eight local Christian and Jewish clergymen who objected to what they considered the "unwise and untimely" protest activities of black citizens. King had smuggled a pen into jail and on scraps of paper, including toilet paper and the margins of the Birmingham *News*, he wrote an eloquent treatise on the use of direct action. His "Letter From Birmingham City Jail" was widely published in newspapers and magazines. In it, King dismissed those who called for black people to wait. The letter resonated with black journalist Carl T. Rowan, who recalled, "My entire journalistic career had embraced a personal war against the gradualists, the whites of power who asked black Americans to wait." Wyatt Walker was empowered by the Birmingham campaign, declaring, "The most important thing that happened, was that people decided that they were not going to be afraid of white folks anymore." He concluded, "Dr. King's most lasting contribution is that he emancipated black people's psyche. We threw off the slave mentality. Going to jail had been the whip which kept black folks in line. Now going to jail was transformed into a badge of honor."

King's "Letter From Birmingham City Jail" (1963) had a national impact. But the Birmingham movement lost momentum because many of the protesters either were in jail or could not risk new arrests. At this juncture James Bevel of SCLC proposed using schoolchildren to continue the protests. Many observers, and some of those in the movement, criticized this idea; King and other leaders, however, believed it was necessary to risk harm to children to ensure their freedom. Thus, on May 2 and 3, 1963, a "children's crusade" involving thousands of youths, some as young as six, marched. This tactic enraged "Bull" Connor and his officers. The police not only arrested the children but flailed away with nightsticks and set dogs on them. On Connor's order, firefighters aimed their hoses at the youngsters, ripping the clothes from their backs, cutting flesh, and tumbling children down the street. In the ensuing days, many of the children and their parents began to fight back, hurling bottles and rocks at their uniformed tormentors. As the violence escalated, white businessmen became concerned, and the city came to the bargaining table.

President Kennedy deployed Assistant Attorney General for Civil Rights Burke Marshall to negotiate a settlement. On May 10, 1963, white businessmen agreed to integrate downtown facilities and hire black men and women. The following night the KKK bombed the A. G. Gaston Motel, where SCLC had its headquarters, and the house that belonged to King's brother, the Rev. A. D. King. Black citizens in turn burned cars and buildings and attacked the police. Only intervention by King and other leaders prevented a riot. White moderates delivered on the promises, and the agreement stuck.

Although SCLC did not win every demand, Birmingham was a major triumph and a turning point in the movement. The summer of 1963 saw protests across the South, with nearly 800 marches, demonstrations, and sit-ins. Ten civil rights protesters were killed and 20,000 arrested as the white South desperately sought to stem the tide. On June 12, 1963, in one of the most tragic losses for the movement, white extremist Byron de la Beckwith gunned down Medgar Evers in the driveway of his home in Jackson, Mississippi. Evers had been the executive secretary of the NAACP's Mississippi organization and the center of a movement in Jackson. His cold-blooded murder dramatized the hatred some white southerners felt and the lengths to which they would go to prevent change.

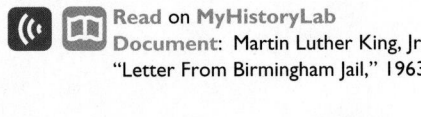

Read on MyHistoryLab
Document: Martin Luther King, Jr., "Letter From Birmingham Jail," 1963

A Hard Victory

21-8 **How did the federal government intermittently support and thwart the long freedom movement?**

The sacrifices in Birmingham and the intensification of the movement throughout the South set the stage for Congress to pass legislation for a Second Reconstruction that would at last fulfill the promise of the first.

The March on Washington

The lingering image of Birmingham and the growing number of demonstrations throughout the South compelled action from President Kennedy. On June 11, 1963, he made his strongest statement about civil rights to the nation: "We face . . . a moral crisis as a country and a people. It cannot be met by repressive police action. It cannot be left to increased demonstrations in the streets. It cannot be quieted by token moves or talk. It is a time to act in the Congress, in your state and local legislative body, and above all, in all our daily lives. A great change is at hand, and our task, our obligation, is to make that revolution . . . peaceful and constructive for all." Kennedy proposed the strongest civil rights bill the country had yet seen; however, despite the public's heightened awareness of discrimination, he could not muster sufficient support in Congress to counter the southern bloc within his own party.

To demonstrate their support for Kennedy's civil rights legislation, a coalition of civil rights organizations—SCLC, NAACP, CORE, SNCC, and the National Urban League—and their leaders resurrected the idea of organizing a march on Washington that A. Philip Randolph had first proposed in 1941. In 1962 Randolph and Bayard Rustin had proposed a march to protest black unemployment. Their initial call received a tepid response; however, after Birmingham the major civil rights organizations reconsidered. Reflecting renewed hope, Randolph christened it a march for "Jobs and Freedom."

On August 28, 1963, nearly 250,000 marchers gathered before the Lincoln Memorial to support the civil rights bill and the movement at large. Throughout the day they sang freedom songs and listened to speeches from civil rights leaders. Finally, late in the afternoon, Martin Luther King, Jr., arose and, casting aside his prepared remarks, delivered an impassioned speech. Most powerfully, King spoke of his vision of the future.

Historian Harvard Sitkoff provides an insightful assessment of the power of King's March on Washington speech by underscoring both its masterful delivery and its declaration of the rights of black people. He declared,

> King's message and majestic delivery made the day historic. At a time when most Americans did not perceive the injustice or the immorality of the nation's racism, King depicted it at its most searing to the millions who watched on television and to the many more millions who had heard it on the radio or would see it excerpted on the evening news. At a time when the sight of black kids and white kids going to the same school inflamed racist mobs, he demanded an end to all barriers separating the races. . . . King confronted white America with the undeniable justice of African-American demands and succeeded in associating black rights with accepted values. . . . No harmless dreamer, the preacher interpreted the vast social upheaval, slaying expectations of gradualism or of moderation if America failed to make good on its promises.

King's words did not still the angry opposition of white southerners. On September 15, 1963, only days after the March on Washington, white racists bombed the 16th St. Baptist Church in Birmingham and killed four girls attending Sunday school: Addie Mae Collins, Denise McNair, Carole Robertson, and Cynthia Wesley. Chris McNair, the father of the youngest victim, pleaded for calm out of the depth of his own pain: "We must not let this change us into something different than who we are. We must be human."

The event shook the nation and, combined with the reaction to Kennedy's assassination on November 22, 1963, set the stage for real change.

The Civil Rights Act of 1964

Kennedy's successor, Lyndon B. Johnson, lobbied hard to pass the landmark Civil Rights Act. Many in the civil rights movement feared that Johnson, a southerner, would back his region's defiance. Nonetheless, only four days after taking the oath of office, Johnson told the nation he planned to support the civil rights bill as a memorial for the slain president. A master politician, Johnson pushed the bill through Congress despite a marathon filibuster by its opponents.

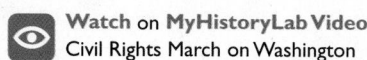

Watch on **MyHistoryLab** Video:
Civil Rights March on Washington

Read on **MyHistoryLab**
Document: John Lewis Speaks at the March on Washington, 1963

Watch on **MyHistoryLab** Video:
Rev. Dr. Martin Luther King Jr's Speech

21-1

21-2

21-3

21-4

21-5

21-6

21-7

21-8

1955–1968
VIOLENCE AND THE CIVIL RIGHTS MOVEMENT

May 7, 1955
Rev. George Lee killed for leading voter registration drive, Belzoni, Mississippi

August 13, 1955
Lamar Smith murdered for organizing black voters, Brookhaven, Mississippi

August 28, 1955
Emmett Louis Till murdered for speaking to white woman, Money, Mississippi

October 22, 1955
John Earl Reese slain by night riders opposed to black school improvements, Mayflower, Texas

January 23, 1957
Willie Edwards, Jr., killed by Klan, Montgomery, Alabama

September 24, 1957
President Eisenhower orders federal troops to enforce school desegregation, Little Rock, Arkansas

April 27, 1959
Mack Charles Parker taken from jail and lynched, Poplarville, Mississippi

May 14, 1961
Freedom Riders attacked in Alabama while testing compliance with bus desegregation laws

September 25, 1961
Voter registration worker Herbert Lee killed by a white legislator, Liberty, Mississippi

April 1, 1962
Civil rights groups launch voter registration drive

April 9, 1962
Roman Ducksworth, Jr., taken from bus and killed by police, Taylorsville, Mississippi

September 30, 1962
Riots erupt when James Meredith, a black student, enrolls at the University of Mississippi; Paul Guihard, European reporter, killed

April 23, 1963
William Lewis Moore slain during one-man march against segregation, Attalla, Alabama

May 3, 1963
Birmingham police attack marching children with dogs and fire hoses

June 12, 1963
Medgar Evers assassinated, Jackson, Mississippi

September 15, 1963
Schoolgirls Addie Mae Collins, Denise McNair, Carole Robertson, and Cynthia Wesley killed in the bombing of the 16th St. Baptist Church, Birmingham, Alabama

September 15, 1963
Virgil Lamar Ware killed during racist violence, Birmingham, Alabama

January 31, 1964
Louis Allen, witness to the murder of a civil rights worker, assassinated, Liberty, Mississippi

21-1
21-2
21-3
21-4
21-5
21-6
21-7
21-8

1955–1968
VIOLENCE AND THE CIVIL RIGHTS MOVEMENT

April 7, 1964
Rev. Bruce Klunder killed protesting construction of a segregated school, Cleveland, Ohio

May 2, 1964
Henry Hezekiah Dee and Charles Eddie Moore killed by Klan, Meadville, Mississippi

June 21, 1964
Civil rights workers James Chaney, Andrew Goodman, and Michael Schwerner abducted and slain by Klan, Philadelphia, Mississippi

July 11, 1964
Lt. Col. Lemuel Penn killed by Klan, Colbert, Georgia

February 26, 1965
Jimmie Lee Jackson, civil rights marcher, killed by state trooper, Marion, Alabama

March 11, 1965
Selma to Montgomery march volunteer, Rev. James Reeb, beaten to death, Selma, Alabama

March 25, 1965
Viola Gregg Liuzzo killed by Klan while transporting marchers, Selma Highway, Alabama

June 2, 1965
Oneal Moore, black deputy, killed by night riders, Varnado, Louisiana

July 18, 1965
Willie Wallace Brewster killed by night riders, Anniston, Alabama

August 20, 1965
Jonathan Daniels, seminary student, killed by deputy, Hayneville, Alabama

January 3, 1966
Samuel Younge, Jr., student civil rights activist, killed in dispute over whites-only restroom, Tuskegee, Alabama

January 10, 1966
Vernon Dahmer, black community leader, killed in Klan bombing, Hattiesburg, Mississippi

June 10, 1966
Ben Chester White killed by Klan, Natchez, Mississippi

July 30, 1966
Clarence Triggs slain by night riders, Bogalusa, Louisiana

February 2, 1967
Wharlest Jackson, civil rights leader, killed when police fire on protesters, Jackson, Mississippi

February 8, 1968
Students Samuel Hammond, Jr., Delano Middleton, and Henry Smith killed when highway patrolmen fire on protesters, Orangeburg, South Carolina

April 4, 1968
Dr. Martin Luther King, Jr., assassinated, Memphis, Tennessee

21-1

21-2

21-3

21-4

21-5

21-6

21-7

21-8

Civil Rights Act of 1964 Federal law banning discrimination in places of public accommodation.

The **Civil Rights Act of 1964** was the culmination of the civil rights movement to that time. The act banned discrimination in places of public accommodation, including restaurants, hotels, gas stations, and entertainment facilities, as well as schools, parks, playgrounds, libraries, and swimming pools. The desegregation of public accommodations irrevocably changed the face of American society. The issue of legally mandated racial separation was now settled. The act also banned discrimination by employers and labor unions on the basis of race, color, religion, national origin, and sex in regard to hiring, promoting, dismissing, or making job referrals. The act had strong provisions for enforcement. Most important, it allowed government agencies to withhold federal money from any program permitting or practicing discrimination. This provision had particular importance for the desegregation of schools and colleges across the country. The act also gave the attorney general the power to initiate proceedings against segregated facilities and schools on behalf of people who could not do so on their own. Finally, it created the Equal Employment Opportunity Commission to monitor discrimination in employment.

Mississippi Freedom Summer

While Congress considered the Civil Rights Act, movement activists renewed their focus on voter registration in the Deep South. In the fall of 1963, many CORE and SNCC workers saw segregation crumbling; however, they knew that without the ballot, African Americans could never drive racist politicians from office, gain a fair hearing in court, reduce police and mob violence, or get equal services from state and local governments. CORE took responsibility for running registration campaigns in Louisiana, South Carolina, and Florida, while SNCC took on the two most repressive states, Alabama and Mississippi. Mississippi was widely known in the movement as the "toughest nut to crack"—the symbolic center of American racism and white violence. By the summer of 1964, national attention had shifted from Alabama to Mississippi, the site of a massive project known as "Freedom Summer."

The voter registration campaign in Mississippi began in late 1963 when Robert "Bob" Moses mobilized the Council of Federated Organizations (COFO), which had been established in 1962 to aid imprisoned Freedom Riders. Moses convinced the members of COFO (CORE, SNCC, SCLC, and the NAACP) to sponsor a mock Freedom Election in Mississippi. On Election Day, 80,000 disfranchised black people voted for COFO candidates. Impressed with the turnout, Moses and other COFO members believed a massive effort to register voters during the summer of 1964 might break the white monopoly on the ballot box.

COFO decided to invite northern white students to participate in the Mississippi project. These students, about 1,000 in all, were to be drawn primarily from the nation's most prestigious universities. This move contradicted the movement's emphasis on black empowerment, but COFO leaders calculated that the presence of elite white students in the Magnolia State would attract increased media attention and pressure the federal government to provide protection.

Shortly after the project began, three volunteers—two white New Yorkers, 24-year-old Michael Schwerner and 21-year-old Andrew Goodman, and a black Mississippian, 21-year-old James Chaney—disappeared. Unknown at the time, Cecil Price, deputy sheriff of Philadelphia, Mississippi, had arrested the three on a trumped-up speeding charge. That evening the young men were delivered to a deserted road where three carloads of Klansmen waited. Schwerner and Goodman were shot to death. Chaney was beaten with chains and then shot.

These events were not publicly known until Klan informers, enticed by a $30,000 reward, led investigators to the earthen dam in which Goodman, Schwerner, and Chaney had been buried. The disappearance of the three nonetheless focused national attention on white terrorism. During that summer, approximately 30 homes and 37 churches were bombed, 35 civil rights workers were shot at, 80 people were beaten, six were murdered, and more than 1,000 were arrested. In the face of this violence, uncertainty, and fear, many SNCC activists rejected Martin Luther King's commitment to nonviolence, the inclusion of white activists in the movement, and the wisdom of integration. Divisions over these issues increased tensions within the movement.

Despite the problems it encountered, the Freedom Summer organized dozens of Freedom Schools and community centers throughout Mississippi. Its efforts mobilized the state's black people to an extent not seen since the first Reconstruction. Many communities began to develop the rudiments of a political movement, one that would grow in coming years.

The Mississippi Freedom Democratic Party

Freedom Summer intersected with national politics at the Democratic Party National Convention in August 1964 in Atlantic City, New Jersey. White Mississippians routinely excluded African Americans from the political process, and Robert Moses encouraged COFO to set up the **Mississippi Freedom Democratic Party (MFDP)** to challenge the state's regular Democratic delegation at the convention. Under the leadership of veteran activists Fannie Lou Hamer, Victoria Gray, Annie Divine, and Aaron Henry, the MFDP held its first state convention on August 6. Approximately 80,000 citizens put their names on the rolls. The convention elected 64 delegates who traveled to the national convention to present their credentials.

The MFDP challenge caused difficulty for the Democratic Party. Many liberals wanted to seat the civil rights delegation, but President Johnson, who was running for reelection, did not want to alienate white southerners, fearing they would vote for Barry Goldwater, his Republican opponent. Liberal Democratic Senator Hubert H. Humphrey, from Minnesota, worked out a compromise calling for Mississippi regulars to be seated if they swore loyalty to the national party and agreed to cast their 44 votes accordingly. The compromise also created two "at-large" seats for MFDP members Aaron Henry and Ed King. The rest of the Freedom Democrats could attend the convention as nonvoting guests.

Martin Luther King, Jr., Bayard Rustin, and other black leaders counseled acceptance of this compromise. Johnson and the Democrats, they argued, had achieved much of the legislative program the movement favored, and if the party were returned to power, they could do much more. But most of the MFDP delegation, fed up with the violence of Mississippi and unwilling to settle for token representation, rejected the compromise. Many members of SNCC turned their backs on liberalism and cooperation with white people of any political persuasion.

Selma and the Voting Rights Act of 1965

The Civil Rights Act of 1964 contained provisions for helping black voters to register, but white resistance in the Deep South had rendered them ineffective. In Alabama, for example, at least 77 percent of black citizens were unable to vote. Their cause was taken up by businesswoman Amelia P. Boynton, owner of an employment and insurance

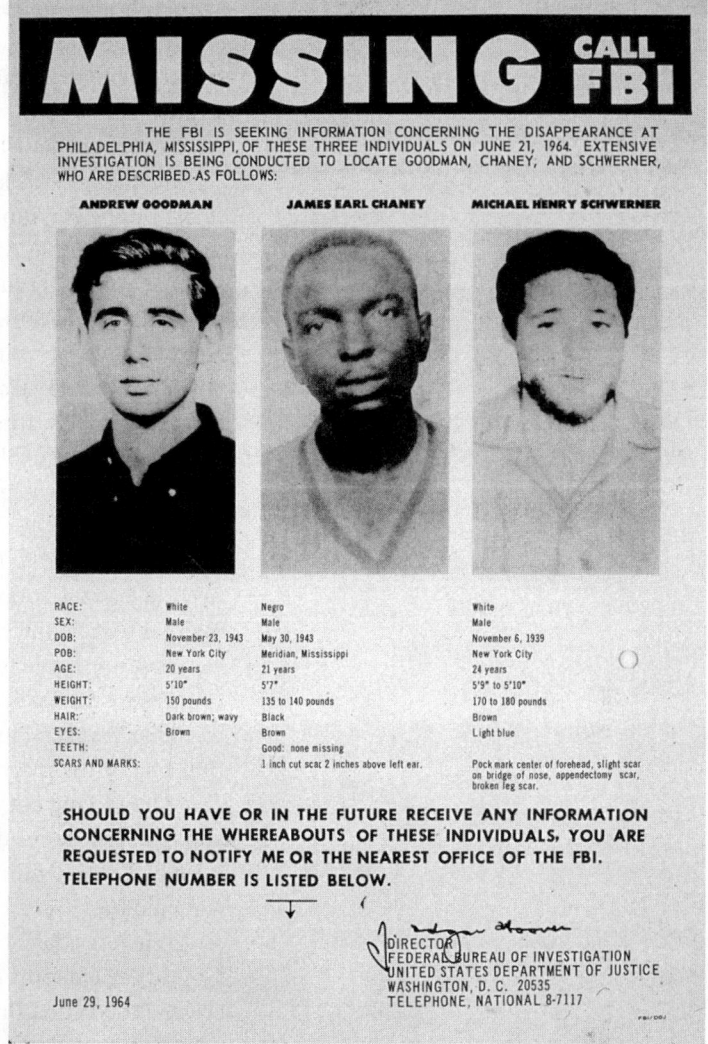

A missing persons poster displays the photographs of civil rights workers Andrew Goodman, James Earl Chaney, and Michael Henry Schwerner after they disappeared in 1964.

Mississippi Freedom Democratic Party (MFDP) Interracial group set up to challenge Mississippi's all-white delegation to the Democratic National Convention in 1964.

Voting Rights Act of 1965 Federal law banning the methods that had systematically excluded African Americans from registering or voting in southern elections.

agency in Selma; her husband; and a high school teacher, the Rev. Frederick Reese, who also led the Dallas County Voters League. These three, with others, fought for black enfranchisement and an end to discrimination. Their struggle would help pass the **Voting Rights Act of 1965**, which finally ended the systematic exclusion of African Americans from southern politics.

Selma's sheriff, James G. Clark, worked to block the voter registration activity sponsored by the Boyntons, Reese, and SNCC suffrage workers. By 1964 fewer than 400 of the 15,000 eligible African Americans had registered to vote in Dallas County. President Johnson refused requests to deploy federal marshals to the county to protect voter registration workers. Seeking reinforcements, the workers sent a call to Martin Luther King, Jr., and SCLC. King came and was arrested. In mid-February 1965, during a night march in neighboring Perry County, 26-year-old Jimmie Lee Jackson was shot as he tried to shield his mother from a beating by a state trooper. His death and the thrashing of several reporters attracted the national media.

SCLC announced plans for a mass march from Selma to Montgomery to begin on Sunday, March 7, 1965. At the forefront of 600 protesters were King; one of his aides, Hosea Williams; and SCNC's chairman, John Lewis. As the marchers approached the Edmund Pettus Bridge, state troopers and Sheriff Clark's county police tear gassed and beat the retreating marchers while their horses trampled the fallen. Captured in graphic detail by television cameras, this battle became known as "Bloody Sunday." Seizing the moment, King and the activists rescheduled a pilgrimage for March 9. The SCLC leader soon found himself in a dilemma. A federal judge who was normally supportive of civil rights had issued an injunction against the march. Moreover, President Johnson and other key figures in the government urged King not to go through with it. King was reluctant to violate a federal injunction, and he knew he needed Johnson's support to win strong voting rights legislation. But the people of Selma and the hundreds of young SNCC workers would probably march even if King did not.

When the day of the march came, 1,500 protesters marched to the bridge singing "Ain't Gonna Let Nobody Turn Me 'Round" and other freedom songs. To their surprise, King crossed the Pettus Bridge, prayed briefly, and turned around. He had made a face-saving compromise with the federal authorities. SNCC workers felt betrayed, and King's leadership suffered. That evening local white people clubbed to death James Reeb, a white Unitarian minister from Boston. His martyrdom created a national outcry and prompted Johnson to act. On March 15 the president, in a televised address to Congress, announced he would submit voter registration legislation. He electrified civil rights activists when he invoked the movement's slogan in his Texas drawl, "We shall overcome."

The protests at Selma and the massive white resistance spurred Congress to pass the Voting Rights Act of 1965, which President Johnson signed on August 6. The act outlawed educational requirements for voting in states or counties where less than half the voting-age population had been registered on November 1, 1964, or where less than half had voted in the 1964 presidential election. It also empowered the attorney general to have the Civil Rights Commission assign federal registrars to enroll voters. Attorney General Nicholas Katzenbach immediately deployed federal registrars in nine southern counties. Within months, they had registered approximately 80,000 new voters. In Mississippi, black registrants soared from 28,500 in 1964 to 251,000 in 1968 (see Map 21–1).

Gaining voting rights made a tremendous difference. Before passage of the act, Fannie Lou Hamer had unsuccessfully challenged the seating of the Mississippi representatives before the U.S. House of Representatives. In 1968 she was selected as a delegate to the Democratic Party convention. To be sure, southern state legislators resisted the act. They instituted a dazzling array of disfranchisement devices such as gerrymandering, at-large elections, more appointive offices, and higher qualifications for candidates. But the era when white supremacy lay at the core of southern politics was over.

Dorothy Irene Height

As a leader of two major black women organizations, the NCNW and the Delta Sigma Theta Sorority, Dorothy Irene Height was one of the most influential women in twentieth-century America.

DOROTHY IRENE HEIGHT (March 24, 1912–April 20, 2010) was born in Richmond, Virginia, to a father, James Height, who was a building and painting contractor, and a mother, Fannie Burroughs, who was a nurse. They migrated to a small town, Rankin, Pennsylvania, where Height graduated from Rankin High School in 1929. A scholarship from the Elks helped her attend college. From the outset she demonstrated a gift for oratory that would facilitate her rise to become one of the great African-American leaders in the struggle for human rights and civic equality in the twentieth century.

Height's father had been active in Republican Party politics, but she refused to be defined by a political affiliation. On March 4, 2004, President George W. Bush presented her with the Congressional Gold Medal. Other presidents, from Harry S Truman to Barack Obama, would seek her council or acknowledge her contributions to the struggle for civil rights. How did an African-American woman earn a living while devoting her life to social justice? The first requirement was an education, which she wasted little time acquiring and spared no effort to attain. Within four years, Height earned both a bachelor's and a master's degree in educational psychology at New York University, and thereafter she continued to take courses at Columbia University and the New York School of Social Work.

She launched her career as a caseworker for the Department of Social Services of New York City at the height of the Great Depression. She became active in New Deal youth programs and found employment with the Young Women's Christian Association (YWCA). In 1937, Mary McLeod Bethune, founder and president of the National Council of Negro Women (NCNW), met Height in New York and invited her to join the NCNW. They shared a long and rewarding friendship. Over four decades, Height combined working for the YWCA with volunteering for the NCNW. Thus, she conjoined her commitment to improving the lives of children with securing greater rights for women and resolving tensions and misunderstandings between black and white women. Height worked closely and tirelessly with Bethune to lobby for jobs for women, greater educational

opportunities for women and men, and food drives for the poor. She spearheaded voter registration drives for black southerners and voter education for black northerners.

Height became the director of the YWCA's Center for Racial Justice in 1965 and remained an employee of the organization until she retired in 1977. Her position with the YWCA enabled her to travel across the globe to train women and observe firsthand the issues that affected them in societies from Haiti to India. In 2000, the YWCA established the Dorothy I. Height Racial Justice Award. The first recipient was President Bill Clinton.

From 1947 to 1956, Height was president of the Delta Sigma Theta Sorority. In 1957, she succeeded Bethune as president of the NCNW, a position she held until 1998. She worked to turn Bethune's dream of a politically empowered, economically secure, well-educated black womanhood committed to social justice and the protection of children into a reality. As leader of two of the largest and most powerful organizations of black women in America, she nurtured generations of black women. These women would prove indispensable to the civil rights movement, as the life and agency of Jo Ann Gibson Robinson, president of the Women's Political Council in Montgomery, Alabama, demonstrated at the time of the Montgomery Bus Boycott in the 1950s.

But gender conventions proved difficult to alter within the black community, and try as she might, Height could not persuade the leaders of the 1963 March on Washington to allow her to speak. The only woman's voice heard on that historic day was that of gospel great Mahalia Jackson. Nevertheless, Height wielded enormous power in both white and black leadership circles in the remaining 50 years of her life. In the 1990s, she received a bank vault of recognitions and awards, including the NAACP's Spingarn Medal (1993), induction into the National Women's Hall of Fame (1993), and the Presidential Medal of Freedom (1994) from Bill Clinton.

Dorothy Height was renown for her quiet dignity and unrelenting determination to speak out on behalf of African-American women, black families, and their communities. Through her mastery of advocacy politics and ability to mobilize educated and resourceful black women, she helped overturn racial second-class citizenship and much of the gender discrimination that forced women into subordinate positions in the American economy. She entered the fray, whether it was to expand educational opportunities, open ballot boxes, or end legal segregation. Her voice never waivered, and she used it with skill and to great effect. At her memorial service, President Barack Obama said of Height, "She deserves a place in our history books. She deserves a place of honor in America's memory." Virtually the entire nation took note of her passing.

21-1

21-2

21-3

21-4

21-5

21-6

21-7

21-8

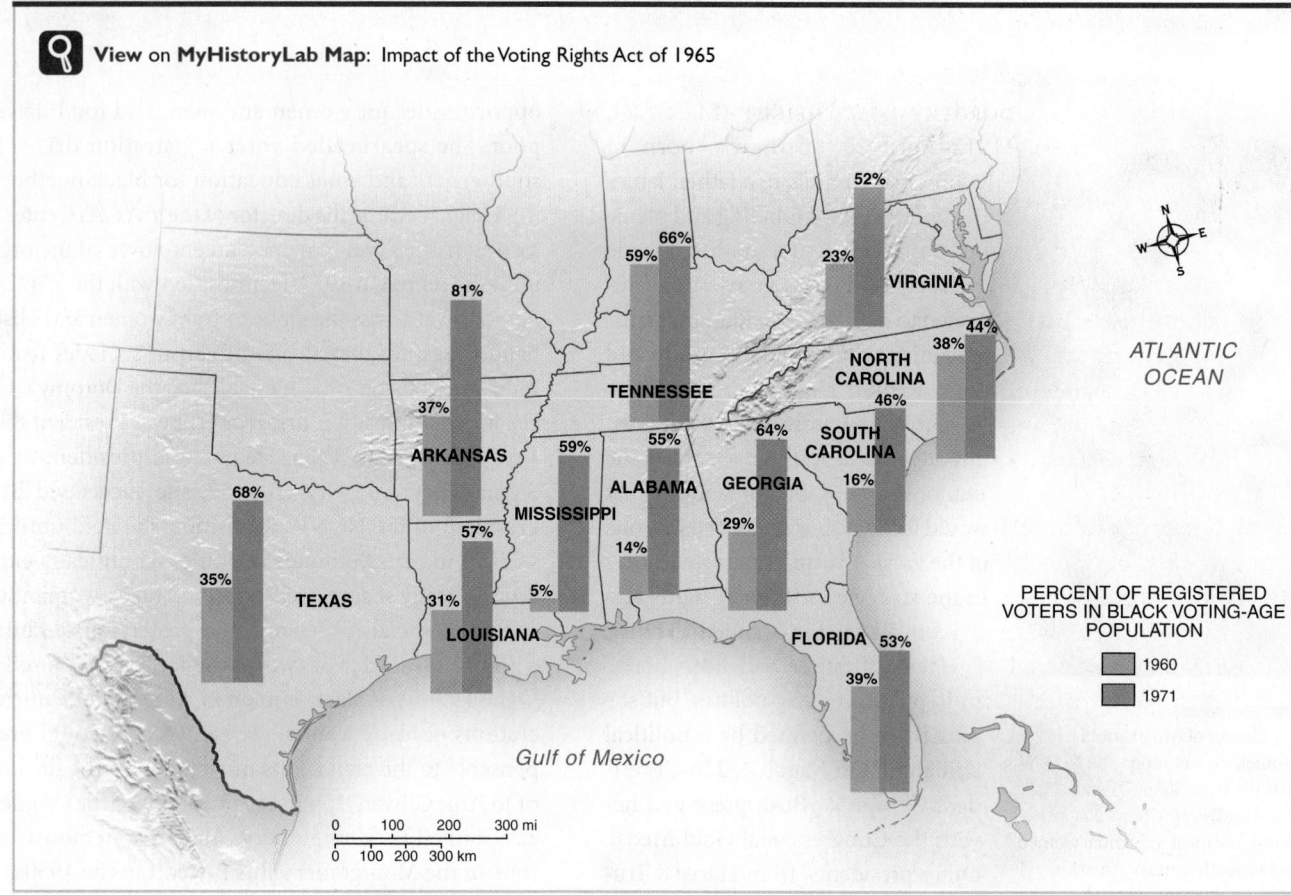

View on **MyHistoryLab Map:** Impact of the Voting Rights Act of 1965

PERCENT OF REGISTERED
VOTERS IN BLACK VOTING-AGE
POPULATION

1960

1971

MAP 21–1 THE EFFECT OF THE VOTING RIGHTS ACT OF 1965
The Voting Rights Act enabled millions of previously disfranchised African Americans in the South to vote.

Why was gaining the right to vote so important for southern African Americans?

CONCLUSION

The two *Brown* decisions ended the legal underpinning of segregation and discrimination and set in motion events that would irrevocably transform the political and social status of African Americans. White southerners resisted the changes *Brown* unleashed, and as their resistance gained momentum, violence against African Americans and their allies exploded.

The civil rights movement successes depended on many factors. The federal government intervened at crucial moments to enact historic civil rights legislation, issue judgments on behalf of the civil rights protesters, and protect the rule of law with federal marshals and soldiers. Black leaders pursued strategies to provoke confrontations that would ensure federal intervention and garner media coverage. For more than a decade, the victorious freedom fighters of the civil rights movement stormed the legal barricades of segregation. The uncompromising struggle of African Americans, their organizations, and their white allies pressured federal officials in the legislative, executive, and judicial branches of government to enact major civil rights legislation, issue executive orders, and deliver judicial decisions that dismantled segregation in the South.

✳ EXPLORE ON MYHISTORYLAB

The Civil Rights Movement

How did conditions for African Americans begin to change in the mid-1900s?

Laws in the South known as "Jim Crow laws"—regulations that banned African Americans and whites from, for example, marrying, dining, going to school, or socializing together—ensured racial discrimination. In the North, segregation undergirded the social structure. However, African-American leaders started to make advancements in their fight for equality in the 1950s and 1960s. Civil rights activists protested across the South, making national headlines. In the industrial cities of the North and West, large numbers of African Americans arrived in the Second Great Migration between 1940 and 1970 as they sought better opportunities than the South afforded them. From these cities, many also began to speak out for an end to racism.

SHIFTS IN AFRICAN-AMERICAN POPULATION IN SELECTED COUNTIES, 1940–1950

County	Change, in Persons	Percent Change
Columbia County, Georgia	−1,108	−20
Cook County, Illinois	+226,822	+60
Los Angeles County, California	+142,672	+94
Quitman County, Mississippi	−2,416	−9
Wayne County, Michigan	+172,122	+70

SOURCE: *1950 Census, Historic GIS Data: Slavery, Citizenship, & Civil Rights, Teaching American History Project, http://www.upa.pdx.edu/IMS/ currentprojects/TAHv3/Slave_Citizen_GIS.html.*

Young black man drinking from a segregated drinking fountain.

✳ Explore the Topic on MyHistoryLab

1. **Cause**   *What challenges did African Americans face during the era of segregation?* Use socioeconomic patterns to consider discrimination.
2. **Comparison**   *In what parts of southern cities did African Americans live?* Map segregation in selected urban centers.
3. **Consequence**   *What was the demographic impact of the Second Great Migration?* Consider the results of this move to the urban North and West.

The victories of this era were far reaching, but as they were achieved, new issues arose that would fracture the movement. Until recently, scholarship concerning the rise and evolution of the civil rights movement focused largely on the South. Impressive new research focuses on the long history of struggles for civil rights and economic justice that occurred during the Great Depression and World War II eras. To be sure, by the advent of the civil rights movement in the South, black residents in northern and western cities, thanks to federal legislation, enjoyed access to public facilities, schools, and jobs in a more diverse economic sector. The civil rights movement has largely been focused on the South because black northerners already had many of the rights granted by the federal legislation of the era. Nonetheless, in all regions, long after the victories of the civil rights movement(s) many black individuals and communities still suffered the negative impact of discrimination and segregation. The future dictated the need for different techniques and new ways of thinking.

CHAPTER TIMELINE

AFRICAN-AMERICAN EVENTS

NATIONAL EVENTS

1954–1958

1954

Supreme Court's *Brown v. Board of Education* decision declares separate but equal education unconstitutional

1955

Supreme Court's *Brown II* decision calls for school districts to desegregate immediately or "with all deliberate speed"

The Interstate Commerce Commission outlaws segregated buses and waiting rooms for interstate passengers

Claudette Colvin arrested for refusing to relinquish her seat to a white woman on a bus in Montgomery

Emmett Till lynched

Rosa Parks arrested for refusing to give up her seat on a city bus, beginning the Montgomery Bus Boycott

1956

The Supreme Court, in *Gayle v. Browder*, bars segregation in intrastate travel

1957

Congress passes the Civil Rights Act of 1957

President Eisenhower enforces integration of Little Rock's Central High School with federal troops

Martin Luther King, Jr., and other religious leaders organize SCLC

1954

First White Citizens Council in Mississippi

1955

The American Federation of Labor and Congress of Industrial Organizations merge to form the AFL-CIO

1956

Segregationists in Congress issue the "Southern Manifesto"

Eisenhower wins second term as president

1960–1965

1960

Black students sit in at Woolworth lunch counter in Greensboro, North Carolina

SNCC founded

Black vote is critical to Kennedy's election

1961

Freedom Riders attacked in Alabama and Mississippi

Kennedy names Thurgood Marshall to the Second Circuit Court of Appeals

Herbert Lee killed in Amite County, Mississippi

1962

COFO is formed

James Meredith desegregates the University of Mississippi with federal support

The Albany Movement fails

Voter Education Project launched

1963

Project C highlights racial injustices in Birmingham; King writes his celebrated "Letter From Birmingham Jail"

Federal government compels Governor George C. Wallace to desegregate the University of Alabama

Medgar Evers murdered

W. E. B. Du Bois dies in Ghana, Africa, at age 95

The March on Washington

1960

John F. Kennedy elected president

1963

Kennedy is assassinated; Lyndon Johnson succeeds to the presidency

1964

Equal Employment Opportunity Commission established

1965

Johnson outlines the Great Society program to attack poverty

CHAPTER TIMELINE

AFRICAN-AMERICAN EVENTS

NATIONAL EVENTS

Martin Luther King, Jr., delivers his "I Have a Dream" speech

Ku Klux Klan bombs the 16th Street Baptist Church in Birmingham, Alabama, killing four girls

Malcolm X breaks with Elijah Muhammad and the Nation of Islam and founds his own movement, Muslim Mosque

1964

SNCC launches the Mississippi Freedom Summer Project to promote voter registration

Twenty-Fourth Amendment to the Constitution outlaws the poll tax

James E. Chaney, Michael Schwerner, and Andrew Goodman murdered in Mississippi

Civil Rights Act of 1964 enacted

The Mississippi Freedom Democratic Party denied seating at the Democratic National Convention

Martin Luther King, Jr., wins the Nobel Peace Prize

1965

Civil rights marchers walk from Selma to Montgomery after violent confrontation in Selma

Voting Rights Act of 1965 enacted

On MyHistoryLab

 Study and Review on MyHistoryLab

REVIEW QUESTIONS

1. What role did "ordinary" or local people play in the civil rights movement? How did children contribute to the struggle for social change?

2. Why did the federal government intervene in the civil rights movement? What were the major pieces of legislation enacted, and how did they dismantle legalized segregation?

3. What were the ideologies, objectives, and tactics of the major civil rights organizations and their leaders?

4. Who were some of the people who lost their lives in the civil rights struggle?

5. What were the major successes and failures of the freedom movement? What intergenerational tensions plagued the movement? How did the movement transform American politics and society?

RECOMMENDED READING

Taylor Branch. *Parting the Waters: America in the King Years, 1954–63.* New York: Simon & Schuster, 1988. Richly researched, lively study that places King at the center of American politics during a transformative decade.

Clayborne Carson. *In Struggle: SNCC and the Black Awakening of the 1960s.* Cambridge, MA: Harvard University Press, 1981.

One of the best historical studies of SNCC and the contributions students made to the civil rights movement.

Vickie Crawford, Jacqueline Rouse, and Barbara Woods, eds. *Women in the Civil Rights Movement: Trailblazers and Torchbearers.* Brooklyn, NY: Carlson Publishing, 1990. An important anthology drawing attention to the women who contributed to the freedom struggle of the 1950s and 1960s.

Phillip Hoose. *Claudette Colvin: Twice Toward Justice.* New York: Farrar, Straus & Giroux, 2009. Essential reading. A splendidly documented book that corrects many erroneous assumptions about the courageous 15-year-old high school student who refused to give up her bus seat on March 2, 1955, in Montgomery, Alabama.

Richard Kluger. *Simple Justice: The History of "Brown v. Board of Education" and Black America's Struggle for Equality.* New York: Knopf, 1976. New ed., 2004. An excellent treatment of the historical events leading up to *Brown* and of the people whose lives were forever changed because of their resistance to Jim Crow segregation. The new edition includes an illuminating assessment of the 50 years since *Brown*.

Steven F. Lawson. *Running for Freedom: Civil Rights and Black Politics in America Since 1941.* 2nd ed. Philadelphia: Temple University Press, 2008. A succinct analysis of the politics, legislative measures, and individuals that figured in the successes and failures of the civil rights movement and recent political developments.

Danielle L. McGuire. *At the Dark End of the Street: Black Women, Rape, and Resistance—A New History of the Civil Rights Movement from Rosa Parks to the Rise of Black Power.* New York: Alfred Knopf, 2010. A revealing and important book that illuminates the organized resistance of black women to resist white male sexual aggression as part of the civil rights movement.

Aldon D. Morris. *The Origins of the Modern Civil Rights Movement: Black Communities Organizing for Change.* New York: Free Press, 1984. An insightful analysis of the mobilization and organizing strategies pursued by diverse communities for social change that paved the way for the modern civil rights movement.

ADDITIONAL BIBLIOGRAPHY

GENERAL OVERVIEWS OF CIVIL RIGHTS MOVEMENT AND ORGANIZATIONS

Robert Fredrick Burk. *The Eisenhower Administration and Black Civil Rights.* Knoxville: University of Tennessee Press, 1984.

Stewart Burns. *Daybreak of Freedom: The Montgomery Bus Boycott.* Chapel Hill: University of North Carolina Press, 1997.

John Dittmer. *Local People: The Struggle for Civil Rights in Mississippi.* Urbana: University of Illinois Press, 1994.

Glenda Elizabeth Gilmore. *Defying Dixie: The Radical Roots of Civil Rights, 1919–1950.* New York: Knopf, 2008.

Risa L. GoluBoff. *The Lost Promise of Civil Rights.* Cambridge: Harvard University Press, 2007.

Lance Hill. *The Deacons for Defense: Armed Resistance and the Civil Rights Movement.* Chapel Hill: University of North Carolina, 2004.

Michael J. Klarman. *From Jim Crow to Civil Rights: The Supreme Court and the Struggle for Racial Equality.* New York: Oxford University Press, 2003.

Nancy MacLean. *Freedom Is Not Enough: The Opening of the American Workplace.* Cambridge, MA: Harvard University Press, 2006.

Manning Marable. *Malcolm X: A Life of Reinvention.* New York: Viking, 2011.

Robert J. Norrell. *Reaping the Whirlwind: The Civil Rights Movement in Tuskegee.* New York: Alfred A. Knopf, 1985.

James T. Patterson. *Brown v. Board of Education: A Civil Rights Milestone and Its Troubled Legacy.* New York: Oxford University Press, 2000.

Charles M. Payne. *I've Got the Light of Freedom: The Organizing Tradition and the Mississippi Freedom Struggle.* Berkeley: University of California Press, 1995.

Belinda Robnett. *How Long? How Long? African-American Women in the Struggle for Civil Rights.* New York: Oxford University Press, 1997.

Amilcar Shabazz. *Advancing Democracy: African Americans and the Struggle for Access and Equity in Higher Education in Texas.* Chapel Hill: University of North Carolina Press, 2004.

Tobin Miller Shearer. *Daily Demonstrators: The Civil Rights Movement in Mennonite Homes and Sanctuaries.* Baltimore, MD: The Johns Hopkins University Press, 2010.

BLACK URBAN POLITICS/WHITE RESISTANCE

Elizabeth Jacoway and David R. Colburn. *Southern Businessmen and Desegregation.* Baton Rouge: Louisiana State University Press, 1982.

Hasan Kwame Jeffries. *Bloody Lowndes: Civil Rights and Black Power in Alabama's Black Belt.* New York: New York University Press, 2009.

Patrick D. Jones. *The Selma of the North: Civil Rights Insurgency in Milwaukee.* Cambridge: Harvard University Press, 2009.

Lisa Levenstein. *A Movement Without Marches: African American Women and the Politics of Poverty in Postwar Philadelphia.* Chapel Hill: University of North Carolina Press, 2009.

Doug McAdam. *Freedom Summer.* New York: Oxford University Press, 1988.

Neil R. McMillen. *The Citizen's Council: A History of Organized Resistance to the Second Reconstruction.* Urbana: University of Illinois Press, 1971.

Heather Ann Thompson. *Whose Detroit? Politics, Labor, and Race in a Modern American City.* Ithaca, NY: Cornell University Press, 2001.

AUTOBIOGRAPHY AND BIOGRAPHY

Daisy Bates. *The Long Shadow of Little Rock: A Memoir.* New York: David McKay Co., 1962.

Taylor Branch. *Pillar of Fire: America in the King Years, 1963–65.* New York: Simon & Schuster, 1998.

Eric R. Burner. *And Gently He Shall Lead Them: Robert Parris Moses and Civil Rights in Mississippi.* New York: New York University Press, 1994.

Katherine Mellen Charron. *Freedom's Teacher: The Life of Septima Clark.* Chapel Hill: University of North Carolina Press, 2009.

Robert S. Dallek. *Flawed Giant: Lyndon Johnson and His Times, 1961–1973.* New York: Oxford University Press, 1998.

Dennis C. Dickerson. *Militant Mediator: Whitney M. Young, Jr.* Lexington: University Press of Kentucky, 1998.

Charles W. Eagles. *The Price of Defiance: James Meredith and the Integration of Ole Miss.* Chapel Hill: University of North Carolina Press, 2009.

James Farmer. *Lay Bare the Heart: An Autobiography of the Civil Rights Movement.* New York: Arbor House, 1985.

Cynthia Griggs Fleming. *Soon We Will Not Cry: The Liberation of Ruby Doris Smith Robinson.* Lanham, MD: Rowman & Littlefield, 1998.

David J. Garrow. *Bearing the Cross: Martin Luther King, Jr., and the Southern Christian Leadership Conference.* New York: William Morrow & Company, 1986.

Henry Hampton and Steve Fayer, eds. *The Voices of Freedom: An Oral History of the Civil Rights Movement From the 1950s Through the 1980s.* New York: Bantam Books, 1990.

Dorothy I. Height. *Open Wide the Freedom Gates: A Memoir.* New York: Public Affairs, 2003.

Chana Kai Lee. *For Freedom's Sake: The Life of Fannie Lou Hamer.* Urbana: University of Illinois Press, 1999.

Genna Rae McNeil. *Groundwork: Charles Hamilton Houston and the Struggle for Civil Rights.* Philadelphia: University of Pennsylvania Press, 1983.

Anne Moody, *Coming of Age in Mississippi.* New York: Dial Press, 1968.

Barbara Ransby. *Ella Baker and the Black Freedom Movement.* Chapel Hill: University of North Carolina Press, 2003.

Jo Ann Gibson Robinson, with David Garrow. *The Montgomery Bus Boycott and the Women Who Started It.* Knoxville: University of Tennessee Press, 1987.

Harvard Sitkoff. *King: Pilgrimage to the Mountaintop.* New York: Hill and Wang, 2008.

Timothy B. Tyson. *Radio Free Dixie: Robert F. Williams and the Roots of Black Power.* Chapel Hill: University of North Carolina Press, 1999.

Donnie Williams and Wayne Greenhaw. *The Thunder of Angels: The Montgomery Bus Boycott and the People Who Broke the Back of Jim Crow.* Chicago: Lawrence Hill Books, 2006.

Hoda M. Zaki. *Civil Rights and Politics at Hampton Institute: The Legacy of Alonzo G. Moron.* Urbana: University of Illinois Press, 2007.

RETRACING THE ODYSSEY

Brown v. Board of Education National Historic Site, Topeka, Kansas. The Sumner and Monroe Elementary Schools compose the *Brown v. Board of Education* National Historic Landmark. The 1954 *Brown v. Topeka Board of Education* decision written by U.S. Supreme Court Chief Justice Earl Warren removed the legal foundation on which the entire system of racial segregation and discrimination in the South was based and reaffirmed the ideal of the equal protection under the law clause in the Fourteenth Amendment to the U.S. Constitution. The *Brown* decision struck down the 1896 *Plessy v. Ferguson* doctrine of "separate but equal." *Brown* was the culmination of a long struggle waged by the NAACP's team of lawyers headed by Thurgood Marshall and dozens of ordinary citizens in local communities.

Birmingham Civil Rights Institute. Exhibits depict the history of the black freedom struggle. The museum chronicles the dramatic and often violent activities that occurred in Birmingham, Alabama, during the 1960s as black protests confronted massive white resistance.

The Lincoln Memorial, Washington, DC. The Lincoln Memorial was built to celebrate President Abraham Lincoln and memorialize the Civil War (1861–1865) that preserved the Union. It possesses a particular relevance and meaning to African Americans. The Lincoln Memorial was the site of the August 1963 March on Washington, during which Martin Luther King delivered his powerful "I Have a Dream" speech.

The Martin Luther King, Jr., Center for Nonviolent Social Change, Atlanta, Georgia. Founded by Coretta Scott King in 1968 as a living memorial dedicated to the preservation and advancement of the work of her husband, the Martin Luther King, Jr., Center for Nonviolent Social Change features exhibits that detail the life and legacy of Martin Luther King, Jr. It contains a unique exhibit of his personal memorabilia. The King Library and Archives contains the world's largest existing collection of civil rights materials.

1965–1980

Black Nationalism, Black Power, Black Arts

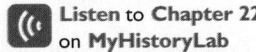

Listen to **Chapter 22**
on **MyHistoryLab**

LEARNING OBJECTIVES

22-1 Why did many African Americans become increasingly militant at the end of the 1960s?

22-2 What factors contributed to and ignited the urban rebellions in the 1960s?

22-3 How did the Vietnam War affect the Great Society and African Americans?

22-4 What was the relationship between the black power movement and black culture?

22-5 What specific policies did President Nixon initiate that affected the civil rights of African Americans?

22-6 What were some of the political accomplishments of the black power movement in the 1970s?

"The future of the Negro is very largely in the hands of the Negro citizen and voter. . . . There is no attempt here to underestimate the forces of resistance, the ignorance, trickery, fear, threats, and physical assault that have been employed and will continue to be employed. . . . Let no man say that it is somehow unfair or unethical for Negro citizens to push politically for their rights as citizens. If it is legitimate to lobby and use political pressure to secure wider markets and fatter profits, what is so wrong with using political power to secure human rights? The answer is "nothing" and Negro Americans should proceed on that basis."

Medgar W. Evers

Black Power . . . a call for black people in this country to unite, to recognize their heritage, to build a sense of community . . . to define their own goals, to lead their own organizations . . . to reject the racist institutions and values of this society. The concept of Black Power rests on a fundamental premise: *Before a group can enter the open society, it must first close ranks.* [emphasis in the original]

Stokely Carmichael and Charles V. Hamilton

When Lyndon B. Johnson became president in 1963 following John F. Kennedy's assassination, he brought to the position impressive political skills and a willingness to use them to help reconcile the racial, social, and economic disparities in American society. Johnson's escalation of America's involvement in Vietnam, however, undermined his domestic agenda. While Dr. Martin Luther King, Jr., intensified his push for jobs and justice for African Americans, a dynamic Nation of Islam minister, Malcolm X, and others questioned whether American racism could be overcome without violent struggle. A younger generation of freedom fighters lost faith in America's promise of justice and equal opportunity for all who played by the rules. Rather, some embraced the black radical tradition and

The raised arm with clinched fist symbolizes both black solidarity and the major shift from the passive resistance of the civil rights movement to the militant consciousness of the black power movement generation.

a nationalist ideology of community empowerment and mobilization to end economic exploitation and disparities in social justice, educational opportunities, and employment. Some also armed for self-defense again police brutality.

At the same time, a white backlash against the gains of the civil rights movement convinced black leaders and scholars—such as Stokely Carmichael and Charles V. Hamilton—to pursue a black power agenda and mobilize black communities to exercise their recently regained voting rights. An emerging community-centered leadership embraced new strategies in the movement for civil rights. They dismissed the inter-racialism of the civil rights movement and found fault with President Johnson's democratic liberalism. Although Martin Luther King was initially ambivalent about black power, it was clear that the winds had shifted direction. The new spirit of change embraced an array of community-level organizers and political figures from Fannie Lou Hamer in Mississippi to Shirley Chisholm in New York, and organizations from the Deacons of Defense in New Orleans to the Black Panther Party in Oakland, California. The venerable race leader, A. Philip Randolph, however, was less charitable to the idea of black power in the black liberation struggle. He called it a "menace to peace and prosperity" and erroneously declared, "No Negro who is fighting for civil rights can support black power, which is opposed to civil rights and integration."

Between 1967 and 1980, the dynamics of the civil rights freedom struggle shifted from protest against segregation, disfranchisement, and discrimination to black mobilization for the election of black officials to public office who would be responsible for meeting the needs and addressing the interests of their community constituents. African-American communities elected an unprecedented number of black politicians as mayors in dozens of America's larger cities. But while witnessing these electoral victories by black officials, the older civil rights movement coalitions fizzled and frayed. Assassins killed Malcolm X in 1965 and both Martin Luther King, Jr., and Robert Kennedy in 1968. Other community organizers and activists were also murdered, including Fred Hampton, deputy chairman of the Illinois Black Panther Party.

The Rise of Black Nationalism

22-1 **Why did many African Americans become increasingly militant at the end of the 1960s?**

President Johnson easily defeated Republican Senator Barry Goldwater in the 1964 election. But his victory proved not to be a mandate for civil rights. In California, for example, voters gave Johnson a decisive win but also approved an amendment to the state constitution that supported the repeal of laws that prohibited housing discrimination. The passage of this law, which was subsequently struck down by the U.S. Supreme Court, reflected white ambivalence to integration. In general elections, white voters also often demonstrated their opposition to civil rights. They elected several Republicans; one, former movie actor Ronald Reagan, became governor of California. In Alabama, white resentment ran even stronger. It is not a coincidence that Alabama Governor George Wallace became a national political figure who deployed virulent opposition to desegregation at this time. Rewarded by favorable responses from many northern white voters in 1968, Wallace planned a full-scale presidential run in 1972 but was shot and left partially paralyzed by a would-be assassin.

As white Americans support weakened for the goals of the civil rights movement, many black Americans searched for, and some turned completely to, the Black Radical Tradition.

Watch on MyHistoryLab Video: "The Movement"

They advocated different strategies as white violence escalated. White thugs terrorized the workers in the Council of Federated Organizations in Mississippi. Floyd McKissick of the Congress of Racial Equality (CORE) and Stokely Carmichael of the Student Nonviolent Coordinating Committee (SNCC) became disillusioned and doubted whether King's moderation, nonviolence, and universalism would secure freedom, justice, and civil equality. Carmichael had argued after the 1964 failure of the Mississippi Freedom Democratic Party that it was time to form an independent black political party. In 1965, after the Selma-to-Montgomery march, he helped found the Lowndes County (Mississippi) Freedom Organization. It became the first political organization in the civil rights movement to adopt the symbol of the black panther.

Black people in northern and western cities lost patience with the slow pace of racial change. Long into the post-1965 era, African Americans confronted the "invisible" racism embedded in American economic, political, social, and educational institutions and challenged the opposition of white people to fair housing, environmental justice, and all policies that required a redistribution of power and resources. In this context, President Lyndon Johnson's "War on Poverty" may be seen as an extension of the black freedom struggle. In particular, black churchmen castigated mainstream white religious groups for their complicity with racism, demanded reparations for slavery, and agitated for substantive power or leadership roles within the governing structures of the National Council of Churches. Black theologians developed a theology that critiqued racism within white religious groups and even called for black reparations. Black feminists also developed a theology that called for greater gender equality in the leadership of black churches and vehemently denounced sexism in the larger society.

Black power transformed black and white leaders of mainstream religious organizations. In 1946, the Federal Council of Churches, composed of Protestants, Catholics, and Jews, pledged to work for "a non-segregated church and a non-segregated society." Between 1963 and 1965, the National Council of Churches (NCC) gave financial and moral support to the civil rights movement. In 1963, the NCC founded its Commission on Religion and Race to support the black freedom movement. Although the Commission was a white-controlled and white-managed operation, three of its eight staff members were African Americans: Anna Hedgeman, J. Oscar Lee, and James Breeden. The NCC supported events such as the March on Washington and lobbied for passage of the Civil Rights Act of 1964 and the Voting Rights Act of 1965.

In 1965, the NCC appointed Benjamin Payton as director of the Commission. Payton, a native of Orangeburg, South Carolina, had been educated at Harvard Divinity School and had earned a Ph.D. at Yale. He had taught at Howard University and was a member of the National Baptist Convention, U.S.A., the largest African-American denomination. Under his stewardship the Commission was incorporated into the Division of Christian Life and Mission and later became part of the NCC's Department of Social Justice that included five other special task forces.

Payton had his own views about how organized religion could address racial problems. He viewed the economic development of black people and their communities as the critical prerequisite to improving national racial relations. In his first address to the NCC, Payton emphasized the need for "a program of economic development to make civil rights real, in housing, employment, education and health care." In July 1966, he convened a small cadre of men that included Gayraud S. Wilmore, who served as the director of the United Presbyterian's Commission on Religion and Race. Out of this gathering emerged the National Commission of Black Churchmen, which became a key mainstream ecumenical church group advocating black power concepts and strategies for the rest of the 1960s. In May 1967, however, the NCC's Department of Social Justice lost some of its momentum and direction when Payton left to become president of Benedict College in Columbia, South Carolina.

The black power movement spurred the creation of black caucuses within predominantly white churches. In February 1968, James Lawson headed the Black Methodists for Church Renewal, a caucus within the United Methodist Church. In the same year, the Black Presbyterians United replaced the Presbyterian Interracial Council. The Episcopal Union of Black Clergy and Laity replaced the interracial Episcopal Society for Racial and Cultural

22-1

22-2

22-3

22-4

22-5

22-6

Unity. By the early 1970s, there were nine such caucuses. Black Roman Catholics insisted that the church demonstrate more respect for African-American patterns of worship. All these black religious groups pressed for more black leaders within their denominations. The stage was set for James Forman's Black Manifesto.

In April 1969, James Forman, a former Chicago schoolteacher renowned for his work with SNCC, addressed the National Black Economic Development Conference in Detroit, sponsored by the Interreligious Foundation for Community Organizations (which was supported by predominantly white churches). Forman demanded that white churches pay $500 million in reparations for their participation in and benefit from American slavery and racial exploitation. His sharply secular critique of American religion precipitated the withdrawal of mainstream white religion groups from active participation in the civil rights movement. Forman's black power rhetoric and revolutionary ideology offended white groups who recoiled at the idea that black and other minority groups wanted to share real power within the white-dominated churches. Relations between black people and Jews steadily deteriorated as countercharges circulated of "Jewish racism" and "black anti-Semitism."

In ways reminiscent of Marcus Garvey in the 1910s and 1920s, Malcolm X (1925–1965) delineated the critical elements or characteristics of the Black Radical Tradition in three speeches delivered in Detroit between 1963 and 1965. He also advocated unity among black people all over the world.

Black studies professor Manning Marable defined black nationalist ideology:

> Black nationalism is a political and social tradition that includes certain characteristics. First, black nationalism advocated black cultural pride and the integrity of the group, which implicitly rejects racial integration. Second, it identifies with the cultures of Africa and advocates either immigrating there or maintaining extensive contacts with Africans. (Of course, black nationalists also advocate interaction between African Americans, African Caribbeans, and Africans on the continent of Africa itself.) Third, black nationalism works toward the construction of all-black social institutions such as self-help agencies, schools, and religious organizations and support for group economic advancement, such as black cooperatives, "Buy Black" campaigns, and efforts to promote capital formation within the African-American community. Finally, black nationalism advances . . . and supports the development of all-black political organizations and protest formations.

Malcolm X, the son of a Baptist preacher, was born Malcolm Little in Omaha, Nebraska, and grew up in Lansing, Michigan. Klan terrorists burned his family's home, and his father was murdered in 1938 when Malcolm was 13. His mother was subsequently committed to a mental institution, and welfare agencies separated the children. Malcolm was sent to a juvenile detention home, quit school after the eighth grade, and moved to Boston to live with his sister. There he became involved in the street life of gambling, drugs, and burglary. He was arrested and sentenced to a 10-year prison term in 1946. During the six-and-a-half years he spent in prison, he embraced the teachings of Elijah Muhammad of the Nation of Islam, renounced his "slave name," and called himself Malcolm X. In 1954, he became minister of Harlem's Temple Number 7. Articulate, charismatic, and courageous, Malcolm rejected both the tenets of nonviolence and racial integration. His words and thoughts resonated with many black residents in northern urban communities. In 1961, Malcolm began publishing *Muhammad Speaks,* the official newspaper of the Nation. In *The Autobiography of Malcolm X,* published in 1965 by the writer Alex Haley of *Roots* fame, Malcolm declared,

> Few white people realize that many black people today dislike and avoid spending any more time than they must around white people. This "integration" image, as it is popularly interpreted, has millions of vain, self-exalted white people convinced that black people want to sleep in bed with them—and that's a lie! Oh you can't tell the average white man that the Negro man's prime desire isn't to have a white woman—another lie!

Malcolm X attracted the attention of an increasingly disillusioned component of the black population. He dismissed the goal of racial integration and considered King's message

22-1

22-2

22-3

22-4

22-5

22-6

👁 **Watch on MyHistoryLab Video:** Malcolm X

22-1

22-2

22-3

22-4

22-5

22-6

Malcolm X (1925–1965) was eloquent, passionate, a courageously outspoken champion of black people, and a critic of American racism. Today he is an iconic figure memorialized in poems, song, films, books, and operas.

🔊 **Listen on MyHistoryLab Audio:** *Message to the Grassroots* by Malcolm X, excerpt

of redemption through brotherly love misguided. Malcolm X's voice and critique of capitalism and white supremacy resonated with those who had experienced so much white violence. "The day of nonviolent resistance is over," Malcolm insisted. He declared that "Revolutions are never based upon love-your-enemy, and pray-for-those-who-spitefully-use-you. And revolutions are never waged by singing 'We Shall Overcome.' Revolutions are based on bloodshed."

Malcolm X's New Departure

Malcolm X's popularity created tensions between himself and the leadership of the Nation of Islam. He grew disillusioned when he learned of Elijah Muhammad's adultery. Elijah Muhammad in turn grew jealous of Malcolm's success. When Malcolm described the Kennedy assassination as a case of "the chickens coming home to roost" (meaning Kennedy was a victim of the same kind of violence that afflicted black people), Elijah Muhammad had ordered him to remain silent. He suspended him for this infraction. Malcolm reacted to the suspension by breaking with the Nation of Islam. He founded his own organization, the Muslim Mosque, Inc. That same year he went on a pilgrimage to Mecca. He changed his name to El-Hajj Malik El-Shabazz, founded the Organization for Afro-American Unity (after the Organization of African Unity), repudiated the Nation of Islam's doctrine that all white people are evil, and began lecturing on the connection between the civil rights struggle in the South and the struggle against European colonialism in Africa. On February 14, 1965, assassins associated with the Nation of Islam killed him as he addressed an audience in Harlem.

Malcolm's militant advocacy of self-defense, of "overturning systems" that deprive African Americans of basic human rights, reflects the long tradition of black radicalism in America dating back to Frederick Douglass and Henry Highland Garnet in the years before the Civil War. The black power movement carried radicalism forward by emphasizing the importance of community-based leaders and of ordinary people mobilizing to secure their best interests through electoral politics.

Stokely Carmichael and Black Power

In 1966 Stokely Carmichael, a native of Trinidad who had been raised in New York City and educated at Howard University, became chairman of SNCC. Later he would abandon the ideal of interracial collaboration and move SNCC toward a stronger embrace of black nationalism. SNCC's few white staffers, including Bob Zellner, who had been with the organization since its inception, left to pursue other activism.

About this time, James Meredith began a one-man "March Against Fear" from Memphis, Tennessee, to Jackson, Mississippi, to encourage black southerners to register and vote. On this march, a white gunman wounded him. SNCC and Carmichael joined with other organizations to complete the march. Carmichael now began to popularize the slogan "black power," which was to become SNCC's rallying cry. "The only way we gonna stop them white men from whippin' us," he announced to a cheering crowd, "is to take over. We been saying freedom for six years and we ain't got nothin'. What we gonna start saying is Black Power." Carmichael and SNCC members spent the spring and summer of 1965 in Lowndes County, Alabama where Carmichael suggested that African Americans should found their own political party. Inspired by the organizing philosophy of Ella Baker, Carmichael believed in the right of ordinary citizens to elect their own leaders and devise strategies to achieve the goals they wanted. They renamed this political party the Lowndes County Freedom Party after the November 1966 elections and selected a snarling black panther as the party logo. Ruth Howard, a SNCC field secretary, described the significance of this logo: "The Black Panther is an animal that when it is pressured it moves back until it is cornered, then it comes out fighting for life or death." Carmichael was specific about what black power meant to black southerners:

> A man needs a black panther on his side when he and his family must endure . . . loss of job, eviction, starvation, and sometimes death, for political activity. . . .
>
> In Lowndes County [Alabama], for example, black power will mean that if a Negro is elected sheriff, he can end police brutality. If a black man is elected tax assessor, he can collect and channel funds for the building of better roads and schools serving black people—thus advancing the move from political power into the economic arena. . . . Politically, black power means what it has always meant to SNCC: the coming-together of black people to elect representatives and to force those representatives to speak to their needs. It does not mean merely putting black faces into office.

When critics attacked black power as reverse racism, Carmichael rejoined that it promoted positive self-identity, racial pride, and independent political and economic power.

As black people became more disillusioned about the slow pace of social change, some questioned whether white people belonged in their organizations. In 1968 CORE followed SNCC's example and ejected its white members, with a resulting loss of financial resources.

In May 1967 Hubert G. Brown became head of SNCC. "H. Rap" Brown, as he became known, raised the militancy of the black power movement's rhetoric, calling white people "honkies" and the police "pigs." In August 1967 Brown told enthusiastic listeners in the black neighborhood of Cambridge, Maryland, that "black folks built America, and if America don't come around, we're going to burn America down." When a fire erupted a few hours later in a dilapidated school in the heart of the city's black community, white firemen refused to fight it. Police charged Brown with inciting a riot and committing arson, but he posted bail and fled. Later he was arrested on other charges.

Read on **MyHistoryLab Document**: Stokely Carmichael Calls for a "Black Power" Movement, 1966

Stokely Carmichael (1941–1998) changed his name to Kwame Turé, a combination of the names of two major African leaders, Kwame Nkrumah and Ahmed Sekou Toure. After he settled in Guinea in 1969, he founded the All-African People's Revolutionary Party.

The Black Panther Party

The most enduring expression of the new black militant political activism was the Black Panther Party for Self-Defense created by Huey P. Newton and Bobby Seale in Oakland, California, in October 1966. Newton and Seale took the name of the party from the black panther symbol of the **Lowndes County Freedom Organization (LCFO)**. The Black Panthers combined black nationalist ideology with Marxist-Leninist doctrines. Working with white radicals, they hoped to fashion the party into a revolutionary vanguard dedicated to ending police brutality. For a few months Stokely Carmichael, who had become estranged from SNCC, was named the party's prime minister. However, Carmichael soon shifted his interest to pan-Africanism. He moved to Guinea in West Africa and changed his name to Kwame Turé. Eldridge Cleaver, the Panthers' minister of education, helped formulate the party's ideology.

Cleaver began writing the autobiographical essays that appeared as *Soul on Ice* in 1968, the year the party dropped "Self-Defense" from its name. Black people, Cleaver maintained, were victims of colonization. Integrationism could not meet their needs. Instead, like other colonized peoples, they had to be liberated. "To achieve these ends," he wrote, "we believe that political and military machinery that does not exist now and has never existed must be

Lowndes County Freedom Organization (LCFO) Political organization founded in 1965.

Black Panther Party founders Huey P. Newton and Bobby Seale. The Panthers advocated a radical economic, social, and educational agenda that made it the target of a determined campaign of suppression and elimination by the police and the FBI.

22-1

22-2

22-3

22-4

22-5

22-6

created. We need functional machinery that is able to deal with these two interrelated sets of political dynamics which, strictly speaking, make up the total political situation on the North American continent." Cleaver and other Panther leaders were arrested after a shoot-out with Oakland police in 1968. Cleaver escaped and fled into exile in Algeria and Cuba. Later, he abandoned his radicalism and became involved with the Republican Party and fundamentalist Christianity upon returning to the United States in 1975.

Police Repression and the FBI's COINTELPRO

The Panthers, imposing in appearance in black leather jackets, berets, and "Afro" haircuts, alarmed white policemen, especially when they armed themselves for self-defense and patrolled their neighborhoods to monitor the police. A series of bloody confrontations in Oakland distracted attention from the Panthers' broader political objectives and community service projects. In Oakland and Chicago, the Panthers arranged free breakfast and healthcare programs, worked to instill racial pride, lectured and wrote about black history, and launched some of the earliest drug education programs. These activities won community support and admiration. The Panthers adopted the slogan "Power to the People."

FBI director J. Edgar Hoover hated the Black Panther Party even more than he disliked Martin Luther King, Jr. Hoover infiltrated, harassed, destabilized, and worked to destroy all black nationalist groups and their leaders. The FBI cooperated with local law enforcement officials to ridicule, undermine, and discredit leaders and members of the Black Panther Party. In August 1967 Hoover distributed a memorandum that detailed the FBI's counterintelligence program against black nationalist groups. The purpose, according to the memo, of this new "counterintelligence (COINTELPRO) endeavor is to expose, disrupt, misdirect, discredit, or otherwise neutralize the activities of black nationalist, hate-type organizations and groupings, their leadership, spokesmen, membership, and supporters, and to counter their propensity for violence and civil disorder." Undercover agents infiltrated the Panthers and provoked violence and criminal acts. Not that the Panthers were saints. Huey P. Newton had a long criminal record. He was imprisoned for murder in 1968 but was acquitted and released, only to be charged with murder and assault again in 1974. After fleeing to Cuba to avoid trial, he returned in 1977 and was again acquitted. He was killed at age 42 in a drug dispute in Oakland in 1989. Still, the FBI and its counterintelligence agents provoked much of the mayhem and violence that became associated with the Panthers. Certainly, COINTELPRO helped shape negative public opinion of black nationalist ideology.

In their effort to destroy the party, law enforcement officials killed an estimated 28 Panthers and imprisoned 750 others. In perhaps the worst incident, police in Chicago killed Fred Hampton and Mark Clark in their sleep in a predawn raid on the Illinois Panther headquarters on December 4, 1969. While the police fired hundreds of rounds, only two shots were fired back from within the apartment.

Prisoners' Rights

Despite such repression, black militancy survived in many forms, including the prisoners' rights movement. One of the Panthers' social programs had focused on the conditions of black prisoners. By 1970 more than half the inmates in U.S. prisons were African American. In New York State, black Americans were around 70 percent of the prison population. Black activists argued that many African Americans were in jail for political reasons and suffered from unfair sentences and deplorable conditions because of racism and social class bias.

Angela Davis, a philosophy professor at the University of California at Los Angeles, became the first black woman on the FBI's Ten Most Wanted list because of her involvement

VOICES   The Black Panther Party Platform

Huey Newton and Bobby Seale's Ten-Point Program reflected their determination to move from the pursuit of civil rights to a radical restructuring of American society along socialist lines, with work and rewards equally shared.

October 1966

Black Panther Party Platform and Program: What We Want, What We Believe

1. We want freedom. We want power to determine the destiny of our Black Community . . .
2. We want full employment for our people . . .
3. We want an end to the robbery of the capitalists of our Black Community . . .
4. We want decent housing fit for shelter of human beings . . .
5. We want education for our people that exposes the true nature of this decadent American society. We want education that teaches us our true history and our role in present-day society . . .
6. We want all Black men to be exempt from military service . . .
7. We want an immediate end to POLICE BRUTALITY and MURDER of Black people . . .
8. We want freedom for all Black men held in federal, state, county and city prisons and jails . . .
9. We want all Black people when brought to trial to be tried in court by a jury of their peer group or people from their Black communities, as defined by the Constitution of the United States . . .
10. We want land, bread, housing, education, clothing, justice, and peace. And as our major political objective, a United Nations supervised plebiscite to be held throughout the Black colony in which only Black colonial subjects will be allowed to participate, for the purpose of determining the will of Black people as to their national destiny.

---

1. **How is the Ten-Point Program similar to the Bill of Rights in the U.S. Constitution? How do they differ?**
2. **How did the Panthers propose to achieve black liberation? Why did they emphasize studying history? How did the Panthers' program conflict with or expand upon that of the older civil rights organizations?**

SOURCE: Clayborne Carson et al., eds., *The Eyes on the Prize Civil Rights Reader: Documents, Speeches, and Firsthand Accounts from the Black Freedom Struggle, 1954–1990* (New York: Viking Penguin, 1991), 346–47.

22-1
22-2
22-3
22-4
22-5
22-6

---

in prisoners' rights. In 1969 UCLA's board of regents refused to renew her contract, citing her lack of a Ph.D., but in fact they objected to her membership in the Communist Party. During the late 1960s, she had worked on behalf of the Soledad Brothers, three prisoners— George Jackson, John Clutchette, and Fleeta Drumgo—accused of murdering a white guard at Soledad Prison. On August 7, 1970, George Jackson's younger brother, 17-year-old Jonathan Jackson, staged a one-man raid on the San Rafael courthouse in Marin County, California, to try to seize hostages to exchange for the Soledad Brothers. In the ensuing shoot-out, he was killed along with two prisoners and a judge. Angela Davis, accused of supplying the weapons for the raid, was charged with murder, kidnapping, and conspiracy. She escaped and lived as a fugitive, but she was eventually captured and spent over a year in jail. After a long ordeal and a national "Free Angela" campaign, a jury acquitted Davis. On August 21, 1971, George Jackson was shot and killed at San Quentin Prison by guards who claimed he was trying to escape.

Across the country, prisoners at Attica, a maximum-security prison in northern New York State, began a fast in memory of George Jackson that erupted into a full-scale rebellion. On September 9, 1971, 1,200 inmates seized control of half of Attica and took hostages. Four days later, state police and prison guards suppressed the uprising. Tom Wicker, a columnist for the *New York Times,* filed this report:

A task force consisting of 211 state troopers and corrections officers retook Attica using tear gas, rifles, and shotguns. After the shooting was over, ten hostages and twenty-nine inmates lay dead or dying. At least 450 rounds of ammunition had been discharged. Four

Listen on **MyHistoryLab** Audio: Angela Davis; Interview from Prison

Although the iconic "Afro" is gone, today Angela Davis continues her forceful advocacy for the rights of prisoners. She serves on the advisory board of the Prison Activist Resource Center and teaches in the Department of the History of Consciousness at the University of California, Santa Cruz.

Read on **MyHistoryLab** Document: Donald Wheeldin Describes Watts Two Years After the 1965 Riot, 1967

hostages and eighty-five inmates suffered gunshot wounds that they survived. After initial reports that several hostages had died at the hands of knife-wielding inmates, pathologists' reports revealed that hostages and inmates all died from gunshot wounds. No guns were found in the possession of inmates.

A state commission, assembled in October 1971 to reconstruct the events at Attica, concluded, "With the exception of Indian massacres in the late nineteenth-century, the State Police assault which ended the four-day prison uprising was the bloodiest one-day encounter between Americans since the Civil War."

The Inner-City Rebellions

22-2 **What factors contributed to and ignited the urban rebellions in the 1960s?**

The militant nationalism and growing embrace of black radicalism reflected growing alienation and anger in America's impoverished inner cities. In 1965, 29.1 percent of black households, compared with only 7.8 percent of white households, lived below the poverty line. Almost 50 percent of nonwhite families lived in substandard housing compared with 18 percent of white families. Despite a drop in the number of Americans living in poverty from 38.0 million in 1959 to 32.7 million in 1965, the percentage of poor black people increased from 27.5 percent to 31 percent. In 1965 the black unemployment rate was 8.5 percent, almost twice the white unemployment rate of 4.3. For black teenagers the unemployment rate was 23 percent compared with 10.8 percent for white teenagers. As psychologist Kenneth Clark declared in 1967, "The masses of Negroes are now starkly aware of the fact that recent civil rights victories benefited a very small percentage of middle-class Negroes while their predicament remained the same or worsened."

The passage of civil rights laws and voting rights legislation did not resolve these social, educational, and economic disparities. This created a fertile environment for the rise in inner-city alienation. As jobs moved to suburbs to which inner-city residents could neither travel nor relocate, inner-city neighborhoods became poorer. School dropout rates reached epidemic proportions, crime and drug use increased, and fragile family structures weakened. These conditions led militants like the Panthers to liken their neighborhoods to exploited colonies kept poor by repressive white political and economic institutions. Few white Americans understood the depths of the black despair that flared into violence each summer between 1965 and 1969, beginning with the Watts rebellion of 1965.

Watts

In the summer of 1965, a section of Los Angeles called Watts exploded. Watts was 98 percent black. Its residents suffered from overcrowding, unemployment, inaccessible healthcare facilities, inadequate public transportation, and crime and drug addiction. Almost 30 percent of Watts' black males were unemployed. The poverty, combined with anger at the often-brutal behavior of Los Angeles' police force in Watts, proved to be an incendiary combination. On August 11, 1965, a policeman pulled over a young black man to check him for drunk driving. The man was arrested, but not before a crowd gathered. The policeman called for reinforcements, and when they arrived, the crowd pelted them with stones, bottles, and other objects. Within hours, Watts was in a total riot.

Governor Pat Brown, a Democrat, sent in the National Guard to restore order, but by the sixth day of the conflagration, Watts had been reduced to rubble and ashes. One reporter commented that Watts looked like Germany at the end of World War II. Thirty-four people had been killed, more than 900 injured, and 4,000 arrested. Total property damage was more than $35 million, equivalent to hundreds of millions of dollars today. The Watts rebellion was the beginning of four summers of uprisings that would engulf cities in the North and Midwest. There were riots in the summer of 1966, but worse ones erupted in Newark and Detroit in 1967.

Watch on **MyHistoryLab Video:**
The Los Angeles Riots

Newark

Newark, New Jersey, had more than 400,000 inhabitants in 1967. As was true in many other urban areas, white flight to the suburbs in the 1950s and 1960s had made Newark a majority black city; nonetheless, it operated on an inadequate tax base and under white political control. The city could not meet its inhabitants' social needs. The school system had deteriorated as unemployment increased. In 1967 Newark had the highest unemployment rate among black men in the nation. As tensions flared and police brutality escalated, white officials paid little attention to black people's complaints. On July 12, after a black cab driver in police custody was beaten, protesters gathered at the police station near the Hayes Homes housing project. When a firebomb hit the wall of the station house, the police charged, clubbing the crowd. This triggered one of the most destructive civic rebellions of the period. During four days of rioting, the police and National Guard killed 25 black people—most of them innocent bystanders, including two children. A white policeman and fireman were also killed. Widespread looting and arson caused millions of dollars in property damage.

Detroit

When Detroit erupted a few days after Newark, it caught everyone by surprise except its inner-city residents. Detroit had seemed like a model of prosperity and interracial accord. Some of the country's most dynamic popular music flowed from Detroit's Motown recording company. Owned by the astute Berry Gordy, Motown was a classic up-by-the-bootstraps success story. Gordy, his wife Raynoma, and their extended family had, by 1967, produced such stars as Diana Ross and Mary Wells. "Before Motown," said Wells, "there were three careers available to a black girl in Detroit—babies, the factories or daywork."

But success like Gordy's was rare among the black migrants and their children, who poured into Detroit during and after World War II. The parents held their disappointment in check, but the children, particularly young men aged between 17 and 35, sought an outlet for their anger and alienation. Some joined the Nation of Islam. Others embraced the Panthers or formed even more radical organizations calling for an all-black nation.

On the night of Saturday, July 23, police raided an after-hours drinking establishment in the black community where more than 80 people were celebrating the return of two veterans from Vietnam. The raid triggered five days of rioting. John Conyers, the black representative for Michigan's First Congressional District, knew many of the people in the area and tried to get them to disperse, but they refused: "People were letting feelings out that had never been let out before, that had been bottled up. It really wasn't that they were that mad about an after-hours place being raided and some people being beat up as a result of the closing down of that place. It was the whole desperate situation of being black in Detroit."

Of the 59 urban rebellions that occurred in 1967, Detroit's was the deadliest. Forty-three black people died, most of them shot by members of the National Guard, which had been sent in by Republican Governor George Romney. But even the National Guard, combined with 200 state police and 600 Detroit police, could not restore order. President Johnson had to order 4,700 troops of the elite 82nd and 101st Airborne units to Detroit. Republicans criticized Johnson's move as designed to embarrass Romney, who was a contender for the Republican presidential nomination in 1968. Johnson vehemently denied the charge. Others argued that Johnson's social welfare policies had raised expectations beyond the country's ability or desire to fulfill them and had subsidized the rioters.

22-1
22-2
22-3
22-4
22-5
22-6

22-1
22-2
22-3
22-4
22-5
22-6

In 1967, Blacks in Detroit expressed their anger and disillusionment about a constellation of social injustices and economic woes.

The Kerner Commission

On July 29, 1967, after the Newark and Detroit riots, Johnson established the National Advisory Commission on Civil Disorders, headed by Illinois Governor Otto Kerner. The commission included two black members, Republican Senator Edward W. Brooke of Massachusetts (elected in 1966 and the first black senator since Reconstruction) and Roy Wilkins, executive director of the NAACP. Explaining why he had set up the commission, Johnson declared,

> The only genuine, long-range solution for what has happened lies in an attack—mounted at every level—upon the conditions that breed despair and violence. All of us know what those conditions are: ignorance, discrimination, slums, poverty, disease, not enough jobs. We should attack these conditions—not because we are frightened by conflict, but because we are fired by conscience. We should attack them because there is simply no other way to achieve a decent and orderly society in America.

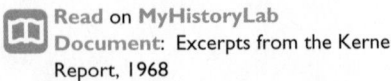

Read on **MyHistoryLab**
Document: Excerpts from the Kerner Report, 1968

In its final report, released in 1968, the Kerner Commission indicted white racism as the underlying cause of the riots and warned that America was "moving towards two societies, one white, one black—separate and unequal. . . . Negroes firmly believe that police brutality and harassment occur repeatedly in Negro neighborhoods. This belief is unquestionably one of the major reasons for intense Negro resentment against the police. . . . Physical abuse is only one source of aggravation in the ghetto. In nearly every city surveyed, the Commission heard complaints of harassment of interracial couples, dispersal of social street gatherings and the stopping of Negroes on foot or in cars without objective basis." The report called for massive government aid to the cities, including funds for public housing, better and more integrated schools, two million new jobs, and funding for a "national system of income supplementation." None of its major proposals was enacted.

Difficulties in Creating the Great Society

The urban rebellions of the late 1960s undercut support for the broadest attack the federal government had yet waged on the problems of poor Americans, what President Johnson

Watch on **MyHistoryLab Video:**
Lyndon Johnson

in his election campaign in 1964 had called "the Great Society." Much of the legislation Johnson pushed through Congress in 1964 and 1965—Medicare, for example, which provided medical care for the elderly and disabled under the Social Security system, or federal aid to education from elementary through graduate schools—remained popular. But the most ambitious Great Society programs—what Johnson called "an unconditional war on poverty"—were controversial and tested the limits of American reform.

Lyndon Johnson was a savvy politician. He had to be to rise from Stonewall, Texas, to the pinnacle of power. But he never lost a deep sympathy for the disadvantaged and the powerless. Entering Congress in 1937, he had been an enthusiastic New Dealer. Elected to the Senate in 1948, he had refused to sign the Southern Manifesto (see Chapter 21) and, as majority leader, had overcome southern filibusters to pass the 1957 and 1960 Civil Rights Acts. As president, he pushed the 1964 Civil Rights Act and the 1965 Voting Rights Act through Congress.

Johnson's concern for the disadvantaged showed itself in the cornerstone of his War on Poverty, the **Economic Opportunity Act of 1964**. This act created an Office of Economic Opportunity that administered programs like Head Start to help disadvantaged preschoolers, Upward Bound to prepare impoverished teenagers for college, and Volunteers in Service to America (or VISTA) to serve as a domestic peace corps to help the poor and undereducated across the country. These programs included community-governing boards on which black men and women gained representation, learning such essential political skills as bargaining and organizing.

The War on Poverty was the first government-sponsored effort to involve poor African Americans directly in designing and implementing programs to serve low-income communities. For example, in the New Careers program, residents of poor neighborhoods found jobs as community organizers, day care workers, and teacher aides. The program provided meaningful work, access to education, and critical resources to poor people so that they would become leaders in their own communities and run for office. The **Community Action Programs (CAPs)** insisted on "maximum feasible participation" by the poor. The Education Act increased federal funding to colleges and universities and provided low-interest student loans.

Johnson faced opposition to CAPs and other Great Society programs. Local politicians, fearing the federal government was subsidizing their opponents and undercutting their power, were especially threatened by programs that empowered the previously disfranchised and dispossessed. Others, reflecting persistent white stereotypes of African Americans, complained that Johnson was rewarding lawlessness and laziness with handouts to the undeserving poor. The black residents of America's inner cities, for their part, had their expectations raised by the promises of the Great Society, only to be frustrated by white backlash and minimal gains. They felt as betrayed by its programs as Johnson's white critics felt robbed by them.

No one will ever know whether Johnson could have won his War on Poverty had he been given the resources to do so. As it turned out, the nation's resources were increasingly diverted into his other war, the war in Vietnam. Statistics tell the story. Government spending, including spending for domestic programs, increased dramatically under Johnson. But most of the money spent on domestic programs during Johnson's presidency, $44.3 billion, went to Social Security benefits, which now included Medicare. Appropriations for the War on Poverty came to only $10 billion. The war in Vietnam, in contrast, consumed $140 billion.

Read on MyHistoryLab Document: President Johnson Calls for a "War on Poverty," 1964

One of the most prominent programs of President Johnson's War on Poverty was the Job Corps, which provided occupational training for poor Americans. In this photo, Johnson speaks with James Truesville at a Job Corps center in Camp Catoctin, Maryland.

Economic Opportunity Act of 1964 Federal law creating the Office of Economic Opportunity and a number of programs aimed at poor communities.

Community Action Programs (CAPs) Anti-poverty programs involving "maximum feasible participation" by the poor themselves.

22-1

22-2

22-3

22-4

22-5

22-6

Johnson and the War in Vietnam

22-3 How did the Vietnam War affect the Great Society and African Americans?

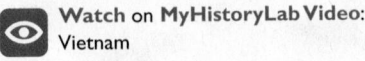

Watch on MyHistoryLab Video:
Vietnam

22-1
22-2
22-3
22-4
22-5
22-6

Vietnam was a French colony from the 1860s until the Japanese seized it during World War II. After the war the Vietnamese communists, led by Ho Chi Minh, declared independence, but the French, with massive U.S. financial aid, fought to reassert their control until they were finally defeated in 1954. In retrospect, it is easy to argue that American policymakers should have been more impressed by the French failure to defeat the communists in Vietnam. But in 1954, with the French pulling out, the Americans arranged a temporary division of the country into a communist-controlled North Vietnam and a U.S.-supported South Vietnam (which, however, contained many communist guerrillas, whom the Americans called "Viet Cong"). The United States ignored the possibility that as guarantor of South Vietnam, it would replace the French as targets for those Vietnamese who were determined to end foreign domination and unify their country.

For nine years, under Presidents Eisenhower and Kennedy, American aid and advisers propped up the corrupt and incompetent South Vietnamese government in Saigon. By the time Johnson became president, only the dramatic escalation of American involvement—the bombing of North Vietnam and the introduction of large numbers of American troops into combat in South Vietnam—could keep the South Vietnamese government in power. Johnson himself doubted the advisability of a wholesale American commitment and did not want a foreign war to distract the public's attention or divert resources from the Great Society programs about which he cared so much. "I knew from the start," Johnson claimed later,

> that I was bound to be crucified either way I moved. If I left the woman I really loved—the Great Society—in order to get involved with that bitch of a war on the other side of the world, then I would lose everything at home. All my programs. All my hopes to feed the hungry and shelter the homeless. All my dreams to provide education and medical care to the browns and the blacks and the lame and the poor. But if I left that war and let the Communists take over South Vietnam, then I would be seen as a coward and my nation would be seen as an appeaser and we would both find it impossible to accomplish anything for anybody anywhere on the entire globe.

And so, half aware he was entering a quagmire but determined to slug through it, Johnson intervened in Vietnam—gradually, massively, and inexorably.

After the North Vietnamese allegedly attacked U.S. destroyers in the Gulf of Tonkin in August 1964, Johnson pushed a resolution through Congress that gave him authority to escalate American involvement in Vietnam. In the spring of 1965, he authorized the bombing of selected North Vietnamese targets, but that failed to stop the North Vietnamese from reinforcing their forces in the south. The American military presence in South Vietnam then grew rapidly. By the end of 1966, more than 385,000 U.S. troops were stationed there and by 1968 more than 500,000.

Black Americans and the Vietnam War

In the mid-1960s, black Americans made up 10 percent of the armed forces. This percentage increased during the Vietnam War. (In 1969, for example, 18.1 percent of active duty soldiers were black.) Black overrepresentation among the U.S. troops in Vietnam resulted, in large part, from draft deferments for college and graduate students who were predominantly white and middle class (such as George W. Bush and Dick Cheney). Black men and women entered the military for many reasons, in addition to the draft. One was patriotism. Another was that the military offered educational and vocational opportunities that the children of the working black poor could not otherwise obtain. Still another was Project 100,000.

❋ EXPLORE ON MYHISTORYLAB
The Vietnam War

What did the war in Vietnam mean for the United States?

Between 1955 and 1975, a civil war raged across Vietnam between the communist government in the north and the weak democracy–dictatorship in the south. In the context of the Cold War, the United States supported the South Vietnamese government, hoping to stop the spread of communism. By the early 1960s, the American government began increasing its troop presence in Vietnam; in 1965, the United States sent its first combat units. American military intervention in Vietnam and the neighboring countries of Southeast Asia grew. As casualties mounted and little military progress was achieved, the intervention became increasingly unpopular at home with the spread of anti-war protests. Some 58,000 American servicemen and servicewomen died before the United States withdrew in 1975. Soon after, the South Vietnamese government fell as the country was united under a single communist government.

Troopers of the 327th, Infantry 101st Air Cavalry, Division patrol the Laotian border during 'Operation, Plain' August, 1968.

22-1

22-2

22-3

22-4

22-5

22-6

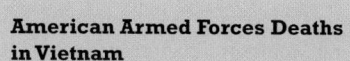

American Armed Forces Deaths in Vietnam	
Year	**Deaths**
1956–1959	4
1960	5
1961	16
1962	53
1963	122
1964	216
1965	1,928
1966	6,350
1967	11,363
1968	16,899
1969	11,780
1970	6,173
1971	2,414
1972	759
1973	68
1974	1
1975	62

SOURCE: *"Statistical Information About Fatal Casualties of the Vietnam War National Archives, National Archives, http://www.archives.gov/ research/military/vietnam-war/casualty-statistics .html#home.*

❋ **Explore** the **Topic** on **MyHistoryLab**

1. **Cause** *What geographic challenges did American forces face in Vietnam?* Map the features that hindered the U.S. military effort.

2. **Response** *What was the significance of various U.S. military operations in Vietnam, especially the Tet Offensive?* Explore the unfolding of the war.

3. **Consequence** *What relationships may have existed between war deaths and other socio-economic factors in an area?* Chart potential correlations and consider underlying reasons.

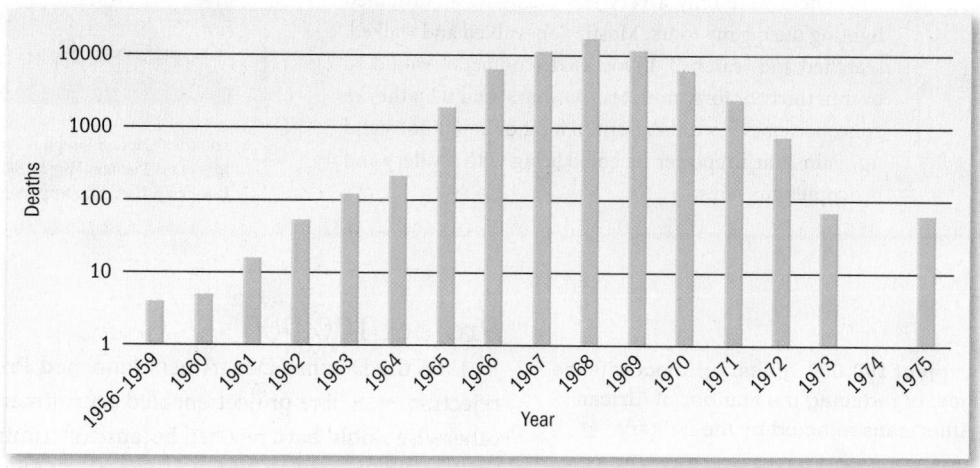

VOICES   They Called Each Other "Bloods"

22-1
22-2
22-3
22-4
22-5
22-6

Captain Joseph B. Anderson, Jr., of Topeka, Kansas, served as a platoon leader at An Khe, Vietnam, from June 1966 to June 1967, and as company commander in Phouc Vinh, Cambodia, from May 1970 to April 1971. His unit in the 1st Cavalry Division was the subject of The Anderson Platoon, *a 1967 French documentary film.*

Shortly after I got to Vietnam, we got into a real big fight. We were outnumbered at least ten to one. But I didn't know it. I had taken over 1st Platoon of B Company of the 12th Cav. We were up against a Viet Cong battalion. There may have been 300 to 400 of them. And they had just wiped out one of our platoons. At that time in the war, summer of 1966, it was a terrible loss. A bloody massacre.

I was an absolute rarity in Vietnam. A black West Pointer commanding troops. One year after graduation, I was very aggressive about my role and responsibilities as an Army officer serving in Vietnam. I was there to defend the freedom of the South Vietnamese government, stabilize the countryside, and help contain Communism. The Domino Theory was dominant then, predominant as a matter of fact. I was gung ho. And I thought the war would last three years at the most.

There weren't many opportunities for blacks in private industry then. And as a graduate of West Point, I was an officer and a gentleman by act of Congress. Where else could a black go and get that label just like that?

Throughout the Cav, the black representation in the enlisted ranks was heavier than the population as a whole in the United States. One third of my platoon and two of my four squad leaders were black. For many black men, the service, even during a war, was the best of a number of alternatives to staying home and working in the fields or bumming around the streets of Chicago or New York.

There were only a very few incidents of sustained fighting during my tours. Mostly you walked and walked, searched and searched. If you made contact, it would be over in thirty or forty minutes. One burst and then they're gone, because they didn't want to fight or could not stand up against the firepower we could bring with artillery and helicopter gunships.

I had a great deal of respect for the Viet Cong. They were trained and familiar with the jungle. They relied on stealth, on ambush, on their personal skills and wile, as opposed to firepower. They knew it did not pay for them to stand and fight us, so they wouldn't. . . .

What was very clear to me was an awareness among our men that the support for the war was declining in the United States. The gung ho attitude that made our soldiers so effective in 1966, 67, was replaced by the will to survive. They became more security conscious. They would take more defensive measures so they wouldn't get hurt. They were more scared. They wanted to get back home.

Career officers and enlisted men like me did not go back to a hostile environment in America. We went back to bases where we were assimilated and congratulated and decorated for our performance in the conduct of the war.

Personally it was career enhancing. A career Army officer who has not been to war during the war is dead, careerwise. I had done that. I received decorations. Two Silver Stars, five Bronze Stars, eleven Air Medals. . . . But in 1978 I decided I did not want to cool my heels for the next eight to ten years to become a general. . . . I resigned my commission, worked a year as a special assistant to the U.S. Secretary of Commerce, and joined General Motors as a plant manager.

The Anderson Platoon won both an Oscar and an Emmy. As time passes, my memory of Vietnam revolves around the film. I have a print, and I look at it from time to time. And the broadness and scope of my two-year experience narrows down to sixty minutes.

1. **How do the experiences of this Vietnam veteran compare with those of black soldiers in World War II?**

2. **Why were African-American men attracted to military service? What benefits did they derive from the military, and what does their disproportionate representation in it suggest about conditions in black communities?**

SOURCE: "Captain Joseph B. Anderson, Jr., Topeka, Kansas," from *Bloods: An Oral History of the Vietnam War by Black Veterans* by Wallace Terry, copyright © 1984 by Wallace Terry. Used by permission of Random House, Inc.

Project 100,000

Project 100,000 Military project with the goal of reducing the number of African Americans rejected by the military.

In 1966 the Defense Department launched **Project 100,000** to reduce the military's high rejection rate. The project enabled recruitment officers to accept applicants whom they otherwise would have rejected because of criminal records or lack of skills. It supplied more than 340,000 new recruits for Vietnam, 136,000 of whom were African Americans. As some have argued, this imbalance made the Vietnam War a white man's war but a black man's fight. Although the recruits were promised training and "rehabilitation," they saw more combat duty than regular recruits.

Johnson: Vietnam Destroys the Great Society

By the end of 1967, the nation seemed to be heading toward total racial polarization. In their rage against economic exploitation and police brutality, some inner-city black people had destroyed their own neighborhoods. Frightened white people, unable to comprehend black anger, rallied behind those who promised to restore order by any means. The two men who, only a few years before, had seemed the most effective advocates of racial reconciliation—Lyndon Johnson and Martin Luther King, Jr.,—were both trying to regain the initiative. Each, tragically, alienated the other.

By 1967 Johnson's situation was untenable. He had escalated the war in Vietnam without convincing many Americans it was worth fighting. Misleading claims about the progress of the war had forfeited public trust and opened what journalists called "the credibility gap." Johnson hoped that, with more bombing and more troops, the Vietnamese communists would give up, but he knew that if Congress had to choose between spending on the war and spending on domestic programs, it would choose the war. After Johnson asked for a tax increase, his Great Society programs met increasing resistance. When, for example, he proposed a special program to exterminate the rats that infested inner-city neighborhoods, congressional opponents turned it into a joke, calling it a "civil rats bill" and proposing to enlist an army of cats.

An even more dramatic example of the ugly mood on Capitol Hill was the House of Representatives' expulsion in 1967 of the most prominent African-American politician in the United States, Adam Clayton Powell, Jr. Pastor of the Abyssinian Baptist Church in Harlem and a longtime civic activist, Powell had first been elected to represent his Harlem district in 1944 and became the foremost champion of civil rights in the House. Because of his seniority he became chairman of the Education and Labor Committee in 1961 and had been instrumental in passing Johnson's education and antipoverty legislation.

Powell gave ammunition to his enemies. He mismanaged the committee's budget, took numerous trips abroad at government expense, and was exiled from his district when threatened with arrest there because of his refusal to pay a slander judgment against him. Yet the sentiment behind his ouster owed much to the dislike he inspired as a champion of minorities and the poor and as a flamboyant black man. The Supreme Court, overruling the House, upheld his right to his seat, and although he lost his chairmanship, Harlem voters kept him in office until his death in 1972.

Despite opposition in Congress, Johnson did not give up on the Great Society. He knew he could initiate no major programs while the Vietnam War lasted, but he continued to push measures, including a law to prohibit discrimination in housing. He also named the architect of the NAACP's attack on segregation, Thurgood Marshall, to the Supreme Court in 1967.

Vietnam trapped Johnson. As the hundreds of thousands of people who demonstrated against the war reminded him, Vietnam was incontestably "Lyndon Johnson's war." It was not, he would have replied, the war he had wanted to fight—that was the war against poverty and discrimination—but he was committed to seeing it through. He believed his and the nation's honor were at stake. Even though objective commentators considered the conflict a stalemate, optimistic reports in 1967, from military commanders and intelligence agents, convinced the president he might yet prevail.

Then, on January 30, 1968, at the start of the Vietnamese New Year (called Tet), communist insurgents attacked 36 of the 44 provincial capitals in South Vietnam as well as its national capital, Saigon, where they

Adam Clayton Powell, Jr. (1908–1972). Beginning in 1954, Powell's Harlem constituency elected him to 11 successive terms in the U.S. House of Representatives. His brilliant leadership of the Education and Labor Committee proved crucial to the successful passage of social reform legislation in the 1960s.

penetrated the grounds of the American embassy. Although American and South Vietnamese forces recaptured all the territory that was lost and inflicted massive casualties on the enemy, the Tet Offensive was a major psychological blow for the American public, deepening the suspicion that the administration had not been telling the truth about the war. Washington was forced to reconsider its strategy.

On March 31, 1968, President Johnson told the nation he would halt the bombing of North Vietnam to encourage the start of peace negotiations, which began in Paris in May. Then, as if an afterthought, he added that he would not seek re-nomination as president. Worn out by Vietnam, frustrated in his efforts to achieve the Great Society, the target of bitter criticism, and dispirited by a poor showing in the New Hampshire primary, Lyndon Johnson ended his public career rather than engaging in a potentially bruising re-nomination battle.

King: Searching for a New Strategy

Like Johnson, Martin Luther King, Jr., was attacked on many fronts. Many white people considered him a dangerous radical. Black militants considered him an ineffectual moderate. His first response to the urban rebellions in 1965 and 1966 had been to move his campaign to the North to demonstrate the national range of the civil rights movement. In 1966 King and the SCLC set up operations in Chicago at the invitation of the Chicago Freedom Movement. King was confident he would receive the support of the city's white liberals and the black community. James Bevel, King's Chicago lieutenant, declared, "We are going to create a new city. . . . Nobody will stop us." His optimism proved unwarranted.

Chicago's powerful, wily Mayor Richard Daley viewed King suspiciously from the outset, but he treated him with respect and cautioned the police not to use violence against King's civil rights demonstrators. Because King's movement depended on provoking confrontation, not much happened until King attempted to march into the white ethnic enclave of Marquette Park and the all-white suburb of Cicero.

The ensuing violence attracted the nation's television cameras. Chicago's white liberals joined with King and Daley in negotiating the Summit Agreement on housing, which amounted to a hasty retreat by King in the face of virulent white rage and black militancy. The Chicago strategy was a dismal failure.

But Chicago reinforced two important lessons for King. First, racial discrimination was more than a southern problem: in Chicago he witnessed an intensity of hatred and hostility that surpassed even that of Birmingham. Second, racial discrimination was inextricably intertwined with the country's economic structure. And so he began to think more critically about the need not only to eradicate poverty but to end systemic economic inequality. "What good is it to be allowed to eat in a restaurant," he remarked, "if you can't afford a hamburger?" In the fall of 1967, he announced plans for his most ambitious and militant project, an integrated, nonviolent "**Poor People's Campaign**" the following spring. According to the plan, tens of thousands of the nation's dispossessed would descend on Washington to focus attention on the disadvantaged in American society. Among other things, King and his aides wanted a federally guaranteed income policy.

Poor People's Campaign Project supported by Martin Luther King involving the march of tens of thousands of poor people on Washington.

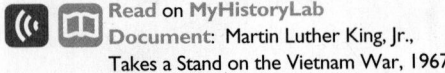
Read on MyHistoryLab
Document: Martin Luther King, Jr., Takes a Stand on the Vietnam War, 1967

King on the Vietnam War

While planning the Poor People's Campaign, King began to attack the war in Vietnam. He rejected what he considered the hypocrisy of the federal government's determination to send black and white men to Vietnam "to slaughter, men, women, and children" while failing to protect black American civil rights protesters in places like Albany, Birmingham, and Selma. His statements that the president was more concerned about winning in Vietnam than winning the "war against poverty" in America turned Johnson against him and further alienated King from many of Johnson's black supporters, including the more traditional civil rights leaders who supported the war. At the same time, the young militants in SNCC, who had already condemned the war, did not rush to embrace him. But King persisted, and by 1968 he had become one of the war's most trenchant critics.

PROFILE Muhammad Ali

Muhammad Ali declared himself "The Greatest," and for many African Americans he was the epitome of the uncompromised and proud black man.

BOXING IS A BRUTAL SPORT. During the 1960s and 1970s, Cassius Clay showed that boxing was also an art, that it could be beautiful, and that the boxer could become a symbol of racial pride, endearing wit, and even love. Born Cassius Marcellus Clay in 1942 in Louisville, Kentucky, Clay won a gold medal in Rome in 1960 as a member of the U.S. Olympic boxing team.

Clay turned the boxing world on its head with audacious assertions of his own greatness as a boxer and beauty as a black man. His defeats of Floyd Patterson and Sonny Liston confirmed the first claim. On February 25, 1964, Clay pounded Liston to become the world heavyweight champion. The next day he announced that he had joined the Nation of Islam and had taken a new name, Muhammad Ali. Explaining his timing of the announcement, he said, "When I joined the Nation in 1961, I figured I'd be pressured if I revealed it, so I kept it quiet for about three years. . . . But after beating Sonny Liston, I was getting more recognition and more power. I revealed it after that fight."

Ali was a master at "playing the dozens," a boasting style that angered his opponents and annoyed white reporters covering his bouts. In 1967, however, it was his refusal to be drafted into the military that incurred the wrath of the boxing establishment and white America. Ali argued that his religion was opposed to military service just as it was against civil rights activism and integration. He was the new black man who refused to accept the white man's rules about how to behave. He embodied the assertive black consciousness that invaded social and cultural life in the 1960s and 1970s.

But most black people also adored Ali for other reasons, recalled basketball player Kareem Abdul-Jabbar, who in 1971 discarded the name Lew Alcindor:

> When Ali announced his refusal to accept the draft, I thought it was a very brave stand. . . . A meeting to help Ali was called by black athletes back in 1967. We let black people around the country know that we supported Ali. I think by that time Black Americans understood that their presence in Vietnam was highly disproportionate to their percentage of the American population and that the front-line casualties were being absorbed by Black Americans in much greater numbers than they should have.

A federal court found Ali guilty of draft evasion, but he was released on bail pending his appeal. Ali immediately became a popular antiwar speaker. In June 1970 the Supreme Court overturned his conviction on the grounds that the FBI had illegally wiretapped his telephone.

Actor Harry Belafonte described Ali in admiring terms:

> He brought America to its most wonderful and its most naked moment. "I will not play in your game of war. I will not kill in your behalf. What you ask is immoral, unjust, and I stand here to attest to that fact. Now do with me what you will," he said. I mean he was, in many ways, as inspiring as Dr. King, as inspiring as Malcolm. Cassius was a black, young American. Out of the womb of oppression he was our phoenix, he was the spirit of our young. He was our manhood. . . . He was the vitality of what we hoped would emerge. . . . the perfect machine, the wit, the incredible athlete, the facile, articulate, sharp mind on issues, the great sense of humor, which was out of our tradition.

In 1974 Ali fought George Foreman to regain his world heavyweight boxing title. Four years later he lost the title to Leon Spinks. He regained it, retired, and then attempted a comeback that ended with his October 2, 1980, loss to Larry Holmes. He was elected to the Boxing Hall of Fame in 1987. In 1996 he lit the Olympic Flame to open the summer games in Atlanta.

22-1

22-2

22-3

22-4

22-5

22-6

King's Murder

King's search for a new strategy led him to a closer involvement with labor issues. In February 1968, while attempting to gain union recognition for municipal workers in Memphis, 1,300 members of a virtually all-black sanitation workers local went on strike and, together with the local black community, boycotted downtown merchants. But Mayor Henry Loeb refused to negotiate. On March 18, 1968, responding to a call from James Lawson, a longtime civil rights activist and the minister of Centenary Methodist Church in Memphis, King went to Memphis to address the striking sanitation workers.

The occasion was marked by violence. Nevertheless, King returned to Memphis on April 3 and delivered his last and perhaps most prophetic speech about seeing the promised land. The next day James Earl Ray murdered King as he stood on the balcony of the Lorraine Motel in Memphis. His assassination unleashed a torrent of civic rage in black communities. More than 125 cities experienced uprisings. By April 11, 46 people were dead, 35,000 were injured, and more than 20,000 had been arrested.

In what seemed to many a belated gesture of racial reconciliation, within days of King's assassination, Congress passed the **Civil Rights Act of 1968**. Proposed by Johnson two years before, the act outlawed discrimination in the sale and rental of housing and gave the Justice Department authority to bring suits against such discrimination.

King's assassination also boosted support for the SCLC's faltering Poor People's Campaign. The campaign began in May when more than 2,000 demonstrators settled into a shantytown they called Resurrection City in Washington, DC. For more than a month, they marched daily to federal offices and took part in a mass demonstration on June 19. On June 24, police evicted them, and the campaign ended, leaving an uncertain legacy.

The Black Arts Movement and Black Consciousness

22-4 What was the relationship between the black power movement and black culture?

The years between 1967 and 1975 witnessed some of the most intense political and cultural discussions in the history of the black freedom struggle. Black power stimulated debate about both the future of black politics in the post–civil rights era and the role of black art and artists in the quest for black liberation. Creative people revisited the long-standing issue of whether black art is political or aesthetic. For a decade, discussion about black culture and identity focused on the relationship between art, the artist, and the political movement within the black community. This period became known as the "**black arts movement**." Among the outstanding poets who helped shape the revolutionary movement, introducing new forms of black writing and delivering outspoken attacks on "the white aesthetic" while stressing black beauty and pride, were Sonia Sanchez, Nikki Giovanni, and Don L. Lee (Haki Madhubuti). One of the best examples of Giovanni's militant poems is "The True Import of Present Dialogue, Black vs. Negro," which appeared in her first collection, a self-published volume titled *Black Feeling, Black Talk* (1967). In a shocking opening line, she asked, "nigger/Can you kill/Can you kill/Can a nigger kill/Can a nigger kill a honkie." The poem continues, "Can you kill the nigger/in you/Can you kill your nigger mind/And free your Black hands to/strangle." Sanchez also captured the era's violence and turbulence. In 1970 she published a major collection of poetry, *We a BaddDDD People.* Of equal significance in the development and evolution of this creative flowering was playwright and poet LeRoi Jones.

The formal beginning of the movement was the founding in 1965 of the Black Arts Repertory Theater by Jones, who changed his name to Imamu Amiri Baraka in 1967. Jones was the bridge that linked the political and cultural aspects of black power. He had been associated with the white avant-garde poets in New York in the 1950s and early 1960s, but he began to change in 1965 from an integrationist to a black cultural nationalist.

The guiding ethos of the black arts movement was the determination of black artists to produce black art for black people and thereby to accomplish black liberation. Baraka

22-1

22-2

22-3

22-4

22-5

22-6

Civil Rights Act of 1968 Federal law banning discrimination in housing.

black arts movement Artistic movement that seeks to promote black art by black artists for black people.

declared, "The Black man must seek a Black politics, an ordering of the world that is beneficial to his culture, to his interiorization and judgment of the world. The Black Artist . . . is desperately needed to change the images his people identify with, by asserting Black feeling, Black mind, Black judgment." In 1968 he coedited with Larry Neal the anthology *Black Fire,* which revealed the extent to which black writers and thinkers had rejected integration in favor of a new black consciousness and nationalist political engagement.

Larry Neal, who was part of the Revolutionary Action Movement, defined this important dimension of the freedom struggle:

> The black arts movement is radically opposed to any concept of the artist that alienates him from his community. Black Art is the aesthetic and spiritual sister of the black power concept. As such, it envisions an art that speaks directly to the needs and aspirations of Black Americans. In order to perform this task, the black arts movement proposes a radical reordering of the western cultural aesthetic. It proposes a separate symbolism, mythology, critique, and iconography. The black arts and the black power concept both relate broadly to the Afro-American's desire for self-determination and nationhood. Both concepts are nationalistic. One is concerned with the relationship between art and politics; the other with the art of politics.

The black arts movement was criticized because of its celebration of black maleness, its racial exclusivity, and its homophobia. It was never a unified movement in the sense that all black artists spoke in one voice. There was creative dissent and competing visions of freedom. In 1970 Maya Angelou published an autobiographical novel, *I Know Why the Caged Bird Sings,* which unveiled her experience with sexual abuse and the silencing of black women within black communities. Other black women writers would create a black women's literary renaissance in the 1970s. Still, prominent integrationist writers agreed with some of the black arts movement's tenets and were converted to its principles.

The works of Langston Hughes, Lorraine Hansberry, Gwendolyn Brooks, and James Baldwin linked the black cultural renaissances of the 1930s, 1940s, and 1950s to the black arts movement. Brooks, for example, stressed the commitment of artists to community and the importance of the relationship between the artist and her audience. She had supported community-based arts programs, and it seemed natural that she should "convert" to a black nationalist perspective during the 1960s and join forces with younger artists.

But the most popular black writer of the era was James Baldwin. Baldwin was an integrationist. In his work he had resisted the simple inversion of racial hierarchies that characterized parts of the black power and black arts movements. He wrote, "I think all theories are suspect, that the finest principles may have to be modified, or may even be pulverized by the demands of life, and that one must find therefore, one's own moral center and move through the world hoping that this center will guide one aright." Yet in many ways, Baldwin was as alienated and angry as some of the artists identified with black arts.

In *The Fire Next Time* (1963), he concluded with a phrase that echoed years later through discussions of the rebellions in Watts, Newark, and Detroit: "If we do not now dare everything, the fulfillment of that prophecy, recreated from the bible in song by a slave, is upon us: 'God gave Noah the rainbow sign, No more water, the fire next time!'"

Baldwin was also unflinching about white racism and had a major impact on public discourse. At one point he told his white readers, "There appears to be a vast amount of confusion on this point, but I do not know many Negroes who are eager to be 'accepted' by white people, still less to be loved by them; they, the blacks, simply don't wish to be beaten over the head by the whites every instant of our brief passage on this planet." And in *No Name in the Street,* Baldwin declared, "I agree with the Black Panther position concerning black prisoners: not one of them has ever had a fair trial, for not one of them has ever been tried by a jury of his peers." He explained, "White middle-class America is always the jury, and they know absolutely nothing about the lives of the people on whom they sit in judgment: and this fact is not altered, on the contrary it is rendered more implacable by the presence of one or two black faces in the jury box."

Imamu Amiri Baraka means "spiritual leader, prince, blessed" in Swahili and is the chosen name of LeRoi Jones. The celebrated "father of the black arts movement" remained prolific, influential, and controversial after five decades of creative engagement in America's "culture war."

((• **Listen** on **MyHistoryLab Audio:** *Song of the Front Yard* by Gwendolyn Brooks

22-1
22-2
22-3
22-4
22-5
22-6

22-1

22-2

22-3

22-4

22-5

22-6

((• **Listen** on **MyHistoryLab Audio:**
"Liberation/Poem" by Sonia Sanchez

Poetry and Theater

The black arts movement had its most significant impact in poetry and theater. The movement had three geographical centers: Harlem, Chicago and Detroit, and San Francisco.

The Chicago-based *Negro Digest/Black World,* edited by Hoyt Fuller and published by John Johnson, promoted the new generation of creative artists. Fuller, a well-connected intellectual with an exhaustive command of black literature, became editor of the monthly magazine in 1961. In 1970 he changed the magazine's name to *Black World* to signal the rejection of "Negro" and the adoption of "black" to designate people of African descent. The new name identified African Americans with both the African Diaspora and Africa itself.

In Detroit, Naomi Long Madgett's Lotus Press and Dudley Randall's Broadside Press republished the previous generation of black poets, notably Gwendolyn Brooks, Margaret Walker, and Sterling Brown. In Chicago, poet and literary critic Don L. Lee, who changed his name to Haki Madhubuti, launched Third World Press, which published many of the black arts poets and writers.

The Chicago–Detroit publishing nexus promoted new poets like Nikki Giovanni, Etheridge Knight, and Sonia Sanchez. These and other poets produced some of the most accomplished and experimental work of the black arts movement. It resonated with the sounds of the African-American vernacular, combining the rhythmic cadences of sermons with popular music and black "street speech" into a spirited new form of poetry that was free, conversational, and militantly cool.

Theater was another prominent genre of the black arts movement. Playwright Ed Bullins edited a special issue of the journal *Drama Review* in the summer of 1968 that featured essays and plays by most of the major activists in black arts, including Sonia Sanchez, Ron Milner, and Woodie King, Jr. This volume became the textbook of black arts. In his plays, Bullins, who was greatly influenced by Baraka, portrayed ordinary black life and explored the inner forces that prevented black people from realizing their own liberation and potential. He showed how racism had deformed the black experience and consciousness. Across the country, local black communities formed their own theater groups, including Val Gray Ward's Kuumba Workshop in Chicago and Baraka's Spirit House Theater in New Jersey. These groups hosted seminars, guest appearances, fashion shows, art exhibits, dance recitals, parades, and media parties.

On the West Coast, in 1969, Robert Chrisman and Nathan Hare launched *The Black Scholar,* the first serious journal to promote black studies. Chrisman compared the black arts movement with the Harlem Renaissance of the 1920s: "More so than the Harlem Renaissance, in which Black artists were always on the leash of white patrons and publishing houses, the black arts movement did it for itself. Black people going out nationally, in mass, saying we are an independent Black people and this is what we produce."

Music

The cultural nationalists in the black arts movement championed modern jazz musicians as icons of the quest for black freedom. Baraka argued that jazz and other black music were the language that black people developed to give uncensored accounts of their experiences. He and other cultural nationalists believed music could promote black identity and encourage the pride that was vital for political struggle. The jazzmen's music was often dense and austere, but it could also be powerfully primitive and dazzlingly complex. Above all, the music appeared to challenge Western conceptions of harmony, rhythm, melody, and tone. In jazz you have to improvise, to create your own form of expression by using whatever information inspires you. The emphasis is not on an original score but on individual articulation.

Cultural nationalists perceived jazz to be a self-consciously engaged, economically independent, politically useful art form. Novelist Ralph Ellison put it most succinctly:

> True jazz is an art of individual assertion within and against the group. Each true jazz
> moment (as distinct from the uninspired commercial performance) springs from a contest
> in which each artist challenges all the rest; each solo flight, or improvisation, represents (like
> the successive canvases of a painter) a definition of his identity: as individual, as member of
> the collectivity and as a link in the chain of tradition.

PROFILE Lorraine Hansberry

PLAYWRIGHT LORRAINE HANSBERRY was, arguably, the artist/activist who spoke most powerfully to three generations of African Americans. Her play *A Raisin in the Sun* has inspired audiences and readers from the 1950s through the civil rights movement to the hip-hop era. Hansberry grew up on the South Side of Chicago and attended the University of Wisconsin, the Art Institute of Chicago, and Roosevelt College (now University) before settling in New York City.

Before achieving national acclaim for *Raisin*, Hansberry worked for Paul Robeson's Harlem newspaper, *Freedom*. In a 1955 essay for the paper, "Life Challenges Negro Youth," she declared, "From the time he is born, the Negro child is surrounded by a society organized to convince him that he belongs to a people whose past is so worthless and shameful that it amounts to no past at all. . . . In a land where the Grace Kelly-Marilyn Monroe monotype 'ideal' is imposed on the national culture, racist logic insists that anything directly opposite—no matter how lovely—is naturally ugly."

In 1953 Hansberry married Robert Nemiroff, but they separated soon after when she told him that she was a lesbian. She and Nemiroff remained close friends and collaborators, however, and the larger world never knew about her sexual identity. Like Bayard Rustin, Hansberry was acutely aware of the homophobia in American society. She disclosed her private life only to a few trusted friends.

In 1965 Hansberry died of pancreatic cancer. Six hundred people attended her funeral, including Malcolm X, James Forman, Nina Simone, Sammy Davis, Jr., Ossie Davis, and Ruby Dee. Martin Luther King, Jr., and James Baldwin sent messages. Paul Robeson delivered a eulogy.

A Raisin in the Sun premiered on Broadway in 1959 to rave reviews. Hansberry explained, "I wrote it between my 26th and 27th birthday. One night, after seeing a play I won't mention, I suddenly became disgusted with a whole body of material about Negroes. Card board characters. Cute dialect bits. Or hip-swinging musicals from exotic scores. . . . Even the most sympathetic novel for the Negro . . . happens to have been built around the most offensive character in American literature—who is Uncle Tom." In *Raisin*, Hansberry captured the tribulations of the Younger family's attempt to move from their crowded apartment in Chicago's Bronzeville to a house in the suburbs and what they hope will be a better life. It is a story of upward mobility running up against American racism. Walter Lee Younger wants to use the money from his father's insurance policy to open a liquor store. His mother wants to buy a house for the extended family. His sister wants the money to help pay her tuition to medical school. Their mother prevails and holds the family together even when a friend swindles Walter Lee out of most of the money, and racist neighbors make it clear that the Youngers are not welcome. At the end of the play, the Youngers move into the new home as a united family even though their future there is uncertain.

In 2004, hip-hop impresario Sean (P. Diddy) Combs revived *Raisin* on Broadway and played the role of Walter Lee that Sidney Poitier had played in the original production. Such was the excitement generated by a play still powerfully resonant 45 years after its premier that the producers recouped their $2.6 million investment within two months. Lorraine Hansberry's writing still inspires artists to deploy their art in the struggle for liberation from the biases and fears that oppress and dehumanize people because of their race, class, gender, and sexual identity.

This outlook explains why Miles Davis's legendary album *Kind of Blue* (1959), one of the most progressive jazz albums ever produced, also became one of the most popular. Davis showed that art could be accessible without sacrificing excellence and rigor. Davis, in the words of one admirer, was able to "dance underwater and not get wet." For black cultural nationalists, Davis projected an image of uncompromising and uncompromised black identity.

Among other celebrated jazz musicians were Archie Shepp, Ornette Coleman, Pharoah Sanders, Eric Dolphy, Thelonious Monk, and John Coltrane. Playwright Ronald Milner described Coltrane as "a man who through his saxophone before your eyes and ears completely annihilates every single western influence." Coltrane also played the deep—and deeply political—blues of "Alabama" written in response to the Birmingham church bombings.

Jazz, however, tended to appeal to intellectuals. Most black people preferred rhythm and blues, gospel, and soul. During the height of the black consciousness movement, black popular musicians gave performances to raise funds and assert racial pride. Aretha Franklin and Ray Charles, for example, allowed SNCC workers to attend their concerts for free. Just as the freedom songs had done, the soul music of the black power era helped unify black people.

No history of the era would be complete without mentioning the performances of the "Godfather of Soul," James Brown; the "Queen of Soul," Aretha Franklin, best known for her powerful rendition of the song "Respect"; and the financial contributions of Berry Gordy of Motown. James Brown's "Say It Loud, I'm Black and I'm Proud" became an anthem for the era. Brown linked commercial marketing to social commentary, confronting American racism with racial pride and righteous indignation. He confessed, "I may not do as much as some other individuals who have made it big," but, "you can bet your life that I'm doing the best I can. . . . I owe it to the black community to help provide scholarships, to help children stay in school, to help equip playgrounds and recreation centers, and to keep kids off the streets." Brown was "totally committed to black power, the kind that is achieved not through the muzzle of a rifle but through education and economic leverage."

Berry Gordy contributed to black freedom struggles both artistically and financially. To support King's Chicago movement, Gordy arranged for Stevie Wonder to give a benefit concert at Soldier Field in Chicago. He contributed to black candidates, the NAACP and its Legal Defense and Educational Fund, and the Urban League.

With Gordy's encouragement, his performers flirted just enough with black radicalism to gain a patina of militancy. During the late 1960s and early 1970s, the musical and lyrical innovations of the Temptations, Stevie Wonder, and Marvin Gaye reflected Motown's politicization. In an address to one of the sessions launching Jesse Jackson's People United to Save Humanity (PUSH) in 1971, Gordy declared, "I have been fortunate to be able to provide opportunities for young people. . . . Opportunities are supposed to knock once in a lifetime, but too often we have to knock for an opportunity. The first obligation we (as black businessmen) have is to ourselves and our own employees, the second is to create opportunities for others." Musician Curtis Mayfield explained simply, "Our purpose is to educate as well as to entertain. Painless preaching is as good a term as any for what we do."

The Black Student Movement

The most dramatic expression of militant assertiveness after 1968 occurred among black college students. The black power generation of students was committed to transforming society and institutions of higher education by agitating for curricula reform and the establishment of Black Studies programs and departments. Some observers describe the period of activism between 1968 and 1975 as the "second phase" of the black students' movement.

The Orangeburg Massacre

In this view, students at southern black colleges launched the first phase in the early 1960s. It began with the sit-ins in Greensboro, North Carolina, and the Freedom Rides and culminated in the Mississippi Freedom Summer of 1964. By 1968, however, many of the student organizations that had grown out of the civil rights movement were invested in mobilizing local communities to overthrow the remaining vestiges of overt discrimination and segregation. The massacre of black students at South Carolina State College in Orangeburg on February 8, 1968, was an appalling demonstration of state violence and a failure of the justice system. Students attending the historically black institution had protested a local bowling alley's whites-only admission policy. When the tension and protests escalated, state officials deployed the highway patrol and National Guard. On the evening of February 8, the students assembled at the front of the campus and taunted the officers. Some threw rocks, bricks, and bottles. One officer was hit by a piece of lumber. Later, without warning, nine highway patrolmen opened fire on the students with shotguns. The officers killed three young men and wounded 28. Most of them were shot in the back. All the officers involved were later acquitted, but a young black activist and SNCC leader, Cleveland Sellers, was convicted of rioting and served nearly a year in prison. He was pardoned in 1993. On February 8, 2001, South Carolina Governor James Hodges apologized to a group of survivors who had assembled in Orangeburg. Since 2008, Dr. Cleveland Sellers has served as president of the traditionally black institution, Voorhees College, in Denmark, South Carolina.

Black Studies

The movement for Black Studies and the transformation of college curriculums owed some of its inspiration to the black power and black arts movements. The Black Studies revolution on campus began with the enrollment of large numbers of black students in predominantly white institutions across the country. These students demanded courses in black history, culture, literature, and art as alternatives to the "Eurocentric" bias of the average university curriculum. Many black students also formed all-black organizations, such as the Black Allied Students' Association at New York University and the Black Organization of Students at Rutgers University.

South Carolina State College Massacre, 1968, Orangeburg, South Carolina. The three young men killed in the Orangeburg Massacre were Henry Smith and Samuel Hammond, both 18, and 17-year-old high school student Delano Middleton. See *Scarred Justice* (2008), a powerful and illuminating PBS documentary film by Judy Richardson.

Black students understood that education was essential to empowerment. In 1967 black students accounted for only 2 percent of the total enrollment at predominantly white colleges and universities. This meant that only 95,000 African Americans were among the approximately five million full-time undergraduates at these schools. Rutgers University in New Jersey provides a case study. Out of 24,000 baccalaureate degrees it awarded between 1952 and 1967, only about 200 went to African Americans. Federal legislation—especially the Civil Rights Act of 1964 and the Higher Education Act of 1965—outlawed discrimination or segregation in higher education, and by instituting an array of financial aid programs, it spurred colleges and universities to recruit black students. Where there had been about 100 black undergraduates at Rutgers in 1965, there were more than 400 by 1968, nearly 3 percent of the undergraduate enrollment.

On the national level, the overall status of black people in education reflected the accomplishments of the classic phase of the civil rights movement, but the black power generation was determined to make its own mark on the struggle. In 1960 only 227,000 black Americans attended the nation's colleges (including those at predominantly black institutions). By 1970, enrollments had increased by 100 percent, and in 1977, 1.1 million black students attended America's universities. This was an almost 500 percent increase over 1960. This generation of students was politically diverse, but they shared the sense of being strangers in a white-controlled environment. Many found the campuses hostile, alien places and discovered little there with which they could identify. They resolved to change this.

At San Francisco State College, Nathan Hare, formerly a professor at Howard University, and black students demanded not only curriculum changes but also the structural transformation of the college. In the 1966–1967 academic year, the Black Student Union orchestrated a strike that involved thousands of students of diverse ethnic and racial backgrounds. The students chose to strike rather than take over buildings so that they could circulate on the campus, increasing their support and maintaining their momentum. Among their demands were the creation of an autonomous degree-granting black studies department and the admission of more black students. The college ultimately created the first black studies department in 1968, with Hare as its head.

Black students also took over administration buildings at other institutions such as Northwestern University, demanding not only that the schools offer more black studies courses and programs and hire more black faculty but also insisting that classrooms and facilities be made available to local black communities. The upheavals that shut down Columbia University in 1968 began when black student members of the Students Afro-American Society and Students for a Democratic Society demonstrated to block construction of a university gymnasium in nearby Morningside Park. The demonstrators argued that the gym would impinge on one of the few parks in Harlem and that the Harlem community vehemently objected to it.

In 1968 Yale University's Black Student Alliance sponsored a symposium to discuss the need, status, and function of Afro-American studies. Conference organizer Armstead Robinson saw it as an attempt to create a viable program of Afro-American studies. In December 1968 the faculty voted to make Yale one of the first major universities in the country to institute a degree-granting African-American studies program. In 1969 Harvard University created an Afro-American Studies Department, and other schools soon followed. In 1969 the Institute of the Black World in Atlanta conducted a project to define the methods and purpose of black studies and then sponsored a black studies directors' seminar. Ron Karenga wrote what remains a major textbook for the new field, *Introduction to Black Studies.* By 1973 some 200 black studies programs existed in the United States. By the late 1980s, several of the programs, such as those at Cornell, Yale, and the University of California, Los Angeles, offered master's degrees in African-American studies. In 1988 Temple University in Philadelphia, under the leadership of Dr. Molefi Kete Asante, became the first university to offer a Ph.D. in African-American studies. In 2002, Michigan State University became the sixth to offer the doctorate in the discipline. In 2006 Northwestern University welcomed its first group of five students into the new graduate program in African-American studies. By 2012 there were at least a dozen doctoral programs in African and African-American Studies.

While there is no universally accepted definition of Black Studies, the discipline has continued to evolve. James E. Turner, founder of Africana studies at Cornell, viewed Black Studies as a collective, interdisciplinary, scholarly approach to the experiences of people of African descent throughout the African Diaspora and the world. History, in black studies, constituted the foundation for analyzing common patterns of life and thought that reflected the social and material conditions of black people. Africana studies or black studies theoreticians have generally agreed on four goals for this new field: (1) it should develop solutions to the problems facing black people in the African Diaspora; (2) it should provide an analysis of black culture and life that challenges and replaces preexisting Eurocentric models; (3) it should promote social change and educational reform throughout the academy; and (4) it should institutionalize the study of black people as a field with its own theories, methods, ideologies, symbols, language, and culture. In short, the first generation of advocates envisioned black studies as a revolutionary, historically grounded, educational reform movement that sought to make the study of African descendants—their culture, problems, belief systems, internationalism, radical traditions, and spirituality—a serious scholarly endeavor with practical implications for improving black people's lives.

The Presidential Election of 1968 and Richard Nixon

22-5 What specific policies did President Nixon initiate that affected the civil rights of African Americans?

In the presidential campaign of 1968, the Democrats provided the excitement but lost the election. In late 1967 Senator Eugene McCarthy of Minnesota entered the race as the anti-war alternative to Lyndon Johnson, Senator Robert Kennedy of New York entered the race in mid-March, after most of the convention delegates had been pledged to Johnson. When Johnson withdrew, these delegates aligned with Humphrey. Whether Kennedy could have gained the nomination will never be known. In the second traumatic assassination of 1968, Robert Kennedy was killed on June 6 in Los Angeles.

A combustible mixture of grief, anger, bitterness, and antiwar sentiment became the fuel for a Chicago explosion. It was the most tumultuous political convention in modern American history, with Chicago policemen clubbing, gassing, and arresting antiwar demonstrators. In November, Republican Richard Nixon narrowly defeated Humphrey.

Of all modern presidents, Richard Nixon is probably the hardest to pin down with neat ideological labels. By the standards of the early twentieth-first century, much of his record seems progressive. He created the Environmental Protection Agency, endorsed an equal rights amendment to the Constitution that would have prohibited gender discrimination, and signed more regulatory legislation than any other president. His naming of Daniel Patrick Moynihan, one of Johnson's experts on social policy, to be his domestic policy adviser illustrates his willingness to innovate in policies affecting African Americans. But Nixon also pursued a "southern strategy" that realigned the Republican Party with the white southern backlash to civil rights and weakened the New Deal coalition.

The "Moynihan Report"

Moynihan first attracted national attention as assistant secretary of labor in the Johnson administration when a confidential memorandum he wrote—loosely organized and full of sweeping generalizations—was leaked to the press. It would later be published as "The Negro Family: The Case for National Action" and is popularly known as the "**Moynihan Report**." Moynihan's guiding assumption was that civil rights legislation, necessary as it was, would not address the problems of the inner city. There, he argued, the breakdown of the "lower-class" black family had led to the "pathology" of juvenile delinquency, illegitimacy, drug addiction, and poor performance in school. He attributed the vulnerability of the black family to "three centuries of almost unimaginable treatment" by white society: exploitation under slavery, the strain of urbanization, and persistent unemployment.

These forces, he argued, weakened the role of black men and resulted in a disproportionate number of dysfunctional female-headed families. In the report's most-often repeated passage, Moynihan declared that the black community had been forced into "a matriarchal structure, [which] because it is so out of line with the rest of American society, seriously retards the progress of the group as a whole, and imposes a crushing burden on the Negro male. . . . Obviously, not every instance of social pathology afflicting the Negro community can be traced to the weakness of family structure . . . [but] once or twice removed, it will be found to be the principal source of most of the aberrant, inadequate, or anti-social behavior that did not establish, but now serves to perpetuate the cycle of poverty and deprivation."

Although based on the work of black scholars, such as E. Franklin Frazier, Moynihan's condemnation of "matriarchy" drew fire. Black social scientists, such as Joyce Ladner, Andrew Billingsley, and Carol Stack, countered that the structure of the black family reflected a functional adaptation that black people had made to survive in a hostile and racist American society. Historians Herbert Gutman and John Blassingame argued that Moynihan underestimated the prevalence of two-parent black families in the past. Although many of the criticisms of the report were deserved, they diverted attention from its positive thrust. Moynihan wanted to eliminate poverty and unemployment in the black community, and he recommended vigorous enforcement of the civil rights laws to achieve equality of opportunity. Moynihan was one of the first policymakers to appreciate how white resentment of the CAPs and the expansion of the welfare rolls would make both programs politically unfeasible.

Intrigued with Moynihan's independence, Nixon told him to develop a plan to assist poor families. Under the **Family Assistance Plan (FAP)** that Nixon unveiled in the summer of 1969, each family of four with no wage earner would receive an annual payment of $1,600 plus $800 of food stamps. With its across-the-board guarantee of income, the

Moynihan Report Report attributing many of the problems of poor black communities to the breakdown of the "lower-class" black family.

Family Assistance Plan (FAP) Plan giving financial assistance to families with no wage earner.

plan eliminated an oppressive welfare bureaucracy and reduced the invidious comparison between "welfare recipients" and everyone else.

Had it passed, FAP would have promoted two-parent families by removing the prohibition against assistance to dependent children whose fathers were alive, well, and living at home. It would also have encouraged work by requiring able-bodied recipients to accept jobs or vocational training and by providing benefits to those accepting low-paying jobs. But although the House approved the plan, the Senate—under pressure from conservatives who objected to any government programs for the poor and from welfare-rights advocates who complained the payments were too low—killed it. Arguably, at least until President Clinton's abortive healthcare plan in the 1990s, Nixon's FAP was the most significant failed initiative in the history of American social policy.

Busing

Yet, however flexible he might have been on many issues, Nixon was acutely aware that he moved in a changed political environment and particularly in a far more conservative Republican Party. In 1968 it was an influx of southern segregationists whom Barry Goldwater had attracted to the Republican Party in 1964 who Nixon had to appease. For example, South Carolina's Senator Strom Thurmond and his allies demanded that Nixon slow down court-ordered school desegregation in the South.

The Nixon administration crafted a southern strategy and embarked on a collision course with civil rights organizations such as the NAACP, which supported busing to achieve school integration. Thus, the major battle over civil rights in the early 1970s was over the federal courts' willingness to implement desegregation goals by busing students across district lines. Nixon, in 1971, advised federal officials to stop pressing to desegregate schools through "forced busing." He argued that such efforts were ultimately "counterproductive, and not in the interest of better race relations."

Educational segregation in the North reflected residential segregation. In Boston, site of some of the most acrimonious busing protests, schools in black neighborhoods received less funding than their white counterparts. Buildings were derelict, overcrowded, and deficient in supplies and equipment, even desks. In 1974 U.S. Judge W. Arthur Garrity ruled in favor of black parents who had filed a class-action suit against the Boston School Committee. The ruling found the committee guilty of violating the equal protection clause of the Fourteenth Amendment. To achieve racial balance in the Boston schools, the judge ordered the busing of several thousand students between mostly white South Boston, Hyde Park, and Dorchester and mostly black Roxbury.

White people who opposed busing organized demonstrations and boycotts to prevent their children from being bused into black communities, as well as to prevent black children from being bused into white schools. During the first week of busing, white students and their mothers clashed with police officers outside South Boston High School. Hostilities continued for weeks despite the arrests of dozens of people and the closing of bars and liquor stores. Sporadic violence persisted for another two years in Boston.

Nixon and the War

Meanwhile, the war in Vietnam seemed to drag on endlessly, with the peace negotiations that had begun in Paris in May 1968 making no apparent progress. Nixon realized that what most Americans disliked about the war was that it was killing their sons and husbands. So in 1969 he began to phase out direct U.S. involvement in the war. This "Vietnamization," he claimed, was made possible by the growing ability of the South Vietnamese to fight for themselves. What Nixon did not say was that the morale of American soldiers was plunging rapidly. Drug abuse among troops was widespread; some soldiers had killed their officers, and some of those incidents had racial overtones. Along with his domestic record, Nixon's promise to "wind down the war" assured his reelection. In 1972 he defeated South Dakota Senator George McGovern in a landslide.

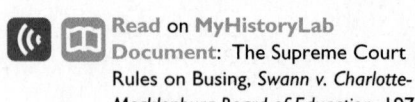

Read on **MyHistoryLab**
Document: The Supreme Court Rules on Busing, *Swann v. Charlotte-Mecklenburg Board of Education*, 1971

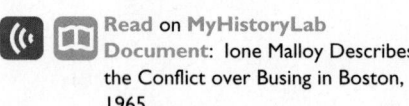

Read on **MyHistoryLab**
Document: Ione Malloy Describes the Conflict over Busing in Boston, 1965

Few in the Nixon administration, however, took South Vietnam's military capability seriously, and Nixon, just as much as Johnson, was unwilling to "lose" Vietnam. Between 1969 and 1971, Nixon stepped up the war. Even as American soldiers were being sent home, he escalated the air war. In Cambodia in 1969–1970, for example, the United States dropped more bombs than it had on all of Asia in World War II.

But each time Nixon escalated the war—in 1970 with a joint American–South Vietnamese invasion of Cambodia, in 1971 with American air support for an invasion of Laos, and in 1972 with the bombing of North Vietnam and the mining of its harbors—opposition to it grew. Antiwar demonstrations kept Nixon off balance and may have deterred him from further escalation.

The most dramatic protests came after the invasion of Cambodia in April 1970, which triggered antiwar demonstrations on many campuses. In one such protest, on May 4, Ohio National Guardsmen shot and killed four white students at Kent State University. The response of students across the country was electric: the first nationwide student strike in American history. Ten days later in Mississippi, the shooting and killing of two black students at Jackson State University attracted much less attention from either white students or the media. Finally, in 1973, the United States and North Vietnam signed a peace agreement. Congress then prohibited the reintroduction of American troops or the resumption of bombing, and in 1974 it began cutting off military aid to South Vietnam. The result was predictable: in 1975 the communists launched another offensive, and South Vietnam collapsed.

Nixon became president in 1969 with popular mandates to restore law and order. The disorder that irritated the American public included many things: the inner-city riots, the antiwar demonstrations and campus protests, and the rise in crime. Responding to this mood, Nixon pushed legislation through Congress that gave local law enforcement officials expanded power to use wiretaps and enter premises without advance warning.

But Nixon's personality—a combination of paranoia and ruthlessness—pushed him beyond what the public would tolerate and even beyond the law itself. He confused criminals with principled protesters and political opponents and decided to punish them all. He created an extralegal ring of burglars, operating out of the White House, to gather incriminating information about his opponents. In June 1972 these burglars were caught breaking into Democratic National Committee headquarters in the Watergate apartment complex in Washington. Full details emerged in a Senate investigation in 1973–1974, and on August 9, 1974, threatened with impeachment, Nixon resigned. His downfall, however, left no one of his stature or with his flexible attitude toward public policy to resist the takeover of the Republican Party by more dogmatic conservatives. One early intimation of this was the difficulty Nixon's successor, Gerald Ford, had in securing the 1976 Republican presidential nomination against the right's new hero, former California Governor Ronald Reagan.

 Read on **MyHistoryLab**
Document: Mayor Maynard Jackson Talks about Race and Politics in Atlanta, 1975

The Rise of Black Elected Officials

22-6 | **What were some of the political accomplishments of the black power movement in the 1970s?**

In the black power movement that followed the civil rights movement, a new generation of black leaders gained prominence. They were determined to mobilize the newly enfranchised black electorate to win political office. After the Voting Rights Act of 1965, Vernon Jordan, director of the Voter Education Project, coordinated registration drives across the South. As he explained, "Too many of these people have been alienated from the political process for too long a time . . . and so we have to . . . teach them what a local government is, how it operates, and try to relate their votes to the things they want."

By 1974 there were 1,593 black elected officials outside the South and 2,455 by 1980. Although black people in northern cities had been able to vote for a century and had been

TABLE 22-1 BLACK POWER POLITICS: THE ELECTION OF BLACK MAYORS, 1967-1990

Cities	Names	Years in Office
Atlanta, Georgia	Maynard H. Jackson	(1974–82) ; (1990–94)
	Andrew J. Young	(1982–90)
Chicago, Illinois	Harold L. Washington	(1983–90)
Cleveland, Ohio	Carl B. Stokes	(1967–72)
Compton, California	Doris A. Davis	(1973–77)
Detroit, Michigan	Coleman A. Young	(1973–93)
Gary, Indiana	Richard G. Hatcher	(1967–87)
Los Angeles, California	Thomas J. Bradley	(1973–93)
Memphis, Tennessee	Willie W. Herenton	(1991–2009)
Newark, New Jersey	Kenneth A. Gibson	(1970–86)
New Orleans, Louisiana	Ernest N. Morial	(1978–86)
New York, New York	David N. Dinkins	(1990–94)
Raleigh, North Carolina	Clarence E. Lightner	(1973–75)
Roanoke, Virginia	Noel C. Taylor	(1975–92)
Washington, DC	Walter E. Washington	(1974–79)
	Marion S. Barry, Jr.	(1980–90); (1994–98)

African American Mayors of Metropolitan Cities with Populations over 50,000

slowly developing political muscle and winning representation in state legislatures and on city councils, they had not been able to command an equal voice in city governance. The rise of black power and the Voting Rights Act, however, signaled a new departure. People now eagerly engaged in the electoral process to achieve the political influence to which their numbers entitled them. In 1967 in Cleveland, where the black population had skyrocketed after World War II, Carl Stokes became the first black mayor of a major American city (see Table 22–1), winning with the support of white business leaders and the solid backing of the black community. In the same year prosecutor Richard G. Hatcher became mayor of Gary, Indiana, where the black population had also increased greatly after the war. Hatcher won by a mere 1,389 votes, garnering 96 percent of the black vote and 14 percent of the white vote.

The Gary Convention and the Black Political Agenda

These victories made possible one of the most significant events of postwar black political history, the Gary National Black Political Convention of 1972. The co-chairs of the convention were Detroit Congressman Charles Diggs, Hatcher, and writer Amiri Baraka. Political scientist Ronald Walters, who helped plan the convention, recalled that various ideological factions had to be placated to make it work: "The most important thing about 1972 was the fact that it was an election year, so it provided the environment for the politics taking place. So you had two groups of people who saw this as an opportunity to make some very important statements. One of these, of course, was the black nationalist movement led by Amiri Baraka, Maulana Karenga, and others at that time." The nationalists interpreted "black power" to mean that black people should control their own communities and create separate cultural institutions distinct from those of white society. These views clashed with those of the black elected officials represented by Stokes and Hatcher. According to Walters, "It was this body of people who really were contending for the national leadership of the black community in the early seventies. And in the seventies this new group of black elected officials joined the civil rights leaders and became a new leadership class, but there was sort of a conflict in outlook between them and the more indigenous, social, grass roots-oriented nationalist movement."

Hatcher observed that "people had come to Gary from communities all over the United States where they were politically impotent, but . . . they went back home and rolled up their sleeves and dived into the political arena." Approximately 8,000 people gathered to develop an agenda for black empowerment. The discussions about bloc voting, the efficacy of coalitions, and the feasibility of a third party inspired scores of individual African Americans to run for local office. The convention was not homogeneous, however, and no unified black consensus emerged.

Discussions over strategies to secure common interests revealed deep-seated internal divisions that allowed ancillary issues to provoke even more impassioned disagreement. Coleman Young and other Michigan delegates walked out to protest a proposal for African Americans to reject "discriminatory" unions and form their own. Others walked out over a resolution condemning Israel for its "expansionist policy" toward the Palestinians. Others argued that "forced racial integration of schools" through busing insulted black students and would cost black teachers their jobs.

Nonetheless, the Gary convention signaled a shift in the political focus of the black community toward electoral politics and away from mass demonstrations and protests. Unity continued to elude subsequent conventions, however, and delegates at the last National Black Convention at Little Rock, Arkansas, in 1974 abandoned the idea of a black political party. Deep ideological differences and institutional cleavages precluded coalitions and cooperation between black nationalists and the rising numbers of black elected officials. These same differences prevented some nationalists and elected officials from taking seriously the 1972 Democratic Party presidential bid of New York Congresswoman Shirley Chisholm.

Shirley Chisholm: "I Am the People's Politician"

Shirley Anita St. Hill was born on November 20, 1924, in Brooklyn, New York, to Charles St. Hill, a factory laborer from Guyana, and Ruby Seale St. Hill, a seamstress from Barbados. She earned a B.A. from Brooklyn College in sociology in 1946 and worked as a nursery school teacher and then as director of two day care centers. In 1949 she married Conrad Q. Chisholm, a private investigator. From 1964 to 1968 she served in the New York State Assembly. In 1968 Chisholm defeated James Farmer, former leader of CORE, to become the first African-American woman to serve in Congress. In 1970 she published her first autobiography, *Unbought and Unbossed*. A second autobiography, *The Good Fight* (1973), described her 1972 campaign for the Democratic presidential nomination—during which she received little support from white women's organizations or from black men. Chisholm retired from politics in 1983. In the late 1960s and early 1970s, she remained an outspoken critic of the Vietnam War and a fierce proponent of the war on poverty.

Black People Gain Local Offices

Despite the demise of the National Black Convention movement, African Americans registered impressive gains in electoral politics. Statistics indicate the success of black politicians. When the leaders first convened the Gary convention, there were 13 African-American members of Congress. By 2010 there were 42. In 1972 there were 2,427 black elected officials, among them Texas state senator Barbara Jordan. By 2001 there were 9,101.

An amendment to the Voting Rights Act in 1975 enabled minorities to challenge at-large voting practices that diluted the impact of bloc voting. This helped increase the number of black elected officials. Districts were redrawn with race as the predominant factor. On November 5, 1985, state senator L. Douglas Wilder was elected lieutenant governor in Virginia, making him the first African-American lieutenant governor in a southern state since Reconstruction. In 1989 he was elected governor, making him the first black governor of any state since Reconstruction.

Shirley Chisholm was outspoken against the Vietnam War and a fierce advocate of women's rights.

22-1

22-2

22-3

22-4

22-5

22-6

VOICES | Shirley Chisholm's Speech to the U.S. House of Representatives

Excerpts from "The Business of America Is War, and It Is Time for a Change," March 16, 1969

"Secretary of Defense Melvin Laird came to Capitol Hill. . . . His mission was to sell the antiballistic-missile insanity to the Senate. . . . Mr. Laird talked of being prepared to spend at least two more years in Vietnam. Two more years, two more years of hunger for Americans, of death for our best young men, of children here at home suffering the lifelong handicap of not having a good education when they are young.

Two more years of high taxes, collected to feed the cancerous growth of a Defense Department budget that now consumes two-thirds of our federal income. Two more years of too little being done to fight our greatest enemies, poverty, prejudice and neglect, here in our own country. Two more years of fantastic waste in the Defense Department and of penny pinching on social programs. Our country cannot survive two more years, or four, of these kinds of policies. It must stop—this year—now. . . .

We Americans have come to feel that it is our mission to make the world free. We believe that we are the good guys, everywhere—in Vietnam, in Latin America, wherever we go. We believe we are the good guys at home,

too. When the Kerner Commission told white America what black America had always known, that prejudice and hatred built the nation's slums, maintain them and profit by them, white America would not believe it. But it is true. Unless we start to fight and defeat the enemies of poverty and racism in our own country and make our talk of equality and opportunity ring true, we are exposed as hypocrites in the eyes of the world when we talk about making other people free.

We are now spending eighty billion dollars a year on defense—that is two-thirds of every tax dollar. At this time, gentlemen, the business of America is war, and it is time for a change."

1. **What reasons does Chisholm give for her opposition to the war in Vietnam?**

2. **What connections does she draw between support for the war and poverty and racism in the United States?**

SOURCE: Warren J. Halliburton, ed., *Historic Speeches of African Americans* (New York: Franklin Watts, 1993). 141–43.

Between 1971 and 1975, the number of African-American mayors rose from 8 to 135, leading to the founding of the National Conference of Black Mayors in 1974. In 1973 Coleman Young in Detroit and Thomas Bradley in Los Angeles became the first African-American mayors of cities of more than a million citizens. Bradley won in Los Angeles even though black people made up only 15 percent of the city's electorate. Ten years later, in 1983, Chicago swore in its first black mayor, Harold Washington. The era of the black elected official had arrived.

Economic Downturn

The 1970s were a decade of recessions and economic instability. Many black people experienced this economic downturn as a depression. During the 1970s, as the gap between the incomes of the upper 20 percent of African Americans and their white counterparts narrowed, the gap between black men and women at the bottom of the economic ladder and their white counterparts expanded. Poor black people were losing ground. In 1969 approximately 10 percent of white men and 25 percent of black men earned less than $10,000 (in 1984 constant dollars). In 1984 about 40 percent of black men between age 25 and 55 earned less than $10,000 compared with 20 percent of comparable white men. Put a different way, between 1970 and 1986, the proportion of black families with incomes of less than $10,000 grew from 26.8 to 30.2 percent. Still, there were some improvements. The black middle class grew. In 1970, 4.7 percent of black families had incomes of more than $50,000. By 1986 the number had almost doubled to 8.8 percent. But, in general, the relative economic status of black workers did not improve.

Black Americans and the Carter Presidency

In 1976 the United States celebrated its bicentennial. Flags flew, and fire hydrants were painted red, white, and blue. Tall ships sailed into New York Harbor from around the world, and there were more parades than anyone could count. For African Americans, it was an important year, but for another reason. For the first time since 1964, the man most of them voted for was elected president—Jimmy Carter, a former governor of Georgia. Ninety percent of African-American voters favored the soft-spoken, religious Democrat over President Gerald Ford. As in 1960, their votes were crucial. Without them, Carter could not have even carried his native South.

Black Appointees

Carter acknowledged his debt to the black electorate by appointing African Americans to highly visible posts. He named Patricia Harris secretary of housing and urban development, making her the first black woman to serve in the cabinet. Carter appointed Andrew Young, former congressman from Georgia and a longtime political ally, ambassador to the United Nations. (Young was forced to resign in 1979.) Clifford Alexander, Jr., became the secretary

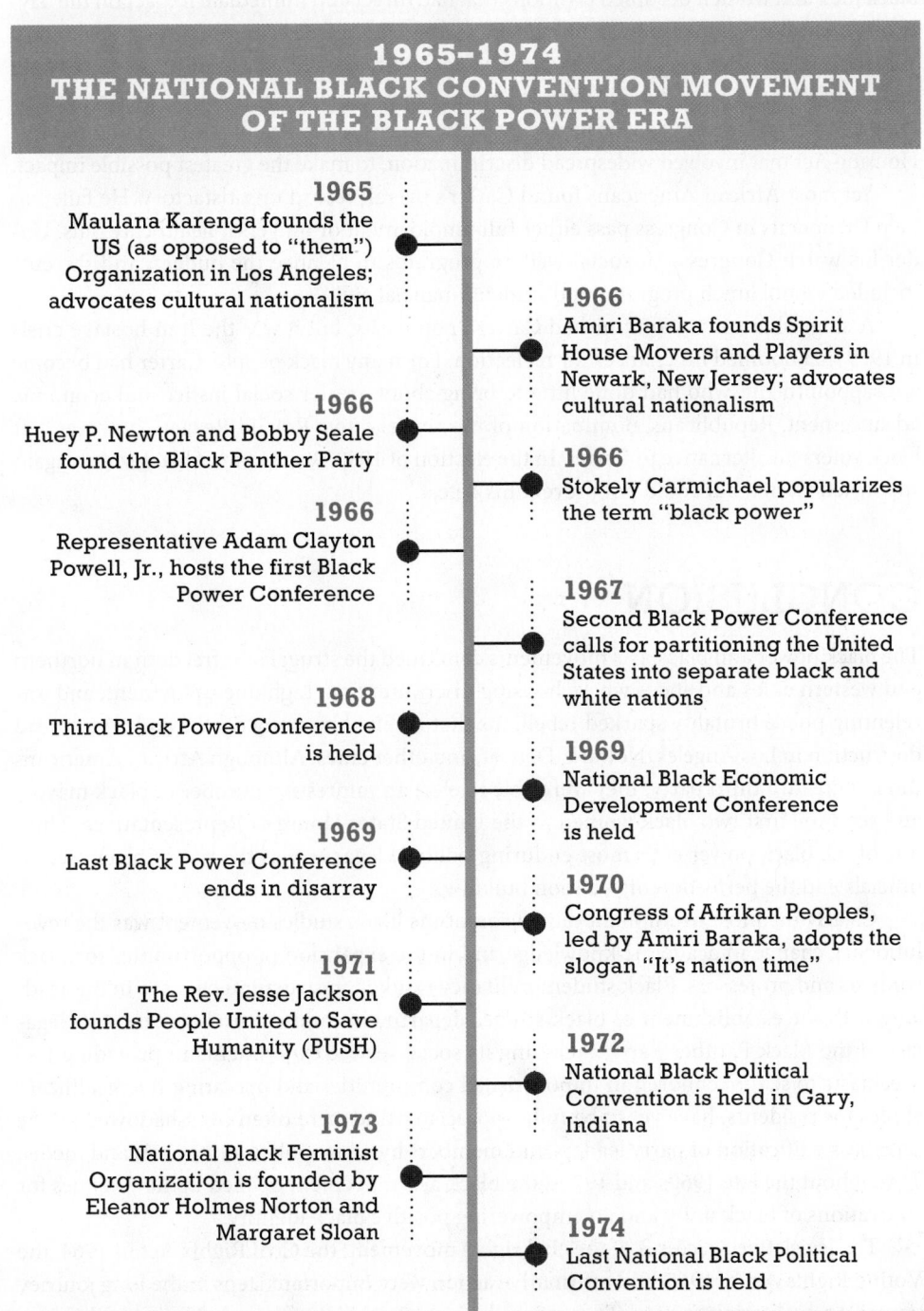

1965–1974
THE NATIONAL BLACK CONVENTION MOVEMENT OF THE BLACK POWER ERA

1965
Maulana Karenga founds the US (as opposed to "them") Organization in Los Angeles; advocates cultural nationalism

1966
Amiri Baraka founds Spirit House Movers and Players in Newark, New Jersey; advocates cultural nationalism

1966
Huey P. Newton and Bobby Seale found the Black Panther Party

1966
Stokely Carmichael popularizes the term "black power"

1966
Representative Adam Clayton Powell, Jr., hosts the first Black Power Conference

1967
Second Black Power Conference calls for partitioning the United States into separate black and white nations

1968
Third Black Power Conference is held

1969
National Black Economic Development Conference is held

1969
Last Black Power Conference ends in disarray

1970
Congress of Afrikan Peoples, led by Amiri Baraka, adopts the slogan "It's nation time"

1971
The Rev. Jesse Jackson founds People United to Save Humanity (PUSH)

1972
National Black Political Convention is held in Gary, Indiana

1973
National Black Feminist Organization is founded by Eleanor Holmes Norton and Margaret Sloan

1974
Last National Black Political Convention is held

22-1

22-2

22-3

22-4

22-5

22-6

of the army. Eleanor Holmes Norton became the first woman to chair the Equal Employ-ment Opportunity Commission (EEOC). Ernest Green, who had been one of the nine stu-dents to desegregate Little Rock's Central High School, was appointed assistant secretary of labor. Wade McCree was appointed solicitor general in the Justice Department. Drew Days III became assistant attorney general for civil rights. Historian and former University of Colorado chancellor Mary Frances Berry was appointed assistant secretary for educa-tion. Carter also named Louis Martin his special assistant, making him the first African American in a position of influence on a White House staff.

Carter's Domestic Policies

There are many ways to judge the significance of the Carter presidency to African Americans. Carter's black appointments were practically and symbolically important. Never had so many black men and women occupied positions that had direct and immediate impact on the day-to-day operations of the federal government. Carter also helped cement gains for civil rights. When Congress passed legislation to stop busing for schoolchildren as a means of integrating the schools, Carter vetoed it. He tried to improve fair employment practices by strengthen-ing the powers of the EEOC. His Justice Department chose cases to prosecute under the Fair Housing Act that involved widespread discrimination, to make the greatest possible impact.

Yet most African Americans found Carter's overall record unsatisfactory. He failed to help Democrats in Congress pass either full-employment or universal healthcare bills. Un-der his watch Congress cut social welfare programs to balance the budget, and the cuts included school lunch programs and student financial aid.

A sluggish economy diminished Carter's popularity, but it was the Iran hostage crisis in 1979 that doomed his chances for reelection. For many black people, Carter had become a disappointment, who had done little to bring about greater social justice and economic advancement. Republicans' nomination of the conservative Ronald Reagan, however, left black voters no alternative to Carter. In the election of 1980, 90 percent of black voters again supported Carter, but could not prevent his defeat.

CONCLUSION

The black power and black arts movements continued the struggle for freedom in northern and western cities and states where housing discrimination, high unemployment, and un-relenting police brutality sparked rebellions that resulted in many deaths and widespread destruction in Los Angeles, Newark, Detroit, and other cities. Although African Americans did not create a third party, they were able to elect an impressive number of black mayors and send the first two black women to the United States House of Representatives. Thus, one of the black power era's most enduring political legacies was the rise of black elected officials and the perfection of coalition building.

Clearly the most triumphant dimension of the black studies movement was the revo-lutionary change in academic knowledge and in the expansion of opportunities for black students and professors. Black student militancy resulted in structural changes in the acad-emy with the establishment of black studies departments and cultural centers. The lega-cies of the Black Panther Party, including its social service experiments in providing free breakfasts to school children in impoverished communities and operating free healthcare clinics for residents, have yet to be fully appreciated and were often overshadowed by the relentless vilification of party leaders and members by white police authorities and media. Throughout the late 1960s and 1970s, the black arts movement opened up new venues for cultivations of black unity and an empowering positive black identity.

The legislative successes of the civil rights movement, the Civil Rights Act of 1964, the Voting Rights Act of 1965, and affirmative action were important steps in the long journey toward an egalitarian society. To varying degrees, Presidents Johnson, Nixon, and Carter attempted to address the needs of the poor. Their efforts produced mixed results, hampered by the disastrous war in Vietnam and massive white backlash against school busing and government-mandated desegregation. In the 1980s, Republicans reaped the benefits of the Democratic Party's disarray, and the plight of the black poor worsened.

Historian and theologian Vincent Harding put it most eloquently:

It may be that the greatest discovery . . . was the fact that there is no last word in the human struggle for freedom, justice, and democracy. Only the continuing word, lived out by men, women, and children who dance and rest, who wrestle with alligators and stand firm before tanks, and presidents, and drug lords and deep, deep, fears. We learn again that the continuing word remains embedded in those who determined not to be moved, who know, against all odds, that they will overcome, will continue to create a more perfect union, a more compassionate world. The world remains with those who discover, in the midst of unremitting struggle, deep amazing powers within their own lives, power from, power for, the planet.

CHAPTER TIMELINE

AFRICAN-AMERICAN EVENTS	NATIONAL EVENTS

1965–1966

1965	**1965**
Malcolm X assassinated	President Johnson authorizes the bombing of North Vietnam
Watts riot	
Voting Rights Act of 1965 enacted	**1966**
1966	National Organization for Women (NOW) formed
Black Panther Party formed	
Stokely Carmichael coins the slogan "black power"	
Martin Luther King's Chicago campaign begins	
Edward Brooke of Massachusetts elected the first black U.S. senator since Reconstruction	
Robert C. Weaver becomes first black cabinet officer	
Strike at San Francisco State University results in first black studies program	

1967–1968

1967	**1968**
Uprisings in Newark, Detroit, and other cities	North Vietnam launches Tet Offensive
Muhammad Ali refuses to be drafted	United States and North Vietnam begin peace talks
Thurgood Marshall confirmed as first black Supreme Court justice	Johnson declines to run for another term
Adam Clayton Powell, Jr., denied his seat in Congress	Robert Kennedy assassinated
1968	Richard M. Nixon elected president
Kerner Commission Report	Secret bombing of Cambodia
Poor People's Campaign in Washington, DC	
Orangeburg Massacre	
Martin Luther King, Jr., assassinated	
Shirley Chisholm elected to the U.S. House of Representatives	
Carl Stokes elected mayor of Cleveland and Richard Hatcher elected mayor of Gary, Indiana	

CHAPTER TIMELINE

AFRICAN-AMERICAN EVENTS	NATIONAL EVENTS

1969–1970

1969
Harvard establishes an Afro-American studies program

Maulana Karenga writes *Introduction to Black Studies*
Black Panther leaders Fred Hampton and Mark Clark killed in Chicago police raid

1970
Jackson State killings
Angela Davis placed on the FBI's Ten Most Wanted list

1970
U.S. incursion into Cambodia
Kent State killings

1971–1972

1971
Jesse Jackson founds PUSH
Busing to achieve integration begins

1972
First National Black Political Convention held in Gary, Indiana

Shirley Chisholm makes a bid for the Democratic presidential nomination

Angela Davis acquitted

1972
Watergate break-in
Nixon reelected president

1973–1974

1973
Thomas Bradley elected mayor of Los Angeles
Coleman Young elected mayor of Detroit

1974
National Council for Black Studies formed

1974
Watergate hearings
Nixon resigns

1975–1976

1975
Antibusing protests in Boston

1977
Andrew Young named ambassador to the United Nations

1975
South Vietnam falls

1976
Jimmy Carter elected president

On MyHistoryLab

 Study and Review on MyHistoryLab

REVIEW QUESTIONS

1. Why did African Americans in Watts, Newark, and Detroit rebel in 1965–1967? What did these rebellions suggest about the value of the civil rights movement victories?

2. How did the visions and ideals, successes and failures of Martin Luther King, Jr., compare with those of Lyndon Johnson? Why were these men at odds with each other?

3. What role did African Americans play in the Vietnam War?

4. In what ways can the presidency of Richard Nixon be considered progressive? Which reforms initiated by President Johnson did Nixon advance once he took office? What was "the southern strategy"?

5. What were the major ideological concerns of the artists of the black arts movement? To what extent did James Baldwin and Amiri Baraka have similar views about art, consciousness, aesthetics, and politics?

6. Why did African Americans not form a third political party? Why was the rise of black elected officials so significant?

7. Why were African Americans disappointed with the presidency of Jimmy Carter?

RECOMMENDED READING

Martha Biondi. *The Black Revolution on Campus*. Berkeley: University of California Press, 2012. Essential reading for a comprehensive understanding of the black studies movement.

Stokely Carmichael and Charles V. Hamilton. *Black Power: The Politics of Liberation in America*. New York: Vintage Books, 1967. One of the most important books of the era of black power.

Lance Hill. *The Deacons for Defense: Armed Resistance and the Civil Rights Movement* Chapel Hill: University of North Carolina Press, 2004. An excellent contribution to black power studies. This is a well-researched and detailed analysis of an important, but often overlooked, organization of armed for self-defense black working class activist leaders.

Robert Dallek. *Flawed Giant: Lyndon Johnson and His Times, 1961–1973*. New York: Oxford University Press, 1998. A definitive biography of Lyndon Johnson with fresh insights, grounded in exhaustive research.

Henry Hampton and Steve Fayer, eds. *Voices of Freedom: An Oral History of the Civil Rights Movement from the 1950s Through the 1980s*. New York: Bantam Books, 1990. Contains the recollections of the key participants in the critical battles and movements of the three decades that transformed race relations in America.

Michael D. Harris. *Colored Pictures: Race and Visual Representation*. Chapel Hill: University of North Carolina Press, 2003. A splendid study of how race has been represented and visualized, with insightful analyses of arts movements and informative discussions of black painters.

Hasan Kwame Jeffries. *Bloody Lowndes: Civil Rights and Black Power in Alabama's Black Belt*. New York: New York University Press, 2009. An essential and important study. It is a thorough, illuminating, and persuasively argued study of the Lowndes County Freedom Organization.

Jama Lazerow and Yohuru Williams, editors. *In Search of the Black Panther Party: New Perspectives on Revolutionary Movement*. Durham, NC: Duke University Press, 2006. A valuable collection of essays providing an overview of the critical intellectual shifts in our understanding of the Black Panther Party.

Alondra Nelson. *Body and Soul: The Black Panther Party and the Fight Against Medical Discrimination*. Minneapolis: University of Minnesota Press, 2011. A remarkable, well-researched, insightful study of the healthcare advocacy work of the Black Panther Party. A valuable addition to black studies scholarship.

Wallace Terry. *Bloods: An Oral History of the Vietnam War by Black Veterans*. New York: Ballantine Books, 1984. One of the best sources for firsthand accounts of the Vietnam War as experienced by black soldiers.

Craig Hansen Werner. *Playing the Changes: From Afro-Modernism to the Jazz Impulse*. Urbana: University of Illinois Press, 1994. An insightful study of the gospel, blues, and jazz impulse among key black writers, including James Baldwin and Leon Forrest, during the post–civil rights movement era.

ADDITIONAL BIBLIOGRAPHY

THE BLACK PANTHER PARTY

Curtis J. Austin. *Up Against the Wall: Violence in the Making and Unmaking of the Black Panther Party*. Fayetteville: University of Arkansas Press, 2006.

Joshua Bloom and Waldo Martin, Jr. *Black Against Empire: The History and Politics of the Black Panther Party*. Berkeley: University of California Press, 2013.

Philip S. Foner, ed. *The Black Panther Speaks*. Philadelphia: Lippincott, 1970.

Toni Morrison, ed. *To Die for the People: The Writings of Huey P. Newton*. New York: Writers and Readers Publishing, 1995.

Kenneth O'Reilly. *Racial Matters: The FBI's Secret File on Black America, 1960–1972*. New York: Free Press, 1989.

Ibram H. Rogers. *The Black Campus Movement: Black Students and the Racial Reconstitution of Higher Education, 1965–1972*. New York: Palgrave/Macmillan, 2012.

Robert Scheer, ed. *Eldridge Cleaver: Post-Prison Writings and Speeches*. New York: Random House, 1969.

Jacobi Williams. *From the Bullet to the Ballot: The Illinois Chapter of the Black Panther Party and Racial Coalition Politics in Chicago*. Chapel Hill: University of North Carolina Press, 2013.

BLACK NATIONALISM, BLACK POWER, AND BLACK POLITICS

Robert L. Allen. *Black Awakening in Capitalist America*. Trenton, NJ: Africa World Press, 1990.

Elaine Brown. *A Taste of Power: A Black Woman's Story*. New York: Pantheon, 1992.

Robert Carr. *Black Nationalism in the New World: Reading the African-American and West Indian Experience*. Durham, NC: Duke University Press, 2002.

Zoe A. Colley. *Ain't Scared of Your Jail: Arrest, Imprisonment, and the Civil Rights Movement*. Gainesville: University of Florida Press, 2012.

James H. Cone. *Martin & Malcolm & America: A Dream or a Nightmare*. Maryknoll, NY: Orbis, 1991.

Theodore Cross. *The Black Power Imperative: Racial Inequality and the Politics of Nonviolence.* New York: Faulkner Books, 1984.

Sidney Fine. *Violence in the Model City: The Cavanagh Administration, Race Relations and the Detroit Riot of 1967.* Ann Arbor: University of Michigan Press, 1989.

James F. Finley, Jr. *Church People in the Struggle: The National Council of Churches and the Black Freedom Movement, 1950–1970.* New York: Oxford University Press, 1993.

Wesley C. Hogan. *Many Minds, One Heart: SNCC'S Dream for a New America.* Chapel Hill: The University of North Carolina Press, 2007.

Richard Iton. *In Search of the Black Fantastic: Politics and Popular Culture in the Post-Civil Rights Era. (Transgressing Boundaries Series: Studies in Black Politics and Black Communities).* New York: Oxford University Press, 2008.

Peniel E. Joseph. *Waiting 'til the Midnight Hour: A Narrative History of Black Power in America.* New York: Henry Holt, 2006.

B. I. Kaufman. *The Presidency of James Earl Carter, Jr.* Lawrence: University Press of Kansas, 1993.

Steven Lawson. *In Pursuit of Power: Southern Blacks and Electoral Politics, 1965–1982.* New York: Columbia University Press, 1985.

Manning Marable. "On Malcolm X: His Message & Meaning." *Open Magazine Pamphlet Series.* Westfield, NJ, November 1992.

Manning Marable. *Malcolm X: A Life of Reinvention.* New York: Viking Press, 2011.

Gordan A. Martin, Jr. *Count Them One by One: Black Mississippians Fighting for the Right to Vote.* Jackson: University of Mississippi Press, 2010.

John T. McCartney. *Black Power Ideologies: An Essay in African-American Thought.* Philadelphia: Temple University Press, 1992.

J. Todd Moye. *Let the People Decide: Black Freedom and White Resistance in Sunflower County.* Chapel Hill: University of North Carolina Press, 2004.

Larry G. Murphy. *Down by the Riverside: Readings in African American Religion.* New York: New York University Press, 2000.

William E. Nelson, Jr., and Philip J. Meranto. *Electing Black Mayors: Political Action in the Black Community.* Columbus: Ohio State University Press, 1977.

Robert A. Pratt. *The Color of Their Skin: Education and Race in Richmond, Virginia, 1954–89.* Charlottesville: University Press of Virginia, 1992.

James R. Ralph, Jr. *Northern Protest: Martin Luther King, Jr., Chicago, and the Civil Rights Movement.* Cambridge, MA: Harvard University Press, 1993.

Wilbur C. Rich. *Coleman Young and Detroit Politics.* Detroit: Wayne State University Press, 1989.

Bobby Seale. *Seize the Time.* New York: Random House, 1970.

Cleveland Sellers, with Robert Terrell. *The River of No Return: The Autobiography of a Black Militant and the Life and Death of SNCC.* New York: William Morrow, 1987.

Stephen G. N. Tuck. *Beyond Atlanta: The Struggle for Racial Equality in Georgia, 1940-1980.* Athens: University of Georgia Press, 2001.

James Melvin Washington. *Frustrated Fellowship: The Black Baptist Quest for Social Power.* Macon, GA: Mercer University Press, 1986.

Michael Vinson Williams. *Medgar Evers: Mississippi Martyr.* Fayetteville: University of Arkansas Press, 2011.

Gayraud S. Wilmore. *Black Religion and Black Radicalism.* New York: Anchor Press, 1973.

BLACK STUDIES AND BLACK STUDENTS

Talmadge Anderson, ed. *Black Studies: Theory, Method, and Cultural Perspectives.* Pullman: Washington State University Press, 1990.

Jack Bass and Jack Nelson. *The Orangeburg Massacre.* 1970. New ed. Mason, GA: Mercer University Press, 2003.

William H. Exum. *Paradoxes of Protest: Black Student Activism in a White University.* Philadelphia: Temple University Press, 1985.

Richard P. McCormick. *The Black Student Protest Movement at Rutgers.* New Brunswick, NJ: Rutgers University Press, 1990.

Albert L. Samuels. *Is Separate Unequal?: Black Colleges and the Challenge to Desegregation.* Lawrence: University Press of Kansas, 2004.

Derrick E. White. *The Challenge of Blackness: The Institute of the Black World and Political Activism in the 1970s.* Gainesville: University of Florida Press, 2011.

CLASS, RACE, AND GENDER

Michelle Alexander. *The New Jim Crow: Mass Incarceration in the Age of Colorblindness.* New York: The New Press, 2010.

Jack M. Bloom. *Class, Race, and the Civil Rights Movement.* Bloomington: Indiana University Press, 1987.

Martin Gilens. *Why Americans Hate Welfare: Race, Media, and the Politics of Antipoverty Policy.* Chicago: University of Chicago Press, 1999.

Cheryl Higashia. *Black Internationalist Feminism: Women Writers of the Black Left, 1945–1995.* Urbana: University of Illinois Press, 2011.

Faith S. Holsaert, Martha Prescod Norman Noonan, Judy Richardson, Betty Garman Robinson, Jean Smith Young, Dorothy M. Zellner, eds. *Hands on the Freedom Plow: Personal Accounts by Women in SNCC.* Urbana: University of Illinois Press, 2010.

Bart Landry. *The New Black Middle Class.* Berkeley: University of California Press, 1987.

Mary Pattillo. *Black Picket Fences: Privilege and Peril Among the Black Middle Class.* Chicago: University of Chicago Press, 1999.

Shirley Sherrod with Catherine Whitney. *The Courage to Hope: How I Stood Up to the Politics of Fear.* New York: Atria Books, 2012.

Kimberly Springer. *Living for the Revolution: Black Feminist Organizations, 1968–1980.* Durham: Duke University Press, 2005.

Heather Ann Thompson. *Whose Detroit?: Politics, Labor, and Race in a Modern American City.* Ithaca: Cornell University Press, 2001.

BLACK ARTS AND BLACK CONSCIOUSNESS MOVEMENTS

James Baldwin. *Notes of a Native Son.* New York: Dial Press, 1955.

_____. *Nobody Knows My Name.* New York: Dial Press, 1961.

_____. *The Fire Next Time.* New York: Dial Press, 1963.

_____. *No Name in the Street.* New York: Dial Press, 1972.

Imamu Amiri Baraka. *Dutchman and the Slave: Two Plays by LeRoi Jones.* New York: William Morrow, 1964.

Samuel A. Hay. *African American Theater: An Historical and Critical Analysis.* Cambridge, MA: Cambridge University Press, 1994.

LeRoi Jones and Larry Neal, eds. *Black Fire: An Anthology of Afro-American Writing.* New York: William Morrow, 1968.

Robin D. G. Kelley. *Thelonious Monk: The Life and Times of an American Original.* New York: Free Press, 2010.

Larry Neal. *Visions of a Liberated Future: Black Arts Movement Writings.* New York: Thunder's Mouth Press, 1989.

Suzanne E. Smith. *Dancing in the Streets: Motown and the Cultural Politics of Detroit.* Cambridge, MA: Harvard University Press, 2000.

Brian Ward. *Just My Soul Responding: Rhythm and Blues, Black Consciousness, and Race Relations.* Berkeley: University of California Press, 1998.

AUTOBIOGRAPHY AND BIOGRAPHY

Imamu Amiri Baraka. *The Autobiography of LeRoi Jones.* New York: Freundlich Books, 1984.

John Carlos and Dave Zirvin; Foreword by Cornel West. *The John Carlos Story: The Sports Moment That Changed the World.* Chicago: Haymarket Books, 2011.

Stokely Carmichael, with Ekwume Michael Thewell. *Ready for Revolution: The Life and Struggles of Stokely Carmichael (Kwame Ture).* New York: Scribner, 2003.

Shirley Chisholm. *Unbought and Unbossed.* Boston: Houghton Mifflin, 1970.

_____. *The Good Fight.* New York: Harper & Row, 1973.

James Farmer. *Lay Bare the Heart: An Autobiography of the Civil Rights Movement.* New York: Arbor House, 1985.

Marshall Frady. *Jesse: The Life and Pilgrimage of Jesse Jackson.* New York: Random House, 1996.

Jimmie Lewis Franklin. *Back to Birmingham: Richard Arrington, Jr., and His Times.* Tuscaloosa: University of Alabama Press, 1989.

Elliott J. Gorn, ed. *Muhammad Ali: The People's Champ.* Urbana: University of Illinois Press, 1995.

Charles V. Hamilton. *Adam Clayton Powell, Jr.: The Political Biography of an American Dilemma.* New York: Atheneum, 1991.

Samuel A. Hay. *Ed Bullins: A Literary Biography.* Detroit: Wayne State University Press, 1997.

Wil Haygood. *King of the Cats: The Life and Times of Adam Clayton Powell, Jr.* Boston: Houghton Mifflin, 1993.

David Remnick. *King of the World: Muhammad Ali and the Rise of an American Hero.* New York: Random House, 1998.

Mary Beth Rogers. *Barbara Jordan: American Hero.* New York: Bantam Books, 1998.

Kathleen Rout. *Eldridge Cleaver.* Boston: Twayne Publishers, 1991.

Bobby Seale. *Seize the Time.* New York: Random House, 1970.

Nancy J. Weiss. *Whitney M. Young, Jr., and the Struggle for Civil Rights.* Princeton, NJ: Princeton University Press, 1989.

RETRACING THE ODYSSEY

Motown Museum, Detroit, Michigan. Birthplace of Berry Gordy's Motown Record Corporation, founded in 1957. The "Motown sound" exemplified the music of such performers as the Jackson 5, Gladys Knight and the Pips, Marvin Gaye, and Stevie Wonder. A sign hangs on the front of the structure, "Hitsville U.S.A.," acknowledging the importance of this state historic site. The museum is composed of two adjoining houses filled with memorabilia of gold record awards, album covers, costumes, and musical instruments. Visitors are able to view in Studio A the original control booth where hits by the Temptations, Supremes, and other artists were recorded.

DuSable Museum of African-American History, Chicago. In 1961 artist Margaret Goss Burroughs opened, in her home, the Ebony Museum, which moved in 1973 to its present location at Washington Park. It is now one of the nation's major museums of black history, life, and culture. It houses an extensive collection of artifacts, art, books, and civil rights documents and sponsors a diverse array of cultural and educational programs. The DuSable Museum is named in honor of Jean Baptiste Pointe DuSable, a Haitian-born immigrant who arrived in Chicago in 1779 and was the first non-Indian to settle in the area.

Southern Poverty Law Center Civil Rights Memorial, Montgomery, Alabama. The Civil Rights Memorial captures the history of the freedom struggle while ensuring that we do not forget the costs so many paid in the ongoing struggle against racism and social inequality.

The Martin Luther King, Jr., National Historic Site, Atlanta, Georgia. The district is composed of Martin Luther King's birthplace and gravesite. The Ebenezer Baptist Church, where three generations of King men served as pastors, along with an informative National Park Service Visitors Center, provides a detailed overview of King's life. Also in the district is the Martin Luther King, Jr., Center for Non-Violent Social Change, which contains King's personal papers and the records of the Southern Christian Leadership Conference in addition to an oral history collection.

The Vietnam Veterans Memorial, Washington, DC. The memorial contains all of the names of Americans who lost their lives in the Vietnam War.

1980–2010

African Americans in the Twenty-First Century

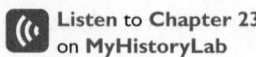

Listen to **Chapter 23** on **MyHistoryLab**

LEARNING OBJECTIVES

23-1	Why are so many African Americans less wealthy and healthy than white Americans?
23-2	What are some of the reasons for continued poverty among African Americans?
23-3	What achievements have African Americans made in the areas of music, literature, and film from the 1980s through the twenty-first century?
23-4	Why has rap music achieved international popularity?
23-5	What is the main philosophy of Afrocentricity?
23-6	What are the strengths and tensions operating within the black church today?
23-7	What are Louis Farrakhan's views and how has he been instrumental in helping African Americans?
23-8	Why has black identity become more complicated in the twenty-first century?

> It is a peculiar sensation, this double consciousness, this sense of always looking at one's self through the eyes of others, of measuring one's soul by the tape of a world that looks on in amused contempt and pity. One ever feels his two-ness,—an American, a Negro; two warring ideals in one dark body, whose dogged strength alone keeps it from being torn asunder.
>
> W. E. B. Du Bois, *The Souls of Black Folk* (1901)

In *The Souls of Black Folk,* W. E. B. Du Bois dreamed of a nation in which black people could be both African and American, embracing their own rich cultural heritage and sharing it with America while becoming full-fledged citizens. This merging of the "two-ness" of the African and American "souls" did not happen in Du Bois's lifetime, but at his death in 1963, the civil rights movement was poised on the edge of its greatest successes. Had Du Bois lived to the dawn of the twenty-first century, he would have been both pleased by the progress made toward fulfilling his dream and saddened by the extent to which the ideals of that dream remain unfulfilled for so many African Americans.

What Du Bois could not have imagined was the globalization of hip-hop, a black youth-generated culture movement that has transformed the world into "hip-hop planet." Hip-hop became the latest of a long series of cultural movements improvised by marginalized but creative black young people determined to refashion empowering images of themselves and to critique the impoverished material conditions of their lives in urban America. They used a wide array of artistic forms to tell the stories of their lives in the early twenty-first century.

In the 2000s, many African Americans advanced to the top ranks of government, the military, sports, entertainment, business, the professions, and academia. The African "soul" that Du Bois urged black Americans to take pride in moved from the shadowy edges of

Co-headlining the "Heart of the City" tour, "Hip-Hip Royalty" Mary J. Blige and Jay-Z brought the house down in Detroit (2008).

American culture to its heart, and black Americans were honored for their contributions to the nation's music, language, and fine arts.

As a result of the legislative successes of the modern civil rights movement, laws now prohibit racial segregation, disfranchisement, and job discrimination. In their wake, millions of black men and women escaped the deep poverty to which nearly all African Americans had been confined when Du Bois wrote *Souls*. Like other Americans, many more black people now complete high school and college and live healthier and longer lives, although white Americans still, on average, earn more and live longer.

Undoubtedly, Du Bois would be appalled by the extreme poverty, poor education, substance addiction, and violent crime that still plague inner-city and rural black populations. But he might not be surprised by the deep racism and ugly stereotyping that continue to define the journey of black people in America, notwithstanding the election of Barack Obama to the presidency of the United States in 2008 and his reelection in 2012.

A "two-ness" dilemma persists a century after Du Bois wrote about "double consciousness," and contemporary scholars, authors, and public intellectuals ponder questions about "post-black" and "post-racial" identities. Such debates are complicated both by the successes African Americans have achieved in recent decades and by demographic and global political changes. Tensions have always festered between a racially defined identity and the many other ways in which African Americans define themselves. Differences of class, color, ethnicity, belief, and region have divided Americans for centuries. Today, other factors further complicate identities, including sexual preference, religious affiliation, immigration status, and political philosophy. Reconciling all these self-understandings within a larger racial identity remains one of the major challenges of the continuing African-American odyssey.

Progress and Poverty:
Income, Education, and Health

23-1 | **Why are so many African Americans less wealthy and healthy than white Americans?**

After the triumphs of the civil rights era, many African Americans made great strides in overcoming the economic and educational disadvantages that had plagued their ancestors. Partly as a result of this progress, they are living longer, healthier lives. Yet, the disparities between the levels of wealth, schooling, and health status of African Americans and the white majority, although narrowed, have persisted. The persistence of black poverty and the social problems associated with it erupted into a major controversy in black communities in 2004 when Bill Cosby used the fiftieth anniversary of the *Brown v. Board of Education* decision to criticize what he termed "irresponsible black poor parents and their delinquent children." Cosby called for greater "personal responsibility" from middle-class black people who, he argued, should put themselves and their children forward as role models for poor African Americans who isolate themselves from the American mainstream and imitate the black inner-city street cultures. Many black commentators objected to this attack and accused Cosby of "airing the black community's dirty laundry."

The late *Ebony* and *Jet* publisher John Johnson.

High-Achieving African Americans

The decades after 1970 witnessed a consolidation of black economic, civic, and political progress and the expansion of a black middle and upper class of professionals, media celebrities, and business entrepreneurs. The success of the black upper class was exemplified by the prominence of highly visible African Americans such as media mogul Oprah Winfrey, Bill Clinton's secretary of commerce Ronald Brown, chairman of the Joint Chiefs of Staff and later secretary of state Colin Powell, and his immediate successor as secretary of state, Condoleezza Rice, and Harvard University professor Henry Louis Gates. To be sure, the ultra-rich remained rare in the black community, but their ranks grew. Winfrey, Cosby, Michael Jackson, Michael Jordan, Jay-Z, and Beyoncé acquired fortunes as entertainers or athletes. Others among the fortunate few include businessman Robert L. Johnson, founder of Black Entertainment Television (BET), who became the first African American to own a professional basketball team, the Charlotte, North Carolina, Bobcats; the late John H. Johnson, publisher of *Ebony* and *Jet* magazines; Berry Gordy, founder of Motown Records; and Russell Simmons, a recording and fashion entrepreneur.

The career of Reginald Lewis illustrates the possibilities open to black people in other industries. Armed with a degree from Harvard Law School, he purchased the McCall Pattern Company in 1984. In 1987 he bought Beatrice Foods, an international packaged goods company, for $2.5 billion. At the time it was the largest leveraged buyout in U.S. history, and Lewis became the wealthiest African American. Before his death in 1993, Lewis gave back to his community by donating millions of dollars to Howard University and the NAACP.

African Americans' Quest for Economic Security

The achievements of the most successful African Americans are impressive, but the increase in job opportunities, income, and wealth for a broad cross section of working African Americans is more significant. Before the 1960s most black men worked in the lower rungs of agriculture, construction, transportation, and manufacturing. Black women predominantly worked in domestic and food service jobs. Few black men or women had a chance to move into higher-paid and more prestigious skilled or managerial positions in the corporate world.

Antidiscrimination laws and affirmative action programs allowed millions of black people to climb up the rungs of career ladders. In 1940, for example, only 5.2 percent of

PROFILE Mark Dean

IN THE 1980S AND 1990S, A PERIOD of urban deindustrialization, working-class black people experienced the highest rate of unemployment in America. To be sure, because of affirmative action policies, more African Americans found employment in skilled positions and in professional occupations. Unlike their white counterparts, however, black unemployed workers at the lower rungs of the job ladder often could not find jobs in the emerging fields such as aerospace technology, electronics, and computer technology that replaced the older industries such as steel.

Despite their small numbers in the computer industry, a few African Americans stood out, none more so than Mark Dean. Dean was born in Jefferson City, Tennessee, in 1957, a year in which African Americans were fighting to end segregation in higher education and state-supported professional schools across the South. Dean's entry into the higher education system was made possible by the civil rights movement, equal opportunity legislation, and affirmative action. He earned a B.S. degree in electrical engineering from the University of Tennessee in 1979, an M.S. degree in electrical engineering from Florida Atlantic University in 1982, and a Ph.D. from Stanford University in 1992.

Before affirmative action, a scientific career such as Dean's would have been hard to imagine in black communities. The 1980s and 1990s witnessed the rise of microcomputers and personal computers. Many businesses were required to hire black employees to obtain government contracts. In 1980 IBM hired Dean. Today he has approximately 40 patents and holds three of the nine patents for IBM's original PC. Dean's work as an IBM chief engineer focused on personal computers. His inventions have changed the way Americans conduct business and manage their lives. In 1995, Dr. Dean was appointed an IBM Fellow, the company's highest technical honor.

Dean, along with colleague Dennis Moeller, developed the Industry Standard Architecture systems bus that allowed add-on devices such as disk drives, keyboards, and printers to be connected to the motherboard of a personal computer. For this innovation, Dean, Moeller, and Robert H. Dennard were inducted into the National Inventors Hall of Fame in 1997. In the same year, Dean was named director of the Austin Research Laboratory and director of Advanced Technology Development for the IBM Enterprise Server Group. Dean's team made important breakthroughs including the testing of the first gigahertz CMOS microprocessor. He also led the team that developed the Blue Gene supercomputer. Dean is a member of the American Academy of Arts and Sciences and the National Academy of Engineering.

---

black men and 6.4 percent of black women worked in white-collar occupations. Today, those figures have risen to 35.3 percent for black men and 62.3 percent for black women. Many black people have moved into jobs in government, education, and banking, and into professions including engineering, law, and medicine.

Middle-class black family income increased dramatically. In 1940 only 1 percent of black families, compared with 12 percent of white families, had incomes at least twice as high as the government's poverty line. By 1998, 50 percent of black families did, compared with 73 percent of white families. The disparity of income between similar families also decreased. In 1960 two-parent black families earned 61 percent as much as two-parent white families, but by 1998 they earned 87 percent as much. This figure is even more impressive because a larger proportion of black people than white people live in the low-wage South. The economic boom of the Clinton presidency, from 1993 to 2001, was particularly beneficial to black people. Although the median income of black families remains well below that of white families, it has risen substantially (see Figure 23–1).

During the 1990s many African-American families narrowed the income gap, yet their average wealth remained far behind that of white families. This was due partly to the long

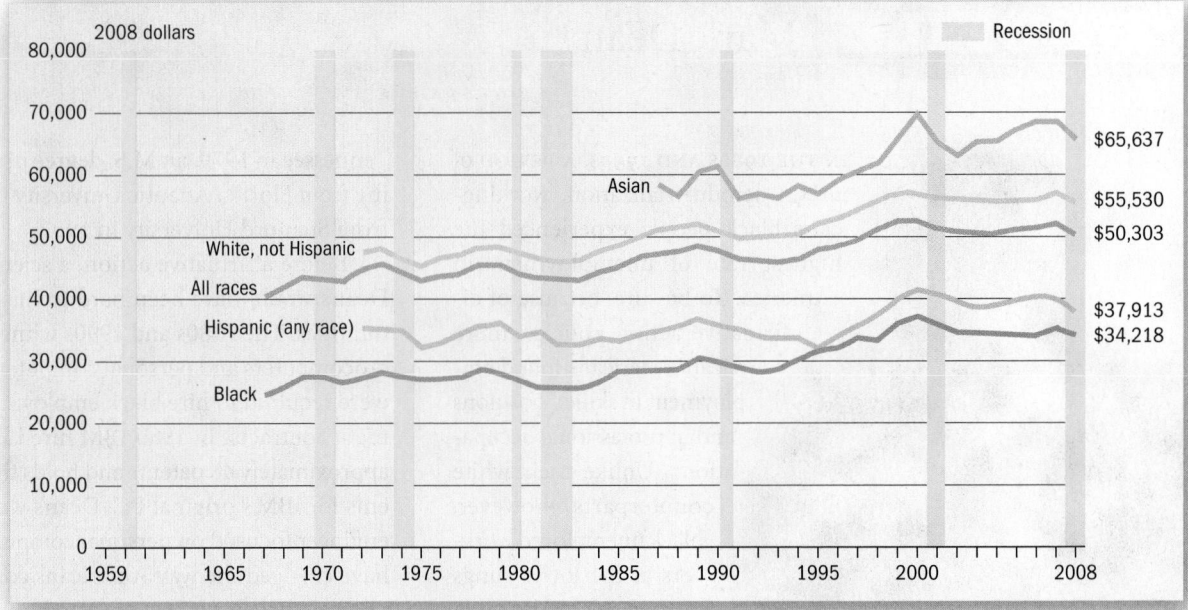

FIGURE 23–1 MEDIAN INCOME OF BLACK, ETHNIC, AND WHITE HOUSEHOLDS, 1967–2011

SOURCE: *U.S. Census Bureau*, Income, Poverty and Health Insurance Coverage in the United States: 2011 *(September 2011)*, 5. *http://www.census.gov/prod/2011pubs/p60-243.pdf.*

heritage of poverty during which most black people accumulated little property or other wealth to pass on to their children. It was also closely tied to differences in the proportions of black and white people who owned their own homes because for most American families, their house is their primary asset. Because of low incomes and systematic discrimination, only 35 percent of African-American families owned their homes in 1950. By 2005, thanks to rising incomes, laws that barred discrimination in housing, and government programs, 46.8 percent of African Americans owned their own homes (the figure for white ownership was 70.7 percent). However, the economic recession that began in 2008 devastated black communities. Unethical bank lending practices along with an array of bad decisions left millions of African-American home owners vulnerable to foreclosures. They had been awarded loans they could not afford to repay, especially when interest rates rose. The economic downturn dramatically increased the unemployment rates among African Americans to percentages unseen since the Great Depression of the 1930s. Almost 16 percent of African Americans were unemployed at the end of 2012 compared to around 7.9 percent of white Americans.

The Persistence of Black Poverty

23-2 **What are some of the reasons for continued poverty among African Americans?**

Although many African Americans enjoyed greater absolute and relative increases in income by the turn of the millennium, too many remained mired in poverty. The poverty rate (in 2010 this meant an annual income below $22,050 for a family of four) for black people had dipped to a low of 22.7 percent during the Clinton boom but rose to 24.5 percent during George W. Bush's presidency and continues to outpace all other groups under President Obama. Equally as alarming, more poor black people remain trapped in inner-city neighborhoods plagued by gang warfare, crime, substance abuse, and HIV/AIDS.

In the urban impoverished communities where so many of the young live, they are cut off from meaningful participation in the social and economic life of the nation and

((•)) **Read on MyHistoryLab**
Document: A Black Sociology
Professor Talks About Teenage
Pregnancy in the Black Community, 1995

TABLE 23–1 BLACK CHILDREN UNDER AGE 18 AND THEIR LIVING ARRANGEMENTS, 1960–2012 (NUMBERS IN THOUSANDS)

Year	Children under 18 Years Old, Total	Two Parents	Living with One Parent			No Parents	
			Total	Mother Only	Father Only	Other Relatives	Nonrelatives
1960	8,649	5,795	1,896	1,723	173	826	132
1970	9,423	5,508	2,996	2,783	213	822	97
1980	9,375	3,956	4,297	4,117	180	999	123
1990	10,019	3,781	5,485	5,132	353	655	98
2000	11,412	4,286	6,080	5,596	484	879	167
2010	11,273	4,424	6,006	5,601	405	740	103
2012	11,196	4,255	6,160	5,687	473	679	102

The increase in the number of children under age 18 living with their mothers only demonstrates the change in the composition of the African-American households in the post-civil rights era. In 2012, most (over 50 percent) black children under age 18 lived with their mothers only. In 1960 only approximately 30 percent of black children lived with their mothers only, while 70 percent lived in two-parent households.

SOURCE: *U.S. Census Bureau, Living Arrangements of Black Children Under 18 Years Old: 1960 to Present, Table CH-3. http://www.census.gov/hhes/families/data/children.html.*

experience fewer educational and other opportunities that might allow them to escape from poverty. More than twice as many 18- and 19-year-old African Americans as 18- and 19-year-old white Americans are either not in school or not working. Another large concentration of black poverty is found in depressed rural areas, especially in the South, where mechanization and declining commodity prices for crops such as cotton, soybeans, and corn have long limited African-American opportunities. Despite cherished myths about rural life, these areas see many of the same social problems as the inner cities. Approximately 40 percent of black rural residents lack high school diplomas as opposed to 20 percent of white rural residents.

The high rate of poverty in the black community disproportionately affects children. In 2008, more than 55 percent of all African Americans under age 18 lived in families with only one parent, generally with their mother (see Table 23–1). This pattern has continued up to 2012 and most black children lived in families at or near the poverty level. Many, if not most, single-parent families headed by females suffer from low incomes, meager public assistance, poor housing, and inferior schools. These conditions handicap children for the rest of their lives, perpetuating poverty from generation to generation. Given their proportion among African-American youth, this is an ominous sign for the future. Marian Wright Edelman, founder of the Children's Defense Fund, captured the plight of the black young when she wrote, "An unlevel playing field from birth contributes to many poor black children getting pulled into a cradle-to-prison-to-death pipeline that we must dismantle if the clock of racial and social progress is to not turn backwards."

Poverty persists among urban African Americans in part because of the national economic restructuring that has occurred since the 1960s. Deindustrialization, relentless advances in labor-saving technology, and the growth of low-wage offshore production have wiped out many jobs that African Americans with limited education and few skills once held. The history of Oakland, California, illustrates this process. In the 1940s and 1950s, Oakland attracted a large black population that was employed in everything from canning food to assembling automobiles. Thousands of black laborers unloaded ships at the ports or worked in the vast yards and repair facilities of the railroads. By the 1960s, however, manufacturing in Oakland was already in flight to lower-wage areas in the United States or overseas; in addition, the port was mechanized, which reduced both the need for longshoremen and the cost of importing foreign goods. Highways, often built through the heart of black business districts, replaced much of Oakland's rail traffic while displacing residents and weakening neighborhoods.

Read on **MyHistoryLab Document**: Exploring America: Growing Inequality

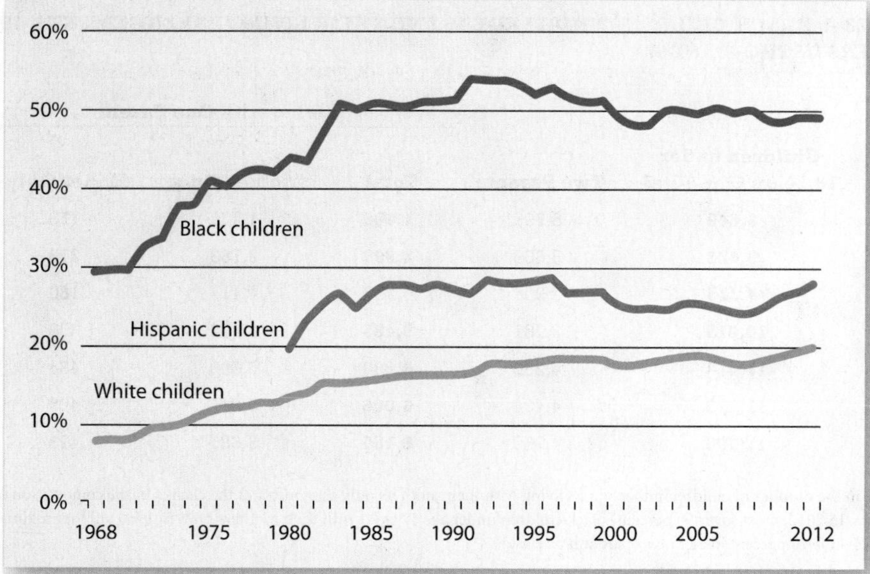

FIGURE 23-2 PERCENTAGE OF CHILDREN UNDER AGE 18 LIVING WITH THEIR MOTHERS, 1968-2012

NOTE: *Direct identification of both parents began in 2007, resulting in the ability to identify children living with two unmarried parents.*

SOURCE: *U.S. Census Bureau,* Current Population Survey, Annual Social and Economic Supplements, 1968–2012. *Figure CH-2-3-4.* http://www.census.gov/hhes/families/files/graphics/CH-2-3-4.pdf

By 2000, Oakland had become a predominantly residential city through which goods made around the globe would flow but in which relatively little was produced or sold. This shift created wealth for some and provided jobs for many middle-class African Americans, but it left many of the once thriving black districts in the city without legitimate work. This paved the way for the rise of drug-related crime that plagued parts of the city. The economic boom of the late 1990s did improve the lot of many inner-city residents, with consequent drops in the rate of crime and poverty in Oakland and elsewhere, but the staying power of this renewal was weakened in the face of the severe recession that began in 2008 and persisted through the end of President Barack Obama's first term (see Figure 23–2).

Impact of the 2008–2010 Economic Recession on Employed Black Women

Read on MyHistoryLab Document: The Bottom of the Economic Totem Pole: African American Women in the Workplace

In 2008, 7 out of 10 mothers with children under age 18 were in the labor force. In 2008 1 out of every 10 women maintaining a family was unemployed, a rate that exceeded the highest rate (9 percent) experienced during the 2001 recession and the "jobless recovery" that followed it. Black and Hispanic women in this group experienced unemployment at rates of 13.3 percent and 11 percent, respectively. White women, including white female heads of household, fared somewhat better than black women in both the 2001 and the 2008 recessions. Black female heads of household started both the 2001 and 2008 recessions with an unemployment rate just under 10 percent, well above the average for all female heads of household. In 2009 the unemployment rate for black female heads of household was 3.7 percentage points higher than it was in 2008.

Extended unemployment benefits, nutrition programs, Medicaid, and tax cuts will bring some immediate relief for these families. Jobs created in education, health care, and child care tend to disproportionately employ women. This will help ensure that as the economy slowly begins to recover, female-headed households will not be left behind.

TABLE 23-2 RATES OF BLACK INCARCERATION

Estimated number of prisoners held in state or federal prison, by gender and race per 100,000 (December 2010).

Males				Females			
Total	White	Black	Hispanic	Total	White	Black	Hispanic
4,791	459	3,074	1,258	257	47	133	77

Estimated number of prisoners held in state or federal prison, by age, gender, and race per 100,000 (December 2010).

Age	Males				Females			
	Total	White	Black	Hispanic	Total	White	Black	Hispanic
20–29	**17,200**	1,618	10,967	4,615	**1,002**	197	481	324
30–39	**21,249**	2,056	13,899	5,294	**1,200**	260	598	342
40–49	**16,139**	1,704	10,388	4,047	**988**	187	528	273
50–59	**9,105**	899	5,680	2,526	**436**	67	226	143
60–64	**2,174**	233	1,262	679	**74**	12	33	29

This table reflects the disproportionately larger number of young African-American males held in prisons and jails compared to white males. The largest number of black women in prison is between 30 and 39 years of age. The largest number of black men is between 30 and 39 years of age.

SOURCE: U.S. Department of Justice, Bureau of Justice Statistics. Prisoners in 2010, *Revised 2/9/12. Appendix Table 14-15.* http://bjs.ojp.usdoj.gov/content/pub/pdf/p10.pdf.

Racial Incarceration

The growth in crime in inner-city communities throughout the 1980s and 1990s combined with a national shift toward aggressive policing and harsher sentencing to vastly increase the imprisonment rates of African-American boys and men. Incarceration became an increasingly common experience for poor young black males, compounding the barriers to advancement they already faced. From 1954 to 2005, the black prison population increased by almost 900 percent, from 98,000 to 910,000. As Table 23–2 shows, while the absolute numbers of both black and white prisoners have begun to fall, African Americans still, in 2011, make up almost half—46 percent—of the nation's prisoners even though only about 12 percent of Americans are black.

Education One-Half Century after *Brown*

Education is the key factor that distinguishes the African Americans who achieve economic success from those who do not. Black rates of school completion have advanced tremendously in the past half century. Many more black youths graduate from high school than ever before. In 1960 only 37.7 percent of African Americans between ages 25 and 29 had completed high school, but by 2007 the U.S. Department of Education estimated that 88.8 percent had completed high school, compared to 93.6 percent for white Americans. Black enrollment in college also rose from a mere 136,000 in 1960 to almost 2 million in 2009. These rates of achievement placed African Americans among the most educated groups of people in the world. African Americans between the ages of 25 and 34 are now more likely than young adults in Canada, France, Italy, and Britain to have completed high school, and they are more likely than those in Italy, Britain, Germany, and France to have completed college.

Yet, despite these encouraging figures, black people who want an education, particularly those in poor inner-city and rural areas, still face severe problems. Schools starved of funds by regressive tax policies and the movement of wealthier people—both black and white—to the suburbs are almost predestined to fail. Affirmative action programs that made a place for African-American students have been cut in many states, resulting in declining enrollments among black students at the top schools. For impoverished black youth, the

Today African-American students pursue education in diverse fields. The Irwin S. Chanin School of Architecture at Cooper Union for the Advancement of Science and Art in New York City offers one path to a brighter future.

combined effect of failing schools and few opportunities results in dropout rates sharply higher than those for more affluent African Americans.

Challenging *Brown*

For over 50 years, conservative groups challenged the meaning and intent of the 1954 Supreme Court decision in *Brown v. Board of Education*. In two 2007 decisions, the justices appointed to the Court by both Presidents Bush moved to end the practice of racial classification as a means to achieve racial diversity in public schools. The two cases involved school assignment plans developed by the boards of education in Seattle, Washington, and in Jefferson County, Kentucky, which includes the city of Louisville. The Seattle school district classified children as white or nonwhite and used this system as the basis for allocating slots to attend the better, or oversubscribed, city high schools. On the other hand, the Jefferson County school district classified children as either black or as "other" and used that system to assign students to elementary schools and to inform decisions about transfer requests.

The Court ruled that both plans violated the Fourteenth Amendment, which guarantees equal protection of the laws. Chief Justice John Roberts, writing the majority opinion, declared, "The way to stop discrimination on the basis of race is to stop discriminating on the basis of race." In a separate opinion, Justice Clarence Thomas insisted, "Racial imbalance is not segregation," adding, "there is no danger of re-segregation."

Joining Roberts and Thomas were Justices Antonin Scalia and Samuel Alito. In his concurring opinion, Justice Anthony Kennedy left open the door for school districts to devise nonracial measures to achieve diversity while limiting the use of racial classification: "Such measures may include strategic site selection of new schools; drawing attendance zones with general recognition of neighborhood demographics; allocating resources for special programs; recruiting students and faculty in a targeted fashion; and tracking enrollments, performance, and other statistics by race."

In a spirited dissent, Justice Stephen Breyer called the majority decision a reversal of precedent and a fundamental weakening of *Brown.* Breyer argued that the majority opinion amounted to a retreat from the principle that allowed local school districts to exercise discretion about the best means to end racial segregation, curb resegregation due to segregated housing patterns, and overcome class division and racial exclusion. (Michigan Congressman John Conyers, chair of the House Judiciary Committee, called the ruling "shameful" and a "step backward" from *Brown.*)

The Court's decisions had affected hundreds of school districts across the country. School systems will now have to struggle to devise their own strategies to avoid or reduce racial concentration, to reverse the wide gaps between white and black students on state tests in reading and math, and to resist the resegregation of schools that has arisen from the growing patterns of housing segregation.

The Health Gap

Read on MyHistoryLab Document: Health Issues in the Black Community, 2005

As in income and education, African Americans have made significant progress toward living longer, healthier lives, but they still suffer greater incidence of disease and mortality for most major illnesses. In 1970, the first year for which we have statistics, life expectancy was 60 years for black men and 68.3 years for black women. By 2009 it had risen to 69.5 and 76.5 years, respectively. Improvements in the quality of care accessible to black people are partly responsible for these increases, but higher infant mortality rates and greater numbers of deaths from diseases kept them well below the 75.7-year life span for white men and 80.8 years for white women.

Cancer and HIV/AIDS infections remain among the greatest threats to black health. African-American men are more likely than white men to develop cancer and die from the disease within five years of diagnosis. Black women have a lower incidence of cancer than do white women, but those black women who do get cancer die at a higher rate from it than white women. Cancer is a complicated disease caused by a variety of factors. Some of the higher rate of its incidence among African Americans is related to risky behaviors common to all impoverished people: smoking, heavy drinking, obesity, and ignorance of health care. A lack of access to insurance or quality health care compounds the impact of these behaviors. Many African Americans also mistrust the healthcare system, while medical workers tend to treat black cancer patients less aggressively than white patients.

African Americans are more likely to have HIV/AIDS than any other group in the United States, as Table 23–3 shows. According to Tavis Smiley's edited volume, *The Covenant with Black America,* published in 2006, "African Americans . . . account for 56 percent annually of new HIV infections. A quarter of these infections are among people under 25 years of age." Among American women, 63 percent of newly diagnosed HIV/AIDS cases are black. Although HIV/AIDS first spread in the United States primarily among gay men, and unprotected sex between men is still the primary form of transmission, only about one-third of African Americans contract the disease in this manner. Most acquire HIV/AIDS through intravenous drug use and unprotected heterosexual sex.

Although African Americans have had high rates of HIV infection from the beginning of the epidemic in the early 1980s, consciousness of this health crisis for black people only began to rise in the 1990s. At first many black leaders declared that the disease affected only gay white men and thus was not a crisis for black communities. This began to change when Los Angeles Lakers' star Earvin "Magic" Johnson told the world he had HIV in 1991. The deaths from AIDS of tennis star Arthur Ashe in 1993 and rapper Eric "Eazy-E" Wright in 1995 also shocked the black community into action.

Identity issues that concerned sexual orientation, feminine and masculine sexual roles, and male/female relationships acquired a new urgency when reports in 2003 and 2012 indicated that African-American women registered more new cases of HIV/AIDS than any other sector of the population. Clearly, heterosexual African-American women sought testing to a greater extent than black men. While women received treatment and understanding, their male partners remained in denial and avoided programs that could prolong their lives. While denying they were gay or bisexual, self-described straight men were having sex with both men and women and were spreading the virus that causes HIV/AIDS to their unsuspecting female partners. Articles in the *New York Times* and in magazines with large

TABLE 23–3 ESTIMATED NUMBER OF DIAGNOSED CASES OF HUMAN IMMUNODEFICIENCY VIRUS (HIV) / ACQUIRED IMMUNODEFICIENCY SYNDROME (AIDS), PER 100,000 IN THE UNITED STATES, 2010

Gender	Black	White
Male	15,444	12,111
Female	6,268	1,733
Total	21,712	13,844

SOURCE: CDC 2012. *HIV Surveillance Report: Diagnoses of HIV Infection and AIDS in the United States and Dependent Areas, 2010, v. 22.* Table 3a. *http://www.cdc.gov/hiv/surveillance/resources/reports/2010report/pdf/2010_HIV_Surveillance_Report_vol_22.pdf*

U.S. Department of Health & Human Services—The Office of Minority Health—"HIV/AIDS and African Americans." http://minorityhealth.hhs.gov/templates/content.aspx?ID=3019.

black readerships such as *Essence* ignited new conversations about black male sexuality. Books also contributed to public dialogue. E. Lynn Harris had done much to expose Down Low behavior in his best-selling novels. In an interview to promote his book *On the Down Low: A Journey into the Lives of "Straight" Black Men Who Sleep with Men,* HIV activist and educator J. L. King declared,

> Many bisexual men choose not to reveal their sexual orientation because they dread the negative fallout that such a disclosure would likely cause. Homophobia is real. We all witness the harsh words and ridicule to which the gay/lesbian community is subjected. Also, there's tremendous normative pressure to keep closeted about any behavior that exists outside the prevailing social and religious norms. Being judged and ostracized isn't something most folks would sign up for, especially not a DL man whose sense of self is intricately linked to his ability to express masculinity and fulfill the traditional gender expectation assigned to men.

The future health of the black community demands open conversation and creative measures to address the HIV/AIDS crisis. That such conversations are now occurring is due in no small measure to the work of gay rights activists and to the support provided to the gay community by President Barack Obama and Vice President Joe Biden, who in spring 2012 announced their support for marriage equality, that is, the right of members of the LBGT communities to marry.

African Americans at the Center of Art and Culture

23-3 What achievements have African Americans made in the areas of music, literature, and film from the 1980s through the twenty-first century?

Cultural triumphs are consistently among the most positive developments for black Americans. Beginning in the 1980s, cultural renaissances emerged in virtually every American community that had a substantial African-American presence. Black consciousness institutions proliferated and flourished. They included black history and culture museums, festivals, expositions, publishing houses, bookstores and boutiques, freedom schools, concerts, theaters, and dance troupes. In 1996 *Publishers Weekly* reported that bookstores specializing in African-American books had increased to more than 200 from only a dozen a few years earlier. By 1994 there were dozens of African-American publishing companies. In 1998 the National Literary Hall of Fame for Writers of African Descent opened at Chicago State University. Black painters used outdoor murals to celebrate the black experience. But with the rise of e-books giant retailers like Amazon, nearly all of the black-owned bookstores had ceased operation by the second decade of the twenty-first century.

During the last days of the civil rights movement, attention shifted to another group of culture workers. Black playwrights were in the vanguard of a cultural explosion that helped revitalize American theater. August Wilson had begun writing overtly political plays in the 1960s and 1970s but focused on broader themes of race and personality as his work matured. His first great success came in 1984 with the Broadway production of *Ma Rainey's Black Bottom,* which explored racism in the music industry. He won praise for his use of the rhythmic and symbolic power of black speech. He had four other plays on Broadway, two of which won Pulitzer Prizes—*Fences* in 1987 and *The Piano Lesson* in 1990. Charles Fuller also made race the center of his plays, attacking stereotypes and exploring the complexity of racial identity in modern America. His best-known play is the 1982 *A Soldier's Tale,* which also won a Pulitzer Prize. It was made into a motion picture titled *A Soldier's Story,* which was nominated for two Academy Awards. George C. Wolfe is a playwright, director, and producer whose achievements helped demolish racial barriers in the theater. His plays, such as *The Colored Museum* and *Jelly's Last Jam,* won critical acclaim, and he received a

Tony Award in 1994 as best director for *Angels in America.* His talent and energy were credited with returning the New York Shakespeare Festival to its former glory when he was its director from 1993 to 2004. Anna Deavere Smith pioneered new forms of theater with her powerful one-woman plays. Her first major success was *Fires in the Mirror,* about tensions between blacks and Jews in Brooklyn's Crown Heights neighborhood. This was followed by *Twilight: Los Angeles, 1992,* a portrayal of the Rodney King riots (see Chapter 24). Smith's achievements in drama and teaching were rewarded with a MacArthur genius grant in 1996.

The new cultural renaissance differed from the black arts movement of the 1960s and 1970s. The contemporary flowering was more inclusive and more appreciative of women artists. It also included the work of openly gay and lesbian artists, such as documentary filmmaker Marion Riggs, choreographer Bill T. Jones, and novelist E. Lynn Harris. Whereas poets and dramatists dominated earlier movements, novelists took center stage in the 1980s. Much of the new work in all fields appealed as much to white audiences as to black, providing insights into the lives of people of African heritage in a predominantly Eurocentric society.

A new wave of African-American women novelists emerged as early as 1977 when Toni Morrison's *Song of Solomon* became a Book-of-the-Month-Club selection, the first by a black author since Richard Wright's *Native Son* in 1940. Then Barbara Chase-Riboud made waves with *Sally Hemings* (1979), a fictional account of a real-life woman who was both slave to and mistress of President Thomas Jefferson. In 1980 Toni Cade Bambara won the American Book Award for *The Salt Eaters.* At least as significant as these individual books was the founding in 1981 of a new publishing house, Kitchen Table: Women of Color Press. Then, in 1982, Alice Walker won the Pulitzer Prize and the American Book Award for *The Color Purple,* which was later made into a movie by director Steven Spielberg, with Whoopi Goldberg in the starring role. In 1987 Rita Dove won the Pulitzer Prize for poetry. In 1993 she became America's poet laureate, and in the same year Toni Morrison became the first African American to win the Nobel Prize for Literature. President Bill Clinton invited Maya Angelou to read one of her poems at his first inauguration. In 2009 President Obama invited Elizabeth Alexander to read a poem at his inauguration.

Critics were not the only ones interested in these works. In 1992 three African-American women novelists—Morrison, Walker, and Terry McMillan—made the *New York Times* best-seller list simultaneously. In 2001 the works of four African Americans made the *Times* best-seller list and revealed the growing appreciation of black literature, biography, and history across the racial spectrum. In 2009 and 2012, several African Americans, including Annette Gordon-Reed, won the Pulitzer Prize. Gordon Reed took the honor for her study *The Hemingses of Monticello: An American Family.* Other black writers and historians whose work has attracted mainstream attention and acclaim include Isabel Wilkerson, Manning Marable, and in 2012 Ayana Mathis for her first novel, *The Twelve Tribes of Hattie.* In the 2000s, African-American performers earned recognition for their work on stage and in film that previous generations would have deemed unthinkable. In 2005, Oprah Winfrey spearheaded a new Broadway production of *The Color Purple,* and more than one million people saw the play in New York before it reopened in Chicago in 2007. Also in 2007, Forest Whitaker won the Academy Award for best actor for his depiction of Uganda's dictator Idi Amin in *The Last King of Scotland,* and Jennifer Hudson won the academy award for best supporting actress in *Dreamgirls,* which was loosely based on the rise of

Toni Morrison accepting the Nobel Prize. One of the most acclaimed writers in the history of U.S. literature, Toni Morrison's (b. 1931 Lorrain, Ohio, as Chloe Ardelia Wofford) novels are, as a Nobel Prize press release put it, "characterized by visionary force and poetic import, [that] gives life to an essential aspect of American reality." Princeton University literary scholar Valerie Smith described Morrison's work as "always steeped in the realities of the political, social, economic, and historical constraints of African American culture." In 1996 Morrison received the National Book Foundation Medal for Distinguished Contribution to American Letters.

23-1
23-2
23-3
23-4
23-5
23-6
23-7
23-8

PROFILE Michael Jackson

23-1

23-2

23-3

23-4

23-5

23-6

23-7

23-8

MICHAEL J. JACKSON was one of the greatest entertainers of the twentieth century. More than any figure of his generation, Jackson helped to make black popular music a global phenomenon. He was born in 1958 in Gary, Indiana, the seventh of nine children of Joseph and Katherine Jackson. His father was a steelworker who molded his sons into a musical group known as the Jackson 5. In 1968, Berry Gordy of Motown Records signed the group, who recorded chart-topping singles including "ABC," "I Want You Back," and "I'll Be There." Michael's voice and showmanship, charisma, and physical attractiveness made him the standout. Jackson attracted legions of fans. At a time when the black family was being maligned and described as "matriarchal" and "broken," the Jacksons represented wholesomeness and a potent blend of patriarchy and talent. Michael became the most beloved black child star of the twentieth century.

In 1976, Michael and his brothers left Motown Records to sign with Epic Records and fired his overbearing father/manager. The following year, Michael joined an all-black cast of *The Wiz* starring former Supremes lead singer Diana Ross. While working on *The Wiz,* the gifted young star impressed the legendary producer and composer Quincy Jones. The two collaborated on Michael's 1979 solo album *Off the Wall*; their subsequent collaboration made musical history and transformed American popular culture. The album *Thriller* (1982) became a phenomenal success. It featured #1 hits like "Billie Jean, the first black video to be shown on MTV, and opened the door for the wider dissemination of and greater appreciation for the music of African-American entertainers.

In 1983, Michael performed on the Motown 25th Anniversary Special and introduced millions of television viewers to his signature dance, The Moonwalk, in which he appeared to defy gravity and walk backward yet land on his toes. This iconic dance and his sequined glove cemented his global celebrity. The young Michael was as shrewd a businessman as he was a mesmerizing performer. In 1985, he purchased the ATV Music Publishing catalog, which contained 251 Beatles songs including "Yesterday" and "Let It Be," for $47.5 million. Today, the catalog is worth 10 times more than Michael's purchase price. Michael gave enormous amounts to charities, especially those devoted to improving the lives of children.

In the 1990s Michael underwent a series of surgeries that altered his features and skin color. The media speculated that he was trying to become a symbol of the universal white male or escape his blackness. But during an interview with Oprah Winfrey in 1993, Michael said that neither was true and that he suffered from a skin disorder that destroyed his pigmentation (a condition known as vitiligo).

There was a downside to his global celebrity. His behavior became increasingly scrutinized and criticized in the world's media. Charges of molestation of underage boys invited outrage and culminated in a sensational trial in California in 2005 in which Michael was acquitted. He left the country and all but ceased to perform. His finances became precarious. In 2008 Michael returned to the United States to restore his reputation and fortune in a planned 50-city world tour. It was not to happen. Because of an apparent drug overdose administered by his personal physician, Michael Jackson died on June 25, 2009. The loss of his creative genius shocked the world. The "King of Pop" was dead, and billions mourned his passing.

First Martin led the struggle that ended Jim Crow racial segregation. Then Malcolm inspired a generation to embrace a positive, empowering racial consciousness. When both Martin and Malcolm were assassinated, Michael Jackson emerged and shattered cultural barriers between the races. The political, social, and cultural transformations that occurred in the last half of the twentieth century were facilitated and inspired by the visionary and creative work of, among others, these heroic African-American men. Each in his own way represented and underscored the humanity of black people as they prepared white America for the 2008 election of Barack Obama as president of the United States.

the Motown singing group the Supremes. Two years earlier Jamie Foxx had won an Oscar for best actor for his role in *Ray,* a film about the singer Ray Charles, and Morgan Freeman won best supporting actor for his role in *Million Dollar Baby.* Playwright Tyler Perry turned his popular plays about the pistol-packing but wise female-in-drag character Madea into box office gold. Tyler Perry's *Madea Goes to Jail* earned $41,030,947 in its opening week in 2009. His media empire continued to expand as did his personal philanthropy and support of President Obama's reelection campaign in 2012. Following the reelection of Obama, Miriam Petty and Northwestern University's Block Museum hosted the first major scholarly conference and roundtable on a college campus to discuss Tyler Perry's films and plays and the ubiquitous Madea character.

The Hip-Hop Nation

23-4   **Why has rap music achieved international popularity?**

Rap was the most commercially successful genre of black music to emerge in the late twentieth century. It became emblematic of the post–civil rights and black power movement generations of African Americans, known collectively as the hip-hop nation. There are many varieties of rap music. At its least complex, rap is a form of rhythmic speaking in rhyme. Hip-hop refers to the backup music for rap that is often composed of excerpts or "samples" from other songs.

Origins of a New Music: A Generation Defines Itself

The rap musical style arose in 1973 in New York City's South Bronx. Its original purpose was to promote musical and dance competitions among the area's inner-city youths, who had few outlets for their creative energies. Rap pioneer Kool Herc (aka Clive Campbell) began using simple raps to cover a mix of beats played from two turntables. At the same time, Afrika Bambaataa developed a political version of rap by merging the ideology of the Nation of Islam with the Black Panthers' cultural nationalism. Bambaataa's Zulu Nation promoted competition in break dancing, rapping, and graffiti art and helped spread rap among poor black and Latino neighborhoods.

The first commercial rap hit, "Rapper's Delight" by the Sugar Hill Gang, came out in 1979 and popularized the term **hip-hop**. This was followed by the rise to stardom of Grandmaster Flash and the Furious Five, which grew out of 1970s funk but added rap vocals and the technique of "scratching"—moving a record back and forth under a needle to produce a rhythmic, jarring sound and manipulating turntable speeds. Much of this music was made primarily for entertainment in the clubs, but some rappers, following the early lead of the spoken-word artists and poets Amiri Baraka, Gil Scott-Heron, and The Last Poets, offered a political critique of American society wrapped in taunting humor.

For African-American youths, whom the world had seemingly left behind and ignored, hip-hop became the most important cultural happening of their lives. It was a creative force in which a dispossessed generation discussed the things that mattered most to them, their lives in cities burdened by racial poverty, heightened violence, and failed schools. In the Reagan years (1981–1989), few middle-class Americans acknowledged the millions left behind in urban decay. Conditions in inner cities worsened during this period, as crack cocaine flooded neighborhoods and gang warfare erupted over drug turfs. The "keeping it real" lyrics of hip-hop artists helped forge a sense of community and common destiny among a trapped generation. As James McBride wrote in *National Geographic* in 2007, hip-hop "is a music dipped in the boiling cauldron of race and class."

 Listen on MyHistoryLab Audio: Zum Zum (Street and Gangland Rhythms) from Beats and Improvisations by Six Boys in Trouble

hip-hop The backup music for rap. It is also the term for the youth culture that developed with the rise of rap music.

Rap Music Goes Mainstream

Ironically, white indifference allowed the first hip-hop entrepreneurs to take control of the production, dissemination, and profits connected with this new music. Russell Simmons saw the potential of rap street music in the mid-1970s and recognized that the mainstream entertainment industry was not aware of it. He became a concert promoter, encouraging early rap groups to stay close to the dress styles and language of the inner-city African-American community. In 1984 he and a partner formed Def Jam Records. Their bands, such as Run-DMC and Public Enemy, became enormously popular, and many of their albums sold millions of copies. Simmons expanded his business to include marketing hip-hop clothing under the label "Phat Farm" and promoting poetry and comedy acts. In 2000 he sold his share of Def Jam for over $100 million. Like Simmons, P. Diddy (aka Sean "Puff Daddy" Combs) found success by working within the mainstream recording industry. Raised in a suburban neighborhood, P. Diddy dropped out of Howard University in 1990 to work for Uptown Records. In 1993 he formed his own company, Bad Boy Records, which was an immediate success.

Commercial success brought new groups to the fore, and the genre expanded. Rap bands such as Run-DMC, which dominated the charts in the mid-1980s, brought the sound to MTV and to a larger public, which soon included white suburban teens. Hip-hop culture quickly spread beyond New York to other African-American urban centers, and each developed a distinctive and often more graphic variant of the original. With the music came changes in clothing style, such as baggy, loose-fitting jeans, that trend-hungry fashion designers quickly adopted.

White suburban youths had always been the wealthiest consumers of hip-hop music and its cultural artifacts. By 2000, hip-hop had become a global cultural force and the source of astonishing profits for men such as Simmons and Combs—and for white-owned business and music companies. The recurrence of the tension between black creativity and white profits fueled new debate. As cultural studies analyst Gregg Tate put it, "Our music, our fashion, our hairstyles, our dances, our anatomical traits, our bodies, our souls continue to be considered ever ripe for the picking and the biting by the same crafty devils who brought you the African slave trade and the Middle Passage."

Gangsta Rap

gangsta rap A genre of rap music characterized by violent and sexist lyrics.

The southern California group N.W.A. (Niggaz wit Attitudes) was one of the most successful new rap bands in the late 1980s. Their 1988 album *Straight Outta Compton* heralded the rise of **gangsta rap**. Its song "Gangsta Gangsta" shocked many with its sexist and violent lyrics. Particularly troubling, however, was the persistent objectification of women in hard-core rap music and films. The widespread use of "bitch" and "ho" by rappers to describe black women reflected broader gender divisions within the black community. Still, many rap bands explicitly rejected hard-core obscenity and violence. Artists like Queen Latifah, for example, avoid denigrating other African Americans even as they promote a message of empowerment for black women and men.

Even more noteworthy was the extent to which hip-hop migrated beyond the United States and became a global cultural force—"hip-hop planet." It influenced music worldwide, particularly across the African Diaspora. France, for example, has a thriving rap music scene. Most of its artists, whose music focuses on ethnic and racial discrimination and social criticism, are of Arab, African, or Spanish descent. Africa, the Caribbean, and Latin America also developed rap that builds on indigenous African music. The ability of rap to combine with other musical forms to create compelling hybrids, together with the global penetration of American popular culture, ensure that hip-hop will continue to thrive and evolve. In the words of *National Geographic*'s James McBride, "Hip-hop remains . . . a cry of 'I am' from the youth of the world."

African-American Intellectuals

23-5   What is the main philosophy of Afrocentricity?

The civil rights and black power movements forced predominantly white academic and cultural institutions to open their doors to African Americans. With a beachhead established, black scholars gained a prominence as public intellectuals unknown in earlier eras. These individuals go beyond their roles as academics to participate in public debate on major issues. In the past, most public intellectuals were white males. Some African Americans, like the formidable W. E. B. Du Bois and novelists Richard Wright, James Baldwin, and Ralph Ellison, were exceptions, but the voices of black intellectuals were seldom heard in the mainstream before the 1960s. In the past five decades, however, many of the most prominent public intellectuals to emerge have been African American. Among them are Cornel West, Henry Louis Gates, Jr., Melissa Harris-Perry, Johnnetta Cole, Beverly Guy-Sheftall, William Julius Wilson, Robin D. G. Kelley, Michael Eric Dyson, and Mary Frances Berry. Their views range across the ideological gamut but they all strive to define black identity in the United States and explore the role of race in its social, economic, and political life. Their emergence and the acclaim accorded to them mark the end of America's long refusal to acknowledge the intellectual accomplishments of African Americans.

Many African-American scholars were connected to the Black Studies programs founded in the late 1960s and early 1970s. Initially marginalized and few in number, these programs now exist in nearly every major university and college. They have become institutionalized—even prized—by institutions that once resisted them. Doctoral degrees in Black Studies are now offered at Northwestern University, Temple University, the University of Massachusetts at Amherst, Harvard, Yale, Michigan State University, and the University of California, Berkeley. Cornell offers a master's degree in the field.

As befits a vibrant intellectual movement, there are several main approaches to understanding the path of African Americans through U.S. history and in contemporary society. Three broad approaches predominate: Afrocentrist; what might be loosely termed an "intersectional" or "inclusionist" approach that has gained prominence more recently as an approach that emphasizes class, sexuality, and gender; and comparative race and diaspora studies.

Afrocentricity

In the 1980s and 1990s, a philosophy of culture referred to as **Afrocentricity** captured wide attention. Afrocentricity had been prominent in the political movement that created black studies, but Temple University professor Molefi Kete Asante gave it a presence and a personality. In the 1980s Asante published three books—*Afrocentricity; Kemet, Afrocentricity and Knowledge;* and *The Afrocentric Idea*—in which he argued that an African-centered perspective was needed to reorient African Americans from the Eurocentric periphery to the center of their own history. In its most extreme form, Afrocentrists argue that much of European civilization originated in Africa, particularly from the culture of ancient Egypt. They also point to evidence of advanced cultures in other parts of Africa to refute assertions of African cultural inferiority.

Many black educators embraced Afrocentricity as a way to celebrate and reclaim a positive African identity and to unite the peoples of the African Diaspora. Afrocentrists rejected the idea of America as a melting pot. Assimilation, they argued, meant rejecting their African cultural

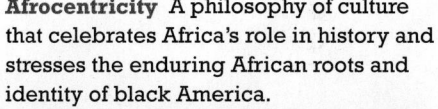

Afrocentricity A philosophy of culture that celebrates Africa's role in history and stresses the enduring African roots and identity of black America.

Molefi Kete Asante changed his name from Arthur Lee Smith in 1973 to better reflect his African heritage. He served as professor and chair of the Department of African American Studies at Temple University from 1984 to 1996. About Afrocentricism, Asante elaborated, "It's a very simple idea. African people for 500 years have lived on the intellectual terms of Europeans. The African perspective has finally come to dinner."

heritage. At the heart of this position is an indictment of American ideas and institutions for their complicity in the long oppression of black people.

Afrocentrists have defended their perspective. Asante explained to his critics, "Afrocentricity is a terribly maligned concept. Afrocentricity is the idea that African people and interests must be viewed as actors and agents in human history, rather than as marginal to the European historical experience—which has been institutionalized as universal." Black historians and social scientists, Afrocentrists argue, must place Africa and its descendants at the center of their studies to increase appreciation of black people's contributions in world history.

Many black scholars, however, insist that Afrocentricity is regressive and fosters self-segregation. Earl Ofari Hutchinson, for example, concedes that Asante's ideas merit attention, but he is skeptical about the claims of some Afrocentrist academics: "In their zeal to counter the heavy handed 'Eurocentric imbalance of history,' some have crossed the line between historic fact and fantasy. They've constructed groundless theories in which Europeans are 'Ice People,' 'suffer genetic defects,' or are obsessed with 'color phobias.' They've replaced the shallow European 'great man' theory of history with a feel-good interpretation of history." White and black critics alike caution that the Afrocentrist desire to fabricate "a glorious past" for black people obscured the truth and fostered a narrow notion of race ill-suited for studying Africans in America.

African-American Studies Come of Age

While the African-American studies department at Temple was the center of the Afrocentric approach and remained one of the largest black studies programs in the nation, many other programs adopted a more ideologically flexible approach. Under the leadership of Henry Louis Gates, Jr., Harvard University followed the integrationist tradition. Gates took charge of the department and the W. E. B. Du Bois Institute in 1991 and attracted leading professors of African-American studies. His goals for the department focused on recovering and making accessible a usable black African and diasporic past. He supports and advocates for a rigorous multidisciplinary study of the black experience: "We're eager to demonstrate that Afro-American studies is an academic department. It is not a place for ethnic cheerleading; it is not a place for a 12-step recovery program to restore your sense of identity. It is a place where one studies an academic discipline in a fashion as rigorous as the study of mathematics or physics, English or history." Apart from intellectual rigor, what held the department together was a belief that race is a malleable category of identity to be analyzed critically and that effective scholarship in the field does not depend on the scholar's racial profile.

As with American intellectual life as a whole, the emergence of scholarship that questioned prevailing gender assumptions also influenced African-American studies. Just as the black studies movement challenged racial ideology, women's studies forced a reconsideration of deeply held gender beliefs while raising historical and social science questions that went unasked in an earlier era. African-American scholars in "womanism" studies, a term Alice Walker popularized to describe the intellectual projects of women of color, pay particular attention to how gender interacted with racial and class hierarchies to shape the historical experiences and contemporary lives of black women. Early journals such as *SAGE* and organizations such as the Association of Black Women Historians, founded by Rosalyn Terborg-Penn and Eleanor Smith, advanced scholarship in black women's studies. Gradually, their scholarly, literary, historical, and polemical works attracted general readers and secured a place in women's studies curricula. As more black women enrolled in college, courses like "Black Women Writers" and "Black Women's History" became part of black studies curricula. The field of black women's history has grown rapidly: scholarly monographs, reference works, anthologies, conferences, and exhibitions have all been devoted to the contribution black women have made to the political struggles and artistic accomplishments of African Americans. In 2007, the journal *Black Women, Gender & Families,* edited by Jennifer Hamer, began as an official organ of the National Council of Black Studies.

23-1
23-2
23-3
23-4
23-5
23-6
23-7
23-8

In 2008 the Organization of American Historians announced the establishment of the Darlene Clark Hine Award for the best book published annually in African American Women's and Gender History. Black woman historian Wanda Hendricks spearheaded the fund-raising effort to make concrete the legitimization of black women's history.

In the 2010s scholars fleshed out definitions and projects illuminating the Black Diaspora framework. Building on the work of Philip Curtin, Colin Palmer, Michael Gomez, Thomas C. Holt, and others, scholars have studied the Atlantic slave-labor economy and compared the centuries-old African-descended communities of the New World with those of more recent African immigrants to Europe. This analysis places African-American history in the context of a global story of movement, citizenship, anti-colonialism and anti-racism struggles, and the quest for belonging. In 2011 and 2012, leaders of African American Studies Departments and programs organized major, well attended, symposia. Yale University's Department of African American Studies coordinated a state of the art conference: "African American Studies: Past, Present and Future." A few months later, Northwestern University's Department of African American Studies brought together students and faculty from the 12 doctoral African American Studies departments and arranged previews of the work of the new generation: "A Beautiful Struggle: Transformative Black Studies in Shifting Political Landscapes—A Summit of Doctoral Programs." The College of Charleston's Avery Center for African American History and Culture hosted the first major black power conference that attracted and featured many of the outstanding young scholars writing a new historiography of black power and black studies. In 2012, the Association for the Study of African American Life and History (founded by Carter G. Woodson in 1915) signaled the recognition and acceptance of black women's history by making "Black Women in American Culture and History" the theme of the annual convention, while the Association of Black Women Historians published a special issue of *Truth* that chronicled the organization's history from 1979 through 2012 and celebrated the work of a generation of black women historians.

Black Religion at the Dawn of the Millennium

23-6 **What are the strengths and tensions operating within the black church today?**

Religion remains at the heart of the African-American experience. Black churches, claiming over 25 million members, remain by far the largest black-controlled institutions in the nation. Houses of worship ranging from storefront operations with a few dozen congregants to "megachurches" with thousands of members are the sinew that binds together nearly every African-American community. The major denominations remain those with roots in the nineteenth century. Among the largest are the African American National Baptist Convention of America, Inc.; the Progressive National Baptist Convention, Inc.; the African Methodist Episcopal (AME) Church; the National Missionary Baptist Convention of America; the Churches of Christ; and the AME Zion Church. Immigration from the Caribbean and Africa has increased African-American membership in some predominantly white denominations. For example, black worshipers make up more than 9 percent of the Catholic Church and over 10 percent of the Episcopal Church. Many African-American Catholics and Episcopalians attend predominantly black churches, so there is still truth in Martin Luther King's observation that "11:00 A.M. Sunday morning is the most segregated hour in America," but progress has been made.

African-American men and women have become leaders within predominantly white denominations since the 1960s. Harold R. Perry was consecrated a bishop in the Roman Catholic Church in 1966, and Wilton Gregory became the first African American to head

Read on MyHistoryLab
Document: Building a Black Christian Community from Scratch, 1999

the United States Conference of Catholic Bishops in 2002. Recognizing the importance of Africans and African Americans to the future of the church, in 1993 Pope John Paul II apologized for the Catholic Church's support of slavery. In 1970 African-American John M. Burgess became the first black bishop to head an Episcopal diocese in America. His leadership in Massachusetts was followed by John T. Walker in Washington, DC, in 1977. African Americans made similar gains in other denominations as churches worked to rid themselves of racist practices.

Despite this continuity with the past and the successes of black religious leaders, African-American religious life has changed in the past several decades. Most African Americans remain Protestants, but demographic and social changes have challenged the mainline denominations. One difficulty is the movement of middle-class parishioners from the close-knit urban communities that once supported churches with people from many different walks of life. Greater levels of education and different life experiences combine with geographical distance to create large suburban megachurches with a distinct character and worship practice. Often Pentecostal, these churches' theology emphasizes the individual's relationship to God. Their ministers speak to the tensions and anxiety of people with stressful lives and careers or with problems such as substance abuse or difficult relationships. They also provide community services for their parishioners.

Perhaps the best-known minister of this new African-American religious tradition is Bishop T. D. Jakes. Starting in 1980 with a 10-member storefront church in Charleston, West Virginia, he built The Potter's House, an enormous ministry with a more than 30,000-member interracial congregation and a 5,000-seat church in Dallas, Texas. Jakes has written best-selling books and produced motion pictures such as *Woman, Thou Art Loosed,* which focused on using religion to heal the psychological wounds of modern society and troubled relationships. He distributes his message through seminars, television broadcasts, and the Internet.

Black Christians on the Front Line

Faced with the problems of the black community and with a changing population, African-American Christians in both traditional and nontraditional religious institutions have developed outreach programs to create supportive communities for the embattled and the vulnerable. Some of the new megachurches are in or near black inner-city communities and remain committed to local action. For example, the Salem Baptist Church in Chicago has over 17,000 members, many of whom patrol neighborhoods to discourage prostitutes and drug dealers. Rev. James T. Meeks led a campaign for an antiliquor referendum to combat the ravages of alcoholism in the community. Many black communities have similar ministries, often with radio and television broadcasts of services.

Rev. Eugene Rivers has developed a different approach from that of the megachurches. Along with former students at Harvard University, he founded the small Azusa Christian Community in a crime-plagued neighborhood in Boston. An evangelical Christian, Rivers believes "the church is the last best hope that black people have." He turned a former crack house into a Christian settlement named the Ella J. Baker House. Its primary goal is to keep children from killing one another. He and fellow black clergy formed the 10-Point Coalition and entered into a partnership with the police. The collaboration helped eliminate juvenile murders for two and a half years. Rivers advocates a pragmatic black nationalism aimed at developing a rich, viable black civil society centered on the church.

Tensions in the Black Church

Tensions have arisen within many black churches over their socially conservative message, patriarchal structure, staid ritual, and lack of social engagement. Gender and sexuality are two key sources of this tension. Along with other conservative Christians, the black church has long advocated the subordination of women to men. Although most black churchgoers are women, men overwhelmingly dominate church leadership. Although a few men and women have always challenged patriarchal assumptions in the churches, only in recent decades has the chorus grown too loud to ignore. As theologian, sociologist, and ordained Baptist minister Cheryl Townsend Gilkes puts it, "The cultural maxim 'If it wasn't for the women, you wouldn't have a church,' rises up against male attempts to exclude, ignore, trivialize, or marginalize women in a number of capacities." Some younger African-American women have left the church because of this marginalization. Others, like Gilkes, have stayed to challenge sexism in individual churches and the denominations.

The AME Church has been at the forefront of this reform. Although the AME has ordained women since 1898, the number of women ministers has only recently become significant. Now 3,000 of the AME's 8,000 ministers are female; in 2000 the church elected Vashti M. McKenzie bishop of its Southern African district. She took the post after a 10-year stint as pastor of Baltimore's Payne Memorial Church, where she increased membership from 300 to 1,700. Upon her election, Bishop McKenzie announced, "The stained glass ceiling has been pierced and broken!" She also connected her achievement to the past efforts of other women. "I stand here tonight," she told the AME convention, "on the shoulders of the unordained women who serve without affirmation or appointment. I don't stand here alone, but there is a cloud of witnesses who sacrificed, died and gave their best." Women's achievements in the churches have not come without conflict, and this promises to be at the center of black religious life in the twenty-first century.

With the support of the Delta Sigma Theta sorority, family, and the Baltimore, Maryland, church community, Vashti Murphy McKenzie broke through "the stained-glass ceiling" (her words) to become the first woman in the history of the AME Church to be appointed a bishop. She is a graduate of the University of Maryland, earned a master of divinity from Harvard University's Divinity School, and earned a doctorate in ministry at the United Theological Seminary in Dayton, Ohio.

Black churches also face conflicts over sexuality. Their theology has traditionally limited legitimate sexual activity to monogamous, heterosexual marriages. Baptist minister and Georgetown University professor Michael Eric Dyson lists the challenges for black Christians over sexuality: "The guilt and shame that result from unresolved conflicts about the virtues of black sexuality. . . . The role of eroticism in a healthy black Christian sexuality. The revulsion to and exploitation of homosexuals. The rise of AIDS in black communities. The sexual and physical abuse of black women and children by black male church members. The resistance to myths of super black sexuality." Of all of these challenges, those surrounding the HIV/AIDS crisis are most pressing but also the most difficult to address, given the church's traditional refusal to do more than denounce, or remain silent about, nontraditional sexualities.

Black Muslims

Although still a relatively small phenomenon among African Americans, Islam has been gaining converts. The Nation of Islam is the best known of the many African-American Muslim groups, but its 20,000 to 40,000 members make up only a small percentage of the estimated 1.5 million black American Muslims. After the death of founder Elijah Muhammad in 1975, his son Warith Deen Muhammad led the Nation of Islam. He eventually left to found the Muslim American Society, the largest group of African-American Muslims, with perhaps 500,000 members. The clarity and discipline of the Muslim faith and the solidarity

African-American Muslims feel with Muslims around the world have attracted an estimated 18,000 converts per year in the United States.

With growing immigration from Islamic countries, African-American Muslims have become more closely connected to the larger trends in Islam. This is evident in the rise of more orthodox Islamic beliefs among American blacks. The attacks on the World Trade Center and the Pentagon on September 11, 2001, and the wars in Iraq and Afghanistan, two Muslim countries, have left many African-American Muslims conflicted. On the one hand, most denounce the attacks and the ideology that led to them. Imam Abdul Malik Mohammed, for example, declared, "While the Muslim World has had the Koran and they have recited the Koran and the Koran has dwelled in their hearts . . . I contend that, in view of circumstances that we have witnessed for many years, Mohammed the Prophet is not known to them." On the other hand, many African Americans are troubled by what they perceive to be an indiscriminate anti-Muslim feeling in the United States and are concerned the nation's war on terror might become a holy war against Islam at home and abroad.

Louis Farrakhan and the Nation of Islam

23-7   **What are Louis Farrakhan's views and how has he been instrumental in helping African Americans?**

Beginning in the 1980s, the Nation of Islam's minister Louis Farrakhan became a potent source of racial division in the United States. Farrakhan was the son of immigrants from the West Indies. As a young man, he attended a black teachers' college in Winston-Salem, North Carolina, but dropped out to become a Calypso singer known as "The Charmer." In 1955, while performing in Chicago, he heard Elijah Muhammad preach. This marked a turning point in his life. After Malcolm X's rupture with Elijah Muhammad and his murder in February 1965, Farrakhan became minister of Harlem Mosque No. 7 and Muhammad's national representative. Farrakhan opposed Warith Muhammad's move to a more orthodox Islam and by 1978 became leader of the Nation. In 1982 he purchased a building to publish the Nation's newspaper, the *Final Call,* and in 1985 he bought and moved into Elijah Muhammad's mansion in Chicago. Under Farrakhan's direction, the Nation developed media ventures, restaurants, clothing stores, and companies to provide security for apartment buildings, distribute soap and cosmetics, and manufacture pharmaceuticals. Farrakhan recruited among poor and marginalized urban African Americans and black prisoners. The national move to the right during the Reagan era complemented the reconstituted Nation's conservative social ideas, which harked back to those that Booker T. Washington advanced in the late nineteenth century. Like Elijah Muhammad, Farrakhan downplayed the struggle for political rights:

> God wants us to build a new world order: A new world order based on peace, justice and equality. Where do we start? . . . Physical separation is greatly feared [by whites], and it is not now desired by the masses of black people, but America is not willing to give us eight or ten states, or even one state. Let's be reasonable. . . . If we cannot go back to Africa, and America will not give us a separate territory . . . we should use the blessings that we have received from our sojourn in America to do for ourselves what we have been asking the whites in this nation to do for us.

Until 1984 most white Americans were barely aware of Farrakhan's existence. In that year, however, he broke the Nation of Islam's long-standing abstention from politics to support Jesse Jackson's bid for the Democratic presidential nomination and ignited a firestorm of controversy. When Jews took offense at Jackson's off-the-record reference to New York as "Hymietown" during a conversation with African-American reporters, Farrakhan, whose Fruit of Islam organization provided security for Jackson's campaign, defended him and

📖 **Read** on **MyHistoryLab Document:** Louis Farrakhan on Education, 2007

Louis Farrakhan and the Nation of Islam. Always controversial, Farrakhan achieved the greatest feat in the history of black mass mobilization, the Million Man March. The actual numbers of black men who heeded his call on October 16, 1995, to attend the Million Man March may forever be in dispute. The figures range from 400,000 to 1.2 million.

made matters worse. On the *CBS Evening News,* Farrakhan warned, "I say to the Jewish people, who may not like our brother. It is not Jesse Jackson you are attacking. . . . When you attack him, you are attacking the millions who are lining up with him. You're attacking all of us. . . . Why dislike us? Why attack our champion? Why hurl stones at him? It's our champion. If you harm this brother, what do you think we should do about it?"

Farrakhan's verbal assaults against Jews, whom he called a principal enemy of African Americans, attracted support from ultra-right-wing anti-Semitic forces and condemnation from Jewish Americans and the Anti-Defamation League. Dredging up anti-Semitic shibboleths reminiscent of Hitler's Germany, Farrakhan blamed Jews for many of the ills plaguing African Americans. Jewish Americans, many of whom had been among the principal allies of African Americans during the civil rights movement, called on African-American organizations and leaders to repudiate Farrakhan and his rhetoric of "Jewish domination and control."

Millennium Marches

In the 1990s Farrakhan reached out to a broader group of African Americans. He called a Million Man March in Washington, DC. Farrakhan framed this march as a "Holy Day of Atonement and Reconciliation . . . to reconcile our spiritual inner beings and to redirect our focus to developing our communities, strengthening our families, working to uphold and protect our civil and human rights, and empowering ourselves through the Spirit of God, more effective use of our dollars, and through the power of the vote."

The estimated 400,000-strong crowd at the October 16, 1995, march made it a symbolic success and generated positive coverage even in the mainstream media. It inspired many black men to become more engaged with their communities and to speak out against oppression. On this occasion, the Nation's conservative philosophy of religion, self-respect, family values, community responsibility, and bootstrap capitalism found a responsive audience. Even though many marchers did not support the Nation's program, the peaceful solidarity of the gathering gave them hope.

Some of the goodwill dissipated, however, when, three months after the march, Farrakhan embarked on a "World Friendship Tour" to Africa and the Middle East. To the consternation of many, he met with the leader of the brutal military regime in Nigeria, General Sani Abacha. At home, Farrakhan's intemperate rhetoric made news, but he failed to forge a coherent strategy to resolve African America's continuing social problems.

Several black intellectuals objected to Farrakhan's conservative ideas, none more effectively than political scientist Adolph Reed, who said that Farrakhan "weds a radical oppositional style to a program that proposed private and individual responses to social problems; he endorses moral repressiveness; he asserts racial essentialism; he affirms male authority; and he lauds bootstrap capitalism. . . . His focus on self-help and moral revitalization is profoundly reactionary and meshes perfectly with the victim-blaming orthodoxy of the Reagan/Bush era."

The Million Man March inspired women to organize their own march. Initiated by two Philadelphia women—Phile Chionesu, a small-business owner, and Asia Coney, a public housing activist—an estimated 300,000 black women gathered in Philadelphia on October 25, 1997, to listen to speeches by California congresswoman and president of the Congressional Black Caucus Maxine Waters, rapper Sister Souljah, and South African activist Winnie Mandela. The march was a celebration, a call to unity, and a forum for black women to denounce domestic violence and inadequate access to quality health care and educational opportunities. The march got less media attention than the Million Man March, perhaps because the organizers were relatively unknown. The march nonetheless symbolized the struggle of black women to be seen and heard in American society and to counter negative stereotypes and derogatory images of black womanhood. Like the Million Man March, there was little in the way of specific policy demands, but the women marchers did gain a feeling of solidarity. As Detroit real estate agent Gloria Graves put it, "I thought that it was very important that we as black women come together in prayer and unity and the belief that we can bring back the family unit that has been lost. I wanted to meet other strong black women who had the same agenda and be united. It has been just great."

Complicating Black Identity in the Twenty-First Century

23-8 Why has black identity become more complicated in the twenty-first century?

The 2000 census counted 281,421,906 Americans, a 13.2 percent increase from 1990. African Americans numbered 34.7 million, or about 12 percent of the total. For the first time in U.S. history, they were no longer the largest minority group: the 35.3 million Americans who identified themselves as Hispanic slightly outnumbered them.

As in the past, most black Americans (54 percent) live in the South; about 19 percent live in the Midwest, 18 percent in the Northeast, and 10 percent in the West. New York City had the largest black population of any urban area at 2.3 million, followed by Chicago at 1.1 million. Detroit, Philadelphia, and Houston were all in the 500,000 to 1 million range. A look beyond these raw numbers, however, reveals important information about the evolving nature of African-American identity in an increasingly multiethnic nation.

For the first time, the 2000 census allowed respondents to choose more than one racial designation for themselves. Since the first census in 1790, the politics of race have shaped such classifications. Before the Civil War, an accurate count of slaves was important because they counted for three-fifths of a person in determining the representation of states in the House of Representatives. Throughout the nineteenth century, fears about miscegenation led census takers to identify individuals as black, white, or mixed race. With the rise of segregation in the late nineteenth and early twentieth centuries, the "one-drop" rule—the belief that any black ancestry, no matter how slight, made a person black—hardened, and the census takers' list of questions dropped the classification of "mulatto." During the early civil rights movement, the American Civil Liberties Union and other groups attempted to remove racial classifications altogether from the census data, reasoning that the only purpose of such distinctions was to disadvantage black people.

The civil rights laws of the 1960s changed the purpose of gathering data by racial classification. Reliable statistics on racial characteristics of people were now necessary to combat discrimination. With the rise of affirmative action programs, identifying oneself as an African American could be beneficial. The black power movement led many to embrace their identity as African Americans and reject the assimilation implied by abandoning racial categories.

In 1977 the Office of Management and Budget addressed the government's need for standard racial categories with its Statistical Policy Directive 15. This set up the familiar racial classifications: white, black, Asian and Pacific Islander, and Native American. "Hispanic" was chosen to denote an ethnicity and could be selected in addition to one of the four racial categories. Because there is no scientific backing for any biological racial distinctions, these categories are bureaucratic approximations of socially relevant distinctions designed to serve administrative needs. They were not necessarily meant to reflect the complex identities of many individuals included in them. For example, "Asian and Pacific Islander" encompasses people from nations with vastly different histories and cultures. The white category includes people descended from Arabs and Turks as well as Europeans. In terms of ethnicity, people now called Hispanic had formerly thought of themselves in terms of national identities, such as Mexican American, Cuban American, and so on, and overlapped with the "black" category for Dominicans and other African-descended people from the former Spanish Caribbean colonies. Over the quarter century after their adoption, these categories became incorporated into identities and social understandings and influenced business and government programs.

Two groups sought to change the categories. The first group saw an end to racial categories as the true legacy of the civil rights movement. These advocates point to the rhetoric of Martin Luther King, Jr., and the language of the Civil Rights Act of 1964, which forbade any discrimination on the basis of race, as evidence of the need to eliminate racial classifications by the government. Some adherents of this view want to abolish the notion of race altogether. They want a color-blind society that they believe will not arrive until a person's race ceases to affect access to education, government programs, or employment. Others who advocate this position, however, are ideological conservatives who want to limit the power of the federal government to redress inequality. They have bankrolled state referendums and court cases to end racial classifications and see this as a way to roll back the gains of the civil rights era.

Those who are biracial also oppose the old classification scheme. Racial mixing is nothing new in America. Many black women slaves were compelled to bear children to their white masters. There have also been consensual sexual relationships and marriages between African Americans and other ethnic and racial groups. The number of such unions and their social acceptance have grown precipitously since the civil rights movement destroyed many of the old racial barriers and the Supreme Court struck down the last **antimiscegenation** laws in *Loving v. Virginia* in 1967. There are now more than 1.5 million mixed-race marriages in the United States and many children growing up in these households. Mixed-race marriages are much more common among younger generations and seem likely to increase rapidly.

antimiscegenation Laws that denied men and women of different racial identities to marry and to risk imprisonment for having sex across the color line during the era of legal segregation.

There is a sharp debate over biracial and multiracial identities in the African-American community. One of the most significant concerns is that fundamental changes in the classification system will undermine the projects they were designed to advance. As poverty researcher John A. Powell put it, "Without racial statistics, we will not know how distributions of resources affect racial and ethnic groups. Without them, racism, which is still very much a part of our society, will be that much more difficult to eradicate, and that much more likely to remain a societal norm." The programs that use these statistics include the Equal Employment Opportunity Act, the Civil Rights Act of 1964, the Voting Rights Act of 1965, the Public Health Act, the Job Partnership Training Act, the Equal Credit Opportunity Act, the Fair Housing Act, and many others. Some argue that offering mixed-race people the option of not being black might undermine the racial solidarity that has been the basis for black advances. As historian Ibrahim K. Sundiata puts it, "The disaggregation of Blacks would drive a wedge into the community that would only increase the isolation of its most disadvantaged members."

Although only 1.8 million Americans opted for the biracial designation in the 2000 census, the existence of the designation raises questions about the nature of racial identity. Clearly racism exists, and black Americans experienced centuries of discrimination that distinguishes them from other groups. But many who would have been considered black under the traditional American system of racial classification no longer think of themselves in the same way and may be increasingly able to assert a multiple identity. Immigration to the United States from Latin America, Asia, and Africa is also undermining what had once been a largely biracial dynamic.

Immigration and African Americans

Because of immigration restrictions and the general oppression of people of African descent in America, few blacks, either from the Western Hemisphere or from Africa, immigrated to the United States before the past few decades. Changes in immigration laws, particularly the landmark 1965 Hart-Cellar Act, which abandoned the racially exclusive restrictions of the past, helped open the door. Military, economic, health, and environmental crises that have roiled Africa and the Caribbean since the 1960s have pushed substantial numbers from these regions through the door. These new black Americans often do not fit their identity neatly into the traditional African-American category.

The number of black immigrants from the West Indies increased dramatically after the 1960s. In the 1950s, only 123,000 Caribbean people immigrated, but during the 1990s nearly one million did so. The Caribbean islands were one of the main areas of importation of African slaves. The islands' sugar production was the economic engine of the Spanish, French, Dutch, and British New World empires into the nineteenth century. These empires all abandoned slavery by the late 1800s, and the retreat of British colonialism from the Caribbean in the twentieth century left many micro-nations largely populated by people of African descent whose cultures have remained more influenced by Africa than was true of black people in the United States. Hence, African cultural practices fused with those of the British in Jamaica, the French in Haiti, and the Spanish in Santo Domingo and Cuba. Although a racial hierarchy is not unknown in these societies, racial identity is less important than class and merit-based achievement. Upon immigration,

In 2003 the New York Haitian American community celebrated the two-hundredth anniversary of the Haitian Revolution. This Haitian flag-waving group of celebrants congregate on the Eastern Parkway in Brooklyn.

mostly to New York, Florida, and other parts of the East Coast, Caribbean immigrants soon learn the importance of race in the United States, but they have also carved out a separate identity from other African Americans. First-generation West Indians tend to have more economic success than native African Americans, in part because employers often favor them. The second generation has often had a more difficult time as discrimination and poor schools take their toll.

Voluntary immigrants from Africa once were few, and before 1980 they were mainly European colonials or North Africans from nations such as Egypt. In the 1950s only 14,000 Africans came to the United States, but during the 1990s over 350,000 arrived. Most of these new immigrants were men and tended to be well educated. Part of their reason for coming to the United States was the destabilization of many African nations and oppression by autocratic regimes.

Black Feminism

The feminist and gay rights movements have challenged traditional ideas of racial identity in recent decades. Both arose as part of the broader "rights revolution" that began with the civil rights movement, but each highlights different aspects of a person's identity—gender or sexuality—in addition to race.

A new wave of feminism in the 1960s and 1970s transformed gender relations. This movement arose, in part, out of the successes of the African-American civil rights struggle. The 1964 Civil Rights Act outlawed sexual as well as racial discrimination in employment. Although this had not been a goal of the civil rights movement at that time and its inclusion was meant, in part, to lessen the prospect that Congress would enact the law, it helped open discussions of gender oppression that had lain dormant for decades. Many white women activists in the Student Nonviolent Coordinating Committee and other civil rights groups became leaders in the emerging feminist movement, often using the same strategies and tactics that had worked to fight racism.

Second-wave feminism achieved many changes. The National Organization for Women, founded in 1966, fought to end job discrimination against women, expand access to safe and effective birth control, legalize abortion, and secure government support for child care. One of the movement's most important early successes was Title IX of the Educational Amendments Act of 1972, which required colleges and universities to ensure equal access for women. Another was the Supreme Court's decision legalizing abortion in 1973 in *Roe v. Wade*. Beyond these victories, the feminist movement opened up choices for women in nearly every aspect of their lives that traditional gender roles had precluded. It also engendered a backlash as conservative men and women fought passage of the Equal Rights Amendment to the Constitution, access to abortion and legalized abortion itself, and sex education in schools.

Black women shaped modern feminism from the start. The core of black feminist thinking is a dual critique of the women's and black liberation ideology. Black women scholars argued that a critique of patriarchy had to include race and class. Whereas white leaders of the women's movement were silent on race, many male leaders in the African-American freedom movement were all too forthright about gender. As Black Panther leader Elaine Brown put it, "A woman in the Black Power movement was considered at best irrelevant. A woman asserting herself was a pariah." Many believed that racial oppression was the primary evil and that feminism either was a distraction or, by encouraging women to be strong and self-reliant, undermined black men's efforts to overcome the emasculating effects of white male power. Black feminists such as Frances Beale countered that racism and sexism had oppressed black women: "It is true that our husbands, fathers, brothers and sons have been emasculated, lynched, and brutalized. They have suffered from the cruelest assault on mankind that the world has ever known. However, it is a gross distortion of fact that black women have oppressed black men."

Responding to sexism in the black power movement, many black women writers and activists sought to make the struggle against sexism as important as that against racism.

23-1

23-2

23-3

23-4

23-5

23-6

23-7

23-8

Between 1973 and 1975, the National Black Feminist Organization (NBFO) articulated many of the concerns specific to black women, from anger with black men for dating and marrying white women; to internal conflict over skin color, hair texture, and facial features; to sexual violence and harassment against black women; to differences in the economic mobility of white and black women. Black feminists also attacked the myth of black matriarchy and stereotypical portrayals of black women in popular culture. Although the NBFO was short lived, it broke the silence black liberation movements had imposed on black women. Black feminists also helped other women talk openly about domestic violence, rape, and sexual harassment in employment. University of California, Los Angeles, law professor Kimberlé Crenshaw summed up their message: "When feminism does not explicitly oppose racism, and when antiracism does not incorporate opposition to patriarchy, race and gender politics often end up being antagonistic to each other and both interests lose."

Gay and Lesbian African Americans

The success of the civil rights movement encouraged gays, lesbians, bisexual, and transgender (LGBT) black Americans to fight openly against the discrimination they had faced for centuries. Their movement was small and quiet until 1969, when gay men at the Stonewall Inn, a bar in New York's Greenwich Village, resisted a police raid. The multiracial crowd's refusal to continue submitting to the kind of police harassment that gays had long been subjected to in the United States sparked an explosion of activism. By the 1980s, many states and cities had decriminalized homosexual behavior and forbade discrimination in employment on the basis of sexuality. Although tensions arose between lesbians and gay men, they worked together to pursue the full range of civil rights heterosexuals enjoy despite persistent opposition from conservative groups.

LGBT African Americans have struggled against their marginality within the larger gay rights movement and homophobia in their own communities. Like the women's movement, the early gay and lesbian rights movement tended to be predominantly white and middle class. Although not explicitly racist, it tended to see racial issues as secondary to or separate from the goal of ending discrimination based on sexual preference.

Despite hostility toward the LGBT rights movement by some African Americans, many black leaders, such as Jesse Jackson, Eleanor Holmes Norton, and John Lewis, and civil rights organizations, such as the NAACP, have embraced its agenda. They do so in part because they accept the analogy between the struggle against repression based on sexual preference and that based on race. The debate between black feminists and gay rights activists, who argue that gender and class identities must be taken into account in political and scholarly analysis, and nationalists, who focus on black identity as primary, continues to rage and will influence our understanding of African-American life in the twenty-first century. As Coretta Scott King put it in a 2002 speech to the National Gay and Lesbian Task Force, "I believe very strongly that all forms of bigotry and discrimination are equally wrong and should be opposed by right-thinking Americans everywhere. Freedom from discrimination based on sexual orientation is surely a fundamental human right in any great democracy, as much as freedom from racial, religious, gender, or ethnic discrimination." In 2008 California voters approved a referendum overturning a decision of the California Supreme Court that had legalized same-sex marriage in the state. To the dismay of the gay community, African Americans were instrumental in passing this referendum, which restricted marriage to unions between a man and a woman. In 2011 President Barack Obama announced his support of same-sex marriage. Over a dozen states have adopted supportive legislation guaranteeing the rights of members of the LGBT community.

VOICES E. Lynn Harris

E. Lynn Harris (1955–2009) was born in Flint, Michigan, and grew up in Little Rock, Arkansas. He was a best-selling writer whose novels explore what it is like to be gay and black in America. His first novel, Invisible Life, *was published in 1991. In this account about his own childhood, Harris is eight years old when he learns a painful lesson about perceptions of sexual difference.*

Easter Sunday, 1964, finally arrived. After my bath, I raced into the tiny room I shared with my two younger sisters and saw the coat laid out on my twin bed. It was red, black, and green plaid with gold buttons. Daddy and I had picked the coat out together at Dundee's Men's Store. I quickly put on my new clothes, and I could see my sisters, Anita and Zettoria, who were five and three, slip on new dresses over their freshly pressed hair. Anita had on a blue taffeta dress, and Shane (our nickname for Zettoria, since her name was so hard to pronounce) had on an identical one in pink. Their dresses were pretty but didn't compare to my coat. After Anita and Shane had accepted their compliments from Daddy, he called me in for inspection. "Where is my little man? Come out here and let Daddy see that new coat," he said. I quickly buttoned up each of the three gold buttons and dashed to the living room for Daddy's endorsement of my outfit. "Look, Daddy. Look at me," I said with excitement as I twirled around like my sisters had a moment before. Suddenly Daddy's bright smile turned into a disgusted frown. What was wrong? Didn't he like my new coat? Had Easter been canceled? "Come here. Stop that damn twirling around," Daddy yelled. I stopped and moved toward Daddy. He was seated on the armless aqua vinyl sofa. Before I reached him, he grabbed me and shouted. "Look at you. You. . . . little sissy with this coat all buttoned up like a little girl. Don't you know better? Men don't button up their coats all the way." Before I could respond or clearly realize what I had done wrong, I saw Daddy's powerful hands moving toward me. His grip was so quick and powerful that I felt the back of my prized coat come apart. A panic filled my tiny body when I saw his hand clutching the fabric. I began to cry as my sisters looked on in horror. I could hear Mama's high heels clicking swiftly as she raced to the living room from the kitchen. "If you don't stop that damn crying, I'm going to make you wear one of your sister's dresses to church." I caught myself and stopped crying. Daddy meant what he said. I would be the laughing stock of the entire neighborhood. . . . I could see all my friends pointing and laughing at me. I don't remember what I wore that Easter Sunday or many Easters that followed. All I recall is that I wasn't wearing a dress, and I remember what my daddy had said to me. I didn't know what a sissy was and why Daddy despised them so. All I knew was that I was determined never to be one.

1. How does Harris's father conceive of masculinity and manhood?
2. Why is this Easter Sunday so important to Harris's self-development and sexual identity?
3. How are Harris's sisters treated differently from him?

SOURCE: From *What Becomes of the Brokenhearted: A Memoir* by E. Lynn Harris. Used by permission of Doubleday, a division of Random House, Inc.

CONCLUSION

The closing of the twentieth century saw remarkable progress for African Americans even as part of the community remained mired in poverty. African Americans still experienced the burden of racism that was so familiar to W. E. B. Du Bois at the nadir of the nineteenth century. Black people confronted those challenges by engaging in collective political action and maintaining predominantly black churches, colleges, and social action groups. The black soul that Du Bois thought had so much to give America now flows freely through its art, language, scholarship, and popular culture, and especially in the Hip-Hop National and International Culture Movement. At the same time, increasing diversity in the ways that African Americans live their lives has led to differences in how individuals understand their identities. Some long for the possibility of asserting those identities in ways not limited by race, sexuality, gender, and class. The tension between racial, class, gender, sexual, and racial-ethnic identities, however, is likely to persist and will profoundly shape the course of the African-American odyssey in the twenty-first century.

CHAPTER TIMELINE

AFRICAN-AMERICAN EVENTS

NATIONAL EVENTS

1960–1969

1964
Civil Rights Act outlaws sexual discrimination in employment

1966
National Organization for Women founded

1969
Stonewall riot in New York

1970–1979

1973
National Black Feminist Organization founded

1978
Louis Farrakhan becomes head of Nation of Islam

1980–1989

1982
Alice Walker and Charles Fuller win Pulitzer Prizes in fiction and drama

1984
Russell Simmons forms Def Jam Records

1987
August Wilson wins Pulitzer Prize for drama

1988
N.W.A.'s *Straight Outta Compton* marks the rise of gangsta rap

1980
Ronald Reagan elected president

1981
Recession settles in; Economic Recovery Tax Act passed

1984
President Reagan reelected

1988
George H. W. Bush elected president

1990–1999

1990
Anna Deavere Smith and August Wilson win Pulitzer Prizes for poetry and drama

1993
Toni Morrison becomes the first black woman to win the Nobel Prize for literature

1995
Million Man March

1997
Million Woman March

1990–1999
1.4 million Caribbean and African immigrants move to the United States

1991
Operation Desert Storm against Iraq

1992
Bill Clinton elected president

1994
Republicans gain control of Congress

1996
Clinton reelected; Clinton signs welfare reform legislation

1998
Clinton impeached by the House of Representatives

1999
Senate acquits Clinton

CHAPTER TIMELINE

AFRICAN-AMERICAN EVENTS

NATIONAL EVENTS

2000–2009

2000

Vashti M. McKenzie elected first woman AME bishop

African-American college enrollment tops 1.5 million

2001

AIDS becomes a leading cause of death among young African-American men

2002

Wilton Gregory heads U.S. Catholic bishops

2004

Carol Moseley Braun and Al Sharpton run for president

Barack Obama elected to U.S. Senate

Condoleezza Rice appointed secretary of state

2009

Barack Obama inaugurated as the forty-fourth president of the United States

President Obama receives the Nobel Peace Prize

Annette Gordon-Reed wins Pulitzer Prize in history

2000

Hispanics become the largest minority group in the United States

George W. Bush elected president

Bush names Condoleezza Rice national security adviser and Colin Powell secretary of state

September 11, 2001

Terrorists demolish the World Trade Center and attack the Pentagon

2004

George W. Bush reelected president

2005

Hurricane Katrina devastates New Orleans

On MyHistoryLab

 Study and Review on MyHistoryLab

REVIEW QUESTIONS

1. What social, economic, and material gains did African Americans make after the civil rights era? Why did some black Americans do better than others during this period? How are tensions surrounding class stratification manifested within the black community?

2. Why do white Americans tend to live longer than black Americans? How has the black community dealt with the problems of HIV/AIDS?

3. Who were some of the most important African-American writers, performers, and social critics in the late twentieth century? What is hip-hop, and what is meant by the term the "hip-hop planet"? What is the relationship between rap music and hip-hop?

4. What are the goals of the Afrocentricity movement? Why is it controversial?

5. Why has the church remained so important to African Americans? How are women's roles changing in the black church?

6. Were the Millenium Marches a success? Why has Louis Farrakhan been so controversial?

7. How has immigration from the Caribbean and Africa affected black America? What factors gave rise to black feminism? What problems do black gays and lesbians face in the black community?

RECOMMENDED READING

Patricia Hill Collins. *Black Feminist Thought: Knowledge, Consciousness, and the Politics of Empowerment.* Boston: Unwin Hyman, 1990. A classic text on black feminist theory and practice by one of black studies' foremost sociologists.

Kent B. Germany. *New Orleans After the Promises: Poverty, Citizenship, and the Search for the Great Society.* Athens: University of Georgia Press, 2007. A well-researched, thoughtful historical study of the successes and failures of the Great Society programs of the 1960s and 1970s that prefigured the Hurricane Katrina disaster in New Orleans in 2005.

Melissa V. Harris-Perry. *Sister Citizen: Shame, Stereotypes, and Black Women in America. For Colored Girls Who've Considered Politics When Being Strong Isn't Enough.* New Haven, CT: Yale University Press, 2011. A brilliant and important study of black women's complicated lives and political struggles.

Richard Iton. *In Search of the Black Fantastic: Politics and Popular Culture in the Post–Civil Rights Era.* New York: Oxford University Press, 2008. A sophisticated and profound study of race, as well as popular culture's impact on American politics. Especially insightful is the chapter on black responses to welfare reform efforts in the 1990s.

Jay-Z. *Decoded.* New York: Spiegel & Grau, 2011. A compelling autobiography by one of hip-hop's most accomplished impresarios. Jay-Z's story is an illuminating merger of art, economics, and politics.

Robin D. G. Kelley. *Yo' Mama's DisFunktional! Fighting the Culture Wars in Urban America.* Boston: Beacon Press, 1998. Powerful essays about America's culture wars and an excellent critique of scholarship about black working-class culture by an elegant and profound scholar.

Philip F. Rubio. *There's Always Work at the Post Office: African American Postal Workers and the Fight for Jobs, Justice, and Equality.* Chapel Hill: University of North Carolina Press, 2010. An illuminating history of black postal workers and their contributions to labor history, postal unions, and civil rights struggles.

Tavis Smiley. *The Covenant with Black America.* Chicago: Third World Press, 2006. A valuable source on the status of African Americans at the dawn of the twenty-first century. It contains useful suggestions for individual and community empowerment programs and strategies.

ADDITIONAL BIBLIOGRAPHY

BLACK CULTURE STUDIES

H. Samy Alim and Geneva Smitherman. *Articulate While Black: Barack Obama, Language, and Race in the U.S.* Foreword by Michael Eric Dyson. New York: Oxford University Press, 2012.

Anthony Bogues. *Black Heretics, Black Prophets: Radical Political Intellectuals.* New York: Doubleday, 2003.

March Christian. "Black Studies in the 21st Century: Longevity Has Its Place." *Journal of Black Studies* 36, no. 5 (May 2006): 698–719.

Jennifer Delton. *Racial Integration in Corporate America, 1940–1990.* New York: Cambridge University Press, 2009.

Melissa Victoria Harris-Lacewell. *Barbershops, Bibles, and BET: Everyday Talk and Black Political Thought.* Princeton, NJ: Princeton University Press, 2004.

Cheryl L. Keyes. *Rap Music and Street Consciousness.* Urbana: University of Illinois Press, 2002.

J. L. King. *On the Down Low: A Journey into the Land of "Straight" Black Men Who Sleep with Men.* New York: Broadway Books, 2004.

Shayne Lee and Phillip Luke Sinitiere. *Holy Mavericks: Evangelical Innovators and the Spiritual Marketplace.* New York: New York University Press, 2009.

Terry McMillan. *Five for Five: The Films of Spike Lee.* New York: Stewart, Tabori & Chang, 1991.

Marcyliena Morgan. *The Real Hip Hop: Battling for Knowledge, Power, and Respect in the LA Underground.* Durham, NC: Duke University Press, 2009.

Mark Anthony Neal. *New Black Man.* New York: Routledge, 2006.

Imani Perry. *Prophets of the Hood: Politics and Poetics in Hip Hop.* Durham: Duke University Press, 2004.

Kevin Powell. *Who's Gonna Take the Weight? Manhood, Race, and Power in America.* New York: Three Rivers Press, 2003.

Riché Richardson. *Black Masculinity and the U.S. South: From Uncle Tom to Gangsta.* Athens: University of Georgia Press, 2007.

Tricia Rose. *Black Noise: Rap Music and Black Culture in Contemporary America.* Hanover, NH: Wesleyan University Press, 1994.

Barbara Dianne Savage. *Your Spirits Walk Beside Us: The Politics of Black Religion.* Cambridge, MA: Harvard University Press, 2008.

T. Denean Sharpley-Whiting. *Pimps Up, Ho's Down: Hip Hop's Hold on Young Black Women.* New York: New York University Press, 2007.

Greg Tate. *Flyboy in the Buttermilk.* New York: Fire-Side, 1992.

Deborah Willis. *Reflections in Black: A History of Black Photographers, 1840 to the Present.* New York: Norton, 2000.

Rhonda Y. Williams. *The Politics of Public Housing: Black Women's Struggles Against Urban Inequality.* New York: Oxford University Press, 2004.

IDENTITY STUDIES

Molefi Kete Asante. *The Afrocentric Idea.* Philadelphia: Temple University Press, 1987.

Sherwin K. Bryant, Rachel Sarah O'Toole, and Ben Vinson III. *Africans to Spanish America: Expanding the Diaspora.* Urbana: University of Illinois Press, 2011.

Dawne Y. Curry, Eric D. Duke, and Marshanda A. Smith, eds. *Extending the Diaspora: New Histories of Black People.* Urbana: University of Illinois Press, 2009.

F. James Davis. *Who Is Black? One Nation's Definition.* University Park: Pennsylvania State University Press, 1991.

Darlene Clark Hine, Trica Danielle Keaton, and Stephen Small, eds. *Black Europe and the African Diaspora.* Urbana: University of Illinois Press, 2009.

E. Patrick Johnson. *Appropriating Blackness: Performance and the Politics of Authenticity.* Durham: Duke University Press, 2003.

E. Patrick Johnson. *Sweet Tea: Black Gay Men of the South, An Oral History.* Durham: Duke University Press, 2009.

Trica Danielle Keaton, T. Denean Sharpley-Whiting, and Tyler Stovall, eds. *Black France/France Noire: The History and Politics of Blackness.* Durham: Duke University Press, 2012.

Tsehloane Keto. *Vision, Identity and Time: The Afrocentric Paradigm and the Study of the Past.* Dubuque, IA: Kendall/Hunt, 1995.

Dwight A. McBride. *Why I Hate Abercrombie & Fitch: Essays on Race and Sexuality.* New York: New York University Press, 2005.

Lisa B. Thompson. *Beyond the Black Lady: Sexuality and the New African American Middle Class.* Urbana: University of Illinois Press, 2009.

Clarence Walker. *You Can't Go Home Again.* New York: Oxford University Press, 2001.

Cornel West. *Race Matters.* Boston: Beacon Press, 1993.

Erin N. Winkler. *Learning Race Learning Place: Shaping Racial Identities and Ideas in African American Childhoods.* New Brunswick: Rutgers University Press, 2012.

RACE, GENDER, AND CLASS

Lois Benjamin. *The Black Elite: Facing the Color Line in the Twilight of the Twentieth Century.* Chicago: Nelson Hall, 1991.

Cassandra Jackson. *Violence, Visual Culture, and the Black Male Body.* New York: Routledge, 2011.

Christopher Jencks. *Rethinking Social Policy: Race, Poverty, and the Underclass.* Cambridge, MA: Harvard University Press, 1992.

Clarence Lang. *Grassroots at the Gateway: Class Politics and Black Freedom Struggle in St. Louis, 1936–75.* Ann Arbor: University of Michigan Press, 2009.

Shayne Lee. *Erotic Revolutionaries: Black Women, Sexuality, and Popular Culture.* Lanham, MD: Hamilton Books, 2010.

Haki R. Madhubuti. *Black Men—Obsolete, Single, Dangerous? Afrikan American Families in Transition: Essays in Discovery, Solution, and Hope.* Chicago: Third World Press, 1990.

Ayana Mathis. *The Twelve Tribes of Hattie: A Novel.* New York: Knopf, 2012.

Harriette Pipes McAdoo, ed. *Black Families.* 4th ed. London: Sage Publishers, 2007.

Jody Miller. *Getting Played: African American Girls, Urban Inequality, and Gendered Violence.* New York: New York University Press, 2008.

Leith Mullings. *On Our Own Terms: Race, Class, and Gender in the Lives of African American Women.* New York: Routledge, 1997.

Steven Shulman, ed. *The Impact of Immigration on African Americans.* New Brunswick, NJ: Transaction Publishers, 2004.

Marshanda Smith, Rose Thevenin, and Ida Jones, eds. *Truth.* www.abwh.org/images/pdf/TruthNewsletter2012.pdf

Celeste Watkins-Hayes. *The New Welfare Bureaucrats: Entanglement of Race, Class, and Policy Reform.* Chicago: University of Chicago Press, 2009.

AUTOBIOGRAPHY AND BIOGRAPHY

Amy Alexander, ed. *The Farrakhan Factor: African-American Writers on Leadership, Nationhood and Minister Louis Farrakhan.* New York: Grove Press, 1998.

E. Lynn Harris. *What Becomes of the Broken Hearted?* New York: Doubleday, 2003.

Nelson Mandela. *Conversations with Myself.* Foreword by President Barack Obama. New York: Farrar, Straus and Giroux, 2010

Joan Morgan. *When Chickenheads Come Home to Roost: My Life as a Hip-Hop Feminist.* New York: Simon & Schuster, 1999.

Charlotte Pierce-Baker. *Surviving the Silence: Black Women's Stories of Rape.* New York: W. W. Norton, 1998.

Randall Robinson. *Defending the Spirit: A Black Life in America.* New York: NAL/Dutton, 1998.

RETRACING THE ODYSSEY

Harpo Studios, Chicago, Illinois. Harpo Studios is a state-of-the-art film production facility created by Oprah Winfrey. It is also the first multimedia complex owned and operated by an African-American woman.

Rock and Roll Hall of Fame and Museum, Cleveland, Ohio. Among the museum's permanent collection of the five hundred songs that most influenced the development of rock and roll are ones by early blues singers: Otis Redding, Chuck Berry, James Brown, Sam Cooke, Ray Charles, Marvin Gaye, and Aretha Franklin. There is a splendid exhibit on the Jackson 5 and on Michael Jackson.

1980–2012

Black Politics from 1980 to the Present: The President Obama Era

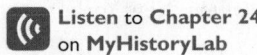

Listen to **Chapter 24**
on **MyHistoryLab**

Dr. Martin Luther King Jr. lies only a few miles from us tonight. Tonight he must feel good as he looks down upon us. We sit here together, a rainbow, a coalition—the sons and daughters of slave masters and the sons and daughters of slaves, sitting together around a common table, to decide the direction of our party and our country. His heart would be full tonight.

We meet tonight at the crossroads, a point of decision. Shall we expand, be inclusive, find unity and power; or suffer division and impotence?

Address by the Rev. Jesse Louis Jackson to the Democratic National Convention, July 19, 1988

If there is anyone out there who still doubts that America is a place where all things are possible, who still wonders if the dream of our founders is alive in our time, who still questions the power of our democracy, tonight is your answer. . . . This is our time, to put our people back to work and open doors of opportunity for our kids; to restore prosperity and promote the cause of peace; to reclaim the American dream and reaffirm that fundamental truth, that, out of many, we are one; that while we breathe, we hope. And where we are met with cynicism and doubts and those who tell us that we can't, we will respond with that timeless creed that sums up the spirit of a people: Yes, we can.

Barack Obama, from his victory speech on November 4, 2008, Chicago, Illinois

The evolution of black politics from the passage of the Voting Rights Act of 1965 to the election (2008) and reelection (2012) of the first black president of the United States, Barack Obama, is best understood in four phases. The first phase was marked by the rise of black elected officials on local and state levels. Especially noteworthy were the elections of numerous black mayors and state legislators. In this first post-civil rights movement phase, the black voting bloc solidified in support of the Democratic Party and pushed for policies that would strengthen their communities and secure their recently won

President Barack Obama enjoys a respite from battles with Republican Congressmen over universal health care to play football with the family dog, Bo. (May 12, 2009).

citizenship rights. The second phase was highlighted by Jesse Jackson's two unsuccessful bids for the Democratic Party's nomination for president in 1984 and 1988 and the efforts of mobilized black communities and their leaders to make the black presence felt on the national level. The third phase witnessed both the rise of black conservatives and the election in 2008 of the first African-American president. The emergence of a fourth phase since 2008 has been characterized by contradictory impulses. While more than 90 percent of black voters supported President Obama's reelection in 2012, black progressives debate whether he has significantly improved the lives of black people. They question Obama's seeming lack of sustained attention to issues that affect African Americans, including chronic economic distress; relentless political assaults (such as the adoption by over 30 states of legislation that restricts voting); the deterioration of black communities; the social, health, and workplace concerns of black women; and shrinking educational opportunities for black children.

Jesse Jackson and the Rainbow Coalition

24-1   **How did Jesse Jackson rise within the Democratic Party?**

In 1983, Jesse Jackson announced his campaign for the presidency of the United States. The first African American to seek the presidential nomination of a major political party was Congresswoman Shirley Chisholm in 1972. Chisholm had little money and only a small organization. Neither her male competitors nor the press took her seriously. Her campaign had nonetheless helped raise the visibility of African-American voters. Although Chisholm won more than 150 votes on the first ballot at the Democratic National Convention, in the male-dominated world of presidential politics, a black man was a more credible contender.

Jackson's preparation for battle was not the traditional climb from one elective office to another. Rather, he rose through the ranks of the civil rights movement, working alongside Martin Luther King, Jr., in the Southern Christian Leadership Conference and heading Operation Breadbasket, an organization that attempted to mobilize Chicago's black poor. After King's death, Jackson founded People United to Save (later Serve) Humanity (PUSH). This Chicago-based organization induced major corporations with large markets in the black community to adopt affirmative action programs. PUSH/Excel, which focused on education, succeeded in raising students' test scores, and the Carter administration gave it a large grant.

In 1983, angered by Ronald Reagan's social welfare and civil rights rollbacks, Jackson and PUSH began a drive to register black voters. Jackson's charismatic style engendered enthusiasm, especially as the Democrats searched for a presidential candidate who could challenge Reagan in 1984.

On November 4, 1983, Jackson declared his candidacy for the Democratic nomination and honed an effective style of grassroots mobilization. He began by appealing to what he would call a "rainbow coalition" of people who felt politically marginalized and underrepresented. The **Rainbow Coalition** was composed of diverse groups, including black people, white workers, liberals, Latinos, feminists, students, and environmentalists. Jackson developed a comprehensive economic policy focusing on tax reform, deficit reduction, and employment. The centerpiece of his plan was "Rebuilding America," a program to coordinate government, business, and labor in a national industrial policy. The Jackson platform was well within the tradition of American liberal reform but far more progressive than anything

Rainbow Coalition Political coalition of African Americans, workers, liberals, feminists, gay people, environmentalists, and others formed by Jesse Jackson in the 1980s.

24-1
24-2
24-3
24-4
24-5
24-6
24-7
24-8
24-9

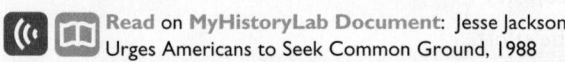

In 1988 Rev. Jesse Jackson addressed the Democratic National Convention. He made two unsuccessful bids for the White House (1984, 1988) but remained a powerful force in the Democratic Party because of his success in registering and mobilizing voters and building coalitions.

his competitors proposed. In January 1984, Jackson gained credentials in international affairs when he traveled to Syria to plead for the release of U.S. Air Force pilot Robert Goodman, who had been held captive there for a year after being shot down in Syrian-controlled airspace. Jackson returned to America in triumph with the freed pilot.

Jackson eventually garnered almost one-fourth of the votes in the Democratic primaries and caucuses and one-eighth of the delegates to the convention. His speech to the convention cemented his position as a voice for progressive change and a spiritual heir to both Martin Luther King, Jr., and Robert Kennedy. Walter Mondale, Jimmy Carter's vice president, who won the nomination, broke new ground when he made Congresswoman Geraldine Ferraro his running mate and the first woman on a major party's presidential ticket. But many Jackson supporters had hoped Mondale would pick Jackson.

In November 1984, black voters overwhelmingly favored the Democratic ticket, but Reagan nonetheless won by a landslide. Mondale carried only his home state of Minnesota and the largely black District of Columbia. Clearly, most white Americans backed Reagan's conservative policies. Undeterred by defeat, Jackson worked to build his Rainbow Coalition, reaching out to a variety of constituencies, including the unemployed, militant trade unionists, small farmers, and gay, lesbian, bisexual, and transgender communities. Perhaps most important, Jackson's campaign registered enough new voters to help Democrats retain control of the House of Representatives in 1984 and regain a majority in the Senate in the 1986 midterm elections.

By the time Jackson announced he would again run for president in October 1987, he had become a serious contender. He won 15 presidential primaries and caucuses and garnered seven million votes, one-third of all those cast. His Rainbow Coalition, however, never materialized. His victories in the primaries were based on mobilizing his black supporters. Almost all of his white support tended to come from college towns. Jackson's campaign strategies, nevertheless, were a precursor to those devised by the strategists for Barack Obama in 2008.

Despite Jackson's voter registration drive and the hopes of the black community, Reagan's vice president, George H. W. Bush, triumphed in the 1988 election. Bush's call for "a kinder, gentler America" was belied by the most memorable feature of his campaign, a polarizing television ad that featured Willie Horton, a black convict who had raped a white woman while on furlough from a Massachusetts prison as part of a program approved both by Bush's opponent Governor Michael Dukakis and his Republican predecessor as governor. Jackson and other black leaders attacked the ad as a blatant appeal to white racism, but it helped elect Bush.

The second phase in the evolution of black politics witnessed both the solidification of black support for the Democrats and the resurgence of a more conservative, increasingly southern-dominated Republican Party that was determined to roll back the progress that civil rights leaders and activists had so painfully won in the 1950s and 1960s. Republican domination was also marked by the emergence of a small but prominent cadre of black neoconservatives. The overwhelming mass of black voters, however, remained bound to the Democratic Party and helped elect William Jefferson Clinton president in 1992 and 1996. Clinton used political appointments and symbolism to maintain black allegiance even as he pursued some policies that black people rejected. Although Republican George W. Bush appointed several African-American conservatives to his cabinets between 2001 and 2008, most black people remained solidly committed to the Democratic Party.

Read on MyHistoryLab Document: Jesse Jackson Urges Americans to Seek Common Ground, 1988

Second Phase of Black Politics

African Americans anticipated that the Clinton victory in 1992 represented the solidification of the Rainbow Coalition of progressive forces that Jesse Jackson had championed.
Clinton was undoubtedly a friend to African Americans, but many of their hopes were only
partly fulfilled. Yet as Donna Brazile—who had worked in Jesse Jackson's campaign and
who, in 2000, would manage Al Gore's doomed race for the White House—asserted, the
Clinton 1990s appeared to be a new era of black power. In retrospect, given what occurred
under President George W. Bush, this may have been true. The conservative triumph in
the 2000 and 2004 elections caused many African-American leaders to reassess black political strategies. The NAACP and other social justice and civil rights organizations crafted
a broad national and international political agenda during the 2004 presidential race. A
new generation of black politicians, such as Barack Obama of Illinois and Governor Deval
Patrick of Massachusetts, addressed the economic, healthcare, education, and security concerns of black and white America in a healing new centrist voice. The 2008 victory that
catapulted Barack Obama into the White House represented the triumph of "Rainbow Coalition" building. The radical right Tea Party faction of the Republican Party won enough
local elections to regain control of the House of Representatives and pursued a strategy of
obstruction that derailed many of the initiatives that the Obama administration advocated
to address the country's fiscal crisis.

The third phase of black politics helped to elect Barack Obama to the presidency and
preserved a Democratic Party majority in the U.S. Senate. In both his 2008 and 2012 election
campaigns, Obama won in no small part because he successfully mobilized black and Latino
voters. Obama represented a new type of black leader, one who, as some argued, was "post-
black" or "post-race," who represented a shift from "color-blind politics" or "pluralism" to a
politics of "hybridity." Both of his presidential campaigns were supported by a majority of
racial minority, women, and gay voters.

The Present Status of Black Politics

In 2007 Senator Barack Obama of Illinois launched his campaign to become the Democratic
presidential candidate, challenging Americans to embrace audacity and hope in the face
of mounting despair and economic anguish. The closing decades of the twentieth century
were characterized by sharp divisions between white and black Americans and between the
Democratic and Republican parties, and by growing economic disparities between working-
class and middle-class Americans and the rich. The conservative right used these years to
create political organizations that supported school prayers, attacked women's reproductive
rights and their right to choose, and denied the civil rights claims of gays, lesbians, and
bisexual and transgendered Americans.

Throughout the 1980s white conservatives nurtured and mobilized their base of disillusioned southerners, alienated northerners, and wealthy elites to reverse liberal-progressive
policies such as affirmative action and reforms epitomized by the Voting Rights Act of 1965.
African Americans, throughout the presidencies of Ronald Reagan and George H. W. Bush
(1981–1993), witnessed a consolidation of Republican Party power. Black American leaders
and community activists developed and adhered to a liberal-progressive agenda that emphasized jobs, universal health care, access to better education, environmental justice, and
freedom of opportunity. African Americans did not develop a race-conscious third party
movement. Instead, black voters overwhelmingly put their hopes in the Democratic Party.

To be sure, the access to greater opportunities in education and employment helped
to fuel growing divisions within black America. Not all black Americans benefited equally
from the gains of the civil rights movement. Fractures along class lines within the black community became more visible. While the ranks of the urban black poor swelled, the growing
black middle and upper class embraced electoral politics to win a greater share in America's
educational, social, and political institutions.

24-1
24-2
24-3
24-4
24-5
24-6
24-7
24-8
24-9

By 2000, a white conservative backlash, combined with inadequate housing, lack of health insurance, resource-starved schools, and reduced funding for welfare and job training programs, dampened the expectations and damaged the health and dignity of many poorer black people. Neither Democrats nor Republicans supported massive urban development and jobs programs for black citizens comparable to the Marshall Plan that had helped rebuild Europe after World War II. In sum, as scholar Nikhil Pal Singh noted, "Despite the growth of a black middle class [during the prosperous 1990s], three decades after the passage of the Civil Rights Act the median net worth of whites—which includes inherited assets as well as income—is a staggering twelve times that of blacks." To be sure, the 2008–2010 recession delivered a major blow to black people in every income bracket, although those in service professions and holding low-skilled jobs fared far worse. The high unemployment of black women-headed households, and the so-called welfare-reform policies pursued during the Clinton presidency, especially devastated families and communities.

Ronald Reagan and the Conservative Reaction

24-2 | How did Reagan and Bush attempt to dismantle the "Great Society" and undermine social welfare programs?

Just as African Americans began mobilizing their communities for full participation in the country's political life in the late 1970s, American politics took a hard turn to the right. This shift had a devastating impact on African Americans, particularly the poor. With the 1980 election of Ronald Reagan (1911–2004) to the presidency, the executive branch sought to curtail civil rights. It reduced welfare programs and staffed key agencies and the federal judiciary with opponents of affirmative action. An overwhelmingly white Republican Party became increasingly entrenched in the South and ended the Democratic Party's' long dominance. The political landscape of the 1980s and 1990s was thus marked by a hardening of ideological conflict between liberal and progressive Democrats on one side and conservative, indeed radical, Republicans on the other.

Ronald Reagan's defeat of Jimmy Carter paved the way for the dominance of the New Right. Reagan possessed charm and the ability to communicate with the American people. His election, however, was the result of more than just personal charisma. Powerful conservative political organizations found a home in the Republican Party. These groups were opposed to equal rights for women, especially their reproduction rights. They sought to overturn Supreme Court decisions protecting the rights of the accused and prohibiting compulsory prayer from the public schools. Many white southerners opposed labor unions, and they joined forces with white northerners who objected to school busing, affirmative action programs, and the tax burden they associated with welfare and entitlement policies.

The King Holiday

Many African Americans invested symbolic importance in making Martin Luther King, Jr.'s birthday a national holiday, elevating him to the stature of George Washington and Abraham Lincoln, both of whom are honored with a holiday. At first Reagan resisted the idea, but he eventually gave in to pressure from African Americans and their white allies. On January 20, 1985, the United States officially observed Martin Luther King, Jr., Day for the first time. In 2011 President Barack Obama unveiled the Martin Luther King, Jr., statue, the first African-American monument on the Washington National Mall.

Dismantling the Great Society

One of the New Right's chief goals was to dismantle the social welfare programs created during and after the New Deal and Johnson's Great Society. From 1981 to 1992, Reagan and George H. W. Bush halved federal grants to cities. As the federal government slashed funds for redeveloping inner cities and constructing public housing between 1980 and 1992, the percentage of city budgets derived from funds from the federal government declined from 14.3 percent to 5 percent. As a result, inner-city neighborhoods where 56 percent of poor residents were African Americans became more unstable. Reagan advanced a trickle-down theory of economics. He believed that if the wealthiest Americans got richer, their increased prosperity and the spending associated with it would percolate through the middle and working classes to benefit the poor. Unemployment statistics soon challenged this theory. By December 1982, the unemployment rate had risen to 10.8 percent, and the rate for African Americans was twice that of white Americans. The annual income of the highest-paid 1 percent of the nation, meanwhile, increased from $312,206 to $548,970 by 1988 (the equivalent of over $1,190,000 a year in 2012).

Reagan and Bush often cloaked their intent to undermine rights-oriented policies by appointing black conservatives to key positions. Reagan chose William Bell, for example, to replace Eleanor Holmes Norton as chair of the Equal Employment Opportunity Commission (EEOC). Bell had few qualifications for the post, and civil rights organizations protested his appointment. Reagan simply replaced Bell the following year with yet another black conservative, Clarence Thomas, who opposed affirmative action. Thomas reduced the commission's staff and allowed the backlog of affirmative action cases to grow to 46,000 and the processing time for a case to increase to 10 months.

Reagan tried to change the direction of the U.S. Commission on Civil Rights (CCR), but in this case he met with resistance. Since its creation in 1957, the commission had been a civil rights watchdog, with no real enforcement powers but with some influence on public opinion. Soon after Reagan took office, the CCR began to issue reports critical of his civil rights policies. Reagan responded by appointing commissioners sympathetic to his perspective. He replaced the commission's chair, Arthur S. Flemming, who was white, with a black Republican, Clarence Pendleton, former executive director of the San Diego Urban League. The vice chair, however, was Mary Frances Berry, a respected civil rights activist and historian whom Carter had appointed and who frequently clashed with the new president. In 1984 Reagan tried to remove Berry from the CCR, but she sued to retain her position. When she won, she became known as "the woman the president could not fire." Nevertheless, the CCR soon declined to insignificance.

Black Conservatives

24-3   **What role did black conservatives play in the Republican Party in the 1980s and 1990s?**

William Bell, Clarence Thomas, and Clarence Pendleton were members of a vocal cadre of black, middle-class, conservative intellectuals, professionals, and politicians who came to prominence during the Reagan years. To augment their influence, the Republican Party nurtured a small, well-educated, articulate cadre of black men and women intellectuals that included Thomas Sowell, Walter Williams, Shelby Steele, Armstrong Williams, Ward Connerly, and, until he broke with them in the late 1990s, Glenn Loury. There was a critical difference, however, between elite black Republican and black Democratic politicians: black Republicans rarely exercised meaningful power within their party. They were expected to embrace the values and support the goals of the white party leaders. In contrast, black Democratic politicians could and often did make their influence felt. Moreover, black Democrats represented a large and essential constituency within the party. Following Obama's victory in 2008, the Republican Party elected black conservative Michael Steele as chair of the Republican National Committee to create an illusion of racial inclusion within the party. Steele

Read on MyHistoryLab
Document: Richard Viguerie, Why the New Right Is Winning, 1981

As a justice on the U.S. Supreme Court, Clarence Thomas has staunchly adhered to conservative values in all of his opinions.

Anita Hill, a law professor at the University of Oklahoma, testified before the U.S. Senate Judiciary Committee confirmation hearings that Supreme Court nominee Clarence Thomas had sexually harassed her. Thomas was confirmed in spite of these sexual harassment charges.

was replaced in 2011 by an even more conservative white chairman who was more closely aligned with the Tea Party insurgents.

The Thomas–Hill Controversy

The role of black conservatives was highlighted when, in 1991, President George H. W. Bush nominated Clarence Thomas to the Supreme Court. Thomas was born in 1948 in rural Georgia. He graduated from Holy Cross College in Massachusetts and Yale Law School. The symbolism of Thomas, who opposed the expansion of civil rights, replacing Thurgood Marshall, the greatest civil rights lawyer of the twentieth century, could not have been more dramatic.

Thomas's nomination precipitated a public display of gender conflict within the black community. While Marshall had been one of the Court's great liberals and a staunch defender of civil rights, Thomas was a black conservative whose record on civil rights did not endear him either to white liberals or many within the black community. His credentials for the Court were questioned. He had served only 15 months as an appellate court judge. Nevertheless, the black community was loath to openly contest his nomination or to challenge the cynical tokenism of the Bush administration. Some civil rights organizations expressed reservations about the Thomas nomination. The Urban League shrewdly declared, "We welcome the appointment of an African-American jurist to fill the vacant seat left by Justice [Thurgood] Marshall. Obviously, Judge Thomas is no Justice Marshall. But if he were, this administration would not have appointed him. We are hopeful that Judge Thomas's background of poverty and minority status will lead him to greater identification with those in America who today are victimized by poverty and discrimination. And [we] expect the Senate, in the confirmation hearings, to explore whether he is indeed likely to do so."

The anticipated easy confirmation process derailed when black law professor Anita Hill appeared before the Senate Judiciary Committee, which heard testimony on Thomas's confirmation. Hill accused Thomas of sexually harassing her when she worked for him at the EEOC.

Both Anita Hill and Clarence Thomas were conservative Republicans, and both had earned law degrees at Yale. Hill did not volunteer to testify about Thomas's sexual harassment. She had answered questions put to her in a confidential investigation. When her answers were leaked to the press, she agreed to appear before the committee. Some senators questioned her character and integrity. Thomas charged that he was a victim of a "high-tech lynching" in the media and that Hill's accusations were false. Although many in the black community supported Thomas, progressive feminists, white liberals, and some black people supported Hill. Activist black women were incensed by the treatment that Hill received from the Senate and were determined to voice their opposition to Thomas's political views. Despite the opposition, Thomas won confirmation to the Court by a narrow 52 to 48 majority. On the Court, Justice Thomas remains an archconservative who unwaveringly votes with the conservative majority. He adamantly opposes affirmative action.

Debating the "Old" and the "New" Civil Rights

24-4 What are the "old" and "new" civil rights?

The Reagan and Bush administrations distinguished between what might be called the "old civil rights law," which they claimed to support, and the "new civil rights law," which they opposed. Developed between the *Brown* decision in 1954 and the Voting Rights Act of 1965, the old civil rights law prohibited intentional discrimination, be it legal segregation in the schools, informal discrimination in the workplace, or racial restrictions on voting. The new civil rights law was concerned with discriminatory outcomes, as measured by statistical disparities, rather than with discriminatory intent. If, for example, black children overall are disproportionately in all-black schools; if the workforce in a given firm, compared with the community in which it is located, is disproportionately white (or male); or if elected officials in a multiracial state or municipality are disproportionately white, discrimination is assumed.

The remedies for such historic discrimination, collectively labeled **affirmative action**, tend to be statistical in nature. They include increasing the number of minority pupils, minority employees, or minority elected officials (by redrawing the districts from which they were elected) to correspond to the percentage of the relevant minority population. In employment (and in admissions to colleges and universities), the methods used in reaching these goals became known as affirmative action "guidelines." Sometimes guidelines were imposed by court order. More often, they were the result of voluntary efforts by legislatures, government agencies, businesses, and colleges and universities to comply with civil rights laws and court rulings.

affirmative action Civil rights policy or program that seeks to redress the effects of past discrimination due to race or gender by giving preference to women and minorities in education and employment.

Affirmative Action

Few civil rights policies in the twentieth century proved more controversial than affirmative action. Many white Americans argue that it runs contrary to the concept of achievement founded on merit and amounts to reverse racial or sexual discrimination. Ironically, because the 1964 Civil Rights Act made gender discrimination in employment illegal, white women were among the major beneficiaries of affirmative action. But its chief advocates have been African Americans who view it as a remedy for centuries of discrimination. The debate over affirmative action not only led to racial polarization, it divided the black community.

President Lyndon Johnson had first used the term "affirmative action" in a 1965 executive order that required federal contractors to "take affirmative action" to guarantee that job seekers and employees "are treated without regard to their race, color, religion, sex, or national origin." In 1969 Arthur A. Fletcher, a black assistant secretary of labor in the Nixon administration, developed the "Philadelphia Plan," in which firms with federal construction contracts were obligated to set and meet hiring goals for African Americans or be penalized. The plan became a model for subsequent "set-aside" programs that reserved some contracts for minority-owned businesses or that favored hiring women and minorities. Setting goals and timetables to achieve full compliance with federal civil rights requirements appealed to large corporations and accounted for the early success of affirmative action initiatives.

The Backlash

Although it produced more litigation, affirmative action in employment proved less controversial than affirmative action in college and university admissions. State higher-education institutions occupied the center of the controversy both because they were narrowly bound by the Fourteenth Amendment's prohibitions against racial discrimination and because they, far more than elite private institutions, were the gateways to upward mobility for many Americans, white and black, Asians, and Latino/as. Nevertheless, both to aid disadvantaged minorities and increase racial and cultural diversity on campus, admissions offices were

24-1
24-2
24-3
24-4
24-5
24-6
24-7
24-8
24-9

VOICES Black Women in Defense of Themselves

24-1
24-2
24-3
24-4
24-5
24-6
24-7
24-8
24-9

Days after Anita Hill appeared before the Senate Judiciary Committee, a group of black women led by Elsa Barkley Brown, Barbara Ransby, and Deborah King raised more than $50,000 to print this statement in the New York Times, *"In Defense of Ourselves." Appearing on November 17, 1991, it was signed by 1,603 black women. Five black newspapers—the* San Francisco Sun Reporter, *the* Los Angeles Sentinel, *the* New York City Sun, *the* Atlanta Inquirer, *and the* Chicago Defender—*also published the declaration.*

As women of African descent, we are deeply troubled by the recent nomination, confirmation and seating of Clarence Thomas as an Associate Justice of the U.S. Supreme Court. We know that the presence of Clarence Thomas on the Court will be continually used to divert attention away from the historic struggles for social justice through suggestions that the presence of a Black man on the Supreme Court constitutes an assurance that the rights of African Americans will be protected. Clarence Thomas's public record is ample evidence that this will not be true. Further, the consolidation of a conservative majority on the Supreme Court endangers the working class people and the elderly. The seating of Clarence Thomas is an affront not only to African American women and men, but to all people concerned with social justice.

We are particularly outraged by the racist and sexist treatment of Professor Anita Hill, an African American woman who was maligned and castigated for daring to speak publicly of her own experience of sexual abuse. The malicious defamation of Professor Hill insulted all women of African descent and sent a dangerous message to all women who might contemplate a sexual harassment complaint.

We speak here because we recognize that the media are now portraying the Black community as prepared to tolerate the dismantling of affirmative action and the evil of sexual harassment in order to have any Black man on the Supreme Court. We want to make clear that the media have ignored and distorted many African American voices. We will not be silenced.

Many have erroneously portrayed the allegations against Clarence Thomas as an issue of either gender or race. As women of African descent, we understand sexual harassment as both. We further understand that Clarence Thomas outrageously manipulated the legacy of lynching in order to shelter himself from Anita Hill's allegations. To deflect attention away from the reality of sexual abuse in African American women's lives, he trivialized and misrepresented this painful part of African American people's history. This country, which has a long legacy of racism and sexism, has never taken the sexual abuse of Black women seriously. Throughout U.S. history Black women have been sexually stereotyped as immoral, insatiable, perverse, the initiators in all sexual contacts—abusive or otherwise. The common assumption in legal proceedings as well as in the larger society has been that Black women cannot be raped or otherwise sexually abused. As Anita Hill's experience demonstrates, Black women who speak of these matters are not likely to be believed. In 1991, we cannot tolerate this type of dismissal of any one Black woman's experience or this attack upon our collective character without protest, outrage, and resistance.

As women of African descent, we express our vehement opposition to the policies represented by the placement of Clarence Thomas on the Supreme Court. The Bush administration, having obstructed the passage of civil rights legislation, impeded the extension of unemployment compensation, cut student aid and dismantled social welfare programs, has continually demonstrated that it is not operating in our best interests. Nor is this appointee. We pledge ourselves to continue to speak out in defense of one another, in defense of the African American community and against those who are hostile to social justice no matter what color they are. No one will speak for us but ourselves.

1. **Why did the African-American women who signed this letter feel they needed to defend themselves?**

2. **Why did they oppose the confirmation of Clarence Thomas to the Supreme Court?**

3. **Why were they unsympathetic to Thomas's claim that he had been a victim of a "high-tech" lynching?**

SOURCE: *New York Times*, November 17, 1991, 53.

forced to employ different admission criteria. Conservatives called these criteria "racial preferences" that promoted unfairness and white resentment.

The case of *Regents of the University of California v. Bakke* reflected the white backlash to affirmative action. The medical school at the University of California, as a form of affirmative action, had set aside 16 of its 100 places in each entering class for disadvantaged and minority students. They were considered for admission in a separate system. A white student named Alan Bakke sued the University for discrimination after it rejected his application. In 1976 the California Supreme Court ruled he should be admitted, but the university appealed to the U.S. Supreme Court, which also ruled in Bakke's favor in 1978. Of the nine justices, five agreed that the university violated Bakke's rights. However, other related legal issues were involved, and the Court split without a majority on nearly all of them. Only one justice declared that affirmative action cases should be judged on the same strict level of scrutiny applied to "invidious" (intentionally harmful) discrimination. All the other justices stated that race-conscious remedies could be used in some circumstances to correct discrimination.

California was at the center of the affirmative action storm because of its multiracial population. In 1995 Republican Governor Pete Wilson ended affirmative action in state employment. In 1996 California voters approved Proposition 209, the so-called California Civil Rights Initiative, which banned all state agencies from implementing affirmative action programs. Ward Connerly, a conservative black entrepreneur, led the campaign for the proposition. Born in 1939 in rural Louisiana, he had earned a B.A. from Sacramento State College and had received over $140,000 from state contracts set aside for minority businesses. Nonetheless, Connerly maintained that affirmative action exacerbated negative stereotyping of African Americans and had failed to address problems of poverty, unemployment, and inadequate education that beset the truly disadvantaged. Instead, it had merely helped those least in need of assistance, especially middle-class white women. Finally, Connerly accepted the broader argument that affirmative action assaulted the concept of individual merit and violated core American values of equality and opportunity.

Fifty-four percent of California voters agreed with Connerly, and the Supreme Court upheld the proposition. Its effect and that of similar laws or court rulings around the nation is now known. The number of African Americans and other protected minorities admitted to the University of California system dropped, and the numbers at Berkeley, the University of California's most prestigious campus, fell precipitously. In both California and Texas, which abandoned affirmative action in its university system after a court challenge, administrators have attempted to assure a diverse student body by offering admission to their top schools to all students in the top ranks of their high school class.

On June 23, 2003, the Supreme Court, in two separate decisions, handed the University of Michigan both a victory, when it upheld the law school's practice of using race as

The majority of African Americans defend affirmative action as a policy designed to open doors to opportunities in employment and education that had been firmly closed during the long era of Jim Crow segregation and discrimination.

24-1

24-2

24-3

24-4

24-5

24-6

24-7

24-8

24-9

1979–2009
SUPREME COURT CASES ON AFFIRMATIVE
ACTION IN EMPLOYMENT

1979
United Steelworkers v. Weber upheld preferential treatment in hiring and training by private firms

1980
Fullilove v. Klutznick upheld government programs that reserved places for minorities

1982
American Tobacco Co. v. Patterson upheld seniority plans in place before 1964 unless discriminatory intent could be shown

1986
Wygant v. Jackson Board of Education rejected a school board's plan for laying off white teachers while retaining less senior black teachers, but it also rejected the Reagan administration position that affirmative action be limited to actual victims of discrimination, thus broadly upholding affirmative action

1986
Local 93 of International Association of Firefighters v. City of Cleveland upheld the promotion of minorities ahead of white applicants with higher test scores and greater seniority

1986
Local 28 of Sheet Metal Workers v. EEOC upheld the order that unions meet minority quotas for membership

1987
U.S. v. Paradise upheld a judicial order imposing racial quotas in hiring and promotions of Alabama state troopers

1987
Johnson v. Transportation Agency of Santa Clara County upheld a plan that promoted women over men

1989
Martin v. Wilks ruled that employees may challenge an affirmative action plan after it has gone into effect. Congress overruled this decision in the Civil Rights Act of 1991

1989
Richmond v. J. A. Croson Co. ruled that the Fourteenth Amendment prohibited set-asides for minority contractors, thus going against the spirit of *Weber* and the letter of *Fullilove v. Klutznick* and implying that all such plans face "strict scrutiny (intense examination)"

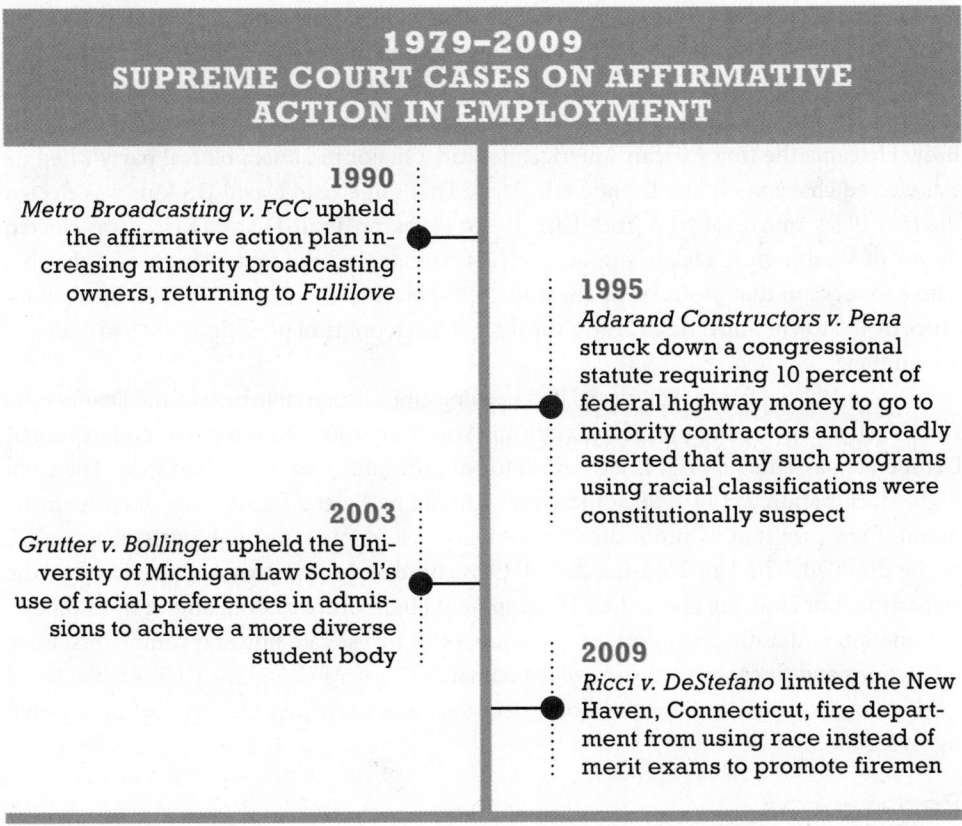

1979–2009 SUPREME COURT CASES ON AFFIRMATIVE ACTION IN EMPLOYMENT

1990
Metro Broadcasting v. FCC upheld the affirmative action plan increasing minority broadcasting owners, returning to *Fullilove*

1995
Adarand Constructors v. Pena struck down a congressional statute requiring 10 percent of federal highway money to go to minority contractors and broadly asserted that any such programs using racial classifications were constitutionally suspect

2003
Grutter v. Bollinger upheld the University of Michigan Law School's use of racial preferences in admissions to achieve a more diverse student body

2009
Ricci v. DeStefano limited the New Haven, Connecticut, fire department from using race instead of merit exams to promote firemen

a criterion in admissions procedures to create a diverse student body, and a defeat, when it banned the university from awarding points based on race as a criterion for admitting undergraduates. In the first case, *Grutter v. Bollinger,* a five-to-four decision declared that the law school could use race to achieve diversity, thus endorsing the *Bakke* decision written by Justice Powell. Justice Sandra Day O'Connor's majority opinion declared that the equal protection clause of the Fourteenth Amendment did not prohibit the law school's narrowly tailored use of race in admissions decisions. She was persuaded that the law school acted out of a compelling interest to obtain the educational benefits that accrued from a diverse student population and meaningful integration. However, writing for the majority in the second case, *Gratz v. Bollinger,* Chief Justice Rehnquist appeared to contradict O'Connor's opinion. Rehnquist maintained that in admitting undergraduates the university crossed the line of what was permissible by giving points to black applicants: "The university's policy, which automatically distributed 20 points, or one-fifth of the points needed to guarantee admission, to every single 'underrepresented minority' applicant solely because of race, is not narrowly tailored to achieve the interest in educational diversity that respondents claim justifies their program."

Black Political Activism at the End of the Twentieth Century

24-5   **What were the focal points of black activism during the Reagan and Bush years?**

The increased participation of black men and women in the upper echelons of the Democratic Party reflected the success of black electoral politics and the internal mobilization of black communities. While in 1964 the nation had only 103 black elected officials, by 1994 there were nearly 8,500. By 2010, 43 African Americans were serving in Congress. In 1988 Representative William H. Gray of Pennsylvania became the first African American to reach the top ranks of congressional leadership, first as chair of the House Democratic caucus and then in 1989 as majority whip of the House of Representatives. In February 1989, Ronald H. Brown became the first African American to lead a major national political party when he was elected chairman of the Democratic Party. That same year, David Dinkins was elected the first black mayor of New York City. In 1990 Sharon Pratt Dixon (Kelly) was elected mayor of Washington, DC, becoming the first woman and the first District of Columbia native to serve in that position. By the mid-1990s, black men and women held the mayor's office in 400 towns and cities. Clearly, the days of black political powerlessness had ended—or had they?

By the 1990s African Americans had become an indispensable base of the Democratic Party. Reflecting the importance of African-American voters to the party, congressional Democrats passed equal rights legislation to solidify gains that blacks had won. The Civil Rights Restoration Act of 1988 authorized withholding federal funds from an entire institution if any program within it discriminated against women, racial minorities, the aged, or the disabled. The Fair Housing Act of 1988 stipulated that either an individual or the Department of Housing and Urban Development could bring a complaint of housing discrimination and authorize administrative judges to investigate housing complaints, issue injunctions and fines, and award punitive damages. These laws and the Civil Rights Act of 1991 were a response to Supreme Court decisions that narrowed the scope of earlier civil rights legislation.

Reparations

While party politics attracted attention, many African Americans focused on specific issues, including reparations for slavery, and the spread of HIV/AIDS in the United States and Africa. In 1969 James Foreman, in his "Black Manifesto," called on America's churches and synagogues to collect $500 million as "a beginning of the reparations due us as a people who have been exploited and degraded, brutalized, killed, and persecuted." Although Foreman's call was widely publicized, churches made no serious effort to respond to his demand. Four years later, Boris Bittker, a Yale Law School professor, argued in *The Case for Black Reparations* that slavery and the persistence of government-sanctioned racial discrimination justified a program to compensate black Americans. Since 1993 black Democratic Congressman John Conyers from Detroit has introduced a bill in every session of Congress—not to pay reparations but to establish a federal commission to investigate slavery and the legacy of racial discrimination. The bill has never come to the floor of the House for a vote.

In 2000 the issue of reparations for slavery received widespread attention when Randall Robinson, founder and president of TransAfrica, published *The Debt: What America Owes to Blacks*. Robinson reasoned that because Jews and Japanese Americans have been compensated for the indignities and horrors they experienced in World War II, African Americans were also due financial indemnification for slavery, "246 years of an enterprise murderous both of a people and their culture." Robinson maintained that many African Americans still bear the scars of slavery in terms of poor housing, inadequate health care, and insufficient educational opportunities. He insists that reparations would remedy the effect of such inequalities. Temple University professor and Afrocentrist Molefi Asante proposed that, instead of "a one-time cash payout," the American government make long-term commitments for "educational, health care, land or property grants, and a combination of such grants. . . . What I have argued for is the establishment of some type of organization that would evaluate how reparations would be determined and distributed: the National Commission of African Americans (NCAA) would be the overarching national organization to serve as the clearinghouse for reparations."

Some black writers and journalists reject arguments that reparations are a realistic resolution of the nation's slave and racist legacy. Two black journalists, William Raspberry and

Juan Williams, objected to the very idea of reparations. Instead, Raspberry favors more investment in education for African Americans, "not because of debts owed to or incurred by our ancestors, but because America needs its citizens to be educated and productive." Williams declared, "The suffering of long-dead ancestors is not a claim check for a bag full of cash. I don't want any money that belongs to any slave. That is obscene. The struggle of African-Americans for civil rights is not about selling out for a check."

TransAfrica and Black Internationalism

Black activism persisted on the international as well as the national front. Much of this effort focused on ending the oppressive conditions of apartheid—the complete social, political, and economic isolation and subjection of black people—in South Africa and its glorification of white racial supremacy.

Randall Robinson, a native of Richmond, Virginia, and a graduate of Harvard Law School who had worked for Michigan Congressman Charles Diggs, sought to link African-American liberation struggles with those that Africans in South Africa and elsewhere waged. In 1977 he founded Trans-Africa to lobby for black political prisoners in South Africa, chief among them Nelson Mandela. In 1984 Mary Francis Berry, Eleanor Holmes Norton, and others joined Robinson for a series of sit-ins at the South African embassy in Washington, DC, during which hundreds were arrested.

The anti-apartheid movement became a major priority for African-American activists. They enlisted the sympathy and help of white Americans on college campuses and pressured universities into divesting their investments in South Africa. Similar pressures were put on corporations, especially those vulnerable to consumer boycotts. In 1986 the Black Congressional Caucus persuaded its colleagues to enact a trade embargo against South Africa and to sustain it over President Reagan's veto.

In 1990, bowing to international pressure, black activism, and a souring domestic economy, South African President F. W. de Klerk removed the ban on the African National Congress, the key opposition party, and ended the 28-year incarceration of Nelson Mandela. Soon thereafter, South Africa became a multiracial democracy, and Mandela was elected its president.

((•)) ▭ **Read** on **MyHistoryLab Document:** Nelson Mandela Speaks after Being Released from Prison, 1990

Nelson Mandela's release from prison was celebrated around the globe as the event that signaled the final days of South Africa's system of racial apartheid.

The Rise in Black Incarceration

24-6   How did general white perceptions of young black men shape trends in criminal justice in the 1990s?

The general white perception of black men as criminals increased following Bush's election. Even during the Democratic Party's resurgence in the 1990s, the perceptions of black youths as criminals acquired potent political currency, resulting in the mass incarceration of young black men and an increase in police brutality and racial profiling. After the disputed 2000 presidential election, the black community became even more aware of the adverse consequences of mass incarceration because many states deny the right to vote to convicted and incarcerated felons, and 1.8 million of the 5.9 million felons and former felons in the United States are black. Researchers have concluded that "If not for disfranchisement . . . the 2000 presidential election would have been reversed, if former felons in a single state (Florida) had had the right to vote." Moreover, black people, especially black men, are incarcerated in astonishingly high numbers. (For the statistics on black incarceration, see Table 23–2 in Chapter 23.)

Reformers have sought to draw attention to the brutal conditions within U.S. prisons, especially the violence and high incidence of inmate rape. Yet they have achieved little. In 1994 Supreme Court Justice Clarence Thomas argued, in voting to dismiss claims that prisons failed to protect inmates, that "prisons are necessarily dangerous places, they house society's most antisocial and violent people in close proximity with one another. Regrettably, some level of brutality and sexual aggression among [prisoners] is inevitable no matter what the guards do . . . unless all prisoners are locked in their cells twenty-four hours a day and sedated."

Policing the Black Community

In March 1991 Los Angeles police pulled Rodney Glen King from his car after a high-speed chase and beat him with nightsticks. A bystander captured the incident on videotape, which television newscasts broadcast repeatedly, fueling long-simmering anger over police brutality among African Americans in Los Angeles. When a jury of 11 white Americans and one Hispanic American acquitted the four police officers involved in the incident of all but one of the charges brought against them, south-central Los Angeles erupted in protest. The verdict highlighted the gulf between the perceptions of white and black Americans about the police and the criminal justice system. Where the mostly white jury had seen the police maintaining law and order, black Americans saw police repression and racism. Altogether, 52 people were killed in the outbreak that followed the verdict. Arsonists and looters devastated much of the community. Thousands of people were injured, 4,000 were arrested, and an estimated half-billion-dollar's worth of property was damaged or destroyed. The four officers were later retried in federal court on charges of violating King's civil rights. This time juries found two of them guilty and acquitted the other two. Meanwhile, a jury in King's civil suit ordered Los Angeles to pay him $3.8 million in damages.

The Rodney King episode resonated with black men across the country. Earl Ofari Hutchinson suggested why:

> Black professionals or business owners still tell harrowing tales of being spread-eagle over the hoods of their expensive BMW's or Porsches while the police ran makes on them and tore their cars apart searching for drugs. In polls taken after the Rodney King beating, blacks were virtually unanimous in saying that they believed any black person could have been on the ground that night being pulverized by the police. These were eternal reminders to the "new" black bourgeoisie that they could escape the hood, but many Americans still considered them hoods.

The videotaped beating of Rodney King by Los Angeles police—shown repeatedly on national television—bolstered charges by African Americans in Los Angeles that they were frequent victims of police brutality. Despite the graphic evidence, the officers were acquitted of using excessive force.

Black Men and White Injustice

Several such high-profile cases focused public attention on the relation of black communities to white police authorities from the 1980s into the 2000s. Police repression was a long-festering cause of tension and hostility that had been behind many of the riots of the 1960s. On November 16, 1992, two Detroit police officers were charged with the murder of Malice Green, a 35-year-old black resident of the city. In 1997 a Haitian immigrant, Abner Louima, was beaten and sodomized while in custody at a Brooklyn police station. In 1999 New York police shot Amadou Diallo, a West African immigrant, 41 times when they mistook his reaching for a wallet for going for a gun. A jury in Albany, New York, acquitted the four police officials charged in the Diallo killing. Also in 2000, Patrick Dorismond (another Haitian immigrant) was shot and killed in New York after he got into an argument with undercover police officers after he refused to buy drugs from them. In 2006 New York police officers killed unarmed 23-year-old Sean Bell, who was on his way to marry the mother of his two children. Apparently Bell was caught in the middle of an undercover sting operation. Police fired at least 50 bullets into his car. In each instance, an enraged black community protested the police profiling as another instance of bias toward black men and one that targeted all minorities for illegal detention. At a protest rally over Bell's shooting, Rev. Al Sharpton declared, "We cannot allow this to continue to happen. We've got to understand that all of us were in that car."

Human Rights in America

In October 1998 the human rights group Amnesty International, known for condemning human rights abuses in countries with repressive governments, reported on police brutality in the United States. The report covered local and state police, the FBI, the Immigration and Naturalization Service, and the prison system. Its contents came as no surprise to most black Americans or, indeed, to any resident of America's poor urban neighborhoods. The report detailed violations of the UN Code of Conduct for Law Enforcement Officials and the UN Basic Principles on the Use of Force and Firearms. Among the violations cited were the following:

- The shooting of unarmed suspects fleeing a minor crime scene
- Excessive force used on mentally ill or disturbed people
- Multiple shootings of a suspect, sometimes after the suspect was apprehended or disabled
- The beating of unresisting suspects
- The misuse of batons, chemical sprays, and electroshock weapons

These violations all involved the misuse of force during arrests, traffic stops, searches, and so forth. The report also cited sexual abuse of prisoners and the denial of food and water to them. The report noted that while most victims of American law enforcement abuse were members of racial and ethnic minorities, most police officers were white.

It is too easy to interpret these findings as showing that American police officers, as a group, are racists who oppress people they do not like. In fact, the issue of police brutality is not nearly so simple. Police officers are under tremendous pressure and live dangerous lives, in part because guns are so widely available in America. No one can be expected to have perfect judgment about using force, and the cumulative effect of years of dealing with violence can destroy a person's sense of perspective and moral equilibrium.

Neither is the problem of crime by black Americans a simple one. The level of crime in black communities is high. The murder rate, for example, for African Americans in 2009 is seven times that of whites, and black victims accounted for 46.9 percent of all those murdered, even though African Americans make up only 12 percent of the population. Over 90 percent of those who murder, rape, and assault black people are black themselves. The murder rate for young black men between the ages of 14 and 17 tripled between 1976 and 1993. Although this rate, like the rate of violent crime in the country in general, has continued to fall since the late 1990s, the security of many African Americans remains imperiled.

Crime devastates black neighborhoods. High crime rates raise the costs of business, driving jobs and investment dollars out of the areas that most need them. Fear of violence leads many in the inner cities to barricade themselves inside their homes. Crime has transformed once vibrant neighborhoods into virtual ghost towns where only the sound of gunfire disturbs the silence of the streets. Filmmaker Spike Lee was shocked in 1994 when he returned to the Brooklyn neighborhood in which he had grown up to shoot his film *Crooklyn*. He found the streets had become so unsafe that the local children he used as extras had to be taught how to play the games he had played growing up in the 1970s because they had never been allowed to play outside. "Nowadays," Lee reflected, "these kids, they'll shoot you dead in a

24-1
24-2
24-3
24-4
24-5
24-6
24-7
24-8
24-9

second and not even think about it. The two big problems are crack and how accessible guns are. And also, you're talking about what Reagan did during his eight years. If I was a parent, I'd be terrified anytime my children left my sight. When I was growing up, I just had to be home by dark." Even Rosa Parks, heroine of the civil rights movement, was not immune to the urban crime wave. In 1994 she was beaten and robbed in her Detroit home by a 28-year-old unemployed black man. Her assailant recognized Parks but assaulted her anyway.

Being disproportionately the victims of crime, most African Americans have looked to the nation's police departments for aid. Because of their growing political power, they have sought, not always successfully, to make the police both responsive to crime and fair in enforcing the laws. One key for changing the behavior of law enforcement officials has been the appointment of black police chiefs.

Black Politics, 1992–2001: The Clinton Presidency

24-7   **Why did African Americans remain supportive of Bill Clinton's presidency and remain loyal Democrats?**

During his first campaign for the presidency in 1992, black Americans welcomed Arkansas Governor Bill Clinton into their churches, schools, and homes. Black citizens and the civil rights leadership embraced Clinton's candidacy against incumbent Republican George H. W. Bush, who had done little to win their loyalty. White Americans, too, were dissatisfied with the Bush presidency. Although he enjoyed high approval ratings in early 1991 following American military success in evicting Iraq from Kuwait in the first Gulf War, by early 1992 his popularity had slumped in the face of an economic downturn. Still, at first, few operatives believed Clinton would unseat Bush.

Shrewdly, however, Clinton positioned himself as a centrist within the mainstream of American politics. This required him to at least appear to place some distance between himself and the liberal-progressive arm of the Democratic Party represented by Jesse Jackson and the Rainbow Coalition. Undeterred by charges of womanizing, draft evasion, and marijuana smoking, Clinton attacked Bush's record and promised to make government more responsive to the needs of Americans. The strategy worked. Clinton won in November 1992 with just 43 percent of the popular vote to Bush's 38 percent and third-party candidate H. Ross Perot's 19 percent. However, Clinton garnered 78 percent of the black vote and 39 percent of the white vote in key states including New Jersey, Michigan, New York, Illinois, and California. The election was not a clear mandate. Although Democrats maintained control of Congress, they gained no seats in the Senate and lost seats in the House. Republicans used the ambiguous outcome to launch a relentless campaign to undermine Clinton's presidency.

Most black people, however, considered Clinton the best president on race issues since Lyndon Johnson. Writer Toni Morrison called

👁 **Watch** on **MyHistoryLab Video:**
The Clinton Years

President William Jefferson Clinton is seen here with members of the Little Rock Nine, who, as teenagers, defied hostile mobs to desegregate Central High School in Little Rock, Arkansas, in 1957. African Americans claimed Clinton as the first black president, given his comfort around black people and the number of African Americans he considered friends.

Clinton the first black president, and in some circles he was called the first woman president because of his support for equal rights for women, both black annd white. Clinton appointed women, including many black women, to 37 percent of the 500 upper-level positions in the White House and federal bureaucracy. During the campaign, he had visited the riot-torn ruins of south-central Los Angeles, played the saxophone on *The Arsenio Hall Show*, and worshiped in black churches, where he was warmly received. In Clinton, black Americans had a friend. Indeed, he named his black friends to his transition team: attorney Vernon Jordan (as cochair), Barbara Jordan, William Gray III, and Marian Wright Edelman, founding president of the Children's Defense Fund. Clinton also created a cabinet that mirrored the diversity of the American population, in some cases—such as Hazel O'Leary as secretary of the Department of Energy, Alexis Herman as secretary of labor, and Ron Brown as secretary of commerce—appointing black people to posts that had nothing to do with race. Clinton also gave to Washington, DC, delegate to Congress Eleanor Holmes Norton the prerogative, normally reserved to U.S. senators, of selecting U.S. district court judges, U.S. marshals, and the U.S. attorney for the District of Columbia. Moreover, not only did Clinton appoint many African-American officials and judges, he was the first American president to visit sub-Saharan Africa.

"It's the Economy, Stupid!"

In 1996 Clinton became the first Democratic president to win a second term since Franklin Roosevelt. Throughout his two terms in office, Clinton focused attention on the economy, a strategy that won grudging support from moderate Republicans. His objective was to strengthen the economy, since a stronger economy would improve economic opportunities for black Americans. In a significant departure from the policies of his predecessors, Clinton increased the taxes of higher-income Americans and pushed for an expansion of the earned income tax credit. His college student-aid program increased federal loan benefits. When Clinton left office in 2001, the country had the lowest poverty rate in 20 years.

Clinton's economic programs were supported by the Congressional Black Caucus (CBC). In 1993 CBC chairman Representative Kweisi Mfume of Maryland and the highest-ranking black congressman, Representative John Lewis of Georgia, delivered the caucus vote that saved Clinton's $500 billion economic budget (the Omnibus Budget Reconciliation Act of 1993) in both the House and the Senate. In return, black congressmen gained financial support for inner cities, poor families, children, and the elderly. For example, Representative Mfume credited the CBC for saving both the $2.5 billion allocation for food stamps that the Senate sought to eliminate and $3.5 billion in funding for empowerment zones in cities and rural areas.

Unemployment plummeted from 7.2 percent when Clinton took office to 4.0 percent when he left it. American businesses created 10 million new jobs, and many black people who feared they would never gain a foothold in the economy found work, some for the first time. Reduced federal spending and the 1993 tax increase helped cut the annual federal deficit in half.

The Welfare Reform Act and "Three Strikes"

Prior to his reelection in August 1996, and to the chagrin of his African-American political base, Clinton opportunistically signed the Personal Responsibility and Work Opportunity Reconciliation Act, a welfare reform bill. African Americans and many white political progressives were disappointed. The legislation combined Clinton's own ideas with those espoused in the Republicans' "Contract with America" blueprint for conservative changes. In 1994, the Republicans used this platform to secure control of both houses of Congress. The main target of the Personal Responsibility Act was Aid to Families of Dependent Children (AFDC), a program created in 1935 as part of the Social Security Act to prevent children from suffering due to the poverty of their parents. Critics claimed AFDC stipends discouraged poor mothers from finding work, that it was responsible for the breakdown of the family among the nation's poor, and that it did little to reduce poverty. They insisted the states did not have enough flexibility in administering welfare. The conservative welfare "reform" measure ended guarantees of federal aid to poor children, turning control of such programs over to the states along with allocations of block grants. The Welfare Reform Act denied benefits to legal immigrants, mandated drastic reductions in food stamp appropriations, and limited families to five years of benefits. It also required most adult welfare recipients to find employment within two years.

There were no good reasons to believe the welfare reform bill would accomplish its sponsors' objectives. Most of the people who would be "encouraged to find work" by having their benefits reduced or cut entirely were among the least employable people in the labor force. A study of individuals terminated from general assistance in Michigan, for example, revealed that as many as two-thirds remained unemployed. As for the bill's effect on families, it is true that most women on welfare had their first children when they were unmarried teenagers, but little evidence indicated that cutting welfare prevented teenage pregnancies. There was, however, evidence that the reforms which targeted improving the collection of child support payments for divorced mothers did reduce welfare costs far more effectively and humanely.

Clinton's support of the welfare act was consistent with his centrist ideology. Furthermore, it immunized him from Republican attacks while leaving black support intact. Clinton endorsed other policies that had a negative impact on African Americans and seemed, at least symbolically, to reassure white moderates. He signed a crime bill that allowed local communities to hire more police officers and build more prisons. He supported the implementation of a "three-strikes" policy of stiffer penalties for those who had at least two prior criminal convictions. Meanwhile, Clinton failed, in the teeth of intense Republican opposition, to enact comprehensive healthcare legislation. With little political alternative, having abandoned a third party political strategy, black support for Clinton remained strong. Clinton won a second term, easily trumping his Republican opponent, Senator Robert Dole of Kansas.

The preliminary results of the new welfare reform strictures indicated that, within a couple of years, half of those who had taken jobs had returned to lives of unemployment, poverty, and quiet desperation. As the economy took a downturn at the end of Clinton's second term, conditions for poor mothers and children deteriorated steadily. The debate over welfare policy receded to the back burner during the 2000 election campaign and disappeared completely after George W. Bush entered the White House.

Black Politics in the Clinton Era

Congressional Republicans and radical conservatives hated Clinton's presidency, and many of them hated Clinton himself. They vowed to take back the White House. Republicans raised huge sums of money and organized local constituencies, especially in the South. The Democrats seemed demoralized and did little to mobilize their base, especially in the black community. Their passivity had predictable results. Many African Americans did not vote in the congressional elections in 1994, and the Democrats lost control of Congress. For the first time in 40 years, the Republicans could implement their conservative agenda, which included rolling back environmental protection policies, reducing taxes for the rich, cutting benefits for the elderly, increasing military spending, establishing the primacy of Christianity over other religions, and advancing white supremacy.

Belatedly awake to the peril of black political alienation, younger Democratic leaders began to fight back. In 1994 Jesse Jackson, Jr., won a seat in Congress from Chicago, held until his resignation in 2012. Jackson outlined a comprehensive social democratic agenda for black America that included full employment, health care, high-quality public education, decent and affordable housing, a safe and sustainable environment, the right to vote, and equality of sexes before the law. Progressive Democrats understood that race was no longer a matter of just black and white people. Many other groups and movements were emerging, including Asian/Pacific Island-Americans, Arab-Americans, and Native Americans. Immigrants, especially migrant workers from Mexico, were forming labor organizations to fight for immigrant rights and social justice. But Democrats were now in the congressional minority, and party leaders seemed loath to knit together these diverse constituencies into viable grassroots organizations and to foster solidarity projects and efforts crucial to social change, such as affordable housing, higher-minimum-wage laws, universal healthcare coverage, and driver's licenses for immigrants.

While Democrats unraveled, Republicans drew strength from the appointment of Kenneth Starr as an independent counsel to investigate allegations surrounding Bill and Hillary Clinton's investment in an Arkansas land development deal known as Whitewater. As the investigations escalated, Clinton became caught up in a sex scandal. He denied sexual involvement with a White House intern, Monica Lewinsky. On December 19, 1998, the Republican majority in the House narrowly voted to impeach Clinton for perjury and obstruction of justice for tampering with witnesses to conceal his relationship with Lewinsky. The Senate, however, refused to convict him, and he remained in office. In the midst of the turmoil, Clinton derived solace from the unwavering support of black people, the CBC, and his friends, including Vernon Jordan and Jesse Jackson.

Black Politics and the Contested 2000 Election

The election of 2000 revealed fault lines of culture and geography, and the changing demographics of race, class, and gender. A gender gap of about 11 percent reflected the fact that men strongly supported Republican candidates and women favored Democratic candidates. The middle of the country and the South voted for Republican Texas Governor George W. Bush. Democratic candidate Vice President Albert Gore, Jr., carried the states of the upper Midwest, the Northeast, and the Pacific coast. Gays and lesbians voted 70 percent for Gore, whereas those who identified themselves as conservative Christians voted 80 percent for Bush. The campaign focused largely on economic issues—social security, taxes, health care, and education.

Black community leaders and organizations worked hard to register voters and increase turnout for the 2000 election. The NAACP, for example, spent $9 million on Operation Big Vote. Organizers even registered more than 11,000 inmates in county jails in the South.

Watch on **MyHistoryLab** Video: The Election of 2000

Gore v. Bush

In a hotly contested election, the outcome hung on one state: Florida. In the end, the Supreme Court, in a five-to-four ruling (*Bush v. Gore*), decided the issue by halting the recount of ballots in Florida. The Court's majority based its ruling on the Fourteenth Amendment's prohibition of states denying citizens equal protection of the law. The Court insisted the recount had to be stopped because the Florida Supreme Court, which had authorized it, had failed to provide uniform standards for determining the intent of the voters. Bush was declared the winner in Florida by fewer than 600 votes, which gave him a four-vote majority in the Electoral College.

Bill Clinton called *Gore v. Bush* "an appalling decision" and compared its impact on African Americans to the infamous *Dred Scott* and *Plessy v. Ferguson* decisions of the nineteenth century. Indeed, African Americans reported serious discrimination and interference with their voting in Florida. A lawsuit in Jacksonville, Florida, claimed that many votes were thrown out as "undervotes" or "overvotes," especially in the four districts with the highest concentration of African Americans in the state. According to the lawsuit, 26,000 ballots were not counted in Duval County, and more than 9,000 of those were cast in largely African-American precincts where Gore had captured more than 90 percent of the vote. Indeed, the U.S. Civil Rights Commission found that tens of thousands of African Americans were disfranchised in Florida. In a draft report, it declared, "African American voting districts were disproportionately hindered by antiquated and error-prone equipment like the punch card ballot system." This meant that more black and low-income voters, who tended to vote Democratic, had their ballots invalidated.

Explore on **MyHistoryLab** Activity: The Election of 2000

The chair of the commission, Mary Frances Berry, wrote in 2001 in the *Journal of American History,*

> The United States Supreme Court helped undermine the pursuit of equal opportunity by African Americans for most of our history. . . . *Bush v. Gore* was so striking, in part, because the 5–4 majority has been assiduous about deference to state courts and states' rights in general. What the Court has done is to remind us that judges have social and political views that are reflected in their decisions. Each side has used the equal protection clause of the Fourteenth Amendment to convey its policy preferences. But, unlike the majority, in cases involving African American voting and the outcome of the 2000 election, the justices in dissent have remained consistent.

Republican Triumph

24-8 How did the events of 9/11, the wars in Iraq and Afghanistan, Hurricane Katrina, and the election of Barack Obama affect black political consciousness?

Watch on MyHistoryLab Video: Politics in the New Millennium

In the 2000 elections, Republicans also retained narrow majorities in Congress. *Gore v. Bush* thus not only put George W. Bush in the White House but also meant that for the first time since 1954, the Republican Party was in control of the presidency and both houses of Congress.

George W. Bush's Black Cabinet

President Bush was aware that few African Americans had voted for him. But this did not prevent him from appointing well-educated, articulate, and accomplished black men and women to key posts. Such appointments tended to mute black criticism and placate white swing voters who disdained racial exclusion. Bush named General Colin L. Powell to be secretary of state. Powell, the son of Jamaican immigrants, had served as chairman of the Joint Chiefs of Staff (1989–1993), the highest military position in the Department of Defense. During his tenure he oversaw Operation Desert Storm, the victorious 1991 Persian Gulf War. Secretary Powell not only assisted in the formulation of foreign policy but also "represented the race." In a speech at Howard University, he expressed pride in his complex role of representing America's universalism on the global stage: "It's just terrific to be able to walk into a room somewhere in Africa, Russia, Asia, and Europe, and you know they're looking at you. You know how they be. They're looking at you and they recognize your position and who you are, and they also recognize that you're black. And it's always a source of inspiration and joy to see people look at me and through me see my country and see what promise my country offers to all people to come to these shores for a better life."

Bush also appointed Condoleezza Rice to be his national security adviser. Rice was the first African American and the first woman to hold this post. During the 2000 election, Rice had formed a strong personal bond with Bush, and this relationship became the foundation of her power in his administration.

In the 2000 campaign, Bush had vowed to reform public education. This was an issue of vital importance to both black and white families. Black parents were especially alarmed over the de facto resegregation of black children in urban schools. Thus, many were heartened when Bush selected black Texan Rod Paige as the secretary of education.

Paige introduced the No Child Left Behind Act, an education reform that Bush ardently embraced. This legislation, signed into law in 2002, required all schools to test students at regular intervals in reading, math, and science. States also had to publish the test results and sanction schools whose students failed to do well on the tests. Implicitly, the measure rejected integration as a primary social policy objective and retreated from mandatory busing while promoting parents' freedom to enroll their children in the schools of their choice through voucher programs.

Some African Americans, such as Anthony Williams, the mayor of Washington, DC, supported the voucher program, arguing that competition with strong schools would force weaker schools to improve their performance. However, Reginald Weaver, the black president of the National Educational Association, argued that the voucher program ignored the needs of most students in poor schools. The No Child Left Behind Act, he said, "gives $13 million to 2,000 kids who are going to voucher school, and $13 million to 27,000 kids to a charter school, and then $13 million to 167,000 other kids. . . . I think it is political, not educational." No Child Left Behind was soon mired in controversy. Critics, including many conservatives, blasted it for setting unrealistic goals and for not including sufficient federal funding to help schools meet the higher standards. In 2007 Congress increased funding under the act, but No Child Left Behind remains controversial, and many critics would still like to see it repealed or substantially modified.

Rod Paige was selected by President George W. Bush to be secretary of the Department of Education. Paige spearheaded a program in which employees of the department volunteered to mentor students in select schools in the District of Columbia. In this 2003 photo, Paige answers questions from students during a visit to the Skinner Magnet Center in Omaha, Nebraska.

September 11, 2001

Americans were stunned on September 11, 2001, when terrorists seized four commercial airliners and crashed them into New York's World Trade Center, the Pentagon in Washington, and rural Pennsylvania. Hundreds of African Americans were among the more than 3,000 people who died that day.

If the debate over reparations dramatized the separate pasts that black and white Americans have experienced, then September 11, 2001, reminded them of their common future. But the sense of national unity did not last. Less than two years later, as the United States prepared to invade Iraq, activist and scholar Manning Marable wrote of the lessons he had learned from the 9/11 tragedy: "No political ideology, no crusade, no belief in a virtuous cause, can justify the moral bankruptcy of terror. Yet, because of the military actions of our own government, any claims to moral superiority have now disintegrated, in the minds of much of the black and brown world."

War

Americans expected President Bush to devise an effective strategy against the Taliban regime in Afghanistan and to destroy Osama bin Laden and the al-Qaeda network, which was responsible for 9/11. The president pledged retribution, and the war in Afghanistan began on October 7, 2001. The Taliban were easily overthrown, but bin Laden and the Taliban leader, Mullah Omar, escaped.

Still, the Bush administration called its Afghan foray a success even though the Taliban launched a new guerrilla war and much of Afghanistan remained in the control of warlords and insurgents. Critics, such as Richard A. Clarke, the former chief counterterrorism adviser to Presidents Clinton and George W. Bush, argued that the Bush administration's real target after 9/11 was not Afghanistan and al-Qaeda but Saddam Hussein's Iraq. Clarke charged that Bush and National Security Adviser Condoleezza Rice had failed to heed the reports of a planned terrorist attack before September 11, 2001. Al-Qaeda, which claimed responsibility for the bombing of U.S. embassies in Kenya and Tanzania in 1998 and for an attack on the USS *Cole* in Yemen in 2000, should have been the national security priority. Rice denied these charges, but early in 2002 the administration began to shift the nation's attention from Afghanistan to Iraq.

24-1
24-2
24-3
24-4
24-5
24-6
24-7
24-8
24-9

The prospect of war in Iraq aroused mass protests at home and vociferous opposition abroad and at the United Nations, which refused to back the United States despite strenuous lobbying led by Secretary of State Colin Powell. In a speech before the UN Security Council in February 2003, Powell argued, based on what turned out to be misleading and possibly distorted intelligence reports, that Saddam not only had weapons of mass destruction but also had ties to international terrorist networks, including al-Qaeda. The Security Council was not convinced and voted against the invasion, but the United States invaded Iraq anyway on March 19, 2003. Only Britain gave it significant support.

As in Afghanistan, victory in Iraq appeared to come quickly, and Bush declared the mission there accomplished when Baghdad was occupied after a few weeks of fighting. However, it proved much easier to overthrow Saddam than to pacify Iraq. The country quickly descended into chaos. Insurgents attacked American occupation forces and those Iraqis who cooperated with them. Critics blasted the administration for failing to develop a coherent peace plan. The war, they charged, had actually strengthened terrorism, while the failure to secure UN support or to find weapons of mass destruction or establish ties between Saddam and al-Qaeda had damaged America's credibility and weakened the fabric of international cooperation.

Black Politics in the Bush Era

Massachusetts Senator John F. Kerry won the Democratic Party's nomination for president in 2004. The war in Iraq dominated other issues, including gay marriage and abortion rights. Kerry selected Senator John Edwards from North Carolina to be his running mate against incumbents George W. Bush and Dick Cheney. While these men campaigned, African Americans registered an important but subtle shift in their status within the Democratic Party as it became clear that they would play a key role in determining the outcome of the election.

The process of political transformation begun in the 1960s peaked in the 2004 presidential primaries. In these contests, African Americans emerged as the most reliable Democratic base and made their views heard and their power acknowledged. They wanted Americans to understand that little divided blacks and whites when it came to regaining the White House from the Republicans. In so doing, African-American leaders skillfully moved away from being considered spokespersons for a small special interest group. In 2004 they demanded acknowledgment of their central role as Democratic standard-bearers. Two of the nine contenders for the Democratic nomination were African Americans: Carol Moseley Braun, former U.S. senator from Illinois, and Rev. Al Sharpton of New York. Braun and Sharpton participated in all of the primary debates before throwing their support to Kerry.

In the spirit of presenting a united front, Braun, Sharpton, and Jesse Jackson addressed the delegates at the Democratic National Convention in Boston. The black star of the convention, however, was the little-known 42-year-old state senator from Illinois, Barack Obama, who was running for the U.S. Senate. Obama's keynote speech, claiming that good and efficient government would improve the life chances of all Americans, catapulted him into the limelight.

Bush's Second Term

On November 4, 2004, Americans reelected George W. Bush by a three-million-vote margin. After the election Colin Powell resigned. In repayment for her loyalty and experience in international affairs, President Bush appointed Condoleezza Rice to replace Powell as secretary of state. However, Bush's popularity soon began to plummet. Scandals rocked the administration. But it was Bush's mishandling of the Iraq War and the fumbling and inadequate federal response in 2005 to the devastation wrought by Hurricane Katrina to parts of the Gulf Coast and the city of New Orleans that defined his second term. In the 2006 midterm elections, the Democrats regained control of Congress. Nancy Pelosi became the first woman Speaker of the House, and several African Americans became chairs of

House committees. Democrats also captured most of the state governorships. Deval Patrick of Massachusetts became the second African American to be elected a governor in history.

The Iraq War

At the outset of his second term, Bush insisted again that America was on the right course in Iraq and that victory would soon be achieved there. Events soon proved him wrong. As the death toll in Iraq mounted—more than 3,500 U.S. troops and tens of thousands of Iraqis had been killed by the summer of 2007—most Americans lost faith in the administration's handling of the conflict, which had become a bloody civil war among Iraq's sectarian and ethnic groups. Civic life in Iraq all but collapsed amid daily suicide bombings, attacks on U.S. troops, kidnappings, murders, and other acts of terrorism. Corruption was rampant. Millions of Iraqis had become refugees. International opinion turned solidly against America.

By 2007, in response to Bush's low poll numbers and the unpopularity of the war, eight Democrats had launched campaigns for their party's presidential nomination. The prospective candidates included a woman, Senator Hillary Rodham Clinton of New York; an African American, Senator Barack Obama of Illinois; and a Hispanic-American, Governor Bill Richardson of New Mexico. This was the most diverse roster of presidential candidates of any party in American history.

Hurricane Katrina and the Destruction of Black New Orleans

Political decisions have consequences. The decision to invade Iraq and the years of combat there, together with questionable appointments to head the agencies charged with providing federal disaster relief, left the government unprepared in August 2005 to deal with the catastrophic devastation Hurricane Katrina caused. Although Katrina also hit the Mississippi and Alabama coasts hard, New Orleans suffered the worst effects. Federal funding for flood control in New Orleans, which is almost completely surrounded by water and part of which lies below sea level, had been reduced by 44 percent since 2001 when Bush took office. State and federal emergency services were so reduced and disorganized that they offered almost no protection from natural disasters. The plan to evacuate New Orleans if a major hurricane threatened the city ignored the fact that most of its poor residents, who were overwhelmingly black, lacked the means to flee. Moreover, one-third (35 percent) of the Louisiana National Guard, who would be needed to furnish aid and keep order in a disaster, was in Iraq.

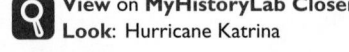

View on MyHistoryLab Closer Look: Hurricane Katrina

What suddenly became apparent to the nation and the world after Katrina struck was that most of the people trapped in New Orleans—abandoned, drowning, rendered homeless, starving, and destitute—were poor and black. New Orleans had been a black-majority city almost since its founding by the French in 1718. Although most black residents of New Orleans had always been poor, the city also had a thriving black professional middle class, private black colleges and universities (Dillard University, Xavier University), and black businesses. Over three centuries, the city's black community had produced a rich culture, famous for its food, music, literature, and artistic heritage. In addition to taking more than 1,500 lives in the city, Katrina damaged or destroyed much of that legacy.

Katrina moved ashore on Monday, August 29, 2005, and caused the highest storm surge in U.S. history. It punctured the levees that protected New Orleans in 53 places and inundated 80 percent of

Many African-American residents in New Orleans found themselves stranded literally and figuratively when the levees broke in the wake of Hurricane Katrina and the federal and state governments failed to provide prompt and sufficient relief and rescue efforts.

the city under 20 feet of water. Most of New Orleans's more affluent residents had escaped before the hurricane hit, leaving behind an estimated 100,000 people to weather the storm. With nowhere else to go and no means with which to get there, thousands of black people made their way to the Louisiana Superdome and the Convention Center, where they found wretched conditions—inadequate food, water, electricity, and poor sanitation. Violence erupted, and chaos loomed. As bad as the hurricane proved to be, the aftermath was worse. As survivors insisted, they were still American citizens and not Third World refugees, as some media figures called them. President Bush cut short his vacation and flew over the wrecked city, but he did not visit New Orleans until September 2, when he praised Michael Brown, the director of the Federal Emergency Management Agency (FEMA), for doing "a heck of a job." Since it was already apparent that FEMA's response and Brown's performance were ineffectual, the president's words outraged the nation—and black people in particular. (Brown was forced to resign on September 12 under relentless criticism.) Hip-hop rapper Kanye West departed from the script of a nationally televised program to raise funds for the displaced victims to charge that "George Bush does not care about black people." His comments made Katrina an "Emmett Till" moment for the hip-hop generation.

In the face of government ineptitude, individuals and groups used their own resources to bring relief to those trapped in New Orleans. Local community organizations mobilized to promote recovery, rebuilding, and renewal. Media stars such as Oprah Winfrey pledged funds to rebuild homes; Jesse Jackson led a caravan to transport hundreds to safety in Chicago. Eleven thousand homeless residents of New Orleans were bused 350 miles away to shelter at the Houston Astrodome. Churches and international relief organizations such as the Red Cross sent supplies, money, and clothes to those who had lost jobs, homes, and loved ones. Universities across the country welcomed students and faculty from historically black institutions, and professional organizations launched book drives to reconstruct libraries.

Yet this aid could not make up for the failure of the government's response. Today, much of residential New Orleans has still not recovered. Whole neighborhoods have disappeared. The city has lost almost a third of its pre-Katrina population. Most of the former residents who have not returned are black people. For the first time in centuries, New Orleans may no longer have a black majority, and in 2010 the city elected its first white mayor since 1978.

Black Politics in the Present Era: Barack Obama, President of the United States

24-9   **In what ways does the election and reelection of Barack Obama represent a triumph of black politics?**

Barack Obama accepted the nomination of the Democratic Party as its presidential candidate on August 28, 2008, in Denver, Colorado. In his acceptance speech, he promised if elected to usher in a new era: "We meet at one of those defining moments—a moment when our nation is at war, our economy is in turmoil, and the American promise has been threatened once more."

Obama versus McCain

The 2008 presidential election campaign was unlike any other in recent American history. The differences between the one-term Illinois Senator Barack Obama and the multi-termed Arizona Senator John McCain quickly became apparent. Obama used his matchless oratorical skills to call for change and inspire hope for a better future. He attacked George W. Bush's failed economic, educational, and social policies relentlessly. He also attacked the administration's rush to war in Iraq, its support for tax cuts for the wealthy, and a series of questionable cabinet appointments and scandals. Obama reminded voters that he had had the good

Read on MyHistoryLab
Document: Barack Obama, A More Perfect Union, 2008

judgment to oppose the Iraq War from the outset. He shrewdly selected Delaware Senator Joseph Biden as his vice-presidential running mate. Biden's 36 years in the Senate and foreign policy expertise made him a formidable candidate in his own right.

To be sure, on occasion both Obama and McCain deployed similar language about change and hope. Both spoke about the need for Americans to bridge their differences, pledged to work to perfect our union, and promised to inaugurate new politics of civility. McCain declared himself a "maverick" who had often opposed Republican policies during his Senate career. He also touted his experience and military background, especially his five years as a prisoner of war in North Vietnam. McCain insisted that he was ready to be commander-in-chief on day one if elected president. In contrast, the Republicans cited Obama's lack of experience and emphasized his "celebrity" to suggest that he was all fluff and little substance. Moreover, McCain predicted that Obama would raise the taxes of middle-class workers and indulge in wasteful spending.

McCain stunned the nation and delighted his supporters by selecting Sarah Palin, the first-term governor of Alaska, as his running mate. McCain believed she would attract white women who were disillusioned by Obama's victory over Hillary Clinton in the Democratic primaries. Palin was the first woman to share a Republican Party presidential ticket. A mother of five children, Palin's opposition to abortion rights, conservative rhetoric, and anti-Washington stand on government spending for pork-barrel projects (although as a mayor and governor she had accepted hundreds of millions of dollars in federal funds for Alaska) enthralled the Republicans' Evangelical Protestant base and energized McCain's campaign. However, Palin failed to win broad support from women, and interviews with journalists quickly revealed her ignorance of political, economic, and foreign affairs and raised doubts about her ability to be president should McCain die in office.

The turning point in the campaign occurred when the nation suffered the worst financial crisis since the Great Depression. McCain suspended his campaign to rush to Washington to help pass a huge federal government rescue plan for Wall Street banks. He tried to assure Americans that the "fundamentals of the economy are strong," though every indicator suggested the opposite. McCain appeared erratic, impulsive, and out of touch. By contrast, Obama seemed calm, steady, reasonable, reliable, and capable. Obama won the three televised debates between the candidates.

More than 120 million Americans voted on November 4, 2008. Approximately 67 million voted for Barack Obama, giving him one of the largest winning percentages in American history. The electoral college registered the extent of the Obama victory. He won 367 electoral votes to McCain's 173. Obama redrew the old electoral blue states/red states map by carrying states in every region of the country, including Virginia and Indiana (which no Democratic presidential candidate had won since 1964) and North Carolina, which the Democrats had not carried since Jimmy Carter won it in 1976 (see Map 24–1). He received an unprecedented 95 percent of the African-American vote.

For many Americans, Obama's victory signaled that "race" or "blackness" was no longer an insuperable barrier to the highest political office. His election heralded the dawn of a new day, the beginning of a new chapter in the United States and in the African-American odyssey. On election night, Obama stood in Grant Park in Chicago and told the world, "If there is anyone out there who still doubts that America is a place where all things are possible, who still wonders if the dream of our founders is alive in our time, who still questions the power of our democracy, tonight is your answer." Echoing Abraham Lincoln, Obama captured the moment:

> In this country, we rise or fall as one nation, as one people. Let's resist the temptation to fall back on the same partisanship and pettiness and immaturity that have poisoned our politics for so long. Let's remember that it was a man from this state who first carried the banner of the Republican Party to the White House, a party founded on the values of self-reliance and individual liberty and national unity.
>
> These are values that we all share. And while the Democratic Party has won a great victory tonight, we do so with a measure of humility and determination to heal the divides that have held

Read on **MyHistoryLab Document**: Dirty Politics in the 2008 Election, 2007

Read on **MyHistoryLab Document**: Darlene Clark Hine, Mystic Chords of Memory

24-1

24-2

24-3

24-4

24-5

24-6

24-7

24-8

24-9

24-1

24-2

24-3

24-4

24-5

24-6

24-7

24-8

24-9

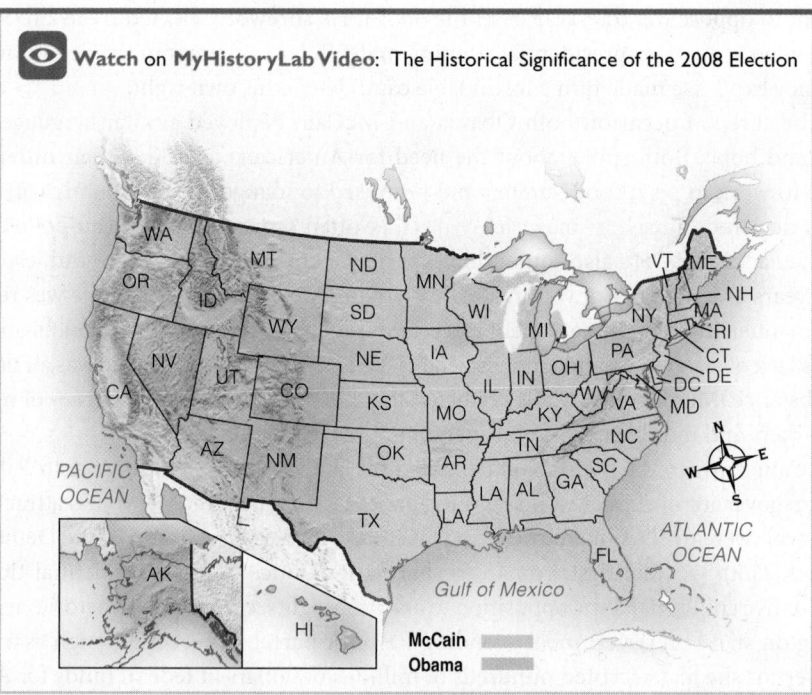

MAP 24–1 ELECTION OF 2008

This map captures the magnitude of Obama's presidential election triumph. It redraws the decades-long alignment of Republican red states and Democratic blue states. In the 2008 election, Americans moved closer to realizing the dream of one nation.

Which southern states most notably voted for Obama?

back our progress. As Lincoln said to a nation far more divided than ours, we are not enemies but friends. Though passion may have strained, it must not break our bonds of affection.

And to those Americans whose support I have yet to earn, I may not have won your vote tonight, but I hear your voices. I need your help and I will be your president, too.

On January 20, 2009, before a global televised audience of billions and before the two million who gathered on the National Mall in Washington, Barack Obama placed his hand on the bible that Abraham Lincoln had used and took the oath of office to become the first black president of the United States of America.

Obama versus Romney

In the 2008 campaign, Obama was helped by the support of his wife Michelle, who became an exceptionally popular and revered first lady. She was an even stronger and more powerful asset in his reelection bid. Again, black social and political icons from Oprah Winfrey and Tyler Perry to Colin Powell ardently supported both of Obama's election bids. Political supporters touted the fact that he had saved the American automobile industry. Others emphasized the national Affordable Health Care Act, the support for rebuilding America's infrastructure, the granting of citizenship to children of illegal immigrants, and his repudiation of the military's anti-gay policy, referred to as "Don't Ask, Don't Tell." Obama raised hundreds of millions of dollars in his second campaign. He used a considerable amount of this money early in the campaign to define the Republican Party candidate Mitt Romney as being hopelessly out of touch with the everyday realities of the lives of most Americans. Romney cemented this depiction in remarks (caught on tape) in which he dismissed 47 percent of Americans as being hopelessly dependent on government handouts and people who refused to take responsibility for their own lives.

PROFILE   Barack Obama

Twice elected (2008, 2012) President Barack Obama secured enactment of the Patient Protection and Affordable Care Act and ended the War in Iraq.

BARACK OBAMA was born in Honolulu on August 4, 1961. His personal history captures the complexity of identity in contemporary America. Obama's father was an immigrant from Kenya who married a white American from Kansas. When his father abandoned the family to complete his studies at Harvard, two-year-old Barack and his mother moved in with her family. In 1967, Obama and his mother relocated with her second husband to Indonesia, where Obama attended both a Roman Catholic and a Muslim school. Obama and his mother later returned to Hawaii, where he lived with his maternal grandparents and completed high school in 1979.

After high school, Obama entered Occidental College in Los Angeles before graduating from New York's Columbia University in 1983. His father, whom he had seen only once in the interim, died in an automobile accident in Kenya before his graduation. After a couple of years in the corporate world, Obama became a community organizer in Chicago, working to start a job placement and training center. His experiences as a community organizer taught him "that meaningful change always begins at the grassroots, and that engaged citizens working together can accomplish extraordinary things." He decided to pursue a law degree "to learn power's currency in all its intricacy and detail."

In 1991 Obama graduated from Harvard Law School, where he was the first African-American editor of the *Law Review*. He returned to Chicago and married Michelle Robinson, a native of Chicago's South Side who had also graduated from Harvard Law School. They have two daughters, Malia and Sasha.

In 1996, Obama was elected to the Illinois State Senate, where he voted to ban racial profiling and supported increased funding for child health care. He also helped pass a law requiring police to videotape interrogations of suspects in all capital crime cases.

In 2004, as a candidate for the U.S. Senate, Obama electrified the Democratic National Convention with an impassioned keynote speech. He declared, to thunderous applause, "The pundits like to slice-and-dice our country into Red States and Blue States. . . . But I've got news for them . . . We worship an awesome God in the Blue States, and we don't like federal agents poking around our libraries in Red States. We coach Little League in the Blue States and have gay friends in the Red States. . . . We are one people." A national political star was born.

In the Senate election, Obama coasted to an easy victory over his Republican opponent, black conservative Alan Keyes. Obama's victory made him the second African-American man to serve in the U.S. Senate in the twentieth century and the second black U.S. senator in Illinois history. The freshman senator wasted no time before opposing the Iraq War. Indeed, Obama had been a consistent critic of the war since the Bush administration first proposed it in 2002.

After months of speculation, in February 2007 Obama announced his candidacy to become the presidential nominee of the Democratic Party. He was a formidable campaigner, raising enormous amounts of money and attracting enthusiastic support from a wide spectrum of Americans. He addressed many of the key issues—the war in Iraq, health care, and public education—that were equally as important to African Americans as they were to others. Yet some African Americans were ambivalent about his candidacy. When asked to explain this, Obama said, "It's interesting that the people who are most hesitant about this oftentimes are African Americans because they feel protective of me. They're either concerned about the attacks I'd be subjected to or they are skeptical oftentimes that America is prepared to elect a black president."

((• **Listen** on **MyHistoryLab Audio:** *The Audacity of Hope* by Barack Obama, excerpt

24-1
24-2
24-3
24-4
24-5
24-6
24-7
24-8
24-9

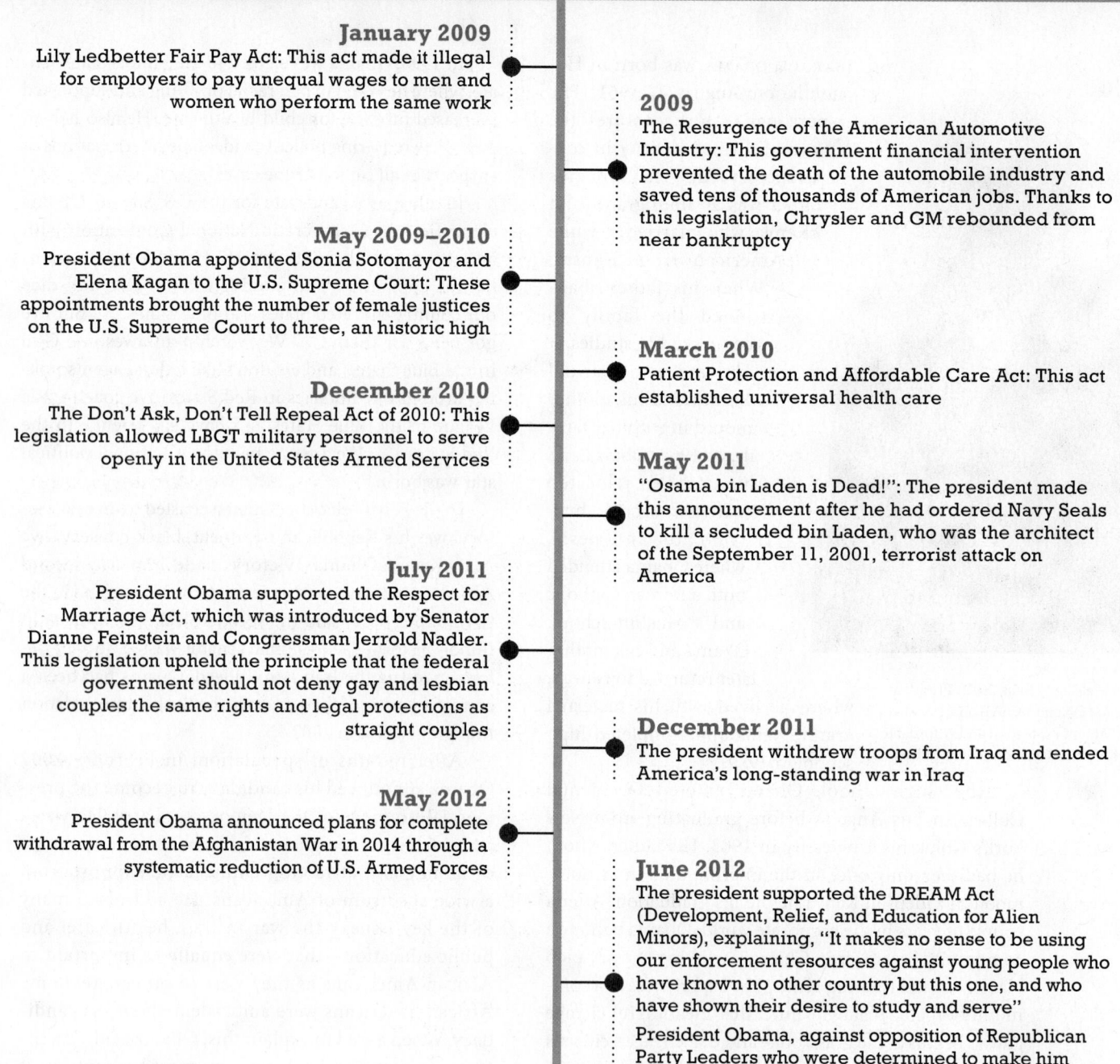

2009 TO 2012
SELECT FIRST TERM ACCOMPLISHMENTS OF PRESIDENT OBAMA

January 2009
Lily Ledbetter Fair Pay Act: This act made it illegal for employers to pay unequal wages to men and women who perform the same work

2009
The Resurgence of the American Automotive Industry: This government financial intervention prevented the death of the automobile industry and saved tens of thousands of American jobs. Thanks to this legislation, Chrysler and GM rebounded from near bankruptcy

May 2009–2010
President Obama appointed Sonia Sotomayor and Elena Kagan to the U.S. Supreme Court: These appointments brought the number of female justices on the U.S. Supreme Court to three, an historic high

March 2010
Patient Protection and Affordable Care Act: This act established universal health care

December 2010
The Don't Ask, Don't Tell Repeal Act of 2010: This legislation allowed LBGT military personnel to serve openly in the United States Armed Services

May 2011
"Osama bin Laden is Dead!": The president made this announcement after he had ordered Navy Seals to kill a secluded bin Laden, who was the architect of the September 11, 2001, terrorist attack on America

July 2011
President Obama supported the Respect for Marriage Act, which was introduced by Senator Dianne Feinstein and Congressman Jerrold Nadler. This legislation upheld the principle that the federal government should not deny gay and lesbian couples the same rights and legal protections as straight couples

December 2011
The president withdrew troops from Iraq and ended America's long-standing war in Iraq

May 2012
President Obama announced plans for complete withdrawal from the Afghanistan War in 2014 through a systematic reduction of U.S. Armed Forces

June 2012
The president supported the DREAM Act (Development, Relief, and Education for Alien Minors), explaining, "It makes no sense to be using our enforcement resources against young people who have known no other country but this one, and who have shown their desire to study and serve"

President Obama, against opposition of Republican Party Leaders who were determined to make him a one-term President, accomplished an impressive array of transformational policies

SOURCE: The White House.

In both the 2008 and 2012 bids, Obama's calm and steadfast demeanor, his eloquent and passionate oratory (at times resonant of the best of black preaching), and his manifest intelligence enabled him to capture the imagination, spirit, and yearning for change in an America weary of war and government incompetence, indifference, and economic insecurity. Prior to the November 2012 election, the fury of Hurricane Sandy wreaked havoc on the lives and property of millions of citizens in New York, New Jersey, Connecticut, and Maryland. Through it all, President Obama remained vigilant, supportive, and on the ground with residents and political leaders including New Jersey Governor Chris Christie,

Read on MyHistoryLab Document:
Barack Obama, Inaugural Address, 2009

PROFILE Michelle LaVaughn Robinson Obama

First Lady Michelle Obama made health, education, safety of children, and military families a top priority on her "Mom-in-Chief" agenda.

THE FIRST LADY OF THE UNITED STATES, MICHELLE LAVAUGHN ROBINSON, was born in Chicago in 1964 to working-class parents. An honor student, she graduated from Chicago's first magnet school for the academically gifted, Whitney Young High School, in 1981 and from Princeton University with a major in sociology and a minor in African-American studies in 1985. In 1988 Michelle earned her law degree at Harvard. In June 1989, she began dating Barack Obama. They married in 1992 and have two daughters, Malia Ann and Natasha (Sasha).

While information about her ancestry is sketchy, her paternal grandparents, Fraser and LaVaughn Robinson, Jr., were part of the Great Migration generation that left the South for northern cities, in this case from South Carolina and Mississippi, respectively. Michelle Obama noted the linked fate of black and white Americans: "Somewhere there was a slave owner—or a white family—in my great grandfather's time that gave him a place, a home that helped him build a life—that again led to me. So who were those people? I would argue they're just as much a part of my history as my great-grandfather."

After three years working in corporate law, in 1991 Michelle became an assistant commissioner of planning and development and a member of Chicago Mayor Richard M. Daley's staff. In early 1993, she became the founding executive director of the Chicago Office of Public Allies, a nonprofit organization that trained young adults for public service. In 2002, she became executive director of community affairs for the University of Chicago Hospitals. In 2007 she took a leave of absence to work on her husband's campaign for the presidency.

For 21 months, she played an invaluable role in humanizing, normalizing, and explaining her husband to a sometimes skeptical public that often questioned his ethnicity, citizenship, religion, experience, and vision and challenged her pride in her country.

Michelle Obama is the nation's first black first lady, and she has indicated that her primary responsibility is to ensure that their daughters grow up as normally as life in the White House allows. In her official capacity, Michelle has focused on the needs of military families, women's efforts to balance work and family, improving public education and nutrition, fighting against childhood obesity—one of her first initiatives was to plant a White House vegetable garden—and serving as a role model for young, marginalized, and disadvantaged Americans.

Michelle, the youngest first lady since Jacqueline Kennedy in 1961, is an important agent of change in American society's perception of black women and a strong role model for all girls and women across the globe. She represents millions of women juggling the demands of career, work, and family.

a Republican. The images of Obama being an active and caring president determined to alleviate suffering and to restore lives were powerful reminders of how much capable and compassionate leadership matters.

On November 6, 2012—after a bitterly contested, long, and costly campaign—the American public voted to retain Barack Obama as president of the United States. One of the most important occurrences during 2012 was the great lengths Republican politicians on both the state and national level went to in order to enact voter identification laws to suppress the black vote and reduce black electoral clout. The voter suppression movement had the opposite effect, however; through unrelenting mobilization, black voters turned out in a higher percentage than any other demographic group to return Obama and his family to the White House. This resilience and determination to keep their hands on the freedom plow bodes well for the future of black politics in America, and by extension across the diaspora. At the dawn of "the Obama Era," African, African-American Studies, and History Professor Paul Tiyambe Zeleza anticipated the emergence of "a more global and nationalistic world," a world that is "impatient with the old injustices and hungry for development, democracy, and self-determination."

24-1

24-2

24-3

24-4

24-5

24-6

24-7

24-8

24-9

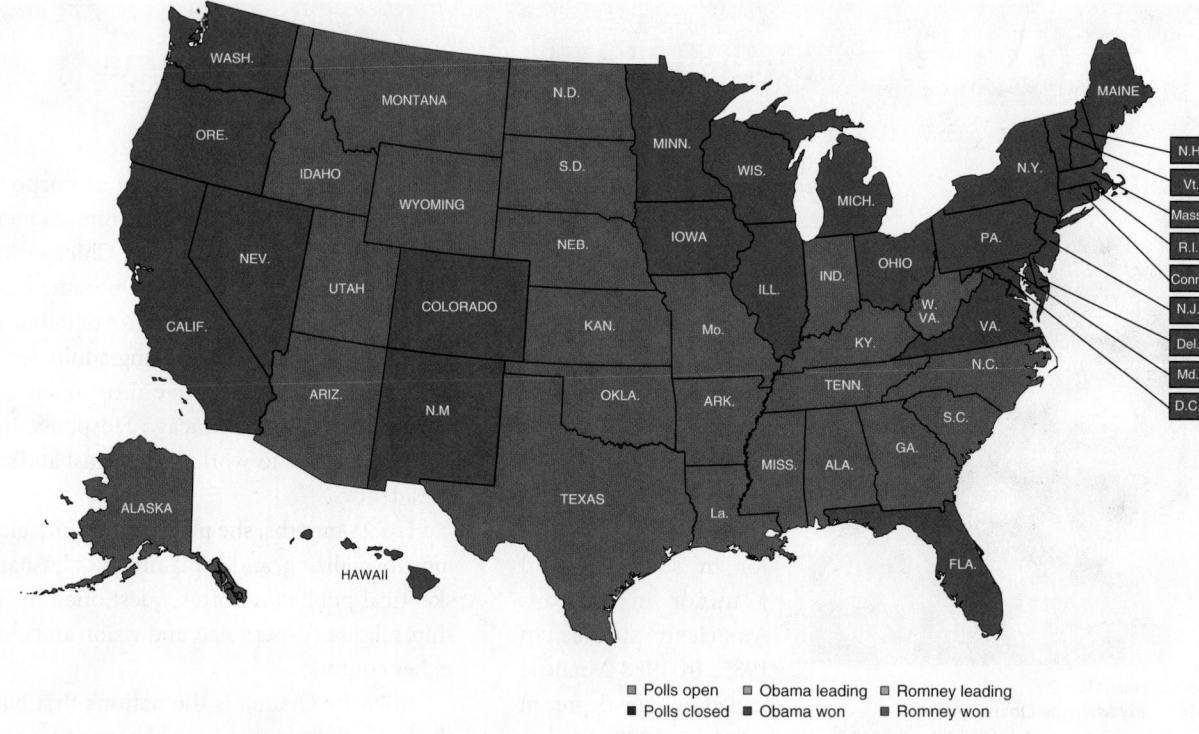

■ Polls open   ■ Obama leading   ■ Romney leading
■ Polls closed ■ Obama won   ■ Romney won

MAP 24–2 ELECTION OF 2012
This map captures the extent of Obama's presidential election triumph. It underscores the realignments of Republican red states and Democratic blue states.

Which states returned to the Republican fold according to the election map?

Factors Affecting the Elections of 2008 and 2012

Many factors contributed to Obama's improbable presidential victories both in 2008 and in 2012. The most important were his skilled, dedicated, and cohesive staff and a mastery of computer technology. His use of the Internet gave him a decisive advantage over Mc-Cain in 2008, and again in 2012 over former Massachusetts Governor Mitt Romney. In both the 2008 and 2012 elections, Obama's campaign staff executed a masterful ground game strategy that increased minority voter turnout. It was the higher black voting rate that, when combined with Hispanic votes and those of Asian Americans, proved decisive in 2012. Obama appealed to millions of new voters in both elections while the white vote continued to decline (see Map 24–2). In 2012, Obama won 80 percent of the non-white vote (including 93 percent of black voters, 73 percent of Asian Americans, and 71 percent of Hispanic voters).

Obama's presidential campaigns were the most technologically and computer-savvy in history. His background as a community organizer, his support of new immigration policies (especially the DREAM Act), and his embrace of the rights of same-sex couples to marry expanded his support in key demographic groups. His grassroots movement of volunteers on local and national levels and the use of celebrity supporters including hip-hop mogul Jay-Z appealed to younger voters while performer Bruce Springsteen attracted white working-class support. The Republican Party's cavalier attitude toward women's concerns, especially the negative remarks by Tea Party candidates challenging women's rights to make their own reproductive decisions, alienated white women voters who turned out in record numbers to support Democratic candidates. In the presidential reelection campaign, white women also voted overwhelmingly for Barack Obama (see Table 24–1).

TABLE 24–1 2012 ELECTION RESULTS: VOTING DEMOGRAPHICS

Total Popular Vote—Obama		65,455,010	**51.0% Wins**
Total Popular Vote—Romney		60,771,703	**47.0%**
Ethnicity	**Percentage**	**Ethnicity**	**Percentage**
Black—Democratic	93%	Black—Republican	6%
Asian—Democratic	73%	Asian—Republican	26%
Hispanic—Democratic	71%	Hispanic—Republican	27%
Other—Democratic	58%	Other—Republican	38%
White—Democratic	39%	White—Republican	59%
Age	**Percentage**	**Age**	**Percentage**
18–29—Democratic	60%	18–29—Republican	37%
30–44—Democratic	52%	30–44—Republican	45%
45–64—Democratic	47%	45–64—Republican	51%
65–100—Democratic	44%	65–100—Republican	56%
Gender	**Percentage**	**Gender**	**Percentage**
Men—Democratic	45%	Men—Republican	52%
Women—Democratic	55%	Women—Republican	44%
Location	**Percentage**	**Location**	**Percentage**
Urban—Democratic	62%	Urban—Republican	36%
Suburban—Democratic	48%	Suburban—Republican	50%
Rural—Democratic	39%	Rural—Republican	59%

SOURCE: CNN, Huffington Post, *and Mail Online.*

CONCLUSION

Jesse Jackson, whose Rainbow Coalition reflected a quest for unity amid diversity, asked at the 1988 Democratic convention, "Shall we expand, be inclusive, find unity and power; or suffer division and impotence?" The Hurricane Katrina disaster in 2005 reminded the black community of how precarious life remained for those trapped in poverty and perched at the intersection of race, class, and gender in America. The 2007 Democratic primary campaign illustrated the political importance of black Americans and the extent to which the Democratic Party had embraced its diverse constituency. African Americans remained committed to a progressive political agenda that emphasized universal health care, quality education, urban economic development, job training, safe environments, an end to racial profiling and police brutality, and reform of the prison-industrial complex that had disfranchised and oppressed so many black Americans and members of other minority groups. It marked another stage in the black odyssey toward freedom and the transformation of American society. In 2008, with the election of Barack Obama and his inauguration on January 20, 2009, to become the forty-fourth president of the United States, black politics came of age.

Few black Americans anticipated the depth of animosity that circulated within the Republican Party and among those whites who supported the rise of the Tea Party. Many Republican politicians vowed to make Barack Obama a "one-term president." They vigorously pursued an obstructionist stand and tried to block every progressive measure that Obama supported or advocated.

The election campaign of 2012 became a referendum on the policies Obama pursued in his first term. The success of the 2012 campaign, and Obama's 51 to 47 percent victory over his opponent Romney, underscored the triumph of coalition politics and the importance of grassroots community organizing and mobilization strategies in the twenty-first century.

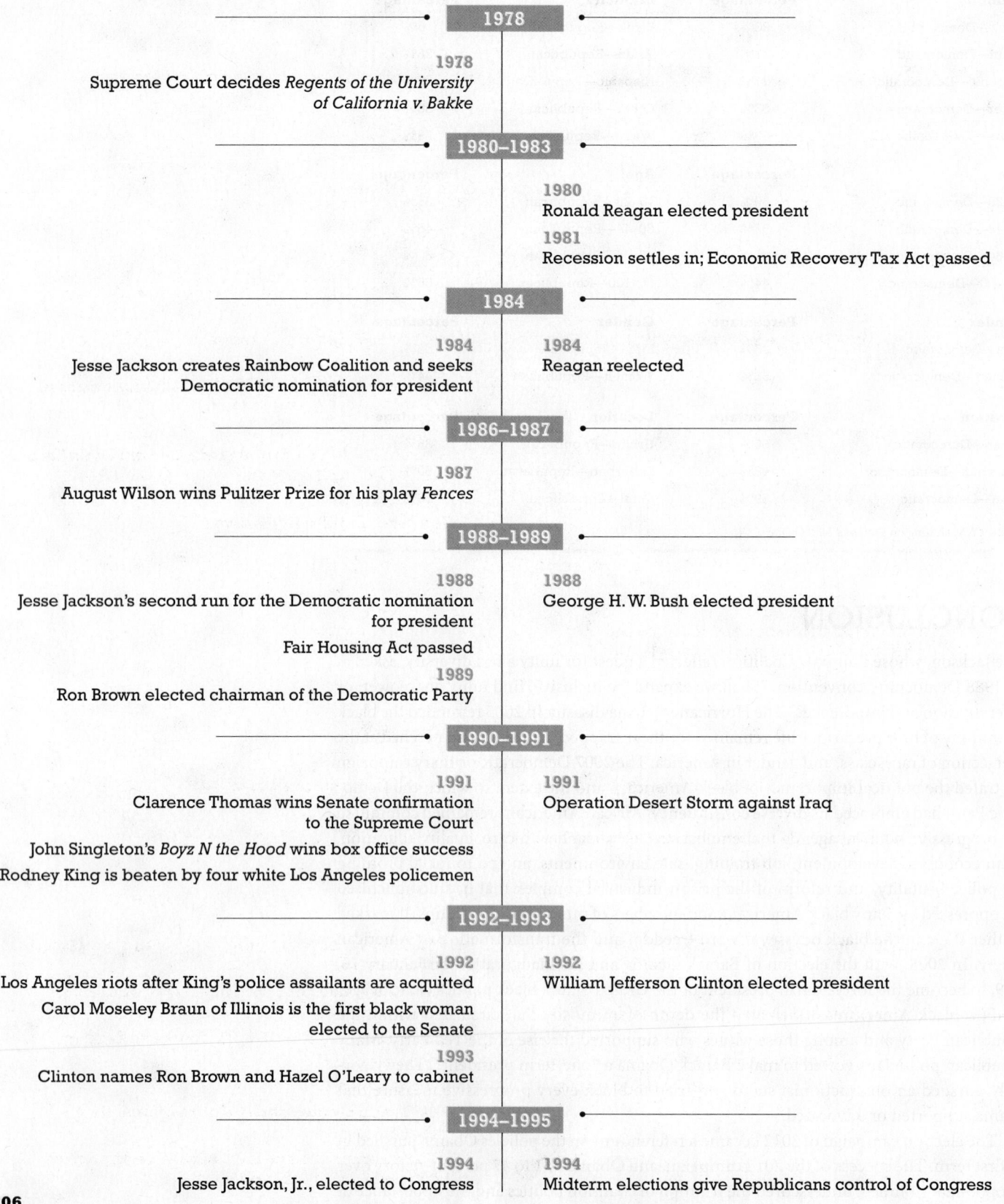

CHAPTER TIMELINE

AFRICAN-AMERICAN EVENTS   **NATIONAL EVENTS**

1978

1978
Supreme Court decides *Regents of the University of California v. Bakke*

1980–1983

1980
Ronald Reagan elected president

1981
Recession settles in; Economic Recovery Tax Act passed

1984

1984
Jesse Jackson creates Rainbow Coalition and seeks Democratic nomination for president

1984
Reagan reelected

1986–1987

1987
August Wilson wins Pulitzer Prize for his play *Fences*

1988–1989

1988
Jesse Jackson's second run for the Democratic nomination for president

Fair Housing Act passed

1989
Ron Brown elected chairman of the Democratic Party

1988
George H. W. Bush elected president

1990–1991

1991
Clarence Thomas wins Senate confirmation to the Supreme Court

John Singleton's *Boyz N the Hood* wins box office success

Rodney King is beaten by four white Los Angeles policemen

1991
Operation Desert Storm against Iraq

1992–1993

1992
Los Angeles riots after King's police assailants are acquitted

Carol Moseley Braun of Illinois is the first black woman elected to the Senate

1993
Clinton names Ron Brown and Hazel O'Leary to cabinet

1992
William Jefferson Clinton elected president

1994–1995

1994
Jesse Jackson, Jr., elected to Congress

1994
Midterm elections give Republicans control of Congress

CHAPTER TIMELINE

AFRICAN-AMERICAN EVENTS

NATIONAL EVENTS

1996

1996
Clinton reelected, signs welfare reform legislation

1998–1999

1998
Clinton impeached

1999
Senate acquits Clinton

2000–2001

2000
Donna Brazile manages the presidential campaign of Al Gore

2000
George W. Bush becomes president

2001
Bush names Condoleezza Rice national security adviser and Colin Powell secretary of state

September 11, 2001
Terrorists demolish the World Trade Center in New York City and attack the Pentagon

October, 2001
United States invades Afghanistan

2002–2003

2003
Supreme Court upholds use of racial preferences in admission to University of Michigan Law School

2002
No Child Left Behind Act

2003
United States invades Iraq

2004–2005

2004
Carol Moseley Braun and Al Sharpton run for president

Barack Obama elected to Senate

Condoleezza Rice appointed secretary of state

2004
George W. Bush reelected president

2005
Hurricane Katrina devastates New Orleans

2006–2013

2006
James Brown dies; Deval Patrick elected governor of Massachusetts

2009
Barack Obama inaugurated as forty-fourth president of the United States

Obama receives the Nobel Peace Prize

Michael Jackson dies

2008
New York Governor Eliot Spitzer resigns and is replaced by David Paterson

Michael Steele elected chairman of Republican Party National Committee

Roland W. Burris replaces Barack Obama as senator

2009
Edward M. Kennedy dies

Barack Obama secures passage of an Affordable Healthcare Act

Sonia Sotomayor becomes first Latina to be appointed to the United States Supreme Court

REVIEW QUESTIONS

1. To what extent and in what key areas did the Reagan and Bush presidencies nullify or dismantle Great Society legislation? How did African Americans respond to the Republican conservative reaction?

2. What was the significance of Jesse Jackson's campaigns for the Democratic presidential nomination? Why did African Americans become so important for the Democratic Party?

3. How did the welfare reform legislation passed under Clinton and George W. Bush's No Child Left Behind Act affect African Americans?

4. Why did affirmative action become so controversial in the 1990s? How did affirmative action in the workplace differ from affirmative action in education?

5. How did the Rodney King case illuminate the differences between how black and white Americans saw the police and the justice system?

6. How did the Hurricane Katrina disaster expose the fault lines of race, class, and gender in American society?

7. Why did Barack Obama defeat John McCain in 2008? Why was Obama's election so significant for African Americans?

RECOMMENDED READING

Martha Biondi. "The Rise of the Reparations Movement." *Radical History Review* 87 (Fall 2003): 5–18. A superb brief historical overview of the black reparations movement from the Civil War to the present era.

Cathy J. Cohen. *The Boundaries of Blackness: AIDS and the Breakdown of Black Politics.* Chicago: University of Chicago Press, 1999. A political scientist's sophisticated and provocative exploration into the social, political, and cultural impact of the AIDS epidemic on the African-American community.

Charles P. Henry, Robert L. Allen, and Robert Chrisman, eds. *The Obama Phenomenon: Towards a Multiracial Democracy.* Urbana: University of Illinois Press, 2011. An excellent anthology

of thought provoking essays covering a range of topics on Obama's first election, public policy, and culture.

Jeremy I. Levitt and Matthew C. Whitaker, eds. *Hurricane Katrina: America's Unnatural Disaster.* Lincoln: University of Nebraska Press, 2009. An excellent collection of essays covering the complexities of the Hurricane Katrina man-made disaster and the consequences of entrenched poverty and governmental ineptitude.

Deborah Gray White. *Too Heavy a Load: Black Women in Defense of Themselves, 1894–1994.* New York: Norton, 1998. A brilliant study by a black woman historian of black women and the community organizations they founded to fight for the ballot, equal opportunities, and an end to sexism and misogyny in black life.

ADDITIONAL BIBLIOGRAPHY

CULTURE AND RACE STUDIES

Michelle Alexander. *The New Jim Crow: Mass Incarceration in the Age of Colorblindness.* New Press, 2010.

Robin D. G. Kelley. *Race Rebels: Culture, Politics, and the Black Working Class.* New York: Free Press, 1994.

Jacob Levenson. *The Secret Epidemic: The Story of AIDS and Black America.* New York: Pantheon, 2004.

Manning Marable. *The Great Wells of Democracy: The Meaning of Race in American Life.* New York: Basic Books, 2002.

Terry McMillan. *Five for Five: The Films of Spike Lee.* New York: Stewart, Tabori & Chang, 1991.

Mary Pattillo, David Weiman, and Bruce Western, eds. *Imprisoning America: The Social Effects of Mass Incarceration.* New York: Russell Sage Foundation, 2004.

Nikhil Pal Singh. *Black Is a Country: Race and the Unfinished Struggle for Democracy.* Cambridge, MA: Harvard University Press, 2004.

Paul Tiyambe Zeleza. *Barack Obama and African Diasporas: Dialogues and Dissensions.* Athens: Ohio University Press, 2009.

BLACK POLITICS AND ECONOMICS

Barry Bluestone and Bennett Harrison. *The Deindustrialization of America: Plant Closings, Community Abandonment, and the Dismantling of Basic Industry.* New York: Basic Books, 1982.

Donna Brazile. *Cooking with Grease: Stirring the Pot in American Politics.* New York: Simon & Schuster, 2004.

Roy L. Brooks, ed. *When Sorry Isn't Enough: The Controversy Over Apologies and Reparations for Human Injustice.* New York: New York University Press, 1999.

Michael K. Brown. *Race, Money, and the American Welfare State.* Ithaca, NY: Cornell University Press, 1999.

Martin Carnoy. *Faded Dreams: The Politics and Economics of Race in America.* Cambridge: Cambridge University Press, 1994.

Dalton Conley. *Being Black, Living in the Red: Race, Wealth, and Social Policy in America.* Berkeley: University of California Press, 1999.

Robert Dallek. *Ronald Reagan: The Politics of Symbolism.* Cambridge, MA: Harvard University Press, 1984.

W. Avon Drake and Robert D. Holsworth. *Affirmative Action and the Stalled Quest for Black Progress.* Urbana: University of Illinois Press, 1996.

Robert Gooding-Williams, ed. *Reading Rodney King: Reading Urban Uprising.* New York: Routledge, 1993.

Lani Guinier. *Tyranny of the Majority: Fundamental Fairness and Representative Democracy.* New York: Free Press, 1995.

Andrew Hacker. *Two Nations: Black and White, Separate, Hostile, Unequal.* Rev. ed. New York: Ballantine Books, 1995.

Fredrick C. Harris. *The Price of the Ticket: Barack Obama and the Rise and Decline of Black Politics*. New York: Oxford University Press, 2012.

Melissa Victoria Harris-Lacewell. *Barbershops, Bibles, and BET: Everyday Talk and Black Political Thought*. Princeton, NJ: Princeton University Press, 2004.

Charles P. Henry. *Jesse Jackson: The Search for Common Ground*. Oakland, CA: Black Scholar Press, 1991.

Anita Faye Hill and Emma Coleman Jordan, eds. *Race, Gender, and Power in America: The Legacy of the Hill–Thomas Hearings*. New York: Oxford University Press, 1995.

James Jennings. *Welfare Reform and the Revitalization of Inner City Neighborhoods*. East Lansing: Michigan State University Press, 2003.

Randall Kennedy. *The Persistence of the Color Line: Racial Politics and the Obama Presidency*. New York: Patheon Books, 2011.

Roland S. Martin. *The First: President Barack Obama's Road to the White House as Originally Reported by Roland S. Martin*. Chicago: Third World Press, 2010.

Douglas S. Massey and Nancy A. Denton. *American Apartheid: Segregation and the Making of the Underclass*. Cambridge, MA: Harvard University Press, 1993.

Adolph Reed, Jr. *The Jesse Jackson Phenomenon: The Crisis of Purpose in Afro-American Politics*. New Haven, CT: Yale University Press, 1986.

Andrea Y. Simpson. *The Tie That Binds: Identity and Political Attitudes in the Post–Civil Rights Generation*. New York: New York University Press, 1998.

Special Issue on Affirmative Action. *Western Journal of Black Studies* 27, no. 1 (Spring 2003).

Thomas J. Sugrue. *Not Even Past: Barack Obama and the Burden of Race*. Princeton, NJ: Princeton University Press, 2010.

The Election Issue. *Souls: A Critical Journal of Black Politics, Culture, and Society* 14, no. 1–2 (January–June 2012).

Ronald W. Walters. *Freedom Is Not Enough: Black Voters, Black Candidates, and American Presidential Politics*. Lanham, MD: Rowman & Littlefield Publishers, 2005.

William Julius Wilson. *The Bridge Over the Racial Divide: Rising Inequality and Coalition Politics*. Berkeley: University of California Press, 1999.

LIBERATION STUDIES

Derrick Bell. *Faces at the Bottom of the Well: The Permanence of Racism*. New York: Basic Books, 1992.

Michael C. Dawson. *Behind the Mule: Race and Class in African-American Politics*. Princeton, NJ: Princeton University Press, 1994.

W. Marvin Dulaney. *Black Police in America*. Bloomington: Indiana University Press, 1996.

David H. Ikard and Martell Lee Teasley. *Nation of Cowards: Black Activism in Barack Obama's Post-Racial America*. Bloomington: Indiana University Press, 2012.

Brenda Gayle Plummer, ed. *Window on Freedom: Race, Civil Rights, and Foreign Affairs, 1945–1988*. Chapel Hill: University of North Carolina Press, 2003.

Randall Robinson. *The Debt: What America Owes to Blacks*. New York: Plume, 2000.

Ytasha L. Womack. Foreward by Derek T. Dingle. *Post Black: How a New Generation Is Redefining African American Identity*. Chicago: Chicago Press Review, 2010.

BLACK CONSERVATIVES

Herman Cain. *This Is Herman Cain!: My Journey to the White House*. New York: Threshold Editions, 2011.

Michael L. Ondaatie. *Black Conservative Intellectuals in Modern America*. Philadelphia: University of Pennsylvania Press, 2009.

Joe Soss, Richard C. Fording, and Sanford F. Schram. *Disciplining the Poor: Neoliberal Paternalism and the Persistent Power of Race*. Chicago: University of Chicago Press, 2011.

Thomas Sowell. *Preferential Policies: An International Perspective*. New York: William Morrow, 1990.

Shelby Steele. *A Dream Deferred: The Second Betrayal of Black Freedom in America*. New York: HarperCollins, 1998.

_____. *A Bound Man: Why We Are Excited About Obama and Why He Can't Win*. New York: Free Press, 2008.

Clarence Thomas. *My Grandfather's Son: A Memoir*. New York: HarperCollins Publishers, 2007.

AUTOBIOGRAPHY AND BIOGRAPHY

Marshall Frady. *Jesse: The Life and Pilgrimage of Jesse Jackson*. New York: Random House, 1996.

John Hope Franklin. *Mirror to America: The Autobiography of John Hope Franklin*. New York: Farrar, Straus and Giroux, 2005.

David Maraniss. *Obama, the Story*. New York: Simon & Schuster, 2012.

Barack Obama. *Dreams From My Father: A Story of Race and Inheritance*. 1995. Reprint, New York: Three Rivers Press, 2004.

Rev. Al Sharpton, with Karen Hunter. *Al on America*. New York: Kensington, 2002.

Rachel L. Swarns. *American Tapestry: The Story of the Black, White, and Multiracial Ancestors of Michelle Obama*. New York: Amistad, 2012.

Richard Wolfe. *Renegade: The Making of a President*. New York: Crown Publishers, 2009.

RETRACING THE ODYSSEY

The *Amistad* Research Center, Tilton Hall, Tulane University, New Orleans. The *Amistad* Center contains manuscripts and art that illuminate the history and culture of diverse ethnic groups and race relations in the United States. Approximately 90 percent of its holdings document the history and records of African Americans' community organizations and struggles. The center also houses records related to religious denominations—Protestant, Catholic, and Jewish. Its art gallery frequently exhibits the work of early black artists such as Aaron Douglas.

CONNECTING THE PAST

The Significance of Black Culture

John Coltrane (1926–1967) was one of the most profound and remarkable jazz musicians in the twentieth century. A master of the tenor and soprano saxophone to be revered for his instrumental improvisation. His most celebrated album, *A Love Supreme* was released in 1965.

IN AN ADDRESS CELEBRATING BLACK HISTORY WEEK in 1935, Kirkland W. Green, Dean of Arts and Sciences at South Carolina State College, declared, "The Negro has traveled through four hundred years of American history amidst thorns of torture, ridicule, scorn, degradation, and shame. These thorns have torn his flesh and wounded his soul. Bathed in blood and tears, he prayed and sang for the coming of a new day when he would come into his own, in possession of his birthright, freedom, recognition of a man's chance—the right to live his best self to fulfill his God given mission. Millions waited for this day and died."

Across the centuries, African Americans created and forged significant black culture movements at pivotal turning points in their long odyssey from slavery to full citizenship. In the twentieth century there were black renaissances in 1920s Harlem and in Chicago from the 1930s through the 1950s against the backdrop of the Great Depression and World War II. Across the United States in the first half of the twentieth century, the cultural achievements of talented black writers and performers made black people feel at home and proud in their new urban environments created by the Great Migration from the rural South to northern and western cities. The southern rural, agricultural-based Negro evolved into first, "The New Negro," then into the "black metropolitan," and finally into empowered members of an "industrial working class" who became activists for social change through their membership in labor unions. At each stage in this evolution or transformation, black cultural workers, artists, writers, and performers forged new weapons that enabled black people to achieve a sense of belonging both to their own community and to the nation as a whole. It also enabled them to shake off the demeaning and dehumanizing stereotype of blackness that centuries of oppression had forced on them.

Indeed, the U.S. government, especially the State Department in the early years of the Cold War against Soviet Communism, recognized this and tried to harness the power and appeal of black culture to win allies in Third World countries. The State Department sponsored international tours and cultural programs by representative black entertainers and spokespersons, including musicians such as Louis Armstrong, Count Basie, and Ella Fitzgerald; painters and writers; actors and dancers like Katherine Dunham; and sportsmen, from Joe Louis to Jackie Robinson, to testify that America was not the most racist country on Earth as depicted in communist propaganda.

In the 1960s and 1970s, the Black Arts Movement flourished in New York, Chicago, Detroit, Los Angeles, and Washington, DC. It was the creative and artistic counterpart to the Civil Rights and Black Power movements. Black musicians produced two strands of art during these decades when the rhythm and blues and soul music of artists like James Brown, Stevie Wonder, and Aretha Franklin flourished alongside the innovative jazz of giants like Miles Davis and John Coltrane.

More recently, the hip-hop cultural movement expressed the hopes and needs of a generation that felt it had received little benefits from the Civil Rights and Black Power movements. Globalization and deindustrialization, which destroyed the jobs that previous generations of black people had depended on, meant that too many black boys and girls of the millennial generation lived in communities with rising rates of poverty and heightened measures of social distress. Because their songs, poetry, body piercings, clothes, body language, movies, paintings, and even humor depicted an alternate reality that few adults could fathom or appreciate, they were repudiated for their use of profanity, sexist language, and seeming glorification of violence.

In each cultural movement of the twentieth and early twenty-first centuries, African-American artists and cultural workers rescued black consciousness from despair and oppression and gave birth to new identities and political awareness. Black cultural innovations reflected resilience and rebirth even when the future seemed most bleak, and the institutional, racist, and ethnic barriers seemed too high to be overcome. Thus, the poems, novels, essays, paintings, and sculpture, and the new styles of music and dance, the changing religious practices and theology, the oratory, and the employment of old and new technology and media emerged just in time to nurture the seeds of progressive black political activism and generate community mobilization, coalition politics, and the creation of empowering communal and individual identities.

Spike Lee, director, and activist, directing one of his ground-breaking films.

At each stage, black culture movements not only helped destroy demeaning racial stereotypes. They also transformed the black community. In the 1990s, the hip-hop movement showcased fundamental human and citizenship rights whose appeal went far beyond the borders of the United States. Hip-hop was enthusiastically adopted by a youth generation across the globe that was battling post-colonial domination, oppressive governments, and economic exploitation, and in the United States had to endure mass incarceration, educational failure, substance addiction, deportation, bullying, and sexual abuse. In other words, hip-hop gave a voice to the disinherited and dispossessed youth not only in the African diaspora, but in Asia, Latin America, the Caribbean, and Europe. But hip-hop was also, at its birth, just plain fun.

Culture is intimately connected with political awareness. The black cultural movements of the twentieth and early twenty-first centuries merged the "double consciousness" that W. E. B. Du Bois talked about in *The Souls of Black Folk* into "better and truer" black selves. Black cultural productions have continually provided new "intellectual equipment" that black people have used to examine, showcase, and discuss the realities and experiences of their lives and dreams. In this way, the lives and art of African-American culture workers have inspired oppressed people around the world.

Black culture has sometimes been dismissed as superficial and inconsequential. Yet the innovative, dynamic, and resonant productions of black artists, musicians, and performers have been in the vanguard of those movements whose appeal cuts across borders and smashes the negative social and political barriers that divide Americans along the fault lines of race, class, gender, and sexuality. The writers, musicians, and artists of the Harlem and Chicago Renaissances humanized black people, raised individual and group pride, and helped expand and preserve democracy for all Americans. They built bridges that connected the resolve of black people in disparate communities, nationally and internationally, to resist and reject dehumanization. Black culture workers from those Renaissances to the creators of the hip-hop movement were not only entertainers and artists. They also strengthened opposition to racial oppression, economic exploitation, political powerlessness, and social injustice. The complex, compelling, and inclusive nature of black culture is one of the great African-American achievements. It deserves to be studied with the same seriousness that we bring to the study of black migration, the struggles for political, social, and economic rights, and the history of sports.

Epilogue

Since the first Africans were brought to America's shores in the seventeenth century, black people have been a constant and distinct presence in America. During the prolonged course of the Atlantic slave trade, approximately 600,000 Africans were sold into servitude in what became the United States. By the outbreak of the Civil War in 1861 there were nearly four million African Americans in the United States. Today black people number over 30 million and make up slightly over 10 percent of the nation's population. Initially regarded merely as an enslaved labor force to produce cash crops, and not as a people who would or could enjoy an equal role in the political and social affairs of American society, African Americans constituted a separate ethnic, racial, and cultural group. For more than two centuries they remained outcasts.

People of African descent developed decidedly ambivalent relationships with the white majority in America. Never fully accepted and never fully rejected, black people relied on their own resources as they created their own institutions and communities. In 1852 Martin Delany declared, "We are a nation within a nation." A half century later, W. E. B. Du Bois observed that the black man wanted to retain his African identity and to be an American as well. "He would not Africanize America, for America has too much to teach the world and Africa. He would not bleach his Negro soul in a flood of white Americanism, for he knows that Negro blood has a message for the world. He simply wishes to make it possible for a man to be both a Negro and an American, without being cursed and spit upon by his fellows, without having the doors of Opportunity closed roughly in his face."

Sometimes in desperation or disgust, some black people have been willing to abandon America or reject assimilation. The slaves who engaged in South Carolina's 1739 Stono rebellion attempted to reach Spanish Florida. From the 1790s to the start of the Civil War, visions of nationhood in Africa attracted a minority of African Americans. During the 1920s, Marcus Garvey and the Universal Negro Improvement Association glorified Africa while seeking black autonomy in the United States. By the 1950s, Elijah Muhammad, Malcolm X, and the Nation of Islam emphasized a separate black destiny.

Yet in spite of the horrors of slavery, the indignity of Jim Crow, and the violence and discrimination inflicted, most African Americans have not rejected America. African slaves accepted elements of Christianity, and their descendants found solace in their spiritual beliefs. Black Americans have embraced American principles of brotherhood, justice, fairness, and equality before the law. The nation within a nation has never been homogeneous. There have been persistent class, gender, and color divisions. There have been tensions and ideological conflicts among black leaders and organizations. Some leaders, such as Booker T. Washington, have emphasized self-reliance and economic advancement, while others, including W. E. B. Du Bois and leaders of the NAACP, have advocated full inclusion in American society.

Furthermore, African Americans have been far more than victims, than an exploited labor force, than the subjects of segregation and stereotypes. They have contributed enormously to the development and character of American society and culture. As slaves, they provided billions of hours of unrequited labor to the American economy. Black people established churches, schools, and colleges that continue to thrive as they demonstrate a willingness to fight and die for their country. African Americans continue to make innovative contributions to art, music, literature, science and technology, athletics, and politics.

Although we are now in the twenty-first century, the long odyssey of people of African descent continues. While African Americans have been and remain "a nation within a nation," the election of Barack Obama in 2008, and his reelection in 2012, represent a remarkable milestone. Michelle Obama gives her husband's presidency an even deeper meaning, as America's first black first lady. Now, with an African-American family occupying the White House, black people will continue to help mold and shape our American civilization.

The Declaration of Independence

When in the course of human events it becomes necessary for one people to dissolve the political bands which have connected them with another and to assume, among the powers of the earth, the separate and equal station to which the laws of nature and of nature's God entitle them, a decent respect to the opinions of mankind requires that they should declare the causes which impel them to the separation.

We hold these truths to be self-evident, that all men are created equal; that they are endowed by their Creator with certain unalienable rights; that among these are life, liberty, and the pursuit of happiness. That, to secure these rights, governments are instituted among men, deriving their just powers from the consent of the governed; that, whenever any form of government becomes destructive of these ends, it is the right of the people to alter or to abolish it, and to institute a new government, laying its foundation on such principles, and organizing its powers in such form, as to them shall seem most likely to effect their safety and happiness. Prudence, indeed, will dictate that governments long established should not be changed for light and transient causes; and, accordingly, all experience hath shown that mankind are more disposed to suffer, while evils are sufferable, than to right themselves by abolishing the forms to which they are accustomed. But when a long train of abuses and usurpations, pursuing invariably the same object, evinces a design to reduce them under absolute despotism, it is their right, it is their duty, to throw off such government and to provide new guards for their future security. Such has been the patient sufferance of these colonies, and such is now the necessity which constrains them to alter their former systems of government. The history of the present King of Great Britain is a history of repeated injuries and usurpations, all having, in direct object, the establishment of an absolute tyranny over these States. To prove this, let facts be submitted to a candid world:

He has refused his assent to laws the most wholesome and necessary for the public good.

He has forbidden his governors to pass laws of immediate and pressing importance, unless suspended in their operation till his assent should be obtained; and, when so suspended, he has utterly neglected to attend to them.

He has refused to pass other laws for the accommodation of large districts of people, unless those people would relinquish the right of representation in the legislature, a right inestimable to them and formidable to tyrants only.

He has called together legislative bodies at places unusual, uncomfortable, and distant from the depository of their public records, for the sole purpose of fatiguing them into compliance with his measures.

He has dissolved representative houses, repeatedly for opposing, with manly firmness, his invasions on the rights of the people.

He has refused, for a long time after such dissolutions, to cause others to be elected; whereby the legislative powers, incapable of annihilation, have returned to the people at large for their exercise; the state remaining, in the meantime, exposed to all the danger of invasion from without and convulsions within.

He has endeavored to prevent the population of these States; for that purpose, obstructing the laws for naturalization of foreigners, refusing to pass others to encourage their migration hither, and raising the conditions of new appropriations of lands.

He has obstructed the administration of justice by refusing his assent to laws for establishing judiciary powers.

He has made judges dependent on his will alone for the tenure of their offices and the amount and payment of their salaries.

He has erected a multitude of new offices and sent hither swarms of officers to harass our people and eat out their substance.

He has kept among us, in time of peace, standing armies, without the consent of our legislatures.

He has affected to render the military independent of, and superior to, the civil power.

He has combined with others to subject us to a jurisdiction foreign to our Constitution and unacknowledged by our laws, giving his assent to their acts of pretended legislation—

For quartering large bodies of armed troops among us;

For protecting them, by mock trial, from punishment for any murders which they should commit on the inhabitants of these States;

For cutting off our trade with all parts of the world;

For imposing taxes on us without our consent;

For depriving us, in many cases, of the benefits of trial by jury;

For transporting us beyond seas to be tried for pretended offences;

For abolishing the free system of English laws in a neighboring province, establishing therein an arbitrary government, and enlarging its boundaries, so as to render it at once an example and fit instrument for introducing the same absolute rule into these colonies;

For taking away our charters, abolishing our most valuable laws, and altering, fundamentally, the powers of our governments.

For suspending our own legislatures and declaring themselves invested with power to legislate for us in all cases whatsoever.

He has abdicated government here by declaring us out of his protection and waging war against us.

He has plundered our seas, ravaged our coasts, burnt our towns, and destroyed the lives of our people.

He is, at this time, transporting large armies of foreign mercenaries to complete the works of death, desolation, and tyranny already begun with circumstances of cruelty and perfidy scarcely paralleled in the most barbarous ages, and totally unworthy the head of a civilized nation.

He has constrained our fellow citizens, taken captive on the high seas, to bear arms against their country, to become the executioners of their friends and brethren, or to fall themselves by their hands.

He has excited domestic insurrections amongst us and has endeavored to bring on the inhabitants of our frontiers, the merciless Indian savages, whose known rule of warfare is an undistinguished destruction of all ages, sexes, and conditions.

In every stage of these oppressions, we have petitioned for redress in the most humble terms; our repeated petitions have been answered only by repeated injury. A prince whose character is thus marked by every act which may define a tyrant is unfit to be the ruler of a free people.

Nor have we been wanting in attention to our British brethren. We have warned them, from time to time, of attempts made by their legislature to extend an unwarrantable jurisdiction over us. We have reminded them of the circumstances of our emigration and settlement here. We have appealed to their native justice and magnanimity, and we have conjured them, by the ties of our common kindred, to disavow these usurpations, which would inevitably interrupt our connections and correspondence. They, too, have been deaf to the voice of justice and consanguinity. We must, therefore, acquiesce in the necessity which denounces our separation, and hold them, as we hold the rest of mankind, enemies in war, in peace, friends.

We, therefore, the representatives of the United States of America, in general Congress assembled, appealing to the Supreme Judge of the world for the rectitude of our intentions, do, in the name and by the authority of the good people of these colonies, solemnly publish and declare, that these united colonies are, and of right ought to be, free and independent states: that they are absolved from all allegiance to the British Crown, and that all political connection between them and the state of Great Britain is, and ought to be, totally dissolved; and that, as free and independent states, they have full power to levy war, conclude peace, contract alliances, establish commerce, and to do all other acts and things which independent states may of right do. And, for the support of this declaration, with a firm reliance on the protection of Divine Providence, we mutually pledge to each other our lives, our fortunes, and our sacred honor.

Proposed Clause on the Slave Trade Omitted from the Final Draft of the Declaration

He has waged cruel war against human nature itself, violating its most sacred rights of life and liberty in the person of a distant people who never offended him; captivating and carrying them into slavery in another hemisphere, or to incur miserable death in their transportation thither. This piratical warfare, the opprobrium of infidel powers, is the warfare of the Christian king of Great Britain. Determined to keep open a market where men should be bought and sold, he has prostituted his negative for suppressing every legislative attempt to prohibit or restrain this execrable commerce.

The Constitution of the United States of America

(with clauses pertaining to the status of African Americans highlighted)

We the people of the United States, in order to form a more perfect union, establish justice, insure domestic tranquility, provide for the common defense, promote the general welfare, and secure the blessings of liberty to ourselves and our posterity, do ordain and establish this Constitution for the United States of America.

Article I

SECTION 1. All legislative powers herein granted shall be vested in a Congress of the United States, which shall consist of a Senate and House of Representatives.

SECTION 2. 1. The House of Representatives shall be composed of members chosen every second year by the people of the several States, and the electors in each State shall have the qualifications requisite for electors of the most numerous branch of the State legislature.

2. No person shall be a representative who shall not have attained to the age of twenty-five years, and been seven years a citizen of the United States, and who shall not, when elected, be an inhabitant of that State in which he shall be chosen.

3. Representatives and direct taxes[1] shall be apportioned among the several States which may be included within this Union, according to their respective numbers, which shall be determined by adding to the whole number of free persons, including those bound to service for a term of years, and excluding Indians not taxed, three fifths of all other persons.[2]

The actual enumeration shall be made within three years after the first meeting of the Congress of the United States, and within every subsequent term of ten years, in such manner as they shall by law direct. The number of representatives shall not exceed one for every thirty thousand, but each State shall have at least one representative; and until such enumeration shall be made, the State of New Hampshire shall be entitled to choose three, Massachusetts eight, Rhode Island and Providence Plantations one, Connecticut five, New York six, New Jersey four, Pennsylvania eight, Delaware one, Maryland six, Virginia ten, North Carolina five, South Carolina five, and Georgia three.

4. When vacancies happen in the representation from any State, the executive authority thereof shall issue writs of election to fill such vacancies.

5. The House of Representatives shall choose their speaker and other officers; and shall have the sole power of impeachment.

SECTION 3. 1. The Senate of the United States shall be composed of two senators from each State, chosen by the legislature thereof,[3] for six years; and each senator shall have one vote.

2. Immediately after they shall be assembled in consequence of the first election, they shall be divided as equally as may be into three classes. The seats of the senators of the first class shall be vacated at the expiration of the second year, of the second class at the expiration of the fourth year, and of the third class at the expiration of the sixth year, so that one third may be chosen every second year; and if vacancies happen by resignation, or otherwise, during the recess of the legislature of any State, the executive thereof may make temporary appointments until the next meeting of the legislature, which shall then fill such vacancies.[4]

3. No person shall be a senator who shall not have attained to the age of thirty years, and been nine years a citizen of the United States, and who shall not, when elected, be an inhabitant of that State for which he shall be chosen.

4. The Vice President of the United States shall be President of the Senate, but shall have no vote, unless they be equally divided.

5. The Senate shall choose their other officers, and also a president pro tempore, in the absence of the Vice President, or when he shall exercise the office of the President of the United States.

6. The Senate shall have the sole power to try all impeachments. When sitting for that purpose, they shall be on oath or affirmation. When the president of the United States is tried, the chief justice shall preside: and no person shall be convicted without the concurrence of two thirds of the members present.

7. Judgment in cases of impeachment shall not extend further than to removal from office, and disqualification to hold and enjoy any office of honor, trust or profit under the United States: but the party convicted shall nevertheless be liable and subject to indictment, trial, judgment and punishment, according to law.

SECTION 4. 1. The times, places, and manner of holding elections for senators and representatives, shall be prescribed in each State by the legislature thereof; but the Congress may at any

---

[1]See the Sixteenth Amendment.
[2]See the Fourteenth Amendment.

[3]See the Seventeenth Amendment.
[4]See the Seventeenth Amendment.

time by law make or alter such regulations, except as to the places of choosing senators.

2. The Congress shall assemble at least once in every year, and such meeting shall be on the first Monday in December, unless they shall by law appoint a different day.

SECTION 5. 1. Each House shall be the judge of the elections, returns and qualifications of its own members, and a majority of each shall constitute a quorum to do business; but a smaller number may adjourn from day to day, and may be authorized to compel the attendance of absent members, in such manner, and under such penalties as each House may provide.

2. Each House may determine the rules of its proceedings, punish its members for disorderly behavior, and, with the concurrence of two thirds, expel a member.

3. Each House shall keep a journal of its proceedings, and from time to time publish the same, excepting such parts as may in their judgment require secrecy; and the yeas and nays of the members of either house on any question shall, at the desire of one fifth of those present, be entered on the journal.

4. Neither House, during the session of Congress, shall, without the consent of the other, adjourn for more than three days, nor to any other place than that in which the two Houses shall be sitting.

SECTION 6. 1. The senators and representatives shall receive a compensation for their services, to be ascertained by law, and paid out of the Treasury of the United States. They shall in all cases, except treason, felony, and breach of the peace, be privileged from arrest during their attendance at the session of their respective Houses, and in going to and returning from the same; and for any speech or debate in either House, they shall not be questioned in any other place.

2. No senator or representative shall, during the time for which he was elected, be appointed to any civil office under the authority of the United States, which shall have been created, or the emoluments whereof shall have been increased, during such time; and no person holding any office under the United States shall be a member of either House during his continuance in office.

SECTION 7. 1. All bills for raising revenue shall originate in the House of Representatives; but the Senate may purpose or concur with amendments as on other bills.

2. Every bill which shall have passed the House of Representatives and the Senate, shall, before it become a law, be presented to the President of the United States; if he approves he shall sign it, but if not he shall return it, with his objections, to that House in which it shall have originated, who shall enter the objections at large on their journal, and proceed to reconsider it. If after such reconsideration two thirds of that House shall agree to pass the bill, it shall be sent, together with the objections, to the other House, by which it shall likewise be reconsidered, and if approved by two thirds of that House, it shall become a law. But in all such cases the votes of both Houses shall be determined by yeas and nays, and the names of the persons voting for and against the bill shall be entered on the journal of each House respectively. If any bill shall not be returned by the President within ten days (Sundays excepted) after it shall have been presented to him, the same shall be a law, in like manner as if he had signed it, unless the Congress by their adjournment prevent its return, in which case it shall not be a law.

3. Every order, resolution, or vote to which the concurrence of the Senate and the House of Representatives may be necessary (except on a question of adjournment) shall be presented to the President of the United States; and before the same shall take effect, shall be approved by him, or being disapproved by him, shall be repassed by two thirds of the Senate and House of Representatives, according to the rules and limitations prescribed in the case of a bill.

SECTION 8. The Congress shall have the power

1. To lay and collect taxes, duties, imports, and excises, to pay the debts and provide for the common defense and general welfare of the United States; but all duties, imports, and excises shall be uniform throughout the United States.

2. To borrow money on the credit of the United States;

3. To regulate commerce with foreign nations, and among the several States, and with the Indian tribes;

4. To establish a uniform rule of naturalization, and uniform laws on the subject of bankruptcies throughout the United States;

5. To coin money, regulate the value thereof, and of foreign coin, and fix the standard of weights and measures;

6. To provide for the punishment of counterfeiting the securities and current coin of the United States;

7. To establish post offices and post roads;

8. To promote the progress of science and useful arts, by securing for limited times to authors and inventors the exclusive right to their respective writings and discoveries;

9. To constitute tribunals inferior to the Supreme Court;

10. To define and punish piracies and felonies committed on the high seas, and offenses against the law of nations;

11. To declare war, grant letters of marque and reprisal, and make rules concerning captures on land and water;

12. To raise and support armies, but no appropriation of money to that use shall be for a longer term than two years;

13. To provide and maintain a navy;

14. To make rules for the government and regulation of the land and naval forces;

15. To provide for calling forth the militia to execute the laws of the Union, suppress insurrections and repel invasions;

16. To provide for organizing, arming, and disciplining the militia, and for governing such part of them as may be employed in the service of the United States, reserving to the States respectively, the appointment of the officers, and the authority of training the militia according to the discipline prescribed by Congress;

17. To exercise exclusive legislation in all cases whatsoever, over such district (not exceeding ten miles square) as may, by cession of particular States, and the acceptance of Congress, become the seat of the government of the United States, and to exercise

like authority over all places purchased by the consent of the legislature of the State in which the same shall be, for the erection of forts, magazines, arsenals, dockyards, and other needful buildings; and

18. To make all laws which shall be necessary and proper for carrying into execution the foregoing powers, and all other powers vested by this Constitution in the government of the United States, or any department or officer thereof.

SECTION 9. 1. The migration or importation of such persons as any of the States now existing shall think proper to admit, shall not be prohibited by the Congress prior to the year one thousand eight hundred and eight, but a tax or duty may be imposed on such importation, not exceeding ten dollars for each person.

2. The privilege of the writ of habeas corpus shall not be suspended, unless when in cases of rebellion or invasion the public safety may require it.

3. No bill of attainder or ex post facto law shall be passed.

4. No capitation, or other direct, tax shall be laid, unless in proportion to the census or enumeration herein-before directed to be taken.[5]

5. No tax or duty shall be laid on articles exported from any State.

6. No preference shall be given by any regulation of commerce or revenue to the ports of one State over those of another: nor shall vessels bound to, or from, one State be obliged to enter, clear, or pay duties in another.

7. No money shall be drawn from the treasury, but in consequence of appropriations made by law; and a regular statement and account of the receipts and expenditures of all public money shall be published from time to time.

8. No title of nobility shall be granted by the United States: and no person holding any office of profit or trust under them, shall, without the consent of the Congress, accept of any present, emolument, office, or title, of any kind whatever, from any king, prince, or foreign State.

SECTION 10. 1. No State shall enter into any treaty, alliance, or confederation; grant letters of marque and reprisal; coin money; emit bills of credit; make any thing but gold and silver coin a tender in payment of debts; pass any bill of attainder, ex post facto law, or law impairing the obligation of contracts, or grant any title of nobility.

2. No State shall, without the consent of the Congress, lay any imposts or duties on imports or exports, except what may be absolutely necessary for executing its inspection laws: and the net produce of all duties and imposts laid by any State on imports or exports, shall be for the use of the treasury of the United States; and all such laws shall be subject to the revision and control of the Congress.

3. No State shall, without the consent of the Congress, lay any duty of tonnage, keep troops, or ships of war in time of peace, enter into any agreement or compact with another State, or with

a foreign power, or engage in war, unless actually invaded, or in such imminent danger as will not admit of delay.

Article II

SECTION 1. 1. The executive power shall be vested in a President of the United States of America. He shall hold his office during the term of four years, and, together with the Vice President, chosen for the same term, be elected, as follows:

2. Each State shall appoint, in such manner as the legislature thereof may direct, a number of electors, equal to the whole number of senators and representatives to which the State may be entitled in the Congress: but no senator or representative, or person holding any office of trust or profit under the United States, shall be appointed an elector.

The electors shall meet in their respective States, and vote by ballot for two persons, of whom one at least shall not be an inhabitant of the same State with themselves. And they shall make a list of all the persons voted for, and of the number of votes for each; which list they shall sign and certify, and transmit sealed to the seat of the government of the United States, directed to the president of the Senate. The president of the Senate shall, in the presence of the Senate and House of Representatives, open all the certificates, and the votes shall then be counted. The person having the greatest number of votes shall be the President, if such number be a majority of the whole number of electors appointed; and if there be more than one who have such majority, and have an equal number of votes, then the House of Representatives shall immediately choose by ballot one of them for President; and if no person have a majority, then from the five highest on the list the said House shall in like manner choose the President. But in choosing the President, the votes shall be taken by States, the representation from each State having one vote; a quorum for this purpose shall consist of a member or members from two thirds of the States, and a majority of all the States shall be necessary to a choice. In every case after the choice of the President, the person having the greatest number of votes of the electors shall be the Vice President. But if there should remain two or more who have equal votes, the Senate shall choose from them by ballot the Vice President.[6]

3. The Congress may determine the time of choosing the electors, and the day on which they shall give their votes; which day shall be the same throughout the United States.

4. No person except a natural born citizen, or a citizen of the United States, at the time of the adoption of this Constitution, shall be eligible to the office of President; neither shall any person be eligible to the office who shall not have attained to the age of thirty-five years, and been fourteen years a resident within the United States.

5. In case of the removal of the President from office, or of his death, resignation, or inability to discharge the powers and duties of the said office, the same shall devolve on the Vice President, and the Congress may by law provide for the case of removal,

---

[5]See the Sixteenth Amendment.

[6]See the Twelfth Amendment.

death, resignation or inability, both of the President and Vice President, declaring what officer shall then act as President, and such officer shall act accordingly until the disability be removed, or a President shall be elected.

6. The President shall, at stated times, receive for his services a compensation which shall neither be increased nor diminished during the period for which he shall have been elected, and he shall not receive within that period any other emolument from the United States, or any of them.

7. Before he enter on the execution of his office, he shall take the following oath or affirmation:—"I do solemnly swear (or affirm) that I will faithfully execute the office of president of the United States, and will to the best of my ability, preserve, protect and defend the Constitution of the United States."

SECTION 2. 1. The President shall be commander in chief of the army and navy of the United States, and of the militia of the several States, when called into the actual service of the United States; he may require the opinion in writing, of the principal officer in each of the executive departments, upon any subject relating to the duties of their respective offices, and he shall have power to grant reprieves and pardons for offenses against the United States, except in cases of impeachment.

2. He shall have power, by and with the advice and consent of the Senate, to make treaties, provided two thirds of the senators present concur; and he shall nominate, and by and with the advice and consent of the Senate, shall appoint ambassadors, other public ministers and consuls, judges of the Supreme Court, and all other officers of the United States, whose appointments are not herein otherwise provided for, and which shall be established by law; but the Congress may by law vest the appointment of such inferior officers, as they think proper, in the President alone, in the courts of laws, or in the heads of departments.

3. The President shall have power to fill up all vacancies that may happen during the recess of the Senate, by granting commissions which shall expire at the end of their next session.

SECTION 3. He shall from time to time give to the Congress information of the state of the Union, and recommend to their consideration such measures as he shall judge necessary and expedient; he may, on extraordinary occasions, convene both houses, or either of them, and in case of disagreement between them with respect to the time of adjournment, he may adjourn them to such time as he shall think proper; he shall receive ambassadors and other public ministers; he shall take care that the laws be faithfully executed, and shall commission all the officers of the United States.

SECTION 4. The President, Vice President, and all civil officers of the United States, shall be removed from office on impeachment for, and conviction of, treason, bribery, or other high crimes and misdemeanors.

Article III

SECTION 1. The judicial power of the United States shall be vested in one Supreme Court, and in such inferior courts as the Congress may from time to time ordain and establish. The judges, both of the Supreme and inferior courts, shall hold their offices during good behavior, and shall, at stated times, receive for their services, a compensation, which shall not be diminished during their continuance in office.

SECTION 2. 1. The judicial power shall extend to all cases, in law and equity, arising under this Constitution, the laws of the United States, and treaties made, or which shall be made, under their authority;—to all cases of admiralty and maritime jurisdiction;—to controversies to which the United States shall be a party;[7]—to controversies between two or more States;—between a State and citizens of another State;—between citizens of different States;—between citizens of the same State claiming lands under grants of different States, and between a State, or the citizens thereof, and foreign States, citizens or subjects.

2. In all cases affecting ambassadors, other public ministers and consuls, and those in which a State shall be party, the Supreme Court shall have original jurisdiction. In all the other cases before mentioned, the Supreme Court shall have appellate jurisdiction, both as to law and fact, with such exceptions, and under such regulations as the Congress shall make.

3. The trial of all crimes, except in cases of impeachment, shall be by jury; and such trial shall be held in the State where the said crimes shall have been committed; but when not committed within any State, the trial shall be such place or places as the Congress may by law have directed.

SECTION 3. 1. Treason against the United States shall consist only in levying war against them, or in adhering to their enemies, giving them aid and comfort. No person shall be convicted of treason unless on the testimony of two witnesses to the same overt act, or on confession in open court.

2. The Congress shall have power to declare the punishment of treason, but no attainder of treason shall work corruption of blood, or forfeiture except during the life of the person attained.

Article IV

SECTION 1. Full faith and credit shall be given in each State to the public acts, records, and judicial proceedings of every other State. And the Congress may by general laws prescribe the manner in which such acts, records and proceedings shall be proved, and the effect thereof.

SECTION 2. 1. The citizens of each State shall be entitled to all privileges and immunities of citizens in the several States.[8]

2. A person charged in any State with treason, felony, or other crime, who shall flee from justice, and be found in another State, shall on demand of the executive authority of the State from which he fled, be delivered up to be removed to the State having jurisdiction of the crime.

---

[7]See the Eleventh Amendment.

[8]See the Fourteenth Amendment, Sec. 1.

3. No person held to service or labor in one State under the laws thereof, escaping into another, shall, in consequence of any law or regulation therein, be discharged from such service or labor, but shall be delivered up on claim of the party to whom such service or labor may be due.[9]

SECTION 3. 1. New States may be admitted by the Congress into this Union; but no new State shall be formed or erected within the jurisdiction of any other State, nor any State be formed by the junction of two or more States, or parts of States, without the consent of the legislatures of the States concerned as well as of the Congress.

2. The Congress shall have power to dispose of and make all needful rules and regulations respecting the territory or other property belonging to the United States; and nothing in this Constitution shall be so construed as to prejudice any claims of the United States, or of any particular State.

SECTION 4. The United States shall guarantee to every State in this Union a republican form of government, and shall protect each of them against invasion; and on application of the legislature, or of the executive (when the legislature cannot be convened) against domestic violence.

Article V

The Congress, whenever two thirds of both Houses shall deem it necessary, shall propose amendments to this Constitution, or, on the application of the legislatures of two thirds of the several States, shall call a convention for proposing amendments, which in either case shall be valid to all intents and purposes, as part of this Constitution, when ratified by the legislatures of three fourths of the several States, or by conventions in three fourths thereof, as the one or the other mode of ratification may be proposed by the Congress; Provided that no amendment which may be made prior to the year one thousand eight hundred and eight shall in any manner affect the first and fourth clauses in the ninth section of the first article; and that no State, without its consent, shall be deprived of its equal suffrage in the Senate.

Article VI

1. All debts contracted and engagements entered into, before the adoption of this Constitution, shall be as valid against the United States under this Constitution, as under the Confederation.[10]

2. This Constitution, and the laws of the United States which shall be made in pursuance thereof; and all treaties made, or which shall be made, under the authority of the United States, shall be the supreme law of the land; and the judges in every State shall be bound thereby, any thing in the Constitution or laws of any State to the contrary notwithstanding.

3. The senators and representatives before mentioned, and the members of the several State legislatures, and all executive and judicial officers, both of the United States and of the several States, shall be bound by oath or affirmation to support this Constitution; but no religious test shall ever be required as a qualification to any office or public trust under the United States.

Article VII

The ratification of the conventions of nine States shall be sufficient for the establishment of this Constitution between the States so ratifying the same.

Done in Convention by the unanimous consent of the States present the seventeenth day of September in the year of our Lord one thousand seven hundred and eighty-seven, and of the independence of the United States of America the twelfth. In witness whereof we have hereunto subscribed our names.

Articles in addition to, and amendment of, the Constitution of the United States of America, proposed by Congress, and ratified by the legislatures of the several States, pursuant to the fifth article of the original Constitution.

Amendment I [First Ten Amendments Ratified December 15, 1791]

Congress shall make no law respecting an establishment of religion, or prohibiting the free exercise thereof; or abridging the freedom of speech, or of the press; or the right of the people peaceably to assemble, and to petition the government for a redress of grievances.

Amendment II

A well regulated militia, being necessary to the security of a free State, the right of the people to keep and bear arms, shall not be infringed.

Amendment III

No soldier shall, in time of peace be quartered in any house, without the consent of the owner, nor in time of war, but in a manner to be prescribed by law.

Amendment IV

The right of the people to be secure in their persons, houses, papers, and effects, against unreasonable searches and seizures, shall not be violated, and no warrants shall issue, but upon probable cause, supported by oath or affirmation, and particularly describing the place to be searched, and the persons or things to be seized.

Amendment V

No person shall be held to answer for a capital or otherwise infamous crime, unless on a presentment or indictment of a grand jury, except in cases arising in the land or naval forces, or in the militia, when in actual service in time of war or public danger; nor shall any person be subject for the same offense to be twice put in jeopardy of life or limb; nor shall be compelled in any criminal case to be a witness against himself, nor be deprived of life, liberty, or property, without due process of law; nor shall private property be taken for public use, without just compensation.

---

[9]See the Thirteenth Amendment.

[10]See the Fourteenth Amendment, Sec. 4.

Amendment VI

In all criminal prosecutions, the accused shall enjoy the right to a speedy and public trial, by an impartial jury of the State and district wherein the crime shall have been committed, which district shall have been previously ascertained by law, and to be informed of the nature and cause of the accusation; to be confronted with the witnesses against him; to have compulsory process for obtaining witnesses in his favor, and to have the assistance of counsel for his defense.

Amendment VII

In suits at common law, where the value in controversy shall exceed twenty dollars, the right of trial by jury shall be preserved, and no fact tried by a jury shall be otherwise reexamined in any court of the United States, than according to the rules of the common law.

Amendment VIII

Excessive bail shall not be required, nor excessive fines imposed, nor cruel and unusual punishments inflicted.

Amendment IX

The enumeration in the Constitution of certain rights shall not be construed to deny or disparage others retained by the people.

Amendment X

The powers not delegated to the United States by the Constitution, nor prohibited by it to the States, are reserved to the States respectively, or to the people.

Amendment XI [January 8, 1798]

The judicial power of the United States shall not be construed to extend to any suit in law or equity, commended or prosecuted against one of the United States by citizens of another State, or by citizens or subjects of any foreign State.

Amendment XII [September 25, 1804]

The electors shall meet in their respective States, and vote by ballot for President and Vice President, one of whom, at least, shall not be an inhabitant of the same State with themselves; they shall name in their ballots the person voted for as President, and in distinct ballots, the person voted for as Vice President, and they shall make distinct lists of all persons voted for as President and of all persons voted for as Vice President, and of the number of votes for each, which lists they shall sign and certify, and transmit sealed to the seat of the government of the United States, directed to the President of the Senate;—The President of the Senate shall, in the presence of the Senate and House of Representatives, open all the certificates and the votes shall then be counted;—The person having the greatest number of votes for President, shall be the President, if such number be a majority of the whole number of electors appointed; and if no person have such majority, then from the persons having the highest numbers not exceeding three on the list of those voted for as President, the House of Representatives shall choose immediately, by ballot, the President. But in choosing the President, the votes shall be taken by States, the representation from each State having one vote; a quorum for this purpose shall consist of a member or members from two thirds of the States, and a majority of all the States shall be necessary to a choice. And if the House of Representatives shall not choose a President whenever the right of choice shall devolve upon them, before the fourth day of March next following, then the Vice President shall act as President, as in the case of the death or other constitutional disability of the President. The person having the greatest number of votes as Vice President shall be the Vice President, if such number be a majority of the whole number of electors appointed, and if no person have a majority, then from the two highest numbers on the list, the Senate shall choose the Vice President; a quorum for the purpose shall consist of two thirds of the whole number of Senators, and a majority of the whole number shall be necessary to a choice. But no person constitutionally ineligible to the office of President shall be eligible to that of Vice President of the United States.

Amendment XIII [December 18, 1865]

SECTION 1. Neither slavery nor involuntary servitude, except as punishment for crime whereof the party shall have been duly convicted, shall exist within the United States, or any place subject to their jurisdiction.

SECTION 2. Congress shall have power to enforce this article by appropriate legislation.

Amendment XIV [July 28, 1868]

SECTION 1. All persons born or naturalized in the United States, and subject to the jurisdiction thereof, are citizens of the United States and of the State wherein they reside. No State shall make or enforce any law which shall abridge the privileges or immunities of citizens of the United States; nor shall any State deprive any person of life, liberty, or property, without due process of law; nor deny to any person within its jurisdiction the equal protection of the laws.

SECTION 2. Representatives shall be apportioned among the several States according to their respective numbers, counting the whole number of persons in each State, excluding Indians not taxed. But when the right to vote at any election for the choice of electors for President and Vice President of the United States, representatives in Congress, the executive and judicial officers of a State, or the members of the legislature thereof, is denied to any of the male inhabitants of such State, being twenty-one years of age, and citizens of the United States, or in any way abridged, except for participating in rebellion, or other crime, the basis of representation there shall be reduced in the proportion which the number of such male citizens shall bear to the whole number of male citizens twenty-one years of age in such State.

SECTION 3. No person shall be a senator or representative in Congress, or elector of President and Vice President, or hold any office, civil or military, under the United States, or under any State, who having previously taken an oath, as a member of Congress, or as an officer of the United States, or as a member of any State legislature, or as an executive or judicial officer of any State, to support the Constitution of the United States, shall have engaged in insurrection or rebellion against the same, or given aid or comfort to the enemies thereof. But Congress may by a vote of two thirds of each House, remove such disability.

SECTION 4. The validity of the public debt of the United States, authorized by law, including debts incurred for payment of pensions and bounties for services in suppressing insurrection or rebellion; shall not be questioned. But neither the United States nor any State shall assume or pay any debt or obligation incurred in aid of insurrection or rebellion against the United States, or any claim for the loss or emancipation of any slave; but all such debts, obligations, and claims shall be held illegal and void.

SECTION 5. The Congress shall have the power to enforce, by appropriate legislation, the provisions of this article.

Amendment XV [March 30, 1870]

SECTION 1. The right of citizens of the United States to vote shall not be denied or abridged by the United States or by any State on account of race, color, or previous condition of servitude.

SECTION 2. The Congress shall have power to enforce this article by appropriate legislation.

Amendment XVI [February 25, 1913]

The Congress shall have power to lay and collect taxes on incomes, from whatever source derived, without apportionment among the several States, and without regard to any census or enumeration.

Amendment XVII [May 31, 1913]

The Senate of the United States shall be composed of two senators from each State, elected by the people thereof, for six years; and each senator shall have one vote. The electors in each State shall have the qualifications requisite for electors of the most numerous branch of the State legislature.

When vacancies happen in the representation of any State in the Senate, the executive authority of such State shall issue writs of election to fill such vacancies: Provided, That the legislature of any State may empower the executive thereof to make temporary appointments until the people fill the vacancies by election as the legislature may direct.

This amendment shall not be so construed as to affect the election or term of any senator chosen before it becomes valid as part of the Constitution.

Amendment XVIII[11] [January 29, 1919]

After one year from the ratification of this article, the manufacture, sale, or transportation of intoxicating liquors within, the importation thereof into, or the exportation thereof from the United States and all territory subject to the jurisdiction thereof for beverage purposes is thereby prohibited.

The Congress and the several States shall have concurrent power to enforce this article by appropriate legislation.

---

[11]Repealed by the Twenty-first Amendment.

This article shall be inoperative unless it shall have been ratified as an amendment to the Constitution by the legislatures of the several States, as provided in the Constitution, within seven years from the date of the submission hereof to the States by Congress.

Amendment XIX [August 26, 1920]

The right of citizens of the United States to vote shall not be denied or abridged by the United States or by any State on account of sex.

Congress shall have the power to enforce this article by appropriate legislation.

Amendment XX [January 23, 1933]

SECTION 1. The terms of the President and Vice President shall end at noon on the 20th day of January and the terms of Senators and Representatives at noon on the 3d day of January, of the years in which such terms would have ended if this article had not been ratified; and the terms of their successors shall then begin.

SECTION 2. The Congress shall assemble at least once in every year, and such meeting shall begin at noon on the 3d day of January, unless they shall by law appoint a different day.

SECTION 3. If, at the time fixed for the beginning of the term of president, the President-elect shall have died, the Vice President-elect shall become President. If a President shall not have been chosen before the time fixed for the beginning of his term, or if the President-elect shall have failed to qualify, then the Vice President-elect shall act as president until a President shall have qualified; and the Congress may by law provide for the case wherein neither a President-elect nor a Vice President-elect shall have qualified, declaring who shall then act as President, or the manner in which one who is to act shall be selected, and such person shall act accordingly until a President or Vice President shall have qualified.

SECTION 4. The Congress may by law provide for the case of the death of any of the persons from whom, the House of Representatives may choose a President whenever the right of choice shall have devolved upon them, and for the case of the death of any of the persons from whom the Senate may choose a Vice President whenever the right of choice shall have devolved upon them.

SECTION 5. Sections 1 and 2 shall take effect on the 15th day of October following the ratification of this article.

SECTION 6. This article shall be inoperative unless it shall have been ratified as an amendment to the Constitution by the legislatures of three-fourths of the several States within seven years from the date of its submission.

Amendment XXI [December 5, 1933]

SECTION 1. The Eighteenth Article of amendment to the Constitution of the United States is hereby repealed.

SECTION 2. The transportation or importation into any State, Territory, or possession of the United States for delivery or use therein of intoxicating liquors in violation of the laws thereof, is hereby prohibited.

SECTION 3. This article shall be inoperative unless it shall have been ratified as an amendment to the Constitution by conventions in the several States, as provided in the Consitution, within seven years from the date of the submission thereof to the States by the Congress.

Amendment XXII [March 1, 1951]

No person shall be elected to the office of the President more than twice, and no person who has held the office of President, or acted as President, for more than two years of a term to which some other person was elected President shall be elected to the office of the President more than once.

But this article shall not apply to any person holding the office of President when this article was proposed by the Congress, and shall not prevent any person who may be holding the office of President, or acting as President, during the term within which this article becomes operative from holding the office of President or acting as President during the remainder of such term.

This article shall be inoperative unless it shall have been ratified as an amendment to the Constitution by the legislatures of three-fourths of the several States within seven years from the date of its submission to the States by the Congress.

Amendment XXIII [March 29, 1961]

SECTION 1. The District constituting the seat of Government of the United States shall appoint in such manner as the Congress may direct:

A number of electors of President and Vice President equal to the whole number of Senators and Representatives in Congress to which the District would be entitled if it were a State, but in no event more than the least populous State; they shall be in addition to those appointed by the States, but they shall be considered, for the purposes of the election of President and Vice President, to be electors appointed by a State; and they shall meet in the District and perform such duties as provided by the twelfth article of amendment.

SECTION 2. The Congress shall have power to enforce this article by appropriate legislation.

Amendment XXIV [January 23, 1964]

SECTION 1. The right of citizens of the United States to vote in any primary or other election for President or Vice President, for electors for President or Vice President, or for Senator or Representative in Congress, shall not be denied or abridged by the United States or any State by reason of failure to pay any poll tax or other tax.

SECTION 2. The Congress shall have power to enforce this article by appropriate legislation.

Amendment XXV [February 10, 1967]

SECTION 1. In case of the removal of the President from office or of his death or resignation, the Vice President shall become President.

SECTION 2. Whenever there is a vacancy in the office of the Vice President, the President shall nominate a Vice President who shall take office upon confirmation by a majority of both Houses of Congress.

SECTION 3. Whenever the President transmits to the President pro tempore of the Senate and the Speaker of the House of Representatives his written declaration that he is unable to discharge the powers and duties of his office, and until he transmits to them a written declaration to the contrary, such powers and duties shall be discharged by the Vice President as Acting President.

SECTION 4. Whenever the Vice President and a majority of either the principal officers of the executive departments or of such other body as Congress may by law provide, transmit to the President pro tempore of the Senate and the Speaker of the House of Representatives their written declaration that the President is unable to discharge the powers and duties of his office, the Vice President shall immediately assume the powers and duties of the office as Acting President.

Thereafter, when the President transmits to the President pro tempore of the Senate and the Speaker of the House of Representatives his written declaration that no inability exists, he shall resume the powers and duties of his office unless the Vice President and a majority of either the principal officers of the executive departments or of such other body as Congress may by law provide, transmit within four days to the President pro tempore of the Senate and the Speaker of the House of Representatives their written declaration that the President is unable to discharge the powers and duties of his office. Thereupon Congress shall decide the issue, assembling within forty-eight hours for that purpose if not in session. If the Congress, within twenty-one days after receipt of the latter written declaration, or, if Congress is not in session, within twenty-one days after Congress is required to assemble, determines by two-thirds vote of both houses that the President is unable to discharge the powers and duties of his office, the Vice President shall continue to discharge the same as Acting President; otherwise, the President shall resume the powers and duties of his office.

Amendment XXVI [June 30, 1971]

SECTION 1. The right of citizens of the United States who are eighteen years of age or older to vote shall not be denied or abridged by the United States or by any State on account of age.

SECTION 2. The Congress shall have power to enforce this article by appropriate legislation.

Amendment XXVII[12] [May 7, 1992]

No law, varying the compensation for services of the Senators and Representatives, shall take effect until an election of Representatives shall have intervened.

---

[12]James Madison proposed this amendment in 1789 together with the ten amendments that were adopted as the Bill of Rights, but it failed to win ratification at the time. Congress, however, had set no deadline for its ratification, and over the years—particularly in the 1980s and 1990s—many states voted to add it to the Constitution. With the ratification of Michigan in 1992 it passed the threshold of the states required for adoption, but because the process took more than 200 years, its validity remains in doubt.

The Emancipation Proclamation

By the President of the United States of America:

Whereas, on the twenty-second day of September, in the year of our Lord one thousand eight hundred and sixty-two, a proclamation was issued by the President of the United States, containing, among other things, the following, to wit:

> That on the first day of January, in the year of our Lord one thousand eight hundred and sixty-three, all persons held as slaves within any State or designated part of a State, the people whereof shall then be in rebellion against the United States, shall be then, thenceforward, and forever free; and the Executive Government of the United States, including the military and naval authority thereof, will recognize and maintain the freedom of such persons, and will do no act or acts to repress such persons, or any of them, in any efforts they may make for their actual freedom.
>
> That the Executive will, on the first day of January aforesaid, by proclamation, designate the States and parts of States, if any, in which the people thereof, respectively, shall then be in rebellion against the United States; and the fact that any State, or the people thereof, shall on that day be, in good faith, represented in the Congress of the United States by members chosen thereto at elections wherein a majority of the qualified voters of such State shall have participated, shall, in the absence of strong countervailing testimony, be deemed conclusive evidence that such State, and the people thereof, are not then in rebellion against the United States.

Now, therefore I, Abraham Lincoln, President of the United States, by virtue of the power in me vested as Commander-in-Chief, of the Army and Navy of the United States in time of actual armed rebellion against the authority and government of the United States, and as a fit and necessary war measure for suppressing said rebellion, do, on this first day of January, in the year of our Lord one thousand eight hundred and sixty-three, and in accordance with my purpose so to do publicly proclaimed for the full period of one hundred days, from the day first above mentioned, order and designate as the States and parts of States wherein the people thereof respectively, are this day in rebellion against the United States, the following, to wit:

Arkansas, Texas, Louisiana, (except the Parishes of St. Bernard, Plaquemines, Jefferson, St. John, St. Charles, St. James Ascension, Assumption, Terrebonne, Lafourche, St. Mary, St. Martin, and Orleans, including the City of New Orleans), Mississippi, Alabama, Florida, Georgia, South Carolina, North Carolina, and Virginia, (except the forty-eight counties designated as West Virginia, and also the counties of Berkley, Accomac, Northampton, Elizabeth City, York, Princess Ann, and Norfolk, including the cities of Norfolk and Portsmouth), and which excepted parts, are for the present, left precisely as if this proclamation were not issued.

And by virtue of the power, and for the purpose aforesaid, I do order and declare that all persons held as slaves within said designated States, and parts of States, are, and henceforward shall be free; and that the Executive government of the United States, including the military and naval authorities thereof, will recognize and maintain the freedom of said persons.

And I hereby enjoin upon the people so declared to be free to abstain from all violence, unless in necessary self-defense; and I recommend to them that, in all cases when allowed, they labor faithfully for reasonable wages.

And I further declare and make known, that such persons of suitable condition, will be received into the armed service of the United States to garrison forts, positions, stations, and other places, and to man vessels of all sorts in said service.

And upon this act, sincerely believed to be an act of justice, warranted by the Constitution, upon military necessity, I invoke the considerate judgment of mankind, and the gracious favor of Almighty God.

In witness whereof, I have hereunto set my hand and caused the seal of the United States to be affixed. Done at the City of Washington, this first day of January, in the year of our Lord one thousand eight hundred and sixty-three, and of the Independence of the United States of America the eighty-seventh.

By the President: Abraham Lincoln
William H. Seward, Secretary of State

Key Provisions of the Civil Rights Act of 1964

An Act

To enforce the constitutional right to vote, to confer jurisdiction upon the district courts of the United States to provide injunctive relief against discrimination in public accommodations, to authorize the Attorney General to institute suits to protect constitutional rights in public facilities and public education, to extend the Commission on Civil Rights, to prevent discrimination in federally assisted programs, to establish a Commission on Equal Employment Opportunity, and for other purposes.

Be it enacted by the Senate and House of Representatives of the United States of America in Congress assembled, that this Act may be cited as the "Civil Rights Act of 1964."

Title I—Voting Rights

SECTION 101 . . . (2) No person acting under color of law shall—

(A) In determining whether any individual is qualified under State law or laws to vote in any Federal election, apply any standard, practice, or procedure different from the standards, practices, or procedures applied under such law or laws to other individuals within the same county, parish, or similar political subdivision who have been found by State officials to be qualified to vote;

(B) deny the right of any individual to vote in any Federal election because of an error or omission on any record or paper relating to any application, registration, or other act requisite to voting, if such error or omission is not material in determining whether such individual is qualified under State law to vote in such election;

(C) employ any literacy test as a qualification for voting in any Federal election unless (i) such test is administered to each individual and is conducted wholly in writing, and (ii) a certified copy of the test and of the answers given by the individual is furnished to him within twenty-five days of the submission of his request made within the period of time during which records and papers are required to be retained and preserved pursuant to title III of the Civil Rights Act of 1960 (42 U.S.C. 1974–74e; 74 Stat. 88): Provided, however, That the Attorney General may enter into agreements with appropriate State or local authorities that preparation, conduct, and maintenance of such tests in accordance with the provisions of applicable State or local law, including such special provisions as are necessary in the preparation, conduct, and maintenance of such tests for persons who are blind or otherwise physically handicapped, meet the purposes of this subparagraph and constitute compliance therewith.

Title II—Injunctive Relief Against Discrimination in Places of Public Accommodation

SECTION 201. (a) All persons shall be entitled to the full and equal enjoyment of the goods, services, facilities, and privileges, advantages and accommodations of any place of public accommodation, as defined in this section, without discrimination or segregation on the ground of race, color, religion, or national origin.

(b) Each of the following establishments which serves the public is a place of public accommodation within the meaning of this title if its operations affect commerce, or if discrimination or segregation by it is supported by State action:

(1) any inn, hotel, motel, or other establishment which provides lodging to transient guests, other than an establishment located within a building which contains not more than five rooms for rent or hire and which is actually occupied by the proprietor of such establishment as his residence;

(2) any restaurant, cafeteria, lunchroom, lunch counter, soda fountain, or other facility principally engaged in selling food for consumption on the premises, including, but not limited to, any such facility located on the premises of any retail establishment; or any gasoline station;

(3) any motion picture house, theater, concert hall, sports arena, stadium or other place of exhibition or entertainment;

(4) any establishment (A)(i) which is physically located within the premises of any establishment otherwise covered by this subsection, or (ii) within the premises of which is physically located any such covered establishment, and (B) which holds itself out as serving patrons of such covered establishment. . . .

(d) Discrimination or segregation by an establishment is supported by State action within the meaning of this title if such discrimination or segregation

(1) is carried on under color of any law, statute, ordinance, or regulation; or

(2) is carried on under color of any custom or usage required or enforced by officials of the State or political subdivision thereof; or

(3) is required by action of the State or political sub-division thereof. . . .

SECTION 202. All persons shall be entitled to be free, at any establishment or place, from discrimination or segregation of any kind on the ground of race, color, religion, or national origin, if such discrimination or segregation is or purports to be required by any law, statute, ordinance, regulation, rule, or order of a State or any agency or political subdivision thereof.

SECTION 203. No person shall (a) withhold, deny, or attempt to withhold or deny, or deprive or attempt to deprive, any person of any right or privilege secured by section 201 or 202, or (b) intimidate, threaten, or coerce, or attempt to intimidate, threaten, or coerce any person with the purpose of interfering with any right or privilege secured by section 201 or 202, or (c) punish or attempt to punish any person for exercising or attempting to exercise any right or privilege secured by section 201 or 202.

Section 204. (a) Whenever any person has engaged or there are reasonable grounds to believe that any person is about to engage in any act or practice prohibited by section 203, a civil action for preventive relief, including an application for a permanent or temporary injunction, restraining order, or other order, may be instituted by the person aggrieved and, upon timely application, the court may, in its discretion, permit the Attorney General to intervene in such civil action if he certifies that the case is of general public importance. Upon application by the complainant and in such circumstances as the court may deem just, the court may appoint an attorney for such complainant and may authorize the commencement of the civil action without the payment of fees, costs, or security. . . .

SECTION 206. (a) Whenever the Attorney General has reasonable cause to believe that any person or group of persons is engaged in a pattern or practice of resistance to the full enjoyment of any of the rights secured by this title, and that the pattern or practice is of such a nature and is intended to deny the full exercise of the rights herein described, the Attorney General may bring a civil action in the appropriate district court of the United States by filing with it a complaint

(1) signed by him (or in his absence the Acting Attorney General),

(2) setting forth facts pertaining to such pattern or practice, and

(3) requesting such preventive relief, including an application for a permanent or temporary injunction, restraining order or other order against the person or persons responsible for such pattern or practice, as he deems necessary to insure the full enjoyment of the rights herein described. . . .

Title III—Desegregation of Public Facilities

SECTION 301. (a) Whenever the Attorney General receives a complaint in writing signed by an individual to the effect that he is being deprived of or threatened with the loss of his right to the equal protection of the laws, on account of his race, color, religion, or national origin, by being denied equal utilization of any public facility which is owned, operated, or managed by or on behalf of any State or subdivision thereof, other than a public school or public college as defined in section 401 of title IV hereof, and the Attorney General believes the complaint is meritorious and certifies that the signer or signers of such complaint are unable, in his judgment, to initiate and maintain appropriate legal proceedings for relief and that the institution of an action will materially further the orderly progress of desegregation in public facilities, the Attorney General is authorized to institute for or in the name of the United States a civil action in any appropriate district court of the United States against such parties and for such relief as may be appropriate. And such court shall have and shall exercise jurisdiction of proceedings instituted pursuant to this section. The Attorney General may implead as defendants such additional parties as are or become necessary to the grant of effective relief hereunder. . . .

Title IV—Desegregation of Public Education

SECTION 401. As used in this title—. . . .

"Desegregation" means the assignment of students to public schools and within such schools without regard to their race, color, religion, or national origin, but "desegregation" shall not mean the assignment of students to public schools in order to overcome racial imbalance. . . .

Survey and Report of Educational Opportunities

SECTION 402. The Commissioner shall conduct a survey and make a report to the President and the Congress, within two years of the enactment of this title, concerning the lack of availability of equal educational opportunities for individuals by reason of race, color, religion, or national origin in public educational institutions at all levels in the United States, its territories and possessions, and the District of Columbia. . . .

Title V—Commission on Civil Rights. . . .
Duties of the Commission

SECTION 104. a. The Commission shall—

(1) investigate allegations in writing under oath or affirmation that certain citizens of the United States are being deprived of their right to vote and have that vote counted by reason of their color, race, religion, or national origin; which writing, under oath or affirmation, shall set forth the facts upon which such belief or beliefs are based;

(2) study and collect information concerning legal developments constituting a denial of equal protection of the laws under the Constitution because of race, color, religion or national origin or in the administration of justice;

(3) appraise the laws and policies of the Federal Government with respect to denials of equal protection of the laws under the Constitution because of race, color, religion or national origin or in the administration of justice;

(4) serve as a national clearinghouse for information in respect to denials of equal protection of the laws because of race, color, religion or national origin, including but not

limited to the fields of voting, education, housing, employment, the use of public facilities, and transportation, or in the administration of justice;

(5) investigate allegations, made in writing and under oath or affirmation, that citizens of the United States are unlawfully being accorded or denied the right to vote, or to have their votes properly counted, in any election of presidential electors, Members of the United States Senate, or of the House of Representatives, as a result of any patterns or practice of fraud or discrimination in the conduct of such election;. . . .

Title VI—Nondiscrimination in Federally Assisted Programs

SECTION 601. No person in the United States shall, on the ground of race, color, or national origin, be excluded from participation in, be denied the benefits of, or be subjected to discrimination under any program or activity receiving Federal financial assistance.

SECTION 602. Each Federal department and agency which is empowered to extend Federal financial assistance to any program or activity, by way of grant, loan, or contract other than a contract of insurance or guaranty, is authorized and directed to effectuate the provisions of section 601 with respect to such program or activity by issuing rules, regulations, or orders of general applicability which shall be consistent with achievement of the objectives of the statute authorizing the financial assistance in connection with which the action is taken. No such rule, regulation, or order shall become effective unless and until approved by the President. Compliance with any requirement adopted pursuant to this section may be effected

(1) by the termination of or refusal to grant or to continue assistance under such program or activity to any recipient as to whom there has been an express finding on the record, after opportunity for hearing, of a failure to comply with such requirement, but such termination or refusal shall be limited to the particular political entity, or part thereof, or other recipient as to whom such a finding has been made and, shall be limited in its effect to the particular program, or part thereof, in which such non-compliance has been so found, or

(2) by any other means authorized by law:

Provided, however, that no such action shall be taken until the department or agency concerned has advised the appropriate person or persons of the failure to comply with the requirement and has determined that compliance cannot be secured by voluntary means. In the case of any action terminating, or refusing to grant or continue, assistance because of failure to comply with a requirement imposed pursuant to this section, the head of the federal department or agency shall file with the committees of the House and Senate having legislative jurisdiction over the program or activity involved a full written report of the circumstances and the grounds for such action. No such action shall become effective until thirty days have elapsed after the filing of such report. . . .

Title VII—Equal Employment Opportunity. . . .

Discrimination Because of Race, Color, Religion, Sex, or National Origin

SECTION 703. a. it shall be an unlawful employment practice for an employer—

(1) to fail or refuse to hire or to discharge any individual, or otherwise to discriminate against any individual with respect to his compensation, terms, conditions, or privileges of employment, because of such individual's race, color, religion, sex, or national origin; or

(2) to limit, segregate, or classify his employees in any way which would deprive or tend to deprive any individual of employment opportunities or otherwise adversely affect his status as an employee, because of such individual's race, color, religion, sex, or national origin.

(b) it shall be an unlawful employment practice for an employment agency to fail or refuse to refer for employment, or otherwise to discriminate against, any individual because of his race, color, religion, sex, or national origin, or to classify or refer for employment any individual on the basis of his race, color, religion, sex, or national origin.

(c) it shall be an unlawful employment practice for a labor organization—

(1) to exclude or to expel from its membership, or otherwise to discriminate against, any individual because of his race, color, religion, sex, or national origin;

(2) to limit, segregate, or classify its membership, or to classify or fail or refuse to refer for employment any individual, in any way which would deprive or tend to deprive any individual of employment opportunities, or would limit such employment opportunities or otherwise adversely affect his status as an employee or as an applicant for employment, because of such individual's race, color, religion, sex, or national origin; or

(3) to cause or attempt to cause an employer to discriminate against an individual in violation of this section.

(d) It shall be an unlawful employment practice for any employer, labor organization, or joint labor-management committee controlling apprenticeship or other training or retraining, including on-the-job training programs to discriminate against any individual because of his race, color, religion, sex, or national origin in admission to, or employment in, any program established to provide apprenticeship or other training. . . .

Other Unlawful Employment Practices

Section 704. (a) It shall be an unlawful employment practice for an employer to discriminate against any of his employees or applicants for employment, for an employment agency to discriminate against any individual, or for a labor organization to discriminate against any member thereof or applicant for membership, because he has opposed any practice made an unlawful employment practice by this title, or because he has made a charge, testified, assisted, or participated in any manner in an investigation, proceeding, or hearing under this title.

(b) It shall be an unlawful employment practice for an employer, labor organization, or employment agency to print or publish or cause to be printed or published any notice or advertisement relating to employment by such an employer or membership in or any classification or referral for employment by such a labor organization, or relating to any classification or referral for employment by such an employment agency, indicating any preference, limitation, specification, or discrimination, based on race, color, religion, sex, or national origin, except that such a notice or advertisement may indicate a preference, limitation, specification, or discrimination based on religion, sex, or national origin when religion, sex, or national origin is a bona fide occupational qualification for employment.

Equal Employment Opportunity Commission

SECTION 705. (a) There is hereby created a Commission to be known as the Equal Employment Opportunity Commission, which shall be composed of five members, not more than three of whom shall be members of the same political party, who shall be appointed by the President by and with the advice and consent of the Senate. One of the original members shall be appointed for a term of one year, one for a term of two years, one for a term of three years, one for a term of four years, and one for a term of five years, beginning from the date of enactment of this title, but their successors shall be appointed for terms of five years each, except that any individual chosen to fill a vacancy shall be appointed only for the unexpired term of the member whom he shall succeed. The President shall designate one member to serve as Chairman of the Commission, and one member to serve as Vice Chairman. The Chairman shall be responsible on behalf of the Commission for the administrative operations of the Commission, and shall appoint, in accordance with the civil service laws, such officers, agents, attorneys, and employees as it deems necessary to assist it in the performance of its functions and to fix their compensation in accordance with Classification Act of 1949, as amended. . . .

Title VIII—Registration and Voting Statistics

SECTION 801. The Secretary of Commerce shall promptly conduct a survey to compile registration and voting statistics in such geographic areas as may be recommended by the Commission on Civil Rights. Such a survey and compilation shall, to the extent recommended by the Commission on Civil Rights, only include a count of persons of voting age by race, color, and national origin, and determination of the extent to which such persons are registered to vote, and have voted in any statewide primary or general election in which the Members of the United States House of Representatives are nominated or elected, since January 1, 1960. Such information shall also be collected and compiled in connection with the Nineteenth Decennial Census, and at such other times as the Congress may prescribe. The provisions of section 9 and chapter 7 of title 13, United States Code, shall apply to any survey, collection, or compilation of registration and voting statistics carried out under this title: Provided, however, that no person shall be compelled to disclose his race, color, national origin, or questioned about his political party affiliation, how he voted, or the reasons therefore, nor shall any penalty be imposed for his failure or refusal to make such disclosure. Every person interrogated orally, by written survey or questionnaire or by any other means with respect to such information shall be fully advised with respect to his right to fail or refuse to furnish such information.

Lyndon B. Johnson July 2, 1964

Key Provisions of the Voting Rights Act of 1965

An Act

To enforce the fifteenth amendment to the Constitution of the United States, and for other purposes.

Be it enacted by the Senate and House of Representatives of the United States of America in Congress assembled, That this Act shall be known as the "Voting Rights Act of 1965."

SECTION 2. No voting qualification or prerequisite to voting, or standard, practice, or procedure shall be imposed or applied by any State or political subdivision to deny or abridge the right of any citizen of the United States to vote on account of race or color.

SECTION 3. (a) Whenever the Attorney General institutes a proceeding under any statute to enforce the guarantees of the fifteenth amendment in any State or political subdivision the court shall authorize the appointment of Federal examiners by the United States Civil Service Commission in accordance with section 6 to serve for such period of time and for such political subdivisions as the court shall determine is appropriate to enforce the guarantees of the fifteenth amendment (1) as part of any interlocutory order if the court determines that the appointment of such examiners is necessary to enforce such guarantees or (2) as part of any final judgment if the court finds that violations of the fifteenth amendment justifying equitable relief have occurred in such State or subdivision: Provided, That the court need not authorize the appointment of examiners if any incidents of denial or abridgment of the right to vote on account of race or color (1) have been few in number and have been promptly and effectively corrected by State or local action, (2) the continuing effect of such incidents has been eliminated, and (3) there is no reasonable probability of their recurrence in the future.

(b) If in a proceeding instituted by the Attorney General under any statute to enforce the guarantees of the fifteenth amendment in any State or political subdivision the court finds that a test or device has been used for the purpose or with the effect of denying or abridging the right of any citizen of the United States to vote on account of race or color, it shall suspend the use of tests and devices in such State or political subdivisions as the court shall determine is appropriate and for such period as it deems necessary. . . .

SECTION 4. (a) To assure that the right of citizens of the United States to vote is not denied or abridged on account of race or color, no citizen shall be denied the right to vote in any Federal, State, or local election because of his failure to comply with any test or device in any State with respect to which the determinations have been made under subsection (b). . . .

(b) The provisions of subsection (a) shall apply in any State or in any political subdivision of a state which (1) the Attorney General determines maintained on November 1, 1964, any test or device, and with respect to which (2) the Director of the Census determines that less than 50 per centum of the persons of voting age residing therein were registered on November 1, 1964, or that less than 50 per centum of such persons voted in the presidential election of November 1964. . . .

(c) The phrase "test or device" shall mean any requirement that a person as a prerequisite for voting or registration of voting (1) demonstrate the ability to read, write, understand, or interpret any matter, (2) demonstrate any educational achievement or his knowledge of any particular subject, (3) possess good moral character, or (4) prove his qualifications by the voucher of registered voters or members of any other class. . . .

SECTION 6. Whenever (a) a court has authorized the appointment of examiners pursuant to the provisions of section 3 (a), or (b) unless a declaratory judgment has been rendered under section 4 (a), the Attorney General certifies with respect to any political subdivision named in, or included within the scope of, determinations made under section 4 (b) that (1) he has received complaints in writing from twenty or more residents of such political subdivision alleging that they have been denied the right to vote under color of law on account of race or color, and that he believes such complaints to be meritorious, or (2) that in his judgment (considering, among other factors, whether the ratio of nonwhite persons to white persons registered to vote within such subdivision appears to him to be reasonably attributable to violations of the fifteenth amendment or whether substantial evidence exists that bona fide efforts are being made within such subdivision to comply with the fifteenth amendment), the appointment of examiners is otherwise necessary to enforce the guarantees of the fifteenth amendment, the Civil Service Commission shall appoint as many examiners for such subdivision as it may deem appropriate to prepare and maintain lists of persons eligible to vote in Federal, State, and local elections. . . . Examiners and hearing officers shall have the power to administer oaths. . . .

Lyndon B. Johnson August 6, 1965

Executive Order 13050 President's Advisory Board on Race

By the authority vested in me as President by the Constitution and the laws of the United States of America, including the Federal Advisory Committee Act, as amended (5 U.S.C. App.), and in order to establish a President's Advisory Board on Race, it is hereby ordered as follows:

SECTION 1. Establishment. (a) There is established the President's Advisory Board on Race. The Advisory Board shall comprise 7 members from outside the Federal Government to be appointed by the President. Members shall each have substantial experience and expertise in the areas to be considered by the Advisory Board. Members shall be representative of the diverse perspectives in the areas to be considered by the Advisory Board.

(b) The President shall designate a Chairperson from among the members of the Advisory Board.

SEC. 2. Functions. a. The Advisory Board shall advise the President on matters involving race and racial reconciliation, including ways in which the President can:

(1) Promote a constructive national dialogue to confront and work through challenging issues that surround race;

(2) Increase the Nation's understanding of our recent history of race relations and the course our Nation is charting on issues of race relations and racial diversity;

(3) Bridge racial divides by encouraging leaders in communities throughout the Nation to develop and implement innovative approaches to calming racial tensions;

(4) Identify, develop, and implement solutions to problems in areas in which race has a substantial impact, such as education, economic opportunity, housing, health care, and the administration of justice.

(b) The Advisory Board also shall advise on such other matters as from time to time the President may refer to the Board.

(c) In carrying out its functions, the Advisory Board shall coordinate with the staff of the President's Initiative on Race.

SEC. 3. Administration. (a) To the extent permitted by law and subject to the availability of appropriations, the Department of Justice shall provide the financial and administrative support for the Advisory Board.

(b) The heads of executive agencies shall, to the extent permitted by law, provide to the Advisory Board such information as it may require for the purpose of carrying out its functions.

(c) The Chairperson may, from time to time, invite experts to submit information to the Advisory Board and may form subcommittees or working groups within the Advisory Board to review specific matters.

(d) Members of the Advisory Board shall serve without compensation but shall be allowed travel expenses, including per diem in lieu of subsistence, as authorized by law for persons serving intermittently in the Government service (5 U.S.C. 5701–5707).

SEC. 4. General. (a) Notwithstanding any other Executive order, the functions of the President under the Federal Advisory Committee Act, as amended, except that of reporting to the Congress, that are applicable to the Advisory Board shall be performed by the Attorney General, or his or her designee, in accordance with guidelines that have been issued by the Administrator of General Services.

(b) The Advisory Board shall terminate on September 30, 1998 unless extended by the President prior to such date.

William J. Clinton June 13, 1997

Glossary Key Terms and Concepts

54th Massachusetts Regiment This all-black volunteer infantry regiment was recruited in the northern states for service with Union military forces in the Civil War. This regiment, made up almost entirely of black men who had been free, was commanded by white officers.

Abolitionists Those who sought to end slavery within their colony, state, nation, or religious denomination. By the 1830s the term best applied to those who advocated immediate rather than gradual emancipation.

Acculturation Change in individuals who are introduced to a new culture.

Affirmative action Civil rights policy or program that seeks to redress the effects of past discrimination due to race or gender by giving preference to women and minorities in education and employment.

African Methodist Episcopal (AME) Church Founded in Philadelphia in 1816, this was the first black church and eventually became the largest independent black church.

Afrocentricists Scholars who view history from an African perspective.

Afrocentricity A philosophy of culture that celebrates Africa's role in history and stresses the enduring African roots and identity of black America.

Age of Revolution A period in Atlantic history that began with the American Revolution in 1776 and ended with the defeat of Napoleonic France in 1815.

Agricultural Adjustment Act (AAA) A federal program that provided subsidies to farmers to grow less to help stabilize prices.

American and Foreign Anti-Slavery Society (AFASS, 1840–1855) An organization of church-oriented abolitionists.

American Anti-Slavery Society (AASS, 1833–1870) The umbrella organization for immediate abolitionists during the 1830s and the main Garrisonian organization after 1840.

American Colonization Society (ACS, 1816–1912) An organization founded in Washington, DC, by prominent slaveholders. It claimed to encourage the ultimate abolition of slavery by sending free African Americans to its West African colony of Liberia.

American Convention for Promoting the Abolition of Slavery and Improving the Condition of the African Race (1794–1838) A loose coalition of state and local societies, dominated by the Pennsylvania Abolition Society, dedicated to gradual abolition.

American Missionary Association This religious organization sent teachers and clergymen throughout the South following the Civil War to tend to the spiritual and educational needs of former slaves. It was instrumental in establishing dozens of schools, including Fisk, Hampton, and Avery.

Amistad A Spanish schooner on which West African Joseph Cinque led a successful slave revolt in 1839.

Animism The belief that inanimate objects have spiritual attributes.

Antimiscegenation Laws that enforced racial segregation at the level of marriage and intimate relationships by criminalizing interracial marriage and sometimes also sex between members of different races.

Asiento The monopoly over the slave trade from Africa to Spain's American colonies.

Assimilation The process by which people of different backgrounds become similar to each other in culture and language.

Barbados An island nation in the Lesser Antilles located to the southeast of Puerto Rico.

Battery Wagner This defensive fortification guarded Fort Sumter near the entrance to Charleston Harbor in South Carolina. It was the scene in July 1863 of a major Union assault by the 54th Massachusetts Regiment, a black unit. The assault failed, but the bravery and valor of the black troops earned them fame and glory.

Benevolent Empire A network of church-related voluntary associations designed to fight sin and save souls. It emerged during the 1810s in relationship to the Second Great Awakening.

Berbers A people native to North Africa and the Sahara Desert.

Black arts movement Artistic movement that seeks to promote black art by black artists for black people.

Black cabinet Informal group of highly placed African-American advisers to President Franklin D. Roosevelt.

Black codes Laws that were passed in each of the former Confederate states following the Civil War that applied only to black people. While conceding such rights as the right to marry, to contract a debt, or to own property, the codes severely restricted the rights and opportunities of former slaves in terms of labor and mobility.

Black Committee An organization of prominent black men in the North who assisted in recruiting African Americans to fight for the Union in the Civil War.

Black English (or African-American Vernacular English) A variety of American English that is influenced by West African grammar, vocabulary, and pronunciation.

Black laws Laws passed in states of the Old Northwest during the early nineteenth century banning or restricting black settlement and limiting the rights of black residents.

Black nationalism A belief held by some African Americans that they must seek their racial destiny by establishing separate institutions and, perhaps, migrating as a group to a location (often Africa) outside the United States.

Black Panther Party Black militant organization set up in 1966 by Huey P. Newton and Bobby Seale.

Black studies Scholarly study of the history and experiences of persons of African descent.

Border ruffians Pro-slavery advocates and vigilantes from Missouri who crossed the border into Kansas in 1855–1857 to support slavery in Kansas by threatening and attacking antislavery settlers.

Brooks-Sumner Affair South Carolina congressman Preston Brooks attacked and severely beat Massachusetts Senator Charles Sumner on the floor of the U.S. Senate after Sumner had denounced the proslavery position of Brooks's uncle, South Carolina Senator Andrew Butler.

Brotherhood of Sleeping Car Porters (BSCP) Black men and women who worked on Pullman passenger coaches on the nation's railroads organized this labor union in 1925 with A. Philip Randolph as its leader. It struggled until the passage in 1935 of the National Labor Relations Act, after which it became one of the most powerful unions within the American Federation of Labor (AFL). In 1978 it was absorbed into the Brotherhood of Railway and Airline Clerks.

Brown v. Board of Education of Topeka   Decision by the Supreme Court in 1954 that overturned the "separate but equal" doctrine.

Brownsville Affair   In 1906, a shooting in Brownsville, Texas, was blamed on black soldiers from the 25th Infantry Regiment. President Theodore Roosevelt summarily dismissed 167 black men from the U.S. Army. Later investigations exonerated the men.

Buffalo soldiers   Four regiments of black soldiers that served with the U.S. Army on the western frontier from the 1870s to the 1890s. The Plains Indians called them the buffalo soldiers.

Call-and-response   An African-American singing style rooted in Africa. A solo call tells a story to which a group responds, often with repeated lyrics.

Carpetbagger   The derogatory term used during Reconstruction to describe northerners who came South following the Civil War to take advantage of political and economic opportunities. They were labeled "carpetbaggers" because they ostensibly carried all of their possessions in a solitary carpetbag.

Cash crop   A crop grown for sale rather than subsistence.

Chattel slavery   A form of slavery in which the enslaved are treated legally as property.

Chicago Renaissance   Flourishing of the arts that made Chicago the center of black culture in the 1940s.

Church of England   A Protestant church established in the sixteenth century as the English national or Anglican church with the English monarch as its head. After the American Revolution, its American branch became the Episcopal Church.

Civil Rights Act, 1866   This act nullified the black codes and made African Americans citizens with the basic rights of life, liberty, and due process. It was passed over President Andrew Johnson's veto. Its main features were subsequently embedded in the Fourteenth Amendment to the Constitution.

Civil Rights Act of 1875   This federal legislation outlawed racial discrimination in public accommodations such as hotels and restaurants, and in transportation, including railroad coaches and steamboats. The Supreme Court invalidated it in 1883.

Civil Rights Act of 1964   Federal law banning discrimination in places of public accommodation.

Civil Rights Act of 1968   Federal law banning discrimination in housing.

Coffle   A file of slaves chained together that was typical of the domestic slave trade.

Colfax Massacre   At least 105 African Americans were murdered on Easter Sunday in 1873 in Colfax, Louisiana, in the single worst episode of racial violence during Reconstruction.

Colored American **(New York, 1837–1842)**   The leading African-American newspaper of its time.

Colored Farmers' Alliance   A large organization of black southern farmers in the 1880s and 1890s that had as many as one million members who agitated for improved conditions and income for black landowners, renters, and sharecroppers.

Committee for Industrial Organization (CIO)   Labor organization that was committed to interracial and multiethnic organizing.

Communist Party   Political party formed to promote communism.

Community Action Programs (CAPS)   Anti-poverty programs involving "maximum feasible participation" by the poor themselves.

Compensated emancipation   Emancipation accompanied by the monetary compensation of former slave owners.

Compromise of 1850   An attempt by the U.S. Congress to settle divisive issues between the North and South, including slavery expansion, apprehension in the North of fugitive slaves, and slavery in the District of Columbia.

Compromise of 1877   This informal arrangement between national Democrats and Republicans settled the disputed presidential election of 1876 by permitting Republican Rutherford B. Hayes to become president while allowing Democrats to complete redemption by taking political control of Louisiana, Florida, and South Carolina.

Confederacy   Association of slave states that left the Union in 1861.

Congress of Racial Equality   Protest group committed to nonviolent direct action.

Conscription law   An 1862 Confederate law defining who was required to provide military service.

Continental Army   The army created by the Continental Congress in June 1775 to fight British troops. George Washington was its commander in chief.

Continental Congress   A representative assembly that first met in October 1775 and served as the de facto central government of the United States during the Revolutionary War.

Contraband   Slaves who escaped to the Union or were captured by Union troops early in the Civil War, who were considered enemy property.

Convict lease system   Southern states and communities leased prisoners to privately operated mines, railroads, and timber companies. These businesses forced the prisoners, who were usually black men, to work in brutal, unhealthy, and dangerous conditions. Many convicts died of abuse and disease.

Cotton gin   A simple machine invented by Eli Whitney in 1793 to separate cotton seeds from cotton fiber. It greatly speeded this task and encouraged the westward expansion of cotton-growing in the United States.

Creole   An American brig on which Madison Washington led a successful slave revolt in 1841.

Creoles   Persons of African and/or European descent born in the Americas.

Crop lien   Black and white farmers purchased goods on credit from local merchants. The merchant demanded collateral in the form of a lien on the crop, typically cotton. If the farmer failed to repay the loan, the merchant had the legal right to seize the crop.

Disfranchisement   White southern Democrats devised a variety of techniques in the late nineteenth and early twentieth centuries to prevent black people from voting. Those techniques included literacy tests, poll taxes, and the grandfather clause as well as intimidation and violence.

Divination   A form of magic aimed at telling the future by interpreting a variety of signs.

Domestic slave trade   A trade dating from the first decade of the nineteenth century in American-born slaves purchased primarily in the border South and sent overland or by sea to the cotton-growing regions of the Old Southwest.

"Double V" campaign   Slogan during World War II that stood for victory over fascism abroad and over racism at home for blacks.

Dred Scott v. Sandford   The 1857 U.S. Supreme Court case that ruled against Missouri slave Dred Scott by declaring that black people were not citizens, that they possessed no constitutional rights, and that they were considered to be property.

Economic Opportunity Act of 1964   Federal law creating the Office of Economic Opportunity and a number of programs aimed at poor communities.

Ellenton Massacre   A conflict in which between 30 and 100 African Americans were killed by marauding white men in September 1876 in Aiken County, South Carolina. The event took place after an alleged assault by a black man on an elderly white woman.

Emancipation Proclamation   Document issued by President Lincoln on January 1, 1863, that freed slaves in areas of the Confederate states not under Union control.

Enforcement Acts   Also known as the Force Acts, these measures were passed by Congress in the early 1870s to undermine the Ku Klux Klan and other terrorist organizations by authorizing the president to use military force and to suspend the writ of *habeas corpus*.

Executive Order 8802   Order issued by President Franklin D. Roosevelt in 1941 banning discrimination in employment in defense industries and the federal government.

Executive Order 9346   Order establishing a new Committee on Fair Employment Practices, with greater resources, and direct oversight by the Executive Office of the president.

Executive Order 9981   Order issued by President Harry Truman in 1948 desegregating the armed forces.

Exodusters   Black migrants who left the South during and after Reconstruction and settled in Kansas, often in all black towns.

Factory   A headquarters for a European company that traded for slaves or engaged in other commercial enterprises on the West African coast.

Fair Employment Practices Committee (FEPC)   A committee created by Franklin Roosevelt to investigate complaints of discrimination.

Fair Play Committee   Organization formed to promote black actors in the movie industry and improve the image of blacks in film.

Family Assistance Plan (FAP)   Plan giving financial assistance to families with no wage earner.

Federal Arts Project   New Deal agency formed to promote the creation of public art.

Federal Elections bill, 1890   A measure, also known as the Force bill, to protect the voting rights of black men in the South by providing federal supervision of elections. It passed in the House of Representatives but failed in the Senate.

Fetish   A natural object or an artifact believed to have magical power; a charm.

Fifteenth Amendment, 1870   This constitutional amendment stipulated that the right to vote could not be denied on account of race, color, or because a person had been a slave.

First Confiscation Act   This 1861 act stated that any slaves used by their masters to benefit the Confederacy would be freed.

First South Carolina Volunteers   This black military unit consisted of former slaves recruited in the South Carolina and Georgia low country in 1862 and 1863 for service with Union military forces in the Civil War.

Fort Pillow   This fort on the east bank of the Mississippi River north of Memphis, Tennessee, was the scene of a massacre of black Union troops as well as some white soldiers and officers by Confederate cavalry in April 1864.

Forty-Niners   The men and women who rushed to California in 1849 after gold had been discovered there.

Fourteenth Amendment, 1868   This amendment ratified during Reconstruction made any person born in the United States a citizen of the United States and of the state in which they lived. It guaranteed citizens the rights of life, liberty, and due process—usually a trial or judicial proceeding—as well as equal protection of the law. It also contained a provision reducing a state's representation in Congress if that state denied the right to vote to any adult males.

Free labor   Mid-nineteenth-century Americans who were free and worked for income or compensation to advance themselves, as opposed to slave labor, which was work done with no financial compensation by people who were not free.

Free papers   Proof of freedom that free black people had to carry at all times in the southern states prior to emancipation. The papers, issued by state governments, identified an individual by name, age, sex, color, height, and so forth.

Free-Soil Party (1848–1853)   An almost entirely northern political coalition opposed to the expansion of slavery into western territories. It included former supporters of the Whig, Democratic, and Liberty parties.

Freedmen's Bureau   Congress established the Bureau of Refugees, Freedmen, and Abandoned Lands in February 1865 to assist black and white southerners left destitute by the Civil War.

Freedmen's Savings Bank   A private financial institution chartered by Congress in 1865. Many black people and organizations deposited funds in the bank, which went bankrupt in 1874.

Freedom Rides   Effort in 1961 to desegregate interstate bus and rail travel.

Freedom suits   Legal cases in which slaves sued their master or master's heirs for freedom.

French and Indian War   A war waged by Great Britain and its American Indian allies against France and its American Indian allies, fought between 1754 and 1763 for control of the eastern portion of North America.

Fugitive Slave Act of 1793   An act of Congress permitting masters to recapture escaped slaves who had reached the free states and, with the authorization of local courts, return with the slave or slaves to their home state.

Fugitive Slave Law, 1850   Part of the Compromise of 1850 that required law enforcement officials as well as civilians to assist in capturing runaway slaves.

Fur trade   A North American colonial industry involving American Indians trapping fur-bearing animals (chiefly beavers) and exchanging their pelts for European products.

Gang system   A mode of organizing labor that had West African antecedents. In this system, American slaves worked in groups under the direction of a slave driver.

Gangsta rap   A genre of rap music characterized by violent and sexist lyrics.

Gary Convention   Meeting of black leaders and organizations in Gary, Indiana, to develop an agenda for black empowerment.

General Order 11   Order threatening retaliation for the mistreatment of black soldiers by Confederate forces.

Grandfather clause   A method southern states used to disfranchise black men. It stipulated that only men whose grandfathers were eligible to vote were themselves eligible to vote. The U.S. Supreme Court invalidated the grandfather clause in 1915.

Great Dismal Swamp   A heavily forested area on the Virginia–North Carolina border that served as a refuge for fugitive slaves during the eighteenth and nineteenth centuries.

Griot   A West African self-employed poet and oral historian.

Guinea Coast   The southward-facing coast of West Africa, from which many of the people caught up in the Atlantic slave trade departed for the Americas.

Habeas corpus   A court order indicating that a person arrested or detained by law enforcement officers must be brought to court and charged with a crime and not held indefinitely.

Hamburg Massacre   White Democrats attacked black Republicans in July 1876 in the village of Hamburg, South Carolina. Five black men were murdered as the Democrats began a violent effort to redeem the state.

Harlem Renaissance   As New York City became a destination for black migrants before, during, and after World War I, most of them settled in Harlem—a large neighborhood in the northern portion of Manhattan Island. By the 1920s it became a center of African-American cultural activities including literature, art, and music.

Harpers Ferry　See John Brown's raid.

Hierarchical　Refers to a social system based on class rank.

Hieroglyphics　A writing system based on pictures or symbols.

Hip-hop　The backup music for rap. It is also the term for the youth culture that developed with the rise of rap music.

Hired their own time　Refers to a practice in which a master allowed slaves to work for wages paid by someone other than the master himself.

House of Burgesses　A representative body established at Jamestown, Virginia, in 1619.

House Un-American Activities Committee (HUAC)　Congressional committee formed to investigate the activities of communists and "communist sympathizers" in America.

Humanism　The belief that human achievement and interests are more important than theological issues.

Hunting and gathering societies　Small societies dependent on hunting animals and collecting wild plants rather than engaging in agriculture.

Immediatism　An antislavery movement that began in the United States during the late 1820s and demanded that slavery be abolished immediately rather than gradually.

Import duties　Taxes on goods brought into a country or colony.

Impressment　During the Civil War, Southern states and the Confederate government required slave owners to provide slaves to work on such public projects as fortifications, roads, and wharves. The owners (not the slaves) were usually compensated for the work.

Incest taboos　Customary rules against sexual relations and marriage within family and kinship groups.

Indentured servant　An individual who sells or loses his or her freedom for a specified number of years.

Indigo　A bluish-violet dye produced from the indigo plant.

Industrial Revolution　An economic change that began in England during the early eighteenth century and spread to Continental Europe and the United States. Industry rather than agriculture became the dominant form of enterprise.

Import duties　Taxes on goods brought into a country or colony.

Jim Crow　Jump Jim Crow was a nineteenth-century dance ridiculing black people that was transformed by the twentieth century into a term meaning racial discrimination and segregation.

John Brown's raid　Brown's raid on Harpers Ferry, Virginia, in October 1859 failed to lead to a major slave insurrection, but it inflamed the controversy over slavery in the North and South.

Joint-stock companies　Primitive corporations that carried out British and Dutch colonization in the Americas during the seventeenth century.

Kansas-Nebraska Act, 1854　Legislation introduced by Democratic Senator Stephen Douglas to organize the Kansas and Nebraska territories. It provided for "popular sovereignty," whereby settlers would decide whether slavery would be legal or illegal.

"Know-Nothing Party"　The nickname applied to members of the American Party, which opposed immigration in the 1850s.

Ku Klux Klan　A secret society founded by former Confederates in Pulaski, Tennessee, in 1866. It transformed itself into a terrorist organization during Reconstruction to drive black and white Republicans from political power in southern states. It disappeared by the late nineteenth century but was revived near Atlanta, Georgia, in 1915 as a powerful, white, Anglo-Saxon, Protestant political force in many states outside the South. It was revived again in the 1950s to oppose the civil rights movement.

Liberty Party (1840–1848)　The first antislavery political party. Most of its supporters joined the Free-Soil Party in 1848, although its radical New York wing maintained a Liberty organization into the 1850s.

Lien　When black and white farmers purchased goods on credit from local merchants, these merchants demanded collateral in the form of a lien on the crop, typically cotton. If the farmers failed to repay the loan, the merchants had a legal right to seize the crop.

Lincoln-Douglas debates　Abraham Lincoln and Stephen Douglas debated seven times in the 1858 U.S. Senate race in Illinois. They spent most of their time arguing over slavery, its expansion, the *Dred Scott* decision, and the character of African Americans. Douglas won the election.

Lineage　A type of clan, typical of West Africa, in which members claim descent from a single ancestor.

Low country　The coastal regions of South Carolina and Georgia.

Lowndes County Freedom Organization (LCFO)　Political organization founded in 1965 by Stokely Carmichael.

Loyalists　Those Americans who, during the Revolutionary War, wished to remain within the British Empire.

Lynching　Killing by a mob without the benefit of a trial or conviction.

Manifest Destiny　A doctrine, prevalent during the nineteenth century, holding that God intended the United States to expand territorially over all of North America and the Caribbean islands, or over the entire Western Hemisphere.

Manumission　The act of freeing a slave by the slave's master.

March on Washington Movement (MOWM)　Movement created by A. Philip Randolph to pressure the federal government to end discrimination in the defense industry and government.

Market revolution　The process between 1800 and 1860 by which an American economy based on subsistence farming, production by skilled artisans, and local markets changed into an economy marked by commercial farming, factory production, and national markets.

Martinique　An island in the eastern Caribbean Sea that was a French sugar-producing colony from the seventeenth into the nineteenth century.

Matrilineal　Descent traced through the female line.

Middle Passage　The voyage of slave ships (slavers) across the Atlantic Ocean from Africa to the Americas.

Militia Act of 1862　The 1862 Act authorizing Lincoln to enlist black soldiers for the military.

Mississippi Freedom Democratic Party　Interracial group set up to challenge Mississippi's all-white delegation to the Democratic National Convention in 1964.

Missouri Compromise, 1820　A congressional attempt to settle the issue of slavery expansion in the United States by permitting Missouri to enter the Union as a slave state, admitting Maine as a free state, and banning slavery in the rest of the Louisiana Purchase north of the 36° 30' line of latitude.

Montgomery Bus Boycott　Refusal of African Americans in Montgomery, Alabama, to ride the city's buses from 1955 to 1957 until the bus lines were desegregated.

Moral suasion　A tactic endorsed by the American Anti-Slavery Society during the 1830s. It appealed to slaveholders and others to support immediate emancipation on the basis of Christian principles.

Moynihan Report　Report attributing many of the problems of poor black communities to the breakdown of the "lower-class" black family.

Nation of Islam　Religious movement that combines Islam with black nationalism.

National Industrial Recovery Act (NIRA)　Federal law intended to promote the revival of manufacturing by allowing for cooperation among industries.

National Negro Congress (NNC)   Organization founded in 1936 to unite African-American protest groups.

Negro National League   A professional baseball league for black players and teams organized in 1912.

New Deal   Set of policies proposed by the Roosevelt administration in response to the Great Depression.

New York City draft riot   In early July 1863, in opposition to the forthcoming military draft, rioting erupted in New York City. Many of the victims were black men, women, and children.

North Atlantic Treaty Organization (NATO)   Military alliance formed to counter the threat posed by the Soviet Union and its allies.

North Star   A weekly newspaper published and edited by Frederick Douglass from 1847 to 1851. *Fredrick Douglass's Paper* (1851–1860) succeeded it.

Northwest Ordinance, 1787   Based on earlier legislation drafted by Thomas Jefferson, it organized the Northwest Territory, providing for orderly land sales, public education, government, the creation of five to seven states out of the territory, and the prohibition of slavery within the territory.

Nuclear family   A family unit consisting solely of one set of parents and their children.

Nullification Crisis (1832–1833)   Situation that arose when the South Carolina legislature declared the United States tariff "null and void" within the state's borders. President Andrew Jackson denounced the action as treasonous and threatened to use military force to uphold national supremacy.

Pan-Africanism   A movement of people of African descent from sub-Saharan Africa in the early twentieth century that emphasized their identity, shared experiences, and the need to liberate Africa from its European colonizers.

Patriarchal   A society ruled by a senior man.

Patrilineal   Descent through the male line.

Patriots   Those Americans who, during the Revolutionary War, favored independence.

Peace Mission Movement   Religious movement led by Father Major Jealous Divine.

Pennsylvania Society for Promoting the Abolition of Slavery (Pennsylvania Abolition Society: 1787–present)   An antislavery organization centered in Philadelphia and based on an earlier Quaker society. Exclusively white, it promoted gradual abolition, black self-improvement, freedom suits, and protection of African Americans against kidnapping.

Peonage   The system that forbade southern farmers, usually sharecroppers and renters, who accumulated debts to leave the land until the debt was repaid—often an impossible task. The U.S. Supreme Court outlawed peonage, but many landowners and merchants still forced farmers to remain on the land.

Philadelphia Female Anti-Slavery Society (1833–1870)   A biracial abolitionist organization aligned with the American Anti-Slavery Society. White Quaker women dominated the society, but it included a significant number of black women.

Pidgin   A simplified mixture of two or more languages used to communicate between people who speak different languages.

Planter elite   Those who owned the largest tobacco plantations.

Plessy v. Ferguson   In 1896 in an eight-to-one decision, the U.S. Supreme Court ruled that segregation did not violate the equal protection clause of the Fourteenth Amendment. The "separate but equal" doctrine remained the supreme law of the land until the 1954 *Brown v. Board of Education* decision overturned *Plessy*.

Polygynous family   A family unit consisting of a man, his wives, and their children.

Polytheism   The worship of many gods.

Poor People's Campaign   Project supported by Martin Luther King involving the march of tens of thousands of poor people on Washington.

Popular sovereignty   A plan in which the residents of a territory (such as Kansas) would vote to legalize or prohibit slavery in that territory.

Populist Party   Also known as the Peoples' Party, the Populists supported inflation; the free and unlimited coinage of silver and gold; government ownership of railroads, telephone, and telegraph companies; and an eight-hour workday. They won state and congressional elections but lost the presidential contests in 1892 and 1896.

Port Royal Experiment   An effort by northern white missionaries, educators, and businessmen in the Sea Islands near Beaufort, South Carolina, to transform former slaves into educated, reliable, and industrious wage earners. Most of the freedmen did not acquire the land they worked.

Preliminary Emancipation Proclamation   Proclamation issued on September 22, 1862, declaring that slaves residing in states still in rebellion on January 1, 1863, would be freed.

Prince Hall Masons   A black Masonic order formed in 1791 in Boston under the leadership of Prince Hall. He became its first grand master and promoted its expansion to other cities.

Project 100,000   Military project with the goal of reducing the number of African Americans rejected by the military.

Race films   Movies made for African-American audiences in the 1930s and 1940s.

Radical Republicans   Members of the Republican Party during Reconstruction who vigorously supported the rights of African Americans to vote, to hold political office, and to have the same legal and economic opportunities as white people.

Rain forest   A dense growth of tall trees characteristic of hot, wet regions.

Rainbow Coalition   Political coalition of African Americans, workers, liberals, feminists, gay people, environmentalists, and others formed by Jesse Jackson in the 1980s.

Reconstruction   The 12 years (1865–1877) following the Civil War during which the former Confederate states were restored to the Union and former slaves became citizens and gained the right to vote and hold political office. It was also a time of violence and terrorism as many southern white people resisted the change in the status of African Americans.

Reconstruction Acts, 1867   Led by Radical Republicans, Congress divided the South into five military districts. Each former Confederate state (except Tennessee) was to frame a new state constitution and establish a new state government. The first Reconstruction Act provided for universal manhood suffrage, which granted the right to vote to all adult males, including black men.

Red Scare   The widespread fear among many Americans in the years immediately after World War I from about 1918 to about 1924 that Russia's 1917 Bolshevik Revolution might result in communists attempting to take over the U.S. government.

Redemption   The term used for the process, often violent, by which white conservative Democrats regained political control of a southern state from black and white Republicans during Reconstruction.

Renaissance   A humanist and artistic movement that began in Italy during the late fourteenth century and spread across Europe.

Rochester Convention, 1853   African-American leaders assembled in Rochester, New York, to discuss slavery, abolition, the recently passed Fugitive Slave Law, and their prospects for life in America.

Savanna   A flat, nearly treeless grassland typical of large portions of West Africa.

Scalawag The derogatory term used during Reconstruction to identify a native white southerner who supported black and white Republicans. They were considered traitors to their people and the Democratic Party.

Scottsboro Boys Nine young African-American men unjustly accused of raping two white women in Alabama in 1931. The Supreme Court overturned their convictions in 1937.

Seasoning The process by which newly arrived Africans were broken in to slavery in the Americas.

Second Confiscation Act The 1862 act freeing all slaves of rebel owners.

Second Great Awakening (1790s–1830s) A widespread religious revival, centered in the North and upper South, that encouraged reform movements.

Secret societies Social organizations that have secret ceremonies that only their members know about and can participate in.

Secularism The belief that the present public welfare should predominate over religion in civil affairs.

Segregation The separation of people based on their race in the use of such public facilities as hotels, restaurants, restrooms, drinking fountains, parks, and auditoriums. In many instances, segregation meant the exclusion of black people.

Semitic Refers to people who speak languages, such as Arabic and Hebrew, native to southwest Asia.

Sharecropping The system following the Civil War in which former slaves worked land owned by white people and "paid" for the use of the land and for tools, seeds, fertilizer, and mules by sharing the crop—usually cotton—with the owner.

Shotgun policy In Mississippi in 1875, white men resorted to violence and intimidation against black and white Republicans to regain political control of the state for conservative Democrats.

Slave codes Legislation enacted between 1660 and 1710 that further defined American slavery as a system that sought as much to control persons of African descent as to exploit their labor. Slaves could not testify against white people in court, own property, leave their master's estate without a pass, congregate in groups larger than three or four, enter into contracts, or marry. They could not, of course, bear arms.

Slave power A term used to indicate the political control exercised by slaveholders over the U.S. government before the Civil War.

Slaver A ship used to transport slaves from Africa to the Americas.

Social Darwinism Derived from Charles Darwin's theory of evolution, Herbert Spencer and William Graham Sumner asserted that life in modern society was competitive and only those individuals who were mentally, emotionally, and physically strong would prevail.

Sons of Liberty A secret American organization formed in the Northeast during the summer of 1765 and committed to forcible opposition to the Stamp Act.

Southern Christian Leadership Conference (SCLC) Organization spearheaded by Martin Luther King, Jr., to provide an institutional base for the civil rights movement.

Southern Homestead Act, 1866 Congress passed this measure that set aside over 3 million acres of land for former slaves and loyal white southerners to farm following the Civil War. Most of the land was not fertile or suitable for agriculture, and the act largely failed.

Southern Regional Council (SRC) Organization that conducted research and focused attention on social, political, and educational inequality in the South.

Spanish Armada A fleet that unsuccessfully attempted to carry out an invasion of England in 1588.

Special Field Order #15 General William Tecumseh Sherman issued this military directive in January 1865. It set aside lands along the coast from Charleston, South Carolina, to Jacksonville, Florida, for former slaves. President Andrew Johnson revoked the order six months later.

Spirit possession A belief rooted in West African religions that spirits may possess human souls.

Student Nonviolent Coordinating Committee (SNCC) Civil rights organization founded by black college students in 1960 at the initiative of Ella Baker.

Syracuse Convention, 1864 A meeting of black leaders in Syracuse, New York, to discuss the future of African Americans following the abolition of slavery. They insisted that black people had earned and deserved the same political and legal rights as white Americans.

Talented Tenth Term coined by W. E. B. Du Bois for the educated black elite of the late nineteenth and early twentieth centuries. The upper 10 percent was supposed to assume responsibility for the leadership and advancement of the remaining 90 percent of African Americans.

Term slavery A type of slavery prevalent in the Chesapeake from the late 1700s to the Civil War in which slaves were able to purchase their freedom from their masters by earning money over a number of years.

Terrell law A Texas law banning African-American participation in the Democratic primary.

The Great Society Programs created in response to the problems of poor Americans championed by President Johnson.

Thirteenth Amendment, 1865 This amendment to the U.S. Constitution outlawed slavery and involuntary servitude.

Three-Fifths Clause A clause in the U.S. Constitution providing that a slave be counted as three-fifths of a free person in determining a state's representation in Congress and the electoral college and three-fifths of a free person in regard to per capita taxes levied by Congress on the states.

Tuskegee Airmen All-black combat air unit during World War II.

Tuskegee Machine As the president of Tuskegee Institute, Booker T. Washington developed an extensive network of contacts that gave him extraordinary influence with white political leaders and philanthropists as well as with black businesspeople, journalists, and college presidents.

Tuskegee Study A medical study by the U.S. Public Health Service of the effects of syphilis on 622 black men. The study ran from 1932 to the 1970s, and the men were given only placebos and no treatment for the disease.

Uncle Tom's Cabin This antislavery novel by Harriet Beecher Stowe was a best seller in the 1850s and it helped inflame the controversy over slavery.

Underground railroad Refers to several loosely organized, semisecret biracial networks that helped slaves escape from the border South to the North and Canada. The earliest networks appeared during the first decade of the nineteenth century; others operated into the Civil War years.

Union League A social and fraternal organization that stirred political interest and support among black and white Republicans in the South during Reconstruction.

Universal Negro Improvement Association (UNIA) Established in 1914 in Jamaica by Marcus Garvey, the UNIA fostered racial pride, African heritage, Christian faith, and economic uplift.

Voting Rights Act of 1965 Federal law banning the methods that had systematically excluded African Americans from registering or voting in southern elections.

Wilmot Proviso A measure introduced in Congress in 1845 to prohibit slavery in any lands acquired from Mexico. It did not pass.

Presidents and Vice Presidents of the United States*

PRESIDENT	VICE PRESIDENT
1. George Washington (1789)	John Adams (1789)
2. John Adams (1797)	Thomas Jefferson (1797)
3. Thomas Jefferson (1801)	Aaron Burr (1801)
	George Clinton (1805)
4. James Madison (1809)	George Clinton (1809)
	Elbridge Gerry (1813)
5. James Monroe (1817)	Daniel D. Tompkins (1817)
6. John Quincy Adams (1825)	John C. Calhoun (1825)
7. Andrew Jackson (1829)	John C. Calhoun (1829)
	Martin Van Buren (1833)
8. Martin Van Buren (1837)	Richard M. Johnson (1837)
9. William H. Harrison (1841)	John Tyler (1841)
10. John Tyler (1841)	
11. James K. Polk (1845)	George M. Dallas (1845)
12. Zachary Taylor (1849)	Millard Fillmore (1849)
13. Millard Fillmore (1850)	
14. Franklin Pierce (1853)	William R. King (1853)
15. James Buchanan (1857)	John C. Breckinridge (1857)
16. Abraham Lincoln (1861)	Hannibal Hamlin (1861)
	Andrew Johnson (1865)
17. Andrew Johnson (1865)	
18. Ulysses S. Grant (1869)	Schuyler Colfax (1869)
	Henry Wilson (1873)
19. Rutherford B. Hayes (1877)	William A. Wheeler (1877)
20. James A. Garfield (1881)	Chester A. Arthur (1881)
21. Chester A. Arthur (1881)	
22. Grover Cleveland (1885)	Thomas A. Hendricks (1885)
23. Benjamin Harrison (1889)	Levi P. Morton (1889)

PRESIDENT	VICE PRESIDENT
24. Grover Cleveland (1893)	Adlai E. Stevenson (1893)
25. William McKinley (1897)	Garret A. Hobart (1897)
	Theodore Roosevelt (1901)
26. Theodore Roosevelt (1901)	Charles Fairbanks (1905)
27. William H. Taft (1909)	James S. Sherman (1909)
28. Woodrow Wilson (1913)	Thomas R. Marshall (1913)
29. Warren G. Harding (1921)	Calvin Coolidge (1921)
30. Calvin Coolidge (1923)	Charles G. Dawes (1925)
31. Herbert C. Hoover (1929)	Charles Curtis (1929)
32. Franklin D. Roosevelt (1933)	John Nance Garner (1933)
	Henry A.Wallace (1941)
	Harry S Truman (1945)
33. Harry S Truman (1945)	Alben W. Barkley (1949)
34. Dwight D. Eisenhower (1953)	Richard M. Nixon (1953)
35. John F. Kennedy (1961)	Lyndon B. Johnson (1961)
36. Lyndon B. Johnson (1963)	Hubert H. Humphrey (1965)
37. Richard M. Nixon (1969)	Spiro T. Agnew (1969)
	Gerald R. Ford (1973)
38. Gerald R. Ford (1974)	Nelson A. Rockefeller (1974)
39. James E. Carter Jr. (1977)	Walter F. Mondale (1977)
40. Ronald W. Reagan (1981)	George H. Bush (1981)
41. George H. Bush (1989)	James D. Quayle III (1989)
42. William J. Clinton (1993)	Albert Gore (1993)
43. George W. Bush (2001)	Richard B. Cheney (2001)
44. Barack H. Obama (2009)	Joseph R. Biden (2009)

* Year of inauguration

Historically Black Four-Year Colleges and Universities

INSTITUTION AND LOCATION	YEAR FOUNDED	LAND-GRANT, PUBLIC, PRIVATE, OR CHURCH-AFFILIATED DENOMINATION
Alabama A&M University, Normal, Alabama	1875	Land-grant
Alabama State University, Montgomery, Alabama	1867	Public
Albany State University, Albany, Georgia	1903	Public
Alcorn State University, Lorman, Mississippi	1871	Land-grant
Allen University, Columbia, South Carolina	1870	AME
Arkansas Baptist College, Little Rock, Arkansas	1884	Baptist
Barber-Scotia College, Concord, North Carolina	1904	Presbyterian
Benedict College, Columbia, South Carolina	1870	Baptist
Bennett College, Greensboro, North Carolina	1873	United Methodist
Bethune-Cookman College, Daytona Beach, Florida	1904	United Methodist
Bluefield State College, Bluefield, West Virginia	1895	Public
Bowie State University, Bowie, Maryland	1865	Public
Central State University, Wilberforce, Ohio	1887	Public
Cheyney University, Cheyney, Pennsylvania	1837	Public
Claflin College, Orangeburg, South Carolina	1869	United Methodist
Clark Atlanta University, Atlanta, Georgia	1988	United Methodist
Concordia College, Selma, Alabama	1922	Lutheran
Coppin State University, Baltimore, Maryland	1900	Public
Delaware State University, Dover, Delaware	1891	Land-grant
Dillard University, New Orleans, Louisiana	1930	Congregational/United Methodist
Edward Waters College, Jacksonville, Florida	1866	AME
Elizabeth City State University, Elizabeth City, North Carolina	1891	Public
Fayetteville State University, Fayetteville, North Carolina	1867	Public
Fisk University, Nashville, Tennessee	1866	United Church of Christ
Florida A&M University, Tallahassee, Florida	1887	Land-grant
Florida Memorial College, Miami, Florida	1879	Baptist
Fort Valley State College, Fort Valley, Georgia	1895	Land-grant
Grambling State University, Grambling, Louisiana	1901	Public
Hampton University, Hampton, Virginia	1868	Private
Harris-Stowe State College, St. Louis, Missouri	1857	Public
Howard University, Washington, DC	1867	Public
Huston-Tillotson University, Austin, Texas	1952	United Church of Christ/United Methodist

(continued)

INSTITUTION AND LOCATION	YEAR FOUNDED	LAND-GRANT, PUBLIC, PRIVATE, OR CHURCH-AFFILIATED DENOMINATION
Jackson State University, Jackson, Mississippi	1877	Public
Jarvis Christian College, Hawkins, Texas	1913	Disciple of Christ Christian Church
Johnson C. Smith University, Charlotte, North Carolina	1867	Presbyterian
Kentucky State University, Frankfort, Kentucky	1886	Land-grant
Knoxville College, Knoxville, Tennessee	1875	Presbyterian
Lane College, Jackson, Tennessee	1882	Christian Methodist Episcopal
Langston University, Langston, Oklahoma	1897	Land-grant
LeMoyne-Owen College, Memphis, Tennessee	1870	United Church of Christ
Lincoln University, Jefferson City, Missouri	1866	Land-grant
Lincoln University, Lincoln, Pennsylvania	1854	Public
Livingstone College, Salisbury, North Carolina	1879	AME
Miles College, Birmingham, Alabama	1908	Christian Methodist Episcopal
Mississippi Valley State University, Itta Bena, Mississippi	1946	Public
Morehouse College, Atlanta, Georgia	1867	Baptist
Morgan State University, Baltimore, Maryland	1867	Public
Morris Brown College, Atlanta, Georgia	1881	AME
Morris College, Sumter, South Carolina	1908	Baptist
Norfolk State University, Norfolk, Virginia	1935	Public
North Carolina A&T State University, Greensboro, North Carolina	1892	Land-grant
North Carolina Central University, Durham, North Carolina	1909	Public
Oakwood College, Huntsville, Alabama	1896	Seventh Day Adventist
Paine College, Augusta, Georgia	1882	United Methodist
Paul Quinn College, Dallas, Texas	1872	AME
Philander Smith College, Little Rock, Arkansas	1877	United Methodist
Prairie View A&M University, Prairie View, Texas	1878	Land-grant
Rust College, Holly Springs, Mississippi	1866	United Methodist
Saint Augustine's College, Raleigh, North Carolina	1867	Episcopal
Saint Paul's College, Lawrenceville, Virginia	1888	Episcopal
Savannah State College, Savannah, Georgia	1890	Public
Selma University, Selma, Alabama	1878	Baptist
Shaw University, Raleigh, North Carolina	1865	Baptist
Sojourner-Douglass College, Baltimore, Maryland	1980	Private
South Carolina State University, Orangeburg, South Carolina	1896	Land-grant
Southern University and A&M College, Baton Rouge, Louisiana	1880	Land-grant
Southern University at New Orleans, New Orleans, Louisiana	1956	Public
Southwestern Christian College, Terrell, Texas	1949	Church of Christ
Spelman College, Atlanta, Georgia	1876	Presbyterian
Stillman College, Tuscaloosa, Alabama	1876	Presbyterian

(continued)

INSTITUTION AND LOCATION	YEAR FOUNDED	LAND-GRANT, PUBLIC, PRIVATE, OR CHURCH-AFFILIATED DENOMINATION
Talladega College, Talladega, Alabama	1867	United Church of Christ
Tennessee State University, Nashville, Tennessee	1912	Land-grant
Texas College, Tyler, Texas	1894	Christian Methodist Episcopal
Texas Southern University, Houston, Texas	1947	Public
Tougaloo College, Tougaloo, Mississippi	1869	United Church of Christ/United Missionary Society
Tuskegee University, Tuskegee, Alabama	1881	Land-grant
University of Arkansas at Pine Bluff, Pine Bluff, Arkansas	1873	Land-grant
University of the District of Columbia, Washington, DC	1977	Public
University of Maryland Eastern Shore, Princess Anne, Maryland	1886	Land-grant
University of the Virgin Islands, St. Thomas, United States Virgin Islands	1962	Public
Virginia State University, Petersburg, Virginia	1882	Land-grant
Virginia Union University, Richmond, Virginia	1865	Baptist
Voorhees College, Denmark, South Carolina	1897	Episcopal
West Virginia State College, Institute, West Virginia	1891	Public
Wilberforce University, Wilberforce, Ohio	1856	AME
Wiley College, Marshall, Texas	1873	United Methodist
Winston-Salem State University, Winston-Salem, North Carolina	1892	Public
Xavier University of New Orleans, New Orleans, Louisiana	1925	Roman Catholic

Photo and Text Credits

CHAPTER 12: The Granger Collection, NYC, 288; Library of Congress, Prints & Photographs Division, [LC-USZ62-117892], 291; PICA 05496, Austin History Center, Austin Public Library, 296; Library of Congress, Prints & Photographs Division, [LC-USZ62-117891], 297; Fotosearch/Getty Images, 298; Library of Congress, Prints & Photographs Division, [LC-USZ62-108067], 299; Library of Congress, Prints & Photographs Division, [LC-USZ62-117139], 306; Library of Congress, Prints & Photographs Division, [LC-USZ62-125422], 309.

CHAPTER 13: Library of Congress, Prints & Photographs Division, [LC-DIG-ppmsca-17564], 314; Library of Congress, Prints & Photographs Division, D.C, LC-USZ62-100971, 315; Library of Congress, Prints & Photographs Division, [LC-USZC4-681], 316; Schomburg Center, NYPL/Art Resource, NY, 319; Schomburg Center, NYPL/Art Resource, NY, 321; Library of Congress, Prints & Photographs Division, [LC-USZ62-119565], 323; Henry Clay Warmoth Papers #752, Southern Historical Collection, Wilson Library, University of North Carolina at Chapel Hill., 323; Library of Congress Prints & Photographs Division, [LC-USZC4-973], 326; Library of Congress, Prints & Photographs Division, [LC-DIG-ppmsca-31598], 336; Bruce Davidson/Magnum Photos, 337.

PART IV: *Images on page 338:* Library of Congress, Prints & Photographs Division, [LC-USZ62-117140]; Library of Congress, Prints & Photographs Division, [LC-USZ62-51555]; National Archives; Library of Congress, Prints & Photographs Division, Detroit Publishing Company Collection, [LC-USZ62-77635]; Library of Congress, Prints & Photographs Division, Carl Van Vechten Collection, [LC-USZ62-42531] *Images on page 339:* Library of Congress, Prints & Photographs Division, Carl Van Vechten Collection [LC-DIG-van-5a52142]; Library of Congress, Prints & Photographs Division, Carl Van Vechten Collection, [LC-USZ62-42529]; U of North Carolina Digital Library & Archives.

CHAPTER 14: Solomon D Butcher/Getty Images, 340; Stock Montage/Getty Images, 346; Bettmann/Corbis, 348; Library of Congress, Prints & Photographs Division, [LC-USZC4-4647], 354; Everett Collection Historical/Alamy, 355; Library of Congress Prints & Photographs Division/[LC-USZ62-26365], 357; Library of Congress, Prints & Photographs Division, Detroit Publishing Company Collection, [LC-D418-8144], 359; Library of Congress, Prints & Photographs Division, [LC-USZ62-116587], 365; Courtesy of SC State Historical Collection & Archives, 362.

CHAPTER 15: Glasshouse Images/Alamy, 370; Library of Congress Prints and Photographs Division [LC-USZ62-120667], 372; Library of Congress, Prints & Photographs Division, [LC-USZ62-49568], 374; Library of Congress, Prints & Photographs Division, [LC-USZ62-106646], 377; Portrait of Reverend H. M. Turner, chaplain of the First U. S. Colored Regiment, 1863 (wood engraving), American School, (19th century)/© Boston Athenaeum, USA/The Bridgeman Art Library, 379; National Archives, 382; Historic Florida/Alamy, 384; Everett Collection/Newscom, 390; National Park Service, 391; Courtesy of the Tennessee State Library and Archives, 394; Bettmann/Corbis, 396; Library of Congress, Prints & Photographs Division, [LC-USZ6-1824], 397; Schomburg Center, NYPL/Art Resource, NY, 393.

CHAPTER 16: *Photos:* Library of Congress, Prints & Photographs Division, [LC-USZ62-64712], 403; Library of Congress, Prints & Photographs Division, [LC-DIG-stereo-1s02155], 406; Library of Congress, Prints & Photographs Division, [LC-USZ62-16767], 409; Bettmann/Corbis, 411; Library of Congress, Prints & Photographs Division, [LC-USZ62-54722] 413; Western Reserve Historical Society, 416; Courtesy of the Queens Borough Public Library, Archives, Lewis H. Latimer Papers, 419; Library of Congress, Prints & Photographs Division, [LC-J601-302], 420; Library of Congress, Prints & Photographs Division, [LC-USZ62-47385], 421; Library of Congress, Prints & Photographs Division, [LC-USZ62-116442], 423; Library of Congress, Prints & Photographs Division, [LC-DIG-ds-00894], 427; Everett Collection Historical/Alamy, 429.

Text: Langston Hughes, The Big Sea: An Autobiography by Langston Hughes, Published A.F. Knopf (1940), 435.

CHAPTER 17: *Photos:* Corbis, 442; Paris Pierce/Alamy, 445; Library of Congress, Prints & Photographs Division, Carl Van Vechten Collection, [LC-USZ62-42498], 449; Bettmann/Corbis, 450; Bettmann/Corbis, 457; Aaron Douglas/Art and Artifacts Division, Schomburg Center for Research in Black Culture, The New York Public Library/Art Resource, NY, 459; Museum of The City of New York/Getty Images, 463; Michael Ochs Archives/Getty Images, 464; National Baseball Hall of Fame & Museum, 465; Everett Collection Historical/Alamy, 461; Chicago History Museum/Getty Images, 470; Mondadori via Getty Images, 471.

Text: "I, Too", from *The Collected Poems of Langston Hughes* by Langston Hughes, edited by Arnold Rampersad with David Roessel, Associate Editor, copyright © 1994 by the Estate of Langston Hughes, 442; "If We Must Die," by Claude McKay, 1919, 456-457; "Red Silk Stockings", from *The Collected Poems of Langston Hughes* by Langston Hughes, edited by Arnold Rampersad with David Roessel, Associate Editor, copyright © 1994 by the Estate of Langston Hughes, 460.

PART V: *Images on page 472:* Library of Congress, Prints & Photographs Division, [LC-USZ62-51950]; Library of Congress, Prints & Photographs Division, Carl Van Vechten Collection, [LC-DIG-ppmsca-10452]; Library of Congress, Prints & Photographs Division, [LC-USZ62-119985]; Library of Congress, Prints & Photographs Division, FSA/OWI Collection, [LC-DIG-fsa-8b29589]; Library of Congress, Prints & Photographs Division, Carl Van Vechten

Collection, [LC-USZ62-102156]; *Images on page 473:* Library of Congress, Prints & Photographs Division, Carl Van Vechten Collection, [LC-USZ62-120855]; Library of Congress, Prints & Photographs Division, Carl Van Vechten Collection, [LC-USZ62-42481]; Library of Congress, Prints & Photographs Division, Carl Van Vechten Collection, [LC-USZ62-109113].

CHAPTER 18: *Photos:* Margaret Bourke-White/Masters/Time Life Pictures/Getty Images, 474; Matilda A. Evans, circa 1897. Photo ID p0278, Legacy Center Archives, Drexel College of Medicine, Philadelphia, 478; Everett Collection Inc/Alamy, 481; Library of Congress, Prints & Photographs Division, [LC-USZ62-119472], 483; Bettmann/Corbis, 488; Washington Bureau/Staff/Hulton Archive/Getty Images, 489; Library of Congress, Prints & Photographs Division, Carl Van Vechten Collection, [LC-USZ62-128514], 491; Library of Congress, Prints & Photographs Division, FSA/OWI Collection, [LC-USE6-D-006321], 492; Library of Congress, Prints & Photographs Division, [LC-USZC4-2028], 493; Everett Collection Historical/Alamy, 495; Bettmann/Corbis, 497; National Archives, 499.

Text: Letter from Dayton Jones of the Federal Emergency Relief Administration to Frank Person, Director of Selection of the Civilian Conservation Corps (1933 to 1942). June 26, 1935., 486-487; Copyrights by The Estate of Langston Huges., 474.

CHAPTER 19: *Photos:* AP PhotoMatty Zimmerman, 505; Library of Congress, Prints & Photographs Division, [LC-USW33-054941-ZC], 506; STF/AFP/Getty Images, 509; Clarice Durham, 513; AP Photo/ASSOCIATED PRESS, 515; The Granger Collection, NYC, 518; Library of Congress, Prints & Photographs Division, Carl Van Vechten Collection, [LC-USZ62-92598], 519; David Lees/Corbis, 521; Hulton Archive/Getty Images, 522; Library of Congress, Prints & Photographs Division, FSA/OWI Collection, [LC-USW3-030278-D], 525; Bettmann/Corbis, 526.

Text: From Collected Poems. Copyright © 1994 by The Estate of Langston Hughes. Reprinted with the permission of Harold Ober Associates Incorporated., 519; Semple Speaks His Mind, By Langston Hughes, Published by Chicago Defender 1943., 519.

CHAPTER 20: Library of Congress, Prints & Photographs Division, [LC-USZC4-4344], 535; Dwight D. Eisenhower Presidential Library & Museum, 540; National Archives, 541; Library of Congress, Prints & Photographs Division, [LC-USZC4-2328], 542; Marie Hansen/Time Life Pictures/Getty Images, 543; National Archives, 543; Moorland-Spingarn Research Center, 546; Library of Congress, Prints & Photographs Division, [LC-DIG-ppmsca-13258], 549; Bettmann/Corbis, 549; National Archives, 551; Robert Maass/Corbis, 554; The Michael Barson Collection, 555; Everett Collection Inc/Alamy, p. 558; Library of Congress, Prints & Photographs Division, FSA/OWI Collection, [LC-USW3-022991-C], 564; Everett Collection Historical/Alamy, 565.

PART VI: *Images on page 566:* Three Lions/Getty Images; Aflo Foto Agency/Alamy; Library of Congress, Prints & Photographs Division,

[LC-USZ62-60139]; AP Photo/Doug Mills; Library of Congress, Prints & Photographs Division, U.S. News & World Report Magazine Collection, [LC-DIG-ppmsc-01266] *Images on page 567:* Library of Congress, Prints & Photographs Division, U.S. News & World Report Magazine Collection, [LC-U9- 32512-12]; Library of Congress, Prints & Photographs Division, U.S. News & World Report Magazine Collection, [LC-DIG-ppmsc-01265]; ITAR-TASS Photo Agency/Alamy.

CHAPTER 21: AP Photo/ASSOCIATED PRESS, 568; Bettmann/Corbis, 571; Carl Iwasaki//Time Life Pictures/Getty Images, 574; ThinkFilm/courtesy Everett Collection, 575; AP Photo/HO, 578; Bettmann/Bettmann Premium/Corbis, 579; St Petersburg Times/ZUMAPRESS/Newscom, 582; Jack Moebes/Historical/Corbis, 583; Bettmann/Corbis, 585; 1964 Steve Schapiro/Black Star/Newscom, 586; Everett Collection Inc/Alamy, 588; MPI/Archive Photos/Getty Images, 595; Express Newspapers/Getty Images, 597; Library of Congress, Prints & Photographs Division, FSA/OWI Collection, [LC-DIG-fsa-8a26761], 599.

CHAPTER 22: *Photos:* Bettman/Corbis, 604; Library of Congress, Prints & Photographs Division, NYWT&S Collection, [LC-USZ62-119478], 608; Bettmann/Corbis, 609; AP Photo, 610; Bettmann/Corbis, 612; Gamma-Keystone/Getty Images, 614; Pictorial Parade/Hulton Archive/Getty Images, 615; Everett Collection Inc/Alamy, 617; AP Photo/Charles Gorry, 619; Pictorial Press Ltd/Alamy, 621; Everett Collection Inc/Alamy, 625; Everett Collection Inc/Alamy, 623 AP Photo, 627; Library of Congress, Prints & Photographs Division, [LC-DIG-ppmsc-01264], 633.

Text: "Ingratitude vs. the NAACP" The Autobiography of Medgar Evers: A Hero's Life and Legacy Revealed Through His Writings, Letters, and Speeches by Myrlie Evers-Williams and Manning Marable, Published by Basic Civitas Books/Perseus Books Group, Cambridge, MA pg 313. Used by permission., 604; "By Any Means Necessary: The Life and Legacy of Malcolm X" by Manning Marable. Speech given at Metro State College, Denver, Colorado, February 21, 1992. By permission of the Estate of Manning Marable., 607.

CHAPTER 23: ZUMA Press, Inc./Alamy, 642; Steven L. Raymer/National Geographic/Getty Images, 644; Michael Macor/San Francisco Chronicle/Corbis, 645; Viviane Moos/Corbis, 650; AP Photo/ASSOCIATED PRESS, 653; AP Photo/Rusty Kennedy, 654; Dr. Molefi Kete Asante, 657; AP Photo/Al Behrman, 661; Scott Olson/Staff/Getty Images, 663; David Grossman/The Image Works, 666.

CHAPTER 24: White House Photo/Alamy, 674; Paul Conklin/PhotoEdit, 676; Mike Theiler/Reuters/Corbis, 680; Bettmann/Corbis, 680; Najlah Feanny/Corbis News/Corbis, 683; Peter Turnley/Corbis, 687; AFP/Getty Images/Newscom, 688; TIM SLOAN/AFP/Getty Images, 690; AP Photo/Nati Harnik, 695; Marko Georgiev/Getty Images, 697; Everett Collection Inc/Alamy, 701; Nancy Stone-Pool/Getty Images, 703; Herb Snitzer//Time Life Pictures/Getty Images, 710; Mary Evans/UNIVERSAL PICTURES/Ronald Grant/Everett Collection, 711.

Index